The raising of Lazarus, from a rare Synaxarium of 1030.
(© Dean Conger/CORBIS)

NEW
CATHOLIC
ENCYCLOPEDIA

NEW CATHOLIC ENCYCLOPEDIA

SECOND EDITION

8

Jud–Lyo

GALE®

THOMSON

GALE

Detroit • New York • San Diego • San Francisco • Cleveland • New Haven, Conn. • Waterville, Maine • London • Munich

in association with
THE CATHOLIC UNIVERSITY OF AMERICA • WASHINGTON, D.C.

The New Catholic Encyclopedia, Second Edition

Project Editors
Thomas Carson, Joann Cerrito

Editorial
Erin Bealmear, Jim Craddock, Stephen Cusack, Miranda Ferrara, Kristin Hart, Melissa Hill, Margaret Mazurkiewicz, Carol Schwartz, Christine Tomassini, Michael J. Tyrkus

Permissions
Edna Hedblad, Shalice Shah-Caldwell

Imaging and Multimedia
Randy Bassett, Dean Dauphinais, Robert Duncan, Leitha Etheridge-Sims, Mary K. Grimes, Lezlie Light, Dan Newell, David G. Oblender, Christine O'Bryan, Luke Rademacher, Pamela Reed

Product Design
Michelle DiMercurio

Data Capture
Civie Green

Manufacturing
Rhonda Williams

Indexing
Victoria Agee, Victoria Baker, Lynne Maday, Do Mi Stauber, Amy Suchowski

While every effort has been made to ensure the reliability of the information presented in this publication, The Gale Group, Inc. does not guarantee the accuracy of the data contained herein. The Gale Group, Inc. accepts no payment for listing; and inclusion in the publication of any organization, agency, institution, publication, service, or individual does not imply endorsement of the editors or publisher. Errors brought to the attention of the publisher and verified to the satisfaction of the publisher will be corrected in future editions.

LIBRARY OF CONGRESS CATALOGING-IN-PUBLICATION DATA

New Catholic encyclopedia.—2nd ed.
  p. cm.
    Includes bibliographical references and indexes.
    ISBN 0-7876-4004-2
    1. Catholic Church—Encyclopedias. I. Catholic University of America.
BX841 .N44 2002
282' .03—dc21
2002000924

ISBN: 0-7876-4004-2 (set)
0-7876-4005-0 (v. 1)
0-7876-4006-9 (v. 2)
0-7876-4007-7 (v. 3)
0-7876-4008-5 (v. 4)

0-7876-4009-3 (v. 5)
0-7876-4010-7 (v. 6)
0-7876-4011-5 (v. 7)
0-7876-4012-3 (v. 8)
0-7876-4013-1 (v. 9)

0-7876-4014-x (v. 10)
0-7876-4015-8 (v. 11)
0-7876-4016-6 (v. 12)
0-7876-4017-4 (v. 13)
0-7876-4018-2 (v. 14)
0-7876-4019-0 (v. 15)

Printed in the United States of America
10 9 8 7 6 5 4 3 2 1

For The Catholic University of America Press

EDITORIAL STAFF

Foreword

This revised edition of the *New Catholic Encyclopedia* represents a third generation in the evolution of the text that traces its lineage back to the *Catholic Encyclopedia* published from 1907 to 1912. In 1967, sixty years after the first volume of the original set appeared, The Catholic University of America and the McGraw-Hill Book Company joined together in organizing a small army of editors and scholars to produce the *New Catholic Encyclopedia*. Although planning for the *NCE* had begun before the Second Vatican Council and most of the 17,000 entries were written before Council ended, Vatican II enhanced the encyclopedia's value and importance. The research and the scholarship that went into the articles witnessed to the continuity and richness of the Catholic Tradition given fresh expression by Council. In order to keep the *NCE* current, supplementary volumes were published in 1972, 1978, 1988, and 1995. Now, at the beginning of the third millennium, The Catholic University of America is proud to join with The Gale Group in presenting a new edition of the *New Catholic Encyclopedia*. It updates and incorporates the many articles from the 1967 edition and its supplements that have stood the test of time and adds hundreds of new entries.

As the president of The Catholic University of America, I cannot but be pleased at the reception the *NCE* has received. It has come to be recognized as an authoritative reference work in the field of religious studies and is praised for its comprehensive coverage of the Church's history and institutions. Although Canon Law no longer requires encyclopedias and reference works of this kind to receive an *imprimatur* before publication, I am confident that this new edition, like the original, reports accurate information about Catholic beliefs and practices. The editorial staff and their consultants were careful to present official Church teachings in a straightforward manner, and in areas where there are legitimate disputes over fact and differences in interpretation of events, they made every effort to insure a fair and balanced presentation of the issues.

The way for this revised edition was prepared by the publication, in 2000, of a Jubilee volume of the *NCE*, heralding the beginning of the new millennium. In my foreword to that volume I quoted Pope John Paul II's encyclical on Faith and Human Reason in which he wrote that history is "the arena where we see what God does for humanity." The *New Catholic Encyclopedia* describes that arena. It reports events, people, and ideas—"the things we know best and can verify most easily, the things of our everyday life, apart from which we cannot understand ourselves" (*Fides et ratio,* 12).

Finally, I want to express appreciation on my own behalf and on the behalf of the readers of these volumes to everyone who helped make this revision a reality. We are all indebted to The Gale Group and the staff of The Catholic University of America Press for their dedication and the alacrity with which they produced it.

Very Reverend David M. O'Connell, C.M., J.C.D.
President
The Catholic University of America

Preface to the Revised Edition

When first published in 1967 the *New Catholic Encyclopedia* was greeted with enthusiasm by librarians, researchers, and general readers interested in Catholicism. In the United States the *NCE* has been recognized as the standard reference work on matters of special interest to Catholics. In an effort to keep the encyclopedia current, supplementary volumes were published in 1972, 1978, 1988, and 1995. However, it became increasingly apparent that further supplements would not be adequate to this task. The publishers subsequently decided to undertake a thorough revision of the *NCE*, beginning with the publication of a Jubilee volume at the start of the new millennium.

Like the biblical scribe who brings from his storeroom of knowledge both the new and the old, this revised edition of the *New Catholic Encyclopedia* incorporates material from the 15-volume original edition and the supplement volumes. Entries that have withstood the test of time have been edited, and some have been amended to include the latest information and research. Hundreds of new entries have been added. For all practical purposes, it is an entirely new edition intended to serve as a comprehensive and authoritative work of reference reporting on the movements and interests that have shaped Christianity in general and Catholicism in particular over two millennia.

SCOPE

The title reflects its outlook and breadth. It is the *New Catholic Encyclopedia,* not merely a new encyclopedia of Catholicism. In addition to providing information on the doctrine, organization, and history of Christianity over the centuries, it includes information about persons, institutions, cultural phenomena, religions, philosophies, and social movements that have affected the Catholic Church from within and without. Accordingly, the *NCE* attends to the history and particular traditions of the Eastern Churches and the Churches of the Protestant Reformation, and other ecclesial communities. Christianity cannot be understood without exploring its roots in ancient Israel and Judaism, nor can the history of the medieval and modern Church be understood apart from its relationship with Islam. Interfaith dialogue requires an appreciation of Buddhism and other world religions, as well as some knowledge of the history of religion in general.

On the assumption that most readers and researchers who use the *NCE* are individuals interested in Catholicism in general and the Church in North America in particular, its editorial content gives priority to the Western Church, while not neglecting the churches in the East; to Roman Catholicism, acknowledging much common history with Protestantism; and to Catholicism in the United States, recognizing that it represents only a small part of the universal Church.

Scripture, Theology, Patrology, Liturgy. The many and varied articles dealing with Sacred Scripture and specific books of the Bible reflect contemporary biblical scholarship and its concerns. The *NCE* highlights official church teachings as expressed by the Church's magisterium. It reports developments in theology, explains issues and introduces ecclesiastical writers from the early Church Fathers to present-day theologians whose works exercise major influence on the development of Christian thought. The *NCE* traces the evolution of the Church's worship with special emphasis on rites and rituals consequent to the liturgical reforms and renewal initiated by the Second Vatican Council.

Church History. From its inception Christianity has been shaped by historical circumstances and itself has become a historical force. The *NCE* presents the Church's history from a number of points of view against the background of general political and cultural history. The revised edition reports in some detail the Church's missionary activity as it grew from a small community in Jerusalem to the worldwide phenomenon it is today. Some entries, such as those dealing with the Middle Ages, the Reformation, and the Enlightenment, focus on major time-periods and movements that cut across geographical boundaries. Other articles describe the history and structure of the Church in specific areas, countries, and regions. There are separate entries for many dioceses and monasteries which by reason of antiquity, size, or influence are of special importance in ecclesiastical history, as there are for religious orders and congregations. The *NCE* rounds out its comprehensive history of the Church with articles on religious movements and biographies of individuals.

Canon and Civil Law. The Church inherited and has safeguarded the precious legacy of ancient Rome, described by Virgil, "to rule people under law, [and] to establish the way of peace." The *NCE* deals with issues of ecclesiastical jurisprudence and outlines the development of legislation governing communal practices and individual obligations, taking care to incorporate and reference the 1983 *Code of Canon Law* throughout and, where appropriate, the *Code of Canons for the Eastern Churches*. It deals with issues of Church-State relations and with civil law as it impacts on the Church and Church's teaching regarding human rights and freedoms.

Philosophy. The Catholic tradition from its earliest years has investigated the relationship between faith and reason. The *NCE* considers at some length the many and varied schools of ancient, medieval, and modern philosophy with emphasis, when appropriate, on their relationship to theological positions. It pays particular attention to the scholastic tradition, particularly Thomism, which is prominent in Catholic intellectual history. Articles on many major and lesser philosophers contribute to a comprehensive survey of philosophy from pre-Christian times to the present.

Biography and Hagiography. The *NCE,* making an exception for the reigning pope, leaves to other reference works biographical information about living persons. This revised edition presents biographical sketches of hundreds of men and women, Christian and non-Christian, saints and sinners, because of their significance for the Church. They include: Old and New Testament figures; the Fathers of the Church and ecclesiastical writers; pagan and Christian emperors; medieval and modern kings; heads of state and other political figures; heretics and champions of orthodoxy; major and minor figures in the Reformation and Counter Reformation; popes, bishops, and priests; founders and members of religious orders and congregations; lay men and lay women; scholars, authors, composers, and artists. The *NCE* includes biographies of most saints whose feasts were once celebrated or are currently celebrated by the universal church. The revised edition relies on Butler's *Lives of the Saints* and similar reference works to give accounts of many saints, but the *NCE* also

provides biographical information about recently canonized and beatified individuals who are, for one reason or another, of special interest to the English-speaking world.

Social Sciences. Social sciences came into their own in the twentieth century. Many articles in the *NCE* rely on data drawn from anthropology, economics, psychology and sociology for a better understanding of religious structures and behaviors. Papal encyclicals and pastoral letters of episcopal conferences are the source of principles and norms for Christian attitudes and practice in the field of social action and legislation. The *NCE* draws attention to the Church's organized activities in pursuit of peace and justice, social welfare and human rights. The growth of the role of the laity in the work of the Church also receives thorough coverage.

ARRANGEMENT OF ENTRIES

The articles in the *NCE* are arranged alphabetically by the first substantive word using the word-by-word method of alphabetization; thus "New Zealand" precedes "Newman, John Henry," and "Old Testament Literature" precedes "Oldcastle, Sir John." Monarchs, patriarchs, popes, and others who share a Christian name and are differentiated by a title and numerical designation are alphabetized by their title and then arranged numerically. Thus, entries for Byzantine emperors Leo I through IV precede those for popes of the same name, while "Henry VIII, King of England" precedes "Henry IV, King of France."

Maps, Charts, and Illustrations. The *New Catholic Encyclopedia* contains nearly 3,000 illustrations, including photographs, maps, and tables. Entries focusing on the Church in specific countries contain a map of the country as well as easy-to-read tables giving statistical data and, where helpful, lists of archdioceses and dioceses. Entries on the Church in U.S. states also contain tables listing archdioceses and dioceses where appropriate. The numerous photographs appearing in the *New Catholic Encyclopedia* help to illustrate the history of the Church, its role in modern societies, and the many magnificent works of art it has inspired.

SPECIAL FEATURES

Subject Overview Articles. For the convenience and guidance of the reader, the *New Catholic Encyclopedia* contains several brief articles outlining the scope of major fields: "Theology, Articles on," "Liturgy, Articles on," "Jesus Christ, Articles on," etc.

Cross-References. The cross-reference system in the *NCE* serves to direct the reader to related material in other articles. The appearance of a name or term in small capital letters in text indicates that there is an article of that title elsewhere in the encyclopedia. In some cases, the name of the related article has been inserted at the appropriate point as a *see* reference: (*see* THOMAS AQUINAS, ST.). When a further aspect of the subject is treated under another title, a *see also* reference is placed at the end of the article. In addition to this extensive cross-reference system, the comprehensive index in volume 15 will greatly increase the reader's ability to access the wealth of information contained in the encyclopedia.

Abbreviations List. Following common practice, books and versions of the Bible as well as other standard works by selected authors have been abbreviated throughout the text. A guide to these abbreviations follows this preface.

The Editors

Abbreviations

The system of abbreviations used for the works of Plato, Aristotle, St. Augustine, and St. Thomas Aquinas is as follows: Plato is cited by book and Stephanus number only, e.g., Phaedo 79B; Rep. 480A. Aristotle is cited by book and Bekker number only, e.g., Anal. post. 72b 8–12; Anim. 430a 18. St. Augustine is cited as in the Thesaurus Linguae Latinae, e.g., C. acad. 3.20.45; Conf. 13.38.53, with capitalization of the first word of the title. St. Thomas is cited as in scholarly journals, but using Arabic numerals. In addition, the following abbreviations have been used throughout the encyclopedia for biblical books and versions of the Bible.

Books

Acts	Acts of the Apostles
Am	Amos
Bar	Baruch
1–2 Chr	1 and 2 Chronicles (1 and 2 Paralipomenon in Septuagint and Vulgate)
Col	Colossians
1–2 Cor	1 and 2 Corinthians
Dn	Daniel
Dt	Deuteronomy
Eccl	Ecclesiastes
Eph	Ephesians
Est	Esther
Ex	Exodus
Ez	Ezekiel
Ezr	Ezra (Esdras B in Septuagint; 1 Esdras in Vulgate)
Gal	Galatians
Gn	Genesis
Hb	Habakkuk
Heb	Hebrews
Hg	Haggai
Hos	Hosea
Is	Isaiah
Jas	James
Jb	Job
Jdt	Judith
Jer	Jeremiah
Jgs	Judges
Jl	Joel
Jn	John
1–3 Jn	1, 2, and 3 John
Jon	Jonah
Jos	Joshua
Jude	Jude
1–2 Kgs	1 and 2 Kings (3 and 4 Kings in Septuagint and Vulgate)
Lam	Lamentations
Lk	Luke
Lv	Leviticus
Mal	Malachi (Malachias in Vulgate)
1–2 Mc	1 and 2 Maccabees
Mi	Micah
Mk	Mark
Mt	Matthew
Na	Nahum
Neh	Nehemiah (2 Esdras in Septuagint and Vulgate)
Nm	Numbers
Ob	Obadiah
Phil	Philippians
Phlm	Philemon
Prv	Proverbs
Ps	Psalms
1–2 Pt	1 and 2 Peter
Rom	Romans
Ru	Ruth
Rv	Revelation (Apocalypse in Vulgate)
Sg	Song of Songs
Sir	Sirach (Wisdom of Ben Sira; Ecclesiasticus in Septuagint and Vulgate)
1–2 Sm	1 and 2 Samuel (1 and 2 Kings in Septuagint and Vulgate)
Tb	Tobit
1–2 Thes	1 and 2 Thessalonians
Ti	Titus
1–2 Tm	1 and 2 Timothy
Wis	Wisdom
Zec	Zechariah
Zep	Zephaniah

Versions

Apoc	Apocrypha
ARV	American Standard Revised Version
ARVm	American Standard Revised Version, margin
AT	American Translation
AV	Authorized Version (King James)
CCD	Confraternity of Christian Doctrine
DV	Douay-Challoner Version

ERV	English Revised Version	NJB	New Jerusalem Bible
ERVm	English Revised Version, margin	NRSV	New Revised Standard Version
EV	English Version(s) of the Bible	NT	New Testament
JB	Jerusalem Bible	OT	Old Testament
LXX	Septuagint	RSV	Revised Standard Version
MT	Masoretic Text	RV	Revised Version
NAB	New American Bible	RVm	Revised Version, margin
NEB	New English Bible	Syr	Syriac
NIV	New International Version	Vulg	Vulgate

J

JUDAH

Fourth son of Jacob by Leah. Judah [Heb. *y^ehûdâ*, praised, object of praise, according to the popular etymology given in Gn 29.35; 49.8, but probably in origin a place name (Noth, 56)], prominent in the Joseph narratives, is the eponymous ancestor of the tribe inhabiting southern Palestine, whence came the family of David.

Patriarch. In the Joseph narratives Judah plays a prominent role; he intervened with his brothers and offered a compromise solution to save Joseph's life (Gn 37.26–28); he stood as surety for Benjamin before Jacob (Gn 43.8–10) and assumed the role of spokesman for the brothers in Egypt (Gn 44.16, 18–34). The narrative of his marital life and his five sons indirectly alludes to the presence of foreign strains in the tribe [Gn 38.1–30; (Bright, 123)].

Tribe. Numerically the largest of the Exodus tribes under Moses (Nm 1.26–27; 26.19–20), Judah, according to the Pentateuchal PRIESTLY WRITERS, traveled east of the meeting tent beside Issachar and Zabulon on the march from Sinai (Nm 2.3–9) and served as the vanguard of the Israelite march through Moab (Nm 10.14). The warlike tribe of Judah (cf. Gn 49.8–9) played a leading role in the conquest of Canaan and, together with Simeon and some lesser clans, gained possession of southern Palestine (Jgs 1.3–20). Bounded on the east by the Dead Sea, on the north by Benjamin and Dan, Judah's territory extended west to the Mediterranean and to the south along a line from the base of the Dead Sea to the Wadi of Egypt and thence to the coast (Jos 15.1–13; 19.2, 9). Unable to expel the Jebusites from Jerusalem and thwarted by the powerful Philistines, Judah was forced to settle in the relatively secure and agriculturally rich central hill country, achieving complete domination of this territory only during the reign of David (Jos 15.63; Jgs 1.1–20; 2 Sm 5.6–10). The Judaites eventually absorbed Simeon and other smaller, previously settled clans into the tribal organization. Their relatively inaccessible land isolated the Judaites somewhat from affairs of their kinsmen (Dt 33.7;

De Vaux, 95). They do not figure in the Israelite coalition force that defeated Sisera's army (Jgs 5). They contributed but one judge, Othniel, to Israelite history (Jgs 3.7–11), though they led the Israelite attack on their Benjaminite kinsmen (Jgs 20.18). Harassment by the PHILISTINES, reflected in the SAMSON narratives (Jgs 15.9–15; cf. also Jgs 3.31; 10.7–9), was their constant preoccupation until David's rout of this foe. During Saul's reign, DAVID, a Judahite, gained many adherents among his tribesmen who, upon Saul's death (*c.* 1000 B.C.), supported him as king (1 Sm 18.16; 2 Sm 2.4). With the fall of Saul's house, David was acclaimed king by all Israel and became the center of Israelite unity (2 Sm 5.5). After the secession of the northern tribes in 922 B.C., as well as during the abortive revolts of Absalom (2 Sm 15.1–18.18) and Sheba (20.1–22), Judah remained faithful to David and his dynasty. Judah, in fact, along with most of Benjamin, became identified with the Southern Kingdom and bestowed on it its tribal name (1 Kgs 12.20). The parallel histories of the kingdoms depict a relationship of constant friction erupting periodically into civil war or tempered in time of common interests to uneasy alliance. Compared to the Northern Kingdom, Judah in size, wealth, and power was of less account. However, in a theological light Judah was important for two reasons: the permanence of the Davidic line, which, as prophetically presented in Jacob's Oracles (Gn 49.10) and confirmed to David (2 Sm 7.12–17), produced Israel's ideal king, the Messiah, and the relative purity of Judah's Yahwism fostered under Isaiah and his successors, which surviving Judah's fall and exile (587–538 B.C.), produced the religious climate for the advent of the Messiah.

Bibliography: G. A. BUTTRICK, ed. *The Interpreters' Dictionary of the Bible*, 4 v. (Nashville 1962), 2:1003–04. *Encyclopedic Dictionary of the Bible*, tr. and adap. by L. HARTMAN (New York 1963), 1225–27. R. DE VAUX, *Ancient Israel, Its Life and Institutions*, tr. J. MCHUGH (New York 1961) 6, 20, 95–97. J. BRIGHT, *A History of Israel* (Philadelphia 1959). M. NOTH, *The History of Israel*, tr. P. R. ACKROYD (New York 1960). Y. AHARONI, ''The Province List of Judah,'' *Vetus Testamentum* 9 (Leiden 1959) 225–246.

[R. BARRETT]

JUDAH HA-NASI

Head of Palestinian Jewry and codifier of the MISH-NAH; b. probably in Galilee, *c.* 135; d. Galilee, *c.* 220. Judah was the son of Simeon II ben Gamaliel II, who was the grandson of GAMALIEL (mentioned in Acts 5.34; 22.3), who was in turn the grandson of Hillel. As the patriarch or head of Palestinian Jewry, Judah received as a permanent epithet the title ha-Nasi (the Prince), originally given to the president of the Great Sanhedrin in Jerusalem. In the Mishnah he is referred to simply as Rabbi (the teacher par excellence), and in the GEMARAH he is often called Rabbenu (our teacher) or Rabbenu ha-kadosh (our saintly teacher). He was instructed in the HALAKAH of the Oral Law by the most famous rabbis of his time, but he summed up his experience as a student, and later as a teacher, in the words: "Much of the Law have I learned from my teachers, more from my colleagues, but most of all from my students" (*Mak.* 10a).

According to his contemporaries, humility and fear of sin were his dominant traits. Although he was very rich, he led a simple and unassuming life because he was convinced that "he who accepts the pleasures of this world is deprived of the pleasures of the world to come" [*Avot de-Rabbi Natan* 28, ed. S. Schechter (New York 1945) 85]. When he succeeded his father as leader of the Jews in Palestine, he established the seat of the patriarchate and the academy, first at Bet Shearim and later at Sepphoris. (Both of these places are within a ten mile radius of Nazareth.) He conducted the patriarchate with royal dignity, and his authority was recognized by the Romans as well as by the Jews. His tomb was discovered in one of the catacombs of Bet Shearim during the excavations made there in 1953 [*Israel Exploration Journal* 4 (1956) 88–107].

Rabbi Judah's greatest and lasting contribution to JU-DAISM was his compilation and codification of the Oral Law in the collection of legal sayings called the Mishnah. Other collected teachings of earlier rabbis had been attempted before his time, but his collection soon eclipsed these and became the sole authoritative expression of the Halakah. Until his time, the traditional interpretation of the Mosaic Law was handed down orally, and hence was known as the Oral Law as distinctive from the written Law of Moses. Judah's revolutionary procedure consisted of recording the Oral Law in writing (in Mishnaic Hebrew). The earlier transmitters of the Oral Law, the Tannaim (repeaters), belonged to different schools that held variant opinions. This resulted in uncertainty as to what was really binding, and the divergent opinions ascribed to the ancient sages could be accepted or rejected at will. Judah's main contribution lay in the judicious selections he made from the copious material at his dispos-

al. Since the publication of his Mishnah at the end of the second or beginning of the third century, the primary pursuit of Jewish sages has been commenting on its contents.

See Also: TALMUD.

Bibliography: W. BACHER, *The Jewish Encyclopedia.* ed. J. SINGER (New York 1901–06) 7:333–33. D. J. BORNSTEIN, *Encyclopaedia Judaica: Das Judentum in Geschichte und Gegenwart.* (Berlin 1928–34) 8:1023–35. L. LAZARUS, *Universal Jewish Encyclopedia* (New York 1939–44) 6: 229–230. K. SCHUBERT, *Lexikon für Theologie und Kirche,* ed. J. HOFER and K. RAHNER (Freiberg 1957–65) 5:889. A. GUTTMANN, ''The Patriarch Judah I: His Birth and Death,'' *Hebrew Union College Annual* 25 (1954) 239–261.

[M. J. STIASSNY]

JUDAISM

The term Judaism admits of various meanings. Rarely, it denotes the identity of an individual Jew (as, ''He is aware of his Judaism'') or an indeterminate bond among all Jews; occasionally, the whole of Jewry; more often, the manifold expression of Jewish history or culture; and commonly, the sum total of commandments, rites, traditions, and beliefs that make up the Jewish religion. Even in its religious signification, the term is not univocal. Taken broadly, it encompasses the life, worship, and faith of the Jewish people of all times, beginning with the Patriarchs and Prophets. More precisely, it refers to the Jewish religion as it developed after the Babylonian Exile. The latter meaning is the topic of this article. (On the older Israelite religion, *see* ISRAEL, 3.)

As Israel's postexilic way, Judaism has known diverse religious experiences, gone through several phases, and expressed itself through a number of currents. There is something unique about it. Fitting none of the usual categories, Judaism is a people religion: a religion limited to one people, and a people so tied to that religion as to exist for and through it. [The word people must not be taken here in a narrow sense. In post-Biblical no less than in Biblical times, Gentiles have sought refuge under the wings of the God of Israel (Ru 2.12). Not only individuals but also a whole people, such as the KHAZARS, have become part of Judaism.] True, not all Jews live by their traditions; still, religion is so woven into the texture of their history that they are tied together by a spiritual bond and not merely by blood.

Birth. Judaism, in the strict sense of the word, was born when, under the leadership of EZRA, the Israelites bound themselves to walk in the ways of God's Torah (Neh 10.29). Probably toward the end of the 5th century B.C. a caravan had brought Ezra from Babylon to Jerusalem. There this priest and scribe began to teach the statutes and ordinances of Torah to those returned from captivity (Ezr 7.10). Thus the industrious scribe—student, knower, and expounder of the Law—took the place of the stormy prophet. As the rabbis have it, with the death of the last Prophets, the Holy Spirit departed from Israel; divine inspiration withdrew, but the men in Israel could still hear ''a small voice [coming from above]'' (*bat qôl*, literally ''daughter of sound,'' i.e., echo; e.g., *Soṭ.* 48b). For fear that the Israelites would not remain constant in the service of the Lord, Ezra ordered them to expel their ''foreign,'' i.e., pagan, wives. The presence of such women threatened faith in and worship of the one God. Ezra was convinced that, as God's ''special possession'' (Ex 19.5), Israel was bound to keep aloof from peoples and lands tainted by idolatry (Ezr ch. 9–10). *See* IDOLATRY (IN THE BIBLE).

Seminal Ideas. Ezra's reform was the starting point of a long development. Seminal forces, small at first and growing slowly, gave Judaism its special character.

God. Prior to the Exile, Israel's belief in the living God—the Lord of history intervening in Israel's life, the One before and above man yet close to him, the One far yet near—had frequently been couched in anthropomorphic language. *See* ANTHROPOMORPHISM (IN THE BIBLE). Without denying God's peerlessness, the anthropomorphisms of Scripture proclaimed Him as the God who loves, seeks, and cares. Postexilic generations, however, must have felt some embarrassment at language that seemed all too human. According to the TARGUMS, it was not God who ''walked in the garden'' (Gn 3.8) but the *memrā*, His word; it was the word, not God Himself, whom Moses called ''a consuming fire'' (Dt 4.24). By the 3d century B.C., the name YAHWEH was considered forbidden to human lips; ADONAI (My Lord) took its place. The Alexandrian Jewish translators of the Old Testament who produced the SEPTUAGINT simply wrote ὁ Κύριος (the Lord). Other circumlocutions were ''the Name,'' ''Heaven,'' or ''Power,'' all of which are echoed in the New Testament: ''hallowed be thy name'' (Mt 6.9), ''the kingdom of heaven'' (Matthew *passim*), ''the Son of Man sitting at the right hand of the Power'' (Mt 26.64).

No matter how deep the emphasis on God's transcendence may have been, Judaism would not be what it is if the intensely personal God had been turned into a remote deity. The later rabbis, too, stressed that God was unlike man, but at the same time they tried to express the warm relationship between God and Israel through concepts such as the SHEKINAH, His indwelling among creatures. The Shekinah was said to go with Israel into exile, to dwell among the people even in their uncleanness, and to weep at the sadness that followed Jerusalem's destruction (*Meg.* 29a; *Yom.* 56b; *Lam. Rabbah* 1.46). In this

Breast Plate for Scroll of Law. (©Hulton-Deutsch Collection/ CORBIS)

concept Judaism developed a counterpoise to the Christian message that God had come in the flesh to carry man's burden.

Israel. With the expulsion of pagan wives under Ezra, there began a growing, though at no time complete, isolation of the Jewish people from its neighbors. From then on, the Biblical belief that Israel was chosen for the sake of all the earth (Gn 12.3) and the noncanonical notion that the world was made for Israel's sake (Assumption of Moses 1.12) rivaled each other. Though the latter may suggest that the heavens and the earth were created for Israel's honor only, this and similar sayings must not be taken with unimaginative literalness. They are often no more than homiletic exaggerations. This one is not necessarily a sign of national vain glory; its underlying thought is rather that the material world is not an end in itself, that all things must serve the salvation of the just (cf. 2 Baruch 15.7)—an eminently Christian idea, too. Nonetheless, there is danger in such affirmations. Though Scripture never tires of proclaiming Israel's unmerited election (e.g., Dt 7.7; Ez 16.3–14), the assumption that it had proved its merit gained ascendancy in postexilic times. A Jewish legend (e.g., *'Avodah Zarah* 2b) has it that Torah was accepted by the chosen people, but only after it had been offered to all the nations and had been

The Western Wall in Jerusalem, the last remains of the Second Temple of Herod. (©David H. Wells/CORBIS)

rejected by them. (On the use of the term Torah without the definite article, see below.)

The terms pagan and sinner were frequently synonymous—a usage that prevailed even in early New Testament times. In his Pentecostal speech Peter reminded the men of Jerusalem that they had crucified Jesus "through the hands of wicked men" (Acts 2.23). The wicked men ("men without the Law," according to the Greek text) are Pilate and his soldiers, all unbelievers in the true God. When Scripture calls Israel God's very own, dearer than all other people (Ex 19.5), it did not pronounce it superior to the Gentiles. No doubt the religious and moral superiority of the Jewish people over the pagan world was real; still, to assert it was not altogether salutary.

"Turn to me and be saved," the Prophet had cried in Yahweh's name to all the ends of the earth (Is 45.22). But the prophetic word announced also a day of vengeance when God would crush the nations in His wrath [Is 63.4, 6; *see* DAY OF THE LORD (ESCHATOLOGY)]. This twofold attitude is heightened in Jewish APOCALYPTIC literature. One vision has it that all Gentiles will become just, worship the one God, and share in the future messianic blessings (e.g., 1 Enoch 10.21); another, that the Messiah will destroy the godless nations, the oppressors

of Israel, with the word of His mouth (e.g., Psalms of Solomon 17.27). One would gravely misunderstand this dire prediction if he forgot that the bitterness spelled out here is common to all peoples trodden under foot.

Torah. Ezra's great work was to teach and expound the Torah. The Torah stands primarily for the Pentateuch, now and then for the entire Old Testament. In later literature, it embraces the whole tradition, written as well as unwritten. (Some scholars distinguish between "the Torah," the five books of Moses, and "Torah"—without the article—the whole body of law built on them by the rabbis, in other words, Biblical and Talmudic law.) A meaningful English rendering of Torah as found in the Bible is "revelation"; its literal sense is "instruction," "guidance." It is God's instruction on what He would have His creature do in order to be just in His eyes, His guidance to Israel on how to follow Him on the road to holiness. The core of this revelation, the Ten Commandments, is surrounded by other laws and norms, statutes, or decrees; "You shall" is their idiom. Since a large part of the Pentateuch is legal in character, Torah came to be understood as law. Such is the translation of the Septuagint and the understanding of later Jewish tradition.

Though not revealed till Sinai, the Law was considered a living being, identical with the wisdom that existed before time (Prv 8.22–31). Like wisdom, the Torah was the craftsman at God's side; it served Him as the plan according to which He created the world (*Ab.* 3.14; *Gen. Rabbah* 1. 1). The Law was perfect and immutable; yet it had to be interpreted, supplemented, and adapted to the exigencies of time. There evolved, then, alongside the written law, sometimes overshadowing it, the unwritten law, "the tradition of the ancients" (Mt 15.2). On the one hand, rules were mitigated so as to make the Law workable; on the other, an ever-higher "fence" was built around it (*Ab.* 1.1)—a protective wall, with stop signs and danger signals, definitions and directives—that, to forestall transgression, left little room for personal decision. Although for the devout the Law was life and joy, the many—those, e.g., whose livelihood depended on the land—found its demands impossible to carry out. As the number of precepts increased, it had to be studied, too, before it could be kept. Hence the unlettered were thought of as the ungodly (see Jn 7.49).

The Final Events. Though the postexilic period was marked by an inner withdrawal from other nations, the ever-widening emigration of Jews to many lands created a vast Jewish DIASPORA whose synagogues became, paradoxically enough, proselytizing centers among the Gentiles. Moreover, foreign invasion and domination, as well as encounter with the two great cultures of Persia and Greece, helped the flowering of certain Biblical seeds, particularly that of hope.

The Prophets had seen the past as herald of the future: the Exodus of old foretelling a new exodus, the reign of David, that of another David (e.g., Is ch. 35; Jer 23.5–6). As time went on, some in Israel looked for a new priest to bring blessing to the people or for a righteous leader who would himself be a source of righteousness. Many others dreamed of a mighty deliverer who would free them from pagan tyranny. Whereas the majority of the people expected a Warrior-Messiah, a scattered few longed for the Chosen One, hidden in God's presence since the beginning of the world and before it, who would soon come in the likeness of a man, yet bearing a face "full of graciousness, like one of the holy angels" (1 Enoch 46.1).

For a long time the glittering magic and morbid sensuousness pervading so much of pagan fantasy about the afterlife had kept Israel from a fuller understanding of the world and life to come. In the centuries preceding the coming of Jesus, however, the hope in a blessed immortality, the bodily resurrection of the just and their share in God's triumph and reign, erupted in many hearts (*see* RESURRECTION OF THE DEAD). Full force was given to the Isaian words: "Your dead shall live, their corpses rise; awake and sing, you who lie in the dust" (26.19).

First Christian Century. These trends did not spring up at the same time, nor were they all universally accepted. In fact, 1st-century Judaism was intensely diversified, full of unrest and strife.

Sadducees. At the center was official Judaism, the small but powerful party of the SADDUCEES. Made up of the leading priests, the notables, the influential and wealthy families, they were defenders of the *status quo.* Clinging to the letter of Scripture, they rejected doctrinal development as well as the oral tradition. Thus the world to come was of little interest to them; they even mocked the hope that the dead would rise (see Mk 12.18–19). But their spiritual tepidity did not hinder them from upholding a rigid and stern jurisprudence. In their self-reliance they thought of man as the captain of his soul, the architect of his fortune (see Josephus, *Ant.* 13.5.9). As they disdained the common people, so were they disdained in turn. Since the grandeur of the Temple was their life, they disappeared with it in A.D. 70.

Pharisees. Pitted against these men of birth were the men of ritual perfection, the PHARISEES, the successors to the HASIDAEANS, those "stout men in Israel" who, at the time of the Machabean uprising, were passionately devoted to the Law (1 Mc 2.42). As their name (*perûšîm,* separated ones) indicates, the Pharisees kept apart from the masses who would not or could not observe the many precepts regarding ritual purity. The pharisaic movement drew its strength from the *ḥăbûrôt,* companies of like-minded men who encouraged one another in the exact fulfillment of the demands made on the pious Israelite: his food, his clothing, the very walls of his house; indeed, his entire life was under the regimen of the Law.

Despite the scrupulous attention the Pharisees gave to the Torah, they believed in a certain evolution of the Torah-bound life and tried to adjust the Law to changing circumstances. They were far from uniform in their interpretation. In the 1st century B.C. there were two great competing schools: the one of the unbending Shammai and the other of the more compassionate Hillel. When confronted, for example, with the authority of truth and its conflict with that sister of love, courtesy, in daily life, the two decided differently. The first would not permit wedding guests to call a homely bride pretty, whereas the latter held that every bride ought to be looked upon as beautiful and praised (*Ket.* 16b-17a). Their differences, mainly of a casuistic nature, were strong enough to produce the byword that "the Torah has become as two Torahs" (*Sanh.* 88b). In the end the camp of moderation prevailed over the more rigid school.

Most of the teachers and preachers, i.e., most of the men who determined the worship of the synagogues in the land, were Pharisees, a fact that explains the influence of the Pharisees on the people despite their aloofness. A saying attributed to the later Rabbi AKIBA BEN JOSEPH is almost a sum of their beliefs: ''All is foreseen, yet free will is given; the world is judged by goodness but all [judgment] is according to the amount of work'' (*Ab.* 3.22). God is sovereign, the Pharisees held, yet man is free. Man is to be judged after death; paradise, purgatory, or hell will then be his lot. In the end God's reign will appear when He will be all in all as the just rise to glory.

Many Pharisees served God faithfully, in genuine devotion, even with a gentle spirit (see Jn 3.1; Acts 5.34; 23.6). When the Gospels charge Pharisees with hypocrisy, this must be taken as prophetic speech, not as a scholarly appraisal of the entire movement, much less of every individual. The Talmud, too, distinguishes between the Pharisees moved by love of God and those driven, knowingly or unknowingly, by love of self (*Soṭ.* 22b). The faults castigated in the Gospels, e.g., those of equating things essential with nonessential or commandment with preference and even confusing one with the other (see Mt 23.16–18), are pitfalls that threaten the life of piety everywhere. Although Jesus and the early Church disagreed with the Pharisees on the function and the interpretation of the Law, they gave new weight and direction to other pharisaic beliefs.

Essenes. Whereas the Sadducees held the center of Judaism and the Pharisees struggled to seize it, the ESSENES deliberately remained at its periphery. Without deciding which of the two is the legitimate heir, one can trace the beginnings of the Essenes, like those of the Pharisees, to the early Hasidaeans (1 Mc 2.42). For some scholars, the term Essenes is a synonym for members of the QUMRAN COMMUNITY; but probably it is a generic name for several kindred groups devoted to an ascetic life. With the monks of Qumran it was a life of obedience, poverty, and chastity; of common study, common worship, and common meals; of strictest submission to the Law, according to a rule. Though they allowed no traffic with the common people, whom they considered unclean and thus enemies of God; though they despised the Sadducees, particularly the high priestly clique, as a band of usurpers; and though they shunned the Pharisees as ''preachers of falsehood'' and ''seekers after smooth things'' (1QH 2.32), the radiance of their lives broke through the walls of their ''cloister.'' For all the tremendous differences of some of their teachings from those of the infant Church, their influence upon the Church was considerable. Yet the community had a sudden end at the hands of Roman legionaries.

Zealots. Another peripheral movement, though a vocal and active one, was that of the ZEALOTS. Zeal for God, His law, and His glory (see Acts 22.3) has always been a distinctive mark of all Jewish piety. The zeal of the Zealots, however, was of a militant kind. Although the Pharisees eagerly awaited the collapse of the Roman Empire, the end of all godless men, and the coming of the messianic reign with its lasting peace, they did not consider it their task to hasten these events. On the contrary, the Zealots, an extreme wing split off from the main pharisaic body, held it their duty to intervene. ''God alone is Lord'' was their creed, and ''Freedom!'' was their battle cry. No one in Israel, they insisted, may obey an emperor who arrogates to himself the homage that is God's due.

The Zealots supported their conviction by violence. Some of them seem to have stabbed their opponents, particularly Jewish collaborators, to death in broad daylight. Because of their favored weapon, concealed in their robes, they were known as dagger men (σικάριοι). As ''underground fighters,'' lawless rebels against the Roman order, they are called λησταί (robbers, bandits, revolutionists) both by the Jewish historian Flavius JOSEPHUS (*Bell. Jud.* 2.253–254) and by the Evangelists (Jn 18.40; Mt 27.38, 44; *see* BARABBAS). Their wrathfulness was the ferment in the people's ''holy war'' against the Romans, whose last procurator, Gessius Florus, had plundered the Temple treasury, probably to make up a tax deficit. This uprising (A.D. 66–73) led to disaster; together with the later one of BAR KOKHBA (132–135), it cost the Jewish people the last vestige of political autonomy and cost Jerusalem its role as the spiritual center of all the Jews wherever they dwelt.

Opposition and Unity. There were other groups at the border of Jewish life, e.g., the penitential movements in the Jordan region, of which John the Baptist's was foremost. The Talmud speaks somewhat disparagingly of those who submerge themselves in water every morning (*Ber.* 22a). There are no exact statistics on the various movements. At the time of Christ, Palestine may have had about 1.5 million Jewish inhabitants, a small number compared to the estimated 4 or 4.5 million Jews already dispersed throughout the Roman Empire (seven percent of its total population). According to Josephus, who describes the major Jewish Sects, the number of Pharisees was 6,000, of the Essenes 4,000 (*Ant.* 13.5.9; 10.6; 17.2.4; 18.1.3–4; 20.9.1; *Bell. Jud.* 2.8.2–14). Although his figures cannot always be relied on, these estimates give at least an idea of the comparative strength of some of the leading movements. But they tell nothing of the extent, much less of the attitude of the people at large, the ''country folk'' (*'ammê hā'āreṣ*). In the New Testament some Pharisees are quoted as saying of them: ''This crowd, which does not know the Law, is accursed'' (Jn

7.49). The opposition among the four major groups was no less fierce. Strangely enough, the Law that united them also separated them. Yet as many-layered and strife-ridden as Judaism was, it was held together by the common confession: "Hear O Israel! The Lord is our God, the Lord alone!" (Dt 6.4).

Rabbinical Judaism. Wishing to have no part in the suicidal revolt of A.D. 66, Jewish Christians retreated to Pella beyond the Jordan. When the Roman army beleaguered the Holy City, Jews in their despair turned on Jews, one group excelling the other in violence. Thousands upon thousands died of starvation and disease, were crucified, deported, or sold into slavery. The ancient estimates of those killed and captured vary from more than half a million to more than a million.

Victory of Pharisaism. One man, however, was able to turn this disaster into a triumph. Before the city fell, Rabbi JOHANAN BEN ZAKKAI had himself carried out in a coffin. He went to the Roman camp and obtained the permission of its commander, Vespasian, to open a school for the study of Torah in the coastal town of Jamnia. This daring move enabled Judaism to survive; or more exactly, it established Pharisaism, rather the school of Hillel, as the foundation of all future forms of Judaism.

Great Bet Din. Rabbi Johanan was joined by other rabbis. Under his presidency, the Great Bet Din (*bet dîn*, house of judgment), a sort of supreme court or council, continued some of the functions of the extinct Sanhedrin. In the course of time it fixed the calendar and the canon of Scripture, from which it rejected the so-called Apocrypha—books contained in the Septuagint, such as Sirach, Tobit, 1 and 2 Maccabees—as well as the Gospels and other "heretical" writings (see Moore, 1:186–187). The Great Bet Din had to tackle also the many problems arising from the fact that at least one third of Torah, the laws pertaining to Temple worship, could no longer be carried out. The groundwork was laid, therefore, for teachings such as these: study of the laws on sacrifice takes the place of the sacrifices themselves; God accepts the former as if the latter had been offered (see *Pes.* K 60b). Since the Temple was destroyed, prayer, "the service of the heart," acquired the atoning power that had resided in the institutions of old. "We have no prophet, no priest, no sacrifice, no sanctuary, no altar to help win forgiveness for us," R. Isaac mourned; "from the day the Temple was laid waste, nothing was left to us but prayer. Lord, hearken then, and forgive" (*Midr. Teh.* 5.7).

Under Johanan's successor, Gamaliel II, Jewish Christians were expelled from the Synagogue by an ingenious strategem. A curse on renegades, heretics, and Nazarenes (i.e., Christians) was introduced into the daily prayers: that they be without hope and stricken from the book of life. No follower of Christ could have repeated this imprecation without committing spiritual suicide.

Talmud. At the turn of the 1st Christian century, Rabbi JUDAH HA-NASI, then head of the Great Bet Din, gathered the oral traditions and probably had them put into writing. The compilation was named MISHNAH for the method applied, i.e., repetition; it contained the important halakic (legal) teachings (*see* HALAKAH) of the preceding generations of rabbis, the Tannaim, or traditioners. The Mishnah soon became the standard work of study and investigation in the academies of Palestine and Babylon. The men who commented on it, the Amoraim, or expositors, produced the GEMARAH, or completion. Both, Mishnah and Gemarah, make up the TALMUD, which is, therefore, basically halakic. Haggadic material, however (*see* HAGGADAH), i.e., spiritual and moral reflections, together with practical counsels, metaphysical speculations, historical narratives, legends, scientific observations, etc., appear in it as well. The Talmud was completed at the end of the 4th century in Galilee and a century later in Babylonia; hence the two versions, the Palestinian and the Babylonian Talmuds. The Talmud is not the only compilation of rabbinic thought. There are, e.g., collections of haggadic commentaries on the Biblical books, the Midrashim (*see* MIDRASHIC LITERATURE).

What makes the understanding of the Talmud difficult is that it is a code of laws, a case book, and a digest of discussions and disputes that went on among various rabbis; interspersed are reflections of every kind; its contents are at times as motley as a daily newspaper. Now and then the opinions recorded are dissimilar or even contradictory. Quite often, the rabbis consider a man ignorant of the Law unworthy of trust, unreliable as witness in a court, unfit to be an orphan's protector. Yet the compilers of the Talmud rejoice in telling of the power a simple man has in heaven. During a drought, Honi (1st century B.C.) drew a circle around himself and said to God, "I swear by Your great name that I will not budge from here until You have mercy upon Your children," and rain fell (*Ta'an.* 23a). Moreover, the Talmud engages in a great deal of casuistry, and all casuistry tends to be tortured; still, in admonishing its readers not to wrong another man through words, it calls moral demands that cannot be codified "things entrusted to the heart" (*Bava Metzia* 58b).

So great is the occasional contrast between rabbinical statements that, in one place, it can be said that the nations' charity is but sin since they practice it for no other reason than to boast; in another, that the Holy Spirit rests on a man, be he Gentile or Jew, according to his deeds (see Montefiore and Loewe, 562–563, 557). Many rabbinic sayings are, therefore, tentative or are located in a definite situation so that evaluation of rabbinic thought is a special science, indeed, an art. It is not only the variety of opinions recorded in the Talmud and other rabbinical literature that hamper their appreciation, but also the style—succinct, telegraphic, often bare to the bone—makes the Talmud inaccessible without a guide. Such guidance was provided by the heads of the two leading rabbinic academies of Babylonia, titled Geonim, "illustrious ones." From the 6th to the 11th centuries their authority was supreme all over Babylonia—which in the meantime had become the center of all Jewry—and thus, for most of that time, in other countries as well. Yet at the very moment the rule of talmudic Judaism seemed unassailable, it was contested by the Karaites, schismatics who, in the 8th century, repudiated the entire rabbinic tradition.

Medieval Thinkers. One who took up the defense of rabbinic Judaism against the Karaites was the Egyptian-born SA'ADIA BEN JOSEPH (882–942), "the father of Jewish philosophy." In his main work, *Beliefs and Opinions,* he propounded the unity of revelation and reason. The new element in his thought is its debt to Moslem theology. Sa'adia thus ushers in a line of medieval thinkers whose thought is born of a meeting with Moslem and Christian theologies, Neoplatonism, or Aristotelianism. With AVICEBRON (IBN GABIROL), in the first half of the 11th century, the focal point of Jewish thought shifts to Spain. According to him all things emanate from God as the first principle, not by necessity but through His loving will. Avicebron's depth may be shown by the climactic stanza of one of his poems:

> When all Thy face is dark, And Thy just angers rise, From Thee I turn to Thee And find love in Thine eyes.

The first to treat Jewish ethics systematically was Avicebron's contemporary IBN PAQŪDA. His *Duties of the Heart* became a guide to the inner life for untold numbers of Jews. Rather than defend Judaism, the poet-philosopher JUDAH ben Samuel ha-Levi (*c.* 1080–*c.* 1145) attempted to show its superiority over Christianity and ISLAM. Although he enjoyed the comforts of "the golden age of Spanish Jewry," he felt that the Jews were in exile and he dreamed of Zion. Jews, he held, bore the sufferings of the world; their restoration to the Holy Land would bring salvation to the entire earth. Yet he sang also: "Would I might behold His face within my heart!/ Mine eyes would never ask to look beyond."

The giant of Spanish-Jewish thinkers was the great Talmudist MAIMONIDES (Moses ben Maimon; 1135–1204). His work is many-sided; what made it original and influential, though at first bitterly opposed by Jews (his *Guide of the Perplexed* was burned), was the

attempt to reconcile Aristotle with Holy Scripture. As a young man, he tried to sum up Jewish faith in 13 principles: (1) God exists and is the Creator of all things; (2) He is one; (3) He is without a body; (4) He is eternal; (5) man is obliged to worship Him alone; (6) the words of the Prophets are to be believed; (7) Moses is the greatest among them; (8) the Torah was revealed by God to Moses; (9) it is unchangeable; (10) God knows all things; (11) He rewards and punishes man according to his deeds; (12) the Messiah will come; and (13) the dead will rise.

Unless he believes in these fundamental principles, a Jew cannot attain everlasting bliss, Maimonides held. Some theologians of his day disagreed with him on the selection of these principles, or on the reduction of Jewish belief to 13 articles, or even on the basic assumption that Judaism possesses dogmas, binding tenets. Still, his "creed" survived the disputes and was eventually embodied—not in its original form but in both a prose and a poetic version of later dates—in the Siddur, the Jewish daily prayerbook. The prose version, by an unknown author, begins with the words: "I believe [*ănî ma'ămîn*] with perfect faith that the Creator, blessed be His name, is the Author and Guide of everything that has been created, and that He alone has made, does make and will make all things." The poetic version by Daniel ben Judah of Rome is known by its first word, *Yigdal,* "Magnified and praised be the living God. . . ."

Significantly, the 13 principles were embodied in the liturgy of the synagogue. Any stress on Jewish faith without an accompanying emphasis on the sacredness of day, week, month, and year distorts the image of Judaism, at whose heart is *ăvōdâ* [(divine) service, (the) work (of honoring God)]. There is no fullness of Jewish life without the SABBATH and the festivals throughout the year—without their joy and their sorrow, without their penitential mood and their delight in God's grace, without Israel's appeal to His mercy and its assurance of His faithfulness, without the remembrance of the past and the expectation of the future. *See* FEASTS, RELIGIOUS; PASSOVER, FEAST OF; BOOTHS (TABERNACLES), FEAST OF; ATONEMENT, DAY OF (YOM KIPPUR); DEDICATION OF THE TEMPLE, FEAST OF; PURIM, FEAST OF.

Cabala. Swift and fragmentary though this survey is, mention must be made, at least, of the sum of Jewish mysticism, the CABALA. Mystical thoughts had appeared intermittently for centuries: in some apocalyptic works as far back as the 2d century B.C., in esoteric teachings found in the oldest midrashic literature, and in early pharisaic speculations on the work of creation and the throne of God, "the Divine Chariot" (see Ezekiel ch. 1). In the 11th century the mystical force so long underground came to the fore. By the 14th century the secrets of a few became the possession of many. In Christian mysticism the longing of the individual believer—irrevocably planted in the community of the faithful—for union with God prevails. In the Cabala (Kabbala) the personal element is hidden; "the Law of the Torah became a symbol of cosmic law, and the history of the Jewish people a symbol of the cosmic process" (Scholem, *On the Kabbalah . . .*, 2). The powerful hold of mystical trends on Jewish life is far greater than is generally assumed.

Among the devotees of cabalistic speculation were men as different as Joseph ben Ephraim CARO (1488–1575), the author of the *Shulchan Aruch* (Set Table); Shabbatai (Sabbatai) Sevi (Zevi; 1626–76), a false Messiah who, after having brought the Jewish masses everywhere to a high pitch of excitement, defected to Islam (*see* SHABATAÏSM); and the Baal Shem Tov (*c.* 1700–60), the founder of the Hasidic movement, whose message of joy, song, and love in God swept across the Jewish communities of eastern Europe. The *Shulchan Aruch,* based on Spanish authorities, such as Maimonides, but neglecting the traditions of central and eastern Europe, sought to fix the Law in all its minutiae forever, as it were. Theoretically, no rabbinic code can be considered final; Halakah is ever in a fluid state. In practice, however, the *Shulchan Aruch* has dominated Jewish life as if it were God's infallible word. Through its unifications of various legal teachings, it became the strongest cohesive bond among Orthodox Jews. But their clinging to demands that have become obsolete made it a barrier, too; thus, even the most legitimate quests for reform were rebuffed.

Modern Times. The experience of having been misled by a "Messiah" who became an apostate and put the Jewish hope to shame was more than many hearts could bear. For a time HASIDISM, with its comfort of God's constant presence in the daily life of every Jew, lifted the Jewish soul to new heights.

Emancipation. Yet the deception was a trauma not to be healed quickly. Weariness set in and the appeal of the outside world became stronger. For centuries Jews had lived within the confines of the GHETTO, whose walls oppressed as well as protected. These walls had given them the chance of leading their own lives; but as they began to tumble, the old life no longer seemed desirable. Not a few Western Jews welcomed the age of ENLIGHTENMENT. Moses Mendelssohn (1729–86), a ghetto-born philosopher, counseled his fellow Jews to adapt themselves to the customs and laws of the countries in which they lived; yet he urged them to remain loyal to the faith of their forefathers. He maintained that Judaism was not a revealed religion, only revealed legislation. He accept-

ed the Mosaic commandments and precepts as given to Jews in a supernatural way, but he recognized no eternal truths save those "comprehensible to human reason and demonstrable by the ability to think."

Cry for Reform. Ever since their loss of national sovereignty, Jews had lived at the fringe of history. All through the Middle Ages they had been a foreign body in a more or less unified society, objects of discriminatory measures, and victims of persecution. Suddenly emancipation—freedom, equality, status, and progress—beckoned before their eyes. An assembly of 110 notables convoked by Napoleon in 1806 marveled at the hidden plans of Divine Providence "changing the form of human affairs, giving comfort to the distressed, and raising the lowly out of the dust" (W. G. Plaut, *The Rise of Reform Judaism*, 72). Again, in 1844, the president of a rabbinic conference held at Braunschweig, Germany, proclaimed: "Let us understand the time and use it . . . [so] that our holy religion, purified of all dross and additions, cleansed of all that is merely local or ephemeral, of all disfigurations which adhere to it, will rise in new glory, to fulfill its mission to mold mankind into one brotherhood" (Plaut, 79).

Two years before, the Society of the Friends of Reform in Frankfurt had declared themselves in favor of unlimited progress in religious matters; they denied any authority to "the collection of controversies, dissertations, and prescriptions commonly called Talmud," and they repudiated the traditional hope of being led back to the land of their forefathers by a messiah. "We know no fatherland except that to which we belong by birth and citizenship," they proclaimed. (See Plaut, 52.)

Reaction. These and similar demands for an updating of Jewish worship, as well as the rejection of the Talmud's perennial authority and the novel actions taken, led to furious controversies. The promoters of the reform were denounced as deceitful or as lacking in scholarship. Bans were imposed by one side, only to be declared null and void by the other. Prohibitions were proclaimed against changing anything in the order of prayer, against using another language than Hebrew in Jewish worship, and against playing an instrument, e.g., an organ, in a synagogue. Observant Jews were warned against traffic with the dissenters; burial was refused to those who deviated from the practices of the past; the innovators were even denounced to the secular authorities. A prominent rabbi counseled the traditionalists of Hamburg: "Go to the government and ask them to humble these wanton people . . . [and to] stay the arm of the evildoers" (Plaut, 36).

Classical Reform in America. In the middle of the 19th century, Reform (Liberal or Progressive) Judaism was brought to the U.S. by German-born rabbis. Before it reached the proportions of the 20th century, it had to struggle, though by no means as hard as in the land of its birth. In 1885, 19 rabbis assembled in Pittsburgh, where they formulated their ideological stance, known as the Pittsburgh Platform, which, interestingly enough, the Central Conference of American Rabbis, the Reform rabbinical organization, never made its own, though the Platform reflected the thinking of its founders.

These were its principles. (1) Every religion is an attempt to grasp the infinite. Judaism presents the highest conception of the God idea. (2) The Bible is the record of the consecration of the Jewish people as priests of the one God and a potent instrument of religious and moral instruction. Though it reflects primitive ideas, modern discoveries are not antagonistic to the doctrines of Judaism. (3) The Mosaic legislation was a necessary system of training for the Jewish people during its national life in Palestine. In the modern world only its moral laws are binding. No ceremonies are to be retained except those of a sanctifying character. Everything not adaptable to modern civilization is to be rejected. (4) The Mosaic and rabbinical laws regarding diet or ritual purity are foreign to modern mental and spiritual outlooks. (5) The modern era of universal culture is a sign that Israel's great messianic hope is about to be realized. Hence, neither a return to Palestine nor a restoration of the ancient sacrificial system is desirable. (6) Judaism is a progressive religion, ever striving to be in accord with the postulates of reason. Christianity has a providential mission in the spreading of monotheistic and moral truths. (7) The soul of man is immortal but belief in bodily resurrection, hell, and paradise is to be rejected as not rooted in Judaism. (8) In the spirit of the Mosaic Law, which strives to regulate the relation between rich and poor, Jews are duty-bound to help solve the modern problems of social justice. (See Davis, 226–227).

Conservative Movement. American Reform Judaism rallied around the Pittsburgh Platform as the instrument that would take Jews "out of medieval darkness into the light of modern progress." But, as had happened in Germany, some reform-minded men felt they could not go all the way with the leaders of the reform. In their eyes the decisive principle of the Platform was the spirit of the age, not that of Jewish tradition. The Law was indeed a living tradition and thus open to change, they argued, but all changes had to be made in harmony with what went before. The totality of Jewish history—past, present, and future—or, as Solomon Schechter (1850–1915), the founder of Conservative Judaism, called it, "Catholic Israel," was ever to be the judge of true development. As the needs of the Jewish people are heeded, Jews dare not

forget the primacy of faith in God and the demands of the Torah.

While thus dismissing a static attitude, the historical school kept a deep reverence for the past and its ways. Its perspective became that of Conservative Judaism. (Its main organizations are the United Synagogue of America and the Rabbinical Assembly of America.) At first glance, it might be considered midway between Orthodoxy and Reform, but its direction is complex. It upholds the rabbinical architecture of life in its entirety, but it interprets it with a certain freedom. It honors the "creed" of Maimonides, but it is responsive to modern critical views. Many of its rabbis see the Messiah as an ideal or an age to come, rather than as a person. The idea of a "universal Israel" and its refusal to stand by any platform or series of tenets make it broad enough to harbor within its ranks the Reconstructionist Movement.

The great concern of Reconstructionism is the survival of the Jewish people; its approach is that of 20th-century pragmatism. In the eyes of Reconstructionists, God is not the supreme being but the process that makes for salvation; to believe is to reckon with life's creative forces as an organic unity and thus give meaning to life; Jewish religious practices are folkways rather than divine demands; and Judaism itself is a civilization of which religion is but a part, however important.

Modified Reform. Half a century after the Pittsburgh Platform, Reform Judaism found it necessary to modify that statement. Therefore, in 1937 the Columbus Platform was issued. Its framers no longer speak of the "God idea" but "of the One, living God, who rules the world through law and love . . . . Though transcending time and space, He is the indwelling Presence of the world." Man is His child and active co-worker. The new declaration still says that "revelation is a continuous process, confined to no one group and to no one age," but it calls the Torah "a depository of permanent spiritual ideas . . . , the dynamic source of the life of Israel." (See Finkelstein, 2:1327–89.) Earlier American Reform rabbis had flatly declared: "We consider ourselves no longer a nation but a religious community, and therefore expect neither a return to Palestine . . . nor the restoration of any of the laws concerning the Jewish State." (See Davis, 227.) Now they see in the rehabilitation of Palestine "the promise of renewed life for many of our brethren. We affirm the obligation of all Jewry to aid in its upbuilding as a Jewish homeland . . . , a haven of refuge for the oppressed [and] a center of Jewish culture and life."

Classical Reform rejected all that was contrary to modern views and habits. The Columbus Platform, however, demands "the preservation of the Sabbath, festivals, and holydays," and "the use of Hebrew, together with the vernacular, in our worship and instruction.'' Thus the way was paved for a deeper appreciation of traditional values and symbols, a move that is paralleled by a slow awakening in some Orthodox Jewish circles to the fact that not all rules or interpretations of the past are absolute and thus unalterable, that change and evil are not necessarily synonymous. Orthodoxy is by no means a monolithic body. It knows several strands, several philosophies of a life ruled by the Law. (Its major organizations are the Rabbinical Council of America and the Union of Orthodox Jewish Congregations of America.)

Differences in Modern Practice. Although the contrasts are less harsh in the 1960s than they were years ago, the differences remain. The traditional service is, except for a few Aramaic interludes, in Hebrew. However, in the typical Reform Temple (the term temple was originally chosen as a substitute for synagogue to disavow hope for the rebuilding of the shrine that was once the pride of Jews) most of the prayers are in the vernacular. Since every congregation is independent, the proportional use of Hebrew and English in Reform and Conservative congregations varies. Traditional Jews will not pray, study Torah, or perform any act of worship unless their heads are covered. If they did otherwise, they would consider it irreverent, to stand slipshod in the presence of the Lord. The Orthodox Jews who follow custom rigidly have their heads constantly covered; at services they like to wear hats, whereas Conservatives use ''yarmulkes'' (Yiddish word for skullcaps), at times of varied colors and beautifully embroidered. Reform Jews wear no head covering, following in this the conventions of Western civilization, where the bared head is a sign of respect.

In Orthodox synagogues men and women are separated. In most Conservative synagogues and all Reform temples they are seated together. In a traditional service Scripture readings and prayers are chanted; in a modernized one, they are recited in a formal manner. In all Orthodox and many Conservative synagogues, priestly descendants (their shoes removed, as was done in the Temple of Jerusalem) chant the Aaronic blessing (Nm 6.22–27) over the people. The cantillation, at times amateurish, may jar a modern musically trained ear. In a reformed service, therefore, the rabbi imparts that blessing. There, as elsewhere, a prevailing criterion is decorum.

On awakening, the pious Jew praises God for having made the new day. He blesses Him for having given him sight, for clothing him, for having renewed his strength, for granting him the power to walk, for putting firm ground under foot. There is a whole system of blessings accompanying the observant Jew throughout the day. (*See* BERAKHOT.) If rightly used, such blessings open his heart to God's nearness and the many manifestations of His

goodness. Yet like all acts to be performed at stated times, they are in danger of becoming routine. Fearing such mechanization or even the ''ritualization'' of religious life, Reform Judaism—mistaking the protests of the Prophets against sacrifices devoid of love as a condemnation of all ritual—has discarded the system of blessings and many other ceremonies as well, although a new appreciation of worship is dawning. Reform Judaism continues to see itself as ''Prophetic Judaism,'' keeping alive the social concern of the Prophets; hence the involvement of many Reform Jews (not to speak here of the commitment of other Jews) in the continuing struggle to obtain social justice.

To consecrate his life to the Lord, the tradition-bound Jew wears, during the morning service, PHYLACTERIES (*t*e*fillîn*) on head and arm near the heart; these are small boxes containing parchment strips with the words of Ex 11.16; 13.1–10; Dt 6.4–9; 11.13–21 and attached to leather straps. At all times, or at least during the morning prayers, he wears the *ṭallît,* a fringed garment used as a prayer shawl. Its purpose is to remind him ''not to follow [his] heart and eyes in lustful urge . . . [but] to be holy to [his] God'' (Nm 15.39–40).

Dietary Laws. Hebrew DIETARY LAWS, too, are meant to hallow a Jew's life. They recall that he lives under the discipline of the Law. Rabbinical tradition requires that animals be slaughtered by a Shoḥet (*šôḥeṭ*), an expert slaughterer who must see to it that the animal dies with the least possible pain and that blood is allowed to flow off freely. The cook, too, must observe certain regulations: the meat is to be cleansed and salted, so that every drop of blood will be drawn out. All vegetables are allowed. Of the animal kingdom, only fish with scales and fins, certain kinds of fowl, and those quadrupeds that chew their food twice and have cloven hoofs are permitted. Meat and dairy products may not be eaten together; hence, two separate kinds of dishes are used, and a six-hour interval must be observed between a meal with meat and one with milk or its derivatives. Reform Judaism has discarded the idea of *kašrût* (fitness), i.e., the laws regulating kosher food, although some of its adherents will, out of a loyalty to parents or to the Jewish past, abstain from pork. While many observant Jews modify the strict requirements of the Law to suit the demands of modern life, they expect their rabbis to observe, in their stead, the traditional rules uncompromisingly.

Bar Mitzvah. Every male child is circumcised. On the Sabbath following his 13th birthday a boy is called up to read publicly the proper passage from the Torah, thus becoming BAR MITZVAH (son of the commandment, man of duty). From that time on, he is obliged to fulfill all the commandments. In quite a few American congregations, there is an equivalent service for 12-year-old girls, called bat mitzvah (daughter of the comandment).

Marriage. A traditional wedding is performed under a *huppâ* (canopy), a symbol of the home, the shelter of the marital state. The ceremony consists of a number of blessings. The first praises God for having created the fruit of the vine, of which both bride and bridegroom partake. After this sharing, the bridegroom places a ring on the bride's finger: "By this ring you are wedded unto me according to the Law of Moses and that of the people of Israel." Whoever officiates, commonly a rabbi, renders thanks to God for creating all things for His glory, fashioning man and woman in His image, making them companions, and granting them joy. He begs for their continued happiness and ties their hopes to the messianic hopes of the Jewish people. At the wedding, a glass is shattered to remind the bridal couple in the midst of joy, as some have it, of the destruction of Jerusalem or, as others interpret it, of the ease with which domestic sanctity and peace can be broken.

Sometime before the wedding, a marriage contract (*keṯûbâ*) is drawn up, and it is read aloud at the marriage ceremony; it contains, among other things, the bridegroom's promise to the bride: "I will work for you. I will honor you. I will support and maintain you as befits a Jewish husband." Complicated rules govern divorce. The *gēṯ,* or bill of divorce, must be drawn up by a recognized scholar. Reform rabbis, however, accept a civil divorce as terminating a Jewish marriage. In the Reform marriage ceremony, *huppâ* and *keṯûbâ* are almost always omitted, as well as the reference to the restoration of the Holy City. Other English prayers, however, for the well-being of the bride and bridegroom, are added.

Death and Burial. As his hour of death approaches, a Jew steeped in the ways of his forefathers admits shame for his sins and asks forgiveness. He begs that his pain as well as his death atone for them, that he be granted the abounding happiness stored up for the just, and that he be admitted to God's presence, where there is fullness of joy. He may appeal to the Lord to take back the soul He lent him in mercy and peace, so that the Angel of Death cannot torment him: "Hide me in the shadow of your wings." He then blesses his children. When the end is truly near, those gathered around him proclaim: "The Lord reigns, the Lord has reigned, the Lord shall reign forever and forever." It is considered a sign of divine favor if a man can die with the profession of faith on his lips: "Hear O Israel! The Lord our God, the Lord is one!"

Several hours after death, the body is washed in a prescribed way and dressed in a white shroud. For a man it is the same garment he wore for the first time as bride-

groom, and later at every New Year's service, on the Day of Atonement, and at the Passover meal. A prayer shawl is wound around his body. All shrouds and coffins have the same simplicity for the rich as for the poor. The moment the coffin is lowered into the grave these words are said: "May he come to his place in peace." If a son buries one of his parents, he prays thus:

> May His great name be magnified and sanctified in the world that is to be created anew, where He will quicken the dead and raise them up to life eternal, where He will rebuild the city of Jerusalem and establish His Temple in its midst, and where He will uproot all alien worship from the earth and restore the worship of the true God.

This KADDISH (*qaddîš,* hallowed) is one of several similar doxologies recited on various occasions. In hallowing the name of God for 11 months, a bereaved son hopes that through the power of praise his beloved parent may find peace in God. The Kaddish does not mention the dead. Yet the mourner's Kaddish is said on every anniversary. Although Jewish tradition frowns on extreme grief—excessiveness is said to imply that the mourner is filled with greater pity than God—the Orthodox rules on various periods of mourning are complicated and quite detailed. Reform Judaism has abandoned most of the practices with which tradition has surrounded the death event, particularly those of mourning, as cumbersome, harsh, and aggravating grief rather than offering solace.

Jews and Jesus. Ever since Jamnia, Judaism has precluded belief in Jesus as the Redeemer. Although some later Jewish teaching developed with Christianity in mind, the Talmudic sages avoided direct discussion of the gospel. The few hostile passages in the Talmud that, according to the opinion of competent scholars, refer to Jesus, do so without naming Him. Moreover, in speaking of Gentiles, rabbinic literature hardly distinguishes between Christians, worshipers of the one, true God, and pagans, worshipers of idols. Maimonides seems to have been the first to hold a mildly positive view of Christ's work. Maimonides (*Mishneh Torah, Hilkhot Melakhim* 11.4) held that Jesus' teaching, like Muḥammad's, "only served to clear the way for the King Messiah to prepare the whole world to worship God with one accord" (cf. So 3.9). Several decades after Maimonides, another rabbi distinguished between the Gentiles referred to in the Talmud and those of his own day. He called his Christian contemporaries "nations restricted by the ways of religion"; and those of which the Talmudic teachers speak, "nations not delimited by the ways of religion." There have been others who spoke of the kindness "the man of Nazareth wrought to the world."

But not till Reform Judaism made its voice heard did Jesus and Christianity—topics shunned till then by most

Jews and even today by some of them—become a matter of investigation. Not until then were such words spoken as those of Sigismund Stern, a German Jewish school teacher of the middle of the 19th century: "Judaism and Christianity must hold out a brotherly hand to each other, for the sake of their common work for mankind . . . . [The Jewish believers] must love their Christian fellow men, not merely as fellow human beings, but feel related to them in faith and bound to them with special ties."

Since then, a new appreciation of the person of Jesus—not to be mistaken, however, for faith in Him as the Christ—has set in. Even a scholar as steeped in tradition as Joseph Klausner (1874–1958) called Jesus a great moral teacher; Claude J. G. MONTEFIORE (1859–1939), the founder of Liberal Judaism in England, saw in Him a new type of prophet; Rabbi Leo Baeck (1874–1956)— the distinguished head of German Jewry at the time of Hitler and one-time president of the World Union for Progressive Judaism—acclaimed Him as the manifestation "of what is pure and good in Judaism." The Conservative theologian Rabbi Milton Steinberg (1903–50) spoke of Him as "an extraordinarily beautiful and noble spirit, aglow with love and pity for men," and the existential thinker Martin Buber (1878–1965) regarded Him as "my great brother." Of the several statements made by American rabbis on this theme, the most interesting are those of Maurice Eisendrath, president of the Union of American Hebrew Congregations, though they carry no official weight. Some consider them eccentric. In 1963 he called on Jews to reappraise their "ofttimes jaundiced view of him in whose name Christianity was established," and in 1965 he asked that Jesus, "this Jewish hero," be incorporated "into our never too overcrowded company of saintly spirits."

Present and Future. The largest Jewish communities are in the U.S., Russia, and Israel. Although the state of Israel guarantees freedom of worship, Orthodoxy so dominates the religious life that it prevents the other branches of Judaism from getting a foothold. Russian Jewry is threatened with spiritual extinction for lack of a sufficient number of synagogues, of religious training, and cultural activities. No attempt has been made to gather exact statistics on the number of the synagogue-affiliated among the 5 ½ million American Jews. Nor is the ratio of Orthodox, Conservative, and Reform membership certain. There were in 1965 more than 1,600 known Orthodox congregations, many of them quite small; the Conservative and Reform synagogues numbered 770 and 640 respectively. In all likelihood, each of the three branches has about one million adherents. According to one estimate, four million avail themselves of the service of the synagogue, at the high points of life.

It is impossible to say what the future holds for the various branches, indeed for the whole of American Judaism. Jews seem to be more exposed than other people to the apathy toward, even the estrangement from, religion that marks much of modern life. There are those who predict that the unprecedented freedom and comfort American Jews enjoy will quench all religious thirst and wipe out most of the marks that distinguish them from their neighbors; after a few generations, they will be little more than "custodians of a museum." There are others, however, who see American Jewish life in flux and who hope for a new flowering, indeed, the emergence of a *Minhag America,* a fresh American-bred expression of the ancient Jewish way.

Christian View of Judaism. Christians have frequently seen Judaism as a "service of death," misapplying the words of St. Paul, who says in 2 Cor 3.6 that "the letter kills but the Spirit gives life," i.e., that the Law, when seen as God's inexorable demands, condemns the sinner to death, whereas grace renews and quickens him. Is the Christian bound to think that Judaism, however much alive empirically, is dead in God's judgment? Or is he bound to believe that God's hand is not shortened and the workings of grace not limited? Every morning the observant Jew remembers man's frailty and dependence, as well as God's sovereign goodness:

> Master of all worlds! Not because of our just deeds do we cast our humble prayers before You but because of Your abundant mercy. What are we? What is our life? What our love? What our justice? What our victory? What our strength? What our might? What are we to say before You, O Lord our God and God of our fathers? Indeed, before Your presence, the mighty are as nothing . . . the wise as without knowledge . . . . Yet, we are Your people, the children of Your covenant, the sons of Abraham Your friend . . . . It is, therefore, our duty to thank, praise, and glorify You . . . . How good is our portion . . . , how great our happiness that early and late, morning and night, twice every day, we may proclaim: Hear O Israel! The Lord is our God, the Lord alone!

There can be no doubt that God's love hovers over those who pray thus. "It is not true," writes Cardinal Liénart, Bishop of Lille, "that Israel, the chosen people of the Old Covenant, has become an accursed people in the New. Actually, the religious destiny of Israel is a mystery of grace, and we Christians ought to ponder it with respectful sympathy" (*Lenten Pastoral* 1960). By encouraging common Biblical and theological studies as well as fraternal dialogue between Christians and Jews, Vatican Council II has clearly shown that it considers Judaism a living faith. (See section on the Jews of the *Declaration on the Church's Relationship to non-Christian Religions,* 1965.)

See Also: JEWS, POST-BIBLICAL HISTORY OF THE; JEWISH PHILOSOPHY.

Bibliography: G. F. MOORE, *Judaism in the First Centuries of the Christian Era: The Age of the Tannaim,* 3 v. (Cambridge, MA 1927–30). C. J. G. MONTEFIORE and H. M. J. LOEWE, eds., *A Rabbinic Anthology, Selected and Arranged with Comments and Introductions* (London 1938; pa. New York 1963). M. KADUSHIN, *The Rabbinic Mind* (New York 1952); *Organic Thinking* (New York 1938). I. EPSTEIN, *Judaism: A Historical Presentation* (Baltimore 1959). D. S. RUSSELL, *The Method and Message of Jewish Apocalyptic* (Philadelphia 1964). G. G. SCHOLEM, *Major Trends in Jewish Mysticism* (3d ed. New York 1954; repr. pa. New York 1961); *On the Kabbalah and Its Symbolism,* tr. R. MANHEIM (New York 1964). W. G. PLAUT, *The Rise of Reform Judaism* (New York 1963–). M. DAVIS, *The Emergence of Conservative Judaism* (Philadelphia 1963). N. GLAZER, *American Judaism* (Chicago 1957). J. B. AGUS, *Guideposts in Modern Judaism* (New York 1954). J. J. PETUCHOWSKI, *Ever Since Sinai: A Modern View of Torah* (New York 1961). L. JACOBS, *Principles of the Jewish Faith* (London 1964). *The Authorised Daily Prayer Book,* ed. H. J. HERTZ (rev. ed. New York 1959). E. GARFIEL, *The Service of the Heart; A Guide to the Jewish Prayer Book* (New York 1958). L. FINKELSTEIN, "The Jewish Religion: Its Beliefs and Practices," *The Jews: Their History, Culture and Religion,* 2 v., ed. L. FINKELSTEIN (3d ed. New York 1960). M. N. EISENDRATH, *Can Faith Survive?* (New York 1964). K. GALLING et al., *Die Religion in Geschichte und Gegenwart,* 7 v. (3d ed. Tübingen 1957–65) 3:978–1000. R. R. GEIS et al., *Lexikon für Theologie und Kirche,* ed. J. HOFER and K. RAHNER, 10 v. (2d, new ed. Freiburg 1957–65) 5:1156–71.

[J. M. OESTERREICHER]

JUDAS ISCAROIT

The Apostle who betrayed Jesus. The name Judas (Ἰούδας) is derived from the Hebrew y^ehudah (Judah), the name borne also by St. JUDE THADDEUS. Iscariot (Ἰσκαριώτης and Ἰσκαριώθ) is usually explained by the equivalent of the Hebrew *'îš-q^erîôt* (man of Carioth); a town of uncertain site in southern Judah called Carioth-Hesron is mentioned in Jos 15.25. Judas was the son of a man named Simon (Jn 6.72; 13.26). Apart from these vague notifications nothing is known about the origin of the man who betrayed Jesus.

Apostleship and Treachery. The New Testament says nothing about the vocation of Judas. His name is simply mentioned with the rest of the Twelve Apostles, always at the end of the list (Mk 3.19; Mt 10.4; Lk 6.16). Undoubtedly he joined the other Apostles on their missionary journeys (Mk 6.7; Mt 10.1; Lk 9.1–2).

No Evangelist gives a character study of Judas. The attempt to determine the crises that led to his defection deals with half knowledge. In Jn 12.6 it is said that Judas was a petty thief and that his hand dipped into the common purse for personal advantage. It seems most probable, however, that the major crisis for Judas was the same as that faced and overcome by the other Apostles, the revelation of a suffering Messiah. This is seen most clearly in Mk 8.31–33. Peter's profession of faith in Jesus as Messiah is followed by Jesus' revelation that "the Son of Man must suffer many things, and be rejected by the elders and chief priests and scribes, and be put to death . . . ." The effect of this statement on the Apostles was appalling. There was no place in their thinking for a suffering Christ. As David's descendant He must be a glorious political king. Peter was so certain of this that he took Jesus aside to remonstrate with Him. And then, even worse, Jesus taught the TWELVE that, not only was He to suffer, but they, too, must follow Him, each with his own cross (Mk 8.34–35). The last half of Mark's Gospel centers on the confusion and fear of the Apostles with regard to Jesus' future suffering (Mk 9.8–11, 30–31; 10.32–34, 43–45; 13.9–13). Judas's courage and faith must have been too weak to accept such a challenge. He traded in his apostleship for the small comforts he could obtain from the common fund.

The seeming waste of perfume at the Bethany anointing disturbed a number of the Apostles (Mk 14.3–9; Mt 26.6–9), but in Jn 12.1–8 Judas is singled out as particularly offended by it. Perhaps this was the final straw for him. Mark immediately follows this incident with the statement: "And Judas Iscariot, one of the Twelve, went to the chief priests to betray him to them" (Mk 14.10). Judas promised to inform the Sanhedrin of a time and place in which Jesus could be seized apart from the crowd: "The chief priests and the Scribes were seeking how they might seize him by stealth and put him to death; for they said, 'Not on the feast, or there might be a riot among the people'" (Mk 14.1–2).

The opportunity arrived during the LAST SUPPER. Jesus was separated from the crowds, and He would soon move down to the olive trees at Gethsemani; night would mask the movement of the Sanhedrin forces. Jesus' response to Judas's plotting was a feeling of intense sorrow. It was one of His own community, one of His particular friends, who was betraying Him. Our Lord's words to and about Judas at the Last Supper are a personalization of Ps 40(41).10: "Even my friend who had my trust and partook of my bread has raised his heel against me." It is this sad truth that is the common element in the varying traditions of Mk 14.20; Mt 26.23–25; Lk 22.21; Jn 13.18–26.

Judas's embrace of Jesus was a tragically clever move to point out Jesus in the darkness of Gethsemani. Luke cannot bring himself to state that Judas actually kissed Our Lord (Lk 22.47–48).

Demons flank the suspended body of Judas Iscariot, Romanesque relief sculpture, Autun Cathedral, France. (©Angelo Hornak/ CORBIS)

Only in Mt 27.3–5 is the story told how Judas rid himself of the blood money by hurling it into the Temple. Matthew's precise specification of the 30 pieces of silver is probably a symbol. Thirty shekels was the assessed value of Zechariah's good shepherd of Yahweh's flock (Zec 11.12–13), and according to Ex 21.32 it was a fine imposed on the owner of an ox that killed a slave.

John's Gospel emphasizes the relationship between Judas and Satan. As the Passion story begins and the conflict between Christ and Satan, between light and darkness, becomes imminent, Judas is the instrument of Satan (Jn 13.2, 27). Judas leaves the supper room to inform the authorities of Jesus' whereabouts that evening; as he does he moves off into the kingdom of darkness: "Now it was night" (Jn 13.30).

Death. There are different accounts of Judas's death in the early Christian writings. According to Mt 27.5 (of which passage there is no parallel in Mark or Luke) he hanged himself. In Acts 1.18 Peter is quoted as saying that Judas fell forward or swelled up (the Greek expression πρηνὴς γενόμενος is of uncertain meaning) and burst open. Papias (early second century) is quoted by a certain Appolinaris as saying that "His [Judas's] flesh became bloated (πρασθείς) to such an extent that he could not walk through a space where a wagon could easily pass. Not even the huge bulk of his head could go through" [Papias Fragment 6, *Partes Apostolici,* F. X. Funk, ed. (Tübingen 1901) 1:360–362]. In this respect Papias agrees with Acts.

Probably both traditions are symbolic. The hanging death mentioned by Matthew refers to 2 Sm 17.23, which says that Achitophel, companion of David and a traitor to him, went and hanged himself. In Jewish tradition Achitophel was the classic example of a traitor. Jesus himself (Jn 13.18; Mk 14.18) applied to Judas Ps 40(41).10, which the rabbis had long understood as referring to Achitophel. Matthew's tradition, therefore, brands Judas, in life and in death, as another Achitophel. He must have died the miserable type of death destined for traitors.

Acts and Papias give us a symbolism based, seemingly, on Wis 4.18–19, which says that sinners shall "become dishonored corpses . . .; for he shall strike them down speechless and prostrate [or swollen: πρηνεῖς]." This tradition states that Judas's death must have been that of a typical sinner. Both Matthew and Acts give, therefore, not the historical circumstances of Judas's death, but its theological meaning.

Bibliography: J. BLINZLER and J. H. EMMINGHAUS, *Lexikon für Theologie und Kirche*, ed. J. HOFER and K. RAHNER (Freiberg 1957–65) 5:1152–54. *Encyclopedic Dictionary of the Bible*, tr. and adap. by L. HARTMAN (New York 1963) 1231–33. R. B. HALAS, *Judas Iscariot: A Scriptural and Theological Study of His Person, Deeds, and Eternal Lot* (Washington 1946). J. DUPONT, "La Destinée de Judas prophetisée par David," *The Catholic Biblical Quarterly* (Washington 1939–) 23 (1961) 41–51.

[N. M. FLANAGAN]

JUDDE, CLAUDE

A representative of the mystical tradition of Jesuit spirituality; b. Rouen, Dec. 19, 1661; d. Paris, March 11, 1735. He entered the Society of Jesus in 1677 at Paris, made his studies there, taught at the Collège de Clermont, and was ordained. He spent his third year of probation at Rouen in 1691. So successful was Judde in his preaching assignments, first in the provinces, then in Paris, that Louis BOURDALOUE wanted the young priest to be his successor and literary executor. His superiors, however, intended Judde to occupy himself with the spiritual formation of young Jesuits. He was instructor of priests in the third year of probation at Rouen (1709–13), and then rector of the Paris novitiate (1713–21), in which office he fulfilled the functions of instructor of the third year of probation and novice master. From 1721 to 1722 he was rector of the Collège Saint-Thomas at Rennes. He died at the professed house at Paris. Judde wrote nothing for publication, but notes made of his retreats and conferences were edited and published posthumously, at first piecemeal but finally in a collection by Abbé Lenoir-Duparc, *Oeuvres spirituelles du P. Judde* (last reissued by Lecoffre, 5 v. Paris 1898–1910). The volumes contain a 30-day retreat, retreats for religious, treatises on confession, prayer, and the Mass, and spiritual exhortations. Judde's importance lies in his continuity with the mystical tradition in Jesuit spirituality, whose chief exponent was Louis LALLEMANT. In the *Spiritual Exercises* of St. Ignatius he found his most characteristic notion, divine liberality calling forth and rewarding human generosity.

Bibliography: *Bibliothèque de la Compagnie de Jésus* 4:863–866; 9:520–521. J. DE GUIBERT, *La Spiritualité de la Com-*

pagnie de Jésus, ed. E. LAMALLE (Rome 1953). R. DAESCHLER, "Un Temoin de la tradition Mystique," *Revue d'ascétique et de mystique* 3 (1922) 224–249; "Le P. Judde et la *tradition mystique*" v. 11 (1930) 17–36.

[F. J. BERGEN]

JUDE, EPISTLE OF

One of the Catholic Epistles of the New Testament. This brief letter of 25 verses is an exhortation to the faithful to remain firm in the face of wicked men who deny Christ. The author tells his readers that the punishment of these men is foreshadowed in the Old Testament (v. 5–7); he illustrates their wickedness by examples drawn from scriptural and other sources (v. 8–13), saying that their judgment was predicted by Henoch (v. 14–16), and their coming, by the Apostles (v. 17–19). He exhorts them to wait for the Lord and to help others (v. 20–23), concluding with a doxology (v. 24–25).

Author and Date. "Jude, a servant of Jesus Christ and brother of James" (v. 1), is almost certainly to be identified with the Jude listed among the "brothers of the Lord" in Mk 6.3. Although this "Jude, brother of James," has, in ecclesiastical tradition, often been identified with the Apostle St. JUDE THADDEUS (Lk 6.16; Acts 1.13; Mt 10.3; Mk 3.18; Jn 14.22), exegetes today, including many Catholics, are inclined to deny this identity for the same reasons that apply in the case of "James, the brother of the Lord" (*see* JAMES, EPISTLE OF ST.). Furthermore, the reference in Jude verse 17 to the Apostles seems to imply that the author did not reckon himself among them. Eusebius (*Ecclesiastical History* 3.19.20; 32.5) quotes Hegesippus as saying that two grandchildren of Jude were arrested under Domitian on the charge of being descendants of David. The cultivated Greek style and certain indications of a relatively late date (e.g., v. 17) lead certain scholars to question (as does the Catholic K. H. Schelkle) or deny the authenticity of the attribution to Jude. However, the literary dependence of 2 Peter on this letter (*see* PETER, EPISTLES OF ST.) cautions against assigning too late a date and, consequently, against too ready a questioning of its authenticity. The destination and place of writing are unknown. Although its canonical status in the early Church is well attested, doubts were occasioned in some quarters by reason of Jude's quoting (in v. 14–15) the apocryphal Book of Henoch. *See* BIBLE.

Occasion and Doctrine. Although the descriptions in the letter are too vague to permit identification of the errors of the wicked intruders, they seem to represent an embryonic form of Antinomian Christian GNOSTICISM, perhaps similar to that underlying Church troubles alluded to in Galatians, Colossians, and the Pastoral Epistles.

The author's chief concern in this short epistle is obviously to warn the recipients of the pressing dangers to faith and morals and thus to protect them from being corrupted. Nevertheless, various points of doctrine are raised or mentioned: the Persons of the Trinity (v. 1, 20, 25), the deposit of faith (v. 3), the existence of good and bad angels (v. 6, 9), the destiny of eternal life (v. 21), and zeal for others' salvation (v. 22–23).

Bibliography: C. BIGG, *Epistles of St. Peter and St. Jude* (*International Critical Commentary*; 2d ed. Edinburgh 1910). G. H. BOOBYER, "Jude," *Peake's Commentary on the Bible,* ed. M. BLACK and H. H. ROWLEY (New York 1962) 1041–42. J. CHAINE, *Les Épîtres catholiques* (2d ed. *Étude bibliques* Paris 1939). R. LECONTE, *Les Épîtres catholiques* (*Bible de Jérusalem*; 42; 2d ed. Paris 1961). J. B. MAYOR, *The Epistle of St. Jude and the Second Epistle of St. Peter* (London 1907). K. H. SCHELKLE, *Die Petrusbriefe, Der Judasbrief* (Herders theologischer Kommentar zum N.T. 13.2; Freiburg 1961). J. CANTINAT, "L'Épître de s. Jude," A. ROBERT and A. FEUILLET, eds., *Introduction à la Bible* (Tournai 1959) 2:602–610. P. FEINE et al., "Der Judasbrief," *Einleitung in das N. T.* (13th ed. Heidelberg 1964) 310–313. J. BLINZLER, *Lexikon für Theologie und Kirche,* ed. J. HOFER and K. RAHNER (Freiberg 1957–65) 5:1155–56. E. FASCHER, *Die Religion in Geschichte und Gegenwart* (Tübingen 1957–65) 3: 966–967. J. B. COLON, *Dictionnaire de théologie catholique,* ed. A. VACANT et al., (Paris 1903–50) 8.2:1668–81. *Encyclopedic Dictionary of the Bible,* tr. and adap. by L. HARTMAN (New York 1963) 1235–36.

[T. W. LEAHY]

St. Jude, 14th-century fresco. (©Francis G. Mayer/CORBIS)

JUDE THADDEUS, ST.

One of the Twelve Apostles. He is called Jude (Gr. Ἰούδας, representing Heb. *yᵉhûdâ*, Judah) in the lists of Lk 6.16 and Acts 1.13; but the corresponding passages of Mt 10.3 and Mk 3.18 have Thaddeus (Θαδδαῖος). In all four passages he is the 11th named. The reason for the use of Thaddeus in Matthew and Mark may lie in a certain care the first two Gospels take not to confuse him with Judas Iscariot. In Jn 14.22 he is called "Judas, not the Iscariot," and in Luke and Acts he is called "Judas of James." Yet the use of Thaddeus in Matthew and Mark is not absolutely constant, for some manuscripts have Lebbeus instead. Both seem to have the same meaning, for Thaddeus from Aramaic *taddai* (Aramaic *tad,* chest) means chesty, and Lebbeus from Hebrew *libbai* (Heb. *leb,* heart) means hearty. Some scholars, however, believe that Thaddeus is a variant of the Greek name Theudas. According to a very early tradition in the Church the James referred to in "Jude of James" is JAMES, son of Alphaeus, and James and Jude are to be identified with the BROTHERS OF JESUS (i.e., His relatives) mentioned in Mt 13.55 and Mk 6.3. Furthermore, since Jude was probably less known, to identify him better his name was associated with that of his brother. This has remained the predominant view among Catholic commen-

tators. But in recent times certain difficulties about this interpretation have been raised. While the expression "Judas of James" used in Lk 6.16 and Acts 1.13 can mean "the brother of James" (under the influence of Jude 1), it is a rare usage. Its ordinary meaning would be "Jude the son of James," and it is precisely in this sense that the same passage uses "James [the son] of Alphaeus." Thus Jude would be the son of an otherwise unknown James. The author of the Epistle of St. Jude, whom Catholic tradition considers the same as Jude the Apostle, calls himself simply "Jude, the servant of Jesus Christ and the brother of James" (v. 1).

The traditional material about Jude Thaddeus's later ministry and martyrdom is completely unreliable. Eusebius (*Ecclesiastical History* 2.40) relates various supposed areas of his preaching, while the Roman Breviary mentions only Mesopotamia and Persia. He is said to have died a martyr, and in art he is represented with a halberd, the instrument of his martyrdom. Mention is made of his grandsons by Hegesippus (Eusebius, *Ecclesiastical History* 3.20.1–5); they were tried and acquitted under Domitian (81–96) and ruled Christian communities of Palestine under Trajan (98–117).

Feast: Oct. 28 (with SIMON THE APOSTLE).

See Also: JUDE, EPISTLE OF ST.

Bibliography: R. LECONTE, *Dictionnaire de la Bible,* suppl. ed. L. PIROT et. al., 4:1288–91. *Encyclopedic Dictionary of the Bible,* tr. L. HARTMAN (New York 1963) 1234–35. J. BLINZLER, *Lexikon für Theologie und Kirche*[2] (Freiburg 1957–65) 5:1154–55. J. CHAINE, *Les Épîtres catholiques* (2d ed. Paris 1939) 269–271. L. CERFAUX, *La Communauté apostolique* (3d ed. Paris 1956) 89–97. A. CHARUE, *Les Épîtres catholiques* in *La Sainte Bible,* ed. L. PIROT and A. CLAMER, 12 v. (Paris 1935–61) 12:375–379. L. TROTTA, *Jude: A Pilgrimage to the Saint of Last Resort* (San Francisco 1998), cult and legends.

[J. A. LEFRANÇOIS]

JUDGE, THOMAS AUGUSTINE

Founder of the Missionary Cenacle; b. Boston, Mass., Aug. 23, 1868; d. Washington, D.C., Nov. 23, 1933. His parents were Irish immigrants. Following education in the public schools, he entered the Congregation of the Mission (Vincentian Fathers) at Philadelphia, Pa., and was ordained there in 1899. Early experience among Latin immigrants and in preaching parish missions awakened his interest in the problem of defections from the Church. To assist the clergy in dealing with this matter, he organized a lay apostolate in Brooklyn, N.Y., in 1909. These lay missionaries, later known as the Missionary Cenacle Apostolate, were successfully established in numerous parishes in New England and the Middle Atlantic states. In 1961 they numbered approximately 2,000 members.

Judge was appointed in 1915 as superior of the Vincentian missions in the Diocese of Mobile, centered at St. Mary's Mission House, Opelika, Ala. From the lay apostles who joined him in this mission field there evolved two new religious congregations. The MISSIONARY SERVANTS OF THE MOST HOLY TRINITY, for priests and brothers, received papal approbation in 1929; the MISSIONARY SERVANTS OF THE MOST BLESSED TRINITY was approved in 1932. These congregations, and their lay missionary associates, known collectively as the Missionary Cenacle, were directed by their founder, who was relieved of his office as superior at Opelika, from 1920 until his death. In 1923 Bp. George J. Caruana of San Juan requested that foundations be established in Puerto Rico. Judge assigned all who could be spared to those missions and personally led them in their initial work. This experience caused him thereafter to give continuing attention to the needs of the Church in Latin America.

Bibliography: J. V. BENSON, *The Judgments of Father Judge* (New York 1934). A. K. WALKER, *Russell County in Retrospect* (Richmond, Va. 1950). A. M. KRAUT, "Thomas Judge and the Catholic Laity in the Rural South," *U.S. Catholic Historian* 8 (1989) 187–98. D. F. O'CONNOR, "America's Pioneer in the Lay Apostolate: Father Thomas Augustine Judge, C.M. (1869–1933)," *Profiles in American Sanctity,* ed. J. N. TYLENDA (Chicago 1982). J. M BLACKWELL, *The Pastoral Ministry of Thomas Augustine Judge and His Role in the Development of a Catholic Lay Apostolate in the United States* (Washington, D.C. 1974).

[L. BREDIGER]

JUDGES (IN THE BIBLE)

The term used in the Book of JUDGES to describe the book's heroes. The word in Hebrew (*šōfēt*) designates one who restores justice or right to someone. Broadly speaking, a judge is one appointed to settle quarrels and assist men to obtain their rights. Yet, even such a fluid concept scarcely justifies applying this term alone to the varying functions described in the Book of Judges. R. de Vaux thinks the title has been wrongly extended to the heroes of the period between Joshua and the monarchy who saved some part of the people from oppression; it would belong properly to the minor judges along with Jephthah (and, probably, Deborah), who combined the judge's office with that of savior. These minor judges were a permanent institution of the tribal federation, elected officials whose function was to interpret Yahweh's law for all Israel and to adjudicate controversial cases between clans.

Actually, the author of the book has included under a generic name (national juridical institution) much more; the great deeds of the major judges, not institutional activities, are the outstanding things in the book. For the Deuteronomist author all judgments are rooted in the historical covenant; justice is God's saving justice. Judges and saviors are equally signs of the divine saving activity in this heroic age. God alone is the ultimate savior; saving activity comes exclusively from Him (Jgs 6.34, 36–37; 7.2, 9, 14–15). Theological considerations, then, probably directed the choice of the title as applied to all the heroes of the book.

Bibliography: R. DE VAUX, *Ancient Israel, Its Life and Institutions,* tr. J. MCHUGH (New York 1961) 143–163. *Encyclopedic Dictionary of the Bible,* tr. and adap. by L. HARTMAN (New York 1963) 1238–39.

[J. MORIARITY]

JUDGES, BOOK OF

Like the Book of Joshua, Judges takes its title from the protagonists in the story. *See* JUDGES (IN THE BIBLE). The theme of the Book of Judges is the recurrent punishment and salvation of Israel under the special providence of God, who raises up saviors, the judges, in time of oppression and oppressors in time of Israel's defection.

Contents and Structure. Judges opens with a bipartite introduction (1.1–3.6), describing political and reli-

Delilah cutting Samson's hair. (©Historical Picture Archive/CORBIS)

gious conditions in the period after Joshua (1.1–36), and setting forth the book's theology (2.1–3.6). The body of the book largely concerns the exploits of the heroic figures whose deeds are extensively recorded—the major judges: Othniel (3.7–11), Ehud (3.12–30), Deborah-Barak (4.1–5.31), Gideon (6.1–9.57), Jephthah (10.6–12.7), and SAMSON (13.1–16.31). Alongside these ''Spirit-designated'' liberators are more shadowy figures, of whom some brief notice is given—the minor judges: Tola (10.1–2), Jair (10.3–5), Ibzan (12.8–10), Elon (12.11–12), Abdon (12.13–15), and perhaps Shamgar (3.31).

Judges 2.6 resumes Joshua 24.28. The long introduction (2.7–3.6) then outlines in a cyclic fashion the themes of the book: sin, anger of God, oppression, salvation, and sin. These motifs are found throughout the book as a schematic formula: At the beginning of the narrative the people sin, they abandon Yahweh and follow false gods,

Yahweh sells them or abandons them to their enemies, they cry to Yahweh.

The body of the narrative that follows is grouped around three main points: God raises up a liberator, a great battle takes place, Israel prevails. The narrative concludes with a twofold element: the enemy is humiliated, the land is at peace. The formulas opening and closing these narratives are rigidly observed, without, however, disturbing the body of the narrative. In the story of Othniel (3.7–11) the pattern is clearly observable. Properly speaking, the story is not a narrative at all. The author has taken a minimum of details from his source and inserted them into the outline. The result is the framework with only two proper names added.

The following structure or arrangement is suggested by the use of recurring formulas. There is a long introductory ''overture'' (2.7–3.6). The themes of the book are enunciated in cyclic fashion. The first part begins with the schematic narrative of Othniel (3.7–11). A simple narrative, Ehud (3.12–30), follows; then the more complex one of Deborah-Barak (4.1–24). The section closes with one of the most ancient Hebrew poems, Canticle of Deborah (ch. 5). The second part begins with a prelude by a prophet (6.7–10). The long GIDEON cycle follows (6.11–8.35), and the section closes tragically with the story of Abimelech (ch. 9), Gideon's son, and the first attempt to establish a monarchy in Israel. The third part begins with a rather long prelude in the form of a dialogue between Yahweh and the people (10.10–16). This is followed by the narrative of Jephthah (11.1–12.7). The saga of Samson (13.1–16.31), which has an ending that is tragical and yet is triumphant, closes this section and the body of the book.

Within this structure, after the story of Abimelech, the list of minor judges was inserted (10.1–5 and 12.8–15). Probably, the insertion was occasioned by the story of Jephthah who combined the office of minor judge with the role of great liberator. The recurring formulas of the book are strikingly absent in this list but there are constant elements in it: the succession, the judge of all Israel, and the duration of the judge's office in apparently artificial numbers, i.e., 23, 22, 6, 7, and 8. The death and place of burial also are noted and sometimes a report of the judge's wealth is recorded. The conclusion of the Jephte narrative (12.7) follows the pattern of this list and not the formula found in all other cases of major judges. Apparently, these minor judges represented a permanent institution of the tribal federation.

The last four chapters of Judges form a double appendix that was added to the structure outlined above: the founding of the sanctuary at Dan (ch. 17–18); the Benjaminite war (ch. 19–21). These sections represent very early traditions. They were not, however, part of the first work of the Deuteronomist editor; the great themes of the body of the book are totally absent here. These traditions were perhaps incorporated to form a link with the following history presented in the Book of Samuel. The double appendix describes the moral and cultural anarchy when, "in those days there was no king in Israel; everyone did what he thought best" (21.25).

Origin. We can distinguish four general stages in the origin and formation of the book.

1. Preliterary stage. Ancient oral traditions circulated embracing hero stories and tribal sagas, some with etiological elements. Very likely these were preserved in cultic centers and in schools of minstrels.

2. Second Stage. Many of these oral stories were probably drawn into cycle form and later still, compiled in writing—probably at the time of David or Solomon.

3. Third Stage. This is the work of the DEUTERONOMISTS writing a religious history of Israel. They used these documents and from them constructed a unity by means of the formulas outlined above in "Structure." These recurring formulas are very similar to the doctrine of Deuteronomy. They reflect the same interpretation of history and the same emphasis on the covenant obligations. Such similarities are the more striking reasons for calling the redactors of the work the Deuteronomists. They found in their sources, linked with the story of Jephte, the list of minor judges, and this, too, was incorporated. The work took place sometime in the 7th century B.C.

4. Fourth stage. At a later date, another hand added the appendix and chapter one.

Chronology. The epoch of Judges extends roughly from 1200 to 1050 B.C. However, the chronological ordering of the book is artificial, as appears from the recurrence of the number 40—the length of a generation—or of its half, 20, or its double, 80. The various wars and oppressions recounted appear to have followed one another. But this ordering is the work of the author, who has fitted originally separate narratives into the framework of a religious history. In point of fact, many of these episodes occurred simultaneously in the various parts of the country. The author had no intention of presenting an organic history, chronologically ordered, of the period between Joshua and Samuel.

Historical Credibility. The Book of Judges is a work of religious history. As such, it has certain characteristics that are, at the same time, limitations, e.g., its scope is practical, not theoretical; it is concerned with the religious meaning of events, with history as a history of salvation. As religious history, it relates both historical facts and their religious aspect. The relation of this religious aspect or meaning demands on the part of the author a certain amount of artistic labor, e.g., selection of events and dialogues. Granted all this, the immediate object of historical examination is the narratives. Are these relations of actual events, or rather simple fictions constructed for religious teaching? The narratives fit well into the whole historical context of this era. Furthermore, the geographical and topographical information in these stories agrees with archeological facts. In general, we can say with a certain amount of confidence that these narratives are not fiction, or, at least, not pure fiction. From the evidence we possess, the basic historical character of these narratives is far more probable than the fictional.

Frequently, the historical credibility of Judges is contested because of the presence of etiological elements in the stories. Etiological tales arise to explain existing customs or landmarks. Objections to the historicity of

Judges suppose that wherever an etiological element is present, the story must be suspect. There certainly were etiological elements in some of the oral traditions. But etiological stories as such were not enumerated among the sources of Judges. To speak of an etiological story or tale assumes that it can be shown that the story came into being through the etiological factor, i.e., that this factor was the creative and determinative element in the story. Such a priority in the formation of these traditions in Judges has not been proved. In addition, the etiological element does not necessarily serve one purpose, namely to explain the origin of customs or curious landmarks. Often such landmarks and customs as well as place names are incorporated into a story in order to ensure the memory of an event. Ultimately the verdict on historical credibility requires objective, external evidence. Literary form of itself furnishes no final test of historicity.

Bibliography: H. CAZELLES, *Dictionnaire de la Bible*, suppl. ed. L. PIROT, et al. (Paris 1928–) 4:1394–1414. A. VINCENT, *Le Livre des Juges* (BJ Paris 1952). L. ALONZO-SCHÖKEL, ''Erzählkunst im Buche der Richter,'' *Biblica* 42.1 (1961) 143–72. *Catholic Biblical Encyclopedia*, ed. J. E. STEINMUELLER and K. SULLIVAN, 2 v. in 1 (New York 1956) 602–03. J. BRIGHT, *A History of Israel* (Philadelphia 1960).

[J. MORIARITY]

JUDGMENT

The operation of the INTELLECT by which something is affirmed or denied of something else or, less properly but frequently, the internal complex expression or PROPOSITION formed by the intellect in judging. Etymologically the word is from the medieval Latin *judicamentum,* like the classical *judicium,* meaning the act of a judge (*judex*) in deciding a question of law or right (*jus*) or in passing sentence. From this the term was extended to moral decisions about right and wrong, to practical estimates and evaluations, and then to the act of deciding about the truth or falsity of a proposition or of making any affirmation or denial (cf. Thomas Aquinas, *Summa theologiae* 2a2ae, 60.1 ad 1). This article presents a historical survey of the notion, an explanation of the doctrine of St. Thomas Aquinas, and a discussion of divergent views in light of that doctrine.

Historical Survey

The philosophical development of the concept of judgment falls naturally into three stages corresponding to the development of ancient philosophy, of scholastic philosophy, and of modern philosophy.

Ancient Philosophy. PLATO has no explicit doctrine of an intellectual operation distinct from direct apprehen-

''Apostles,'' detail of the fresco ''Last Judgment'' by Pietro Cavallini, S. Cecilia in Trastevere, Rome.

sion, but he does speak of an act or faculty of decision, of assessing or evaluating (κρίσις), not only in matters of action and prudence but also in regard to fact and truth (*Rep.* 582AD; *Theaet.* 201B; *Gorg.* 526C; *Leges* 658A, 950B). ''Opinion'' (δόξα), in his usage, has some of the meaning of judgment. It is an intellectual act, as opposed to sensation (αἴσθησις), and connotes belief or assent. It may mean an assessment of what is, and thus be true or false (*Rep.* 478B; *Theaet.* 201AB; *Soph.* 263A–264B; *Meno* 97B, 98C).

ARISTOTLE expressly distinguishes two operations of the intellect on the basis of their objects. The first is ''the understanding of indivisibles,'' or ''simples,'' i.e., of single uncompounded terms or intelligible contents; in this the question of truth or falsity does not arise. The second is a certain association of intelligible contents separately apprehended, which will necessarily be either true or false (*Anim.* 430a 25-b5; *Interp.* 16a 13; *Meta.* 1027b 17–23, 1051b 2–26, 33–35).

The Stoics devoted much discussion to judgment and the proposition (ἀξίωμα), which they defined as a complete utterance that is either true or false (Diogenes Laertius, *Lives* 7.65–66; Cicero, *Tusc.* 1.7.14, *De fato* 10.20): Truth and error, they held, do not belong to disconnected notions but to notions combined in a judgment. Yet it is

"Last Judgement," 11th-century Roman Benedictine School painting by Giovanni and Niccolo.

not the simple combination of concepts that they stress but assent. Judgment is basically the referring of an image received in sensation to an external thing. Though there are some irresistible perceptions, which clearly and distinctly represent a real thing as it really is and constitute the criterion of truth (Sextus Empiricus, *C. math.* 7.244; Cicero, *Acad.* 2.12.37–38, 1.11.41; Diogenes, *Lives* 7.51), nevertheless assent is usually in man's power and thus voluntary (Sextus, *C. math.* 8.397; Cicero, *Acad.* 1.14.40, 2.12.37; *De fato* 19.43). *See* STOICISM.

Scholastic Philosophy. In the Middle Ages the general lines of Aristotle's doctrine were commonly followed. Judgment was referred to as the second operation of the intellect or as *compositio et divisio*. Varying degrees of emphasis were put upon the compositive, the assentient, and the existential aspects. (For the doctrine of St. Thomas Aquinas see below.)

In later SCHOLASTICISM, FERRARIENSIS, interpreting St. Thomas, taught that judgment is in a certain way a reflective act since it implies the comparison of a QUIDDITY apprehended by the intellect with the thing about which it is apprehended, and the pronouncement of conformity or disconformity (*In C. gent.* 1.59.6). F. SUÁREZ denied that judgment is reflexive and held that the direct act that constitutes it has two aspects that are not really distinct operations: the combination of two previously apprehended terms and the acceptance of this combination as representative of the thing (*De anim.* 3.6.3–4). JOHN OF ST. THOMAS maintained that the operations of forming the proposition and of assenting to it as true of the thing are distinct and that the latter is judgment taken formally (*Phil. nat.* 11.3 ad 2).

Modern Philosophy. R. DESCARTES too emphasized the aspect of assent. Holding with the supposedly traditional view that judgment consists in the affirmation or denial of one idea or another and that only here are truth and error found, he nevertheless insisted that this is more than the perception of a relationship between concepts: it is an activity of accepting and approving the association made; and because all activity depends upon the will, the assent of judgment is voluntary and free and is, in fact, an act of the will rather than of the intellect (*Princ. phil.* 1.32, 34, 6; *Med.* 4).

T. HOBBES took a nominalistic view of judgment, regarding it as the joining of two names that belong to the same thing (*Leviathan* 1.7; cf. 1.5). Truth is merely "the right ordering of names in our affirmations" (1.4).

J. LOCKE paid much more attention to the association of ideas than to affirmation or negation. For him, knowledge is "nothing but the perception of the connexion and agreement or disagreement and repugnancy of any of our ideas" (*Essay Concerning Human Understanding* 4.1.2). Knowledge is certain. Judgment is of the same character except that it is sometimes contrasted with knowledge as being only probable or presumed perception (4.14.3–4; 4.6.13).

D. HUME too was concerned more with the association of ideas than with judgment as such. For him, "ideas" are only faint images left by sensory impressions (*Treatise of Human Nature* 1.1.1). In an important note on the *Treatise* he finds fault with the traditional division of the operations of the mind into conception, judgment, and reasoning and says that these operations "all resolve themselves into the first," which is conception or simple apprehension (1.3.1 n).

T. REID rejected the "ideal system"—the doctrine of ideas as substitutes for things—of Descartes, Locke, and Hume. Though he agreed with Hume in rejecting the traditional "division of the powers of the mind" (*Essays on the Intellectual Powers* 1.7), rather than reduce judgment to simple apprehension he made judgment come first. Sensation, taken absolutely, is held to be "necessarily accompanied by a belief in its present existence." Simple apprehension is defined as "a sensation imagined or thought of" (*Inquiry into the Human Mind* 2.3). Because "sensation must go before memory and imagination," he argues that "it necessarily follows that apprehension accompanied with belief and knowledge must go before simple apprehension . . . , so that here, instead of saying that the belief or knowledge is got by putting together and comparing the simple apprehensions, we ought rather to say that simple apprehension is performed by resolving and analyzing a natural and original judgment" (*ibid.* 2.4).

Though the point is not clear in I. KANT, there are indications that he too considers judgment to precede apprehension or conception. Understanding is the awareness of a unity (*Critique of Pure Reason* B89–90) and is primarily or essentially judging (B93–94, 141). This must be done by means of concepts, and the basic concepts or categories are derived from the forms of judgment (B94, 378). Kant even asserts that distinct concepts presuppose judgment just as complete concepts presuppose ratiocination. This leaves the possibility, however, that at least indistinct concepts do not come after judgment but that judgment and concepts arise together, one being impossible without the other. The division of "judgments" from which Kant derives the categories more properly belongs to a study of propositions. But there is a twofold prior division that belongs to the very manner of judging. Judgments are a posteriori if derived from experience and a priori if independent of experience (B1–2). They are analytic when the predicate is contained in the concept of the subject and synthetic when the predicate adds to the subject something not contained in its concept (B10–11). Kant's theoretical doctrine is devoted chiefly to examining how a priori synthetic judgments are possible (B14–24).

Reacting against the opinion of judgment as a mere association of images or ideas, which he thought to be almost universally held, F. BRENTANO distinguished between representation and acceptance or assent [*Vom Ursprung sittlicher Erkenntnis*, ed. O. Kraus (Hamburg 1955) 15–16]. And he interprets the "is" of all propositions as expressing directly actual existence [*Von der Klassifikation der psychischen Phänomene* (Leipzig 1911) 53–63].

Doctrine of St. Thomas Aquinas

The doctrine of St. THOMAS AQUINAS on judgment may be exposed in terms of his teaching on composition through comparison, on the distinct function of terms, on the affirmation of concrete existence, and on truth and falsity.

Composition Through Comparison. Judgment is commonly referred to by St. Thomas as *compositio et divisio,* combining and separating (*In 3 anim.* 11.746–747; *In 6 meta.* 4.1232; *In Boeth. de Trin.* 5.3; *In 1 anal. post. 1.4*). By it the natures apprehended in the first operation are associated or dissociated (*In 1 perih.* 1.3–4). This second operation would not be needed were it not for the imperfection of man's simple APPREHENSION, which is abstractive, attaining only a single partial aspect of the thing at a time (*Summa theologiae* 1a, 58.4; *C. gent.* 1.58, 2.98; *De ver.* 8.4 ad 5). Common intelligible traits are grasped without the individualized subject in which they are found (*Summa theologiae* 1a, 85.1, 12.4; *In 2 anim.* 12.377); the nature is first known only confusedly and indeterminately, i.e., generically, without its specific characteristic (*Summa theologiae* 1a, 85.3, 14.6; *In 1 phys.* 1.7; *C. gent.* 2.98); the substantial nature is known without the accidents (*Summa theologiae* 1a, 85.5; *In 7 meta.,* 5.1379; *De ver.* 2.7); the accidents are grasped separately (*In 2 phys.* 3.5; *In 1 perih.* 10.4); and the quiddity, or essence, is understood without the particular act of existing (*esse*) that it has in reality (*De ente* 3; *Quodl.* 8.1).

To know the thing as it is in reality, a single whole, one and concretely existing, one must have an operation that reintegrates the intelligible aspects of the thing and signifies it as existing. This requires a comparison, the establishment of a relation, which is the unity of its terms. Correlatives are known together (*C. gent.* 1.55; *In 4 sent.* 15.4.2.5 ad 3; *De pot.* 7.10 ad 4; *De ver.* 2.3 sed. contra 2). So when the data of apprehension are seen to be relat-

ed, they are seen as one (*De ver.* 13.3; *Summa theologiae* 1a, 58.2; *Quodl.* 7.2). This comparison is judgment, "combination and separation." As an operation it is always a combination or composition, though from the standpoint of the apprehended natures it is either composition or separation according as they are perceived to belong together or not (*In 1 perih.* 3.4). Composition is a form of union (*De ver.* 2.7 ad 3; *De pot.* 7.1 ad 10) by which distinct things are made one. By the compositive act of the intellect the various yields of apprehension are united into a single intelligible whole (*In 3 anim.* 11.747; *In 6 meta.* 4.1241; *In 3 sent.* 14.1.2.4; *De ver.* 8.14; *Summa theologiae* 1a, 58.2). By judging and forming a proposition the intellect restores natures to subjects and accidents to substances (*De ver.* 2.7; *Summa theologiae* 1a, 14.14, 85.5), thus reestablishing the condition in which things exist (*In 3 sent.* 27.1.1 ad 5).

Distinct Function of Terms. The two elements joined in judgment do not stand on the same footing and perform the same function. One, which represents the thing to be understood (and stands as the subject in the proposition formed), is regarded as determinable in human thought; the other, which signifies what one understands about the thing (and stands as the predicate in the proposition), is determining. The two elements are therefore related as material and formal principles respectively (*In 9 meta.* 11.1898; *In 1 perih.* 8.11, 10.23; *De ver.* 8.14 ad 6; *Summa theologiae* 1a, 16.2; 3a, 16.7 ad 4, 9 ad 3). The hylomorphic composition of the proposition represents the real composition or unity of the thing known and the condition in which it exists.

When the apprehended aspects of the thing are connected in their very notions or essence, the judgment is *per se,* or essential. When the connection is not essential but only factual or existential, the judgment is *per accidens,* or accidental (*In 1 anal. post.* 13.2, 10.2–7, 33.4–9; *In 5 meta.* 9.886–888; *In 4 meta.* 2.548, 554; 7.622–635; *De pot.* 8.2 ad 6, 9.4; *In 1 perih.* 5.9; *De fallaciis* 10). In the latter case the connection must be perceived through the SENSES. In the former, though the notions are abstracted from sense representations, the connection itself is intelligible, and knowledge of it does not depend upon this presentation.

Because in judging one says that the subject *is* the predicate, he establishes an identity between them (*In 5 meta.* 11.908; *Summa theologiae* 1a, 85.5 ad 3). The kind of identity, however, is not the same in essential and in accidental judgments. In those that are essential the identity is formal (*In 3 sent.* 11.1.4 ad 6); that is, the two intelligibilities are grasped as being in whole or in part the same (*ibid.* 10.1.1.2; *De ente* 2; *In 7 meta.* 2.1288, 3.1328; *De pot.* 8.4 ad 2). In accidental judgments the identity, being only factual, is merely an identity in subject or supposit (*In 3 sent.* 22.1.2, 11.1.4 ad 6, 12.1.1 ad 6; *Summa theologiae* 1a, 85.5 ad 3), for the thing apprehended in the subject and in the predicate is the same (*De pot.* 8.2 ad 6). This identity in the thing is signified by the verbal composition (*C. gent.* 1.36). The unity of the thing founds the composition made in understanding (*ibid.; De ente 3*). The judgment, accordingly, by combining a subject and a predicate distinguished in apprehension, signifies a real unity and a rational diversity (*Summa theologiae* 1a, 13.12; *C. gent.* 1.36).

Affirmation of Concrete Existence. Just as the real existence of a composite being results from the composition of its elements (*De pot.* 7.1; *In 9 meta.* 11.1903; *In 1 sent.* 23.1.1, 38.1.3), so the existence will be signified in thought when a corresponding composition of the apprehended elements is effected in judging. Consequently, the second operation is concerned with the existence of the thing, whereas the first operation is concerned with its essence (*In Boeth. de Trin.* 5.3; *In 1 sent.* 19.5.1 ad 7, 38.1.3). This does not mean that apprehension has no reference to existence (for the essence is the manner in which existence is exercised) or that every judgment is directly a judgment of existence (for in an attributive judgment the direct intent is to assign an attribute). But the verb "to be" that is used to effect the composition, and is called the copula (*In 9 meta.* 11.1900; *In 5 meta.* 9.895–896; *Quodl.* 9.3; *C. gent.* 1.12; *In 1 sent.* 33.1.1 ad 1; *De nat. gen.* 2), even when attributive, retains the meaning of existence. For the subject is said to exist in the way signified by the predicate. "This paper is white" means "This paper exists in a white way." The predicate signifies a form had by the subject; form is the principle of existence; and for each form had there is an act of existing (*In Boeth. de hebdom.* 2.27; *Summa theologiae* 1a, 75.6, 42.1 ad 1; *De prin. nat.* 2). "To be" is the ultimate act of things and the act in which composite beings have their reality. The verb "to be" used without qualification signifies only actual existence; but it also, when followed by an attribute, signifies composition, because it signifies existence with the form attributed (*In 1 perih.* 5.22, 9.4). It need not, however, always signify existence in the real order (outside the mind); it suffices that it signify the type of existence appropriate to the subject, for truth is fulfilled in the mind (*In 1 sent.* 19.5.1 and ad 5).

Truth and Falsity. Because judgment signifies existence, it always involves TRUTH or FALSITY (*In 3 anim.* 11.748, 760; *In 6 meta.* 4.1224, 1225, 1227, 1236; *In 1 perih.* 3.2, 6.9). For "true" means that what is *is,* and that what is not *is not;* and "false" means just the reverse (*In 4 meta.* 17.740, 736; 16.721; *C. gent.* 1.59, 62). And it is in judging that one says that something is or is not, is so or is not so. For not only is something known about

a thing, but it is also applied to the thing, setting up a relation or comparison between one's knowledge and the thing (*C. gent.* 1.59). When an intelligible character is apprehended about some thing, the intellect, being spiritual and self-luminous, is conscious of its act of apprehending and of its reference to the object; it thereby knows the conformity of its concept (used as the predicate in judging) to the thing (*De ver.* 1.9; *In 3 sent.* 23.1.2 ad 3; *In 1 perih.* 3.6, 9; *In 6 meta.* 4.1236). The judgment made contains implicitly the affirmation that the thing is as the intellect has conceived it. Thus there is here the known conformity required for formal truth (*In 1 perih.* 3. 6, 9; *Summa theologiae* 1a, 16.2; *In 1 sent.* 19.5.2).

Judgment accordingly implies assent, which is adherence to a proposition as true (*De ver.* 14.1). By expressing the "is" (or "is not") of judgment man commits himself to the truth or falsity of the composition he makes, and in this his knowledge is completed (*C. gent.* 1.59).

Discussion of Divergent Views

The diversity of views mentioned in the historical survey may now be discussed in terms of the doctrine of St. Thomas. This is done in three stages, the first treating views in modern philosophy; the second, disputes in scholastic philosophy; and the third, the special theory of Brentano.

Modern Views. The view that judgment is a mere association of ideas arises in Locke and Hume largely from their empiricism and their inadequate distinction of "ideas" from sensory images and impressions, along with their psychologism and their rather automatic view of the association of images. Hobbes's association of names rests on a similar empiricist basis. The genuine intellectual nature of judgment is obscured, if not denied; judgment is deprived of its distinctive feature: the conscious reference of the representations of things to the things they represent; assent is slighted; and the relevance of truth and falsity to judgment is made accidental. This is especially evident in Hume's reduction of judgment to simple apprehension. (*See* EMPIRICISM; PSYCHOLOGISM.)

Reid's interpretation of judgment as preceding apprehension, while taking account of assent and identifying judgment with it, is possible only because, retaining a strong empiricism, he makes assent consist in a mere acceptance of sense impressions. Assent thus appears not to be an intellectual activity at all, and judgment implies no reflection upon a CONCEPT formed and reference back to the real.

Kant, in seeming to make judgment anterior to conception, overlooks the necessity of first deriving from the thing known some intelligible character or nature and then referring it to the thing. And even within his system it is hard to see how there can be any conscious subsumption of phenomena organized in sensibility under a mental form of synthesis unless that form is in some sense preconceived.

In holding that all assent in judgment is an act of the will and is free (thus going even beyond the Stoics), Descartes excessively generalized a very true observation: many of a person's judgments are in fact free. This is true of all judgment based upon testimony, whether human or divine, because the evidence is only extrinsic and not found in the proposition itself to which assent is given. It is true also in judgments in which the evidence had is insufficient or less than compelling, as in opinionative judgments. In judgments in which the evidence is sufficient, a distinction must be made. When the evidence is mediate and the judgment is made as a result of reasoning, the judgment, and the assent, is free as regards the exercise of the act (i.e., carrying out the reasoning process or not), but not, if the reasoning is actually done, as regards "the object," i.e., the conclusion (*Summa theologiae* 1a2ae, 17.6). For the process, with the mediate evidence that it brings, is compelling. It is in this latter sense that St. Thomas says that the assent of science is not subject to free choice (*Summa theologiae* 2a2ae, 2.9 ad 2). In regard to immediate evidence, as is had in FIRST PRINCIPLES, assent is necessary not only as regards the object but even as regards the exercise if the intellect is used at all (*Summa theologiae* 1a, 82.2; 1a2ae, 17.6), for these principles are implicit in every judgment that is made (*In 4 meta.* 6.605).

Scholastic Disputes. In the dispute involving Ferrariensis, Suárez, and John of St. Thomas, Suárez correctly rejected any reflex act as the initial act of reason; for a reflex act always presupposes an antecedent direct act. But he incorrectly attributed the rejected view to Ferrariensis, who did not place assent in reflex judgments but rather in direct judgments, which nevertheless imply and suppose a reflection upon the apprehension of the predicate. Nor did Suárez, in holding that judgment consists primarily in the conjunction of concepts, deny or exclude assent. He says that the composition is made by "passing judgment." But what judgment is passed upon, in his view, is the fact that one concept belongs to the other. This does not sufficiently explain why the conjunction is made and neglects reference to the thing of which the concepts are formed. The distinction made by John of St. Thomas (in opposition to this view of Suárez) between the formation of the proposition (or the recognition of the composition) and assent to it as two really distinct acts requires some qualification. When a proposition is proposed by another, it is true that one first recognizes the

proposition before assenting to it. But when one forms a proposition oneself, the assent is not distinct from the formation of the proposition. For the proposition is not formed until one places the "is" or "is not" of the copula; and when one places these, by that very fact he assents to the truth of the proposition. One does admittedly form *questions* without assenting. But a question is not a proposition in the technical sense any more than an interrogative sentence is declarative. A proposition is declarative or assertive; it is an assertion, a statement, an enunciation; and this implies commitment and assent.

A more recent dispute is that among contemporary Thomists on the role of judgment in the knowledge of existence. Taking the statement of St. Thomas that simple apprehension deals with essence and judgment with existence, some of his followers have held that existence is known only in judgment and that there is no concept of existence [É. Gilson, *Being and Some Philosophers* (2d ed. Toronto 1952); R. J. Henle, "Existentialism and Judgment," *American Catholic Philosophical Association. Proceedings of the Annual Meeting* 21 (Baltimore 1946) 40–51]. Others have disputed this, holding that existence is known in simple apprehension and in a concept, even though the knowledge is completed and the existence is joined with its subject in judgment [L. M. Régis, "Gilson's *Being and Some Philosophers,*" *The Modern Schoolman* 28 (St. Louis 1950–51) 111–125]. Still others have held that, though a judgment of existence precedes the concept of existence, a concept is formed in an indirect way, in which it is treated somewhat as if it were an essence (J. Maritain, *Existence and the Existent,* New York 1949). The words of St. Thomas can also be taken to mean that existence is not expressly signified in the simple apprehension of things, as it is in judgment, though it is implicitly connoted.

Brentano's Theory. Finally, Brentano's contention that every proposition, because it expresses or implies "is," is existential correctly calls attention to the fact that existence is signified in every judgment; but it exaggerates in supposing that the existence signified is always real and actual and that the direct intent of the judgment is always to signify existence unqualified. This clearly does not fit the case when the subject is a logical being, as in the judgment that "a syllogism is made up of three propositions"; for a syllogism cannot have real existence. And even when the subject designates a real being but is taken universally and the proposition is attributive, this interpretation is inapplicable; for example, "Man is a social being." Here, though the existence in question is real rather than logical, it is not the actual existence of man or of men but the possible or hypothetical existence that is meant: "If man exists, then man is social." And the direct intent of this proposition is not to affirm existence but to assign an attribute. It is not the bare fact of existing that is primarily meant but rather the manner in which the existence, if had, is exercised. Directly existential judgments are rather rarely made; for it is only when the existence of something is doubtful or brought into question that one stops to affirm it explicitly.

See Also: UNDERSTANDING (INTELLECTUS); KNOWLEDGE, CONNATURAL; KNOWLEDGE, PROCESS OF.

Bibliography: M. J. ADLER, ed., *The Great Ideas: A Syntopicon of Great Books of the Western World,* 2 v. (Chicago 1952); v.2, 3 of *Great Books of the Western World* 1:835–849. P. H. J. HOENEN, *Reality and Judgment According to St. Thomas,* tr. H. F. TIBLIER (Chicago 1952). F. H. PARKER and H. B. VEATCH, *Logic as a Human Instrument* (New York 1959). R. W. SCHMIDT, ''Judgment and Predication in a Realistic Philosophy,'' *The New Scholasticism* 29 (Washington 1955) 318–326. F. M. TYRRELL, ''Concerning the Nature and the Function of the Act of Judgment,'' *ibid.* 26 (1952) 393–423. J. LEBACQZ, ''Apprehension or Assent?'' *Heythrop Journal* 5 (Oxford 1964) 36–57. F. A. CUNNINGHAM, ''Judgment in St. Thomas,'' *The Modern Schoolman* 31 (1954) 185–212.

[R. W. SCHMIDT]

JUDGMENT, DIVINE (IN THE BIBLE)

The belief that God is judge of all men is found throughout Scripture. Judgment is sometimes manifested in this life, but when the belief in an afterlife appears, God is seen primarily as eschatological judge. *See* ESCHATOLOGY (IN THE BIBLE). In the New Testament much emphasis is placed upon the bestowal of the divine prerogative of judgment upon Christ. This article will investigate the concept of God as judge, the particular judgment, and the general judgment.

God as Judge. The concept of God as a judge, imposing divine decisions upon men, is an idea that Israelite religion shared with surrounding pagans. The power that all religions generally attribute to their gods is best illustrated by the prerogative of judging, of issuing decrees and verdicts from which there is no appeal. The Biblical concept of judgment, however, can be clearly understood only in relation to the idea of justice, for it was the primary duty of a judge ''to do justice'' (*see* JUSTICE OF GOD; JUSTICE OF MEN). A man is just (*saddīq*) if he is in a right relationship with God and his fellow men. Since this righteousness is necessary to regulate all the affairs of life, it can be described as the highest value in life. By Western standards just conduct is considered as behavior conforming to an established ethical norm with absolute claims. In the Old Testament, however, conduct was measured not by an ideal norm but by the fulfillment of the various claims exacted by specific relationships with other men. Men move in many different relationships—familial, national, economic—each of which carries with it particular demands.

There is, furthermore, the special relationship of man with God; here again the just man is the one who fulfills the claims placed upon him by this relationship. In turn, God shows forth His justice, His righteous acts, when He is faithful to the role which He Himself established in relation to Israel. God fulfills the claims of this relationship particularly when He acts as judge. Numerous texts appeal to the divine decisions: ''The Lord judge between you and me'' (Gn 16.5; *see also*: Jgs 11.27; 1 Sm 24.13). So closely are justice and judgment related that the two terms are constantly linked in Biblical texts, becoming almost a literary cliché [Am 5.7; Ps 35(36).7; 93(94).15; 139(140).13].

Basically, the notion of judging means settling a dispute, making things right. Inasmuch as one of the disputants was right and the other wrong, to judge came to mean to help a man obtain his rights [Ps 74(75).8] or to condemn a man (Ez 7.3; 8.27). Many of the Psalms of complaint envision the suppliant pleading before God to do justice, i.e., to recognize the requirements of the divine relationship with His servant by vindicating the servant before his enemies [Ps 25(26).1; 34(35).24; 42(43).1].

The vindication of the just man through God's judgment brought with it condemnation of the unjust adversary; hence judgment is sometimes equated with punishment or condemnation: ''He will do judgment on the nations, heaping up corpses'' [Ps 109(110).6; *see also*: 7.12; 118(119).84; Ez 25.11].

Particular Judgment. Because of development of thought concerning the resurrection of the dead and afterlife, ideas on God's judgment of the individual underwent a good deal of change during the Biblical period. Separate sections on particular judgment in the Old Testament and in the New Testament will make this evolution clear.

In the Old Testament. Particular judgment in the sense of a divine pronouncement determining an individual's fate after death is not found in the Old Testament. The prevailing view of a RETRIBUTION operative within the limits of the present life prevented such an understanding until quite late, when the ideas of resurrection (*see* RESURRECTION OF THE DEAD) and immortality had taken hold of Jewish thought. The judgment of God had to be exercised here and now by recognition of a man's works and the recompense proper to them. Prosperity, posterity, longevity—these were the signs of God's favorable judgment upon a man [Ps 1.1–3; 36(37).18–25; 54(55).23; Prv 22.4]. To live wretchedly and to be cut off from life early without descendants were regarded as evidence of God's judgment against a man [Jb 15.20–21; Ps

139(140).12; Wis 3.18–19]. For the just and unjust alike the judgment was lived out in this life.

Reality belied the traditional picture, however. The Psalmist might say, "Neither in my youth, nor now that I am old, have I seen a just man forsaken nor his descendants begging bread" [Ps 36(37).25], but from early times Israel could also ask, "Why do the wicked prosper?" [Jer 12.1; *see also*: Psalms 36(37) and 72(73)]. In such questioning the justice of God is not doubted; this divine attribute is always assumed: "Does God pervert judgment, and does the Almighty distort justice?" (Jb 8.3). Even the cynical assertions of the Book of ECCLESIASTES about a like fate for the good and the wicked are counterbalanced by the author's insistence that "God will bring to judgment every work" (Eccl 12.14; *see also*: 3.17).

To see God's justice achieved was more difficult, however, and the gap between theory and observable fact produced genuine pain. The answers varied from dogged repetition of the traditional view to the cynical assertion that "it is all one! . . . Both the innocent and the wicked he destroys" (Jb 9.22). The answer of an immortality of reward or punishment following a personal judgment was not reached until a century and a half before Christ.

If some texts seem to suggest a personal judgment after death, this is doubtless because the developed doctrine of a later time is read into them. For example, Sir 21.9 suggests the fires of hell: "A band of criminals is like a bundle of tow; they will end in a flaming fire," but the words indicate merely the speedy destruction of the wicked by comparing them to swift-burning tow. Mention of the pain, decay, and corruption in store for man (Jb 17.14; 21.26; Is 14.11; 66.24) means no more than the fate common to all men. (*See* AFTERLIFE, 2.) Even the texts that speak of God's repaying a man on the day of his death according to his deeds (Sir 11.26) refer to retribution in this life, which may, however, be deferred until the day of death.

The prerogative of judging is closely associated with Yahweh's power as king. Justice and judgment are the foundations of His throne [Ps 96(97).2]. The divine judgment is not limited to Israel, for the entire earth is under His sway: "Rise, O God; judge the earth, for yours are all the nations" [Ps 81(82).8; *see also*: 104(105).7; 1 Sm 2.10; Jer 25.31]. God is especially the protector of the rights of the poor, the widow, and the orphan [Jb 36.6; Ps 67(68).6; 81(82).3; Is 1.17]. All the judgment exercised by the Israelite king is regarded as the gift of the Lord, from whom all right judgment comes [Ps 71 (72).1–2; Is 9.6].

From God's decisions there is no appeal, and Israel recognizes the justice of His verdict: "By a proper judgment you have done all this because of our sins" (Dn 3.29; *see also*: Tb 3.2–5; Ez 7.8). Every man will be judged according to his works (Wis 3.10; Ez 7.8). This doctrine of individual responsibility is developed especially in Ez 18.1–32; 33.10–20. As divine pronouncements, His decrees possess a binding force like that of the commandments, with which they are often associated: "They shall live by my statutes and carefully observe my decrees" (Ez 37.24).

Beginning with Genesis, God's judgment upon wickedness is spelled out in almost every book of the Old Testament, from the punishment of ADAM and EVE to the fate of the soldiers in the army of the Machabees (2 Mc 12.40–42). The moral will of the Lord permeates all of life; He is not indifferent to His creatures' disobedience, and He never leaves the guilty unpunished (Na 1.2–3; 1 Chr 21.7). Indeed there is often a disconcerting association between evil-doing and swift judgment: "Her was wicked in the sight of the Lord, so the Lord killed him" (Gn 38.7).

Numerous proverbs in the SAPIENTIAL BOOKS show the Lord weighing a man's heart: "The eyes of the Lord are in every place, keeping watch on the evil and the good" (Prv 15.3; *see also*: 16.2). Nothing escapes His impartial and just scrutiny (Prv 16.11); the nether world and the abyss lie open before Him; "how much more the hearts of men" (Prv 15.11; *see also*: Sir 18.1).

In the New Testament. The notion of divine judgment is continued and expanded in the New Testament. Since the ideas of the resurrection of the body and immortality were well developed by the time of Christ, God's definitive judgments, both particular and general, were regarded as taking place after death. Meanwhile, both the good and the wicked will continue to grow until the harvest (Mt 13.30, 40). There are no clear references to individual judgment in the Gospels; passages such as "Of every idle word men speak, they shall give account on the day of judgment" (Mt 12.36) can refer to either a particular or general judging. The particular judgment is implied in the story of Lazarus and the rich man (Lk 16.19–31). References to judgment occur always within the context of admonitions to penance and good works. Only repentance can save a man from the wrath to come (Mt 3.7–10; Lk 3.7–9). To avoid the dread sentence no price is too great: "It is better for thee to enter life maimed or lame, than, having two hands or two feet, to be cast into the everlasting fire" (Mt 18.8; *see also*: Mk 9.42–46). See HELL (IN THE BIBLE). In the light of coming judgment men are urged to enter by the narrow gate leading to life (Mt 7.13–14; Lk 13.24–30); to lay up lasting treasure in heaven (Mt 6.20); and for the sake of heaven to rejoice in suffering (Mt 5.12).

In his Epistles St. Paul reminds his hearers that "we shall all stand at the judgment seat of God" (Rom 14.10; *see also*: Acts 24.25; Heb 9.27–28). In 2 Cor 5.10 he speaks of judgment before the tribunal of Christ.

General Judgment. The theme of a judgment upon all men on the last day is a common one in Scripture. In both the OT and the NT it is often referred to as the DAY OF THE LORD.

In the Old Testament. The concept of general judgment in the OT occurs usually in the form of divine verdicts upon cities, tribes, or peoples in terms of punishment here on earth for their crimes. There is no doubt that events like the deluge (Gn 6.5–8.19) or the destruction of Sodom and Gomorrah (Gn 19.1–29) are presented as God's moral judgment upon human wickedness. The Book of JUDGES is built upon the often-repeated pattern of sin, punishment, repentance, and delivery. The prophetic writings in particular abound in harsh threats of the judgment awaiting the men and nations who continue to defy the Lord by the evil of their ways (Am 1.3–2.16; Ez 38.21–22; etc.). After the division of the kingdom, Amos threatened Israel and her neighbors with divine punishments for their manifold crimes (Am 1.4–6.14). Other prophets, too, direct their oracles against the pagan nations, reminding them of God's judgment to come (Is 13.1–19.25; Jer 46.1–51.64; Ez 25.1–32.32). These nations will feel God's wrath because of their crimes and because they have rejoiced over the desecration of the Temple and over Judah's downfall.

Although God will punish the arrogance of the pagans toward His chosen people, He nevertheless permits this conduct as His judgment upon faithless Israel: "I will chastise you as you deserve; I will not let you go unpunished" (Jer 46.28; *see also*: 17.4; 25.8–11). He uses the pagan nations as a rod for the punishment of His chosen ones (Is 10.5–11). Utter ruin and exile are the historical forms in which the Lord's judgments were expressed.

One of the earliest features of MESSIANISM in Israel was the expectation of "the day of the Lord," a time when God's destiny for His people would be fully and finally realized. This day of shame and destruction for Israel's enemies would bring corresponding triumph and prosperity to Israel. But the prophets question this understanding; Amos asks, "What will the day of the Lord mean for you? Darkness and not light!" (Am 5.18). This day will be "exceedingly terrible" (Jl 2.11), a day "of wrath and burning anger" (Is 13.9). These and similar texts are often applied to the general judgment at the end of the world; *see also*: Ez 30.1–19; So 1.2–2.15.

As messianism developed, the prophetic vision of judgments upon individual nations and upon Israel be-

came cosmic in scope: God's judgment would be a definitive intervention in history at the end of time (Dn 8.17), marked by devastation and destruction as preludes to a new order of things (Dn 2.31–45; 7.11–14, 17–27). In this apocalyptic literature the end of time is preceded by resurrection from the dead; the good will live forever, but everlasting horror and disgrace will be the lot of the wicked (Dn 12.2). The tribunal will pronounce against all the enemies of God and give to the just possession of the kingdom (Dn 7.9–18, 21–23, 26–27).

In the New Testament. Many specific references to the general judgment at the end of the world at the return of Christ occur in the New Testament. The most dramatic account of the general judgment is found in Mt 25.31–46; *see also*: Mk 13.14–27. The Judge, the standard of judgment, and the rewards and punishments are vividly described. At that time the SON OF MAN will render to everyone according to his conduct (Mt 16.27); it will be more tolerable for Tyre and Sidon than for unbelievers (Mt 11.22–24; Lk 10.14); and the men of Nineve will rise in judgment against an unbelieving generation (Mt 12.41; Lk 11.32).

The judgment of condemnation is invariably linked with fire: John the Baptist warns that the bad tree will be cast into unquenchable fire (Mt 3.10; Lk 3.17; *see also*: Mt 18.8–9; Mk 9.42–47). Jesus uses the same metaphor in Mt 7.19, as well as in the parable of the wheat and weeds (Mt 13.30, 40–42). Buried in hell, the rich man longs for a single drop of water (Lk 16.22–24). In Matthew's classic description the wicked are committed to the fires intended for the Devil and his angels (Mt 25.41–46).

For the just the final judgment will be a vindication and often a reversal of their situation in this life; on that day they will take possession of the kingdom (Mt 25.34) and receive a hundredfold with life everlasting (Mt 19.29–30). The ideas of the kingdom of God and judgment are closely associated: John preaches that the kingdom is at hand (Mt 3.2), and one can enter it only through repentance (Mt 3.7–8), which is also the condition for a favorable judgment. Further, a man's attitude toward the kingdom is often mentioned in terms applicable to the final judgment: "Not everyone who says to me, 'Lord, Lord,' shall enter the kingdom of heaven" (Mt 7.21). Finally, the kingdom in its full glory will be established only on the day of judgment, when the good will be separated from the wicked.

The general judgment is most often depicted as a single aspect of the PAROUSIA, the glorious return of Christ (Mt 16.27; 19.28–29; Lk 9.26). Historically, Catholic piety has often emphasized the judgment to the neglect of other features, such as the definitive establishment of

God's kingdom and the inauguration of a new order of creation (*see* CREATION, 1). In the Parousia it is Christ who judges, but there are also texts which state that it is the Father who repays (Mt 6.4, 18; Lk 18.7) and that it is Christ who bears witness for the just (Mt 10.32).

John speaks of judgment in terms similar to those of the Synoptics (Jn 5.27, 29; 12.48), but in some passages a new note is found: judgment has already occurred (Jn 5.25; 12.31). In this realized eschatology the believer ''does not come to judgment, but has passed from death to life'' (Jn 5.24), while the wrath of God rests upon the unbeliever (Jn 3.36; see also 3.18). The twofold theme of light and life [*see* LIFE, CONCEPT OF (IN THE BIBLE)] in his Gospel is closely linked with judgment: ''Now this is the judgment: The light has come into the world, yet men have loved the darkness rather than the light, for their works were evil'' (Jn 3.19); and ''he who is unbelieving towards the Son shall not see life, but the wrath of God rests upon him'' (Jn 3.36). John speaks of judgment having been committed to the Son (Jn 5.22, 27, 30; 9.39), but he also states that Jesus has not come to judge, but to save (Jn 3.17; 12.47). *See* JOHN, GOSPEL ACCORDING TO ST.

The Epistles also speak of the last day when ''God will judge the hidden secrets of men through Jesus Christ'' (Rom 2.16; *see also*: Acts 17:31; 1 Pt 4.5). The role of Christ as judge is emphasized in all the texts; usually the judgment is spoken of in connection with the second coming of Christ (2 Thes 1.7–10; 2 Tm 4.1), when pronouncement will be made on both the living and the dead (Acts 10.42; 2 Tm 4.1; 1 Pt 4.5).

Since the judgment will manifest God's justice, St. Paul speaks of it as ''the revelation of the Lord Jesus'' (2 Thes 1.7). The day of the Lord described by the prophets becomes for him ''the day of our Lord Jesus Christ'' (1 Cor 5.5; 2 Cor 1.14). The unexpectedness of God's visitation should prompt watchfulness (1 Thes 5.1–11) and perseverance in good works. The reward of the just is ''to be ever with the Lord'' (1 Thes 4.17), but the Lord will pour out his wrath upon sinners (Rom 2.5–10), slaying them with the breath of His mouth and the brightness of His coming (2 Thes 2.8).

Reflecting the traditions of the late apocalyptic writing of the Old Testament, the Book of Revelation emphasizes the resurrection of the dead before the final judgment (11.11), the utter destruction of God's enemies (ch. 6, 8, 9), the coming of Christ for judgment (14.7, 14–20), and the establishment of a new order of happiness and bliss for the elect (20.4–6).

Bibliography: *Encyclopdeic Dictionary of the Bible,* tr. and adap. by L. HARTMAN (New York 1963)1241–47. A. PAUTREL and D. MOLLAT, *Dictionnaire de la Bible,* suppl. ed. L. PIROT (Paris 1928–) 4:1321–94. F. BÜCHSEL and V. HERNTRICH, G. KITTEL, *Theologisches Wörterbuch zum Neuen Testament* (Stuttgart 1935–) 3:920–955. J. SCHMID, *Lexikon für Theologie und Kirche,* ed. J. HOFER and K. RAHNER, 10 v. (2d, new ed. Freiburg 1957–65); suppl., *Das ZweiteVatikanische Konzil: Dokumente und kommentare,* ed. H. S. BRECHTER et al., pt. 1 (1966) 4:727–731. F. HORST and H. CONZELMANN, *Die Religion in Geschichte und Gegenwart,* 7 v. (3d ed. Tübingen 1957–65) 2:1417–21. W. EICHRODT, *Theology of the Old Testament,* tr. J. A. BAKER (Philadelphia 1961–) 1:381–391, 457–471. P. HEINISCH, *Theology of the Old Testament,* tr. W. G. HEIDT (Collegeville, MN 1950) 259–280. G. VON RAD, *Old Testament Theology,* tr. D. STALKER (New York 1962–) 1:370–383. W. COSSMANN, *Die Entwicklung des Gerichts-Gedankens bei den alttestamentlichen Propheten* (Giessen 1915). M. GOGUEL, *Le Jugement dans le N. T.* (Paris 1942) 5–20. J. A. T. ROBINSON, *Jesus and His Coming* (London 1957); ''The *Parable* of the Sheep and the Goats,'' *New Testament Studies* 2 (1955–56) 225–237. C. H. DODD, *The Interpretation of the Fourth Gospel* (Cambridge, England 1953) 201–212. F. V. FILSON, *St. Paul's Conception of Recompense* (Leipzig 1931). H. BRAUN, *Gerichtsgedanke und Rechtfertigungslehre bei Paulus* (Leipzig 1930).

[A. SUELZER]

JUDGMENT, DIVINE (IN THEOLOGY)

The theological treatment of divine judgment (1) considers it as it has been understood and expressed in the tradition of the Church, and then (2) goes on to a synthesis of the theology of divine judgment.

IN CATHOLIC TRADITION

The tradition of the Church continued the Biblical teaching on divine judgment and clarified some aspects of it that were obscure in the sacred text. The continuation of the Biblical teaching is especially noteworthy in the different professions of faith or creeds of the Church. From the very earliest, nearly all of them explicitly mention the fact that Christ is to come again to judge the living and the dead. One sees this in the Apostles' Creed in its varied early forms, in the so-called Athanasian Creed or *Quicumque* (H. Denzinger, *Enchiridion Symbolorum* 76), in the Nicene Creed (Denzinger 125), in the Creed of Constantinople I (Denzinger 150), in the Creed of Epiphanius (Denzinger 42, 44), and in many others in later centuries.

General Judgment. In distinction to the particular judgment, the general judgment occupied the primary place in the teaching and reflection of the early Church. It influenced Christian thought in many different ways. Athenagoras in the 2d century argued from the justice of God's judgment to the need for a resurrection of the body. He reasoned that if judgment were passed only on the soul, and the body were left dissolved forever into its constitutive elements, then God's judgment would be lacking in justice. For the one who practiced virtue or wickedness, the one who must be rewarded or punished through judgment, is the whole human person, body and soul, not the soul by itself. Hence, the very justice of the divine judgment requires the resurrection [*Res.* 20; TU 4.2: 73].

St. Irenaeus, Bishop of Lyons in the latter part of the 2d century, writing against the Gnostic heretics and defending the doctrine of the resurrection, saw the coming of Christ itself as a work of judgment, for He comes "for the fall and the resurrection of many" (Lk 2.34). He brings ruin to those who refuse to believe in Him and resurrection to those who believe and do the Father's will. His coming thus separates people from one another and judges between them on the basis of their response to Him. The Father embraces all people in His loving providence, but human persons by their choices consent either to believe or to disobey and thus range themselves on the right hand or the left hand of the Word of God (*Haer.* 5.27–28).

St. Hippolytus in the early years of the 3d century considered Christ's exercise of judgment at the last day as His final accomplishment of the mission confided to Him by His Father. The just and the unjust are brought before Him, to whom all judgment has been committed. He then passes the just judgment of the Father upon all, giving to each person that which is deserved in accordance with the person's deeds [*Graec.* 3; TU 20.2: 141].

In the opening years of the 4th century Lactantius expressed a view peculiar to himself, that only persons who have been somehow introduced into the religion of God will be judged. All the rest he maintained (through an inaccurate exegesis of Ps 1.5) are already judged and condemned. Those who have known God must be judged on the basis of whether their deeds have been in conformity with the truth that was granted them or not. The good deeds will be weighed against the evil, and whichever prove the heavier will determine the person's eternal lot [*Instit.* 7.20; *Corpus scriptorum ecclesiasticorum latinorum* 19:647–649].

Such testimonies to the Church's uninterrupted faith in the last judgment could be multiplied indefinitely. These, however, may suffice as examples of how this faith profoundly influenced the Christian view of life and of man's relationship to God.

Particular Judgment. The greatest area of clarification of the scriptural doctrine on judgment concerns the particular judgment of each individual made at the moment of death. Scripture never speaks explicitly of this judgment and in general says very little about the "intermediate state," the condition of the soul between death and resurrection. (The most important passages are Wisdom ch. 3–5; Lk 16.19–31; 2 Cor 5.6–9; and Phil

Last Judgment Portal of the Cathedral of Notre Dame, Paris, scenes of the Blessed and the Damned, commissioned by Maurice de Sully, Bishop of Paris, in 1163; completed mid-13th century. (©Adam Woolfit/CORBIS)

1.21–23.) But it is in developing the meaning of the few places that are found that the Church came to formulate an explicit doctrine on the particular judgment.

Early Centuries. In the very early ages of the Church there was much hesitation about affirming that before the resurrection and final judgment anyone was admitted to the face-to-face vision of God. The roots of this hesitation seem to have been two: the strong emphasis in Scripture on the judgment of the last day as the time when each person will receive an appropriate reward or punishment; and the teaching of the Revelation (20.1–6) on a millennium, which some interpreted as an actual 1,000-year reign of Christ upon earth at the end of time, just before the last judgment (*see* MILLENARIANISM). But in spite of this hesitation no one among orthodox Christians questioned that at death the period of trial for the human person is over. And though at first they did not use the term judgment, yet the Fathers clearly taught that from the moment of

The End Times, from "Liber Chronicarum," woodcut print, compiled by Hartmann Schedel. (©Historical Picture Archive/ CORBIS)

death onward the good and the wicked are definitively separated from one another.

St. Justin shortly after the middle of the 2d century expressed the opinion in his *Dialogue with Trypho the Jew* that at death the souls of the good and wicked are given separate dwelling places, the place of the good being better than that of the wicked. Here they await the day of the great judgment (5; PG 6.488).

Tatian, writing about the same time, distinguished between death and dissolution. The soul that does not know the truth both dies and is dissolved with the body. Later, however, it must rise at the end of the world to receive undying death in punishment. But the soul that has knowledge of God does not die, though for a time it is dissolved [*Orat.* 13; TU 4.1:14]. This appears to mean that the souls of the wicked are not only separated from the body but are annihilated until the last day, whereas the souls of the good are separated for a time from the

body but remain in existence. In any event, it implies that a judgment of God upon them takes place at death.

In the opening years of the third century Tertullian considered that all souls except those of the martyrs are consigned to the lower regions. Here, however, there is an anticipation of the judgment to come. For the good experience refreshment and consolation; and the evil, punishment and pain. The martyrs are at once given entrance into paradise with Christ [*Anim.* 55, 58, CSEL 20:388, 394–395; Res. 43, CSEL 47:88–89].

St. Hilary of Poitiers in the following century used the parable of the rich man and Lazarus (Lk 16.19–31) to warn sinners that hell will receive them at once at the moment of death. They are not to cajole themselves into thinking that they will have some respite before their punishment begins. Though the last day brings the judgment of eternal blessedness or eternal punishment, death meanwhile is governed by its own laws, which determine that either ABRAHAM'S BOSOM or a place of torment is to be the waiting place for that day [*In psalm.* 2.49; CSEL 22:74].

Writing around the year 420, St. Augustine spoke explicitly of a judgment that awaits the soul as soon as it leaves the body, and he distinguished this from the great judgment to come after the resurrection. He, too, appealed to the parable of the rich man and Lazarus and regarded any denial of such a judgment as an obstinate refusal to listen to the truth of the gospel [*Anima* 2.4.8; CSEL 60:341]. But he was not sure if this means that the just see God face to face before the resurrection [*Retract.* 1.13.2; CSEL 36:67].

Intermediate State. The question of the intermediate state, and by implication the particular judgment, did not enter the solemn teaching of the Church in an ecumenical council until the Second Council of Lyons in 1274. The occasion for this treatment was a reunion with the Orthodox Churches of the East. During the time of the schism the West had come to hold firmly the doctrine of a particular judgment immediately after death, followed at once by the reward of heaven, or the temporary purification of PURGATORY, or the punishment of hell. The East, on the other hand, had no universal doctrinal uniformity in this matter. Consequently, the profession of faith of this Council contained the doctrine held in the West, though it did not use the expression "particular judgment" [Denzinger 856–859]. This judgment is clearly implied, however, in the just assignment of rewards or punishments straightway after death. The same thing is to be said of another Council of reunion, that of Florence in 1439 [Denzinger 1304–06]. The doctrine of the Council of Florence was confirmed in 1575 by Pope Gregory XIII, when there was again question of restoring communion between the East and the West [Denzinger 1986], and once more in 1743 by Benedict XIV in a profession of faith for the Eastern Maronite Christians, which expressly mentioned the first eight ecumenical councils and then Florence [Denzinger 1468] and Trent.

Benedictus Deus. One other important document on the intermediate state deserves special mention in connection with the particular judgment. It is the apostolic constitution (*see* BENEDICTUS DEUS [Denzinger 1000–02]) issued by Benedict XII in 1336 to set at rest certain doubts and questions that had been raised by the preaching of his immediate predecessor, John XXII. In a series of sermons given toward the end of 1331 and the beginning of 1332 at Avignon, Pope John had maintained as his opinion that until the resurrection no one enjoyed the intuitive vision of the divine essence. This was contrary to the common belief of the faithful and aroused much commotion. The Pope established a commission of cardinals and theologians to investigate the question, and they showed the Pope that his opinion was a departure from the Catholic faith. He retracted his opinion in writing just before his death in 1334. His successor, then, after a more complete examination of the whole matter issued a strict dogmatic definition of faith. He taught solemnly that the BEATIFIC VISION of God is granted to the just directly after death (of after purgatory, when this is necessary). Those dying in mortal sin are likewise at once punished in hell. As is most evident, this teaching involves a particular judgment of God, separating the just from the impenitent sinners and giving to each what is due.

Reformers. The early Protestant reformers did not assume a completely clear position on the intermediate state. Luther at one time held that with very few exceptions all souls sleep unconscious until the day of judgment [Letter to Amsdorf, Jan. 13, 1552; *Luther's Works,* v.48 (Philadelphia 1963) 361]. But it is not certain that he thereafter continuously affirmed this. Calvin, on the other hand, opposed the Anabaptist position that maintained that all souls sleep until the resurrection. He taught that though all things are held in suspense until the appearance of Christ the Redeemer, still the souls of the pious, having ended their time of battle, enter into blessed rest and await joyfully the promised glory, and the reprobate suffer such torments as they deserve [*Instit.* 3.25.6; ed. J. T. McNeil, 2 v. (Philadelphia 1960) 2:996–998]. They did not therefore completely deny a particular judgment for each soul at death. The Church issued no special new decree regarding their positions except to reaffirm the doctrine on purgatory [Denzinger 1580, 1820], which had been expressly opposed, and which of course implies a doctrine of particular judgment.

Since that time no documents of major importance have appeared relative to the particular judgment. It is a doctrine universally taught and believed throughout the Catholic Church, though only implicitly contained in its solemn definitions and declarations of faith. It is likewise held by many Protestant and Orthodox Christians.

THEOLOGY OF DIVINE JUDGMENT

This will be considered under four heads: (1) the essential idea of divine judgment as the act of God by which God achieves the divine purposes through the creature's free response to divine initiative; (2) the continuous judgment of God as the divine activity of government in executing the unfolding plan of providence; (3) the particular judgment of God as a special focus of the divine judging activity of God upon each individual in the moment of death; (4) the general judgment of God as the final consummating act of God in Christ, achieving the purpose of creation.

Essential Idea. One may proceed on the basis of all that is revealed in Sacred Scripture about divine judgment and of the meditation of the Church upon this revelation as it is manifested in the writings of the Fathers and teaching of the magisterium.

Description. This judgment may be described as God's vindication of the divine purposes in the face of the free activity of rational creatures. There is never any question of God's judgment falling upon irrational creatures, except in an analogical or symbolic fashion, as in Christ's cursing of the barren fig tree; for in the final analysis what they do is wholly determined either by the natures they have received from God (these natures variously interacting among themselves) or from the use to which they are put by the actions of free creatures. Thus, in a schematic fashion, God's judgment may be regarded as the third moment in the dialogue between God and God's free creatures that constitutes salvation history. The first moment is that of God's free, loving, merciful initiative. It embodies the divine creative purpose to share in the goodness and happiness of God with a society of angels and human beings united to God and to one another in vision, love, and joy. This divine initiative is of its nature prior to all created existence and activity. The second moment is that of the creature's free response to this loving initiative. In its response the creature either freely consents to act according to God's purpose, or in a greater or lesser degree rejects it and thus estranges itself from God and God's intentions. The third moment is God's reassertion of the divine purpose in the face of this created free response, no matter what it was; here God vindicates effectively the divine intentions and brings them to realization in a way that is somehow shaped by the creature's response. God passes judgment upon free created activity and thereby completes what God intends to achieve.

From this description of divine judgment, its effects may be listed as four: to destroy, to purify, to perfect, and to separate. God's judgment destroys the sinful response that rejected the divine initiative. This destruction does not mean annihilating the creature or making the creature's response not to have been, but it ultimately frustrates the evil intention of the sinner by somehow making this sinful purpose serve God's own merciful design. God's judgment purifies the imperfect response by removing what is unacceptable. Here there is a partial destruction in something that is fundamentally good. The latent selfishness and disorder of the creature's free activity is effectively, though perhaps painfully, eliminated from its final results. Where the response to God's initiative has been one of total acceptance, the judgment of God brings the creature's activity to full perfection. God's judgment perfects by realizing in the creature and through it the complete good aimed at by the loving, divine initiative. Finally, the judgment of God separates sometimes slowly, sometimes suddenly, but always as a manifestation of mercy and justice, those who consent to submit freely to God from those who refuse.

There is a special Christian orientation of divine judgment that needs to be mentioned even in this very general preliminary description. In the cross and Resurrection of Christ God has already passed a definitive judgment upon the totality of Christ's work, and it is a judgment of mercy. Christ is the center of God's creative and redemptive plan. He is the new head under whom all things are summed up (Eph 1.10). Christ freely responded in obedience and love to the Father's merciful disposition for the liberation of humankind from sin. The Father passed a judgment of mercy and eternal life upon all humankind in raising Jesus from the dead and constituting Him the effective source of the world's final glorification *within* the created world itself. From now on there is no other way in which the justifying and glorifying judgment of God falls upon an individual except in and through Christ. The last age has already begun in Him; it will be manifested and realized in all people when Christ comes again to judge the living and the dead.

Definition. Divine judgment may be essentially defined as the activity of God's intellect and will whereby God accomplishes the divine purposes in the created world according to the free responses of creatures to his prior loving initiative in the order of nature and grace. It is an act of the divine intellect, since God hereby knows the free response of the creature, the goodness or badness of that response, the consequences that follow from it, and the way it can be fitted into the divine plan. It is an act of the divine will because in judgment God effectively determines to order the free act of the creature and its consequences to God's own purposes. Judgment is thus the essential act of divine government, the effective execution of the plan of divine providence.

This understanding of judgment allows one then to make a threefold division. (1) The continuous judgment of God upon each and every free creaturely response to God's initiative. In this sense it may be said that human beings are living always under the divine judgment and that everything that happens is in some way a consequence of the judgment of God. But the full meaning of this continuous judgment of God remains to be revealed at the last day. (2) The particular judgment of God upon the individual at the moment of death. Here the judging activity of God comes to a special focus, since the individual at death makes a final, complete, irreversible response to God's loving initiative. (3) The general judgment of God upon the totality of created things. Here is the ultimate focus of the divine judging activity. God brings to final perfection the whole divine work, the universe, according to the entire history of creaturely response to God's merciful designs. All other divine judgments are integrated into this last universally consummating act, which establishes the whole of creation in its final form and sustains it forever as the perfect embodiment of divine wisdom and power and love.

Continuous Judgment of God. Human beings, both as individuals and as societies, live under the continuous judgment of God. Every free response they make to God's loving initiative is at once judged by God and related to the achievement of the divine purposes. During the period of mortal life, when the creature's choice is capable of reform and development, God's judgment also contains within it a further initiative of love. God does not simply judge what has been done but continues to invite to a fuller participation in the divine life, through a call to repentance or to further growth.

Upon Individuals. One can consider the continuous judgment of God upon individuals as it affects four different classes: repentant sinners, unrepentant sinners, the just who are endeavoring to do good, and the just who are growing careless. The judgment of God upon sin is always a destructive judgment, rendering it ultimately futile in its rebellious purpose. But as mercy tempers this judgment, God invites the sinner to destroy his own evil deed through repentance. The sinner, of course, is completely incapable of repenting and accomplishing this destruction through his own power. It is God who must draw the sinner to appreciate the disorder of his life and to reject it. This judgment of mercy leading to interior repentance was objectively passed on all sinners in the death of Christ upon the cross, "because when as yet we were sinners, Christ died for us" (Rom 5.8–9). It is applied to the individual sinner through faith in Christ, through fear of God's just punishments, confidence in God's mercy, sorrow for sin, and determination to follow God's will in the future. God then pronounces a further judgment upon the repentant sinner; this judgment is called JUSTIFICATION. By it God makes the unjust person just, the enemy a friend, and thereby accomplishes the divine purposes in accordance with the response the creature has made to God's initiative. It must be emphasized that in this manifestation of saving justice God goes far beyond anything the repentant sinner is entitled to. No response the sinner has made to grace has given him any claim upon God. God's justifying judgment is a triumph of mercy, a supreme demonstration of loving kindness. This judgment was objectively passed upon all repentant sinners in the Resurrection of Christ from the dead, "who was delivered up for our sins, and rose again for our justification" (Rom 4.25). As the sinner has died to sin with Christ's death upon the cross, so he has risen to a new life in Christ's Resurrection.

When the sinner refuses to repent, persistently rejecting the light offered by God and resisting the attraction of God's GRACE, the judgment of God is to blind the sinner and to harden the sinner's heart. This is not a positive action on God's part; it means the withdrawal of the graces that the sinner has been refusing to accept. The immediate result of this judgment of God is the sinner's experience of personal weakness. The sinful condition is deepened and the misery of the sinner's plight forces itself upon his awareness. But even here God's mercy is at work, for the darkness and unrest that take possession of the sinner's heart are intended by God to lead to an awareness of the need for repentance and forgiveness. They are designed to break through the barrier of the sinner's resistance, not by violence or coercion, but by making the sinner taste the bitterness of this voluntary estrangement from God. It might be thought that God could more easily overcome this resistance by dazzling the sinner with the brightness of divine light and drawing him with a virtually irresistible sweetness of attraction toward what is good and holy. And it seems at times that God does act in this way in the beginning of a sinner's conversion. But one who is moved toward good in this way is still largely self-seeking; and if it is only on these terms that such a person will do what God commands, this is not really serving God but oneself. Thus, the normal judgment of God upon the unrepentant sinner is to harden and blind the sinner so that the realization of his personal insufficiency may prepare him for conversion and justification. A person may persist in trying to satisfy his deep personal need by the pursuit of power, pleasure, and fame through an exertion of energy that can end only in despair. To refuse the light is to close one's being to the advance of God's grace; and this hardening is a pre-

lude to everlasting fixity in sin, everlasting darkness, everlasting despair—not because God so intended it, but because the sinner has made anything else impossible.

The judgment of God upon the just person who continuously responds in adoring love to the initiative of God's grace is to further sanctify and draw such a person further into FRIENDSHIP WITH GOD, that is, with the Holy Trinity. This judgment of God is not always an immediately pleasant experience. Our Lord said that His Father is a vinedresser who prunes the branches that bear fruit in order that they may bear more fruit (Jn 15.2). The judgment of God, while rewarding with a more abundant life those who seek God in forgetfulness of merely selfish concerns, acts also to promote a further selflessness, a deeper humility, a freer pursuit of the sovereign good. This, too, is a mingling of mercy with justice in the execution of judgment.

The just person who begins to retreat into the selfishness he once renounced is also an object of God's judgment. God gradually lets such a one experience a deep personal weakness and insufficiency, generally in small ways at first, to enable the person to learn from lesser falls the imminent danger of a greater fall. But if he continues to fail to live according to the measure of divine life the God has given, the judgment of God will be to desert him just as he has been deserting God. A halfhearted response to grace will prove insufficient to enable a person to remain essentially faithful to God, and a serious lapse will follow as a consequence of God's judgment. Once again, this judgment of God contains within it an initiative of mercy: to make the careless one realize the danger of the situation and amend his life so as to grow as God wishes.

In these judgments of God upon individuals according to their responses to his initiative one can discern the general characteristic effects of judgment noted above. God in justifying the repentant sinner, hardening the unrepentant sinner, sanctifying further the fervent just person, and gradually deserting the careless just person is destroying sin, purifying what is imperfect, perfecting what is good, and thus separating those who respond to him in adoring love from those who refuse to do so.

Upon Societies. Sacred Scripture makes it clear that God's continuous judgment falls not only on individuals as such but also on societies. The earliest concepts of divine retribution that one finds in the Hebrew Scriptures reflect this fact. A man's faithfulness or unfaithfulness had its repercussions also upon his descendants. Groups and nations were condemned or rewarded by God for their corporate actions. Later insistence upon a greater measure of personal responsibility modified but never destroyed the earlier point of view. It remains true that where one can identify a common action and a common responsibility one can speak of a judgment of God upon the group as such. This consideration opens up vast fields for trying to understand God's action in the world; but the treatment here will confine itself to some theological observations about the continuous judgment of God upon the Church, upon civil societies, upon families, and upon other human associations in general.

It may seem strange to speak of the Church as such coming under the judgment of God. The Church is the MYSTICAL BODY OF CHRIST, vivified by the Holy Spirit, charged with the mission and authority of Christ to teach, govern, sanctify, and save all people, divinely preserved from error in its teaching, assured of an unfailing existence until the end of time. This description might lead one to assume that though individual members of the church may come under divine judgment, the Church as such is rather to be regarded as one with the divine Judge. It is true that what is divine in the Church, what is purely and simply the action of God's merciful and redeeming love, does not come under divine judgment. But whatever in the Church involves in any way a human, free response to God does come under the judgment of God. The fact that the Church has authority from Christ does not mean that this authority will always be exercised in the best possible way. The fact that the Sacraments give grace from the power of Christ at work in them does not mean that sacramental discipline is always the one best calculated for the upbuilding of the Church. The fact that the Church cannot universally err in matters of faith and morals does not mean that it will always insist on the most significant truths or interpret them to the world in the way best suited to enlighten it. In all these ways and many more the Church as such through its leaders and its members can fail to respond properly to God's initiative within it. Or to put the matter positively, in all these areas each generation of the PEOPLE OF GOD is called upon to prove itself loyal to the covenant God has made with it in the blood of His Son.

The continuous judgment of God upon the Church does not directly affect its external success or temporal well-being; for these are not matters that are directly involved in its mission. But the Church as such will live a fervent life of faith, worship, unity, love, and apostolic concern as a consequence of God's judgment upon a submissive response of the Church's members to the guidance of the divine Spirit within the Church. Or else, the Church can experience division, formalism, defections, apostolic ineffectiveness, and scandal as God's judgment on those who seek the things that are their own and not the things of Jesus Christ. No one in the Church can be excused of responsibility before God as judge because of a particular position within the community; nor can the Church as a whole expect that, no matter what its re-

sponse to God may be, its mission will be as abundantly fruitful and its witness to the world as unambiguously clear just because God is at work within it.

The continuous judgment of God likewise rests upon civil society, for this too is an instrument of divine providence for realizing God's purposes. Occasionally natural disaster or prosperity can reflect the judgment of God, as one sees illustrated in the Hebrew Scriptures. But normally the judgment of God will be seen in what directly touches the inner well-being of the society itself, in the presence or absence of tranquillity, opportunities for personal development, respect for law and civic officials, confidence in the organs of government, a tradition of genuine regard for the rights of others, and whatever else knits a people together for continuing and effective cooperation for the welfare of all. To the extent that a citizenry willingly conforms to the order of reason that manifests God's will, to that extent they as a whole will experience the tranquillity of order that is peace. It is true that there is question here largely of the working out of the natural laws of social relations; but these laws express the divine initiative on the natural level, and their built-in sanctions represent God's effective judgment on the same level.

Families, especially where these are constituted by a sacramental union, occupy a special place in God's plan and fall in a special way under God's judgment. The frequent blessings in the Hebrew Scriptures on families as such make this fact clear. But, once again, it would be a mistake to see God's judgment on a family chiefly in things that are external to it, in its wealth, social status, or even its health. Rather, to the extent that the family strives to live together in unselfish love and to worship God together in gratitude and trust, its members will as a group know the contentment that comes from God's approving judgment; and as they are negligent or disobedient in these areas, they will experience God's judgment in domestic strife, jealousy, suspicion, and unhappiness.

All other human societies and institutions follow the same pattern. Where the members genuinely cooperate for the establishment of a common good, the society will flourish, and all will benefit from the common good established by their combined efforts. But where the body of members begin to seek their own selfish aims, the institution is on its way to failure and dissolution. God's judgment upon societies as such is necessarily realized in temporal results, for these societies do not as such have an unending existence. The individual members of these societies, of course, will be judged eternally according to their individual responsibilities. A given society can exist through many generations of members, and a later generation may experience the full force of the judgment of God upon the corporate actions of an earlier generation.

For by joining themselves to this society and by ratifying in their attitudes what was determined by their ancestors, they assume the responsibility, not individually but corporately, of what was done earlier. Hence, for example, it is not incongruous that the Church at Vatican Council II should have expressed repentance and asked pardon for the faults of an earlier generation of Catholics that had contributed to the disunity of the Church [*Decree on Ecumenism* 7; *Acta Apostolicae Sedis* 57 (1965)97].

Particular Judgment of God at Death. Since divine judgment is the activity by which God achieves the divine purposes through the free responses made by creatures to God's gracious initiative, there are two moments of special focus for this activity, as was noted earlier. These are the moment of death, when the human person's response to God becomes total and definitive, and the moment of Christ's Second Coming, when the purposes of God are brought to final realization. The judgment of the individual at the moment of death is called the particular judgment.

Sources of Data. As was explained in the section on divine judgment in Catholic tradition, the existence of the particular judgment as a special instance of divine activity is attested only indirectly but certainly in Sacred Scripture and the documents of the Church. It is implied in the truths that at death the good and the wicked are straightway rewarded or punished for their choices during life and that these rewards and punishments are definitive (except for purgatory, which is a transitional state in preparation for the reward of heaven). Scripture makes this clear in the parable of the Rich Man and Lazarus (Lk 16.19–31) and in St. Paul's desire to die and be with Christ (Phil 1.21–23; 2 Cor 5.6–9). Besides the testimony of the early Fathers, who always insist on a separation of the good and evil immediately after death but are not always clear that this results at once in definitive rewards and punishments, there is especially to be noted in this connection the apostolic constitution *Benedictus Deus* in which was solemnly defined the truth that the good after death (or after purgatory, if that is necessary) receive without delay the eternal beatific vision of God and that the wicked dying in mortal sin likewise without delay begin the punishment of hell [Denzinger 1000–02].

In the Soul. A certain type of devotional literature and popular preaching has pictured the particular judgment as a kind of judicial process, where accusations are made and a defense is offered, where one's guardian angel and patron saints plead the cause of the one being judged against the indictment leveled against the person by devils intent on carrying the soul off to hell. Meanwhile, Christ listens to both sides and at length pronounces a just sentence from which there is no appeal.

However helpful this may be to foster a proper attitude toward the seriousness of the particular judgment, it does not correspond to the way in which God's judgment is passed and the sentence executed. The particular judgment takes place wholly within the individual soul by the power of God's mind and will, which effectively and definitively joins the final dispositions of the soul with their appropriate realization. The soul in the moment of death is all that the free choices of a lifetime have made it. The dispositions of the soul in this moment sum up all the responses to God's initiative it has ever made (*see* DEATH, THEOLOGY OF). The soul is therefore voluntarily related to God and all creation in a certain definite manner. It is fitted to occupy a certain place in the plan of God. God's judgment both makes clear to the soul what it has made of itself and gives it that place in the total design of divine wisdom and love that the soul is suited to fill. In a sense the soul judges itself; for in the light of the divine judgment the soul inescapably recognizes and affirms what it has become and what it deserves, and by an internal impulse growing out of this condition it is carried toward its destiny, St. Thomas observes, in much the same way as a heavy object is carried earthward and a light object heavenward.

Definitive. The particular judgment at death is definitive and irrevocable. During life the individual has been under the continuous judgment of God. But this has always been somewhat provisional, never totally definitive so long as the human response was intrinsically mutable and the divine initiative capable of still different approaches and manifestations. The consummating judgment of God upon the human person in death is no longer provisional but completely definitive. It resumes in itself and ratifies the whole continuous judgment of God made throughout the person's life. All the partial achievements of the divine purpose in respect to this individual become united in a total achievement, for the good of God's whole plan and for the weal or the woe of this individual depending on the basic option manifested in his life and made firm in death.

One who during life has been led by the Spirit of God (cf. Rom 8.11), who has repented of all personal sins and through the power of Christ made satisfaction for them, and who in death has perfectly assimilated the dying of Christ, experiences the particular judgment as God's action as completely perfecting and fulfilling. God is the ultimate cause of salvation, and here is finally united to the creature who now experiences intuitive vision, unfailing love, and selfless joy. By the divine judgment God assumes the soul irreversibly and wholly into the kingdom of God.

For one whose fundamental attitude is one of love of God, but who bears the stains of lesser sins or has failed to respond fully to that grace which would lead him to deeper union with Christ and help in making satisfaction for the grievous sins that have been forgiven him, the particular judgment is experienced first as a purifying action of God, one that removes and repairs what is disordered within the soul. Theologians generally distinguish purgatory and the particular judgment, but this distinction should not lead one to separate them. Purgatory is the state or condition established by the judgment of God considered as a purifying action to complete the work of grace in preparing the soul for heaven. It is generally thought that created agents are in some way the instruments of God's judgment in accomplishing this purification. But what or how this is so is not entirely clear. In any event, the ultimate purifying force is precisely the judgment of God upon the soul. The soul likewise experiences within the purifying judgment of God the immensity of God's love and the fundamental approval given its life. It is drawn to undergo in peace and perfect willingness the process that strips it of all selfishness and introduces it into everlasting blessedness.

The soul of one who dies in sin, rejecting to the last the offer of God's mercy and the invitation to repentance, experiences the particular judgment as a divine rejection, a destroying force rendering futile the self-centered goals it has refused to renounce. It must be emphasized that the individual who is lost is the ultimate cause of his own destruction. For the ultimate evil to be found in this final result is not traceable to any deficiency in God or God's activity but to the deficiency of the individual in his free response to God. God's judgment of destruction upon the individual is not the ultimate reason why a human person is lost (the individual person bears this responsibility); but it is God's affirmation of achieving the divine ultimate purpose not only in spite of, but somehow even through this rebellious individual who has chosen to be excluded from personal participation in the enjoyment of the divine good in the city of the blessed. God's action reduces this soul to the status of a mere thing, a means to an end, deprived by its own choice of the special dignity attaching to itself as person. The soul is given what it has in the last analysis really been choosing: itself, in isolation from God and in disorder with respect to the rest of the world—and this is the essential meaning of hell. And it thereby becomes through a tragic paradox an eternal witness to the fact that God is the source of all good, for cut off from God it has nothing in which it can finally rest. It witnesses also to the supreme worthiness of God to be loved, for having freely refused to love God it finds itself justly and by its own choice fixed in eternal misery.

Thus the particular judgment as it is passed on each individual at the moment of death separates finally the good and the evil. Under this action of God the world in

the course of time is assuming the definite shape and structure of personal relations it will have forever.

Time and Place? Questions are sometimes raised about the time and place of the particular judgment. Some think of an interval between death and judgment when the soul is being transported to a heavenly tribunal. But such considerations spring from a too vivid imagination that attempts to picture sensibly what is wholly spiritual. The judgment of God takes place precisely at the moment of death, when the soul is separated from the body and begins to operate independently of matter. The separated soul has no spatial relationships to the material world, and so the question as to the place of the particular judgment is not a wholly intelligible one. Suffice it to say that the particular judgment does not so much occur in a place as it effectively puts the soul in a place, i.e., a state that is heaven, purgatory, or hell.

General Judgment of God. The continuous judgment of God and all particular divine judgments are ordered to the final, great consummating act of God in the general judgment when God brings all the divine, merciful designs to full realization.

Establishment of Heavenly Society. It might seem at first thought that the general judgment is a kind of anticlimax, that everything has already been decided in the sum of particular judgments, and that all one has here is a sort of public resumé of the many private acts of judgment that have been passed on all individuals in the course of history. But this is to miss the perspective of the divine purpose. It is noteworthy that Sacred Scripture frequently mentions the general judgment and nowhere explicitly mentions the particular judgment. For what God intends is not simply to save a large number of isolated souls, who thereafter happen to form themselves into a heavenly society. What God intends primarily is to establish this heavenly society, this family of persons joined to the Persons of the Holy Trinity and to one another in everlasting knowledge, love, and joy. The definitive establishment of this society is had in the general judgment.

The difference between the particular and general judgment and the importance of both can be further understood by recognizing that at one level each human person is an individual created being, while at another level each individual is also part of the total order of the universe, part of God's total design. The particular judgment consummates each person precisely in terms of its individuality, in that person's individual relationship to God, in the loneliness of the moment of death. The general judgment consummates the whole universe and the individual person along with it as a part, in that person's social relationship to all other things, in the great gathering together of all human persons at the resurrection.

It is not sufficient to distinguish these judgments by saying that in the particular the human person's soul is judged and in the general the body also. This is true enough, but it does not at all account for the greater importance of the general judgment in Holy Scripture. Human bodies are judged at the general judgment, because in the realization of God's plan human nature is reintegrated, and all human beings in their complete human personalities as body-soul composites are given the places in God's total work that their free responses to God's prior initiative have fitted them to occupy.

Some theologians have spoken of the need for a further general judgment in addition to the particular because human beings need to be judged with regard to all the consequences of their acts, and these may well continue long after the individual's death, even until the end of the world. Thus it would not be possible to judge them completely at the moment of death; another judgment at the end of time is required for all. Although there is some truth to this way of looking at things, by itself it does not seem conclusive. Strictly speaking, a person is responsible only for the consequences he foresees and intends in some way, not for everything that happens to follow upon his free choices. Hence, the individual can be judged at death for the consequences for which he is strictly responsible, and cannot really be judged at all for the other consequences. The element of truth, however, in this way of looking at the matter would seem to lie in the fact that one does influence others by one's personal choices in ways that reach across time and place and help to constitute a corporate response of humankind to the total initiative of God's love. This corporate response is indeed judged by God at the end of time. It is, of course, a response that divides humankind into two groups, those who accept this initiative and those who reject it. God's judgment forms one group into the city of God, and casts the other into outer darkness.

Names and Aspects. This judgment at the end of time has a number of different names that serve to underline various aspects of it. It is called God's judgment, because the Holy Trinity, Father, Son, and Holy Spirit together, are through their common divine act the supreme cause of the final perfection of the universe; it is a judgment passed by all of them (though by each in a way appropriate to His position within the Trinity), and it achieves the divine purpose by rewarding and punishing according to the response given the Trinitarian initiative.

It is called also the judgment of Christ. Our Lord in His humanity exercises the role of judge as one who has received this power from His Father. The New Testament and tradition are unanimous in giving Him this function. There is no opposition between a judgment of the Holy Trinity and a judgment of Christ. The Holy Trinity judges through the judgment of Christ. It is His, an activity truly proceeding from His human intellect and will, but endowed with a divine efficacy as belonging to a Divine Person within the Trinity. The act of judging is, indeed, Christ's last and greatest act as savior of mankind. Here, as will be considered presently, the glorified head of all creation completes the work assigned Him in the moment of His Incarnation.

This judgment is called the general judgment, since it embraces all human beings, good and bad, the living and the dead. The latter expression, which occurs in Scripture (Acts 10.42; 2 Tm 4.1; 1 Pt 4.5) and is found in nearly all professions of faith (Apostles' Creed, Nicene Creed, etc.), has two possible meanings. It may mean those spiritually alive and spiritually dead, and thus be the same as the good and the wicked. Or it may mean those who are physically alive at His coming and those who have already died, but are now raised to life. In any event, it is intended as a comprehensive formula to show that all people are subject to Christ's judgment.

This judgment is also called the last or the final judgment, since it is completely definitive. It does not look forward to any other judgment by which what is done here may be completed, modified, or set aside. Beyond lies only the sustaining power of God, upholding forever what is here established.

Apocalyptic Descriptions. One is accustomed to associate the general judgment with other events at the end of time, notably Christ's Second Coming and the resurrection of the dead. Following the imagery of Scripture, one thinks of Christ coming on the clouds of heaven in great glory. The dead are raised by His power to a never-ending union of body and soul. And all are gathered before Him, the good on one side, the wicked on the other, to hear the fateful words of His welcome or banishment. In times past, too, it was a subject of some speculation just where this gathering together of all people would take place. Many spoke of the valley of Josaphat, relying on an expression found in the Prophet Joel (Jl 4.2).

But one must recognize that Scripture in these places is using a symbolic language to help people understand the greatness of this concluding intervention of God in human history. Neither Christ's Ascension into heaven nor His Second Coming should be thought of in terms of local motion simply visible to the eye. Christ "ascends" into heaven by entering into His glory, by being raised from the dead and completely filled in His humanity by the power of the Holy Spirit, by being associated as man in God's supreme Lordship over all creation. He "comes again" when by an exercise of His fullness of power He makes Himself present in the world, transforming it and bringing it to the state of its final perfection.

One Consummating Intervention. Scripture gives indications that the Second Coming, resurrection of the dead, and last judgment are really only diverse aspects of one single consummating divine intervention. Christ executes judgment in raising all humans from the dead, some to a resurrection of life, others to a resurrection of judgment (in John's customary sense of "condemnation," Jn 5.25–29). Christ comes in the act of raising people from the dead (cf. 1 Cor 15.22–23; Phil 3.20–21). Christ judges by His coming [cf. 2 Tm 4.1 (in many Greek and Latin MSS); Heb 9.27–28]. Admittedly the places here referred to do not clearly state the identity affirmed above, but they suggest a radical unity that prompts the theologian to look more deeply into the matter.

In general a divine coming is based on an exercise of divine power that produces some new effect. Thus, the Holy Spirit comes as God infuses sanctifying grace or increases it within human persons. Hence, having recognized that Christ's Second Coming is not simply a matter of local motion and visible manifestations, one perceives that this coming, this new presence of His, is in function of a new exercise of His power producing a new effect. Thus He comes in power to the whole world when He effects a consummating transformation of all humankind. He does this by raising all people from the dead, "by exerting the power by which He is able also to subject all things to Himself" (Phil 3.21). And in effecting the resurrection of all people He gives to each a bodily condition that reflects the state of the soul in each case. Those who are united to God in the life of divine grace manifest in their bodies the glory of divine adoption. They "shine forth like the sun in the kingdom of their Father" (Mt 13.43). Those souls that are dead in sin are united to a body that rather possesses and imprisons them than is possessed by them as an instrument of self-expression and life. Individuals who are alive at this Second Coming of Christ will not undergo death as a separation of body and soul; for as St. Paul wrote, "We shall not all sleep, but we shall all be changed" (1 Cor 15.51). They will experience the moment of total commitment that death involves, and their bodies will be changed to accord with their inner relationship to God.

Christ Our Lord in causing this resurrection and transformation of all people is in effect judging them. He is realizing in the totality of humankind God's gracious and loving purpose according to the response that every person has made to that purpose. Each and all are brought to the final state of relationship to God, to one another, and to all of creation, that has been shaped by their individual and collective responses to God's initiative. "Then comes the end, when He delivers the kingdom to God the Father, when He does away with all sovereignty, authority and power . . . that God may be all in all" (1 Cor 15.24, 28).

Victory and Purification. In this act of judging, which is at once Christ's Second Coming and the cause of humankind's resurrection, Our Lord reduces to utter powerlessness and futility all that is opposed to the self-giving, creative love of God. Fallen angels and condemned humans are compelled by the inner consequences of their rebellion to glorify the power and wisdom and goodness of God in the justice of their punishment. This judgment is likewise a purification for those just who are alive at the coming of Christ but are not perfectly prepared for heaven. For them, particular judgment and general judgment coincide, and the purification of purgatory is here accomplished. St. Paul described this purifying effect of Christ's judgment in the special case of some who were preaching in Corinth from unworthy motives; he made the supposition, without however actually affirming it, that they would be alive at the coming of Christ. In this case, the FIRE OF JUDGMENT will test the quality of each person's works; if a person's work burns such a one will suffer loss, "but will personally be saved, yet so as through fire" (cf. 1 Cor 3.10–15).

But most important, Christ's judgment in the glorious resurrection of the saints completes the building of the new Jerusalem. In these human beings and in the faithful angels, God's intention to share the joy of the divine Trinitarian life with created persons who relate to God in adoring love is triumphantly achieved. These persons together constitute the society of the blessed, the bride of the Lamb (Rv 21.9), "the everlasting kingdom of our Lord and Savior Jesus Christ" (2 Pt 1.11).

This theological view of the general judgment does not destroy the beautiful imagery of Scripture but helps one to see the reality that lies behind it. The coming of Christ in glory upon the clouds, His voice calling all people from the grave, the assembling of all before Him to hear His sentence—all the meaning of these images is found in that totally transforming action by which Christ makes Himself present to all people, raising them from the dead, and assigning to each and all their places in the perfectly realized plan of God.

Revelation in Judgment. Finally, the general judgment is a public divine intervention making known to all the justice of God's judgment. "Therefore, pass no judgment before the time, until the Lord comes, who will both bring to light the things hidden in darkness and make manifest the counsels of hearts; and then everyone will have his praise from God" (1 Cor 4.5). This revelation will be for the glory and joy of the saved and for the shame and sorrow of the lost. It is not clear whether the blessed in a single instant will receive complete knowledge of the whole plan of salvation as it was worked out in detail, or simply that this knowledge will be perfectly available, to be acquired as they wish in an ever deepening fashion throughout eternity. Those condemned to hell will not perceive this plan with the same fullness; their knowledge will be only such as to impress upon them the isolation they have brought upon themselves, the responsibility they bear for their own condition, and the triumph of God's purposes in spite of and even through their rebellion.

The revelation of the forgiven, secret sins of the just will not be a source of embarrassment for them. For along with these sins there will be manifested the sorrow they conceived for them, the penance they did for them, and the humble acceptance of God's forgiveness that they received for them. They will rejoice that God's mercy is revealed so strikingly in their regard, to the glory of Christ and the joy of the blessed.

Christ at the moment of the Incarnation received from the Father the commission to redeem fallen humanity, to head a new race of human beings vivified by the Holy Spirit, to establish an eternal kingdom where God's love may enrich forever those He has made His sons and daughters. All the events of the terrestrial and glorified life of Christ are directed to the fulfillment of this commission, which is finally perfectly executed in the moment of the general judgment. The action of Christ in subduing all enemies is at last brought to a close by this act of power and justice and love. His work done, the Son will deliver the kingdom to God the Father; and as all things are then subject to Christ and Christ is subject to the Father, there will begin the everlasting kingdom of the Father, where God is all in all (cf. 1 Cor 15.24–28).

See Also: JUDGMENT, DIVINE (IN THE BIBLE); END OF THE WORLD; ESCHATOLOGY (IN THEOLOGY); HEAVEN, (THEOLOGY OF); HELL (THEOLOGY OF); KINGDOM OF GOD; MAN; PAROUSIA; RESURRECTION OF CHRIST; RESURRECTION OF THE DEAD; ESCHATOLOGY, ARTICLES ON.

Bibliography: J. RIVIÈRE, *Dictionnaire de théologie catholique* 8.2:1721–1828. Ibid., Tables générales 2:2705–19. J. HAEKEL et al., *Lexicon für Theologie und Kirche* 2 4:726–737. N. J. HEIN et al., *Die Religion in Geschiche und Gegenwart,* 3 2:1415–23. W. PESCH and A. WINKLHOFER, *Handbuch theologischer Grundbegrifle,* ed. H. FRIES 1:483–491. M. and L. BECQUÉ, *Life after Death,* tr. P. HEPBURNE-SCOTT (New York 1960). R. GARRIGOU-LAGRANGE, *Life Everlasting,* tr. P. CUMMINS (St. Louis 1952). R. W. GLEASON, *The World to Come* (New York 1958). R. GUARDINI, *The Last Things,* tr. C. E. FORSYTH and G. B. BRANHAM (New York 1954). A. WINKLHOFER, *The Coming of His Kingdom,* tr. A. V. LITTLEDALE (New York 1963). C. DAVIS, *Theology for Today* (New York 1962) 294–306. K. RAHNER, *Theological Investigations* (London, 1966–) 4:323–346. *Texte und Untersuchungen zur Gerschiste der altchristlichen Literatur* (Berlin 1882–). *Corpus scriptorum Christianorum latinorum,* (Vienna 1866–). *Acta Apostolicae Sedis,* (Rome 1909–).

[J. H. WRIGHT]

JUDICAËL OF QUIMPER, ST.

King of Brittany; d. *c.* 647–658. There are many legendary reports about the life of this saint, the last independent king of Brittany. According to the *Chronicle of Fredegar* (*see* FREDEGARIUS), King Dagobert I (d. 639), while staying at Clichy, sent messengers to the Bretons demanding "that they make amends promptly for what they had done amiss and submit to his rule." Judicaël came quickly to Clichy bearing gifts, and with the aid of Dagobert's treasurer ELIGIUS, later bishop of Noyon, and the referendary OUEN OF ROUEN, the two monarchs arrived at an amicable solution (*Gesta Dagoberti* 38). The *Vita S. Mevenni* records that Judicaël later became a BENEDICTINE monk at the Abbey of Saint-Jean-Baptiste, later called Saint-Méen-Gaël [L. H. Cottineau, *Répertoire topobibliographique des abbayes et prieurés,* 2 v. (Mâcon 1935–39) 2:2810] while St. Mevennus (d. 617) was still abbot; there he lived an exemplary life and died with a reputation for sanctity (*Acta Sanctorum,* June, 5:89). According to other reports, however, Judicaël became a monk to escape an assassination plot, but later returned to the world, claimed his throne, married, and begot many children, and only toward the end of his life returned to religious life. In any event, his cult was clearly established by the tenth century, when his name appeared in the Litany of All Saints at Reims, and it became widespread in the Middle Ages.

Feast: Dec. 17; Dec. 16 (Diocese of Quimper).

Bibliography: J. MABILLON, *Acta sanctorum ordinis S. Benedicti,* 9 v. (Paris 1668–1701) 2:542. F. PLAINE, "Vita S. evenni," *Analecta Bollandiana,* 3 (1884) 142–158. *Monumenta Germaniae Historica, Scriptores rerum Merovingicarum* (Berlin 1826–) 2.2:160, 416. *The Fourth Book of the Chronicle of Fredegar,* ed. and tr. J. M. WALLACE-HADRILL (New York 1960) 66. *Gallia Christiana,* v.1–13 (Paris 1715–85), v.14–16 (Paris 1856–65) 14:1019–20. A. LE GRANDE, *Les Vies des saints de la Bretagne armorique* (Rennes 1901) 711–713. F. DUINE, *La Métropole de Bretagne* (Paris 1916) 30. A. M. ZIMMERMANN, *Kalendarium Benedictinum: Die Heiligen und Seligen des Benediktinerordens und seiner Zweige,* 4 v. (Metten 1933–38) 3:448–449. *Histoire de l'église depuis les origines jusqu'à nos jours,* ed. A. FLICHE and V. MARTIN (Paris 1935–) 5:306. J. L. BAUDOT and L. CHAUSSIN, *Vies des saints et des bienheureux selon l'ordre du calendrier avec l'historique des fêtes* (Paris 1935–56) 12:538–544. J. M. WALLACE-HADRILL, *The Long-Haired Kings* (New York 1962) 222.

[H. DRESSLER]

"Vicar's Tribunal in Naples," 18th century. (©Archivo Iconografico, S.A./CORBIS)

JUDICIAL VICAR (OFFICIALIS)

In the canonical system the highest judicial power is vested in the Supreme Pontiff, who has the right to reserve to himself certain particular cases (*Codex iuris canonici* c. 1405 §1; *Codex Canonum Ecclesiarium Orientalium* c. 1060 §1). In a diocese, the natural judge is the diocesan bishop (*Codex iuris canonici* c. 1419 §1; *Codex Canonum Ecclesiarium Orientalium* c. 1066 §1), who constitutes one tribunal with the judicial vicar, or chief judge, of his court (*Codex iuris canonici* c. 1420 §2; *Codex Canonum Ecclesiarium Orientalium* c. 1086 §2).

History. The idea of the judicial vicar or officialis has deep historical roots. In the very early days of the Church it was common for the bishop to use priests for the spiritual ministry and deacons for the direction of temporalities. From the middle of the 4th century the archdeacon occupied a very important position in church administration. His was the duty of finding clerics, educating them, approving them, and presenting them to the bishop for ordination. Moreover, he took care of the treasures and income of the Church. At times he was commissioned to make visitations of the diocese for the bishop. From the 6th century on we find he even had jurisdiction in criminal cases. In the 11th century most of

the larger dioceses were divided into districts with an archdeacon in charge of each. The most important of these was the archdeacon of Rome. Gradually the jurisdictional power of archdeacons was recognized as ordinary and not too dependent upon the authority or jurisdiction of the bishop. They held synods, conducted courts, named and invested pastors, and established penalties against clerics. Appeals were made from their tribunals to the tribunal of the bishop.

In the 12th century bishops had to curb the power of the archdeacons; they did so by establishing the institution of rural deans or vicars. In Rome a vicar general or officialis was named. He had voluntary and noncriminal jurisdiction along with the jurisdiction of the archdeacon. In many regions of Germany, Spain, and France only voluntary jurisdiction would be given to this new office of vicar general. Jurisdiction in noncriminal cases was given to another who was named the officialis. The power and juridical figure of the archdeacon gradually fell into desuetude. The Council of Trent reduced the office to practically nothing (session 24, cap. 3, 20; session 25, cap. 14).

What grew up from particular law in certain places was made universal and an obligation of common law in the Latin Church by the 1917 Code of Canon Law, namely, that jurisdiction in judicial matters, separate and apart from that of the vicar general, would be committed to a new office, that of officialis.

Appointment, Qualifications, and Jurisdiction. Canon Law directs the diocesan bishop to select a judicial vicar who will enjoy ordinary authority for making judgments. He is to be an individual other than the vicar general, unless the smallness of the diocese or the lack of cases persuades the bishop that this office can be assigned to the vicar general (*Codex iuris canonici* c. 1420 §1; *Codex Canonum Ecclesiarium Orientalium* c. 1086 §1).

The judicial vicar constitutes one tribunal with the bishop of the place; he cannot judge cases that the bishop reserves to himself (*Codex iuris canonici* c. 1420 §2; *Codex Canonum Ecclesiarium Orientalium* c. 1086 §2). He must be a priest no younger than 30 years of age, of good character, and if he is not a doctor of canon law he must at least hold a licentiate in that science (*Codex iuris canonici* c. 1420 §4; *Codex Canonum Ecclesiarium Orientalium* c. 1086 §4). He is appointed for a definite time (*Codex iuris canonici* c. 1422; *Codex Canonum Ecclesiarium Orientalium* c. 1088 §1). His office does not cease but perdures during the vacancy of a see (*Codex iuris canonici* c. 1420 §5; *Codex Canonum Ecclesiarium Orientalium* c. 1088 §2). The jurisdiction of the judicial vicar is ordinary (*Codex iuris canonici* c. 1420 §1; *Codex Canonum Ecclesiarium Orientalium* c. 1086 §1). Since he constitutes one and the same tribunal with the bishop of the place, there is no appeal from his sentence or decision to the bishop; the appeal must be made to the authority to which a decision of the bishop himself would be appealed.

Functions. Since practically all the cases before a diocesan tribunal today are marriage cases, the work of the judicial vicar is to prepare, study, and judge pleas for nullity brought before the court on any of the grounds described in church law for such a nullity plea. The formal cases, or those involving people who have been married in what appears to be a valid marriage, are heard and tried before a panel of three judges. The judicial vicar or his associate, the adjutant judicial vicar, usually presides at such a panel.

Bibliography: R. NAZ, *Dictionnaire de droit canonique*, ed. R. NAZ (Paris 1935–65) 6:1105–11. J. ABBO and J. HANNAN, *The Sacred Canons* (2d ed. St. Louis 1960) 2:759–760. E. FOURNIER, *L'origine du vicaire-général et des autres membres de la curie diocésaine* (Paris 1940). M. LEGA and V. BARTOCETTI, *Commentarius in iudicia ecclesiastica iuxta Codicem iuris canonici*, 3 v. (Rome 1950) 1:112. A. COUSSA, *Epitome praelectionum de iure ecclesiastico orientali*, 2 v. (Grottaferrata 1948) 1:320–327.

[J. S. QUINN]

JUDITH, BOOK OF

The Book of Judith relates the story of the heroic and devout Hebrew woman, Judith, who singlehandedly saved her city and country from the enemy. The content, text, canonicity, and literary form of the book are discussed in this article.

Content. NEBUCHADNEZZAR, who is described as king of the Assyrians, dispatches his chief general, Holofernes, to punish the Western countries for refusing to pay tribute to him. The general so terrifies his enemies that they hasten to submit. The Hebrews, however, fearing for the safety of their temple, resist. After a long siege of Bethulia by Holofernes's forces, the famished inhabitants urge their governor to surrender. At this point, the beautiful and wealthy widow, Judith, indignant because of the people's lack of confidence in God, initiates her own plan. After a lengthy prayer, Judith enters the Assyrian camp, explaining that she is a deserter. Holofernes, lured by Judith's beauty, invites her to his tent to eat and drink. When Holofernes is overcome by excessive drink, Judith decapitates him and returns to Bethulia with the severed head. The next day the besieged put the confused enemy to flight. So highly acclaimed is Judith that the high priest comes from Jerusalem to honor her. The book ends with the Canticle of JUDITH and an account of her last days. The Vulgate adds a note concerning a holy day instituted in remembrance of the victory.

Text. The original Hebrew (or Aramaic) text of the Book of Judith has been lost. Of the three recensions of the Greek, the best is represented by codices Alexandrinus, Vaticanus, and Sinaiticus. The translation of St. JEROME in the Vulgate is based on an Aramaic text and takes into account the readings of the Old Latin Version; it is about one-fifth shorter than the Greek text (LXX). There exist also a few Hebrew renderings of the text and a number of midrashic résumés of late date. It has long been assumed that the Hebrew versions were mere translations of the Vulgate, but the careful study of A. M. Dubarle has shown that this supposition is unfounded; it is more probable that the existing Hebrew texts depend upon an Aramaic text similar to that used by St. Jerome.

Canonicity. Although never accepted as canonical by official JUDAISM, the deuterocanonical story of Judith was popular enough to merit reading at the feast of Hanukkah (*see* DEDICATION OF THE TEMPLE, FEAST OF), the date of its introduction into that liturgy, however, is not known. As part of the Greek Scriptures, the Book of Judith was used by the early Church. It has been argued that St. Paul alludes to Jdt 8.14 (LXX) in 1 Cor 2.10–11, and there may be a reminiscence of Jdt 15.10–11 in Lk 1.42, 48. Although St. Jerome did not accept the book's canonicity (and he was by no means alone), he admitted that it was "read" by the Church. The Church terminated all doubts by affirming the inspired character of the book at the Council of Trent.

Literary Form. Catholic scholars have long manifested reserve in accepting the Book of Judith as a historical work. The prevailing tendency today is to classify this work as an edifying fiction or as an apocalypse. The most serious objection to the factual content of the book arises from the difficulty in identifying the Nebuchadnezzar who is called "king of the Assyrians who reigned in NINIVEH" (Vulg 1.5; LXX 1.1). It would be naive to view this statement as a crude error concerning the Babylonian King Nebuchadnezzar. The statement represents either an obvious declaration that the author is not dealing with facts, or that he is employing pseudonyms. The view that Nabuchodonosor in this passage represents some other king has been the most popular explanation among Jewish and Christian exegetes alike until recent times. Of the various candidates proposed, Christian writers have favored the Persian King Artaxerxes III (*see* PERSIA); Jewish tradition has leaned toward one of the Seleucid kings. The German scholar Gottfried Brunner, basing his conclusions on the Behistun inscription of DARIUS I, identifies the Nebuchadnezzar of the Judith narrative with a certain Araka, a pretender to the fallen Babylonian throne. According to Brunner, Araka, who styled himself Nebuchadnezzar IV, probably established himself in the Syrian city of Ninus-vetus (whence Nineveh) until he

Biblical illustration of the Story of Judith and Holofernes. (©Historical Picture Archive/CORBIS)

was crushed by Darius I. Such an identification might support a literal interpretation of the narrative, but it raises new problems without eliminating all the old ones. The high priest in the Judith narrative is Joachim (LXX 4.6–8; 15.8; the Vulgate gives the name first as Eliachim [4.5–10], but then as Joachim [15.9]). Such a figure should certainly be identifiable. A succession of high priests is listed in ch. 12 of Nehemiah. A Joachim does appear in that list, but he is too early to have been a contemporary of Artaxerxes III and too late to have held office when Araka was posing a threat to Darius I. It has been suggested, therefore, that the Joachim in the Book of Judith is the high priest Alcimus of the Maccabean times (1 Mc 7.5–25; 2 Mc 14.3–26), who, according to Josephus, was also called Ἰάκειμος. There are also references in the text that point to the Maccabean era, e.g., the Sanhedrin (LXX 4.8; 11.14; 15.8).

The geographical background of the narrative is as difficult to understand as its historical framework. There have been many scholarly attempts to locate the strategic citadel of Bethulia, but from the evidence thus far obtained it must be concluded that under the name of Bethulia no such place ever existed. The name, of course, has been diversely interpreted. The simplest explanation is probably the correct one: it is a transliteration of the Hebrew word for "virgin" (*b^etûlâ*), and is, like the name Judith (Heb. *y^ehûdît,* "Jewess"), symbolic.

This confusing mixture of historical allusions, of which only the most important have been indicated, on the one hand, suggests that Dubarle and others are correct in judging that the Book of Judith has undergone extensive revision; and, on the other, indicates rather clearly that the present book does not pretend to present a historical account. Some exegetes see in the narrative a historical event that forms the nucleus around which the author has composed a free narrative with elements gathered from various periods of Israelite history. There is no agreement, however, concerning precisely what that event was. Consequently, the majority of exegetes consider the narrative a parable dressed in historical clothing. The parable seems to be a demonstration of the truth found in the words of the Jewish enemy Achior: "But if there be no offense of this people in the sight of their God, we cannot resist them, because their God will defend them; and we shall be a reproach to the whole earth" (Vulg 5.25; LXX 5.21; cf. words of Judith, Vulg 9.15–16; LXX 9.11). The story of Judith illustrates this truth in a striking manner, for it is a woman who singlehandedly defeats the formidable enemies of her people.

The points of contact with the forces of irreligion depicted in Ezekiel (ch. 38), Daniel (ch. 7–8, 10–11), and the New Testament Revelation of St. John (ch. 13, 17) are obvious, and it is for this reason that the parable of Judith has also been called an apocalypse. The Judith narrative is history, parable, apocalypse—all these things woven together by a gifted and inspired craftsman who will probably remain forever unknown.

See Also: MIDRASH.

Bibliography: A. BARUCQ, tr., *Judith* (*Bible de Jérusalem,* 43 v., each with intro. by the tr. [Paris 1948–54]; single v. ed. of the complete Bible [Paris 1956] 14; Paris 1959). A. MILLER and J. SCHILDENBERGER, eds. and trs., *Die Bücher Tobias, Judith und Esther* (Bonn 1940–41). Y. M. GRINTZ, *Sefer Yehudith* (Jerusalem 1957). J. STEINMAN, *Lecture de Judith* (Paris 1953). P. F. ELLIS, *The Men and the Message of the Old Testament* (Collegeville, Minn. 1963) 523–530. A. LEFÈVRE, *Dictionnaire de la Bible,* suppl. ed. L. PIROT et al. (Paris 1928–) 4:1315–21. C. C. TORREY, *The Apocryphal Literature* (New Haven, Conn. 1945). A. M. DUBARLE, "Les Textes divers du livre de Judith," *Vetus Testamentum* 8 (1958) 344–373; "La Mention de Judith dans la littérature ancienne, juive et chrétienne," *Revue biblique* 66 (1959) 514–549. R. HARRIS, "A Quotation from Judith in the Pauline Epistles," *Expository Times* 27 (1915–16) 13–15. G. BRUNNER, *Der Nabuchodonosor des Buches Judith* (Berlin 1959). H. CAZELLES, "Le Personnage d'Achior dans le livre de Judith," *Recherches de science religieuse* 39 (1951–52) 125–137. J. E. BRUNS, "Judith or Jael," *Catholic Biblical Quarterly* 16 (1954) 12–14. P. W. SKEHAN, "Why Leave out Judith?" *Catholic Biblical Quarterly* 24 (1962) 147–154; "The Hand of Judith," *Catholic Biblical Quarterly* 25 (1963) 94–110.

[J. E. BRUNS]

JUDITH, CANTICLE OF

The Canticle of Judith is a triumphal hymn celebrating Judith's victory over the Assyrian army, presented as the Lord's apocalyptic day of judgment on His enemies. It is found in ch. 16 of the Book of Judith, vv. 2–21 in the Vulgate, 1–17 in the Septuagint (*see* JUDITH, BOOK OF). Like the Canticle of MIRIAM and the Canticle of Deborah, it praises Yahweh for the crushing defeat He inflicted on the enemies of His people. A more careful analysis of this canticle shows its literary relationship to other Biblical passages as well. The prelude (vv. 1–2 following the versification of the Septuagint) and the concluding paean (vv. 13–17) are modeled on the so-called enthronement Psalms [Ps 46(47); 92(93); 94–98(95–99)] especially Ps 97(98). The body of the hymn (vv. 3–9) describes the events that motivated its composition and should be compared with 2 Kgs 18.9–19.37 and Jgs 5.24–27. The apocalyptic tenor of v. 17 is strikingly reminiscent of Is 66.24, and some regard it as proof that the story of Judith is to be understood as an apocalyptic parable (Steinmann, 118). The most interesting question raised by the canticle is whether it antedates the rest of the book in which it is found. Just as the Canticle of Deborah is much older than the prose account that precedes it (Jgs 4.1–28), so, also, may the case be here. However, if this view is accepted, it does not alter the prevailing opinion that "Judith, the daughter of Merari" is a pseudonymous characterization. There is considerable alternation of voices in the canticle: v. 4 appears to be the sentiment of Yahweh; vv. 5–10 that of an observer who is neither Judith nor the Lord; vv. 11–12 the words of Judith, who, however, assumes here a matriarchal, if not regal, role. This technique, not uncommon in the Psalms, may indicate a liturgical *Sitz im Leben* for the canticle or, alternatively, a composite origin.

Bibliography: F. ZORELL, "Canticum Judith," *Verbum Domini* 5 (1925) 329–332. H. L. JANSEN, "La Composition du chant de Judith," *Acta Orientalia* 15 (1937) 63–71. J. STEINMANN, *Lecture de Judith,* in *Bible de Jérusalem,* 43 v. (Paris 1948–54) 1953, 115–119. A. E. COWLEY, "The Book of Judith," *The Apocrypha and Pseudepigrapha of the Old Testament in English,* ed. R. H. CHARLES et al., 2 v. (Oxford 1913) 1:242, 246–247, 265–267.

[J. E. BRUNS]

JUDITH OF NIEDERALTAICH, BL.

Widow and recluse; d. before 800. There is considerable debate regarding the identity of Judith and her companion, St. Salome. They may have been cousins (or Judith the aunt of Salome) of Anglo-Saxon royal lineage, who lived for a considerable period as recluses under Abbot Walther (or Walker) in Oberaltaich-am-Donau. A later tradition identifies Salome as Edburga, daughter of King Offa of Mercia, who was exiled for accidentally poisoning her husband and befriended by the Bavarian widow, Judith. Relics of both were later disinterred and buried near the altar of St. Giles. It is thought that their bodies came to Niederaltaich on the occasion of the destruction of Oberaltaich by the Hungarians.

Another report states that the two recluses lived in NIEDERALTAICH about 1100. The altar of St. Giles is here rather than in Oberaltaich, and Walker was abbot here from 1069 to 1098. According to this version, while in the neighborhood of Regensburg after a pilgrimage to the Holy Land Salome became blind, allegedly in answer to prayer, asking for this affliction to escape from sinful proposals. She lived by begging. Once she fell into the Danube and was rescued by a passing ship, which took her to Passau. Afflicted with leprosy, she was recommended to the abbot of Niederaltaich, who had a recluse's cell built for her beside the monastery church. Here she was found by her blood relative and childhood playmate, Judith, who having been widowed young and having likewise gone to Jerusalem, had searched for Salome. With permission of the abbot and the chapter Judith was then also given a cell by the church of Niederaltaich. Both women worked as servants in the monastery. Both died before the end of the 11th century, Salome first. The biography dates from the 13th or 14th century. It claims that both bodies were interred in a common shrine before the altar of St. Giles; they have since been lost.

Judith and Salome were venerated in monastic martyrologies and in art but had no liturgical cult.

Feast: June 29.

Bibliography: *Bibliotheca hagiographica latina antiquae et mediae aetatis,* 2 v. (Brussels 1898–1901) 2:1081, 7465. *Acta Sanctorum* (Paris 1863—) 5:492–498. A. M. ZIMMERMAN, *Kalendarium Benedictinum: Die Heiligen und Seligen des Benediktinerorderns und seiner Zweige* (Metten 1933–38) 2:374, 376. R. BAUERREISS, *Kirchengeschichte Bayerns* (St. Ottilien 1949–55) 2:113; *Lexikon für Theologie und Kirche,* ed. J. HOFER and K. RAHNER (Freiburg 1957–65) 5:1180.

[G. SPAHR]

Adoniram Judson.

Bibliography: F. WAYLAND, *Memoir of . . . Rev. Adoniram Judson,* 2 v. (Boston 1853). E. JUDSON, *Life of Adoniram Judson* (New York 1883). C. ANDERSON, *To the Golden Shore: The Life of Adoniram Judson* (Boston 1956).

[R. K. MACMASTER]

JUDSON, ADONIRAM

Baptist missionary; b. Malden, MA, Aug. 9, 1788; d. at sea, April 12, 1850. He was the son of a Congregationalist minister. While studying for the ministry at Andover Seminary, MA, in 1810, he and several other students determined to devote themselves to the foreign missions. Their petition led to the establishment of the American Board of Commissioners for Foreign Missions. Judson was ordained at Salem, MA, Feb. 6, 1812, and sailed for India 13 days later. On shipboard his views on the necessity of faith before baptism changed. Upon arriving in Calcutta, India, he and his bride, Ann Hasseltine Judson, were rebaptized by English Baptist missionaries. In 1813 the Judsons went to Burma and opened a mission in Rangoon. The mission prospered, but in June 1824 Judson was imprisoned for 18 months, and in 1827 he moved his station to Maulmain. He published a complete translation of the Bible in Burmese (1840) and an English-Burmese dictionary (1849).

JUGAN, JEANNE, BL.

Known in religion as Marie of the Cross, foundress of the Little Sisters of the Poor; b. Oct. 25, 1792, Petites-Croix (near Cancale), Brittany, France; d. Aug. 29, 1879, Pern, France.

After the death of her fisherman father, Joseph Joucan, when she was four, her mother, Marie Horel, supported the six children as a farm laborer and taught them the faith. At 16, Jeanne, the youngest child, became a kitchen maid to a charitable family. The mistress, Viscountess de la Choue, took her on visits to the sick and poor. At 25, Jugan joined the third order of the Heart of the Admirable Mother (founded by St. John EUDES), gave away her meager possessions, and began working in a hospital, but after six years of exhausting work she returned to domestic service. Realizing that she could do more, she then devoted herself entirely to the poor, especially widows.

Bl. Jeanne Jugan.

Hospital work and domestic service had prepared Jugan for giving hospitality to the aged in Saint-Servan. She was aided by two other women, Virginie Tredaniel and Marie Jamet, to whom Abbé Augustin Marie Le Pailleur had given a rule and a charge to care for an elderly blind woman, Anne Chauvin. All four women lived together in Jugan's home and elected her superior, May 29, 1842. Eventually a benefactor purchased an abandoned convent for the Little Sisters. These women, and others who assisted them, begged daily for the needs of the elderly in their care. The sisters ate what was left after feeding their guests. Houses were soon established in Rennes, Dinan, Tours, and Angers. Although Jugan was reelected superior (Dec. 8, 1843), she was suddenly replaced (Dec. 23, 1843) by 23-year-old Marie Jamet through the action of Le Pailleur. No recognition of her role as foundress came during her lifetime. After receiving a petition from the people of Saint-Servan, the French Academy made her recipient of one of its annual awards for virtue (December 1845) in appreciation of her heroic charity in caring for the poor. In 1852 the congregation was officially

recognized, and she was sent to the motherhouse for the remaining 27 years of her life, without an active role in the growth of the community.

Her contemporary Charles Dickens wrote: "There is in this woman something so calm, and so holy, that in seeing her I know myself to be in the presence of a superior being. Her words went straight to my heart, so that my eyes, I know not how, filled with tears."

It was not until 1893 that Jugan was recognized as the founder of the congregation whose rule was approved by PIUS X in 1907. In beatifying Jugan (Oct. 3, 1982) Pope JOHN PAUL II said: "I give thanks to the Lord for bringing about what Pope JOHN XXIII had so rightly hoped for and PAUL IV so ardently desired," the beatification of Jugan.

Feast: Aug. 30.

Bibliography: G. M. GARRONE, *Poor in Spirit*, tr. A. NEAME (London 1975). A. HELLEU, *Jeanne Jugan, Foundress of the Little Sisters of the Poor*, tr. M. A. GREY (St. Louis 1942). P. MILCENT, *Jeanne Jugan: Humble So as to Love More*, tr. A. NEAME (London 1980). F. TROCHU, *Jeanne Jugan*, tr. H. MONTGOMERY (Westminster, Md. 1950). *Acta Apostolicae Sedis* (1984) 346–49. *L'Osservatore Romano*, Eng. ed. 42 (1982) 9–10.

[T. F. CASEY/K. I. RABENSTEIN]

JULIAN OF CUENCA, ST.

Patron and second bishop of Cuenca; b. Burgos, Castile, *c.* 1113–38; d. January 28, *c.* 1208. He taught theology in Palencia and became archdeacon of Toledo (1182). In 1196 he was made bishop of Cuenca, a city taken from the Moors in 1177 and granted a famous charter (*fuero*) *c.* 1190. He drew up (*c.* 1200) the constitution of the cathedral chapter, later revised by Cardinal Gil ALBORNOZ. His *vita* and miracles have separate and obscure origins. He was an exemplary frontier bishop, known for pastoral visits and almsgiving and the feeding of the poor in person. He triumphed over temptations to gluttony, avarice, and sensuality proffered by the devil and twice miraculously provided grain for Cuenca. The cures reported at his shrine made Cuenca a place of pilgrimage. In 1589 Julian's name was included in the Roman Martyrology.

Feast: Jan. 28.

Bibliography: B. ALCÁZAR, *Vida . . . de San Julian* (Madrid 1692). *Acta Sanctorum* January 3:509–512. M. LÓPEZ, *Memorias históricas de Cuenca*, ed. A. GONZÁLEZ PALENCIA, 2 v. (Cuenca 1949–53) v.1. R. DE LUZ LAMARCA, *San Julian en Goya y el Greco* (Cuenca 1992). A. RUIZ, *Dictionnaire d'histoire et de géographie ecclésiastiques*, ed. A. BAUDRILLART (Paris 1912–) 13:1088–91. G. BÖING, *Lexikon für Theologie und Kirche*, ed. J. HOFER and K. RAHNER, 10 v. (2d, new ed. Freiburg 1957–65) 5:1197.

[E. P. COLBERT]

JULIAN OF ECLANUM

Fifth-century bishop and Pelagian theologian; b. Eclanum, Italy, 380; d. Sicily, c. 455. The son of Memorius, Bishop of Eclanum, Julian married (between 400 and 404) Ia, a woman mentioned by St. PAULINUS OF NOLA in the *Epithalamium* he dedicated to Julian. On the death of his wife, Julian joined the clergy of his native diocese and succeeded his father as bishop. He had an excellent knowledge of Latin and Greek, keen logic, and a fine secular and theological formation. He became a supporter of PELAGIUS, and in 418 he attacked the *Epistola tractoria* of Pope ZOSIMUS, in which Pelagius and Celestius were definitively condemned. Julian was deposed and expelled from Italy. He stopped in Sicily to gain supporters, then traveled in the Orient, where he was received by THEODORE OF MOPSUESTIA and NESTORIUS. Having tried in vain to regain his see, he taught letters in an obscure village in Sicily and died there under Valentinian III without being reconciled with the Church. However, until the 9th century his tomb had the inscription: "Here lies Julian a Catholic bishop."

Of his writings only these are incontestably authentic: four books to Turbantius; three letters; and eight books to Florus. He was answered in three different works by AUGUSTINE of Hippo. Julian's teaching is definitely heterodox. He reduced grace to a simple, protective, divine assistance, or a modality extrinsic to the soul. He practically denied the solidarity of the human race in Adam's sin. However, some of his ideas on the relation between the natural and supernatural orders and between liberty and grace must be seen as legitimate in the dogmatic and historical context of the age in which he wrote. This is the basis of recent attempts to rehabilitate Julian as both a philosopher and a theologian.

Bibliography: *Patrologia Latina* (Paris 1878–90) 21:959–1104. *Patrologia Latina* Suppl. 1 (1958) 1571–72, bibliog. B. ALTANER, *Patrology* (New York 1960) 442–443. G. BOUWMANN, *Des Julian von Aeclanum Kommentar* (Analecta biblica 9; 1958). J. FORGET, *Dictionnaire de théologie catholique*, ed. A. VACANT (Paris 1903–50) 8.2: 1926–31. H. I. MARROU, *Historisches Jahrbuch der Görres-Gesellschaft* 77 (1958) 434–437. F. REFOULÉ, *Recherches des sciences religeuses* 52 (1964) 42–84, 233–247.

[J. BENTIVEGNA]

JULIAN OF HALICARNASSUS

MONOPHYSITE bishop and leader of the allegedly radical heretical faction; d. after 527. After being expelled from his see at Halicarnassus in Caria by the Byzantine Emperor JUSTIN I in 518, Julian fled to Alexandria, where he became the principal exponent of so-called aphthartodocetism. This aberration from orthodox doctrine maintained that Christ's body was essentially incorruptible (ἄφθαρτος) and that His Passion and death were real but were the result of a free and extraordinary choice of His will, whereby He conferred passivity on His naturally incorruptible body. Opponents called the Julianists also "Phantasiastae" (those who teach that Christ had merely a phantom or apparent body). R. Draguet, in a minority opinion on the evidence, believes that Julian was fundamentally orthodox and that his use of extreme monophysitic terms may be applied to Christ's humanity in a broadly moral sense. Julian's prime opponent was SEVERUS OF ANTIOCH, a moderate Monophysite against whom Julian wrote four works, of which numerous fragments in Syriac and Greek have survived. Some of Julian's letters are extant also, but a commentary on Job seems to be erroneously attributed to him.

Bibliography: R. DRAGUET, *Julien d'Halicarnasse et sa controverse avec Sévère d' Antioche sur l'incorruptibilité du corps du Christ* (Louvain 1924). M. JUGIE, "J. d'H. et Sévère d'Antioche," *Échos d'Orient* 24 (1925) 129–162, 256–285. P. PEETERS, *Analecta Bollandiana* 43 (1925) 422–424. E. STEIN, *Histoire du Bas-Empire*, tr. J. R. PALANQUE 2:233–235.

[R. J. SCHORK]

JULIAN OF LE MANS, ST.

Bishop; dates unknown. According to the episcopal lists, he was the first bishop of Le Mans. His vita, written at the request of Bishop Avesgaud (d. 1036), has no historical value. Bishop BERTRAM OF LE MANS (d. 616) provided the earliest reference to a Bishop Julian of Le Mans when he made a bequest "to the basilica *S. Juliani Episcopi.*" He stated that this basilica, on the right bank of the Sarthe, had been built over Julian's tomb near the basilica of Saint-Victor. When both these churches were abandoned, Bishop ALDRIC OF LE MANS transferred the remains of his predecessors to the recently built west choir of his cathedral and dedicated the altar to them (June 21, 835). In time Julian replaced Saints GERVASE AND PROTASE as titular saint of the east choir. Bishop Mainard (d. 968) ordered a silver reliquary for his remains. Fulk of Anjou, leaving for Jerusalem, invoked the protection of St. Julian for his son Geoffrey and his lands (1128). Julian was made patron of the cathedral in 1158; he is represented in several of its stained–glass windows. In 1254 his remains were translated to the cathedral's Gothic choir. Julian is also honored at Bayeux, at Paderborn, southern England, and even in Russia.

Feast: Jan. 27

Bibliography: L. DUCHESNE, *Fastes épiscopaux de l'ancienne Gaule*, 3 v. (2d ed. Paris 1907–15) 2:312–335. C. GIRAULT, "Le Tombeau de Saint Julien au Pré," *Province du Maine*, ser. 2, 33

(1953) 49–59, esp. 53. *Congrès archéologique de France* 119 (1961) 18–23, 60, 100–102. A. MUSSAT, *Le Style gothique de l'Ouest de la France* (Paris 1963). L. RÉAU, *Iconographie de l'art chrétien,* 6 v. (Paris 1955–59) 3.2:769–771. H. LECLERCQ, *Dictionnaire d'archéologie chrétienne et de liturgie,* ed. F. CABROL, H. LECLERCQ and H. I. MARROU, 15 v. (Paris 1907–53) 10.2:1461–74.

[J. CAMBELL]

JULIAN OF NORWICH

Anchoress, author of *Sixteen Revelations of Divine Love;* b. 1342; d. probably between 1416 and 1423. Her anchorhold was attached to the church of SS. Julian and Edward at Conisford, Norwich. That she was still enclosed there in 1416 is attested by a bequest to ''Julian, Recluse at Norwich'' in the will of Lady Suffolk of that date. A bequest in 1423 to a male anchorite, occupying this same anchorhold, indicates the *terminus ad quem* for Julian's death date. The various editions of Butler's *Lives of the Saints* list her as ''Blessed'' under the date of May 13, and some Benedictine calendars [e.g., *Corona Sanctorum Anni Benedictini* (Ramsgate 1947)] give her the title of ''Saint.'' There is no reputable historical evidence that there was any persistent *cultus* to her, even of a local nature; her reputation for holiness seems to be based entirely on her *Revelations,* if one excludes the brief reference to her by Margery KEMPE of Lynn, who described her as an expert in giving good counsel. It is not known whether Julian was her proper name, or whether she adopted it after her enclosure at St. Julian's Church. It is unlikely that she was ever a member of the Benedictine community at Carrow Abbey, which is located near Norwich.

Apart from bequests in two other wills dated 1404 and 1416, which also refer to her as the anchoress of St. Julian's, all that is known of her she tells herself in her book of *Revelations:* ''These revelations were shewed to a simple unlearned creature living in this mortal flesh in the year of our Lord 1373, on the 13th day of May. And when I was 30 years old and a half, God sent me a bodily sickness . . . .'' She goes on to say that she was thoroughly and completely cured of her illness; and that the figure of Christ on the cross became alive before her eyes. This was the first revelation or ''shewing''; 14 others followed on the same day, six concerned with Our Lord's passion, the remaining eight with other spiritual truths, and the last with the indwelling of the Blessed Trinity in the soul. The allegation that her sickness was a form of nervous hysteria, and the inference that the revelations were due to a diseased or disordered imagination, has been satisfactorily refuted by Paul Molinari, SJ.

Julian has left two separate accounts of her revelations: a shorter version, probably written soon after her experience, and a longer narrative, the result of more than 15 years of prayer and meditation on the shewings, during which time she received more light on them. Both versions are written in the first person and follow the chronological order of the shewings. The tone of her narrative is informal and conversational: it is a record of personal experience rather than a theological treatise. The purpose and content of the *Revelations* concern the knowledge of God and of ourselves: what we are by Him, in nature and in grace; what we are in our sinfulness and weakness. The knowledge of God granted to Julian was of His love: it is courteous, homely, intensely personal. To explain its intimate nature she has recourse to the unusual image, not to be found in any of the Fathers except St. Anselm, of the mother and the child.

In her development of the doctrine of the Mystical Body, man's incorporation into Christ, she may have owed something in expression to her contemporary Walter HILTON, an Augustinian canon; even the psychology she uses to expose the human relationship to the Father in Christ is a simplified Augustinianism (there were Austin Friars at Norwich). But if one looks for the real source of her theology of incorporation into Christ it can be found nowhere else than in St. Paul, just as for her teaching on the mystery of the divine indwelling one must go back to St. John. The account of her *Revelations* is regularly punctuated by concern with the problem of sin and damnation, which appeared to her to conflict with divine love and goodness, and the assurance that all shall be well. The various formulations and solutions to this problem impart a highly artistic structure to her book, which falls into four sections (ch. 1–27; 28–43; 44–65; 66–86).

Although she says repeatedly that her revelations were granted for the profit of all her fellow Christians, her audience is effectively reduced to those who ''deliberately choose God in this life for love.'' She is particularly concerned for the ''little and the simple—those who for love hate sin and dispose themselves to do God's will.'' The title of the first printed edition of the shorter version of her *Revelations,* ''Comfortable Words for Christ's Lovers,'' is extraordinarily apt. Like Julian's own homely language, it gives no immediate clue to the profundity and wealth that is embodied in her mystical doctrine.

Bibliography: Editions. JULIAN OF NORWICH, *The Shewings of Julian of Norwich,* ed. G. R. CRAMPTON (Kalamazoo, Mich. 1994); *The Revelation of Divine Love in Sixteen Showings Made to Dame Julian of Norwich,* tr. M. L. DEL MASTRO (Liguori, Mo. 1994); *Revelations of Divine Love (Short Text and Long Text),* tr. E. SPEARING, intro. and notes A. C. SPEARING (Harmondsworth, Eng. 1998); *Revelations of Divine Love, Translated from British Library Additional Manuscript 37790; The Motherhood of God: An Excerpt, Translated from British Library Manuscript Sloane 2477,* intro., interpretive essay, and bibliography F. BEER (Rochester, N.Y. 1998). **Studies.** P. MOLINARI, *Julian of Norwich: The Teaching of* *a 14th-Century Mystic* (London 1958). D. KNOWLES, *The English Mystical Tradition* (New York 1961) 119–137. F. C. BAUERSCH-MIDT, *Julian of Norwich and the Mystical Body Politic of Christ* (Notre Dame, Ind. 1999). S. J. MCENTIRE, ed., *Julian of Norwich: A Book of Essays* (New York 1998). J. M. NUTH, *Wisdom's Daughter: The Theology of Julian of Norwich* (New York 1991). B. PEL-PHREY, *Julian of Norwich: Christ, Our Mother* (Wilmington, Del. 1989). G. M. JANTZEN, *Julian of Norwich: Mystic and Theologian* (New York 1988).

[J. WALSH]

JULIAN OF SPEYER

Known also as Julianus Teutonicus, early Franciscan poet, liturgist and musician; d. Paris *c.* 1250. As a youth he left his home of Speyer, the imperial city in the upper Rhine valley, for the new University of Paris to study music. Before long he was promoted to *magister cantus* (master of song) at the court of the French king. In Paris sometime after 1227 he joined the brothers of Saint Francis of Assisi in their new center of studies. For over 20 years he served the student brothers of the Franciscan Order at the "Grand Couvent des Cordeliers." His task was to oversee the proper singing of the Divine Office and to correct mistakes in public reading during the liturgy, meals, and other community gatherings. Trained in the rhythmic tradition he composed two Offices with musical notation for FRANCIS OF ASSISI and ANTHONY OF PADUA. The former, dating from *c.* 1231–32, was later included in the *Ordinal* of HAYMO OF HAVERSHAM and became widely used throughout the Latin Church until the liturgical reform of Pius V in the 16th century. Much of the textual composition of the Office is drawn from THOMAS OF CELANO's *Life of St. Francis*, but it further develops the significance of the stigmata. Shortly after the composition of these two versions of the Divine Office, Julian wrote two lives, *Life of St. Francis* and *Life of St. Anthony*. The former likewise draws from the work of the same title composed earlier by Thomas of Celano. Julian's life about the saint from Assisi is much shorter and, as it was written for the formational needs of his younger brothers in Paris, it is more pastoral and practical, intimately connected with the liturgical themes of the Divine Office for Francis of Assisi.

Bibliography: R. ARMSTRONG, W. HELLMANN, W. SHORT, eds., "Divine Office of St. Francis," in *Francis of Assisi: Early Documents*, v. 1 (New York 1999), 311–360; "Life of St. Francis," *ibid.*, 363–420; bibliography. J. MISKULY, "Julian of Speyer: Life of St. Francis," *Franciscan Studies* 49 (1989), 93–117. J. STRAYER, ed., "Rhymed Offices," in *Dictionary of the Middle Ages*, v. 10 (New York 1988), 366–377.

[J. A. W. HELLMANN]

JULIAN OF TOLEDO, ST.

Theologian, archbishop of Toledo, Jan. 29, 680 to March 690; b. *c.* 642; d. Toledo, 690. He was born into a converted Jewish family and educated in the cathedral school of Toledo under EUGENE II (III) and his successor St. ILDEFONSUS. Julian presided over the 12th to 15th Councils of Toledo (681, 683, 684, and 688). His angry reaction when his first *Apologeticum fidei,* dealing with the recently condemned Monothelite heresy, was criticized by Roman theologians in 684 provides evidence of an increasing isolation from Rome on the part of the Spanish Church. Julian's theology was orthodox, and there was no final break with Rome. As primate of Spain, Julian increased the importance of his see and played a part in late Visigothic politics.

Only five of the 17 works mentioned by Julian's biographer survive, together with a short *Elogium Ildefonsi* and a poem recently recovered. They reveal an original mind and a wide range of achievement, which includes controversy (the *De sextae aetatis comprobatione,* to prove to the Jews the coming of Christ, and the *Apologeticum de tribus capitulis,* sent to Rome in 686—the first *Apologeticum* is lost); the *Prognosticum futuri saeculi,* a manual on the future life, which enjoyed immense influence in the Middle Ages; and the *Anti-keimena seu liber de contrariis,* a forerunner of ABELARD's *Sic et Non.* The *Historia Wambae* and the *Ars grammatica* (the latter, if not by Julian, certainly by one of his disciples) display a deep knowledge of the classics.

Julian possessed a remarkable library, which may have included a few patristic texts in Greek. Julian was the author of a revision of the HISPANA, the Spanish collection of Canon Law, and he revised the MOZARABIC, or Spanish Liturgy. He received cultus in Toledo (by 858), where he was buried in the church of St. Leocadia, and was commemorated in the later calendars of Silos and Oña. Apparently there were relics of Julian at San Millán de la Cogolla and at Oviedo.

Feast: March 8.

Bibliography: *Opera omnia,* v.2 of *SS. PP. Toletanorum quotquot extant opera,* ed. F. A. LORENZANA Y BUTRÓN (Madrid 1785) 1–384, repr. *Patrologia Latina,* ed. J. P. MIGNE, 217 V., indexes 4 v. (Paris 1878–90) 96:452–818. FELIX OF TOLEDO, *Vita, ibid.* xv–xxii, repr. *Patrologia Latina,* 96:444–452. M. C. DÍAZ Y DÍAZ, *Index scriptorum lationorum medii aevi Hispanorum,* 2 v. (Salamanca 1958–59). B. BISCHOFF, "Ein Brief Julians von Toledo über Rhythmen, metrische Dictung und Prosa," *Hermes,* 87 (1959) 247–256. A. VEIGA VALIÑA, *La doctrina escatológica de San Julián de Toledo* (Lugo 1940). F. X. MURPHY, in *Mélanges Joseph de Ghellinck,* v.1 (Gembloux 1951) 361–373, Monothelitism; "J. of T. and the Fall of the Visigothic Kingdom in Spain," *Speculum,* 27 (1952) 1–27. J. MADOZ, *Estudios eclesiásticos,* 26 (1952) 39–69; "Fuentes teologico-literarias de S. J. de T.," *Gregorianum,* 33 (1952)

399–417. J. N. HILLGARTH, "El *Prognosticum futuri saeculi* de S. J. de T.," *Analecta Sacra Tarraconensia,* 30 (1957) 5–61, bibliog; "St. J. of T. in the Middle Ages," *Journal of the Warburg and Courtauld Institutes,* 21 (1958) 7–26.

[J. N. HILLGARTH]

JULIAN SABAS, ST.

Monk; b. Heliopolis, Syria, *c.* 300; d. Osrhoene, 377 or 380. Theodoret (*History of the Monks,* 2) says that he lived first in a hermit's cell on the banks of the Euphrates and then in a cave in the desert of OSRHOENE, between Antioch and the Euphrates, where he gathered a group of disciples. He went to Sinai and built a church on the rock where the Lord was said to have appeared to Moses. He appeared in Antioch in the reign of VALENS (364–378) to refute Arian claims that he agreed with them and then retired to Osrhoene. In *Acta Sanctorum* Dec., Propyl. 21,231; 461, he is identified with St. Julian the Monk and St. Julian the Hermit (Roman MARTYROLOGY (RM) Jan. 14, June 9, and Oct. 18).

Feast: Jan. 17 (RM and Greek Synaxarion); Oct. 18.

Bibliography: *Acta Sanctorum* Nov., Propyl. 398–400. THEODORET, *Historia Ecclesiastica, Patrologia Graeca,* ed. J. P. MIGNE, 161 v. (Paris 1857–66) 82: 1305–24. J. L. BAUDOT and L. CHAUSSIN, *Vies des saints et des bienheureux selon l'ordre du calendrier avec l'historique des fêtes* (Paris 1935–56) 1:352–353.

[J. VAN PAASSEN]

JULIAN THE APOSTATE

Roman Emperor (361–363); b. *c.* 331; d. June 26, 363. He was the son of Julius Constantius, the half brother of Constantine the Great. His mother Basilina died shortly after his birth in 331; his father perished in 337 in the slaughter that brought into power the illegitimate branch of Constantine's descendants. The fraternal rivalries within the family shaped Julian's whole life. With his brother Gallus, Julian lived precariously and in obscurity, chiefly at Macellum in Asia Minor. His tutor Mardonius, probably a pagan, introduced him to the best aspects of Hellenistic culture. At Macellum Julian also read extensively in Christian literature, received baptism, and even served as lector in church. Most of the Christian clergy he knew, such as Eusebius of Nicomedia and George of Cappadocia, for example, were Arians.

When Gallus became Caesar in 351, Julian was allowed to travel and study. Libanius and other teachers strengthened his love of Greek culture. Contact with the theurgist Neoplatonist, Maximus of Ephesus, led to Julian's secret apostasy from Christianity *c.* 351; he was

Julian the Apostate, 19th century. (©The Granger Collection)

also initiated into the cult of Mithra. The fall of Gallus in 354 endangered Julian, who was summoned by Constantius II to the West, where he lived under surveillance. In 355 Constantius, with no sons of his own, appointed Julian Caesar with jurisdiction over the West. In battles against the Germans during the next five years Julian showed true military skill. In 360 his soldiers proclaimed him Augustus, in a mutiny. Constantius died in 361, with civil war imminent and Julian was accepted as sole emperor. He spent his reign in the East. Except for minor administrative measures, he concerned himself with religion and the war that he waged against the Persians and in which he eventually died.

The mainspring of Julian's abhorrence of Christianity was his cultural conservatism. He was completely devoted to Greco-Roman civilization and thought he was mystically called to rescue it from an alien, uncouth Christianity. Disinclined to persecution by force, he proclaimed toleration for all Christian sects, revoked all special privileges, removed Christians from political office, and forbade them to teach the classical curriculum of the schools. He exiled St. ATHANASIUS and refused to come to the defense of NISIBIS because of its Christian population. In his work, *Against the Galileans,* he expounds his anti-Christian position. Positively, his religious program envisioned a rejuvenated paganism with Neoplatonism as an intellectual base and a reformed priesthood modeled on the Christian clergy. His efforts met with complete apathy, however. He wrote four minor philosophical works. His letters and the satirical *Misopogon* offer additional insights into a noble but erratic character.

Bibliography: K. GROSS, *Lexicon für Theologie und Kirche*, ed. J. HOFER and K. RAHNER (Freiburg 1957–65) 5:1195–96. H. DÖRRIE, *Die Religion in Geschichte und Gegenwart* 3:1060–61. E. STEIN, *Histoire du Bas-Empire*, tr. J. R. PALANQUE, 2 v. in 3 (Paris 1949–59). G. RICCIOTTI, *Julian the Apostate* (Milwaukee 1960).

[R. H. SCHMANDT]

JULIANA OF LIÈGE, BL.

Also known as Juliana of Mont–Cornillon; promoter of the Feast of Corpus Christi; b. Rétinne, near Liège, *c.* 1191–92; d. Fosses, near Namur, April 5, 1258. She joined the Canonesses Regular at Mont-Cornillon, where she became prioress in 1222. As a result of a vision in 1209, she had become one of the earliest protagonists for a feast of the Blessed Sacrament. Her local bishop, Robert of Torote (1240–46), ordered the celebration of this feast on the Thursday following the octave of Trinity Sunday. She persuaded John of Cornillon to compose a preliminary Office for the feast [*cf.* C. Lambot and I. Franson, *L'Office de la FêteDieu primitive* (Maredsous 1946)]. Then cardinal legate HUGH OF ST. CHER extended its celebration to Germany, Bohemia, and Poland (1252). But her zeal earned her enemies and she was forced to leave Cornillon, seeking shelter among the BEGUINES of Namur. Six years after Juliana died at Saint–Fevillen in Fosses, URBAN IV, a former archdeacon at Liège, urged by Eve of Liège, extended the celebration of CORPUS CHRISTI to the whole Church. Juliana's cult as a beata was confirmed in 1869.

Feast: April 5.

Bibliography: *Acta Sanctorum,* April, 1:442–475. E. DENIS, *La Vraie histoire de sainte Julienne de L.* (Tournai 1935). G. SIMENON, *J. de Cornillon* (Brussels 1946). E. W. MCDONNELL, *Beguines and Beghards in Medieval Culture* (New Brunswick, N.J. 1954). A. BUTLER, *The Lives of the Saints,* rev. ed. H. THURSTON and D. ATTWATER, 4 v. (New York 1956) 2:37–38.

[J. J. SMITH]

JULIANISTS (APHTHARTODOCETISM)

Heresy concerned with the incorruptibility of Christ's body. Among the Monophysites who took refuge in Egypt when JUSTIN I became emperor in 519 was JULIAN OF HALICARNASSUS, a strong partisan of SEVERUS OF ANTIOCH. Julian and Severus disagreed on the question of the incorruptibility of Christ's body. Severus maintained that the value of Christ's sacrifice on the cross would be null if His body were not capable of corruption. Julian denied this, saying that Christ was not subject to the effects of original sin. While Christ's sufferings were real, they were due to an act of His will which made it possible for His body to experience death, though it was naturally not subject to suffering or corruption. This disagreement caused a split among the Egyptian Monophysites. The Julianists accused the Severans of maintaining that Christ's body was corrupted in the tomb. The Severans called the Julianists "aphthartodocetists," because they believed the body of Christ to be a mere appearance, and consequently not corruptible; furthermore, they attributed to the Julianists radical heresies, such as that of the Actistetae who affirmed that the body of Christ, as well as His divinity, was uncreated. Under Gaianus, patriarch of Alexandria, the Julianist heresy spread quickly through Egypt, establishing itself in Ethiopia, Syria, Mesopotamia, Albania, and Armenia, and in the mid-6th century it seemed about to prevail in the East. Although eventually absorbed by strict Monophysitism, it caused the further disintegration of that belief into various sects. Toward the end of 564, Emperor JUSTINIAN I, evidently under the influence of the bishop of Joppa in Palestine, issued an edict affirming that the body of Christ was by nature incorruptible and impassible, whereupon the Patriarch Eutychius of Constantinople protested and was deposed on Jan. 31, 565. Led by ANASTASIUS, patriarch of Antioch, the patriarchs of Alexandria and Jerusalem also resisted, and on the death of the Emperor the Justinian cause ended.

Bibliography: R. DRAGUET, *Julien d'Halicarnasse et sa controverse avec Sévère d'Antioche sur l'incorruptibilité du corps du Christ* (Louvain 1924); *Dictionnaire de théologie catholique*, ed. A. VACANT et al., 15 v. (Paris 1903–50) 8.2:1931–40. M. JUGIE, "Julien d'Halicarnasse et Sévère d'Antioche," *Échos d'Orient* 28 (1925) 129–162, 257–285. E. STEIN, *Histoire du Bas-Empire*, tr. J. R. PALANQUE, 2 v. in 3 (Paris 1949–59) 1:233–235, 685–687.

[G. A. MALONEY]

JULIUS I, ST., POPE

Pontificate: Feb. 6, 337 to April 12, 352. Papal history enters a new phase with Julius. From his pontificate onward, scholars have far more information to work with, including papal documents; they also have accurate dates. A vacancy of four months occurred between the death of Mark and Julius' election as Bishop of Rome, described by the *Liber pontificalis* as "a Roman by birth, whose father was Rusticus." The date of the new Pope's consecration is known from the Liberian catalogue, the date of his burial from the *Depositio Episcoporum*.

His election coincided roughly with the death of Constantine the Great (May 22), and marked, in the Arian struggle, the beginning of a new phase characterized on the part of the Roman See by a more vigorous participation which apparently had not been possible while the Emperor lived. The death of Constantine meant the end, for the time being, of any uniform imperial policy toward the Church. Of his three sons who shared the Empire, two, Constantine II and Constans, followed the Council of NICEA while Constantius, who obtained the East, favored the Arian party. Constantine II permitted the return of Athanasius from exile, an act that prompted EUSEBIUS OF NICOMEDIA, now bishop of Constantinople, and the Arian-sympathizing Eastern bishops to try to have Athanasius ousted again. They sent a delegation to Julius with the acts of the council at Tyre (335) in an attempt to obtain his approval for what had been done there and to win recognition for Pistus, the Arian intruder in Alexandria. When Julius informed him about the opposition of the Eusebian party, Athanasius vindicated himself of the charges made against him in a great council in Alexandria and notified Julius and the other bishops in a synodal letter (338).

Before the envoys from Athanasius arrived, the leader of the Eusebian delegation, Macarius, departed from Rome, leaving his assistants, Hesychius and Martyrius, behind. When confronted by the refutation of Athanasius, they suggested that the pope summon a general council to settle the matter. Julius accepted the idea and wrote to both sides in this sense. Meanwhile Athanasius had to flee Alexandria when the Eusebians forcibly installed a new Arian intruder, Gregory of Cappadocia, in place of Pistus (339). Athanasius protested his expulsion in an encyclical that prompted Julius to send legates to the Eusebians summoning them to a council in Rome (340). After delaying the papal representatives in Antioch for a long time, the Eusebians refused the summons, and the legates returned to Rome with their negative reply (341).

The letter of the Eusebians is interesting for the light it throws on Eastern attitudes toward the primacy. While confessing that "the Roman church was entitled to the honor of all, because it was the school of the Apostles and was from the beginning the metropolis of religion," they found fault with Julius for transgressing the canons by disregarding their council at Tyre and communicating with Athanasius. This would be a common Eastern attitude for centuries, honoring Rome's antiquity and apostolicity, but not feeling obliged to agree with or follow the papacy on all matters. The Roman council, attended by Athanasius, Marcellus of Ancyra, and other bishops driven from their sees by the Eusebians, was held without the Eusebians (June 10, 341). The case of Athanasius was

(l to r) Pope Cornelius, Pope St. Julius I, and Bishop Lepodius, right side detail of 12th-century mosaic in the apse of the church of S. Maria in Trastevere, Rome.

again examined, and he and the other bishops were ordered restored to their sees.

The reply of Julius to the Eusebians (341) is called "a masterpiece of episcopal diplomacy" because of its admirable combination of firmness and conciliation. The pope refuted their charges and found their reasons for not attending the Roman council unconvincing. It was not he, but they, who had violated the canons by deposing Athanasius without reference to Rome. It is interesting that Julius bases his intervention not on the Petrine privilege to which later popes would appeal, but on ecclesiastical custom (canons), and that he discreetly refers to the collegial character of episcopal authority: "You should have written to us all, so that justice might be determined by all. For the sufferers were bishops and prominent churches, which the Apostles themselves had governed. And why were we not written to about the church of the Alexandrians? Are you ignorant that the custom was first to write to us, and then for justice to be determined from here?"

The last sentence probably refers to the special tie binding the Church of Alexandria to Rome, but the Roman decision remained without effect.

In a council at Antioch held later the same year and presided over by Constantius himself (the so-called Dedication Council), the deposition of Athanasius was confirmed; Gregory was recognized as bishop of Alexandria; and Arian formulas were adopted. The Council of SARDICA (Sofia), at which Julius was represented by the legates Archidamus and Philoxenus, was called to find a way out of the impasse (343), but ended in disagreement. After issuing a synodal letter addressed to all the bishops condemning Athanasius and Marcellus of Ancyra and excommunicating Julius as the cause of "all the evil," the Eusebians, who refused to join their Western colleagues, departed for home. The remaining bishops, under the presidency of Hosius, once again vindicated Athanasius and passed several canons intended to regulate appeals to Rome. These remained a dead letter, however, owing to the refusal of the Eusebians to recognize the council and, probably, a cause of their restrictive nature. They are interesting, nevertheless, as evidence of the persistence of the belief that the Roman primacy was based on Peter: "in order to honor the memory of blessed Peter . . . ."

After the death of the intruder Gregory, Athanasius was able to return to his see with the permission of Constantius, and he brought with him a letter to the Alexandrians from Julius (346). The remaining years of the pontificate of Julius were relatively quiet. He had the satisfaction of receiving the submission of two prominent Arians, Ursacius of Singidunum (Belgrade) and Valens of Mursa (347), who withdrew their allegations against Athanasius at a council in Milan and before the Pope in person in Rome. Unfortunately, they soon reverted to their old ways.

The *Liber pontificalis* attributes to Julius a decree, possibly contemporary, regarding the organization of the archives and chancery (*scrinium*) of the Roman Church on the imperial model, in which mention is made for the first time of the *primicerius notariorum;* to this Pope it attributes also the construction of several churches including the two city churches later known as SS. Apostoli and S. Maria in Trastevere (*titulus Iulii*), as well as a ceremonial hall in the Lateran Palace (*basilica Iulii*), later demolished to make way for the medieval Hall of Councils. An anonymous author known as the CHRONOGRAHER of 354 recorded that Rome observed the birth date of Jesus on December 25, but indicates that the practice had been known since 336. This means that Julius was the first pope to celebrate Christmas on the now traditional day, a practice followed by other Western churches and by most Eastern ones. Julius was buried in the cemetery of Calepodius on the Via Aurelia, but the exact location of his tomb is unknown.

Feast: April 12.

See Also: ARIANISM.

Bibliography: ATHANASIUS, *Apologia contra Arianos,* 25: 282–291, 343–347. *Clavis Patrum latinorum,* ed. E. DEKKERS (Streenbrugge 1961) 1627. *Patrologiae cursus completus, series latina;* suppl., ed. A. HAMMAN (Paris 1957–) 1:191–192. *Liber pontificalis,* ed. L. DUCHESNE (Paris 1886–92, 1958) 1:205–206; 3:81–82. É. AMANN, *Dictionnaire de théologie catholique,* ed. A. VACANT et al., (Paris 1903–50) 8.2:1914–17. H. LECLERCQ, *Dictionnaire d'archéologie chrétienne et de liturgie.* ed. F. CABROL, H. LECLERCQ and H. I. MARROU (Paris 1907–53) 13.1:1199. E. SCHWARTZ, *Gesammelte Schriften,* ed. H. D. ALTENDORF, 5 v. (Berlin 1938–62), v.4. R. U. MONTINI, *Le tombe dei Papi* (Rome 1957) 92–93. R. VIELLIARD, *Recherches sur les origines de la Rome chrétienne* (Mâcon 1941; repr. Rome 1959) 68–69. H. HESS, *The Canons of the Council of Sardica, A.D. 343* (Oxford 1958). E. FERGUSON, ed., *Encyclopedia of Early Christianity* (New York 1997) 2:644–645. W. GESSEL, "Das primatiale Bewüsstsein Julius I," *Festschrift H. Tüchle* (Paderborn 1975) 63–74. H. JEDIN, ed., *History of the Church* (New York 1980) 2:35–41. J. N. D. KELLY, *Oxford Dictionary of Popes* (New York 1986) 29–30. C. PIETRI, *Roma Christiana* (Rome 1976) 187–237. G. FERNÁNDEZ HERNÁNDEZ, "La autenticidad de los cánones del sínodo sardicense en los años 343–344: una polémica historiogràfica," *Anuario de Historia de la Iglesia* 6 (Pamplona 1997) 305–7. N. STANEV, "Le concile de Sardique de 343: étape nouvelle dans la lutte des idées au IVe siècle," in *Thracia 11. Studien in honorem Alexander Fol* (Serdicae 1995) 455–62. M. VINZENT, ed., *Markell von Ankyra. Die Fragmente—der Brief an Julius von Rom,* (Leiden 1997).

[J. CHAPIN]

JULIUS II, POPE

Pontificate: Nov. 1, 1503, to Feb. 21, 1513; b. Giuliano Della Rovere, Albisola (near Savona) in the Republic of Genoa in 1443; d. Rome. His father, Raffaello, was a brother of Pope SIXTUS IV (Francesco Della Rovere). While his uncle was Franciscan minister general, Giuliano studied with the Franciscans in Perugia and was ordained. It is uncertain if he entered the Franciscan order. When his uncle became pope in 1471, he was named bishop of Carpentras and made cardinal priest of St. Peter in Chains. Eventually, he held eight bishoprics, was archbishop of Avignon, and was granted many abbeys and benefices. From 1480 to 1482 Giuliano served as legate *a latere* to France, showing great skill in composing the differences between Louis XI and Maximilian of Austria over the Burgundian inheritance. When Sixtus IV died, Cardinal Della Rovere, partly by simony, secured the election of Battista Cibò, who took the name of INNOCENT VIII. Della Rovere's influence, therefore, continued and he became a rival of Cardinals Borgia and Sforza. The

Monument of Pope Julius II by Michelangelo and his atelier, the Church of St. Peter in Chains, Rome. (Alinari-Art Reference/Art Resource, NY)

election of Rodrigo Borgia as ALEXANDER VI in 1492 was a reverse for him. Except for brief shows of reconciliation, Della Rovere was hostile to Alexander VI and usually resided away from Rome.

Della Rovere and Charles VIII. Just prior to the invasion of Italy by Charles VIII, Della Rovere fled to France with the belief that Church reforms might be achieved with the King's support. He accompanied Charles VIII into Italy, and, on Dec. 31, 1494, sought his backing for the convocation of a council to depose Alexander VI on the grounds of his having won the election of 1492 through bribery. When Charles VIII negotiated and signed a treaty with Alexander in 1495, Della Rovere became disillusioned with the French and returned to Avignon.

The Borgia Peril. In 1498 a reconciliation with Alexander VI was effected, when Della Rovere's diplomatic services helped to secure Charlotte d'Albret, sister of the King of Navarre, as a bride for Cesare Borgia. This peace ended in 1502 when Cesare attacked the Duke of Urbino where Francesco Della Rovere, the cardinal's nephew, stood in line of succession to the dukedom. During the following year Della Rovere remained far from Rome, spending part of the time in France. There Louis XII, considering the cardinal as friendly to French interests, granted him the abbey of Chiaravalle near Milan. The death of Alexander VI in August 1503 made the cardinal's return to Rome possible. The rallying of the Romans against Cesare Borgia's troops, and the illness of Cesare himself, saved the conclave from Borgia intimidation. Although Della Rovere was unable to obtain the election for himself, he frustrated the attempt to elect Cardinal d'Amboise. The election of the sickly Cardinal Piccolomini as PIUS III was followed by a pontificate of less than a month. Thereupon, by extensive promises to Cesare Borgia, and with bribes, Della Rovere was unanimously elected pope.

Julius II sought to repair the damage inflicted on the Church by the Borgias. He determined to recover territories lost to the Papal State, to achieve financial solvency, to strengthen administration, to eliminate simony, and to reduce nepotism. Believing that papal authority might best be enhanced by increased temporal power, he stressed territorial conquest, skillful diplomacy, and external glory. He was determined to recover territories alienated by his predecessors or occupied in the months immediately following the death of Alexander VI. The dukedom of the Romagna had been bestowed upon Cesare Borgia, and the Venetians had moved in on these papal lands in 1503. Julius II used persuasion with the Venetians, who relinquished some of these Romagna holdings but continued to hold Rimini and Faenza. In

September 1506 the Pope obtained the surrender of Gian Paolo Baglioni, Lord of Perugia, and expelled Giovanni Bentivoglio from Bologna. But the Venetians continued to deny the restitutions the Pope demanded.

Military Alliances. In 1508 the Emperor Maximilian made war on Venice and joined Louis XII of France in the League of Cambrai against the republic. In 1509 the Pope entered the league and issued a bull of excommunication and interdict. After the Venetians were defeated at Agnadello in May 1509, papal troops regained Rimini, Faenza, and other lost territories. By the beginning of 1510, after Julius II had received freedom of trade and navigation, and confirmation of ecclesiastical rights in Venetian territory, he became reconciled with the republic and lifted the excommunication. But neither France nor the Emperor wished to make peace. At that point the French threat to Italy led the Pope to form an alliance with Venice and Spain.

The first countermove of Louis XII was to convoke a synod at Tours in which the French bishops revived the ancient Gallican claims. Louis XII then, in agreement with the Emperor, promoted in the name of a group of rebel cardinals the calling of a council at Pisa. This act led Julius II to call the Fifth Lateran Council in 1511. Meanwhile, the Pope turned against the Duke of Ferrara, who was supporting the French. Papal troops occupied Modena in 1510 and took Mirandola in January 1511. These successes were offset by the loss of Bologna in May and the recapture of Mirandola. In August, however, Julius reconciled the powerful Roman families of Colonna and Orsini so that he had the nearly unanimous backing of the Roman nobility. Furthermore, the Holy League (Venice, Spain, and the papacy) was formally completed in October 1511. Before the end of the year England joined this combination. In April 1512, the league was defeated at Ravenna by Gaston de Foix. But the French victory was brief. Cardinal Schiner, leading Swiss forces on behalf of the league, took Cremona and Pavia and then, in June 1512, secured the surrender of Milan. The congress of the league met in Mantua and awarded Milan to Maximilian Sforza. At the end of 1512 Italian affairs in general were still unsettled except for the withdrawal of the French. While the league congress was deliberating in Mantua, the Medici returned to Florence, from which they had been ousted. Although territorial problems remained unresolved when Julius II died in February 1513, he had enlarged the territory and power of the Papal State. Some hailed him as the "Liberator of Italy."

Reforms and the Lateran Council. A bull, published in 1510 but dated Jan. 14, 1505, voided any papal election tainted with simony. This bull was confirmed in February 1513, a few days before Julius' death, by the

Fifth Lateran Council (*see* LATERAN COUNCILS). Julius also renewed the bull of Pius II forbidding appeal from a pope to a council. It was he, too, who granted a dispensation enabling Prince Henry of England, later HENRY VIII, to marry CATHERINE OF ARAGON. Julius was aware of the need for reform in the Church and indicated this when the Lateran Council opened in May 1512. But the Council became preoccupied with the problems associated with France and with the uncanonical council of Pisa-Milan. The latter council, which had been poorly supported, left Pisa for Milan and then, in 1512, moved to Lyons where it lost the sponsorship of France and came to an end. Administratively Julius II carefully supervised magistrates through a governor and vicechamberlain and defined more precisely legal and procedural distinctions between lay and ecclesiastical cases. He required, annually, strict audits of accounts, and he reorganized the college of notaries. He effected a monetary reform, increased papal revenue by the sale of curial offices, and restored a treasury left almost empty by the Borgias. For these among other reasons Jacob Burckhardt described him as "Savior of the Papacy."

Patron of Arts. He was a patron to Michelangelo, Raphael, Bramante, and others. He began building the new basilica of St. Peter's with plans by Bramante. He commissioned, among other works by Michelangelo, the frescoes on the vault of the Sistine Chapel. He assigned to Raphael the paintings of the Stanze della Segnatura. He beautified Rome and carried out much construction throughout the Papal State. He helped found the Vatican Library. In the courts of Saint Damasus and the Belvedere he provided the beginnings of a great collection of ancient sculpture.

Bibliography: L. PASTOR, *The History of the Popes from the Close of the Middle Ages,* (London–St. Louis 1938–61) 6. M. BROSCH, *Papst Julius II und die Gründung des Kirchenstaates* (Gotha 1878). E. RODOCANACHI, *La Première renaissance: Rome au temps de Jules V et de Léon X* (Paris 1912); *Histoire de Rome: Le pontificat de Jules II* (Paris 1928). J. KLAZKO, *Jules II* (Paris 1898). A. LUZIO, *Isabella d' Este di fronte a Giulio II negli ultimi tre anni del suo pontificato* (Milan 1912). E. GAGLIARDI, "Julius II, der Schöpfer des Kirchenstaates," *Deutsche Rundschau* 149 (1911) 262–275. F. VERNET, *Dictionnaire de théologie catholique,* ed. A. VACANT et al., 15 v. (Paris 1903–50; Tables générales 1951–) 8.2:2667–86. G. B. PICOTTI, *La politica italiana sotto il pontificato di Giulio II* (Pisa 1949). F. X. SEPPELT, *Geschichte der Päpste von den Anfängen bis zur Mitte des 20 Jh.* (Leipzig 1931–41) 4:394–408. A. SCHIAVO, "La cappella vaticana del coro e vicende dei sepolcri di Sisto IV e Giulio II," *Studi Romani* 6 (1958) 297–307. C. SHAW, *Julius II: The Warrior Pope* (Oxford 1988). I. CLOULAS, *Julius II* (Paris 1990). F. GILBERT, *The Pope, His Banker, and Venice* (Cambridge, Mass. 1980). J. D'AMICO, *Renaissance Humanism in Papal Rome* (Baltimore 1983).

[D. R. CAMPBELL]

"Pope Julius III," by Scipione Pulzone.

JULIUS III, POPE

Pontificate: Feb. 7, 1550, to March 23, 1555; b. Giovanni Maria Ciocchi del Monte, Rome, Sept. 10, 1487. Born into a family of lawyers, he studied jurisprudence in Perugia and Bologna, after completing his humanistic instruction under the tutelage of Raffaelo Lippo Brandolino in Rome. He undertook theological training at the direction of the Dominican Ambrosius Catharinus and became a chamberlain of Julius II. In 1511 he succeeded his uncle, Antonio del Monte, in the archiepiscopal See of Siponto, and on Feb. 16, 1513, preached the sermon at the fifth session of the Fifth Lateran Council (1512–17). He became bishop of Pavia in 1520 and served two terms as governor of Rome during the pontificate of Clement VII. In 1534 PAUL III appointed him vicelegate of Bologna, Romagna, Parma, and Piacenza, and auditor of the Apostolic Camera. He was created a cardinal priest with the title of SS. Vitalis, Gervase, and Protase on Dec. 22, 1536, and, on Oct. 5, 1543, he was raised to cardinal bishop of Palestrina. Having been chosen as copresident of the Council of Trent with Cardinals Marcello Cervini (later MARCELLUS II) and Reginald POLE, he opened the council on Dec. 13, 1545. His opposition to the anti-Roman policies of Emperor Charles V, and especially his influence in moving the council to Bologna, made him unpopular in Germany. As a result his chances of election to succeed Paul III in the conclave of Nov. 29, 1549, were blocked by imperial veto, until a compromise of French and Farnese cardinals secured his majority. To achieve this accord he made an election capitulation in which he promised to cede Parma into the control of Ottavio Farnese. Parma later became a central issue that involved Julius in the Hapsburg-Valois power struggle. Ottavio allied himself with French interests in Northern Italy and signed a treaty with Henry II on May 27, 1551. This drove the Pope to support Charles V at the risk of a French schism. He declared the fief of Parma vacant and sent an army, commanded by his nephew, Giambattista del Monte, to join the forces of Ferrante Gonzaga, Governor of Milan. The combined armies were to overthrow the French who invaded the Romagna from Mirandola, reduced Crevalcore, occupied Castro, and threatened Ravenna. At the failure of these armies, Julius was forced into a truce on April 29, 1552, that restored Castro to the papacy but placed Farnese in possession of Parma for a two-year period.

The Parma war and the Lutheran wars in Southern Germany hindered the continuance of the Council of Trent, which Julius ordered resumed on May 1, 1551, with Cardinal Marcello Crescenzi as president. The opposition of Henry II and his loyal bishops led to its suspension on April 15, 1552. Although the council was stalled, Julius continued efforts at Church reform. As early as 1550 he appointed a commission of Cardinals Domenico de Cupis, Gian Pietro Caraffa (later Paul IV), Francesco Sfrondato, Marcello Crescenzi, Innocenzo Cibo, and Reginald Pole to prepare a schema of reform. He wrote more than 50 briefs on reform, and on Sept. 16, 1552, he initiated a program to control the conferring of benefices, the relationships between regular and secular clergy, monastic discipline, clerical dress, and changes in curial administration. He planned a bull to implement these measures, but his death prevented its publication. He encouraged the newly formed Society of Jesus, whose constitution he confirmed on July 21, 1550, and at the suggestion of St. Ignatius of Loyola he founded the Collegium Germanicum to train German priests in Rome on Aug. 31, 1552, giving it an annual endowment. He was interested in the expansion of the faith in the Indies, Far East, and the Americas, and worked toward the reunion of the Chaldean Nestorians in Mesopotamia, and the Copts of Abyssinia. He named the Jesuit João NUNES BARRETO, first Patriarch of Abyssinia with Melchior Carneiro and Andrew Oviedo as his coadjutors, to win the favor of Negus (emperor) Claudius of Abyssinia. Upon the accession of Catholic Mary Tudor to the throne of England in 1553, he appointed Cardinal Reginald Pole as legate and adviser to the Queen, and by 1555 complete restoration of papal supremacy was achieved by a proclamation of Parliament.

A Renaissance Pope, Julius was a generous patron of humanism, and during his pontificate he placed Galeazzo Florimonte, Romolo Amaseo, and Paolo Sadoleto in his chancery; received the homage of Paolo Giovio, Pietro Aretino, and Lorenzo Davidico; appointed Marcello Cervini as Vatican Librarian and reformed the Roman University; appointed Michaelangelo chief architect of St. Peter's and named Giovanni Pierluigi da Palestrina its choir master. Besides building the Church of St. Andrew to commemorate his escape from death during the Sack of Rome in 1527, he erected the luxurious Villa Giulia at the Porta del Popolo, where he resided during his later years. A policy of vacillation and excessive nepotism cloud his pontificate. He was extravagant with gifts to his relatives and created a scandal by bestowing a cardinal's hat on a youth of 17, who was adopted by his brother, Baldovino del Monte.

Bibliography: L. PASTOR, *The History of the Popes from the Close of the Middle Ages* (London–St. Louis 1938–61) 13:1–335 with full bibliography. A. FLICHE and V. MARTIN, eds., *Histoire de l'église depuis les origines jusqu'à nos jours* (Paris 1935–) 17:105–145. H. JEDIN, *History of the Council of Trent*, tr. E. GRAF, (St. Louis 1957–60) v.1. G. SCHWAIGER, *Lexikon für Theologie und Kirche*, ed. J. HOFER and K. RAHNER, 10 v. (2d, new ed. Freiburg 1957–65) 2 5:1205–06. A. NOVA, *The Artistic Patronage of Julius III (1550–1555)* (New York 1968). P. PARTNER, *Renaissance Rome, 1500–1555* (Berkeley 1976). *Epistolae ad Principes. Leo X–Pius IV (1513–1565)* ed, L. NANNI (Vatican City 1993). C. GUTIERREZ, *Trento, un problema (1552–1562)* (Madrid 1995). P. PRODI and W. REINHARD, eds. *Il Concilio di Trento e il moderno* (Bologna 1996).

[E. D. MCSHANE]

JULIUS AFRICANUS, SEXTUS

Father of Christian chronography; b. Roman colony, Jerusalem, *c.* 160; d. *c.* 240. Destined for a military career, he accompanied the Emperor Septimius Severus on his campaigns in Osrhoene in 195 and was in close contact with the royal house at Edessa. He also attended lectures by the Christian teacher Heraclas in Alexandria and was influenced by the *Stromata* of CLEMENT OF ALEXANDRIA. About 220 he became prefect of Emmaus-Nicopolis, a subdivision of Palestine, and in 224 the Emmaus colony sent him to plead its case before the Emperor.

At Rome, Alexander Severus gave him the task of organizing the public library housed in the Pantheon. It seems that he was spiritual adviser to the Empress-Mother, Mamaea. Later tradition has it that he became a bishop, but it is unlikely that he was even a priest. With his friend ORIGEN, he corresponded about scriptural questions.

His main extant works are the *Chronicles* and the *Kestoi*. There are also two letters. The *Chronicles* appeared in 221 and provide a chronological list of sacred and profane events from creation to A.D. 220. This first Christian "history of the world" became a main source for EUSEBIUS OF CAESAREA and subsequent historians. The work comprised five books, of which only fragments remain. Computing 5,500 years between creation and the birth of Christ, Julius expressed his belief that the Second Coming would take place in the year 6000, thus giving a chiliastic turn to the work. His use of sources was scarcely critical.

The *Kestoi* (i.e., "embroideries") is an encyclopedic miscellany in 24 books, of which large fragments are extant. It is dedicated to the Emperor Alexander Severus, and its subject matter ranges from medicine, science, and agriculture to magic and war. This work was written after the *Chronicles* and contains a strange mixture of Christianity and superstition.

One of the two letters is addressed to Origen and deals with the authenticity of the story of Susanna (Dn 13.1–64); it exhibits a sounder critical sense, and the entire text is extant. There are only fragments of the second letter. It was addressed to ARISTIDES, and in it Julius attempts to harmonize the Mathaean and Lucan genealogies of Christ.

Bibliography: M. J. ROUTH, ed., *Reliquiae Sacrae*, 5 v. (2d ed. Oxford 1846–48) 2:238–309, chronicles. B. P. GRENFELL and A. S. HUNT, eds., *The Oxyrhynchus Papyri*, 3 v. (London 1903) 36–41, *Kestoi*. É. AMANN, *Dictionnaire de théologie catholique*, ed. A. VACANT et al. (Paris 1903–50) 8.2:1921–25. J. QUASTEN, *Patrology* (Westminster MD 1950) 2: 138–140. H. GELZER, *Sextus Julius Africanus und die byzantinische Chronographie*, 2 v. (Leipzig 1880–98). W. REICHARDT, ed., TU 34.3 (1909), letters. W. A. OLDFATHER and A. S. PEASE, *American Journal of Philology* 39 (1918) 405–406, *Kestoi*. F. GRANGER, *Journal of Theological Studies* 34 (1933) 157–161, Library; 35 (1934) 361–368, Western Text. E. H. BLAKENEY, *Theology* 29 (1934) 164–169, Letter to Origen.

[P. W. LAWLER]

JUMIÈGES, ABBEY OF

Former Benedictine abbey, in Upper Normandy, west of Rouen, Archdiocese of Rouen (Latin, *Gemmeticum*). It was founded on the Seine in 654 by Clovis II at the urging of Queen BATHILDIS. The first abbot, PHILIBERT, established the monastery under the LUXEUIL observance, built three churches (Notre Dame, Saint-Pierre, Saint-Germain), the cloister buildings, and the abbey walls. He organized the abbey's commercial port on the Seine. The abbey, already called "Jumièges the Almsgiver," enjoyed its first period of real prosperity from the 8th through the early third of the 9th century. At this time the BENEDICTINE rule replaced the Luxeuil observance; the monastery had several hundred monks, students, domes-

Papyrus fragment from book 18 of "Kestoi," by Sextus Julius Africanus, written between 221–276 A.D., discovered in Oxyrhynchus, Egypt.

tics, and serfs. After the Norman plunderings (841, 845, 851), Jumièges was abandoned by the monks, who fled to Haspres (near Cambrai, France). It was temporarily restored in 940 by Duke William Longsword of Normandy, with monks from Poitiers; it was permanently restored *c.* 1010 by Abbot WILLIAM OF SAINT-BÉNIGNE OF DIJON and his disciple Thierry. The church of Notre Dame, rebuilt in Romanesque style, was consecrated in 1067; it was enhanced *c.* 1250 by the addition of an ogival choir, and its transept was rebuilt during the 14th century. The church of Saint-Pierre was restored during the same years. The abbey's second period of prosperity lasted from 1050 to 1340, during which time Abbot Gontard (1048–95) promoted the abbey's intellectual life, organized a scriptorium (which developed a school of miniature painters), and procured manuscripts. Abbot Alexander (1198–1213) gave further impetus to education and reorganized the scriptorium. Abbot William of Rouen (1239–1259) increased the abbey's manuscript holdings by gift and purchase. Excessive papal taxation, accumulation of debts, and pillaging during the Hundred Years' War led to a decline, but the abbey was restored by Jean de la Chaussée (1431–62). In 1516 the Reform of CHEZAL-BENOÎT was introduced. From 1524 to 1539 Abbot François de Fontenay restored the buildings and the church of Notre

Abbey of Jumieges. (©Julia Waterlow; Eye Ubiquitous/CORBIS)

Dame and built a new cloister of unusual richness in flamboyant ogival style, but he was succeeded by commendatory abbots who were both greedy and litigious. In 1562 the abbey was plundered by the Protestants. The MAURIST Reform was introduced in 1616 and Jumièges produced many Maurist scholars, e.g., C. F. Toustain and R. P. Tassin. But only 20 monks remained at Jumièges in 1730; it was abolished during the French Revolution. The library became the nucleus of the municipal library of Rouen; the archives were sent to Yvetôt, but in 1827 were returned to Rouen. The local pastor would not accept Notre Dame for his parish church, and it was allowed to go to ruin by its owner, as were the convent buildings.

Bibliography: *Chartes de l' abbaye de Jumièges (v. 825 à 1204) conservées aux archives de la Seine-Inférieure,* ed. J. J. VERNIER, 2 v. (Paris 1916); *Histoire de l'abbaye royale de Saint-Pierre de Jumièges,* ed. J. LOTH, 3 v. (Rouen 1882–85). *Vita Filiberti, Monumenta Germaniae Historica: Scriptores rerum Merovingicarum* (Berlin 1826–) 5:568–606. L. A. JOUEN, *Jumièges, histoire et légendes, ruines et reliques* (Rouen 1954). D. KNOWLES et al., "Jumièges et l' Angleterre," *Jumièges: Congrès scientifique du XIIIe centenaire, Rouen, 10–12 juin 1954,* 2 v. (Rouen 1955) 1:259–313.

[P. COUSIN]

JUNG, CARL GUSTAV

Psychiatrist, founder of the school of analytical psychology; b. Kesswyl, Switzerland, July 26, 1875; d. Zurich, Switzerland, June 6, 1961. After receiving his medical degree from the University of Basel, he obtained training in psychiatry from individuals such as Pierre Janet, Eugen Bleuler, and Sigmund Freud. He held staff positions at the Burgholzli Mental Hospital in Zurich and at the University of Zurich. About 1913 he gave up all of his formal institutional affiliations to devote his life to clinical practice, training, research, and writing. Beginning a regular correspondence with Freud in 1906, which ended when he terminated his relationship with Freud in 1913, Jung became closely associated with the psychoanalytical movement and with Freud himself. From the date of its founding in 1910 and until 1914, Jung served as president of the International Psychoanalytical Association. In 1909 Jung and Freud made a historical trip to Clark University in Worcester, Mass., to present a lecture series.

However, in spite of Freud's great confidence in him and their close friendship, Jung began to persist in disagreeing with Freud in many areas. Not only did he feel that Freud's theory of the libido, centering around sexuality, should be broadened to include other drives, such as the urge for power, but also he felt that Freud's theory of the unconscious was too limited. He postulated the concept of a "collective" unconscious that was the seat of archetypes—inherited predispositions reflecting symbolically the entire history of man.

Among his other noteworthy contributions was his personality typology. It suggested that along the basic attitudinal spectrum of introversion-extraversion, in combination with the four functions of thinking, feeling, intuition, and emotion, eight modal personality types existed.

Of particular interest to Thomistic scholars was his concept of INDIVIDUATION, which encompassed the ultimate growth and fulfillment of the individual into a "total spiritual being." It is predicated heavily on the concept of self-responsibility in contrast to Freud's emphasis on a biological-historical determinism.

In the area of DREAM interpretation he believed that the "manifest" content of the dream can be interpreted quite literally in the context of the aspirations for the future of the individual, while Freud stressed the "latent" meaning of the dream as symbolic representation of the now unconscious past.

One interesting aspect of Jung's orientation is that as a youth he had a desire to study archeology; although he eventually became a psychiatrist, his general approach to the understanding of man was archeological. For example, his methodical studies of cultures of the past, for clues to symbols that could be used in support of his theory of archetypes and his concept of the collective unconscious, would appear to reflect his archeological background. Yet, in his approach to psychotherapy, he was much more likely to be concerned with the conscious—present and future—than was Freud, whose theory of the repetition compulsion suggested that man was acting out repeatedly the influences of the first few years of life.

Jung was a prolific writer, and much of his thinking, from his spelling out of a theory of personality to a morass of metaphysical speculations, can be found in his many books and articles.

Bibliography: C. G. JUNG, *Collected Papers on Analytical Psychology* (New York 1917); *Contributions to Analytical Psychology* (New York 1928); *Psychological Types* (New York 1923); *Modern Man in Search of a Soul* (New York 1933); *Psychology and Religion* (New Haven 1938; repr. 1960); *The Integration of Personality* (New York 1939); *Über Psychische Energetik und das Wesen der Träume* (2d rev. ed. Zurich 1948); *Von den Wurzeln des Bewusstseins* (Zurich 1954); *Memories, Dreams, Reflections*, ed. A. JAFFÉ, tr. R. and C. WINSTON (New York 1963). R. I. EVANS, *Conversations with Carl Jung and Reactions from Ernest Jones* (Princeton 1964). C. S. HALL and G. LINDZEY, *Theories of Personality* (New York 1957). R. L. MUNROE, *Schools of Psychoanalytic Thought* (New York 1955).

[R. I. EVANS]

JUNGMANN, JOSEF

Jesuit authority in homiletics and aesthetics; b. Münster, Westphalia, Nov. 12, 1830; d. Innsbruck, Nov. 25, 1885. In 1850 he began his philosophical and theological studies at the German College in Rome and upon their completion in 1855 he was ordained. Two of his brothers also studied at the German College and became priests. His brother Bernard (1833–95) was a lecturer at the University of Louvain and wrote on a wide variety of philosophical and theological topics. On May 5, 1857, Josef entered the Society of Jesus. In 1858, even before the end of his novitiate, he was made professor of homiletics in the reestablished faculty of theology at the University of Innsbruck. He remained at the University lecturing in homiletics and catechetics for many years, exercising an extraordinary influence over the many students who came under his direction. A prolific author of books and articles, he is particularly well known for his specialized treatises on homiletics, aesthetics, and devotion to the Sacred Heart. [For a commentary on Jungmann's work, see Croce's article in *Zeitschrift für katholische Theologie* (1958) 193–199.] Jungmann's principal works are: *Theo-*

rie der geistl. Beredsamkeit (2 v. 1877–78; Michael Gatterer, the author's colleague, edited a fourth and much abbreviated edition in 1908 excluding the section on catechetics); *Die Schöneit und die schöne Kunst* (1886), re-edited under the title of *Aesthetik* (2 v. 1884); *Zur Verehrung U.L. Frau* (1879); *Die Andacht zum hl. Herzen Jesu u. die Bedenken gegen dieselbe* (1885); *Das Gemüt und das Gefühlsvermögen der neueren Psychologie* (1885); and the *Gefahren belletristischer Lecture* (1872).

Bibliography: C. SOMMERVOGEL, *Bibliotèque de la Compagnie de Jésus*, 11 v. (Brussels-Paris 1890–1932) 4:884–885. L. KOCH, *Jesuiten-Lexikon: Die Gesellschaft Jesu einst und jetzt* (Paderborn 1934); photoduplicated with rev. and suppl., 2 v. (Louvain-Heverlee 1962) 944.

[C. SEVILLA]

JUNGMANN, JOSEF ANDREAS

Austrian Jesuit, inspirer of the liturgical and catechetical renewal; b. Sand near Taufers, South Tirol (pre–World War I Austria), Nov. 16, 1889; d. Innsbruck, Jan. 26, 1975. After theological studies in the diocesan seminary of Brixen, S. Tirol, he was ordained on July 27, 1913. His work as assistant pastor in Niedervintl and Gossensasz, before becoming a Jesuit, Sept. 13, 1917, contributed substantially to the basically pastoral orientation of his later scientific work. From 1925 at the University of Innsbruck, he taught pastoral theology, catechetics, and liturgy until 1963, with an interruption from 1938 to 1945 when Hitler closed the theology faculty of the university. Jungmann was also editor (1926–63) of *Zeitschrift für katholische Theologie* (again with an interruption, 1938–45). After having contributed through his writings to creating the general theological and pastoral climate for Vatican Council II, he was chosen, Aug. 25, 1960, to be a member of the conciliar Preparatory Commission. He continued his intensive and dedicated work during the council as a highly esteemed *peritus* of the Commission for Liturgy and after the Council as consultor of the Consilium (the commission entrusted with the implementation of the Constitution on the Liturgy).

Superb mastery of his subject; penetrating, well-balanced, and impartial judgment; an exceptional gift of inspiration for sound and timely developments within the church, especially in the fields of liturgy and preaching; deep respect for the achievements of others who engaged in the same field of studies; and his proverbial modesty—all won Jungmann many friends and enthusiastic admirers. *Festschriften* of his colleagues, friends, and former students on his 60th, 70th, and 80th birthdays, as well as honors conferred by his country, manifested the great and general appreciation of him and his work. Jungmann's special talent consisted in letting the past teach an understanding and right evaluation of the present and point to right solutions for the future. Although outstanding in historical research, he was never lost in its details nor did he ever pursue history for its own sake. Solid historical research was for him the indispensable tool for a right assessment of the present condition of the Christian community and its need for genuine, penetrating renewal. His deep faith and his imperturbable adherence to the Church did not prevent him from seeing clearly and presenting with respectful objectivity unhealthy and harmful trends and developments of the past in Christian worship and preaching. The mere fact that, e.g., the leaders of the Church authorized and contributed to an ever-decreasing active participation of the people in the official worship of the Church, does not prove that this development was healthy and guided by the Holy Spirit. It is the special merit of Jungmann that, with his thorough historical studies combined with deep understanding of the conditions of authentic historical development, he undermined any simplistic interpretation of the Church's guidance by the Holy Spirit and opened the way to the needed thorough reform. At first many, including also prominent leaders of the Church, considered Jungmann to be unorthodox; but soon the weight of his incontestable reasons and also his modest and prudent presentation achieved general recognition and admiration. Without the self-sacrificing work of forerunners like Jungmann the reform as initiated by Vatican II could never have happened.

Writings. Although his 1924 doctoral thesis (never published) dealt with the catechesis on grace in the early Church, the field of Jungmann's special studies was liturgy and in particular the history of the Latin liturgy and the problems of an authentic liturgical renewal. His very first book *Die Stellung Christi im liturgischen Gebet* (1925; tr. *The Place of Christ in Liturgical Prayer,* 1965) is a masterpiece of his own method. Through a thorough study of the official worship of the Church it delineates, although only implicitly, the much-needed renewal of devotional prayer. Similarly, he paved the way for the timely renewal of the rites of penance in *Die lateinischen Buszriten* (1932). His *Die liturgische Feier. Grundsätzliches und Geschichtliches über Formgesetze der Liturgie* (1938; 4th rev. ed. 1965) is a precious study on the nature and form of authentic liturgical celebration outside of sacramental liturgy; it appeared in English as *The Liturgy of the Word* (1966). In *Gewordene Liturgie* (1940) the best of Jungmann's numerous articles reached a larger audience. Jungmann used the academic exile imposed by Hitler for preparing his main work, which made him suddenly world famous, *Missarum Sollemnia. Eine genetische Erklärung der römischen Messe* (2 v., 1948; 5th ed.

1965). It was soon translated into all major European languages: the complete English translation of F. A. Brunner, *The Mass of the Roman Rite* (2 v., New York 1950) was followed by an abridgement by C. Riepe (1 v., New York 1959). Probably more than any other single book, *Missarum Sollemnia* prepared for and favored the conciliar reform of the Latin liturgy. Another significant work was *Der Gottesdienst der Kirche* (1955, 3d ed. 1962; tr. *Public Worship,* 1957). The lectures Jungmann gave in the summer of 1949 at the University of Notre Dame appeared first in English as *Early Liturgy to the Time of Gregory the Great* (1959; Ger. 1967). *Liturgisches Erie und pastorale Gegenwart* (1960) collects articles and conferences of general interest into one volume. The last two books, *Christliches Gebet im Wandel und Bestand* (1969) and *Messe im Gottesvolk. Ein nachkonziliarer Durchblick durch Missarum Sollemnia* (1970) are the crowning conclusion of an extremely rich and intensive literary activity: 304 books and articles, not counting some 800 shorter reviews of books. After Jungmann's death *The Mass, an Historical, Theological and Pastoral Survey* (1976) was published.

Because his masterful research and towering authority were almost exclusively in the history of liturgy and liturgical renewal, one may easily overlook Jungmann's momentous contribution to the renewal of catechesis and preaching. He is the acknowledged initiator and most prominent exponent of the second phase of modern catechetics known as kerygmatic renewal. It led to a shift of emphasis from method to content in all forms of the ministry of the Word. The kerygmatic approach means that any authentic announcing of God's word to young and old alike must concentrate on the good news of salvation by which God challenges sinful man to a new life in Christ. How biblical, liturgical, and kerygmatic renewal must be seen and actualized as partial aspects of a thorough integral pastoral renewal Jungmann showed best in his classic *Die Frohbotschaft und unsere Glaubensverkündigung* (1936); abridged English ed. *The Good News Yesterday and Today,* 1962, tr. W. A. Huesman, with essays, ed. J. Hofinger, appraising its contribution to pastoral renewal. When the book appeared it was so much ahead of the times that only swift withdrawal from the market could save it from ecclesiastical condemnation. But it had served its purpose. Hardly any other book anticipated and prepared for Vatican II's pastoral renewal as much as Jungmann's controversial book. During the council, without any further opposition, its revised edition appeared: *Glaubensverkündigung im Lichte der Frohbotschaft* (1963; Eng. tr. *Announcing the Word of God,* 1967). Great influence was also exerted by *Katechetik. Aufgabe und Methode der religiösen Unterweisung* (1953; 5th ed. 1968; tr. *Handing On the Faith,* 1959). His

Christus als Mittelpunkt religiöser Erziehung (1939) brings out the central position of Christ in genuine catechesis.

Bibliography: B. FISCHER and H. B. MEYER, eds., *J. A. Jungmann, Ein Leben für Liturgie und Kerygma* (Innsbruck 1975) 156–207. J. HOFINGER, ''J. A. Jungmann,'' *Living Light* 13 (1976) 350–359. F. X. ARNOLD and B. FISCHER, eds., *Die Messe in der Glaubensverkündigung* (Freiburg 1950; 2d ed. 1953). B. FISCHER and J. WAGNER, eds., *Paschatis Sollemnia. Studien zu Osterfeier und Osterfrömmigkeit* (Freiburg 1959). For Jungmann's 80th birthday, a separate issue of *Zeitschrift für katholische Theologie* 91 (1969) 249–516.

[J. HOFINGER]

JUNILIUS AFRICANUS

Ancient exegete and Quaestor Sacri Palatii under the Emperor Justinian I in the years A.D. 541 to 549. Birth and death dates are unknown, although it seems certain that he died before A.D. 550. An African, he entered the imperial service and rose to one of the highest offices. How he acquired a considerable knowledge of theology and Scripture is not indicated in the scanty sources available on his life and work. His friend, Primasius, Bishop of Hadrumentum, having learned through him of the existence of an introduction to scriptural exegesis composed in Greek by the Persian Paul, who had been trained at the Syrian School of NISIBIS, urged Junilius to translate the work into Latin. His *Instituta regularia divinae legis,* in two books and cast in dialogue form, is a free translation or adaptation of the original Greek. The work reflects essentially the method of exegesis and general outlook of THEODORE OF MOPSUESTIA, but its Nestorian tendencies have been exaggerated. Cassiodorus mentions Junilius's ''Introduction'' with praise in his *Institutes* (1.10), and the work had considerable influence in the early Middle Ages.

Bibliography: H. KIHN, *Theodor von Mopsuestia und Junilius Africanus als Exegeten* (Freiburg 1880); this work contains a critical text of the *Instituta.* O. BARDENHEWER, *Geschichte der altkirchlichen Literatur* (Freiburg 1913–32) 5:334–336. L. PIROT, *Dictionnaire de théologie catholique,* ed. A. VACANT et al. (Paris 1903–50) 8.2:1971–76. E. STEIN, ''Deux questions de Justinien et l'emploi des langues dans ses novelles,'' *Bull. Acad. Roy. de Belgique* (Lettres) 23 (1937) 365–390. M. L. W. LAISTNER, ''Antiochene Exegesis in Western Europe during the Middle Ages,'' *Harvard Theological Review* 40 (1947) 19–31.

[M. R. P. MCGUIRE]

JURA, FATHERS OF

The Fathers of Jura is a monastic community founded by St. Romanus and his brother St. Lupicinus at Condat in the French Jura region. Romanus (b. *c.* 400) was trained in the monastery of AINAY and went to Condat (now Saint–Claude) to become a hermit. He was soon joined by Lupicinus. Their holiness was so edifying that others came in great numbers to join them, and the two were obliged to found the new monastery of Leuconne (now St. Lupicin), as well as a convent for cloistered nuns, La Beaume, the site of the present village of Saint–Romain–de–la–Roche. The rule first followed by these monks was a composite, drawn from other existing rules and adapted to their own situation and needs. Time was given every day to prayer and reading; manual labor was stressed. In the beginning each monk lived in a separate cell, but at the time of St. EUGENDUS, the second successor to Lupicinus, there was a common building for sleeping and for eating. Clothing and food were simple. From earliest times the monastery enriched the district with temporal benefits as well as spiritual. Plantations, gardens, and mills sprang up in the area through the work of the monks. Intellectual labor also was encouraged, and under St. Eugendus, Greek and Latin were taught and manuscripts were transcribed. Lupicinus also wielded social and political influence, not hesitating to have recourse to the civil authority of the region in order to help his neighbor.

St. Romanus died *c.* 463–464 and was buried in the convent church at La Beaume. St. Lupicinus governed the monks until his death in 480. There are two biographies of these saints, one by St. GREGORY OF TOURS in the *Liber vitae patrum,* and an anonymous *Vita patrum Jurensium.* This latter is from the early 6th century, and was always considered authentic until Quesnel found apparent inconsistencies in it. However, these have been explained by L. Duchesne in his *La Vie des Pères du Jura,* where he urged that the traditional value of the vita be recognized.

Feast: St. Romanus: Feb. 28; St. Lupicinus: March 21.

Bibliography: *Acta Sanctorum* Feb. 3:743–754. *Monumenta Germaniae Historica: Scriptores rerum Merovingicarum* (Berlin 1826–) 3:131–153. L. DUCHESNE, ''La Vie des Pères de Jura,'' *Mélanges d'archéologie et d'histoire* 18 (1893) 3–16. G. A. A. HANOTAUX, *Histoire de la nation française,* 15 v. (Paris 1920–35) 6:58. H. LECLERCQ, *Dictionnaire d'archéologie chrétienne et de liturgie,* ed. F. CABROL, H. LECLERCQ, and H. I. MARROU, 15 v. (Paris 1907–53) 8.1:430–438. A. BUTLER, *The Lives of the Saints,* rev. ed. H. THURSTON and D. ATTWATER, 4 v. (New York 1956) 1:438–439. É. BROUETTE, *Lexikon für Theologie und Kirche²,* ed. J. HOFER and K. RAHNER, 10 v. (2d, new ed. Freiburg 1957–65) 9:24–25.

[G. E. CONWAY]

JUST PRICE

This article does not treat in detail the many complexities of modern price JUSTICE, but attempts only to state generally accepted moral principles governing the just price. These principles are meant to apply to staple commodities bought and sold in the open market; they do not necessarily apply to rare articles or occasional private transactions.

Notion of a Just Price. The price of a thing is its value in terms of money. Value, in this context, is the capacity of goods to satisfy human wants. Money is the medium of exchange; it serves as a general standard of value for all goods. Fundamentally, then, the just price is the true money value of the commodity, a price that can buy other commodities having a capacity for satisfying human wants equal to that of the commodity sold. The whole concept of commutative justice is based on the idea of equality. Modern commerce, though very complex, is rooted in the same idea of equality. It aims at allowing a person to obtain the equal of what he gives. This idea of equality is not opposed to the idea of profit; a person is entitled to the fruit of his industry or ingenuity. One may profit without violating justice, but justice sets limits on the methods by which profit may legitimately be gained.

Determination of the Just Price. The problem facing the moralist is this: How can the equal capacity of commodities for satisfying human wants be calculated? Extreme answers to this question must be rejected. One extreme view holds that each commodity has a fixed money value that van be exactly determined at any given time. This view must be rejected, since it is impossible to determine human needs and desires with precision; these needs vary widely from person to person, and from time to time, and depend on too many purely psychological factors, such as taste and fashion. Another extreme view is that all value so depends on the whims of individual buyers that any price they are willing to pay is just. This position must be rejected because it is immoral; it would thwart the very idea of money as a medium of exchange, of trade as a function of society, and of commutative justice as a moral virtue.

In opposition to such views, the traditional, NATURAL LAW theory maintains that the just price should be determined not by the usefulness of a commodity to this or that individual, but to men generally. The price should represent the judgment of the general buying public on the value of a particular commodity. This judgment is expressed in the open market, where buyers and sellers freely compete with one another and establish in the process a true equality between the capacities of different commodities to satisfy human wants. The competitive price

is, then, the natural (or common) price that will drive out all other prices. Wherever there is pure competition, this competitive price will be the just price. This competitive or common price is not static. Neither is it exactly determinable, but may range between a highest and a lowest limit. Within this range any price could be considered just.

Legal Price. At times, in order to protect the interests of both buyers and sellers and to offset attempts to raise or lower prices artificially, public authority may consider it necessary to establish a legal price. In this case, value is set at a particular level and an adequate price for a commodity or service is fixed by law. Moralists agree that this legal price, where established, is the just price. However, deviations is considerably better (or worse) than the standard item, or if the established price is no longer observed by most people with the tacit consent of the public authority.

In pricing things for which there is no established market to furnish a common estimate of value, or no legal price, justice depends on the judgment of appraisers experienced in such transactions. This is sometimes called the conventional price because it is formed by compact or agreement. Moralists hold that a just price for things whose value is uncertain is reached when both parties to the bargain freely and honestly consent to it. There is agreement among Catholic moralists that: (1) It is against justice, in ordinary circumstances, to demand more than the legal price permits; (2) To sell above the highest just price or to buy below the lowest is a violation of justice.

Bibliography: J. MESSNER, *Social Ethics: Natural Law in the Modern World*, tr. J. J. DOHERTY (St. Louis 1957). V. A. DEMANT, ed., *The Just Price: The Medieval Doctrine and Its Possible Equivalent Today* (London 1930). P. BOVEN, *Le Prix normal* (Paris 1924). O. VON NELL–BREUNING, *Lexicon für Theologie und Kirsche*, ed. J. HOFER and K. RAHNER (2d, new ed. Freiburg 1957–65) 8:719–721. A. MICHEL, *Dictionnaire de théologie catholique*, ed. A. VACANT et al., 15 v. (Paris 1903–50; Tables générales 1951) 15.2:2625–31.

[D. LOWERY]

JUSTICE

The complete integration of love and justice is the chief characteristic of Christian moral doctrine besides its Christocentric orientations. It is through love of God and neighbor that the kingdom of God is achieved within us. And yet this love cannot be authentic unless the Christian also continually attempts to form the external world by the same dynamic force. Only thus does man honestly respond to the justice that God has gratuitously given him. This article therefore considers the relation between the justice received from God and the cardinal virtue of justice, and then the relation of justice to love. It then distinguishes, without unduly separating, the basic moral attitude of justice from objective right and especially from legal right, and with this as a background considers the various species and characteristics of justice.

Justice, Love, and Right (Ius)

From a theological point of view, justice among men is not primary. The primacy belongs rather to God's own sovereign justice, bestowed on and thus obligating man as a creature, justifying sinners with utter gratuity, making them just and simultaneously, with and through gratuitous justice, making them capable of a newer and ''better justice.'' Theologically prior to justice among men is the awareness that the ''justice'' owed to God in a thousand ways is an absolutely free and yet absolutely binding love involving a man totally. In the biblical-theological view, justice among men deserves the name justice in the full sense only if it is accomplished with a view toward God in that love and thanksgiving and obedience are owed to God absolutely.

In this respect biblical thought is fundamentally different from the anthropocentrism of Aristotelian and Stoic thought. The relation of man to God is far different from a relation between equals, and it involves far more than a strict equality between giving and receiving. And yet in the relation of man to God the essential structure of all genuine justice is verified. Man in his totality, with whatever good there is in him, is a gift of God, a gift in person. And in the life of grace God gives man His most personal love. In the relation of man to God it is therefore a question of the original and absolute duty of ''justice'' that finds expression in piety and in the worship of God. ''What can I give to the Lord for all that He has given me?'' (Ps 115.12). The exemplar of justice is Jesus, who in His sacred humanity gave Himself up to the Father for man's redemption from that most fundamental injustice: sin. Speaking to the Baptist of the baptism of penance that He would finally achieve on the Cross, Christ said, ''. . . it becomes us to fulfill all justice'' (Mt 3.15). God's superabundant fidelity and love make man perpetually indebted, and man cannot presume ever to even accounts. ''When you have done everything that was commanded you, say, 'We are unprofitable servants; we have done what it was our duty to do''' (Lk 17.10).

The worship of God that man as a creature and a member of the family of God can offer to the Creator and the Father must be the most righteous possible. But the Christian must be extremely careful to avoid self-righteousness and self-satisfaction, precisely on the basis of justice. Worshipful justice makes one aware that ''he who is just, let him be just still'' (Rv 22.11).

If, after the manner of the Pharisee, the notion of justice among men, which is basically measured in terms of objective equality, is univocally applied to the relation of man to God, then authentic religion is greatly endangered. The situation must be reversed: that better justice demanded by, and owed to, God should serve as model and mollifier of justice among men, which tends toward a certain rigidity if it is not thus spiritualized and purified. Justice among men will become a genuinely Christian virtue only if it is an extension of that grateful justice that is owed to God.

Justice and Love. The question of the point of departure and the point of view is decisive for a specifically Christian and a truly human understanding of justice. If one looks first to external relations and sees them as objective and regards personal relations, on the contrary, as ''merely'' subjective, then justice becomes mere external order. Connected with this is the view that considers man as primarily a possession of the state, which overemphasizes the juridical order. But if the person, with his essential relation to the Thou and the We, is taken as the point of departure, and if the personal community is considered above all in terms of the intimate community of the family, then, with complete necessity, love is seen as primary and justice is the mediator in the personal order of love, preserving the capacity of the person for love. The theological viewpoint decisively corroborates this position: God is love, and every revelation of His justice, all His justifying action, speaks primarily of His love.

If one treats justice one-sidedly in terms of material goods (acquisition, property, exchange), then only with difficulty can he arrive at a comprehensive view. The person has rights that stand on a much higher plane than property rights. To another, not his goods but his personal dignity and personal rights are due before all else. But without love—i.e., without that attitude that is directed to the person as such—the most sublime rights of the person and of the community cannot be fully and authentically recognized at all. On the other hand, the fulfillment of the duties of justice directly related to measurable values clears away many obstacles that stand in the way of love—although indirectly the person must indeed always be cointended as the bearer of these rights. Thus the basic ontological order is love, then justice; but, in terms of the gradual achievement of order, the order may be justice, then love.

When it is a case of an order imposed from without and enforceable by sanction, then justice is directly intended and love only indirectly. Civil society or a financial undertaking cannot synthesize love and justice in the same way as the intimate community of marriage. But when men intend to order their common undertakings in a human way, then justice must place itself at the service of the community, and thus at the service of love. But love does not render superfluous or cancel out either justice in the material order, which measures according to the most exact standards possible, or the external order of law. These orders of justice must remain as long as all men have not yet achieved the perfection of love, i.e., as long as this world lasts. It is significant that in the opinion of many of the Church Fathers and theologians the necessity of a juridical order stems principally from original sin.

In considering the relation of love and justice, the following basic propositions must come into play: (1) Love is more basic than justice. (2) Love best guarantees the fulfillment of justice; and, correspondingly, failure in justice points to a failure of love. (3) The aim of justice must be achieved in the spirit of love. (4) Love gives clear vision and full extension to justice. (5) When there is question of one's own activity, one who bases himself on love considers primarily not the minimum requirements of justice but the actual needs of his neighbor and of the community; and when there is question of claims against or the imposition of burdens on others, he is above all careful to demand no more than that to which he has clear title. (6) Love is always prepared to suspend one's own rights for the good of another, assuming, of course, that the rights are such that they can be given up without damage to one's own integrity and that of the community. That love is indeed great that considers whatever is here and now obstructive to one's neighbor and the community as no longer a right at all, demonstrative legal title and honest acquisition to the contrary notwithstanding. For love there is a clear distinction between abstract right and the actual need for that right.

Every duty in justice is a duty in love, for every external order must be simultaneously informed by the personal dynamic force of order, which is love. And yet not every duty in love is strictly a duty in justice. Before God, the duties of love are no less binding than the duties of justice. Yet much more than the duties of justice, the duties of love are measured by the progress of the person in good. It is only through growth in love that one gradually comes to recognize better the real and exalted demands of the chief commandment: to love God and one's neighbor "according to the measure of the gifts of grace." This is not true of justice in the same measure. Here there is a clear contrast with the universally binding minimum standards. Here there is likewise a basis for the fact that systems of instruction in moral theology that are chiefly concerned with what one must demand of everyone in the confessional depend on the tract "Right and Justice" rather than on the description of the essence of love.

Justice and Right. In considering justice further, one must distinguish three facets: (1) the basic attitude (virtue) of justice that is a constant disposition to give to each his due; (2) the objective right (*ius*) that is owed objectively to each person and community, either on the basis of divine law or on the basis of the just legislation of the Church or of the State; and (3) the statute itself. Basic moral insight and the virtue of prudence are concerned with seeing what is due, not only abstractly and universally but also concretely, here and now. However, the virtue of justice facilitates the unbiased search for objective right and—this is its main function—determines the will to acknowledge and fulfill that right. The legislation of the Church and of the State is necessary. In part it merely corroborates what is due on the basis of divine law; in part it more carefully determines that which answers to the nature and calling of man in any given historical situation; and in part it represents a selection from among many possible legitimate arrangements, so that it might guarantee a common life and activity that are orderly and peaceful.

A purely mechanical fulfillment and application of the positive law without the control of the virtues of prudence and justice make life in society unworthy of man and, in the long run, unjust as well. When it comes to considering positive (legislated) law, one must first ask whether it answers to the objective requirements of justice. A positive law can entail injustice either if it violates the demands of divine law (natural or revealed)—in which case compliance is not allowed—or if it is basically neither necessary nor actually useful—in which case prudence determines, with the well-being of the community and of the person in mind, whether compliance or noncompliance is better. A law may be initially just, but because of altered circumstances it can become useless and unjust. In a situation in which the authority is duly constituted and functioning properly, one's decision should favor the law whenever there is real doubt. But when the authorities are either totally incapable or completely criminal, critical sense must be employed. The virtue of prudence will normally be exercised in determining whether and in what way the application of the law in the concrete circumstances of the here and now corresponds to true justice. Without *EPIKEIA*, without dispensation or the responsible excusing of oneself from the law itself or from its literal fulfillment when circumstances require it, compliance with positive law cannot truly correspond for any length of time to the virtue of justice.

The individual approaches the full realization of the basic virtue of justice only by constantly striving for it. Similarly, there is an essentially dynamic character to the science of human rights and of legislation. Consider, for example, the cases of slavery and of racial integration. There was a time when the abolition of slavery was utopian, when the immediately pressing duty was the mitigation of the condition of the slaves. (Of course this does not imply blamelessness in the fact that the recognition of the complete abolition of slavery as the only solution in keeping with the dignity of man came so late in history.) The same is true of the complete integration of the various races.

The Virtue of Justice and Its Subspecies

According to the common definition of St. THOMAS AQUINAS, the virtue of justice is "the strong and firm will to give to each his due" (ST 2a2ae, 58.1). This does not imply that to each exactly the same is due. Apart from commutative justice, which aims at complete parity between what is given and what is due in return (give and take), justice demands an equality of proportion. Only in matters in which one is equal to the other is there question of exact equality; in cases in which men differ the degrees and types of right must be distinguished. Indeed, the subspecies of justice are distinguished according to the types, the bearers, and the executors of right.

Commutative Justice. In *iustitia commutativa* the private person as well as groups (communities as moral persons) are the bearers of right. The aim of this right is the utility of both parties who exchange their goods or services. Commutative justice demands that one strive for a fair standard of giving and receiving in return. It forbids encroaching on the rights of others. Basic violations of commutative justice are theft, fraud, unjust damage.

General, or Legal, Justice. In *iustitia generalis,* or *legalis,* the community is the bearer of rights. This right intends the common good. Its fulfillment is the work of official agencies of the community, as well as of each individual member. The legislative authorities exercise legal justice through the promulgation of laws that further the common good. The government in its executive officials achieves it by the sensible use of existing just laws and by taking whatever measures are necessary for the common good. And every member of civil society exercises it by backing good legislation and government (through voting, influencing public opinion, and the like) and by intelligently obeying the existing laws for the sake of the common good. For St. Thomas, the complete range of moral virtues is seen from the perspective of general, or legal, justice, which subordinates every legitimate activity to the common good (ST 2a2ae, 58.5). In this way he considers it as the chief of all moral virtues, for the common good takes precedence over that of the individual (ST 2a2ae, 58.12). This indicates the essentially social—and ultimately the salvific-social—perspective of

Christian morality. However, the common interpretation of legal justice is not so broad.

Distributive Justice. *Iustitia distributiva* intends the good of each individual as a member of the community. In feudal times and still more in the age of absolutism, it seemed that the governmental agency alone exercised this virtue. In a democratic age it evidently affects every citizen not only to the extent that the just distribution of burdens or privileges is a matter of concern to each but also to the extent that each should actively assert his influence to that end. Every individual has basic rights within the community that the community as a whole and each of its agencies and members must recognize. One sins against distributive justice by stirring up and advocating group and class egoism.

Legal and distributive justice have a certain proportion to each other: the more the individual devotes his powers to the common good, so much the more must the community also devote to his good. And yet this basic proposition should not be exaggerated, nor should it be considered in terms of commutative justice, for the fundamental relation between community, group, and individual is not that of mere service and reward. Rather, as in an organism, special care is due to the weak member. And the powerful are bound to renounce all privileges, however they may have been obtained, that infringe on the basic rights and the true good of the other members of the community.

Social Justice. In the age of privileged classes and even more in the age of individualism, doctrinal presentations of distributive (and also legal) justice ignored a perspective that has been added in the 20th century, namely, that of justice of the common good, or social justice. *Iustitia socialis* has become recognized as a new and important subspecies of the virtue of justice since Pius XI's encyclical *Quadragesimo anno.* It includes both legal and distributive justice, and yet its chief concern is not so much strict legal rights and duties as it is the natural rights of the community, its members, and the member communities of the family of nations in their relations to one another.

In keeping with the pressing question of the just social position of the worker, the notion of social justice was first applied basically and primarily to the relation between the owner of capital, the entrepreneur, and the worker as members of various social groups. Among other things, that meant the worker should be paid as a member of a family; that the shares of wages and profits, the allotment of the social products to each, should be computed with an eye toward the good of the industry, the general economy, and the social order.

In an age of steadily increasing economic complexity, of countless interrelations, and a solidarity that extends far beyond particular industries, indeed beyond national economies, it becomes much more apparent than in the ages of household and city economy that the principles of commutative justice alone are entirely insufficient. There is much more involved in every transaction than mere exchange between private parties, for every transaction presupposes countless prior transactions on the part of the society. And ultimately it is not merely a question of transactions and prior transactions. A truly realistic view of justice, achieved only gradually in the modern age, envisions above all the community of persons naturally established by God: the common family of all mankind. Every talent and all possessions are bestowed by God with a view toward the totality. The person unfolds to the highest level of his being only in solidarity. Every form of justice is included in and presupposed by social justice, but in the latter case it is always a question of rights and duties that derive from the nature of the human community and of the person. Transactions are not primary. It is rather the social nature of man that is primary, the encompassing social purpose of all earthly goods, and also the abilities of the person.

The Family. Social justice encompasses every community from the family to the community of nations. The child as a person and as a member of the human community has inalienable rights—above all, the right to life (and that indeed from the moment of conception), the right to be born into a wholesome family (from which follow the immorality of extramarital intercourse and a whole set of community obligations for safeguarding the family), and the right to education and support. Every community, from the family on up to the state and the community of nations, has to attend to and, as far as possible, to protect these rights. Because of their parenthood, because of their place in the community, parents owe to the child all that is requisite for healthy physical and spiritual development and for membership in human society. This social obligation depends on their means and on their ability to work, but first and most basically on the fact that they are parents. Similarly, on the basis of his belonging to the family, the child has the obligation, to the extent that it is possible within the family, to be concerned with the progress of the family in every regard and above all to show love for his parents in return for their love. But this is not a debt that could be paid off on the basis of commutative justice. It is the response required by the very nature and position of the child as a member of the family. And it becomes real and urgent also if—and perhaps only if—other members of the family are remiss.

Civil Government. Beginning with the smaller groups and next higher communities and extending on up to the state and the community of nations, the government has the duty of safeguarding the inalienable rights of each member of the community. Such rights would be, for example, the rights to life, security, intellectual and religious freedom, and the opportunity to work according to one's capacity, so long as one does not forfeit one or the other of these rights by wrongdoing, thus bringing into play penal justice.

Social justice demands that neither the person nor the group be deprived of its proper functions. On the contrary, the fundamental principle of subsidiarity—a typical expression of social justice—requires the higher community, from the family on up, to do all that it can to preserve the functional integrity of the lower community and the person and also, if necessity forces it to take over the lower role, to reestablish it, having taken on this function only temporarily and as a substitute measure. Conversely, the person and the group must be constantly prepared to preserve the functional integrity of every higher group and of society as a whole at their own levels.

International Community. In the mid-20th century the solidarity of the community of nations has strongly come to the fore. Through the development of modern technology and culture, nations have grown more closely together and now demonstrate in very many ways that the general welfare of each nation individually and of all nations collectively are closely linked. Catholic social teaching (above all, *Mater et Magistra, Pacem in terris,* and the Constitution of Vatican Council II *On the Church and the Modern World*) has made a decisive contribution to the further development of a worldwide view of common welfare justice. The nations especially favored by nature and history are obliged to come to the aid of the poor nations seeking further technological and cultural advancement, until the poor nations reach their full functional capacity and corresponding autonomy within the community of nations. Aid for development and promoting practicable possibilities for emigration are not charitable ''alms'' but rather actual demands of the social order and duties in justice for the sake of peace. Such help should not be made to depend on repayment, which is often quite impossible.

Boundaries between Justice and Love. Social justice presupposes deep insight into the social nature of man and into the essential purpose of the different types of community. The boundaries between justice and love are drawn strictly or more loosely, depending on the situation. Much of what was seen in the past as a mere ''duty of love'' or as gratuitous almsgiving is now clearly seen as a requirement of social justice if one considers the essential solidarity of the family of mankind. This advancement approximates the view of the Church Fathers (despite differences in social and economic structures and in the tasks at hand), who, moreover, saw this essential solidarity not from the viewpoint of justice among men but from the perspective of divine justice and evangelical love. Finally, social justice can endure in its full breadth and height only in terms of faith in God, the giver of all good gifts, and in the unity of the human race in God's sight. It is the familial justice of the creatures of God and the children of God, the basic attitude of the "family of God."

Such an approach to social justice in no way allows men to be self-satisfied after the manner of those who are just according to the law. It is an essentially dynamic view that keeps them aware of the perpetually approximative and imperfect character of every fulfillment. It attempts to take the next step that is historically possible at any given time.

Penal Justice. *Iustitia vindicativa* is the temperate will to restore violated justice and order through punishment proportionate to the violation and to the exigencies of the social order. It is above all a virtue proper to superiors and judges, who, in meting out punishment, should aim only at the furtherance and protection of the common good (public order and safety, confidence in justice and the sense of right). But it is also a virtue of the subject who is prepared to undergo due punishment if necessary and a virtue of other members of the community who contribute to the restoration of violated justice and order (*see* VENGEANCE).

Characteristics of Justice. The obligations of justice can be strictly and objectively determined, at least in their basic form, without regard to the gifts and the particular level of virtue of each individual, even if the process of determination is conditioned by change and history. In the case of justice, it is not directly and primarily a question of personal relations but of the order of possessions and goods—always, of course, with a view toward the person and the community. However, as regards goods, not only material goods should be considered but also the higher cultural goods—indeed, even truth, fidelity, and honor—insofar as they concern the necessary functioning of communal life. In contrast to legal right, it is a peculiarity of the virtue of justice that it is never fully enforceable, even though a certain measure of enforceability is required by the very nature of justice. The limits of enforcement are set by the clearly discernible rights and by the nature of the common welfare, which can be very much endangered by the excessive use of force; for it is a question of the common welfare that has as its very center the spirit of liberty that moves men to the free fulfillment of what is just.

Bibliography: E. BRUNNER, *Gerechtigkeit* (Zurich 1943). G. DEL VECCHIO, *Justice: An Historical and Philosophical Essay*, ed. A. H. CAMPBELL, tr. LADY GUTHRIE (New York 1953); *Philosophy of Law*, tr. T. O. MARTIN (Washington 1953). A. DESCAMPS, *Les Justes et la justice dans les évangiles et le christianisme primitif hormis la doctrine proprement paulinienne* (Louvain 1950). B. HÄRING, *The Law of Christ: Moral Theology for Priests and Laity*, tr. E.G. KAISER (Westminster, Md. 1961–). F. HEIDSIECK, *La Vertu de justice* (Paris 1959). V. HEYLEN, *Tractatus de iure et iustitia* (5th ed. Mechlin 1950). H. MERSCHMANN, *Die dreifache Gerechtigkeit: Grundgedanken der scholastischen Gesellschaftslehre* (Recklinghausen 1946). J. MESSNER, *Social Ethics: Natural Law in the Modern World*, tr. J. J. DOHERTY (new ed. St. Louis 1964). R. NIEBUHR, *Love and Justice*, ed. D. B. ROBERTSON (Philadelphia 1957). J. PIEPER, *Justice*, tr. L. E. LYNCH (New York 1955). P. TILLICH, *Love, Power, and Justice* (New York 1960).

[B. HÄRING]

JUSTICE, DOUBLE

The early reformers taught that the sinner is justified, or declared righteous, by the imputation of the justice, or righteousness, of Jesus Christ. Even though the justified man's sins are forgiven, they remain in him; but God does not reckon them to him because of the merits of the Savior. In Catholic doctrine, on the other hand, JUSTIFICATION is an internal sanctification of the sinner, who voluntarily receives from God an infusion of GRACE and the VIRTUES. The one and only formal cause of justification is inherent, or inhering, justice, also called "sanctifying grace." By this inherent justice sins are forgiven and blotted out, even though CONCUPISCENCE, which is not punishable, remains.

In the discussions of the sixth session of the Council of Trent on the justification of the sinner, a compromise theory, that of double justice, was proposed by Girolamo SERIPANDO, superior general of the Augustinians and afterward cardinal. A primitive form of this opinion had been defended prior to Trent by a few Protestant and some Catholic theologians. Chief among the latter were John Gropper of Cologne and Gasparo Contarini, a Venetian, created cardinal in 1535.

The doctrine of double justice was so named because it taught two formal causes of justification, both the inherent justice held by Catholics and the imputed righteousness held by Protestants. The proponents of this opinion argued that inherent justice is imperfect and that the works of the just man, marred with faults and imperfections, are not worthy of heaven. To become completely righteous before God and to be able to appear at the tribunal of the divine judge clothed in righteousness and with sufficient merit of eternal life, a person needs more than internal sanctification. The justified sinner needs also a special application of the merits of Christ by way of imputation. The application or imputation is not, however, purely forensic or external but includes a formal effect, namely, the insertion of the just man into the Body of Christ as one of its members.

The fathers of the Council of Trent, in approving the decree on justification, decisively rejected the doctrine of double justice in chapter seven: "Finally the only formal cause [of justification] is the 'justice of God, not the justice by which He is Himself just but the justice by which He makes us just'" (H. Denzinger, *Enchiridion symbolorum*, ed. A. Schönmetzer, 1529). Furthermore, the necessity of a special imputation of Christ's merits for the fullness of the merits of the just is excluded in chapter 16: "It must be believed that nothing else is wanting to the justified [besides the constant influx of Christ in His members] for them to be considered as having fully satisfied the divine law by their works . . . and as having truly merited the eternal life which they will attain in due time . . . for the justice that is said to be ours because it inheres in us and justifies us is likewise God's justice because He has put it in us through the merit of Christ" (H. Denzinger, *Enchiridion symbolorum* 1546–47). The condemnation in canon ten shows both that Christ's righteousness is the meritorious cause of justification and that Christ's righteousness is neither its single formal cause nor one of two formal causes.

Bibliography: H. JEDIN, *Papal Legate at the Council of Trent: Cardinal Seripando,* tr. F. C. ECKHOFF (St. Louis 1947). A. BRIVA, "El problema de la doble justificación en la escuela de Colonia," in *Semana española de teología* 18, 1958 (Madrid 1961) 19–44. P. PAS, "La Doctrine de la double justice au concile de Trente," *Ephemerides theologicae Lovanienses* 30 (1954) 5–53. C. E. MAXCEY, "Double Justice, Diego Laynez, and the Council of Trent," *Church History* 48 (1979) 269–78. P. SCHÄFER, "Hoffnungsgestalt und Geganwart des Heiles: Für Disjussion um die doppelte Gerechtigkeit auf dem Konzil von Trent," *Theologie und Philosophie* 55 (1980) 204–29. E. ARNOLD, "'Triplex iustitia': The Sixteenth Century and the Twentieth," in *Christian Authority: Essays in Honor of Henry Chadwick,* ed. G. R. EVANS (Oxford 1988) 204–23. A. E. MCGRATH, *Iustitia Dei: A History of the Doctrine of Justification* (Cambridge 1998).

[T. J. MOTHERWAY/C. MALLOY]

JUSTICE OF GOD

The concept of God's justice is discussed here as it evolved in the Bible and as it has been developed in Christian theology.

In the Bible. The concept of justice has a special meaning in the Old Testament and this meaning is carried over into the New Testament, particularly into Paul's Epistle to the Romans.

In the Old Testament. In ordinary usage one thinks of the "justice of God," as either vindictive justice, that is, the justice whereby God punishes sinners, or as distributive justice, that is, the justice by which he both punishes sinners and rewards the just. However, the Hebrew concept of justice must be clearly discerned lest one read modern notions into it. Therefore we must examine the Hebrew word *ṣedâîâh* (justice or righteousness) and its relationship to *hesed* (loyalty) and *'ĕmet* (fidelity).

The use of parallelism in the Old Testament poetry makes it often quite clear what words these writers considered to be synonymous. Thus, the consoling message of Deutero-Isaiah (40–66) justice (*ṣedâîâh*) and salvation (*tešûâ*) appear quite frequently together. God is said to be "a just and saving God" (Is 45.21) or "I am bringing on my justice, it is not far off, my salvation shall not tarry" (Is 46.13, also 51.5). In the Psalms God's justice is often paralleled or associated with his salvation, his truth or fidelity and his mercy (Ps 35,36.6–7, 39,40.11, 70,71.15, 102,103.17). In both Deutero-Isaiah and the Psalms God's justice, equivalent by parallelism to his salvation, is described as something to be revealed (Ps 97,98.2). This understanding is important for the interpreting the Letter to the Romans.

In the Old Testament the justice of God is often bestowed on the just man, whereas the wrath of God is reserved for the sinner. Thus Mi 7.9 states: "The wrath of the Lord I will endure because I have sinned against him. He will bring me forth to the light; I will see his justice." In Ps 84 and 85 such terms as wrath, anger, vexation (v. 3–5) are opposed to such terms as kindness, truth, peace, salvation and justice (v. 9–11).

In the Old Testament, then, the justice of God is neither vindictive nor distributive but salvific, and it is founded upon God's covenantal commitment to Israel. God is just in that he is abidingly faithful to his freely made promises of salvation and deliverance. Hence such terms as justice, salvation, fidelity and truth are easily interchanged in the Old Testament (Ps 97,98.2–3, Dt 32.4).

In the New Testament. Within the Old Testament the messianic era was foreseen as the establishment of God's perfect salvific justice (Is 9.6, 11.3–9; Jer 23.6). Yet, within the New Testament, it is limited, almost exclusively, to the Letter to the Romans (see Mk 1.15 with Is 40.13). While Paul discusses a common theme in both Galatians and Romans, the concept of justice does not appear in the former. Because Paul was writing to the Galatians within the polemical atmosphere of the Judaizers, he probably avoided the term "justice" since, within contemporary Jewish thought, it had come to assume the connotation of the impartial distribution of rewards and punishments in accordance with legal norms. Instead he uses ἐπαγγελία (promise) (see Gal 3–4) for the basis of the gratuitous gift of salvation. Nonetheless, from within the Old Testament environment one can readily equate "promises of God" (Galatians) with "justice of God" (Romans). There are five principal texts to be considered in Rom 1.17; 3.5, 21–22, 25–26; 10.3. Luther interpreted Rom 1.7 to denote that attribute of God whereby he is just and punishes the sins of the unjust. However, such an interpretation is dubious.

Rom 1.17 is placed within the context of God being faithful to his covenantal promise of salvation, whereby God vindicates his justice. In this verse the justice (δικαιούνη) of God is revealed in the preaching of the gospel. Moreover, in Rom 1.18 the "wrath [ὀργή] of God" is likewise "revealed." In accordance with the Old Testament this places Rom 1.17–18 in continuity with the distinction of justice as salvific deliverance and wrath as God's justice against "all ungodliness and wickedness."

Rom 3.5: "But if our wickedness shows forth the justice of God . . . is God unjust to inflict wrath on us?" This verse is again placed within convenantal theology. Even if Israel does not remain faithful, God will not break his bond. Israel's infidelity will serve only to make God's fidelity even more merciful. Thus Paul establishes three antitheses: infidelity – fidelity (3.3); injustice – justice (3.5); and falsehood – truth (3.7). Once again the justice of God is his fidelity and truth to his covenantal promises despite the infidelity of man, which, of course, begets his wrath.

Rom 3.21-22: "But now the justice of God has been manifested apart from the law, although the law and the prophets bear witness to it, the justice of God through faith in Jesus Christ for all who believe." Thus God's justice is manifested negatively "apart from the law" and yet positively "through faith in Jesus Christ." In 3.20 Paul alludes to Ps 142,143.2 where justice is used in the sense of salvific deliverance, for it is parallel to fidelity and opposed to divine judgement. Once again, then, Paul uses the term in its foundational Old Testament sense of divine covenantal fidelity for salvation.

Rom 3.25–26: ". . . Christ Jesus, whom God has put forward as an expiation by his blood, to be received by faith. This was to show God's justice, because in his divine forbearance he had passed over former sins; it was to prove at the present time that he himself is just and that he justifies him who has faith in Jesus." This text has always caused exegetical difficulties, especially because of the enigmantic phrase that God "had passed over [τὴν πάρεσιν] former sins." The Old Testament usage elucidates the phrase and its context. God and man were bound together in a covenantal bond, but man broke his side of the covenant by sin and therefore nullified the entire relationship. Yet God did not allow man's sin to free him from his own commitment. Rather, he "passed

over" these sins, not in regard to punishment, but in regard to covenant nullification. He himself remained faithful and even merciful. His fidelity showed the greatness of his own justice in bringing man the promised salvation even after man's repudiation of its advent by the sins of covenant infidelity. Such salvation, indeed, is precisely to give man a share in the divine justice so that man himself now remains in an eternal covenant with God through Christ. God's justice was manifested through the expiation of sin through the blood of Jesus and so believers are justified, that is, acquire the justice of God, through faith in him.

Rom 10.3–4: "For, being ignorant of the justice that comes from God, and seeking to establish their own, they did not submit to God's justice. For Christ is the end of the law, that every one who has faith may be justified." Again, the Old Testament meaning of God's justice is evident in these verses. The Pharisaic attempt to obtain salvation by works of the Law showed that they did not understand the salvation (the justice of God) offered to them by God, that is, salvation initiated only by the gratuitous gift of God and accepted through faith. Therefore they did not submit to the justice of God, that is, his salvific deliverance now made manifest in Christ and accepted in faith.

In both the Old Testament and Paul the primary meaning of divine justice is God's merciful fidelity to his promises. This finds its culmination in Jesus Christ through whom the justice of God is revealed and through whom the believer is made just. However, for those who refuse the justice of God through Jesus Christ, God's just wrath will come upon them at the end of time (Rv 16.5–7; 19.2).

See Also: JUSTIFICATION; REDEMPTION (IN THE BIBLE); RETRIBUTION; GRACE (IN THE BIBLE).

Bibliography: R. ADAMIAH, *Justice and History in the Old Testament* (Cleveland 1982). R. B. HAYS, s.v. "Justification," *The Anchor Bible Dictionary* (New York 1992). S. LYONNET, "De 'Iustitia Dei' in Ep. Ad Rom," *Verb Dom*, 25 (1947) 23–34, 118–121, 129–144, 193–203, 257–263. J. PIPER, *The Justification of God* (Grand Rapids, Mich. 1983). J. RUWET, "Misericordia et Justitia Dei in V.T.," *Verb Dom*, 24 (1947) 35–42, 89–98.

[D. M. CROSSAN/T. G. WEINANDY]

In Theology. Within systematic theology there are four interrelated notions of the justice of God. The first pertains to God's perfection in that he is perfectly just in himself. Thus the justice of God is the absence and impossibility of any moral disorder within himself. God's justice is thus equivalent to his infinite holiness and perfect goodness (Aquinas, *Summa theologiae*, I.21.1.ad 3 and 4). (*See* HOLINESS OF GOD).

Secondly, the justice of God in himself is the foundation and cause of the justice or righteousness within sinful humankind. Augustine states that as God shares his wisdom with humankind, because he is wisdom itself, so also he, who is just in himself, gives to humankind justice "when he justifies the godless (Rom 4.5)" (*De Trin.* 14.15). The Council of Trent, quoting Augustine, declares the same: "The only formal cause [of our justification] is 'the justice of God, not the justice by which he is himself just, but the justice by which he makes us just'" (Denzinger, *Enchiridion symbolorum,* 1529). Or again: "The justice that is said to be ours because it inheres in us is likewise God's justice because he has put it in us through the merit of Christ" (Denzinger 1546) (*See* JUSTIFICATION).

Thirdly, the theological concept of God's justice is most broadly applied to God's action towards creation and particularly towards human beings in so far as he renders to each and all their due. Aquinas designates this "retributive justice" or "commutative justice." As a ruler or the head of a family justly gives to each member what is due, "so the order of the universe, which is manifest in both physical nature and in beings endowed with a will, shows forth God's justice" (*S.T.,* I.21.1). Aquinas approvingly quotes Dionysius: "We must need see that God is truly just in seeing how he gives to all existing things what is proper to the condition of each; and preserves the nature of each one in the order and with the powers that properly belong to it" (*Div. Nom.,* 8.4). Thus God "exercises justice when he gives to each thing what is due to it by its nature and condition" (*S.T.,* I.21.1.ad 3). God's justice then is placed within his overall providential and orderly care for the whole of creation.

Fourthly, God's justice pertains to his response to the free moral actions of human beings. God "will render to every man according to his works" (Rom 2.6; see Mt 16.27). "For God is not so unjust as to overlook your work and the love which you showed for his sake in serving the saints, as you still do" (Heb 6.10). Thus, "God rewards those who seek him (Heb 11.6, see Denzinger, 2122). Paul, having kept the faith, is confident that "henceforth there is laid up for me the crown of righteousness, which the Lord, the just judge, will award to me on that Day, and not only to me but also to all who have loved his appearing" (2 Tm 4.6–7, see Denzinger 1545). Aquinas states: "Justice, therefore, in God is sometimes spoken of as the fitting accompaniment of his goodness; sometimes as the reward of merit" (*S.T.,* I.21.1.ad 3). He then equally approves Anselm's statement: "When you punish the wicked, it is just, since it agrees with their deserts; and when you spare the wicked, it is also just; since it befits your goodness" (*Pros.,* 10). The magisterium more often refers to God's justice as the punishment due to sin than to the reward due to merit (see Denzinger, 621, 1672, 2216, 3781). Augustine states that

God "can condemn no one without demerits, because he is just" (*C. Julian.* 3.18.35). Yet he also speaks of God's justice with regard to the retribution of both good and evil—"making good or bad use of their free will, they are judged most justly" (*Spir. et litt.* 33.58); or of the reward to be rendered for merits that the just judge will render (see *Grat. et lib. arb.* 6.14). Moreover, it should be noted that God's justice is not arbitrary. God justly rewards those who have freely cooperated with his grace and he justly, depending upon the seriousness of the sin, punishes or even condemns unrepentant sinners, for sin itself justly demands such condemnation which God justly sanctions (see Aquinas, *S.C.G.,* 3.140). Within our sinful world the misuse of power, or greed, or lust, or hatred and prejudice cause horrendous and appalling injustice by violating the authentic dignity and just rights of human beings. Because this world's justice cannot possibly make right such injustices, Christians look then to the day when Jesus will come in glory for finally he will redress all wrongs and set all things right. All will proclaim: "Just are you in these your judgments . . . true and just are your judgments" (Rv 16.5–7, 19.2). God's justice will then reign forever.

God's justice does not conflict with his mercy, nor does his mercy diminish his justice. Both are part of God's absolute goodness. Aquinas states: "The communicating of perfections, absolutely considered, appertains to goodness; in so far as perfections are given to things in proportion, the bestowal of them belongs to justice . . .; in so far as God does not bestow them for his own use, but only on account of his goodness, it belongs to liberality; in so far as perfections given to things by God expel defects, it belongs to mercy" (*S.T.,* I.21.3). Justice demands mercy. "The Lord does deeds of justice . . . He knows of what we are made, he remembers that we are dust" (Ps 102/103.6, 14). God's justice demands that he act mercifully towards sinners and his mercy is always enacted in accordance with his justice. Thus, the Father, in his loving mercy, sent his Son into the world not to condemn it but that those who believe might rightfully possess eternal life (Jn 3.16–17). In mercy God justly condemned sin through the cross of Christ so that humankind might be justified through faith in him (Rom 3.21–26). Aquinas holds that "mercy does not destroy justice, but in a sense is the fullness thereof" (*S.T.,* I.21.3.ad 2). God mercifully renders to humankind more than it justly merits and he mercifully punishes humankind less than it justly deserves (see *S.T.,* I.21.4 and ad 1). (*See* MERCY OF GOD)

See Also: JUDGMENT, DIVINE (IN THE BIBLE); JUDGMENT, DIVINE (IN THEOLOGY); PUNISHMENT; SANCTION; SANCTION, DIVINE; GOD, ARTICLES ON.

Bibliography: T. AQUINAS, *Summa Theologiae*, I.21; *Summa Contra Gentiles*, 3.140. B. DAVIES, *The Thought of Thomas Aquinas* (Oxford 1992). H. KÜNG, *Justification* (New York 1964).

[T. G. WEINANDY]

JUSTICE OF MEN

The concept of man's justice is discussed here as it evolved in the Bible and as it has been developed in Christian theology.

In the Bible. After treating the fundamental themes concerning the justice of men found in the OT, consideration will be given to the perfection of man's justice in the NT.

In the Old Testament. In the covenantal theology of Israel the term *ḥesed* (fidelity) applied to both parties of the agreement, to both God and man. The term justice (*ṣedāqâ* or δικαιοσύνη) had the same duality of application: the justice of God meant His fidelity to His covenantal promises, and the justice of man meant basically and originally his fidelity to his side of the mutual commitment. That man, then, was just who fulfilled completely all the stipulations of the covenant, which consisted of the Ten Commandments and all their applications to everyday life and to new situations that constituted the case law of the Pentateuch. An example from the life of David makes this meaning clear. While Saul was pursuing David, the latter got a chance to kill him but refrained from doing so because Saul was still "the Lord's anointed." Afterward Saul admitted that David was "more just" than he, for David had shown him kindness whereas he had shown him evil (1 Sm 24.18). David was just, i.e., faithful to his king, even while the latter attempted to kill him.

In the prophetic indictment of Israel for covenant infidelity, i.e., for idolatry and the social injustices that proceeded from ignoring the covenant, it was often simply of Israel's injustice that the Prophets spoke, for the term summed up the idea of covenant disobedience. Thus Amos, having condemned the extravagant cult (Am 3.14) and social evil of Israel (4.1), pinpointed his indictment by saying, "Woe to those who turn judgment to wormwood and cast justice to the ground!" (5.7).

Especially were those who exercised the office of judge in Israel obliged to judge justly, i.e., according to covenantal law and its casuistic specifications, and not to allow respect of persons or bribery to contaminate their decisions (Dt 1.16–17; 16.19–20). But beyond the justice or injustice of human judges was the judgment of God; one of the functions of the Temple according to Solomon's dedication prayer was to have been to serve as a place of vindication for the wrongly accused who came into God's presence to swear to their innocence (1 Kgs 8.31–32).

The theme of God's ultimate vindication of the justice of the wrongly accused appears quite frequently also in the Psalms, e.g., 25(26).1; 34(35).23–24, and especially 23 (24).3–5, where the justice that was rewarded is described as belonging to one "whose hands are sinless, whose heart is clean, who desires not what is vain, nor swears deceitfully to his neighbor." The picture of the just man as one who kept covenant fidelity with his God (in practice, the Ten Commandments) appears in greater detail in Psalm 14(15) in a kindred context; such a man could dare to approach the Temple and enter the presence of God. The counterpart of the just man was the rich extortioner described in Jer 22.13–17. (*See* JUSTICE OF GOD.)

In such a context of justice, equated with the covenant fidelity whereby man lived out the results of his commitment to Yahweh, the justice of the coming Messiah is to be understood. Against the background of the increasing infidelity of the Davidic dynasty, Isaiah announced a new Davidic monarch who would rule with justice and fidelity to the covenant. He himself, the messianic monarch, would live in justice with God and procure justice for others by judging them according to the covenant (Is 9.6; 11.2–5; 16.5). Jeremiah spoke of a new covenant between God and His people, one that they would keep (Jer 31.31–34); but he also promised at the same eschatological era ("days are coming" in 23.5; 31.27, 31; 33.14–18) a new David to reign in justice (23.5; 33.15).

The restoration and fixation of the Mosaic Law that took place after the exile still retained the ancient covenantal framework. Israel's obligation to the divine commands grew intrinsically and organically from its new being as "my people" (cf., e.g., Joshua ch. 24 with Nehemiah ch. 9). In the solemn renewal of the covenant, the author of Neh 9.13–14 stressed the Mosaic Law within the usual historical prologue to the establishment of covenant obligation, and he then interpreted Israel's former infidelity in terms of disobedience to this Law (Neh 9.16, 26, 29, 34). The newly inspired Israelites made and signed a binding covenant (9.38), which was interpreted as meaning to take an oath, under the penalty of a curse, that they would walk in the Law of God, given by Moses, God's servant, and would be careful to observe all the Lord's commands, His ordinances, and His statutes (10.29–30). The just man and his justice would henceforth be more and more described in terms of obedience to law as a means to attain fidelity to the covenant. Yet, even in Psalm 118(119), the praise of fidelity to the Law, the Psalmist knew full well that it was only in so far as God came into an individual's life that he was thereafter enabled to observe the Law ("Give me discernment, that I may observe your law and keep it with all my heart," v. 34). This thinking is summed up succinctly in Ps 1.2, which sees the just man as one who "delights in the law of the Lord and meditates in his law day and night." Such a theme is far from the thinking of the Pharisee who sought justice by keeping precepts; he should rather have kept precepts because he had found justice, or better, because justice had found him. Once sacred law became disconnected from its basis in divinely given covenantal being, it tended to proliferate indiscriminately in multiple interpretations and applications, and since its vital core was now dead, it became eventually an insufferable burden for the believer. By the time of the NT the Mosaic Law had fallen into such a state in the hands of the Pharisaic theologians.

In the New Testament. The problem of the justice of men in the NT coincides with that of JUSTIFICATION. At the time of Jesus the spiritual authorities of the people of God had lost an understanding of divine law as the day-to-day specification of their covenant commitment, even to the point where their interpretation was now in open conflict with the Ten Commandments themselves (Mt 15.1–9). Thus, one of the first things Jesus had to do in preparing His disciples for the arrival of the kingdom was to warn them that "unless your justice exceeds that of the Scribes and Pharisees, you shall not enter the kingdom of heaven" (Mt 5.20). Jesus' new justice is described in Matthew ch. 5–7; it was spiritual and interior, but, above all, it was based on the fact that the believer saw God as his Father and sought to act according to such an existential situation (Mt 5.48; 6.4, 6, 18). The justice of the kingdom of God was based, in other words, on a new and perfect relationship with God, which Jesus mediated to mankind as Moses had mediated the ancient covenant at Sinai. With the new covenant came a new law, and when the new law conflicted, in the Pharisaic interpretation, with the old Law, Jesus did not hesitate to place mercy and love before such an explicit law as that commanding rest on the Sabbath (Mk 3.1–6).

St. Paul was embroiled even more formally and theologically in the same controversy. The Pharisaic position was known to him from within, and he set out to oppose it in Galatians, on a rather personal level, and in Romans, on a more theoretical basis. There had been, he argued, only one justice (justification) for man and that was offered gratuitously to man by God's merciful love and was accepted as such by faith; this was as true for Abraham as for those living after Christ (Gal 3.6–18; 4.21–31; Rom 4.1–25; 9.6–9). Neither in the OT nor in the NT could a man attain justification, i.e., become just, by observing a set of precepts, however divine and holy they may have been. Paul's teaching was a direct polemic against the Pharisaic position that was in danger of passing, through Pharisee converts, into the early Church. But Paul also insisted in the moral section of almost all his Epistles and equally clearly in the doctrinal part of Romans (e.g., ch. 5 and 8) that the justice that man accepted by faith, which was a share in God's own fidelity to Himself (Rom 3.26), was a baptismal commitment that resulted in the life lived in the risen Lord (Gal 2.20; Col 3.1–4).

James stressed the last point even more strongly, possibly because of a misunderstanding of Paul existing among some of the Apostle's converts. The act of faith had to lead to a life of charity or it could hardly be termed faith; it was dead faith (Jas 2.14–26). In a polemic with the Pharisees it was necessary for Paul to stress the absolute gratuity of the first moment of transition from sin to grace whereby the justice of men was established; but in the polemic of James, possibly with negligent Christians, it was necessary to talk rather of the daily commitment that flowed organically from the gift of faith. The same teaching appears in Jn 1.17, where Christ brings into this world for mankind the power of abiding covenant fidelity, which then overflows for mankind in love (1 Jn 2.29; 3.16–18; 4.7–11).

Bibliography: *Encyclopedic Dictionary of the Bible,* tr. and adap. by L. HARTMAN (New York 1963), from A. VAN DEN BORN, *Bijbels Woordenboek* 1254–55. A. DESCAMPS and L. CERFAUX, *Dictionnaire de la Bible,* suppl. ed. L. PIROT et al. (Paris 1928–) 4:1417–1510. W. KORNFELD and H. VORGRIMLER, *Lexikon für Theologie und Kirche,* ed. J. HOFER and K. RAHNER, 10 v. (2d, new ed. Freiburg 1957–65) 4:711–713. A. DESCAMPS, *Les Justes et la justice dans les évangiles et le christianisme primitif hormis la doctrine proprement paulinienne* (Louvain 1950).

[D. M. CROSSAN]

In Dogmatic Theology. Justice of men may be understood either as the moral virtue that regulates man's actions regarding other people and by which he renders each one his due (justice considered as a cardinal virtue or as a special virtue; *see* JUSTICE), or in a broader sense as designating rectitude in man himself, in his inner disposition, his higher powers being submissive to God and his lower powers to the higher in such a manner that he finds himself in right order with regard to God, to his neighbor, and to himself (*Summa theologiae* 1a2ae, 113.1; *De ver.* 28.1). In a word, it is the state of man in which he is what he should be. It is in this sense, closely akin to the biblical concept of the just man and identical with the meaning of the term in the phrase ORIGINAL JUSTICE, that justice is considered here.

Gift of God. This justice of men is a gift of God's GRACE and the fruit of justification. Of himself man is unable to be what he should be. St. Augustine and the anti-Pelagian councils inspired by him, when they were confronted by the naturalism of Pelagius, asserted the doctrine that only God's grace in Christ makes men just (see H. Denzinger, *Enchiridion symbolorum,* ed. A. Schönmetzer [32d ed. Freiburg 1963] 225–227). The Council of Trent in its decree on justification restated and developed the doctrine. Neither the Law nor nature, it said, can bestow justice, but only the grace of God through Christ, man's redeemer (H. Denzinger, *Enchiridion symbolorum* 1521–25). Hence "the justice that is said to be ours because it inheres in us and justifies us is likewise God's justice because He gave it to us through the merit of Christ" (H. Denzinger, *Enchiridion symbolorum* 1547; cf. 1529).

This justice is an objective reality in man (H. Denzinger, *Enchiridion symbolorum* 1529), different for different persons (*ibid.*), susceptible to growth and meant to grow by GOOD WORKS in keeping the Commandments (H. Denzinger, *Enchiridion symbolorum* 1535). It is the contrary of the state of sin or of injustice (H. Denzinger, *Enchiridion symbolorum* 1528): "Every sin, insofar as it entails insubordination of reason to God, may be called injustice contrary to . . . justice" (*Summa theologiae* 1a2ae, 113.1 ad 1). Accordingly, only those who live in the state of grace are just; they only are what they should be according to the will of God. This supernaturalism excludes every form of naturalism, past or present.

This doctrine rests on a double basis. First, without this divine gift of justice, all men are sinners, having either ORIGINAL SIN or personal SIN or both. Historically this is the more explicit reason for the doctrine of St. Augustine and the councils of his time; it is also the explicit teaching of Trent, which allows no middle state between sin and justice (cf. H. Denzinger, *Enchiridion symbolorum* 1528, 1524). A second and more basic reason is that in the present world economy all men are called to the supernatural DESTINY that no one can attain without grace; and so no one is just in God's eyes unless he lives in grace. The justice or righteousness of those who are not in grace is but justice in a relative sense, *secundum quid.* But it is a doctrinal deviation repudiated by the Church to say "that the 'justice' of infidels is injustice or sin" (cf. H. Denzinger, *Enchiridion symbolorum* 1925). Only Christian justice is justice in the full sense of the term, *simpliciter.* St. Augustine did not say more when he spoke of the good works and virtues of infidels as sins and vices because they are without faith and grace: their justice is only apparent, not real; it does not effectively help them toward SALVATION.

The justice of men, justice of Christians, applies to "being" before it applies to "doing." It is not merely a matter of keeping the law; the Church condemned the legalistic concept of justice proposed by Baius (H. Denzinger, *Enchiridion symbolorum* 1942, 1969–70; *see* BAIUS AND BAIANISM); keeping the Commandments is only a sequel to the state of justice. But objective justice of its nature requires just works, or subjective justice. On being follows doing. In terms of Christian grace, INCORPORATION IN CHRIST postulates imitation of Christ.

Imperfection of Man's Justice. This justice, however, in the redemptive economy of grace is incomplete and imperfect. It never reaches the level of perfection that it had in the state of original justice. First of all, vigilance and struggle are required to persevere in justice; no one can be victorious in the struggle with the flesh, the world, and the devil without the help of grace (cf. H. Denzinger, *Enchiridion symbolorum* 1541). Even with the help of grace, man is not able to avoid every venial sin—not without a special privilege such as was given to the Blessed Virgin (H. Denzinger, *Enchiridion symbolorum* 1573). Furthermore, from the existence in the just of CONCUPISCENCE common theological doctrine concludes that without the help of actual grace man is unable to keep the natural law for long and to avoid every mortal sin. Man's justice does not take away his congenital debility. Awareness of this is a constant reminder to man that his justice is not the fruit of his own effort only but a gift of God.

Current theology of grace expresses the traditional doctrine of men's justice by saying that justice is one of the formal effects of sanctifying grace. This means that they, and only they, who live in the state of grace are what they should be according to the will of God. In fact, only they who share in Christ's grace are on the way to salvation and effectively living in the right order established by God, namely, the SUPERNATURAL ORDER.

See Also: ELEVATION OF MAN; GRACE, ARTICLES ON; MAN; PELAGIUS AND PELAGIANISM; SALUTARY ACTS; SUPERNATURAL.

Bibliography: R. LEMONNYER and J. RIVIÈRE, *Dictionnaire de théologie catholique,* ed. A. VACANT et al., 15 v. (Paris 1903–05) 8:2:2042–2227. *Dictionnaire de théologie catholique,* Tables générales (1951–) 1:1844–68. J. HASPECKER et al., *Lexikon für Theologie und Kirche,* ed. J. HOFER and K. RAHNER, 10 v. (2d, new ed. Freiburg 1957–65) 4:977–1000. R. SCHNACKENBURG et al., *ibid.* 8:1033–50. J. WANG TCH'ANGTCHE, *Saint Augustin et les vertus des païens* (Paris 1938).

[P. DE LETTER]

JUSTIFICATION

The doctrine of God's justification of the sinner is treated under five headings: 1. In the Scriptures, 2. In Classical Theology, 3. In the Sixteenth Century, 4. From Trent to Vatican II, 5. After Vatican II.

Council of Trent, painting by Hermanos Zuccarelli, c. 1560–1566. (©Archivo Iconografico, S.A./CORBIS)

IN THE SCRIPTURES

In the Old Testament. The word for justification has a juridical and forensic connotation. The verb *ṣādaq* means "to be just" or "to be not guilty" in the juridical sense. The causative form *hiṣdîq* means "to justify," and this usually intends the obtaining of justice for one unjustly accused, justification as vindication. This justification whereby the accused is declared innocent before the tribunal is supposed to conform to reality as far as the judge can decide. In Dt 25.1, for example, two men litigate before the law and "a decision is handed down to them acquitting the innocent party and condemning the guilty party." It is strictly enjoined, however, "The innocent and the just you shall not put to death, nor shall you acquit [justify] the guilty" (Ex 23.7). Quite often the main value of this external juridical justification is seen as a vindication of interior innocence before God, and it is God who has requited this innocence by the judge's decree [Ps 25 (26).1; 34 (35). 23–24] In the Septuagint

(LXX) δικαιόω is used for *hiṣdîq* of the Hebrew OT, and the meaning changes slightly. The emphasis of the Hebrew word was rather negative or, better, liberative in that it denoted the juridical declaration of forensic, though presumably factual, innocence; but the Greek term meant "to give justice," either of acquittal for the innocent or of condemnation for the guilty.

The use of *hiṣdîq* in Is 53.11 deserves special attention: "Through his suffering, my Servant shall justify many, and their guilt he shall bear." This is explained in the next verse: "And he shall take away the sins of many, and win pardon for their offenses." The Servant is not merely a judge who declares "the many" juridically acquitted before a human tribunal. By his suffering he obtains pardon and remission of their sins before God; and so he "justifies" them in reality. Otherwise the justification would be a declaration of innocence without foundation in fact, which is always a heinous crime in the OT. This is a unique use of *hiṣdîq*, for the general OT usage reserves the term for the actually innocent; here it is used for the action whereby sinners are rendered innocent by pardon. The Servant alone can do this, since God accepts his atonement as having redemptive and justifying value. There is a similar case in Dn 12.3: "But the wise shall shine brightly like the splendor of the firmament, and those who lead the many to justice shall be like the stars forever." Here the wise men have taught sinners how to live justly before God and so have brought them to forgiveness of their sins in God's sight, that is, to justification.

The recovered Hebrew text of Sir 42.1–2 is to be translated as: "But of these things be not ashamed lest you sin through human respect of the law of the Most High and his precepts or of the judgment, so as to justify him who is guilty." The Greek δικαιῶσαι τὸν ἀσεβῆ, might be taken, in the neutrality of the Greek δικαιόω ("acquit" or "condemn"), as meaning, "to condemn the wicked." But the Hebrew le haṣdîq rāšā' means that one must not fear man so as to justify an evil man by acquittal. Thus, in the OT it is always wrong "to justify" (hiṣdîq) the guilty, to declare them innocent, unless they have become just before God. Only God can do this. Any declaration of justification that does not conform to inner reality is sinful and must never be done by a human judge, as of course it is never done by the divine Judge.

In Jesus Christ's Teaching. As it is reported in the NT, the early preaching of Jesus, especially to the group of the disciples, stressed the difference between the δικαιοσύνη (justification) of the Pharisees and that which the disciples were to have. In Matthew ch. 5–7 the theme of the initial section, immediately after the exordium of the Beatitudes, is conveyed in the words, "unless your justice exceeds that of the Scribes and Pharisees, you shall not enter the kingdom of heaven" (5.20). Justice has a wide sense in this context and is almost equivalent to holiness. It is not restricted to the precise passage from sin to holiness; it rather denotes a mode of life in union with God. There follow five examples from the Mosaic Law, and Jesus's interpretation is contrasted with the customary one on murder (5.21–26), adultery (5.27–28), oaths (5.33–37), revenge (5.38–42), and love (5.43–48). The justice that will belong to the approaching kingdom must be spiritual, interior, and based on God's forgiving love.

The second section follows the same pattern. The theme appears in Mt 6.1: "Take heed not to do your good [δικαιοσύνη] before men, in order to be seen by them; otherwise you shall have no reward with your Father in heaven." This is developed with regard to three basic works of piety, alms (6.2–4), prayer (6.5–6), and fasting (6.16–18). Rather than the idea of justification (6.2, 5, 16)

or holiness that the Pharisees are said to demand, Jesus requires an interior bond between the believer and God, not an external manifestation that others would see. In this context the term "justice" is used in a wide sense that does not evoke a juridical statement of innocence but a life of innocence or holiness that is led before God. No doubt the declarative idea is still present, for one should presume that God pronounces the innocent holy and guiltless before the divine tribunal.

The same theme appears more clearly in Lk 16.15: "You are they who declare themselves just [οἱ δικαιοῦντες ἑαυτοὺς] in the sight of men, but God knows your hearts." In Luke 18 the Pharisee proclaims himself innocent before the divine tribunal: "O God, I thank you that I am not like the rest of men" (18.11), while the publican simply prays: "O God, be merciful to me a sinner!" (18.13). But the publican "went down to his home justified rather than the other" (18.14). This parable throws light on the statement of Jesus: "I have come not to call the just, but sinners" (Mk 2.17b; Mt 9.13b). It is not for those who consider themselves justified, but for those who need justification that Jesus has come. Already in the life and preaching of Jesus there was a clash with the Pharisees on justification, at least on the practical rather than the theoretical level. In a similar polemical situation, St. Paul will explore the implications of this teaching more theoretically.

The Doctrine of Paul. In order to understand the Pauline understanding of justification it is necessary to appreciate the anti-Pharisaic polemic within which it was forged and to take careful note of the precise meaning that the term came to have in the controversy.

Originally the law of MOSES had been given to Israel in the framework of a covenantal relationship with Adonai, their God. Suzerainty treaties in the Near East of Mosaic times formulated the obligations of vassal states to their imperial overlord in terms of a reciprocal bond created by some anterior action of the latter upon them. Such a format was used for the Ten Commandments and thence for all the cases that flew logically from them. This meant that Adonai proclaimed a covenant with the Israelites, who then were given a new being, that of "my people," based on a mutual commitment between them and God. The divine law was seen as a formulation and specification of Israel's being as the people of God (Ex 19.1-6; Lv 19.2).

In Pharisaic thought, however, the covenant basis came to be obscured by an expanding system of laws and prescriptions. As a result the mass of Mosaic legislation took on the appearance of a burden, an obligation forced upon the people from outside. The faithful, exact, and minute fulfillment of these many prescriptions tended to become the basis for union with God, the cause rather than the effect of relationship with Adonai. Instead of fidelity to obligation being a result of God's grasping the existence of Israel, fidelity appeared to be the cause of Israel's grasping of God, the means becoming the end, and the effect the cause.

In order to combat the delusion that one can be just and holy by exact fulfillment of Torah, Paul drew attention to the precise moment when one passes from the state of sin to that of holiness before God. He understood the Pharisees' teaching from within since be had been formally trained in their schools. In Phil 3.6 he states: "as regards the justice of the Law, I was blameless." That is, in light of the Pharisaic norm that justification arises from a flawless fulfillment of all the law's requirements, he was perfect. In such a perspective we really accomplish our own justification, if at least God has given us the necessary legal precepts. Paul repeatedly refers to this as justification "in" or "from" or "by" the Law and/or its works (Gal 2.21; Rom 3.20; 8.3: 10.5: 11.31). Since, however, Paul's thought developed under the influence of his growing theological acumen in the vicissitudes of his apostolic mission, his ideas can be followed in chronological sequence.

Decision at Jerusalem. Peter had baptized the centurion Cornelius, who had not accepted the obligations of Torah. He had done so at the command of the Holy Spirit (Acts 10.1–11.18). On his first missionary journey, Paul also made many Gentile converts (Acts 13.12, 48). The question of the value of the Mosaic Law for Christians was then inevitably raised. There were converted Pharisees who regarded circumcision and the whole Torah as necessary to Christian life (Acts 15.1, 5). The conclusion reached at Jerusalem, however, was that the Gentiles could not be bound by the Mosaic Law as necessary to salvation because salvation comes through Christ alone (Acts 15.6–12; Gal 2.1–16).

Controversy at Antioch. The decree of Acts 15.13–29 may have been sent by James to ANTIOCH at some later date than the first decision in Acts 15.1–12, since Paul behaved in his churches as if it did not exist (1 Cor 5.1–8; 8.1–13). It may have been a special concession to the churches of Syria, intended to enable Jews and Gentiles to live and eat together, and to intermarry. In any case it seems to have provided the occasion of the disagreement between Paul and Peter at Antioch (Gal 2.11–21). Paul used the incident to give a clear formulation of his position: "We know that one is not justified by the works of the Law, but by the faith of Jesus Christ. Hence we also believe in Christ Jesus, that we may be justified by the faith of Christ, and not by the works of the Law, because by the works of the Law no one will

be justified" (Gal 2.16). Justification cannot be at the same time by the works of the Law and by faith in Christ. Paul argues that Peter has already committed himself to the latter belief, in keeping with Acts 10–11 and 15, and his action in Antioch belies it. By faith in Christ the believers receive a new existence, a new life, and it is in virtue of this new being that they should act (Gal 2.20–21). The statement in Galatians may have been more clearly expressed at the time of its recall than in its first formulation, but already in Antioch Paul realized that justification by the works of the Law is radically opposed to justification by immersion in the dying and rising of Christ.

Galatians and Romans. The controversy over justification reaches a climax in these Epistles. Although the date of Galatians is disputed, the closeness of its theme and language to those of Romans makes it likely that both were written in the same period toward the end of Paul's third missionary journey. Galatians was composed to offset the action of some Judaeo-Christians who came to the churches of Galatia and argued for the continuing value of the Mosaic Law and accordingly of justification through the works of the Law (Gal 3.1–6). It is plausible that the problems that had come to a head in Galatia and that Paul had dealt with vehemently and rather personally led him to bring attention to the question in a formal letter. Romans was then composed to explain the conclusions he had reached and to present them to the intended sphere of his future activity (Rom 15.22–33). In this explanation the controversy moved to a deeper level as Paul argued that there was, is, and can be only one way of justification, the gratuitous gift of divine forgiveness offered in Christ and received in faith and baptism. The works of the Law never effected justification, which is always by faith in the promises of God, whether these concern the Messiah to come or the One who has come. The way of justification in Christ is firmly rooted in the OT, which, Paul argues, his opponents—Judaeo-Christians who bring justification by works of the Law into the communities led by Paul—have not understood, any more than they have understood the teaching of Christ. Sharpened by this controversy, Paul's thought has turned to the first moment when the sinner is made just. Is this moment brought about by the works of the unjustified in obedience to Torah? or by an act of faith, the humble acceptance of the gratuitous gift of divine mercy, forgiveness, and life? Paul's demonstration hinges on three antitheses.

(1) Adam and Christ. The basic antithesis does not appear in the more pointed polemic of Galatians, but in the fuller exposition of Romans. Scripture and human experience show that before the coming of Christ both pagans (Rom 1.18–32) and Jews (2.1–3, 20) were sinners before God; the entire world lacked and longed for justifi-

cation. It is only from the "justice of God" (3.21, 22, 25, 26a), that is, from God's fidelity to the covenantal promise of salvific deliverance, that the believer is justified. The key phrase is in 3.26b: "so that [God] might be just [δίκαιον] and justifying [δικαιοῦντα] the one who believes in Christ." Justification precedes any consideration of how the justified live out their life and salvation, united with the risen Lord, in anticipation of their bodily resurrection. This justification is based exclusively on God's fidelity to the promises; it is purely gratuitous and cannot be gained by human works. Though foretold in the OT it cannot be obtained by the works of the Law or by any works (3.21–22). Received in faith, it is no mere intellectual assent to a set of propositions, but a commitment of one's entire being to the centrality of the death and resurrection of Christ in God's salvific plan (3.23–24). Only by such an act of faith related to baptism (see Gal 3.26–29; Rom 6.3–5; Col 2.12 and cf. Gal 2.16–20 with Rom 6.3–9) is one brought from sin to justice and holiness.

In order to offset the view of justice obtained through the works of the Law, Paul used the term "justification" to denote precisely the transition from sinner to saint. Adam's sin brought sin into the world for all his descendants, who then compounded it by their personal sins. Reversely, Christ brought justice. Having received it in baptismal faith, the justified believers now live a life that is not their own but that of the risen Lord. With Adam as with Christ, Paul does not envisage only the moment of fall or of justification, but also the entire realm and life of sin or salvation that ensue from that moment (Rom 5.1–21). Both justification and salvation are purely gratuitous gifts, the former by faith alone, the latter as the believer's entire life lived in the risen Lord. It is the works-in-Christ of the justified that concern Paul in the second section of almost all his letters. The Adam-Christ parallel is also developed in 1 Cor 15.45–49 (earlier than Romans) and in Eph 4.22–24. The antithesis makes it clear that the gift of justification is the beginning of the life of salvation, the climax of which will be bodily resurrection in Christ (Phil 2.6–11; 3.20–21).

(2) Abraham and Christ. In Gal 3.6–18, 29; 4.21–31 and Rom 4.1–25; 9.6–9, Paul uses the example of Abraham to show that the only justification ever offered, even in the OT, was by faith, whether in the Christ to come or in the Christ who has come. There never was a way of justification by legal works. The core of the argument is the citation of Gn 15.6 in Gal 3.6 and Rom 4.3: "Abraham believed the Lord, who credited the act to him as justice [εἰς δικαιοσύνην]." The primary transition, the moment of justification (of the aorist ἐλογίσθη in Gn 15.6 with the aorist δικαιωθέντες in Rom 5.1 that denotes the instant of baptismal faith), was not achieved by works of the Law, for the Law was not given until much later (Gal 3.15–18), or indeed by any one of Abraham's works (Rom 4.1–5). Abraham was justified by God's gratuitous promise, which he only had to believe.

According to Paul, Abraham's example was already seen in the OT as the model for all future justification. In Gal 3.8 Paul cites Gn 12.3; 18.18 in the LXX version ("In you shall all the nations of the earth be blessed") rather than in the original Hebrew ("In you shall all the nations of the earth invoke blessings on one another," that is, by saying, "May you be as blessed as Abraham"). The citation is seen as a prophecy that eventually the Gentiles will receive the blessing of justification after the manner of Abraham, by faith-acceptance. This line of thought is further developed in Rom 4.18–22. Abraham believed the angel's prophecy that new life would come from his and Sara's old bodies; and Christians believe that just as God brought Jesus from the dead to glorified life, so they will themselves be raised from death in sin to life in grace. A second point emerges in Rom 4.9–12. Abraham received the promise and was justified by faith before submitting to ritual circumcision. He was therefore justified while in uncircumcision, as in Gn 17. (This tradition of the Pentateuchal priestly writers is more recent than the Yahwist tradition of Gn 15 that relates to the same event). Here again Abraham's case shows that the Gentiles can be justified in uncircumcision, without the works of the Law. In summary, the OT itself knows only of justification by faith, the acceptance of God's free gift. And this is what God promised to extend to all humankind through a unique descendant of Abraham (Gal 3.15–18).

(3) Moses and Christ. In Gal 3.19–29 and more fully in Rom 4.13–16; 7.1–23 Paul examines the relationship of the Mosaic Law and its works to justification by faith. Torah was originally given by God as part of a covenant framework, and its precepts were the specification and objective statement of the relation between "your God" and "my people," by virtue of which those who had been freed from EGYPT by the divine will were made God's own people. However, the Mosaic Law that Paul knew, however divine, holy, and sacred, was not the divine gift that had fed the prophetic zeal. Shorn of its covenantal basis, the Law had turned into an intolerable burden imposed on human liberty from without, by external pressure and compulsion. The Law of God, so conceived and practiced, strengthens Paul's thesis. Far from producing justification, which it could never do in any case, the Mosaic Law, as Paul knew it and as much of Israel's past could show, had occasioned a disobedience that imprisoned Israel under the wrath of God. Now, however, the way of escape was opened. In the gift of God in Christ Jesus, the disciples receive in baptismal faith a justifica-

tion that brings them to a new being in union with the risen Lord (Col 1–4). And such "justification into life" (δικαίωσιν ζωῆς, Rom 5.18) gives the justified a continuing holiness in union with the Lord (Rom 8).

The Epistle of James. At first glance the teaching of the Epistle of James seems diametrically opposed to the view of justification that is explained in Galatians and Romans. Paul states, "But we know that man is not justified [δικαιοῦται] by the works of the Law, but by the faith of Jesus Christ" (Gal 2.16), and again, "For we reckon that one is justified by faith independently of the works of the Law" (Rom 3.28). James, however, says: "You see that by works one is justified [δικαιοῦται], and not by faith only" (Jas 2.24). While the vocabulary is exactly the same—"justified," "works," "faith"—the statements seem to be clear contradictions. Even the OT example used by Paul to support his thesis of justification by faith alone is adduced by James to show that justification is by faith and works. Paul had cited Abraham as witness, using Gn 15.6 in both Gal 3.6 and Rom 4.3. In Jas 2.21–23, however, the author takes the same Gn 15.6 as a prelude to Gn 22, so that Abraham's faith in the promised posterity is "made perfect" by his obedient willingness to sacrifice Isaac, in whose descendants the promises should come to fulfillment. Actually, however, the very argument from Abraham clarifies the quite different meanings that Paul and James give to the same vocabulary.

The teaching of Paul may at times have been deliberately abused as an excuse for license rather than as a mandate for the liberty of the children of God. His teaching on the Parousia (see 2 Pt 3.16), and, more to the point, his teaching on justification seems to have led some to conclude that life after justification could be lived in any manner whatever. In 1 Cor 6.12, "all things are permissible" reads like the slogan of such an attitude, taken up by Paul in order to reject it. In Rom 3.8 and 6.1, Paul speaks of those who calumniate his teaching in such a manner. James may well be writing specifically against people who were using Paul's oral catechesis as an excuse for sin or indifference. Freed from the Mosaic Law, justified by baptismal faith, they no longer recognized any obligations. Paul, however, taught that the justified must live a life consonant with union with the risen Lord.

James, in this perspective, is not talking of the "works of the Law," an expression the Epistle never uses. Instead he insists on the works one must do after baptismal justification lest justification become a lie. Justification then designates the entire life rather than merely the initial moment when one has received the gift of divine life. James is interested in the works of the justified Christian, like charity (Jas 2.14–17), and he makes exact-

ly the same point as 1 Jn 3.16–18: "Let us not love in word, neither with the tongue, but in deed and truth." This was also what Paul intended by "faith which works through charity" (Gal 5.6).

There is thus no fundamental contradiction between Paul and James. Were it not for their use of the same vocabulary in differing senses the question might never have arisen. When James says, "Of his own will he has begotten us by the word of truth, that we might be, as it were, the first-fruits of his creatures" (Jas 1.18) his teaching converges with that of Paul. When both are read in conjunction against the OT background of the term "justification" the Biblical doctrine appears in its fullness. No human forensic tribunal can justify a person who is guilty before it, for this would be a perversion of justice. The presumption is always that a tribunal justifies a person falsely accused, who is thus proclaimed not guilty (OT). But even the OT knows that things are quite different with God, who is able to "justify" the guilty when the divine sentence forgives their sins. Such a divine action brings about an inner change in being for the person concerned, or else the Judge of all the world would have acted unjustly (cf. Is 53.4–12).

Paul works in a situation of anti-Pharisaic polemic. He argues that the justification whereby God declares a sinner holy is not effected by human fidelity to the prescriptions of Torah. The sinner is justified only by the gratuitous gift of divine forgiveness. On the one hand, Paul stresses quite forcefully that thereafter the justified person lives a life of love in the risen Lord. Justification and salvation are free divine gifts, as are life and holiness. The moment of justification is by faith alone, and the life in Christ that follows is by faith that works through Christ's charity. On the other hand, James is in a different polemical situation as, most likely, he argues against a libertarian interpretation of Paul's teachings. Faith is not a dead act of mere lip service. It must be lived out as Christian, otherwise of course it was not there from the beginning, and there was merely an exterior semblance of it.

Bibliography: G. KLEIN, *Die Religion in Geschichte und Gegenwart*, 6 v. (3d ed. Tübingen 1957–63) 5: 825–828. A. DESCAMPS and L. CERFAUX, *Dictionnaire de la Bible*, suppl. ed., ed. L. PIROT et al. (Paris) 4:1417–1510. B. R. LEMONYER, *Dictionnaire de théologie catholique*, ed. A. VACANT et al., 15 v. (Paris 1903–50) 8.2:2043–77. G. E. MENDENHALL, *Law and Covenant in Israel and the Ancient Near East* (Pittsburgh 1955). S. DUPONT, *Les Béatitudes. 1. Le problème littéraire: Les deux versions du Sermon sur la montagne et les Béatitudes* (Louvain 1958). H. KÜNG, *Justification: The Doctrine of Karl Barth and a Catholic Reflection*, tr. T. COLLINS et al. (New York 1964). J. REUMANN, *Righteousness in the New Testament, with Responses by Joseph A. Fitzmyer and Jerome D. Quinn* (Philadelphia 1982).

[D. M. CROSSAN/G. H. TAVARD]

IN CLASSICAL THEOLOGY

In the present context "classical theology" designates the theology of the patristic and medieval periods, chiefly in the West, with the understanding that the Eastern and Oriental Churches went through a distinct development while the Western Church struggled with the implications of the theology of St. AUGUSTINE. Briefly, justification is understood to be a gift from God, conveyed in faith and baptism, by which the faithful are moved from the state of injustice or sinfulness called original sin, eventually compounded by personal sins, to a state of justice or righteousness in God's eyes. While Eastern Christianity did not emphasize justification but drew attention to its fulfillment in sanctification and deification, Western Christianity explored the passage from sin to justice, along with its moral implications for the Christian life. To see the meaning of this doctrine in its proper context one ought (1) to locate it in the Christian message, (2) to sketch its historical development and show the main influences that went into its making, (3) to expound the doctrine of the scholastics and the theological explanation of it, mainly according to the mind and principles of Thomas Aquinas.

Setting of the Doctrine in the Christian Message. The Christian kerygma is centered on the Good News that salvation is offered in Christ to all human persons. The Word Incarnate became the Redeemer through his life, passion, death, and resurrection, bringing the forgiveness of sins to fallen humanity, and restoring the life of grace which anticipates the glory of heaven. Justification is the application of Christ's redemption to the individual believer.

Accordingly, the doctrine of justification presupposes the revelation of the fall. All men and women, Jesus and Mary excepted, are burdened with an inherited sinfulness when they come into this world. The universal reign of sin, the result of both original and personal sin, makes them incapable of being naturally just in the eyes of the Creator. Human sinfulness entails the forfeiture of the life of grace and a congenital weakness, called concupiscence, in seeking and doing what is right. Since no human person is just by nature and his personal efforts, justification must be God's gift. Christ's overcoming of the Fall opens the way to justification. By his earthly life, passion, death, and resurrection, Jesus took away the sins of the world and restored the original justice lost by the fall. The redemption of humanity, however, still has to be applied to particular persons as their personal redemption through the forgiveness of their sins and the undeserved gift of grace. Justification is the opening of this process. It is inseparable from Jesus Christ the Redeemer and from the Holy Spirit, the Sanctifier.

Christ's redemptive mission continues in and through the Church, which may be understood analogically as the primary sacrament of Christ. The Church fulfills its mission by preaching the gospel, administering the sacraments, whose primary minister is Christ himself, and generally leading the faithful in the way of holiness.

Infants can be saved and receive grace and glory through baptism, without their personal involvement. Morally adult persons, however, are not saved without their consent. Justification requires true conversion, so that adults must freely ask for baptism. When they fall again into personal sin they can be forgiven when, sinful and repentant, they meet again with Christ and God in contrition, normally by way of the sacrament of Reconciliation. In justification Creator and creature, God's grace and the human will, are one. The restoration of the sinner through justification, however, is not completed in this life. The gifts that are constitutive of the life of grace are restored, but not all of those which, like the gift of "integrity," could facilitate and stabilize it. Concupiscence remains. As it restores the life of grace, justification is a beginning. Sanctification, however, is imperfect and always precarious since it can be undone by mortal sin. It is at the same time perfectible, capable of growth in grace. Only at the consummation of redemption at the Second Coming of Christ, in the Parousia at the end of time, will all the lost gifts be restored. The fulfillment of justice and holiness is for the next world, when grace is changed into glory.

Historical Development before St. Augustine. The idea of and even the term "justification" originated with St. Augustine. Later on the medieval scholastics speculated about their meaning and implications.

Before Augustine elements of the doctrine of justification are found primarily in the catechesis and liturgy of Christian initiation, in which baptism is prominent, and secondarily in the penitential discipline. Even before explicit awareness of the fallen state was expressed in the doctrine of original sin in the controversies provoked by Pelagianism early in the fifth century, the beginning of Christian life through the sacraments of initiation was commonly seen under the two aspects of forgiveness of sin and participation in the life of Christ.

The Greek Fathers emphasized the second aspect as they explained θειοποίησις, deification, but they were aware that baptism remits sin. The Latins, without overlooking the new life in Christ which begins in Baptism, focused attention on the forgiveness of sin. While the Greeks spoke of the indwelling Spirit, or the Logos of God, or the Holy Trinity as the source of divinization, more than of the transformation that the indwelling brings about, the Latins did the reverse. They paid more attention to the human transformation than to the divine indwelling, to the effect than to the cause. They concentrated on the state following baptism, as contrasted with the state that preceded it, more than on the mode of passage from sin to faith and justice.

As the early Fathers of the Church understood it, the human condition steers a middle course between the Manichean view of matter and flesh as evil, and the Stoics' belief that there is by nature a spark of the divine in all human persons. Even though sin is now forgiven, sharing in the divine nature is not a natural datum but a pure gift of God.

Augustine and Pelagianism. The occasion for the bishop of Hippo to formulate the doctrine of justification came in his reaction to Pelagius's denial of the absolute need of the grace of Christ to be good and to do the right thing. Pelagius, a fashionable spiritual director in the city of Rome, taught that the soul is so endowed with free will that it is perfectly able to do what is good by itself. The asceticism he promoted denied fundamental sin and the absolute need for grace. His followers blamed the influence of Manicheeism for the doctrine of original sin. Each person, they maintained, is good and able to persevere in justice thanks to a good use of God's gifts through the free will.

Against this overt naturalism Augustine reaffirmed the absolute need of Christ's grace for redemption. Humans are born in sin and cannot be just unless they are justified by the grace of Christ. Justification is not only the forgiveness of sin. It is also a shield against future sin. Yet justifying grace does not remove all the consequences of the fall of Adam. Concupiscence remains after baptism, if no longer as guilt, at least as a tendency to exclusive self-love: *transit reatu remanet actu*. Justification requires a human consent that is itself enabled by God's grace. No human person left to the resources of nature can do anything that is not affected by inordinate self-love, which inevitably vitiates all thoughts and actions. Even those that seem to be virtuous need to be purified by healing grace. This sort of working with God may be summed up as having a living faith, the sort of faith that inspires hope and charity, all of which is God's gift.

In Augustine's mind, as in that of his contemporaries, justifying grace is grace taken as a whole, without the later distinctions between actual and habitual grace. The reason for its necessity derives primarily from the fallen state of humankind. Grace has both a healing and an elevating function that Augustine, like the Greeks, also spoke of as divinization, though this aspect of grace was hardly prominent in the course of the anti-Pelagian polemics. At the time, the distinction between the natural and the supernatural was not explicit, so that Augustine

envisaged the human condition as it is, in its actual existence. When he affirmed human working with grace he was satisfied that grace restores the will to the perfection it had before sin, and he made no attempt to show how grace and free will can share a common action. Lastly, keeping the grain of truth contained in Manicheeism, Augustine was not blind to the disorder of concupiscence that remains after baptism. This Augustinian teaching on justification *in facto esse* rather than *in fieri*, in its achieved reality rather than in its becoming, was the first systematic Western formulation of the Christian condition after baptism. It was to have a far-reaching influence on later Latin theology.

The most important element in the doctrine, decisive for all further development, is that righteousness is God's gift. It is a sharing in the justice of God, justice and mercy being one when God saves those who deserve to be condemned. The gratuity of salvation is central. All initiative in the process of justification comes from God alone. When, as in the writings of the monk John Cassian, remnants of Pelagianism, later called Semi-Pelagianism, suggested that at times God's grace awaits a sinner's positive gesture toward justification, Augustine objected that the beginning of faith, including the very assent of the mind to the message of salvation, is, no less than any subsequent growth and maintenance or perseverance of justification, totally God's gift and grace.

Augustine's influence in the West was decisive in shaping its doctrine on justification, with its negative stress on the remission of sin, its positive stress on the total gratuity of God's gift, and also, echoing Augustine's view of the consequences of the Fall, on the precariousness of human holiness. It should be noted, however, that decrees of Council II of Orange (529) against the Semi-Pelagians were mostly unknown to medieval theologians between the ninth century, when Archbishop Hincmar of Rheims quoted them in the predestinarian controversy against Gottschalk, and the sixteenth century, when they were incorporated in the canonical collection of Peter Crabbe in 1538. St. Thomas himself did not know this council, even when in his later works he distinguished between the position of Pelagius and that of his followers.

In any case the influence of Augustine has been considerably less in the Christian East than in the West. The Greek Fathers after Augustine remained reluctant to call sin a state that is independent of the personal will, and they continued to stress the doctrine of divinization.

Scholastic Theology. The transition from the patristic to the scholastic theology of justification took from the eighth to the twelfth century. It brought about the predominance of a very different mentality in the formulation of doctrine. The Fathers' pastoral and practical approach made way for a speculative and academic one. The main problem before the schools related to the connection between the negative and the positive sides of justification, between the forgiveness of sin and the infusion of grace. Is this connection merely factual, known from revelation and tradition? Or is it necessary in the first place? Investigation of this problem led the scholastics to study not merely the state of justification in contrast with the state of sin, but also the very process that leads from the one to the other. This study was facilitated by the use of Aristotelian philosophy and the gradual elaboration of various concepts regarding sin and grace such as act, habit, change, mutation in the light of formal and material causality. The question thus became: How and why does the habitual state or habit of sin give way to the state or the habit of grace?

The several schools that took up the problem were generally marked by either intellectualism or voluntarism. The first is characteristic of the thought of St. THOMAS AQUINAS. In the realism of his theory of intellectual knowledge, which he regarded as valid even when bearing on supernatural realities, he applied the general metaphysics of mutation to the changeover from sin to grace, which he then identified as the expelling of one form by the infusion of a new one. He thus could see an organic and necessary correlation between remission of sin and infusion of grace and, in another aspect, between God's action and the human response. In this perspective justification involves both the negative and the positive aspects, as well as divine and human actions. It is a complex event that is wrought by God and accepted by the sinner, in which habitual sin is expelled from the soul by the infusion of the new form that is grace. Other questions regarding the degree of grace infused or the persistence of concupiscence Thomas explained in a similar way, not merely in light of God's disposition but also from the point of view of the human reception of grace. This disposition, in his mind, is expressed in the very nature of divine causality: *Scientia Dei causa rerum*. The theology of justification thus moves to the objective or ontological level. This basic trust in the realism of our intellectual knowledge of supernatural realities sets theology a new task as the *fides quaerens intellectum* of St. Anselm functions in light of the synthesis of Augustinianism and Aristotelian metaphysics that is St. Thomas's achievement.

The other trend, voluntarism, was favored in the Franciscan School. It was based on Bonaventure's determination that Goodness (*bonum*) rather than Being (*esse*) is the primary name of God. The forgiveness of sin and the infusion of grace are connected by the will, that is, the goodness of God. Yet they are not identical and they need not coincide. As John Duns Scotus reflected that the connection is not due to the contradiction between sin and

grace, but simply to God's will, he identified grace and charity, which must be one when given to the sinner as they are one in God. Habitual sin was then seen as an orientation to punishment (*ordinatio ad poenam*), and grace as a sanctifying power that is given when the sinner is accepted by God (*acceptatio Dei*). Consequently, the organic structure of justification appeared in another light than in the theology of Thomas Aquinas. Since God's will is the cause of all that is (*voluntas Dei causa rerum*), it is also the sole reason for the correlation of the remission of sin and the infusion of grace.

WILLIAM OF OCKHAM took one further step. He not only saw God's decree as the only reason for the connection between the negative and the positive aspects of justification. Because he denied the capacity of the human intellect to know reality as it is, he attributed a merely nominal value to concepts, including the theological notions of justice and justification. He then logically concluded that God could have decreed otherwise. By absolute divine power (*de potentia absoluta*) grace could have been given without sins being forgiven, although it is not so given in the actual order of creation and redemption (*de potentia ordinata*). The distinction of these two divine powers and the ensuing orders became a fundamental principle of nominalist theology.

Such a voluntarism was not compatible with the organic concept of justification that Thomas Aquinas had elaborated or with the realism of the Thomist conception of grace. If human concepts cannot be relied upon to express supernatural realities truly, though imperfectly, God's will, which is the reason why things are what they are, can be known only by revelation. In this case the human intellect cannot be trusted to know the truth, a situation that brought about a gradual shift of attention from ontology to psychology in theological circles. The basic question became, not ''what is reality?'' but, ''what do we think of it?'' The data of tradition, in this perspective, needs to be supported by the evidence of experience. Thus the nominalist theology of justification and grace opened the way to the notion that justification of the sinner is a purely forensic act of God, decreed indeed by the divine will, yet totally external to the person. In this case one could logically entertain the thought that God not only could, but would proclaim the sinner just without necessarily abolishing the sin. This became in the sixteenth century one of the basic problems of the Reformation.

IN THE SIXTEENTH CENTURY

The Reformers. The Protestant theology of justification has a twofold origin in the life and teaching of Martin LUTHER (ca.1483–1546). Negatively, it derives from his experience of sinfulness and of the ineffectiveness of the ascetical practices in his life as an Augustinian friar. Positively, it is the fruit of his discovery that the justice of God to which St. Paul refers is not a sentence of condemnation, but the merciful justice by which God forgives and declares the sinner just. Faith in Christ, and not the works of the law or anyone's personal works, justifies from sin. The main points of doctrine in the Lutheran theology of justification corresponded to Luther's personal experience. Human efforts, words, and works are of no avail. Only the grace of God made known through Christ justifies and saves. Christ covers the sinner with his own justice, which is then imputed to the sinner. Since justification comes entirely from God and not from anything that is human, one may say that the justified sinner remains fundamentally sinful, even when, as they should, the believers do follow Christ in performing works of holiness. These works are the fruit of divine grace and have no merit of their own.

When Luther turned to the medieval doctrine of justification in the form that nominalism had given it, he simply had to repudiate what was belied by his experience and by his understanding of the Pauline teaching. Neither good works nor merits are the way to justification. It is an illusion to think that the human person is able freely to cooperate with God at any moment of the process of salvation. Luther did not repudiate medieval theology as a whole. He even found conceptions that were germane to his own in the writings of the Rhineland mystics, notably Johannes Tauler and the anonymous author of the book to which he gave the title *Theologia deutsch*. From the standpoint of ecclesiology, justification, because it is the key to salvation, is the article where the Church stands and falls (*articulus stantis et cadentis ecclesiae*). From the standpoint of morality and the proper Christian behavior, it does not change what sinners remain in themselves because of the resilience of concupiscence after forgiveness. The sinner is nonetheless seen by God as just, because included by faith in the very justice of Christ, thus being at the same time just and sinful (*simul justus et peccator*). From the standpoint of methodology, justification is the principle of discernment between truly Christian and Pelagian or Semi-Pelagian systems of salvation.

This basic understanding of justification was incorporated by Melanchthon in article four of the Confession of Augsburg (1531): "Men cannot be justified before God by their own strength, merits, or works, but are freely justified for Christ's sake through faith." In keeping with this the Formula of Concord in 1581 declared: "Nevertheless they [the faithful] through faith on account of the obedience of Christ . . . are pronounced good and just and reputed as such, even though by reason of their corrupt nature they are sinners to this point and so remain as long as they bear this mortal body" (*Solida Declaratio*, 3.16; *Die Bekenntnisschriften der evangelisch-lutherischen Kirche* 921).

When John CALVIN composed his *Institutio christianae religionis* (five editions, each longer than the previous one, from 1536 to 1559), he systematized the Lutheran doctrine of justification in his own original way. While he tied together justification and election, he also balanced the power of grace with the necessity of good works in proof of justification. However, the central doctrine of his systematic theology is, rather than justification, the interior testimony of the Spirit who assists the faithful when they read the Scriptures. In addition, the doctrine of justification was increasingly absorbed in Calvin's conviction that all humans, when they are created, are destined to heaven or to hell by a divine decree (double predestination), which is nonetheless just for being antecedent to their creation.

Similar doctrines of justification had also been formulated, in partial dependence on Luther, by Ulrich Zwingli in Zurich and Martin Bucer in Strasbourg. Heinrich Bullinger, Zwingli's successor in Zurich, endorsed Calvinist formulations in the Second Helvetic Confession (1566). The doctrines that were passed on to most of the later Reformed Churches, however, had been hardened by the Synod of Dort (1617–1618), where the dominant accent was placed on predestination and the invincibility of grace.

The Council of Trent. The Council of TRENT, called to respond to the Protestant Reformation, formulated the Catholic doctrine of justification at its sixth session (1547). The decree *De justificatione impii* (DS 1520–83) is in two parts. The first part explains the doctrine in 16 chapters. Thirty-three canons condemn various doctrines that may or may not have been taught as such by the Reformers, not one of whom is named in the conciliar texts.

The Tridentine decree set the problem of justification in a broad Trinitarian and sacramental context, even as it made use of Aristotelian categories of causality. It identified the final cause of justification as the glory of God and of Christ, and the life eternal to be given to the justified. The efficient cause is God's gracious mercy. The meritorious cause is Our Lord Jesus Christ, who redeemed the faithful through the passion and the cross. The instrumental cause is baptism, the sacrament of faith, received in fact or in desire (DS 1529; cf. DS 1524), along with the sacrament of penance, also received in fact or in desire for the recovery of grace lost by post-baptismal personal sin (DS 1542; decree De *sacramento paenitentiae*, session XIV, 1551, DS 1677). The formal cause is the justice of God by which he makes us just (DS

1529). The Trinitarian aspect of justification is thus indicated, though not explained at length. The Father, the Word of God, and the Holy Spirit have a role in it (DS 1525–30). Justification creates a new relation or union with God the Father, with Christ, and with the Holy Spirit. This is called God's indwelling in the soul.

The decree on justification essentially sums up and reformulates the doctrine of the preceding centuries, particularly that of the councils of Carthage against Pelagianism and of Orange against Semi-Pelagianism. Nothing substantial has in fact been added to the Church's teaching since Trent, except for what a better understanding of Martin Luther's teaching made possible after the Second Vatican Council. Justification implies a real remission of sins (DS 1528) and not merely their nonimputation (cf. DS 1561), although concupiscence persists after baptism (cf. DS 1515). It brings about an interior renewal that is the fruit of grace and divine gifts (DS 1528), even if this origin cannot be detected at the psychological level (cf. DS 1533, 1562–65). It implies the sinner's voluntary acceptance of the divine grace and gifts (DS 1528). This assent to God is the fruit of prevenient grace, so that one may truly speak of a preparation for justification (DS 1526).

The immediate context of justification is no other than the universal redemption wrought by Christ, who came to reconcile creation with God, and whose grace when applied to individual believers justifies them in the eyes of God (DS 1521–23). The initiative comes from God's grace and not from human free will, although it does require human assent (DS 1524–27). Along with Semi-Pelagianism this rules out deterministic views for which divine grace would be totally irresistible (DS 1554). That justification "is not only the remission of sins but also a sanctification and an interior renovation by the willing reception of grace and gifts" (DS 1528) implies three dogmatic principles, regarding the remission of sins, sanctification, and the acceptance of grace.

Remission of Sins. For the Council of Trent whatever is truly and properly sin is taken away rather than merely brushed over or not imputed to the guilty (DS 1515). Redemption in Christ entails liberation from sin (DS 1522) when it is applied to the faithful as their justification (DS 1523). This does not mean that concupiscence has disappeared. As was said in the decree of session V on original sin (1546), concupiscence remains after baptism, "to be struggled against, though it has no power over those who do not consent to it and who, by the grace of Jesus Christ, strenuously resist it" (DS 1515). While it is not sin properly so called, it comes from sin and inclines to it. Thus the council affirmed the reality of the remission of sin in baptism, while it also recognized the imperfection of the baptized as long as concupiscence has not been stifled.

Sanctification. The Christian is made interiorly holy and is renewed through a willing reception of the divine grace and gifts (DS 1528) by which the faithful are consecrated to God and know themselves to be a new creation. In justification they are reborn and receive justifying grace (DS 1523). Grace and charity, infused in the soul, inhere in it (DS 1561). "The only formal cause [of justification] is the justice of God, not that by which God is just, but by which God makes us just so that when endowed with it we are renewed by God in the spirit of our mind" (DS 1529). Such a formula undoubtedly implied that justification is not purely forensic and that it does bring about a true change in the justified: "Not only are we held to be, but we are truly called and are just." Thus sanctifying grace is received as a gift that is intended to be permanent and places the faithful in the state of grace.

As it referred to the *only* formal cause of justification, the Tridentine decree implicitly excluded the notion of "double righteousness." That justification is the fruit of two formal causes—God's justice imputed to the believer and a human justice based on good works—had been proposed in 1542 at the Regensburg Colloquy and agreed upon by Melanchthon and Cardinal Gasparo Contarini, though it was immediately rejected by both Luther and Pope PAUL III. It was put before the Council of Trent by Cardinal Seripando. The council, however, did not accept it. Instead, it held that the imputation of God's justice, which is also the application of the merits of Christ, takes place in the gift of faith, hope, and love to the baptized. Through the merits of Christ's Passion, the justification of the impious unites them to Jesus Christ, through whom they receive the theological virtues of faith, hope, and love (DS 1530; 1561). The council considered grace and love to be inseparable, although it did not decide whether they are distinct or identical, so as not to favor either of two opinions that were held at the time by Catholic theologians. The interior renewal, "whereby from unjust one becomes just, and from enemy friend" (DS 1528), includes the reception of grace along with faith, hope, and love as gifts from God through the merits of Christ.

Free Acceptance. The reception of God's grace and gifts is not forced upon sinners (DS 1528). It is accepted in a free personal movement toward God in living faith (DS 1531), a faith that is manifest in hope and in love (DS 1530). Repentance is cited among the acts that dispose to justification (DS 1526). It is active in the process and at the moment of justification (cf. DS 1559). It is necessary to those who fall into sin after justification (DS 1542), and there is no remission of personal sins after baptism without penance and contrition. Thus the teaching of Trent implies repentance as one element in the sinner's willing reception of God's grace and gifts.

Related Conciliar Teachings. Regarding the gift of justice in justification the conciliar decree added several other points that are not without importance. First, grace is granted in varying degrees to various persons, depending on the Holy Spirit's good pleasure and each person's dispositions (DS 1529). This teaching on the inequality of grace sets aside the error of Pelagius and of some of the Protestants who claimed equal justice for all. Second, justice or grace is capable of increasing and is intended to increase as the faithful strive for perfection and make their way toward holiness. It grows in proportion with the good works that the just do when, by God's grace, they keep the commandments (DS 1535, 1574, 1582). Third, against what they took to be "the vain confidence of the heretics," the Tridentine bishops denied that the fact of one's own justification could be a point of faith: "No one can know with the certainty of faith, which cannot admit of error, that one has obtained God's grace" (DS 1533; cf. 1562). They did not, however, exclude the possibility of a moral certitude of being in grace, as was maintained in Scotist theology. Fourth, Trent rejected the absolute predestination of the elect and a predestination of others to evil (DS 1540, 1565–67), as also the possibility, outside of a private revelation, of having an antecedent certainty of one's final perseverance (DS 1541).

It should be noted, although this did not affect the substance of what they taught, that the council fathers assumed that as they preserved the old notion of merit their doctrine differed substantially from the Lutheran teaching that justification is by faith alone. Likewise, as they affirmed that grace can be lost, and is actually lost by every mortal sin and not only by infidelity (DS 1544, 1572), they thought that they contradicted the belief, held by some of the "Spiritual Reformers," that once it is given by God, justice cannot be lost again.

FROM TRENT TO VATICAN II

The Tridentine decree on justification considerably influenced later Catholic theology, being used as the central bulwark against what the theologians of the Counter-Reformation identified as the errors of the Reformers. This influence led to a rehabilitation of the realist trend in the organic concept of justification that had been developed in Thomism, although Scotist ideas were not systematically ignored. A typical example in this regard is Suarez's notion of the physical, though not metaphysical, incompossibility of the state of sin and the state of grace. Suarez toned down Thomist realism without disregarding it altogether. The Tridentine teaching further determined two emphases in the subsequent theology of justification. Its description of the interior renewal of the soul invited keeping the Aristotelian image of grace as a form that inheres in the soul. Its teaching on the voluntary acceptance of grace led to a pastoral insistence on the free cooperation of the faithful with grace. The point of debate in Catholic theology, however, shifted from habitual or sanctifying grace to actual grace. There were heated discussions between followers of the Dominican Dominic Bañez (1528–1604) and of the Jesuit Luis de Molina (1535–1600) regarding the nature of actual grace and the relations between free will and grace in human action.

The reaction to the Reformation led to exaggerations. Because they saw created grace as a form in the soul some authors tended to treat it as a thing and to overlook its essentially relative character, constant dependence on uncreated grace, the Holy Spirit. Moreover, a emphasis on free cooperation focused undue attention on human merit and led to giving a disproportionate importance to actual grace over sanctifying grace and uncreated grace. When they were not engaged in polemics with one another or against the Reformers and the theologians of Protestant Orthodoxy, the Catholic theologians of the seventeenth and eighteenth centuries generally restated the Tridentine teaching in light of the classical commentators of Thomas Aquinas, although some, following Suarez, incorporated various aspects of the Scotist perspective in their syntheses. In any case, apologetic and polemic concerns with Protestantism led them to stress the lifelong process of sanctification rather than its beginning in justification, and to focus the theology of justification on the passage from sin to grace.

Protestant Scholasticism. In the Protestant schools of the seventeenth century theological reflection became somewhat distant from the religious experience of the great Reformers. The writings of Luther were treated as source books that needed to be exegeted rationally in light of the inter-Lutheran agreement embodied in the Formula of Concord (1581). In this process many theologians turned to Aristotelian categories and logical tools in spite of Luther's misgivings about philosophy. The theology of justification tended to become a theory of conversion, one theme among many, rather than the very heart of thought and piety and the key to theology. The various aspects of the experience of justification repentance and faith, sense of unworthiness and evidence of divine filiation followed one another instead of coalescing. The nine-volume *Loci theologici* of Johann Gerhard (1582–1637) represents the acme of Lutheran orthodoxy. Like their counterparts in Roman Catholicism these theologians sought out Scripture and tradition for arguments that could lead, with the help of rational logic, to a systematic understanding of doctrine. Similar systems were built up by Reformed theologians, who found their chief inspiration in Calvin's *Institutio christianae religionis* and their doctrinal standards in the Calvinist Confessions, especially the Second Helvetic Confession (1566) and the

Westminster Confession (1646), and often also in the decisions of the Synod of Dort.

Pietism and Revivalism. In reaction to the rather dry intellectualism of Protestant orthodoxy, the rise of Pietism brought about a renewal of the theology of justification. Already in the sixteenth century the spiritual Reformers, many of them Anabaptists, understood faith to be an interior illumination coming from the Spirit. In England George Fox (1624–1691) and the Quakers carried this to an extreme that rendered the Church superfluous for those attentive to the Inner Light in their heart. Under the influence of Philip SPENER (1635–1705) in Germany, a drastic shift took place in systematic theology. The emphasis came to be placed on faith experienced as an overwhelming moment of conversion rather than on the dialectic of sin and righteousness. With Count Nikolaus von Zinzendorf (1700–1760) and the Moravian communities, religion became a mystical experience in which fear is absorbed in the assurance of salvation. Conversion was taken to be a complete transformation manifested in warm fervor. The theology of justification amounted to a description of the personal experience of conversion and rebirth. In the eighteenth and nineteenth centuries, similar pietistic emphases led, in the American colonies, to the enthusiastic revivals of the Connecticut valley, which in turn, through the Holiness movement of the nineteenth century, inspired a Pentecostal turnabout in communities where the centrality of Scripture gave way to that of the interior Spirit outwardly manifested.

The Wesleyan Reaction. The theology of justification that was developed in the seventeenth century by the Caroline divines of the Church of England incorporated many ideas from the Catholic tradition. The exclusivity of faith (*sola fides*) that had been at the heart of the Reformation was delicately balanced by the conviction that, as Augustine had observed, God does not save sinners against their will. In this case faith is a divine gift that needs so to be accepted as to act as a condition of justification. There thus crept into English theology a strong emphasis on the human work that is involved in the process of justification, sanctification, and salvation. In the eighteenth century, however, the philosophy of deism and the spread of varieties of Arianism in some sections of the Church of England had the effect of stifling the fruits of Caroline theology in many areas of the British Isles. A reaction, largely inspired by continental pietism, led to a powerful Evangelical movement, as may be seen in the life of John WESLEY (1703–1791), the initiator of Methodism.

Wesley, who had turned to piety as a student in Oxford and had visited the Moravien societies in Germany, found that his work as an Anglican priest, especially in the years he spent in Georgia, was largely a failure. He suddenly discovered the cause of this failure on May 24, 1738, at Aldersgate in London, when he found what had hitherto been missing in his life and ministry. As he listened to a lecture on the Epistle to the Romans he "found his heart strangely warmed" and underwent a profound conversion. As Wesley described it in his diary, this conversion was focused on a sense of personal salvation: "I felt I did trust in Christ, Christ alone, for my salvation; and an assurance was given me that he had taken away my sins, even mine, and saved me from the law of sin and death." Until this moment Wesley's work had been unknowingly self-centered. From that time on it was Christ-centered, and inseparably tied to a search for perfection on the model of biblical holiness. This implied a recovery of the centrality of justification by faith alone. But it also introduced a personal assurance of salvation in the theology of justification. What has been called "the Wesleyan reaction" in the evolution of Protestantism was indeed a restoration of justification by faith, without any condition on the human side, yet with an added dimension of awareness that had not been featured in the theologies of Luther or Calvin. By the same token, Wesley brought the necessity of good works back to the center, not indeed as conditions of salvation, but as necessary manifestations of effective justification. From this arose a new focus on moral conversion in Christian life and pastoral guidance, which became a feature of the Evangelical movements and revivals of the nineteenth century.

Schleiermacher and Liberal Protestantism. In the history of the Protestant Churches, the Wesleyan and Evangelical movements had to struggle with another fruit of the eighteenth century: the liberal Protestantism that grew out of the philosophy of the Enlightenment and in which the theology of justification lost its centrality. In 1799, as he defended religion against its "cultured despisers," Friedrich Schleiermacher (1768–1834) identified it with an intuitive sense of total dependence on a transcendent principle that believers call God. In light of this basic human experience he presented the Christian doctrines, in 1821 (*The Christian Faith*), as so many aspects of the human dependence on God as this is revealed in Jesus Christ. Faith is the Christian religious consciousness. It sees the historical Christ as the highest exemplification of total dependence on God. In this perspective justification is examined as the "second theorem" that explains and explores the "doctrine of regeneration" (109). Following conversion, which is the "first theorem" (108), it implies the forgiveness of sins and recognition of the converted as a child of God. Thus entering into living fellowship with Christ in his "kingly office," the believer is in a changed relation to God. This new Christian self-consciousness implies awareness of "the communication of the Spirit" (121).

As it was inspired by, but often went beyond, Schleiermacher, much of Protestant theology in the later nineteenth century took a turn toward a "liberalism" that was in danger of dilution into a sort of religious rationalism. The Christian message could then hardly be distinguished from the promotion of a humanist morality at the service of human progress and civilization. The Reformation doctrine of justification could hardly survive in such a context.

Neo-Orthodoxy. Liberal theology inevitably provoked reactions, and eventually a rehabilitation of the theology of justification. Albrecht Ritschl (1822–1889) was the first to attempt to restate the doctrine of justification by faith alone in its traditional sense, though without restoring it to the central place it had with Martin Luther. In his "dialectical" or existential theology, Søren KIERKEGAARD (1813–55) reemphasized both the centrality of the Word and the paradoxical character of the faith that justifies. Following World War I, the Swiss theologian Karl BARTH (1886–1968), in the second edition of his *Commentary on the Epistle to the Romans* (1921), formulated a powerful restatement of the theology of justification, which he brought back to centrality in his multivolume *Church Dogmatics* (1932–1967). He particularly insisted on the ties between justification and the work of Christ. The *sola fides* that is the means of justification implies *solus Christus* as the agent. It is the doctrine of Christ, and not only justification by faith alone, that is the *articulus stantis et cadentis ecclesiae*. As was shown, among others, by Hans Urs von Balthasar and Hans Küng, Barth's theology of justification is in close agreement with the Catholic tradition at its best. Barth's reflection comes near to the Catholic conviction on the ineffectiveness of all human effort unaided by grace.

The Neo-Scholastic Theology of Justification. Catholic theology in the twentieth century did not particularly stress the doctrine of justification. In light of the neo-scholasticism that had been advocated by LEO XIII and inserted in canon law as the official theology of seminaries (1917 CIC, canon 1366 2), the standard view was focused, on the one hand, on an interpretation of the Tridentine decree that overstressed its anti-Protestant bias and, on the other, on a systematic reading of the *Summa theologiae* of Thomas Aquinas (I II, q.113) that tended to ignore its historical conditioning.

In this neo-scholastic perspective, justification includes true remission of sins and removal of the state of sin, that is, the original sin that is made worse by the *habitus* created by repetitions of sinful actions. God does not consider a person just without making that person just, for it is God's knowledge of reality that causes it to be. Habitual sin is a permanent and guilty turning away from God as the supernatural goal of the creature. Its removal requires a reorientation to God, a voluntary deprivation or permanent rejection of the obstacles that impede the human striving for God. Since this cannot be done without grace and the accompanying gifts, the cessation or removal of sin implies the restoration of grace and gifts that will enable the sinner's reconversion to God. As God alone gives grace, so God alone forgives sin. The infusion of grace and gifts therefore means that a sinner recovers an habitual orientation to God as supernatural and final end. By grace, through faith, in hope and in love, the Christian effectively looks to God for salvation. Striving toward this supernatural end is the fruit of a dynamic principle that has its origin in God's gift and its setting in human nature, thus raising the human person to supernatural dignity.

The grace and gifts bestowed in justification activate the soul and its faculties in their obediential potency before God's action. Endowed with this deifying dynamism the sinner is just according to God's salvific will. Whether seen negatively as remission of sins or positively as infusion of grace, conversion implies free cooperation and a personal relationship with God that is necessarily voluntary. Removal of sin and reception of grace require the turning away from sin that is called repentance (contrition when it is total, attrition when incomplete), and a free turning to God in living faith, that is, faith with hope and charity. This voluntary cooperation in justification entails an awareness of moving away from sin and turning to God.

Justification is thus seen as the instantaneous changeover of a repentant sinner who is moved by God from sin to grace. As God forgives sin and infuses grace, the believer feels contrition and accedes to grace in faith, hope, and love (S.T. I–II, q.113, a.1; a.7–8). That the change in justification happens in an instant, however gradual and slow may have been its preparation, follows from the Aristotelian principle that the loss of one form is the gain of another (*corruptio unius est generatio alterius*). The cessation of the state of sin is the inception of the state of grace, and vice versa (S.T. I–II, q.113, a.7).

This analysis raises questions regarding the relations (1) between God's action and human cooperation, (2) between the forgiveness of sin and the infusion of grace as two aspects of a single divine act, and (3) between the components of human cooperation: contrition and faith with hope and charity. The solution, again, comes from the mutual priority and causality that scholastic philosophy identified as the law of every real change or mutation. In the line of formal causality the introduction of a new form determines, or causes, or is prior to, the cessation of the previous form. In the line of dispositive or material causality, however, the cessation of the previous form causes, or is prior to, the introduction of the new form. A new form is gained because a previous one is lost, and conversely a previous form is lost because a new one is gained. Sin is remitted because grace is infused, and grace is infused because sin is remitted, ''because'' expressing formal and dispositive causality, not efficient causality.

(1) God's Action and Human Cooperation. God is the mover and the repenting sinner is being moved, but as a free being that moves itself, that is, not without willing cooperation. The infusion of grace is prior to the human response and causes it by way of formal causality. Inversely, human free cooperation or voluntary reception is prior to the infusion of grace in the line of dispositive or material causality. Being the last disposition for grace, the acceptance of it causes the infusion of grace by making its reception possible. God's action and human cooperation condition one another in different ways; they do not hinder or oppose one another. The reception of grace presupposes a receptive soul, disposed for grace, this disposition being itself caused by grace itself.

(2) Remission of Sin and Infusion of Grace. That sin is forgiven because grace is infused, and grace infused because sin is forgiven, shows the metaphysical impossibility of separating the forgiveness of sin and the infusion of grace. It would be self-contradictory for God to infuse grace without forgiving sin, or to forgive sin without infusing grace. This seems to preclude a merely declarative, imputative, or forensic justification. It also excludes the incompossibility of sin and grace, as though God could *de potentia absoluta* (but does not *de potentia ordinata*) give grace while sin remains, or forgive sin without giving grace.

(3) Contrition and Faith with Charity. Perfect contrition exists when repentance is totally inspired by faith enlivened by the pure love of God. As such it is the final disposition of a repentant sinner for the gift of grace. Love for God in turn causes repentance to be true contrition. Contrition is perfect because of love, while as ultimate disposition it makes God's gift of love possible. Contrition and love condition one another; and this mutual conditioning enables them to coexist at the instant of justification. That contrition perfected by charity constitutes the human cooperation with God in justification implies that it is the only one way to be effectively ready for the infusion of grace, both in and outside the sacrament. Since there can be only one ultimate disposition for one form, only contrition is the sinner's final disposition for grace. The difference between sacramental and extrasacramental justification is accidental, regarding only the manner in which this ultimate disposition comes about.

Whence a trend in modern sacramental theology that so requires proper dispositions in the recipient of grace that it no longer accepts what used to be the common opinion, namely, that the sacrament makes up for imperfect dispositions.

Three systematic conclusions seem to follow that were generally accepted in the last decades before Vatican Council II:

(1) Justification is always relatively imperfect since grace is normally given while concupiscence remains. Were grace infused in the human soul by virtue of a natural disposition without free acceptance by each person, it would entail the restoration of natural, prelapsarian integrity. Because of the persistent attraction of evil it is possible for the just to lose grace, and morally impossible to remain in sanctifying grace and avoid all grave sin without the help of actual grace.

(2) Since the acceptance of the divine grace and gifts is indispensable to justification, a justified sinner may, by virtue of his awareness of repentance, faith, hope, and love, be also aware of grace received. There is normally, however, no direct evidence of the supernatural aspect of these dispositions and of grace itself, though the analysis of psychological dispositions may well show signs of the passage from sin to grace. One such sign is true contrition, which entails the effective resolution to abstain from sin. These signs may be sufficient to provide a moral certitude of being in the state of grace.

(3) The Council of Trent affirmed that justification entails relationships with God, Christ, and the Holy Spirit (DS 1525, 1529–1531) that are called in spiritual writings the indwelling of the Holy Trinity in the soul of the just. Since created grace and its gifts flow from uncreated grace, the indwelling Three Persons are directly involved in justification. Although the scholastic perspective points to created grace as the only formal cause and the only form of justification, uncreated grace, the Holy Spirit, may be likened to a ''quasi-form'' as the soul's indwelling Guest.

Pastoral Implications. Pastoral theology cannot be indifferent to the doctrine on justification, especially in the Thomist understanding that became standard in neoscholasticism.

Since a kind of cooperation with justifying grace is irreplaceable, sincerity and genuineness in religious practice are imperative. Without repentance perfected by charity, which includes faith and hope, no justification and no genuine religious life are possible. Whether one is justified by God in or outside the reception of a sacrament there is no substitute for the change of heart that bears fruit under grace. Thomism identifies this change of heart with contrition perfected by love. Sacramental grace, especially in the sacraments of initiation and of reconciliation, contributes to this contrition. This has inspired the insistence of contemporary moral theology and pastoral practice on the sacramental life.

The remains of concupiscence in the justified entail that it is not possible to live in grace without struggle and watchfulness. Unless they are assisted by healing grace, the justified are unable to remain in the state of grace. Because this help is always offered by God they can indeed persevere. Distrust of self, however, should go along with trust in God's never-failing grace, thus creating a spiritual equilibrium that is not always easy to obtain or maintain.

Since classical THOMISM finds an ontological change in the process of justification, some psychological repercussions of it may be perceived. Nevertheless the forgiveness of sin and the infusion of grace cannot be identified with the psychoanalytical resolution of a guilt complex and its attending peace of soul. Therapeutic methods are helpful in their own line, yet foreign to metaphysics and still more to the remission of sin by the pure gift of divine grace. While psychoanalysis may eventually free a person for a willing response to grace, it is no substitute for the theological return to God that is justifying grace.

AFTER VATICAN II

Neither Vatican I nor Vatican II had occasion to debate the doctrine of justification. Vatican II, however, created conditions in which Catholic theologians could take a new look at the doctrine of the Reformers, especially in the context of the bilateral dialogues with Lutherans and with Anglicans that were started in the wake of the council. Despite the anti-Protestant interpretation of the Tridentine decree that prevailed through the Counter-Reformation, a better knowledge of Luther by Catholic scholars in the mid-twentieth century and the ecumenical impetus coming from John XXIII opened what turned out to be unexpected possibilities for the overcoming of traditional polemics. It was in fact already apparent in theology on the eve of Vatican II that there was a convergence between Martin Luther's view of the Christian as *simul justus et peccator* and the Catholic teaching that concupiscence remains in the justified. What the Protestant view calls sinfulness in the justified bears some similarity to the inclination to evil that Catholic theology names concupiscence. Likewise, the Protestant idea that the justified relate to Christ and God in a trustful faith that initiates a conversion of life does not contradict the Catholic idea that created grace structures the state of the justified as a complex of new relationships with the Three divine Persons. It is because these relationships are real that created grace is needed to give them an objective setting in human life. Thus it was pos-

sible even before the ecumenical opening of Vatican II to present the Catholic doctrine on justification in a perspective that was closer to the position of the Reformers than had been the case in the heyday of the Counter-Reformation.

The bilateral dialogues that started in 1965 between Lutherans and Catholics paid attention early to the question of justification and to the frequent assumption that there is a contradiction between the Catholic and the Lutheran notions. Already in 1972 the International Joint Lutheran/Roman Catholic Commission noted in its statement, "The Gospel and the Church," that "a far-reaching agreement on the doctrine of justification appears possible." Both sides had to take account of the modern context of the question. Modern culture born of the Enlightenment, the FRENCH REVOLUTION, and the industrial and technological advances of the nineteenth and twentieth centuries requires a new language and, to a large extent, a new method for the presentation of the Christian faith and its theology. In 1963 the Lutheran World Federation meeting in Helsinki had found itself unable to arrive at a consensus on the contemporary meaning of justification. Its concluding document, *Justification Today,* recognized that modern culture is more concerned with the global meaning and conditions of life than with Luther's original questions, how to find a gracious God and how to be just in God's eyes. It reaffirmed the centrality of justification for Christian faith, while admitting the urgency of new expressions of the doctrine that would be attuned to the emerging theologies of Africa and of Asia.

Lutheran reflection in the last decades before the third millennium tended to go in two general directions. On the one side, some authors presented justification in light of an existential hermeneutics, often influenced by the *Systematic Theology* of Paul Tillich. Justification is then seen as the divine response to the conundrum of sinful existence. On the other side, others, who remained closer to Luther and the confessional books, saw justification as a passage from death to life which ought to act as a "metaprinciple" behind all Christian affirmations and actions, and in the light of which all Christian institutions and theologies should be assessed. Among Catholics the multiplication of unbiased studies on Martin Luther and a better knowledge of the sixth session of the Council of Trent gave rise to a new appreciation of the Reformer's intents and actions.

The effect of these developments was keenly felt when the official dialogues began to deal at length with the problem of justification. In 1983, "Lutherans and Catholics in Dialogue" in the United States issued a common statement on the topic. This document and the supporting material describe the situation between the churches in and after the sixteenth century, and survey the convergence of thought that is manifest in recent developments. Its concluding "declaration" (nn. 161–164) attempts to do justice both to Luther's central insight and to the decrees of Trent. It amounts to a modern formulation of the doctrine of justification. In this text "the gospel" is identified with the proclamation of "God's creative graciousness offered to us and to everyone for healing and reconciliation." It is an "undeserved gift which is granted and made known in faith." Furthermore, justification is acknowledged to be the heart of Christian life and the critical principle for all theology and life in the Church.

In 1987, the second commission of the Anglican-Roman Catholic International Consultation (ARCIC-II) issued an agreed statement, "Salvation in the Church," in which justification was set in the broad context of the traditional theology of salvation. No difference was found between the Catholic and the Anglican doctrines. Furthermore, in 1985 unofficial consultations that took place in Germany reached the conclusion that the anathemas of the Council of Trent against the doctrines of the Lutheran Reformation, especially in regard to justification by faith, have become for the most part obsolete, and that many of them in any case had condemned doctrines that were not those of the Lutheran Reformation. The question was pursued by an ad hoc study group of nine Catholic theologians, who presented their report to the Holy See in 1994. This in turn led to a largely unexpected ecumenical breakthrough, in the form of an agreement between the Lutheran World Federation and the Pontifical Council for the Promotion of Christian Unity concerning the Tridentine canons on justification. The text of this agreement was finalized in 1997 after extensive consultations in the Lutheran and Catholic churches. In the city of Augsburg on Aug. 31, 1999, officials of the Lutheran World Federation (LWF) and of the Catholic Church (Cardinal Edward Cassidy and several bishops) signed a statement that supported the "Joint Declaration on the Doctrine of Justification." The text declared:

> Consensus in basic truths of the doctrine of justification exists between Lutherans and Catholics. . . . The earlier mutual doctrinal condemnations do not apply to the teaching of the dialogue partners as presented in the Joint Declaration. . . . Lutherans and Catholics will continue their efforts ecumenically in their common witness to interpret the message of justification in language relevant for human beings today, and with reference both to individual and social concerns of our times.

This solemn agreement, the first of its kind in the history of the ecumenical movement, is limited to the under-standing of justification by faith. Neither does it answer all the questions raised reciprocally by Protestants and Catholics since the Reformation; nor does it speak for all Lutherans since there are some Lutheran churches that remain outside the LWF. In addition, a few churches of the LWF have not approved the text, and a number of theologians in Germany have even protested against it. Nonetheless, the document and its signing have two major theological consequences. First, the theologies of justification that developed during the Counter-Reformation and in neo-scholasticism have become untenable in the Catholic Church, at least insofar as they involve a misunderstanding of some basic Lutheran tenets. Second, Catholic theology is now committed to making a common effort with Lutheran theologians to work out together the implications of the "Joint Declaration" for the life of the churches.

Bibliography: J. RIVIÈRE, *Dictionnaire de théologie catholique*, ed. A. VACANT et al. (Paris 1903–50) 8:2042–2227. A. VACANT et al, ed. *Dictionnaire de théologie catholique*, 15 v. (Paris 1903–50) Tables générales 2:2782–96. H. ROCKERT, *Die Rechtfertigungslehre auf dem Tridentinischen Konzil* (Bonn 1925). M. PIETTE, *John Wesley in the Evolution of Protestantism* (New York 1937). W. CANNON, *The Theology of John Wesley, with Special Reference to the Doctrine of Justification* (Nashville 1946). W. DETTLOFF, *Die Lehre von der acceptatio divina bei I. D. Scotus* (Werl 1954). H. KÜNG, *Rechtfertigung: Die Lehre Karl Barths und eine katholische Besinnung* (Einsiedeln 1957) bibliog. 288–304. J. OLAZARAN, *Documentos inéditos Tridentinos sobre la justificacion* (Madrid 1957). K. RAHNER, *Schriften zur Theologie* (Einsiedeln 1954–1962) 4:237–271. O. E. BORGEN, ed., *John Wesley. An Autobiographical Sketch of the Man and His Thought, Chiefly from His Letters* (Leiden 1966). B. HÄGGLUND, *The Background of Luther's Doctrine of Justification in Late Medieval Theology* (Philadelphia 1971). G. H. TAVARD, *Justification: An Ecumenical Study* (New York 1983). H. G. ANDERSON, T. A. MURPHY, J. A. BURGESS, eds., *Justification by Faith: Lutherans and Catholics in Dialogue VII* (Minneapolis 1985). A. E. MCGRATH, *Justitia Dei. A History of the Christian Doctrine of Justification,* 2 v. (Cambridge 1986). H. MEYER and G. GASSMANN, eds., *Rechtfertigung im Oekumenischen Dialog* (Frankfurt-am-Main 1987). ARCIC-II, *Salvation and the Church* (London 1987). *Justification by Grace through Faith. Joint Declaration on the Doctrine of Justification. Study Resources for Congregations and Parishes* (Ottawa 1999).

[G. H. TAVARD/P. DE LETTER]

JUSTIN I, BYZANTINE EMPEROR

Reigned July 1, 518 to Aug. 1, 527; b. near the fortress of Bederiana in Thrace, *c.* 450, a Latin-speaking area which had suffered from Hunnic and Ostrogothic invasions that had made life difficult for the peasantry. In the reign of the emperor, Leo (457–474), Justin, along with two other young farmers from Bederiana, set out for Constantinople with only some parched bread in their pockets, and once there, they found that Leo was creating a new palace guard, the *Excubitores*, that was intended to counterbalance the Germanic troops in the city. The three young farmers were enrolled. We hear nothing further of Justin's companions, but he himself rose through the ranks and under the emperor, Anastasius I, he became the count, that is, commander of the Excubitors. When Anastasius I died suddenly in 518, Justin was chosen emperor even though he was already an old man, and uneducated, although it is unlikely that he was completely illiterate. His wife, Lupicina, whom he had purchased as a slave, freed and married, became empress, taking the more genteel name, Euphemia. He had no children, but as his fortunes rose, he brought his nephews to the capital and saw to it that they received an education.

One of these, Flavius Petrus Sabbatius, the son of his sister, he adopted with the name Justinian. By 518, Justinian was already a guardsman in the Scholarians, the largely ornamental imperial guard, and he became his uncle's right-hand man, so much so that Justin's reign was considered by some contemporaries as part of Justinian's. The empress, Euphemia, disapproved of THEODORA (1), and Justinian could not marry her before Euphemia's death (*c.* 523). Four months before his own death, Justin made Justinian co-emperor.

At the start of his reign, Justin, who recognized the supremacy of Rome in matters of dogma, was determined to end the impasse over the *Henotikon* of the emperor, Zeno. It was promulgated to reconcile the Monophysites and the Chalcedonians, but instead it resulted in the ACACIAN SCHISM (484–519), which divided the churches of Rome and Constantinople. After a year of negotiation, Justin met the demands of Pope Hormisdas and union with Rome was restored. During the negotiations, a group of monks from Scythia Minor (Dobrudja) went to Rome with Justinian's approbation to seek Hormisdas's approval of a compromise known as Theopaschitism, but Hormisdas rejected their formula. Later, however, (March 15, 533) Justinian would publish his own acceptance of Theopaschitism and Pope John I would in turn agree to it (March 25, 534). Justin took vigorous measures against the Monophysites in Syria. The patriarch of Antioch, Severus, and more than 50 bishops were deposed. In spite of Pope Hormisdas's urging, however, Justin would not extend the persecution to Egypt, where Monophysitism was deeply entrenched.

In 523 to 524, Justin moved against the Arian heretics in the Eastern empire, intending to consecrate the wealthy Arian churches as Catholic, probably with the aim of eliminating ARIANISM. In Italy, Theoderic, the king of the Arian Ostrogoths, reacted angrily, commanding Pope John I to go to Constantinople to intercede with Justin and Justinian. The pope was received in Constantinople with high honors, and while there, he performed a coronation ceremony for Justin, thereby recognizing Justin as his sovereign. Imperial policy towards the Arians remained tolerant for the next ten years, until after the Byzantine reconquest of Africa. But Theoderic's suspicions were aroused, and when Pope John returned to Italy, he threw him into prison, where he died on May 18, 526.

Justin launched the age of Justinian, which was his greatest achievement, and he has been overshadowed almost completely by his successor. But his own career was remarkable; he rose from the humblest beginnings and brought his family into positions of power and influence. At the start of his reign he showed a degree of independence. For example, his abrupt reversal of Anastasius's pro-Monophysite policy and his submission to Pope Hormisdas was his own decision, though it was supported by the empress, Euphemia, and perhaps with less enthusiasm, by Justinian. In his final years, when he was old and ill, he fell completely under Justinian's domination.

Bibliography: E. STEIN, *Histoire du Bas-Empire* (Amsterdam 1949) 2:219–273. J. B. BURY, *A History of the Later Roman Empire from the Death of Theodosius I to the death of Justinian, A.D. 395–565* (London 1923) 2:16–23. A. H. M. JONES, *The Later Roman Empire, 284–602. A Social, Economic and Administrative Survey,* 3 v. (Oxford 1964). A. A. VASILIEV, *Justin the First* (Cambridge, MA 1950) the basic work. J. A. S. EVANS, *The Age of Justinian: The Circumstances of Imperial Power* (London 1996) 96–110. G. GREATREX, "Justin I and the Arians," *Studia Patristica* 34 (2001) 72–81.

[J. A. S. EVANS]

JUSTIN II, BYZANTINE EMPEROR

Justin II, Byzantine Emperor, the son of Justinian I's sister, Vigilantia, reigned nominally from Nov. 14, 565 to his death Oct. 5, 578. However his wife, Sophia, a niece of the empress, Theodora, took over the reins of power when he suffered a mental breakdown, and she persuaded Justin I, in a brief moment of lucidity, to appoint the count of the Excubitors, Tiberius, as emperor on Dec. 7, 574.

On his accession, Justin reversed Justinian I's policy of appeasing the empire's enemies on the frontiers with subsidies. In 572, he repudiated the peace treaty Justinian had negotiated with the Persians ten years earlier, and refused further subsidies, with the result that war was renewed. After some initial success, the Byzantines suffered disastrous defeat, losing the fortress of Daras to Persia. It was the news of this loss that triggered Justin's insanity. Sophia was forced to buy peace. Justin also ended the subsidies Justinian I had made to the Avars, but after the Byzantine debacle on the Persian frontier, the Avar khan was able to extort a generous payment. The Avars consolidated their control north of the Danube, helping the Lombards to destroy the Gepids, and then pushing the Lombards to leave for Italy in 568. The Lombard invaders found Italy ill-prepared; Justin could not spare reinforcements and the able but autocratic Narses, who had conquered the Ostrogoths (552) and might have organized resistance, had been dismissed on the eve of the invasion.

For six years, Justin and Sophia, who were initially sympathetic to the Monophysites, tried to find a solution to the schism between them and the orthodox, but in vain. Finally (March 22, 571), Justin turned to persecution and issued a comprehensive creed which all bishops, priests and monks had to sign or go to prison. Justin also brought about a short-lived union of the Armenian church with Constantinople at the start of his reign, when the Armenian Christians in Persian-controlled Persarmenia were hard pressed by Persian Zororastrians, and sought his help. He is supposed to have fixed Christmas to December 25, but it still fell on Jan. 6, in 1601.

Bibliography: A. A. VASILIEV, *A History of the Byzantine Empire* (Madison, WI 1952; repr. 1964). A V. CAMERON, "The Empress Sophia," *Byzantion* 45 (1975) 5–21; "The Artistic Patronage of Justinian II," *Byzantion* 50 (1980) 62–84.; "The Early Religious Policies of Justin II," *Studies in Church History* 13 (1976) 51–67. P. GOUBERT, *Byzance avant l'Islam I* (Paris 1951). H. TURTLEDOVE, "Justin II's Observance of Justinian' Persian Treaty of 562," *Byzantinische Zeitschrift* 76 (1983) 292–303.

[J. A. S. EVANS]

JUSTIN MARTYR, ST.

Christian philosopher and apologist; b. Flavia Neapolis (Shechem, modern Nablus, in Samaritan territory) of Greek parents; d. Rome, *c.* 165. His father was Priscus; his grandfather, Bacchius. With various teachers at Ephesus he studied philosophy: Stoic, Peripatetic, Pythagorean, and finally Platonist. His quest was for religious truth, and Platonism spoke of the vision of God. But an old Christian by the seashore undermined his Platonism, spoke of the Old Testament Prophets, and converted him to Christianity. He had already been impressed by the martyrs. For a time he taught Christian philosophy in Ephesus, but left soon after 135. He next appears in Rome, teaching at his house, apparently on the Viminal. He disputed with the Cynic philosopher Crescens. About 165 he was delated to the city prefect Rusticus and martyred for his faith. In the ninth century he was introduced in the martyrology of FLORUS OF LYONS on April 13. Leo XIII transferred him to April 14. The Greek Acts of Justin's martyrdom rest on contemporary record and survive

St. Justin Martyr, woodcut.

in a good MS tradition. In Byzantine times many works circulated under his name; but from the three collections of writings ascribed to him in MSS (Paris. Gr. 451, dated 914; Paris. Gr.450, dated 1364; and a Strassburg codex of *c.* 1300 destroyed in 1870), criticism allows as authentic only the two apologies and the *Dialogue with Trypho the Jew,* a corrupt text of which is transmitted by Paris. Gr. 450. *Apologia II* is a supplement to *Apologia I,* which was addressed to Antoninus Pius soon after 150. The *Dialogue,* purporting to represent a debate at Ephesus in 135, was written after *Apologia I.* To *Apologia I* Justin appended a rescript of Hadrian of 124; this document is genuine.

Justin and Philosophy. As a Christian philosopher, Justin adopted the philosopher's cloak. He describes his conversion from Platonism to Christianity in such a way as to imply that there is no sharp discontinuity between them: Christianity fulfills the highest aspirations of Plato. Justin regards both the Bible and Plato as agreed: that God is transcendent, unchangeable, incorporeal, impassible, beyond time and space; that the world is created (Justin does not say created out of nothing); and that the soul is akin to God and has free will. Not, indeed, that Plato is always right: he mistakenly thought that the soul is naturally immortal and undergoes transmigration. But Plato correctly saw the deceit in pagan cult and myth. So Christianity can have no compromise with pagan religion, but has much in common with the best philosophers. Accordingly, Justin presents his faith as a virtually corrected Platonism, expressed in forms suitable for universal apprehension even by the uneducated, and elevated above the uncertainties of human reasoning by the gift of supernatural revelation. An almost equal optimism appears in Justin's estimate of STOICISM, excellent in its ethical teaching, but mistaken in adopting materialism, pantheism, and cosmic fatalism.

Justin has two ways of explaining how philosophers have found the truth. First, they have studied the Old Testament, whence they learned, e.g., of punishment hereafter. The reference to the divine triad in the second (pseudo-) Platonic epistle shows that Plato had learned from Moses of the mystery of the Trinity. (So Justin first attests the coming together of the Christian Trinity with late Platonic speculation.) Because the divine oracles are obscure and because allegory can be penetrated only through inspiration from the divine Author, the philosophers have erred. For example, the Stoic belief in a cycle of cosmic conflagrations "misunderstands" the fire of God's judgment. Second, the philosophers have also discovered truth independently of the Biblical revelation. Christ, the divine LOGOS, is the universal reason, the "seminal logos" in which all rational beings participate; therefore seeds of truth are found in everyone endowed with reason, particularly in the most gifted. Disagreements among philosophers show that each has but a partial apprehension; Christ is the whole Logos. Socrates, like Abraham, was a "Christian before Christ." Justin implies the thesis developed by CLEMENT OF ALEXANDRIA that philosophy is God's gift to the Greeks, a preparation for the gospel parallel to the Old Testament.

Justin's philosophy is eclectic, not in the sense of seeking to reconcile everyone and everything, but in taking the Biblical revelation as the criterion of truth and welcoming all philosophy compatible with it. In fact, the philosophy of the educated public he addresses is already a fusion of Stoic ethics and Platonic metaphysics. The distinctive and original feature of his thought lies in his conception of a divine plan in history, bringing together the Old Testament and the highest aspirations of the Greeks as two tributaries of the great river of Christianity. As a thinker, Justin should not be overestimated, but he was as good a Platonist as most of his pagan contemporaries; it is a measure of his impact that the anti-Christian writer CELSUS took him very seriously. Of the three classical arguments of ancient apologetics (miracles, prophecies, and the spread of the gospel), the argument from prophecy is prominent in Justin's armory, not only in the *Dialogue with Trypho the Jew,* but also in *Apologia I* addressed to the emperor (*see* APOLOGETICS).

Justin's Theology. Justin's Platonism seriously affects his theology of the relation between the Father and the Logos. Arguing against Trypho's thesis that Biblical monotheism excludes the honor in which Christians hold Jesus, Justin replies that the theophanies of the Old Testament imply the existence of "another God," "other than the Father in number, not in will"; for the supreme Father is too remote and transcendent to be in direct contact with this world. The presuppositions of the argument had been made commonplace by PHILO JUDAEUS, but it is not certain that Justin had read Philo. The presuppositions were later exploited by ARIANISM until Justin's legacy was finally purged by Augustine's *De Trinitate.*

Because Justin is distinguishing "Father" and "Son" as God transcendent and God immanent, he remains unclear about the work of the Holy Spirit, who (he says) is "in the third rank," except as inspiring the Prophets. Apart from his Logos theology, Justin is the most eloquent representative of the popular theology of the second century with its characteristic credal stress on the historic facts of Redemption—passionately opposed to the DOCETISM and GNOSTICISM that spiritualized away both the historicity of the gospel and the hope of resurrection, and acutely aware of the conflict with MARCION's denial that the Old Testament God is Father of Jesus Christ. Justin wrote a treatise against Marcion that is lost. He insists that the Incarnation is the culmination of the Creator's plan. Christ as Logos is the agent in creation, manifesting Himself to the Patriarchs, and finally taking of Mary our entire manhood: body, reason, and soul. To the Pauline typology of Adam and Christ, Justin adds the analogy of Eve with Mary, seeing in this "recapitulation" a proof of the unity of Old and New Testaments and the continuity of creation and Redemption. Here Justin contributed much to the thought of Irenaeus and Tertullian. Anti-Gnostic polemic may also be seen in his eschatology: preceded by Elijah as forerunner, Christ will return to a renewed Jerusalem for 1,000 years until the final resurrection. Justin thinks it heresy to hold that souls ascend to heaven immediately at death. A toleration that he extends to fellow Christians who do not accept the virgin birth is not accorded to those who deny millennial hopes.

Church and Sacraments. Though undeveloped, Justin's doctrine of the Church stresses unity and universality. The Church is the true Israel, vindicated against rival sects by being the object of persecution. The Romans ought to recognize an ally in it and suppress the heretics. To dispel pagan suspicion that the Sacraments are black magic Justin describes Baptism and the Eucharist. His account is noteworthy for references to pagan analogies (e.g., a Mithraic initiation ceremony with bread and water), which Justin explains as diabolical counterfeits.

(DEMONOLOGY is prominent in Justin's world view.) Baptism, which is washing with water in the name of the Trinity, signifies remission of sins, regeneration, "illumination," and transference from necessity to freedom. The weekly Eucharist is thanksgiving for both creation and Redemption. After readings from Prophets and Apostles, a sermon, prayers, and the kiss of peace, the "president" is given bread and wine mixed with water (the stress on dilution meets pagan gossip about Christian inebriation) and offers a long prayer of thanksgiving. The deacons distribute the Eucharist to the baptized, who receive it not as bread and drink, but as Jesus' flesh and blood. They also take the Sacrament to absent members.

Justin is a crucial witness to the emerging New Testament corpus. He cites synoptic sayings as from "the apostles' memoirs," probably using a synoptic gospel harmony that his follower TATIAN enlarged to include St. John. Justin's tradition included a few apocryphal points and sayings diverging from canonical forms. The Apocalypse he regards as the work of the Apostle John. He never names St. Paul but has many echoes of several Epistles, including Hebrews. He is the first certain writer to use Acts. His knowledge of St. John's Gospel is probable.

Justin was not translated into Latin before 1554. His influence is marked above all in IRENAEUS, TERTULLIAN, HIPPOLYTUS, and ORIGEN, who built on foundations laid by him. Between the Apostles and Irenaeus he is much the greatest figure.

Feast: April 14; June 1 among the Greeks.

Bibliography: JUSTIN MARTYR, *The Dialogue with Trypho,* tr. A. L. WILLIAMS (New York 1930), well-annotated translation. E. J. GOODSPEED, *Die ältesten Apologeten* (Leipzig 1914), critical apparatus misleading. R. KNOPF and G. KRÜGER, *Ausgewählte Märtyrerakten* (3d ed. Tübingen 1929). W. SCHMID, "Die Textüberlieferung der Apologie des Justin," *Zeitschrift für die neutestamentliche Wissenchaft und die Kunde der älteren Kirche* 40 (1941) 87–138. C. ANDRESEN, *Logos und Nomos: Die Polemik des Kelsos wider das Christentum* (Berlin 1955); *Die Religion in Geschichte und Gegenwart.* 6 v. (3d ed. Tübingen 1957–63) 3:1076. H. WEY, *Die Funktionen der bösen Geister* (Winterthur 1957). W. PANNENBERG, "Die Aufnahme des philosophischen Gottesbegriffs," *Zeitschrift für Kirchengeschichte* 70 (1959) 1–45. K. GROSS, *Lexicon für Theologie und Kirche,* 5:1225–26. J. QUASTEN, *Patrology* (Westminster, Md.) 1:196–219, bibliog.

[H. CHADWICK]

JUSTINA OF AREZZO, BL.

Baptized Francuccia Bezzoli; BENEDICTINE nun, ANCHORITE; b. Arezzo, Italy; d. there, Mar. 12, 1319. She entered the convent of Santa Maria del Ponte in her native city at the age of 13 and later, with the permission of her

Justinian I, relief portrait by Gaetano Cecere.

superiors, left the convent and joined an anchoress named Lucia living in a cell near Civitella. She remained there alone after the death of her companion, until blindness forced her return to Arezzo, where she lived for another 20 years exhibiting great patience and prayerfulness. Her cult was confirmed in 1890, and her relics are kept in Santo Spirito in Arezzo. She is invoked in cases of blindness and for other diseases of the eyes.

Feast: March 12.

Bibliography: *Acta Sanctorum,* Mar. 2:238–241. *Spicilegium monasticum* 1 (Rome 1896) 19–34. A. M. ZIMMERMANN, *Kalendarium Benedictinum: Die Heiligen und Seligen des Benediktinerorderns und seiner Zweige* 1:318, 322. A. M. ZIMMERMANN, *Lexikon für Theologie und Kirche²* 5:1226. A. BUTLER, *The Lives of the Saints* 1:578–579.

[C. R. BYERLY]

JUSTINIAN I, BYZANTINE EMPEROR

Reigned 527 to 565; legislator, theologian, restorer of the Roman Empire, b. Tauresium, probably modern Caricin Grad, 482, d. Constantinople, Nov. 14, 565.

Flavius Petrus Sabbatius Justinianus was the son of an obscure Thracian named Sabbatius and of a sister of the future emperor JUSTIN I. His native tongue was Latin and his family Catholic, and evidently unquestioning supporters of the Chalcedonian Creed. He received a good education thanks to his uncle Justin, who served in the guard under the emperors Leo I and Anastasius, rising to the rank of Count of the Excubitors, and at some point Justin adopted him: hence the name "Justinianus." At the time of Justin's enthronement (July 1, 518), Justinian was a *candidatus* (the name refers to his white uniform) in the Palatine guard known as the Scholarians, and he immediately became a *comes illustris* and Justin's close counselor. He supported Justin's policy of repairing relations with the papacy, which had developed into open rupture under Anastasius, and on March 28, 519, the ACACIAN SCHISM was finally healed and Rome and Constantinople were reconciled. He lent support to the Scythian monks who tried to get Pope Hormisdas to accept the Theopaschite formula as orthodox, and though Hormisdas refused, his successor Pope John I was to prove amenable. On the assassination of his rival Vitalian, he became a commander of the troops in Constantinople (*magister militum praesentalis*) in July 420, and the next year, he became consul and celebrated his inauguration with magnificent games. His marriage to THEODORA had to be postponed until after the death of Empress Euphemia, who disapproved of Theodora's earlier life as an actress and prostitute. On April 1, 527, the ailing Emperor Justin gave him the title of Augustus, and on April 4, the patriarch Epiphanius crowned him coemperor. Theodora (d. June 548) was associated with him as Augusta. Perhaps because of their humble origins, the imperial couple encouraged elaborate court ceremonial, and Theodora in particular insisted on all the marks of reverence which were her due.

Imperial Reorganization. On the death of Justin I (Aug. 1, 527), Justinian became sole emperor, and commenced a plan of repair and restoration on the political, religious and legislative fronts. The empire was gravely menaced by barbarian incursions from without and by heresies in the Christian church from within. He reorganized the military, and overthrew the Vandal kingdom in Africa (533–534), and reorganized civil and ecclesiastical affairs in new African prefecture. He destroyed the Ostrogothic kingdom in Italy (535–552) and when so-called "Endless Peace" (533) with Persia collapsed after seven years, he continued the Persian War with varying degrees of success. The Persian destruction of Antioch in 540 marked the low point of imperial fortunes in the east, and the arrival of bubonic plague, which reached Constantinople in 542, drastically reduced the empire's manpower resources. In 530, Justinian recognized Harith, the sheik of the Christian Arab clan known as the Ghassanids, as phylarch and ally, and entrusted the defense of the south Syrian frontier to him. In Egypt, where the First Cataract had marked the southern frontier since the time of the emperor Diocletian, Justinian closed the temple of Isis at Philae in 537, and after 543, the three Nubian kingdoms to the south of Philae were converted to Christianity. In the Crimea, civil war broke out after Grod, the king of the "Huns" (proto-Bulgars) came to Constantinople for Christian baptism (528) and on his return was killed in an anti-Byzantine insurrection aroused by the pagan priests who were incensed at Grod's efforts to spread Christianity in his realm. Justinian moved quickly to safeguard Bosporus in the Crimea and made it a center of resistance to the Huns. In the Balkans where there were constant invasions by raiding parties of proto-Bulgars and Slavs, he built numerous forts and places of refuge and prevented any permanent settlements of Slavs south of the Danube.

Justinian almost lost his throne to an uprising (Jan. 13–18, 532) known as the Nika revolt from the battle cry *nika* ("conquer!") which the rebels used. The Blues and the Greens, the colors of the two major groups of chariot-racing fans in the Hippodrome, allied against him, took control of the streets and set fire to large areas of Constantinople. Justinian and his court were on the point of taking flight when Empress Theodora rallied them to make a final effort. Belisarius and Mundo, a Gepid prince who had entered Justinian's service, led out their troops, caught the rebels massed in the Hippodrome where they were acclaiming Anastasius' nephew Hypatius as emperor, and massacred them. Some 30,000 were reportedly slain. The revolt had won the support of much of the Constantinople senate, and once it collapsed, Justinian needed to fear no more opposition from that quarter. The fire had destroyed the center of the city, including the Theodosian church of HAGIA SOPHIA, and Justinian seized the opportunity to rebuild magnificently. He employed the architects Anthemius of Tralles and Isidore of Miletus to build a new Hagia Sophia, a domed basilica that pushed the limits of contemporary engineering skill. An earthquake on Dec. 14, 557 opened a fissure in the dome, and the following spring (May 7) the dome collapsed, almost killing the masons who were repairing it. The church was restored according to the plans of Isidore the Younger, who made the dome higher so as to reduce its outward thrust. The old patriarchal cathedral of Hagia Eirene was also destroyed in the Nika riots and was rebuilt, though the rebuilt church was burned again in 564. The Holy Apostles church, built by CONSTANTIUS II, was unharmed by the Nika riots, but it had fallen into disrepair and was completely rebuilt (536). Tradition attributed its construction to Theodora. It provided the model for San Marco in Venice with its five cupolas.

Religious Policy. Deeply interested in theology and convinced that, as emperor and vicegerent of God, he possessed authority over matters of religion, he undertook to repress pagans, heretics, and Samaritans, and unlike previous emperors, he lumped Jews together with other non-believers, even though Judaism was still a *religio licita*. However in practice he seems not to have extended his repressive measures to the Jews, and archaeology reveals that in Palestine, his reign was a golden age of synagogue building in spite of the law forbidding Jews to construct new synagogues. He ruled that the Scriptures could be read in synagogues either in Greek or the local language of the congregation, but he prohibited use of the *Mishnah*. His repression of paganism was harsh: he deprived pagans of the right to teach or inherit and in 529, he closed down the Neoplatonic Academy in Athens which had become an intellectual center for pagan revival. Justinian's reign marks the end of the long, unequal struggle between Christianity and paganism. Samaritan revolts in 529 and 556 were suppressed savagely; the 529 revolt reportedly left 100,000 Samaritans dead or enslaved, and deprived large areas of Palestine of cultivators. After a vain effort to convert the Manichees, Montanists, Macedonians (PNEUMATOMACHIANS) and Ophites, he persecuted them. The Montanists resisted vigorously, some of them shutting themselves up in their churches and setting them on fire.

At the instance of Theodora, who was herself Monophysite, and a Monophysite advocate at the imperial court, Justinian softened the repressive measures applied during the reign of Justin I. In 532, he held a colloquy at Constantinople between the moderate Monophysites who looked to the exiled patriarch of Antioch, Severus, as their leader, and representative Catholic bishops, and personally presided over the third session in a vain attempt to find an agreement. He published his own confession of faith in the form of an edict (March 15, 533) which was based on the Theopaschite formula that stated that one of the Trinity suffered in the flesh, and persuaded Pope JOHN I to accept it. When the Sleepless Monks (*Akoimetoi*), tireless champions of the Chalcedonian Creed, protested, the pope excommunicated them.

In 535, Empress Theodora arranged for the installation of two new patriarchs: Theodosius as successor to Timothy IV of Alexandria (February 10), and Anthimus, bishop of Trebizond as successor to Epiphanius (d. June 5) of Constantinople. Anthimus was considered Catholic but Theodora knew that in fact, he was sympathetic to Monophysitism, and when he met Severus, the two easily came to an agreement. However in March 536, Pope Agapetus arrived in Constantinople as an emissary of the Ostrogothic king Theoderic, and he convinced Justinian of the error of his ways. The pope excommunicated and deposed Anthimus and consecrated Mennas as patriarch. Severus fled to Egypt, and Theodora protected Anthimus by hiding him in the women's quarters of the Great Palace, where he was discovered after her death (548). Agapetus' sudden death (April 22) did nothing to lessen Justinian's new resolve to enforce orthodoxy. A synod (May 2–June 4) confirmed Mennas as patriarch and condemned both Anthimus and Severus, and Justinian undertook to repress Monophysitism throughout the empire, not excepting Egypt (Aug. 6, 536). Theodosius, the Monophysite patriarch whom Theodora supported, had retained his see for almost 17 months, but only with the help of imperial troops, for his position was challenged by the Julianists, a.k.a. Aphthartodocetists, a more radical wing of the Monophysites. Now he was summoned to Constantinople where the emperor urged him to accept the Chalcedonian Creed, and when he refused, he was replaced by a Chalcedonian patriarch. Theodosius was sent off to the fortress of Derkos in Thrace with some 300 Monophysite clergy, but Theodora soon secured more comfortable quarters for them in the Palace of Hormisdas next to the Great Palace, and there he lived until his death in 566, recognized by the Monophysites after Severus' death as their leader. In 541, when the Ghassanid phylarch Harith approached Theodora with a request for a Monophysite bishop for his tribe, Theodosius, with Theodora's blessing, consecrated two monks, Theodore as metropolitan of Bostra and Jacob Baradaeus as metropolitan of Edessa. Jacob, before his death (578) in turn consecrated 27 metropolitan bishops and some 100,000 clergy, thus creating a Monophysite hierarchy separate from the Chalcedonians, who became known as "Melkites" after the Semitic word for "king".

The "Three Chapters." While Rome was under siege by the Goths (537–538), Empress Theodora had Pope SILVERIUS I deposed by Belisarius on suspicion of treason, and Vigilius I, who had promised Theodora to be more flexible, was chosen in his place. Vigilius' nuncio (*apokrisarios*) in Constantinople, Pelagius, later Pope PELAGIUS I, became Justinian's counselor. His position as favorite adviser, however, was usurped by two Origenist monks from Palestine, THEODORE ASCIDAS and Domitian, who caught Justinian's attention when they came to Constantinople in 536 to take part in a synod. Pelagius served an an imperial appointee at the synod of Gaza which replaced Paul, the Melkite patriarch of Alexandria with Zoïlus (late 539) and on his return to Constantinople, he convinced Justinian to write a long treatise against Origenism in the form of an edict (543), which all five patriarchs signed. Thus Pelagius had the satisfaction of annoying Theodore Ascidas as well as striking a blow for orthodoxy. But when Pelagius left for Rome (late 543), Theodore riposted by convincing Justinian that a road to reconciliation with the Monophysites lay in the condemnation of the person and writings of THEODORE OF MOPSUESTIA, certain works of Theodoret of Cyrrhus and a letter by Ibas of Edessa. Theodoret and Ibas had been supporters of Nestorius, but after the Council of Chalcedon, they had been brought into communion, thus providing grounds for the Monophysite charge that Chalcedonianism was really only NESTORIANISM. All three had died at peace with the Church.

In early 544, Justinian published his edict against the THREE CHAPTERS. However, for the Monophysites it was irrelevant, for it failed to condemn the Council of Chalcedon, and for the Catholics it was disconcerting, for it appeared to attack the doctrine of Chalcedon. The Roman see in particular viewed the Three Chapters edict as a challenge to papal authority, and opposition was particularly strong in Africa which had now been liberated from the Vandals. The patriarchs of Constantinople, Alexandria and Antioch signed the edict under protest. But Pope Vigilius, aware of the strength of the opposition in the Latin West, refused, and Justinian resorted to strong-arm tactics. Vigilius was arrested while saying mass in the church of S. Cecilia in Trastevere and taken to Constantinople (Jan. 27, 547). Under pressure, Vigilius gave Justinian and Theodora secret assurances that he would condemn the Three Chapters, and in April 548, issued a *Iudicatum* which anathematized the Three Chapters that at the same time upholding Chalcedon. There was a storm of protest from the western bishops, and Justinian, who could not afford western alienation at this point while the Byzantine conquest of Italy was still in the balance, allowed Vigilius to abrogate his *Iudicatum* in return for a secret promise to work for the condemnation of the Three Chapters (August 550).

Pope Vigilius. In preparation for the council, Justinian tried to win over the African bishops. Reparatus of Carthage was intransigent, and Justinian arranged for him to go into exile on a trumped-up charge of treason, and his fate so impressed Firmus of Numidia that he signed the Three Chapters edict. But the remaining two African bishops would not give way. In July 551, Justinian published a theological tract condemning the Three Chapters that he had prepared with Theodore Ascidas, but Vigilius threatened to excommunicate anyone who accepted it, and on being menaced, took refuge in the church of SS. Peter and Paul, the twin of SS. Sergius and Bacchus which still stands in Istanbul near the site of the Palace of Hormisdas. Justinian sent a posse of notables there, including Belisarius, to arrest the pope, but he resisted and the onlookers intervened when the posse tried to drag him off. However, on the night of Dec. 23, 551, Vigilius crossed the Bosporus to the basilica of S. Euphemia together with the two African bishops who would not sign

the Three Chapters edict, and there sought asylum. The pope returned to Constantinople on June 26, and the patriarch and bishops in turn reiterated their support of the Creed of Chalcedon. Meanwhile, Justinian's agents set to work in Africa and they were effective. Reparatus was replaced as bishop of Carthage by a more flexible prelate and used a combination of force and persuasion to win over the African clergy.

Mennas died suddenly (Aug. 24, 552) and was replaced swiftly by the abbot Eutychius. In July 551, Justinian had replaced the Melkite patriarch of Alexandria with Apollinaris, and in December 552, Eustachius became patriarch of Jerusalem. In a meeting between the pope and the patriarchs (Jan. 6, 553), Vigilius was given a profession of the faith of the patriarchs and asked to preside at a forthcoming ecumenical council. Vigilius agreed but suggested to Justinian that the Latin West could not be properly represented unless a synod were held in Italy or Sicily. Justinian rejected this proposal, as well as the suggestion of a preparatory commision where the pope and his aides could not be outvoted by the Eastern patriarchs.

In March 553, Justinian convoked a synod at the request of monks from Palestine where a fierce struggle between the Origenist and the strictly Chalcedonian monasteries had developed after the death of the doughty Chalcedonian archimandrite of the Judaean lauras, Mar Saba (533). In this synod, Justinian had 15 anathemas promulgated against Origenism and the isochritic doctrines, and the pope concurred. Justinian also demanded a final decision about the Three Chapters from the pope and sent him copious documentation. Yet the pope demurred, and when the Fifth Ecumenical Council at Constantinople opened in Hagia Sophia (May 5, 553), the pope did not attend.

Council of Constantinople. Justinian left the presidency of the council to the patriarchs but a letter from him was read out at the opening session, wherein he laid down a program of procedure, reminded the bishops that they had already agreed to the condemnation of the Three Chapters, and deplored Vigilius' refusal to participate. At his suggestion, several deputations waited on the pope, and he yielded so far as to publish his *Constitutum I*, wherein he condemned the doctrines attributed to Theodore and Theodoret, but avoided any condemnation of the three churchmen under indictment. Justinian refused to accept the *Constitutum*, commenting that if Vigilius condemned the Three Chapters, it was superfluous, and if he justified them, he was condemning himself. He informed the seventh session of the Council that he had removed the pope's name from the diptychs, and he also presented the bishops with documents containing the secret assurances he had received from Vigilius in 547 and 550. In condemning Vigilius, he declared, he was not breaking with the See of Rome but only with the incumbent, thereby making a distinction which was first made by Pope LEO I (440–461). The council condemned the pope and in its final session (June 2) it promulgated 14 anathemas that were taken almost literally from Justinian's edict of July 551. It also included Origen among the group of heresiarchs.

Hoping the pope would give way, Justinian published the council's condemnation only on July 14, and then he began a campaign of pressure until the pope surrendered, sending a letter of submission (December 8) to the Patriarch Eutychius. Justinian demanded a formal statement, and on Feb. 23, 554, Vigilius published his *Constitutum II* wherein he repudiated his former decisions and condemned both the doctrines and the authors of the Three Chapters. In return, Justinian gave heed to the pope's petition on behalf of Italy which was ruined by war and plague, and on Aug. 13, 554, he issued the Pragmatic Sanction, regulating ecclesiastical, economic and political affairs in Italy. It was an effort to restore the social fabric of Italy as it had existed before the Gothic War, and it was for the most part a futile effort.

Vigilius was already an ill man, suffering from a kidney stone, when he surrendered and on his way back to Rome, he died at Syracuse (June 7, 555). He had fought a good fight to preserve authority of Rome, but the Italian clergy did not forgive his surrender, and he was refused interment in St. Peter's basilica where the other sixth century popes were buried. Knowledge of Greek had by this time faded badly in the west, and hence many of the Latin clergy who defended the Three Chapters so fiercely could not read them. If they had, they might have realized that Justinian had a point: the Three Chapters did smack of heresy. But the Latin West saw the Three Chapters dispute as a challenge to the Creed of Chalcedon and the supremacy of the pope, and it fought back with all its might. The condemnation of the Three Chapters had no effect on the Monophysite dispute. In 557, Justinian called Jacob Baradaeus and a large selection of his followers to Constantinople for a colloquy, but it achieved nothing.

Aftermath of the Council. In a surprise move, Justinian offered the papal throne to Pelagius, a stout defender of Vigilius whose *In defensione trium capitulorum*, written the previous year, had strongly opposed Justinian's condemnation of the Three Chapters. The condition was that Pelagius now agree with the condemnation, and Pelagius accepted. He returned to face hostility in Italy, but imperial troops under Narses' command maintained firm control, and he was ordained bishop of Rome on Easter Sunday, 556, in St. Peter's basilica, by two bishops and a presbyter, since the usual complement of three bishops willing to perform the ceremony could not be found. Yet little by little Pelagius managed to impose his authority south of the Po River. Milan, north of it, remained estranged until the Lombard invasion (568). In Africa Justinian exiled and imprisoned recalcitrant prelates and his tactics bore fruit. Justin II's first edict sent the exiles back to their sees with the provision that they avoid any "novelties". Their passion was spent.

When Theodore Ascidas died (January 558), the bishop of Joppa in Palestine, whose name is unknown, took Theodore's place as Justinian's advisor, and he pointed out that if Justinian could not win over those Monophysites who followed the teachings of Severus, why not approach the follower of Severus' rival, Julian of Halicarnassus who preached the incorruptibility of Christ's body and were known as Aphthartodocetists? Justinian was not immediately won over. In 562, he published an edict reasserting the Chalcedonian doctrine. But near the end of 564 he promulgated an edict declaring orthodox the doctrine of Julian of Halicarnassus that Christ's body was incorruptible and incapable of suffering. Eutychius, the patriarch of Constantinople, refused his assent and was arrested (Jan. 22, 565) and deposed by a synod (Jan. 31, 565). He was replaced by John of Sirimis, who seems to have convinced Justinian that he would be willing to assent to his Aphthartodocetist decree, but he would not be the first of the patriarchs to do so. The other patriarchs, Apollinaris of Alexandria, Anastasius of Antioch and Macarius of Jerusalem, all resisted, and Justinian's death on November 14 averted a major crisis. JUSTIN II immediately cancelled Justinian's decree.

Legislation. Justinian promulgated a cluster of laws intended to bring about religious conformity. His first such law (*Cod.Just.* I. 5. 12) dates to 527, while he was still co-emperor with Justin I, and it was followed by a group of laws against pagans, heretics, and Samaritans. These laws were extended to include Jews, though he does not appear to have enforced the laws against Judaism any more rigorously than his predecessors. At the same time, he attacked the social inequities of the empire with exemplary vigor. Laws governing slavery were simplified. Freedmen should conduct themselves as free citizens, he asserted, and though he safeguarded the rights of former masters as patrons of their freed slaves, he ruled that the demands of the patron must be reasonable. However he did nothing to better the condition of the *adscripticii coloni*, tenant farmers bound to their lessors under conditions little different from slavery. By now, free tenant farmers had practically disappeared and Justinian recognized only the freehold farmer and the adscript tenant, who was a serf and could break his tie to his landlord only if he became a bishop. He passed laws against prostitution, he wiped out many of the legal disabilities of actors and actresses, and passed regulations governing dowries and ante-nuptial donations. The old custom of divorce by mutual consent was prohibited; instead he gave legal recognition to a list of just causes. The rights of women to hold property was put on an equal footing with the rights of men.

By way of ecclesiastical legislation, he passed laws requiring clerical celibacy and regulating accession to the episcopate (*Cod. Just.* I. 3.41; *Just. Novel.* 6.1). Bishops were instructed to retrench their ordinations, for churches were spending more than their income on the stipends of their clergy. He regulated the conduct of monks and clergy, forbade them to attend the Hippodrome, legislated the control of property for convents and monasteries, and forbade the alienation of Church goods. He gave prefects and provincial governors the right of surveillance over ecclesiastical abuses and excluded persons accused of murder, adultery or rape from the right of asylum in church. On the other hand, bishops were authorized to act against governors to right injustice when necessary (*Cod. Just.* I. 41.33; *Novel.* 8.8) and juridical processes against clerics and monks were put exclusively into the hands of bishops unless referred to the emperor himself. This was a period when the only source of justice in the outlying parts of the empire was often only the local bishop.

Justinian's great achievement, however, was his code of laws. On Feb. 13, 528, he summoned a ten-man commission chaired by John the Cappadocian to update the old Gregorian and Hermogenian Codes, as well as the Theodosian Code published a century earlier. The aim of the new code was to limit the ingenuity of lawyers who would produce obscure constitutions as precedents in order to win a point even when it did not conform to the general law. The new code came into effect in April 529. Twenty months later, Justinian set up another commission to undertake the collection of jurists' law, that is, the writings of private specialists in jurisprudence as opposed to imperial edicts, constitutions and responses. The commissioners had to scan 1,528 books written by Roman lawyers from the first to the fourth centuries. Heading the commission was the brilliant Tribonian, probably a product of the Beirut Law School who was "Quaestor of the Sacred Palace." The *Nika* riots cost Tribonian his quaestorship, but the commission continued its labors with Tribonian still its chair, and the whole work was completed in three years and published (Dec. 16, 533). It was called the *Digest* or in Greek, the *Pandects*.

At the same time as the *Digest* a new textbook for law students (the *Institutes*) was published. It was written by Dorotheus, the dean of the Beirut Law School, and Theophilus, a professor of the Constantinople Law School, both members of the commission chaired by Tri-

bonian who also supervised the writing of the Institutes. Like the *Digest*, Justinian gave the *Institutes* the force of law. It now became clear that the Code of 529 needed updating, and Tribonian, Dorotheus and three lawyers set to work on a second edition. It was published on Nov. 14, 534. This edition superseded the Code of 529, known as the *Codex vetus*, which has not survived.

In the Constitution (*Cordi nobis est*) which prefaced the promulgation of the Code in 534, Justinian indicated that he planned a collection of his subsequent laws under the title *Novellae Constitutiones,* but he never carried out this plan. But there were unofficial collections, the oldest of which is an abridged Latin version made for use in Italy and containing no novels later than 555. The fullest is a collection of 168 constitutions, which also contains some by Justin II and Tiberius II and hence is no earlier than the reign of Tiberius II. It gives each novel in its original language, which is usually Greek. The third is the *Authenticum*, where the latest entry dates to 556. It gives Greek originals in literal Latin translation and contains 134 Novels. Noteworthy is the use of Greek. In Justinian's reign, Latin ceased to be the exclusive language of law.

Justinian's Building Program. We are usually well-informed about Justinian's buildings because Procopius of Caesarea, better known as the author of the *History of the Wars of Justinian*, which chronicled events of the wars up until 552, wrote a panegyric describing them. The *Peri Ktismaton*, in Latin, the *De aedificiis*, begins with Justinian's buildings in Constantinople in the first book, and then in the remaining five books, undertakes to describe his building program throughout the empire. Italy is omitted, but Justinian built little there. The church of San Vitale in Ravenna, which contains famous mosaics of Justinian and Theodora on the two side-walls of the chancel, was dedicated in 547. But it was begun while Ravenna was still the capital of the Ostrogothic kingdom in Italy, and it was paid for by a local banker, Julius Argentarius. In Constantinople, pride of place goes to the great church of Hagia Sophia, which still stands. Also surviving, and used as a mosque, is SS. Sergius and Bacchus near the Palace of Hormisdas where Justinian and Theodora lived before Justinian became emperor. Justinian joined it to the imperial palace, and Theodora used it as a monastery and refuge for Monophysite churchmen. SS. Sergius and Bacchus may have been used for Monophysite services, and its twin, SS. Peter and Paul, which was joined to SS. Sergius and Bacchus by a common exonarthex, may have been used for the Latin rite. Outside Constantinople, he rebuilt Antioch which was sacked by the Persians in 540, and rebuilt his birthplace Tauresium with the new name, Justiniana Prima, and he made its metropolitan an archbishop, giving him the same rank as the metropolitans of Ravenna and Carthage. Procopius' panegyric reveals Justinian's concern for building churches to the glory of God, forts and walls to defend his subjects, and wells and aqueducts to assure a water supply. In the Balkans Procopius lists over 600 sites where Justinian built or improved defenses, many of them simply places of refuge where the inhabitants of the surrounding area could go for safety when invaders threatened.

Conclusion. Justinian's reign was a period of change, and in spite of his efforts, he left the empire in a more precarious position when it ended than when it began. Part of the reason was bad luck. The economy was expanding under the reign of Anastasius (d. 518) and the expansion continued under Justin I and Justinian until the epidemic of bubonic plague, which broke out first in Egypt, moved up the eastern Mediterranean coast and reached Constantinople in 542. From there it traveled westward, reaching Italy and France by 543 and even reaching Ireland the following year. There was a second outbreak in Constantinople in 558. This was bubonic or bubo-septicaemic plague, spread by fleas living on rodents, not the more deadly pulmonary type which is directly communicable to another person, for Procopius who describes the symptoms in detail notes that those who cared for plague victims did not necessarily contract the disease. Nonetheless it cut the population base drastically. One estimate is that the empire's population in 600 was only 60 percent of what it was in 500.

The empire's resources became overextended. It is the general view that Justinian's ambition to restore the Roman Empire in the western Mediterranean was responsible for this. But the reconquest at first went well. Justinian made a peace intended to last indefinitely with Persia (533), for which he paid an indemnity of 11,000 gold pounds and, trusting that the Persian king Khusro would keep his word and he would have no cause for alarm on his eastern frontier, Justinian sent an expedition of modest size led by the young general Belisarius against the Vandal kingdom in North Africa in 533. The conquest was easy and Belisarius returned to Constantinople to celebrate a triumph. In 535 Belisarius led an even smaller force against Sicily, which fell easily. On December 31, Belisarius entered Syracuse. Next year he invaded Italy. The offensive went well at first; on Dec. 9, 536, Belisarius entered Rome without a fight, for Pope Silverius urged the Romans to open the city gates to him. But the Goths regrouped, and subjected Rome to a terrible siege that lasted until mid-March 538. Quarreling among the Byzantine general staff hampered the campaign, and when Belisarius finally took Ravenna in 540, it was because he tricked the Ostrogoths into believing that if they surrendered the city to him, he would rebel against Justinian

and declare himself independent ruler in Italy with Gothic support. When Belisarius returned to Constantinople, he received a cool welcome.

The 540s were grim. In 540 Khusro broke the Endless Peace and invaded Syria, sacking Antioch and collecting ransoms from other cities. In Italy, the Goths rallied under a new king, Baduila, and the war dragged on until 552. The plague drained the empire of manpower and Justinian had to rely more upon barbarian recruits. In Africa there was unrest. The war of reconquest, which was launched when times were prosperous, overextended the resources of the empire. Still, Justinian could not resist an opportunity for more conquest in the west. In 551, a Visigothic noble, Athanagild, rebelled against the Visigothic king and appealed for help to Justinian. Justinian sent an army, which helped obtain the kingdom for Athanagild, but then the Byzantines declined to leave. The Byzantines remained in Spain until c. 624. Nonetheless the criticism that Justinian neglected the defense of his eastern provinces in order to concentrate on his western conquests is not justified. Justinian refused to commit large numbers of troops to the Gothic War in Italy in the 540s. Not until 551 did he send the eunuch Narses to Italy with sufficient resources to win the war in Italy, and the Goths were finally destroyed in two battles fought in 552.

Justinian's activities and accomplishments reveal a man of incredible energy and acute intelligence: his subjects spoke of him as the "Emperor who never sleeps" (John Lydus, *De magistratibus* 3.55). He was a tireless reformer in a society that was hostile to innovation. To quote his own words, he spent day and night reflecting on measures which were pleasing to God and useful to his subjects (*Novel* 8, preface). His reign is notable for the number of brilliant generals who served under him, such as Belisarius, the eunuch Narses, the Armenian Sittas who became Justinian's brother-in-law, and his cousin Germanus whose career suffered from Theodora's antipathy until her death. His praetorian prefect John the Cappadocian carried through administrative reforms ruthlessly until he ran afoul of the empress Theodora who contrived his downfall. Justinian spent prodigiously and taxed heavily; Evagrius (4.30) writing after his death, thought him greedy for money, but a generous builder of churches, orphanages, homes for the aged and hospitals for the sick. He believed it was his mission, as vicegerent of God, to unify Christian belief and to that end, he pursued heretics and sought to find a formula that was common ground for the Chalcedonian Catholics and the Monophysites. Contemporaries wondered at his partnership with Theodora, for she was Monophysite and championed the Monophysite cause. Procopius in his *Secret History*, an invective wherein he claimed to reveal the depravity of Justinian and Theodora as well as Belisarius and his wife Antonina, thought that Justinian and Theodora pretended to disagree in order to stir up trouble. More likely Justinian realized the value of having a loyal opposition, for as long as the Monophysites had an ally at court, they did not spawn any separatist movement. Whatever their theological differences, Justinian had no doubt of Theodora's loyalty.

According to the panegyrist Corippus, Justinian spent his last years in his religious preoccupations (*In laudem Justini* 2.265–267). The end of his reign was disturbed by a number of attempted rebellions. The aged Belisarius was implicated in one of the these, but since there was no proof of his guilt, in July 563, he was rehabilitated. He died in March 565, eight months before Justinian. His last service to the empire was to organize the defense of Constantinople against an incursion of the Kutrigur Huns in 559. Justinian himself died in his sleep without warning on the night of November 14 or 15, and his death averted a theological crisis. For all his contradictions and failures, he was probably the greatest of the Byzantine emperors.

Bibliography: J. B. BURY, *A History of the Roman Empire from the Death of Theodosius I to the Death of Justinian,* 2 v. (London 1923). W. SCHUBART, *Justinian und Theodora* (Munich 1943). R. BROWNING, *Justinian and Theodora,* 2nd ed. (London 1987). P. CHUVIN, *A Chronicle of the Last Pagans,* tr. B. A. ARCHER (Cambridge, Mass. 1990). A. CAMERON, *Circus Factions: Blues and Greens in Rome and Byzantium* (Oxford 1976). C. DIEHL, *Justinien et la civilisation byzantine* (Paris 1904). J. A. S. EVANS, *The Age of Justinian: The Circumstances of Imperial Power* (London 1996). idem, *The Empress Theodora: Partner of Justinian* (Austin, Tex. 2002). W. H. C. FREND, *The Rise of the Monophysite Movement: Chapters in the History of the Church in the Fifth and Sixth Centuries* (Cambridge 1972). G. GREATREX, ''The *Nika* Riot: A Reappraisal,'' *Journal of Hellenic Studies* 117 (1997) 60–86. A. H. M. JONES, *The Later Roman Empire 284–602,* 3 v. (Oxford 1964). F. MAFFEI, *Edifici di Giustiniano nell'ambito dell'impero* (Spoleto 1988). J. MOORHEAD, *Justinian* (London 1994). C. PAZDERNIK, '''Our Most Pious Consort Given us by God': Dissident Reactions to the Partnership of Justinian and Theodora, A.D. 525–548,'' *Classical Antiquity* 13 (1994) 256–281. B. RUBIN, *Das Zeitalter Iustinians* 2 v. (Berlin 1960). E. STEIN, *Histoire du Bas-Empire,* tr. J. R. PALANQUE, 2 v. in 3 (Paris 1949–59) 2: 275–780. P. N. URE, *Justinian and His Age* (Harmondsworth 1951).

[J. A. S. EVANS]

JUSTINIAN II, BYZANTINE EMPEROR

With his father's death in 685, Justinian II became Byzantine emperor at the age of 17. The first years of his reign were successful ones for the Byzantine Empire. The Caliph 'Abd al-Malik, faced with internal problems and the possibility of new Byzantine attacks, renewed his peace treaty with more favorable terms for the Byzantines. The caliph not only increased the amount of yearly tribute paid to the Byzantines, but also agreed to share the income from Armenia, Iberia, and Cyprus. Justinian, in return, resettled the Mardaites, who had been raiding the countryside in Syria and Lebanon, in western Asia Minor and the Peloponnese. In 688, Justinian led a successful military expedition against the Slavs who were settled in the eastern regions of the empire. In 692 Justinian renewed attacks on the Arabs but suffered a setback when a large number of Slavs who had been recently drafted into his army deserted, leading to a Byzantine defeat.

Justinian continued the religious policy of his father, Constantine IV, and attempted to bring about a reconciliation between Rome and Constantinople. He was the first emperor to place the image of Christ on his coinage, along with the motto *servus Christi*. Justinian, however, was soon at odds with the papacy since he was not willing to agree to the supremacy of the Roman see over the see of Constantinople. In an effort to resolve the conflict, he convened the Trullo council in 692, which was also known as the Quinisext council since it dealt with matters discussed at the fifth and sixth ecumenical councils. While the council addressed a wide range of subjects, such as church organization and clerical marriage, its most significant judgment was when it emphasized the equality of the Constantinopolitan and Roman sees. Pope Sergius I, however, upheld the position that the Roman see was superior to all others and rejected all the council's canons. Justinian attempted to militarily enforce the council's decision and ordered the arrest of the pope, but the Roman populace and local troops prevented this.

While he enjoyed early success, the latter part of Justinian's reign was not popular with the people. Heavy taxation and his disregard for the senate led to a successful coup in 695 that elevated Leontius to the throne. Leontius then had Justinian's nose and tongue slit and exiled him to Cherson. Justinian's mutilation led to his nickname *rhinotmetos*, ''cut'' or ''slit nose'', and he supposedly wore a gold nose over the disfigurement to hide it. During his exile, the city authorities became concerned that Justinian was plotting to regain the throne and decided to send him to Constantinople. Receiving word of this, Justinian fled to the Khazars and was received by their khan with great hospitality and eventually married the khan's sister, who took the name Theodora. Learning of his actions, the Byzantines sent envoys to the Khazars to demand that they give up Justinian. The khan eventually relented and agreed to hand over Justinian to the envoys. Justinian, learning of the betrayal, fled to the Bulgars who agreed to support him in his effort to regain the throne. In 705, Justinian arrived outside Constantinople with a large army of Bulgars and Slavs. Since the defenses of Constantinople proved to be too formidable for a frontal assault, Justinian entered the city through the aqueducts and was able to seize control and regain his throne. He then had his wife Theodora, who became the first foreign Byzantine empress, and their son Tiberius join him in Constantinople.

In 711, in an effort to stop the Khazars' encroachment on Byzantine territory, Justinian sent a successful military expedition against the city of Cherson. This expedition also gave him the opportunity to punish the city for his poor treatment during his exile. After the punitive expedition departed from Cherson, the city immediately revolted. When the Byzantine force returned in an effort to retake the city, it was unable to do so. Soon the besieging fleet and army switched sides and joined the revolt against Justinian and proclaimed Philippicos as emperor. Justinian was forced to flee and traveled to Asia Minor in an effort to raise military support. He was unable to gain any backing and was soon killed and his head was removed and sent to Rome and Ravenna for display.

Bibliography: F. GÖRRES, "Justinian II und das römische Papsttum," *Byzantinische Zeitschrift* 17 (1908) 432–54. J. F. HALDON, *Byzantium in the Seventh Century: The Transformation of a Culture* (Cambridge 1990). W. E. KAEGI, JR. *Byzantine Military Unrest, 471–843: An Interpretation* (Amsterdam 1981). G. OSTROGORSKY, *Geschichte des byzantinischen Staates* (Munich 1963). A. N. STRATOS, *Byzantium in the Seventh Century* (Amsterdam 1968). W. TREADGOLD, *A History of Byzantine State and Society* (Stanford 1997).

[R. S. MOORE]

JUSTINIANUS, ST.

Hermit and martyr; probably of noble Breton origin; d. Isle of Ramsey (off Pembrokeshire, now Dyfed) or Isle of Man, *c.* 530–540. Having come to Wales early in the sixth century, Justinianus (Stinan or Jestin) lived in a hermitage on either the Isle of Ramsey or the Isle of Man. Accounts of his martyrdom differ; he is variously reported to have been murdered by three companions, slaves or pirates. John CAPGRAVE, author of *Nova legenda Angliae,* is the first to produce a vita of Justinian; but his editor (*Acta Sanctorum,* Aug., 4:636) complained that Justinianus was too little known; no compiler of Breton saints, not even Albert le Grand, included his name. Nevertheless, his name was included in several Welsh calendars and a church at Llanstinan (near Fishguard) is dedicated to him.

Feast: Aug. 23 or Dec. 5.

Bibliography: *Acta Sanctorum,* Aug., 4:633–636. *Bibliotheca hagiographica latina antiquae et mediae aetatis,* 2 v. (Brussels 1898–1904; suppl. 1911) 1:4576. J. L. BAUDOT and L. CHAUSSIN, *Vies des saints et des bienheureux selon l'ordre du calendrier avec l'historique des fêtes* (Paris 1935–56) 8:431–432.

[M. C. HILFERTY]

JUSTUS OF CANTERBURY, ST.

First bishop of Rochester, fourth archbishop of Canterbury; d. Nov. 10, 627. A member of GREGORY I's second missionary group, which arrived in England in 601, he was consecrated bishop for west Kent in 604 by AUGUSTINE OF CANTERBURY and established his see at ROCHESTER, where St. Andrew's was built as his cathedral. He was driven from his see *c.* 617 during a pagan reaction, but was received back after a year in Gaul. He succeeded MELLITUS (d. April 24, 627) as archbishop of CANTERBURY. The chief accomplishment of his primacy was the consecration of PAULINUS OF YORK in 625 as missionary bishop for Northumbria. The opening of this mission resulted eventually in the founding of the second primatial see at YORK. Justus was buried in the church of Saints Peter and Paul, Canterbury (*see* SAINT AUGUSTINE, ABBEY OF).

Feast: Nov. 10.

Bibliography: BEDE, *Historia Ecclesiastica* 1.29; 2.3–9, 18. *Councils and Ecclesiastical Documents Relating to Great Britain and Ireland,* ed. A. W. HADDAN and W. STUBBS, 3 v. in 4 (Oxford 1869–78) 3:72–81. W. BRIGHT, *Chapters of Early English Church History* (3d ed. Oxford 1897). W. STUBBS, *A Dictionary of Christian Biography,* ed. W. SMITH and H. WACE, 4 v. (London 1877–87) 3:592–593.

[R. D. WARE]

JUSTUS OF TIBERIAS

Jewish historian and Josephus's rival in connection with the Jewish war against the Romans; fl. in the 1st Christian century. What little is known of his life and works is derived almost entirely from the writings of Flavius JOSEPHUS (*Life* 343, 354–358, 390–393, 410), with whom he had strong differences. The recipient of a Greek education and favorably inclined to Greco-Roman culture, Justus joined his father, Pistus, perhaps unwillingly, at Tiberias in the general Jewish revolt against the Romans (A.D. 66). His part in the insurrection is not clear, and Josephus may well have been responsible for the local uprising; apparently each accused the other of complicity with the Romans to remove the blame from himself, or perhaps neither was very zealous for the Jewish cause. Shortly after the outbreak, Justus fled to AGRIPPA II at Beirut. Denounced before Vespasian, he was ordered to be executed by Agrippa but instead he was imprisoned. After being freed and again imprisoned, he eventually gained the favor of Agrippa, who appointed him as his secretary. When he was later found incompetent and unreliable, he was expelled.

Among the books Justus is reported to have written is a *History of the Jewish War,* which was published probably about 25 years after the end of the war (A.D. 70), for he would hardly have criticized Agrippa II so severely, as Josephus claimed he did, before the king's death (*c.* 93). Josephus, in his *Life,* contradicts the contentions and facts of Justus's presentation and thus gives an idea of the contents of his rival's work. The knowledge that some of the Church Fathers had of Justus was derived probably from the prejudiced statements of Josephus, rather than from Justus's own writings. According to PHOTIUS, another work of Justus was a *Chronicle of the Jewish Kings* from Moses to Agrippa II, of which perhaps the *History of the Jewish War* was a part. Jerome (*De viris illustribus* 14) ascribes to Justus a short commentary on the Scriptures.

Bibliography: H. LUTHER, *Josephus und Justus von Tiberias* (Halle 1910). E. SCHÜRER, *A History of the Jewish People in the Time of Christ,* tr. J. MACPHERSON et al., 5 v. (Edinburgh 1897–98) 1.1:65–69, with bibliog., 92; 2.3:222. F. JACOBY, *Paulys Realenzkylopädie der klassischen Altertumswissenschaft* (1919) 10.2:1341–46. S. KRAUSS, *Jewish Encyclopedia,* ed. J. SINGER (New York 1901–06) 7:398–399. A. SCHALIT, *Encyclopedia Judaica* (Berlin 1928–34) 9:623–626. J. SCHMID, *Lexikon für Theologie und Kirche* ed. J. HOFER and K. RAHNER (Freiburg 1957–65) 5:1230.

[R. KRINSKY]

JUSTUS OF URGEL, ST.

Bishop of Urgel, Catalonia, Spain; b. Valencia(?); d. Urgel(?), after 546. According to ISIDORE OF SEVILLE (*De viris illustribus,* 33–34), he had three brothers: Bishops Justinianus, of Valencia; Nifridius, of Egara; and Elpidius, of an unknown see. Justus signed the acts of two councils: Toledo II, in 527; and Lerida, in 546. His allegorical explication of the CANTICLE OF CANTICLES (Song of Songs), in which he alludes to the persecution of the Church in Spain by Arian Visigoths, is introduced by a letter to the Metropolitan Sergius of Tarragona, another to the Deacon Justus, and a prologue to the reader. His sermon on the feast of St. VINCENT OF SARAGOSSA was used in the Mozarabic liturgy. He was entered in the Roman MARTYROLOGY in 1586.

Feast: May 28.

Bibliography: *Patrologia Latina,* ed. J. P. MIGNE, 217 V., indexes 4 v. (Paris 1878–90) 67:961–994. B. DE GAIFFIER, "Les Notices Hispaniques du martyrologe Romain," *Analecta Bollandiana,* 58 (1940) 84; "Sermons Latin en l'honneur de S. Vincent antérieurs au Xᵉ siècle," *ibid.,* 67 (1949) 278–280.

[E. P. COLBERT]

JUTTA, BL.

Benedictine abbess, sister of Count Meginhard of Spanheim; b. *c.* 1090; d. Disibodenberg (Diessenberg),

near Kreuznach, Germany *c.* 1136. Jutta (Judith) became a recluse near the monastery of Disibodenberg (*Mons St. Disibodi*) and in 1106 was joined by St. HILDEGARD OF BINGEN, who was then eight years old. Other noble women soon gathered there, and Jutta presided over them as prioress until her death. She was succeeded by St. Hildegarde, who said that Jutta "overflowed with the grace of God like a river fed by many streams."

Feast: Dec. 22.

Bibliography: "De s. Hildegarde," *Acta Sanctorum,* Sept. 5:679–701. *Analecta Bollandiana* 27 (1908) 341. A. SILVAS, *Jutta and Hildegard: The Biographical Sources* (University Park, PA 1999). J. MAY, *Die heilige Hildegard von Bingen* (Munich 1911) 14–31. A. BUTLER, *The Lives of the Saints* 4:597–598. W. BÖHNE, *Lexikon für Theologie und Kirche²* 5:1230–31. J. L. BAUDOT and L. CHAUSSIN, *Vies des saints et des bienheureux selon l'ordre du calendrier avec l'historique des fêtes* 12:616.

[J. C. MOORE]

JUTTA OF FUCHSSTADT, BL.

Cistercian abbess; d. *c.* 1250. She lived at Essleben in an independent community of pious women who, wishing to order their religious life according to a rule, obtained permission from the bishop of Würzburg to found the Cistercian convent of Heiligenthal (Lower Franconia). Jutta (or Julitta) served as its first abbess (1234–50). She was buried before the high altar of the convent church, to which many made pilgrimages. Her grave was opened with the approval of the bishop in 1664 and again in 1897. Her most striking relic was an arm to which was attached a golden cup from which the sick drank and were cured; it came into the possession of Julius Hospital in Würzburg in 1579, but is now lost.

Feast: Nov. 29.

Bibliography: M. WIELAND, "Kloster Heiligenthal," *Cistercienser-Chronik* 124 (1899) 161–164; 125 (1899) 201–202. A. M. ZIMMERMANN, *Kalendarium Benedictinum: Die Heiligen und Seligen des Benediktinerordens und seiner Zweige* 3:372, 373. S. LENSSEN, *Hagiologium cisterciense* 1:313. E. KRAUSEN, *Die Klöster des Zisterzienserordens in Bayern* (Bayerische Heimatforschung 7; Munich 1953) 48.

[D. ANDREINI]

JUTTA OF SANGERHAUSEN, ST.

Widow, patroness of Prussia; b. Sangerhausen, Thuringia; d. Kulmsee, Prussia, May 12, 1260. Though drawn to the religious life, Jutta (or Judith) married, acquiescing to the wishes of her parents. After her husband died during a pilgrimage to the Holy Land, she entrusted their children to religious houses, divided her goods among the poor, and set out to help the sick and distressed. She settled in Prussia in 1256 on the Kulmsee, as an anchoress (*see* ANCHORITES), and nursed the sick, especially the leprous. Her spiritual directors were Blessed JOHN LOBEDAU and Bishop Heidenreich. Like Lobedau she is remarkable for her devotion to the SACRED HEART OF JESUS. She was buried in Kulmsee cathedral.

Feast: May 5.

Bibliography: *Acta Sanctorum,* May, 7:593–604. H. WESTPFAHL, *Jutta von Sangerhausen* (Meitingen 1938). C. KROLLMANN, *Altpreussische Biographie* (Königsberg 1941) 1:315. H. HOFFMANN, *Helden und Heilige des Deutschen Ostens* (Lippstadt 1953) 72–74.

[D. ANDREINI]

K

KAAS, LUDWIG

Center Party representative in German Reichstag, prothonotary apostolic; b. Trier, Germany, May 23, 1881; d. Rome, April 15, 1952. After studying in Rome he was ordained (1909) and then studied law at Bonn under Ulrich Stutz. In 1918 he became professor of canon law in Trier. He was elected in 1919 to the National Assembly as a CENTER PARTY delegate and later sat on the Prussian Privy Council (*Staatsrat*). Under the Weimar Republic he was a representative in the Reichstag from 1920, where his main interest was in foreign affairs. He was a member of the German delegation to the League of Nations (1926) and at the London and Paris conferences. He did not, however, support strongly Gustav Stresemann's foreign policy. Kaas advocated the liberation of the Rhineland and the formation of this region as a state within the German Republic. As chairman of the Center party from 1928 until its dissolution in 1933, Kaas upheld Heinrich Brüning as chancellor, disassociated the party from collaboration with the Socialists, and urged coalition with the rightist German Nationalists. When the Nazis came to power (1933), Kaas was one of those mainly responsible for the passage of the enabling act that permitted Hitler as chancellor to assume dictatorial powers. Kaas was a friend of the nuncio Cardinal Eugenio Pacelli (later PIUS XII) and was his close adviser in the negotiations leading to the concordat of 1933. From 1933 Kaas, a prothonotary apostolic *di numero partecipanti* since 1929, lived in Rome, where he became secretary of the Congregation of ST. PETER'S BASILICA. In this position he directed until his death the archeological investigations under the basilica that led to very important discoveries concerning the burial place and remains of St. Peter.

Bibliography: A. WYNEN, *Ludwig Kaas* (Trier 1953). J. N. MOODY, ed., *Church and Society* (New York 1953) 325–583. E. EYCK, *A History of the Weimar Republic,* tr. H. P. HANSON and R. G. L. WAITE, 2 v. (Cambridge, Mass. 1962–63), v. 2. G. SCHREIBER, *Staatslexikon* 4:747–750; *Lexikon für Theologie und Kirche,* ed. J. HOFER and K. RAHNER (Freiburg 1957–65) 5:1233. A. L. C. BULLOCK, *Hitler: A Study in Tyranny* (rev. ed. New York 1958).

[M. A. GALLIN]

KADDISH

A Jewish prayer that is often referred to as the prayer for the dead since it is customary for the Jewish mourner to recite it in the synagogue thrice daily for 11 months after the death of a parent or close relative. Its text, however, does not contain words of supplication for the dead but only exaltation and glorification of the Holy Name, in line with the teachings of the sages that one should praise God equally for the good and for the evil that befall him, even in the time of deepest mourning.

The Kaddish (Aramaic *qaddîš,* "holy," i.e., hallowed be the great name of the Lord), first mentioned in the tractate *Soferim,* originated as a closing doxology to a haggadic discourse in study houses of the Jewish community in Babylonia, and was composed in Aramaic, the vernacular of that time, except for one section in Hebrew. The first part of the text was taken from Ez 38.23, and other sections were added in later eras. The second part is from the 1st century. The last paragraph, beginning with the *Oseh Shalom* (He who makes peace), is taken from the *Shemoneh Esreh* [18 (blessings)], and the *Al Yisrael veRabbanan* (Unto Israel and the rabbis) was added in medieval times. Today it is recited also after the study of the oral law and as a doxology with congregational response at the end of prayers in the synagogue. Of even greater importance than the body of the text is the congregational response: "May His Great Name be praised for all Eternity." The Talmud (*Sotah* 49a) states: "Since the destruction of the Temple the world has been sustained by the Kedushah [proclamation of God's holiness] of the liturgy and the *Yehe Shemeh Rabba* [May His Great Name . . .] of the haggadic discourse. Happy the King who is thus lauded in His house!" (Berakhot 3a). The repetition of the AMEN (verily, truly) represents affirmation, acceptance, and faith. Ten men are needed to recite the Kaddish.

The Kaddish has several different forms, each used for a different purpose: (1) Kaddish ha-Gadol (the great Kaddish), known also as the Burial Kaddish, is the mourner's first recitation of the Kaddish. It is a prayer of faith in resurrection of the dead, and so it is called also Kaddish of Resurrection (*Tehiyat ha-Meytim*). (2) Kaddish de Rabbanan (rabbis' Kaddish) is a tribute of praise, arranged to be recited after learning the oral Law, especially haggadic material; it is also a prayer for the rabbis. (3) Kaddish de Sheliah Tzibbur (Kaddish of the deputy of the community) is the congregational Kaddish recited by the cantor at public prayer (*see* CANTOR IN JEWISH LITURGY). This form has two divisions, the Half Kaddish (Hatzi-Kaddish) and the Full Kaddish [Kaddish Shalem including Tithkabbel (May it be acceptable)], each of which is inserted in specific places in the regular congregational prayers. (4) Kaddish Yatom (Orphan's Kaddish), called also the Mourner's Kaddish (Kaddish Abelim), is recited by the orphan for an 11-month period. The 10 forms of praise are parallel to the Ten Commandments.

The regular recitation of the Orphan's Kaddish produces a special kind of mystic benefit. The earliest reference to this was in a legend wherein Rabbi AKIBA BEN JOSEPH met a spirit in the guise of a man carrying wood; the spirit told Akiba that the wood was for the fire in GEHENNA, in which he was burned daily in punishment for having maltreated the poor while he was a tax-collector, and that he would be released from his awful torture if he had a son to recite the Bareku (bless ye) and the Kaddish before a worshiping assembly that would respond with the praise of God's name. On learning that the man had utterly neglected his son, Akiba cared for and educated the youth, so that one day he stood in the assembly and recited the Bareku and the Kaddish and released his father from Gehenna (*Maseket Kallah* 11.11). At first, the Kaddish for deceased parents was recited a full year; later the time was reduced to 11 months, since it was considered unworthy to have such an opinion of the demerit of one's father. The custom of reciting this Kaddish was extended to include the Yahrzeit (anniversary of death) as well.

Bibliography: J. SCHICK, *The Kaddish* (New York 1928). D. DE SOLA POOL, *The Kaddish* (New York 1909; repr. 1929); *Universal Jewish Encyclopedia* 6:273–275. P. BIRNBAUM, *A Book of Jewish Concepts* (New York 1964) 537–539. J. H. HERTZ, ed. and tr., *The Authorized Daily Prayer Book* (rev. ed. New York 1948). J. D. EISENSTEIN, *Jewish Encyclopedia* 7:401–405. M. E. JERNENSKY and A. NADEL, *Encyclopedia Judaica* 9:734–742. R. R. GEIS, *Lexikon für Theologie und Kirche*, ed. J. HOFER and K. RAHNER, 10 v. (2d new ed. Freiburg 1957–65) 5:1238. E. LEVI, *Yesodot Ha-Tefilah* (Tel Aviv 1963), in Hebrew. I. JACOBSON, *Netiv Binah* (Tel Aviv 1964–) 1:365–373, in Hebrew.

[E. SUBAR]

KAFKA, MARIA RESTITUTA, BL.

Baptized Helena, nurse, martyr of the Franciscan Sisters of CHRISTIAN CHARITY ("Hartmannschwestern"); b. May 10, 1894, Hussowitz-Brunn, Moravia (now Brno, Czech Republic); d. March 30, 1943, Vienna, Austria. Helena Kafka was the sixth daughter of a cobbler who moved the family to Vienna while she was still a child. During her teens she began working as a sales clerk, then as a nurse, which put her into contact with the nursing Hartmannschwestern. She took the name "Restituta" upon entering the congregation (1914). Sr. Restituta was a skilled surgical nurse (1919–39), but also gained a reputation for championing the cause of those in need: the poor, the oppressed, and the unjustly accused—even a Nazi doctor.

Following the Anschluss (March 1938), she was an outspoken opponent of Adolf Hilter. She was arrested on Ash Wednesday 1942 for replacing the pictures of Hitler in each room of a new hospital wing with crucifixes and refusing to remove them. On Oct. 28, 1942, she received the death sentence for treason. Upon being offered her freedom in exchange for leaving the order, she refused. For the next five months, until the order of decapitation was executed, Sr. Restituta nursed other prisoners without regard to political affiliation.

On April 6, 1998, her martyrdom was declared. In the Plaza of Heroes in Vienna in front of the balcony where Hilter announced the Anschluss of Austria, Pope John Paul II beatified Kafka on June 21, 1998.

Feast: Oct. 29 (Franciscans).

Bibliography: P. RONAI, *Schwester Maria Restituta Kafka* (Innsbruck 1998).

[K. I. RABENSTEIN]

KAGAWA, TOYOHIKO

Japanese social reformer and Protestant leader; b. Kobe, July 10, 1888; d. Tokyo, April 23, 1960. After being orphaned at the age of four, he was raised by an uncle and aunt in Awa and Tokushima. When he became a Christian in his teens, he was disinherited, but with the help of missionaries he studied at the Presbyterian College in Tokyo (1905–08). From 1910 to 1924 he spent all but two years in a small hut in the slum section of Kobe, called Shinkawa. Disturbed by the poverty and misery of the area, he went to the United States to pursue at Princeton University further studies in social techniques (1914–16) and then founded the Labor Federation (1918) and the Farmers' Union (1921). Kagawa was arrested during the rice riots of 1919 and the shipyard strikes of

1921, but he agitated successfully for universal manhood suffrage and modification of laws against trade unionism. In 1923 he was asked to supervise relief and social work in Tokyo. Within a year he reorganized entirely the Bureau of Social Welfare. His book *Across the Death Line* (1920), which drew on his experiences, won him enormous popularity. This and other books drew the attention of the Japanese government to the appalling conditions in the slums. Kagawa insisted that a reorganization of the world's economic structure through cooperative enterprise was necessary to realize the Christian ideal of the social order. Besides founding the Anti-War League (1928), he started the Kingdom of God Movement (1930) to promote the conversion of Japan. He established credit unions, schools, hospitals, and churches on the cooperative principle. On five occasions he visited the United States to gain support for his social reform projects. His pacifism caused his imprisonment in 1940, but he was released after World War II and became a leader in the attempt to adapt democratic institutions to Japan. Among the more important of his numerous writings, with dates of their translation into English, are *The Religion of Jesus* (1931), *Christ and Japan* (1934), *Songs of the Slums* (1935), *Meditations on the Cross* (1936), *Brotherhood Economics* (1934), and *Behold the Man* (1941).

Bibliography: W. AXLING, *Kagawa* (8th ed. rev. New York 1946). *Kagawa nijû seiki no kaitakusha* (Tokyo 1960), Kagawa, a pioneer of the 20th century, ed. at Meiji Gakuin University.

[A. SCHWADE]

KAKUBILLA, ST.

Called also Cacucabilla, Cacucilla, Cucacilla, and other names, a mythological, popular saint of the 15th century. Her name, reminiscent of Colum–cille (*see* CO-LUMBA, ST.), goes back to St. COLUMBAN, who was invoked against demons and in thunderstorms. In Germany the Latin ending *–illa* made the saint a woman, who was invoked against rats and mice. In the "Book of Remedies of Wolfsturn" one may find the curious advice: "Against rats write these words on four places in the house: *Sanctus*(*?*) *Kakukakilla*." In the later Middle Ages the blessing formulas consider this saint as masculine in Tyrol, and as feminine in Styria, Thuringia, Alsace, and Sweden. There is a portrait of a saint with two mice and with the title Cutubilla in the abbey church of Adelberg in Württemberg; the picture is of no historical value, but of ethnological interest. Similar pictures are found in Uppland, Sweden, dating from *c.* 1500. These, however, represent an abbess, probably confused with the abbess St. GERTRUD OF NIVELLES. The name Kakubilla has superstitious and magical implications.

Bibliography: H. BÄCHTOLD–STÄUBLI, ed., *Handwörterbuch des deutschen Aberglaubens*, 10 v. (Leipzig 1927–42) 4:913–914. *Zeitschrift des Vereins für Votkskunde* 1 (1891) 321, 444; 2 (1892) 199–201; 8 (1898) 341–342. W. STAMMLER, *Münster* 13.10 (1960), bibliog.; *Lexikon für Theologie und Kirche*² 5:1254–55. J. BRAUN, *Tracht und Attribute der Heiligen in der deutschen Kunst* (Stuttgart 1943).

[V. H. REDLICH]

KALĀM

The science of Muslim theology. This article discusses its meaning, origin and development, content, nature and method.

Meaning. *Kalām* means speech, utterance, discourse; *'ilm al-kalām* is speech or discourse par excellence, i.e., the speech of those who discuss God and the things of God, or, according to some, the science that treats of God's attribute of speech. The latter was one of the first questions discussed by Muslim theologians, and so all theological discussion came to be called *kalām*. The theologians are called *mutakallimūn* (speakers, discoursers). Ibn Khaldūn (d. 1406) defines *kalām* as "a science which furnishes the means of proving the dogmas of the faith by rational arguments and of refuting the innovators who, in matters of belief, depart from the doctrine followed by the ancients and the partisans of tradition. The very essence of these dogmas is the profession of God's unicity." This definition, like most others, brings out the essentially defensive and polemic nature of Muslim theology.

Origin and Development. The specifically Islamic sciences all derive from the Qur'ān and its influence. The Qur'ān is for Islam a divine and autonomous datum in the strictest sense. But its meaning was not always clear, and the first efforts at exegesis reveal two tendencies, one literalist and the other rational, which continued to characterize Muslim thought in general, and *kalām* in particular. Political quarrels over the Caliphate gave rise to the factions, later sects, of the Khārijites (secessionists), the SHĪ'ITES, and the Murji'a (those suspending judgment). The theological points involved were faith and its relation to works, and the juridical position of the Muslim grave sinner.

Umayyad Period (661–750). The transfer of the capital of Islam to Damascus led to the first real encounter of Muslims with Christian theological thought. SS. Sophronius, Andrew of Crete, and John of Damascus all date from the Arab period of Damascus. The two main points discussed were predestination (*qadar*) and whether the Qur'ān is created or uncreated. In Persia, the encounter with dualism led to polemic on God's unicity, His existence, and His attributes.

'*Abbāsid Period (750–1258).* The constitution of *kalām* as an autonomous science came early in this period. Non-Arab, especially Persian, influences were very important. The foundation of the Basra and Kufa schools of grammar affected exegesis of the Qur'ān and in this and other ways influenced *kalām.* The formation of the principal systems of jurisprudence (*fiqh*) also left its mark on the mentality and method of many *mutakallimūn,* since these were usually also jurists (*see* ISLAMIC LAW). But the most important factor in the shaping and development of *kalām* was the influence exercised by the translation into Arabic, through Syriac or directly from the Greek, of the principal philosophical works of Greek antiquity. Moreover, Islam now had to face all kinds of ''heterodoxies,'' such as materialism and MANICHAEISM. To reply to their adversaries, Muslim doctors threw themselves into the fray, and the resulting first significant school of *kalām* was that of the MU'TAZILITES. These were the real founders of *kalām.* They were succeeded by the Ash'arite schools, and Ash'arism finally came to be identified with ''orthodoxy'' (*see* ASH'ARĪ, AL-). The role played by such other schools of *kalām* as the Māturīdites, Zaydites, and Shī'ites is difficult to evaluate, since their works have not been sufficiently studied.

Content. The chief questions discussed by the *mutakallimūn* may be indicated by a brief analysis of the *Tamhīd* of al-Bāqillānī (d. 1013). The first two chapters are a rudimentary epistemology and ontology leading to an important third chapter on God's existence and attributes. Chapters 4 to 9 are polemics against materialists, astrologers, dualists, Magians, Christians, and Brahmins. Chapters 10 to 11 discuss the prophethood of Muḥammad and his signal miracle of the inimitable Qur'ān. Chapters 12 to 15 are a polemic against the Jews, and chapter 16 is directed against the corporealists (who made God a body). This leads to a theoretical discussion of attributes and their nature in chapters 17 to 19. The uncreatedness of the Qur'ān is defended in chapter 20. Chapter 21 details Mu'tazilite views, and chapter 22 returns to the divine attributes. Chapter 23 is on the beatific vision. In chapters 24 to 35 various aspects of the divine will, predestination, and human acts are discussed. Chapters 36 to 39 deal with faith and the status of the sinner in this life and the next. The Prophet Muḥammad's intercession is the subject of chapter 40. The long concluding section is a discussion of the authenticity of tradition and of the caliphate, with a long defense of the legitimacy of the first four caliphs.

Nature and Method. The history of *kalām* and the study of the texts at hand make it very clear that *kalām* is primarily a defensive and polemic apology aimed at refuting adversaries and solving doubts. It is never conceived as a means of penetrating more profoundly into the data of revelation. Thus al-Ghazzālī, whose *Iqtiṣad* is one of the finest works of *kalām,* is inclined to minimize the importance of *kalām* and to restrain its use to those who need a remedy against doubts about the faith. The real theological problem of Islam is not that posed by *kalām,* but rather that evoked by the rigid Ḥanbalite insistence on the absolute transcendence of the one God. *Kalām,* therefore is Muslim theology in an actual, but rather restricted, sense.

The theological sources of the *mutakallimūn* are: texts of the Qur'n, always the weightiest proofs; ISLAMIC TRADITIONS (*ḥadīth:* the words and acts of Muḥammad as reported by his companions and handed down by oral transmission); and rational arguments. Consensus (*ijmā'*) is sometimes appealed to, but it is more a source of jurisprudence. Philological, or grammatical, arguments and subtleties are often involved in the interpretation of Qur'ān texts and of traditions. As *kalām* developed, the use of rational argument became more prominent and the relatively simple analogies of the early authors were more and more replaced by Aristotelian logic and the formal syllogism. Philosophy as such was never very popular in Islam, but the later *mutakallimūn* gave much attention to questions that were more philosophical than theological. The professional philosophers, such as Averroes and MAIMONIDES, had a very poor opinion of the reasoning of the *mutakallimūn.*

Kalām and Catholic Theology. There are two reasons why at least some Catholic theologians should not neglect *kalām.* The first is that a sympathetic knowledge of ISLAM, unclouded by passion or prejudice, must include knowledge of this discipline, which has played so important a role in the direction and development of Islamic religious thought. This scarcely needs elaboration, and the theologian is the one best equipped to gain and evaluate such knowledge. The second reason may be summed up in the fact that it is an important area of ''comparative theology.'' The significance of this has been brought out well by M. M. Anawati and L. Gardet.

Knowledge of the nature and methods of *kalām* can help the Catholic theologian to a deeper appreciation of his own theology. It can also suggest further questions that must be asked in Catholic as well as in Islamic theology. And it can lead to a dialogue conducted not in the spirit of *kalām* perhaps, but in a sympathetic spirit that may be permanently fruitful.

Bibliography: L. GARDET and M. M. ANAWATI, *Introduction à la théologie musulmane* (Paris 1948). I. GOLDZIHER, *Vorlesungen über den Islam* (2d ed. Heidelberg 1925); *Le Dogme et la loi de l'Islam,* tr. F. ARIN from the 1st ed. (Paris 1920). A. S. TRITTON, *Muslim Theology* (London 1947). W. M. WATT, *Free Will and Predestination in Early Islam* (London 1948). A. J. WENSINCK, *The Muslim Creed* (New York 1932). MAS'ŪD IBN 'UMAR, AL-TAFTĀZĀNĪ, *A*

Commentary on the Creed of Islam, tr. E. E. ELDER (New York 1950), commentary on the creed of al-Nasafī. AL-GHAZZĀLĪ, *Iqtisād* (*El justo medio en la creencia*) tr. M. ASIN-PALACIOS (Madrid 1929), includes summary translations of some of his other works. IMĀM EL ḤARĀMEIN, *El-Irchad,* ed. and tr. J. D. LUCIANI (Collection du centenaire de l'Algerie; Paris 1938).

[R. J. MCCARTHY/EDS.]

KALANDS BRETHREN

Confraternities of the Calends, so called because of their custom of holding divine services on the first of the month (*calendae*). They were an ecclesiastical society whose members, both clerical (*domini*) and lay (*fratres*), were under the direction of a clerical dean; they existed for the purpose of providing for burials and suffrages for the dead and also for mutual help in economic and legal difficulties. The custom of celebrating the first of the month is of pagan origin, but early in the Middle Ages this custom was directed toward special suffrages and Masses for the dead; e.g., Conrad of Hochstaden, Archbishop of Cologne, referred in 1260 to canons who were negligent in the matter of *lunationes mensium, aut Kalendae, seu obitus fidelium.* In the 13th and 14th centuries the Kalands spread throughout the northwestern part of Germany, with heaviest concentration in Westphalia, and were usually connected with cathedrals and chantries. Membership in the Kalands differed according to individual statutes, some groups being composed exclusively of priests or clerics, others of clerics and laymen, but most commonly of clerics, laymen, and women. Membership was usually limited to 12 persons, a good reputation being an essential requirement for acceptance. During the Reformation the Kalands suffered almost total disintegration, and during the secularization that followed they disappeared, leaving hardly a trace. They are still preserved in Münster (cathedral, since 1300), Wiedenbrück, (chantry, since 1343), and Wüllen (parish church, since 1357).

Bibliography: L. VON LEDEBUR, ''Die Kalandsverbrüderungen in den Landen Sächsischen Volks–Stammes'' *Märkische Forschungen von dem Verein für Geschichte der Mark Brandenburg* 4 (1850) 7–76. R. STAPPER, ''Der grosse Kaland am Dom zu Münster,'' *Westfälische Zeitschrift* 86 (1929) 82–96. F. FLASKAMP, *Die Kalands–Brüderschaft zu Wiedenbrück,* 2 v. (Münster 1957–59). R. PREISING, *Der Werler Kaland* (Werl 1958).

[M. F. LAUGHLIN]

KĀLĪ

One of the names of the Mother Goddess in Hinduism. She is the consort of Śiva, and is known in her auspicious aspect as Umā or Pārvatī, but in her terrible aspect

The goddess Kali. (Victoria & Albert Museum, Crown Copyright/Art Resource, NY)

as Durgā or Kālī. She is represented as a four-armed woman with her tongue lolling out; she is garlanded with skulls and dancing on the body of her prostrate lord. Yet, this fearful goddess is worshiped all over India as the Great Mother, and especially in Bengal, she has inspired intense devotion. She was celebrated in exquisite poetry by Rāmprasād Sen in the 18th century; and Rāmakrishna, the ''saint'' of modern Hinduism, was her devotee, regarding her as the eternal manifestation of the Supreme Being. Her cult is distinguished by the sacrifice of goats; the Kālī Ghat in Calcutta is the center of these rites.

See Also: HINDUISM and its bibliography.

[B. GRIFFITHS]

KALINOWSKI, RAFAŁ OF ST. JÓZEF, ST.

Baptized Józef (Joseph), engineer, freedom fighter, Discalced Carmelite (OCD) priest, ''martyr of the confessional''; b. Sept. 1, 1835, at Vilna, Lithuania; d. Nov. 15, 1907, at the Carmel in Wadowice, Poland.

Born in Lithuania to an aristocratic Polish family, Kalinowski entered the military in 1853 and studied civil engineering at the Academy of Military Sciences, St. Petersburg. Thereafter he was appointed to the fortress at Brest Litowski, Belarus, where he was charged with overseeing the building of the railway line between Kurst and Odessa. His success in that task led to his promotion to captain about the time the Russian Army occupied Poland (1863). Although he desired to devote himself to charity, as a Polish patriot, he accepted the position of minister of war in Vilna and participated in the uprising (1863) against the Russian occupation. He was captured in 1864 and condemned to death. Later his sentence was commuted to ten years' exile in Siberia. The first four years were spent in a desolate labor camp, where he became known as a man of boundless charity and serenity. Fellow prisoners sought him out for spiritual advice. He was freed in 1874, but since he was forbidden to live in any major Polish city, he went to Paris, where he became tutor to Prince August Czartoryski, who later became a Salesian priest.

In 1877 he was received into the Austrian Carmelites, taking the name Rafał of St. Józef and was ordained priest in 1882. Thereafter he began his work of restoring the Discalced Carmelites in Poland, especially in Czerna, Krakow, and Wadowice, where he a founded a monastery (1892) and served as its prior. His primary apostolate centered on the confessional. His gift of charity made him a much sought spiritual director, but he also taught novices and served in other capacities. Among his spiritual sons is St. Albert CHMIELOWSKI.

His spiritual life is marked by continual prayer fed by austerity and silence. He also longed and worked for Christian unity. He wrote several books on Carmelite spirituality. Kalinowski is buried at Czerna.

Pope JOHN PAUL II, who was born in Wadowice and tried to become a Carmelite, beatified Kalinowski in 1983 at Krakow, Poland. When Kalinowski was canonized by the same pope (Nov. 17, 1991), he was the first Carmelite friar to be so honored since John of the Cross in 1726.

Feast: Nov. 19 (Carmelites).

Bibliography: *Acta Apostolicae Sedis* 76 (1984) 1045–1047. *L'Osservatore Romano,* English ed., no. 28 (1983) 9–10. S. ADAMC-ZYK, *Niespokojne serce* (Krakow 1983). R. BENDER, *Powstaniec-zakonnik [ojciec] Rafał Kalinowski* (Warsaw 1977). J. GALOFARO, *Al Carmelo attraverso la Siberia* (Rome 1960). C. GIL, *O. Rafał Kalinowski* (Krakow 1979). R. KALINOWSKI, *Listy* (Lublin 1978). S. T. PRASKIEWICZ, *St. Raphael Kalinowski: An Introduction to His Life and Spirituality,* tr. T. COONAN, M. GRIFFIN, and L. SULLIVAN (Washington 1999).

[K. I. RABENSTEIN]

KANSAS, CATHOLIC CHURCH IN

Part of the Louisiana Purchase, the area that is now Kansas was annexed to the United States in 1803. Having been part of the Missouri Territory until 1821, it remained unorganized until formation of the Indian Territory in 1832. The Kansas-Nebraska Act (1854) established the territories of Kansas and Nebraska, and on January 29, 1861, Kansas became the 34th state to enter the Union. Its 81,815 square miles are at the geographic center of the continental United States, with Nebraska to the North, Missouri to the East, Oklahoma to the South, and Colorado to the West.

At the time of the Louisiana Purchase, Shawnee, Osage, Potawatomi, Quivira, Kaw (Kansa), Ottawa, Cherokee, and many other Native American tribes occupied the territory. During the nineteenth century, thousands of Native Americans were relocated to Kansas, and then to Oklahoma. When Kansas attained statehood, it held a population of about 110,000—mostly settlers from the South and New England and immigrants from Germany, Russia, Sweden, and England. By that time, nearly all Native Americans had been pushed into Oklahoma. In the year 2000, Kansas had a total population of 2,688,418, of whom 86.1% were white, 7.0% Hispanic, 5.7% black, 1.7% Asian, and only 0.9% Native American.

Early History. On June 29, 1541, Franciscan Friar Juan de Padilla (*c.* 1490–1542) crossed the Arkansas River near present-day Dodge City with Spanish conquistador Francisco Vásquez de Coronado (*c.* 1510–1554). After celebrating the first Mass in what is now the United States, he separated from Coronado and began evangelizing the Quivira. A monument stands near Saint Rose's Church, Council Grove, at the site believed to be the place where he became the protomartyr of the United States at the hands of a rival tribe.

Father Charles DE LA CROIX (1792–1869) made the next attempt to evangelize Kansas when he traveled to the Neosho River and converted many of the Osage (1822), but it was the Jesuits who established a lasting presence. Beginning in 1827, Father Charles VAN QUICKENBORNE, S.J. (1788–1837) journeyed repeatedly from St. Louis to evangelize the Native Americans of northeast Kansas—primarily Osage, Peorias, Weas, and Pienkishaws. He established Saint Francis Xavier mission for the Kickapoo near Leavenworth in 1836 but abandoned it in 1847. Father Christian Hoecken, S.J. (1851) established a mission for the Pottawatomie at Sugar Creek (1839), where Saint Rose Philippine DUCHESNE (1769–1852) and the Religious of the Sacred Heart founded a school for girls (1841). In 1847, when the Pottawatomies moved to their new reservation west of present-day Topeka, the missionaries followed and established Saint Mary's Jesuit Mission with Saint Mary's College, which they operated until 1967, and in 1978 sold to the schismatic Society of Saint Pius X. In 1846, the Jesuits established a mission for soldiers at Fort Scott, and then in 1847, Fathers John Schoenmakers, S.J. (1807–1883) and John Bax, S.J. (1817–1852), along with three lay brothers, established Osage Mission at St. Paul, both in southeast Kansas. Osage Mission included Saint Ann's Academy for girls, run by the Sisters of Loretto from Kentucky.

Pius IX established the ''Vicariate Apostolic East of the Rocky Mountains to Missouri'' in 1851. He gave care of this territory to Bishop Jean-Baptiste Miège (1851–1874), who resided at Saint Mary's Mission. With over one million square miles of land, the territory stretched from the Rocky Mountains to the Missouri River, and from Texas to Canada. A year after the Kansas-Nebraska Act allowed white immigration, Miège established Leavenworth as his episcopal city. There were 700 Catholics, six complete churches, three under construction, 11 stations, and eight priests. Pius IX divided the vicariate in 1857, leaving Miège with just the Kansas Territory. Even in this smaller territory, covering the vast land remained a considerable challenge. To this end, Father Philip Colleton (1821–1876) organized a circulating library of 250 volumes, and Miège brought various religious orders to Kansas, including Benedictine monks (Atchison 1858), Sisters of Charity (Leavenworth 1858), Benedictine Sisters (Atchison 1863), and Carmelite priests (Leavenworth 1864). These religious men and women established schools and took of the care of parishes and missions. Bishop Miège consecrated the Leavenworth Cathedral of the Immaculate Conception (1868) and attended the Vatican Council (1869–70) before he resigned in 1874.

Bishop Louis Mary Fink (1877–1904) succeeded Miège and promoted Catholic immigration to Kansas, bringing German, Polish, Croatian, Slovak, Slovenian, Lithuanian, and Irish immigrants who established ethnic parishes. The Homestead Act (1862)—granting 160 acres of land to each settler—and the building of railroads led to a tripling of the Kansas population from 107,206 in 1860 to 364,399 in 1870. In the aftermath of the Civil War, the Black population also rose and Holy Epiphany parish was established in Leavenworth as the first African-American parish west of St. Louis (1874). At Fink's request, the Holy See established Leavenworth as a diocese on May 22, 1877, a suffragan of St. Louis. At the time, it included 45,000 Catholics, 60 priests, 80 churches and chapels, one abbey, seven colleges, 20 parochial schools, an orphanage, and a hospital.

It was Fink's vision to establish a system of ''Christian forts'' throughout Kansas following the military

Archdiocese/Diocese	Year Created
Archdiocese of Kansas City in Kansas	1952
Diocese of Dodge City	1951
Diocese of Salina	1887
Diocese of Wichita	1887

model. These would be places of refuge for Catholics and especially the clergy who often traveled long distances in their ministerial activities. He brought Franciscan friars to Emporia (1878) and Ursuline sisters to Scipio (1896). The most notable example of these was, however, Saint Fidelis Friary at Victoria, established in 1878 by Capuchin Friar Anastasius Joseph Mueller (d. 1878), who died two months after founding the friary. The Capuchins expanded the friary to include the Capuchin school of philosophy (1903), Hays Catholic College (1908), Saint Anthony's Hospital in Hays (1909), and the nationally known ''Cathedral of the Plains'' (1912). The friary with the ''cathedral'' still stands as a landmark for travelers on Interstate 70. The Capuchin friars of Missouri, Kansas, and Colorado formed the Mid-American Province of Saint Conrad (1977), with a novitiate in Victoria.

At Fink's request, the Holy See divided the diocese in 1887, establishing the Dioceses of Concordia in northwest Kansas under Bishop Richard Scannell (1887–1890) and Wichita, which occupied the southern half of the state, under James O'Reilly (d. 1887), who died before his installation, and who was replaced by Bishop John Joseph Hennessy (1888–1897). The Church of Our Lady of Perpetual Help was made the cathedral in Concordia, and in Wichita, Saint Aloysius church was designated the pro-cathedral until the dedication of the Cathedral of the Immaculate Conception (1912). The last Indian raid in Kansas occurred that year and the railroads flourished. Quarantine laws had stopped the cattle trail drives from Texas in 1885, and harsh winters in 1886 and 1887 had disastrous effects on cattle. Land values had risen 400% from 1881–1887, so a crash in 1887 drove many settlers from the land making room for immigrants. These immigrants came largely from around the Great Lakes, especially Illinois and Ohio, and from Germany. Unlike in most other states, women in Kansas were able to vote in municipal, school, and bond elections, and Susanna Medora Salter (1860–1961) served as America's first Woman Mayor in Argonia, Kansas.

Twentieth Century. When Scannell was transferred to Omaha, Bishop Henessey of Wichita was named administrator of Concordia until the 1897 appointment of Thadeus Butler (1833–1897), who died in Rome before his installation. John Francis Cunningham (1898–1919)

Skyline of Topeka, Kansas. (Greater Topeka Chamber of Commerce)

was then named the second bishop of Concordia. Immigration continued through the turn of the century, bringing more challenges for the Church. As communities grew and moved due to flooding, railroads, or changes in county seats, churches were needed that could hold larger congregations and withstand the Kansas weather. Many of the earlier wooden buildings had since been destroyed by fire, flood, or wind, so new churches were built of stone, many of which remain in use, especially in rural communities.

Father Francis Clement Kelly, pastor of Immaculate Conception parish, Lapeer, Michigan and later Bishop of Oklahoma City and Tulsa (1924–1948), gave a lecture to Catholics at Argonia in southwestern Kansas. The following day, moved by their inability to build a church, he addressed Bishop Hennessy who suggested that he form an extension society to collect money for needy parishes. Therefore, in 1904, Father Kelly established the Catholic Church Extension Society of the United States of America (CCES). One of the society's earliest projects was Saint Anthony's chapel car, a 72-foot railroad car with a chapel that seated 50, sleeping quarters for the missionaries and a porter, a kitchen with refrigerator, and a library. On June 22, 1907, it left Wichita on its first mis-

sionary journey stopping first in Wellington, Kansas the following day; Father Tom McKernan (1881–1959) celebrated a Mass at which Bishop Hennessy preached. Those two, along with organist George Hennessey (no relation to the bishop), a representative of the CCES, and a porter traveled throughout the Diocese of Wichita administering the sacraments, praying vespers, and leading various devotions. They made a tour through the South before leaving the chapel car in New Orleans with the CCES. The overwhelming success prompted the Extension Society to construct a second, larger car, but it did not serve in Kansas due to new anti-pass laws which prevented the pass courtesy that the chapel car had previously enjoyed from the railroads.

Due in part to the great demand for wheat in Europe, the 1910s and 1920s were a time of economic prosperity for Kansas. Bishops Thomas F. Lillis (1904–1910) and John Ward (1911–1929) of Leavenworth; Hennessy, and August J. Schwertner (1921–1939) of Wichita; and Cunningham and Francis J. Tief (1921–1938) of Concordia placed great emphasis on education. In addition to the high schools these bishops established throughout the state, Tief founded Marymount College at Salina in 1922, which, four years later, was the first school in the state to offer degrees to women, and Ward founded Saint Mary's College at Leavenworth in 1923.

However prosperous times may have been in the first two decades of the century, the following decade brought disaster. In 1929, the Great Depression reduced the demand for crops while production remained high. The following year brought dust storms in which violent winds at times carried the fertile Kansas soil over 100 miles before dropping it, covering roads, railroad tracks, and farm machinery. Hot summers, cold winters, floods, and grasshopper swarms devastated Kansas' agriculture throughout the 1930s. During the depression, the emphasis on education continued with Bishop Cunningham establishing Saint Joseph's College and Military Academy at Hays in 1931. Bishop Schwertner established 16 religious vacation schools in 1929, with 737 students, and 19 more in 1930, with a total of 1,469 students. He also established religious correspondence schools for children who lived far from a church, and in 1929, the Sisters College, a branch of the University of Wichita, was opened at the cathedral to train teachers, with 129 sisters enrolled. The following year, radio station KFH aired the Catholic Radio Hour to further these educational efforts, and in the 1930s, the Confraternity of Christian Doctrine was begun in all three dioceses.

Expansion and Change. Because of its location on the Missouri River and the presence of railroad lines, Kansas City grew rapidly. As a result, Bishop George Donnelly (1947–1950) moved his see from Leavenworth to Kansas City, Kansas in 1947, shortly after his installation. He made Saint Peter's church his cathedral.

Clyde Cessna (1879–1954), during the winter of 1916–17, and Walter Beech (1891–1951), in 1932, began constructing planes on assembly lines in Wichita, setting the stage for a great turning point in state history. With the entry of the United States into World War II (1939), the demand for military aircraft brought thousands of workers to Wichita from surrounding rural areas and other states; in the 1940s, the population of Wichita grew from 114,966 to 168,279. Further growth came for Wichita with the activation of McConnell Air Force Base in 1951. While at the beginning of World War II there were only eight parishes in the city, by 1960, there were 17. In that same time, only seven parishes were established elsewhere within the 1960 diocesan boundaries, three of which were near the Air Force base. Expansion of Fort Riley infantry camp and Air Force bases in Salina and Walker brought rapid growth to those towns. The Kansas population, and by consequence, the Church, was becoming more and more urban.

As populations grew and shifted, Bishop Frank A. Thill (1938–1957) moved his see from Concordia to the

Exterior view of cupola of Catholic church with golden dome and cross, Kansas City. (©Kevin R. Morris/CORBIS)

larger Salina where better access to railroads facilitated travel for himself and his priests; he named Sacred Heart church his new cathedral. Bishop Frederick W. Freking (1957–1965) dedicated the current Sacred Heart Cathedral, built in a grain elevator motif, in 1962. Also due to this rapid growth, Bishop Mark K. Carroll of Wichita (1947–1963) petitioned that the Diocese of Wichita be split. The Holy See granted his request and in 1951 established the Diocese of Dodge City with Bishop John B. Franz (1951–1960) its first ordinary. In 1961, Dodge City became the first diocese in the United States and the second in the western hemisphere to honor Mary as its patroness under the title of Our Lady of Guadalupe, and the Cathedral of Our Lady of Guadalupe was dedicated in 2001. A year after the establishment of the Diocese of Dodge City, Kansas was made an ecclesiastical province with Kansas City as its metropolitan see.

In 1954, Bishop Carroll announced the project he considered to be his "greatest ambition," the establishment of Chaplain Kapaun Memorial High School in Wichita, which he opened two years later. A priest of the Diocese of Wichita from Pilsen, Kansas, Chaplain Emil Kapaun (1916–1951) had served as an army chaplain in both World War II and the Korean Conflict. He died in a prisoner of war camp hospital in Pyoktong, Korea. In

1971, the high school merged with Mount Carmel Academy to form Kapaun Mount Carmel High School. In 1965, Archbishop Hunkeler (1951–1969) opened Savior of the World Minor Seminary with 66 freshmen and 31 sophomores from various dioceses. However, decreasing enrollment and the shortage of priests to serve on its faculty forced Archbishop Ignatius Strecker (1969–1992) to close the seminary in 1987. The facility was then converted into the Savior Pastoral Center. With the rapid cultural changes that came about in the 1950s and 1960s, the dioceses of Kansas felt the need to reevaluate their ministries. Dodge City held its first synod in 1957. Wichita held a synod the following year, its first since 1898, and Salina held its first in 1962. Diocesan Councils of Catholic Women were established in Wichita and Salina in 1958 and in Dodge City in 1962. As the number of priests in all four dioceses decreased in the years following Vatican Council II, new efforts were made to meet the spiritual needs of the faithful. In Salina, in 1975, Bishop Cyril J. Vogel (1965–1979) began "Team Ministry," a group of three priests who together staffed six parishes (though each retained canonical responsibility for two of them). The model was continued, though individual priests were transferred into and out of the team, and eventually, women religious were included, thus initiating their role as "pastoral associates" in the diocese. In Dodge City, Bishop Eugene Gerber (1976–1982) began a permanent diaconate program in 1978 that produced seven deacons, ordained in the winter of 1983–84. Bishop Gilmore (1998–) reestablished the program in 1999, and in December 2000 ordained six Hispanic men. He hoped that they could help the diocese meet the growing demand for Hispanic ministry that arose as Mexican laborers immigrated to the area to work in meat packing plants. In addition, priests have been recruited for ministry in the state from Burma, Vietnam, and the Philippines.

Wichita received international attention in 1991 when the pro-life organization Operation Rescue organized the "Summer of Mercy," a six-week series of demonstrations, rallies, and protests. Operation Rescue leaders arrived in Wichita on July 15 and immediately began protesting in front of Wichita's three abortion clinics by praying, singing, and physically blocking entrances. Those six weeks saw over 2,000 arrests and cost local and county governments over $500,000. The Summer of Mercy culminated on August 24 with a rally at which Bishop Gerber encouraged the 40,000 people present to continue their peaceful efforts against abortion. At the same time, the National Organization for Women held a counter-rally drawing only 5,000 pro-choice advocates. As the counter-rally disbanded, a group calling themselves "Rural America For Life" jammed Wichita traffic for three hours as their tractorcade moved through the city with 300 farm vehicles sporting pro-life signs. The Summer of Mercy breathed new life into the pro-life movement in Wichita, throughout the state, and other parts of the country. The diocese has seen lasting effects as the abortion issue has remained a source of unity, drawing adults and especially youth to greater participation in the life of the Church.

Catholic health care in Kansas has been led by the Sisters of the Sorrowful Mother of the Third Order of Saint Francis, who started Saint Francis Hospital in Wichita in 1889. By 1969, with 860 beds, it had become the second largest Catholic hospital in the nation. In 1995, the hospital merged with Saint Joseph's Hospital, for which the Sister's of Saint Joseph had assumed responsibility in 1925, forming the Via Christi Regional Medical Center with over 1,500 beds at the two campuses.

Since the Second Vatican Council, all four dioceses have put a new emphasis on the universal call to holiness. Bishop Gerber, while in Dodge City, introduced RENEW (1981) to promote family and small group prayer and scripture study. Later, in that same diocese, Bishop Stanley G. Schlarmann (1983–1998) promoted Teens Encounter Christ and the Cursillo movement. Catholics in the diocese participated in Cursillo weekends in Texas beginning in 1962 until 1988 when the first weekend was held in the diocese at Lakin. Though normally conducted in Spanish, the diocese has also held weekends in English. Bishop George K. Fitzsimons (1984–) established a RENEW Office (1985) and an Office of Lay Ministry (1986) for the Diocese of Salina, and Archbishop Strecker directed every parish in the Archdiocese of Kansas City to establish a parish council and finance committee in order to promote lay involvement. The archdiocese also became home to a large number of active Serra Clubs, an international organization that supports vocations.

After being transferred to the Diocese of Wichita in 1982, Bishop Gerber promoted various programs to deepen spirituality among the laity, including Teens Encounter Christ and the Totus Tuus Summer Catechetical Program, which has served all four dioceses of Kansas as well as parishes in Colorado, Nebraska, Oklahoma, Missouri, Georgia, and Wisconsin since its beginning in 1987. Bishop Gerber also made a strong effort to promote Eucharistic devotion, which was enthusiastically received in parishes throughout the diocese. Archbishop Keleher (1992–) did similarly in Kansas City.

Bibliography: The Archdiocese of Kansas City in Kansas, *The Archdiocese of Kansas City in Kansas: 150 Years of Faith 1850–2000* (Strasbourg, France 2000). M. P. FITZGERALD S.C.L, *Beacon on the Plains* (Leavenworth, KS 1939). M. F. LAHEY, *Har-*

vest of Faith: History of the Diocese of Salina, 1887–1987 (Dallas, TX). J. M. MOEDER, *History of the Diocese of Wichita* (1963). I. J. STRECKER, *The Church in Kansas 1850–1905: "A Family Story"*. A. TONNE, *The Story of Chaplain Kapaun: Patriot Priest of the Korean Conflict* (Emporia, KS 1954). T. WENZL, *A Legacy of Faith, A History of the Diocese of Dodge City* (Newton, KS 2001).

[D. MARSTALL]

KANSAS CITY, ARCHDIOCESE OF

Metropolitan see embracing 21 counties in the northeastern part of Kansas, an area of 12,524 square miles, with the Dioceses of Dodge City, Salina, and Wichita, all in Kansas, as suffragan sees. The Archdiocese of Kansas City (*Kansanopolitana*) was established as the Diocese of Leavenworth on May 22, 1877, was changed to Kansas City on May 10, 1947, and it became an archdiocese on Aug. 9, 1952. At the beginning of the 21st century, Catholics comprised about 20 percent of the total population.

Early History. Catholicism in Kansas dates from 1541, when the Coronado expedition arrived, accompanied by the Franciscan Juan de PADILLA, who lost his life while preaching to Native American tribes. In 1820, Sans Nerf, head chief of the Osage, appealed to Bp. Louis William DuBourg of St. Louis to visit or send them missionaries. Rev. Charles de la Croix was sent in 1822. That same year DuBourg went to Washington to ask the U.S. government to subsidize four missionaries whom he proposed to send to the Osages. His proposal was approved by Secretary of War John C. Calhoun, then in charge of Native American affairs, who promised an annual subsidy of $800.

Although the Kickapoo mission, founded in 1835 by Charles Van Quickenborne, SJ, lasted only four years, it became the center from which the two focal missions were later established among the Osages and Pottawatomies. From Osage Mission School, founded by John Schoenmakers, SJ, in 1847, and from St. Mary's Pottawatomie mission, founded by Christian Hoecken, SJ, in 1848, the Jesuits first ministered to surrounding Indian tribes and later sought out scattered white frontiersmen. Their itinerant circuits covered most of Kansas as it is now constituted. As secular priests arrived to assume responsibility for established parishes, the Jesuits gradually withdrew from the mission field. However, the zeal of Fathers John Bax, Paul Ponziglione, Philip Colleton, and Louis Dumortier had opened the frontier to the Catholic Church, making it known and respected not only by Catholics but by non-Catholics also.

The religious of the Sacred Heart, including Mother Phillipine DUCHESNE, opened a school for Native American girls among the Pottawatomies in 1841. The Sisters of Loretto arrived at Osage mission in 1847, to establish the first permanent boarding school on Kansas soil.

At the request of the Seventh Provincial Council of Baltimore, Pius IX, on July 19, 1850, erected the vicariate apostolic of Native American Territory, which included the present states of Kansas, Nebraska, Oklahoma, parts of North and South Dakota west of the Missouri River, Wyoming, Montana, and Colorado. John B. MIÈGE, SJ, professor of moral theology at St. Louis University, was consecrated bishop of Messine and first vicar apostolic of the new jurisdiction. He made St. Mary's mission in Kansas his residence, and the log cabin church there served as his cathedral until August 1855, when he moved to Leavenworth, a promising city in the newly organized Kansas Territory. On horseback or by wagon, Miège visited the Native American villages, military forts, trading posts, and growing towns of his vast mission, which was reduced in size in 1857 when Nebraska was organized into a separate vicariate.

Miège invited the Benedictine and Carmelite fathers, the Benedictine sisters, and the Sisters of Charity, to the mission fields in his vicariate. The Sisters of Charity opened the first orphanage in Kansas (1863) and the first hospital in Leavenworth (1869). Among the first secular priests to enter the apostolate in Kansas were Theodore Heimann, a German priest who later joined the Carmelites, J. H. Defourri from France, and Ambrose T. Butler from Ireland. Daniel Hurley, the first Native American ordained in Kansas (1877), exerted an important influence on the growth of the Church there.

Ecclesiastical Administration. In 1871, Louis M. FINK, OSB, was consecrated bishop of Eucarpia and auxiliary to Bishop Miège, whom he succeeded upon Miège's resignation in 1874. When Leavenworth was elevated to the status of diocese in 1877, Fink administered the entire state of Kansas, which then included 65 priests, 88 churches, three "colleges," four academies, one hospital, one orphanage, and 13 parochial schools with 1,700 pupils. During the next ten years, the building of roads and railroads, generous government land policies, and the settlement of the Native American issue on the frontier attracted immigrants; and Irish, Germans, Belgians, and French established colonies throughout the diocese. The German-Russians who settled in Ellis and Rush counties in the late 1890s left an enviable cultural heritage to the Church in Kansas. Those who worked among them included the Capuchin Fathers, Sisters of St. Agnes, and Sisters of St. Joseph of Concordia.

At Fink's suggestion, the Diocese of Leavenworth was divided and the western section constituted the Dioceses of Concordia and Wichita, Aug. 2, 1887. The areas of the three dioceses were redistributed in 1897 when boundaries were adjusted. Fink continued to administer Leavenworth until his death in 1904, when he was succeeded by Thomas F. Lillis, who was consecrated on Dec. 27, 1904, and governed the see until his transfer to the Diocese of Kansas City, Mo., in 1910. John Ward, consecrated third bishop of Leavenworth on Feb. 22, 1911, ruled until his death in 1929, when his coadjutor, Francis Johannes, succeeded to the see, which he headed until his death in 1937. Paul C. Schulte's administration, begun in 1937, was terminated by his transfer to the Archdiocese of Indianapolis in 1946, when George J. Donnelly succeeded him in Leavenworth. A year later the see was changed to Kansas City where, following Donnelly's death in 1950, Edward J. Hunkeler became successively bishop (1951) and archbishop (1952). When Hunkeler retired in 1969, he was succeeded by Bishop Ignatius J. Strecker, Bishop of Springfield-Cape Girardeau, who was Archbishop of Kansas City from 1969 until his retirement in 1993. In 1993, Bishop James P. Keleher, Bishop of Belleville was installed as Strecker's successor.

Institutional Development. In the expansion of its parochial and secondary school systems, the archdiocese pioneered in the central Catholic high school movement in the U.S. in the early 20th century. Catholic institutions of higher learning in the archdiocese included Donnelly College (Kansas City), St. Mary College (Leavenworth) and Benedictine College (Atchison), established, July 1, 1971, as a merger between St. Benedict's College, directed by the Benedictine monks; and Mt. St. Scholastica College, directed by the Benedictine Sisters.

Bibliography: P. BECKMAN, *The Catholic Church on the Kansas Frontier, 1850–1877* (Washington 1943). R. J. BOLLIG, *History of Catholic Education in Kansas, 1836–1932* (Washington 1933). Garraghan JMUS. W. W. GRAVES, *Life and Letters of Fathers Ponziglione, Schoenmakers and Other Early Jesuits at Osage Mission* (St. Paul, Kan. 1916). T. H. KINSELLA, *A Centenary of Catholicity in Kansas 1822–1922* (Kansas City 1921). M. E. THOMAS, *Footprints on the Frontier* (Westminster, Md. 1948). THE ARCHDIOCESE OF KANSAS CITY IN KANSAS, *The Archdiocese of Kansas City in Kansas: 150 Years of Faith 1850–2000* (Strasbourg, France 2000).

[M. E. THOMAS/EDS.]

KANSAS CITY-ST. JOSEPH, DIOCESE OF

The Diocese of Kansas City was established Sept. 10, 1880; the Diocese of St. Joseph, March 3, 1868. After some territorial alterations throughout the state of Missouri, the two dioceses were redesignated as the Diocese of Kansas City-St. Joseph (*Kansanopolitana-Sancti Joseph*), Aug. 29, 1956. It is a suffragan of the Archdiocese of St. Louis.

Early History. The first bishop of St. Joseph was John J. Hogan, who was consecrated Sept. 13, 1868; he was transferred to the new See of Kansas City in 1880, but remained administrator of St. Joseph until 1893. His successors in Kansas City were Thomas F. Lillis (1913–38) and Edwin V. O'Hara (1939–56); Bp. Maurice F. Burke of Cheyenne, Wyo., was transferred to St. Joseph (1893–1923), and was succeeded there by Francis Gilfillan (1923–33) and Charles H. LeBlond (1933–56). On Sept. 11, 1956, Bp. John P. Cody, coadjutor of St. Joseph since 1954, was appointed to succeed O'Hara in the redesignated Diocese of Kansas City-St. Joseph. Bishop Charles H. Helmsing of Springfield-Cape Girardeau, Mo., became the ordinary of Kansas City-St. Joseph on Jan. 27, 1962, following Cody's transfer (Aug. 10, 1961) to New Orleans, La. Following Helmsing's retirement in 1977, Bishop John J. Sullivan of Grand Island, Nebr. was transferred to Kansas City-St. Joseph on June 27. Upon his retirement on Sept. 9, 1993 he was succeeded by Bishop Raymond J. Boland who was transferred from Birmingham, Alabama.

The earliest Catholics of the diocese were French traders and their Native American wives and children, then German and Irish immigrants. Among the first European families to settle in what is now the site of Kansas City was François and Berenice Chouteau who offered their time and money to build Kansas City's first church, for some time known as "Chouteau's Church." They were instrumental in preserving the faith for themselves and the other members of the small community at the big bend of the Missouri River until they secured a resident priest.

Early clergy included Frs. Charles de la Croix (1822) Anthony Lutz (1828) and various Jesuit missionaries (1827–1875) The first resident priest to serve the area that is now Kansas City was Benedict Roux from Lyons, France, who was sent to St. Louis by the Society for the Propagation of the Faith and then appointed (1833) to the frontier settlement by Bp. Joseph Rosati. The first resident pastor of Independence, Mo., was Bernard Donnelly, who served from 1845 to his death in 1880 as missionary to much of the territory now comprising the diocese. He was pastor of the pioneer parish in Kansas City and was personally responsible for the establishment of the first Catholic school, hospital, orphanage, and cemetery in Kansas City.

Twentieth Century. Following Vatican II, the diocese, under the leadership of Bishop Helmsing was involved in several ecumenical projects, the most significant of which was the signing of a Covenant with the Episcopal Diocese of West Missouri. Further implementation of the Council came under Bishop Sullivan who was interested in lay ministry development. In 1978 the Center for Pastoral Life and Ministry was established for the purpose of preparing a well trained cadre of lay pastoral ministers. (In 1995 the Center' formation program, New Wine, was published by Paulist Press for use throughout the United States.)

In the mid 1960s, mission outreach began with the sending of priests to serve in four parishes in Bolivia all of which were subsequently turned over to indigenous clergy and pastoral workers. Efforts continued with the growth of "sister parish" relationships developed during the last two decades of the 20th century. Delegations traveled to sister parishes in Mexico and Central America for mutual learning, sharing and faith development.

Typical of many dioceses in the 20th century, growth in Catholic population and the establishment of parishes and institutions to serve their needs flourished through the mid 1960s. With the great cultural shifts and racial tensions following this period, many priests, religious and lay leaders were active in promoting civil rights both locally and nationally. Nevertheless, the diocese was not immune from "white flight" from the inner city and the economic hardships developing in rural America necessitating the closure and consolidation of numerous parishes from the 1970s to the early 1990s. In the latter half of the 1990s, the trend changed and several new parishes were established to accommodate the Catholic population.

At the dawn of the 21st century the Catholic population in the diocese numbered about 13 percent of the total population, distributed across 85 parishes and 15 missions. This included a growing presence of Hispanic and Vietnamese Catholics. Among Catholic institutions of higher education are Conception Seminary College (1886), Rockhurst University (1910) and Avila College (1916). *The National Catholic Reporter,* originally started as a national edition of the diocesan newspaper, is headquartered in Kansas City. *The Catholic Key* is the diocesan newspaper.

Bibliography: W. J. DALTON, *The Life of Father Bernard Donnelly* (Kansas City, Mo. 1921). G. J. GARRAGHAN, *Catholic Beginnings in Kansas City, Missouri* (Chicago 1920); ed., "Selected Letters from the Roux Correspondence, 1833–34," *American Catholic Historical Review* 4.1 (Washington 1918) 84–100. J. HOGAN, *Fifty Years Ago: A Memoir Written in 1898* (Kansas City, Mo. 1907). J. P. O'HANLON, *Life and Scenery in Missouri: Reminiscences of a Missionary Priest* (Dublin 1890). J. E. ROTHENSTEINER, *History of the Archdiocese of St. Louis* (St. Louis 1928). J. J. SCHLAFLY, *Light in the Early West* (New York 1959); "Birth of Kansas City's Pioneer Church," *Missouri Historical Review* 44 (1950) 364–372. W. KUENHOF, "Catholic Church Annals in Kansas City, 1800–57," *American Catholic Historical Review* 3.2 (1917) 326–335.

[J. J. SCHLAFLY/G. M. NOONAN]

Immanuel Kant. (Archive Photos)

KANT, IMMANUEL

German philosopher of outstanding ability and influence; b. Königsberg, East Prussia, April 22, 1724; d. there, Feb. 12, 1804. Kant's father was a harness maker of ability. The spiritual climate of his family was that of orthodox Lutheranism intermingled with pietistic elements. Kant himself never traveled farther than the province of Königsberg; he left the city but seldom, and then only for short stays in the country. He began his graduate studies in 1740 at the University of Königsberg and earned his doctorate in philosophy there in 1755. His *Habilitationsschrift* at the university was a work on the first principles of metaphysics. He remained an instructor until 1770, when he was appointed ordinary professor of logic and metaphysics. Kant was popular and much esteemed as a professor at the university; after 1781, in fact, he came to be recognized as one of the most famous men of his time. His way of life was always simple and rigorously ordered; he spent his days working seriously and with a sense of duty that may be characterized as stoic. Although he had no family of his own, he had the inclination and the time for sociability, and in spite of a weak physical constitution he lived to old age.

Development and Works. The line development of Kant's philosophical activity may be seen in his works.

There is a clear contrast between two periods: from the years 1769/1770 and on his precritical thought gradually gave way to his critical philosophy. During the precritical period Kant mainly followed the thought patterns of the rationalist Enlightenment, proceeding along the paths traced by G. W. LEIBNIZ and C. WOLFF. At the same time he somehow transcended this movement by taking into account the irrationalistic philosophy of emotions that he had learned from the work of J. J. ROUSSEAU. Again, he manifested strong interest in mathematics and the natural sciences; here he had high regard for Sir Isaac Newton, whom he considered his master. Chief among the works of this period are his *Natural History and Theory of the Heavens* (Königsberg 1755; tr. W. Hastie in *Kant's Cosmogony,* Glasgow 1900) and *Der einzig mögliche Beweisgrund zu einer Demonstration des Daseins Gottes* (Königsberg 1763). In the latter work he attempts to develop a proof of God's existence that is completely a priori. This proof gives a new foundation for causal thinking and thus develops the true sense of the cosmological and teleological proof of God's existence. However, the rational surface current lost some of its force because of the irrational undercurrent. The following words are indicative of this trend: "It is absolutely necessary to convince oneself of the existence of God; but it is not equally necessary to demonstrate it." This formulation already contains a foreboding of the critical period.

In the second phase of Kant's philosophical development, the irrational element gains the upper hand and rational metaphysics disappears. As Kant himself expresses it, he was roused from his "dogmatic slumber" through Hume's remarks on the law of causality. D. HUME maintained that the necessity that, according to traditional metaphysics, links the effect to its cause and ultimately leads to the first cause cannot be inferred either from the connection of concepts (a priori) or from experience (a posteriori). This position was taken up by Kant, who extended the argument to all necessary connections between concepts and, in so doing, raised the general question as to the possibility of experience and science and, above all, of metaphysics. Kant endeavored to solve this problem in his main work, the *Critique of Pure Reason* (Riga 1781, 2d ed. 1787; tr. N. K. Smith, 2d ed., London 1933). The *Prolegomena to Any Future Metaphysics* (Riga 1783; tr. P. Carus, rev. L. W. Beck, New York 1950) gives a short introduction and a synthetical presentation of this work. To the investigation of the theoretical realm (the field of knowing) Kant added the study of the practical realm (the field of moral action). Thus his main ethical work was titled the *Critique of Practical Reason* (Riga 1788; tr. L. W. Beck, Chicago 1949); three years previously, as a precursor to this, Kant had published his *Groundwork of the Metaphysics of Morals* (Riga 1785;

tr. H. J. Paton, London 1950). His *Critique of Judgment* (Berlin 1790; tr. J. H. Bernard, 2d ed. London 1931) is intimately connected with the two great critiques just mentioned. It deals with the faculty that plays an intermediary role between knowing and willing and that he identifies as judgment and feeling in one; its contents show that it deals with aesthetics and critical teleology. To the critique of religion Kant devoted his *Religion within the Limits of Reason Alone* (Königsberg 1793; tr. T. M. Greene and H. H. Hudson, Glasgow 1934). His *Metaphysics of Ethics* (Königsberg 1797; tr. J. W. Semple, 3d ed. Edinburgh 1886) deals with problems of ethics and the philosophy of law. Finally, the *Opus postumum* (Tübingen 1920, 1938) gives a valuable glimpse into Kant's ultimate development and into the transition from his thought to German IDEALISM.

Philosophy of Criticism. Criticism is Kant's original achievement; it identifies him as one of the greatest thinkers of mankind and as one of the most influential authors in contemporary philosophy. But it is important to understand what Kant means by criticism, or critique. In a general sense, the term refers to the cultivation of reason by way of "the secure path of a science" (B xxx). More particularly, its use is not negative but positive, a fact that finds expression in the famous sentence: "I have therefore found it necessary to deny knowledge in order to make room for faith" (B xxx). Correspondingly, its negative use consists in not allowing oneself to "venture with speculative reason beyond the limits of experience" (B xxiv). Thus criticism removes the decisive hindrance that threatens to supplant or even to destroy the "absolutely necessary practical employment of pure reason . . . in which it [pure reason] inevitably goes beyond the limits of sensibility" (B xxv). Accordingly, the critique guarantees a secure path for science by confining speculative reason to its own limits and by giving practical reason the complete use of its rights—rights that thus far had not been recognized.

Place in the History of Ideas. Kant, being confronted with the two extremes of RATIONALISM and EMPIRICISM, set for himself the task of creating a synthesis between them. As he saw it, rationalism operates in the sphere of innate ideas, with their analytical and therefore aprioristic necessity; this necessity, however, is not based on experience and consequently does not apply to reality itself. On the other hand, empiricism starts completely from experience and thus (it seems) from reality, but it arrives only at a posteriori and therefore synthetic statements that lack necessity. Kant sought to unite the concept and experience; he sought a necessity that extends to the order of objective reality and an order of objective reality that in itself contains necessity. This interpenetration finds its expression in judgments that are a priori and yet synthetic, on the one hand, and synthetic and yet a priori, on the other. Kant thought that he could attain this goal only by way of a "changed point of view" (B xvi) referred to as a "Copernican revolution." On the supposition, thus far considered to be valid, that "all our knowledge must conform to objects" (*ibid.*), a priori judgments that enlarge man's knowledge synthetically are impossible. Here one needs the opposite assumption, according to which "we suppose that objects must conform to our knowledge" (*ibid.*); only in this way are we able "to have knowledge of objects a priori, determining something in regard to them prior to their being given" (*ibid.*). Consequently, "we can know a priori of things only what we ourselves put into them" (B xviii); this means that the process of knowing a priori "has to do only with appearances, and must leave the thing-in-itself as indeed real per se, but as not known by us" (B xx). Since, however, all of metaphysics aims at the thing-in-itself, speculative reason, by which, as has been said, we "never transcend the limits of possible experience" (B xix), is unable to rise to the metaphysical level.

Critique of Knowledge. Kant perfects his criticism of knowledge in the *Critique of Pure Reason,* which moves from transcendental aesthetics to transcendental logic; and, within the latter, from transcendental analytics to transcendental dialectics. *See* TRANSCENDENTAL (KANTIAN). Throughout, the investigation revolves around the synthetic a priori judgments that have already been mentioned; these are synthetic insofar as they extend knowledge through a predicate that is not contained in the concept of the subject; they are a priori insofar as they have a necessary and universal validity, and this previous to any actual experience of individual cases. All of this, however, leads to the question: "How are a priori synthetic judgments possible?" (B 19). To put it more accurately, these judgments are questioned as to the conditions for their possibility; such conditions, on the terms of the Copernican revolution, can be found only in the subject. Kant here develops his transcendental method, a method by which he transcends a priori knowledge and arrives at the level of the conditions for its possibility, which are already marked out in the subject.

Mathematics and natural science, for him, have already followed the certain path of science. Thus, as he points out in detail, they contain a number of synthetic a priori judgments that are valid without further discussion. Consequently, one has to prove not that they are valid, but how their accepted validity is possible. To explain this, Kant goes back to the distinction between matter and form in human knowledge. The matter coincides with sensation; this is "the effect of an object upon the faculty of representation, so far as we are affected by it" (A 19); only in this way "can the object be given to us"

(*ibid.*). Matter, taken a posteriori as unordered multiplicity, has as its opposite complement form, "in which alone the sensations can be posited" and connected "in certain relationships" (A 20); this form must "lie ready for the sensations a priori in the mind" (*ibid.*). At this point one must explain the three domains of a priori forms.

First is the region of sense knowledge. This is the field of "receptivity" by which "we are affected by the objects" (A 19); "objects are given to us by means of sensibility, and it alone yields us intuitions" (*ibid.*). Now, that intuition is called empirical "which is in relation to the object through sensation" (A 20) and which therefore is based on received impressions. By way of contrast, a pure intuition is that in which "there is nothing that belongs to sensation" (*ibid.*); it is "the pure form of sensibility" (*ibid.*) and is actuated in the mind a priori, even without a given object. Correspondingly, transcendental aesthetics is "the science of all principles of a priori sensibility" (A 21); but these are two, "namely, space and time" (A 22), and they are the conditions for the possibility of the a priori synthetic judgments of mathematics. Space is more particularly the form of the external sense faculties, i.e., "the subjective condition of sensibility, under which alone outer intuition is possible for us" (A 26). Time, on the other hand, is "the form of inner sense, that is, of the intuition of ourselves and of our inner state" (A 33). Again, time is "the formal a priori condition of all appearances whatsoever," because the external representations also "belong, in themselves, as determinations of the mind, to our inner state" (A 34). To space and time is ascribed an "empirical reality" (A 35), that is, an objective validity, as the conditions that alone enable man to perceive objects; in the same way they have a "transcendental ideality" (A 36) insofar as they are "merely conditions of our sensibility" and cannot, in any way, be ascribed to "things as they are in themselves" (*ibid.*). Thus, it is true, they "make a priori synthetic propositions possible," but these "apply to objects only in so far as objects are viewed as appearances, and do not present things as they are in themselves" (A 39).

Second is the area of reason. As "spontaneity [in the production] of concepts," reason cooperates with the sense faculties, which are "receptivity for impressions"; through these impressions the object is "given," whereas through reason it is "thought" (A 50). Knowledge can arise "only through their union," for "thoughts without content are empty, and intuitions without concepts are blind" (A 51). Everything depends on the pure concepts; in these "there is no mingling of sensation," and they concern only "the form of the thought of an object in general" (A 50–51). Thus transcendental analytics consists in the "dissection of the faculty of understanding itself" insofar as, in this faculty, the pure concepts as in "their birthplace," have been located and prepared in an a priori way (A 65–66). It is thus that the synthetic a priori judgments of natural science are explained with regard to their possibility. Here the question is how to seek pure concepts on the basis of a single principle and how to "determine in an a priori manner their systematic completeness" (A 67). Because reason reaches only to "the mediate knowledge of an object" (A 68) or judgments, it constitutes "a faculty of judgment" (A 69). The elementary forms of judgment are outlined in it; from the point of view of "the mere form of understanding" they can be classified "under four heads, each of which contains three moments" (A 70). Coordinated to these are the 12 "pure concepts of understanding" (e.g., substance, causality, etc.) "which apply a priori to objects of intuition in general" (A 79); as "the true, primary concepts of the pure understanding" they are called "the categories" (A 81). To the process of educing them is linked transcendental deduction, which shows that the categories are "conditions of the possibility of experience and are therefore valid a priori for all objects of experience" (B 161). However, objects must be understood not as things in themselves, but as "appearances in space and time" that are determined by the categories (B 168–169). "Consequently, there can be no a priori knowledge, except of objects of possible experience" (B 166). Subject to the same limitations are the principles that teach reason (being the potency for judging) how "to apply to appearances the concepts of understanding" (A 132). To these principles belong the "principle of succession in time in accordance with the law of causality: All alterations take place in conformity with the law of the connection of cause and effect" (A 189, B 232).

Third is the study of the intellect, which is the concern of transcendental dialectics. Here the synthetic a priori judgments of metaphysics are examined as to their possibility. The question is not how they are possible, but simply whether they are possible. Kant's answer is that they are not. Here his concern is to show the "transcendental illusion" (A 297); it is a "natural and inevitable illusion" (A 298), and thus it has been able to lead metaphysics astray until now. The critique must be applied to "transcendental principles" that, in contrast to "immanent" principles, lead man to go beyond "the limits of possible experience" (A 295). At the basis of these principles one finds "transcendental ideas," designed by reason in an a priori and necessary fashion; "no object adequate to the transcendental idea can ever be found within experience"; "for they view all knowledge gained in experience as being determined by an absolute totality of conditions," by "an absolute whole" (A 327), or even by "an unconditioned [reality]" (A 323), whereas "no experience is unconditioned" (A 326). From the different ways of drawing conclusions, Kant gathers that there are three and only three ideas, namely, the soul as "the absolute (unconditioned) unity of the thinking subject," the world as "the absolute unity of the series of conditions of appearance," and God as "the absolute unity of the condition of all objects of thought in general" (A 334). These ideas "never allow of any constitutive employment . . . as supplying concepts of certain objects" (A 644). In other words, the objects that are outlined in these ideas are never recognized through them; for ideas that go as far as the thing-in-itself remain empty, because the intellectual intuition that complements them and reaches out into the realm of the thing-in-itself has not been given to man. Or, one should say, man's "nature is so constituted that our intuition can never be other than sensible" (A 51). On the other hand, these same ideas have an "indispensably necessary, regulative employment" insofar as they put before the intellect the "form of a whole of knowledge" and in this way "determine a priori for every part its position and relation to the other parts" (A 644–645). This delimitation of their use is opposed by the "sophistications" that rise "from the very nature of reason" (A 339) and claim to form a bridge from ideas to their corresponding objects. The four paralogisms intend to proceed "from the transcendental concept of the subject" to a science "concerning the nature of our thinking being" (A 340, 345). Just as "rational psychology" (A 342) is impossible, so also is "rational cosmology" (A 408). When the latter is attempted as "the absolute totality . . . of conditions for any given appearance" (A 340), reason is entangled in the four antinomies (e.g., the limitation vs. the boundlessness of the universe in space and time). In like fashion, there can be no rational theology (A 631); for all three kinds of proof for the existence of God are inconclusive (A 590). "The physico-theological proof . . . rests upon the cosmological proof, and the cosmological upon the ontological [proof]" (A 630), which itself suffers from an illegitimate transition from the realm of concepts to the realm of reality. What is left of God is only the "transcendental ideal" as the "concept of all reality" and "the complete determination of things," "without requiring that all this reality be objectively given and be itself a thing" (A 580).

Critique of Morality. Whereas the theoretical reason, or strict knowledge, can use ideas only in a regulative manner and concepts only within the realm of the PHENOMENA (in contrast to the NOUMENA), practical reason, or morality, goes on to the objective use of ideas and to extending the application of concepts to the noumena. Here Kant finds a basic fact, a given reality beyond any doubt: the CATEGORICAL IMPERATIVE as the "fundamental law of pure practical reason." It is: "So act that the maxim of your will could always hold at the same time as the principle of a universal legislation" (*Critique of Practical Reason;* ed. Cassirer, 5:35). This "synthetic proposition a priori" is not based on "any pure or empirical intuition"; but it presents itself as something that "forces itself upon us" (36). In it the "pure will" is conceived as "determined by the mere form of the law" (35); on the other hand, "the material of volition," being the "object of a desire," takes away morality (38). As opposed to this "heteronomy," one finds "autonomy" to be "the sole principle of all moral laws" (38), and in this principle pure reason is "originally legislative" (36). Moral acting is not only conditionally, viz, "to make a desired effect possible," but it is "unconditionally commanded" (36). Therefore, it is "not limited to human beings" but extends to all rational beings, even "the Infinite Being" (37); however, it presents itself only to man as an "obligation" whose fulfillment brings him closer to the holiness of the Divine Being.

By reason of the unconditional or absolute quality of the moral law, pure reason is authorized to make "an extension in its practical use which is not possible to it in its speculative use" (57). In this way Kant arrives at the postulates, which are not "theoretical dogmas but presuppositions of necessarily practical import." They do not expand "speculative knowledge, but they give objective reality to the ideas of speculative reason" (143); here the pure will shows itself as "belonging to a pure intelligible world" (57). "These postulates are those of immortality, of freedom affirmatively regarded (as the causality of a being so far as he belongs to the intelligible world), and of the existence of God" (143). They evoke assent not through insight, but through "pure practical faith." One says: I will those things that correspond to the postulates to be reality, "I stand by this and will not give up this belief" (155). At this point "my interest inevitably determines my judgment because I will not yield anything of this interest" (*ibid.*). Thus the practical metaphysics of faith, for which room had been made by abolishing the theoretical metaphysics of pure knowledge, is shown by Kant to be the center of gravity in human thought.

Critique of Aesthetic Experience. This critique deals with the transition that constitutes the ultimate unity of reason. Here the faculty of judgment forms "a middle between understanding and reason" (*Critique of Judgment;* ed. Cassirer, 5:245). In like manner "the feeling of pleasure or displeasure" stands "between the faculties of knowledge and desire" (*ibid.*). The reflective (as opposed to the determining) power of judgment rises from "the particular" to "the universal" (248). In this it is guided by the a priori principle of "finality," which, however, reflects only on the "nexus of phenomena in nature," and should not be ascribed to nature itself (249). Finality is

also found in the fact that nature is in keeping with the "need of understanding" to discover repeatedly the comprehensive principles in the apparently "heterogeneous laws" and phenomena of nature (255–256). The fulfillment of this need gives "a very appreciable pleasure"; even "the feeling of pleasure . . . is determined by a ground which is a priori and valid for all men: and that, too, merely by virtue of the reference of the object to our faculty of cognition" without considering the practical finality attached to the faculty of desire (256).

More particularly, one must distinguish the aesthetic judgment from the teleological judgment (262). The first consists in "the faculty of estimating formal finality (otherwise called subjective) by the feeling of pleasure or displeasure"; the latter refers to "the faculty of estimating the real finality (objective) of nature by understanding and reason" (262). More precisely, "the aesthetic representation of finality" is present when the representation of an object is "immediately coupled with the feeling of pleasure" (258). But this pleasure is caused through the fact that "the conformity of the object to the cognitive faculties" is "brought into play in the reflective judgment" and establishes a harmonious interplay, particularly between the imagination and the intellect (258–259). The object with whose representation "pleasure is also judged to be combined necessarily" is called beautiful; "the faculty of judging by means of such a pleasure (and so also with universal validity)" is taste (259). Accordingly, "the beautiful is that which, apart from a concept, pleases universally" (289) or "is cognized as object of a necessary delight" (311), and this "apart from any interest" (279) or "apart from the representation of an end" (306), which would appeal not to feeling but to desire.

Critique of Religion. According to Kant, religion consists in the "recognition of all duties as divine commands" (*Critique of Practical Reason,* 140); this, however, does not mean that they are "arbitrary and contingent ordinances of a foreign will" (*ibid.*). He who fulfills the obligation out of consideration of God, out of "fear or hope," falls into a heteronomy that "would destroy the entire moral worth of the actions" (*ibid.*). However, the moral law orders man to strive after "the highest possible good," and one must follow this law without self-interest and purely as an obligation (*ibid.*). This highest good includes "the greatest degree of moral perfection" and the "greatest happiness" corresponding to it (141). But because only "a holy and beneficent Author of the world" is able to guarantee such a correspondence, it is possible for one to hope for the highest good only when his will is in accord with God's will (*ibid.*). It is only in this sense that obligations, though they are "essential laws of any free will, . . . must [still] be regarded as commands of the Supreme Being'' (140). Religion is ultimately ''the disposition, accompanying all our actions, to perform these as though they were being executed in the service of God'' (*Religion within the Limits of Pure Reason;* ed. Cassirer, 6:346). All religious activity (e.g., prayer) reduces to this; everything that goes beyond it is characterized by Kant as ''a superstitious illusion'' (345). Only such a religion based on reason and restricted to the field of morals is permitted; only this constitutes the true core of the Christian religion of revelation, which degenerates into ''practical superstition'' and ''clericalism'' (325–327) when it pretends to be more than it is.

Critical Appraisal. With the ability of a genius, Kant aspired to create a grand synthesis between sense knowledge and intellectual knowledge and between man's theoretical and practical activity. He developed his transcendental method in order to achieve this synthesis. In this undertaking he was able to attain noteworthy results: the unity of human cognition, its necessity and universality, the significance of the a priori, the absoluteness of the moral imperative, the foundation of existence in the metaphysical order, and the transcendental problematics. Yet Kant's synthesis, taken as a whole, failed. It did so because he remained too much subject to the limitations of his own historical situation and, therefore, was not able to go deep enough and penetrate to ultimate depths.

From the point of view of M. Heidegger, one may summarize Kant's failure in his being unaware of BEING. How much Kant succumbs to this is clearly shown by his distinction between reason and intellect. The reason is rightly considered the faculty that, by way of fundamental concepts or categories, permeates sensible phenomena; this is equivalent to the *ratio* of St. THOMAS AQUINAS and its corresponding QUIDDITY, or *quidditas rei materialis.* Kant's intellect, on the other hand, reaches out into the metaphysical realm with its three ideas, but is never able really to penetrate it. The basis for this restriction lies in intellect's having lost, for Kant, its proper orientation toward being as all-inclusive—an orientation that enables man to enter the metaphysical realm in the first place. For St. Thomas, on the contrary, *intellectus* is intrinsically ordered to *ens,* which is grounded in *esse.* In this connection, Kant considers intellect as completely excluded from any form of intellectual INTUITION, whereas for St. Thomas *intellectus* participates in such intuition through its grasp of being, but without having it as such. Consequently, in St. Thomas's view man enters into the realm of the absolute on the theoretical level; here he is in communication with all other intelligent beings, including the divine mind. Kant relegates all this to the practical realm alone.

The transcendental method can be carried through in a way that goes beyond Kant himself to arrive at being as the primary condition for the possibility of human knowledge, and even of all human action. This basic idea has far-reaching consequences. The proof for God's existence is somehow precontained in the orientation of intellect toward being; thus does theoretical metaphysics become possible. Being, too, enables a priori knowledge to reveal rather than conceal, as it must do for Kant. Again, the formal objects of the soul's faculties for St. Thomas correspond to Kant's forms; thus knowledge through categories is not restricted to that which is ''for man,'' but opens up to that which is ''in itself.'' Finally, the absoluteness of the moral imperative also receives its foundation in being, and thus theory and practice are brought into harmony and unity.

See Also: KANTIANISM; NEO-KANTIANISM; CRITICISM, PHILOSOPHICAL; AGNOSTICISM; UNDERSTANDING (INTELLECTUS).

Bibliography: Works. *Gesammelte Schriften,* 22 v. (Berlin 1902–42), critical ed. sponsored by the Prussian Academy of Sciences. *Immanuel Kants Werke,* ed. E. CASSIRER, 11 v. (Berlin 1912–18). General studies. F. C. COPLESTON, *History of Philosophy* (Westminster, Md. 1946–1963) v.6. J. D. COLLINS, *A History of Modern European Philosophy* (Milwaukee 1954). S. VANNI ROVIGHI, *Introduzione allo studio di K.* (2d ed. Milan 1951). M. CAMPO, *La genesi del criticismo kantiano* (Varese 1953–). V. MATHIEU, *La filosofia trascendentale e l'''Opus postumum'' di K.* (Turin 1958). H. J. DE VLEESCHAUWER, *La Déduction transcendantale dans l'oeuvre de K,* 3 v. (Antwerp 1934–37); *L'Évolution de la pensée kantienne* (Paris 1939). K. VORLÄNDER, *I. Kant: Der Mann und das Werk,* 2 v. (Leipzig 1924). M. WUNDT, *Kant als Metaphysiker* (Stuttgart 1924). J. MARÉCHAL, *Le Point de départ de la métaphysique,* v.3 (3d ed. Paris 1944) v.5 (2d ed. 1949). Catholic and fundamental. M. AEBI, *K.s Begründung der ''Deutschen Philos''* (Basel 1947). G. MARTIN, *I. Kant: Ontologie und Wissenschaftstheorie* (Cologne 1951). Tulane University, *A Symposion on K.* (New Orleans 1954). J. B. LOTZ, ed., *Kant und die Scholastik heute* (Pullach 1955). H. HEIMSOETH, *Studien zur Philosophie I. Kants* (Cologne 1956). F. DELEKA, *I. Kant: Hist.-krit. Interpretation der Hauptschriften* (Heidelberg 1963). Theoretical philosophy. M. HEIDEGGER, *K. und das Problem der Metaphysik* (Bonn 1929); *Die Frage nach dem Ding* (Tübingen 1962). C. NINK, *Kommentar zu K.s Kritik der reinen Vernunft* (Frankfurt 1930). H. J. PATON, *K.s Metaphysics of Experience* (New York 1936). F. GRAYEFF, *Deutung und Darstellung der theoretischen Philosophie K.s* (Hamburg 1951). H. W. CASSIRER, *Kant's First Critique* (New York 1954). R. P. WOLFF, *Kant's Theory of Mental Activity* (Cambridge, Mass. 1963). Practical philosophy. G. KRÜGER, *Philosophie und Moral in der kantischen Kritik* (Tübingen 1931). R. DAVAL, *La Métaphysique de Kant* (Paris 1951). A. R. DUNCAN, *Practical Reason and Morality* (London 1957). H. J. PATON, *The Categorical Imperative* (3d ed. London 1959). J. SCHMUCKER, *Die Ursprünge der Ethik Kants in seinen vorkritischen Schriften und Reflektionen* (Meisenheim 1961) Catholic and fundamental. Aesthetics. W. BIEMEL, *Die Bedeutung von Kants Begründung der Ästhetik für die Philosophie der Kunst* (Cologne 1959). Philosophy of religion. J. HASENFUSS, *Die Grundlagen der Religion bei Kant* (Würzburg 1927), Catholic. B. JANSEN, *Die Religionsphilosophie Kants* (Berlin 1929), Catholic.

[J. B. LOTZ]

KANTIANISM

The philosophy of criticism developed by I. KANT and his followers. Since Kant's thought is exposed in the article devoted to him, this article concentrates on his first followers and opponents, the impact of his thought on his contemporaries, and its later influences on German idealism, neo-Kantianism, and neoscholasticism.

Characteristics. Kantianism was influenced by the preceding movements of EMPIRICISM, RATIONALISM, and the philosophy of the ENLIGHTENMENT, and through them was led to formulate a profound synthesis of their views. In the process, it limited the speculative or theoretical reason to the area of possible experience. Accordingly, it conceived human knowledge as arriving at necessary and universally valid judgments by way of a priori forms, but it held that these judgments refer only to the appearances or PHENOMENA. The NOUMENA or things-in-themselves were conceived as remaining hidden, although their reality was never questioned by Kant. Another conclusion drawn from this was the impossibility of a metaphysics in the Kantian theory of knowledge; the ideas that reason forms when conceptualizing metaphysical reality have only a regulative function with respect to the knowledge of phenomena and have no constitutive or objective meaning. Thus man is not able to grasp the corresponding objects of these ideas.

In Kantianism, the practical reason or the purely rational will has a greater role to play than the theoretical reason. This role expresses itself in a CATEGORICAL IMPERATIVE that is plainly unconditional and thus absolute. The imperative is exclusively determined by the form of the law that the pure will gives itself in virtue of its autonomy (*see* ETHICAL FORMALISM). For the Kantian, he who lets himself be guided by concretely defined motives lapses into a heteronomy that destroys the ethical nature of his action. Because of its indeterminateness the ethical imperative embraces not only man but in general all intelligent beings. Consequently, it opens the way to the intelligible world, to the noumena and the thing-in-itself. This is the basis for the possibility of a practical metaphysics that rests upon a belief required by ethical considerations but that does not increase man's speculative knowledge.

The term criticism is often used as a synonym for Kantianism (*see* CRITICISM, PHILOSOPHICAL). But usually criticism is taken in the more strict sense of a critical theory of knowledge; it represents only the first and basic part of Kantianism, according to Kant's own words: "Criticism constitutes rather the preliminary organization necessary for arriving at a solid, scientific metaphysics" (B xxxvi). Its opposite is DOGMATISM, wherein pure reason develops itself "without a previous criticism of its own capacity" (B xxxv). In the fullest sense of the word, Kantianism designates not only the philosophical work of Kant himself but also the further development of the intellectual movement he started. This development led to a series of different interpretations because of the intrinsic tensions that existed within Kant's own thought.

Early Adherents. Among the early proponents of Kantianism the most important was K. L. Reinhold (1758–1823), who introduced Kant's thought to a wide audience; his popular *Briefe über die kantische Philosophie* (1786–87) were particularly effective, and through his efforts Jena became a center of studies on Kant. In his *Versuch einer neuen Theorie des menschlichen Vorstellungsvermögens* (Jena 1789) he applied himself to the dualism of sense knowledge and reason, both of which stood side by side in Kant's work without further reduction. Reinhold looked for their common origin and thought this to be the imagination. Thus he prepared the way for J. G. Fichte.

S. Maimon (1753–1800) focused attention on Kant and contributed heavily to a further cultivation of his thought with some penetrating and profound works. He rejected the thing-in-itself as a delusion or fiction of consciousness; multiplicity as given corresponds, for him, to the inner capacity of human thought itself and therefore need not be reduced to some thing independent of mind.

J. S. Beck (1761–1840) likewise turned against the thing-in-itself. When Kant affirms that things affect the subject, for Beck this must be understood as a purely didactic accommodation to dogmatically inclined readers. Thus both Maimon and Beck explained Kant's thought in a one-sided, idealistic way while suppressing its realistic elements.

In contrast to these authors C. G. Bardili (1761–1808) developed his abstruse "rational realism" that prepared the way for the ideas of F. W. J. Schelling and G. W. F. Hegel by reducing the real world and the ideal world to their unity in the ABSOLUTE. Kantianism was defended also by many scholars in Holland, France, and England.

Opponents. The critical discussion that had already started among the followers of Kant was brought to a focus by his opponents. Among the independent critics must be included C. Garve (1742–98). As early as 1782 Garve published a review of the first edition of the *Critique of Pure Reason*, which he interpreted in the sense of Berkeley's idealism and came to overlook its realistic elements. In the second edition Kant replied to this by bringing out more clearly the realistic features of his work. Garve also furnished a critical study of Kantian moral philosophy that still merits the attention of scholars.

Under the inspiration of J. Locke and of G. W. Leibniz, D. Tiedemann (1748–1803) defended the objective validity of man's knowledge of reality, and in this opposed himself to Kant. J. A. Eberhard (1739–1809) also stood out among the followers of Leibniz; it was against his attacks that Kant wrote a special essay "on a discovery that would make it possible to dispense with every new criticism of pure reason on the basis of an older one" (Königsberg 1790).

The skeptic G. E. Schulze (1761–1833) argued in a penetrating way against Kantianism. In his *Aenesidemus* (Helmstädt 1792), he attacked the Kantian thing-in-itself on the grounds that the very affection that it produces, which Kantians regard as necessary, is impossible in the terms of their philosophy. Besides, he criticized the fact that Kant attributed logical validity to subjective forms; from this, for him, Hume's PSYCHOLOGISM would be the only reasonable consequent.

Influence on Contemporaries. Under this heading are discussed thinkers who did important intellectual work on their own and in so doing came into dispute with Kantian doctrines.

J. G. HAMANN, who was on friendly terms with Kant and with J. G. Herder and F. H. Jacobi, rejected the dualism Kant assumed to exist in the source of human knowledge. This dualism, for Hamann, bespeaks an untenable one-sidedness that is the product of reason and its distinctions; moreover, it is refuted by language, through which reason attains its own sensible existence. Intellectual knowledge should be replaced by the individual certainty of faith, which enables the mysteries of Christianity to become a living experience.

F. H. JACOBI clearly analyzed the difficulty inherent in Kant's doctrine of the thing-in-itself. By holding that the affection of the senses results from the thing-in-itself, Kantians apply the relation of cause and effect (which, according to Kantianism, is valid only within the world of phenomena) to the realm of the thing-in-itself. In virtue of sense perception Jacobi himself was immediately convinced of the existence of real things. With Kant he assumed that the theoretical reason is confined to finite and experiential things. While rejecting the Kantian doctrine of the metaphysical postulates, he defended an immediate perception of transcendental reality; this he called faith and claimed it is achieved by reason. Kant took a position against this view in his treatise *Was heisst, sich im Denken orientieren?* (Berlin 1786).

J. G. HERDER did not do justice to Kant in his bitter *Metakritik* (Riga 1799) of the transcendental analytics. Against Kant's gross dualism of matter and form and of nature and freedom, he asserted their essential unity and gradual development. Language, for him, testifies strongly against the apriorism of Kant; space and time are concepts derived from experience.

J. C. F. Schiller studied Kant's major works and particularly the *Critique of Judgment.* Under Kant's influence he wrote his important work *Über Anmut und Würde* (Leipzig 1793); in this he attacked the heart of the Kantian doctrine on duty because it could lead to a gloomy asceticism. Moral dignity, for him the surging of the spirit above nature, is complemented by moral grace, which is the harmony between spirit and nature, between duty and inclination. In opposition to this Kant observed that along such lines EUDAEMONISM could easily creep into moral doctrine.

J. W. GOETHE occupied himself especially with the *Critique of Judgment* and admitted that it gave him the philosophical basis for his "creations, actions, and thoughts." He praised the work for giving its due both to nature and to art.

Later Influences. The philosophical work of Kant remained so fundamental for succeeding thinkers that not one who took his work seriously could avoid discussing it. Every competent mind thus felt Kant's influence, either positively or negatively, and the stimulating effect of his work has not yet been exhausted.

German Idealism. Kantianism was further developed, overcome, and at first supplanted by the vast speculative systems of German IDEALISM; one may call this an "elevating process" (in Hegel's terminology a *Vorgang des Aufhebens*) wherein, of course, not all the basic elements of Kantian thought were preserved, e.g., the finite character of human knowledge. Idealism received its decisive stimulus from the tensions that were typical in Kant's thought. The search went beyond sense knowledge and reason, appearance and the thing-in-itself, experiential and metaphysical reality, the theoretical and the practical, and nature and freedom toward an underlying, unifying principle that was ultimately found in absolute reality. From a methodological point of view this evolving idealism should be characterized as transcendental, insofar as it refers to Kant's transcendental problematics that he himself projected into the metaphysical realm. *See* TRANSCENDENTAL (KANTIAN). Its essentially dialectical method may also have been anticipated in Kant, particularly in the "logical requirements and criteria of all knowledge of things in general" (B 114) where the three steps of unity, multiplicity, and reduction of multiplicity to unity emerge. More specific details may be seen in considering the three principal authors of German idealism, viz, Fichte, Schelling, and Hegel.

J. G. FICHTE intended merely to bring Kant's basic insight to its logical and systematical conclusions; but

Kant's idea differed sharply from Fichte's *Wissenschaftslehre.* More precisely, Fichte started with the practical reason and tried to develop this through transcendental deduction and also to derive from it the theoretical reason with its categories. The thing-in-itself, for him, coincides with the pure Ego or subject and its moral activity, and from this all else (except God) results. This amounts to an idealism that eliminates the realistic element proper to Kant's thought.

F. W. J. SCHELLING aimed in a conscious and determined way at completing and thus surpassing Kant; to this effect his thought went back beyond that of Fichte. Following the example of Kant's three *Critiques,* he divided his transcendental philosophy into a theoretical and a practical philosophy, the unity of which he perfected with his doctrines on the finality of nature and of art. In doing so Schelling gave new emphasis to the *Critique of Judgment.* Against the background of the identity of nature and spirit, it is art that constitutes the highest union of freedom and necessity. Schelling departed from Kant not only as to content but also as to method by raising intellectual INTUITION to the status of being fundamental to philosophical activity.

G. W. F. HEGEL focused on theoretical philosophy and therefore put the *Critique of Pure Reason* in the foreground. His principal objection against Kant was that Kant did not go beyond the intellect, which was unable to reconcile oppositions. Hegel himself believed that he could achieve a comprehensive mediation of antitheses by way of reason; in this way the categories could be expanded beyond the phenomena and raised to the point where absolute reality could manifest itself. As to methodology, Hegel advocated intellectual intuition against Kant and with Schelling, but held that intuition presents itself only in the dialectical movement of the mind, a point on which he differed from Schelling.

Neo-Kantianism. After idealism began to wane, German philosophy lost itself to a large degree in POSITIVISM, MATERIALISM, and HISTORICISM. The first signs of renewal came from K. Fischer (1824–1907), E. Zeller (1814–1908), and O. Liebmann (1840–1912), who started the movement back to Kant; each chapter of Liebmann's book ended with the words: "Therefore, one must return to Kant." NEO-KANTIANISM, which was influential for several decades before waning in the 20th century, developed from these endeavors. It emphasized, in a somewhat one-sided way, Kant's theory of knowledge and of science. Basic to this movement was the conviction that the scientific content of reality was exhaustively dealt with by the particular sciences; therefore, the only possible task for philosophy was to develop a theory of science by investigating its nature and presup-

positions. The Marburg school restricted its field of investigation more to the natural sciences and arrived in this way at an extreme form of idealism that no longer permits anything to be given in advance, but admits only whatever is produced or established by consciousness (H. Cohen, P. Natorp, and E. CASSIRER). The Baden school, on the other hand, was concerned with the historical sciences of culture and art and developed from this study its theory of values (W. Windelband, H. Rickert, and H. Münsterberg). H. Vaihinger founded the *Kantstudien* (1896) and the *Kantgesellschaft* (1904). The metaphysical element in Kant also came gradually into sight as some thinkers sought not to destroy, but to provide a new foundation for, metaphysics in line with Kant's principles (Liebmann, F. Paulsen, and above all M. Wundt). The ontological aspect of Kant's thought was worked out by G. Martin and H. Heimsoeth.

Traces of Kant's continued influence persisted in the PHENOMENOLOGY of E. HUSSERL, particularly in his transcendental reduction and in constituting of essences; in the realism of N. HARTMANN, developed in opposition to neo-Kantianism, and particularly in Hartmann's conception of metaphysics as pure problematics; and finally, in the EXISTENTIALISM of K. Jaspers, especially in the limits ascribed to knowledge and in his metaphysics of philosophical faith.

Neoscholasticism. At first scholastic thinkers adopted a negative attitude toward Kant, seeing him mainly as one who opposed realism, founded idealism, and destroyed the proofs for the existence of God. The scholastic theory of knowledge developed in opposition to Kant's theories; based on realism, it argued for a rational metaphysics. A more positive view of Kantian philosophy asserted itself only gradually; its pioneers were, in France, A. G. SERTILLANGES and A. Valensin and, in Germany, B. Jansen, T. Steinbüchel, and E. Przywara. The real breakthrough, however, was achieved by J. MARÉCHAL, who elaborated Kant's metaphysical theory of cognition and established a lively confrontation with a more profoundly understood THOMAS AQUINAS. In particular, Maréchal, taking over the transcendental problematics and method and perfecting them far beyond Kant, indicated the correlation between Kant's a priori forms and Aquinas's formal objects, and unfolded the dynamism of the human mind. He made use of Aquinas to show that the tendency that for Kant discloses the metaphysical world only at the stage of practical reason is already inherent in theoretical reason. In scholastic circles Maréchal's interpretation of Kant met with much opposition but with even more approval; it opened up a new road that was taken and further extended by many authors, who proposed their own emendations. In this field new suggestions have been offered by M. Heidegger, who considers the *Critique of Pure Reason* as the foundation of metaphysics. These ideas have been crystallized in the *Mélanges Maréchal* as well as in *Kant und die Scholastik heute* (ed. J. B. Lotz).

Appreciation. For a critique of Kantianism, the reader is referred to the article on Kant himself. The point that touches the heart of the criticism is that the finite human mind is infinite to the extent that it arrives at being pure and simple, penetrates into the essences of sensible things, grasps the inner, objective reality, and finally discloses metaphysical reality, still within the sphere of theoretical knowledge. In the *Critique of Pure Reason* nothing but a faint trace of this infinity can be found. Only in the *Critique of Practical Reason* does it emerge, and this because the metaphysical realm is made accessible by the absolute character of the moral imperative, There, however, the infinity in man's autonomy is just as much overdone as it is weakened in Kant's faith regarding the metaphysical postulates. The succeeding development of Kantianism evolves around the same issues: it oscillates between the extreme infinity of the German idealists and the more or less extreme theories of finitude advocated by other Kantians.

See Also: NEO-KANTIANISM; HEGELIANISM AND NEOHEGELIANISM.

Bibliography: A. RIEHL, *Der philosophische Kritizismus,* 2 v. (Leipzig 1876–1887). R. KRONER, *Von Kant bis Hegel,* 2 v. (2d ed. Tübingen 1961). V. DELBOS, *De Kant aux postkantiens* (Paris 1940). J. VUILLEMIN, *L'Héritage kantien et la revolution copernicienne: Fichte, Cohen, Heidegger* (Paris 1954). V. VERRA, *Dopo Kant: Il criticismo dell'età preromantica* (Turin 1957). M. WUNDT, *Kant als Metaphysiker* (Stuttgart 1924). *Mélanges Jos. Maréchal,* 2 v. (Brussels 1950). J. B. LOTZ, ed., *Kant und die Scholastik heute* (Pullach 1955).

[J. B. LOTS]

KARDEC, ALLAN

Pseudonym of Hippolyte Léon Denizard Rivail, exponent of Spiritism; b. Lyons, France, Oct. 3, 1804; d. Paris, March 31, 1869. He was the son of the lawyer Jean Baptiste Antoine Rivail and began his studies in Lyons and completed them in Yverdun, Switzerland, in the famous institute of PESTALOZZI, with whom he became a collaborator. Kardec received a bachelor's degree in sciences and letters, became a fine linguist, and early devoted himself to his duties as a teacher. Already in 1828 he began to publish didactic works of arithmetic, geometry, grammar, chemistry, physics, astronomy, and physiology. In 1832 he married Amelia Boudet.

Early in his youth he dedicated himself with enthusiasm to mesmeric magnetism and hypnotism, applying magnetic passes to the sick, from which activity arose his reputation of also being a doctor. In December 1854 he became interested in the phenomenon of the dancing table, a careful observation of which led him to discover two important peculiarities, impossible, he then thought, to be explained by the blind force of magnetism: (1) the table denoted intelligence and, therefore, the cause of the movements must be intelligent; (2) this intelligence was autonomous, independent of the persons who placed their hands on the table, and, therefore, must originate from a cause intelligent, different, and invisible. For this reason he concluded: (1) that neither animal magnetism by itself, nor the presences of persons, could be sufficient and adequate causes of the intelligent gyrations of the table; and (2) that the other extracorporeal intelligence, present and engaging interest, though invisible, must be a spirit. Thus arose the idea of SPIRITISM, a neologism created by Kardec to indicate the perceptive and provocative communicability with the spirits (souls of the dead). From this point he dedicated himself with extraordinary vigor and persistence to the evocation and consultation of the spirits, because it seemed to him that in this way he was able to aid others and to definitely resolve the moral and religious problems of humanity.

On April 18, 1857, the first edition of *Le livre des esprits contenant les principes de la doctrine spirite* appeared in the form of 1018 questions (formulated by him) and answers (supposedly "according to the instructions given by the superior spirits with the confluence of diverse mediums"). With that book arose the codified Spiritism of a religious character that still exists today (*see* BRAZIL). In 1861 he published another fundamental work for the spiritual movement, the book of mediums (or the "guide of evocators"). In 1864 appeared the Gospel according to Spiritism; in 1865, a book about heaven and hell; and in 1868, one about miracles and prophecies. Other works were published after his death. In 1857 he initiated the *Revue Spirite,* and in 1858 he founded the Society of Spiritual Studies. By the decree of the Holy Office of April 20, 1864, all his works were prohibited. Every movement initiated by Kardec was characterized by necromancy and reincarnation.

[B. KLOPPENBURG]

KARLOWSKA, MARIA, BL.

Foundress of the Sisters of the Good Shepherd of Divine Providence; b. Sept. 4, 1865, Stupówka (now Karlowo near Gziezno), Poland; d. March 24, 1935, Pniewita, Poland. The eleventh child of Matthew Karlowska and Eugenia Dembinski, Maria attended school in Poznán, where her family had moved after her birth. Following the death of her parents (1882), Maria worked in her sister's tailor shop, where she met a prostitute. Maria came to understand that her mission was to work for the moral and social rehabilitation of prostitutes and to tend to those suffering from venereal diseases. Her ministry attracted a number of like-minded women. Together they founded the Good Shepherd Sisters in 1894. That same year, with financial help from Duchess Aniela Poluticka, Maria established the Good Shepherd Institute in Winiary (near Poznán) to care for prostitutes. Both Prussian and Polish civil authorities commended Karlowska's work, which continues today in seven Polish educational institutions for girls and women, three homes for single mothers, and a rehabilitation center. Karlowska's cause for beatification started in 1965. She was declared venerable on July 11, 1995, and on March 8, 1997, a miracle attributed to her intercession was approved. She was beatified by John Paul II on June 6 1997 (Feast of the Sacred Heart), at Wielka Krokiew Arena, Zakopane (near Kraków), Poland.

Feast: June 5.

Bibliography: M. KARLOWSKA, *Wybór pism Marii Karlowskiej*, ed. J. R. BAR (Warsaw 1981). *L'Osservatore Romano,* English edition, no. 29 (1995): 5.

[K. I. RABENSTEIN]

KARLSTADT, ANDREAS RUDOLF BODENSTEIN VON

German theologian and reformer; b. Karlstadt am Main, *c.* 1480; d. Basel, Switzerland, Dec. 24, 1541. Karlstadt (or Carlstadt), one of Luther's earliest supporters, was educated at the Universities of Erfurt and Cologne. In 1505 he was professor of Thomistic philosophy at the University of Wittenberg; three years later he was made a canon at the collegiate church. His initial work, *De Intentionibus, Distinctiones sive Formalitates Thomistae,* marks him as one of the strongest adversaries of the *via moderna* in this university. After obtaining the doctorate in theology in 1510, he was made *professor ordinarius* of sacred theology. Two years later, at the insistence of Frederick the Wise, he was sent to Rome, where within a few months he obtained a doctorate in canon law and civil law. Upon returning from Rome, he published an attack on the abuses of the papal court entitled *Concerning Papal Sanctity.* He also launched an attack on scholastic theology. In September of 1516 he published 151 theses that repudiated the traditional Catholic doctrine on grace and free will. In 1518 he replied to Johann ECK's attack on Martin Luther by maintaining the supremacy of Scripture over tradition and patristic writings. He later engaged

the Ingolstadt professor in the famous Leipzig debate. Karlstadt was mentioned in Leo X's bull of excommunication *Exsurge Domine* (June 15, 1520) against Luther. During this early period of the Reformation, Karlstadt became one of the most prominent of the early Lutheran exegetes. He denied the Mosaic authorship of the Pentateuch and divided the Scripture into three categories based upon relative certainty of authorship, *De Canonicis Scripturis* (1520). Unlike Luther, he did not reject the authorship of the Epistle of St. James. In 1521 he was invited by King Christian II of Denmark to introduce the reform into that country, but the hostility of the nobility and the clergy forced him to return to Wittenberg, where he continued his polemical writings, denouncing monastic vows, celibacy, and the Catholic doctrine of the Eucharist. He anticipated Luther in rejecting much of the liturgy of the Mass, and he was the first of the early reformers to marry. The iconoclastic disturbance that occurred in Wittenberg during Luther's absence and that was instigated by the Zwickau prophets, can be traced indirectly to his attacks on the externals of divine worship (*see* MÜNZER, THOMAS; ANABAPTISTS).

When expelled from Wittenberg in 1524, he wandered throughout Germany associating himself for a time with the Anabaptists in Holstein and Friesland. After 1530 he settled in Zurich and was later recommended by Heinrich BULLINGER to a position at the University of Basel. Here he was directly involved in a struggle with the humanists in an attempt to raise the academic standards of the university. In 1536 at the invitation of Martin BUCER, he represented the city council at Strassburg in a final attempt to reconcile the Lutheran and Zwinglian factions on the question of the Real Presence. Karlstadt's importance lies in the fact that he was the real author of the Eucharistic controversy that later divided the Protestant movement. It was a result largely of his influence that the Swiss reform movement was converted to the Sacramentarian position. His role was more that of a nonviolent visionary, a spiritualist, rather than a man of affairs. Although opposed to the ancient Church, he had nothing substantial to put in its place.

Bibliography: *Karlstadts Schriften aus den Jahren 1523–25,* ed. E. HERTZSCH, 2 v. (Heidelberg 1956–57). E. HERTZSCH, *Die Religion in Geschichte und Gegenwart,* 7 v. (3d ed. Tübingen 1957–65) 3:1154–55; *Karlstadt und seine Bedeutung für san Luthertum* (Gotha 1932). K. SCHOTTENLOHER, *Bibliographie zur deutschen Geschichte im Zeitalter der Glaubensspaltung, 1517–85,* 6 v. (Leipzig 1933–40; repr. Stuttgart 1956–58, v. 7 1962–) 9616–49. T. FREY, *Das Rheintal zur Zeit der Glaubensspaltung* (Altstätten 1947). O. VASELLA, *Lexikon für Theologie und Kirche,* ed. J. HOFER and K. RAHNER, 10 v. (2d, new ed. Freiburg 1957–65) 5:1363–64. H. BARGE, *Andreas Bodenstein von Karlstadt,* 2 v. (Leipzig 1905). F. L. CROSS, *The Oxford Dictionary of the Christian Church* (London 1957) 237.

[J. P. DOLAN]

KARMA

A term literally meaning "action," it came to be used in Hindu doctrine to signify the chain of cause and effect by which every action necessarily produces a given effect, not only in the physical but also in the moral order. This chain of cause and effect was believed to extend beyond the individual life-span, so that each man's character and fortune is determined by his past action or *karma* in a previous life. Thus, every soul has its own *karma,* which it inherits from the past, and continues to create new *karma* by its actions in the present. Nevertheless, by good works, especially of a religious nature, and by refraining from all harmful action, it is possible to destroy the effects of past *karma* and to avoid acquiring new. Accordingly, though one's life, character, and above all one's position in society are largely determined by *karma,* an element of freedom is left. The goal of every soul is ultimately to be set free from *karma* and to attain liberation (*mokṣa*) from the wheel of time (*saṁsāra*). Hence, though there is an element of fatalism in the doctrine of *karma,* it is rightly contended that it leaves a place for freedom and morality.

See Also: INDIAN PHILOSOPHY; HINDUISM.

[B. GRIFFITHS]

KARNKOWSKI, STANISLAW

Archbishop of Gniezno and primate of Poland 1581–1603; b. May 10, 1520; d. Lowicz, Poland, June 8, 1603. In 1567, he was appointed bishop of Włocławek. Here he began his life–long effort to revivify Catholic life and worship. Karnkowski summoned a diocesan synod in 1568 to implement the Tridentine reforms. As a patron of the Jesuits, he aided their work, and it was with his encouragement that Jacob Wujek, SJ, translated the Bible into Polish. Karnkowski also founded seminaries in Gniezno and Kalisz as centers of reform. In 1579 he made a collection of synodal laws published as the *Constitutiones synodorum metropolitanae ecclesiae Gneznensis provincialium.* Politically, he favored Henry of Valois as king of Poland; later on, he also supported Stephen BÁTHORY and Sigismund III Vasa who became kings of Poland during his lifetime. Karnkowski's vigorous leadership and support of reform did much to strengthen the church and reclaim many for Catholicism in the second half of the 16th century.

Bibliography: *Cambridge History of Poland,* ed. W. F. REDDAWAY et al., 2 v. (Cambridge, Eng. 1941–50). B. STASIEWSKI, *Lexicon für Theologie und Kirche,* ed. J. HOFER and K. RAHNER, 10 vol. (2nd ed. Freiburg 1957–65) 5:1372–73.

[F. J. LADOWICZ]

KASPER, KATHARINA

Foundress of the POOR HANDMAIDS OF JESUS CHRIST; b. Dernbach, near Montabaur (Unterwesterwald), Germany, May 26, 1820; d. there, Feb. 2, 1898. Katharina, who came from a poor, pious family, founded her religious congregation in her native village in 1848 to care for the sick. It received diocesan approval in 1851. From 1858 the congregation's apostolate broadened to include teaching. Mother Maria (Katharina's name in religion), who served as superior general until her death, saw her first house opened in the U.S. (1868). During the KULTURKAMPF she went to England to establish houses (1875). By 1898 the Poor Handmaids had almost 2,000 members in 193 houses, including 286 sisters in 27 houses in the U.S. In 1950 her remains were moved to the chapel in the motherhouse in Dernbach. The Roman decree introducing her beatification cause was issued in 1946.

Bibliography: W. P. MEYER, *Heiliges Magdtum vor Gott: Mutter Maria Kasper* (Wiesbaden 1933). G. T. MEAGHER, *With Attentive Ear and Courageous Heart: A Biography of Mother Mary Kasper* (Milwaukee 1957).

[N. BACKMUND]

KASSAB, NIMATULLAH AL-HARDINI YOUSEF, BL.

Baptized Youssef Girgis (Joseph George) Kassab, scholar, priest of the Maronite Rite; b. 1808 at Hardine, Caza de Batroun, northern Lebanon; d. Dec. 14, 1858, at Kfifan Monastery, Lebanon.

Son of Girgis Kassab and Maryam Raad, Youssef attended the monastery school of Saint Antony Abbot at Houb (1816–22). On Nov. 1, 1828, he joined the Lebanese Maronite Order of Monks at Saint Antony at Qozhaya. He took the name, Brother Nimatullah ("Grace from God"). Following a two-year probation and profession at Qozhaya (Nov. 14, 1830), he studied theology at the Monastery of Keprianos and Yustina in Kfifane.

From the time of his ordination by Bishop Semaan Zouein (Christmas Day 1835) until his death, Nimatullah was involved in the formation of new priests as director of the scholasticate (1938–45) and a professor of moral theology at Bharsof (1847–50) and Kfifan (1835–38, 1853–56), where one of his students was Sharbel Maklouf (canonized by Pope Paul VI, Oct. 9, 1977). Nimatullah served as administrator of the monastery of Our Lady of Tamiche (1847–50) and as assistant general for three terms (1845–48, 1850–53, 1856–58). He refused appointment to the office of abbot general, although he was the recognized master of spirituality in the order. Despite suffering through two civil wars (1840 and 1845), Nimatullah remained unshaken in faith and invariably charitable in his interactions with others until his death from pleurisy aggravated by the cold. Saint Sharbel Makhlouf was among the brothers who attended his deathbed.

Nimatullah's body was reburied in his monastery church at Kfifan (May 18, 1996), where many miracles occurred. He was declared venerable by John Paul II on Sept. 7, 1989, and beatified by John Paul II, May 10, 1998.

Feast: Dec. 14 (Maronites).

Bibliography: D. ATTWATER, *Saints of the East* (New York 1963) 180–84. O. ELIAS, *The Blessed Nimatullah Kassab Al-Hardini* (Beirut 1998). *Acta Apostolicae Sedis* 12 (1998) 599.

[K. I. RABENSTEIN]

KASTL, ABBEY OF

Originally a Benedictine abbey in the Diocese of Eichstädt, Upper Palatinate, Holy Roman Empire; located between Amberg and Neumarkt on the Lauter River. Kastl (Castl, Castellum, Castelbergenses) was founded in 1098, and endowed by Berengar I of Sulzbach, Frederick of Hapsburg, and Luitgard of Kastlberg, widow of Diepold I of Nordgau. Paschal II placed Kastl under papal jurisdiction in 1102. These privileges were confirmed and expanded by Innocent II in 1139 and by Gregory IX in 1233. In 1163 Emperor Frederick I Barbarossa placed Kastl under imperial protection. At the instigation of Bishop Gebhard III of Constance, Kastl was settled by Abbot Theodore and 12 of his monks from Petershausen. The monks of Kastl, being advocates of the Hirsau reform, brought the Hirsau constitution to a number of monasteries under their jurisdiction. Houses at Reichenbach, Plankstitten, Ahausen, Heidenheim, and Wülzburg (including its convent of nuns) embraced the Hirsau-Kastl reform. The most vigorous growth of Kastl's estates and commercial interests took place under Abbot Herman (1322–56), whose loyalty to Louis of Bavaria and whose friendship with the Wittelsbach landlords served as a strong foundation for reform as well. Herman's reforms, inspired by Benedict XII's bull *Summi magistri* (1336), were responsible for the first stirrings of monastic revival and improvement at Kastl and its daughter houses. Later, in 1378, Abbot Otto Nortweiner codified the constitutions of Kastl. The *Consuetudines Castellenses*, based on reform movements at Monte Cassino, Hirsau, and Erfurt and influenced by the writings of Benedict of Aniane, Bernard of Clairvaux, Peter Damian, and Benedict XII, inspired Benedictine ascetical and liturgical reform throughout the 15th century. Joining ranks with the younger Bursfeld congregations, the Kastl reform movement spread throughout southern Germany. The deteriorating political situation within the empire eventually thwarted the growth and influence of Kastl. Dynastic wars over succession, the Knights' War, the Peasants' War, and the Reformation itself brought decline, division, and destruction. Shortly after the Count Palatine Otto Henry embraced Calvinism, his son and successor, Frederick III, suppressed Kastl in 1563. Not until 1636, one year after the treaty of Prague, did the Elector Maximilian of Bavaria restore Kastl and confide it to the Jesuits. When the latter were suppressed in 1773, Kastl eventually came under the jurisdiction of the Knights of St. John of Jerusalem (1782–1808). Kastl itself was suppressed for the last time in 1808 as a result of the Napoleonic reform.

Bibliography: C. WOLFF, *Lexikon für Theologie und Kirche*, ed. J. HOFER and K. RAHNER, 10 v. (2d, new ed. Freiburg 1957–65) 6:14–16. L. H. COTTINEAU, *Répertoire topobibliographique des abbayes et prieurés*, 2 v. (Mâcon 1935–39) 1:1507–08.

[P. S. MCGARRY]

KATERKAMP, JOHANN THEODOR HERMANN

Catholic theologian and church historian; b. Ochtrup, Westphalia, Jan. 17, 1764; d. Münster, Westphalia, June 9, 1834. After his ordination as priest in 1787, Katerkamp was recommended by his university professor Clemens Becker as private tutor for the family of the imperial princes of Droste-Vischering in Münster. He thus became one of the youngest members of the Münster circle of scholars around the Princess Amalia GALLITZIN, a circle that included such men as Franz von FÜRSTENBERG, B. OVERBERG, and Von Stolberg. From 1797 until the princess's death in 1806 Katerkamp lived in her home. He began his public work only in 1809 when he was named provisional professor of church history at the University of Münster. Then in 1819 he was appointed ordinary professor of church history, canon law, and patrology at Münster. Katerkamp was the author of the first major Catholic Church history of modern times. This was his principal work; it was influenced by and followed entirely the spirit of F. L. von Stolberg's 15-volume *Geschichte der Religion Jesu* (1806–18).

See Also: HISTORIOGRAPHY, ECCLESIASTICAL.

Bibliography: Works. *Kirchengeschichte*, Intro. and 5 v. (Münster 1819–34), to 1153; *Über den Primat des Apostels Petrus und seiner Nachfolger* (Münster 1820), also under the title *Friedrich Leopolds Grafen zu Stolberg historische Glaubwürdigkeit im Gegensatz zu Herrn Dr. Paulus' kritischer Beurteilung seiner Geschichte; Denkwürdigkeiten aus dem Leben der Fürstin A. von*

Gallitzin, mit besonderer Rücksicht auf ihre nächsten Verbindungen, Hemsterhuys Fürstenberg, Overberg und Stolberg (Münster 1828; 2d ed. 1839). Literature. H. BROCKMAN, ''Trauerrede'' in *Zeitschrift für Philosophie und katholische Theologie* 3 (1834) 113–132. A. B. LUTTERBECK, *Allgemeine deutsche Biographie* 15:452–453. *Realenzyklopädie für protestantische Theologie* 10:179–180. P. BRACHIN, *Le Cercle de Münster (1779–1806) et la pensée religieuse de F. L. Stolberg* (Lyons 1951). E. REINHARD, *Die Münsterische ''Familia sacra''* (Münster 1953). E. HEGEL, *Lexikon für Theologie und Kirche* ed. J. HOFER and K. RAHNER (Freiburg 1957–65) 6:57–58.

[H. RUMPLER]

KATZER, FREDERICK FRANCIS XAVIER

Third archbishop of the Milwaukee, WI, Archdiocese; b. Ebensee, Austria, Feb. 7, 1844; d. Fond du Lac, WI, July 20, 1903. He spent his boyhood in Gmunden and studied at the seminary in Freinberg, near Linz, Austria. As a student he joined a group of volunteers for the Minnesota missions in the United States, but when all could not be accepted there, Katzer entered St. Francis Seminary for the Milwaukee Diocese. Bp. John M. Henni ordained him on Dec. 21, 1866, and appointed him professor in the seminary. In this capacity, he composed an allegorical drama, *Der Kampf der Gegenwart* (The Battle of the Present), dealing with Europe's social problems. When F. X. Krautbauer of Milwaukee was appointed bishop of Green Bay, WI, in 1875, he took Katzer with him and later appointed him rector of the cathedral and vicar-general. When Krautbauer died suddenly, Katzer was named his successor and consecrated on Sept. 21, 1886, by Abp. Michael Heiss.

Leadership of the campaign for repeal of the Bennett Law (1889) passed to Katzer at the death of Heiss in 1890. Catholic opinion regarding the state law, which made education compulsory and prescribed the use of English in instruction, was divided. Despite Catholic disunity, the Heiss-Katzer crusade succeeded, and the law was repealed following the 1890 election.

Meanwhile the death of Archbishop Heiss in March 1890 had left the Milwaukee Archdiocese vacant. Fearing that Katzer might be named to it, some priests, desiring a more American metropolitan, tried to prevent his appointment. Abp. John Ireland advised Gibbons that Katzer was ''thoroughly German and thoroughly unfit to be an archbishop.'' At the archbishops' meeting in Boston (July 1890), Katzer was set aside in favor of Bp. John L. Spalding of Peoria as the metropolitans' first choice for Milwaukee. Nevertheless, Rome, passing over other candidates, appointed Katzer on Jan. 30, 1891. Fully aware of the strained situation, Gibbons, at the conferring

of the pallium in Milwaukee, warned of the dangers of dissension and nationalism. The sermon was hailed by those who regarded Katzer's appointment as a distinct triumph for the German-American element in the Church, but settlement of the German question was still remote.

Katzer was an ardent supporter of the legislation of the Third Plenary Council of Baltimore concerning Catholic grade schools. With other German Catholics he was critical of Ireland's advocacy of the Faribault plan and was irked at Rome's toleration of it. In addition, he looked with disfavor on the 14 points that Abp. Francesco Satolli delivered to the American archbishops in 1892 to settle the school controversy. In regard to secret societies, Katzer likewise espoused the stricter view. When the election of 1896 raised the question of socialism, Katzer let it be known that he did not favor William Jennings Bryan, fearing that social revolution would follow from the free coinage of silver. In contrast to some churchmen who gloried in Catholic loyalty during the war with Spain in 1898, Katzer observed silence. But after Leo XIII issued his letter on Americanism, Katzer, together with his suffragans, dispatched a letter of thanks to the Holy Father affirming that the condemned errors were more widespread than many cared to concede. Four years later, Katzer died. His remains were interred in the Chapel-in-the-Woods cemetery at St. Francis Seminary.

Bibliography: C. J. BARRY, *The Catholic Church and German Americans* (Milwaukee 1953). B. J. BLIED, *Three Archbishops of Milwaukee* (Milwaukee 1955). F. LOIDL, *Erzbischof Friedrich Xavier Katzer* (Vienna 1953).

[B. J. BLIED]

KAZEL, DOROTHY

Ursuline nun and missionary; b. Cleveland, Ohio, June 30, 1938; d. San Pedro Nonualco, El Salvador, Dec. 2, 1980. The only daughter of Joseph and Malvina (Kazlawskas) Kazel, Dorothy grew up in a predominately Lithuanian neighborhood on Cleveland's East Side. She graduated from Notre Dame Academy in 1957 and subsequently worked as a medical secretary, taught third grade, and became engaged. Deciding that marriage was not for her, she entered the Ursuline Community on Sept. 8, 1960, and became a novice the next year, taking the name Sister Laurentine, a prophetic choice since an Ursuline martyred during the French Revolution bore that name. Later Kazel resumed her baptismal name. She made final vows in August of 1968.

During the next few years, she earned B.A. and M.A. degrees and was certified as a school counselor. Sister Kazel was appointed to the Cleveland Diocesan Latin

American Mission team in July of 1974 to serve a five-year term in El Salvador. After a period of orientation in Costa Rica, she was assigned to the parish of Nuestra Señora de Guadalupe in Chirilagua. Later she was transferred to the parish of San Carlos Borromeo in La Union, and finally to the parish of the Immaculate Conception in La Libertad. In those parishes, Dorothy assisted with the liturgy, prepared children for First Communion, helped train lay catechists, taught reading, and instructed women in basic nutrition and child care.

As political unrest and violence escalated in 1977, Kazel continued her ministry undaunted by danger. She took on the additional tasks of transporting the dispossessed to refugee camps, helping bury the slain, and counseling survivors. When Archbishop Oscar Romero was murdered in March of 1980, Kazel, deeply affected, wrote to U.S. President Jimmy Carter to express concern that U.S. money was being used to intimidate and exterminate thousands of innocent people.

Her five-year term drawing to a close, Kazel offered to remain one more year to help the Cleveland team's new recruits. Shortly afterwards, on the evening of Dec. 2, 1980, she and her co-worker, lay missionary Jean Donovan, drove their van to El Salvador international airport to pick up Maryknoll Sisters Ita Ford and Maura Clarke. As the four women drove toward La Libertad, five Salvadoran national guardsmen abducted them, drove them to a deserted area, tortured and raped them, then shot and left them by the roadside for strangers to bury in a common grave. Dorothy's body was returned to Cleveland for burial, where her wake was held at the Ursuline motherhouse. After the Mass of the Resurrection was celebrated on December 9 at St. John Cathedral, she was laid to rest in the Ursuline community plot in All Souls Cemetery, Chardon, Ohio.

International public outrage at the murder of the churchwomen became so great that the Salvadoran government ultimately arrested the guardsmen. Yet almost four years passed before they were tried, found guilty, and sentenced to 30 years in prison.

The people of El Salvador venerate the memory of Kazel. Her heroic sacrifice has helped raise the consciousness of Americans to an awareness of the intolerable plight of El Salvador's poor. Through her death Kazel has accomplished what she had set out to do in life.

Bibliography: A. CARRIGAN, *Salvador Witness: The Life and Calling of Jean Donovan* (New York 1984). D. C. KAZEL, *Alleluia Woman: Sister Dorothy Kazel, O.S.U.* (Cleveland 1987).

[M. F. HEARON]

KAZIMIERCZYK, STANISLAW YOUSEF, BL.

Augustinian canon regular of the Lateran of Corpus Christi; b. 1433 at Casimiria, near Krakow, Poland; d. there, May 3, 1489. Stanislaw, son of Soltyn Matthias and Jadwiga, attended the local schools before studying at the Jagiellonian University of Krakow. After joining the canons regular of the Lateran of Corpus Christi (1456), professing his vows, and completing his studies for the priesthood, he was ordained. Thereafter, he served the community in many roles, including novice master and subprior. However, he is remembered for his defense of the faith against John HUS and John WYCLIF, his devotion to the Blessed Sacrament, concern for the poor and sick, and preaching. Some of his written sermons and lectures have survived the destruction of World War II. His body now rests in the church of the Corpus Christi. John Paul II recognized his ancient cultus, April 18, 1993, following the issuance of the *decretum* Dec. 21, 1992.

Bibliography: *Acta Apostolicae Sedis* (1993) 549.

[K. I. RABENSTEIN]

KEANE, AUGUSTUS HENRY

Journalist; b. Cork, Ireland, June 1, 1833; d. London, Feb. 3, 1912. He studied for the priesthood in Ireland and at Rome's Propaganda Fide College (renamed in 1962 the Pontificia Università Urbaniana), but did not proceed beyond minor orders. His flair for languages and anthropological research, already evident in Rome, grew with studies at the Catholic University in Dublin, where he received a B.A. degree. He also devoted himself to journalism, and, in 1862, took over the editorship of the weekly *Glasgow Free Press* (1851), the only Catholic newspaper published in Scotland. In 1864 he became its proprietor.

The religious situation in southwest Scotland was complex and explosive. In 1862, more than 200,000 Irish-born Catholics had settled in southwest Scotland; they had left Ireland in the two previous decades as a result of the famine and lived mainly in and around Glasgow. This sudden expansion brought the organization of Scottish Catholicism almost to a breaking point. Differences of national temperament and politics between the immigrants and the native clergy led to misunderstandings and strife; the *Free Press* had begun by 1859 openly to champion the grievances of the immigrants against the alleged partiality of the Scottish vicars apostolic. Though he had taken over the *Free Press* with expressions of loyalty to ecclesiastical authority, Keane soon began a virulent attack on Bp. John Murdoch, the vicar apostolic resident in Glasgow; on his successor, Bp. John Gray; and on all native-born Scots priests. This attack increased in violence until 1868, when the newspaper was condemned by the Congregation for the Propagation of the Faith; the *Free Press* ceased publication in that year.

The *Free Press* incident is important in the development of the Church in modern Scotland: the very real threat of schism it produced made it clear that the Church in Scotland badly needed reorganization. The result was the reestablishment of the Scottish hierarchy in 1878. After the suppression of the *Free Press,* Keane devoted himself to academic pursuits and contributed extensively on ethnology, geography, and allied subjects to learned journals and encyclopedias. For some years he was professor of Hindustani at University College, London, and, in 1897, received a Civil List pension of £50 "for his labours in the field of ethnology." The fact that he was cremated would seem to indicate that he had given up the practice of his faith.

[D. MCROBERTS]

KEANE, JOHN JOSEPH

Archbishop, first rector of The Catholic University of America; b. Ballyshannon, Donegal, Ireland, Sept. 12, 1839; d. Dubuque, Iowa, June 22, 1918. He was one of the five children of Hugh and Fannie (Connolly) Keane. When John was seven years old, the family emigrated to St. John, New Brunswick, Canada, and then moved to Baltimore, Md., in 1848. After graduating from Calvert Hall, Baltimore, in 1856 and working for firms in Baltimore for three years, he entered St. Charles' College, Ellicott City, and later St. Mary's Seminary in Baltimore. He was ordained on July 2, 1866, by Archbishop Martin J. Spalding, who assigned him to St. Patrick's Church, Washington, D.C.

During the 12 years that he labored in Washington as an assistant, he was an enthusiastic promoter of the temperance movement and was instrumental in the formation of the Catholic Total Abstinence Union of America (1872), as well as the Catholic Young Men's National Union (1875), the Carroll Institute (1873), and the Tabernacle Society in Washington. The zeal and ability he displayed in furthering the objectives of these organizations and in working for the welfare of all classes in the parish attracted the notice of his superiors, who obtained his appointment on March 31, 1878 to the Diocese of Richmond, Va., as its fifth bishop. It soon became clear that all within the jurisdiction of the new bishop had a claim on his attention and care. By lecturing throughout the diocese to Protestant groups, he lessened prejudice against

the Church. Despite opposition, he persisted in an endeavor to instruct African Americans in the Church's teachings, eventually recording some gains among them. From the beginning of his episcopal career, he fostered devotion to the Holy Spirit, publishing in 1880 *A Sodality Manual for the Use of the Servants of the Holy Ghost.*

Rectorship at Catholic University. After the Third Plenary Council of Baltimore (1884), he became more influential in ecclesiastical affairs. In May of 1885, as a member of the committee appointed by the council to found a Catholic university in the United States, he entered wholeheartedly into the work of collecting for the proposed institution. He and Bishop John Ireland of St. Paul represented the committee in obtaining the Holy See's approval for the establishment of The CATHOLIC UNIVERSITY OF AMERICA in Washington, D.C. He was relieved of the care of the Richmond diocese on Aug. 14, 1888, to devote all his energy to the founding of the university, which opened Nov. 13, 1889, with Keane as its first rector. Within a few years he gained a national reputation as an administrator and as an interesting and powerful orator, widely quoted in newspapers. At the same time, he became more clearly identified with the so-called liberal or progressive members of the American hierarchy through active participation in controversial matters. He had a part in preventing the condemnation of the KNIGHTS OF LABOR and in influencing Roman authorities to set aside many of the demands that the Germans had made in the Abbelen memorial (*see* ABBELEN, PETER). He was active in the controversy over the school question and over Cahenslyism (*see* CAHENSLY, PETER PAUL), in obtaining full and suitable representation of the Catholic Church at the Chicago Parliament of Religions, and in advocating the rapid Americanization of Catholic immigrants. Consequently, he incurred the enmity of prominent ecclesiastics who made up the conservative party in the American Church, as well as of conservatives in Europe who had an interest in American Church affairs. Roman authorities, who were kept fully informed about his activities (which were frequently represented as indicating dangerous liberalism), gradually lost confidence in him and in his ability to retain the support of Catholics of all national origins for the university. On Sept. 15, 1896, Leo XIII removed him from the rectorship and offered him a choice of honorable positions.

Later Career. He accepted his banishment from the institution that owed to him, more than to any other prelate, its existence and spirit. To counteract the impression that he and his progressive friends were held in disfavor by their ecclesiastical superiors because of his dismissal from the university, he accepted the Holy Father's invitation to work in Rome. He was raised to archiepiscopal rank and appointed a consultor of the Congregation of the

Propaganda and of the Congregation of Studies. For two and one half years he lived simply in two rooms at the Canadian College, serving in Rome and elsewhere in Europe the interests of the American Church and of his friends. In the controversy known as Americanism that raged in Europe from 1897 to 1899, he was attacked in an unprincipled manner by critics who pictured him "as a rationalist, throwing all dogma over to modern ideas." He engaged in an exhausting battle in Rome to counteract this endeavor to destroy his good name and won a victory. At the request of the governing board of The Catholic University of America, he was released in 1899 from his duties in Rome to devote a year to procuring donations from wealthy Catholics in the United States, since the institution was then in financial difficulty. He entered upon the familiar paths of former years with some enthusiasm and with modest success. While he was engaged in this work, the Archdiocese of Dubuque became vacant and his friends urged the Holy See to name him to the post. After considerable delay, he received the appointment on July 24, 1900.

He considered the appointment to Dubuque a satisfactory answer to those who had been attacking him for several years and became engrossed in the administration of the archdiocese. He devoted particular attention to the development of Loras College, and he gave all the Catholic educational institutions of the archdiocese new inspiration and impetus. During his tenure, 12 new academies for girls and two for boys were constructed. He carried on an effective campaign against alcoholism and its attendant evils throughout his administration, forming in 1902 an Archdiocesan Total Abstinence Union. By the year 1909 he became aware of a loss of physical vigor and of some impairment of his faculties. When an attempt to have a coadjutor or an auxiliary appointed for Dubuque failed, Keane sent his resignation to the pope, who accepted it on April 3, 1911. He lived at the cathedral rectory until his death. Many of his lectures were published, and articles by him on various topics appeared in the *Catholic World, American Ecclesiastical Review, American Catholic Quarterly Review* and the *North American Review.*

See Also: AMERICANISM.

Bibliography: J. J. KEANE, *Onward and Upward,* comp. M. F. EGAN (Baltimore 1902). P. H. AHERN, *The Life of John J. Keane, Educator and Archbishop 1839–1918* (Milwaukee 1955); *The Catholic University of America, 1887–1896: The Rectorship of John J. Keane* (Washington 1949).

[P. H. AHERN]

John Keble. (Archive Photos)

KEBLE, JOHN

Anglican theologian, leader of the OXFORD MOVEMENT; b. Fairford, England, April 25, 1792; d. Bournemouth, March 29, 1866. He was the son of John and Sarah (Maule) Keble. After study at Corpus Christi College, Oxford, he was elected a fellow of Oriel College (1811). Ordained to the Anglican priesthood in 1816, he renounced his tutorship at Oriel in 1823 and devoted the rest of his life to parochial work, principally at Hursley. He maintained contact with Oxford, however, holding a professorship of poetry there (1831–41). Among the Oxford students who were converted to his HIGH CHURCH views was Richard Hurrell FROUDE, who acted as intermediary in drawing Keble and John Henry NEWMAN together. Newman regarded Keble's sermon, "National Apostasy," delivered at Oxford on July 14, 1833, as the beginning of the Oxford Movement. Keble's contributions to the movement included a book of poetry, *The Christian Year* (1827), which portrayed the Church as the visible channel of invisible grace; seven of the *Tracts for* the Times; and a translation of St. Irenaeus for the *Library of the Fathers*. He also helped to edit Froude's *Remains* (1837) and the *Works* of Richard Hooker (1836). After Newman's conversion Keble continued his sermons in defense of TRACTARIANISM and advocated the adoration of the sacred species in his work, *On Eucharistical Adoration* (1857). His influence on the Oxford Movement was exerted chiefly through his qualities as a humble pastor. Keble College at Oxford was named for him in 1869.

Bibliography: G. BATTISCOMBE, *John Keble: A Study in Limitations* (New York 1964). J. T. COLERIDGE, *A Memoir of the Rev. John Keble* (London 1869).

[T. S. BOKENKOTTER]

KEDERMYSTER, RICHARD

Abbot of the Benedictine monastery of Winchcombe and a man of some influence in the reign of Henry VIII; b. Worcestershire?, England, date unknown; d. Winchcombe, Gloucestershire, 1531. Kedermyster entered the abbey of Winchcombe as a novice at the age of 15 and at 19 went to study at the Benedictine House, Gloucester Hall, in Oxford. Four years later he was recalled to Winchcombe, and in 1487 he was elected abbot. He was an exact observer and reformer of the discipline of the house and was famous as a scholar and promoter of learning. He made frequent visits to Oxford and in 1500 took the degree of D.D. Kedermyster became well known as a preacher and often preached before Henry VIII. In 1512 he was sent with Bp. John FISHER and others to the Lateran Council convened by Julius II. In 1514 he preached his famous sermon that attacked the Act of 1512 depriving minor clerks of "benefit of clergy" and thereby sparked off a controversy in which current anticlerical feeling played an important part. Kedermyster was a keen antiquarian, and in 1532 he compiled a register, since lost, of the early documents of his abbey. In 1521 he published his *Tractatus contra M. Lutheri,* and in 1525 he resigned the abbacy.

Bibliography: *The Victoria History of the County of Gloucester,* ed. W. PAGE (London 1907–). T. COOPER, *The Dictionary of National Biography from the Earliest Times to 1900*, 63 v. (London 1885–1900 10: 1185.

[M. M. CURTIS]

KEEGAN, ROBERT FULTON

Administrator; b. Nashua, NH, May 3, 1888; d. New York City, Nov. 4, 1947. He was educated in New York City at Cathedral College and St. Joseph's Seminary; he

was ordained on Sept. 18, 1915. After receiving (1916) his M.A. in sociology at The Catholic University of America, Washington, D.C., he was appointed (1919) by Abp. Patrick J. Hayes to be the first executive director of New York's Catholic Charities. Under Keegan's direction, Catholic Charities became the largest voluntary charitable organization in the United States. He unified its diverse and overlapping welfare agencies, broadened their base of financial support, expanded their technical and professional services, and improved their standards of operation. The social agencies of the Archdiocese of New York became recognized leaders in the field of welfare, and there was a nationwide awakening of diocesan responsibility in the field of charity. Keegan also obtained the cooperation of public and nonsectarian agencies, many of which elected him as their president. In 1933 he was named pastor of Blessed Sacrament Church, New York City. He subsequently became a papal chamberlain (1929), domestic prelate (1937), and prothonotary apostolic (1940).

Bibliography: E. R. MOORE, *Roman Collar* (New York 1950).

[G. A KELLY]

KEELY, PATRICK CHARLES

19th-century American church architect (variously Kiely, Keily); b. Ireland, either Kilkenny, Aug. 9, 1816, or Thurles, Aug. 9, 1820; d. Brooklyn, N.Y., Aug. 11, 1896. Presumably trained under his architect-father, he migrated to the U.S. in 1841. Between 1847 and 1892 he designed 16 Catholic cathedrals and an estimated 500 to 700 other churches. The cathedrals of Rochester, N.Y., Chicago, Ill., Boston, Mass., Providence, R.I., and Erie, Pa., and St. Francis Xavier Church in New York City are among his best-known works. In general his structures are"preaching churches"—broad for their length, with large, unobstructed interiors and often stark and naïve but monumental exteriors. Their style is neo- or "Victorian" Gothic, a decadent adaptation of medieval architecture that became widespread in both Europe and America in the 19th century. In 1884 Keely received the second Laetare medal conferred by the University of Notre Dame, Ind.

Bibliography: H. F. and E. R. WITHEY, *Biographical Dictionary of American Architects* (Los Angeles 1956). F. W. KERVICK, *Architects in America of Catholic Tradition* (Rutland, Vt. 1962). H. L. WILSON, *The Cathedrals of Patrick Charles Keely* (Master's diss. unpub. Catholic University of America 1952), valuable critique. W. A. DALY, *Patrick Charles Keely: Architect and Builder* (Master's diss. unpub. Catholic University of America 1934), uncritical but useful for chronology.

[P. GOETTELMAN]

KEHR, PAUL FRIDOLIN

Protestant historian of the papacy; b. Waltershausen (Thuringia), Germany, Dec. 26, 1860; d. Wässerndorf, near Würzburg, Nov. 9, 1944. Kehr began his academic career as a collaborator on the *Monumenta Germaniae historia* and taught at Marburg in 1893. In 1895 he was nominated to the chair in medieval history at Göttingen. In 1896 he suggested that the Academy of Göttingen carefully collect and publish all pontifical documents preceding the reign of Innocent III (1198). He proposed that all such documents, edited and unedited, recensions, originals, and copies, in all the archives of Europe, be investigated critically and scientifically. The resulting project came to be known as the *Regesta Pontificum Romanorum*. The organization for the reporting of these documents was planned along regional and diocesan lines. Kehr's first volume was published in Rome (1906). It and the volumes that followed were consistently notable for their precision and meticulous methodology. For his impressive achievement in shedding further light upon the growth and development of the papacy, PIUS XI (1931) financially assisted Kehr in founding the "Pius-Stiftung für Papst-Urkunden und mittelalterliche Geschichts-forschung." Since his death additional volumes have appeared. As present, *Italia Pontifica* has reached eight volumes; *Germania Pontificia,* three volumes. Similar collections for France, England, Portugal, and Spain either have appeared or are in preparation.

Bibliography: W. HOLTZMANN, *Deutsches Archiv für Erforschung des Mittelalters* 8 (1950) 26–58. O. VASELLA, *Lexikon für Theologie und Kirche,* ed. J. HOFER and K. RAHNER, 10 v. (2d, new ed. Freiburg 1957–65) 6:102–103.

[B. F. SCHERER]

KELLER, JAMES G.

Founder of The CHRISTOPHERS; b. Oakland, California, June 27, 1900; d. New York City, Feb. 7, 1977. Educated in public schools and for seven years at St. Patrick's Seminary, Menlo Park, California he joined Maryknoll in September of 1921. Most of his studies during the major seminary years were at The Catholic University of America (bachelor of sacred theology, 1924, and master of arts, 1925). He was a member of the Maryknoll class of 1925 and was ordained on Aug. 15, 1925 at his parish church, St. Francis de Sales in Oakland. He founded The Christophers in 1945 out of the conviction that each person can do something, with God's help, to change the world for the better. The name "Christopher" taken from the Greek meaning "Christ-bearer," sums up the missionary character of the movement.

Tirelessly Keller proclaimed the Christopher ideal that "everyone can change the world" by stimulating others to show personal responsibility and individual initiative in raising the standards of all phases of human endeavor. He stressed in particular those fields of influence that affect the common good of all—government, education, labor-management relations, literature and entertainment. His book, *You Can Change the World,* published in 1948, was a best seller. To bring the message of positive, constructive action to the widest audience possible, he launched *Christopher News Notes*—published seven times a year, sent gratis to 750,000 persons; weekly radio and television programs; a one-minute inspirational radio spot broadcast daily; a yearly Christopher book; a daily newspaper column called "Three Minutes a Day"; and the Christopher Awards—in recognition of writers, producers, and directors in literature, motion pictures, and television whose works attest to the highest values of the human spirit. To accentuate the positive as the Christopher objective, he adopted as the Christopher motto the Chinese proverb, "Better to light one candle than to curse the darkness"; the Prayer of St. Francis as the Christopher Prayer; and stressed the biblical injunction from St. Paul, "Be not overcome by evil, but overcome evil with good" (Romans 12.21). A man of prayer, great hope and vision, he was consumed with the idea of reaching as many people as he could in his lifetime with the love and truth of Christ. A victim of Parkinson's Disease, he retired as director of The Christophers in 1969, but remained as consultant up until the last year of his life.

Bibliography: J. G. KELLER, *To Light a Candle; The Autobiography of James Keller, Founder of the Christophers* (New York, 1963).

[THE CHRISTOPHERS/EDS.]

KELLEY, FRANCIS CLEMENT

Bishop, founder of the Extension Society; b. Prince Edward Island, Canada, Nov. 24, 1870; d. Oklahoma City, Oklahoma, Feb. 1, 1948; the son of John Kelley, a merchant, landowner, and senior partner in the firm of Ely & Kelley, and Mary (Murphy) Kelley, the daughter of an Irish political exile. Kelley attended Laval University in Quebec, where he studied at Nicolet Seminary and was ordained a priest on August 24, 1893, for the Diocese of Detroit, Michigan. Kelley was appointed pastor of Lapeer parish. In 1905, he founded the Catholic Church Extension Society of the United States, and was elected its president. The following year, its headquarters, and Kelley himself, transferred to Chicago, Illinois; there for 19 years he presided over the society, raising its receipts to almost $1 million annually.

Kelley founded and edited the quarterly *Extension Magazine,* featuring articles on home mission activities and fiction by Catholic writers. Under his direction, the magazine had more than 3 million paid subscribers. Not merely a gifted editor, Kelley was a popular lecturer and author of more that a dozen books. His two most prominent works were: *Blood Drenched Altars* (1935), a controversial account of the church in Mexico; and *The Bishop Jots It Down* (1939), an autobiography written, it has been said, with the encouragement of H. L. Menken.

Kelley was widely active in war and diplomacy. He served as chaplain in the Spanish-American War; and as a diplomat, Kelley represented the bishops of Mexico during the World War I Peace Conference in Paris. He initiated unofficial negotiations in Paris with Premier Vittorio Orlando of Italy for a settlement of the Roman question, and two years after the peace conference, was sent to England by the Vatican to settle postwar difficulties over German and Austrian missions. As president of the Extension Society, Kelley represented the Mexican bishops during the Carranza Revolution and established St. Philip Neri Seminary at Castroville, Tex., for exiled Mexican seminarians and clergy, while collecting money for their relief. Similarly, he was active in raising funds to assist the Archdiocese of Vancouver, Canada, in times of financial crisis.

In 1924, he was named bishop of Oklahoma City and Tulsa, Oklahoma. During his episcopate, Kelley successfully resisted the agitation of the Ku Klux Klan and continued his mission work as "the Extension Bishop." Under his care the infant diocese grew to maturity.

Bibliography: J. P. GAFFEY, *Francis Clement Kelley and the American Catholic Dream.* 2 vols. Bensenville, Ill., 1980. M. J. OBERKOETTER, O.S.B. "A Bio-Bibliography of Bishop Francis Clement Kelley, 1870–1948." M.A. thesis, Rosary College, River Forest, Ill., 1955.

[E. A. FLUSCHE]

KELLS, ABBEY OF

Former Irish abbey in present-day Kells, County Meath, Ireland, about 40 miles northwest of Dublin. In 807, after IONA had been sacked three times by the Vikings, Cellach transferred the primacy of the Columban league of churches to Kells (Cenannas), a mainland foundation of COLUMBA OF IONA. However, the Vikings struck at Kells also, and its church (built *c.* 804) was destroyed. Another church (now called Colum Cille's, or Columba's, House) was built in 814. About 848 the Pictish King Kenneth mac Alpin seems to have tried to withdraw the churches in Scotland from the primacy of Kells, endeavoring to set up Dunkeld as the metropolis there. Kells was pillaged once again in 899 and five times in the 10th century. In the 12th century the primacy passed from

Kells to Derry, and at Kells the Columban rule was replaced by that of the CANONS REGULAR OF ST. AUGUSTINE. The modern Protestant church in Kells occupies the site of the original monastic foundation, of which there remain five 10th-century IRISH CROSSES, a round tower, and St. Colum Cille's House. The Rolls of Chancery of Ireland, 31 Henry VIII, contain the instrument (dated Nov. 18, 1539) under which Kells was surrendered to the crown. The famous *Book of Kells* belonged to Kells, and on the blank spaces of this *evangeliarium* were copied certain charters of the abbey. These are of considerable interest and provide important information about the organization of one of the principal monastic churches at a period of decline, when the old order was being replaced by the new diocesan system. The Crozier of Kells is preserved in the British Museum.

Bibliography: M. ARCHDALL, *Monasticon hibernicum* (London 1786) 541–548, complete but must be checked with later eds. of sources used. ADAMNAN, *The Life of St. Columba,* ed. W. REEVES (Dublin 1857) 387–389. J. F. KENNEY, *The Sources for the Early History of Ireland,* v. 1, *Ecclesiastical* (New York 1929). 1:445, 753–756, with a synopsis of the charters of the *Book of Kells* and bibliog. E. H. L. SEXTON, *A Descriptive and Bibliographical List of Irish Figure Sculptures of the Early Christian Period* (Portland, Maine 1947) 174–191. E. SULLIVAN, *The Book of Kells* (5th ed. New York 1952) 20–22. H. G. LEASK, *Irish Churches and Monastic Buildings,* 3 v. (Dundalk, Ire. 1955–60) 1:32–34. M. and L. DE PAOR, *Early Christian Ireland* (2d ed. New York 1960).

[C. MCGRATH]

KELLS, BOOK OF

The *Book of Kells* is a vellum Gospel book profusely and brilliantly decorated, one of the greatest achievements of European decorative art, produced in the Columban mission field, perhaps at Iona, 775–800. It is now at Trinity College, Dublin. The decoration builds on the earlier tradition of the books of DURROW and LINDISFARNE, but belongs to a later, more elaborate, sophisticated, and baroque phase. In addition to the pages representing the Evangelist symbols, it has pages of fantastic ornament with spreads of minute and intricate color work and pen drawing; great ornamental monogram pages; heavily ornate canon tables; and illustrative pages depicting the arrest of Christ, the Virgin and Child, the temptation of Christ, and other subjects. A brilliant series of inhabited or zoomorphic initials, all different, runs through the text. The ornamental text passages in capitals have become almost illegible. The human figure, foliate motifs, and marginal genre subjcts, such as the otter and salmon or cat and mice, appear.

At least four, perhaps five, different artists can be distinguished, and their work varies in style and quality but the palette is consistently rich. In the elaborate canon tables the symbols of the Evangelists replace their names over the columns. The book appears to have been regarded primarily as a medium of unrestricted artistic creation. The text is mixed, and it is poorly set out and full of mistakes, though in an ornamental half–uncial hand of great beauty.

Bibliography: *Codex Cenannensis,* ed. E. H. ALTON and P. MEYER, 3 v. (New York 1950–51). S. F. H. ROBINSON, *Celtic Illuminative Art in the Gospel Books of Durrow, Lindisfarne and Kells* (Dublin 1908). E. SULLIVAN, *The Book of Kells* (New York 1955). F. O'MAHONY, ed., *The Book of Kells: Proceedings of a Conference at Trinity College Dublin, 6–9 September 1992* (Aldershot, Eng. 1994). G. HENDERSON, *From Durrow to Kells: The Insular Gospel–books, 650–800* (New York 1987). C. FARR, *The Book of Kells: Its Function and Audience* (London 1997).

[R. L. S. BRUCE–MITFORD]

KELLY, GERALD ANDREW

Jesuit moral theologian; b. Denver, Colo., Sept. 30, 1902; d. Kansas City, Mo., Aug. 2, 1964. After receiving his elementary and secondary education in Denver, he entered the Society of Jesus at Florissant, Mo., in 1920. He obtained his bachelor's and master's degrees in arts at St. Louis University, where he also received his licenciate in theology. He was ordained in 1933 and took his doctorate in theology at the Gregorian University in Rome in 1937.

For 26 years Kelly taught moral theology to Jesuit scholastics at St. Mary's College, St. Mary's, Kansas. At summer sessions he gave courses to nuns and laity at Marquette, St. Louis, and Creighton Universities, at Rockhurst College, and at St. Mary's College, Notre Dame, Ind. On many and various occasions he addressed assemblies of priests, nuns, physicians, nurses, and students in different parts of the United States. He was managing editor of the *Review for Religious* (1942–59).

His approach to moral problems was thoroughly scientific and his solution was always solidly based upon principles clearly seen and lucidly expounded. He was an independent thinker who respected points of view different from his own, but he did not hesitate to disagree with others when the occasion demanded it. If he could not solve a problem, he frankly said so. He had the ability to simplify complex problems without oversimplifying them and to deal with profound matters without recourse to jargon or complicated language. He was at his best in his treatment of medico-moral problems, and he was chairman of the committee that formulated the ethical code of the Catholic Hospital Association. He received the Cardinal Spellman award for theology for 1953.

Among his writings were *Modern Youth and Chastity* (1941), *The Good Confessor* (1951), *Guidance for Re-*

Dr. Herbert Parke, the Chief Librarian of Dublin's Trinity College, holds the Book of Kells before a backdrop depicting the book's illumination of the Virgin Mary, Nov. 1, 1961. (©Hulton-Deutsch Collection/CORBIS)

ligious (1956), *Medico-Moral Problems* (1957), *Moral Theology under Pius XII* (with John C. Ford, SJ, 1957), *Contemporary Moral Theology* (with John C. Ford, SJ, v. 1, 1958; v. 2, 1963). His critical summaries of current developments in moral theology published between 1946 and 1952 in *Theological Studies* were of considerable value to theologians and students, and his many articles in the *Linacre Quarterly* were helpful especially to physicians and nurses.

[C. MCAULIFFE]

KELLY, MICHAEL VINCENT

Author of books and articles on pastoral theology, religious education, and rural life; assistant superior general of the Basilian Fathers (1922–36); b. Adjala, Ontario, Canada, July 31, 1863; d. Toronto, Ontario, July 24, 1942. The son of Irish immigrants, he was educated at St. Michael's College, Toronto, and at the University of Toronto (B.A. 1887). He entered the Congregation of Priests of St. Basil at Beaconsfield, England, and was ordained at Toronto Sept. 21, 1891. Kelly's special interest was the parochial ministry. Among his books are: *Zeal in the*

St. John Kemble.

Classroom (Toronto 1922); *Some of the Pastor's Problems* (Toronto 1923); *Remarked in Passing* (Toronto 1934), reminiscences on his 70th birthday; *First Communicant's Catechism* translated into Slovak and Spanish; and in collaboration with Canon J. B. Geniesse, *Efficax Antidotum ad Matrimonia Mixta Praecavenda* (Rome 1923).

Bibliography: *Basilian Annals 1* (July 1943) 22–25. M. V. KELLY, *The Kellys of Monasterevan and Adjala* (Toronto 1942).

[R. J. SCOLLARD]

KEMBLE, JOHN, ST.

Priest, martyr, *alias* John Holland; b. Rhyd y Car Farm, St. Weonards, Herefordshire, England, 1599 or 1600; d. Hereford, Aug. 22, 1679. The Kembles were an old Wiltshire family. Sometime in the 1620s, John was smuggled abroad to the English College at Douai where he was ordained on Feb. 23, 1625. On June 4 he was sent home to his native district as a missionary. He made his headquarters at Pembridge Castle, the home first of his brother George, then of his nephew Captain Richard Kemble, who saved Charles II's life at the Battle of Worcester. With the help of the Jesuits, John established mission centers throughout Herefordshire and Mon-

mouthshire. The persecution was less severe in the reign of Charles I than in that of James and he worked in comparative safety. Nevertheless, Monmouthshire headed the list of recusant convictions for the 29 counties of the southern division in the first 15 years of Charles I's reign. In 1649 John paid a visit to London, presumably on ecclesiastical business. He returned home and continued his missionary labors throughout the Commonwealth. He took no part in politics but ministered to the existing Catholics and converted many Protestants.

The storm broke in 1678, when Titus Oates revealed his "popish plot" (*see* OATES PLOT). Everywhere priests were arrested and dragged up to London to confront Titus. Sometimes he fitted them into his "plot," sometimes he did not bother. The result was the same—execution. Kemble's friends urged him to hide, but he refused. Although over 80, he was arrested in November and taken to Hereford jail. His captor was Captain Scudamore, whose wife and children were Catholics and members of his flock. After three months' imprisonment, during which the prison governor sketched his portrait, John was brought to trial and sentenced to be hanged, drawn, and quartered as a seminary priest. On Apr. 23, 1679, he was sent with David LEWIS for examination by Oates. John was suffering from a malady that made riding particularly painful, but he was nevertheless strapped to a horse and brought up to London. There, neither Titus Oates nor his associate, Bedloes, was able to bring any charge against the two priests. They were offered life and liberty to disclose details of the nonexistent plot to no avail. On May 28 they were ordered back to their respective jails. When the undersheriff arrived to take John to execution on Aug. 22, the martyr asked for time to finish his prayers, and smoke a last pipe, and have a last drink. (Hence the expressions "Kemble pipe" and "Kemble cup" for the last pipe or drink of a sitting). At Widemarsh Common, before a huge crowd, John denied the plot and made a last profession of faith. He was allowed to hang till dead before they quartered him. He was beatified on Dec.15, 1929, and canonized by Paul VI on Oct. 25, 1970 as one of the Forty Martyrs of England and Wales.

Feast: Aug. 22; Oct. 25 (Feast of the 40 Martyrs of England and Wales); May 4 (Feast of the English Martyrs in England).

See Also: ENGLAND, SCOTLAND, AND WALES, MARTYRS OF.

Bibliography: R. CHALLONER, *Memoirs of Missionary Priests,* ed. J. H. POLLEN (rev. ed. London 1924; repr. Farnborough 1969), 555–57. B. CAMM, *Forgotten Shrines* (St. Louis 1910). M. V. LOVEJOY, *Blessed John Kemble* (Postulation pamphlet; London 1960).

[G. FITZ HERBERT]

KEMP, JOHN (KEMPE)

Cardinal, archbishop of Canterbury; b. near Ashford, Kent, c. 1377; d. Canterbury, March 22, 1454. He attended Merton College, specializing in Canon Law. He was appointed a member of the ecclesiastical courts, and in 1415 became dean of the Court of ARCHES, having been made vicar-general of Abp. Henry CHICHELE of Canterbury the year before. Henry V made him chancellor of Normandy and keeper of the privy seal in 1418. MARTIN V provided him with the bishopric of Rochester on June 21, 1419. He was translated to Chichester, Feb. 28, 1421, only to accept papal provision for his translation to the bishopric of London the same year. He became archbishop of York, July 20, 1425. The king employed him on numerous diplomatic missions abroad, e.g., at the Council of BASEL and at Arras, and found him a strong supporter at home, for, as chancellor (1426–32), Kemp sided with Henry BEAUFORT against Duke Humphrey of Gloucester. EUGENE IV recognized Kemp's abilities by creating him a cardinal priest in 1439. This caused a conflict with Abp. Chichele of Canterbury, for a cardinal of whatever rank had precedence over an archbishop. On July 21, 1452, Kemp became archbishop of Canterbury after having been continuously in the king's service during his 27 years at York. He is buried at Canterbury. There are no extant writings of Kemp. Although his diplomatic activity cannot have been conducive to exercising ecclesiastical influence, there is no evidence to suggest that he neglected his pastoral or episcopal duties. His career reflects the multifarious responsibilities of a competent higher ecclesiastic in the later Middle Ages.

Bibliography: W. F. HOOK, *Lives of the Archbishops of Canterbury,* 12 v. (London 1860–84) v.5. R. F. WILLIAMS, *Lives of the English Cardinals* 2 v. (London 1868) 2:110–123. A. B. EMDEN, *A Biographical Register of the University of Oxford to A.D. 1500* 2: 1031–32. W. ULLMANN, ''Eugenius IV, Cardinal Kemp, and Archbishop Chichele,'' *Medieval Studies, Presented to Aubrey Gwynn, S.J.* (Dublin 1961).

[W. ULLMANN]

KEMP, THOMAS

Bishop of London; b. c. 1414; d. March 28, 1489. He owed his early advancement to his uncle, Cardinal John KEMP. After taking his M.A. and B.Theol. at Oxford, he became canon of Lincoln in 1433. Rapid preferment followed in the Archdiocese of York, where his uncle was archbishop, and Thomas became canon of York (1435), and archdeacon of York (1436–42) and of Richmond (1442–48); he was also archdeacon of Middlesex (1449). On Henry VI's recommendation, he was provided by Nicholas V to the See of London on Aug. 21, 1448, de-

spite Henry's later change of mind. Consecrated by his uncle on Feb. 8, 1450, he held the see until death. He was king's clerk and chaplain by 1443, and he was among the bishops who tried to mediate between Henry VI and the Yorkists before the Battle of Northampton (1460). Afterward he played little part in politics. He was a considerable benefactor of Merton College, Oxford, and of the university, where he helped to finance the Divinity School and the building of the library.

See Also: OXFORD, UNIVERSITY OF.

Bibliography: Manuscript Register, Guildhall Library, London. A. B. EMDEN, *A Biographical Register of the University of Oxford to A.D. 1500,* 3 vol. (Oxford 1957–59) 2:1032–34.

[C. D. ROSS]

KEMPE, MARGERY

English mystic and author of *The Book of Margery Kempe,* the oldest extant autobiography in English; b. Lynn, Norfolk, c. 1373; d. sometime after 1439. The daughter of John Brunham, who was five times mayor of Lynn, she married John Kempe, burgess, in 1393. Vain and ambitious, she tried to support her extravagances by trade, first by brewing, then by a horsemill. The failure of both undertakings, together with an attack of madness suffered after the birth of her first child, turned her gradually to prayer and penance. The madness, which did not recur, was cured, she tells us, by a vision of Christ seated on her bed and saying: ''Dowtyr why hast thou forsakyn me and I forsoke never the.''

In 1413, having borne her husband 14 children, she separated from him by mutual consent, to live a religious life in the world. Soon after, having visited many English shrines and holy persons (among them Julian of Norwich), she set out for the Holy Land. On her return journey she spent six months in Italy (1414–15), where she was better understood than among the English pilgrims, who did not appreciate her unusual vocation—''boystrous'' crying, exclusively religious conversation, and rebuke of her neighbors' faults. Throughout her life she suffered taunts of Lollardy that occasionally developed into formal accusations. In 1417–18 she visited Santiago de Compostela. In 1425 she returned to Lynn to nurse her husband until his death in 1431. Thereafter, she traveled to Norway and Danzig (1433–34).

Unable to write herself, she had set down by the aid of two clerks, c. 1431–38, a vivid and frank account of her travels, temptations, mystical experiences, and deep compassion for sinners. Her book, known only in extracts till 1934, when a manuscript was discovered in the Butler-Bowden family, has undoubted value as a literary and human document, and as a picture of medieval life. Margery herself remains a controversial figure: by some considered a victim of religious mania; by others, a genuine mystic.

Bibliography: *The Book of Margery Kempe,* critical ed. S. B. MEECH and H. E. ALLEN (*Early English Text Society* 212; 1940); modernized version ed. W. BUTLER-BOWDON (New York 1944). E. I. WATKIN, ''In Defense of Margery Kempe,'' *Poets and Mystics* (New York 1953) 104–135. D. KNOWLES, ''Margery Kempe,'' *The English Mystical Tradition* (New York 1961) 138–150. L. COLLIS, *Memoirs of a Medieval Woman: The Life and Times of Margery Kempe* (New York 1983).

[M. N. MALTMAN]

KEMPTEN, ABBEY OF

Former royal BENEDICTINE monastery in the present-day town of Kempten (the old Roman *Campodunum*), Bavaria, Germany. It was founded by SANKT GALLEN *c.* 725 as a small cell, and by 752 it was a nondependent, royal, proprietary, Benedictine monastery with the right of free election of abbot. It was favored by CHARLEMAGNE and his consort Hildegard, who was considered a foundress. Its first monastic buildings probably imitated the style of Sankt Gallen. Kempten organized the evangelization of the Algäu. The Hungarians destroyed the old abbey in 926, and the monks moved to a hill west of the town (at the site of the east wing of the residence now there). Reformed under Bp. ULRIC OF AUGSBURG, it had ties with the GORZE-TRIER-EINSIEDELN circle, and, in the 12th century, with the HIRSAU-FRUTTUARIA-SANKT-BLASIEN group. In 1213 the abbatial territory was given the status of a county; the abbot was invested with pontificalia in 1238. He was made a prince of the empire in 1360, and thenceforth Kempten accepted only noblemen as monks. In 1419 it gained EXEMPTION. The 15th and 16th centuries saw the beginnings of reform, but the inroads of the Swabian nobility, peasant uprisings in 1491 and 1525 with looting of church and monastery, strife with the town, and the REFORMATION made reform ineffective. The famous printing press whose tradition is maintained by the Kösel publishing house was established at Kempten in 1593. Prince-Abbot Johann Euchar von Wolfurt (1616–31) saw the abbey looted by Swedes and townsmen in the Thirty Years' War. Under Roman Giel of Gielsberg, elected abbot in 1639 at the age of 27, Kempten joined the Lorraine Benedictine congregation (1649) and the Swiss congregation (1664), and with Christophorus of Schönau from Einsiedeln as subprior (at the request of the bishop of Constance and the nobility), the cloisters and church were rebuilt after 1651. The original church dated from the 10th to the 11th centuries; its interior and exterior baroque reconstruction and expansion were not completed until *c.* 1742; the old parish church of St. Lawrence still shows the influence of Sankt Gallen. When Kempten was dissolved in 1803, it ceded its holdings (18 square miles occupied by 42,000 people) to the state of Bavaria.

Bibliography: L. H. COTTINEAU, *Répertoire topobibliographique des abbayes et prieurés,* 2 v. (Mâcon 1935–39) 1:1510–11. R. HENGGELER, *Profess-buch der fürstlichen Benediktinerabtei unserer lieben Frau zu Einsiedeln* (Monasticon-Benedictinum Helvetiae 3; Einsiedeln 1934). K. HALLINGER, *Gorze-Kluny,* 2 v. (*Studia anselmiana* 22–25; Rome 1950–51). J. ROTTENKOLBER, *Geschichte des hochfürstlichen Stiftes Kempten* (Munich 1933); *Geschichte des Allgäus* (Munich 1951). A. SCHÄDLER, ed., *1200 Jahre Stift Kempten* (Kempten 1952). H. TÜCHLE, *Kirchengeschichte Schwabens,* 2 v. (Stuttgart 1950–54). F. ZOEPFL, *Das Bistum Augsburg und seine Bischöfe im Mittelalter* (Munich 1955). *Festschrift zur 900-Jahr-Feier des Klosters, 1056–1956,* ed. G. SPAHR (Weingarten 1956). N. LIEB, *Rokoko in der Residenz von Kempten* (Kempten 1958).

[G. SPAHR]

KENNA, JOHN EDWARD

U.S. senator; b. Kanawha County, Va. (later W. Va.), April 10, 1848; d. Washington, D.C., Jan. 11, 1893. His father, Edward Kenna, was an Irish immigrant, and his mother, Margery Lewis, came from a prominent Virginia family. His childhood was spent in southern Missouri, where frontier conditions did not permit even an elementary education. In 1864 Kenna joined Gen. Joseph O. Shelby's Confederate forces and stayed with them until their surrender at Shreveport, La., in 1865. Kenna then returned to West Virginia, studied for three years at St. Vincent's College, Wheeling, and was admitted to the bar in 1870. That year he married Rosa Quigg; after her death he married Anna Benninghaus in 1876. In 1872 he was chosen prosecuting attorney for Kanawha County, and in 1875 he became justice *pro tempore* of the circuit court of his district. He was elected in 1876 to the national House of Representatives. After three terms in the House, he was elected to the U.S. Senate, where he served from 1883 until his death. In Congress Kenna sought Federal aid for improved navigation along the Kanawha River and advocated Federal regulation of railroads. As a leader of the Democratic party, he was chairman (1886, 1888) of the Democratic Congressional Committee and a spokesman in the Senate for the administration of President Grover Cleveland. He defended Cleveland's power to remove appointed officials from office and supported his demand for tariff reform in 1887.

[V. P. DE SANTIS]

KENNETH (CANICE) OF DERRY, ST.

Patron of Diocese of Ossory, Ireland; b. Glengiven, County Derry, 521 or 527 (Annals of Ulster); d. 599 or 600 (Annals of Ulster) or 603 (Annals of Inisfallen). Kenneth (Canice or Cainnech), one of the most famous early Irish saints, was born of poor parents. He studied at the great Irish monastic schools of Clonard and Glasnevin and later at St. Cadoc's, Llancarvan in Wales. He returned to Ireland and made his principal monastic foundation at Aghaboe, County Laois. One of his many foundations, that of Kilkenny, Ireland, later replaced Aghaboe as the principal church of Ossory. As a friend of COLUMBA OF IONA, Kenneth also traveled and preached extensively in Scotland. He had a Hebridean island foundation on Inchkenneth, not far from Iona. Devotion to the saint became widespread in Scotland, where he is known as Kenneth. In Ireland today "Canice" is preferred. He is invoked in some early Continental litanies of saints. St. Adamnan's biography of Columba pictures Kenneth's luminous personality.

Feast: Oct. 11.

Bibliography: *Vitae sanctorum Hiberniae,* comp. C. PLUMMER, 2 v. (Oxford 1910) 1:152–169. J. F. KENNEY, *The Sources for the Early History of Ireland:* v.1, *Ecclesiastical* (New York 1929) 1:394–395, 409. L. GOUGAUD, *Les Saints irlandais hors d'Irlande* (Louvain 1936). D. D. C. POCHIN MOULD, *Scotland of the Saints* (London 1952). ADAMNAN, *Adamnan's Life of Columba,* ed. and tr. A. O. and M. O. ANDERSON (London 1961).

[D. D. C. POCHIN MOULD]

KENOSIS

The INCARNATION is described as a humiliation or emptying (Greek κενόω) in Phil 2.7. The whole passage (2.5–11) is important because it is one of the great Christological texts of the New Testament and because it has been cited in support of a modern theory on the Incarnation known as kenoticism.

In Phil 2.5–11 Paul is probably quoting a hymn sung in the Palestinian Churches. As L. Cerfaux has shown, the movements of the third and fourth strophes (v. 7b and v. 9) are patterned on the Deutero-Isaian picture of the suffering and glorified Servant of the Lord (Is ch. 53; *see* SUFFERING SERVANT, SONGS OF). The words "every tongue shall confess that Jesus Christ is Lord [κύριος]" is a brief act of faith like Rom 10.9 and 1 Cor 12.3 (*see* LORD, THE). Despite a wide variation in the interpretation of individual words and phrases, the mainstream of patristic exegesis is unanimous in seeing in this text a scriptural proof of the divinity of Christ, of His real and complete humanity, and of the unity of His Person.

The modern kenotic theory of the Incarnation began with Evangelical theologians in Germany in the 19th century. It was taken up by some Anglicans and Russian Orthodox. Common to all the types of kenotic theology is the thesis that the divine Word relinquished some or all of His divinity in becoming man: that He surrendered His omnipotence, His divine omniscience, His omnipresence; that He lost consciousness of His divinity; or even that He ceased to be God from the moment of the Incarnation until the Resurrection. For the kenotic school of theology there is no other way of reconciling a really human experience in Our Lord with belief in His divinity.

P. Henry's brilliant and exhaustive evaluation of kenotic theology makes the following points: the whole weight of impartial scholarship is against the kenotic interpretation of Phil 2.5–11; in all of Christian antiquity there is no trace of kenoticism in interpreting this passage; it is metaphysically impossible for God to change. On the other hand, a positive refutation of kenoticism must reckon with the questions it has raised. Was the human condition in all its fullness (e.g., the agony of decision) experienced by Our Lord? If so, what is to be said about such traditional theological assertions as that of Christ's foreknowledge?

See Also: JESUS CHRIST (IN THEOLOGY).

Bibliography: P. HENRY, *Dictionnaire de la Bible,* suppl. ed. L. PIROT, et al. (Paris 1928–) 5:7–161. A. GAUDEL, *Dictionnaire de théologie catholique,* ed. A. VACANT, 15 v. (Paris 1903–50; Tables générales 1951–) 8.2:2339–49. F. LOOFS, J. HASTINGS, ed., *Encyclopedia of Religion & Ethics,* 13 v. (Edinburgh 1908–27) 7:680–687. L. CERFAUX, *Christ in the Theology of St. Paul,* tr. G. WEBB and A. WALKER (New York 1959). C. GORE, *The Incarnation of the Son of God* (Bampton Lectures; London 1891). D. G. DAWE, "A Fresh Look at the Kenotic Christologies," *Scottish Journal of Theology* 15 (1962) 337–349.

[J. M. CARMODY]

KENRAGHTY, MAURICE

Irish martyr; b. Kilmallock, date unknown; d. Clonmel, Tipperary, April 30, 1585. He was a silversmith's son. After earning his bachelor of theology degree abroad, Kenraghty became chaplain to Gerald, 16th Earl of Desmond. During Desmond's rebellion Kenraghty was captured in Sept. 1583 by Murtough MacSweeney, one of Lord Roche's mercenaries, and imprisoned in Clonmel. During Passiontide, 1585, Victor White, a citizen of Clonmel, bribed Kenraghty's jailer to release him for one night to administer the Sacraments. The jailer, however, betrayed them; White was arrested, but Kenraghty escaped. Apparently he surrendered himself in return for the release of White and was condemned to death for high treason. When he was offered pardon if he acknowledged the spiritual supremacy of the queen, he declined and was hanged, drawn, and quartered.

Bibliography: D. MURPHY, *Our Martyrs* (Dublin 1896). R. BAGWELL, *Ireland Under the Tudors*, 3 v. (London 1885–90). R. D. EDWARDS, *Church and State in Tudor Ireland* (New York 1935).

[J. G. BARRY]

KENRICK, FRANCIS PATRICK

Archbishop, author; b. Dublin, Ireland, Dec. 3, 1796; d. Baltimore, Md., July 8, 1863. He was the elder son of Jane (Eustace) and Thomas Kenrick, a successful scrivener. The second son, Peter Richard, became the first archbishop of St. Louis. Francis was educated in local schools under the tutelage of his pastor and uncle, Richard Kenrick, known as the Vincent de Paul of Dublin. At the age of 18 he went to Rome to study for the priesthood at the College of the Propaganda, where he made a brilliant record in Scripture and theology. On April 7, 1821, he was ordained by Abp. Alfonso Frattini, and shortly thereafter he volunteered for the American mission in Kentucky.

His first assignment was to teach theology, Church history, and liturgy at St. Joseph's Seminary, Bardstown, Ky. He also taught history and Greek in the college department. During these years he laid the foundation that made him the foremost theological scholar in the American Church. He was also pastor of the local congregation and acted as secretary to Bp. Benedict FLAGET. When named a preacher of the 1826 Jubilee Year, he quickly won acclaim throughout his diocese as an apologist ready to defend the teachings of the Church by either the spoken or written word. In 1828 his answer to an attack on the Real Presence was published as the *Letters of Omega and Omicron on Transubstantiation* (Louisville 1828). The following year he went to the First Provincial Council of Baltimore as Flaget's theologian and was chosen secretary of that assembly. Among the Council's problems was the difficulty with lay trustees in Philadelphia, which had proved too much for the aged Bp. Henry CONWELL. The Council persuaded Rome to name Kenrick coadjutor of Philadelphia with full jurisdiction; on June 6, 1830, he was consecrated titular bishop of Arath in the Bardstown cathedral by Flaget.

Ordinary of Philadelphia. In 1830 the PHILADELPHIA diocese included the states of Pennsylvania and Delaware and what was known as West Jersey. Although Conwell had asked that Kenrick be named his coadjutor, the young bishop met with opposition from his superior when he tried to assume the administration. This situation was not fully remedied until Conwell's death in 1842, when Kenrick succeeded him as ordinary of Philadelphia.

One of Kenrick's first acts as coadjutor in Philadelphia was to attack the trustee problem by placing St. Mary's Church under interdict until the lay trustees recognized his episcopal authority to name pastors. The following year (1832) he convoked the first diocesan synod, which enacted legislation that prevented the recurrence of trusteeism in the diocese; the policy was adopted by other American bishops. Two later synods, in 1842 and 1847, ensured uniformity of discipline and faced the problems arising from increasing immigration. The work of the bishop, his priests, and the Sisters of Charity, during the cholera epidemic in Philadelphia, including the use of St. Augustine's school as a hospital, won goodwill for the Church.

Kenrick was interested in helping the poor, and he used the royalties from his writings for this purpose. He promoted the temperance movement, but would not sponsor Father Theobald Mathew's program because he thought that it slighted the necessary spiritual means. Because he refused to become politically involved in the Irish Freedom Movement, he was not so popular as some of his Irish contemporaries in the American hierarchy. The diocesan newspaper the *Catholic Herald,* which he founded with the assistance of Michael HURLEY, OSA, and Father John Hughes, the future archbishop of New York, avoided purely political questions and was criticized for its conservative policy, even in Church affairs. The bishop refused to preside at the Masonic funeral of Stephen Girard from Holy Trinity Church, but he permitted burial in Holy Trinity cemetery without the benefit of clergy because Girard's sudden death had prevented his reconciliation with the Church.

During the early years of his administration, Kenrick founded St. Charles Borromeo, the diocesan seminary. To supply textbooks for his seminarians he wrote four volumes of *Theologica Dogmatica* (Philadelphia 1834–40) and three volumes of *Theologia Moralis* (Baltimore 1860–61). At the time of his promotion to Baltimore he had translated all of the New Testament and most of the Old. Among his works defending the Church against the attacks of non-Catholics are *The Primacy of the Apostolic See Vindicated* (Philadelphia 1845) and *The Catholic Doctrine on Justification* (Philadelphia 1841). *A Treatise on Baptism and a Treatise on Confirmation* (Baltimore 1852) stressed the necessity of sacramental Baptism and the normal manner of receiving the Holy Spirit in opposition to Quaker and some Baptist teachings.

He fostered a parochial school system that embraced half of the parishes in the diocese and encouraged the founding of the Augustinian college (University), Villanova (1842), and the Jesuit college, St. Joseph's (1851), as well as several private academies and convent schools. He successfully contested compulsory attendance at instructions based on the King James Version of the Bible in Philadelphia public schools. Although he wanted the children of each sect to be permitted to read their own Bible, his stand was distorted into the calumny that "the Catholic bishop wants to take the Bible out of the public schools." This served as an inflammatory note for the Native-American riots of 1844 in which St. Michael's and St. Augustine's churches were burned and St. Phillip's destroyed. Despite criticism, Kenrick restrained his angry flock from retaliation. By temporarily closing the churches in the troubled areas and turning over the keys of church properties, he placed the burden of protection on the civil authorities. His moderation saved bloodshed, and in the public reaction against the "church-burners" he received many noted converts into the Church.

In the 21 years of his administration of Philadelphia, Kenrick made 19 visitations by stagecoach and horseback over a territory extending from Lake Erie to Cape May, N.J., and from the southern boundary of New York to the eastern boundary of West Virginia, an area equal to that of England, Scotland, and Wales. During his rule the number of churches increased from 22 to 92, priests from 35 to 101, and the Catholic population from 35,000 to 170,000, even though the new Diocese of Pittsburgh had removed the western part of the state from Philadelphia's jurisdiction.

Archbishop of Baltimore. On Aug. 3, 1851, Kenrick was promoted to the See of Baltimore. The following year he presided over the First Plenary Council as apostolic delegate. At the request of Pius IX in 1853, he collected the opinions of the American bishops concerning a definition of the doctrine of the Immaculate Conception and was in Rome for its promulgation in 1854. Through his efforts the Forty Hours devotion was introduced into the U.S. As he had done in Philadelphia, he encouraged each parish to found its own school. In Baltimore he completed his translation of the Sacred Scriptures and continued his contributions to scholarly periodicals.

Kenrick was considered the leading American moral theologian of his generation. During the Civil War, he held the opinion that the institution of slavery under certain protective conditions was not in itself immoral. As the leader of the American hierarchy he stated his position in an address on Christian patriotism in which he taught that national loyalty should prevail over state patriotism. This teaching was not popular with many Marylanders dedicated to the South. Because of his policy of aloofness from all political entanglements, he was disturbed by the pro-Southern editorial policy of Baltimore's *Catholic Mirror*. It seems that his death was hastened by reports of the slaughter at Gettysburg. His cause for canonization was being considered by the

Church authorities of Philadelphia when it was decided instead to promote that of his successor, John Neumann, who was beatified in 1963.

Bibliography: H. J. NOLAN, *The Most Reverend Francis Patrick Kenrick* (*Catholic University of America Studies in American Church History* 37; Washington 1948). J. J. O'SHEA, *The Two Kenricks* (Philadelphia 1904). F. E. TOURSCHER, ed., *The Kenrick-Frenaye Correspondence, 1830–1862* (Philadelphia 1920); *Diary and Visitation Record of Rt. Rev. Francis Patrick Kenrick* (Lancaster, Pa. 1916).

[H. J. NOLAN]

KENRICK, PETER RICHARD

First archbishop of St. Louis, author; b. Dublin, Ireland, Aug. 17, 1806; d. St. Louis, Mo., March 4, 1896. Upon completion of his education at St. Patrick's College, Maynooth, Ireland, he was ordained on March 6, 1832. A year later he traveled to Philadelphia at the invitation of his elder brother, Francis Patrick, the bishop of that diocese. There he became rector of the cathedral, president of the seminary, and vicar-general. It was during this time that he also published *The New Month of Mary* (1840), *The Validity of Anglican Ordinations* (1841), and *The Holy House of Loretto* (1842). On Nov. 30, 1841, he was named coadjutor bishop of St. Louis and was consecrated in Philadelphia by Bishop Joseph ROSATI of St. Louis. Rosati then left for Haiti, under the commission of Gregory XVI, sending Kenrick to administer the St. Louis diocese in his absence. When Rosati died on Sept. 25, 1843, Kenrick became bishop of St. Louis. On Jan. 30, 1847, Pius IX raised St. Louis to an archdiocese, appointing Kenrick as its first archbishop. It was almost two years, however, before Kenrick received the pallium, and another year before he had suffragan sees assigned to him.

Kenrick's lengthly tenure in St. Louis was characterized by an impressive growth of the area and of the Church. During his time, the population of the city rose from 20,000 to 500,000; the Catholic population of the see, from 100,000 to 200,000, although the size of the archdiocese was substantially reduced. The number of priests increased from 75 in the early 1840s to 350 near the end of the nineteenth century; parishes increased from 39 to 165. Part of this growth in parishes was made possible by the bank that Kenrick established to help finance diocesan programs; he managed and supervised the bank until the late 1860s. After the Civil War, Missouri adopted the so-called Drake constitution, which forbade any clergyman from preaching or solemnizing marriages without first taking an oath of loyalty to the State. When one of his priests was imprisoned for failing to take the oath, Kenrick appealed the case to the U.S. Supreme Court, which overruled two previous decisions of Missouri courts that the oath was constitutional.

Kenrick played an active role in VATICAN COUNCIL I as one of the leaders of the minority party that opposed the definition of papal infallibility. He not only held that definition was inopportune because it would keep interested non-Catholics from the Church and possibly cause a schism within it, but, theoretically, he believed that papal pronouncements were infallible only if the bishops of the world concurred in them. For these reasons, he vigorously opposed the definition of papal infallibility as understood by the majority in the council and published in Naples his *Concio,* a pamphlet that represented the general views of the minority. Following the definition, the pamphlet was condemned by the Congregation of the Index, but it did not appear on the list of prohibited works.

While in Rome, Kenrick asked the cardinal prefect of the Congregation of Propaganda Fide for a coadjutor. Approximately one year after his return from the council, he consecrated Patrick J. Ryan, who had been serving as administrator of the archdiocese. For reasons not altogether clear from extant sources, Ryan thereafter performed all episcopal functions in the archdiocese and governed it with the assistance of the vicar-general. Meanwhile Kenrick, though still retaining the powers of governing, went into what was equivalent to retirement. For 12 years Ryan ordained, confirmed, made the parish visitations, and dedicated the churches, until 1884 when he was appointed archbishop of Philadelphia. With Ryan's departure from St. Louis, Kenrick abandoned his retirement and once again took up the customary episcopal duties. He also attended the Third Plenary Council in Baltimore (1884).

In the early 1890s the pastors of St. Louis petitioned Cardinal James Gibbons for a coadjutor; the Holy See named Bishop John J. Kain of Wheeling, who arrived in St. Louis on Aug. 23, 1893, and was made administrator on December 14. On May 21, 1895, the Holy See appointed him archbishop of St. Louis and named Kenrick titular archbishop of Marcianopolis.

It was characteristic of Kenrick to formulate an opinion and then stand by it. Incidents throughout his life indicate that he was independent in his thinking and strong-willed. When he first asked for a coadjutor, for instance, he did so against the advice of his brother, Francis Patrick, then archbishop of Baltimore. When the proposition to publish his brother's revised English version of the Sacred Scriptures was introduced at the Second Plenary Council of Baltimore (1866), Peter Kenrick was its chief opponent. At the time of the Civil War, he refused to allow the U.S. flag to be flown from his cathedral as some other bishops had done. He was so generally suspect for his Southern sympathies that Secretary of State William Seward questioned Archbishop John Hughes of New York about having Kenrick removed from his see by the Vatican.

A judgment concerning such resolute independence is difficult to make and is complicated by the fact that much of Kenrick's correspondence has been lost; at times what is available is not conclusive and may even be contradictory. For 54 years he acted as administrator, as bishop, and then as archbishop of St. Louis; Pius IX called Kenrick ''a great man'' and Leo XIII referred to him as ''a noble man and a true Christian bishop.''

Bibliography: J. E. ROTHENSTEINER, *History of the Archdiocese of St. Louis,* 2 v. (St. Louis 1928). H. J. NOLAN, *The Most Reverend Francis Patrick Kenrick, Third Bishop of Philadelphia, 1830–1851* (Washington 1948).

[J. LEIBRECHT]

KENTIGERN (MUNGO), ST.

Bishop of Glasgow, Scotland, and apostle of the ancient British kingdom of Strathclyde; d. *c.* 612. Very little is known for certain about him. Of the five known sources of his life that describe his mother as the British princess Theneuu and recount his miracles, his friendship with St. Servanus, and his meeting with St. COLUMBA, none is earlier than the 12th century. The two main sources are the *Life* written by an anonymous cleric for Bishop Herbert of Glasgow (1147–64) and that written by Jocelin of Furness for Bishop Jocelin of Glasgow (1175–99). It is suggested, however, that both these authors drew on earlier *Lives,* one of which was composed shortly after the saint's death. That he was bishop of Glasgow and labored in the Clyde Valley can hardly be doubted.

Feast: Jan. 14 (formerly Jan. 13).

Bibliography: *Acta Sanctorum,* Jan. 2:97–103. K. H. JACKSON, ''The Sources for the Life of St. Kentigern,'' in *Studies in the Early British Church,* by N. CHADWICK et al. (Cambridge, Eng. 1958) 273–357. J. MACQUEEN, ''Yvain, Ewen, and Owein ap Urien,'' *Transactions of the Dumfriesshire and Galloway Natural History and Antiquarian Society,* 33 (1954–55) 107–131; 36 (1959) 175–183. R. B. HALE, *The Beloved St. Mungo, Founder of Glasgow* (Ottawa 1989). JOCELINUS OF FURNESS, *Saint Mungo: Also Known as Kentigern,* ed. I. MACDONALD (Edinburgh 1993).

[L. MACFARLANE]

KENTUCKY, CATHOLIC CHURCH IN

By 2000, Catholics constituted about 10 percent of the population in the state of Kentucky. In addition to the

Holy Land area near Bardstown, the greater numbers of these lived in cities along the Ohio River that had received significant inflow of German and Irish immigrants in the 19th century. They are concentrated in Louisville, Owensboro, Covington, Henderson and Paducah. In many areas of Kentucky, especially in the south and east, it is not uncommon to find only one Catholic congregation per county. There are four Catholic jurisdictions in the state: the Archdiocese of Louisville, and the dioceses of Covington (1853), Owensboro (1937), and Lexington (1988).

Early History. The early Catholics in Kentucky were a resourceful group of pioneers. Initially without priests, their earliest parishes were gathered by laity. Their first seminary (St. Thomas) had its beginnings on a flatboat coming down the Ohio River. One of their first colleges (St. Mary's) began life in an old distillery building. One of their pioneer priests was Stephen BADIN, the first priest ordained in the United States.

In 1808 Pope Pius VII established America's first inland diocese at Bardstown in Nelson County, Kentucky. Nelson, Marion and Washington counties came to be known as Kentucky's "Catholic Holy Land." The designation results both from the history of the area as well as from its ongoing institutions—such as St. Joseph's Proto-Cathedral, numerous parishes, three large motherhouses of sisters and the Abbey of Gethsemani. The sizable population of Catholics in the area is something of a rarity in the rural South.

The first Catholics in Kentucky came almost entirely from Maryland, including the William Coomes family and Dr. George Hart, who settled at Harrodsburg in 1775. Dr. Hart was one of the first physicians, and Mrs. Coomes conducted the first elementary school in Kentucky. The first Catholic colony, consisting of 25 families led by Basil Hayden, came in the spring of 1785 to establish the Pottinger Creek settlement, a few miles from Bardstown. Before Kentucky was admitted to the Union in 1792, there were at least six distinct colonies settled on the creeks in an arc around Bardstown. The first priest to be assigned to Kentucky by Bishop John Carroll was an Irish Franciscan, Charles Whelan, who, in the fall of 1787, accompanied a group from Maryland. A controversy over his salary, issuing in a court case, forced Whelan to leave Kentucky after two-and-a-half years of service. In 1791 Rev. William De Rohan arrived with a group from North Carolina. Under his direction, the Pottinger Creek Catholics built a log chapel, named variously Holy Cross and Sacred Heart, which was the first Catholic place of worship in Kentucky. However, his ministry, unauthorized by Carroll, soon met with many difficulties, and De Rohan was deprived of his faculties. Thereafter, he taught

Archdiocese/Diocese	Year Created
Archdiocese of Louisville	1937
Diocese of Covington	1853
Diocese of Lexington	1988
Diocese of Owensboro	1937

in various Catholic settlement schools, and resided at St. Thomas Seminary, where he died in 1832.

In 1793, Rev. Stephen T. Badin, the first priest to be ordained in the United States, with Rev. Michael Barrieres arrived in Kentucky from Baltimore. On the first Sunday in Advent, Badin said Mass in the home of Denis McCarthy at Lexington; he remained in the Scott County settlement for more than a year before moving to Pottinger's Creek. Three miles from the chapel at Holy Cross, he purchased a farm, which he named St. Stephen's. From this place (later the site of the motherhouse of the Sisters of Loretto), Badin directed Catholic life for the next 15 years. Among the 70,000 Kentuckians in 1793 Badin estimated there were about 300 Catholic families, to whom he alone ministered until February 1797, when Carroll sent Rev. Michael Fournier to his aid. Two years later, Rev. Anthony Salmon joined them, and shortly after, Rev. John Thayer of Boston was added to the group. However, Salmon was killed by a fall from his horse in 1799, and in 1803 Fournier died and Thayer departed, leaving Badin alone once again.

In 1805 help arrived in the person of the Belgian priest, Charles NERINCKX, who soon began the erection of Holy Mary, the first of ten churches he was to build in less than ten years. The Dominican, Edward D. FENWICK, also arrived that spring to look for land; a year later he returned with three English confreres, Samuel T. Wilson, William R. Tuite, and Robert A. Angier, to establish the first foundation of the Dominican Order in the United States at Springfield. By 1807 they had enrolled 12 boys in their seminary, and two years later they dedicated St. Rose Church, a brick structure. In 1809 the Dominicans opened St. Thomas College, the first Catholic college in the West, which for 20 years provided a classical education for many prominent Southerners, including Jefferson Davis. With Nerinckx, there had also come into Kentucky in 1805 a group of Trappist monks, led by Dom Urbain Guillet. After a short stay with Badin, the monks moved to a farm on Pottinger's Creek and finally bought land on the Green River in Casey County, where they began a free school for boys, the first Catholic school in Kentucky. In 1809 Dom Urbain transferred the group to the Illinois country after seven priests and eight brothers had died in the attempt to found the community in Kentucky.

Diocese. As early as October 1804, Carroll asked Badin for a report on the possibility of establishing a diocese in Kentucky; every year thereafter Badin discussed the idea with the bishop. In 1807 the missionary recommended that the see be located at Bardstown and the first incumbent be Benedict FLAGET. Among the names submitted to Rome by Carroll were Flaget, Badin (whom some, including the Dominicans, feared might be selected), Wilson, and Nerinckx. In 1808 Rome finally acted, creating Baltimore an archdiocese with suffragan sees at Boston, New York, Philadelphia, and Bardstown.

Flaget. Flaget, shocked by his nomination to Bardstown, tried to refuse the office, going to France to plead with his Sulpician superiors for support in his stand. However, when the Pope ordered him to accept, he gave up his resistance and spent his time in France gathering recruits for his new diocese. Upon their return, Archbishop Carroll consecrated Flaget on November 4, 1810, in Fells Point, Maryland, and the following May the new bishop set out for Kentucky.

Immediately after his installation in Bardstown on June 9, 1811, he began a visitation of the Kentucky congregations organized by Badin and Nerinckx. On December 21, 1811, Flaget ordained Chabrat at St. Rose, the first ordination in Kentucky and in the West. Three miles from Bardstown, on the Thomas Howard plantation, he established St. Thomas Seminary, and by 1816 a brick church was erected there. In 1812 two distinctly American sisterhoods were founded: the Sisters of LORETTO and the Sisters of Charity of Nazareth, both of which flourished, staffing schools, orphanages, and hospitals throughout the diocese and the country. In 1822 another native Kentuckian sisterhood, the Dominican Sisters of St. Catharine, was formed by Wilson at St. Rose, Springfield. The order later spread to conduct hospitals, a college, and grade and high schools.

The first diocesan synod was called by Flaget on February 20, 1812; five seculars and three Dominican priests attended. This period also marked the beginning of the dispute between Badin and Flaget over Church lands. Title to practically all land was held by Badin, who had purchased many acres with his own money or funds he had personally borrowed. The bishop thought that Badin should turn over to him all titles, with no conditions; Badin argued that Flaget should at least assume the outstanding debts. Since Canon Law was not clear on the subject and Carroll would make no decision, the matter went unsettled and was partly the cause of Badin's departure for Europe in 1819. On his return nine years later, Badin performed missionary work in various states, returning frequently to Kentucky, where in later years he was again invested with the title of vicar-general. The

land question was evidently settled when Badin made the transfer in his last will.

During his long episcopate, Flaget's visitations took him to Catholic settlements throughout a vast territory that ultimately embraced not only Kentucky, but also Tennessee, Indiana, Missouri, Ohio, Illinois, Wisconsin, and Michigan. He administered Confirmation, settled disputes over TRUSTEEISM, negotiated with Indian commissioners, and directed the progress of the Church. In 1816 Flaget blessed the cornerstone of St. Joseph's Cathedral in Bardstown, which was dedicated on August 8, 1819. The first cathedral west of the Alleghenies, it has been named a national monument by the Federal government. A seminary was opened next to the cathedral and the seminarians moved from St. Thomas to Bardstown. In the fall of 1819 Rev. George Elder founded St. Joseph's College in the basement of the seminary, and within a year another building was necessary to accommodate the students. In 1821 Rev. William Byrne founded St. Mary's College near Lebanon on property acquired by Nerinckx, who had intended it for the establishment of a brotherhood. As there were only two members for the proposed community, the college remained there and in 1833 was entrusted to Jesuits Peter Chazelle and Nicholas Petit. Four years later, it was granted a charter by the state, and the next year a novitiate was opened there. The Jesuits kept this college until 1846 when they left to accept St. John's College, Fordham, New York City, on the invitation of John Hughes, later archbishop of New York. Two years later a group of Jesuits from Missouri entered the diocese, serving in Bardstown and establishing a free school and St. Aloysius College in Louisville. In 1868 the Jesuits again left the diocese.

In 1832 when Flaget decided to resign his see, Rome designated his coadjutor, John David, whom he had consecrated in 1819, as his successor. However, the uproar that ensued in Catholic Kentucky led the Holy See to reverse the action, and the see was returned to Flaget. On July 20, 1834, when Chabrat was consecrated as the second coadjutor of Bardstown, many of the priests, especially the faculty of St. Joseph College, were opposed to this promotion. Although there remained a great deal of unrest and dissatisfaction, Chabrat made no major blunders and satisfactorily directed the diocese during the several years Flaget was in Europe. Failing eyesight caused Chabrat to retire to France in 1846; he died at Mauriac, November 21, 1868.

When Flaget made his first *ad limina* visit to Rome in 1836, he petitioned for the removal of the see from Bardstown to Louisville. This was done in 1841, four years after the boundaries of the diocese had been reduced to the single state of Kentucky. Bishop David died

July 12, 1841, in Nazareth, Kentucky, and was buried there.

Soon after Martin J. SPALDING's return from Rome in 1834 he joined the faculty of the seminary and the college in Bardstown and initiated the publication of the first Catholic periodical of Kentucky, a monthly literary magazine, the *St. Joseph College Minerva*. After a year it was succeeded by a weekly newspaper, the *Catholic Advocate* under Benjamin J. Webb, which was to last 15 years before merging with the Cincinnati paper.

Flaget's invitation to the French sisters of the Institute of the Good Shepherd was accepted in 1843 when they established a house in Louisville. In December 1848, a colony of 40 Trappists purchased 1,600 acres in Nelson County from the Sisters of Loretto. This foundation of Gethsemani, which was raised to the rank of abbey in July 1850, gave the diocese seven religious communities. Flaget consecrated Martin J. Spalding coadjutor bishop of Louisville on Sept. 10, 1848. The following year the cornerstone of the new Cathedral of the Assumption in Louisville was blessed. When Flaget died on Feb. 11, 1850, he was 87 and had been a priest for 62 years and a bishop for almost 40. Buried first in the garden of the Good Shepherd convent, his remains were later transferred to the crypt of the cathedral in Louisville.

Flaget was succeeded by his coadjutor, Bishop Martin John Spalding who served until 1864 when he was transferred to Baltimore. In 1853 the diocese of Covington was erected by separating the eastern part of Kentucky from Louisville.

The Civil War took its toll on Catholic institutions in the state. The colleges and academies of the Holy Land were especially hard hit in their enrollments. St. Joseph's College in Bardstown had to close and was commandeered for a military hospital. Train accommodations were in such short supply that Bishop Martin John Spalding was once required to ride back to Louisville in a baggage car with soldiers' corpses.

In the years after the war, the turbulent administration of Bishop William George McCloskey began (1868–1909). At Rome during the Vatican Council, he long opposed the declaration of papal infallibility as inopportune, eventually joining the large number who accepted it. At home he managed to quarrel frequently and publicly with his priests as well as with many of the religious communities in the diocese. He once placed the motherhouse of the Sisters of Loretto under interdict over an insurance issue. During these disputes a number of priests left the diocese, perhaps the best known was the intellectual John Lancaster Spalding (1840–1916), nephew of bishop Martin John Spalding and later first bishop of Peoria.

In the late 19th and early 20th centuries, the state was home to a group of lively and talented Catholic laity: Colonel Patrick Henry Callahan (1866–1941), an early national figure in furthering social justice issues as elucidated by papal social encyclicals; poet Elvira Sydnor Miller (1860–1937); writer Charles T. O'Malley (1851–1910); John Whallen (1850–1913) and James Whallen (1851–1930), brothers, who ran the Democratic political machine in Louisville; and Colonel Matt Winn (1861–1941) who turned the Kentucky Derby into an international event. Additionally, in this era there was Daniel Rudd (1854–1933), a national black lay leader who helped to bring together congresses of African American Catholics in the 1890s. He grew up in the area, moved away, but was buried at Bardstown.

The Catholic Church in Kentucky has had a long, venerable tradition with academic institutions. Five Catholic higher education centers stand proudly in the commonwealth today: Spalding University opened in 1920 in Louisville as Nazareth College, continuing an educational tradition of the Sisters of Charity of Nazareth dating back to 1814. St. Catharine Junior College at Springfield was founded by the Dominican Sisters in 1931. Bellarmine College in Louisville, established in 1950, merged with the city's Ursuline College in 1968. Bellarmine, a university since 2000, hosts the international Thomas Merton Studies Center. Covington is home to Thomas More College, originally founded as Villa Madonna in 1921. Brescia University in Owensboro began in 1925 as a junior college for women on the grounds of the motherhouse of the Ursuline Sisters of Mount St. Joseph.

Bibliography: J. A. BOONE, ed., *The Roman Catholic Diocese of Owensboro, Kentucky* (Owensboro 1995). T. D. CLARK, *A History of Kentucky* (Lexington 1977). C. F. CREWS, *An American Holy Land* (Wilmington 1987). J. HAYDEN, ed., *This Far by Faith: The Story of Catholicity in Western Kentucky* (Owensboro 1987). L. HARRISON and J. KLOTTER, *A New History of Kentucky* (Lexington 1997). J. H. SCHAUINGER, *Cathedrals in the Wilderness* (Milwaukee 1952). M. R. MATTINGLY, *The Catholic Church on the Kentucky Frontier, 1785–1812* (Washington, D.C. 1936). P. E. RYAN, *History of the Diocese of Covington, Kentucky* (Covington 1954). M. J. SPALDING, *Sketches of the Early Catholic Missions of Kentucky* (Louisville 1844). B. WEBB, *The Centenary of Catholicity in Kentucky* (Louisville 1884).

[V. P. MCMURRY/C. F. CREWS]

KENYA, THE CATHOLIC CHURCH IN

A temperate, humid, agricultural country located in equatorial East Africa, the Republic of Kenya is bordered on the southeast by the Indian Ocean, on the south by Tanzania, on the west by UGANDA, on the north by ETHIO-

Capital: Nairobi.
Size: 224,960 sq. miles.
Population: 30,339,770 in 2000.
Languages: English, Kiswahili; indigenous languages are spoken in various regions.
Religions: 8,495,135 Catholics (28%), 2,901,780 Muslims (10%), 11,529,112 Protestants (38%), 70,980,073 indigenous beliefs (23%), 315,670 other (1%).

Archdioceses	Suffragans
Kisumu	Bungoma, Eldoret, Homa Bay, Kakamenga, Kisii, Kitale, Lodwar
Mombasa	Garissa, Malindi
Nairobi	Kericho, Kitui, Machakos, Nakuru, Ngong
Nyeri	Embu, Meru, Marsabit, Muranga

The is an apostolic vicariate at Isiolo. The region also has a military ordinariate.

PIA, on the northeast by SUDAN and on the east by SOMALIA. A former British crown colony, Kenya was granted extensive internal autonomy in 1960, following years of ethnic unrest and bloodshed. It achieved independence as a Commonwealth nation on Dec. 12, 1963. With a landscape that ranges from mountain peaks to arid plains to coastal lowlands, Kenya is noted for its wildlife and its rivers. Coffee and tea are among the country's main exports. While natural resources in the region include veins of gold, rubies and garnets, Kenya's economic growth is founded primarily on agriculture, as well as the manufacture of small consumer goods, agricultural processing, cement and tourism. Kenyans are primarily a tribal people representing Kikuyu, Luhya, Luo, Kamba, Kisii, Kalenjin, Meru and other African peoples. The life expectancy for an adult Kenyan male was under 47 years in 2000.

Church History. In Kenya's Great Rift Valley some of the earliest hominid fossil remains have been discovered by paleontologists. Arabs settled the region in the 7th century, remaining near the Kenyan coast to allow for trade. Portuguese traders appeared along that same coastal region from 1498 onward, but systematic Christian evangelization of Kenya's native peoples— predominately the Masaii and Kikuyu, who entered the region in the mid-18th century— was begun by Protestant missionaries in 1844. This Protestant influence increased after 1887 when Kenya fell under the control of the British East Africa Company. The HOLY GHOST FATHERS entered the region from Tanganyika in 1892, and Kenya became subject to the Prefecture Apostolic of Zanzibar (vicariate in 1906). The CONSOLATA MISSIONARY Fathers came in 1902, the MILL HILL MISSIONARIES in 1904 and ST. PATRICK'S MISSIONARY SOCIETY in 1953. Native apathy, language difficulties and Muslim influences in the country's coastal areas presented formidable obstacles to evangelization efforts, but Catholicism grew, especially through its promotion of education.

In 1920 Kenya became a British crown colony. Improved by railways to enhance trade, portions of the country were set apart for the exclusive habitation of the many British who immigrated to Africa. Ultimately native Kenyans, let by nationalist leader Jomo Kenyatta, de-

manded equal representation in government, as well as a dismantling of the social constructs separating the races. This rising nationalism led to the Mau Mau movement of the 1950s, during which time many African Christians were killed. Even during World War II and the Mau Mau terrorism, Church efforts among Kenyan natives continued, and conversions, particularly among the Kikuyu, increased. Providing the continued opportunity for Kenyans to receive a basic education certainly ranked among the most praiseworthy charitable efforts of the Kenyan Catholic Church during the 20th century.

In 1953 the Church hierarchy was established, and Nairobi, the capital, became the seat of an archdiocese and metropolitan see for the country. At the time of Kenya's independence in 1963 about 10 percent of the inhabitants were Muslims, 20 percent were Christians (including 820,000 Protestants) and the rest practiced indigenous beliefs that sometimes incorporated Christian elements.

Kenyatta, who served as the first president of the new republic, died in 1978, and Daniel arap Moi succeeded to power. Unpopular, inefficient and corrupt, Moi's government sparked further unrest and a failed coup attempt before he agreed to elections in 1991. His continued victory in multiparty elections held during the 1990s did nothing to stabilize Kenyan politics, and ethnic violence continued. In 1998 the U.S. Embassy in Nairobi was bombed, leaving numerous victims; the Church played an active role in alleviating the suffering that followed this tragedy. Despite the government corruption throughout the country, Kenya's Catholic Church leaders continued to speak out against poverty, ethnic prejudice and other social issues that threatened the quality of life in Kenya into the 21st century. Among the most vocal of these leaders were Archbishop of Nairobi Raphael Ndingi Mwana a' Nzeki and Father John Kaiser, a Mill Hill Missionary. Father Kaiser was murdered in August of 2000, his death believed to be a consequence of his outspoken

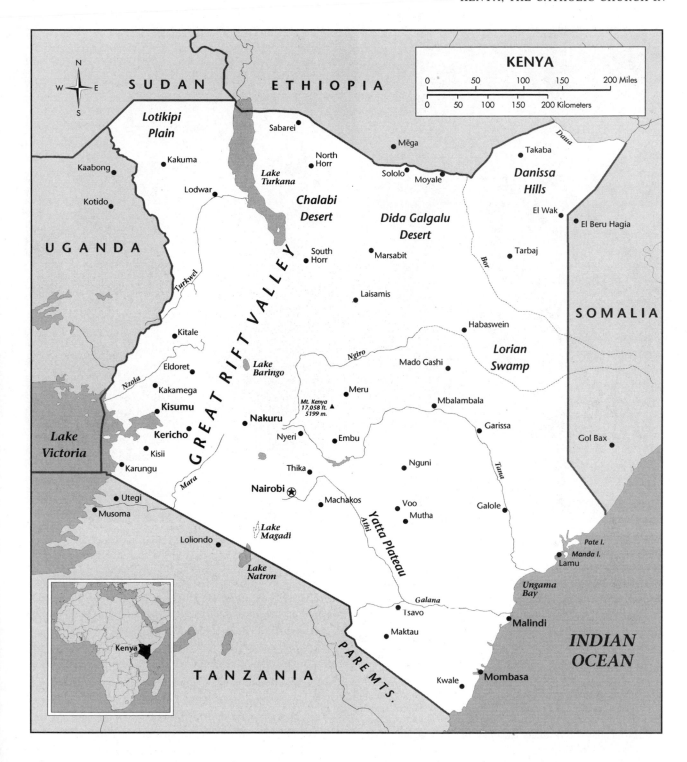

KENYA

attacks against the government; investigations into his death were continually stalled by the police.

Despite the controversy surrounding his administration, Moi advocated many social policies in line with Catholic doctrine. For example, in 1996 he prohibited the teaching of sex education in Kenyan schools. While the government continued to respect religious freedom, it ac-

tively restricted some non-worship activities of the Church. In April of 2000 police broke up a gathering of Catholics in a Laikipia Church on the grounds that the participants were suspected freedom fighters. Ecumenical efforts by the Church in Kenya included the creation of the Inter-Faith Peace Movement, bringing together Muslims, Catholics, Hindus and Protestants; despite such efforts, clashes between Muslims and Christian sects were

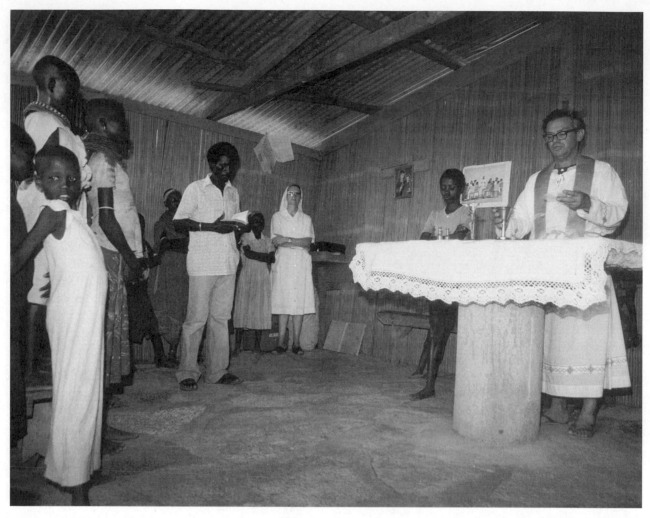

Members of the el-Molo tribe attend Mass at the Catholic Mission in Loiyangallani, Kenya. (©Jeffrey L. Rotman/CORBIS)

reported throughout the 1990s, and in 1996 a basilica in Nairobi was desecrated by fundamentalist Christians.

By 2000 Kenya had 607 parishes tended by 860 secular and 877 religious priests, 609 brothers and 3,773 sisters. Over 220,000 baptisms were performed in the country during 1999.

Bibliography: K. INGHAM, *A History of East Africa* (London 1962). R. OLIVER, *The Missionary Factor in East Africa* (London 1952). *Bilan du Monde* 2:545–551. *Annuario Pontificio* has annual data on all dioceses, vicariates and prefectures. For additional bibliography, *see* AFRICA.

[J. J. O'MEARA/EDS.]

KEOGH, JAMES

Editor, theologian; b. Enniscorthy, Ireland, Feb. 4, 1834; d. Pittsburgh, Pa., July 10, 1870. He immigrated to the U.S. with his parents in 1841 and settled at Pitts-

burgh. Keogh received his doctorate in philosophy (1851) and theology (1855) from the College of the Propaganda, Rome, and was ordained on Aug. 5, 1856. He returned to Pittsburgh, where he served as convent chaplain and pastor of a mission church at Latrobe, Pa. In 1857 Bp. Michael O'Connor appointed him professor of dogmatic theology at St. Michael's Seminary, Glenwood, Pa. He became president of the seminary in 1863 and acted also as secretary to Bp. Michael Domenec, CM, and as editor of the diocesan newspaper, the *Pittsburgh Catholic*. Disagreement over the management of the seminary and the editorial policy of the newspaper caused him to resign his offices in 1865. He then lectured in theology at St. Charles Seminary, Philadelphia, Pa., and became the first editor of the *Philadelphia Catholic Standard*, founded in 1866. He was one of the secretaries of the Second Plenary Council of Baltimore (1866), and was considered for the post of American representative in the preparatory work for Vatican Council I. He was acquiring some reputation as a lecturer and contributor to the *Catholic World* when ill-health forced his retirement to Pittsburgh in 1868.

Bibliography: A. A. LAMBING, *A History of the Catholic Church in the Dioceses of Pittsburgh and Allegheny* (New York 1880).

[J. J. HENNESEY]

KEOGH, JOHN

Often called the father of the Newman apostolate in the U.S.; b. Philadelphia, Nov. 29, 1877; d. there, Oct.14, 1960. He was ordained in 1909 for the Archdiocese of Philadelphia, and in 1913 was appointed first full-time chaplain to Catholic students at the University of Pennsylvania, where the first Newman club had been formed 20 years earlier. In 1917 Keogh became first national chaplain of the Federation of College Catholic Clubs, later known as the National Newman Club Federation. Keogh remained national chaplain until 1935. During these years, at his own expense he crossed the U.S. many times, urging bishops to provide Newman programs for Catholic students at secular colleges and universities. He often met with opposition. He was abused, criticized, ridiculed, and scolded for being "opposed to Catholic education"; yet eventually he won his point by the logic of his position and the persistence of his zeal. Although named pastor of a large Philadelphia parish, St. Gabriel's, in 1938, he maintained an active interest in the national Newman movement. He was one of the founders of the John Henry Cardinal Newman Honorary Society and in 1945 became its chaplain, a post he held until his death. He rarely missed a national Newman convention, and was an active member of the Newman Chaplains' Association from the time it was established in 1950. In the 50th year of his priesthood, Keogh was made a domestic prelate by Pope Pius XII. That same year he became the first priest to receive the Cardinal Newman Award, a citation normally given to a Catholic layman. Though remembered best for his pioneer work in the Newman apostolate, Keogh for many years was also president of the Catholic Total Abstinence Union.

[C. W. ALBRIGHT]

KEOUGH, FRANCIS PATRICK

Bishop of Providence, RI, archbishop of Baltimore, MD; b. New Britain, CT, Dec. 30, 1889; d. Washington, D.C., Dec. 8, 1961. The second son of Irish immigrants, Patrick and Margaret (Ryan) Keough, he attended parochial school in his native city and began his studies for

James Keogh.

the priesthood at St. Thomas Seminary, Hartford, Connecticut. In 1911 he was sent to the Sulpician Seminary at Issy, France, but he returned after the outbreak of World War I and continued his theological studies at St. Bernard's in Rochester, New York. He was ordained for the Hartford diocese on June 10, 1916. For three years he did parochial work; thereafter, until his appointment to Providence (Feb. 10, 1934), he was engaged in special diocesan assignments as institutional chaplain, director of the Society for the Propagation of the Faith, assistant chancellor, and secretary to the bishop. Keough was consecrated in his see city on May 22, 1934, by the newly appointed Apostolic Delegate, Abp. Amleto Cicognani, later cardinal and Vatican secretary of state. During his 13 years as ordinary of a heavily Catholic state, Keough founded a minor seminary, used his knowledge of French to soften differences that had risen between the French-speaking and English-speaking members of his flock, and employed his financial talents to overcome entirely the heavy debts burdening the diocese at his arrival. Despite his reluctance to leave his native New England, he was appointed to the nation's premier see Nov. 29, 1947, and was installed in Baltimore's basilica-cathedral by Archbishop Cicognani on Feb. 24, 1948.

Keough's new position of prestige led to numerous major appointments to the National Catholic Welfare

Conference, where he had already served in many secondary posts. He played a decisive role in the issuance of the historic 1958 statement of the American Catholic hierarchy against racial discrimination. Always concerned about the needy, he built a residence for the elderly (Stella Maris) and a consolidated home for deprived school-age children (Villa Maria); he also took the initial steps for constructing a new St. Vincent's Infant Home and an adjacent maternity care residence (Villa St. Louise). His major building project was the construction (1954–59) of an $8 million cathedral from funds bequeathed by a Baltimore merchant, Thomas O'Neill. This Cathedral of Mary Our Queen became the metropolitan center on Sept. 21, 1959. Two years later the archbishop was buried beneath its main altar.

As a retiring man of childlike piety and conservative temperament, Keough preferred a gradual and quiet approach in solving the practical problems that completely absorbed his energies. Declining health, which began with a major illness in 1954, and the preoccupations of overseeing the construction of the new cathedral considerably restricted the general productivity of his later years.

[J. J. GALLAGHER]

KEPLER, JOHANN

Astronomer, mathematician, discoverer of the three laws of planetary motion; b. Weil der Stadt, Germany, Dec. 27, 1571; d. Regensburg, Germany, Nov. 15, 1630.

He was the son of Heinrich and Katharina (Guldenmann) Kepler. The Keplers, Lutherans in a predominantly Catholic city, were craftsmen, although their ancestors belonged to the minor nobility. Kepler attended German and Latin elementary schools, the Maulbronn seminary, and the Tübingen seminary, passing the master's examination in theology in 1591 but continuing at the university. There, Michael Maestlin, although following Ptolemaic astronomy in his writings, taught Kepler the essence of the Copernican theory.

Not his support of that doctrine, but his doubts about the interpretation of the Sacraments and his unwillingness to condemn the Calvinists completely, caused Kepler to incur his teachers' disfavor. In 1594, having been recommended by them as the best available candidate because of his mathematical and astronomical knowledge, Kepler became a mathematics teacher at the Protestant seminary in Graz, Austria.

In 1595 Kepler, believing that nothing in nature was created by God without a plan and influenced by Pythag-

oras, Plato, and others, suddenly thought of a geometrical structure of the universe that accounted for the number of planets and their relative distances from the sun by circumscribing the five regular solids about the planet spheres. The *Mysterium Cosmographicum* (1596), describing this, attracted the favorable attention of Tycho Brahe.

Kepler sought a parallax of the fixed stars. He could accept neither Tycho's geo-heliocentric system, which he considered a compromise, nor the enormous diameter of the sphere of fixed stars necessitated by a moving earth. He studied chronological problems, magnetism, the inclination of the ecliptic, and the weather, seeking the stars' influence on it. He planned his later work on the world harmony, noting Copernicus's allusion to the symmetry in the visible universe, and finding the regular solids as the basis of musical harmony. To test his theories, Kepler needed Tycho Brahe's accurate observations.

When the Counter Reformation triumphed in Graz, Kepler, although among those ordered to leave, received permission to return, possibly because of his friendship with the Catholic Bavarian chancellor. He never became Catholic and upheld the Augsburg Confession (*see* AUGSBURG, CONFESSION OF).

Work with Tycho Brahe. When Graz became unbearable, Kepler accepted Tycho's invitation to visit him near Prague, and he finally moved there with his wife and stepdaughter. The two astronomers first met on Feb. 4, 1600. Kepler was assigned work on the Mars observations but did not obtain precise values for the eccentricities of the planet orbits and their distances from the sun that he needed to test his theories, nor was he granted access to the bulk of Tycho's observations.

When Tycho died on Oct. 24, 1601, Kepler succeeded him as imperial mathematician but at a lower and infrequently paid salary. Now all of Tycho's observations were at his disposal. Without acceding to Tycho's dying request to present the planetary motions in accordance with the Tychonic system, Kepler, whenever possible, showed where this system agreed with the observations.

Laws of Planetary Motion. Kepler believed that within the sun there was a force that moves the planets, their motion being so much the quicker the nearer they are to the sun. Using Tycho's observations of Mars, as though observing the earth from there, Kepler calculated the eccentricity of the earth's orbit, discovering that at the aphelion and the perihelion, and presumably everywhere, the speed of the earth is inversely proportional to its distance from the sun. Dividing half the earth's circular orbit into 180°, he calculated and added together the distances to the sun of each of these little arcs. Correct distances of the earth from the sun provided correct distances from Mars. His use of Mars was fortunate because of its large eccentricity.

His calculations resulted in the discovery (1602) of the second law of planet motion (the radius vector describes equal areas in equal times) and (1605) of the first law (planets move in ellipses with the sun at one focus), both announced in 1609 in the *Astronomia Nova*. Kepler replaced the geometrical systems with a dynamic one and abandoned the 2,000-year old principle of uniform circular motion. Under William GILBERT's influence Kepler explained the deviation in radius vector by considering the planets as composed of magnetic filaments; one end of each filament was attracted by the sun, the other repelled.

In the *Ad Vitellionem* (1604) Kepler explained the inverted image on the retina, improved the formula for refraction, and discussed the apparent diameters of the celestial bodies and of eclipses. This book is important in the history of infinitesimal calculus, as are his *Astronomia Nova* and his work on the shapes of wine casks (Latin, 1615; German, 1616) in which he replaced Archimedes' "exhaustion method" by a direct method and contributed to the theory of regular solids.

Kepler described the 1604 nova in German and Latin tracts. He placed it among the fixed stars, thought it an agglomeration of heavenly material, and considered its appearance to be God's manner of exhorting men. The comet of 1607 received similar treatment.

Galileo's *Sidereus Nuncius* (1610) drew a favorable reply from Kepler, whose *Dioptrice* (1611) gave an exhaustive treatment of the passage of light through lenses.

In 1611 Kepler's wife and one of his three children died. The emperor, deposed in 1611, died early in 1612. Thereupon, Kepler moved to Linz, remaining as district mathematician until 1626. During that time he remarried; fathered six children; witnessed his mother's witch trial; and published the *Epitome of Copernican Astronomy* (1618, 1620, 1621), the *World Harmony* (1619), which announced the third planet law (the squares of the times of the revolution of two planets are to each other as the cubes of their mean distances from the sun), a work on logarithms, and other tracts. He worked on the *Somnium* (1634), begun in Tübingen, describing a journey to the moon and the earth viewed from there, and completed the *Rudolphine Tables* (1627), based on Tycho's observations but on the Copernican-Keplerian system of the universe.

His last years were spent in Ulm and in Sagan, in Wallenstein's employ. He died while seeking funds owed him by the Imperial Treasury.

Johann Kepler.

Bibliography: M. CASPAR, *Kepler,* tr. and ed. C. D. HELLMAN (New York 1959); ed., *Bibliographia Kepleriana* (Munich 1936).

[C. D. HELLMAN]

KERBY, WILLIAM JOSEPH

Sociologist, writer, editor, and organizer of Catholic social work; b. Lawler, Iowa, Feb. 20, 1870; d. Washington, D.C., July 27, 1936. Kerby had the advantage of unusually devoted Catholic parents, Daniel and Ellen (Rochford). His father was able to personally teach him the rudiments of Latin and Greek, and his mother schooled him in personal service to the needy. For his secondary and college training, he was sent to St. Joseph's College, now Loras College, Dubuque, Iowa. Afterward he studied for the priesthood at St. Francis Seminary, Milwaukee, Wis., and was ordained in Dubuque on Dec. 21, 1892. He was then sent to the Catholic University of America, where he obtained the licentiate in theology in 1894, returning to teach at the college in Dubuque in that year.

When Catholic University decided to introduce sociology into its curriculum, it invited him to take charge of the subject. He was sent to Europe in 1895, attended Bonn and Berlin universities, and received his doctorate in social and political science from Louvain in 1897. That fall he began his long career with the department of sociology at the Catholic University.

Kerby's interpretation of sociology was strongly influenced by his great concern for the welfare of the needy and the underprivileged. His major impact was therefore in social service, an area that in those days was not sharply distinguished from sociology. It has been truly said that he deserves the title of founder of scientific social work among the Catholics in the United States. He was a moving spirit in the organization of the National Conference of Catholic Charities in 1910. From 1911 to 1917 he edited the *Saint Vincent de Paul Quarterly.* He was also a prime mover in organizing the first Catholic school for social workers. Moreover in books, such as *The Social Mission of Charity,* in numerous periodical articles, in his work as editor of the *American Ecclesiastical Review,* and especially in his personal contacts he deeply impressed his generation.

On April 19, 1934 Kerby was made a domestic prelate. By this time his health had begun to fail and he had resigned as head of the department of sociology at the Catholic University. He was able to continue many of his activities up to the last.

Bibliography: J. J. BURKE, ''The Rt. Rev. William J. Kerby: An Appreciation,'' *Ecclesiastical Review* 95 (1936) 225–233.

[P. H. FURFEY]

KERGUIN, JEANNE MARIE, ST.

In religion Marie de Ste. Nathalie (or Mary of the Nativity), martyr, religious of the Franciscan Missionaries of Mary; b. May 5, 1864, Belle-Isle en Terre, Brittany, France; d. July 9, 1900, Taiyüan, China. Born into a peasant family, Jeanne Marie assumed responsibility for household duties following her mother's death. In 1887, she was received into the novitiate of the Missionaries of Mary, where she worked on the farm and joyfully attended to menial chores. Following her novitiate she was assigned to Paris, then Carthage—where she fell ill—then Rome. Although her health was still a concern, she was sent to China in March 1899, where she was beheaded a little more than a year later during the Boxer Rebellion. She was beatified by Pius XII with her religious sisters by Pope Pius XII, Nov. 24, 1946, and canonized, Oct. 1, 2000, by Pope John Paul II with Augustine Zhao Rong and companions.

Feast: July 4.

Bibliography: G. GOYAU, *Valiant Women: Mother Mary of the Passion and the Franciscan Missionaries of Mary,* tr. G. TEL-

FORD (London 1936). M. T. DE BLARER, *Les Bse Marie Hermine de Jésus et ses compagnes, franciscaines missionnaires de Marie, massacrées le 9 juillet 1900 à Tai–Yuan–Fou, Chine* (Paris 1947). L. M. BALCONI, *Le Martiri di Taiyuen* (Milan 1945). *Acta Apostolicae Sedis* 47 (1955) 381–388. *L'Osservatore Romano,* Eng. Ed. 40 (2000): 1–2, 10.

[K. I. RABENSTEIN]

KERN, JAKOB FRANZ, BL.

Baptized Franz (Francis) Alexander Kern, Norbertine priest; b. April 11, 1897, Vienna; d. there, Oct. 20, 1924. One of three children of a working-class family, Kern discerned a call to the priesthood at an early age. He was in the minor seminary at Hollabrunn hoping to become a diocesan priest, when his studies were interrupted by the outset of World War I. He was drafted (1915) and sent to Vöklabruck for officer training. As an officer in the Austrian Army with the Fourth Tyrolean Imperial Fusiliers, he was severely wounded on the Italian Front (Sept. 11, 1916). After recuperating in Salzburg for nearly a year, he resumed his seminary studies, but was recalled to military duty until the end of the war. Thereafter, he recommenced with his training for the archdiocesan priesthood. Upon hearing that Father Isidor Bogdan Zahrodnik, a Norbertine, had left his monastery for the schismatic Czech National Church, Jakob felt an inward compulsion to complete his training as a priest. He entered the Premonstratensian Abbey of Geras, northwest of Vienna near the Czech border, to begin his novitiate (1920). On July 23, 1922, with a dispensation because he had not taken his final vows, Brother Jakob was ordained in Saint Stephen's Cathedral, Vienna. He developed complications from his war injuries that debilitated him. On the day he was to make his solemn profession, he died during a second surgery. Kern's mortal remains are preserved in a small silver casket in a chapel adjacent to the Norbertine abbey church at Geras. He was beatified by Pope John Paul II in the *Heldenplatz* at Vienna, June 21, 1998.

Feast: Oct. 20.

Bibliography: P. VOGEL, *Drei Aarauer Pioniere* (Zurich 1980). H. J. WELDINGER, *Jakob Kern,* tr. H. S. SZANTO (Silverado, Calif. 1998). *Sühnepriester Jakob Kern* (Graz 1960). *L'Osservatore Romano,* Eng. ed. 29 (1995) 5; 25 (1998) 2.

[K. I. RABENSTEIN]

KERSUZAN, FRANCOIS MARIE

Bishop, Haitian patriot; b. Grandchamp, Brittany, March 25, 1848; d. Morne Lory, Haiti, July 1935. He was ordained in 1871 and served in the cathedral of Port-au-Prince until 1884. He was auxiliary bishop of Port-au-Prince and titular bishop of Hippa from 1884 to 1886. In 1886 he became bishop of Cap-Haitien. After 1925, illness made it impossible for Kersuzan to administer his diocese. In 1929 he retired, and as titular archbishop of Sergiopolis he spent the rest of his life in prayer, especially devoted to Our Lady of Perpetual Help.

After the death in 1890 of Archbishop Hillion of Port-au-Prince, Kersuzan was the only bishop in Haiti. He undertook a strong campaign against superstition and voodoo. He organized a Catholic league against it and founded an official journal of the league, *La Croix*. He was a firm believer in education as essential to true Christian life. In 1904 he founded the secondary school, or the Collège Notre Dame du Perpétuel Secours, where he spent his last years.

In 1903 Bishop Kersuzan's name was proposed to Rome by the provisional government for the archbishopric of Port-au-Prince when Archbishop Tonti was sent as apostolic nuncio to Brazil. However, he was not acceptable to General—and President—Nord Alexis and his wife, so the appointment was not made.

When the city of Cap-Haitien was threatened with disaster in the political upheavals of 1888, the bishop began his role as its defender. He remained the protector of citizens and officials, of prisoners and of suspects, through the wild revolutionary days after 1902 and the American occupation which began in 1915. During the occupation he was the only bishop in contact with the United States authorities. He made a trip to the U.S. in 1918, and he gave a deposition before the McCormick Commission in 1921, both times to explain the situation of the Church in Haiti. Thus he became the representative of the Haitian people. Kersuzan was a zealous apostle of the devotion to Our Lady of Perpetual Help, which became widespread in Haiti. He was buried in the cathedral of Cap-Haitien.

Bibliography: J. M. JAN, *Collecta pour l'histoire du diocese du Cap-Haïtien* 2 v. (Port-au-Prince 1958).

[J. M. JAN]

KERYGMA

The solemn and public proclamation of salvation in Christ made in the name of God to non-Christians; it was accompanied by an appeal to signs and wonders to dispose the hearers to faith, conversion, and a return to God.

New Testament and Early Church. In the New Testament the word is used in its verbal form (κηρυσσεῖν) some 61 times to describe the proclamation of the kingdom of God and of the "gospel of God, which he had promised beforehand through his prophets in the holy Scriptures" (Rom 1.2). Kerygma (κάρυγμα) was employed in an almost technical sense by the New Testament authors to signify the manner in which an authorized preacher, kērux (κῆρυξ), announced the truth that "the kingdom of God has come upon you" (Mt 12.28; Lk 11.20). The message consists essentially in proclaiming Christ dead and risen from the dead (cf. Rom 8.34) as the SON OF GOD "who gave himself for our sins, that he might deliver us from the wickedness of this present world" (Gal 1.4).

The content of the kerygma is the gospel of Christ (cf. Mk 1.14), what is to be believed (Rom 10.18), or simply the logos, or word (Acts 17.11; 2 Tm 4.2). Jesus had announced the coming of the kingdom with His call for repentance (Mk 1.15). The central object of the apostolic kerygma was Christ (Acts 8.5; 19.13; 1 Cor 1.23), in whom, according to the prophecies, is salvation (2 Cur 1.19–20). It was the cross with the implication of the Resurrection (1 Cor 1.23; Rom 8.17) and Christ's return as judge (Acts 10.42).

The earliest exponents of the Christian faith had worked out a distinct way of presenting the fundamental convictions of their religion. The Christian preacher thought of himself as the divinely authorized announcer, or herald, of very important news after the manner of John the Baptist (Mt 3.1–2; Mk 11.30–33). The preacher recounted the life and work of Jesus Christ in brief form, demonstrating that in Christ's conflicts, sufferings, death, and Resurrection, the divinely guided history [*see* SALVATION HISTORY (HEILSGESCHICHTE)] of mankind had reached its climax. God Himself had now most personally intervened in the history of mankind to inaugurate His kingdom on earth. This announcement was bracketed between that of the fulfillment of the Old Testament prophecies and the new Christian community's, or Church's, eschatological destiny in the Second Coming of the Savior to reader judgment. The preacher sought to convince his hearers that they were now confronted by God Himself as represented in His kingdom and that they stood liable to immediate and inescapable judgment. They had only to accept His invitation to embark on a new life wherein through God's mercy they would be unburdened of past delinquencies and have the opportunity of enjoying a new relationship with God, in the Lord Christ Jesus.

This apostolic kerygma is exemplified in the speech attributed to Peter on Pentecost (Acts 2.14–39; cf. 4.812), in which the Apostle, appealing to "what was spoken through the prophet," described Jesus of Nazareth as a man approved by God, who had been "delivered up by the settled purpose and foreknowledge of God.'' He was crucified by the hands of lawless men but was raised by God from death and made LORD and Christ; exalted by the right hand of God, He poured forth through the Holy Spirit what was seen and heard. This was followed by an exhortation to repeat and be baptized in the name of Jesus Christ unto the remission of sins.

A similar formula is revealed in St. Paul's letter to the Romans (1.1–4; 2.16; 8.34; 10.8–9). Paul announces the ''gospel of God, which he had promised beforehand through his prophets,'' concerning the Son, Jesus Christ, who was from the seed of David; who died and was raised from the dead; who was declared Son of God with power according to the Spirit of holiness; who is at the right hand of God; and through whom God will judge the secrets of men. It was completed with the assurance: ''For if thou confess with thy mouth that Jesus is the Lord, and believe in thy heart that God raised him from the dead, thou shalt be saved'' (Rom 10.9).

Dogmatic Theology. The modern attempt to reintroduce the kerygmatic element into the study and teaching of THEOLOGY centers on the proclamation of the mystery of the faith as an invitation to direct commitment to Christ, to efficacious and dynamic actualization. This is in contrast to that kind of systematic study which focuses more contemplatively on a series of topics, or concepts. The latter is necessary as a safeguard of orthodoxy and for the fashioning of a structure to encompass the full content of the faith and to serve as a basis of theological development, but it sometimes tends to static conceptualism. Kerygmatic theology emphasizes charismatic witness under the immediate stimulus of the Holy Spirit to the dynamic presence of Christ in the Church.

The kerygma may indicate the act of proclamation or the thing proclaimed, i.e., the content of the kerygma, or both, so that in some manner the past salvific event becomes present as a call to FAITH and obedience. K. Rahner has brought together all the notes of kerygma cited above. It is the living proclamation of the word of God in the Church by a divinely (through the Church) empowered and designated preacher, in such a way that this word—uttered by the preacher in the strength of the Spirit unto faith, hope, and charity as an evangelical offer of salvation and as a power that binds and judges—makes itself present with the actuality of the ''now'' presence characteristic of salvation history *in Christo Jesu*, from the beginning to the end (of time). This word the hearer, with the strength of the same Spirit, can receive in faith and love, the spoken and the heard having become a word-event.

Kerygma finds its widest expression in the prophetic ministry of the whole body of the Church, most common-

ly expressed in preaching. It attains its highest signification in the Church's sacramental (and liturgical life, where word and action join, and here especially in the Eucharistic celebration (1 Cor 11.26).

Bibliography: H. SCHÜRMANN and K. RAHNER, *Lexikon für Theologie und Kirche,* ed. J. HOFER and K. RAHNER, 10 v. (2d, new ed. Freiburg 1957–65) 6:122–126. G. FRIEDRICH, G. KITTEL, *Theologisches Wörterbuch zum Neuen Testament* (Stuttgart 1935) 2:705–734; 3:682–717. J. OEHLER, *Paulys Realenzyklopädie der klassischen Altertumswissenschaft,* ed. G. WISSOWA, et al. (Stuttgart 1893–) 11.1 (1921) 349–357. H. OTT, *Die Religion in Geschichte und Gegenwart,* 7 v. (3d ed. Tübingen 1957–65) 3:1250–54. C. H. DODD, *The Apostolic Preaching and Its Developments* (New York 1937; repr. 1962). D. GRASSO, *L'annuncio della salvezza* (Naples 1965). A. OEPKE, *Die Missionspredigt des Apostels Paulus* (Leipzig 1920). K. H. RENGSTORF, *Apostolat und Predigtamt* (2d ed. Stuttgart 1954). H. SCHLIER, *Wort Gottes* (Würzburg 1958). C. F. EVANS, *Journal of Theological Studies* 7 (1956) 25–41. Z. ALSZEGHY and M. FLICK, *Gregorianum* 40 (1959) 671–744. J. MCKENZIE, *Theological Studies* 21 (1960) 183–206. A. RÉTIF, *Nouvelle Revue Théologique* 71 (1949) 910–922.

[F. X. MURPHY/E. F. MALONE]

KERYGMATIC THEOLOGY

The systematic study of theological truths within a structure that can directly and immediately serve to prepare for and promote the preaching of the truths of revelation to the Christian people (A. de Villalmonte). The modern movement for a kerygmatic theology seeks to orientate scientific theology to Christian life and apostolate, and thereby to bring about an interaction of theology and apostolic action.

Kerygmatic theology can mean any organic statement of Christian truth that includes in its scope the goals of the pastoral activity of the Church. It includes those theological systems that, while primarily representing a scientific position, contain its methodological characteristics, e.g., the Christocentric organization of M. Scheeben, M. d'Herbigny, and É. Mersch and the existential problematic of K. Rahner. In its strictest sense, the term applies to a systematic structuring of the revealed data as the ''good news'' of SALVATION in Christ. The organization of doctrinal and theological content follows closely the presentation of salvation history given by God in Sacred Scripture, setting each doctrinal statement and religious or moral commandment within the framework of God's saving action.

The concern of kerygmatic theology is primarily pedagogical. This pedagogy is *historical,* advancing through the moments of salvation from Abraham to Jesus Christ, and within the New Testament through the deepening revelation of God and His work in the Person and work of Jesus Christ. It is *Christocentric,* setting forth

God's providential purpose and plan to prepare for and manifest Jesus Christ. It is *reasonable*, for it employs a systematic presentation of its own with a progressive and concentric illumination of this mystery in fundamental themes: the promise, the alliance, the faithfulness of God; His holiness, His justice and love, His wisdom; and, finally, Jesus Christ, Son of God and son of man, Word of life, and head of a new humanity, founder and consummator, together with the Holy Spirit, of the definitive kingdom of God.

Because a kerygmatic theology exists to nourish a missionary preaching, it is a theology of *value.* The value content of a doctrinal truth controls the conceptual structuring of the theological synthesis, so that the dominant value is perceptible throughout the total corpus of Christian truth, and in every part of the corpus, particularly through a thematic organization, e.g., as it is nuanced in Sacred Scripture in the major themes of covenant, word, etc. The statement and arrangement of the many particular truths reveal and reinforce the dominant value.

The concern for value results in a synthesis that is concrete rather than abstract, historically situated rather than scientifically and speculatively organized. Salvation history provides the principle of synthesis, revealing and preserving the inherent value. By relating Christian truth with a personal meeting with Christ in Scripture and liturgy, expressed in a life of worship and service, there is both an experience and a reinforcement of the meaningful value of the Christian proclamation.

Symbolism is used to convey value, and the value-symbol relation explains the central position of the man Jesus Christ and His history in a kerygmatic synthesis. The relation highlights as well the demand for a theology and a catechesis adaptable to the psychological and cultural needs of the individual.

An early attempt to establish a theology independent of SCHOLASTIC THEOLOGY met with a strong disapproval, principally because of its inherent ambiguity, imprecision, and limited intellectual scope. The middle position expressed principally by J. Jungmann and K. Rahner found general acceptance: (1) the goals of theology and preaching are different; (2) every full Christian theology is kerygmatic; (3) the technical and scholastic precision of scientific theology is necessary; (4) this must be complemented by a kerygmatic synthesis.

See Also: CHRISTOCENTRISM; KERYGMA; SALVATION HISTORY (HEILSGESCHICHTE); SYMBOL IN REVELATION; THEOLOGY.

Bibliography: K. RAHNER, *Lexikon für Theologie und Kirche,* (Freiburg 1957–66) 6:126. G. E. CARTER, *The Modern Challenge to Religious Education,* ed. W. J. REEDY (New York 1961). J. HOF-INGER, *The Art of Teaching Christian Doctrine* (2nd ed. Notre Dame, Ind. 1962). J. A. JUNGMANN, *The Good News Yesterday and Today,* ed., abr., and tr. W. A. HUESMAN (New York 1962); *Handing on the Faith,* rev. and tr. A. N. FUERST (New York 1959). A. DE VILLALMONTE, *La teología kerigmática* (Barcelona 1962).

[E. F. MALONE]

William Henry Ketcham.

KETCHAM, WILLIAM HENRY

Missionary; b. Summer, Iowa, June 1, 1868; d. Washington, D.C., Nov. 14, 1921. Ketcham, born of non-Catholic parents, was received into the Church in 1885 while a student in St. Charles College, Grand Couteau, La. He was ordained on March 13, 1892, at Guthrie, Okla., and served at first as pastor to the settlers and indigenous people in the northern Native American territory, then as a missionary to the Choctaw. He made many converts to the Church in Oklahoma and organized 18 new congregations, six parish churches, and four schools. In 1901 Ketcham was appointed by the U.S. hierarchy as director of the Bureau of Catholic Indian Missions; he served in this capacity for 20 years. The Native American missions had been crippled by the withdrawal of Federal subsidies and the passage of restrictive legislation inspired by American Protective Association agitation. Ketcham helped to eliminate these policies and established, by appeal to the U.S. Supreme Court, the right of natives to use tribal funds for the education of their children in mission schools. He placed the missions on a satisfactory financial basis and stimulated mission work by his frequent visits. In 1912 Pres. William Howard Taft, recognizing Ketcham's influence among the natives, appointed him a member of the U.S. Board of Commissioners of Indian Affairs. During the next decade, Ketcham was responsible for many improvements in the facilities and operation of Federal schools and hospitals for Native Americans.

[J. B. TENNELLY]

KETTELER, WILHELM EMMANUEL VON

German bishop, pioneer in Catholic social thought; b. Münster, Westphalia, Dec. 25, 1811; d. Burghausen, Upper Bavaria, July 13, 1877.

Career. After completing legal studies he entered government service as a law clerk (1835), but left it (1838) in protest against Prussia's treatment of Abp. Clemens von Droste zu Vischering of Cologne in the CO-LOGNE mixed marriage dispute. He became a member of the circle of Joseph von GÖRRES in Munich, where Bp. Karl Von Reisach of Eichstätt influenced him to study for the priesthood. During his theological studies in Munich (1841–44) he was much influenced by Johann MÖHLER, Karl Windischmann, and Ignaz von DÖLLINGER. After ordination he served as a chaplain in Beckum (1844–46), pastor in Hopsten (1846–49), and dean at St. Hedwig's Church in Berlin (1849–50). This pastoral experience made him keenly aware of the material as well as the spiritual needs of his parishioners. His conviction grew that concern for their social betterment was inseparable from the care of their souls.

As bishop of Mainz, from May 20, 1850, until his death, Ketteler came to be recognized as the spiritual leader of German Catholics; his interest in social questions won general and deep respect. At the National Assembly in Frankfurt (1848) Ketteler was a representative and attracted considerable attention by his speech commemorating the victims of the September revolt. This address contained his basic notions on political and social topics. As a member of the German Reichstag (1871–72)

he opposed unequivocally the beginnings of the KULTUR-KAMPF. During the following years he was the leading Catholic spokesman and defender of the Church's rights. Ketteler was a cofounder of the Bishops' Conference that began in Fulda (1867) and he was mainly responsible for making it a permanent institution. At VATICAN COUNCIL I he opposed the definition of papal infallibility as inopportune and claimed that the assumptions, conditions, and scope of infallibility should be explained with greater precision in relation to the episcopal office. Ketteler was increasingly recognized as a key figure in the Church for opposing current LIBERALISM and LAICISM and their effects on marriage, education, the family, and economic life, and for upholding the primacy of religious factors as constructive and spiritualizing forces. Ketteler strengthened his case by his utilization of all the modern means at his disposal, by his determination and energy, and by his ability to transform weak, indolent priests infected with liberalism into united and determined clerics. He fulfilled his episcopal duties selflessly, earnestly, and forcefully.

Social Program. Four stages can be distinguished in the ever-widening influence of Ketteler's social program. First came his appeal for social reform in a speech delivered in Frankfurt (1848). At the Catholic congress (*Katholikentag*) held the same year in Mainz, and soon after, in his Advent sermons in the cathedral, Ketteler expounded the Church's position on social questions. This was the year when MARX and ENGELS issued the *Communist Manifesto*. The second stage came with Ketteler's book on Christianity and the labor problem, *Die Arbeiterfrage und das Christentum* (1864), which was based on a thorough investigation of socialist literature and Christian social principles as expounded by St. Thomas Aquinas. A third stage appeared with Ketteler's sermon on the worker problem, in which he proposed concrete reforms (July 25, 1869). The final stage was reached in his sermon (September 1869) at the episcopal conference in Fulda. In this, his most significant pronouncement, Ketteler spoke on the Church's social and charitable obligations to the working class and tried to rouse the interest of his fellow bishops by defining the essentials of the problem. Ketteler emphasized that the natural law and Christian fraternal charity contradicted current economic liberalism and its view that economic life was a war waged by each man against all others. As this system developed, according to Ketteler, it resulted in many places in the growth of a working class that was spiritually and morally crippled and inaccessible to Christian influence. Liberalism, he pointed out, contradicted human dignity, because God intended to bestow the goods of this world for the support of all mankind; liberalism opposed the divine plan for the procreation and education of men by means of the family; and, even worse, it neglected Christian precepts concerning love of neighbor. Ketteler argued that the Church must intervene and fulfill its mission to save the souls of working-class persons, and to release them from a proximate occasion of sin that often rendered the observance of Christian duties almost impossible. His final appeal was for a changed Christian outlook on social thought and for legislative reforms. This was an opportune time to enact social legislation in Germany and the initiative in this direction was taken (1877) by Count Ferdinand von Galen, Ketteler's nephew, in the Reichstag. Unfortunately, this proposal was not enacted into law until 1891; yet Ketteler's name remained closely linked from the beginning with Germany's much-admired social legislation and its safeguards for workers in illness, disability, and old age.

At the *Katholikentag* in Mainz (1871) Ketteler's address on "Liberalism, Socialism, and Christianity" revealed the false ideas rooted in contemporary social thought and proposed the possibility of correcting them by Christian ideas that would eradicate the evils in current views without sacrificing anything good in them. Ketteler's pastoral letter (February 1876) on religion and social welfare stressed religion's cultural role in the proper regulation of modern social life.

A. F. Lennig, J. B. Heinrich, C. Moufang, P. L. Haffner, and others at Mainz who came under Ketteler's influence, continued his theological ideas and social program later in the 19th century and spread them throughout Catholic Germany. Leo XIII's encyclical *RERUM NOVARUM* (1891) was so much indebted to Ketteler that the pope referred to him as "my great predecessor" and admitted that he had learned much from him.

Bibliography: Works. *Predigten,* ed. J. M. RAICH, 2 v. (Mainz 1878); *Briefe,* ed. J. M. RAICH (Mainz 1879); *Hirtenbriefe,* ed. J. M. RAICH (Mainz 1904); *Ausgewählte Schriften,* ed. J. MUMBAUER, 3 v. (2d ed. Munich 1924); *Die grossen sozialen Fragen der Gegenwart,* ed. E. DEUERLEIN (Mainz 1948). **Biographies.** O. PFÜLF, 3 v. (Mainz 1899). G. GOYAU (Paris 1907). F. VIGENER (Munich 1924). T. BRAUER (Hamburg 1927). W. FRANZMATHES (Mainz 1927). L. LENHART (Kevelaer 1936). **Literature.** L. LENHART, *Seelennot aus Lebensenge: Das Problem "Lebensraum und Sittlichkeit" nach Bischof von Ketteler* (Mainz 1933); J. HÖFER and K. RAHNER *Lexicon für Theologie und Kirche* (Freiburg 1957–65) 6:128–130. P. TISCHLEDER, *Der Totalismus in der prophetischen Vorausschau W. E. v. Kettelers* (Mainz 1947). R. AUBERT, "Mgr. K., évêque de Mayence et les origines du catholicisme social," in *Collectanea Mechliniensia* 32 (1947) 534–539. F. S. NITTI, *Catholic Socialism,* tr. M. MACKINTOSH (2d ed. New York 1895). J. J. LAUX (G. METLAKE, pseud.) *Christian Social Reform: Program Outlined by Its Pioneer, William Emmanuel, Baron von Ketteler* (Philadelphia 1912). W. E. HOGAN, *The Development of Bishop W. E. v. K's Interpretation of the Social Problem* (Washington 1946). G. G. WINDELL, *The Catholics and German Unity, 1866–1871* (Minneapolis 1954). C. BAUER, *Staatslexicon,* H. SACHER, ed. 4:953–957.

[L. LENHART]

KEVENHOERSTER, JOHN BERNARD

Bishop, first vicar apostolic of the Bahama Islands; b. Alten-Essen, Prussia, Nov. 1, 1869; d. Bahama Islands, Dec. 9, 1949. He was the son of Bernard Kevenhoerster, an architect and contractor, and Agnes Plantenberg. The family left Germany in 1881 to settle in the German-speaking parish of St. Joseph, Minneapolis, Minn., where John attended St. Joseph's School until 1883. In 1887 he began his studies for the priesthood at St. John's Abbey, Collegeville, Minn., and entered the novitiate on July 25, 1892. He made his vows as a Benedictine a year later and was ordained on June 24, 1896. In October 1907, he was appointed pastor of St. Anselm's Parish, Bronx, N.Y., where he built a school, opened one of the first public playgrounds in the city, and constructed a church modeled after the Hagia Sophia. On Dec. 3, 1929, he was made vicar forane of the Bahamas, where he served for 20 years as a missionary of the poor. After becoming domestic prelate and prefect apostolic in 1932, he was consecrated bishop on Dec. 21, 1933. By the time the Bahamas became a vicariate apostolic in 1941, Kevenhoerster had introduced 19 churches and missions, 14 grammar schools, St. Augustine's Priory School, and the Bahamian teaching sisterhood. In 1946 Kevenhoerster was honored as an assistant at the pontifical throne.

[B. J. HOWARD]

KEVIN, ST.

Irish monastic founder; b. near Dublin, Ireland; d. Glendalough, June 3, 618. Kevin (Coemgen) received the rudiments of education from three ascetics, possibly at Killnemanagh, near Tallaght, and retired to a deserted place called Hollywood, near Blessington, where he stayed until sought out by many disciples. He retired to Glendalough (the Two Lakes) and on a hillock built a beehive cell. When his whereabouts was discovered Kevin realized that he could not in conscience ignore his disciples, and Glendalough became a monastic center *c.* 570 with Kevin as abbot. A church of wood was built on a mountain ledge, close to the community, who lived in huts. At his death, Kevin was laid to rest beside the little church, later known as Rigferta, "royal graves." When the space beneath the mountain ledge became too cramped the monastery proper was moved to a larger site half a mile down the valley, where a new church dedicated to St. Kevin was erected with other churches to a total of ten. In the penitential season Kevin retired to a crude stone cell above the upper lake still known as "St. Kevin's Bed." Glendalough was made an episcopal see in 1111, but is now part of Dublin. It was famous as a place of pilgrimage on St. Kevin's day until well into the 19th century.

Saint Kevin's Church, Glendalough, Ireland. (©Michael St. Maur Sheil/CORBIS)

Feast: June 3.

Bibliography: C. EDMONDS, *The Catholic Encyclopedia,* ed. C. G. HERBERMANN et al., 16 v. (New York 1907–14; suppl. 1922) 4:92. "Vita Sancti Coemgeni," *Vitae sanctorum Hiberniae,* ed. C. PLUMMER, 2 v. (Oxford 1910) 1:234–257. *Acta Sanctorum,* June, 1:303–315. J. F. KENNEY, *The Sources for the Early History of Ireland:* v.1, *Ecclesiastical* (New York 1929) 1:403–404. J. RYAN, *Irish Monasticism* (London 1931). W. DELIUS, *Geschichte der irischen Kirche* (Munich 1954). M. and L. DE PAOR, *Early Christian Ireland* (New York 1958). M. RODGERS, *Glendalough: a Celtic pilgrimage* (Harrisburg, Pa. 1996).

[J. RYAN]

KEYS, POWER OF

The glorified Christ's possession of "the key of David" (Rv 3.7) symbolizes His royal authority in the messianic kingdom. So, in Isaiah 22.22, the giving of the "key of the House of David" expresses the idea of the authority to be conferred on Eliakim, chosen to be master of the royal palace. In rabbinic literature the "giving of keys" consistently means the granting of authority, as to a steward placed over his master's household (H. L. Strack and P. Billerbeck, *Kommentar zum Neuen Testament* 1:736). Jesus denounces the Scribes and Pharisees, because having the "key of knowledge" (Lk 11.52) they have "shut the kingdom of heaven against men" (Mt 23.13).

In the light of canonical and extracanonical parallels, it seems certain that Mt 16.19a means not that St. PETER is to be the "gate-keeper of heaven," but that Christ will confer on him vicarious authority over His household on earth, that is, over the Church that He promises to build on him as on a rock. For it is "on earth" that Peter will exercise his power of BINDING AND LOOSING (Mt 16.19bc). The keys that Christ will give to Peter are the keys of the kingdom of heaven, in the sense that Peter's authoritative decisions will bind men in conscience; on

Christ Giving the Keys to Saint Peter, painting by Vincenzo di Catena, 1517. (©Archivo Iconografico, S.A./CORBIS)

their acceptance of his teaching of the gospel and his direction in the way of SALVATION will depend their entrance into the KINGDOM OF GOD for all eternity.

See Also: AUTHORITY, ECCLESIASTICAL; OFFICE, ECCLESIASTICAL; POPE; PRIMACY OF THE POPE

Bibliography: J. JEREMIAS, *Theologisches Wörterbuch zum Neuen Testament* (Stuttgart 1935) 3:749–53. H. VON CAMPEN-HAUSEN, "Die Schlüsselgewalt der Kirche," *Evangelische Theologie* 4 (1937) 143–69.

[F. A. SULLIVAN]

KHAZARS

The Khazars were an ethnic group, belonging to the Turkish peoples, who, toward the end of the second century of the Christian Era, had settled in the region between the Caucasus and the lower Volga and Don Rivers, and in the following centuries, after a series of victories over the Byzantines, the Persians, and the Arabs, established a powerful kingdom in southeastern Asia. At the beginning of the eighth century, dynastic ties bound the Khazars more closely to Constantinople, which led to a limited spread of Christianity among them. They also be-

came acquainted with Judaism from the numerous Jews who lived in the Crimea and along the Bosphorus. When the Byzantine emperor, Leo the Isaurian, persecuted the Jews in A.D. 723, many Jews found refuge in the Khazar kingdom, and their influence was so great that, around the middle of the eighth century, the king of the Khazars and many of the Khazar nobility accepted the Jewish faith. According to a widespread legend, the conversion of the Khazars to JUDAISM followed a religious discussion in which their king was particularly impressed by the arguments of Jewish theologians.

After the conversion of the leading Khazars to Judaism, many Jews, including several Jewish scholars, migrated to the Khazar kingdom, where they kept in touch with the intellectual centers of the Jewish world, especially those in Mesopotamia and Palestine. The literary sources indicate explicitly that the Khazars acknowledged the authority of the Talmud; hence, they must not have been affected in religious matters by the Karaites.

The Khazars' acceptance of Judaism coincided with a period of peaceful development in their history, when they focused their attention on the strengthening of their power at home and on the extending of their political influence abroad. They thus established new commercial centers of importance at various places throughout their sphere of influence, and in these places, as well as in their older cities, such as Itil in the delta of the Volga, and Samkarsh and Tamatarcha on the Bosphorus, the Jewish element formed an important part of the population. At Semender on the Caspian Sea, a viceroy of the Khazars, who was likewise a convert to Judaism, had his headquarters. Although the most important posts among the Khazars were held by families which had been converted to Judaism, there reigned in Khazaria a spirit of religious toleration such as was rarely to be found at the time in Christian or Moslem countries.

In the last third of the ninth century, the Khazar kingdom suffered considerably from the incursions of another Turkish people, the Petchonegs. Meanwhile, since the Russians occupied the region at the delta of the Dnieper and even attacked Constantinople, the Byzantines were forced, for the sake of mutual defense, to strengthen their friendly relations with the Khazars. The task of doing this was entrusted to Cyril, the later apostle of the Slavs, who used the opportunity to further an effort to win the Khazars to Christianity. At the beginning of the tenth century, however, the Byzantines allied themselves with peoples who were hostile to the Khazars, and among these people, too, they sent their Christian missionaries. The Khazar king was once more able to avert the threatened invasion of his land, but he put an end to the vaunted religious toleration in his realm. After this failure of the Byzantines in their efforts to weaken the Khazars, they induced the Russians to undertake a military campaign against them. The Russian grand duke, Igor, captured the city of Samkarsh and the Khazar cities in the Crimea, but he was then defeated, together with his Byzantine allies, by the Khazars. Yet the Russians' advance could not be checked forever. Between A.D. 964 and 969 they overran most of the region where the Khazars had been settled. Many of the Khazars withdrew into the remote steppes and especially into the inaccessible mountain country of the Caucasus. From here their king appealed to various Muslim countries for help, offering them in return his willingness to become a Muslim himself.

For some centuries several sections of the former kingdom of the Khazars preserved a certain amount of political independence, and in these regions the Khazar people remained loyal to their Jewish faith. However, when the Crimea was later conquered by the Tartars, most of the remaining Khazars embraced Islam, while the others were absorbed, partly by the Rabbanite and partly by the Karaite communities of Jews. Yet the so-called Mountain Jews of modern times are in part descendants of the ancient Khazars. Some Khazar elements seem to have entered Hungary, too, at an early date in the train of the Magyars, who were akin to the Khazars and once belonged to their kingdom.

Although the European Jews in the first Christian millennium had some knowledge of the existence of a Jewish kingdom in Khazaria, they did not have much precise information about it. The Spanish-Jewish scholar and statesman, Ḥasdai Ibn Shaprut, who lived around the middle of the tenth century, sent a letter to King Joseph of the Khazars in which he asked several definite questions about this people. The king's answer, written in Hebrew, was cited by various medieval authors and was also used by Judah Ben Samuel HA-LEVI in his *Kuzari* (about A.D. 1100). Toward the end of the nineteenth century, a copy of this letter was discovered among the documents that were found in the GENIZA of the synagogue of Old Cairo, together with other documents concerning the Khazars. Their contents largely corroborate the data already known about this people from the Armenian, Byzantine, and Arabic historians.

Bibliography: J. BRUTZKUS, *Encyclopaedia Judaica: Das Judentum in Geschichte und Gegenwart,* 10 v. (Berlin 1928–34) 5:337–350. R. W. ROGERS, *The Jewish Encyclopedia,* ed. J. SINGER, 13 v. (New York 1901–06) 4:1–7. J. STARR, *Universal Jewish Encyclopedia,* 10 v. (New York 1939–44) 6:375–378. A. YARMOLINSKY, ''The Khazars: A Bibliography,'' *Bulletin of the New York Public Library* (Sept. 1938), rev. ed. printed separately (New York 1939).

[K. HRUBY]

KHOMĨAKOV, ALEKSEĬ STEPANOVICH

Leader of the early Slavophile ideologists and most influential Russian Orthodox lay theologian of the 19th century, poet; b. Moscow, May 1, 1804; d. of cholera on his estate near Riazan, Sept. 23, 1860. Khomĩakov was a very versatile and erudite member of the landed gentry, and he was intimately acquainted with leading intellectuals at home and abroad. He was well read in the Greek Fathers, but the chief influence on his thought came from the German romantic and idealist philosophers then popular in Russia. He studied literature at the University of Moscow and wrote verse tragedies (e.g., *Ermak,* 1832). After two ventures in a military career (1822 and 1828) and some study of art, he married in 1836. He vigorously argued for the abolition of serfdom, for intellectual freedom, and for the curtailment of censorship.

In contrast to the secularist Westernizers who believed that Russia should adopt European ideas and institutions such as a representative assembly, Khomĩakov, a religious populist, advocated the preservation and strengthening of Russia's ancient patriarchal traditions as embodied in the peasant collective village or commune.

He held that history's movement was caused by the clash of two forces, the Iranian principle of spiritual and moral freedom and the Kushite principle of material and logical necessity. The former characterized Russia, the latter predominated in the West. The Slavophiles, not to be confused with the later political Pan-Slavists, asserted that Western civilization was doomed to extinction because it was based on juridicism, rationalism, and materialism.

According to Khomíakov, Roman Catholicism had turned Christianity into a state by its absorption of Roman law and its exaltation of a legalistic hierarchy. This hierarchy, apart from and above the faithful, culminated in a despotic papacy. It possessed an enforced external unity without inner freedom. Protestantism was a logical continuation of Catholic rationalism and had achieved only an unprincipled freedom without unity, which is license. The Russian Orthodox people alone, i.e., the peasants in their communes, as distinct from the upper classes and the institutional hierarchic Church, had preserved Christianity in its pure form and was destined to lead other nations into a new Christian era because of its Christian character. The superiority of the Russian Orthodox people was attributed to the spirit of *sobornost,* Khomíakov's main contribution to theology. *Sobornost* is derived from the Slavonic word for "catholic" in the Nicene Creed and variously translated as integrality, communality, collegiality, or collectivity. *Sobornost* effects the harmonious blending of inner freedom and unity, of the individual and society, in a living organic body whose members are bound together by mutual love under the sole headship of Christ; this love is the Holy Spirit. *Sobornost* is also the criterion of truth, which resides not in the decisions of the hierarchy, nor even of an ecumenical council, but in acceptance by the whole Christian community united in mutual love.

See Also: RUSSIAN THEOLOGY; SLAVOPHILISM.

Bibliography: A. S. KHOMÍAKOV, *Polnoe sobranie sochineniĭ,* 8 v. (Moscow 1900), collected works. A. GRATIEUX, *A. S. Khomíakov et le mouvement slavophile,* 2 v. (Paris 1939). P. BARON, *Un Théologien laïc orthodoxe russe au XIXᵉ siècle* (*Orientalia Christiana Analecta* 127; Rome 1940). P. K. CHRISTOFF, *An Introduction to Nineteenth-Century Russian Slavophilism: A Study in Ideas* (The Hague 1961–) v. 1. N. V. RIASANOVSKY, *Russia and the West in the Teaching of the Slavophiles* (Cambridge, Mass. 1952).

[W. J. MCBREARTY]

KIERKEGAARD, SØREN AABYE

Danish philosopher and theologian, influential Protestant thinker of the 19th century, commonly considered the precursor of EXISTENTIALISM; b. Copenhagen, May 5, 1813; d. Copenhagen, Nov. 4, 1855.

Søren Aabye Kierkegaard.

Early Formation. Søren was the seventh and last child of an elderly couple. His father, who had started life as a shepherd lad in the Jutland moors, retired at the age of 40 from a prosperous hosier business in Copenhagen. In his later years he was given to melancholy, particularly after losing his wife and five of his children within two years. This melancholy left a deep impression on the young Kierkegaard, as did the strict pietistic education he received at home. A secret guilt in his father's life, which he discovered as a theology student, affected Søren profoundly. A later diary entry about an unidentified man records: ". . . the terrible thing about this man, who once when he was a small boy, as he tended his sheep on the Jutland heath, suffering greatly, starving and in want, stood up upon a hill and cursed God—and this man was unable to forget it when he was 82 years old." When confronted with this text after Kierkegaard's death, Peter, his only surviving brother, exclaimed: "This is the story of our father and ourselves."

After this "great earthquake" in his life, Kierkegaard became convinced that a curse rested upon his family, that it was to be "wiped out by the powerful hand of God." A period of dissipation and estrangement from his father followed. Four years later, a religious conversion coincided with a family reconciliation. Shortly afterward Kierkegaard passed his final examinations in theology and wrote a doctoral Dissertation *On the Concept of Irony* (1841); in contrast to his later works, this betrays the strong influence of HEGEL.

Along with his father's influence, another event was to determine Kierkegaard's spiritual evolution. In 1840 he betrothed himself to a 17-year-old girl, Regine Olsen. A year later, realizing that he was psychologically unfit for marriage, he broke the engagement. This unhappy love affair initiated one of the most prodigious literary careers in history. Initially Kierkegaard tried to clarify his personal problems and to understand their meaning in the larger context of human existence. All his early works allude to his relationship with Regine and contain cryptic messages for her.

Published Works. In 1843 he published *Either-Or,* a compendious work in two volumes. Although it appeared under a pseudonym, the book made its author famous immediately. In the next three years 14 more works followed: *Repetition* (1843), *Fear and Trembling* (1843), *The Concept of Dread* (1844), *Prefaces* (1844), *Philosophical Fragments* (1844), *Stages on Life's Way* (1845), *Concluding Unscientific Postscript* (1846), and seven sets of *Edifying Discourses,* published under his own name to accompany the other pseudonymous writings. After 1846 Kierkegaard's creativity slackened, although he was still to publish three major works: *The Works of Love* (1847), *Sickness Unto Death* (1849), and *Training in Christianity* (1850). During this period he also wrote the greater part of his diary.

In 1846 he came under attack from the *Corsair,* a Copenhagen satirical weekly that he had challenged in a newspaper article. For almost a year the ridicule and low wit of the *Corsair* made him an object of derision all over Denmark.

Kierkegaard's last two years were marked by a violent conflict with the Danish National Church, which he felt had betrayed the message of the Gospel by its compromising attitude. He carried on his onslaught in a self-published periodical, the *Instant.* In the middle of this attack he fainted on the street and was brought to the Frederikshospital, where he died from an unknown disease in the spinal marrow.

Freedom and Choice. Kierkegaard has rightly been called the father of modern existentialism. Man for him is essentially FREEDOM, and he constitutes himself in his free CHOICE. Already in his first major work, *Either-Or,* Kierkegaard describes life as a choice between an aesthetic attitude in which man drifts along from one pleasure to another, and an ethical one in which freedom determines itself by a self-imposed acceptance of law and duty. The aesthete refuses to commit himself to anything permanent (marriage, a profession) lest he limit the infinite possibilities of his SELF; but since the real self of a free being can be constituted only by a self-choice, he does not "exist" in the full sense of the word. The ethical man, on the contrary, accepts the limitations of his choice and thus becomes a real PERSON.

Yet, as Kierkegaard shows in his two subsequent works, *Repetition* and *Fear and Trembling,* the ethical choice is not final. Sooner or later the ethical man will be faced by the predicament of a transcendent power that prevents him from fully realizing his freedom. Just as Job, in spite of his exemplary life, lost all his possessions, so man in his striving toward self-realization has to cope with powers beyond his control. How will he do this? He cannot simply ignore them. Much less can he abandon his moral autonomy by forfeiting his freedom in blind resignation. But to maintain simultaneously both freedom and TRANSCENDENCE would seem to be a task that is impossible.

Faith and Subjectivity. This is made even more difficult by freedom's intrinsic deficiency. In accordance with the Protestant interpretation of the ORIGINAL SIN, which he analyzed in *The Concept of Dread,* Kierkegaard claims that man is essentially unable to fulfill the law of his own being. The ethical attitude, therefore, cannot be final in the constitution of the self. This fact is illustrated by the Biblical story of Abraham, who received a divine order to sacrifice his son and thus to "suspend" the ethical law. The realization of the ethical universal, the immanent law of a nature identical for all men, cannot be the highest achievement of freedom, as Hegel claimed. Only religious faith enables man to reconcile immanent freedom with the acceptance of a transcendent reality placing him in a position of dependence, for in faith alone can he consistently assert his insufficiency and the certainty to overcome this insufficiency with the help of a higher power. It was faith that allowed Abraham to ascend Mt. Moria, and yet to believe that in his posterity all generations would be blessed. The ultimate stage in the constitution of the self is, therefore, not the mere choice of the self, but a choice that includes the self's dependence on the transcendent. To become an authentic self, man must commit himself to God; for he is, in his very essence, a dynamic relation to God. To choose or not to choose is no longer the only alternative for freedom; a more basic one is to choose or to choose "before God." In *Stages on Life's Way,* Kierkegaard thus describes the three possible attitudes of man with respect to his self: the aesthetic, the ethical, and the religious.

In his most technical works, *Philosophical Fragments* and *Concluding Unscientific Postscript,* Kierkegaard further elaborates the relation between freedom and faith. If the self is essentially freedom, then its highest truth must be subjective; that is, a truth that is not entirely given but becomes true only after having gone through an appropriation process of the WILL. That existential certainty is acquired only through personal commitment is illustrated by the attitude of Socrates, who staked his life for an objectively uncertain affirmation. But this is precisely what faith does: the transcendent by its very nature is never objectively certain—yet it is an integral part of man's relation to himself. Man therefore must make it certain by his subjective commitment to it. Since the highest existential truth is the most subjective, and since subjectivity increases as objective certainty decreases, Christian faith is the highest existential truth, for its object is not merely uncertain to objective reason—it is repellent. Indeed, according to Kierkegaard's Protestant interpretation, Christianity teaches that man is untrue in his very being, and consequently, that even his subjectivity is bound to be unauthentic. While natural faith is paradoxical, Christianity is absolutely paradoxical, or, from the point of view of reason, absurd. Yet, by the same token, Christianity is the highest truth of existence, for it brings man to an inwardness that is deeper than his own subjectivity.

Influence and Critique. Kierkegaard is one of the most provocative of Christian thinkers. His influence on philosophers, particularly Heidegger and Sartre, and on theologians, Protestant and Catholic alike, can be compared with that of Augustine and Pascal. His most important contribution to modern thought is his definition of the self as freedom, by which man becomes a self-constituting being. Yet equally important is his insistence that this self is, in its very center, dependent on God. For Catholics, the most objectionable part of his thought is his radical individualism. Catholics also find themselves unable to accept a notion of SIN that totally disconnects the link between Creator and creature, and the subjectivism that this implies in the theology of faith.

See Also: EXISTENTIALISM; IRRATIONALISM; EXISTENTIAL THEOLOGY.

Bibliography: Danish Editions. *Samlede Vaerker,* ed. A. B. DRACHMANN et al., 20 v. (3d ed. Copenhagen 1962); *Papirer,* ed. P. A. HEIBERG et al., 20 v. (Copenhagen 1909–48). *Breve og Aktstykker vedrørende Søren Kierkegaard,* ed. N. THULSTRUP, 2 v. (Copenhagen 1953–54). English Translations. Almost all of Kierkegaard's works have been translated into English; complete and up-to-date bibliography of these translations can be found in W. LOWRIE, *Kierkegaard,* 2 v. (New York 1962). Secondary Studies. J. D. COLLINS, *The Mind of Kierkegaard* (Chicago 1953). H. DIEM, *Kierkegaard's Dialectic of Existence,* tr. H. KNIGHT (Edinburgh 1959). L. K. DUPRÉ, *Kierkegaard as Theologian* (New York 1963). H. ROOS, *Søren Kierkegaard and Catholicism,* tr. R. M. BRACKET (Westminster, Md. 1954). D. F. SWENSON, *Something about Kierkegaard,* ed. L. M. SWENSON (rev. and enl. Minneapolis 1945). E. HIRSCH, *Kierkegaard-Studien,* 2 v. (Gütersloh 1933). W. RUTTENBECK, *Sören Kierkegaard: Der Christliche Denker und sein Werk* (Berlin 1929). P. MESNARD, *Le Vrai visage de Kierkegaard* (Paris 1948). J. WAHL, *Études Kierkegaardiennes* (2d ed. Paris 1949).

[L. DUPRÉ]

KILDARE, ABBEY OF

Former Irish monastery in Kildare, County Kildare (*Cill Dara,* "the church of the oak tree"), Ireland. Its foundation by St. BRIGID dates probably from the transition period between the death of St. Patrick and the rise of the great monastic founders, that is, *c.* 460 to 520. Church organization was still incomplete, and Brigid found herself the most important Christian personage in a large part of the province of Leinster. To provide for the spiritual needs of the people, she induced the bishop, Conlaed, to leave his hermit life and take up residence in a house beside the convent for women she had already founded at Kildare. This was the beginning of the double MONASTERY there, the only one of its kind in Ireland. Brigid and her successors as abbess of Kildare exercised jurisdiction over the faithful in the neighborhood with the approval of the successors of St. Patrick in ARMAGH. The long line of abbesses continued to 1171; a corresponding list of abbots, bishops, and other officials shows that the men's monastery retained its identity into the 12th century. When Kildare became an Episcopal see in 1111, it gradually shed its earlier monastic character. GIRALDUS CAMBRENSIS speaks of the Book of Kildare, which seems to have compared with the Book of KELLS, but this is lost. Only the monastic round tower remains of the abbey buildings.

Bibliography: J. F. KENNEY, *The Sources for the Early History of Ireland,* v. 1, *Ecclesiastical* (New York 1929) 356–364. *The Annals of Ulster,* ed. and tr. W. M. HENNESSY and B. MACCARTHY, 4 v. (Dublin 1887–1909). *Chronicum Scotorum,* ed. W. M. HENNESSY (Rerum Britannicarum medii aevi scriptores 46; 1866). *The Annals of Inisfallen,* ed. and tr. S. MACAIRT (Dublin 1951). *Annals of the Four Masters,* ed. and tr. J. O'DONOVAN, 7 v. (2d ed. Dublin 1856).

[J. RYAN]

KILIAN OF AUBIGNY, ST.

Irish hermit in France; d. 670. Little is known of the career of Kilian (originally Chillen). He is said to have been returning from a pilgrimage to Rome when he met St. FARO, bishop of Meaux, who found him a site for a hermitage at Aubigny near Arras. Here Kilian spent the rest of his life and was later venerated as a saint. St. Faro was also responsible for settling the Irish St. FIACRE in the same part of France.

Feast: Nov. 13.

Bibliography: J. F. KENNEY, *The Sources for the Early History of Ireland: v.1, Ecclesiastical* (New York 1929) 1:492–493. L. GOUGAUD, *Les Saints irlandais hors d'Irlande* (Louvain 1936). A. BUTLER, *The Lives of the Saints,* rev. ed. H. THURSTON and D. ATTWATER, 4 v. (New York 1956) 4:330–331. T. Ó FIAICH, *Gaelscrinte i gCein* (Dublin 1960) 52–53.

[D. D. C. POCHIN MOULD]

KILIAN OF WÜRZBURG, ST.

Bishop and martyr; b. Ireland (according to strong local tradition, at Mullagh, County Cavan), *c.* 640; d. Würzburg, Germany, July 8, 689. According to the older and more trustworthy *passio* Kilian (or Chilianus) was already a bishop when he left Ireland with 11 companions and reached the residence of the pagan Thuringian duke, Gozbert, at Würzburg. Having decided to evangelize this region, he reputedly traveled to Rome for papal approval in the autumn of 686. The account of this journey and of his meeting with Pope CONON is certainly unhistorical. He converted many in Franconia and Thuringia, including Duke Gozbert, whom he persuaded to separate from Geilana, his brother's widow. In revenge Geilana had Kilian murdered along with two of his fellow missionaries, the priest Coloman (Kolonat) and the deacon Totnan. Their relics were solemnly transferred by BURCHARD, first bishop of Würzburg, to the new cathedral on July 8, 752, and are now enshrined in the Neumünster, erected over the spot where, according to tradition, the martyrdom took place. Much controversy has centered on the dating and reliability of the *Passio Prima* and *Secunda* that deal with the saint's life, but A. Bigelmair dates the *Passio Prima* to 752 and accepts it as historical, though with an accretion of legend.

Feast: July 8.

Bibliography: **Sources.** *Monumenta Germaniae Historica, Scriptores rerum Merovingicarum* (Berlin 1826–) 5:711–728. *Acta Sanctorum,* July, 2:599–619. J. MABILLON, *Acta sanctorum ordinis S. Benedicti,* 9 v. (Paris 1668–1701) 2:951–953. **Literature.** N. MOORE, *The Dictionary of National Biography from the Earliest Times to 1900,* 63 v. (London 1885–1900) 4:363–364. F. EMMERICH, *Der heilige Kilian, Regionarbischof und Märtyrer, historisch-kritisch dargestellt* (Würzburg 1896). A. BIGELMAIR, "Die Gründung des Bistums Würzburg," *Würzburger Diözesangeschichtsblätter,* 2 (1934) 1–18; "Die Passio des heiligen Kilian und seiner Gefährten," *Herbipolis jubilans: 1200 Jahre Bistum Würzburg* (Würzburg 1952) 1–25. J. DIENEMANN, *Der Kult des heiligen Kilian im 8. und 9. Jahrhundert* (Würzburg 1955). A. GWYNN, "New Light on St. Kilian," *The Irish Ecclesiastical Record,* 88 (1957) 1–16. K. FIRSCHING, *Die deutschen Bearbeitungen der Kilianslegende unter besonderer Berücksichtigung deutscher Legendarhandschriften des Mittelalters* (Würzburg 1973). W. DETTELBACHER, *Die Kilianimesse zu Würzburg* (Würzburg 1977), cult. L. K. WALTER, *St. Kilian: Schrifttumsverzeichnis zu Martyrium und Kult der Frankenapostel und zur Gründung des Bistums Würzburg* (Würzburg 1989). F.-L. GANZ, *Dich loben, dir danken—: 1300 Jahre Mission und Martyrium der Frankenapostel Kilian, Kolonat und Totnan: das Buch der Diözese Würzburg zum Jubiläumsjahr* (Würzburg 1990).

[T. Ó FIAICH]

KILMARTIN, EDWARD J.

Jesuit priest and theologian of liturgy; b. Portland, Maine, Aug. 31, 1923; d. Boston, Massachusetts, June 16, 1994. Kilmartin entered the Society of Jesus in 1941 and was ordained in 1954. Having prepared to teach petroleum engineering in the ill-fated Jesuit mission in Baghdad, Iraq, Kilmartin next earned a doctorate in dogmatic and ecumenical theology under J. Witte at the Gregorian in Rome (1958). He was recalled suddenly to the Jesuit theologate in Weston, Massachusetts, to teach a course in sacramental theology, where he collaborated on *New Testament Abstracts.* This originally temporary assignment led to 19 years' teaching of historical-systematic theology specializing in sacraments—the final nine after Kilmartin relocated to Cambridge, Massachusetts. From 1975 to 1985 Kilmartin directed the doctoral program in Liturgical Studies at the University of Notre Dame. In 1985 he was appointed professor ordinarius of liturgy at the Pontifical Oriental Institute, Rome, and named professor emeritus in 1994. Summer-school teaching at Marquette, San Francisco, Notre Dame, and Creighton universities and in Australia acquainted numerous students with his theological method.

The work of the WORLD COUNCIL OF CHURCHES on eschatology and baptism, eucharist, and ministry provided a special focus at the beginning and near the end of Kilmartin's theological career. At Notre Dame he directed dissertations in Protestant and Catholic liturgical traditions. As member for 19 years of the Roman Catholic-Orthodox dialogue in the United States (for 13 years executive secretary) and active participant in the Oriental-Orthodox dialogue over the same period, he pursued a lifelong interest in the traditions of the undivided churches of the first millennium with a view to recovering common perspectives. Kilmartin was a principal drafter of the Roman Catholic response to the Lima Document, above all the section on eucharist, for the Secretariat for Promoting Christian Unity. He was also consulted by the Congregation for the Doctrine of the Faith.

Kilmartin's thought was stimulated by key themes of European theology: Odo CASEL's *Mysterientheologie,* anamnesis, the active presence of Christ, and pneumatology. He rooted his theology in New Testament and early liturgical sources, painstakingly analyzing them and integrating the gains made especially by the Germans J. Betz, K. RAHNER, A. Häussling, L. Lies, and H. B. Meyer.

Christian Liturgy (1988), his major work, presents a post-Rahnerian systematic theology of liturgy for which D. Coffey provides the trinitarian model. His work established parameters for and a method of systematic theology of liturgy in which the response of faith and the sacraments are brought back in all respects to their trinitarian foundations.

The major contributions of Kilmartin include: an articulation of liturgy's relation to the Trinity and the consequences of the personal missions of Christ and the Holy Spirit; a eucharistic theology that, inspired by early church and patristic sources, relates this data to contemporary confessional and ecumenical questions; and a critical analysis of Christomonistic theologies of eucharist and ministry for their failure to incorporate pneumatology and ecclesiology. Up to his death he investigated areas where official Roman theology could fruitfully dialogue with Eastern and Western liturgical traditions.

Bibliography: A complete bibliography and curriculum vitae is found in M. A. FAHEY, ''In Memoriam: Edward J. Kilmartin, SJ (1923–1994),'' *Orientalia Christiana periodica* 61 (January 1995). On ecumenism and ecclesiology: ''Reception in History: An Ecclesiological Phenomenon and Its Significance,'' *Journal of Ecumenical Studies* 21 (1984) 34–54; *Culture and the Praying Church: The Particular Liturgy of the Individual Church* (Ottawa 1990). On eucharist and ministry: ''Apostolic Office: Sacrament of Christ,'' *Theological Studies* 36 (1975) 243–64; ''Ecclesiastical Office, Power and Spirit,'' *Proceedings of the Catholic Theological Society* 37 (1982) 98–108; ''The Active Role of Christ and the Holy Spirit in the Sanctification of the Eucharistic Elements,'' *Theological Studies* 45 (1984) 225–53; ''A Catholic Response to Lima 1982,'' *One in Christ* 21 (1985) 204–16; ''The Official Vatican Response to BEM: Eucharist,'' *Ecumenical Trends* 17 (1988) 37–40; ''The Catholic Tradition of Eucharistic Theology: Towards the Third Millennium,'' *Theological Studies* 55 (1994) 405–57. On systematic theology of liturgy: *Christian Liturgy: Theology and Practice. Part I: Systematic Theology of Liturgy* (Kansas City, Mo. 1988); ''Sacraments as Liturgy of the Church,'' *Theological Studies* 50 (1989) 527–47.

[M. M. SCHAEFER]

KILWINNING, ABBEY OF

Former Benedictine monastery of the Tironian congregation (*see* TIRON, ABBEY OF) at Kilwinning, Ayrshire, within the Diocese of Galloway, Scotland. The identity of the founder and the date of foundation remain obscure. Kilwinning (Kylwynnyn and other variants) was long thought to have been founded by Hugh de Moreville in 1140, but recent evidence points rather to his son Richard's having founded it sometime between 1162 and 1189. Records mention the church of St. Vinin or Wynnin there in 1184 (Kilwinning itself meaning the ''cell or church of Wynnin''), but the first reference to it as an abbey is dated 1202–07. Kilwinning, a daughterhouse of

Kelso Abbey, was well endowed by private and royal benefactors, and judging by its fine remains, must have been one of the most graceful and impressive abbeys in the country by the mid-13th century. It was largely destroyed by Reformers in 1561 and was erected into a free barony for William Melville in 1592. It is now a ruin.

Bibliography: W. MACLEOD, ''Collections Towards a History of the Abbey of K.,'' *Archaeological and Historical Collections Relating to the Counties of Ayr and Wigton,* 1 (1878) 115–222. D. E. EASSON, *Medieval Religious Houses: Scotland* (London 1957) 59. G. W. S. BARROW, ''From Queen Margaret to David I: Benedictines and Tironians,'' *Innes Review,* 11 (1960) 22–38.

[L. MACFARLANE]

KINDEKENS, PETER

Founder of the American College of Louvain; b. Denderwindeke, Belgium, date unknown; d. Detroit, Michigan, March 23, 1873. Before his ordination on Sept. 24, 1842, he offered his services to bishop Peter Paul LEFEVERE of Detroit. On coming to the United States, he became Lefevere's vicar-general. He served as director of St. Thomas Seminary, Detroit, which opened in 1846, and designed the new cathedral in Detroit, begun in 1845. In 1856 he was sent to Rome to represent Lefevere in a controversy with the REDEMPTORISTS of the diocese. There, on behalf of archbishop Francis P. KENRICK of Baltimore, Maryland, Kindekens inquired into the possibility of establishing an American College at Rome. Conditions there were unfavorable, but it seemed possible to found a similar college at Louvain, Belgium. On his return to America, Kindekens sent a circular letter to the bishops of the United States proposing this idea. Bishops Lefevere and Martin J. SPALDING adopted the project, and Kindekens was sent to Louvain early in 1857 to establish the college. During his two and a half years as rector, he purchased a house and property, opened the seminary, and obtained financial support from Belgian and German donations. He admitted at least 30 students and sent nine to the missions of America, most of them to the Diocese of Detroit. In 1860 he surrendered his office to John DE NEVE and returned to his duties as vicar-general of Detroit.

Bibliography: J. D. SAUTER, *The American College of Louvain, 1857–1898* (Louvain 1959). G. PARE, *The Catholic Church in Detroit, 1701–1888* (Detroit 1951).

[J. D. SAUTER]

AL-KINDĪ, 'ABD AL-MASIḤ

Supposed author of what is now being recognized as a pseudonymous apology in Arabic for the Christian faith. The work purports to be the contemporary record of a controversy held in 819 before the Caliph al-Ma'mūn on the relative worth of Christianity and Islam.

The parties to the controversy are a Muslim, 'Abdallah ibn Ismā'īl al-Hāshimī, and a Nestorian Christian, al-Kindī. The bulk of the work is al-Kindī's reply to a letter of the former. Al-Hāshimī in this letter, after showing a surprising familiarity with a number of Christian practices and persons and revealing a preference for Nestorians over Jacobites, appeals to his Christian friend to embrace ISLAM. Specifically he urges on him: prayer to the one God after the example of Abraham "the first Muslim," confession of MUḤAMMAD's prophetic dignity, observance of RAMADAN, the pilgrimage to MECCA, the holy war, belief in the general resurrection, abandonment of the Trinity and Holy Cross, and the attractiveness of the Moslem moral code and its effective sanctions.

Al-Kindī deals with these items in detail. He denies that Abraham was a Muslim. From being a pagan, he became, through God's intervention, a believer long before Muḥammad. It has been noticed that al-Kindī's treatment of God's unicity draws largely and even verbatim on the Jacobite Abu Ra'ita.

Al-Kindī treats Muḥammad's prophetic dignity with harshness and biting irony. He contrasts unfavorably the holy war and the wars of the Old Testament; Muḥammad's teaching of mercy and his practice of force and immorality. He charges that Muḥammad lacks true prophecy and miracles and that the spread of Islam has the marks of falsehood.

In discussing the QUR'ĀN he makes bold to distinguish three kinds of law: divine, brought by Christ; natural or rational, brought by Moses; and Satanic, brought by Muḥammad. In this context he develops what has been called the first sketch of a critical history of the Qur'ānic text. He accepts none of the claims made for the book—its miraculous language and probative worth—and is indignant at God's being made responsible for Muḥammad's decisions and practices.

The pilgrimage to Mecca is classed with pagan ceremonies and contrasted with prayer in the Christian holy places. Circumcision is denied a religious character. The holy war is held to be opposed to Christian love. On these and similar grounds al-Kindī rejects al-Hāshimī's appeal and makes his own counterappeal.

The work is probably later than 819. Evidence supporting this includes the use of Abu Ra'ita (third decade of the 9th century); the argument against Muḥammad's name being on the throne of God suggests a controversy in the days of al-Ṭabarī (d. 923); and parallels with a work of Ibn al-Rāwandī (d. 910). It would seem then to belong to the 10th century. The pseudonymous character would explain how it was tolerated. The preference for Nestorians suggests a Nestorian author. Known and used by medieval Europeans, it was first printed in London in 1880.

Bibliography: L. MASSIGNON, *Encyclopedia of Islam*, ed. M. T. HOUTSMA et al., 4 v. (Leiden 1913–38) 2:1080. G. GRAF, *Geschichte der christlichen arabischen Literatur*, 5 v. (Vatican City 1944-53); *Studi e Testi* 118, 133, 146, 147, 172 2:135–145.

[J. A. DEVENNY]

AL-KINDĪ, ABŪ YŪSUF YA'QŪB IBN-ISḤĀQ

First outstanding scholar of Arab descent, hence his honorific title *Faylasüf al-'Arab* (the philosopher of the Arabs). His surname indicates descent from the noble South Arabian tribe of Kindah.

Life. Al-Kindī was born about 801 in al-Kūfah (Kufa), Iraq, where his father was a governor under the 'Abbāsids. He studied at Baghdad, where he flourished and died about 873. As a young man he held positions in the courts of al-Ma'mūm (813–833) and al-Mu'taṣim (833–842), whose son he tutored. He dedicated some of his works to his pupil. Baghdad was then not only the political but also the intellectual capital of Islam. It was especially noted as a center of translation from Hindu through Persian, and from Greek through Syriac into Arabic. Al-Kindī himself is credited with translating, among other Greek works, those of Ptolemy; but recent research seems to indicate that he, whose philosophical vocabulary shows many Syriacisms, depended upon translations made by Christian Syrians, whose Arabic he may have revised. The philosophy he developed was eclectic, concerned primarily with reconciling and combining—in Neoplatonic fashion—the views of Plato and Aristotle. He followed the Neo-Pythagoreans in attaching mystic values to numerals, making mathematics the basis of science, especially of physics, and in not excluding medicine. In his moral philosophy he shared with his contemporaries, the Mu'tazilites, the views of Socrates on virtuous living and the deprecation of luxury.

Al-Kindī is ranked among the 12 greatest minds of Islam, but he was more encyclopedic than creative. His industry and literary activity contributed to the early diffusion of Greek learning and Persian-Indian science. Hardly a known scientific field—mathematics, physics, optics, medicine, astrology, geography, music, logic, poetry, or theology—was alien to his pen.

Works. For the celebration of al-Kindī's 1,000th anniversary in Baghdad (1962), Richard J. McCarthy, SJ, published a list of 361 titles attributed to him [*Al-Taṣānīf al-Mansūbah ilā Faylasūf al-'Arab* (Baghdad 1962)]. The list begins with a work on philosophy and ends with one on swords. A short treatise by him on the manufacture of swords was published on the same occasion ['*Aml al-Suyūf* (Baghdad 1962)]. One treatise in the list deals with the art of cooking. In the titles, the names of Socrates, Aristotle, Plato, Euclid, Archimedes, Ptolemy, Hippocrates, and Galen appear, some more than once. Most of the works are treatises, some still in manuscript form, others now lost; a few may be spurious. Those extant in Latin are perhaps more numerous than those in Arabic. Alkindus, as he was designated in Latin, was well known to scholars throughout medieval times, but in the Arab world his influence waned after the 10th century. He was eclipsed by other Arab-Muslim philosophers both in Spain and in the East. Perhaps some of his books were lost when the conservative Caliph al-Mutawakkil (847–861) restored orthodoxy, disgraced and humiliated him, and seized his library. It was to the school of translators that flourished in Toledo under the patronage of Archbishop Raymond that the Latin world owed its knowledge of this Arab philosopher. GERARD OF CREMONA (d. 1187) was especially interested in al-Kindī, as was John of Seville (Joannes Hispalensis), a Christian convert from Judaism. At least some of the medical translations by Gerard of Cremona were included in the *De medicinarum compositarum gradibus investigandis,* published at Strassburg in 1531. In it al-Kindī propounds the extraordinary theory that mathematics is the basis of composite medicine and that doxology is a mathematical art. Alchemy, then considered an important science, was deprecated by al-Kindī. He did not believe it possible to transform base metal into gold or silver (the chief preoccupation of alchemists in his day). In Arabic the first large collection of al-Kindī [*Rasā'il al-Kindī al-Falsafīyah,* ed. Muḥammad 'Abd-al-Wahhāb abū-Rīdah (Cairo)], containing 25 philosophical treatises, was not published until 1950–53.

One of al-Kindī's principal works dealt with geometrical and physiological aspects. Based on the optics of Euclid in Theon's recension, it was rendered into Latin as *De aspectibus* and was widely used in both Latin and Arabic until superseded by the greater work of Alhazen (Ibn al-Haytham). In his treatise, al-Kindī discusses the passage of light in a straight line and the process of vision directly, or through a looking glass. He recognizes that while in smell, taste, hearing, and touch the sense receives impressions from outside objects, in the case of vision the sense grasps its object instantaneously and in an active manner. In a treatise, extant in Latin, on the blue color of the sky he recognizes the effect of atoms of dust and vapor.

The earliest Arabic works on music that have come down to us are the five compiled by al-Kindī. They contain a determination of pitch and a description of rhythm (*īqā'*) as a constituent of Arab music, indicating a knowledge of measured song, or mensural music, in Islam centuries earlier than in Christendom. In music, which he renders as *mūsīqī* in Arabic, he was clearly indebted to the Greeks, as he was in other fields, such as astronomy. Although celebrated as an astrologer, he dealt with exact astronomical measurements.

Primarily a natural philosopher, al-Kindī devoted works to the soul (*nafs*), the intelligence ('*aql*), and to the relationship of the two. To him the world as a whole was the work of an external force, the divine intelligence. Between God and the world of matter lay the world of the soul. The human soul is an emanation of this world soul. Purely Islamic issues did not escape his attention. In one treatise he takes up the question of *tawḥīd,* the dogma of the unity of God, and in other works he attempts to refute both dualists and disbelievers.

Bibliography: T. J. DE BOER, *The History of Philosophy in Islam,* tr. E. R. JONES (London 1903). C. BROCKELMANN, *Geschichte der arabischen Literatur,* 2 v. (2d ed. Leiden 1943–49) 1:230–231. G. SARTON, *Introduction to the History of Science,* 3 v. in 5 (Baltimore 1927–48) 1:559–560. A. NAGY, *Die philosophischen Abhandlungen des Ja'qūb ben Ishāq al-Kindī Beiträge zur Geschichte der Philosophie und Theologie des Mittelalters* 2.5 (1897).

[P. K. HITTI]

KINDNESS

Gentleness, compassion, beneficence, the opposite of malevolence. Originally it seems to have indicated an attitude likely to be found among persons related by blood, but the modern designation is broader. Moreover, family affection, when too exclusive, can become a vice. In any case, the term came to be applied generally to an attitude and behavior toward people at large.

Though some elements of this human characteristic found favor with the Greek moralists, its present ethical position flows quite directly from OT and NT sources. It is considered as a divine attribute (1 Sm 20.14). In the teachings of Jesus the kind and forgiving spirit is made a condition of receiving divine mercy and forgiveness. Kindness in the sense of love is extended even to enemies (Mt 5.44). Just as in OT times there prevailed a special law of HOSPITALITY for strangers and travelers, so too in the early Christian Church hospitality and kindness to strangers was held in esteem. In fact, St. Paul made it one of the qualifications for selection for the episcopacy (1 Tm 2.2).

In describing virtuous actions St. Paul was frequently given to an abundant use of synonyms and to redundancy. Thus in speaking of the fruits of the Spirit (Gal 5.22–23), he sometimes used kindness in place of benignity or meekness. Again in 1 Cor 13.4 he lists kindness as one of the many attributes of the charitable man. Thus, for the moralist, kindness is considered in relationship with charity.

Since charity is love, it impels one to will the good of others in an efficacious manner. Hence, any general activity in which charity expands into practical exercise is kindness. Normally such activity takes into consideration the spiritual and bodily needs of neighbors. Thus, kindness extends to sinners who have a special claim to those gestures of compassion that prove helpful in restoring them to the community of saints. Such gestures are seldom misunderstood as approbation of sin itself. (*See* CHARITY.)

Bibliography: B. OLIVIER, "Charity," *The Virtues and States of Life*, ed. A. M. HENRY, tr. R. J. OLSON and G. T. LENNON (*Theology Library* 4; Chicago 1957) 127–208. G. KELLY, "On the Duty of Loving the Neighbor, Especially Enemies," *Review for Religious* 7 (1948) 299–312.

[W. HERBST]

KINGA, ST.

Also known as Cunegund or Kunigunde, princess (sometimes referred to as "queen") of Malopolska (Little Poland), widow, consecrated virgin of the Poor Clares; b. 1224, Hungary; d. July 24, 1292, Stary Sacz (also Sandeck, Sandecz, or Sandez), Poland.

Kinga was the daughter of King Bela IV of Hungary, Arpad Dynasty, and his wife, Maria, daughter of Emperor Theodorus Lascharis of Constantinople. Among the religious luminaries of her lineage are her sisters, Saint MARGARET OF HUNGARY (d. 1270) and Blessed Jolenta of Hungary (d. 1299); her great-aunt, Queen Saint HEDWIG of Silesia (d. 1243); her aunt, Saint ELIZABETH OF HUNGARY (1207–31); her uncle, Blessed Ludwig IV of Thuringia (1200–27); and her cousin, Blessed Gertrude of Altenberg (d. 1297).

Kinga's position required her to marry (1239) Boleslaw II, sovereign of Lesser Poland (Krakow, Sandomire, and Lublin). Tradition relates that by mutual consent the couple pledged vows of perpetual continence before their bishop and their marriage was never consummated. Throughout her married life, Kinga continued to engage in prayer, mortification, and personal charity. Her spirituality was influenced by her contemporaries, the Dominican Saint HYACINTH (d. 1257) and the Blesseds, Bronisława (d. 1259), Sadok (d. 1260), and Salomea (d. 1268). At Boleslaw's death (1279), Kinga sold her possessions to relieve the poor, then took the veil at Stary Sacz Abbey, which she had built for the Poor Clares.

While Pope Alexander VIII approved Kinga's cultus as a beata in 1690 and she was declared patroness of Poland and Lithuania in 1695, her cause for canonization required reintroduction and her heroic virtues were declared on July 3, 1998. She was canonized by Pope John Paul II at Stary Sacz, Poland, June 16, 1999.

Feast: July 24 (Poland); July 27 (Franciscans).

Bibliography: *Blogoslawiona Kinga: zyciorys, zbiór modlitw*, ed. J. R. BAR (Warsaw 1985). R. PICO, *Vita della venerabile Cunegonde, reina di Polonia*, based on data collected by A. BZOWSKI (Rome 1633). *Vita sanctae Kyngae ducissae Cracoviensis* (Tarnów 1997).

[K. I. RABENSTEIN]

KINGDOM OF GOD

The biblical expressions "Kingdom of God," "Kingdom of Christ," and "Kingdom of Heaven," all roughly equivalent, refer to three different aspects of the divine lordship or sovereignty over creation. Greek *basileia*, Hebrew *malkuth*, Aramaic *malkutha*, all connote these three aspects: a territory or space governed by a king (= kingdom); a king's activity or time of governing (= reign); the office or function of being a king (= kingship). Because this biblical formula is central to Jesus' way of conceiving the relationship between God and the world, God and humankind, it has become a major theme of biblical theology.

The Kingdom of God in the Scriptures

Old Testament. The formula "Kingdom of God" only begins to emerge in the later books of the Hebrew Bible, for example, 1 Chronicles 28:5 (*malkut Yhwh*) and 2 Chronicles 13:8 (*mamlechet Yhwh*); confer, Psalms 45:6–7; 22:28; 145:11–13; Wisdom 10:10. It becomes the dominant theme of the book of Daniel, the apocalyptic book par excellence of the OT, where almost every chapter culminates in its proclamation. The theme is also present in the literature of the Qumran sect, particularly in the War Scroll, which shares the same apocalyptic outlook as Daniel. In Daniel, the two most important chapters for our purposes are 2 (the dream of the statue of four metals plus clay) and 4 (the night vision of the four beasts). The four metals and four beasts represent four world empires or kingdoms, followed by the kingdom of God. These chapters thus represent a theological interpretation of world history. The crucial verses for Jesus and the NT are Daniel 7:13–14: "I saw one like a son of man coming with the clouds of heaven. And he came to the Ancient of Days and was presented before him. To him was given dominion and glory and kingship [= kingdom], that all peoples . . . should serve him.'' This scene takes place in heaven and presents a transfer of royal power from a senior god to a younger god whose kingdom will be universal. This text is a basis for the NT doctrines of the kingdom, Christology, the Trinity and the Church (= ''the saints of the Most High'' in Daniel 7:18, 22, 27), besides giving a theology of history and a foundation for Christian involvement in the struggles for greater social justice and peace. Its importance can thus hardly be overestimated. This list of theological topics shows also the implications of the kingdom theme. In this sense apocalyptic is ''the mother of Christian theology'' (Käsemann).

In the earlier periods of Israelite literature the formula ''Kingdom of God'' is not common. Much is uncertain in the conceptual development, but one thing is clear: ''Kingdom of God'' grows out of the older idea that ''God is king'' (*Yahwe malach*). This older formula can have an anti-monarchical or a pro-monarchical sense. God, and no man, is king: this is the old theocratic notion found in Judges 8:22–23; 9:1–5, esp. vv. 7–15 (M. Buber). Or: God is king, and David is his earthly representative. The divine king can also fit into the priestly theology of a beneficent creation. Yet the expression is hardly present in the Pentateuch (Ex 15:18; Nm 23:21; perhaps Dt 33:5, all poetic texts). God as king takes the side of the hungry, prisoners, the oppressed, the blind, resident aliens, widows and orphans (Ps 146). He protects those without other social protection. As such, he is intended as the model for earthly kings. The prophet Ezekiel takes a radical turn: God as king punishes his disobedient people by sending them into exile (Ez 20, esp. v. 33). The Deuteronomistic historian is generally critical of the Israelite monarchy (1 Sm 8 and 12). Deutero-Isaiah softens these harsh views: God will now lead his people back to the land, in a new exodus (Is 4:2; 43:14–15, 25; 52:7–8). The disappointments after the return, especially the Seleucid persecutions and its martyrs, led religious reflection to a more radical apocalyptic and messianic hope for a new divine intervention that would replace the world empires and Judea's Temple state. This hope for a definitive reign of God on earth is expressed in Daniel (see above), but also in many pseudepigrapha (Assumption of Moses, Ethiopic Enoch), as well as much of the Qumran literature, for example, the War Scroll, where the mention of Michael shows the link with Daniel.

The kingdom of God and the Messiah are strongly present in rabbinic literature and the targums, written down one or several centuries after the close of the NT canon but often containing traditions current in earlier times. In this literature it is customary to refer to the kingdom as the kingdom of heaven (lit. ''of the heavens'').

This usage is also present in Matthew. ''Heaven'' here functions as a reverent circumlocution for God. It is a mistake to identify this variant formula with heaven, and thereby cut off any connection between the kingdom hope and this earth, an error made by several church fathers (see below).

New Testament. During the 20th century it was common to say that the announcement of the near coming of the kingdom of God was the central message of the preaching of Jesus. This view has been challenged by the ''third quest'' for the historical Jesus (M. Borg, J. D. Crossan, B. L. Mack), which classifies Jesus as a saintly sage rather than as an apocalyptic prophet. But, based on our earliest sources, Q and Mark (not the Gospel of Thomas), it will be the view held in this article.

Jesus' public ministry begins with this announcement (Mk 1:15; Mt 4:17; Luke 4:18–19, citing Is 61:1–2, gives a good idea of the social justice implications of the kingdom, without employing the term; the same may be said for Rv 5:12). The kingdom is also to be the main message of the preaching of Jesus' disciples: Mt 10:7 par Lk 9:2 (Q). The prayer Jesus taught his disciples has as its center the petition that ''thy kingdom come . . . to earth, as it [already] is in heaven'' (Mt 6:20; Lk 11:2 [Q]). This prayer implies that the kingdom is *not yet* fully realized on earth; it is to come in its fullness in the near future, as a divine gift. The parallel clause ''thy will be done'' suggest that the kingdom means that God's will be done. This moral content is then clarified as essentially justice (Mt 6:33). The petition also implies that the kingdom already exists in its fullness in heaven, even if not yet on earth. Still, in the healing and exorcizing ministry of Jesus the kingdom is already present (Matthew 12:28; Luke 11:20 [Q]), in sign, by anticipation, in germ. The kingdom is the content and purpose of the parables (Mk 4:11, 26, 30). It is the goal of death and the motive for ethical practice (Mk 9:1, 47). It must be approached as a child and is far from the rich (Mk 10:14–15, 23–25). One who knows that the greatest commandment is to love God and neighbor is near to it (Mk 12:34). The eucharistic meal anticipates it and looks forward to it (Mk 14:25). The man who takes care of the body of Jesus is one who seeks the kingdom (Mk 15:43). Thus the kingdom of God is the ultimate horizon of the preaching of Jesus, the highest value, the goal of history.

The two later synoptic gospels add some further developments. Matthew's gospel can be analyzed in such a way that from start to finish its second major theme (alongside the principal theme, the story of Jesus) is the kingdom of God. Even the infancy gospel becomes a mortal contest between two rival claimants to the throne. Matthew contributes two special emphases. The first is the close connection between eschatology (kingdom) and ethics. Entrance or admission to the kingdom becomes the reward for ethical action, the struggle for social justice. The kingdom is the first and last reward in the beatitudes (Mt 5:3, 10). The point is most powerfully made in the last judgment scene, proper to Matthew (25:31–46, esp. vv. 34–36). The second special emphasis is the relation between the kingdom and the church. Matthew 16:17–19 asserts that there is a connection between kingdom and church, that leaders in the church hold the keys to the kingdom, and, implicitly, that our relationship to the leaders has some bearing on our eternal destiny. The church is not the kingdom, nor is it heaven, but it is the path to them—that is, a gathering of those who look forward to them. The church is a sign of the kingdom's partial presence; she is at the service of the kingdom, its proto-sacrament.

Luke's contributions to the kingdom theme are: (1) the description in 4:16–30; (2) the kingdom as the object of preaching (Lk 4:43; 8:1; 9:2, 11, 60, 62; 16:16; Acts 8:12; 19:8; 20:25; 28:23, 31); (3) the mysterious *entos hymon* of Luke 17:21b. Today this is usually translated: "The kingdom of God is in the midst of you," but in the past it was translated as "within you." This older translation ignores the context and the plural pronoun, and was sometimes used to make the kingdom a purely, private, interior, mystical affair, in the spirit of John 14:23. (4) The book of Acts begins (1:3, 6) and ends (28:31) with the kingdom hope; as the church waits for it, she is consoled by the gift of the Holy Spirit (1:8; 2:1–4).

Both Paul and the book of Revelation present a kind of timetable of the last events (1 Thes 4:13–18; 1 Cor 15:20–28; Rv 20:1–10); these schedules in large measure are harmonious, but only Revelation 20 gives a figure for the duration of the kingdom in its fullness on earth: a thousand years, the millennium. This figure must be understood as symbolic, meaning "a long time." 2 Peter (3:1–14) tries to keep up the hope for the kingdom in view of its delay. The Gospel of John on the whole represents a shift away from the hope for the kingdom to come to earth. It displaces Christian hope to a hope for eternal life, already now on earth, and then in heaven. But it still maintains a hope for the return of Christ to earth (14:3, 18, 28), and mentions the kingdom explicitly in 3:3, 5, and in 18:36. This last verse has often been badly translated, but the New Revised Standard Version corrects the errors: the kingdom does not originate on earth, but it is intended to come here.

Summarizing the biblical message, we may say that the kingdom is a (1) social, (2) political, (3) personal, (4) universal, (5) divine gift to redeemed humanity.

The Kingdom of God in Church History

Church fathers. There are four main currents of interpretation of the kingdom of God in the patristic period. (1) The *apocalyptic* or eschatological interpretation, the only one exegetically defensible, continues in the first centuries and culminates in St. Irenaeus. Its features have already been described in the biblical section above. (2) The *spiritual-mystical* current begins with Origen. It identifies the kingdom either with heaven, or with Christ himself, or with the immortality of the soul, or with grace and charity in the soul. (3) The *political* current begins when the persecution of Christians by the Roman empire ceases, and the emperor Constantine refounds the empire as Christian (312). The theologian Eusebius of Caesarea saw this surprising shift as a fulfillment of biblical prophecy. For him the empire had become the kingdom of God on earth, the emperor was the Son of man, and he had the right to govern not only the state but also the church (caesaropapism). This view prevailed in the eastern or Byzantine empire till 1453. After that, its claims passed to the czars of Moscow. The western empire was revitalized in 800 with Charlemagne and continued till 1806, in frequent tension with papal claims. The imperial or political model continued in central Europe in various guises until 1918, and took a brief (1933–1945) demonic form in Hitler's Third Reich. Similar ideas were present in other parts of Europe (England, France) and spread to the new world (for example, America as redeemer nation). Military religious orders like the Knights of Malta, born during the crusades, symbolize this model inside the Church today. (4) About a century after Eusebius, St. Augustine developed the ecclesial model for interpreting the kingdom of God. On this view, the kingdom is found already now imperfectly in the church on earth, and will be found perfectly in the future in heaven. This concept was later expanded to reinforce papal claims to superiority over the emperors. Although biblically weak, this view at least helped preserve the religious character of the concept.

Medieval period. In the middle ages, these four lines of interpretation continued to compete with one another. The kingdom ceased to be a central object of reflection for the great scholastic theologians except in connection with the ideas of Joachim of Fiore. In meditating on the scriptures, he arrived at the idea of a history of salvation in three states or ages: the state of the Father (OT); the state of the Son (NT); and the state of the Holy Spirit in the future, when all God's people would be contemplatives under an angelic pope. Joachim's ideas were radicalized by Franciscan Spirituals, notably Gerard of Borgo San Donnino. Saints Bonaventure and Thomas Aquinas both attacked this challenge to the abiding form of the church. Joachim's ideas were later picked up by Protestant radical reformers and then by Romantic idealist philosophers like Schleiermacher and Schelling. The German Dominican school of Rhineland mysticism meanwhile developed the idea of the kingdom as identical with God.

Modern period. In the early modern period, the kingdom vision continued to inspire utopian political thinkers like St. Thomas More and Tommaso Campanella, scientists like Newton and Priestley, explorers like Columbus, and missionaries like A. Viera. Rationalist philosophy (Descartes to Hume) ignores it. The "hero" of the story of the kingdom in modern thought (up to 1892) is Immanuel Kant. In one of his last works, *Religion within the Limits of Reason Alone* (1793), he devotes a chapter to the kingdom as a model "ethical commonwealth." This he conceived as a kingdom of virtue. The tendency is moralizing, even Pelagian, as though we build the kingdom ourselves, rather than receive it as a gift of God. Kant's views had a great influence on what was later called "culture Protestantism" in Europe (Harnack) and on the Social Gospel movement in America (Rauschenbusch). More violent strains appeared in Marxism and in Nietzsche's aristocratic-radical reaction to Marx.

In 1892, a major rediscovery of the biblical message of the kingdom as a social gift of God occurred in a little book by Johannes Weiss, *Jesus' Proclamation of the Kingdom of God*. Weiss's break with Kantian moralism was aggressively promoted by Albert Schweitzer in his studies of Jesus and Paul. Catholic exegetes, at first blocked by censors, were able to receive this discovery starting with R. Schnackenburg's book of 1958, just in time to influence the second Vatican Council. This exegetical rediscovery was also exploited in systematic theology by Jürgen Moltmann, *Theology of Hope* (1964), and J. B. Metz. Latin American liberation theology is another application of kingdom-centered theology.

Because of the use of the kingdom theme in the current theological discussion of the possibility of salvation of believers in non-Christian religions (see esp. the work of Jacques Dupuis), recent magisterial documents have devoted increasing attention to it: *Redemptoris missio* (all of chap. 2), *Dialogue and Proclamation*, and *Dominus Iesus*. Biblically, there seems to be no justification for using the kingdom as a means to bypass the church in the present eon of salvation. But the precise contours of the kingdom as it will come in its fullness with the return of Christ in the future cannot now be exhaustively determined.

The theme of the kingdom of God, made central by Daniel and Jesus, offers a powerful vision of hope for the future of this world in God's plan of salvation, which intends to realize the values of justice, peace, love, and joy (Rom 14:17). It is one of the several master themes of the Bible. This theme is dangerous to the extent that we forget that it is *God's* kingdom, his to bring when he judges that we are ready to receive it. People of hope can only prepare the way of the Lord. The struggle for social justice, which the promise of the kingdom inspires, needs to be sustained by faith and prayer, by life in community and persevering study.

Bibliography: J. BRIGHT, *The Kingdom of God* (Nashville 1953). K. KOCH, *The Relevance of Apocalyptic* (London 1972). J. WEISS, *Jesus' Proclamation of the Kingdom of God* (Philadelphia 1971). R. SCHNACKENBURG, *God's Rule and Kingdom* (New York 1963). B. T. VIVIANO, *The Kingdom of God in History* (Wilmington 1988). J. FUELLENBACH, *The Kingdom of God* (Maryknoll 1995). J. RATZINGER, *The Theology of History in St. Bonaventure* (Chicago 1971).

[B. T. VIVIANO]

KINGS, BOOK(S) OF

Name and Division. In the Hebrew Bible, the books of 1–2 Kings are one continuous book, called simply "Kings." The ancient Greek translation, the Septuagint (LXX), split the text into two books, as it did as well with the preceding book, "Samuel." It then named the four resulting books 1–4 Kingdoms. The Vulgate, translated by Jerome in the fourth Christian century, followed the LXX, though it drew slightly closer to the Hebrew tradition by naming the books 1–4 Kings. Although the Protestant tradition moved even closer to the Hebrew by naming the books 1–2 Samuel and 1–2 Kings, Roman Catholic tradition retained the practice of the Vulgate until the mid-twentieth century. This resulted in the confusing situation of 1–2 Kings in Protestant translations being the same as 3–4 Kings in Roman Catholic versions. Since the encyclical *Divino Afflante Spiritu* (1943), however, when Pope Pius XII urged Roman Catholic biblical translators to base their work on the original language texts rather than on the Latin Vulgate, Roman Catholic Bibles, like Protestant ones, title the four books 1–2 Samuel and 1–2 Kings. The artificiality of the division between 1 and 2 Kings is nevertheless clear, since the last three verses of 1 Kings contain the formulaic introduction to the reign of Ahaziah, which is continued and completed in 2 Kings 1.

Content and Organization. The two Books of Kings tell the story of the Israelite monarchy from the accession of Solomon, son of David (around 960 B.C.), through the division of the single Davidic realm into the two kingdoms of Israel in the north and Judah in the south, to the destruction of both kingdoms: Israel fell to the Assyrians in 722 B.C., Judah to the Babylonians in 587 B.C.. A brief addendum tells of the release of Jehoiachin, exiled king of Judah, from Babylonian prison in 562 B.C. (2 Kgs 25:27–30). Coverage of this four-century period is not even. The narrative treats some decades very extensively (e.g., the forty-year reign of Solomon takes eleven chapters to recount) and other decades very briefly (e.g., the forty-one-year reign of Jeroboam II is summarized in seven verses). The overall arrangement of the books is roughly symmetrical, and follows a concentric pattern that centers on the history of the northern kingdom's Omrid dynasty (see Savran, 148):

1. The Reign of Solomon (1 Kgs 1–11)
2. Separate establishment of the northern kingdom (1 Kgs 12–14:20)
3. Summaries: kings of north and south (1 Kgs 14:21–16:20)
4. The Omrid dynasty
   a. Foundation of the dynasty in violence (1 Kgs 16:21–28)
   b. Omrid kings, especially Ahab, and the prophets, especially Elijah (1 Kgs 16:29–2 Kgs 1:18)
   c. Elisha succeeds Elijah as prophet (2 Kgs 2)
   d. Omrid kings, especially Jehoram (sometimes abbreviated to Joram), and the prophets, especially Elisha (2 Kgs 3:1–9:13)
   e. Destruction of the dynasty in violence (2 Kgs 9:14–11:20)
5. Summaries: kings of north and south (2 Kgs 11:21 [= Hebrew 12:1]–16:20)
6. Destruction of the northern kingdom (2 Kgs 17)
7. The southern kingdom to its destruction (2 Kgs 18–25)

Within this overall organization, the narrator uses a regular pattern for the recital of the history of the divided kingdoms. He tells the whole story of each king in turn, in order of accession to the throne, irrespective of whether that king ruled over the northern kingdom or the southern. The result is indeed a history of the *kings*, as the Hebrew text says, and not of the *kingdoms*, as the LXX would have it. The pattern is not theologically innocent. By it, the narrator reminds us that the division of Israel into two *political* units was indeed God's will (1 Kgs 11:29–39; 12:15), even if its fragmentation into separate *religious* bodies was due to human sin (1 Kgs 12:26–31; 13:33–34). The narrator's strategy thus balances the unity of God's people with the duality of the kingdoms God has assigned them to.

From the death of Solomon on (1 Kgs 11:41–43), with few exceptions, each king's reign is recounted according to the same pattern. Each regnal account begins with a formulaic introduction that comprises (a) a synchronization of the new king's year of accession with the regnal year in the other kingdom; (b) the king's age at accession (for kings of Judah only); (c) the length of the

king's reign and his capital city; (d) the name of the king's mother (for kings of Judah only); and (e) a rather less formulaic theological evaluation of the king. Each regnal account ends with a formulaic conclusion that (a) refers the reader to other sources and (b) notes the death and burial of the king and the name of his successor (some of this information may be left out if it has already been given, for instance, in reporting an assassination). Between the introduction and conclusion, summary accounts usually describe a single noteworthy event of the reign. But even longer treatments, such as the reign of Ahab, begin and end with the formulas (see 1 Kgs 16:29–30; 22:39–40). The pattern is rarely disrupted, and few passages are situated *between* regnal accounts (1 Kgs 16:21–22; 2 Kings 2; 2 Kgs 13:14–25).

History of the Text. Clearly, 1–2 Kings as we have them today cannot predate the latest event they describe, the release of Jehoiachin from prison in 562 B.C.. However, most scholars believe that the present text is based on one or more earlier editions of the history that derive from the reign of Josiah (about 640–609 B.C.) or perhaps even Hezekiah (about 715–687 B.C.). Furthermore, the authors of 1–2 Kings refer their readers to three older sources, unfortunately not extant today ("The Book of the Acts of Solomon," 1 Kgs 11:41; "The Book of the Chronicles of the Kings of Israel," 1 Kgs 14:19 and *passim*; and "The Book of the Chronicles of the Kings of Judah," 1 Kgs 15:23, and *passim*). Whether these sources were based on official court records from the two kingdoms, or perhaps even constituted such court records themselves, is a matter of conjecture. Passages like 1 Kgs 4:2–6, 8–19 may indicate that the authors had (indirect?) access to archival records, and story cycles like 2 Kgs 2:19–8:6 may originate in anecdotes passed on in prophetic circles.

Kings as History. Despite the authors' possible use of older records, scholars today hesitate over the value of 1–2 Kings as reliable history. In general terms, most would agree with the panoramic sweep of the tale: a single kingdom, divided, and eventually conquered by the great Mesopotamian empires of Assyria and Babylon. But the particulars of the account are much less certain. Paucity of external corroboration (such as documentary evidence from other contemporary cultures or archaeological evidence from Israel) makes it difficult to judge the accuracy of the books' historical claims. Careful reading of the text reveals that the authors had no compunction about "adjusting" the historical data for their own purposes. For instance, details in 1 Kgs 4:22–23 surely originally described the "provisions" supplied by the Israelites (4:7), not the "tribute" exacted from vassal states (4:21). A second example concerns the invasion of Judah by the Assyrians toward the end of the eighth century (2

Kings 18–19). Difficulties reconciling the biblical narrative with Assyrian records suggest that the biblical authors have either conflated two different versions of one invasion or combined independent accounts of two separate incursions. On the level of individuals, the uncertainty is even more cogent. The intransigence of Elijah, the evil of Jezebel, the piety of Hezekiah—surely these owe as much or more to the authors' sense of dramatic portrayal as they do to historically reliable biography.

Kings as Theology. The key to the Books of Kings is to understand them as a theological interpretation of history. The presenting issue of 1–2 Kings is to explain the dismal failure of the monarchic experiment in Israel. The presenting issue of the entire Deuteronomistic History, of which 1–2 Kings is the last major section, is to explain the dismal failure of Israel's experience in the Promised Land, from their arrival under the leadership of Joshua to their departure by Assyrian and Babylonian dispersion. And the explanations are thoroughly theological: violation of the covenantal obligations toward God resulted in imposition of punishments foreseen in the covenant itself (see Dt 27–28, especially 28:36, 64).

Each king receives a theological evaluation at the end of the formulaic introduction to his reign. Northern kings are condemned without exception, usually for following "the sin of Jeroboam"—that is, worship of the golden calves the first northern king set up at sanctuaries in Dan and Bethel. The authors deem this idolatry, although historically Jeroboam's shrines were almost certainly dedicated to the true God of Israel, who was understood to be enthroned invisibly on the golden calves (just as he was enthroned invisibly on the cherubim— winged lions?—in the Temple at Jerusalem). The condemnations of northern kings become progressively more severe, reaching their nadir with Ahab (1 Kgs 16:30–33). After the fall of the northern kingdom in 722 B.C., the authors interrupt the historical recital to reflect on the cause of Israel's destruction, their abandonment of Yahweh (2 Kgs 17:6–23).

Some of the southern kings, too, are condemned, though many receive qualified praise. Praise is given for fidelity to God; praise is qualified for "failing to remove the high places"—that is, sanctuaries that were presumably dedicated to Yahweh but that the authors of Kings considered heterodox, because, in their view, the Temple in Jerusalem was the sole legitimate place to offer sacrifice to Yahweh. Only two southern kings receive unqualified praise, Hezekiah (2 Kgs 18:3–4) and Josiah (2 Kgs 22:2), both for their fidelity to Yahweh following the model of King David. The purely theological basis of the authors' evaluations is clear when one considers their treatment of Manasseh, whose reign was the longest of

any king of either kingdom. His policies seem to have preserved peace in the land throughout his long reign (though at the expense of vassalage to Assyria); but the authors of Kings dismiss him in less than a chapter, and deem his idolatry so evil that not even the pieties of Josiah could atone for it (2 Kgs 24:3).

A further indication of the theological spirit of Kings is the important and pervasive presence of prophets and prophetic material. The concentric structure of 1–2 Kings (see above) centers on a moment of prophetic succession, as if the whole history of Israel pivots on the bearers of God's word, rather than on the deeds of mere kings. History is driven by that Word. It is spoken in prophecy and realized in fulfillment events (see, among more than forty examples, 1 Kgs 11:31–39 and 12:15; 1 Kgs 13:2 and 2 Kgs 23:15–16; 1 Kgs 21:19 and 22:38; 1 Kgs 19:15–16 and 2 Kings 8:7–15; 9:1–13). Even the behavior of Yahweh himself reflects the importance of prophets: he speaks several times (twice in dreams) to King Solomon, but with one exception God never speaks directly to anyone but prophets after that.

Reading Kings Today. The enduring message of 1–2 Kings is its claim that the Word of God is the driving force of human history. There is no perfect, inevitably right form of human government; even those human institutions established by divine dispensation are vulnerable to the weaknesses and sins of the human beings who embody them in our world. But beneath the vacillations of men and women, behind the vagaries of kings and nations, around and above the vicissitudes of human history, the Word of God is at work and will ultimately prevail.

Bibliography: J. A. MONTGOMERY, *The Books of Kings, International Critical Commentary,* ed. S. R. DRIVER et al. (Edinburgh 1951). J. GRAY, *I & II Kings* (Philadelphia 1970). R. D. NELSON, *The Double Redaction of the Deuteronomistic History* (Sheffield 1981). C. CONROY, *1–2 Samuel, 1–2 Kings* (OTM; Wilmington 1983). G. H. JONES, *1 and 2 Kings* (NCBC; Grand Rapids 1984). B. O. LONG, *1 Kings* (FOTL; Grand Rapids 1984). S. J. DEVRIES, *1 Kings* (WBC; Waco 1985). T. R. HOBBS, *2 Kings* (WBC; Waco 1985). R. NELSON, *First and Second Kings* (Atlanta 1987). G. SAVRAN, "1 and 2 Kings," in *The Literary Guide to the Bible,* ed. R. ALTER and F. KERMODE (Cambridge, Mass. 1987); 146–64. M. COGAN and H. TADMOR, *II Kings* (New York 1988). I. W. PROVAN, *Hezekiah and the Books of Kings* (BZAW; Berlin 1988). J. T. WALSH and C. R. BEGG, "1–2 Kings," in *The New Jerome Biblical Commentary* (Englewood Cliffs, N.J. 1990), §10. B. O. LONG, *2 Kings* (FOTL; Grand Rapids 1991). S. L. MCKENZIE, *The Trouble with Kings* (SVT; Leiden 1991). S. W. HOLLOWAY, "Kings, Book of 1–2," in *The Anchor Bible Dictionary* (New York 1992); 4:69–83. G. N. KNOPPERS, *Two Nations under God* (Atlanta 1993). A. BRENNER, *A Feminist Companion to Samuel and Kings* (Sheffield 1994). I. W. PROVAN, *First and Second Kings* (NIBCOT; Peabody, Mass. 1995). J. T. WALSH, *1 Kings* (Berit Olam; Collegeville 1996). T. FRETHEIM, *First and Second Kings* (Louisville 1999). R. L. COHN, *2 Kings* (Collegeville 1999).

[J. T. WALSH]

KINGSHIP IN THE ANCIENT NEAR EAST

A purely secular view of Near Eastern kingship that does not take into account the special relationship existing between king and deity is destined to be found myopic. In ancient Egypt, Mesopotamia, and Israel the king was the representative of the deity on earth. It is very important, therefore, to determine the nature of this association in order to understand better the concept of kingship in the respective countries. After treating of kingship in ancient Egypt, Mesopotamia, and Israel, this article will conclude with a consideration of the Israelite concept of the ideal king of the future.

Relation of King to Deity in Ancient Egypt. The fundamental concept of Egyptian kingship was that the king or pharaoh was a superhuman being, a god from birth, begotten by the sun god and first King RA (RE) and metaphysically one with all of the great gods. In his different ministerial capacities he incarnated the gods Horus, Seth, and Osiris. As the personification of the gods, he ruled by divine decree and meted out justice by divine wisdom. The beneficial relations between heaven and earth resulting from the king's union with the gods were reactivated yearly at the principal festivals, especially the all important "Sed festival." On that occasion the king took part in a cultic drama in which he ritually overcame death and chaos by resurrecting in triumph and thus generated prosperity for the land and its people during the coming year.

Relation of King to Deity in Ancient Mesopotamia. In ancient Mesopotamia the king was the earthly viceroy of the national god, but he was not considered divine as were the pharaos. He was a mortal, made to carry a superhuman charge placed upon him by the gods—a "big man" as his Sumerian title 1u-ga1 signifies. There are some scattered examples of kings using the divine ideogram before their names, but these graphic signs are not enough to establish a common concept of deification.

The king did take on characteristics of a deity, but only intermittently, as for instance at the New Year festival. It was then that he substituted for the national god in the enacted ritual drama and renewed his superhuman endowments, while also restoring harmony and fruitfulness to nature temporarily disturbed by the change of seasons. Nature's renewal in the spring was looked upon as the result of a sacred marriage (hierogamy) between the mother goddess, represented ritually by a priestess, and the king, made to play the part of the divine bridegroom.

The Mesopotamian king is said to be "adopted, nursed, and reared" by the gods. He is "holy" by virtue of his familiarity with the gods, and thereby partakes of "eternity, splendor, and glory." He is likened to the different gods, especially the sun god and the resurrected fertility god, Tammuz; yet he ever remains the earthly steward of the deities—a mortal like all men.

Whereas in Egyptian ideology the king's role of representing the gods was particularly emphasized, in Mesopotamia more stress is placed upon the king's representation of his people before the divine throne. Once again, at the prominent New Year festival the king, as the representative of the congregation, ritually effected the resuscitation of the "dead god" by bringing him the assistance he needed. The people also through their king "descended to the dead god," temporarily confined to the nether world, and by a further ritual effected a reversal of mood that brought the god back to the world of the living. Thus conjoined to their king, the people would be assured a new period of fertility for the coming year. Even in such a ritual, the king is never a god. He is temporarily "fused" with divinity, imbued with the god's destiny, experience, and life giving powers that he, in his turn, imparts to the society he represents.

On the basis of such ideas, advocates of the so-called "Myth and Ritual School" of comparative religion conclude to a common "ritual pattern" in the king ideology of the entire ancient Near East. This theory revolves about the divine figure of the king, especially in his cultic function at the great cyclic festivals. The king is of divine origin. He suffers, dies, returns to life, conquers the monsters of chaos, and in the annual repetition of these sacred acts becomes a source of prosperity and blessing for his people. Israelite kingship is said to be patterned on this ideology.

As ingenious as the "Ritual Pattern Theory" may be, most Biblical scholars today view it as an unproved hypothesis, wanting seriously in Biblical evidence, and, on the whole, underestimating the distinctive qualities of Israel's religion.

Relation of the King to Yahweh in Ancient Israel. Although Israel's monarchical structure was in some ways influenced by the "king ideology" of neighboring nations, the theistic concept of Yahweh's kingship was and always remained such a basic tenet of Israel's religion that kingship took on properties quite distinct from the ideologies of Egypt and Mesopotamia.

For one thing, kingship in Israel was integrated into a theocratic system in which Yahweh alone was considered king and absolute ruler of the universe (Ex 15.18; 19.6; Nm 23.21; 1 Sm 8.7; 12.12; Jgs 8.23); the human king was but His earthly regent. As a matter of fact, there was strong feeling against the introduction of the monarchy from the very outset; it appeared too restrictive of the free and independent traditions inherited from Israel's migrant days, and what was more objectionable, it was too closely allied with the Canaanite way of life.

The theocratic structure of the people of God was based on the Sinai covenant [*see* COVENANT (IN THE BIBLE)]. In their attempt to settle the promised land the Israelites encountered steady opposition from hostile neighbors, and it soon became clear there was need of effective centralized action; the Israelite tribes needed a leader (1 Sm 8.20). It was then that a new "royalized" covenant was established between Yahweh and the Davidic dynasty; the latter, however, always representing and embodying the people Israel by virtue of the Biblical concept of "corporate personality." The king becomes Yahweh's viceregent, and in contrast to Yahweh, Israel's real king, the human position of the king is clearly delineated.

In Israel there is no indication at all of the earthly king's divinization. He did enjoy a privileged position as God's viceroy on earth, it is true. He became "the Lord's anointed" (1 Sm 16.6; 2 Sm 1.14) and "prince" (Hebrews *nāgîd*) over Israel (1 Sm 9.16; 10.1; 13.14); he was changed into "another man" (1 Sm 10.6, 9), and as such he was endowed with the "spirit" (*rûaḥ*) of Yahweh (1 Sm 10.6, 10; 11.6; 16.13) and treated as inviolable (1 Sm 24.7; 31.4; 2 Sm 1.4). He became Yahweh's adopted son: "This day I have begotten thee" (Ps 2.7). In a critically troublesome passage he is even called *'ĕlōhîm* (God), and his throne is regarded as eternal [Ps 44 (45).7]. Such extravagant phraseology depicting the close association between God and the king really proves nothing more than that the king of Israel existed by virtue of Yahweh's will and was His earthly representative. The hyperbolic expressions so common to oriental *Hofstil* (court style) cannot be taken too literally. They indicate the preeminent role of the king, but always as subordinated to God.

Furthermore if the kings were considered quasidivine, it is difficult to explain why the Prophets reprimanded them so harshly and frequently for their dereliction of covenant duties, and for neglecting to fulfill their obligations as servants of God and of the people (Dt 17.14–20; 1 Sm 13.8–15; 15.26; 2 Sm 5.12; 1 Kgs 11.31–39; 18.17–19; 21.17–24; Jer 22.15–17).

As God's earthly viceroy, the king became a purveyor of divine blessings for the people and their land. He was their source of strength [Ps 89(90).18], their breath of life (Lam 4.20), and therefore had to be protected in the interests of the nation (2 Sm 18.3). His position entitled him to universal sovereignty [Ps 2.8–9; 71(72).8–11; 88(89).26–28], establishing justice in the world [Ps 44 (45).4–8; 71 (72).1–4], and destroying his enemies [Ps 2.9; 20(21).9–14]. Even the fertility of the land was as-

cribed to his association with Yahweh, the source of all life [Ps 71(72).3, 16].

Israel's Ideal King of the Future. An important phase in the historical development of Israelite kingship was Yahweh's promise, delivered through the Prophet Nathan, that the Davidic dynasty would remain forever [2 Sm 7.8–16; 1 Chr 17.7–14; Ps 87(88).3–5, 20–38]. This assertion was the basis of future eschatological hopes for a new kingdom and an ideal king, and in this regard also Israelite kingship differed radically from the kingship patterns of Egypt and Mesopotamia.

A tension arose when this promise came into contact with the harsh empirical reality of the utter failure of the monarchy in both Israel and Judah. Many of the kings had so often abandoned their covenant obligations, and appeared so unworthy of their privileged position that there arose within the prophetic movement, especially in Isaiah of the late 8th century B.C., the hope for an ideal king, one who would embody and revive the qualities of David of old: a king of peace and justice (Is 9.1–6), animated by the spirit of the Lord (Is 11.2), one who would restore the earth to her paradisaical harmony and bliss (Is 11.6–9). This future MESSIAH was depicted in various images by the classical prophets down through the centuries.

With the fall of Jerusalem in 587 B.C. and the dissolution of the monarchy, the hopes and aspirations for a future king were marked by a profound change. Israel was chastened by the humiliating experience of the Babylonian Exile [Lam 4.20; Ps 88(89).39–52], and although the first pioneers who returned to Jerusalem were stimulated temporarily by the hope of a new Davidic "branch" (Zec 3.8–10; 6.9–14), the Israelite hope for the future focused more on the KINGDOM OF GOD than on one specific individual. Yet at the threshold of the New Testament, Judaism was awaiting a Messiah king who would free Israel from foreign oppression and bring about lasting peace in the world.

See Also: MESSIANISM.

Bibliography: R. LABAT, *La Caractère religieux de la royauté assyro-babylonienne* (Paris 1939). H. FRANKFORT, *Kingship and the Gods* (Chicago 1948). C. R. NORTH, ''The Religious Aspects of Hebrew Kingship,'' *Zeitschrift für die neutestamentliche Wissenschaft und die Kunde der älteren Kirche* 50 (1932) 8–38. J. DE FRAINE, *L'Aspect religieux de la royauté Israélite; L'Institution monarchique dans l'A. T. et dans les textes mésopotamiens* (Rome 1954). S. MOWINCKEL, *He That Cometh*, tr. C. W. ANDERSON (Nashville 1956) 21–95; *The Psalms in Israel's Worship*, tr. D. R. APTHOMAS, 2 v. (Nashville 1962) 1:50–61. H. CAZELLES, ''Mito, rituale, e regalità,'' *Bibbia e Oriente* 2 (1960) 121–35. K. H. BERNHARDT, *Das Problem der altorientalischen Königsideologie in A. T., unter besonderer Berücksichtigung der Geschichte der Psalmenexegese dargestellt und kritisch gewürdigt* (Vetus Testamentum suppl. 8; 1961). *Encyclopedic Dictionary of the Bible*, tr. and adap. by L.

HARTMAN (New York 1963), from A. VAN DEN BORN, *Bijbels Woordenboek* 1282–86.

[E. J. CIUBA]

KINLOSS, ABBEY OF

Former CISTERCIAN Abbey of St. Mary within the county and old diocese of Moray, Scotland. Founded by DAVID I in 1150 or 1151, it was colonized from MELROSE. Much of the abbey's later, unquiet history was faithfully recorded and preserved by the learned Italian humanist John Ferreri, who taught classics there at the invitation of its greatest abbot, Robert Reid, subsequent bishop of Orkney (1541). Erected into a temporal lordship for Edward Bruce in 1601, the abbey is now a ruin.

Bibliography: J. FERRERI, *Historia abbatum de Kynlos* (Edinburgh 1839). J. STUART, ed., *Records of the Monastery of Kinloss* (Edinburgh 1872). J. M. CANIVEZ, ed., *Statuta capitulorum generalium ordinis cisterciensis ab anno 1116 ad annum 1786,* 8 v. (Louvain 1933–41) 8:287. D. E. EASSON, *Medieval Religious Houses: Scotland* (London 1957) 65.

[L. MACFARLANE]

KINO, EUSEBIO FRANCISCO

Missionary, explorer, and cartographer; b. Segno, Italy, Aug. 10, 1645; d. Magdalena, Ariz. (then Mexico), March 15, 1711. Called the "Apostle of Sonora and Arizona," Kino changed his family name, spelled Chino or Chini, to Quino or Kino. In his prayers for recovery from a nearly fatal illness in 1663, he promised St. Francis Xavier that he would assume the name Francisco, enter the Society of Jesus, and devote himself to the missions. Two years later, he joined the Jesuit province of Upper Germany. While engaged in ecclesiastical studies, chiefly at Innsbruck and Ingolstadt, he also familiarized himself with astronomy and mathematics as necessities for the Chinese missions. His association with Germany during these years have led some historians to class him as a German under the name Kühn. Finally in 1678, after repeated petitions, Kino was assigned to a group being assembled in Spain for missions in American and Asia. Since their destinations were not explicit, he and a fellow Jesuit drew lots; the pious gamble chose his destination as Mexico.

Kino voyaged from Genoa to Cádiz, only to endure a two-year delay in Spain—a delay that permitted him to study the comet of 1680. He sailed from Cádiz in January of 1681 and landed at Vera Cruz, Mexico, in May. In Mexico City he published a pamphlet containing his observations on the comet, which were attacked by the Mexican scholar and former Jesuit novice, Carlos Sigüenza y Góngora. Meanwhile Kino had left Mexico City to serve as a royal cosmographer and Jesuit superior on the Atondo expedition of 1683 to Lower California. He wrote reports, crossed this reputedly "large island" from Gulf shore to Pacific coast, and drew maps which he sent to Europe. Drought caused the abandonment of his missionary and colonizing venture in 1685.

Pimería Alta, a vast region extending over modern northern Sonora and southern Arizona, was the scene of Kino's endeavors from 1687 until his death. Establishing his headquarters at Mission Dolores in 1687, he founded missions in the San Miguel, Magdalena, Altar, Sonóita, Santa Cruz, and San Pedro valleys. He baptized 4,500 Pimas, promoted cattle raising, and established missions on the sites of many modern towns and cities. He rode thousands of miles, traveling north from Dolores as far as the Gila and Colorado Rivers. His was the first clearly recorded description of the Casa Grande of the Gila. His enthusiastic letters and reports on Lower California helped the Jesuits to return there in 1697. Kino himself was retained at Primería even though royal decrees directed him to go to California with the missionary Juan Salvatierra; his missions sent cattle and other supplies to the new posts across the Gulf.

In 1700, while constucting the first mission of San Xavier del Bac, he became convinced that California was not an island when he noticed blue shells that he had originally seen on California's Pacific coast side. Two expeditions to the lower Colorado strengthened his opinion, and his maps did much to prove the fact to Europe. He planned to open a road around the head of the gulf, but it was not until generations later that Juan de Anza and Junípero Serra made it a reality. In 1711 the dedication of a chapel in honor of St. Francis Xavier brought Kino to his mission at Magdalena, and he died there.

Bibliography: E. S. KINO, *Kino's Historical Memoir of Pimería Alta,* tr. and ed. H. E. BOLTON (Berkeley 1948). E. J. BURRUS, ed., *Kino Reports to Headquarters* (Rome 1954). H. E. BOLTON, *Rim of Christendom: A Biography of Eusebio Francisco Kino, Pacific Coast Pioneer* (New York 1936; repr. 1960).

[J. A. DONOHUE]

KIRBY, LUKE, ST.

English martyr; b. probably near Richmond, Yorkshire, England, *c.* 1548; d. Tyburn (London), May 30, 1582. Cardinal William Allen calls him a master of arts of Cambridge, but this is uncertain. However, he was educated as a non-Catholic and, crossing to Douai, he was received into the Church at the English College, where he was ordained on Sept. 19, 1577. From Douai he went the next year to Rome to continue his studies. On Apr. 18, 1580, along with (St.) Edmund CAMPION, he set out for England. He left Rheims on June 16, but he was captured immediately on landing at Dover and was taken to London and imprisoned in the Gatehouse. On Dec. 4, 1580, he was transferred to the Tower, where he was subjected to the ''Scavenger's Daughter,'' a double iron hoop that enclosed and contracted the body. On Nov. 16, 1581, he was tried at Westminster Hall with Edmund Campion, Ralph SHERWIN, and Alexander BRIANT. Although he was condemned with his companions for complicity in a fictitious plot in Flanders, his execution was delayed until May 30 the following year. During this interval he was kept in chains. Before he was hanged, drawn, and quartered, he protested his innocence of any conspiracy against the Queen. Kirby was beatified by Leo XIII on Dec. 29, 1886, and canonized by Paul VI on Oct. 25, 1970.

Feast: May 28; Oct. 25 (Feast of the 40 Martyrs of England and Wales); May 4 (Feast of the English Martyrs in England).

See Also: ENGLAND, SCOTLAND, AND WALES, MARTYRS OF.

Bibliography: B. CAMM, ed., *Lives of the English Martyrs Declared Blessed by Pope Leo XIII in 1866 and 1895,* 2 v. (New York 1904–14) 2:500–522. M. T. H. BANKS, *Blessed Luke Kirby* (Postulation Pamphlet; London 1961). A. BUTLER, *The Lives of the Saints* 2:415–416. R. CHALLONER, *Memoirs of Missionary Priests,* ed. J. H. POLLEN (rev. ed. London 1924; repr. Farnborough 1969).

[G. FITZ HERBERT]

KIRCHER, ATHANASIUS

German archeologist; b. Geisa (Fulda), May 2, 1601; d. Rome, Oct. 30, 1690. He joined the Society of Jesus at 17 and later taught mathematics and philosophy at the Jesuit college in Würzburg. He was ordained in 1628. During the THIRTY YEARS' WAR he was forced to go to Avignon (1632), but two years later he settled in Rome, where he taught mathematics, physics, and Oriental languages. He later devoted all his attention to archeology, especially to the interpretation of hieroglyphics found in ancient monuments and ruins. He also did some work in physics, where he is credited with the construction of convergent mirrors and projectors. The Kircher Museum that he founded in the Roman College was taken over by the state in 1870. He wrote many books about different subjects, among them: *Specula melitensis encyclica* (Mesina 1638); *Ars magna lucis et umbrae* (Rome 1645); *Musurgia universalis* (Rome 1650); *Magnes sive de arte magnetica libri tres* (1640); *Itinerarium extaticum* (1656); *Iter extaticum II* (1657); *Lingua aegyptiaca resti-*

Athanasius Kircher.

tuta (Rome 1664); *Mundus subterraneus* (Amsterdam 1664, 3d ed. 1671); *Polygraphica seu artificium linguarum* (Rome 1665); *Latium, id est, nova et parallela Latii descriptio* (Rome 1671).

Kircher's place in science rests primarily on his extensive writings, which give a picture of scientific understanding in the 17th century. He was a man of his time, and many of his statements have been shown to be uncritical or incorrect, but the charge of scientific falsification, which has been leveled against him, has not been substantiated.

Bibliography: K. BRISCHAR, *Athanasius Kircher: Ein Lebensbild* (Würzburg 1877). *P. Athanasii Kircheri vita a semetipso conscripta* (Augsburg 1684). L. KOCH, *Jesuiten-Lexikon: Die Gesellschaft Jesu einst und jetzt* (Paderborn 1934); photoduplicated with rev. and suppl., 2 v. (Louvain-Heverlee 1962) 2:983–984.

[E. T. SPAIN]

KIRK, KENNETH ESCOTT

Anglican bishop of Oxford, theologian; b. Sheffield, England, Feb. 21, 1886; d. Oxford, June 8, 1954. Educated at Sheffield Royal Grammar School and at St. John's, Oxford, Kirk graduated (1908) with first class honors and became assistant to the professor of philosophy at University College, London (1909–12). He received holy orders in 1913, and devoted the rest of his life, except for an interval as military chaplain during World War I, to an academic career at Oxford. In 1927 he became regius professor of moral and pastoral theology, and canon of Christ's Church, Oxford. He delivered the Bampton Lectures in 1928. From 1937 to his death he was bishop of Oxford. Kirk was an Anglo-Catholic in the liberal tradition of Charles GORE and the *LUX MUNDI* school. He contributed to *Essays Catholic and Critical* (1926), a symposium that accepted the findings of critical scholarship in a way that would have seemed temerarious to earlier generations of Tractarians, but that was by 1926 taken for granted by most progressive Anglo-Catholics. Kirk was also one of the most prominent Anglican moral theologians of his day. His main publications were: *A Study of Silent Minds* (1918), *Some Principles of Moral Theology* (1920), *Conscience and Its Problems* (1927), *The Vision of God* (Bampton Lectures 1928), *The Threshold of Ethics* (1933), *The Crisis of Christian Rationalism* (1935), *The Epistle to the Romans* (Clarendon Bible, 1936), *The Ministry of Absolution* (1947), and *The Coherence of Christian Doctrine* (1950). Kirk edited and contributed to *Personal Ethics* (1934) and the *Apostolic Ministry* (1946).

Bibliography: E. W. KEMP, *The Life and Letters of Kenneth Escott Kirk* (London 1959).

[W. HANNAH]

KIRK, RUSSELL AMOS

Man of letters and political theorist; b. Plymouth, Michigan, Oct. 18, 1918; d. Piety Hill, Mecosta, Michigan, April 29, 1994. Russell Kirk was the son of Russell and Marjorie (Pierce) Kirk. He received a B.A. from Michigan State University (1940); an M.A. from Duke University (1941); and a D.Litt. from St. Andrews University, Scotland (1952). He married Annette Courtemanche in 1964 and was the father of four children.

Kirk achieved national prominence and a broad permanent following with the publication of *The Conservative Mind: From Burke to Santayana* (1953). This was followed by 29 other books, including studies of John Randolph of Roanoke, Edmund Burke, and T. S. Eliot. Notable among his many publications are *Academic Freedom* (1955), *Eliot and His Age* (1971), *The Roots of the American Order* (1974), *Decadence and Renewal in the Higher Learning* (1978), *The Conservative Constitution* (1990), and *The Politics of Prudence* (1993). The author of a long-running column "From the Academy" in the *National Review*, Kirk founded the quarterly review, *Modern Age*, in 1957 and in 1960 *The University Bookman*, which continues under the editorship of his wife.

Throughout his career Kirk devoted his intellectual energy to studying the philosophical roots and principal documents of the Anglo-American tradition of political theory. A convert to Catholicism shortly before his marriage in 1964, he was convinced that all political problems, in the last analysis, are religious and moral problems. "At heart," he wrote, "all social questions are exercises in ethics; and ethics in turn depend on religious faith." He believed that religion, particularly Christianity, is the key to restoring the harmony of a properly ordered society.

"Purveyor of Immutable Truths." A defender of the principle of subsidiarity, Kirk stressed the need to preserve local communities against the leveling tendency of big government and big business. Judging the modern university to be the instrument for the inculcation of the secular philosophy of the Enlightenment, he was a consistent critic of American higher education. For decades he waged war against administrators and faculty members whom he regarded as corrupting the American university by lowering standards of achievement and by failing to respect inherited traditions.

Kirk was convinced that cognitive claims cannot always be immediately adjudicated, that the process of judging can be complicated, and consequently, that if standards are not to be trivial, they must transcend the present and rest upon the best judgments available. His conservative mind reflected his study and appreciation of classical antiquity, i.e., Plato, Aristotle, Seneca, Cicero, Livy, and Pliny. He was convinced that nature is intelligible, that the human mind is capable of ferreting out its secrets, and that time-transcending standards can be adduced and employed. Kirk wanted to be known as "a purveyor of immutable truths."

Hailed as the "father of the conservative movement," Kirk's contribution to letters was widely recognized. He was awarded numerous honorary degrees and was the recipient of the Ingersoll prize for scholarly writing (1984) and the Presidential Citizen's Medal (1989). He was a Fulbright Lecturer, a Guggenheim Fellow, a Senior Fellow of the American Council of Learned Societies, a National Endowment for the Humanities Constitutional Fellow and a Distinguished Fellow of the Heritage Foundation.

Bibliography: A bibliography of Kirk's writings is available from the Intercollegiate Studies Institute, 14 South Bryn Mawr Avenue, Bryn Mawr, PA 19010. For a tribute to his work, see *The Unbought Grace of Life,* ed. J. E. PERSON (Peru, IL 1994).

[J. DOUGHTERY]

Kirkstall Abbey from the Northwest. (©Historical Picture Archive/CORBIS)

KIRKMAN, RICHARD, BL.

Priest and martyr; b. Addingham, West Riding, Yorkshire, England; d. hanged, drawn, and quartered at York, Aug. 22, 1582. He studied at the seminaries of Douai and Rheims prior to his presbyterial ordination on Holy Saturday 1579. In order to disguise his priestly nature, Kirkman served as tutor in the household of Robert Dymoke, hereditary Champion of England (d. in Lincoln gaol for his faith, Sept. 11, 1580), at Scrivelsby, Lincolnshire. Fr. Kirkman was eventually discovered and arrested, Aug. 8, 1582. He was arraigned shortly thereafter for being an illegal priest and confined to a turret cell with Bl. William LACEY. For the last 12 days of his earthly life, Richard was held in a verminous underground dungeon. He was beatified by Pope Leo XIII on Dec. 9, 1886.

Feast of the English Martyrs: May 4 (England).

See Also: ENGLAND, SCOTLAND, AND WALES, MARTYRS OF.

Bibliography: R. CHALLONER, *Memoirs of Missionary Priests,* ed. J. H. POLLEN (rev. ed. London 1924; repr. Farnborough 1969). J. H. POLLEN, *Acts of English Martyrs* (London 1891).

[K. I. RABENSTEIN]

KIRKSTALL, ABBEY OF

Former CISTERCIAN monastery near Leeds, England, in the ancient See of YORK. Kirkstall was a daughter-house of FOUNTAINS ABBEY and thus in the line of descent from CLAIRVAUX. It was founded in 1147 by Henry Lacy as an offering of thanksgiving for his recovery from a severe illness. The original foundation was at Barnoldswick, on the Lancashire side of Yorkshire. In 1152, however, the monastic community was translated to its permanent site at Aierdale, near Leeds, and built there the abbey dedicated to the Blessed Virgin Mary. The abbey flourished during the later Middle Ages until the dissolution of all monastic communities in England in the 16th century. It was surrendered to HENRY VIII on Nov. 22, 1540. The buildings that have survived constitute a fine example of the Norman Gothic style of the mid-12th century.

Bibliography: Sources. M. V. CLARKE and N. DENHOLM-YOUNG, ''The Kirkstall Chronicle, 1355–1400,'' *The Bulletin of the John Rylands Library* 15 (1931) 100–137. *Fundacio abbathie de Kyrkestall,* ed. E. K. CLARKE (Thoresby Society 4; Leeds 1895) 169–208. Literature. W. DUGDALE, *Monasticon Anglicanum* (London 1655–73); best ed. by J. CALEY et al., 6 v. (1817–30) 5:526–552. A. MULREADY and C. COPE, *An Historical, Antiquarian and Picturesque Account of Kirkstall Abbey* (Leeds 1827). L.

JANAUSCHEK, *Origines Cistercienses,* v. 1 (Vienna 1877) 93–94. L. H. COTTINEAU, *Répertoire topobibliographique des abbayes et prieurés,* 2 v. (Mâcon 1935–39) 1:1521. D. KNOWLES, *The Religious Houses of Medieval England* (London 1940), *passim.* D. KNOWLES, *The Monastic Order in England, 943–1216* (2d ed. Cambridge, Eng. 1962) *passim.*

[J. BRÜCKMANN]

KIRLIN, JOSEPH

Pastor, author; b. Philadelphia, PA, March 20, 1868; d. Philadelphia, Nov. 26, 1926. He was educated by the Christian Brothers at La Salle College, Philadelphia, receiving an A.B. in 1886. That fall he began to study for the priesthood at St. Charles Seminary, Overbrook, PA, and continued at The CATHOLIC UNIVERSITY OF AMERICA, Washington, D.C. He was ordained on Dec. 17, 1892, and obtained a bachelor's degree in sacred theology the following year. While assistant at St. Patrick's Church, Philadelphia, he published the *Life of Most Reverend Patrick John Ryan* (1903), planned as part of a complete history of the Catholic Church in Philadelphia. By 1909 he had completed his large volume, *Catholicity in Philadelphia,* a work rich in facts about the Colonial and Revolutionary periods. Kirlin was disappointed with the indifferent reception this book received, and later turned to devotional writing. In 1920, when he was named a papal chamberlain, he began to contribute to *Emmanuel,* the magazine of the national Priest's Eucharistic League. From his monthly articles there grew a trilogy of works: *One Hour with Him* (1923), *Our Tryst with Him* (1925), and *With Him in Mind* (1926). Kirlin preached and lectured widely on the Eucharistic movement. His sermons were published posthumously in 1929 as *Christ the Builder.* His *Priestly Virtue and Zeal,* also appearing in 1929, was a study of the Curé of Ars. Shortly before his death Kirlin accepted the presidency of the Catholic University Alumni Association and that of the American Catholic Historical Society. He had long been pastor of the Most Precious Blood Parish, which he founded in Philadelphia in 1907.

[H. J. NOLAN]

KIRSCH, JOHANN PETER

Church historian, archeologist, and pioneer in the history of papal finances; b. Dippach, Luxemburg, Nov. 3, 1861; d. Rome, Feb. 4, 1941. Kirsch made his seminary studies and was ordained in Luxemburg in 1884. In residence at the Campo Teutonico, Rome, from 1884 to 1890, he came under the influence of G. B. de ROSSI, J. HERGENRÖTHER, H. S. DENIFLE, F. X. KRAUS, and P. Bat-

Johann Peter Kirsch.

tifol; and in 1888 he became director of the Institut der Görresgesellschaft. Professor of patrology and Christian archeology at Fribourg from 1890 to 1932, he was named rector of Istituto Pontificio di Archeologia Cristiana at Rome by Pius XI in 1926, and a prothonotary apostolic in 1932.

In his scholarly activity he specialized in methodical research and provided a deeper understanding of the Reformation through his *Die Finanzverwaltung des Kardinalkollegiums im XIII. und XIV. Jahrhundert* (Münster 1895) and *Die päpstlichen Kollectorien in Deutschland während des XIV. Jahrhunderts* (Paderborn 1894). He was editor of the fourth to sixth editions of Hergenröther's *Handbuch der allgemeinen Kirchengeschichte,* and he joined with Bigelmair, Greven, and Veit in publishing a new church history (4 v. Freiburg 1930–49). He was coeditor with A. Ehrhard of *Forschungen zur christlichen Literatur-und Dogmengeschichte* from 1900. He investigated early Christian places of worship, especially in their relation to the liturgy, published *Die römischen Titelkirchen* (Paderborn 1918), *Der stadtrömische christliche Festkalender im Altertum* (Münster 1924), *Die Stationskirchen des Missale Romanum* (Freiburg 1926), and contributed 249 articles to the *Catholic Encyclopedia.*

Bibliography: O. PERLER, *Zeitschrift für Kirchengeschichte* 35 (1941) 1–3. J. SAUER, *Historisches Jahrbuch der Görres–Gesellschaft* 61 (1941) 467–474. G. BELVEDERI, *Rivista di archeologia cristiana* 18 (1941) 7–21. E. MOLITOR, *Mgr. J. P. Kirsch* (Luxembourg 1956). *The Catholic Encyclopedia and its Makers* (New York 1917) 92–93.

[E. MOLITOR]

KISMET

Arabic-Turkish term for fate, destiny. The original meaning of the Arabic word *qismah, qismat,* was distribution; later it came to mean lot, portion; in the third stage, which is a Turkish adaptation, it received the specific meaning of the lot that is destined for every man. The earliest use of the word in English was in 1849 by E. B. Eastwick in *Dry Leaves,* 46: "One day a man related to me a story of kismet or destiny." In Turkish the word kismet is usually an expression of a practical fatalism that accepts the blows of fate with resignation (*see* FATE AND FATALISM). Hence it is not to be confused with the word *qadar,* which is an expression of the theological doctrine concerning PREDESTINATION. The words *charkh* and *falak* in Persian and Turkish literature express almost the same sentiment: irrational and inevitable influence exercised by the spheres. It is interesting to notice that such a doctrine, which might seem to paralyze human endeavor, has had among the Muslims precisely the opposite effect. It has been the chief inspiration of the great courage that won for their religion its early triumphs and made it one of the great spiritual powers of the world.

Bibliography: *Encyclopedia of Islam,* ed. M. T. HOUTSMA et al. (Leiden 1913–38) 2:1041. For other meanings of the word in Turkish, *see* E. LITTMANN, *Morgenländische Wörter im Deutschen* (2d ed. Tübingen 1924), and E. MARGAURDSEN, *Das Wesen des Osmanen* (Munich 1916) 100. For the interpretation of *qadar, see* E. E. SALISBURY, "Muhammadan Doctrine of Predestination and Free Will," *The Journal of the American Oriental Society* 8 (1864–66) 152.

[P. KUJOORY]

KISS OF PEACE

The kiss as an expression of fraternal love and peace derives from several New Testament epistles in which the faithful are urged to salute one another with the kiss of love, or holy kiss. (1 Pt 5:14, Rom 16:16, 1 Cor 16:20, 2 Cor 13:12). Many scholars believe that there is reference here to a liturgical rite. In the middle of the 2nd century it is clearly referred to by Justin Martyr as a liturgical act (I Ap 1:65).

The kiss of peace was used in many circumstances that called for a special expression of charity, such as the welcoming of the newly baptized into the Christian community and the reconciliation of penitents. But it has been most widely practiced in the celebration of the Eucharist. In the early centuries, it took place before the Canon and usually before the Offertory (see Ap. Trad. 4). While the kiss of peace has retained its ancient position in the Christian East until today, in the West it was transferred to the end of the Canon before 417 (Innocent I, *Epist. Ad Decentium* 1; *Patrologia Latina,* ed. J. P. Migne, 217 v., indexes 4 v. (Paris 1878–90) 20:553), apparently in order to associate it with the expression of fraternal peace in the LORD'S PRAYER. Later it became a part of the rite of communion as a sign of unity and bond of love.

The kiss of peace was extended to all the faithful up to the end of the Middle Ages (Innocent III, *De sacro altaris Mysterio* 6.5; *Patrologia Latina* 217:909). Originally it seemed to have been done with the mouth (Ap. Trad. 22). In the latter part of the Middle Ages we find the substitution of an embrace for the clergy and the circulation of an object to be kissed by the faithful, at first the paten or a liturgical book, such as the Missal or the Gospel Book, later a crucifix, a reliquary, or an object called the osculatorium or peace–board, which was often a piece of wood with a cross inscribed, but sometimes a highly decorated object of precious metal or ivory.

The liturgical reforms of Vatican II gave the kiss of peace a new lease on life. The 1969 General Instruction of the Roman Missal exhorted the people to express their love for one another and beg for peace and unity in the Church in the exchange of peace according to the "customs and mentality of the people" as determined by the local conference of bishops (*General Instruction of the Roman Missal,* n.56[b]). This could take the form of an embrace or handshake (as is the usual practice in North America), a bow (as is customary in many parts of the Far East) or even a kiss done with the mouth according to the ancient usage (in many parts of Europe and Latin America).

Bibliography: J. A. JUNGMANN, *The Early Liturgy* (South Bend, Ind. 1959). G. DIX, *The Shape of the Liturgy* (2nd ed. London 1945). G. W. WOOLFENDEN, "'Let Us Offer Each Other the Sign of Peace'—An Enquiry" *Worship,* 67 (1993) 239–252. L. E. PHILLIPS, "The Kiss of Peace and the Opening Greeting of the Pre–anaphoral Dialogue," *Studia Liturgica,* 23 (1993) 177–186. R. CABIÉ, "Le rite de la paix," in *Les Combats de la paix* (Toulouse 1996) 47–71.

[B. I. MULLAHY/EDS.]

KITBAMRUNG, NICHOLAS BUNKERD, BL.

Baptized Benedictus, priest, martyr; b. *c.* Jan. 31, to Feb. 28, 1895, on a sampan in the Nakhon Chaisri district (mission of Bangkok), Thailand; d. Jan. 12, 1944, near Ban Han, Thailand. One of six children of converts to the faith, Joseph Poxang and Agnes Thiang Kitbamrung, Nicholas entered the minor seminary of Hang Xan at thirteen. He completed his studies at Penang (Malaysia) Seminary and was ordained in Assumption Cathedral, Bangkok, by Bishop René Perros (Jan. 24, 1926).

He began his pastoral work as assistant at Bang Nok Kheuk, Samut Songkhram province, where he also taught catechesis to Salesian seminarians and Thai to the priests establishing a mission in Thailand. He was transferred to Phitsanulok (1928), where he taught the language to his newly arrived pastor and learned a Chinese dialect (Hakka) himself. In 1930, he was sent as a missionary to North Vietnam and Chiang Mai (northern Thailand) to strengthen the faith of those who had left the Church due to privation. At the end of that mission, he was assigned to the Khorat District to engage in catechesis and re-evangelization of lapsed Catholics. He began evangelizing virtually unexplored lands along the border of Laos in 1937.

He was arrested as a French spy (1941) during the war between France and Indochina and sentenced to ten years' imprisonment. While incarcerated, Nicholas contracted tuberculosis, which was aggravated by maltreatment. Nevertheless, he continued to minister to his fellow inmates and baptized many of them before his death. When his illness became severe he was left in a hospital to die because he was a Catholic.

The decree of martyrdom in his cause was promulgated, Jan. 27, 2000. He was beatified by John Paul II on March 5, 2000. Patron of Thailand.

Bibliography: *L'Osservatore Romano,* Eng. ed. (March 8, 2000) 1, 2–3.

[K. I. RABENSTEIN]

KITTEL, GERHARD

German Evangelical NT scholar, son of Rudolph KITTEL; b. Breslau, Sept. 23, 1888; d. Tübingen, July 11, 1948. He taught at Kiel (1913–17), Leipzig (1917–21), Greifswald (1921–26), Tübingen (1926–39), and Vienna (1939–43). He devoted himself principally to a study of the Jewish background of the NT, maintaining that the Jewish element of the primitive community prevailed over the Hellenistic. In 1931 he organized and became the first editor of the monumental *Theologisches Wörterbuch zum Neuen Testament.* Following the example of H. Cremer and G. Koegel and the suggestions of A. Schlatter, he insisted on tracing the semantics of every word; this entailed a study and combination of its secular usages

in classical Greek and Koine with its religious significance in the Septuagint and its Hebrew background. His little book, *Die Judenfrage* (Stuttgart and Berlin 1933), numerous articles in anti-Semitic magazines, and collaboration with Eugen Fischer in *Das antike Weltjudentum* (1943) caused his imprisonment by the Allies after World War II and forced his retirement to the Benedictine Abbey of Beuron.

Bibliography: W. F. ALBRIGHT, "Gerhard Kittel and the Jewish Question in Antiquity," *History, Archaeology and Christian Humanism* (New York 1964) 229–240.

[L. A. BUSHINSKI]

KITTEL, RUDOLF

German Protestant OT scholar, best known by his critical edition of the Hebrew Bible; b. Eningen, Württemberg, March 28, 1853; d. Leipzig, Oct. 20, 1929. Kittel became professor of Old Testament studies in Breslau (1888) and in Leipzig (1898). As a theologian who believed in divine revelation, in his three-volume *Geschichte des Volkes Israel* (v.1, 6th ed. Gotha 1923; v.2, 7th ed. *ibid.* 1925; v.3, Stuttgart 1927–29) he rejected the natural-evolutionism of J. WELLHAUSEN and set forth the inner spiritual history of Israel while also showing its relationship to the history of other religions of the ancient Near East. He was the first to make extensive use of archeological discoveries in connection with the history of Israel, and he also employed these to good effect in his controversy with Friedrich Delitzsch over PANBABYLONIANISM. Independent historical and theological judgment is likewise characteristic of his *Religion des Volkes Israel* (Leipzig 1921, 2d ed. 1929) and his commentaries on several books of the Old Testament: Psalms, Judges, Samuel, Kings, Chronicles, and Isaiah. His indispensable *Biblia Hebraica* was prepared with the assistance of several fellow specialists (Leipzig 1905–06; 3d ed., P. Kahle, ed., *ibid.* 1929–37).

Bibliography: J. HEMPEL, *Zeitschrift der deutschen morgenländischen Gesellschaft* 84 (1930) 78–93. E. KUTSCH, *Die Religion in Geschichte und Gegenwart,* 7 v. (3rd ed. Tübingen 1957–65) 3:1626–27. O. KAISER, *Lexikon für Theologie und Kirche,* ed. J. HOFER and K. RAHNER, 10 v. (2d, new ed. Freiburg 1957–65) 6:310–311.

[V. HAMP]

KJELD, ST.

Danish noble, whose cult is confined to Denmark; b. Venning, near Randers, Denmark, *c.* 1105; d. Viborg, Sept. 27, 1150. After a pious youth Kjeld (Ketillus or Exuperius) became a canon regular at the Cathedral of Our Lady in Viborg, at the urging of Bishop Eskil of Viborg (d. 1132). On completing his studies he became provost of the cathedral, but lost this office because his generosity was considered excessive. Following a trip to Rome (1148–49) he was reinstated by EUGENE III. Kjeld had preached the expedition of 1147 against the Wends and was planning to devote himself to the Slavic missions when he died. The Danish bishops, especially Archbishop ABSALON OF LUND, sought but failed to obtain his canonization from CLEMENT III. The pope, however, allowed the archbishop to establish Kjeld's cult in his own see on July 11, 1189. Kjeld was venerated especially in Jutland, and was the patron of a guild at Viborg and of a chapel in Viborg's cathedral. His reliquary was burned in 1726.

Feast: July 11.

Bibliography: *Vitae sanctorum danorum,* ed. M. C. GERTZ (new ed. Copenhagen 1908–12) 251–283. T. GAD in *Kulturhistorisk leksikon for nordisk middelalder,* ed. J. DANSTRUP (Copenhagen 1956–) 8:435–437. A. OTTO, *Lexikon für Theologie und Kirche,* ed. J. HOFER and K. RAHNER, 10 v. (2d, new ed. Freiburg 1957–65) 6:311–312.

[L. MUSSET]

KLESL, MELCHIOR

Austrian cardinal and statesman; b. Vienna, Feb. 19, 1552; d. Wiener-Neustadt, Sept. 18, 1630. Son of a Protestant banker, Klesl (Khlesl, Klesel) was 16 when, together with his family, he was converted to Catholicism by the Jesuit G. Scherer, one of the best known preachers of his time. He studied philosophy at the University of Vienna. In 1579 he received his doctorate, was ordained, and appointed provost of St. Stephen and chancellor of the University of Vienna. As such he became instrumental in carrying out the previous ordinance of Ferdinand I, when it was renewed by Emperor Rudolph II in 1581; this forbade Protestants either to teach or to take academic degrees in the University of Vienna. The following year Klesl was appointed councilor of the bishop of Passau for lower Austria. Thus began his lifetime work of bringing Catholicism back to Austria. In 1588 he was appointed administrator of the Diocese of Wiener-Neustadt, and in 1590 he was made the chairman of the Reformation Commission for all the towns and cities other than Vienna. He brought back to the Church, at least outwardly, a number of Austrian towns, among them Neustadt. The chief obstacle to his work was the lack of well-qualified priests. In 1598 he was made bishop of Vienna and in 1615 a cardinal. Chancellor to the Archduke Matthias (1599), he became in 1611 head of his privy council. When Matthias became emperor (1612), Klesl conducted most of the imperial business. At the beginning of the disorders in Bohemia, Klesl at first counseled against the concessions to the Protestants. It was upon his advice that Matthias, in a letter of March 21, 1618, rejected their complaints as unjustified, forbade their intended meetings, and threatened the originators with legal proceedings. Later, however, Klesl reversed himself and tried to reconcile the contending religious parties. In order to remove the chief obstacle to the war policy, the Archduke Ferdinand, who suspected Klesl of being opposed to his candidacy for the imperial throne, and the Archduke Maximilian of Tyrol, probably supported by the Spanish ambassador Oñate, had the cardinal arrested (July 20, 1618) and conveyed to Amras castle near Innsbruck. A few days later he was brought to the castle of Innsbruck, and from there to the monastery Georgenberg near Schwaz. Through the intercession of the pope he received permission to go to Rome (1622). He returned to Vienna in 1627.

Bibliography: J. VON HAMMER-PURGSTALL, *Khlesls . . . Leben . . . ,* 4 v. (Vienna 1847–51). B. CHUDOBA, *Spain and the Empire, 1519–1643* (Chicago 1952). K. H. OELRICH, *Lexikon für Theologie und Kirche,* ed. J. HOFER and K. RAHNER, 10 v. (2d, new ed. Freiburg 1957–65) 6: 339–340, bibliog. M. RITTER, *Allgemeine deutsche Biographie* (Leipzig 1875–1910) 16:167–178. G. MECENSEFFY *Die Religion in Geschichte und Gegenwart,* 7 v. (3d ed. Tübingen 1957–65) 3:1664.

[J. FELICIJAN]

KLEUTGEN, JOSEPH

Philosopher and theologian; b. Dortmund, April 9, 1811; d. Kaltern (Tyrol), Jan. 13, 1883. He entered the Society of Jesus in 1834, taking the name Peters to avoid conflict with the Prussian government. From 1837 until 1843 he taught ethics at the University of Freiburg. Many consider Kleutgen responsible for the restoration of the use of the scholastic method in German Catholic philosophical and theological circles. His *Die Theologie der Vorzeit* (3 v. Münster 1853–60) and *Die Philosophie der Vorzeit* (2 v. Münster 1860–63) are representative works. While inveighing against the errors of G. HERMES, A. GÜNTHER, and J. FROHSCHAMMER, and repudiating the philosophies of I. KANT, G. W. F. HEGEL, and F. SCHELLING, these studies set forth Catholic principles of philosophy and theology in the traditional scholastic form, especially as interpreted and employed by F. SUÁREZ. During VATICAN COUNCIL I Kleutgen served as theologian for the bishop of Paderborn and took part in the formulation of the dogmatic constitution *De fide catholica.* In 1878 Leo XIII named him prefect of studies and professor of dogmatic theology at the Gregorian University in Rome. It is said that Kleutgen was instrumental in the composition of the first draft of the famous encyclical on the doctrine of St. Thomas, *AETERNI PATRIS*, issued by Leo XIII in 1879. He was able to complete only the first of his projected eight-volume work entitled *Institutiones theologicae,* namely, *De ipso Deo* (Regensburg 1881).

[C. R. MEYER]

KLOSTERNEUBURG, MONASTERY OF

A monastery of Augustinian canons on the Danube, Archdiocese of Vienna, Austria. Established *c.* 1100 with secular canons, it was transferred to Augustinians in 1133. Margrave St. LEOPOLD III (*c.* 1075–1136) and Abp. Conrad II of Salzburg endowed the monastery richly and in 1114 began the building of its monumental church. The monastery, always one of the most important spiritual and artistic centers in Austria, defended papal interests in the Middle Ages, and in 1359 its provost received the right to wear pontificals. As a rich monastery it had political prominence, and as the burial place of Leopold it was the religious center of the country. Theological disciplines were cultivated from the beginning, and in the 15th century cartography and astronomy were studied. After declining during the Reformation, it was brought back to Catholicism under the strong direction of the emperors and in a 16th-century renaissance it reestablished the Bohemian monasteries of Třebon and Borovany. In 1730 Charles VI began a gigantic, still unfinished monastery-residence modeled after the ESCORIAL. During World War II under the Nazis, the monastery was suppressed.

The provosts of the monastery include OTTO (1126–32), later bishop of Freising; Bl. HARTMANN (1133–40), later bishop of Brixen; and Cardinal Friedrich PIFFL (1907–13), later archbishop of Vienna. Pius PARSCH (1884–1954), institutor of the popular liturgical movement, and Romanus Scholz (1912–44), an Austrian resistance hero, were canons of Klosterneuburg. The interior of the Romanesque church (1114–36) with Gothic towers was rebuilt in 17th-century baroque. St. Leopold's chapel, originally the chapterhouse, includes the famous enamel altar by Nicholas of Verdun (1181), a great bronze chandelier (1120–30), and beautiful glass paintings of the 14th and 15th centuries. A Gothic cloister (13th–14th century) and a baroque emperor's ''palace'' with a marble hall (1730–40) are noteworthy. The library of 160,000 volumes and 1,256 MSS, the archives, the famous treasure containing the Austrian archducal crown (1616), and a gallery with many Gothic paintings are of great value. The 95 members of 1914 were reduced to 65 in 1964. The monastery serves 26 parishes with 135,000 souls. It has a theological academy founded in 1768, a school for boys and a choir school, and editorial and publishing facilities. It engages in farming, forestry, and the cultivation of vineyards. Pilgrims come to the shrine of St. Leopold for his feast (November 15). The monastery has published the bimonthly *Bibel und Liturgie* since 1926.

Bibliography: *Jahrbuch des Stiftes Klosterneuburg,* 9 v. (1908–20; NS 1961–). *Klosterneuburger Kunstschätze* (1961–). B. ČERNIK, *Das Augustiner-Chorherrenstift Klosterneuburg* (Vienna 1958). F. RÖHRIG, *Lexikon für Theologie und Kirche,* ed. J. HOFER and K. RAHNER, 10 v. (2d, new ed. Freiburg 1957–65) 6:349–350. H. FILLITZ, ed., *Beiträge zur Kunstgeschichte und Archäologie des Frühmittelalters* (Graz 1962).

[F. H. RÖHRIG]

KLUPFEL, ENGELBERT

Theologian; b. Wipfeld near Würzburg, Jan. 18, 1733; d. Freiburg im Breisgau, July 8, 1811. He was baptized Andrew, but took the name Engelbert when he entered the Augustinian Order in 1751. After philosophical studies (1751–58) at Fribourg (Switzerland), Erfurt, Freiburg, and Constance, he taught philosophy and theology (1763–67) in the order's houses at Oberndorf (Neckar), Mainz, and Constance. In 1767 he was named professor of theology at the University of Freiburg im Breisgau and remained there until 1805. In his *De statu naturae purae* (Freiburg 1768) and *De eximiis dotibus humanae naturae ante peccatum* (Freiburg 1769), he embraced the teaching on grace of the young Augustinian school begun by H. NORIS. Despite his being influenced by the spirit of his times in the denial of papal infallibility, his two-volume work *Institutiones theologiae dogmaticae* (Vienna 1789) is free of rationalistic errors; it was prescribed as the official theological manual for Austria. His purely positive theological method, in reaction to scholasticism, developed valuable insights for the history of dogma. Also noteworthy are his *Christus Dominus sacerdos* (Freiburg 1772) and *Nova bibliotheca ecclesiastica Friburgensis* (7 v. Freiburg 1775–90); in the latter he attacks the rationalism of J. S. Semler.

Bibliography: W. RAUCH, *Engelbert Klüpfel, ein führender Theologe der Aufklärungszeit* (Freiburg 1922). H. HURTER, *Nomenclator literarius theologiae catholicae,* 5 v. in 6 (3d ed. Innsbruck 1903–1913); v.1 (4th ed. 1926) 5.1:651–654. F. LANG, *Lexikon für Theologie und Kirche,* ed. J. HOFER and K. RAHNER, 10 v. (2d, new ed. Freiburg 1957–65) 6:355.

[A. ZUMKELLER]

KNIGHT, WILLIAM, BL.

Lay martyr; b. *c.* 1572 at South Duffield, Hemingbrough, Yorkshire, England; d. Nov. 29, 1596, hanged, drawn, and quartered at York. On coming of age he claimed from his Protestant uncle property left to him by his father, Leonard Knight. When his uncle denounced him to the authorities for being a Catholic, he was immediately arrested. In October 1593, Knight was remanded to York Castle, where BB. William GIBSON and George ERRINGTON were already confined. A certain Protestant clergyman, also a prisoner, arranged to gain his freedom by feigning a desire to become a Catholic. He won the confidence of Knight and his two companions, who explained the faith to him. With the connivance of the authorities, he was directed to Bl. Henry ABBOT, then at liberty, who endeavored to find a priest to reconcile him to the Church. Thereupon Abbot was arrested and, together with Knight and his two comrades, sentenced to death for persuading the clergyman to embrace Catholicism—an act of treason under the penal laws. He was beatified by Pope John Paul II on Nov. 22, 1987 with George Haydock and Companions.

Feast of the English Martyrs: May 4 (England).

See Also: ENGLAND, SCOTLAND, AND WALES, MARTYRS OF.

Bibliography: R. CHALLONER, *Memoirs of Missionary Priests,* ed. J. H. POLLEN (rev. ed. London 1924). J. H. POLLEN, *Acts of English Martyrs* (London 1891).

[K. I. RABENSTEIN]

KNIGHTS OF ALCÁNTARA

One of three chief military orders in Spain, established in the 12th century to fight the Moors. The order was known initially as that of San Julián del Pereiro. The first evidence of its existence is a charter from King Fernando II of León (Jan. 1176), addressed to the community settled at Pereiro on the borders of León and Portugal. In December of the same year Pope ALEXANDER III gave his approval to the community. The settlement at Pereiro may date from 1167 as suggested by INNOCENT III's bull of 1207 referring to the possessions that the order had held for 40 years or more. LUCIUS III's bull of 1183 indicates that the knights followed a mitigated BENEDICTINE RULE as a dependency of Cîteaux. Sometime before 1187 they were affiliated to the Order of Calatrava. About the same time they transferred their chief seat to Trujillo in the Kingdom of Castile where it remained until the Moors captured Trujillo in 1195. In 1218 the Order of Calatrava ceded the fortress of Alcántara (on the Tagus River near the Portuguese frontier) to the Knights of San Julián. Henceforth they were known as the Order of Alcántara. The master of Calatrava retained the right to visit Alcántara ''according to the Order of Cîteaux.'' The organiza-

tion and customs of Alcántara were similar to those of the Order of Calatrava. The Knights of Alcántara played an active role in the reconquest of Extremadura and Andalusia, but in the later medieval centuries, from 1318 onward, their energies were diverted increasingly by internal dissension and by involvement in domestic politics. This prompted King Ferdinand V and Queen Isabella, who had seen the loyalty of the master vacillate from Spain to Portugal and back, to assume administration of the order in 1494 with papal permission. Pope ADRIAN VI in 1523 annexed the mastership of the crown in perpetuity. Since 1546 the knights have been permitted to marry. Although Charles V and other rulers underwent the year of probation and became professed members in the order, the original spirit was gradually lost. The order survives today as an honorary society of noblemen.

Bibliography: A. DE TORRES Y TAPIA, *Cronica de la Orden de Alcántara,* 2 v. (Madrid 1763). J. F. O'CALLAGHAN, ''The Foundation of the Order of Alcántara, 1176–1218,'' *Catholic Historical Review* 47 (1961–62) 471–486. *Bullarium ordinis militiae de Alcántara* (Madrid 1759). A. FOREY, *The Military Orders from the Twelfth to the Early Fourteenth Centuries* (Toronto 1992).

[J. F. O'CALLAGHAN]

KNIGHTS OF COLUMBUS

A fraternal benefit society of Catholic men chartered by the state of Connecticut in 1882. For over its 115 years the Order has responded to the myriad needs of the local churches in the United States, Canada, Mexico, Puerto Rico, and the Philippines. This article traces the origins of Columbianism as a force in the Church and society with particular focus on its character as a Catholic antidefamation society.

History. Michael J. McGivney was the New Haven priest who founded the Knights of Columbus in 1882. He was an unassuming pious priest who easily elicited the trust of the laity. Concerned with the strong appeal of the prohibited secret societies among Catholic youth and with the plight of the widows and children suffering the loss of the breadwinner, he was eager to form a fraternal insurance society imbued with deep loyalties to Catholicism and to the American experience.

In October of 1881 McGivney and a small group of laymen decided to establish an independent society rather than become a branch of one of two existing Catholic benefit societies. In early February 1882 they placed their order under the patronage of Christopher Columbus. According to the few surviving documents, the Columbian motif represented the group's Catholic consciousness. Columbus was the symbol. By portraying the navigator's landing at San Salvador as the Catholic baptism of the na-

Knights of Columbus headquarters, New Haven, Connecticut.
(©G.E. Kidder Smith/CORBIS)

tion, the Knights were asserting religious legitimacy. Just as the heirs of the Pilgrims invoked the Mayflower as the Protestant symbol of their identity as early Americans, so the Knights invoked the Santa Maria as the symbol of their self-understanding as Catholic citizens. On March 29, 1882 the Order was incorporated in the State of Connecticut. One of the charter members invoked the cause of Catholic civil liberty when he asserted that the order's patron signified that, as Catholic descendants of Columbus "[we] were entitled to all rights and privileges due to such a discovery by one of our faith."

For the first ten years insurance was a mandatory feature of membership in the order. In 1892 non-insurance or associate membership was established, which meant that candidates for knighthood could be drawn to the order unfettered by economic ties. When the order expanded into Massachusetts in 1892, Columbianism became more explicit. The quadricentennial of Columbus's landfall, the rise of another wave of anti-Catholicism in the form of the American Protective Association and the expansionist policies of the leadership fostered the development of Columbianism. The general spirit of patriotism, culminating in the Spanish American War, also animated the order's character. From New England the order expanded throughout the nation. By 1905 the

Knights were in every state in the Union, five provinces of Canada, Mexico, the Philippines, and were poised to enter Cuba and Puerto Rico. The causation for this enormously successful period of expansion is primarily due to the way in which the Knights conveyed through their ceremonials their strong sense of American Catholic identity. In a sense, the ceremonials provided the candidates for knighthood with a rite of passage from old world ties to loyalty to the new republic. Basic to their ethos was the prevailing notion of manliness, that gender construction manifested in fraternal sentiments and muscular Christianity.

The Knights extolled Catholic unity and struggled against the divisive character of ethnic particularism. Though the leaders were all second-generation Irish-Americans, they were realists on the ethnic issue. Hence, they allowed the establishment of the Teutonic Council for German-American Knights and of the Italian-American Ansonia Council, both of which were instituted in Boston during the 1890s.

Activities. In accord with the order's anti-defamation character, it instituted in 1914 the Knights of Columbus Commission on Religious Prejudices. The latter was mandated "to study the causes, investigate conditions and suggest remedies for the religious prejudice that has been manifest through the press and rostrum." Under the chairmanship of Patrick Henry Callahan, then K. of C. state deputy of Kentucky and a wealthy industrialist known for his capital-labor profit-sharing plan, the commission followed its mandate to the letter. As an antidote to prejudices Callahan especially promoted the papal encyclical of 1891, *Rerum Novarum.*

Columbian lay activism manifested itself in a new field of work in 1916 when U.S. troops were stationed along the Mexican border. After learning of the needs for recreational and religious centers, the order established sixteen buildings from the Gulf of Mexico to the Gulf of California for the social needs of all soldiers and for the religious needs of Catholics.

As a result of this experience, the Knights offered such services to the U.S. government when it entered World War I in April 1917. American and Canadian K. of C. "Huts" with signs saying, "Everyone Welcome, Everything Free," were established in the training camps and eventually in Europe and Asia, even to the remote area of Siberia. The order raised one million dollars during the first year. As a result of a joint drive with the Y.M.C.A., the Jewish Welfare Board, the Salvation Army, and others, the order received over thirty million dollars for its War Camp Fund.

After the war, the Knights established employment bureaus throughout the country to find jobs for veterans.

They also provided college scholarships for returning servicemen and set up evening schools for veterans and all others interested in academic and vocational advancement. In January 1924 there were sixty-nine evening schools with an enrollment of more than 30,000 students. The Knights received numerous commendations for war and reconstruction work, but the greatest tribute was demonstrated by the more than 450,000 men who joined the order between 1917 and 1923.

During the 1920s Columbianism expressed itself in a variety of new programs. In response to those historians who stressed an economic interpretation of American history, who disregarded the idealism of the revolutionary period, and who ignored the contributions of the various non-Anglo-Saxon immigrant groups, the order established the K. of C. Historical Commission. The commission was charged with the responsibility "to investigate the facts of history, to correct historical errors and omissions, to amplify and preserve our national history to exalt and perpetuate American ideals and to combat anti-American propaganda by means of pamphlets . . . and by other proper means and methods as shall be approved by the Supreme Assembly." Under the direction of Edward McSweeney, a former trade unionist and immigration officer on Ellis Island, the commission awarded prizes for the best historical monographs. Works of such scholars who later earned national reputations, as Samuel Flagg Bemis and Allan Nevins, were published by Macmillan in the Knights of Columbus Historical Series.

In the autumn of 1922, McSweeney designed a unique set of historical studies entitled, "The Knights of Columbus Racial Contribution Series." Three monographs were published in this ambitious series: *The Gift of Black Folk* by W. E. B. DuBois; *The Jews in the Making of America* by George Cohen; and *The Germans in the Making of America* by Frederick Franklin Schrader. In his introduction to each of these books, McSweeney summarized the history of immigration to America, the waves of nativism, anti-Catholicism, anti-Semitism, and the persistence of racial prejudice in the life of the nation.

In 1921 Pope Benedict XV called upon Columbianism's Catholic anti-defamation character to respond to religious prejudice in Rome. The pope elaborated on how anti-Catholic propaganda was a strong factor in the Protestant evangelization of Rome and the degree to which it threatened to break down Roman youth's loyalties to the Church.

Within a year after this historic audience, the order had appointed a commission for the order's Roman project, had established a one-million-dollar Italian Welfare Fund through a per capita tax on the membership, had received permission to construct recreation centers from Benedict's successor, Pope Pius XI, and had contracted the services of a Roman engineer and architect, Enrico Galeazzi. Between 1924 and 1927 the order opened five recreation centers, the most significant of which was St. Peter's Oratory, adjacent to Vatican City. In the 1930s this program was absorbed into the Catholic Action movement.

During the Great Depression the Knights revived their antisocialism, a crusade that included a social justice component. At the Supreme Council meeting in August 1937, held in San Antonio, the crusade was unanimously endorsed by the delegates. Supreme Knight Martin Carmody reported that the *Daily Worker*, the official voice of the American Communist Party, had frequently vented "its wrath against the Knights of Columbus." Shortly after the convention, the Supreme Board of Directors approved Carmody's proposal to hire an anti-Communist lecturer, George Hermann Derry, who had been a member of the K. of C.'s Historical Commission and who had recently resigned as president of Marygrove College in Detroit. Derry's lecture program, which was subject to the prior approval of the hierarchy, included a general public address sponsored by local Knights and an address to the clergy of the diocese on anti-Communist leadership.

The administration of Luke E. Hart (1953–64), John K. McDevitt (1964–1977), and Virgil C. Dechant, are identified with the modernization of the order within the context of its traditional loyalty to Church and country. Hart laid the basis for the modern insurance program that was later greatly refined by Virgil Dechant. Hart's conservatism on racial and labor issues alienated many members of the order and the hierarchy. McDevitt led a movement to reform the policy governing admissions to local councils, thereby engendering racial integration. By this policy and by cosponsoring a Human Rights Congress at Yale and fostering other programs related to social justice, McDevitt restored the confidence of the hierarchy in the order's direction. In general, John McDevitt's administration represents a synthesis of modern fraternalism and traditional faith.

Virgil C. Dechant's administration reflects his command of the insurance programs, his policy to modernize the structures of the international headquarters in New Haven, his commitment to infuse a strong social service component into the order's fraternalism, his positive response to the needs of the American Church mediated by the bishop, and his deep loyalty to the Vatican represented by the order's contributions to the pope's charities, and the Vatican's needs for architectural restoration and artistic beatification.

Under Dechant's leadership the order has experienced considerable growth. In 2001 there were 1.7 million Knights located in more than 13,000 councils. With twenty-five billion dollars of insurance in force and with the widespread programs of the order, entailing contributions of nearly $92.2 million by Supreme, state, and local councils in 1989, and almost twenty-three million man-hours given to community service during that year, the Knights of Columbus still experience the vitality of their original mission to respond to the needs of the Church and to witness to the unique character of the Catholic experience in America.

Upon the retirement of Virgil Dechant at the age of 70 in October 2000, Carl Anderson, the Supreme Secretary, was elected Supreme Knight by the Supreme Board of Directors. Formerly the Dean of the John Paul II Institute for Marriage and Family, Anderson brings a theological dimension to his leadership. His columns in *Columbia* include a religious message in a popular idiom. Since a year later the amount of insurance in force reached the record level of $42 billion, Anderson reveals a command of that vital aspect of the Order.

Bibliography: The papers of the order are located in the Archives of the Knights of Columbus in New Haven, Connecticut. C. J. KAUFFMAN, *Faith and Fraternalism The History of the Knights of Columbus*, rev. ed (New York 1992); *Columbianism and the Knights of Columbus* (New York 1992).

[C. J. KAUFFMAN]

KNIGHTS OF DOBRIN

One of the twelve religious MILITARY ORDERS of knighthood that came into being between 1100 and 1300 and one of the three of German origin. It was founded by Duke Conrad of Masovia and Bp. CHRISTIAN OF PRUSSIA, who patterned the new brotherhood after the Order of the KNIGHTS OF THE SWORD of Livonia. In August 1228 a certain Bruno, together with 14 knights, were invested into the new order. These ''new'' Knights of Dobrin may actually have been former members of the Order of the Brothers of the Sword. Duke Conrad endowed them with Dobrin castle in Prussia on the Drweca River, hence the name, Knights of Dobrin. The knights were most likely Germans. Their habit consisted of a white mantle with a red cross. The new order, however, had little opportunity to develop. The Prussians were greatly annoyed by the news of its foundation and attacked Dobrin castle in strength and surrounded it so closely that none of its inhabitants dared to venture far beyond its ramparts. When Duke Conrad was forced to cede Prussia to the TEUTONIC KNIGHTS, the Order of Dobrin lost its reason for existence and applied to the Holy See for permission to merge with the Teutonic Order. On April 19, 1235, permission was granted. A group of knights, however, refused to accept

the merger, and ten of them were still living under the protection of Duke Conrad *c.* 1240. After this date the Order of Dobrin disappeared completely from history, and its possessions, following a short litigation, became the property of the Teutonic Knights.

Bibliography: T. HIRSCH et al., eds., *Scriptores rerum Prussicarum*, 5 v. (Leipzig 1861–74), v.1, main source. M. TUMLER, *Der Deutsche Orden im Werden, Wachsen und Wirken bis 1400* (Vienna 1955; 2d ed. 1965). A. FOREY, *The Military Orders from the Twelfth to the Early Fourteenth Centuries* (Toronto 1992).

[G. GROSSCHMID]

KNIGHTS OF LABOR

A U.S. labor organization founded in 1869 at Philadelphia, Pa., by Uriah S. Stephens (1821–82); it was the most successful effort of its kind up to that time and exercised maximum influence from 1877 to 1887. In 1871 Stephens, an abolitionist who had studied for the Baptist ministry before becoming a tailor and labor leader, adopted the name Noble and Holy Order of the Knights of Labor for his secret organization. Ten years later the order dropped ''Noble and Holy'' from its official title, eliminated its oath of secrecy, and revised its ritual. Combining advanced social theories with practical objectives, the Knights advocated laws for improved safety regulation, mechanics' liens, the eight-hour workday, public ownership of utilities, and the regulation of child labor. Convict leasing was opposed. Although arbitration, instead of strikes, was advanced strongly, a strike fund was soon started. Women were encouraged to organize, and equal pay for both sexes for equal work was advocated. The order's stated objective was the organization of every department of productive industry; it became an advocate of industrial union, in contrast with its earlier emphasis on craft unions. The Knights were committed also to a system of producer cooperatives, an activity that proved unprofitable and contributed to the eventual decline of the organization. After Terence Vincent Powderly succeeded Stephens as grand master workman of the order (1879), membership increased to 700,000 (1886), and the Knights emerged successful in a number of strikes, including that against the Missouri Pacific railroad. However, the Chicago Haymarket Square riot in May 1886 was used widely to discredit the Knights, although they took no part in it.

The attitude of Catholic clergy was an important factor in the rising and waning fortunes of the organization. Many parish priests, fearing possible socialistic or violent influences, often opposed such unions. The Knights were condemned by the hierarchy of Canada on the grounds of secrecy, but Cardinal James Gibbons of Baltimore,

Md., was convinced of the merits of labor organizations and obtained assurance against condemnation from Rome. In 1891 Leo XIII's encyclical *RERUM NOVARUM* strongly supported the cardinal's position. When Powderly retired (1893), the Knights' difficulties with the Church had ceased; but other labor unions, more in touch with the changing times, were coming to the fore. In 1917 the Knights of Labor officially disbanded.

Bibliography: H. J. BROWNE, Catholic University of America, *Studies in American Church History: The Catholic Church and the Knights of Labor* 38 (Washington 1949). N. J. WARE, *The Labor Movement in the United States, 1860–1895* (New York 1929). J. R. COMMONS et al., eds., *A Documentary History of American Industrial Society*, 10 v. (Cleveland 1909). J. T. ELLIS, *The Life of James Cardinal Gibbons*, 2 v. (Milwaukee 1952).

[J. W. COLEMAN]

KNIGHTS OF MALTA

The Sovereign Military Order of the Hospital of St. John of Jerusalem, of Rhodes, and of Malta, commonly called the Knights of Malta or Knights Hospitaller, a religious and knightly order dating from the 11th century.

History of the Order. Whatever its possible antecedents, the order began in Jerusalem in a hospice-infirmary for pilgrims founded by Blessed Gerard (d. 1120) before the First CRUSADE. Together with the adjoining church, the hospice was dedicated to St. John the Baptist and served by a religious confraternity following a variant of the rule of St. AUGUSTINE. Gerard was its first rector. After the formation of the kingdom of JERUSALEM this confraternity received approbation in a bull of PASCHAL II, February 15, 1113 (P. Jaffé, *Regesta pontificum romanorum* 6341), which also ensured to the new order the protection of the Holy See and the right of freely electing Gerard's successors without interference from any other authority, ecclesiastical or lay. Succeeding popes confirmed and enlarged these privileges. Gerard's successors were styled masters and then grand masters of the hospital. Under its second head, Raymond de Podio (du Puy), the order acquired its military-chivalric character because of the need to defend pilgrims and the Christian kingdom against Muslim attacks.

The growing prestige of the order brought it great donations, especially the TEMPLAR properties granted to it by the Holy See in 1312. Throughout its extensive possessions, East and West, it spread a network of *domus hospitales* for the service and defense of pilgrims. These were grouped into bailiwicks, priories, and grand priories. The failure of the Crusades forced the order to abandon the Holy Land; in 1310 it acquired the island of RHODES, becoming a territorial state and a naval power

Coat of arms embellishing one of the tombs of the Knights of St. John of Jerusalem, St. John's Cathedral, Valletta, Malta. (©Adam Woolfitt/CORBIS)

patrolling the eastern Mediterranean against the Muslim assault. In the 14th and 15th centuries the order was divided into national units called Tongues (*Langues*). The advance of Islam, now led by the OTTOMAN TURKS, could not be arrested. After four unsuccessful Turkish attacks, the Sultan Süleyman I the Magnificent conquered Rhodes in 1522 and forced the Knights to retreat to the West. In 1530 the Emperor CHARLES V ceded to them the sovereign possession of the islands of Malta, Gozo, and Camino, as well as Tripoli in North Africa. Malta's strategic position between the Christian and the Moslem world enabled the order to block Islam's advance toward the heart of Christendom. This island was subjected to violent Ottoman attacks especially in 1551, 1565 (the Great Siege), and 1644. Galleys of the order took part in the Battle of LEPANTO (1571), which broke the Ottoman tide. On Malta the order reached the height of its power. Grandiose fortifications made the island impregnable. The order's navy became one of the most powerful in the Mediterranean and waged incessant war on the Ottomans and the Barbary pirates.

The REFORMATION deprived the order of its English and of many of its German possessions, and during the 17th and 18th centuries the Knights experienced a period of decline. Growing nationalism in the West clashed with the order's supranational character, and finally the FRENCH REVOLUTION, hostile both to the Church and to the Knights Hospitaller, despoiled the order in France and advanced irresistibly toward its Mediterranean holdings. Greek Orthodox Russia, however, motivated by the Russian Emperor Paul I's personal admiration for the Knights, his abhorrence of the Revolution, and Russia's very practical perennial drive toward the Mediterranean, appeared ready to oppose France. The *rapprochement* that resulted was sealed in the Convention of Jan. 15, 1797, between the Grand Master de Rohan and Paul I, establishing a new grand priory of the order in Russia. This foundation was formed in part from the Polish grand priory, which, in the partitions of Poland, had fallen under Russian control. In November 1797, under the new Grand Master Ferdinand von Hompesch, Paul I was proclaimed protector of the order. The French reply was the seizure of Malta. On his way to Egypt, NAPOLEON I moved on the island in violation of the order's internationally guaranteed neutrality, and on June 12, 1798, the island fell to the French. Hompesch and the convent removed to Trieste under Austria's protection. Russia's reply to this seizure of Malta was to produce a claim to it. On September 6, 1798, profiting by the indignation aroused by the surrender of Malta, the Russian grand priory proclaimed Hompesch deposed; on September 21, Paul assumed the "supreme direction" of the order; on November 7 the Russian grand priory proclaimed him grand master and on November 24 he accepted that dignity and the sovereignty over Malta implied by it. On January 8, 1799, he announced the formation (December 10, 1798) of another "Grand Priory of Russia" for non-Catholics.

Despite Paul's pressure the Holy See refused to recognize him as grand master. Recognition came from many of the knights and from European governments, however, and on July 6, 1799, the Court of Vienna forced Hompesch to abdicate. Thus *de facto,* if not *de jure,* Paul I was the head of the order. By September 1800 the British had taken Malta from the French; Paul I was murdered (March 23, 1801), and his son and successor Alexander I assumed protection of the order. Laying no claims to the grand mastership, he called for a canonical election of a new grand master. With the approval of PIUS VII the Bailiff John Baptist Tommasi became grand master on February 9, 1803, and was recognized by the allied powers and by Russia. In 1803 Alexander I tacitly abandoned the protectorship of the order; in 1810 the order's properties were confiscated by the crown; and in 1817 a decision of the Russian cabinet, sanctioned by the Emperor, declared that the order no longer existed in Russia. The Grand Master Tommasi had died in 1805, and an in-

terregnum followed, during which the order was ruled by lieutenants. In 1834 the convent was finally moved to Rome. LEO XIII restored the grand mastership in the person of the Lieutenant Ceschi a Santa Croce (1879–1905), who was succeeded by the Grand Masters Thun-Hohenstein (1905–31) and Chigi della Rovere Albani (1931–51). The position of the order vis-à-vis the Holy See was defined anew, January 24, 1953, by a commission of cardinals appointed by PIUS XII. John XXIII (June 24, 1961) approved the new Constitutional Charter of the order.

The Knights of Malta have also had a second order, the Hospitaller Sisters of St. John of Jerusalem, still existing in Spain and Malta, but no longer under the grand master's jurisdiction.

Status. The order is a religious community of lay men and women, and chaplains, whose aims are the sanctification of its members, service of the faith and of the Holy See, and welfare work. It is also the oldest order of chivalry in existence, composed of both religious and lay knights and of other associates, and is internationally recognized as sovereign. In its latter capacity it deals with the Papal Secretariate of State and maintains diplomatic relations with the Holy See and a number of states in both hemispheres. The sovereign aspect of the order enables it to carry on its religious and charitable activities freely on a worldwide scale. Like chivalry itself, the order has been traditionally an institution of the nobility, but in modern times, its membership includes Catholics on the basis of merit as well as birth.

Classes of Members. Its members are divided into three classes: (1) the knights of justice and professed chaplains, forming the religious and directive core, and bound by religious vows, both simple and solemn; (2) the knights of obedience and donates of justice, who promise to strive toward Christian perfection in their lives; the "donates" are not knights, but persons who have served the order; (3) the lay members and secular chaplains, subdivided into knights and dames of honor and devotion, honorary conventual chaplains, knights and dames of grace and devotion, magistral chaplains, knights and dames of magistral grace, and donates of devotion. Several grades require proof of nobility in addition to other qualifications; others require merit alone. Within them, the higher ranks of grand cross or bailiff may be acquired. Cardinals are traditionally invested with the insignia of bailiffs grand cross of honor and devotion.

Territorially the order is now divided into five grand priories (Rome, Lombardy-Venetia, Naples-Sicily, Bohemia, Austria) and 26 national associations including two of master knights, i.e., knights of magistral grace. In the U.S. Members not belonging to either priories or associations are *in gremio religionis,* depending directly on the grand master in Rome. The supreme head of the order is the grand master, elected for life from among the solemnly professed knights of justice, with papal approval. In his absence the order is ruled by a lieutenant. The grand master has the title of prince and is equal in rank to a cardinal. He is styled most eminent highness and is internationally recognized as a chief of state. He governs the order with the assistance of the sovereign council; the supreme assembly is the general chapter convoked at regular intervals. For the elections of grand master or lieutenant the complete council of state is convoked. The pope is represented in the order by a cardinal *patronus.* The order's headquarters and the grand master's residence (the convent) are at the Malta Palace in Rome.

Activities. The order's principal charitable activities fall into the following categories: (1) Hospital work: the order maintains a great number of hospitals, clinics, medical and research centers, and dispensaries in various parts of the world.(2) Care for the wounded in war and peace: it operates first-aid centers and maintains a number of ambulance corps, equipped with hospital facilities, trains, and transport planes. (3) Relief work for refugees and the needy.

The spiritual character of the order is founded on the mixture of its religious and chivalric ideals. Its service of Christ and of the unfortunate, its honor, courtesy, and *noblesse oblige* have lost none of their worth with the passage of time. The blending of these two aspects in the military-monastic orders of the Crusades helped to spiritualize military valor on the model of its ideal, the soldier of Christ.

Bibliography: F. DE HELLWALD, *Bibliographie méthodique de l'ordre souv. de St. Jean de Jérusalem* (Rome 1885). E. ROSSI, *Aggiunta alla bibliographie méthodique de l'ordre souv. de St. Jean de Jérusalem de F. de Hellwald* (Rome 1924). G. BOTTARELLI and M. MONTERISI, *Storia politica e militare del sovrano ordine di S. Giovanni di Gerusalemme, detto di Malta,* 2 v. (Milan 1940). J. M. DELAVILLE LE ROULX, *Cartulaire général de l'ordre des Hospitaliers de St. Jean de Jérusalem,* 4 v. (Paris 1894–1906). T. MICHEL DE PIERREDON, *Histoire politique de l'ordre souverain de St. Jean de Jérusalem (ordre de Malta) 1789–1955,* 2 v. (2d ed. Paris 1956–63). E. E. HUME, *Medical Work of the Knights Hospitallers of St. John of Jerusalem* (Baltimore 1940). J. H. VAN DER VELDT, *The Ecclesiastical Orders of Knighthood* (Washington 1956).J. A. BRUNDAGE, ''A Twelfth-Century Oxford Disputation concerning the Privileges of the Knights Hospitallers,'' *Mediaeval Studies* 24 (Toronto-London 1962) 153–160. *Constitutional Charter of the Sovereign Military Hospitaller Order of St. John of Jerusalem of Rhodes and of Malta* (Rome 1961). Order of Malta, *Livre blanc* (Rome 1962). H. J. A. SIRE, *The Knights of Malta* (New Haven 1994). R. MCHUGH, *The Knights of Malta: 900 Years of Care* (Dublin, Ireland: 1996).

[O. P. SHERBOWITZ-WETZOR/C. TOUMANOFF/EDS.]

KNIGHTS OF MONTESA

A military order established June 10, 1317, by Pope JOHN XXII at the request of King JAMES II OF ARAGON. The order received the properties of the TEMPLARS and of the KNIGHTS OF MALTA in the Kingdom of Valencia and had its chief seat at Montesa near Játiva. The knights were subject to the rule and customs of the Order of CALATRAVA, whose master, accompanied by the abbot either of Santes Creus or Valldigna, was obliged to visit Montesa annually. Only in 1319 did the master of Calatrava implement the pope's instructions and confer the habit on the first knights of Montesa. The Cistercian general chapter of 1321 incorporated Montesa into the Order of CÎTEAUX in accordance with the papal bull, and authorized the abbot of Santes Creus to send monks to care for the spiritual needs of the knights. Statutes enacted by the masters of Calatrava (1326, 1331, and 1353) and by the Cistercian abbots of MORIMOND (1444 and 1468) give a clear picture of the organization and customs of Montesa. In 1400 Pope BENEDICT XIII, at the request of King Martin of Aragon, united the Order of San Jorge de Alfama to Montesa. Several masters of Montesa performed distinctive services in the international policy of the kings of Aragon. In 1587 Pope Sixtus V annexed the mastership to the crown in perpetuity.

Bibliography: H. DE SAMPER, *Montesa ilustrada,* 2 v. (Valencia 1669). A. L. JAVIERRE MUR, *Privilegios reales de la Orden de Montesa en la Edad Media* (Madrid 1945). *Enciclopedia de la Religión Católica* 5: 577–578.

[J. F. O'CALLAGHAN]

KNIGHTS OF PETER CLAVER

A predominantly African-American Catholic fraternal organization founded Nov. 7, 1909 at Mobile, Ala., by three Black laymen (Gilbert Faustina, Frank Collins and Frank Trenier) and four Josephite fathers (Revs. Conrad F. Rebesher, John H. Dorsey, Samuel J. Kelly and Joseph P. Van Baast), and placed under the patronage of St. Peter Claver. It was incorporated on July 12, 1911. The organization was later extended to include fourth-degree knights (1917), junior knights (1917), ladies auxiliary (1922), and junior daughters (1930). The constitutions of the national council were revised nine times (1925, 1929, 1936, 1948, 1951, 1971, 1979, 1989, and 1999). The Ladies' Auxiliary was recognized as a division of the National Council at Galveston, Texas in August of 1926, and the Junior Knights recognized as a division of the National Council from Oct. 1, 1935 onwards. The order operates in over 56 archdioceses and dioceses throughout the United States.

The purpose of the order is to render service to God and to the Church by promoting the brotherhood of man, especially through spiritual and corporal works of mercy and various other Catholic activities. Historically, the order operated mutual aid, thrift, social, educational and poverty-alleviation programs, and supported endeavors promoting desegregation in the South and the extension of suffrage to African Americans. The order continues to collaborate in mutual projects with the National Advancement of Colored People, National Council of Negro Women, National Council of Catholic Women, Urban League, Sickle Cell Anema Foundation, Xavier University Development and Expansion Fund, The Sr. Thea Bowman Black Catholic Educational Foundation, The International Alliance of Catholic Knights, the National Black Catholic Congress, and National Black Clergy and National Black Sisters' Conferences. Besides offering educational scholarships and financial aid, the order supports a variety of charitable appeals. It contributed $100,000 toward the construction of Our Mother of Africa Chapel in the National Shrine of the Immaculate Conception, Washington, D.C. that was dedicated at the closing liturgy of the 8th National Black Catholic Congress in August of 1997.

The order has had 13 supreme knights: Gilbert Faustina (1909–26), Louis Israel (1926–40), Alphonse Auguste (1941), John H. Clouser (1941–46), J. Roland Prejean (1946–52), Beverly V. Baranco, Jr. (1952–58), Eugene B. Perry (1958–64), Shields G. Gilmore, Jr. (1964–1970), Ernest Granger, Sr. (1970–76), Murray J. Frank (1976–1982), Chester J. Jones (1982–88), Paul C. Condoll (1988–1994) and A. Jackie Elly (1994–). In the Ladies' Auxiliary, there have been ten Supreme Ladies: Mrs. M. L. Lunnon (1926–28), Mrs. A. R. Aubry (1928–1952), Mrs. E. B. Jones (1952–1958), Mrs. Inez Y. Bowman (1958–1964), Mrs. Thelma P. Lombard (1964–70), Mrs. Florence W. Lee (1970–1976), Mrs. Elise LeNoir Morris (1976–1982), Mrs. Consuella M. Broussard (1982–1988), Mrs. Dorothy B. Henderson (1988–1994) and Ms. Leodia Gooch (1994–).

The first official journal of the order was the *Shield*, which commenced publication in November of 1910. In 1922, it was renamed the *Claverite*, and since 1974 it is published semi-annually. The headquarters of the order is located at 1825 Orleans Ave., New Orleans, LA 70116.

[E. B. PERRY/EDS.]

KNIGHTS OF ST. GEORGE

A Catholic fraternal society organized in Pittsburgh, Pa., in 1880 with the approval of Bp. John Tuigg (1876–89). The original purpose of the order was to form a large, well-organized society capable of offering effective assistance to the many German immigrant families that were settling in the Pittsburgh area at that time. The movement began among members of St. Martin's parish, a German national parish in Pittsburgh. In the fall of 1880 a constitution was adopted, and the order took as its official title the German Roman Catholic Knights of St. George. On Jan. 8, 1881, a civil charter was obtained in Allegheny County, Pa. In addition to various social and charitable works, the knights gave financial aid to seminarians and sponsored the lay retreat movement. At one time, they also published a periodical called *Knight of St. George*.

[R. A. KLINEFELTER]

KNIGHTS OF ST. JAMES

Military religious order under the patronage of the Apostle James, established Aug. 1, 1170, in Cáceres, Spain, by Pedro Fernandes and companions. King Fernando II of León, realizing the value of such an order for the defense of his recent conquests in Extremadura, ceded Cáceres to the order. Thus the order was known initially as that of Cáceres, although the Moslems soon reconquered the town. In 1171 the knights concluded a pact with the archbishop of SANTIAGO DE COMPOSTELA, who placed them under the Apostle's protection and received their master as a canon of the cathedral chapter. Meanwhile, Fernando II, who was later to be considered one of the founders, continued his generous donations to the order. At the same time the order acquired properties in Portugal, Castile, and Aragon, and by 1184 even held property in France, England, and Carinthia. ALEXANDER III gave his approbation to the new order in 1175, stipulating that a convent of clerics under the direction of a prior should be responsible for its spiritual welfare. A general chapter was to be held each year, and 13 councilors were to elect the master, who served for life. The knights, following the Rule of St. AUGUSTINE, were allowed to marry under certain conditions. In addition to the master, the principal officers were the priors of León and Uclés and the commanders entrusted with the administration and defense of the order's encomiendas.

Uclés, lying east of Toledo, was the order's principal seat in the Kingdom of Castile, and frequently the order was known by that name. The order contributed substantially to the Reconquest in all the Hispanic kingdoms, though its major holdings were located in Extremadura, the Campo de Montiel, and Andalusia. It soon became the wealthiest of all the peninsular military orders, and in the later Middle Ages the mastership became a prize avidly sought by powerful personages.

Some of the leading figures of 15th century Castilian politics, viz, Enrique, nephew of King Enrique III, Alvaro de Luna, Beltrán de la Cueva, and Juan Pacheco, Marquess of Villena, all enjoyed the power, prestige, and revenues attached to the mastership. To curb this threat to monarchical authority, King Ferdinand V and Queen Isabella, with papal approval, annexed the mastership to the crown in 1493. In 1523 Pope Adrian VI united the mastership to the crown in perpetuity.

Bibliography: *Bullarium ordinis sancti Jacobi,* ed. A. F. AGUADO et al. (Madrid 1719). J. LOPEZ AGURLETA, *Vida del venerable fundador de la Orden de Santiago,* 2 v. (Madrid 1731). C. GUTIÉR-REZ DEL ARROYO, *Privilegios reales de la Orden de Santiago* (Madrid 1946). A. FOREY, *The Military Orders from the Twelfth to the Early Fourteenth Centuries* (Toronto 1992).

[J. F. O'CALLAGHAN]

KNIGHTS OF ST. JOHN

A semimilitary fraternal organization incorporated by a special act of the Legislature of the state of New York on May 6, 1886, as the Roman Catholic Union of the Knights of St. John. The name of the organization was changed by another special act on Feb. 20, 1896, to Knights of St. John, for the purpose of admitting to membership persons of all rites of the Catholic Church. The order was founded under the protection of St. John the Baptist, patron of the HOSPITALLERS OF ST. JOHN OF JERU-SALEM, who were organized in the 12th century as a military order to protect pilgrims to the Holy Land from attack by the Turks and to assist those wounded or taken ill while traveling.

Among the objectives of the modern Knights of St. John were: to foster a feeling of fraternity among its members; to improve their moral, mental, and social condition; to aid and support members and their families in case of need; and to participate in a special way in the functions of the Catholic Church. The knights wore their uniforms when they exercised their privilege of serving as escort at the more important liturgical, ceremonial, and official functions of the Church and on many civic occasions. The central governing body, called the supreme commandery, comprised grand commanderies covering a given geographical area. The grand commanderies were made up of local commanderies, generally affiliated with a parish, and district commanderies, usually contained within a diocese.

[R. C. NOONAN/EDS.]

KNIGHTS OF THE FAITH

Knights of the Faith was a Catholic and royalist secret society in France during the Restoration period. Its

15th-century tomb slab from one of the knights of St. James, housed within the chapel of Villar de Donas, Santiago de Compostela, Spain. (©Adam Woolfitt/CORBIS)

founder was Ferdinand de Bertier, whose father, the last *intendant* of Paris, was slaughtered by a revolutionary mob (July 22, 1789). Convinced that FREEMASONRY was responsible for the FRENCH REVOLUTION and his father's death, Bertier decided to fight it with its own methods. To this end he created in 1810 a kind of counter–Masonry dedicated to the defense of throne and altar. The hierarchy of the *Chevaliers de la Foi,* as they were known, comprised the following grades: charity member (Associé de Charité), equerry, hospital knight, and knight of the Faith. Only the last grade knew the full scope of the organization. In each civil department of France members formed a "banner." The society was governed by a council of nine members presided over by a grand–master, Viscount (later Duke) Mathieu de Montmorency. The Holy See refused to approve it as a military religious order. In the last months of the rule of Napoleon I, the Knights prepared public opinion for the return of the Bourbons, and were instrumental in arranging the royalist coup in Bordeaux (March 12, 1814) that helped to convince the Allied governments of the feasibility of restoring the old dynasty. After 1815, the society organized the ultraroyalist party that fought bitterly against the moderate policies of Louis XVIII and his favorite minister Élie Decazes. At the end of 1822, when royalists came to power, two knights, Montmorency and Joseph de Villèle, entered the ministry. When their protector, Charles X, became king (1824), they were able to press their reactionary and religious program. Villèle tried to rule the majority of the elected chamber by using the vote of some 100 members affiliated to the Knights, although other leading knights disagreed with him because they considered the outcry against the congregation injurious to religion. One of these organizations was confused with the other because notable Rightist political figures such as Montmorency, Armand de Polignac, and Ferdinand de Bertier belonged to both of them. To end this mix-up and weaken Villèle's position, the founders dissolved the knights (January 1826). In a way, the Knights of the Faith prefigured the later OPUS DEI.

Bibliography: G. DE BERTIER DE SAUVIGNY, *Un type d'ultraroyaliste: Le Comte Ferdinand de Bertier et l'énigme de la Congrégation* (Paris 1948).

[G. DE BERTIER DE SAUVIGNY]

KNIGHTS OF THE HOLY SEPULCHER

Formally known as The Equestrian Order of the Holy Sepulchre of Jerusalem (*Ordo Equestris Sancti Sepulcri Hierosolymitani*), the Knights of the Holy Sepulcher is a confraternity of persons bound together solely by the pious custom of receiving knighthood at the Holy Sepulcher in Jerusalem. Legend attributes the foundation of the Knights of the Holy Sepulcher to GODFREY OF BOUILLON, one of the leaders of the First CRUSADE, who, after the conquest of Jerusalem in 1099, was elected *Advocatus sancti sepulchri*. Historical data to support this account are entirely lacking. The Knights of the Holy Sepulcher ought not to be confused with the Canons Regular of the Holy Sepulcher, nor are they to be thought of as a military religious order similar to the TEMPLARS or the KNIGHTS OF MALTA. The origin of the confraternity can be traced to the above-mentioned devotion, which was practiced by many pilgrims to the Holy Places.

Technically members of the knightly class—but often in fact, not—those so knighted in Jerusalem could be described as Knights of the Holy Sepulcher. At first, knighthood was always conferred by a member of the knightly class. The FRANCISCANS, to whom Pope Clcm-

ent VI entrusted the custody of the Holy Land in 1342, always conferred the *benedictio militis* and, in the absence of a knight, even the accolade upon prospective knights. At the close of the 15th century, the superior of the Franciscan monastery in Jerusalem assumed the title of grand master of the Holy Sepulcher and was so recognized by the Holy See. In 1847 Pope Pius IX accorded the title to the Latin patriarch of Jerusalem, with authority to admit knights to the confraternity. From 1907 to 1928 the popes held the grandmastership, which is now given to one of the cardinals. In 1868 and again in 1949, 1962, and 1977 the popes promulgated statutes for the knights. At present the knights are organized in five classes: knights of the collar, knights grand cross, commanders with plaque, commanders, and knights. Investiture has been open to women since 1868. The insignia are a white cape and a red enameled cross of Jerusalem.

Bibliography: M. H. A. D'ASSEMANI, *The Cross on the Sword: A History of the Equestrian Order of the Holy Sepulchre of Jerusalem* (Chicago 1944). X. DE BOURBON–PARMA et al., *Les Chevaliers du Saint–Sépulcre* (Paris 1957). G. TESSIER, "Les Débuts de l'Ordre du St. Sépulcre en Espagne," *Bibliothèque de l'École des Chartes* 116 (1958) 5–28.

[J. F. O'CALLAGHAN]

KNIGHTS OF THE SWORD

Known also as the Brothers of the Sword and as the Livonian Knights, one of the 12 religious MILITARY ORDERS of knighthood that came into being between 1100 and 1300, and one of the three of German origin. It was founded in 1201, either by Abbot Theoderic of Riga or by Bp. ALBERT I of Riga. The order was confirmed by Pope Innocent III in 1204. The brother knights were to be called *Milites Christi de Lyvonia,* but they were commonly referred to as Brothers of the Sword. Their rule was that of the TEMPLARS; their habit was the white mantle with a red cross and a red sword behind it pointing up. The purpose of the new order was to convert the heathen Esths and Livs of Livonia, both obstinately pagan. The Knights of the Sword merged with the Teutonic Knights on May 12, 1237, thereby extending considerably the sphere of interest of the latter. This merger merely added to the already great political confusion and complex political hierarchy of Livonia: the master of the Brothers of the Sword, the representative of the TEUTONIC KNIGHTS, the archbishop of Riga, and the estates of Livonia all exercised simultaneous and conflicting jurisdiction over that territory. The Brothers of the Sword, unrestricted by their merger with the Teutonic Knights, continued their skirmishes with Poland, Lithuania, and the Russian states. Untamed, they never took on the semireligious characteristics of the Teutonic Knights, but, true to their name, continued to live by the sword until Nov. 8, 1561, when, pursuant to an agreement between the Land Master Gotthard Kettler and the archbishop of Riga, William of Brandenburg, Livonia became a part of Lithuania. The Knights of the Sword were dissolved then.

Bibliography: F. G. VON BUNGE, *Der Orden der Schwertbrüder* (Leipzig 1875). M. TUMLER, *Der Deutsche Orden im Werden, Wachsen und Wirken bis 1400* (Vienna 1955; 2d ed. 1965). F. BENNINGHOVEN, *Der Orden der Schwertbrüder* (Cologne 1964). A. FOREY, *The Military Orders from the Twelfth to the Early Fourteenth Centuries* (Toronto 1992).

[G. GROSSCHMID]

KNOLL, ALBERT

Theologian; b. Brunico, Italy, July 12, 1796; d. Bolzano, Italy, Mar. 30, 1863. He entered the Capuchins in 1818, and later taught theology for 27 years and was a definitor general of his order from 1847 to 1853. His literary activity covered three areas: dogma, Canon Law, and pastoral theology. His outstanding theological work was *Institutiones theologiae dogmaticae generalis* (Innsbruck 1852). This work was accorded an extraordinary reception in seminaries because of its orthodoxy, clarity of method, and abundance of proofs; it went through 15 editions from 1852 to 1904. A more ample treatment of theology was given in *Institutiones theologiae theoreticae* (6 v. Turin 1853–59); it enjoyed 12 editions from 1862 to 1892. In the field of Canon Law he wrote an exposition of the Franciscan rule, *Expositio Regulae Fratrum Minorum* (Innsbruck 1850), which is regarded as official by the Capuchins. There were five editions in Latin, two in Spanish, and one in Italian. In addition, he left two courses on preaching, *Predigten für die Sonntage* (Bressanone 1867), that were published four times in German and three times in Italian.

Bibliography: É. D'ALENÇON, *Dictionnaire de théologie catholique,* ed. A. VACANT et al, 14 vol. (Paris 1903–50) 1.1:664–666.

[M. DE POBLADURA]

KNOW-NOTHINGISM

A form of NATIVISM which flourished in the 1850s, expressing itself principally in the political activity of the American or Know-Nothing party.

Heavy German and Irish immigration, chiefly Catholic, in the years 1830 to 1860 evoked an outburst of nativism expressed in various cities by propaganda and riots against foreigners and "papists." It became political with the organization of nativists in local and state (e.g.,

Know-Nothing Party 1844 campaign ribbon. (©David J. & Janice L. Frent Collection/CORBIS)

Louisiana in 1841) elections. The cities of New York in 1844 and Boston in 1845 were carried by the American-Republican or Native American party who had the support of the Whigs. But the latter eventually withdrew their support and the party disappeared from the national scene in 1847.

The Know-Nothing party then developed from several nativist secret societies, a few of which merged under the leadership first of Charles B. Allen of New York and later of James W. Barker. Known originally as the Order of the Star-Spangled Banner, the organization and proceedings were secret and every member was sworn to know nothing about them when questioned. The party first entered politics indirectly by supporting the nativistic nominees of existing parties, and by 1852 the success of this maneuver was becoming evident. Election frauds in the older parties strengthened Know-Nothing opposition to foreigners and Catholics, leading to the demand that 21 years' residence in the U.S. be required before an alien could become a citizen, and even then he could not hold public office. Other proposals sought to deny all rights to the foreign-born and to their children, unless educated in public schools.

In 1854 the Know-Nothing party officially became the American party and won some startling victories. Its candidates were elected to the governorships of Massachusetts and Delaware; carried the state legislatures in several New England states and in Maryland, Kentucky, and California; and obtained five seats in the Senate and 43 in the House of the 34th Congress. However, factions soon developed over tariff and land problems and especially over the slavery question, with the consequent decrease of the party's power. In 1856 a national platform that included anti-alien and anti-Catholic planks was presented, and Millard Fillmore, who was also the Whig candidate, was nominated for the presidency. The Know-Nothings dedicated themselves to "place in offices of honor, trust or profit . . . none but native-born Protestant citizens" and swore to oppose all "foreign influence, Popery, Jesuitism and Catholicism." Abraham Lincoln's comment on this bigotry was: "When the Know-Nothings get control, the [Declaration] will read: 'all men are created equal except Negroes, and foreigners, and Catholics.'" Although the American party polled about 25 per cent of the popular vote in 1856, it received the electoral vote of only one state, Maryland.

After 1857 the party lost ground, so that by 1859 only the border states supported it. Such vestiges as remained in 1860 were absorbed into the Constitutional Union and Republican parties. The same year marked Know-Nothingism's disappearance as a local political power. Thereafter, many of the Know-Nothing gains were reversed; for example, the New York legislature, which under Know-Nothing influence had passed the Putnam Bill of 1855 forbidding Catholic bishops to hold property in their own names, quietly repealed the measure in 1863.

Public opinion never fully supported the forces of Know-Nothingism, particularly in regard to the immigrant and Catholic citizen, although Know-Nothing views on nonsupport for sectarian schools continued to be upheld. As a short-lived phenomenon of the 1850s, this singular movement did not withstand the test of time and its force was dissipated before it became too dangerous. Although a similar spirit of racial and religious intolerance was revived sporadically in such organizations as the KU KLUX KLAN, few of these had much political vitality.

Bibliography: A. R. BILLINGTON, *The Protestant Crusade, 1800–1860* (New York 1938). F. X. CURRAN, *Major Trends in American Church History* (New York 1946). M. T. GEARY, *A History of Third Parties in Pennsylvania, 1840–1860* (Ph.D. Thesis, CUA, Washington 1938). J. HIGHMAN, *Strangers in the Land: Patterns of American Nativism, 1860–1925* (New Brunswick, N.J. 1955). L. D. SCISCO, *Political Nativism in New York State* (New York 1901). W. D. OVERDYKE, *The Know-Nothing in the South* (Baton Rouge 1950).

[M. L. FELL]

KNOWLEDGE

Variously defined as the act by which one becomes the other in an intentional way; the act by which one is aware of something in thought, with or without the aid of the senses; the habit or ability to recall such an act; or the matter that is the object of such an act or habit. This article discusses the common notion of knowledge, its definition and characteristics, its various classifications, and the problem it poses—all from the viewpoint of Thomistic philosophy. For other views, *see* KNOWLEDGE, THEORIES OF.

Common Notion. Knowledge rarely presents itself as a problem to the average person; he simply takes it for granted as something that in some way puts him in contact with things other than himself. He also recognizes it as something unique, even though he may not be able to define it or even to describe it articulately. This inability stems, in part, from his discerning so many different types of knowledge; for example, seeing, imagining, remembering, and reasoning can all be included under his notion. He knows facts and he knows persons; he knows his business or profession; he knows some science and some philosophy; he knows how to do certain things and how to achieve particular goals. Yet with all this he also has experience of imperfect knowledge, of ignorance, of error and mistakes, both in himself and in others.

Although such a notion of knowledge generally suffices for the average person, the philosopher cannot be satisfied with it. He must come to grips with knowledge in its proper nature and its general and detailed classifications. Reflecting upon knowledge, he notes that it poses problems: what are the processes through which it occurs; does it have any validity; what is the possibility of attaining certitude? Such questions open broad areas for investigation; yet they present such difficulty that opposed and often contradictory theories of knowledge continue to have their expositors and defenders.

Definition and Characteristics. St. THOMAS AQUINAS defined knowledge in the following terms: "The noblest way of possessing a thing is to possess it in an immaterial way, that is, by possessing its form without its matter; and this is the definition of knowledge" (*In lib. de caus.* 18). He thus calls attention to the fact that knowing means possessing something and making it one's own, but in a unique and peculiar way. To know a thing means not to make it one's own in a material or bodily way, but rather to make its form one's own. Since FORM is the perfection or determination that is distinctive in a thing and that makes it to be what it is, knowledge is making one's own the perfection of something else; the knower adds to his own perfection the perfection of another.

This definition he explains more fully by noting that the perfection a thing has in virtue of being what it is also limits it by differentiating it from other things whose perfections it lacks (De ver. 2.2). In order that there be a remedy for this type of imperfection, some beings have knowledge; this enables the perfections of one thing to be found in another. The ability to possess the perfection of other things while remaining oneself is precisely the perfection of the knower as knower. For St. Thomas, in fact, the natural end and purpose of man's existence is to have, through knowledge, the perfections of the entire universe: "The ultimate perfection to which the soul can reach is that in it there be found the whole order of the universe and its causes. This, according to the philosophers, is the ultimate end of man" (ibid.).

Knowledge as Perfection. Such a view of knowledge eliminates the possibility that knowledge be a physical or mechanical process. It is, on the contrary, a perfection that can be found only in living things; these alone have the ability to perform immanent or self-constructing operations, i.e., actions that increase rather than decrease the perfection of the agent. More particularly, it is only in the animal kingdom that this ability is found. Here it culminates in the intellectual knowledge of man, who, although limited as a creature, is nonetheless open, through knowledge, to unlimited perfection.

Knowledge is said to be an action or an operation just as LIFE is said to be a motion or a self-motion. According to St. Thomas, however, these expressions are "more by way of example than of definition" (In 2 anim. 1.219). Ontologically, knowledge is neither an action nor a MOTION; it belongs rather in the category of QUALITY (see CATEGORIES OF BEING; ACTION AND PASSION). Knowing, therefore, is not doing something but becoming something. It is a self-modification brought about precisely by the objective possession of some thing other than oneself. The knower's being is expanded by the addition of a perfection previously not possessed, yet contributed by something else that has lost nothing in the giving. There has been no change such as occurs when matter receives a new form while losing an old one, but form, itself a perfection, has had new perfection added to it, and thus has been modified and perfected cognitively.

Subject and Object. It is not surprising that the capacity to share in the being of other things and make their perfections one's own should present mysterious facets and paradoxes. Knowledge, for example, forces itself upon man's attention as a number of activities occurring within him that are at the same time related to things outside him, which are thereby brought into his field of consciousness. The paradox here is that of SUBJECT and OBJECT. Knowledge never occurs except in the framework of this subject-object relatedness. Apart from knowledge, the subject has not as yet begun to be a subject but remains only an organism or a person; the object, also, has not yet begun to be an object, but is simply a thing, sensible or intelligible but not yet known. A being is constituted an object only by some relation that it begins to have to some living thing having the power of knowing.

Neither subject nor object can ever be viewed as absolutes, but only as related; otherwise knowledge itself is eliminated. This makes it necessary to reject the contemporary view of the cognitive relationship as one of self as opposed to nonself, each being regarded as an absolute. When one attempts to explain knowledge on this basis, the explanation is prejudiced and divorced from reality. Actually, in knowledge subject and object are intelligible only by correlative reference.

Interiority and Exteriority. No sooner has one become assured of the IMMANENCE and interiority of knowledge as an operation proceeding from a living being, an operation having its roots in IMMATERIALITY and thus completely different from any kind of motion in matter, than he must face its opposing characteristic, viz, its exteriority, its relation to something other than the self. The paradox of subject and object is continued and deepened, a fact that tortures the modern mind into a flight to some kind of IDEALISM wherein the mind supposedly creates its own object. But this will not do; it solves nothing and it eventually makes all knowledge unintelligible and impossible, whereas in experience knowledge is a most stubborn fact that refuses to be sequestered and quarantined in the mind as in a prison. The solution to this part of the paradox is a recognition that the object is quite real; that there is no knowledge without an object to which a subject becomes related through some type of INTENTIONALITY. This means that a cognitive power is a living relation to the object that stimulated it and thereby set off the act of cognition. In this the object has neither a real relation to the subject nor any real dependence on it, although St. Thomas does maintain that the subject has a real relation to the object as that which is measured to the measure (De pot. 7.10). While using this expression, however, St. Thomas warns that the word "measure" is not to be taken quantitatively, but rather in an analogous way as relating to being and to truth (In 5 meta. 17.1003).

Consciousness. In some theories, knowledge is identified with CONSCIOUSNESS. Despite their close connection, the two are not the same. Consciousness is a state of greater or lesser awareness in a cognitive being; as such, it should not be substantialized and made a reality in itself. A conscious act is an act of knowledge that involves knowing one's internal operations and dispositions and oneself as subject to them. These operations may in turn be acts of knowledge, but they may also be noncognitive acts, such as wishing or walking. It is also possible that knowledge occur without consciousness, as happens when one dreams or experiences an external sensation during sleep. Consciousness and knowledge are simultaneous when one knows an object and at the same time is aware of himself as knowing it. It may further be noted that analytically consciousness can be distinguished into sensory and intellectual; yet in the concrete, man has only one unified human consciousness that embraces both simultaneously.

Truth and Certitude. In the simplest act of knowledge, simple APPREHENSION, the measuring by the object is effected automatically, with the result that apprehensive knowledge is always true and allows no room for error. This is not remarkable; it means simply that when an object is presented to a knowing power, it will be known as presented. The possibility of FALSITY and ERROR arises as soon as one begins to rearrange and unify his knowledge through judgments that apply a predicate to a subject. TRUTH is had as a property of knowledge when JUDGMENT is in harmony with being as it is in reality; otherwise falsity is present. Similarly, a judgment is said to be certain when it is enunciated with no fear of error, and merely probable when one is inclined to regard what he proclaims as true while recognizing that the opposite is also possible (*see* CERTITUDE).

Classification. Knowledge may be classified from many different points of view. On the basis of origin, natural knowledge, achieved by the unaided use of human cognitive powers, may be distinguished from supernatural knowledge, which derives from some divine assistance given in revelation. Knowledge gained by the unaided use of man's resources includes the greater part of human knowledge, taken in a quantitative sense, and is responsible for the development of all the sciences and arts, with the exception of sacred theology. From the standpoint of the objects that man can know, the fundamental division is that into SENSE knowledge and intellectual knowledge. Sense knowledge arises from the immediate impact of bodily things upon the sense organs of sight, hearing, taste, smell, and touch. When elaborated by such internal senses as the IMAGINATION, MEMORY, and the COGITATIVE POWER, the content of sense knowledge becomes the basis for intellectual knowledge, the

characteristic of which is its abstractness—a freedom and disengagement from all the conditions of material existence (*see* ABSTRACTION).

Intellectual Knowledge. Whereas sense knowledge is a perfection common to both animals and men, intellectual knowledge is specific to man; indeed, it is the hallmark of humanity. It enables man not merely to know—all animals can do this—but to know abstractly, in a detached and absolute fashion. Such knowing has no counterpart in the senses, which depend on bodily organs and are limited by them and their conditions. Intellectual knowledge alone is properly called thinking, since it alone can present objects to man in the abstract mode free from the limitations and conditions of matter, time, and place. Intellectual knowledge alone, grasping not the external appearances or surface qualities of things but their very essence, penetrates to the inner reality of things and reveals in some degree what they are, rather than what they look like, taste like, or feel like. Because of this, the object of intellectual knowledge is said to be the being of things (*see* INTELLECT). The wide extension of this object opens up to man the possibility of knowing things above the material order, even though the source of such knowledge always remains in sensory experience.

The product of intellectual apprehension is called the IDEA or CONCEPT. At first imperfect and representative of only a limited part of the reality that is their object, ideas or concepts are perfected by series of judgments and reasoning processes. Through these, intellectual knowledge expands itself and becomes more completely representative of reality. Utilizing such processes, men have gradually developed all their sciences and arts, culminating in the natural wisdom of METAPHYSICS and the supernatural wisdom of sacred theology.

Supernatural Knowledge. The possibility of supernatural knowledge, i.e., knowledge unavailable to man by his own natural cognitive powers, is precisely the possibility of God's making known to man certain truths he could not discover by himself. A gratuitous denial of the possibility of revelation is certainly unwarranted; the acceptance of the fact of revelation is something else, but this is not the concern here. While it usually presupposes assent to the rational truths of natural religion, FAITH properly so-called is not to be identified with a natural acceptance; it is in itself supernatural and a gift of God. St. Paul describes the origin of supernatural knowledge with these words: "God who at sundry times and in divers manners spoke in times past to the fathers by the prophets, last of all in these days has spoken to us by his Son, whom he appointed heir of all things, by whom also he made the world" (Heb 1.1–2). This supernatural knowledge, accepted by faith, has been elaborated into a series of conclusions and implications that is properly the science of sacred THEOLOGY.

Actual and Habitual Knowledge. Because the sum total of a man's knowledge is not always in the forefront of his consciousness, a distinction must be made between actual and habitual knowledge. At any given moment, the activity of man's cognitive powers is producing in him actual knowledge; yet some of his powers are capable of preserving knowledge and recalling it when the objects previously known are no longer present. Although the external senses are stimulated only by objects actually present, one may have habitual knowledge both in the internal senses, e.g., in the imagination or memory, and in the intellect. This habitual knowledge is preserved through qualities that are more or less permanent, such as the PHANTASM on the sensory level and the idea on the intellectual. The ability to recall these at will in any particular case varies greatly and may be influenced by a wide array of situations and circumstances.

Intuitive and Discursive Knowledge. Another distinction is that between knowledge that is immediate or intuitive and that which is mediate or dicursive. In the first type, the knowledge arises either from the direct contact of the external senses with their objects or the direct intellectual grasp of a proposition whose terms are seen to be necessarily related (*see* INTUITION). In the second, there is a progression from one or more propositions to another whose truth is recognized as being based on, and implicated with, the proposition already known (*see* REASONING). This can occur in two ways: when the process is from the particular to the general, from facts to laws or causes, it is called INDUCTION; its opposite, DEDUCTION, arises from general propositions and proceeds to their particular application. A further distinction may be mentioned in connection with the inference involved in mediate knowledge. When the inference proceeds from cause to effect, it is said to be a priori; when the procession is from effect to cause, it is a posteriori.

Problem of Knowledge. Knowledge has always raised questions for the inquiring mind, and these questions take different forms depending upon the point of view of the inquirer. The psychologist, for example, wants to know what knowledge is and how it originates (*see* KNOWLEDGE, PROCESS OF). The logician searches for the laws that govern exact thinking and that must be followed if truth is to be attained (*see* LOGIC). All such questions about knowledge, however, point toward the major problem of the value of knowledge. The solution of this and its attendant problems is the primary concern of EPISTEMOLOGY.

It has been frequently taken for granted that before anyone can enter the temple of wisdom, he must begin with a critique of knowledge to determine, at the beginning, whether or not his ideas correspond with reality. This method was inaugurated by R. DESCARTES and I. KANT, and perfected by their followers. So deeply were their disciples convinced of its necessity that they tended to make the problem of the critique of knowledge not merely the preliminary question but the entire content of philosophical investigation.

Actually, however, it is impossible to begin all investigation with a critique of knowledge, if only because a critique of knowledge presupposes both a psychology and a metaphysics. Man does not first know knowledge; he first knows things. St. Thomas points out that all man's knowledge originates from knowledge of FIRST PRINCIPLES, and that these arise directly from sense experience (*De ver.* 10.6). All human knowledge is thus based on the certitudes of immediate EVIDENCE, and these form the foundation of all knowledge on both the sensory and intellectual levels. The first object of man's knowledge is the material world in which he lives, the material bodies that present themselves to his senses as the subjects of continual changes and movements. And the value of this knowledge is guaranteed by the immediate contact of the senses with their proper formal objects in material things. No bridge from subject to object is either necessary or possible. The contact is immediate and direct.

Validity of Sensation. There can be no proof, moreover, that such is the origin of human knowledge; proof must proceed from something more fundamental, and nothing can be more primitive or fundamental than the primary knowledge of the senses. Proof, again, requires a middle term. There is none here; nor can there be. While immediacy of the evidence makes proof unnecessary, however, one may give an indirect indication of its validity by observing that the lack of any one of the senses deprives a man of all the knowledge that particular sense might have apprehended. A man born blind, for example, knows nothing of color, and no amount of teaching will help him in this regard; color for him is unimaginable and unthinkable, a clear indication that the materials of knowledge come only through the experience of the senses.

Besides this indirect indication of the validity of sense knowledge, it is possible to defend this validity positively by a direct analysis of SENSATION itself. St. Thomas makes such an analysis in the *Summa theologiae* in answer to the question: ''Whether there is falsity in the senses?'' He there states: ''The affection of the sense is its sensation itself. Hence from the fact that sense reports as it is affected, it follows that we are not deceived in the judgment by which we judge that we experience sensation'' (*Summa theologiae* 1a, 17.2 ad 1). When, therefore, one is aware of his senses reporting contact with an object, he can have infallible assurance that he is really sensing something, and sensing it as it is, no matter what, on further analysis, its nature might turn out to be. For it may be taken as certain that no legitimate distinction between appearance and reality can make whatever appears to be be itself unreal. If there is an appearance to the senses, there is a reality appearing; the alternative is to face the contradiction, that a sensation could terminate in nothing, and that nothing can appear. To sum up, if man senses, he senses something; and if he senses something, he must sense it as it is. The seeming alternative, that is, to sense nothing, is an absurdity; the only alternative is not to sense at all.

Validity of Intellection. There is no doubt, then, that all man's knowledge begins with the senses, but man is also clearly aware that it does not end there. His intellect is a different and higher power of knowledge that utilizes the content provided by the senses to expand and elaborate his knowledge into ideas, judgments, and reasoning processes. Analysis of his experience forces him to recognize intellectual knowledge as different and more perfect than sensory knowledge, although it does not force him to conclude that the intellect operates separately and in isolation from the senses. The PERSON is a strict unity and so is human knowledge. Yet the component of knowledge supplied by the senses differs from that of the intellect. The knowledge of the senses is restricted to the external and sensible qualities of things, while intellectual knowledge grasps the essences, the intimate natures of things. One sees, for example, the color, shape, size, and position of a house, but it is only by intellectual knowledge that he begins to understand what a house is, that is, a structure used to shelter human living and working. In short, whereas the senses are concerned only with the sensible phenomena, the intellect penetrates to the nature, the very being of the object.

The analysis of knowledge, therefore, reveals that human knowledge exists on two distinct levels that complement and complete each other. In man they are bound together in such close unity that together they grasp the same object, an object that is at once sensible and intelligible. In this close association with the senses is to be placed the critical foundation of the validity of intellectual knowledge. This knowledge begins and derives from the content provided by the senses, without which the intellect would have no object, and therefore no operation.

Since the proper object of the intellect is being, the intellect manifests itself as a living relation to being, to the real. What man grasps intellectually is not the PHENOMENA of things, but the determinations hidden under the phenomena, though manifested by them, and characterizing the ESSENCE of the thing. The validity of such intellectual apprehension has a parallel in the necessary validity of sensory apprehension. St. Thomas uses and applies the analogy when he answers the question: "Whether the intellect can be false?" He writes: "For, every faculty as such is per se directed to its proper object, and things of this kind are always the same. Hence so long as the faculty exists, its judgment concerning its own proper object does not fail. . . . Hence as regards simple objects not subject to composite definitions we cannot be deceived unless we understand nothing whatever about them" (*Summa theologiae* 1a, 85.6). Just as color is necessarily perceived by sight, so being is necessarily understood by intelligence. The intellect knows the thing in its being, and it knows it as it is. Intellectual knowledge is valid in apprehension because the light of the intellect penetrates to the REALITY of the object and cannot avoid doing so.

Validity of Judgment. A more formidable problem arises concerning the validity of the JUDGMENT, since it is here that truth or falsity is properly found. Because it is in this intellectual act that the first indemonstrable principles are known, the judgment furnishes the basic foundation for the truths of every science and both wisdoms. Thus St. Thomas maintains that, in its origin, all knowledge consists in becoming aware of the first indemonstrable principles (*De ver.* 10.6). These principles are simply the primary mental assents at which the mind naturally and necessarily arrives in its inspection of reality, both in terms of the general modes of being common to everything and the special modes of being proper to the different kinds of things in man's experience. The judgments relating to the general modes of being concern the TRANSCENDENTALS; these are the origin of all the principles and conclusions of METAPHYSICS. The judgments relating to the special modes of being concern the categories or various types of reality found concretized in things; these are the origin of all principles and conclusions of SCIENCE (*SCIENTIA*). The ultimate test of the truth of any judgment, then, can only be the analytic resolution of that judgment back to first principles. For this reason St. Thomas can say: "There is never falsity in the intellect if resolution back to first principles be rightly carried out" (*De ver.* 1.12). The human intellect does not learn these principles, nor does it assume them; it arrives at them naturally, necessarily, and immediately upon knowing the terms that make them up. The mind thus attains truth and certitude by grasping first principles, and then proceeding from these to conclusions. This does not mean that from these principles all knowledge can be deduced, but only that before anything can be deduced, they must be admitted and applied.

All judgments take place as the result of a unifying mental process that adds, to a concept already possessed, some new characteristic. It is well to note that a judgment does not take place by comparing mentally two different concepts and seeing these as compatible or not. A judgment is an assent, a dynamic act of the mind that occurs after a REFLECTION on a composite concept that itself results from a composite phantasm. The connection between the two elements, known simultaneously in the composite concept and seen as possible in the apprehension, is affirmed in the judgment, which is a dynamic statement of the conformity between mind and reality. This is, in turn, the known conformity of the bond between the elements of the composite concept in the mind and the make-up of the object in reality.

This analysis of the act of judgment is the very core of St. Thomas's critical theory and his solution to the problem of knowledge. Judgment is the touchstone of all truth, the bridge that closes the gap between mind and reality. Using it, man's intellect can penetrate the secrets of matter and unravel the mysteries of the universe. He can detect the order in the world and put order into his life and his relations with others. He can know the natural law and even the eternal law of God as the ultimate rule of his action. Thus the power of judgment leads him upward to the life of the spirit and ultimately to God Himself.

See Also: EPISTEMOLOGY.

Bibliography: G. A. DE BRIE, *Bibliographia philosophica, 1934–1945* (Brussels 1950–) 2:130–165. V. J. BOURKE, *Thomistic Bibliography, 1920–1940* (St. Louis 1945) 2216–2741. L. M. RÉGIS, *St. Thomas and Epistemology* (Milwaukee, Wis. 1946); *Epistemology,* tr. I. C. BYRNE (New York 1959). W. O. MARTIN, *The Order and Integration of Knowledge* (Ann Arbor, Mich. 1957). J. MARITAIN, *Distinguish to Unite; or, The Degrees of Knowledge,* tr. G. B. PHELAN (New York 1959). R. HOUDE and J. P. MULLALY, eds., *Philosophy of Knowledge* (Philadelphia 1960). G. VAN RIET, *L'Épistémologie thomiste* (Louvain 1946). J. PÉGHAIRE, *Regards sur le connaître* (Montreal 1949).

[G. C. REILLY]

KNOWLEDGE, CONNATURAL

Knowledge through connaturality is an act of the INTELLECT and is, like other forms of knowledge, an immanent activity whereby the knowing subject goes out and mingles in the life of others without ceasing to be himself. Unlike the rational, discursive knowledge characteristic of the sciences and philosophy, however, connatural knowledge is not achieved primarily through concepts and by way of DEMONSTRATION. It is rather a knowledge resulting from an interaction between sensitivity and affectivity, intellect and will, knowing and loving. It is thus a type of knowledge caused in some way by the unitive tendencies of man's appetites, in particular his rational appetite, or WILL. As knowledge, it is essentially an act of the intellect; as connatural, it involves APPETITE and will. Because it is a mode of knowing involving desire as well as intellect, it is a highly personal act, evidencing in the concrete that knowing is an act of the whole man, of a person, who knows through his intellect but whose knowledge is affected, at times intrinsically, by noncognitive factors. Again, unlike rational, discursive knowledge, connatural knowledge is directed to the concrete individual, not to the abstract universal.

History. This type of knowledge, which is perhaps best illustrated in the saying from the *Imitation of Christ* (1.1), "I would rather feel contrition than know how to define it," has a rich philosophical heritage. Aristotle implicitly recognized it when he distinguished between the rational, scientific knowledge of moral questions and the knowledge of these questions based on virtuous habits within the person, maintaining that in moral matters virtue is more certain than science (*Eth. Nic.* 1143b 11–13) and that "virtue and the good man are as such the measure of each thing" (*ibid.* 1176a 17). Connatural knowledge was implied also by PSEUDO-DIONYSIUS, who maintained that the spiritual man knows divine things not only because he has learned them but also because he "suffers" them.

The medieval schoolmen did not work out explicit theories of connatural knowledge, but they recognized it as a genuine mode of knowing. The discussions of man's moral conduct and his spiritual life, particularly in St. THOMAS AQUINAS, suggest the lines along which a more formal analysis of this type of knowledge can be developed. Aside from the Renaissance commentators on St. Thomas, in particular JOHN OF ST. THOMAS, philosophers of the modern period paid little attention to this mode of human knowledge. The emphasis on inter-subjectivity in recent existential and phenomenological thought has helped redirect inquiry into this subject. Interest in it is reflected in J. H. Newman's distinction between notional and real knowledge, a distinction further elaborated by M. Blondel, and in H. Bergson's opposition of the knowledge characteristic of scientific inquiry to that achieved in INTUITION. The question of connatural knowledge has engaged a number of contemporary Thomists, particularly in discussions of ethical and aesthetic questions. Among those who have given much thought to this subject are T. Gilby, J. P. ROUSSELOT, R. O. Johann, B. Miller, and, in particular, J. Maritain.

Connaturality. The connatural is whatever is fitting to or in accord with nature (Thomas Aquinas, *Summa theologiae* 1a2ae, 26.1 ad 3). It refers to a linking or union of two natures (and is thus distinct from the natural), and it is a linking that springs from something intrinsic to the natures involved. Knowledge is itself a nature, and, as a nature, is distinct from the nature of the knowing subject. Yet it is fitting for man to know; this act is "in accord" with his nature. Thus, in a loose sense, one can say that knowledge itself is connatural to man. Moreover, one can apply the term connatural to whatever is fitting or proper either to the act of knowing itself, or to the faculties of knowledge, e.g., the intellect, or to the agent or subject of knowledge, the human person. Thus it is connatural for man's knowledge to be objective and to be derived from the senses: in this sense the term connatural is predicated of the act of knowledge as such. Again, acts of knowing, even in the speculative order, become connatural to a person whose intellect has been strengthened through habits or virtues inclining him to judge easily in certain areas of judgment. In this way one who has acquired the speculative habit of mathematics, for example, is connaturalized to making judgments in mathematical questions. This is a type of connatural knowledge called by Maritain an intellective mode, one "by way of knowledge."

The type of knowledge usually referred to as connatural is knowledge through affective inclination, a knowledge wherein the connaturality influences not only the manner in which knowledge takes place but also what is known. It is a knowledge wherein "love passes into the condition of the object," as John of St. Thomas put it (*Curs. theol.* In 1am2ae, 70.18.4.11). It is the type of knowledge characteristic of the good man in his judgments of moral questions, of the mystic with regard to divine things, of the artist with respect to his work. Connatural knowledge in the strict sense, then, refers to judgments that are based not "on the perfect use of reason," but rather on an inclination or affinity of the knowing subject to the object known, an inclination caused by affective factors within the knower (cf. ST 1a, 1.6 ad 3; 1a2ae, 68.1 ad 4; 2a2ae, 45.2–3).

Knowledge and Love. To see how knowledge through affective connaturality takes place, it is necessary to consider the relation between knowledge and desire and the effect of love on knowledge. The intellect itself is an appetite: it has a native desire or inclination for perfect union with being—for the concrete, the individual, the whole substance—and for a union greater than that attainable through concepts and discursive thought. The need for discourse reveals the imperfection of man's intellect and of his inability to grasp reality in an all-embracing intuitive vision. His intellect, moreover, has an elicited appetite, the will, which goes out to the goods presented by reason and draws him to things even more than does reason (cf. ST 1a2ae, 22.2). The object known

is present to the intellect as a representation existing in a spiritual way, as an intentional SPECIES joining intellect to thing. But this is not enough for love; "in the intellect the object is present in a specific likeness, but in the will . . . as a motive principle" (*C. gent.* 4.19), or, as Gilby puts it, objects are present to the intellect as meanings, but they are present to the will as magnetic forces (35).

There is, then, pressure on the intellect, both by reason of its native drive and by reason of the love it elicits, to a closer union with the real, with being. Intellect and will are spiritual powers of the same person; and because they are spiritual, they "mutually contain each other" (ST 1a, 16.4 ad 1) and interact. Not only does the will act on the intellect as an efficient cause, moving it to acts of knowledge, but it also acts on the intellect as a formal cause, intrinsically modifying the act of knowledge. As St. Thomas says, "the lover is not content with a superficial knowledge, but strives to enter into everything that belongs to the beloved"; he does not rest with an external and superficial attachment, but longs for a perfect and intimate possession (ST 1a2ae, 28.2). In this interaction of intellect and will, there is built up within the knowing subject, the person, an inclination or connaturality toward the object of his affections. Even his love can be said to discern "by causing discernment in the reason" (ST 2a2ae, 47.1 ad 1).

This type of knowledge is well described in the words of John of St. Thomas: "Love experiences its object with a sort of loving taste . . . . In this way the one loving takes on the very condition of his object, that is, through the effective experience the object is rendered more conformed, more proportioned and united to the person, more suitable to him. For this reason the intellect is carried toward the object as something experienced, as brought into agreement with it" (*Curs. theol.* In 1am2ae, 70.18.4.11). Because the object of connatural knowledge is so attuned, as it were, to the knowing subject, the type of knowledge achieved is in some ways similar to one's knowledge of oneself. And one's self-knowledge is not essentially dependent on concepts or representations: "For the mind to attend to itself . . . a representation is not necessary. It is enough that the essence of the soul is present to the mind and is perceived through its activity" (*De ver.* 10.8). Representations and concepts are conditions, antecedents, and byproducts of one's CONSCIOUSNESS of oneself, but are not formal constituents of self-knowledge itself (cf. ST 1a, 87.1).

The same reasoning is analogously true of man's knowledge of things through affective connaturality, as illustrated by the chaste man's knowledge of chastity, by a father's loving knowledge of his son, by a mystic's knowledge of God, by the poet's knowledge of his art.

As knowledge, connaturality pertains to the intellect, but as connatural it introduces noncognitive factors and shows the truth of the Thomistic dictum that it is man, a person, who knows, not a disembodied intellect.

See Also: KNOWLEDGE; JUDGMENT; FIRST PRINCIPLES; SYNDERESIS.

Bibliography: B. MILLER, *The Range of Intellect* (London 1961). T. GILBY, *The Poetic Experience* (New York 1934). R. O. JOHANN, *The Meaning of Love* (Westminster, Md. 1955). J. MARITAIN, *Creative Intuition in Art and Poetry* (New York 1955); *Distinguish to Unite, or The Degrees of Knowledge,* tr. G. B. PHELAN (New York 1959); *The Range of Reason* (New York 1952). A. HAYEN, *L'Ordre philosophique de Saint Thomas,* v.2 of *La Communication de l'être d'aprés Saint Thomas d'Aquin* (Paris 1957–).

[W. E. MAY]

KNOWLEDGE, GIFT OF

The gift of the Holy Spirit that perfects the work of faith by enabling the believer to appreciate rightly the relation of created things to his supernatural, ultimate end. Faith, unassisted by this gift, that is, acting under ordinary grace, knows that all things are ordered to God. The gift of UNDERSTANDING moves the mind to penetrate this truth more deeply than is possible to faith alone. To this penetration achieved by understanding, the gift of knowledge adds a judgment on how the things of earthly experience are related to the supernatural order. The judgment is intuitive in that it is immediate and bypasses the ordinary discursive steps by which faith operates. It develops in the soul a connaturality for such judgment. Without conscious reflection, the believer is immediately certain of how the realities he meets are related to eternal life.

See Also: HOLY SPIRIT, GIFTS OF; UNDERSTANDING, GIFT OF.

Bibliography: B. FROGET, *The Indwelling of the Holy Spirit in the Souls of the Just,* tr. S. A. RAEMERS (Westminster, Md. 1950). A. ROYO, *The Theology of Christian Perfection,* ed. and tr. J. AUMANN (Dubuque, Iowa 1962) 378–383. R. CESSARIO, *Christian Faith and the Theological Life* (Washington, D.C. 1996). S. PINCKAERS, *The Sources of Christian Ethics,* tr. M. T. NOBLE (3d rev. ed.; Washington, D.C. 1995). THOMAS AQUINAS, *Summa theologiae* 2a2ae, 8–9.

[P. F. MULHERN]

KNOWLEDGE, INFUSED

Infused knowledge is that knowledge that is not acquired by personal effort nor by the instruction of others, but rather is produced directly in a created mind by some angelic or divine illumination. Its distinguishing characteristic is its mode of acquisition and not its subject matter, which can be either natural or supernatural truths. Infused knowledge should also be distinguished from connatural knowledge, such as the angels are sometimes presumed to possess, in that infused knowledge is not necessarily or inseparably associated with the intellect endowed with it.

Whatever is to be said of an angel's ability to infuse knowledge into other minds, there is no doubt that God can do so. To what extent He actually does so is more difficult to determine. Theologians plausibly assume some infusion of knowledge is involved in the initial revelation of supernatural truths such as that given to Adam, the Patriarchs, the Prophets, and so on. Though Scripture often describes God or His angelic messengers as speaking audibly, or appearing in some physical guise, to man (Gn 3.8–9; 4.6; 18.1; 22.11, 15–19; Ex 3.4), it also mentions internal communications of God, or an angel, coming "in a dream by night" (Gn 20.3; Mt 1.20; 2.13, 22). In such instances God could "speak internally" or work directly upon the mind (cf. 2 Cor 12.1–4). Even if God imparted knowledge by audible sounds, some inner illumination would be required to make the recipient certain that God Himself is speaking.

Theologians commonly teach not only that Christ's human soul enjoyed the beatific vision from the first moment of its creation but also that Christ's human mind was infused with the highest possible degree of natural and supernatural knowledge. Texts like that of Luke 2.52 are referred either to the external manifestation of this knowledge or to Christ's experimental knowledge, viz, that acquired through the medium of His mental faculties and bodily senses.

Before human evolution came to be widely accepted, Adam was generally cited as another instance where natural knowledge was infused. Created in the full bloom of manhood, so the argument went, he must be endowed with such knowledge as befitted his status as head of the human race. This would include not only the primitive supernatural revelation but also at least such natural knowledge as a mature man would require. But if man is viewed in an evolutionary context, the need for infused natural knowledge is less apparent. Since man's mental development, however, is ordinarily linguistically conditioned, where no previous language existed some infused knowledge would still seem to be required.

Infused knowledge frequently figures in the rich and varied speculations of scholastic philosophers and theologians as to how angelic spirits or departed souls communicate with one another or acquire new knowledge, particularly about the material universe.

Bibliography: A. MICHEL, *Dictionnaire de théologie catholique,* ed. A. VACANT et al., 15 v. (Paris 1903–50; Tables générales 1951–) 1.1:371; 8.2:2028; 14.2:1653–57. THOMAS AQUINAS, *Studia theologiae,* 3a, 11. *Sacrae theologiae summa,* ed. Fathers of the Society of Jesus, Professors of the Theological Faculties in Spain, 4 v. (Madrid), v. 1 (5th ed. 1962), v. 2 (3d ed. 1958), v. 3 (4th ed. 1961), v. 4 (4th ed. 1962); *Biblioteca de autores cristianos* (Madrid 1945–) 3:1, 265–304.

[A. B. WOLTER]

KNOWLEDGE, PROCESS OF

Knowledge is a most ordinary human experience, while at the same time it is a most mysterious one. We know instinctively what it is, but we cannot clearly define it. With eyes open at day, we see countless objects. We know them; we hear, smell, taste, and touch things; we imagine some and remember others. We make affirmations and denials; we plan for the future; we try to solve problems. All the time, we are aware of doing these things, thus we are conscious of the many forms of knowing that can occupy the human mind: sense knowledge, both exterior (seeing and hearing) and interior (imagining and remembering); and intellectual knowledge, both direct (affirming, reasoning) and indirect or reflexive (awareness of affirming or of reasoning).

Acquisition of Knowledge. How do we acquire such knowledge? Philosophers do not agree on an answer (*see* KNOWLEDGE, THEORIES OF). Here we consider only the Thomistic explanation of the origin of knowledge, first discussing this as a simple approximation to the thought of St. THOMAS AQUINAS, then correcting and deepening the explanation in the light of recent scholarship and a more penetrating study of Aquinas's doctrine.

Sense Knowledge and Abstraction. According to some exponents of THOMISM, all human knowledge comes entirely from the SENSES. Through the senses, especially those of seeing and of hearing, man knows many material objects. For example, I have seen countless trees in my life. They have provided me with sensations—green, hard; with perceptions—this maple tree, that oak; and with the IDEA of tree—a woody perennial with a single trunk—that is universal and applies to all trees, here and everywhere, present, past, and future, real and possible. How does one pass from many concrete, individual trees, all different, to a single and universal idea of tree? Through the process of ABSTRACTION, which may be explained as follows: The countless trees we know have some characteristics in common, whereas other characteristics belong only to one tree, or to a few trees. We drop the latter characteristics, keeping only those that are found in every tree. This seems to imply that the universal idea of tree is present in every perception of a tree, but hidden under many characteristics that do not strictly belong to it. We remove these accidental characteristics; we extract or abstract from the individual image or perception the underlying universal idea.

As a rough approximation, this interpretation is correct, but it can easily be taken in an empirical way, implying that man's INTELLIGENCE is merely passive in the formation of ideas. Such an empiricism logically leads to materialism, for if the intelligence receives its ideas passively from the material objects of sense experience, it must be a material power. How can material objects act upon an immaterial faculty? If the reply is that human intelligence is not merely passive, since it actively abstracts the universal idea from the senses or from the phantasm, that reply raises another difficulty. If to abstract means to make a choice between common features that will be kept in the universal idea and accidental features that will be dropped, this supposes that the intellect knows all the features among which it must choose. This idea implies that man's intellect knows the singular, material individual; that it is directly affected by the concrete, material aspects of reality. This is not the teaching of Aquinas.

Activity of Intellect. A closer study of St. Thomas's thought reveals his position to be as follows: The human INTELLECT is not a purely passive faculty in the formation of ideas, but contributes something of its own. With everything it comes to know, man's intelligence affirms that it is something, a being. A fuller description of that being comes from the senses. Thus it follows that man does not attain the universal idea gradually and inductively, as described above. The first contact of intelligence with a material object produces at once a universal idea. This might be simply the idea of "something big and green." Such a concept is actually a composite of intellectual and sense data. It is a universal idea, for it applies to an indefinite number of possible objects, yet it can be particularized by a pointing finger that says, in effect: "Something big and green, over there." We see, therefore, that abstraction does not involve the extraction of a thing's hidden ESSENCE from its many accidental features, but rather the fact of referring a unity supplied by the intellect to a multiplicity offered by the senses.

Types of Knowledge. Man's knowledge involves both sensation and intellect, and these two elements always go together. Man never has a sensation without a corresponding idea; he never has an idea without a sensation or image that is the residue of former sensations.

SENSATION gives man knowledge of concrete aspects or qualities of individual, material objects, e.g., colors, sounds, and odors. When such qualities are organized so as to constitute a unity in space and time, the result is a PERCEPTION. For instance, I perceive this house, that man. Such perceptions are stored away in the IMAGINA-

TION and the memory. Thus, even when I do not see the house before my eyes, I may have a distinct individual representation of it—an image that I may recognize as referring to a real house previously perceived—known as a memory image.

When I perceive, imagine, or remember a tree, I can also say: "That is a tree." This statement itself represents intellectual knowledge. It implies that I have a CONCEPT of tree; even though I refer at present to this individual oak, my perception applies equally to innumerable other trees, and thus is universal (*see* UNIVERSALS). Also, when I state: "This is a tree," I affirm something. I perform an act of JUDGMENT, the central act of human knowledge affirming (or denying) something of something else; this reflects my contact with extramental reality, for it states that an objective state of affairs corresponds to my subjective representation.

Immateriality. The previous section described lower to higher types of knowledge. It is also useful to start by considering knowledge first as it occurs in God. For a Thomist, God not only possesses knowledge; He *is* knowledge. In other words, God is consciousness; He is supreme and fully luminous self-awareness, and since God is also infinite and pure BEING, it follows that being in its fullness is consciousness, self-awareness, and knowledge. Looking at knowledge from this viewpoint, we no longer ask: How is it possible that some beings know? Instead we ask: How is it possible that some beings do not know? Since God, who is infinite being, is also infinite knowledge, being and knowledge seem to go together, and this is so. The degree of knowledge a being possesses corresponds to the degree of being with which it is endowed. The more it is being, the more and the better it knows. Conversely, whatever limits the being of things limits also their power of knowing, but being is limited by POTENCY, especially the potency known as MATTER. Thus, the more a being is material, the weaker is its power of knowing. The basis of all knowledge is therefore IMMATERIALITY.

This may be further explained as follows. By and of itself being is self-luminous and conscious. When more and more limited by matter, it gradually loses this self-luminosity. Because animals are more material than men, their knowledge is inferior to human knowledge, while plants, being even more material than animals, possess no knowledge, although even they have some activities that are akin to knowing, such as their ability to collect from the soil and air exactly what they need for life and growth, building the specialized tissues needed for their vital activities.

Form in Knowledge. In the act of knowledge, two features require explanation: immanence and objectivity.

Immanence obtains when the object as known exists in some way in the mind of the knowing subject. Objectivity is the feature of knowledge by which the object is recognized as existing outside the knowing subject and as distinct from it.

Immanence. Thomists explain the immanence of knowledge as follows: Every material object possesses many forms—usually one substantial form and a multiplicity of acccidental forms. The substantial FORM makes the object be what it is, whereas the accidental forms make it be such and such a thing of this kind. Thus, a young black cat is a cat because of its substantial form, and it is young and black because of its accidental forms of age and color. In the process of cognition, these forms, while existing physically or ontologically in the extramental object, enter the knowing subject and become, intentionally, his own forms. They do not become the forms of that subject physically, since this would make the subject become ontologically whatever he knows—e.g., a man would thus become a young black cat—but the forms become intentionally his, and he becomes intentionally whatever he knows.

This phenomenon is referred to as the intentional presence of the object in the knowing subject. Intentional is here not opposed to real, but rather to physical. While forms are really present in the knowing subject, they are in that subject not as the subject is in its natural reality, but they inform it as it is actually in the act of knowing. Intentional existence is the existence of something in a knowing power precisely as such. St. Thomas explains that this presence differs from the presence of an accident in the substance that underlies it, and from the presence of the substantial form in primary matter. Both the union of substance and accident and that of form and matter result in a third reality differing from its two components. The intentional union, however, is more intimate. Through it the faculty becomes the other, as other, while still remaining itself; through it the subject knows the other as other. The forms that come to be intentionally present in knowing faculties are known as intentional species (*see* SPECIES, INTENTIONAL; INTENTIONALITY).

Objectivity. The problem of OBJECTIVITY has attracted less attention than immanence in traditional Thomism. The intentional species explains how the knower becomes in some way what he knows. Yet, since the forms thus become his own forms, it seems that he should know them as his own; what requires explanation is how, through them, he can know the other as other, i.e., as non-subject, as object.

It is not enough to say that the subject is aware that these forms come from objects outside, for this begs the question. He knows that they come from objects outside only because he knows such objects as "not himself"; how then does he know them as "not himself"? Again, it is not enough to appeal to the physical CAUSALITY of the object upon the knowing power. Such causality is undeniable, at least on the sense level, but it does not fall directly under conscious awareness.

To answer the question, one must distinguish the objectivity of the sense powers from that of the intellect. It seems evident, from their behavior, that animals are aware of objects, i.e., of things as distinct from themselves, yet they do not seem to know objects as objects; they are not aware of things in their environment as distinct in being from themselves. Several reasons lead to this conclusion. First, to know things as different entities from themselves, animals must know being as such; but the senses do not attain being formally as being, but in a material way. Next, to know objects as objects and nonsubjects, animals must be aware of themselves as subjects; but to know oneself as a subject supposes reflection, which is proper to spiritual faculties. Finally, if animals knew objects as such, they would designate them, refer to them, give them names; they would talk and use language.

Animal vs. Human Objectivity. How then do animals know that things are distinct from themselves? It seems that they know objects only as spatially distinct from their own bodies. Kant's explanation of this kind of objectivity is that space is the a priori form of external sensation. While maintaining, against him, that real space exists outside knowing subjects, we can agree that space as man knows and sees it—the dimensions in which material objects are contained—is an a priori form. Animals, too, must have such an a priori intuition of space. By that intuition an animal notices that objects occupy positions that are not its own position, and thus knows them as spatially distinct from itself. Man has great difficulty in understanding such mere spatial objectivity because, although he too perceives it in sense perception, for him it is always backed by an ontological distinction that is discerned by his intellect.

How this ontological distinction can be known has been explained by Joseph MARÉCHAL, who accounts for the objectivity of human knowledge by the dynamism of the intellect. Knowledge does not simply happen to man's intellect. The intellect wants to know; it has an appetite for the forms of objects and strives toward cognition of these forms; but the term of its striving is known as other, distinguished from the striving subject, and thus is objectified. Objects are known as such, as ontologically distinct from man, because their forms fulfill the intellect's natural appetite for being and intelligibility.

Knowledge of Knowing. Man not only knows objects, he also knows that he knows them. He is aware of being aware, conscious that he is conscious. This fact, important in that many thinkers insist upon it as the note that distinguishes man from animals, is undeniable. He who attempts to deny it, affirms it in his very denial; for how can he know that he does not know, except that, in examining his own knowledge—and thus knowing it—he does not discover in it any self-knowledge?

Knowledge of knowing is a special kind of knowledge. It is intuitive; that is, it uses no intermediary concepts (*see* INTUITION). Man knows the universal nature of tree or of justice only in, and through, the concept of tree or of justice. On the other hand, when he is aware that he knows, he does so directly and immediately, without a *species expressa* or a concept. The fact that man possesses such complete self-reflection constitutes the best proof of the immateriality of the human intellect, and also of the immateriality of the human soul (*see* REFLECTION; SOUL, HUMAN, IMMORTALITY OF).

See Also: KNOWLEDGE; EPISTEMOLOGY.

Bibliography: THOMAS AQUINAS, *Summa theologiae* 1a, 14; 54–58; 84–89. J. F. DONCEEL, *Philosophical Psychology* (2d ed., rev. New York 1961). R. E. BRENNAN, *Thomistic Psychology* (New York 1941). J. E. ROYCE, *Man and His Nature* (New York 1961). H. REITH, *An Introduction to Philosophical Psychology* (Englewood Cliffs, N.J. 1956). P. ROUSSELOT, *The Intellectualism of Saint Thomas,* tr. J. E. O'MAHONY (London 1935). B. J. F. LONERGAN, *Insight: A Study of Human Understanding* (New York 1957).

[J. F. DONCEEL]

KNOWLEDGE, SOCIOLOGY OF

The study of the relation between products of the mind and existential conditions. The basic assumption of the study is that the development of thought is not independent of the concrete situation in which it takes place. This connection being assumed, the sociology of knowledge aims at defining its nature, whether in general terms or with reference to specific events. The field, therefore, embraces both a theory and a method of investigation; in either case, it differs from disciplines such as EPISTEMOLOGY and ETHICS that focus their attention on the internal coherence, logical antecedents, and final value of a given system. The sociological approach shifts the focus from the intrinsic validity to the external origin and consequences of knowledge, from the objective content of a proposition to the subjective dispositions of its proponents. The distinction between the two approaches is certainly not easy; not seldom one finds sociologists moving from premises and reaching conclusions that are proper to the philosophy of knowledge (*see* KNOWLEDGE, THEORIES OF).

Sometimes studies in this field give the term knowledge so broad a meaning as to make it virtually equivalent to CULTURE (in the anthropological sense). So understood, the sociology of knowledge tends to encompass in its object all kinds of mental products, from folklore to law and technology. In this sense, it may include the contributions of the French school, e.g., Émile DURKHEIM (1858–1917), Lucien Lévy-Bruhl (1857–1939), Marcel Mauss (1872–1950), and Marcel Granet (1884–1940), which investigated the correspondence between mentality and social structures, especially among primitives.

Central Problem. In principle, there is no reason why sociological analysis should be limited to one rather than to another type of knowledge; except for certain forms of mysticism, learning and COMMUNICATION always occur in a social situation and can, therefore, be analyzed in terms of the concrete conditions of their occurrence. In point of fact, however, students have concentrated mostly on political thought, economic doctrines, social ethics—in a word, on knowledge that implies systematic value judgments with respect to interpersonal relations and human institutions in industrial society.

Two reasons, one theoretical, the other historical, may explain the tendency to concentrate on the history of social thought. It is generally assumed that natural and mathematical sciences are relatively independent of the historical situations in which they develop, at least insofar as the very content of the scientific propositions is concerned. Historically, the sociology of knowledge is rooted in the works of social philosophers and reformers whose main concern has not been to institute a systematic analysis of knowledge as such, but to prove the dependence of political ideologies on class interests and economic structures. This trend is best expressed in the writings of Karl MARX (1818–83) and Friedrich ENGELS (1820–95). Actually, the Marxian doctrine of the ideology as a superstructure has played a determining role in the emergence and the initial orientation of the sociology of knowledge. This influence explains also the original tendency to correlate the development of thought with socioeconomic factors much more than with natural conditions, with the cultural milieu rather than the physical environment. Special importance is attributed to a thinker's identification with a status group, whether based on education, prestige, wealth, political power, ethnic or religious affiliation.

All these factors—physical, demographic, economic, sociocultural—constitute the "existential conditions" involved in the development of thought. The most controversial point in the sociology of knowledge is the definition of the nature of this relation. For some, the relation is strictly causal; for others, it is functional or merely symbolic. Often enough, the same author uses different and ill-defined words, such as "correspondence," without giving a definite interpretation of this relation, either theoretically or—even less—on the basis of substantive findings. On the whole, the tendency has been to stress much more the dependence *of* thought *on* the existential conditions rather than the reverse side of the relation. With the passing of the years, however, the tendency has been to interpret this dependency less and less in a deterministic way; this trend coincides with a progressive shift from a philosophical to a stricter empirical approach.

Development. The problems raised by the sociology of knowledge are very old; one could trace them back to Francis BACON (1561–1626) and his famous theory of the *Idola* or even further to the SOPHISTS' interpretation of the social origin of law and religion. Formally, however, the very name of the discipline first appeared at the beginning of the 20th century, in an article by Wilhelm Jerusalem, "Soziologie des Erkennens" (*Die Zukunft*, May 1909). The most significant contributions belong to the period between the two world wars; they are mostly in German, and prefer the name *Wissens-soziologie*. Particularly important are the works of Max SCHELER (1874–1928) and Karl Mannheim (1893–1947).

Scheler rejected the Marxian theory of the complete dependence of thought on economic conditions; at the same time, he decried the idealistic view of history as the constant unfolding of the Mind. For him there could be no one-way dependence but only an orderly interaction between the "ideal factors" (the realm of transcendental values) and the "real factors" (racial, economic, demographic, and political conditions). He defined the sociology of knowledge as the study of such interaction as has actually occurred in specific historical periods, and he found most appropriate to this investigation the phenomenological approach of Edmund HUSSERL (1859–1938), intended to detect the incarnation of the essence (*Wesen*) in the concrete existence (*Dasein*). Scheler's works, including his *Versuche einer Soziologie des Wissens* (1924), are philosophical rather than sociological in orientation.

Mannheim is probably the best-known exponent of the discipline, especially for his *Ideologie und Utopie* (1929). He combined in his eclectic system the Marxian views with the spiritual trends of German HISTORICISM. He saw all political thought, the proletarian no less than the bourgeois, as existentially conditioned. To him this "total conception" of ideology did not necessarily invalidate the objectivity of knowledge, since each social group develops a particular *Weltanschauung* that is neither false nor entirely true; full truth, he believed, would come from the synthesis of the various points of view.

Ideologies aim at maintaining well-established positions; the "utopia," on the contrary, is a doctrine promoting social progress, a prophecy embodied in a powerful historical movement. In his view, the rise of SCIENTISM marked the end of the utopian mentality, hence the risk of stagnation. The sociology of knowledge therefore had a twofold function: to understand the idea systems relative to the various groups and epochs and to restore confidence in the transforming role of ideas in history. Mannheim considered these two functions to be strictly intertwined, so that the same discipline could appear as both an objective method of investigation and a new philosophy of social renewal; each function (*verstehen or erklären*) he assigned to a socially free elite (*eine freischwebende Intelligenz*) having a role in many respects similar to that of the Marxian proletariat.

In the U.S., the sociology of knowledge gained status after 1930, as a result of the translation of German studies and some original works, such as P. A. Sorokin's *Social and Cultural Dynamics* (4 v. New York 1937–41). Sorokin's work offers two significant features: a theoretical stand for the dependence of socioeconomic structures on the major value premises in a given culture and a methodological effort to analyze statistically the cultural products of several centuries in order to detect the types of value orientation prevailing in the various epochs. It is difficult to say how much American sociology has contributed to the field, since much research may bear on the problems of the sociology of knowledge without being formally included under the name or within the theoretical framework of the discipline. In this respect, it is possible to cite studies of mass communication; social stratification; cultural change; and, in general, research on one or the other aspect of knowledge, e.g., the sociology of law, RELIGION, art, or education. As a whole, American contributions to this sociological field are mostly methodological, intended to supply a better definition of basic concepts (e.g., existential condition, cultural integration, ideology) and a better definition of particular areas of investigation in order to test the sweeping generalizations that characterized the beginnings of the sociology of knowledge.

Bibliography: F. ADLER, "The Range of Sociology of Knowledge," in *Modern Sociological Theory in Continuity and Change,* ed. H. BECKER and A. BOSKOFF (New York 1957) ch. 13. H. O. DAHLKE, "The Sociology of Knowledge," in *Contemporary Social Theory,* ed. H. E. BARNES et al. (New York 1940) ch. 4. P. KECSKEMETI, "Introduction" to K. MANNHEIM, *Essays on the Sociology of Knowledge* (New York 1952). J. J. MAQUET, *The Sociology of Knowledge: Its Structure and Its Relation to the Philosophy of Knowledge,* tr. J. F. LOCKE (Boston 1951) with bibliog. R. K. MERTON, *Social Theory and Social Structure* (Glencoe, Ill. 1957) ch. 12–13. W. STARK, *The Sociology of Knowledge: An Essay in Aid of a Deeper Understanding of the History of Ideas* (Glencoe, Ill. 1958). L. WIRTH, "Preface" to K. MANNHEIM, *Ideology and Utopia: An Introduction to the Sociology of Knowledge,* tr. L. WIRTH and E. A. SHILS (New York 1936). P. BERGER and T. LUCKMANN, "Sociology of Religion and Sociology of Knowledge," in *Sociology and Social Research* 47 (1962–63) 417–427. P. L. BERGER and T. LUCKMAN, *The Social Construction of Reality* (Garden City, N.Y. 1966).

[P. TUFARI]

KNOWLEDGE, THEORIES OF

Theory of knowledge is an area of philosophical speculation concerned with the nature, conditions, and/or first principles of knowledge in general and also, according to some authors, with the truth-value, or reliability, of knowledge in general. The expression "theory of knowledge" is used interchangeably with the term EPISTEMOLOGY by some authors, but others, particularly in Europe, mean something else by the latter term—usually a critique of modern scientific knowledge (cf. *Enciclopedia filosofica* 1:1942). Theory of knowledge is among the more controversial areas in philosophy, there being serious disagreement among the different philosophical traditions over the selection and correct formulation of the problems to be considered. Disagreement exists also over the question of whether theory of knowledge should precede and control, or follow and be controlled by, METAPHYSICS and psychology.

Scholastic philosophers generally prefer the second alternative, both because their conception of being and knowing requires that a theory of knowledge rest on something more basic than itself, and also because there is a strong tendency, discoverable in history, for the first alternative to lead to some kind of skepticism.

This article traces the historical development of theories of knowledge from early times to the present, treating successively of the Greek origins of the problem, medieval theories of knowledge, knowledge in modern thought, and contemporary views of knowledge. Systematic analyses, from the viewpoint of scholastic philosophy, of various problems associated with the theory of knowledge are treated elsewhere (*see* KNOWLEDGE; SENSE KNOWLEDGE; CERTITUDE; TRUTH).

Greek Origins of the Problem

Like many problems in philosophy, the problem of knowledge received its earliest formulation and a variety of solutions among the Greeks, the most important of whom include Parmenides, Democritus, Socrates, Plato, and Aristotle.

Parmenides. Questions concerning the nature and conditions of knowledge first assumed importance in the philosophy of PARMENIDES (fl. *c.* 485 B.C.). Parmenides's predecessors had concerned themselves, from the very beginning of GREEK PHILOSOPHY (*c.* 585 B.C.), with cosmological questions concerning the basic material from which the familiar things of experience are made and concerning the process whereby such things undergo change. That there is a plurality of things undergoing change these thinkers took as an obvious fact. The starting point of Parmenides's thought seems also to have been this plurality, but he found that a more basic affirmation about reality is that it exists. Being is and nonbeing is not. Determined to discover the ultimate implications of this intuition, Parmenides said that being cannot come to be (since being "is" and what "is" cannot come to be) and must therefore be eternal, in the sense of beginningless. Moreover, change must be an appearance only, since change means becoming, and neither being (because it simply "is") nor nonbeing (because it is nothingness) can become. In a conclusion that influenced the subsequent history of Greek thought about being and knowledge, Parmenides declared that being is eternal and changeless.

This intuition controls Parmenides's theory of knowledge. Corresponding to the duality that he introduces between being (or true reality) and appearances, he also introduces a duality between knowledge, the object of which is being and in which alone is to be found truth, and another, corrupted or limited kind of cognition called *doxai* (Gr. δόξαι), a term often translated, somewhat misleadingly, as "opinions," that rather means one's perceptions of the plural and changing appearances of being. A similar duality is introduced by Parmenides between reasoning, which, because it achieves knowledge about true reality, is the higher way; and sensation, which, tied down to the appearances of plurality and change, leads to perplexity and poor discernment. The ordinary cognition of all men is one in which knowledge and *doxai* are mixed, and it is only in rare moments of inspiration and illumination that men—a few men—have cognitions in which things are seen from the standpoint of the timelessness and changelessness of being.

Atomists and Sophists. The theory of knowledge of the Greek atomistic school (5th century B.C.) was a continuation of Parmenides's doctrine on knowledge, in spite of the fact that, at first glance, a world conceived in terms of a plurality of atoms would seem to have little in common with the Parmenidean world. The best known representative of this school, DEMOCRITUS of Abdera, distinguishing between reality (eternal and changeless atoms moving through the void) and appearances (the changing configurations of atom-groups making up the familiar world), concluded that, since no one perceives the atoms, knowledge of reality is impossible. One has only *doxai*, which were explained as private sensations resulting from atoms impinging upon the cognitive organs.

While Democritus's theory of knowledge restricted cognition to *doxai*, his Parmenidean background was strong enough to move him to regard such cognition as superficial and second best; a genuine knowledge of true reality, were it possible, would be better. It was left for the SOPHISTS to take the logical step of declaring that, if *doxai* alone constitute the cognition possible for man, then there is hardly any basis for depreciating and regarding as second best this kind of cognition. Among the Sophists, Protagoras (*c.* 49 to 420 B.C.) eliminated the Parmenidean notion of truth—i.e., stable knowledge of eternal, changeless being—on the ground that it was useless and therefore quite irrelevant in the matter of living one's life wisely and well. Truth, therefore, if it is to be found anywhere, will have to be found in one's ever-changing *doxai*, one's perceptions of the appearances. This doctrine was taken by some to mean that the way in which things happen to appear to an individual is the way they actually are, for him, and that therefore truth is relative to each individual.

Socrates, Plato, and Aristotle. Against this background, SOCRATES, whose chief interest was virtue (identified, for him, with knowing how to live wisely and well), saw that the Sophists' notion of truth made virtue impossible, since ever-changing *doxai* provided no dependable guides for living well. Accordingly, Socrates sought to discover from the changing, particular appearances of things some permanent and universally valid meanings in terms of which there could be a genuine knowledge of being and hence some basis for making wise decisions.

Socrates's project was carried further by his major disciple PLATO, who agreed that *doxai* were not a satisfactory guide for living well. Only genuine knowledge could be a satisfactory guide. Accepting the Parmenidean doctrine that knowledge means knowledge of being and that being is eternal and changeless, Plato concluded that behind the familiar world of changing sensible things—appearances—there is an archetypal world of Forms (Ideas) which, eternal and changeless, provide the stability needed for objects of knowledge. In spite of the ever-changing character of the material world about which there can be only *doxai*, genuine knowledge of permanent and universally valid meanings—and therefore a basis for making wise decisions—is possible, because of the existence of the Forms. These Forms were said by Plato to be known by the soul prior to its imprisonment in the body, and during its earthly life the soul's knowledge is simply recollection.

ARISTOTLE, while agreeing with Parmenides and Plato that stability is a necessary requisite for an object of knowledge, rejected Plato's tendency to locate this stability in a separate world of Forms and insisted that, since all knowledge begins with sensible things, there must be something stable in these themselves. This was explained in terms of the Aristotelian hylomorphic doctrine, according to which every sensible substance is a composite of a determinable principle (matter) in virtue of which the substance can change, and a determining principle (form) in virtue of which the substance is what it is (*see* MATTER AND FORM). Accordingly, while a sensible substance can change, nevertheless to the extent that it ''is'' it is stable; hence it is being and is knowable—its stability, being, and knowableness resulting from its form. The knower's knowledge was explained by Aristotle in terms of the knower abstracting the form of the known object, so that the knower's knowledge is not something that represents the known object; it actually is the known object (*see* ABSTRACTION).

Later Greeks. Among later Greek philosophers, the Stoics viewed knowledge as consisting in impressions on the soul brought about through sense perceptions of particular things. The Epicureans located truth basically in sensation, which they reduced, after the manner of Democritus, to particles striking the cognitive organs. The Skeptics repudiated all claims to knowledge and truth, but their skepticism was aimed at destroying philosophies and not at paralyzing practical life.

See Also: SKEPTICISM; PYRRHONISM; CYNICS; STOICISM; EPICUREANISM; NEOPLATONISM.

Bibliography: General introductions. A. H. ARMSTRONG, *An Introduction to Ancient Philosophy* (Westminster, Maryland 1957). J. BURNET, *Greek Philosophy: Thales to Plato* (London 1914; reprint 1932). F. C. COPLESTON, *History of Philosophy:* v.1: *Greece and Rome* (Westminster, Maryland 1946; 2d ed. 1950). J. OWENS, *A History of Ancient Western Philosophy* (New York 1959). J. I. BEARE, *Greek Theories of Elementary Cognition from Alcmaeon to Aristotle* (Oxford 1906). Particular philosophers. G. VLASTOS, ''Parmenides' Theory of Knowledge,'' *American Philological Association, Transactions and Proceedings* 77 (1946) 66–77. *Plato's Theory of Knowledge,* tr. F. M. CORNFORD (London 1935). N. GULLEY, *Plato's Theory of Knowledge* (New York 1962). W. D. ROSS, *Plato's Theory of Ideas* (Oxford 1951); *Aristotle* (5th ed. London 1953) 136–165, 215–21. M. M. PATRICK, *The Greek Sceptics* (New York 1929). M. DE CORTE, *La Doctrine de l'intelligence chez Aristote* (Paris 1934).

[F. R. ELLIS]

Medieval Theories of Knowledge

From such origins in Greek philosophy, theories of knowledge were extensively developed by the early medievals and the schoolmen. Under the sway of Platonism, writers such as St. Augustine, Boethius, St. Anselm, and Abelard set the stage for the later scholastic theories. Aristotle's influence, transmitted by Arab thinkers such as Avicenna and Averroës, added a further dimension to medieval thought. These currents fused in the *hochscholastik* period, and brought forth various solutions to the problem of knowledge, as proposed principally by St. Bonaventure, St. Thomas Aquinas, John Duns Scotus, and William of Ockham.

Christian Platonists. Like Aristotle, medieval scholars inherited a noetic that derived from Plato and, often enough, succeeded in becoming Aristotelians without altogether ceasing to be Platonists. Knowledge, for instance, was specified by its certitude. The stability of knowledge, they were tempted to think, must be founded on the object known, but the changing singular seemed a poor candidate for the role. Still, permanent structures are discerned in things. To grasp their essences, a Platonic mind has but to concentrate forces that are weakened when dispersed among sensibles. A Platonic being is intelligible of itself and hardly needs modification by the intellect. What is required is rather an ethical purification of the one who knows.

St. Augustine. St. AUGUSTINE surmounted a crisis of skepticism in his youth with the reflection that to err is to exist and to reject an error is to proclaim truth (*Civ.* 11.26; *Lib. arb.* 2.3.7). He urged the mind in search of true knowledge to turn from deceptive externals and to collect her forces, to enter within herself where the mind must recognize that she is under the rule of a higher light (*Vera relig.* 39.72), that truth is the mind's discovery, not her construction (*Doctr. christ.* 2.32.50; *Lib. arb.* 2.12.34; *Civ.* 11.25), and that this higher light, one for all minds, inferior to nothing, and eternally immutable, is an illumination that flows from and reveals God (*Lib. arb.* 2.13.36–37). Although St. Paul is an indispensable guide into the mysteries of ultimate truth (*Conf.* 7.21.27), Plato can teach man to turn within and to allow love, the ''weight'' of the soul (*Epist.* 157.2.9; *Conf.* 13.9.10), to bear her above the dissipation of sensual involvement. Sensation is much more a matter of the soul's attention than of corporeal passivity (*Musica* 6.5.9).

St. Augustine proposes a crucial role for memory. With mind and will, a Trinitarian vestige in man, memory renders the eternal exemplars accessible to the mind (*Trin.* 12.15:25). Citing Vergil to show that there can be a memory of the present (*ibid.* 14.11.14), Augustine holds that by memory man retains the past and also sees the present in the light of the exemplars to which the apex of the soul is always present. But he is careful to disclaim a prior existence of the human soul (*Civ.* 11.23; *Retract.* 1.4.4).

Boethius. BOETHIUS claimed that he had cultivated what Augustine had sown (*Trin.*), but to say nothing of his personal genius, he added to his knowledge of Plato a technical training in the philosophy of Aristotle and, despite (or perhaps because of) his knowledge of both, thought they could be reconciled (*Lib. de interp. ed.* 2.2). Knowledge is proportioned to the capacity of the knower (*Consol.* 5 prosa 4, 6) and also to the object known (*In Porphy. dial.* 1; *Trin.*), for knowledge is possible only to the extent that knower and known can coincide in their grade of being. The object of man's highest knowledge is the "intellectible," a term coined by Boethius to designate what is one and the same of itself, always consistent in its own divinity, and never grasped by sense, but only by mind and intellect (*In Porphy. dial.* 1).

The second level of knowledge and thus of being is that of the "intelligibles." Here man proceeds "by thought and understanding concerning the First Intellectible" to grasp the causes of the sublunar sphere and the human soul itself, that soul which, at first an "intellectible," has lost caste by the contamination of body and has become an "intelligible" (*ibid.*).

A third level of speculative knowledge discerns the natures and attributes of bodies by prescinding from their matter (*ibid.*). God, the object of theology, the supreme degree of speculative knowledge, is approached by man in "intellectual" fashion (*intellectualiter*). Intelligible objects, superior to bodies although in contact with them, are approached by way of "discipline" (*disciplinaliter*), the rationalizing proper to man; a procedure that results in mathematics. Corporeal natures, "rationally" (*rationaliter*) considered, are the objects of physics (*Trin.*). Because he has fallen, man cannot know without rationalizing; but because he is a fallen god, an "intellectible," he need not despair of wisdom.

In sensation, the soul is active (*Consol.* 5.4 prosa 5) and, taken to the letter, Boethius more than once invoked the preexistence of souls to explain knowledge (*Consol.* 3.11 prosa 12; *In Porphy. dial.* 1). But these remarks are in the spirit of Platonic myth-making, inspired by man's present state, rather than descriptions of the historic past.

Erigena. One of the most daring applications of dialectic to Christian faith is that of JOHN SCOTUS ERIGENA: since to know God is salvation, ignorance must be the same as damnation (*De praed.* 17.9). Because nature is "everything that is and everything that is not" (*De div. nat.* 1), the knowledge of nature is radically theological. "Nature creating, but not created" is God, the divine Ideas are "nature creating and created." The World is "nature, not creating, but created" and the goal of the great return, when God will be all in all, is God qualified as "nature neither creating nor created" (*ibid.*). Thus all knowledge, with all being, is treated under the title "On the Division of Nature."

St. Anselm. By his use of the old truth that God is "that than which a greater cannot be conceived" to establish that God necessarily exists, ANSELM OF CANTERBURY posed a sign of contradiction for all succeeding speculation. For those who accept his world, the *Proslogion* argument is irrefutable, but for those who live in another world, the reasoning remains unconvincing (*see* ONTOLOGICAL ARGUMENT). This means less than Anselm had a strange theory of truth and knowledge, than that his consciousness of reasoning in the presence of truth and its participations rendered all theories superfluous. Unparticipated truth is being itself, and Anselm's world is no more a world of beings than a world of truths.

Peter Abelard. ABELARD came to the problem of knowledge impressed by the radical singularity of each individual and by man's inability to recognize in a general concept the individuals of which, nonetheless, it can be predicated. Man knows things, it seemed to him, in three ways: by sensation, when a thing is present; by imagination when, in its totality, a thing is the object of the soul's attention; and by intellection, when the soul attends to some detailed aspect of that thing. Like an artist, the knower holds his material with one hand and shapes it with the other. He works over what is grasped by sense or imagination to discern the forms that exist together, but that can be thought apart. Sensation requires corporeal instruments, but is primarily the work of the soul (*Logica 'Ingred.,' Gloss. in Perih.*).

The Arabian Aristotle. With access to Aristotle, there was a shift in the problematic. No longer deplored as an obstacle to knowledge, sensation was accredited as its sole starting point. At once receptive to what sense can deliver and active in dematerializing that content to fit it for intellectual assimilation, intellect implies two powers. As capable of adaption to the forms of other things, intellect is passive. As capable of rendering the potentially intelligible material singular actually intelligible, intellect is "agent." This much is surely in Aristotle, but where did the Stagirite intend to locate these powers?

Arabian commentators took firm positions where the text of Aristotle left some latitude. The intelligence responsible for providing the human knower with suitably immaterial forms is an astronomical deity, styled by Avicenna the "Giver of Forms" or the "Intellect in effect" and by Averroës, the "Agent Intellect." Both hold it is one for all men.

Avicenna. The soul may be, as Avicenna would have it, the very essence of man (*De anim.* 1.1), but for all Aristotelians, soul is the form of the body, and here Avicenna betrays some uneasiness with Aristotle. For to be a form of matter, Avicenna remarked, defines a function of the soul rather than its nature (*ibid.*). As in potency to receive such forms, the intellect of man is "material," by which he meant "passive," not "corporeal." As possessed of forms, but not adverting to them, intellect is "habitual"; as actually knowing that it knows, intellect is "in effect," or, in terms that remind one that intelligible forms come to man from above, it is "borrowed" (*accommodatus*) and "acquired" (*adeptus*). "The Giver of Forms, totally and always 'in effect,' is to our minds what the sun is to our sight." Not only the source of intelligible forms for human intellects, the Giver of Forms has a second right to his title. This Intelligence provides matter under the sphere of the moon with the constituent forms it is prepared to receive and thus brings new beings into existence.

Averroës. Averroës agreed with Avicenna that there is a "passive" intellect by which a man is capable of receiving intelligible forms from above, but this he described as corporeal imagination, destined to perish at the death of the individual who possesses it. The union of the separate Agent Intellect with the passive one engenders a third intellect that Averroës termed "material," since it too is passive. This third intellect is as little the possession of the individual as light reflected from a body is part of that body. Hence there is no ground in the uncorruptibility of intellect for the immortality of the human individual. All that is individual is corruptible, and all that is incorruptible is both radically separate from matter and one for all men. As the Agent Intellect is one for all men, so too the material intellect is one for the entire race. The highest cognitive faculty that pertains to the individual is the corporeally rooted, and therefore perishable, "passive intellect" or "imagination."

If this is the last word of philosophy, then it is a wisdom incompatible with Christian faith in personal immortality. The "prophetic intellect," source of the illumination that has resulted in that "miraculous" work, the Qu'rān, reinforces the decision of modern scholarship that the *Three Impostors* (Moses, Jesus, and Muḥammad), attributed to Averroés, is a forgery, but it was not enough to defend him from persecution by the Islamic theologians of his own day (*In de anima* 3.4, 5). *See* INTELLECT, UNITY OF; DOUBLE TRUTH, THEORY OF; ARABIAN PHILOSOPHY.

Aristotle and the Christians. The dangers implicit in the Arabian development of Aristotelian thought were quickly recognized by the schoolmen of the 13th century. Correctives were soon forthcoming, with various repudiations of Aristotle and with a pronounced revival, in some quarters, of the doctrines of St. Augustine.

St. Bonaventure. His intimate knowledge of Aristotle's text notwithstanding, St. BONAVENTURE was little inclined to abandon the pathways of his Christian masters

for those of Aristotle. The content of knowledge as garnered through sensation and the intellect can be described in Aristotelian terms, but certitude specifies genuine knowledge and this, as St. Augustine knew and Aristotle did not know, is the fruit of a divine ILLUMINATION. Neither the created mind that knows, nor the created object known, can be the source of the universality, necessity, and immutability of "certitudinal" knowledge. The divine attributes these terms evoke are the ultimate ground of knowledge (*In 2 sent.* 7.2.2.1).

Faced with the two-edged risk of ascribing too much to creatures or too much to God, Bonaventure never hesitated to follow the dictates of his piety and to choose the explanation that gives most to God. But not everyone, not even every Franciscan, in the 13th century was content with this solution. Is the divine illumination the same as the general concurrence of God with creatures, or is it a special help? Does divine illumination pertain to the order of nature or to the order of grace? The Franciscans found it increasingly difficult to know with Aristotle and to be certain with Augustine, and the temptation was not always resisted to transfer the problem from philosophy to theology.

St. Thomas Aquinas. The most important of those who declined to accept a piety that exalts the Creator by positing intrinsic deficiencies in creation was St. THOMAS AQUINAS. With the balance that is one of his chief glories, however, he admitted that whether, with Plato and Augustine, one says that the intelligibles are participated from God, or, with Aristotle and himself, that what is participated is the very light that renders things intelligible, "does not matter much" (*De spir. creat.* 10 ad 8). The light of reason implanted in man by God, the natural power of the human mind that Aristotle had called the "agent intellect," is "as it were, a certain similitude of Uncreated Truth" (*De ver.* 11.1). As Augustine had found much to christen in Plato, Aquinas found the Aristotelian panoply of knowledge within the created structure of man. Intellect, with its passive and active powers, belongs within the human soul. As truly the form of body for Aquinas as for Aristotle, the soul is the single form of man's being and man is profoundly one, for all his wealth of powers. The human soul is by nature incorruptible and a being (*hoc aliquid*) in its own right, destined to inform a body, but capable of surviving the dissolution of death because by nature incapable of dissolution.

On the other hand, Aquinas had many reservations on how much man can know. His acceptance of the Aristotelian cosmos, for instance, is provisional; although this is a good account of how things seem (*apparentia salvarentur*), men may find another that will do as well. For all his "demonstrations," Aristotle was handling as truths what are but hypotheses (*In 2 cael.* 17). In philosophy, where, in principle, the human intellect "penetrates to the essence" (*Summa theologiae* 1a2ae, 31.5), the essential principles, substantial forms—indeed, the essence of even a fly—all remain in fact unknown to man (*In 1 anim.* 1.15; *De spir. creat.* 11 ad 3; *Symb.* 1). The theologian too must resign himself to a modest accomplishment: the most profound moment in his knowledge of God is the realization that men are ignorant of Him (*De pot.* 7.5 ad 14). Within these limitations, content with knowledge consonant with man's limited being, Aquinas developed both philosophical and theological knowledge.

His successors were less patient. Removing from knowledge whatever fails to meet the highest standard of certitude and working under the shadow of the Parisian condemnations of 1270 and 1277, they relinquished one proposition after another and assigned to belief what they had thought could be known. To preserve what knowledge might be salvaged, they set out on a road that could end only by restricting knowledge to immediate experience.

Scotus and Ockham. John DUNS SCOTUS accepted Aristotelian abstraction, but his "absolute quiddities," known to be real because they move the intellect, a thing that nonbeing cannot do, are traces, it has been said, of the eternal "reasons" of Augustine (Gilson, 766). To his mastery of Aristotle's theory of knowledge, Scotus added a distinction between man's intuitive knowledge of what exists as such and his abstractive knowledge of common natures that, of themselves, remain indifferent to existence. WILLIAM OF OCKHAM borrowed this terminology, but opposed the doctrine.

For Scotus, to have intuitive knowledge of a nonexistent is a contradiction (*Rep. Par.* 3.14.3.12), whereas for Ockham, the two knowledges differ intrinsically (*seipsis different*) and it is within the absolute power of God to cause intuitive knowledge of what does not exist in man. This is Ockham's way of saying that it is not a contradiction to have intuitive knowledge of a nonexistent (*Quodl.* 6.6). Abstractive knowledge cannot be concerned with common natures, for the Ockhamist reason that they are gratuitous constructions, unfounded in the real world. Ockham reserves abstractive knowledge for man's grasp of the objects he represents to himself in their absence. Owing to the absolute divine power, even intuitive knowledge is open to the danger of error. If this is so, man's last resource is not even theology. It is faith, as faith was Ockham's final resort. Because faith and knowledge are not identical, their marriage had been possible, but now men began to refuse the name of knowledge to whatever falls short of the absolute certitude

possibly only to Absolute Spirit (Pieper, 145). Noetic fatigue could hardly go further.

See Also: DIALECTICS IN THE MIDDLE AGES; UNIVERSALS.

Bibliography: É. H. GILSON, *History of Christian Philosophy in the Middle Ages* (New York 1955). J. PIEPER, *Scholasticism,* tr. R. and C. WINSTON (New York 1960). R. P. MCKEON, ed. *Selections from Medieval Philosophers,* 2 v. (New York 1929–30). WILLIAM OF OCKHAM, *Philosophical Writings,* ed. P. BOEHNER (New York 1957).

[E. A. SYNAN]

Knowledge in Modern Thought

Modern philosophy, commonly regarded as having begun with René Descartes (1596–1650), developed theories of knowledge having all the characteristics of the new scientific age. Descartes and G. W. Leibniz tried to reduce the complexities of human understanding to basic formulae; British empiricists tried to restrict human knowledge to only what could be measured and empirically observed. Even Immanuel Kant was deeply impressed by the creative scientific hypothesis that apparently brought understanding of reality and explained experience without being based on it; and, in his elaborate theory of knowledge described in *The Critique of Pure Reason* (1781), Kant presented human knowledge as taking place largely through a priori forms that shape the human understanding and differentiate it from the divine. For G. W. F. Hegel consciousness evolving in rich complexity ultimately constitutes the divine; and this theme was developed in the 19th century by A. Schopenhauer and others.

Descartes and Leibniz. In the philosophy of René DESCARTES, the act of knowledge is central. Seeking a solid basis for his entire system and through a methodic doubt questioning the existence of everything he could not know with certitude, he finally selected his consciousness of thinking as the most self-evident and irrefutable principle possible. "I think, therefore I am." But, if his own existence was implied by his thought, then he must be a substance whose whole nature or essence was thought. "I realized," he writes, "that this substance of myself had no need of a place or any material thing in order to exist. The result was that I,—that is, the soul by which I am what I am—is entirely distinct from my body." Unsettled too by the obscurity of sensation, Descartes rejected the reports given by the senses about the world. Man must believe the world is real; he possesses no demonstrable certitude of its reality.

Gottfried Wilhelm LEIBNIZ continued the same philosophical development. Discoverer of the infinitesimal calculus, Leibniz was attracted by the rigor of the mathematical method of deduction from definitions. Why, he asked, cannot this method be applied to metaphysics as well as to mathematics? Asserting that man's notions of substance, cause, and unity arise out of interior reflection (rather than from sense experience), Leibniz thought that all knowledge of the world could be explained if one conceived of all bodies as being composed of monads, i.e., immaterial, animated units depending directly upon God for existence. The soul and body, although composed of different kinds of monads, work in harmony, forming one being. Man's concept of space arises from the thought of monads coexisting in some relationship; his concept of time arises from the notion of events happening together or successively. Briefly, the world could be best understood, not through sense experience, but through reflection upon the nature of the MONAD and its infinite possibility of order and perfection under divine direction.

Hobbes and Locke. The British empiricists reacted against such reasoning. To Thomas HOBBES, all philosophy begins with sense experience, and philosophy's only function is to explain it. Universal ideas cannot be abstracted from experience; they are simply common names standing for particular things. Colors, sounds, odors, and other qualities are subjective and nonscientific, since they have significance only to an individual, stimulated sensory organ. The "objective" world of bodies in motion is meaningful since they can be measured. Surprisingly, Hobbes speaks of human willing as a form of motion, and describes degrees of human intelligence as traceable to differences in dynamic forces.

Another Englishman, John LOCKE, shared Hobbes's conviction that philosophy should begin with sense experience, but, unlike Hobbes, he did not think that it should end there. Making the nature of human knowledge the central focus of his philosophy (his principal work was *Essay concerning Human Understanding*), Locke denied that any ideas are innate. Man's concepts of space and time arise from experience; and although color, sound, and other sensations are not simple reproductions of identical qualities in bodies around him, nevertheless they are objective since they are caused by such bodies. Man can at least infer the existence of bodies from such sensations and call them the unknown substrate of accidents, since he cannot be certain to what extent the substances that cause these sensations possess the qualities corresponding to them. Locke extended this principle to intellection: one knows only his ideas of objects directly, and can merely infer the existence of objects from the fact that he has ideas of them. But how can one be certain that his ideas correspond with their objects? How can he be cer-

tain that there are any objects at all? These were the questions posed by his critics.

Berkeley and Hume. Anglican Bishop George BERKELEY answered such questions for himself and his followers by asserting that there are no objects. All of man's ideas come directly from God. There is no need of a world; for if Locke's substance is unknown and unknowable, it is also unnecessary. *Esse est percipi* ("to be is to be perceived") was the basic theme of Berkeley's philosophy. Human ideas have their correspondent reality in the divine ideas found in the mind of God. Physical laws of nature do not constitute an adequate explanation of experience; they are generalizations but not explanations of what has happened. The ultimate explanation of nature, or rather of the experience that constitutes nature, is to be found in metaphysics, which teaches that God constantly pours ideas into minds and in this sense continually creates the world.

David HUME shared Bishop Berkeley's doubts about the reality of substance. If, as Locke says, the substrate of accidents is unknown, why postulate its existence? The ultimate cause of impressions is beyond explanation. "It will always be impossible to decide with certainty whether they arise immediately from the object or are produced by the creative power of the mind or are derived from the author of our being." He felt that all of human knowledge could be reduced to two kinds of sense impressions: faint, general images, and vivid, individual phantasms. Intellectual or abstract knowledge were excluded. Universal ideas are in reality the general terms with which particular sense images are associated.

Hume rejected any kind of a generalization. Since there is no particular sense quality (i.e., a color or sound) to indicate that a being is an effect, this is unverifiable by the senses and should be rejected. All that can be asserted about causality, he argues, is what is observable, and this is that a certain sequence of events can be seen to take place whereby one event follows another. What follows another in time is called an effect. But there is nothing in any object (such as its contingency) that can prove that it is an effect, i.e., caused by another.

Hume considered his own person to be not a substance but a mass of sensations: "When I enter most intimately into what I call myself I always stumble on some particular impression or other." Hence, he concluded that his self is constituted by "bundles or collections of different perceptions which succeed each other . . . and are in a perpetual flux and movement."

Kant's Criticism. Describing himself as being roused from his dogmatic slumber by the writings of Hume, Immanuel KANT wrote his masterpiece, *The Cri-*

tique of Pure Reason, explicitly to save science (especially the laws of mathematics and physics) and morality in general. Admitting that knowledge begins with sense experience, Kant denied that it must end there. In fact (he argues) all of sense experience is conditioned by space and time. Being the condition of sense experience, space and time cannot themselves be explained by such experience. They must be a priori forms of human sensation. For this reason, he continues, metaphysics, or the knowledge of being as it is in itself, should be based not on experience but rather on what conditions experience in human understanding. In *The Critique of Pure Reason,* Kant attempted to effect what he called a Copernican revolution in philosophy: truth would henceforth be considered as the conformity, not of the intellect with an object, but of the object with the intellect. In other words, philosophy would concern itself not with making certain that its concepts corresponded with an objective reality; its task would be to see that human experience corresponded with the nature of concepts and categories that constitute human understanding.

A later work on morality, *The Critique of Practical Reason* (1788), insisted that since one cannot discover any objective moral law in nature, he must be guided by an innate concept of holiness, expressed in the maxim "So act that the maxim of your will can always be valid as a principle making universal law."

Hegel and Schopenhauer. Of the great German thinkers following Kant, Georg Wilhelm Friedrich HEGEL was undoubtedly the greatest If, as Kant averred, consciousness must conclude that thought is purely formal and regulative, should one not go further and maintain that intelligence itself must be considered as absolute? If one cannot know the thing in itself (*das Ding an sich*) as Kant was forced to admit, why should he concern himself with it? Cannot consciousness supply its own content, as well as its own form? Thus, the ultimate duality between thought and being, between subject and object can be dissolved. In a transcendent identity of thought and being, of subject and object, would arise spirit (*Geist*), which, containing contradictory ideas, transforming them by generating their opposites, would finally synthesize them in a higher form including both. This Hegeltan triad—constituting a dynamic dialectic—K. MARX was later to borrow and exploit in his own system of materialism (*see* MATERIALISM, DIALECTICAL AND HISTORICAL).

Arthur SCHOPENHAUER continued the tradition of Hegelian idealism. Conceiving philosophy's task as the explanation of conscious experience, he asserted that principles of becoming govern sense experience; principles of being are the basis of mathematical concepts and constructs; and, finally, principles of knowing form the foundation of logical categories. Hence, all of knowledge is determined by innate principles.

Yet Schopenhauer did not entirely lose the Kantian nostalgia for the world as it is in itself. Although it can never be known, Schopenhauer writes, its existence cannot be questioned by man's deepest instinct. The phenomenal world (the world as it appears) is a world of conflict; the noumenal world (the world as it is in itself) is a world of peace, and the soul yearns for it. Suffering and sympathy lead man away from the phenomenal world to the noumenal world, and the human spirit finds its highest act in heroic self-renunciation.

Twentieth-Century Views

In the 20th century, disillusionment with Hegelian philosophies of the Absolute Spirit gave rise to the study of knowledge as a purely human act. Neo-Kantians abandoned the quest for "the thing-in-itself" (which Kant had said could be known only by a divine mind) and, while insisting that the only meaningful knowledge would be that of an object as it appears, asserted that the highest type of knowledge is the provisional explanation scientists give of reality. Under the leadership of Edmund Husserl, phenomenologists held that judgment about the actual existence of reality can be suspended; it is sufficient to describe simply what appears to consciousness. Existentialists, such as J. P. Sartre (1905–1980), flatly denied that one can know what a thing is in itself; in itself a thing has no essence. It is sufficient to know that a thing is, for its entire meaning is imposed upon it by man. Logical analysts insisted that no statement is meaningful if its elements cannot be verified by the senses; and since man is only too prone to confuse what he experiences with irrelevant materials drawn from grammar and religious beliefs, all his statements should be purified by being subjected to rigorous logical analysis.

Bergson and Dilthey. Impatient with the self-destructive tendencies in German idealism, philosophers of France were moved to construct systems emphasizing the dynamic aspects of consciousness. To Henri BERGSON, the essence of reality is not being but becoming. Against Kant, he denied that time is an a priori condition of experience; it is, instead, the very essence of experience. Time should not be excluded from metaphysics; metaphysicians should try to understand the primary role that time plays in human experience and in the universe itself. All matter is in motion; consciousness itself may be said to be constituted by time and motion since it is continually evolving. In fact, all things can be said to be part of the *élan vital,* the surging flow of life toward higher forms of freedom and consciousness. The ordinary function of intelligence consists in devising means whereby human life can progress; its highest act, however, is the intuition whereby the intelligence understands its relationship with God and its destiny of transcending present limitations.

Eminent German philosophers, such as Wilhelm DILTHEY, had similar philosophical ideas. Dilthey reacted against Kantian and Hegelian philosophy as being systems of static concepts, and characteristically suggested that philosophy should be viewed as a form of history, since history alone can express experience as a living whole.

Neo-Kantians. A group of German philosophers at Marburg, calling themselves Neo-Kantians, thought that ordinary knowledge is nonscientific and nonphilosophical. Epistemology should restrict itself to examination and evaluation of the philosophical implications of the methods and statements of positive sciences. Herman Cohen (1842–1918), the most distinguished proponent of the Marburg school, felt that since scientific explanations of phenomena are based upon intellectual constructs, all reality (i.e., all phenomena) might be reduced to laws of reason. Hence, the ultimate explanation of reality would be found in logic, rather than in metaphysics. Wilhelm Windelband (1848–1915), founder of the Baden school, developed a similar theory of epistemology, stressing the importance of subjective cultural values in human experience. He maintained that the truth value of judgments is determined by their correspondence with indemonstrable values that the mind has by its nature and expresses in its logic, ethics, art, and religion.

Phenomenologists. Edmund HUSSERL is frequently called the founder of the phenomenological method, which stresses the importance of returning to things themselves. In perception, a thing is present to consciousness. It is a phenomenon; it appears to man. To avoid the conflict between the realists and the idealists, Husserl asserted that it is sufficient to say simply that the thing appears; one can suspend judgment as regards its existence. And since essence determines the meaning of an object, its actual existence is relatively unimportant to consciousness. By describing what appears, the phenomenologist gets at the essence, and this is what matters. (*See* PHENOMENOLOGY.)

Neorealists and Naturalists. Neorealism did not accept this view, however. Its adherents asserted that it is possible and highly important to affirm trans-subjective reality. In England, Bertrand RUSSELL is frequently considered to be a neorealist—although his views changed considerably over the years. He insisted that philosophy should ask hard, matter-of-fact questions about the data that empirical science provides about existing objects. Philosophy would not be a science at all were it not for

the fact that, while clarifying the concepts of empirical science, it constructs a purely formal logic; yet its laws, like those of science, have no more than high probability. In the United States, George SANTAYANA was frequently numbered among the neorealists, although his views were quite opposed to those of Lord Russell. Santayana maintained that substance is external to consciousness, and, although constant assumes various shapes that consciousness understands through modifications in space and time. What lies behind space, time, and substance is unknowable.

Alfred North WHITEHEAD is sometimes called a realist, for his interest in empirical science and its methods made him sympathetic to Russell's views. However, Whitehead held that philosophy can and should go beyond science. It should embrace all of human experience, including art and religion. Although philosophy must begin with experience, it is not constrained within its limits; actually, even so-called material bodies are but convenient concepts enabling one to explain experience. The world is made up, not of things, but of events—the central event being the act of consciousness, which contains the past and anticipates the future.

In the United States, the term naturalist was applied to the school initiated by John Dewey. Defining thought as the reaction of the intelligence to the doubtful as such, Dewey emphasized the nature of thought as inquiry, rather than understanding or contemplation. Thought and learning must be active, rather than passive. To him the methods of empirical science, of affirmation and varification through experiment, were the only valid sources of certainty. Although he had been educated in a strongly Hegelian environment and had been a Hegelian himself for a brief period, he developed a contempt for what he called "idealistic speculation." He considered metaphysics a harmful pastime, and accepted ethical ideals as real only if they succeeded in moving men to constructive action in society. The highest function of human intelligence takes place when, understanding the present, the mind employs itself in the service of society to realize its ideals in the future. No value is absolute or terminal. New and higher values will always appear. Hence, all knowledge must be provisional. Absolute certitude is not only impossible; it is illusory even to desire it.

Neopositivists and Analysts. Neopositivism is a name frequently applied to the philosophy of the Vienna Circle, represented in the United States by Rudolph Carnap (1891–1970) and Hans Reichenbach (1891–1953), two German émigrés. Reverencing logic as the philosophical science par excellence, neopositivists restricted the role of philosophy to analysis of scientific methods and procedures. Ludwig WITTGENSTEIN, in his *Tractatus*

Logico-Philosophicus (1921), often called the ''neopositivist Bible,'' asserted that universal statements cannot possibly be based upon the intellectual knowledge of natures or intellectual abstraction. They are simply shorthand symbols of many individual facts or events. Consequently, it is meaningless to speak of a metaphysics or ethics arising from a consideration of the nature of being or the nature of man and society. (*See* LOGICAL POSITIVISM.)

Closely allied with neopositivism and sometimes identified with it is the analytical school represented by A. J. Ayer (1910–1989) and Gilbert Ryle (1900–1976). In *Language, Truth and Logic* (1936), Ayer proclaims the principle of verification whereby nothing can be considered as true if it cannot be immediately verified by sense experience. The concept of substance is regarded as having arisen out of grammar, i.e., the need to have a subject for predicates; and metaphysics in general is presented as a word game inferior to poetry, since the poet realizes that he is working in the realm of imagination whereas the philosopher does not. Ryle's work, *The Concept of Mind* (1949), presents philosophy as a system of linguistic analysis whose burden is to clarify general statements. ''Philosophy is the replacement of category-habits by category disciplines''; that is, philosophy should concern itself, not with trying to divide being into categories (as Aristotle and Kant attempted to do) but rather with establishing a systematic explanation of the categories themselves.

Existentialists. Another school of thought, EXISTENTIALISM, derives its name from the fact that its proponents stressed the importance of existence over essence. Plato, they alleged, made ideas or essences the supreme concern of philosophers. Almost all philosophers who have followed him have been ''essentialists,'' constructing their systems out of ideas, essences, and definitions. But an essence as such has no reality. The Universal man does not exist. It is men who exist—existing individuals, not general essences.

Kierkegaard. Søren KIERKEGAARD is generally acknowledged to be the father of existentialism. Danish-born and inheriting beliefs that man is essentially evil, with an intellect so darkened that he can know nothing of God and His laws except what he learns through blind faith, Kierkegaard attacked Hegelianism and German idealism as empty rationalisms without any relevance to life. Human lives are ruled, not by logic, but by God, whose providence is incomprehensible and whose acts (such as His command to Abraham to kill Isaac) are seemingly absurd. Philosophy should not discourse about natures and essences; this is metaphysical make-believe. The world is constituted of individual existing beings without any intelligible interrelationship.

Jaspers. Karl Jaspers (1883–1969), a Protestant, can also be classified as an existentialist, although, unlike Kierkegaard, he had no aversion to philosophy as a system, as his three-volume *Philosophie* (1932) indicates. In the spirit of Kierkegaard, he described the self as being basically consciousness of the self as sin. But, consciousness is existence, and existence is consciousness, since meaningful relationships can exist only through the act of knowledge. Moreover, one cannot talk about subject and object in the act of knowledge as though they had no relationship. What is called object is already assimilated to the subject and has no meaning without the subject. For Jaspers, the term existence includes both subject and object, even though he seems to accentuate the role of subject by describing the manner in which existence exercises liberty through the creation of values.

Marcel. Gabriel Marcel (1889–1973), regarded frequently as a Catholic existentialist, conceived of human life as a continuing encounter with God, a dialogue beginning in time and enduring in eternity. Without denying that the intellect can know the nature of man, Marcel (like Martin Buber, the Jewish existentialist) insisted that each man is unique and his ultimate meaning to be found in his incommunicable personality, rather than in the nature he shares with others.

Heidegger. Martin Heidegger (1889–1976) and Jean Paul Sartre were the two most influential 20th-century existentialists. Heidegger, once a Catholic, later an atheist, and still later a theist, outlined his principal ideas in *Sein und Zeit* (1927). Rejecting the classical inquiry into being as such, Heidegger begins with a study of what he describes simply as *Dasein.* Although Heidegger himself believed that *Dasein* defies translation, some felt that its general notion can be conveyed through the phrase ''individual consciousness.'' It is this kind of being that has primacy; all other beings exist for consciousness. It is consciousness that gives meaning to all objects; it makes all serve its purposes and its projects. Moreover, since human consciousness is open to knowledge of all things, its potential enrichment is limited only by death; in fact, consciousness can be described as ''freedom until death,'' i.e., consciousness can become all things until death cuts it short.

Sartre. Overtly atheistic, Sartre similarly centered his system in human consciousness, which he described as ''nothingness'' in *L'Etre et le néant* (1943), since consciousness finds its entire meaning in what it knows, and paradoxically is meaningless unless it is consciousness of something other than consciousness. However, the intellect does not come upon a world constituted of fixed essences, since there are no essences but only existents. Every object stands alone. Each object is unique, non-related to other objects, hence absurd. An object can be defined only as the totality of its possible or actual phenomenological aspects; but the phenomenological aspects of any object are determined by the needs, desires, and values of each consciousness.

According to Sartre, the essence of consciousness is becoming. Were it to cease becoming, it would cease to be; and, although this potentiality immanent within consciousness gives it life and movement, it condemns it to the restless existence of being forever a projection into a nonexistent future (for the future as such never is).

Concluding Evaluation. Most historians of philosophy agree that the foregoing disputes over the nature of knowledge have arisen from an over-simplification of human understanding. Constituted as it is of both abstract and concrete elements, man's knowledge is subject to two kinds of analysis and development. The idealists seem to have concentrated on the abstract elements in human knowledge; for them knowledge soon becomes a matter of concepts and definitions. Empiricists, on the other hand, have concentrated on the concrete elements of human knowledge in a laudable effort to "stay in the real world"; but, ironically, their world of reality seems to be without meaning, as the existentialists have been quick to point out.

Any adequate theory of knowledge must, it seems, consider human knowledge as the complex operation of an intellectual substance that is the form of a human body. Unless the human soul had sense organs and formed perceptions from which to abstract its concepts, it could not know any existing thing. Thus, abstract knowledge cannot be viewed entirely apart from its empirical origins; otherwise it will lose its existential significance. On the other hand, empirical knowledge cannot be viewed entirely apart from the common elements that are discoverable within it; otherwise it will lose its full intelligibility.

Scholastic and Greek theories of knowledge do, in fact, have many concerns found also in modern theories. For example, scholastic philosophers are usually careful to point out that the intellect rarely knows the essences of material substances completely. Hence, man's knowledge of such substances is normally provisional, and subject to revision. In his commentaries on the logical writings of Aristotle, St. Thomas Aquinas notes how frequently one must rely upon nominal or provisional definitions, and he expresses as well the continuing need of logical analysis of terms in judgments.

In any event, there are as many theories of knowledge as there are theories of man, for EPISTEMOLOGY itself is always shaped by basic views regarding the nature of the human soul and of the reality that surrounds man— of which he is a part. (*See* MAN; SOUL, HUMAN.)

See Also: AGNOSTICISM; CONCEPTUALISM; CRITICISM; DOGMATISM; EMPIRICISM; EXEMPLARISM; FIDEISM; IDEALISM; MATERIALISM; NOMINALISM; PHENOMENALISM; POSITIVISM; PRAGMATISM; RATIONALISM; REALISM; RELATIVISM; SENSISM; SOLIPSISM; TRADITIONALISM.

Bibliography: I. M. BOCHEŃSKI, *Contemporary European Philosophy,* tr. D. NICHOLL and K. ASCHENBRENNER (Berkeley 1956). J. D. COLLINS, *A History of Modern European Philosophy* (Milwaukee 1954). *History of Philosophy;* v. 4: *Descartes to Leibniz* (Westminster, Maryland 1958). L. M. RÉGIS, *Epistemology,* tr. I. C. BYRNE (New York 1959). M. J. ADLER, ed. *The Great Ideas: A Syntopicon of Great Books of the Western World,* 2 v. (Chicago 1952); v.2, 3 of *Great Books of the Western World* 1:880–920. P. PRINI, *Enciclopedia filosofica,* 4 v. (Venice-Rome 1957) 2:813–40. R. EISLER, *Wörterbuch der philosophischen Begriffe,* 3 v. (4th ed. Berlin 1927–30) 1:389–95.

[R. W. MULLIGAN]

KNOWLES, DAVID

English monk, historian; b. on the feast of St. Michael, Sept. 29, 1896 at Eastfield, Studley, in Warwickshire; d. Nov. 21, 1974 in Chichester. Christened Michael Clive, he received the name David as a Benedictine. Knowles' scholarly reputation rests principally on his work as a historian of pre-Reformation English monasticism; his *opus magnum* is *The Monastic Order in England; a History of its Development from the Times of St. Dunstan to the Fourth Lateran Council, 943–1216* (Cambridge 1940; 2d ed., 1963). The 3-volume *The Religious Orders in England* (Cambridge 1956, 1957, 1959) completed his history of the religious orders in England up to and inclusive of the Reformation; this work is not of the same exceptional stature as his *Monastic Order.*

Knowles was educated in the school at DOWNSIDE ABBEY where he became a novice in 1914 and where he pronounced simple vows in 1915 and solemn vows in 1918. From 1919 to 1922 he studied classical languages and philosophy at Cambridge as a member of Christ's College. He was ordained a priest on July 9, 1922. During the academic year of 1922–1923 he studied theology at Sant' Anselmo, Rome. Upon his return to Downside Abbey, Dom David took up a number of duties, e.g., as teacher of classics in the school, temporary novice master in 1928, and master over the junior monks from 1929 to 1933. He became the editor of the *Downside Review* to which he made many contributions. His first book, *The American Civil War . . .* (Oxford 1926) was the result of a lifelong enthusiasm, but he never visited North America, despite many invitations to lecture.

Dom David was the leader of a group of monks at Downside who sought to initiate a new foundation of a contemplative character. Permission for this foundation was refused by the abbot of Downside and by the Congregation of Religious (1934). As a result, Father David lived from 1933 to 1939 in a form of exile at Ealing Abbey, London. In 1939 the tension of these years culminated in a nervous breakdown. Without permission Father David left the jurisdiction of Downside, an action which resulted in a canonical suspension. Later Abbot Cuthbert Butler (now Bishop Butler) arranged for Dom David's position to be regularized as an exclaustration, a condition which perdured until his death. This arrangement made it possible for Dom David to live outside his monastery and yet remain a Benedictine in good standing. Despite this tragedy in his life, Dom David always deeply cherished his calling as a Benedictine and he maintained an affection for Downside Abbey. The monks of Saint Leo Abbey, Florida, reissued Dom David's booklet, *The Benedictines* . . . (Saint Leo, Florida 1962), which had appeared years before (London 1929; reprinted New York 1930) because these monks considered this essay to be the ''nearly perfect exposition'' of Benedictine monasticism.

Knowles' reputation as historian was spreading. In November of 1941 he was awarded the honorary degree of Doctor of Letters by Cambridge, and in 1944 he became a Fellow of Peterhouse and thereafter his ascent up the ladder of academic success was rapid: university lecturer at Cambridge in 1946, professor of medieval history in 1947, and, in 1954, Regius Professor of Modern History in the University, a position he held until his retirement in 1963.

Father David was a man of slight physical build but with an intense and strong inner spirit. He was quiet and even austere, but possessed a gentle humor. His inner strength made possible his extraordinary productivity, but it also had a hand in the tragedy of his life. Moreover, this quiet strength was discernible in his carefully prepared and dignified lectures which held both seasoned scholars and undergraduates spellbound. Father David, as he was known to his friends, was a reserved man, but this reserve did not prevent his warmth and charm from coming through clearly in his lectures and especially in personal conversation and correspondence.

As an author David Knowles was perhaps the finest stylist of modern historians writing in English. He wrote to be clear and he always was so; yet his writings were rich in apt figures of speech and in literary allusions. He may have been at his very best in his assessment of character, a topic that he took up in his now-famous inaugural lecture as Regius Professor. However, at times he demanded too much of those about whom he wrote, as he did of himself, a characteristic that no doubt played a part in difficulties with his abbey. His characterizations of Thomas BECKET, BERNARD OF CLAIRVAUX, Lord Macaulay, Cardinal GASQUET, and Dom Edward Cuthbert BUTLER are modern classics in character evaluation.

Throughout his life, Father David was intensely interested in the life and study of mysticism. In the former he had a personal abiding interest. His writings on mysticism, however, are narrow in scope and not of the same caliber as his work as a monastic historian. The personal quality of his passion for mysticism may have prevented his writings on it from achieving the quality of his historical writings.

Bibliographies of Father David's writings indicate the exceptional productivity of a monk whose way of life was both highly disciplined and austere. He continued to be prolific in his years of retirement. What did emerge in his later years was a firmly conservative concern over the changes taking place in the Catholic church and in what he considered to be its crisis of authority. He expressed this concern avidly and eloquently in a number of articles written in retirement. Dom David composed an autobiography which will not be published in the near future nor will it be accessible to researchers until a later date, a decision made by his literary executors. In considering the life of David Knowles as a monastic historian, one cannot escape a comparison with Dom Jean MABILLON, the 17th-century Maurist whom he so admired. In addition, what Dom David wrote of Dom Edward Cuthbert Butler (1858–1934) is surely an even more apt description of himself: ''[H]e will long be remembered as the most remarkable English Benedictine scholar and historian of his time'' (*The Historian and Character and Other Essays* [Cambridge 1963] 362).

Bibliography: For lists of the writings of Knowles, 1919–1962: D. KNOWLES, *The Historian and Character and Other Essays* (Cambridge 1963) 363–373; for 1963–1974 with supplement for 1932–1962: A. STACPOOLE, ''The Making of a Monastic Historian—III,'' *Ampleforth Journal* 80 (1975) 51–55. Biographical studies: C. N. L. BROOKE, ''David Knowles, 1896–1974,'' *Proceedings of the British Academy* 61 (1976) 439–477 K. J. EGAN, ''Dom David Knowles (1896–1974),'' *American Benedictine Review* 27 (1976) 235–246. W. A. PANTIN, ''Curriculum Vitae,'' in D. KNOWLES *The Historian and Character* . . . xvii–xxviii. A. STACPOOLE, ''The Making of a Monastic Historian—I, II, III,'' *Ampleforth Journal* 80, Parts I and II (1975) 71–91; 19–38: 48–55.

[K. J. EGAN]

KNOX, JAMES ROBERT

Cardinal archbishop of Melbourne, curia official, papal legate; b. Bayswater, a suburb of Perth in Western Australia, March 2, 1914; d. Rome, June 26, 1983.

One of three children born to John Knox, an immigrant from Kilkenny, Ireland, and the former Emily Walsh, who died when James was still a child. He attended local schools but was forced to interrupt his education in order to help support the family during the Depression years. When later he sought to enter the seminary, he applied to the abbot at the distant Abbey Nullius of New Norcia, then a suffragan See of Perth, in the hope of joining the small group of priests already incardinated in this widespread rural diocese. (At the time, the archdiocese of Perth did not have a seminary, and depended entirely on applicants from Irish seminaries for its clergy.) Knox completed his secondary education at St. Ildephonsus' College in New Norcia, and in 1935 he began studies at the abbey seminary. Later he joined other Australians at the Propaganda Fidei in Rome where he was ordained on Dec. 22, 1941. He remained in Rome during World War II, earning a doctorate in theology, and he did graduate studies in canon law. In 1945 he joined the staff at Propaganda Fide becoming vice-rector in 1947.

The year 1948 marked the beginning of his career with the Vatican diplomatic corps. Working in the Secretariat of State, he developed a friendship with Archbishop Giovanni Battista Montini, who was to become Pope PAUL VI, that endured through the years. Named to the *Camerieri Segreti Soprannumerati* (Chaplains to His Holiness), Monsignor Knox was appointed secretary to the apostolic delegation in Japan in 1950. In 1953, he was consecrated titular archbishop of Melitene and named Apostolic Delegate to Eastern and Western British Africa with his residence at Mombasa (Kenya). During his four years in that position many native African priests were nominated as bishops. In 1957, Knox was appointed Apostolic Internuncio to India and Apostolic Delegate to Burma and Ceylon (Sri Lanka). In the ten years he served as representative of the Holy See in the Indian subcontinent, a period that spanned the duration of the Second Vatican Council, Archbishop Knox was instrumental in creating many new dioceses and in the development of religious communities in both the Oriental and Latin rites, including the MISSIONARIES OF CHARITY founded by Mother Teresa.

Post Vatican II. In 1967, then 53 years old, Knox was appointed to succeed Justin Simonds, as archbishop of Melbourne in his native Australia. During the six years he served in that see, Knox instituted a long list of reforms in the spirit of Vatican II: the division of the archdiocese into regions under the pastoral care of three auxiliary bishops; the naming of eleven episcopal vicars; the reorganization of the provincial seminary at Clayton; the adaptation of the sanctuary of the cathedral to conform with the liturgical requirements of Vatican II; the establishment of the Melbourne Education Board and Parish Education boards as well as the Catholic Education Commission of Victoria; the introduction of recurrent funding from federal government sources in 1970; the funding of non-government teachers' colleges and the amalgamation of the existing Catholic colleges into the Institute of Catholic Education; the establishment of additional regional secondary schools and the creation of 20 new parishes with parish schools in each. He fostered missionary endeavors in the archdiocese and supported missionary projects in New Guinea and Venezuela through the Melbourne Overseas Mission. In February of 1973 Melbourne hosted the Fortieth International Eucharistic Congress.

At the Consistory of March 5, 1973, Pope Paul VI nominated Knox to the College of Cardinals, and six months later called him to Rome to become the prefect both of the Sacred Congregation for the Discipline of the Sacraments and of the Sacred Congregation for Divine Worship. It was Knox's task to merge these two dicasteries into one. In 1975 Paul VI approved the formation of the new Congregation for Sacraments and Divine Worship, with Knox as prefect and Archbishop Antonio Innocenti as secretary. In addition to his responsibilities as prefect of the Congregation for Sacraments and Divine Worship, Knox was an active member of other congregations, and on several occasions he served as special envoy of both Paul VI and John Paul II. In May of 1981, Pope John Paul II appointed him the first president of the newly formed Pontifical Council for the Family.

His health began to decline in the summer of 1982, but he continued his work. Stricken with a circulatory failure in May of 1983, while attending a meeting of the Congregation for Oriental Churches, Cardinal Knox died a few weeks later. He is buried in St. Patrick's Cathedral in Melbourne.

Bibliography: *Annuario Pontificio,* 1945; 1946; 1949; 1950; 1953; 1954; 1958; 1968; 1974; 1975; 1982; 1983. *Official Directory of the Catholic Church in Australia,* 1969–70; 1981–82; 1985–86. *L'Osservatore Romano,* June 27–28, 1983; July 2, 1983. *L'Osservatore Romano* (Eng.) July 4, 1983; July 11, 1983.

[W. A. MULLINS]

KNOX, JOHN

Scottish Protestant reformer; b. near Haddington, East Lothian, 1513; d. Edinburgh, Nov. 24, 1572. Of his early life, little is recorded. His family for several generations had been retainers of the house of Bothwell. The Universities of St. Andrews and Glasgow claim him as a student, but definite proof of his attendance is lacking. A recent document asserts that he was ordained by Bp. William Chisholm of Dunblane on April 15, 1536. During the next decade he performed the duties of notary apostolic in the Archdiocese of St. Andrews and acted as tutor to the children of some East Lothian lairds who patronized the leading Protestant preacher of the day, George WISHART.

Conversion to Evangelicalism. During this period, Knox became a convert to the "new Evangel," and in the winter of 1545–46 he himself carried a "two-handed sword" before the preacher. When Wishart was put to death for heresy at St. Andrews (March 28, 1545–46), a group of disaffected gentry assassinated Cardinal David Beaton, Chancellor of Scotland, and occupied the archepiscopal castle at St. Andrews. On April 10, 1547, Knox and his pupils joined the "Castilians," a group of devout and radical Protestants. The group soon recognized Knox's ability as a controversialist preacher and commissioned him to undertake the public preaching of the new doctrines. Knox began preaching in the castle and parish kirk of St. Andrews. When the French fleet captured the castle on July 30, 1547, Knox was taken captive with the others and remained aboard a French galley for 19 months. Released early in 1549, Knox made his way to England and became a licensed preacher, first at Berwick, then at Newcastle, and finally in London, where he was one of the six chaplains to the young King, Edward VI. His intervention in the preparatory discussions for the revised BOOK OF COMMON PRAYER is responsible for the inclusion of the "Black Rubric" in the service (when approaching the Lord's Supper, "no adoration is intended or ought to be done"). Knox turned down the offer of the bishopric of Rochester, for he shrewdly foresaw that Catholic Mary Tudor would succeed to the throne.

Exile at Geneva. When that event occurred (1553), Knox fled to the Continent, where he preached in various English Protestant colonies. He visited Dieppe several times, but his principal place of sojourn was that "perfect school of Christ," Calvin's Geneva. There was a short visit to Scotland in 1555, "at the end of the harvest," when he claims to have laid the small beginnings of a Protestant church. The French Queen-Regent of Scotland, Mary of Guise, constrained by the pressure of international politics, had allowed religious toleration. Before long the political and religious climate changed, and Knox, now married to the English Marjory Bowes (spring 1556), returned to Geneva. The Protestant nobles in Scotland invited Knox (May 1557) to return to minister to them, but by the time he reached Dieppe they had changed their minds. This vacillation brought about a change in Knox's political thinking. Hitherto following Calvin, he had advocated moderation and nonviolence in dealing with "idolatrous" rulers. Then, in 1558, he published several pamphlets asserting that punishment of

John Knox.

"idolatry" and "blasphemy" in rulers "doth not appertain to kings and chief rulers only but also to the whole body of that people and to every member of the same" and that this duty extends to deposing and punishing rulers who are "tyrants against God and against his truth known." In these pamphlets Knox provided the ideology for the revolution that was shortly to be accomplished in Scotland.

Return to Scotland. Some Protestant nobles and lairds, after pledging themselves "to maintain, set forward and establish the most blessed word of God and his Congregation" (December 1557), invited Knox to return to Scotland. He landed on May 2, 1559, joined the forces of the Congregation at Perth, and on May 11, in the parish kirk of St. John, he preached the sermon that led to the "casting down" of the town churches and the wrecking of the religious houses in the neighborhood. In June the coast towns of Fife and the primatial city of St. Andrews were purged by the army of the Congregation: Stirling, Linlithgow, and Edinburgh were visited in turn. On June 10, 1560, the whole resistance of the Catholic and French party collapsed with the death of the Queen-Regent, Mary of Guise. The Treaty of Edinburgh, in July, eliminated the French and created a situation where the Lords of the Congregation, with English help, could now dominate Scotland. The illegal "Reformation Parliament," held in August, abolished the jurisdiction of the pope in Scotland and prohibited the celebration of Mass, together with all doctrine and practice contrary to the Confession of Faith, which was now adopted.

Knox was the architect of the new ecclesiastical system. Although the Confession of Faith, drawn up by him and his associates, was accepted, the Book of Discipline, which sought to redistribute the temporal possessions of the medieval Church in accordance with the needs of the new Protestant regime, was rejected. Knox was appointed minister of Edinburgh, and during the tumultuous years of the personal reign of MARY STUART, QUEEN OF SCOTS, he made the pulpit of the collegiate kirk of St. Giles a focal point in the political and religious life of the kingdom. In March 1564, now a widower in his 50s, he contracted his second marriage, with Margaret Stewart, the 16-year-old daughter of Lord Ochiltree. After the assassination of the regent, James Stewart, Earl of Moray (1570), Knox's health began to decline. He was buried in the kirkyard of St. Giles.

During his lifetime, Knox was known chiefly as a powerful and inspiring preacher with a strong sense of his personal vocation as a prophet. His posthumous fame rests mostly on his *History of the Reformation in Scotland,* an extremely biased but vigorous and dramatic specimen of 16th-century Anglo-Scottish prose. From this work and from his other writings, especially the Confession of Faith, can be pieced together the main elements of Knox's theological teaching. His contribution lay not in original thought; his works instead repeated Protestant teachings, but in a lively idiom that inspired his admirers. In his early Protestant years, due no doubt to the influence of Wishart, Knox accepted the Zwinglian views of a symbolic presence of Christ in the Eucharist. Later at Geneva his theological tenets were molded into Calvinism, and his antipathy to traditional Catholic doctrine concentrated on the rejection of the sacrificial character of the Mass and of the real presence of Christ in the Eucharist. Among his writings are: *The First Blast of the Trumpet against the Monstrous Regiment of Women* (1558), a diatribe against Mary of Guise; *Treatise on Predestination* (1560); *English Metrical Psalter* (1564).

See Also: SCOTLAND, CHURCH OF.

Bibliography: Works, ed. D. LAING, 6 v. (Edinburgh 1846–64); *History of the Reformation in Scotland,* ed. W. C. DICKINSON, 2 v. (New York 1949). A. LANG, *John Knox and the Reformation* (London 1905). T. MCCRIE, *The Life of John Knox,* 2 v. (Edinburgh 1812; 1 v. ed. Inverness 1960). D. MCROBERTS, ed., *Essays on the Scottish Reformation, 1513–1625* (Glasgow 1962). E. S. C. PERCY, *John Knox* (London 1937). G. MACGREGOR, *The Thundering Scot* (Philadelphia 1957). M. SCHMIDT, *Die Religion in Geschichte und Gegenwart,* 7 v. (3d ed. Tübingen 1957–65) 3:1686. A. J. G. MACKAY, *The Dictionary of National Biography From the Earliest Times to 1900,* 63 v. (London 1885–1900; repr. With corrections, 21 v., 1908–09, 1921–22, 1938; suppl. 1901–) 11:308–328. R. MASON, ed., *John Knox and the British Reformations* (Aldershot UK. 1998). J. MCEWEN, *The Faith of John Knox* (Richmond 1961). J. G. RIDLEY, *John Knox* (New York 1968). D. SHAW, ed., *John Knox: A Quartercentenary Reappraisal* (Edinburgh 1975).

[D. MCROBERTS]

KNOX, RONALD ARBUTHNOTT

Author, biblical scholar; b. Kibworth, England, Feb. 17, 1888; d. Mells, England, Aug. 24, 1957. The youngest son of the Anglican bishop of Manchester, he was educated at Eton and Balliol College, Oxford. He took Anglican orders in 1910 and became chaplain of Trinity College, Oxford. A strong Anglo-Catholic, he introduced as many Roman practices as possible, a policy that brought him into conflict with the Anglican bishops. He carried his satirical gifts into religious controversy and satirized the latitudinarian views of some of his Anglican fellow clergy in brilliant parodies of Dryden and Swift. Increasingly dissatisfied with his Anglican position, in 1917 he was received into the Catholic Church, detailing his reasons in his *Spiritual Aeneid* (1918).

He made his theological studies at St. Edmund's, Ware, and was ordained in 1919. He taught at St. Edmund's until 1926 when he was appointed chaplain to the Catholic students at Oxford University, a post he held until immediately before the outbreak of World War II. His major literary work of that period was *Let Dons Delight* (1939), a series of imaginary conversations at intervals of 50 years in an imaginary Oxford common room.

Knox found that life at Oxford was too full of interruptions to his literary work. Convinced that the great work to which he was called was the production of a modern English Bible, he withdrew from his chaplaincy and other activities. His Bible (the New Testament, 1944; the Psalms, 1947; the Old Testament, 1948; complete edition, 1955) was a masterpiece of English style. Prominent among his later works was *Enthusiasm* (1950), a study of religious vagaries. In his last public appearance, he delivered the Romanes Lecture at Oxford on "Translation" in June of 1957.

Other than those mentioned above, his numerous volumes include *Other Eyes Than Ours* (1926), *The Belief of Catholics* (1927), *Essays in Satire* (1928), *Caliban in Grub Street* (1930), and *Broadcast Minds* (1932).

Bibliography: E. WAUGH, *Monsignor Ronald Knox* (Boston 1959).

[C. HOLLIS]

KNOXVILLE, DIOCESE OF

The Diocese of Knoxville was established on Sept. 8, 1988. The Most Reverend Anthony J. O'Connell, D.D., was appointed its first bishop. When O'Connell was appointed bishop of Palm Beach in 1999, he was succeeded by Msgr. Joseph E. Kurtz of the Diocese of Allentown. With an area of 14,242 sq. miles, the diocese comprises 36 counties in the eastern portion of the state of Tennessee and is situated in a rural area where some of the poorest counties in the nation are located. At the beginning of the 21st century, Roman Catholics comprised around two percent of the total population, distributed in 43 parishes and two missions. The diocesan newspaper is *The East Tennessee Catholic*.

[F. X. MANKEL/EDS.]

KNUDSON, ALBERT CORNELIUS

Methodist minister, Old Testament scholar and theologian, known especially for his synthesis of personalistic philosophy with a systematic Christian theology; b. Grandmeadow, Minn., Jan. 23, 1873; d. Aug. 28, 1953. He was the son of Rev. Asle Knudson, and he studied at the University of Minnesota, Minneapolis (A.B. 1893); Boston University, Mass. (S.T.B. 1896, Ph.D. 1900); and the German Universities of Jena and Berlin (honorary Th.D. 1923). After teaching briefly at the Universities of Denver, Colo., and Baker, Baldwin City, Ks, and at Allegheny College, Meadville, Pa., he began his long career in Boston University School of Theology as professor of Hebrew and Old Testament exegesis (1906). From 1921 to 1943 he was professor of systematic theology and served also as dean from 1926 to 1938.

In theology, he defended an independently valid religious a priori, alongside Immanuel Kant's speculative, ethical, and aesthetic a prioris. He developed his theological system in deliberate relation to the theologies of Friedrich SCHLEIERMACHER and Albrecht RITSCHL, on the one hand, and the personalistic philosophy of Borden Parker Bowne, on the other (*see* PERSONALISM). His books included *Religious Teaching of the Old Testament* (New York 1918), *The Doctrine of God* (New York 1930), *The Doctrine of Redemption* (New York 1933), and *The Validity of Religious Experience* (New York 1937).

[L. H. DE WOLF]

KNUTSON, KENT SIGVART

Theologian and president of American Lutheran Church (ALC); b. Goldfield, Iowa, Aug. 7, 1924; d., Minneapolis, March 12, 1973. After receiving a B.S. in chemical engineering in 1947 from Iowa State University, he worked briefly for an oil company, but then entered Luther Seminary, St. Paul, and received the B.D. there in 1951. The same year he married Norma Arnesen of Brooklyn, N.Y., and they became the parents of four children, in addition to adopting two Korean children.

He pursued graduate studies from 1951 to 1954 at Columbia University and Union Theological Seminary in New York, receiving a Ph.D. in 1961. In 1954 he was ordained by the Evangelical Lutheran Church, one of the churches that joined in 1960 to form the ALC. After serving as pastor of Our Saviour Lutheran Church in Staten Island, N.Y. (1954–58), he joined the faculty of Luther Seminary, teaching systematic theology and serving (1960–69) as director of graduate studies. In 1969 he became president of Wartburg Seminary, Dubuque. At the 1970 ALC convention, where he supported the decision to ordain women, Knutson was elected as the second ALC president, succeeding Fredrik Schiotz the following January. Knutson was a participant in the Lutheran-Catholic dialogues in the U.S. from their beginning in 1965, and in the international Lutheran-Anglican talks. He was a member of the executive committee of the Lutheran World Federation and the central committee of the World Council of Churches at the time of his death. He had also served as author and editor of theological publications. In the fall of 1972 he became fatally ill with what physicians diagnosed as Jakob-Creutzfeldt disease, a rare disorder of the central nervous system. He had perhaps contracted the disease in New Guinea during a tour of Asian mission stations the previous summer.

[T. EARLY]

KODALY, ZOLTAN

Hungarian composer and musicologist; b. Kecskemét, Hungary, Dec. 16, 1882; d. Budapest, March 6, 1967. From his early years Kodaly acquired musical culture through his parents and from singing in the Catholic cathedral in Nagyszombat (now Trnava, Slovakia), where his father, a railway official, was stationed several years. But Kodaly also began to absorb the folk music of the countryside, and after studies at the University of Budapest and the Academy of Music there, he received his doctorate (1906) by presenting a thesis on Hungarian folk music.

After brief studies in Berlin and Paris, where he was influenced by Debussy, he taught (1907–41) at the Budapest Academy. With Béla Bartók (1881–1945), a friend and collaborator, he collected thousands of Hungarian folk songs. Some were published in 1906 and 1921, and they served as the basis of the *Corpus Musicae Popularis Hungaricae,* begun in 1951. Kodaly also published a scholarly treatment, *Folk Music of Hungary,* (1937), and made extensive use of Hungarian folk melodies in his own compositions. His varied output included such religious works as *Psalmus Hungaricus* (1923), a setting for a 16th century poet's version of Psalm 55; *Te Deum of Budavar* (1936), written for the 250th anniversary of Buda's liberation; and *Missa Brevis* (1945), which Kodaly conducted at its U.S. premier in 1946.

Kodaly devoted much of his efforts to improving musical education for children, and his theories in this field gained international influence. World War II was a difficult period for Kodaly, but he successfully defied Nazi demands that he divorce his Jewish wife. In the postwar years he held a number of government and cultural posts, and received Hungary's Kossuth Prize in 1952 and 1957. He also made several trips to other countries during those years, lecturing, conducting, and attending international conferences.

Bibliography: L. EOSZE, *Zoltan Kodaly* (London 1962), tr. I. FARKAS and G. GULYAS. F. BÓNIS, "Beobachtungen zum schaffensprozess in Kodálys *Psalmus Hungaricus,*" *Kirchenmusikalisches Jahrbuch,* 75 (1991) 93–105. J. BREUER, *A Guide to Kodály* tr. M. STEINER (Budapest 1990). K. DOMMETT, "Zoltán Kodály," in *International Dictionary of Opera,* ed. C. S. LARUE, 2 v. (Detroit 1993) 694–696; "Háry János" in *International Dictionary of Opera,* ed. C. S. LARUE, 2 v. (Detroit 1993) 584–585. L. EÖSZE, "Zoltán Kodály," in *The New Grove Dictionary of Music and Musicians,* ed. S. SADIE, v. 10 (New York 1980) 136–145. I. KECSKEMÉTI, *Kodály, the Composer: Brief Studies on the First Half of Kodály's Oeuvre* (Kecskemét 1986).

[T. EARLY]

KOHLMANN, ANTHONY

Defender of the seal of confession and of religious freedom; b. Kaiserberg, Alsace, July 13, 1771; d. Rome, Italy, April 11, 1836. After his theological studies and ordination at Fribourg, Switzerland, he joined (1796) the Congregation of the Fathers of the Sacred Heart. After transferring (1800) to the Society of Jesus then existing in Russia, he joined (1804) the Georgetown College community, Washington, D.C., and frequently made missionary excursions into Pennsylvania and Maryland. From 1808 to 1815 he served in New York; under his direction the foundations of old St. Patrick's were laid, a school was established on what later became the site of the new cathedral, and a school for girls was opened under the Ursulines (1812). While rector of St. Peter's in 1813, Kohlmann undertook to return goods stolen by a penitent. When the owner, James Keating, urged the court to com-

pel Kohlmann to reveal the name of the penitent, four Protestant judges of the Court of General Sessions upheld Kohlmann's defense of secrecy of the confessional. Referring to article 38 of the state constitution, the Protestant defense lawyer, Richard Riker, asked: "Where is the liberty of conscience to the Catholic, if the priest and the penitent be thus exposed?" The controversy attracted attention throughout the country; New York and other states soon passed special protective legislation.

Kohlmann returned to Georgetown (1815) and was later assigned (1824) to the Gregorian University, Rome, where the future Leo XIII was one of his students. He served as consultor to the College of Cardinals and to various congregations of the Holy See. During his last days he was confessor at the Gesú, where he died.

Bibliography: A. P. STROKES, *Church and State in the United States,* 3 v. (New York 1950).

[T. O. HANLEY]

KOLBE, FREDERICK CHARLES

South African educator, poet, and author; b. Paarl, Cape Province, 1854; d. Cape Town, Jan. 12, 1936. He was the son of a Westphalian (German) Protestant missionary who had married the daughter of a member of the London Missionary Society. At the University of Cape Town he won a scholarship for law studies in London, where he was converted to Catholicism; Cardinal Henry Manning sent him to the English College in Rome, where he was ordained in 1882. Back in South Africa, he began a life of teaching and lecturing in addition to his pastoral duties. He not only expended much time and energy in actual teaching in Cape Town Catholic schools, but he pioneered in improving Catholic teacher education. As a member of the board of governors of the University of Cape Town and the University of the Cape of Good Hope (where he was also an examiner), he sought to create centers of intensive teacher training; he long but fruitlessly advocated the foundation of a Catholic university for South Africa.

At the request of the hierarchy, Kolbe founded (1891) the *South African Catholic Magazine* and until 1909 (except for two short intervals) was its editor and chief contributor. Never an organ of official Catholic opinion, it had as its chief aim the defense of the faith, although it carried many articles of general interest. Kolbe frequently defended Aristotelian-Thomistic education, then under attack by the scientists of the day, a stand that led him to a lengthy criticism of Newman's *Grammar of Assent.* After 1908 he devoted himself exclusively to evaluating the efforts of the Catholic schools so as to stimulate them to greater excellence. By 1898 his hearing was steadily failing, and he was suffering progressive loss of sight, but he remained a leading figure in Catholic education and in South African university circles. He confessed to being "penlazy," and many of his articles are merely transcribed lectures. His *The Art of Life,* however, was once considered the most perfect piece of prose by a South African. His three volumes of poems, mostly devotional and didactic, never won much acclaim, although his most famous poem, "Out of the Strong Came Sweetness," is in almost every anthology of South African literature.

Kolbe's range of interests was large; he inherited a love for botany and mountaineering from his father, he had an extensive knowledge of Shakespeare, and his insights into the psychology of education were notable. Catholics often referred to him as the "Newman of South Africa"; his close friend, Gen. Jan Christian Smuts, called him "South Africa's showpiece."

Bibliography: W. E. BROWN, *The Catholic Church in South Africa from Its Origins to the Present Day* (New York 1960).

[J. A. BELL]

St. Maximilian Kolbe. (AP/Wide World Photos)

KOLBE, MAXIMILIAN, ST.

Franciscan priest, evangelizer, "martyr of charity"; b. Jan. 8, 1894, Zdunska Wola, Poland; d. Aug. 14, 1941, in Oświęcim (Auschwitz), Poland. Baptized Raymond Kolbe, he took the religious name Maximilian when he entered the Conventual Franciscan Order's novitiate on Sept. 4, 1910. Having professed simple vows as a friar on Sept. 5, 1911, and solemn vows on Nov. 1, 1914, he was ordained a priest in Rome, Italy, on April 28, 1918. While still a seminarian in Rome, on Oct. 16, 1917, he founded the *Militia Immaculatae,* a movement promoting evangelization through Marian consecration. Returning to Poland in 1919, he soon initiated a mass media apostolate to further the work of evangelization. In 1922, he launched the publication *Rycerz Niepokalanej* (Knight of the Immaculate), whose monthly circulation would grow to one million issues by 1939. His publishing apostolate expanded to include three additional journals and one daily newspaper.

Though debilitated by tuberculosis, Kolbe founded a massive Franciscan friary and evangelization center, *Niepokalanów* (City of the Immaculate) near Warsaw in 1927 and a similar one in Nagasaki, Japan, in 1930. He labored at the Japanese mission for six years. He was regarded as an innovator in religious life, entrusting key responsibilities to nonordained friars trained in various specialties of the apostolate.

As guardian of Niepokalanów during the Nazi occupation of Poland, Kolbe welcomed more than 1,500 displaced Jewish refugees, ministering to them with such sensitivity that he even provided for their celebration of Jewish religious feasts. He was arrested by the Gestapo on Feb. 17, 1941, after publishing an article entitled "Truth." First imprisoned at Pawlak jail in Warsaw, he was transported to Oświęcim (Auschwitz) concentration camp on May 28, 1941. Though beaten, tortured, and subjected to extra punishment because he was a priest, Kolbe constantly encouraged his fellow prisoners to love their enemies: "Hatred destroys; love alone creates." In late July 1941, a prisoner escaped from his barracks. In retaliation, the Nazis selected ten individuals for execution. One of the condemned, Franciszek Gajcwniczek, cried aloud that he had a wife and children. Moved by the plight of this family man, Kolbe stepped forward to take Gajowniczek's place. The Nazi commandant Fritsch allowed the substitution. Consigned with the other nine to a subterranean cell, Kolbe survived without food or water for nearly two weeks, until the Nazis dispatched him and the other survivors with lethal injection. On Oct. 17, 1971 Pope Paul VI beatified him and, on Oct. 10, 1982, Pope John Paul II canonized him with the title "Martyr of Charity."

Feast: Aug. 14.

Bibliography: D. DEWAR, *Saint of Auschwitz* (San Francisco 1982). J. DOMANSKI, *I dati storici della vita del P. Massimiliano M. Kolbe* (Rome 1973); *For the Life of the World: Saint Maximilian and the Eucharist* (Libertyville, Ill. 1993). L. M. FACCENDA, *One more gift* (West Covina, Calif. 1990); *Symbiosis—contemplation and action* (West Covina, Calif. 1991). A. FROSSARD, *"Forget Not Love": The Passion of Maximilian Kolbe* (Kenosha, Wisc. 1977; San Francisco 1990). B. HANLEY, *Maximilian Kolbe* (Notre Dame, Ind. 1982). JOHN PAUL II, *Massimiliano Kolbe, patrono del nostro difficile secolo* (Vatican City 1982). S. C. LOSRIT, *The last days of Maximilian Kolbe* (New York 1981). H. M. MANTEAU-BONAMY, *La Doctrine mariale du père Kolbe* (Paris 1975), Eng. tr. R. ARNANDEZ, *Immaculate Conception and the Holy Spirit* (Kenosha, Wisc. 1977). A. RICCIARDI, *St. Maximilian Kolbe: Apostle of Our Difficult Age* (Boston 1982). A. ROMB, ed., *The Kolbe Reader: The Writings of St Maximilian M. Kolbe, OFM Conv.* (Libertyville, Ill. 1987); *Maximilian Kolbe: authentic Franciscan* (Libertyville, Ill. 1990). P. TREECE, *A Man for Others: Maximilian Kolbe Saint of Auschwitz, In the Words of Those Who Knew Him* (San Francisco 1982). M. WINOWSKA *The Death Camp Proved Him Real*, (Kenosha, Wis. 1971), Eng. tr. of *Secret de Maximilien Kolbe* (Paris 1971).

[J. E. MCCURRY]

KÖLLIN, CONRAD

Dominican apologete and early Thomistic commentator; b. Ulm, Germany, *c.* 1476; d. Cologne, Aug. 26, 1536. Köllin (Kollin, a Colle, Kolyn), the son of an undertaker, entered the Order of Preachers in 1492, eight years after the entry of his brother Ulrich (1469–1535). He studied philosophy and theology at Ulm, then matriculated at the University of Heidelberg in 1500. After serving as *biblicus* (1501), bachelor of the *Sentences* (1503), and master of students (1505), he became a master of theology in 1507. The same year he was elected prior of the Dominican community and became dean of the theology faculty of the university. At that time he began his lectures on the *Summa theologiae* of St. Thomas Aquinas. At the insistence of the theology faculties of Heidelberg and Cologne, and with the permission of Cardinal T. de Vio CAJETAN, then master general, Köllin published his most important theological work, a commentary on the la2ae of the *Summa* (Cologne 1512). His other contributions to moral theology include *Speculum vitae* (Cologne 1518) and *Quodlibeta* (Cologne 1523). His influence led to the introduction of the *Summa theologiae* as the standard theological textbook in place of the *Sentences* of Peter Lombard.

Köllin was probably the most important Catholic theologian in Germany at the time of the Reformation. He energetically defended Catholic doctrine against the teaching of the Lutherans in his *Eversio Lutherani Epithalamii* (Cologne 1527) and *Adversus caninas Martini Lutheri nuptias* (Tübingen 1530). From 1528 until his death he was inquisitor for the ecclesiastical provinces of Mainz, Trier, and Cologne.

Bibliography: J. QUÉTIF and J. ÉCHARD, *Scriptores Ordinis Praedicatorm*, 5 v. (Paris 1719–23) 2.1:100. J. WILMS, Der *Kölner Universitätsprofessor Konrad Köllin* (Cologne 1941). N. PAULUS, *Die deutschen Dominikaner im Kampfe gegen Luther, 1518–1563* (Freiburg 1903) 111–134.

[J. HENNESSEY]

KOLPING, ADOLF, BL.

Pioneer German Catholic social leader; founder of the Kolping Societies *(Gesellenvereine);* b. Kerpen, near Cologne, Dec. 8, 1813; d. Cologne, Dec. 4, 1865. Kolping was the son of a shepherd, Peter Kolping, and Anna Maria Zurheyden. He apprenticed as a shoemaker. While working 12 hours a day he prepared himself for institutions of higher learning by teaching himself. He was graduated from the Marzellengymnasium at the age of 24, and then studied at the Universities of Munich and Bonn (1841–44). After his ordination at Cologne in 1845, he was assigned to the struggling industrial city of Elberfeld, where he was impressed by the effects of the new capitalism. He joined a youth organization founded by a teacher, Johann Gregor Breuer, became its president in 1847, and, after two years of successful effort, began to be called "father of the journeymen." This organization was his model when, in 1849, he was transferred to the Cologne cathedral and founded there a Catholic association of journeymen. Even in his lifetime his "Kolping Families" *(Kolpingwerke)* spread throughout Europe and to America; at his death he was mourned by some 26,000 members in 400 different branches.

Kolping's spiritual character was formed by his family, his early sacrifices, and hard work. On the intellectual level he encountered at Munich the heritage of Johann Michael Sailer (1751–1832), for whom religion was the basis of all education. The social teachings of Franz von Baader (1765–1841) likewise left their mark upon his program. Professors who influenced him especially were Josef Görres, Ignaz Döllinger, and Friedrich Windischmann. Kolping deliberately opposed the intellectual tendencies of his age. He was a leader against the rationalism and antisocial individualism then found in the social and political spheres as liberalism among the upper classes and socialism among the lower. Nevertheless, he developed no system, but became a man of action.

Kolping recognized the new value of work and achievement in the transition from the feudal to the modern social order, as well as the importance of the education of the individual for the attainment of this value. He furthered the education of the young people in his association, which he wanted to have recognized as "a people's academy in the people's style." At the same time, he demanded occupational efficiency, saying, "Religion and work are the golden foundation of the people."

Kolping's strength as an educator lay in his fostering of those attitudes that enable individuals to achieve something by their own power and to improve their social position. His purpose extended to raising the intellectual and spiritual status of the whole working class. In 1849, Kolping was appointed vicar of the Cologne cathedral and began to write and speak extensively to promulgate the ideas of the Gesellenverein, defend the rights of workers, and awaken Catholics to their socio-political responsibilities. Kolping used the money generated by his writings to found several periodicals: *Rheinische Kirchenblatt*, *Feierstunde*, and *Vereinsorgan* (1850–54), *Rheinischen Volksblätter für Haus, Familie, und Handwerk* (from 1854), the *Katholischer Volkskalender* (1850–53), *Kalender für das katholische Volk* (1853–66). The so-called German "John Bosco" or "Journeymen's Father" died at age 51 and was buried in the Minoritenkirche, Cologne.

At his beatification Oct. 27, 1991, Pope John Paul II called Kolping the "precursor of the great social encyclicals." He described the blessed as a man who "stood with both feet planted firmly on the ground, and was oriented toward heaven."

Bibliography: *Schriften. Kölner Ausgabe*, Vol. I: Documents, Diary, Poems, ed. H. J. KRACHT (Cologne 1975; 2d ed. 1981); Vol. II: Letters, ed. M. HANKE (Cologne 1976); Vol. III-V: Social Statements and the Gesellenverein, ed. R. COPELOVICI et al. (Cologne 1985–87); Vol. VI: Pictures from Rome, ed. H. J. KRACHT (Cologne 1986). *Briefe*, ed. M. HANKE and R. COPELOVICI (Cologne 1991). *Kolping und sein Werk*, ed. Generalsekretariat der kath. Gesellenvereine (Cologne 1920). Literature. T. BRAUER, *Kolping* (Freiburg 1923, Kevelaer 1935). A. BUETTNER, *Kolping Der Mann Gottes: Priester des Volkes* (Cologne 1937). V. CONZEMIUS, *Kolping Der Gesellenvater aktuell, damals und heute* (Fribourg-Hamburg 1982). C. FELDMANN, *Adolf Kolping: Für ein soziales Christentum* (Freiburg 1991). H. FESTING, *Kolping und sein Werk. Ein Überblick über Leben und Wirken des großen Sozialreformers sowie über die Entwicklung seines Werkes bis heute* (Freiburg 1981); *Was Kolping für uns bedeutet* (Freiburg 1985). H. GRANVOGL, *Kolping und die christliche-soziale Bewegung* (Augsburg 1987). M. HANKE, *Sozialer Wandel durch Veränderung des Menschen. Leben, Wirken und Werk des Sozialpädagogen Kolping* (Mülheim 1974). H.-J. KRACHT, *Kolping: Ein Mann von gestern mit Ideen für morgen* (2d. ed. Essen 1972); *Kolping: Sozialpädagoge und Erwachsenenbildner* (Cologne 1977); *Adolph Kolping: Priester, Pädagoge, Publizist im Dienst christlicher Sozialreform* (Freiburg 1993). R. MÜLLER, *Adolf Kolping: Visionär und Reformer* (Freiburg 1991). L. PERRIDON, *Gesellschaftspolit. Bedingungen der Arbeit Kolpings* (Augsburg-Munich 1978). T. REMPE, *Kolping: Grundsätze zur Pädagogik und Organisation seines Werkes* (Cologne 1975). B. RIDDER, *Person und Leben Kolpings in Urkunden und im Urteil von Zeitgenossen* (Cologne 1960). G. RITZERFELD, *Kolping* (Cologne 1963). S. G. SCHÄFFER, *Kolping, der Gesellenvater. Ein Lebensbild* (Münster 1880, 1882, reprinted Paderborn 1894, Cologne 1927, 1947, 1952, 1961). *Acta Apostolicae Sedis* (1991) 1064. P. STEINKE, *Leitbild für die Kirche* (Paderborn 1992). H. J. WIRTZ, *Katholische Gesellenver-*

eine und Kolpingsfamilien im Bistum Münster 1852-1960 (Münster 1999). *Acta Apostolicae Sedis* (1991) 1064.

[H. FISCHER]

KOLPING SOCIETY, CATHOLIC

A socio-religious organization for promoting the development of the individual and family, founded in Cologne, Germany, in 1849 by Adolph Kolping, a priest of the archdiocese. Through its "Kolping Houses," which serve as centers of activity of the local branches and also as familial homes with boarding facilities for out-of-town members, it fosters a sense of belonging and friendship through spiritual, educational, social, and charitable programs.

Kolping was ordained on April 13, 1845, in the Minoriten Church in Cologne, which later became the center of his foundation and his final resting place. He became interested in the work that bears his name during his first priestly assignment at Elberfeld in the Rhineland where he was director for a small group of young Catholics organized as a friendship society. After his transfer to Cologne, he organized the first group of young workers on May 6, 1849. The organization soon spread over Central Europe; by 1865, the time of his death, Kolping's societies spread throughout many countries of the world.

The first Kolping societies in the United States were organized in 1859. The present national organization, The Catholic Kolping Society of America, was constituted in 1923 and affiliated to the International Kolping Society. Historically, its houses in New York and Los Angeles served as boarding houses for young men in transition. Its activities are organized in and around the many Kolping Houses, where members and friends gather and interact within the framework of the Christian Gospel.

Bibliography: M. I. FIEDERLING, *Adolf Kolping and the Kolping Society of the United States* (Chicago 1941). F. J. WOTHE, *Adolf Kolping: Leben und Lehre eines grossen Erziehers* (3d ed. Recklinghausen 1952). J. NATTERMANN, *Adolf Kolping als Sozialpädagoge* (Meiner 1926).

[H. A. KREWITT/EDS.]

KÖNIG, FRANZ BORGIA

Cardinal, archbishop of Vienna; b. Aug. 3, 1905, Rabenstein, Lower Austria into a farmer's family, the eldest of 10 children. He attended the grammar school of the Benedictine Monastery of Melk, and in 1927 went on to Collegium Germanicum-Hungaricum in Rome, where he

Franz Borgia Cardinal König. (Archive Photos.)

studied philosophy (Ph.D., 1930) and theology (Ph.D., 1936) and was ordained to the priesthood on Oct. 29, 1933. During his stay in Rome he also studied old Persian religions and languages at the Pontifical Institute Biblicum. After his return to his home diocese of Sankt Pölten, Lower Austria, he served as chaplain in smaller parishes and then as curate to the cathedral. His teaching career began in 1945 with an appointment to lecture in religious studies at the University of Vienna; from 1948 to 1952 he taught moral theology at the University of Salzburg. He published widely in the field of comparative religion, his chief work being the three-volume *Christus und die Religionen der Erde* (1948). In 1952 he was elected titular bishop of Liviade and appointed coadjutor of Sankt Pölten, with right of succession. Continuing his work in religious studies he compiled his *Religionswissenschaftliches Wörterbuch* (1956) and was appointed editor for the second edition of the *Lexikon für Theologie und Kirche* (10 vols). Pope Pius XII appointed him archbishop of Vienna in 1956, and two years later he was created cardinal, with the title of S. Eusebio, by

Pope John XXIII. He was also the ordinary for Greek-rite Catholics living in Austria and, from 1959 to 1968, military vicar of Austria. In 1959 Cardinal König founded the Afro-Asian-Institute in Vienna as a platform for intercultural and interreligious exchange between the Christian West and the newly emancipated Afro-Asian countries. This spontaneous experiment gave him a clear vision and firm attitude at the Second Vatican Council regarding religious freedom (declaration *Dignitatis Humanae,* 1965) and interreligious dialogue (declaration *Nostra Aetate,* 1965). König was appointed to the Central Preparatory Commission of the Second Vatican Council and for the first session served in the Theological Commission. Karl Rahner was his *peritus* at the council.

In 1965 Pope Paul VI appointed Cardinal König president of the Secretariat for Non-Believers, a position he held until 1980. A concern for dialogue—ecumenical, interreligious, church-state—was the hallmark of his public activity. In Austria he tried to heal the wounds of civil war and the dissent of pre-war Austria (Austrofascism vs. Austro- Marxism) by reconciling trade unions and socialists with the church. A breakthrough was achieved by his lecture at the General Assembly of the Austrian Trade Unions 1973, "Kirche und Gesellschaft." His first diplomatic contacts with eastern churches under communist oppression resulted in a profound ecumenical engagement with Orthodoxy and Old Oriental Churches from which the foundation "Pro Oriente" took its origin (1964). The resulting mutual visits and free theological exchange bore rich fruit, including the "Vienna Formula" (1993), which cleared old misunderstandings in Christology by a commonly accepted definition of the natures and person of Christ with a large impact on interecclesial relationships. The global dimension of the gospel's message led Cardinal König to cooperate with the Congregation of World Mission in Rome (1968). He also made notable attempts to engage in dialogue with scholars. In 1968 he offered an attempt to reconcile natural sciences and Christian faith with "Der Fall Galilei." He also helped to found the "Institut für die Wissenschaften vom Menschen" (1983), which since that time has held biennial seminars with the pope at Castel Gandolfo. In 1985 Cardinal König resigned his archbishopric. For the next five years he served as president of "Pax Christi International."

It is widely held that Cardinal König took the lead in advancing the candidacy of Karol Wojtyła in the 1978 conclave that elected him as Pope John Paul II.

Bibliography: A. SCHIFFERLE, *Geduld und Vertrauen: Franz Kardinal König—Texte und Gespräche.* (Freiburg 1995).A. FENZL and R. FÖLDY, eds. *Franz Kardinal König. Haus auf festem Grund.* (1994). F. KÖNIG, *Appelle an Gewissen und Vernunft* (1996).J.

KUNZ, ed. *Kardinal Franz König: Ansichten eines engagierten Kirchenmannes.* (1991).

[P. BSTEH]

KONINGS, ANTHONY

Redemptorist moral theologian; b. Helmond, near 's-Hertogenbosch, in the Low Countries, Aug. 24, 1821; d. Ilchester, Maryland, June 30, 1884. Konings entered the REDEMPTORIST congregation and was professed on Nov. 6, 1843, and ordained on Dec. 21, 1844. He served as professor of moral theology and Canon Law in the Redemptorist house of studies at Wittem, Holland, and became provincial of the province of Holland (1865–68). In 1870 he accepted an assignment that brought him to the U.S., where he taught moral theology and Canon Law in the Redemptorist seminary at Ilchester, Maryland, and quickly became a consultant to American bishops and priests in difficult questions involving theological and canonical principles and practice. He wrote a number of tracts and articles on these subjects and two highly appreciated books: *Theologia moralis S. Alphonsi in compendium redacta et usui ven. cleri americani accomodata* (Boston 1874, six later editions) and *Commentarium in facultates apostolicas . . . ad usum ven. cleri americani* (New York 1884). This work was revised by J. Putzer in 1893 and had a 5th edition in 1898.

Bibliography: J. A. HANDLEY, *The Catholic Encyclopedia,* ed. C. G. HERBERMANN et al, 16 vol. (New York 1907–14) 8:689–690. M. DE MEULEMEESTER et al., *Bibliographie générale des écrivains Rédemptoristes,* 3 vol. (Louvain 1933–39) 2:227–228; 3:333.

[A. SAMPERS]

KOREA, MARTYRS OF, SS.

Also known as Andrew Kim Tae-gon and Companions, and Paul Chong Hasang and Companions; d. in Korea, 1839, 1846, 1866, and 1867. During his 21st international pastoral visit, Pope John Paul II canonized 103 of the estimated 8,000–10,000 martyrs of Korea on May 6, 1984, in its capital Seoul. This marked the bicentennial of Christianity in Korea and the first canonization ceremony held outside the Vatican. After noting the uniqueness of the Korean Catholic community in the history of the Church, he said: "The death of the martyrs is similar to the death of Christ on the Cross, because, like his, theirs has become the beginning of new life."

The canonized Korean Martyrs are 103 Catholics first beatified in two groups: 79 martyrs who died during the Choson dynasty (1839–46) were beatified in 1925; 24 martyred in 1866–67 were raised to the altar in 1968.

St. Andrew Kim Tae-gon.

Among the group were 10 French missionaries (3 bishops and 7 Paris Society of Foreign Missions [MEP]), 46 Korean men (1 priest, 1 seminarian, 25 lay catechists, and 19 other laymen), and 47 Korean women (15 virgins, 11 married women, 18 widows, and 3 of unknown marital status; 3 of them were catechists). They ranged in age from 13 to 78. Most of the canonized saints were beheaded, but 17 were hanged or strangled, 10 expired in prison, and 7 died under torture. Their common feast is September 20 on the General Roman Liturgical Calendar.

The names of the two martyrs listed in the liturgical calendar are Andrew Kim Tae-gon, the first Korean priest, and Paul Chong Hasang, a renowned lay leader.

Andrew Kim Tae-gon, b. Tchoung-tcheng Province, Korea, Aug. 21, 1821; d. near Seoul, Korea, Sept. 16, 1846, was born into Korean nobility. Kim's father Ignatius Kim, and grandfather, In-He Kim (d. 1814) died for the faith. After his baptism (1836) Andrew went with two other Korean youths to seminary in Macau, China, where he remained until 1842. He then set out for his native land, but not until his third attempt and after many difficulties did he succeed in entering the closely guarded Hermit Kingdom, as Korea was known, by way of Manchuria (1845). In 1844 he was ordained a deacon, and in 1845 he crossed the Yellow Sea and was ordained a priest in Shanghai, becoming the first native Korean priest. He returned to Korea in company with Bp. Jean Ferréol, the vicar apostolic, and Fr. A. Daveluy. In 1846 Kim was assigned to arrange for the entrance of more missionaries by some water routes that would elude the border patrol. During this process he was arrested, imprisoned, tortured, and finally beheaded at the Han River near Seoul, the capital. The body was exposed publicly for three days, according to the custom, before burial at the site of execution. After 40 days the Catholics were able to obtain the remains and bury them on Mi-ri nai Mountain about 35 miles distant. In 1949 the HOLY SEE designated him the principal patron of the clergy of Korea.

Paul Chong Hasang (Cheong), seminarian, lay catechist, d. Sept. 22, 1839 (age 45), hanged outside the small west gate in Seoul. Paul was one of the lay leaders of the early Korean Church. His father, leader of the confraternity of Christian doctrine, and his uncle were martyred in the Shin-Yu persecution of 1801. Following in their footsteps, Paul gathered the scattered Christians and labored to strengthen the infant Korean Church. He traveled nine times to Beijing as a servant to the Korean diplomatic mission in order to petition the bishop of Beijing to send priests to Korea. Because his plea fell on deaf ears, he appealed directly to Rome in 1925, which led to the dispatch of French missionaries. He also wrote to the prime minister a short apologetic *(Sang-Je-Sang-Su)* on Christian doctrine and its harmony with national values in the hope of ending the persecution of Christians. Paul was one of the three men sent by Maubant to Macau for seminary training; he was martyred, however, prior to ordination. His mother, Cecilia, and sister died for their faith shortly thereafter.

The earliest missionaries to Korea are also included among the martyrs canonized: Laurent Joseph Marius Imbert, bishop; b. 1786, Marignane (Bouches-du-Rhône), France; Pierre Philibert Maubant, b.1803 in Vaussy (Calvados); Jacques Honoré Chastan, b. 1803 in Marcoux (Basses-Alpes). Imbert entered the MEP in 1818, was ordained in 1819, and went to China (1820) after ordination, where he labored as a missionary until he became the second vicar apostolic of Korea (1837) and the first one to enter the country. Preceding him were two French confreres, Maubant and Chastan. Maubant was ordained in 1829, joined the MEP in 1831, and set out for Korea in 1832. He entered the country in 1836, the same year as Chastan, who was ordained in 1826, joined the MEP in 1827, and went to Thailand before his assign-

ment to Korea (1832). Since the Hermit Kingdom did not admit foreigners and did not tolerate Christians, the three men, the only priests then in the country, could not engage openly in their apostolate. An edict, issued in April 1839 was followed by fierce persecution. Bishop Imbert (whose Korean name was Bom) found it necessary to flee from Seoul, the capital, in June. He remained in hiding until betrayed by a renegade Christian and seized by the authorities (August 11). From his prison in Seoul he sent to his two priests a controversial letter that directed them to come forward. Maubant (Ra in Korean) and Chastan (Cheong) came as directed. The three were tried, tortured, and sentenced to military execution. After they had been beheaded at state expense at a public and solemn ceremony in Sae Nam Do near Seoul (Sept. 21, 1839), their heads were suspended in public to terrify Christians. Their mortal remains are enshrined at Samsong-san, near Seoul.

Besides these men, the following other martyrs were canonized. They are listed by their given name together with their date of death and age at the time of death.

Agatha Chon Kyong-hyob (Kyung-Hyun Jeon, Tiyen), virgin; d. Sept. 26, 1839 (52), beheaded outside the small west gate.

Agatha Kim A-gi (Up-Yi Kim), widow; d. May 24, 1839 (65); beatified 1925.

Agatha Kwon Chin-i (Jin-Yi Kwon), housewife; d. Jan. 31, 1840 (21), beheaded at Dang-Gogae.

Agatha Yi (Lee), virgin; d. Jan. 9, 1840 (17), hanged at Po Chung Ok.

Agatha Yi Kan-nan (Gan-Nan Lee), widow; d. Sept. 20, 1846 (32), hanged at Po Chung Ok.

Agatha Yi Kyong-i (Kyung-Yi Lee), virgin; d. Jan. 31, 1840 (27), beheaded at Dang-Gogae.

Agatha So-Sa Lee, widow; d. May 24, 1839 (55), beheaded outside the small west gate.

Agnes Kim Hyo-ju (Hyo-Joo Kim), virgin; d. Sept. 3, 1839 (23), beheaded outside the small west gate. She was imprisoned with her sister Columba Kim.

Alexius U Se-yong (Se-Young Woo); d. March 21, 1866 (21), beheaded at Saenam-To, then was displayed.

Andrew Chong Hwa-gyong (Hwa-Kyung Jung; Cheong; Tjyeng), lay catechist; d. Jan. 23, 1840 (33), hanged at Po Chung Ok.

Anna Kim Chang-gum (Jang-Keum Kim), widow; d. July 20, 1839 (50), beheaded outside the small west gate.

Anna Pak A-gi (Ah-Ki Park), housewife, May 24, 1839 (56), beheaded outside the small west gate.

Antoine Daveluy, French bishop; d. March 30, 1866 (49) beheaded at Kalmaemot, then the head was displayed as a warning to other Christians. He entered Korea with Andrew Kim Tae-gon and Bp. Ferréol in 1845. In 1862 he baptized 40 catechumens in the Christian refuge now called Han-Ti (meaning "mass grave") in the Palgong Mountains. Later all the Christians of the village were massacred in a surprise attack and buried together. Daveluy was responsible for establishing a press to print catechisms and for collecting and preserving information on those martyred. He edited the first Korean-French dictionary, which authorities burned together with other Christian books. In an attempt to spare other Christians, Daveluy turned himself in. From jail he wrote to Aumaitre and Martin Huin suggesting the same course of action. He was consecrated auxiliary to Bp. Berneux (1856) and martyred with Aumaitre, Huin, and Joseph Chang Chu-gi just three weeks after becoming the 5th apostolic vicar of Korea.

Anthony Kim Song-u (Sung-Woo Kim), lay catechist, d. April 29, 1841 (46), strangled in prison at Dang-Gogae for harboring foreign priests in his home. Two of his brothers were also martyred.

Augustine Pak Chong-won (Jong-Won Park), lay catechist; d. Jan. 31, 1840 (48), beheaded at Dang-Gogae.

Augustine Yi Kwang-hon (Kwang-Hun Lee, Ni), lay catechist; d. May 24, 1839 (52), beheaded outside the small west gate.

Augustine Yu Chin-kil (Jin-Kil Yoo, Ryou, Nyou); d. Sept. 22, 1839 (48), beheaded outside the small west gate.

Barbara Cho Chung-i (Zung-Yi Cho), housewife; d. Dec. 29, 1839 (57), beheaded outside the small west gate.

Barbara Ch'oe Yong-i (Young-Yi Choi), housewife; d. Feb. 1, 1840 (22), hanged at Dang-Gogae.

Barbara Han A-gi (Ah-Ki Han), widow; d. May 24, 1839 (47), beheaded outside the small west gate.

Barbara Kim, widow; d. May 27, 1839 (34) in prison.

Barbara Ko Sun-i (Soon-Yi Ko), housewife; d. Dec. 29, 1839 (41), beheaded outside the small west gate.

Barbara Kwon Hui (Hee Kwon), housewife; d. Sept. 3,1839 (45), beheaded outside the small west gate.

Barbara Yi (Jung-Hee Lee, Yong-h'ui), widow; d. Sept. 3, 1839 (40), beheaded outside the small west gate. She is the aunt of Barbara Yi Chong-hui (infra) and sister of Magdalene Yi Yong-h'ui.

Barbara Yi Chong-hui (Jung-Hee Lee), virgin; d. May 27, 1839 (14) in prison. Her aunts Barbara Jung-Hee Lee and Magdalene Yi Yong-h'ui were martyred several months later.

Bartholomew Chong Mun-ho (Moon-Ho Jung), county governor; d. Dec. 23, 1866 (65), beheaded at Jun Joo (ChonHo), where he is buried.

Benedicta Hyon Kyong-nyon (Kyung-Ryung Han; Hyen), lay catechist; d. Dec. 29, 1839 (45), beheaded outside the small west gate.

Catherine Chong Ch'ol-yom (Chul-Yom Jung; Cheong), housewife; d. Sept. 20, 1846 (29), hanged at Po Chung Ok.

Catherine Yi (Lee), widow; d. Sept. 26, 1839 (56) in prison.

Charles Cho Shin-ch'ol (Shin-Chul Cho, Tjyo); d. Sept. 26, 1839 (46), beheaded outside the small west gate.

Charles Hyon Sok-mun (Seok-Moon Hyun, Hyen), lay catechist; d. Sept. 19, 1846 (49), decapitated and head displayed at Seoul. Bishop Imbert entrusted the care of the Korean Christians to Charles before the deaths of the three priests.

Cecilia Yu So-sa (Ryou), widow and mother of Paul Chong Hasang and Elizabeth Chong Ch'ong-hye; d. Nov. 23, 1839 (78) in prison.

Columba Kim Hyo-im, virgin; d. Sept. 26, 1839 (25), imprisoned, pierced with red hot awls, scorched with burning coals, then beheaded outside the small west gate.

Damian Nam Myong-hyok, lay catechist; d. May 24, 1839 (37) beheaded outside the small west gate. He was a model husband and father.

Elizabeth Chong Ch'ong-hye (Jung-Hye Jung; Cheong), virgin, younger sister of Paul Chong Hasang; d. Dec. 29, 1839 (42), beheaded outside the small west gate.

Francis Ch'oe Kyong-hwan (Kyung-Hwan Choi, Tchoi), lay catechist; d. Sept. 12, 1839 (34) in prison. Francis is the father of Korea's second native priest, Thomas Yang-Up Choi. During the Gihae persecution his family was arrested. His youngest son starved to death in his mother's arms in prison; four of his sons, however, survived to witness the beheading of Francis's wife, Maria Song-Rye Yi, the year following his death (1840). Although his sons did not die for the faith, they suffered becoming exiled beggars. In 1849 Fr. Yang-Up Choi returned to his homeland to pray at his father's grave near AnYang in the village of DamBae-Gol.

Ignatius Kim Che-jun (Je-Joon Kim), father of Andrew Kim and lay catechist; d. Sept. 26, 1839 (43), beheaded outside the small west gate.

John Baptist Chon Chang-un (Jang-Woon Jeon), vendor and publisher; d. March 9, 1866 (55), beheaded outside the small west gate.

John Baptist Nam Chong-sam (Jong-Sam Nam), regional governor; d. March 7, 1866 (49), beheaded outside the small west gate of Seoul. Chong-sam was renowned as a just government official. Before his arrest and martyrdom he resigned his position and retired to Myojae because he could not offer sacrifice to his ancestors in good conscience. He is remembered as a model of chastity, charity, and poverty.

John Baptist Yi Kwang-nyol (Kwang-Ryul Lee), technician; d. July 20, 1839 (44), beheaded outside the small west gate.

John Pak Hu-jae (Hoo-Jae Park), merchant; d. Sept. 3, 1839 (40), beheaded outside the small west gate.

John Ri Mun-u (Moon-Woo Lee), lay catechist; d. Feb. 1, 1839 (31), hanged at Dang-Gogae. He was a Korean layman who wrote a still extant letter from prison; beatified 1925.

John Yi Yun-il (Yoon-Il Lee), lay catechist; d. Jan. 21, 1867 (43), beheaded at Kwan-Duk Jung in TaeKu. In 1987 his body was translated to the Lourdes Grotto at TaeKu, where Pope John Paul II stopped to pray in 1984.

Joseph Chang Chu-gi (Joo-Ki Jang), lay catechist and teacher of Chinese literature; d. March 30, 1866 (63). The first Korean seminary was established in his home in 1856. One room was used as a classroom and dormitory; the other as a rectory. He was decapitated and his head displayed at Kalmaemot for trying to protect the Christians hidden in his pottery kiln, which had been used by the Christians as a place of worship and to support themselves once they were dispossessed of family and property for their religion.

Joseph Chang Song-jib (Sung-Jip Jang, Tjyang), brother of Anthony Sung-Woo Kim; d. May 26, 1839 (53) strangled in prison at Po Chung Ok.

Joseph Cho Yun-ho (Yoon-Ho Cho), farmer; d. Dec. 23, 1866 (18) died at Jun Joo.

Joseph Im Ch'i-baek (Chi-Baek Im, Rim), Seoul boatman; d. Sept. 20, 1846 (42) hanged at Po Chung Ok.

Julietta Kim, virgin; d. Sept. 26, 1839 (55), beheaded outside the small west gate.

Just Ranfer de Bretennières, French priest; d. March 7, 1866 (28), decapitated, head displayed at Seoul.

Lawrence Han I-hyong (Yi-Hyung Han), lay catechist; d. Sept. 20, 1846 (47), hanged Po Chung Ok.

Lucy Kim, virgin; d. July 20, 1839 (21) outside the small west gate.

Lucy Kim (II), widow; d. Sept. 26, 1839 (70) in prison.

Lucy Pak Hui-sun (Hee-Soon Park), virgin; d. May 5, 1839 (38), beheaded outside the small west gate.

Louis Beaulieu, French priest; d. March 7, 1866 (26), decapitated and head displayed at Seoul.

Luke Hwang Sok-tu (Seok-Du Hwang), lay catechist; d. March 30, 1866 (53), beheaded then displayed at Kalmaemot. Luke was the brilliant coworker of Bishop Daveluy. He translated the Bible into Korean and wrote catechetical material for publication.

Magdalena Cho, virgin; d. Sept. 26, 1839 (32) in prison.

Magdalena Han Yong-i (Young-Yi Han), widow; d. Dec. 29, 1839 (55), beheaded outside the small west gate.

Magdalena Ho Kye-im (Gye-Im Her; He Kye-im, Ho), housewife; d. Sept. 26, 1839 (66), beheaded outside the small west gate.

Magdalena Kim Ob-i (Ah-Ki Lee), widow; d. May 24, 1839 (52), hanged outside the small west gate.

Magdalena Pak Pong-son (Bong-Son Park), widow; d. Sept. 26, 1839 (43), beheaded outside the small west gate.

Magdalena Son So-byok (So-Byuk Son), housewife; d. Jan. 31, 1840 (39), hanged at Dang-Gogae.

Magdalena Yi Yong-dok (Young-Duk Lee), virgin; d. Dec. 29, 1839 (27), beheaded outside the small west gate.

Magdalena Yi Yong-h'ui (Young-Hee Lee), virgin; d. July 20, 1839 (30) outside the small west gate. She is the sister of Barbara Yi.

Maria Pak K'un-agi (Keum-AhKi Park), housewife; d. Sept. 3, 1839 (53), beheaded outside the small west gate. Her husband, Philip Kim, was also martyred but is not numbered among these saints.

Maria Won Kwi-im (Gui-Im Won, Ouen), virgin; d. July 20, 1839 (21), beheaded outside the small west gate.

Maria Yi In-dok (In-Duk Lee), virgin; d. Jan. 31, 1840 (22), hanged at Dang-Gogae.

Maria Yi Y'on-hui (Yeon-Hee Lee), wife, mother, member of a simple form of religious sisterhood; d. Sept. 3, 1839 (35), beheaded outside the small west gate.

Mark Chong Ui-bae (Eui-Bae Jung), lay catechist; d. March 11, 1866 (71), decapitated and head displayed at Seoul.

Martha Kim Song-im (Sung-Im Kim), widow; d. July 20, 1839 (49), outside the small west gate.

Martin Luc (Luke) Huin, French priest; d. March 30, 1866 (30), beheaded and head displayed at Kalmaemot.

Paul Ho Hyop (Im Her, He, Heo), soldier; d. Jan. 30, 1840 (45), hanged at Po Chung Ok.

Paul Hong Yong-ju (Young-Joo Hong), lay catechist; d. Feb. 1, 1840 (39), beheaded at Dang-Gogae.

Perpetua Hong Kum-ju (Keum-Joo Hong), widow; d. Sept. 29, 1839 (35), beheaded outside the small west gate.

Pierre Aumaitre, French priest of MEP; d. March 30, 1866 (29), beheaded at Kalmaemot.

Peter Cho Hwa-so (Hwa-Seo Cho), farmer; d. Dec. 13, 1866 (51), beheaded at Jun Joo.

Peter Ch'oe Ch'ang-hup (Chang-Hoop Choi), lay catechist; d. Dec. 29, 1839 (52), beheaded outside the small west gate.

Peter Ch'oe Hyong (Hyung Choi), lay catechist; d. March 9, 1866 (52), beheaded outside the small west gate.

Peter Chong Won-ji (Won-Ji Jung), farmer; d. Dec. 13, 1866 (20), beheaded at Jun Joo.

Peter Hong Pyong-ju (Byung-Joo Hong, Kong), lay catechist; d. Jan. 31, 1840 (42), hanged at Dang-Gogae.

Peter Kwon Tug-in (Deuk-In Kwon, Kouen), producer of religious goods; d. May 24, 1839 (34) in prison outside the small west gate.

Peter Nam Kyong-mun (Kyung-Moon Nam), soldier, lay catechist; d. Sept. 20, 1846 (50), hanged at Po Chung Ok.

Peter Son Son-ji (Seon-Ji Son), lay catechist; d. Dec. 13, 1866 (46), beheaded at SupJungYi with Bartholomew Chong Mun-ho. Their bodies rest at Chon Ho in the north Cholla province.

Peter Ho-Young Lee, lay catechist; d. Nov. 25, 1838 (35) in prison.

Peter Won-Seo Han, lay catechist; d. Dec. 13, 1866 (20), beheaded at Jun Joo.

Peter Yi Myong-so (Myung-Seo Lee), farmer; d. Dec. 13, 1866 (45), beheaded at Jun Joo.

Peter Yi Tae-ch'ol (Dae-Chul Yoo, Ryou, Ryau), youth; d. Oct. 31, 1839 (13) at Po Chung Ok. Little Peter had presented himself to the magistrates, proclaiming that he was a Christian. The judges were horrified at his tortures. Fearing the popular opinion would turn again the authorities, his executioners strangled him after his return to prison.

Peter Yu Chong-nyul (Jung-Ryung Yoo), lay catechist; d. Feb. 17, 1866 (29) at PyungYang (now in North Korea).

Pierre-Henri Dorie, French priest; d. March 7, 1866 (27), beheaded at SaeNamTo and head displayed.

Protasius Chong Kuk-bo (Kook-Bo Jung, Cheong), noble and maker of musical instruments; d. May 20, 1839 (40) in prison at Po Chung Ok. He apostatized under torture and was released. Later he regretted his weakness, gave himself up to the authorities, and died from his torments.

Rosa Kim, widow; d. July 20, 1839 (55), beheaded outside the small west gate.

Sebastian Nam I-gwan (Yi-Kwan Nam), lay catechist; d. Sept. 26, 1839 (59), beheaded outside the small west gate.

Simeon Berneux, French bishop; d. March 7, 1866 (52), beheaded.

Stephen Min Kuk-ka (Geuk-Ga Min), lay catechist; d. Jan. 30, 1840 (53), hanged at Po Chung Ok.

Susanna U Sul-im (Sul-Im Woo), widow; d. Sept. 20, 1846 (43), hanged at Po Chung Ok.

Teresa Kim, widow; d. Jan. 9, 1940 (44) hanged at Po Chung Ok.

Teresa Kim Im-i (Yim-Yi Kim), virgin; d. Sept. 20, 1846 (35), hanged at Po Chung Ok.

Teresa Yi Mae-im (Mae-Im Lee), housewife; d. July 20, 1839 (51), outside the small west gate.

Thomas Son Cha-son (Ja-Sun Son), farmer; d. March 30, 1866 (22), hanged at Gong Joo.

Bibliography: *Acta Apostolicae Sedis* 17 (1925) 366–69. *L'Osservatore Romano*, English ed., no. 20 (1984) 5–6, 20. C. DALLET, *L'Histoire de l'Eglise de Corée* (1874) 118–185. *Documents relatifs au martyrs de Corée*, 2 v. (Hong Kong 1924). C. A. HERBST, "Unless the Grain of Wheat First Die . . . ," *American Ecclesiastical Revue* 139 (1958) 331–337; "The Bishop Dies," *ibid.* 138 (1958) 149–157; "Korea's Martyr-Patron," *ibid.* 137 (1957) 330–341. K. D. KIM, *Life of Kim Dae Kun* (Seoul 1960), in Korean. A. LAUNAY, *Martyrs français et coréens* (1925). S. A. MOFFETT, *The Christians of Korea* (New York 1962). M. W. NOBLE, *Victorious Lives of Early Christians* (Seoul 1933).

[C. A. HERBST/K. RABENSTEIN]

KOREA, THE CATHOLIC CHURCH IN

Located on the eastern coast of the Asian continent, the Korean peninsula borders on China in the north and

Capital: The capital of North Korea is P'yongyang; the capital of South Korea is Seoul.
Size: 46,609 sq. miles (north); 38,022 sq. miles (south).
Population: 21.2 million (north); 46.4 million (south). The people are racially homogeneous except for a few ethnic Japanese and a small number of Chinese.
Languages: Korean; English is taught in schools in the south.
Religions: 49% are Christian, 47% Buddhist, 3% Confucian, and 1% Shamanist, Ch'ondogyo (Religion of the Heavenly Way) and other in the south. Buddhism and Confucianism dominate in North Korea with some Christians and followers of the Ch'ongdogyo.

is surrounded by the Yellow Sea to the east and the Sea of Japan to the west. Politically the peninsula is divided into the Democratic People's Republic of Korea in the north and the Republic of Korea in the south. The *Annuario Pontificio* treats Korea as a single entity.

The Korean peninsula, mostly mountainous and poorly endowed with natural resources, was unified politically from the 7th century onward. Bitter experiences with invaders led the kingdom to close its doors to all foreigners except Chinese at the end of the 16th century. For the next 250 years or so Korea was known as the Hermit Kingdom. From 1910 until 1945 it was annexed to Japan. In 1948 North Korea came under communist rule, and the ensuing civil war between North and South Korea (1950–53) ended in a stalemate. Subsequent rapprochement between the North and South resulted in in a marked reduction in border tensions, limited family reunion meetings, reopening of rail connection and closer trade ties. For his peacemaking efforts, Kim Dae Jung, the first Catholic to be President of South Korea, was awarded the 2000 Nobel Peace Prize.

Korean Religion. The earliest form of Korean religion exhibits close affinity with the nature cults of north-central Asia and may be described as animism. It embodied a belief in the existence of numerous spirits and demons in the sky and on earth, in the sun, moon, and stars, and in mountains and rivers. Ancestor worship is a marked feature of the old native religion, and there is a belief in a High God (Hananim), identified with the firmament, or heaven. The shaman (mutang) has had so central a role since prehistoric times that the native Korean religion may well be called shamanism. Even after the coming of Confucianism and Buddhism, shamanistic beliefs and practices continued to flourish, and they are still very much alive in modern Korea, especially in the countryside.

Confucianism was introduced from China as early as the 1st century B.C., and gave strong support to the native ancestor worship. It exercised a marked influence on Ko-

rean culture and government until it was eclipsed by Buddhism from the 4th and 5th centuries A.D. Neo-Confucianism spread from China into Korea several centuries later and in 1392 was adopted as the official religion of the Korean state under the Wang Dynasty. Despite the official supremacy of Confucianism until the Japanese occupation of Korea beginning in 1910, Buddhism continued to have an important place in the religious life of the people. The severe measures employed by the Japanese in the 1930s and during World War II to suppress all forms of religion in Korea that were regarded as inimical to Japanese imperial policy and their efforts to introduce Shintoism were marked largely by failure even before the recovery of Korean independence in 1945.

Among the numerous non-Christian sects that developed especially during the Japanese domination and since 1945, Ch'ondogyo (Religion of the Heavenly Way) deserves mention. Formerly known as Tonghak (Eastern Learning), Ch'ondogyo is an indigenous Korean religion that was founded by Ch'oe Cheu in 1860. It is a syncretic blend of Buddhism, Confucianism, Taoism, shamanism and Roman Catholicism.

Origins of the Catholic Church in Korea. During the Japanese invasion of Korea from 1592 to 1599, some Koreans were baptized, probably by Japanese Christian soldiers. Koreans were among the Christians put to death during the severe persecutions in Japan early in the 17th century: 9 of the 205 martyrs beatified in 1867 were Koreans (*see* JAPAN, MARTYRS OF). Attempts at Christian evangelization were frustrated by Korea's refusal to permit contacts with the outside world except for an annual embassy to pay a tax to the overlords of the imperial court in Beijing. Christian literature, obtained from the Jesuit missionaries there on these occasions, was brought back to Korea. In 1777 a group of educated Koreans began to study these books, and one of the scholars advised Yi Sung Hun, a member of the annual delegation of 1783, to contact the missionaries in Beijing. There he was baptized by Jean de Grammont, a Jesuit previous to the suppression of the order, and took the name Peter. Upon his return to Seoul he soon converted his influential friends Yi Pyok (baptized John Baptist) and Kwon Il Shin (Francis Xavier). The first church was located in the home of Kim Bom Ou in Myongdong. So successful was the apostolate of these first converts that James Chu, a Chinese priest who managed to enter the country secretly (1794), found 4,000 Catholics, none of whom had ever seen a priest. By 1801, when Father James Chu and 300 others were put to death for their faith, the Church had grown to 10,000.

Growth under Persecution. In 1831 the country was removed from the jurisdiction of the Diocese of Beijing and placed under the newly created Vicariate Apostolic of Korea, which was entrusted to the Paris Foreign Mission Society (MEP). Bishop Barthilemy Bruguière, the first vicar apostolic, died in 1835 before reaching Korea. Pierre Maubant, his companion, arrived in 1836 and was soon joined by another priest, Jacques Chastan, and by the second vicar apostolic, Laurent Imbert. These three MEP missionaries were martyred in the persecution of 1839, leaving Korea without priests until 1845, when Andrew Kim Te-gon, the first Korean priest, arrived from China with Father Daveluy and Bp. Jean Ferriol. Thomas Choi, the second native priest, arrived in 1849. In 1857 Korea had 7 priests for its 15,000 Catholics, and counted 1,924 baptisms; and in 1866 it had 12 priests for 23,000 Catholics. The first century of the Catholic Church in Korea was one of growth in the face of persecutions, which became particularly severe in 1801, 1839, 1846, and above all from 1866 to 1869, when some 10,000 Catholics were put to death. The final royal decree against Catholicism appeared in 1881, but it was not seriously enforced. During his pastoral visit to Korea in 1984 Pope John Paul II canonized the first Korean priest Andrew Kim Te-gon, the seminarian Paul Chong Pasang and 111 others who died in the persecutions (*see* KOREA, MARTYRS OF).

The Church since 1883. Religious freedom was granted in 1883 when Korea was opened to foreigners, and a period of steady growth followed. Bishop Felix Ridel, who had escaped from the 1866 persecution, returned as vicar apostolic in 1877. He was soon arrested, but French and Japanese pressure effected his release. Ridel sent 22 Koreans to Malaya to prepare for the priesthood and began building red-brick churches in the Western style. The cathedral in Seoul was begun in 1888. The Sisters of St. Paul (Chartres) arrived in 1888, and the Benedictines in 1908. The seminary at Seoul opened in 1891. In 1901 a riot on the island of Cheju, fomented by jealous shamans, resulted in the massacre of 700 Catholics. Two Paris Foreign Mission Society (MEP) priests, who had baptized hundreds there, narrowly escaped death.

Korea had 77,000 Catholics in 1911 when the Vicariate Apostolic of Seoul was divided to create that of Taikyu. As the Church grew, other vicariates were erected. Paul Ro, who became bishop of Seoul in 1942, was the first native bishop. Another Korean, F. Hong, became bishop of P'yongyang in 1944. The Korean War seriously disrupted the Church. In sections that were invaded by Communists, persecutions occurred: bishops and priests were imprisoned and put to death; Bp. Patrick Byrne, one of the Maryknoll Missioners, perished during a forced march. In South Korea, the Catholic Church experienced tremendous growth after 1953. Very little is known about

Metropolitan Sees	Suffragans
Kwangju	Cheju, Chongju
Seoul	Ch'unch'on, Hamhung (North Korea), Inch'on, P'yongyang (North Korea), Suwon, Taejon, Wonju
Taegu	Andong, Ch'ongju, Masan, Pusan

There is also a territorial abbacy at Tokwon.

the Church in North Korea since then. In 1962, when the Korean hierarchy was established, three ecclesiastical provinces were created Kwangju, Seoul and Taegu.

The Impact of Vatican II. The Catholic Church in Korea in the 1960s and 1970s was strongly influenced by the Second VATICAN COUNCIL. The use of the vernacular in the Mass and the liturgical reforms were eagerly embraced. The Catholic Conference of Korea had the documents of the council and many explanatory works translated quickly into Korean. Since there had been a lack of materials for religious education, these materials filled a vacuum. In the 1970s Korea became a sending Church. The Korean Foreign Mission Society was founded in 1975, and religious institutes of women began to send missionaries abroad. By 1992 Koreans had also joined such foreign missionary societies as the Columbans and Guadalupe Missioners. Koreans were serving as missionaries in Papua-New Guinea, Taiwan, and several countries of Africa and South America. In addition, many Korean priests and religious were serving Koreans living abroad, especially those living in the United States. This post-conciliar period coincided with a period of economic expansion in South Korea that had begun in the late 1950s. The rapid economic development, led by a strong central government that favored large monopolistic corporations (chaebols), involved much exploitation and injustice. To mobilize the population for this development effort, and to counter North Korea's strong military, the central government employed a strong anti-communist stance and pervasive control of the media and squelched opposition. Thus, the main challenges to the Church during the 1970s and 1980s were issues of justice and human rights. Bishop Daniel Tji of Wonju and Cardinal Kim, Archbishop of Seoul, became outspoken critics of the regime and a group of clergy formed the Catholic Priests' Association for Justice.

Changing Status. In the 1980s the Catholic Church enjoyed high prestige in South Korean society. It was considered urban and modern. Its churches and liturgies

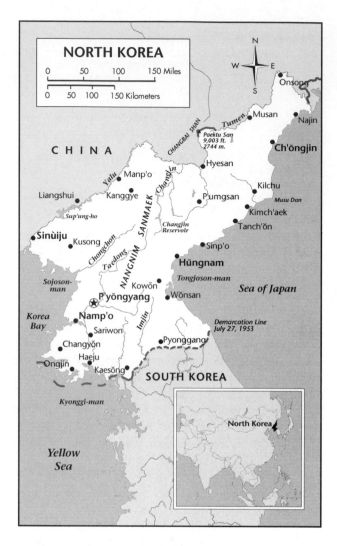

NORTH KOREA

0   50   100   150 Miles
0   50   100   150 Kilometers

CHINA

Onsong

Tumen

Musan

Najin

Paektu San
9,003 ft.
2744 m.

Ch'ŏngjin

Hyesan

Manp'o

Kilchu

P'umgsan

Musu Dan

Liangshui

Kanggye

Kimch'aek

Sup'ung-ho

Changjin
Reservoir

Tanch'ŏn

Sinŭiju

Kusong

Sinp'o

Hŭngnam

Tongjoson-man

Sojoson-man

Kowŏn

Sea of Japan

P'yŏngyang

Wŏnsan

Korea
Bay

Namp'o

Demarcation Line
July 27, 1953

Sariwon

Changyŏn

Pyonggang

Haeju

Ongjin

Kaesŏng

SOUTH KOREA

Kyonggi-man

North Korea

Yellow
Sea

gave Koreans a sense of awe and of the divine. The Koreanization of the clergy and visible involvement of Catholic priests and laity, especially young people, in the struggle for justice lent credibility to the whole Church. Priests in general became regarded as trustworthy persons, and Cardinal Kim was perceived by many as the most trustworthy person in the nation. Furthermore, the sense of insecurity following the Kwangju massacre helped turn many Koreans to religion. The Catholic laity, organized in the parishes into neighborhood groups or into lay organizations such as the Legion of Mary, were zealous in evangelizing the non-Christian Koreans. The Church enhanced its prestige by holding two huge events involving papal visits: the two hundredth anniversary of the birth of the Catholic Church in Korea, held in 1984, and the Eucharistic Congress in 1989. These large celebrations fitted in with the mood of the nation hosting the Asian Games in 1986 and the Olympic Games in 1988.

Ecumenical Collaboration. From the 1990s onwards, Christians comprised almost half of the South Korean population, and are strongly represented in all parts of society. This was the result of Christianity's rapid growth after religious freedom was granted in 1883. A sizeable proportion of Christians are Presbyterians and Methodists, followed by the Roman Catholics. Charismatic movements have attracted many Korean Christians. The Protestant charismatics have often formed around a charismatic leader, such as the case of Cho Yonggi, founder of the Full Gospel Central Church in 1958, which grew rapidly to over 250,000 members by the 1980s and eventually began sending out missionaries internationally. In other cases charismatic healers have set up prayer houses for faith healing, and have attracted huge numbers of the sick or of penitents. In the Catholic Church the charismatic movement is much more subdued and has for the most part been incorporated into the parish or diocesan structure. On the other hand, suspicious private revelations have influenced many of the Korean faithful, both Protestant and Catholic, and several Catholic priests have been suspended for promoting them.

Ecumenical collaboration between Protestants and Catholics in Korea has been slow for a number of reasons. Catholics and Protestants use a different name for God. They have produced a common translation of the New Testament, but it has been adopted widely only in the Catholic Church. The Catholic Church is generally tolerant and open, but many Protestant groups attack the Catholic Church, and some even attack other Protestant churches. This divisiveness is often associated with competition for members. One of the few areas of ecumenical collaboration has been among Christians engaged together in the social movements for justice.

Bibliography: C. DALLET, *Histoire de l'Église de Corée*, 2 v. (Paris 1874). E. FOURER, *La Corée: Martyrs et missionaires* (Nancy 1895). *The Catholic Church in Korea* (Hong Kong 1924). F. DE-MANGE, "Centenaire de l'érection de la Corée en Vicariat Apostolique (1831-1931)," *Revue d'histoire des missions* 8 (1931) 387-415. COREANUS, "La Préhistoire de l'Église de Corée," *ibid.* 11 (1934) 203-220. J. LAURES, "Koreas erste Berührung mit dem Christentum," *Zeitschrift für Missionswissenschaft und Religionswissenschaft* 40 (1956) 177-189, 282-287. YU HONG-NYOL, *History of the Catholic Church in Korea* (Seoul 1962), in Korean. C. KIM and J. CHONG, *Catholic Korea Yesterday and Today* (Seoul 1963), in Korean. W.E. BIERNATZKI, *Korean Catholicism in the 1970s: A Christian Community Comes of Age* (New York 1975). NYUNG KIM, *The Politics of Religion in South Korea, 1974-1989: The Catholic Church's Political Opposition to the Authoritarian State* (Pullman WA 1993). J.G. RUIZ DE MEDINA, *Origenes de la Iglesia católica coreana desde 1566 hasta 1784* (Rome 1986). Kwangju Archdiocese Catholic Justice and Peace Research Institute, *Hankuk Kat'olik Kyohoiwa Sowoichung Kurigo Sahoi Undong* (Kwangju 1990). KWANG CHO, *Hankuk Chunjukyo 200 Nyun* (Seoul 1989). SOK WU CH'OI, *Hankuk Chunjukyohoiui Yoksa* (Seoul 1982). OK HUI KIM, *Hankuk Chunjukyo Yosongsa* (Masan 1983).

[C. A. HERBST/M. S. PARK/EDS.]

KOŠICE, MARTYRS OF, SS.

Melichar Grodziecký, Marek Križín, and Stefan Pongrácz; priests, martyrs; d. Sept. 7 and 8, 1619 at Košice in the far eastern portion of Slovakia; beatified 1905; canonized by Pope John Paul II, July 2, 1995 at the airport of Košice.

Košice was a Calvinist stronghold in the early seventeenth century. These martyrs came from three countries in order to offer the sacraments to Catholics who were otherwise without priests. The king's deputy petitioned the Jesuits to send priests to tend to the minority population and gratefully housed the two respondents in his official residence outside the city. Protestant antipathy toward Catholicism increased. Upon hearing that the Calvinist prince of Transylvania was approaching Košice under Georg I Rákóczi, the Jesuits hurried back to the city to be with their flock and were joined by the canon Križín. On the morning of September 7, soldiers tried to force them into apostasy. Upon their refusal, the priests were brutally beaten and killed. Their bodies were thrown into a sewage ditch, where they remained for six months before a pious countess was given permission to bury them. Immediately after death, they became the objects of veneration. Their relics are now housed in the Ursuline church at Trnava, Croatia.

Melichar Grodziecký, also known as Melchior Grodech or Grodecz, Jesuit priest; b. ca. 1584, in Grodziec (a village between Biesko and Cieszyn), Silesia, Poland. Melichar was born into a noble family and had Bishop John of Olomouc as an uncle. Melichar was educated by the Jesuits at Vienna, Austria. After joining the Society of Jesus at Brno, Moravia (1603), which was founded by his uncle John, he studied philosophy and theology, was ordained (1614), and worked as a teacher in Prague. At the outbreak of the Thirty Years' War, he passed through Moravia and Slovakia, finally settling in Košice. Following the initial beating, Fr. Melichar was stripped, tortured, and finally he was mercifully beheaded.

Marek Križín, also known as Mark Crisin, Korosy, or Križevčanin, diocesan priest, administrator of Széplak Abbey; b. 1588 at Križevci, Croatia. Born into a noble Croatian family, he was educated by the Jesuits in Vienna and Graz, where he earned a doctorate in philosophy, and at the Germanicum (1611–1615) in Rome. Following ordination in Rome, he ministered for two years in his homeland. Then his former professor in Graz, Cardinal Pázmány, appointed him head of the Trnava seminary and a canon of the Esztergom Cathedral (Hungary). In 1619, he accepted assignment as administrator of the property of the former Benedictine abbey of Krásna near Košice in the hope of stimulating the faith there. In the face of persecution he remained at the service of his

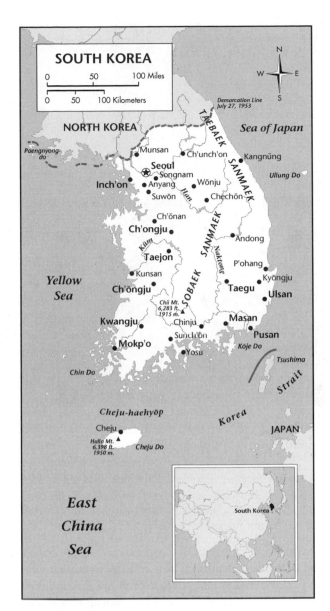

flock, offering an example of fidelity to Christ. Križín, to whom the attention of the soldiers had first turned, suffered the same tortures as Grodziecký. When Križín fainted from the pain, he was beheaded.

Stefan (Stephen) Pongrácz, Jesuit priest; b. ca. 1582 at Alvincz Castle, Transylvania, Hungary. Born into a noble family, he studied classics in his homeland, then attended the Jesuit College at Cluj, Romania, and abandoned the prospect of a brilliant, secular career in order to enter the Society of Jesus at Brno, Moravia (1602), where he first met Grodziecký. Following his studies in philosophy at Prague (Bohemia) and theology at Graz (Austria), he was ordained in 1615. He taught for a time at the Jesuit college at Humenné, Slovakia, before accepting the invitation to minister in troubled Košice. Despite

Exterior of The Immaculate Conception Cathedral, Seoul, South Korea.

savage and prolonged torture, Pongrácz' was alive when the soldiers threw him into the sewage ditch with his dead companions. He suffered in pain for another 20 hours before giving up his spirit.

During the canonization ceremony the Holy Father noted: ''This canonization was also an important ecumenical event, as was evident both at my meeting with representatives of the Protestant denominations and during my visit to the place that commemorates the death of a group of the faithful of the Reformation.'' He prayed at the monument commemorating their death.

On first glance it is difficult to reconcile Pope John Paul II's efforts toward Christian unity and this canonization of three martyrs of the Reformation. But as he explained it in his homily:

> Today's liturgy invites us to reflect on the tragic events of the early seventeenth century, emphasizing, on the one hand, the senselessness of violence relentlessly visited upon innocent victims and, on the other, the splendid example of so many followers of Christ who were able to face sufferings of every kind without going against their own consciences. Besides the three Martyrs of Košice many other people, also belonging to Christian confessions, were subjected to torture and suf-

fered heavy punishment; some were even put to death. How can we fail to acknowledge, for example, the spiritual greatness of the 24 members of the Evangelical Churches who were killed at Presov? To them and to all who accepted suffering and death out of fidelity to the dictates of their conscience the Church gives praise and expresses admiration. . . . May [the example of the three new saints] renew in their fellow citizens of today a commitment to mutual understanding.

Feast: Sept. 7 (Jesuit calendar).

Bibliography: *L'Osservatore Romano,* English edition, 27 (1995): 1–3; 28 (1995) 6, 11; 29 (1995) 9. J. N. TYLENDA, *Jesuit Saints and Martyrs* (Chicago 1998) 290–292.

[K. I. RABENSTEIN]

KOSTISTK, GEREMIA OF VALACHIA, BL.

Also known as Jeremiah or Jeremy of Valachia, and Ieremia Stoica, Capuchin; b. June 29, 1556, Zaro, Romania; d. March 5, 1625, Naples, Italy. Leaving his friary in Romania to travel to Naples, Geremia startled the locals by living in imitation of Christ for forty years. He was known for his spiritual wisdom and fraternal love for the poor and sick to whom he ministered selflessly. He fell ill while tending the sick and died at age sixty-eight. Pope John Paul II beatified him on Oct. 30, 1983, as the first Romanian so recognized officially.

Feast: May 8.

Bibliography: F. S. TOPPI, *Spirito francescano nel beato Geremia Stoica da Valacchia, Studi e Ricerche Francescane* (1984) 127–42. *Acta Apostolicae Sedis* 76 (1984): 550–53. *L'Osservatore Romano,* Eng. ed. 46 (1983): 6–7.

[K. I. RABENSTEIN]

KOSTKA, STANISLAUS, ST.

Patron of Poland; b. Rostkovo, Poland, Oct. 28, 1550; d. Rome, Italy, Aug. 15, 1568. He was the second of seven children, born into the high Polish nobility. His training at home was religious, exacting, and firm. At 14 he and his elder brother Paul enrolled in the Jesuit college in Vienna. Stanislaus's early desire for holiness intensified and he showed great constancy in his practice of prayer and penance. This annoyed Paul who treated Stanislaus with brutality. Stanislaus seemed to receive some unusual spiritual favors. On one occasion, when seriously sick, he saw angels, attended by St. Barbara, patron of his sodality at school, bringing him Holy Communion. He also beheld the Blessed Virgin, holding the Christ Child and advising him to enter the Society of Jesus. The Jesuit superior at Vienna was reluctant to admit him into the society because of the possible wrath of his father, so Stanislaus decided to apply elsewhere. He left Vienna and, after successfully eluding his brother, who pursued him, he walked to Dillingen in Germany where he met St. Peter CANISIUS, the German provincial. Canisius sent him to Rome where he was admitted to the novitiate of St. Andrew on Oct. 28, 1567, by the General, St. Francis BORGIA. In the ten remaining months of his life all were impressed by his earnest and childlike fervor. In early August of 1568, he seemed to foresee his death. On the tenth he became ill and died within the week. He was canonized in 1726.

Feast: Nov. 13.

Bibliography: D. BARTOLI, *Compendio della vita del B. Stanislao Kostka,* ed. C. GROSSI (Turin 1925). J. E. KERNS, *Portrait of a Champion: A Life of St. Stanley Kostka* (Westminster, Md. 1957). J. MAJKOWSKI, *Saint Stanislaus Kostka. A Psychological Hagiography* (Rome 1972). U. UBALDINI, *Analecta Bollandiana,* 9 (1890) 360–378.

[W. V. BANGERT]

A priest and nuns stand amid a group of toddlers outside Maryknoll Kindergarten in Seoul, Korea, 1946. (©Horace Bristol/CORBIS)

KOUDELKA, JOSEPH MARIA

Bishop; b. Chlistovo, Bohemia, Dec. 8, 1852; d. Superior, Wis., June 24, 1921. At 13, after education at the college at Klattau, Bohemia, he immigrated with his parents to the U.S. and settled near Manitowoc, Wis. He continued his studies at St. Francis Seminary, Milwaukee, Wis., became a naturalized citizen, and was ordained Oct. 8, 1875. After pastoral work at St. Prokopius Church, Cleveland, Ohio, until 1882, he served (1882–83) as editor of *Hlas*, a Bohemian magazine published in St. Louis, and then returned to Cleveland as pastor of St. Michael's (1883–1907), where he built the parish church and school.

He prepared the first, second, and third readers (in German) for Bohemian schools (1882), wrote a short history of the Catholic Church for Catholic schools (1905), and compiled prayer books for adults and children. He spoke German, Polish, Bohemian, and English and had a command of the classical languages. When Bp. Ignatius Horstmann asked for an auxiliary bishop in Cleveland to care for the foreign populace, especially the Slavic peoples, Koudelka was appointed Nov. 29, 1907, and consecrated bishop of Germanicopolis Feb. 25, 1908. He was the first auxiliary bishop of special jurisdiction appointed in the U.S., and he served in Cleveland until Sept. 4, 1911, when he was transferred to Milwaukee as auxiliary to Abp. S. G. Messmer.

On Aug. 1, 1913, Koudelka was appointed second bishop of the Diocese of Superior, where, during his eight-year administration, ten parish churches, 22 missions, three hospitals, two high schools, five elementary schools, two industrial schools, and one orphanage were built. The Catholic population increased from 53,130 to 57,514; the number of priests serving the diocese, from 86 to 98. Among the most noted buildings erected under Koudelka was the St. Joseph Orphanage in Superior, with its imitation baroque chapel, much of which was financed by the missions and retreats Koudelka gave across the nation. He was buried at St. Michael's, his former parish in Cleveland, and his remains are interred in St. Mary's cemetery there.

[V. E. RUSH]

KOWALSKA, FAUSTINA, ST.

Baptized Elena (or Helena), in religion Maria Faustina (Polish: Faustyna), visionary, virgin of the Congregation of the Blessed Virgin Mary of Mercy; b. Aug. 25, 1905, at Głogowiec (west of Łodz), Poland; d. Oct. 5, 1938, at Kraków.

Known as the apostle of Divine Mercy, Faustina was the third of ten children (six survived infancy) in a poor family. Although she had only two years of formal education, her diaries exhibit profound insight. She was baptized at St. Casimir's, Swinice Warckie; at age 7 (1912), she first heard Jesus in an inner locution inviting her to strive for perfection. In 1922, she expressed a desire to

The embroidered drapery with an image of sister Faustina Kowalska hangs on the facade of St. Peter's Basilica April 30, 2000. Pope John Paul II made her his first canonization of the Catholic Jubilee year. (©APF/CORBIS)

enter the convent, but, because her parents needed her financial help, she worked as a housekeeper in Aleksandrów, Łodz, and Ostrówek. At age 29, she first attempted to enter a convent in Warsaw, but was turned away. Following a vision of the suffering Christ, she entered the Sisters of the Blessed Virgin Mary of Mercy Aug. 1, 1925, and changed her name. After her postulancy at a vacation house and novitiate in Kraków, she made her temporary vows April 30, 1928. Faustina professed her final vows in 1933 before Bishop Stanislaus Rospond of Kraków. Thereafter, she served her sisters as an unassuming cook, gardener, and porter in the congregation's houses at Kraków, Płock, and Vilnius.

On Feb. 22, 1931, in Płock, Faustina had a vision of Jesus, asking her to promote the Second Sunday of Easter as a celebration of Divine Mercy and spread the devotion throughout the world. After a psychiatric assessment certified Faustina's mental health, Father Michael Sopocko, her spiritual director, arranged for artist Kazimierowski to render a painting of her vision of Jesus as the merciful savior with streams of red and white light shining from his heart. Faustina kept a journal of her mystical experiences. Only a few of her superiors, her confessor, and spiritual director knew of her visions, revelations, hidden stigmata, and gifts of ubiquity, reading souls, and prophecy. A poor translation of her nearly 700-page diary was condemned by the Vatican in 1958. However, when popular veneration of Faustina continued, Cardinal Karol Wojtyła had it re-translated, which resulted in the ban's removal April 15, 1978, six months before his election to the papacy. In visions Christ also asked the humble sister to propagate the Chaplet of Divine Mercy, veneration of the Divine Mercy image inscribed ''Jesus, I trust in You,'' and the remembrance of his death each day at 3 P.M.

Faustina, the inspiration for the Polish Apostles of Divine Mercy, died from tuberculosis. The movement comprised of priests, religious, and laity has spread to 29 countries. Pope John Paul II made a pilgrimage to Faustina's tomb at the Sanctuary of Divine Mercy in Kraków-Łagiewniki June 7, 1997, where she died and which the young Wojtyła visited daily before work at the Solvay factory.

Her cause for beatification was reopened in Rome Jan. 30, 1968. Faustina was both beatified April 18, 1993, and canonized April 30, 2000, by John Paul II, whose lifelong efforts to propagate devotion to the Divine Mercy (see DIVES IN MISERICORDIA, 1980) culminated when he officially declared April 30, 2000, that the Second Sunday of Easter would also be designated ''Divine Mercy Sunday'' throughout the Church.

Feast: Oct. 5.

Bibliography: Writings by St. Faustina: *Diary: Divine Mercy in My Soul* (3d rev. ed. Stockbridge, Mass. 2000); *Revelations of Divine Mercy: Daily Readings from the Diary of Blessed Faustina Kowalska,* ed. G. W. KOSICKI (Ann Arbor, Mich. 1996). Literature about St. Faustina: J. BURKUS, *Gaila minios* (Hot Springs, Ark. 1983). G. W. KOSICKI, *Now Is the Time for Mercy* (Stockbridge, Mass. 1991); *Meet Saint Faustina* (Ann Arbor, Mich. 2001). MARIAN FATHERS, *The Promise* (Stockbridge, Mass. 1987). S. MICHALENKO, *The Life of Faustina Kowalska* (Ann Arbor, Mich. 1999). C. M. ODELL, *Faustina: Apostle of Divine Mercy* (Huntington, Ind. 1998). S. URBANSKI, *Zycie mistyczne błogoslawionej Faustyny Kowalskiej* (Warsaw 1997).

[K. I. RABENSTEIN]

KOZAL, MICHAŁ, BL.

Bishop, martyr of Dachau; b. Sept. 27, 1893, Ligota (now Nowy Folwark near Poznán), Poland; d. Jan. 26, 1943, Dachau Concentration Camp. Kozal was born into a devout peasant family. Following his ordination to the priesthood (1918), he held parish assignments while teaching in Catholic secondary schools. In August 1939, Kozal was appointed by Pope Pius XII auxilary bishop of Wloclawek, Poland, then named bishop. During the short time between his consecration and arrest in which he could celebrate only a single Mass, Kozal was responsible for sending to safety Stefan Wyszynski. Kozal was arrested by the Gestapo on Nov. 7, 1939 as part of the Nazi drive to eradicate the Polish intelligentsia and elite. He was held for a time in a Wloclawek prison, then sent to a convent in Lad. Following stops in Szczeglin and Berlin, Kozal was interned at Dachau (April 25, 1941). For the next two years he secretly celebrated Mass whenever possible and ministered to his fellow prisoners. He was killed with an injection of carbolic acid. Bp. Kozal was beatified at Warsaw, Poland, by John Paul II, June 14, 1987.

Feast: June 14.

Bibliography: S. BISKUPSKI, *Meczénskie biskupstwo ksiedza Michala Kozala; bararzynstwo hitlerowskie w walce z Kósciolem Katolickim w Polsce* (2d. ed. Warsaw 1955). T. BOJARSKA, *Cierniowa mitra* (Warsaw 1971). W. FRATCZAK, *Biskup Michal Kozal: zycie-meczénstwo-kult* (Warsaw 1987). F. KORSZYNSKI, *Un vescovo polacco a Dachau* (Brescia 1963). *Nuremberg War Crimes Trial Proceedings,* v. 4, 511. *L'Osservatore Romano,* Eng. ed. 23 (1987): 12.

[K. I. RABENSTEIN]

KOZKA, KAROLINA, BL.

Virgin martyr for purity, lay woman; b. Aug. 2, 1898, Wal-Ruda, Poland; d. there Nov. 18, 1914. The fourth of the eleven children of the farmers Jan Kozka and Maria Borzecka, vivacious Karolina developed an intense prayer life at an early age. She was dragged into the woods and killed by one of the occupying Russian soldiers after she rejected his advances. When her body was found nearly three weeks later, it was interred in the churchyard at Zabawa (Dec. 6, 1914). Her relics were translated in November 1917 and a cross erected at the execution site. Pope John Paul II beatified her at Tarnów, Poland, June 10, 1987.

Bibliography: *Acta Apostolicae Sedis* (1987) 739. *L'Osservatore Romano,* Eng. ed. 29 (1987) 3–5.

[K. I. RABENSTEIN]

KÓZMÍNSKI, HONORAT, BL.

Baptized Florence Wenceslaus John Kózmínski (or Kózmínskiego), also known as Honorat a Biala, architect, Capuchin, founder; b. Oct. 16, 1829, Biala Podlaska, Poland; d. Dec. 16, 1916, Nowe Miasto, Poland. Kózmínski was the second of four children of an affluent architect and his pious spouse. Following in his father's footsteps, he studied architecture at the Warsaw School of Fine Arts. Kózmínski's faith failed at his father's death in 1845, but was reinvigorated during his internment (1846–47) on a false charge of treason against the Russian occupation and subsequent illness. He became a Capuchin December of 1848, received the name Honorat, and was ordained Dec. 8, 1852. Thereafter he preached and served as spiritual director in Warsaw. Under the Russian occupation, he founded more than 20 associations and congregations, including the Circles of the Living Rosary and the Sister Servants of Mary Immaculate (1878). Most of these groups were reorganized by the Polish hierarchy in 1908. Among the surviving organizations is the Franciscan Sisters of Saint Felix of Cantalice (FELICIANS), founded by Mother Angela TRUSZKOWSKA under the spiritual direction of Blessed Honorat, who witnessed the dedication of the initial Felician sisters on Nov. 21, 1855. Although Honorat was placed under house arrest at Zakroczym monastery during the Russian period of suppression, he continued to provide spiritual direction. From 1892 to 1895, Kózmínski ministered at Nowe Miasto until he was appointed commissary for the Polish Capuchins. He died following a painful illness. Pope John Paul II beatified Honorat Oct. 16, 1988.

Bibliography: *Dziedzictwo bl. Honorata Kózmínskiego,* ed. H. I. SZUMIL and G. BARTOSZEWSKIEGO (Sandomierz 1998). C.-C. BILLOT, *Honorat Kozminski* (Blois, France 1982). W. KLUZ, *Ziarnko gorczycy: o Honorat Kózmínski OFMCap* (Warsaw 1987). F. DA RIESE PIO X, *Onorato Kózmínski da Biala Podlaska: un polacco che visse sempre in piedi* (Rome 1976). M. SZYMULA, *Duchowóśc zakonna: duchowóśc zakonna wedlug nauczania bl. Honorata Kózmínskiego* (2d. ed. Warsaw 1999). M. A. WERNER, *O. Honorat Kóz-*

mínski, kapucyn (Poznan 1972). *Acta Apostolicae Sedis* (1988) 1173.

[K. I. RABENSTEIN]

KRAMP, JOSEPH

Liturgist; b. Kerpen, Rhineland, June 19, 1886; d. Frankfurt, June 14, 1940. He joined the Society of Jesus in 1905. During World War I he served as a chaplain in German army hospitals. For a short while he taught in Bombay but returned to Germany because of poor health. From 1928 to 1940, though he lived the life of a quiet scholar in Frankfurt, he exerted an especially strong influence on the Catholic German youth movement. In the field of his special competence, pre-Tridentine theology, he published ten major and minor works, several of which have been translated. He won international recognition for his work *Eucharistia* (Freiburg 1924; English tr. St. Paul, Minn. 1926). In it he offers the first analysis of the late medieval changes of attitude toward the Eucharist. His published writings also include: *Die Opferanschauungen der römishen Messliturgie* (Regensburg 1920), *Mess. liturgie and Opfergedanken* (Regensburg 1921), and *Messliturgie und Gottesreich* in three volumes (Freiburg 1921). A great part of his endeavor was given to a study of the Liturgical Year. Avoiding the then prevalent tendency to moralize, his method consisted in a careful analysis of the liturgical texts. His books also show a remarkable eschatological tendency long before this became common in the writings of other liturgists. Unfortunately, because of his daring interpretation of the sacrificial character of the Mass, he was excluded from academic offices.

[H. A. REINHOLD]

KRAUS, FRANZ XAVER

Church and art historian; b. Trier, Germany, Sept. 18, 1840; d. San Remo, Italy, Dec. 28, 1901. He was ordained in 1864; he became professor of the history of Christian art at Strassburg in 1872, and of Church history at Freiburg im Breisgau in 1878. As a leader of the liberal wing of Catholic scholars, he criticized the centralization of Church government and the Ultramontanes (see ULTRAMONTANISM) and attempted to provide a reconciliation between Catholicism and modern culture, as well as between Church and State in the KULTURKAMPF difficulties. He was a Dante scholar and essayist who raised Christian archeology and art history to independent disciplines in Germany. His diaries are important for the history of the Church in the 19th century. His *Lehrbuch der*

Kirchengeschichte went through four editions (Trier 1872–96) during his lifetime. He produced the two-volume *Realencyklopädie der christl. Altertümer* (Freiburg 1883–86); the *Geschichte der christl. Kunst* in two volumes (Freiburg 1895–1900), and several studies of ancient Christian art and inscriptions in Alsace-Lorraine and the Rhineland. His diaries (*Tagebücher*) were published by H. Schiel (Cologne 1957).

Bibliography: C. BRAIG, *Zur Erinnerung an F. X. Kraus* (Freiburg 1902). H. SCHIEL, *Im Spannungsfeld von Kirche und Politik: F. X. Kraus* (Trier 1951); *F. X. Kraus und die Katholische Tübinger Schule* (Ellwangen 1958). H. TRITZ, ''F. X. Kraus und P. M. A. Hughes,'' *Spicilegium Historicum Congregationis SSmi Redemptoris* 11 (1963) 182–232.

[H. SCHIEL]

KRAUTH, CHARLES PORTERFIELD

Lutheran leader and theologian; b. Martinsburg, Va., March 17, 1823; d. Philadelphia, Pa., Jan. 2, 1883. After education at Gettysburg College and Theological Seminary, Pa., where his father, Charles Philip Krauth, was professor, he became pastor of churches in Maryland, Virginia, and Pennsylvania. In 1859 he moved to Philadelphia, where he was made editor of the *Lutheran,* and in its weekly columns he championed the conservative teachings and practices that were characteristic of the confessional revival of the mid-19th century. Krauth was a man of great learning and contributed to a variety of theological journals. When the Lutheran Theological Seminary was founded in Philadelphia (1864), he was elected professor of systematic theology. He was the leading organizer and first president of the General Council (1867), into which he hoped to gather all the conservative synods of English-, German-, and Scandinavian-speaking Lutherans in North America. Although his hope was only partially realized, his leadership was widely respected. His position was set forth in his major work, *The Conservative Reformation and its Theology* (1872). Besides teaching theology, Krauth was professor of philosophy at the University of Pennsylvania, Philadelphia, during his last 15 years.

Bibliography: A. SPAETH, *Charles Porterfield Krauth,* 2 v. (v.1 New York 1898; v.2 Philadelphia 1909).

[T. G. TAPPERT]

KREISLER, FRITZ

Composer and violin virtuoso; b. Vienna, Feb. 2, 1875; d. New York City, Jan. 29, 1962. He was a musical wonder child whose talent was fostered by his parents,

Fritz Kreisler. (©Hulton-Deutsch Collection/CORBIS)

Anna and Samuel Severin Kreisler, and his teachers, including Anton Bruckner and Leo Delibes. He won the Vienna Conservatory's gold medal for violin as a boy of ten, and the Paris Conservatory's grand prize at 12; at 13 he made his New York debut. Later, while working toward recognition as an adult artist, he became acquainted with Johannes BRAHMS and Joseph Joachim, whose influence on him was lasting. Kreisler's Berlin debut took place in 1899, and for the next 60 years he brought violin virtuosity to audiences the world over. In 1939 he settled in America, and in 1943 he became a U.S. citizen. He retired from the concert stage in 1950 but continued to play for charitable causes, as had been his lifelong custom. His funeral took place at St. John the Evangelist Church, New York City.

Loved by audiences and revered by critics and colleagues, Kreisler also enriched the violin repertory as composer and arranger. Early in his career he published as transcriptions of 17th- and 18th-century masters, such as Vivaldi and Couperin, works that were later revealed to be his own. He composed concertos, chamber music, violin and piano solos, operettas, and cadenzas for Mozart, Beethoven, and Brahms concertos. His best-known works are *Caprice viennois, Liebesfreud, Tambourin chinois,* the operetta *Apple Blossoms,* and the Quartet in A-minor.

The Benedettini Room in the Kremsmünster Abbey Library. (©Massimo Listri/CORBIS)

Bibliography: L. P. LOCHNER, *Fritz Kreisler* (New York 1951). M. PINCHERLE, *The World of the Virtuoso,* tr. L. H. BROCKWAY (New York 1963). *New York Times* (Jan. 30, 1962) 1:4. H. JANCICK, *Die Musik in Geschichte und Gegenwart,* ed. F. BLUME (Kassel-Basel 1949–) 7:1742–43. *Baker's Biographical Dictionary of Musicians,* ed. N. SLONIMSKY (5th, rev. ed. New York 1958) 869. AMY BIANCOLLI, *Fritz Kreisler: Love's Sorrow, Love's Joy* (Portland 1998). D. M. RANDEL, ed., *The Harvard Biographical Dictionary of Music* (Cambridge 1996) 467. B. SCHWARZ, "Fritz Kreisler" in *The New Grove Dictionary of Music and Musicians, vol. 10,* ed. S. SADIE, (New York 1980) 249–250. N. SLONIMSKY, ed. *Baker's Biographical Dictionary of Musicians, Eighth Edition* (New York 1992) 963.

[M. FITZGIBBON]

KREMSMÜNSTER, ABBEY OF

Benedictine abbey on the Krems River in the Diocese of Linz, north central Austria; dedicated to St. Agapitus. Established (777) by Duke Tassilo III of Ba-

varia with monks from Mondsee (founded before 748) and under the Carolingians from 788, it evangelized and colonized among the Slavs. Magyar invasions ended an era of brilliance, and the abbey came under the bishops of Passau *c.* 917. GORZE reforms were introduced under Abbots Sigmar (1013–40) and Dietrich (1066–85); the HIRSAU reform, under Ulrich III (1173–82). A strong Cistercian influence appeared under Friedrich von Aich (1275–1325), and Kremsmünster, with its scriptorium and famous historian Bernard (d. 1326), reached its peak. The 15th-century MELK reform brought humanist influences. In 1549 the abbey school became a Gymnasium. Monastic and intellectual life was strengthened under Erhard Voit (1571–88), Johann III (1588–1600), Alexander a Lacu (1601–13), and Anton Wolfradt (1613–39). Baroque buildings were begun under Erenbert Schrevogel (1669–1703), and the observatory was constructed (1748–58). The learned baroque poet-dramatist Simon Rettenpacher (d. 1706) illustrates Kremsmünster's activities in music and liturgical drama in the 17th and 18th centuries. A few monks remained during the Nazi occupation of the abbey (1941–45). The library of 100,000 volumes has 400 MSS; the science and art collections are noteworthy. The treasure includes the 8th-century Tassilo chalice and candlesticks and the *Codex millenarius.*

Bibliography: *Monumenta Germaniae Historica: Necrologia* (Berlin 1826–) 4:197–238. *Monumenta Germaniae Historica: Scriptores* 9:544–554; 25:610–678. T. HAGN, *Urkundenbuch für die Geschichte des Benediktiner Stiftes Kremsmünster, seiner Pfarreien und Besitzungen vom Jahre 777 bis 1400* (Vienna 1852); *Wirken der Benedictiner-Abtei Kremsmünster* (Linz 1848). *Festschrift zum 400jährigen Bestande des öffentlichen Obergymnasiums der Benedictiner zu Kremsmünster, 1549–1949* (Wels 1949). A. KELLNER, *Musikgeschichte des Stiftes Kremsmünster* (Kassel 1956). L. H. COTTINEAU, *Répertoire topobibliographique des abbayes et prieurés*, 2 v. (Mâcon 1935–39) 1:1529–30. O. L. KAPSNER, *A Benedictine Bibliography: An Author-Subject Union List*, 2 v. (2d ed. Collegeville, Minn. 1962) 2:222. W. NEUMÜLLER, *Lexikon für Theologie und Kirche*, ed. J. HOFER and K. RAHNER, 10 v. (2d, new ed. Freiburg 1957–65) 6:602.

[D. ANDREINI]

KRIŽANIĆ, JURAJ

The "Father of Pan-Slavism"; b. Oberh, Croatia, *c.* 1617; d. near Vienna, 1683. He attended the Jesuit Gymnasium in Zagreb from 1630 to 1636, studied philosophy at the University of Graz, Austria, and theology at Bologna and Rome, and after his ordination in September 1642, received a doctorate in theology. He prepared himself for the mission in which he had long been interested, converting the Russians to Catholicism. In 1647, after two years in Croatia, he traveled to Warsaw, Smolensk, and Moscow, and then went to Poland for two years. Subsequently he arrived at Vienna and visited Constantinople with an Austrian diplomatic mission. In Rome in 1652, he wrote several treatises in Latin about Russia and the Orthodox. Without permission of the Office of Propaganda he left Rome for Vienna, and by April 1659 he was in the Ukraine. In September 1659, he concealed his identity as a Catholic priest, went to Moscow, and worked for a time as a translator for the government of Tsar Alexis. In January 1661, he was exiled to Tobolsk, Siberia, where he wrote several books, notably a grammar of a proposed general Slavic language, and *Politika,* which appealed to the Tsar to unite all Slavs against the Germans. In March 1676 he was released and went to Vilna to join the Polish Dominicans. He died as a chaplain in the Polish army of King John III Sobieski during the Turkish siege of Vienna in the summer of 1683. Several of his books were published in Russia where he was hailed as a significant writer and an advocate of the ideal of Slavic solidarity.

Bibliography: P. G. SCOLARDI, *Krijanich: Messager de l'unité des chrétiens et père du panslavisme* (Paris 1947). M. B. PETROVICH,

John Joseph Krol. (Catholic News Service)

"Juraj Križaniç: A Precursor of Pan-Slavism," *American Slavic and East European Review* 6. 18–19 (1947) 75–92.

[G. J. PRPIC]

KROL, JOHN JOSEPH

Cardinal, archbishop of Philadelphia; b. Cleveland, Ohio, Oct. 26, 1910; d. Philadelphia, Pa., Mar. 3, 1996. The fifth child of John Krol Sr., a stone cutter by trade, and Anna Pietruszka, Krol received his early education at St. Hyacinth's elementary school and the Cathedral Latin School in Cleveland. Upon graduation from high school in 1927, he found employment as a meat cutter in a local market. He eventually answered God's call to the priesthood, began his studies at St. Mary's College, Orchard Lake, Mich., and completed them at St. Mary's Seminary in Cleveland. He was ordained on Feb. 20, 1937 at St. John's Cathedral in Cleveland by Bishop Joseph SCHREMBS. His first and only parochial assignment followed at Immaculate Heart of Mary Parish in Cleveland. The following year he was sent to Rome for studies in canon law. With the outbreak of World War II, he was recalled to the United States and assigned to the CATHOLIC UNIVERSITY OF AMERICA, where he completed a doctorate in CANON LAW.

In 1942 Krol returned to Cleveland and the chair of canon law at St. Mary's Seminary. At the same time, he functioned as defender of the bond, vice-chancellor, and eventually chancellor of the diocese. In 1948 he was elected president of the Canon Law Society of America. Pope PIUS XII created him Papal Chamberlain in 1945 and Domestic Prelate in 1951. In 1953 Monsignor Krol was named auxiliary bishop of Cleveland and titular bishop of Cadi. He chose as his episcopal motto *Deus Rex Meus,* a heraldic pun on his own name (*krol* is Polish for "king").

In 1960 Pope John XXIII announced his intention of summoning an ecumenical council. Bishop Krol was named to the preparatory commission on bishops and the government of dioceses. As the council years unfolded he would go on to be appointed one of the five undersecretaries of the council. He was also a member of the central coordinating committee of the council. Before the council convened, Krol was named to succeed Cardinal O'Hara as tenth ordinary of the Archdiocese of Philadelphia. He was installed on March 22, 1961. On the same day as his appointment to Philadelphia, the archdiocese was split to create the diocese of Allentown.

Archbishop Krol arrived in Philadelphia at a time of social and demographic change. Of the 39 parishes he founded, all but five were in the suburbs; of 16 parishes closed or consolidated, all but two were within the city of Philadelphia. One of Archbishop Krol's chief priorities was Catholic education. During his tenure St. Charles Borromeo Seminary received full accreditation for its college program. A student apostolate program was introduced, and a school of religious studies for religious and laity was founded. Despite the decline in enrollment during the 1970s, Krol maintained a viable archdiocesan school system. One of his most successful efforts to raise funds for the schools was the foundation of BLOCS (Business Leaders Organized for Catholic Schools). This was a non-sectarian community business effort to raise money for Catholic schools as a recognition of their value to the whole community. In 1963 Archbishop Krol was named chairman of the Education Department of the National Catholic Welfare Conference (NCWC). In 1965 he was elected vice-chairman of the administrative board of the NCWC. When the NCWC gave way to the newly organized NCCB/USCC, he was elected vice-president of the NCCB and president of the same body in 1971. As spokesman for the Catholic bishops he testified against nuclear arms and the arms race before Congress during the deliberations on the SALT Treaty of 1979.

Archbishop Krol was a strict constructionist with regard to the liturgical reforms of the Second Vatican Council. One innovation he consistently opposed was that of Saturday evening Mass. To the end of his life he battled for the sanctity of Sunday observance. In matters ecumenical, he was among the leaders of the American hierarchy. In 1964 he founded the Archbishop's Commission on Human Relations with a twofold mandate of directing the archdiocesan ecumenical movement and of promoting racial harmony in cooperation with other faith groups. His ecumenical efforts brought him recognition from the Mason's Golden Slipper Square Club in 1966 when they granted him their Brotherhood Award. In 1967 he received the first John Wesley Ecumenical Award. In 1968 he was given the Human Relations Award of the National Conference of Christians and Jews.

On June 26, 1967 Pope Paul VI named Krol to the College of Cardinals, the same day that Archbishop Karol Wojtyła received the red biretta. Krol's titular church was Santa Maria della Mercede e Sant' Adriano. He was appointed to the Congregation for the Evangelization of Peoples and the Congregation for Oriental Churches. He also served on the Prefecture of Economic Affairs of the Holy See.

In 1976 Cardinal Krol and the archdiocese hosted the Forty-first International Eucharistic Congress. During his tenure the cardinal diligently pursued the causes of Philadelphia's local heroes of the faith. He saw the canonization of St. John Neumann, CSSR, fourth bishop of Philadelphia, in June of 1977. In 1964 he opened the cause of Mother Katherine Drexel, foundress of the Sisters of the Blessed Sacrament, which ultimately led to her canonization in October of 2000.

Cardinal Krol participated in the two historic conclaves of 1978 that elected Popes John Paul I and John Paul II. In October of 1979 he welcomed John Paul II to Philadelphia on the journey that would take the pontiff to New York, Boston, Chicago, Des Moines, and Washington D.C.

Much still remains to be known about the historic collaboration between Pope JOHN PAUL II and President Ronald Reagan in the downfall of Communism in Poland during the 1980s, but there have been credible reports that the line from the Vatican to the White House ran through Philadelphia and Cardinal Krol.

The Cardinal retired from his archdiocesan duties on Feb. 11, 1988. During his retirement years, he was a moving force behind the Papal Foundation that was set up in 1988 to ease the financial burdens of the Holy See in the wake of the Banco Ambrosiano collapse. Cardinal Krol died at the archepiscopal residence on the feast day of Mother Katherine DREXEL. He is interred in the crypt of Philadelphia's Cathedral Basilica of Sts. Peter and Paul.

Bibliography: J. F. CONNOLLY, *The History of the Archdiocese of Philadelphia* (Philadelphia 1976). *The Catholic Standard* *and Times* vol. 100 (March 1996). *The American Catholic Who's Who* (Washington 1980).

[THOMAS J. MCMANUS]

KROMER, MARTIN (CROMER)

Polish bishop, humanist, historian, and diplomat; b. Biecz, near Cracow, 1515; d. Heilsberg, East Prussia, March 23, 1589. After studying at Cracow, Bologna, and Rome, he served as secretary to Bp. Gamrat of Cracow and to Prince (later King) Sigismund II August. During these years he wrote his *De origine et rebus gestis Polonorum* (1555), a history of Poland from early times down to 1506. From 1557 to 1564 he was ambassador of King Sigismund II August (1548–72) at the Imperial Court of Ferdinand I. He also served on diplomatic missions to Rome and Trent. His great work *Polonia sive de situ, populis, moribus, magistratibus et republica regni Poloniae,* appeared in 1577. He became coadjutor of Ermland (Warmia) in 1569, and succeeded as bishop in 1579. He convoked a number of synods during his tenure as bishop. Pastoral visitations, ecclesiastical reforms, and several new foundations increased under his direction. A patron of the Jesuits, he fought the Lutheran and Calvinist reformers. Kromer also wrote several books in Polish, German, and Latin for liturgical use in his diocese. He continued his lifetime interest in music, already begun in 1534 when he published *De musica figurata.* His interest in Greek and Roman studies continued throughout his life, and a translation of St. John Chrysostom's sermons was one of his early works. His own polemical writings, sermons, and catechism were written in Polish.

Bibliography: E. M. WERMTER, *Lexikon für Theologie und Kirche,* ed. J. HOFER and K. RAHNER, 10 v. (2d, new ed. Freiburg 1957–65) 6:648–649. A. EICHHORN, *Der ermländische Bishof Martin Kromer. . .* (Braunsberg 1868). A. BORRMANN, *Ermland und die Reformation 1523–1772* (Königsberg 1912). *Cambridge History of Poland,* ed. W. F. REDDAWAY et al., 2 v. (Cambridge, Eng. 1941–50).

[F. J. LADOWICZ]

KU KLUX KLAN

Two secret organizations in the U.S. have used this name. The original Klan was formed as a Southern response to Radical Reconstruction. The modern society traces its ancestry to the intolerance of the Know-Nothing Movement and the American Protective Association. The second Klan was directed against African Americans, Jews, Catholics, and other, more recent, immigrant groups. It has also been a self-appointed guardian of Americanism and of a fundamentalist code of morality.

In May 1866, six Confederate veterans in Pulaski, Tenn., formed a social club, deriving its name from the Greek word *kyklos,* or circle. When its ghostly disguises and macabre ritual unexpectedly proved frightening to blacks, Southerners discerned in the Klan a means of resistance to carpetbag-scalawag regimes supported by the votes of African-Americans. At Nashville, Tenn., in 1867, the Invisible Empire, Knights of the Ku Klux Klan, was organized under the former Confederate cavalry leader Nathan Bedford Forrest as grand wizard. The empire was divided into realms (states governed by grand dragons), provinces (counties governed by grand titans), and dens (local units governed by grand cyclopses). A prescript setting forth the aims of the order referred to chivalry and patriotism but meant the reestablishment of white supremacy.

During the height of its reign, from 1868 to 1871, the Klan could boast of a membership of 550,000. In white robes and masked by hoods, Klansmen rode at night to terrorize African-Americans with ghostly tricks. When fear did not succeed, lynching, whipping, and other forms of violence were employed. Congress responded in 1871 by enacting the Ku Klux Act, designed to break up the organization. But the Klan had already begun to decline, as its leaders became alarmed at irresponsible criminal acts protected by Klan secrecy. The Klan disbanded locally, however, only after its purpose was accomplished or when it became possible to work openly for its objectives. Not until 1877 did the Klan entirely disappear, leaving behind a legend of heroic defense of Southern rights.

In 1915, on Stone Mountain, near Atlanta, Ga., a second Ku Klux Klan was founded by Col. William J. Simmons. As imperial wizard, Simmons developed an elaborate ritual and nomenclature based on that of the old Klan. In 1921 a professional publicity man, Edward Young Clarke, was hired to build up the membership. With the help of Elizabeth Tyler, Clarke conducted a campaign that enrolled five million members by 1924. The Klan's sudden appeal can be ascribed to post–World War I developments: extreme nationalism, economic depression, moral breakdown, and antiradical hysteria. The Klan blamed each of these problems on one of its numerous targets—African-Americans, Jews, Catholics, foreigners, violators of the Klan's moral code—and offered as antidote a self-advertised gentile, Protestant, American, white man's organization.

As the society grew, its activities were no longer confined to parading and cross burning. The New York *World* revealed lynchings, mutilations, tar-and-feather parties, and assorted varieties of violence that could be traced to the Klan. A moral scandal involving Clarke and

Ku Klux Klan members marching down Pennsylvania Avenue in Washington, D.C., 1920s.

Mrs. Tyler was unearthed, and the disclosure of huge profits from the sale of memberships and costumes cast doubt on the promoters' motives. Simmons, Clarke, and Tyler were ousted when a Texas dentist, Hiram Wesley Evans, became imperial wizard. Under Evans the Klan concentrated its efforts upon attaining political power. Governors in Georgia, Alabama, and Texas furthered Klan interests, while in Oregon a Klan-dominated legislature enacted a law against parochial schools.

The Klan never enjoyed lasting influence at the national or even state level. Its principal power lay in local politics, and even there the society soon began to disintegrate. The Klan was discredited by the conviction of its Indiana grand dragon on a charge of murder and undermined by the return of prosperity and the collapse of postwar reaction. It retained enough strength to play a role in the defeat of Alfred E. Smith in the election of 1928, but by 1930 its membership had fallen to 30,000. During the 1930s the Klan tried to recoup its fortunes by attacking Bolshevism, which it virtually equated with such labor unions as the CIO, but by 1944 the order was forced to dissolve to elude payment of $685,000 in federal taxes. In 1946 Dr. Samuel J. Green revived the order, but met with effective resistance when most states enacted anti-Klan legislation and the U.S. Department of Justice placed the Klan's name on its subversive list. After Green's death the invisible empire split asunder. The Klan revived to some extent because of the Supreme Court antisegregation decision of 1954 and the nomination of a Catholic presidential candidate in 1960. However, it has been largely supplanted by the White Citizens Councils, which generally denounce Klan secrecy and terrorism. The Klan's status today is one of widespread disrepute.

Bibliography: E. M. COULTER, *The South During Reconstruction 1865–1877* (Baton Rouge 1947). H. CARTER, *The Angry Scar* (Garden City 1959). J. M. MECKLIN, *The Ku Klux Klan* (New York 1924). S. F. HORN, *Invisible Empire* (Boston 1939). A. S. RICE, *The Ku Klux Klan in American Politics* (Washington 1962). W. H. FISH-

ER, *Invisible Empire: A Bibliography of the Ku Klux Klan* (Metuchen, N.J. 1980).

[J. L. MORRISON]

KUHN, JOHANNES

Theologian; b. Wäschenbeuren, Germany, Feb. 19, 1806; d. Tübingen, May 8, 1887. He studied theology at the University of Tübingen and was ordained in 1831. At Munich he studied philosophy under F. SCHELLING. He was professor of the exegesis of the New Testament at Giessen in 1832, and at Tübingen in 1837. From 1839 to 1882 he was professor of dogma at Tübingen. In 1856, he became a permanent member of the state tribunal, and in 1868, a member of the Board of Peers. As a philosophically endowed and skilled dialectician, he wrote *Das Leben Jesu* (Mainz 1838), against D. F. Strauss's *Leben Jesu Kritisch bearbeitet*. His most famous work is the four volume *Katholische Dogmatik* (Tübingen 1846–68). Kuhn showed the development of each truth of faith in accordance with the historical character of revelation, and sought to understand it speculatively through the dialectics that he had shaped in his discussions with G. W. F. HEGEL (d. 1831). Revelation is given us in Scripture and tradition; the norm of Christian faith is living tradition. Through opposition to heresies, faith develops in a dialectical process that is not only logical but also real and historical, and that eventually brings opposites to a real unity. The scientific dialectic of dogmatic theology proceeds from a knowledge of facts to a knowledge of their necessity.

Bibliography: P. SCHANZ, "Zur Erinnerung an Johannes E. von Kuhn," *Theologische Quartalschrift* 69 (1887) 531–598. F. A. SCHALCK, *Dictionnaire de théologie catholique*, ed. A. VACANT, 15 v. (Paris 1903–50; Tables générales 1951–) 8.2:2377–79. R. VATTER, *Das Verhältnis von Trinität und Vernunft nach Johannes E. von Kuhn* (Speyer, Ger. 1940). J. R. GEISELMANN, *Die lebendige Überlieferung als Norm des christlichen Glaubens* (Freiburg 1959); *Lexikon für Theologie und Kirche*, ed. J. HOFER and K. RAHNER, 10 v. (2d, new ed. Freiburg 1957–65) 6:656–657.

[J. R. GEISELMANN]

KULTURKAMPF

Church-State conflict in Prussia and other states in GERMANY, in Austria, and in Switzerland (1871–90). It became known as the Kulturkampf (struggle for civilization) after Rudolf Virchow, an atheist and materialist scientist, thus described it (Jan. 17, 1873) in the Prussian Landtag, where he represented the German Liberal party. The term is misleading because the struggle developed from a complex of causes.

Antecedents. The dispute began in Prussia and had its main center there. This predominantly Protestant terri-

tory had been the scene of a major Church-State conflict concerning mixed marriages during the 1830s (*see* COLOGNE, MIXED MARRIAGE DISPUTE IN). King Frederick William IV (1840–61) ended this disagreement, and for the duration of his long reign granted considerable freedom to Catholics, permitting the Church to prosper. For nearly three decades after the settlement of the Cologne affair, Prussian Catholics enjoyed a liberty superior to that in most other sections of Germany, although intolerance continued to be the rule in many German principalities under Protestant rulers. State control of religion was common, even in Catholic states such as Bavaria. From about the mid-19th century, however, opposition to the Church in Prussia was on the increase from diverse quarters and for a variety of reasons. Part of it was confessional. Protestant hostility tended to subside until 1850, but became much more pronounced after that because of growing Catholic activity and demands for further liberties. The marked progress of ULTRAMONTANISM, the increasing influence of the PAPACY in Germany and elsewhere, and finally the solemn definitions of papal primacy and infallibility at VATICAN COUNCIL I (1870) disturbed many Protestants. So did the writings of DÖLLINGER and others against Luther and the Reformation. The growing practice of recruiting membership in various kinds of societies along sectarian lines further separated Protestants and Catholics. There were unfounded fears of an imminent Catholic offensive.

German LIBERALISM became very hostile to Catholicism. After the revolution in 1848, liberalism in Germany developed along lines more philosophical than political and fell under the influence of HEGELIANISM and its views on the unlimited power of the state. The liberal outlook was materialistic and antiecclesiastical. To speed the process of laicizing society, secularizing education, and eliminating all religious influences from public and private life, the liberals advocated a return to Prussia's former practices of state control over religion. Middle-class financial and industrial interests, strong supporters of liberalism, objected also to the progressive social views of Bp. Wilhelm von KETTELER and the CENTER PARTY. The naturalistic liberal view of the world and of man was so diametrically opposed to the Catholic one that the struggle between them could be regarded, in part at least, as a Kulturkampf. The SYLLABUS OF ERRORS (1864) served to widen the gulf between liberals and Catholics.

Nationalistic and political factors were also part of the background of the Kulturkampf. In the drive to unify Germany, Catholics favored the inclusion of Austria, whereas Protestants sided with Bismarck in the successful move to eliminate this great Catholic power from united Germany and to make Protestant Prussia the leading state. Germanism was portrayed as the equivalent of Protestantism and Prussianism.

Solidarity among Catholics increased with the mounting offensive against them. Prussian Catholics took the lead in organizing themselves for political, social, and religious purposes. The formation of the Center party in 1870 was the best-known manifestation of this trend. One of its effects, however, was to stimulate the opposition.

Otto von Bismarck was the person most responsible for inaugurating the Kulturkampf. His motives were both religious and political. He misunderstood and disliked Catholicism as a religion, and a number of political considerations reinforced his opposition. Catholics were the chief opponents to his plans for uniting Germany, but excluding Austria. During the Franco-Prussian War some Catholics in southern Germany sympathized openly with France. In Alsace-Lorraine many of the Catholic clergy opposed incorporation into the new German Empire. Catholic nostalgia for a "Great Germany" did not disappear in 1870. Catholics throughout Germany showed themselves wary of a Protestant emperor. Bavarians voiced suspicions that unification under the Hohenzollerns aimed to convert all Germans into Prussians and Lutherans.

Bismarck's suspicions about Catholic patriotism increased when the clergy in Silesia advocated the use of the Polish language in confessional schools and resisted Germanization. Bismarck wanted a centralized state, but Catholics inclined toward a federated one. Their particularist views were understandable because Catholics were a minority group in the Empire as a whole, but they won political support among Protestants in Hanover and elsewhere. The Center party was sufficiently powerful to challenge the chancellor's dominance. The Catholic Church, Bismarck thought, should be subject to state control, like other religious groups. In his foreign policy Bismarck believed it advantageous to ally himself with the new Kingdom of Italy. The Center party, however, pressed for intervention in the ROMAN QUESTION to bring about the restoration of the STATES OF THE CHURCH. Bismarck condemned this policy as preferring the welfare of the pope to that of the fatherland. He denounced the Center as a state within a state and as a gathering of enemies of the Empire. The chancellor tried to destroy the Center by having the Holy See disavow the party, and when this attempt failed, he resorted to open conflict with Catholics. In doing so he had the support of the liberals and of many Protestants.

The Conflict. The Kulturkampf began with the abolition of the Catholic bureau in the Prussian ministry of education and public worship (July 8, 1871).

Prussia. The government began to support the OLD CATHOLICS in their conflicts with the hierarchy. In August, Bismarck ordered normal schools and school inspection in Alsace-Lorraine removed from the control of the Catholic clergy and placed under lay supervision. The Pulpit Law (*Kanzelparagraph*) was enacted (Nov. 28, 1871) by the Reichstag, placing severe penalties on criticisms of the state from the pulpit. Tension increased when Pius IX refused to accept Cardinal Gustav Hohenlohe as the first ambassador of the Empire to the Holy See. This rebuff led Bismarck to remark (May 15, 1872): "We shall not go to Canossa."

Upon the proposal of Adalbert Falk, Prussian minister of education and public worship, a law was passed (March 1872) in the Prussian Landtag that subjected all schools to state inspection. Bismarck sought primarily to terminate anti-German activities by priests in Silesia, but the Center party saw this as an opening wedge to secularize education completely, a step the liberals had been advocating. In June all religious were excluded from public education in Prussia, and the Reichstag ordered all Jesuits expelled from the empire within six months (July 4, 1872). As a result, more than 500 members of this order went into exile. When Pius IX protested (December 1872), Bismarck severed diplomatic relations with the Vatican. In 1873 the Redemptorists, Vincentians, Holy Ghost Fathers, and Religious of the Sacred Heart fell under the same ban as the Jesuits.

In 1873 the Prussian Landtag promulgated a series of laws in May—hence the name May Laws. They placed priestly training under close government supervision and required seminarians, who must be German nationals, to study three years in a German university and to submit to state examinations in literature, history, and philosophy. Clerical appointments by bishops were subjected to government veto, and restrictions were placed on episcopal powers of excommunication and of discipline, although appeals could be made from episcopal decisions to a newly created civil tribunal.

One effect of these May Laws was to unify Catholics. Prussian bishops refused to cooperate in carrying out this legislation. Priests supported their bishops, even though many of them were fined and imprisoned. The Center party increased greatly its representation in the Landtag and Reichstag. Archbishop Mieczysław LEDÓCHOWSKI was arrested and exiled for opposing the teaching of the catechism in German to Polish children. The archbishop of Cologne and the bishop of Trier were also arrested. A second set of May Laws, in 1874, made recalcitrant bishops and priests liable to deposition and exile. During vacancies caused by their removal, their offices were to be administered in accordance with the Prussian government's directives. Pius IX declared the May Laws null and void (February 1875). An attempt by a Catholic to assassinate Bismarck (July 1874) was utilized by the chancellor to try to discredit the Center party and to justify further measures against Catholics. Civil marriage was made obligatory in Prussia (February 1875), and later in other German states. In April of 1875, the Landtag passed the so-called Bread-basket Law, which permitted the state to suspend all financial grants in dioceses where the law was not obeyed. In May all religious, except those engaged in hospital work, were expelled. In June all Church property was confiscated, and title to it was transferred to lay trustees elected by the parishioners. By 1877 thousands of parishes had lost their pastors, and nine of the twelve Prussian bishops were in exile. Although some bishops were able to administer their dioceses secretly through delegated priests, the disruption of Church life was very serious.

The height of the Kulturkampf came in 1875. Catholic resistance remained firm; yet Ludwig WINDTHORST prevented an extremism in the Center party and in the growing Catholic press that would preclude negotiation and compromise with Bismarck. By 1875 there was no longer likelihood of an alliance of German Catholics with Austria against the empire. Then, too, the coalition of national liberals and conservatives that had supported Bismarck lost its coherence, and the socialists emerged as a new political enemy that Bismarck had to take into account. Emperor William I favored a more moderate policy. Pope Leo XIII (1878–1903) proved more conciliatory than his predecessor, and the papal nuncio at Munich began conversations to end the strife. Bismarck slowly gave way, but he was reluctant to repeal the May Laws outright, and he insisted upon the Center party's cooperation on certain military issues. Falk was dismissed in 1879, and his successor was given wide discretionary powers to alleviate the May Laws. German Catholics resented the exclusion of Windthorst and other Center leaders from the negotiations in Vienna between Prussia and the Vatican. Restoration of diplomatic relations with the Holy See came in 1882. In 1886 and 1887 the May Laws were modified to the satisfaction of Catholics. Other anti-Catholic measures were repealed in 1890 and 1891, but it was not until 1904 that the section of the law expelling Jesuits was rescinded, and not until 1917 was the anti-Jesuit legislation completely abrogated.

Elsewhere in Germany. Some other German states followed Prussia's example. Baden, which had introduced restrictions on Catholics in the 1860s, enacted laws similar to Prussia's concerning clerical education and appointments. It required all primary schools to operate as interdenominational ones (*Simultanschule*) and assisted the Old Catholics. Although Baden did not copy Prussia's

severity in enforcing these laws, the Archdiocese of Freiburg remained vacant from 1868 to 1881. Hessen-Darmstadt introduced interdenominational schools, but the other measures patterned on Prussia's were not strictly enforced. Baden and Hessen-Darmstadt repealed their Kulturkampf laws between 1880 and 1886. In Catholic BAVARIA, Johann von Lutz, the liberal minister of education (later premier), started the Kulturkampf in close cooperation with Bismarck. Bavaria aided the Old Catholics, established *Simultanschule,* and until 1890 reverted to the type of state control of the Church (Staatskirchentum) prevalent in the 18th century.

Austria. A Kulturkampf began in Austria before 1870. In 1868 the liberals under Prime Minister Count Franz von Beust transferred marriage jurisdiction to civil courts, secularized the administration of public schools, and undermined the public position of the Church. In 1870 the government used the definition of papal infallibility as a pretext to abrogate the concordat of 1855. The liberals also cultivated the Old Catholics and impeded the Jesuits. In 1874 a set of May Laws passed the Austrian parliament that seriously affected the Church's legal position, restricted the rights of religious orders, placed Church funds under State supervision, and imposed upon bishops the obligation of notifying the state concerning ecclesiastical appointments. Pius IX sharply condemned the legislation, and Cardinal Joseph von RAUSCHER, Bp. Joseph Fessler, and Bp. Franz von RUDIGIER offered resistance. Since the enforcement of these measures was not severe, the Austrian bishops were divided, and a serious Church-State conflict was averted. When the liberal parties lost their influence (1879), much of the damage to the Church was soon undone.

Switzerland. In Switzerland, Catholics were in a difficult situation after the military defeat of the Sonderbund in 1847. The Jesuits were subsequently banned and monasteries were closed. The Syllabus of Errors and the definition of papal infallibility incensed Protestants and led them to enter a bitter onslaught against the Church. Old Catholics received government protection and were allowed to form the Christian Catholic Church (1875); in Protestant cantons they were given many Catholic churches for their use. In Basel, Bp. Eugène LACHAT was expelled for proceeding against priests who refused to accept the decrees of Vatican Council I. In Bernese Jura, where protest was strongest against the expulsion, priests faithful to their bishop were forced from their parishes and replaced by Old Catholic priests. At Geneva, Bp. Gaspard MERMILLOD was similarly deposed and expelled (1873) for attempting to establish an episcopal see in the city. In 1874 the federal constitution was revised to prohibit the establishment of new dioceses or monasteries without the federal government's consent. Jesuits and other religious orders were expelled from the entire country. The papal nuncio was asked to leave (1874), and diplomatic relations with the Holy See were severed until 1884. Civil marriage became obligatory; and schools, interdenominational. One effect of this repression was to draw Swiss Catholics closer together. Leo XIII began negotiations, seeking a settlement, and in 1883 Mermillod was able to return. Religious peace gradually returned.

Conclusion. The Kulturkampf caused much suffering for the Church, but it was not a success. Moral victory lay with the Catholics, who emerged more closely united and much more attached to Rome. Unfortunately, Catholics tended to develop the ghetto mentality of an oppressed minority and to remain aloof from the higher cultural life. For the state, the Kulturkampf had the bad effect of estranging millions of Catholic citizens for some decades.

Bibliography: A. CONSTABEL, *Die Vorgeschichte des Kulturkampfes: Quellenveröffentlichung aus dem deutschen Zentralarchiv* (Berlin 1956). G. GOYAU, *Bismarck et l'Église: Le Kulturkampf,* 4 v. (Paris 1911–13). J. B. KISSLING, *Geschichte des Kulturkampfes im Deutschen Reiche,* 3 v. (Freiburg 1911–16). G. FRANZ, *Kulturkampf: Staat und katholische Kirche in Mitteleuropa von der Säkularisation bis zum Abschluss des preussischen Kulturkampfes* (Munich 1954). E. SCHMIDT-VOLKMAR, *Der Kulturkampf in Deutschland, 1871–90* (Göttingen 1962), reviewed by J. K. ZEENDER, *Washington Catholic Historical Review* 50 (1965) 601–602. P. SATTLER, ''Bismarcks Entschluss zum Kulturkampf,'' *Forschungen zur brandenburgischen und preussischen Geschichte* 52 (1940) 66–101. R. MORSEY, ''Bismarck und der Kulturkampf,'' *Archiv für Kulturgeschichte* 39 (1957) 232–270. E. WEINZIERL-FISCHER, ''Bismarcks Haltung zum Vatikanum und der Beginn des Kulturkampfes,'' *Mitteilung des österreichischen Staatsarchivs* 10 (1957) 302–321. R. AUBERT, *Le Pontificat de Pie IX* (*Histoire de l'église depuis les origines jusqu'à nos jours* 21; 2d ed. Paris 1964). H. BORNKAMM, ''Die Staatsidee im Kulturkampf,'' *Historische Zeitschrift* 170 (1950) 41–72, 273–306, also sep. pub. (Munich 1950). E. JESTAEDT, *Der Kulturkampf im Fuldaer Land* (Fulda 1960). G. G. WINDELL, *The Catholics and German Unity, 1866–71* (Minneapolis 1954). K. S. PINSON, *Modern Germany: Its History and Civilization* (New York 1954) ch.9. E. EYCK, *Bismarck and the German Empire* (London 1950). F. A. ARLINGHAUS, ''The Kulturkampf and European Diplomacy,'' *Washington Catholic Historical Review* 28 (1943) 340–375; ''British Public Opinion and the Kulturkampf in Germany 1871–75,'' *ibid.* 34 (1949) 385–413. M. O. KOLBECK, *American Opinion on the Kulturkampf* (Washington 1942). L. P. WALLACE, *The Papacy and European Diplomacy 1869–78* (Chapel Hill, N.C. 1948). F. ENGEL-JANOSI, *Österreich und der Vatikan, 1846–1918,* 2 v. (Graz 1958–60) v.1. J. WODKA, *Kirche in Österreich* (Vienna 1959). K. EDER, *Der Liberalismus in Altösterreich* (Vienna-Munich 1955). T. SCHWEGLER, *Geschichte der Katholischen Kirche in der Schweiz* (2d ed. Stans 1943). F. STROBEL, *Die Jesuiten und die Schweiz im 19. Jahrhundert* (Olten 1954). A. LINDT, *Protestanten, Katholiken, Kulturkampf* (Zurich 1963), for the Kulturkampf in Switzerland. E. DANCOURT, *Scènes et récits du Kulturkampf dans le Canton de Berne* (St. Maruice 1921). R. W. LOUGEE, ''The Kulturkampf and Historical Positivism,'' *Church History* 23 (1954) 219–235. H. RAAB, *Staatslexikon,* ed. GÖRRES-GESELLSCHAFT (Freiburg 1957–63) 5:181–185. K. KUPISCH, *Die Religion in Geschichte und Gegenwart* (Tübingen 1957–65) 4:109–115. N. MIKO, *Lexikon für Theologie und Kirche,* ed. J. HOFER and K. RAHNER (Freiberg 1957–65) 6:673–675.

[H. W. L. FREUDENTHAL]

KUNDIG, MARTIN

Priest, cathedral rector, civic leader; b. Switzerland, Nov. 19, 1805; d. Milwaukee, WI, March 6, 1879. He attended schools at Einsiedeln and Lucerne, Switzerland; Rome, Italy; and Bardstown, KY. He was ordained on Feb. 2, 1829, for the Diocese of Cincinnati, Ohio. After spending three years in southern Ohio, he was transferred to Detroit, MI, where he founded parishes and was active in civic affairs. During a cholera epidemic in 1834 he set up relief services, among them a hospital. He became superintendent of the poorhouse for Wayne County, and his interest in free public schools gained him an appointment as a regent of the University of Michigan, Ann Arbor. In 1842 he went to Wisconsin, where he helped newcomers, especially the English-speaking, by guiding their land purchases and organizing societies. At his initiative, temperance societies were formed in Milwaukee and the city received such favorable notice that the hierarchy recommended it as the headquarters of a new diocese. Among his civic interests were the promotion of easier attainment of citizenship for immigrants, better harbor facilities, and education. The first free public school in Wisconsin was opened June 16, 1845, in the basement of St. Mark's Church, Kenosha, of which he was the pastor. He also planned a trade school in connection with Bishop's Hall at the cathedral in Milwaukee. The builder of 22 churches in southeastern Wisconsin and rector (1859–79) of the cathedral, he served also for 30 years as vicar-general under Bp. John Martin Henni.

Bibliography: P. L. JOHNSON, *Stuffed Saddlebags: The Life of Martin Kundig, Priest* (Milwaukee 1942).

[P. L. JOHNSON]

KUNIGUNDE, GERMAN EMPRESS, ST.

German empress also known as Cunegunda; b. *c.* 980; d. convent of Kaufungen, Hesse, Germany, March 3, 1033 or 1039. The daughter of Count Siegfried of Luxembourg, Kunigunde married Duke Henry IV of Bavaria, the future Emperor HENRY II, *c.* 998. She was crowned queen at Paderborn on Aug. 10, 1002, and on Feb. 14, 1014, she was crowned empress by Pope BENEDICT VIII in Rome. She helped and counseled Henry II in affairs of government and repeatedly represented him during his absences. When he founded the Diocese of Bamberg

(1007) she presented her dowry as the financial basis for its establishment. After the emperor's death (1024) she retired to the convent in Kaufungen that she had founded earlier (1017). She is buried at her husband's side in the cathedral of Bamberg. Her vita, written *c.* 1199, is rich in miraculous accounts, for example, that she walked unharmed on 12 red-hot plowshares. Since their marriage was childless, a legend arose that she and the emperor had vowed perpetual virginity. Her cult as a virgin in the Diocese of Bamberg and in other places where she had been active has Marian overtones. Kunigunde was canonized on March 29, 1200.

Feast: March 3, also Sept. 9 (Diocese of Bamberg).

Bibliography: S. HIRSCH, *Jahrbücher des deutschen Reichs unter Heinrich II,* 3 v. (Berlin 1862–75). Vita, *Monumenta Germaniae Historica, Scriptores* (Berlin 1826–) 4:821–824. J. BRAUN, *Tracht und Attribute der Heiligen in der deutschen Kunst* (Stuttgart 1943) 447–450. R. KLAUSER, *Der Heinrichsund Kunigundenkult im mittelalterlichen Bistum Bamberg* (Bamberg 1957). *Lexikon für Theologie und Kirche,* ed. J. HOFER and K. RAHNER, 10 v. (2d, new ed. Freiburg 1957–65) 6:680–681. A. BUTLER, *The Lives of the Saints,* rev. ed. H. THURSTON and D. ATTWATER, 4 v. (New York 1956) 1:470–471. EBERNANT OF ERFURT, *Heinrich und Kunegunde,* ed. R. BECHSTEIN (Stuttgart 1860, repr. Amsterdam 1968). G. BEZZENBERGER, *Leben und Legende der Kaiserin Kunigunde* (Kassel 1982). B. NEUNDORFER, *Leben und Legende: die Bildwerke am Grab des Kaiserpaares Heinrich und Kunigunde im Bamberger Dom* (Bamberg 1985). K. GUTH, *Die heiligen Heinrich und Kunigunde: Leben, Legende, Kult und Kunst* (Bamberg 1986). *Kunigunde: eine Kaiserin an der Jahrtausendwende,* ed. I. BAUMGÄRTNER (Kassel 1997).

[F. DRESSLER]

KUNO OF TRIER, ST.

Archbishop; b. Pfullingen, Swabia, Germany, 1016; d. Ürzig, June 1, 1066. Kuno (or Conrad) was cathedral provost under his uncle, Archbishop ANNO II of Cologne, under whose influence HENRY IV named Kuno archbishop of Trier (1066), investing him with ring and staff. The people and clergy of Trier objected to this violation of their electoral rights, and a force under Count Theoderich, the protector of Trier, captured Kuno at Bitburg, en route to his coronation. After two weeks' imprisonment at Ürzig on the Moselle River, he was killed by a vassal of Theoderich. Bishop Theoderich of Verdun brought the body to Tholey monastery, where Kuno was venerated as saint and martyr, although his cult did not spread.

Feast: June 1.

Bibliography: THEODERICH VON THOLEY, *Vita et passio, Monumenta Germaniae Historica, Scriptores* (Berlin 1826–) 8:212–219. G. MEYER VON KNONAU, *Jahrbücher des Deutschen Reiches unter Heinrich IV. und Heinrich V.,* 7 v. (Leipzig 1890–1909)

v.1. R. MARTINI, *Die Trierer Bischofswahlen vom Beginn des zehnten bis zum Ausgang des zwölften Jahrhunderts* (Berlin 1909). J. HEYDENREICH, *Die Metropolitangewalt der Erzbischöfe v. Trier bis auf Baldewin* (Marburg 1938).

[D. ANDREINI]

KUTTNER, STEPHAN GEORGE

Historian of canon law, researcher, university professor; b. Bonn, Germany, March 24, 1907. Kuttner studied at the Universities of Frankfurt, Freiburg, and Berlin where he received a LL.B. in 1928 and a J.U.D. in 1930. He served for a short time as assistant in the Berlin University Law School (1929–32). Forced to flee Germany in 1933 because of Hitler's pogrom of the Jews, Kuttner made his way to Rome, entering the Catholic Church on Aug. 15, 1933. The following year he became research associate at the Vatican Library, a position he held from 1934 to 1940. Immersing himself in the study of medieval canon law, Kuttner laid the foundation for his future career. In 1937 he published *Repertorium der Kanonistik (1140–1234),* the first extensive catalogue of manuscripts from the *Decretum of Gratian* to the *Decretals of Gregory IX.* From 1937 to 1940 he also served as an associate professor *Utriusque Juris* at the Pontifical Institute (now the Lateran University). At the outbreak of World War II Kuttner and his family found asylum in the United States and acquired citizenship in 1945.

After two years as visiting professor of the History of Canon Law at the Catholic University of America in Washington, D.C., Kuttner was appointed ordinary professor in 1942, the first lay person to hold a regular appointment on the pontifical faculty of canon law. In 1964 he accepted an invitation from Yale University to become the T. Lawrason Riggs Professor of Roman Catholic Studies. His final academic move was to the University of California at Berkeley in 1970 as director of the Robbins Collection of Canon Law and professor (1975 emeritus) in residence.

Kuttner was founder and co-editor (1943–71) of *Traditio,* a journal of studies in ancient and medieval history, thought and religion (now published at Fordham University) and editor of *Seminar* (1943–56) devoted to Roman law studies. He was also founder and president of the Institute of Medieval Canon Law from 1955 to 1991, when he was named chairman of the board. He edited publications of the Institute, the *Bulletin of Medieval Canon Law* (from 1971 to 1991), and the *Monumenta iuris canonici* in three series: glosses, canonical collections, and proceedings of international congresses (1965–).

Upon receiving the "Role of Law" award from the Canon Law Society of America in 1978 Kuttner stated:

Capital: Kuwait City.
Size: 6,880 sq. miles.
Population: 1,973,572 in 2000.
Languages: Arabic; English is widely spoken.
Religions: 157,800 Catholics (.8%), 1,677,536 Muslims (85%), 138,236 (14.2%) practice other faiths.

I owe my career only to my stubborn conviction that for the knowledge of canon law it is necessary to know how canon law developed over the centuries, and that it is a crucial point in this development to know the riches of canonical thought of the middle ages which are to a great part hidden in manuscripts. . . . But that there is this connection between the history of the Church and the law of the Church has to me always been a key to my own passion for my own work (CSLA Proceedings 40 [1977] 161–62).

On Feb. 11, 1993 Dr. and Mrs. Kuttner were present for the inaugural lecture instituting ''The Stephan Kuttner Distinguished Chair in Canon Law'' at the Catholic University of America.

Bibliography: Variorum Reprints (London) has collected many of Kuttner's essays. In each of the three volumes there is a retractationes section in which he corrects and updates the original articles: *The History of Ideas and Doctrines of Canon Law in the Middle Ages* (1980), 11 studies in English and French, including ''Harmony from Dissonance: An Interpretation of Medieval Canon Law'' (Wimmer Lecture, 1956) and ''Cardinalis: The History of a Canonical Concept''; *Medieval Councils, Decretals, and Collections of Canon Law* (1980), 13 studies in French, English, and German; *Gratian and the Schools of Law, 1140–1234* (1983) 10 studies in English, French, German, and Italian, including with E. RATHBONE, ''Anglo-Norman Canonists in the Twelfth Century''; *Kanonistische Schuldlehre von Gratian bis auf die Dekretalen Gregors IX: systematisch auf Grund der handschriftlichen Quellen dargestellt, Studi e Testi 64* (Vatican City 1935, reprint 1961); *Repertorium der Kanonistik (1140–1234): Prodromus corpus glossarum, Studi e testi 71* (Vatican City 1937); *L'Edition romaine des conciles généraux et les actes du premier concile de Lyon* (1940); *Decreta septem priorum sessionum Concilii Tridentini* (1945); KUTTNER and RELZE, eds., *A Catalogue of Canon and Roman Law Manuscripts in the Vatican Library, Studi e Testi 322, 328* (Vatican City 1986).

[J. E. LYNCH]

KUWAIT, THE CATHOLIC CHURCH IN

The State of Kuwait is an independent monarchy located on the northwest coast of the Persian Gulf. It is bounded by Iraq on the northwest, and Saudi Arabia on the west and south. An arid, desert territory, Kuwait'

economy depended primarily upon the fishing off its long coastline until the discovery of oil within its borders in April 1938, and the material and social progress brought about by oil revenues quickly transformed life throughout the country. Major inland oil fields are located in Al Wafrah and Maqwâ to the south of Kuwait City, and Al Bahrah and Sabriya to the northeast; other oil is pumped from offshore platforms. Containing ten percent of the world's petroleum reserves, Kuwait ranked first in crude oil production in the Middle East and fourth in the world.

Kuwait's population is composed chiefly of Kuwaiti and other Arabs, who are ethnically closer to Iraqis than to the Arabs of the peninsular hinterland. South Asians and Iranians account for just over ten percent of the population. Except for small communities of Jews, Hindus, Christians, and Parsi, the population is evenly divided between Sunni and Shi'a Muslim, and almost half the country's residents are immigrants.

The ruling al-Sabah family, Sunni Muslims of Bedouin descent, gained power in Kuwait in 1756, shortly after the founding of the principality. The sultanate became an ally of Great Britain through a treaty signed by Muvarak in 1899, and Britain extended its relationship to that of protectorate in January 1914. Kuwait's boundaries with Saudi Arabia were defined by a treaty ratified in 1934. The sultanate became a sovereign state in June 1961, after a claim by Iraq to Kuwaiti territory was repulsed, and Kuwait joined the United Nations two years later.

In 1971 the defense pact between Kuwait and Great Britain expired, leaving Kuwait to pursue a neutral position in international matters. However, its natural wealth remained a temptation to neighboring Iraq, which invaded Kuwait on Aug. 2, 1990. After a seven-month occupation during which thousands of Kuwaitis were killed or taken hostage, U.S. and other forces entered the region, repulsing the Iraqi Army in the Gulf War. Cleanup costs following the war were astronomical due to the necessity of cleaning up the oil leaked after Iraq sabotaged over 700 oil wells throughout Kuwait. In 1992 the country held its first parliamentary elections, allowing radical and other opposition groups to extend their influence.

Although the Kuwaiti constitution of Nov. 11, 1962, granted freedom of religion, it also proclaimed Islam to be the religions of the state, and the government placed restrictions on religious activities as required by Islamic law. While tensions continued to flare between the country's two Muslim factions, relations between Muslims and Christians remained amicable. The Catholic Church was permitted to operate openly in Kuwait, although the government prohibition against evangelical efforts limited its presence to administering primarily to the foreign-born workers residing in the country. Most of these workers, employed by the oil industry, were Philippine Catholics who had immigrated to the region with their families.

An Apostolic Vicariate of the Roman Catholic Church is located in the capital city of Kuwait, and a Patriarchate of the Roman Orthodox or Eastern-rite Church is also present. Between the two Catholic churches, Kuwait contains four parishes administered by nine priests. Bibles and other religious materials are legally imported into Kuwait through the Book House Company, Ltd. In 1969 diplomatic relations were established between the Vatican and the Kuwaiti government; by late 1996 a nunciature was situated in the country, followed, in March 2000, by a permanent mission.

Bibliography: *Bilan du Monde* 2:551–552. L. LOCKHART, "Outline of the History of Kuwait," *Journal of the Royal Central Asian Society* 34 (1947) 262–274.

[A. JAMME/EDS.]

KYRIE ELEISON

An acclamation, immediately following the penitential rite in the Roman Rite of the Mass, which praises the Lord and implores his mercy (General Instruction of Roman Missal, 30). In the Roman Rite, the text comprises two basic invocations: "Kyrie eleison" (Lord, have mercy) and "Christe eleison" (Christ, have mercy). In the Eastern Christian liturgical tradition, the acclamation "Kyrie eleison" is used extensively, especially as a congregational response in the many litanies scattered throughout the eucharist and the divine office. In its pre-Christian context, the acclamation "Kyrie eleison" was widely used in civic and religious ceremonies, often as an acclamation of the munificent benevolence and mercy of the Roman emperor.

The Kyrie first appeared in the Mass as the response of a litany in the Antioch-Jerusalem liturgy after the middle of the 4th century. From there it passed to Rome early in the 5th century. Toward the end of the 5th century a litany was codified by Pope Gelasius (492–96), inserted into the entrance rite of the Mass; it is known as the *Deprecatio Gelasii* [for the critical text, see B. Capelle, "Le Kyrie de la messe et le pape Gélase," *Revue Bénédictine* (Maredsous 1884–) 46 (1934) 126–44]. This litany was still sung at Mass during the time of Pope Gregory the Great (d. 604). However, Gregory made some historically important changes in its form. On ordinary days and on the Sundays after Pentecost and Epiphany, the customary invocations to be intoned by the clerics were omitted and only the response *Kyrie eleison* was sung. A

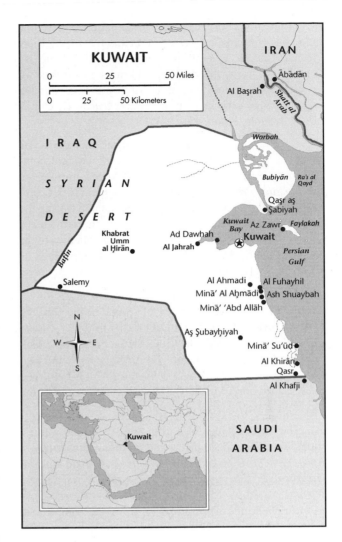

further modification made by Pope Gregory was the insertion of the *Christe eleison* [Gregory the Great, *Ep. 9* 26, in *Monumenta Germanae Historica: Epistolae* (Berlin 1826–) 2:59].

Over time, this limited use of the full Gelasian invocations on greater feasts disappeared entirely. The Kyrie as an independent entity was very early joined to the end of the stational litany. In such cases, the Kyrie of the Mass was omitted [*Ordo Romanus* 11 (1143), *Patrologia Latina*, ed. J. P. Migne (Paris 1878–90) 78:1039]. This usage is retained in the present Easter Vigil, where the litany replaces the entrance action, and its Kyrie is the Kyrie of the Mass. Originally, the number of invocations was not fixed in the Roman Rite of the Mass. *Ordo Romanus I* (*circa* 700) directs the Kyrie to be sung until the Pope gave the signal to stop. The early 9th century *Ordo Romanus IV* (St. Armand) specified that nine invocations were to be sung, giving rise to the traditional ninefold Kyrie.

Originally a congregational acclamation, by the time of the first Roman *Ordo* (*Ordo Romanus 1* 9, ed. Andrieu, 2:84), the *schola* was the only performer of the Kyrie. By the 12th century, the two semichoruses of clerics—of which the *schola* formed a part—simply alternated in the singing of the nine invocations (*Liber usuum O. Cist. 2* 62, *Patrologia Latina* 166:1435).

The first musical witnesses indicate that the Kyrie melodies had achieved a high degree of musical complexity by the 10th century. The oldest such witnesses are the *Kyriale, Troparium,* and *Sequentiarium* (10th century) of St. Martial in Limoges (Paris B.N. lat. 887) and the *cantatorium* (10th or 11th century) from the same place (Paris B.N. lat. 1118). Among the elaborate settings found in the St. Martial *Kyriale* are the Kyries listed as numbers 3 to 6 in the *Graduale Romanum*.

Many of these elaborate melodies were the direct outgrowth of the appearances of tropes in the 9th and 10th centuries (Anglès, 126). Kyrie 10 in the *Graduale Romanum* began with the trope *Alme Pater,* of which only the first verse is extant today. Blume has published 158 complete tropes (*Analecta hymnica* 47:43–216). The total rises to approximately 175 with the inclusion of the incomplete examples.

The first evidence of a troping of the Kyrie was afforded by Amalarius of Metz and represented as follows: *Kyrie eleison, Domine Pater, miserere; Christe eleison, miserere qui nos redemisti sanguine tuo; Kyrie eleison, Domine, Spiritus Sancte, miserere* (*De off. eccl.3* 6, *Patrologia Latina* 105:1113). None of the song books contain this trope, but the trope *Alme domine* is similarly constructed (*Analecta hymnica* 47:163).

The names given by medieval MSS for the troped *Kyrie* are numerous. The *Winchester Troper* describes the troped Kyrie as follows: "Incipiunt laudes preces, quae voce latina hoc resonant: Miserere tuis, O Christe, misellis" (see Blume, *Analecta hymnica* 47:1). Besides the term *laudes preces,* early French sources used the terms *prosulae, prosae,* or *versus ad Kyrie eleison.* An important distinction in the Kyrie tropes is that found between the *rahmen* (surrounding) tropes (new musical and textual material that precedes or follows the original Kyrie setting or separates the groups of three) and the *textual* tropes (i.e., textual interpolations, laid out syllabically on the single notes of disaggregate melismatic settings of the Kyrie). The *rahmen* trope is generally rather rare, whereas the *textual* trope is found very frequently. Only the MSS Paris B.N. lat. 887 and 1118 show a mixture of both types; all the other MSS know only the one or the other type of Kyrie trope.

The notation of the *textual* tropes in the MSS is varied. Usually, each acclamation is notated twice, in a troped and an untroped version—one under the other. In the St. Gall MSS, the melismatic version is notated first and is followed by the troped version. In the St. Martial family MSS, the troped version is placed first and is followed by the melismatic version. From this double style of notation, one might conclude to a corresponding difference in performance. Ursprung, however, interprets this double notation as implying that one semichorus sang the melisma while the other simultaneously sang the troped version, the two choirs then coming together on the word *eleison* (*Die Kath. Kirchenmusik* 57). Handschin, on the other hand, denies this possibility of "combining heterogeneous material" [*New Oxford History of Music,* ed. J. A. Westrup (New York 1957–) 2:166].

Of some 493 MSS studied, a total of 226 chant melodies have been found for the Kyrie (Melnicki, 13). Their musical form can be divided into three main groups: (1) AAA—the simplest form based on litanic models and comprising about one-fifth of all the melodies; (2) ABA—*Da capo* form, also comprising one-fifth of the melodies (see Kyries 2, 5, 11, and 18 in *Grad. Rom.*); (3) ABC—the latest of the three, although its oldest specimens date from the 10th century (see Kyrie 9 in *Grad. Rom.*). Within the third group, extremely varied forms developed. Among these developed forms is the following example: AXA; BXB; CXC. The X in each of the three sets may either be the same in each case as XXX, or as XYX, or finally as XYZ (see Kyries 3, 6, 9, and *ab lib.* 1–6 in *Grad. Rom.*).

The most ancient version in common usage today is that of the Vatican Kyrie 18. Vatican Kyrie 15 and 16 also are very early and form a special group with Kyrie 18. Among the earlier versions, the final invocation often descends to provide the tone for the Gloria. Kyrie 16 provides an example of this trait as it descends to E—the first tone of Gloria 15.

Modality was not a strict concept for the musical settings of the Kyrie. The Kyrie was not linked to a psalm tone as a canon of modality. Similarly, heterogeneous transmission of the melodies made them less susceptible to the modal canons of the theoreticians.

The modality of the medieval settings of the Kyrie was built principally on the final. Hence it is more helpful to speak of D, E, F and G modes. Among these, the most popular were the G and D modes. The D mode is found most frequently in French sources; the G mode is found most frequently in Italian sources. Very popular in German sources was a loosely knit group of E-mode melodies using a triadic structure (E-G-H, or C). Only in the 12th century (*Narbonne Troper,* Paris B.N. lat. 778) were all the Kyries arranged according to modes. Here, too, the larger modal groups were distinguished into authentic and plagal modes.

The differences between the musical settings of the Kyrie and those of the Propers for the Mass are very marked. The settings of the Proper have a very strong melodic unity, whereas those of the Kyrie tend to be largely regional in character. Out of the 226 settings cited by Melnicki, only 26 are international in character (Melnicki, 14–26). For the Propers, the medieval MSS show an almost unbelievable uniformity in the transmission of both the melody and the neume groupings, while the transmission of the Kyrie settings shows a substantial number of melodic variants and discrepancies in the melismatic neume groupings from region to region. The Kyrie melodies also have stylistic characteristics that are manifestly different from the musical settings of the Propers: transposition, episodic melodic material, motif repetition, and eventually signs of a strong influence exerted by the popular Sequence, *Estampie,* and *Lai-Leich* forms.

Bibliography: H. ANGLÈS, ''Gregorian Chant,'' *New Oxford History of Music*, ed. J. A. WESTRUP, 11 v. (New York 1957–) 2:126–27. *Analecta hymnica* (Leipzig 1886–1922) v.47, ed. C. BLUME and H. M. BANNISTER. C. CALLEWAERT, ''Les Étapes de l'histoire du Kyrie,'' *Revue d'histoire ecclésiastique* 38 (1942) 20–45. *Graduale Romanum* (Tournai 1961). J. HANDSCHIN, ''Trope, Sequence, and Conductus,'' *New Oxford History of Music* 2:128–74. J. A. JUNGMANN, *The Mass of the Roman Rite,* tr. F. A. BRUNNER, 2 v. (New York 1951–55) 1:333–46. M. MELNICKI, *Das einstimmige Kyrie des lateinischen Mittelalters* (Regensburg 1955). B. STÄBLEIN, *Die Musik in Geschichte und Gegenwart* ed. F. BLUME (Kassel-Basel 1949–) 7:1931–46. O. URSPRUNG, *Die katholische Kirchenmusik* (Potsdam 1931). P. WAGNER, *Einführung in die gregorianischen Melodien*, 3 v. (Leipzig) v.2 (2d ed. 1912); repr. (Hildesheim 1962). D. A. BJORK, ''The Kyrie Trope,'' *Journal of the American Musicological Society* 33 (1980) 1–41. D. A. BJORK, ''Early Settings of the Kyrie Eleison and Problems of Genre Definition,'' *Journal of the Plainsong and Medieval Music Society* 3 (1980) 40–48. P. DE CLERCK, *La prière universelle dans les liturgies latines anciennes: témoignages patristiques et textes liturgiqques* (Münster 1977). J. F. BALDOVIN, *The Urban Character of Christian Worship: The Origins, Development, and Meaning of Stational Liturgy* (Rome 1987). J. F. BALDOVIN, ''Kyrie eleison and the Entrance Rite of the Roman Eucharist,'' *Worship* 60 (1986) 334–47.

[C. KELLY/EDS.]

L

LABADIE, JEAN DE

Founder of the Labadists; b. Bourg, near Bordeaux, Feb. 13, 1610; d. Altona, Feb. 13, 1674. He was educated by the Jesuits at Bordeaux, then entered the Society of Jesus and was ordained in 1635. As a teacher and preacher he gained considerable renown, and he was esteemed for his piety. However, he imagined himself to have visions and revelations and a call to reform the Catholic Church. He fell seriously ill and after recovering asked for and received permission to leave the Society of Jesus. As a diocesan priest he labored at Bordeaux, Paris, Amiens, and Abbeville. Finally, after a stormy career, he embraced Protestantism at Montauban on Oct. 16, 1650. The delight of the reformers at so illustrious a recruit seems to have been tempered when Labadie now tried to reform them. His failure here ended in the formation of a sect of his own about 1670. Labadie thought that man, through contemplation, would see all things in God. Thus the Scriptures are not necessary; rather the Holy Spirit will inspire man. Labadie rejected infant Baptism and denied the Real Presence in the Eucharist. He minimized the observance of the Lord's Day. The semicommunistic society of his followers died out about 1732.

Bibliography: G. FRANK, *The New Schaff-Herzog Encyclopedia of Religious Knowledge*, ed. S. M. JACKSON (Grand Rapids, Mich. 1951–54) 6:390–392. L. MARCHAL, *Dictionnaire de théologie catholique*, ed. A. VACANT et al. (Paris 1903–50) 8.2:2383–85.

[H. J. MULLER]

LABARUM

The name given to the banner of Emperor CONSTANTINE I, an adaptation of the Roman cavalry standard (*vexillum*) with the pagan emblems replaced by Christian symbols. After his victory at the Milvian bridge (313), Constantine made the labarum the imperial flag of the western Empire, and from 324, for the entire Roman Empire. It was accompanied by an honor guard of 50 soldiers, outstanding for their bravery and devotion to the Christian faith (Eusebius, *Vita Constantini* 1.26).

Eusebius stated that the labarum was designed by Constantine himself on the day after his alleged vision of the cross. The banner consisted of a long gilt spear with a transverse bar forming a cross, crowned with a wreath of gold and precious stones enclosing the CHI-RHO monogram of Christ with a square purple banner inscribed ΤΟΥΤΩ NIKA ("by this sign conquer") and embroidered with precious stones interlaced with gold hanging from the cross-bar. There were medallions of the Emperor and his sons immediately above this banner (Eusebius, *Vita Constantini* 1.26). The labarum is pictured on Constantinian coins from 314. Variants of the original labarum were supplied to all legions; the variety of design, together with the constancy of the essential parts, can be seen upon comparison of several preserved Constantinian coins. After a period of brief eclipse during the reign of Emperor Julian (361–363), the labarum was brought back to a place of honor by Jovian and housed in the imperial palace in Constantinople. The significance of the labarum transcends its use as the first Christian military standard. In effect it proclaimed that Constantine, aware of the bankruptcy of the old psychological stimuli to geopolitical solidarity, was calling on the labarum to provide a new stimulus and rallying point; and it meant that Christianity was agreeing to ride at the head of a huge organized military force and share the fortunes of an earthly power.

Bibliography: EUSEBIUS, *Vita Constantini* 1.26–31; *Hist. eccl.* 9.9.2. H. GRÉGOIRE, *Byzantion* 4 (1927–28) 477–482. H. LECLERCQ, *Dictionnaire d'archéologie chrétienne et de liturgie*, ed. F. CABROL, H. LECLERCQ, and H. I. MARROU (Paris 1907–53) 8.1:927–962. J. J. HATT, *Latomus* 9 (1950) 427–436.

[A. G. GIBSON]

LABASTIDA Y DÁVALOS, PELAGIO ANTONIO DE

Mexican archbishop and scholar; b. Zamora, Michoacán, March 21, 1816; d. Coacaleco, Tlalnepantla, Feb.

The Emperor Honorius Holding a Labarum, leaf of a 5th-century ivory diptych in the Cathedral at Aosta, Italy.

4, 1891. He was ordained on Nov. 10, 1838, and received his degree in Canon Law in 1839. He became a professor of literature, philosophy, and Spanish. In the Michoacán curia he held the offices of prosecutor and judge of wills and inheritances, chaplaincies, and pious works. Santa Anna proposed him for the Puebla Diocese. He was appointed in Rome on March 23, 1855, and consecrated on July 8 by the bishop of Michoacán, Clemente de Jesús Munguía. When the Plan of Ayutla was promulgated, Labastida was accused of attacking the government from the pulpit, and he went into exile in Havana. From there he went to live in Rome. In his travels he visited Palestine, Egypt, and India. When Maximilian of Austria heard the bishop was in Europe, he asked to see him to obtain more exact information on the Mexican political situation; so Labastida, bishop of monarchist leanings, visited the future emperor in Miramar. On March 19, 1863, Labastida was appointed archbishop of Mexico, returning there on October 12. He was named to the imperial regency but soon resigned. In 1865 he made pastoral visits to

Tierra Caliente and the valley of Toluca. On Feb. 5, 1867, on the invitation of Pope Pius IX, he went to Rome, where he remained because of the new political unrest in Mexico, taking part in Vatican Council I as a member of the commission on ecclesiastical discipline. When the Council was suspended, he returned to Mexico City on May 19, 1871, and took up his episcopal duties in a political climate dominated by Liberals. He secured approval for the coronation of the statue of Our Lady of Guadalupe. The president of Mexico, Porfirio Díaz, presented him with a crozier on the 50th anniversary of his ordination (1888) and atttended the bishop's funeral three years later. Labastida left a large number of sermons, pastoral letters, decrees, and funeral orations.

Bibliography: J. T. BASURTO, *El Arzobispado de México* (Mexico City 1944). E. VALVERDE TÉLLEZ, *Bio-bibliografia eclesiástica mexicana* (1821–1943), 3 v. (Mexico City 1949).

[L. MEDINA-ASCENSIO]

LABAT, JEAN BAPTISTE

Dominican missionary, author; b. Paris, 1663 or 1664; d. Paris, Jan. 6, 1738. Professed in Paris April 11, 1685, he later lectured in Nancy. From 1694 to 1705 he was active in the islands of Martinique and Guadeloupe in the Lesser (French) Antilles, first as priest then as procurator, superior, and finally as apostolic prefect. As a missionary he was generous, commercially astute, inventive, and a defender of French interests against foreign rivals. Through his outstanding military efforts, he liberated Martinique from the British expedition, led by Sir Christopher Codrington in 1703. His superiors recalled him to France, where instead of granting him recognition for his work, the government through intrigues and misrepresentation confined him to a cloister in Toul without a trial, and he was not allowed to resume his island voyages. Released after intervention by the Dominican superior general, he traveled extensively in Spain and Italy, and was allowed to return to Paris after the death of Louis XIV (1715). There he wrote his famous memoirs. In 1727 he was made procurator for the Dominican superior general. He was a perceptive observer with many interests. His accounts of foreign countries were sincere, candid, and objective, but often diffuse. In addition to the *Nouveau voyage aux Isles de l'Amerique* (6 v., Paris 1722), which has been often translated and edited, and *Voyages en Espagne et en Italie* (8 v., Paris 1730), Labat wrote of West Africa (5 v., Paris 1728), Guinea (4 v., Amsterdam 1728), and Syria-North Africa (7 v., Paris 1735).

Bibliography: M. A. LAMARCHE, *Le Père Labat au l'humour d'un savant,* 1664–1738 (Montreal 1938). J. RENNARD, *Le Père Labat aux Antilles* (Paris 1927).

[B. M. BIERMANN]

LABBE, PHILIPPE

French scholar and Jesuit; b, Bourges, July 10, 1607; d. Paris, March 17, 1667. Philippe Labbe was born into a middle-class family whose professional connections were with the law. After entering the Society of Jesus (Sept. 28, 1623), Labbe taught the upper classes at the Jesuit college in Bourges. He soon abandoned teaching for ambitious projects of research, many of which remained unfinished at the time of his death. Many of his works were compilations, dealing with a variety of disciplines and comprising numerous volumes. Every year he produced one or more works. Labbe, like other of his contemporaries, was given to stating controversial opinions and to defending them vigorously in print. He spoke of Protestants and the intolerance typical of his century. *De scriptoribus ecclesiasticis quos attigit card. Robertus Bellarminus* (Paris 1660) is a criticism of a bibliography of ecclesiastical authors in which Labbe censured certain Protestant writers. Labbe's learning was extensive. His scholarly interests included hagiography, ecclesiastical and secular history, heraldry, antiquities, geography, and Greek prosody. In some fields his learning was sound, and certain of his works have been useful to subsequent generations of scholars. For a complete list of his publications (some 80 titles), see C. Sommervogel et al., *Bibliothèque de la Compagnie de Jésus,* 11 v. (Brussels-Paris 1890–1932).

In *Pharus Galliae Antiquae* (Moulins 1644), Labbe bitterly criticized a similar account by Sanson. The dispute that ensued reached such proportions that the Chancellor of France, Pierre Séguier, Duc de Villemor, had to intervene and pacify the irate scholars. Labbe was responsible for the first plan of a history of Byzantium, *De Byzantinae historiae scriptoribus* (Paris 1648). This work was his most precious contribution to historical studies and the most useful to posterity. *Aristotelis et Platonis graecorum interpretum types hactenus editorem* (Paris 1657) is the plan of a work devoted to the history of Greek and Roman philosophy. *Claudii Galeni Vita* (Paris 1660) and *Claudii Galeni chronologium eloquim* (Paris 1660) are basic works on the life of Galen. Labbe attempted a historical concordance that is useful to the study of French history, *L'Abrégé royal de l'alliance chronologique de l'histoire sacrée et profane* (Paris 1651). Another major and lasting contribution is his collection of councils, *Sacrosancta concilia ad regiam editionem exacta . . .* (Paris 1671–72). This particular work comprised eight volumes and was completed by G. Cossart.

Bibliography: H. HURTER, *Nomenclator literarius theologiae catholicae,* 5 v. in 6 (3d ed. Innsbruck 1903–13) 4:184–190. C. SOMMERVOGEL et al., *Bibliothèque de la Compagnie de Jésus,* 11 v. (Brussels-Paris 1890–1932) 4:1295–1328; 9:561–563. L. KOCH, *Jesuiten-Lexikon: Die Gesellschaft Jesu einst und jetzt* (Paderborn 1934) 2:1053–54.

[C. HOLMES]

LABERTHONNIÈRE, LUCIEN

French Modernist philosopher and theologian; b. Chazelet (Indre), Oct. 5, 1860; d. Paris, Oct. 6, 1932. After ordination (1886) as a member of the ORATORIANS, he became a professor of philosophy at the College of Juilly (1887). He came under the influence of BOUTROUX, at the Sorbonne, where he continued his studies. In his preoccupation with reconciling philosophy and religion, his thinking was influenced by BLONDEL, PASCAL, and MAINE DE BIRAN. He was appointed superior at the École Massillon in Paris (1898) and of the college of Juilly (1900). From 1905 until 1913 he edited *Annales de la philosophie chrétienne.* As a follower of Blondel's immanence theories and a severe critic of Church authority and of SCHOLASTIC PHILOSOPHY (but not that of St. THOMAS AQUINAS), he developed a pragmatic personalist view of religion called moral dogmatism. His *Essais de philosophie religieuse* (1903) and *Le Réalisme chrétien et l'idéalisme grec* (1904) were put on the Index in 1906. The *Annales* and two of his other works, *Le Témoignage des martyrs* (1912) and *Sur le chemin du Catholicisme* (1913), were placed on the Index in 1913. When he was subsequently forbidden to publish his writings, he obeyed but continued to write. His *Études sur Descartes* and *Études de philosophie cartésienne,* published posthumously, were placed on the Index in 1936 and 1941, respectively. His private life was exemplary, and he died at peace with the Church, after receiving the Last Rites.

Bibliography: M. M. D'HENDECOURT, *Essai sur la philosophie du Père Laberthonnière* (Paris 1947). E. CASTELLI, *Laberthonnière* (Milan 1927). J. P. GOLINAS, *La Restauration du Thomisme sous Léon XIII et les philosophies nouvelles: Études de la pensée de M. Blondel et du Père Laberthonnière* (Washington 1959). I. DANIELE, *Enciclopedia filosofica,* 4 v. (Venice-Rome 1957) 2:1760–62.

[F. M. O'CONNOR]

LABORANS

Cardinal, canonist, and theologian; b. Pontorma, near Florence; d. most likely Rome, *c.* 1190. He studied at Frankfurt and received the rank of magister at the University of Paris. He held the post of *canonicus* at Capua before 1160. In 1173 he became cardinal deacon of S. Maria in Porticu and in 1180 cardinal priest of S. Maria in Trastevere. He belonged to the school of canonists known as the DECRETISTS, in that their main concern was to comment on the *Decretum* of GRATIAN. He is the author of several works, the most famous being his *Codex Compilationis*. This work, finished in 1182, was the result of 20 years of labor on his part. It is an attempt at rearranging Gratian's *Decretum* in a more logical order, with the addition of new materials such as decretals of Innocent II, Eugene III, Alexander III, and the canons of the Third Lateran Council. Laborans is also the author of three theological treatises: *De vera libertate* (1144–61); *Contra Sabellianos* (1180–90); and *De relativa praedicatione personae in divinis* (1180–90). He was apparently influenced by the school of Gilbert of Poitiers in his theological work.

Bibliography: S. KUTTNER, *Repertorium der Kanonistik* (Rome 1937) 267–268. G. LEBRAS, *Dictionnaire de théologie catholique*, ed. A. VACANT et al., 15 v. (Paris 1903–50; Tables générales 1951) 8.2:2388.

[J. M. BUCKLEY]

LABOREM EXERCENS

Pope John Paul II's encyclical on labor, dated Sept. 14, 1981. The intermediate occasion for the encyclical was the ninetieth anniversary of *RERUM NOVARUM*, Pope Leo XIII's social encyclical of 1891—the start of what has come to be known as "papal social thought." *Laborem exercens* defined the human being as "worker." Humans differ from animals because humans alone must create the conditions of their survival and well-being by labor. The encyclical significantly expanded the notion of work. John Paul II indicated that labor does not refer principally to industrial labor, as it tended to do in previous encyclicals, but included agriculture, clerical, scientific, service-oriented and intellectual work (nn. 1, 4).

The encyclical presented Catholic social teaching as a radical critique of communism and capitalism. Oppression and inequality in the world are caused by a disorder in the organization of labor. While capital (including the mechanical means of production and the natural resources made available for production) is "the result of labor" (n. 12), i.e., accumulated labor, and therefore should be united with labor and serve labor, in actual fact capital has organized itself against labor in Western society.

The encyclical formulated the fundamental principle of "the priority of labor over capital." In today's world in which industries are interconnected and related to public institutions, capital is meant to serve the entire laboring society. State ownership of the industries in itself offers no guarantee that the priority of labor over capital will be respected. The encyclical defended private ownership of productive goods, but added that ownership,

whether private or public, is always conditional. "Isolating the means of production as separate property in order to set it up in the form of capital in opposition to labor—and even to practice exploitation of labor—is contrary to the very nature of these means . . . because the only legitimate title to their possessions is that they should serve labor" (n. 14).

Laborem exercens argued that the dignity of labor is such that laborers are entitled to co-own the goods they produce and thus share in the decisions regarding the use of these goods. Workers are also entitled to share in the decisions concerning the work process. According to John Paul II, workers are meant to be "the subjects," the fully responsible agents, of production. The encyclical encouraged all movements that seek to extend workers' participation in ownership and management. (At the time the encyclical appeared there was still hope that the union movement Solidarity would transform Polish society).

What strategy must be adopted to transform the economic systems of West and East so that the priority of labor be respected?

> To achieve social justice in the various parts of the world, in the various countries and in the relationship between them, there is a need for ever new movements of solidarity of the workers and with the workers. . . . The Church is firmly committed to this cause, for it considers it to be its mission, its service, a proof of its fidelity to Christ, so that it can truly be the Church of the poor (n. 8).

This radical teaching was reinstated in the "Instruction on Christian Freedom and Liberation" (March 1986), published by the Congregation for the Doctrine of the Faith: "The serious socio-economic problems which occur today cannot be solved unless new fronts of solidarity are created: solidarity among themselves, solidarity with the poor to which the rich are called, solidarity among the workers and with the workers" (n. 89).

Bibliography: For the text of *Laborem exercens*, see *Acta Apostolicae Sedis* (1981): 57–647 (Latin); *Origins* 11, no. 15 (Sept. 24, 1981): 225, 227–244 (English); *The Pope Speaks* 26 (1981): 289–336 (English). For commentaries and summaries of the encyclical, see: G. BAUM, *The Priority of Labor* (New York 1982). D. DORR, *Option for the Poor* (Maryknoll, N.Y. 1983). J. W. HOUCK and O. F. WILLIAMS, eds., *Co-creation and Capitalism: John Paul II's "Laborem Exercens"* (Washington, D.C.: University Press of America, 1983).

[G. BAUM]

LABOURÉ, CATHERINE, ST.

Mystic, inaugurator of the MIRACULOUS MEDAL devotion; b. Fain-les-Moutiers, Burgundy, France, May 2,

1806; d. Enghien-Reuilly Convent, Paris, Dec. 31, 1876. Zoé, as she was baptized, was the ninth of 17 children of Pierre Labouré, a prosperous farmer, and Madeleine Louise Gontard (d. 1815). She received no formal education, but frequent Communion, daily Mass, and hours of prayer nurtured her desire to enter religious life. From the age of 12 she managed the household for her father and brothers. In 1828 her father tried to discourage her vocation by sending her to Paris to work as a waitress in his brother's café. Unhappy there, she fled to relations in Châtillon-sur-Seine, where she entered the Daughters of Charity of St. Vincent de Paul (January 1830) and took Catherine as her name in religion. At the novitiate in Rue du Bac, Paris, she soon experienced visions of St. Vincent de Paul's heart. Repeatedly she enjoyed the visible presence of Jesus in the Blessed Sacrament. According to Catherine, she was awakened on the night of July 18, 1830, by her guardian angel, who led her to the chapel. There Our Lady appeared and, while Catherine knelt at her knee, sat and talked for two hours, giving spiritual advice, predicting world calamities, and speaking of a mission for Catherine. In a second apparition (Nov. 27, 1830) this mission was revealed when the novice beheld a picture of Mary standing on a globe with light streaming from her hands. Around the Virgin were the words in French: "O Mary, conceived without sin, pray for us who have recourse to thee." After manifesting the miraculous medal, Mary entrusted to Catherine the inauguration of the devotion to it. A third vision (September 1831) was to the same effect. Catherine confided her experience only to her confessor, M. Aladel, who obtained permission from the archbishop of Paris to have the medal struck (1832). In 1836 an archdiocesan commission canonically approved the authenticity of the visions.

Catherine was sent to Reuilly, Paris (January 1831), and worked there for the remaining 46 years of her life, tending the aged and laboring in other humble occupations. Her mystical experiences continued. She had a mysterious vision of the cross (c. 1847) and made remarkable prophecies. To her superiors, however, she seemed "insignificant" and "cold, even apathetic." Not until May 1876 did Catherine reveal her visions to her superiors, and then in order to expedite a statue requested by Mary. Her incorrupt body lies in the chapel of the motherhouse on Rue du Bac, Paris. She was beatified May 28, 1933, by PIUS XI, and canonized July 27, 1947, by PIUS XII.

Feast: Nov. 28.

Bibliography: J. I. DIRVIN, *St. Catherine Labouré of the Miraculous Medal* (New York 1958). O. ENGLEBERT, *Catherine Labouré and the Modern Apparitions of Our Lady,* tr. A. GUINAN (New York 1959). R. LAURENTIN and P. ROCHE, *Catherine Labouré et la médaille miraculeuse: documents authentiques: 1830–1876* (Paris 1976). R. LAURENTIN, *The Life of Catherine Labouré,* tr. P. INWOOD (London 1983). *Siegeszug der wunderbaren Medaille,* ed. W. DURRER (Jestetten 1983). Franciscan Friars of the Immaculate, *"You Will Make This Known . . ."* (New Bedford, MA 1998).

[J. I. DIRVIN]

LABRE, BENEDICT JOSEPH, ST.

The "beggar of Rome" and promoter of the FORTY HOURS DEVOTION; b. Amettes, France, March 25, 1748; d. Rome, Italy, April 16, 1783. He was the eldest of 15 children of a village shopkeeper. At the age of 12 he was sent to study with his uncle, the parish priest of Érin, at whose home he became so interested in Scripture and the saints that he tended to neglect more practical studies. After they had both selflessly devoted themselves to the care of the sick during a local epidemic, his uncle died of cholera, and Benedict's ambition then became entrance into an austere religious order. At the age of 18 he set out on foot for La Trappe, but was told upon arriving that he was too young. Although he was later several times accepted by the Carthusians and the Cistercians, his eccentricities and poor health prevented his becoming an apt subject for community life.

In 1770, Benedict started on a pilgrimage to Rome, walking all the way and living on alms. His last letter to his parents mentioned his intention of joining an order in Italy, but he apparently abandoned this plan in favor of a different and unusual vocation: to live the evangelical counsels as a wanderer in the midst of the world. For the next six years his life was one of continual pilgrimages to all the principle shrines of Europe. He visited Loreto, Assisi, Bari, Einsiedeln, Aix, Compostela, and others. He made himself homeless, traveled everywhere on foot, normally slept on the bare ground, and had no possessions except a ragged cloak and a few books. Living on alms, he frequently shared what he received with other beggars. He took no care of his body, and this neglect became a source of mortification and, to Benedict's delight, induced contempt. In the course of his journeys, he often spent hours before some wayside shrine or days in a remote church absorbed in prayer. Hardships, inclement weather, and calumnies were borne with equanimity and joy.

After 1776, Benedict settled in Rome. His nights were spent in the ruins of the Colosseum and his days in various churches. He particularly loved Forty Hours and sought out churches where the devotion was being observed. His increasing ill health finally forced him to take lodging in a poor house. Early in 1783 he fell ill and peacefully died during Holy Week. He was immediately popularly proclaimed a saint, and devotion to the "beggar of Rome'' and the ''saint of the Forty Hours'' spread rapidly throughout the entire Church. He was canonized in 1883 by LEO XIII.

Feast: April 16.

Bibliography: J. MANTENAY, *St. Benoît Labre* (Paris 1908). L. BRACALONI, *Il Santo della strada: Benedetto Giuseppe Labre* (Rome 1946). F. GAQUÈRE, *Le saint pauvre de Jésus-Christ, Benoît-Joseph Labre* (new ed. Avignon 1954). A. BUTLER, *The Lives of the Saints,* rev. ed. H. THURSTON and D. ATTWATER, 4 v. (New York 1956) 2:106–108. A. BEILLIARD, *Amettes-en-Artois, Saint Benoît–Joseph Labre: itinéraire* (Amettes 1973). J. RICHARD, *Le vagabond de Dieu: saint Benoît Labre* (Paris 1976). A. DHÔTEL, *Saint Benoît Joseph Labre* (Paris 1983). P. DOYÈRE, *Benoît Labre, ermite pèlerin* (Paris 1983). Centre d'histoire religieuse de Lille, *Benoît Labre: errance et sainteté, histoire d'un culte,* ed. Y. M. HILAIRE (Paris 1984). G. VILLARUBIAS, *Amettes, sanctuaire et village d'Artois* (Amettes, France 1985).

[W. E. LANGLEY]

LABRIOLLE, PIERRE DE

Historian, Latin scholar, and patrologist; b. Asnières, near Paris, June 18, 1874; d. Nantes, Dec. 28, 1940. After classical studies in Paris, he taught at Laval University in Montreal, at the Collège Stanislas in Paris, at the lycée in Rennes, and at the University of Fribourg in Switzerland (1904–19), and was associated with the University of Poitiers and the Sorbonne in Paris, (1926–40). In 1916 he entered the Académie des inscriptions et belles lettres. His patristic studies began with short biographies of SS. Vincent of Lérins (1906), Jerome (1907), and Ambrose (1908). After a dissertation at Fribourg on the sources for the history of MONTANISM (1910), he published *La Crise montaniste* (Paris 1913). His *Histoire de la littérature latine chrétienne* (1910, Eng. tr. H. Wilson, 1925), was re-edited by G. BARDY (2 v., Paris 1947). He founded the *Bulletin d'ancienne littérature et d'archéologie chrétienne* (Paris 1911—). He revived the study of patristics in French universities; his fame rests particularly on the texts he edited and his translation of several of Augustine's works for the Budé series. *La Réaction païenne* (to Christianity) appeared in Paris in 1934, and he contributed to volumes three and four of *Histoire de l'Église* (1936–37) of A. FLICHE and V. MARTIN.

Bibliography: J. ZEILLER, *Revue des études latines* 19 (1941) 55–61. A. HAMMAN, *Lexikon für Theologie und Kirche,* ed. J. HOFER and K. RAHNER (2d, new ed. Freiburg 1957–65) 6:721.

[F. X. MURPHY]

LA CAVA (SS. TRINITÁ), ABBEY OF

Benedictine monastery near Salerno, Italy. It was founded in 1011 by St. ALFERIUS and enlarged by his sec-

ond successor, Abbot PETER PAPPACARBONE (1079–1123), who built the church that was consecrated by Pope Urban II in 1092. Cava became the center of a flourishing Benedictine congregation inspired by the usages of CLUNY, where Alferius and Peter had stayed for some time. Endowed with a considerable number of holdings and dependencies, including several seaports, the abbey established a closely knit network of trade relations with Africa and the eastern Mediterranean and extended its influence through all of Italy, from Milan to Sicily. By the middle of the 13th century, Cava's power began to decline; becoming involved in the wars between the houses of Anjou and Aragon, it lost many holdings on the mainland, and in 1282 Pope MARTIN IV forced the abbey to cede its Sicilian holdings to Aragon. Its abbot was one of the most influential dignitaries at the royal court of Naples, and in consequence by 1394 Cava came to be ruled by bishops, selected at will by the popes from among the secular clergy, and with results for the abbey that can be readily imagined. The monastery lost its Calabrian holdings in 1410; Pope Eugene IV introduced COMMENDATION in 1431. In 1492, when the monks remaining at Cava proved refractory to reform, the commendatory abbot Cardinal Oliviero Carafa removed them and substituted monks of the Reform Congregation of St. Justina (*see* BENEDICTINES), in favor of whom he renounced his commendation. The consequent abrogation of episcopal authority at Cava resulted in local disorders and pillaging, leading to the erection (1513) of the Diocese of Cava, distinct from the abbey. The monastery was closed from 1807 to 1815 and then suppressed in 1866; the monks, however, were left as ''custodians,'' a step that preserved monastic buildings and the library from destruction. Today the abbot *nullius* of Cava has a territory of 22 parishes and about 25,000 inhabitants; the abbey belongs to the Benedictine Cassinese Congregation. In the library, besides documents of historical importance, there are preserved a Gothic Bible of the 14th century, a codex of Lombard law, and more than 600 incunabula. Four abbots are honored as saints: Alferius (1011–50), Leo I of Cava (1050–79), Peter (1079–1123), and CONSTABILIS (1123–24). Their veneration, authorized by Pope Sixtus V in 1589, was reconfirmed by Leo XIII in 1893. Another eight are blessed: Simeon (1141), Falco (1146), Marinus (1170), Benincasa (1194), Peter II (1208), Balsamon (1232), Leonard (1255), and Leo II of Cava (1268–95).

Bibliography: *Chronicon Cavense,* L. A. MURATORI, *Rerum italicarum scriptores, 500–1500,* 25 v. in 28, ed. G. CARDUCCI and V. FIORINI (2d, new ed. Città di Castello 1900–) 7:913–962. *Annales Cavenses, Monumenta Germaniae Historica: Scriptores* (Berlin 1826–) 3:185–197. *Codex diplomaticus Cavensis,* ed. M. MORCALDI et al., 8 v. (Naples-Milan 1874–93). P. GUILLAUME, *Essai historique sur l'abbaye de Cava* (Cava 1877). L. H. COTTINEAU, *Répertoire topobibliographique des abbayes et prieurés,* 2 v. (Mâcon 1935–39) 1:635–637. P. SCHMITZ, *Dictionnaire* *d'histoire et de géographie ecclésiastiques*, ed. A. BAUDRILLART et al. (Paris 1912–) 12:21–24. G. PENCO, *Storia del monachesimo in Italia* (Rome 1961).

[I. DE PICCOLI]

LACEY, WILLIAM, BL.

Priest and martyr; b. Horton, near Settle, West Riding, Yorkshire, England; d. hanged, drawn, and quartered at York, Aug. 22, 1582. William Lacey, a gentleman who held a distinguished position under the Crown until *c.* 1565, was step-father to two sons, Arthur and Joseph Cresswell, who became Jesuits. For 14 years he and his wife suffered persecution as recusants, including imprisonment at Hull. After the death of his wife, Lacey studied at the English College in Rheims (1580–81) and, under a special dispensation because he had been married twice, was ordained priest at Rome in 1581. He visited Loreto (May 10, 1581) en route back to England. The following year he was arrested in York Castle (July 22, 1582) after hearing a Mass said by the soon-to-be apostate Thomas Bell. After enduring the hardships of imprisonment in a dungeon, he was arraigned (August 11), condemned, and confined until his death. He was beatified by Pope Leo XIII on Dec. 9, 1886.

Feast of the English Martyrs: May 4 (England).

See Also: ENGLAND, SCOTLAND, AND WALES, MARTYRS OF.

Bibliography: B. CAMM, ed., *Lives of the English Martyrs,* (New York 1905), II, 564–88. R. CHALLONER, *Memoirs of Missionary Priests,* ed. J. H. POLLEN (rev. ed. London 1924; repr. Farnborough 1969), I, 16–17. J. H. POLLEN, *Acts of English Martyrs* (London 1891).

[K. I. RABENSTEIN]

LA CHAIZE, FRANÇOIS DE

Jesuit confessor of Louis XIV; b. Château d'Aix (Loire), Aug. 25, 1624; d. Paris, Jan. 20, 1709. He studied at the Jesuit college of Roannes, entered the novitiate in Avignon in 1639, was ordained in 1656, and in 1658 made his profession in Lyons, where he taught philosophy and was later rector and provincial. From 1675 to his death he was confessor of LOUIS XIV, coming to the court when Louis was giving public scandal by living with the Duchess of Montespan. La Chaize's policy of mildness rather than strictness was in time justified by the complete conversion of the king. His influence was long preponderant on the Council of Conscience, where he assisted the king in the appointment of bishops. He took a position akin to that of the bishops in the difficulties between Louis, and Innocent XI, who, inclined toward a strict stand, was displeased with La Chaize. He advised against extreme measures against Jansenists and Protestants.

Bibliography: G. GUITTON, *Le Père de La Chaize, confesseur de Louis XIV,* 2 v. (Paris 1959). J. BRUCKER, *La Compagnie de Jésus* (Paris 1920).

[P. BLET]

LACHAT, EUGÈNE

Bishop of Basel; b. Montavon (Berne), Switzerland, Oct. 14, 1819; d. Balerna (Ticino), Nov. 1, 1886. After completing his philosophical and theological studies in Albano in Italy, he was ordained (1842) and then worked as a missionary in Italy until 1844, when he went to Alsace. In 1850 he became pastor in Grandfontaine (Berne), and in 1855, dean in Delémont. As bishop of Basel (1863–84), he headed the largest see in the seven cantons during a period of radicalism characterized by constant infringements on ecclesiastical matters. At VATICAN COUNCIL I, Lachat spoke in favor of papal infallibility. As a result, the Swiss press violently attacked him. Open battle, the KULTURKAMPF, broke out when Lachat inflicted ecclesiastical censures on the few priests who refused to admit the defined doctrine of papal infallibility. Lachat was declared deposed by the governments of five of the seven cantons in which his diocese lay (Jan. 29, 1873) and was expelled from his residence (April 16, 1873). For the next 12 years he directed his see from exile in Lucerne, where he erected a seminary (1882). At the wish of Pope LEO XIII, he resigned his bishopric (1884). He was made titular archbishop of Damietta and apostolic administrator of Ticino (1885), and he erected a seminary in Lugano, where he was buried in the church of S. Maria degli Angeli.

Bibliography: P. VAUTREY, *Histoire des évêques de Bâle,* v.2 (Einsiedeln 1886) 559–635. D. FERRATA, *Mémoires,* v.1 (Rome 1920) 69–184. J. FOLLETÊTE, *Un Évêque jurassien* (Paris 1925). T. SCHWEGLER, *Geschichte der katholischen Kirche in der Schweiz* (2d ed. Stans 1943). A. CHÈVRE, ''Mgr. Eugène Lachat, évêque de Bâle: Á Propos d'un centenaire 1863–1963,'' *Zeitschrift für Schweizerische Kirchengeschichte,* 58 (1964) 119–133.

[J. B. VILLIGER]

LACHELIER, JULES

French Catholic idealist philosopher; b. Fontainebleau, May 27, 1832; d. there, Jan. 18, 1918. After graduation from the École Normale Supérieure, he studied philosophy privately under Félix Ravaisson (1813–1900). From 1864 to 1875 he taught philosophy at the École Normale Supérieure, but resigned because of a secret fear of disturbing his students' faith. He served in the university administration from 1875 to 1910, but his influence on young professors of philosophy remained great, and perdures through the 20th century.

Lachelier's idealism, Platonist and Leibnizian rather than Kantian, is based on the incompatibility of realism with absolute scientific determinism. The latter demands absolute homogeneity of all parts of matter, and therefore excludes any qualitative diversity whereby individual things can have distinct existence. Hence absolute scientific determinism implies that its object is purely mental. Mechanism thus proceeds from mind, but from impersonal mind that cannot be other than the object it thinks. Mechanical necessity is therefore a purely intelligible object of mathematical physics, from which all sensible qualities and distinct bodies, whether living or nonliving, are absent.

Impersonal mind does not stop at this level of abstract thought. Rather, by a pure act of instinct, it organizes distinct bodies harmoniously into a cosmos. By producing a world of real bodily units, impersonal mind itself becomes real through its real object.

Yet impersonal mind cannot be other than its object, which is still blind instinct. To become intellectual thought, impersonal mind reflects on itself and sees that it is the act whereby all things have being and truth. This creative act is man's intellectual judgment in which he judges the world of instinct to be true being. The human intellect, however, can only apply its judgment to instinctive finality that antedates it and to which it must passively conform. Since passive conformity is contrary to the nature of mind, the possibility remains that Pure Thought (God) may exist independently of human sense consciousness. God's existence is an unverifiable possibility, however, because experience is sufficiently explained without it.

In criticism, one should note that Lachelier's idealism was based on an absolute mechanical determinism later rejected by the physical sciences. His argument against natural units resembles the common scholastic argument that natural units are composed of primary matter and substantial form. To the extent that he acknowledged the human mind's passivity to the instinctive cosmos, Lachelier was a realist.

See Also: IDEALISM

Bibliography: *Oeuvres,* 2 v. (Paris 1933). *The Philosophy of Jules Lachelier,* tr. E. G. BALLARD (The Hague 1960). L. MILLET, *Le Symbolisme dans la philosophie de Lachelier* (Paris 1959), excellent bibliog. E. G. BALLARD, "Jules Lachelier's Idealism," *Review of Metaphysics,* 8 (1954–55) 685–705. R. A. POWELL, *Truth or Absolute Nothing: A Critique of the Idealist Philosophy of Jules Lachelier* (River Forest, Ill. 1958). A. G. SERTILLANGES, *Le Christianisme et les philosophies,* 2 v. (Paris 1939–41). V. MATHIEU, *Enciclopedia filosofica,* 4 v. (Venics–Rome 1957) 2:1766–68.

[R. A. POWELL]

LACOMBE, ALBERT

Missionary; b. St. Sulpice, Montreal, Canada, Feb. 28, 1827; d. Midnapore, Alberta, Canada, Dec. 12, 1916. He was the son of Albert and Agathe (Duhamel) Lacombe. After ordination on June 13, 1849, he first exercised his ministry at Pembina, North Dakota (1849–51) and then returned to Canada as a curate in Berthierville (1851–52). He offered his services to Bp. Alexandre TACHÉ, OMI, of Red River, and went with him to Saint Boniface in 1852. From there he left for Edmonton and worked among the Cree and métis of Lake LaBiche, wintering at Fort Edmonton. In 1853 he took up residence at Lake St. Anne and visited Fort Jasper, and in 1855 he undertook an extensive trip to Small Slave Lake and Peace River. Upon his return to Lake St. Anne he joined the Oblates of Mary Immaculate and made his profession on Sept. 28, 1856. He founded the mission of St. Joachim in Edmonton (1858), and with Taché he determined the site of St. Albert mission, which bears his name (1861). From 1865 to 1872 he roamed the Plains and evangelized the Cree and Black Feet, founding (1866) St. Paul of the Cree in Brosseau, Alberta, the first attempt at agricultural colonization of the natives of the West.

He was named an official government intermediary during Louis RIEL's revolution (1873–74), served as pastor in Winnipeg (1874–80), attended to the care of the construction gangs of the Canadian Pacific railroad, and succeeded in preventing the Black Feet from slaughtering the workers (1883). Because of this he was named president of the Pacific for one hour when the first train arrived in Calgary in 1884. He founded the first industrial school for indigenous peoples at Dunbow, Alberta (1884), and opened a hospital (1893) and a school (1898) at Blood Reserve. From 1886 to 1892 he was a member of the Board of Education of the Northwest Territories. He founded a colony for the métis at St. Paul, Alberta, the source of many parishes. Between 1893 and 1895 he was frequently sent to the government at Ottawa to see justice done in the Catholic school question of the West. He was part of the government commission entrusted with making a treaty with the natives (1899) and traveled to Hungary (1900) and to Austria (1904) to enlist Ruthenian rite priests. In 1909 he founded a hospital at Midnapore, Alberta. He was the author of many important works in the native language.

Bibliography: K. HUGHES, *Father Lacombe: The Black-Robe Voyageur* (New York 1911). *Le Père Lacombe . . . d'après ses* *memoires . . . par une soeur de la Providence* (Montreal 1916). P. E. BRETON, *The Big Chief of the Prairies: The Life of Father Lacombe* (Montreal 1956).

[G. CARRIÈRE]

LACORDAIRE, JEAN-BAPTISTE HENRI

Dominican preacher, refounder of Dominican Order in France; b. May 12, 1802, Recey-sur-Ource (Burgundy); d. Nov. 21, 1861, Sorèze. His father, a physician like many of his ancestors, died when Jean-Baptiste was only four. His mother was deeply committed to providing the best care and education for her four children. At the lycée Lacordaire attended, he came under the influence of a bright but unbelieving teacher. Within a short time, the impressionable young student lost his Catholic faith. He had, however, acquired a love of the ideals of the French Revolution, liberty, equality, and fraternity, which would endure throughout his life. In 1819 Lacordaire entered the law school at Dijon, where his exceptional talent for public speaking blossomed. Early in his law school career, Lacordaire was very much influenced by the writings of J. J. ROUSSEAU on religious and political issues. He adopted a deistic understanding of God and saw religion, especially Christianity, as important because of its social utility. He parted company with Rousseau's political views after he became involved with a group of conservative, monarchist, and mostly Catholic students known as the *Société d'Études*. This group, founded in 1821, strongly supported the Bourbon Restoration. Influenced by these students, Lacordaire rejected Rousseau's notion of the social contract and instead committed himself to government based on a constitutional monarchy because it alone seemed capable of maintaining a balance between liberty and authority. As a result of his association with this predominantly Catholic group, Lacordaire became increasingly open to Catholicism and preoccupied with questions of religious faith. He completed law school at Dijon and moved to Paris in 1822 in order to begin a legal apprenticeship.

Conversion and Early Priesthood. Although Lacordaire's legal career in Paris got off to a bright and promising start, he was very troubled interiorly. He suffered from the Romantic melancholy that was typical of his generation, from the Romantic need for religious belief that was frustrated by the inability to believe. His "cold" reason seemed to rule out religion while his Romantic imagination, his "extremely religious soul," yearned to believe. By early 1824, it was apparent that his heart would be the victor. He wrote to a friend: "Would you believe it, I am every day growing more and more a Christian." His conversion to Catholic Christianity was soon completed. He described it in this Romantic fashion: "I remember having read the Gospel of Matthew and having cried one night: when one cries, one soon believes." From the beginning, his Catholic faith was profoundly related to his concern for the betterment of society. He believed that society could only have balance, just laws, authentic progress, and perfection through the Catholic Church.

Lacordaire entered the Sulpician seminary near Paris on May 12, 1824. Despite misgivings by seminary officials about his political views, which were untypical of French priesthood candidates of his era, he was ordained as a priest of the archdiocese of Paris on Sept. 22, 1827 by Archbishop de QUÉLEN. He was soon offered an important position in Rome but declined becoming instead chaplain of a Visitation convent. He received a supplementary assignment in 1828 when he was appointed assistant chaplain of a secondary school. These two tasks allowed him ample opportunity to pursue the study of theology. By the end of the 1820s Lacordaire was seriously considering the possibility of becoming a missionary to the United States because of its separation of church and state. He had received an offer from Bishop John Dubois of New York, an exile from revolutionary France, to become vicar general of his diocese and rector of the diocesan seminary.

Political Involvement. In 1830, Lacordaire abandoned any plans to leave France for the United States when he joined with Félicité LAMENNAIS, a priest who was one of the leading ultramontanists and Catholic political liberals in France, and a few others of like mind in the project of reconciling the Catholic Church and modern liberal society. They decided to fight for the cause of "God and liberty" by publishing a nationally distributed Catholic daily newspaper called *L'Avenir*. From the first issue of Oct. 16, 1830, the editors sought the support of all, Catholic or not, who believed in freedom of religion, education, and the press. They also argued that church and state should be free from mutual interference. The newspaper also advocated the freedom of religious orders to exist. *L'Avenir* soon found itself confronted by enemies on all sides. Secular liberals distrusted Catholic liberals. The predominantly conservative Catholic population of France distrusted liberals of every kind. The bishops, who were generally Gallican, disliked both the ULTRAMONTANISM and the political liberalism of Lacordaire, Lamennais et al. The editors, fearing that *L'Avenir* would be unable to survive such widespread opposition, decided to appeal to Pope GREGORY XVI for support. They believed that their staunch ultramontanism would bolster their case. They were mistaken: the pope issued the encyclical *Mirari vos* (Aug. 15, 1832), condemning

L'Avenir, without mentioning it by name, and its entire project of reconciling Catholicism with such modern ideas as separation of church and state and freedom of religion and the press. The editors promptly accepted the papal condemnation and permanently ceased publication of their newspaper. In 1833, Lacordaire quietly resumed his chaplaincy at the Visitation convent.

Beginning of Preaching Career. Lacordaire's brilliant preaching career began in early 1834 with a series of conferences given to the students of the Collège Stanislas in Paris at the suggestion of Frédéric Ozanam. As his reputation grew, more adults than young students came to these conferences. Among his attentive listeners were such literary figures as CHATEAUBRIAND and Victor HUGO. His audience was impressed by the eloquence, enthusiasm, and commitment that he brought to his presentation of religious themes. To a generation that loved liberty, Lacordaire spoke of it as a tree that God himself had planted in the Garden of Eden. However, some of the clergy denounced him to the archbishop of Paris as a preacher of novelties rather than of orthodox Christianity. Consequently, Archbishop de Quélen suspended his conferences but later dramatically vindicated Lacordaire by giving him the prestigious task of preaching the 1835 Lenten conferences at Notre Dame Cathedral. In his sermons there, he expressed his concern for the social problems of his era and offered Christianity as the only adequate solution to these problems. He continued his popular and influential preaching at Notre Dame during Lent of 1836. At the conclusion of those conferences, he resigned from his preaching position at Notre Dame and retreated to Rome for study and meditation.

Dominican Vocation. During a retreat made with the Jesuits in Rome in May 1837, Lacordaire began to seriously think about the possibility of becoming a religious. In August of that year, he discussed the possibility of refounding the Dominican Order in France with Prosper Guéranger, who was himself engaged in restoring the Benedictine Order in France. Lacordaire was very impressed with the Dominican emphasis on preaching and with the order's democratic structure. He definitively decided to join the Order of Preachers during a retreat in France at the Abbey of Solesmes in June 1838. To win public approval for the restoration of an order that was still technically illegal in France, he wrote his *Essay on the Re-Establishment in France of the Order of Preachers* in which he eloquently appealed to his compatriots' love of liberty for support of an institution that he believed had historically been characterized by liberal and democratic constitutions. With two French recruits, Lacordaire began his novitiate year at the Dominican convent of La Quercia near Viterbo, Italy, in April 1839. He wrote an important *Life of St. Dominic* while still a nov-

ice. After completing theological studies in Rome, he returned to France where, on Feb. 14, 1841, he preached from the pulpit of Notre Dame Cathedral in his Dominican habit to an immense congregation which included Archbishop de Quélen as well as many government officials. Lacordaire continued to preach throughout France and Belgium, even resuming his acclaimed conferences at the Parisian cathedral. During the revolutionary year of 1848, he served briefly as a deputy of the National Assembly. The Dominican Order officially restored the Province of France in 1850 in recognition of the great growth in vocations and the establishment of new convents in that country during the 1840s. Lacordaire was appointed as provincial.

Alexandre Jandel, one of Lacordaire's early recruits, was appointed head of the Dominican Order in 1850 by Pope Pius IX. Long-standing differences between the two friars on questions of religious observance soon surfaced. Jandel emphasized the necessity for a strict and rigorous interpretation and observance of the Dominican constitutions while Lacordaire emphasized an ''admirable freedom'' at the heart of Dominican life which allowed for mitigations in the observance for the sake of the primary end of the order, preaching. In 1852, the issue of the night office brought the two superiors into open conflict. Jandel believed that, according to the constitutions, the office of Matins could be celebrated no later than three a.m. Lacordaire had instructed the friars of his province to celebrate that office at four a.m. in order to allow for adequate sleep, given the demands of their ministries. Jandel then informed the superiors in the French province that he was revoking Lacordaire's directive.

In 1852, Lacordaire, who had always been concerned about the religious education of the young, founded a men's community of Third Order Dominican teachers. Two years later, he accepted responsibility on behalf of the Dominicans for an historic boys' college at Sorèze near Toulouse. He made himself the head of that school, a post that he held for the rest of his life. When his term as provincial ended in 1854, he became more deeply involved in the direction of the college while continuing to do some preaching. He was elected provincial for the second time in 1858. His failing health led to his resignation as provincial in August 1861. On Nov. 21, 1861, he died at Sorèze.

Bibliography: H. LACORDAIRE, *Essay on the Re-Establishment in France of the Order of Preachers (Mémoire pour le Rétablissement en France de l'Ordre des Frères Precheurs)*, ed. S. TUGWELL (Chicago 1983); *La liberté de la parole évangélique: écrits, conférences, lettres,* textes choisis et présentés par A. DUVAL et J.-P. JOSSUA (Paris 1996). P. BATTS, ''Lacordaire's Understanding of 'Restoration' in Relation to his Refounding of the Dominican Order in 19th Century France'' (D.Th. diss., St. Paul University [Ottawa] 1999). B. BONVIN, *Lacordaire-Jandel, la Restauration de* *l'Ordre Dominicain en France après la Revolution* (Paris 1989). B. CHOCARNE, *The Inner Life of Père Lacordaire,* trans. A. DRANE (New York 1879). J. T. FOISSET, *Vie du R. P. Lacordaire,* 2 vols. (Paris 1870). H. D. NOBLE, *La vocation dominicaine du P. Lacordaire* (Paris 1914). L. C. SHEPPARD, *Lacordaire: A Biographical Essay* (New York 1964).

[P. M. BATTS]

LACROIX, CLAUDE

Jesuit moral theologian; b. Dahlem, Luxembourg, April 7, 1652; d. Cologne, June 1 or 2, 1714. He entered the Society of Jesus at Trier in 1673 and was ordained in 1684. For three years he taught philosophy at Cologne, and then taught moral theology at Münster and Cologne. His great work *Theologia moralis* (8 v. Cologne 1707–14) was a commentary on the *Medulla theologiae moralis* of Hermann BUSENBAUM and itself became one of the outstanding theological works of the 18th century. It went through 25 editions in 50 years and won for Lacroix the reputation of being one of the finest moralists of his age. One of the later editions (1757), however, served as a focal point of the opposition of the Jansenists to the Jesuits and was condemned by the parliament of Paris and publicly burned at Toulouse.

Bibliography: C. SOMMERVOGEL, *Bibliothèque de la Compagnie de Jésus* (Brussels-Paris 1890–1932) 4:1347–54. H. HURTER, *Nomenclator literarius theologiae catholicae* (Innsbruck 1903–13) 4:911. P. BERNARD, *Dictionnaire de théologie catholique* (Paris 1903–50) 8.2:2424.

[J. C. WILLKE]

LA CROSSE, DIOCESE OF

The Diocese of La Crosse (*Crossensis*), suffragan of the metropolitan See of MILWAUKEE, was established March 3, 1868, upon recommendation of the Second Plenary Council of Baltimore, and embracing that half of the state of Wisconsin north and west of the Wisconsin River. Subsequent subdivisions erecting the Diocese of Superior (1905) and Madison (1946) reduced the original territory to 15,070 square miles. The resulting territory spans 19 counties in West-Central Wisconsin. Approximately 30 percent of the population is Catholic. The diocesan Catholic population grew steadily throughout the history of the diocese, aided initially by German and Irish immigration, and subsequently by heavy pockets of Polish immigration. After leveling off for a couple of decades, the Catholic population again began to increase in the 1990s as a result of the influx of large number of Mexican immigrants.

Bishops. When the first bishop, Bavarian-born Michael HEISS, was consecrated in 1868, the diocese had 18 priests, 47 small churches, and a Catholic population of about 30,000. By 1880, when he was transferred to Milwaukee, the number of priests had increased to 59 and the number of churches had more than doubled, while the Catholic population showed an increase of 50 percent. The second bishop, Kilian C. Flasch, also Bavarian-born, was rector of St. Francis Seminary in Milwaukee in the years before his consecration as the second bishop of La Crosse in 1881. During his ten-year episcopate there was a marked increase in the number of churches and educational facilities within the diocese.

The third bishop of La Crosse, James Schwebach, who was Flasch's vicar-general, was consecrated in 1892. Schwebach was born in Platen, Luxembourg, in 1847, immigrated to the United States in 1864, and, after completing his studies at St. Francis Seminary, Milwaukee, was ordained in 1870. Under his episcopacy the expansion of Catholic activity kept pace with the increase of population. A continuous program of construction of churches and the establishment of a diocesan high school marked his episcopate.

Alexander J. McGavick, a former auxiliary of Chicago, Ill., was appointed the fourth bishop of La Crosse in 1921. Despite his own poor health, the economic depression of the 1930s, and the outbreak of World War II, McGavick erected 38 new buildings, including a number of high schools. John P. Treacy, who had been appointed coadjutor with right of succession in 1945, became the fifth ordinary of the diocese in July 1946, two years before the death of McGavick. To encourage priestly vocations Treacy established Holy Cross Seminary, overlooking the Mississippi River south of La Crosse. Treacy also built a new cathedral, placing it under the patronage of St. Joseph the Workman.

After Treacy's death in 1964, Bp. Frederick W. Freking of Salina, Kans., was appointed sixth bishop of La Crosse in 1965. Freking oversaw the implementation of postconciliar reforms in the diocese. John J. Paul, a priest of the diocese, was ordained an auxiliary bishop in 1977, eventually becoming the seventh bishop of La Crosse in 1983. Bishop Paul implemented an aggressive recruitment program for the diocesan clergy. By the time of his resignation in 1994, the number of diocesan seminarians had rebounded to more than 30.

Raymond L. Burke, another native son of the diocese, served on the Apostolic Signatura in Rome before his ordination as the eighth bishop of La Crosse in 1995. An ardent defender of the family farm, Bishop Burke was named President of the Board of Directors of the National Catholic Rural Life Conference in 1996. His episcopate was marked by several major building projects. In December of 1999 he unveiled plans to build a large pilgrimage shrine southeast of La Crosse in honor of Our Lady of Guadalupe, scheduled for completion in 2004. He held a diocesan synod to mark the Jubilee Year 2000.

Bibliography: H. H. HEMING, ed. *The Catholic Church in Wisconsin* (Milwaukee 1895–98). L. RUMMEL, *History of the Catholic Church in Wisconsin* (Madison 1976).

[J. E. BIECHLER/D. SAKOWSKI]

LACTANTIUS

Lucius Caelius (or Caecilius) Firmianus, Christian apologist; b. North Africa, *c.* 240; d. *c.* 320. As a pagan he was a pupil of ARNOBIUS the Elder and long a teacher of rhetoric; he was officially invited to teach at Nicomedia during Diocletian's reign. It is uncertain when he became a Christian, but in the persecution of 303 he lost his official position and was impoverished. He seems to have moved to the West (*c.* 305), may have lived in Gaul, and probably returned to the East (311–313). In his old age (*c.* 317) in Trier, he became tutor to Crispus, Constantine's son.

None of his works survive except those connected with Christianity. The *De Opificio Dei* (303–304) is a demonstration of divine providence based on the wonders of human anatomy. The *Divinae institutiones* in seven books, completed by 313, was written to refute attacks on Christianity by a philosopher and a high official (Hierocles)—and other past or future traducers of Christianity. In this work Lactantius attacks paganism and philosophy; discusses Christianity, justice, true worship, and true religion; and deals extensively with eschatology. In pursuing his goal, the union of true religion and true wisdom, possible only in Christianity, he makes little use of Scripture but relies on pagan prophets, such as the SIBYLLINE oracles and Hermes Trismegistus. His quotations of Scripture depend largely on Cyprian's *Testimonia*. In *De ira Dei* (*c.* 314) he counters the notion that God is indifferent, showing that His anger toward the wicked corresponds to His favor to the good. *De mortibus persecutorum* (*c.* 318), which shows the evil fate of those who had persecuted Christians, is an important historical source for the period after 303. Its authorship is no longer questioned. Lactantius's *Epitome* of his *Institutiones* and a poem on the PHOENIX are also extant.

In style Lactantius is the most classical of the early Christian Latin authors. He uses pagan authors, especially Cicero, Lucretius, and Vergil. Jerome says that his writing is "like a stream of Ciceronian eloquence," and in the Renaissance he was called the "Christian Cicero." He has little to say of Christian doctrine and institutions and is of little value as a theologian. "Would that he had been able to establish our teaching as well as he demolished that of others," said Jerome.

Bibliography: *Opera Omnia,* ed. S. BRANDT and G. LAUBMANN, 2 v. in 3 (*Corpus scriptorum ecclesiasticorum latinorum* 19, 27.1, 27.2; 1890, 1893, 1897); *De la mort des persécuteurs,* tr. and ed. J. MOREAU, 2 v. (*Sources Chrétiennes* 39; 1954); *De ira Dei,* tr. and ed. H. KRAFT and A. WLOSOK (Darmstadt 1957); *Divinarum institutionum epitome,* tr. and ed. E. H. BLAKENEY (London 1950). R. PICHON, *Lactance* (Paris 1901), fundamental. A. WLOSOK, *Laktanz und die philosophische Gnosis* (Heidelberg 1960); "Zur Bedeutung der nichtcyprianischen Bibelzitate bei Laktanz," *Studia Patristica* 4.2 (*Texte und Untersuchungen zur Geschichte der altchristlichen Literatur* 79; 1961) 234–250. J. STEVENSON, "The Life and Literary Activity of Lactantius," *ibid.,* 1.1 (*Texte und Untersuchungen* 63; 1957) 661–677. J. QUASTEN, *Patrology* 2:392–410. D. R. S. BAILEY, "Lactantiana," *Vigiliae christianae* 14 (1960) 165–169.

[J. STEVENSON]

LACUNZA Y DÍAZ, MANUEL DE

Chilean theologian and Scripture scholar; b. Santiago, Chile, July 19, 1731; d. Imola, Italy, July 18, 1801. On Sept. 7, 1747, he entered the Society of Jesus and in 1755, he was ordained. On the expulsion of the Jesuits from Spain and its colonies in 1767, he went to Italy, where he led a retired life dedicated to meditation and study. This resulted in a book that later became famous, *Venida del mesías en gloria y majestad,* finished in 1790. It circulated in manuscript form before it was published in Cádiz, Spain, in 1812. It was later published in London, Mexico, Paris, and elsewhere, and translated into various languages. Lacunza used the pseudonym Juan Josafat Ben Ezra. The book had, even among the Jesuits, fervent admirers as well as strong opponents. It was finally banned by the Holy Office on Sept. 6, 1824, and again on July 11, 1941, this time with specific reference to the book's moderate MILLENARIANISM. This was considered a fatal blow to the book among Catholics, although many of them, like Menéndez Pelayo, believed before 1941 that the condemnation did not refer to millenarianism per se but rather to statements against the Roman Curia or statements offensive to the Fathers of the Church or in praise of Judaism. Among Protestants the book has become a symbol for some adventist sects. Lacunza's good faith and proper intentions cannot be doubted, although his mental health is questionable. His great reputation in Chile is based upon the depth of his thought, expressed in a polished style.

Bibliography: A. F. VAUCHER, *Une Célébrité oubliée: Le padre Manuel de Lacunza y Díaz* (Collonges-sous-Salève, Switzerland 1941). F. MATEOS, "El padre Manuel de Lacunza y el milenarismo," *Revista chilena de historia y geografía* 115 (1950) 134–161.

[F. MATEOS]

LACY, EDMUND

Bishop of Exeter; d. Chudleigh, Devonshire, Sept. 18, 1455. The son of Stephen Lacy of Gloucester, he was a fellow of University College, Oxford, by 1391; he became doctor of theology in 1414. However, he was called ''the king's clerk'' and enjoyed royal patronage on a moderate scale from 1400. He may have been attached to Henry (V), Prince of Wales, for he became dean of the chapel in the royal household soon after Henry's accession in 1413. Lacy resigned this office and ceased to attend the king after his consecration as bishop of HEREFORD in 1417. He was translated to EXETER in 1420, and for the remainder of his life he generally resided in the diocese. In 1435 Lacy was excused from attending parliaments and councils because of a long-standing disease of the shin bones (*Cal. Patent Rolls 1429–36* 453). This affliction may have occasioned his promotion of the therapeutic cult of St. Raphael, for whose feast he composed an Office to be observed in Exeter Cathedral and the collegiate churches of Crediton and Ottery St. Mary; he eventually secured its observance in Hereford and York Cathedrals as well. Lacy's tomb in Exeter Cathedral is said to have been the scene of many miraculous cures [U. M. Radford, ''The Wax Images Found in Exeter Cathedral,'' *The Antiquaries Journal* 29 (1949) 164–168].

Bibliography: Lacy's registers have been pub. Hereford, ed. A. T. BANNISTER (Canterbury and York Society; London 1918); Exeter, register of institutions, ed. F. C. HINGESTON-RANDOLPH (Devon and Cornwall Record Society; Exeter 1909). For his Exeter common register, ed. G. R. DUNSTAN (Canterbury and York Society; London 1963–). A. B. EMDEN, *A Biographical Register of the University of Oxford to A.D. 1500* (Oxford 1957–59) 2:1081–83.

[R. L. STOREY]

LADISLAUS, KING OF HUNGARY, ST.

Reigned 1077 to July 29, 1095; b. Poland, *c.* 1040; d. Nitra, Czechoslovakia. The son of King Béla I of Hungary and a daughter of the Polish King Mesko II, Ladislaus (László, Lazlo, or Lancelot) was elected king against his will after the death of his brother King Geisa I. His cousin Solomon, aided by Emperor HENRY IV, rebelled against him. When Solomon revolted a second time with the aid of heathen Cumans, Ladislaus defeated them and finally unified his kingdom. In 1083 he successfully promoted the canonization of King STEPHEN I of Hungary, EMERIC OF HUNGARY, and GERARD OF CSANÁD. In 1091 he founded the bishopric of Zagreb, later annexing Croatia and Bosnia outright. Ladislaus did not subscribe to the GREGORIAN REFORM although in the INVESTITURE STRUGGLE he sided with the pope and with Rudolph of Swabia. He married Agnes (sometimes called Adelaide),

the daughter of Rudolph. He introduced a new law code for his kingdom. Priests were allowed to marry, but remarriage was forbidden. The Diet at Szabolcs marked a step toward a deepened religious life among both clergy and laymen. He died while preparing for the First CRUSADE, and he was buried in the cathedral that he had built in Oradea (Romania). In 1192 he was canonized by CELESTINE III.

Feast: June 27.

Bibliography: *Acta sanctorum* June 7:284–294. G. FEJÉR, *Codex diplomaticus Hungariae,* 43 v. (Budapest 1829–44) v.1. S. L. ENDLICHER, ed., *Rerum Hungaricarum monumenta arpadiana* (Sankt Gallen 1849). P. VON VÁCZY, *Die erste Epoche des ungar. Königtums* (Budapest 1935). *Vies des saintes et des bienheureux selon l'ordre du calendrier avec l'historique des fêtes* 6:461–463. A. BUTLER *The Lives of the Saints* rev. ed. (New York 1956) 2:654–655. P. J. GÁL, *Idvezlégy, kegyelmes Szent László kerály, Magyarországnak édes oltalma* (Budapest 1999), legends.

[J. PAPIN]

LADISLAUS OF GIELNIÓW, BL.

Franciscan popular missionary; b. *c.* 1440, Gielnów, Diocese of Gniezno, Poland; d. May 4, 1505 (feast, May 4, September 25). After being educated in Cracow, he entered the FRANCISCAN Order. Pious and filled with apostolic zeal, Ladislaus in his pastoral activities followed the example of JOHN CAPISTRAN. In 1487 he became provincial of the Polish Bernardine province; he founded a new observant convent that became a center of missionary activity for Lithuania. He excelled as a poet, whose works were devoted to the Passion of Christ and to Our Lady, in whose honor he introduced a special form of rosary. He was beatified on Feb. 11, 1750, by BENEDICT XIV, and in 1753 he was proclaimed a patron of Poland, the city of Warsaw, and Lithuania.

Bibliography: *Acta Sanctorum* May 1 (1863) 565–620. *Masarykův slovník naučný,* 7 v. (Prague 1925–33) 4:291. C. BOGDALSKI, *Bernardyni w Polsce,* v.2 (Krakow 1933) 93–142, the Bernadines of Poland. B. STASIEWSKI, *Lexikon für Theologie und Kirche,* ed. J. HOFER and K. RAHNER, 10 v. (2d, new ed. Freiburg 1957–65) 6:728.

[J. PAPIN]

LAETUS, ST.

Hermit; fl. at Micy, sixth century. The sole primary source for his life is the largely legendary vita composed in the 10th century on the model of the vita of St. Viator of Sologne (sixth century) written in the ninth century. Whether Laetus was ever ordained or remained a deacon is uncertain. He was a monk in the monastery at Micy under the abbot AVITUS, and then went into a forest area north of Orléans as a hermit. The place where he died was later called Saint-Lié in his honor. In 943 Ermentheus, bishop of Orléans, transferred his relics to Pithiviers, France. In the late Middle Ages he was venerated, among other places, at Laon, Paris, and Orléans.

Feast: Nov. 5.

Bibliography: *Bibliotheca hagiographica latina antiquae et mediae aetatis* (Brussels 1898–1901) 2:4672. *Acta sanctorum* Nov. 3:67–79. A. M. ZIMMERMANN, *Kalendarium Benedictinum* (Metten 1933–38) 3:264–265. A. PONCELET, ''Les Saints de Micy,'' *Analecta Bollandiana* 24 (1905) 1–104, esp. 61–71, 98–103.

[M. R. P. MCGUIRE]

LAFARGE

A family of distinguished U.S. artists and authors founded by Jean Frédéric de la Farge, a refugee from Revolutionary France, who arrived in the United States in 1807 and settled near the present LaFargeville in upper New York State, and his wife Louisa, daughter of emigré Louis François Binsse de St. Victor (1774–1884), a miniaturist.

John. Artist and author; b. New York, March 3, 1835; d. Providence, R. I., Nov. 14, 1910. A son of Jean Frédéric and Louisa, he attended St. John's College (now Fordham University), New York City, and graduated (1853) from Mt. St. Mary's College, Emmitsburg, Md. He was preparing for law, but went to Paris (1856) and enrolled briefly in Thomas Couture's studio, apparently without any notion of becoming an artist. He met French intellectuals through his cousin, the literary critic Paul Bins, Comte de St. Victor (1825–81), encountered the Pre-Raphaelites in England, and haunted the art galleries. He came under the influence of William Morris Hunt, a Couture disciple, at Newport, R.I. in 1859 and began a serious interest in art. His early works were chiefly landscapes that somewhat anticipated impressionism as well as *plein-air* painting.

Never robust after a serious illness in the 1860s, LaFarge nevertheless served on the committee set up to establish the Metropolitan Museum of Art in New York City. Shortly thereafter he began mural painting and, through his collaboration with architects, realized a fusion of building and decorative arts for the first time in the United States. His work appears in Trinity Church, Boston, planned with the architect H. H. Richardson; the Capitol, St. Paul, Minnesota; the Supreme Court building in Baltimore; the Church of the Ascension, New York City (probably his masterpiece); and in private New York mansions. His experiments in stained-glass design, which led to the invention of ''opaline'' glass and the creation of the jewel-like ''Peacock Window'' in the art museum at Worcester, Massachusetts, brought new life to this supposedly dead medium. He was also in the vanguard of European and U. S. artists who evinced interest in the art of the Pacific Islands. His voyage to Japan and the South Seas with his close friend Henry ADAMS in 1886 occasioned an important series of water colors. In 1899 he ''incited'' Adams to visit Chartres with him to study the windows, about which Adams philosophizes in his classic *Mont-Saint-Michel and Chartres.*

LaFarge was a stimulating writer and lecturer. His *Considerations on Painting* (1895) originated as lectures at New York's Metropolitan Museum. In 1897 he published *An Artist's Letters from Japan* and a monograph on the Japanese artist Hokusai (1760–1859). LaFarge possessed, according to Adams, the most complex mind in the United States. To the art critic Royal Cortissoz, his biographer, he stated: ''Painting is, more than people think, a question of brains.'' This attitude probably reveals both the strength and weakness of his work; in certain of his murals, for example, the desired effect is somewhat marred by an overly meticulous regard for detail. His achievement was substantial, however, both in his own works and in his influence.

LaFarge married (1860) Margaret Mason, granddaughter of Commodore Matthew C. Perry and great-granddaughter of Benjamin Franklin, and fathered nine children; among them were Christopher Grant, John Louis Bancel, and John.

Bibliography: R. CORTISSOZ, *John LaFarge* (Boston 1911). J. LAFARGE, *The Manner Is Ordinary* (New York 1954). S. ISHAM, *History of American Painting* (New York 1927). O. W. LARKIN, *Art and Life in America* (rev. ed. New York 1960). H. ADAMS, *The Education of Henry Adams* (Boston 1961).

[F. GETLEIN]

Christopher Grant. Eldest son of John, architect; b. Newport, R. I., Jan. 5, 1862, d. Saunderstown, R. I., Oct. 11, 1938. After two years at the Massachusetts Institute of Technology and a two-year apprenticeship with H. H. Richardson, he formed (1886) a partnership with George L. Hains, and their Romanesque design won the competition for the cathedral of St. John the Divine, New York City. He devoted most of his time and talent to this project until, after the completion of the choir in 1907, all work was halted, a new competition held, and the firm of Cram, Goodhue, and Ferguson was selected to complete the cathedral in Gothic style. Although bitterly disappointed, LaFarge continued to serve his profession, not only with distinguished designs, but also as a fellow, director, and vice president of the American Institute of Architects and as chairman of the advisory committee of the architecture schools at Columbia University in New York City and the Massachusetts Institute of Technology. As a member of the American Institute of Architects Committee for Education, he visited schools of architecture, lecturing on cultural aspects of the profession. Other La-Farge designs are the Fourth Presbyterian Church, New York City; the U.S. Naval Hospital, Brooklyn; buildings for the New York City Zoological Society (of which he was a founder); St. Paul's Church, Rochester, N. Y.; the Houghton Memorial Chapel, Wellesley College, Wellesley, Massachusetts; the Parkhard Memorial Library, Salt Lake City, Utah; the Morgan Building and Williams Memorial, Trinity College, Hartford, Connecticut; and St. Matthew's Cathedral, Washington, D.C. He was the husband of Florence Bayard Lockwood and father of poet, novelist, and architect Christopher Grant (1897–1956) and writer and social scientist Oliver Hazard Perry (1901–1963).

Bibliography: J. LAFARGE, *op. cit.*

[P. GOETTELMANN]

John Louis Bancel. Second son of John, artist and designer; b. Newport, R. I., Sept. 23, 1865; d. Mount Carmel, Conn., Aug. 14, 1938. After a year at the University of Pennsylvania School of Medicine, a serious eye infection caused him to abandon this study in 1885. He turned to art, and after a brief apprenticeship in his father's New York studio, he studied in Europe for 12 years. He maintained close association with his father in the latter's business affairs. His major art work was related to church architecture and public buildings and included murals, mosaics, and stained glass; but he was known as well for his landscapes and figure painting. His most outstanding piece is the mosaic of the coronation of the Virgin Mary in the chapel of Trinity College, Washington, D.C. Other notable creations are the four altarpieces for the Church of the Immaculate Conception at Newport (his earliest commission); and mural decorations for the National Shrine of the Immaculate Conception in Washington, D.C.; St. Charles Seminary, Catonsville, Maryland; Sacred Heart Chapel, St. Paul, Minnesota; St. Aidan's Chapel, New Haven, Connecticut; and the New Haven public library. Examples of his work in stained glass are found in the Sacred Heart Chapel in St. Paul and the Church of Our Lady of Mount Carmel, Mount Carmel, California. He served with the Connecticut State Commission on Sculpture and with the national competitions jury sponsored by the U.S. Treasury Department for the decoration of government buildings. Yale University awarded him an honorary B. F. A. in 1917. He was a member of the National Institute of Arts and Letters, the National Society of Mural Painters, the New York Water Color Club, Liturgical Arts Society (president), and hon-

orary member of the American Institute of Architects. He married Mabel Hooper in 1898 and they had four children: Louis Bancel, Edward Hooper, Henry Adams, and Thomas Sergeant LaFarge. Thomas Sergeant (1904–1943), an assistant to his father, was lost at sea during World War II.

Bibliography: J. LAFARGE, *op. cit. New York Times* (Aug. 15, 1938) 15:1, obituary.

[D'A. MCNICKLE]

John. Third son of John, editor, journalist, founder of the Catholic interracial movement in the United States; b. Newport, R. I., Feb. 13, 1880; d. New York City, Nov. 24, 1963. His early education was largely private; he entered Harvard College in 1897 and graduated in 1901. He studied for the priesthood at the University of Innsbruck, Austria, where he was ordained on July 26, 1905. He entered the Society of Jesus on Nov. 12, 1905, at Poughkeepsie, New York, and after two years of noviceship taught for a year at Canisius College in Buffalo and later at Loyola College in Baltimore. Two years of study at Woodstock College in Maryland earned him an M. A. in philosophy, but ill health forced him to abandon hope of reviewing theology. One year was spent as chaplain in the penal and hospital institutions of New York City, followed by 15 years of pastoral labor in the Jesuit missions in Charles and St. Mary's counties in southern Maryland. It was there he witnessed first hand racial prejudice and exploitation of the blacks. This period was interrupted for a year (1916–17) by studies in ascetical theology at St. Andrew-on-Hudson in Poughkeepsie. In August of 1926 he was appointed an associate editor of *America,* the national Catholic weekly review, a position he held until his death, except for two years as executive editor and four years as editor in chief.

Upon his return to New York City in 1926, LaFarge began his long apostolate for interracial justice in the pages of *America,* on the lecture platform, and principally through the formation of the Catholic Interracial Councils and their organ, the *Interracial Review.* The forerunner of this body had been the Catholic Laymen's Union, a group of Afro-American Catholics brought together by LaFarge to develop a program of spiritual formation and study of race relations. On Pentecost Sunday 1934 the union expanded into the first Catholic Interracial Council. In 1958 the 40 such councils established across the country held their first national convention in Chicago and established the NATIONAL CATHOLIC CONFERENCE FOR INTERRACIAL JUSTICE, with offices in Chicago and New York. The conference has been a strong voice for the Catholic position on civil rights and has widened the influence LaFarge first gave to the movement. The previous year (1937) LaFarge published *Interracial Justice: A*

Study of the Catholic Doctrine of Race Relations in which he condemned racism as sinful.

LaFarge was also chaplain of the LITURGICAL ARTS SOCIETY from its foundation in 1933, of the St. Ansgar's Scandinavian Catholic League, and of the Catholic Laymen's Union, all of New York. At various times he was an officer of the Catholic Association for International Peace and of the National Catholic Rural Life Conference.

Besides his signed and unsigned contributions to *America,* he contributed to *Études* (Paris), *Civiltà Cattolica* (Rome), *Criterio* (Argentina), *Stimmen der Zeit* (Munich), *Streven* (Brussels), *De Linie* (Amsterdam), the *Month* (England), as well as numerous American reviews. In 1947 he delivered the Dudleian Lecture at Harvard University Divinity School and the Phi Beta Kappa oration at the Harvard College commencement of 1954. In 1958 he lectured in French at the Cours International of the Benedictine Monastery of Toumliline, Morocco. In 1961 he was a traveling consultant in Germany for the U.S. Department of State. Of his frequent book reviews, some two or three a month for about 35 years, most appeared in *America,* but some also appeared in *Thought, Interracial Review, New York Times, Saturday Review, New York Herald Tribune,* and other publications. He also wrote several pamphlets for the America Press.

LaFarge was a fellow of the National Academy of Arts and Sciences (Boston), a member in 1947 of Panel VII (Rockefeller Brothers Report on Foreign Policy), and one of the 147 electors of the National Hall of Fame (New York University, 1960). He was the recipient of many awards, among them the American Liberties Medallion of the American Jewish Committee and the annual Campion Award of the Catholic Book Club. He published two autobiographical works, *The Manner Is Ordinary* (1954) and *Reflections on Growing Old* (1963). His other works include *Jesuits in Modern Times* (1927), *The Race Question and the Negro* (1953), *The Catholic Viewpoint on Race Relations* (1956), and *An American Amen* (1958).

Bibliography: J. LAFARGE, *op. cit. America* 109 (Dec. 7, 1963) 725. *Publishers Weekly* 184 (Dec. 9, 1963) 27–28. R. HECHT, *An Unordinary Man: A Life of John LaFarge, S.J.* (Metuchen, N.J. 1996) D. SUTHERN, *John LaFarge and the Limits of Catholic Interracialism* (Baton Rouge 1996). M. W. NICKELS, *The Federated Colored Catholics: A Study of Three Varied Perspectives on Racial Justice as Represented by John LaFarge, William Markoe, and Thomas Turner* (PhD Dissertation, Catholic University of America 1975).

[P. S. HURLEY]

LAFAYETTE, DIOCESE OF

The Diocese of Lafayette (*Lafayettensis*), Louisiana, suffragan of the metropolitan See of New Orleans, comprises the civil parishes of Acadia, Evangeline, Iberia, Lafayette, St. Landry, St. Martin, St. Mary, and Vermilion in western Louisiana, a total of 5,777 square miles. The diocese was erected Jan. 11, 1918, by Pope Benedict XV, with Jules B. Jeanmard as its first bishop. Catholics number about 65 percent of its population. There are 121 ecclesiastical parishes and 32 missions.

The early history of the area is part of the history of the Archdiocese of NEW ORLEANS. When Lafayette was chosen as the seat of a new diocese in 1918, St. John the Evangelist parish church became the cathedral. The first bishop, Jules B. Jeanmard, who was the first Lousiana-born priest to become a bishop, and who had served as chancellor and administrator of New Orleans, was consecrated at St. Louis Cathedral, New Orleans, Dec. 8, 1918. He took possession of the new see December 12, and remained its ordinary until his resignation on March 13, 1956; he died on Feb. 23, 1957. Under Jeanmard's 38 years as ordinary several more parishes were created, schools established, and lay involvement in programs of Catholic Action was stressed through religious instruction, spiritual conferences, and retreats. Sodality, scouting, and the retreat movements encouraged the faith of young Catholics and promoted vocations to the priesthood and religious life. Institutions founded by Jeanmard such as St. Mary's Children's Home (1924), staffed by the Most Holy Sacrament Sisters, Our Lady of Lourdes Hospital (1949), run by the Sisters of St. Francis of Calais, and Immaculata Seminary (1948), staffed by the Marist Fathers, helped to aid the physical and spiritual welfare of the growing diocese. Diocesan sponsorship of radio and, later, television programs in French and English, and a local newspaper were encouraged. In 1934 Jeanmard welcomed the first Black priests ordained by the Society of the Divine Word.

Bishop Maurice Schexnayder, who had been consecrated auxiliary Feb. 22, 1951, succeeded Bishop Jeanmard on May 24, 1956. Upon his resignation in 1972, Bishop Gerard L. Frey was transferred from Savannah, Georgia, and appointed the third Bishop of Lafayette. The Rev. Harry J. Flynn was appointed coadjutor to Bishop Frey in 1986 and became the fourth Bishop of Lafayette in 1989. When Bishop Flynn was elevated to Coadjutor Archbishop of Minneapolis-St. Paul in 1994, Bishop Edward J. O'Donnell was installed as the fifth bishop in 1994.

Bibliography: Archives, Diocese of Lafayette; R. BAUDIER, *The Catholic Church in Louisiana* (New Orleans 1939).

[R. E. TRACY/M. G. GUIDRY]

LA FERTÉ, ABBEY OF

First daughter abbey of CÎTEAUX (Latin, *Firmitas*), founded in 1113 in the Diocese of Châlon-sur-Saône (now Autun) by the counts of Châlon, who donated a fourth of the forest of Bragny. Under the administration of the first abbot, Philibert, the domain was enlarged by donations from noblemen of the region. In 1120 the number of religious was large enough to enable the abbot, Opizo, to found the first Cistercian house outside France, the abbey of Tigliedo, located south of the Alps in the province of Genoa, the Diocese of Acqui. In 1124 the third abbot, Peter, was promoted to the archbishopric of Tarentaise. That same year the abbey of Locedio was founded from La Ferté in Piedmont in the Diocese of Vercelli. In 1132 the abbey of Maizières was founded in Burgundy in the Diocese of Châlon (modern Diocese of Dijon). When the general chapter at Cîteaux in 1191 learned that the abbeys of Lombardy had held a separate chapter, it requested that the Abbey of La Ferté make an inquiry there summoning all the abbots in order to forbid such reunions. A struggle for power within the Cistercian Order continued between the abbot of Cîteaux and the first four daughter abbeys, La Ferté, PONTIGNY, CLAIRVAUX, and MORIMOND (all founded by St. STEPHEN HARDING; d. 1134). Innocent III checked the controversy (1215), but it flared up again in 1265, to be settled by Clement IV's bull *Parvus fons* (P. Cousin 375). In 1207 the abbey of Barona was founded in Lombardy in the Diocese of Pavia. The last daughter abbey, Saint-Serge, was founded in Syria in 1235. The monastery was built on a grand scale by the abbot Simon (1208–29). Several of its daughter abbeys founded still other houses, and the Abbey of La Ferté eventually had a filiation of 16 monasteries.

When the Peace of Brétigny (1360), between France and England, came to an end, La Ferté was plundered and ravaged by roving companies of mercenaries. In 1415 the duke of Burgundy, John the Fearless, fortified the abbey with a moat and two walls. In 1439 the general chapter designated the abbot, John, along with three other abbots, to attend the Council of Florence as the representatives of the order from France. In 1562, during the Wars of Religion, the abbey was plundered by the Huguenots. Several years later (1567) Admiral de Coligny seized La Ferté; the abbey was pillaged and burned. Abbot Claude Petit (1677–1710) rebuilt the monastery, preserving the 13th-century church, adding to it a new contemporary façade. At the beginning of the French Revolution there were only about 15 religious left at La Ferté. The buildings were sold, and the library was scattered. Today all that remains of the monastery is the 18th-century abbatial palace.

Bibliography: Sources. G. DUBY, *Recueil des pancartes de l'abbaye de la Ferté-sur-Grosne, 1113–1178* (Paris 1953). T. HÜMPFNER, "Exordium Cistercii cum summa cartae caritatis et fundatio primarum quattuor filiarum Cistercii," *Analecta Sacri Ordinis Cisterciensis* 2 (1946) 119–145. *Statuta capitulorum generalium ordinis cisterciensis,* ed. J. M. CANIVEZ, 8 v. (Louvain 1933–41). Literature. J. L. BAZIN, "Notice historique sur l'abbaye de la Ferté-sur-Grosne," *Mémoires de la Société d'histoire et d'archéologie de Châlon-sur-Saône* (1895) 1–70. A. A. KING, *Cîteaux and Her Elder Daughters* (London 1954) 106–147. B. STÜRZER, "La Ferté-sur-Grosne," *Cistercienser-Chronik* 7 (1895) 225–231, 257–264, 289–296, 321–334, 353–360. K. SPAHR, *Lexikon für Theologie und Kirche,* ed. J. HOFER and K. RAHNER, 10 v. (2d, new ed. Freiburg 1957–65) 6:729.

[M. A. DIMIER]

LAFITAU, JOSEPH FRANÇOIS

Jesuit author and missionary in New France; b. Bordeaux, Jan. 1, 1681; d. there, July 3, 1746. He entered the Society of Jesus in 1696 and in 1711 he was sent to New France (Canada), where for several years he labored among the Iroquois at Sault Saint Louis. After his recall to France in 1717 he spent his remaining years as a professor and writer. One of his better-known works, familiar to historians and anthropologists, is the two-volume treatise *Moeurs des sauvages Américains comparés aux moeurs des premiers temps* (Paris 1724), which went through several editions and translations. This is an excellent source work and contains penetrating observations on the liquor traffic of the French traders with the natives. Shortly after his return to France he published also a work on ginseng, species of which had been found in Canada, and was responsible for spreading knowledge of this medicinal root among Europeans. Another major work, *Histoire des déouvertes et conquêtes des Portugais dans le Nouveau Monde* (Paris 1733), was later translated into Portuguese. This work is a disappointment to an Americanist hoping for contemporary and historical insights into the story of colonial Brazil; the author interprets the "Nouveau Monde" as including the Orient and devotes his study primarily to Portuguese enterprise in that area, rather than to the New World of the Americas. Lafitau was also one of the contributors of his day to the important Jesuit periodical of the 18th century, *Mémoires de Trévoux.*

Bibliography: L. KOCH *Jesuiten-Lexikon: Die Gesellschaft Juse einst und jetzt* (Louvain-Heverlee 1962) 1056–57.

[J. F. BANNON]

LAFLÈCHE, LOUIS FRANÇOIS RICHER

Canadian bishop; b. Ste. Anne de la Pérade, Quebec, Canada, Sept. 4, 1818; d. Three Rivers, Quebec, July 14,

1898. He attended Nicolet College, Quebec; was ordained in 1844; and went as a missionary to the Northwest. In 1846 he accompanied Rev. (later Abp.) A. A. TACHÉ to La Crosse island, where he distinguished himself by his rapid mastery of the native languages and was the first to reduce the language of the Mantagnas to a grammatical form. After being named titular bishop of Arath (1849), he was ill for five years and begged for a release from the episcopate, suggesting that Taché take his place. In 1851 at Turtle Mountain, N.Dak., he directed the defense of 60 people of mixed native and European descent against 2,000 Sioux who kept them under siege for two days (July 13 and 14). The Sioux finally withdrew, convinced that the Great Spirit was guarding the small band. He returned to Canada (1856) and taught at Nicolet, where he was named president of the college (1859). In 1866 he was appointed coadjutor of Three Rivers and in 1870, succeeded to the see. He was an able administrator and an eloquent orator, whose weekly sermons dealt with the great social and politicoreligious questions of the time. His writings include five volumes of pastoral letters as well as *Quelques considerations sur les rapports de la société civile avec la réligion et la famille* (Montreal 1866) and *Conferences* (Three Rivers 1885). He is considered as one of the fathers of French Canadian nationalism.

Bibliography: *Généalogie des familles. Richer de LaFlèche et Hamelin* (Desauliers 1909). R. RUMILLY, *Monseigneur Laflèche et son temps* (Montreal 1938). A. G. MORICE, *Dictionnaire historique des Canadiens et Métis français de l'Ouest* (Quebec 1908). J. P. A. BENOÎT, *Vie de Mgr. Taché,* 2 v. (Montreal 1904).

[C. W. WESTFALL]

LAGNY-SUR-MARNE, ABBEY OF

Former royal BENEDICTINE abbey in the canton of Lagny, arrondissement of Meaux (Seine-et-Marne), France; in the old Diocese of Paris, present-day Meaux (Lat. *Latiniacum*). It was founded *c.* 644 by (St.) FURSEY, a noble Irishman, on land belonging to Archambaud, mayor of the palace under Clovis II. Burned by the NORMANS, it was restored during the 10th century. In 933 the abbots became the counts of Lagny. Thanks to the protection of the counts of Champagne and the kings, as well as to the friars of Champagne and Brie, which were held in Lagny, the abbey became very prosperous. In 1396 Abbot Peter II started the construction of a new abbey church, of which only the choir was erected. In 1485 the abbey was placed in COMMENDATION. In 1512, under the cardinal of Narbonne, it underwent the reform of Saint-Martin-des-Champs. In 1562 it was plundered by the Huguenots. The MAURIST reform of 1641 included Lagny among its member abbeys. When the abbey was suppressed by the FRENCH REVOLUTION, it was paying £9,000 to the commendatory abbot and £7,000 to the 15 or 16 religious who were living there. The abbey church is now used as a parish church; the monastic buildings have been appropriated for municipal use.

Bibliography: BEAUNIER, *La France monastique,* v. 1 of *Abbayes et prieurés de l'ancienne France,* ed. J. M. L. BESSE, 12 v. (Paris 1905–41). L. H. COTTINEAU, *Répertoire topobibliographique des abbayes et prieurés,* 2 v. (Mâcon 1935–39) 1:1538–39.

[H. TARDIF]

LAGRANGE, MARIE JOSEPH

Outstanding Scripture scholar, b. Bourg-en-Bresse (Ain), France, March 7, 1855; d. Saint-Maximin (Var), France, March 10, 1938. After attending the minor seminary at Autun, Albert Lagrange studied in Paris, where he obtained a doctorate in law in 1878. He spent one year at Saint-Sulpice and then joined the Dominicans, receiving the habit in 1879 and the religious name Marie-Joseph at Saint-Maximin. Because the Dominicans were then expelled from France, he finished his studies at Salamanca and was ordained at Zamora on Dec. 23, 1883. He taught history and philosophy at Salamanca and Toulouse, and four years later (in 1888) he took up oriental studies at the University of Vienna. When he had been there two years, he was sent to Jerusalem to set up a Biblical school. He arrived in Jerusalem on March 10, 1890. The Ecole Pratique d'Études Bibliques opened its doors on November 15 of that year (*see* ÉCOLE BIBLIQUE). His articles on inspiration (1895–96) in the *Revue biblique,* founded in 1892, showed him to be a rare combination of theologian and Biblical scholar. In 1900 a new project, the *Études bibliques,* was announced; Lagrange's own contribution (*Juges,* 1903) was the first to appear in this series.

A paper on the sources of the Pentateuch, read to him at an international congress held in Fribourg (1897), and the publication of his Toulouse lectures under the title of *La Méthode historique* (1903) led to such bitter criticism that in 1907 he turned to work on the New Testament; his *S. Marc* appeared in 1911. The mention of his name in a consistorial decree—a disciplinary measure and not a doctrinal censure—resulted in his leaving the École from September 1912 to June 1913. World War I (1914–18) obliged him to leave the Holy City, but in Paris he saw to the regular appearance of the *Revue biblique.* His commentaries on Romans and Galatians were written in this period.

His commentaries on Luke, Matthew, and John appeared at regular intervals (1921, 1923, 1925), and his most popular work, the *Gospel of Jesus Christ,* in 1928. In 1935 ill health forced Lagrange to leave Jerusalem for France where he died three years later at the age of 83. He was buried at Saint-Maximin, but in 1967 his body was brought back to Jerusalem where it was interred in the Basilica of Saint Stephen.

A complete bibliography of Father Lagrange's writings contains 1,786 items. Some of his other important books are: *Études sur les religions sémitiques* (1903), *Éclaircissement sur la méthode historique* (1905 *pro manuscripto*), *La Genèse* (1906 *pro manuscripto*), *La Messianisme chez les Juifs* (1909), *Synopsis evangelica graece* (1926), *Le Judaïsme avant Jésus-Christ* (1931), *Histoire ancienne du canon du NT* (1933), *Critique textuelle—La Critique rationnelle* (1935), *Critique historique—Les mystères: L'Orphisme* (1937). His last article, entitled "L'Authenticité mosaïque de la Genèse et la théorie des documents," was completed on his deathbed.

The name Lagrange is rightly associated with the twentieth century revival of Catholic interest in the Bible and almost alone lifted Catholic Biblical studies out of mediocrity. The encyclical *DIVINO AFFLANTE SPIRITU* (1943) mentions his École Biblique with approval.

Bibliography: F. M. BRAUN, *The Work of Père Lagrange,* tr. R. T. A. MURPHY (Milwaukee 1963). F. L. CROSS, *The Oxford Dictionary of the Christian Church* (London 1957) 779. M-J. LAGRANGE, *Père Lagrange, Personal Reflections and Memoirs,* tr. H. WANSBROUGH (New York, 1985).

[R. T. A. MURPHY/EDS.]

LAICISM

Etymologically and historically, the term "laicism" suggests a movement wherein the laity seek to take over clerical functions and to comport themselves in civil life without taking into account the Church's prescriptions and teachings. This concept ill accords with laicism as it is known nowadays. Among the contemporary partisans of laicism are men who have never belonged to the Catholic Church and who are sometimes strangers to all religious affiliation. Yet these men are called "laymen." While remaining outside the Church and even while rising up against it, they retain a name borrowed from the ecclesiastical vocabulary. Thereby laicism avows its origins; it can be born only in Catholic countries. Often it is confused with ANTICLERICALISM, which anteceded it and is a negative and popular form of it. "Laicism" and "laicist" are terms belonging to the Catholic armory of combat; the opposing camp speaks only of *"laïcité"* and laic (*laïque*). To give precision to these vague notions, distinctions are necessary.

Marie Joseph Lagrange.

Early Manifestations. The various forms of laicism can be grouped and examined from two viewpoints, institutional and political.

Institutional. The distinction between clerics and laity in the Church is of divine institution. To deny this or to try to dilute it is to adopt a laicist position. Such happened in MONTANISM, which accorded more authority to prophets than to priests and bishops. Although they separated from the Roman Church, the Montanists retained, from the third to the fifth centuries, a hierarchy of an unusual kind, since it very probably included women. Among the numerous medieval heresies, those of the CATHARI and WALDENSES exalted those Christians whom they termed "spiritual" and regarded as priests those who passed as "morally perfect." According to John WYCLIF, only the predestined are truly priests. Attitudes of this type remained hesitant and confused; while abandoning the hierarchy they attempted to retain at least some elements of it.

Luther and Calvin, however, were well aware of what they denied. In his *Open Letter to the Christian Nobility* (1520) Luther termed oversubtle and hypocritical the teaching that pope, bishops, priests, and monks are called to the ecclesiastical state; whereas princes, lords, artisans, and peasants are called to the lay state. All

Christians, according to him, belong to the ecclesiastical state; all are consecrated priests by Baptism. Calvin affirmed that there is only one priest, Jesus Christ, and two Sacraments, Baptism and the Eucharist; all the other Sacraments, including Holy Orders, are merely "false sacraments."

QUESNEL, along with some 18th–century Jansenists, revived certain ideas of Edmond RICHER in order to transform them into laicist Richerism by equating priests and bishops, laymen and priests. To the laymen, in Quesnel's view, belong a determining role in the excommunication of bad Christians, in the election of pastors, and in the confirmation of doctrinal definitions. These ideas inspired the authors of the CIVIL CONSTITUTION OF THE CLERGY (1790).

Political. St. Ambrose once had to remind Theodosius that the emperor was "in the Church and not above the Church." After the conversion of Constantine, however, the Roman emperors watched over the Church and considered themselves "bishops of those outside." Later the barbarian kings were likewise invested with ministerial roles. The episcopate was then said to be in the hands of the king, who intervened in the recruiting of bishops, convoked councils, and alone gave legal force to synodal decrees. When kings were consecrated, their power appeared still more clearly to be a necessary prolongation of ecclesiastical authority. Not without reason did E. Amann and A. Dumas, authors of the seventh volume of *Histoire de l'Église* (ed. A. Fliche and V. Martin), subtitle this tome *The Church in the Power of the Laity, 888–1057,* because bishops were elected both by the clergy and by prominent lay personages. During this period, temporal rulers often did not await the choice of the clerical electors; rather they imposed their own candidates on them. The emperor and certain kings conferred INVESTITURE on abbots and bishops by cross and ring. All the energy of Pope Gregory VII (1073–85) was required to curb this invasion of laicism (*see* INVESTITURE STRUGGLE).

Less than two centuries later, the continual claims by civil rulers against the ecclesiastical world found support in a laity better instructed and more conscious of its rights. This new lay spirit developed by means of a philosophy inspired by Aristotle's political theories and was strengthened subsequent to the gaining of communal liberties, which were often won despite clerical opposition that occurred, in Flanders, Italy, France, and Germany.

This outlook was revealed blatantly in the conflict between Pope BONIFACE VIII and King PHILIP IV, the Fair, of France. It was to sustain Louis IV, the Bavarian, that MARSILIUS OF PADUA composed the *Defensor pacis,* which John XXII condemned (1327). According to the *Defensor pacis* the Church is only the totality of the faithful believers who invoke the name of Christ; the State should reserve to itself the choice of candidates for the priesthood, nominations to pastorates and other benefices, control of religious teaching by priests, surveillance over devotional practices, and payment of salaries to the clergy, who should no longer have any possessions. The Western Schism, OCKHAMISM, and the revival of the study of Roman Law provided a convergence of circumstances that facilitated the return of the episcopate to the power of rulers. The papacy had to make concessions. Thanks to a concordat concluded in 1516 with Pope Leo X, the king of France obtained control over all consistorial benefices; he could expect thereafter to have as bishops and abbots only men devoted to him.

The French government went further; without breaking with the Holy See, it conducted a "lay policy." Thus, it did not hesitate to ally with the Turks in order to escape from the menace that threatened the immense empire of Charles V. Ignoring the "testament of Adam" and the ALEXANDRINE BULLS that divided newly discovered lands between Spain and Portugal, France conquered colonies in virtue of the natural law, which gives unpossessed lands to the first occupant. Without admitting freedom of conscience, France granted to Protestants freedom to practice their religion in the Edict of NANTES (1598). In manifold ways (foreign alliances, colonial affairs, domestic government), profane interests were thereby divorced from religious interests. Each Catholic ruler in Europe imitated the king of France and pretended to be "emperor in his kingdom" and to enjoy all the same privileges that the emperors of the HOLY ROMAN EMPIRE enjoyed.

The 18th Century. As a result of the Eastern Schism in the 11th century and the Protestant Reformation in the 16th, two large groups detached themselves from Rome; but both of them continued to honor God through Jesus Christ. Some modern Catholic states, however, repudiated Christianity and even enfranchised themselves from all religion. The initiative was taken by France during the FRENCH REVOLUTION. Preparing the way for dechristianization in this upheaval were government regulations that removed from the clergy the charge of civil registers of Baptisms, marriages, and burials; granted authorization for divorce; and permitted, even encouraged, priests and religious to marry. Dechristianization was carried through in 1793 when the French Revolutionary calendar replaced the Gregorian; and all churches in Paris were closed to Catholic services and transformed into temples devoted to the cult of the goddess of REASON—a measure that was extended to the provinces. Gatherings of the faithful were forbidden as suspect. Infractions of these laws were punishable with imprisonment and death. By 1795 the French Republic recognized no cult.

The 19th Century. The laws that struck at religious in Spain (1820, 1835), Portugal (1834), and Piedmont (1855, 1866) did not spring from a plan of laicization. The policy in France under the Third Republic, however, carried through in stages from 1879, seemed to follow a preconceived design. Anticlericalism had for more than 50 years fostered animosity against religion, but this type of anticlericalism was sentimental. The preparation of French anticlerical plans, however, was the work of thinkers. Its roots were (1) the rationalistic SPIRITUALISM of such men as Victor COUSIN, Pierre Janet, and Joseph Ernest RENAN, who admitted the existence of God, but rejected all religion; (2) the atheistic PERSONALISM of Charles Renouvier, who deified man and recommended the practice of a morality independent of all authority; and (3) the positivism of Auguste COMTE and Hippolyte TAINE, who rejected theology and metaphysics as outmoded disciplines of a bygone age.

Three essential steps can be distinguished in French laicism. The first concerned public elementary education, since it suppressed religious education (1882) and then removed from the schools the religious men and women engaged in this work (1886). Legislation required that teaching be lay or neutral. Jules Ferry, author of the law of March 28, 1882, knew well what he sought, for he declared: "My aim is to organize humanity without God and without king." René Viviani, a deputy in a position to know the will of the anticlerical majority, stated in the Chamber of Deputies: "There is talk about neutrality in the schools, but it is time to say that educational neutrality has been only a diplomatic lie. . . . We have never had any other design than to make an antireligious university."

The 20th Century. The second step consisted of the dissolution and spoliation of French religious congregations (1901–04). This was open warfare. Voltaire had earlier approved this tactic when he congratulated King Frederick II of Prussia for his proposal to get rid of monks in his realm; he wrote to him: "Your idea of attacking Christian superstitition through the monks is that of a great captain." This passage was quoted in the Chamber of Deputies during the discussion in the law of associations, an enactment known as the Waldeck-Rousseau law, which was very liberal in all other respects save those concerning religious congregations. In the judgment of Ferdinand Buisson, the Waldeck-Rousseau law was the most decisive anticlerical act since the laicizing of the schools, the first public act engaging the republic in a basic conflict with the Church, a conflict up to then characterized by many armistices, peace treaties, and tacit compromises. Viviani did not dissimulate when he admitted in the Chamber of Deputies to the applause of his friends: "We are face to face not only with these

ardent and bellicose congregations. . . . We are . . . face to face with the Catholic Church." Another deputy declared in 1903: "We are combating religion and all religions, religious sentiment, and all religious dogmas."

These thoughts coincided with those of Justin Émile Combes, who was then president of the council. It was he who applied the law of 1901, forced religious to go into exile or become secularized, and caused the enactment (1904) of a law that forbade all former members of congregations to teach. The third step in laicization, likewise Combes's work, was the law separating the Church from the State (Dec. 9, 1905). The churches in question were the Catholic, Protestant, and Jewish—the three "confessions" recognized since the time of Napoleon I. The goods of the Catholic Church were ordered to be passed over to special associations called *"cultuelles,"* made up of laymen and distinct from the hierarchical organization. When Pius X forbade (1906) the recognition of these associations, the government left the churches at the disposition of the faithful (1907), but seized episcopal residences, seminaries, etc. (1908). Thus the spoilation of the dioceses and parishes followed upon the confiscation of religious houses (1903).

In Portugal, after the republic was proclaimed (Oct. 5, 1910), it required but a few months to accomplish what had taken France 25 years. In MEXICO, the constitution of 1917 gathered a complete program of laicism into a single article that, among other things, arrogated to the State all authority in religious matters, denied all legal character to dioceses and parishes, ordered the goods of religious to be seized, and deprived candidates to the priesthood of the right to vote. Under the dictatorship of Pres. Plutarco Elias CALLES, priests could not exercise their ministry without legal authorization (1926), and churches were abandoned or transformed into museums, prisons, and garages. All religious services ceased. This situation lasted until 1936.

Previous to the outbreak of civil war in 1936, SPAIN had for five years engaged in the establishment of a laicism inspired by French legislation. The constitution of 1931 declared that the State had no official religion, envisaged the expulsion of the Jesuits without explicitly naming them, permitted divorce, secularized cemeteries, etc. A decree dissolved the Jesuits (1932), and a law suppressed the other religious institutes (1933), but the republic did not have time to establish the state monopoly over education foreseen in the constitution. The official atheism in all countries under communist rule implies the introduction of laicism sooner or later.

Numerous Church documents condemned antireligious laicism as contrary to the Church's rights and to the natural law. The texts of many papal pronouncements can be found in the work by Ehler and Morrall cited in the bibliography. Laicism does not exist automatically wherever Church and State are separated. In Chile, e.g., the separation was regarded by Pius XI in 1925 as a friendly union. The same can be said of the U.S. because of the strict application of its Constitution.

To avoid equivocation, defensive laicism can be distinguished from aggressive. The former is the heir of past monarchies; it can appeal for support to the Gospel, which prescribes rendering to Caesar the things that are Caesar's and to God the things that are God's (Lk ch. 20 and 25); this is the laicism of liberal states that respect religions and at the same time carefully preserve the greatest possible independence. Aggressive laicism ignores God or denies His existence and strives to consign Him to oblivion. This is the laicism of totalitarian states that persecute all religions; this is the ''plague of our epoch'' denounced by Pius XI in the encyclical *QUAS PRIMAS* (1925).

Bibliography: E. M. ACOMB, *The French Laic Laws, 1879–1889* (New York 1941). H. X. ARQUILLIERE, *L'Augustinisme politique* (2d ed. Paris 1955), L. CAPÉRAN, *Histoire contemporaine de la laïcité française,* 3 v. (Paris 1957–61); *L'Invasion laïque* (Paris 1935). P. H. CARON, *L'État contre l'Esprit: Laïcisme ou christianisme* (Paris 1955). *Chiesa e stato,* 2 v. (Università cattolica del Sacro Cuore; Milan 1939). S. Z. EHLER and J. B. MORRALL, eds. and trs., *Church and State through the Centuries* (Westminster, Md. 1954), contains documents. B. EMONET, *Dictionnaire apologétique de la foi catholique,* ed. A. D'ALÈS (Paris 1911–22) 2:1767–1810. G. DE LAGARDE, *La Naissance de l'esprit laïque au déclin du moyen âge,* 5 v. (3d ed. Louvain 1956–63). A. LATREILLE, *L'Église catholique et la révolution française,* v.1 (Paris 1946). O. GIACCHI, *Lo stato laico* (Milan 1947). É. LECANUET, ''Les Pères du laïcisme en France,'' *Le Correspondant* 277 (1919) 420–444. J. LECLER, *The Two Sovereignties: A Study of the Relationship between Church and State* (New York 1952), tr. from French. M. LIGOT, *Laïcisme et Laïcité* (Paris 1926). L. V. MÉJAN, *La Séparation des Églises et de l'État* (Paris 1959). L. L. RUMMEL, ''The Anticlerical Program as a Disruptive Factor in the Solidarity of the Late French Republics,'' *American Catholic Historical Review* 34 (1948–49) 1–19. J. B. TROTABAS, *La Notion de laïcité dans le droit de l'Église catholique et de l'État républicain* (Paris 1961). G. WEILL, *Histoire de l'idée laïque en France au XIXᵉ siècle* (Paris 1929). *Dictionnaire de théologie catholique,* ed. A. VACANT et al., (Paris 1903–50) Tables générales, 2857–62.

[C. BERTHELOT DU CHESNAY]

LAICIZATION (LOSS OF THE CLERICAL STATE)

In canon law, laicization is an act by legitimate authority that takes away from a cleric the lawful use, except for emergencies, of the power of orders; deprives him of his rights, privileges, and clerical status; and renders him juridically equivalent to a lay person. Church law clearly points out that laicization in no way affects the power of orders, not even those that are clearly of ecclesiastical origin; rather, the action touches on the lawful use of the power of orders. There are three ways in which a cleric loses the clerical state: (*a*) by judicial sentence or administrative decree that declares the invalidity of sacred ordination; (*b*) by a penalty of dismissal legitimately imposed for some crime specified in church law; or (*c*) by a rescript or letter of the Apostolic See, as for example, the priest who desires to leave active ministry and live as a lay person, either with or without marriage (see CIC 290 and CCEO 394).

Historically, the Catholic Church divided clergy into major and minor clerics. The first category consisted of *sacerdotes,* that is, bishops and priests, along with deacons; the second category comprised those tonsured clerics receiving the minor orders of PORTER, acolyte, LECTOR, and exorcist. Since 1972, laicization applies only to deacons, presbyters, and bishops.

Examples of laicization occurred more frequently in history among those with minor orders. A minor cleric who freely married, or joined the military without permission, or without legitimate cause ceased to wear ecclesiastical dress and tonsure and did not resume them within a month after warning automatically incurred laicization. Likewise, religious minor clerics automatically incurred laicization if dismissed from their institute. Church law provided that laicization be imposed in the case of a minor cleric guilty of external carnal sins and the religious minor cleric whose profession is declared invalid due to fraud. Voluntary instances of laicization took place when the minor cleric informed his ordinary that he wished to return to the lay state, and the decree of the same ordinary ordering the return of a cleric whom he judged unsuitable for advancement to major orders.

Ecclesiastical law did not envision the voluntary departure from active ministry by major clerics, as for example, priests. Involuntary departure as a penalty, however, appeared in church history and law. The distinction between deposition and degradation may be found in the Decretals of Gregory IX (*Decretales Greg. IX,* c. 27, *De verborum significatione,* lib. V, tit. 40). In either case, the focus of the penalty was upon the use of an individual's power through ordination.

Laicization is connected in canon law with the theological principle that once Holy Orders have been validly received, they constitute an indelible character on that person that can never be invalidated. The loss of the juridical status of a cleric does not mean that a person becomes ''unordained,'' but rather that he loses the right to the lawful exercise of orders and he loses all the privileges and obligations (except that of celibacy) of a cleric.

The most significant effect of the loss of the clerical state is the prohibition from exercising the power of orders and the subsequent deprivation of all offices, functions, and any delegated power.

1917 Code of Canon Law. There were no commonly known procedures for voluntary departure or laicization in the 1917 code. One reason may be that dispensations from the priestly vow of celibacy were not granted. Prior to 1970, the law and the practice for a laicized priest was that he retain his obligation to celibacy. For example, a decree dated April 18, 1936, from the Sacred Penitentiary stated that for the Latin Church "dispensation from [sacred celibacy], in past times, was hardly ever granted, and according to the present discipline is never given, even in danger of death" (AAS 28 [1936] 242). From 1939 to 1963, such dispensations were granted in 315 instances. Since that time, the number of dispensation requests rose into the thousands. When such a dispensation from celibacy is requested and granted by the supreme authority of the Church, it always includes the loss of the clerical state and significantly restricts the person's ability to participate in public church functions.

The 1917 code contained procedures for involuntary loss of the clerical state. The distinction between the two penalties of deposition and degradation found expression in CIC canons 2303 and 2305. Both penalties could be inflicted only for offenses specified as punishable by these penalties under the law of the code. In addition to the case mentioned in canon 2305, §2, the 1917 CIC lists five others in which the law warrants the imposition of the penalty of degradation (see canons 2314, §1, 3°; 2343, §1, 3°; 2354, §2; 2368; and 2388, §1). Deposition, while leaving in effect the obligations arising from the reception of sacred orders, carried a suspension from offices and ineligibility for offices and positions in the Church. Degradation includes deposition, perpetual deprivation of the right to wear ecclesiastical garb and the reduction of the cleric to the lay state whereby the cleric was relieved of the obligations of the clerical state, except that of observing celibacy.

Changes were introduced in the wake of Vatican Council II. The first may be classified as terminological while the second concerns the development of procedures governing voluntary departures and later involuntary departures from the clerical state. The major moments of this change may be marked by the norms issued by the Holy See, especially those of 1980; the revision of church law in 1983; the norms issues in 1988 by *Pastor bonus* and subsequent directives.

Vatican Council II. The Church altered its view of the clerical state as a result of the insistence of the Second VATICAN COUNCIL on the fundamental equality of all the People of God. The change is clear with respect to membership. Entrance into the clerical state, according to the 1917 Code of Canon Law, came about with the reception of tonsure followed by the minor orders. With the suppression of both of these entrance rites in 1972 by the *motu proprio Ministeria Quaedam* (AAS 64 [1972] 529–534), ordination to the diaconate marks one as a cleric. Therefore, the present discipline on the loss of the clerical state applies only to deacons, presbyters, and bishops. The change is equally clear with respect to the loss of the clerical state. The material on the loss of the clerical state in the 1917 code was entitled "The Reduction of Clerics to the Lay State," which clearly implied the inferiority of the laity. The use of "loss of the clerical state" and "return to the lay state" more accurately reflect the conciliar emphasis on equality, which became one of the principles guiding the revision of the code. Vatican II deliberations pointed to the difference between involuntary and voluntary loss of the clerical state, but left the implementation to the Holy See.

At the request of many bishops at Vatican Council II, Pope Paul VI launched a twofold approach to the question of procedures for voluntary departure from active ministry. On one hand, church teaching would continue to explore the great value placed on priestly celibacy in the Latin Church (CLD 7:92–95). On the other hand a special 18 member commission was formed in the Congregation for the Doctrine of the Faith. They set forth on Feb. 2, 1964, an instruction announcing their exclusive competence to deal with petitions for the return of priests to lay status, dispensed from all obligations of the clerical state, including celibacy (CLD 7:1002–1015).

The Congregation for the Doctrine of the Faith instituted in 1964 a procedure whereby the gathering of information with respect to a petition take place by a strictly judicial process through ecclesiastical court authorities under the local ordinary. Each dispensation request, after examination by the special commission was reserved to the pope. The policy required two items: the dispensed priest live outside the area of his previous priestly ministry and any celebration of canonical marriage was to be privately celebrated and witnessed by the ordinary. The same congregation replaced this first procedure on Jan. 13, 1971. Preparation of a petition no longer required judicial procedure, which was replaced by an administrative and pastoral procedure of data-gathering. Presentation of a petition to Rome need no longer be made necessarily by the local ordinary. Instead, the responsible agent was the petitioner's personal superior—the bishop in the case of his diocesan priest, the major superior in the case of religious priest. The new norms required that the laicized priest refrain not only from strictly priestly functions, but also from certain specified functions often associated with priestly ministry, e.g., the function of homilist and the office of rector, spiritual director, or professor in seminaries, theology faculties, and similar institutes. Further, he should not hold the position of religion teacher, nor the office of principal of a Catholic school. Restrictions on the externals of a marriage ceremony of the laicized priest were generally retained as in the instruction of 1964. (AAS 63 [1971]:303–312 or CLD 7:117–121).

Eighteen months later the congregation gave authentic clarification to some doubts arising in the 1971 norms in a circular letter of June 26, 1972. Laicization should never be the first, but only the last resort in salvaging a disintegrated priestly commitment; and ordinaries are encouraged to use every means to help prevent a priest from seeking a dispensation on impulse, in a state of depression, or without truly mature and solid motivation. Once dispensed and canonically married, the former priest may never be readmitted to the exercise of orders, but the dispensed priest, if unmarried and convinced that he mistakenly sought laicization may apply to the Holy See and seek the recission of his laicization. The circular letter reminded bishops that they may not resort to the emergency powers granted them by canon 81 of the 1917 code to dispense a priest from celibacy since the office of priesthood involves the public order and the common good; a priest is not free to set it aside at his own discretion once he has freely accepted it (AAS 64 [1972] 641 or CLD 7:121–124).

Procedures and Norms after 1980. On Oct. 14, 1980, the Congregation for the Doctrine of the Faith issued a letter to all local ordinaries and moderator generals of clerical religious institutes "on the mode of procedure in the examination and resolution of petitions which look to a dispensation from celibacy" (AAS 64 [1972]:1132 or CLD 9:92–96). Appended to the letter were eight procedural norms to be followed in the instruction of each case.

The norms adopt a position that a dispensation is a relaxation of the law in a particular case and should never be viewed as a right; that is, a dispensation from priestly celibacy is anything but an inevitable, almost automatic, result of an administrative process. The norms presumed that before applying, each petitioner already has used all the resources available to solve his problems, i.e., the help of priestly brothers, friends and relatives as well as counseling by spiritual and psychological experts. The norms attempt to stress the individuality of each case and the need to develop an approach that addresses the uniqueness of the petition being prepared. Therefore, the norms must always be interpreted in the light of guidance found in the congregation's letter. Paragraph five of that letter, for example, speaks of cases of priests who long abandoned the priestly life, cannot withdraw from their present state and wish to sanate it; cases of those who should not have received priestly ordination because they lacked due sense of freedom or responsibility, or because the competent superiors were not able, at the proper time, to judge in a prudent and sufficiently suitable manner whether the candidate was really fit to live his life perpetually in celibacy dedicated to God.

The 1983 Code of Canon Law identifies three ways by which a member of the clergy can lose his juridical status as a cleric and thus be returned to the lay state. Canon 290 states that a cleric loses the clerical state by: (1) a juridical decision or administrative decree that declares the invalidity of sacred ordination; (2) the legitimate infliction of the penalty of dismissal; and (3) a rescript of the Apostolic See that is granted to deacons for serious reasons only and to presbyters for only the most serious reasons. Except for the case of the declaration of the invalidity of sacred ordination (c. 290) laicization does not entail, and is distinguished from, a dispensation from the obligation of celibacy (c. 291).

The theology of orders determines that which is necessary for the validity mentioned in canon 291, namely requirements of the minister, candidate, their intentions, and liturgical form. Procedures for claiming the invalidity of orders are found in canons 1708–1712. The loss of the clerical state by imposition of the penalty of dismissal (c. 291) requires a careful procedure as outlined in canons 1717–1731 and can be imposed only for reasons identified in the law. Similar to the 1917 code, the new code cites six instances: cc 1364, §2; 1367; 1370, §1; 1387; 1394, §1; and 1395. Such an imposed penalty is considered an expiatory one, that is, it is meant to repair or compensate for damage done to the ecclesial community. It can never be inflicted automatically or by decree, but must be imposed.

Pastor bonus. Pope John Paul II transferred competence for dispensation requests to the Congregation for Divine Worship and the Discipline of the Sacraments under articles 63 and 68 of the Apostolic Constitution on the Roman Curia, *Pastor bonus,* of June 28, 1988. Competence for cases submitted prior to this date were retained by the Congregation for the Doctrine of the Faith. The competency called for by *Pastor bonus* was confirmed in a letter of Feb. 8, 1989 (*Notitiae* 25 [1989] 485). All petitions of secular and religious clerics in Latin or other Churches sui juris in common law or mission territories come to this congregation. Further clarification on competency occurred in a July 25, 1989, letter to the Congregation for Institutes of Consecrated Life and Societies of Apostolic Life regarding dispensations from the obligations arising from the ordination to the diaconate by religious men (*Notitiae* 26 [1991] 53–54).

Since *Pastor bonus,* a number of practical instructions on processing laicization petitions became available. "Documents Necessary for the Instruction of a Case for the Dispensation from the Obligations of Priestly Celibacy" was issued by the Congregation for Divine Worship and Discipline of the Sacraments in April 1991 (*CLSA Roman Replies & Advisory Opinions* [1991] 2–4). The next year the congregation issued "Loss of the Clerical State by a Deacon and a Dispensation from All the Obligations of Ordination" through Archbishop Daniel Pilazczyk, May 11, 1992 (*CLSA Roman Replies & Advisory Opinions* [1992] 6–11). Finally, a circular letter was sent on June 6, 1997, to all ordinaries and superiors concerning the laicization of priests and deacons (*Origins* 27/11 [Aug. 28, 1997] 169, 170–172).

The Effects of the Loss of the Clerical State. While more attention focuses on the procedures on loss of the clerical state, there are a number of consequences applicable to all three modes. CIC canon 292 and CCEO canon 395 state that one who loses the clerical state is no longer bound by its obligations but also no longer enjoys its rights (cc. 279–289). With the exception stated in canon 976, one who loses the clerical state is forbidden the exercise of sacred orders. It is necessary therefore to examine individual rescripts for restrictions imposed on the departing cleric.

A Return to the Clerical State. The present law of the Church provides for such a possibility with CIC canon 293 and CCEO canon 398. "A cleric who loses the clerical state cannot be enrolled among clerics again except through a rescript of the Apostolic See." No further procedures are set forth. As a commentary on this topic, one might consult M. Souckar, "Return to Ministry of Dispensed Priests," *Jurist* 54 (1994) 605–616.

Bibliography: POPE PAUL VI, "Tradition of Priestly Celibacy Reaffirmed (Feb. 2, 1969)," *Canon Law Digest [CLD]* 7:92–95; "Reduction to Lay State: Norms," *CLD* 7:1002–1015; "Reduction to Lay State: Circular Letter to Ordinaries (Jan. 13, 1971)," *CLD* 7:117–121; "Reduction to Lay State; Procedural Norms; Interpretation (June 26, 1972)," *CLD* 7:121–124; "Reduction to Lay State: Norms (Oct. 14, 1980)," *CLD* 9:92–96; "Documents Necessary for the Instruction of a Case for the Dispensation from the Obligations of Priestly Celibacy," *CLSA Roman Replies & Advisory Opinions* (Washington, D.C. 1991) 2–4; "Loss of the Clerical State by a Deacon and a Dispensation from All the Obligations of Ordination," *CLSA Roman Replies & Advisory Opinions* (Washington, D.C. 1992) 6–11; "Circular Letter to All Ordinaries and Superior (June 6, 1992)," *Origins* 27:11 (Aug. 28, 1997) 169, 170, 172. J. E. LYNCH, "Loss of the Clerical State," *The Code of Canon Law: A Text and Commentary,* ed. J. A. CORIDEN, et al. (New York/Mahwah, N.J. 1985) 229–238. F. J. SCHNEIDER, "Loss of Clerical State," *New Commentary on the Code of Canon Law,* ed. J. P. BEAL et al. (New York/Mahwah, N.J. 2000) 382–392. M. SOUCKAR, "Return to Ministry of Dispensed Priests," *Jurist* 54 (1994) 605–616.

[A. ESPELAGE]

LAÍNEZ, DIEGO

Theologian; b. Almazán, Spain, 1512; d. Rome, Jan. 19, 1565. Upon completing his humanistic studies at Soria and Sigüenza, he studied philosophy and one year of theology at Alcalá (1528–33), and received a master in arts (1532). In 1533 he continued his studies at the University of Paris, attracted there also by the desire to know IGNATIUS OF LOYOLA.

After having made the spiritual exercises, he along with six companions pronounced vows at Montmartre on Aug. 15, 1534. This was the nucleus of the Society of Jesus. He was ordained June 24, 1537, and spent the rest of his life in Italy, preaching and teaching. The Company of Jesus having been canonically established on Sept. 27, 1540, he and his companions made their solemn profession in it (April 22, 1541). His wisdom, prudence, and learning made him a confidant of Ignatius. Laínez was successively provincial in Italy (1552), vicar (1556), and general (1558) of the Company.

Though dedicating himself constantly to the study of the sacred sciences, Laínez was one of the great men of the Catholic reform, active in both preaching and teaching. He acquired a truly extraordinary reputation before popes and outstanding churchmen of his time. At his death, PIUS V said that the Church had lost one of its best experts.

The best-known activity of Laínez was his participation in three periods of the Council of Trent, in the first two as papal theologian, in the third as Council father. He arrived at Trent toward the end of the fifth session and intervened in the discussion on justification. Especially decisive was his refutation of G. SERIPANDO on twofold justification and the certitude of the state of grace. He worked on the redaction of an index of Protestant errors about the Sacraments prior to the seventh session. He also spoke on Penance and Purgatory. During the second period (1551–52) Laínez intervened in important discussions on the Real Presence, Penance, and the Sacrifice of the Mass. No less influential were his reform decrees drawn up in collaboration with dogmatic theologians. During the third period (1562–63) he spoke on the Mass, Communion under both species for the laity (which he opposed), Holy Orders, the jurisdiction, reform and residence of bishops, abuses in the clerical state, and annulment of clandestine marriages. He used his prestige to obtain the Council's approbation of the Company of

Jesus. On the 400th anniversary of the Council (1963) it was recalled that Laínez was one of the leading figures in the Council's work.

At the request of Peter Canisius and Emperor Ferdinand I, Ignatius entrusted Laínez with the compilation of a theological work to meet the needs of the times. Because of the demands of the apostolic ministry, he was unable to finish it. Only notes and rough drafts were left behind.

Bibliography: D. LAÍNEZ, *Disputationes Tridentinae*, ed. H. GRISAR, 2 v. (Innsbruck 1886). J. H. FICHTER, *James Laynez, Jesuit* (St. Louis 1944). C. SOMMERVOGEL, *Bibliothèque de la Compagnie de Jésus* (Brussels-Paris 1890–1932) 4:1596–1600. P. BERNARD, *Dictionnaire de théologie catholique* (Paris 1903–50) 8.2:2449–50. M. SCADUTO, *Storia della Compagnia di Gesù in Italia*, v.3, *L'Epoca di Giacomo Laínez: Il governo 1556–1565* (Rome 1964). F. CERECEDA, *Diego Laínez en la Europa religiosa de su tiempo, 1512–1565*, 2 v. (Madrid 1945–46).

[J. M. DALMAU]

LAITY, CANON LAW

The 1983 Code of Canon Law is unique in the history of Church legislation in the prominence it gives to lay members of the Christian Faithful. In the 1917 Code, laity were mentioned in two canons. One stated that laity had a right to receive from clergy the spiritual goods of the church and the second prohibited laity from wearing clerical dress unless they were seminarians. The 1983 Code, as the canonical articulation of Vatican II, is conspicuously different in its approach to and inclusion of laity. Most notably, reflecting the teaching of Vatican II, book II of the Code, ''The People of God,'' is restructured to begin with a treatment of the Christian faithful, clergy and laity alike, their place in the Church their obligations and rights (cc. 204–223), and then the rights and obligations of the lay Christian Faithful in particular (cc. 224–231). In addition, laity are the particular concern of the final section of book II, ''Associations of the Christian Faithful'' (cc. 298–329).

Particularly significant in the canons on all the Christian Faithful are: the statement that all the baptized share in Christ's priestly prophetic and royal functions and in the mission ''which God has entrusted to the Church to fulfill in the world'' (c. 204 § 1); all the Christian Faithful enjoy ''true equality regarding dignity and action'' by which each one builds up the body of Christ (c. 208 § 1); that each one has the right and duty to lead a holy life (c. 210) and receive the spiritual goods of the Church, especially the word of God and the sacraments (c. 213); all are at liberty to join together in associations, by their own initiative, for purposes of ''charity or piety or for the promotion of the Christian vocation in the world'' (c. 215).

Two stipulations of the 1983 Code, both radical departures from the former Code, form the basis for much lay involvement in the inner life of the Church. First, laity are eligible to hold ecclesiastical offices (cc.145, 228 §1) and second, laity may cooperate in the exercise of the power of governance (c. 129). Many questions surround the scope and implementation of these canons, especially the second, and study of them is ongoing.

In addition to these pervasive provisions of the law, laity are specifically mentioned with respect to a number of activities to which they may be invited by the hierarchy. A qualified lay person may serve as chancellor of a diocese (c. 483), or in a variety of marriage tribunal positions, including judge (cc. 1421, 1428, 1435), or on diocesan or parish finance councils (cc. 492–494, 537) or pastoral councils (c. 512). Some laity on a diocese must be invited to participate in a diocesan synod (c. 463). When there is a dearth of priests, laity may be entrusted with participation in the pastoral care of a parish (c. 517, § 2). All qualified laity may be invited to serve as experts and advisors to bishops and pastors (c. 228 §2).

In the liturgical life of the church, lay men may be permanently installed as lectors or acolytes (c. 230 § 1). All qualified lay persons may be invited to serve as readers, commentators, cantors (c. 230 § 2), and when warranted because of need, laity may be invited to preach, preside at prayer, confer baptism and distribute the Eucharist (c. 230 § 3). Laity may be delegated to assist at weddings (c. 1112), administer sacramentals (c. 1168), preach in churches (c. 766), and be commissioned as missionaries (c. 784) or catechists (c. 785)

In virtue of their own proper role in the mission of the Church received in baptism, laity share in the Church's teaching office by witnessing to the gospel in their lives (c. 759) and by having concern for catechesis (c. 774 § 1). From the same baptismal foundation, laity share in the Church's sanctifying office through their active participation in liturgical celebrations, especially the Eucharist (c. 835 § 4).

Those lay persons who are married receive particular attention in the 1983 Code. A married couple, in living out their vocation, are to build up the people of God (c. 226, § 1). Those couples who are also parents have the obligation and right to educate their children in the faith (c. 226 § 2). This role of parents with respect to the faith formation of their children is repeated and emphasized a number of times, especially in the canons on sacramental preparation (For instance, see cc. 851, 868, 872, 890, 914, 1063, 1°). In circumstances other than sacramental preparation, the role of parents is no less diminished. They are to set an example of faith for their children by word and example (c. 774 § 2) and are given a ''most grave duty and primary right'' to care for their children in all aspects of life, physical, social, moral, cultural and religious (c. 1136; see also cc. 793 and 1252).

Despite the significant changes clearly seen from the 1917 Code to the 1983 Code, there are some weaknesses. First, many of these statements on laity, especially the enumerations of the obligations and rights, are so new to the law that they are neither fully implemented nor fully understood. Related to this is concern that the enumerated rights are not sufficiently complemented with structures for the vindication of rights. Also, authors have noted the Code's omission of the role of charism in determining a lay person's activity within the Church (see *AA* 3; *LG* 12, 13), which raises significant canonical questions about the foundation of lay ministries undertaken.

Bibliography: J. BEAL, et al., eds., *New Commentary of the Code of Canon Law* (Mahwah 2000). F. MCMANUS, ''Laity in Church Law: New Code, New Focus,'' *The Jurist* 47 (1987) 11–31. E. PFNAUSCH, ed., *Code, Community, Ministry* (Washington, DC 1992). *Lay Ecclesial Ministry: The State of the Questions* (Washington, DC 1999).

[E. RINERE]

LAITY, FORMATION AND EDUCATION OF

In the context of Christian belief and discipleship, formation can be understood as a continuing, lifetime process by which one grows into the likeness of Christ, according to God's will and under the guidance of the Holy Spirit. The task of formation of the lay faithful, whether viewed as a responsibility of the individual or as a ministry of the community for its members, is considered critical for the development of ''a living, explicit, and fruitful confession of faith'' (*General Directory for Catechesis*, 82).

Numerous references to the importance of formation appear in the documents of the Second Vatican Council (e.g., *Apostolicam actuositatem*, 28–32) and in postconciliar documents (e.g., *Christifideles laici*, 57–63). *Christifideles laici* (57) urges that formation be placed among the priorities of a diocese's plan of pastoral action. The U.S. Bishops underscore this direction and assert that attention to adult faith formation will render all Church ministries more fruitful (*Our Hearts Were Burning within Us: A Pastoral Plan for Adult Faith Formation in the United States,* pp. 12–14).

Formation is situated within the renewal of the Church as a means to an end. Conciliar and postconciliar teaching envisions a laity who are witnesses to Christ: well-formed in faith, enthusiastic, capable of leadership in society and in the Church, filled with compassion, and working for justice. Formation is a tool for achieving these outcomes.

The fundamental purpose of lay formation is a clearer discovery of one's vocation and a greater willingness to live it so as to fulfill a mission of discipleship within the broader communion and mission of the Church. Because it aims to bring about a unity of faith and life, formation encompasses and integrates such activities as catechesis, religious education, and various types of pastoral training. Formation has several interrelated dimensions: spiritual, doctrinal, and the cultivation of human values.

Formation takes place at many levels and through a variety of methods. Noting that formation is an ecclesial activity in the Church and by the Church, *Christifideles laici* (61–62) mentions as typical places of formation the ''domestic church'' of the family, the diocese and parish, small church communities, schools, groups, associations, and movements. Each of these agents plays an appropriate and complementary role in the total endeavor. Formation efforts in the United States include also parish religious education programs for adults in general, for catechists, and for parents preparing their children for sacraments. Every year the RCIA/Catechumenate enrolls thousands of adults seeking baptism or full communion with the Church or simply returning to the practice of their faith. Parish or diocesan-sponsored renewal programs and Scripture study groups often provide a systematic process of faith formation for many adults. For others, a process of formation is integral to their membership in a small Church community, an apostolic movement or association of the Christian faithful (*Codex iuris canonici* c. 298ff), a secular institute or third order, or an associate program connected to a religious congregation. Catholic colleges and universities, as well as some seminaries, offer undergraduate and graduate degrees to lay people in theology, canon law, religious studies, and pastoral ministries.

In the United States particularly, the postconciliar flourishing of lay ministries has led to an increase in the number and variety of education and formation programs conducted by diocesan agencies, academic institutions, and some Catholic organizations. The distinguishing characteristic of these programs is their focus on equipping lay men and women for designated roles of service and leadership in the public ministries of the Church. Programs are designed for both full- and part-time participants. Diocesan formation programs typically involve two or three years of part-time study and offer a certificate of completion at the end. Some diocesan programs are affiliated with a local college, university, or seminary and enable a student to earn an academic degree. Programs sponsored by institutions of higher learning typically offer a masters degree (e.g., M.A. or M.Div.) upon completion. Between 1985 and 2000 the number of persons enrolled in diocesan and academic programs of lay ministry formation grew from 10,500 to more than 30,000. Women account for a little over 60 percent of the total enrollment.

A significant effort in lay formation is carried out by the Hispanic Catholic community in the United States through diocesan lay leadership programs, lay movements, and a network of regional pastoral institutes, e.g., the Mexican American Cultural Center (MACC), the Southeast Pastoral Institute (SEPI), and the Northeast Pastoral Formation Institute. There are more than 20 such institutes, each serving several dioceses in a geographic region.

[H. R. MCCORD]

LAITY, THEOLOGY OF

The theology of the laity flows from a total ecclesiology that highlights the sacraments of baptism, confirmation, and Eucharist in its consideration of membership, functions, rights, duties, and mission of the faithful. The Second VATICAN COUNCIL was unprecedented in its reflection upon and articulation of the identity, role, and spirituality of the laity in the Church and in the world. This renewal of ecclesial thought and practice was due to an emphasis on: the biblical theme of the Church as the People of God, the dignity and equality of the members of the Church that is rooted in baptism, and the common sharing in the threefold mission of Christ as priest, prophet, and king.

Term and Concept. The terms ''lay'' or ''laity'' are derived from the Greek terms *laos theou,* meaning simply the people, and *laikos,* meaning the mass of common people in contrast to their leaders. The Scriptures only use the term *laos.* In the Septuagint, the term *laos* is used to distinguish the people from their rulers or leaders, such as prophets, princes, and priests (Is 24:2; Jer 26:11). But *laos* is also used in the Septuagint to denote the election of Israel from among the nations as God's chosen race and special possession (Ex 19:4–7; Dt 7:6–12). This sense is used later in the New Testament to affirm that all Christians are chosen, called, and predestined as the People of God (1 Pt 2:9–10; Eph 1:4–5).

The term *laikos,* on the other hand, is used neither in the Septuagint nor in the New Testament. In fact, it was not used until 95 A.D. in the patristic source of *I Clement* 40.5. In later Christian usage, however, *laikos*

became the pejorative term for the mass of common, often uneducated, people, as distinguished from the clergy, monastics, and religious of the Church. In this development, the sense of consecration, election, and call of the laity was almost forgotten.

The Second Vatican Council rediscovered the New Testament nuance of the concept of laity, *laos,* in its *Dogmatic Constitution on the Church* (*LG*). This document gave a typological description of the laity employing not only the negative sense, that laity are neither clergy nor religious, but also the positive sense of their call, election, and consecration by God. ''The faithful who by Baptism are incorporated into Christ, are placed in the People of God, and in their own way share the priestly, prophetic, and kingly office of Christ, and to the best of their ability carry on the mission of the whole Christian people in the Church and in the world'' (*LG* 31).

Development of the Theology of the Laity. The conciliar theology of the laity, as articulated in the documents *LG, The Decree on the Apostolate of the Laity,* and *The Pastoral Constitution on the Church in the Modern World,* is based on a foundation of preconciliar biblical, theological, and liturgical developments. The liturgical movement, begun in the early 20th century, promoted the full, conscious, and active participation of all the baptized as essential to the proper celebration of the liturgical life of the Church. The laity were viewed no longer as passive recipients of the liturgy celebrated by the clergy, but rather as active participants in the sacramental worship of the Church. Another important factor in the development of the conciliar theology of the laity was the theology of the Church as the Body of Christ, as taught by Pope Pius XII (*Mystici Corporis* 1943). This Pauline and patristic image of the Church highlighted both the unity and diversity of the members of the Body and the common responsibility for the mission of the Church. Similarly, the 20th-century renewal of biblical studies helped to shape a theology of the laity. The study of the New Testament ecclesiologies of the Church as the People of God and the New Israel demonstrated the communal aspect of the Church, which is integral for any theology of the laity. Finally, the apostolic movements of the 20th century, particularly Catholic Action, were the pastoral context for articulating the mission of the laity as a full sharing in the salvific mission of the Church.

Conciliar Theology. As a result of these developments, a new theology of the laity began to emerge. The difficulty in formulating a theology of the laity is that it presupposes a whole ecclesiology in which the mystery of the Church is given in all its dimensions, including the full ecclesial reality of the laity. This shift in ECCLESIOLOGY is exactly what happened at the Second Vatican

Council. It was the first council to treat the laity from a theological, rather than an exclusively canonical, point of view.

The conciliar ecclesiology can be found in *LG*. This document speaks of the laity in two places: in chapter 2, "The People of God," and chapter 4, "The Laity." Based on the theological and biblical foundation of chapter 2, chapter 4 presents a description of the identity and role of the laity in the context of a total ecclesiology. This renewed ecclesiology enabled the council to speak of the laity from the perspective of their relation to the mystery of the Church itself and to the Church's mission. This document clearly presents the laity as part of the Church, rather than as a mere appendage or addition to the Church. The laity are not simply the object of the ministry of the clergy. In terms of mission, the laity are not merely cooperators in the hierarchy's apostolate, but rather full sharers in the one mission of Christ.

The fundamental equality and dignity of the Christian existence of all the members of the People of God is affirmed within the common matrix of baptismal identity. From this common baptism flows an incorporation into the Church and a common vocation to holiness. Through confirmation, all the baptized are deputed to share in the mission of the Church. According to *LG*, baptism, confirmation, and holy orders imprint a sacramental character that are both instruments of grace as well as juridical signs giving visible structure to the People of God. From these characters, which are based on sacramental configuration to Christ, flows a functional diversity within the People of God. Within the one mission of the Church, there is a diversity of roles. All the members of the People of God, therefore, share in the activity of the Church, and not just the clergy or religious.

Vocation and Mission of the Laity. The two fundamental concepts in the conciliar theology of the laity are the vocation or identity of the laity and the mission or role of the laity. According to the conciliar ecclesiology, the identity or vocation of the laity must be properly understood before the roles, mission, and function of the laity can be treated. The vocation of the laity is described in *LG* #31 and the mission of the laity is described in #33. A further elaboration of the mission of the laity can be found in *The Decree on the Apostolate of the Laity* (*AA*), specifically sections #2 and #3, which are founded upon the theology of *LG*. *AA* sought to give the laity a renewed sense of responsibility in the life of the Church by stressing their active participation in its saving mission.

A typological, rather than ontological description of the laity is given in *LG* #31. The council gave a proximate genus for the laity, that is, what they have in common with all of the other members of the faithful, as a point of departure for reflecting on their vocation. This common matrix is the baptismal character, which includes the fundamental dignity and equality of all the faithful and a common responsibility for carrying out the mission of the Church. The laity, like clergy and religious, have their own sharing in the threefold offices of Christ as priest, prophet, and king.

This section also gave a description of the specific difference of the vocation of the laity, that is, what belongs properly and exclusively to them, namely, their secular character. The laity seek for the Kingdom of God in temporal affairs. The description itself admits that the clergy and religious engage in secular activities, but their competence is not specifically related to the world, as is the laity's. The conciliar ecclesiology, therefore, views the secular character of the vocation of the laity as something more than sociological, it is in fact part of the theological description of the laity.

The mission of the laity is described in *LG* #33. The council affirmed that the apostolate of the laity is a sharing in the salvific mission of the Church itself, and not simply a sharing in the apostolate of the hierarchy, which was the popular pre-conciliar definition. The laity, according to the council, have both the right and the responsibility to participate in the Church's mission to the world as well as the right and responsibility to contribute to the Church's inner life and organization.

Section #2 of *AA* states that there are two aspects to the mission of the Church: to make all people sharers in Christ's redemption and to order the whole world in relationship to Him. The laity participate in both of these aspects by exercising their apostolate in both the Church and the world. Once again, the council is affirming that it is not only the hierarchy who engage in the apostolate, but rather all the members of the faithful have the right and duty to engage in apostolic activity. Within the one mission of the Church, there is a diversity of ministry, according to this section. Among the members of the Church there is a basic equality, yet a functional diversity. All the faithful share in the threefold offices of Christ as priest, prophet, and king, and therefore all have their own responsibility in the mission of the People of God.

The dogmatic basis for the mission of the laity is the sacraments of baptism and confirmation (*LG* #33; *AA* #3). These sacramental characters depute the laity for their mission in the Church and in the world. The laity are commissioned by Christ Himself through these sacraments, and thereby receive the right and duty to exercise the apostolate. The laity, therefore, do not need any special delegation or deputation from the hierarchy in order to labor for the sanctification and growth of the Church and the renewal of the temporal order in general terms, since they are deputed by the Lord Himself. The sacramental identity of the laity, which flows from baptism and confirmation, is nourished by the Eucharist since it communicates that love which is the soul of the apostolate.

The laity's participation in the royal priesthood of believers is another aspect of their sacramental identity (*AA* #3). Along with the ministerial priesthood, the common priesthood of the laity is a true participation in the one priesthood of Christ. Drawing upon the teaching of 1 Peter 2, the council demonstrates that each member of the Church, by reason of their baptism and confirmation, is consecrated into a royal priesthood and a holy people. The mission of those so consecrated consists in offering spiritual sacrifices through everything they do and giving witness to Christ throughout the world. The priestly character of this mission consists in communicating the grace of Christ's redeeming sacrifice to the world.

The secular character of the laity gives their mission its uniqueness (*LG* #33; *AA* #2). Typically, although not exclusively, the lay apostolate is exercised in and through direct concern with secular affairs. Because of their secular character, the laity make the Church present and operative in the world in a way distinct from that of the clergy or religious. There are certain circumstances and places, according to the council, where the Church can be the salt of the earth only through the laity. The secular character of the laity is not merely concerned with physical presence in the world—since every member of the Church is in the world in this sense—but with a living presence that involves commitment and immersion in the temporal order. The laity are described not simply as representatives of the Church to the world, but rather, they are the Church in the world. They are the witnesses and living instruments of the mission of the Church through their engagement in temporal affairs. The Christian penetration of the temporal order implies apostolic activity. The council affirms the redemptive value of the daily activities of the laity in the family, workplace, school, and society. The laity, empowered by the Spirit of Christ, exercise their apostolate typically amidst the affairs of the world as a kind of leaven. Because of their secular character, the laity are the Church in the heart of the world, and therefore they bring the world into the heart of the Church.

The mission of the laity includes not only their activities in the world, but also their participation in the inner life and organization of the Church. *LG* #33 states that the laity can take on a direct form of cooperation in the apostolate of the hierarchy. This organized form of apostolic activity is not specifically described in this section, but it could include liturgical roles, preaching, ecclesiastical administration, works of mercy, etc. This coopera-

tion in the apostolate of the hierarchy can take on an even more direct form, through deputation. These offices are functions, which properly belong to the hierarchy, but can be fulfilled by the laity in a case of necessity through deputation for a spiritual purpose.

This mission of the laity is carried on through the three theological virtues of faith, hope, and charity (*AA* #3). These three virtues, poured into the faithful by the power of the Holy Spirit, are the motivating force of their apostolate, and bring with them the new command of love. This new command of love given to the Church by the Lord is fulfilled in bringing the message of salvation to others. This apostolate of communicating eternal life to all is the obligation of all the faithful, and not an additional responsibility for only certain members of the Church. Besides the theological virtues, charisms of the Holy Spirit are also given to the laity for the exercise of their apostolate. Charisms are special gifts given according to the needs of the Church that complement the sacraments and ministries. The reception of these charisms brings with it the right and duty to exercise them by responding to the grace bestowed by the Spirit.

Postconciliar Developments. The most important papal document on the theology of the laity since the Second Vatican Council was Pope John Paul II's Apostolic Exhortation, *The Lay Members of Christ's Faithful People* (*CFL*), issued Dec. 30, 1988. This exhortation was the result of the 1987 Bishops' Synod whose theme was "The Vocation and Mission of the Laity in the Church and in the World Twenty Years after the Second Vatican Council."

The theme of the vocation of the laity is described in *CFL* #9–15, with the key sections being #9 and #15, where the question of the identity of the laity is specifically raised. The mission of the laity is described in *CFL* #23–24, which deal with the ministries, offices, roles, and charisms of the laity.

The pope does not offer a new dogmatic definition or description of the laity, but rather, he returns to the conciliar typological description. In *CFL* #9, two elements of the conciliar teaching are highlighted, the baptismal identity of the laity and their unique secular character. Baptism brings about a newness of life, which is a regeneration in the life of the Son of God, an incorporation into His Body, the Church, and an anointing in the Holy Spirit. After this reflection on baptismal identity, the pope then describes the secular character of the laity. Although all the members of the Church have a secular character because the Church itself has an authentic secular dimension, the laity have their own manner of realization and function within this common secular character. The pope explains how the world is the place, in sociological and theological terms, in which the laity receive their call from God. The laity, because of their secular character, are to be a leaven in the world, sanctifying the world from within by fulfilling their own particular duties.

The mission of the laity is presented by the pope in *CFL* #23–24 as flowing from their vocation. The Church is an organic *communio,* characterized by the presence of both a diversity and a complementarity of vocations, states of life, ministries, charisms, and responsibilities. The Holy Spirit is the source of both the diversity and complementarity. Within this *communio,* there is a fundamental equality and dignity of all the baptized in acting for the edification of the Church. The mission of each member of the faithful is determined by their specific sacramental identities, vocations, and charisms received from the Holy Spirit. The laity participate with all the faithful in the threefold offices of Christ and therefore share in the priestly, prophetic, and kingly mission of Christ. Within this one mission of Christ, the roles, offices, and ministries of the laity find their source in the sacramental identity flowing from baptism and confirmation.

The ecclesiology of the Second Vatican Council brought about a new age of the laity. Twenty years later, the 1988 apostolic exhortation on the laity provided a further elaboration of the fundamental themes of the vocation and mission of the laity in the Church and in the world. From these developments emerges the need for renewed understandings of: the spirituality of the laity, their rights and duties according to canon law, the possibilities for lay ministry, and the necessity of spiritual and educational formation of the laity.

Bibliography: "Dogmatic Constitution on the Church, The Decree on the Apostolate of the Laity," in *Vatican Council II, the Conciliar and Post-Conciliar Documents,* ed. A. FLANNERY (New York 1975). POPE JOHN PAUL II, *Christifideles Laici, Acta Apostolicae Sedis* 81 (1989) 393–521 (Eng. tr., "On the Vocation and Mission of the Lay Faithful in the Church and in the World," *Origins* 18 [1989] 561–595). Y. CONGAR, *Lay People in the Church* (London 1957). P. COUGHLIN, *The Hour of the Laity* (Philadelphia 1989). L. DOOHAN, *The Lay-Centered Church* (Minneapolis 1984). A. FAIVRE, *The Emergence of the Laity in the Early Church* (New York 1990). A. HAGSTROM, *The Concepts of the Vocation and Mission of the Laity* (San Francisco 1994). F. KLOSTERMANN, "The Laity," in *Commentary on the Documents of Vatican II,* v. 1, ed. H. VORGRIMLER (New York 1969) 231–252; "Decree on the Apostolate of the Laity," in *Commentary on the Documents of Vatican II,* v. 3, ed. H. VORGRIMLER (New York 1969) 273–404. K. B. OSBORNE, *Ministry: Lay Ministry in the Roman Catholic Church* (New York 1993). R. PARENT, *A Church of the Baptized* (New York 1987). K. RAHNER, "Notes on the Lay Apostolate," in *Theological Investigations,* v. 2 (London 1963) 319–352. E. SCHILLEBEECKX, *The Layman in the Church and Other Essays* (New York 1963); *The Mission of the Church* (New York 1973).

[A. A. HAGSTROM]

LAITY IN THE MIDDLE AGES

Specific study of the laity in the MIDDLE AGES has until recently been neglected. Standard works of reference seldom treat separately or even mention "lay" thought and influence. There is much research yet to be done, so what shall be attempted here is an interpretive study under the following headings: (1) definition of the term *laicus* in the Middle Ages; (2) the two powers—cleric and lay, Church and State; (3) the laity and the Church's teaching authority and jurisdiction; (4) the social order; (5) LAY SPIRITUALITY; and (6) conclusion.

Definition. The term *laicus* in the Middle Ages took on a strongly juridical, institutional meaning. As an antonym of *clerus* it became synonymous with "one under authority" or "one who was unconsecrated" as against the consecrated authorities, the clerics. The great medieval authors had little time for the layman; when they did mention him, it was usually to stress his subordination to the clergy or to note his excesses. This negative attitude contrasted sharply with the use and meaning of the term λαός in the NT and λαϊκός in the early Church, where it meant a member of the people of God, one who was baptized, and thus referred to clergy and laity alike. By the 11th century the dualistic concept of membership in the Church was strengthened by the GREGORIAN REFORM ideals, which fostered specific religious virtues for all clerics, e.g., the common life and CELIBACY. GRATIAN crystallized this attitude in the influential text *Duo sunt genera Christianorum* (*Corpus iuris canonici* C.12 q.1 c.7); there are *two* kinds, for religious are included with the clerics. The distinguishing mark of the clergy was the TONSURE; it marked the recipient's submission to ecclesiastical jurisdiction and brought him many advantages not possessed by laymen. Consequently, many of the laity took the tonsure or entered minor orders (*see* HOLY ORDERS), whose original specific function was gradually rejected. We may cite, for example, the instance of Arras, in which a group of married bankers and merchants took the tonsure to escape secular justice against their financial misdoings. Abuse of clerical immunity from secular jurisdiction became common, for the test of membership of the clergy was hard to apply and literacy became the criterion. Extreme claims arising from this confusion, e.g., Thomas BECKET's defense of criminous clerks and the bull *CLERICIS LAICOS* of BONIFACE VIII, injured the cause of the Church in the eyes of the laity.

The Two Powers. Throughout the Middle Ages the laity were regarded as inferior to the clergy. Such texts as Dt 22.10, "You shall not plow with an ox and an ass harnessed together," were cited as proof that the laity should not be brought into ecclesiastical matters. Thus, the Synod of Seville (619) forbade laymen to serve as stewards or as ecclesiastical judges (*Corpus iuris canonici* C.16 q.7 c.22). But the reality was far different. In the matter of episcopal elections in the early Church, the laity approved of the candidate elected by the clergy. Then the lay ruler, apart from the consecration, consolidated the whole process by taking it into his own hands. His influence predominated until the 11th century. Thus Richard I of Normandy had his son Robert elected to Rouen; his nephew Hugh, to Bayeux; and another nephew, John, to Avranches. The Gregorian reformers tried, though unsuccessfully, to restore the ancient discipline. Despite the eventual control exercised by the CATHEDRAL chapter and later by the papacy, episcopal elections continued to be subject to pressure by the lay rulers.

Much of this interference arose from the nature of the relationship between CHURCH and State in the Middle Ages. The Church, which occupied a favorable position in the Western kingdoms, treated the lay powers as an instrument to fulfill its mission. Churchmen often invoked lay help, e.g., in the deposition of "unjust" rulers (thus, the Emperor HENRY IV), in the CRUSADES against the infidels, or in the suppression of heresy, as in the wars against the ALBIGENSES (1208–1330). GREGORY VII expressed these ideas in his two letters to Abp. Hermann of Metz in 1076 and 1081 (*Reg.* 4.2, 8.21). Popes, such as INNOCENT III and INNOCENT IV, and other prelates often exercised great influence over lay rulers. Papal authority in Italy and its spiritual influence elsewhere frustrated the so-called medieval Empire (*see* HOLY ROMAN EMPIRE).

Although lay rulers benefited from ecclesiastical recognition, such as sacral ANOINTING, they did not accept hierocratic claims unless these suited their purposes. Moreover, they quickly converted the concept of a duty to help the Church into a right to do so. The lay princes generally favored the dualism of the primitive form of the Gelasian theory (*see* GELASIUS I, POPE), but extreme polemicists, such as the ANONYMOUS OF YORK, could reverse the roles completely (cf. *Monumenta Germaniae Historica: Libelli de lite* 3.667).

In practice, the distinction between Church and State was an obvious one throughout the Middle Ages. So great was the lay threat to the independence of the Church that the latter was forced to define its position in every way. Its great wealth was the special object of lay ambition. Ultimately, by the 11th century, this resulted in the virtual feudalization of the Church. The PROPRIETARY CHURCH system and lay ownership of TITHES were widespread abuses, which caused even supposedly extreme hierocratic churchmen to distinguish between the Church, as divine and clerical, and the State, as temporal and lay.

Canonically, the clerical reaction to lay intrusion was consistent and absolute (cf. *Corpus iuris canonici* C.16 q.7 cc.1–43). Secularization of church property was prohibited. Laymen were excluded from ecclesiastical administration with some exceptions, e.g., the *seniores laici* in the African Church in the 4th and early 5th century. In fact, lay interference, especially in the use and disposition of CHURCH PROPERTY, lasted throughout the Middle Ages. Much of the interference was the result of willing consent by the clergy, e.g., the employment of laymen as collectors of tithes, as agents and bailiffs for cathedral chapters, as lawyers to represent Church interests in the secular courts, and as bankers for the papacy and lesser ecclesiastical units. Lay intrusion was particularly strong after 1300, for the canonists and theologians failed to deal with the problems generated by the economic changes of the time. They continued to repeat the ancient formulas when they should have dealt anew with such urgent matters as the "right" of the State to tax Church wealth or its responsibility to care for the poor. There had been some exceptions, as when Innocent III accepted the already existent alienation of tithes to laymen, except for the parish clergy's quarter, and when the various national clergy made payments of grace in lieu of taxation. However, from 1300 onward ecclesiastical finance caused a great dial of suspicion and dispute.

Papal finances in particular roused lay hostility, so that in the 16th century pretended financial abuses were commonly regarded as a major cause of the REFORMATION. This was a major propaganda victory for the lay rulers. In fact, the papacy had been most powerful financially only until the early 14th century. Papal assets gradually fell into lay hands, so that on the eve of the Reformation the greater part of papal income came from the Italian patrimony and not from abroad (*see* STATES OF THE CHURCH).

These disputes enlivened the Middle Ages and, toward the end, took place in an atmosphere of ANTICLERICALISM. But this was not always so. Before 1300 in all the major conflicts there were laymen and clergy on both sides. Gregory VII often appealed to the laity against recalcitrant clergy, and the Emperor Henry IV enjoyed the support of the clergy of the Empire against the pretender Rudolf. Mutual interests and prevailing opinion drew Church and State together. The laity could not conceive of a society without the Church, and from this the medieval Church drew its greatest strength. In the last resort the Church depended on the lay powers for the enforcement of its "rights," the *libertas Ecclesiae*.

Laity, the Magisterium, and Church Jurisdiction. With few exceptions, notably heretics and Jews, the laity wished to live and die within the body of the Church. The Church carried the grave responsibility of presenting the true faith, which it elected to fulfill by developing its institutions and sacramentology, to the detriment, some would say, of the charismatic or prophetic ministry. Thus, no treatise emerged from the Middle Ages on the place of the laity within the Church; in fact, there is no treatise *De ecclesia* as such until the *De regimine christiana* of JAMES OF VITERBO. Of course, the laity had some function within the sacramental system, especially in the administration of the Sacrament of MATRIMONY and, in times of necessity, of BAPTISM. Certain pious practices, e.g., LAY CONFESSION, approved by THOMAS AQUINAS (*In 4 sent.* 17. 3.3.2 ad 1), helped to bridge the gap between clerics and laymen. The concept of lay participation in offering the sacrifice of the Mass *with* the priest was not lost (cf. PETER DAMIAN, *Patrologia Latina* 145:237). But these were exceptions and do not refute the generalization that the role of the people in the medieval Church was essentially a passive one. Lay poverty and ignorance were chiefly responsible for the laity's never achieving an ''apostolate'' or a ''theology,'' making it impossible for the educated clergy to propose a cooperative role, except that of the material sword, the arm of the Church. The office of preaching was rigorously denied to laymen (cf. Leo I, *Patrologia Latina* 54:1045–46; *Corpus iuris canonici* D.23 c.29; X 5.7.12, 13; VI⁰ 5.2.2); women especially were forbidden to preach.

These prohibitions were generally successful until *c.* 1100, when the intellectual Renaissance and the economic revolution of the 12th and 13th centuries produced a new type of layman, the forerunner of the humanist and the *civis,* and a new class of people, the urban proletariat. These new laymen came up against the ancient prohibitions. The gap between them and the clergy widened, and their aspirations went elsewhere, especially into the medieval heresies, until the coming of the friars (*see* MENDICANT ORDERS) helped redress the balance.

The heresies (there were really only two main groups, the WALDENSES and the CATHARI) were largely lay movements that were strong in the towns. They were evangelical, anticlerical, and inspired by the concepts of the ''primitive church'' and the ''community of believers.'' Both stressed lay preaching and apostolic poverty (*see* POVERTY MOVEMENT). The Waldenses in particular encouraged Bible reading in the vernacular and lay confession. Not surprisingly, the heretics succeeded so long as they had support of the lay rulers, who used the threat of heresy to secure economic concessions from the Church. Ultimately the lay princes were forced to ally with the Church to suppress heresy because the doctrine of lay individualism threatened their own theocratic basis as well as the hierocratic structure of the Church (cf. Second Lateran, c.23; *Conciliorum oecumenicorum decreta* 178).

Various methods of suppression were tried, including force and persuasion. The rise of the friars, initially with strong lay orientation, partly succeeded in winning back the laity who had been lost to the parish clergy. But in Canon Law the property of obstinate heretics was confiscable (cf. Innocent III, *Vergentis in senium,* March 25, 1199; A. Potthast, *Regesta pontificum romanorum inde ab a. 1198 ad a. 1304* 643; *Corpus iuris canonici* X 5.7.10). This decided the lay rulers, especially the lords of northern France, who then forced the Church into the long wars against their southern neighbors, the so-called crusade against the Albigenses.

The final adoption of force and the use of the INQUISITION as the prime instrument for the suppression of heresy may be linked with the failure of the noble attempt by St. FRANCIS OF ASSISI to channel lay fervor into the service of the Church. Francis' great merit was to have recognized a vital truth, viz, that in certain situations the people must be consulted and their needs linked with those of the Church. Unfortunately, the subsequent institutionalization of the FRANCISCANS was a sign that the Church was not prepared to pay a sufficiently high price to retain the allegiance of the masses, i.e., a religious order with a predominantly lay character. After 1242 no lay brother could be appointed to offices in the order (*see* ELIAS OF CORTONA).

The conflict between lay and cleric was heightened by lack of understanding on the part of the clergy. Although the Church recognized lay competence in secular affairs (Fourth Lateran, c.42; *Conciliorum oecumenicorum decreta* 229), its whole approach was prejudiced by regarding the lay state as a concession to human weakness (cf. *Corpus iuris canonici* C.12 q.1 c.7). The laity reacted by hostility, which led to the common clerical observation that ''they [the laity] are opposed to us'' (cf. commentary of HOSTIENSIS, *Corpus iuris canonici* X 3.30.17).

In practice the conflict was generally one of jurisdiction (the independence of Church courts, clerical immunity from secular courts, the right of the Church to try laymen for certain offenses) and administration (the distribution and use of Church property, and appointment to Church offices). On these matters the Church left no doubt that the laity should not interfere. The (false) decretal *Nulla facultas* of Pope Stephen was widely cited in support (cf. First Lateran c.8; *Conciliorum oecumenicorum decreta* 167).

There was also a great deal of agreement and cooperation, e.g., in the medieval councils and synods to which the laity were generally summoned for technical advice, publicity, or aid in executing certain decrees. Hostiensis stated that laymen should be present when their own causes, marriage, or matter of faith were being treated but absent during discussion of ecclesiastical matters or clerical faults. In the 15th century Panormitanus (*see* TUDESCHIS, NICOLAUS DE) gave two examples of the use of lay *periti* at general COUNCILS. The idea of excluding laymen from councils did not emerge until after the Council of TRENT.

The Social Order. The medieval Church performed many of the welfare functions of the modern State, for ecclesiastics recognized the principle that the Church's wealth was not for the sole use of the individual cleric but for the good of the Church as a whole. Such welfare services included provision for HOSPITALS, the poor, pilgrims and travelers, and education. But the canonists failed to adjust their teaching fully in the light of the economic and social changes of the period after 1300. This left the Church unprepared for the emergence of the concept of the *civis,* or citizen, which replaced the term *laicus.* It signified a diminution in the social functions of the Church and called for a realignment of traditional distinctions.

In this respect, the most notable deficiency of the Church was the failure to provide a system of education for the masses. [*See* EDUCATION.] This is not the same as saying that there were no educated laymen in the Middle Ages. It is commonly but mistakenly supposed that once the classical tradition of the early Church in the West had passed, an educated laity had also disappeared, and that especially from the 9th to the 12th century only clerics could read and write. Riché gives many examples to prove the contrary, concluding that the equation *laicus = illiteratus* was valid only in the sense of one who does not know Latin. In any case, certain professions, e.g., law and medicine, had a strong lay tone throughout the Middle Ages (cf. Fourth Lateran, c.18; *Conciliorum oecumenicorum decreta* 220). In Italy the tradition of a lay culture was never entirely abandoned, and it began to flower again in the 11th century. Throughout Europe instruction for children did exist, although the teaching was a clerical monopoly until the 13th century. The earliest lay-controlled schools were those conducted by heretics.

However, the rise of the learned layman as a prominent figure in society dates from the early 12th century onward, and educated laymen flourished in the Roman law schools and universities of southern Europe. Laymen were even admitted to the Canon Law schools and included such canonists as the eminent JOANNES ANDREAE (1270–1348), Petrus de Ancharano (1330–1416), and Laurentius de Ridolfis (d. *c.* 1450). But lay education was directed principally to secular subjects. There was nothing in the later Middle Ages to equal lay influence in the early Church, when a large number of the Fathers began their theological work as laymen, e.g., SS. Cyprian, Basil, Gregory Nazianzus, Jerome, and Augustine. Significantly, the majority of these belonged to the Eastern Church, where the tradition of the lay theologian had never died. Institutionalism in the West led to the idea that the study of the sacred sciences belonged to the clergy, and that of the profane to the laity.

Changes in the social and educational status of the laity resulted from the economic expansion of the 12th and 13th centuries, and the Church played a role in these developments. One view is that the Church encouraged "good" business (cf. the JUST PRICE and the prohibition of USURY). Another is that the Church hindered commercial growth by such restrictions. Both views need revision. In the early Middle Ages the economy was mainly at subsistence level, so the Church could treat economic matters in severe condemnatory terms because little was at stake. But in the expansion period her teaching was modified to suit new conditions: usury laws were revised, the just price was in fact merely the market price, and business became respectable. If anyone suffered it was the Church, which frequently was the victim of the layman's pursuit of profits. At the end of the Middle Ages economic collapse and discontent among the lay rulers and merchant classes led them to attack the Church's wealth as a cure for economic ills and even, finally, to embrace the Reformation.

Lay Spirituality. In the Western Church the general lack of an educated laity left the people cut off from the main stream of religious thought. The language of the Church was Latin, which proved difficult for the barbarian and pagan masses who had entered the former Roman provinces. Such people could not, initially, provide a firm foundation for the faith, so the Church established its unity upon the clergy, the sacramental system, and Canon Law. There was thus little opportunity for a positive lay contribution to the spread of the faith. For several centuries the sorry lot of the masses, victims of frequent plagues, famine, a high mortality rate, and low life expectancy, made it impossible for the Church to do more than preach satisfaction for sin (*see* PENITENTIALS) and to encourage prayer in the form of the cult of some local saint. In any case piety was associated with asceticism, and marriage was at its best a concession to human weakness. From about 1000 some changes were noticeable. Marriage as a Sacrament was stressed; devotion to the humanity of Christ and to Mary, His Mother, the elevation and adoration of the Blessed Sacrament, PILGRIMAGES to Rome and the Holy Land, religious drama and literature, vernacular translations of the Bible, as well as the physical expansion of the Church (parish churches, cathedrals, monasteries, built principally by laymen and financed by lay donations) witness to a remarkable growth of lay piety that was genuine, intense, and widespread. In 1215 the Fourth LATERAN COUNCIL (c.21; *Conciliorum Oecumenicorum Decreta* 221) obliged every Christian of the age of reason to receive the Sacraments of Penance and the Eucharist at least once a year. Finally, the coming of the friars helped spread religion in the cities and towns. If this enthusiasm failed to remain orthodox and gave place in the later Middle Ages to SUPERSTITION and heresy (see, e.g., J. WYCLIF, J. HUS, M. LUTHER), the responsibility lay elsewhere.

Conclusion. Throughout the medieval period there were definite modifications in the status and influence of the laity within the Church. The most marked change is noted after 1300, when lay hostility to the papacy, anticlericalism, and a lay spirit emerged (see MARSILIUS OF PADUA, *Defensor pacis*). Contact with Renaissance HUMANISM, the growth of the State, the philosophical skepticism of NOMINALISM, the spread of lay education, the effects of endemic plague, especially of the Plague of 1348, the Hundred Years' War, the AVIGNON PAPACY, the WESTERN SCHISM, CONCILIARISM, the spread of heresy and popular revolts such as the Peasants' Revolt of 1381 in England, made the period from 1300 to 1500 an age of transition. Yet canonists and theologians failed to note these things. The general councils merely reiterated earlier prohibitions and in doing so increased the gap between the laity and the clergy. On the eve of the Reformation, the Fifth LATERAN COUNCIL (1512–17) had nothing to say concerning the social and religious aspirations of the masses, apart from the bull for reform of the *MONTES PIETATIS* (*Conciliorum Oecumenicorum Decreta* 601–603).

The great merit and achievement of the medieval Church was that it had been able to inspire the masses to fervor and enthusiasm. But its negligence in directing these emotions into worthwhile and respectable objectives and, essentially, its failure to educate the laity were momentous defects for which the Church was to pay a heavy price.

Bibliography: P. THOMAS, *Le Droit de propriété des laïques sur les églises et le patronage laïque au moyen âge* (Paris 1906). A. TEETAERT, *La Confession aux laïques dans l'Église latine depuis le VIIIe jusqu'au XIVe siècle* (Paris 1926). J. HASHAGEN, *Staat und Kirche vor der Reformation: Eine Untersuchung der vorreformatorischen Bedeutung des Laieneinflusses in der Kirche* (Essen 1931). J. HUIZINGA, *The Waning of the Middle Ages* (London 1924; pa. Garden City, NY 1954). É. LESNE, *Les Écoles de la fin du VIIIe siècle à la fin du XIIe* (Lille 1940). J. E. DOWNS, *The Concept of Clerical Immunity* (Catholic University of America Canon Law Studies 126; Washington 1941). M. J. HUGHES, *Women Healers in Medieval Life and Literature* (New York 1943). S. RUNCIMAN, *The Medieval Manichee: A Study of the Christian Dualist Heresy* (Cambridge, Eng. 1947). P. DELHAYE, "L'Organisation scolaire au XIIe siècle," *Traditio* 5 (1947) 211–268. Y. M. J. CONGAR and F. VARILLON, *Sacerdoce et laïcat dans l'Église* (Paris 1947). R. A. KNOX, *Enthusiasm: A Chapter in the History of Religion* (New York 1950). O. KOEHLER, "Der Laie im katholischen Kirchenrecht," *Stimmen der Zeit* 146 (1949–50) 43–53. P. G. CARON, "Les *Seniores laici* de l'Eacute;glise africaine," *Revue internationale des droits de l'antiquité* 6 (1951) 7–22. É. AMANN and A. DUMAS, *L'Église au pouvoir des laïques* (A. FLICHE and V. MARTIN, eds., *Histoire de l'église depuis les origines jusqu'à nos jours* 7; 1948). A. SIGUR, "Lay Cooperation with the Magisterium," *Jurist* 13 (1953) 268–297. L. LEITMAIER, "Der Laie in der Kirche im Mittelalter und im 20. Jahrhundert," *Zeitschrift der Savigny-Stiftung für Rechtsgeschichte, Kanonistische Abteilung* 39 (1953) 28–45. G. B. BORINO, "L'investitura laica del decreto di Nicolò II al decreto di Gregorio VII," *Studi gregoriani*, ed. G. B. BORINO 5 (1956) 345–359. G. DE LAGARDE, *La Naissance de l'esprit laïque au déclin du moyen âge*, 5 v. (3d ed. Louvain-Paris 1956–63). H. I. MARROU, *A History of Education in Antiquity*, tr. G. LAMB (New York 1956). G. PHILIPS, *The Role of the Laity in the Church*, tr. J. R. GILBERT and J. W. MOUDRY (Chicago 1956). N. R. C. COHN, *The Pursuit of the Millennium* (London 1957). Y. M. J. CONGAR, *Jalons pour une théologie du laïcat* (3d ed. Paris 1964); Eng. *Lay People in the Church*, tr. D. ATTWATER (Westminster, MD 1957). E. H. KANTOROWICZ, *The King's Two Bodies* (Princeton 1957). I. ORIGO, *The Merchant of Prato* (New York 1957). R. B. BROOKE, *Early Franciscan Government: Elias to Bonaventure* (Cambridge, Eng. 1959). R. J. COX, *A Study of the Juridic Status of Laymen in the Writing of the Medieval Canonists* (Catholic University of America Canon Law Studies 395; Washington 1959). H. MAISONNEUVE, *Études sur les origines de l'Inquisition* (2d ed. Paris 1960). H. GRUNDMANN, *Religiöse Bewegungen im Mittelalter* (2d ed. Hildesheim 1961). D. KNOWLES, *The English Mystical Tradition* (New York 1961). W. ULLMANN, *Principles of Government and Politics in the Middle Ages* (New York 1961). J. LECLERCQ et al., *La Spiritualité du moyen-âge* (Paris 1961). S. C. NEILL and H. R. WEBER, eds., *The Layman in Christian History* (Philadelphia 1963). P. RICHÉ, "Les Bibliothèques de trois aristocrates laïcs carolingiens," *Moyen-âge* 69 (1963) 87–104. K. MÖRSDORF, *Lexikon für Theologie und Kirche*, ed. J. HOFER and K. RAHNER (Freiburg 1957–65) 6:733–741. D. HERLIHY, *Women, Family, and Society in Medieval Europe* (Providence 1995).

[J. GILCHRIST]

LAKE, KIRSOPP

Biblical scholar; b. Southampton, England, April 7, 1872; d. Pasadena, Calif., Nov. 10, 1946. After education at St. Paul's School and Lincoln College, Oxford, he was ordained (1896) to the Anglican ministry and made curate of St. Mary the Virgin, Oxford. While there he wrote one of his most important works, *The Text of the New Testament* (1900). In 1904 he joined the University of Leiden, Netherlands, as a professor of New Testament exegesis. Three years later he published *Historical Evidence for the Resurrection of Jesus Christ,* in which he cast doubt on the evidence of Christ's physical resurrection. In 1914 he went to Harvard University in the U.S., becoming successively professor of early Christian literature, Winn professor of ecclesiastical history (1919–32), and professor of history (1932–37). Lake's early scholarly work was historical, dealing particularly with St. Paul and the Acts of the Apostles. He later did important work in textual criticism and succeeded in identifying the Lake Group of manuscripts as part of the library used by Origen in commentaries written at Alexandria and Caesarea. Among his other publications are *Earlier Epistles of St. Paul* (1911), which emphasizes the influence of Hellenistic religions on primitive Christianity; *Stewardship of Faith* (1915), which was attacked by Roman Catholics as a denial of the divinity of Christ; and *Beginnings of Christianity* (5 v. 1920–32), written in collaboration with F. J. Foakes Jackson, an imposing introduction to the Acts of the Apostles.

[E. DELANEY]

LALLEMANT, JACQUES PHILIPPE

Theologian; b. Saint-Valéry-sur-Somme, Sept. 18, 1660; d. Paris, Aug. 24, 1748. He entered the Society of Jesus in 1677, and spent most of his life combating Jansenism. Of his 31 published works the following are the most important: *Journal historique des assemblées tenues en Sorbonne pour condamner les Mémoires de la Chine* (Paris 1700), seven letters concerning the controversy about the CHINESE RITES, and *Réponse aux nouveaux écrits de MM. des missions étrangères contre les jésuites* (Paris 1702); *Jansenius condamné par l'Église, par luimême et par ses défenseurs et par saint Augustin* (Brussels 1705), an abridged history of the judgments of the Church against the teachings of C. O. JANSEN; *Le Véritable esprit des nouveaux disciples de saint Augustin* (4 v., Brussels 1705); *Le P. Quesnel séditieux et hérétique dans ses Réflexions morales sur le Nouveau Testament* (Brussels 1704); and *Réflexions morales avec notes sur le Nouveau Testament traduit en français* (12 v., Paris 1713–25).

Bibliography: C. SOMMERVOGEL, *Bibliothèque de la Compagnie de Jésus* (Brussels-Paris 1890–1932) 4:1387–1400. J. CARREYRE, *Dictionnaire de théologie catholique* (Paris 1903–50) 8.2:2456–59.

[P. BROUTIN]

LALLEMANT, LOUIS

French Jesuit authority on the spiritual life; b. Châlons-sur-Marne, Oct. 30?, 1587; d. Bourges, April 5, 1635. We know little about the ancestry and infancy of Lallemant. He was the son of a magistrate in the service of the king of France in the province of Champagne. He was sent as a boarding student to the Jesuit college at Bourges where he gave evidence of a precocious and solid piety.

He entered the novitiate at 18, and pronounced his solemn vows Oct. 28, 1621. He then became professor of philosophy and of theology, later master of novices and, of special importance, instructor of tertians, charged with the spiritual formation of the Jesuits making an additional year of novitiate after having finished their studies and before beginning their apostolic ministries.

Lallemant himself did not write, but one of his students gathered notes that were preserved, arranged, and published in Paris (1694) by Pierre Champion, SJ, almost 60 years after Lallemant's death. This book was entitled *La Vie et la doctrine spirituelle du P. Louis Lallemant de la Compagnie de Jésus*. It contains a biography, written by Champion, and an addition, made up of notes taken at the conferences of Lallemant by his disciple J. J. SURIN. Despite the difficult critical problems posed by such a manner of transmission and composition, we can regard the *Doctrine spirituelle* as the true thought of Lallemant.

In this work he insists on purity of heart, on docility to the direction of the Holy Spirit. Under the influence of the Spiritual Exercises he teaches the discernment of spirits, that is, the discovery of the action and of the will of God, recognized in everyday life through the movements of the heart. He insists as well on the gifts of the Holy Spirit and on union with Our Lord in prayer. He poses the classic problem of the relation between prayer and action. For him, prayer ought to lead to a disinterested contemplation, but it ought also to prepare for apostolic action, nourish it, and submit it to the light of the Holy Spirit. Action, on the other hand, ought to lead us to God and be a constant stimulus to prayer. This is an apostolic spirituality: prayer and action are the means of becoming a true apostle. "The final point of the highest perfection in this world is zeal for souls."

Lallemant inspired a double set of disciples: mystical writers, such as J. Rigoleuc and J. J. Surin; and heroic missionaries, such as Bl. Julien Maunoir and St. Isaac Jogues.

Bibliography: L. LALLEMANT, *La Vie et la doctrine spirituelle du Père Louis Lallemant* (2d ed. Paris 1961), introd. and notes by F. COUREL. J. DE GUIBERT, *La Spiritualité de la Compagnie de Jésus*, ed. E. LAMALLE (Rome 1953), a sure and precise general view of Lallemant. H. BRÉMOND, *Histoire littéraire du sentiment réligieux en France depuis la fin des guerres de religion jusqu'à nos jours* (Paris 1911–36) 5:3–65. A. POTTIER, *Essai de théologie mystique comparée: Le Père Louis Lallemant et les grands spirituels de son temps*, 3 v. (Paris 1927–29). P. BOUVIER, *Dictionnaire de théologie catholique* (Paris 1903–50) 8.2:2459–64. F. COUREL, *Lexikon für Theologie und Kirche* (Freiburg 1957–65) 6:753. J. JIMÉNEZ, "En torno a la formación de la *Doctrine spirituelle* del P. Lallement," *Archivum historicum Societatis Jesu* 32 (1963) 225–292.

[F. COUREL]

LALOR, TERESA, MOTHER

Foundress of the American Visitandines; b. Ballyragget, County Kilkenny, Ireland, *c.* 1769; d. Washington, D.C., Sept. 9, 1846. While on a visit to Philadelphia, Pa., in 1797, Alice Lalor and two other young women cooperated with Rev. Leonard Neale in founding what was to become the first American house of the VISITATION NUNS. In 1799, when Neale was transferred to Georgetown (Washington, D.C.), they followed. They lodged first with a group of refugee Poor Clare nuns, but they later moved into their own quarters and adopted a quasi-Jesuit rule given them by Neale. "The Pious Ladies," as they were known, obtained the Visitation rule, and Mother Teresa took her vows on Dec. 28, 1816. The free school for girls that she established, as well as the sisterhood itself, prospered after initial difficulties. The school assumed a national character, and the sisterhood expanded to Mobile, Ala., in 1832 and to Baltimore, Md., in 1837. After almost 20 years as superior, Mother Teresa relinquished her office in 1819 and spent her remaining days in the ranks of her community.

Bibliography: J. B. CODE, *Great American Foundresses* (New York 1929). G. P. and R. H. LATHROP, *A Story of Courage: Annals of the Georgetown Convent of the Visitation* (Cambridge, Mass. 1895).

[J. B. CODE]

LAMAISM

Mahāyāna Buddhism first entered Tibet from India in the 7th century. In the 8th century it became "Lamaism" through local developments and absorption of many native religious elements. Several sects came into being. Most of the lamas (*bla-ma,* "superior") were married and wore red garments, hence the name Red Church. In the 8th century Tibet became a powerful empire, a development helping the consolidation of Lamaism. Contrary to original Buddhist doctrine, Lamaism developed into a theistic religion with many gods and demons, and an elaborate ritual with spells, incantations, and prayer formulas. Under the Mongol dynasty in China (13th and 14th centuries), Lamaism wielded much influence at the court and made its first entry into Mongolia.

Reformed Lamaism. Tsong-kha-pa (1357–1419), a native of northeastern Tibet, started a reformation and restored celibacy of the monks. His sect, *dGe-lugs-pa,* "the virtuous," became known as the Yellow Church, because of its yellow garments. It was centered around Lhasa. In 1577 Tsong-kha-pa's third successor was invited to visit Mongolia. On this occasion, a Mongol prince bestowed upon him the title Dalai Lama—"Ocean, or Universal,

lama"; he thus became the third Dalai Lama, and his successors have ever since borne that title. He died in Mongolia, in 1588. The fourth Dalai Lama was a Mongol (1589–1616). The most famous one was the fifth, Ngagdbang-bLo-bzang (1617–82). The 14th Dalai Lama went into exile in India in 1959.

The Mongol journey and the subsequent revival of Lamaism in Mongolia brought added prestige to the Yellow Church in Tibet: in due time it supplanted almost entirely the earlier sects (about 90 percent of the lamas were of the Yellow Church), and the Dalai Lama became temporal ruler as well as supreme religious head. From Mongolia, Lamaism spread into southern Siberia, and with the Mongol emmigration of the 17th century, into southern Russia.

The Dalai Lamas. The Dalai Lamas are believed to be incarnations ("Living Buddhas") of the *bodhisattva Avalokiteshvara,* "Looking with mercy upon the world." Another hierarch of great importance was the Panchen Lama, a reincarnation of Amitābha Buddha. Theoretically of equal rank with the Dalai Lama, he was often subordinated to him, but after China had established supremacy over Tibet in the 18th century, it was Chinese policy to exploit their rivalry. At one time an important Lamaist hierarch was located in Urga (now Ulanbator), Outer Mongolia.

The sacred writings of Lamaism are called *Kandjur* (*bKa-'gyur*), "translation of precepts," in 108 volumes, mostly from the Sanskrit, and *Tanjur* (*bsTan-'gyur*), "translation of commentaries," comprising commentaries and various treatises, in 225 volumes.

See Also: BUDDHISM.

Bibliography: L. A. WADDELL, J. HASTINGS, ed., *Encyclopedia of Religion and Ethics* 13 v. (Edinburgh 1908–27) 7:784–789. C. A. BELL, *The Religion of Tibet* (Oxford 1931). H. HOFFMANN, *Die Religionen Tibets* (Freiburg 1956). G. REGAMEY, "Die Religion Tibets," *Christus und die Religionen der Erde,* ed. F. KÖNIG (2d ed. Vienna 1916): 3:307–317.

[H. SERRUYS]

LAMB OF GOD

This subject is dealt with here first exegetically and then, on that basis, theologically. Finally, the iconography will be considered.

Exegesis. The origin of this title given to Christ (Jn 1.29–36) is difficult to determine. It can perhaps be traced to Isaiah ch. 53, where the Servant of Yahweh is compared to a lamb (v. 7), and Acts (8.32) applies this text explicitly to Christ. There it is said that He *bears* our sins

A Lamb of God stained glass window at the Chapel of the Holy Ghost Hospital. (©Dave Bartruff/CORBIS)

(Is 53.6, 11–12); but by itself this text is incapable of explaining the expression, for in John, Christ is not said to be like a lamb; He is the lamb; what is more, the lamb of God. He does not bear the sins of others; He takes them away. However, the entire account of the baptism of Christ, within the framework of which John places the proclamation made by the Baptist (cf. Jn 1.31–34 and Mt 3.16–17) directs one's search toward the Servant of Yahweh. The divine revelation, "This is my beloved Son, in whom I am well pleased," and the descent of the Spirit (Mt 3.16–17 and parallels) and Jn 1.34 (with the variant "he is the chosen one," which seems original) recall clearly the prophecy of the Servant of Yahweh, Is 42.1 [cf. O. Cullmann, *The Christology of the New Testament,* tr. S. Guthrie and C. Hall (rev. ed. Philadelphia 1963)]. C. F. Burney, following C. J. Ball, has pointed out that the Aramaic word *ṭalya'*, which like the παῖς of the Septuagint, signifies boy, young man, and servant, also signifies lamb. The studies of J. Jeremias render very plausible

the explanation that the meaning of the expression can be found in the twofold signification of the word *ṭalya'* and that the original form of the expression was "Behold the Servant of God" (Cullmann, B. Gärtner, M. E. Boismard, R. Schnackenburg), a saying much easier to explain, coming from the lips of the Baptist, than the expression Lamb of God. B. Gärtner states that the Targum of Psalm 117(118) in fact gives to the Davidic Messiah the title to *ṭalya'*, taken by turn in the twofold sense of servant and of lamb. All this would indicate that the Johannine account is Aramaic in origin, moreover that the translation of *ṭalya'* into ἀμνός was intentional and not the result of an error.

The meaning of the title is to be sought not in the concept that the Baptist may have had of the Messiah, since the expression as it came from his lips probably had another form; it is to be sought in the fourth Gospel. However, the fourth Gospel appears to a number of exegetes, with the evidence growing [cf. F. X. Durrwell, *The*

Resurrection: A Biblical Study, tr. B. Sheed (New York 1960); B. Gärtner *John 6 and the Jewish Passover* (Lund 1959)], as a paschal Gospel. The symbolism underlying the title is that of the lamb of sacrifice, and not of the daily sacrifice, but of the paschal sacrifice. The final evocation of the paschal lamb (Jn 19.36), when the Evangelist's account reaches its culminating point, explains the proclamation at the beginning (1.29). The primitive liturgy (cf. 1 Cor 5.7–8), the coinciding of the death of Christ with the paschal feast of the Jews, probably contributed to giving this title to Christ.

Theology. For St. John the title of Lamb of God is of great theological importance. This springs from the fact that the whole Gospel account is enclosed between this proclamation of Jesus as lamb of God and the evocation of the prefigurative lamb (1.29 and 19.36); also from the fact that John emphasizes (18.28; 19.14, 31) the coincidence between the immolation of the prefigurative paschal lamb and the Hour of Christ when the destiny of Christ is accomplished and His whole being is revealed (8.28), and when He is presented to men as the object of their faith (3.14–15; 12.32; 19.35, 37). It can be concluded, then, that the paschal lamb was for St. John a privileged image to express the mystery of Christ.

Salvific Transcendence. In its form, the title is close to others in the fourth Gospel that express the transcendence of Christ. Just as Jesus is not like bread, a vine, a shepherd, etc., but indeed is the Bread, the Vine, the Shepherd, etc., so that no others can be so named, in the same way He is not only like a lamb, He is the Lamb. This transcendence is emphasized by the addition "of God," which expresses not only the divine origin and character (cf. "the bread from heaven," "the bread of God" 6.32–33), but also the sacrificial consecration in God. Christ is the victim of the true sacrifice. There is on this point as on others [cf. C. Spico, *L'Épître aux Hébreux* (Paris 1952) 1:109–138] a certain resemblance between Johannine thought and that of the Epistle to the Hebrews.

The transcendence of Christ is, according to St. John, essentially salvific, so that in Him one cannot separate the mystery of the Incarnation from that of the Redemption. Christ says: "I Am" (8.28, 58); but ordinarily He adds a predicate signifying that He Is for men (the bread, the vine, the resurrection and the life). The title Lamb of God makes it clear and precise that this salvific mystery is sacrificial. One can say that the mystery of Redemption, the paschal mystery, is for St. John inherent in that of the Incarnation.

Just as Christ is from the beginning "the bread from heaven," "the shepherd," etc., and just as He becomes so in plenitude only by His sacrifice (6.52; 10.11), so also He is from the beginning called the lamb (1.29)—from the beginning there is in Him the sacrificial consecration (10.36)—but He becomes so in plenitude only in death. The salvific Incarnation is realized in plenitude only by passage through death, and it is as immolated that Christ continues forever when, in glory, the mystery of the salvific Incarnation has reached its plenitude (cf. Rv 5.6).

Sanctification in God. This title also sheds light on the nature of the redemptive sacrifice. The paschal rite was a sacrifice of communion (cf. 1 Cor 5.7–8); the meal was an essential element of it. Understood by St. John by means of the symbolism of the paschal lamb, the sacrifice of Christ is not presented in the manner of a substitution, where the victim bears the sins of others and expiates them by undergoing their punishment. Contrary to Isaiah 53.6, 11–12, it is not said that the Lamb bears but that He takes away sin. Just as, according to St. John, darkness is dispelled by the Word that is light, and death by communion with Him who is the bread of life, the resurrection, so also sin is destroyed by communion with the Lamb, by participation in the sanctity proper to His sacrifice.

For the sacrifice is, in the eyes of John, a sanctification in God (17.19). Sanctified from the beginning (10.36), Christ comes to the plenitude of His sanctification in His death (17.19), where He is caught up into the glory of God (13.32) and where He shares this sanctification with His own (17.19).

It is therefore vain to pose the question: Is it by His innocence (Lagrange) and by His holiness (Boismard) or rather is it by His sacrifice that the Lamb abolishes sin? It is certainly through His sacrifice, according to St. John, that sin is abolished (1 Jn 1.7; 2.2; 4.10), but in this sacrifice is the plenitude of the sanctification of Christ by God.

Sin, therefore, is abolished by the sanctity of Christ in His sacrifice and by communion with Him. So the Apocalypse shows the faithful washing their garments in the blood of the Lamb (7.14). Christ not only merits the pardon of sin, He is Himself the expiation (1 Jn 2.2; 4.10), that is, the abolition of sin. This is in conformity with the idea of the Old Testament, according to which it is the holiness of God that expiates the sins of men in the sacrifice. A confirmation that sin is expiated by Christ immolated and by communication with His holiness is found in the fact that the Lamb of God is characterized by the presence of the Holy Spirit in Him (1.29–34), that Christ is designated once again as the Lamb of God at the moment when from His opened side issued the water, symbol of the Holy Spirit (19.33–36; cf. 7.37–39), and that it is in the Spirit that sins are forgiven (1.33; 20.22–23).

The theology of the Lamb is taken up again in the Apocalypse. Heaven is the place proper to the sacrifice of the Lamb (5.6). Christ is there forever immolated (5.6). All that is said of Christ: Lord, judge, fullness of the Spirit of God, pastor of the Church and its spouse—all this is said of Him in so much as He is the lamb immolated. The paschal sacrifice belongs to His very being, and the faithful are saved by communion with this Lamb immolated.

Bibliography: R. SCHNACKENBURG, *Lexikon für Theologie und Kirche*, ed. J. HOFER and K. RAHNER (Freiberg 1957–65) 6:768–769, bibliog. E. LOHSE, *Die Religion in Geschichte und Gegenwart* (Tübingen 1957–65) 4:218–219. *Encyclopedic Dictionary of the Bible*, tr. and adap. by L. HARTMAN (New York 1963) 1297–99. M. E. BOISMARD, *Du baptême à Cana* (Paris 1953).

[F. X. DURRWELL]

Iconography. The symbol of the Lamb shows up very early in Christian iconography. Behind the representation, which underwent only slight modification throughout history, lies a wealth of theology. The lamb first appears, it seems, with representations of the Good Shepherd, but by the fourth century the lamb became an independent symbol, without the figure of Christ. Both the symbol and the idea behind it derive from Scripture: the eating of the paschal lamb and the saving power of its blood (Ex ch. 12); the comparison of the Servant of the Lord to a lamb (Is ch. 53); and John the Baptist's reference to Christ as the Lamb of God (Jn 1.29–36).

The symbolic lamb began to appear in the apses or façades of basilicas, on sarcophagi, and on smaller pieces of art. In ancient Christian portrayals of paradise one sees the lamb on the mountain, with four streams (the four Gospels) flowing to the four ends of the earth (SS. Cosmas and Damian, Rome). Frequently six lambs were added on either side, representing the Apostles or the faithful. In the apse of old St. Peter's, Rome, the lamb is depicted as in Rv 5.6–10, standing in a triumphant, redeeming position in front of the cross. In A.D. 692 a small restriction was placed on the symbolic representation of the lamb. The Council of Trulla, held in the Eastern Church, forbade the representation of the lamb to take the place of the body of Christ on the cross.

In the baptistery of the Lateran, one sees the lamb depicted as the source of the fruits of Baptism. The Lateran also shows the lamb, according to an image in the Revelation, resting on the scroll with seven seals, holding a victorious banner, and adored by the 24 elders and the four living creatures. All of these representations, with minor differences, are found in Italy, Spain, France, and Germany as far back as the fourth century. Somewhat later the lamb was associated with the holy sacrifice of the Mass and with the Passion by having the lamb appear with a chalice; this chalice is sometimes receiving a stream of blood from the wounded side of the lamb. The symbolic use of the lamb continued through the Middle Ages, but during this later period deterioration crept in. The lamb, for instance, became the base for pillars and doorposts or was pictured led by Mary as its shepherdess. Today the lamb symbol is modeled mostly upon very early types.

Gradually the lamb was also used in art forms and in other instruction media of the Church as a symbol of purity, humility, holy simplicity, patience, and still other virtues; e.g., St. Agnes is shown with the lamb (purity).

With regard to liturgical music and recitation, the term Lamb of God is prominent in the Latin rite. The lamb, apparently representing Christ as the victorious Redeemer, is cited in the Mass and in litanies. Some of these Mass texts reach as far back as the fourth century. In the Byzantine liturgy the sacramental bread bears the figure of the lamb; and in order to signify the sacrifice and death of the victim Christ, the lamb is cut into four parts. A popular sacramental is the AGNUS DEI (Latin for Lamb of God), wax blessed every seven years by the Pope. It has a very interesting history and is used as a reminder of God's special blessing.

In the Western Church as far back as the seventh century (Sacramentary of Bobbio) one finds a blessing of a lamb that was to be eaten at the Easter meal. The *Rituale romanum* contains the blessing of the lamb. In the Eastern Church there was some hesitation to accept this blessing of the lamb, but by the Middle Ages it was received into their rituals.

To appreciate the lamb symbol adequately, one must be acquainted with the nature and peculiar habits of the lamb. Unfortunately, many people today are almost entirely ignorant of these, as well as of the special mode of pasturing sheep in seminomadic areas like Palestine.

See Also: RESURRECTION OF CHRIST, 2; SUFFERING SERVANT, SONGS OF SATISFACTION OF CHRIST.

Bibliography: E. MANGENOT, *Dictionnaire de théologie catholique*, ed. A. VACANT et al., (Paris 1903—50) 1:576–585. V. H. ELBERN et al., *Lexikon für Theologie und Kirche*, ed. J. HOFER and K. RAHNER (Freiberg 1957–65) 6:766–768. R. SCHNACKENBURG, *ibid.* 768–769. H. LECLERCQ, *Dictionnaire d'archéologie chrétienne et de liturgie.* ed. F. CABROL, H. LECLERCQ and H. I. MARROU (Paris 1907–53) 1:877–905. *Proceedings of the Precious Blood Study Week*, 2 v. (Rensselaer, Ind. 1957–60), index s.v. ''Lamb.''

[V. M. OBERHAUSER]

LAMBACH, ABBEY OF

Benedictine abbey near the former Diocese of Passau, now Linz, in upper Austria, founded *c.* 1040 by

Count Arnold II of Wels-Lambach for 12 secular canons, and placed under the patronage of the Assumption. In 1056 Arnold's second son, Bp. ADALBERO OF WÜRZBURG (1045–90), summoned BENEDICTINE monks from Münsterschwarzach. Lambach became a reform center that influenced ADMONT, MELK, SANKT LAMBRECHT, etc. In the 12th century Lambach developed a distinguished school of painting, writing, music, and theater that flourished into the baroque period. The monastery was a transshipment center for salt. In the 15th century the Melk reform was introduced at Lambach, Pontificals were granted to the abbot (1459), and Lambach monks were made abbots of Schotten in Vienna and NIEDERALTAICH. The abbey enjoyed close relations with the new Universities of Vienna and Salzburg. It suffered loss of holdings and decline of discipline because of schism and wars (especially in 1626 and 1632), despite generally competent abbots from 1585 to 1725. The Lambach monk Florentius Müller worked among London Catholics while chaplain to Prince Starhemberg. The extant abbey church dates from 1652–56, the monastic buildings from 1664. Lambach artists included Altomonte and the brothers Carlone and Koloman Felner (1818). Lambach was dissolved for two months in 1784. However, by the second half of the 19th century it was once again flourishing. It was dissolved by the National Socialists (1941–45). Today it conducts both a middle school and a school of agriculture and administers four parishes.

Bibliography: L. H. COTTINEAU, *Répertoire topobibliographique des abbayes et prieurés,* 2 v. (Mâcon 1935–39) 1:1542–43. K. HALLINGER, *Gorze-Kluny,* 2 v. (*Studia anselmiana* 24–25; 1951). W. LUGER, *Die Benediktinerabtei Lambach* (Linz 1952). S. LEIDINGER, *900 Jahre Lambach* (Linz 1956). N. WIBIRAL et al., "Die Freilegungsarbeiten im ehemaligen Westchor der Stiftskirche von Lambach," *Oesterreichische Zeitschrift für Kunst und Denkmalpflege* 14 (1960) 1–24.

[G. SPAHR]

LAMBERT, LOUIS ALOYSIUS

Priest, editor, publicist; b. Charleroi, Pa., April 13, 1835; d. Newfoundland, N.J., Sept. 25, 1910. He attended St. Vincent's College, Latrobe, Pa., and the St. Louis archdiocesan theological seminary, Carondelet, Mo. After ordination on Feb. 11, 1859, for the Diocese of Alton, Ill., he did pastoral work in Cairo, Alton, and Shawneetown, Ill. Five months after the outbreak of the Civil War, Lambert enlisted as U.S. Army chaplain and saw action at Fts. Henry and Donelson and at the Battle of Shiloh before his resignation took effect on April 16, 1862. He returned briefly to Shawneetown and was reassigned to Cairo, where he held the pastorate of St. Patrick's church from 1863 to 1868.

With the permission of his bishop, he next went to New York to teach for the Paulist Fathers, whose community he considered joining. Deciding against this, he secured excardination from the Diocese of Alton on May 20, 1869, and was adopted by Bp. Bernard John MCQUAID as a priest of the Diocese of Rochester, N.Y. There he held posts as administrator and pastor. In 1877, while stationed at St. Mary's, Waterloo, NY, he founded the diocesan weekly *Catholic Times,* which he edited until 1880, when he became involved in a controversy with his ordinary, Bishop McQuaid. He was subsequently transferred to Scottsville, N.Y., where he was pastor of Assumption church until his death.

He founded and edited the *Catholic Times* of Philadelphia (1892–94) and edited the *Freeman's Journal* of New York (1895–1910), in which he renewed the controversy with McQuaid by highly literate (and often unfair) attacks. An able linguist, Lambert translated several works into English. One, Paul Merz's *Thesaurus Biblicus,* or *Handbook of Scriptural Reference* (Waterloo, NY 1800), was the first Catholic scriptural concordance published in the United States. Another of his translations was August Kerckhoff's *Grammar of Volapük* (New York 1888). His *Notes on Ingersoll* (Buffalo 1887) definitively refuted the then current rationalistic preachments of the "great agnostic," Robert Green Ingersoll (1822–99). These internationally popular books and his subsequent *Christian Science before the Bar of Reason* (New York 1908) inspired Lambert's fellow Catholics to call him the "American Newman." As a result he was much in demand as an essayist, lecturer, and literary editor. In 1892 the University of Notre Dame, South Bend, Ind., bestowed on him an honorary doctorate of laws.

Bibliography: Archives of The Catholic University of America. Archives of the Dioceses of Rochester and Belleville. The National Archives, Washington, D.C. A. H. GERMAIN, *Catholic Military and Naval Chaplains, 1776–1917* (Washington, D.C. 1929). F. J. ZWIERLEIN, *Life and Letters of Bishop McQuaid,* 3 v. (Rochester 1925–27). G. N. SCHUSTER, *Dictionary of American Biography,* ed. A. JOHNSON and D. MALONE, 20 v. (New York 1928–36; index 1937; 1st supplement 1944; 2nd supplement 1958) 10:557–558.

[R. F. MCNAMARA]

LAMBERT DE LA MOTTE, PIERRE

Missionary; b. La Boissière, France, Jan. 28, 1624; d. Juthia, Thailand, June 15, 1679. He was ordained Dec. 27, 1655, and went to Rome to take part with F. PALLU in negotiations for vicars-apostolic under the jurisdiction of the Congregation for the Propagation of the Faith. With Pallu he founded the Paris Missions seminary in 1658. In 1659 he was made titular bishop of Beirut, vicar-apostolic of Cochin China, and apostolic administrator of southern China. He set out in 1660; crossed Egypt, Persia, and India on foot; and reached Siam in 1662. He and Pallu, finding the condition of the missions disheartening, prepared instructions for missionaries that were adopted by the Congregation for the Propagation of the Faith. He founded a seminary in Siam and ordained two Vietnamese priests in 1668. Then he visited Tonkin (northern Vietnam), where he ordained four priests and held a synod to govern the parochial apostolate. He founded the congregation of the LOVERS OF THE HOLY CROSS for women in Vietnam (*Amantes de la Croix, Dòng Mênh Thánh Giá*) in 1670.

Bibliography: J. GUENNOU, *Les Missions étrangères* (Paris 1963).

[H. PROUVOST/EDS.]

LAMBERT OF MAASTRICHT, ST.

Bishop and martyr; d. Liège, Sept. 17, 705 or 706. Born of wealthy parents, Lambert grew up under the supervision of his uncle, Theodard of Maastricht, whom he succeeded as bishop in 672. Shortly afterward the incompetent Childeric II, king of Austrasia, was assassinated. In the upheaval that followed, Lambert fled to the monastery of STAVELOT while an intruder took his place as bishop. After seven years of exile, Lambert was restored to his see by the new mayor of the palace, Pepin II of Heristal. Later the bishop had to upbraid Pepin for an adulterous affair. In the conflict over the immunity of his church, Lambert was murdered by his adversary, Count Dodo. Popularly venerated as a martyr in France, Westphalia, and Holland, Lambert is honored as the patron of the city of Freiburg im Breisgau, Germany.

Feast: Sept. 17.

Bibliography: *Acta Sanctorum* September 5:518–617. J. L. BAUDOT and L. CHAUSSIN, *Vies des saints et des bienheueux selon l'ordre du calendrier avec l'historique des fêtes,* ed. by The Benedictines of Paris, 12 v. (Paris 1935–56) 9:361–364. *Bibliotheca hagiographica latina antiquae ct mediae aetatis,* 2 v. (Brussels 1898–1901; suppl. 1911) 2:4677–94. A. BUTLER, *The Lives of the Saints,* ed. H. THURSTON and D. ATTWATER, 4 v. (New York 1956) 3:579–580. H. LERCLERCQ, *Dictionnaire d'archéologie chrétienne et de liturgie,* ed. F. CABROL, H. LECLERCQ and H. I. MARROU, 15 v. (Paris 1907–53) 9.1:623–625; 10.1:955–963. A. M. ZIMMERMANN, *Lexikon für Theologie und Kirche,* ed. J. HOFER and K. RAHNER, 10 v. (2d, new ed. Freiburg 1957–65) 6:758. J. DE BORCHGRAVE D'ALTENA et al., eds., *Trésors d'art Saint Remacle, Saint Lambert* (Stavelot 1968).

[J. E. LYNCH]

LAMBERT OF SAINT-OMER

Encyclopedist; d. *c.* 1125; A canon at Saint-Omer as his father, Onulf, had been before him, Lambert was the author of an encyclopedia of general knowledge, the *Liber floridus (Patrologia Latina* 163:1003–31), completed in 1120. His work is a compilation of extracts from authorities, both ancient and contemporary, usually unacknowledged; it embraces most fields of learning, including history, geography, mathematics, astronomy, natural history, grammar, and orthography. His sources included Pliny, Seneca, Publilius Syrus, Orosius, Macrobius, Paulinus of Nola, Jerome, Isidore, Gregory of Tours, Rabanus Maurus, Peter the Painter, Einhard, Bede, and others. The work has many illustrations, maps, plans, and genealogical trees. There is much repetition of information. Nothing is known of Lambert's career. He is sometimes confused with LAMBERT OF SAINT-BERTIN, who is certainly a separate identity, but the two may have belonged to the same monastery of Sithiu, i.e., SAINT-BERTIN.

Bibliography: The original MS of the *Liber floridus* is Ghent 92, s. xii. On the illustrations in this MS, see V. VAN DER HAEGHEN, ''Le Manuscrit gantois du *Liber floridus* et ses illustrations, XIIe siècle,'' *Bulletijn der Maatschappij van Geschieden Oudheidkunde te Gent* 16 (1908) 112–118. For other MSS, see Manitius 3:241–244. L. DUCHESNE, ed., *Liber Pontificalis* (Paris 1886–1892) 1:clxxxv–clxxxvii. L. V. DELISLE, ''Notice sur les manuscrits du *Liber floridus''* in *Notices et extraits des manuscrits de la Bibliothèque nationale et autres bibliothèques* 38.2 (1906) 577–791. J. M. DE SMET, ''L'Enégète Lambert, écolâtre d'Utrecht,'' *Revue d'histoire ecclésiastique* 42 (1947) 103–110. B. SMALLEY, *The Study of the Bible in the Middle Ages* (2d ed. Oxford 1952).

[P. B. CORBETT]

LAMBERT OF SAINT-BERTIN

Abbot; b. *c.* 1060; d. Saint-Bertin, June 22, 1125. Born of a noble family, Lambert entered the Abbey of SAINT-BERTIN *c.* 1070. There he taught grammar, philosophy, theology, and music. Having become abbot in 1095, he made energetic reforms in the monastery and brought it under the CLUNIAC REFORM. A contemporary account of his life (*Monumenta Germaniae Historica,* Scriptores 15:946–953) records that he wrote sermons on the Old Testament; disputations on free will, predestination, and grace; and *questiones* on natural science. His letters to ANSELM OF CANTERBURY are extant (*Patrologia Latina* 158:1083; 159:72, 171), as are the verses exchanged with REGINALD OF CANTERBURY [ed. F. Liebermann, *Neues Archiv der Gesellschaft für ältere deutsche Geschichtskunde* 13 (1888) 528, 531–534]. The identification of Lambert with LAMBERT OF SAINT-OMER made by M. E. Taillar, J. Tessier, and R. Ceillier has been denied by

L. Duchesne, L. Delisle, and M. Manitius, *Geschichte der lateinischen Literatur des Mittelalters.*

Bibliography: H. DE LAPLANE, *Les Abbés de Saint-Bertin,* 2 v. (Saint-Omer 1854–55). *Liber pontificalis* 1:clxxxv–clxxxvi. L. DELISLE, *Notice sur les manuscrits du Liber floridus* (Paris 1906). O. HOLDER-EGGER, *Neues Archiv der Gesellschaft für ältere deutsche Geschichtskunde* 32 (1907) 524–525. O. BLED, ''L'École bertinienne,'' *Bulletin de la société des anti-quaires de la Morinie* 14 (1923) 99–115. M. MANITIUS, *Geschichte der lateinischen Literatur des Mittelalters* (Munich 1911–31) 3:241–244.

[P. B. CORBETT]

LAMBERT OF SPOLETO, GERMAN EMPEROR

Ruled April 30, 892, to Oct. 15, 898; son of Guido III of Spoleto and the Lombard Princess Agiltrude; d. Marengo, Italy, in a hunting accident. Having been associated with his father as king of Italy in 891 and crowned emperor by Pope FORMOSUS in 892, he became sole ruler on his father's death in 894. From his father he inherited a conflict with Berengar I of Friuli. An expedition against him by Arnulf, the German emperor, in 895, prompted by an appeal from Formosus, resulted in the capture of Rome from Agiltrude, acting for her son. Arnulf was crowned emperor by Formosus but was incapacitated by illness and returned to Germany. The death of Formosus and an agreement with Berengar enabled Agiltrude and Lambert to re-enter Rome in 897. To satisfy the enemies of Formosus, Pope STEPHEN VI condemned and degraded the exhumed body of the dead pope in a macabre postmortem trial. Agiltrude and Lambert had left the city, and the measure of their responsibility for this profanation is still debated. In a papal election later that year Lambert pronounced in favor of pacification by supporting JOHN IX. The Synod of Ravenna in 898 affirmed Lambert's power over Rome and the STATES OF THE CHURCH and issued a series of reforming decrees, which he incorporated in a capitulary. An attempt at resistance by Adalbert of Tuscany was crushed.

Bibliography: P. BREZZI, *Roma e l'Impero medioevale (774–1252)* (Bologna 1947). G. FASOLI, *I re d'Italia, 888–962* (Florence 1949). C. G. MOR, *L'età feudale,* 2 v. (Milan 1952–53). F. ZOEPFL, *Lexikon für Theologie und Kirche,* ed. J. HOFER and K. RAHNER (Freiburg 1957–65) 6:759.

[C. E. BOYD]

LAMBERTENGHI OF COMO, GEREMIA, BL.

Priest of the Franciscan Third Order Regular, called the Martyr of the Cloister because of his exceptional practice of penance; b. of a noble family at Como, Italy, 1440; d. convent of Valverde (Forlí), Mar. 25, 1513. From early youth he showed devotion to Christ's Passion and a love of austerity. In his 20th year he entered the convent of St. Donato, near Como. After ordination, he was appointed to the office of preacher, vicar, and prior in various communities. His apostolic dedication to these duties did not diminish his observance of the rule nor decrease the intensity of his penances. It is recorded that he used an iron chain to discipline his body and often took his rest lying in a coffin through which he had driven 100 nails. There is testimony of his miraculous power before and after death. His body, still uncorrupt, now rests in the Cathedral of Forlí.

Bibliography: R. PAZZELLI, *Il Terz'ordine Regolare di S. Francesco* (Rome 1958).

[V. PETRICCIONE]

LAMBERTINI, IMELDA, BL.

Virgin; b. Bologna, Italy, *c.* 1321; d. near Bologna, May 12, 1333. Born of a noble family, she entered the Dominican cloister of Valdipietra near Bologna. Since she was under 12, then the required age for First Communion, her ardent request for Holy Communion was denied. On Ascension Day 1333, when the nuns received Communion, Imelda, then 11 years old, remained in her place. Suddenly, it was reported, the Sacred Host appeared above her head. The priest gave it to the child, whose First Communion was also her last, for she died in the rapture of her thanksgiving. She was beatified in 1826, and in 1910 was proclaimed the patroness of first communicants.

Feast: May 13.

Bibliography: *Acta Sanctorum* May 3:181–183. Daughters of St. Paul, *Her Dream Came True; The Life of Bl. Imelda Lambertini* (Boston 1967). *Année dominicaine,* Sept 2 (Lyon 1900) 527–545. A. BUTLER, *The Lives of the Saints* (New York 1956) 2:301.

[M. J. FINNEGAN]

LAMBETH CONFERENCE

The consultative assembly of bishops of the entire Anglican Communion that are held at approximately ten-year intervals at Lambeth Palace, London, under the presidency of the Archbishop of Canterbury. The initiative for these gatherings came from the bishops of Canada, who were disturbed by the liberal theology of *Essays and Reviews* (1860) and of Bp. John Colenso who petitioned in 1865 for a council representative of Anglicans throughout the world. Despite initial misgivings, especially in England, Abp. Charles Longley of Canterbury agreed to convene an assembly, provided that it issued no declaration of faith and no canons or decisions binding on the Church, but confine itself to counsel and encouragement. Since its inauguration, the Lambeth Conference has been a purely informal and consultative gathering of all Anglican episcopal leaders without jurisdictional power; but they have contributed greatly to Anglican unity and cohesion. Their recommendations lack binding force until enacted by local hierarchies in local synods of convocations.

The authority of Lambeth within the Anglican Communion is entirely moral, in the sense of being advisory, rather than legislative and jurisdictional. For this reason the conference normally expresses its corporate mind on issues confronting the church in documents that are commended to Anglicans throughout the world for study. These statements are commonly taken into account by the legislative and policy-making bodies of the individual member churches as being expressive of the mind of the church.

The Lambeth Conference has been criticized by some Anglicans on two counts: it consists solely of bishops, and it meets only once every decade. Since its inception until the end of the 20th century, there have been thirteen conferences. The 1968 conference took positive action to provide a fully representative pan-Anglican body made up of bishops, clergy, and laity that could meet more frequently. The result was the establishment of the Anglican Consultative Council in October 1969. In 1988, for the first time the Lambeth Conference included the full Anglican Consultative Council and episcopal representatives from churches in communion with Canterbury, namely the churches of Bangladesh, North India, South India and Pakistan, and the Old Catholic Churches of the Union of Utrecht.

Bibliography: R. T. DAVIDSON, ed., *The Lambeth Conferences of 1867, 1978 and 1888* (New York 1896). H. RYAN, "Lambeth '68, a Roman Catholic Theological Reflection," *Theological Studies* 29 (1968) 597–636. G. F. LYTLE, *Lambeth Conferences Past and Present* (Austin, Texas 1989). V. K. SAMUEL, and C. SUGDEN, *Lambeth: A View from the Two Thirds World* (London 1989).

[W.H. HANNAH/C. E. SIMCOX/EDS.]

LAMBETH QUADRILATERAL

The four articles stating, from the Anglican point of view, the essentials for a reunited Christian Church: acceptance of Scripture, the Apostles' and Nicene Creed, the two Sacraments of Baptism and the Eucharist, and "the historic Episcopate." It was first proposed by the

Protestant Episcopal Church in the U.S. in its General Convention held in Chicago in 1886, and adopted by the LAMBETH CONFERENCE of 1888. There have been some variations in the wording of these points. The Lambeth Conference of 1888 declared that Scripture contained "all things necessary to salvation" and that the two Sacraments were ordained by Christ himself; the Chicago declaration of the Protestant Episcopal Church in the U.S., in its general convention of 1886, had omitted these qualifications. The four points must be understood in connection with other Anglican statements, among which was the report of the Joint Commission on Approaches to Unity in the American Episcopalian General Convention of 1949. It contained declarations on the Eucharistic sacrifice and on the other Sacraments as "sacramental rites of mysteries." Some Anglican statements also interpret acceptance of the Nicene Creed as involving recognition of the first six ecumenical councils. The subject of episcopacy has been discussed at subsequent Lambeth Conferences and other church unity gatherings.

Bibliography: R. T. DAVIDSON, *The Five Lambeth Conferences* (New York 1920). R. M. BROWN and D. H. SCOTT, eds., *Challenge to Reunion* (New York 1963). J. R. WRIGHT, ed. *Essays on the centenary of the Chicago-Lambeth Quadrilateral 1886/88-1986/88: Quadrilateral at One Hundred* (London 1988).

[B. LEEMING/EDS.]

LAMBING, ANDREW ARNOLD

Priest, author, historian; b. Manorville, Pa., Feb. 1, 1842; d. Wilkinsburg, Pa., Dec. 24, 1918. He was the third child of Michael Anthony and Anne (Shields) Lambing. He entered St. Michael Seminary, Glenwood, Pa., in 1863, and was ordained on Aug. 4, 1869, by Bp. Michael Domenec, CM, of Pittsburgh, Pa. First assigned to St. Francis College, Loretto, Pa., he later held appointments in Pennsylvania at Pittsburgh (1873–85) and Wilkinsburg (1885–1918). He was active in diocesan affairs, serving as fiscal procurator, censor of books, and president of the diocesan school board. As a writer, he contributed articles to newspapers and to such magazines as *Ave Maria* and *American Ecclesiastical Review*. His religious works that gained wide popularity included *The Orphan's Friend* (1875), *The Sunday-School Teacher's Manual* (1877), *The Sacramentals* (1892), *Come Holy Ghost* (1901), *The Immaculate Conception of the Blessed Virgin Mary* (1904), and *Fountains of Living Water* (1907). Lambing was an authority on early western Pennsylvanian history. He wrote *A History of the Catholic Church in the Dioceses of Pittsburgh and Allegheny* (1880), which, with its critical essay on sources, was a landmark in American Catholic historiography. He founded (1884) the Ohio Valley Catholic Historical Society, the first organization of its kind. In July 1884 he edited the first American Catholic historical quarterly, *Historical Researches in Western Pennsylvania, Principally Catholic,* retitled *American Catholic Historical Researches* (1886). He also translated *The Baptismal Register of Fort Duquesne, 1754–1756* (1885); contributed to *History of Allegheny County* (1889) and *Standard History of Pittsburgh* (1898); helped to edit *A Century and a Half of Pittsburgh and Her People* (1908); and wrote *Brief Sketch of St. James' Roman Catholic Church, Wilkinsburg, Pa.* (n.d.) and *Foundation Stones of a Great Diocese* (1912). In 1915 Lambing was elevated to the rank of domestic prelate.

Bibliography: M. M. HAMMILL, *The Expansion of the Catholic Church in Pennsylvania* (Pittsburgh 1960).

[M. C. SCHROEDER]

LAMBRUSCHINI, LUIGI

Cardinal, papal secretary of state; b. Sestri Levante (Genova), Italy, May 16, 1776; d. Rome, May 12, 1854. After completing his early studies at S. Margherite Ligure, he joined the BARNABITES and took his vows (Nov. 18, 1794). His philosophical studies were made at Macerata and his theological course at Rome, but the installation of the Roman Republic caused him to transfer to Genoa. Subsequent to his ordination (Jan. 1, 1799), he taught in various colleges of the Barnabites. In 1814 he began a career of intense activity in the Roman Curia. He was appointed consultor (August 1814) and then secretary (March 1816) in the Congregation of Extraordinary Ecclesiastical Affairs. As theological consultor he collaborated with the secretary of state Cardinal Ercole CONSALVI in concluding concordats with Tuscany (1815) and Naples (1818) and in many other ecclesiastical matters of special importance. As vicar-general for Cardinal Francesco Fontana, he helped restore Barnabite colleges suppressed during the Napoleonic epoch in Italy. He was appointed archbishop of Genoa (1819) and nuncio to France (November 1826), while retaining the See of Genoa until 1830. In the Paris nunciature (1827–31) he demonstrated decisively his opposition to LIBERALISM and to popular sovereignty. He was opposed to the July Revolution and remained loyal to the Bourbons, but he was hostile toward the house of Orléans. The new French government demanded his recall (1831).

Upon returning to Rome, Lambruschini, who had meanwhile been named titular archbishop of Beirut (July 5, 1830), was created a cardinal (Sept. 30, 1831). He became prefect of the Congregation of Regular Discipline (1832) and then prefect of the Congregation of Studies (1835). From 1832 he served also in the Congregation of

Andrew Arnold Lambing. (Archive Photos, Inc.)

Extraordinary Ecclesiastical Affairs. In January 1836 GREGORY XVI appointed him secretary of state, a post he held until the pope's death (June 1, 1846). At the papal conclave in 1846 Lambruschini received 15 votes in the first ballot. PIUS IX selected him as a member of the Congregation of State. Lambruschini also conducted the diplomatic arrangements with Russia for the concordat signed Aug. 3, 1847.

Toward the end of 1848 he fled Rome for Naples, where he was often consulted by Pius IX, who was in exile at Gaeta. After the fall of the short-lived Roman Republic, Lambruschini returned to Rome and served as prefect of the Congregation of Rites, secretary of briefs, librarian of the Roman Church, and bishop of Porto and S. Rufina, and of Civitavecchia. His role was very important in the preparation of the decree defining the Immaculate Conception (1854).

Lambruschini's knowledge of philosophy and theology was vast. He showed himself always an intransigent conservative and a strenuous defender of the Church's doctrines and of the Holy See's rights. He did not, however, comprehend contemporary problems. He realized the need for better education of the clergy, but he did not understand how the clergy could be dedicated to the instruction and education of all the faithful. In general he mistrusted all innovations in cultural, spiritual, ecclesiastical, political, and social areas.

Bibliography: L. LAMBRUSCHINI, *La mia nunziatura di Francia,* ed. P. PIRRI (Bologna 1934). A. GIAMPAOLO, "La preparazione politica del cardinale L. . .," *Rassegna storica del Risorgimento* 18 (1931) 81–163. G. BOFFITO, *Scrittori Barnabiti,* 4 v. (Florence 1933–37) 2:312–336. J. GRISAR, "Die Allokution Gregors XVI vom 10. Dez. 1837," in *Gregorio XVI Miscellanea Commemorativa,* 2 v. (Rome 1948) 2:441–560. P. DROULERS, "La Nonciature de Paris et les troubles sociaux-politiques sous la Monarchie de juillet," in *Saggi storici intorno al Papato dei professori della Facoltà di storia ecclesiastica* (*Miscellanea historiae pontificiae* 21; Rome 1959) 401–463. L. M. MANZINI, *Il cardinale L. Lambruschini* (*Studi e Testi* 203; 1960).

[L. PASZTOR]

LAMBTON, JOSEPH, BL.

Priest, martyr; b. 1569 at Malton, Yorkshire, England; d. July 24, 1592 (?), at Newcastle-on-Tyne. This second son of Thomas Lambton and his wife Katharine Birkhead of West Brandon, Durham, studied at the English College in Rheims (1584–89) and in Rome (1589–92). Ordained at age 23 in 1592, he was sent to the English Mission and was arrested upon landing at Newcastle with Bl. Edward WATERSON. As was usual for the execution of a popish priest, he was hung, but cut down alive before the final phase of the sentence: drawing and quartering. The reprieved felon who acted as his hangman refused to complete the sentence, which was at last carried out by a Frenchman practicing as a surgeon at Kenton. Lambton was beatified by Pope John Paul II on Nov. 22, 1987 with George Haydock and Companions.

Feast: July 27; May 4 (Feast of the English Martyrs in England).

See Also: ENGLAND, SCOTLAND, AND WALES, MARTYRS OF.

Bibliography: Catholic Record Society's Publications (London, 1905–), V, 212, 228, 231, 293. R. CHALLONER, *Memoirs of Missionary Priests,* ed. J. H. POLLEN (rev. ed. London 1924). J. H. POLLEN, *Acts of English Martyrs* (London 1891).

[K. I. RABENSTEIN]

LAMENNAIS, HUGUES FÉLICITÉ ROBERT DE

French priest, writer, philosopher, apologist for ultramontanism, and pioneer of Catholic liberalism; b. Saint-Malo (Ille-et-Vilaine), France, June 19, 1782; d. Paris, Feb. 27, 1854.

Early Career. He came from a well-to-do, upper-middle-class family of Brittany. His grandfather added to the family name the title de La Mennais. Félicité signed his name F. de La Mennais until his alignment with the democratic movement led him to adopt the signature F. Lamennais. During his early years he steeped himself in the works of ROUSSEAU and other rationalistic authors of the French ENLIGHTENMENT, and became indifferent to religion. The influence of his brother Jean de LAMENNAIS was instrumental in restoring his Catholic faith (1804). Félicité began a serious private study of religious problems. In collaboration with his brother he wrote *Réflexions sur l'état de l'Église en France au XVIIIᵉ siècle* (1809) and *Tradition de l'Église sur l'institution des évêques* (1814). He was ordained in 1816 without attending a seminary. Thereupon he devoted himself to apologetic studies with the aim of restoring to the Church the self-confidence it had lost during the FRENCH REVOLUTION. He intended also to provide a religious basis for civil society in the spirit of Joseph de MAISTRE, Louis de BONALD, and other defenders of tradition. Both purposes were evident in his widely acclaimed *Essai sur l'indifférence en matière de religion* (4 v. 1817–23) in which he claimed that certitude must be sought in the *raison générale* or *sens commun,* the common conviction of men in general. This norm he valued as a participation in the divine omniscience and, therefore, infallible. A "natural" belief in the testimony of humanity, according to this outlook, is the basis of certitude (*see* TRADITIONALISM). Lamennais further asserted that the highest expression of truth comes from the Church. This reasoning was defective because it confused cause with effect and concluded that certitude for the individual results from the "common sense," whereas the "common sense" results from the totality of individual certitudes. Despite this shortcoming the book provided a powerful attack on widespread religious indifference. The author's fame spread quickly throughout Europe.

La Chesnaie, a country house acquired in 1799 by the two brothers, was the center from which Félicité diffused his ideas. He began there a campaign to restore society from a state that seemed to him to be verging on dissolution. In 1828 he founded the short-lived Congregation of St. Peter, designed to inaugurate a new type of religious institute more flexible in its organization than existing religious orders. It combined a broader outlook on the world with a training, considered better suited to modern needs, that introduced members to the founder's ideas concerning the revival of Christianity.

Catholic Liberalism. From his study of history Lamennais became convinced that union with the civil power does not aid religion. He concluded that a Catholic revival would occur only when the Church was liberated from dependence on the state and its Bourbon rulers. Soon he thought of allying Catholicism with liberalism (*see* LIBERALISM, RELIGIOUS). In his book *De la religion considérée dans ses rapports avec l'ordre politique et civil* (2 v. 1825–26) his views on the proper relation between the spiritual and temporal powers opposed those of GALLICANISM and upheld those of ULTRAMONTANISM. A second book, *Des progrès de la révolution et de la guerre contre l'Église* (1829), insisted that the Church utilize the fundamental liberties granted by the government in the charter and abandon all claims to a privileged position, thereby accepting, at least *de facto,* the liberal notion of the state instead of the traditional Christian one.

The revolution of 1830 in France convinced Lamennais of the correctness of his ideas. To propagate them he started (1830) a newspaper, *L'Avenir,* which became the voice of Catholic liberalism. Its motto was ''God and Liberty.'' GERBET, GUÉRANGER, LACORDAIRE, MONTALEMBERT, ROHRBACHER, and other disciples of Lamennais were on the distinguished list of collaborators. In his belief that liberty and Christianity were equally necessary, Lamennais appealed to both liberals and Catholics to accept ''everybody's right to do anything that is not against right.'' *L'Avenir* sought complete religious liberty, freedom for the Church in education, freedom of the press and of association, universal suffrage, and governmental decentralization. Basing its stand on the legal one of common law, even where the Church's rights were concerned, *L'Avenir* advocated complete separation of Church and State. It held that the state must keep aloof from all religious groups and exercise no authority over them, but must respect the liberty of each of them. As a result the French CONCORDAT OF 1801 should be abolished, episcopal nominations left to the Church, and the clergy removed from the public payroll. *L'Avenir* publicized a campaign for educational and religious liberty organized by the *Agence générale pour la défense de la liberté religieuse,* founded by Lamennais in 1828. The intent was to bring before the civil courts every encroachment on the Church's liberty.

L'Avenir was concerned with such delicate problems, and its harsh denunciations of opposing views aroused the hostility of the government and the bishops, most of whom were Gallicans who owed their appointments to the provisions of the concordat. Several bishops publicly opposed some methods of *L'Avenir,* such as open controversy and recourse to trials in the civil courts, and some of its ideas, such as those on liberty, democracy, popular sovereignty, and complete separation of Church and State. Thereupon the number of subscribers to *L'Avenir* declined rapidly.

Condemnation. With a crisis inevitable Lamennais, Lacordaire, and Montalembert departed (December 1831) for Rome to submit their program to the pope. After a formal audience with GREGORY XVI, the trio returned to France, leaving behind for examination a memoir that exposed their ideals. Meanwhile several French bishops had forwarded to Rome a document called the ''Censure of Toulouse,'' which requested the condemnation of certain propositions extracted from the writings of Lamennais. The French and Austrian governments also applied pressure on Rome to gain a condemnation of doctrines and activities that were regarded as subversive of the state. Notwithstanding this pressure the Vatican conducted a more careful study than Lamennais realized. At its conclusion Gregory XVI issued the encyclical *Mirari vos* (Aug. 15, 1832); its warnings against the evils of the age contained implicitly a censure of *L'Avenir.* In a letter to Lamennais Cardinal PACCA revealed that the Holy See was grieved with the editors mainly because: (1) they had taken it upon themselves to deal publicly with very delicate questions that should be handled only by the heads of the Church and the State; (2) their doctrines on civil and political liberty tended of their nature to foment a spirit of revolt; (3) their views on liberty of worship and of the press were exaggerated and contrary to the Church's teachings and practice; and (4) their suggestion of collaboration between Catholics and all who wanted to work for liberty was most disturbing to the pope.

The Roman censure was justifiable because *L'Avenir* failed to make the necessary distinctions in its defense of complete separation of Church and State. The LIBERALISM with which an alliance was sought regarded religion as merely a personal question, a subjective matter; and this outlook led inevitably to RELATIVISM and INDIFFERENTISM. The term liberalism recalled to Catholic minds the excesses of the French Revolution; yet Lamennais failed to distinguish between the true and the false in liberal ideology. He neglected also to make essential reservations in proclaiming his alliance with the liberals. *L'Avenir*'s editors did not accept the philosophical bases of secular liberalism or the indifferentism to which *Mirari vos* reduced these bases, but they gave the impression of doing so by making the concessions they did and by taking positions that led logically to what was legitimately objectionable in the liberal standpoint. This impression was strengthened by the polemical expressions utilized by the editors and by the failure to disassociate the paper's views on liberty and democracy from the violently anti-Catholic, secular bias that characterized many champions of these ideals.

It was a profoundly disappointed Lamennais who drafted an act of submission on behalf of the editors of

L'Avenir and of the council of the *Agence générale* (Sept. 10, 1832), but it cannot be proved that this submission was insincere. During the following two years, however, Lamennais changed his attitude toward the papacy and transferred his campaign to the purely secular level by avoiding the theological aspects of questions. Contributing to his subsequent tragedy was the inconsiderate attitude of Bishops D' ASTROS and De Lesquen. Lamennais was required to reiterate his submission four more times. Finally he became embittered and abandoned all priestly functions (January 1834).

Four months later he published *Paroles d'un croyant,* which bitterly denounced political tyranny. The book exercised a baneful influence despite its condemnation in the encyclical *Singulari nos* (July 15, 1834) as undermining the entire civil order. In *Affaires de Rome* (1836–37) Lamennais made a serious but incomplete attempt to justify himself. The book was placed on the Index (Feb. 14, 1837). By this time Lamennais had abandoned the Church and his former associates had broken with him. Five more of his works were also placed on the Index between 1838 and 1846.

Last Years. The solution of the growing social question and the defense of democracy were his chief concerns in his remaining years. Regeneration of society had, to be sure, ever been his constant driving force; it gave consistency to the seeming contradictions in the various periods of his career. He was not strictly a socialist even though his views at times approached socialism. His conviction was that mankind was approaching a regime in which the working class would predominate. He sympathized with the proletariat and believed in its moral superiority over other classes. After the revolution of 1848 he was elected to the Chamber of Deputies, but the effect of his brief term in the legislature was disillusionment. Soon he retired from public life. His last important publication was a translation of Dante's *Divine Comedy;* its lengthy introduction may be considered his spiritual and intellectual testament. His faith deteriorated into a strange mixture of Christianity, pantheism, and naturalism. He died unreconciled with the Church.

Appraisal. Scholarly studies in mid-20th century have tended to recognize the great merit and significance of Lamennais in many fields. Despite the failure of his priestly vocation and the imprudence and inaccuracy of some of his proposals, he has exercised profound influence on Catholicism. He supplied a new impetus to Catholic apologetics, demonstrated the need for an improved program of clerical studies, and did more than anyone else to popularize ultramontanism and to weaken Gallicanism among the French clergy. His attempt to obtain the active participation of the laity in the Church's de-

fense was laudable. It was with him that the reconciliation of the Church with democracy began. He pioneered in social Catholicism by seeking to satisfy popular longings for social justice. In his impetuosity he went too far and too fast. Several of his ideas reappeared, however, in mitigated form later in the 19th century. Outside France Lamennais exercised considerable influence as an apologist. His notions of liberty were utilized by the Church later in its struggles for emancipation. Among the more prominent Catholics influenced by Lamennais were DÖLLINGER and Görres in Germany, GIOBERTI and ROSMINI-SERBATI in Italy, BALMES and DONOSO CORTÉS in Spain, Malou and Van Bommel in Belgium, J. G. LeSage ten Broek in the Netherlands, WISEMAN in England, and O'CONNELL in Ireland.

Bibliography: H. TALVART and J. PLACE, *Bibliographie des auteurs modernes de langue française (1801–)* (Paris 1928–) 11:167–229. F. DUINE, *Essai de bibliographie de F. R. de Lamennais* (Paris 1923). **Works.** *Oeuvres complètes,* 12 v. in 6 (Paris 1836–37). There is a mediocre Eng. tr. of the first v. of the *Essay on Indifference in Matters of Religion* by H. E. STANLEY (London 1895); *Oeuvres posthumes,* ed. E. D. FORGUES, 3 v. (Paris 1856–59); *Paroles d'un croyant: 1833* (Paris 1834), critical ed. Y. LE HIR (Paris 1949), Eng. *The People's Prophecy,* tr. C. REAVELY (London 1943); *Articles de l'Avenir,* 7 v. (Louvain 1831–32); *Essai d'un système de philosophie catholique* (Paris 1834), critical ed. Y. LE HIR (Rennes 1954); *Correspondance inédite entre L. et le baron de Vitrolles,* ed. E. FORGUES (Paris 1886); *Lettres inédites de L. à Montalembert,* ed. E. FORGUES (Paris 1898). C. F. MONTALEMBERT, *Lettres à L.,* ed. G. GOYAU and P. DE LALLEMAND (Paris 1932). **Literature.** C. BOUTARD, *Lamennais: Sa vie et ses doctrines,* 3 v. (Paris 1905–13). F. DUINE, *L.: Sa vie, ses idées, ses ouvrages* (Paris 1922). P. DUDON, *L. et le Saint-Siège (1820–1834)* (Paris 1911). A. R. VIDLER, *Prophecy and Papacy: A Study of L., the Church and the Revolution* (New York 1954), excellent. F. J. VRIJMOED, *L. avant sa défection, et la Néerlande catholique* (Paris 1930). C. CARCOPINO, *Les Doctrines sociales de L.* (Paris 1942). Y. LE HIR, *L. écrivain* (Paris 1948). R. REMOND, *L. et la démocratie* (Paris 1948). J. B. DUROSELLE, *Les Débuts du catholicisme social en France, 1822–1870* (Paris 1951). A. DANSETTE, *Religious History of Modern France* (New York 1961) v.1. A. GAMBARO, *Sulle orme del L. in Italia* (Turin 1958–). J. R. DERRÉ, *L.: Ses amis et le mouvement des idées à l'époque romantique* (Paris 1962). C. CONSTANTIN, ''Libéralisme catholique,'' *Dictionnaire de théologie catholique,* ed. A. VACANT et al., 15 v. (Paris 1903–50; Tables Générales 1951–) 9.1:506–629. A. FONCK, *ibid.* 8.2:2473–2526 I. DANIELE, *Enciclopedia filosofica,* 4 v. (Venice-Rome 1957) 2:1786–88.

[R. BOUDENS]

LA MENNAIS, JEAN MARIE ROBERT DE, VEN.

Religious founder; b. Saint-Malo (Ille-et-Vilaine), France, Sept. 8, 1780; d. Ploërmel (Morbihan), Dec. 26, 1860. Jean, the brother of Hugues Félicité de LAMENNAIS, was ordained in 1804. After serving as curate and teacher, he retired because of ill health to La Chesnaie, a country home belonging to his family. There he guided his brother toward ecclesiastical studies and collaborated with him by doing the research for *Reflexions sur l'état de l' Église en France au XVIIIe siècle* (1808) and *Tradition de l'Église sur l'institution des évêques* (1814), and the translation for *Guide spirituel* (1809). In 1814 Jean became secretary to Bishop Caffarelli of Saint-Brieuc and then vicar-general of the diocese. He was also active in organizing and conducting parish missions and in starting confraternities. In 1819 he founded a group of teaching brothers that joined in 1820 with another group, founded also in Brittany in 1816 by Gabriel DESHAYES, to form the BROTHERS OF CHRISTIAN INSTRUCTION OF PLOËRMEL. Until his death Jean administered this congregation and the Daughters of Providence of Saint-Brieuc, which he founded in conjunction with Marie Anne Cartel (1818). Called to Paris in 1822 as vicar-general of the grand almoner of France, he participated in the nomination or transfer of some 40 bishops, but repeatedly declined to accept the episcopal dignity for himself.

After returning to Brittany (1824) La Mennais centered his educational and other apostolic activities in Ploërmel. He founded the Priests of St. Méen (1824), which soon became the Congregation of St. Peter, and placed his brother in charge of it (1828). Félicité's apostasy terminated the brief existence of this congregation and caused Jean unwarranted humiliations as well as personal sorrow, but it did not curb his apostolic labors. He guided François Mazellier with his congregation, which fused with the MARIST BROTHERS in 1841. He acted also as adviser to Jacques Dujarié and Basil MOREAU in the founding of the Holy Cross Brothers. His cause for beatification was introduced in 1911 and the antepreparatory congregation on his virtues was held in 1946.

Bibliography: A. P. LAVEILLE, *Jean-Marie de La Mennais (1780–1860)*, 2 v. (Paris 1903). A. MERLAUD, *Jean-Marie de La Mennais* (Paris 1960).

[E. G. DROUIN]

Ven. Jean Marie Robert De La Mennais.

LAMENT, BOLESLAWA MARIA, BL.

Foundress of the Missionary Sisters of the Holy Family; b. July 3, 1862, Lowicz, Poland; d. Jan.29, 1946, Bialystak, Poland. Lament is remembered for persevering in charity during difficult times. She began her work by establishing organizations in her home town to care for the ill and abandoned, which led to the founding of the Missionary Sisters of the Holy Family (1905). The sisters soon spread to St. Petersburg, Mohilev, and Zytomierz. The turmoil of World War I and subsequent civil unrest forced Lament to reestablish her missions three times. Before her death the congregation extended to Pinsk, Vilnius, and Bialystak. Long before the Second Vatican Council, Lament labored for Christian unity. She was beatified at Boleslawa, Poland by John Paul II, June 5, 1991.

Bibliography: B. LAMENT, *Wybór pism Boleslawy Lament*, ed. R. J. BAR (Warsaw 1976).

[K. I. RABENSTEIN]

LAMENTABILI

A decree of the Holy Office (July 3, 1903), approved *in forma communi* by Pius X (July 4), which lists 65 condemned propositions. These cover, such areas as the Church's right to interpret Scripture, Biblical inspiration, the historicity of the Gospels, the meaning of revelation, the preservation of Christology, the fact of the Resurrection, the origin of the Church and the Sacraments from Christ, the objectivity of dogma, and dogma's harmony with history. Modernism, the movement aimed at, was officially so named in the encyclical *PASCENDI* (Sept. 8, 1907). Some of the propositions have a sense not intended by many Modernist writers. But the decree purposely remains on an impersonal level, and the propositions are condemned precisely in the sense in which they are stated. The decree gives no precise qualifications to the vari-

The "wailing wall" in Jerusalem. The old orthodox Jews are praying and teaching the youngsters the Lamentations on Jeremiah. (©Bettmann/CORBIS)

ous assertions beyond the term "errors." The carefully worded propositions are by no means as conservative as a cursory reading might infer. Many of the condemnations contain echoes of a memoir on the writings of LOISY prepared for Cardinal Richard of Paris to be submitted to the Holy Office. It is generally agreed that certain of the propositions also reflect the writings of G. TYRRELL, E. LE ROY, and A. HOUTIN.

Bibliography: *Acta Sanctorum Sedis* 40 (1907) 470–478. H. DENZINGER, *Enchiridion symbolorum,* ed. A. SCHÖNMETZER (Freiburg 1932) 3401–66. Eng. tr. V. A. YZERMANS, *All Things in Christ* (Westminster, Md. 1954). J. RIVIÈRE, *Le Modernisme dans l'Èglise* (Paris 1929).

[J. J. HEANEY]

LAMENTATIONS, BOOK OF

This book appears in the Vulgate (Vulg) after Jeremiah, but in the Greek Septuagint it is usually found after ch. 5 of Baruch. In Hebrew tradition it is the fifth book of "The Writings," and is entitled "How" (the book's first word).

Author. Scholars are unanimous today in denying its authorship to Jeremiah. In the past many attributed it to him because of the lamentations he wrote for Josiah (2 Chr 35.25), but neither the style nor the contents reflect his authorship. Many differences exist between Jeremiah and Lamentations, e.g., in Jer. 37.7 the Prophet knew that Egypt could not help Israel, but the author of Lam 4.17 records his disappointed hope in Egypt's aid. The five poems were very likely not even written by the same author. They reflect the conditions in Judah during the period following the destruction of Jerusalem in 587 B.C. and received their present form before Jerusalem's restoration.

Form and Content. The first four Lamentations are studied literary creations, acrostic in form and having a peculiar rhythm characteristic of the *gênâ* (elegy or dirge), each line having three accented syllables followed after a pause by two more. The fifth Lamentation is a supplication with a three-plus-three meter and in the Vulg is entitled *The Prayer of the Prophet Jeremiah.*

The first four poems have an acrostic form, i.e., the first word of each verse begins with a consecutive letter of the Hebrew alphabet. The fifth poem has as many verses as the letters in the alphabet, but is not acrostic. The first three poems have three-line stanzas, but the fourth has two-line stanzas. Each line of each stanza in the third poem begins with the same letter, i.e., three lines with *aleph* in the first stanza, three with *beth* in the second, etc. The 16th letter (*'ayin*) and the 17th letter (*pē*) are reversed in ch. 2–4. This alphabetic confusion is an indication that the poems were written independently, and when they were compiled they had already a form so fixed as to preclude any correction.

The acrostic form was used as a pedagogic device, symbolizing completeness and suggesting the totality of grief and sorrow for sin, and thus instilling hope. It may also have served a mnemonic purpose.

Following H. Gunkel's analysis of Hebrew psalmody, three literary types are found in Lamentations, the communal lament, the individual lament, and the funeral dirge. The first, second, and fourth poems are essentially funeral dirges; the fifth poem is a communal lament, while the third, while resembling a personal lament similar to Jeremiah's "Confessions" (e.g., Jer 11.18–12.6), contains elements also of the communal lament. The national calamity that struck Judah in 587 B.C. required all the resources of the poet to express his emotion. He therefore sometimes used all three types in the same poem. Thus in the funeral dirges of ch. 1, 2, and 4 there are also elements of the communal and the personal lament.

The dirges express the destitution of Jerusalem and Judah after the ravages of the Babylonian conquest. The poems contrast in graphic images the present humiliation and devastation with past glory and favor. They indict the priests and Prophets for their poor leadership in failing to warn Judah of her sin and coming judgment. Suffering is shown as a purifying agent for Israel's faith and as leading the Israelites to a consciousness of their sin.

Bibliography: Commentaries. G. RICCIOTTI (Turin 1924). M. HALLER (Tübingen 1940). A. F. KNIGHT (Torch Bible Comment; London 1955). E. J. CROWLEY (Pamphlet Bible Ser. 29; New York 1962). A. GELIN (*Bible de Jérusalem,* 43 v., each with intro. by the tr. [Paris 1948–54]; 23; 1951). A. GELIN and A. S. HERBERT in *Peake's Comment, on the Bible,* ed. M. BLACK and H. H. ROWLEY (New York 1962) 563–567. Literature. A. GELIN, *Dictionnaire de la Bible,* suppl. ed. L. PIROT et al. (Paris 1928–) 5:237–251. N. K. GOTTWALD, *Studies in the Book of Lamentations* (Chicago 1954).

[C. MCGOUGH]

LAMORMAINI, WILHELM

Jesuit administrator and teacher; b. Duchy of Luxembourg, Dec. 29, 1570; d. Vienna, Feb. 22, 1648. He received his doctorate at Prague, entered the Society of Jesus in 1590, and was ordained in 1596. From 1600 he

taught philosophy and theology at Graz; he became rector of the Jesuit college there in 1614. He was in Rome between 1621 and 1623 and then went to Vienna to become father confessor and spiritual counselor to the Emperor FERDINAND II. As such, he played a significant role in conjunction with Ferdinand's efforts to renew Hapsburg power and Catholic strength in the Holy Roman Empire, in particular with respect to the administration of the Edict of RESTITUTION (1629) and the elimination of Duke Albrecht von WALLENSTEIN in 1634. After the death of Ferdinand in 1637, Lamormaini became rector of the University in Vienna, and between 1643 and 1645 he was provincial of the Austrian province of the Society of Jesus. There he was noted for encouraging the growth of Jesuit institutions in the Empire and strengthening the Church in the Hapsburg lands. Part of his biography of the emperor, *Ferdinand II, Romanorum Imperatoris virtutes,* was published in 1638.

Bibliography: A. POSCH, "Zur Tätigkeit und Beurteilung Lamormains," *Mitteilungen des Instituts für Österreichische Geschichtsforschung* 63 (1955) 375–390; *Lexikon für Theologie und Kirche,* ed. J. HOFER and K. RAHNER (Freiburg 1957–65) 6:769. C. SOMMERVOGEL, *Bibliothèque de la Compagnie de Jésus* (Brussels-Paris 1890–1932) 4:1428–31.

[T. T. HELDE]

LAMPLEY, WILLIAM, BL.

Lay martyr; b. probably at Gloucester, England; hanged, drawn, and quartered there, Feb. 12, 1588. He was tried for persuading some of his relatives to "popery," but offered leniency if he would conform to the new religion. Upon his refusal he was sentenced to be hanged, drawn, and quartered, an unusual punishment for a layman. He was beatified by Pope John Paul II on Nov. 22, 1987 with George Haydock and Companions.

Feast of the English Martyrs: May 4 (England).

See Also: ENGLAND, SCOTLAND, AND WALES, MARTYRS OF.

Bibliography: R. CHALLONER, *Memoirs of Missionary Priests,* ed. J. H. POLLEN (rev. ed. London 1924). J. H. POLLEN, *Acts of English Martyrs* (London 1891). D. DE YEPES, *Historia Particular de la persecución de Inglaterra* (Madrid 1599).

[K. I. RABENSTEIN]

LAMPS AND LIGHTING, EARLY CHRISTIAN

Few exact data exist regarding the use of lamps and lighting in the primitive Christian house churches (*see* BA-

SILICA); but two elements were present: (1) the use of artificial light for utilitarian or prudential reasons during the night vigil services and the evening liturgies as indicated in 1 Cor 11.21; need to repudiate pagan calumnies concerning debauchery at Christian worship services. (2) Light was employed also for specifically liturgical purposes. The first element accounts for the instance reported in Acts 20.7–8, and the frequent symbolico-homiletical references to lighting equipment in Rv 1.12; 4.5; 11.4 imply the second element.

When worship services began to be held in the CATACOMBS, the two elements were combined—to honor the martyrs and to supply constant illumination. The utilitarian and liturgical elements are succinctly combined in the phrase in the *Testament of Our Lord:* "all places should be lighted both for symbolism and for reading." For this purpose small terra-cotta lamps, plain or decorated with Christian symbols, were used, as is attested by the numerous discoveries in the catacombs.

The transition to a daytime use of lights no longer serving any utilitarian purpose at liturgical functions was a gradual one. There is some evidence of a protest among the 4th-century Fathers against a practice disturbingly redolent of pagan customs and unjustified by need or usefulness (Lactantius, *Institut. Div.,* 6.2; Jerome, *Contra Vigilantium,* 6; Gregory of Nazianzus, *Orat.,* 5.35).

An inventory of the furnishings of the church of Cirta, dating from the early 4th century, lists seven silver lamps, two chandeliers, seven small brass candelabra with lamps, and 11 lamps with chains to hang them by. Lamps and chandeliers began to be presented to individual churches in the early 4th century (*Liber pontificalis* 1: 173–176).

The Constantinian Peace of the Church (313) and the subsequent enhancement of the status of Christian churches brought a great development in lighting. PAULINUS OF NOLA and PRUDENTIUS are most valuable informants. Paulinus speaks of a perpetual light (*continuum scyphus argenteus aptus ad usum; Patrologia Latina* 61:539). This source from which all lamps could readily be lighted when desired had a utilitarian purpose. It also served as watch light against thieves and cannot be considered as indicative of a special cult of the Blessed Sacrament. Paulinus himself introduced colored candles whose papyrus wick gave off a heady perfume while burning (*Patrologia Latina* 61:467). Prudentius comments enthusiastically on the richness of the lighting in Christian churches (*Patrologia Latina* 69:819, 829). Constantine I presented to the Lateran two sets of seven 10-foot bronze candelabra and hanging *coronae* (*phari, canthari, stantarea*) with as many as 120 dolphin-shaped branches, each supporting one or more lamps (*Liber pontificalis* 1:173–176).

Jerome speaks of the "custom, through all the churches of the East, that when the Gospels are to be read, lights are kindled, though the sun is already shining, not indeed to dispel darkness but to show a token of joy" (*Contra Vigilantium* 7). Eusebius of Caesarea indicates the use of candles at funeral ceremonies when he writes that Constantine's body lay in state and "they lighted candles on golden stands around it . . ." (*Vita Const.* 4.66); and Constantius's *Vita S. Germani* says that at the funeral of this 5th-century bishop of Auxerre "the multitude of lights eclipsed the rays of the sun and maintained their brightness even through the day" (20.24). The burning of candles and lamps before martyrs' relics probably developed from this funeral custom and was already practiced in Jerome's day (*Contra Vigilantium* 6).

All early representations of the Last Supper show a lamp hanging over the table; and the Jerusalem pilgrim (*c.* 550), author of the *Breviarius,* was shown the alleged original. The Syrian Narsai (d. 512) has a description of the liturgy remarking that "the altar stands crowned with beauty and splendor and upon it is the Gospel of life and the adorable wood . . . the censors are smoking, the lamps shining" [R. H. Connolly, *Liturgical Homilies of Narsai* (Cambridge 1909) 12]. By this time, use of lamps and candles around, but apparently not actually on, the altar had become universal.

In the course of the 5th century, bronze began to be substituted for more precious metals; but the ecclesiastical lighting equipment was among the last to make the substitution.

See Also: LIGHT, LITURGICAL USE OF.

Bibliography: H. LECLERCQ, *Dictionnaire d'archéologie chrétienne et de liturgie,* ed. F. CARROLL, H. LECLERQ, and H. I. MARROU, 15 v. (Paris 1907–53) 2.2:1834–42; 3.1:210–215; 4.2:1726–30. A. WECKWERTH, *Lexikon für Theologie und Kirche,* ed. J. HOFER and K. RAHNER, 10 v. (2d new ed. Freiburg 1957–65) 6:990–991; *Zeitschrift für Kirchengeschichte* 69 (1958) 71–76. H. SCHNELL, *Das Münster,* v.1 (Münster 1947) 103-.

[A. G. GIBSON]

LAMY, BERNARD

Oratorian philosopher and theologian; b. Le Mans, France, June 1640; d. Rouen, Jan. 29, 1715. He entered the order Oct. 17, 1657, and was ordained in 1667. Appointed to teach philosophy at the University of Angers (1673–75), he distinguished himself by his adherence to CARTESIANISM and his attacks on ARISTOTELIANISM, the only philosophy authorized by the Sorbonne and Louis XIV. He tried to explain the transubstantiation by the Cartesian theory of extension, and he questioned the divine origin of the royalty. As a result he was forbidden to teach and was exiled near Grenoble. But after eight months he was sent to teach at the seminary in Grenoble, where he wrote most of his works. In 1686 he began teaching at the seminary of Saint-Magloire in Paris. But a great controversy arose over publication of his *Harmonia, sive concordia quatuor evangelistarum* (1689), in which he worked out a new chronology of the life of Christ, asserting that He could not have celebrated the Passover on the day before His death; and he was sent to Rouen. He wrote also on rhetoric, *L'Art de parler* (1675), which was translated into English, and *Réflexions sur l'art poétique* (1678), and on arithmetic, geometry, mechanics, and optics. He wrote studies on the New Testament and several treatises on Christian education. His masterpiece is *Démonstration de la vérité et de la sainteté de la morale chrétienne.* He was a disciple of N. MALEBRANCHE and helped to develop his philosophy in France.

Bibliography: F. GIRBAL, *Bernard Lamy de l'Oratoire* (Paris 1964). J. CARREYRE, *Dictionnaire de théologie catholique* (Paris 1903–50) 8.2:2550–52. J. F. DRISCOLL, *The Catholic Encyclopedia*, ed. C. G. HERBERMANN (New York 1907–14) 8: 771–772. F. GIBRAL and P. CLAIR, *Entretiens sur les sciences* (Paris 1966), critical edition.

[F. GIRBAL]

naissance de soi-même. In it he interpreted several passages by Malebranche as endorsing quietism, which provoked Malebranche to reply, denying the assertion. Lamy advocated OCCASIONALISM against Leibniz's theory of a preestablished harmony and was answered by Leibniz (*Philosophische Schriften,* 4:572–595). He wrote polemics on monastic studies, against the Jesuits (*Plaintes de l'apologiste des bénédictins,* 1699), and on rhetoric (*Réflexions sur l'éloquence,* 1700; *La rhétorique trahie par son apologiste,* 1704). He wrote *Réflexions sur le traité de la prière publique* against J. J. Duguet (1649–1733). In his philosophical works Lamy was inspired largely by Malebranche, particularly in *Les premiers éléments des sciences . . .* (Paris 1706). He refuted Spinoza in *Le nouvel athéisme renversé* (Paris 1696). He wrote also *L'incrédule amené à la religion par la raison* (Paris 1710) and *De la connaissance et de l'amour de Dieu* (Paris 1712).

Bibliography: R. P. TASSIN, *Histoire littéraire de la congrégation de Saint-Maur* (Brussels 1770) 351–367. F. BOUILLIER, *Histoire de la philosophie cartésienne,* 2 v. (3d ed. Paris 1868) 2: 363–373. G. RODIS-LEWIS, *Le Problème de l'inconscient et la cartésianisme* (Paris 1950) 200–238. C. ROSSO, *Enciclopedia Filosofica* 2:1792. J. BAUDOT, *Dictionnaire de théologie catholique* (Paris 1903–50) 8.2:2552–55. D. MISONNE, *Lexikon für Theologie und Kirche,* ed. J. HOFER and K. RAHNER (Freiburg 1957–65) 6:770.

[G. RODIS-LEWIS]

LAMY, FRANÇOIS

Benedictine philosopher; b. Montereau, Diocese of Chartres, 1636; d. Saint-Denis, April 4, 1711. At first a military man, Lamy in 1659 entered the order at Saint-Maur after a duel. He taught a Cartesian philosophy, although not without difficulties, at Saint-Maur (1670), Saint-Quentin, and Soissons (1672–73). He taught theology at Saint-Germain-des-Prés (1674–75) and then went to live in the solitude of Saint-Bale in the Diocese of Meaux, where he came into contact with BOSSUET. From 1687 to 1689 he was prior of Rebais. Because of his adherence to CARTESIANISM he was prohibited from teaching by order of the king in 1689; he retired to Saint-Denis until his death. Although his works were generally of a polemic nature, he easily reconciled himself with his adversaries. He criticized P. NICOLE in *Réflexions sur le Traité de la grâce générale* (MS 3217, Archives of Port-Royal, Amersfoort, Netherlands). His discussions with Bossuet regarding the infinite satisfaction deriving from the sufferings of Christ may be found in *Correspondance de Bossuet* [ed. C. Urbain and L. Levesque (Paris 1909–23) 456]. He effected a reconciliation between Bossuet and N. MALEBRANCHE after the appearance of the latter's *Traité de la nature et de la grâce,* which Lamy himself had attacked. Lamy's chief work is *De la con-*

LAMY, JOHN BAPTIST

First archbishop of SANTA FE, N.M.; b. Lempdes, Puy-de-Dôme, France, Oct. 11, 1814; d. Santa Fe, Feb. 13, 1888. His parents were Jean and Marie (Dié) Lamy, of old and respected families of the district.

Early Career. After studies in the seminaries of his home diocese of Clermont-Ferrand, Lamy was ordained in 1838. Some months later he was recruited for the American missions by bishop J. B. PURCELL of Cincinnati, Ohio. He was appointed (1850) to the new vicariate apostolic of New Mexico. His jurisdiction then embraced most of what later became New Mexico, Arizona, and the eastern settled part of Colorado, an area annexed by the United States in 1846 and established as a formal Territory in 1850. Lamy was consecrated in St. Peter's Cathedral, Cincinnati on Nov. 24, 1850, by M. J. Spalding, then Bishop of Louisville, Kentucky. To avoid the perils of the Santa Fe Trail between Missouri and his see, Lamy sailed down to New Orleans, Louisiana, and then started from the Texas coast up to Santa Fe. After suffering shipwreck and many other hardships, he reached Santa Fe on Aug. 9, 1851, and was enthusiastically received by the people. He soon learned, however, of the hostility of the local clergy, who regarded him as a foreign intruder. Making the hazardous 800 mile journey to Durango, Mexico, Lamy conferred with the former ordinary of the territory, bishop Antonio Zubiria, who not only received him kindly, but wrote a strong letter to the New Mexico clergy, enjoining them to accept the new order.

Ordinary of Santa Fe. The need for educational institutions and an adequate clergy were among Lamy's major concerns when he returned to Santa Fe on Jan. 10, 1852. While attending the First Plenary Council of Baltimore (1852), he succeeded in recruiting four Sisters of LORETTO from Kentucky, who returned to Santa Fe with him to open an academy and motherhouse and lay the foundations for Catholic education throughout the entire territory. When the vicariate was erected into the Diocese of Santa Fe on July 29, 1853, as a suffragan of St. Louis, Missouri, Lamy, as ordinary, continued his efforts to further the progress of the Church in the vast area of his jurisdiction. Lamy, renowned for his frequent journeys over the perilous Santa Fe Trail in search of loans and donations and of additional priests and teachers, was largely responsible for reestablishing the faith in the Southwest. His trips to Europe to recruit more young priests and seminarians met with considerable success, as did his patient handling of a few dissident native clergy and a strange lay flagellant society, the Penitentes. By 1865 he could report to Rome that, where he had found only ten priests in 1850, he now had 37 priests and six theologians in minor orders; 45 new churches and chapels had been built, and 18 or 20 ancient ones repaired; and there were four convent schools conducted by the Loretto Sisters and three by the Brothers of the Christian Schools. Six of the priests were natives ordained by Lamy, who had started a seminary to accommodate native vocations as well as seminarians from abroad.

New priests and seminarians from France continued to arrive periodically, to augment the clergy staffing distant Tucson, Arizona, and Denver, Colorado, as well as New Mexico proper. Lamy also welcomed the first Jesuits from Naples, Italy (1867), as well as the Sisters of Charity from Cincinnati (1865), who founded the first hospital and orphanage in the far West. The extent of the diocese, and of Lamy's burden, were very much lessened in 1868 with the creation of the Vicariates Apostolic of Colorado and Arizona, with two of his best priests, Joseph MACHEBEUF and John B. Salpointe, as their first bishops. With the help of a French architect, Lamy planned to replace the adobe Church of St. Francis, erected in 1714, with a new cathedral in the French Romanesque architecture of the cathedral in his native Clermont. The structure was still incomplete when it was dedicated in 1886 as the Cathedral of San Francisco de Asis.

When the Holy See erected Santa Fe into an archdiocese Feb. 12, 1875, Lamy became its first archbishop. By 1884, Lamy's age and failing health led Rome to give him Salpointe as coadjutor. When Lamy resigned his see a year later and was appointed titular archbishop of Cyzicus, he retired to a secluded ranch north of Santa Fe; early in 1888 he was brought back to town, where he died peacefully.

A memorial resolution, passed by the Territorial Congress of New Mexico in 1888, paid tribute to the esteem in which Lamy was held by Catholic, Protestant, and Jewish citizens for his personal work in promoting every type of civic and cultural improvement in the Territory. The place of his final retirement later became an exclusive resort called "Bishop's Lodge," where his little chapel remained as a memorial to him. In 1915 a heroic bronze statue of him was unveiled in front of his cathedral; the first governor and major officials of the new state of New Mexico took active part in the ceremonies. Willa Cather's novel, *Death Comes for the Archbishop* (1927), was based on his career. During World War II, New Mexico named a liberty ship "Archbishop Lamy," and in 1950 the archdiocese observed a Lamy Centennial, with appropriate ceremonies in the cathedral, and the founding of a Lamy memorial parish of St. John the Baptist in Santa Fe.

Bibliography: J. B. SALPOINTE, *Soldiers of the Cross* (Banning, California 1898). A. CHAVEZ, *Archives of the Archdiocese of Santa Fe, 1678–1900* (Washington 1957). P. HORGAN, *Lamy of Santa Fe, His Life and Times* (New York 1975).

[A. CHAVEZ]

LANCELOTTI, GIOVANNI PAOLO

Canonist and teacher; b. Perugia, 1522; d. Perugia, Sept. 23, 1590. He received his doctorate in law in Perugia in 1546 and soon became professor of law there. His classes followed the division of the *Corpus iuris civilis Institutiones* into persons, things, and actions, instead of the usual method of pure commentary on the Decretals. On invitation of PAUL IV he went to Rome to edit his class notes in a canonical volume that would correspond to the Institutes of Justinian. His hope was for his work to receive the force of law through official approbation and to be attached to the authentic collections of the Decretals. Neither Paul IV nor his successor PIUS IV would give the desired approbation. The work was, therefore, published privately in Perugia in 1563 under the title *Institutiones iuris canonici, quibus ius pontificium singulari methodo libris quatuor comprehenditur*. It received wide diffusion in the schools. Other works include: *De Comparatione iuris pontificii et caesarei et utriusque interpretandi ratione* (Lyons 1674), *Index rerum Corporis iuris canonici* (Rome 1580), *Rebularum in universo pontificio iure libri tres* (Perugia 1587).

Bibliography: R. NAZ, *Dictionnaire de droit canonique*, ed. R. NAZ (Paris 1935–65) 6:333. A. E. VAN HOVE, *Commentarium Lovaniense in Codicem iuris canonici* (Mechlin 1928) 1:384–385. *Die Geschichte der Quellen und der Literatur des kanonischen Rechts* (Graz 1956) 3.1:451–453. A. M. STICKLER, *Historia iuris canonici latini* (Turin 1950) 365–366.

[H. A. LARROQUE]

LANCICIUS, NICHOLAS (LECZYCKI), VEN.

Jesuit ascetical writer; b. Nesvizh (Nieswiesz), Lithuania, Dec. 10, 1574; d. Kaunas (Kovno), Lithuania, March 16, 1652. Through his constant study of apologetic writings he was converted from CALVINISM. Two years later, Feb. 17, 1592, he entered the Society of Jesus at Cracow. He studied at Rome under R. BELLARMINE and F. SUÁREZ. After his ordination in 1601, he worked with Niccolò Orlandini seeking documents for the history of the society. When Orlandini died in 1606, Lancicius became the spiritual father of the Roman College. After 1608 he was in Poland, where he taught Hebrew, Scripture, and theology at the Academy of Wilna. He was then made the rector of the college at Kalisz (Kalisch) and Cracow, and was provincial of the Lithuanian Province (1631–35). During these years of administration he was able to keep up a direct apostolate among the people as well as to write ascetical works and books on the spirit and organization of the Society of Jesus. Among his principal works are: *De meditationibus rerum divinarum, De condicione boni superioris, De efficacia S.mae Eucharistiae ad profectum spiritualem in virtutibus, De praxi divinae praesentiae,* and *De praestantia instituti S.J.* In 1650 Bollandus published his collected works (2 v. Antwerp). These have often been re-edited in whole or in part, and a number have been translated into various languages.

Bibliography: G. FELL, *Wetzer und Welte's Kirchenlexikon,* 13 v. (2d ed. Freiburg 1882–1903) 7:1378–81. L. KOCH, *Jesuiten-Lexikon: Die Gesellschaft Jesu einst und jetzt* (Paderborn 1934) 1071–72. H. HURTER, *Nomenclator literarius theologiae catholicae* 3:1216–17. C. SOMMERVOGEL, *Bibliothèque de la Compagnie de Jésus, Bibliothèque de la Compagnie de Jésus* (Brussels-Paris 1890–1932) 4:1446–55. B. A. BALBINUS, *Vita venerabilis patris Nicolai Lancicii* (Prague 1690). J. DE GUIBERT, *The Jesuits: Their Spiritual Doctrine and Practice,* tr. W. J. YOUNG, ed. G. E. GANSS (Chicago 1964) 330–331.

[R. M. BUSH]

LAND, PHILIP S.

Jesuit priest, professor, social activist; b. Montreal, Canada, June 13, 1911; d. Washington, D.C., Jan. 20, 1994. Land was born the fifth of seven children. The family eventually settled in Tacoma, Washington, where Land attended the Jesuit high school Bellarmine Prep before entering the Society of Jesus in August 1929. During philosophy studies in Spokane, Washington, he was exposed to New Deal social programs and to Catholic social teaching. While teaching high school in Tacoma from 1936 to 1939, he became a popular speaker on social justice topics. Following his theology studies and ordination to the priesthood, he pursued a Ph.D. in economics, studying at St. Louis University and Columbia.

In 1950, Land joined the staff of the Institute of Social Order in St. Louis, doing social research, writing and teaching. He helped to create the review Social Order. From 1953 to 1954 he served on the editorial staff of *America* magazine in New York.

In January 1956, Land was called to Rome to teach economics at the Gregorian University, where he served in full- or part-time capacity for twenty years. In 1967 he joined the staff of the newly-founded Pontifical Commission Justice and Peace, working there under the leadership of Joseph Gremillion. Land left Rome in 1976 after his opposition to *HUMANAE VITAE* led to his dismissal from the Vatican delegation to the United Nations (UN) Population Conference in Bucharest [1974] and ended his effectiveness at the Commission Justice and Peace. He joined the staff of the Center of Concern in Washington, D.C., where he worked as a senior researcher and writer until his death.

Intellectual Journey. The life work of Land reflects a singular commitment to social justice that can be traced to his encounters with victims of the 1929 stock market crash who came to the doors of the Jesuit novitiate in Los Gatos, California, hungry and homeless. Land's intellectual journey saw him break free from the early strong influence of the German Catholic social thinkers Heinrich Pesch and Gustav GUNDLACH. He opened himself to more biblically based, theological approaches to social teaching and gradually came to embrace the insights of praxis-based liberation theology, the Rahnerian shift to the subject, ecotheology, and feminist theology. He argued forcefully that this intellectual evolution constituted an authentic retrieval of Thomas Aquinas' vision of prudence and practical wisdom.

During his years at the Commission Justice and Peace, Land made several important contributions to the Church's work for justice. He played a key role in the foundation of SODEPAX, a joint commission of the Vatican and the World Council of Churches to address issues of society, development and peace. He helped to conceptualize and organize the commission, securing George Dunne, SJ, to be its first director.

In 1970 Land served as the principal staff person for the synod Justice in the World and the major drafter of its document. In that capacity, he fought single-handedly to save the passage insisting that the Church should not speak about injustice unless it is willing to recognize its own injustice. In addition he was instrumental in preparing and distributing a study guide and background materials for the synod document, including highlights of the MEDELLÍN Conference of bishops held in 1968 in Colombia. Thus, under Land's leadership, foundational liberation themes were made available to the whole Church for the first time.

As part of the Vatican delegation to the UN, Land was also responsible for getting language about the "obligation of the nation or nations toward the international common good under the guidance of international social justice" into the UN charter.

During his eighteen years at the Center of Concern, Land's activities ranged from marching in demonstrations to teaching and lecturing to scholarly research and publication. His major writings include a reflective and careful defense of the US bishops' pastoral letter on the economy entitled *Shaping Welfare Consensus* and his semi-autobiographical reflections on the evolution of Catholic social thinking in the thirty years after Vatican II, *Catholic Social Thought: As I Have Lived It, Loathed It and Loved It.*

Bibliography: P. LAND, *Catholic Social Teaching: As I Have Lived It, Loathed It and Loved It* (Chicago 1995); *Eco-Theology* (Washington, D.C. 1991); "Toward a New Methodology in Catholic Social Teaching," in *The Logic of Solidarity: Commentaries on Pope John Paul II's Encyclical on Social Concern,* G. BAUM and R. ELLSBERG, eds. (New York 1989); *Shaping Welfare Consensus: U.S. Catholic Bishops' Contribution* (Washington, DC 1988); "The Lordship of Christ and Economic Structures," in *Above Every Name: The Lordship of Christ and Social Systems,* T. CLARK, ed. (New York 1980).

[J. E. HUG]

LANDA, DIEGO DE

Franciscan missionary and bishop; b. Cifuentes, Guadalajara, Spain, date unknown; d. Mérida, Yucatán, April 29, 1579. He was professed as Friar Minor in the Convento de los Reyes, Toledo. In 1549, soon after ordination, he went to Yucatán to serve as missionary to the Maya. He quickly achieved mastery of the Maya language, of which he composed a grammar, now lost; and during his missionary labors in major centers of the native population he acquired comprehensive knowledge of preconquest Maya culture. For several years he administered the mission in the pueblo of Izamal, where he began

construction of a large church and friary. In 1561 he was elected first minister provincial of the newly established Franciscan province of St. Joseph of Yucatán and Guatemala.

From May to July 1562, Landa made a sweeping inquisitorial investigation of survivals of native religion in the Tutul Xiu district of Mani and adjacent areas. In this inquiry, for which he had active collaboration of the Spanish alcalde of Yucatán, physical torture was employed to elicit testimony and confessions from many Indians. The recorded testimony revealed substantial evidence of continuing practice of idolatry and human sacrifice by baptized Mayans, including prominent leaders. Francisco de Toral, OFM, first resident bishop of Yucatán, who arrived in August 1562, severely criticized Landa's stern measures on the grounds that they were unjust and impolitic in a new mission area.

Landa's authority to conduct the inquiry was also questioned in several quarters. In 1563 Landa returned to Spain to defend his actions before the royal court. The crown referred the case for review and decision to the minister provincial of the Franciscan province of Castile, who in turn called for opinions from a distinguished panel of canonists and civil lawyers. This group concurred that Landa, as minister provincial in Yucatán, had legal authority to conduct inquisitorial proceedings prior to the arrival of Bishop Toral by virtue of Pope ADRIAN VI's *Omnímoda* of 1522, which granted quasiepiscopal powers to prelates of mendicant orders in America in areas without a resident bishop. They also expressed general agreement that the conditions faced by Landa in 1562 had warranted stern remedial measures. In 1569 the minister provincial absolved Landa of all charges of which he had been accused.

In April 1572, PHILIP II presented Landa to the Holy See as bishop of Yucatán, successor of Toral (d. April 20, 1571). The papal bulls of appointment were issued on Nov. 17, 1572. A year later (October 1573), Landa took possession in Mérida. The most significant feature of his episcopate was his sustained effort, illustrated by unpublished documentation in the Archivo de Indias, Seville, to alleviate exploitation of the Maya by the local officials, the colonists, and the encomenderos.

During his residence in Spain in the 1560s, Landa wrote the *Relación de las cosas de Yucatan,* his most enduring claim to fame. The only extant MS (not the original version, which has not been found) of this treatise on Maya antiquities is now preserved in the Academy of History, Madrid. Publication of an incomplete text of this MS, with a French translation, by Brasseur de Bourbourg in 1864, stimulated renewed interest in Maya civilization by European and American scholars. Since 1864 at least eight editions of the *Relación* in Spanish, French, and English have appeared. Landa's discussion of the Maya calendar and his representations of month and day glyphs have facilitated decipherment of a considerable part of the known corpus of Maya hieroglyphic writings and inscriptions. His Maya ''alphabet'' has not proved too useful as a research tool. In many other respects, however, the *Relación* has been a major source of great value for modern students of Maya life, society, and religion in pre- and postconquest times.

Bibliography: *Landa's Relación de las cosas de Yucatan,* ed. and tr. A. M. TOZZER (Cambridge, Mass. 1941). D. LÓPEZ COGOLLU-DO, *Historia de Yucatan* (Madrid 1688 and later eds.). C. CARRILLO Y ANCONA, *El obispado de Yucatan,* 2 v. (Mérida de Yucatan, Mex. 1892). F. V. SCHOLES and R. L. ROYS, ''Fray Diego de Landa and the Problem of Idolatry in Yucatan,'' Carnegie Institute of Washington, *Cooperation in Research* (Washington 1938) 585–620.

[F. V. SCHOLES]

LANDELIN, SS.

Two saints of the seventh century.

Landelin (Landolin), fl. early seventh century, a hermit and possibly a missionary laboring near the site of the future Abbey of Ettenheimmünster in Baden, near Freiburg im Breisgau. He apparently suffered a violent death, and he is honored as a martyr at Ettenheimmünster, Strasbourg, and Freiburg im Breisgau.

Feast: Sept. 21.

Landelin of Crespin and LOBBES, abbot; d. *c.* 686. He was a Frankish noble, who, according to FOLCWIN OF LOBBES in his *Gesta abbatum Lobiensium* (*Monumenta Germaniae Historica Scriptores* (Berlin 1826–) 4:56), was converted from a life of robbery by Bp. St. Autbert of Cambrai (d. *c.* 669) and founded the monastery of Lobbes (654) at the site of his former crimes (Hainaut, Belgium) as well as the Abbey of Crespin (670, Department of Nord, France), and perhaps the monasteries of AULNE (656 in Hainaut) and Walers-en-Faigne (657 in Hainaut) also.

Feast: June 15.

Bibliography: Landelin, or Landolin. J. VAN DER STRAE-TEN, *Analecta Bollandiana* 73 (1955) 66–97, life; *ibid.,* 97–118, text. *Bibliographica hagiographica latina antiquae et mediae aetatis* 2:4699. A. ZIMMERMANN, *Kalendarium Benedictinum* (Metten 1933–38) 2:313–315. A. ZIMMERMANN, *Lexikon für Theologie und Kirche,* ed. J. HOFER and K. RAHNER (Freiburg 1957–65) 6:772–773. **Landelin.** *Acta sanctorum* June 3:538–544. A. POTTHAST, *Bibliotheca historica medii aevi* 2:1417. *Bibliographica hagiographica latina antiquae et mediae aetatis* 2:4696–98; suppl. No. 4698a. U. BERLIÈRE, *Monasticon belge,* v.1 (Bruges 1890).

[C. DAVIS]

LANDÉVENNEC, ABBEY OF

Dedicated to St. Guénolé (Gwenole); belonging to Benedictines of the Congregation of Subiaco, in Landévennec, Finistère, Brittany, France; Diocese of Quimper. It was founded *c.* 480 by St. Guénolé, born in Brittany of parents who had migrated from Wales (SS. Fracan and Guen). His brothers Jacut and Guéthénoc and sister Clervie also are venerated as saints. Educated by ''the eminent master'' St. Budoc on the island of Lavret, Guénolé and 11 monks settled on the barren island of Topepig for three years before moving to Landévennec. Feasts of St. Guénolé are celebrated on March 3 (his death, 532?) and April 28 (translation). SS. Guenaël and Judul were early successors of Guénolé. The 6th-century Celtic usages of IONA (St. COLUMBA or Columbcille) were abandoned under Abbot Matmonoc on the order of Louis I the Pious (818). Gurdistan (Wrdisten), under whom the abbey prospered, wrote the vita of St. Guénolé *c.* 880.

Norman invasions drove the monks to Montreuil-sur-Mer with the relics of their founder (914). They returned under John, ally of Duke Alan Twisted Beard, liberator of Brittany (936–939); the relics stayed at Montreuil until they were destroyed in 1793. Several times burned and pillaged (14th–16th century), the abbey became commendatory on the death of Jean du Vieux Chastel (1522), last of the 51 regular abbots. It was reformed by MAURISTS (1636), but the Jansenist crisis of 1718 was fatal. The last commendatory abbot, Bp. Conen de Saint-Luc of Quimper, suppressed the title of abbot and incorporated the abbey into his mensal revenue (1784). The last monks were dispersed in 1791, and the buildings were demolished in the early 19th century.

In the 18th century the abbey's domain included eight priories and nomination to ten parishes. Prior Audren de Kerdrel founded the Société d'Histoire de Bretagne (1684). François Delfau (1637–76), critic of COMMENDATION, was exiled from SAINT-DENIS to Landévennec. Subprior François Louvard was a noted Jansenist (1696). Louis Le Pelletier (d. 1733) compiled a Breton dictionary.

In 1950 Louis-Felix Colliot, third abbot of Kerbénéat (built in 1878), purchased Landévennec, and in 1958 the community of Kerbénéat moved to new buildings in Landévennec. The church was consecrated in 1965, at which time the abbey had a hostel for men's retreats, published the bulletin *Pax* every three months, and had assembled a Breton library and a museum of Landévennec history. MSS of the 9th, 10th, and 11th centuries attributed to Landévennec are in Quimper, Oxford, Cambridge, Copenhagen, and New York. A 17th-century necrology of Landévennec has been edited by A. Oheix (*Bulletin diocésain d'histoire et d'archeologie de Quimper* 1913).

The Abbey of Landévennec: the ruins of the medieval abbey.

Bibliography: N. MARS, "L'Extinction du titre abbatial de Landévennec en 1784," *Association Bretonne* 69 (1960). P. DE LA HAYE, *L'Abbaye de Landévennec* (Châteaudun 1958). L. H. COTTINEAU, *Reépertoire topobibliographique des abbayes et prieurés*, 2 v. (Mâcon 1935–39) 1:1549–50. H. LECLERCQ, *Dictionnaire d'archéologie chrétienne et de liturgie*, ed. F. CABROL, H. LECLERCQ, and H. I. MARROU, 15 v. (Paris 1907–53) 8.1:1237–56. J. TEMPLÉ, *Catholicisme. Hier, aujourd'hui et demain*, ed. G. JACQUEMET (Paris 1947–) 5:323–324. N. MARS, "Histoire du royal monastère de S. Guénolé de Landévennec (MS of 1648)," *Pax* (1956–61).

[G. OLLIVIER]

LANDINI, FRANCESCO

Blind poet-organist of the *ars nova* era; b. Fiesole, Italy, *c.* 1325; d. Florence, Sept. 2, 1397. His father was the painter Jacopo del Casentino. Francesco, blinded by smallpox in early childhood, probably studied music under Jacopo da Bologna, developing a prodigious mem-ory and great skill at improvisation. He also worked in philosophy and astrology, and supported the theories of WILLIAM OF OCKHAM. He was crowned poet laureate at a Venetian festival in 1364. At least nine of his musical compositions are known to be settings of his own verses, and many anonymous verses he set are possibly his. Although he was for many years organist at the Basilica of San Lorenzo, Florence, his only surviving organ piece is an arrangement of one of his own love songs. An account book of Andrea de'Servi shows that he was paid for five motets, but no sacred works of his are known today. He is considered the most prolific *ars nova* composer of 14th-century Italy. There survive 12 madrigals, a *caccia,* and 142 *ballate* set for voices and instruments in two or three parts. Both his portrait in the Squarcialupi Codex (Florence, Bibl. Medicea Laurenziana, Pal. 87) and his tombstone at San Lorenzo show a blind figure holding a small lap-organ or *organetto,* on which he could accom-

The Abbey of Landévennec: the new abbey buildings completed in 1958.

pany his own singing, as described in Giovanni da Prato's *Il Paradiso degli Alberti* (1389).

Bibliography: *Works,* ed. L. ELLINWOOD (Cambridge, Mass. 1939). F. VILLANI, *Liber de Civitatis Florentiae Famosis Civibus,* ed. G. C. GALLETTI (Florence 1847). L. SCHRADE, ed., *Polyphonic Music of the Fourteenth Century,* 4 v. (Monaco 1956–58) v. 4. L. ELLINWOOD, "The Fourteenth Century in Italy," *New Oxford History of Music,* ed. J. A. WESTRUP, 11 v. (New York 1957–) 3:77–80. N. PIRROTTA, *Die Musik in Geschichte und Gegenwart,* ed. F. BLUME (Kassel-Basel 1949–) 8:163–168. P. GARGIULO, ed., *Dolcissime Armonie: nel sesto centenario della morte di Francesco Landini* (Florence 1997). M. P. LONG, "Francesco Landini and the Florentine Cultural Élite," in *Early Music History 3: Studies in Medieval and Early Modern Music,* ed. I. FENLON (Cambridge, Eng. 1983) 83–99; "Landini's Musical Patrimony: A Reassessment of Some Compositional Conventions in Trecento Polyphony," *Journal of the American Musicological Society,* 40 (1987) 31–52. N. SLONIMSKY, ed., *Baker's Biographical Dictionary of Musicians* (8th ed. New York 1992) 1002. K. VON FISCHER, "Francesco Landini," in *The New Grove Dictionary of Music and Musicians,* ed. S. SADIE, v. 10 (New York 1980) 428–434.

[L. ELLINWOOD]

LANDO, POPE

Pontificate: July or Nov. 913 to Mar. 914. A Roman of Sabinian ancestry, Lando was one of several popes created in the tenth century by the house of Theophylactus. Pope FORMOSUS had appointed the original THEOPHYLACTUS as *vestararius* (or *vestiarius*), an office of considerable influence and importance in the control of the temporalities of the Holy See. In Rome Theophylactus held the titles of consul and senator—a distinction shared by his wife THEODORA and his daughters THEODORA and MAROZIA. These women dictated the election of papal candidates for half a century, and thus gave grounds for the legend that in this period of history a woman wore the tiara (*see* JOAN, POPESS, FABLE OF). Like most popes of this tragic era, Lando enjoyed a very brief pontificate. During the six months of his tenure nothing good or evil is recorded of the papacy. It is probable that Lando was simply the instrument of the Roman aristocracy, especially the elder Theodora. He was succeeded by JOHN X.

Bibliography: *Liber pontificalis*, ed. L. DUCHESNE (Paris 1886–92) 2:239. P. JAFFÉ, *Regesta pontificum romanorum ab condita ecclesia ad annum post Christum natum 1198*, ed. S. LÖWENFELD (repr. Graz 1956) 1:448. LIUTPRAND, *Antapodosis, Monumenta Germaniae Historica: Scriptores rerum Germanicarum* (Berlin 1826–) v. 41. H. K. MANN, *The Lives of the Popes in the Early Middle Ages from 590 to 1304* (London 1902–32) 4:147–148. A. FLICHE and V. MARTIN, eds., *Histoire de l'église depuis les origines jusqu'à nos jours* (Paris 1935) 7: 32–34. R. BENERICETTI, *La cronologia dei Papi dei secoli IX–XI secondo le carte di Ravenna* (1999) 35–36. S. SCHOLZ, *Lexikon für Theologie und Kirche* 6 (3d. ed. Freiburg 1997). J. N. D. KELLY, *Oxford Dictionary of Popes* (New York 1986) 121.

[P. J. MULLINS]

LANDOALD, ST.

Missionary to the Low Countries; d. Wintershoven, near Maastricht, Netherlands, 668. According to the legendary life produced by HERIGER OF LOBBES in the 10th century, Landoald was a Roman priest, descended from a Lombard family. When Pope (St.) MARTIN I sent him with a party of missionaries to help St. AMANDUS, the Apostle of the Belgians, Landoald evangelized the territory between the Meuse and the Schelde. In that district he made his headquarters at Wintershoven, where he built a church dedicated by St. Remaclus, *c.* 659. The remains of Landoald were discovered in 980 at Wintershoven and translated to Ghent.

Feast: March 19.

Bibliography: *Bibliographica hagiographica latina antiquae et mediae aetatis* 2:4700-10. *Acta sanctorum* March 3:35–47. *Monumenta Germaniae Historica Scriptores* (Berlin 1826–) 15.2:599–611. L. VAN DER ESSEN, *Étude critique . . . des saints mérovingiens de l'ancienne Belgique* (Louvain 1907) 357–368. É. DE MOREAU, *Histoire de l'Église en Belgique* (2d ed. Brussels 1945–) 1:312; 2:254, 272–273, 286, 322, 397. *Vies des saintes et des bienheuruex selon l'ordre du calendrier avec l'historique des fêtes* 3:424–425. A. BUTLER, *The Lives of the Saints* (New York 1956) 1:634–635.

[C. P. LOUGHRAN]

LANDRY (LANDRICH), SS.

Landry of Paris, bishop of Paris from 650 to *c.* 656; d. *c.* 660. He succeeded Andebert and distinguished himself by his charity during the famine of 651. The foundation of the HÔTEL-DIEU DE PARIS is attributed to him. The only known charter of his episcopate concerned the abbey of Saint-Denis-en-France. This document is lost, but it is mentioned in the privilege of Clovis II, dated

June 22, 654, to which the bishop affixed his signature. The relics of St. Landry were preserved in the church of Saint-Germain-l'Auxerrois in Paris, where they had been deposited in 1171. These relics, enclosed in a silver reliquary, were destroyed in 1798.

Feast: June 10.

Landry of Soignies, abbot, bishop; d. *c.* 730. He was the son of St. VINCENT MADELGARIUS and St. WALDETRUD. He became abbot of Soignies (Hainaut, Belgium) and of Hautmont (Nord, France). He was a missionary bishop in the region of Brussels, particularly "in Meltis castellum," now Melsbroek, Belgium. The lists of bishops for Metz or Meaux either are very inaccurate or outrightly contradict any attempt to insert his name within their lists. Landry is very probably the person to whom Marculfus dedicated his *Formulae*. His relics are in the collegiate church of Soignies. There is a local cult to him there as well as at Melsbroek. His vita was written in Soignies in the 11th century or earlier.

Feast: April 17.

Bibliography: *Acta sanctorum* June 2:289–291. *Gallia Christiana* 7:24–25. U. CHEVALIER, *Répertoire des sources historiques du moyen-âge. Bibliographie* (Paris 1905–07) 2:2752. L. DUCHESNE, *Fastes épiscopaux de l'ancienne Gaule* (Paris 1907–15) 2:472. A. BUTLER, *The Lives of the Saints* (New York 1956) 2:518–519. *Acta sanctorum* April 2:483–488. L. VAN DER ESSEN, *Étude critique . . . des saints merovingiens* (Louvain 1907) 288–291. A. M. ZIMMERMANN, *Kalendarium Benedictinum: Die Heiligen und Seligen des Benediktinerorderns und seiner Zweige* (Metten 1933–38) 2:64, 66. J. L. BAUDOT and L. CHAUSSIN, *Vies des saintes et des bienheureux* (Paris 1935–56) 4:413–414; 6:177–79.

[É. BROUETTE]

LANDULF

A member of the *capitanei* (the Italian noble class) in 11th-century Milan, leader of the Patarines from *c.* 1056 through the early 1060s; b. Milan; d. the early 1060s (exact date is unknown). While ARIALDO preached in the countryside, Landulf covered the city. Together, they formed a powerful team, exhibiting sincerity, efficiency, gentleness, and most of all a good strategic plan for their quest of reforming the Church of Milan.

Dressed shabbily, Landulf, with a persuasive voice, preached reform to the people like a demagogue. As early as 1057 he could be heard addressing the people as follows: "For light flatters darkness, all blind are affected, because the blind are your leaders. But now can the blind lead the blind? Is it not both who are falling down in a pit?"

On his way to Rome during the pontificate of STEPHEN IX to join Arialdo, Landulf was wounded at Piacenza. (It seems that the Patarine movement branched throughout Lombardy, especially at one of the Lombard cities, Piacenza, where Bishop Dionigo tried to drive them from his city; thus it can be assumed that Landulf received his wound in one of the skirmishes there.) Shortly afterward, his strength was weakened further by consumption. Thus, he had to withdraw from the Patarine effort. After his death his brother, ERLEMBALD, replaced him in the reform movement.

Bibliography: ARNULF, "Gesta archiepiscoporum Mediolanensium," *Monumenta Germaniae Historica* Scriptores (Berlin 1826–) 8.1–31. U. BALZANI, *Le cronache Italiane nel medio evo* (2d ed. Milan 1900). S. M. BROWN, "Movimenti politico-religiosi a Milano ai tempi della Pataria," *Archivo-storico Lombardi*, ser. 58, 6 (1931) 227–228. H. E. J. COWDREY, "The Papacy, the Patarenes and the Church of Milan," *TRHS*, ser. 5, 18 (1968) 25–48. LANDULF SENIOR, "Historia Mediolanensis," *Monumenta Germaniae Historica* Scriptores (Berlin 1826–) 8.32–100. F. MEDA, "Arialdo ed Erlembaldo," *La scuola cattolica e la scienze Italiana,* ser. 2, 10 (1895) 535–552. J. P. WHITNEY, *Hildebrandine Essays* (Cambridge 1932) 143–157.

[P. M. LEVINE]

LANDULF OF ÉVREUX, ST.

Bishop; d. before 614. Very little is known about this saint except that he was bishop of Évreux, and that *c.* 600 he exhumed the relics of St. TAURINUS (late fourth century), the first bishop of Évreux, and built a church in his honor. Other biographical embellishments are taken from the *Vita s. Taurini,* a forgery dating from the ninth century, supposedly the work of a disciple of the saintly Bp. DEODATUS OF NEVERS. Reputed miracles were added to the vita in the 10th and 11th centuries. According to these accounts even before becoming bishop, Landulf had been informed by heavenly voices about the relics of his holy predecessor. After Landulf assumed the episcopal office, a great ray of light reportedly indicated the very spot where he was to seek for the body of St. Taurinus. In spite of these uncertainties, the local cult of Landulf is one of long standing.

Feast: Aug. 13.

Bibliography: *Gallica Christiana* 11:567. *Acta sanctorum* Aug. 3:96. J. L. BAUDOT and L. CHAUSSIN, *Vies des saintes et des bienheureux* (Paris 1935–56) 8:320. E. JARRY, *Catholicisme* 4:848–849. C. DUCHESNAY, *Dictionnaire d'histoire et de géographie ecclésiastiques* (Paris 1912) 16:210.

[H. DRESSLER]

LANFRANC

Archbishop of CANTERBURY; b. Pavia, *c.* 1005; d. Canterbury, May 24, 1089. After studying and practicing

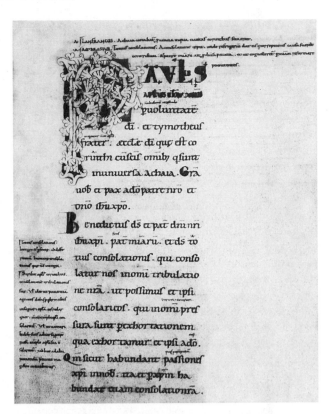

12th-century manuscript page of "St. Paul's First Epistle to the Corinthians," translated by John Wesley, with marginal glosses of Lanfranc and St. Ambrose, (Bib. Vat. Cod. Lat. 143, fol. 67v).

civil law at Pavia he became a student of the liberal arts and theology under BERENGARIUS at his school in Tours (1035). He excelled in dialectic and opened his own school at Avranches in 1039, but suddenly entered the destitute Benedictine abbey of BEC in 1042 to become a monk, and later prior, under Abbot HERLUIN OF BEC. There he founded a school that became known throughout Europe; St. ANSELM OF CANTERBURY, IVO OF CHARTRES, and the later Pope ALEXANDER II were among his pupils. As a dialectician and theologian Lanfranc wrote glosses on the Epistles of St. Paul, the *Collationes* of Cassian, and other works, concentrating, like Berengarius, on a thorough study of the words of the text. In the Eucharistic controversies he defended the orthodox position against Berengarius at the councils of Rome and Vercelli (1050), at Tours (1059), and in his *Liber de corpore et sanguine Domini* (*c.* 1059–62). While at Bec he became an adviser to William, Duke of Normandy, the future WILLIAM I OF ENGLAND, who in 1063 made him abbot of his new foundation, St. Stephen's at Caen. Against his inclination and only on papal order Lanfranc was consecrated archbishop of Canterbury, Aug. 29, 1070. He proved himself an effective but cautious reformer. Unlike GREGORY VII, Lanfranc agreed with William that the reform of the English Church was the king's responsibility. However, Lanfranc's reforms concerning clerical celibacy, marriage, and cathedral chapters, and his use of Norman churchmen brought the English Church into close contact with the GREGORIAN REFORM movement on the Continent. His most important innovation was the creation of separate courts of ecclesiastical jurisdiction. He introduced pre-Gregorian collections of Canon Law into England and infused new vitality into English monasticism. Lanfranc asserted his supremacy over the archbishop of YORK, but H. Böhmer's thesis that he forged documents to support his primacy has been disproved [E. Hora, "Zur Ehrenrettung Lanfranks. . ." *Theologische Quartalschrift*, 3 (1931) 288–319]. While he had the full confidence and support of William the Conqueror, relations with William's successor. William (II) Rufus, soon became difficult. Lanfranc's life as a scholar, prelate, and statesman as well as his lapidary letters reveal an agile, orderly mind and a determined, practical disposition. The monks who lived with Lanfranc, such as St. Anselm, GILBERT CRISPIN, and EADMER OF CANTERBURY, testify to his fatherly care, kindness, and humility.

Bibliography: Works. *Opera omnia*, ed. J. L. D'ACHÉRY (Paris 1648); *Opera . . . omnia*, ed. J. A. GILES, 2 v. (Oxford 1844). *Patrologia Latina*, ed. J. P. MIGNE (Paris 1878–90) 150. LANFRANC, *The Monastic constitutions*, ed. and tr. D. KNOWLES (New York 1951). Sources. "Acta Lanfranci" in J. EARLE, *Two of the Saxon Chronicles Parallel*, ed. C. PLUMMER, 2 v. (Oxford 1892–99) 1:287–292. GILBERT CRISPIN, *Vita Herluini* in *Gilbert Crispin*, ed. J. A. ROBINSON (Cambridge, Eng. 1911) 87–110. A. LE PRÉVOST, ed., *Ordericus Vitalis: Historia ecclesiastica*, 5 v. (Paris 1838–55) 2:126, 209–213; 3:309; 5:382. WILLIAM OF MALMSBURY, *Gesta Pontificum Anglorum*, ed. N. E. S. A. HAMILTON (*Rerum Britannicarum Medi: aevi scriptores* [New York 1964-]) 52:37–73. M. CRISPIN, "Vita beati Lanfranci," *Patrologia Latina* 150:19–58. Literature. A. J. MACDONALD, *Lanfranc: A Study of His Life, Work and Writing* (2d ed. London 1944). É. AMANN and A. GAUDEL, *Dictionnaire de théologie catholique* 8.2:2558–70. Z. N. BROOKE, *The English Church and the Papacy* (Cambridge, Eng. 1931). D. KNOWLES, *The Monastic Order in England, 943–1216* (Cambridge, Eng. 1962) 107–144. F. M. STENTON, *Anglo-Saxon England* (2d ed. Oxford 1947). N. F. CANTOR, *Church, Kingship, and Lay Investiture in England, 1089–1135* (Princeton 1958). F. L. Cross, *The Oxford Dictionary of the Christian Church* (London 1957) 783–784. J. GODFREY, *The Church in Anglo-Saxon England* (Cambridge, Eng. 1962). R. W. SOUTHERN, "Lanfranc of Bec and Berengar of Tours," *Studies in Medieval History Presented to F. M. Powicke*, ed. R. W. HUNT et al. (Oxford 1948) 27–48; "The Canterbury Forgeries," *English Historical Review* 73 (1958) 193–1226; *Saint Anselm and His Biographer* (New York 1963). D. C. DOUGLAS, *William the Conqueror* (Berkeley 1964).

[B. W. SCHOLZ]

LANG, ANDREAS

Benedictine abbot of Michelsberg (Bamberg, Germany); b. Staffelstein (Upper Franconia) *c.* 1450; d. Oct. 23, 1502. He became the third in a series of reform abbots of his monastery (1483), restoring the discipline of the Bursfeld reform and initiating the abbey's second period of flourishing. He also improved the material situation of his abbey, reorganizing its economic management and restoring the buildings of church and cloister. Interested in learning himself, he took special care to assist the monastery's school and library. His local reform activity made him influential in the general chapters of the Bursfeld Congregation. He collected materials on the history of the bishopric of Bamberg, on the history of the Michelsberg abbey, and on the saints of the Benedictine order. He wrote a number of works on these topics, notably his *Catalogus sanctorum ordinis sancti Benedicti*. Manuscripts of his writings survive in the Staatsbibliothek and the Staatsarchiv at Bamberg.

Bibliography: F. DRESSLER, *Lexikon für Theologie und Kirche*, ed. J. HOFER and K. RAHNER (Freiburg 1957–65) 6:782. *Der Catalogus sanctorum O.S.B. des Abtes Andreas von Michelsberg*, ed. J. FASSBINDER (Bonn 1910).

[C. G. NAUERT, JR.]

LANG, MATTHÄUS

German statesman, churchman, and humanist; b. Augsburg, 1468; d. Salzburg, March 30, 1540. A member of a burgher family, he studied law at Tübingen and pursued humanistic studies at Ingolstadt and Vienna. He entered the imperial service as a secretary and soon rose to a position of power and influence; his unquestioned talent and loyalty commended him to Emperor Maximilian I. He reached the high point in his diplomatic career when he acted as the emperor's representative in the negotiations leading to the League of Cambrai (1508), the reconciliation with the pope (1512), and the marriage treaties with the Jagellonians, concluded at the Congress of Vienna (1515). The great influence he had as the emperor's chief adviser made possible his especially rapid rise in the ecclesiastical hierarchy: provost of the Augsburg chapter (1500), bishop of Gurk (1505), cardinal (1512), and archbishop of Salzburg (1519). He was ordained and consecrated bishop only in 1519. Maximilian's death brought the period of his involvement in imperial politics to a close, and he devoted much of his energy to the governing of Salzburg. He was soon confronted by powerful demands for social and religious change; during the PEASANTS' WAR (1524–25) he was able to repress revolt in his territory only by securing the help of the Swabian League. The strong measures he took to halt the spread of the Reformation were paralleled by his effort to carry out a program of reform within the Church, which constituted one of the first tangible signs of the Catholic reform in Germany. Gifted and ambitious, he was not popular with his contemporaries, many of whom were troubled by his nonaristocratic origin; yet his achievements as imperial adviser and diplomat, prince-archbishop of Salzburg, and patron of the arts were of a very high order.

Bibliography: *Allgemeine deutsche Biographie* (Leipzig 1875–1910) 20:610–613. H. WIDMANN, *Geschichte Salzburgs*, v.3 (Gotha 1914) 1–72. J. WODKA, *Lexikon für Theologie und Kirche*, ed. J. HOFER and K. RAHNER (Freiburg 1957–65) 6:783.

[W. B. SLOTTMAN]

LANGDON, JOHN

Bishop of Rochester; b. Kent, England; d. Basel, Switzerland, Sept. 30, 1434. In 1398 Langdon became a Benedictine at Christ Church, CANTERBURY, where he was subprior by 1411. In that year, while studying at Canterbury College, Oxford, he incepted as doctor of theology. He served on a university commission examining the works of John WYCLIF (1411) and continued to be prominently engaged in the suppression of heresy. In 1419 King Henry V tried in vain to obtain Langdon's PROVISION to the Norman See of Lisieux, but he was provided to Rochester in 1421. As the appointment of regular clergy to bishoprics was then rare in England, Langdon's promotion to the See of ROCHESTER was a recognition of his outstanding qualities: he was a zealous champion of orthodoxy and a distinguished preacher (he twice preached before the convocation of Canterbury). He compiled a now lost *Anglorum chronicon*. He was abroad in 1422–23, probably in Italy (*Cal. Patent Rolls 1422–29*, 82; *Cal. Close Rolls 1422–29*, 482, 484), and he may have attended the Council of Siena. Langdon was appointed to the king's council in 1430 (Public Record Office, Exchequer Warrants for Issues 47.322) and served on an embassy to treat for peace with King Charles VII of France in 1432. He was an English representative at the Council of BASEL.

Bibliography: C. L. KINGSFORD, *The Dictionary of National Biography from the Earliest Times to 1900* (London 1885–1900) 11:538–539. *A Biographical Register of the University of Oxford to A.D. 1500* (Oxford 1957–59) 2:1093–94.

[R. L. STOREY]

LANGHORNE, RICHARD, BL.

Lay martyr; b. Bedford, England, *c.* 1635; d. hanged, drawn, and quartered at Tyburn (London), July 14, 1679. Richard, son of the barrister William Langhorne and Lettice Needham, was himself admitted to the Inner Temple, November 1646, and the bar in 1654. He married a Protestant woman, Dorothy Legatt. Langhorne suffered persecution. He was arrested for the first time on June 15, 1667, but was later released. He was not so fortunate the second time, Oct. 7, 1678, when he was arrested in connection with the fallacious Titus Oates Plot. Without examination he was committed to Newgate Prison, where he was kept in solitary confinement for eight months. On June 14, 1679, he was brought before the bar at the Old Bailey and found guilty based on the perjury of several witnesses. Although he was offered a pardon if he confessed his guilt and disclosed the property of the Jesuits, he persisted in declaring his ignorance of any conspiracy. Thus, he was condemned to execution. His last words were to the hangman were "I am desirous to be with my Jesus. I am ready and you need stay no longer for me." He was beatified by Pius XI on Dec. 15, 1929.

Feast of the English Martyrs: May 4 (England).

See Also: ENGLAND, SCOTLAND, AND WALES, MARTYRS OF.

Bibliography: R. CHALLONER, *Memoirs of Missionary Priests*, ed. J. H. POLLEN (rev. ed. London 1924; repr. Farnborough 1969), II, 388. J. H. POLLEN, *Acts of English Martyrs* (London 1891).

[K. I. RABENSTEIN]

LANGLEY, RICHARD, BL.

Gentleman, lay martyr; b. Grimthorpe (?), Yorkshire, England; hanged, drawn, and quartered at York, Dec. 1, 1586. As the son of Richard Langley of Rathorpe Hall (Walton) and Joan Beaumont of Mirfield, Richard inherited several estates including Grimthorpe, Rathorpe, and Ousethorpe near Pocklington in the East Riding of Yorkshire, which was his primary home. He married Agnes Hansby of New Malton with whom he had one son and four daughters. He created hiding places on his estates for refugee priests. The existence of an underground retreat at Grimthorpe was revealed to the president of the North, who dispatched (Oct. 28, 1586) a group of civil, military, and Protestant religious authorities to search his properties. Two priests were arrested at Grimthorpe and Langley himself seized at Ousethorpe. All were taken to York prison and arraigned. During his trial, the sympathetic jury was dismissed and another empaneled. Although his guilt was never established by the evidence, Langley was convicted and sentenced to death for harboring illegal priests. His friends requested and were denied the opportunity to bury him honorably. Langley was beatified by Pius XI on Dec. 15, 1929.

Feast of the English Martyrs: May 4 (England).

See Also: ENGLAND, SCOTLAND, AND WALES, MARTYRS OF.

Bibliography: R. CHALLONER, *Memoirs of Missionary Priests,* ed. J. H. POLLEN (rev. ed. London 1924; repr. Farnborough 1969), I, 120. H. FOLEY, *Records of the English Province of the Society of Jesus* (London 1878), III, 735; (London 1880), VI, 316. J. MORRIS, ed., *The Troubles of Our Catholic Forefathers Related by Themselves,* 3 v. (London 1872–77). J. H. POLLEN, *Acts of English Martyrs* (London 1891).

[K. I. RABENSTEIN]

LANGRES, COUNCILS OF

Several assemblies held at the diocesan seat of Langres, in northeast France. In 859 bishops from the Provinces of Lyons, Vienne, and Arles met at Langres and revised the canons on predestination made at VALENCE in 855. A few weeks later this new version was proposed by REMIGIUS of Lyons to the council at Savonnières (C. J. Von Hefele, *Histoire des conciles d'après les documents originaux,* tr. and continued by H. Leclercq, 4:216–217, 1336). Other Langres councils included the provincial council for Lyons held in 830, mentioned in a donation charter (*ibid.* 4:82). A charter of 883 speaks of a diocesan synod held at Langres in that year (*ibid.* 4:1356), and in 1116 two further synods were assembled, one with a papal legate, the archbishop of Vienne, copresiding with the bishop of Langres (*ibid.* 5:558).

Bibliography: J. RATH, *Lexikon für Theologie und Kirche,* ed. J. HOFER and K. RAHNER, 10 v. (2d, new ed. Freiburg 1957–65).

[R. KAY]

LANIGAN, JOHN

Irish ecclesiastical historian; b. Cashel, County Tipperary, 1758; d. Finglas, near Dublin, July 7, 1828. He was the son of Thomas Lanigan, a schoolmaster, and Mary Anne Dorkan. In 1776 Archbishop Butler of Cashel sent him to the Irish College, Rome, where he was ordained. One of his professors in Rome had been Pietro Tamburini, on whose advice he went to the University of Pavia, where he became professor of Hebrew, Sacred Scripture, and ecclesiastical history. In 1786 he was pressed to attend the synod of Pistoia, where Tamburini played a very prominent part, but he refused. He continued to teach at Pavia, and published some books on Scripture studies, of which the most significant was *Institutionum Biblicarum pars prima* (1793). In 1794 the university conferred on him its doctorate of divinity.

He returned to Ireland when Napoleon's troops occupied Pavia in 1796. Because of his associations with Tamburini he was suspected of JANSENISM by some Irish bishops, and was refused assistance in the Diocese of Cork, where he had landed, and in his native Diocese of Cashel. He made his way to Dublin, where he was helped by a fellow student of his Roman days, Martin Hugh Hamill, the parish priest of Francis Street, and by the Capuchins in Church Street.

In 1798 he was offered the chair of Sacred Scripture in St. Patrick's College, Maynooth, on the proposal of Archbishop O'Reilly of Armagh, seconded by Abp. John T. Troy of Dublin. However, Bishop Moylan of Cork, with what certainly seems to have been excessive zeal, demanded that he be asked to subscribe to an anti-Jansenist formulary then commonly tendered to French refugee clergy. Lanigan was resentful of this demand, and the proposed appointment fell through.

On May 2, 1799, he was appointed "translator, editor and corrector of the press" by the Royal Dublin Society, and in 1808 he became its librarian. In this same year he was one of the founders of the short-lived "Gaelic Society of Dublin." The fruit of his personal studies was *An Ecclesiastical History of Ireland from the First Introduction of Christianity among the Irish to the Beginning of the Thirteenth Century,* published in four volumes in 1822. Lanigan wrote his work despite failing health. It showed his wide reading and trenchant style and judgment, and marked a great advance on anything previously published on the subject. Although recent scholarship has dated it, it is still useful.

Bibliography: T. COOPER, *The Dictionary of National Biography from the Earliest Times to 1900* (London 1885–1900) 11:576–578. W. J. FITZPATRICK, *Irish Wits and Worthies: Including Dr. Lanigan, His Life and Times* (Dublin 1873). H. F. BERRY, *A History of the Royal Dublin Society* (London 1915).

[P. J. CORISH]

LANSPERGIUS, JOHANNES JUSTUS

Carthusian spiritual writer; b. Landsberg, Bavaria, 1490; d. Cologne, Aug. 10, 1539. He entered the Charterhouse of St. Barbara at Cologne in 1509, and except for the period from 1530 to 1535, when he was prior at Jülich, his life was spent at Cologne. At that time St. Barbara's was a notable center of religious fervor, and Lanspergius was one of its leading representatives. He exercised a wide influence by preaching, writing letters, circulating prayers and devout treatises, and giving spiritual direction. Two of the earliest Jesuits, Peter FABER and St. Peter CANISIUS, came under his influence. Lanspergius was convinced that the only effective remedy for the evils of his day—the Reformation period—consisted in enkindling, preserving, and increasing the fire of divine love in the souls of men. His writings, which were numerous, were addressed to a varied public. He wrote a treatise on perfection for interior souls, sermons and homilies, counsel for Christian gentlemen, letters to nuns, and exhortations for sinners. He was an eloquent apostle of devotion to the SACRED HEART. All the essentials of that devotion can be found in his letter to a monk of his own monastery [*Lanspergii Opera Omnia* (Montreuil 1890) 4:138–139]. As a means of promoting this devotion, he edited the *Revelations* of St. Gertrude of Helfta (Cologne 1536).

Bibliography: J. J. LANSPERGIUS, *An Epistle of Jesus Christ to the Faithful Soul,* tr. P. HOWARD, ed. MONK OF PARKMINSTER (London 1926). S. AUTORE, *Dictionnaire de théologie catholique* (Paris 1903–50) 8.2:2606–09. R. BAUERREISS, *Lexikon für Theologie und Kirche,* ed. J. HOFER and K. RAHNER (Freiburg 1957–65) 6:779. H. C. MANN, "Chronicles of Cologne Charterhouse," *Pax* 47 (1957) 13–19, 59–64, 95–98, 134–139; 48 (1958) 50–55, 86–92; 51 (1961) 66–71.

[B. DU MOUSTIER]

LANTBERT OF FREISING, ST.

Bishop of Freising; d. Sept. 19, 955 or 957. He is supposed to have been descended from the count of Sempt and to have been attached to the cathedral even before his elevation. Lantbert was appointed bishop of Freising in 937 or, according to other sources, on Aug. 28, 938, and presided in that see during the period of the Hungarian incursions and of domestic opposition to OTTO I. A document of Otto I confirmed the donation of the Abbey of Moosburg and of estates in Vöhringen from 950. Lantbert was present at a synod of Augsburg in 952. He has been venerated since the 11th century, and his cult has been officially recognized in Freising Diocese since the 15th century. His biography owes much to the legend of St. NICHOLAS of Myra; e.g., Lantbert is supposed even as a child to have denied himself milk and other nourishment on certain days of the week; three blind men are alleged to have received their sight from drinking the surplus milk. The legend also reflects the Hungarian invasion: the Hungarians are supposed to have come to Freising, ravaged the city for six days, and burned down the churches of St. Vitus and St. Stephen together with the rest of the city, the cathedral alone being spared because of a thick fog that hid it from the enemy. Other sources state that the Hungarians had indeed set fire to the cathedral but that the fog put it out. In either case, the deliverance was ascribed to the prayers of the bishop, who is therefore usually represented in art as praying in front of the cathedral with the city of Freising in flames about him.

Feast: Sept. 18 or 19.

Bibliography: J. E. STADLER and F. J. HEIM, *Vollständiges Heiligen-Lexikon,* 5 v. (Augsburg 1858–82) v.3. J. A. FISCHER, *Lan-tbert von Freising, 937–957, der Bischof und Heilige* (Munich 1959).

[G. SPAHR]

LANTERI, PIO BRUNONE

Founder of the Oblates of the Virgin Mary; b. Cuneo, Italy, May 12, 1759; d. Pinerolo (Torino), Aug. 5, 1830. After leaving the Carthusians because of ill health, he studied for the secular priesthood and was ordained, and soon after he received the laureate in theology at the University of Turin (1782). In order to devote himself entirely to apostolic and charitable activities in Turin, he refused all ecclesiastical benefices and offices. He was especially active in the Amicizia Cristiana, an association founded by Nikolaus von Diessbach, SJ, to utilize the press and secret gatherings for the benefit of the Church, much as the Freemasons were using them against the Church. Lanteri was very successful as a spiritual guide to university students, seminarians, young soldiers, and workers. He was a stanch supporter of PIUS VII during the pope's years of imprisonment by Napoleon I; as a result he was exiled from Turin (1811–14). Together with Giovanni Reinaudi, he founded a religious congregation of priests, the Oblates of the Virgin Mary (1815), which received the Holy See's approval (1826) and which numbered 200 members in 1963. Lanteri established in Turin (1817) the Amicizia Cattolica to counteract the Protestant biblical societies of London by distributing Catholic devotional literature. Soon this organization absorbed all the functions of the Amicizia Cristiana but abandoned its secrecy. It was the prototype for lay Catholic organizations in Italy. Lanteri also promoted the education and formation of the clergy, preached retreats in the Ignatian method, and spread the writings of St. Alphonsus Liguori. Save for a few devotional works that appeared in print, Lanteri's writings remain in manuscript form. The decree introducing his beatification cause in Rome was issued in 1952.

Bibliography: T. PIATTI, *Un precursore dell'Azione Cattolica: Il servo di Dio P. B. Lanteri* (2d ed. Turin 1934). I. FELICI, *Una bandiera mai ripiegata. P. B. Lanteri, fondatore dei PP. Oblati, precursore dell'Azione Cattolica* (Pinerolo 1950). L. CRISTIANI, *Un Prêtre redouté de Napoléon: P. B. Lanteri* (Nice 1957). *Acta Apostolicae Sedis* 44 (1952) 883–887.

[F. G. SOTTOCORNOLA]

LANTRUA, GIOVANNI OF TRIORA, ST.

Franciscan priest, martyr; b. Triora (Savona), Italy, March 15, 1760; d. Changsha (Hunan), China, Feb. 7,

1816. After joining the Franciscans (1777), he was ordained (1784) and then served as superior of various houses in Tarquinia and Velletri until he left for China (1798). A long delay in Lisbon and a difficult sea voyage delayed his arrival at Macau until 1800. During a period of political upheavals and religious persecutions, he exercised a zealous apostolate in the Provinces of Hunan, Hupeh, and Kiangsi from 1802 until his arrest in July 1815. After six months of imprisonment and torture, he was put to death by strangulation. His remains were transported to Macau (1819) and later to Rome, where they rest in the church of S. Maria in Aracoeli. He was beatified by Pope Leo XII (May 27, 1900) and canonized (Oct. 1, 2000) by Pope John Paul II with Augustine Zhao Rong and companions.

Feast: Feb. 3.

Bibliography: *Acta Apostolicae Sedis* 39 (Rome 1947) 213–221, 307–311. G. ANTONELLI, *Un martire di Cina, il b. G. da Triora* (Rome 1900), J. L. BAUDOT and L. CHAUSSIN, *Vies des saints et des bienheureux selon l'ordre du calendrier avec l'historique des fêtes,* ed. by the Benedictines of Paris, 12 v. (Paris 1935–56); v. 13, suppl. and table générale (1959) 2:317–318.

[J. KRAHL]

LAODICEA

Nine different cities were called Laodicea in antiquity; those in Phrygia, in Pisidia, and on the northern seacoast of Syria are the more significant.

Laodicea in Phrygia Pacatiana, also known as Laodicea near Lycus, was founded by Antiochus II and named after his wife. In spite of disastrous earthquakes, particularly in Nero's time, Laodicea was prosperous and noted for the quality of the woolen clothing it produced. Friendly relations with Smyrna, Hierapolis, Pergamum, and Nicomedia and the city's location on the main trade route from Ephesus to the East contributed to its affluence. A well-organized Jewish community lived in the city.

Christianity came to Laodicea in Apostolic times. St. Paul (Col 4.12–17) mentions the Church here and its zealous Epaphras, but a Pauline epistle to the Laodiceans is disputed. By the end of the 1st century the Church was an important one in Asia Minor, to which St. John (Rv 3.14–22) gave stern admonitions. Between 165 and 170 a synod met at Laodicea to discuss the EASTER CONTROVERSY (Eusebius, *Ecclesiastical History* 4.26.3). Polycrates in sending the synod's decisions to Pope St. VICTOR I calls Sagaris, the martyr bishop of Laodicea, one of the "great luminaries of Asia" (*ibid.* 5.24.5). A council convened in the city (*c.* 360) and formulated important canons for the discipline of the clergy and laity, and for the liturgy. The much-discussed canon 60 lists the books of the Old and New Testaments omitting Judith, Tobit, Sirach, Maccabees, and Revelation. The bishopric of Laodicea became the metropolitan see of Phrygia with numerous suffragans. In the 12th and 13th centuries Turks and Mongols destroyed the city; its ruins have not yet been excavated.

Laodicea in Pisidia (*Laodicea Combusta* or *Catacecaumene*), the modern Yorgan Ladik, was located on the main trade route from Ephesus to the Euphrates. Little is known about the city's early Christianity, but numerous Greek inscriptions dating from 350 to 450 show its vigorous growth. In 1908 the sepulchral inscription of Marcus Julius Eugenius (d. *c.* 332), Bishop of Laodicea, was discovered. In his epitaph written by himself the bishop says that he was the son of Cyrillus Celer; served the governor of Pisidia in a military capacity; married a senator's daughter, Gaia Julia Flaviana; suffered for the faith because of Maximinus's command to offer sacrifice; and came to Laodicea, where he was chosen bishop and held that office for 25 years, during which he rebuilt the church and adorned it with paintings and statues.

Laodicea on the northern seacoast of Syria was a port city founded by Seleucus I and named after his mother. Hellenistic cults survived long in this region, and no bishops are listed before the middle of the 3rd century. APOLLINARIS, whose Christological errors went undetected for some time, became bishop there in 362. A synod met in Laodicea in 481 to deal with matters concerning Stephen of Antioch. Justinian I renovated the church of St. John in this city. Because of its strategic location Laodicea frequently bore the brunt of military expeditions from the Byzantines, Arabs, and Crusaders but was never completely destroyed. On April 28, 1961, Laodicea became the seat of the Melchite archbishop.

Bibliography: É. BEURLIER, *Dictionnaire de la Bible,* ed. F. VIGOUROUX 4.1:86–87 (Paris 1895–1912). W. M. RAMSAY, *The Cities and Bishoprics of Phrygia,* 2 v. (Oxford 1895–97). E. HONIGMANN, *Paulys Realenzyklopädie der klassischen Altertumswissenschaft,* ed. G. WISSOWA et al. 12.1 (Stuttgart 1924). 712–724. C. M. KAUFMANN, *Handbuch der altchristlichen Epigraphik* (St. Louis 1917) 249–251. H. LECLERCQ, *Dictionnaire d'archéologie chrétienne et de liturgie* (Paris 1907–53) 8.1:1321–23. *Monumenta historica Societatis Jesu,* v.1 (Rome 1932). B. KÖTTING, *Lexikon für Theologie und Kirche,* (Freiburg, 1957–66) ed. J. HOFER and K. RAHNER 6:793–95.

[H. DRESSLER]

LAOS, THE CATHOLIC CHURCH IN

The Lao People's Democratic Republic is a landlocked country in southeast Asia, bordered on the northwest by Burma and China, on the northeast and east by

VIETNAM, on the south by CAMBODIA and on the west by THAILAND (formerly Siam). The region's terrain is characterized by rugged mountains, plateaus and the alluvial plains of the Mekong River which serves as Laos' western border. Heavily forested and with a tropical climate, it weathers monsoons, a summer rainy season and a winter dry season. Agricultural products include rice, corn, tobacco and tea, while natural resources consist of timber, gypsum, gold, gemstones and tin.

Formerly part of French Indochina, Laos became a constitutional monarchy in 1947 and gained independence in 1949. For the next decade Laos experienced continual political unrest and sporadic civil war among rightist, neutralist and communist-backed Pathet Lao factions, and by the 1960s communists controlled the government. Laos was bombed by the United States during the Vietnam War between 1965–69, and it was proclaimed a republic in 1975. A majority of Laotians are ethnic Lao, the principal lowland inhabitants who are also the most dominant politically and culturally.

Early History. Originally inhabited by Tai from China, Laos joined Thailand as part of the kingdom of Lan Xang in the 14th century, and by 1550 Buddhism had been established as the predominant religion. Lan Xang went into decline in the 17th century, a result of dynastic conflicts. Italian Jesuit Giovanni Leira entered Vientiane c. 1630. In 1666 Louis Laneau, the first vicar apostolic of Siam (1673–96), successfully evangelized a Laotian village in Siam, near Ayuthia. The receptivity of these people to the Gospel moved Laneau to send missionaries into Laos and to compose *Instructions aux missionnaires du Laos,* a remarkable missiological document. The Siamese revolution of 1688 prevented the continuation of the Laos mission, and it would not be revived until the late 19th century, although challenging terrain continued to hamper evangelization efforts through the 20th century.

In the late 18th century, Siam established hegemony over much of what is now Laos. The region was divided into principalities centered on Luang Prabang in the north, Vientiane in the center and Champassak in the south. Following its colonization of Vietnam, the French supplanted the Siamese and began integrating all of Laos into the French empire. The Franco-Siamese treaty of 1907 defined the present Lao boundary with Thailand.

In the 19th century the Laotians dwelling in the northern region around Sam Neua, near the border of Vietnam, were evangelized to a certain extent from western Tonkin (Hanoi). Missionary efforts also originated from Cambodia (1852), although they were ultimately unsuccessful. Most of the missionary endeavor in eastern

Capital: Vientiane.
Size: 91,430 sq. miles.
Population: 5,497,459 in 2000.
Languages: Lao, French, English; tribal dialects are spoken in various regions.
Religions: 43,765 Catholics (.8%), 3,298,475 Buddhists (60%), 21,650 Protestants (.3%), 1,649,237 animists (30%), 484,332 with no religious affiliation.
Apostolic vicariates: Luang Prabang, Paksé, Savannakhet, and Vientiane.

Laos started from Ubon in 1881. Two Ubon priests of the PARIS FOREIGN MISSION SOCIETY (MEP), Jean Prudhomme and François Guéguo discovered a forbidden traffic in slaves and began to ransom hundreds of them. Between 1881 and 1887 nine Christian communities of former slaves were established, and a strong movement of conversions followed, although it could not be fully exploited for lack of apostolic workers. From the right bank of the Mekong, Prudhomme relocated in 1883 to the left bank, where the French, now installed in Cochin China and Cambodia, extended their protectorate in 1893 over the kingdoms of Luang Prabang and Vientiane, thereby giving rise to modern Laos. Conversions diminished along the right bank of the Mekong, but increased along the left bank. The first chapel opened in Vientiane in 1896 and the first permanent residence in 1910. The Vicariate Apostolic of Laos, embracing Laos and eastern Siam, was created in 1899 when there were 8,000 Catholics and 2,000 catechumens in the entire area. Not until 1929 did a missionary begin to work in the northern section around Luang Prabang.

The 20th Century and Beyond. During World War II Japanese forces occupied French Indochina, including Laos. King Sisavang Vong of Luang Prabang declared independence from France on July 19, 1949, just prior to Japan's surrender, and a nationalist fervor gripped the region. In September of 1945, Vientiane and Champassak united with Luang Prabang to form an independent government under the Lao Issara ("Free Laos") banner. The movement, however, was short-lived. Within six months French troops had reoccupied the country and conferred limited autonomy on Laos following elections for a constituent assembly.

During the first Indochina war between France and the communist movement in Vietnam, Prince Souphanouvong formed the Pathet Lao ("Land of Laos"), a communist resistance group. Laos was not granted full sovereignty until the Geneva Peace conference, held in 1954 following Vietnam's defeat of the French. Following elections held in 1955, the first coalition government was formed, led by Prince Souvanna Phouma. It col-

LAOS

0   100   200 Miles

0   100   200 Kilometers

lapsed in 1958, amidst increased polarization of the political process, and rightist forces took over the government, which operated in tandem with a constitutional monarch.

In 1960 paratroop captain Kong Le seized Vientiane in a coup and formed a neutralist government in hopes of ending the fighting. The new government, again led by Souvanna Phouma lost power to rightist forces under General Phoumi Nosavan that same year. Subsequently, the neutralists allied themselves with the communist insurgents and won the support of the USSR. General Nosavan began receiving aid from the United States.

A second Geneva conference (1961–62) established the independence and neutrality of Laos. Unfortunately, shortly afterward, both sides accused each other of violating the terms of the agreement, and with superpower support on both sides, civil war resumed and the increasing U.S. and North Vietnamese military presence in the country drew Laos into the second Indochina war (1954–75). For nearly a decade the region was devastated by what some considered the worst bombing of the

20th century, as U.S. troops attempted to destroy the supply lines along the Ho Chi Minh Trail in eastern Laos.

By 1963 Laos contained three vicariates: Ventiane (created in 1952 from the Prefecture of Ventiane and Luang Prabang, erected in 1938), Luang Prabang (part of the Vicariate of Ventiane until 1963), and Savannaket (1963, called the Prefecture, 1950–58, and then Vicariate of Thakkek, 1958–63). Ventiane and Luang Prabang, in the north, were confided to the Oblates of Mary Immaculate, who first came in 1937; Savannaket was entrusted to the MEP. Despite the fact that Buddhism has been named the state religion, Laos's three vicariates encompassed 28,000 Catholics, 82 religious and 6 secular priests, 48 brothers and 124 sisters. In the country's 45 Catholic schools were enrolled 8,000 students.

The Church under Communism. The war in Laos had drastic consequences for the Church. In 1972 the country's communist party renamed itself the Lao People's Revolutionary Party (LPRP) and became part of a new coalition government in 1973, shortly after the Vientiane cease-fire agreement. Nonetheless, the political struggle between communists, neutralists and rightists continued. The fall of Saigon, Vietnam and Phnom Penh, Cambodia to communist forces, in April of 1975 hastened the decline of the coalition in Laos. Months after Vietnam's communist victories, the Pathet Lao entered Vientiane. On Dec. 2, 1975 the King of Laos abdicated his throne and the LPDR set about establishing a communist state.

Once in power, the Pathet Lao took control of the media and set about arresting and imprisoning many military leaders and members of the former government. In a centralized society, the Laotian economy began to falter, and ten percent of the country—including many lowland Lao and ethnic Hmong—became refugees. Of these people, most were eventually resettled in other countries, including the United States, China and Thailand, although by 1999 29,000 Hmong and lowland Lao had returned to Laos. Most political prisoners were released by the government during the early 1980s. While a new constitution enacted in 1992 embodied more liberal social policies, including freedom of religion, the communist government continued its policy of control.

Into the 21st Century. By 2000 Laos had 29 parishes and fewer than 20 priests at work among the faithful, and the Church maintained its greatest influence in the central and southern provinces, while northern regions were more resistant to minority faiths. Tending to humanitarian needs were 79 sisters, who were prohibited from any evangelization. While the state did not recognize the

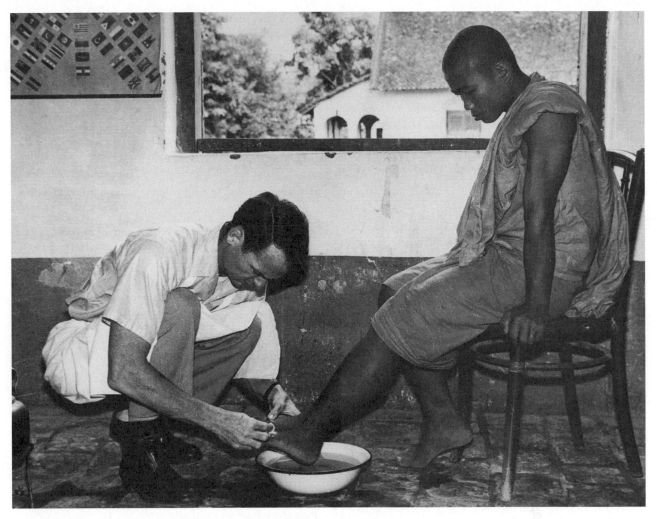

American doctor and missionary Tom Dooley cares for a Laotian Buddhist monk. Dr. Dooley was one of the founders of a medical mission in Laos. (©Bettmann/CORBIS)

Vatican, a papal nuncio from Bangkok coordinated efforts by Laotian missions to provide aid to the region's lepers and disabled persons. Catholic schools continued to be banned by the government, as party cadres continued their antagonism to "foreign" religions, in 1997 going so far as to demand a list of those believing in Jesus. All religious groups were required to report to the government's Department of Religious Affairs in the Lao Front for National Construction, a group mandated by the constitution to discourage "all acts . . . creating division of religion or creating division among the people." Buddhism was voted into law as the state religion in 2000, although its practice was inhibited along with that of minority faiths. Despite the government's efforts to reform the nation's economic base, Laos continued to rely on aid from the International Monetary Fund and other sources, Japan being its largest donor nation.

In February of 1999 Vientiane Bishop Jean Khamse made the first ad limina visit to Pope John Paul II in over four decades. Asked about the status of the Laotian Church, Bishop Khamse commented that "the Church in Laos is like an infant, an infant saved from the waters." With little infrastructure and few priests, the Church gained most support from animists, for whom Catholicism was seen as a psychological liberation from the superstitions of tribal faiths. Efforts at evangelization in Laos, Khamse added, required a contemplative dimension and missionaries "must be witnesses of Jesus who love's the people around them."

Bibliography: M. BERTHÉAS, *La Mission du Laos* (Lyons 1909). E. PAPINOT, "Cinquante ans d'apostolat au Laos (1881–1931)," *Revue d'historie des missions,* 8 (1931) 337–352. *Le missioni cattoliche: Storia, geographia, statistica* (Rome 1950) 271–272. *Bilan du Monde,* 2:553–555. *Annuario Pontificio* has data on all diocese.

[J. GUENNOU/EDS.]

LAOZI (LAO-TZU)

In English, "Venerable Master" or "Old Master." An honorific title for a mysterious Chinese philosopher and Daoist (Taoist) sage, supposed author of the *Daode Jing (Tao Te Ching* in English: "The Classic of The Way and Virtue"), venerated as the deity known as Taishang laojun (Tai-shang Lao-Chün, in English "Highest Venerable Lord") or Huanglao jun (Huang Lao-Chün, in English "Yellow Venerable Lord") by the adherents of Daoism (Taoism), lived apparently in the period circa 500–400 B.C. during the Zhou (Chou) Dynasty.

What little is known about his life comes from the account of his supposed life in the *Shiji (Shi Chi*, "Records of the Historian"), written by the Chinese historian Sima Qian (Ssu–ma Ch'ien) around 100 B.C. According to him, Laozi's family name was Li, his supposed given name was Er Dan (Erh Tan, in English "long ears," probably a reference to the traditional Chinese symbol of wisdom and longevity rather than a reference to the sage's real name). Apparently, he worked as an archivist at the Zhou imperial court, before leaving in disillusionment and making his way westward in search of wisdom. Scholars are divided as to the historicity of Sima Qian's account of the alleged encounter between Laozi and CONFUCIUS at the Zhou court, in which Laozi berated Confucius for his arrogance and lack of understanding; many scholars have attributed that account to subsequent anti–Confucian polemics of the Daoists.

Some scholars have questioned Sima Qian's attribution of the authorship of the *Daode Jing* to Laozi, as there is no mention of an author in all extant versions of the *Daode Jing*. Sima Qian had recounted a legend in which Laozi, weary of living and heading westward in search of wisdom, penned down his philosophy at the request of the "Keeper of the Pass" (i.e., frontier guard). Contemporary textual analysis of the received text points to the existence of several redactional layers. Although the received text is traditionally divided into 81 chapters of 5,000 characters, the earliest extant manuscripts—the Guodian text (circa 300 B.C.) and the Mawang dui (Ma–wang Tui) texts (168 B.C.)—while preserving the contents of the work albeit in an inverted order, suggest that the original was probably a continuous work of some 5,400 characters, in all likelihood written or edited by a single author.

The *Daode Jing* presents the Dao as a nameless, undefinable, spontaneous, eternal, cyclical and ever–changing cosmological essence. It advocates that one engages in "non–action" (*wu–wei*) to be in harmony with the Dao. Here, "non–action" is not mere passivity, but rather, taking only those actions that would be in harmony with the cosmological ordering of things in the Dao.

The utopian society which the *Daode Jing* presents is one of harmony between ruler and ruled, in which the Sage–Ruler embodies *wu–wei* as a way of governing, viz., governing behind the scenes in a manner that the subjects are not even aware that they are being governed. This philosophy has attracted many adherents both in the Far East and in the Western world, making the *Daode Jing* the most translated ancient Asian treatise in the European languages in the 19th and 20th centuries.

See Also: CHINESE PHILOSOPHY.

Bibliography: M. KALTENMARK, *Lao–tzu and Taoism* (Stanford 1969). W. T. CHAN, *A Source Book in Chinese Philosophy* (Princeton 1963) 136–176. K. Y. CH'EN, *Lao–tzu: Text, Notes, and Comments* (San Francisco 1981). D. C. LAU, tr. *Chinese Classics: Tao Te Ching* (Hong Kong 1982). A. C. GRAHAM, *Disputers of the Tao* (LaSalle, IL 1989). E. WONG, *Lao–tzu's Treatise on the Response of the Tao* (San Francisco 1993). R.G. HENRICKS, tr. *Lao–tzu's Tao Te Ching: A Translation of the Startling New Documents Found at Guodian* (New York 2000).

[J. Y. TAN]

LAPIDE, CORNELIUS A.

The Latin form of his Dutch name, Cornelis Cornelissen van den Steen, voluminous exegete; b. Bocholt, Province of Limburg, Belgium, Dec. 18, 1567; d. Rome, March 12 (or 11), 1637. After studying theology at Douai and Louvain, Lapide entered the Society of Jesus in 1592 and was ordained three years later. He taught Sacred Scripture for 40 years, first at Louvain (1596–1616) and then at the Roman College (1616–36). His lively lectures, rich in topical allusions and pleasant irrelevancies, delighted students. His prodigious commentaries, covering the entire Bible with the exception of Job and Psalms, appeared steadily from 1614 to 1645. Supported abundantly by quotations from Church Fathers and later interpreters, his exegesis frequently included not only the literal sense of a passage but the allegorical, tropological, and anagogical meanings as well. His knowledge of Hebrew, Greek, and Latin, of theology, Church history, and the classical philosophers and natural historians (especially Aristotle and Pliny), and his intense industry, fervor, and awareness of problems of the day, all combined to produce commentaries highly esteemed by his contemporaries and posterity. He saw his greatest work, *Commentaria in omnes Divi Pauli Epistolas* (Antwerp 1614), go through 11 of its eventual 80 editions. The entire listing of his works and their editions fills 15 columns in the *Bibliothèque de la Compagnie de Jésus.* Two notable editions of his complete works, with commentaries on Job (by J. de PINEDA) and Psalms (by St. Robert BELLARMINE) added, are the Malta edition (1843–46) in 10 volumes and the Paris edition (1859–63) in 22 volumes. A large part of his exegesis was included by J. P. Migne in his *Cursus S. Scripturae* (Paris 1837–45) v. 5–20.

Bibliography: C. SOMMERVOGEL, *Bibliothèque de la Compagnie de Jésus*, (Brussels-Paris 1890–32) 4:1511–26. H. HURTER, *Nomenclator literarius theologiae catholicae* (Innsbruck 1903–13) 3:787–789. R. GALDOS, ''De scripturisticis meritis P. Cornelii a Lapide,'' *Verbum Domini* 17 (1937) 39–44, 88–96; ''De canonibus exegeticis apud P. C. a L.,'' *ibid.* 146–152; ''Nel Terzo Centenario della morte di C. a L.,'' *La civilta cattolica* 88.3 (1937) 204–218. J. SCHMID, *Lexikon für Theologie und Kirche*, ed. J. HOFER and K. RAHNER (Freiburg 1957–65) 3:58. G. HEINRICI, *Realencyklopädie für protestantische Theologie* 4:289–291.

[T. T. TAHENY]

LAPINI, ANNA MARIA

Foundress of the Poor Daughters of the Holy Stigmata of St. Francis; b. Florence, Italy, May 27, 1809; d. there, April 15, 1860. At her father's urging, Anna Maria Fiorelli relinquished her desire to enter religious life and married Giovanni Lapini (1835). Her husband caused her much grief by his immoral conduct and unbelief, but she led him back to a Christian life before his death (1844). In 1848 she founded the Stigmatine Sisters, who followed the rule of the Third Order of St. Francis and labored to educate poor and abandoned girls. Anna and her companions received their habits in 1850. The Holy See's approval came in 1888. By 1961 the congregation numbered 1,255 members in 123 houses, mostly in Italy. Anna's religious life was one of great poverty and suffering caused by ill health, misunderstanding, and unfair hostility. The cause for Anna's beatification was formally introduced in Rome in 1918.

Bibliography: A. MARTINI, *Suor A. Lapini, fondatrice delle Suore Stimmatine* (Florence 1937). M. RICCI, *Anna Lapini* (4th ed. Florence 1937). *Acta Apostolicae Sedis* 10 (1918) 99–102.

[F. G. SOTTOCORNOLA]

LAPSI

From the Latin word for ''fallen,'' the Christians who fell from the faith in the persecution of Decius (249–251). They were of three kinds: *sacrificati,* those who offered sacrifice to the pagan gods; *thurificati,* those who burned incense at a pagan religious ceremony; and *libellatici,* those who obtained certificates stating they had sacrificed, though they had not done so. While there had always been apostates, the *lapsi* formed a problem because of their great number and the desire most had of being readmitted to communion in the Church even while the persecution continued. Church leadership differed in the solution of the problem. In Rome NOVATIAN leaned

Ven. Luis de La Puente, 17th-century engraving.

toward a rigoristic treatment, denying penance and reconciliation, at least until after the persecution; in Carthage many *lapsi* had recourse to confessors of the faith for their intercession and received *libelli pacis,* or requests that the bishops admit them to communion. Bishop Cyprian decided on a synod to solve the problem in Carthage, and Pope Cornelius did the same in Rome. Reconciliation was extended to the *libellatici* and to the *sacrificati* in danger of death who had already begun to do penance.

Bibliography: CYPRIAN, *Epist.* 5–56; *Laps.* B. POSCHMANN, *Paenitentia secunda* (Bonn 1940) 368–397. K. RAHNER, *Zeitschrift für katholische Theologie* 74 (1952) 257–276, 381–438. H. LECLERCQ, *Dictionnaire d'archéologie chrétienne et de liturgie,* ed. F. CARROLL, H. LECLERQ, and H. I. MARROU, 15 v. (Paris 1907–53) 5.1: 1067–80; 9.1:78–79, 81–85.

[F. HAUSER]

LA PUENTE, LUIS DE, VEN.

Jesuit spiritual writer; b. Valladolid, Nov. 11, 1554; d. there, Feb. 16, 1624. La Puente studied arts and letters at the University of Valladolid and later pursued courses in theology with the Dominicans. He entered the Society of Jesus on Dec. 2, 1574, and later made his tertianship under the direction of Balthasar Alvarez, SJ. He was regent of studies and professor of theology in Oviedo and Valladolid from 1596 to 1599. He dedicated almost the whole of his life to administration and spiritual direction. He served as rector in Vallagarcia and twice in Valladolid (1594–96, 1601–02), as novice master in Villagarcía (1585–89, 1593–94, 1599–1601) and in Medina del Campo (1592–93), and as spiritual director in Valladolid and Salamanca (1589–92, 1597–99).

He is remembered chiefly for his spiritual writings. The specific characteristic of his spirituality was its paternal spirit. This quality La Puente appears to have acquired through the gift of wisdom, and it enabled him to inspire in his disciples a clear perception of the spiritual world. In his writings he appears not only as a theologian of depth but as a spiritual master as well. His knowledge of the Scriptures, soundness of doctrine, and clarity of expression are remarkable. His spirituality seems to spring from his insight into the theological foundations of the truths about which he wrote. However, he misused symbolism, made frequent use of an artificial interpretation of the Scriptures, and the pace in the development of his ideas was often too slow.

Among his principal writings was *Meditaciones de los Misterios de nuestra fe* (*Meditations on the Mysteries of our Faith*, 2 v., Valladolid 1605). More than 260 complete or partial editions of the *Meditations,* including translations into many languages, are known to have been published. The *Meditations* begin with a study of the end of man and the four last things, continue with the life of Christ, and end with a masterful consideration of the divine attributes. The introduction to the *Meditations* is a "short, clear and precise summary of mental prayer, the most complete and delightful treatise on prayer ever written." (C. M. Abad, 152).

Guía espiritual (*Spiritual Guide*, Valladolid 1609), a work not as well known as La Puente's *Meditations,* is more profound and sublime in doctrine. It treats of the contemplative life in its various practices (including mystical exercises) and the active life, in the consideration of which great emphasis is laid upon mortification. In this work La Puente revealed himself not only as a mystic but as a learned theologian able to present his doctrine with accuracy and precision.

De la perfección del cristiano en todos sus estados (*On Christian Perfection in the Different States of Life*, 4 v., Valladolid 1612–16) is one of the first treatises on spirituality to be based upon the perfection of the different states of life. Perfection is considered in its relation to the Sacraments. The book treats of the spiritual perfection to which God calls the Christian in Baptism and the perfection signified in Confirmation and Holy Orders, and there follows an application of these principles to the different states of life. It includes a treatment of the necessity and kind of civil obedience expected of the Christian, and it dwells upon the perfection proper to married life.

Expositio moralis et mystica in Canticum Canticorum (2 v., Cologne 1622) is a spiritual and mystical commentary on the Song of Songs. Its value does not lie in its exegesis of the text, which is too symbolic and contrived, but in the spiritual doctrine that it sets forth, especially that with regard to grace, the Mystical Body, and contemplation.

La Puente is also remembered for his *Vida del Padre Baltasar Alvarez* (*The Life of Father Balthasar Alvarez*, Madrid 1615) and his *Sentimientos y avisos espirituales* (*Spiritual Counseling and Dispositions*, Seville 1671).

Bibliography: C. SOMMERVOGEL et al., *Bibliothèque de la Compagnie de Jésus* (Brussels-Paris 1890–1932) 6:1271–95. I. IPARRAGUIRRE, *Répertoire de spiritualité ignatienne* (Rome 1961), with detailed bibliog. C. M. ABAD, *Vida y escritos del V. P. Luis de La Puente* (Comillas 1957), best biog.; *El V. P. Luis de La Puente: Sus libros y doctrina espiritual* (Comillas 1954), analysis of works. J. DE GUIBERT, *The Jesuits: Their Spiritual Doctrine and Practice,* tr. W. J. YOUNG, ed. G. E. GANSS (Chicago 1964).

[I. IPARRAGUIRRE]

LARA PUENTE, SALVADOR, ST.

Martyr, lay youth; b. Aug. 13, 1905, Berlin, Súchil, Archdiocese of Durango, Mexico; d. Aug. 15, 1926, Puerto de Santa Teresa near Zacatecas. Like his cousin St. David ROLDÁN, he abandoned his studies at Durango seminary in order to assist his family financially. While working for a mining company, he remained active in pastoral work, Mexican Youth for Catholic Action (president), and the National League (secretary). He was arrested and shot with his cousin, after witnessing the assassination of their pastor BATIZ and Manuel MORALES. Salvador was both beatified (Nov. 22, 1992) and canonized (May 21, 2000) with Cristobal MAGALLANES [*see* GUADALAJARA (MEXICO), MARTYRS OF, SS.] by Pope John Paul II.

Feast: May 25 (Mexico).

Bibliography: J. CARDOSO, *Los mártires mexicanos* (Mexico City 1953). V. GARCÍA JUÁREZ, *Los cristeros* (Fresnillo, Zac. 1990).

[K. I. RABENSTEIN]

LARKE, JOHN, BL.

Priest, martyr; d. hanged, drawn, and quartered at Tyburn (London), March 7, 1544. For most of his life, Fr.

Larke was rector of St. Ethelburga's, Bishopsgate, London (1504–42). For some of that time he was rector of Woodford, Essex (1526–27). Chancellor (St.) Thomas MORE nominated him as rector of Chelsea, a position Larke held from March 29, 1530 until his attainder. He was indicted Feb. 15, 1543 for refusing to acknowledge the royal supremacy in spiritual matters. Charged with him were BB. Fr. John IRELAND, German GARDINER, and John HEYWOOD (who recanted on the hurdle). Their heads and quarters were buried under the gallows. He was beatified by Pope Leo XIII on Dec. 9, 1886.

Feast of the English Martyrs: May 4 (England); March 11 (Diocese of Brentwood).

See Also: ENGLAND, SCOTLAND, AND WALES, MARTYRS OF.

Bibliography: B. CAMM, ed., *Lives of the English Martyrs,* (New York 1904), I, 541–47. R. CHALLONER, *Memoirs of Missionary Priests,* ed. J. H. POLLEN (rev. ed. London 1924; repr. Farnborough 1969). J. H. POLLEN, *Acts of English Martyrs* (London 1891).

[K. I. RABENSTEIN]

LARKIN, JOHN

Jesuit, educator; b. Newcastle-on-Tyne, England, Feb. 2, 1801; d. New York City, Dec. 11, 1858. He was born of Irish parents who sent him at an early age to Ushaw College, Ushaw, England, where he studied under the noted historian, John Lingard. After a trip to India, Larkin entered the Seminary of Saint-Sulpice in Paris; he was ordained in 1827. About 1830 he went to teach philosophy at the Sulpician College in Montreal, Canada, and in 1841 he entered the Society of Jesus in Louisville, KY. In 1846 he came with his fellow Jesuits from Mt. St. Mary, KY, to staff St. John's College, Fordham, NY, founded five years before by Bp. John Hughes. Larkin served as vice president for a year and, in 1847, he was appointed president of a college that was being planned in New York City. Having borrowed the money to purchase a Protestant church, he opened a school in its basement, but the building was destroyed by fire on Jan. 22, 1848. While looking for another site, he received a letter from the archbishop of Quebec, informing him of his appointment to the See of Toronto. With the permission of his superior, Larkin went to Europe and successfully petitioned to have his designation as bishop rescinded. After making his third year of probation at Laon, France, he became president of St. John's College, Fordham, in 1851. He left St. John's in 1854 and went to England, where he was engaged in parochial work. In 1857, in the U.S., he served as parish priest at St. Francis Xavier's Church, New York City, where he died the following year.

Duke Francois-Alexandre-Frederic de La Rochefoucauld-Liancourt.

Bibliography: T. G. TAAFE, *A History of St. John's College, Fordham* (New York 1891).

[V. C. HOPKINS]

LA ROCHEFOUCAULD

An ancient French aristocratic family, originating in the town of La Rochefoucauld (Charente), well known since the 12th century and presently divided into three branches: the main branch of the La Rochefoucaulds and the families of the Ducs of Estisse and De Doudeauville.

François de, cardinal; b. Paris, Dec. 8, 1558; d. Sainte-Geneviève, Feb. 14, 1645. François, orphaned at the age of four by the death of his father on the battlefield, was reared by an uncle, Jean de la Rochefoucauld, Abbot of Marmoutier, and educated at the Jesuit College of Clermont. Appointed abbot of Tournus at the age of 15, he proved himself, despite his youth, an excellent ecclesiastical administrator. He finished his theological and classical education in Rome, and became bishop of Clermont (1584). Protestantism was very strong in his diocese, but the young bishop was successful in reconquering it fully for Catholicism. He did not participate in the religious wars of his age, but he refused to recognize HENRY IV as King of France till the latter's conversion to Catholicism. Subsequently, close relations were established between the bishop and the monarch. Bishop de La Rochefoucauld became cardinal on the personal intervention of Henry IV at Rome (1607). The cardinal was a deeply respected adviser to the court during the minority of Louis XIII. Appointed bishop of Senlis, he was sent to Rome as royal ambassador. As a diplomatist, he supported the decrees of the Council of Trent, with strong reservations, however, since he was deeply attached to the Gallican Church and the interests of the French monarchy. In 1618 he became great almoner of France, abbot of Sainte-Geneviève in 1619, and then president of the State Council. Two years later, he resigned as president, and consecrated himself to the reform of religious orders. He founded the Congregation of Sainte-Geneviève, known also as the Congregation of France. He was also vice dean of the College of Cardinals.

François de, litterateur, moralist, known first as the Prince of Marsillac; b. Paris, Sept. 15, 1613; d. Paris, March 17, 1680. As a youth, he participated in various military campaigns and in the continuous intrigues of his aristocratic world against Cardinal de Richelieu. He even played a part in the plot of Cinq-Mars. This was the beginning of a series of political adventures, plots, and rebellions first against Richelieu, then against Mazarin. During the Fronde, he unsuccessfully plotted the murder of Cardinal de Retz and, in the battle of the Faubourg of Saint-Antoine, he was seriously wounded and lost his eyesight for a short period. After 1653 La Rochefoucauld lived in retirement and devoted his time to writing his *Mémoires* and *Maximes morales*. The most celebrated and witty women of his age, Mmes. de Sablé, de Lafayette, and de Sévigné were his constant companions. Louis XIV showered him with royal favors. His *Mémoires* were first published in 1662 in Cologne, although the author disavowed this edition. This work, republished in 1817, is a revelation concerning the history of the Fronde. The original title of the *Maximes* is *Reflections ou sentences et maximes morales;* the Saint-Beuve edition (1853) is considered the best. Voltaire said that the *Maximes* with their high literary value, their deep intellectual honesty, and their precise style greatly contributed to the development of the French sense of taste.

Rochefoucauld-Bayers, François Joseph de la, Bl., bishop of Beauvais; b. Angoulême, March 28, 1755; d. Paris, Sept. 2, 1792. A representative of the clergy in the States General of 1789, he defended the privileges of the clergy and the court. Soon he and his brother Pierre Louis, Bishop of Senlis, were declared "enemies to the constitutional monarchy." The two prelates fled to their sister, the Abbess of Soissons (Marie-Charlotte de la Rochefoucauld). Unwilling to compromise their sister, they returned to Paris. There Rochefoucauld-Bayers, Bishop of Beauvais, was arrested and jailed in the infamous prison of Carmes. Soon his brother, the bishop of Senlis, was arrested also and detained in the same jail. Both were murdered during the general massacre of political prisoners on Sept. 2, 1792.

Feast: Sept. 2

Bibliography: G. DE LA ROCHEFOUCAULD, *Un Homme d'église et d'état. . .: Le Cardinal F. de la Rochefoucauld* (Paris 1926). M. BISHOP, *The Life and Adventures of Rochefoucauld* (Ithaca 1951). É. MAGNE, *Le Vrai visage de La Rochefoucauld* (Paris 1923). P. CARON, *Les Massacres de Septembre* (Paris 1935). *Acta Apostolicae Sedis* (1926) 415–425. S. SKALWEIT, *Lexikon für Theologie und Kirche*, ed. J. HOFER and K. RAHNER, 10 v. (2d, new ed. Freiburg 1957–65) 6:799–800.

[E. GONDA]

LA RUE, PIERRE DE

Renaissance church composer (called also Peter van Straten, Petrus de Vico, Pierchon); b. probably Tournai, Belgium, *c.* 1460; d. Courtrai, Nov. 20, 1518. He was a singer and member of the Brotherhood of Our Lady,'s Hertogenbosch (1489–92), and a chaplain and singer of the Burgundian-Hapsburg court at Brussels and Malines (1492–1516) where he served Maximilian of Austria, Philip the Fair, Margaret of Austria, and Charles V. He participated in many journeys of the court, including those to Spain in 1501–02 and 1506. In 1516 he took up residence at the chapter of Notre-Dame Cathedral, Courtrai, where he held a canonry, and died there. His known compositions include 31 Masses, 7 Mass movements, 7 Magnificats, 23 motets, and about 35 secular songs to French and Flemish texts. Most of his works survive in MS, among them splendidly illuminated choirbooks of the Netherlands court chapel and the Papal chapel. Petrucci printed a volume of five of his Masses, the *Misse Petri de la Rue* (Venice 1503).

La Rue's compositions are notable examples of Franco-Flemish polyphony and are distinguished by their rhythmic and contrapuntal intricacy and their great expressiveness. He was held in high regard by his royal employers and by fellow musicians, and his works continued to be cited in treatises throughout the 16th century. Most important are the Masses, among them a requiem for low voices, a six-part *Missa Ave sanctissima Maria* in triple canon (parodying a motet variously attributed to Verdelot and to La Rue himself), and two canonic Masses on the popular *cantus firmus, L'Homme armé.*

Bibliography: Modern eds. *Liber Missarum*, ed. A. TIRABASSI (Malines 1941), seven Masses from a MS in Royal Library, Brus-

sels. *Monumenta musicae Belgicae,* v. 8 *Drie missen,* ed. R. B. LEN-
AERTS and J. ROBIJNS (Antwerp 1960). *Documenta polyphoniae
liturgicae Sanctae Ecclesiae Romanae,* ed. L. FEININGER (Rome
1947–), ser. 1B, no. 1, one Mass. *Das Chorwerk,* ed. F. BLUME, v.
3 (1930), chansons; v. 11 (1931), Requiem; v. 91, motets. M. PICK-
ER, ed., *The Chanson Albums of Marguerite of Austria* (Berkeley
1965). J. ROBYNS, *Pierre de la Rue, circa 1460–1518: Een biobibliographische studie* (Brussels 1954). N. DAVISON, ''The Motets
of Pierre de la Rue,'' *Musical Quarterly* 48 (1962) 19–35. W. RUB-
SAMEN, *Die Musik in Geschichte und Gegenwart,* ed. F. BLUME
(Kassel-Basel 1949–) 8:225–239. G. REESE, *Music in the Renaissance* (rev. ed. New York 1959). N. DAVISON, ''*Absalom fili mi* Re-
considered,'' *Tidschrift van de Koninklijke Vereniging voor
Nederlandse Muziekgeschiedenis,* 46 (1996) 42–56. J. E. KREIDER,
''The Masses for Five and Six Voices by Pierre de la Rue'' (Ph.D.
diss. Indiana University 1974). H. MECONI, ''Style and Authenticity
in the Secular Music of Pierre de la Rue'' (Ph.D. diss. Harvard University 1986). D. M. RANDEL, ed., *The Harvard Biographical Dictionary of Music* (Cambridge, Mass. 1996) 485. N. SLONIMSKY, ed.,
Baker's Biographical Dictionary of Musicians (8th ed. New York
1992) 1012. M. STAEHELIN, ''Pierre de La Rue,'' in *The New Grove
Dictionary of Music and Musicians,* ed. S. SADIE, v. 10 (New York
1980) 473–476.

[M. PICKER]

LA SALETTE

Village in the Diocese of Grenoble, southeast
France. Since the apparition of the Blessed Virgin to two
children there on Sept. 19, 1846, it has been a major pilgrimage shrine. The apparition occurred while Melanie
Mathieu-Calvat, age 15, and Maximin Giraud, age 11,
poor peasants with almost no secular or religious education, were herding cows on a mountain above La Salette.
They were startled by the appearance in a globe of brilliant light of a beautiful Lady resplendently attired but
weeping. She gave them a message, which they could
hardly have invented, ''to all her people'': unless there
should be repentance from widespread religious apathy,
she would be forced to let fall the arm of her Son. The
children were told to pray, and each was entrusted with
a secret.

Initial disbelief in the apparition soon gave way. In
the glen where the episode had taken place a spring began
to flow, and miraculous cures associated with its waters
began to multiply. Bishop Philibert de Bruillard of Grenoble began a canonical inquiry of the children and the
miracles. After five years of silence he gave an official
judgment that the apparition had all the characteristics of
truth and that the faithful had grounds for believing in it,
inasmuch as the events could not be explained except by
divine intervention and the testimony of the miracles was
superior to men's objections. Devotion to Our Lady of La
Salette was therefore authorized. Subsequent popes since
Pius IX, to whom the children made known the secrets,
have confirmed La Salette and the cult. Leo XIII made

Bishop de Bruillard's church (1852–64) a minor basilica
(1879). A proper Mass and Office was granted in 1942.

From the first, objections had been raised by anticler-
icals, clerical liberals, and sincere people on grounds of
mendacity and the uncouth nature of the children; but the
objections ignored the exhaustive episcopal investigation. St. John VIANNEY, the Curé of Ars, who had accepted the account, interpreted an interview with Maximin as
a denial of the apparition; but, following two favors received through the intercession of Our Lady of La Salette, he publicly renewed his belief the year before his
death (1858). The fact that neither Maximin nor Melanie
subsequently became manifest saints led some people to
doubt the apparition, the authenticity of which is independent of the persons to whom it was revealed. ''Our Lady
left me as I was,'' said Maximin, who died a holy death
in nearby Corps at the age of 40. Melanie, who died in
1904, made several efforts to become a religious in Grenoble, Darlington (England), and Marseilles; in 1867 she
went to live in south Italy, returned to France (1884), and
again to south Italy, attending Mass daily. Neither Maximin nor Melanie ever repudiated any part of their account.

Bibliography: L. J. AUBIN, ''La Salette,'' *Catholic Encyclope-
dia* Suppl. II (New York 1922). L. CARLIER, *Histoire de
l'apparition de la Mère de Dieu sur la montagne de La Salette*
(Paris 1941). J. JAOUEN, *La Grace de La Salette* (Paris 1946). J.
BEEVERS, *The Sun Her Mantle* (Westminster, Md. 1953). J. S. KEN-
NEDY, *Light on the Mountain* (New York 1953). L. BASSETTE, *Le
Fait de La Salette* (Paris 1955). W. B. ULLATHORNE, *The Holy
Mountain of La Salette* (4th ed. London 1855).

[H. M. GILLETT]

LA SALETTE, MISSIONARIES OF OUR LADY OF

(MS, Official Catholic Directory #0720); a congregation of priests and brothers devoted to preaching missions and retreats, conducting shrines and centers of
devotion to Our Lady, working in the foreign missions,
and caring for parishes.

Beginnings. The Missionaries of Our Lady of La Salette had their origin in the group of diocesan priests organized in 1852 by Bp. Philibert de Bruillard of Grenoble,
France, to serve at the church being erected on the mountain of La Salette, on the spot of the apparition of the
Blessed Virgin Sept. 19, 1846. The first three members,
P. Burnoud, M. Sibillat, and A. Denaz, began their work
in May 1852 and were joined the following spring by P.
Bonvallet and P. Archier. Although Denaz was the first
to express a desire for religious life, he died before the
first profession, when six of his companions took their

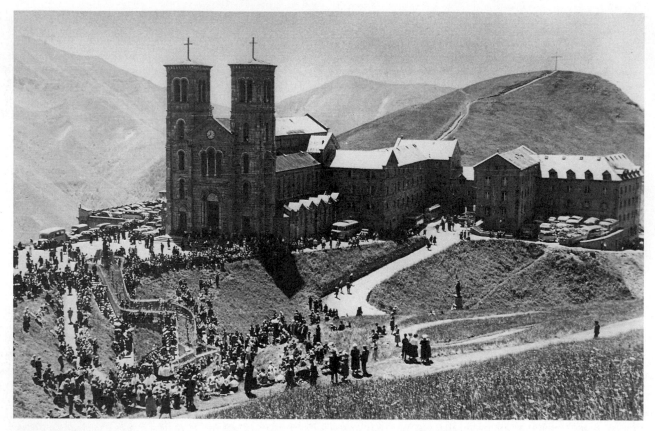

Exterior of pilgrimage church, La Salette, southeast France.

vows on Feb. 2, 1858, the foundation day of the congregation.

The first rule was merely an outline drawn up by the vicar-general of the diocese; however, Revs. Sylvain Giraud and Pierre Archier soon crystallized the nature, purpose, and spirit of the congregation. Giraud, who had entered the congregation in November 1858 and was appointed novice master in 1862, wrote *La Pratique de la Dévotion à Notre Dame de la Salette* (1863) and *De la Vie d'Union avec Marie* (1864). His books embodied the spirit and spirituality of the congregation. Between 1858 and 1876, however, two tendencies developed within the community—one for a contemplative, Trappist-like life, and the other for an active apostolate. A chapter in 1876, which elected Archier as superior, firmly oriented the congregation toward the active apostolate.

Development. In 1876 Archier opened a minor seminary and sought the approval of Rome for the congregation. LEO XIII gave the first decree of approbation in May 1879; the rule was finally approved in 1926. In June 1880 the first band of missionaries left for Norway, and five years later, three of the group were ordained, the first in Norway since the Reformation. In 1881 the major seminary was moved to Switzerland and in 1896 to Rome.

Two priests were sent to the U.S. in 1892 to begin a foundation at Hartford, Conn.; in 1899 missionaries departed for Madagascar.

In 1901, when all French foundations were lost to the congregation through governmental legislation, the care of the basilica and the pilgrimage on the mountain of La Salette reverted to the bishop. After World Wars I and II, however, the former foundations were reestablished and new ones begun; the fathers returned to La Salette in 1943. The first foundation in Rome dates from 1896, when some seminarians were sent there to complete their studies.

American Foundations. In 1902 at the request of Bp. Thomas Beaven of Springfield, Mass., five Swiss priests were sent to Cracow, Poland, to learn the language to prepare them to minister to Polish immigrants in the U.S. This led to a Polish province and foundations in the U.S. and Argentina.

Bp. Lawrence McMahon welcomed the two priests who were sent to Hartford, where a number of priests, seminarians, and lay brothers joined them. Encouraged by the hierarchy, the U.S. province also entered actively into parish work. In 1937 the mission territory of Arakan,

Burma (eventually also the Prome-Thayetmyo district) was given to its care. In 1927 the basis for a new province was laid with the purchase of property in Enfield, N.H., to serve as a minor seminary for the French-speaking in New England and Canada. In 1958 the western part of the U.S., two foundations of the Polish province (Olivet, Ill., and Milwaukee, Wis.), and five in Canada, was established as a separate province, with provincial residence at St. Louis, Mo.

The generalate is in Rome. There are three provinces in the U.S.: the Province of Our Lady of Seven Dolors (1934) with its headquarters in Hartford, Conn.; the Province of the Immaculate Heart of Mary (1945) with its headquarters in Attleboro, Mass.; the Province of Mary Queen (1958) with its headquarters in St Louis, Mo.; and the Province of Mary, Queen of Peace (1967) with its headquarters in Twin Lakes, Wis.

Bibliography: J. JAOUEN, *Les Missionnaires de Notre Dame de la Salette* (Les Grands Ordres Monastiques et Instituts Religieux 43; Paris 1953). J. P. O'REILLY, *The Story of La Salette* (Chicago 1953). L. BASSETTE, *Le Fait de la Salette* (Paris 1955).

[J. A. LEFRANCOIS/EDS.]

Bp. Philibert de Bruillard.

LA SALLE, ROBERT CAVELIER DE

French explorer; b. Rouen, France, Nov. 22, 1643; d. Texas, March 19, 1687. In 1658 he went to Paris, where he became a Jesuit novice, but finding himself unsuited to this kind of life, he left the society. He sailed for New France (1666), arriving at Montreal, where the Sulpicians granted him a seigneury on the island of Montreal, which he named Saint Sulpice in honor of his benefactors; Saint Sulpice later became the town of La Chine. La Salle's curiosity was aroused by the natives' tales of a great river to the southwest that flowed, no one knew how far, in a southerly direction. He spent two years learning eight Native American dialects and gaining practical experience with French homesteaders and native hunters in the Canadian terrain. In 1668 he approached Gov. Rémy Courcelle and the intendant, Jean Baptiste Talon, who authorized a trip for exploration, but advanced no funds and delegated no authority to draw upon state resources for any assistance. Unlike J. Cartier, La Salle had to finance his own exploring ventures; he obtained funds for the journey by selling to the Sulpicians the land they had given him earlier. At Courcelle's suggestion, the Sulpicians under Dollier de Casson sent a few of their number with La Salle to preach to the Native Americans. After exploring the Ohio River, the French penetrated into Lake Michigan and discovered the upper Illinois River. In 1672 La Salle was sent out by L. de B. Frontenac, governor of New France, to arrange a meeting with the native tribes. It was held the following summer on the site of present-day Kingston, Ontario, at the junction of Lake Ontario and the St. Lawrence River, where Frontenac advised the tribes of his intentions to build a fort and trading post. La Salle was made commandant (1673) of the fort, named after Frontenac, and, after receiving a patent of nobility from Louis XIV, began (1675) to develop it as a trading post. In the autumn of 1677 he returned to France to obtain sanction for a proposed expedition in search of the Mississippi; he received authorization to erect at his own expense two forts, one at the mouth of the Niagara and one at the southern extremity of Lake Michigan. In return for these efforts, Louis XIV granted him exclusive right of the buffalo hide trade in the Mississippi region.

After his return to Fort Frontenac (1678), La Salle set out on his second trip of exploration, during which he succeeded (1682) in descending the Mississippi from its junction with the Illinois to the Gulf of Mexico at present-day New Orleans. He took possession of the whole area, which he named Louisiana. When he returned to France (1683) and discovered that war between Spain and France was imminent, he recognized that, since Spanish-controlled Mexico was relatively close to the regions he had recently penetrated, New Orleans could serve as a strategic base for military operations against Mexico.

Moreover, the northern portion of Mexico contained rich gold and silver mines that would greatly increase French wealth. At Versailles, on April 14, 1684, Louis XIV sanctioned La Salle's plan and gave some state aid to the enterprise, which, however, met with trouble from the outset. La Salle was unsuccessful in his attempt to locate the mouth of the Mississippi by sailing from France directly to the Gulf of Mexico, and his four ships carrying potential settlers finally landed on the southern coast of Texas. The captains of the ships refused to cooperate with the unfortunate La Salle, who was shot and killed on March 19, 1687. The settlers fell victims to the natives, who spared only the children, who later were adopted by the Spaniards in Mexico. Of the 300 people who had set out from France on July 24, 1685, only five escaped the natives and made their way to New France.

La Salle's expeditions did not enjoy the full support of the French government, which was more interested in a thorough development of the St. Lawrence area and felt that exploration took men away from this goal. Despite this, the famous explorer added to European knowledge of North America and greatly extended French sovereignty there.

Bibliography: P. CHESNEL, *History of Cavelier de La Salle, 1643–1687: Explorations in the Valleys of the Ohio, Illinois and Mississippi,* tr. A. C. MEANY (New York 1932). W. J. ECCLES, *Frontenac: The Courtier Governor* (Toronto 1959). *The Encyclopedia of Canada,* ed. W. S. WALLACE, 6 v. (Toronto 1935–37) 6:75–76. L. V. JACKS, *La Salle* (New York 1931). F. PARKMAN, *The Discovery of the Great West* (Toronto 1962). *Royal Fort Frontenac,* comp. and tr. R. A. PRESTON (Toronto 1958). J. L. RUTLEDGE, *Century of Conflict: The Struggle between the French and British in Colonial America* (Can. Hist. Ser. 2; Garden City, N.Y. 1956).

[F. BOLAND]

LASANCE, FRANCIS XAVIER

Writer of Catholic devotional works; b. Cincinnati, Ohio, Jan. 24, 1860; d. there, Dec. 11, 1946. After education at Xavier College, Cincinnati, and St. Meinrad Abbey, Ind., he was ordained May 24, 1883, by Abp. William Henry ELDER of Cincinnati. During the next seven years Lasance served as curate and pastor at Kenton, Reading, Dayton, Lebanon, and Monroe—all in the Cincinnati Archdiocese. Poor health forced him to give up parish work in 1890; from then until his death he lived a retired, semi-invalid existence, writing numerous devotional works on the Mass and the Eucharist; editing and compiling several missals; and publishing numerous spiritual books, especially for religious and children. He was the author of about 30 works, including *Thoughts on the Religious Life* (1907), *My Prayer Book* (1913), *Reflec-*

tions for Religious (1920), *Our Lady Book* (1924), and *New Missal for Every Day* (1932).

[J. Q. FELLER]

LAS CASAS, BARTOLOMÉ DE

Spanish Dominican author and "Apostle to the Indians"; b. Seville, 1474; d. Madrid, 1566. The son of a merchant who had accompanied Columbus on his second voyage, Las Casas himself went to America in 1502 with Governor Ovando, and was ordained in Española. After his own experience as an encomendero in Cuba, he gave up colonizing to undertake the reform of a colonial system whose inhumanity disgusted him. From 1515 to 1522 both in Spain and in America, he tried to win approval for a series of projects that, without ignoring the just interests of the Crown and of good colonists, would lead to the elimination of the disastrous practices of the encomienda system and military conquest and would foster peaceful colonization and the Christianization of the native tribes. The results hardly came up to his hope and when his last attempt, thwarted by circumstances and his own imprudence, ended bloodily, Las Casas withdrew from society and entered the Dominican Order (1523).

After a long retreat, which gave him the opportunity to study theology and to plan his great works, Las Casas resolutely resumed his interrupted activity, directing his efforts toward evangelical conquest. He played a decisive role in the defeat of the rebel cacique Enriquillo in Española; he attempted a missionary venture, opposed by the authorities, in an unpacified area of Nicaragua; and, above all, he laid careful plans for a peaceful entry into Guatemala—in Tezulutlán, the Land of War. In Spain after 1540, Las Casas devoted himself to far-reaching demands for reform that produced some favorable results. As implacable in his accusations as he was fertile and persuasive in his suggestion for remedies, he is considered primarily responsible for the famous New Laws of 1542–43, which reorganized the Council of the Indies, established new *audiencias,* provided for the gradual suppression of the encomienda system, prohibited enslavement of native peoples, and decreed new regulations for discoveries and conquests. These laws were not a complete success, and the colonial world opposed them strongly. As bishop of Chiapa, Las Casas returned to America in 1544 to take part in the struggle himself. He did not even succeed in enforcing the New Laws in his own diocese, but received a slightly warmer reception from the natives of the "Land of War," where he and his fellow DOMINICANS founded a mission called Vera Paz.

His final return to Spain in 1547 did not mean retirement for the tireless old man. About 1550 he engaged in

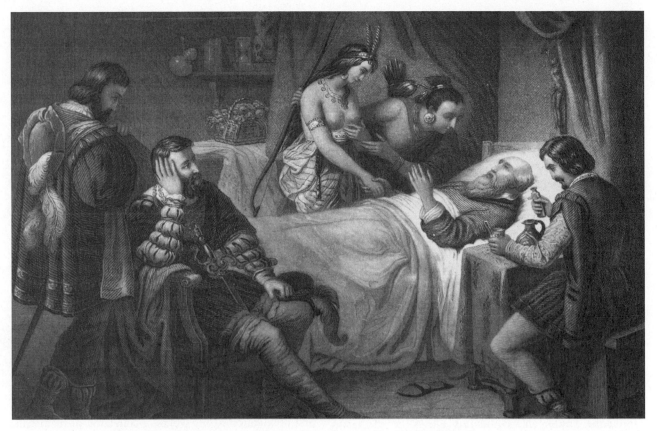

Bartolomé de Las Casas is visited by two native converts in this early engraving. (Archive Photos)

his famous controversy with Sepúlveda on the question of wars of conquest in the Indies. Some years later he was actively opposing the continuation of the encomienda system, and up until his death he was the zealous advocate of the native peoples, seeking redress of their grievances. During these last years, as well as earlier in his career, his chief weapon was his pen. His extensive writings were all connected with his reform projects. He wrote three major works: *De unico vocationis modo,* a Latin treatise on the theory of the evangelical conquest; *Apologética historia,* a detailed description of the abilities of native peoples; and *Historia de Las Indias*; a condemnation of 30 years of poor colonial policy. He wrote also many doctrinal treatises, letters, memorials, and pamphlets, of which the most famous, *Brevísima relación de la destrucción de las Indias,* is also the most stern indictment of the cruelty of the CONQUISTADORES. Because of its sensationalism it was immediately translated into other languages and widely circulated. It was in large part responsible for the development of the "Black Legend," the consequences of which still exist and have fallen back in part upon Las Casas himself. Despite this, history must note the human compassion in Las Casas's ideals.

Bibliography: *Obras escogidas,* ed. J. PÉREZ DE TUDELA BUESO, 5 v. (Madrid 1957–58). R. MENÉNDEZ PIDAL, *El padre las Casas, su doble personalidad* (Madrid 1963). M. M. MARTINEZ, *Fray Bartolomé de las Casas: Padre de América* (Madrid 1958). M. GIMÉNEZ FERNÁNDEZ, *Bartolomé de las Casas,* 2 v. (Seville 1953–60). L. HANKE, *The Spanish Struggle for Justice in the Conquest of America* (Philadelphia 1949). H. R. WAGNER and H. R. PARISH, *The Life and Writings of Bartolomé de las Casas* (Albuquerque, NM 1967). J. FRIEDE and B. KEEN, *Bartolomé de las Casas in History: Toward an Understanding of the Man and His Work* (De Kalb, Ill. 1971). G. GUTIÉRREZ, *Las Casas: In Search of the Poor of Poor of Jesus Christ* (Maryknoll, N.Y. 1993).

[A. SAINT-LU/EDS.]

ŁASKI, JAN AND JAN (LASCO)

Uncle and nephew. Jan, chancellor and primate of Poland; b. Łaski, Poland, 1456; d. Kalisz, Poland, May 19, 1531. After completing his education in Poland and abroad, he held various spiritual offices, becoming chancellor in 1503. In 1505 he compiled the "Łaski Statutes," the first official edition of Polish law. In 1510 he became archbishop of Gniezno, and thereby, primate of Poland. An ardent foe of the TEUTONIC KNIGHTS, he sought to annex East Prussia to Poland. At the Fifth LATERAN COUNCIL he defended Poland's rights to Prussia, at which time Pope Leo X conferred upon him and his successors in the archiespiscopal See of Gniezno the title of *legatus natus.* At Łaski's request Pope Leo X ordered the grand master of the Teutonic Knights to pay homage to the king of Poland. He later opposed the Peace of Cracow (1525), by which the grand master, in return for this homage, received the king's recognition of the secularization of Prussia. From 1526 onward, Łaski's influence at court began to decline. Toward the end of his life, he was suspected of aiding the Turks through his nephew Jerome. In 1530 Pope Clement VII ordered him to Rome to explain his actions, but he was prevented from leaving the country by King Sigismund. Łaski was a vigorous foe of Lutheranism. Even before the COUNTER REFORMATION, which began in Poland under his aegis, he laid particular stress on the need for Church reform, especially in the selection and training of parochial clergy and in the general enlightenment of the faithful. Throughout his life he stressed discipline, morals, and clerical zeal. He edited a number of editions of canonical decrees and statutes.

Jan, religious reformer, nephew of the above Jan; b. Łaski, Poland, 1499; d. Pinczów, Jan. 8, 1560. He began his early education at Cracow under the guidance of his uncle and later studied in Rome and Bologna. He was ordained in 1521. From 1524 to 1526, he traveled throughout western Europe and befriended Huldrych ZWINGLI, Guillaume FAREL and Desiderius ERASMUS; the last-mentioned left him his library. On the death of his uncle (1531), he returned to western Europe, residing principally in Frankfurt and Liège, where he came further under the influence of the Protestants and where he later married. He was then appointed superintendent of Church affairs in Emden, in East Friesland, which he quickly turned into a "northern Geneva" and where he established one of the first compulsory educational systems in Europe. The Emden catechism was in great part his work. In 1550 he accepted the invitation of Thomas CRANMER to visit England, where he became the head of the congregation of Protestant refugees of Austin Friars in London. In this position, he influenced the development of Puritanism, and to a lesser degree that of Anglicanism. On the accession of Mary Tudor, he settled in Denmark, then in Emden, and eventually in Frankfurt. From Frankfurt he addressed three letters to King Sigismund August and to the Polish nobility, in which he called upon them to introduce the Reformation into Poland. At the request of the Polish Calvinists, he was permitted to return to Poland, where he unsuccessfully sought to win the king and the Lutherans to Calvinism. He settled in Little Poland, where he quickly became the head of the Calvinists. He spent his last years in organizing schools and in improving existing translations of the Bible.

Bibliography: H. DALTON. *John A. Lasco* (London 1936). B. STASIEWSKI, *Reformation und Gegenreformation in Polen* (Münster 1960); *Lexikon für Theologie und Kirche,* ed. J. HOFER and K. RAHNER, 10 v. (2d, new ed. Freiburg 1957–65) 6:803–804. v. FALKENROTH, *Die Religion in Geschichte und Gegenwart,* 7 v. (3d ed. Tübingen 1957–65) 4:236.

[E. KUSIELEWICZ]

LASSO, ORLANDO DI

Distinguished Renaissance polyphonist of the Franco-Flemish tradition; b. Mons (Hainaut), Flanders, 1530 or 1532 (evidence favors 1532); d. Munich, June 14,1594. The original name was probably Roland de Lassus, Latinized as Orlandus Lassus, but the composer himself preferred the Italian form. After being choirboy at St. Nicholas in Mons, at age 12 he was brought to the court at Palermo and later to Milan by Ferdinand Gonzaga, Viceroy of Sicily. From 18 to 21 he was in the service of the Marquis of Terza at Naples, and in 1553 was appointed choirmaster at St. John Lateran in Rome, which position he held for a little more than a year. At that time he must have become acquainted with PALESTRINA, then choirmaster at the Julian Chapel and in 1555 Lasso's successor at the Lateran. After visits to England and France, he spent two years (1555–56) in Antwerp supervising the first publication of his works, a collection of madrigals, chansons, and motels that display remarkable versatility and accomplishment. Called to the Bavarian court of Albert V at Munich in 1556, he served in the ducal chapel as a tenor singer and then, after 1563, as chapelmaster. In 1558 he married Regina Wäckinger, who gave him four sons and two daughters. He was knighted in 1570 by Maximilian II, and in 1574 by Pope Gregory XIII. That same year he was offered a post at the French court by Charles IX, but the offer was quickly voided by the king's death later that year. Among Lasso's Munich pupils was Giovanni GABRIELI, who served and studied under him from 1575 to 1579. Lasso's later years were darkened by ill health and melancholia.

Lasso was one of the most prolific of major composers. Of some 1,250 known works, his most important are the motets, which constitute about half the total and rank him, along with Josquin DESPREZ and Palestrina, among the greatest Renaissance masters. He also composed over 50 Masses, more than 100 Magnificats, four Passions, and a wide variety of liturgical pieces. His hundreds of Italian, French, and German songs include many excellent examples of their kind. Lasso's style is rooted in the expressive, firmly wrought polyphony of his older countrymen, Desprez and Jacobus CLEMENS NON PAPA. It appears fully matured in his *Primo Libro de Motetti* (Antwerp 1555), wherein not only his mastery of imitative polyphony for five and six voices is displayed, but also a remarkable sensitivity to the text and ability to express it through music. Influence of the chromatic experiments of RORE and VICENTINO is revealed in the early *Prophetiae Sibyllarum.* His style is identified with *musica reservata* (music "reserved" for the understanding of connoisseurs) by his humanist friend Samuel Quickelberg in commenting on the composer's monumental cycle of penitential psalms. On the whole, Lasso's music is more harmonically oriented than Palestrina's, and is more apt to display dramatic and extraordinary effects that anticipate the baroque idiom.

Most of Lasso's Masses are parodies based on motets, madrigals, and chansons by himself and others. His Masses, unlike his motets, cannot compare with Palestrina's for richness of invention and spiritual power. As Lasso aged, the exuberance and harmonic color of his earlier work gave way to a more austere, somber style "affording a profounder pleasure to the mind and ear," as he wrote in the preface to his last motet collection (1593). His final work, the cycle of spiritual madrigals *Lagrime di S. Pietro* (1595), illustrates the introspection of his late style. In 1604 Lasso's sons, Rudolph and Ferdinand, brought out virtually the entire corpus of his motets as the *Magnus opus musicum.* This served as the basis for the *Sämtliche Werke* of which 21 of a projected 60 volumes were published.

See Also: LITURGICAL MUSIC, HISTORY OF, 4

Bibliography: *Sämtliche Werke,* ed. F. X. HABERL and A. SANDBERGER, 21 v. (Leipzig 1894–1926), motets and most of the secular music; Neue Reihe (new ed. Kassel 1961–64), 4 v. to date, containing miscellaneous motets and secular pieces, the 4 Passions, and 17 Masses; *Septem Psalmi poenitentiales,* ed. H. BÄUERLE (Leipzig 1906); *Lagrime di S. Pietro,* ed. H. J. THERSTAPPEN, in *Das Chorwerk,* ed. F. BLUME, 34, 37, 41 (Wolfenbüttel 1936); *Prophetiae Sibyllarum* (ibid.) 48 (1937); *Musica Sacra,* ed. F. COMMER, v. 5–12 (Regensburg 1839–87), Masses and liturgical pieces. W. BOETTICHER, *Orlando di Lasso und seine Zeit, 1532–1594* (Kassel 1958–); *Die Musik in Geschichte und Gegenwart,* ed. F. BLUME (Kassel-Basel 1949–) 8:251–292. E. LOWINSKY, *Das Antwerpener Motettenbuch Orlando di Lasso's . . .* (The Hague 1937). J. R. MILNE, *Grove's Dictionary of Music and Musicians,* ed. E. BLOM, 9 v. (5th ed. London 1954) 5: 59–82. G. REESE, *Music in the Renaissance* (rev. ed. New York 1959). D. CROOK, *Orlando di Lasso's Imitation Magnificats for Counter- Reformation Munich* (Princeton, N.J. 1994). R. FREEDMAN, "The Lassus Chansons and Their Protestant Listeners of the Late Sixteenth Century," *Musical Quarterly,* 82 (1998) 564–585. F. KÖRNDLE, "Lassos Musik zum *Vltimum Judicium,*" *Die Musikforschung,* 53 (2000) 68–70. M. LESSOIL-DAELMAN, "Les jeux numériques dans les *Psaumes de la Pénitence* de Lassus," *Revue Belge de Musicologie,* 49 (1995) 47–78. H. LEUCHTMANN, "Orlando di Lassos Bußpsalmen," *Musik und Kirche,* 66 (1996) 273–278. D. R. MELAMED, "Who Wrote Lassus's Most Famous Piece?," *Early Music,* 26 (1998) 6–22. J. T. WINEMILLER, "Lasso, Albrecht V, and the Figure of Job: Speculation on the History and Function of Lasso's *Sacrae lectiones ex propheta Iob* and Vienna Mus. Ms. 18.744," *Journal of Musicological Research,* 12 (1993) 273–302.

[M. PICKER]

Orlando di Lasso. (©Bettmann/CORBIS)

LASSO DE LA VEGA, RAFAEL

Bishop in Gran Colombia during the independence period; b. Santiago de Veraguas, Panama, Oct. 21, 1764; d. Quito, Ecuador, April 6, 1831. He belonged to an honorable family. He was educated in the seminaries of Panama and Santafé de Bogotá, in whose University of Santo Tomás he received a doctorate in canon law. He was ordained in 1792 and served in a parish in Bogotá, teaching at the same time in the university as professor of Latin. He became canon of the metropolitan cathedral of Bogotá and of the cathedral of Panama. Ferdinand VII presented him as bishop of Mérida, and he was confirmed by the papal bull of March 8, 1815. As an appointment of the restored Ferdinand VII, Lasso de la Vega worked against the independence movement and suspended priests who supported it. However, when the break with Spain was accomplished, he changed his position and supported the victorious Bolívar. In 1821, after the signing of the Constitution of Cúcuta, he left his congregation in Mérida and took an active part in the legislative work of the new republic of Colombia. He was a senator in 1823–24 and was selected vice president of the Congress. He undertook to promote contacts between the new nation and the Roman Curia. His letter to Pius VII of Oct. 20, 1821, on the political events in the New World, revealed the problems of the American revolution to the pope and was the

Mosaic of the Last Supper, 6th century, S. Apollinare Nuovo, Ravenna.

beginning of diplomatic relations between the Vatican and the new republics. In 1828, on the petition of the president of Colombia, he was promoted by Leo XII to the bishopric of Quito.

[E. J. CASTILLERO]

LAST SUPPER, ICONOGRAPHY OF

Symbolic representations of the Last Supper appear in the earliest Christian art. Aside from these, the iconography of the Last Supper usually takes the form of one of three scenes: the washing of the feet of the Apostles; the discovery of the treachery of Judas; and the Communion of the Apostles.

Symbolic Representations. Until the Edict of Milan (313), virtually all references to the New Testament in the art of the CATACOMBS are symbolic. Representations of the Last Supper, however, are unusually abundant in the catacomb of St. Callisto, Rome (early 3d century). The fish and bread are shown together, sometimes filling a tripod. During this period, in the same underground cemetery, seven places provided with bread and fish are shown spaced out around the table. It is, on the one hand, an exact recollection of the *refrigerium* or funerary meal and, on the other, a reference to the Eucharist, though not to the Last Supper. In the famous Greek chapel of the Roman catacomb of Priscilla, one of the guests is already shown (*c.* 150; *see* AGAPE) making the gesture of *fractio panis*; the figure, however, is not to be interpreted as that

of Christ. As soon as the Church attained its freedom, references to the Last Supper become more explicit. In a colonnaded sarcophagus (350–380; Musée Lapidaire Chrétien, Arles), Christ is in the midst of six Apostles, the two closest of whom offer him bread and fish. The symbolic articles survived beyond the art of the catacombs. In Rome on the bas-relief of the door of S. Sabina (*c.* 425–430) Christ is represented twice. In the upper part He is shown blessing seven baskets of bread, and in the lower portion, He is blessing seven pitchers of wine.

The Washing of the Feet. The first of the three scenes (Jn 13.1–17) is very important, since it prefigures the Sacrament of Penance and appropriately precedes that of the Eucharist, or Communion. This purification of the Apostles, sometimes referred to as the "Baptism of the Apostles," constituted a theme that was perfect for the decoration of lavabos in the sacristy and the cloister (1705, wood lavabo by Giovanni Giuliani; Cistercian Abbey, Heiligenkreuz). In this scene, Christ remains standing in Byzantine art (6th-century evangeliary, archbishop's residence, Rossano; 11th-century mosaic, Daphni), whereas in Western art he customarily kneels before Peter (12th-century cloister capital, Moissac; façade relief, St.-Gilles-du-Gard). Though the washing of the feet has never been a very popular scene in Christian iconography, nevertheless it persisted long after the Council of Trent. Later representations include those of Claude Vignon (1653, Nantes Museum), Jean-Honoré Fragonard (1754, cathedral of Grasse), and Ford Madox Brown (1852; Tate Gallery, London).

The Treachery of Judas. The discovery of the treachery of Judas has been widely represented in Western art. It permitted, in every case, the most incisive psychological study and the most dramatic setting (1495–97; fresco by Leonardo da Vinci, S. Maria delle Grazie, Milan). A few rare examples show Christ and his disciples standing (late 13th century; central tympanum, west façade, cathedral of Strasbourg). In the art of the first millennium of our era, the C-shaped table perpetuated the memory of the Roman triclinium (520–530, mosaic, San Apollinare Nuovo, Ravenna; 6th-century evangeliary, Rossano). This arrangement of the triclinium does not reappear until much later, under the influence of archeological preoccupations (1678, painting by Jean Baptiste de Champaigne; Lyons Museum). Beginning in the Romanesque period, the guests are seated around a rectangular table; Christ commonly occupies the center of the long side, and Judas, isolated, is opposite him. Judas is identified by one or more of the following characteristics: in the vast majority of cases he holds a purse; frequently he holds his hand toward the plate or swallows the piece of bread, dipped in wine, which Christ extends to him (1394, panel painting by Bertram de Minden; Hanover

Last Supper, late-13th-century sculpture, detail of the west facade tympanum, Cathedral at Strasbourg, Germany.

Museum). At this precise moment, the devil sometimes enters into his mouth in the form of a toad or a red winged creature, in order to illustrate the words of St. John: *tunc introivit in eum Satanas* (*c.* 1215, Psalter of Blanche of Castille; Bibliothèque de l'Arsenal, Paris); or he steals a fish, proof of his gluttony (1181; ambo of Nicholas of Verdun, Klosterneuberg). In contrast to the bright haloes of the other Apostles, that of Judas is black or absent (1305, fresco by Giotto; Scrovegni Chapel, Padua). Titian was the first to place the table on a slant, to suggest a much greater depth (*c.* 1544; Ducal Palace, Urbino). Accepting this ingenious arrangement, Tintoretto plunged the scene into darkness pierced with difficulty by a flaring lamp (1594; S. Giorgio Maggiore, Venice).

Communion of the Apostles. The Communion of the Apostles is a theme especially well represented in Byzantine art (Gospel Book of Rabbula, 586; Laurentian Library, Florence). Christ is represented twice, since six Apostles advance toward him to receive the bread and six others to receive the wine; all are standing. In Western art, Christ is represented once and He alone remains standing. The Apostles kneel, and the Virgin also, if she is present. Among the rare examples may be cited a fresco by Fra Angelico (1432–42; Convent of St. Mark, Flor-

ence), a panel by Justus of Ghent (1474; Pinacoteca, Urbino), and a fresco by Luca Signorelli (1512, Cortona cathedral). Western artists have sometimes evoked the institution of the Eucharist by means of the blessing of the bread and of the wine (Consecration). This is the case with Dirk Bouts (1464–70; church of St. Peter, Louvain), who enriched the theme by means of four prefigurations borrowed from the Old Testament: the sacrifice of Melchisedec to Abraham, the harvest of the manna in the desert, Elijah comforted by an angel, and the Jewish Passover.

Bibliography: O. SCHMITT, ed., *Reallexikon zur deutschen Kunstgeschichte* (Stuttgart 1933–). M. VLOBERG, *L'Eucharistie dans l'art* (Grenoble 1946). E. H. KANTOROWICZ, "Baptism of the Apostles," *Dumbarton Oaks Papers* 9–10 (1956) 205–251. L. RÉAU, *Iconographie de l'art chrétien*, 6 v. (Paris 1955–59) 2.2.

[V. DENIS]

LASUÉN, FERMÍN FRANCISCO DE

Franciscan missionary; b. Vitoria, Cantabria, Spain, June 7, 1736; d. Carmel, Calif., June 27, 1803. He was the son of Lorenzo and María Francisca (de Arasqueta) de Lasuén. He became a Franciscan (1751) and as a deacon volunteered for the missions of the New World. Upon arriving in Mexico (1759), he entered the Apostolic College of San Fernando. After serving the missions of the Sierra Gorda (1762–67), he went to Baja California until 1773, building the mission of San Borjas. Traveling overland to the missions of Upper California, Lasuén reached San Diego (1773) and was assigned to Mission San Gabriel until 1775, when he became the personal chaplain to Commander Rivera at Monterey. Fray J. Serra sent him to found Mission San Juan Capistrano, but his assignment there was cut short by the Native American revolt at San Diego. After the restoration of peace he was placed in charge of San Diego until 1785, when he was chosen president of the missions of Upper California, with headquarters at Mission San Carlos, Carmel. Between 1786 and 1798, Lasuén founded nine missions, bringing the total established since 1769 to 18. He was vicar forane, ecclesiastical judge, and military vicar for the bishop of Sonora, in whose jurisdiction California lay, and from 1795 he was commissary of the Holy Office of the Inquisition. Under Lasuén the number of missionaries increased from 18 to 40; between 1784 and 1802 baptisms rose from 5,800 to 33,717, and the number of converts living at the missions, from 4,646 to 15,562. Mission buildings increased, and stone churches such as San Carlos and San Gabriel were erected.

Though adhering to principles, Lasuén was diplomatic in his relationships with the civil and military authorities. The explorers G. Vancouver, J. P. Lapérouse, and C. Malaspina, who met him at Monterey, proclaimed him a model padre and president. Their combined appraisal of him, together with that of later historians such as G. Bancroft and C. E. Chapman, show Lasuén to have been a pious, learned, agreeable, dignified, unobtrusive, and benevolent apostle, who through the quiet force of his character built up the missions spiritually, economically, and architecturally. His numerous writings were confined to missions matters and are concise in style. Lasuén is interred at Carmel Mission church.

See Also: CALIFORNIA, CATHOLIC CHURCH IN; SAN FRANCISCO, ARCHDIOCESE OF.

Bibliography: Archives, Santa Barbara Mission. Archives, Archdiocese of San Francisco. Archivo General de la Nación, Mexico City. Missions San Gabriel, San Diego, and San Carlos, Calif., Church Registers. H. H. BANCROFT, *History of California,* 7 v. (San Francisco 1884–90). C. E. CHAPMAN, *A History of California: The Spanish Period* (New York 1928). Z. ENGELHARDT, *The Missions and Missionaries of California,* 4 v. (2d ed. San Francisco 1929); *San Diego Mission* (San Francisco 1920). M. J. GEIGER, *The Life and Times of Fray Junípero Serra,* 2 v. (Washington 1959). F. KENNEALLY, *Writings of Fermín Francisco de Lasuén,* 2 v. (Washington 1965).

[M. GEIGER]

LAS VEGAS, DIOCESE OF

From 1931 to the establishment of the Diocese of Las Vegas (*Dioecesis Campensis*) in 1995, all the state of Nevada was in the jurisdiction of the Diocese of Reno. In October 1976, Pope Paul VI, in recognition of the growth in population and importance of the southern part of the state where the majority of Catholics lived, redesignated it as the diocese as Reno-Las Vegas. In 1995 when Pope John Paul II re-formed Reno as a separate diocese, Bishop Daniel Walsh who had been bishop of Reno-Las Vegas was appointed to the new diocese of Las Vegas. In May 2000 Bishop Walsh was transferred to the diocese of Santa Rosa and a year later Joseph A. Pepe was installed in Guardian Angel Cathedral as the second bishop of Las Vegas.

The Las Vegas diocese consists of Nevada's five southernmost counties. The diocesan newspaper is the *Desert Clarion.* It is a suffragan see of the Province of San Francisco.

[M. CUNNINGHAM]

LATEAU, LOUISE

Stigmatic; b. Bois d'Haine, Belgium, Jan. 29, 1850; d. there, Aug. 25, 1883. She came of poor parents. Her health seems to have been good until she was savaged by a cow when she was 13. From that time she suffered successively from abscesses, throat trouble, neuralgic pains, and blood-spitting and was several times believed to be dying. She also began to have visions, and in 1868 she was gradually stigmatized, the wounds in the side, feet, and hands appearing one after the other and bleeding on Fridays, when she also fell into ecstasy. On the other days of the week she continued to work, but she ate practically nothing, and from spring 1871 onward was unable to take any solid food. She drank very little and later, it is alleged, nothing at all. In 1876 she became bedridden and from then on is believed to have lived only on Holy Communion. She also developed other faculties generally associated with stigmatization such as clairvoyance and hierognosis, that is, discernment of blessed objects and of the authenticity of relics.

The phenomena aroused great interest throughout Belgium and elsewhere, and in 1868 an ecclesiastical commission was appointed to investigate them. Its members subjected Louise to severe tests including the "recall," that is, the termination of an ecstasy or trance by a mental or oral command, and by making her work on Fridays in an unsuccessful attempt to prevent the phenomena from appearing. The German physician, Prof. R. Virchow, considered her a fraud, but on the other hand, the Belgian Academy of Medicine, after a lengthy investigation, confessed themselves unable to explain the phenomena naturally (*See* STIGMATIZATION).

Bibliography: M. DIDRY and A. WALLEMACQ, *Belgian Mystic of the Nineteenth Century: Louise Lateau of Bois-d'Haine, 1850–53,* tr. F. IZARD (London 1931); *La Stigmatisée belge: La servante de Dieu, Louise Lateau, de Bois-d'Haine* (3d ed. Louvain 1947). A. THIÉRY, *Nouvelle Biographie de Louise Lateau d'après les documents authentiques,* 3 v. (Louvain 1915–21).

[H. GRAEF]

LATERAN

The term Lateran may refer to one building or the entire group of buildings that stand on the Monte Celio in ROME. They comprise mainly: (1) the Basilica of St. John Lateran, which is the episcopal seat of the pope as bishop of Rome; (2) the Baptistery; and (3) the Lateran Palace, which at one time served as the residence of the popes. The Lateran has been the site for five major church councils (1123, 1139, 1179, 1215, 1512–1517) and several minor ones. Under the LATERAN PACT of 1929 the Lateran enjoys diplomatic immunity but not extraterritoriality (arts. 13, 15). The Lateran serves as a museum and as the cathedral and central offices for the Diocese of Rome. Renovations and restorations have been carried out by many of the popes throughout the centuries until the present.

Although the present architecture is largely late 16th century onward, the buildings retain some foundations, architectural detail, and decoration that illustrate the long and varied history of the Lateran both before and during its Christian period (from the 4th century onward). Originally the site had been occupied by the palace of the Laterani, a noble Roman family. Eventually it became imperial property and finally passed to the Emperor Constantine through his wife Fausta (the *domus Faustae*). Constantine, pursing his policy of recognizing Christianity as the official religion of the Empire, donated the property with an ample patrimony to the Church. This event would be recalled several times over the subsequent centuries to reinforce the prestige of the Lateran. The height of its influence as a residence was in the Middle Ages until the time of the Avignon papacy. Subsequently the Vatican replaced the Lateran as the residence of the popes and the administrative center of the Holy See. However, on the feast of St. John the Baptist in 1962 John XXIII (1958–1963) announced the transfer of the offices for the Vicariate of Rome to the Lateran Palace. He transferred the Lateran Museum from the Vatican to the Lateran Palace in 1963.

Basilica. The Basilica of St. John Lateran is one of the four great patriarchal basilicas of Rome. It is the oldest and the first in rank (*Mater et Caput Omnium Ecclesiarum Urbis et Orbis*). Originally it was known as the Church of the Savior, and only later was it dedicated to John the Baptist. The first basilica was probably an adaptation by Constantine of the already existing basilica or great hall of the palace (Jerome, *Ep.* 73; *Patrologia Latina* 22:692). The subsequent architectural history is marked by numerous occasions of destruction followed by renovation, the principal causes being fire, earthquake, and neglect. There was an earthquake that damaged the apse in 443, the Vandal attacks occurred in 455; restoration was undertaken by Leo I (440–461) around 460. During the 8th century the Saracens attacked the basilica, and Adrian I (772–795) renovated it. Severe damage caused by earthquake in 896 was repaired by Sergius III (904–911) in 905. After that the Lateran retained its typical medieval form for four centuries. There is a tradition that St. Francis of Assisi appeared to Innocent III (1198–1216) in a dream to support the crumbling Lateran. At the end of the 13th century a Gothic renovation took place in 1290 under Nicholas IV (1288–1292), especially through the work of the artists Giacomo Torriti and Giacoma di Camerino. In 1308 the Lateran burned and was partly rebuilt by Clement V (1305-1314) and John XXII (1316–1334); it was burned again in 1360 and later restored by Urban V (1362–1370). It was not therefore surprising that under the impact of these and later changes, both the early and the medieval features of the basilica have disappeared almost entirely. But old drawings and paintings preserve a picture of the monumental character of the former edifice.

The main characteristics of the Constantinian basilica were the large apse rising above the bishop's throne; the altar as the center of worship, seen through the great triumphal arch at the west end of the central nave—the church was rectangular in shape and divided by rows of columns that ran from east to west; and by the arcades and four side aisles formed by the columns. The roof timbers were open. In front was an atrium surrounded by colonnades with a fountain in the center. The façade had three windows and was embellished with mosaics. Generally the early basilica is said to have lacked a transverse nave until one was added under Clement V (1305–1314), but now Josi, Krautheimer, and S. Corbett think otherwise. They refer to a closed, tripartite nave. There was no crypt or *confessio*. The main walls of the central nave originally rested on 30 granite pillars, in time replaced by columns of masonry. The upper walls had mosaics with scenes from the Old and New Testaments. Toward the front a clerestory of 16 windows on each side opened onto the timber framework of the lower side roofs; the side aisles were divided by 21 smaller pillars on each side. Although the altar formerly occupied the position customary in basilicas, i.e., in the center of the chord of the apse, successive rebuildings and extensions added to the transverse nave and placed the choir beyond the altar. Above the altar is the BALDACHINO, resting on four marble columns; it was erected in 1369 but appears somewhat incongruous in the present baroque interior. Traditionally the basilica was richly decorated, hence the title *Basilica Aurea* given by Gregory I (590–604). Of the decoration the most famous were the mosaics of the semicircular apse. The main mosaic, representing Christ the Redeemer, was venerated throughout the Middle Ages. It was reworked in the 13th century and when the old apse was destroyed in 1878 to enlarge the church, the mosaics were reerected in the new apse.

During the Avignon papacy most of the basilica was ruined by two fires and was collapsed by an earthquake. As a result many wanted St. Peter's Basilica to become the primatial church. However, Gregory XI (1370–1380) issued a bull from Avignon in 1372 affirming the Lateran's primacy. When Gregory returned to Rome in 1377 he had to live at the Vatican because the Lateran was in poor condition and it lacked security. Martin V (1417–1431) sent a clear signal about the Lateran's importance when he restored it and provided a place for his burial there. He also installed the cosmatesque pavement in 1425. Eugenius IV (1431–1447) continued some renovations and constructed a new monastery for the Augustinian order of canon regular. Both Martin V and Eugenius IV reaffirmed the Lateran's primacy. Sixtus IV (1471–1484) affirmed the primacy of the Lateran by soliciting donations during the Holy Year of 1475. In preparation for the Holy Year of 1500 Alexander VI (1492–1503) had work done in the interior, including a fresco above the Holy Door and the triumphal arch that separates the nave from the transept. Julian II (1503–1513) had limited renovations done in preparation for the Lateran Council in 1512. Leo X (1513–1521) initiated restoration of the Lateran baptistery.

Pius IV (1559–1565) launched extensive renovations. Most the changes during his reign were done on the exterior, especially the transept façade and the roof. Pius V (1566–1572) continued the renovations and extinguished the rivalry of primacy with a bull in 1569 giving the Lateran this distinction. Freiburg highlights the importance of the twin towers and the transept façade as restoring the imperial majesty and spiritual primacy that the Lateran possessed during the Constantinian period. Gregory XIII 1572–1585) completed projects (the Aurelian wall portal, Via Appia Nuova, Via Merulana) of Pius IV and constructed another road in preparation for the Holy Year of 1575. This road began at from the north piazza, continued past the Porta Metronia to the Porta San Sebastiano, where it intersected with the Via Appia Antica.

Freiburg points out that these changes made the Lateran the centric point in a radiating scheme that facilitated access to three of the four churches Holy Year pilgrims were required to visit.

Sixtus V (1585–1590) continued the theological influence of renovations that he accomplished in the Lateran Palace. He wanted to emphasize the sacraments, especially the Eucharist. A new benediction loggia was built on the north transept façade of the basilica by Domenico Fontana. Under Clement VIII (1592–1605) renovations occurred in two phases: construction of the new transept ceiling, restoration of the high altar, the ciborium, and the *confessio* chapel (1592–1596) and a new chapel, with material from the Pantheon, and expansion of the transept (1597–1600). The full baroque remodeling and decoration were executed by Francesco Borromini under Innocent X (1644–1655), especially from 1646 to 1649. A new curtain wall concealed the old brickwork, and the former columns were enclosed in huge pilasters with great statues in front. Alexander Galilei built the main facade in 1735. Finally during the reign of Leo XIII (1878–1903) came the choir with extended apse.

Originally outside the basilica there were seven oratories for the deacons of the church. These were eventually worked into the church itself. The devotion of visiting the seven altars gave rise to the similar devotion found in other Roman churches.

The Baptistry. Next to the basilica, in the southwest corner of the Piazza di San Giovanni, is the octagonal baptistery, begun by Constantine on the site of the baths belonging to the former palace of the Laterani. Excavations have discovered a hot spring structure with a network of underground passages. There is evidence of an earthquake in 191. A circular room was found constructed between 300 and 312. There is a decorated mosaic pavement from the 4th century and graffiti with the Christian cross. In the interior of the baptistery are eight porphyry columns that support an architrave on which are eight smaller columns, which in turn support the octagonal drums of the lantern. Originally, detached from the basilica, the BAPTISTERY was entered through the portico of St. Venantius consisting of a vestibule in which two large porphyry columns leading still stand and which was formerly approached by a colonnade of smaller porphyry columns leading from the church. The grandeur of the baptistery expressed the solemnity with which Baptism was received in the early church. Hilary (461–468) added the two Johannine chapels; on the west side is that of John the Baptist with its bronze doors taken from the Baths of Caracalla, and on the east, that of the Evangelist. John IV (640–642) built a third oratory in honor of St. Venantius and other Dalmatian martyrs. Here the mosaics are 7th century and, when compared with earlier mosaics, they illustrate the decline in this art form.

Gregory XIII (1572–1585) made extensive renovations to the baptistery. Restorations in the interior included new windows, repairs to the marble revetment of the walls, and fresco decoration—all lost in later interventions. Freiburg states these renovations highlighted the baptistery's historical prominence given by the baptism of Constantine. During the reign of Gregory XIII baptism was once again regularly performed in the Lateran baptistery on the feasts of Easter and Pentecost. Gregory also revived the tradition of conferring confirmation there immediately after the baptismal ceremony. Clement VIII (1592–1595) renovated the chapels around the central octagon.

The Lateran Palace. The imperial residence was given by Constantine to Melchiades, the Bishop of Rome. The Lateran Palace provided a location for the residence (including a library and archives) and central administration of the church for almost 1,000 years. Julian II (337–352) created the Holy Scrinium as a repository for literary and theological writings. St. Jerome mentioned the scrinium in a 4th century letter. Hilarius I (461–468) built two libraries at the palace. Gregory the Great (590–604) mentions that he placed his sermons at Lateran. The condition of the palace declined over the next two hundred years as construction work focused on new churches to honor martyrs. John VII (705–707) planned to restore it or move the papal residence to the Palatine Hill. The palace was finally restored by Zacharias (741–752). Mandel describes how he embellished and enlarged the palace after the imperial palace at Constantinople, with a great tower, known as the *Torre degli Annibaldi*; a new porch before the palace archives; and a new *triclinum* on the *piano nobile*, also known as the Basilica Zacharia, complete with a map of the world. The impetus to maintain and beautify the papal residence was carried on by Leo III (795–816), who built two more *triclinia*; restored the long corridor connecting the second *triclinium*, also known as the *Sala del Concilio*, to the basilica; and dedicated an oratory to the Archangel Michael. Work continued on the palace during the pontificates of Gregory IV (827–844), Leo IV (847–855), and Sergius III (904–911). Callistus II (1119–1124) built a chapel dedicated to St. Nicholas and Innocent II (1130–1143) built two new rooms. Innocent III (1198–1216) further enlarged the residence with more rooms and an oratory to express the grandeur of the papacy. An earthquake damaged the Lateran in 1227. Boniface VIII (1294–1303) built the Palazzo Nuovo and the Benediction Loggia. The Lateran palace was destroyed by fire in 1308 and 1309. During the Avignon period (1309–1377)

another earthquake in 1349, and a fire in 1361, further damaged the residence.

After the Avignon period the abysmal condition of Lateran Palace led to the papal residence being moved to the Vatican, where it remains to the present. However, restoration on the Lateran palace began to take place during the reign of Julius II (1503–1513) in preparation for the Fifth Lateran Council. Sixtus V (1585–1590) constructed a new Lateran Palace. Mandel describes the layout of the Lateran Palace and the frescoes of the four main halls (Hall of the Popes, Hall of the Emperors, Hall of the Apostles, and the Hall of Constantine), the five Old Testament rooms dedicated to Samuel, David, Solomon, Elijah and Daniel), the papal chapel and antechapel, the Hall of the Obelisks, the Hall of Gloria, and the four rooms of the private papal apartment. Sixtus V also had the *Scala Sancta*, a staircase of 28 steps made of Tyrian marble covered with wood, moved to the present site where they lead to the *Sancta Sanctorum*, the old private chapel of the popes in the Lateran Palace. An Egyptian obelisk was excavated from the Circus Maximus in 1586 and transferred to the piazza of the Lateran. Recent studies have demonstrated that Sixtus V's construction and decoration of a palace with imperial dimensions sought to emphasize the spiritual imperium of the pope.

Subsequent popes have made wonderful improvements. Innocent X (1644–1655) commissioned Borromini in 1646 to make additions and Alexander VII (1655–1667) restored the Oratory of the Blessed Sacrament in 1662. Pius IX (1846–1878) undertook some restorations in 1853 but he also desired to construct 14 chapels in the Sancta Sanctorum to correspond with the Stations of the Cross; Pius X (1903–1914) approved this project in 1909. Pius XI (1922–1939) approved plans to build a chapel for the Holy Year of 1925. The Lateran Museum and the Vicariate offices of Rome were moved from the Vatican to the second floor of the Lateran Palace by John XXIII (1958–1963) to restore the Lateran's historic role in the diocese. He also initiated excavations of the Lateran in 1961 that were completed in 1968 under Paul VI (1963–1978).

Bibliography: JOHN THE DEACON, *Liber de ecclesia Lateranensi, Patrologia Latina* 194:1543–60. P. F. KEHR, *Regesta Pontificum Romanorum. Italia Pontificia* (Berlin 1906–35) 1:22–35. A. L. FROTHINGHAM, *The Monuments of Christian Rome from Constantine to the Renaissance* (New York 1908). P. LAUER, *Le Palais de Latran* (Paris 1911). R. A. LANCIANI, *Wanderings through Ancient Roman Churches* (New York 1924). H. LECLERCQ, *Dictionnaire d'archéologie chrétienne et de liturgie*, ed. F. CABROL, H. LECLERCQ, and H. I. MARROU (Paris 1907–53) 8.2: 1529–1887. E. JOSI, "Scoperte nella Basilica Costantiniana al Laterano," *Revista di archeologia cristiana* 11 (1934) 335–358. R. KRAUTHEIMER, "La Façade ancienne de Saint-Jean de Latran à Rome," *Revue Archéologique* 6th ser., 5 (1935) 231–235. A. M. COLINI, *Storia e topo-*

grafia del Celio nell'antichità (Atti della Pontificia Acccademia Romana di Archeologia, ser. 3, Memorie 7; 1944). F. W. DEICHMANN, *Frühchristliche Kitchen im Rom* (Basel 1948). J. DE BLASI, *Le 4 basiliche patriarcali dell'Anno Santo* (Florence 1949). R. ELZE, "Die päpstliche Kapelle im 12. und 13. Jahrhundert," *Zeitschrift der Savigny- Stiftung für Rechtsgeschichte, Kanonistidche Abteilung* 36 (1950) 145–204; "Das 'Sacrum Palatium Lateranense' im X. und XI. Jht.," *Studi gregoriani* 4 (1952) 27–54. E. JOSI et al., "Note Lateranensi," *Revista di archeologia cristiana* 33 (1957) 79–98; 34 (1958) 59–72. L. VOELKL, "Archäologische Funde und Forschungen," *Römische Quartalschrift für christliche Altertumskunde und für Kirchengeschichte* 55 (1960) 101–121; *Lexikon für Theologie und Kirche*, ed. J. HOFER and K. RAHNER (Freiburg 1957–65) 6:813–815. D. FONTANA, *Della transportatione dell'obelisco Vaticano et delle fabriche di Nostre Signore Papa Siste V* (Rome 1604; reprinted Milan 1978). A. SCHIAVO, *The Lateran Palace and Baptistery* (Rome 1969). G. PELLICCIONI, *Le nuove scoperte sulle origini del Battistero Lateranense* (Rome 1973). C. MANDEL, *Sixtus V and the Lateran Palace* (Rome 1994). J. FREIBURG, *The Lateran in 1600: Christian Concord in Counter-Reformation Rome* (New York 1995). A. ROCA DE AMICIS, *L'Opera di Borromini in San Giovanni in Laterano: gli anni della Fabbrica 1646–1650* (Rome 1995). L. DONADONO, *Scala Santa a San Giovanni in Laterano* (Rome 2000).

[J. GILCHRIST/C. KOSANKE]

LATERAN COUNCILS

The Lateran basilica was from early times the particular cathedral of the bishop of Rome; and from 313, in the reign of Emperor CONSTANTINE I THE GREAT, the Lateran palace provided a meeting place for many councils convened by papal authority. Among these, although the councils held in 649, 769, 823, 1059, 1102, 1105, 1110, 1112, and 1116 have a notable place in conciliar history, it is the meetings of 1123, 1139, 1179, 1215, and 1512 to 1517 that are of outstanding importance. They are traditionally known as the First, Second, Third, Fourth, and Fifth Lateran Councils respectively, and have ecumenical status in the Western Church [*see* COUNCILS, GENERAL (ECUMENICAL)].

First (1123). The First Lateran (9th ecumenical) Council was convoked by Pope CALLISTUS II in December 1122, and sat from *c.* March 18 to April 6, 1123. Its historical context was the settlement of the INVESTITURE STRUGGLE by the Concordat of WORMS on Sept. 23, 1122, and the *instrumenta* of Worms were read and ratified at the Council. About 300 archbishops and bishops and perhaps 600 abbots from the Western Church were present. No record of the Council's deliberations has survived; but 22 (or, by some reckonings, 25) canons were promulgated, and various particular affairs were transacted, such as the canonization of CONRAD OF CONSTANCE (d. 976), the granting of the PALLIUM to Archbishop Adalbero of Bremen-Hamburg, and the ventilation of the Canterbury and YORK dispute over primacy in England. The canons

themselves mostly restated earlier rulings (notably those of the Council of Reims in 1119), and ranged from general principles applicable to the whole Church to matters of immediate or regional interest, many of them being later subsumed into the *Decretum* of GRATIAN. They dealt principally with ordinations, offices, and spiritual ministrations; with clerks; and with the protection of churches, property, persons, and places. More precisely, they may be classified according to their definitions on the following topics: simoniacal ordinations (1), appointments to ecclesiastical offices (2), ordinations by the antipope Gregory VIII (6), episcopal control of the granting of the cure of souls (7), communion of clerks with excommunicates (9), the consecration of uncanonically elected bishops (10), spiritual ministrations by monks (17), appointment of parish priests by the bishop (18), monastic subjection to the bishop (19), cohabitation of clerks with women (3), clerical concubinage and marriage (21); safeguards for church property (4), protection of church offerings—especially of certain Roman churches (14), protection of church goods (20), alienation of church property by intruders (22), protection of Benevento in the papal patrimony (8) and of the Porticians in the Leonine City (12), indulgences for Crusaders and protection for their families (11), protection of pilgrims and merchants (16), the Truce of God (13), the laws of consanguinity (5), and false coining (15). The work of the Council was therefore the confirmation of peace in Christian society, the establishment of order and discipline within the Church, and the eradication of abuse. It holds a significant place in the history of the Church reform that had originated in the previous century (*see* GREGORIAN REFORM).

Second (1139). The double election of Pope INNOCENT II and Anacletus II (*see* PIERLEONI) in 1130 inaugurated a period of schism that ended only with the latter's death in 1138. To affirm the recovered unity of the Church and also to deal with doctrinal and disciplinary problems, Innocent convened a plenary synod in the Lateran during April 1139. This Second Lateran (10th ecumenical) Council was attended by a large and widely representative assembly of between 500 and 1,000 archbishops, bishops, and abbots, including some from the East. The opening address by the Pope announced the deposition of the adherents of his former rival, the excommunication of Roger II of Sicily, and the condemnation of the heretical followers of PETER OF BRUYS and ARNOLD OF BRESCIA. The Council promulgated 30 canons and dealt with, among other matters, the canonization of Sturmi, first abbot of Fulda. The canons repeated a large number of definitions from the Council of Reims (1131), which itself had been influenced by that of Clermont-Ferrand (1130); and most of them were later included in

The 12th-century cloister of the Basilica of St. John Lateran, Rome, by Vassallettus and Petrus Cosmati. (Alinari-Art Reference/Art Resource, NY)

Gratian's *Decretum.* Continuing the work of First Lateran, this legislation marks a consolidation of the reform program dating from the previous century, its canons dealing with doctrine and authority, the rights of bishops, clerks, religious, churches, and other related topics. In particular, the Council defined on the following questions: annulment of many elections by the antipope and his adherents (30); sanctions against those condemning the Eucharist, infant baptism, the priesthood, and marriage (23); prohibition of payment for Confirmation, Extreme Unction, and burials (24); the nonreception of excommunicates by bishops (3); the nonspoliation of the property of dead bishops and clerks (5); the consultation of monks and canons regular in episcopal elections (28); clerical dress and behavior (4); married clerks and those with concubines (6); marriage after solemn vows of chastity (7–8); the prohibition of study of civil law and medicine by religious (9); protection of clerks, monks, pilgrims, merchants, and others (11); priests' sons and the

service of the altar (21); nuns failing to live by their rules (26) or chanting in choir with monks or canons regular (27); the protection of clerks from violence (25: *Si quis suadente*); simony (1–2); lay ownership of churches or tithes (10), inherited benefices (16); lay grants of benefices (25); the Truce of God (12); the prohibition of usury (13); tournaments (14); cross bows and archery (29), incendiarism (18–20); and false penitence (22).

Third (1179). Like the Council of 1139, the Third Lateran (11th ecumenical) Council followed the ending of a long period of schism that in this instance had begun with the contested election of Pope ALEXANDER III in 1159, was maintained through a series of three antipopes supported by the Emperor FREDERICK I BARBAROSSA, and was effectively ended with the papal-imperial agreement at Venice in 1177. A surviving list of the Council's participants, the first of its kind, records the attendance of about 300 bishops and numerous abbots. Regional rep-

Interior of the Basilica of St. John Lateran, Rome, showing 17th-century decorations by Francesco Borromini. (Alinari-Art Reference/Art Resource, NY)

resentation was impressively wide, including, besides Italian prelates, those from France, Germany, England, Ireland, Scotland, Dalmatia, Spain, Denmark, Hungary, and the Crusaders' States. In addition there were envoys from many Christian rulers. The Council sessions were held on March 5, 14, and 19, 1179, and 27 canons were promulgated. The Council, both for its circumstances and its achievements, occupies an important place in the history of Canon Law: it was the first ecumenical council in the period of *ius novum,* and was presided over by the first of the great canonist popes, Alexander III, the former Rolando Bandinelli. The canons of the Council were widely disseminated and were promptly taken into the new collections of DECRETALS, from which they passed into *Compilatio prima* (*see* QUINQUE COMPILATIONES ANTIQUAE) and finally into the official Canon Law in the Gregorian *Decretales* (*see CORPUS IURIS CANONICI*) of 1234. The opening canon (*Licet de vitanda*) embodied a ruling of permanent historical importance in that it required a two-thirds majority of the cardinals in all future papal elections (*see* POPES, ELECTION OF); the second annulled the ordinations of the antipopes Victor IV, Paschal II, and Callistus III. The remaining canons dealt mainly with disciplinary matters concerning clerks and with abuses and sanctions. The principal topics can be grouped

as follows: the canonical age requirement for bishops and other officials (3); the necessity of a title before ordination (5); benefice collation (8); occupations forbidden to clerks (12); majority decisions in ecclesiastical communities (16); prohibition of more than one rector in a single church (17); the provision of cathedral schools with free instruction (18); clerical and church immunities (19); appellate jurisdiction (6); injunctions against excessive procurations (4); simony (7); pluralism (13); and clerical vices (11); regulations concerning the TEMPLARS, HOSPITALLERS (9) and CISTERCIANS (10), and provision of religious services for lepers (23); tournaments (12); the Truce of God (21); and protection for clerks, monks, pilgrims, merchants and others (22); sanctions against those cooperating with Saracens and pirates (24), against usurers (25), Jews and Saracens (26), Cathari, Brabançons, and other mercenaries (27). The Council therefore marked a further important stage in the development of papal legislative authority and of Church reform, and prepared the way for the still more important legislation of Pope Innocent III in the Council of 1215.

Fourth (1215). The Fourth Lateran (12th ecumenical) Council marks the high point of medieval papal legislation and is sometimes called "the Great Lateran Council" or simply "the Great Council." It is generally considered the most important council before the Council of TRENT.

Background and Sessions. Projected for many years by Pope INNOCENT III, but delayed by the numerous vexatious problems with which the Pope was confronted, the Council was formally announced in a bull of April 19, 1213. "In accordance with the practice of the ancient fathers," archbishops and bishops from all parts of the Church, in East and West, were invited, together with the heads of religious orders and clerical communities and Christian secular rulers. Many letters of invitation are recorded in the papal registers. Great care and preparation were devoted to securing the widest possible representation at the Council and to ensuring its success. When at last the Council assembled in November 1215, there were present more than 400 archbishops and bishops, of whom about 70 were either primates or archbishops, including the Latin patriarchs of Constantinople and Jerusalem, together with the delegates of those of Alexandria and Antioch. The bishops came from every part of the Western Church, including Bohemia, Hungary, Poland, Lithuania, and Estonia. Also present were more than 800 abbots and priors, as well as the envoys of Emperor FREDERICK II and the Latin Emperor of Constantinople; of the kings of France, England, Aragon, Sicily, Hungary, Cyprus, and Jerusalem; of princes, magnates, cities, and communes. There were, however, no representatives from the Greek Church in the East, though these were invited. The Council was opened on November 11 with a solemn address by the Pope on the text *Desiderio desideravi hoc Pascha manducare vobiscum ante patiar* (Lk 22.15). Immediately after the Pope, the patriarch of Jerusalem spoke on the misfortunes of the Holy Land. The bishop of Agde spoke next on the problem of the ALBIGENSES in the south of France. The choice of these two speakers suggested the major problems with which the Council was concerned.

In addition to the inaugural session, further meetings were held on November 20 and 30, and many questions were debated both at and between the sessions. Two problems in particular engaged the Council's attention: the promotion of a new Crusade following the unsatisfactory outcome of the Fourth CRUSADE of 1204 and the recrudescence of heresy. The Council sought the establishment of peace and unity throughout Christendom as a prerequisite for the new Crusade (a four-year peace was imposed on Christian peoples and the bishops were commanded to reconcile all enemies) and fixed the starting date at June 1, 1217; the obligation of preaching and supporting the Crusade was enjoined on all prelates and Christian rulers, protection and privileges were decreed for the crusaders, and a three-year impost of one-fortieth of their income was laid on the clergy. But Innocent's hopes were destined to be unfulfilled in this matter; with his death on June 16, 1216, the necessary unity and interest were soon dissipated. As for the problem of heresy, the doctrines of the CATHARI (or Albigenses) and, to a lesser extent, those of the WALDENSES were condemned, though neither sect was specifically named in the official decrees. Of particular importance in this context were the conciliar definitions touching on the Cathari, including a solemn statement of orthodox faith, later incorporated in the Gregorian *Decretales* of 1234 as the opening text. Procedural rules were drawn up for the repression of heresy, and crusading privileges were extended to those taking part in the campaigns against the heretics. In addition, the position of those schismatic Greeks reunited with the apostolic see was the subject of an important decree (4). The Council was concerned also with many other spiritual and political questions: the general state of the Church, touching on dogmatic, disciplinary, and juristic questions; the moral well-being of the Church in its clergy, religious, and laity. Matters of political or regional interest dealt with at the Council included the confirmation of Frederick II as emperor of the West; the granting of the conquered part of the county of Toulouse to Simon de Montfort l'Amaury in recognition of his role against the Albigenses; the confirmation of the Pope's earlier rejection of MAGNA CARTA, which was judged by Innocent to have been extorted by the magnates from King JOHN and therefore invalid; the confirmation of Archbishop STEPHEN LANGTON's suspension;

the jurisdictional claims of the primate of Toledo; and many other disputes and problems within the provinces of the Western Church. A proposal that the central machinery of papal administration should in future be supported financially by regular payments from the Church as a whole was opposed by a majority and therefore frustrated: this action is an indication of a measure of consultation and consent in the Council's deliberations.

Canons. The Council promulgated 70 canons (or *capitula*) and one crusading decree. The canons were soon after incorporated in *Compilatio quarta* (of the *Quinque Compilationes antiquae*), together with decretals from the closing years of Innocent's pontificate, and later passed with very few exceptions into the *Decretales* of 1234. Certain canons established dogmatic definitions and sacramental obligations that have remained in force to the present day: the opening canon (*Firmiter credimus*) included the profession of Catholic faith mentioned above, and is especially important for its definitive Eucharistic doctrine of TRANSUBSTANTIATION; the second canon condemned the teachings of JOACHIM OF FIORE and AMALRIC OF BÈNE, and the third dealt with heretics, their protectors and episcopal INQUISITION; the fifth asserted the order of patriarchal precedence after the Roman see to be: Constantinople, Alexandria, Antioch, and Jerusalem; the 21st canon (*Omnis utriusque sexus*) bound all Christians of the age of reason to receive annually the Sacraments of Penance and the Eucharist. For their spiritual and canonical importance the greater number of the canons can be classified according to several main themes: the Sacraments and spiritual ministrations; Church order, organization, and reform; ecclesiastical benefices and property; and judicial, procedural, and penal questions. As for the Sacraments and spiritual ministrations, the Council legislated on all the Sacraments except Confirmation: annual confession and Communion (21); Extreme Unction (20) and the care of the dying, with the obligation of doctors to consider the spiritual needs of their patients (22); episcopal elections (24–25); episcopal responsibility for worthy appointments and the requisite qualities of character and learning for priests and holders of benefices (26–27, 30); abuses in connection with the celebration of the Mass and divine services (17); the nonprofanation of churches (19); and marriage questions (50–51), including the reduction of the prohibited degrees of consanguinity from seven to four (52). For the promotion of Church order, organization, and reform, the Council pronounced on bishops and, among other matters, their powers of excommunication (47) and absolution (49), exactions and procurations (65, 33–34) and the nonprolongation of episcopal vacancies (23); on clerks in regard to their benefices, tonsure, behavior, and neglect of spiritual duties (14–18), their nonparticipation in secular administration and relations with feudal superiors (43, 45); and the provision for cathedral schools with free instruction (11); repeating the legislation of the 1179 Council; on monks and religious, enjoining that no new orders be founded (13) and that triennial general chapters be held in each ecclesiastical province for houses not so organized already (12: *In singulis regnis*), on tithe exemptions and payments (56), on privileges enjoyed during interdict (58), and other questions (cf. 59–60, 64). Relating to ecclesiastical benefices and church property, the Council dealt with the resignation of benefices (28); the abuse of pluralism (29); the canonical requirements for collation to benefices (30); the nonhereditability of benefices and the prohibition of the illegitimate sons of canons succeeding to their fathers' churches (31); incomes, taxes, imposts, procurations, and so forth (32–34); vicarages (32); prohibition of lay alienation of church property (44); regulations for the exposition of relics; and curbing the abuses of indulgences (62). Judicial, procedural, and penal matters were inevitably a concern of the great jurist Pope, and were regulated by canons on the procedure for the inquiry into and punishment of offenses, while stressing the need of prudence (9); the prohibition of the blessing of hot water and hot iron for judicial ORDEALS (18); the safeguarding of the rights of clerks from lay usurpation and the prohibition of clerks from involvement in secular justice (42); on courts of justice and appellate procedure (48); the prohibition of lay persons from being appointed arbitrators in spiritual matters (40); consideration of objections raised against judges (48); and penalties for all forms of SIMONY, relating to consecrations, ordinations, the reception of religious, for raising interdict, and undue exactions for burials and marriages, with the reminder that lay persons were to pay their accustomed dues (63–66).

The closing "chapters" of the Council dealt specifically with the Jews and their place in Christian society: no Christian was to have commerce with usurious Jews (67); both Jews and Saracens were to wear a distinctive dress to mark them off from Christians, and Jews were forbidden to appear in public in Holy Week to avoid risk of insult to Christians at that time (68); they might exercise no public function involving power over Christians (69); and Jews willingly seeking baptism were first to abandon their own rites (70). This legislation against the Jews, which in part continued and restated Alexander's work in the Third Lateran Council, must be seen in the context of contemporary society and in the special circumstances of the Council's preoccupation with the misfortunes of the Holy Land and a new Crusade.

The Great Lateran Council, whose canons were for the first time promulgated in the name of the Pope, is aptly considered a culminating point in the history of medieval papal legislation and leadership of Christendom, with its concern for all problems of the universal Church and every class of person in the *Societas Christiana*.

Fifth (1512–17). The First Lateran to the Council of VIENNE, CONCILIARISM found its expression in the Councils of PISA, CONSTANCE, and BASEL. The reemergence of papal monarchical authority after Basel did not, however, entail the eclipse of conciliar ambitions: an attempt to reopen the Council of Basel in 1482 was a failure, but academic interest in the conciliar doctrines survived and secular princes at times employed the threat of a council to bring pressure to bear on the pope. It was in the midst of the conflict between the French King Louis XII and Pope JULIUS II, and because of Julius's failure to implement his promise to convene a council, that a group of disaffected cardinals meeting in Milan summoned a council to convene in Pisa, with the support of the French King and Emperor Maximilian. The council assembled (a month late) on Nov. 1, 1511, in the presence of four cardinals, the proxies of three others, two archbishops, 14 bishops, five abbots, procurators of three French universities, canonists, and theologians. Sessions one to three (1511) were held in Pisa where the decrees of Constance and Basel were reissued, sessions four to eight (1511–12) in Milan where Julius II was suspended from office, and sessions nine and ten (1512) in Asti and Lyon respectively where the council asserted its legitimacy.

It was in response to this *conciliabulum* of Pisa, known also as the Council of Pisa II, that Julius II convoked the Fifth Lateran (18th ecumenical) Council for April 19, 1512. The Council was announced in the bull *Sacrosanctae Romanae ecclesiae* of July 18, 1511, which condemned the projected council of the schismatic cardinals and justified the Pope's own delays. As a result of the French victory at Ravenna on April 11, 1512, the Council opened later than intended, on May 3, 1512. The ecumenical status of the Fifth Lateran Council has been questioned through the centuries, but is at present generally accepted. According to the count of the master of ceremonies, the inaugural session was attended by 16 cardinals and 83 mitred prelates. Later, following the death of Julius II and the reconciliation of his successor with the French, the number attending the Council rose to 23 or 24 cardinals and 122 prelates at the eighth session, on Dec. 19, 1513.

The Council was conceived within the framework of the great papal assemblies of the Middle Ages, and was held in Rome under papal presidency. Its decrees were issued as papal bulls or constitutions having conciliar approval. In addition to condemning the work of the *conciliabulum* of Pisa, the Council was concerned to condemn the PRAGMATIC SANCTION of Bourges. There were 12 sessions in all, the final one being on March 16, 1517. The death of Julius II had intervened on Feb. 21, 1513, and the succession of Pope LEO X had facilitated French adherence to the Council, as mentioned above. The first five sessions (May 10, 1512 to Feb. 16, 1513) dealt primarily with Pisa II and the Pragmatic Sanction of Bourges, the Emperor repudiating the actions of Pisa II at the third session. The fifth session declared papal elections would be null if they were tainted with simony (*Cum tam divino*). Under Leo X, three commissions were set up to deal with general peace, Church reform, the preservation of the faith, and the extinction of schism. The eighth and ninth sessions (Dec. 19, 1513, and May 5, 1514) registered respectively the disavowal of Pisa II by the ambassadors of Louis XII and a document testifying to the submission of the French bishops. The eighth session confirmed an earlier papal bull regulating the Curia's taxation system (*In apostolici culminis*) and included a dogmatic definition on the individuality of the human soul, against the teachings of Pietro POMPONAZZI; the ninth session pronounced on reforms touching the choice of bishops, monasteries held in trust by secular clergy, pluralities, ecclesiastical dress, blasphemy, and clerical immunity (*Supernae dispositionis*). Three important measures of the 10th session (May 4, 1515) dealt with *MONTES PIETATIS* (pawn shops) to aid the poor, episcopal liberties and dignities, and the pre-publication censorship of printed books; the 11th session (Dec. 19, 1516) was concerned with preaching, exemptions of religious, abrogation of the Pragmatic Sanction of Bourges, and approval of the Concordat of Bologna. The concluding session (March 16, 1517) decided for a Crusade against the Turks and the imposition of a three-year tax on all benefices.

The deliberations and enactments of the Council testify to an awareness of the principal abuses in the Church and a concern on the part of some Church leaders for reform. Several measures were well designed to deal with these problems, but there proved to be little zeal in making them effective, and the Church was soon confronted with protestations far more perilous.

Bibliography: General. G. TANGL, *Die Teilnehmer an den allgemeinen Konzilien des Mittelalters* (Weimar 1922). H. E. FEINE, *Kirchliche Rechtsgeschichte,* v. 1, *Die katholische Kirche* (4th ed. Cologne 1964). H. JEDIN, *Ecumenical Councils of the Catholic Church,* tr. E. GRAF (New York 1960). P. HUGHES, *The Church in Crisis* (New York 1961). G. LE BRAS et al., *Histoire du droit et des institutions de l'Église en Occident,* v. 7 *L'Âge classique (1140–1378): Sources et théorie du droit* (Paris 1965). R. FOREVILLE, "Procédure et débats dans les conciles médiévaux de Latran (1123–1215)," *Revue historique de droit français et éranger,* 42 (1964) 122–23; *Histoire des conciles oecuméniques, v. 6 Latran I, II, III, et Latran IV* (Paris 1966). M. MOLLAT, *Les conciles Latran I a Latran IV* (Louvain 1974). **First Council.** J. D. MANSI, *Sacrorum Conciliorum nova et amplissima collectio,* 31 v. (Florence-Venice 1757–98); reprinted and continued by L. PETIT and J. B. MARTIN 53 v. in 60 (Paris 1889–1927; repr. Graz 1960–) 21:277–304. C. J. VON HEFELE, *Histoire des conciles d'après les documents originaux,* tr. and continued by H. LECLERCQ, 10 v. in 19 (Paris 1907–38) 1:630–44. A. FLICHE and V. MARTIN, eds., *Histoire de l'église depuis les origines jusqu'à nos jours* (Paris 1935–) 8:391–95. F. VERNET, *Dictionnaire de théologie catholique,* ed. A. VACANT et al., 15 v. (Paris 1903–50) 8.2:2628–37. R. NAZ, *Dictionnaire de droit canonique,* ed. R. NAZ, 7 v. (Paris 1933–65) 6:344–45. R. BÄUMER, *Lexikon für Theologie und Kirche,* ed. J. HOFER and K. RAHNNER, 10 v. (2d, new ed. Freiburg 1957–65) 6:815–16. **Second Council.** *Sacrorum Conciliorum nova et amplissima collectio,* 21:525–46. *Histoire des conciles d'après les documents originaux,* 5.1:721–38. *Histoire de l'église depuis les origines jusqu'à nos jours,* 9.1:137–39. F. VERNET, *Dictionnaire de théologie catholique,* 8.2:2637–44. R. NAZ, *Dictionnaire de droit canonique,* 6:346–47. R. BÄUMER, *Lexikon für Theologie und Kirche,* 6:816. **Third Council.** *Sacrorum Conciliorum nova et amplissima collectio,* 22:209–467. *Histoire des conciles d'après les documents originaux,* 5.2:1086–1112. *Histoire de l'église depuis les origines jusqu'à nos jours,* 9.2:156–74. M. PACAUT, *Alexandre III* (Paris 1956) *passim.* F. VERNET, *Dictionnaire de théologie catholique,* 8.2:2644–52. R. NAZ, *Dictionnaire de droit canonique,* 6:347–49. R. BAUMER, *Lexikon für Theologie und Kirche,* 6:816. **Fourth Council.** *Sacrorum Conciliorum nova et amplissima collectio,* 22:953–1086. *Histoire des conciles d'après les documents originaux,* 5.2:1316–98. A. LUCHAIRE, *Innocent III,* 6 v. (Paris 1906–08). *Histoire de l'église depuis les origines jusqu'à nos jours,* 10:194–211. S. KUTTNER, *Repertorium der Kanonistik* (Rome 1937) (*Studi et Testi* 71) 369–71. S. KUTTNER, "Johannes Teutonicus, das vierte Laterankonzil und die Compilatio quarta," *Miscellanea Giovanni Mercanti* (Rome 1946) v. 5 (*Studi et Testi* 125; 1946) 608–34. H. TILLMANN, *Papst Innocenz III* (Bonn 1954). A. GARCÍA Y GARCÍA, "El Concilio IV de Letrán (1215) y sus comentarios," *Traditio,* 14 (1958) 484–502. F. M. POWICKE and C. R. CHENEY, eds., *Councils and Synods,* 2.1 (Oxford 1964) 47–49. F. VERNET, *Dictionnaire de théologie catholique,* 8.2:2652–67. R. NAZ, *Dictionnaire de droit canonique,* 6:349–53. R. BÄUMER, *Lexikon für Theologie und Kirche,* 6:816–17. S. KUTTNER and A. GARCÍA Y GARCÍA, "A New Eye-witness Account of the Fourth Lateran Council," *Traditio,* 20 (1964) 115–78. F. ROBB, "The Fourth Lateran Council's Definition of Trinitarian Orthodoxy," *Journal of Ecclesiastical History,* 48 (1997): 22–43. C. SMALL, "The Fourth Lateran Council of 1215: A Turning Point in the History of Medieval Europe," *Religious Studies and Theology,* 11 (May-September 1991): 66–78. **Fifth Council.** *Sacrorum Conciliorum nova et amplissima collectio,* 32:649–1002. *Histoire des conciles d'après les documents originaux,* 8.1:339–375, 396–548. *Histoire de l'église depuis les origines jusqu'à nos jours,* 15:164–65, 187–89. H. JEDIN, *History of the Council of Trent,* tr. E. GRAF, v. 1–2 (St. Louis 1957–60), v. 3 (in prep); *Geschichte des Konzils von Trient,* 2 v. (Freiburg 1949–57; v.1, 2d ed. 1951) F. VERNET, *Dictionnaire de théologie catholique,* 8.2:2667–86. R. NAZ, *Dictionnaire de droit canonique,* 6:353–56. R. BÄUMER, *Lexikon für Theologie und Kirche,* 6:817–18. N. H. MINNICH, *Lexikon für Theologie und Kirche,* ed. M. BUCHBERGER (3d ed. Freiburg 1993) 6:670–71; *The Fifth Lateran Council (1512–1517)* (Aldershot, Hampshire 1993). O. DE LA BROSSE, in *Latran V et Trente, Historie des conciles oecuméniques,* 10 (Paris 1975), 13–114, 397–98, 411–33. P. B. T. BILIANIUK, *The Fifth Lateran Council (1512–1517) and the Eastern Churches* (Toronto 1975).

[C. DUGGAN/N. H. MINNICH]

LATERAN PACTS

Lateran Pacts refer to the treaty, financial agreement, and concordat between the Holy See and the Kingdom of Italy, signed Feb. 11, 1929, in the Lateran Palace.

Diplomatic Preliminaries. Subsequent to the seizure of the STATES OF THE CHURCH (1870), succeeding popes protested against this procedure as unjustified and refused to accept the Law of GUARANTEES. The Italian government persisted in its unwillingness to cede to the papacy any territory or to permit international mediation. Immediately after his election (Feb. 6, 1922) PIUS XI indicated his eagerness to terminate the long, embittered situation by appearing on the front balcony of St. Peter's Basilica to impart his blessing, a gesture unknown since 1870. With the triumph of Fascism (1922) Mussolini soon gave proof of a similar desire. Proposals to reform ecclesiastical legislation were introduced (1925) by the minister of justice, Alfredo Rocco, but were withdrawn when Pius XI declared that he could not recognize statutes ''unless preceded by proper negotiations and agreements with the Holy See and Us.''

Discussions that finally succeeded began on Aug. 5. 1926, between Domenico Barone, an official representing Italy, and Francesco Pacelli, legal adviser to the Holy See (and brother of the later Pius XII), authorized by the pope as Vatican representative. Their numerous meetings until 1929 were held in unviolated secrecy. Pius XI, who followed the proceedings very attentively and personally supervised all details, insisted from the start on ''recognition of the absolute sovereignty of the pope over the territory to be assigned to him.'' His interests throughout were motivated clearly by religious considerations, as those of Mussolini were by political ones.

Treaty. The treaty, consisting of a preamble and 27 articles, definitively and irrevocably settled the ROMAN QUESTION. It recognized the Holy See's absolute, visible independence and sovereignty, even in international relations. Italy affirmed the Catholic religion as the sole religion of the state, although restrictions were not imposed on other religions. VATICAN CITY was created as an independent state with its own defined territory over which the Holy See could exercise exclusive, absolute, sovereign jurisdiction, free of interference from the Italian or other governments. The treaty also admitted the right of Vatican City to issue coinage and stamps, send and receive diplomatic representatives, and govern as citizens those with fixed residence within its border. Italy guaranteed to the tiny state (108.7 acres) an adequate water supply, a link with the Italian railway system and the construction of a station within Vatican City, and connections with the telegraph, telephone, and postal services of the outside world. Various details of relations between Italy and Vatican City were arranged in other clauses.

The person of the pope was held to be sacred and inviolable. Offenses against him by deed or word were held punishable in Italian law and similar in gravity to offenses against the king. Central corporate entities of the Church were also exempted from all governmental interference.

Italy recognized the Holy See's full proprietary rights over the patriarchal basilicas of St. John Lateran, St. Mary Major, and St. Paul; also over several other churches and buildings in Rome and over the papal palace at CASTEL GANDOLFO. These also were granted extraterritoriality and immunities were given to foreign embassies, although they were part of Italian territory.

The Holy See declared its desire to remain aloof from temporal disputes between nations and from international congresses convoked to settle such disputes, unless the contending parties jointly appeal to its mission of peace. As a result Vatican City is always to be considered neutral and inviolable territory. Aircraft flights of any kind over it were prohibited. The Holy See recognized the Kingdom of Italy under the Savoy dynasty with Rome as its capital. Both parties declared the Law of Guarantees abrogated.

Financial Settlement. By a special convention constituting an integral part of the treaty (although in an appendix to it), Italy undertook to compensate the Apostolic See for its loss of the States of the Church and possessions therein. In view of Italy's economic situation, the pope reduced his legitimate claims for indemnity and settled for 750 million lire in cash and 1 billion lire in 5 percent negotiable government bonds.

Concordat. The concordat, with a preamble and 45 articles, accompanied the treaty as a necessary complement and sought to regulate in detail the status of religion and the Church in Italy. It guaranteed to the Church free exercise of its spiritual power and free, public exercise of worship. The government promised to prevent occurrences in Rome at variance with the city's sacred character. Freedom was assured the Holy See, bishops, and priests in the exercise of their religious functions. The rights of the Holy See to communicate freely with the Catholic world and to publish instructions in any language were admitted. The Holy See could also select archbishops and bishops in Italy after presenting the names to the government for possible objections. However, newly appointed bishops were obliged to take an oath of loyalty to the state. The ecclesiastical authorities were to award benefices, but Italian benefices must be given to Italian citizens; and the government was to receive previous notice of appointments to parochial benefices. The government abolished the *exequatur* and *placet*. Priests and religious were exempted from military service and jury duty. The basilicas of the Holy House at Loreto, St. Francis of Assisi, and St. Anthony at Padua and their administration were ceded to the Holy See, which was also given control of the catacombs in Rome and elsewhere in Italy.

The state recognized the civil effects of the Sacrament of Matrimony. It also agreed to have religious instruction given in public elementary and secondary schools by ecclesiastically approved priests, religious, or laymen. Religious associations and confraternities received state approval, as did auxiliary organizations of Catholic Action. Prohibition was renewed against ecclesiastics or religious who might wish to enroll or engage in political parties.

Aftermath. Almost unanimous enthusiasm greeted the pacts in Italy and elsewhere. Negotiations at times had threatened to break down completely, and the final texts embodied compromises. For Italy, however, it was a relief to end a situation injurious throughout the world to the reputation of the kingdom since its foundation. Mussolini's prestige was enhanced. The pacts were for the Holy See a great improvement over the unilateral Law of Guarantees, which gave no assurance of permanence. If Vatican City contained only a minute fraction of the area of the former States of the Church, Pius XI insisted that its size was adequate. The pontiff was especially pleased with the Concordat, by which, he said, "Italy was given back to God, and God to Italy." International guarantees were lacking in the accords, but the pope believed them useless. Early in the deliberations the question of associating other nations with the agreements was discussed and quickly dismissed. Between the date of signing the pacts and that of formal ratification (June 7), Pius XI criticized some of Mussolini's comments, especially those asserting full rights of the Fascist party over Italian youth.

During the Fascist regime many attacks were made against Catholic Action in defiance of the Concordat. The most serious conflict arose in 1931 over the charge that Catholic youth associations were engaging in political rather than religious activities. Basically the difficulties were the result of the Fascist pretension to exclusive control of all youth organizations. Pius XI also condemned the racial laws (1937), imitations of Hitler's, as a breach of the Concordat.

The Lateran Pacts outlived the overthrow of Fascism and the kingdom. After Italy became a republic (1944), the pacts were embodied in the new constitution, with the support of Communist and Socialist as well as of Christian Democratic deputies.

Bibliography: *Acta Apostolicae Sedis* 21 (1929) 209–295. A. MERCATI, *Raccolta di Concordati . . .* (Rome 1954) 2:84–133. *Treaty and Concordat between the Holy See and Italy: Official Documents* (Washington 1929) has the original text and English tr. of the pacts. F. PACELLI, *Diario della Conciliazione* (Vatican City 1959). C. A. BIGGINI, *Storia inedita della Conciliazione* (Rome 1942). D. A. BINCHY, *Church and State in Fascist Italy* (New York 1941). V. DEL GIUDICE, *La Questione romana e i rapporti tra Stato e Chiesa fina alla Conciliazione* (Rome 1947). N. TRIPODI, *I Patti Lateranesi e il Fascismo* (Bologna 1959). F. M. MARCHESI, *Il Concordato italiano dell'll febbraio 1929* (Naples 1960).

[A. RANDALL]

LATERAN PACTS 1985

On June 3, 1985, with the exchange of ratifications between the Holy See and the Italian government, the Concordat of Feb. 18, 1984, went into effect. This agreement between the Vatican and the Italian State amounts to a revision of the original Concordat which formed a part of the LATERAN PACTS of Feb. 11, 1929. Over the course of time it had become outdated in several areas. The Concordat of 1985, which probably will be referred to commonly as the "Revised Lateran Pacts," retained some of the fundamental provisions of the earlier agreement.

The revised Concordat consists of a Preamble, 14 Articles and an Additional Protocol which is to be regarded as an integral part of the agreement. There is also a Protocol of Approval to which both parties affixed their signatures on Nov. 15, 1984, and which regulates the norms governing ecclesiastical goods.

Outline of the Pact. The Preamble explains why the Holy See and the Government of the Italian Republic thought it necessary and opportune to modify the old Concordat. Since 1929, many changes had occurred in the political and social order which dictated such a modification. Additionally, developments brought about by the Second VATICAN COUNCIL on the subject of relations between Church and State likewise demanded change. There had been for several decades in Italy a political regime vastly different from that of the period of the original Pacts. After the Second World War, the nation had adopted a new Constitution and it was therefore both necessary and desirable to revise the Concordat in order to bring it into closer harmony with the Italian Constitution. The Constitution of 1948 included the principle, from the original Lateran Pacts, that "modifications of the [Lateran] Pacts, accepted by both parties, do not require a revision of the Constitution." This principle was important to both the Italian government and the Holy See in reaching their decision to revise the Lateran Pacts rather than simply abolish them completely. Such radical action would have required a change in the Constitution which, quite understandably, would have entailed a far more

Façade of St. John Lateran Cathedral, Rome. (©Ruggero Vanni/CORBIS)

complex process. The new Concordat retains throughout its text the above-mentioned principle.

In the very first article of the Concordat, the Government of the Italian Republic and the Holy See reaffirm that the State and the Catholic Church are, each in its proper order, independent and sovereign. Furthermore, each party commits itself to respect fully that principle in their mutual relations and they pledge reciprocal cooperation in promoting the good of citizens and the country. The Church, for its part, acknowledges the independence and sovereignty of the State in temporal affairs and binds itself not to interfere in those matters which are proper to the State. On the other hand, the State concedes that the Church is truly independent and sovereign in the spiritual and religious order.

In its Pastoral Constitution on the Church in the Modern World, *Gaudium et spes,* the Second Vatican Council dealt with the question of relations between the Church and the political community. The Council document stated:

> The political community and the Church are autonomous and independent of each other in their own fields. Nevertheless, both are devoted to the personal vocation of man, though under different titles. This service will redound the more effectively to the welfare of all insofar as both institutions practice better cooperation according to the local and prevailing situation . . . For man's horizons are not bounded only by the temporal order; living on the level of human history he preserves the integrity of his eternal destiny (n. 76).

While the State refrains from expressing judgments of a religious, spiritual or moral value, it does recognize that humanity has certain needs which lie beyond its scope and which the State, of itself, cannot adequately meet. At the same time, the State acknowledges that the Church can accomplish much for the good of the country. This occurs, for example, whenever the Church contributes to the uplifting of the moral tone of the citizenry, or through its acts of charity towards the impoverished in society. The Concordat makes it improbable to think of the Church and State as completely distinct one from the other. Reciprocal ignorance and mutual disinterest have been replaced by a healthy harmony which requires each party to meet with each other and to work together for the common good.

It is highly significant that in the Concordat's Additional Protocol both sides agreed that "the Catholic Church is no longer to be regarded as the only State religion." Such was the arrangement sanctioned by the original Lateran Pacts, but now the concept of a State religion implies that there exists a confessional State which is Catholic. This would be inconsistent with the teaching of the Second Vatican Council where it is declared that the Church does not desire any privileged position vis-à-vis the political community (cf. *Gaudium et spes*, n. 76).

In the second article of the Concordat, the Italian Republic recognizes that the Church enjoys ample freedom in carrying out its pastoral, educational and charitable mission of evangelization and sanctification. This Article takes into account the broad scope of the Church's mission which is not confined merely to worship but includes, among others, the tasks of educating its members and performing charitable acts. When the Church establishes its own schools, whether for the formation of its clergy or for the education of young people, it does so to fulfill its own proper mission and not to supplement the State's educational system.

In regard to the appointment of bishops, article three abrogates the practice previously in force whereby candidates for episcopal appointment had to be presented by the Holy See to the government for notification, in case it had some objection. The requirement of bishops to take an oath of fidelity to the State before the President of the Republic has also been dropped. The fourth article exempts priests, deacons and religious in vows from military service, allowing them to select some form of civil service instead in times of national emergency.

The revised Concordat, in its fifth article, assures that houses of worship cannot be occupied, expropriated or demolished by the State except for grave cause and only with the prior consent of the competent ecclesiastical authority. Additionally, in this article, the right of sanctuary is upheld.

Sundays and other religious feasts determined by both parties are officially recognized holidays according to article six. Article seven guarantees that ecclesiastical institutions and associations receive treatment identical to any other association, without discrimination or privi-

lege. The State acknowledges that institutions established or approved according to Canon Law possess a true juridical personality within society.

The most profound innovations of the Revised Concordat can be found in article eight which treats of marriage. In contrast to the original Concordat, no mention is made here of marriage as a sacrament. This is consistent with the fact that the State no longer holds that the Catholic religion is the religion of the State. The Concordat states only that the State recognizes the civil effects of marriage contracted according to the norms of Canon Law, provided that certain conditions are met. Whereas in the 1929 Concordat, sentences of nullity of marriage and dispensations from *ratum et non consummatum* marriages received ratification by the State, the Revised Concordat stipulates that only nullity cases will have this effect when one of the parties to the marriage formally requests it. At this point in the Concordat, the Holy See sought to reaffirm its teaching on marriage and wished to emphasize the solicitude which the Church has in safeguarding the dignity and the values of the family. Such a declaration is understandable in the context of legislation which had been passed in recent years that permitted divorce and abortion in Italy.

Article nine guarantees the Church the right to establish its own schools. An important element of this article is the norm governing the teaching of religion in the public schools. "The Italian government, acknowledging the value of religious culture and taking into consideration the fact that Catholicism forms a part of the historical patrimony of the Italian people, will continue to permit the teaching of religion in the public schools at every level except at the university level." The right to choose whether a pupil will receive religious training in the public school is left to the parents or the students at the time of their enrollment.

Although recognized by the State, those institutions of formation in ecclesiastical disciplines that have been established in accord with Canon Law fall under the sole competency of the ecclesiastical authority. Article eleven guarantees the exercise of religious freedom to those whose personal liberty is in some way restricted, as in the case of people in hospitals, nursing homes, prisons, the armed forces, etc. The State will appoint ecclesiastics for this service upon presentation by competent Church authority. The Holy See and the Italian Republic have also agreed to collaborate in preserving the historical and artistic patrimony which they share. The final two articles of the Concordat reiterate a constant theme, that of collaboration between the two parties. These articles call for a spirit of collaboration and conclude that not every single situation can be foreseen by the present agreement.

Thus, the door is left open for further negotiations, always in a collaborative way, should these prove necessary in the future.

Relevance. Finally, we may ask what is the importance of this Concordat for the Church in Italy? First, it does allow the Church greater freedom. The Church in Italy is now able to exercise that *libertas ecclesiae* it has received from Christ. This is the ultimate purpose of establishing an agreement between Church and State. Secondly, the Church reaches out to the State and obligates itself to collaborate to a greater extent in the promotion of the well-being of the citizenry. In the words of *Gaudium et spes,* "whatever truth, goodness, and justice is to be found in past or present human institutions is held in high esteem by the Church . . ." (n. 42). Thirdly, the Church cannot be dependent on the State as it strives to fulfill its own mission. Thus, there is an urgent need to involve the laity in a far greater way and to make the Catholic community understand that it must support its clergy and institutions. The important matter of the teaching of religion in the schools can no longer be taken for granted. Parents and children are now called upon to make an active choice for this institution.

For the Church in Italy, the Revised Concordat signifies greater freedom but at the same time it implies on the part of the Church a greater effort to collaborate with the Italian government. Of particular importance is the notion that the Church must now rely more and more on itself for its own mission.

In addressing Mr. Bettino Craxi, then President of the Italian Republic, Pope John Paul II referred to the Revised Concordat as "an instrument of harmony and collaboration." The Concordat, he noted, "is situated now in a society characterized by free competition of ideas and by pluralistic articulation of the various social components. It can and must constitute an element of promotion and growth, fostering the profound unity of ideals and sentiments by which all Italians feel themselves to be brothers in the same homeland."

Bibliography: Text of the Revised Concordat *La Civiltà Cattolica* I (1984) 470–478 [Italian]. F. LOMBARDI, "I nuovi rapporti tra la Chiesa e lo Stato in Italia," *ibid.,* 479–494. G. DE ROSA, "Che cosa cambia in Italia dopo la revisione del Concordato?" *ibid.,* 176–187. Address in *L'Osservatore Romano,* English edition (August 19, 1985): 6–7, contains addresses in English on the concordat by A. CASSOROLI, B. CRAXI, and JOHN PAUL II.

[P. LAGHI]

LATHROP, ALPHONSA, MOTHER

Author, foundress of the Servants of Relief for Incurable Cancer; b. Lenox, Mass., May 20, 1851; d. Hawthorne, N.Y., July 9, 1926. The youngest child of Nathaniel and Sophia (Peabody) Hawthorne, Rose was taken as an infant to Liverpool, England, where her father served as U.S. consul. The family subsequently spent two years in Italy before returning to Concord, Mass., in 1860. In 1871 Rose married George Parsons Lathrop in London. They lived in New York City until Lathrop moved to Boston as assistant editor of the *Atlantic Monthly.* During these years, Rose wrote verses and short stories that appeared in the *Independent, Harper's Bazaar,* the *American, Scribner's, Appleton's Journal,* and *St. Nicholas;* a book of poems, *Along the Shore,* was published in 1888. In 1876 a son, Francis Hawthorne Lathrop, was born, but he died of diphtheria in 1881. Received into the Catholic Church in 1891 by Alfred Young, CSP, the Lathrops collaborated on *A Story of Courage* (1894), a history of the Georgetown Sisters of the Visitation. At this time, however, Lathrop's increasing intemperance led his wife, with the vicar-general's permission, to leave him. Learning from Young of a young seamstress sent to Blackwell's Island to die of cancer, Mrs. Lathrop determined to devote her life to serving victims of this disease. After training for three months at the New York Cancer Hospital, she began work on the lower east side of the city. For financial assistance she depended on persons who learned of her plans from the articles she wrote. She also found time to publish her *Memories of Hawthorne* (1897).

Her husband died in 1898 and in 1899 Clement Theunte, OP, received Mrs. Lathrop and her associate, Alice Huber, as Dominican tertiaries. As Sister M. Alphonsa and Sister M. Rose, they made their first vows on Dec. 8, 1900, and established the Dominican Congregation of St. Rose of Lima, incorporated as the Servants of Relief for Incurable Cancer (*see* DOMINICAN SISTERS). As the community grew, its work expanded. The motherhouse, novitiate, and a cancer home were established at Hawthorne, and aid for patients was secured through Mother Alphonsa's magazine, *Christ's Poor,* and through her series of published reports.

Bibliography: K. BURTON, *Sorrow Built a Bridge: A Daughter of Hawthorne* (New York 1937). T. MAYNARD, *A Fire was Lighted: The Life of Rose Hawthorne Lathrop* (Milwaukee 1948). M. JOSEPH, *Out of Many Hearts* (Hawthorne, N.Y. 1961), unpub. biog.

[M. L. C. DUNN]

LATIMER, HUGH

Bishop of Worcester and most influential preacher of the early English Reformation; b. Thurcaston, Leicestershire, date uncertain but perhaps 1492; d. Oxford, Oct.

16, 1555. He came of yeoman stock, and was educated at Cambridge, elected Fellow of Clare Hall (1510), and awarded the master of arts degree in 1514. The following year he was ordained. He remained at the university for more than 20 years and came to occupy a position of prominence and influence there, being appointed a university preacher and chaplain (1522). His disputation for the bachelor of divinity degree in 1524 was an attack on Melanchthon's teachings. Soon thereafter, however, he became a leader of the group of Cambridge reformers who had come under the influence of Erasmus and Martin Luther. He preached on behalf of an authorized English translation of the Bible and took a leading part in supporting Henry VIII against papal claims in the matter of the King's marriage. He likewise preached in defense of the royal supremacy.

In 1535 Latimer was made bishop of Worcester. As a Member of Parliament he voted for the suppression of the lesser monasteries. He also gave strong support to the government's destruction of the shrines. In 1539 he resigned his see, believing that this was the King's wish. In the changing religious scenes of this period, Latimer experienced varying fortunes. He had been charged with heresy in the reign of Henry VIII and had been forced to recant. He had served as the King's chaplain and shortly after had been imprisoned and forbidden to preach. In 1548 he formally rejected the doctrine of transubstantiation. As court preacher under Edward VI he exercised a great influence on the formation of Protestant thinking in England. When Queen Mary Tudor came to the throne he was charged with heresy, brought to trial, condemned, and burned at the stake with Nicholas RIDLEY.

Bibliography: *Works,* ed. G. E. CORRIE, 2 v. (Cambridge, Eng. 1844–45). A. G. CHESTER, *Hugh Latimer, Apostle to the English* (Philadelphia 1954). M. SCHMIDT, *Die Religion in Geschichte und Gegenwart*[3] 4:238–239.

[D. J. GUNDERSON]

LATIN (IN THE CHURCH)

At the time of the first Pentecost the inauguration of the Church the most commonly spoken languages in Jerusalem were ARAMAIC, GREEK, and Latin. Natives of the city knew Aramaic (a later dialect of Hebrew) as their birthright. From the fourth century B.C. onward, Greek had been the most important language of commerce and communication throughout the Mediterranean; as a consequence, many speakers of Aramaic were more comfortable reading the Holy Scriptures in what amounted to the vernacular i.e., Greek available in the Septuagint, a translation intended for those no longer fluent in the earlier Hebrew. Latin arrived as a language of irrepressible polit-

Mother Alphonsa Lathrop.

ical force first under Pompey in 67 B.C. and finally, after some reorganization, in the days of Augustus, who in A.D. 6 combined Judaea and Samaria into a single Roman province. The inscription placed above the head of Jesus at his crucifixion was written, as John attests, ''in Hebrew, in Latin, in Greek'' (19.20).

The ubiquity of *koine,* or ''common,'' Greek during the Hellenistic Age (from the death of Alexander in 323 B.C.) and the reality of Roman control of the Italian peninsula (from 264 B.C.) with a South largely inhabited by Greek immigrants together meant that even the Latin-speaking Romans found it profitable to learn Greek as a second language. The plebeian Roman soldier, however lacking in formal education, would acquire Greek when on duty abroad; those of the patrician class at home who entered public service saw that Greek was a necessary part of their training. Quintilian, the Roman teacher of rhetoric, notes (*ca.* A.D. 95.) that public servants had for several generations used the exercise of translation from Greek into Latin to sharpen their verbal facility. Consequently, when Peter came from the Greek environment of Jerusalem to Rome he found among people high and low a fully bilingual community where the newborn Church could continue to use the worldwide language of Greek.

Hugh Latimer. (Archive Photos)

Greek is the original language of the New Testament from Paul's Letter to the Galatians (*ca.* 49) to the Second Letter of "Peter" (*ca.* 100–125); it is the tongue of the earliest Christian Fathers from Clement of Rome to Eusebius and beyond; it is the language of the Eucharistic liturgy and other formal rites as prescribed by the early Church. The NICENE CREED is a Greek document.

Beginnings of Ecclesiastical Latin

The first missionaries from Rome to the world found in the province of Africa (annexed in 146 B.C. after the last of the Punic Wars) a vast territory centered on a reconstructed Carthage, whose inhabitants spoke both the mother tongue Punic, or Phoenician and Latin, the language of their Roman administrators, but very little Greek. As a result, it was convenient for these bilingual missionaries to use Latin when spreading the Gospel to the Africans. Africa is the source of the earliest Church record originally composed in Latin, the Acts of the Scillitan Martyrs (180), in the form of a Roman legal procedure, from which (§12) we gather most importantly that a Latin version of the Bible (including the letters of Paul) was by then in circulation. Here in north Africa, the anonymous translators of the Bible showed the way to TERTULLIAN (*ca.* 160 –*ca.* 225), the earliest Christian writer in Latin whose works are extant. By the start of his ca-

reer, the Latin-speaking community through its vernacular liturgies had already become familiar with hundreds of words now standard in Christian terminology, e.g., *angelus, baptisma, blasphemus, daemonium, ecclesia, ethnicus, eucharistia, extasis, martyr, Paracletus, prophetia, annuntiatio, gratia, peccator, persecutor, sacramentum, saeculum.* Tertullian's unforced use of these terms assumes their long familiarity. In addition, he may be given credit for extending Christian vocabulary; his background in law, and its necessary training in Greek, equipped him as a coiner of words from Greek into Latin (e.g., *exomologesis, christianismus*) as well as from Latin resources (e.g., *vivificatio, trinitas*). In his day, Christians and non-Christians alike sought mastery of *declamatio,* a speech-writing exercise on set topics practiced in the schools of rhetoric. Thus as an apologist of the early Church, he was able use his secular education to defend Christianity.

Latin Translations of the Bible

The earliest translation of the Bible from Greek into the vernacular, i.e., Latin, grew out of an understandable pastoral concern: the people's immediate need to hear the Word of God preached in their own tongue. But the style and language of the "Old Latin" versions of the Bible made for unusual works of Latin since they preserved both the Semitic thought and the Greek expression of the originals. The Old Latin New Testament is filled with "loan translations," i.e., attempts at putting not only the thought of the original into a different tongue, but also its idiomatic syntax. However odd such a Grecized Latin may have sounded to the uneducated flocks of north Africa, nevertheless, the bilingual missionaries, as their shepherds, very early on through their preaching and exegesis fostered an enduring devotion to the expression as well as to the thought of the Good News in Latin. At the core of many primitive Christian liturgies was the reading of the Latin Bible, a circumstance which soon made familiar that which was once odd.

Toward the end of the fourth century, when in the West Latin had overtaken Greek as the language of the Church, there existed various forms of a Latin Bible in Christian communities across Europe as well as in Africa. The time had come for the compiling of a uniform edition to serve the needs of a widespread, ever more Greekless, Church of the West. So thought Pope DAMASUS, who in 382 asked Sophronius Eusebius Hieronymus, or JEROME, to begin this enormous task. The Pope's insight embraced not only the recognition of the need for uniformity, but more significantly, the realization that Latin had become the *de facto* official language of the Western Church; he had seen in his lifetime the use of Greek in the Eucharistic liturgy its last major use finally give way to Latin.

Urged on (after the death of the pope) by bishops Cromatius and Heliodorus, Jerome translated the Old Testament books from the original Hebrew not from the Septuagint, itself a translation. (Some OT books, such as Baruch and Wisdom, probably unseen by Jerome, have come down to us only in Old Latin translations from the Septuagint.) Looking both to preserve and correct as much as he could of the time-honored Old Latin versions, Jerome carefully emended the Latin of the Psalms by comparing it to the Greek of the Septuagint (while also making an entirely new rival translation of the Psalms directly from the Hebrew), but only slightly refurbished the Old Latin of the New Testament, often simply transposing phrases to conform to the word order of the Greek original. For instance, he corrected *et pax in terra* "and peace on earth" to *et in terra pax* "and on earth peace" (καὶ ἐπὶ γῆς εἰρήνη) (Lk 2.14). Jerome's ideal was to serve both the *Hebraea veritas* and the *Graeca veritas* the authentic Hebrew of the Old Testament and the authentic Greek of the New. Nevertheless, he anticipated (rightly) that for his troubles some would call him a *falsarius sacrilegus* "sacrilegious falsifier." Only gradually, over the next 300 years, did the Old Latin version yield ground to Jerome's Vulgate, or "published," edition of the Latin Bible. Not one of the many Bible quotations in the sixth-century work, *Instituta Regularia Divinae Legis,* by Junillus, comes from the Hieronymian VULGATE. Furthermore, the existence of at least one ninth- and one twelfth-century manuscript containing excerpts from the Old Latin translation of 2 Maccabees 7 bears witness to the fact that religious culture, once firmly established, changes but slowly. In 1546, the Council of TRENT at last gave formal approval to the work of Jerome and his successors; the Vulgate had finally become the *editio typica,* or official version, of the Hebrew and Greek originals. It was revised under the auspices of Pope Sixtus V (1589) and Pope Clement VIII (1592, 1593, 1598). The Nova Vulgata, the current *editio typica,* made its appearance in 1979.

Two Levels of Ecclesiastical Latin

Among the earliest Latin Fathers were men trained in rhetoric and the sophisticated literature of classical Latin and Greek; nevertheless, they did not hesitate to apply their secular skills to defend or explain Christianity despite the fact that its basic texts were couched in a graceless Latin derived from a rude Greek. Such Latin Fathers include Tertullian, Minucius Felix, Lactantius, and, of a later generation, Ambrose, Jerome, and Augustine. Because their works of apologetics and exegesis added to the fund of basic Christian texts, ecclesiastical Latinity was of two kinds: one that produced original works by known authors, where the genius and power of

St. Jerome. (Archive Photos)

the language was free to speak out boldly on every page, and another an anonymous and earlier kind that timidly fulfilled the confining task of nearly verbatim translation of the sacred books, a too cautious Latin which the early Fathers found themselves in the uncomfortable position of having to support. The unknown translators' respect for the sacred original and fear of paraphrase had at least initially restrained the proper use of Latin in the Church. (In contrast, Quintilian earlier praised translation as an exercise that gave Latin speakers free rein in turning the thought of a Greek original into idiomatic Latin.) Jerome exemplifies the tension between the two Latins: "What does Horace have to do with the Psalter? Maro with the Gospels? Cicero with the Apostle [Paul]?" (Letter XXII, 29). Despite Jerome's love of the choice language and style of classical literature, ironically, because of his work in revising the Old Latin translations of the Bible, his name is virtually the only one attached to them. But next to his classical library brought to the desert from Rome, he could point with satisfaction to the *bibliotheca Christi,* "the library of Christ" (Letter LX, 10): Tertullian, Cyprian, Lactantius, Hilary of Poitiers, Minucius Felix, Victorinus, Arnobius. AUGUSTINE, a native speaker of Punic, versed in rhetoric and the classics, both spoke and wrote a powerful Latin as a second language, and yet he, too, accepted the fact that the literal translations of the Bible had left no room for the display of an idiomatic, if not eloquent, style. The Greek sacred corpus, to begin with, had not been written in the elegant dialect of Plato but instead in the later *koine,* the common Greek of its time; the anonymous Latin translators, unconscious of literary history, wrote in the Vulgar Latin of their time, one far removed from the Ciceronian ideal. Of this both Jerome and Augustine were fully aware. Later Christian Doctors, such as THOMAS AQUINAS, were wholly uninhibited by the question of the levels of Latinity. The language of Aquinas addresses human knowledge and divine revelation in a clear and beautiful manner, proving that ecclesiastical Latin can be the vehicle of powerful philosophical thought.

Latin Superseded as the Vernacular but Maintained by the Church

The partition of the Roman Empire (330) and the dissolution of its western half (early fifth century) accelerated an inevitable process: Latin both began to forget itself and continued to remember itself. When it proceeded unconsciously to change, former Latin-speaking provinces no longer in communication with a centripetal Rome (indeed, in his last days Constantine ruled from Constantinople) each began to develop imperceptibly a local dialect from the prevalent but now moribund tongue of their former rulers. By the end of the sixth century, these local vernaculars were on the way to becoming the Romance languages: Romanian, Italian, French, Spanish, Portuguese, Romansch. One example of the transformation will suffice: we can say that by 1100 with the appearance of *Le Chanson de Roland* the process in Gallia, now France, was fairly well complete; Latin, unchecked, had become French. But when Latin remained conscious of its long history, aided by the unyielding sameness of the written-down word and among Christians by the desire of the Church to preserve rather than to innovate, it took on the role of a second language of the learned class. Educated men of the Middle Ages looked before and after upon two worlds: they might choose to speak or not an emerging patois, such as French or Italian, while at the same time in their formal studies they strove to emulate the style of Cicero, that paragon of classical Latinity, and aimed for a public career where a more formal Latin, written or spoken, was required. The Frankish scholar Einhard (*ca.* 770–840), educated in the Thuringian monastery of Fulda with its excellent classical library, wrote the Latin biography of Charlemagne in a clear imitation of the style of Cicero and the manner of Suetonius. Departures from the classical norm reveal him as a man of his day, conversant with legal and ecclesiastical texts important to his life and work. Literate Christians over many centuries could read Latin in its highest form in Cicero or Virgil, and still cherish the now no longer strange Latin of the Bible with its close imitation of constructions peculiar to Greek. As time passed, however, and the new vernacular languages became firmly established, the uneducated faithful were no longer so well served by Latin. In Italy, for example, DANTE ALIGHIERI, after much hesitation, chose to write his *Commedia,* not in Latin, now limited to scholars, but in Italian, the tongue understood by all. Translations of the Latin version of the Bible (in whole or substantially so) into the various European vernaculars came relatively early: Anglo-Saxon, *ca.* 1000; Anglo-Norman, *ca.* 1350; French, 13th century; German, early 15th century; Swedish, 15th century; Italian, 1472; Spanish, 1478; Dutch, 1545. These several vernacular translations, designed to serve pastoral needs, all appeared before the opening of the Council of Trent (1545 1563). As a Counter-Reformation measure, the council gave a unique place to the Vulgate translation of the Bible by declaring it divinely inspired, thus ensuring for the time that translations would continue to be made from this Latin version. The use of Latin in the Eucharistic liturgy confirmed by the bull, *Quo Primum,* promulgated by Pope Pius V in 1570 moreover continued well into the twentieth century. From the sixteenth century onward, Latin was sharply perceived as a sacral language, one entirely set apart from the vernacular. The use of Latin passed from a pastoral function to a canonical one.

Characteristic Features of Liturgical Latin

The most remarkable stylistic features in the Roman liturgy were taken from the old tradition of pre-Christian Rome. In the canon of the Mass the striking use of parallelism, the polished sentence structure, the accumulation of synonyms, and the almost legal precision in the expression are all very closely related to the ancient Roman prayer style. Furthermore, in the canon and in the presidential prayers there is a certain predilection for ancient Roman religious terms, which are sometimes even preferred to the equivalent words of the Christian vocabulary. Thus, for example, the ancient Roman word *preces* (which occurs together with *precatio* and *deprecatio* in the early liturgical texts) partly replaces *oratio,* the early Christian word for "prayer." Next to the early Christian *orare,* "to pray," we find the old Roman *precari. Beatitudo* is used more often than the early *refrigerium,* a word derived from popular usage. Official terms from the Roman tradition, such as *pontifex* and *antistes,* are found beside *episcopus; praesul* another old Roman word beside *presbyter*. These pre-Christian elements had been neglected by the earliest Christian communities, but by the end of the fourth century any Christian texts that were not translations freely availed themselves of Latin's wide scope. Christians educated in rhetoric, such as Ambrose, fully conscious of the history of the language and the classical models such as Cicero, did not hesitate to compose liturgical texts replete with rhetorical devices (e.g., parallelism, tricolon, isocola, antithesis, chiasmus, synchysis, and paradox) and sophisticated rhythmical clausulae. Such a text is the glorious Exsultet, believed to be the work of Ambrose.

The Ambrosian Hymn

In the same period in which the Latinization of the Roman liturgy was completed, the Western Church was enriched by a new literary form: the so-called Ambrosian hymn. Although HILARY OF POITIERS was the first in the West to introduce hymns on Greek and Syrian models, it was AMBROSE who fully realized the potential of such a popular form of communication. So completely was Ambrose's name associated with these hymns that the genre itself, taken up by many successors, early on was styled the "Ambrosian hymn." The canonical hours as prescribed by the rule of Benedict of Nursia made constant use of Ambrosian hymns, very many of which are still to be found in the Roman Breviary. The ones generally considered to be the work of Ambrose are "Aeterne rerum Conditor," "Deus Creator omnium," "Jam surgit hora tertia," and "Veni Redemptor gentium." All are in quantitative measures (quatrains of iambic diameter); all reinforce points of Christian dogma.

The Curial Style

When the Western Church was becoming more and more consolidated, the papal Curia gradually took the place of much temporal authority, finally even adopting many of its outward forms. In this combining of the ecclesiastical and the secular, there slowly developed a papal chancery language and style that even today continues to look to classical Latin as its model for its official documents. In its purely ceremonial form for example in proclaiming various honors the Latin used can be nearly inscrutable. In papal bulls, however, it often demonstrates a notable clarity, power, and grace; such a Latin is regarded as the guide when papal documents are translated into the world's dominant languages.

The Triumph of the Vernacular

Since the Second Vatican Council (1962 1965), the Church has borne witness to the fact that the message of the gospel is not language-specific, that it transcends all languages, including Latin. Although the council's Constitution on the Sacred Liturgy declared that "the use of the Latin language is to be preserved in the Latin rites," it was left open to "the competent territorial [i.e., national] ecclesiastical authority . . . to determine whether, and to what extent, the vernacular language is to be used" (36). The result has been that, although Latin continues to hold an honored place, it has in the celebration of the Eucharist throughout the world been superseded by the various living languages of the people "for the sake of a better comprehension of the mystery being celebrated" (*General Instruction of the Roman Missal,* intro., §12). To such an extent has Latin declined in importance that the official hymn of the Jubilee Year 2000 appeared in several vernacular tongues, but not in Latin.

Such a rapid reversal could not have been anticipated by Pope John XXIII in February 1962 when, before the opening of Vatican II later that year, he issued *Veterum Sapientia,* his Apostolic Constitution on promoting the study of Latin. In this bull John repeated the sentiments of his predecessor, Pius XI, who (in 1922) had praised Latin as universal, immutable, and non-vernacular.

The movement away from Latin to the national languages was well underway at the time of the promulgation (in 1969) by Pope Paul VI of the *Missale Romanum* in its most comprehensive reworking since the sixteenth century. This revision (the *Novus Ordo Missae*) was in keeping with the general norms set forth in the Constitution on the Sacred Liturgy, 34 36, of the Second Vatican Council. The General Instruction of the Roman Missal (GIRM) and the Missal itself, including the *Ordo Missae cum populo,* took its more precise form in 1975, and now has the force of law. In his *motu proprio Ecclesia Dei* (1988), Pope John Paul II renewed permission for the use of the Roman Missal of 1962 (the 400-year-old legacy of the Council of Trent) which he first granted in his universal indult of 1984, *Quattuor abhinc annos.* Thus today the liturgy of the Eucharist may be celebrated in Latin in two forms, that of the Missal of 1962 and that of 1975 these provisions occurring, however, in the much larger context of the now prevalent use of the vernacular.

The waning of Latin is further marked in the differences between the Code of CANON LAW of 1917 and that of 1983. While the 1917 Code prescribed classroom lectures in Latin, the 1983 Code states that "the program for priestly formation is to make provision that the students are not only carefully taught their native language but also that they are well skilled in the Latin language" (can. 249); in the contemporary American seminary/college, this latter requirement may be fulfilled in two semesters. The 1983 Code, first promulgated in Latin, is freely available to the clergy in the vernacular.

At the start of the third millennium, Greek had been for so long as a former predominant language of the Church, that it was worthy of the utmost respect and serious study. Scholars of philosophy and history know that familiarity with the Greek and Latin sources, not to mention the Hebrew, affords a priceless perspective on the Church and its mission. But the uniqueness of the Latin language over the course of eighteen centuries has been in its changing roles. Originally, Latin was adopted as a pastoral measure to communicate the message of Christ in a language understood by most of the Christian people. Later, the mark of catholicity led Church leaders to emphasize the need for one enduring tongue, Latin, which could be reliably studied and interpreted for the faithful throughout the world. Finally, the process having come full circle, current pastoral concerns have permitted the option of liturgical practice in the vernacular. Although Latin is no longer the common tongue, nevertheless it retains an honored place as the sacral and canonical language of the Church.

Bibliography: P.-M. BOGAERT, "La Bible Latine des Origines au Moyen Âge: Aperçu Historique, État des Questions," *Revue Théologique de Louvain* 19 (1988) 137 159, 276 314. A. BUGNINI, *The Reform of the Liturgy, 1948 1975,* tr. M. J. O'CONNELL (Collegeville, Minn. 1990). F. DI CAPUA, *Il Latino Letterario Medievale e lo Stile della Curia Romana* (Rome 1948). E. DEKKERS and A. GAAR *Clavis Patrum Latinorum* (3rd ed. Turnhout 1995). B. FISCHER, *Biblia Sacra iuxta Vulgatam Versionem* (3rd ed. Stuttgart 1983). H. J. FREDE, *Kirchenschriftsteller: Verzeichnis und Sigel,* Vetus Latina 1/1 (4th ed. Freiburg 1996). M. T. GIBSON, *The Bible in the Latin West,* The Medieval Book 1 (Notre Dame 1993). M. G. HAESSLY, *Rhetoric in the Sunday Collects of the Roman Missal* (St. Louis 1938). R. E. LATHAM, comp. *Revised Medieval Latin Word-List from British and Irish Sources* (Oxford 1965). B. LÉCUREUX, *Le Latin, Langue de l'Église* (2nd ed. Paris 1998). E. LÖFSTEDT, *Late Latin* (Cambridge, Mass. 1959). F. MANTELLO, and A. G. RIGG, *Medieval Latin* (Washington, D.C. 1996). C. C. MARTINDALE, *The Prayers of the Missal* (New York 1937). B. M. METZGER, "The Latin Versions," 285–374, *The Early Versions of the New Testament* (Oxford 1977). C. MOHRMANN, *Liturgical Latin, Its Origin and Character* (Washington, D.C. 1957). L. R. PALMER, *The Latin Language* (3rd ed. London 1961). JOHN XXIII, apostolic constitution *Veterum Sapientia* (22 Feb. 1962). PAUL VI, apostolic constitution *Missale Romanum* (3 April 1969). JOHN PAUL II, motu proprio *Ecclesia Dei* (2 July 1988). J. QUASTEN and A. BERARDINO, *Patrology,* 4 vols. (Westminster, Md. 1950). F. J. E. RABY, *A History of Christian-Latin Poetry in the Middle Ages* (Oxford 1953). L. D. STEPHENS, "Syllable Quality in Late Latin Clausulae," *Phoenix* 40 (1986) 72 91. K. STRECKER and R. B. PALMER, *Introduction to Medieval Latin* (Zurich and Berlin 1957).

[J. F. COLLINS]

LATIN EMPIRE OF CONSTANTINOPLE

Latin Empire of Constantinople is the modern name for the state created on the ruins of the Byzantine Empire by members of the Fourth CRUSADE in 1204; it endured until 1261. To contemporaries, it was known as Imperium Constantinopolitanum or as Romania.

After the capture of Constantinople on April 13, 1204, the crusaders, roughly half Venetian and half French, Flemings, and north-Italians, established a commission of 12 to elect a new "emperor" who would replace the former Byzantine Emperor. Baldwin of Flanders was chosen; when in 1206 he perished in Bulgarian captivity, he was succeeded by his brother Henry of Hainault (emperor 1206–1216), the ablest of the Latin Emperors. After his death, a succession of ineffectual rulers ended in the weak reign of Baldwin II (1240–1261, died 1273).

The Latin Empire borrowed some trappings of the Byzantine Empire: the coronation ceremony, the imperial purple boots, and certain titles. However, it was essentially a feudal monarchy. Its vassal states included the Kingdom of Thessalonike, the Principality of Achaia, and the Duchy of Athens, as well as the fiefs of individual knights in the vicinity of Constantinople. Uniquely among medieval feudal realms, it had a form of written constitution. Each new emperor was required to swear to abide by three documents: the pre-Conquest treaty of March 1204 which provided for the election of a new ruler and a division of the expected spoils, an agreement made in October 1204 which parceled out the territories of the former Byzantine Empire, and a treaty of October 1205 between the then-regent Henry and the Venetians which regulated the latter's responsibilities to the emperor. In fact, a council consisting half of feudal vassals of the emperor and half of Venetians had to consent to any significant civil or military action of the Latin Emperor; it proved a hindrance for most emperors.

Rival states shortly appeared on former Byzantine territory, founded by members of previous Byzantine ruling families. In Trebizond, a branch of the Comneni family established itself under Georgian protection. At Nicaea and in northwest Anatolia, Theodore Laskaris, son-in-law of the former emperor Alexius III Angelus, created a state which eventually superseded the Latin Empire. In Epirus (in northwest Greece), an illegitimate son of John (Angelus) Doukas took the name of Michael Angelus Comnenus Doukas and established a state which for a while threatened the Latin Empire. The so-called "Second Bulgarian Empire" was the greatest immediate danger: in 1205, Baldwin I was captured, imprisoned, and killed (1206) by its ruler Ioannitsa or Kaloyan (d. 1207). His successor, John Asen II (1218–1241), was alternately ally and enemy of the Latin emperors, and effectively arbiter of the empire's destiny. After John Asen's death, the Lascarids of Nicaea acquired most of the territory in

Thrace that John Asen had taken from the Latins. In 1259, Michael VIII Palaeologus overthrew the Lascarids, and on July 25, 1261, his general, Alexius Strategopoulus, seized Constantinople. The Byzantine Empire was reinstituted in its old capital, on a restricted basis, but destined to last until the Turkish conquest of 1453.

Because in 1204 the imperial crown had gone to Baldwin I, a Fleming, the Venetians were entitled to choose a patriarch for Constantinople; they picked Thomas Morosini, a subdeacon of noble Venetian descent. Pope Innocent III, although displeased that he had not been consulted, consented to the choice. Innocent and later popes tried to minimize the Venetian control of the Latin Patriarchate, with little success. While the upper clergy were Venetian or French, the parish priests remained Greek. For the most part, they submitted to rule by the Latin bishops, but remained at heart loyal to the Greek church, specifically to the Orthodox Patriarch chosen at Nicaea in 1208, whose successor returned to Constantinople in 1261.

While Dominican and Franciscan friars attempted missionary activity among the Greek population, few were willing to follow them. The violence, greed, and oppression of the victorious crusaders, and of the Latin clergy, alienated the Greeks. Only Emperor Henry of Hainault, by his moderation and outstanding justice, won support among the populace. His successors arrogantly disdained the Greeks. The principal result of Latin rule in Constantinople was to solidify Orthodox hostility to the Western Church.

Bibliography: R. WOLFF, "The Latin Empire of Constantinople, 1204–1261," in *A History of the Crusades*, ed. K. SETTON, 2nd ed., vol. II (Madison 1969), 187–233. R. L. WOLFF, *Studies in the Latin Empire of Constantinople* (London 1976). M. ANGOLD, *Church and Society in Byzantium under the Comneni, 1081–1261* (Cambridge 1995). D. E. QUELLER and TH. MADDEN, *The Fourth Crusade: The Conquest of Constantinople*, 2nd ed. (Philadelphia 1997). D. J. GEANAKOPLOS, *Emperor Michael Palaeologus and the West 1258–1282: A Study in Byzantine-Latin Relations* (Cambridge, Mass. 1959).

[C. M. BRAND]

LATIN RITE

The Latin Rite, or Latin Church as it is called in canon 1 of the Code of CANON LAW, is the part of the Church that follows the ROMAN RITE in liturgy, has its own special canonical discipline, and is subject to the bishop of Rome as patriarch of the West. (*See* ROME, PATRIARCHATE OF.)

History. At the beginning of the Christian Era, the disciplinary rules of the Church varied from one country to another and even from one community to another. Ecclesiastical laws applicable to a particular area were formulated only during the fourth and fifth centuries with the development of the PATRIARCHATES.

Early Development. Endowed with jurisdiction over a specified and often large territory, the patriarchs enjoyed a wide autonomy in most matters of administrative and disciplinary order. Juridically the preeminence of the patriarchal sees over areas was recognized for the first time at the Council of Nicaea I (c. 6) in 325, confirmed by the Council of Constantinople I (c. 2) in 381, and reconfirmed by the Council of Chalcedon (c. 28) in 451. Constantinople I and Chalcedon extended the patriarchal privilege to the See of Constantinople and to the See of Jerusalem. The patriarchs of Alexandria, Antioch, Constantinople, and Jerusalem became the chiefs of all the bishops of Egypt and the Near East, their jurisdiction corresponding roughly to the *Praefectura Orientis* created by Diocletian for the East. The Western prefectures of the empire, Italy, Gaul, and Illyricum, made up the Roman patriarchate. Each patriarchate organized itself, held synods, enacted laws, and created its own particular canonical discipline.

Notwithstanding the decree of Nicaea, in the fourth and fifth centuries the Roman patriarchate did not wield a very wide authority outside Italy and especially outside the ten suburbicarian provinces of the city of Rome, where the pope exercised all the powers of a true metropolitan. A progressive centralization in the administrative and disciplinary order was to come in the West, but in the sixth century such centralized power as becomes a real patriarch was not exercised by the bishop of Rome in the Latin Church. Rome did not seem to care very much for the title of patriarch, contenting itself with the attributes of primacy.

Before St. Leo the Great (440–461), a few steps were taken tending toward administrative and disciplinary centralization under Rome. Legates of the pope were sent to certain troubled areas in the Church, as in the case of the creation of the Vicariate Apostolic of Illyricum and of the establishment of the short-lived Vicariate Apostolic of Arles in France. But nearly everywhere in the Western Church—in northern Italy, in Spain, in Africa—the local authorities retained practically all jurisdiction in the administrative order.

Definitive Establishment. The pontificate of St. Leo marked real progress toward centralization, although the onslaught of the barbarians marching through southern Europe did bring about a pause in the unifying movement. Yet the trend revived with new vigor after the conversion of England by missionaries who were sent by Rome and remained under the influence of the Roman

Church. Indirectly, through the English monks, the authority of the pope even in matters of discipline was increased all over Europe. From England came the apostles of Germany, the ecclesiastical counselors of the first Carolingians, and the whole centralizing movement that, ridding the Latin Church of all the complications brought about by local primacies and national churches, was to unite in the hands of the bishop of Rome many of the powers exercised previously by the local Churches.

Although in most countries (e.g., Africa, Spain, and France) for several centuries the local episcopacies enjoyed a large measure of autonomy in administrative and disciplinary matters, even in those days great authority was attributed to Rome. The intervention of the bishop of Rome as head of the Western Church was not infrequently solicited to solve thorny or more difficult problems of a local nature. Some of the appeals to Rome against certain decisions of metropolitans and particular synods are well known: the affair of Bishop Marcianus of Arles (the right to excommunicate a bishop recognized as belonging to the bishop of Rome by the bishops of Gaul and of Carthage), the case of the Spanish bishops of Mérida and Astorga (a deposed bishop appealed to Rome against the synodal sentence condemning him), and the controversy centering around St. Cyprian in Africa. Nevertheless, at the time of St. Leo the Great, centralization in the Western Church had made very little headway; and Rome, which did not intervene in episcopal ordinations, particular councils, and the like, had no power comparable to that exercised by Alexandria over Egypt.

Among the causes that contributed considerably to increase the power of the bishop of Rome and to consolidate the centralizing trend in administrative matters were two initiatives of major importance. The pope began to take a more direct hand in cases concerning the erection and division of dioceses. Examples of such interventions can be traced as far back as the fourth and fifth centuries in Italy, in Burgundy, and in Gaul; but the intervention of Rome later became a more regular practice. At the end of the eleventh century, such interventions constituted an accepted principle of canon law. The right to erect, unite, or divide dioceses was reserved to the pope, as evidenced from a letter of Urban II written in 1092 to the archbishop of Reims: "Solius etenim Apostolici est Episcopatus conjugere, conjunctos disjungere aut etiam novos constituere," a rule reiterated by Innocent III and recorded in the decretals (*Corpus iuris canonici* [Leipzig 1879–81; repr. Graz 1955] X 1.1.7).

Another measure taken by the pope was equally conducive to the strengthening and the extension of the centralizing power of Rome in disciplinary matters. By the institution and the establishment of *legati a latere* (*legati missi, legati nati, legati nuntii*) in different areas of Christendom with the power to act in the name of the pope, the bishop of Rome intervened directly in the affairs of local Churches. Several of these legations, originally called vicariates apostolic, go as far back as the sixth century, and many were added in the following centuries. During the great crusade undertaken by the popes in the eleventh century for the reformation of the clergy and the faithful, these vicars were used to apply the program of reformation and further the interests of the Roman see.

Later Development. By the end of the twelfth century, the Latin Church already possessed an imposing and very comprehensive disciplinary system, built up gradually over the years since Constantine and his edict granting full liberty to Christianity. A vast arsenal of laws, enacted by local synods, by general and particular councils, and by the popes in their decretals constituted a huge collection of juridical rules adapted to the needs of a large society and provided the Western Church with a powerful and effective instrument of government. One thing remained to be done: Such a massive conglomeration of canonical rules, accumulated during centuries, needed unification, coordination, and systematization to clarify the existing law and to eliminate repetitions, contradictions, and useless or obsolete prescriptions. This was the work of Gregory IX (1227–41), who appointed St. Raymond Penafort to codify the ecclesiastical canons and prepare a new collection, the Decretals of *GREGORY IX*, which would be the only authentic collection in the Latin Church. Later the decretals became part of the *CORPUS IURIS CONONICI*, a monumental digest of laws, containing the particular discipline of the Latin rite, under which Western Christendom was governed until 1918 and whose principles are embodied in the present Code of CANON LAW.

Apart from its liturgy, which, even after the changes decreed by Vatican Council II, is quite different from that of the Eastern Churches, the Latin rite differs considerably from the others in its canonical discipline. The more striking and more commonly noted differentiations are the celibacy of the clergy, the use of unleavened bread at the Eucharist, and the distribution of Holy Communion under one species. But there are more fundamental and broader differences, which touch on practically all the aspects of ecclesiastical discipline and government. Many of the powers reserved to the bishop of Rome and exercised by him in the Latin Church are within the ordinary jurisdiction of the metropolitans or the patriarchs of the Eastern churches.

See Also: ROME; PAPACY.

Bibliography: C. H. TURNER, *Studies in Early Church History* (Oxford 1912). P. BATIFFOL, *La Paix constantienne et le catholi-*

cisme (2d ed. Paris 1914); *Le Siège apostolique (359–451)* (Paris 1924). L. M. O. DUCHESNE, *Histoire ancienne de l'Église*, 3 v. (Paris 1906–10); *L'Église au VIᵉ siècle* (Paris 1925); *Origines de culte chrétien* (5th ed. Paris 1925). A. HERMAN, ''De conceptu ritus,'' *Jurist* 2 (1942) 333–345. A. PETRANI, *De relatione iuridica inter diversos ritus in Ecclesia catholica* (Turin 1930). H. DAUSEND, *Das interrituelle Recht im Codex iuris canonici* (Görres-Gesellschaft, Veröffentlichungen der Sektion für Rechts- und Staatswissenschaft 79; Paderborn 1939). G. MICHIELS, *Normae generales juris canonici*, 2 v. (2d ed. Paris-Tournai-Rome 1955); *Principia generalia de personis in ecclesia* (2d ed. Paris 1955). F. X. WERNZ and P. VIDAL, *Ius canonicum*, 7 v. in 8 (Rome 1933–1951).

[A. CARON/EDS.]

LATINA THEOLOGY

Latina theology represents a body of theological writings rather than a self-designated theological movement. Latina theologians begin with particular aspects of the Latina/o experience and offer distinct interpretations of that experience. In nascent form, Latina theology does not divide easily into clear sub-groups. Within the category of ''Latina theology,'' three distinguishable theological commitments emerge. First, a number of Roman Catholic Latina theologians either explicitly identify their work as feminist or, if not, they privilege gender, as well as culture and ethnicity, as primary categories in the development of theology. A second group identify their work as primarily ''pastoral.'' This group, largely Roman Catholic, endeavors to interpret contemporary Latina/o experience through the lens of history, with the purpose of responding more effectively to the immediate pastoral concerns of the Latina/o community. Finally, Protestant Latinas, incorporate some aspects of the previous two groups while also privileging the distinctiveness of Protestant faith experience.

Origins and Sources. Latina theology is an outgrowth and expression of the long history of an evolving consciousness on the part of women in Latin culture. This consciousness or critical recognition arises from the lived experience of gender, culture, race and class inequities, coupled with the lived experience of enduring faith. Short of this understanding, Latina theology can be misinterpreted as emerging exclusively in reaction to the white women's movement and theology, and in reaction to Latin American liberation theology. While these have undeniably made their contributions, Latinas' own history of struggle has played as prominent a role in the development of Latina theology. Latina consciousness can be found, for example, in the writings of the Mexican nun Sor Juana Inés de la Cruz (1648–1695); in the memoirs of 19th and 20th century Latinas (e.g. Doña María Inocencia Pico, Nina Otero-Warren); and in accounts of the Chicano Movement of the 1960s.

Some expressions of Latina theology espouse, along with white feminist theologies, a rejection of the patriarchal social system. But for Latina feminist theologians, the distortion of human nature concerns not only gender but also race and class. With Latino theologians, Latina feminist theologians share a critique of the subordination of Latinas/os to whites and the subordination of economically poor people to those of the middle and upper economic strata.

LIBERATION THEOLOGY, in both its Latin American form (e.g. Gustavo Gutierrez, Ignacio Ellacuria, Jon Sobrino) and its Third World feminist form (e.g. Elsa Tamez, Ivone Gebara, Virginia Fabella), constitutes one of the primary sources for Latina theology. Much of Latina theology attempts to interpret the idea of a ''preferential option for the poor'' as a preferential option for Latinas and to respond to the question, ''What would theology look like if it was genuinely life-giving for Latinas?'' Some expressions of Latina theology emphasize the promotion of the full humanity of Latina women; others focus less on gender believing that the liberation of the Latina/o community as a whole will adequately promote the full humanity of Latinas.

Distinct Forms. The first of the three forms, feminist or gender conscious Latina theology, is varied. Cuban-born Ada María Isasi-Díaz, along with collaborators, originated *Mujerista theology* in the mid-1980s. This theology assumes a preferential option for Latina women by encouraging the development of their moral agency and by giving public voice to Latinas' theological insights. Ethnography, a method used to further the reflective knowing processes of Latinas, characterizes this approach to Latina theology. In contrast, María Pilar Aquino (Mexican-born) terms her theology *Latina feminist theology*. It bears a strong liberationist orientation and draws on philosophy and on various social science disciplines. Her theology highlights the connections between Latin American feminist theology, Latin American liberation theology, and U.S. feminist theology. Along with these theologians, other Latina scholars have made important contributions. These are Jeanette Rodríguez-Holguin, Gloria Loya, Nancy Pineda-Madrid, and Michelle González. Not all of these theologians identify themselves as feminists but all privilege the category of gender in their work.

Pastoral theologies constitute the second form of Latina theology. Above all these theologies concern themselves with how to witness to, and communicate the faith to, Latinas/os in this historical moment. They investigate, among other ministerial foci, questions of catechesis, spiritual growth, liturgical practice and the practice of the church. They strive to respond to the contemporary pastoral needs of Latinas/os. Significant contributions have been made by Ana María Pineda, Anita de Luna, Ana María Díaz-Stevens, Marina Herrera, Rosa María Icaza, María de la Cruz Aymes, Carmen Nanko and Dominga Zapata.

Protestant Latinas form the third and final group. In drawing upon the Protestant faith experience and church practices, these theologians examine the meaning of the term *evangelica/o*, and provide a new interpretation of the experience of *mestizaje* (mixing of two realities), namely the experience of being both "Hispanic" and "Protestant." Key contributions have been made by Daisy Machado, Loida I. Martell-Otero, Teresa C. Sauceda and Elizabeth Conde-Frazier.

See Also: FEMINISM; FEMINIST THEOLOGY; WOMANIST THEOLOGY.

Bibliography: M. P. AQUINO, *Our Cry for Life: Feminist Theology From Latin America* (Maryknoll, NY 1993). M. P. AQUINO, D. MACHADO and J. RODRÍGUEZ, eds., *Religion, Feminism and Justice: A Reader in Latina Feminist Theology* (Austin, TX 2001). A. M. ISASI-DÍAZ, *Mujerista Theology* (Maryknoll, NY 1996); *En La Lucha: Elaborating a Mujerista Theology* (Minneapolis 1993). J. D. RODRÍGUEZ and L. I. MARTELL-OTERO, *Teología en Conjunto: A Collaborative Hispanic Protestant Theology* (Louisville 1997).

[N. PINEDA-MADRID]

LATITUDINARIANISM

A name at first applied to those 17th-century members of the Church of England who, while not skeptics, were indifferent to creeds, ritual practices, and church organization, and who set much store by personal prayer and holy living. Eventually, however, the name came to be applied to those members who combined an attendance at Sunday worship services with various degrees of rationalism and agnosticism.

Latitudinarianism is a product of two streams of thought in the 17th century. The first was an increasing distrust of religious polemic; the theological controversies of the 16th century had generated political controversy and wars. In the second place, a growing interest in scientific experiment put a premium on reason and downgraded respect for authority and tradition.

The influence of these currents of thought was seen in a handful of scholars who became known as the CAMBRIDGE PLATONISTS. Though members of the Church of England, they were strongly influenced by PURITANISM. They refused to concern themselves with doctrine, ritual, and organization, and stressed the importance of prayer, meditation, and godly living. Their views became increasingly popular in the late 17th century, but not with-

out some change of emphasis. The result among many socially prominent churchmen in the 18th and 19th centuries was a divorce between preaching and practice. This state of religion stimulated the rise of EVANGELICALISM and METHODISM.

Though the term latitudinarian became obsolete in the 19th century, its ideas remained powerful and served to encourage the Broad Churchmen of a later age in their work of adapting religion to what they considered to be the demands of a modern and scientific age.

Bibliography: G. P. H. PAWSON, *The Cambridge Platonists and Their Place in Religious Thought* (London 1930). G. R. CRAGG, *From Puritanism to the Age of Reason: A Study of Changes in Religious Thought within the Church of England, 1660 to 1700* (Cambridge, Eng. 1950).

[E. MCDERMOTT]

LATOMUS, BARTHOLOMAEUS (STEINMETZ)

Humanist and controversialist; b. Arlon, Luxembourg, *c.* 1490; d. Koblenz, Germany, Jan. 3, 1570. As a result of humanistic studies at Freiburg im Breisgau (1517), he became acquainted with ERASMUS and traveled with him through Alsace in 1521. After teaching philosophy in Trier and Cologne, he was named professor of Latin eloquence at the Royal College of France (1534), and he taught there until called to Trier by the new elector, Ludwig Von Hagen, to act as his counselor. His work against the Reformers is exemplified in a letter written to Johann Sturm of Strassburg, which, along with Sturm's reply, is found in *Epistolae duorum amicorum B. Latomi et J. Sturmii . . .* (Strassburg 1540, 1566). Latomus became involved in controversy with Martin BUCER, who tried to introduce the reform into Cologne. Against him he wrote *B. Latomi adv. M. Buccerum . . .* (Cologne 1545) and *Refutatio calumniosarum insectationum M. Bucceri . . .* (Cologne 1546). He accompanied his archbishop to Speyer, Worms, and Regensburg; and in 1557 he returned to Worms to publish the *Spaltung der Auspurchischen Confession* (Schism of the Augsburg Confession), a work that involved Latomus in more controversy with Petrus Dathenus (1531/32–88), a Calvinist minister. As a result of a later polemical exchange with Jakob Andreä, Latomus wrote *De docta simplicitate primae Ecclesiae* (Cologne 1559).

Bibliography: L. ROERSCH, "Barthélemy Latomus, le premier professeur d'éloquence latine au Collège royal de France," *Bulletins de l'Académie royale de Belgique,* 3d ser. 14 (1887) 132–176. R. STUPPERICH, *Die Religion in Geschichte und Gegenwart* (Tübingen 1957–65) 4:239. E. AMANN, *Dictionnaire de théologie catholique* (Paris 1903–50) 8.2:2624–26, with bibliog.

[G. J. DONNELLY]

LATOMUS, JACOBUS

Louvain theologian; b. Cambron, Hainault, *c.* 1475; d. Louvain, May 29, 1544. Latomus (Jacques Masson) became a doctor in theology at Louvain in 1519, and was rector there in 1537. He aroused the humanists by his attack on the Erasmian school in *De trium linguarum . . . dialogus* (Antwerp 1519), although he did not name ERASMUS. That humanist defended the necessity of knowledge of the languages of Scripture as a basis for true theology in his *Apologia refellens suspiciones . . .*, and St. THOMAS MORE supported Erasmus in his letter to Edward Lee, mentioning Latomus (Rogers, *Correspondence*, 75.414). From 1520 on Latomus wrote against the reformers, defending the decree of Louvain in 1520 against Luther's ideas in *Articulorum doctrinae F. Martini Lutheri . . .* (Antwerp 1521), and after a series of exchanges: *De primatu Romani Pontificis . . .* (Antwerp 1525). He wrote tracts against Johannes Oecolampadius, Beatus Rhenanus, Jean Gerson, Bartholomew Batnus, and William Tyndale. His works, collected by his nephew, J. Latomus, were published at Louvain (1550). The controversial writings of Latomus, though marred by the defects of the time, mark progress from decadent scholasticism to the development of a genre that Bellarmine perfected.

Bibliography: H. HURTER, *Nomenclator literarius theologiae catholicae* (Innsbruck 1903–13) 1:1447–48. E. AMANN, *Dictionnaire de théologie catholique* (Paris 1903–50) 8.2:2626–28. F. NÈVE, *Biographie nationale de Belgique* 11:425. J. ÉTIENNE, *Lexikon für Theologie und Kirche*, ed. J. HOFER and K. RAHNER (Freiburg 1957–65) 6:822. R. STUPPERICH, *Die Religion in Geschichte und Gegenwart* (Tübingen 1957–65) 4:239. P. KALKOFF, *Die Anfänge der Gegenreformation in den Niederlanden*, 2 v. (Halle 1903).

[G. J. DONNELLY]

LA TOUR DU PIN, CHARLES HUMBERT RENÉ (MARQUIS DE LA CHARCE)

French Catholic social thinker; b. Arrancy (Aisne), April 1, 1834; d. Lausanne, Switzerland, Dec. 4, 1924. He was a descendant of an illustrious family, began his career as an officer, and took part in military campaigns in the Crimea, Italy, and Algeria. When taken prisoner during the War of 1870, he was interned at Aix-la-Chapelle with Albert de Mun. Together they came upon Émile Keller's condemnation of LIBERALISM [*L'Encyclique du eight décembre 1864 et les principes de 1789* (Paris 1865)] and the social doctrine of Wilhelm Emmanuel von KETTELER. Seeing in liberalism and social injustice the causes of the French defeat, La Tour du Pin wished to combat these forces, especially after the experience of the Commune. Maurice Maignen's circle of Catholic workers gave him the desired tool.

Toward the end of 1871 there was born the movement of Catholic workers' circles that multiplied encounters between employers and workers under the presidency of a member of the "ruling class." The republican government soon began to harass the circles. La Tour du Pin, who kept in close contact with Frédéric le Play, wished to give them a corporativist character. In 1877 he was named military attaché to Vienna, where he met the Comte de Chambord and continued his social studies with the Austrian Social Catholics. His work was published in his movement's official organ, *L'Association catholique*. Raised to the rank of colonel, he retired from the army in 1882 to devote himself to his estate at Arrancy and to the movement.

La Tour du Pin played an important role in the studies undertaken by the Fribourg Union that prepared the way for RERUM NOVARUM (1891). He greatly influenced Albert de Mun's legislative projects and strongly encouraged Léon HARMEL in the transformation of his enterprise and in his appeal to Christian employers. He took an interest in the founding of the Catholic Association of French youth by the Comte de Roquefeuile. He favored the introduction of the agricultural syndicates in 1884. His closest followers were Henri Lorin, founder of the Semaine sociales de France, and the deputy, H. de Gailhard-Bancel. In 1891 he published his *Aphorismes de politique social.*

The RALLIEMENT, which he refused to accept, and the decline of the circles isolated him. His influence narrowed, and he turned to ACTION FRANÇAISE. His wife's death and the German invasion that drove him out of Arrancy saddened his declining years.

La Tour du Pin was the thinker among the early Social Catholics, exerting considerable influence on the entry of the state and the Church into social questions between 1880 and 1895. He repudiated liberalism and sought to transform society, in accord with God's will, into an organic whole, a "body social" based on the family and not on the individual, on property, on work, and having the king at its head.

Bibliography: *Vers un ordre social chrétien: Jalons de route* (Paris 1929), essays of La Tour du Pin. E. BOSSAN DE GARAGNOL, *Le Colonel de La-Tour-du-Pin d'après lui-même* (Paris 1934). C. BAUSSAN, *La Tour du Pin* (Paris 1931). R. SÉMICHON, *Les Idées sociales et politiques de La-Tour-du-Pin* (Paris 1936). A. CANALETTI GAUDENTI, *Un corporativista cattolico: Renato de La Tour du Pin* (Rome 1935). H. ROLLET, *L'Action sociale des catholiques en France* (Paris 1948). R. TALMY, *René de la Tour du Pin* (Paris 1964).

[H. ROLLET]

LATOURETTE, KENNETH SCOTT

Professor of Missions and Oriental History at Yale University (1921–53); b. Oregon City, OR, 9 Aug. 1884; d. there, 26 Dec. 1968. After serving for approximately a year on the faculty of Yale in China at Changsha, he returned to the United States and taught at Reed College (1914–16), Denison University (1916–21), and finally at Yale where he also became chairman of the religion department and director of graduate studies. He was recipient of a number of honorary doctorates, and served as president of the American Society of Church History and the American Historical Association. In 1951, he was elected President of the American Baptist Convention.

From the moment he responded to the call of the Student Volunteer Movement and became a missionary, his life was dominated by a concern for missions. Motivated by this deep concern, Latourette became a pioneer in both the history of missions and East Asian history. His work in both these areas opened a new phase in historical studies, and many of his more than eighty monographs and numerous articles continue as standard, authoritative works. His major work is a seven volume *History of The Expansion of Christianity,* completed in 1945.

Latourette has often been criticized for being a "tireless chronicler," excessively imbued with a concern for "objective" history, and lacking depth theologically. Though there is truth to these criticisms, it must be remembered that his historiographical method was the product of his age. It must also be pointed out that Latourette was trained as a historian, not a theologian. Although his historical treatment was governed more by sociological than theological considerations, he clearly made an invaluable contribution—perhaps more than any other U.S. scholar—to ground Christianity in universal history.

Bibliography: W. C. HARR, ed., *Frontiers of the Christian World Mission since 1938: Essays in Honor of Kenneth Scott Latourette* (New York 1962). K. S. LATOURETTE, *Beyond the Ranges: An Autobiography* (Grand Rapids 1967). L. MOORE, JR., "Beyond the Ranges—The Autobiography of Kenneth Scott Latourette," *Hartford Quarterly Review* 8.4 (Summer 1968) 77–95. W.R. HOGG, "Kenneth Scott Latourette 1884–1968: Interpreter of the Expansion of Christianity," in *Mission Legacies: Biographical Studies of Leaders of the Modern Missionary Movement,* eds. G.H. ANDERSON et al, (Maryknoll, 1994), 416–27. A. PFEIFFER, "Kenneth Scott Latourette: A Description and Assessment of His Historical Analysis of the Spread of Christianity in the First Five Centuries," *Logia* 7 (1998) 19–24.

[J. K. LUOMA]

LA TRAPPE, ABBEY OF

Or Maison-Dieu Notre Dame de la Trappe (Lat., *Domus Dei de Trappa*), Cistercian abbey founded in 1140 near Mortagne, France, in the Diocese of Séez, by Rotrou III, count of Perche. The first religious were monks from Breuil-Benoît of the Congregation of SAVIGNY, sent there by the founder. In 1147 the Congregation of Savigny joined the order of CÎTEAUX as a filiation of CLAIRVAUX. The abbey prospered during the administration of Bl. Adam. During the 14th century the abbey was burned by the English. Commendatory abbots in the 16th century brought a spirit of relaxation to the community. Later one of them, Armand le Bouthillier de RANCÉ, renounced his worldly life, took the religious habit, and spent his novitiate in the Abbey of Perseigne in the Province of Maine. In 1664 he became a regular abbot at La Trappe. After meeting with much initial resistance, he was able to reestablish discipline. Thus the TRAPPIST reform began; it was adopted by several monasteries of the order. During the French Revolution, Augustin de Lestrange, master of novices, left with a group of monks to seek refuge outside France, first in Switzerland at the Carthusian convent of La Valsainte. Later he traveled through Europe, attracting many vocations. He returned to France in 1815 and was able to restore the Abbey of La Trappe. The present monastery, rebuilt in 1895, is still occupied by the reformed CISTERCIANS.

Bibliography: *Cartulaire de l'abbaye de Notre-Dame de la Trappe* (Alençon 1889). H. DE CHARENCEY, *Histoire de l'abbaye de la Grande-Trappe*, 2 v. (Mortagne 1896–1911). L. F. DU BOIS, *Histoire civile, religieuse, et littéraire de l'abbaye de la Trappe* (Paris 1824). H. TOURNOÜER, *Bibliographie et iconographie de la Maison-Dieu, N.-D. de la Trappe* (Mortagne 1894). *Odyssée monastique: Dom A. de Lestrange et les Trappistes pendant la Révolution* (Soligny-la-Trappe 1898). M. A. DIMIER, *La Sombre Trappe: Les Légendes et la vérité* (Paris 1946).

[M. A. DIMIER]

LATTER-DAY SAINTS, CHURCH OF JESUS CHRIST OF

Also called the Mormon Church, founded in upstate New York on April 6, 1830, by Joseph SMITH (1805–44), who reported divine visitations. In 1830 he published the *Book of Mormon,* claiming to have translated it from plates of gold given him by the angel Moroni, purportedly a record of God's dealings with the ancestors of the American Indians, alleged to have been Hebrews who came in three migrations to the New World. Mormonism was one product of the religious revivalism and turmoil characteristic of upstate New York in that period.

Historical Development. From 1831, with the founding of a Mormon community at Kirtland, Ohio, to 1844, when Joseph Smith was murdered by a mob in Carthage, Ill., the church had a stormy history. In those years, four attempts were made to build a community embodying Mormon ideals and giving expression to the group's separate existence. At Kirtland, the effort led to financial disaster. At Independence and Far West, Mo., two more attempts were made. After some success, the Mormons attracted the opposition of their neighbors and were driven out in violence and bloodshed. Their initial successes, northern manners, religious peculiarities, claims to make the area a holy land of their religion, and favorable attitudes toward the indigenous peoples combined to elicit Missourian hostility. They were driven from Independence in the winter of 1833–34 and went into Clay County, from which they were shortly asked to leave. In Far West, which they then founded, a similar pattern of success, hostility, and expulsion followed. Joseph Smith estimated losses of $2 million in Missouri, and the final expulsion in a small-scale "Mormon War" cost some 40 lives, all but one or two of them Mormon.

Mormon efforts in the Middle West were most successful on the east bank of the Mississippi River in Illinois at Nauvoo, which soon became an attractive city of about 15,000. This accomplishment issued in a second "Mormon War." In Nauvoo, rumors concerning the secret practice of polygamy contributed to antagonism, as did the palpable evidence of Mormon size and power. In the violence that ensued, Joseph Smith and his brother Hyrum were murdered by the mob, and after considerable tension and some open fighting, the Mormons were driven out. They commenced evacuation of Nauvoo in sub-zero weather in February of 1846.

There followed a period of discouragement and dissension. Several groups broke off at this time, one of which later formed the Reorganized Church of Jesus Christ of Latter Day Saints. Brigham YOUNG (1801–77) took over the church leadership and organized migration across Iowa to the banks of the Missouri River, where he established winter quarters. After a season of great suffering, Young organized the Mormon trek to the West, and on April 7, 1847, he left with a party of 148 for the Valley of the Great Salt Lake, Utah. They arrived on July 22, and two days later Young entered the valley.

Thus began the Mormon migration to and settlement of the intermountain region. Thousands came by wagon train, handcart, and later by railroad. The Mormons developed their settlement on a planned basis, and the church "called" people to establish communities in irrigable valleys throughout the region. By the time of Young's death in 1877, the Mormons had established 357 Settlements, and Utah had a Mormon population of about 140,000. Settlement and emigration continued. By 1900 some 90,000 immigrant converts had been brought from Europe.

The Mormon communities succeeded in Utah, but the conflict with gentile opinion and government authorities continued. When in 1857 Pres. James Buchanan sent Federal troops under Gen. A. S. Johnston, the issue nearly came to open conflict. Gradually the lines of antagonism were drawn around the two issues of Utah's admission to the Union and polygamy, which had been practiced openly in Utah since 1852. In 1863 Congress passed the Morrill Law, forbidding polygamy, which the Supreme Court upheld in 1879. In 1882 the Edmunds Act was passed, followed in 1887 by the Edmunds-Tucker Act. These laws were more stringent; the latter dissolved the church as a corporation. Anti-Mormon sentiment was aroused among the small but significant non-Mormon group in Utah, and in the nation generally. With about 200 members in jail, the Mormons capitulated and in the constitutional convention of 1887 supported the outlawing of polygamy. In September of 1890, Church President Wilford Woodruff (1807–98) renounced polygamy as effective church teaching, and in 1896 Utah was admitted to the Union. There followed a period of accommodation, and Mormonism strove for and achieved acceptance and respectability. However, a small dissident and excommunicated sect advocating and practicing polygamy continues to exist in Utah.

Mormonism's most striking achievement was settlement of the arid terrain of the intermountain West. This achievement finds its most appropriate monument in the establishment of irrigation as the basis for agriculture. The Mormons displayed both the cooperation and the discipline necessary for this accomplishment. By 1865 there were over 1,000 miles of canals in Utah, and by 1946, some 8,750 miles.

Basic Doctrinal Position. Mormonism is based upon Joseph Smith's claim that contemporary revelation began with his divine election as prophet-founder of the Mormon Church. The Book of Mormon, the Doctrine and Covenants, and the Pearl of Great Price, alleged revelations of the founder, are accepted, with the Bible, as scripture. The first claims to be a miraculously translated pre-Columbian scripture; the second contains revelations announced by Joseph from time to time, including that establishing polygamy; the third allegedly contains lost parts of the Pentateuch, some of which was transcribed by Smith from papyri, Smith's writings, and articles of Mormon belief.

While the Book of Mormon is a work obviously Christian in tenor, the later teachings introduced a number of innovations. These include the doctrine of human existence in a previous spirit world, a finite developing God, baptism for the dead, an interpretation of the Trinity as tritheism, marriage for time and eternity, humanity's eternal progression to god-like status, and polygamy. Mormonism emphasizes worldly virtues of a distinctively American kind: optimism, self-improvement, hard work, and respect for law. Recreation is highly valued and organized by the church, and abstinence from coffee, tea, tobacco, and liquor is enjoined. The importance of the family is stressed. The Mormons also hold that the U.S. enjoys a special providential position in the world and that its Constitution has been divinely inspired. Millennialism has long been an integral part of Mormon doctrine, and in one form or another remains of some significance.

Organizational Structure. Church structure is complex with a hierarchical priesthood embracing all males deemed worthy. There are two levels of priesthood: the lesser Aaronic priesthood with its stages of deacon, teacher, priest, and bishop; and the Melchizedek order, which contains two higher ranks—seventies, to which men are advanced after mission experience, and high priest. Important leaders on all levels are high priests. For a long time, admission to the priesthood was only opened to white European males, and this caused some internal protest and complications in external relations. In 1978, this decision was reversed, and it was held that ''all worthy male members of the church may be ordained to the priesthood without regard for race or color.''

The local unit is the ward; several wards comprise a stake. The ward is led by an unpaid leader who is called a bishop and is assisted by two counselors, this triumvirate form being characteristic of all offices of executive importance. While there is great rank-and-file participation, direction is centralized and authority comes strictly from the top down. Most officers are unpaid. At the top is the church presidency made up of the First President and his two counselors and the Council of the Twelve Apostles, which has selected a number of assistants. The top 24 officials are known as the General Authorities. The church is highly organized and characterized by tremendous activism. Large numbers of young men and some young women go on two-year missions at their own expense. The church conducts a large welfare organization that farms land by volunteer labor; it also has a Genealogical Society connected with temple work for the dead that activates many older people.

The Mormon Church continues to grow, and by the end of the 20th century it had more than five million members. The church is a dominant influence in Utah, where it represents a bulwark of conservatism and has contributed people of importance nationally in a wide number of fields. It is supported by payment of tithes and has large business investments.

Bibliography: W. A. LINN, *The Story of the Mormons* (New York 1902). L. L. BENNION, *The Religion of the Latter-Day Saints* (rev. and enl. Salt Lake City 1940). W. R. CROSS, *The Burned Over District: The Social and Intellectual History of Enthusiastic Religion in Western New York, 1800–1850* (Ithaca 1950). L. NELSON, *The Mormon Village: A Pattern and Technique of Land Settlement* (Salt Lake City 1952). K. YOUNG, *Isn't One Wife Enough?* (New York 1954). T. F. O'DEA, *The Mormons* (Chicago 1957). L. J. ARRINGTON, *Great Basin Kingdom: An Economic History of the Latter Day Saints, 1830–1900* (Cambridge, Mass. 1958). W. MULDER and A. R. MORTENSEN, eds., *Among the Mormons: Historic Accounts by Contemporary Observers* (New York 1958). F. S. MEAD, S. S. HILL and C. D. ATWOOD, eds., *Handbook of Denominations in the United States*, 11th ed (Nashville 2001).

[T. F. O'DEA/EDS.]

LATVIA, THE CATHOLIC CHURCH IN

Located in eastern Europe, the Republic of Latvia borders the gulf of Riga on the north, ESTONIA on the northeast, LITHUANIA on the south and the Baltic Sea on the west. Comprised of lowlands, Latvia boasts a continental climate, with moderately cold winters. Its terrain rises in the eastern lake region, and most of the country is well forested. Natural resources include amber, peat, limestone and dolomite, while hydropower from the Dvina River provides half the region's energy needs. Crops include various grains, sugar beets, potatoes, vegetables and dairy products.

Under the domination of German, Polish, Swedish and then Russian governments for many centuries, Latvia gained independence briefly in 1918 before becoming incorporated into the USSR in 1944. In 1991, the region achieved independence, and has since attempted to boost its sagging economy through privatization of its industrial base and the development of trade with the rest of Europe. In the wake of decades of Soviet occupation, ethnic Latvians constitute barely 52 percent of the country's population, while Russians make up about a third of the total. Conflicts over the citizenship status of the Russian population continued to be of concern to the Russian Federation in 2000.

The Early Church. Named for the Lettish people, who originally inhabited the region, Latvia was invaded by Swedes and Russians between 900 and 1000; by the 12th century the Latgali, Kurši, Sēli and Zemgali tribes were settled there. Each tribe had its own administration and state, the strongest of which was Gersika, the Latgalian state on the Daugava River, adjacent to the state of Novgorod. Gersika was Christianized through Byzantium, giving early Latvian religious terminology its Slavonic characteristic. The faith spread throughout the region, reaching Riga, then home to Livonians and Germans. Augustinian canon St. Meinhard founded a church and chapel of canons in 1180 at Ikškile, southeast of Riga, and became the first bishop of Livonia in 1186. AL-BERT I became Riga's first bishop in 1201 and there established the KNIGHTS OF THE SWORD, who, together with the Order of the Cross, conquered most of the eastern Baltic. Riga was suffragan to Bremen until 1214. Innocent III (1198–1216) made the see exempt, and in 1255 it became a metropolitan see.

Reformation to Communism. Albert (Hohenzollern) of Prussia, grand master of the TEUTONIC KNIGHTS, secularized the ecclesiastical territory to form the first Duchy of Prussia and introduced LUTHERANISM into Latvia *c.* 1530. Interior weaknesses brought Livonia (modern-day Latvia and Estonia) to its political downfall. War with Russia, from 1558 to 1582, devastated the region and it split into two parts, Vidzeme and Latgola, both of which fell under Polish rule from 1561–1629. The Swedish took Vidzeme in 1629; Latgola remained in Polish hands until 1772, when Russia acquired it in the partition of Poland; Kurzeme became the independent Duchy of Kurland in 1721. Under Polish rule, Latgola remained Catholic according to the principle of *cuius regio, eius religio,* with the Dominicans and Jesuits contributing greatly to its spiritual and cultural growth (*see* DACIA).

Under Czarist rule, until it won independence in 1918, Latvia was under constant pressure to conform to Russian ways, including eschewing the Latin rite for the Roman Orthodox faith. Roman letter type was banned in 1865 with the purpose of annihilating both Catholicism and the native tongue. This ban was not lifted until 1904, when Latgalian literature finally began to develop. During the ban, books became scarce and were either written by hand or were smuggled in from Tilsit. The prayer book, studied privately at home, was the sole means of education. A strong nationalist sentiment remained throughout the country. Chief among those who advocated against the Russification of the faith were P. Miglinīks (1850–83), A. Jurdžs (1845–1925), K. Skrynda (1875–1919), A. Skrynda (1881–1933), F. Kemps (1876–1952), N. Rancāns (1870–1933), and F. Trasuns (1864–1926).

In 1918, with the collapse of the Russian Empire following World War I, the Latvian provinces united and declared their independence. After a period of chaos under a Bolshevik occupation (1918–20) during which Catholics were persecuted, the region gained political stability. Tsarist rule had left Latvia with a shortage of priests, many of its churches destroyed by the war, and its leading laymen dead from a typhoid epidemic. Within ten years the country had rebuilt its industry and had progressed in all areas of life, including matters of faith. The Congress of Latvian Catholics met in Rezekne in

Capital: Riga.
Size: 24,600 sq. miles.
Population: 2,404,926 in 2000.
Languages: Lettish, Lithuanian, Russian.
Religions: 500,000 Catholics (23.5%), 190,000 Orthodox (8%), 400,000 Lutheran (16%), 12,500 Protestants (.5%), 5,100 other (.23%), 1,297,326 without religious affiliation.
Archdiocese: Riga, with suffragans Liepaja, Jelgāva, and Rēzekne-Aglona.

1917 and adopted a resolution to form one state but to retain local autonomy, freedom in religious matters and the use of High Latvian. Under Pope BENEDICT XV the diocese of Riga was restored, and churches were rebuilt. Seminarians who had once prepared for the priesthood at the seminary in St. Petersburg, now attended seminaries in Aglyuna, Riga or in western European universities. In 1939, when Latvia's population was less than two million, 60 percent of Latvians were Lutheran, 25 percent Catholic, six percent Greek Orthodox and five percent Jewish.

In 1920 a Catholic political party was formed that took an active role in policymaking until 1934, when a *coup d'état* led by the fascist Karlis Ulmanis led to the abolishment of all political parties, as well as curtailment of freedom of speech and of the press. A highly centralized totalitarian regime was established that lasted until 1940. Despite the change in government, the Church continued to function in the country, and religious such as the Marian Fathers worked in Vilāni, and the Capuchins in Skaistkaine and Riga. Sisters of the Poor Child Jesus, from Austria, conducted a girl's high school in Jaunaglyuna, while Sisters of the Holy Cross and Sisters of the Sacred Heart of Jesus also performed humanitarian services. The first papal nuncio to Latvia was Antonio Zecchini (1922–35). Antonio Arata became nuncio in 1935 but was expelled in 1940, as the country entered another phase of its history.

The Church under Communism. In June of 1940 the Red Army entered and occupied Latvia. Devastation followed, as Catholic institutions were suppressed and priests and laymen arrested, threatened and tortured. The Lutheran Church's educational functions were also curtailed and most theological institutes were closed. Massive deportations created such havoc that many Latvians welcomed the arrival of invading German forces in June of 1941. The policy of the German occupying government toward the Church was ambivalent: not to destroy and not to help. While their policy toward the faith was viewed favorably in comparison to that of Russia, the mass killings of Latvian Jews that occurred during the Holocaust presented a moral challenge to the Church.

LATVIA

0   25   50 Miles

0   25   50 Kilometers

Irves aurums   *Kolkas Rags*   Salacgriva   *Burtnieku Ezers*   ESTONIA   *Pskovskoye Ozero*

Valka   Valga   Pskov

Gulf of Riga   Limbaži   **Valmiera**   Alūksne

Ventspils   *Stende*   Smiltene

Usmas Ezers   Talsi   Cēsis   Gulbene   RUSSIA

Baltic Sea   *Venta*   *Gauja*   Sigulda   Balvi   *Velikaya*

Kuldīga   Tukums   Jūrmala   **Riga**   ▲ *Gaizina 1,020 ft. 311 m.*   Ostrov

Pāvilosta   *Lietupe*   Ogre   *Lubānas Ezers*

Saldus   Dobele   **Jelgava**   Kegums   *Aiviekste*   *Malta*

Liepāja   Grobiņa   Pļaviņas   Costiņi   Rēzekne

Auce   Bauska   *Daugava*   **Jēkabpils**   *Rēznas Ezers*

Rucava   *Memele*   Zalve

iauliai   **Daugavpils**

LITHUANIA   Navapolatsk

Latvia

BELARUS

Once Soviet forces returned in October of 1944, following the end of World War II, the government's disregard of the Church drastically changed, and Catholics were rigidly watched and persecuted. With their bishops exiled or in Siberia, about 100 pastors and nearly 100,000 Latvian laymen fled the country, while massive deportations between 1945 and 1953 sent of thousands of others to Siberia or other remote areas of the USSR. Prohibitive taxes were levied against the Church, and in 1948 religious instruction in churches was banned by the Soviets. At the same time all Church properties were nationalized. The Lutheran and, to a lesser extent, Orthodox Churches in Latvia also suffered from repression and flight to the West, although the Soviet regime was somewhat less active in controlling the Lutheran Church because it lacked a well-organized national-religious dissident movement. Nonetheless the regime's intensification of antireligious propaganda after 1957 continued to have a detrimental effect on all faiths within Latvia.

The Fall of Communism to Present. With the rise of Soviet leader Mikhail Gorbachev to power in 1985, the most egregious restrictions on religion were quickly relaxed, and by 1989 virtually all legal restrictions on the Church had been removed. In March of 1990, with the fall of communism in Eastern Europe, the Latvian government proclaimed independence, and the international community recognized an independent Latvian republic in 1991. The new constitution preserved the right of religious freedom, and as an established faith, the Catholic Church received tax benefits and other privileges. Although the majority of the Christian population in Latvia were members of the Lutheran Evangelical Church, Catholics formed a majority in sections of eastern Latvia. The Orthodox Church was also active in the country. In 1996, consideration of a Vatican proposal to reestablish the 1922 Concordat between the Holy See and Latvia was undertaken, although other churches in the country objected to the possibility of the Catholic Church gaining favored status. The Church also requested permission to establish a faculty of theology at the then nondenominational University of Latvia.

By 2000 there were 214 parishes tended by 88 diocesan and 21 religious priests in Latvia. In addition, 80 sisters worked within the country. Encouraging Church leaders to take an active role in promoting Catholic unity, Pope John Paul II recalled his trip to the region in 1993 and noted during a September of 1999 meeting with Latvian bishops that ''indifference and religious relativism'' were among those aspects of society that most threatened the country's Catholic population. By 2000 efforts were underway to establish an ecumenical dialogue in Latvia.

Bibliography: R. WITTRAM, *Die Religion in Geschichte und Gegenwart,* 7 v. (3d ed. Tübingen 1957–65) 1:850–856; ed., *Baltische Kirchengeschichte* (Göttingen 1956). L. ARBUSOW, *Die Einführung der Reformation in Livonia, Estonia und Kurland* (Halle 1921). A. BILMANIS, *A History of Latvia* (Princeton 1951). M. HELLMANN, *Das Lettenland im Mittelalter* (Cologne 1954). M. BOURDEAUX, *Land of Crosses* (Chulmleigh UK 1980). A. LIEVEN, *The Baltic Revolution: Estonia, Latvia, Lithuania, and the Path to Independence* (New Haven CT 1993). R. J. MISIUNAS and R. TAAGEPERA, *The Baltic States: Years of Dependence 1940–1990* (2d ed. Berkeley 1993). V. S. VARDYS, ''Human-Rights Issues in Estonia, Latvia, and Lithuania,'' *Journal of Baltic Studies,* 12 (fall 1981) 275–98; *Lexikon für Theologie und Kirche,* eds., J. HOFER and K. RAHNER, 10 v. (2d, new ed. Freiburg 1957–65) 6:986–987.

[L. LATKOVSKI/EDS.]

LAUD, WILLIAM

Archbishop of Canterbury; b. Reading, England, Oct. 7, 1573; d. London, Jan. 10, 1645. Laud, the only son of a clothier, matriculated at Oxford in 1589 and was ordained in 1601. He held modest chaplaincies and was vicar of Stanford for one year. In 1608 he was awarded his doctorate in divinity, cultivated his interest in Arabic, and preached before James I. Laud abhorred extremism. He regarded Puritans with disfavor and disliked Roman Catholicism. He believed strongly in episcopacy, order, and uniformity in religious worship. He wanted a strong and united national church, energetic and resolute, purged of sects, schisms, and slackness, and decorous and disciplined. Laud was short, red-faced, tactless, testy, and profoundly convinced of the rectitude of his own reform policies. He had an authoritarian temper and, unfortunately, he tried to force upon the PURITANS the religion of tradition-minded Anglicans. He believed in the full exercise of the royal prerogative and was accordingly rewarded by a series of promotions—from the deanery of Gloucester to the bishopric of St. David's. When James died in 1625, Laud was 52. His real predominance in the Church of England was only beginning.

The new king, Charles I, admired and respected the much older prelate. Laud became bishop of Bath and Wells, and then dean of the chapel royal, privy councilor, bishop of London, and chancellor of Oxford. Again, by

Icon of Our Lady of Latvia.

the King's good grace, he was elevated to the archbishopric of Canterbury, the highest ecclesiastical office in the realm. The new archbishop was insensitive to the many diverse elements that made up the disorderly and deteriorating ecclesiastical establishment. In trying to enforce ceremonial uniformity he incurred the wrath of the Puritans because he submerged their religious practices and violated their most cherished prejudices. The English dispute over ceremonial and ritual—bowing, surplices, the position of the communion table—was sharply intensified when Laud accompanied the King to Scotland in 1633 and the fateful decision was made to ask for the acceptance of the English Prayer Book and official liturgy in that Presbyterian country. The request was regarded as an outrageous foreign interference in Scottish affairs. Scottish resistance was immediate and was followed by a futile English invasion to compel obedience.

After 11 years of personal rule, Charles summoned Parliament. As soon as it convened in 1640, the 3-week Short Parliament complained bitterly about Laud's religious despotism and the King's illegal taxation. It was

William Laud, print after a painting by Anthony Van Dyke.

dismissed. The Scots successfully invaded England and the Long Parliament (1640–60) had to be called into session. Angry and vindictive, it proceeded against the King's principal political adviser, Thomas Wentworth, Earl of Strafford, and imprisoned Archbishop Laud under a charge of treason. Strafford was summarily executed (1641), but several years passed before Laud, then an old man of 72, was brought to trial. While it was alleged that the archbishop had sought to subvert the foundations of Church and State, the charge could not be sustained and Commons proceeded against Laud by an ordinance of attainder. He was brought to the scaffold on Tower Hill, protesting that he was guilty of no offense that deserved the death penalty, rejecting the muddled accusation that he tried to bring in popery, and affirming his loyalty to English Protestantism.

Bibliography: H. R. TREVOR-ROPER, *Archbishop Laud, 1573–1645* (London 1940). R. P. T. COFFIN, *Laud, Storm Center of Stuart England* (New York 1930). S. R. GARDINER, *The First Two Stuarts and the Puritan Revolution, 1603–1660* (New York 1928 D. MATHEW, *The Age of Charles I* (London 1951). C. V. WEDGWOOD, *The King's Peace, 1637–1641* (New York 1956); *The King's War, 1641–1647* (New York 1958). M. J. HAVRAN, *The Catholics in Caroline England* (Stanford, Calif. 1962).

[J. J. O'CONNOR]

LAUDA SION SALVATOREM

The opening words of a sequence composed *c.* 1264 by St. THOMAS AQUINAS for the Mass of CORPUS ET SANGUINIS CHRISTI. It is one of the four great hymns on the Holy Eucharist by the Angelic Doctor, the others being *PANGE LINGUA GLORIOSI*, *SACRIS SOLEMNIIS*, and *VERBUM SUPERNUM PRODIENS*. Together they set forth in cogently clear yet beautiful language the fundamental doctrinal teachings of the Church on the Real Presence. *Lauda Sion salvatorem* was written at the request of Pope Urban IV when the Feast of Corpus Christi was first established, and it was intended for the sequence of the Mass of the feast. Although the work was once ascribed to St. BONAVENTURE, the authorship of Aquinas is today beyond dispute. Thomas uses the prevalent accentual rather than the older classical quantitative meter, and in addition to rhyme abundant use is made of alliteration and assonance. It follows rather closely the form in which ADAM OF SAINT-VICTOR did many of his sequences, especially the beautiful *Laudes crucis attollamus*. It is a dogmatic poem and never wanders from the correct scholastic terms in its closely reasoned stanzas, but even so it cannot fail to make an impression by its grand and deeply moving style. *Sion* in the first verse is the Church or the people of God, who are summoned to sing the praises of the life-giving Sacrament. The old PASSOVER is replaced by this new feast, the commemoration of which is explained, where Christ himself figures as the sacrificial lamb. Much the same theme is developed by the same author in his *Summa Theologiae* (ST 1a2ae, 73–83) as is found in the seventh and later stanzas of the poem. Topics such as transubstantiation, the nature and dogma of the Sacrament, and the mystery and faith involved are all treated clearly and forcefully. The last strophe expresses the hope that the congregation of the faithful will eventually be gathered together for a heavenly feast in the company of the saints. The author of the plainsong melody of the *Lauda Sion salvatorem* is not known but is supposed by some scholars to have been St. Thomas himself. The melody, however, dates from the 12th century, and possibly even earlier.

Bibliography: Text, *Analecta hymnica* 50:584–585. G. MORIN, "L'Office cistercien pour la Fête-Dieu comparé avec celui de saint Thomas d'Aquin," *Revue Bénédictine* 27 (1910) 236–246. E. DUMOUTET, *Corpus Domini: Aux sources de la piété eucharistique médiévale* (Paris 1942). O. HUF, *De Sacramentshymnen van den Hl. Thomas van Aquino* (Liturgische Studien 4; Maastricht 1924). G. A. BURTON, "The Liturgical Poetry of St. Thomas," *St. Thomas Papers* (Cambridge, Eng. 1925) 285–298. F. TRUCCO, *San Tommaso d'Aquino poeta della santissima Eucaristia* (Sarzana 1928). M. GRABMANN, *Die Werke des hl. Thomas von Aquin* (3d ed. Münster 1949) 317–324. C. LAMBOT, "L'Office de la Fête-Dieu," *Revue Bénédictine* 54 (1942) 61–123. M. BRITT, ed., *The Hymns of the Breviary and Missal* (new ed. New York 1948) 166–188. R. BUSA, *S. Thomae Aquinatis hymnorum ritualium varia specimina* *concordantium* (Milan 1951). F. J. E. RABY, *A History of Christian-Latin Poetry from the Beginnings to the Close of the Middle Ages* (Oxford 1953) 402–414. F. CALLAEY, *L'origine della festa del Corpus Domini* (Rovigo 1958). J. SZÖVÉRFFY, *Die Annalen der lateinischen Hymnendichtung* (Berlin 1964–65) 2:246–251.

[W. C. KORFMACHER]

LAUDABILITER

Papal bull defining the rights of the English king in Ireland. JOHN OF SALISBURY states in his *Metalogicon* (1159) that on the occasion of his visit to ADRIAN IV at Benevento between November 1155 and July 1156, the latter, at his request, granted to Henry II of England the "hereditary possession" of Ireland; he proceeds to mention documentation then in existence as proof of this as well as a ring of investiture, preserved in the public treasury, which he, John, had conveyed from the pope to the king. Historians do not question John's veracity, and GIRALDUS CAMBRENSIS later published in *Expugnatio Hiberniae* (2.5) a papal bull, *Laudabiliter,* which he states was the document given to John. Its contents have been summarized by M. P. Sheehy: "To the King of the English, Pope Adrian IV sends his approval of the king's intention to enter Ireland for the purpose of improving the state of religion. While propagating the faith the king should respect the rights of the Apostolic See—particularly her rights over islands—and the rights of Irish Church leaders." The science of diplomatics shows that the document is no forgery and points to its having been issued during the reign of Adrian IV. The bull, however, does not grant to Henry II "hereditary possession" of Ireland. Nevertheless, in the succeeding centuries, when reference is made to Henry's sovereignty in Ireland, *Laudabiliter* is the document cited. Although the bull is frequently mentioned in official documents issued in Rome, it is clear that the papal chancery knew of it only by report and neither confirms nor denies its existence. Most modern historians believe that some such document conferring hereditary possession did exist, although it has been since lost.

Bibliography: *Laudabiliter et satis,* ed. M. P. SHEEHY, in *Pontificia Hibernica* (Dublin 1962) 15–16. M. P. SHEEHY, "The Bull *Laudabiliter:* A Problem in Medieval Diplomatics and History," *Galway Archaeological and Historical Society Journal* 29 (1961) 45–70. J. WATT," *Laudabiliter* in Medieval Diplomacy and Propaganda," *Irish Ecclesiastical Record* 87 (1957) 420–432. J. F. O'DOHERTY, "Rome and the Anglo-Norman Invasion of Ireland," *ibid.* 42 (1933) 131–145. P. JAFFÉ, *Regesta pontificum romanorum ab condita ecclesia ad annum post Christum natum 1198,* ed. S. LOWENFELD (Graz 1956) 10056. A. EGGERS, *Die Urkunde Papst Hardians IV. für König Heinrich II. von England über die Besetzung Irlands* (Berlin 1922).

[C. MCGRATH]

LAUDOMAR, ST.

Hermit and abbot; d. Chartres, *c.* 590. Of the extant *vitae*, the shortest, first edited by Mabillon, was written probably by a disciple soon after the saint's death. Laudomar (Lomer or Launomar) received his early training from the priest Chirmirius. He was ordained and performed pastoral duties at Chartres for some years. He then withdrew to the solitude of La Perche, where he lived as a hermit. His reputation for sanctity and for the miracles ascribed to him attracted so many disciples and reverent admirers that he left La Perche and founded the monastery of Curbio (*c.* 570), becoming its first abbot. His relics were eventually taken to Blois, where the monastery named in his honor, Saint-Lomer, was built in 924.

Feast: Jan. 19.

Bibliography: *Bibliographica hagiographica latina antiquae et mediae aetatis* 2:4733–40. J. S. MABILLON, *Acta sanctorum ordinis S. Benedicti* (Venice 1733–40) 1:317–327. *Gallica Christiana* 8:1350–53. A. M. ZIMMERMANN, *Kalendarium Benedictinum* (Metten 1933–38) 1:104. S. A. BENNETT, *Dictionary of Christian Biography* 3:628.

[M. R. P. MCGUIRE]

LAUDS

The morning hour of the Divine Office. The term "lauds" is derived from its nature as praise (laud) and from the *Laudes* or the three Psalms (148, 149, 150) that always concluded its psalmody until the reform of Pius X (d. 1914). Because it is the Church's morning prayer, its more ancient Latin names made reference to that fact, for example, *matutinum, matutinum officium, matutini hymni, matutina solemnitas.*

Early morning, with its wonderful freshness and stillness, is a time of day especially suited to the praise of God. When human beings and nature once again awaken and undergo their daily "resurrection," it is natural for all to rejoice anew in life and light and to acclaim the beneficent creator of all things. The rising sun has traditionally been looked on as a symbol and reminder of the Lord's Resurrection. Over time, the hour of Lauds evolved into a beautiful and solemn service of morning praise.

Resurrection thoughts are very evident in the antiphons, where the Alleluia (the resurrection acclamation par excellence) occurs frequently. This is preeminently true on Sunday, the Lord's day, when both the resurrection day and resurrection hour coincide at Lauds. On Easter Sunday there is a triple coincidence of this basic Christian motif. The climax of Lauds' praise comes at the Gospel canticle, the Benedictus, Zechariah's joyful "filled with the Holy Spirit" hailing the dawn of the day of salvation. At the beginning of each new day of grace and redemption the Church loves to greet her risen Lord and Savior as the divine Sun, the *oriens ex alto*.

Lauds was the fruit of a slow, persistent development. The first Christians, converted Jews, made no attempt at an immediate break with Judaism. It was to be expected that they would continue to follow Jewish prayer practices. There was prayer thrice daily in the synagogues; these services consisted of instructional Scripture readings and of prayer. The Shema and the 18 benedictions were said at the morning and evening hours. It is considered probable that the Lord's Prayer, advocated thrice daily for Christians by the Didache, had already supplanted the Shema in apostolic times.

All the early Christian writers who spoke of times of prayer, such as, Cyprian (d. 258) and Clement of Alexandria (d. *c*. 215), mentioned morning prayer (Cyprian, *De oratione dominica* 35; Clement, *Stromata* 7.7). Tertullian, at the beginning of the third century, did not hesitate to call the morning and evening prayers "legitimate prayers" (*De oratione* 25). Some say "legitimate" means prescribed, but does not demand a public service. Others say it means that these prayers were in conformity with a custom already well established, if not a veritable law, and that they were kept regularly by the Christian community, in short, were liturgical. The work of Tertullian's contemporary, Hippolytus of Rome, tends to bear out the judgment that morning prayer was kept regularly by the Christian community. It describes an early morning assembly every day at places designated by the bishop at which the presbyters and deacons gave instruction and then there were prayers (*Apostolic Tradition* 39, 41). The faithful were urged, not obliged, to attend. The instruction was quite likely given in connection with a reading from Holy Scripture. This is the most important and detailed early witness to an organized service in the morning. From such lessons and prayers the liturgical hour of Lauds eventually took form.

During the peace that followed Constantine's edict of toleration in 313, the Church everywhere soon appointed times of prayer for her rapidly growing community. Lauds and Vespers became canonically established hours of prayer throughout Christendom. Research has brought to light a striking uniformity throughout the Church in the basic structure of these hours. Lauds commonly had Psalm 63 and the *Laudate* Psalms, a Scripture reading with explanation, a hymn (inserted somewhat later), *Preces* (a litany of intercessions for the needs of the Church), and the concluding prayer and blessing by the presiding bishop or priest.

St. Benedict described the basic arrangement of Lauds already in his 6th–century Rule (ch. 12 and 13).

His is the first complete account of the daily organization of the Office. He himself acknowledges that he is following the Roman Church, that is, the practice of the communities, more or less regular, that served the Roman basilicas at that time. Even the titular churches of Rome, served by the secular clergy, very probably had much the same Office for Lauds.

By the middle ages, Lauds consisted of introductory versicles, five Psalms and antiphons, a short Scripture reading, a hymn, a versicle, the Benedictus, *Preces* on penitential days, an oration, and the concluding versicles. Unlike most of the other hours, Lauds had specially selected Psalms. Of set purpose, they are Psalms of praise and often contain nature motifs. The first Psalm of Lauds (except on penitential days) was always one in praise of God's kingship, and in the New Testament context this means the kingship of the risen Christ. In at least one of the next two Psalms there was some reference to morning. On Sundays and great feasts, the Old Testament canticle that follows is the Benedicite (Canticle of the Three Young Men); it called on all creation to join in praise of the Lord. Lastly came one of the *Laudate* Psalms that have praise as their dominant characteristics. The 1971 revision of the Liturgy of the Hours has preserved much of the classical structure of Lauds. Lauds or Morning Prayer begins with an introductory versicle, followed by a morning hymn. The number of psalms and canticles has been reduced to three: a psalm, an Old Testament Canticle, and a psalm of praise. Next comes a short Scripture reading, a responsory, the Canticle of Zechariah (*Benedictus*), intercessory prayers (*preces*), the Lord's Prayer, closing prayer, and a blessing.

Bibliography: P.F. BRADSHAW, *Daily Prayer in the Early Church: A Study of the Origin and Early Development of the Divine Office* (London 1981). G. GUIVER, *Company of Voices: Daily Prayer and the People of God* (New York 1988). R. TAFT, *The Liturgy of the Hours in East and West: The Origins of the Divine Office and Its Meaning for Today*, 2nd rev. ed. (Collegeville 1993).

[G. E. SCHIDEL/EDS.]

LAUDUS (LÔ), ST.

Bishop; b. perhaps at St. Lô, Normandy, France; d. *c*. 568. He became bishop of Coutances *c*. 523 and attended the synods of Orléans in 533, 538, 541, and 549, as well as the funerals of St. Paternus (d. 563) and St. Marculf (d. 558). He was a friend of St. Melanie of Rennes (d. *c*. 535). As patron saint of Coutances, he has his own Office; and in the Mass, his own Sequence and Preface. There is evidence that his cult existed also at Bayeux, where he was perhaps buried, at Rouen, and at Angers in the ninth century, when his vita was written.

Feast: Sept. 22 (Coutances and Sarum calendar); Sept. 25 (Bayeux).

Bibliography: *Acta sanctorum* Sept. 6 (1863) 438–448. E. W. BÖHNE, *Lexikon für Theologie und Kirche*, ed. J. HOFER and K. RAHNER (Freiburg 1957–65) 6:827. V. LEROQUAIS, *Les Sacramentaires et les missels manuscrits des bibliothèques de France* (Paris 1924) 3:380. E. A. PIGEON, *Vies des saints du diocèse de Coutances et Avranches* 2 v. (Avranches 1892) 113–172. L. DUCHESNE, *Fastes épiscopaux de l'ancienne Gaule* (Paris 1907–15) 2:238. J. L. BAUDOT and L. CHAUSSIN, *Vies des saintes et des bienheureux* (Paris 1935–56) 9:464–465.

[V. I. J. FLINT]

LAUNOY, JEAN DE

Theologian; b. Valdesie, France, Dec. 21, 1601; d. Paris, March 10, 1678. Launoy studied philosophy and theology at the College of Navarre in Paris, of which he became the historian. Receiving a licenciate and doctorate in 1634, he was ordained a priest in 1636. As an historian he developed an extreme form of criticism, pointing out the false attributions of works and the unchecked assertions of the martyrologium. He admitted neither the identity of Denis, Bishop of Paris, with the Areopagite, nor the legend according to which St. Magdalen would have taken refuge at Sainte-Baume. In his books and letters he developed a strong and coherent form of Gallicanism, rejecting the infallibility of the Roman pontiff and professing the superiority of the general council.

In 1649, he took part in the controversy concerning the author of the *Imitation of Christ:* according to him, the author was not Thomas à Kempis, but Gersen, Abbot of Vercelli. He defended NICHOLAS OF CLAMANGES who was posthumously attacked by his adversaries, and he published his unedited works. He also took part in a controversy about DURANDUS OF SAINT-POURÇAIN'S theory of the divine action on human beings. He did not favor the Immaculate Conception or the Assumption of the Blessed Virgin, and took part in literary controversies on these issues. Although opposed to the Jansenists, he encouraged frequent communion and considered attritionism authorized by Trent.

He was excluded from the Faculty of Theology of Paris for his refusal to subscribe to the censure of A. Arnauld (1656). In his *Regia in matrimonium potestas* (Paris 1674), he claimed that Christian marriage was only a civil contract and was exclusively under the jurisdiction of the state. His works were issued in 10 volumes, *Joannis Launoii opera omnia* (Geneva 1731–33).

Bibliography: J. CARREYRE, *Dictionnaire de théologie catholique*, ed. A. VACANT et al., (Paris 1903–50) 9.1:2–6. P. FÉRET, *La Faculté de théologie de Paris et ses docteurs les plus célèbres.*

Époque moderne (Paris 1906). A. G. MARTIMORT, *Le gallicanisme de Bossuet* (Paris 1953). J. M. GRES-GAYER, *Le Jansénisme en Sorbonne, 1643–1656* (Paris 1996); *Le gallicanisme de Sorbonne, 1656–1688* (Paris 2001).

[G. MOLLAT/J. M. GRES-GAYER]

LAURA

A laura is a colony of monks leading semieremitical lives in separate huts grouped around a central building (*coenobium*) near a church. The monks were subject to a spiritual father and gathered on Saturday and Sunday for the communal celebration of the liturgy. Often the anchorites had to pass a period of probation in the *coenobium*. Laura is most commonly used with reference to 4th–century Palestinian MONASTICISM, the first monastery there having been founded by St. Chariton (*c.* 350) at Pharan, northeast of Jerusalem. However, the first monks of Egypt, especially those of Scete, patterned their semieremitical life on that of the laura also, as did monks of Syria, Mesopotamia, Gaul, Italy, Ireland, Britain, and as they do in Russia to this day (*see* ATHOS, MOUNT). It represents a mid–stage between the life of the recluse and the fully cenobitic life developed by St. PACHOMIUS. St. Euthymius (377–473) and his disciple St. SABAS (439–532) founded the most famous Palestinian lauras. In 483 Sabas established also, southeast of Jerusalem, the Great Laura (known as Mar Saba), which still stands today; and in 507, the New Laura.

Bibliography: S. VAILHÉ, "Les premiers monastères de Palestine," *Bessarione* 3 (1897–98) 39–58, 209–225; 4 (1898) 193–210. H. LECLERCQ, *Dictionnaire d'archéologie chrétienne et de liturgie,* ed. F. CABROL, H. LECLERCQ, and H. I. MARROU, 15 v. (Paris 1907–53) 8.2:1961–88. H. G. EVELYN–WHITE, ed., *The Monasteries of the Wadi n' Natrûn,* 3 v. (New York 1926–33) 3:3–9. F. VAN DER MEER and C. MOHRMANN, *Atlas of the Early Christian World,* ed. and tr. M. F. HEDLUND and H. H. ROWLEY (New York 1958) 15, 17, 34, 35, 170–171.

[M. C. MCCARTHY]

LAUSIAC HISTORY (PALLADIUS)

A history of the desert Fathers, written about 419–420 by Palladius, Bishop of Helenopolis, who dedicated it to Lausus, the royal chamberlain at the court of Theodosius II. The work gives the biographies of the monks of Egypt, Palestine, Syria, and Asia Minor, many of whom Palladius had met in his sojourn in those countries. At one time he had attempted the solitary life himself, so he knew whereof he spoke. Of the historical validity of much of the work there can be no doubt; some of the stories he heard second hand, and of these we may be less certain. Palladius presented no theory of asceticism, he merely reported what he saw. If he tells of a backsliding monk or a fallen nun, he shows how the defection happened through pride or through abstention from the Liturgy and the Sacraments. It is a rich document for the history of monasticism, and it spread throughout the East. So popular a work was soon translated into Latin and many Oriental languages.

Bibliography: J. MEURSIUS, ed. (Leiden 1616). C. BUTLER, ed., 2 v. (*Texts and Studies* 6.1–2; Cambridge, Eng. 1898–1904) critical ed. For Butler's notes on this ed. *see Journal of Theological Studies* 22 (1920–21) 21–35, 138–155, 222–238. R. T. MEYER, ed. and tr. (*Ancient Christian Writers,* ed., J. QUASTEN et al. [Westminster, Md.-London 1946–] 34; 1965). J. QUASTEN, *Patrology* (Westminster, Maryland 1950–) 3:177–179. H. RAHNER, *Lexikon für Theologie und Kirche,* ed. J. HOFER and K. RAHNER (Freiberg 1957–65) 5:390–391. E. HONIGMANN, *Patristic Studies* (*Studi e Testi* 173; 1953) 104–122. C. E. BUTLER, *The Lausiac History of Palladius: A Critical Discussion together with Notes on Early Egyptian Monachism* (Hildesheim 1967). G. FRANK, *The Memory of the Eyes: Pilgrims to Living Saints in Christian Late Antiquity* (Berkeley 2000).

[R. T. MEYER]

LAUZON, PIERRE DE

Jesuit missionary; b. Poitiers, France, Sept. 26, 1687; d. Quebec, Canada, Sept. 5, 1742. He joined the Society of Jesus in France, Nov. 24, 1703, and was ordained and sent to Canada about 1716. He studied the Huron and Iroquois languages at L'Ancienne Lorette near Quebec and was then assigned to the Sault St. Louis (Caughnawaga) mission near Montreal. He served the Iroquois until 1721, when he went to the College of Quebec as professor of hydrography for a year. In response to the entreaties of the Iroquois and to allay their resentment at the news of a garrison taking up winter quarters at Sault St. Louis, Lauzon was sent back to his former mission (1722), was named its superior (1723), and ably directed the post for nine years. In 1732, when he was appointed superior of the Jesuits in Canada, he automatically became rector of the College of Quebec, where he remained for seven years. On a visit to France to seek help (1733), he brought back Rev. Jean Pierre Aulneau, who was martyred at Lake of the Woods in 1739. Upon completion of his term of office, Lauzon rejoined his old mission at Caughnawaga in 1739, but ill health caused his recall to Quebec two years later. Although sometimes known as Jean, Lauzon signed his name Pierre in official documents.

[G. CARRIÉRE]

LAVAL, FRANÇOIS DE MONTMORENCY, BL.

First bishop of Québec, Canada; b. April 30, 1623, Montigny-sur-Avre, France; d. May 6, 1708, Québec, Canada.

François Laval was the third son of Hughes de Laval, knight and lord of Montigny, and of Michelle de Péricard. As a younger branch of the Montmorency, his family bore its arms as well as those of the Lavals on its blazon. The coat of arms, engraved on a stone in the old church of Montigny-sur-Avre, is still extant, as is the lordly manor of the family. At age nine, Laval entered the royal college of La Flèche, a renowned Jesuit institution, where he began preliminary studies for the priesthood. Ten years later he transferred to the Jesuit Collège de Clermont in Paris for theological courses. While there he also frequented the Caen Hermitage, a house for closed retreats founded by Jean de Bernières-Louvigny, famous mystic and spiritual director who influenced his spiritual development. During Laval's prolonged studies, his father and two older brothers in turn were killed in 1645 while pursuing their military careers. Despite these trials and the material responsibility for his family, he was ordained in 1647 before renouncing his patrimonial rights. Already a canon in the cathedral of Évreux from the age of 12, he became its archdeacon soon after his ordination and diligently performed the functions of these offices until his resignation in 1654 to enter a hermitage in Caen.

His candidacy for the office of first bishop of New France was supported by the JESUITS and the French court, and on June 3, 1658, Rome named him vicar apostolic with the title of bishop of Petrea, *in partibus infidelium.* Despite the intrigues of some French bishops, he finally received episcopal consecration Dec. 8, 1658, feast of the Immaculate Conception, to which he later consecrated his cathedral. The young bishop departed from La Rochelle on April 13, 1659, and after a brief stop at Percé, landed on June 16 at Québec, where the small colony received him with great joy. He immediately set about organizing the Canadian Church, until then without a real leader. Leaving the apostolate of the Native Americans to the Jesuits, he entrusted the care of the French colonists to the few secular priests. To guarantee a supply of diocesan priests, both from the colony and from his mother country, he founded the Seminary of Québec in 1663, a community designed not only to form priests but to provide lodgings for those worn out by their ministry. He soon associated this seminary to that of the Paris Foreign Mission Society and in 1668 he added a minor seminary. Laval undertook pastoral visits in his huge diocese, traveling great distances on snowshoes in winter and by canoe when the rivers were free of ice. Despite obstacles and infringements of the civil authority on the ecclesiastical domain, the Canadian Church grew rapidly and became firmly united. In 1674, after prolonged negotiations, made difficult by the GALLICANISM of the French episcopacy, Laval secured the erection of the Diocese of Québec. It was immediately subject to Rome and had jurisdiction over all the lands discovered by the French in North America.

From the beginning the bishop was aware of the disorders caused by the traffic of alcohol in the colony, particularly its tragic consequences among the natives. He energetically fought the abuses of the traders, who were often protected by the governor and his counselors, and even by the French court, and on three different occasions he went directly to the king to plead for the spiritual and temporal interests of the colony. He supported existing religious communities, helped in new foundations in the cities and countryside, and tried to manage the Recollect Franciscans, who returned to Canada through the intervention of the civil authorities. His great concern for education led him to consolidate the Seminary of Québec, which was already providing several Canadian priests. After securing for it a beautiful plot of land, he generously contributed to the construction of its buildings, one of which, dating from 1678, still exists. To ensure its future he acquired vast *seigneuries* and ceded to it all their goods. He also founded the School of Arts, Trades, and Agriculture of St. Joachim, eight leagues from Québec, and helped to open primary schools. On orders from the court he even tried instructing natives in his minor seminary.

By visits and ordinances he stimulated individual and community piety. Devotions to the Virgin and Ste. Anne de Beaupré (the well-known pilgrimage spot dates from his time) flourished, as well as to the Holy Angels and the Holy Family, whose confraternity and feast were instituted by his mandate. New France was the first country in the world to have an Office of the Holy Family. The fervor of the French establishments was remarkable and was imitated by some of the natives, among whom high mysticism was discovered, as with the young Iroquois maid Kateri TEKAKWITHA. Laval himself solemnly baptized Daniel GARAKONTHIE, Onondaga chief. In 1688, weakened by cares, labors, and infirmities, Laval resigned and was replaced by Bp. J. B. de Saint-Vallier. The "old bishop" retired to his seminary, spending his time in prayer, works of mercy, and, frequently, at pontifical functions during his successor's long absences. Their differences over policy was a hard trial for the older man.

After Laval's death his reputation for sanctity kindled piety, and extraordinary favors were granted through his intercession. His cause of canonization was begun in

Bl. François de Montmorency Laval. (Archive Photos)

1878, introduced in Rome in 1890, and reached a decisive stage in the 1960 decree proclaiming the heroic nature of his virtues. He was beatified by John Paul II June 22, 1980. Laval's remains lie in a funeral chapel in the Seminary of Québec, a pilgrimage site.

Feast: May 6 (Canada).

Bibliography: *La positio de la cause* (Rome 1956), a collection of known letters. *Quebecen. beatificationis et canonizationis ven. servi Dei Francisci de Montmorency-Laval Episcopi Quebecensis 1708: altera nova positio super virtutibus ex officio critice disposita* (Rome 1956). N. BAILLARGEON, *Le séminaire de Québec sous l'épiscopat de Mgr de Laval* (Québec 1972). É. BÉGIN, *François de Laval* (Québec 1959). G. E. DEMERS, *Mgr. de Laval* (Montréal 1951). É. GERVAIS, *Le Vén. François de Montmorency-Laval* (Montréal 1952). A. H. GOSSELIN, *Vie de Monseigneur de Laval*, 2 v. (Québec 1890; new ed. 1906); *Au pays de Mgr de Laval: letters de voyage* (Québec 1910). H. HOUSSART, *Mgr. de Laval vu par son serviteur* (Québec 1961). C. DE LA ROCHEMONTEIX, *Les Jésuites et la Nouvelle-France au XVIIme siècle*, 3 v. (Paris 1895–96). A. VACHON, *François de Laval* (Montréal 1980). *Acta Apostolicae Sedis* (1981) 235–58. *L'Osservatore Romano*, Eng. ed. 26 (1980) 10–11.

[H. PROVOST/ K. I. RABENSTEIN]

LAVAL, JACQUES DÉSIRÉ, BL.

Doctor, priest of the Congregation of the Holy Heart of Mary (now merged with the Holy Ghost Fathers);

apostle of Mauritius; b. Sept. 18, 1803, Croth, Diocese of Évreux, Normandy, France; d. Sept. 9, 1864, Port-Louis, Mauritius.

Laval, the son of a lawyer with extensive land holdings and a pious mother who tended the needy, owned his own farm by age 13. After attending local schools, he completed his secondary studies at Évreux, then studied the humanities in Paris, theology at Saint Stanislaus College in Évreux, and medicine in Paris, where he earned a doctorate at the Sorbonne Aug. 21, 1830. He opened a successful medical practice in Saint-André near Évreux, while serving as captain of the national guard and maintaining a large household. He returned to the practice of the faith following a riding accident in 1835. That summer he decided to continue his theological studies at Saint-Sulpice Seminary in Paris, where he became acquainted with François Libermann.

Laval was ordained a priest in 1838 and decided to join Libermann in a single mission for the welfare of Black slaves. Until they established their mission, Laval administered the parish of Pinterville, Évreux Diocese. During the summer of 1841, Laval donated his entire wealth to Libermann, joined the Congregation of the Holy Heart of Mary, and accompanied the newly appointed bishop to the island of Mauritius. Thus, on Sept. 11, 1841, Father Laval, whose companions remembered him as "the saint who always says he does nothing," began his 23 year ministry to a parish of 80,000. He is responsible for baptizing 67,000 emancipated slaves and instituting works for economic, social, and technical development on the island.

Laval's cause for canonization was opened in 1918. In the first beatification ceremony presided over by John Paul II, April 29, 1979, he was raised to the altars as a blessed. Patron of slaves.

Bibliography: Works. J. D. LAVAL, *Extraits de sa correspondance*, ed. J. LÉCUYER (Paris 1978); *Le Serviteur de Dieu, Jacques-Désiré Laval, de la Congr. du St. Espirit et du St. Coeur de Marie* (Paris 1912). Literature. J. ACKING, *Père Laval* (Port Louis 1986). B. BOCAGE, *Le Père Jacques Laval: un saint de chez nous* (Pacy-sur-Eure, France 1989). F. DELAPLACE and M. PIVAULT, *Le Père Jacques-Desirè Laval, Apôtre de L'ile Maurice* (Paris 1932). J. FITZSIMMONS, *Father Laval* (London 1973). J. MICHEL, *Les auxiliaires laïcs du bienheureux Jacques Laval, apôtre de l'île Maurice* (Paris 1988). J. T. RATH, *Jakob Laval, der Apostel von Mauritius* (Dormagen 1978). *Acta Apostolicae Sedis* 72 (1980) 154–57. *L'Osservatore Romano*, Eng. ed. 19 (1979) 6–7.

[K. I. RABENSTEIN]

LAVAL, MARTYRS OF

A group of 19 beatified victims of the FRENCH REVOLUTION, martyred in 1794. The martyrs (14 secular and one religious priest, three religious women, and one lay woman) were among the many whom the revolutionists put to death for religious reasons in the area of the present *département* of Mayenne in western France, whose capital is Laval.

At Laval 14 priests, arrested at various times in the preceding months, were guillotined (Jan. 21, 1794) for refusing to subscribe to the CIVIL CONSTITUTION OF THE CLERGY, to which two of them had previously subscribed with restrictions. They were: René Ambroise (b. 1720), Jacques André (b. 1763), François Duchesne (b. 1736), André Duliou (b. 1727), Jean Gallot (b. 1747), Louis Gastineau (b. 1727), François Migoret-Lambardeère (b. 1728), Julien Morin de la Girardière (b. 1733), Julien Moulé (b. 1716), Joseph Pellé (b. 1720), Augustin Philippot (b. 1716), Pierre Thomas (b. 1729), Jean Baptiste Turpin du Cormier (b. 1732), and Jean Baptiste Triquerie (b. 1737), a Conventual Franciscan.

Jacques Burin (b. 1756) was imprisoned in 1791 after reading publicly, with approval, Pius VI's condemnation of the Civil Constitution, to which he had subscribed with reservations a few months previously. After his release he disguised himself as a merchant and continued his priestly ministrations until he was shot to death in an ambush at Champgenêteux (Oct. 17, 1794). His murderer rejoiced when a chalice, found on Burin's person, indicated that his victim was a priest.

Françoise Mézière (b. 1745), a very pious laywoman and teacher, was guillotined at Laval (Feb. 5, 1794), after being apprehended while caring for wounded Vendean soldiers. At Ernée the guillotine made martyrs of two sisters belonging to the congregation of *Charit é de la Chapelle-au-Riboul*. For refusing to take the prescribed oath, Françoise Tréhet (b. 1756) was executed March 13, 1794, and Jeanne Véron (b. 1766), seven days later. On June 25, Sister St. Monica (Marie Lhullier, b. 1744), an illiterate lay sister belonging to the congregation of the Hospital Sisters of the Mercy of Jesus, was executed at Laval for refusing to take the oath condemned by the Church.

All 19 were beatified June 19, 1955.

Bibliography: E. CESBRON, *Les Martyrs de Laval* (Rennes 1955). J. L. BAUDOT and L. CHAUSSIN, *Vies des saints et des bienheueux selon l'ordre du calendrier avec l'historique des fêtes*, ed. by The Benedictines of Paris, 12 v. (Paris 1935–56) 13:105–114.

[M. LAWLOR]

LA VALETTE, JEAN PARISOT DE

Grand Master of the Knights of St. John of Jerusalem (known also as KNIGHTS OF MALTA after 1523); b. Toulouse, 1494; d. Malta, Aug. 21, 1568. La Valette, member of a great French noble family, entered the Order of the Knights of St. John and fought the Muslims in North Africa and on the Sicilian coast. After his unanimous election as grand master of the order in 1557, he managed to restore its finances, and he cooperated with the viceroy of Sicily in an attempt to capture Tripoli. Mismanagement of the expedition by the viceroy resulted in disaster from which La Valette contrived to save some of the expeditionary force. He also built up the Maltese fleet and secured official representation for his order at the Council of Trent. The Turkish Sultan Suleiman II determined to destroy the measures taken for the strengthening of Malta. As a result of La Valette's indomitable leadership the cavaliers and mercenary soldiers on the island were brought to a high degree of readiness. The Turkish attack began on May 18, 1565, with the arrival of 159 vessels of war carrying at least 30,000 Janissaries and Spahis, with artillery and food supplies, to oppose the some 9,000 members of the island garrison. The invaders effectively laid siege to the fortress of San Elmo, but the Grand Master for a time defeated their efforts. La Valette invented a new weapon made up of wooden circles soaked in alcohol and oil, which were then covered with cotton, saltpeter, and gunpowder. These circles, lighted and flung amidst the attackers, burned them alive. Despite heroic resistance the fort fell on July 23. The Muslims then besieged San Angelo, the main citadel of the island. The Turkish commander mounted an attack on the island fortress of St. Michael where the cavaliers of the order had withdrawn; he lost thousands, and the fortress successfully resisted the attack. Finally, with the Sicilian viceroy as commander a substantial force came (September 1) to La Valette's assistance. The Turkish commander fled with the besieging army but changed his mind and returned. However, La Valette had acted promptly and in the interval had destroyed the siege machines and trenches the Muslims had constructed.

Pius IV offered La Valette a cardinal's hat, which he refused. Later, the Turks planned another invasion but ships from Malta destroyed the Turkish arsenal at Constantinople. La Valette rebuilt the fort of San Elmo and started the construction of a new city (modern Valletta). When contributions for this enterprise from western Europe failed, copper coins were struck to carry on the work so that there would be no delay; these coins appropriately carried the device *non aes, sed fides*. In his later years La Valette's vigorous administration was troubled by rebellion among the Spanish cavaliers on the island and by what he considered to be ingratitude on the part of Pope Pius V, who, instead of permitting La Valette to nominate his own candidate for the leadership of the order's grand priory in Rome, appointed a papal nephew to the post.

Bibliography: J. A. THOU, *Historiarum sui temporis* (Paris 1604). J. P. E. JURIEN DE LA GRAVIÈRE, *Les Chevaliers de Malte et la Marine de Philippe II,* 2 v. (Paris 1887). R. A. VERTOT, *Histoire des Chevaliers Hospitaliers de S. Jean de Jerusalem,* 5 v. (Paris 1726). P. DE BOURDEILLE, SEIGNEUR DE BRANTÔME, *Grands capitaines françois,* v.3–4 of *Oeuvres complètes,* 11 v. (Paris 1864–82). E. W. SCHERMERHORN, *Malta of the Knights* (London 1929). E. D. S. BRADFORD, *The Great Siege* (New York 1962). R. COHEN, *Knights of Malta 1523–1798* (New York 1920).

[S. J. T. MILLER]

LA VANG, OUR LADY OF

Our Lady of La Vang, in Vietnamese, is *Đức Mẹ La Vang,* also known as Our Lady of Vietnam. Located in the Hai Lang district in the Quảng Trị region, La Vang is about 60 km north of Hứ. On Aug. 17, 1798, King Cảnh Thịnh issued an edict ordering the immediate execution of all Catholics in his realm. As persecution erupted, a group of Catholic refugees from neighboring villages escaped into the jungles of La Vang. According to the received tradition, one night, a beautiful and radiant lady with a compassionate countenance appeared to the frightened and starving refugees by a huge, old tree as they were praying for deliverance from their persecutors and protection from wild beasts. Calling herself the ''Blessed Mother'' (*Đứ Mẹ*), she comforted and encouraged them to keep their faith in Jesus Christ, taught them how to collect herbs in the forest as medicine, and promised to intercede to her Son on their behalf.

When the persecution subsided, a cult to the Blessed Virgin grew at the spot of the tree, drawing Catholics and non–Catholics alike. In 1820, a small shrine was built at the foot of the tree by her devotees. In 1825, the first church of Our Lady of La Vang was built at the spot of her apparition with land and monetary donations from the nearby villages of Thach Hản, Cổ Thành, and Ba Trừ. In 1866, the local bishop rebuilt and enlarged the church. Destroyed by anti–Catholic radicals in 1885, construction of a new church began in 1886, and the church was consecrated in 1901. By the 1920s, this building proved too small. In 1923, construction began on a new edifice which was consecrated on Aug. 22, 1928 with 20,000 pilgrims in attendance. In 1959 La Vang was officially declared the National Shrine of Our Lady of Vietnam, marking 300 years of the Church's presence in Vietnam. On Aug. 22, 1961, Pope John XXIII elevated this shrine to a minor basilica. In 1972, at the height of the Vietnam War, the basilica was completely destroyed by Communist bombardment, save for the shrine of Our Lady of La Vang, which miraculously survived intact. On Aug. 15, 1993, in his address to Vietnamese–American youth during World Youth Day in Denver, Colorado, Pope John

Paul II entrusted the Vietnamese Catholic Church under the protection of Our Lady of La Vang.

Despite repeated requests, the Communist authorities refused permission to rebuild the destroyed basilica. Nevertheless, the triennial Marian Days pilgrimage to the shrine grew in size in the late 1980s and 1990s, gathering in the public square in front of the existing shrine. The 200–year anniversary celebration of the apparition in 1998–99 drew more than 200,000 pilgrims from across Vietnam, despite official restrictions barring overseas Vietnamese from participating. In the U.S., devotion to Our Lady of La Vang was promoted by the CONGREGATION OF THE MOTHER CO–REDEMPTRIX (*Dòng Đồng Công*). Their annual Marian Days pilgrimage celebration every August, mirrored after the traditional Marian Days pilgrimage to La Vang, drew an estimated 50,000 Vietnamese Catholics to Carthage, Missouri each year.

[V. T. PHAM]

LAVANOUX, MAURICE ÉMILE

Artist, editor, critic; b. New York, N.Y., June 10, 1894; d. New York, N.Y., Oct. 21, 1974. He received a bilingual education, studying in Montreal (1906–11), at Columbia University (1912–17), and Atelier Laloux, Paris (1919–20). A volunteer for military service in the French army in World War I, he worked in the offices of Gustaf Steinback and of Maginnis and Walsh, Boston, as draftsman and researcher, acquiring vast experience in the planning and construction of churches. In 1928 he invited a group of architects, artists, and clergymen interested in liturgical arts to several meetings at Portsmouth Priory, Newport, R.I.; from this emerged the Liturgical Arts Society. In 1932 he launched *Liturgical Arts Quarterly* with Harry Lorin Binsse as managing editor. Lavanoux served as editor and secretary until the magazine was discontinued in 1972 for lack of funds.

During the 40 years that he published the *Quarterly* Lavanoux became internationally respected among artists and scholars associated with the liturgical movement. He lectured on church art and architecture in universities and seminaries throughout the United States, Canada, and in Europe. His world travels were constantly geared to the study of new developments in the field and the establishment of personal contacts that might enrich editorial contributions to the *Quarterly*. It gradually took on an international character that provided leadership throughout the Church. Early, too, Lavanoux associated his work with the ecumenical movement, and he became highly respected in Protestant and Jewish circles.

While almost all of his publishing energies were focused on the *Quarterly,* a considerable opus in itself,

Lavanoux also edited A. Henze's and T. Filthout's *Contemporary Church Art* (1956) and contributed an important introduction to A. Christ-Janer's and M. M. Foley's, *Modern Church Architecture* (1962). He served on juries for competitions sponsored by the American Institute of Architecture, the Cardinal Lercaro Awards, and Columbia and Princeton Universities' schools of architecture. He also served as advisor to architecture students at Columbia. He was consultant on many ecclesiastical buildings and contributed articles to many magazines.

While his years of enforced retirement following the discontinuance of the *Quarterly* were fraught with disappointment, he continued to work for the improvement of standards in liturgical art and assumed the editorship of *Stained Glass* magazine. He also threw himself more energetically than ever into the work of the Contemporary Christian Art Gallery (New York City). Following his quiet death at home, tributes appeared in many journals, both religious and secular. While many stressed that Vatican Council II and its Constitution on the Sacred Liturgy to which he had substantially contributed had put the seal on his life's work, he himself had felt that the work was just beginning.

[C. J. MCNASPY]

LAVATER, JOHANN KASPAR

Swiss theologian, philosopher, and poet: b. Zurich, Nov. 15, 1741; d. there, Jan. 2, 1801. He attended schools in his native town and began Protestant theology in 1759. As early as 1763, however, he was turning from the ENLIGHTENMENT's rationalistic conception of religion to the ideas of the *Sturm und Drang* period. He became parson at the church of St. Peter, Zurich, in 1786. A writer of deep feeling and vivid imagination, he won wide fame by his religious writing, his *Schweizerlieder* (1767), and especially his four-volume *Physiognomische Fragmente zur Beförderung der Menschenkenntnis und Menschenliebe* (1775–78), in which he attempted to analyze the character of man through an intuitive interpretation of bodily structure. This occasioned his reputation throughout Europe and led to extensive correspondence with great contemporaries such as GOETHE, Johann HERDER, and Johann HAMANN. Lavater first sympathized with the French Revolution but later protested its excesses. Ironically, he died of wounds sustained while acting as stretcher-bearer at the battle of Zurich (Nov. 26, 1800).

Lavater's belief in Christ was manifested in an undogmatic and emotional piety, as is evident in *Christliche Lieder* (1776–80), the four-volume *Aussichten in die Ewigkeit* (1768–78), and the four-volume *Pontius Pilatus oder die Bibel im Kleinen* (1782–85). Yet his attempt to confirm by logic his shakily based convictions led to tensions between his religious experience and theology and his yearning for a constant, earthly manifestation of God, hence his uncritical interest in mesmerism and spiritism and his passion for detecting miracles. He rebutted atheism with untiring clerical fervor; he was generally tolerant of Catholics, and his friendship with Bp. J. M. SAILER led some to believe that he was a crypto-Catholic.

Bibliography: *Ausgewählte Schriften*, ed. J. K. ORELLI, 8 v. (Zurich 1841–44), 4 v. (3d ed. Zurich 1859–60). C. JANENTZKY, *Johann Caspar Lavater* (Frauenfeld 1928). M. LAVATER-SLOMAN, *Genie des Herzens: Die Lebensgeschichte Johann Caspar Lavaters* (5th ed. Zurich 1955). O. VASELLA, *Lexikon für Theologie und Kirche*, ed. J. HOFER and K. RAHNER (Freiburg 1957–65) 6: 840–841.

[J. B. KELLER]

LAVELLE, LOUIS

French philosopher; b. Saint-Martin-de-Villeréal (Lot-et-Garonne), July 15, 1883; d. there, Sept. 1, 1951. An *agrégé* in philosophy in 1909, he taught at the Lycée Fustel de Coulanges at Strasbourg and defended his thesis for the doctorate of letters in 1921. Shortly thereafter he started teaching at the Sorbonne, and in 1930 edited the philosophy chronicles of *Le Temps*. In 1934, with his friend René LE SENNE, he founded the movement known as philosophy of the spirit, which aimed at a renewal of metaphysics in reaction to positivism and classical rationalism. Named inspector general of national education, then professor at the Collège de France in 1941, in 1947 he was elected to the Académie des Sciences morales et politiques. He profoundly influenced not only his students but also the general public; an architect of ideas, he added to the fullness and flexibility of his thought a purity of language and charm of style that are in the best tradition of MALEBRANCHE and the French moralists. He lived in conformity with what he taught, closely uniting his spiritual with his intellectual life. One of his last writings ends on this characteristic note: "We should tremble with joy every morning at the thought that we have another day to love God."

The point of departure for Lavelle was an analysis of being, founded on an experience that includes and transfigures the sensible. From this he drew the title for his thesis, *Dialectique du monde sensible* (Strasbourg 1921). In his general ontology, being and reality were first identified; subsequently Lavelle discovered a pure act at the heart of being and finally divine love at the source of this act. More and more merging being with subjectivity, he later described the real as contained within the plenitude of being and as existing only for finite subjects. The real, in his thought, gradually merged with cosmicality and tended to reduce itself to objectifiable phenomena.

Being is participated; man is separated from it by an interval that God eternally crosses but that man finds inseparable from temporal ambiguity, from freedom of negation, and from the possibility of evil. Participated act does not merge with the participating act that gives rise to human freedoms. Although he relentlessly defended the univocity of being, Lavelle sought to avoid PANTHEISM. "Participation," he wrote, "does not have the extinction of the part in the whole as an ideal, but the formation of a spiritual society from the parts with themselves and with the whole" [*De l'Acte* (Paris 1937) 165]. The endless fecundity of the divine act that invites man to renew himself in it shapes Lavelle's optimism.

Applied to the analysis of categories—specifically to that of time—and with its many kinds of values, this philosophy expresses itself as a highly developed system. Yet its very richness leaves one undecided over its final meaning; one wonders whether it is legitimate to establish such a complete equality between religion and philosophy and wishes that Lavelle had given a fuller analysis of intersubjective causality.

Bibliography: M. MANNO, *Enciclopedia Filosofica* 2:1820–26. P. LEVERT, *L'Être et le réel selon Louis Lavelle* (Paris 1960). W. PIERSOL, *La Valeur dans la philosophie de Louis Lavelle* (Paris 1959). J. ÉCOLE, *La Métaphysique de l'être dans la philosophie de Louis Lavelle* (Paris 1957).

[M. NÉDONCELLE]

LAVELLE, MICHAEL JOSEPH

Vicar-general, educator; b. New York City, May 30, 1856; d. there, Oct. 17, 1939. He was the eldest of four children of Patrick and Rose (Fitzsimons) Lavelle, both Irish-born. After study at Manhattan College, New York City (A.B., 1873; M.A., 1875), he was ordained at St. Joseph's Seminary, Troy, NY, June 7, 1879, by Bp. Edgar P. Wadhams of Ogdensburg, NY. Lavelle was assigned to St. Patrick's Cathedral, New York City, where he spent all his priestly life and was appointed rector in May of 1887. Under his rectorship the cathedral, opened for public worship a month before his ordination, was gradually completed. Lavelle was a close friend of Abp. Michael A. Corrigan, and vicar-general (1902–18) of New York under Cardinal John Farley, and again (1934–39) under Cardinals Patrick Hayes and Francis Spellman. For half a century Lavelle was the best-known priest in the diocese, much in demand as a public speaker, and chairman of innumerable committees.

Lavelle founded Cathedral High School, the first free Catholic high school in the city, in 1905 (chartered 1910).

Charles Martial Allemand Lavigerie, in clerical vestments.

He was one of the founders of the Catholic Summer School at Plattsburg, NY, its president (1896–1903), and chairman (1924–39) of its Board of Trustees. He founded the Catholic Institute for the Blind (now the Lavelle School for the Blind), and was one of the three organizers of the Federation of Catholic Societies, which later merged into the National Catholic Welfare Conference. He was honored as domestic prelate in 1904 and as prothonotary apostolic in 1929.

[F. D. COHALAN]

LAVIGERIE, CHARLES MARTIAL ALLEMAND

Cardinal, archbishop of Algiers and of Carthage, founder of the White Fathers and the White Sisters; b. Bayonne, France, Oct. 31, 1825; d. Algiers, Nov. 26, 1892. His father held a position in the customs, and his mother was the daughter of the director of the royal mint at Bayonne. Lavigerie owed his early religious formation to the influence of the clergy of Bayonne and of Monsignor Félix A. P. DUPANLOUP. During his studies at Saint-Sulpice in Paris he formed a friendship with the Sulpician Charles Baudry, a leader among French ontologists. Baudry's theological learning, as well as his vigorous ideas about political morality and spirituality, left a deep mark upon Lavigerie. His consciousness of his missionary vocation began in those formative years. After his ordination in 1849 he obtained doctorates in letters (1850) and in theology (1853) and was made associate professor of ecclesiastical history at the Sorbonne, becoming titular of the chair in 1857. In that same year his responsibilities were further increased, for he took under his direction the *Oeuvre des écoles d'Orient*. In the discharge of his duties in connection with this position he made, in 1860, at the time of the massacres in Syria, a trip to the East that left a lasting imprint upon his missionary thought. As an auditor of the Rota (1861–63), finding it necessary to take a stand upon the Roman question, he favored a general solution to the difficulties of the Holy See by a renewal of the spirit, the methods, and the organization of Church government. Elevated to the See of Nancy in 1863, Lavigerie was able in the space of four years to bring about a notable reform. He sought particularly to raise the intellectual level of the clergy and to bring his priests into contact with contemporary society.

His nomination to the See of Algiers in 1867 enabled him at last to realize his missionary vocation. From the time of his promotion, his apostolic vision reached far beyond the confines of his diocese and embraced the whole of continental Africa. His first care was to obtain from the reluctant French government freedom to exercise the apostolate among the Algerian Muslims. This brought the archbishop into conflict with the governor, Marshall MacMahon, but in 1868 he succeeded in obtaining from Napoleon III the assurance that no obstacle would be put in the way of the works of charity undertaken by the Church. In 1868 Rome made Lavigerie apostolic delegate of western Sahara and the Sudan. During this time he laid the foundations of the Society of Missionaries of Africa (the White Fathers). This was conceived as an institute of secular priests living in community; it was to be apostolic in its purpose and Ignatian in the character of its spirituality, and its members, in conformity with the spirit Lavigerie had shown from the beginning, were to adapt themselves in every respect compatible with Christian faith and morals to the life and mentality, of the Africans among whom they worked. The Missionary Sisters of Our Lady of Africa, founded in 1869, was a religious society of women with the same missionary objective and sharing the same spirit of accommodation.

At Vatican Council I the archbishop, after associating himself with a third party of accord that sought to reconcile the differences between those who favored the definition of papal infallibility and those who thought it inopportune, gave his *placet* to the constitution *Pastor aeternus.*

In 1873 Lavigerie established his missionaries in the Sahara and in Kabylie. Always interested in the reunion of Churches, he founded in 1877 at St. Anne of Jerusalem a Greek Melchite seminary and entrusted it to his missionaries. In this he was motivated by a desire to increase among Eastern Catholics an esteem for their culture and a respect for their theological, canonical, and liturgical traditions.

In 1878 he founded the missions of equatorial Africa and his responsibilities as apostolic delegate were extended to include that area. Without personally visiting this new field he provided for the restoration of the practice of the primitive Church with regard to the catechumenate. When Tunisia was occupied by the French in 1881, Lavigerie was named apostolic administrator of that area, and he established many foundations in his new jurisdiction.

Leo XIII made him a cardinal in 1882, and two years later gave him the title of archbishop of Carthage and primate of Africa. From the same pope he received two missions. The first, an official one, was to stir up world opinion on the subject of African slavery. In compliance with the Pope's wish, Lavigerie began a resounding campaign, the echoes of which reached Europe and America. The conference of the great powers at Brussels in 1890 adopted proposals with regard to the best method of achieving the abolition of slavery that were in large part in conformity with suggestions Lavigerie had made, but that this was effected through the influence of the suggestions is less certain.

The second mission, an unofficial one, was to rally French Catholics to the support of the republican regime in France so as to overcome the anticlerical majority in parlement and make it possible to change the laws that barred the way to a *rapprochement* between France and the Holy See. Lavigerie, who from the accession of Leo XIII had actively upheld the French policy of the Holy See, launched the *ralliement* by proclaiming before a large assembly of officials in Algiers on Nov. 12, 1890, the obligation of French Catholics to adhere to the republican form of government. This famous *toast d'Alger* angered French monarchists, who criticized Lavigerie severely and heaped vituperation upon him. The cardinal replied with his spirited *Lettre à un catholique,* in which he attacked the claims of the pretenders and even went so far as to suggest that monarchy was an outgrown institution. But the *Lettre à un catholique* is only one document among others of equal importance and the

antimonarchism he expressed in it is only one, and a secondary, aspect of his thought on the *ralliement.*

Apostolic zeal, a sense of the contemporary realities, and a constant concern for the reform of the Church were the most distinctive traits of the personality of Lavigerie.

Bibliography: L. BAUNARD, *Le Cardinal Lavigerie,* 2 v. (Paris 1898). J. BOUNIOL, *The White Fathers and Their Missions* (London 1929). G. D. KITTLER, *The White Fathers* (New York 1957). J. DE ARTECHE, *The Cardinal of Africa: Charles Lavigerie,* tr. M. MITCHELL (London 1964). J. TOURNIER, *Le Cardinal Lavigerie et son action politique, 1863–1892* (Paris 1913); *Bibliographie du cardinal Lavigerie* (Paris 1913). S. C. WELLENS, *La Societé des Missionaires d'Afrique* (Louvain 1952). F. RAUSCHER, *Die Mitarbeit der einheimischen Laien am Apostolat in den Missionen der Weissen Väter* (Münster 1953). G. DINDINGER, ''Missionsschrifttum von und über Kardinal Lavigerie,'' *Miscellanea Pietro Fumasoni-Biondi* (Rome 1947) 107–191, bibliog. X. DE MONTCLOS, *Lavigerie, le Saint-Siège et l'Église, 1846–1878* (Paris 1965); *Le Toast d'Alger, 1890–1891* (Paris 1966).

[X. DE MONTCLOS]

LAW

A principle that connotes order, whether this be the order of the physical universe or that of morality. In a more specific sense, law is the rule and measure of human acts and relations. This article deals with the general concept of law as it underlies the juridical order, which pertains to the sphere of morality. It explains how law is a principle of order, analyzes the classical definition of law proposed by St. THOMAS AQUINAS, and discusses his view of the relationship that obtains between law and ethics. Other conceptions of law are treated in other articles (*see* LAW, PHILOSOPHY OF; NATURAL LAW).

Principle of Order. Although the term law is used in all sciences, it is employed sometimes in a speculative and sometimes in a practical sense. Examples of laws that are formulations of the speculative reason are the law of gravitation, the law of conservation of energy, and the law of diminishing returns. Those that proceed from man's practical reason, on the other hand, are normative principles that regulate human activities and relationships. While both kinds of law have the connotation of order, regularity, and predictability, they serve as principles of order in different ways corresponding to the different operations of the speculative and the practical reason.

The speculative reason has TRUTH for its object, whereas the practical reason has the GOOD for its end. The former deals with causes and effects, with facts and factual relationships, whereas the latter deals with ends and means, with values and their relative importance. This difference in their subject matters has important consequences relative to the order or regularity they establish when formulating laws. As St. Thomas notes, "since the speculative reason is busied chiefly with necessary things, which cannot be otherwise than they are, its proper conclusions, like the universal principles, contain truth without fail. The practical reason, on the other hand, is busied with contingent things, about which human actions are concerned, and consequently, although there is necessity in the general principles, the more we descend to matters of detail the more frequently we encounter defects" (*Summa theologiae* 1a2ae, 94.4). The recognition of the kind of necessity associated with the order of practical reason enables one to avoid the extremes of dogmatism, which claims absolute validity for all conclusions of moral law, and relativism, which denies validity even to its fundamental principles.

Thomistic Definition. St. Thomas defines law as "an ordinance of reason for the common good, made by him who has care of the community, and promulgated" (*Summa theologiae* 1a2ae, 90.4). This definition contains four essential elements: (1) reason, (2) the common good, (3) lawmaking authority, and (4) promulgation, to which are usually added sanction and enforcement.

Reason. Since law is a rule and measure whereby man is induced to act or restrain from acting, it is evidently a product of practical reason. The will of the competent authority must also be present to set the lawmaking process in motion; but what is made must accord with some rule of reason to have the nature of law. The will of the sovereign is the efficient cause of the law, while reason is its formal cause. Thus, reason is intrinsic to law; will, however necessary genetically, remains nonetheless an extrinsic factor. For St. Thomas, the common saying that the will of the sovereign has the force of law should be understood only of a will that is in accord with reason, for "otherwise the sovereign's will would savor of lawlessness rather than of law" (*ibid.* 90.1 ad 3). And according to Henry de BRACTON, "there is no true kingship where will, and not the law, wields dominion" (*De legibus,* 5b).

Common Good. The COMMON GOOD is the final cause of law. In the case of the eternal law, this is the good of the whole of creation under the governance of divine providence. In the case of the natural law, the common fountainhead of ethics and jurisprudence, it is man's ultimate happiness, which consists in the perfection of the human person, mutual friendship between man and man, and friendship with God (*Summa theologiae* 1a2ae, 99.1 ad 2). In the case of human law, it is the well-being of the people and the public welfare of the political community.

Since the natural law forms an essential part of human law, the ends of the natural law are capable of being furthered by human law. Human law can protect and implement the natural rights of man, which have been enumerated by Pius XII as follows: "The right to maintain and develop physical, intellectual, and moral life, and in particular the right to a religious training and education; the right to worship God, both in private and in public, including the right to engage in religious works of charity; the right, in principle, to marriage and to the attainment of the purpose of marriage, the right to wedded society and home life; the right to work as an indispensable means for the maintenance of family life; the right to the free choice of a state of life, and therefore of the priestly and religious state; the right to the use of material goods, subject to its duties and social limitations" [Christmas Broadcast, 1942; *Atti e Discorsi di Pio XII,* 6 v. (Rome 1942) 4:320–321].

Authority. AUTHORITY is the efficient cause of law. The very existence of law implies the existence of a lawmaker. God is the sole author of the eternal law, as also of the natural law, which He has ingrained in man's nature. All systems of human law thus contain, in varying proportions, a natural-law element and a positive-law element. The former is not made by man but only declared by him, whereas the latter is man-made.

The constitutions of modern states indicate where the lawmaking power of each state is lodged. According to St. Thomas, sovereign powers belong ultimately to the people, and the government exercises them merely in a representative capacity. This theory of popular sovereignty was the basis of his maintaining that custom not only can obtain force of law but can even change or abrogate an existing law: "For . . . the consent of the whole people expressed by a custom counts far more in favor of a particular observance than the authority of the sovereign, who has not the power to frame laws, except as representing the people" (*Summa theologiae* 1a2ae, 97.3 ad 3).

Promulgation and Enforcement. These constitute the material cause of law. Nowhere is the realistic temper of St. Thomas more manifest than in his maintaining that shared knowledge is essential to the notion of law. "Wherefore, in order that a law obtain the binding force which is proper to law, it must need be applied to the men who are to be ruled by it" (*Summa theologiae* 1a2ae, 90.4). Such application is usually effected in two stages: by promulgation, when a law is officially declared or made public, and by divulgation, when knowledge of it is effectively disseminated so that it becomes commonly known. In a similar spirit one may add that the rule or measure must be effectively sanctioned and enforced for it to become a complete, existential law.

Law and Ethics. For St. Thomas, the primary precept of the natural law is "Good is to be done and evil avoided.'' Applied to the field of human relations, this may be stated: "Love thy neighbor" and "Do injury to no one." The first is the Golden Rule of Christ, whereas the second is basically Confucius's maxim, "Do not do to another what you would not like to have done to yourself." Long before St. Thomas, Ulpian had formulated the threefold precepts of law as "to live honestly, to injure no one, and to render each his due."

Such precepts are common to both law and ETHICS. Yet in actual practice the juridical standard of honesty seems to fall short of the ethical standard. Again, as more than one jurist has pointed out, not everything that is lawful is honorable. Why this duality of standard between ethics and law? Must man choose one and disregard the other? Confucius, for instance, preferred ethics to law: "If you guide the people by laws and keep them in order by penalties, they will merely try to avoid the penalties, but will have no sense of honor. If you guide them by moral virtues and keep them in order by inculcating good manners, they will not only keep their sense of honor but be reformed in and out" [*Analects of Confucius,* ed. and tr. A. Waley (London 1938) 2.3]. On the other hand, the legalists of ancient China extolled the law and dismissed ethics as subversive to the public order of the state.

In St. Thomas's view, law and ethics are equally necessary; the apparent duality of their standards can be seen to merge in a higher unity. The end of both law and ethics is to make man good, teaching him to practice virtue and refrain from vice. But ethics impels man through an internal principle, while law compels him through an external principle (*Summa contra gentiles* 3.127). Although "the purpose of human law is to lead men to virtue, it can do so only step by step, not abruptly" (*Summa theologiae* 1a2ae, 96.2 ad 2). Prudence dictates that human law not lay upon the multitude of imperfect men the burdens that can be carried only by those already advanced in virtue. To compel the rank and file to refrain from all evil is liable to induce them to commit yet greater evils, for "he that violently bloweth his nose, bringeth out blood" (Prv 30.33). This is why "human law does not prohibit everything that is forbidden by the natural law" (*Summa theologiae* 1a2ae, 96.2 ad 2).

Nor should the law prescribe all moral duties indiscriminately, but only those that bear directly upon the common good, such as good faith and fair dealing in human transactions. It would be imprudent to impose on all men the cultivation of the virtues required for their personal perfection, even if this were possible. Human law can contribute toward moral perfection only in an indirect way, by preserving peace and order and fostering the freedom that is required for the cultivation of VIRTUE.

See Also: LAW, DIVINE POSITIVE.

Stele depicting King Hammurabi receiving the Law from the god Shamash, basalt, c. 1780 B.C. (©Gianni Dagli Orti/CORBIS)

Bibliography: A. M. MOSCHETTI, *Enciclopedia filosofica,* 4 v. (Venice-Rome 1957) 2:1843–45. R. EISLER, *Wörterbuch der philosophischen Begriffe,* 3 v. (4th ed. Berlin 1927–30) 1:540–548. F. LAU, *Die Religion in Geschichte und Gegenwart,* 7 v. (3d ed. Tübingen 1957–65) 2:1531–33. H. SCHUSTER, *Lexikon für Theologie und Kirche,* ed. J. HOFER and K. RAHNER (Freiburg 1957–65); suppl., *Das Zweite Vatikanishe Konsil: Dokumente und Kommentare,* ed. H. S. BRECHTER et al. (1966) 4:822–824. J. C. H. WU, *Cases and Materials on Jurisprudence* (St. Paul 1958). R. POUND, *Outlines of Lectures on Jurisprudence* (5th ed. Cambridge, Mass. 1943).

[J. C. H. WU]

LAW, ANCIENT NEAR-EASTERN

Written laws have come down from various countries and peoples of the ancient Near East: Sumeria, Babylonia, Assyria, the land of the Hittites (Asia Minor), and Israel. From Egypt no written laws have been preserved. Israelite law is treated elsewhere in this encyclopedia. (*See* LAW, MOSAIC.)

General Characteristics. In the ancient Near East, where even literary texts were composed orally, oral legal tradition and customary law preceded written law, so that the texts of at least some laws were already more or less fixed before they were written down. All the written laws have much in common. Their style is usually "casuistic," as it has been called: "When such or such a case presents itself, this or that must be done." This formula makes it very probable that the written laws originated from precedents, i.e., judicial decisions that were extended to similar cases. The laws never lay down any basic principles, but nearly always regard particular cases or situations in which men may come into conflict with each other or which are liable to be brought before the judges or judicial courts. Sometimes the legislator imposes general measures, e.g., when he determines the prices of important articles, the amount of rent to be paid in such or such a circumstance; but these regulations too are to be applied in individual relations. There is no marked difference between *ius* (human law) and *fas* (divine law), between public and private, civil and penal law. The idea of revealed law is absent, though a code such as that of Hammurabi may receive religious sanction (see below on the Code of Hammurabi). There is no order in the laws of the codes, nor in the compilations of laws for private use. A series of some paragraphs may be arranged around a common subject (judicial matter); a peculiar expression in one of them may be a key word for a sequence of other paragraphs. But there are no large subdivisions, no logical or systematic conception of the law considered as a whole.

There is no evidence that the codes that have survived were universally applied in the juridical practice of the territories for which they had been given. The lawgivers proclaimed their ideals in their codes, hoping that these would be put into practice everywhere, but they could not enforce them everywhere. Such laws were certainly applied by the kings themselves, if anyone brought a complaint before their own courts. But nobody was obliged to appear in court before the king unless he was called, nor was everybody able to do so. Local judges might have applied other judicial principles with the consent of the parties concerned. This is quite clear from many legal documents from the time of Hammurabi, which are often not in accordance with the principles of the Code of Hammurabi. The ancient Near-Eastern states were not like modern states in this respect, nor did their governments function as modern governments do. The king was the defender of the state and the supreme commander of its armies and levies; he was the supreme judge, whose special duty was to protect the weak; he often performed cultic functions. (*See* KINGSHIP IN THE ANCIENT NEAR EAST.) But no ancient Near-Eastern government or king ever thought of drawing a blueprint of the state and society and promulgating laws in order to realize this ideal. This fact also determined the character of the laws, which do not state or develop basic principles, but merely mention a number of cases in which situations of conflict may arise in civil life and then state what is to be done in such cases. A marked preponderance is given to laws concerning social and family life. The peoples for whom the laws were given were urban societies dependent primarily on agriculture.

In the following paragraphs a conspectus is given of the various collections of laws or legal codes that have been preserved, but no detailed analysis can be given in this limited space, because the laws were not drawn up according to clear principles or in a logical order.

Sumerian Laws. The oldest known laws naturally come from the oldest known civilization—the Sumerian. Besides the indirect evidence from several cuneiform tablets recording legal matters, such as decisions given in lawsuits (di-tilla tablets), that from three collections furnishes knowledge of Sumerian laws as such: (1) entries in the *ana ittišu* series; (2) the Code of Ur-nammu; (3) the Code of Lipit-Ishtar.

Entries in the ana ittišu Series. The bilingual (Sumerian-Akkadian) series ("dictionary" texts) known from its opening Akkadian entry as the *ana ittišu,* a collection of legal terms drawn up for the use of Babylonian scribes, contains 12 paragraphs, in two separate groups, of Sumerian laws with Akkadian translation. Although the preserved tablets of this series were written in the 7th century B.C. for the library of Assurbanipal (Asshurbanipal) at Nineveh, the laws themselves are probably at least as old as the Third Dynasty of Ur (*c.* 2060-1950). The first six paragraphs are commonly known as Sumerian Family Laws because they state the penalties attached to repudiation of one member of a family by another: a father or mother by a son, a son by a father or mother, a husband by a wife, a wife by a husband. (For the text and translation, see Driver and Miles, *The Babylonian Laws,* 2:308–313.)

Closely related to these Sumerian Family Laws are the nine laws on the tablet from the Old-Babylonian period published by A. T. Clay as No. 28 of his *Miscellaneous Inscriptions in the Yale Babylonian Collection* [Yale Oriental Series 1 (New Haven 1915) 18–27].

Code of Ur-nammu. A tablet from the Old-Babylonian period published in transliteration and translation by S. N. Kramer [*Orientalia* 23 (1954) 40–51] preserves the first section of the Code of Ur-nammu, first king (*c.* 2060–2043 B.C.) of the Third Dynasty of Ur. The extant portion of the prologue, in which this king refers to certain historical events of his reign, shows that this is an official code of laws in the technical sense. Official legal codes of ancient Mesopotamia place the corpus of laws between a prologue and an epilogue, both of a religious nature, in which the royal legislators speak of their authority as having been received from the gods and in which they invoke the gods in curses to punish the violators of the laws. In this code, the Sumerian King Urnammu, after attributing his kingship and victories to the high gods, states that he was appointed by them ''to establish justice in the land.'' By this expression is meant the protection of the poor and weak and the maintenance of the traditional customs and rights of the various social classes by the authority of the king. Of the laws themselves only seven are partially preserved on the tablet. Most of them are concerned with bodily injuries done to one man by another.

Code of Lipit-Ishtar. Although composed in the early post-Sumerian period by Lipit-Ishtar, the fifth king of the Semitic Dynasty of Isin (c. 1983–1733 B.C.), this code is still written in Sumerian. Large parts of it have been preserved on seven clay tablets, almost all from Nippur. The most complete publication of the text is by F. R. Steele [*American Journal of Archeology*, Concord, NH 52 (1948) 425–450]. An English translation of it is given by S. N. Kramer (J. B. Pritchart, *Ancient Near Eastern Texts Relating to the Old Testament*, 159–161). Between the usual prologue and epilogue, the extant 38 laws treat of the hiring of boats, real estate, slaves, defaulting on taxes, inheritance and marriage, and rented oxen.

Babylonian Codes. In taking over the culture of the Sumerians almost in its entirety, the Akkadian-speaking Semites of ancient Mesopotamia also continued the Sumerian laws, not only in substance, but even in their formulation, so that the earliest Babylonian laws may be regarded as more or less translated from the older Sumerian laws, with certain adaptations for current conditions. The Old-Babylonian laws have been preserved particularly in two codes, that of the kingdom of Eshnunna and that of Hammurabi, King of Babylon.

Code of Eshnunna. The city of Eshnunna (modern Tell Asmar) was the capital of an Amorrite kingdom in the Diyala region east of Baghdad that flourished between the end of the Third Dynasty of Ur (c. 1950 B.C.) and the rise of the empire founded by Hammurabi (1728–1686 B.C.). Knowledge of this code comes from two tablets found in the 1945 and 1949 archeological excavations at Tell Abu Harmal, a small site near Baghdad, which in ancient times was an outpost of the kingdom of Eshnunna. Both partly mutilated tablets are private copies, with certain small variants, of an earlier, already somewhat corrupt copy of the original code. The copies

reduced the prologue merely to a date formula and apparently omitted the whole epilogue. Since one of the tablets was written during the time of King Dadusha of Eshnunna, who reigned a generation before Hammurabi, and the other tablet is a little older, the original code, which is in Akkadian, must have been composed several generations before the Akkadian Code of Hammurabi. Its relationship in age with the Code of Lipit-Ishtar is uncertain. The text was published by A. Goetze [provisionally in *Sumer* 4 (1948) 63–102, and definitively, with translation and full discussion, in *Annual of the American Schools of Oriental Research* 31 (1956)]. In the first edition of the text, on which Goetze's English translation (J. B. Pritchard, *Ancient Near Eastern Texts Relating to the Old Testament* 161–163) is based, the name of the king who composed the code was read as Bilalama, one of the early kings of Eshnunna, but this reading proved untenable. The name of the author of the code is unknown.

The 60 extant laws of this code treat of maximum prices (1–2), hiring a wagon (3), boats (4–6), wages of farm workers and the hire of a donkey (7–11), trespass and unlawful entry (12–13), business transactions (13–21), unlawful distraint (22–24), engagement and marriage (29–30), defloration of a slave girl (31), raising of children by others than their parents (32–35), deposit (36–37), sales and purchases (38–41), bodily injury (42–48), slaves (49–52), damage caused by animals or falling masonry (53–58), divorce (59), and neglect in guarding a house (60). A remarkable feature of the code is that many of the laws are formulated, not in the usual casuistic style (''If . . . , then . . .''), but as apodictical statements: ''One kor of barley is priced at one shekel of silver; three qa of very light oil are priced at one shekel of silver,'' etc.

Code of Hammurabi. The most important and best preserved of all the law codes of the ancient Near East is the Code of HAMMURABI (HAMMURAPI), sixth king (1728–1686 B.C.) of the First Dynasty of Babylon. It is inscribed in Old-Babylonian monumental script on a diorite STELE, 7 ½ feet high. Although the date formula of Hammurabi's second regnal year is ''The year he enacted the law of the land,'' the code as inscribed on the stele must represent a later revision, because the Prologue mentions several events of the King's later years. Originally the stele stood in the temple of E-sagila at BABYLON. It was carried off to Elam as war booty, probably in the 12th century B.C. In 1902 it was found by French archeologists in the course of their excavations at Susa and published, with a French translation, in the same year by Vincent Scheil [*Memoires de la delegation en Perse* 4 (Paris 1902)]. The stele is now in the Louvre Museum, Paris. On top of the obverse is a bas-relief depicting the King standing in worship before the enthroned sun-god

Shamash, who is also the god of justice. It is sometimes stated that the scene portrays Shamash as giving the law to Hammurabi, but there is no basis for this, either in the bas-relief or in the text. Shamash holds out in his right hand the staff and ring as symbols of his divine authority. In the prologue and epilogue of the inscription the King thus expresses his relationship to Shamash: "I, Hammurabi, am the king of justice [i.e., just king], to whom Shamash has bestowed the right things [*kīnātim*] . . . obedient to Shamash . . . to rise like Shamash over the people . . . at the command of Shamash, the great judge of the heavens and the earth, to make justice shine forth in the land" (reverse 25.95–98; obverse 2.23; 1.40; reverse 24.82–88). Similarly described is the relationship between the King and Marduk, the national god of Babylon (e.g., obverse 5.14–24). Nowhere is it stated that Shamash or Marduk gave the laws of the code to Hammurabi. The king, it is true, derived his authority to legislate and judge from the gods, but the law was his own; it was not a revealed law, like the law of Israel.

The stele is inscribed on the reverse as well as the obverse, and the whole text is almost perfectly preserved except for 16 lines at the bottom of the obverse. These lines were obliterated, most likely by the Elamites, who intended, but never carried out the plan to put an inscription of their own in this place. However, certain parts of the text of these lines can be restored from copies that had been made on clay tablets of various parts of the inscription. These tablets also duplicate, with variant readings, parts of the code that are preserved on the stele. The most complete publication of these tablets as well as the text of the stele itself, with a Latin translation, is by A. Deimel [*Codex Hammurabi* (Rome 1930; 3d rev. ed. by A. Pohl and R. Follet, Rome 1950). An English translation of it by T. J. Meek is given in J. B. Pritchard, *Ancient Near Eastern Texts Relating to the Old Testament*, 163–180].

The Code of Hammurabi is essentially a compilation of the older laws and customs of ancient Mesopotamia, most of them going back to Sumerian times. Hammurabi boasts that he rendered the Sumerian laws into the language of his people, classical Old Babylonian: "When Marduk sent me to rule the people and govern the land, I established right and justice [*kittam u mišaram*] in the language of the land, thereby promoting the people's welfare" (5.14–24).

The prologue is concerned mostly with recounting the benefits that Hammurabi bestowed on his country, particularly the various favors given to the different temples throughout the land. The epilogue, after briefly reviewing the achievements of the King, is taken up with curses on those who violate the laws or damage the stele.

The large, central part of the inscription contains the laws. In modern editions these are divided into 282 sections. The individual laws are often joined in logical groups, but there is usually but little logical sequence between the various groups. The principal groups of laws are concerned, in this order, with: false accusations; retraction of judgment by judges; theft; kidnapping; fugitive slaves; burglary; robbery; ransoming of captives; substitution of conscripts; property of soldiers; rent; irrigation; fields; orchards; loans; sale of fermented liquor; debts; embezzlement; slander; marriage; sexual crimes; inheritance; legitimation of children; adoption; substitution of another child by a wet nurse; maltreatment; damage done by a surgeon; houses and ships; cattle; damage done by cattle; theft of grain, seeds, and farm tools; hiring of people and animals; cattle breeding; and slaves. The social classes are distinguished in the code: the *awēlū*, citizens with full rights and full responsibility; the *muškēnū*, free men with limited rights and responsibilities; and the *wardū*, slaves. The laws presuppose a very highly developed civilization, basically agricultural, but with considerable commerce.

Since the period of Hammurabi corresponds roughly with the period of the Israelite patriarchs, the relationship between his code and the Mosaic Law has often been discussed. There are undoubtedly a few similarities that help to elucidate certain Old Testament customs, such as the husband of a childless wife begetting children in her name by the wife's slave girl (cf. par. 144–147 with Gn 21.9–14). The similarities, however, are due to the same juridical customs throughout the ancient Semitic milieu, not to any borrowings by the Israelites from Babylonian laws. In general, the material culture envisioned by the Code of Hammurabi was much higher than that of the Israelites either in the patriarchal period or in the Mosaic period. One of the closest resemblances, even in words, between the code and the Mosaic Law is in the laws of retaliation ("an eye for an eye, a tooth for a tooth"; cf. par. 196–197, 200 with Ex 21.23–25; Lv 24.19–20; Dt 19.21). But these are instances of ancient tribal customs that had almost died out in the Babylonia of Hammurabi's time.

Neo-Babylonian Laws. A school tablet (writing exercise in a scribal school) published by F. E. Peiser [SB-Münch 18 (1889) 823–828] contains 16 laws, of which only 9 are intelligible. The tablet was written in the Neo-Babylonian period (626–539 B.C.) and apparently represents the legal customs of this time. But these laws are probably not extracts from any code in the strict sense. The best preserved are concerned with marriage customs. (An English translation by T. J. Meek is given in J. B. Pritchard, *Ancient Near Eastern Texts Relating to the Old Testament* 197–198.)

Assyrian Laws. In addition to a few fragmentary tablets with laws from the Old-Assyrian trading post of

Kanes (modern Kultepe) in eastern Asia Minor, dating from the first centuries of the 2d millennium B.C., a considerable corpus of Middle-Assyrian laws are known from tablets found by the German archeologists who excavated (1903–14) the ancient city of ASSUR (modern Qal'āt Sherqāt). These tablets, now in the Staatliches Museum, Berlin, were published by O. Schroeder [*Keilschrifttexte aus Assur verschiedenen Inhalts* 1.7 (Leipzig 1920)]and E. F. Weidner [*Archiv für Orientforschung* 12 (1937) 50–52]. Although the tablets date from the 12th century B.C., the laws themselves are probably a few centuries older. About 116 laws, some of them of considerable length, can be reconstructed from the tablets. They contain prescriptions on sacrilege, theft and receipt of stolen goods, assault, murder, rape, slander, abortion, flight of married women, adultery, marriage, divorce, debt and surety, veiling of women, widows and wives of prisoners of war, sorcery, bodily injuries, deflowering of a virgin, manner of inflicting corporal punishment, sale of real estate, irrigation, sale of slaves, animals, theft, shipping, blasphemy, hereditary rights, etc.

The laws on women, marriage, and sexual crimes are the longest in this compilation. Characteristic of Assyrian law is the common infliction of corporal punishment, on women as well as on men, such as flogging with from 20 to 50 stripes, and amputations of various parts of the body. In contrast, penalties in Babylonian law are mostly in the form of fines. Incarceration as a penalty was not practiced in the ancient Near East. Many of the Assyrian laws are more complicated and less clearly worded than the Babylonian laws. Moreover, they give more consideration to subjective factors, such as intention, knowledge, and ignorance. (An English translation of the Middle-Assyrian laws by T. J. Meek is given in J. B. Pritchard, *Ancient Near Eastern Texts Relating to the Old Testament*, 180–188.)

Hittite Laws. Two of the many tablets found in the archeological excavations from 1906 to 1912 of the Hittite capital on the site of modern Bogazköi contain part of a collection of Hittite laws from the middle of the 2d millennium B.C.. Each tablet contains 100 legal paragraphs, formulated casuistically in a short and clear manner. Reference is made to a similar third tablet, but this has not been recovered.

The text contains various prescriptions on: maltreatment and murder, sorcery, mutilations, kidnapping, fugitive slaves, divorce, marriage, hiring of men and animals, feudal estates, stealing of cattle, damage to cattle, burglary, incendiarism, agriculture, theft of animals, prices, wages, bestiality, other sexual crimes, etc.

Of special interest is the fact that in many of the paragraphs more than one version of the law is given. The more recent version represents a later stage of legislation or customary law, and the compiler was interested in differences of local customs. The collection was compiled in a disorderly fashion, the same legal matters often being treated again in different places. (An English translation of the Hittite laws by A. Goetze is given in J. B. Pritchard, *Ancient Near Eastern Texts Relating to the Old Testament*, 188–197.)

Egyptian Laws. There are good reasons for thinking that the ancient Egyptians possessed written laws, even though these have not been preserved. Diodorus Siculus (*Bibliothecae Historicae* 1.25), who wrote between 60 and 30 B.C., states that in the great Egyptian courts of justice a number of scrolls containing the text of all the laws were laid before the judges. On a representation of a court of justice of the 18th Dynasty (1570–c. 1304 B.C.) 40 long objects, probably law scrolls, lie on four mats at the feet of the vizier Rechmerê. [See A. Erman, *Aegypten und aegyptisches Leben im Altertum* (Tübingen 1922) 158.] Diodorus also gives the names of six famous Egyptian lawgivers whose laws were handed down in writing. The oldest, according to him, was Mneus, who received his laws from Mercury (i.e., the Egyptian god Thot, the god of the order of the world, the heavenly judge, the scribe of the gods, etc.). The other legislators were Sasyches, Sesostris, Bocchoris, Amasis, and Darius the Persian. If Diodorus is correct, the Egyptians ascribed at least to some of their laws a heavenly, i.e., a revealed origin. On a stone erected by Horemheb (second half of the 14th century B.C.) a very worn copy of a royal decree is given. In the 1940s a law in demotic writing was found at Hermopolis, but it has not yet been published.

Bibliography: G. R. DRIVER and J. C. MILES, *The Assyrian Laws* (Oxford 1935); *The Babylonian Laws,* 2 v. (Oxford 1952–55). E. NEUFELD, *The Hittite Laws* (London 1951). J. M. P. SMITH, *The Origin and History of Hebrew Law* (Chicago 1931). F. HROZNY, *Code Hittite provenant de l'Asie Mineure* (Paris 1923). J. LEROY, *Introduction à l'étude des anciens codes orientaux* (Paris 1944).

[J. VAN DER PLOEG]

LAW, DIVINE POSITIVE

The law given by God to man in addition to the NATURAL LAW. Whereas the natural law is promulgated in the very structure of his being and is discernible by natural reason alone, the existence and content of divine positive law is known only by revelation. It is not altogether identifiable, however, with revealed law, because revelation embraces some laws of the natural order, which man could know by his own unaided reason but which God has nevertheless revealed in order that they might be grasped more readily and surely. Divine positive law includes the primitive law given by God in Paradise and after the Fall, the law of the Old Testament given through Moses and the Prophets (*see* LAW, MOSAIC), and the law of the New Testament revealed through Christ. The judicial and ceremonial precepts of the Mosaic Law were abrogated either on the death of Christ, or on Pentecost when the new law was solemnly promulgated, but its moral precepts were confirmed and promulgated anew in the law of Christ.

Bibliography: THOMAS AQUINAS, *Summa theologiae* 1a2ae, 91.4, 98–108. B. HÄRING, *The Law of Christ,* tr. E. G. KAISER, v.1 (Westminster, MD 1961) 237–238. A. MOLIEN, *Dictionnaire de théologie catholique,* ed. A. VACANT, 15 v. (Paris 1903–50; Tables générales 1951–) 9:887–889.

[P. K. MEAGHER]

LAW, MOSAIC

Law has a most important place in the religion of the OT. The first five books of the Bible, called by Christians the PENTATEUCH, are called the Torah (*tôrâ,* law) by the Jews. The first of them, Genesis, contains only history; the fourth, Leviticus, only laws; the three other books, Exodus, Numbers, and Deuteronomy, contain history, laws, and discourses of Moses. The Pentateuch was the first book to be canonized by Judaism; it is the only holy book of the Samaritans. Its importance has been paramount for the history and development of the Jewish religion.

Nature of Israelite Law. The greatest difference between OT law and ancient Oriental law lies in its character of having been revealed. It is stressed that the Law is an expression of God's will, which has to be revealed to become known. Yahweh, the God of Israel, did not primarily reveal articles of faith to be believed, but commandments to be obeyed. The word *tôrâ* etymologically means instruction. The underlying idea is that man has been created by God and therefore must serve Him; but in order to be able to do so, he must know His will. God's revelation is His instruction to Israel how to serve Him. In the Greek Septuagint *tôrâ* is usually translated by νόμος (law), a translation that has become universal; but it should be borne in mind that for Israel the *tôrâ* meant more than law now means.

The importance of law in Israel appears from the fact that the Hebrew language possesses many synonyms for *tôrâ,* which, though originally of different meanings, came finally to include this meaning (word, prescription, commandment, custom, testimony, etc.). For the pious Israelite the Law has never been a yoke, but a supreme privilege: it enables him to conform his life to the divine ordinances and so to give intrinsic value to his deeds.

Therefore, it is his duty and his privilege to study the Law in order to know it always better.

Growth of Mosaic Law. The laws of the Pentateuch were not all given at once to Israel, nor all during the life of Moses. ''At present there is no longer anyone . . . who does not admit the progressive growth of the Mosaic laws caused by the social and religious conditions of later times'' [*Acta Apostolicae Sedis* 40 (Rome 1948) 45–48]. Old laws were expanded and adapted to new circumstances; new paragraphs and new laws were added; the existing laws were gathered in various collections or codes before the whole was compiled in the Pentateuch in its present form. This process went on from the time of Moses until after the end of the Babylonian Exile (538 B.C.).

Not all the laws are explicitly represented as revealed to Moses; e.g., those of Deuteronomy are nearly all formulated as prescriptions given by Moses, who was invested with divine authority (Dt 5.31–33). A part of the laws are formulated in the casuistic style of ancient Near-Eastern LAW, but many of them are formulated apodictically as divine commandments. This apodictic form is characteristic of Israelite law and reveals its nature [especially the form of the Decalogue: ''Thou shalt (not) . . .'' etc.]. But there is also a mixture of both styles in various ways and there are other formulations. The laws are often accompanied by religious considerations, because the Law as a whole is thought to be a divine instruction. Most of the law paragraphs have a direct religious meaning, and in this they differ from the other laws of the ancient Near East.

Relation of Law to Covenant. It is clear that Israel borrowed a part of the material of its legislation, not only in civil but also in religious matters, from the common Near-Eastern civilization; yet it pervaded its law with its own spirit, the spirit of the ''fear of Yahweh.'' The Law was closely connected also with the COVENANT Israel had concluded with God; the covenant was conditioned on the fulfillment of the Law by the people. The nature of the covenant was that of a free pact between Yahweh and Israel, but Israel would have been far from blameless if it had not accepted the covenant and its law offered by God. Therefore in later times the people felt itself bound not only by act of the forefathers, but by the very revealed will of God.

In the postexilic period the importance of the Law grew more and more; it was identified with the idea of divine wisdom as revealed to men (Bar 3.37–4.4; Sir 24.22–27). The scrolls of the Law became and still are an object of veneration in the Jewish synagogue.

Various Collections of Laws. Different collections of laws, among which are at least two codes, can be clearly distinguished, each of them having its own literary history. The most important ones are briefly analyzed or characterized below.

Decalogue. The basic law of the Ten COMMANDMENTS is quoted twice (Ex 20.2–17; Dt 5.6–21) in forms not completely identical; this shows that in the course of time even the text of this fundamental law received secondary additions. The Mosaic origin of the Decalogue has been disputed in modern times, though without cogent reasons.

Book of the Covenant. The group of laws in Ex 20. 22–23.33 is a true code, the (modern) name of which, BOOK OF THE COVENANT, has been taken from Ex 24.7. It contains a series of casuistic laws of the common Oriental type (21.18–22.16), which may have antedated the time of Moses, and a number of typically Israelitic statutes that contain certain important moral principles (e.g., 23.1–3, 6–9). The section in 21.12–22.16 seems to have been arranged according to a plan: crimes committed by a man against the life or bodily integrity of his fellow man; injuries done by a beast; damage caused to the property of a man. In the second part of the Book of the Covenant we find a series of various religious prescriptions and of some moral or humanitarian precepts. The historical circumstances in which the law was given are clearly indicated in the context; the promulgation of it was followed by the conclusion of a covenant. The code was destined for people possessing flocks and devoted to agriculture, but they do not presuppose a seminomad population only.

Book of Deuteronomy. Chapters 12 to 26 of the Book of DEUTERONOMY form a code also. The laws are preceded by discourses of Moses, recalling God's guidance of the people in history and inculcating the scope and general meaning of the Law: to serve God as his chosen people, distinguished and separated from all the peoples of the earth. The Greek name Δευτερονόμιον (second law), based on a faulty translation of mišnēh hattôrâ (copy of the law) in Dt 17.18, was taken to mean that the book contains the second legislation of Moses given to the people at the end of the 40 years of wandering through the desert. Though no convincing argument can be produced to disprove the fact of a second legislation by Moses, the book in its present form is certainly of a much later date, probably of the 8th or 7th century B.C., and may have received even later additions. Most likely Deuteronomy is the book of the Law found in the temple in 622 B.C. (2 Kgs 22.3–23.24). In its present form it is a code, clearly with reform tendencies, for a sedentary people living in towns and villages, in which the rights of various groups of socially weak people are defended. The paragraphs are given without much order; systematically reviewed, they

may be said to contain: religious precepts, especially the law of centralization of the cult; laws that regulate institutions of public interest, such as kingship, prophecy, Levites, justice, war; measures taken to protect common interests of the nation, the town, and the family; measures to protect easily oppressed persons and even animals. In the discourses of Moses, the Decalogue and some other precepts of a general nature, such as the love of God (Dt 6.4), are quoted.

Priestly Code. Large portions of Exodus and Numbers and the whole of Leviticus have received the modern name Priestly Code from the supposedly priestly character of its legislation, which is for the greater part concerned with ritual matters: sacrifices, the cult, purity and impurity, etc. As a whole it is not a true code, but the name given to a collection of laws from various times. Many of them are ancient, others date from the time of the Exile (587–538 B.C.) or even later. Special mention should be made of the Law of HOLINESS (Lv ch. 17–26), considered by modern scholars to be the most ancient collection in the Priestly Code. It ends with a long epilogue of a general character, promising rewards, and menacing with punishments. (*See* PRIESTLY WRITERS, PENTATEUCHAL.)

Undue importance has been given by some scholars to the so-called cult Decalogue of Ex 34.10–26. It presents a problem to exegetes, but apparently consists of extracts from older laws. The Pentateuch does not contain all the laws and customs observed in Israel. From other Biblical passages, several other laws may be reconstituted [see J. van der Ploeg, *The Catholic Biblical Quarterly* 13 (Washington 1951) 42].

Bibliography: J. VAN DER PLOEG, "Studies in Hebrew Law," *The Catholic Biblical Quarterly* 12 (Washington 1950) 248–259, 416–427; 13 (1951) 28–43, 164–171, 296–307. J. M. P. SMITH, *The Origin and History of Hebrew Law* (Chicago 1931). G. ÖSTBORN, *Tora in the Old Testament: A Semantic Study,* tr. C. HENTSCHEL (Lund 1945). H. H. ROWLEY, "Moses and the Decalogue," *The Bulletin of the John Rylands Library* 34 (Manchester 1951–52) 81–118. L. WATERMAN, "Pro-Israelite Laws in the Book of the Covenant," *American Journal of Semitic Languages and Literatures* 38 (Chicago 1921–22) 36–54. J. MORGENSTERN, "The Book of the Covenant," *Hebrew Union College Annual,* 5 (Cincinnati 1928) 27–81. H. CAZELLES, *Dictionnaire de la Bible,* suppl. ed. L. PIROT, et al. (Paris 1928–) 5:497–530. M. NOTH, *Die Gesetze im Pentateuch* (Halle 1940). A. ALT, *Die Ursprünge des israelitischen Rechts* (Leipzig 1934). W. STODERL, *Das Gesetz Israels nach Inhalt und Ursprung,* v.1 of *Beiträge zur Einleitung ins Alte Testament* (Marienbad 1933). W. KORNFELD, *Studien sum Heiligkeitsgesetz* (Vienna 1952). L. M. SCHMÖKEL, *Das Angewandte Rechte im Alten Testament* (Leipzig 1930).

[J. P. M. VAN DER PLOEG]

LAW, PHILOSOPHY OF

The part of philosophy that studies the nature of LAW, with particular reference to the origins and ends of civil law and the principles that should govern its formulation. The study may be elaborated systematically in the context provided by a particular philosophical school, or it may be elaborated historically in light of the teachings of various schools. This article adopts the former method and discusses, from the viewpoint of Christian (or scholastic) philosophy, the following topics: law and force, authority and law's origin, inadequate theories of the nature of law, justice and law, the end of law, historical sources of the realist conception of law, and present needs in legal theory.

Law and Force. Law is addressed to persons for the purpose of directing their conduct. It develops as one aspect of human culture and tends to become significant with the expansion of commerce. Because it functions as a directive, its subject matter involves the respect due to the person when property is apportioned for man's use. At times throughout history the priorities have become inverted, and law has tended to become so identified with property that persons who have been dissatisfied by a prevailing property distribution have revolted against the law.

Although its appeal is primarily to human reasoning power and its technique relies chiefly on persuasion, law has often been associated with the implementation of state power and spoken of as if it were identical with force. Properly, law is the alternative to force; resort to force usually signifies the failure of law to persuade. Again, resort to force, especially when applied in the protection of property, tends to associate the notion of law with fear rather than with confidence. Observance of law is thereby reduced to avoidance of punishment. The statement of the rule shifts from ''do right,'' to ''do what you will, but do not get caught''; and payment of a prescribed penalty is accepted as the equivalent of fulfilling the law. The result obviously is not the same, and may be neither desired nor desirable.

Traditionally law and liberty were spoken of together, not law and fear. To ascertain the sequence of events that caused freedom to be displaced by conformity, one must examine the relationship of law to authority. This in turn raises questions about the origin and source of law.

Authority and Law's Origin. Repeatedly Sacred Scripture is cited for the observation that all AUTHORITY is from God. Kings anointed with ecclesiastical blessings, after solemn promises to rule ''under God and the law'' —in Bracton's phrase, who adds, ''for the law makes the king'' (fol. 5b; ed. T. Twiss, *Rerum Britannicarum medii aevi scriptores* 1:39)—have sometimes presumed to translate the inspired words into terms of their own, such as ''the divine right of kings,'' with the Stuarts in England, or ''l'état, c'est moi,'' with Louis XIV of France. The people, unable to reconcile arbitrary royal decrees with the scriptural admonition, revolted against the kings and left the exegesis of the words to the Church, as if the Church were outside the realities of human experience. Those who have subsequently aspired to govern in place of the kings have often widened the breach instead of reconciling their assumption of authority with Holy Writ. The question not yet satisfactorily answered, for governors and governed alike, is basically epistemological, viz, In what form can the authority that is from God be recognized?

The unanswered question is philosophical, and not merely doctrinal or theological, for those outside the organized Christian Church are equally affected by authority and are equally subject to the conditions of life as to a universal law. The Code of Hammurabi, the Mosaic Code, the customary law of India and of China, the laws of Solon and Draco among the ancient Greeks, the highly developed early law of the Romans—which retained its significance centuries later in the Code of Justinian—all indicate that law itself is close to the essence of man. When Justinian began his Code in the name of the Blessed Trinity, he added a Christian sanction to the work of the Roman jurists, without thereby excluding much that was formulated by pagans before the Christian Era began. The fact that the specific forms of law differ in various times and places is evidence of different conditions and degrees of comprehension, not of enclaves exempt from the universal law. The task of philosophy is to examine the relationship between human conduct and the observed universal order, and to give a satisfactory account of that relationship. It may begin with the theory of knowledge, with the question of how the natural law becomes known, but it ultimately must extend to the actual situation of man in his universe.

Natural Law, Truth, and Being. The notion of NATURAL LAW has become less clear the more it has been discussed. Indeed so contradictory are some of the theories attributing authority to the natural law that the term has become divisive. Repudiated though it may be on this account, the notion of natural law has survived through so many centuries that some reconsideration of its underlying signification is needed.

As the pursuit of TRUTH is the primary motivation in scientific discovery, so it is primary in ascertaining how the human mind participates consciously in the universal law. Human laws may be created, i.e., formulated or given shape, by men as a result of observations, inferences, and conclusions, and expressed not in stone or paint but in determinations, decisions, and judgments. To the extent that these judgments conform to the actually existent order of NATURE, they are acceptable as an expression of truth, but to the extent that some elements may not conform, they are subject to revision in a manner similar to the conclusions of physical scientists. Truth is in the judgment, but not the whole truth, unless the judge is omniscient. Inventiveness and resourcefulness in utilizing findings of fact can enrich the creativity of judgment, but excesses of imaginative construction must be brought into agreement with the actual conditions of human existence.

As truth is the ultimate criterion of the way things are, and therefore is interchangeable with BEING as known by the intellect, so the GOOD is the criterion of choice at the level of the will, and therefore is interchangeable with being as the ultimate goal of motivation and desire. Again, as truth is interchangeable with being in one aspect and as good is interchangeable with being in another, so both the true and the good are interchangeable with each other (*see* TRANSCENDENTALS). Yet human comprehension of truth is prior to knowledge of the good, since one cannot choose what he does not know. To act in accordance with CONSCIENCE, then, means to make a decision consistent with the degree of knowledge of being one has attained; this, in fact, is indicated in the etymology of the term, *con* (or *cum*) and *scientia*.

Nature and Person. The point of view from which a human being observes reality is necessarily personal. By definition, adopted from BOETHIUS, a PERSON is an individual substance of a rational nature. Without investigating the quantitative implications of INDIVIDUALITY or the metaphysical significance of SUBSTANCE, attention may be focused on nature and the qualification of rationality. The term nature incorporates persons into the totality of existence, since nature refers to the essence of things that exist in the universe. The most important element in the notion of person, therefore, is being; nothing that lacks existence, no matter what its potentialities, can be a person. Beyond this, a person is distinguishable from other things by his ability to reason. Personality acquires a unique dignity or value because of its essential rationality. It is this quality of reasonableness, limited though it may be, in each individual substance, that is primary. To it all evidence, argument, and proof are directed; from it every conclusion, determination, and judgment is derived. Indeed, it is on the distinction of the rationality of persons that the similarities and differences between universal law and its human formulations are based.

The universal law unceasingly challenges man to new discoveries of its essence and manifestations. However, his capacity to reapportion the latter is admittedly conditional, and functions usually through COMMUNICATION with other persons. It is obvious that the movement of fish in the sea continues independently of man's word, whereas the course of action of employers and employees alike may be changed by the announced decision of an economist, perhaps, or a human lawgiver. The difference between the two cases has not always been clearly stated, and an exaggerated mechanism in human affairs has led to confusion in the history of jurisprudence.

Scriptural Basis. Just as the notion of authority in Sacred Scripture has been cited repeatedly in connection with government and liberty, so the original words used in the inspired text have been referred to again and again, even in recent times. In English translation, the natural law is "written in the heart" (Rom 2.15). This, of course, is a figure of speech that conveys an ineffable truth in everyday language and is not expected to be taken literally. Yet it presents a difficult problem of interpretation. The words used actually challenge the reasoning human mind to discover the nature, or essence, of man and to act according to that nature. This challenge has often been acknowledged, but not successfully met. It is obvious that knowledge and judgment are involved, but intelligence alone is insufficient; in fact, the heart suggests motivation, and choice as well. The entire essence of man, and the impact of the rest of existence upon his struggle for survival and identity, are implied. Small wonder that the explanations so far suggested in philosophy reflect little more than the characteristics of the different schools that have offered them.

Inadequate Theories. Among the inadequate theories sometimes presented, determinism has had much to say about law and the natural order. It can be found throughout the history of ideas in one form or another. In modern times it has become familiar through the triad, or troika, of G. W. F. HEGEL, who presented the dialectic of thesis, antithesis, and synthesis as if it were an inevitable sequence of events. In the governments in which Hegel's theory has been dominant, it has resulted in a revolting loss of freedom. Moreover, the exalted conceptualism that characterized Hegel's speculations cannot claim general acceptance, for in it man's ability to choose is left out of account.

Mechanicism and Positivism. Mechanicists also, impressed by the repetitiveness of the physical order, have adhered generally to a determinism, but appeared less assured as mid-20th-century explorations into the atom disclosed unexpected discontinuities in nature. Their confidence in mechanical rigidity was replaced by uncertainty to such an extent that many suspended judgment while awaiting further findings.

POSITIVISM had a particularly strong influence in legal theory after the mid-19th century, but, like determinism began reviewing its dogmas. When judgments are confined to narrow interpretations of written legal documents, public or private, too many of the verifiable facts of life are left out of account, with results that are more abstract than realistic. Furthermore, identification of the rule of law with its hopefully automatic enforcement has placed an exaggerated emphasis on punishment rather than on correction. Positivists, who consistently accorded priority to power at the expense of justice in the legal order, were sufficiently shocked by unsatisfactory results of their theory to turn again to science for greater precision. But with physics and chemistry becoming less predictable, they shifted attention from atoms to cells and looked toward the life sciences, so-called, for help. Sociology proved disappointing its tendency to subordinate individuals to the pressures of mass society had been offset by concern for the protection of human rights under law. Psychology was more favored, but exaggerated emphasis on the "can't helps" of human existence and on comparable irrationalities seemed to be calling forth deeper quests. Until positivists abandon the imperialistic notion that law is to be identified with command, and with the power to enforce command, resistance was anticipated from those uncommitted to their sphere of influence, national or international.

Unwarranted Assumptions. Another unsatisfactory emphasis in philosophy, found even in the basically sound realistic school, has proved disadvantageous for the development of law. This is the tendency to proceed on the basis of unwarranted assumptions. Deductions from a priori premises that cannot be verified must, no matter how insistently repeated, be excluded in the interests of truth. The ultimate criterion of the true and the good is what the Creator has actually created, not what any limited human mind presumes to be true or accepts on hearsay evidence. It is necessary to know what has been previously thought in order to avoid repeating errors and to conserve facets of truth. However, since no human being is omniscient or able to verify everything by personal experiment, man must develop critical powers to avoid the acceptance of half-truths. Law depends for its advancement on a humble conscience, but not on an uncritical one. Yet the temper of criticism should be prudent, judicious, kind, and constructive, since love, as St. Paul teaches, is the fulfillment of the law (Rom 13.10).

Justice and Law. A striking feature of postmodern thought is the somewhat general omission of JUSTICE from theories about the legal order. Law is mentioned in connection with commands, sanctions (i.e., penalties added to a breach), demands, rights, expectations, duties, freedoms—especially freedom of expression (even when

this amounts to engaging in the business of spreading mental, as opposed to physical, poison for profit)—conformed or regimented behavior, and even coexistence. The notion of justice seemed to have disappeared. In fact, H. Kelsen, a writer on jurisprudence, published his collected essays under the title *What is Justice?* (Berkeley 1957), thus recalling Pontius Pilate's comparable question to Christ, "What is Truth?" (Jn 18.38). Clearly, the notion of justice needed to be reasserted in legal theory.

Lex, or legislative enactment, was distinguished in Roman law from *ius,* or right, and *ius,* in turn, was distinguished from *iustitia,* the rendering to each his own. European languages have preserved the distinction by retaining two words for law, but the English language has obscured the difference by using one word to convey both meanings. A consciousness that the difference is significant appears in modern legal literature, however, where some attention is devoted to the "is" and the "ought" of law. Among influential positivists only the "is" mattered, as already existent; the "ought" was left to those who speculated on the nonexistent or the imagined. Hegelians and evolutionists, concerned as much with "becoming" as with "being," were somewhat more receptive to the notion of what the law "ought" to be, although, if they were also determinists, their interest in the "ought" would appear inconsistent. It was a new concern for realism in American law in the 1920s that began again to inquire whether the law that "is" corresponds adequately with the facts of life and to inquire further whether, insofar as it does not, changes should be considered. The neorealists [e.g., K. N. Llewellyn, *Jurisprudence* (Chicago 1962)] opened the way for a reconsideration of the relation of law to right, without quite reviving the notion of justice.

Writers in Europe [e.g., G. del Vecchio, *Justice* (New York 1953)], influenced perhaps by Immanuel Kant, questioned anew the meaning of justice. Following Kant's classification of law under the practical reason, praxis, or the will aspect of human activity, which takes from the intellectual judgment its natural priority—T. E. Davitt, *The Nature of Law* (St. Louis 1951) contrasted Ockham and Suárez with Aquinas and Bellarmine on the distinction here—these 20th-century writers stressed the CATEGORICAL IMPERATIVE. They reemphasized the golden rule of action—do unto others as you would be done unto—and suggested that the most important word here is "others." They then drew the inference that justice pertains exclusively to others, thereby giving law a modern sociological connotation. The result was quite different from the traditional notion of justice, which is the notion of rendering to each person what is his own.

It is to the merit of the older definition, however, that it takes account of the necessities of human existence. It sees the proper function of law as an instrument of justice, which undertakes to assure to each living person whatever he actually needs in order to attain the fullness of existence of which he is capable. The right, or *ius,* or what the law "ought" to express, is, in the traditional view, not the post-Kantian wish or expectation concerning what others should do to one, but rather whatever human existence actually requires—one's own, or anyone else's—and this whether one is conscious of that need or not. Such a notion of justice is much closer to the universal order that confronts the intellect than is any theory that separates intellect from will and identifies law with the will. VOLUNTARISM, in minimizing the importance of both judgment and justice for law, is unable to reconcile satisfactorily the double aspect under which law functions, viz, as science and as art. Indeed, it fails even to account adequately for the scriptural definition of natural law as that which is "written in the heart."

End of Law. Just as the relation of law to authority raises questions about the origins and sources of both law and lawgiver, the relation of law to justice calls for a consideration of the purpose, or end, of law. Unless the latter be explained in terms of existence, or being, the entire law-giving activity proceeds on unsound premises. This is why natural philosophy, metaphysics, epistemology, and natural theology are as important for an adequate philosophy of law as are ethics or theories of the state. Yet these latter have claimed what amounts to a monopoly in speculations about law.

The fact that ETHICS and law are both concerned with conduct, and refer to the natural law in formulating directions, led to much confusion in jurisprudence. Theories of the relationship extend from those who hold that law should implement ethical decisions by force to those who hold that law is entirely unrelated to ethics. Although the ultimate goal for both is the good, their functions are quite different. Ethics directs toward the best possible conduct of which each human being is capable, whereas law is satisfied with the minimum that is acceptable to a majority in a community. This is not to say that law is public and ethics private, since law relies on conscience in private decisions as fully as ethics does in public affairs. The tasks are parallel and may at times coincide, but they are not identical. Confusion usually comes from identifying law with force, while ignoring law's reliance on judgment and persuasion in arriving at decisions.

Among the features of law that perhaps can most easily be left to legal experts are the procedures and techniques through which the law is made applicable to particular situations. Practically the entire course of studies in university law schools is devoted to these details. Moreover, legal terminology, unlike that of the physical sciences and the arts, is not generally understood by those in other intellectual pursuits. It is generally true also that the significance of law for life, which is seldom mentioned in the law schools, receives little attention in other departments of the modern university.

Historical Sources. The cultural void notable in juridical studies by the mid-20th century was not always characteristic of university teaching. Not only do the great *summae* of learning provide chapters on law, but there is evidence also of interchanges of expert opinion throughout Western Europe. Nor were the teachers unique in making important contributions to juridical thought. Heads of government have left monumental contributions as well.

The work of three 13th-century rulers in particular can provide the foundation for a much-needed comparative study of law. All three were kings, and they were closely associated in blood or friendship. St. LOUIS IX OF FRANCE was so concerned for lawyers that he built the beautiful Sainte-Chapelle near the law courts of Paris for their religious devotions. Alfonso X, King of Castile, patronized the collection of laws known as *Siete Partidas,* whose influence is still found in the southwestern United States. And Edward I of England has come to be called the English Justinian, because the common law reached such heights before his reign was over that the great modern jurist Maitland could speak of that era as "the golden days of the common law" [F. Pollock and F. W. Maitland, *The History of English Law before the Time of Edward I* (Cambridge, England 1895) 1:112].

This was the same century that saw not only the drafting of Magna Carta by the archbishop of Canterbury, STEPHEN LANGTON; but also the *Summa* of the English Franciscan ALEXANDER OF HALES at the University of Paris, with its section *De legibus;* the incomparable treatise of the cleric-judge Henry de BRACTON, *De legibus et consuetudinibus Angliae;* and the *Summa theologiae* of St. THOMAS AQUINAS at Paris, with its special chapter, *De legibus.*

Preceding this flowering were centuries of legal experience paralleling the growth of Christian thought. In the patristic era all the important writers, from TERTULLIAN to BOETHIUS and ISIDORE OF SEVILLE, many of whom were jurists, made significant contributions. Undoubtedly the *sic et non* dialectic of ABELARD influenced the development of adversary procedure; similarly, the harmonization of conflicting canons by Gratian showed the way for systematic treatises (*see* GRATIAN, DECRETUM OF). The Saxon contribution spread from the Christian renaissance in the time of BERNWARD OF HILDESHEIM, through the laws of ALFRED THE GREAT of England, to the *Sachsenspiegel,* which served as prototype for various collections of laws known by such titles as *speculum* and *spicilegium* (mirror of the justices). The impetus given to revived Roman-law studies at Bologna and Padua by MATILDA OF TUSCANY is perhaps better known. In the Scandinavian countries, the beginnings of maritime law at the island of Wisby is attested by the ruins of the churches that served to guarantee good faith. The laws of Oléron, no less than the Visigothic Code, were shaped in the Spanish peninsula. Irish monks brought the knowledge of the Brehon laws to the Continent. The Norman development was particularly noteworthy, the archbishops of Canterbury from St. ANSELM OF CANTERBURY to Thomas BECKET, at least, and Anglo-Norman jurists such as VACARIUS having found a convenient crossroads for the exchange of ideas at the Abbey of Bec in Normandy. Materials are thus plentiful for a new synthesis of the relations of law to life as these unfolded in the ages of faith.

From this jurisprudential heritage, Thomas MORE, F. de VITORIA, F. Suárez, Sir Edward Coke, F. BACON, H. GROTIUS, and J. Selden were able to draw when solving problems posed by the exploration of the American continent. In recent times, modern jurists such as R. von Ihering, E. Ehrlich, and G. Radbruch, in Germany; F. Gény, M. Hauriou, and G. Rénard, in France; and F. W. Maitland, in England, raise questions of grave philosophical import, but a hollow echo is heard in reply. The popes alone, from Leo XIII to John XXIII and Paul VI, have pointed out directions for an acceptable meeting-place for law and life. Justice, human dignity, subordination of force continually reappear in encyclical letters, but the universities for the most part pay little heed.

Present Need. Perhaps the greatest need is a corrective for the popular identification of law with prohibitions. Law is not essentially negative. The revealed Mosaic Code itself begins positively, and only afterward becomes negative by way of clarification. Instead of the view of law as obstructionist, the truly creative tasks that require great originality of mind must be emphasized. Law functions as a science, in arriving at its judgments, but it functions also as an art, in giving expression to choice and in decision-making. To the extent that a person glimpses an aspect of truth, or selects an aspect of good, as an authoritative guide to human conduct and formulates the result cogently, he participates in the creativity of the universal order. Through his work the truth as being becomes more intelligible, and the good as being is seen to be more desirable. And when a person to whom the law is directed accepts the application in good conscience, adopting the true and the good as his own, he also participates in the creativity of the universal order by way of responsibility or self-government. In fact, exclusion from participation, itself the deprivation of a good, is really a punishment. Law's constructive function in relation to human conduct is thus what earns for law its place of honor in the learned world, a place acknowledged in the medieval universities to be second to philosophy and theology alone.

See Also: LAW; NATURAL LAW.

Bibliography: Sources. THOMAS AQUINAS, *Summa theologiae* 1a2ae, 90–97. H. DE BRACTON, *De legibus et consuetudinibus Angliae,* ed. and Eng. tr. T. TWISS, 6 v. (*Rerum Britannicarum medii aevi scriptores,* 244 v. (London 1858–96; repr. New York 1964–) 1878–83). H. G. RICHARDSON, *Bracton: The Problem of His Text* (London 1965). Encyclical letters on the reconstruction of the social order. LEO XIII, *Rerum novarum* (1891). PIUS XI, *Quadragesimo anno* (1931). PIUS XII, *Summi pontificatus* (1939). JOHN XXIII, *Mater et magistra* (1961); *Pacem in terris* (1963). Pastoral Letter of the archbishops and bishops of the United States, signed by Cardinal James Gibbons, Sept. 26, 1919 (NCWC; Washington, DC 1920), drafted by E. A. PACE, on the reconstruction of the social order after World War I. Studies. T. F. T. PLUCKNETT, *A Concise History of the Common Law* (5th ed. Boston 1956). C. H. MCILWAIN, *The Growth of Political Thought in the West* (New York 1932; repr. 1955). R. O'SULLIVAN, *Christian Philosophy in the Common Law* (Westminster, Maryland 1942). M. T. ROONEY, *Lawlessness, Law, and Sanction* (Washington 1937). J. C. H. WU, *Fountain of Justice* (New York 1955); *Cases and Materials on Jurisprudence* (St. Paul 1958), useful bibliography. E. BODENHEIMER, *Jurisprudence: The Philosophy and Method of the Law* (Cambridge, Massachusetts 1962), objective account of modern views. Periodicals. *Index to Legal Periodicals* (New York 1908–). *Index to Foreign Legal Periodicals* (London 1960–). *Catholic Lawyer* (New York 1955–). *Natural Law Forum* (Notre Dame, Indiana 1956–). *World Justice* (Louvain 1959–).

[M. T. ROONEY]

LAW, WILLIAM

High Anglican ecclesiastic and spiritual author; b. Kings Cliffe, Northamptonshire, 1686; d. there, April 9, 1761. He was the son of a grocer. He entered Emmanuel College, Cambridge, in 1705. After ordination, he was elected a fellow of his college in 1711 and taught at Cambridge until the accession of George I in 1714, when he was suspended from his degree and deprived of his fellowship for his Jacobite sympathies. From 1727 to 1737, Law resided with the family of Edward Gibbon, grandfather of the historian, as tutor and as spiritual guide for the family and their friends, among whom were Archibald Hutcheson and John and Charles WESLEY. After 1743 Hutcheson's widow and Gibbon's sister joined Law at Kings Cliffe in a life of simplicity, devotion, and prayer inspired by ideals set forth in Law's *Serious Call to a Devout and Holy Life* (1728). They maintained two small schools and used their considerable incomes for charity. Law was the ablest High Church writer of his day: direct, simple, and logical in his exposition of Christian ideals.

His influence was limited, however, because he wrote in opposition to the prevailing tendencies of his time. In the Bangorian Controversy of 1716–17, he opposed the party supported by the crown. He wrote forcefully against deism at a time when the deist and rationalist approach to religious studies, popularized by John LOCKE, was in its heyday. In 1726 he wrote a work condemning the contemporary theater.

Law had always been interested in such late medieval mystics as THOMAS À KEMPIS, TAULER, and RUYSBROECK, whose influence appears in the *Serious Call*. He advocated a full Christian life, with attention to meditation, ascetical practices, and moral virtues, especially those of daily life—everything being directed to the glorification of God. The *Serious Call* was the most influential spiritual work, apart from *Pilgrim's Progress,* after the English Reformation. In 1737 Law fell under the influence of the Moravian mystic Boenler and the German Jacob BÖHME. His later works, *The Spirit of Prayer* (1749–50) and *The Spirit of Love* (1752–54), which emphasize the indwelling of Christ in the soul, led the Wesleys to break with him, although they continued to admire him. Law's doctrine tended toward the Quaker conception of the Inner Light.

Bibliography: *Works,* 9 v. (London 1892–93). S. H. GEM, *The Mysticism of William Law* (London 1914). L. STEPHEN, *Dictionary of National Biography from the Earliest Times to 1900* (London 1885–1900) 11:677–681. J. B. GREEN, *John Wesley and William Law* (London 1945). E. W. BAKER, *A Herald of the Evangelical Revival* (London 1948). M. SCHMIDT, *John Wesley,* tr. N. P. GOLDHAWK (London 1962) 1. M. SCHMIDT, *Die Religion in Geschichte und Gegenwart* 4:245. F. L. CROSS, *The Oxford Dictionary of the Christian Church* (London 1957) 791.

[B. NORLING]

LAW IN CHRISTIAN LIFE

According to the New Testament, God created man in and for Christ (Eph 1.3–14; Col 1.15–17) to take him up into His Trinitarian life (cf. Jn 17.20–24). With his nature, man received (Gn 2.17) his basic structure, norm of activity (ontological NATURAL LAW: Rom 2.14–15). Regenerated into a new creature (Gal 6.15; 2 Cor 5.17), he concretely tends to the beatific vision according to a new norm (ontological supernatural law) that incorporates the natural law. As a redeemed sinner, his march toward the end should be a "paschal ascent" following the Savior through the Cross to the Resurrection (Mt 16.24; Col 2.6; Heb 10.19–25). In anticipation of the incarnate "Way," Christ (Jn 14.6), God enlightened man's darkened conscience by a positive (Mosaic) law or economy, the revealed embodiment of a Divine "Way" (cf. Ps 118, 119). (*See* LAW, MOSAIC). Not containing the WORD, it could not justify by its own works (Gal 2.16; Rom 3.28) or supply inner strength (Gal 3.21; Rom 7.16–24). Observed without FAITH, it turned into a "letter" that kills (2 Cor 3.6–11; 1 Cor 15.56), into a prosecutor unveiling man's sinfulness (ἁμαρτία: Rom 3.20; 7.7) and thus became instrumental to transgression (παράβασις: Rom 4.15; Gal 3. 19).

Christ, Man's Living Law. Christ both completes and terminates the economy of the law (Mt 5.17; Rom 10.4; Gal 3.25), for He is the Incarnate "Way" to all truth (Jn 14.6). From within (Jn 14.15–24; Rom 8.9–11; Gal 2.20; 1 Jn 5.11–13) Christ through His Spirit moves His members and guides them. By Himself and through His Spirit (Rom 8.2–4), *He is their living law* (St. Thomas, *In 8 Rom*), supplying the strength to observe it (Gal 5.16–25). Borne up by love (Rom 5.5; 1 Jn 5.3), the Christian as such does not feel compelled by exterior laws (Jas 1.25); he may not, indeed, transgress these, for he observes them eminently with the liberty and generosity of God's children (Gal 4.5–7; Rom 8.14–17). Qua Christian, man does not sin (Gal 5.16; 1 Jn 3.6, 9; 5.18); even, beyond strict obligation, he is invited to acts of supererogation (e.g., the counsels, cf. 1 Cor 7.7, 25–38); he is to tend to perfection (Mt 5.48; 19.21). In case he draws back from love, he is still compelled by the external law, which protects him from falling below a vital minimum of love (cf. 1 Tm 1.9; Gal 5.16–23). Jesus has been a "doctor" and law-giver (cf. Mt 5–7; 11.29–30; 23.10); He has given His new commandments (Jn 15.12–17; 1 Jn 3.22). After Him, the Apostles too give precepts in their epistles. Christ's law (Gal 6.2; 1 Cor 9.21), however, constitutes man's very liberty in action, because it frees man from the slavery of any other (Gal 5.1, 13, 18; Rom 6.14).

Law of Charity. Basically the Christian law is the law of love (Mt 7.12; Mk 12.28–34; Rm 13.8–10; Gal 5.13–14; 1 Jn 4). Indeed, it canalizes man's tendency to the End loved as a good (*Summa theologiae* 1a2ae, 1.3–8), and its driving force and its revealer—God in Christ—is love (1 Jn 4.8, 16). A real love proves and expresses itself in deeds (cf. Jn 14.15; 1 Jn 5.3): the acts of all the virtues, chiefly of fraternal charity (1 Jn 4.12, 20–21), mediate and determine specifically the basic tendency of love-charity in the various fields of moral activity (moral objects) and in the different active powers (subjective aspect, cf. *Summa theologiae* 2a2ae, 23.8: *caritas . . . forma virtutum*). As for its content, the Christian law "fulfills" and elevates the structures—and the commandments—of the natural law, giving them their concrete, supernatural finality. It sets aside the precepts that are specifically Jewish (cf. Gal 2.14–21; 4.10–11; 6.12), creates a new hierarchy of moral values (Mt 5), and adds the structures—and commandments—of the "new creation" (Trinitarian, sacramental, ecclesial). It leads directly to the following of Christ (Mt 16.24; 1 Cor 11.1). It is perceived by the reason elevated by faith and is lived in the Christian community (Acts 2.42–47; 4.32–35). In the Christian dispensation, explicit laws (canonical, civil, international) remain necessary; but their "letter" receives its meaning, inspiration, and obligation from the (individual and social) Christian dynamism proper to the members of Christ and springing from Christ Himself.

With the complete, divinized man for immediate criterion and with the God-Man for ultimate criterion, it judges of the morality of human laws according to absolute truth: above Caesar stands God and the Wisdom of His Word (cf. Prv 8.15).

See Also: AUTHORITY, ECCLESIASTICAL; CANON LAW; COMMANDMENTS, TEN; FREEDOM, SPIRITUAL; KINGDOM OF GOD; LAW, DIVINE POSITIVE; OFFICE, ECCLESIASTICAL; SOCIETY (THEOLOGY OF).

Bibliography: P. BLÄSER, *Lexikon für Theologie und Kirche*, ed. J. HOFER and K. RAHNER (Freiberg 1957–65) 4:825–826. G. GILLEMAN, *The Primacy of Charity in Moral Theology,* tr. W. F. RYAN and A. VACHON (Westminster, Md. 1959) 253–279 and *passim.* E. HAMEL, "Loi naturelle et loi du Christ," *Sciences Ecclésiastiques* 10 (1958) 49–76. B. HÄRING, *The Law of Christ,* tr. E. G. KAISER, 3 v. (Westminster, Md. 1961) 1:227–285. S. LYONNET, "Liberté du Chrétien et loi de l'Esprit selon S. Paul," *Christus* (1954) 6–27; *Les Épîtres de saint Paul aux Galates, aux Romains* (BJ 38; 1953), annotations.

[G. A. GILLEMAN]

LAWRENCE, ANTIPOPE

Pontificate: Nov. 22, 498 to 499, 502 to 506. At the death of ANASTASIUS II in November 498, the Roman community split between those who wanted to continue the dead pope's conciliatory policies toward the Byzantine empire and the Patriarchate of Constantinople and those who wanted to return to the hardline approach of GELASIUS I (492–496). Most clergy favored a hard line and chose the deacon Symmachus (Nov. 22, 498–July 19, 514); a minority of the clergy, but the bulk of the aristocracy favored conciliation and chose the archpriest Laurentius. Neither faction could prevail, and so both appealed to the Ostrogothic, Arian king of Italy, Theodoric (493–516), which meant that a heretical barbarian would choose the bishop of Rome. Theodoric decided that Symmachus had more support at Rome and so sided with him. Laurentius accepted the decision, withdrew his candidacy in February of 499, and put his name first on the list of clergy supporting the decrees of a synod held by Symmachus. He also graciously accepted a bishopric in Campania.

However, his supporters would not accept defeat. In 502 they went to Theodoric to charge Symmachus with unchastity and misuse of funds. Symmachus retaliated by turning on Lawrence, who gave up his bishopric and fled to the Ostrogothic capital at Ravenna. The king ordered a synod to judge the case against Symmachus, who was exonerated, but by then Lawrence's supporters controlled much of Rome, and he returned to the city and occupied the Lateran basilica, forcing Symmachus to retire across the Tiber and hold court in St. Peter's basilica. For four years Lawrence's had the stronger position, but Theodoric's relations with Constantinople steadily declined, and he had less tolerance for a pro-Byzantine pope. In 506 the king forced Laurentius to leave the city, and Symmachus promptly excommunicated him. Lawrence retired to an estate owned by one of his supporters, and he died there a year later.

Bibliography: H. JEDIN, *History of the Church* (New York 1980) 2:620–621. J. N. D. KELLY, *Oxford Dictionary of the Popes* (New York 1986) 52. P. LEEWELLYN, "The Roman Church during the Laurentian Schism: Priests and Senators," *Church History* 45 (1978) 417–4278. J. MOOREHEAD, "The Laurentian Schism: East and West in the Roman Church," *Church History* 47 (1978) 125–136. J. RICHARDS, *Popes and Papacy the Early Middle Ages* (London 1979) 69–99.

[J. F. KELLY]

LAWRENCE, ST.

Roman deacon and martyr; d. Rome, probably 258. Lawrence and four clerics were put to death, probably by the sword, during the persecution of Valerian (258), four days after the martyrdom of Pope SIXTUS II and his four deacons. The legendary details of his passion, such as the parting words of Sixtus predicting Lawrence's martyrdom four days later and Lawrence's last joke to the judge while being roasted on the gridiron— *Assam est; versa, et manduca!* (it is well done; turn it over and eat it)— were known to DAMASUS, AMBROSE, PRUDENTIUS, and AUGUSTINE. These details may have come into the legend as a result of the cult of the Phrygian martyrs described by the historians SOCRATES and SOZOMEN. The feast of St. Lawrence is noted in martyrologies as early as the beginning of the fourth century; the church built over his tomb became one of the seven principal churches of Rome and a favorite place for Roman PILGRIMAGES. His cult spread rapidly through Christendom. His intercession is credited with a decisive victory over the Magyars on the Lechfeld in 955 and the victory of St. Quentin in 1557.

Feast: Aug. 10.

Bibliography: A. BENVENUTI PAPI, *Il Diacono Lorenzo tra storia e leggenda,* ed. C. BATTIGELLI BALDASSERONI (Florence

1998). N. WIREKER, *The Passion of St. Lawrence*, ed. and tr. J. M. ZIOLKOWSKI (Leiden 1994). D. W. RUSSELL, *La Vie de Saint Laurent: An Anglo-Norman Poem of the Twelfth Century* (London 1976). R. PAFFEN, *Der Streit um das Laurentiushaupt* (Mönschengladbach 1970). V. L. KENNEDY, *The Saints of the Canon of the Mass* (Vatican City 1938). P. FRANCHI DE' CAVALIERI, "S. Lorenzo e il supplicio della graticola," *Römische Quartalschrift für Christliche Altertumskunde und für Kirchengeschichte* (Freiburg 1887–) 14 (1900) 159–176. *Acta Sanctorum* Aug. 2:485–532.

[J. BRÜCKMANN]

LAWRENCE, ROBERT, ST.

Carthusian martyr; b. probably in Dorsetshire, date unknown; d. Tyburn, May 4, 1535. He received his LL.B. degree from Cambridge in 1508, and, according to Thomas Wriothesley, Earl of Southhampton, was once chaplain to the Duke of Norfolk. After his profession at the London Charterhouse, he succeeded Bl. John HOUGHTON as prior of Beauvale (1531). At the appearance of the decree of May 15, 1535, announcing Henry VIII as Supreme Head of the English Church, Lawrence went to London for the advice of Prior Houghton. He accompanied Houghton and Bl. Augustine WEBSTER, Prior of Axholme, in a visit to Thomas Cromwell for a modified form of the decree that they could accept in conscience. They were imprisoned in the Tower together with Bl. Richard Reynolds, a Bridgettine of Syon. On April 20 they were examined by royal commissioners and sent to Westminster Hall for trial. They pleaded innocent of any seditious opposition to the king, but were declared guilty by a jury that hesitated for two days until compelled to act by Cromwell. On May 4 in the company of Bl. John Haile, the aged vicar of Isleworth, these protomartyrs were set on hurdles and dragged to Tyburn, where they suffered the penalty of treason. They were hanged, cut down while alive, eviscerated, and quartered. In 1936 a benefactor attributing his restoration to health to Lawrence's intercession erected a small chapel in the Catholic church at Eastwood near Beauvale, to which the former altarstone of Beauvale priory was restored in 1940. The ruins of Lawrence's lodging are still preserved.

Feast: May 4; Oct. 25.

Bibliography: Contemporary accounts by M. CHAUNCY, "De B.B. Martyribus Carthusiensibus in Anglia," ed. F. VAN ORTROY, *Analecta Bollandiana* 14 (1895) 268–283; "Martyrum Monachorum Carthusianorum in Anglia Passio minor," ed. F. VAN ORTROY, *ibid.* 22 (1903) 51–78; *Passion and Martyrdom of the Holy English Carthusian Fathers*, tr. A. F. RADCLIFFE (New York 1936). L. HENDRIKS, *London Charterhouse, Its Monks and Its Martyrs* (London 1889). E. M. THOMPSON, *The Carthusian Order in England* (New York 1930). L. E. WHATMORE, *Blessed Carthusian Martyrs* (London 1962).

[L. E. WHATMORE]

LAWRENCE JUSTINIAN, ST.

Spiritual writer, bishop, and first patriarch of Venice; b. Venice, 1381; d. there, Jan. 8, 1456. At the age of 19, after a spiritual crisis, he entered the Canons Regular at San Giorgio on the island of Alga, near Venice. The community became a congregation of secular canons living a common life and was approved in 1404. Lawrence Justinian (Lorenzo Giustiniani) was elected superior at Vicenza in 1407, and held the same office at San Giorgio in Alga for four terms (1409–21), and afterward he was four times elected general of the congregation (1424–31). In 1433 he was named bishop of Castello by EUGENE IV, and in 1451 he was transferred to the See of Venice. He was distinguished for the simplicity and poverty of his personal life, but was eminently, even heroically, liberal in the practice of charity toward others. He was noted also for the intensity of his apostolic zeal. His writings, the composition of which paralleled the different stages of his career, comprise 15 doctrinal works and a collection of sermons.

His doctrinal works fall into two groups. The first, concerned with the religious life, began with his *Lignum vitae* (1419) and ended with *De compunctione et complanctu christianae perfectionis* (1428), although the central work, which sums up all the others, was *De casto connubio Verbi et animae* (1425). The second group, which grew out of his apostolic activities, began with *De spirituali animae interitu* (1425) and culminated with *De institutione et regimine praelatorum* (c. 1450). Throughout these works there is a basic unity in the form of a dominant theme, that of Eternal Wisdom, which was derived from his mystical experience.

His conversion from the world and his entrance into the monastery was due to a vision of Eternal Wisdom that called to him to be taken as a spouse (see *Fasciculus amoris* 16). All spiritual paths develop from that as a progressive possession of Incarnate Wisdom in the ever more profound assimilation of the knowledge attained through love, until the soul becomes, in the light of Wisdom, a new creature, which is made to the image of the Incarnate Word and espoused to Wisdom by love.

His teaching on the apostolate, included in the second group of writings, presupposes the foregoing doctrine and is a logical development of it. Only he can be a true apostle who has attained a true and proper union with Wisdom. The Incarnate Word will infuse into such a one His own sentiments and desires for the salvation of neighbor, and the soul will correspond to this by giving testimony of the love it bears. The apostolate is nothing other than the communication of that same Wisdom; it is a diffusion of truth permeated by love. The apostle, whose work is on the efficacious level of the supernatural, not only does not impoverish, but actually enriches himself, by communication.

Much of the figure of Lawrence Justinian remains still to be brought to light. Hagiographical works about him, from that of the Bollandists to that of P. La Fontaine, are defective because of their dependence on the first life written by Bernardo Giustiniani, the nephew of the saint; and complementary studies of importance, such as those of I. Tassi and G. Cracco, have been few. The same can be said of his spirituality, for the different authors have treated only of its collateral aspects, whereas the sapiential theme constitutes the central and personal element in Lawrence Justinian's mystical doctrine and in his teaching on the apostolate. He was canonized by ALEXANDER VIII in 1690.

Feast: Sept. 5 (episcopal consecration).

Bibliography: Biographical. B. JOANNES, *De beato Laurentio Justiniano, primo patriarcha veneto, Acta Sanctorum* Jan. 1 (1643) 551–563. A. REGAZZI, *Notizie storiche edite ed inedite di S. Lorenzo Giustiniani* (Venice 1856). P. LA FONTAINE, *Il primo Patriarca di Venezia* (3d ed. Venice 1960). B. GIUSTINIANI, *Vita B. Laurentii Justiniani Venetiarum Proto Patriarchae,* with Ital. tr. (Rome 1962). **Special studies.** G. CRACCO, "La fondazione dei Canonici secolari di S. Giorgio in Alga," *Rivista di storia della chiesa in Italia* 23 (1959) 70–88. S. G. MANTESE, *S. Lorenzo Giustiniani priore del Monastero di S. Agostino in Vicenza, in Miscellanea in memoria ed onere di Mons. F. M. Mistrorigo* 1 (Vicenza 1956) 719–757. I. TASSI, *Ludovico Barbo* (Rome 1952). S. TRAMONTIN, *S. Lorenzo Giustiniani nell'arte e nel culto della Serenissima* (Venice 1956). *S. Lorenzo Giustiniani, protopatriarca di Venezia nel V centenario della morte: 1456–1956* (Venice 1959). F. COLASANTI, *San Lorenzo Giustiniani nelle raccolte della Biblioteca nazionale marciana* (Rome 1981). **On the writings of the saint.** S. TRAMONTIN, *Saggio di bibliografia Laurenziana* (Venice 1960). A. COSTANTINI, *Introduzione alle opere di S. Lorenzo Giustiniani* (Venice 1960). N. BARBATO, *Ascetica dell'orazione in S. Lorenzo Giustiniani* (Venice 1960). F. DE MARCO, *Ricerca bibliografica su S. Lorenzo Giustiniani* (Rome 1962). G. DI AGRESTI, *La Sapienza, dottrina di spiritualità e di apostolato in S. Lorenzo Giustiniani* (Rome 1962). G. GEENE, *Praerogativa Doctoris Ecclesiae in operibus S. Laurentii Justiniani* (Rome 1962). S. GIULIANI, *Vita e dottrina* (Rome 1962). A. HUERGA, *Presencia de las Obras de S. Lorenzo Giustiniani en la Escuela de la Oracion* (Rome 1962). T. PICCARI, *Note marginali al libello del dottorato di S. Lorenzo Giustiniani* (Rome 1962). M. L. FAY, *Episcopal Asceticism in the Thought of Saint Lawrence Justinian* (Rome 1970). P. M. SPOLETINI, *Il De contemptu mundi di s. Lorenzo Giustiniani* (Rome 1971). G. M. PILO, *Lorenzo Giustiniani: due imprese pittoriche fra Sei e Settecento a Venezia, San Pietro di Castello e Santa Maria delle Penitenti* (Pordenonesi 1981), iconography.

[G. DI AGRESTI]

LAWRENCE OF BRINDISI, ST.

Capuchin preacher, doctor of the church; b. Brindisi, July 22, 1559; d. Lisbon, Portugal, July 22, 1619. He was baptized Julius Caesar, and after the death of his devout, middle class parents, William and Elizabeth (Masella) Russo, he was sent to Venice for his education. In 1575 he entered the Venetian province of the Capuchin Friars Minor, receiving the name Lawrence. He completed his ecclesiastical studies at the University of Padua, where he developed his great gift of languages by learning Hebrew, Greek, German, Bohemian, Spanish, and French.

Eminent Preacher. After his ordination in 1582, he preached with success throughout Northern Italy and beyond the Alps. Much of his effectiveness was due to his homiletic use of the Bible. Eleven of his 15–tome *Opera Omnia* contain sermons and homilies rich with scriptural allusions. To his vast audiences he strove to communicate his devotion to the MOTHER OF GOD. He extolled her Immaculate Conception, her Assumption, and other prerogatives with a splendor of thought scarcely ever heard before. The 84 sermons of his *Mariale* (*Opera Omnia.* v.1) employ the Bible, tradition, the Fathers, theology, and the liturgy to magnify her name, and form a complete, solid tract in MARIOLOGY.

Apostle and Diplomat. Between 1599 and 1602, and again from 1606 to 1613, he came to grips with militant Protestantism in Bohemia, Austria, and Germany. In these lands, he established the Capuchin Order and reclaimed numerous Protestants for the church. At Stuhlweissemburg (Székesfehérvár) in Hungary in 1601, he played a momentary but decisive role in halting the Muslim advance of Mohammed III. When appointed by Emperor Rudolf II as chief chaplain to the outnumbered and disheartened Christian forces, Lawrence rode before the army holding aloft the cross and urging his men to victory. It was his skill as a veteran diplomat that welded the Catholic League in 1610. In 1614 he was instrumental in achieving peace between Spain and Savoy. The journey that ended with his death was a mission to Philip III of Spain on behalf of the people of Naples, who were oppressed by their tyrannical viceroy P. Giron, Duke of Osuna. Lawrence escaped Naples disguised as a Walloon soldier, found the Spanish king at Lisbon, and was successful in his mission. It was in Lisbon that his last illness overcame him. His host, Don Pedro de Toledo, carried his body back to Spain, and interred it in the Church of the Poor Clares at Villafranca del Bierzo in the Diocese of Astorga.

Administrator. In addition to these activities, Lawrence was almost continuously a major superior, serving the order as provincial of Tuscany (1590–92), Venice (1594–96), Switzerland (1598), and Liguria (1613–16). He was commissary general in Bohemia and Austria (1599–1602; 1606–10), and Bavaria–Tirol (1611–13), as well as definitor–general 1596, 1599, 1613, and 1618.

When the chapter of Capuchins in 1602 elected him superior general for three years, the order had become one of the main forces of the Catholic Restoration, numbering 9,000 friars in 34 provinces spread throughout Italy, France, Belgium, Switzerland, and Spain. He visited most of these areas on foot, preaching to large gatherings en route. His permanent affect, like that of St. Bonaventure, was one of stabilization, as he strove to balance the rigor of primitive Capuchin life with the needs of the apostolate.

Author. The admirable edition of Lawrence's *Opera Omnia,* published by the Venetian Capuchins at Padua between 1928 and 1956, comprises ten volumes in quarto distributed in 15 majestic tomes. Characteristic of the work is its abundant use of sacred scripture based on a perfect command of the original tongues. His mastery of Hebrew was such that when Clement VIII appointed him preacher to the Jews, rabbis took him for one of their own turned Christian. His qualities as an exegete appear in his *Explanatio in Genesim* (*Opera Omnia* v.3), a literal exposition of the first 11 chapters of Genesis.

At Prague in 1607 he undertook his most extensive work, *Lutheranismi hypotyposis* (*Opera Omnia* v.2), to meet the challenge of the Protestant theologian, Polycarp Leyser. This original and thorough refutation of Lutheranism is important for its ecclesiology and first hand information about Luther's personal life and teaching. It was never published because of Brindisi's lack of leisure and Leyser's death. As a fair controversialist Lawrence refused to "fight against the dead and make war on shadows."

St. Lawrence served the church as scriptural theologian, popular preacher, missionary, polemicist, religious superior, and diplomat. His achievements in the post–Tridentine restoration of Catholicism earned him, in the words of Benedict XV, "a truly distinguished place among the most outstanding men ever raised up by Divine Providence to assist the Church in time of distress" [*Acta Apostolicae Sedis* 11 (1919) 268].

Lawrence was beatified by Pius VI on May 23, 1783, and canonized by Leo XIII on Dec. 8, 1881. John XXIII declared him a Doctor of the Universal Church, March 19, 1959.

Feast: July 23.

Bibliography: A. DA CARMIGNANO, *St. Lawrence of Brindisi,* tr. P. BARRETT (Westminster, Md. 1963). J. HAAS, *The Theological Significance of Some Biblical Symbols in the Mariale of St. Lawrence of Brindisi* (Rome 1994), bibliography. A. M. DI BRENTA, "San Lorenzo da Brindisi Dottore Apostolico," *In Santi e Santita nell'Ordine Cappuccino,* trans. M. D'ALATRI (Rome 1980) 121–151. *Saint Lawrence of Brindisi, Doctor of the Universal*

St. Lawrence of Brindisi, oil painting by Pietro Labruzzi, at the Convent of the Capuchins, Florence-Montughi, Italy, 1610.

Church: Commemorative Ceremonies, v. 2 (Washington, D.C. 1961).

[T. MACVICAR]

LAWRENCE OF CANTERBURY, ST.

Benedictine(?) monk, second archbishop of CANTERBURY; d. Feb. 2, 619. Probably already a priest, Lawrence accompanied St. AUGUSTINE OF CANTERBURY in the first Anglo-Saxon mission that arrived in Kent (597). Having returned to Rome, he brought additional missionaries to England in 601; and upon Augustine's death (May 26, 604 or 605), having already been consecrated by Augustine himself, he succeeded as archbishop. During his tenure there was a serious anti-Christian reaction c. 617, and reputedly he was restrained from abandoning England only by a dream in which he was scourged by St. Peter. Under his leadership there was no expansion of the Church in England and continued efforts to reconcile Celtic Christians to his authority proved fruitless. He was buried beside Augustine in the church of SS. Peter and Paul, Canterbury (ST. AUGUSTINE'S ABBEY).

Feast: Feb. 3 (Dioceses of Westminster and Southwark).

Bibliography: BEDE, *Historia Ecclesiastica* 1.27, 33; 2.4–7. A. W. HADDAN and W. STUBBS, eds., *Councils and Ecclesiastical Documents Relating to Great Britain and Ireland,* 3 v. in 4 (Oxford 1869–78) 3:61–70. W. BRIGHT, *Chapters of Early English Church History* (3d ed. Oxford 1897). F. M. STENTON, *Anglo-Saxon England* (2d ed. Oxford 1947) 106–113, 125, 127. C. J. GODFREY, *The Church in Anglo-Saxon England* (New York 1962).

[R. D. WARE]

LAWRENCE OF DURHAM

Prior, writer; b. Waltham, England, before 1100; d. France, March 17, 1154. Sometime before 1128, Lawrence became a Benedictine monk at Durham, where he taught Aelred of Rievaulx (*see* AELRED, ST.; DURHAM, ANCIENT SEE OF). His learning and holiness won him the office of precentor and, under Bp. Geoffrey Rufus (1129–41), that of chaplain palatine. The controversy following the death of Rufus in which Lawrence was exiled by William Cumin, usurper of the see, is described in his *Dialogi.* Having been recalled, Lawrence succeeded as prior of Durham in 1149. When the monks elected Hugh Pudsey as bishop in 1153, the choice was contested by HENRY MURDAC OF YORK, BERNARD OF CLAIRVAUX, and others, whereupon Lawrence and several other delegates went to Rome to petition the consecration of Pudsey. ANASTASIUS IV recognized Hugh, granting at the same time Lawrence's request for an indulgence for pilgrims to the shrine of St. CUTHBERT OF LINDISFARNE.

Bibliography: Works. *Acta sanctorum* Feb. 1:172–185; *Dialogi Laurentii Dunelmensis,* ed. J. RAINE (Durham 1880). M. L. MISTRETTA, ed., *The Hypognosticon of Lawrence of Durham* (New York 1941). A. HOSTE, "A Survey of the Unedited Work of Lawrence of Durham . . ." *Sacris erudiri* (1960) 249–265. **Literature.** C. L. KINGSFORD, *The Dictionary of National Biography from the Earliest Times to 1900* 11:689–691. M. MANITIUS, *Geschichte der lateinischen Literatur des Mittelalters* 3:816–820. J. DE GHELLINCK, *L'Essor de la littérature latine au XIIᵉ siècle* 2:214, 220.

[M. L. MISTRETTA]

LAWRENCE OF RIPARFATTA, BL.

Dominican reformer and preacher; b. Ripafratta, near Pisa, Italy, March 23, 1373 or 1374; d. Pistoia, Italy, Sept. 28, 1456. He was a leading figure in the Dominican reform begun by Bl. RAYMOND OF CAPUA. When, under the influence of John DOMINICI, he joined the Dominican Reformed Congregation of Italy, he was about 23 years old and already a deacon. Professor of philosophy and theology at the priories in Fabriano and Pistoia for many years, he served also as prior at Fabriano (1411) and at Pistoia (1438). The opinion that at Cortona he was the novice master of St. ANTONINUS, Bl. Peter Capucci, Bl.

Fra Angelico (*see* FIESOLE, GUIDO DA), and Fra Benedetto, and that he served for a time as vicar-general of the Reformed Congregation, lacks documentary evidence. He was noted for his austerity and works of mercy, and was the counselor of St. Antoninus while the latter was bishop of Florence. PIUS IX approved his cult in 1851.

Feast: Sept. 28.

Bibliography: *Acta sanctorum* Oct. 1:42. A. BUTLER, *The Lives of the Saints* (New York 1956) 3:671. S. ORLANDI, *Il beato Lorenzo da Ripafratta* (Florence 1956).

[R. M. BEISSEL]

LAWRENCE OF SPAIN

A native of the Iberian Peninsula; b. place and date unknown; d. Dec. 15, 1248. From 1210 to 1215 he taught at the University of Bologna, where he wrote his works. He studied Roman law under Azo. Although an expert in both laws, it is not certain that he taught more than Canon Law. Among his disciples were TANCRED of Bologna and probably BARTHOLOMEW OF BRESCIA. He is called Magister Laurentius and Laurentius Magister Scholarum in documents of the cathedral of Orense (Spain) of 1214, 1215, and 1218, where he was bishop from 1218 or 1219 to 1248. His activities both within and outside the Diocese of Orense are attested by local documents and by various bulls from Honorius III, Gregory IX, and Innocent IV that are addressed to Lawrence himself or mention him.

The following works, all still in manuscript, are known: (1) *Apparatus* to Gratian's *Decretum* (in a very poor manuscript tradition, since Lawrence's glosses are mixed up with those of other authors and much material not belonging to him carries his siglum). The *Glossa Palatina* (1210–15) is probably his work. Particular mention must be made of the Laurentiustype, that is, a large series of manuscripts of the *Decretum* from the 14th century, in which a great part of the contents of the *Glossa Ordinaria* is attributed to Lawrence. (2) *Apparatus* to the treatise *De poenitentia* of the *Decretum,* which was to become almost wholly a part of the *Glossa Ordinaria.* (3 and 4) Glosses on *Compilationes I and II* (before 1210). (5) *Apparatus to Compilatio III* (this must not be identified with the *Seruus appellatur,* as Gillmann alleged against Post, but with the *Hoc non aduerto,* as Nörr has shown). Although it is not certain that he commented on *Compilatio V,* it is quite possible that he wrote a gloss on the decrees of the Fourth Lateran Council (1215), since a number of glosses with Lawrence's siglum appear in the apparatus of JOANNES TEUTONICUS. He is considered one of the most important figures in the classical period of medieval Canon Law (*see* DECRETISTS; QUINQUE COMPILATIONES ANTIQUAE).

Bibliography: A. GARCÍA, *Laurentis Hispanus* (Rome 1956), with bibliog. A. M. STICKLER, "Kanonistik," *Lexikon für Theologie und Kirche,* ed. J. HOFER and K. RAHNER (2d, new ed. Freiburg 1957–65) 5:1289–1302; "Laurentius Hispanus," *ibid.* 6:832. K. W. NÖRR, "Der Apparat des Laurentius zur Compilatio III," *Bulletin of the Institute of Research and Study in Medieval Canon Law* (*Traditio* 17 1961) 542–543. R. WEIGAND, *Die bedingte Eheschliessung im kanonischen Recht* (Munich 1963), *passim.* J. GRÜNDEL, *Die Lehre von den Umstaänden der menschlichen Handlung im Mittelalter* (Münster 1963). G. POST, "The So-called Laurentius-Apparatus to the Decretals of Innocent III in Compilatio III," *The Jurist* 2 (1942) 5–31.

[A. GARCÍA]

LAWRENCE OF THE RESURRECTION

(Herman, Nicholas), Discalced Carmelite lay brother and mystic; b. Herimesnil, Lorraine, France, 1611; d. Paris, Feb. 12, 1691. After 18 years in the army and some service as aide to William de Fuibert, treasurer of the king of France, he took the habit of the Discalced Carmelites as a lay brother in Paris. He remained there as a humble cook for 30 years, being relieved of this duty only because of blindness. He died in the French capital with a reputation for holiness.

The few writings that Lawrence left include only simple spiritual notes and a few edifying letters. After Lawrence's death, Joseph de Beaufort, vicar-general of the Diocese of Paris under Cardinal Noailles, gathered these spiritual notes, letters, and many unwritten sayings of the lay brother, publishing them under the title *Abrégé de la vie . . . maximes spirituelles, lettres,* etc. (Paris 1691). From this basic collection came: *Maximes spirituelles* (Paris 1693), and *Moeurs et entretiens du Frère Laurent . . . avec la practique de la présence de Dieu* (Chalons 1693). The fame of these writings was considerably diminished among French Catholics because Mme. de GUYON attempted to justify her illuministic theories with the writings of Lawrence; however, his prestige increased among Protestants, especially after the pseudomystic Pierre Poiret published the *Maximes* in Heidelberg in 1710.

Bibliography: N. HERMAN, *La Pratique de la présence de Dieu* (new ed. Paris 1934); *Practice of the Presence of God,* tr. D. ATTWATER (Springfield, Ill. 1962); *Practice of the Presence of God,* tr. M. D. CAMERON (Westminster, Md. 1945). FAUSTINO SGDA. FAMILIA, "Práctica de la Presencia de Dios por Fr. Lorenzo de la Resurreccion. Un poco de historia," *El Monte Carmelo* 34 (1930) 408–411.

[O. RODRIGUEZ]

LAWRENCE OF VILLAMAGNA, BL.

Franciscan preacher; b. Villamagna, Abruzzi, Italy, May 15, 1476; d. Ortona, Italy, June 6, 1535. He belonged to the noble family of the Mascoli whose members occupied positions of importance in the Kingdom of the Two Sicilies during the 15th and 16th centuries. While still very young he overcame the violent objections of his father and entered the Franciscan Order at the Friary of Our Lady of Grace in Ortona. In the course of his theological training he showed himself a brilliant student. After his ordination he specialized in preaching, which occupied most of his remaining years. He preached with remarkable success in almost every city in Italy. His impassioned eloquence drew large crowds wherever he spoke, and he was generally acknowledged as one of the masters of sacred eloquence of his time. Several miracles were attributed to him during his life. He became ill while preaching the Lenten course at Ortona in 1535, died soon after, and was buried in the friary church there. The veneration tendered him by the faithful was confirmed by PIUS XI in 1923.

Feast: June 9.

Bibliography: *Acta Sanctorum* 15 (1923) 170–173. *Acta Ordinis Fratrum Minorum* 25 (1906) 127–130. G. D'AGOSTINO, *Vita del B. Lorenzo da Villamagna* (Lanciano 1923).

[C. J. LYNCH]

LAWRENCE O'TOOLE, ST.

First Irish archbishop of Dublin; b. near Castledermot(?), County Kildare, 1128; d. Eu, Normandy, Nov. 14, 1180. Lawrence (Lorcán O'Tuathail) was of the royal family Uí Muiredaig (which at that time had lost the right of succession); its patrimony was the southern part of Kildare, with stronghold at Mullaghmast. While yet a boy, Lawrence spent some time as a hostage with the notorious Diarmait Mac Murchada. He was committed to the care of the bishop of GLENDALOUGH, of which his grandfather, Giolla Comgaill, had been *comarba Coemgin,* or lay head. There, at the age of 25, he became abbot (1148–54). On the death of the bishop, Gilla na Naomh, Lawrence, then 29, declined an invitation to succeed him. But he was prevailed upon in 1162 to be consecrated the first archbishop of Dublin. The circumstances of his consecration marked a definite break with Canterbury.

As archbishop, Lawrence reformed the canons of Christ Church (Dublin) by introducing the Aaroasian rule, which he himself embraced. He was a fearless upholder of the rights of the Church. He attended synods at Athboy (1167), Cashel (1172), Dublin (1177), and Clonfert (1179), when many grave abuses were corrected. In

1179 also he set off for the Third LATERAN COUNCIL; when he stopped in England on his way to Rome, HENRY II made him swear not to infringe upon the rights of the English crown in Ireland. Lawrence, however, secured from ALEXANDER III papal protection for Dublin and its five suffragan sees and was appointed papal legate for Ireland. He played an important part as intermediary between the Irish and the Norman invaders in 1170 and 1171; in 1175 he negotiated the Windsor Treaty for Ruaidhrí O'Conchobhair, high king of Ireland. But he found it necessary in 1180 to return to England with the son of the high king to treat further on behalf of Ruaidhrí. This time he was ignored by Henry II and was forbidden to return to Ireland. When the king departed for Normandy, Lawrence followed him still hoping to make peace between him and Ruaidhrí. However, he died at Eu. He was canonized by HONORIUS III in 1226.

Feast: Nov. 14.

Bibliography: A. LEGRIS, *Saint Laurent O'Toole . . . archevêque de Dublin* (Rouen 1914). J. F. O'DOHERTY, *Laurentius von Dublin und das irische Normannentum* (Dublin 1934); ''St. Laurence O'Toole and the Anglo-Norman Invasion,'' *The Irish Ecclesiastical Record* 50 (1937) 449–477, 600–625; 51 (1938) 131–146. M. V. RONAN, ''St. Laurentius, Archbishop of Dublin: Original Testimonies for Canonization,'' *ibid.* 27 (1926) 347–364; 28 (1926) 247–256, 467–480. A. GWYNN, ''Saint Lawrence O'Toole as Legate in Ireland (1179–1180),'' *Analecta biblica* 68 (1950) 223–240. C. PLUMMER, ''Vie et miracles de S. Laurent, archevêque de Dublin,'' *ibid.* 33 (1914) 121–186. J. RYAN, ''The Ancestry of St. Laurence O'Toole,'' *Reportorium novum* 1 (1955) 64–75. D. FORRISTAL, *The Man in the Middle: St Laurence O'Toole, Patron Saint of Dublin* (Dublin 1988). J. HENNIG, ''The Place of the Archdiocese of Dublin in the Hagiographical Tradition of the Continent,'' *ibid.* 45–63, esp. 54–59.

[C. MCGRATH]

LAWS, CONFLICT OF

Conflict of laws is a clashing of the demands of one law with those of another. Strictly speaking, no true conflict of laws is possible; and laws, like rights, are not subject to collision. This follows from the fact that law is a dictate or ordinance of reason, and right reason cannot contradict itself. When two laws are in apparent conflict, one will be more authoritative than the other; and the less authoritative law ceases to be an ordinance of reason and to that extent becomes, in effect, no law. In a case of apparent collision of laws, therefore, the conflict should be resolved by determining which of the conflicting obligations is superior to the other, and the superior obligation should be deemed to prevail and the lesser to yield before it. If it is impossible to discover which obligation is superior, a person can in good conscience give priority to whichever obligation he pleases, for the conflicting law

in that case would be doubtful, and a doubtful law does not oblige.

When precepts in conflict pertain to different categories of law, the precept of a higher law prevails over that of a lower law. Thus, the natural law takes precedence over positive law, divine positive law over human law, and ecclesiastical over civil law. Although a conflict of civil and ecclesiastical law is possible, troublesome occurrences of it are infrequent under contemporary circumstances. Civil governments for the most part seek to avoid making laws regarding religious matters, and the Church abstains from legislation about matters that rightly fall under civil authority. In matters of common interest, the Church generally shows a willingness, when nothing essential to its mission is concerned, to negotiate and to compromise in order to avoid a conflict. Rights that the Church claims are not commonly urged in face of existing conflict of law, as, for example, in the case of the clerics' immunity from military service [*Codex iuris canonici* (Graz 1955) c. 120.3]. Where the civil law forbids the marriage of a man and woman of different races or declares such marriages to be invalid, ecclesiastical authority can generally avoid difficulties with the civil authority by not exercising its right to perform the marriage and by advising the couple instead to go to another state where the ceremony can be legally performed.

When conflicting precepts pertain to the same category of law, the general rule is that the more important, urgent, or necessary law rightfully prevails. Thus a law defending a greater good has priority of claim over a law defending a lesser good, and obligations in justice should take precedence over obligations arising only from charity, except in cases in which a neighbor is in extreme need. This does not mean that justice is greater than charity. On the contrary, justice is among the prime requirements of charity, and the urgency of its claims depends upon the fact that charity demands that they be respected. When justice and charity are opposed in a context such as this, the sense is that a claim based upon justice (and charity) is more exigent than a looser claim based only on charity.

Bibliography: B. HARING, *The Law of Christ: Moral Theology for Priests and Laity,* tr. E. G. KAISER, (Westminster, Md. 1961—) 1:227–285. R. F. BEGIN, *Natural Law and Positive Law* in *Catholic University of America Canon Law Studies* 393; 1959). K. FUCHS, *Lex naturae: Zur Theologie des Naturrechts* (Dusseldorf 1955). J. FUNK, *De jure naturali transcendente jus positivum* (Kaldenkirchen 1947). J. A. MCHUGH and C. J. CALLAN, *Moral Theology,* rev. E. P. FARRELL, 2 v. (New York 1958) 1:284–294.

[P. K. MEAGHER]

LAXISM

The moral system according to which a person in a doubt of conscience about the morality of a certain course of action, may safely follow the opinion for liberty provided that it possesses any probability whatsoever. This system, or certain individual solutions logically following from it, found favor with a number of 17th–century theologians, such as Juan SÁNCHEZ, Tommaso TAMBURINI, and Juan CARAMUEL. The fundamental principle of this system was condemned by Innocent XI in 1679. The condemned proposition read: "Generally, when we do anything relying on probability, whether intrinsic or extrinsic, however slight, provided it is not beyond the bounds of probability, we are always acting prudently" (Denz 2103). Many particular errors of laxism also were condemned by the Holy See in the 17th century (Denz 2021–25; 2101–67). No Catholic theologian accepts laxism today. This system is based on the idea that the law of God is something to be evaded, rather than to be lovingly observed when its existence is practically certain, as is surely the case when the opinion for liberty is only slightly probable.

See Also: MORALITY, SYSTEMS OF; DOUBT, MORAL; CONSCIENCE; REFLEX PRINCIPLES.

Bibliography: D. M. PRÜMMER, *Manuale theologiae moralis,* ed. E. M. MÜNCH (Barcelona 1945–46) 1:343. J. AERTNYS and C. A. DAMEN, *Theologia moralis,* 2 v. (Turin 1947) 1:101. H. NOLDIN, *Summa theologiae moralis,* ed. A. SCHMITT, 3 v. (Barcelona 1945) 1:234.

[F. J. CONNELL]

LAY CONFESSION

An avowal of sins, made to a layman (one in no sense in Orders), in order to obtain forgiveness. As a practice, it existed in certain areas and at certain times in the Church. Doctrinally, however, no authoritative teacher has ever held that the layman has the power to absolve sacramentally. Yet the practice showed high esteem for the value of confession in the process of repentance, that was still developing in those times. As a religious fact, lay confession pertains historically to three different periods, and to both the Greek and Latin Churches, although in different fashions.

1st to 4th Centuries. Not only deacons, but Christians without hierarchical rank sometimes acted as confessors. The laymen belonged to a class called "saints" (*les spirituels*); it was a kind of charismatic order, enjoying special graces and gifts, including the power to hear confessions, even to absolve (among many witnesses are Tertullian-Montanist, Clement of Alexandria, and Origen). This class, functioning alongside the hierarchy, was involved in an abusive practice, that may have developed out of a faulty interpretation of Jn 20.22–23. It at least paralleled a practice in some of the monasteries of the time, where the "saints" filled the role of confessor. However, during this period, for grave sins, the penitent was obliged to submit to the bishop in public penance.

4th to 13th Centuries. The proximate origin of lay confession in this period was twofold: originally, it was an extension of the monastic practice of confession, prescribed by both SS. Basil and Columbanus; later, it accompanied the doctrinal development of Penance: the obligation of confession gradually increased, as the burden of external penances gradually diminished.

The Greek Church. The bishop, always the principal director of souls, the confessor par excellence, delegated ordained priests to assist in the work. Oriental Christians added the requirement of clairvoyance and holiness to constitute a true director of souls. Confessors without priestly Orders began when the monks extended their work as spiritual fathers and confessors beyond the cloister. Probably earlier, but surely in the eighth and nineth centuries, the monks moved out among the people. Impressed by the monks' distinctive garb, celibacy (which the secular clergy had refused at Nicaea), and asceticism, the people turned to the monks enthusiastically for direction, confession, and even remission. The monks were judged the "saints" par excellence, and soon they completely replaced the secular clergy in the ministry of Penance. This abuse was complained of by Emperor Baudouin (13th century) and opposed doctrinally by Balsamon, but the monk confessors without Orders multiplied from the tenth to the 12th centuries at Alexandria, Constantinople, and Antioch.

The Latin Church. Here the practice dates from the 11th century. Previously, mortal sins were confessed to bishops and priests only. Although they always remained the only official ministers of the Sacrament, confession to laymen, in cases of necessity, was in general usage by the 13th century. Prime sanction came from *Liber de vera et falsa poenitentia* 10.25: "So great is the power of confession, that if no priest is available, confess to your neighbor" (*Patrologia Latina*, ed. J. P. Migne [Paris 1878–90] 40:1122). With the prestige of Augustine's name, the opinion won acceptance. Where previously the penitent was permitted (Lanfranc) to confess lesser sins (St. Bede, Raoul Ardent) to laymen, now he was said to be obliged to confess both lesser and grave sins (Lombard, Alain de Lille, St. Thomas in early writings) to a layman; St. Bonaventure held such a confession to be permitted, but not obligatory.

To this period belong several abuses that grew out of the practice. For example, Innocent III, in an apostolic letter, condemned and ordered the extirpation of the practice of certain Cistercian abbesses who preached publicly and heard the confessions of their subjects.

13th Century and After. Theologians asked, What is the value of a confession to a layman? Is it a Sacrament? All schools agreed that it was not formally sacramental, because it was made to one who could not absolve. With this reservation, it may be stated that the Augustinian school inclined to a sort of sacramental value; for St. Thomas it was sacramental in some way, but not completely; and for the Franciscans, not sacramental at all. Scotus, teaching that priestly absolution is the essence of Penance, questioned whether lay confession was even licit.

Its Disappearance. Lay confession disappeared because of three factors: (1) the nature of the Sacrament was better grasped and made explicit; (2) heretical teachers attempted to use the practice as an argument to claim the power of remission for all men (H. Denzinger, *Enchiridion symbolorum*, ed. A. Schönmetzer [Freiburg 1963] 1260); and (3) the official action of the Church at the Fourth Lateran Council made annual confession to one's own priest a matter of precept (*Enchiridion symbolorum,* 810). The final blow came from the definition of the Council of Trent: there can be no sacramental character to any confession made to a layman (*Enchiridion symbolorum,* 1684, 1710). By the middle of the 16th century, the practice had already disappeared in Spain, although it continued to be mentioned in other places (England, for example).

See Also: PENANCE, SACRAMENT OF; CONFESSOR.

Bibliography: P. GALTIER, *De paenitentia* (new ed. Rome 1956). 186, 533. E. VACANDARD, *Dictionnaire de théologie catholique*, ed. A. VACANT et al. (Paris 1903—50) 3.1:838–894. P. BERNARD, *ibid.*, 894–926. A. TEETAERT, *La Confession aux laïques dans l'Église latine depuis le VIIIᵉ jusqu'au XIVᵉ siècle* (Paris 1926).

[J. A. SPITZIG]

LAY CONGRESSES, AMERICAN CATHOLIC

Held in Baltimore, MD (1889), and Chicago, IL (1893), and attended by Catholic lay delegates from all over the U.S. for the purpose of considering various social problems affecting the Church. The Catholic Congress of 1889 was held on November 11 and 12 at the Concordia Opera House, Baltimore, in conjunction with the centennial celebration of the American hierarchy. The suggestion for such a convention of laymen came from Henry F. Brownson, son of Orestes Brownson; and despite the initial opposition of Cardinal James GIBBONS, who doubted the wisdom and timeliness of a congress, the idea quickly won the support of several members of the hierarchy, including Abp. John IRELAND OF ST. PAUL, Minn. William J. ONAHAN, chairman of the committee on organization, was assisted by the historian John Gilmary SHEA. Brownson was chairman of the committee on papers to be read at the congress. After a solemn opening in the Baltimore cathedral, about 1,500 delegates reassembled at the Concordia to hear 14 papers, including Shea's "Catholic Congresses," Brownson's "Lay Action of the Church," and Charles J. Bonaparte's learned address on "The Independence of the Holy See." Among the resolutions adopted at the congress were those denouncing Mormonism, divorce, secret societies, socialism, and communism. Catholic social and benevolent societies, the Catholic press, and Catholic education were commended; and the delegates pledged their loyalty to the pope and demanded temporal freedom for the Holy See. Finally, they agreed that a second lay congress should be held in Chicago during the Columbian celebration (1892–93).

The second Catholic Congress, which met in Chicago in early September 1893, was organized by Abp. Patrick FEEHAN of Chicago and William J. Onahan. During the three-day gathering, 18 papers touching on a variety of subjects, including capital and labor, Church and State, the independence of the Holy See, temperance, and Catholic education were read, but without discussion. The more prominent speakers at the congress included Gibbons, Abp. F. Satolli, Edgar H. Gans, Maurice Francis Egan, and George Parsons Lathrop. Resolutions similar to those of 1889 were adopted, but no plans were made for a third congress.

These two Catholic congresses, both of which were looked on with favor by the Holy See and a majority of the American hierarchy, foreshadowed a closer cooperation between the clergy and the laity in the U.S. Archbishop Ireland stated at the conclusion of the Baltimore congress that he hoped the hierarchy, heretofore unaware of the laity's potential, would put "so much talent, so much strong faith" to good use. Seventy-five years later, the bishops assembled at Vatican Council II debated Ireland's suggestion and through legislation reemphasized the interdependence of the clergy and laity within the Church's structure.

Bibliography: *Souvenir Volume of the Centennial Celebration and Catholic Congress* (Detroit 1889). J. T. ELLIS, *The Life of James Cardinal Gibbons*, 2 v. (Milwaukee 1952).

[J. Q. FELLER]

LAY SPIRITUALITY

Describing lay spirituality is a formidable task, not least because the very concept is in doubt. It has been asserted that lay spirituality is simply basic Christian spirituality *sine addito* and thus ought not be treated as a separate subject. Some have argued that there is not just *one* lay spirituality but *many* reflecting the diverse contexts of the lay vocation. For example, might not the married require a different spirituality than the single, the worker than the professional, the member of a lay ecclesial movement than a tertiary? Still others are hesitant to delineate a lay spirituality for fear of reviving past tendencies to treat laity as second class citizens and their spirituality as somewhat inferior to that of clerics and religious.

Despite these concerns, a convergence of ideas regarding lay spirituality has emerged since the Second Vatican Council. While there are diverse ways of living the lay vocation, some fundamental and unifying components can be identified. This article explores the foundations for a lay spirituality in the New Testament, reviews the historical data in order to see how lay spirituality has evolved, and discusses the impact of the Second Vatican Council and post-conciliar developments. By way of conclusion, some key elements for a lay spirituality in the twenty-first century are suggested.

New Testament Foundations. Although it is clear that Jesus instituted a structured community (Mt 16–18) and St. Paul described different roles within the body of Christ (cf. 1 Cor 12, Rom 12), the New Testament as a whole precludes the idea of distinct spiritualities for diverse members of the Church, and consequently any notion of a specific lay spirituality. The word *laikos* is not even found in the New Testament; rather the Greek substantive is used to describe an entire people consecrated to God through baptism who together become "a chosen race, a royal priesthood, a holy nation, God's own people (*laós*)" (1 Pt 2:9). All the baptized, without distinction, are called to holiness.

The primordial and fundamental spirituality for all the baptized, according to the New Testament, is one of Christian discipleship. Through a continual process of conversion which manifests itself in conformity to Jesus Christ, the disciple seeks the Kingdom by doing the will of the Father (Mt 6:33), living the beatitudes (Mt 5:1–11), joining the community in celebration of the Eucharist (Acts 2: 46) and embracing an evangelical life of service to others (Mt 25: 35–36). This radical new life is brought about through the action of the Holy Spirit, enfolding the believer into *koinonia* with other believers (2 Cor 13:14) and the very life of God (Rom 5:5). This spirituality is for the laity; this spirituality is for every Christian who struggles with the tension of living in the world but being not of the world (Rom 12–13).

A Brief Historical Survey.

From the Early Church to the Middle Ages. The spirituality of the early Church was decisively informed by a dichotomy between the Church and world. Until the peace of Constantine (313), persecution and exclusion from civil society marked Church life. In a community characterized by internal cohesion against a hostile world, the model of sanctity for all the baptized was the martyr. Convinced that the End Times were at hand, these martyrs embraced a costly discipleship in imitation of Christ, identifying with his perfect martyrdom. Among the first martyrs were many laity, including Blandina (d. Lyon, 177 A.D.) and Perpetua and Felicitas (d. Carthage, 203 A.D.).

Notwithstanding the certainty that the world around them was vanishing, some of the early Christians grappled with how best to incarnate the Gospel in a pagan society. An early manifestation of this dilemma is found in the *Epistle to Diognetus* (c.150–200 A.D.): "Christians are not distinguished from the rest of humanity by either country, speech or customs. They do not live in cities of their own; they use no peculiar language, they do not follow an eccentric manner of life. . . .They reside in their own countries, but only as aliens; they take part in everything as citizens, and endure everything as foreigners. Every foreign land is their home, and every home a foreign land" (*Epistola Diognetus* V, 1–5 *passim*). This anonymous letter exhorts Christians to embrace their responsibilities in the world, "for God has appointed them to so great a post" (V, 9). They are to become for the world what the soul is to the body. Just as the soul animates the body, so Christians are called to bring the life of Christ to the world.

Mindful of the true source of their strength in God, Christians from the earliest time gathered on the first day of the week to celebrate Eucharist. Here again, the incarnational and eschatological dimensions of spirituality are united as the memorial of the death and resurrection of Christ is joined with joyous expectation of Christ's return. It was common to consider Sunday not only the first day of the week, but also the Eighth Day, for it was not only the beginning of time, but an anticipation of the festal gathering at the end of time (St. Basil, *On the Holy Spirit*, 27, 66; SC 17,484–485).

In addition to the Eucharist, early Church Fathers encouraged presbyters and laity alike to pray daily either alone or with others. Tertullian's treatise *On Prayer* (c. 198–204 A.D.), counsels every Christian to pray not only at the beginning and end of each day, but also at the third, sixth and ninth hours, and even at night. Further, he suggests that Christians pray before meals, before going to the baths, as well as when they entertain guests (chapters

25–27). The *Apostolic Constitutions*, written in Greek by a Syrian around 380 A.D., specifically instructs bishops to encourage lay participation in communal prayer: "When you teach, bishop, command and exhort the people to frequent church regularly, morning and evening every day, and not to forsake it at all, but to assemble continually and not diminish the Church by absenting themselves and making the Body of Christ lack a member. . . . But especially on the Sabbath, and on . . . the day of the resurrection of the Lord, meet even more diligently, sending up praise to God . . ." (*Apostolic Constitutions*, book II, 59).

To these directives, John Chrysostom (344–407 A.D.) and Gregory the Great (540–604 A.D.) added familiarity with the WORD of God. Chrysostom's reply to a skeptical lay person is telling: "You say, 'I am not a monk'. . . But in this you have made a mistake, because you believe that Scripture concerns only monks, while it is even more necessary for you faithful who are in the midst of the world" (*In Matthaeum* V, 5). Gregory makes a similar point in a letter (c. 595 A.D.) to the physician of the emperor who was too busy to read Sacred Scripture everyday. "What is Sacred Scripture if not a letter from Almighty God to his creatures? If you find yourself away on a journey and you receive a letter from the Emperor, . . . you would not go to bed, until you knew what the Emperor had to say to you. The Emperor of heaven, the Lord of all humanity and of angels, has written you a letter regarding your life. . . and you do not show any impatience in reading this letter. . . . Find a way every day to meditate on the words of your Creator. Learn to discover the heart of God in the word of God" (*Registrum Epistola L.* V, 46).

Even in this early period, a spirituality common to all the baptized nourished by the Eucharist, prayer and Sacred Scripture had to compete with an emerging wedge between the clergy and the laity. The first use of the word *laikos* is found in Clement's letter to the Corinthians with the enigmatic statement that "the layman is bound by lay ordinances" (40, 5). While scholars debate Clement's precise meaning, it is clear that the use of the term is isolated; it does not occur again until the mid-second century. By this time, the laity are distinguished from clerics in the writings of CLEMENT OF ALEXANDRIA (d. *c.* 215 A.D.), Origen (d. *c.* 254 A.D.) and CYPRIAN (d. *c.* 258 A.D.). By the beginning of the third century, this division becomes widely accepted, leading to both a distinctive lay spirituality and in some cases its denigration as inferior to that of the cleric.

In addition to the dichotomy between clergy and laity, the rise of monasticism, which itself began as a lay movement, had an adverse effect on lay spirituality. In the period after Constantine, the monk and the virgin replaced the martyr as models of Christian perfection. Although monasticism's positive and valid emphasis on virginity and *fuga mundi* as a spiritual path remains a vital gift to the Church, there was an accompanying negative proclivity to undervalue the married state and to suggest that Christian perfection for ordinary lay women and men consisted in an imitation, insofar as possible, of the monastic lifestyle.

Another line of thought detrimental to the idea of lay spirituality came from AUGUSTINE OF HIPPO's (354–430) teaching on ORIGINAL SIN. In his anti-Pelagian writings, Augustine taught that Adam's sin was passed on from one generation to the next through the inordinate concupiscence intrinsic to sexual intercourse. Though Augustine's teaching is complex and needs to be understood in the diverse contexts of his writings, without a doubt, his works, as interpreted through the centuries, have cast a dark shadow on human sexuality and marriage. Since marriage is one key element that distinguishes most lay persons from the monk or virgin, the ideal of a common spirituality of all the baptized further recedes.

Notwithstanding these developments, one can find in Augustine positive and constructive contributions to lay spirituality. For example, precisely in his teaching on baptism, Augustine says, "Let us rejoice and give thanks: we have not only become Christians, but Christ himself . . . Stand in awe and rejoice: We have become Christ" (*In Ioann. Evang. Tract.* 21,8). This statement along with many others in the Church Fathers, especially those surrounding the preparation of catechumens and the mystagogical catechesis for the newly baptized, are significant resources for developing a lay spirituality firmly rooted in the sacraments of initiation.

The Middle Ages. Unfortunately, in the Middle Ages these treasures from the Church Fathers remained largely obscured. The canonist, GRATIAN (*c.* 1189) epitomizes a prevalent attitude towards the laity when he delimits two types of Christians: clerics (and also monks), involved in spiritual activities, and laity, consigned to temporal affairs. For Gratian, the lay state is a concession to human weakness for "these are allowed to possess temporal goods . . .They are allowed to marry, to till the earth, to pronounce judgements on men's disputes and plead in court, to lay their offerings on the altar, to pay their tithes: and so they can be saved, if they do good and avoid evil" (*Corpus iuris canonici* C. 12, q.1 c.7). This common outlook, when combined with the fact that most of the laity were uneducated, led to a minimalist approach to lay spirituality. Gradually, lay spirituality became coterminous with simply keeping the commandments. It must be said, however, that our access to the actual spiritual life of the laity during this time is obscured by the fact that the vast majority, being illiterate, had no means to leave their thoughts to posterity.

Yet here again there are counter-trends. Earlier, Charlemagne (r. 768–814), the first layman of the new empire, both lived and promoted a spirituality appropriate for the laity, emphasizing the relationship between prayer and the need for Christian formation (cf. *General Monition* of 789). Later, in the twelfth century, various lay movements that promoted chastity, simplicity, poverty and manual work became popular. These movements were sometimes prone to error, either by exaggeration or imprecise theological formulations which led to suspicion on the part of the institutional Church. Among them were the *mulieres sanctae* in the low countries, commonly known as the BEGUINES. These women lived a committed Christian life, either alone or in community, without entering a monastery or marrying. The development of lay confraternities like the *Humiliati* in Lombardy and of the Tertiaries connected with various mendicant orders provided new ways of living the lay vocation in the midst of the world. Some outstanding medieval lay saints include ANGELA OF FOLIGNO (*c.* 1248–1309), CATHERINE OF SIENA (1347–1380) and FRANCES OF ROME (1384–1440), though their status as laity is often neglected.

For those laity not connected with a particular counter-movement, the liturgical year provided a spiritual framework in which everyday activities were conducted. Liturgical feasts and fasts marked the turning of the seasons and proclaimed the sacredness of time. Other positive elements include popular devotions focused on the humanity of Christ, a profound reverence for the presence of Christ in the Eucharist, pilgrimages to Rome and the Holy Land, a greater accessibility to Sacred Scripture, and a more developed devotion to the Virgin Mary. Marriage, though still not fully appreciated as a path to Christian perfection, was at least recognized as one of the seven sacraments. In addition, all Christians of the age of reason were not only encouraged, but required to receive the Sacrament of Penance and the Eucharist at least once a year (cf. Fourth Lateran Council c. 21; *Conciliorum Oecumenicorum Decreta* 221).

The waning of the Middle Ages brings a further development in lay spirituality. With increased literacy the laity were able to gain a new level of participation in the life of the Church. For example, in late medieval England, the popularity of Books of Hours or primers, monastic in origin, and devotional books allowed some lay Christians to take greater initiative in their own spiritual formation.

From the Reform to Modern Times. The Catholic response to the Protestant Reformation had both negative and positive consequences for lay spirituality. Negatively, an increased insistence on the hierarchical character of the Church relegated the laity to the lowest rung. Positively, however, many developments in the Counter-Reformation helped the laity discover God in their daily lives. IGNATIUS OF LOYOLA's (1491–1556) *Spiritual Exercises*, written when he was still a layman, brought spirituality out of its monastic confines into the heart of the world. The first spiritual treatise written specifically for the laity was *The Introduction to the Devout Life* written by FRANCIS DE SALES (1567–1622). His preface explains that ''Nearly everybody who has written about the spiritual life has had in mind those who live apart from the world, or at least the devotion they advocate would lead to such retirement. My intention is to write for those who have to live in the world and who, according to their state, to all outward appearances have to live an ordinary life'' (p. 1). Addressing himself primarily to noble women, de Sales insists that they too are called to holiness, to the fulness of Christian perfection, seeking the will of God in ordinary activities.

If Francis de Sales offered the first spirituality of the laity, Vincent Pallotti (1795–1850) offers significant insights into the mission of the laity. His spirituality, focused on *Caritas Christi urgens* (2 Cor 5:14), is rooted in the compelling love of Christ which draws all Christians, clerical and lay, to participation in the mission of the Church. Pallotti envisioned a universal apostolate as a collaborative and complementary effort uniting clergy, religious and laity.

Along similar lines, Vincent Pallotti's contemporary John Henry NEWMAN (1801–1890) sought to retrieve the biblical notion that every Christian has a vocation and mission. This idea is most beautifully expressed in a personal meditation: ''God has created me to do Him some definite service; He has committed some work to me which He has not committed to another. I have my mission—I never may know it in this life, but I shall be told it in the next. . . . I am a link in a chain, a bond of connection between persons. He has not created me for naught. I shall do good. I shall do His work'' (Meditations on Christian Doctrine, March 7, 1848 in *Meditations and Devotions*). Of course, Newman was fully aware that for laity to participate in the mission of the Church, greater attention to formation in the faith was needed. ''I want a laity. . . who know their religion and who enter into it, who know just where they stand, who know what they hold, and what they do not, who know their creed so well that they can give an account of it, who know so much of history that they can defend it. I want an intelligent and well-instructed laity'' (Newman, *Lectures on the Present Position of Catholics in England*, Longmans Green 1924, p. 390).

A layman who well fits Newman's ideal of an intelligent and well-instructed laity is Frédéric OZANAM (1813–1853), who served the poor as part of the Society of Saint Vincent de Paul. This married man and father juggled family commitment, active service of those in need, and a career as a professor. He demonstrated that it is possible for a committed lay person to live a radical evangelical life in the midst of the world. In a letter to his wife, Ozanam offers a vision of discipleship within marriage. "Then Providence led you into my path, and I offered you the sharing of a life poor, for long and perhaps ever obscure, but sanctified, ennobled by the cultivation of all that is beautiful. I offered you . . . the tenderness of a heart which had never belonged to anyone but you" (*Letters*, p. 357). Ozanam stands out as an exemplar of lay sanctity, although full appreciation of what lay holiness might mean will be delayed until the next century.

The Impact on Early Twentieth Century Developments on Lay Spirituality. For Catholic lay spirituality in the twentieth century all roads lead to and from the Second Vatican Council. In the first half of the century various trends of spiritual revival and theological reflection retrieved the biblical centrality of baptism and the Church as the People of God. This retrieval would have great and positive effects on a new appreciation of the lay vocation and mission. Careful attention to pre-conciliar developments reveals that the Second Vatican Council's teaching on the laity is as much a point of arrival as a point of departure. This becomes evident by tracing the insights into the lay apostolate developed in the teachings of Pius X, Benedict XV, Pius XI and Pius XII, especially with regard to CATHOLIC ACTION. Within theological circles, the great milestone is Yves Congar's *Jalons pour un théologie du laïcat* (1953). Also important were the effects of the liturgical movement and advances in Biblical scholarship. In sum, the emerging theology of the pre-conciliar period aimed at a more positive description of the laity, stressing that the lay mission comes directly from Christ through baptism. All of these elements will affect the spirituality of the laity as fostered at and after the Second Vatican Council.

Combined with developments in theology, the twentieth century has also seen the birth of various and diverse initiatives to promote lay spirituality, sometimes in the form of movements, new communities and associations. The Young Christian Worker Movement, begun in 1912 by the Belgian priest, Joseph Cardign, helps young working class men and women develop a spirituality that integrates faith and life through its threefold discernment process of see, judge and act. *OPUS DEI*, founded in 1928 by the Spanish priest Josemaría Escrivá, became a personal prelature in 1982. It proposes to help ordinary people discover paths to sanctity in their everyday life. Other movements or associations respond to specific challenges. Chiara Lubich's FOCOLARI movement, begun in 1943, seeks to overcome the modern sense of isolation by providing a communal experience of unity with God and others. Another effort to combat isolation, particularly intense for handicapped women and men, is Jean Vanier's L'Arche which began in 1964 and offers a community of love and healing. In all of their diversity, these various initiatives, of which only a few have been mentioned here, desire to promote a spirituality that acknowledges the universal call to holiness and encourage lay women and men to live an evangelical life in the midst of the world.

The Influence of Vatican II on Lay Spirituality. The Twentieth Century renewal made itself felt in the Second Vatican Council's deliberations on how best to present the nature of the Church in *Lumen Gentium*. The monumental decision to begin with the whole people of God (*Lumen Gentium* 9–17) before reflecting on the hierarchy (*Lumen Gentium* 18–29) and laity (*Lumen Gentium* 30–42) sets the framework for a total ecclesiology which recognizes both the equality of all the members of the Church and the fundamental unity of the *communio Christifidelium*. While charisms, roles and functions differ, all the baptized share the same dignity and ultimate call to communion with the Triune God. The consequences of this approach for the spirituality of the laity are four. First, the laity are not relegated to the margins of the Church, but through their baptism enter into a life of communion that incorporates them into the Christ. Second, the lay state is presented as a genuine path to holiness and is in no way a concession to human weakness. Third, through baptism and confirmation the laity participate in the priestly, prophetic and kingly office of Christ, which is an expression of their vocation and mission in the Church and in the world. Finally, the dualistic notion that clerics and religious are concerned only with the sacred while the laity are concerned only with the temporal is rejected. The entire Church is called to be a sacrament of salvation in the world.

While firmly rejecting dualism, *Lumen Gentium* holds that the distinguishing mark of the lay vocation and mission is its secular character (*Lumen Gentium* 31). As the conciliar teaching unfolds, it becomes clear that the secular character is understood not merely as an anthropological or sociological reality, but as a profoundly theological reality. *Lumen Gentium* examines the existential situation in which lay people live out their baptism and respond to God's call. It is identified as primarily in the midst of the world—in the context of family life, work, civic responsibilities. These concrete situations of everyday life present opportunities for growth in holiness

(*Lumen Gentium* 41) and are how the laity participate in the one mission of Christ. They are to become like a leaven in the world (cf. *Lumen Gentium* 31, AA 2).

The Pastoral Constitution on the Church in the Modern World, *Gaudium et spes*, encourages all Christians—laity, priests and religious— to see religious and temporal activities as one vital synthesis and to guard against a split between faith and life. Specifically, regarding the laity, the Council Fathers caution that those who neglect family, work and responsibilities in society place their eternal salvation in jeopardy (GS 43). Family life and faith are to be united, and work, far from separating one from Christ, is a path for living out one's baptism. (AA 4). This emphasis on the integration of faith and life is one of the key contributions of the Second Vatican Council to lay spirituality.

Post Conciliar Developments. Six post conciliar developments deserve mention. Foremost are the 1987 synod dedicated to the vocation and mission of the laity in the Church and the world, and the publication of the post-synodal apostolic exhortation, *Christifideles laici* (*CL*, 1988), by John Paul II. *Christifideles laici* is closely related to the two other post-synodal apostolic exhortations that followed it, *Pastores dabo vobis* (1992) and *Vita Consecrata* (1996). Taken together, they celebrate the diverse vocations in the Church in the context of an ecclesiology of communion.

The primary strength of viewing lay spirituality within an ecclesiology of community is the priority given to *being* before *doing*. The laity are described more in terms of who they are rather than what they do. This approach also emphasizes that the sacraments of initiation are an entrance into communion with the Triune God. The theme of communion has the further value of retrieving the Pauline insistence on the diversity and complementarity of the various charisms and ministries in the Church.

Another important theme of *Christifideles laici* is its promotion of a full integration of spiritual and secular activity. Using an image from the Gospel of John (John 14), John Paul II notes that, "the branch, engrafted to the vine which is Christ, bears its fruit in every sphere of existence and activity. In fact, every area of the lay faithful's lives, as different as they are, enters into the plan of God, who desires these very areas be the 'places in time' where the love of Christ is revealed and realized for both the glory of the Father and service of others" (*Christifideles laici* 59). *Christifideles laici* also makes explicit the paradigm shift that had already taken place in the documents of the Second Vatican Council. Instead of referring to the "laity," *Christifideles laici* consistently refers to "the lay faithful," or "lay Christians"—*Christifideles laici*—

those faithful who have been incorporated into Christ by baptism. Here, the lay faithful are not characterized by their relationship to priests, but by their relationship to the person and work of Jesus Christ.

Second, *Christifideles laici* recognizes not only the secular character of the lay vocation, but also the gift that lay participation in ecclesial activities has been to the Church (*Christifideles laici* 23). Already in the post-synodal exhortation, *Evanglii Nuntiandi* (1975), Paul VI stated that the laity "are being called, to cooperate with their pastors in the service of the ecclesial community, to extend and invigorate it by the exercise of different kinds of ministries according to the grace and charisms which the Lord has pleased to bestow upon them" (*Evanglii Nuntiandi* 73). Developing a theology and a spirituality that recognizes these legitimate ecclesial lay ministries is a major task for the twenty-first century.

Third, the pontificate of John Paul II has given great attention to the spirituality of marriage and the family, beginning with the apostolic exhortation, *Familiaris consortio* (1981). Taking up this challenge to develop a spirituality appropriate for couples and their families, a variety of institutes have emerged. What unites these initiatives is the conviction that the relationships between husband and wife, between parents and children, provide an authentic path for spiritual growth. In particular, the virtues traditionally associated with asceticism are here expressed in the mutual self-gift inherent in the struggles and joys of marital and family life. A deeper understanding of this relatively new area of lay spirituality will require an interdisciplinary approach that takes into account not only theological insights, but also philosophical, psychological and sociological data. Concomitant with this urgent need for a marital and family spirituality is the development of a spirituality of those who are single—whether through choice, widowhood or as a result of broken marriages.

Fourth, the rapid growth of ecclesial movements, associations and other more spontaneous groupings has opened up new contours of lay spirituality. Such diverse groups as the Cursillos de Cristiandad, Charismatic Renewal, the Neocatechumenal Way, Communion and Liberation and Worldwide Marriage Encounter witness to the desire of many laity to enter into a deeper Christian commitment with others who share the same vision. In addition to more formal movements and associations, small Christian communities, sometimes referred to as basic ecclesial communities, have flourished in various parts of the world, often among the poorest of the poor. These groups not only develop solidarity amongst their members through common prayer and reflection on Sacred Scripture, but also explore how GOSPEL values can transform society. Each ecclesial movement, association or initiative makes its own contribution to the development of lay spirituality and together they are a sign of the SPIRIT working to renew the Church. *The Code of Canon Law* provides guidelines for the various categories of associations in the Church (cf. canons 215, 298–329).

Fifth, there are recent attempts to promote a spirituality of the workplace. Since most lay women and men spend a major portion of their day in economic activity, the theological significance of human work must be considered. Work is embraced not exclusively for personal and familial needs, but also to serve society and to cultivate resources for the common good. A Christian spirituality of work accents the inherent dignity of labor, but does not define a person by his or her occupation. (*GS* 35, *LE* 26). A full approach this spirituality will aim to connect work, leisure and worship.

Finally, a survey of the twentieth century would not be complete without mentioning the renewed appreciation of martyrdom for lay spirituality. When the Commission for the New Martyrs published its findings in March 2000, among the 12,692 new martyrs listed were 2,351 lay men and women. These are representative of the countless unknown laity who died for their faith in this century. This development provides a needed corrective to past tendencies to identify radical discipleship almost exclusively with clerical or monastic models. Remembering those men and women who lived their baptismal commitment to the full can expand and enrich the spiritual landscape of the entire Church.

Towards a Lay Spirituality in the Twenty-first Century. In light of past developments, some guidelines for a lay spirituality in the twenty-first century can be ascertained. First, every consideration of lay spirituality begins with the conviction that all the baptized are called to radical Christian discipleship. Jesus is the paradigm of every Christian vocation and it is in conformity to Christ that one's relationship with the Triune God, with the Church and with the world, is discerned. Since to be a follower of Jesus is to be baptized into his life and death, there can be no second class Christians. The future of lay spirituality presumes the universal call to holiness by virtue of the sacraments of initiation.

Second, even within a new context, the traditional building blocks of lay spirituality provide a firm foundation. The laity, living out their baptism within the sacramental life of the Church, are challenged to experience the Eucharist as the font and summit of their spirituality. This celebration flows into a eucharistic way of life, a life lived in thanksgiving, praise of God and self-giving love to God and to others. This eucharistic way of life finds nourishment in prayer grounded in meditation of Sacred Scripture. The task, however, is to find creative ways to assist laity in rediscovering the centrality of the sacraments, Sacred Scripture and prayer in a fragmented and frenetic society where the link between faith and life is under constant threat.

Third, the secular character of the lay vocation is gaining in importance in the twenty-first century. The challenges of globalization, environmental stewardship and cultural diversity will require new ways to actualize the Gospel of Jesus Christ. Like the early Christians, the baptized of the future will be called not to abandon the world, but to transform it in light of the KINGDOM OF GOD. Theirs will be an incarnate spirituality, always supporting whatever promotes the dignity of the human person and courageously resisting all that is contrary to Gospel values. As followers of the Crucified One, the lay faithful must be in solidarity with the poor, promoting a faith that does justice.

Fourth, the future of Catholic lay spirituality is inseparable from Vatican II's irrevocable commitment to ecumenism and inter-religious dialogue. A mature spirituality strives for full visible unity among Christians, while celebrating the *communio* already shared through baptism. In addition, those living in religiously pluralistic societies are challenged to integrate the proclamation of the Gospel of Jesus Christ with respectful openness to neighbors of different religious convictions. With nonbelievers whose lives are often marked by ethical values and a sincere search for truth, the laity are called to embody a culture of dialogue.

Finally, since lay spirituality is no longer to be seen as a watered down form of monastic spirituality, new models of sanctity need to be promoted. Some past exemplars have already been mentioned in this article. The Church will benefit from more models of lay sanctity, including canonized married saints, recognized precisely because they bear signs of holiness in and through their lay vocation, as husbands, as wives, as mothers, as fathers, as workers, as politicians.

In conclusion, those exploring the potential of lay spirituality will encounter not only the burdens of the past, but the genuine riches of the tradition. The postconciliar era has proved to be a springtime for the lay vocation, but whether the Church will reap the full measure of the harvest will depend upon laity taking responsibility in forging their own paths to sanctity. Too often in the past, family and work responsibilities have prevented them from carving out large block of sacred time and sacred space for spiritual activities. In reality, however, all time and space have a sacred dimension for they are shot through with God's presence. Salvation is worked out precisely in and through relationships at home, at work, and in the marketplace. The challenge in the twenty-first century is for laity to discover extraordinary grace ever active in their ordinary lives.

Bibliography: G. ANGELINI, et.al. *I laici nella Chiesa.* Collana di teologia pratica, 6. (Torino 1986). A. ANGEL, "Principios fundamentales para una teología del laicado en la Eclesiología del Vaticano II," *Gregorianum* 68 (1987):103–155. A. W. ASTELL, ed. *Lay Sanctity, Medieval and Modern* (Notre Dame 2000). A. "LAICO" BARUFFO, S. DE FIORES and T. GOFFI, eds. *Nuovo dizionario di spiritualità,* Cinisello Balsamo (Milano 1985). Y. CONGAR, "Laic et laïcat." *Dictionnaire de spiritualité ascétique et mystique, doctrine et histoire,* M. VILLER, C. BAUMGARTNER, A. RAYEZ, eds. (Paris 1937–1994). Y. CONGAR, *Lay People in the Church: A Study for a Theology of Laity,* Eng trans. D. ATTWATER (London 1985). Revised and updated ed. of *Jalons pour une théologie du laïcat* (Paris 1964). Y. CONGAR, *Ministères et communion ecclésiale* (Paris 1971). Y. CONGAR, "My Pathfindings in the Theology of Laity and Ministry," *Jurist* 32 (1972)169–188. E. DAL COVOLO, F. BERGAMELLI, E. ZOCCA, M. G. BIANCO, *Laici e laicità nei primi secoli della Chiesa* (Milan 1995). I. DE LA POTTERIE, "L'origine et le sens primitif du mot laïc." *Nouvelle Revue Théologique* 80 (1958): 40–853. E. DREYER, "A Spirituality of the Laity: Yes or No," *Spirituality Today* 38 (1986) 197–208. I. DOOHAN, *The Lay Centered Church: Theology and Spirituality* (Minneapolis, MN 1984). L. DOOHAN, *The Laity: A Bibliography* (Wilmington 1987). E. DUFFY, *The Stripping of the Altars: Traditional Religion in England 1400–1580* (New Haven and London 1992). J. DUPUIS, "Lay People in Church and World," *Gregorianum* 68 (1987) 347–390. K. J. EGAN, "The Call of the Laity to a Spirituality of Discipleship," *The Jurist* 47 (1987): 71–85. E. DIAZ, J. ANTONIO, *La espiritualidad de los laicos en una eclesiología de comunión* (Madrid 1992). A. FAIVRE, *Les laïcs aux origines de l'Eglise* (Paris Centurion, 1984). A. FAIVRE, "Naissance d'un laïcat chrétien: Les enjeux chrétiens d'un mot," *Freiburger Zeitschrift für Philosophie und Theologie* 33 (1986) 391–429. J. FONTAINE, "The Practice of Christian Life: The Birth of the Laity," *Christian Spirituality: Origins to the Twelfth Century,* B. MCGINN, J. MEYENDORFF, and J. LECLERCQ, eds. (New York 1985), 453–491. W. H. C. FREND, "Early Christianity and Society, A Jewish Legacy in the Pre-Constantinian Era," *Harvard Theological Review* 76 (1983) 53–71. W. H. C. FREND, "Blandina and Perpetua: Two Early Christian Heroines," *Les Martyrs de Lyon,* Colloques Internationaux du Centre Nationale de la Recherche Scientifiques, 575 (Paris 1978) 167–177. W. H. C. FREND, "The Church of the Roman Empire, 313–600," *The Layman and Christian History: A Project of the Department on the Laity of the World Council of Churches,* ed. S. C. NEILL and H.-R. WEBER (Philadelphia 1963) 57–87. B. FORTE, *Laicato e laicità* (Genova 1986). R. GOLDIE, "Lay, Laity, Laicity: A Bibliographical Survey," *The Laity Today* 26 (1979) 107–144. R. GOLDIE, "L'Avant-Concile des 'Christifideles laici.'" *Revue d'Histoire Ecclésiastique* 88 (1993) 131–171. R. GOLDIE, *From a Roman Window: Five Decades: The World, The Church and the Catholic Laity,* (Blackburn, Victoria 1998). M. JOURJON, "Les premiers emplois du mot laïc dans la littérature patristique," *Lumière et Vie* 65 (1963) 37–42. C. O'DONNELL, "Diognetus, Epistle to" and "Laity," *Ecclesia: A Theological Encyclopedia of the Church* (Collegeville 1996). D. ORSUTO, "Discovering the Extraordinary in the Ordinary: Towards a Christian Marital Spirituality, *INTAMS Review* 7 (2001) 3–12. O. PASQUATO, *I laici in Giovanni Crisostomo: Tra Chiesa, famiglia e città* (Roma 1998). PONTIFICIUM CONSILIUM PRO LAICIS, "Movements in the Church" *Laity Today* (Vatican City, 1999). A. PREWWINTERS, "Who Is a Lay Person?" *The Jurist* 47 (1987): 51–70. R. TAFT, *The Liturgy of the Hours in East and West* (Collegeville 1986). G. THILS, "Les laïcs: A la récherche d'une définition," *Revue théologique de Louvain* 19 (1988) 191–196. A. VAUCHEZ, *The Laity in the Middle Ages,* ed. D. E. BORNSTEIN, trans. M. J. SCHNEIDER, (Notre Dame and London 1993). K. WAAIJMAN, "Lay Spirituality," *Studies in Spirituality* 10 (2000) 5–20.

[D. ORSUTO]

LAYMANN, PAULUS

Canonist; b. Arzl, near Innsbruck, 1574; d. Constance, Nov. 13, 1635. He entered the Society of Jesus in 1594 after completing his juridical studies, and was ordained in 1603. He taught philosophy at the University of Ingolstadt until 1609. He taught theology in a house of his institute in Munich from 1609 to 1625, and Canon Law at the University of Dillingen from 1625 to 1632. He was acknowledged as one of the era's great experts in Canon Law and moral theology. His works number 35 and are enumerated in Sommervogel. The most important of these works, used as a seminary text through many editions until the 18th century, is *Theologia Moralis in quinque libros partita* (Munich 1625). His *Jus Canonicum seu Commentaria in libros decretales* (3 v., Dillingen 1666–98) was published after his death.

It has been falsely asserted that he approved extreme measures in the treatment of witnesses in witchcraft cases. This charge was based on the *Processus juridicus contra sagas et veneficos,* which was attributed to him. It has now been accepted that this was not his own work because of the more lenient measures he suggests in his *Theologia Moralis* and *Jus Canonicum.*

Bibliography: C. SOMMERVOGEL et al., *Bibliothèque de la Compagnie de Jésus* (Brussels-Paris 1890–1932) 4:1582–94. H. HURTER, *Nomenclator literarius theologiae catholicae* (3d ed., Innsbruck 1903–13) 3:884–886. A. VAN HOVE, *Commentarium Lovaniense in Codicem iuris canonici 1,* v.1–5 (Mechlin 1928–); v.1, Prolegomena (2d ed. 1945) 1:537. E. JOMBART, *Dictionnaire de droit canonique,* ed. R. NAZ (Paris 1935–65) 6:366. F. X. WERNZ, *Ius decretalium,* 6 v. (Rome 1898–1905) 1:320.

[T. F. DONOVAN]

LAZARUS

The name of two men in the New Testament. The Greek form of the name, Λάζαρος, is based on an abbreviated form of the Hebrew name, 'el'āzār (God has helped).

Lazarus of Bethany. He is mentioned only in John (ch. 11–12). He was the brother of Mary and Martha (the former distinct from St. MARY MAGDALENE) and a friend of Jesus (Jn 11.1–2, 11). Jesus had a special affection for

The Tomb of Lazarus. (©Historical Picture Archive/CORBIS)

him (11.3, 36), and often received hospitality at his house (Lk 10.38–40). Shortly before Our Lord's last visit to Jerusalem Lazarus died; when Jesus was informed of his death He delayed two days; He then came to Bethany and raised Lazarus from the dead, although Lazarus had been four days in the tomb (Jn 11.1–44). This resulted both in the conversion to Christ of many who had witnessed the miracle (11.45), and in the determination of the enemies of Jesus to do away with both Jesus and Lazarus (11.46–53; 12.10–11). Lazarus last appears at a banquet given in honor of Jesus (12.1–8), apparently the same banquet that Matthew and Mark place at the house of Simon the Leper six days before the Crucifixion (Mt 26.6–13; Mk 14.3–9). There is no trustworthy evidence on the later life or on the death of Lazarus. Some scholars [e.g., F. V. Filson, *Journal of Biblical Literature* 68 (1949) 83–88] have made futile attempts to identify Lazarus with "the disciple whom Jesus loved" of the Fourth Gospel, even though Lazarus was not one of the TWELVE, to whom the "beloved disciple" obviously belonged.

In his customary fashion John surrounds the Lazarus incident with symbolism. The raising of Lazarus from the dead is the seventh and last of the Johannine "signs." Jesus had shown Himself to be the light of the world by restoring sight to the blind (John ch. 9); now He appears as the life of the world by restoring Lazarus to life: "I am the resurrection and the life . . ." (Jn 11.25). Natural life is the pledge of the supernatural life that is bestowed by the glorified Christ after His own death and Resurrection. It is noteworthy that the Synoptic Gospels make no mention of Lazarus, although they describe other raisings from the dead (Mk 5.21–43; Lk 7.11–17;.)

Modern Bethany is called El-'Azariyeh, the Arabic form of the Latin word *Lazarium*, which became the fourth-century Christian name for the little village that gradually surrounded the church built above the reputed tomb of Lazarus.

Lazarus the Poor Man. In one of His parables (Lk 16.19–31) Jesus gave the name Lazarus to the man who lay sick and miserable at the rich man's gate, longing in vain for "the crumbs that fell from the rich man's table"; when both men died, Lazarus was borne by angels to ABRAHAM'S BOSOM, to dine at the messianic banquet table, but the rich man went to torments in HADES. This is the only New Testament parable in which a character is given a name. Perhaps Jesus did so here to show that Lazarus put his trust in God's help, as the name signifies. The rich man is popularly called Dives, which is merely the Latin word for "rich man." He is called Neues (Ninive?) in the early MS *P75*, and Phinees in the Sahidic (Coptic) version. Despite the use of a personal name in this parable, the characters in it were obviously not historical. However, in the Middle Ages the poor man of the parable became St. Lazarus, the patron of beggars and lepers (known also as lazars).

Bibliography: *Encyclopedic Dictionary of the Bible*, tr. and adap. by L. HARTMAN (New York 1963) 1315. J. MICHL, *Lexikon für Theologie und Kirche*, ed. J. HOFER and K. RAHNER (Freiburg 1957–65) 6:845–846. G. STÄHLIN, *Die Religion in Geschichte und Gegenwart* (Tübingen 1957–65) 4:246–247. P. RENARD, *Dictionnaire de la Bible*, ed. F. VIGOUROUX (Paris 1895–1912) 4.1:137–141. R. DUNKERLEY, *New Testament Studies* 5 (1958–59) 321–327. W. CADMAN, "The Raising of Lazarus," *Studia Evangelica*, ed. K. ALAND (Berlin 1959) 423–434. W. WILKINS, "Die Erweckung des Lazarus," *Theologische Zeitschrift* 15 (1959) 22–39. J. MARTIN, "History and Eschatology in the Lazarus Narrative," *Scottish Journal of Theology* 17 (1964) 332–343. H. J. CADBURY, "A Proper Name for Dives," *Journal of Biblical Literature* 81 (1962) 399–402.

[E. MAY]

LAZARUS THE CONFESSOR, ST.

Stylite and monastic founder; b. near Magnesia, 968; d. Mt. Galesius, Nov. 8, 1054. As a child Lazarus felt an attraction for the Holy Land and made several abortive attempts to go there. Finally he succeeded and at first took up the life of a solitary, then entered the monastery of St. Sabas near Jerusalem, where he was ordained a priest. In the neighborhood of Ephesus he founded three monasteries: one in honor of the Savior; another in honor of the Resurrection; and the Theotokos, or Mother of God, Monastery on Mt. Galesius. As a stylite living in a hut on a column near the monastery church, he directed the monastic life. He composed a rule for the monks, laying out their spiritual and temporal tasks, and insisted on special care for the poor and indigent. His vita was written by GREGORY II CYPRIUS; a second life was written by an unknown monk named Gregory in the 14th century (*Biblioteca hagiographica Graeca*, ed. F. Halkin, 979).

Feast: Nov. 7.

Bibliography: *Biblioteca hagiographica Graeca*, ed. F. HALKIN (Brussels 1957) 979, 980, 980e. *Acta Sanctorum* (Antwerp 1643– ; Venice 1734– ; Paris 1863–) Nov. 3:502–608. H. DELEHAYE, *Les Saints stylites* (Brussels 1923) 106–116, 131, 160. *Synaxarium ecclesiae Constantinopolitanae. Propylaeum ad Acta sanctorum novembris*, ed. H. DELEHAYE (Brussels 1902) 203–204.29, 211–212.43, 826.31.

[P. ROCHE]

LEA, HENRY CHARLES

American Protestant publisher and historian; b. Philadelphia, Pa., Sept. 19, 1825; d. Philadelphia, Oct. 24, 1909. He was the son of Isaac Lea (d. 1886), a distinguished scientist of Quaker descent, and of the Catholic-born Frances Ann Carey. He early displayed a remarkable diversity of interests, writing with equal facility in the fields of chemistry, biology, botany, modern and classical literature, and politics. But his reputation rests upon his historical works, written later in life, and dealing almost exclusively with the customs and institutions of the medieval Church. Lea tackled vast subjects with a breadth of conception, industry, attention to detail, and soberness of style that brought critical acclaim from scholars as distinguished and diverse as Lord ACTON, F. W. Maitland, and Bishop Mandell CREIGHTON, but his works are marred by a slipshod and confusing system of reference and by strong anti-Catholic prejudice. Although in part they remain of fundamental value today, particularly in the treatment of legal procedures, many facets of his historical writings have been superseded by later research. His chief works are *An Historical Sketch of Sacerdotal Celibacy in the Christian Church* (Philadelphia 1867; rev. and enl. ed. Boston 1884; rev. in 2 v. New York 1907), *A History of the Inquisition of the Middle Ages* (3 v. New York 1888; rev. ed. London and New York 1906), *A History of Auricular Confession and Indulgences in the Latin Church* (3 v. Philadelphia 1896), *A History of the Inquisition of Spain* (4 v. New York and London 1906–1907), and *The Inquisition in the Spanish Dependencies* (New York 1908).

Bibliography: P. M. BAUMGARTEN, *Henry Charles Lea's Historical Writings* (New York 1909). E. S. BRADLEY, *Henry Charles Lea* (Philadelphia 1931), contains exhaustive bibliog. E. A. RYAN, "The Religion of Henry Charles Lea," in *Mélanges Joseph de Ghellinck, S.J.*, 2 v. (Gembloux 1951) 2:1043–51.

[J. V. FEARNS]

LEADERSHIP CONFERENCE OF WOMEN RELIGIOUS IN THE U.S.A. (LCWR)

History. During the Holy Year 1950, major superiors from the entire world gathered in Rome to participate

Church mural showing St. Lazarus rising from the dead Bethany, Jordan. (©Hanan Isachar/CORBIS)

in the First General Congress of the States of Perfection. For women major superiors of the U.S.A. this meeting began a chain of events leading to the establishment of the Leadership Conference of Women Religious of the U.S.A., initially known as the Conference of Major Superiors of Women in the U.S.A. (CMSW). In 1952 the Holy See established a commission of General Superiors of Orders of Men and Women. The first committee for women religious in the U.S. planned the National Congress of Religious of the U.S.A., held in South Bend in 1952. That same year participants in the meeting also attended the First World Congress of Mothers General in Rome. All these events furthered the movement toward a national conference. In 1956 the first statutes of CMSW were adopted; the following year the first chairperson of the organization was elected. In 1959 the Holy See gave the Conference formal approbation.

In the late 1960s and the early years of the 1970s the membership of the Conference of Major Superiors of Women Religious (CMSW) manifested, in striking contrast, the different viewpoints prevalent in the American Church on what constitutes authentic adaptation and renewal. The resultant tension between religious superiors of different theological orientations was one of the char-

acteristics of the CMSW during these years. So sharp was the contrast that many believed both the role and existence of the Conference were in jeopardy. Movements among the rank and file of American sisters made the point that the formal organization of superiors, the CMSW, could not speak for the generality of the sisters. New organizations arose attempting to speak for sisters of all communities, the "grass roots," on questions of social and religious concern, in particular the National Association of Women Religious (NAWR). Another organization, the *Consortium Perfectae Caritatis*, was begun by superiors who believed that CMSW was promoting a form of renewal of religious life that they judged as dissonant from the directives of the Church.

In an effort to clarify its nature and purpose, the Conference initiated a project known as the *Sisters Survey*. Through a questionnaire disseminated in 1967, data were collected on: the changing structures of religious orders; preferred apostolic services, life styles and theologies; and participation in adaptation/renewal processes after Vatican II. Participating in the study were 139,000 sisters, from 301 different congregations. In 1969, it commissioned a thorough managerial study of the organization. This study became the occasion of extended dialogue among the membership on the objectives of the Conference as well as on the most effective structures to attain these purposes.

As a result of this study the Conference was reorganized in 1971 and a number of new committees were created. The superiors, expressing a different concept of their role, voted to change their corporate title to Leadership Conference of Women Religious (LCWR). Associate membership status was granted to representatives of a number of national organizations. The bylaws of LCWR were revised in 1971 to reflect these changes and were approved by the Sacred Congregation for Religious and Secular Institutes in 1972. In 1989 the bylaws were again revised and again approved by the Congregation for Institutes of Consecrated Life and Societies of Apostolic Life (CICLSAL). Although LCWR worked hard for several years to resolve the internal tensions resultant upon conflicting theologies of religious life represented by the membership, the dissenting superiors formed a separate group. They requested and received recognition in 1992 from the Congregation for Institutes of Consecrated Life and Societies of Apostolic Life (CICLSAL) as the Council of Major Superiors of Women Religious (CMSWR).

Structure and Organization. The Conference, as an organization with pontifical status, exercises moral power in relationship to its members. The autonomy of each congregation is preserved. The Conference possesses authority sufficient for its organizational purposes. Membership in the LCWR is open to the chief administrative officers of all institutes, provinces and regions of women religious in the U.S. and territorial possessions. The current membership is drawn from approximately 300 congregations. The primary purpose of the Conference is to "promote a developing understanding and living of religious life" in three areas: (1) assisting members "personally and communally to carry out more collaboratively their service of leadership in their congregations in order to accomplish further the mission of Christ in today's world"; (2) "fostering dialogue and collaboration among religious congregations within the Church and the larger society"; and (3) collaborating with "groups concerned with the needs of society, thereby maximizing the potential of the Conference for effecting change" (Bylaws Art. II, Section 1).

Organizationally the LCWR is divided into 15 geographic regions. The members gather annually in national assembly, which constitutes the legislative body of the Conference. Between assemblies a national board and the executive committee of that board govern the LCWR. The board is composed of five national officers, one representative from each region and the executive director.

Henry Charles Lea. (Archive Photos)

The Conference is administered by a national secretariat located in Silver Spring, Maryland. The LCWR works in close collaboration with the Conference of Major Superiors of Men (CMSM). It maintains liaison relationships with various committees of the NCCB/USCC as well as with a number of other national organizations that share similar values and goals. As a symbol of its concern for the world community and its need to know that community, the LCWR has secured nongovernmental status through the Office of Public Information at the United Nations.

Projects and Activities. From its inception the LCWR has manifested five priorities in its programs and activities: the development of an apostolic spirituality which sees religious as vitally involved in the mission of the Church, action for justice, the fullest participation of women in ecclesial and civic life, the promotion of leadership and collaboration with other groups of similar orientation. LCWR emphasizes three goals as expressions of its enduring priorities: to develop effective religious leadership, to foster a transformed religious life and to articulate our evolutionary understanding of its underlying spirituality, and to collaborate with others in effecting systemic change for justice. In addition to concern for the growth and development of communities of American women religious, the LCWR has devoted much of its energy and resources to promoting service to the needs of the world. Together with a continuing commitment to traditional ministries of education and health care, LCWR has given increased attention to newer ministries for women religious, such as the parish team ministry, better housing conditions, service to the migrant workers or campus ministries. The LCWR also continues its commitment to supporting a fuller role for women and their gifts in service to the Church and to the world, in keeping with calls from the U.S. bishops and from Pope John Paul II.

Over the years the LCWR has maintained relationships with CICLSAL through an annual meeting. They have related as well with the United States Conference of Catholic Bishops (USCCB) and with the American Conference of Major Superiors of Men (CMSM) through a variety of structures. Initially relationships were through liaison committees. In 1988 after two years of planning, a "mixed commission" of bishops, CMSM representatives and LCWR representatives was established as the Tri-Conference Commission. Each organization had five members. The purpose of the Commission was to assist and advise all three conferences by coming together for consultation and collaboration on issues and programs of mutual interest. The group also served as the board for the National Religious Retirement Office (NRRO). With the recognition of CMSWR as a canonical body, the LCWR initiated an invitation to them to join the Commission. The newly expanded and renamed commission held its first meeting in November 1994 as the Commission on Religious Life and Ministry.

Bibliography: *Bylaws of the Leadership Conference of Women Religious of the United States of America* (Washington, D.C. 1972). L. A. QUINONEZ, *New Visions, New Roles: Women in the Church: Leadership Conference of Women Religious of the United States* (Washington, DC 1975). M. M. MODDE, *A Canonical Study of the Leadership Conference of Women Religious (LCWR) of the United States of America* (J.C.D. dissertation, The Catholic University of America, Washington, D.C. 1977). F. R. ROSENBERG, *Women and Ministry: A Survey of the Experience of Roman Catholic Women in the United States: A Project Undertaken for the Ecclesial Role of Women Commission of the Leadership Conference of Women Religious* (Washington, DC 1980). *The Role of U.S. Religious in Human Promotion: A Joint Project of the Conference of Major Superiors of Men, and of the Leadership Conference of Women Religious* (Washington, DC 1984).

[M. D. TURNER/P. M. BOYLE/S. DELANEY]

LEAGUE, THE HOLY

French leagues were religious and political organizations designed as a countermeasure to the Reformation. They started on a local basis to oppose and combat more effectively the action of the HUGUENOTS. Early Catholic leagues, formed in Toulouse (1563), Angers (1565), Dijon (1567), Bourges, and Troyes (1568), were restricted to the towns and composed of royalist burghers. The movement was taken over by the nobility in 1576 with the formation of the Sainte Ligue. In the formulation of the League's program the decisive event was the Treaty of Beaulieu ("Peace of Monsieur") of May 6, 1576. Marshal d'Humières, governor of Peronne, Roye, and Montdidier—who organized in Picardy the first league to be dominated by the aristocracy—refused to give Peronne to Henry, Prince of Condé, one of the Huguenot leaders, who had been appointed governor of Picardy under the terms of the treaty. D'Humières's goal was not simply defense of the Catholic religion, but also revolt against royalty. Outside the province the movement was spread by the lawyer Pierre David and the Jesuit Jean Mathieu; in Paris it was organized by Pierre Hennequin and the Des Labruyère (father and son). Despite the official declaration of obedience to Henry III, who became the nominal chief of the League, its most zealous new recruits were antiroyalist. The League became a tool of the nobles, who were intent on promoting their own ends at the expense of the crown.

Leadership of the Duke of Guise. The first public action of the League took place at the first States-General at Blois (November to December 1576) when both the nobility and the clergy demanded revocation of the Treaty of Beaulieu and the suppression of heresy by armed force. Henry III capitulated by passing the Edict of January (1577) and joining the League. During the two wars of religion between 1576 and 1580 his influence and authority in the Catholic camp rapidly diminished: Henry, Duke of GUISE, became the real leader of the Catholic party and set his sights on the throne of France. It became the League's aim to depose the House of Valois. Its members were afraid that Henry III might appoint Henry de Navarre, a Huguenot, as his successor. A secret committee of five (expanded to 16 in early 1587) was formed in Paris; its members were concerned with pro-League propaganda, the recruitment of adherents, the arming of Parisians, and the establishment of links with the major French towns. Cardinal de Bourbon was declared the League's official candidate for the throne. Henry de Guise, with the League's strong backing—his strongest support came from extremist elements within the party—turned to foreign alliances (one of the chief reasons for the League's later demise) and concluded a formal alliance with PHILIP II OF SPAIN (Treaty of Joinville, 1584). The purpose of the alliance was to destroy heresy in France and the Netherlands, and upon the death of Henry III to crown Cardinal de Bourbon. Guise's reputation was further enhanced during the eighth war of religion (1585–89) in which he personally defeated German troops at Vimory and at Auneau in 1587 (*see* WARS OF RELIGION). The war was a series of successes for the League: these included the taking of a number of fortified towns in the east (Metz, Toul, Verdun, etc.) to bar a possible Protestant invasion from abroad. By the Treaty of Nemours (July 1585) Henry III surrendered to the League, canceling all previous measures of toleration. The only major defeat suffered by the League was at the battle of Coutras (Oct. 20, 1587) in which Joyeuse was beaten by Navarre.

Defying the king's orders, on May 9, 1588, Guise went to Paris (where he was acclaimed "King of Paris") to press him to introduce into France the Inquisition and the decrees of the Council of Trent (1545–63). The latter rejected all forms of compromise between Protestantism and Catholicism. The 30,000 men mustered by the League, and kept in readiness to support Guise's claims against the royalty, were ready to destroy the 6,000 Swiss soldiers called into the city by the King on May 12 ("Day of the Barricades"). Henry III fled to Chartres and through the Edict of Union (July 10) made far-reaching concessions: he granted places of surety to the Leaguers, made Guise lieutenant general of the kingdom, and promised to call the States-General.

Dual Character of the League. The second States-General, held at Blois (September to December 1588), was entirely dominated by the League; the overall national interest was to be sacrificed to the religious need, and the king was to yield to the representatives of the people. The dual character of the League was thus revealed: a religious movement against Protestantism combined with a joint reaction of aristocratic and democratic elements against royal absolutism. Humiliated and angered by the States-General, Henry III broke with the League and had Henry de Guise and his brother Charles murdered (Dec. 23 and 24, 1588). Taking over the League, the Duke of Mayenne assumed the presidency of its general council, consisting of 40 members. He received financial aid from Philip II of Spain and sought the support of Rome. The League ruled Paris in open revolt against the monarchy. Henry III, in alliance with Henry de Navarre, was about to begin the siege of Paris when he was assassinated by Jacques Clément (Aug. 2, 1589). The royalist army recognized Navarre as heir to the throne; all patriotic elements acclaimed him as the national leader. He soon fostered an alliance between the Huguenots and the moderate Catholics against the Leaguers. The latter, refusing to recognize him as Henry IV, proclaimed the aged Cardinal de Bourbon as Charles X (1590). A division within the League followed: some wanted Mayenne as successor to the throne; others backed Philip II, who claimed the throne on behalf of his daughter Isabella, offspring of his marriage with Elizabeth de Valois; some supported

Charles Emmanuel, Duke of Savoy. The League vigorously opposed Henry IV while he was reconquering the country and, despite Henry's victories—he defeated Mayenne at Arques (September 1589) and at Ivry (March 1590)—had some successes.

Decline in Power. Henry IV's final victory at the siege of Paris was delayed by Alexander Farnese, Duke of Parma, one of Philip II's generals. Combining forces with Mayenne, Farnese managed to break the blockade and bring provisions into the city. During Mayenne's absence from Paris, the government of Sixteen took violent measures, killing some members of the *parlement* and terrorizing the *politiques* by drawing up proscription lists. Upon his return, Mayenne had four of the Sixteen executed; others went into hiding and the revolutionary government of the League in Paris came to an end. Cardinal de Bourbon died in 1591. At the States-General in 1593, an attempt was made to deal with the question of succession. The assembly rejected the candidature of Isabella of Spain on the ground of the Salic law. The solution was offered by Henry IV, who abjured the reformed religion at Saint-Denis (July 25, 1593). The great majority of Catholics declared themselves on his side; among the first towns to do so were Meaux, Pontoise, Orléans, Bourges, and Lyon. Charles de Cossé, Count of Brissac, governor of Paris, having received a gift of 200,000 livres and a marshal's baton, led the king into the city on March 22, 1594. Gifts amounting to 32 million livres bought the allegiance of the dukes of Mayenne, Guise, Elbeuf, Nemours, Epernon, and Joyeuse. The League melted away. In September 1595 Henry IV was granted the papal absolution. Only the Duke of Mercoeur resisted the king in Brittany until March 1598.

Bibliography: M. WILKINSON, *A History of the League or Sainte Union 1576–1595* (Glasgow 1929). I. V. LUCHITSKII, *Documents inédits pour servir à l'histoire de la Réforme et de la Ligue* (Paris 1875). P. LE ROY et al., *Satyre Ménippée de la vertu du Catholicon d'Espagne . . .* (Paris 1594), a contemporary parody of the States-General of 1593. H. DE L'ÉPINOIS, *La Ligue et les papes* (Paris 1886). P. ROBIQUET, *Paris et la Ligue sous le règne de Henri III* (Paris 1886). C. LABITTE, *De la démocratie chez les prédicateurs de la Ligue* (2d ed. Paris 1865). S. GOULART, ed., *Mémoires de la Ligue. . .*, rev. C. P. GOUJET, 6 v. in 4 (Amsterdam 1758).

[W. J. STANKIEWICZ]

LEANDER OF SEVILLE, ST.

Bishop and organizer of the Spanish Church; b. probably Cartagena, Spain; d. Seville, *c.* 600. Leander (Leandro) was the older brother of three other saints, FLORENTINA; FULGENTIUS, later bishop of Écija; and ISIDORE, whose education he personally supervised. He became a monk and was chosen (*c.* 577) to be archbishop of Seville. For 20 years he was the most important ecclesiastic in Spain. He persuaded the Arian King Leovigild's two sons, HERMENEGILD (*c.* 579) and Reccared (587), to embrace the Catholic faith. In 589 he presided over the Third Council of TOLEDO, at which the Visigoths officially embraced Catholicism. Leovigild had forced Leander to leave Spain (579–80) because of the part he had played in the conversion of Hermenegild, but whether Leander approved of Hermenegild's rebellion against his father is uncertain. He spent his years of exile at Constantinople, where he met the future pontiff, GREGORY I THE GREAT, and urged him to write his *Moralia,* or commentary on Job. The two corresponded in later years, and Gregory sent the pallium to Leander, the first bishop in Spain to receive this privilege.

Only two of Leander's writings are extant: the sermon he preached at the Third Council of Toledo, in which he expressed the joy of all at the end of religious disunity in the country, and *De institutione virginum,* written at the request of his sister Florentina. The latter is concerned with the virtues that nuns should practice and the dangers they should avoid. It is one of the gems of medieval ascetical literature.

Feast: Feb. 27.

Bibliography: LEANDER OF SEVILLE, *De institutione virginum,* ed. A. C. VEGA (Escorial 1948). U. DOMÍNGUEZ, *Leandro de Sevilla y la lucha contra el arrianismo* (Madrid 1981). L. NAVARRA, *Leandro di Siviglia: profilo storico-letterario* (L'Aquila 1987). *Leandri Hispalensis episcopi, De institutione virginum et contemptu mund: léxico latino-español,* ed. M. MARTÍNEZ PASTOR et al. (Hildesheim 1998). B. ALTANER, *Patrology* (Span. ed.) appendix 14–15. A. C. VEGA, *Lexikon für Theologie und Kirche,* ed. J. HOFER and K. RAHNER (Freiburg 1957–65) 6:847–848. A. BUTLER, *The Lives of the Saints,* 4 v. (New York 1956) 1:432–433.

[S. J. MCKENNA]

LEBANON, THE CATHOLIC CHURCH IN

The Lebanese Republic is located in the Middle East, and is bordered on the north and east by Syria, on the southeast by the Israeli-occupied Golan Heights, on the south by Israel and on the west by the Mediterranean Sea. Two Mountain ranges dominate the region, separated by the fertile Al Biqa' valley. In medieval times the mountains served as a refuge for religious minorities, such as the Maronites in the north and the Druzes in the south, as well as for political dissidents, their rugged heights discouraging communication with the East while the sea invited contact with the West. In antiquity the slopes of Mt. Lebanon provided fir, pine, cedar and other hardwood trees sought by Egyptian pharaohs and Assyrian emperors for building palaces, temples and boats in their treeless lands. The offshore waters of Tyre and Sidon yielded murex, the source of the precious purple dye that gave the Phoenicians ("purple red") their Greek name.

Gaining its political independence from the French in 1943 under a mandate from the League of Nations, Lebanon maintained social and political stability during the mid-20th century. In 1975 the region was engulfed by civil war, which continued for 16 years before ending in 1991 with the Ta'if Accord. While Israel, Syria and Damascus continued to maintain a military presence in the region, Lebanon attempted to return to relative stability, resuming multiparty elections and attempting to restore its weakened economy.

Early History. While maintaining their Semitic identity under Egyptian, Assyrian, Neo-Babylonian and Persian suzerainties, the Lebanese became Hellenized *c.*350 B.C. Christianity reached southern Lebanon during Jesus's lifetime, and Christ Himself reached the district of Tyre and Sidon (Mt 15.21). Returning from Greece *c.* A.D. 56, St. Paul landed at Tyre, where stood an established church that some consider to be the earliest church in Lebanon. That of Sidon, where Paul stopped on his way to Rome, evidently came next. Books of martyrs abound with names of Lebanese victims of persecution. Emperor Constantine's conversion to Christianity resulted in the demolition of the temple at Afqah and the conversion of the temple of Hadad (Jupiter) at Baalbek (Heliopolis) into a church. Throughout the Roman-Byzantine period Lebanon enjoyed relative peace and security under the *Pax Romana,* while benefitting from participation in a worldwide market. This was reflected in increased population—hitherto limited to the maritime lowlands, which spread inland and attained a new density.

Arab conquests began in 633 and engulfed the entire region, except for the mountains. While Arabic quickly spread, it did not displace the Aramaic dialect of Syriac in some areas until the 17th century; the dialect was still in use in Maronite liturgy in 2000. Beginning in the mid-7th century Mu'āwiyah, founder of the UMAYYAD dynasty and his successors paid a weekly subsidy to Christian bands in north Lebanon that eventually evolved into the Maronite community. These Christians provided the first Crusaders with guides and later furnished the Latin Kingdom of Jerusalem with a contingent of archers. When Muslim rule returned in the 13th century, such acts would receive retribution, as Mameluke sultans ravaged the community and decimated its population. After the Crusades neighboring Syria and Palestine adopted a generally Muslim aspect. In 1584 Pope Gregory XIII established a special college in Rome for Maronite clergy.

The Druzes entered southern Lebanon in about 1020 as dissident Muslims and spread northward, where Fakhr-al-Dīn II al-Ma'nī and Bashīr II al-Shihābi ruled almost independently. The Maronite-Druze wars fought from 1842 to 1860 resulted in an autonomous Lebanon under a Christian Ottoman governor-general. World War I ended this privileged status, and World War II ended the French mandate. By the early 20th century a number of Eastern Patriarchs, including the Maronite, Syrian Catholic, Armenian Catholic and Armenian Orthodox, had their principal residences in Lebanon.

Bibliography: H. LAMMENS, *La Syrie: Précis historique,* 2 v. (Beirut 1921). N. A. ZIADEH, *Syria and Lebanon* (New York 1957). A. H. HOURANI, *Syria and Lebanon* (New York 1946). P. K. HITTI, *Lebanon in History* (2d ed. New York 1962). R. RISTELHUEBER, *Les Traditions françaises au Liban* (2d ed. Paris 1925).

[P. K. HITTI]

Capital: Beirut.
Size: 3,799 sq. miles.
Population: 3,578,100 in 2000.
Languages: Arabic, French, English.
Religions: 1,073,420 Catholics (30%), 2,218,400 Muslims (62%), 286,280 Protestants (8%).
Ecclesiastical organizations: The Latin-rite Church in Lebanon has an apostolic vicariate in Beirut. In addition, a number of Eastern churches in communion with Rome are present in the region. The Maronite Catholic Church has a patriarchate at Antioch, archeparchies at Antélias, Beirut, Tripoli, and Tyre, and eparchies at Baalbek-Deir el-Ahmar, Batrun, Jbeil, Joubbé-Sarba and Jounieh, Saida, and Zahleh. A patriarchate for the Armenian Catholic Church is located in Cilicia, with an eparchy in Beirut. The Greek Melkite Church has patriarchates in Beirut-Gibail and Tyre, the latter with suffragans at Baniyas, Saida, and Tripoli, as well as eparchies at Baalbek and Zahlah. The Syrian Catholic Church has a patriarchate at Antioch, with an eparchy located in Beirut. An eparchy for the Chaldean Catholic Church is located in Beirut.

In 1943 the Lebanese Republic was born, and for three decades thereafter peace and prosperity characterized the region. Christians and Muslims shared equal political power and ecumenical dialogue between all faiths continued to take place. Universities and seminaries, long the center for Christian intellectual activity, trained many of the clergy, not only for Lebanon but for other countries in the Middle East as well. The University of St. Joseph of Beruit, administered by the Jesuits and the University of the Holy Spirit of Kalik, administered by the Order of Lebanese monks, both with pontifical faculties, continued to flourish. Publishing houses in Lebanon produced liturgical texts, catechetical resources and works of theology.

War in the Middle East. While Lebanon's stable political situation and strategic location aided its economic growth and gained it influence within the Middle East, problems soon surfaced. Over time the government fell into the hands of conservative Christians, leaving the substantial Muslim population without political representation and influenced by the growing tide of Islamic fundamentalism. Balancing the interests of so many religious communities and cultures was bound to suffer serious strain under the tensions prevalent in the Middle East.

As the Arab-Israeli conflict escalated to the south, thousands of Palestinian Muslims crossed the border north into Lebanon, among them heavily armed militants who used Lebanon to stage attacks on Israel. In 1958 U.S. troops landed in Beirut to break up a Muslim rebellion. Finally, in April of 1975 civil war broke out between the Christian militia and Muslim groups supporting the Palestinian cause, resulting in the deaths of thousands of Christians and the loss of homes, churches, schools, convents and monasteries. In addition, several hundred thousand Christians were forced to flee from the region.

Despite an April of 1976 cease-fire declared by Lebanese president, Suleiman Franjieh, fighting continued and two years later Israel invaded southern Lebanon in an effort to destroy Palestinian bases. These forces returned in 1982 to force the evacuation of the Palestine Liberation Organization (PLO) headquarters in West Beruit. Two months of bombing ended when U.S. and European troops were deployed to protect Palestinian and Muslim civilians. Still the violence in West Beirut continued: president-elect Bashir Gemayel was assassinated, the Christian militia massacred Palestinian refugees, fighting erupted between Christian and Druze militias, hostages were taken and terrorist attacks on international peacekeeping forces and other Westerners resulted in the withdrawal of Western forces.

The Lebanese army finally gained control of Beirut and a peace was reached in 1991. By the close of the fighting, 140,000 had been killed, 300,000 wounded, 800,000 lost their homes and 950,00 left Lebanon, most of them Christians. 175 communities were destroyed. Hundreds of churches were gone, most of them Catholic, and almost a third of the region's Catholic schools had been closed. A third of the population remaining in Lebanon were left without jobs.

In 1992 a new government was elected that attempted to restore the country economically and socially. Under the peace, the president, prime minister and speaker of parliament were required to be Maronite Christian, Sunni Muslim and Shi'a Muslim, respectively, as a way of preserving political balance. In 1998 Emile Lahoud became Lebanon's new president. In 1995 Pope John Paul II convened a synod to aid bishops in their task of healing the many wounds caused by the violence of the war, al-

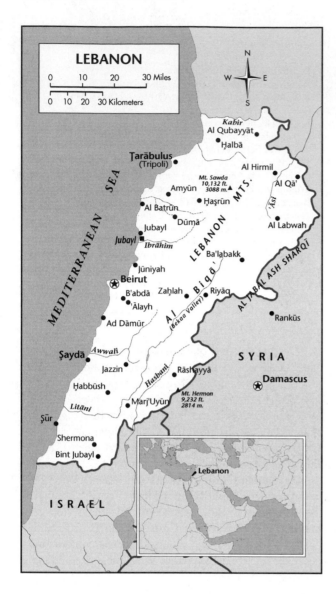

LEBANON

0   10   20   30 Miles

0   10   20   30 Kilometers

though this meeting engendered new controversy when several bishops criticized the existence of an Israeli militarized "security zone" in South Lebanon. Four years later Beirut hosted a meeting of Middle East and North African Church leaders as they addressed the future of the Catholic Church in an increasingly fundamentalist Muslim world.

Into the 21st Century. Despite the devastation of the late 20th century, Lebanon remained the one country in the Middle East where Islam and Christianity were able to encounter each other as equals. Minor religious groups included Protestants, Syrians (*Suryān,* Orthodox and Catholic), Nusayri and Jews, all of which were encouraged by the government to participate in interfaith dialogue. Greek Melkite Catholics, an Orthodox group that split with Rome in the 18th century, was among the nine partriarchal sects active in Lebanon by 2000. In ad-

dition, followers of five Muslim sects and 11 Christian denominations made their home in the region.

By 2000 there were over 990 parishes serving various Catholic denominations in Lebanon, and 740 diocesan and 622 religious priests tended them. The Church operated over 300 trilingual (Arabic, French, English) primary and secondary schools for the benefit of the Lebanese community, and their students accounted for 30 percent of the nation's students. Almost 3,000 sisters worked among the religiously diverse Lebanese community, serving the educational and humanitarian needs of all people, no matter what their faith.

Bibliography: P. K. HITTI, *Lebanon in History: From the Earliest Times to the Present* (London 1967). K. S. SALIBI, *The Modern History of Lebanon* (Westport, CT 1976); *Cross Roads to Civil War: Lebanon 1958–1976* (Delmar, NY 1976). P. DIB, *History of the Maronite Church,* tr. S. BEGGIANI (Beirut 1971).

[S. BEGGIANI/EDS.]

LEBBE, FREDERIC VINCENT

Priest, promoter of Chinese Catholic journalism, founder of missionary and indigenous religious congregations, advocate of adaptation to Chinese culture and of the establishment of a Chinese hierarchy; b. Ghent, Belgium, Aug. 19, 1877; d. Chongquing, China, June 24, 1940. The eldest son of a Belgian Catholic father and a French-English convert mother, he entered the Congregation of the Missions (the Vincentians) in 1895. Fired by a desire to be a missionary and martyr, he went to Beijing, China, with Msgr. A. FAVIER, Vicar Apostolic, in 1901. He was ordained there the same year.

From the beginning of his missionary work, Lebbe was convinced the missioner should become a Chinese to the Chinese. Hence he lived, spoke, wrote, and dressed as a Chinese. Remarkable success in the country missions brought him to Tianjin, where he strove for widespread conversions by public lectures for intellectuals, by forming associations of Catholic laymen for the propagation of the faith, and by establishing a Catholic press. With the help of Ying Lien-chih, a Catholic layman and former editor of a Chinese newspaper, and some other writers, in 1912 he started the first Catholic weekly in China, *Kuang I Lu* (Public Benefit Record). Success was immediate, and its rapidly increasing circulation brought it to areas outside of Tianjin. It proved to be an informative and powerful force during the first public elections and in the forging of the Constitution.

Lebbe's next step (1916) was a great journalistic success, a large Catholic daily, *I Shih Pao* (People's Welfare Daily). Within three months it was the leading newspaper in North China and compared favorably with others in accuracy of news reporting and independence of judgment. Lebbe contributed a daily chat on religion and a column of answers to religious questions. Editions in Beijing and Shanghai soon appeared, and a woman's weekly, a magazine for missionaries, and a children's weekly followed. Lebbe strongly recommended such use of the press in his suggestions to Rome on missionary methods.

Many of Lebbe's ideals seemed vindicated by Benedicts XV's apostolic epistle on missionary methods, *Maximum illud* (1919), and in 1926, six Chinese priests, recommended by Lebbe, were consecrated bishops. In Europe he established the priests' Society of Auxiliaries of the Missions and the International Women's Auxiliaries; in China, he gave impetus to Chinese monasticism and established the Little Brothers of St. John and the Little Sisters of St. Teresa. He died during the Sino-Japanese War due to harsh treatment by Chinese communists. The Chinese government proclaimed a day of mourning in his honor, and it also published an official decree acknowledging and praising his work.

Bibliography: *Recueil des Archives Vincent Lebbe,* 5 vols. (Louvain 1982–86). J. P. LECLERCQ, *Vincent Lebbe: Der Apostel des modernen China* (Vienna 1965). J. P. WIEST, ''The Legacy of Vincent Lebbe'' *International Bulletin of Missionary Research* 23 (1999): 33–37.

[A. R. O'HARA]

LEBON, JOSEPH

Twentieth-century patrologist, Orientalist, and theologian; b. Tamines, Belgium, Dec. 18, 1879; d. Namur, June 12, 1957. After following a course of studies in the diocesan institutions of Namur, Lebon was ordained on Aug. 10, 1903. He earned a doctorate at Louvain on July 14, 1909, with a dissertation (*Le Monophysisme sévérien,* Louvain 1907) that has been acknowledged as the standard history of the Monophysite Christology, then succeeded P. Ladeuze as professor of New Testament theology and patrology at the university. In December of 1918 he obtained the chair of the history of theology in the Middle Ages, and in 1920 he began to teach courses in Armenian culture. From 1932 to 1941 he taught Syriac languages and literature; and from 1942 to 1949, the introduction to the theology of the Orthodox churches.

Although Lebon devoted attention to other subjects, such as Christian of Stablo and Heriger of Lobbes, and published several studies on MARIOLOGY, his main interest was centered on the Fathers of the Church and the development of Christology in the patristic age. Introduced to the study of MONOPHYSITISM by J. Chabot, Lebon published a remarkable series of editions and studies dealing

Monumental Archway of Ancient Tyre, Lebanon. (©Paul Almasy/CORBIS)

with SEVERUS OF ANTIOCH (ed. *Contra impium Grammaticum, Orationes ad Nephalium, Correspondence with Sergius the Grammarian*); PHILOXENUS OF MABBUGH (*Textes inédits*); and a revised study of the Monophysite Christology (1951). He contributed a number of articles to the *Revue d'histoire ecclésiastique* and *Muséon* in which he identified works of THEODORET OF CYR and the *florilegia* of TIMOTHY AELURUS, Severus of Antioch, and Ephrem of Antioch, and contributed monographs to a critical edition of the works of ATHANASIUS of Alexandria. He studied the definitions of faith at the Councils of Ephesus (431), Nicaea I (325), and Constantinople I (381) as well as that of Chalcedon (451). With J. de Ghellinck, he founded the *Spicilegium Sacrum Lovaniense.* An indefatigable and exact scholar, he collaborated on a number of projects in the field of Oriental patrology and was a mainstay in the continuation of the *Corpus Scriptorum Christianorum Orientalium,* a joint effort of the University of Louvain and The Catholic University of America.

Bibliography: G. BARDY, *Annua Nuntia Louvaniensia* 5 (1948):56–75. *Bibliographie académique* 7 (1934–54):301–303. J. COPPENS, *Ephemerides theologicae Lovanienses* 33 (1957): 672–675. A. M. CHARUE, *Revue diocésaine de Namur* 11 (1957): 335–344. A. VAN ROEY, *Revue d'histoire ecclésiastique* 52 (1957): 1023–26.

[F. X. MURPHY]

LEBRETON, JULES

Theologian and church historian; b. Tours, March 20, 1873; d. Neuilly-sur-Seine, July 6, 1956. He entered the Society of Jesus at Canterbury, England, in 1890. Following his juniorate he taught Greek and Latin for four years (1895–99). He completed his studies in philosophy and theology in Jersey, Fourvière, and Canterbury, and was ordained in 1903. In the meantime, he had presented two theses on Latin syntax to the Sorbonne for the *doctorat ès lettres* and received his degree in 1901. The first thesis, *Études sur la langue et la grammaire de Cicéron* (Paris 1901), remains a valuable contribution to its field. The solid training in classical philology and its method as well as that in theology was to stand him in good stead in his future career. In 1905 he was appointed a professor of dogmatic theology in the Faculty of Theology at the Institut Catholique in Paris, and two years later the new rector, A. Baudrillart, gave him the chair of the history of Christian origins in the same faculty, a post that he held, apart from a long illness (1912–17), until his retirement in 1943. In 1910, with L. de Grandmaison, SJ, he founded the scholarly *Recherches de Science religieuse,* to which for over 30 years he contributed his invaluable *Bulletins* on the history of Christian origins. He was a frequent contributor also to *Études* and other journals. Among his numerous books and articles, several must be given special mention. His magistral *Les Origines du Dogme de la Trinité,* v. 1 *Les Origines* (Paris 1910), appeared in the midst of the Modernist crisis and demonstrated that sound and objective historical and theological criticism could be combined with uncompromising orthodoxy. In 1927 the sixth edition appeared under the new title *Histoire du Dogme de la Trinité: des Origines au Concile de Nicée,* v. 1 *Les Origines.* The second volume, *De saint Clément à saint Irenée,* was published the following year. Other preoccupations prevented the continuance of the work as originally projected. In 1931 Lebreton published his *La Vie et l'Enseignement de Jésus-Christ Notre Seigneur* (2 v. Paris 19th ed. 1951), which immediately took its place as one of the leading scholarly works on Our Lord. He collaborated with J. Zeiler on the first two volumes of Fliche-Martin, *Histoire de l'Église* [*L'Église primitive* and *De la fin du second siècle à la paix constantinienne* (Paris 1934, 1935)], a work that marks an epoch in ecclesiastical historiography. Among his later contributions are *Lumen Christi. La Doctrine Spirituelle du Nouveau Testament* (Paris 1947), *Tu Solus Sanctus. Jésus-Christ vivant dans les Saints. Études de Théologie Mystique* (Paris 1948), the article "Contemplation dans la Bible" (*Dictionnaire de Spiritualité* 2.2:1645–1716), and the article "Jésus-Christ" (*Dictionnaire de la Bible, Supplément* 4:966–1073). There is a complete list of all Lebreton's publications, including translations of his books into other languages to 1950, in *Mélanges Jules Lebreton* 2:446–477. His work throughout reveals a phenomenal breadth and depth of learning, meticulous accuracy, and an attitude that is critical but at the same time reverent and strictly orthodox.

Bibliography: *Dictionnaire de théologie catholique, Tables générales* 15 v. (Paris 1903–50) 2:2925–27. R. D'OUINCE, "Le Père Jules Lebreton (1873–1956)," *Études* 290 (1956) 274–280. *Mélanges Jules Lebreton,* 2 v. (*Recherches de science réligieuse* 39–40; 1951–52).

[M. R. P. MCGUIRE]

LEBUFFE, FRANCIS PETER

Author, editor; b. Charlestown, S.C., Aug. 21, 1885; d. New York City, May 27, 1954. He was the son of Adolphe F. and Mary (Guillemin) LeBuffe. After receiving his early education at Gonzaga College, Washington, D.C., he entered the Society of Jesus (1901) and studied at Poughkeepsie, N.Y., and at Woodstock, Md., where he was ordained on June 28, 1915. A physical collapse prevented sustained work for three years, after which he became regent (1920–22) of the School of Law at Fordham University, N.Y., and published a book on jurisprudence. He was dean of the Fordham University School of Social Service from 1923 to 1926, when he joined the staff of *America* and also became managing editor of *Thought.* After 1939 he devoted his time to writing in New York City. Besides several books, he published hundreds of articles and pamphlets on current topics and devotional subjects. He possessed varied interests and was the founder of the Eastern Jesuit Philosophical Association and the Jesuit Anthropological Association; president of the Catholic Anthropological Conference; director of the Catholic Press Association; moderator of the Catholic Evidence Guild; and regional director of the sodalities of the Blessed Virgin.

[F. X. CURRAN]

LEBUINUS (LEBWIN), ST.

Benedictine, Anglo-Saxon missionary to Germany; d. Deventer, *c.* 780. Lebuin(us) or Lebwin is the Latin form of the Old English Liafwin, "dear friend." A monk of the Abbey of RIPON, where he was ordained, Lebuinus was one of the many monks to follow St. BONIFACE and his companions to Europe to carry on the work of conversion. After their martyrdom, according to his earliest biographer, Lebuinus was divinely inspired to preach to the Franks and SAXONS near the river Ysel, and thus to continue the work of St. WILLIBRORD OF UTRECHT. Sometime after 754 he sought out St. GREGORY OF UTRECHT, who directed him to the territory of the Frisians bordering on Westphalia, sending one of Willibrord's disciples, Marchelm (Marculf?), with him. Lebuinus was gladly received into the household of the widow Abarhilda, who helped him build a chapel across the river from Deventer. Later he built a church in Deventer itself.

In his attempt to convert the Frisians and Saxons Lebuinus underwent many persecutions. His church was burned by the Westphalians and their allies, and his Frisian converts scattered. With the help of friends he rebuilt the church and continued his preaching. Among his friends and acquaintances were many chieftains, particularly Folcbert of the Village of Sudberg, who with his son Helco protected Lebuinus. At that time the Saxon chieftains met once a year at Marklo on the Weser with their freedmen and serfs to confirm their laws and to hold court. Against the advice of Folcbert, who feared that he would anger the pagan assembly, Lebuinus appeared at one such meeting robed in full canonical vestments and carrying a cross in one hand and a book of the Gospels under his arm. Announcing himself as a messenger of God, he informed the assembly that if they would accept God's commands, He would confer benefits upon them and preserve them in their liberty. If not, He would send a king to vanquish them, despoiling them of lands and possessions and leading them into slavery. Although the elders in the group tried to deter them, the immediate reaction of the younger Saxons was to wrench stakes from the fence to cast at Lebuinus. In the midst of the melee Lebuinus disappeared. All then agreed that they had been unjust and decided that if they listened to messengers from the Normans, Slavs, and Frisians, in justice they should listen to a messenger from God. After that meeting, the Saxons allowed Lebuinus to travel unharmed wherever he wished to preach throughout their territory.

After his death Lebuinus was buried in his own church in Deventer. Shortly afterward the Saxons, after searching vainly for his body, burned the church and laid the village waste. Albricus, successor to Gregory at Utrecht, sent St. LUDGER to restore the place and rebuild the church. According to report, Lebuinus appeared to Ludger in a dream and told him where his body lay. His body and the Gospels discovered with it, written probably in his own hand, were still in Deventer in a church bearing his name in 882 when it was again destroyed, this time by the Normans. The relics of St. Livinus (whose feast also is on November 12) are probably those of Lebuinus.

Feast: Nov. 12 (primarily in the Netherlands).

Bibliography: *Patrologia Latina,* ed. J. P. MIGNE (Paris 1878–90) 132:877–894, by HUCBALD OF ST. AMAND, *c.* 900. *Analecta Bollandiana* 34–35 (1915–16) 306–330; 39 (1921) 306–330; 70 (1952) 285–305. W. BÖHNE, *Lexicon für Theologie und Kirche,* ed. J. HOFER and K. RAHNER (Freiburg 1957–65) 6:870. A. M. ZIMMERMANN, *Kalendarium Benedictinum,* (Metten 1933–38) 3:286–289, 297–298. *Monumenta Germaniae Historica: Scriptores* 30.2:789–795, an early Life of St. Lebuinus on which Hucbald of St. Amand's version is based. C. H. TALBOT, ed. and tr., *Anglo-Saxon Missionaries in Germany* (New York 1954) 229–234, tr. of the Life in the *Monumenta Germaniae Historica: Scriptores* above. S. BARING-GOULD, *The Lives of the Saints,* 16 v. (new ed. Edinburgh 1914) 13:306–307. A. BUTLER, *The Lives of the Saints,* ed. H. THURSTON and D. ATTWATER (New York 1956) 4:324.

[M. E. COLLINS]

LE CAMUS, ÉTIENNE

French cardinal; b. Paris, 1632; d. Grenoble, Sept. 12, 1707. As the son of an illustrious noble family, he was, in the traditional manner, marked early for a clerical career, although he showed no personal inclination for the religious life. Through family connections he became an almoner of the king, holding office from 1653 to 1669. This phase of his life was marked by dissipation and constant scandal. He came under the influence of Bossuet and retired from court to place himself under the spiritual tutelage of the austere and Jansenist-tainted Nicolas PAVILLON, bishop of Alet. In 1671 Le Camus became bishop of Grenoble, having first refused the office on the grounds that the past notoriety of his life might cause scandal. His sanctity while he was a bishop was legendary: he underwent extraordinary fastings, slept on straw, and shunned ostentation of all kinds. The affection and respect he showed to Protestants in his diocese resulted in an exceptional number of conversions years before the revocation of the Edict of Nantes. He staunchly opposed the violence later employed against Protestants. In 1686 he received the red hat as a sign of papal approval. But it was without the king's presentation, for it had been intended by King Louis XIV for his own favorite, Harlay, Archbishop of Paris.

Bibliography: É. LE CAMUS, *Lettres,* ed. A. M. P. INGOLD (Paris 1892); *Lettres inédites,* ed. C. FAURE (Paris 1933). L. CEYSSENS, *Lexikon für Theologie und Kirche,* 10 v. (Freiburg 1957—) 6:871. É. APPOLIS, *Le "Tiers parti" catholique au XVIIIᵉ siècle: entre Jansénistes et Zelanti* (Paris 1960). J. ORCIBAL, *Louis XIV contre Innocent XI* (Paris 1949).

[L. L. BERNARD]

LE CLERC, ALIX, BL.

Foundress with St. Peter Fourier of the Congregation of Notre Dame; b. Remiremont, Lorraine, France, Feb. 2, 1576; d. Nancy, France, Jan. 9, 1622. A dream of the

Bl. Alix Le Clerc, engraving.

Blessed Virgin wearing the habit of the future Congregation of Notre Dame induced youthful Alix Le Clerc to sacrifice the pleasures of a wealthy bourgeois family and, at the direction of her pastor, Peter FOURIER, to organize a community dedicated to the free education of youth. Fourier drafted the first constitutions, which were provisionally approved in 1598, confirmed in 1617, and finally approved by Pope URBAN VIII in 1628. Alix braved the difficulties of new foundations, false accusations, and public humiliations; she persevered in constant, appalling, corporal penances and still maintained equanimity and personal charm. Her cause for canonization was introduced in 1899. She was beatified on May 4, 1947. Alix's work lives on not only in her own congregation, but in the Canadian Congregation de Notre Dame founded in 1650 by St. Marguerite BOURGEOYS, who was inspired by the work of the earlier society. The Canonesses Regular of St. Augustine were reformed on the Notre Dame pattern by Fourier. The School Sisters of Notre Dame founded in 1833 also follow the Rule of Fourier.

Feast: October 22.

Bibliography: R. BAZIN, *Take This Child,* tr. M. A. GELSON (Boston 1948). M. S. L. WEST, *Blessed Alix Le Clerc* (London 1947).

P. DE GONNEVILLE, *La Mère Alix Le Clerc* (Paris 1947). A. BUTLER, *The Lives of the Saints,* 4 v. (New York 1956) 1:59–63.

[M. P. TRAUTH]

LE CLERC, JEAN

Arminian theologian and biblical scholar; b. Geneva, March 19, 1657; d. Amsterdam, Jan. 8, 1736. Le Clerc (Clericus) studied at Grenoble and Saumur and came under Arminian and Socinian influence. His first work, *Epistolae theologiae* (1679), written under the pseudonym Liberius de St. Amore, was directed against what he called scholastic errors on the major dogmas. He proposed to restate them in scriptural and historical terms. In 1684 he was named professor of philosophy, later of ecclesiastical history, in the Remonstrant Seminary in Amsterdam. He attacked Nicholas Malebranche in part two of a collaborative work, *Entrétiens sur diverses matières de théologie* (1685). Beginning the same year, in *Sentiments de quelques théologiens de Holland,* he engaged in a series of anonymous or pseudonymous published exchanges (1685–87) with Richard Simon, attacking his plan of a polyglot Bible and ascribing the historic portions of the Pentateuch to King Josiah. He also denied the divine inspiration of certain other books. He made a new edition of the apostolic Fathers and edited three major encyclopedias of literature, including *Bibliothèque universelle et historique* (26 v. 1686–93). From 1728 to his death he suffered paralysis and the loss of memory and voice.

Bibliography: J. CARREYRE, *Dictionnaire de théologie catholique,* 15 v. (Paris 1903–50) 9.1:105–107. J. P. DE BIE and J. LOOSJES, eds., *Biographisch woordenboek van protestantsche godgeleerden in Nederland* (The Hague 1919–49) 2:83–104.

[G. H. WILLIAMS]

LE CLERC DU TREMBLAY, FRANÇOIS

Better known by his religious name, Father Joseph of Paris, intimate adviser of Cardinal RICHELIEU and thus called the *éminence grise;* b. Paris, Nov. 4, 1577; d. Rueil, near Paris, Dec. 18, 1638. As the son of a magistrate and a noblewoman, he studied at the University of Paris and began a military career but, after travels in Italy and England, entered the Capuchin novitiate in Orléans in 1599. He was ordained in 1604, and was subsequently professor of philosophy, master of novices, and provincial of Touraine. He was also a preacher and devoted himself to the reform of religious orders. In 1617 he obtained from Rome the brief confirming his foundation of the reformed Benedictine nuns of Notre Dame du Calvaire (Calvairiennes) with convents in Angers, Paris, and elsewhere, for whom he composed instructions and spiritual works until his death.

True to the spirit of St. Francis, his spirituality is characterized by love of Christ crucified, and his first political interest was to rouse Christian princes to reconquer the tomb of Christ. He wrote an epic on the Crusades. But, unable to rely on the position of Spain, he put all his trust in a France strong within and without. In contact with the royal court from 1615, he favored the political rise of Richelieu, who, when head of the royal council, made him his most intimate counselor and trusted aid. Richelieu even sent him to the Diet of Regensburg, where he is credited with having frustrated the plan of FERDINAND II to have his son elected to succeed him as emperor.

Father Joseph wrote works in defense of Richelieu's policy, composed instructions for diplomats and generals, and at times revived the cardinal's own courage, making known to him the visions of his reformed nuns. Richelieu wanted to make him his successor and asked the cardinalate for him. As prefect of French missions in the Levant, which he fostered actively, he also concerned himself with other Capuchin missions. He left many spiritual writings, among which are *Exercice des bienheureux practicables en terre par les âmes dévotes* (1610) and *Introduction à la vie spirituelle* (1626).

Bibliography: *Lexicon Capuccinum* (Rome 1951) 870–873. JOSEPH DE PARIS, *Lettres et documents . . . concernant les missions étrangères (1619–38)*, ed. G. DE VAUMAS (Lyon 1942). G. FAGNIEZ, *Le Père Joseph et Richelieu (1577–1638)*, 2 v. (Paris 1894) fundamental. L. DEDOUVRES, *Politique et apôtre: Le Père Joseph . . .*, 2 v. (Paris 1932). É. D'ALENÇON, *Dictionnaire de théologie catholique*, ed. A. VACANT et al., (Paris 1903—50) 8.2:1530–33. Bonaventura v. M., *Lexikon für Theologie und Kirche*, ed. J. HOFER and K. RAHNER (Freiberg 1957–65) 5:1133–34.

[P. BLET]

LECLERCQ, HENRI

Benedictine scholar, archeologist, and historian of the early Church; b. Tournai, Belgium, Dec. 4, 1869; d. London, March 23, 1945. A naturalized French citizen, Henri Leclercq d'Orlancourt entered the Benedictines and was professed in the Abbey of Solesmes in 1896. With Dom Fernand CABROL, he transferred to Farnborough, England, and was ordained in 1898. In 1924 he was incardinated into the Diocese of Westminster and became an oblate of the Abby of St. Mary, Paris, and chaplain to the Sisters of Sion in London.

This indefatigable scholar, who spent the major part of his career in the British Museum, was the assistant and

heir to the great editions inaugurated by his mentor, Dom Cabrol. He collaborated on the first volumes of the *Monumenta Ecclesiae liturgica,* 4 v. (Paris 1904–12) and *Les Martyrs: Recueil des pièces authentiques sur les martyrs,* 15 v. (Paris 1903–24) and wrote *L'Afrique chrétienne,* 2 v. (Paris 1904) and *L'Espagne chrétienne,* 2 v. (Paris 1906), *Manuel d'archéologie chrétienne,* 2 v. (Paris 1907) and *Histoire du déclin et de la chute de la monarchie française,* 10 v. (Paris 1921–40). All these works are remarkable for the author's ability to synthesize the latest results of scholarship on these subjects. This talent he utilized in carrying on almost alone the edition of the *Dictionnaire d'archéologie chrétienne et de liturgie,* 15 v. (1907–53), which he inherited from Dom Cabrol and for which he had prepared the final articles for volume 14. The work was completed by H. I. Marrou. While his archeological scholarship has been severely criticized as being a not always accurate compilation, particularly in the description of monuments, and while his prejudices are obvious, the *Dictionnaire d'archéologie chrétienne et de liturgie* is an invaluable source for studies of Christian antiquity.

Leclercq also translated and revised C. J. von HEFELE's monumental history of the councils, *Histoire des conciles,* 10 v. (Paris 1907–38), and published *Saint-Benoît sur Loire* (4th ed. Paris 1925), *S. Jérôme* (Louvain 1927), *L'Ordre Bénédictine* (Louvain 1930), *La Vie chrétienne primitive* (Louvain 1928), *Ferdinand Gaillard, "maître-graveur"* (Paris 1934), and *A Chronicle of Social and Political Events from 1610 to 1914* (Oxford 1937).

Bibliography: G. DRIOUX, *Revue d'histoire ecclésiastique* 40 (194–45): 384. E. KIRSCHBAUM, *Lexicon für Theologie und Kirche,* 10 v. (Freiburg 1957–65) 6:872. L. BROU, *Ephemerides liturgicae,* 60 (1946): 198–199. A. FERRUA, "Il Dictionnaire d'archéologie chrétienne et de liturgie," *La civiltà cattolica* 89.1 (1938): 67–72; 90.4 (1939): 172–175.

[F. X. MURPHY]

LECLERCQ, JEAN

Benedictine, monastic scholar; b. Jan. 31, 1911, Avesnes, France; d. Oct. 27, 1993, Clervaux. In 1927 he sought admission to the Abbaye Saint-Maurice in Clervaux, Luxembourg, but was initially refused because he asked to be a simple monk rather than a priest. He was finally received into the community in 1928 and was ordained to the priesthood in 1936. From 1933 to 1937 he studied theology at the Collegio S. Anselmo in Rome where he was influenced by Anselm STOLZ, whose work *Theologie der Mystik* contained themes that Leclercq eventually developed and disseminated to a wide audience in his numerous books and articles. He completed his dissertation, begun in Rome, at the Institut Catholique in Paris in 1940. During the Second World War he lived at the motherhouse of French monasticism at Ligugé. By 1944 he had published his dissertation on John of Paris as well as nineteen articles. With the encouragement of Étienne Gilson, he turned his attention away from scholastic theologians to the medieval monastic authors, including PETER OF CELLE, PETER THE VENERABLE, and JOHN OF FÉCAMP. In 1948 the procurator general of the CISTERCIAN Order commissioned Leclercq to prepare a new critical edition of the works of St. Bernard, a project that occupied him for many years, brought him into close contact with Cistercian houses, constituted his most important contribution to medieval studies, and inspired numerous other books and articles. He was the most prolific medievalist of the second half of the twentieth century. He taught at both S. Anselmo and the Gregorian University in Rome. Following the Second VATICAN COUNCIL, while not relinquishing his scholarly research, he devoted himself to monastic renewal as he traveled to numerous monasteries throughout the world, even to Africa, Asia, South America, and the South Pacific. He was as much loved in monastic cloisters as he was admired in academic circles for his keen intellect, prodigious memory, and an enthusiastic and joyful personality.

Bibliography: J. LECLERCQ, *Memoirs: From Grace to Grace* (Petersham, Mass. 2000). E. R. ELDER, ed., *The Joy of Learning and the Love of God: Studies in Honor of Jean Leclercq* (Kalamazoo, Mich. 1995). M. MARTIN, ''A Bibliography of the Works of Jean Leclercq,'' in *The Joy of Learning,* 415– 498. E. JEAUNEAU and M. SHEEHAN, ''Hommage à dom Jean Leclercq,'' *Studia Monastica* 33 (1991) 379–388. A. LIMAGE CONDE, ''Dom Jean Leclercq y las letras monásticas,'' *Studia Monastica* 32 (1992) 315–359.

[R. K. SEASOLTZ]

LECTIONARIES, I: HISTORICAL

Lectionary is the term used broadly to refer to any book of biblical passages indicated for liturgical celebration. The individual readings are also known by the Latinate *lections* or by the Greek technical term *pericope* (a ''snippet'' of a biblical book). The history of the evolution of the pericopal system is complicated. This article will focus on the Jewish context, general development, typology, and illustration of the lectionaries for Mass in the West through the Missal of Pius V (1570). Further historical detail is covered in PERICOPES. The revision and development of the Lectionary for Mass after the Second Vatican Council is treated under LECTIONARIES, II: CONTEMPORARY ROMAN CATHOLIC and LECTIONARIES, III: ECUMENICAL.

Jewish Use of the Scriptures. The reading of passages from the Scriptures was one of the elements of worship continued by Christians from Jewish liturgical practice (Lk 4:16–21; Acts 13:27). Jewish communities developed an extensive order of scriptural passages designated to be read at the weekly Sabbath services. Nevertheless, the earliest information about which readings were used and how they were read in synagogues dates to the 6th century A.D. Norman Bonneau, following C. Perrot, has explored the evidence. The liturgical action revolved around various prayers and readings, but the high point was the reading from Torah (known in the Greek Septuagint as the *Pentateuch* in reference to its five books). The Babylonian tradition divided the Torah into 54 sequential segments that were read over a one-year cycle of Sabbaths. The Palestinian tradition read the Torah in 154 sequential segments extending over a three-year cycle of Sabbaths. The one-year Babylonian tradition prevailed and is used in synagogues today. In addition to the first reading from the Torah, each Sabbath synagogue service also included a second reading selected from what the Jewish tradition identifies as the prophets. Joshua, Judges, 1 and 2 Samuel, 1 and 2 Kings constituted the ''early prophets''; Isaiah, Jeremiah, Ezekiel and the 12 Minor Prophets constituted the ''later prophets.'' The reading from the prophets (called *haftorah,* Aramaic for ''dismissal'') was chosen to amplify and comment upon the reading from Torah. Every year, the Jewish calendar feasts of Passover (*Pesach*), Pentecost (*Shavuot*), and Tabernacles (*Sukkoth*) interrupted the sequence of Torah readings. Even if these feasts did not fall on the Sabbath, they nevertheless required the reading, at least on contiguous Sabbaths, of passages consonant with the event the feasts celebrated. In these cases the normally prescribed sequential excerpt from the Torah, with its accompanying prophetic reading was set aside. The major liturgical feasts, then recurring in a yearly cycle, interrupted the weekly cycle of Sabbaths. By the 6th century A.D. the Jewish tradition of lectionaries exhibited the following features: a sequential reading from the Torah, paired with a *haftorah* from the prophets, interrupted by special readings at the annual high feasts, proclaimed at the weekly Sabbath synagogal service.

Within the Bible itself, there is evidence for the practice of selecting special readings for major occasions. Deuteronomy 31:9–11, Nehemiah 8:18, and 2 Kings 23:1–3 are but three examples where texts were read on major celebrations in the Temple at Jerusalem. These passages suggest the temple liturgy at times of high liturgical feasts and are valuable for establishing the practice for the selection of special readings for the yearly feasts as well as the pairing of prophets to readings from Torah.

Early Christian Use of the Scriptures. References found in the Acts of the Apostles attest to regular Sabbath readings that were firmly established and practiced widespread: "For in every city, for generations past, Moses has had those who proclaim him, for he has been read aloud every Sabbath in the synagogues" (15:21). Luke relates how Jesus visited the synagogue in Nazareth on the Sabbath and read from the prophet Isaiah (4:15–21), which may suggest the emerging system of *haftorah*. Many Jewish scholars posit that it was not until after the destruction of the Temple in A.D. 70 that the synagogue was transformed from a place for study of Torah to a place of ritual reading of Torah.

Further references within the New Testament attest to the early Christian use of the Hebrew Scriptures in their worship, especially the psalms (Eph 5:18–20; Col 3:16). Scripture was also read for community edification and instruction (1 Tm 4:13). These texts, however, do not mention the Sunday Eucharist. Furthermore, it is not clear that Paul's injunctions to read his letters (1 Thes 5: 27; Col 4:16) refer to liturgical gatherings.

The earliest witness of the use of Scripture at liturgy dates to the mid-2d century at the time of Justin Martyr: "On the day which is dedicated to the sun, all those who live in the cities and who dwell in the countryside gather in a common meeting, and the Memoirs of the apostles and the writings of the prophets are read as long as time permits. Then, when the reader has finished, the president verbally gives a warning and appeal for the imitation of these good examples" (1 *Apol* 67).

Ways of Reading the Bible. The early church had coextensive systems of improvisation, continuous reading, and fixed readings. Scholars today emphasize that as far as liturgical readings in the early period were concerned, improvisation was the rule, with readings selected by the bishop according to occasion. As the canon was taking shaping, there was also a degree of variety among the churches as to what books were read; for example, in some churches The *Shepard of Hermas* or Clement of Rome's letters were read; while in others, Revelation was omitted.

Continuous reading or *lectio continua* was also a method used in the ancient Church. A related manner involves semicontinuous reading, whereby some passages are omitted. The most obvious example is to be found in the voluminous patristic commentaries on the Old and New Testaments, some of which provide transcription of homilies on the Scripture readings given in the liturgy or for catechesis. From the 4th century on there are letters and sermons of St. Ambrose and St. Augustine that reveal certain books were reserved to certain liturgical seasons: at Milan, as at Constantinople, the books of Job and Jonah were read during Lent. In Africa, Genesis took up part of this season, and the Acts of the Apostles was read during Easter time. In the middle of the 5th century, ac-

cording to the testimony of Gennadius of Marseilles, Venerius, the bishop of Marseilles, drew up the first authoritative lectionary determining the pericopes proper to the particular feasts and seasons, but it excluded ferial days. The first complete lectionaries date only from the 7th century.

The first evidence of fixed readings for liturgy is related to the development of the liturgical year and to a lesser degree, the local church in which the liturgy was celebrated. The introduction of annual feasts, seasons, and martyrs, is correlated to specially selected biblical books and fixed passages that were deemed appropriate to the mystery being celebrated. This method sometimes is referred to as an *eclogadic* reading (Greek *eklogé*, "what is selected"), where a passage is excerpted from a longer narrative context. Often a typological reading was used for the selection of the passages.

The type and number of readings at liturgy varied from region to region. In the Antiochene tradition, for example, there were two lessons from the Law and the Prophets (akin to synagogal practice) followed by one from the epistles or Acts and finally one from the Gospels (*Apostolic Constitutions*, 8.5.11). The use of three lessons, one OT and two NT, was far more common, as witnessed by the custom in Gaul and Spain until the 7th century and in the ancient Masses in Milan. In Rome, the system of three readings was simplified to two by the 7th century, when the custom was to have two readings on Sundays (NT and Gospel) and one OT reading and the Gospel on serial weekdays. Liturgical vigils for feasts such as Pasch and Pentecost included several longer readings from the OT and NT.

Methods of Indication. Four methods developed and were used coextensively to indicate the biblical pericopes to be proclaimed at the liturgy. The first, the simplest, was simple notes or symbols written in the margins of the books of the Bible to help the reader find the proper passage. From this grew the second method of compiling lists called *capitularies*. There are three types of capitularies: lists of epistles (sometimes including the Old Testament), lists of Gospel readings, and lists that combined the two. The list would give the liturgical day and the specific *incipit* (beginning verse) and *explicit* (ending verse) of the reading or in the case of the Gospels, the appropriate Eusebian section. The division of the Bible into chapters and then verses evolves only in the late Middle Ages. Scholarship has determined that the choice of epistle readings and of Gospel readings developed and circulated separately. The lists came to be combined, but as Vogel points out, more by chance than design. A third type of organization involved giving the whole text of the particular reading, rather than just the beginning and ending.

A fourth system developed that gives the readings with the prayers of the sacramentary (e.g., *Casinensis* 271).

Terminology. Historians of the liturgy note that there is no precision used to described the types of lectionary. The difficulty in classification of the historical manuscripts resides in the fact that books in the Middle Ages were custom made and thus differed one from the other depending upon the design of the scribe or the desire of the one placing the order. Following T. Klauser, complete lists of non-Gospel readings or books with the non-Gospel reading given are referred to as *epistolaries*. Complete lists of Gospel readings or Gospel readings given in full are generally called *evangeliaries*. The term ''Mass Lectionary'' refers to documents that contain both series of epistles and Gospels. The term *comes* (or *liber comitis*) is used in the manuscript tradition to refer to both lists of epistles as well as documents that give the epistles in full, but not Gospels. The term *comes* is alternatively explained as derived from *comma,* meaning a ''selection,'' or *comes,* meaning a ''companion'' to the whole Bible. Likewise, the term ''lectionary'' retains its general sense, and one encounters such terms as *lectionarius epistolarum* or *lectionarius evangeliorum*. As the full missal (*missale plenarius*) (*see* MISSAL, ROMAN) developed beginning in the 9th century, the readings contained in the epistolary and evangelary were combined with the prayers of the sacramentary and the antiphons into a single book. With the development of the Missal, the readings for the Mass were subsumed into one book along with the mass prayers and chants, rendering the Lectionary redundant.

Further Types of Lectionaries. In the early Middle Ages a variety of liturgical books emerged in response to the liturgical needs and roles of the time. The diverse parts performed by the various ministers were distributed accordingly. Therefore, prayers that the priest had to pray at the altar were in one book, while the readings to be read by reader or Gospels for the deacon were contained in another, and a different volume of antiphons was prepared for the choir. There were also lectionary collections that contained either extracts from the Fathers or historical narratives about the martyrs and other saints, which were read aloud as lessons in the Divine Office. Sometimes collections were made containing just the extracts to be used in choir. Other times a large volume of patristic homilies (known also as a homilary or *sermonarium*) or historical matter was employed, in which certain passages were marked to be used as lessons. This last custom seems more particularly the case with regard to the short biographical accounts of martyrs and other saints. In this connection the word *legenda* in particular is of common occurrence. The *legenda* (also called *passionarium*) is a collection of narratives of variable length, in which are recounted the life, martyrdom, translation, or miracles of the saints. This usually forms a large volume, and the order of the pieces in the collection is commonly, though not necessarily, that of the calendar. A few *legendæ* come down from the early Middle Ages, but the vast majority of those now preserved in libraries belong to the 11th, 12th, and 13th centuries.

Manuscript Evidence. The oldest surviving liturgical documents containing information on the nature and arrangement of the readings in the liturgy date to the 6th century. They are preserved in the manuscripts of Wolfenbüttel (Herzog-August Bibl., cod. *Weissenburgensis* 76; *c.* 500, Gaul) and at Fulda (Hess. Landesbibl. *Cod. Bonif.* 1; *c.* 545, Capua). Another early sacramentary is the *Codex Velseri,* ms. lat. 3514, of the Royal Library at Munich, written probably before 700. When these books were used in choir during Office the reader either read certain definitely marked passages, indicated by markings of which our existing manuscripts constantly show traces, or, in the earlier periods especially, he read on until the abbot or priest who presided gave him the signal to stop. After the 13th century, however, this type of book was much more rarely transcribed in favor of a complete lectionary with passages *in extenso*.

Illustration of the Books of Readings. During the Middle Ages considerable artistic attention was given to the illumination of books for Mass readings. E. Palazzo calls particular attention to this tradition. The Gospel Book was especially suited to elaborate decoration both with the exterior binding and the interior illustrations indicating the privileged place Sacred Scripture had in the liturgy. In the Middle Ages the Book of the Gospels was carried in procession through the church to the ambo where the deacon read from it. In medieval inventories and catalogs of church libraries and treasuries, the books of readings were called such things as ''golden book,'' ''golden text with ivory cover and precious stones,'' or ''three books adorned with gold and precious stones'' (*liber aureus, textus aureus cum tabulis eburnea et gemmis, libri III auro et gemmis ornati*), terms indicating their great value both materially and spiritually. The books of Gospels, with or without *capitulare,* then the evangeliaries, are the two main books that were illustrated. The Carolingian books of Gospels commonly have full-page paintings of the four evangelists serving as sumptuous dividers between the four Gospels. The tables of canons indicating the scriptural pericopes to be read are often framed in beautiful arches inspired by paleo-Christian subjects, such as the fountain of life and symbolic birds. The Evangeliary of Godescalc (781–183; Paris, B.N., new acq. lat. 1203), named for the scribe who signed the colophon and written for Charlemagne in the court scriptorium, contains paintings of the evangelist as well as those of the *Majestas Domini* and the fountain of life grouped together at the beginning of the book. The Gospel text is written in gold and silver letters on a purple parchment, indicating the regal destiny of this manuscript.

The Ottonian period witnessed a change in illustration of the lectionaries, especially the evangeliary. Certain scriptoria, such as Reichenau, distinguished themselves for the highly ornate evangeliaries with well-worked-out iconographic cycles adopted from the earlier Carolingian books. Most of the Ottonian evangelaries are based upon a christological cycle, which originate in biblical illustration drawn from the sacramentaries. Special attention was devoted to images of Gospel parables, similar to the iconographic tradition of the Byzantine books of the same period. The Ottonian tradition carried through in later books of readings from the Romanesque period, especially in books of German provenance. After the 12th century, the evangeliary and lectionary would diminish in artistic importance in favor of the missal and pontifical. Compared to the evangeliaries, the epistolaries never received the same important decoration during the Middle Ages.

Tridentine Liturgical Reform. One fruit of the liturgical reform of the Council of Trent was a pruning, organization, and standardization of the calendar and lectionary systems. Norman Bonneau has examined the reading assignments of the 1570 Missal of Pius V in its 1955 edition. There was a one-year cycle of readings consisting of 138 difference biblical passages. Each Sunday and feast day had two readings, the Epistle and the Gospel. The OT was read as the ''Epistle'' only on three occasions: Epiphany, Good Friday, and the Easter Vigil. The Gospel of Mark was read 4 times; Matthew, 22; Luke, 21; and John, 14 times, primarily in the Easter Season, Christmas, and Lent. There were two minor instances of *lectio continua* for the Gospels, and a number of short ones for the epistles.

As for the weekday cycle, the scriptural passages for weekday Eucharist in the Missal of Pius V were derived from the Sunday Eucharist without reference to liturgical feast or season. After the Council of Trent when the Roman Missal was being prepared, the suggestion was made and rejected that three weekday readings be provided as a choice when the Sunday reading had to be repeated. A precedent for this practice existed in the sacramentaries from the 8th century to the second half of the 19th century for masses on Wednesdays and Fridays. The ferial Masses of Lent had no reading of an epistle in the strict sense of the word. A pericope (part of a scriptural text used as a liturgical reading) from the Old Testament always took its place. Even though certain Masses,

those of the Ember Wednesdays and of the Wednesdays of the Great Scrutiny, had three readings, they still had no epistle, since the first two readings were taken from the Old Testament. The Masses of the Ember Saturdays had, by way of exception, five readings from the Old Testament before the Epistle; but this distribution was not from earlier practices—the old Roman lectionaries had either four or six readings; the reading from Daniel and the Canticle of the Three Young Men is a Gallican addition (*see* EMBER DAYS). In reducing the number of the readings from 12 to four, the *Ordo* of the Easter Vigil as revised during the pontificate of Pius XII reestablished the practice of the time of Gregory the Great, leading to the reading first from the Law then the Prophets, followed by the Apostle (Paul), and the Gospel.

By way of comparison, in the other rites of the Latin West, the method of organization varied from the Roman system. In the AMBROSIAN RITE of Milan and MOZARABIC RITE of Toledo in Spain, there were usually three readings, as in the ancient Gallican liturgy. St. Ambrose indicates the traditional order: ''First the Prophet is read, and the Apostle, and then the Gospel'' (*In psalmum CXVIII*, 17, 10, *Patrologia Latina*, ed. J. P. Migne, 271 v., indexes 4 v. [Paris 1878–90] 15, col. 1443). Various indications, in particular the number of Collects given in the early substrate of the Gelasian Sacramentary, allow a presumption that this was also the practice of the Roman Church before St. Gregory the Great. If this is the case, then the liturgies of Milan and Toledo are the guardians of the universal tradition of the West.

Readings for the Divine Office. The lectionary for Mass is distinguished from the lectionary for the Divine Office (Liturgy of the Hours). The Bible furnishes the broad contours of the Office with its psalmody, singing of the canticles of the Old and New Testaments, and the continuous reading of the Scriptures. Longer and more difficult texts, and even entire books, are read in the Office. This would not be possible at Mass. Given the difference in the cycles of Office and Mass, the different length of the readings, and the continuity of the readings within each service, the Scripture readings for the Office were not harmonized with the lectionary for Mass until Vatican II.

Although the Church has always given a large place in the Divine Office to the reading of the Bible, the place for this reading is not the same in all rites. The day Hours, including Lauds and Vespers, had only ''little chapters,'' vestiges of longer readings. During the papacy of Pius XII a new Latin version of the Office was prepared using the entire Bible with a more abundant use of the New Testament. Vatican II continued the reform of the Office and it was thus that the Constitution on the Liturgy decreed that Matins "shall be made up of fewer psalms and longer readings" (SC 89c). In 1964 when the Consilium met to implement the liturgical reforms of Vatican II, two guidelines were approved: no day without a reading from Scripture; and the Bible readings of the Office are to complement those of the Mass. Pope Paul VI promulgated the new Liturgy of the Hours in 1970 but it was not published until February 1971. The initial plan was to have two volumes: the first to contain the Psalter, the Ordinary, and the Commons; and the second volume the readings, thus constituting a true lectionary. In the end, it was decided that this format would be unwieldy. Therefore, the new Office comprises four self-contained volumes. Regarding the cycle of Scripture readings, originally a two-year cycle was planned. In view of the practical difficulties entailed, it was finally decided to include only a one-year cycle in the books containing the Liturgy of the Hours and to leave the second year of the cycle to a supplement. The supplement as a fifth volume has yet to appear.

Bibliography: P. BERNARD, "La question du nombre des lectures à la messe dans le rit romain jusqu'au VIIᵉ siècle: Quelques réflexion à propos d'un ouvrage récent," *Bibliothèque de l'École des Chartes* 151 (1993) 185–192. N. BONNEAU, *The Sunday Lectionary: Ritual Word, Paschal Shape* (Collegeville, Minn. 1992). A. CHAVASSE, *Les lectionnaires romaines de la messe au VIIᵉ et au VIIIᵉ siècle. Sources et dérivés,* 2 v. Spicilegii friburgensis Subsidia 22 (Fribourg 1993); "Les plus anciens types du lectionnaire et de l'antiphonaire romains de la messe," *Revue Bénédictine* 62 (1952) 3–94; "L'évangéliaire romain de 645: un recueil. Sa composition (façons et matériaux)," *Revue Bénédictine* 92 (1982) 33–75; "Aménagements liturgiques à Rome au VIIᵉ et au VIIIᵉ siècle," *Revue Bénédictine* 99 (1989) 75–102; "Évangéliaire, épistolier, antiphonaire et sacramentaire. Les livres romains de la messe aux VIIᵉ et VIIIᵉ siècles," *Echos d'Orient* 6 (1989) 177–225; "Après Grégoire le Grand. L'organisation des évangéliares au VIIᵉ et au VIIIᵉ siècle," in *Rituels. Mélanges offerts au P. Gy, OP,* (Paris 1990) 125–130. For a complete list of his works, as well as a treatment of his life and career, see "Hommage à M. le Pr Chavasse," *Recherches de science religieuse* 58 (1984). M. JOHNSON, *Bibliographia Liturgica: Bibliographie der Nachschlagewerke für Liturgiewissenschaft* (Rome 1992). K. GAMBER, *Codices liturgici latini antiquiores,* (Spicilegii Friburgensis subsidia, v. 1; Freiburg 1988). T. KLAUSER, *Das römische Capitulare evangeliorum* (Münster 1935). G. MORIN, "Le plus ancien Comes ou Lectionnaire de l'Eglise romaine," *Revue Bénédictine* 27 (1910) 41–74. H. P. NEUHEUSER, *Internationale Bibliographie "Liturgische Bücher": eine Auswahl kunsthistorischer und liturgiewissenschaftlicher Literatur zu liturgischen Handschriften und Drucken* (Munich 1991). É. PALAZZO, *A History of Liturgical Books from the Beginning to the Thirteenth Century* (Collegeville, Minn. 1993). C. PERROT, "The Reading of the Bible in the Ancient Synagogue," *Mikra: Text, Translation, Reading, and Interpretation of the Hebrew Bible in Ancient Judaism and Early Christianity,* ed. M. J. MULDER (Philadelphia 1988) 137–159. C. VOGEL, *Medieval Liturgy: An Introduction to the Sources Translated and Revised by William Storey and Niels Rasmussen* (Washington, D.C. 1986). G. G. WILLIS, "The Kalendar and Lectionary," in *A History of the Early Roman Liturgy,* ed. G. G. WILLIS (London 1994).

[M. S. DRISCOLL]

LECTIONARIES, II: CONTEMPORARY ROMAN CATHOLIC

Readings from Holy Scripture constitute an essential element of the Sacred Liturgy. Recognizing the importance of integrating the readings into all the rites of public worship, especially the Eucharistic liturgy, the Fathers of the Second Vatican Council in the *Constitution on the Liturgy, Sacrosanctum Concilium* (SC) declared that "Sacred Scripture is of the greatest importance in the celebration of the liturgy. For it is from it that lessons are read and explained in the homily, and psalms are sung. It is from the Scriptures that the prayers, collects and hymns draw their inspiration and their force, and that actions and signs derive their meaning" (SC 24). Further, the council mandated a reform of the liturgy that would promote an appreciation for the Scriptures by providing the faithful with "more ample, more varied and more suitable" readings at every Mass (SC 35), by opening up treasures of the Bible "more lavishly so that richer fare may be provided for the faithful at the table of God's Word. In this way, a more representative part of the Sacred Scriptures will be read to the people in the course of a prescribed number of years" (SC 51).

First *Editio Typica* of the Lectionary for Mass. As a part of the overall reform of the liturgy the Second Vatican Council ordered that the lectionary be revised, thereby increasing the number of pericopes from Sacred Scripture, particularly from the Old Testament. These new inclusions would be accommodated by the creation of a three-year cycle of Sunday readings and a two-year cycle of daily readings. Since the shift from the existing annual cycle to the new multiyear cycles was such a vast and important undertaking, Study Group (*Coetus*) 11 was engaged for the purpose of creating a suitable preliminary study for the enterprise. They created a preliminary weekday lectionary (*ordo lectionum per ferias*), which had a providential twofold effect: the appetite of the faithful was whetted for a broader taste of Sacred Scriptures; and valuable guidelines were yielded, based on the experience, for the compilation of the definitive set of readings.

In response to the council's directives, and in collaboration with *Coetus* 11, a revised Lectionary was prepared by the Consilium for the Implementation of the Constitution on the Sacred Liturgy under the title *Ordo Lectionum Missae.* The *editio typica* of the new Lectionary, approved by Pope Paul VI in the Apostolic Constitution *Missale Romanum* (April 3, 1969) and published by a letter from Benno Cardinal Gut, prefect of the Sacred Congregation for Divine Worship on Pentecost Sunday

(May 25, 1969), provided only the appropriate biblical citations for the particular celebrations.

First Edition in English Translation. The desire for greater variety in the readings was stimulated by the introduction of the vernacular languages. Repetition of the same readings—especially on weekdays, when the Scriptures of the preceding Sunday were read over and over, and in the Commons—created boredom and were not effective in promoting prayer. The Consilium for the Implementation of the Constitution on the Sacred Liturgy therefore sent a letter of publication that directed episcopal conferences to prepare vernacular editions of the *Ordo Lectionum Missae* in accordance with the consilium's 1969 instruction on vernacular translations.

The National Conference of Catholic Bishops (NCCB) in the United States published such an edition and decreed its mandatory use in the dioceses of the United States beginning with the first Sunday of Advent, Nov. 29, 1971. The biblical texts used for this edition were from the New American Bible (NAB), a translation first commissioned by the Bishops' Committee for the Confraternity of Christian Doctrine in 1944. For the next two decades, some 50 scholars of the Catholic Biblical Association labored to produce a translation of the Bible from its original languages and the oldest extant texts.

The English edition of the Lectionary, which appeared in 1970, contained the complete texts of the biblical readings and chants for the liturgy of the word in the celebration of the Mass. In addition to the texts, indices and tables indicating the use of the years in the cycle of readings provide the rationale for the arrangement of readings in the pattern of this Lectionary. For English speakers throughout the world a joint commission was established in 1963 known as the INTERNATIONAL COMMISSION ON ENGLISH IN THE LITURGY that was entrusted with the responsibility of producing English translations of liturgical texts.

Second Edition of the Lectionary for Mass. The Holy See issued a second typical edition of the *Ordo Lectionum Missae (editio typica altera),* which was approved by Pope John Paul II and published by a decree from James Cardinal Knox, Prefect of the Sacred Congregation for the Sacraments and Divine Worship on Jan. 21, 1981. The primary goal of the second edition of the Lectionary for Mass was the production of a book displaying the greatest possible fidelity to the biblical text. Being aware of the limitations of the English language, and acting in accord with *Dei Verbum*—The Constitution on Divine Revelation—which teaches that "since the Word of God must be readily available at all times, the Church, with motherly concern, sees to it that suitable and correct translations are made into various languages, especially

from the original texts of the sacred books," a working group, comprised of representatives of the Congregation for the Doctrine of the Faith, the Congregation for Divine Worship and the Discipline of the Sacraments, and the NCCB, sought a lectionary that would faithfully convey the meaning of the Greek and Hebrew scriptures. The second edition of the Lectionary for Mass (LFM) for use in the dioceses of the United States was approved by the NCCB on June 20, 1992, and confirmed by the Congregation for Divine Worship and the Discipline of the Sacraments on Oct. 6, 1997.

As with its first edition, the revised Lectionary for Mass was based on the 1970 New American Bible. The 16 years of private and liturgical use of this translation, as well as subsequent advances in biblical scholarship, led to the revision of its translation of the New Testament in 1986. The revised Lectionary for Mass therefore employs the 1986 edition of the Revised New Testament and the 1970 edition of the Old Testament, including the Psalms.

Of concern to the editors of the revised Lectionary for Mass was the development of a common scriptural vocabulary. By the preferential use of NAB vocabulary and phrases in the translation of titles (*tituli*) found above readings and in the first lines (*incipits*) of all readings, the editors attempted to develop consistent biblical-liturgical terms.

Certain changes to the base text were made both for increased precision and in the interest of accurately conveying a horizontally inclusive scriptural term as well as for greater ease in proclamation. In the first category may be included the following kinds of examples: "their holocausts" was changed to "their burnt offerings" (LFM 118); "a smoking brazier" was changed to "a smoking fire pot" (LFM 27); "seahs of flour" was changed to "measures of flour" (LFM 108C).

Two concerns were raised in a second category of inclusive language: the problem in the English language for a true generic term when referring to humanity, and the preponderance of masculine images and pronouns in reference to God. With attention to the principle of demonstrating maximum possible fidelity to the sacred text, the working group adopted three base versions for the lectionary. First, the 1986 Revised New Testament of the NAB was chosen as a translation whose primary concern was fidelity to what the text says. When the meaning of the Greek is inclusive of both sexes, the translation seeks to reproduce such inclusivity insofar as this is possible in normal English usage, without resort to inelegant circumlocutions or neologisms that would offend against the dignity of the language. Second, the working group adopted the 1970 Old Testament of the NAB, which was then modified for accuracy in rendering certain collective nouns and for the particular demands of public proclamation. Third, the working group adopted the 1970 translation of the NAB Psalter rather than the 1991 revision of this work. Because of previous critiques by Roman congregations of the 1991 translation, the working group concluded that the 1991 Psalter was unacceptable for liturgical use.

The 1989 NCCB Criteria for the Evaluation of the Use of Inclusive language in Scriptural Translations noted that the revealed word of God consistently uses a masculine reference for God. Hence, the working group avoided any use of vertical inclusivity in rendering scriptural texts.

The introduction to the second edition of the Lectionary for Mass was considerably expanded and opens with an extended theological reflection, based on conciliar and postconciliar teachings, on the significance of the Word of God in liturgical celebration. Following the example of Christ, who himself read and proclaimed the Scriptures, the liturgy is both founded on the Word of God and sustained by it. Through a variety of liturgical celebrations and other gatherings, the Word of God enriches the Church through the "unfolding mystery of Christ" in the liturgical year, while the liturgy itself enriches the word with new meaning and power. In this process all of Christ's faithful through the liturgy respond collectively and individually to the working of the Holy Spirit.

See Also: LECTIONARIES I: HISTORY; LECTIONARIES III: ECUMENICAL.

Bibliography: A. BUGNINI "The Lectionary of the Roman Missal," *The Reform of the Liturgy 1948–1975* (Collegeville, Minn. 1990) 406–425. É. PALAZZO, *A History of Liturgical Books from the Beginning to the Thirteenth Century* (Collegeville, Minn. 1993). C. VOGEL, *Medieval Liturgy: An Introduction to the Sources,* tr. and rev. by W. STOREY and N. RASMUSSEN (Washington, D.C. 1986). C. WIÉNER, "The Roman Catholic Eucharistic Lectionary," *Studia Liturgica* 21.1 (1991) 2–13. N. BONNEAU, *The Sunday Lectionary: Ritual Word, Paschal Shape* (Collegeville, Minn. 1998). E. NÜBOLD, *Entstehung und Bewertung der neuen Perikopenordnung des Römischen Ritus für die Messfeier an Sonn-und Festtagen* (Paderborn 1986).

[M. S. DRISCOLL]

LECTIONARIES, III: ECUMENICAL

In 1969 the Roman Catholic Church issued its *Ovdo lectionum Missae* (*see* LECTIONARIES, II: CONTEMPORARY). This lectionary provided a three-year cycle of Scripture readings for use during liturgical worship on the Sundays of the Catholic liturgical year, a two-year cycle of readings for the weekdays, readings for the Proper and Common of saints, and a selection of readings for ritual and votive Masses and Masses for various occasions. This system of readings was prepared in order to fulfill a mandate of the Second Vatican Council, which called for the provision of a richer share of God's word through the use of a more representative portion of Scripture during worship than had previously been the case. The effect of the Sunday lectionary in particular is that in the course of three years Catholics experience virtually the entire New Testament and a substantial selection of the Old Testament in their weekly worship.

Ecumenical Adoption. In the years immediately following the appearance of the Roman Lectionary, a number of churches in the United States and Canada adopted and adapted the Sunday portion of this lectionary to their particular denominational needs. Before the end of the 1970s the three-year lectionary (as it came to be called) existed in several major denominational forms in addition to the Roman Catholic: Episcopalian, Lutheran, Presbyterian, and United Methodist. Each of these was constructed essentially upon the principles of selection and arrangement of the 1969 Roman Catholic system of readings. Differences, where they existed, were for the most part the result of calendar questions or editorial matters, for example, the question of where to begin and end specific readings.

In the decade that followed, North American Christians benefitted from an ecumenical development that has perhaps been insufficiently recognized. On a given Sunday and in different denominational assemblies largely similar and frequently identical passages of the Bible were proclaimed and preached.

Interest in ecumenical lectionaries went beyond North America. The Joint Liturgical Group (JLG), an ecumenical association of eight churches in Great Britain, developed a lectionary that uses a two-year cycle of readings and that divides the Sundays of the year into a threefold thematic scheme.

Common Lectionary. Building upon this development, the CONSULTATION ON COMMON TEXTS (CCT) sponsored a conference on the lectionary in 1978 to determine whether it would be possible to seek greater consensus in the matter of the lectionary. The conference delegates voted unanimously in favor of seeking as much consensus as possible with the three-year lectionary. At the request of the conference participants, the CCT established a project committee of biblical and liturgical experts to carry out several specific recommendations of the conference: to produce a common calendar for the Christian year that would include common terminology for the days of the year; to produce a consensus table of readings and psalms for the Sundays of the three-year lectionary and for a few special days or feasts; and to include in this table a more representative selection of readings from the Old Testament in order to balance the nearly exclusive use of prophetic and narrowly typological passages in the Roman Lectionary.

In 1983 the CCT released the fruits of this labor under the title *Common Lectionary: The Lectionary Proposed by the Consultation on Common Texts.* This proposal was recommended to the churches and interested individuals for a period of trial use and study. On the basis of recommendations received, the CCT was to revise its proposed system of readings and calendar and then make it available in a final version for the churches. The U.S. National Conference of Catholic Bishops voted overwhelmingly to participate in the trial use of the *Common Lectionary* in selected parishes, but this action did not receive the necessary Vatican approval.

The *Common Lectionary* was an order of readings, not a printed lectionary, for use on Sundays and a few special days of the Christian liturgical year. The following were its major principles: (1) It incorporated the basic calendar and structure of three readings and psalm in the Roman lectionary; (2) the Gospel pericopes were maintained as given in the existing versions of the three-year lectionary (this was the area of least divergence between denominational systems of readings); (3) the New Testament pericopes of the existing three-year lectionaries were largely accepted, with some lengthening and minor textual arrangement; (4) the principle of semi-continuous reading, already present in the second readings and Gospel readings on the Sundays following Pentecost, was extended to the Old Testament reading on a number of the Sundays following Pentecost. This made possible the reading of major narratives from the Old Testament; (5) more selections from the minor prophets and from Wisdom literature were included.

The *Common Lectionary* was for the most part a careful harmonization of the slight variations in readings that existed in the major versions of the three-year lectionary. The semi-continuous reading of the Old Testament readings on some of the Sundays following Pentecost was the only real innovation in this lectionary proposal. Its extension to the first reading in this part of the lectionary has not meant, however, the abandonment of the typological relationship between the first reading and the Gospel, a major premise of the three-year lectionary on Sundays. A broad harmony between the two has been maintained and thus the topological principle retained, though not on a Sunday-by-Sunday basis. The narrative material that this arrangement made possible included, for Year A, 20 Sundays of selections from the

Pentateuch (beginning with Abraham's call and concluding with Moses' death); for Year B, 14 Sundays of the Davidic narrative (from David's anointing to his death); for Year C, 10 Sundays of the Elijah-Elisha narrative (beginning with Solomon's dedication of the Temple and concluding with Elisha's death).

Revised Common Lectionary. In 1983 the CCT, JLG, and other ecumenical liturgical associations joined with the INTERNATIONAL COMMISSION ON ENGLISH IN THE LITURGY (ICEL) to form the ENGLISH LANGUAGE LITURGICAL CONSULTATION (ELLC). From its inception, the ELLC played an active role in fostering the development of an international ecumenical lectionary based on feedback received from the use of the *Common Lectionary.* The fruit of its endeavors was a revised edition published under the title *Revised Common Lectionary* (RCL), which incorporated much of the feedback and suggestions received from the trial use of the *Common Lectionary.*

The RCL retained the foundational three-year cycle of the Roman Lectionary, with a virtually identical liturgical calendar. The NT epistle and gospel readings are almost always the same. There are two major differences between the RCL and the Roman Lectionary. First, in the OT readings in ordinary time, the RCL abandons the Roman typological model in favor of a broader system which links the Patriarchal and Mosaic narratives (i.e., from Genesis to Judges) for Year A (Matthew), the Davidic and Wisdom narratives for Year B (Mark), and a broad selection of Major and Minor Prophets (Elijah, Elisha, Amos, Hosea, Isaiah, Jeremiah, Joel and Habbakuk) for Year C (Luke). Second, an attempt was made in the RCL to include women and their role in salvation history by providing texts about women never heard on Sunday before. In the Roman Lectionary these readings are found in the two-year weekday lectionary cycle, and not in the three-year Sunday cycle.

The RCL was widely adopted by major Protestant churches worldwide, making it a truly ecumenical lectionary. Some of the churches that officially adopted the RCL include the American Baptist Churches in the United States of America, the Anglican Church of Australia, the Anglican Church of Canada, the Christian Church [Disciples of Christ], the Christian Reformed Church in North America, the Church of England, the Anglican Church in South Africa, the Evangelical Lutheran Church in America (ELCA), the Evangelical Lutheran Church in Canada, the Presbyterian Church in Canada, the Presbyterian Church in the United States of America, the United Church of Canada, the United Church of Christ, and the United Methodist Church.

Bibliography: *The Revised Common Lectionary* (Nashville, Tenn. 1992). C. J. SCHLUETER, ''The Gender Balance of Texts from the Gospels: The Revised Common Lectionary and the Lutheran Book of Worship," *Currents in Theology and Mission* 20 (June 1993) 177–186. P. C. BOWER, *Handbook for the Revised Common Lectionary* (Louisville, Ky. 1996). J. C. ROCHELLE, "Notes on the Revised Common Lectionary," *Currents in Theology and Mission* 23 (Feb. 1996) 29–37.

[J. M. SCHELLMAN/EDS.]

LECTIONARY FOR MASSES WITH CHILDREN

The *Lectionary for Masses with Children* (LMC) adapts the Roman Lectionary for Mass (1981) to the needs and capacities of pre-adolescent children. The aim of the LMC is to nourish the faith of children and lead them to full participation in the worship of the whole assembly. The translation of the scriptures used is the Contemporary English Version (CEV), a translation from the original languages prepared specifically for children by the American Bible Society.

The publication of a LMC follows the recommendation of the Directory for Masses with Children published by the Congregation for Divine Worship (no. 43) and approved by Pope Paul VI in 1973. The National Conference of Catholic Bishops of the United States approved the *Lectionary for Masses with Children* in November 1991 and the Apostolic See granted permission for an experimental use of the lectionary in 1992. The LMC is best understood within the broader context of the Directory, the General Instruction of the Roman Missal, and the Introduction to the Lectionary for Mass.

Principles and Directives. Part One of the Introduction of the LMC reflects on the importance of the celebration of the word of God for the formation of the community. Part Two provides basic principles for liturgies of the word with children: 1) the Gospel is always read; 2) a liturgical dismissal is used when children occasionally celebrate a separate liturgy of the word; 3) and a homily by the priest or an explanation of the readings by one of the adults is given at Masses with children.

Part Three discusses the purpose and provides foundational principles. This section also underlines some basic principles of liturgical catechesis such as the formative influence of liturgy; the need to involve children in the actions of the liturgy as well as to appeal to the intuitive nature of children through the use of ritual elements and symbols; and the liturgy of the word is ritual prayer and not an instructional session. The final section of part three includes catechetical notes on the relationship of the lectionary to the liturgical year and on the way in which the Church's calendar expresses and shapes Christian identity.

Part Four treats "Particular Issues" connected with the liturgy of the word celebrated with children. It examines the place of celebration, objects used in celebration, the importance of the use of music, and the need to preserve the common format of the full assembly in the liturgies for children.

The LMC may be used at Sunday Masses when there are large numbers of children present along with adults (although proper balance and consideration for the entire assembly requires that LMC should not be used exclusively or even preferentially), at a separate liturgy of the word with children, or at other liturgical celebrations within the context of the liturgical year. On Christmas Day, Epiphany, Sundays of Lent, Easter Sunday, Ascension, and Pentecost, the universal lectionary takes precedence. The readings from the children's lectionary may be used only when the celebration of the liturgy of the word for the children is held in a place apart from the main assembly.

The Content of the Lectionary. The LMC follows the content and arrangement of readings for the three cycles of Sundays, the proper of seasons, solemnities, and feasts of the Lord in the Roman Lectionary. All three readings for Sunday are included when they are suitable for use with children. At least one reading is always given in addition to the Gospel and common texts for sung responsorial psalms are included.

Sets of readings that reflect the liturgical and theological motifs of the major seasons are provided for weekdays of the year (seasons and Ordinary Time). The final section of the lectionary is comprised of Gospel acclamations for weekdays in Ordinary Time, the Proper of the Saints, Common of the Saints, ritual Masses and Masses for special occasions.

Bibliography: C.K. DOOLEY, *To Listen and Tell: Introduction to the Lectionary for Masses with Children with Commentary* (Washington, DC 1993). P. MAZAR and R. PIERCY, *A Guide to the Lectionary for Masses with Children* (Chicago 1993).

[C. DOOLEY]

LECTOR

Historically, the lector was the second of the minor orders leading to the priesthood. Readings from the sacred books are an important part of Christian worship. Originally, this task was entrusted to lay persons, but by the end of the second century it had become the function of a special order. As time went on, however, the lectorate lost its importance. In the Western Church the reading of the Epistle and Gospel was reserved to the subdeacon and the deacon respectively.

By the apostolic letter, *Ministeria quaedam*, dated Aug. 15, 1972, Pope Paul VI suppressed, among other things, the minor order of the lector. Under present legislation, only men may be instituted into the ministry of lector by the ordinary (see CIC canon 230 §1). Requirements for admission into the ministry of lector are: (1) the presentation of a petition freely made out and signed by the aspirant to the ordinary who has the right to accept the petition; (2) a suitable age and special qualities to be determined by the episcopal conference; (3) a firm will to give faithful service to God and the Christian people (Paul VI *Ministeria quaedam* VIII). The lector is appointed and instituted to fulfill the following functions in the liturgy: (1) to read the lessons from sacred Scripture, except for the Gospel, in the Mass and other liturgical celebrations; (2) to recite the psalm between the readings when there is no psalmist; (3) to present the intentions for the General Intercessions in the absence of the deacon or cantor; (4) to direct the singing and the participation of the faithful. The lector "may also instruct the faithful for the worthy reception of the sacraments," (and) "take care of preparing other faithful who by a temporary appointment are to read the Scriptures in liturgical celebrations" (ibid. V). To assure the authenticity of this ministry's exercise, *Ministeria quaedam* directed episcopal conferences to set suitable intervals "interstices" which "should be observed between the conferring of the ministries of lector and acolyte whenever more than one ministry is conferred on the same person" (ibid. X). The NCCB set the interval between the two institutions as six months at its regular meeting in November 1973. While institution in the lay ministries is required before diaconal ordination, it is not limited to candidates for the order of deacon or priest. However, the exclusion of women from institution in the ministry of lector has made of this office a step before ordination in the U.S. and in many other countries, much as the former minor order of lector was a step on the way to priesthood. Both women and men without formal institution may fulfill all the functions of a lector by temporary designation under the provisions of CIC canon 230 §2.

Bibliography: M. ANDRIEU, "Les Ordres mineurs dans l'ancien rite romain," *Revue des sciences religieuses* 5 (Strasbourg 1925) 232–274. W. CROCE, "Die niederen Weihen und ihre hierarchische Wertung," *Zeitschrift für katholische Theologie* 70 (Vienna 1948) 257–314. *The Institution of Readers*, Eng. tr., ICEL (Washington, D.C. 1976). Bishops' Committee on the Liturgy, *Study Text III, Ministries in the Church: Commentary on the Apostolic Letters of Pope Paul VI, "Ministeria quaedam" and "Ad pascendum"* (Washington, D.C. 1974); *Newsletter* 11 (1975) 4. *Notitiae* 60 (1971) 20.

[T. J. RILEY/J. A. GURRIERI/EDS.]

LEDESMA, PEDRO DE

Thomistic theologian; b. Salamanca, *c.* 1550; d. Salamanca, Sept. 9, 1616. After becoming a Dominican in 1563, he taught theology for more than 40 years at Segovia, Avila, and Salamanca where he occupied the chair of Durandus (moral theology and liturgy) from 1604, and the second chair of St. Thomas (dogmatic theology) from 1608. Ledesma was noted for his great erudition, virtuous life, and defense of the absolute Thomism of BAÑEZ. He is unjustifiably named a forerunner of PROBABILISM. Among his works are: *De divinae gratiae auxiliis* (1611); *De magno matrimonii sacramento* (1592); *De divina perfectione* (1596); *Primera parte* and *Segunda parte de la Summa* (1598), a two-volume commentary on the sacramental theology of St. Thomas; and the *Doctrina Christiana* (1598).

Bibliography: J. QUÉTIF and J. ÉCHARD, *Scriptores Ordinis Praedicatorum* (New York 1959) 2.1:404–405. D. CHENU, *Dictionnaire de théologie catholique,* ed. A. VACANT et al. (Paris 1903–50) 9:126–127. A. MICHELITSCH, *Kommentatoren zur Summa Theologiae des hl. Thomas v. Aquin* (Graz 1924) 53, 163.

[M. MARKOWSKI]

LEDÓCHOWSKA, MARIA TERESA, BL.

Foundress of the Sodality of St. Peter Claver for African Missions (now the MISSIONARY SISTERS OF ST. PETER CLAVER); b. Loosdorf, Austria, April 29, 1863; d. Rome, July 6, 1922. She was the daughter of Count Antonius Kalka-Ledóchowski, the sister of Wladimir LEDÓCHOWSKI, superior general of the Jesuits, and (Bl.) Urszula LEDÓCHOWSKA and niece of Cardinal Miecysław LEDÓCHOWSKI. After living at Salzburg in the court of the grand duchess of Tuscany (1885–90), Countess Ledóchowska came under the influence of Cardinal Charles LAVIGERIE and dedicated herself entirely to the abolition of slavery and to the evangelization of Africa. In 1894 she founded a religious congregation to aid the missions of Africa directly or indirectly. For the remainder of her life she acted as the sodality's superior general. She recognized the importance of the press for the mission apostolate and started the periodical *Echo of Africa*. The polyglot printing plants that she established have published millions of copies of catechisms and other religious works in native languages. She was beatified Oct. 19, 1975 by Paul VI.

Bibliography: *Maria Terésa Ledóchowska i misje: praca zbiorowa,* eds. B. BEJZE, J. GUCWY, and A. KOSZORZA (Warsaw 1977). V. BIELAK, *The Servant of God, Mary Theresa Countess Ledóchowska, Foundress of the Sodality of Saint Peter Claver* (2d ed. St. Louis, Mo. 1944). M. and G. MAGNOCAVALLO, *Vita della fedel*

Serva di Dio Maria Teresa Contessa Ledóchowska (Rome 1940). G. PAPÁSOGLI, *Maria Teresa Ledóchowska* (Rome *c.* 1950). M. WINOWSKA, *Allez dans le monde entier: l'appel de Marie-Thérèse Ledochowska* (Paris 1975).

[P. MOLINARI]

LEDÓCHOWSKA, URSZULA (URSULA), BL.

Baptized Julia Maria, founder of the Ursuline Sisters of the Agony of Jesus in Gethsemane; b. April 17, 1865, Loosdorf, Austria (now Lipnica Murowana near Tarnów, Poland); d. May 29, 1939, Rome, Italy. Urszula was born into a privileged family of Count Antonius Kalka-Ledóchowski and his Swiss wife; the sister of Maria Teresa LEDÓCHOWSKA and Wladimir LEDÓCHOWSKI, superior general of the Jesuits; and niece of Cardinal Miecysław LEDÓCHOWSKI. Following financial setbacks the family moved to Saint Poelten (1873), where her father died two years later. Urszula founded a congregation of Ursulines, known as the Gray Ursulines, at Pniewy (near Poznán). She shared the benefits of her privileged family life by caring for and teaching young people. In 1907, she left Krakow to work in St. Petersburg, Russia. Three years later she moved the boarding school for Polish girls from St. Petersburg to Karelia, Finland, until she herself left Russia for Scandinavia (1914). After receiving papal approbation from Benedict XV following the war, the Gray Ursulines spread throughout Poland and beyond. Urszula was called to Rome by the Holy See, where she inspired many Catholic institutions. She was beatified by Pope John Paul II, June 20, 1983, at Poznán, Poland.

Feast: May 29.

Bibliography: T. BOJARSKA, *W imie trzech krzyzy: opowiesc o Julii Urszuli Ledóchowskiej i jej zgromadzeniu* (Warsaw 1981). J. LEDÓCHOWSKA, *Zycie dla innych: blogoslawiona Urszula Ledóchowska* (Poznán 1984). *Acta Apostolicae Sedis* (1987) 1264–68. *L'Osservatore Romano,* Eng. ed. 27 (1983) 10–11.

[K. I. RABENSTEIN]

LEDÓCHOWSKI, MIESCYSŁAW HALKA

Polish cardinal, archbishop, count; b. Górki, near Klimontów, Poland, Oct. 29, 1822; d. Rome, July 22, 1902. After attending the Gymnasiums in Radom and Warsaw, he continued his higher studies in Warsaw and Rome and obtained doctorates in theology and canon law. In 1845 he was ordained. After several years of service in the papal Secretariate of State, he was appointed *audi-* *tor* in the nunciature in Portugal. From 1855 to 1860 he was apostolic delegate extraordinary in Colombia and Chile. After his consecration as a titular bishop on Nov. 3, 1861, he served as nuncio in Belgium (1861–66). On December 8, 1866, Pope Pius IX named him archbishop of Gniezno and Poznań (German, Gnesen and Posen). In this office he showed special concern for the proper training of his clergy and the care of souls. At VATICAN COUNCIL I he was a member of the commission dealing with dogmatic questions. In 1870 he journeyed to Versailles to induce Otto von Bismarck to support the restoration of the STATES OF THE CHURCH. When the KULTURKAMPF in Prussia endangered Polish Catholicism, Ledóchowski dedicated the archbishoprics of Gniezno and Poznań to the Sacred Heart of Jesus. He insisted that religion be taught in Polish and permitted religious instruction in German only for the highest classes of the Gymnasium. Because of his failure to observe the May Laws issued by the Prussian government, he was fined 30,000 taler (about $90,000). On Nov. 24, 1873, the governor of the Province of Posen demanded his resignation from his episcopal office. Upon his refusal, he was arrested on Feb. 3, 1874 and interned at Ostrów. The Prussian court for ecclesiastical affairs ordered his removal from office and forced the cathedral chapter to elect a successor, but the archbishop's authority actually increased during his detention (1874–76). Pope Pius IX called him ''the brave defender of the faith'' and upon making him a cardinal (1875) compared him with John FISHER. After his release, he was forbidden to reside in his sees or in the neighboring provinces. When he issued regulations for his archdioceses from Rome, he was again fined by the German government for ''usurpation of episcopal rights.'' During the negotiations leading to the settlement of the Kulturkampf, he resigned from his archbishoprics (February 1886). Meanwhile, beginning in 1883 he had been serving in the papal Secretariate of State; in 1885 he was made secretary of papal briefs. He was a highly respected member of several Roman congregations and served as prefect of the Congregation for the PROPAGATION OF THE FAITH (1892–1902). He was skeptical of the efforts of the Holy See to reach an understanding with Russia and even expressed opposition. In 1927 his remains were transferred from Rome to the cathedral of Poznań.

Bibliography: J. B. KISSLING, *Geschichte des Kulturkampfes im Deutschen Reiche,* 3 v. (Freiburg 1911–16). W. KLIMKIEWICZ, *Kardynal Ledóchowski na tle swej epoki, 1822–1902,* 2 v. (Cracow 1938–39). E. WINTER, *Russland und die slawischen Völker in der Diplomatie des Vatikans, 1878–1903* (Berlin 1950). A. MERCATI and A. PELZER, *Dizionario ecclesiastico,* 3 v. (Turin 1954–58) 2:621–622. G. MARON, *Die Religion in Geschichte und Gegenwart,* 6 v. (Tübingen 1957–63) 4:261–262.

[B. STASIEWSKI]

LEDÓCHOWSKI, WLADIMIR

Superior general of the JESUITS; b. Loosdorf, Austria, Oct. 7, 1866; d. Rome, Dec. 13, 1942. He was the son of Count Antonius Kalka-Ledóchowski, the brother of Maria T. LEDÓCHOWSKA, and the nephew of Cardinal Miecysław LEDÓCHOWSKI. During his secondary school studies at the Theresianum in Vienna, he was a page for the Austrian empress. After studying law for a year at the University of Cracow, he began to study for the secular priesthood in 1885 at Tarnów and continued them at the Gregorian University in Rome. In 1889 he joined the Jesuits and was ordained in 1894. He was appointed successively writer, superior of the residence in Cracow, and then rector of the college there, vice-provincial (1901) and provincial (1902) of the Galicia province. He acted as assistant for the German assistancy from 1906 until Feb. 11, 1915, when he was elected the 26th superior general of the order. During his term in this post (1915–42) assistancies increased in number from five to eight; provinces, from 26 to 50; missions, from 29 to 46; missionaries, from 971 to 3,785; members from 16,946 to 26,588. Ledóchowski was responsible also for the new codification of the order's constitutions after the promulgation of the Code of Canon Law; the reorganization of the superior general's curia; changes in the *RATIO STUDIORUM*; the notable impetus given to the Jesuit institutions of higher studies in Rome, including the Pontifical Oriental Institute and the Russian College (which was confided to the Jesuits during Ledóchowski's generalate); the promotion of publications, especially scientific ones; the vigorous impulse to the work of the SPIRITUAL EXERCISES, to sodalities of the Blessed Virgin, and to the APOSTLESHIP OF PRAYER. His numerous letters and instructions to Jesuits promoted IGNATIAN SPIRITUALITY. Ledóchowski was noted for keen perception, knowledge of men and of conditions throughout the world, spiritual firmness, and indefatigable labor.

Bibliography: *Selected Writings of Father Ledóchowski* (Chicago 1945). L. KOCH, *Jesuiten-Lexikon; Die Gesellschaft Jesu einst und jetzt* (Paderborn 1934) 1085–1088. J. H. SLATTERY, "In Memoriam: VI. Ledóchowski," *Woodstock Letters* 72 (1943): 1–20. G. CASSIANI INGONI, *Il p. W. Ledóchowski* (Rome 1945), uncritical.

[P. MOLINARI]

LEE, EDWARD

Archbishop of York (1531–44); b. Kent, *c.* 1482; d. York, Sept. 13, 1544. He was the son of Richard Lee, a country gentleman of Delee Magna, Kent. He was a bachelor of arts and fellow of Magdalen College, Oxford, and then received his M.A. from Cambridge in 1504. After a succession of ecclesiastical positions at Wells, Norfolk, and Lincoln, he became King Henry VIII's chaplain in 1518 and was groomed by Cardinal Thomas Wolsey for diplomatic service. From 1517 to 1520, this boyhood friend of Thomas More carried on a sharp literary controversy with Erasmus over the latter's revised version of the New Testament. Lee accused Erasmus of plagiarism, and the quarrel has led historians to describe Lee as an opponent of the new learning. Lee, however conservative in literary and religious matters, was never an obscurantist or a reactionary. He served King Henry VIII on several diplomatic missions to Austria (1523), Spain (1529), and Bologna (1530). His rapid promotions to king's almoner, the archdeaconry of Colchester, chancellor of Salisbury, and finally the archbishopric of York in 1531 were due in large measure to his efficient service. The archbishop supported King Henry VIII in his opposition to papal claims in English affairs, but he was very uncomfortable with Henry's doctrine of royal supremacy over the Church and refused to sign an agreement calling the king's first marriage void from the beginning (1533). When taken prisoner during the Pilgrimage of Grace (1536) and fearful for his life, Lee swore an oath supporting the rebellion. He later opposed the rebels, and despite royal annoyance at his somewhat hasty action retained the approval of Thomas Cromwell. A disciplinarian, the archbishop kept good order in his archdiocese. He loyally supported the Act of Six Articles in 1539 and issued new statutes for the governing of York. An opponent of Lutheranism and of Tyndale's Bible, Lee, like Bishops Stephen Gardiner, Cuthbert Tunstall, and Edmund Bonner, was a Henrician doctrinal conservative who once confessed that he owed "all things save his soul" to the king. These bishops observed the tradition of obedience to the king and state, a principle universal to Tudor England and one that had a marked effect on conservative and reformer alike.

Bibliography: W. HUNT, *The Dictionary of National Biography from the Earliest Times to 1900*, 63 v. (London 1885–1900) 11:788–790. P. HUGHES, *The Reformation in England*, rev. ed. 3 v. in 1 (New York 1963). L. B. SMITH, *Tudor Prelates and Politics, 1536–1558* (Princeton 1953).

[P. S. MCGARRY]

LEEN, EDWARD

Educator, retreat master, and spiritual writer; b. Abbeyfeale, Ireland, Aug. 17, 1885; d. Dublin, Nov. 10, 1944. Edward Thomas Leen grew up in a deeply religious family, which produced three priests, including Archbishop James Leen, CSSp, of Mauritius. Educated at Rockwell College, Cashel, he made his profession in the Congregation of the Holy Ghost at Chevilly, France, in

1909. After studying philosophy at University College, Dublin, he went to Rome in 1912, where he earned his doctorate in theology *summa cum laude* at the Gregorian University and earned the Pius X gold medal for excellence in dogmatic theology. After working for two years as a missionary in Nigeria, he returned to Dublin and became dean of studies and subsequently president of Blackrock College. He played a prominent role in the founding of the Missionary Sisters of the Holy Rosary (1924). In 1930 he joined the staff of the Spiritan Senior Seminary in Ireland, of which he became president in 1939. In the same year he made a tour of the United States, lecturing and preaching in many places. He was happy to note, "Far from finding people who were materialistic in their outlook, I have come in contact with a spirituality which has astounded me, and I would say abashed me."

A widely read spiritual writer, Leen established his reputation with a series of books that appeared rapidly after 1935. His spiritual outlook was deeply influenced by Dom Marmion, OSB, and Francis Libermann, CSSp. All his writings are thoroughly centered on Christ and present a synthesis of Christian wisdom, linking the person's own spiritual life to that of Christ.

His philosophy of Christian humanism, expounded in *What Is Education?* (1943), gave rise to many controversies, but its plea that catechetical instruction take a psychological rather than logical approach and stress God's love and mercy rather than His justice has finally been heard. His other works are *Progress in Mental Prayer* (1935); *In the Likeness of Christ* (1936); *The Holy Ghost* (1937); *Why the Cross?* (1938); *The True Vine and Its Branches* (1938); *The Church Before Pilate* (1939); and *The Voice of a Priest*, ed. by Bernard J. Kelly, CSSp (1946).

Bibliography: M. O'CARROLL, *Edward Leen, C.S.Sp.* (Westminster, Md. 1953).

[H. J. KOREN]

LEEUW, GERARDUS VAN DER

Protestant theologian, leading representative of the phenomenological interpretation of religion; b. The Hague, March 18, 1890; d. Utrecht, Nov. 18, 1950. He was a professor at the University of Groningen from 1918 to 1950, but he also served as minister of education, art, and science, from 1945 to 1946. In his thought, he was influenced by N. Söderblom, R. Otto, L. Lévy-Bruhl, and R. Bultmann. He was concerned primarily with the systematic description of the phenomenon of religion, in which the history of religion had a central place. In his treatment of the primitive mentality, he made a sharp distinction between the primitive and the modern. He found no place for God in the earliest form of religion, but he maintained that this form was based on *Mana*. He was an artist as well as a scientist. Many of his students have made contributions in the religious aspects of music, dance, and drama. His concept of the primitive was criticized by his successor at Groningen, T. P. van Baaren, in his book *Wij Mensen* (Utrecht 1960).

Bibliography: Works. *Phänomenologie der Religion* (Tübingen 1933; 2d ed. 1956); Eng. *Religion in Essence and Manifestation,* tr. J. E. TURNER (London 1938); *Inleiding to de phaenomenologie von de godsdienst* (Haarlem 1948); German tr. with rev., *Einführung in die Phänomenologie der Religion* (Gütersloh 1957); *Vom Heiligen in der Kunst* (3d ed. *ibid.* 1957); Eng., *Sacred and Profane Beauty,* tr. D. F. GREEN (New York 1963). Literature. J. HAEKEL, *Lexikon für Theologie und Kirche,* 10 v. (Frieburg 1957–65) 6:875. G. LANCZKOWSKI, *Die Religion in Geschichte und Gegenwart,* 6 v. (Tübingen 1957–63) 4:262. F. SIERKSMA, *Prof. Dr. Gerardus van der Leeuw* (Amsterdam 1951).

[H. M. M. FORTMANN]

LEFEBVRE, MARCEL

Missionary, bishop of Tulle (France), titular archbishop and superior general of the HOLY GHOST FATHERS; b. Tourcoing, France, Nov. 29, 1905; d. Martigny, Switzerland, March 25, 1991. Marcel Lefebvre was one of eight children of René and Gabrielle Lefebvre. Madame Lefebvre, a pious but demanding mother who predicted that her son Marcel would play a "great role" in the church, died in 1938. Marcel's father, a rigid disciplinarian with monarchist political views, was active in the French underground during World War II. Captured by the Nazis, he died in Sonnenburg Prison at age 62 in 1944.

Marcel studied for the priesthood at the French seminary in Rome. After receiving degrees in philosophy and theology, he was ordained on Sept. 21, 1929 and subsequently appointed to the working-class parish of Marias-de-Lomme, an industrial suburb of Lille, France. Three years later, through the influence of his older brother René, a priest member of the Holy Ghost Fathers, Marcel joined the same congregation. He was sent to Gabon, where he served as rector of a seminary and in various missionary apostolates in French Equatorial Africa.

Lefebvre returned to France in 1945 to head the training school of the Holy Ghost Fathers at Mortain. Two years later he returned to Africa, was ordained a bishop, and named vicar-apostolic of Dakar by Pope Pius XII. In September 1948, Lefebvre was appointed apostolic delegate for the whole of French-speaking Africa, a position he held for the next 11 years. He returned again to

France in 1959 and was appointed bishop of the diocese of Tulle by Pope John XXIII. In 1962, when he was elected superior general of the Holy Ghost Fathers, the pope named him titular archbishop of Synnada in Phrygia.

Between 1960 and 1962, Archbishop Lefebvre served on the Central Preparatory Commission charged with producing the schemata presented at the Second Vatican Council. Although he later professed that he approached Vatican II with high hopes and an open mind, his work on the Preparatory Commission quickly led to disillusionment. During the Council debates, Lefebvre's opposition to the new theological currents intensified. He was a founder of the International Group of Fathers (Coetus Internationalis Patrum) an organization of conservative prelates who maneuvered to uphold tradition against the liberal-progressive elements pressing for change. Lefebvre sided with the conservatives in all the major Council debates and refused to sign the conciliar documents on the Church in the Modern World (*Gaudium et Spes*) and the Declaration on Religious Liberty (*Dignitatis Humanae*).

Seminary at Econe. In 1968 Lefebvre resigned as head of the Holy Ghost Fathers in a dispute with members of the Chapter General over reform of the order in keeping with the Council directives. He then moved to Rome to retire but, by his own account, was sought out by a group of young men who were looking for someone to direct them in traditional priestly formation. Lefebvre, who had previously directed a small group of conservative seminarians to the French seminary in Rome, subsequently encouraged them to pursue their studies at the University of Fribourg in Switzerland. He abandoned this course of action when he became convinced that the university—like the Church itself—was "infected" with modernism. In June 1969 he gained permission from Bishop Charriere of Fribourg to establish a house for seminarians and with the approval of Bishop Adam of Sion, Lefebvre obtained a large house belonging to the canons of Saint Bernard in the canton of Valias, Switzerland. This property became the Econe seminary, opening formally on Oct. 7, 1970. The following month, Bishop Charriere canonically established Lefebvre's priestly fraternity as the *Fraternité Sacredotale de Pie X* (the Society of Saint Pius X)—named after the Pope known as the "scourge of modernists."

Lefebvre's seminary quickly developed a reputation as a traditionalist stronghold committed to the Tridentine rite, to Thomistic theology, and to a general repudiation of the reforms of Vatican II. In the fall of 1974, in response to Lefebvre's escalating critique of the Council and continuing use of the (then prohibited) Tridentine Mass, and in response to pressures from French bishops

Archbishop Marcel Lefebvre speaking during the public Mass marking the 50th anniversary of his ordination, Paris, 1979. (AP/Wide World)

who opposed Lefebvre's "rebel seminary," the Vatican announced an investigation of Econe. On November 21, in reaction to the "scandal" occasioned by remarks made by the two Belgian priests who carried out the visitation, Lefebvre issued an acerbic declaration denouncing the neo-modernist and neo-Protestant tendencies that were contributing to the "demolition of the Church, to the ruin of the priesthood, to the destruction of the Holy Sacrifice of the Mass and the sacraments, to the disappearance of religious life, and to naturalist and Teilhardian teaching in universities, seminaries, and catechetics. . . ." Lefebvre renounced the new Mass as the preeminent symbol of all postconciliar trends opposed to "orthodoxy and the never-changing Magisterium." He pronounced Vatican II "entirely corrupt" and asserted that fidelity to the true Church could only be assured by a "categorical refusal" of the Council.

In February 1975, Lefebvre was asked to go to Rome for a "discussion" with curia officials. Shortly after the meeting, his Declaration was condemned as "unacceptable on all points." In spite of this reprimand, a public rebuke by Pope Paul VI, and an order to close his seminary, Lefebvre continued his traditionalist initiatives. On July 22, 1976 he was officially suspended *a divinis* for refusing a direct Vatican order prohibiting ordinations. Defying the suspension in August, the ''rebel archbishop'' gave a controversial and emotional sermon during a public and previously planned Mass at Lille. He denounced the ''bastard sacraments,'' the ''adulterous union of the Church with the Revolution,'' and the ecumenical dialogues with Protestants—while reiterating the call for the re-establishment of the temporal power of the Church wherever possible.

For the next 12 years, communication between Lefebvre and the Vatican remained open. The archbishop corresponded with Pope Paul VI and his successors and answered various doctrinal queries from the Vatican. While these discussions proceeded without resolve, Lefebvre's priestly fraternity steadily expanded its international network of traditionalist publishing enterprises, chapels, schools, priories, and seminaries. Lefebvre traveled extensively on behalf of the Society, giving spiritual conferences to his priests and supporters and bringing the traditional sacraments to beleaguered groups of traditionalist Catholics.

Excommunication and Death. Following the election of Pope John Paul II (1978) the atmosphere in Rome regarding the ''Econe affair'' turned more conciliatory. Lefebvre met personally with John Paul II on Nov. 18, 1978. Although the expectation of rapprochement was high, negotiations between Lefebvre and the Vatican remained at an impasse throughout the 1980s. In 1983, Lefebvre retired as superior general of the Society and chose Father Franz Schmidberger, a German priest, as his successor.

While appearing publicly irenic and willing to reach some accommodation with Church officialdom, Lefebvre continued to equivocate on his position on Vatican II and on the doctrinal integrity of the new (Novus Ordo) Mass. In October 1983, he increased pressure on the Vatican by intimating that he would ordain an episcopal successor, with or without papal permission.

Aging and in ill health, Lefebvre renewed this threat again in 1987 during the June ordinations at Econe when he announced his ''Operation Survival'' for tradition. A new round of Vatican negotiations ensued, culminating the following year in the archbishop's signing a May 5, 1988 protocol granting him much of the substance of his previous demands: official recognition of the Society, semi-independence from diocesan bishops, and permission to continue to use the Tridentine liturgy. On the critical issue of a successor, Lefebvre received permission to ordain one bishop.

The long-sought solution to the ''Econe problem'' proved short-lived, however. Lefebvre promptly with-

drew his assent to the protocol the following day. Insisting that the Vatican was stalling and had not collaborated effectively, he demanded a June 30 date for the ordinations and the right to ordain more than one episcopal successor. These demands were refused. Lefebvre, in turn, proceeded with his plans to ''perpetuate tradition'' in spite of a flurry of last minute Vatican pleas. On June 30, 1988, under a tent church constructed in the shadow of his flagship seminary in Econe, he ordained four of his priests as bishops. Lefebvre and his new bishops incurred immediate excommunication—along with Bishop Antonio de Castro Mayer of Campos, Brazil, a longtime supporter of Lefebvre's, who attended the ordinations.

Following his excommunication, Lefebvre's contact with the Vatican diminished, although several overtures were undertaken from Rome to reopen the conversation. Through his writing and public pronouncements, Lefebvre maintained that his excommunication was ''absolutely null and void.'' His denunciations of Vatican II, the conciliar Church, the de-Christianization of society, and the subversion of Catholicism by a cabal of Freemasons, communists, and liberal and modernist forces within it continued unabated.

In the early hours of March 25, 1991, following surgery for the removal of an abdominal tumor, Marcel Lefebvre died in Martigny in the Canton of Valais near Econe, Switzerland.

Archbishop Lefebvre's serene and tranquil public demeanor and deep personal piety belied a resolute and doctrinaire mind. His many years of seminary and episcopal experience sharpened his administrative acumen and political sagacity in dealing with the internal affairs of his expanding priestly fraternity and with Vatican officials. To his opponents and detractors he was an incorrigible reactionary whose conservative religious views and rigid ecclesiology paralleled the *ancien regime* political thinking of France's extreme right-wing elements. From the magisterial perspective Lefebvre became a recalcitrant and disobedient servant who refused to recognize an ecumenical council, broke the bonds of ecclesial unity, and led his followers into a schism because of his ''incomplete and contradictory'' notion of the Church's living tradition.

To many of his supporters, however, the French archbishop was a ''saint,'' a modern day Athanasius, an instrument of Providence who heroically exposed the ''false spirit'' of Vatican II and who acted to save the Church from its betrayal by a modernist bureaucracy and the forces of subversion that had long conspired against it.

Throughout his controversy with the Vatican, the ''rebel archbishop'' presented his actions in the rhetoric of classical sectarianism: as pristine and uncorrupted initiatives through which he and his supporters alone maintained continuity with the true faith. He died professing that he had done no more than "hand down" what he had received by his own training and ecclesial mandate.

Bibliography: Y. CONGAR. *Challenge to the Church: The Case of Archbishop Lefebvre* (Huntington IN 1976). J. HANU, *Vatican Encounter: Conversations with Archbishop Lefebvre,* trans. E. Shosberger (Kansas City KS 1978). M. DAVIES, *Apologia Pro Marcel Lefebvre,* Vols. I, II, III (Dickinson TX 1980, 1984, 1988). M. LEFEBVRE, *A Bishop Speaks: Writings and Addresses, 1963-1975* (Edinburgh n.d.); *I Accuse the Council* (Dickinson TX 1982); *An Open Letter to Confused Catholics* (Herefordshire, England 1986). F. LAISNEY, *Archbishop Lefebvre and the Vatican, 1987-1988* (Dickinson TX 1989). W. DINGES, "Roman Catholic Traditionalism," in M.E. MARTY and R.S. APPLEBY, eds., *Fundamentalisms Observed,* Vol. I (Chicago 1991): 66-101. *The Angelus* XI:7 (July 1988); XIV:5/6 (May/June 1991).

[W. D. DINGES]

LEFEVERE, PETER PAUL

Bishop, missionary; b. Roulers, Bruges, Belgium, April 29, 1804; d. Detroit, Mich., March 4, 1869. He was the son of Charles and Albertine (Muylle) Lefevere. After study at the Lazarist seminary in Paris, he was sent to Missouri, where he completed his theology at The Barrens in Perryville. He was ordained by Bishop Gabriel Rosati of St. Louis, Mo., on Nov. 20, 1831, and then was pastor for seven years in Salt River, a parish covering eight stations in Missouri, four in Illinois, and two in Wisconsin. His work earned him appointment as administrator and coadjutor of Detroit, and he was consecrated on Nov. 21, 1841. He began his episcopate in a diocese that was disorganized and financially distressed. Lefevere recruited priests from Belgium, and in 1844 he introduced the Daughters of Charity, the first of a number of teaching sisterhoods to come to Michigan. To bring discipline to clergy and laity, he issued the first set of diocesan statutes (1843) and held the first diocesan synod (1859). Against much opposition, he secured for himself and his successors the ownership of church property. He also promoted the cause of temperance, particularly among the Indians. Beyond the diocese, he founded, with Bishop John Lancaster Spalding, the American College at Louvain, Belgium, and sent priests from Detroit to be its first four rectors. Lefevere had come to a territory that contained only 25 churches and 18 priests; he left, at his death, 160 churches and 88 priests in the lower peninsula of Michigan alone.

Bibliography: R. H. CLARKE, *Lives of the Deceased Bishops of the Catholic Church in the United States,* 4 v. (New York 1887–89).

[E. P. ATZERT]

LEFÈVRE D'ÉTAPLES, JACQUES

Humanist Aristotelian, Biblical and patristic scholar; b. Étaples, Picardy, *c.* 1461; d. Nérac, French Navarre, March 1536. He was educated at the University of Paris (B.A., 1479). Lefèvre lectured on philosophy at the Collège Cardinal Lemoine from *c.* 1490 until he retired from active teaching in 1508. Between 1508 and 1520 he continued his scholarly work at the abbey of Saint-Germain-des-Prés under the patronage of the abbot Guillaume BRIÇONNET, subsequently bishop of Meaux. In June 1521 Briçonnet called him to Meaux to participate in a comprehensive program of diocesan reform. His chief contribution was a French translation of the New Testament (1523) and Psalms (1524). The fortuitous coincidence of the Meaux experiment with the first penetration of Lutheranism in France focused the attention of the faculty of theology on his works. In 1523 a committee of theologians detected 11 errors in his commentary on the Gospels. When summoned to appear before the Parlement of Paris on suspicion of heresy, Lefévre fled to Strasbourg in the late summer of 1525. He was recalled by Francis I in 1526 and appointed librarian at Blois and tutor of the King's children; he finished translating the Bible under royal protection and published it in a single volume at Antwerp in 1530. He passed his last years in tranquil retirement at the court of Marguerite d'Angoulême, Queen of Navarre.

Lefévre's principal intellectual interests were the philosophy of Aristotle, the Pauline Epistles, patristic literature, and the tradition of medieval Christian mysticism. By means of translations, commentaries, introductions, and paraphrases he recovered, or so his contemporaries believed, both the precise meaning of the works of Aristotle and the true elegance of their style. From Aristotle he urged his readers to turn to a reverent study of Scripture, guided by the Fathers. He himself edited a variety of patristic texts and undertook a major program of Biblical research and commentary: on the Psalms (1509), St. Paul (1512), the Gospels (1522), and the Catholic Epistles (1527). But it was in the mystics that Lefévre found the most satisfying nourishment of his own piety. He published works of Richard of Saint-Victor, Elizabeth of Schönau, and Hildegarde of Bingen; seven books by Raymond Lull; and Ruysbroeck's *De ornatu spiritualium nuptiarum.* Lefévre crowned his Aristotelian, patristic, and Biblical scholarship with a variety of speculative mysticism derived from the two thinkers who influenced him most profoundly, Pseudo-Dionysius and Nicholas of Cusa. After 1519 Lefévre moved toward a more self-consciously Biblical theology. He read Luther with sympathetic interest. A common devotion to St. Paul gives their doctrines of justification a superficial resemblance, while direct Lutheran influence can be detected in his last works. But he remained too attached to Catholic sentiment and practice and too committed to the image of human liberty and dignity in Aristotle and the Greek Fathers to break with tradition.

See Also: ARISTOTELIANISM; RENAISSANCE PHILOSOPHY; MYSTICISM; HUMANISM.

Bibliography: É. AMANN, *Dictionnaire de théologie catholique,* ed. A. VACANT, 15 v. (Paris 1903–50; Tables générales 1951–) 9.1: 132–159. A. RENAUDET, *Préréforme et humanisme à Paris pendant les premières guerres d'Italie, 1494–1517* (2d ed. Melun 1953). M. MANN, *Érasme et les débuts de la Réforme française, 1517–1536* (Paris 1934). E. F. RICE, ''The Humanist Idea of Christian Antiquity: Lefévre d' Étaples and His Circle,'' *Studies in the Renaissance* (New York 1954–) 9 (1962) 126–160. G. BEDOUELLE, *Lefèvre d'Étaples et l'intelligence des écritures* (Geneva 1976). J. LEFÈVRE D'ÉTAPLES, *The Prefatory Epistles of Jacques Lèfevre d'Étaples* (New York 1972). E. F. RICE, ''Jacques Lèfevre d'Étaples and the Medieval Christian Mystics,'' in *Florilegium Historiale,* J. G. ROWE and W. H. STOCKDALE, eds. (Toronto 1971).

[E. F. RICE]

LEGATES, PAPAL

Papal legates are clerics sent by the pope into a particular nation, with or without ecclesiastical jurisdiction, with or without diplomatic character, to treat, on his behalf, of the Church affairs entrusted to them.

Papal Prerogative of Legation. It is the right of the Roman pontiff, independent of all civil authority, to send legates into every part of the world. Because the pope unites in himself two distinct sovereignties, the spiritual and the temporal, he enjoys the right of legation by a twofold juridical title. It is, however, in virtue of the mandate received from the divine founder of the Church that the right to send legates is eminently his. The primacy, or the pope's supreme, full, and immediate jurisdiction in the universal Church requires, as a logical consequence, that it be so. This refers primarily to the right of *internal* legation—the legation concerned with the jurisdictional relations of the pope with local churches and subordinate ecclesiastical authorities in the world. The pope enjoys further the right of *external* legation—the legation concerned with the Church's international activities and her relations with civil governments. External legation is the right of all independent states and, in general, of all subjects of international law, that is, of any international institution having an independent and autonomous personality within the international community. The Church is such a universal juridic entity or society juridically perfect. This is so although it lacks, or may at times lack (as do other atypical international entities, such as the United Nations), certain characteristics typical of states. For a great number of centuries the Church has

been so considered. Thus, as a subject of international law, it was consistently permitted, even when deprived of its temporal power, the performance of acts belonging exclusively to the competence of universal juridic entities. Among these acts is the uncontested exercise of external legation, passive and active.

Early History. There were practical applications of the papal right of internal legation as early as the 4th century, when the popes began sending representatives to general and particular councils and, as vicars apostolic, to remote provinces of the Church. From the 5th century through the middle of the 8th, other legates were being sent by Rome, in what may be considered the first manifestations of the papal right of external legation. These apocrisiaries, or *responsales* (papal agents and observers), were to act as papal representatives at the imperial court in Constantinople. The first of these was sent by Leo I. Their function was to keep Rome posted on the happenings at the court and in the eastern regions of the Empire and to convey the pope's instructions on the Church's doctrinal and disciplinary matters, as well as on questions affecting Italy.

Diplomatic legates of a special kind, called *legati missi* (literally, ''legates sent''), made their appearance about the 9th century. Their importance and prestige grew when, in the 11th century, their legations, both to courts of princes and to particular Church dignitaries, began to be entrusted to cardinals—who were then given greater power and the higher title of *legati a latere* (legates sent from the pope's side, as it were). The Middle Ages brought still another category of legates—the *legati nati* (native legates or born legates), so called because they were not sent from Rome but received their role, chiefly a jurisdictional one in matters strictly ecclesiastical, as incumbents of some illustrious episcopal see, such as Canterbury, York, Rheims, Cologne, Prague, or Toledo. There, and in surrounding territories, these residential archbishops represented the pope and acted in his name. The papal emissaries for final purposes were another kind of medieval legate (*nuntii et collectores iurium, redituum et omnium bonorum Camerae Apostolicae*). Their chief task was to collect alms and tithes of princes and the faithful and forward them to Rome and otherwise raise funds for the support of the Holy See and its activities. Their range of duty extended beyond the financial until, not infrequently, it included negotiations and transactions of a diplomatic nature with local political authorities.

The modern nuncios and nunciatures trace their origins to one or more of these types of legates. They derive their name and pattern from the last mentioned—the *nuntii* and *collectores.*

Modern Development. The first nuncios and nunciatures in the modern sense date from the close of the 15th century. According to some, the first papal agent on a permanent basis was Francisco de Prats, Alexander VI's emissary to Spain from 1492 to 1503. Others say Angelo Leonini, sent to Venice in 1500 by the same pope, was the first nuncio. These and others who may then have been called nuncios were certainly true emissaries of the popes. Whether they were nuncios in the strict sense (papal officers sent as ambassadors to a foreign court on a permanent basis with authority to treat any question affecting the pope and the princes) is not clear, for the term "nuncio" was still used in a broad sense at the time and could indifferently describe an envoy sent on either an extraordinary or an ordinary mission. At any rate, before the Reformation there were nunciatures in Vienna, Paris, Madrid, Lisbon, and Naples. More were added after the Protestant Revolt, in Cologne (1582), Brussels (1577), and other northern cities.

In 1584, Gregory XIII (1572–85) strengthened the system of papal diplomacy, giving it organic structure and a body of well-defined regulations. For the first time, the distinctive role, attributions, and economic treatment of the various kinds of papal diplomatic agents (nuncios, internuncios, legates, etc.) were clearly defined. This reorganization was instrumental in ushering in the golden era of Church diplomacy. But soon after the Treaties of Westphalia (1648) came a period of decline that lasted for more than two centuries. There was a notable amelioration in the period between World Wars I and II, as all over the world nunciatures, internunciatures, and apostolic delegations grew in number and prestige. After World War II, numerous and active representations were established in Asia and Africa. For the list of all papal missions, diplomatic and nondiplomatic, as well as of all civil diplomatic missions accredited to the Holy See, see the latest edition of *Annuario pontificio,* the book prepared and issued annually by the Vatican Secretariate of State.

Functions. Paul VI in the *motu proprio* of June 24, 1969, *Sollicitudo omnium Ecclesiarum,* redefined the meaning and function of papal legates. They are ecclesiastics, especially bishops, who are entrusted with the task of personally and stably representing the pope in various countries and regions. The term "legate" applies to a number of different kinds of officials. Apostolic delegates are the personal representatives of the pope to local Churches. NUNCIOS, pronuncios, or internuncios represent the Holy See to the civil governments of the territories in which they serve as well as to the local Church there. Occasionally a papal mission is appointed to deal with a specific issue in a given country. Both lay people and clerics can be sent as delegates or observers to international conferences; these, too, are papal legates; but

their office is not treated in detail in general canonical legislation.

A legate expresses the pope's concern for the good of the nation in which he serves, especially with respect to questions of peace and the development of peoples. He is charged with protecting the legitimate interests of the Church in her dealings with the civil government. Occasionally and bearing in mind the advice of local bishops, he enters into negotiations with the civil government about questions of concern to both CHURCH AND STATE. Within the limits of his mandate and in close association with the bishops and patriarchs of the region, the legate promotes ecumenical dialogue. Being under the direction of the cardinal secretary of state and the prefect of the Council for the Public Affairs of the Church, the legate reports directly to them about all his activities.

Other duties of the legate are more closely allied with internal affairs. He informs the Holy See about the spiritual condition of the local Church and communicates and interprets papal documents and curial deliberations to the local Church. He is the facilitator of the process whereby candidates for the episcopacy are selected; and he forwards their names to the proper Roman dicasteries, together with an accurate indication of which candidate seems most suitable. The legate also has the duty of studying the question of the creation, division, and suppression of dioceses. He will inform the proper Roman dicastery of the episcopal conference's recommendations on the matter.

The legate is advised to give generous assistance and counsel to individual residential bishops. Although not himself a member of the national episcopal conference, he generally attends its sessions. He is to be notified in advance of its agenda and is to inform the Holy See about it. The legate exercises similar functions with respect to religious superiors and the national conferences of religious. Whenever no official delegate or observer has been appointed to an international conference within his territory, the legate is to pursue the business of the conference, informing the Holy See of its progress. Delegates or observers at an international conference are to complete the mission entrusted to them after consulting with the legate in whose territory they happen to be.

The legation (offices of the papal legate) itself has certain legal privileges. It is exempt from the jurisdiction of the local Ordinary and the legate can grant faculties for use in the oratory of the legation. The legate has the right to bless the people and to celebrate the Liturgy of the Hours in all churches within his territory. He takes precedence over all patriarchs, archbishops, and bishops within his territory, but not over cardinals. All of these rights aim at making clear the dignity of the office of the legate and at enabling him to perform his duties more easily.

Bibliography: A. WYNEN, *Die päpstliche Diplomatie geschichtlich und rechtliche dargestellt* (Freiburg im Br. 1922). P. BREZZI, *La diplomazia pontificia* (Milan 1942). G. PARO, *The Right of Papal Legation* (Catholic University of America Canon Law Studies 211; Washington 1947). P. SAVINO, *Diplomazia ecclesiastica* (Rome 1952). E. L. HESTON, "Papal Diplomacy: Its Organization and Way of Action," *The Catholic Church in World Affairs,* ed. W. GURIAN and M. A. FITZIMONS (Notre Dame, Ind. 1954). G. DE MARCHI, *Le nunziature apostoliche dal 1800 al 1956* (Rome 1957). D. STAFFA, *Le delegazioni apostoliche* (Rome 1959). R. A. GRAHAM, *Vatican Diplomacy* (Princeton 1959). I. CARDINALE, *Le Saint-Siège et la diplomatie* (Paris 1963). J. ABBO and J. HANNAN, *The Sacred Canons,* 2 v. (2d ed. St. Louis 1960) 1:265–270. PAUL VI, *Sollicitudo omnium ecclesiarum, Acta Apostolicae Sedis* 61 (Rome 1969) 471–484.

[J. A. ABBO/J. G. JOHNSON]

LE GAUDIER, ANTHONY

Jesuit theologian and spiritual writer; b. Château-Thierry, France, Jan. 7, 1572; d. Paris, April 14, 1622. At the age of 17 Le Gaudier entered the Society of Jesus in Belgium (Sept. 4, 1589). As a Jesuit, he exhibited an exceptional talent for directing the spiritual lives of his fellow religious. This was so true of his life as a professor of scripture at Pont-à-Mousson and as a professor of moral theology at La Flèche and at Verdun that Le Gaudier was eventually made master of novices and of tertians, and he served as rector at Liège and at Paris. It was during his years as rector in Paris (1618–21) that he published his works on the spiritual life. Written originally in Latin, they were translated into French and other languages. They include *De sanctissimo Christi Jesus Dei et hominis amore paraeneticum in quo ejus amoris causae praxis et fructus exponuntur* (Pont-à-Mousson 1619), *De vera Christi Jesus Dei et hominis imitatione* (Paris 1620), *De Dei praesentia* (Paris 1620), and *Praxis meditandi a B. P. Ignatio Societatis Jesu fundatore traditae explicatio* (Paris 1620). However, Le Gaudier's outstanding contribution to Catholic asceticism, *De natura et statibus perfectionis* (Paris 1643), was published posthumously.

Bibliography: C. SOMMERVOGEL, *Bibliothèque de la Compagnie de Jésus,* 11 v. (Brussels-Paris 1890–1932) 3:1265–68. J. DE GUIBERT, *The Jesuits: Their Spiritual Doctrine and Practice,* tr. W. J. YOUNG (Chicago 1964). J. J. MCCANN, *Contemplation and the Mixed Life according to Antonius Le Gaudier, S.J.* (Manila 1951). H. DE GENSAC, *Revue d'ascétique et mystique* 39 (1963) 172–195, 338–360.

[V. A. LAPOMARDA]

LÉGER, PAUL-EMILE

Cardinal, archbishop of Montreal, missionary; b. St. Anicet, Quebec, April 26, 1904; d. Montreal, Nov. 13, 1991. Léger was the son of Ernest and Alva (Beauvais) Léger. Required to leave school at an early age because of ill health, he apprenticed first as a butcher and then as a mechanic before he resolved one Christmas morning to be a priest. He was accepted by the Société de St. Sulpice and proceeded with his priestly studies at Montreal's Grand Séminaire.

Ordained in 1929, Léger was sent for further studies to the Institut Catholique in Paris. He spent some years in Japan establishing a new seminary in Fukuoka. After a term as rector of the Pontifical Canadian College in Rome, he was appointed archbishop of Montreal in 1950.

In 1953, Léger was created a cardinal by Pope Pius XII. A member of the preparatory commission for the Second Vatican Council and a confidant of Popes John XXIII and Paul VI, Léger was identified with the leading progressives of the Council—Alfrink, Suenens, and Lercaro. He spoke eloquently of the primacy of love over law and repeatedly reminded the hierarchy that the laity, particularly in the area of sexual morality, had an indispensable role to play in the life of the Church. They must be listened to, he argued, and their experience and wisdom given heavy weight by Church authorities.

In 1967, Léger amazed the world by resigning as archbishop of Montreal. He exchanged the vermilion robes of the cardinal prince for the white soutane of the missionary priest. He reasoned: "I have reached the age when a certain sclerosis of soul and body sets in. The spur must be used to get out of the rut." He went to work among the lepers of Cameroon.

Bibliography: K. BELL, *A Man and his Mission: Cardinal Léger in Africa* (Scarborough 1976). J. DUGGAN, *Paul-Emile Léger* (Don Mills 1981). L. LACHANCE, *Le prince et les lépreux* (Montreal 1972). P. E. LÉGER, *Les origines de l'homme: Conférence prononcée a l'Université de Montréal* (Montreal 1961).

[M. HIGGINS]

LEGES ROMANAE BARBARORUM

Leges romanae barbarorum is a comprehensive term employed for the law codes issued by the Germanic kings, from the middle of the 5th century A.D., for their subjects of Roman origin. They are the *Lex Romana Visigothorum, Lex Romana Burgundionum*, and *Lex Romana Curiensis.* Whether the Visigoths had put out an earlier *Codex Theodoricianus c.* 458 to 466 for the population living under their traditional Roman law is a disputed question. The personal principle was still in force at that time, i.e., Romans and Germans lived under a different law; although both were under the same German royal rule. Gradually the territorial principle dominated, i.e., the same law for all subjects, a step that was closely connected with Romanization. The extant sources (*leges*) reflect in part this development, since at first one finds side by side *Leges Romanae* for the Romans and *Leges Barbarorum* for the Germans, but later one finds a merging of the two into a common code of law for both elements of the population. For example, on the one hand, the prohibition of marriage between Goths and Romans was abolished under King Leovigild (568–586), and the abandonment of Arianism for Catholicism by the Goths under Leovigild's successor, Reccared I (586–601), was of basic significance for the process of legal unification. On the other hand, among the other Gothic peoples, e.g., the Ostrogoths (so in the kingdom of Theodoric between A.D. 493 and 507), the law was the same for Romans and Germans from the outset.

The Roman law in the *Leges Romanae* constituted what was known as a vulgar law. It was no longer on the level of classical jurisprudence and was somewhat primitive and crude. No distinction was made anywhere between ownership and possession. The drafting of the *Leges* was done by members of the clergy and laymen trained in Roman law. However, it is possible, often very clearly, to trace the respective roles of the royal chanceries and the Church in the legislation. At times the influence of the Roman vulgar law was so strong that it all but suppressed German national law. The latter then maintained itself outside the *Leges* as customary law over a long period. During the high Middle Ages in Spain, for example, in a land once held by the VISIGOTHS, it even received a written form in the so–called *Fueros*.

Bibliography: R. BUCHNER, *Die Rechtsquellen* in W. WATENBACH, *Deutschlands Geschichtsquellen im Mittelalter. Vorzeit und Karolinger,* Hefte 1–4, ed. W. LEVISON and H. LÖWE (Weimar 1952–63) Beiheft 1953. K. VON AMIRA and K. A. ECKHARDT, *Germanisches Recht,* v.1 (4th ed. Berlin 1960). H. MITTEIS and H. LIEBERICH, *Deutsche Rechtsgeschichte* (9th ed. Munich 1965). *Estudios visigóticos,* v.2 *El Codigo de Eurico* (Rome 1960) ed. and tr. A. D'ORS.

[H. THIEME]

LEGION OF MARY

An international association of lay Catholics founded in Dublin, Ireland (1921), for the spiritual advancement of its members and the general intensification of Catholic life. On Sept. 7, 1921, a small group of lay people, stimulated by an awareness of the Christian vocation to be a witness and urged on by the writings of the popes, met with their parish priest in St. Nicholas of Myra parish, Dublin, to discover some practical means of translating their discussions on the doctrine of the MYSTICAL BODY OF CHRIST and the writings of St. Louis Marie GRIGNION DE MONTFORT into concrete action in the service of others. The system of lay apostleship that eventually became known as the Legion of Mary was influenced also by the ST. VINCENT DE PAUL SOCIETY, which was extremely active in Dublin during the 1920s. During the next 40 years the original group of the Myra Street meeting multiplied worldwide. In addition to the active members of the Legion of Mary, there are also auxiliary members who render the Legion a service of prayer. The Legion was first established in the U.S. in 1931.

Membership. The Legion admits any practicing Catholic of at least 18 years of age. (A junior system, differing only in the adaptation of the work to adolescents, parallels the senior organization and prepares the young for membership in the senior group). The Legion demands high standards of Christian life, but only after the member is enrolled and not as a prerequisite for admission; the method employed consists of prayer and active work in the apostolate. Consequently, the two most fundamental requirements for membership are (1) attendance at the weekly meeting, where the Legion prayers, spiritual reading, and guidance by the spiritual director form the member and (2) the performance of a substantial amount of assigned apostolic work each week. Discipline, very much a part of the ideal of membership, is measured by the individual's adherence to the system; in addition, each member has a personal responsibility to recruit new members, both active and auxiliary. The Legion seeks to undertake any and every form of social service and evangelical outreach. The visitation of homes is the most characteristic work of the Legion members.

Organization. The nomenclature employed, derived from ancient Roman military usage, designates the individual unit or cell as a praesidium, a district of two or more praesidia as a curia, the governing body for a country or region as a senatus, and the supreme governing body as the concilium. The higher governing bodies come into existence only as the multiplication of praesidia requires them. As the number of praesidia in an area increases, the curias, composed of the officers of the various praesidia, are multiplied and in turn are governed by a higher council, the comitium. Several comitia are supervised by a senatus, which answers directly to the highest council in the system, the concilium, whose headquarters are in Dublin. This tight supervision of the lower groups by the governing councils, together with the standard handbook accounts for the remarkable uniformity throughout the world.

Bibliography: LEGION OF MARY, *The Official Handbook of the Legion of Mary.* F. DUFF, *Miracles on Tap* (Bay Shore, NY 1962), by the founder of Legion of Mary. L. C. MORAND, *The Character of the Legion of Mary in the Law of the Church* (London 1955). L. J. SUENENS, *Theology of the Apostolate of the Legion of*

Mary (Westminster, MD 1954). F. J. RIPLEY and F. S. MITCHELL, *Souls at Stake* (New York 1948).

[T. P. CARROLL/EDS.]

LEGIONARIES OF CHRIST

A clerical congregation established in Mexico City in 1941 by Marcial Maciel, a priest from Cotija, Michoacán. During the religious persecution in Mexico in 1936, Maciel, then a 16-year-old seminarian, felt called to start a religious congregation of priests. On Jan. 3, 1941, under the auspices of Francisco Gonzáles Arias, bishop of Cuernavaca, he founded the Legion of Christ and opened the Sacred Heart Apostolic School with a group of 13 boys.

In 1946 Maciel opened a second Apostolic School and the first novitiate in Comillas, Santander, Spain. On May 25, 1948, the Holy See granted the legion the *nihil obstat* necessary for the canonical establishment of a diocesan congregation. The Holy See elevated it to pontifical status with the Decree of Praise (*Decretum laudis*) on Feb. 6, 1965 and gave definitive approval of its constitutions on June 29, 1983.

Regnum Christi. Meanwhile, in 1949 Father Maciel founded Regnum Christi, an apostolic movement dedicated to the service of humanity and the world. It includes laity, men and women, deacons and priests. The association reminds its members of their responsibility, rooted in baptism, to make faith the driving force in their daily lives and to undertake organized apostolic activity. The Regnum Christi Movement is inspired by the charism of its founder and is closely allied with the Legionaries of Christ.

In 1950 the Legion of Christ moved its general headquarters to Rome and established a Center for Higher Studies. In 1958 the Legionaries, with the support of Mexican Catholics, built the church of Our Lady of Guadalupe adjacent to the Generalate. The legion has centers of formation in Mexico, Spain, Italy, Ireland, and the United States. Its U.S. headquarters are in Cheshire, Conn.

Bibliography: J. GARCIA, ''Legionari di Cristo'' and ''Marcial Maciel,'' *Dizionario degli Isituti di Perfezione*, 5 v. (Rome 1978). M. MACIEL, *Integral Formation of Catholic Priests* (Hamden, Conn. 1998).

[J. GARCIA]

LEGITIMACY OF CHILDREN (CANON LAW)

Legitimacy, in its ordinary sense, means that a person has been conceived from a valid marriage. Thus a person conceived or born outside of valid wedlock, or born, but not conceived, of a valid marriage would be illegitimate according to the natural law. This same principle would apply if such a person was conceived and born of a marriage that was thought, at least by one party, to be valid, but in fact was not. However, legitimacy in canon law is not so narrowly defined. The Church broadens the definition by considering as legitimate those born of a union that is thought to be valid but in reality is not.

Definition. Church law considers as legitimate those born or conceived of a valid or putative marriage (*Codex iuris canonicis* c. 1137). This definition includes not only those naturally legitimate, but also gives a juridic legitimacy to those born of a putative marriage, that is, a marriage thought to be valid by at least one of the parties.

For a marriage to be valid it is required that there existed no invalidating impediment to the marriage, that true matrimonial consent is given, and that the required form of marriage is followed. It must be noted that a marriage is usually not described as putative for a Catholic party if he has not followed the Catholic form of marriage. (*See* MARRIAGE LEGISLATION [CANON LAW].)

The church law enumerates certain presumptions. First of these is that the husband of the woman is the father of her child unless the contrary is proved by clear evidence (*Codex iuris canonicis* c. 1138 1). Another is that a child born at least 180 days after the celebration of the marriage or within 300 days after conjugal life has been dissolved is presumed to be legitimate (*Codex iuris canonicis* c. 1138 2).

Legitimation of Children. The Holy See may change the status of an illegitimate child and declare him or her legitimate. The reasons the Church might so decree are for the good of the child, the parents, and society. A child is also legitimated by subsequent valid or putative marriage of his or her parents (*Codex iuris canonicis* c. 1139).

There is an additional way of legitimatizing children. Illegitimate persons may become fully legitimate by a radical sanation (*Codex iuris canonicis* c. 1161; *Corpus canonum ecclesiarum orientalium* c. 848). A radical sanation is an extraordinary means of convalidating a marriage. It dispenses from impediments, dispenses from the renewal of consent, and, by a fiction of law, the canonical effects of the marriage are retroactive. One of these effects is the legitimation of the offspring. This is legitimation in its fullest sense; it is as if the child were born of a valid marriage. The effect reaches back to the time when the parties first exchanged true matrimonial consent. Thus, any children conceived or born after this first consent are to be considered legitimate.

Effects. Under the 1917 Code of Canon Law, there were several instances where persons who were illegitimate were barred from certain ecclesiastical dignities and offices. Illegitimacy would have prohibited a man from entering a seminary because illegitimacy made him irregular to receive Orders (1917 *Codex iuris canonicis* c. 984, 1°). An illegitimate man would have also been restricted from the cardinalate (1917 *Codex iuris Canonicis* c. 232 §2, 1°), the episcopacy (1917 *Codex iuris Canonicis* c. 331 §1, 1–) and the office of abbot or prelate nullius (1917 *Codex iuris Canonicis* c. 320 §2). Illegitimate persons could not have been elected to the office of major superior in religious institutes (1917 *Codex iuris Canonicis* c. 504).

There are no effects of illegitimacy in the 1983 Code of Canon Law. The Church maintains the distinction in canon law, although it has little practical importance.

Bibliography: J. ABBO and J. HANNAN, *The Sacred Canons* (St. Louis 1960) 2:1114–17. H. A. AYRINHAC and P. J. LYDON, *Marriage Legislation in the New Code of Canon Law* (New York 1957) 1114–17. T. L. BOUSCAREEN and A. C. ELLIS, *Canon Law* (Milwaukee 1957) 1154–60. G. I. MCDEVITT, *Legitimacy and Legitimation* (Catholic University of America Canon Law Studies 138; Washington 1941). T. P. DOYLE, in J. A. CORIDEN et al., *The Code of Canon Law: A Text and Commentary* (New York 1985) 810–811. L. A. ROBITAILLE in J. P. BEAL et al., *New Commentary on the Code of Canon Law* (New York 2000).

[A. SWIFT]

LE GOBIEN, CHARLES

French Jesuit, founder of the *Lettres édifiantes* an important source of information on the history of Catholic missions; b. Saint-Malo, Dec. 20, 1653; d. Paris, March 5, 1708. He entered the Society of Jesus on Nov. 25, 1671. After teaching for a number of years in Jesuit schools in Tours and Alençon, he became procurator for the Chinese mission. To arouse interest in the work of the Jesuit missionaries, in 1697 he published a letter on the progress of religion in China. That was followed in 1698 by a history of the Chinese emperor's edict in favor of Christianity with an explanation of the CHINESE RITES honoring Confucius and the dead, and next by an account in 1700 of the Catholic missions in the Marianas Islands. Then in 1702, Gobien began the *Lettres édifiantes,* an annual publication of selected letters from Jesuit missionaries in China and the East Indies. He continued as editor of the first eight volumes. The entire collection of 36 volumes was reissued about four times; and M. L. Aimé-Martin published an abridged French edition entitled *Panthéon Littéraire* (1838–43). Some of the letters were translated into English in 1714 and German in 1720.

Bibliography: C. SOMMERVOGEL, *Bibliotèque de la Compagnie de Jésus,* 11 v. (Brussels-Paris 1890–1932) 3:1512–1515; 9:417; 12:1124. C. CARY-ELWES, *China and the Cross: A Survey of Missionary History* (New York 1957).

[J. V. MENTAG]

LEHMKUHL, AUGUST

Jesuit moralist; b. Hagen, Westphalia, Sept. 23, 1834; d. Valkenburg, Holland, June 23, 1918. He taught scripture and later moral theology at Maria Laach. He then taught at Ditton Hall, England, until 1880, when he returned to the Continent and devoted himself exclusively to writing. In 1883 he published his major work, the *Theologia Moralis* (2 v. Freiburg). In it he applied the principles of St. THOMAS AQUINAS and St. ALPHONSUS LIGUORI to contemporary problems in moral theology. It has gone through numerous editions and revisions. His other major work was his *Casus Conscientiae* (2 v. Freiburg 1902–04). In the area of social and economic justice he wrote *Arbeitsvertrag und Streik* (Freiburg 1899); *Die Soziale Not und der Kirchliche Einfluse* (1892); and *Die Internationale Regelung der Sozialen Frage* (Freiburg 1893). In these and other articles he was a pioneer in attempting an exact and scientific analysis of sociopolitical problems from the viewpoint of moral theology. He was an ardent defender of many of the demands of the working class.

Bibliography: G. GUNDLACH, *Staatslexicon,* H. SACHER, ed. (Freiburg 1957–) 5:335–336.

[R. M. BUSH]

LEHODEY, VITAL

Trappist Cistercian ascetico-mystical author; b. Hambye, France, Dec. 17, 1857 (Baptized Alcime Jude); d. Abbey of Bricquebec, Diocese of Coutances, May 6, 1948. After ordination to the priesthood on Dec. 18, 1880, Lehodey spent nine years in diocesan ministry before entering the Trappist Cistercian Abbey of Bricquebec, where he took the religious habit and received the name Vital, on Aug. 15, 1890. Appointed prior upon his simple profession on Aug. 20, 1892, he became superior *ad nutum,* on Nov. 1, 1893; and, thanks to an indult permitting anticipation of his solemn profession, he was elected abbot on July 8, 1895. Reasons of health forced his resignation in 1929.

The fruits of Lehodey's progressive liberation from a somewhat rigoristic pessimism characteristic of his milieu are found in three major works. *Les Voies de l'oraison mentale* (Paris 1908; *The Ways of Mental Prayer,* Dublin 1912), notable for its clarity and solid the-

Gottfried Wilhelm von Leibniz.

ology, marks a return to a mystical tradition sadly neglected in the aftermath of the quietist and Jansenist controversies. The *Directoire spirituel* (Bricquebec 1910; *A Spiritual Directory for Religious,* New Melleray 1932, Gethsemani Abbey 1946), is a revision of the order's *Directoire* of 1869, the excessive pessimism of which is tempered by a new insistence on the primacy of charity and contemplation. *Le Saint abandon* (Paris 1919; *Holy Abandonment,* Dublin 1934) is universally recognized as a classic on this subject.

Bibliography: ''*Dom Vital Lehodey, 1857–1948,*'' *Collectanea Ordinis Cisterciensium Reformatorum* 10 (1948) 155–161. I. VALLERY-RADOT, *La Mission de Dom Vital Lehodey* (Paris 1956), Eng. adaptation by N. KINSELLA, *Flight and Pursuit: The Mission of Dom Vital Lehodey* (Dublin 1962).

[C. WADDELL]

LEIBNIZ, GOTTFRIED WILHELM VON

German philosopher, polyhistorian, and court adviser; b. Leipzig, July 1, 1646; d. Hanover, Nov. 14, 1716.

Life. Leibniz studied law, mathematics, and philosophy at Jena and Leipzig. There he became acquainted with, and was influenced by, the works of Aristotle and the scholastics, especially F. SUÁREZ, as well as contemporary mechanistic theories in the natural sciences. At 17 he wrote *De principio individui* (Lcipzig 1663); at 20 he received the degree of doctor of laws in Altdorf, near Nuremberg. In 1667 Leibniz entered the service of the Archbishop-Elector of Mainz, J. P. Schönborn, who wielded considerable influence in the political life of the times. Leibniz spent the years from 1672 to 1676 as a diplomat in Paris, where he came into contact with prominent scientists, philosophers, and theologians, among them C. Huygens, E. Mariotte, N. MALEBRANCHE, E. W. Tschirnhaus, and A. ARNAULD. Between his duties in Paris, he managed to go to London, where he corresponded with members of the Royal Society. On his return to Germany, he sought out and conferred with B. SPINOZA in Holland. While in Paris, Leibniz invented the infinitesimal calculus, which I. Newton had also discovered. Then, from 1776 on, Leibniz was court adviser and librarian for the Duke of Braunschweig-Lüneburg at Hanover, where he worked on the history of the Guelfs and made an excellent series of source studies. He carried on an extensive correspondence with leading figures in the Church, in science, and in politics, discussing even such practical economic matters as mining, water supply, and land cultivation. He set himself especially to the task of organizing science, founded the Society (later Academy) of Science at Berlin, and negotiated similar plans for Petersburg and Vienna. He interested himself also in the spread of Christianity and worked toward reuniting the two great Christian denominations. He was a Protestant by persuasion; however, toward the end of his life he became a solitary, opposed even to his own church.

Doctrines. The distinctive philosophical teachings of Leibniz may be discussed under the headings of logic and theory of knowledge; metaphysics and theodicy; and ethical, political, and religious theory.

Logic and Theory of Knowledge. Leibniz here adopted a rationalistic approach, combining in one synthesis the theory of recollection of Plato, the eternal law concept of the Stoics—which, for St. Paul, is written in the hearts of men (Rom 2.15)—the theory of the active intellect of the scholastics, the notion of the divine spark of the mystics, and the innate ideas of R. DESCARTES. However, one cannot represent these innate ideas as ''the public proclamations of a magistrate inscribed on a particular tablet.'' They are nothing more than the understanding or reason itself judging between true and false on the basis of immanent, aprioristic faculties and principles. The senses are also required, but only as a blind man requires a cane. They offer man only the occasion for the exercise of understanding, which alone can throw light on the concept and without which sensation remains empty.

Leibniz therefore distinguishes between two types of truth, factual truth (contingent truths or truths of fact and existence) and real truth (truths of essences). Only the latter are truths in the strict sense of the word; the former are obscured by the senses. Man must have recourse to the principle of SUFFICIENT REASON (*ratio sufficiens*) in making judgments; i.e., he can justify the connection between subject and predicate only if there is sufficient ground for doing so. Since not all interrelationships between things are accessible to sense experience, factual truths are only probabilities, properly speaking, and not real truths, which are always universally valid, necessary, and eternal. For a mind to be able to penetrate all relations it must resolve factual truths into real truths, as if everything that could accompany an essence were already contained in its concept. The divine mind may see in this way, but Leibniz would have had the human mind operate thus also. For this reason, he attempted to resolve facts into necessary truths and sense data into concepts by means of a typical rationalist oversimplification.

Moreover, this feature of his philosophy was one over which he was most enthusiastic. He referred to the process of reducing factual knowledge to necessary conceptual relations as the *ars combinatoria* or *characteristica universalis*. One could, he thought, establish characteristic symbols or figures for all existing things and develop an algebraic art of comprehension on the basis of a mathematical calculus. Thus with Raymond LULL he became a forerunner of modern logistics (*see* LOGIC, SYMBOLIC). He hoped in this way to be able to resolve all controversies and intellectual disputes. He also conceived his *ars combinatoria* as of help in spreading the faith. "For if missionaries can be led to use this language, they can establish the true religion that stands in complete harmony with reason and one need no longer fear defections from religion in the future."

Metaphysics and Theodicy. The central concept of Leibniz's metaphysics is the MONAD. He devised his theory while enlarging upon Descartes's notion of substance. If the body, as Descartes had said, is extension only, then something of the essence, namely, its capacity for activity, is not accounted for. Substance must then be a unit of action, *un être capable d'action.* This unit of action might be regarded as an aggregate of forces, but this would have no reality if the substance itself were not real. On the other hand, substance cannot be extended, because it would admit of infinite divisibility and thus fail to be an ultimate force unit. Hence, substances must be extended, not as a mathematical point, but as an ultimate unit of a psychical nature, a monad. "Monads are then the real atoms of nature; in short, they are the elements of things."

The function of the monad is representation; every force, including the will, is a type of representation—but this too is a radical simplification. There is a differentiation in the intensity of representations; this extends from the most unconscious (in pure or "empty" monads) to conscious representation that approaches perception and thought (as in plants and animals), to that of self-conscious being (as in human souls), and finally to that of the divine monad, who mirrors all things with the utmost clarity because He is pure act (*actus purus*). The ascent from absolutely motionless monads to pure act is, according to Leibniz, an unbroken continuum, for nature admits of no gaps (*lex continui*), a principle that also underlies the infinitesimal calculus.

Every monad reflects the universe, and this without external stimuli. "Monads have no windows." For this reason, all monads have a similar content and harmonize with one another without having to interact causally: they are ruled by a preestablished harmony like that of two clocks that are set and wound together but run independently. Nevertheless, the differentiation of intensity in the representations serves as a principle of INDIVIDUATION. Without this, all substances would be identical—the principles of the identity of indiscernibles.

Since for Leibniz the monad took the place of the atom, he can be regarded as taking account of modern mathematical and mechanistic thought, which he knew, and also of classical metaphysics, whose teachings on FORM and ENTELECHY he further advanced by combining them with the monad concept. He recognized that there are not only parts in nature—and mechanism took account of these alone—but also unities and associations and ends that were included in the concept of entelechy. Thus each monad comprehends other monads under it and organizes them into a unity. The human soul is such a monad substance. One finds such entelechies in the whole range of the organic, but surprisingly also in the inorganic. God is the monad of monads; He is the substance that makes all other substances possible.

By this teaching Leibniz attempted to avoid Spinoza's concept of undifferentiated substance, since his monad theory preserved individuality and particularly the human person with his freedom and self-determination. He went too far, however, for his reduction of the atom to something psychical or spiritual could not account for the nature of bodies. Although he regarded EXTENSION as a *phenomenon bene fundatum,* he actually was teaching a type of PANPSYCHISM. The implied DYNAMISM is too one-sided, for it is necessary that force be opposed to something that is not force in order for it to be intelligible.

As for God's being the monad of all monads, this put Leibniz more in accord with tradition, where God is regarded as the Form of forms and PURE ACT. He also adopted the standard proofs for the existence of God, even the ONTOLOGICAL ARGUMENT. There are difficulties in his teachings, however, for he conceived God as having created the best of all possible worlds (*see* OPTIMISM), and thus seemed to endanger God's freedom. Leibniz felt that he had not done so, asserting the best possible worlds included EVIL. In his THEODICY he justified this by distinguishing between metaphysical, physical, and moral evil. The first is nothing more than the finitude of the world. Physical evil he equated with pain; God wills this indirectly as punishment for guilt, on the one hand, and for the greater good He wills to draw from it, on the other. He does not will moral evil as such, but permits it because man is free. Leibniz also sought to justify revelation in his theodicy. It never contradicts real truth, the truth of reason; it can, however, go beyond reason and especially beyond factual truth, which itself is without necessity. A similar stand was taken by a contemporary, J. A. COMENIUS.

Ethical, Political, and Religious Theory. Leibniz opposed T. HOBBES in advocating the reasonableness, the wisdom, and the goodness proper to God's order. Man is the being he is because of his spirit and freedom, and his habitat is the realm of spirit where God is both sovereign and father. This perfection must be served by both the law and the state. Law consists in wise and good order, with God as well as with man. If right were to be sought only in utility or in power, God would not differ from an all-powerful devil, Leibniz's philosophy of law stands in contrast with the utilitarianism of Hobbes, S. Pufendorf (1632–94), and C. Thomasius. He had a strong following, however, in R. Boscovich, J. F. Herbart, B. Bolzano, G. Teichmüller (1832–88), and R. H. LOTZE; he also influenced E. Becher (1882–1929) and A. N. WHITEHEAD.

See Also: RATIONALISM.

Bibliography: Major works. *Discours de métaphysique* (1686) and *La Monadologie* (1714), Eng. *Discourse on Metaphysics, Correspondence with Arnauld, and the Monadology,* tr. G. R. MONTGOMERY (La Salle, Ill. 1962); *Système nouveau de la nature . . .* (1695); *Nouveaux essais sur l'entendement humain* (1704); Eng. tr. A. G. LANGLEY (2d ed. Chicago 1916); *Essais de shéodicée* (Amsterdam 1710); *Principes de la nature et de la grâce* (1714). Editions. *Opera philosophica,* ed. J. E. ERDMANN, 2 v. (Berlin 1839–40; repr. 1959); *Die philosophischen Schriften,* ed. C. I. GERHARDT, 7 v. (Berlin 1875–90; repr. Hildesheim 1960–61); *Sämtliche Schriften und Briefe,* ed. Preussische Akademie der Wissenschaften (Berlin 1923–). Literature. F. C. COPLESTON, *History of Philosophy* (Westminster Md. 1946–), v.4. J. HIRSCHBERGER, *History of Philosophy,* tr. A. N. FUERST, 2 v. (Milwaukee 1958–59). Y. BELAVAL, *Leibniz: Initiation à sa philosophie* (Paris 1962). H. W. B. JOSEPH, *Lectures on the Philosophy of Leibniz* (Oxford 1949). L. COUTURAT, *La Logique de Leibniz après des documents inédits* (Paris 1901; rept. Hildesheim 1961). B. RUSSELL, *A Critical Exposition of the Philosophy of Leibniz* (new ed. London 1937). K. HILDEBRANDT, *Leibniz und das Reich der Gnade* (The Hague 1953). H. G. ALEXANDER, ed., *The Leibniz-Clark Correspondence* (Manchester, Eng. 1956). J. O. FLECKENSTEIN, *G. W. Leibniz: Barock und Universalismus* (Munich 1959). A. WILDERMUTH, *Wahrheit und Schöpfung: Ein Grundriss der Metaphysik des G. W. Leibniz* (Winterthur 1960). J. JALABERT, *Le Dieu de Leibniz* (Paris 1960). G. MARTIN, *Leibniz: Logik und Metaphysik* (Cologne 1960). H. M. WOLFF, *Leibniz: Allbeseelung und Skepsis* (Bern 1961).

[J. HIRSCHBERGER]

LEIDRADUS OF LYONS

Archbishop of Lyons; b. in the ancient Province of Noricum; d. Soissons, France, Dec. 28, 817. A cleric in Salzburg *c.* 790, Leidradus through his friend ALCUIN received an invitation to CHARLEMAGNE's court, where he was Alcuin's favorite disciple. In 797 or 798 he succeeded Ado as archbishop of Lyons. His consecration was delayed until 799 because in 798 Charlemagne sent him with THEODULF OF ORLÉANS as *missi dominici* to Narbonnaise Gaul, a commission immortalized by Theodulf's charming poem, *Contra judices,* where he praises Leidradus's rare ability, exceptional good sense, and eminent virtue. An important contribution of Leidradus's episcopate, his struggle against ADOPTIONISM, took him to Spain in 798, where he attended the Council of Urgel in 799. One source, based on Jerome de la Higuera's report of *c.* 810, which states that he had the happiness of converting ELIPANDUS OF TOLEDO and Felix of Urgel, is probably erroneous. Leidradus's work in Lyons rescued that see from the sad conditions resulting from the Muslim occupation during the 731–734 period and subsequent confiscations by CHARLES MARTEL in 737 (*see* CAROLINGIANS).

Leidradus's achievements were solid, and he recounts them in a letter to Charlemagne (ed. H. Leclerq, *Dictionnaire d'archéologie chrétienne et de liturgie* 10:235–237, with a Fr. tr.). He described them because he feared death might interrupt his program, which he wished Charlemagne to carry out. He had reformed the chant, using as a model the plainsong of Metz taught by a cleric from that see (*see* CHRODEGANG OF METZ), and his own lectors and chanters were so well trained that they could teach others. He promoted the transcription of numerous manuscripts, but he was especially the restorer of churches and monasteries: St. John the Baptist (the cathedral), St. Nizier, St. Mary, St. Eulalia, and the convent of St. George, Île-Barthe, a monastery on an island in the Saône. In imitation of Bishop Chrodegang, he organized his clergy into a college of canons, priests, and deacons, whom he attached to the Baptistery of St. Stephen, designating them as *fratres sancti Stephani.* The episcopal family thus produced continued until the twelfth century, and a school for training young clerics was attached to it. Someone, perhaps Leidradus himself, added to this letter a summary account of each church and monastery according to the number of its inhabitants and their social rank; there are 727 *colonicas* (cultivated estates) and 33 *absas* (vacant ones). Perhaps the list, specific and detailed, was what Charlemagne expected, and the letter may have been a clever move to make him favorable to the attached report because of his esteem for Leidradus. Besides the letter to Charlemagne, Leidradus wrote a theological treatise for the emperor entitled *Liber de sacramento baptismi* (ed. E. Dümmler, *Monumenta Germaniae Historica: Epistolae* 4:539–540) and a short treatise on the accompanying ceremony of renouncing the devil (*ibid.* 540–541). A letter of consolation to his sister (*ibid.* 544–545) is also preserved. After the death of Charlemagne, the bishop retired to the monastery of Saint-Médard at Soissons, where he died.

Bibliography: *Patrologia latina*, 217 v. (Paris 1878–1890) 99:853–886. *Monumenta Germaniae Historica: Epistolae* 4:539–546. J. POURRAT, *L'Antique école de Leidrade* (Lyons 1899); *L'Université catholique* 31 (Lyons 1899): 161–182. M. MANITIUS, *Geschichte der lateinischen Literatur des Mittelalters* 3 v. (Munich 1911–31) 1:249, 380, 381, 386–390, 392, 394, 538, 541. L. DUCHESNE, *Fastes épiscopaux de l'ancienne Gaule,* 3 v. (Paris 1907–15) 2:171–172. É. AMANN, *Dictionnaire de théologie catholique,* 15 v. (Paris 1903–50) 9.1:195–196. H. LECLERCQ, *Dictionnaire d'archéologie chrétienne et de liturgie,* 15 v. (Paris 1907–53) 10.1:232–244. B. WALCHER, *Lexicon für Theologie und Kirche,* 10 v. (Freiburg 1957–) 6:926.

[C. M. AHERNE]

LEIGH, RICHARD, BL.

Priest, martyr; *alias* Garth or Earth; b. ca. 1561, Cambridgeshire, England; hanged at Tyburn (London), Aug. 30, 1588. Leigh, ordained in Rome (1586), returned to England in 1587 to minister in London, where he was arrested and exiled. Soon after his second arrival he was again captured and imprisoned in the Tower of London (June 1588). He irrefutably betrayed himself as a Catholic by answering questions put to another who was under examination and was condemned for his priesthood. He was executed together with BB. Edward SHELLEY, Richard FLOWER, John Roche, and St. Margaret WARD. Leigh was beatified by Pius XI on Dec. 15, 1929.

Feast of the English Martyrs: May 4 (England).

See Also: ENGLAND, SCOTLAND, AND WALES, MARTYRS OF.

Bibliography: R. CHALLONER, *Memoirs of Missionary Priests,* ed. J. H. POLLEN (rev. ed. London 1924; repr. Farnborough 1969). J. H. POLLEN, *Acts of English Martyrs* (London 1891).

[K. I. RABENSTEIN]

LEISNER, KARL FRIEDRICH WILHELM MARIA, BL.

Priest, martyr; b. Feb. 28, 1915, Rees am Niederrhein, Westphalia, Germany; d. Aug. 12, 1945, Planegg (near Munich). Karl's parents, Wilhelm Leisner and Amalie Falkenstein, moved to Kleve in 1921, where he attended the local public school. He studied philosophy and theology at the Borromeo College in Münster (1934–36); theology at Freiburg in Breisgau (1936–37) and Münster (1937–39). While at the university, his bishop commissioned him as diocesan leader of youth groups from 1934 to 1936. To circumvent Nazi control, Karl taught his charges the catechism on excursions. His education was interrupted for six months in 1937 by mandatory national agricultural service in Sachsen and Emsland. During this period he again opposed Nazi regulations by organizing Sunday Mass for fellow workers. Leisner entered Münster's diocesan seminary in 1938 and was ordained deacon March 25, 1939 by Bishop Clemens Augustinus Graf von Galen.

While recuperating from tuberculosis in the sanitarium at St. Blasien, Schwarzwald, he was arrested Nov. 8, 1939, for offhandedly expressing regret that an assassination attempt against Hitler had failed. He was held in the prison of Freiburg from 1939 to 1940, then incarcerated in Mannheim's prison. After Mannheim, he was taken to the concentration camps at Sachsenhausen and Dachau Dec. 24, 1940. On Dec. 17, 1944, French Bishop Gabriel Piguet of Clermont-Ferrand secretly ordained Leisner to the priesthood at Dachau. Father Leisner furtively celebrated Mass for the first and only time on Dec. 26 in the barrack's chapel. Dachau was liberated by Allied troops May 4, 1945. Leisner, suffering the effects of tuberculosis and imprisonment, died a few months later at the age of 30 in a sanitarium at Planegg near Munich.

In 1966 his body was exhumed from his grave in Kleve and placed in the Martyrs Crypt in the Xanten cathedral. His cause was opened in Rome March 15, 1980. Among the documents examined were his diary with entries from March 23, 1927 through July 25, 1945, and about 130 substantial letters, which provide insight into his spirituality. He was beatified June 23, 1996, by John Paul II during his third pastoral visit to Germany.

Bibliography: *Christus meine Leidenschaft, Karl Leisner, sein Leben in Bildern und Dokumenten,* ed. W. HAAS (Kevelaer 1985); *Karl Leisner: Mit Christus leben. Gedanken für jeden Tag,* ed. W. HAAS (Kevelaer 1979). O. CESCA, *Castelo no tormenta, Carlos Leisner* (Santa Maria, Brazil 1963). C. FELDMANN, *Wer glaubt, muss widerstehen: Bernhard Lichtenberg-Karl Leisner,* 3d ed. (Freiburg 1996). R. LEJEUNE, *K. Leisner: Wie Gold geläutert im Feuer* (Strassburg 1988). O. PIES, *Stephanus heute, Karl Leisner, Priester und Opfer.* (Kevelaer 1951). J. SCHMIEDL, *Karl Leisner:*

Leben für die Jugend (Vallendar-Schönstatt 1996). *L'Osservatore Romano,* English edition, no. 26 (1996) 1–3.

[K. I. RABENSTEIN]

LEISURE

Leisure is an analogous term, for its import changes from person to person and from CULTURE to culture. The leisure of a university professor, for instance, no doubt differs from the leisure of his young student. The term, however, has similar resonances for both: joyful feelings of FREEDOM, fulfillment, and significance. Both intuitively recognize the truth of Aristotle's dictum that men are unleisurely only to gain leisure (*Ethica Nicomachea,* 1177 b).

An examination of the leisure-time pursuits of different cultures makes the analogous nature of leisure even more apparent. Although the resonances of freedom, fulfillment, and significance remain, the concrete embodiments of these sentiments vary widely—an afternoon in a Manhattan art gallery differs both in tone and content from a native religious festival. Leisure, then, is not a simple essence but rather a category of activity defined by a SOCIETY's view of what constitutes man's true happiness. It can be examined in its richest context only when it is related to all other values of a society. This is best done by viewing leisure in its social function, i.e., by considering what leisure does for society and how it is related to each major social institution (the family, the state, the economy, etc.). The relationship between leisure and the institutions that universally arise to meet society's recurrent problems of continuity, cooperation, and survival will be seen more easily after leisure has been functionally defined and located within the Western humanistic tradition.

Relation to Work. Leisure is often defined functionally as the opposite of labor, but this definition is inadequate for two reasons. First, the word has received a modicum of clarity by being distinguished from mere recreation (the renewal of energies for more efficient work) and from free time (any time set apart from the exigencies of toil). Although the worker receives no pay for his use of free time or recreation, these two concepts actually stand in close relation to work itself. Recreation and free time find their justification as propaedeutics for work. From a purely business point of view, Sunday worship and the coffee break are qualitatively the same: they both contribute to making better workers for the enterprise.

The second reason that leisure cannot expeditiously be defined as the opposite of work is that the actual boundary between labor and leisure is sometimes difficult to fix. Philosopher Yves Rene Simon speaks of how work is meant to be a delight rather than toil when he says "work is essentially joyful but it involves the permanent foundation of the possibility of pain." When a carpenter goes about his daily tasks he indeed labors. But may a lawyer who makes artistic cabinets for his own pleasure be categorized as a man of work or as a man of leisure? It is an observable fact that some men expend more energy at their so-called leisure activities than they do at their jobs. Expenditure of energy, then, cannot be the criterion. Nor, in the light of the example, can the activity in itself be the norm for distinguishing work from leisure.

This refractoriness to definition is rooted in the fact that labor is also socially defined. Since the same activity can be labor in one situation and not in another, one must conclude that labor is a concept that does not refer merely to the nature of human activity, but also to the social structure in which this activity is performed. Since the labor structure changes in the course of history, the meaning of the word labor changes with this development. The underlying characteristic of all the various manifestations of labor is that labor is always incorporated into a system of services done with a certain regularity. The performance of these services does not depend solely upon the freedom of the working individual.

Transcendent Character. Leisure, on the other hand, is of an entirely different order. It enables man to transcend the social matrix of economic production and routine social duties so that he can consider the significance of things and perform significant acts. Such a social category is possible because society itself, through its hierarchy of values, can recognize and decree that man has a dignity transcending the ordinary demands of social interaction. Thus J. Pieper includes within the comprehension of the term leisure "the philosophical act, the religious act, the aesthetic act, and, of course, the effect of love and death, or some other way in which man's relation to the world is convulsed and shaken—all these fundamental ways of acting belong naturally together, by reason of the power which they have in common of enabling a man to break through and transcend the workaday world" (*Leisure* 95).

Leisure, then, is time spent in activities intimately and causally connected with the highest powers of man (*see* PERFECTION, ONTOLOGICAL). These activities have no other purpose than the individual's fullest self-realization. What this human perfection involves concretely and what activities further its achievement are matters of cultural definition. At the sociological level, therefore, the important consideration is that norms of human perfection are operative in any society, whether

Christian or Marxist, for example, and the time available for uninterrupted and single-minded pursuit of the ideal norm is leisure time.

Commentators usually portray the Greek tradition of leisure, for example; as highly intellectualist with a heavy emphasis on CONTEMPLATION and a bias against action. This linking of intellect and leisure is understandable in the light of the Greek linking of the intellect with man's perfection. Aristotle concluded that the life of the intellect is the best and most pleasant for man because the intellect, more than anything else, is the man (*see* INTELLECTUAL LIFE). He stressed that all noncontemplative activities are encased in a productive system: they are means used to gain further goals. But contemplation frees man from any instrumental system and is "loved for its own sake; for nothing arises from it apart from the contemplating, while from practical activities we gain more or less apart from the action" (*Ethica Nicomachea*, 1177 b).

In modern society contemplation is not considered the highest realization of man's powers nor the pinnacle of knowledge and thus, even in the Greek sense, it can no longer be considered as the only act worthy of the term leisure. Science, for example, as Werner Heisenberg and others point out, is innately a form of activity in which the answers to questions in nature are not simply found, but provoked by the active attitude of the investigators. Even before the impact of science, the Christian emphasis on love of neighbor and the priority of deeds over words, the stress on the unity of thought and action, did much to shift the Western perspective on the perfection of man from a primarily intellectualist to a more integral conception.

Universality. Although the Greeks reflected on leisure more than any other people, leisure was not unknown outside their tradition. In fact, leisure is a cultural universal. Even non-industrial peoples are capable of producing some excess of goods over the minimum demands of necessity. The ceremonial exchange of goods and the extension of credit by one tribesman to another show that not only entire groups, but individuals within these groups, may possess surpluses over immediate needs. They translate their economic surpluses, however small, into social leisure that is enjoyed primarily but not entirely by the members of the community who are supported by this excess wealth. Besides this, from the standpoint of the depth and intangible richness of a human life, it is not hard to see that non-industrialized people of the past, or present, provided they are not penurious and not involved in dehumanized work, may in their daily life enjoy more constant leisure than those in industrialized and technological societies. Heidegger says that the ten-

dency in these latter groups has been "to look upon the world primarily as a fund of energy." This has produced a shallowness of meaning and an understanding of leisure as mere diversion. Similarly, Gabriel Marcel has said apropos the often technocratic modern world that "a great tragedy with the world today is that life is no longer loved but taken as something to be gotten through."

The empirical fact of the universality of leisure can be intelligibly explained by a systematic functional analysis of society. Viewed as a whole, any successful society must solve four major functional problems: (1) adaptation to its environment, accomplished for the most part by economic institutions; (2) goal setting, the task of political institutions; (3) management of the tension generated by the possible conflict between an individual's desires and capabilities and society's demands and requirements, a contribution made largely by the family and other primary groups; and (4) the integration or harmonization of all the different institutions that are meeting the problems of adaptation, goal setting, and management of tension. The integrative function is performed when the social system, through a religion or ideology, explains itself to itself. There must be a broad general consensus as to the worth of the system and the justness of its demands, if relatively smooth interaction is to be possible. The implications of this analysis are apparent: if the integrative function is necessary for a society, as both theoretical analysis and empirical findings indicate, then much leisure is necessary for some members of the society, and some leisure is necessary for all members. The formulation of values and their effective transmission to the population and, equally important, the internalization of these crucial values demand at least some degree of freedom from toil.

Leisure, then, appears in every society precisely because it is a prerequisite for the formation and survival of a society. Some have seen the development of a leisure class simply as a parasitical growth undermining the efficiency of a society. Historically, leisure has frequently been twisted into a shield of privilege. Analysis confined to these phenomena, however, is inadequate to the explanation of leisure. First, consensus makers and transmitters of values are functionally required by all societies. Second, leisure can never be entirely limited to one social class, for the members of a society must, to some degree, have the time and opportunity to internalize the core values of the society. Because of the plasticity of the human organism, internalization is never merely passively receptive but rather a dynamic process of acceptance and ratification. Rejection of values is also a possibility and, under certain conditions, is one of the important sources of social change.

Acceptance or rejection of values involves necessary reference to an ego-ideal, and it is this reference to some standard of human perfectibility that roots the functional analysis of leisure well within the traditional conception of the term. Thus the foregoing analysis of the integrative function of leisure, with its concomitant emphasis on values and concept of human perfectibility, turns out to be very Greek in its theoretical structure. The concrete results in application to a specific society can nevertheless be very non-Hellenic. A society could channel most of its energies into solving one functional problem, such as economic adaptation, and give relatively little consideration to the problem of explaining the significance of this productive activity and its relation to the perfection of its citizenry.

American Patterns. For example, most commentators observe that American leisure patterns are competitive in tone and pervaded with puritanical doubts that are resolved only by justifying leisure as earned by work or as necessary for continued work. Many Americans fear retirement not because of economic worries but simply because of a gnawing fear that their idleness will lower their prestige in a work-oriented society that confers status only on active producers. In a word, leisure in America can be viewed as strongly affected by economic functions and characterized by the need for mere tension release rather than engagement in significant activity. Leisure's relation to the integrative function is less pronounced. This analysis is in tune with the often heard remark that America is long on means but short on ends. Still, this tendency has been reducing in American society in the last 50 years, as evidenced by a 2001 IPSOS poll contrasted with one taken by Gallup in 1955. The recent poll shows considerably less interest in work itself and in leisure for the purpose of resting one for work and correspondingly more interest in leisure as contributive of meaning and wellness in one's life. One may wonder, of course, how much this developing appreciation for leisure is a refinement of self-occupied pleasures and health and how much it represents a greater openness to spiritual joy and to an embracive generosity to other persons.

Despite America's poor history with regard to the social evaluation of leisure, some observers are optimistic about future leisure patterns. Although American leisure is strongly influenced by economic values, the economic sphere itself is undergoing radical change. With the spread of AUTOMATION and the increase of managerial jobs, work can become more of an expression of human creativity and initiative. If this is the case, then leisure and work can be identified on the deepest level: the achieving of human perfection. For if work is increasingly characterized by intelligence, initiative, and responsibility, it will become more an expression of human creativeness and will be very close to those activities that the Greeks termed leisure. This is, of course, highly conjectural. Work, since it does to some degree tie one to a system, can never be an expression of complete initiative and responsibility. Work and leisure will perhaps be closer partners in the future, but they will remain, to some degree, distinct. According to traditional Western philosophy, this distinction is rooted in the very nature of man. For it is man's nature to be part of a social system, to be an individual member of a species, and yet to transcend the system as a person, as an end in himself.

Philosophical Remarks. In a more philosophical and spiritual vein, leisure can be viewed as a sense of deep restfulness and presence to life: to nature, other persons, one's self, and God. It can become a contemplative act in which one realizes that in spite of the hustle and bustle of life there is time to learn, love, laugh, and enjoy. Like every virtue it is ultimately both a gift from God and an expression of our freedom. Its presence in daily life draws us beyond mere toil and goal-fixation, beyond perfectionism and toward real perfection and sanctity. It carries us beyond all forms of acquisitiveness and lust, mere egoistic planning and daydreaming, and needless worry into briefer and longer periods of delight in the ordinary and innocent pleasures of body and soul, in the expression of our creative energies, and in the contemplation of God. In this deepest, truest, and most humane form of leisure we are enabled to step out of the tyranny of worldly tasks and goals into a foretaste of eternity. In Charles Pèguy's poem "Sleep" God says to the worker who resents the need to sleep that "I have it against you a little because you have it against my creature sleep. The world has told you never to put off till tomorrow what you can do today. But I, God, tell you: Never do today what you can put off until tomorrow. Blessed is he who puts off."

Bibliography: ARISTOTLE, *Ethica Nicomachea,* J. PEIPER, *Leisure: The Basis of Culture,* tr. A. DRU (New York 1952; rev. 1964), invaluable speculative introductions S. DE GRAZIA, *Of Time, Work and Leisure* (New York 1962). P. TEILHARD DE CHARDIN, *The Divine Milieu* (New York 1960). H. ARENDT, *The Human Condition* (Chicago 1958). T. VEBLEN, *Theory of the Leisure Class* (London 1898; pa. New York 1954). N. ANDERSON, *Work and Leisure* (New York 1961). H. DURANT, *The Problem of Leisure* (London 1938), E. O. SMIGEL, ed., *Work and Leisure* (New Haven 1963). R. DENNEY and M. L. MEYERSON, "A Preliminary Bibliography on Leisure," *American Journal of Sociology* 62 (1956–57) 602–615. W. KERR, *The Decline of Pleasure* (New York 1962). G. MARCEL, *Being and Having,* tr. K. FARRER (London 1949). T. WINNIFRITH and C. BARRETT, eds., *The Philosophy of Leisure* (New York 1989).

[J. R. KELLY/R. E. LANE]

LE JAY, CLAUDE (JAJUS)

Theologian; b. Mieussy, near Geneva, 1504; d. Vienna, Aug. 6, 1552. Le Jay followed his friend Peter FABER to Paris and there earned a master's degree in arts in 1534; he made solemn profession with St. Ignatius in 1541. With Salmeron and Canisius he earned a doctorate at Bologna, and in 1542 he was sent by Paul III to Germany, where he lectured on the scriptures at Ingolstadt. His clear theological mind was enlisted by Cardinal O. TRUCHSESS VON WALDBURG both before and during the Council of Trent. At the Synod of Salzburg he greatly aided the Catholic cause by clearly indicating that the denial of papal primacy was itself heresy. At Trent he was one of the two theologians charged with drafting the decree on sacred scripture and tradition.

Bibliography: C. SOMMERVOGEL *Bibliothèque de la Compagnie de Jésus,* 11 v. (Brussels-Paris 1890–1932) 4:765.

[A. ROCK]

LEJEUNE, JEAN

French Oratorian and preacher; b. Dôle, in Franche-Compté, 1592; d. Limoges, Aug. 19, 1672. Lejeune was the son of a successful lawyer, councilor of the parlement of Dôle, and member of a well-known family distinguished for careers in law and renowned for piety. He studied theology at the University of Dôle and had settled down as a canon of Arbois when he came under the influence of Pierre de Bérulle, founder of the French Congregation of the Oratory. In 1611 Lejeune renounced his canonry and entered the Oratory; after serving briefly as director of the seminary at Langres, he devoted the rest of his life to preaching. The next few years saw Lejeune preaching Advent and Lenten courses, missions, and sermons throughout France. He quickly became known as a most persuasive orator, notable for his unusual ardor and an exceptionally popular style. At age 37 he was struck blind in the midst of a Lenten course at Rouen, but he continued to engage in preaching as much as ever with the aid of a devoted confrere, Lefevre, who acted as his companion.

Lejeune soon acquired the nickname of Le Père Aveugle (the blind father), and his handicap served to increase and strengthen his apostolate rather than to diminish it. He was noted for his life of mortification and acquired a reputation for sanctity, so that Lamy could praise him for preaching by his manner of life more than by his style of oratory.

In 1662 he published in Toulouse a collection of 362 sermons, which was later republished under the title they now bear, *Le Missionaire de L'Oratoire* (Lyons 1825–27). The sermons deal with the usual topics in a rather unpretentious style without polemics. They do suffer from faults common in the seventeenth century, especially from lengthy classical citations and a somewhat unusual manner of presentation. In a typical sermon, Lejeune would first state the theme of his discourse and then proceed to prove the thesis by successive arguments from Sacred Scripture, from the Fathers of the Church, and from natural reason, so that his talks greatly resembled classroom presentations of theological theses.

In general, he avoided controversial issues and tended to confine himself to the exposition of fundamental Catholic doctrine. Even so, he was personally criticized and shared in the suspicion of Jansenism generally directed toward the French Oratory. Selections of his sermons were translated into Latin and published under the title *Johannis Junii deliciae pastorum* (Mainz 1667).

Bibliography: G. GOYAU, *Histoire religieuse,* v. 6 of G. A. A. HANOTAUX, *Histoire de la nation française,* 15 v. (Paris 1920–35). A. MOLIEN, *Dictionnaire de théologie catholique,* 15 v. (Paris 1903–50) 9.1:196–197.

[A. J. CLARK]

LEJEUNE, JÉRÔME

Physician, research scientist, member of the Pontifical Academy of Sciences, first president, Pontifical Academy for Life; b. Montrouge, France, 1927; d. Paris, France, April 3, 1994. Jérôme Lejeune studied at the University of Paris, earning a doctorate in medicine in 1951 and a doctorate in science in 1960. While in his early thirties, he worked at the Centre National de la Recherche Scientifique, the French government laboratory. At age thirty-one, he discovered the chromosomal abnormality that causes Down Syndrome, a form of mental retardation. This seminal discovery opened the door to an increase in the field of genetic research known as clinical cytogenetics that deals with disorders resulting from chromosomal abnormalities.

Lejeune showed that in Down Syndrome, the extra chromosome was a marker for biochemical imbalance. Although he never produced a way to prevent the condition, he devised several protocols for its treatment and was able in most cases to improve the intelligence of his patients. He also identified the occurrence of thyroid deficiency in fifty percent of his patients under five. By treating the thyroid deficiency, he was able to improve his patients' intelligence and activity quickly and permanently. He also discovered other conditions caused by chromosomal abnormalities (e.g., the deletion of the short arm on the fifth pair of chromosomes in Cri du Chat syndrome). At the time of his death, he was treating amino acid deficiencies in his patients.

While professor of fundamental genetics at the René Descartes University, he also ran a department at the institute of genetics and treated patients at the Hospital for Sick Children in Paris. Lejeune continued his research and treatment of Down Syndrome children from around the world even when government funding for his work was withdrawn.

His work did not go unrecognized, and he was honored in many countries. In France, he was a member of the sociological section of the Academy of Moral and Political Sciences; in the United States, he was a member of the American Academy of Arts and Sciences, having spent several years in the United States. He worked with the United Nations scientific committee on congenital abnormalities, and he was a member of many academies of science worldwide.

Christian Faith. Lejeune's Christian faith was the bedrock of both his personal and his public life, and he never compromised the fundamental belief that all human life is sacred from conception to natural death. When Lejeune began research into Down Syndrome, he was one of several scientists working on the problem in Europe. With the advent of legalized abortion, the attitude of the medical profession changed. Research became concentrated on what has been described as "search and destroy": most modern research is concerned with finding a quick and efficient test to spot a child with Down Syndrome as early as possible in pregnancy in order that the child may be aborted. By the mid-1970s Lejeune was one of few scientists in Europe still trying to find a cure or an amelioration for the Down Syndrome children.

In 1974 he was made a member of the Pontifical Academy of Sciences and in the 1980s he was in great demand by Pope John Paul II for information and advice on the many disturbing developments in genetics, such as embryo experimentation and genetic engineering. They became close friends. When the pope established the Pontifical Academy for Life, he invited Lejeune to become its first president, although the pope knew that Lejeune was dying. Lejeune was a great leader in the prolife movement, serving as chairman of Laissez-les vivres, president of the Society for the Protection of Unborn Children (SPUC), and founding member of the World Federation of Doctors Who Respect Human Life.

Bibliography: J. LEJEUNE, *Les Chromosomes humains* (Paris 1965); *Concentration Can* (San Francisco 1992).

[M. WHITE]

LELOUTRE, JEAN LOUIS

Missionary; b. Morlaix. France, Sept. 26, 1709; d. Nantes, France, 1772. After ordination at the seminary of the Paris Foreign Mission Society in 1737, he was sent to Canada to the parish of Annapolis, Nova Scotia, but he was detained in Louisbourg, Cape Breton Island. He was named as missionary to the Acadian Micmacs (Nova Scotia) and arrived in Schubenacadie in 1738. In 1745 he returned to Louisbourg as military chaplain. Following a trip to France, he resumed his missionary work among the Micmacs in 1749. In 1754 he was named vicar-general of Quebec. He was taken prisoner by the English after the fall of Ft. Beausejour and was deported to the Island of Jersey (1758–63). After the Treaty of Paris he was released; he returned to France, where he became involved in arrangements for the settlement of the Acadians at Belle-isle-en-mer, Canada.

Bibliography: N. M. ROGER, "The Abbé Le Loutre," *Canadian Historical Review* 11 (1930): J. B. BREBNER, *New England's Outpost* (New York 1927). J. C. WEBSTER, *The Career of Abbé Le Loutre* (privately printed; Shediac, N.B. 1933).

[G. CARRIÈRE]

LE MAISTRE, ANTOINE AND ISAAC

Brothers who were prominent in the history of JANSENISM, particularly as *solitaires* of PORT-ROYAL.

Antoine, lawyer and writer; b. Paris, May 2, 1608; d. Port-Royal, near Paris, Nov. 4, 1658. He was the son of Isaac Le Maistre, a master of requests, and of Catherine Arnauld, a sister of the reformer of Port-Royal, Angélique Arnauld. After acquiring a brilliant legal reputation, he came under the influence of Jean Duvergier de Hauranne, Abbé Saint-Cyran and withdrew to Port-Royal in 1637. Antoine was known to his contemporaries primarily for his legal speeches, which were already famous when he published them in 1657. Afterward, Antoine used his eloquence to vindicate his fellow-Jansenists. He defended Saint-Cyrian in a spirited letter to Cardinal Richelieu in 1638, and again in the *Apologie pour feu M. l'ábbe de Saint-Cyrian* (Paris 1642). He produced several other polemics, devotional works, and translations.

Isaac, spiritual director and writer, better known as Le Maistre de Saci (Sacy; anagrams of Isaac); b. Paris, March 29, 1613; d. Pomponne, Jan. 4, 1684. In 1637 he retired with his brother to Port-Royal. After his ordination in 1649, he became spiritual adviser to the other *solitaires*. With the imposition of Alexander VII's "formulary" in 1661, he fled from Port-Royal, was imprisoned from 1666 to 1668 in the Bastille, and spent most of his later life in exile. Isaac did much to popularize Jansenism in France by letting it speak through his many translations of the Scriptures and Church Fathers. Among his best-known works was *Traduction du Noveau Testament*, 2 v. (Amsterdam 1667), which was condemned by Clement IX in 1669. His life's work was to initiate *La sainte Bible en latin et en français,* 32 v. (Paris 1687–1702).

Bibliography: G. DELASSAUT, *Le Maistre de Sacy et son temps* (Paris 1957). J. CARREYRE, *Dictionnaire de théologie catholique,* ed. A. VACANT et al., 15 v. (Paris 1903–50) 9.1:198–202. *Biographie universelle,* ed. L. G. MICHAUD, 45 v. (Paris 1843–65) 24:65–66; 37:196–198.

[J. Q. C. MACKRELL]

LE MASSON, INNOCENT

Carthusian author; b. Noyon, Dec. 21, 1627; d. May 8, 1703. He entered the Carthusian order at Mont-Renaud in 1645, and became prior there 18 years later. In 1675 he became prior of Grande-Chartreuse and general of the order. The following year his monastery was destroyed by fire, and he designed the new buildings of Grande-Chartreuse. He reconstituted the archives and produced *Annales Ordinis Cartusiensis,* later known as *Disciplina Ordinis Cartusiensis* (ed. Montreuil, 1894). It is a commentary on the rules and a vindication of the order from accusations of relaxation made by Abbé de Rancé. Le Masson also stimulated the composition of the real annals of the order by Dom Le Couteulx (8 v. ed. Montreuil, 1887) and of the collection by Dom Le Vasseur of biographies of saintly Carthusians, *Ephemerides Ordinis Cartusiensis* (5 v., ed. Montreuil, 1890). He prepared a new edition of the rules that had been approved by Rome in 1688. During his administration, he himself controlled and disposed many things, and centralized authority into the hands of the general; sometimes his ideas were out of harmony with authentic Carthusian traditions.

He preserved Carthusian spirituality from dangers of JANSENISM, ordering books suspected of the heresy to be gathered up from the charterhouses and sent to the head house, where he burned them. He wrote a *Directorium Novitiorum* and several treatises for the young monks' instruction. They are sound in doctrine, clear and pithy, and illustrated by apt examples. His Carthusian sources for these were GUIGO II, Adam of Cryburgh, LUDOLPH OF SAXONY, DENIS THE CARTHUSIAN, and Johannes Justus LANSPERGIUS; he borrowed also from Thomas à Kempis (*The Imitation of Christ*) and from St. FRANCIS DE SALES.

Le Masson combated QUIETISM, particularly among the Carthusian nuns whose houses he himself visited. He composed the *Semaine du Sacré-Coeur* for them.

Bibliography: C. M. BOUTRAIS, *La Grande Chartreuse par un Chartreux* (9th ed. Grenoble 1964). J. P. MARTIN, "La Doctrine spirituelle de Dom Innocent Le Masson," *Revue d'ascétique et de mystique* 17 (1936): 368–396; 18 (1937): 45–64. S. AUTORE, *Dictionnaire de théologie catholique,* 15 v. (Paris 1903–50) 9.1:202–208.

[B. DU MOUSTIER]

LEME DA SILVEIRA CINTRA, SEBASTIÃO

Second Brazilian cardinal; b. Espirito Santo do Pinhal, São Paulo, Jan. 20, 1882; d. Rio de Janeiro, Oct. 17, 1942. After becoming a priest on Oct. 10, 1904, he served in São Paulo as assistant pastor, seminary professor, director of the Catholic daily, *A Gazeta do Povo,* and cathedral canon. He was consecrated auxiliary bishop to Cardinal Joaquim ARCOVERDE DE ALBUQUERQUE CAVALCANTI, of Rio de Janeiro, in 1911. In 1916 he became archbishop of Olinda, Pernambuco, where he actively supported the press and religious instruction. He did much to promote priestly vocations and Eucharistic weeks, founded the Catholic Confederation to coordinate Catholic Action associations, and rebuilt the cathedral and episcopal palace. His pastoral letter of 1916 on religious ignorance and its remedies aroused nationwide concern for its frankness in the treatment of religious indifference and the inefficiency of the Catholic majority.

As coadjutor bishop of ailing Cardinal Arcoverde, he launched, in 1923, the Catholic Confederation of Rio de Janeiro, which, together with the significant manual, *Acão Católica,* set the policy of future Catholic Action. The same year he was the president of the first National Eucharistic Congress, which invigorated the Catholicism of Rio de Janeiro. In 1924 he was instrumental in reopening the diocesan seminary, which had been closed for 16 years. He organized spiritual retreats for the laity, instituted the Social Week of Catholic Action in 1928, and promoted the construction of the huge statue of Christ the Redeemer overlooking the city from Mount Corcovado. Dom Leme succeeded Arcoverde as archbishop of Rio de Janeiro in 1930 and went to Rome to receive the cardinal's hat. During his difficult term, he sought to attack directly the evils already outlined in his 1916 pastoral letter, and his principal fighters were intellectuals transformed into defenders of the faith. These intellectuals, stimulated by the cardinal, associated themselves with the "Centro Dom Vital" and the periodical *Ordem,* founded by Jackson Figueiredo, and extended their influence into various sectors of national life.

During the revolution fostered by the state of São Paulo against Getúlio Vargas in 1932, Leme acted with diplomatic decision. The cardinal obtained promises from the Constitutional Assembly for the abolition of certain anti-Catholic laws and their replacement by Catholic ones. He founded the Catholic Electoral League (LEC), which supported candidates who attacked divorce and secularism in the schools and who favored chaplaincies for the Armed Forces and hospitals. Owing to pressure from the cardinal's Catholic Confederation, women received the right to vote, and the Constitution of 1934 acquired a Christian foundation. Leme organized and was named papal legate of the important Brazilian Plenary Council of 1939, which modernized ecclesiastical legislation for the Church in Brazil. His last important act was the foundation of the Catholic University of Rio de Janeiro in 1941.

Bibliography: L. PESSOA RAJA GABAGLIA, *O cardeal Leme, homem de coração* (Rio de Janeiro 1945). G. SCHUBERT, ed., *A província eclesiâstica do Rio de Janeiro* (Rio de Janeiro 1948). I. M. R. DO SANTO ROSARIO, *O cardeal Leme* (Rio de Janeiro 1962).

[I. SILVEIRA]

LEMIRE, JULES

French priest and legislator; b. Hazebrouck (Nord), April 23, 1853; d. Hazebrouck, March 7, 1928. As a young teacher he was impressed by the social doctrines of Frédéric le Play and Cardinal Henry Edward MANNING; he dedicated to Manning his book *Le Cardinal Manning et son oeuvre sociale* (Paris 1893). In 1893 he was elected as a Christian Democratic deputy from his native department in opposition to a conservative. Soon after, he was wounded in the Chamber of Deputies during an anarchist uprising. He projected the image of a progressive priest—a "democratic pastor"—and sat in the assembly with the anti-clerical party on the left during the open conflict between Church and State. His candidacy for reelection was first disapproved and then forbidden by the archbishop of Cambrai. In 1914, when he was triumphantly reelected and named vice-president of the Chamber of Deputies, he refused the latter office but incurred ecclesiastical suspension nonetheless. This was lifted in 1916 by Benedict XV. Lemire remained in the position of deputy until his death.

Lemire dedicated his oratorical talent and his zeal to spreading the doctrine of *RERUM NOVARUM* and the ideals of Christian democracy. He established innumerable workers' gardens. In the Chamber of Deputies, he addressed himself to the defense of the family in opposition to the individualistic conception of the Code Civil. Indefatigable in his interventions, he helped to secure the first family benefits: civil service allowances, marriage assistance, and the protection of family property against unjust seizure. He was the first to petition for the establishment of a ministry of labor. In 1901 he encouraged the priests' congress of Bourges to introduce young priests to the social teaching of the popes and its early accomplishments. In his last years he was an outstanding mayor of his own town of Hazebrouck.

Bibliography: J. DORIGNY, *L'Abbé Lemore: Sa carrière parlementaire* (Paris 1914). J. R. and G. RÉMY, *Une grande figure et un grand coeur: L'Abbé Lemire* (Paris 1929). C. DROULERS, *Chemin faisant avec l'Abbé Lemire* (Paris 1929).

[H. ROLLET]

LEMKE, PETER HENRY

Missionary; b. Rhena, Mecklenburg, Germany, July 27, 1796; d. Carrolltown, Pa., Nov. 29, 1882. His parents, J. Martin and Friederike Lemke, sent him to the Lutheran cathedral school at Schwerin, Germany, in 1811. Later he attended the University of Rostock, Mecklenburg-Schwerin, and received his license as a Lutheran minister in 1820. After reading the works of Martin Luther in 1823, Lemke lost his faith. He then went to Regensburg, Germany; there he was converted to Catholicism in 1824 and was ordained on April 11, 1826. He began his American missionary career under Bishop Francis P. Kendrick of Philadelphia, Pa., in 1834. The next year he was sent to assist Demetrius Gallitzin, the prince priest of Loretto, Pa. Here in western Pennsylvania Lemke bought land and founded Carrolltown. On Feb. 2, 1853, as Father Henry, he pronounced his Benedictine vows at the Priory of St. Vincent, Latrobe, Pa. In 1855 he moved to Doniphan City in the Kansas Territory, becoming the forerunner of the Benedictines at Atchison, Kans. In 1858 he revisited Europe and wrote a biography of Gallitzin. After holding pastorates in Elizabeth, N.J. (1861–77), he retired to Carrolltown.

Bibliography: P. BECKMAN, *Kansas Monks: A History of St. Benedict's Abbey* (Atchison, Kans. 1957) 9–43. A. A. LAMBING, *Ave Maria* 19 (1883) 41–45; 68–71; 110–113; 128–132; 141–143.

[R. J. MURTHA]

LEMOS, TOMÁS DE

Theologian; b. Rivadavia, Spain, c. 1546; d. Rome, Aug. 23, 1629. With Diego ÁLVAREZ, De Lemos was chosen to represent officially the Dominican position in the dispute over the nature of efficacious grace. A papal commission had voted to censure 61 propositions in Luis de MOLINA's *Concordia liberi arbitrii cum gratiae donis.* Since subsequent efforts at reconciling the two positions had proven futile, Clement VIII (d. 1605) brought the Jesuit defendants and their accusers face to face. Clement VIII and Leo XI (d. 1605) died without reaching a decision. Under Paul V (d. 1621) the cardinals voted to condemn 42 propositions of Molina, but no final decision was ever reached. Throughout the discussion Tomás de Lemos made a trenchant presentation of the Augustinian-Thomistic position. At the close of the dispute, he refused a bishopric offered him through the King of Spain and retired to the Roman priory of Santa Maria sopra Minerva.

His part in the 47 discussions was subsequently published in the *Acta omnia congregationum ac disputationum* (Louvain 1702). His own famous work *Panopolia gratiae* (4 v., Liége 1676) was attacked by the Inquisition but vigorously defended by the Dominicans.

Bibliography: J. QUÉTIF and J. ÉCHARD, *Scriptores Ordinis Praedicatorum* (New York 1959) 2.1:461–464. M. D. CHENU, *Dictionnaire de théologie catholique,* ed. A. VACANT et al. (Paris 1903–50) 9.1:210–211.

[W. D. HUGHES]

Vladimir Ilich Lenin, painting by Valentin Aleksandrovich Serov.

LENIN, N.

Pseudonym of Vladimir Ilich Ulyanov, founder of the Russian Bolshevik party, first head of the Soviet Union; b. Simbirsk (now Ulyanovsk), April 22 (N.S.), 1870; d. Gorki, near Moscow, Jan. 21, 1924. The talents of young Vladimir, son of a school inspector, were recognized early by the director of his gymnasium, F. M. Kerensky, father of Alexander Kerensky, who became head of the provisional government after the revolution of 1917. In May of 1887, an older brother, Alexander, was executed for participation in a populist attempt to assassinate Czar Alexander III. In June of 1887, the family moved to Kazan, where Vladimir entered the university law school. He joined an illegal student circle and, to avoid arrest, left the university. The czarist police soon took him into custody, however, and he was exiled to the village of Kokuschkino. In the fall of 1888 he was allowed to return to Kazan, where he joined the Marxist circle under the leadership of Fedoseev. In 1891 he took his bar examination in St. Petersburg and returned to practice law in Samara (now Kuibyshev), where the family had moved in 1889. He founded the first Marxian circle in the city in 1892, demanding from the members unquestioning subordination to his dictates. In August of 1893, he returned to the capital.

Lenin's first monograph, circulated privately in 1894, was entitled "Who Are the 'Friends of the People' and How Do They Fight Against Social Democrats?" It was directed against the populist organization. In April of 1895, he traveled for the first time to Western Europe to make contacts with emigré Marxists who had established themselves in Geneva as the "Liberation of Labor" group. He returned to Russia in September of 1895 and united most of the existing Marxist groups in St. Petersburg into one organization, the "Union for the Struggle for the Liberation of the Working Class." In December of that year he was arrested and jailed, and in February of 1897 he was exiled for three years to Eastern Siberia. There he continued to write and to discuss the problems of the Russian Marxists with other exiled revolutionaries. He wrote pamphlets for his followers at home and prepared a monumental work, *The Development of Capitalism in Russia* (1897). To hide his identity he adopted in 1900 the pseudonym N. Lenin.

Foundation of the Bolshevik Party. After emigrating to Western Europe in July 1900, Lenin began in December the publication in Germany of his first newspaper, *Iskra* (The Spark), which was smuggled to the Russian empire. It was at his insistence that the second congress of the Russian Socialist Democratic Labor Party was convened in Brussels and London during the summer of 1903 (the founding congress had been held at Minsk in 1898). A bitter discussion about the structure of the party led to a split between the *Bolshinstvo,* (i.e., majority, hence *Bolsheviks,*) and the *Menshinstvo,* (i.e., minority, hence, Mensheviks). The next year Lenin started his own Bolshevik newspaper, *Vperyod* (Forward). The Bolsheviks played only a very small role during the Russian revolution of 1905. Lenin returned to the Russian capital in November of that year but, realizing the weakness of the Marxists, he eventually fled again to Switzerland and later moved to Paris. His main preoccupation from 1907 to 1912 was with polemics against the Mensheviks and all other elements that opposed his views. In 1912, the Bolshevik party was formed as an independent political organization at a conference in Prague. Later in the year Lenin moved to Cracow, Poland, where he convened the Bolshevik Central Committee. It was at this meeting that he decided to utilize the national enmity between the Russians and the non-Russians for revolutionary Bolshevik strategy. At the outbreak of World War I he was arrested by the Austrian police but managed to return to Switzerland where, together with G. Zinoviev, he established the headquarters of Bolshevik agitation.

The Soviet Revolution. When the czarist empire collapsed, during the revolution of February and March of 1917, Lenin returned to Russia and immediately demanded ''All Power to the Soviets.'' He called for an immediate end to the war, distribution of land to the peasants, and the right of all nations of the former Russian empire to self-determination, including secession from Russia. In July he provoked a revolt against the provisional government, but the Bolsheviks were quickly defeated. Lenin went into hiding in Finland. By September, however, the St. Petersburg Soviet (elected council) was under Bolshevik control. Trotsky, who had joined Lenin's forces early in 1917, became its chairman. During the night of November 7–8, the Bolsheviks gained control of St. Petersburg and forced the provisional government to capitulate.

The first Soviet government was formed on November 8. Its cabinet was called the Council of People's Commissars, and Lenin was its chairman. The secret police, the *Cheka,* was organized. Lenin ordered the nationalization of property. In January of 1918, he dispersed the constituent assembly. In March he signed the Brest-Litovsk Peace Treaty with the Central Powers. When the non-Russian nations proclaimed their independence, Lenin ordered the Red Army to invade and conquer them. In March of 1921, however, he reversed his policy of integral socialism (''war communism'') and initiated the New Economic Policy, interpreted by many as a retreat from Marxist principles and a return to partial private ownership. On May 26, 1922, he suffered a stroke, and only temporarily regained his health. One of his last major concerns was the role of Joseph Stalin, whom he wanted removed from his position as general secretary of the Party.

Bibliography: V. I. LENIN, *Selected Works,* 2 v. in 4 (Moscow 1952). D. SHUB, *Lenin* (New York 1950). D. W. TREADGOLD, *Lenin and His Rivals* (New York 1955). B. D. WOLFE, *Three Who Made a Revolution* (New York 1948).

[M. S. PAP]

LENT

From the Anglo-Saxon *Lencten,* meaning springtime, Lent is the 40–day period of prayer, penance, and spiritual endeavor in preparation for Easter. Lent is not an end in itself; it exists only to lead to the paschal feast and so can be rightly understood only in the light of Easter. Easter gives meaning to Lent and shows it for what it is: the great paschal retreat of the Church. ''The season of Lent has a twofold character: primarily by recalling or preparing for the celebration of Christian Initiation and by penance, it disposes the faithful, who more diligently hear the word of God and devote themselves to prayer, *to celebrate the Paschal Mystery*'' (*Constitution on the Sacred Liturgy* 109).

History. In the first three centuries, the period of fasting in preparation for the paschal feast did not exceed a week at the most; one or two days was the usual limit. Irenaeus of Lyons declares that in some places the faithful fasted on only one day, in others two days, and in still others, for 40 consecutive hours (Eusebius, *Eccesiastical History* 5:24; *Patrologia Graeca.* ed J. P. Migne [Paris 1857–66] 20:503). The third or fourth century *Apostolic Tradition* prescribes a two-day fast (33; B. Botte, ed., *La Tradition apostolique de saint Hippolyte: Essai de reconstitution* [*Liturgiegeschichtliche Quellen und Forschungen,* Münster 1909–40] [1963] 79).

The first mention of a period of 40 days occurs in the fifth canon of the Council of Nicaea (325), although some scholars dispute whether Lent is meant there. There is no question about the existence of the 40–day fast later on in that century, however, for St. ATHANASIUS often alluded to it in his festal letters. The Council of Laodicaea (360) expressly commanded its observance, and by the end of the fourth century the 40–day fast, called *tessarakosté* in Greek and *quadragesima* in Latin, was observed everywhere throughout both East and West.

Fasting. The custom may have originated in the prescribed fast of candidates for Baptism; it is certain that the catechumenate had a great deal to do with the formation of Lent. The number 40 was suggested no doubt by Christ's 40–day fast in the desert. The manner of reckoning the 40 days, however, varied in the different Churches. As a rule, the East spread Lent over seven weeks with both Saturday and Sunday exempt from fasting, whereas in the West there was a six–week period with only Sundays exempt. As a result there were only 36 actual fasting days, a situation that the Western Church remedied in the seventh century by adding four days beginning with Ash Wednesday. In the fourth century, however, the concern was not so much about whether there were 40 actual fasting days or not; the approach was to the season as a whole. The emphasis was not as much on the fasting as on the spiritual renewal that the preparation for Easter demanded. It was simply a period marked by fasting, but not necessarily one in which the faithful fasted every day. However, as time went on, more and more emphasis was laid upon fasting, and consequently there is apparent a more precise calculation of the 40 days.

During the early centuries (from the fifth century on especially) the observance of the fast was very strict. Only one meal a day, toward evening, was allowed; flesh meat and fish, and in most places even eggs and dairy products, were absolutely forbidden. Meat was not allowed even on Sundays. However, from the nineth century on the practice began to be considerably relaxed. The time for the one evening meal was anticipated so that by the 15th century it was the general custom even for religious to have this meal at noon. Once that was generally accepted, the way was opened for a collation in the evening, which by the 13th century included some light food as well as drink. The prohibition against fish was removed during the Middle Ages, while dispensation permitting the use of dairy products came to be more general.

In the course of the last few centuries the Holy See has granted other more substantial mitigations of the law of fasting. Meat was allowed at the principal meal on Sundays, then gradually on the weekdays, Friday always excepted. The trend to greater emphasis on other forms of penitential works than fasting and abstinence, particularly on exercises of piety and the works of charity, found legislative expression in the apostolic constitution *Poenitemini* of Pope Paul VI (Feb. 17, 1966). According to this constitution, abstinence is to be observed on Ash Wednesday and on all Fridays of the year that do not fall on holy days of obligation, and fasting as well as abstinence is to be observed on Ash Wednesday and Good Friday.

Spirit. The popular idea of Lent, which prevailed until well into the 20th century was that it was a time of prolonged meditation upon the Passion, with special emphasis upon Christ's physical sufferings. This view finds little support in the texts of the Lenten liturgy, and in any case it must be abandoned in the light of Vatican Council II's insistence that the season of Lent has the twofold character: by recalling or preparing for Christian Initiation and Penance to dispose the faithful for a celebration of the Paschal Mystery. Furthermore, the *Constitution on the Sacred Liturgy* declares that it is important to impress upon the minds of the faithful not only the social consequences of sin, but also the true nature of the virtue of penance as leading to the detestation of sin as an offense against God.

Lent is unquestionably a time of penance, of asceticism, of spiritual discipline. However, making these things ends in themselves can obscure the real purpose of Lent, as is demonstrated in the sermons of the Fathers, especially St. Leo, and in the liturgy itself. The accumulated evidence of Christian tradition in this regard shows without any doubt that the real aim of Lent is, above all else, to prepare Christians for the celebration of the death and RESURRECTION OF CHRIST. This celebration is not a matter only of commemorating the historical fact of the redemption of the human race, but even more of an anamnetical *reliving* the mystery of Redemption in all its fullness. Consequently, the better the preparation, the more effective the celebration will be. One can effectively relive the mystery only with purified mind and heart. The purpose of Lent is to provide that purification by weaning all of humanity from sin and selfishness through self-denial and prayer, by creating in them the desire to do God's will and to make His kingdom come by making it come first of all in their hearts.

Lent is then a collective retreat of 40 days, a time when one tries to live in the spirit of his Baptism, a time of penance in the ancient sense of repentance, *metanoia,* change of heart and mind, conversion.

Once Lent was established in the fourth century, it quickly became associated with Christian Intiation, since Easter was the great baptismal feast. It was the time when those catechumens who would be baptized at the Easter feast were more immediately prepared for that Sacrament. Not only those who were to be baptized, but all Christians prepared themselves for Easter. The Lenten season consequently developed into a time of spiritual renewal for the whole Church and a more profound initiation into the mystery of Christ. The whole Church renews her spiritual youth, and the necessary prelude to this rejuvenation is the awakening of the consciousness of Baptism, of realizing what it means to be baptized. This explains the prominence of the themes of Baptism, new life, and Redemption in the Lenten liturgy.

Lent is especially consecrated to the purification of the heart. This purification is accomplished first of all by sorrow for sin, compunction of heart, and penance, but also involves the positive element of growth in virtue. The Church often insists upon fasting from sin and from vice during these 40 days; in fact bodily fasting is the symbol of this true internal and spiritual fast as well as the means to attain it. True conversion, which is the aim of Lent, means forsaking sin and sinful ways. The Lenten Office reminds us of this every day: "Return to me with your whole heart, with fasting and weeping and mourning; rend your hearts and not your garments says the Lord Almighty" (Joel 2.12–13 from the "little chapter" for Terce). The bodily fasting and self-discipline in which all Christians engage during this time has for its main purpose to give them that control over themselves that they must have to purify their hearts and renew their lives. We are not only to fast from sin, but by our very fasting, pursue holiness. The Gospel pericopes of this season present the person of Christ as the model and source of all holiness. These passages focus attention upon Him and inspire the Christian to follow in His steps.

This conversion from sin and compunction of heart should take place at the very beginning of Lent and not be deferred to the end of the season. Lent is not intended to be a kind of preparation for the Easter Confession. On the contrary, the original ideal was that Confession was made before Lent began. The penance was imposed on Ash Wednesday and penitents guilty of very serious sins were excluded from the Eucharist until they were absolved on Holy Thursday. The whole Lenten season is the time for penance, which means sorrow for sin and conversion to God. A further reason for confessing grave sins before Lent begins is that the Eucharist plays an important part in bringing about that purification of heart that is the goal of the Lenten observance.

Stational Mass. Historically, the importance of Lent in the Church year was emphasized by the fact that each day in this season had its proper Mass and STATIONAL CHURCH. No other season of the year is distinguished in this manner. Furthermore, these Mass formularies (with the exception of the Thursday Masses, which were added in the eighth century) are among the most ancient in the Missal, going back at least to the time of Gregory the Great (d. 606).

The reason there is a proper Mass for each day in Lent is that the Christian community at Rome was accustomed to gather in a designated church to participate in the pope's Eucharistic celebration. This custom emphasized both the unity of the Christian community and the importance of Lent as a time of special prayer. It showed too that Lent is not an individualistic affair, but a corporate action that involves the whole community. The Church at Rome instinctively felt that the solemn corporate offering of the Holy Eucharist by the whole community gathered around its chief shepherd was the ideal way of observing Lent.

After these ferial Masses had been in large part eclipsed for many centuries, Pius X took the first step to restoring them to their original dignity by permitting the Masses of those days to be said even on feast days (below the rank of second class). In the 1955 reforms of Pius XII, all feasts under second class rank are reduced to commemorations leaving the ferial Mass and Office in possession of the day. This gave a renewed prominence to the temporal cycle over the sanctoral, reversing a tendency that began in the Middle Ages and that obscured the fact that the liturgical year is primarily the celebration of the work of Redemption.

The texts of the ferial Masses show strong influence of the themes of the Lenten season: penance, conversion, return to God, sorrow for sin, redemption, the Passion, and especially Baptism. The fact that Lent was the great baptismal retreat of the Church and the last stage of the catechumenate has greatly affected the liturgy of the season.

The last week of Lent is called HOLY WEEK; the theme of the Masses during this time is the Lord's messianic mission achieved by means of His Passion. The prayers continue to refer to fasting, but most of the chants are drawn from those Psalms that allude to the voice of Christ in His Passion. The Gospels during this time present the Passion as a growing conflict between Christ and His enemies. The Office during Passiontide is remarkable chiefly for the hymns that sing the triumph of the cross: the *Pange lingua* of Prudentius and the *Vexilla Regis* of Venantius Fortunatus.

Historically, the Lenten Masses have several other features that set them apart. The most notable are the *Oratio super Populum* and the absence of the Alleluia in the Christian West. The first of these is simply the ancient collect of blessing that concluded every Mass. Gregory the Great dropped this from the Mass during the rest of the year, but retained it for the ferial days during Lent and made it a prayer for penitents. In the 1969 liturgical revisions, the ancient form of collect of blessings was fully restored. In the Latin Church, the Alleluia is so intimately associated with the joy of Easter that it was natural it should be dropped out during so penitential a season as Lent. The Christian East has always kept the use of the Alleluia throughout the Sundays of Lent, on the basis that every Sunday is a celebration of the Lord's celebration, the season of Lent notwithstanding.

Bibliography: E. FLICOTEAUX, *Le Sens du carême* (Paris 1956). H. FRANKE, *Lent and Easter* (Westminster, Md. 1955). T. J. TALLEY, *The Origins of the Liturgical Year* (Collegeville, 1991); A. J. MARTIMORT, ed. *The Church at Prayer IV: The Liturgy and Time* (Collegeville 1986); A. NOCENT, *The Liturgical Year, v. 2 Lent* (Collegeville 1977). A. ADAM, *The liturgical year : its history & its meaning after the reform of the liturgy* (New York 1981).

[W. J. O'SHEA/T. KROSNICKI/EDS.]

LENTINI, DOMENICO, BL.

Priest of the Diocese of Tursi-Lagonegro (formerly Policastro); b. Nov. 20, 1770, at Lauria, Potenza, Italy; d. there Feb. 25, 1828. The youngest of the five children of Macario Lentini and Rosalia Vitarella, Domenico (Dominic) Lentini studied in the seminary at Salerno and was ordained in 1794. In addition to his ministry in Lauria, he taught literature, philosophy, and theology to young people in his home without monetary compensation. He preached and catechized throughout the diocese and spread the devotion to Our Lady of Sorrows. He is called the ''precursor to the Curé d'Ars'' (St. John VIANNEY) because of his willingness to make himself available to hear confessions and his gift of reading hearts. He practiced personal austerity in order to provide charity to the poor, and frequent penances in the spirit of reparation. Lentini was beatified on Oct. 12, 1997 by Pope John Paul II.

Feast: Feb. 25.

Bibliography: *Acta Apostolicae Sedis* 20 (1997): 999. *L'Osservatore Romano*, English edition, no. 42 (1997): 1–2. G. REALE, *Domenico Lentini, santo di paese* (Reggio Calabria 1977).

[K. I. RABENSTEIN]

LENZ, DESIDERIUS

Benedictine architect and sculptor who founded the school of BEURONESE ART; b. Peter Lenz, in Haigerloch, March 12, 1832; d. Beuron, Jan. 28, 1928. After a sculpture course at Munich Academy (1850–58), Lenz was professor at the Nuremberg Artistic Handicrafts School until 1862. He studied in Italy until 1865 and was profoundly influenced by Egyptian art through the publications of the Egyptologist K. R. Lepsius. In 1872 he entered Beuron as artist oblate and was sent to Monte Cassino for his novitiate; he took vows in 1878 (subdiaconate, 1891; choir monk, 1892). Lenz together with Gabriel (Jakob) Wüger founded the Beuron art school in 1894; its purpose was to achieve a renewal of sacred art in a time of overriding naturalism. For this purpose Lenz developed an aesthetic geometry based on his observation of Egyptian art. In his studies he sought for the primordial dimensions of the human body, in order to create a ''dogma-grounded religious art,'' which was his understanding of ancient art. In this spirit, between 1868 and 1871, Lenz built and decorated with frescoes the St. Maur Chapel near Beuron aided by his friends Gabriel Wüger and Luke (Fridolin) Steiner. In 1872 he remodeled the baroque Beuron monastery church, eliminating the high altar with J. A. Feuchtmayer's ''Assumption.'' In later years Lenz and the Beuron school planned and directed extensive projects in the Abbey of Monte Cassino. Frescoes were painted in the tower (1876–80, 1885–93), and the crypt was decorated with mosaics (1898–1913). Decorations were carried out also in the churches of Maredsous, Belgium (1892), and of Emmaus (1881–91) and St. Gabriel (1891–99) in Prague.

Bibliography: D. LENZ, *Zur Ästhetik der Beuroner Schule* (2d ed. Beuron 1927). G. SCHWIND, *P. Desiderius Lenz* (Beuron 1932). M. DREESBACH, ''P. Desiderius Lenz von Beuron: Theorie und Werk,'' *Studien und Mitteilungen zur Geschichte des Benediktinerordens und seiner Zweige* 68 (1957): 95–183; 69 (1958): 5–59. S. MAYER, *Beuroner Bibliographie, 1863–1963* (Beuron 1963) 161–164.

[U. ENGELMANN]

LEO, LEONARDO

Baroque composer of opera and church music (full name: Lionardo Oronzo Salvatore de Leo); b. San Vito degli Schiavi (near Brindisi), Italy, Aug. 5, 1694; d. Naples, Oct. 31, 1744. In 1709 Leo began his musical studies at the Conservatorio Santa Maria della Pietà dei Turchini in Naples. While he was still a student, his first sacred opera (1712) was successfully performed there. He was a supernumerary organist of the royal chapel from 1713, and, after the death of A. SCARLATTI in 1725, he became first organist. As choirmaster for the royal chapel from 1744, Leo composed Mass propers for the Sundays of Lent in A CAPPELLA style to replace the *concertato* music previously favored. At the time of his death, Leo was *primo maestro* at the Conservatorio di Sant' Onofrio (where he began teaching in 1739) and at the Turchini (where he had been *secundo maestro* 1734–37 and *primo maestro* from 1741 on). Among his students were JOMMELLI, Piccini, and Traetta. Leo's importance arises partly from his activity in the Neapolitan *opera seria* tradition (he was also one of the creators of the comic opera) and partly from the contrapuntal innovations in his church music (Masses, Magnificats, motets, etc.). The well-known, eight-voice *Miserere*, for two choirs and basso continuo (ed. H. Wiley Hitchcock, St. Louis 1961), may have drawn other Neapolitan composers to the *a cappella* style. A number of instrumental works (organ, harpsichord, cello) have also been preserved.

Bibliography: H. HUCKE, *Die Musik in Geschichte und Gegenwart*, ed. F. BLUME (Kassel-Basel 1949–) 8:622–630. E. J. DENT, *Grove's Dictionary of Music and Musicians*, ed. E. BLOM, 9 v. (5th ed. London 1954) 5:131–135. R. EITNER, *Quellen-Lexikon der Musiker und Musikgelehrten*, 10 v. [Leipzig 1900–04; New York n.d. (1947)] 6:134–138. Leo's sacred music is repr. in several standard collections. There is no complete modern ed. G. H. HARDIE, ''Leonardo Leo (1694–1744) and His Comic Operas *Amor vuol sofferenze* and *Alidoro*'' (Ph.D. diss. Cornell University, 1973). H. HUCKE,

Leo I, Byzantine Emperor. (Archive Photos)

"Leonardo Leo" in *The New Grove Dictionary of Music and Musicians, vol. 10*, ed. S. SADIE (New York 1980) 666–669. D. M. RANDEL, ed., *The Harvard Biographical Dictionary of Music* (Cambridge 1996) 497. N. SLONIMSKY, ed., *Baker's Biographical Dictionary of Musicians, Eighth Edition* (New York 1992) 1038–1039. S. R. VAN NEST, "Leonardo Leo's F Major *Dixit Dominus*: An Edition and Commentary" (D.M.A. diss. University of Missouri at Kansas City, 1997).

[R. STEINER]

LEO I, BYZANTINE EMPEROR

Reigned from 457 to 474; b. Thrace, *c.* 400; d. Constantinople, 474. A tribune commanding Selymbria, Leo was presented to the troops in Constantinople as the new emperor upon the death in 457 of MARCIAN by the Alan Patrician Aspar. Accepted by the Senate, he was crowned by Patriarch ANATOLIUS, in the first such ceremony recorded in Byzantine history.

When informed of the anti-Chalcedonian intrigue by Julian of Cos, apocrisiarius for Pope Leo I in Constantinople, the new emperor sent an imperial decree to the Oriental metropolitans upholding the orthodox faith (*Acta Conciliarum Oecumenicorum* 2.5:12.8 and 75.28). Under the influence of Monophysite agitation (particularly that of the usurper bishop of Alexandria, TIMOTHY

AELURUS, installed after the murder of Proterius on March 29, 457), and of Aspar, Leo exhibited some hesitation in his attitude toward the Council of CHALCEDON and was importuned by letters from Pope LEO I to himself and Bishop Anatolius.

He decided against a council to revise the Chalcedonian decisions, and he sent a circular inquiry to the Oriental metropolitans, asking whether Chalcedon should be upheld and Timothy Aelurus recognized as bishop of Alexandria (Evagrius, *Hist. Eccl.* 2.9). The metropolitan synods, except that of Pamphylia. voted in favor of Chalcedon and against Timothy, as did the renowned ascetics Symeon STYLITES, John of Cyr, and Baradatus. The results of these consultations, which attested the unity of the episcopate, were published and a policy of rigorous repression of the anti-Chalcedonians inaugurated. Timothy Aelurus was banished to Gangra in Paphlagonia (spring of 460) and the intruder Peter the Fuller (469–471) was deposed from Antioch on the complaint of Bishop Martyrius. A law forbade monks to leave their monasteries unless sent as procurators and prohibited their participation in doctrinal quarrels (*Codex Just.* 1.3.29). In 469 Leo condemned simony in episcopal elections (*ibid.* 1.3.30), having in mind Patriarch Gennadius (458–471) and the collusion of the 80 bishops who attended his installation. Unsuccessful in the repression of the VANDALS in Africa (461–468), he turned against the Arians after the death of Aspar (471).

The unique manuscripts of the Latin translation of the *Codex Encyclius,* which is apparently a second version made by the monk Epiphanius for CASSIODORUS, is mutilated and contains the responses of only 20 provinces to Leo's circular inquiry (*Acta Conciliarum Oecumenicorum* 2.5:24–98).

Bibliography: T. SCHNITZLER, *Im Kampfe um Chalcedon* (Analecta Gregoriana 16; 1938). E. SCHWARTZ, *Publizistische Sammlungen zum Acacianischen Schisma* (*Abhandlungen der Bayerischen Akademie der Wissenschaften* N.S. 10 (Munich 1935–). C. MOELLER, *Das Konzil von Chalkedon: Geschichte und Gegenwart,* A. GRILLMEIER and H. BACHT, eds. 3 v. (Würzburg 1951–54) 1:651–668. F. HOFMANN, *ibid.* 2:24–35. R. HAACKE, *ibid.* 108–112. H. BACHT, *ibid.* 257–261. A. J. FESTUGIÈRE, ed., *Les Moines d'Orient* (Paris 1961–) 2:87–161. E. STEIN, *Histoire du Bas-Empire,* 2 v. in 3 (Paris 1949–59) 1:354–362. F. DÖLGER, *Lexicon für Theologie und Kirche,* 10 v. (Freiburg 1957–65) 6:961.

[H. CHIRAT]

LEO III, BYZANTINE EMPEROR

March 25, 717, to June 18, 741; b. Germaniceia, northern Syria, *c.* 675. Leo was transferred with his parents to Thrace by JUSTINIAN II. He first came into prominence in 705, when he helped Justinian regain his throne.

Justinian rewarded him with the title of *spatharius* and later sent him on a mission to the Caucasus. Anastasius II appointed him *strategus* of the Ametolikon theme, but when Anastasius was overthrown, Leo rebelled and in 717 seized the throne for himself. His reign is known for two important developments: the checking of the expansion of the Arabs and the launching of ICONOCLASM. When Leo shattered the Arab siege of Constantinople in 717, he saved the empire as a whole; and when he defeated them in 740 at Acroinon, he saved Asia Minor. Iconoclasm, launched in 726 (*see* GERMANUS I, PATRIARCH), plunged the empire into a controversy that lasted more than a century; it also brought about a rift with Rome that had serious consequences. For it was as a result of this rift that Leo III removed Sicily, Calabria, and Illyricum (732–733) from the jurisdiction of the papacy and placed them under that of the Byzantine PATRIARCHATE (*see* ANASTASIUS, PATRIARCH OF CONSTANTINOPLE; GREGORY III, POPE). Leo III was also a reformer. He issued a new legal code, the *Ecloga,* and made several administrative changes, but the important social and economic reforms formerly attributed to him are no longer considered to have been his work.

Bibliography: K. SCHENK, *Kaiser Leo III* (Halle 1880). G. OSTROGORKSY, *History of the Byzantine State* (Oxford 1956) 133–147.

[P. CHARANIS]

LEO V, BYZANTINE EMPEROR

Emperor from 813 to 820; iconoclast; d. Constantinople, 820. Leo was of Armenian descent. He served as a general in Anatolia under Michael I and caused that emperor's defeat and deposition by withholding the support of his troops in a battle against the Bulgarians at Versinikia, near Adrianople on June 22, 813. When proclaimed emperor, he assured the patriarch of Constantinople NICEPHORUS I (806–815) of his orthodoxy before entering the capital. After his coronation on July 11, 813, however, he refused to give the patriarch a written assurance of his orthodox faith.

Upon the death of the Bulgarian King Krum on April 13, 814, the siege of Constantinople was raised, and Leo arranged a 30-year peace treaty with the new Bulgarian Khan Omortag (winter of 815–816). He had already initiated the second period of ICONOCLASM, which lasted from 814 to 843. He set up a commission of six to justify the iconoclastic theology in a document that repudiated the making, existence, and veneration of images (Pentecost, 814); exiled Patriarch Nicephorus for his opposition (March 13, 815); installed Theodotus as the new patriarch; and convoked a synod in the Hagia Sophia (April

of 815) to confirm the decisions of Constantine V's council of 754 and condemn the justification of the use of images defined by the Council of NICAEA II (787).

He persecuted bishops Joseph of Thessalonika, Peter of Nicaea, Michael of Synnada, Euthymius of Sardis, and Anthony of Dyrrachium for their opposition to his iconoclastic policy. THEODORE THE STUDITE appealed to Pope PASCHAL I and asked the intervention of the Carolingian King Louis the Pious; and the Studite monk Thaddeus and THEOPHANES THE CONFESSOR died in exile in 818.

Leo's iconoclastic policies, however, were not as stringent as those of his predecessors, and he made a number of converts among the monks who had previously been the strongest upholders of the orthodox position. On the Vigil of Christmas, supporters of Michael II the Amorian (820–829) assassinated Leo in the palace chapel. His reign, despite his iconoclasm, is regarded as one of the more efficient in Byzantine history.

Bibliography: F. DÖLGER, *Corpus der griechischen Urkunden des Mittelalters und der neueren Zeit,* series A, *Regesten* (Munich 1924–32) 1:47–49. P. J. ALEXANDER, *The Patriarch Nicephorus of Constantinople* (New York 1958) 77–80, 111–147, 222. G. OSTROGORSKY, *Studien zur Geschichte des byzantinischen Bilderstreites* (Breslau 1929) 46–60. V. GRUMEL, *Les Regestes des actes du patriarcat de Constantinople,* (Kadikoi-Bucharest 1932–) 1.2:29–41. S. RUNCIMAN, *A History of the First Bulgarian Empire* (London 1930) 61–74.

[H. CHIRAT]

LEO VI, BYZANTINE EMPEROR

Reigned: Aug. 30, 886 (coemperor Jan. 6, 870), to his death on May 11, 912; b. Constantinople?, Sept. 19, 866; d. Constantinople; surnamed "the Wise" during his own lifetime. He was the second son of the emperor Basil I, and the eldest by Basil's marriage to Eudocia Ingerina. Although contemporary sources maintained that his real father was Basil's predecessor, Michael III, Leo never admitted his dubious parentage, and the translation of the body of Michael III to the capital was rather an act of political reconciliation than one of filial concern. He received a careful, mainly literary and theological education. Imprisoned for three years on charges of conspiracy against his father, he survived several conspiracies and revolts during his own reign. His private life was marred by the premature deaths of his first three wives, Theophano Martinakiou, Zoe Zaoutzaina, and Eudocia Baiane, and of two, perhaps even all three of his children by them. In September 905 a male heir, the future Constantine VII, was born by his mistress Zoe Karbounopsina, whereupon Leo uncanonically married for a fourth time. In the ensuing crisis in church-state relations, known as the "Tetragamy affair," he first had the support of Patriarch Nicholas I Mystikos, who subsequently, changed his mind. He was exiled and replaced by the emperor's spiritual father, EUTHYMIUS I. In March 907 a council of the representatives of Rome and the other patriarchates accorded Leo dispensation, although he had to observe penance. After his death, but with his prior consent, his brother the emperor Alexander restored Nicholas to the patriarchal throne. Reconciliation of the rival church parties became possible only in 920 and led to the promulgation of the *Tomus Unionis,* which was the official condemnation and prohibition of fourth marriages in the future (including the regulation of third marriages) and a declaration of the union of the Church.

In the belief that as God's chosen and omnipotent representative on Earth the emperor is responsible for the welfare and guidance of his subjects, Leo consistently pursued imperial control of internal affairs, including his officials, the aristocracy, the military, the guilds, and the church. To this end, one of his first acts after his accession was the deposition of Patriarch Photios and the appointment of his own brother Stephen. He was especially active in the improvement of the efficiency of the state, as several works published during his reign bear witness. They include *Cletorologion* of Philotheos, which is about government administration, and the *Book of the Prefect,* which discusses commerce. His legislative activity was remarkable. It included the completion of the *Sixty Books* (i.e., a great corpus of Roman law, a later version of which came to be known as the *Basilica*), the promulgation of 117 *Novels* and the compilation of the *Procheiron.* His government had the support of worthy administrators, especially Stylianos Zaoutzes, who was prominent in the early years of the reign. Leo was a successful diplomat, and during a period of continuous warfare he was able to stabilize of the empire despite some important defeats by the Bulgars (896) and Arabs (the loss of Taormina in 902, the sack of Thessalonica in 904, and the annihilation of the fleet of Himerios in 911–12). His armies had some success in the field, although Leo did not lead them himself, but his military policies, especially his diplomacy, contributed to the establishment of a balance of power on the eastern and western fronts.

Under Leo the court was a flourishing cultural and intellectual center. He himself was an author, and his literary production includes his *Novels,* two military treatises, homilies and orations (including a funeral oration on his parents), hymnography, and a monastic treatise. Various works, most notably two collections of oracles, were later attributed to him and maintained his posthumous fame as a prophet. Several depictions of Leo survive, and he can probably be identified as the emperor prostrating himself before Christ in the famous narthex mosaic of St. Sophia, Constantinople.

Bibliography: P. NOAILLES and A. DAIN, *Les Novelles de Léon VI le Sage* (Paris 1944). A. DAIN, *Leonis VI Sapientis Problemata* (Paris 1935). Tactica: *Patrologia Graeca,* ed. J. P. MIGNE, 161 v. (Paris 1857–66) 107, 672C–1120, and in part R. VÁRI, *Leonis Imperatoris Tactica* I–II.1 (Budapest 1917–22). A. VOGT and I. HAUSHERR, *Oraison funèbre de Basile I par son fils Léon VI le Sage* (Rome 1932). Homilies: *Patrologia Graeca,* ed. J. P. MIGNE, 161 v. (Paris 1857–66) 107, 1–298, and Akakios, *Levonto' tou' sofou' panhgurikoi; lovgoi* (Athens 1868). Monastic treatise: A. PAPADOPOULOS-KERAMEUS, ed., *Varia Graeca Sacra* (St. Petersburg 1909) 213–253. H. J. W. TILLYARD, "JEwqina; jAnastavsima. The Morning Hymns of the Emperor Leo," *Annual of the British School at Athens* 30 (1932) 86–108; 31 (1933) 115–147. F. CICOLLELA, "Il carme anacreontico di Leone VI," *Bollettino dei Classici* ser. III, 10 (1989) 17–37. P. KARLIN-HAYTER, *Vita Euthymii Patriarchae CP* (Brussels 1971). C. MANGO, "The Legend of Leo the Wise," *Zbornik Radova Vizantoloskog Instituta* 6 (1960) 59–93; repr. in his *Byzantium and Its Image* (London 1984) no. XVI. G. OSTROGORSKY, *History of the Byzantine State,* tr. J. HUSSEY (2d ed. New Brunswick, N.J. 1969; several repr.) 233–261. J. GROSDIDIER DE MATONS, "Trois études sur Léon VI," *Travaux et Mémoires* 5 (1973) 181–242. A. SCHMINCK, *Studien zu mittelbyzantinischen Rechtsbüchern* (Frankfurt 1986). T. ANTONOPOULOU, *The Homilies of the Emperor Leo VI* (Leiden, New York 1997). S. TOUGHER, *The Reign of Leo VI (886–912)* (Leiden, New York, Cologne 1997).

[T. ANTONOPOULOU]

LEO I, POPE, ST.

Pontificate: 440 to 461, called the Great, Doctor of the Church; b. probably Tuscany, the son of Quintianus, c. 400; d. Rome, Nov. 10, 461.

Life. Leo was deacon under Pope Celestine I (422–432), apparently entrusted with the care of the poor, and was possibly the acolyte mentioned as a Roman messenger to Africa by St. Augustine (*Epist.* 191.1). During the early difficulties over Nestorianism, he requested John CASSIAN to prepare a treatise, *De Incarnatione Domini* (430), sending him documents from the papal chancery (*praef.*). He was appealed to by CYRIL OF ALEXANDRIA for aid in curtailing the ambition of Juvenal of Jerusalem in 431 (Leo, *Epist.* 119.4). He was probably among the *rectores romanae ecclesiae* who drew up the syllabus on grace appended to the Letter of Pope Celestine to the bishop of Marseilles (P. Jaffé, *Regesta pontificum romanorum ab condita ecclesia ad annum post Christum natum 1198*, ed. F. Kaltenbrunner, 381) in which decisions of previous popes and synods in Africa are cited for the Church's doctrine (*Patrologia Latina* 45:175–660). PROSPER OF AQUITAINE credited Leo with strengthening the stand of Pope SIXTUS III in 439 against Julian of Eclanum (*Chronicles.* an. 439). Apparently at the request of the court of Ravenna, Leo was sent to Gaul

Proscenium arch view of Pope Leo I dissuading Attila, King of the Huns, from wrecking Rome after the destruction of Aquileia. (Archive Photos)

in the spring of 440 to mediate the quarrel between the Patrician Aetius and the Pretorian Prefect Albinus (Prosper, *Chronicles*. an. 441). During his absence, Sixtus died (Aug. 19, 440), and the populace elected Leo, who returned to Rome and was consecrated bishop on Sept. 29, 440. In the sermon he preached on the occasion, Leo thanked the assembled clergy and populace for the confidence placed in him "absent on a long journey" (*Ser.* 1); and in four anniversary sermons at annual synods he described the bishops as "equal in the episcopacy, and in infirmities," but guided by "Peter in the person of Peter's successor" (*Ser.* 3.3), who is the "primate of all the bishops" (*ibid.* 4). He acknowledged the universal priesthood of the faithful presided over by Christ, whom the bishop of Rome represents, taking the place of Peter. Christ gave such great power to him whom he made ruler (*principem*) of the whole Church so that "if anything is properly done or directed by us in our time" it is to be attributed to the activity of him to whom it was said,

"And you converted, confirm your brethren" (*Ser.* 4.2–4). Finally, Leo saw Peter functioning in the person of the pope (*Ser.* 5.2–4).

As bishop of Rome Leo dedicated himself to the priestly duty of preaching (*sacerdotalis sermonis officium*), and sermons of his for the whole liturgical cycle have been preserved: 10 for Christmas, eight for Epiphany, 12 for Lent, 19 on the Passion, two for Easter, two for the Ascension, three for Pentecost, one on the Feast of St. Peter, and another for St. Lawrence, 22 for the Ember days, which he says are celebrated four times a year (*Ser.* 19.2), when the faithful fast on Wednesday, Friday, and Saturday and celebrate the vigil of Sunday at St. Peter's. Six sermons (*de collectis*) describe the distribution of alms to the poor as an Apostolic institution to offset pagan superstition (*Ser.* 6–11), and a sermon on Rome's deliverance, apparently from Genseric in 455, testifies to survivals of astrology, the circus, and pagan spectacles (*Ser.* 84). Leo reproved the custom of bowing toward the sun and condemned as *paganitatis spiritu* the notion that December 25 marks the rise of the New Sun rather than the birth of Christ (*Ser.* 27.4). He was also active in seeking to preserve the peace of his parishioners. He met with Attila the Hun at Mincio in Northern Italy and was successful in persuading him to withdraw from Italy. In 455, after Rome had been sacked by Genseric over a period of two weeks, he persuaded him to vacate the city with no further loss of life or property. In his efforts against heresy he prosecuted the Manichees (*Ser.* 9.4; *Epist.* 7) and condemned the Monophysites who had come to Rome with merchants from Egypt (*Ser.* 9.4; 96.1), the Pelagians (*Epist.* 1), and many other heretics.

To the bishops of the ten provinces of central and southern Italy under papal jurisdiction (corresponding in area to that of the civil *vicarius Urbis*), Leo commended the *decretalia constituta* of his predecessors and demanded notification of election, with approbation and consecration in Rome, and attendance at the annual synods. He specified liturgical, canonical, pastoral uniformity, gave rules for the Church's patrimony (Jaffé, 414–417), and sent aid to Sicily after the Vandal invasion.

Milan, which was the imperial capital of the West, functioned, particularly under St. Ambrose, as the seat of the metropolitan for the seven North Italian provinces. But this did not prevent Leo from asserting his authority here. For example he ordered a synod at Milan (451) to accept his *Tome to Flavian*; he vindicated the rights of Bishop Septimus of Altinum against the bishop of Aquileia (Jaffé, 398, 399), but congratulated Bishop Januarius of Aquileia for vigilance (*ibid.* 416), and in March 458 he settled a moral problem for Nicetas of Aquileia, ruling in favor of returned captives of war whose wives had taken a second husband in good faith (*ibid.* 536).

In dealing with the universal Church Leo was equally assertive. On July 27, 444, he acknowledged the succession of DIOSCORUS as patriarch of Alexandria, spoke of the papal *principatus apostolicus*, and urged uniformity in canonical and liturgical practice (*ut fide et actibus congruamus*; Jaffé, 406). When the Eutychian troubles began in Constantinople, Leo chided Bishop FLAVIAN for his delay in referring the matter to Rome, but supported him by sending his *Tome to Flavian* and legates to the Council of EPHESUS in 449; he later castigated the council as *illud Latrocinium*, that Robber Synod. He appealed in vain to Theodosius II to have its proceedings reversed, and on the accession of Marcian as Co-emperor with Pulcheria in August 450 he wrote to congratulate them. Though he preferred no council or one in Italy, he accepted Marcian's convocation of the Council of CHALCEDON and sent to it legates and his *Tome*. Though he refused to accept the jurisdictional ordination of canon 28, which gave Constantinople primacy in the Orient after Rome as the "New Rome," he finally confirmed the council's doctrinal decisions (453) and kept in close contact with the Emperor and, despite hesitations, with Anatolius the Patriarch and his own *apocrisiarius*, Julian of Cos, for information and action in attempting to have the council's decisions accepted among the Monophysite clergy and monks of Egypt, Palestine, and Syria. He kept abreast of ecclesiastical movements in the Orient, accepted the prerogative of Alexandria to set the annual date for Easter as of Nicene determination, and asserted papal rights over Eastern Illyricum, despite the claims of Constantinople. On the death of Marcian (457), the pope entered into cordial relations with Emperor Leo the Thracian, tolerated his hesitation to accept the pope's counsel regarding the support of Chalcedon, and encouraged him to safeguard the true faith even by intimidating or deposing bishops. In Africa, Pope Leo insisted upon the preservation of ecclesiastical statutes in the choice of bishops and in the resolution of scandals and disputes among clerics and bishops; but he cautioned great moderation, particularly under the Vandal vexations.

When Hilary of Arles, who had interfered in the affairs of many dioceses in Gaul and, in a synod in Rome discussing one of his interventions, withstood Leo to the face, Leo proved just but intransigent. He had Hilary confined to his diocese by an imperial edict (*Novel. Valent.* 17: July 8, 445) in which Emperor Valentinian III acknowledged the papal primacy. With his vicar in Illyricum, Anastasius of Thessalonica, Leo was almost brutal when he discovered that Anastasius had acted precipitously in dealing with his suffragans. "I gave you power as my vicar, but did not invest you with the *plentitudo potestatis*," said Leo, again recommending moderation in the use of power, and conceded that in governance, some things must be severely repressed, others, tolerated.

Doctrine. In regard to faith, Leo wrote no treatise, but he described the process of achieving faith: "We are led to the faith as it is proclaimed in the Gospel story and by prophetical instruments; so that we cannot hold as ambiguous what has been announced by so many oracles." The testimony of the Apostles renders Christ present: "We see what they saw; touch what they touched" (*Ser.* 64.1; 73.1). He maintained that the Church and Christ do not live in the past: "Not in history alone do we know these things, but in virtue of present achievements" (*Ser.* 63.6). God adorns his body the Church with innumerable charismatic gifts (*Ser.* 63.7). In the body of Christ (*Ser.* 25.5; 46.3) sanctified by the Holy Spirit (*Ser.* 75.5), the members are held together by a *consortium gratiae* (*Ser.* 89.5) excluding those who will not accept its belief and practice. It is the Holy Spirit who instructs in the Scriptures, and although frequently the mystery of the message is difficult to understand, there is never need for doubt (*Ser.* 66.1). Even the attack of heretics can render faith clearer and stronger through the assistance given the faithful by the Holy Spirit in overcoming difficulties (*Epist.* 102.1; 104.1). The Apostles' Creed is a "brief and perfect confession of the Catholic faith" (*Epist.* 31.4) and has already refuted the Nestorians and Eutychians. Leo expressed some hesitation before the *ratiocinatio humana* (*Ser.* 26.2) and the *argumenta mundanae doctrinae* (*Ser.* 69.5), placing his reliance in the mystery of the Redemption. He warned against the philosophical attempt to limit God to categories of space and time.

Adam's fall was occasioned by the temptation of the devil and the human desire for angelic honors (*Ser.* 25.5; 30.6). But God in his mercy prepared a remedy from the beginnings of the universe (*primordia mundi*; *Ser.* 22.1), sending a singular physician from the heavens, announced by great signs and prophecies (*Ser.* 12.1), His Son, the same in nature as man but sinless, and thus, as man, a perfect image and likeness of God (*Ser.* 64.2; *Epist.* 59.4). Born of a Virgin, Christ retained the paternal glory (*Ser.* 22.2). He is *homoousios,* of same substance as the Father, and consubstantial with his Mother as man (*Ser.* 30.6). Thus he has been able to accomplish human redemption (*Ser.* 56.1; *Epist.* 35.1), which neither the Mosaic Law nor the Prophets could achieve (*Ser.* 23.3). The cross of Christ is thus a sacrament or mystery, and the altar is for the oblation of humanity through this salutary Host (*Ser.* 55.3), and is for all men at all times (*Ser.* 23.4).

Human redemption unto liberty should be exercised in observance of evangelical discipline in the works of mercy and the love of justice, which have been perfected and augmented by the Savior (*Ser.* 63.5; 92.1). Human dignity, given by Christ, is supported by Grace so that the person can love what God loves and abstain from what displeases God (*Ser.* 94.2), who gives both the desire for doing good to the will, and efficacy to the action placed (*Ser.* 38.3). While humanity recognizes the revolt of concupiscence, the person should still be more conscious of his regeneration in Christ through Baptism and the Sacraments (*Ser.* 90.1; 18.1; 98.1).

In Baptism the contagion of the ancient damnation is burnt out, so that the human person becomes the body of Christ (*Epist.* 59.4). While the person is still in the body, there is no need for despair since correction is to be hoped for by all (*Ser.* 34.5).

Lent is the time for expiating faults both grave and small through penance (*Ser.* 43.3; 45.1). Fasting, almsgiving, and prayer, particularly in unison with the Church, are the principal means of obtaining pardon; for the tears of the penitent through the apostolic key open the gates of God's mercy (*Ser.* 49.3), since penance disarms God's justice (*Ser.* 92.1). This pardon is exercised through the power of the keys confided to the bishops, who should exhort to penance and apply forgiveness most mercifully, particularly to those in danger of death (*Epist.* 108.2; *Ser.* 5.5).

The Eucharist is the sacrament of Christ's body and blood, fulfilling the sacrifice once for all, offered to God (*Ser.* 54.3). It should be received with faith so that there is no doubt in the mind of those answering *Amen* as to the reality of the body and blood of Christ that they receive (*Ser.* 91.30; *Epist.* 69.2). Leo spoke of the *chrismatio* of the baptized, whom the "Sign of the Cross makes kings and the unction of the Holy Spirit makes priests" (*Ser.* 4.1), and he mentioned the *clarior ordo levitarum* (deacons), the greater dignity of priests, and the *sacratior unctio sacerdotum* (bishops; *Ser.* 69.7; 66.2). He distinguished between the three hierarchical orders (*Epist.* 12.5) and mentioned subdiaconate, all four orders being subject to the law of continence (*Epist.* 14.4).

Ecclesiastical Governance. In the government of the Church, Leo set down norms of propriety and moderation whereby, the onus of evil being lifted, a differential in correction is required; for certain things are to be tolerated, others, cut out (*Epist.* 12.15). The Church should ever apply moderation, acting severely with the obdurate, but quickly giving forgiveness to those who repent and strive for correction (*Epist.* 30.1). Nevertheless, care must be taken to preserve the *statuta* of the Apostolic See and the decrees and authority of the canons (*Epist.* 1.1). The bishops form a society of charity, throughout the whole world preserving the integrity of communion (*Epist.* 80.1), and this fraternal union in charity and peace is served by the confession of one faith (*Epist.* 130.2).

Leo conceded that the emperor, whose subject he was as a Roman, was endowed with *regalia potentia* and *sacerdotalis industria* (*Epist.* 115.1; 116). He attributed to Leo the Thracian both a royal and sacerdotal spirit (*mens*; *Epist.* 155.2) and reminded him of his care for the universal church. In the end, however, Leo conceded that there was fundamental difference between imperial politics and the administration of the Church, each having its own proper function.

Of Leo's writings only 96 sermons and 173 letters (of which 20 are considered spurious and 30 were written to him) have survived. It is certain that Leo had Prosper of Aquitaine as secretary and that in the composition of papal documents the curial style was achieved by experts. Leo's sermons are of his own composition, but they exhibit an extremely polished antithetical style that indicates they were refashioned before publication. However, they are excellent instruments of the exhortation to sanctity, with scriptural foundation and an ecclesiastical awareness that enters deeply into the supernatural mystery of salvation, which Leo accommodated to the everyday needs and interests of his people on a liturgically effective plane. Considerable research has been done on the sacramentaries to ferret out Leo's contribution to the liturgical life of the Church; but in this field few certainties have been attained. What is certain is that the sacramentary bearing his name is a compilation of orations and prefaces of the Mass made in the sixth century. Although the Leonine Sacramentary is not wholly Leonine, it still remains as the oldest extant form of the Roman Missal. Leo's greatness is assured in the fundamentally spiritual approach he exercised in his daily pastoral instruction for the sanctification of his people. He is admittedly the greatest administrator of the ancient Church, the man who truly amalgamated ecclesiastical procedure with Roman law and put a juridical structure under the Roman primacy that has withstood the toll of 16 centuries. But his true significance resides in his doctrinal insistence on the mystery involved in Christ and the Church and in the supernatural charisms of the spiritual life accorded to man in Christ and in His body the Church. In keeping with this concept, Leo firmly believed that everything he did and said as pope for the governance of the Church was participated in by Christ, the head of the mystical body, and concurred in by St. Peter, in whose place Leo acted (*cujus vice fungimur*).

Feast: April 11, June 28; (Greek Church, Feb. 18).

Bibliography: *Patrologia latina*, ed. J. P. MIGNE (Paris 1878–90) v.54–56. A. CHAVASSE, ed. *Leo Magnus Tractatus*, (Turnhout 1987). R. DOLLE, *Sources Chrétiennes*, ed. H. DE LUBAC et. al (Paris 1941) 22, 49. E. HUNT, tr. *Letters* (New York 1957). E. SCHWARTZ, *Acta conciliorum oecumenicorum* 2.4. *Clavis Patrum latinorum*, ed. E. DEKKERS (2d ed. Stenbrugge 1961) 1656–61. E. CASPAR, *Geschichte de Papsttums von den Anfängen biz zur Höhe der Weltherrschaft* (Tübingen 1930–33) 1:423–564. H. SCHIPPER and J. VAN OORT, *Sermons and Letters against the Manicaheans: Selected Fragments* (Turnhout 2000). C. SILVA-TAROUCA, "Nuovi studi sulle antiche lettere dei papi," *Gregorianum* 12 (1931) 3–56, 349–425, 547–598; *Epistulae contra Euthchis haerisin* (Rome 1934–5); "La tradizione manoscritta del Tomus Leonis," *Studi dedicati alla memoria di Paolo Ubaldi* (Milan 1937) 151–170. M. KRABBLE, ed. *Epistuala ad Demetriadem de vera humilitate* (Washington DC 1965). J. LECLERQ, ed. *Sermons* (Paris 1964). B. ALTANER, *Patrology*, tr. H. GRAF (New York 1960) 417–422. P. BATIFFOL, *Dictionnaire de théologie catholique,* ed. A. VACANT et al. (Paris 1903–50) 9.1:218–301. H. LIETZMANN, *Paulys Realenzyklopädie der klassischen Altertumswissenschaft*, ed. G. WISSOWA et. al. 12.2 (1925) 1962–73. H. ARENS, *Die Christologische sprache Leos des Grossen: analyse des Tomus an den Patriarchen Flavian* (Freiburg 1982). P. BARCLIFT, "The Shifting Tones of Pope Leo the Great's Christological Vocabulary," *Church History* 66 (1997): 221–39; and "Predestination and Divine Foreknowledge in the Sermons of Pope Leo the Great," *Church History* 62 (1993): 5–21. L. CASULA, *La cristologia di San Leone Magno: il fondamento dottri-nale e soteriologico* (Milan 2000). Y. M. DUVAL, "Quelques emprunts de saint Léon á Saint Augustin," *Mélanges de science religieuse* 15 (1958) 85–94; *Journal of Theological Studies* 11 (1960) 83–84. F. DI CAPUA, *Il ritmo prosaico nelle lettere dei papi*, 3 v. (Rome 1937–47). G. M. DURAND, "Leon le Grand," *Revue des Sciences Philosophiques et Theologiques* 69 (1985): 577–610. W. J. HALLIWELL, *The Style of Pope St. Leo the Great* (Catholic University of America, *Patristic Studies* 59; 1939). C. CALLEWAERT, S. *Léon le Grand et les textes du Léonien* (Steenbrugge 1954). A. FIELD, *The Binding of the Strong Man: the Teaching of St. Leo the Great in a Modern Version.* (Ann Arbor, MI 1976). A. P. LANG, *Leo der Grosse und die Texte des Altgelasianums* (Steyl 1957). P. GALTIER, A. GRILLMEIER and H. BACHT, *Das Konzil von Chalkedon: Geschichte und Gegenwart* (Würzburg 1950–54)1:345–387. F. HOFMANN, *ibid.* 2:24–35. E. STEIN, *Histoire du Bas–Empire*, tr. J. R. PALANQUE (Paris 1949–59) 1:309–362, 572–579. O. HORN, *Petrou Kathedra: der Bischof von Rom und die Synoden von Ephesus (449) und Chalcedon* (Paderborn 1982). A. GUILLAUME, *Jeûne et charité. . .chez s. Léon le Grand* (Paris 1954). M. B. DE SOOS, *Le Mystère liturgique d'après s. Léon le Grand* (Mènster 1958). N. JAMES, "Leo the Great and Prosper of Aquitane: A Fifth Century Pope and His Advisor [texts]," *Journal of Theological Studies* 44 (1993): 554–84; and, "Was Leo the Great the author of Liturgical Prayers?" *Studia Patristica* 26 (1993): 35–40.

[F. X. MURPHY]

LEO II, POPE, ST.

Pontificate: January 681, to July 3, 683. A Sicilian by birth, he was competent in both Greek and Latin. In accord with the decree of Emperor CONSTANTINE IV Pogonatus that the electoral certificate of Pope AGATHO's successor be sent to Constantinople for ratification, Leo's election shortly after Agatho's death on Jan. 10, 681, was announced to Constantine by March 681. Confirmation, however, was not received at Rome until July 682, thus delaying Leo's consecration by the bishops of Ostia, Porto, and Velletri to August 682. On Dec. 13, 681, the emperor had forwarded for papal approbation the acts of the Council of CONSTANTINOPLE III that condemned Monothelitism. Leo ratified the synodal decisions sometime after Sept. 1, 682, but explained that Pope HONORIUS I's only fault in regard to Monothelitism lay in his permissive attitude toward the heresy. At the same time papal letters were written to the Spanish hierarchy, to King Ervigio, a Count Simplicius, and Abp. Quiricus of Toledo; they contained a partial Latin translation of the acts of the Council and the request that they be subscribed to and their teaching promulgated. The privilege of Mar. 1, 666, whereby the Church of RAVENNA had been declared AUTOCEPHALOUS by Emperor CONSTANS II was withdrawn by Constantine IV, and the Emperor directed the archbishop–elect of Ravenna to go to Rome for his consecration. In turn Leo exempted the archbishop from the traditional taxes incidental to consecration.

Feast: July 3.

Bibliography: *Patrologia Latina*, ed. J. P. MIGNE (Paris 1878–90) 96:387–420. *Liber pontificalis*, ed. L. DUCHESNE (Paris 1886–92) 1:359–362,377–379. P. JAFFÉ, *Regesta pontificum romanorum ab condita ecclesia ad annum post Christum natum 1198*, ed. P. EWALD (repr. Graz 1956) 1:240–241; 2:699, 741. F. DÖLGER, *Corpus der griechischen Urkunden des Mittelalters und der neueren Zeit* (Munich 1924–32). J. D. MANSI, *Sacrorum Conciliorum nova et amplissima collectio* (Florence-Venice 1757–98) 11:713–922, 1046–58. H. K. MANN, *The Lives of the Popes in the Early Middle Ages from 590 to 1304* (London 1902–32) 1.2:49–53. É. AMANN, *Dictionnaire de théologie catholique,* ed. A. VACANT et al. (Paris 1903–50) 9.1:301–304. E. CASPAR, *Geschichte des Papsttums von den Anfängen bis zur Höhe der Weltherrschaft* (Tubingen 1930–33) 2:610–619. O. BERTOLINI, *Roma di fronte a Bisanzio e ai Longobardi* (Bologna 1941). J. HALLER, *Das Papsttum* (Stuttgart 1950–53) 1:338–342. A. BREUKLAAR, *Biographisch–Bibliographisches Kirchenlexikon* 4 (Herzberg 1992). FULLER, A., "A propos de la nouvelle édition des actes du sixième concile oecuménique (Constantinople III)," *Revue des Études Byzantines* 52 (1994) 273–86. G. SCHWAIGER, *Lexikon für Theologie und Kirche* 3d ed. (Freiburg 1997). B.S. SODARO, *Santi e beati di Calabria* (1996) 71–74. J. N. D. KELLY, *Oxford Dictionary of Popes* (New York 1986) 78–79.

[H. G. J. BECK]

LEO III, POPE, ST.

Pontificate: Dec. 26, 795 to June 24, 816. Son of a non-noble and perhaps non-Roman family, Leo made a career in the papal administration, eventually becoming a cardinal priest and an important official in charge of the personal possessions of the pope. Elected pope with the support of the clerical party in Rome and perhaps uncertain of his position in the eyes of the Roman aristocracy, Leo quickly sent a letter to CHARLEMAGNE asking renewal of the Frankish-papal friendship alliance. The new pope also sent the keys to the tomb of St. Peter and the standards of the city of Rome along with a request that the king send an official to accept oaths of obedience and loyalty from the Romans. At least symbolically, these acts suggested that the pope recognized some special status for the king extending beyond the role of protector of the Papal State. Charlemagne indicated his willingness to renew the friendship alliance, but he also made clear in somewhat ominous terms his conception of the relationship between king and pope: As king, his was the responsibility to take whatever measures were necessary to defend the true faith against external attacks by pagans and infidels and to enhance its practice and restrain its detractors within the Christian community, while it was the pope's responsibility to pray for the success of the king in his efforts to safeguard and promote the Church.

Leo was soon in need of a protector, this time from within the Papal State. Almost from the beginning of his pontificate, there was unrest among the nobility in the Papal State stemming from what was perceived as the harshness of the papal administration. In April 799 a band of dissidents, led by a papal official who was a nephew of Leo's predecessor, Pope ADRIAN I, attacked Leo while he participated in a religious procession. They sought to render him unfit for office by blinding him and cutting out his tongue. Rescued from that fate by supporters, including Frankish agents, Leo was summoned to Paderborn to meet with Charlemagne. His enemies also appeared there to bring charges of adultery and perjury against Leo. Charlemagne ordered the pope back to Rome, escorted by Frankish bishops and counts. At the Frankish court there was growing concern about the seriousness of the crisis and a sense that only Charlemagne was in a position to guarantee the welfare of Christendom. Once back in Rome, Leo was reinstalled as pope. The Frankish officials who escorted him undertook an investigation of the charges against the pope, but the final settlement of the case was left to Charlemagne, who arrived in Rome in late November 800. He summoned a synod of Frankish and Roman dignitaries to examine the charges against Leo. That body took the position that no earthly authority was qualified to judge the Vicar of Christ. Instead, on December 23, Leo appeared before another synod and cleared himself by swearing on oath that he was innocent of the charges against him.

On Christmas Day 800, during Mass at St. Peter's, Leo placed a crown on the head of Charlemagne while the assembled crowd acclaimed him "emperor of the Romans." Songs praising Charlemagne as emperor (the *laudes*) were intoned and the pope prostrated himself before the new emperor. The responsibility for and the implications of this momentous event have long been debated. Despite a claim made later by Charlemagne's biographer, Einhard, that the king would not have attended Mass that day had he known what was going to happen, the evidence leaves little doubt that the event was jointly planned by pope and king. In view of the tenuous position of the pope at the moment and of Charlemagne's usual mode of action, perhaps it can be assumed that the king was the prime mover. The coronation offered advantages for both. To Charlemagne and his advisers the new title was one befitting the king's accomplishments and his exalted place in Christendom, and it reinforced the ideology of rulership being shaped at the Frankish court. As emperor Charlemagne's legal position in the Papal State was clearer than that defined by his previous title of *patricius Romanorum*. His new title gave him a status equal to that of the emperor in Constantinople. For Leo the coronation established on a clearer basis a legal authority capable of dealing with the enemies of the pope within the Papal State as well as his external enemies. That aspect of the coronation became obvious when early in 801 Charlemagne tried the conspirators, found them guilty of treason under Roman law, and sentenced them to death, a sentence commuted to exile at the request of Leo. Leo's role in bestowing the imperial crown served to exalt papal authority and acted as a precedent for later papal claims to rights in the selection of emperors. Some contemporaries claimed that in 800 the imperial office was vacant because a woman, the Empress IRENE, occupied the throne. But despite Byzantine suspicions to the contrary, Charlemagne and Leo had no intention of usurping the crown of the eastern emperors or of transferring the office from new Rome back to old Rome. Instead they created a second empire comprised of all who were loyal to the Roman faith and its guardians, the pope, and the emperor in the West. The coronation linked the pope and the emperor in the West more closely together in guiding the Christian people, but it also posed the issue of which held the superior authority.

After 800 Leo remained on friendly terms with Charlemagne despite occasions when the pope complained about the intrusion of Frankish agents into papal affairs. Although the Roman Church provided models for the shaping of Christian life in Charlemagne's empire, the emperor continued to act as the directive force in renewing religious life in his realm without deferring to the pope. Charlemagne paid no heed to the pope in matters relating to his imperial title, which the pope had played some part in creating. In 806 he arranged for his own succession by dividing his empire among his three sons without reference to the imperial office; perhaps Leo was informed of the emperor's intention in this matter when he visited Francia in 805–806, but that was the extent of papal involvement. In 813 Charlemagne himself crowned as emperor his one surviving son, Louis the Pious, again acting without papal participation. Charlemagne carried on his long struggle to gain recognition from Constantinople for his imperial title without any significant participation by the pope; only when the treaty successfully ending that quest was worked out in 812 was Leo given a copy of it. Leo was able to act independently in some religious affairs, not always with the emperor's approval. He stoutly resisted Charlemagne's efforts to gain papal approval for the introduction of the *filioque* clause into the text of the Nicene Creed used in the Roman liturgy. Leo did cooperate with Charlemagne and his theologians to end the heresy of ADOPTIONISM in Spain.

Although most of his attention was focused on his own Papal State and the Frankish court, Leo was able to exert influence in other areas. He played an important role in establishing the ecclesiastical organization of Bavaria. He collaborated with Charlemagne in restoring King Eardulf of Northumbria to his throne, in disciplining the archbishop of York for his intrigues against Eardulf, and in restoring territory to the jurisdiction of the

archbishop of Canterbury that had been detached by Pope ADRIAN I. Dissident factions in the Byzantine Church, especially one led by THEODORE THE STUDITE, repeatedly appealed to Leo for help against alleged abuses by Byzantine emperors and patriarchs; Leo usually tried to be conciliatory in these cases, in part because he was conscious of Charlemagne's ongoing effort to gain from Constantinople recognition for his imperial office. These cases indicate that Leo sustained his position as primate in Christendom, albeit vaguely defined and in spite of the towering shadow of Charlemagne and his CAESARO-PAPISM.

With the tacit consent of Charlemagne, Leo ruled the papal state as a sovereign. He was active in increasing papal revenues in order to continue the rebuilding the city of Rome and its churches, an effort made possible in part by generous gifts from Charlemagne. Despite the benefits his pontificate brought to Rome and the Papal State, his regime continued to meet resistance. The end of his pontificate was marked by another rebellion followed by a rural uprising, both vigorously suppressed by the papal administration. Amidst indications that he was less inclined toward the papacy than was his father, Emperor Louis the Pious was sufficiently concerned about the situation in the Papal State to order an investigation and then to summon the king of Italy, Bernard, to settle the problem. The Republic of St. Peter still needed a protector, one increasingly called upon to settle disturbances within the papal state threatening its existence.

Feast: Jan.12.

Bibliography: Sources. *Le Liber Pontificalis,* ed. L. DUCHESNE, 3 v., 2d ed. (Paris, 1955–1957) 2: 1-48 (Eng. tr. in *The Lives of the Eighth-Century Popes (Liber Pontificalis). The Ancient Biographies of Nine Popes from A.D. 715 to A.D. 817,* trans. with intro. R. DAVIS, (Liverpool 1992) 173–230. *Regesta Pontificum Romanorum ab condita ecclesia ad annum post Christum MCXCVIII,* ed. P. JAFFÉ, 2 v., 2d ed. (Leipzig 1885–1888) 1: 307–316. *Annales regni Francorum,* a. 799–801, ed. F. KURZE, *Monumenta Germaniae Historica: Scriptores rerum Germanicarum in usum scholarum* (Hannover 1895) 106–116 (Eng. tr. in *Carolingian Chronicles. Royal Frankish Annals and Nithard's Histories,* tr. B. W. SCHOLZ [Ann Arbor, Mich. 1970], 77–82). *Epistolae selectae pontificum Romanorum Carlo Magno et Ludowico Pio regnantibus scriptae,* ed. K. HAMPE, *Monumenta Germaniae Historica: Epistolae* v. 3 (Berlin 1899) 58–68. *Leonis III. Papae Epistolae X,* ed. K. HAMPE, *Monumenta Germaniae Historica: Epistolae,* v. 3 (Berlin 1899) 85–104. *Annales Laureshamenses,* a. 801, ed. G. PERTZ, *Monumenta Germaniae Historica: Scriptores* (Hannover 1826) 39. *Karolus Magnus et Leo Papa. Ein Paderborner Epos von Jahre 799,,* ed. J. BROCKMANN, with studies by H. BEUMANN, F. BRÜNHOLZ, and W. WINKLEMANN, Studien und Quellen zur westfälischen Geschichte 5 (Paderborn, 1966). *Alcvini sive Albini Epistolae,* ed. E. DÜMMLER, *Monumenta Germaniae Historica: Epistolae,* v. 2 (Berlin 1899) 1–493. **Literature.** L. DUCHESNE, *The Beginnings of the Temporal Sovereignty of the Popes, A.D. 754–1073,* tr. A. H. MATTHEW (London 1908) 112–125. F. X. SEPPELT, *Geschichte des Papsttums. Eine Geschichte der Päpste von den Anfängen bis zum*

Tod Pius X, v. 2: *Das Papsttums im Frühmittelalter. Geschichte des Päpste von Regierungsantritt Gregors des Grossen bis zum Mitte des ll. Jahrhundert* (Leipzig 1934)184–199. É. AMMAN, *Histoire de la Église depuis les origines jusqu'a nos jours*, ed. A. FLICHE and V. MARTIN 6 (Paris 1947) 153–203. J. HALLER, *Das Papsttums: Idee und Wirklichkeit*, vol. 2: *Der Aufbau* (Basel 1951) 16–39. W. ULLMANN, *The Growth of Papal Government in the Middle Ages. A Study in the Ideological Relation of Clerical to Lay Power* (London 1955) 87–118. W. MOHR, ''Karl der Grosse, Leo III und der römische Aufstand von 799,'' *Archivum Latinitatis Medii Aevi et Bulletin Ducange,* 20: 39–98. W. OHNSORGE, ''Zur Frage der griechischen Abstammung des Papstes Leo III,'' *Deutsches Archiv für Erforschung des Mittelalters* 23: 188–190. F. KEMPF, H.-G. BECK, E. EWIG, and J. A. JUNGMANN, *The Church in the Age of Feudalism,* tr. A. BIGGS, Handbook of Church History, ed. H. JEDIN and J. DOLAN, v. 3 (New York and London 1968) 84–102. H.-G. BECK, ''Die Herkunft des Papstes Leo III.,'' *Frühmittelalterliche Studien* 2: 131–137. V. PERI, ''Leone III e il *Filioque*. Ancora un falso e l'autentico simbolo Romono,'' *Rivista di storia e litteratura religiosa* 6: 266–297. W. H. FRITZE, *Papst und Frankenkönig. Studien zu den päpstlichfränkischen Rechtsbeziehungen von 754 bis 824,* Vorträge und Forschungen, Sonderband 10 (Sigmaringen 1973) *passim,*, especially 46–48. R. FOLZ, *The Imperial Coronation of Charlemagne,* tr. J. E. ANDERSON (London 1974). M. KERNER, ''Der Reinigungseid Leos III. Von Dezember 800. Die Frage seiner Echtheit und der frühen kanonistischen Überlieferung. Eine Studia zum Problem der päpstlichen Immunität im früheren Mittelalter,'' *Zeitschrift des Aachener Geschichtsvereins* 84–85, 131–160. L. WALLACH, ''The Genuine and the Forged Oaths of Pope Leo III,'' and, ''The Roman Synod of December 800 and the Alleged Trial of Leo III,'' in *Diplomatic Studies in Latin and Greek Documents from the Carolingian Age* (Ithaca, N.Y., and London 1977) 299–327, 328–352. R. KRAUTHEIMER, *Rome: Profile of a City, 312–1308* (Princeton, NJ 1980) 109–142. O. HEGENEDER, ''Der *crimen maiestatis,* der Prozess gegen die Attentäter Papst Leo III. und die Kaiserkrönung Karls des Grossen,'' in *Aus Kirche und Reich: Studien zu Theologie, Politik und Recht im Mittelalter. Festschrift für Friedrich Kempf zu seinem fünfundsiebzigsten Geburtstag und Füfzigjährigen Doktorjubiläum,* ed. H. MORDEK (Sigmaringen 1983) 55–79. T. F. X. NOBLE, *The Republic of St. Peter. The Birth of the Papal State, 680–825* (Philadelphia 1984) 291–299. V. PERI, ''Il *Filioque* nei magisterio Adriano I e di Leone III. Une plaausible formulazione del dogma,'' *Rivista di storia della chiesa in Italia* 41 (1987) 5–25. P. LLEWELLYN, ''Le contexte romain du couronnement de Charlemagne. Le temps de l'Avent de l'année 800,'' *Le Moyen Age* 96: 209–225. P. DELOGU, ''The Rebirth of Rome in the 8th and 9th centuries,'' in *The Rebirth of Towns in the West, A.D. 700–1050,* ed. R. HODGES and B. HIBLEY, CBA Research Reports 68 (London 1988) 33–42. J. FRIED, ''Ludwig der Fromme, das Papsttum und die fränkischen Kirche,'' in *Charlemagne's Heir. New Perspectives on the Reign of Louis the Pious (814–840),* ed. P. GODMAN and ROGER COLLINS (Oxford, 1990) 231–273. L. P. ERMINI, ''*Renovatio murorum*. Tra programma urbanistico et restauro conservativo: Roma e il ducato Romano,'' in *Committenti e produzione artistico-letteraria nell'alto medioevo occidentale,* 2 v., Settimane di studio del Centro italiano di studi sull'alto medioevo 39 (Spoleto 1992) 2: 485–530, and figures 1–36. P. LLEWELLYN, *Rome in the Dark Ages* (London 1993) 141–172, especially 150–156. P. ENGLEBERT, ''Papstreisen ins Frankenreich,'' *Römische Quartalschrift für christliche Altertumskunde und Kirchengeschichte* 88: 77–113.

[R. E. SULLIVAN]

The Assumption of the Virgin, Pope St. Leo IV at left, detail of a 9th-century fresco in the basilica of S. Clemente, Rome.

LEO IV, ST. POPE

Pontificate: Jan. 847 to July 17, 855. Of Roman origin, Leo became a Benedictine monk as a youth. Pope GREGORY IV called him to service in the Lateran administration, and Pope SERGIUS II made him a cardinal priest. At the time of his election the Papal State was in dire need of strong leadership. It was torn by internal strife resulting from what many perceived as oppressive misgovernment by papal officials during the pontificate of Sergius II. It was recovering from a Saracen raid in 846, which witnessed the sack of the basilica of St. Peter and the ravaging of countryside surrounding Rome. As a consequence of the Treaty of Verdun in 843, which divided the previously unified Carolingian Empire into three competing kingdoms, it remained to be seen who would serve as St. Peter's protector. The new Pope's response to these challenges opened the way for a remarkable expansion of papal prestige during the next three decades.

Leo IV's first concern was the defense of Rome against the Saracens. He undertook to strengthen the existing city walls and to ensure the future safety of St. Peter's by constructing a wall enclosing the basilica and its associated ecclesiastical structures, and by attaching the enclosure to the city's main fortifications. This project, requiring four years (848 to 852) and a vast outlay of money and labor, created the Leonine city (*Civitas Leonina*), a stronghold which for centuries to come served as a place of safety for the papacy. Leo took steps to improve the fortifications of port cities guarding the papal state, especially those at the mouth of the Tiber. He even built a new city, Leopolis, as a refuge for the inhabitants of Centumcellae (Civita-vecchia) who were in danger of Saracen attack. In 849 the Pope was instrumental in organizing a naval campaign by the combined fleets of the cities of Naples, Amalfi, and Gaeta that, with the aid of a storm, inflicted a major defeat on a Saracen fleet preparing to attack Rome. All of these efforts played an important part in elevating papal prestige and marked a significant contribution to a larger effort that, during the last half of the ninth century, prevented the Saracen occupation of southern and central Italy.

Leo IV's relationship with his Frankish protectors was outwardly orderly, but often marked by tensions. Within the already established framework marking Frankish-papal relationship, Leo recognized Emperor LOTHAIR I as his overlord. Lothair, who resided in Aachen after he succeeded Louis the Pious as emperor in 840, increasingly entrusted directions of affairs in Italy to his son, Louis II, who served as king of Italy until 850, when at the request of Lothair I he was crowned co-emperor by Pope Leo IV, thus affirming once again the role of the papacy in authenticating the assumption of the imperial office. The authority of Lothair I and Louis II in Rome continued to be defined by the *Constituto Romana,* an accord reached in 824 between Pope Eugenius II and the Carolingian government. In general, Leo IV respected its provisions, which defined for the Papal State a privileged position within the Empire. However it also placed limits on papal sovereignty and allowed the emperor specific rights in the governance of the Papal State, rights that Louis II was inclined to press. Yet Leo IV guarded his ability to control the governance of the Papal State. He challenged unwarranted intrusions of his protector's agents into affairs rightly belonging to the pope as governor of the Republic of St. Peter. Recent analysis of his benefactions in Rome reveal that he worked hard to keep the favor of nobles whose support was required to assure continued papal control over the Papal State, but who were increasingly resentful of the Frankish presence in Rome. He was especially concerned with instituting reforms; a Roman synod of 853 issued a series of canons aimed at limiting the involvement of the Roman clergy in secular affairs, defining and enforcing the spiritual responsibilities of clerics, improving clerical education and morals, and protecting church property. Leo's efforts to maintain control of affairs in the Papal State and to improve the quality of governance not only set him at occasionaly odds with Emperor Louis II, but also met opposition from a circle of educated nobles centered around a certain Bishop Arsenius of Orte and his nephew, Anastasius the Librarian. Although Arsenius and his circle were primarily interested in personal power, they also

nurtured aspirations of restoring Rome to its ancient role as political capital of world. These nostalgic dreams inclined them toward Emperor Louis II as a more suitable ruler of Rome than Pope Leo IV. Anastasius reflected this inclination when he sought the protection of Louis II after Leo's dissatisfaction with his exercise of his priestly duties caused him to flee Rome. Despite Leo's repeated sentences of excommunication intended to force his return to Rome, Anastasius remained with Louis II and was widely viewed as the Emperor's choice to succeed Leo.

Leo IV's activities extended beyond defense of the Papal State against external enemies and resistance to its absorption into the Carolingian Empire. A careful analysis of his correspondence, surviving only in fragments, suggests that by the middle of the ninth century the bishop of Rome was increasingly viewed as an authority to whom those seeking guidance in the conduct of religious life, broadly defined, might turn.

Most often Leo IV was asked to intervene in cases involving the actions taken by powerful ecclesiastical potentates in the exercise of their offices. On the basis of complaints from various sources, he was forced to take firm action to curb the efforts of Archbishop John of Ravenna to escape Roman control. In response to appeals to Rome Leo challenged the actions of Archbishop Hincmar of Reims on various issues: excommunicating a vassal of Emperor Lothair I for violating his marriage vows; threatening to excommunicate Emperor Lothair I; and acting on decisions concerning the legality of episcopal ordinations reached in local councils held without papal participation or approval. In these cases the Pope ruled that Hincmar had exceeded his canonical authority and was subject to correction by the higher authority of the bishop of Rome. On the basis of appeals by the injured parties, Leo IV challenged the authority of Patriarch Ignatius of Constantinople for his action in deposing three Sicilian bishops. Leo died before the cases involving Hincmar and Ignatius were fully resolved, but his actions reflected an expanded definition of papal authority.

On occasion Leo IV confronted secular rulers. Emperor Lothair I's requested that Leo designate Hincmar as papal vicar of Gaul and Germany. Leo refused, stating that another already had that honor. In 853 Alfred, the young son of King Ethelwulf of Wessex, appeared in Rome as a pilgrim; Leo anointed him as future king and adopted him as his spiritual son by serving as his godfather. The Pope reprimanded the duke of Brittany for his treatment of the bishops of Brittany who resisted the duke's efforts to promote political independence from the West Frankish kingdom by establishing an autonomous Breton metropolitan see free from the jurisdiction of the archbishopric of Tours. Leo IV responded to still other appeals to Rome by sending instructions intended to provide proper direction in matters of ecclesiastical discipline to inquiring parties; such instructions went to a bishop in Africa, to bishops in England, and to bishops in Brittany.

In the responses coming from Rome to an ever widening circle in the Christian world, a certain message began to emerge, a message by no means new, but articulated again in terms reflecting new realities. Ultimate authority in ecclesiastical affairs rested in the hands of bishops. Their decisions were subject to appeal to the bishop of Rome who had a right to render final, binding judgments on the issues at stake. So too were the decisions of bishops sitting in council subject to approval and correction by the pope. The judgments of the bishop of Rome became, in effect, additions to the body of canon law, thereby expanding Rome's right to legislate for the entire Church. The bishop of Rome had the authority to take whatever action he deemed necessary to assure the safeguarding of the faith and proper Christian discipline. In brief, Leo IV's actions in these cases gave powerful impetus to a hierarchical view of governance of the Christian establishment, with the vicar of St. Peter placed at the apex of the hierarchy in possession of the final authority to assure that God's will would prevail.

Aside from his efforts to strengthen the defenses of Rome, Leo IV took a strong interest in rebuilding and beautifying churches in Rome and elsewhere in the papal state. In this respect he earned an important place among the late eighth– and early ninth–century popes who created the medieval city of Rome. His biography notes that he made important changes in the Roman liturgy, did much to encourage the development of Church music, and was famous as a preacher.

Feast: July 17.

Bibliography: Sources: *Le Liber Pontificalis* ed. L. DUCHESNE, 3 v., 2nd ed. (Paris 1955–1957), 2: 106–139; Eng. tr. *The Lives of the Ninth-Century Popes (Liber Pontificalis)* R. DAVIS (Liverpool 1995) 99–159. *Regesta Pontificum Romanorum ab condita ecclesia ad annum post Christum MCXCVIII*, ed. P. JAFFÉ, 2 v., (2d ed. Leipzig 1885–1888) 1: 329–339. *Epistolae selectae Sergii II, Leonis IV, Benedicti III pontificum Romanorum*, ed. A. VON HIRSCH-GEREUTH, *Monumenta Germaniae Historica: Epistolae* (Berlin 1899). *Der Konzilien der karolingischen Teilreiche, 843–859*, ed. W. HARTMANN, *Monumenta Germaniae Historica: Concilia*, (Hannover 1984). *Annales Bertiniani*, a, 868, ed. G. PERTZ, *Monumenta Germaniae Historica*, Scriptores rerum Germanicarum in usum scholarum (Hannover 1888); Eng. tr. in *The Annals of St.-Bertin*, tr. J. L. NELSON (Manchester 1991). **Literature:** L. DUCHESNE, *The Beginnings of the Temporal Sovereignty of the Popes, A.D. 754–1073*, tr. A. H. MATTHEW (London 1908) 144–152. F. X. SEPPELT, *Geschichte des Papsttums. Eine Geschichte der Päpste von den Anfängen bis zum Tod Pius X* v. 2 (Leipzig 1934) 223–240. É. AMANN, *Histoire de l' Église depuis les origines jusqu'a nos jours*, ed. A. FLICHE and V. MARTIN (Paris 1947) 6:280–288. R. KRAUTHEIMERR,

Rome: Profile of a City, 312–1308 (Princeton, N.J. 1980) 109–142. P. DELOGU, ''The Rebirth of Rome in the 8th and 9th Centuries,'' in *The Rebirth of Towns in the West, A.D. 700–1050*, ed. R. HODGES and B. HIBLEY (London 1988) 33–42. W. HARTMANN, *Die Synoden der Karolingerzeit im Frankenreich und in Italien, Konziliengeschichte, ed. W. BRANMÜLLER (Paderborn 1989). P. LLEWELLYN, *Rome in the Dark Ages* (London 1993)141–172. K. HERBERS, *Leo III. und das Papsttum in der Mitte des 9. Jahrhunderts: Möglichkeiten und Grenzen päpstlicher Herrschaft in der späten Karolingerzeit* (Stuttgart 1996).

[R. E. SULLIVAN]

LEO V, POPE

Pontificate: July to September 903; the successor of BENEDICT IV; from Arden. A simple priest from Priapi, in the district of Ardea, Leo was not a member of the Roman clergy when elected pope. After three months in office he was imprisoned and killed by Christopher, cardinal priest of S. Damaso, who succeedcd him as pope (antipope?) from September 903 to January 904. Christopher, in turn, was deposed and executed by SERGIUS III. Leo's only recorded act is found in a bull issued in the interest of the canons of the church of Bologna. A legend of Breton origin identifies him with a Benedictine, St. Tugdual, who as a pilgrim to Rome was reputedly elected pope.

Bibliography: P. JAFFÉ, *Regesta pontificum romanorum ab condita ecclesia ad annum post Christian natum 1198*, ed. S. LÖWENFELD (2d ed. Leipzig 1881–88; repr. Graz 1956) 1:444; 2:746. *Liber pontificalis*, ed. L. DUCHESNE, v. 1-2 (Paris 1886–92), v. 3 (Paris 1958) 2:234. H. K. MANN, *The Lives of the Popes in the Early Middle Ages from 590 to 1304*, 18 v. (London 1902–32) 4:111. J. HALLER, *Das Papsttum*, 5 v. (2d, rev. ed. Stuttgart 1950–53) 2:193, 545–546. F. X. SEPPELT, *Geschichte der Päpste von den Anfängen bis zur Mitte des 20. Jh.* (Munich 1955) 2:346, 434. A. FAVÉ, ''S. Tugdual pape,'' *Bull. de la Societé archéol. du Finistère* (Quimper 1897–98) 91–95. É. AMANN, *Dictionnaire de théologie catholique*, ed. A. VACANT et al., 15 v. (Paris 1903–5) 9.1:316. K. HERBERS, *Biographisch-Bibliographisches Kirchenlexikon*, 4 (Herzberg 1992). S. SCHOLZ, *Lexikon für Theologie und Kirche*, 3d ed. 6 (Freiburg 1997). J. N. D. KELLY, *Oxford Dictionary of Popes* (New York 1986) 118–119.

[O. J. BLUM]

LEO VI, POPE

Pontificate: May or June 928 to Dec. 928 or Jan. 929; b. Rome. The son of the *primicerius* Christopher, he was a priest of St. Susanna at the time of his promotion. He was elected by MAROZIA and her party and succeeded to the papacy at the deposition of Pope JOHN X, who died in prison in the CASTEL SANT 'ANGELO. Almost nothing is known of his brief pontificate. He seems to have followed the policy of his predecessor, and one surviving bull was directed to the bishops of Dalmatia, ordering them to obey their archbishop, John of Spalato, to whom Leo had granted the pallium.

Bibliography: P. JAFFÉ, *Regesta pontificum romanorum ab condita ecclesia ad annum post Christum natum 1198,* ed. S. LÖWENFELD (repr. Graz 1956) 3579. *Liber pontificalis,* ed. L. DU-CHESNE (Paris 1886–92) 2:242. H. K. MANN, *The Lives of the Popes in the Early Middle Ages from 590 to 1304* (London 1902–32) 4:188. P. BREZZI, *Roma e l'Impero medioevale* (Bologna 1947). F. X. SEPPELT, *Geschichte der Päpste von den Anfängen bis zur Mitte des 20. Jh.* (Munich 1954–59) 2:355, 434. S. SCHOLZ, *Lexikon für Theologie und Kirche* 3d. ed. 6 (Freiburg 1997). H. ZIMMERMANN, *Biographisch–Bibliographisches Kirchenlexikon,* 4 (Herzberg 1992). J. N. D. KELLY, *Oxford Dictionary of Popes* (New York 1986) 122.

[O. J. BLUM]

LEO VII, POPE

Pontificate: Jan. 936 to July 13, 939; b. Rome. A priest of St. Sixtus and probably a Benedictine, he was promoted to the papacy by Alberic II, on whose favor he was wholly dependent. Together they promoted the reform of GORZE and the CLUNIAC REFORM. At Leo's invitation Abbot ODO OF CLUNY came to Rome, where he was effective both as a peacemaker and as a stimulator of spiritual revival. Leo's surviving letters indicate his interest in CLUNY and SUBIACO, whose rights he confirmed, and in the rebirth of Christian life in France. He sent the PALLIUM to ADALDAG of Bremen–Hamburg (*c.* 937) and appointed Abp. Frederick of Mainz apostolic vicar and legate for all Germany, charging him with the reform of the clergy of every rank. His advice to Frederick regarding the Jews was something less than permissive: he forbade their forced conversion but allowed Frederick to expel them from the cities unless they accepted the Christian faith.

Bibliography: P JAFFÉ, *Regesta pontificum romanorum ab condita ecclesia ad annum post Christum natum 1198,* ed. S. LÖWENFELD (repr. Graz 1956) 1:455–457; 2:706, 747. *Patrologia latina,* ed. J. P. MIGNE (Paris 1878–90) 132:1065–88. *Neues Archiv der Gesellschaft für ältere deutsche Geschichtskunde* 10 (1885) 380–386. *Liber pontificalis,* ed. L. DUCHESNE (Paris 1886–92) 2:244. H. K. MANN, *The Lives of the Popes in the Early Middle Ages from 590 to 1304* (London 1930–32) 4:205–207. E. BOURGEOIS, "L'assemblée de Mersen 847," in *Mélanges Paul Fabre. Études d'histoire du Moyen Age* (Geneva 1972) 72–100. P. BREZZI, *Roma e l'Impero medioevale* (Bologna 1947). G. SCHWAIGER, *Lexikon für Theologie und Kirche,* ed. J. HOFER and K. RAHNER (Freiburg 1957–65) 6:949. H. ZIELINSKI, "Zur Aachener Königserhebung von 936," *Deutsches Archiv für Erforschung des Mittelalters* (1972) 210–222. H. ZIMMERMAN, *Biographisch–Bibliographisches Kirchenlexikon,* 4 (Herzberg 1992). J. N. D. KELLY, *Oxford Dictionary of Popes* (New York 1986) 123–124.

[O. J. BLUM]

LEO VIII, POPE

Pontificate: Dec. 4, 963 to March 1, 965; b. Rome. A man of blameless character, Leo was still a layman holding the office of *protoscriniarius* when Emperor OTTO I chose him to become pope. He was elected at the Roman synod at which the absentee JOHN XII was deposed and was consecrated on Dec. 6, having been promoted to all orders in one day without observing the canonical interstices. Leo was the first pope to be installed according to the new liturgy introduced into Italy by the reforming Otto. His tenure in Rome remained uncertain; and on Jan. 3, 964, the Romans, incited by John XII, rioted against the Emperor and his papal appointee. The uprising was crushed in a bloody encounter with imperial troops. After Otto departed for Spoleto, John returned, took the city, and at a synod in St. Peter's (Feb. 26, 964) reciprocated by excommunicating and deposing Leo, who had fled to Otto's court. John died suddenly on May 14, and the impetuous Romans elected the cardinal deacon Benedict *Grammaticus,* who took the name BENEDICT V. On June 23, Otto reentered Rome and reinstated Leo, whose pontificate was thenceforth uneventful after Benedict had been deprived, degraded, and deported to Hamburg (965). Three supposed Leonine documents, the *Privilegium minus, the Privilegium maius,* and the *Cessatio donationum (Monumenta Germaniae Historica: Constitutiones* 1:665–678), the last purporting to restore a number of papal territories to Otto and his wife, Adelaide, are forgeries of the period of the INVESTITURE STRUGGLE.

Bibliography: P. JAFFÉ, *Regesta pontificum romanorum ab condita ecclesia ad annum post Christum natum 1198,* ed. S. LÖWENFELD (repr. Graz 1956) 1:467–470. *Liber pontificalis,* ed. L. DUCHESNE (Paris 1886–92) 2:250. C. J. VON HEFELE, *Histoire des conciles d'après les documents originaux,* tr. H. LECLERCQ (Paris 1907–38) 4:609–626. H. K. MANN, *The Lives of the Popes in the Early Middle Ages from 590 to 1304* (London 1902–32) 4:260–281. É. AMANN, *Dictionnaire de théologie catholique,* ed. A. VACANT et al. (Paris 1903–50) 9:317–320. T. KLAUSER, "Die liturgischen Austauschbeziehungen . . ." *Historisches Jahrbuch der Görres–Gesellschaft* 53 (1936) 186–189. M. ANDRIEU, "La Carrière ecclésiastique des papes," *Revue des sciences religieuses* 21 (1947) 109–110. F. X. SEPPELT, *Geschichte der Päpste von den Anfängen bis zur Mitte des 20. Jh.* (Munich 1954–59) 2:369–372, 435. B. GEBHARDT, *Handbuch der deutschen Geschichte,* ed. H. GRUNDMANN (Stuttgart 1954–60) 1:184–185. W. ULLMANN, *The Growth of Papal Government in the Middle Ages* (2d ed. New York 1962). E.D. HEHL, *Lexikon für Theologie und Kirche* 3d. ed. 6 (Freiburg 1997). K. JORDAN, "Ravennater Fälschungen aus den Anfängen des Investiturstreites," *Ausgewählte Aufsätze zur Geschichte des Mittelalters* (1980) 52–74. I. S. ROBINSON, "Zur Entstehung des Privilegium Maius Leonis VIII papae," *Deutsches Archiv für Erforschung des Mittelalters* 38 (1982) 26–65. H. ZIMMERMANN, *Biographisch–Bibliographisches Kirchenlexikon* 4 (Herzberg 1992). J. N. D. KELLY, *Oxford Dictionary of Popes* (New York 1986) 127–128.

[O. J. BLUM]

LEO IX, POPE, ST.

Pontificate: Feb. 2, 1049 to April 19, 1054; b. Bruno of Egisheim, Egisheim, Alsace, June 21, 1002. Leo's reign marks the beginning of true papal reform and of the liberation of the Church from both the Roman nobility and German imperial entanglements. As a young cleric, he saw military service in Lombardy, replacing his aged bishop in the muster of Emperor CONRAD II. A blood relative of Conrad, he owed to him his later appointment as bishop. He was consecrated in the See of Toul, Sept. 9, 1027. Influenced by the principles of monastic reform of CLUNY and Lorraine, he reformed the monasteries of St. Aper, MOYENMOUTIER, REMIREMONT, and Saint-Dié, which were under his patronage. As bishop, he also held many visitations and synods. Bruno was elected pope at Worms by his cousin, the Emperor Henry III, and was crowned in St. Peter's. His biographer, HUMBERT OF SILVA CANDIDA, states that he accepted only after the acclamation of the Roman clergy and people. Experienced in administration, he introduced fresh policy carried out by young reformers from Lorraine: HUGH OF REMIREMONT; Frederick of Lorraine, later STEPHEN IX; and especially Humbert, his "secretary of state" and author of his important papers. Hildebrand, later GREGORY VII, also began his career in Rome during Leo's pontificate.

After his coronation, Leo spent no more than six months in Rome. Traveling through Italy, Germany, France, and as far as Hungary, he projected an image of the papacy in action to those for whom the pope had been only a name, sometimes one of ill repute. He held 12 synods at Rome, Bari, Mainz, Pavia, Reims, and elsewhere, and issued decrees against simony and clerical marriage. He granted papal security to monastic property, honored the relics of saints, and canonized GERARD OF TOUL. At Vercelli in 1050, he condemned BERENGARIUS OF TOURS for his teachings on the Eucharist.

Working harmoniously with Henry III, Leo could be styled the "Imperial Vicar for Italy." His policy, stimulated by the DONATION OF CONSTANTINE, of opposing by force the Norman devastation of southern Italy made the German court uncooperative and aroused the antagonism of MICHAEL CERULARIUS, Patriarch of Constantinople. With ragged recruits from Germany and Italy, Leo engaged the Normans at Civitate on June 18, 1053, but was defeated and then honorably detained near Bari. In January 1054, he sent a mission under Humbert to the Byzantine Emperor, CONSTANTINE IX, proposing a triple alliance of the papacy, Byzantium, and the Empire against the Normans. But irresponsible acts by Humbert and Cerularius on this occasion aggravated the chronically strained relations between the churches, which led eventually to the denouement of 1204 (*see* EASTERN

SCHISM). Leo did not live to direct these events. Broken by defeat and weakened, perhaps by malaria, he was carried to Rome and died in St. Peter's, where he was buried.

Feast: April 19.

Bibliography: Sources. *Acta Apostolicae Sedis,* April 2:648–665. J. MABILLON, *Acta sanctorum ordinis S. Benedicti,* v.9 (Paris 1668–1701; 2d ed. Venice 1733–40) Saec 6.2:47–81. *Bibliotheca hagiographica latina antiquae et mediae aetatis,* 2 v. (Brussels 1898–1901; suppl. 1911) 4818–29. *Analecta Bollandiana* (Brussels 1882–) 25:258–297. *Patrologia Latina,* ed. J. P. MIGNE, 217 v. (Paris 1878–90) 143:465–798. P. JAFFÉ, *Regesta pontificum romanorum ab condita ecclesia ad annum post Christum natum 1198,* ed. S. LÖWENFELD et al., 2 v. (2d ed. Leipzig 1881–88; repr. Graz 1956) 1:529–549. P. F. KEHR, *Regesta Pontificum Romanorum. Italia Pontificia,* 8 v. (Berlin 1906–35) 8:8–10. C. J. C. WILL, *Acta et scripta* (Leipzig 1861). Literature. A. MICHEL, *Humbert und Kerullarios,* 2 v. (Paderborn 1924–30); "Die folgenschweren Ideen des Kardinals Humbert," *Studi gregoriani,* 1, ed. G. B. BORINO (Rome 1947) 65–92; "Die Anfänge des Kardinals Humbert," *Studi gregoriani,* 3, ed. G. B. BORINO (Rome 1948) 299–319. L. SITTLER and P. STINTZI, *S. Léon IX, le pape alsacien* (Colmar 1950). J. HALLER, *Das Papsttum,* 5 v. (2d, rev. ed. Stuttgart 1950–53) 2:286–296. V. GRUMEL, "Les préliminaires du schisme de Michel Cérulaire," *Revue des études byzantines,* 10 (Paris 1952) 5–23. H. TRITZ, "Die Hagiographischen Quellen zur Geschichte Papst Leos IX," *Studi gregoriani,* 4, ed. G. B. BORINO (Rome 1952) 191–364, R. MAYNE, "East and West in 1054," *Cambridge Historical Journal,* 11 (Cambridge, Eng. 1953–55) 133–148. H. G. KRAUSE, *Das Papstwahldekret von 1059* (Rome 1960). D. M. NICOL, "Byzantium and the Papacy in the 11th Century," *The Journal of Ecclesiastical History,* 13 (London 1962) 1–20. J. DREHMANN, *Papst Leo IX. Und die Simonie* (Hildesheim 1973). E. PETRUCCI *Ecclesiologia e politica di Leone IX* (Rome 1977). M. L. JACOTEY, *Bruno, pape alsacien ou Saint Léon IX* (Remiremont 1984). J. N. D. KELLY, *Oxford Dictionary of Popes* (New York 1986) 147. J. DAHLHAUS, "Leo IX," *Lexikon für Theologie und Kirche,* third ed. (Freiburg 1996) 6:825–825. M. PARISSE, ed., *Vita Leonis noni,* French trans by M. GOULLET (Paris 1997).

[O. J. BLUM]

LEO X, POPE

Pontificate: March 9, 1513, to Dec. 1, 1521; b. Giovanni de'Medici, Florence, Dec. 11, 1475. As the second son of Lorenzo the Magnificent, he was destined for high Church service from an early age. Giovanni received the tonsure before reaching the age of eight and became the cardinal deacon of Santa Maria in Dominica at 13. He was educated at his father's court by the humanists Marsilio FICINO, Angelo Poliziano, and Giovanni and PICO DELLA MIRANDOLA, who instilled in him a lifelong interest in learning; later at Pisa he studied theology and Canon Law (1489–91). In 1492, still in his teens, he became a member of the College of Cardinals and took up residence in Rome. At the death of Lorenzo de'Medici (1492), he returned to Florence and lived with his elder brother Pietro. In the same year Cardinal de'Medici took

Pope Leo X with the cardinals Giulio de'Medici (later Pope Clement VII) and Luigi de Rosai, portrait by Raphael, 1518.

part in the conclave that elected, without his vote, Alexander VI. During SAVONAROLA'S "reign of Virtue" he was living in Florence and he left only when the Medicis were sent into exile in November 1494. Expelled from his native city, the 19-year-old cardinal, who was considered clever and wise, visited France, the Netherlands, and Germany. Not until May 1500 did he return to Rome, where he buried himself in literature and the arts and developed a love for music and the theater that he never lost. In 1503, when his brother Pietro died, he became the head of the Medici family. The death of Alexander VI brought the Sacred College of Cardinals together in September of the same year, and only the aging and ailing PIUS III could gain the necessary two-thirds vote. When he died 26 days later, the cardinals resumed their deliberations. Cardinal Giulio della Rovere emerged from the conclave as JULIUS II. In October 1511 the Pope appointed Cardinal Giovanni de'Medici legate of Bologna and Romagna. The following year, when Florence supported the schismatic council at Pia, Julius ordered him to attack his native city at the head of a papal army. But the Florentines engineered a bloodless revolution allowing the Medicis to return on September 14, 1512, Giovanni then became the real power in Florence, though his younger brother Giuliano actually held the first place in the Republic.

Election to the Papacy. The death of Julius II during the night of February 20–21, 1513, resulted in the seven-day conclave that opened March 4. The College was not at full strength since the rebellious cardinals who were holding a council at Pisa were excluded. The remaining 25 cardinals were not divided in any major rivalries, but were desirous of a peace-loving successor to the deceased soldier-pope. As a result, Cardinal de'Medici, who was supported by the younger cardinals, and finally by the senior members as well, since they believed his ill health would lead to a short pontificate, emerged from the conclave with the required votes. The 37-year-old cardinal received Holy Orders on March 15, was consecrated bishop two days later, and was crowned on the 19th. Leo X was the personification of the Renaissance in its most humanistic form. He befriended the humanists, spending not merely the vast sums accumulated by his predecessor and all that he could raise, but mortgaging the papacy to the extent of 400,000 ducats. His love of art, music, and the theater again made Rome the cultural center of the Western world. He vigorously advanced the construction of St. Peter's Basilica and collected books, manuscripts, and gems, with little regard for price. The scandals of the Borgia era were not to be found in Medici Rome. Leo knew how to enjoy life, but not at the expense of piety. Before hunting, one of his greatest loves, he always attended Mass, and on occasions even celebrated the Mass himself. Never one to overwork, he would escape from Rome for months at a time to relax in the country.

Fifth Lateran Council. The early years of the pontificate of Leo X witnessed the culminating work of the Fifth Lateran Council (*see* LATERAN COUNCILS). The Council had been called by Julius II to offset the council called in Pisa. Nine cardinals, most of them French, had gathered at Pisa and issued a summons for an ecumenical council to meet in that city in 1512. Alienated by Julius's foreign policies and his autocratic manners, they wished to curtail the absolute power of the pope by invoking the decree of the Council of Constance that required councils to be called every ten years. Julius had met this challenge swiftly and effectively by convoking an ecumenical council of his own to meet at the Lateran in July 1511. The Pisa group was supported almost exclusively by the French and Germans, who were unable to come to agreement because both insisted on managing Church affairs within their respective national boundaries. When Emperor Maximilian believed that Pisa II would lead to schism, he withdrew his support and opened negotiations leading to his recognition of the Lateran Council, which opened on May 3, 1512. The death of Julius within nine months left the bulk of the work of the council to his successor, Leo X.

The Council was poorly attended from the beginning, and of the 80 to 90 bishops present, the majority were Italian. Its main objectives were peace within the Christian world, a crusade against the Turks, and internal reforms. The decrees of this Council were primarily disciplinary. Under the heading of reform the Council discussed most matters treated at Trent some 40 years later. That little came out of the deliberations of the Lateran Council is explained in part by the lack of urgency that, as the result of the Protestant Revolt, characterized Trent. Nevertheless there were attempts at reform. Strict rules were drawn up for cardinals and other members of the Curaia; although the Pope violated them even before the Council adjourned. Preachers were warned against criticism of the hierarchy, and a system was approved for the censorship of printed books. The standard condemnations against pluralism and absenteeism were reissued, but it was made clear that dispensations might be granted to circumvent this prohibition. The Council's only major decision concerning faith was to condemn the neo-Aristotelian doubts about the immortality of the soul. The Council ended on March 16, 1517, a scant six months before Martin Luther posted his attack on indulgences.

Foreign Policies. Leo X was not only the head of the universal Church, but also, and often primarily, the temporal ruler of the States of the Church. In addition, as head of the house of Medici, he controlled the Florentine Republic. The major diplomatic problem facing Leo when he ascended the throne was the removal of foreign influence and dominance from the peninsula. France's interest in Italy arose from the claims of Charles VIII to Naples. His successor, Louis XII, added to this a title to Milan. At the beginning of 1513 the French, in alliance with the Venetians, were attempting to regain Milan and Naples. Leo found himself at war as an ally of Emperor Maximilian I, Ferdinand I of Spain, and Henry VIII of England in the League of Mcchlin (April 5, 1513). The league suffered initial setbacks, but at the battle of Novara (June 6) the French were decisively defeated. The peace signed between Louis XII and the papacy included the withdrawal of French support from the Pisan council, bringing it to an inglorious end (December 1513).

Concordat with Francis I. The death of Louis XII (1515) brought the ambitious and energetic Francis I to the throne of France. The new King immediately revived his predecessor's claims to Milan and Naples and crossed the Alps at the head of an army that was victorious at the battle of Marignano (September 14, 1515). Leo negotiated a settlement, followed by a secret conference with Francis at Bologna in December of the same year. The groundwork was laid here for a long overdue understanding on Church-State relations. The new Concordat, written into the bull *Primitiva* (August 18, 1516) and promulgated as law in France the following year, clarified the relationship between King and Pope. The King was given the right to nominate all bishops, abbots, and priors, while the Pope reserved for himself the nominations to vacant benefices *in curia* and certain other benefices. While in practice the King's nomination amounted to appointment, in theory the Pope always had the power to veto an undesirable candidate. This settlement lasted until the French Revolution in 1789.

Imperial Election. The death of Ferdinand of Aragon in 1516 brought his young and energetic grandson Charles to the throne. Then in 1519 Charles's paternal grandfather, Emperor Maximilian, died. When both Charles and Francis I made a bid for the imperial title, the Pope supported the French King. However, Leo quickly veered in the direction of Frederick the Wise of Saxony, the protector of Martin Luther, until the contest was settled in June 1519, with the election of Charles V. The Pope then gravitated toward Spain.

Leo was also plagued by real and rumored domestic problems and intrigues. To cope with these difficulties and to enhance the grandeur of the Medici family he practiced nepotism. He appointed as archbishop of Florence, and then as cardinal and vice chancellor of the Holy See, his cousin Giulio de'Medici (later CLEMENT VII). The Pope's younger brother, Giuliano, and his nephew, Lorenzo, were named Roman patricians. In 1517 the failure of a conspiracy to poison the Pope by several discontented members of the College of Cardinals resulted in the execution of Cardinal Alfonso Petrucci and the imprisonment and punishment by fines of Cardinals Adriano Castellesi, Francesco Soderini, Raffaello Riario, and Bandinello Sauli, as well as far-reaching changes in that Sacred College. Notable among these was the publication on July 1, 1517, of the names of 31 new cardinals.

St. Peter's Indulgence. The construction of St. Peter's in Rome, the planned crusade against the Turks, the war with France and Spain, patronage of the arts, and the various other ever-increasing expenses of the papacy caused Leo X to search constantly for new sources of revenue. One of these, by no means new, was the preaching of indulgences. Julius II had authorized an indulgence to support the building of St. Peter's. Leo renewed the indulgence; although it was so unpopular in Germany, because the local princes resented the flow of money out of northern Europe, that it was being preached in only a few German dioceses by 1514. The death of Archbishop von Gemmingen of Mainz in March 1514 left one of Germany's wealthiest archdioceses vacant. ALBRECHT OF BRANDENBURG, already archbishop of Magdeburg and bishop of Halberstadt, immediately advanced his candidacy, but was unable to raise the 14,000-ducat installation tax for

Mainz and the 10,000 ducats required for the papal dispensation for the plural holding of sees. In an arrangement with the banking house of Jacob Fugger, the full amount would be advanced to the papacy at once if the new archbishop would allow indulgence preachers to go into his, as yet untouched, dioceses. One-half of the sums accumulated from the indulgences would go to the Fuggers, the other half to Rome. Leo X looked favorably on the profitable proposition, and on March 31, 1515, he issued the bull authorizing the indulgence to be preached in the Archdioceses of Mainz and Magdeburg. It was not until January 1517, that the Dominican friar Johann TETZEL began preaching.

Luther's 95 Theses. It was a direct reaction to Tetzel's preaching that led Martin LUTHER to post his 95 theses on the church door of Wittenberg castle. A summary of Luther's ideas was sent to Rome early in 1518. The Pope instructed the Augustinian general, Gabrielle della Volta, to silence the monk, but the attempt was unsuccessful. The diplomatic move to win over Luther's protector, Frederick the Wise of Saxony, by sending him the Golden Rose was likewise futile. After the Leipzig debates between Johann ECK and Luther (1519), Leo issued the bull *Exsurge Domine* (June 15, 1520), which condemned Luther on 41 counts. When Luther publicly burned the bull on December 10, he was excommunicated in the bull *Decet Romanum Pontificem* (January 3, 1521).

Luther's teachings were by no means confined to Germany. In England Henry VIII reacted by writing a defense of the seven Sacraments, for which the Pope bestowed upon him the title Defender of the Faith (October 11, 1521). Reaction in Scandinavia was more negative. Giovannangelo ARCIMBOLDI, the papal nuncio to the Danish court of Christian II, had been expelled (1520) because of his political activities, and Christian invited Lutheran theologians to Copenhagen. Leo acted promptly and sent a new nuncio, the Minorite Francesco de Potentia, who temporarily restored harmony.

The Lutheran challenge was not the only one to trouble the reign of Leo X. The dispute between Johannes Pfefferkorn and Johann Reuchlin became the concern of the papacy in September 1513. Pfefferkorn had begun a campaign to confiscate Jewish literature as subversive of faith and was opposed by Reuchlin and other humanists. The Pope referred the matter to the local bishops, who handed down a decision in favor of Reuchlin in March 1514. An appeal to Rome resulted in Leo's reversing the decision; Reuchlin was silenced.

The entangled international wars and alliances, together with the turbulence of domestic politics, explain in part why Leo was not more vigorous in suppressing the heretical and schismatical movements in northern Europe. He was perhaps, the last of the Renaissance popes who looked upon the papacy as primarily a temporal monarchy.

Bibliography: LEO X, *Regesta . . . Leonis X . . . e tabularii Vaticani manuscriptis voluminibus,* ed. J. HERGENRÖTHER (Freiburg 1884–). P. GIOVIO, *Historia sui temporis,* 2 v. (Florence 1550–52); *Vita Leonis X* (Florence 1548, 1551), earliest account of his life. W. ROSCOE, *Life and Pontificate of Leo X,* 2 v. (London 1853). D. GNOLI, *La Roma di Leone X* (Milan 1938). L. PASTOR, *The History of the Popes from the Close of the Middle Ages* (London-St. Louis 1938–61) v.7–8, bibliog. F. X. SEPPELT, *Geschichte der Päpste von den Anfängen bis zur Mitte des 20 Jh.* (Leipzig 1931–41) 4:408–426. H. M. VAUGHAN, *The Medici Popes* (New York 1908). G. B. PICOTTI, *La Giovinezza di Leone X* (Milan 1928). E. P. RODOCANACHI, *Le Pontifical de Léon X, 1513–1521* (Paris 1930). G. K. BROWN, *Italy and the Reformation to 1550* (Oxford 1933). G. TRUC, *Léon X et son siècle* (Paris 1941). H. JEDIN, *History of the Council of Trent,* tr. E. GRAF, (St. Louis 1957–60) v.1. R. AUBENAS and R. RICARD, *Histoire de l'église depuis les origines jusqu'à nos jours,* 15, ed. A. FLICHE and V. MARTIN (Paris 1951). G. MOLLAT, *Dictionnaire de théologie catholique,* ed. A. VACANT et al., 15 v. (Paris 1903–50; Tables générales 1951–) 9.1:329–332: G. SCHWAIGER, *Lexikon für Theologie und Kirche,* ed. J. HOFER and K. RAHNER, 10 v. (2d ed. Freiburg 1957–65) 6:950–952, bibliog. S. BEDINI, *The Pope's Elephant* (Lisbon 1997). C. FALCONI, *Leone X* (Milan 1987). A. FERRAJOLI, *Il ruolo della Corte di Leone X* (Rome 1984). *Epistolae ad Principes. Leo X–Pius IV (1513–1565),* ed. L. NANNI (Vatican City 1992). C. BRESNAHAN MENNING, *Charity and State in Late Renaissance Ithaca* (Ithaca, N.Y. 1993).

[J. G. GALLAHER]

LEO XI, POPE

Pontificate: April 1 to April 27, 1605; b. Alessandro Ottaviano de' Medici, Florence, June 2, 1535. His mother, Francesca Salviati, of a collateral branch of the ruling Florentine family, objected to her son's vocation, and he was not ordained until after her death. For 15 years he served in Rome as the ambassador of Grand Duke Cosimo of Tuscany. Gregory XIII named him bishop of Pistoia in 1573, archbishop of Florence in 1574, and cardinal in 1583. Clement VIII appointed him his legate to France in 1596 in the hope of improving the situation of Catholics under King Henry IV. He became cardinal-bishop of Albano in 1600 and was transferred to Palestrina two years later. At the same time he was named prefect of the Sacred Congregation of Bishops and Regulars. His election to the papacy with French support was predicted by Philip Neri, his close friend during his years as Tuscan ambassador in Rome. Sixty-two cardinals met in the conclave of 1605. Ten votes were given to the Jesuit Cardinal Robert BELLARMINE; 20 were cast for the historian from the Oratory, Cardinal Caesar BARONIUS, who, after receiving 37 votes in the second scrutiny, urged his friends not to vote for him. The election then went to Alessandro de' Medici. During his short pontificate Leo XI, who adopted the name of his uncle Leo X, initiated changes in the system of voting in conclave, settled the conflict between the clergy of Castile and Léon and the Jesuits, assisted Emperor Rudolf II in the Turkish War, and purchased the Villa Medici on the Pincio in Rome.

"*Monument of Pope Leo XII,*" *sculpture by Giuseppe De Fabris,1836, located in the Basilica of St. Peter, Rome.* (Alinari-Art Reference/Art Resource, NY)

turn to practices abandoned during the French occupation proved distasteful to the populace of the Papal States and intensified their desire for greater self-determination and lay administration.

Education was regulated by the bull *Quod divina sapientia* (1824), which created some uncertainty about Leo XII's attitude concerning the relation between science and religion. The Pope also restored the Gregorian University to the Jesuits.

Across the Atlantic, James WHITFIELD was appointed to succeed Ambrose Marechal as archbishop of Baltimore (1828). The Pope also named an administrator in Philadelphia in 1826 to aid Bp. Henry CONWELL, who had yielded to demands that the laity name their own pastors (*see* TRUSTEEISM). Two vicariates apostolic were formed in 1825, one for Mississippi and the other for Alabama and Florida. Louisiana was divided into the Dioceses of New Orleans and Saint Louis in 1826.

Leo XII was more conciliatory in dealing with the European powers than with his own subjects. He ardently desired to strengthen alliances with sovereigns; yet he did not hesitate to send a critical letter to Louis XVIII complaining against the restoration governments and their dealing with enemies of the Church. He was sympathetic with Hugues Félicité de LAMENNAIS and the protest of ultramontanism against the prevailing GALLICANISM. While rejoicing at the restoration in SPAIN, he resisted the royal demand that he recognized its right of *PATRONATO REAL* over the newly independent lands of Latin America. The NETHERLANDS were tense because of Protestant and Catholic frictions, which had been aggravated by Belgian independence movement leaders; yet Leo XII concluded a concordat with King William I (1827). During this pontificate Catholic EMANCIPATION came close to achievement in Great Britain and Ireland; the emancipation act was passed April 13, 1829.

Leo XII tried to suppress the growing forces of LIBERALISM and sympathized with monarchs who were seeking to restore the conditions of the *ancien régime*.

Bibliography: J. SCHMIDLIN, *Papstgeschichte der neuesten Zeit, 1800–1939* (Munich 1933–39) v.1. J. LEFLON, *La Crise révolutionnaire, 1789–1846* (A. FLICHE and V. MARTIN, eds., *Histoire de l'église depuis les origines jusqu'à nos jours* 20 [Paris 1949]). E. E. Y. HALES, *Revolution and Papacy, 1769–1846* (Garden City, N. Y. 1960). P. PASCHINI and V. MONACHINO, eds., *I. Papi nella Storia*, 2 v. (Rome 1961) 2:887–898, P. DE LETURIA, *Relaciones entre la Santa Sede e Hespanoamérica*, 3 v. (Rome 1959) v.2, 3. R. COLAPIETRA, *La formazione diplomatica di Leone XII* (Rome 1966). R. COLAPIETRA, *La chiesa tra Lamennais e Mettenich Il Pontificato di Leone XII* (Brescia 1963). J.D. HOLMES, *The Triumph of the Holy See* (London 1978). M. CARAVALE and A. CARACCIOLO, *Lo stato pontificio da Martino V a Pio IX* (Turin 1978).

[T. F. CASEY]

LEO XIII, POPE

Pontificate, Feb. 20, 1878, to July 20, 1903; b. Gioacchino Vincenzo Pecci, Carpineto (Frosinone), central Italy; March 2, 1810.

Prepapal Career. He was the sixth of seven sons of Col. Ludovico Pecci and Anna Prosperi Buzi. His family was noble but by no means wealthy. After his early education at the Jesuit college in Viterbo (1818–24), he studied at Rome in the Romain College (1824–32). Admitted in 1832 to the Accademia dei Nobili ecclesiastici, he pursued studies in theology and in civil and Canon Law at the University of the Sapienza (1832–37). In 1837 he was ordained and was appointed a domestic prelate. In January of 1838, Gregory XVI, who had remarked his courage during the cholera epidemic of the previous year, appointed him apostolic delegate to Benevento in the STATES

OF THE CHURCH. There Msgr. Pecci proved energetic in controlling banditry and the intrigues of the liberals. Transferred to the same function in Perugia (1841), he faced similar problems. By his capable administration and economic improvements, building roads and establishing a savings bank for farmers, he won the affection of the populace.

Consecrated titular archbishop of Damietta, he went to Belgium as nuncio in January of 1843. The most delicate question confronting him was that of education. Pecci supported the bishops and Catholic politicians in opposition to Prime Minister Nothomb, who wished to confer on the government the right of naming members of "University Juries." So discontented was the king at the defeat of this project that he demanded the recall of the nuncio, whose attitude had helped check the entente between moderate liberals and Catholics known as unionism.

Pecci's three years in Brussels were of considerable importance in developing his later outlook as pope. They represented his sole contact with industrial Europe, save for brief sojourns in the Rhineland, London, and Paris. Conditions in Belgium led him to reflect on the situation of Catholics elsewhere who lived under political regimes with liberal institutions.

Quitting Brussels (May 1846) Pecci went to Perugia, where he remained as archbishop until 1878. He showed special interest in clerical formation. Under the auspices of his brother Joseph, a Jesuit and professor at the seminary, he favored the renewal of THOMISM and established the Academy of St. Thomas in 1859. During the revolutionary events of 1859–60 he reaffirmed the legitimacy of the papal temporal power and protested firmly but not abusively the religious policy of the Italian government. At VATICAN COUNCIL I he voted with the majority, but was not an outstanding member. Cardinal ANTONELLI, secretary of state, believed Pecci's policies hostile to his and kept him from Rome. The archbishop's pastoral letters (1876–77) on the Church and civilization, emphasizing that the Church must enter the current of modern civilization, drew wide attention. A cardinal from 1853, he became camerlengo in the Roman Curia (Sept. 9, 1877) while retaining his see. At the conclave following Pius IX's death, he was *papabile* as candidate of the moderates. After receiving 19 votes on the first ballot, compared with six given to the next most favored choice, Cardinal BILIO, he emerged as pope after the third ballot, with 44 of the 61 votes.

Pontificate. Leo XIII's pontificate, foreseen as a brief transitional one, lasted more than 25 years and came to be ranked among the most significant in recent times because of his numerous teachings, acts of initiative, and

Pope Leo XIII. (Kean Collection/Archive Photos)

exceptional prestige. Patient, conciliatory, and wise in choosing opportune solutions to problems and then abiding by them, the pontiff displayed a strong will and calm energy in his actions.

In line with Pius IX he favored devotion to the SACRED HEART. His encyclical *Annum Sacrum* (May 25, 1899) consecrated the whole human race to the Sacred Heart. Nine encyclicals concerned devotion to the Blessed Virgin MARY and to the ROSARY. The encyclical *Auspicato concessum* (Sept. 17, 1882) renewed the Franciscan Third Order.

Missions received much attention. Leo's pontificate coincided with the apogee of colonialism. To speed the abolition of African slavery he published two encyclicals, *In plurimis* (May 5, 1888) to the Brazilian hierarchy, and *Catholicae Ecclesiae* (Nov. 20, 1890). A concordat (June 23, 1886) restrained the king of Portugal's right of *padroado* in India solely to Portuese possessions (*see* PATRONATO REAL; GOA). In the same year the pope established the hierarchy in India. The Congregation for the

Propagation of the Faith reorganized the missions in China, but the French protectorate over Catholics in China would not permit (1886) the erection of a nunciature in Beijing.

Leo XIII had high hopes of reunion with the Oriental and Slavic Churches. Bishop STROSSMAYER urged the Pontiff to display his interest in them. The encyclical *Grande munus* (Sept. 30, 1880) recalled the Holy See's approval of the apostolic methods of SS. CYRIL AND METHODIUS. The Eucharistic Congress in Jerusalem (1893) and the apostolic letter *Orientalium* (Nov. 30, 1894), which dealt with rites questions, reaffirmed hope for reunion, which did not materialize.

A papal commission was appointed (1895) to study ANGLICAN ORDERS. The apostolic letter denying their validity (*APOSTOLICAE CURAE,* Sept. 13, 1896) discouraged prospects for union with ANGLICANISM.

In the intellectual order the encyclical *AETERNI PATRIS* (Aug. 4, 1879) was decisive in importance. Urged by his brother Cardinal Joseph Pecci and by Father LIBERATORE, Leo XIII sought renewal of philosophical thought in the Church on the basis of Thomism and an assurance of sound doctrinal teaching in seminaries. In Thomism he perceived the body of thought that he wished used in opposition to LIBERALISM on the political and social planes. The reorganization of the Roman Academy of St. Thomas (1886), the nomination of MERCIER to a chair of Thomism at Louvain (1882), the condemnation (1887) of propositions extracted from the works of ROSMINI-SERBATI, who had a following in northern Italy, were all part of the program to restore Thomism.

The opening of the VATICAN ARCHIVES in 1881 to historians demonstrated concretely Leo XIII's eagerness to promote scholarly research.

The encyclical *PROVIDENTISSIMUS DEUS* (Nov. 18, 1893) explained the paths open to biblical exegesis. The creation (1902) of the PONTIFICAL BIBLICAL COMMISSION marked a stiffer policy, a solicitude for watching over the labors of exegetes at the time MODERNISM was developing.

The organization of society and the relations between CHURCH AND STATE called forth the famous encyclicals *DIUTURNUM* (June 29, 1881), *IMMORTALE DEI* (Nov. 1, 1885), *LIBERTAS* (June 20, 1888), and *Sapientiae christianae* (Jan. 10, 1890), which reaffirmed the condemnations of the principles of liberalism by Gregory XVI and Pius IX. They recalled also the divine origin of AUTHORITY and the proper union between Church and State, both "perfect" societies. The encyclicals further demonstrated that the Church is not hostile to any form of government. Also they contrasted "legitimate and honest liberty" with "immoderate liberty" that refuses all reference to God and admits the coexistence of diverse cults. Especially did the pope urge Catholics to accept existing institutions in view of the COMMON GOOD, to participate in political life, and to make use of the liberal institutions of the press and the parliamentary systems of government in the interest of the Church.

Social questions were also the topic of papal encyclicals that gained wide attention even from unbelievers. *Quod Apostolici muneris* (Dec. 28, 1878) condemned socialism. *Arcanum* (Feb. 10, 1880) defined the Christian concept of the FAMILY. *RERUM NOVARUM* (May 15, 1891), published three years after the letter to Cardinal GIBBONS concerning the KNIGHTS OF LABOR, was Leo XIII's most important social pronouncement. Directed against socialism and economic liberalism, it drew its inspiration from the Catholic social studies at the Union of Fribourg and imparted a strong impulse to the Christian Social Movement (*see* SOCIAL THOUGHT, PAPAL).

Christian Democracy arose in Belgium, France, and Italy. The encyclical *Graves de communi re* (Jan. 18, 1901) accepted the term Christian Democracy, but denied to it all political significance by defining it as "beneficent Christian action in favor of the people."

Leo XIII and States. The policy of the pope and his successive secretaries of state (FRANCHI, NINA, JACOBINI, RAMPOLLA) was dominated by the contrast between an intransigent attitude on the ROMAN QUESTION and a search for a solution to the conflicts with various governments that had arisen at the close of Pius IX's pontificate.

No sooner was Leo XIII elected than he protested against the situation confronting the pope in Rome. After several attempts at conciliation failed, he despaired of a settlement of the Roman Question by direct negotiations with the Kingdom of Italy. From this point of view the year 1887 and the appointment of Cardinal Rampolla as secretary of state were decisive. Henceforth the pontiff sought in vain to pose the problem on an international plane, placing his hopes in Germany after the KULTURKAMPF subsided, and then in France. For Italian Catholics he maintained the policy of *NON EXPEDIT*, requiring abstention from political elections. Italian Catholics developed a civil sense, however, by social action in the Opera dei Congressi.

The Kulturkampf ended in Germany after long negotiations. The Center Party wanted the complete abolition of the May Laws. Leo XIII was content with partial, compromise settlements in 1880 and 1883. Only in 1887 was there formal revision of the May Laws.

In Belgium and France the pope had to withstand a reign of ANTICLERICALISM. The Belgian school law

(1879) occasioned a conflict that led to the rupture of diplomatic relations with the Vatican in June of 1880. Despite this, Leo XIII invited intransigent Belgian Catholics to accept the constitution of their country. It was in this period that a truly Catholic party was formed whose success at the polls (1884) resulted in the renewal of diplomatic relations.

In France Leo XIII urged moderation on Catholics at the time of the vote on the lay laws. After hopes for a restored monarchy proved vain and Boulangism failed, the pope pressed French Catholics to accept the Third Republic. From the Algiers Toast pronounced by Cardinal LAVIGERIE (Nov. 12, 1890) to the encyclical *Au Milieu des sollicitudes* (Feb. 16, 1892), he promoted the RALLIEMENT. This policy was stalemated, at least for a while, by dissensions among French Catholics, by their attitude on the Dreyfus case and by the new wave of anticlericalism that led to the vote (1901) on the Law of Associations and to the accession of Combes as premier.

Relations were strained with Austria-Hungary, which was particularly defiant of Cardinal Rampolla. Improved Vatican relations with Russia, a condition for reunion with the Orthodox Churches, disturbed the court of Vienna.

Leo XIII on many occasions expressed his favorable sentiments toward the United States. He followed closely the growth of Catholicism there, as he made clear by naming Msgr. SATOLLI as apostolic delegate (1893) and by the encyclical *Longinqua* (Jan. 6, 1895). Disputes over AMERICANISM were ended by the letter *TESTEM BENEVOLENTIAE* (Jan. 22, 1899).

Relations with Latin American nations improved. In 1899 an important council met in Rome representing the Church of this area.

Leo XIII envisioned an important role for the papacy in international affairs. On many occasions he recalled the Church's mission as peacemaker and pointed out the costs of an armed peace. His sole success, however, was the Roman mediation (1885) in the dispute between the German empire and Spain over the Caroline Islands. When the Hague Peace Conference met in 1899, the pope was not invited because of the opposition of the Italian government. Thus the Roman Question prevented the papacy from enjoying its sought-after international role.

Papal prestige, symbolized by the white, ascetic silhouette of Leo XIII, considerably increased during his pontificate. Commentaries from the entire world at the time of the pope's death gave proof of this. Despite setbacks, Leo XIII's pontificate planted seeds that were eventually to grow into an abundant harvest.

Bibliography: Sources. *Acta Sanctae Sedis*, v.11–35. (Rome 1878–1903). *Acta Leonis XIII*, 24 v. (Rome 1881–1905). *The Great Encyclical Letters of Pope Leo XIII* (New York 1903). A. MERCATI, *Raccolta di Concordati* (Rome 1954) 1:1001–91, [72]–[90]. A. SIMON, ed., *Documents relatifs à la Nonciature de Bruxelles* (Brussels 1958); *Lettres de Pecci, 1843–46* (Brussels 1959). M. C. CARLEN, *Dictionary of Papal Pronouncements, 1878–1957* (New York 1958). Literature. C. T'SERCLAES, *Le Pape Léon XIII*, 3 v. (Paris 1894–1906). D. FERRATA, *Mémoires* (Paris 1922). E. SODERINI, *Il pontificato di Leone XIII*, 3 v. (Milan 1932–33); tr. B. B. CARTER, v.1 *The Pontificate of Leo XIII* (London 1934), v.2 *Leo XIII, Italy and France* (1935), v.3 not tr. G. GOYAU, *Dictionnaire de théologie catholique*, ed. A. VACANT et al. (Paris 1903–50) 9.1:334–359. J. SCHMIDLIN, *Papstgeschichte der neuesten Zeit, 1800–1939* (Munich 1933–39) v.2. K. S. LATOURETTE, *Christianity in a Revolutionary Age: A History of Christianity in the 19th and 20th Centuries* v.1. H. DANIEL-ROPS, *L'Église des révolutions: Un Combat pour Dieu, 1870–1939* (*Histoire de l'Église du Christ* 6.2; Paris 1963). A. DANSETTE, *Religious History of Modern France*, tr. J. DINGLE (New York 1961) v.2. É. LECANUET, *L'Église de France sous le Troisième République* (Paris 1930–31) v.2–4. A. C. JEMOLO, *Church and State in Italy, 1850–1950*, tr. D. MOORE (Philadephia 1960). F. FONZI, *I cattolici e la società italiana dopo l'unità* (Rome 1953). F. ENGEL-JANOSI, *Österreich und der Vatikan, 1846–1918*, 2 v. (Graz 1958–60) v.1. E. WINTER, *Russland und die slawischen Völker in der Diplomatic des Vatikans 1878–1903* (Berlin 1950). C. CRISPOLTI and G. AURELI, eds., *La politica di Leone XIII da Luigi Galimberti a Mariano Rampolla* (Rome 1912). F. MOURRET, *Les Directions politiques, intellectuelles, et sociales de Léon XIII* (Paris 1920). A. CHIH, *L'Occident "chrétien" vu par les Chinois vers la fin du XIXᵉ siècle, 1870–1900* (Paris 1962). R. ESPOSITO, *Leone XIII e l'oriente christiano* (Rome 1960). R. AUBERT, "Aspects divers du néo-thomisme sous le pontificat de Léon XIII," *Aspetti della cultura cattolica nell'età di Leone XIII*, ed. G. ROSSINI (Rome 1961) 133–227; *Lexikon für Theologie und Kirche*, ed. J. HOFER and K. RAHNER (Freiburg 1957–65) 6:953–956. G. PELL, *Rerum novarum: One Hundred Years Later* (Boston 1992). P. FURLONG and D. CURTIS, eds., *The Church Faces the Modern World: Rerum novarum and its Impact* (United Kingdom 1994). M. LAUNAY, *La papauté à l'aube du XXe siècle: Léon XIII et Pie X (1878–1914)* (Paris 1997).

[J. M. MAYEUR]

LEO LUKE, ST.

Abbot; b. Corleone (Coriglione), Sicily, *c.* 885; d. Monteleone in Calabria, *c.* 980. While very young he became a monk at the Abbey of St. Philip in Argira. Some years later (*c.* 940) Arab raids and the generally usettled conditions led him to accompany many other monks to the interior of Calabria. After a pilgrimage to Rome, he became a disciple of St. Christopher of Collesano (d. *c.* 955), the founder of a monastery near Monteleone, and succeeded him as abbot, a position he held for more than 20 years until his death. His cultus has never been confirmed.

Feast: March 1.

Bibliography: *Acta Sanctorum* March 1:97–102. D. PERRI, *Note agiografiche sul protettore di Vibo Valentia, S. Leoluca abate* (Vibo Valentia, Italy 1947), see review in *Bollettino della badia greca di Grottaferrata* 2 (1948): 231–234. S. BORSARI, *Il monache-*

simo bizantino nella Sicilia e nell'Italia Meridionale prenormanne (Naples 1963) 53.

[G. T. DENNIS]

LEO MARSICANUS

Also known as *Ostiensis,* monk and chronicler of MONTE CASSINO; b. *c.* 1046; d. May 22, 1115. At the age of 14 Leo entered Monte Cassino, where he subsequently became abbey librarian. In 1101 PASCHAL II named him cardinal bishop of Ostia. Leo has been called the most important medieval Italian historian. He is the author of the reliable *Chronica Casinensis monasterii* from St. Benedict to 1057; Guido and the unreliable Peter the Deacon of Rome continued it to 1139. Leo's other works include *Historia peregrinorum, Vita S. Mennatis, De consecratione ecclesiarum a Desiderio et Oderisio in Monte Cassino aedificatarum.*

Bibliography: Sources. *Monumenta Germaniae Historica: Scriptores* (Berlin 1826–) 7:574–727. L. A. MURATORI, *Rerum italicarum scriptores, 500–1500,* 25 v. in 28 (2nd new ed. Città di Castello 1900–) 4:151–628. **Literature.** M. MANITIUS, *Geschichte der lateinischen Literatur des Mittelalters,* 3 v. (Munich 1911–31) 3:546–549. H. W. KLEWITZ, "Petrus Diaconus und die Montecassiner Klosterchronik des Leo von Ostia," *Archiv für Urkundenforschung* 14 (1935) 414–453. W. SMIDT, "Die vermeintliche . . . Urgestalt der Chronik Leos," *Quellen und Forschungen aus italienischen Archiven und Bibliotheken* 28 (1938) 286–297. P. SCHMITZ, *Histoire de l'ordre de Saint Benoît,* 7 v. (Maredsous 1942–56) v. 2, 5.

[V. GELLHAUS]

LEO OF ASSISI (BROTHER LEO)

Secretary, companion, and confessor of FRANCIS OF ASSISI; b. end of 12th century; d. Assisi(?), Nov. 14–15, 1271. Francis affectionately called him *Frate pecorella di Dio* because of his innocence and candor. The only extant holographs of Francis, i.e., a letter preserved in Spoleto and the *Laudes creatoris* with the blessing from Nm 6.24 on the reverse, in Sacro Convento, Assisi, were written for Leo. After the death of Francis, Leo conflicted sharply with ELIAS OF CORTONA, but soon retired to a hermitage and spent the rest of his life writing in defense of what he considered the authentic ideas of Francis. Attributed to him are the *Vita b. Aegidii, Liber de intentione s. Francisci,* and *Verba s. Francisci;* the *Speculum perfectionis* and *Legenda trium sociorum* are most probably not his.

Bibliography: *Vita* in *Analecta Franciscana* 3 (1897) 65–74. L. OLIGER, "Liber exemplorum Fratrum Minorum saeculi XIII," *Antonianum* 2 (1927) 203–276. L. LEMMENS, ed. *Documenta antiqua Franciscana,* 3 v. (Quaracchi Florence 1901–02) v. 1; "Die

Schriften des Br. Leo von Assisi," *Miscellanea Francesco Ehrle* 5 v. *Studi e Testi* (1924) 37–41 3:25–48. A. MACDONELL, *Sons of Francis* (London 1902) 95–112. FRANCIS OF ASSISI, *The Writings,* ed. P. HERMANN, tr. B. FAHY (Chicago 1964). L. HARDICK, *Lexikon für Theologie und Kirche,* ed. J. HOFER and K. RAHNER (Freiburg 1957–65) 6:956. O. ENGLEBERT, *St. Francis of Assisi: A Biography* (Chicago 1966).

[M. F. LAUGHLIN]

LEO OF CAVA

Name of two abbots of the Benedictine Abbey of LA CAVA, outside Salerno, Italy.

Leo I, St., from Lucca in Tuscany; d. July 12, 1079. Leo was designated successor by Abbot ALFERIUS, the founder of Cava, at the moment of his death in 1050. He is known almost uniquely through the vita by Abbot Hugh of Venosa in Apulia, former monk of Cava, who wrote his biography (*c.* 1140) along with the lives of Alferius and Leo's successors, PETER PAPPACARBONE and CONSTABILIS. The vita presents Leo as a humble and charitable man, dedicated to the relief of the poor and oppressed, and thus in constant conflict with the vindictive and cruel Gisulf II, Prince of Salerno (1052–77). It is reported that Leo was rewarded with visions of the Mother of God. The archives of Cava contain many documents outlining donations made to Cava during his abbacy. Toward the end of his life he selected as coadjutor and successor Alferius's nephew Peter. This choice aroused dissension and hostility because of the strictness of the new abbot. Leo's immemorial cult was approved by Pope Leo XIII in 1893.

Feast: July 12.

Leo II, Bl.; d. Aug. 19, 1295. After becoming abbot of Cava in 1268, he followed the example set by his namesake and predecessor. In 1274 he took part in the Council of Lyons, stopping at CLUNY on his way there. He encouraged the development of the Cava SCRIPTORIUM and both the monastery's beautiful cloister and the chapel of San Germano (decorated with GIOTTO paintings), which he built, are extant. Despite numerous endowments, the abbey suffered a notable loss during his reign when it was compelled to give up all its holdings in Sicily in 1282. His cult was approved by Pope Pius XI in 1928.

Feast: Aug. 19.

Bibliography: L. A. MURATORI, *Rerum italicarum scriptores, 500–1500,* 25 v. in 28 (Milan 1723–51; 1748–71) 6.5:11–16, thirteenth-century manuscript at Cava. P. GUILLAUME, *Un monaco ed un principe del secolo XI* (Naples 1876); *Essai historique sur l'abbaye da Cava d'après des documents inédits* (Naples 1877)

29–43, 170–182. P. LUGANO, *I santi padri Cavensi* (Naples 1932) 13–15, 48–51.

[I. DE PICCOLI]

LEO OF ST. JOHN

Carmelite of the Touraine Reform; b. Rennes, France, July 9, 1600; d. Paris, Dec. 30, 1671. He was a man of prodigiously extensive interests and accomplishments. He promoted reform within his own order and held all its most important offices, except that of general. He was a friend of Richelieu and later of Mazarin, whose policies he generally supported, in spite of his connections with the devout party. Although Leo was a conciliator in the Jansenist conflict, he was nevertheless attacked violently by Arnauld. He maintained important political, religious, and intellectual relations with the royal family, great statemen, the nobility, the intellectuals, St. Vincent de Paul, Innocent X, and many cardinals. He was a precursor of Bossuet and wrote a remarkable *Traité de l'éloquence Chrétienne* (in *Année royale*, 1, Paris 1655). He entered successfully into the controversy with the Calvinists. His *L'Économie de la vraie religion* (Paris 1643), was an important work, whose apologetic, completely different from that of Pascal, and foreshadowing Malebranche, took its inspiration from medieval Augustinian rationalism, notably that of Raymond Lull. A Dionysian and Augustinian, Leo can neither be listed among the Thomists nor among the "devout humanists." He was a major instrument in spreading Bérulle's spirituality.

Bibliography: C. DE VILLIERS, *Bibliotheca carmelitana*, 2 v. in 1 (Rome 1927) 2:235–246. P. ANASTASE DE S. PAUL, *Dictionnaire de théologie catholique*, 15 v. (Paris 1903–50) 9.1:394–396. J. P. MASSAUT, "Léon de Saint-Jean . . . prédicateur et théologien encyclopédique," *Carmelus* 8 (1961): 27–62; "Autour de Richelieu et de Mazarin: Le carme Léon de Saint-Jean et la grande politique," *Revue d'histoire moderne et contemporaine* 7 (1960): 11–46; "Thomisme et augustinisme dans l'apologétique du XVIIᵉ siècle," *Revue des sciences philosophiques et théolgiques* 44 (1960): 617–638; "Humaniste ou augustinien? Le carme Léon de Saint-Jean et l'antiquité classique," *Revue des études augustiniennes*, Aug. 7 (1961): 373–388.

[J. P. MASSAUT]

LEO OF VERCELLI

Bishop of Vercelli (998–999), poet, imperial logothete, and trusted adviser of Otto III; d. Vercelli, April 10, 1026. His origin, whether German or Italian, is disputed. In 997 he was the colleague of Gerbert (see SYLVESTER II) in the palace chapel of OTTO III. In 998 he accompanied Otto to Italy, where he remained for the rest of his life in the service of three German emperors. His legal training gave him an influential role as imperial judge and redactor of legislation. He probably drafted Otto III's capitularies on church property, although their substance should probably be ascribed to Gerbert. He drew up the diploma whereby Otto gave eight counties to the Roman Church. At the Council of Pavia in 1022 he rendered similar services to Emperor HENRY II. As bishop he regarded himself as an imperial official, a "bishop of the empire." He energetically enforced the imperial decrees reintegrating Church property and governed the counties of Vercelli and Santhià conferred upon him by Otto III. He opposed Arduin of Ivrea, leader of the opposition to Otto and claimant to the Italian crown after his death. His loyalty to Henry II of Germany contributed largely to Henry's ultimate victory. Extremely versatile, Leo on occasion expressed his imperialist enthusiasm in Latin verses that showed considerable literary skill.

Bibliography: K. STRECKER, ed., *Monumenta Germaniae Historica: Poetae*, (Berlin 1826–) 5.2:476–489. H. BLOCH, "Beiträge zur Geschichte des Bischofs Leo von Vercelli und seines Zeit," *Neues Archiv der Gesellschaft für ältere deutsche Geschichtskunde* 22 (1896): 13–136. M. MANITIUS, *Geschichte der lateinischen Literatur des Mittelalters*, 3 v. (Munich 1911–31) 2:511–517. E. N. JOHNSON, *The Secular Activities of the German Episcopate, 919–1024* (Lincoln, Neb. 1932). M. UHLIRZ, "Die italienische Kirchenpolitik der Ottonen," *Mitteilungen des Instituts für österreichische Geschichtsforschung* 48 (1934): 201–321, *passim.*

[C. E. BOYD]

LEO THAUMATURGUS, ST.

Bishop of Catania, Sicily, and miracle worker; b. probably at Ravenha, *c.* 703; d. *c.* 785. As bishop of Catania, he enjoyed universal respect. He was invited to Constantinople to the courts of Emperor Leo IV and of Emperor Constantine VI, who solicited his intercession.

Feast: Feb. 20.

Bibliography: *Acta Sanctorum* Feb. 3 (1865) 226–229. *Synaxarium ecclesiae Constantinopolitanae. Propylaeum ad Acta sanctorum novembris* 479. *Bibliotheca hagiographica Graeca* 3:981. H. G. GECK, *Kirche und theologische Literatur im byzantinischen Reich.*

[M. C. HILFERTY]

LEOBARD, SS.

The name of two saints of the sixth and seventh centuries.

Leobard (Liberd) of Tours, Benedictine recluse of Auvergne; d. *c.* 593. After the death of his parents, who had wanted him to marry, he lived for 22 years as a recluse in the Diocese of Tours under the spiritual direction of GREGORY OF TOURS, who also wrote his life. Leobard founded the Abbey of MARMOUTIER and was its first abbot.

Feast: Jan. 18 (Roman MARTYROLOGY); Feb. 13 (Tours).

Leobard of Maursmünster, abbot, disciple of Waldebert, known also as Liuberat in the necrology of Reichenau, founded the Abbey of Maursmünster; d. *c.* 660.

Feast: Dec. 31; Feb. 25.

Bibliography: *Acta Sanctorum* 2:562–563. GREGORY OF TOURS, *Opera,* in *Patrologia Latina,* 217 v. (Paris 1878–90) 71:1092–96. *Monumenta Germaniae Historica: Scriptores rerum Merovingicarum,* (Berlin 1826–) 1.2:741. J. L. BAUDOT and L. CHAUSSIN, *Vies des saints et des bienheureux selon l'ordre du calendrier avec l'historique des fêtes* 12 v. (Paris 1935–56) 1:369–370.

[O. L. KAPSNER]

LEOBIN OF CHARTRES, ST.

Bishop of CHARTRES, 544– *c.* 556. From detailed information furnished by the vita, written most probably by his successor, Caletric (557– *c.* 567), but reworked in the ninth century, Leobin is one of the best known of the early bishops of Chartres. He entered the monastery of St. Hilary at Poitiers, where he subsequently became cellarer and acquired a reputation for strict enforcement of monastic regulations and for zeal in his studies. Apparently forced to leave St. Hilary's because of the hostility of certain monks, he visited a number of monasteries from the region of the Loire to Lerins. Subsequently, St. AVITUS OF VIENNE made him abbot of Brou. In 544, he was elected bishop of Chartres, and, although not the founder of its episcopal school, he did much to develop it. An active participant in the synods of Orléans (549) and Paris (552), he was one of the judges who deposed Saffaracus, bishop of Paris.

Feast: March 14; Sept. 15 (translation feast).

Bibliography: *Bibliotheca hagiographica latina antiquae et mediae aetatis,* 2 v. (Brussels 1898–1901) 2:4847. *Acta Sanctorum,* March 2:344–349. *Monumenta Germaniae Historica: Auctores antiquissimi* (Berlin 1826–) 4.2:73–82. H. LECLERCQ, *Dictionnaire d'archéologie chrétienne et de liturgie,* 15 v. (Paris 1907–53) 3.1:1021–25. A. PONCELET, ''Les Saints de Micy,'' *Analecta Bollandiana* 24 (1905): 1–104, esp. 25–31.

[M. R. P. MCGUIRE]

LEODEGAR OF AUTUN, ST.

Bishop and martyr, also known as Léger; b. *c.* 616; d. forest of Sarcing, near Arras, France, Oct. 2, 678. Descended from a noble Frankish family, he was archdeacon at Poitiers under his uncle Didon (d. 673) and then abbot of SAINT-MAIXENT for at least six years until he was called to the court of Neustria by BATHILDIS, regent there since 657. Through the queen's influence he became *c.* 663 bishop of AUTUN, an important Burgundian see struggling to maintain its autonomy. He had the cathedral restored, brought about the translation of the relics of St. Symphorian (second century), and convened a synod. The kingdom, however, was thrown into chaos when Chlotar III (d. 673) came of age and Bathildis retired to the convent of CHELLES, leaving power to Ebroinus (d. 681), the mayor of the palace. Neustria and Burgundy thus had the same king but each remained a separate kingdom. When Ebroinus attempted to assert universal authority, the Burgundian nobles revolted, led by Leodegar. In March (or May) of 673, young Chlotar died, and Ebroinus tried to impose Theodoric III (d. *c.* 691) as king, but the nobles had him shorn and the mayor was exiled to LUXEUIL. Childeric II (d. 675), king of Austrasia since 662, became the sole monarch for the three kingdoms. Accused of plotting against the king, Leodegar also was exiled to Luxeuil, but upon the assassination of Childeric in the fall of 675 and the return of Theodoric, both Leodegar and Ebroinus were liberated. Leodegar returned to Autun, where Hermanarius restored to him his usurped see, and Ebroinus became more active than ever. Ignoring Wulfoad, the mayor of the palace, he proclaimed Clovis III king in Austrasia and assumed power in his name. At Crécyen-Ponthieu he captured King Theodoric, who had been thought dead, and laid siege to Autun. Fasting, alms, and processions were of no avail, and at length, Leodegar gave himself up to prevent a sack of the city. Under the false indictment of having had a hand in the assassination of Childeric, Leodegar was blinded and his tongue was cut out. In September of 678 he appeared at the royal palace before a synod that degraded him; he was then dragged off to the forest of Sarcing, where he was beheaded.

Desiderius, bishop of Chalons, and Waimer, count of Champagne, Leodegar's enemies, were condemned by the Synod of Mâlay even before his death, and Ebroinus was assassinated in the spring of 681. Nothing now stood in the way of a rehabilitation, and an assembly of bishops proclaimed Leodegar a martyr. His remains were translated *c.* 682 to Saint-Maixent by Abbot Audulf (d. 682), and a basilica was erected under his patronage near the abbot's house. During the NORMAN invasions the relics were transferred from one place to another, but a part of them was returned *c.* 930. Many churches in France and Belgium bear his name, and he is especially honored in the Dioceses of Autun and Poitiers. He is invoked for diseases of the eyes, and he is depicted in art as a bishop holding in one hand an auger, the instrument used in his blinding.

Feast: Oct. 2.

Bibliography: *Patrologia Latina,* 217 v. (Paris 1878–90) 96:373–376. *Monumenta Germaniae Historica: Scriptores rerum Merovingicarum* (Berlin 1826–) 5:249–362. *Acta Sanctorum* Oct. 1:355–463. CAMERLINCK, *St. Léger* (Paris 1910). H. LECLERCQ, *Dictionnaire d'archéologie chrétienne et de liturgie* 15 v. (Paris 1907–53) 8.2:2460–93. J. L. BAUDOT and L. CHAUSSIN, *Vies des saints et des bienheureux selon l'ordre du calendrier avec l'historique des fêtes* 12 v. (Paris 1935–56) 10:39–43. L. RÉAU, *Iconographie de l'art chrétien,* 6 v. (Paris 1955–59) 2:796–797. A. MUSSAT, *Le Style gothique de l'Ouest de la France* (Paris 1963) 370–371 and plate ivii/a. D'ARCO SILVIO AVALLE, *Monumenti prefranciani. Il Sermone di Valenciennes e il Sant Lethgier,* ed. R. ROSANI (Turin 1967). *Bibliotheca hagiographica latina antiquae et mediae aetatis,* 2 v. (Brussels 1898–1901) 4850–4856. A. M. ZIMMERMANN, *Kalendarium Benedictinum: Die Heiligen und Seligen des Benediktinerorderns und seiner Zweige,* 4 v. (Metten 1933–38) 3:125–129. R. DU MOULIN-ECKART, *Leudegar, Bischof von Autun* (Breslau 1890).

[J. CAMBELL]

LEÓN, LUIS DE

Augustinian friar, theologian, exegete, poet, philosopher; b. Aug. 15, 1527, Belmonte (Cuenca), Spain; d. Aug. 23, 1591. Luis was the first-born son of Lope de León and Ines de Varela; the family was of lesser nobility (hidalgos) of Jewish descent. Luis spent his childhood in Madrid and Valladolid and, after 1541, in Salamanca where he studied canon law at the prestigious university there. On Jan. 29, 1544, he made his profession as an Augustinian friar at the Convento San Agustin in Salamanca. He studied arts at that convento (1544–1546) and then theology at the University of Salamanca under such teachers as Melchor Cano, Domingo Soto, and Mancio del Corpus Christi. He became proficient in Latin, Greek, and Hebrew, later studying Scripture and Semitic languages at the University of Alcala de Henares (1556–1557). It was in 1557 that he delivered his famous *Discurso de las Duenas,* an oratorical piece of high literary quality and profound religious insight. Continuing his theological studies at Salamanca, he earned the licentiate and masters in theology in 1560. From 1561 to 1565, while holding the Chair of St. Thomas ''in opposition,'' he explicated a number of questions from Aquinas's *Summa Theologiae,* among them *De religione, De simonia, De iuramento,* and *De fide.* At about the same time, at the request of his cousin Isabel de Osorio, a nun at the convent of Sanctus Spiritus in Salamanca, he began the translation of and commentary on the Hebrew text of the ''Song of Songs.'' A friar who cleaned Luis's cell pilfered a copy and what had been intended for private use

Seventh-century crypt of the church dedicated to and built over the interred remains of St. Leodegar of Autun, Saint-Maixent, France.

received unexpectedly wide publication. The ''Song of Songs'' (Cantar de Cantares) is a brilliant display of Luis's talent. His Spanish version of the Hebrew text is a unique and unprecedented expression of the theme of divine love.

In 1563 Luis was named definitor of the Order of St. Augustine in the Province of Castille. He held the Durando Chair at the University of Castille from 1565 to 1573. During this time the impassioned academic disputes between the Augustinians and the Dominicans grew more heated. Fray Luis considered in his *De Incarnatione* (1566–1567) how best to reconcile the freedom of Christ with the mandate for redemption received from His Father. In 1571 he lectured on Aquinas's *De Legibus,* adding a number of significant new ideas, namely, the development of the concept of the common good and an examination of the juridical nature of the Law of Nations.

In 1571 Bartolome de Medina censured Fray Luis in 17 propositions presented to the Council of the Inquisition. The case was examined and in March of 1572 Fray Luis was imprisoned in Valladolid. In that same year Martin Martinez de Cantalapiedra and Alfonso Gudiel were also imprisoned, accused of ''hebraizing tendencies.'' While imprisoned, the three professors collaborated on an effort to incorporate into scriptural interpretation the advances and insights made possible by linguistics and the study of ancient classical civilization. The Inquisition questioned Fray Luis about his Jewish ancestry, about his translation of the ''Song of Songs,'' and about his critique of the Latin Vulgate translation. In 1575 Mancio del Corpus Christi delivered a finding favorable to Fray Luis's teaching, and in December of 1576 he was absolved from all accusations of heresy and restored to his university chair at Salamanca. In subsequent years he was appointed to the chair of moral philosophy (1578) and then the chair of Scripture (1579), which he held until his death.

Fray Luis was a born poet whose verses extol beauty, goodness, and peace, but also expresses pain, sadness, and restlessness. His odes are elegant, short, and simple. Forty years after his death, his verses were published by Francisco de Quevedo in *Obras propias, y traducciones latinas, griegas, y italianas* (Original Works and Translations from Latin, Greek and Italian). His literary work reaches its highest point in *De los nombres de Cristo* (On the Names of Christ). Published in 1583 and again in 1585, this work offers an extensive introduction to biblical, patristic, philosophical, and theological thought. His sources range from Horace to the Psalms, from Plato to Augustine, from Cicero to the Neoplatonists, and from the Church Fathers to the Hebrew exegetes. He adopted the literary form of a Renaissance Christian dialogue. The interlocutors are three Augustinians from the Convento de Salamanca, Sabino, Marcelo, and Juliano, who converse on the fundamental names attributed to Christ in the scriptures. In another work popular with newlyweds of the day, *La perfecta casada* (The Perfect Spouse) (1583), he draws the picture of a sixteenth-century woman in light of the Book of Proverbs. It shows an awareness of feminine psychology and the influence of the Renaissance humanist Luis Vives's *De institutione feminae christianae* (1524). The *Comentario al libro de Job* (Commentary on the Book of Job), begun in prison, was never finished. Another Augustinian friar added a conclusion and published it in 1779. In this work, possibly his most autobiographical, Fray Luis occupies the place of Job and his dramatic experience of sin and abandonment.

Fray Luis also promoted reform of the Augustinian Order by his work *Forma de vivir* (Way of Living) (1589) and in his role as prior and provincial counselor. He advanced reform of the Carmelite Order and was the first publisher of the works of Teresa of Avila (1588). He died nine days after being elected provincial. His remains rest in an urn in the Chapel of the University of Salamanca.

Bibliography: Works. *Obras completas castellanas*, prologue and notes by P. FELIX GARCIA, rev. ed. by R. LAZCANO, 5th ed. in 2 v. (Madrid 1991); *The Names of Christ*, tr. M. DURAN and W. KLUBACK (New York 1974). *A Bilingual Edition of Fray Luis de León's La perfecta casada, The Role of Married Women in Sixteenth-Century Spain*, ed. and tr. J. A. JONES and J. SAN JOSE LERA (Lewiston-Queenston-Lampeter 1999). *Poesias completas. Obras propias en castellano y latin y traducciones e imitaciones latinas, griegas, biblico-hebreas y romances*, ed. C. CUEVAS (Madrid 1998); *Cantar de los Cantares de Salomon*, ed. J. M. BLECUA (Madrid 1994). **Literature.** G. BARRIENTOS, *Fray Luis de León y la Universidad de Salamanca* (San Lorenzo de El Escorial 1996). J. CASTILLO VEGAS, *El mundo juridico en Fray Luis de León* (Burgos 2000). V. GARCIA DE LA CONCHA and J. SAN JOSE LERA, eds., *Fray Luis de León: Historia, Humanismo y Letras* (Salamanca 1996). I. JERICO BERMEJO, *Fray Luis de León: La Teologia sobre el articulo y el dogma de fe (1568)* (Madrid 1997). R. LAZCANO, *Fray Luis de León, un hombre singular* (Madrid 1991), Eng. trans. in *Augustinian Heritage* 39 (1993): 3–77. R. LAZCANO, *Fray Luis de León. Bibliografia. Segunda edicion, actualizada y ampliada* (Madrid 1994). F. J. PEREA SILLER, *Fray Luis de León y la lengua perfecta. Linguistica, cabala y hermeneutica en ''De los nombres de Cristo''* (Cordoba 1998). J. PEREZ, *El humanismo de Fray Luis de León* (Madrid 1994).

[R. LAZCANO]

LEONARD OF PORT MAURICE, ST.

Renowned preacher, ascetic; b. Paul Jerome Casanova, in Porto Maurizio, Liguria, Italy, Dec. 20, 1676; d. Rome, Nov. 26, 1751. As a youth, Paul was sent to Rome and educated at the Jesuit Collegium Romanum. In 1697 he became a Franciscan of the *Riformella* instituted by Bl. Bonaventure of Barcelona. When assigned in 1709 to the retreat of Monte alle Croci in Florence, he initiated his 40-year apostolate of preaching popular missions, retreats, and Lenten courses and of promoting the devotion of the Way of the Cross. He also founded the retreat of Incontro near Florence. His collected works of sermons, correspondence, spiritual directives, and treatises were published in two editions (13 v. Rome 1853–54; 5 v. Venice 1868). His remains are preserved in S. Bonaventura al Palatino, Rome. He was beatified in 1796 and canonized in 1867. In 1923 he was declared patron saint of popular missionaries.

Feast: Nov. 26.

Bibliography: LEONARD OF PORT MAURICE, *Prediche e lettere inedite a cura del P. Benedetto Innocenti* (Quaracchi-Florence 1915). B. M. DONATIELLO and K. SOLTÉSZ, ''San Leonardo da Porto Maurizio. Lettere e documenti inediti,'' *Studi Francescani* 94, 3-4 (1997) 353–425. M. BIGARONI, ''Lettere inedite di San Leonardo da Porto Maurizio,'' *Archivum Franciscanum historicum* 64 (1971) 172–196. G. CANTINI, *S. Leonardo da P. M. e la sua predicazione* (Rome 1936).

[J. B. WUEST]

LEONARDI, JOHN, ST.

Founder of the CLERKS REGULAR OF THE MOTHER OF GOD; b. Diecimo, near Lucca, 1541?; d. Rome, Oct. 9,

1609. Leonardi, who came from a working-class family, was apprenticed to a druggist. After his ordination *c.* 1572, he immediately began to train lay leaders and catechists, and in 1579 he formed the CONFRATERNITY OF CHRISTIAN DOCTRINE. He published a compendium of Christian doctrine (Lucca 1574) that remained in use until the nineteenth century. In 1574 Leonardi founded his religious congregation, which received episcopal approval in 1583, papal approbation in 1595, and became an order proper, the Clerks Regular of the Mother of God, in 1621. Leonardi inaugurated four additional religious orders, reformed several others, was cofounder in 1603 of a seminary for foreign missions, and fulfilled several important missions. He himself died after nursing his brethren through an influenza epidemic. John Leonardi was beatified in 1861 and canonized in 1938. His relics are enshrined at Santa Maria in Campirelli, Rome.

Feast: Oct. 9.

Bibliography: *S. Giovanni Leonardi, Fondatore dei Chierici Regolari della Madre di Dio,* ed. Members of the Ordine della Madre di Dio (Rome 1938). F. FERRAIRONI, *Tre Secoli di storia dell'Ordine della Madre di Dio* (Rome 1939). A. BUTLER, *The Lives of the Saints,* 4 v., rev. ed. (New York 1956) 4:65.

[M. P. TRAUTH]

LEONIDES, ST.

Martyr, father of ORIGEN; b. place unknown, 150–160?; d. Alexandria, 202 (203?) during the persecution under Septimius Severus. It is unlikely that Leonides was a bishop; however, he was an excellent husband and father and a man of profound faith who took care to teach Holy Scripture to his seven sons. Origen, his eldest son, encouraged him to remain firm in his faith while in prison and not to be concerned about his family. His goods were confiscated after he was beheaded.

Feast: April 22.

Bibliography: EUSEBIUS, *History Ecclesiastical* 6:1–2 in *Patrologia Graeca,* 161 v. (Paris 1857–66) 20:524–525. JEROME, *De vir. ill.,* 54 in *Patrologia Graeca,* 161 v. (Paris 1857–66) 23:664. *Acta Sanctorum* April 3:10–11. J. L. BAUDOT and L. CHAUSSIN, *Vies des saints et des bienheureux selon l'ordre du calendrier avec l'historique des fêtes,* 12 v. (Paris 1935–56) 4:564–566.

[J. VAN PAASSEN]

LÉONIN

The first significant composer of the Notre Dame school; dates and places of birth and death unknown (in Latin, Leoninus). An avant-garde composer of the late 12th century, he was the first polyphonist to create music of such compelling style and beauty that it was sung both in his own country and elsewhere in Europe. His works were immediately performed in his local cathedral, Notre Dame of Paris (whose cornerstone had been laid in 1163), and he was commissioned to set the cycle of solo parts of the Alleluia and Gradual of the Mass and some responsorial parts of the Office for feasts and for the whole liturgical year. The resulting compilation was the famous *Magnus liber organi* . . . . He composed for two voices in techniques known as *organum* and *clausula* and was probably the first contrapuntist to work out his lines in a series of repeated rhythmic patterns called *modi.*

Bibliography: W. WAITE, *The Rhythm of Twelfth-Century Polyphony* (New Haven 1954), contains transcription of his works. H. TISCHLER, ''A Propos the Notation of the Parisian Organa,'' *Journal of the American Musicological Society* 14 (Boston 1961) 1–8. H. HUSMANN, ''The Origin and Destination of the Magnus liber organi,'' *Musical Quarterly* 49 (New York 1963) 311–330. H. COUSSEMAKER, *Scriptorium de musica medii aevi nova series* 4 v. (Paris 1864–76) 1:342. G. REESE, *Music in the Middle Ages* (New York 1940). *New Oxford History of Music,* ed. J. A. WESTRUP v.2 (New York 1957–). I. D. BENT, ''Léonin'' in *The New Grove Dictionary of Music and Musicians,* vol. 10, ed. S. SADIE, (New York 1980) 676–677. D. M. RANDEL, ed., *The Harvard Biographical Dictionary of Music* (Cambridge 1996) 498. N. SLONIMSKY, ed., *Baker's Biographical Dictionary of Musicians,* 8th ed. (New York 1992) 1040.

[E. THURSTON]

LEONINE COMMISSION

As a consequence of the encyclical *Aeterni Patris* (1879), a commission was formed in 1880 for preparing new editions of the writings of St. Thomas Aquinas and was named after Pope Leo XIII. A committee of three cardinals headed by the Dominican Thomas Zigliara inaugurated the enterprise. The pope had desired texts corrected from the best manuscripts that could be rapidly published for use in the Thomistic revival. However, the commission soon realized that a study of all extant manuscripts alone could produce definitive editions, so that in 1893 it became a project solely of the Dominican Order. The Leonine editions are highly regarded, their editorial method set new standards, and they have significantly contributed to the development of medieval textual criticism.

In the first period (to 1930) the *Summa theologiae* and the *Summa contra Gentiles* were completed, together with Aristotelian commentaries on logic and natural philosophy. When the commission had practically become defunct, the Order launched a revival in 1948, and besides the original group sections were founded in Spain, Canada, and the United States. In this second period sixteen editions were brought to completion, some winning the greatest acclaim. Now at the opening of a new century almost all the experienced researchers have ceased their labor, so that another beginning commences with new recruits. Although the membership has always chiefly been composed by Dominicans, as Leo XIII insisted, lay scholars have been associated with the project and have been editors of some texts. At present two non-Dominicans are full members. The American Section, located at the Dominican House of Studies, Washington, D.C., has as its projects the *Sententia libri Metaphysicae*; the *Scriptum*, the Third Book of the *Sentences* of Peter Lombard; and the *Quaestio disputata De spiritualibus creaturis* (now published). The *St. Thomas Aquinas Foundation* contributes financial assistance.

The state of the edition at present is as follows. Tomes that have been published:

t. 1 v.1 *Expositio libri Perhermenias*, 1882, new ed. 1989;

t. 1 v.2 *Expositio libri Posteriorum Analyticorum*, 1882, new ed. 1989;

t. 2 *In Aristotelis libros Physicorum*, 1884;

t. 3 *In Aristotelis libros De caelo . . . Meteorologicorum*, 1886;

t. 4–12 *Summa theologiae*, 1888–1906;

t. 13–15 *Summa contra Gentiles*, 1918–1930;

t. 16 *Indices in tomos 4–15*, 1948;

t. 22 *QD De veritate*, 1970–1976;

t. 23 *QD De malo*, 1982;

t. 24 v.1 *QD De anima*, 1996;

t. 24 v.2 *QD De spiritualibus creaturis*, 2000;

t. 25 *Quaestiones De quolibet*, 1996;

t. 26 *Expositio super Iob*, 1965;

t. 28 *Expositio super Isaiam*, 1974;

t. 40–43 *Opuscula I–IV*, 1967–1979;

t. 45 v.1 *Sententia Iibri De anima*, 1984;

t. 45 v.2 *Sententia libri De sensu*, 1985;

t. 47 *Sententia libri Ethicorum*, 1969;

t. 48 *Sententia libri Politicorum*, 1971;

t. 50 *Super libros Boetii De Trinitate, De hedomadibus*, 1992.

In various stages of preparation:

t. 17–20 *Scriptum Super IV Sententiarum*

t. 21 *QD De potentia*

t. 24, 3 *QD De virtutibus*, etc.

t. 30 *Super Matthaeum*

t. 31 *Super Ioannem*

t. 32–35 Super *Epistolas Pauli Apostoli*

t. 44 *Opuscula V*

t. 46 *Sententia libri Metaphysicae*

t. 49 *Super liberum De causis, Super librum Dionysii divinis nominibus.*

Tomes not begun:

t. 27 *Super Psalmos*

t. 29 *Super Ieremiam et Threnos*

t. 36–39 *Glossa continua super Evangelia (Catena aurea)*

Bibliography: G. M. GRECH, ''The Leonine Edition of the Works of St. Thomas Aquinas,'' in *From an Abundant Spring*, The Walter Farrell Memorial Volume of *The Thomist* (New York 1952) 218–258. L. J. BATAILLON, ''L'Édition léonine des oeuvres de saint Thomas et les études médiévales,'' *Atti dell'VIII Congresso Tomistico Internazionale* 1 (1981) 425–464. P. M. DE CONTENSON, ''Documents sur les origines et les premières années de la commission léonine,'' in *St. Thomas Aquinas, 1274–1974; Commemorative Studies* (Toronto 1974) 2:331–388.

[J. F. HINNEBUSCH]

LEONINE PRAYERS

The prayers ordered by Leo XIII to be said kneeling (and usually in the vernacular) after low Mass; they comprised the Hail Mary (three times), *SALVE REGINA*, (Hail Holy Queen) with versicle, response and oration, and a prayer to St. Michael the Archangel. To these the addition of an ejaculatory prayer to the Sacred Heart was recommended by St. Pius X in 1904. Although prayers of this kind had been in use in the Papal States since 1859, Leo XIII extended them to the whole church on Jan. 6, 1884. In 1886 a slight change was made in the oration and it was then that the St. Michael prayer was added. The prayers were first ordered because of loss of the Papal States, but after the 1928 LATERAN Treaty, Pius XI ordered them recited for Russia. After various curtailments, they were suppressed on Sept. 26, 1964.

Bibliography: R. E. BRENNAN, ''The Leonine Prayers,'' *American Ecclesiastical Review* 125 (Washington, DC 1951) 85–94.

[F. A. BRUNNER/EDS.]

LEONINE SACRAMENTARY

The popular, though incorrect name for the earliest surviving collection of Roman Mass formularies and ordination prayers that scholars have called the Sacramentary of Verona (*Sacramentarium Veronense*). The name ''Leonine Sacramentary'' is misleading, since it is neither a sacramentary, nor was it composed by Pope Leo I. More accurately, it is a compilation of individual *LIBELLI MISSARUM* in a single manuscript. It is a *unicum*, i.e., it exists in a single MS, Codex LXXXV (80) of the Chapter Library at Verona. E. A. Lowe dates it, on palaeographical grounds, as written in the first quarter of the 7th century. J. Bianchini published it in 1735, in v.4 of his *Anastasius Bibliothecarius,* under the title *Sacramentarium Leonianum*. In 1748 L. A. Muratori reedited it under the same title, but in 1754 J. A. Assemani, who gave it the title *Sacramentarium Veronense, vulgo Leonianum,* edited it again. In 1896 C. L. Feltoe published a handy, but inaccurate, edition, with the old title. The most recent edition is that of K. Mohlberg, who has rightly again called it *Sacramentarium Veronense* (Rome 1956).

Description. The contents of this book are exclusively Roman, at least in origin. They are not a well-ordered whole, but a random collection of Mass prayer formularies, grouped under the months of the year. The first part of the MS is missing, and as it is today, it begins in the middle of April. It contains more than 1,300 formularies, but for relatively few occasions. The feast of SS. Peter and Paul, for instance, has no fewer than 28 Masses, while that of St. Lawrence has 14. Although the material is Roman, the Sacramentary was not compiled for use at Rome.

Authorship. Various theories have been put forward to explain its origin. E. Bourque and A. Stuiber, in *Libelli Sacramentorum Romani* (Bonn 1950) conjectured that it is a collection of Roman *Libelli Missarum* preserved in the Lateran Archives. Many of these may well have dated from the pontificate of Damasus. More recently, Schmidt has put forward the hypothesis that one of the immediate sources of this Sacramentary is a somewhat elusive collection of prayers that he calls the *Sacramentarium Tabularii Papalis* and that he attributes to Pope Gelasius. Interesting as this theory is, some may well think that it supposes a too logical development. The more common view is that the *Veronense* is a collection of Roman *Libelli Missarum* put together by a provincial bishop anxious for Roman formularies. G. Lucchesi has suggested that its calendar is that of the See of Ravenna and that its compiler may have been Maximianus, archbishop from 546 to 557. But Lowe thinks that Verona is possibly its place of origin.

Bianchini gave his edition the title *Sacramentarium Leonianum* because he was convinced that Leo I was its author. However, C. Callewaert (d. 1943) has made a comparison of the literary parallels between the text of the Sacramentary and the writings of Leo. He has shown that some parallels do exist, but the difficulty is to interpret these. There are three possible explanations: (1) that in his writings Leo is making use of liturgical texts familiar to him from use, (2) that someone familiar with Leo's writings made use of phrases from them in composing the prayers, and (3) that in fact Leo wrote the prayers. Callewaert preferred the third explanation, but in this he may have been a little hasty, since F. L. Cross has shown that the first solution might be considered equally probable ["PreLeonine Elements in the Proper of the Roman Mass" *Journal of Theological Studies* 50 (1959) 191–197]. Nor is the second explanation impossible: in at least two places in the Gregorian Sacramentary someone has used the language of St. Gregory the Great in composing (after his lifetime) prayers for liturgical use. Callewaert observed that not all the formularies in the *Veronense* could be attributed to Leo, but he maintained that Leo was the creator of the style of liturgical prayer found in the *Veronense*. J. H. Crehan, in reviewing the excellent study of Leonine formularies by A. P. Lang, was inclined to the opinion that Leo did, in some instances, quote from earlier liturgical prayers in his writings. Further scrutiny of the text of the *Veronense* and the literary output of Popes Gelasius and Vigilius (537–555) has led such scholars as B. Capelle, C. Coebergh, and A. Chavasse to attribute much of this Sacramentary to these popes. How much of the actual material in the *Veronense* can be attributed to Leo is, therefore, still not known with certainty.

C. Vogel summarizes the scholarly consensus as follows: (1) the *Veronense* is not a sacramentary, properly, speaking, but a private collection of *libelli missarum* deriving, in the first instance, from the Lateran archives. Several of the *libelli* appeared to have been rearranged and adapted for use in the various Roman *tituli*. (2) Most of the *libelli* were composed in the 5th or 6th centuries. (3) The apparent disorganized state of the collection stems not so much from the compiler's carelessness or inexperience, as from his obsession with keeping intact the various groupings of masses as he had found them. (4) The compiler worked outside Rome. (5) The *libelli* reveals the oldest prayer formularies of the Roman Rite: *preces* (consecratory formulae), *oratio fidelium* (prayer of the faithful) and *orationes* (brief prayers after the chants, the readings and at the conclusion of morning and evening prayer). (6) The *Veronense* was compiled at a time when the desire to collect all the documents of the popes was manifesting itself in the Latin Church (Vogel, *Medieval Liturgy*, 43).

Bibliography: Critical Edition. *Sacramentarium Veronense* (Cod. Bibl. Capit. Veron; LXXXV: formerly LXXX) ed. L.C. MOHLBERG, L. EIZENHÖFER, P. SIFFRIN, Rerum Ecclesiasticarum Documenta, Series Maior, Fontes 1 (Rome 1956, 1966). **Commentaries.** P. BRUYLANTS, *Concordance Verbale du Sacramentaire Léonien* (Louvain 1948). D. M. HOPE, *The Leonine Sacramentary: A Reassessment of Its Nature and Purpose* (Oxford 1971). A discussion of the problems concerning St. Leo the Great and the *Leonianum* together with the relevant bibliog. is in E. DEKKERS, "Autour de l'oeuvre liturgique de s. Léon le Grand," *Sacris erudiri* 10 (1958) 363–398. G. LUCCHESI, *Nouve note agiografiche Ravennati: Santi e riti del Sacramentario Leoniano a Ravenna* (Faenza 1943). A. P. LANG, *Leo der Grosse und die Texte des Altgelasianums* (Steyl 1957); "Leo der Grosse und die liturgischen Texte des Oktavtages von Epiphanie," *Sacris erudiri* 11 (1960) 12–135; "Anklänge an Orationen der Ostervigil in Sermonen Leos des Grossen," *ibid.* 13 (1962) 281–325. For overview and further bibliographies, see: C. VOGEL, *Medieval Liturgy: An Introduction to Sources* (Washington, DC 1986); and E. PALAZZO, *A History of Liturgical Books:*

From the Beginning to the Thirteenth Century (Collegeville, Minn. 1998).

[H. ASHWORTH/EDS.]

LEONIUS, BL.

Benedictine abbot and reformer in the Low Countries, noted for works of charity; d. Oct. 26, 1163. Leonius, descended from an old Flemish family, was educated at Anchin by the Benedictines, whom he joined at the age of 22. Influenced by his teacher Alvisius, Leonius adopted the ideals of the CLUNIAC REFORM. He was prior at Hesdin, and in 1131 he was made abbot of Lobbes, where he served until 1137, when he became abbot of SAINT-BERTIN. There he established a school of higher religious studies. Leonius took part in the Second CRUSADE and was a friend of its preacher, BERNARD OF CLAIRVAUX.

Feast: Jan. 26, and Feb. 6 or 7.

Bibliography: *Acta Sanctorum* Oct. 11:792–794. *Monumenta Germaniae Historica: Scriptores* 13:661–666; 21:323–331. *Patrologia Latina*, ed. J. P. MIGNE (Paris 1878–90) 182:585–590 (letters from St. Bernard to Leonius). W. LAMPEN, *Lexikon für Theologie und Kirche*, 10 v. (2d, new ed. Freiburg 1957–65) 6:967. A. M. ZIMMERMANN, *Kalendarium Benedictinum: Die Heiligen und Seligen des Benediktinerorderns und seiner Zweige* 1:130, 132–133. M. A. BORELLI, A. MERCATI and A. PELZER, *Dizionario ecclesiastico* 2:647.

[R. BALCH]

LEONTIUS OF BYZANTIUM

Sixth-century Byzantine monk and theologian; b. probably in Constantinople, *c.* 500; d. Constantinople, 543. Leontius entered (*c.* 520) the monastery called the New Laura in Palestine with his spiritual master, Nonnus, a disciple of the Origenist monk EVAGRIUS PONTICUS (d. 399). After coming to Constantinople in 531, Leontius remained there until at least 536, defending the Council of CHALCEDON against the MONOPHYSITES. In 532 he was an observer at a colloquy between Orthodox and Monophysites (*see* HYPATIUS OF EPHESUS) and in 536 was present at the council in Constantinople that banished the Monophysites. Leontius became the nucleus of an Origenistic Chalcedonian party, led after 537 by his friend THEODORE ASCIDAS. In 537 Leontius was in Palestine, where he defended Origenism against the attacks of the Orthodox, but he returned to Constantinople about 540, when the controversy was referred to the emperor. The Origenistic Chalcedonians lost, and in 543 JUSTINIAN I condemned ORIGENISM. However, just before his death (543) Leontius's polemic against THEODORE OF MOPSUESTIA seems to have launched the campaign that led to the condemnation of the THREE CHAPTERS at the Council of CONSTANTINOPLE I (553). Three works of Leontius are extant: *Three Books against the Nestorians and Eutychians; A Resolution of the Arguments Advanced by Severus* [of Antioch]; and *Thirty Chapters against Severus.* He is perhaps the author of *Against the Frauds of the Apollinarians.*

The Christology of Leontius translated the heretical Christology of Evagrius Ponticus into the terms of the formula of the Council of Chalcedon: Jesus Christ, one person (hypostasis) in two natures. For Leontius as for Evagrius Ponticus, Jesus Christ is the one spirit or intellect (*nous*) of the intellectual and immaterial world who did not fall and so remains united to the Word of God in the vision of God. In the Incarnation this *nous,* Jesus Christ, joins himself to a body and so in one person unites two natures, the Word of God and man. This Christology had no future; but Leontius's concept of an enhypostasized being (ἐνυπόστατον), that is, a being that finds its hypostasis or existence in its union with a being of a different nature, was developed later by MAXIMUS THE CONFESSOR and JOHN DAMASCENE.

Bibliography: *Patrologia Graeca* 86:1267–1396, 1901–76. F. LOOFS, *Leontius von Byzanz* in *Texte und Untersuchungen zur Geschichte der altchristlichen Literatur* (Berlin 1882–) 3.1–2; 1887. F. DIEKAMP, *Die origenistischen Streitigkeiten im 6. Jahrhundert* (Münster 1899). V. GRUMEL, *Dictionnaire de théologie catholique,* 15 v. (Paris 1903–50) 9.1:400–426. M. RICHARD, *Revue des sciences philosophiques et théologiques* 27 (1938): 27–52; *Revue d'histoire ecclésiastique* 35 (1939): 695–723; *Mélanges de science religieuse* 1 (1944): 35–88; *Revue des études byzantines* 5 (1947): 31–66. E. SCHWARTZ, ed., *Kyrillos von Skythopolis* in *Texte und Untersuchungen zur Geschichte der altchristlichen Literatur,* (Berlin 1882–) 49.2; 1939. B. ALTANER, *Theologische Quartalschrift* 127 (1947): 147–165. D. B. EVANS, *Leontius of Byzantium* (Doctoral diss. unpub. Harvard Divinity School 1966).

[D. B. EVANS]

LEONTIUS OF FRÉJUS, ST.

Bishop, patron of Fréjus (France); b. probably Nîmes, late fourth century; d. Fréjus, *c.* 432. He was consecrated bishop of Fréjus before 419 and remained there until his death. The local tradition that holds that he went as an apostle into Germany (432–442) is historically doubtful. He supported St. HONORATUS OF ARLES in the foundation of the monastery at LÉRINS. John CASSIAN dedicated the first ten *Collationes* to him. He is among several bishops of Gaul who received a joint letter from BONIFACE I in 419 (P. Jaffé, *Regesta pontificum romanorum ab condita ecclesia ad annum post Christum natum 1198*; 349) and from CELESTINE II in 431 (Jaffé 381).

Feast: Dec. 1 (Fréjus); Dec. 5 (Nîmes).

Bibliography: S. LE NAIN DE TILLEMONT, *Mémoires pour servir à l'histoire ecclésiastique des six premiers siècles,* 16 v. (Paris 1693–1712) 12:468–470, 476–477, 676–679. *Gallia Christiana* v. 1–13 (Paris 1715–85) v. 14–16 (Paris 1856–65) 1:420–421. J. B. DISDIER, *Recherches historiques sur saint Léonce* (Draguignan 1864). L. DUCHESNE, *Fastes épiscopaux de l'ancienne Gaule,* 3 v. (Paris 1886–92; 2d ed. Paris 1907–58) 1:285. J. L. BAUDOT and L. CHAUSSIN, *Vies des saints et des bienheureux selon l'ordre du calendrier avec l'historique des fêtes,* 12 v. (Paris 1935–56) 12:25–27.

[G. E. CONWAY]

LEONTIUS OF JERUSALEM

Sixth-century monk and theologian. Leontius belonged to the party of Neochalcedonians, or Cyrillian Chalcedonians. He is known only from two works, composed probably during the reign of JUSTINIAN I, before the outbreak of the controversy over the THREE CHAPTERS (*c.* 544), *Contra Monophysitas,* and *Adversus Nestorianos.* Leontius insisted that the Christological formula of the Council of CHALCEDON (451), stating that Jesus Christ is one person (hypostasis) in two natures, could be interpreted only by means of the Christology of CYRIL OF ALEXANDRIA. Therefore he identified the one hypostasis of Jesus Christ with one hypostasis of the Trinity, that is, with the Word of God, who was incarnate in Jesus Christ. His *Contra Monophysitas* defends this position against the Monophysites and against SEVERUS OF ANTIOCH, whereas the longer *Adversus Nestorianos* defends it against his orthodox Chalcedonian critics: the strict Dyophysites of the tradition of the school of Antioch, as well as, it seems, the Origenistic Chalcedonians (*see* LEONTIUS OF BYZANTIUM).

Because Justinian I was a Cyrillian Chalcedonian, it has been suggested that Leontius was the emperor's theological adviser and that he, and not Leontius of Byzantium, was the Leontius present at the colloquy of 532 between the orthodox and the Monophysites and at the council of 536. Although as a Cyrillian Chalcedonian Leontius stood in the mainstream of the development of Eastern orthodox Christology, his work seems to have been little used in later times.

Bibliography: *Patrologia Graeca* 86:1395–1902. M. RICHARD, *Mélanges de science religieuse* (1944) 35–88. C. MOELLER, in A. GRILLMEIER and H. BACHT, *Das Konzil von Chalkedon: Geschichte und Gegenwart,* 3 v. (Würzburg 1951–54) 1:686–687, 701–704. *Ephemerides theologicae Lovanienses* 27 (1951): 467–482.

[D. B. EVANS]

LEOPOLD III OF AUSTRIA, ST.

Margrave of Austria; b. Gars, Austria, *c.* 1075; d. Nov. 15, 1136. Leopold was educated by St. ALTMAN OF PASSAU. Because of his loyalty during the INVESTITURE STRUGGLE, Pope INNOCENT II called him "Son of St. Peter." Leopold later changed his allegiance to Emperor HENRY V and married Henry's daughter Agnes. Two of his six sons were the historian OTTO OF FREISING and Archbishop Conrad II of Salzburg. In 1108 Leopold refounded the monastery of the canon regulars in KLOSTERNEUBURG, and in 1133 (not 1135), the Cistercian abbey HEILIGENKREUZ. He also founded the Benedictine monastery of Kleinmariazell and placed the monasteries of MELK and Klosterneuburg directly under papal jurisdiction. He laid the foundations of Austria's greatness and also of its ecclesiastical provincialism. In 1125 he gave up his claim to the German throne. Buried in the crypt of Klosterneuburg, he was canonized in 1485 and declared the national patron of Austria in 1663; his feast is a national holiday. He is pictured in a suit of armor with a flag and the model of a church (miniatures published by V. O. Ludwig, Klosterneuburg, Vienna 1951).

Feast: Nov. 15.

Bibliography: Sources. *Chronicon pii marchionis,* in *Monumenta Germaniae Historica: Scriptores* (Berlin 1826–) 9:609–613. H. FICHTENAU and E. ZÖLLNER, eds., *Urkundenbuch zur Geschichte der Babenberger in Österreich,* v. 1 (Vienna 1950) 2–14. **Literature.** H. PFEIFFER and B. CERNIK, *Catalogus codicum manuscriptorum qui in bibliotheca canonicorum regularium s. Augustini Claustroneoburgi asservantur* (Klosterneuburg 1925). V. O. LUDWIG, *Der hl. Leopold* (Innsbruck 1936). *Sankt Leopold: Festschrift des Augustiner Chorherrenstiftes Klosterneuburg,* ed. S. WINTERMAYR (Klosterneuburg 1936). G. WACHER, *Leopold der Heilige und Klosterneuburg vom 12–20 Jahrhunderts.* (Diss. Vienna 1949). H. HANTSCH, ed., *Gestalter der Geschichte Österreichs* (Innsbruck 1962). *Leopold III. und die Babenbergerzeit,* ed. H. LAMPALZER (Vienna 1985). F. RÖHRIG, *Leopold III. der Heilige, Markgraf von Österreich* (Vienna 1985). M. KASTL, *Das Schriftwort in Leopoldspredigten des 17. und 18. Jahrhunderts* (Vienna 1988). J. WODKA, *Kirche in Österreich* (Vienna 1959) 79–85, 419.

[V. H. REDLICH]

LEOPOLD OF GAICHE, BL.

Franciscan; b. Gaiche, Italy, 1732; d. Monteluco, April 2, 1815. He became a Franciscan in 1751, was ordained in 1757, and taught philosophy and theology. In 1768 he began 47 years of missionary activity in Umbria and the Papal States, in the manner of St. LEONARD OF PORT MAURICE. He was elected provincial (1781–84) but continued to preach, and he built in Monteluco a retreat for missionaries, of which he became guardian. When Napoleon seized the Papal States and suppressed religious houses, Leopold withdrew to a hut. He was imprisoned briefly for his refusal to take an oath to the new regime. After Napoleon's fall in 1814, Leopold returned to Monteluco and spent his last years in prayer. He wrote a *Diario delle S. Missioni*. He was beatified by Leo XIII, on March 3, 1893.

Feast: April 2.

Bibliography: M. A. HABIG, *Franciscan Book of Saints* (Chicago 1959). G. FUSSENEGGER, *Lexikon für Theologie und Kirche*, ed. J. HOFER and K. RAHNER, 10 v. (2d, new ed. Freiburg 1957–65) 6:970.

[R. BARTMAN]

LEOPOLDINEN STIFTUNG (LEOPOLDINE SOCIETY)

An Austrian mission society organized in 1828 in Vienna through the efforts of Frederick Résé, a German missionary who joined the U.S. Diocese of Cincinnati in 1824. While in Europe in 1828 to solicit funds for his diocese, Résé obtained an audience with Emperor Francis I, who granted permission for the new mission society; the following year the society received official approbation from Pope Leo XII. Patterned after the French Society for the PROPAGATION OF THE FAITH, established in Lyons in 1822, the Austrian organization was called Leopoldinen Stiftung to honor St. Leopold, an Austrian medieval margrave, and to memorialize the emperor's daughter Leopoldina, who died as empress of Brazil in 1826.

Members of the organization were required to pray for the missions and contribute a weekly alms to be used exclusively for America. Funds thus collected were sent to headquarters in Vienna, where they were then distributed to needy bishops and religious communities in the U.S. Contributions to America had totaled more than $436,000 by 1861, after which the activity of the society declined sharply. It ceased to exist in 1921, and by then the total contributed was $709,114. The generous financial assistance was augmented by valuable gifts of church goods and, more important, numerous Austrian recruits for the American missions, including the future Bishop (later Blessed) John NEUMANN of Philadelphia; the future Bishop Frederic BARAGA of Marquette; Father Caspar Rehrl, founder of the Sisters of St. Agnes; Father Joseph SALZMANN, founder of St. Francis Seminary in Milwaukee; Father Francis X. PIERZ of Minnesota; Father John Stephen RAFFEINER of New York; and many others. Coinciding with the period of expansion of church and nation into the Ohio and Mississippi valleys, this foreign mission aid proved more effective in strengthening Catholicism than the bare facts indicate, and served to arouse nativist opposition.

From the outset the society published missionary data; its annual reports, *Berichte der Leopoldinen Stiftung im Kaiserthume Oesterreichs*, presenting financial statements and letters from missionaries, which featured especially the work among the native and immigrant groups of the U.S., still constitute an important source of American Church history. Of historical value also is Canon Josep Salzbacher's *Meine Reise nach Nord-Amerika im Jahre 1842*, published after he, as editor of the *Berichte*, visited the U.S. to investigate charges of unfairness that had been reaching Europe regarding the distribution of aid.

Bibliography: B. J. BLIED, *Austrian Aid to American Catholics, 1830–1860* (Milwaukee 1944). T. ROEMER, *Ten Decades of Alms* (St. Louis 1942).

[B. J. BLIED]

LEPANTO, BATTLE OF

The battle of Lepanto was an engagement fought between the Christian and Turkish fleets on Oct. 7, 1571. It was the last great naval battle under oars. The capture of Constantinople by Mohammed II (1430–81) in 1453 ended the Eastern Roman Empire and opened the Balkans and Hungary to further conquest. It also established Turkey as the dominant maritime power in the Mediterranean. Turkish galleys raided the coasts of the Italian peninsula; Syria, Egypt, Tripoli, and Tunisia acknowledged the Sultan as overlord; Rhodes, after a valiant defense by the Knights of St. John, was captured in 1522.

Occasion for War. To protect her valuable trade with Eastern ports, Venice had tried to maintain a strategic neutrality in the continual Christian-Turkish warfare, but when Sultan Selim II (1566–74) demanded the surrender of Cyprus (1570), the Venetian senate appealed to Pope Pius V. The pope succeeded in organizing resistance to the Muslims and assembled a fleet to meet at Messina in 1571 under the command of Don Juan of Austria, half-brother of Philip II of Spain. Spain would pay one-half, Venice one-third, and the pope one-sixth of the total expense of the operation. Of a total of 206 galleys, Venice furnished 108, Naples 29, Genoa 14, Spain 13, the Pope 12, and Malta 3. This was a period of transition in naval weaponry. The larger vessels had guns in their bows, and the fighting men were archers or musketeers, but were provided with swords for the hand-to-hand fighting that usually ended a battle. In the Christian fleet there were also six large galleasses, each mounting 20 guns and a large crew of musketeers. In the plan of Don Juan two of these ships were to move ahead of his three squadrons. In all, there were about 80,000 men under his command. The Turks held a distinct superiority with a

Allegorical representation of the ''Battle of Lepanto,'' fresco by Giorgio Vasari and Daniele da Volterra in the Sala Regia of the Palazzo Vaticano, Rome.

fleet of 220 to 230 galleys, 50 to 60 galeots (smaller, oared vessels), and 120,000 soldiers and rowers; these last were Christians captured at sea or in shore raids. The rowers in the Christian fleet were either captive Muslims, convicted criminals promised freedom after victory, or hired for the campaign. Pius V sent a legate and chaplains to Messina, together with a blue banner for the flagship, showing Christ crucified. After the blessing of the legate, the ships sailed from Messina harbor.

Encounter. Don Juan passed down the Greek coast on the morning of Oct. 7, 1571, and spied the Turks in the Gulf of Lepanto, 20 miles east of the southern tip of Ithaca. The Venetian admiral, Agostino Barbarigo, took position on the northern end of his squadron while the 53 galleys formed a line abreast, heading east. Don Juan visited each of the 62 galleys in his center squadron early in the morning, holding a crucifix aloft. His flagship, the "Reale," with 60 oars, 300 rowers, and 400 fighting men, was placed in the center of the line. The papal admiral, Marco Antonio Colonna, was on Don Juan's right, the Venetian admiral, Sebastian Veniero, the most experienced seaman of the fleet, on his left. Two of the 38 galleys of the reserve squadron under the command of the Spanish Marquis de Santa Cruz were directly astern. The wind, favorable to the Turks at dawn, fell before the battle. The two northern Turkish squadrons advanced abreast, suffering slight damage from the four galleasses. Mohammed Scirocco, Viceroy of Alexandria, attacked the galley of Barbarigo. Other galleys passed through shallow water and attacked the vessel on her side and stern. Opening the visor of his helmet, Barbarigo was struck in the eye by an arrow that pierced his brain. His nephew, Marino Contarini, boarded the ship with reinforcements, drove off the Turks, and was mortally wounded. The Venetian and Spanish fighting men reorganized, swept the deck of the Egyptian flagship with musketry fire, and charged over her bow with pikes and swords, killing Scirocco and capturing the ship.

The Turkish commander-in-chief, Admiral Ali Pasha, led his center squadron with 95 galleys. His flagship, the "Sultana," flying a white flag embroidered with verses from the Qu'ran, carried 100 archers and 300 musketeers. Steering for the "Reale," flagship of Don Juan, it fired three cannon at point-blank range, and striking almost bow on, cut into the Spanish galley. The "Sultana" rode higher in the water, and Turks poured down onto the deck of the "Reale," which would have been captured had not Admiral Colonna maneuvered to ram the "Sultana," and Santa Cruz joined with reinforcements. The "Sultana" was captured and Ali Pasha slain in battle. Meanwhile Giovanni Andrea Doria made an error in handling his 53 galleys of the right squadron. Instead of heading eastward, in line with the other squadrons, Doria

turned to the south to prevent envelopment of his seaward flank. Uluch Ali, with 60 galleys and 30 smaller craft, countered and drew Doria farther away from the center squadron. The nearest Christian galleys were overwhelmed, and the flagship of the Knights of St. John was captured. The prompt action of Santa Cruz and Don Juan saved the squadron, and Uluch Ali abandoned his captives and fled with 15 galleys. About 35 other Turkish galleys reached Lepanto, taking with them one captured galley.

Results of the Battle. Aside from those burned, sunk, or wrecked, 117 Muslim galleys, six galeots, 117 large cannon, and 250 smaller ones were divided among the victors. Twelve thousand Christians were released from slavery; nearly 9,000 Christians were killed or died of wounds. Twice this number, including Don Juan, Colonna, Santa Cruz, and Veniero recovered from their wounds. The heroic dead included Venetian Admiral Barbarigo and 16 galley captains, a papal galley captain, 60 Knights of St. John, and many Spanish noblemen. The Turks lost 30,000. The pursuit of Uluch Ali was begun, but the difficulties of preparing the galleys with less than three hours of daylight remaining were too great. The victory though impressive was not decisive, because it was not effectively followed up. Venetian power in the Mediterranean continued to wane in favor of the Turks, when in 1573 Venice sued for peace and abandoned Cyprus. Nevertheless, the Battle of Lepanto was celebrated throughout Europe as a decisive Christian victory and became the subject for artistic and literary invention.

Bibliography: J. P. E. JURIEN DE LA GRAVIÈRE, *La Guerre de Chypre et la bataille de Lépante,* 2 v. (Paris 1888). L. COLOMA, *The Story of Don John of Austria,* tr. A. M. MORETON (New York 1912). W. L. RODGERS, *Naval Warfare Under Oars* (Annapolis 1939). R. C. ANDERSON, *Naval Wars in the Levant* (Princeton 1952). A. MACIA SERRANO, *Lepanto* (Madrid 1971). J. BEECHING, *The Galleys at Lepanto* (New York 1982).

[J. B. HEFFERNAN]

LÉPICIER, ALEXIS

Cardinal, theologian; b. Vaucouleurs, France, Feb. 28, 1863; d. Rome, May 20, 1936. At the age of 15 Lépicier left France and joined the Servite Order in London. After completing his studies at various priories of the Order in England and at the Seminary of Saint-Sulpice, Paris, he was ordained in London, in September of 1885. Two months later he was called to Rome by his superior general to study at the Propaganda Fide, where he earned doctorates in theology and philosophy. In 1890 he returned to England as master of novices.

In 1892 at the age of 29 he was appointed by Leo XIII to the chair of dogmatic theology left vacant by his former professor, Francesco Satolli, who had been appointed first apostolic delegate to the United States. Lépicier held this post for 21 years, until he was elected superior general of the Servites in 1913. The prodigious theological work of these years culminated in his *Institutiones theologicae dogmaticae ad textum S. Thomae Concinnatae* (25 v.). His tract *De Beata Virgine Maria Matre Dei* (5 eds.) was one of the earliest scholastic treatments of Marian theology. His writings influenced the neoscholastic revival. In addition to a busy teaching career, Lépicier filled positions in five Roman Congregations and was assigned to various commissions. Moreover, he undertook long journeys in the interest of the Curia. In 1912 he was apostolic visitor in Scotland and upon his return to Rome he was made delegate to that country without the obligation of residence.

In May of 1924 he was consecrated archbishop of Tarsus and sent as apostolic visitor to India, where he remained for nearly two years. In 1927 he traveled to Abyssinia and Eritrea as visitor. In December of 1927 Pius XI made him a cardinal, and the following year he became prefect of the Congregation of Religious.

Bibliography: A. M. LÉPICIER, *Le Cardinal Lépicier, des servites de Marie,* 2 v. (n.p. 1946).

[J. M. RYSKA]

LEPIDI, ALBERTO

Dominican philosopher and theologian; b. Popoli (Abruzzi), 1838; d. Rome, 1922. He taught theology in the spirit of St. Thomas Aquinas at Flavigny (1870), Louvain (1874), and Rome (1885). His lectures were a curious mixture of Aristotelian Thomism and Greco-Christian mysticism. His critical examination of ONTOLOGISM as taught by N. MALEBRANCHE and V. GIOBERTI, *Examen philosophicotheologicum de ontologismo* (Louvain 1874), clearly asserts the teaching of St. Thomas on the origin of ideas, the nature of knowledge, and the natural knowledge of God. His *Elementa philosophiae Christianae* (3 v. Paris and Louvain 1875–79) follows Aquinas for the most part, but deviates somewhat on the real distinction between essence and existence in creatures and on the use of Anselm's ontological argument to demonstrate the existence of God. He wrote also a critical study of I. Kant's doctrine of pure reason: *La critica della ragion pura secondo Kant* (Rome 1894). In 1897 he resigned the chair of theology at the College of St. Thomas in Rome to become master of the sacred palace. In 1905 he wrote a short dogmatic explanation of the cult of the Eucharistic Heart of Jesus, which was edited by E. HUGON (Paris 1926). Lepidi is remembered as a prominent contributor to the neoscholastic movement for

his work in reorganizing the course of theological studies for the Dominicans, especially in the French province.

Bibliography: G. SESTILI, *Il p. Alberto Lepidi e la su filosofia* (Turin 1930). *Enciclopedia filosofica* (Venice-Rome 1957) 2:1886. H. HURTER, *Nomenclator literarius theologiae catholicae* (Innsbruck 1903–13) 5.1:1260.

[F. J. ROENSCH]

LE PLAT, JODOCUS

Canonist; b. Mechelen, Nov. 18, 1732; d. Koblenz, Aug. 6, 1810. He became professor of canon law at Louvain in 1775. Prior to this time he had already achieved notoriety in opposing the doctrine of the Pauline Privilege, which had the support of Benedict XIV and many illustrious theologians. He became a supporter of JOSEPHINISM, which he introduced into Belgium. This incited such displeasure that he was forced in 1787 to flee to Holland, where he was received by the Jansenists with whom he collaborated in the *Nouvelles Ecclesiastiques.* He became rector of the Canon Law School in Koblenz in 1806. He secured the publication of the *Commentaire* of Van Espen on the *Decretum,* endeavoring to show the apocryphal canons. His other works include *Institutionum iurisprudentiae ecclesiasticae* (1780); *Canones et Decreta S. S. oecumenici et generalis concilii Tridentini* (Antwerp 1779); *Dissertatio de sponsalibus et impedimentis matrimoniorum* (1783); *Monumentum concilii Tridentini* (Louvain 1781–87).

Bibliography: R. NAZ, *Dictionnaire de droit canonique,* 7 v. (Paris 1935–65) 6:401–402.

[H. A. LARROQUE]

LEPROSY (IN THE BIBLE)

Leprosy, also known as Hansen's disease, is the only sickness whose traditional complex of social, legal, religious, and hagiographical aspects have made its history inseparable from that of the Bible and the Church. It is also unique in that the treatment, cure, and rehabilitation of millions of victims are seriously impeded today by widespread errors concerning it, which are historically associated with the Bible and the Church.

Nature of True Leprosy. Hansen's disease is a chronic infectious sickness caused by a rod-shaped acid-fast bacillus, *Mycobacterium leprae,* discovered by G. A. Hansen in Bergen, Norway, in 1873. It chiefly affects the skin, mucous membranes of the upper respiratory tract, eyes, and certain peripheral nerves. The disease is neither congenital nor hereditary. Its exact mode of transmis-

Elisha Cures Naaman of Leprosy. (©Historical Picture Archive/CORBIS)

sion—probably direct contact—remains unknown. Only a small percentage of persons having prolonged contacts with patients contract the disease. A natural immunity, therefore, appears to prevail in most people, dependent on unexplored racial or genetic factors. Hansen's disease is considered less infectious than tuberculosis. Its average incubation period is about three years, but it may be shorter or longer. Apart from indeterminate and border-line cases, the two main types, presumably based on high or low resistance, are: (1) tuberculoid, having few bacilli, but with nerve involvement causing anesthesia, paralysis of some muscles, and disintegration of toe and finger bones; these so-called closed cases are considered noninfectious except during reaction, and often result in spontaneous recovery (''burnt-out cases''); and (2) lepromatous, characterized by lesions and swellings containing numerous bacilli, expecially on the face (''leonine face'') and in the upper respiratory tract and vocal cords, with frequent eye-involvement; these so-called

open cases are infectious. Often decades after infection, death usually results, not from the disease itself, but from secondary infections and other causes. Until the 20th century, leprosy was thought to be highly contagious and generally incurable.

So-called Leprosy in the Bible. Before discussing the Biblical disease that has been traditionally called leprosy, it is good to consider the evidence concerning the existence of genuine leprosy in the ancient world during Biblical times.

Modern medical historians, notably G. Sticker, have disproved often repeated errors concerning leprosy in pre-Christian times that have resulted from mistranslations of generic ancient terms unaccompanied by clinical descriptions. The oldest recognizable reference to Hansen's disease occurs in the Indian medical treatise *Sushruta Samhita,* compiled in its present recension about 600 B.C., but including more ancient traditional knowledge. The term *kushta* in the still older Vedas and Laws of Manu designates skin diseases in general. In Chinese medical literature, leprosy is not recognized until 500 to 300 B.C. and clinically described only in A.D. 200 to 300 by Hua T'o.

Of direct relevance to the problem of so-called leprosy in the Bible is the still confused history of Hansen's disease in ancient Egypt. References in the Ebers medical papyrus (*c.* 1550 B.C.) to sicknesses named *aat* and *uchedu* have been mistranslated as leprosy. B. Ebbell's identification of "Chon's swelling" as leprosy has been rejected by leprologists J. Lowe and Dharmendra; G. Grapow, a leading expert on ancient Egyptian medicine, has not thoroughly analyzed the problem. A. Bloom has shown that the terms used by Flavius JOSEPHUS (*Contra Apionem,* 1.26) and other writers to designate a disease that allegedly afflicted the people of Israel in Egypt under Moses do not refer to leprosy. Bloom also reports no evidence of leprosy in ancient Egyptian statuary and art that clearly depict other sicknesses. As to skeletons and mummies, he records only one case indicating leprosy, but it came from a Christian cemetery of the Christian era. In 1962 V. Møller-Christensen examined 18,000 human remains from ancient Egypt, Palestine, and Europe, but found no trace of Hansen's disease older than *c.* A.D. 500. Lucretius' reference to *elephas morbus* (*De rerum natura,* 6.1112)—if it means genuine leprosy, a disputed point—would prove only that it existed there in the first century B.C., which no one denies.

Evidence of Hansen's disease in the Middle East before the armies of Alexander the Great probably imported it from India is limited to a few references to unidentified skin diseases in Herodotus and in Persian and Babylonian texts. In Palestine, the only hint is a "leonine face" of the Egyptian god Bes on a Canaanite jar of *c.* 1411 to 1314 B.C. found at Beth-San (Bethshan) in 1925. It would therefore seem probable that cases of Hansen's disease were sporadic rather than endemic in the Near East during the millennium between Moses and Alexander the Great, i.e., in Old Testament times.

In the Old Testament. Concordances list up to 83 references in both the Old Testament and the New Testament to various forms of the Hebrew root *ṣr'* and the Greek words λέπρα and λεπρός that are inaccurately translated as leprosy, leper, or leprous in modern Bibles. The root of the Hebrew noun *ṣāra'at* that is used in the Old Testament (often accompanied by *nega',* "blow," "plague") probably means etymologically affliction, prostration, or defilement; hence it designates, according to the context, a condition of ritual or cultic uncleanliness manifested in certain skin disorders and blemishes or in incrustations of fungi or molds in linen, leather, or stones.

Explicit rules for the priests on how to diagnose *ṣāra'at* in human beings are given in Lv 13.1–46; however, modern translations of clinical terms in that chapter are confusingly disparate. The affliction called *ṣāra'at* was diagnosed from the following symptoms: subcutaneous lesions with hairs turning white (Lv 13.3), spreading lesions (Lv 13.7–8), lesions with ulceration (Lv 13.11), secondary infections with ulceration (Lv 13.15), deep-seated lesions spreading from a healed ulcer (Lv 13.22) or from the healed scar of a burn (Lv 13.25, 27), spreading lesions on scalp or chin or forehead (Lv 13.30, 36, 43). Superficial local skin infections that improved or failed to spread after a quarantine of a week or two were not considered *ṣāra'at* (Lv 13.6, 23, 28, 34, 37, 39). Moreover, a man in whose skin *ṣāra'at* developed into a generalized eruption covering the entire body that later healed by desquamation (scaling) was declared clean (Lv 13.12–13,16–17).

Once a man was diagnosed as having *ṣāra'at,* he had to keep his clothes rent and his head bare, muffling his beard and calling out, "unclean" (Lv 13.45); he was obliged also to dwell outside the camp (Lv 13.45; Nm 5.2; 12.15) or in a separate house (2 Chr 26.21) "as long as the sore is on him" (Lv 13.46). When a priest found that the *ṣāra'at* had healed, the man underwent an expiatory rite of purification (Lv 14.1–32). Another rite was prescribed for the purification of houses in which *ṣāra'at* of walls had not spread after replastering (Lv 14.49–53).

Nine other passages shed helpful light on the Old Testament concept of *ṣāra'at*: Ex 4.6–7 (Moses' hand); Lv 22.4 (disqualification for the priesthood); Nm 5.2 (isolation); Nm 12.9–14 (Miriam); 2 Sm 3.29 (Joab); 2 Kgs 5.1–14, 27 (Naaman and Gehazi); 2 Kgs 7.3–11 (four outcasts of Samaria); 2 Chr 26.17–23; See Also 2 Kgs 15.5 (King Azariah) and Dt 24.8–9, which merely stresses Leviticus ch. 13–14 and Nm 12.10. These texts demonstrate that *ṣāra'at* in human beings referred to skin disorders that might be disfiguring and serious (Nm 12.12), and chronic or even lifelong (2 Kgs 7.3;2 Chr 26.21), but they might also be cured or cleansed (Lv 13.12; Lv 14.3; 2 Kgs 5.14). In several instances they are described as a sign (Ex 4.6–7) or punishment (Nm 12.9–10; 2 Sm 3.29; 2 Kgs 5.27; 2 Chr 26.17–23) inflicted by God, as were other maladies (Dt 28.21–22, 27, 35, 59).

As a stain or blemish, *ṣāra'at,* like other sources of defilement, e.g., touching a corpse (Nm 19.11–22), rendered a person technically "unclean," i.e., temporarily impure or unholy, hence unacceptable in proximity to the ark of the covenant, which could be approached only by the pure and unblemished (*see* PURE AND IMPURE).

Scholars disagree as to whether *ṣāra'at* was contagious in a hygienic sense, because of the failure of some to make the necessary distinction between bacterial infection, unknown as such in the Bible, and the cultic concept of uncleanliness. The latter was highly contagious (Leviticus ch. 11–15)—but only among Israelites (Mishnah, *Negaim,* 3.1). The case of the Gentile Naaman (2 Kgs 5.1) proves that ṣāra'at was not considered medically infectious. Nevertheless, it is obvious that the Levitical regulations had an effective prophylactic influence.

Almost without exception, modern leprologists agree that the symptoms of ṣāra'at do not resemble those of Hansen's disease. Stressing the omission of such characteristic features as anesthesia, leonine face, hoarseness, blindness, mutilations, slow evolution, and incurability, leprologists suggest that ṣāra'at designated skin disorders of various kinds, including leucoderma, vitiligo, psoriasis, eczema, yaws, sycosis or *tinea barbae,* ringworm of the scalp, or impetigo, as well as fungi and molds. Consequently, they conclude that Hansen's disease is not described in the Old Testament. However, owing to the sporadic presence of genuine leprosy in the Near East in early Old Testament times and its gradual spread in late Old Testament centuries, some of its victims may have been included among those diagnosed as having ṣāra'at. Incidentally, Job's skin disorder is not called by that name and was probably *scabies crustosa,* according to H. P. Lie. The passing allusions to sāra'at in the writings of the QUMRAN COMMUNITY and the extended dermatological treatise *Negaim* in the Mishnah serve to underline the persistence of the cultic aspect.

Of crucial importance to an understanding of ṣāra'at is the choice of the Greek word λέπρα (Latin *lepra*) by the learned rabbis who made the Greek translation, known as the Septuagint (LXX), of the Pentateuch in the third century B.C. at Alexandria, which was then a Hellenistic scientific center. The Hippocratic and later Greek medical writings apply λέπρα to curable scaling skin affections such as vitiligo and psoriasis. The standard Greek term for genuine leprosy, significantly appearing only after 250 B.C. (and not in Hippocrates) was έλεφαντίασις, later Latinized as *elephantiasis Graecorum.*

In the New Testament. Following the pattern of the LXX, λέπρα was used to designate cases of ṣāra'at in the New Testament, with a direct reference to the Levitical rules in Mk 1.44 and to Naaman in Lk 4.27. Stressing the cultic aspect, cures were called cleansing (καθαρίζω: Mk 10.8;11.5; Mk 1.40–42: Lk 4.27: 17.14), excepting that of the grateful Samaritan, for whom Luke the physician used healing (ίάομαι: Lk 17.15). These cleansings were one of the messianic signs (Mt 10.8; 11.5). Of significance for the future was the detail that Jesus "had compassion on and touched" the outcast (Mk 1.41; See Also Mt 8.3; Lk 5.13). Also noteworthy was his befriending

of "Simon the leper" (Mt 26.6; Mk 14.3). The beggar Lazarus is described as being covered with sores (Lk 16.20), but as with Job, he is not called λεπρός (leprous). Outside the Gospels, there is no mention of any form of leprosy in the New Testament.

Noting that none of the passages in the Gospels supply clinical descriptions, leprologists conclude that the *lepra* of the New Testament, being the equivalent of the ṣāra'at of the Old Testament, was not Hansen's disease. However, it is more probable, since genuine leprosy was endemic in the Near East in the first Christian century, that some of its victims may have been included among those diagnosed as having *lepra.* In any case, whatever the particular disease was, the instantaneity of the cures effected by Christ testifies to their miraculous nature.

Bibliography: General. V. KLINGMÜLLER, *Handbuch der Hautund Geschlechtskrankheiten* 10.2 (Berlin 1930) 4–21. K. GRÖN, *ibid.* 806–842. G. STICKER, *ibid.* 23 (1931) 264–642. E. JEAN-SELME, *La Lèpre* (Paris 1934) 9–67. A. WEYMOUTH (I. G. COBB), *Through the Leper-squint: A Study of Leprosy from Pre-Christian Times to the Present Day* (London 1938). J. LOWE, "Comments on the History of Leprosy," *Leprosy Review* 18 (1947) 54–64. Antiquity. B. EBBELL, "A Contribution to the Earliest History of Leprosy," *International Journal of Leprosy* 3 (1935) 257–263. DHARMENDRA, "Leprosy in Ancient Indian Medicine," *ibid.* 15 (1947) 424–430. M. YOELI, "A 'Facies Leontina' of Leprosy on an Ancient Canaanite Jar," *ibid.* 30 (1962) 211–214. V. MOLLER-CHRISTENSEN, "The Origin and Antiquity of Leprosy," *ibid.* 31 (1963) 562. A. BLOOM, *La Lèpre dans l' ancienne Ègypte et chez les anciens hébreux. La Lèpre dans la Bible* (Cairo 1938). H. GRAPOW, *Grundriss der Medizin der alten Agypter,* 7 v. (Berlin 1954–61). O. K. SKINSNES, "Leprosy in Society," *Leprosy Review* 35 (1964) 21–35, 106–122, 175–182. Bible. H. P. LIE, "On Leprosy in the Bible," *ibid.* 9 (1938) 25–31, 55–67. F. C. LENDRUM, "The Name 'Leprosy,'" *American Journal of Tropical Medicine and Hygiene* 1 (1952) 999–1008. *Leprosy and the Bible* (pamphlet; London 1961), repr. of four articles from *The Bible Translator* 11 (1960) 10–23, 69–80, 80–81; 12 (1961) 75–79. R. G. COCHRANE et al., in J. HASTINGS and J. A. SELBIA, eds., *Dictionary of the Bible* (Edinburgh 1942–50) (1963) (rev. ed. New York 1963) 575–578. W. LEIBRAND, *Lexikon für Theologie und Kirche,* ed. J. HOFER and K. RAHNER (Freiberg 1957–65) 1:1115–16. *Encyclopedic Dictionary of the Bible,* tr. and adap. by L. HARTMAN (New York 1963) 1322–23.

[R. BROWN]

LE QUIEN, MICHEL

Dominican theologian and historian of the Eastern Church; b. Boulogne-sur-Mer, Oct. 8, 1661; d. Paris, March 12, 1733. After studying at Plessis College, Paris, Le Quien entered the Dominican Order, in which he served as librarian of the convent of Saint-Honoré in Paris and devoted his career to scholarly pursuits. He mastered Hebrew, Greek, and Arabic; assisted scholars; and was a friend of Bernard de MONTFAUCON and the

MAURISTS. He published *Défense du texte hébreu et de la version Vulgate* (Paris 1690), in which he attempted to establish the integrity of the text. In his *Panoplia contra schisma Graecorum* (Paris 1718), published under the pseudonym Stephanus de Altamura Ponticensis, he took issue with the historical arguments advanced by Patriarch Nectarius of Jerusalem against the papal primacy and opposed the validity of Anglican Orders in a bitter controversy (91725–31) with P. Le Courayer. He produced the still standard though incomplete edition of St. JOHN DAMASCENE's *Opera omnia* (2 v. Paris 1712; *Patrologia Graeca* v.94–96) and *Oriens Christianus* (3 v., posthumous, Paris 1740). The latter work is a synthesis of the history of the Oriental patriarchates and bishoprics with an account of the Latin bishops who occupied those sees after the Crusades. His ambitious plan to include in this work the *Notitiae episcopatuum* and catalogues of the Eastern and African monasteries and of the African hierarchy had to be abandoned. Le Quien also wrote a monograph on Boulogne-sur-Mer and left unfinished an edition of the *Opera omnia Leontii Byzantini*.

Bibliography: H. LECLERCQ, *Dictionnaire d'archéologie chrétienne,* 15 v. (Paris 1907–53) 8.2:2592–96. J. CARREYRE, *Dictionnaire de théologie catholique,* 15 v. (Paris 1903–50) 9.1:441–443. H. ENGBERDING, *Lexikon für Theologie und Kirche,* ed. J. HOFER and K. RAHNER, 10 v. (Freiburg 1957–65) 6:974. S. VAILHÉ, *The Catholic Encyclopedia,* ed. C. G. HERBERMANN et al., 16 v. (New York 1907–14; suppl. 1922) 9:187–188.

[J. BEAUDRY]

Tower of the Abbey of Lérins. (©John Heseltine/CORBIS)

LERCHER, LUDWIG

Theologian; b. Hall, Austria, June 30, 1864; d. Innsbruck, Aug. 5, 1937. He became a Jesuit in 1891 and professor of theology at the University of Innsbruck in 1899. Through his lectures and writings he exercised great influence on the formation of the clergy. His chief work, *Institutiones theologiae dogmaticae,* 4 vols. (Innsbruck 1924–34), combines a solid presentation of theology with an emphasis on its ascetical relevance.

Bibliography: *Lexikon für Theologie und Kirche,* 10 v., ed. J. HOFER and K. RAHNER, (Freiburg 1957–65) 6:974. F. LAKNER, "Die dogmatische Theologie an der Universität Innsbruck, 1857–1957," *Zeitschrift für katholische Theologie* 80 (1958): 101–141.

[J. BEUMER]

LÉRINS, ABBEY OF

Cistercian monastery on the island of St. Honoratus, one of a group of islands off the southeast coast of France, opposite Cannes. In about 410 HONORATUS OF ARLES and a companion settled on the abandoned and desolate site as hermits. They were joined by other men with similar ideals, and soon a monastic community came into being, probably somewhat similar to a Palestinian laura. Its importance as a spiritual center is attested to by the names of the saints and bishops who were monks or visitors there in the first century of its existence. Among the monks were Maximus and Faustus of Riez, Caesarius and Virgilius of Arles, Eucherius of Lyons, and Lupus of Troyes; among the visitors were Vincent of Lérins, Salvianus of Marseilles, Patrick of Ireland, and Augustine of Canterbury. The early rule, possibly unwritten, in any case has not survived. There are some indications that it strongly influenced St. Benedict when he wrote his Rule, which in its turn was officially adopted by Abbot Aigulf (*c.* 660). A massacre of the monks (*c.* 732), when the island was occupied by the Saracens, brought an end to the first period of monastic life at Lérins. A restoration took place when the invaders were driven out (975), and the 11th century was a time of great material and spiritual prosperity. Numerous foundations along the whole Mediterranean coast and to the north spread the heritage of Lérins. This period of prosperity came to an end in 1464 when the pope replaced the regular abbot with a commendatory one. This was a death blow to the moral greatness of the abbey and also prepared its material ruin. One of these commendatory abbots, A. Grimaldi, bishop of Vence, united Lérins to the Italian Cassinese Congregation (1515), but the reformation that might have taken place because of this was impeded by the continual difficulties raised by the French kings and bishops over the foreign affiliation. The abbey was suppressed by royal decree in 1786 and its buildings sold at auction in 1791. In 1859 Monsignor Jordany, bishop of Fréjus, purchased the island and gave it to the Cistercian Congregation of Senanque, which established a community (1871) and eventually its headquarters there. Several remains of the earlier monasteries still exist: the so-called seven chapels, probably going back to very early days; an old cloister from the 8th century; and a defensive tower from the Middle Ages.

Bibliography: H. MORIS, *L'Abbaye de Lérins. Histoire et monuments* (Paris 1909). H. MORIS and E. BLANC, *Cartulaire de l'abbaye de Lérins*, 2 v. (Paris 1884–1905). A. C. COOPER-MARSDEN, *The History of the Islands of the Lérins* . . . (Cambridge, Eng. 1913). C. L. CRISTIANI, *Lérins et ses fondateurs* (Paris 1946). H. LECLERCQ, *Dictionnaire d'archéologie chrétienne et de liturgie* 8.2:2596–2627. L. H. COTTINEAU, *Répertoire topo-bibliographique des abbayes et prieurés* 1:1588–90. D. MISONNE, *Lexicon für Theologie und Kirche* 2 6:975–976.

[C. FALK]

LEROQUAIS, VICTOR MARTIAL

Specialist in liturgical manuscripts; b. Saint-Germain-de-Tallevende, France, Sept. 7, 1875; d. Paris, March 1, 1946. Having studied at Vire and Sommervieu, he studied theology at Saint-Sulpice. Ordained in Paris on June 9, 1900, he became assistant pastor at Lisieux and later (1906–12) pastor of Bény-sur-mer. As he explained the Mass to the children of his parish, he decided to learn more about liturgical manuscripts and to write a history of the Latin Mass. With some difficulty he obtained leave of his bishop, Msgr. Lemonnier, and began to work at the Bibliothèque Nationale in Paris. Here he remained, apart from trips to provincial libraries. At his own expense, which he met by selling his furniture and books, he published a series of inventories in which he described the Sacramentaries, Breviaries, Pontificals, and Psalters found in French public libraries: *Les Sacramentaires et les missels manuscrits des bibliothèques publiques de France* (Paris 1924); *Les Livres d'heures manuscrits de la Bibliothèque Nationale*, 3 v. (Paris 1927); *Les Bréviaires manuscrits des bibliothèques*

publiques de France, 6 v. (Paris 1934); *Les Pontificaux manuscrits des bibliothèques de France,* 4 v. (Paris 1937). He taught courses at the École Pratique des Hautes Études and gave a series of lectures at the École des Chartes. He was also a member of the Henry Bradshaw Society.

Bibliography: J. LECLERCQ, *Revue du moyen-âge latin* 2 (1946): 126–128. J. PORCHER, *Scriptorium* 1 (1946–47): 170–172. F. COMBALUZIER, *Ephemerides liturgicae* 60 (1946): 389–395.

[N. HUYGHEBAERT]

LE ROY, ALEXANDER

Alexander Le Roy was born (1854) of humble means in Normandy, a farmer's son. An unusually gifted student, he planned to be a parish priest but transferred to the Spiritans, the missionary Congregation of the Holy Ghost (1874), his heart set on Africa. Suddenly, before ordination (1876), his health failed, perhaps explaining his subsequent appointment not to the rigors of Africa but to the classroom: to Réunion in the Indian Ocean (1877), to central France (1878), and to Pondicherry, India (1880). Improved health and a change of Congregational leadership brought a new appointment, and he finally arrived in Bagamoyo, East Africa (1881), bursting with energy and about to develop prodigiously wide-ranging interests.

He doubly liberated African slaves: once freed, they continued the habit of dependency, so he made them responsible for their own farms and livelihood, thus promoting their self-respect. He also traveled widely, making, in his words, "numerous journeys with more or less prolonged sojourns from Somaliland to Mozambique . . . from Kilimanjaro [climbing above 16,500 feet] to the Maasai plains." He was constantly and avidly accumulating information, writing, criticizing the colonial régime, and becoming *persona non grata* for his pains.

Effectively expelled by the German authorities, he returned to Paris (1892), and was appointed vicar apostolic of the two Guineas (stretching from Sénégal in West Africa to the Cape of Good Hope). Within three years—and with formidable administrative skills—he reorganized the vicariate, only to be elected superior general (1896). For three decades, Le Roy would lead the Spiritans. He had already championed the formation of catechists in his vicariate. His unpublished study *The Catechists in the Missions* urged lay catechists both to spread the Gospel in a predominantly Islamic society and create Christian communities; and he deemed premature the huge effort to train a native clergy. He also founded the Missionary Sisters of the Holy Ghost (1921) to work across French and Portuguese Africa. As the first superior general with African experience he would leave a distinctively African stamp on the congregation, whose numbers doubled to over 2000 during his tenure.

His encouragement inspired both scholarship and missionary zeal, and he left a rich scholarly legacy. In his fifties he became the first incumbent of the Chair of the History of Religions at the Institut Catholique de Paris (his inaugural lectures becoming his sympathetic and still-in-print textbook *The Religion of the Primitives*). His bibliography fills ten pages and includes exploration, geography, cartography, ethnology, ethnography, biography and autobiography, including: *Le T.R.P Frédéric Le Vavasseur* (Paris, n.d); v. 5 of Piolet, J. (editor), *Les Missions Catholiques Françaises au XIX siècle*; "Le rôle scientifique des missionaires" *Anthropos* 1 (1906) 3–10; *The Religion of the Primitives* (New York, 1969); *Au Kilema-Ndjaro*, 4th Edition (Paris 1928) and *Directoire Général des Missions* (Paris 1930). Failing health precipitated his resignation (1926), yet Le Roy recovered and enjoyed twelve more years of life. The sickly twenty-year-old survived to be an octogenarian, dying in Paris (1938), aged 84.

Bibliography: E. BAUR and A. LE ROY, *Voyage dans L'Oudoé, L'Ouzigoua et L'Ousogara* (Tours 1899). H. KOREN, *The Spiritans: A History of the Congregation of the Holy Ghost* (Pittsburgh 1958).

[A. J. GITTINS]

LE ROY, ÉDOUARD

French Catholic philosopher and mathematician; b. Paris, June 18, 1870; d. Paris, Nov. 1, 1954.

Le Roy developed the evolutionary philosophy of Henri BERGSON in the direction of a Christian "psychistic" idealism, and succeeded to Bergson's chair at the Collège de France in 1921. In holding that theoretical science is only a system of symbols and not a penetration into ultimate reality, he opposed philosophies that tended to substitute abstract concepts for an intuition of life. Even dogmatic statements have a limited function that is negative (to prevent error) and practical (to engender religious attitudes and action). They provide no direct insight into God's inner life. Le Roy believed that, unlike static concepts, life is always on the move. The process of evolution begins with a diffused cosmic energy that is latently psychic; life is manifested when this energy is concentrated in organisms of growing complexity. The biological realm of organisms is transcended when man appears, and thenceforth evolution is continued in the realm of spirit, or the noösphere—while remaining always subject to God's transcendent and continuously cre-

ative action. The resulting phenomenology of evolution bears many resemblances, in thought and terminology, to notions later expressed by Le Roy's close friend and associate, Pierre TEILHARD DE CHARDIN.

Bibliography: Works. *Dogme et critique* (Paris 1907); *Les Origines humaines et l'évolution de l'intelligence* (Paris 1928); *La Pensée intuitive*, 2 v. (Paris 1929–30); *Le Problème de Dieu* (Paris 1930); *La Pensée mathématique pare* (Paris 1960), posthumously. **Literature.** I. DANIELE, *Enciclopedia filosofica*, 4 v. (Venice-Rome 1957) 2:1888–90. A. G. SERTILLANGES, *Le Christianisme et les philosophies,* 2 v. (Paris 1939–41) 2:402–419.

[J. M. SOMERVILLE]

LES DUNES, ABBEY OF

Former Cistercian abbey (Latin, *Dunae*), located near Coxyde, Belgium, in the former Diocese of Thérouanne (presently the Diocese of Bruges). This abbey, founded in 1107 by the hermit Léger, was attached *c.* 1120 to the Norman Abbey of SAVIGNY. The abbot Fulk, successor of Léger, placed the monastery under St. BERNARD and retired to CLAIRVAUX. Under the administration of the abbot, Bl. Idesbald, the abbey gained many domains along the coast. The abbot of Les Dunes was chief of the *wateringues;* that is, he had charge of the maintenance of the dikes. From Les Dunes, Clairmarais, near Saint-Omer, and TER DOEST, not far from Bruges, were founded. The abbey raised sheep for their wool. At the beginning of the 13th century a new monastery was built for a community of 400 religious. During the 16th century, because of the wars and internal strife, the abbey faced serious financial difficulties. In 1566 and 1578 the abbey was ravaged by Protestants. Abbot Bernard Campmans (1623–42) transferred the community to a new monastery at Bruges, from which the monks were evicted by the French Revolution. Since 1841 the abbey buildings have housed the major seminary of Bruges. Recent excavations at Coxyde have brought to light a large part of the monastery.

Bibliography: A. BUT, *Cronica et cartularium monasterii de Dunis*, ed. F. VAN DE PUTTE (Bruges 1864); *Cronica abbatum monasterii de Dunis* (Bruges 1839). *Statuta capitulorum generalium ordinis cisterciensis*, ed. J. M. CANIVEZ, 8 v. (Louvain 1933–41). L. JANAUSCHEX, *Origines Cistercienses* (Vienna 1877) 51. M. A. DIMIER, "L'Église de l'abbaye des Dunes," *Bulletin monumental* 112 (1954) 243–251; *Dictionnaire d'histoire et de géographie ecclésiastiques*, ed. A. BAUDRILLART et al. (Paris 1912–) 14:1039–1044. J. DE VINCENNES, *L'abbaye des Dunes: Saint Idesbald* (Charleroi 1956). P. SCHITTEKAT, *Sous les dunes de Coxyde* (Brussels 1960). A. JANSSENS DE BISTHOVEN, *De abdij van de Duinen te Brugge* (Bruges 1963).

[M. A. DIMIER]

LE SENNE, RENÉ

French philosopher; b. Elbeuf-sur-Seine, July 8, 1882; d. Paris, Oct. 1, 1954. He was a student at the École Normale Supérieure in 1903 and *agrégé* at the University of Paris in 1906; he defended his dissertation for a doctorate of letters in 1930. He then taught at the Lycée Louis-le-Grand, was named professor at the Sorbonne in 1942, and was admitted to the Académie des Sciences morales et politiques in 1948. With Louis LAVELLE he established the collection *Philosophie de l'Esprit* in 1934; he also directed the *Logos* and *Caractères* collections of the Presses Universitaires de France and presided at the International Institute of Philosophy in 1952 and 1953.

His thought is dialectical, like that of O. Hamelin (1856–1907), whose method he reformed and enlarged. It begins with relation and not with being, as does Lavelle's, and seeks not so much an explanation of the world as salvation of the person. The privileged relation for Le Senne is duty, to which he devoted his doctoral dissertation (*Le Devoir,* Paris 1930); dialectic itself is a duty, as duty is a dialectic. Duty encroaches upon intelligence, but man must allow himself to be stimulated by contradiction everywhere and surmount it. "At the provocation of the irrational," he writes, "the self answers with courage." This courage must be inventive, for the work of awareness never ends; it cannot establish itself alongside Infinity, which unceasingly moves reflection and makes it pass alternately from an obstacle to a value (*Obstacle el Valeur,* Paris 1934). This is why the moral treatise he published presents both exemplary lives, such as those of Socrates and Jesus, and analyses of concepts (*Traité de morale générale,* Paris 1942).

Le Senne opposed reasoning to lived experience; yet the opposition he referred to as "the ideo-existential relation" is a call to live thought and to think life. Value thus reaches man from two directions, each of which preserves the image of the other. A sort of refraction, or diffraction, of value into life follows this; it is manifested by a "double *cogito*"—reflection, surpassing its given determinations, centers itself in the self and in God. There is no self without God and no God without self, except asymptotically.

Le Senne's vision of the world is harsher than that of Lavelle; he insists on the interhuman bond, but on condition of seeing in it a work in common rather than a mystical intimacy. The opacity and the conflicts of nature contaminate value itself, as one sees in the example of war, where hostility rests on the devotion of each belligerent to one same value, that of country. There is no solution to this APORIA except an increasing fidelity to the solidarity itself of values. Thence the condemnation of all fanaticisms, not because they are intense but because they are exclusive; thence also the refusal to give privilege to any particular value, not even charity. God alone is the perfectly determining and indeterminable value for all determined values. Even in future life Le Senne seemed to await a sort of perpetual purgatory that made him say: "To die is to move one's furniture."

Besides his philosophical work, Le Senne is noteworthy for his interest in characterology (*Traité de caractérologie,* Paris 1946). He conceived of character as the mental skeleton of man and not as a bundle of virtualities that could be equated with his person. He also rethought and deepened the distinction G. Heymans (1857–1930) proposed between primary character, which is changeable, and secondary character, which retains all the reverberation that goes on within it.

Bibliography: C. ROSSO, *Enciclopedia filosofica,* 4 v. (Venice- Rome 1957) 2:1891–1894. G. BERGER, *Notice sur la vie et les travaux de René Le Senne, 1882–1954* (Paris 1956). J. PAUMEN, *Le Spiritualisme existentiel de René Le Senne* (Paris 1949).

[M. NÉDONCELLE]

LESEUR, ÉLISABETH

Spiritual writer; b. Paris, Oct. 16, 1866; d. Paris, May 3, 1914. She was the eldest of five children of a cultivated background, and attended a small private school. In July of 1889 she married Félix Leseur, a doctor who had lost his faith through reading the fashionable atheist literature then current in France. To unsettle his wife's moderate Catholicism, he gave her Renan's *Vie de Jésus.* Paradoxically, the book awakened her dormant faith, and her *Spiritual Journal* begins at this point.

Adopting as her motto, "Each soul that perfects itself perfects the world," she proceeded to make her life ever more ascetic, interior, and hidden. Her greatest trial arose from the fact that Félix, whom she deeply loved, did not share her spiritual adventure. Her apostolate was an indirect one: she never preached and never sought religious discussion. The hallmarks of her dealings with souls were affability, delicacy, silence, and individual encounter.

Since childhood she had suffered from hepatitis, and she was often forced to receive visitors from a chaise longue. In March of 1911, she offered her life for Félix's conversion. Soon after, her illness was diagnosed as generalized cancer and she died at the age of 48 with no apparent sign of change in Félix.

In 1917, however, her husband was reconciled to the faith and, at the age of 62 he was ordained a Dominican priest, thus fulfilling Élisabeth's prophecy that he would one day be "Père Leseur." He spoke throughout Europe and frequently referred to her *Journal,* which had been published in 1917. He died in February of 1950.

Her cause for beatification has been introduced in Rome.

Bibliography: M. L. HERKING, *Elisabeth Leseur Nous Parle* (Paris 1955). J. VERBILLION, "The Silent Apostolate of Elizabeth Leseur," *Cross and Crown* 11 (1959): 28–45.

[J. VERBILLION]

LESOTHO, THE CATHOLIC CHURCH IN

The Kingdom of Lesotho is located in Africa, completely surrounded by the Republic of SOUTH AFRICA. A mountainous region, it consists of highland plateaus, rising to hills and thence to mountains at its perimeter. Featuring a temperate climate, Lesotho's natural resources consist primarily of water and pasture land from which its small farming concerns raise corn, wheat, barley, sheep and goats. Between 45 and 65 percent of the adult male labor force travel to South Africa to work in the mines, sending home a portion of their pay to their families. Lesotho also has a small reserve of diamonds, as well as small quantities of minerals.

Welded together from scattered Basotho tribes by Chief Moshesh in 1820, Lesotho resisted European claims until 1871, when it was annexed to the Cape Town colony. From 1884 to 1966 it was a British protectorate administered by a high commissioner, together with SWAZILAND and BOTSWANA (formerly Bechuanaland). Following over two decades of military rule, the region established a constitutional government in 1993. Lesotho is inhabited primarily by a single tribe, the Basotho, which has helped it maintain peace.

History. The first Catholic mission was established in 1862 by the OBLATES OF MARY IMMACULATE from the Vicariate Apostolic of Natal. Having sought the help of the British as a means of avoiding Dutch incursions, Basuto Chief Moshesh welcomed them and chose the site for the mission, later called Roma, which benefited from the efforts of Father Joseph Gerard (beatified 1988). The Prefecture Apostolic of Basutoland, created in 1894, became a vicariate apostolic in 1909. In 1924 the Oblates established at Roma a seminary, and in 1945, Pius XII University College. In 1951, when the South African hierarchy was established, the vicariate became the diocese of Maseru. In 1961 Maseru was made an archdiocese and metropolitan see for Basutoland, its first archbishop the great-grandson of Moshesh. In 1963 the University College became nondenominational, but the Oblates remained in charge of Pius XII College.

Capital: Maseru.
Size: 11,716 sq. miles.
Population: 2,143,140 in 2000.
Languages: Sesotho, English, Zulu, Xhosa.
Religions: 1,114,440 Catholics (52%), 107,160 Muslims (5%), 642,780 Protestants (30%), 27,860 without religious affiliation.
Archdiocese: Maseru, with suffragans Leribe, Mohale's Hoek, and Qacha's Nek.

In 1959 the Church helped to found the Basotholand National Party (BNP), which was instrumental in the region's move toward independence. In 1966 Lesotho became an independent constitutional monarchy, its national assembly working with the region's tribal chiefs. By the late 1970s, under BNP leadership, Lesotho was able to stabilize its economy, but strains on its small economy increased due to the steady influx of South African refugees seeking escape from their country's racist apartheid policies; Lesotho's international airline flights were not subject to the scrutiny or control of South African police. A military government gained power in 1986, whereupon the national assembly was dissolved and replaced by a military council that ruled with the king. A democratic constitution was enacted in a bloodless coup in 1991 and elections held two years later.

In addition to its active role in the nation's health care system, one of the reasons for the predominance of the Catholic faith in the region was the early establishment of a network of Church-run schools, which by 2000, with over 490 primary and 75 secondary schools, accounted for 75 percent of all schools in the country. Lesotho's bishops were members of the South African Bishops' Conference, an organization that worked diligently to bring about racial peace and justice in the whole region. Theological disputes between Catholic and Lesotho's evangelical Protestant leaders made ecumenical efforts rare, although during a 1996 ad limina visit with Pope John Paul II the bishops were exhorted to engage in such outreach.

By 2000 there were 78 parishes tended by over 50 diocesan and 80 religious priests. Other religious included approximately 45 brothers and 600 sisters, who cared in particular for those families whose breadwinner's worked in South Africa. Beginning in the mid-20th century, the Church in Lesotho adopted some elements of local culture, such as tribal call-and-response singing, in its services and performed services in the native language. The pope urged that such "inculturation" be controlled so that Church doctrine be interpreted correctly. Catholics continued to wield political influence at the beginning of the 21st century, due to both their relative af-

LESOTHO

0   25   50 Miles
0   25   50 Kilometers

SOUTH AFRICA

Libono
Butha-
Buthe
Leribe
Peka
Mapoteng
Teyateyaneng
Maseru
Mazenod
Roma
Morija   Marakabeis
Tsa-Kholo
Malealea
Mafeteng   Semonkong
Sekake
Mohales
Hoek
Mount
Moorosi
Quthing

Letseng-la Terai
Mokhotlong
Thabana
Ntlenyana
11,425 ft.
3482 m.
Thaba-Tseka
Sehonghong

MALOTI MTS.
Malibamatso
Matsoku
Orange
Senqunyane
Makhaleng
Tsedike

DRAKENSBERG RANGE

SOUTH AFRICA

Orange
Tina

Rhodes

Barkly
East

N
W E
S

Bashee
Kraai

Lesotho

fluence and their position as a majority voice in the dominant BNP.

Bibliography: W. E. BROWN, *The Catholic Church in South Africa,* ed. M. DERRICK (New York 1960) 207–223. *Annuario Pontificio* (1965) 235, 266. *Bilan du Monde,* 2:120–123. For additional bibliography, *see* AFRICA.

[J. E. BRADY/EDS.]

LESSING, GOTTHOLD EPHRAIM

German critic, dramatist, leading exponent of the *Aufklärung;* b. Kamenz, in Oberlausitz (Saxony), Jan. 22, 1729; d. Braunschweig, Feb. 15, 1781. He was the son of a Lutheran pastor and attended the celebrated school of St. Afra in Meissen (1741–46). He then entered the University of Leipzig, where, at the wish of his father, he studied first theology, then medicine. But his main interest was in philosophy and literature. His early play, *Der*

junge Gelehrte, was produced at Leipzig in 1748 by the company of actors under the direction of Caroline Neuber (1697–1760). When this company failed in the same year, Lessing, who had become surety for its debts, fled to Berlin to escape his creditors. There he again wrote plays: *Der Freigeist* (1749), under the influence of the French comedy, and *Die Juden* (1749), which foreshadowed the themes of his later play *Nathan der Weise.* He also became a literary and dramatic critic; his essays were published in the short-lived journal *Beiträge zur Historie und Aufnahme des Theaters* (1749–50; with Christlob Mylius, 1752–54), the *Berliner Privilegierte Zeitung,* and the *Vossische Zeitung* and its supplement, *Das Neueste aus dem Reiche des Witzes,* of which he was editor in 1751.

In 1751–52, after having studied for his master's degree in Wittenberg, Lessing was again in Berlin, where he published the first volumes of his collected works (*Schriften,* 6 v., 1753–55, which included the lyrics and epigrams originally published as *Kleinigkeiten* in 1751). Lessing's second review of drama, *Die theatralische Bibliothek,* was published from 1754 to 1758. In collaboration with Moses Mendelssohn (1729–86) he published *Pope, ein Metaphysiker!* (1755), an essay that defines the distinct roles of poet and philosopher. He frequently changed his residence in the following years: he was at Leipzig (1755–58), where he formed a close friendship with the poet Ewald Christian von Kleist (1715–59); at Berlin (1758–60); Breslau (1760–64), as secretary to the governor, General Tauentzien; Berlin (1765–67); Hamburg (1767–68); and in Italy (1768–70). In 1770 he accepted the position of court librarian at Wolfenbüttel in Braunschweig, where, except for a visit to Vienna and Italy in 1775, he remained until his death. In 1776 he married a widow, Eva König, who died in childbirth the following year.

Influence as Critic. Lessing, in whom the German ENLIGHTENMENT found its culmination and German classicism its most eminent precursor and teacher, has been called the foremost critic of his time. His essay on the nature of the fable, prefixed to the collected edition of his *Fabeln* (1759), distinguishes the kinds of action proper to fable, drama, and epic. Perceptive criticisms of contemporary authors, among them Klopstock and Wieland, are to be found in the 54 letters he contributed to the journal *Briefe, die neueste Literatur betreffend,* published in Berlin (1759–65), with Moses Mendelssohn and Friedrich Nicolai (1733–1811), the latter a bookseller and writer of rationalistic literature. Especially noteworthy is the seventeenth letter, in which Lessing strove to free German literature from its subjection to the artificial rules of French pseudoclassicism by reinterpreting the classical tradition of the ancients and pointing the way to a

LESSING, GOTTHOLD EPHRAIM

proper appreciation of Shakespeare. In *Laokoon oder Über die Grenzen der Malerei und Poesie* (1766) he defined the boundaries between the plastic arts, which portray objects in space, and literature, which portrays events in time.

As dramatic critic of the newly established National Theater in Hamburg, Lessing published the *Hamburgische Dramaturgie* (1767–68). Intended originally as a series of reviews of plays performed at the National Theater, these essays became in point of fact vehicles for the expression of Lessing's own dramatic theory, which, though largely derivative, exerted a major influence on 18th-century drama in Germany and in Europe generally. In them he again strove to break the tyranny of French pseudoclassicism in Germany and to create a German national drama based on a correct interpretation of Aristotle's dramatic theory of the unities. Out of Lessing's feud with the antiquarian Christian Adolf Klotz (1738–71), professor at the University of Halle, arose the *Briefe antiquarischen Inhalts* (1768–69) and the admirable essay *Wie die Alten den Tod gebildet* (1769).

Dramatic Work. Lessing's interest in the theater was not confined to criticism. Besides the plays already mentioned, he is author of a one-act tragedy *Philotas* (1759) and of the more important *Miss Sara Sampson* (1755), the first significant tragedy of middle-class life (*bürgerliches Trauerspiel*) in German literature. Based on English models (especially George Lillo's *Merchant of London,* 1731), this play gave practical expression to Lessing's revolt against Johann Christoph Gottsched (1700–66), the chief patron of French pseudoclassicism in Germany. In *Minna von Barnhelm* (1767), a play whose setting was the Seven Years' War, Lessing wrote the first German national drama of modern times, the first play in which a soldier (the hero, Major von Tellheim) has an honorable role. It is also the first masterpiece of German comedy, in which the comedy has its logical source in the events themselves, and the events in the characters who portray them; it is still popular in Germany. Lessing likewise gave Germany its first political tragedy, *Emilia Galotti* (1772), an indictment of corruption and immorality among the petty princes of absolutism.

Lessing's last drama, *Nathan der Weise* (1779), belongs more properly among the theological polemics precipitated by his publication, in *Beiträge zur Geschichte und Literatur* (1773–81), of selections from the *Apologie oder Schutzschrift für die vernünftigen Verehrer Gottes* by Hermann Samuel Reimarus (1694–1768). To the ensuing controversy between orthodoxy and rationalism belong Lessing's *Anti-Goeze* (1778), a rebuttal of his most vehement opponent, the Hamburg pastor Johann Melchior Goeze (1717–86), and *Nathan der Weise,* in which

Gotthold Ephraim Lessing.

Lessing, forbidden by the Braunschweig government to continue his strife with orthodoxy, returned to his "old pulpit," the stage, and pleaded for religious tolerance; the play's parable of the three rings reflects his rejection of the concept of one true religion. *Die Erziehung des Menschengeschlechts* (1780) is an essay that contains his doctrine of an organic religious evolution away from revealed religion and toward a future rational religion to succeed Judaism and Christianity. *Ernst und Falk: Gespräche für Freimaurer* (1777, 1780) is a group of five dialogues in which Lessing renewed his plea for religious and political tolerance. Mention should be made also of the volume of *Rettungen* (1753–54), in which Lessing sought to vindicate earlier victims of theological bigotry, and of the publication of a previously unknown manuscript of BERENGARIUS OF TOURS, a work Lessing found in the Wolfenbüttel library.

Bibliography: Works. First ed. by his brother K. G. LESSING et al., 31 v. (Berlin 1771–1825); ed. K. LACHMANN, 13 v. (Berlin 1838–40); ed. W. STAMMLER, 2 v. (Munich 1959); ed. H. KESTEN, 2 v. (Frankfurt 1962). Studies. K. G. LESSING, ed., *Gotthold Ephraim Lessings Leben nebst seinem noch übrigen literarischen Nachlasse,* 3 v. (Berlin 1793–95). J. SIME, *Lessing: His Life and Writings,* 2 v. (London 1877). E. SCHMIDT, *Lessing: Geschichte seines Lebens und seiner Schriften,* ed. F. SCHULTZ, 2 v. (4th ed. Berlin 1923). H. KESTEN, *Gotthold Ephraim Lessing: Ein deutscher Moralist* (Mainz 1960). W. KOSCH, *Deutsches Literatur-Lexikon,* ed. B. BERGER

NEW CATHOLIC ENCYCLOPEDIA

(Bern 1963) 246–248. H. B. GARLAND, *Lessing: The Founder of Modern German Literature* (2d ed. New York 1962).

[M. F. MCCARTHY]

LESSIUS, LEONARD

Theologian; b. Brecht near Antwerp, Oct. 1, 1554; d. Louvain, Jan. 15, 1623. His family name was Leys. The early loss of his parents produced in him a sobriety and profound introversion that were to last throughout his life and to give impetus to his proclivity toward prayer and serious study. Destined by his uncle for a career in business, Leonard instead won a scholarship at the University of Louvain at the age of 13. There he took courses in arts and philosophy, preparatory to becoming a Jesuit. He distinguished himself by winning the first place in his class. In June of 1572 he was assigned to teach philosophy at the College of Douai. At the same time he began to study theology on his own initiative. He was ordained in 1580 and made prefect of studies at Douai the following year. Later, he was given a sabbatical in Liège and then sent to Rome, where he continued his theological studies under Bellarmine and Suárez. Returning to Belgium in 1584, he taught theology at the University of Louvain. There he shocked some of the older professors by substituting in his classes the *Summa* of St. Thomas for the customary *Liber Sententiarum* of Peter Lombard.

From 1564 one of the professors at the university, Michael du Bay (Baius), had been teaching a doctrine suspected by some as being tainted with heresy (*see* BAIUS AND BAIANISM). When some of Lessius' lectures had a tone quite antithetic to the ideas of their master, Baius's followers presented a garbled version of the young Jesuit's theses to the university authorities for scrutiny. Lessius was accused of reviving SEMI-PELAGIANISM. At the instigation of P. Tolet, the university issued a condemnation of 31 of the supposed propositions of Lessius. In 1586 Lessius published his *Theses theologicae,* in which he defended the doctrine he was really teaching. A bitter quarrel between the Baianists and Jesuits ensued; Lessius maintained such composure that even his opponents were constrained to express their admiration for him. Eventually, at the request of Sixtus V (d. 1590), the doctrine of Lessius was examined by a commission of theologians and found to be in accord with Catholic dogma.

During his lifetime as a teacher, Lessius published a great number of works, many of which went through several editions even in various languages. Most famous of all was his treatise *De justitia et jure* (Louvain 1605). The book deals in great detail with the morality of contracts, buying and selling, fair prices, wages, market manipulations, problems of exchange, exploitation of newly discovered lands and their resources, etc. Outstanding in this work was the then novel opinion that taking of interest on loans of money is not in itself sinful. The division of Christianity through the multiplication of sects did not escape his notice or pen; on this question he wrote *Quae fides et religio sit capessenda* (Antwerp 1609). He also compiled a theological treatise *De providentia numinis et animi immortalitate* (Antwerp 1613). Lessius' masterful defense of papal authority is not extant today because his superiors, fearful of confiscation and reprisals by the king of France, restricted the circulation of this work.

His defense of MOLINISM in his famous work on efficacious grace, *De gratia efficaci* (Antwerp 1610), caused quite a controversy among the Jesuits (*See* GRACE, EFFICACIOUS). At first the book was approved by the Jesuit general's office, but later Aquaviva, the Jesuit general, censured it because it failed to distinguish clearly enough the difference between sufficient and efficacious grace. In virtue of holy obedience Lessius was commanded by the general to emend his original text in accordance with propositions dictated to him by Aquiviva. Lessius complied.

Representative of Lessius' spirituality is his little series of meditations called *De summo bono et aeterna beatitudine hominis* (Antwerp 1620). His cause for beatification has been introduced.

Bibliography: C. H. CHAMBERLAIN, ''Leonard Lessius,'' *Jesuit Thinkers of the Renaissance,* ed. G. SMITH (Milwaukee 1939). C. VAN SULL, *Léonard Lessius, S.J.* (Louvain 1930). R. BÄUMER, *Lexikon für Theologie und Kirche,* ed. J. HOFER and K. RAHNER, 10 v. (Freiburg 1957–65) 6:981–982. C. SOMMERVOGEL, et al., *Bibliothèque de la Compagnie de Jésus,* 11 v. (Brussels-Paris 1890–1932) 4:1726–1751. P. BERNARD, *Dictionnaire de théologie catholique,* 15 v. (Paris 1903–50) 9.1:453–454; 7.2:2135–2145.

[C. MEYER]

LESTONNAC, JEANNE DE, ST.

Foundress of the COMPANY OF MARY (ODN); b. Bordeaux, France, 1556; d. there, Feb. 2, 1640. She was the niece of the philosopher Michel de MONTAIGNE. Jeanne married Gaston de Montferrand in 1573 and bore seven children. In 1603, six years after her husband's death, she entered the Cistercian convent at Les Feuillants, Toulouse. Her health failed after ten months, and she left the convent upon the advice of her superiors. She then devoted herself to charitable works in which she was joined by several friends. From this group she founded her religious congregation for the education of girls, approved by PAUL V in 1607. Mother de Lestonnac governed the congregation until 1622 when, through malicious gossip, she was discredited and replaced as superior. After bearing this trial and subsequent humiliations with heroic patience and confidence in God, she was vindicated in 1624. Her last years were devoted to assisting new foundations and to revising the order's constitutions. She was buried in Bordeaux, but her body was found preserved in 1822 at the solemn translation of her remains. She was declared venerable in 1834, beatified by LEO XIII on Sept. 23, 1900, and canonized by PIUS XII on May 15, 1949.

Feast: Feb. 2.

Bibliography: P. HOESL, *In the Service of Youth,* tr. J. CARR (London 1951). V. MERCIER, *La Vénérable Jeanne de Lestonnac* (Paris 1891). F. SOURY-LAVERGNE, *Chemin d'éducation: sur les traces de Jeanne de Lestonnac* (Chambray 1985). C. TESTORE, *Ste. Giovanna de Lestonnac di Montferrant-Landiras* (Rome 1949).

[M. G. MCNEIL]

LE TELLIER, CHARLES MAURICE

Archbishop of Reims; b. Turin, 1643; d. Reims, February 22, 1710. His father was the chancellor Michel, and his brother François, the Marquis of Louvois. From his childhood an ecclesiastical career was planned for him. From the time of his ordination, he expressed strong Gallican views. At the age of 25 he was named coadjutor of François Barberini, Archbishop of Reims, and at 28 he became Barberini's successor. Further honors included his being named a councilor of state in 1679 and a commander of the Order of the Holy Spirit in 1688. As a very active Gallican, he opposed the Jesuits. His library of more than 50,000 volumes was renowned; this he bequeathed to the abbey of Sainte-Geneviève. He presided over the general assembly of the French clergy in 1700. Most of his writings deal with diocesan administration, but he wrote also against the Molinists and Jansenists. He administered his diocese excellently. Contemporaries describe him as haughty. His manuscripts are collected in the Bibliothèque Nationale, having been given in 1718 by his nephew to the King's library.

Bibliography: J. GILLET, *Charles-Maurice Le Tellier, archevêque-duc de Reims* (Paris 1881). H. J. P. FISQUET, *La France pontificale,* 21 v. (Paris 1864–73) 14:190–193. L. DE R. SAINT-SIMON, *The Memoirs of the Duke of Saint-Simon,* tr. B. ST. JOHN, 4 v. in 2 (New York 1936). *Biographie universelle,* ed. L. G. MICHAUD, 45 v. (Paris 1843–65) 24:358–359. J. CARREYRE, *Dictionnaire de théologie catholique,* ed. A. VACANT, 15 v. (Paris 1903–50; Tables générales 1951–) 9.1:454–456.

[D. R. CAMPBELL]

LE TELLIER, MICHEL

Confessor of King LOUIS XIV, theologian; b. Vire, France, Dec. 16, 1643; d. La Flèche, France, Sept. 2, 1719. Though he published significant books between 1685 and 1708, his historical importance was a result of his influence upon King Louis XIV after 1708. He entered the Jesuits in 1661, and for 28 years taught humanities, philosophy, and biblical exegesis at Louisle-Grand in Paris. He became rector of this college. He was Jesuit provincial when, in 1708, he was chosen as the king's confessor after Father La Chaise's death. Before this he had written in defense of Jesuit practices in China in allowing Confucian rites to their Chinese converts. He wrote also against JANSENISM and against Pasquier Quesnel's *Reflexions morales;* and he was associated with the publication of the *Mémoires de Trevoux.* It was at his insistence that the king ordered Port-Royal destroyed. He also worked to bring about the condemnation of Quesnel's book in Rome and to obtain the publication of the bull *Unigenitus* in France. He was openly hostile to Cardinal Louis Antoine de NOAILLES. Upon Louis XIV's death, he was sent first to Amiens, then to La Flèche. Harsh judgments of him were written by the Janscnists, by partisans of the Duke of Orleans, and by Saint-Simon.

Bibliography: L. ANDRÉ, *Les Sources de l'histoire de France, XVIIᵉ siècle* (Paris 1932). A. BROU, *Les Jésuites de la légende,* 2 v. (Paris 1906–07). G. PLANTAVIT DE LA PAUSE, *Lettres sur le confessorat du Père Le Tellier,* ed. I. DE RECALDE (Paris 1922). C. SOMMERVOGEL et al. *Bibliothèque de la Compagnie de Jésus,* 11 v. (Brussels-Paris 1890–1932) 7:1911–1919. J. CARREYRE, *Dictionnaire de théologie catholique,* 15 v. (Paris 1903–50) 9.1:456–458. L. DE R. SAINT-SIMON, *The Memoirs of the Duke of Saint-Simon,* tr. B. ST. JOHN, 4 v. in 2 (New York 1936).

[D. R. CAMPBELL]

LE THORONET, ABBEY OF

Former Cistercian abbey of Provence, France, founded in 1136 in the Diocese of Fréjus by Raymond Bérenger, count of Barcelona and marquis of Provence. The monks came from Mazan in the region of Viviers and settled first in Tourtour. The abbey took the name of Florège and was later transferred to nearby Thoronet. On the island of Porquerolles an abbey founded from Thoronet was destroyed by the Saracens in 1160. During the 16th-century THIRTY YEARS' WAR the monks temporarily left the abbey. During the French Revolution the monastery was suppressed and the buildings were sold. The most famous abbot was Bl. Fulk, a former troubadour, who became bishop of Toulouse in 1205. In 1854 the French government purchased the buildings and restored them.

Bibliography: L. ROSTAN, ''Étude d'archéologie comparée: trois abbayes de l'Ordre de Cîteaux, Silvacane, Thoronet, Senanque,'' *Bulletin monumental,* 18 (1852) 111–121. M. AUBERT, ''L'Abbaye du Thoronet,'' *Congrès archéologique de France* 95

(1932) 224–243. R. BÉRENGUIER, *L'Abbaye cistercienne du Thoronet* (Lille 1955). M. A. DIMIER and J. PORCHER, *L'Art cistercien* (Paris 1962).

[M. A. DIMIER]

LEUBUS, ABBEY OF

Cistercian monastery near Wohlau, Silesia, Diocese of Breslau. It was founded in 1150 as a Polish Benedictine monastery and was taken over by CISTERCIANS from PFORTA in 1163. In about 1175 the Romanesque church was consecrated. The Gothic monastery church and prince's chapel were constructed between 1300 and 1340; and the baroque renovation, distinguished by the magnificent paintings of Michael Willmann (d. 1706), dates from the period, 1695 to 1740, after the destruction of the monastery by the Swedes (1632). The harmony of its style and the grand scale on which it was built (it measured almost 800 feet across the front) make it a remarkable example of German BAROQUE. The hall of princes and the library with their magnificent paintings and stucco work are especially important. Leubus was a significant cultural center and as such contributed to the Germanization of Silesia. Several foundations were made from Leubus: Mogila near Cracow (1222), Heinrichau (1227), and Kamenz in Silesia (1239). The monks splendidly illuminated their manuscripts, antiphonals, graduals, and missals (13th and 14th century, now in the city library of Breslau) and influenced, to a great extent, the development of Silesian engraving. In 1810 the monastery was suppressed by King Frederick William III of Prussia and became a mental institution. Since 1945 the monastery and church (which were plundered) have stood empty.

Bibliography: Sources. J. G. BÜSCHING, *Die Urkunden des Klosters Leubus* (Breslau 1821). W. WATTENBACH, *Monumenta Lubensia* (Breslau 1861). Literature. F. HANUS, *Die ältere Geschichte der Zisterzienser-Abtei Leubus in Schlesien bis zur Mitte des 14. Jahrhunderts* (New York 1947). G. GRUNDMANN, *Schlesische Barockkirchen und Klöster* (Lindau 1958).

[A. SCHNEIDER]

LEUREN, PETER

Canonist; b. Cologne, Germany, May 13, 1646; d. Coblenz, Germany, Nov. 16, 1723. On April 13, 1633, he joined the Society of Jesus. He received his doctorate in theology at Treves, Germany (1679). He was named rector of the Jesuit College in Coblenz. The following are his principal works about Canon Law: *Forum beneficiale* (Cologne 1704), a complete study on the law of benefices; *Vicarius episcopalis* (Cologne 1708; Venice 1709),

a treatise on the practical problems of the vicar-general; and *Forum ecclesiasticum* (Mainz 1717; Augsburg 1720; Venice 1729; Augsburg 1757), a general presentation of Canon Law according to the teaching of ancient and modern authors.

Bibliography: J. FOLLIET, *Dictionnaire de droit canonique,* ed. R. NAZ, 7 v. (Paris 1935–65) 6:419. J. F. VON SCHULTE, *Die Geschichte der Quellen und der Literatur des kanonischen Rechts,* 3 v. in 4 pts. (Stuttgart 1875–80; repr. Graz 1956) 3.1:155–156.

[L. R. KOZLOWSKI]

LEUTFRED (LEUFROY), ST.

Founder of the abbey of La Croix–Saint–Ouen (later, La Croix–Saint–Leufroy) of Évreux; d. 738. Born of good parentage near Évreux, he studied at Chartres at the suggestion of St. OUEN. After a short teaching career, he suddenly left his family and went to live at the monastery of Cailly under the direction of a hermit. Finally, having gone to Rouen, he put himself under the direction of the Irish monk Sidonius, from whom he received the monastic habit. He became the friend of St. Ansbert. After returning to his own country, he ruled the house he had founded until his death. In 851 his relics were translated for the first time; later during the 9th century, when the monks had to flee the Normans, they carried the relics to the church of SAINT–GERMAIN–DES–PRÉS (PARIS). In 1222 they were again brought to the La Croix–Saint–Ouen.

Feast: June 21.

Bibliography: *Acta Sanctorum* June 5:91–100. *Monumenta Germaniae Historica: Scriptores rerum Merovingicarum* 7.1:1–18. M. COENS, *Analecta Bollandiana* 41(1923) 442–446. J. B. MESNEL, *Saint Leufray, abbé de la Croix,* fasc. 6 of *Les Saints du diocèse d'Évreux* (Évreux 1912–81). A. M. ZIMMERMANN, *Kalendarium Benedictinum: Die Heiligen und Seligen des Benediktinerordens und seiner Zweige* 2:343. J. L. BAUDOT and L. CHAUSSIN, *Vies des saints et des bienheureux selon l'ordre du calendrier avec l'historique des fêtes* 6:339–341. A. BUTLER, *The Lives of the Saints* 2:610.

[É. BROUETTE]

LE VACHER, JEAN

French missionary and consul, martyred in North Africa; b. Écouen, France, March 15, 1619; d. Algiers, July 28, 1683. After being ordained in the Congregation of the Mission in 1647, he was sent the same year by St. VINCENT DE PAUL as a missionary to the Christian slaves in Tunis. During his stay in North Africa, he was French consul in Tunis from 1648 to 1653 and from 1657 to 1666, becoming prefect apostolic of Tunis in 1648, vicar apostolic of Tunis in 1650, and vicar-general of Carthage in 1651.

After spending two years in France, he returned to Algiers in 1668 and was named vicar apostolic of Algiers, Tunis, Tripoli, and Morocco; in 1677, he became French consul in Algiers. His life of apostolic heroism in Africa terminated when a French force bombarded Algiers in 1683. Le Vacher refused firmly to renounce his faith and was bound to the mouth of a cannon, which was then fired. Beatification proceedings began on July 6, 1923.

Bibliography: L. MISERMONT, *Le Plus grand des premiers missionaires de saint Vincent de Paul* (Paris 1935). R. STREIT and J. DINDINGER, *Bibliotheca missionum* (Freiburg 1916–) 16:728–733, 924.

[M. A. ROCHE]

LEVADOUX, MICHAEL

Missionary; b. Clermont in Auvergne, France, April 1, 1746; d. Puy, France, Jan. 13, 1815. He entered the Society of Saint-Sulpice at Paris in 1774 and taught at the seminary in Limoges until 1791. When John CARROLL decided to establish the first American seminary in Baltimore, Md. (1791), under Sulpician direction, Levadoux sailed from Saint Malo with the first group of Sulpicians sent by their superior general, Jacques André Emery. As treasurer, Levadoux assisted in the administration of St. Mary's Seminary for one year. In June of 1792 Carroll assigned Levadoux to do missionary work in Illinois. For four years with the help of another Sulpician, Gabriel RICHARD, Levadoux ministered to the French settlements at Cahokia, Kaskaskia, and Prairie du Rocher. When the Catholic Church in Michigan became part of the Baltimore jurisdiction, Carroll transferred Levadoux to Detroit (1796) as pastor of St. Anne's parish. Ill health forced Levadoux to leave Detroit in the spring of 1802, and after a year's residence at St. Mary's in Baltimore, he returned to France.

Bibliography: G. W. PARÉ, *The Catholic Church in Detroit, 1701–1888* (Detroit 1951). P. K. GUILDAY, *The Life and Times of John Carroll,* 2 v. (New York 1927).

[T. O. WOOD]

LEVI BEN GERSON

Jewish philosopher, physician, and astronomer, known also as Ralbag, Gersonide, and Master Leo of Bagnols (Languedoc); b. Orange, France, 1288; d. 1344. He spent his life alternately in Orange, Perpignan, and Avignon, where the popes were residing. He is the most famous teacher of the philosophical school that followed the spirit initiated by MAIMONIDES, as well as the best among the Jewish writers of the fourteenth century. Although he had talent for the theological, natural, medical, astronomical, and speculative sciences, he became outstanding by virtue of his writings about religious philosophy and exegesis.

His first works are *The Book on Comparison* and *The Book of Numbers,* but his masterpiece has the title *Wars of the Lord,* which his detractors called *Wars Against the Lord* because of some slightly rationalistic tendencies in its author. Gerson's principal philosophical ideas reside particularly in this work. The subjects treated are numerous and diversified: the immortality of the soul, prophecy, God's omniscience, providence, the heavenly bodies, and creation. The book also contains a whole treatise on astronomy, the calculations and observations of which make him a precursor of Kepler.

Despite edifying reflections, Gerson's exegesis has a pronounced rationalistic flavor inasmuch as it does violence to biblical texts and Jewish beliefs in order to adapt them to Aristotelian philosophy. This is quite different from the procedure of St. Thomas Aquinas, who in the preceding century had adapted the same philosophy to Christian dogma. More precisely, Gerson was interested especially in reconciling religion and philosophy by proceeding, not with the hypotheses of Maimonides, but with an impartial and purely critical spirit cleansed of all religious prejudice. He anticipated Spinoza, who also would seek the truth for its own sake and outside of every historical consideration. "Our law," Gerson said, "is not despotic. It does not seek to make us accept error as though it were truth. It seeks especially to lead us to the knowledge of the truth." Going beyond the positions held by the Jewish philosophers who came before him, Gerson was the first to attack the dogma about creation ex nihilo by recognizing the existence of a primary matter that he deemed so formless as to make it equivalent to the "nothing" referred to in the cited dogma.

The success of his exegesis resulted not so much from his philosophical ideas as from the charm of his style and, even more so, from the reflections for moral practice he placed at the end of each chapter in the Bible. These reflections or *Toalioth* enjoyed great popularity and underwent many editions. Yet Gerson did not have great influence on Judaism, the orthodox members of which at times accused him of heresy. He had more success with Christian scholars, indeed, to the extent that Pope CLEMENT VI had him translate from Hebrew into Latin his treatise on astronomy and his study about the instrument he had invented.

See Also: JEWISH PHILOSOPHY; SCIENCE (IN THE MIDDLE AGES).

Bibliography: I. HUSIK, *A History of Medieval Jewish Philosophy* (New York 1959); *Encyclopaedia Judaica: Das Judentum in*

Geschichte und Gegenwart, 10 v. (Berlin 1928–34) 7:324–338. G. VAJDA, *Introduction à la pensée juive du moyen âge* (Paris 1947). J. CARO, *Kritische Untersuchungen zu Levi ben Gersons Widerlegung des aristotelischen Zeitbegriffes* (Würzburg 1935). E. L. EHRLICH, *Lexikon für Theologie und Kirche,* ed. J. HOFER and K. RAHNER, 10 v. (Freiburg 1957–65) 6:995.

[A. BRUNOT]

LEVIATHAN

Leviathan is a mythical sea monster of ancient folklore. Ancient tablets discovered at UGARIT in the 1930s have confirmed the mythical background of Leviathan, or *lôtān,* as he is known in these texts ("the coiled one," from the root *lwy,* to turn or twist). In these texts, where he is called the "fleeing serpent" and "coiled serpent," exactly as in Is 27.1 and Jb 26.13, he is pictured as a seven–headed, evidently serpentlike monster that is slaughtered by BAAL or his consort Anat [*see* J. B. Pritchard, *Ancient Near Eastern Texts Relating to the Old Testament* (Princeton 1955) 137, 138]. It is unfortunate that the nature and activity of the monster are not more prominent in the extant narratives, which, it may be noted, are not cosmogonic in nature.

According to the Old Testament [Ps 73(74).14] it is not Baal, but Yahweh, who crushed the many–headed Leviathan and fed him to the sharks. The context of the reference in this Psalm shows that here also Leviathan is pictured as a sea monster and seems to indicate that he was destroyed before the organization of the universe (v. 16–17). There is an allusion to the myth, though an obscure one, also in Jb 3.8. In Is 27.1 the apocalyptist, basing himself on Leviathan's double attribute ("fleeing serpent" and "coiled serpent"), seems to have made two monsters out of one and used them to symbolize unidentified political enemies that will be destroyed in eschatological times (cf. Rahab as a symbol of Egypt). In Jb 40.25–41.26 is found a lengthy description of Leviathan, the terrible monster of the deep. The author seems to have found his inspiration in the crocodile for most of the traits he attributes to Leviathan, but some of them he has drawn from his own imagination (e.g., 41.10–13). In this passage, as well an in Ps 103(104).26, Leviathan has been in large part "demythologized" and merely designates a marine animal, awesome to man, perhaps, but a plaything to Yahweh.

Bibliography: H. GUNKEL, *Schöpfung und Chaos in Urzeit und Endzeit* (2d ed. Göttingen 1921). O. KAISER, *Die mythische Bedeutung des Meeres in Ägypten, Ugarit, und Israel* (Berlin 1959). J. L. MCKENZIE, "A Note on Psalm 73(74):13–15," *Theological Studies* 11 (1950) 275–282.

[L. F. HARTMAN]

LEVIRATE MARRIAGE (IN THE BIBLE)

The term levirate marriage, from the Latin *levir* meaning husband's brother or brother-in-law, refers to marriage between a widow and her deceased husband's brother. If a married man died without a son, his brother was to marry the widow. The practice is reflected in three Old Testament texts: Gn 38.6–11, the Book of Ruth, and Dt 25.5–10.

The purpose of the law in Deuteronomy was to prevent loss of family property by the widow's marrying outside the clan. The law applied only to the case of brothers who had lived together and worked common property. The levirate marriage would insure issue to the deceased and pass the inheritance to the firstborn of the new union. Later, levirate law applied only if no child was born, since daughters could inherit (Nm 27.8; 36.6–7). If the brother-in-law refused to marry, his sister-in-law took off his sandal publicly and spat in his face because he refused to build up his brother's house (Dt 25.7–10). In Ruth, in default of a brother-in-law, other relatives had the duty of marrying the widow in order of nearness of kinship to her. Both widow and relative could refuse to marry in this case without disgrace (Ru 3.10; 3.13).

In Mt 22.23–28; Mk 12.18–23; Lk 20.27–33, the question put to Christ about a widow's marrying seven brothers reflects the levirate law. Though not found in the Code of Hammurabi, the custom was known also among the Assyrians and Hittites. Here death during engagement also brought the law into effect [J. B. Pritchard, *Ancient Near Eastern Texts relating to the Old Testament* (Princeton 1955) 182; 196].

Bibliography: P. CRUVEILHIER, "Le Lévirat chez les Hébreux et chez les Assyriens," *Revue biblique* 34 (Paris 1925) 524–546. M. BURROWS, "Levirate Marriage in Israel," *Journal of Biblical Literature* 59 (Boston 1940) 23–33. R. DE VAUX, *Ancient Israel, Its Life and Institutions,* tr. J. MCHUGH (New York 1961) 37–38.

[R. H. MCGRATH]

LEVITATION

The suspension of a material body in the air without any visible support, in apparent opposition to the law of gravity. There seems to be little doubt concerning the fact of levitation, but it has not been scientifically proved that this type of bodily suspension surpasses the psychophysical powers of nature. Levitation of human bodies or of inanimate objects has been reported in the lives of the saints, in cases of diabolical intervention, in spiritualistic seances, and in certain psychotic seizures. The three possible causes of levitation are God (directly or through the agency of angels), the devil (with God's permission), or some force or power of nature as yet unknown. Among the numerous canonized saints who experienced levitation, the following are the most renowned: SS. TERESA OF AVILA, JOSEPH OF CUPERTINO, CATHERINE OF SIENA, Philip NERI, Peter Alcántara, PAUL OF THE CROSS, JOHN BOSCO, Peter CLAVER, and Gemma GALGANI. Levitation is not admitted as one of the miracles required for the canonization of a saint, though it may be considered a testimony of a person's heroic sanctity.

Bibliography: J. MARÉCHAL, *Studies in the Psychology of the Mystics,* tr. A. THOROLD (London 1927). A. FARGES, *Mystical Phenomena Compared with Their Human and Diabolical Counterfeits,* tr. S. P. JACQUES (London 1926). J. G. ARINTERO, *The Mystical Evolution in the Development and Vitality of the Church,* tr. J. AUMANN, 2 v. (St. Louis 1949–51). A. ROYO, *The Theology of Christian Perfection,* tr. and ed. J. AUMANN (Dubuque 1962). H. THURSTON, *The Physical Phenomena of Mysticism,* ed. J. H. CREHAN (Chicago 1952). A. WIESINGER, *Occult Phenomena in the Light of Theology,* tr. B. BATTERSHAW (Westminster, Md. 1957).

[J. AUMANN]

LEVITES

Members of an Israelite tribe set aside for the service of the Lord. In the development of this institution over several centuries, there were many changes as evidenced by the divergent picture of the Levites in various Biblical traditions.

Origin of the Name. Many scholars agree that the word Levi (Heb. *lēwî*) was not a personal name but designated primarily a functional class, the sons of Levi (*benē lēwî*), with Levi probably only their quasi-fictitious eponymous ancestor. If the word is derived from the Hebrew root *lwh,* it could come from either of two meanings: (1) "to associate with, to be attached to," a meaning suggested by the word play at Levi's birth (Gn 29.34) and by the phrase, "they will be associated" (*weyillāwû*) with AARON, used in Nm 18.2, 4; or (2) "to be given over as a pledge, to be consecrated," a meaning found in Minaean inscriptions, from the root *lw',* used for persons consecrated to a divinity. Some scholars (e.g., R. De Vaux *Ancient Israel, Its Life and Institutions,* tr. J. McHugh (New York 1961) 358–359, 369–370), however, favor an origin in a personal name (perhaps a short form of Levi-El, attached to God), and Levite as primarily a *nomen gentilitium,* a descendent of Levi.

Early Secular History. The treacherous attack of Levi and Simeon on Shechem (Gn 34.1–31) and their later condemnation by Jacob (49.5–7) are seen by many as ancient tradition concerning these two tribes in central Palestine before the conquest under Joshua. According to this theory, elements of these tribes met with some disaster in the area of Shechem and were forced southward. Simeon eventually lost its identity within the tribe of Judah, while the tribe of Levi, after the sojourn in Egypt, won a new lease on life by assuming the priestly functions of all the tribes. That the tribe of Levi had a secular history can hardly be doubted, since Levi is included on an equal footing with the other tribes in ancient lists, e.g., Gn 46.8–27. It is also quite certain that Levite elements were in Egypt, for this tribe has many names of Egyptian origin, including that of MOSES. Although in Jacob's Oracles there is no mention of any priesthood in the oracle on Simeon and Levi (Gn 49.5–7), there is no reason to reject the Biblical connection between the secular and priestly tribe of Levi.

Levites as a Priestly Tribe. It is difficult to untangle the Biblical traditions of the Levitical priesthood. That the Levites were set aside for the service of the sanctuary at an early date is clear, but when this happened and how it was related to Aaron's priesthood are problems. As late as the early monarchy, the Levites did not have exclusive control of priestly functions, for non-Levitical priests existed, e.g., the son of the Ephraimite Micah (Jgs 17.5), the Ephraimite Samuel (1 Sm 1.1–20; 7.9), and David's sons (2 Sm 8.18). Micah, however, preferred a Levite priest when he was able to engage the services of one (Jgs 17.7–13).

Tradition ascribes the origin of the Levitical priesthood to Moses. Because of their part in carrying out the command of Moses to kill the idolaters of the golden calf, the Levites were "dedicated to the Lord" (Ex 32.27–29). In Moses' Oracles a relatively long oracle is given to Levi as the tribe that is entrusted with priestly functions: the use of the Urim and Thummim, the teaching of the law, and the offering of sacrifice (Dt 33.8–11). In both of these passages the Levites are detached from family ties. They are no longer a secular tribe to be counted with the others (Nm 1.47–49); they have no share in Israel (Dt 18.1–2). In Canaan they are allotted no territory (Jos 13.14, 33) but are given instead the Levitical cities (Nm 35.1–8; Jos 21).

Granted a preconquest Levitical priesthood, when did the distinction between priestly and nonpriestly Levites arise? It is still the common opinion that the Book of DEUTERONOMY insists on the same priestly rights for all the Levites. If there is any distinction, it is based on circumstances; the Levites at the central sanctuary function and receive their stipend (Dt 18.1–5), while those living elsewhere do not function, unless they visit the central shrine (18.6–8), and therefore depend on the charity of the people (14.27–29). Probably the Levites who were able to act as priests at the many local shrines after

Simeon and Levi Killing the Men of Hamor's City. (©Historical Picture Archive/CORBIS)

the conquest found themselves at a growing disadvantage: first by the official sanctuary at Jerusalem with its Zadokite clergy, and then by the centralization of cult under Ezekiel and Josiah. Later the distinction became not only a fact but also law.

Later Functions of Levites. In the idealized restoration of Ezekiel there are the priest sons of Zadok who serve the altar and the Levites who serve the Temple (Ez 44.10–31). The Pentateuchal PRIESTLY WRITERS make a clear division between Aaron and his sons, the priests, on the one hand, and the Levites ''given'' to serve Aaron, on the other (Nm 16.1–18.24). This division probably reflects the end of a long process: the final supremacy of the Aaronic claim over the Levites. The difference can be seen in Deuteronomy (Dt 10.8), where the Levites carry the ark, and in the priestly writers (Nm 4.15), where the Levites approach the ark only after it has been veiled by the priests.

With the return of the exiles under EZRA and NEHEMIAH, there are distinct families of priests, Levites, singers, doorkeepers, and Temple servants or oblates (Ezr 2.36–58); but it was not until later, in the additions to the work of the Biblical CHRONICLER, that the singers and doorkeepers were incorporated into the Levites and traced back to the three sons of Levi in rather artificial genealogies (1 Chr 6.18–22). The oblates, or Nathinim (Heb. *n^etînîm*, given), who were originally slaves or foreigners employed in the pre-exilic Temple, gradually disappeared after the Exile; and the Levites took over their function. The Levites had other important functions, acting as clerks, judges (1 Chr 23.4), and teachers (Neh 8.7–9; 2 Chr 17.8–9).

Bibliography: *Encyclopedic Dictionary of the Bible*, tr. and adap. by L. HARTMAN (New York 1963) 1326–30. R. DE VAUX, *Ancient Israel, Its Life and Institutions*, tr. J. MCHUGH (New York 1961) 358–371, 388–394, 544–545. G. HÖLSCHER, *Paulys Realenzyklopädie der klassischen Altertumswissenschaft*, ed. G. WISSOWA et al., 12.2 (1925) 2155–2208. A. LEFÈVRE, *Dictionnaire de la Bible* supplement, ed. L. PIROT et al. (Paris 1928–) 5:389–397. D. R. JONES, J. HASTINGS, and J. A. SELBIA, eds., *Dictionary of the Bible* (New York 1963) 793–797. H. H. ROWLEY, "Early Levite History and the Question of the Exodus," *Journal of Near Eastern Studies* 3 (1944) 73–78. G. E. WRIGHT, "The Levites in Deuteronomy," *Vetus Testamentum* 4 (1954) 325–330. J. A. EMERTON, "Priests and Levites in Deuteronomy," *ibid.* 12 (1962) 129–138.

[O. BUCHER]

LEVITICUS, BOOK OF

The third book of the Bible, called in Hebrew by its initial word *wayyiqrā'* (and he called), takes its English name from the Latin translation of the Greek title λευιτικόν (βιβλίον), "the Levitical book," because much of the book is concerned with the cultic duties of the Levitical priesthood. The division of the book, its origin and date of composition, and its contents are treated in this article.

Divisions. The book has five main divisions: sacrifice ritual (ch. 1–7), ordination ceremony (ch. 8–10), legal purity laws (ch. 11–15) with accompanying atonement ritual (ch. 16), Holiness Code (ch. 17–26), and redemption of offerings (ch. 27).

Origin and date. This book developed within the sacerdotal circles and is the major work of the priestly tradition (*see* PRIESTLY WRITERS, PENTATEUCHAL). Although profoundly influenced by the cultic directives of Moses, the Book of Leviticus has a protracted history of composition that precludes its being attributed to any single person. Many of its laws are very ancient; some of them were adapted from Canaanite practices during the early centuries of the Hebrew occupation of Palestine. Preserved mainly at local sanctuaries, these laws existed primitively in detached form or in small independent collections.

The more proximate history of the book dates from the final years of the Hebrew monarchy before the fall of Judah in 587 B.C. when the Holliness Code was edited by the clergy of Jerusalem (*see* HOLINESS, LAW OF). This important collection of earlier material exerted great influence on subsequent work of the priestly school, notably, the remainder of the Book of Leviticus and the Book of Ezekiel. The Book of Leviticus in its present form is post-exilic, i.e., after 538 B.C. and is concerned largely with the liturgy of the restored Temple. At that time the priestly authors re-edited the Holiness Code and added the ritual of sacrifice, rite of ordination, laws of legal purity, and the ceremonial for the Day of Atonement, with chapter 27 appended at a still later date. The literary setting of this legislation at the foot of Sinai, under the aegis of Moses, pointed to its ultimate source and spirit and gave the book its authoritative character.

Content. Chapters 1 to 7 delineate the various types of sacrifice: the HOLOCAUST, wherein the entire victim was burned on the altar; the cereal offering, frequently an adjunct to the animal offering; the PEACE OFFERING, divided into thanksgiving, VOTIVE, and free will offerings, wherein one part of the victim was completely burned and the other cooked and eaten by priest and offerer; the SIN and guilt offerings, made in expiation for sin, with part of the victim burned and the remainder either destroyed or consumed by the priests. In addition to outlining the ritual, these chapters underscore the rights and duties of priest and layman in sacrificial matters. [*See* SACRIFICE, III (IN ISRAEL).]

Although as a whole this book consists of laws and regulations, there are two small narratives, namely, the account of the ordination of AARON and his sons, and the death of Aaron's sons, Nadab and Abihu (ch. 8–10). The elaborate account of how Aaron and his sons were ordained is intended less as factual history than as a norm regulating the ordinations of priests. The untimely death of Aaron's two sons illustrates the seriousness of intermingling the SACRED AND THE PROFANE in acts of cult.

Legal purity, given extensive treatment in chapters 11 to 15, was strictly required of a people wholly dedicated to the Lord. Objective uncleanness, communicable to both persons and things, arose from eating certain animals or touching their dead bodies, childbirth, various skin diseases, sexual disturbances, and such corrupting elements as mildew or moss. These categories, often reflecting primitive taboos, underscored the necessity of unmarred integrity in every aspect of life. To remedy uncleanness, purification rites were demanded. (*See* PURE AND IMPURE.) Similar rites, applicable to the sinful uncleanness of the entire community, constituted the ceremony for the Day of Atonement (ch. 16). [*See* ATONEMENT, DAY OF (YOM KIPPUR).]

The Holiness Code (ch. 17–26), the original nucleus of the Book of Leviticus, stresses the importance of moral and legal sanctity in Israel as a reflection of Yahweh's own sacredness. The book's appendix, chapter 27, treats sacred vows and tithes and their accepted commutation.

Bibliography: H. CAZELLES, *Le Lévitique*, (Bible de Jérusalem 3; 1951); *Dictionnaire de la Bible*, suppl. ed. L. PIROT et al. (Paris 1928–) 5:497–530. M. NOTH, *Das Dritte Buch Mose* (Das Alte Testament Deutsch 6; Göttingen 1962). G. H. DAVIES, *Interpreter's Dictionary of the Bible*, 4 v. (New York 1962) 4:117–122. G. AUZOU, "Connaissance du Lévitique," *Cahiers Sioniens* 7 (1953) 291–319. R. DE VAUX, *Ancient Israel, Its Life and Institutions* (New York 1961) 439, 460–464, 507–510. A. S. HERBERT, *Worship in Ancient Israel* (Richmond 1959).

[R. J. FALEY]

The Offering of the Jews, taken from Leviticus 1 and 6, painting by the Master of the Gathering of Manna. (©Francis G. Mayer/ CORBIS)

LEWES, PRIORY OF

Former Benedictine monastery, in present-day Lewes, Sussex, England. Founded between 1078 and 1081 by William de Warenne, earl of Surrey, and his wife, Gundreda, it was the earliest Cluniac foundation in England. It was dedicated to St. Pancras. The original community, sent by St. HUGH OF CLUNY, consisted of three monks and a prior. By the terms of the foundation charter the prior was to be nominated by the abbot of CLUNY from among the three best monks in the house, precedence being given to the abbots of Cluny itself and of La CHARITÉ-SUR-LOIRE. The abbots of Cluny had few rights of oversight of Lewes and her dependencies, which came to number a dozen monasteries and cells. In 1351 Lewes bought a charter of denization from King Edward III to secure immunity from royal control; and in 1410 the abbot of Cluny appointed John Burgherst, prior of Lewes, vicar-general of all the Cluniac houses in England, a measure that caused resentment in those communities that had not been founded directly from Cluny. In 1480 Pope SIXTUS IV exempted Lewes from the jurisdiction of Cluny and placed it directly under the Holy See. The house was surrendered to King HENRY VIII on Nov. 11, 1537, and the church and monastery were demolished by Giovanni Portinari and his assistants between Feb. 16 and April 11, 1538. The lands were given to the Cromwell family.

Bibliography: R. GRAHAM, "The English Province of the Order of Cluny in the 15th Century," *Transactions of the Royal Historical Society*, 4th ser., 7 (1924) 98–130. *Victoria History of the County of Sussex*, ed. W. PAGE, v. 2 (London 1927). D. KNOWLES, *The Monastic Order in England, 943–1216* (2d ed. Cambridge, Eng. 1962) 151, 153, 154–158, 281–282. D. KNOWLES, *The Religious Orders in England* (Cambridge, Eng. 1948–60) 2:159–160, 167–168; 3:280, 285, 350, 384.

[B. HAMILTON]

LEWIS, CLIVE STAPLES

Literary historian, Christian apologist, scholar, critic, writer of science fiction and children's books; b. Belfast, Ireland, Nov. 29, 1898; d. the Kilns, Headington, England, Nov. 22, 1963. His father was Albert James Lewis, a solicitor; his mother Florence Augusta Hamilton. They had two sons, Warren and Clive, who at an early age changed his name to "Jack." Before he was 10 his mother died of cancer, and the two boys were on their own, being somewhat estranged from their father. In 1917 Lewis prepared for entrance into Oxford University but World War I found him commissioned as a second lieutenant in the Somerset Light Infantry. He arrived at the front line trenches on his 19th birthday Nov. 29, 1917, soon afterwards seeing service at Fampoux and Monchy, and was wounded at Mt. Bemechon, near Lillers, in April 1918.

He returned to Oxford in January 1919 and on June 25, 1925, was elected to official fellowship in Magdalen College as tutor in English Language and Literature. He remained at Oxford until 1954. Passed over for the Merton Chair of English Literature in 1947 and defeated in 1951 for the Professorship of Poetry, he finally accepted in 1954 the Professorship of Medieval and Renaissance Literature at Magdalene College in Cambridge. Soon after, Oxford awarded him an honorary fellowship.

In 1956 Lewis married Joy Gresham Davidman, who died in 1960 of bone cancer. Lewis described this most difficult experience in *A Grief Observed* (1961).

Prior to 1929 Lewis had considered himself an atheist or at least an agnostic, and had published two books of poetry in that vein, but his conversion to theism in 1929 and to Christianity in 1931 resulted in his first book on apologetics: *The Pilgrim's Regress* (1933). Using John Bunyan's classic as a model, Lewis enucleated one of his major themes: the idea of longing, disquietude, yearning, *Sehnsucht*, for the eternal which no earthly thing can satisfy since our hearts are restless for the Eternal. Following Saint AUGUSTINE, the PSEUDO-DIONYSIUS, and Pascal, Lewis asserts that earthly pleasures, being unsatisfactory, can only point to an everlasting heavenly pleasure. This theme is repeated in the *Chronicles of Narnia* (1950–56), a series of children's books treating traditional topics but translating them into an imaginary kingdom of people and animals. Aslan, the lion and king of beasts, represents a Christ figure.

Lewis's two most popular works are *The Screwtape Letters* (1942), a series of letters from the devil to his undersecretary in hell, Wormwood, on how to win a Christian from the fold, and *Mere Christianity* (1952), a summation of talks from the British Broadcasting Series that made Lewis famous during World War II.

Elsewhere, Lewis deals with the imperatives of the moral law, and in *The Abolition of Man* (1943) asserts that ethical commands (the Tao) are not merely written in the heart, but into the very structure of the universe itself. *The Great Divorce* (1945) records a series of conversations between various visitors from hell who are allowed to make an excursion to heaven, and for the most part decide not to remain there. *The Problem of Pain* (1940) contains some interesting analyses of evolution, primitive societies, animal pain, and the existence of hell. Various kinds of love (*The Four Loves* 1960), prayer (*Letters to Malcolm: Chiefly on Prayer* 1964), insights into the Psalms (*Reflections on the Psalms* 1958), and theological questions on sin and redemption arising on other planets not yet or about to be tempted (*Out of the Silent Planet* 1938; *Perelandra* 1943; and *That Hideous Strength* 1945), are just a few of the many topics which Lewis dealt with. Some consider his best work to be the novel *Till We Have Faces* (1956), a story of the soul based on the Greek legend of Psyche.

Lewis is widely remembered not so much for his scholarly expertise in medieval and Renaissance English literature (brilliantly demonstrated in the *Oxford History of English Literature* 1966), but for his popular writings in defense of traditional Christianity, and in this he is not infrequently compared to G. K. CHESTERTON and Hilaire Belloc. Quite orthodox in content but very original in style it is their direct "ad hominem" approach which has helped to make his books so lasting in their appeal.

Bibliography: H. CARPENTER, *The Inklings* (London 1978). M. J. CHRISTENSEN, *C. S. Lewis on Scripture* (Waco, Tex. 1979). J. R. CHRISTOPHER and J. K. OSTLING, *An Annotated Checklist of Writings About Him and His Works* (Kent, Ohio 1974). J. T. COMO, ed., *C. S. Lewis at the Breakfast Table and other Reminiscences* (New York 1979). C. DERRICK, *C. S. Lewis and the Church of Rome* (San Francisco 1981). W. GRIFFIN, *Clive Staples Lewis: A Dramatic Life* (San Francisco 1986). W. HOOPER, *Past Watchful Dragons: The Narnian Chronicles of C. S. Lewis* (New York 1979). C. C. KILBY, *The Christian World of C. S. Lewis* (Grand Rapids, Mich. 1964). G. MEILAENDER, *The Taste for the Other. The Social and Ethical Thought of C. S. Lewis* (Grand Rapids, Mich. 1978). R. L. PURTILL, *C. S. Lewis' Case for the Christian Faith* (New York 1981). C. WALSH, *C. S. Lewis: Apostle to the Skeptics* (New York 1949); *The Literary Legacy of C. S. Lewis* (New York 1979). W. L. WHITE, *The Image of Man in C. S. Lewis* (Nashville 1969). J. R. WILLIS, *Pleasures Forevermore. The Theology of C. S. Lewis* (Chicago 1983).

[J. R. WILLIS]

LEWIS, DAVID (CHARLES BAKER), ST.

Welsh martyr, b. Monmouthshire, 1617; d. Usk, Wales, Aug. 27, 1679. His father, Morgan Lewis, was a Protestant; his mother, Margaret Pritchard, a Catholic; David was the only one of his parents' nine children to be brought up a Protestant. He was educated at the Royal Grammar School, Abergavenny, and from the age of 16, at the Middle Temple. After three years there he went abroad as tutor to the son of Count Savage. At Paris he became a Catholic, then entered the English College, Rome, on Nov. 6, 1638. He was ordained in 1642 and became a Jesuit novice two years later. In 1646 he was sent to England, but shortly afterward was recalled to become confessor at the English College. In 1648 he left again for South Wales, where he worked until his death, "a zealous seeker after lost sheep . . . and so charitable to his indigent neighbors that he was commonly called the father of the poor."

He went about mostly at night and on foot. His headquarters were at Cwm, a small hamlet between Monmouth and Hereford; twice he was superior of this district. During the Oates persecution Cwm was sacked, and the library there taken to Hereford Cathedral, where it is now. Lewis hid at Llanfihangel Llantarnam. He was betrayed by Dorothy James, the wife of his apostate servant: she boasted that she would "wash her hands in Mr. Lewis' blood and have his head to make porridge of, as a sheep's head." On Sunday, Nov. 17, he was found in his refuge as he was about to say Mass. He was committed to Monmouth jail, and kept there until Jan. 13, 1679, when he was taken to Usk. He was tried at the March assizes at Monmouth, and condemned for his priesthood, chiefly on the evidence of James and his wife.

Before the sentence was carried out, he was made to ride to London with John KEMBLE, to be questioned on the OATES Plot by the Privy Council. On his return, he was executed on August 27, at Usk, close to the site of the present Catholic church. The official executioner refused to perform his task and fled; a convict, a bungling amateur, was bribed to take his place with a promise of freedom. When threatened with stoning by sympathetic onlookers, he too ran away, and a blacksmith was finally employed. On the scaffold Lewis made a stirring address in Welsh. He was buried in the Protestant churchyard at Usk, where his traditional grave, outside the west door of the church, is today a place of pilgrimage. He was beatified by Pius XI on Dec. 15, 1929, and canonized by Paul VI in 1970.

Feast: Aug. 27.

Bibliography: T. P. ELLIS, *Catholic Martyrs of Wales* (London 1933). H. FOLEY, ed., *Records of the English Province of the Society of Jesus*, 7 v. (London 1877–82) 5.2:912–931. A. BUTLER, *The Lives of the Saints*, rev. ed. H. THURSTON and D. ATTWATER (New York 1956) 3:424–426. J. GILLOW, *A Literary and Biographical History or Bibliographical Dictionary of the English Catholics from 1534 to the Present Time* (London–New York 1885–1902) 4:205–209. R. CHALLONER, *Memoirs of Missionary Priests*, ed. J. H. POLLEN (rev. ed. London 1924).

[G. FITZHERBERT]

LEWIS, EDWIN

Methodist theologian and pioneer in mediating the European neo-orthodox movement to America; b. Newbury, England, April 18, 1881; d. Morristown, N.J., Nov. 28, 1959. At age 19 he went to Newfoundland, Canada, and entered the ministry. In 1904 he moved to the United States, where he served pastorates in North Dakota, New Jersey, and New York. Lewis received his higher education at several schools; he earned his A.B. (1915) at New

York State College, Albany, and his Th.D. (1918) at Drew Theological Seminary, Madison, N.J. At Drew he was professor of systematic theology for 35 years. Lewis's first book, *Jesus Christ and the Human Quest* (1924), revealed him as an evangelical liberal. His *A Christian Manifesto* (1934) indicated a shift; he proclaimed the gospel as understandable only in terms of revelation, comprehensible only as an act of faith. His reorientation developed from intensive Bible study while coediting the *Abingdon Bible Commentary* combined with the influence of crisis theologians whom he both expounded and criticized. His persistent, basic sympathy with the concerns of liberals, however, prevents his being identified with radical NEO-ORTHODOXY. In retirement beginning in 1951, he lectured widely, wrote 60 articles for *Harpers' Bible Dictionary,* and completed his 12th and 13th books.

[R. STOODY]

LEWIS, FRANK J.

Businessman and philanthropist; b. Chicago, IL., April 9, 1867; d. there, Dec. 21, 1960. He was the son of William and Ellen (Ford) Lewis, Irish immigrants. Before he was 20 he had not only learned the roofing trade but had also organized a tar products company that eventually became one of the nation's leading producers of roofing and paving materials and of coal tar chemicals as well. Later he served as chairman of the board of directors of the Federal Reserve Bank of Chicago; he also held directorships in several large corporations. At 60, Lewis withdrew from active participation in the business world and dedicated the following 33 years to philanthropy and Catholic charities. He made substantial contributions, totaling millions of dollars, to the Catholic Church Extension Society; to the Lewis Memorial Maternity Hospital, Chicago; to St. Ambrose College, Davenport, Iowa; and to De Paul University and Loyola University, Chicago. Lewis College, in Lockport, IL., was named after him in 1934. His philosophy of life was expressed in his statement that "God gives a man money so that he will share it with others. Ownership of money is stewardship." He received many honorary degrees from colleges and universities and was honored by the papacy by being made a Knight of St. Gregory, a Knight Commander of St. Sylvester, a Knight Commander of the Order of Pius IX, and a Papal Count of the Holy Roman Empire.

[P. KINIERY]

LEXINGTON, DIOCESE OF

The diocese of Lexington (*Lexingtonensis*) was established Jan. 14, 1988, by Pope John Paul II. At its inception the diocese comprised fifty counties of central and eastern Kentucky that had formerly been part of the diocese of Covington and the archdiocese of Louisville. Eighty percent of the diocese is in the area of Kentucky designated by an act of Congress as "Appalachia."

The Most Reverend J. Kendrick Williams, a native of Athertonville, Kentucky, auxiliary bishop of the diocese of Covington, was installed March 2, 1988 as Lexington's first bishop, in the newly designated Cathedral of Christ the King. Bishop Williams took the lead in fostering good ecumenical relations. He served as an advisory committee member for the Bible Belt Study conducted by the Catholic University of America, as a member of the American Board of Catholic Missions, and as episcopal representative to the Southern Baptist/Roman Catholic Conversation and the Bishops' Committee for Ecumenical and Inter-religious Affairs.

The Lexington diocese with the support of the Extension Society and other agencies fosters a missionary outreach, especially in the mountains of eastern Kentucky, a region where historically Catholics are few and far between. The diocese supports a sizeable Catholic Center at the University of Kentucky in the see city and promotes the Newman apostolate in several other cities where there are colleges and universities. In 2000 the diocese had 59 parishes ministering to some 45,000 Catholics.

[M. K. SEIBERT/C. F. CREWS]

LEXINTON, STEPHEN DE

Cistercian reformer, abbot, founder of the Cistercian College at the University of Paris; b. Lexinton, Nottinghamshire, England, between 1190 and 1196; d. Ourscamp Abbey, Oise, France, March 21, 1260. He came from a distinguished family: his father, Richard of Lexinton, had three other sons, Robert, a judge (d. 1250), John, a royal clerk and keeper of the great seal (d. 1257), and Henry, Bishop of Lincoln (d. 1258). Stephen was intended for the Church and was sent to study in Paris and then in Oxford under EDMUND OF ABINGDON. In 1215 King John appointed him to a canonry in Southwell, Nottinghamshire, but in 1221 Stephen chose to become a CISTERCIAN monk at QUARR, Isle of Wight. In 1223 he was made abbot of Stanley Abbey in Wiltshire, and in 1227 he was sent to reform the Cistercian abbeys in Ireland. Finding them in a disgraceful state, he was forced to use the drastic remedy of suppressing the whole filiation of MELLIFONT, placing those abbeys under the visitation and supervision of a number of English houses, a system that lasted until 1274 when the filiation was restored. In 1229 he was appointed abbot of SAVIGNY, and in 1235 he played an important part in resolving the difficulties that had risen between the abbot of CÎTEAUX and the four abbots of CLAIRVAUX, LA FERTÉ, PONTIGNY, and MORIMOND. In 1241 he was summoned to Rome and narrowly escaped being captured with the other Cistercian abbots by Emperor FREDERICK II. When Abbot William of Clairvaux died in captivity, Stephen was elected to succeed him (1243). In 1245 he undertook his most controversial action, that of founding a Cistercian house of studies, the Collège St. Bernard, at the University of Paris. MATTHEW PARIS says that Stephen was deposed because of this action by the abbot of Cîteaux in 1256. Paris's statement has been challenged, but C. H. Lawrence has recently proven that there can be no doubt but that Stephen was actually deposed, and furthermore, that despite the strong support of Pope ALEXANDER IV, who ordered that he should be restored to office and thought of promoting him to an English archbishopric (probably York), he retired to Clairvaux's daughter house of Ourscamp, where he died. A register book of his early letters up to 1241 has survived and is printed in *Analecta Sacri Ordinis Cisterciensis* 2 (1946): 1–118; 8 (1952): 181–378.

Bibliography: A. B. EMDEN, *A Biographical Register of the University of Oxford to A.D. 1500,* 3 v. (1957–59) 2: 1140–1141. C. H. LAWRENCE, ''Stephen of Lexington and Cistercian University Studies in the Thirteenth Century,'' *The Journal of Ecclesiastical History* 11 (1960): 164–179.

[D. L. BETHELL]

LEZANA, JUAN BAUTISTA DE

Carmelite canonist, theologian, and historian; b. Madrid, Nov. 23, 1586; d. Rome, March 29, 1659. He made his profession of vows in Madrid in December of 1602. After studying philosophy at Toledo, he pursued his theological courses at houses of his order and at the Universities of Salamanca and Alcalá. He came under the influence of Michael de La FUENTE. Lezana lectured to Carmelite students on Aristotle and Aquinas, and took charge of studies for the order at Toledo. In 1625 he attended the general chapter in Rome, and he remained in that city the rest of his life. Again put in charge of studies, he lectured in theology at the Carmelite house of studies of Santa Maria in Traspontina. For 16 years he also taught metaphysics at the Roman Sapienza. He was made a consulter of the Congregation of the Index by URBAN VIII and a consulter of the Congregation of Rites by INNOCENT X. He refused a bishopric. In 1658 ALEXANDER VII appointed him procurator general of his order, and he held various titular provincialates besides acting as counselor to a number of priors general, a position for which he several times received some votes. Lezana was an ex-

emplary religious, dedicated to the observance of the common life, and very assiduous in prayer and study. An indefatigable writer, he published works on asceticism, Canon Law, Mariology (he was an apologist for the Immaculate Conception), theology, and history, besides works of translation. His writings have been influential, highly respected, and widely diffused. However, the first three volumes of his *Annales sacri, prophetici, et Eliani Ordinis Beat. Virginis Mariae de Monte Carmeli . . .* (4 v., Rome 1645–56) are concerned with the so-called history of the Carmelite Order up to the twelfth century, although the order was not founded until *c.* 1200. Nevertheless, these volumes are a witness of the seventeenth-century beliefs of the CARMELITES about their past. The fourth volume takes the history up to 1513 and contains some important documentation. An unfinished fifth volume supposedly preserved in the archives of the order in Rome cannot be traced.

Bibliography: C. DE VILLIERS, *Bibliotheca carmelitana,* ed. G. WESSELS, 2 v. in 1 (Rome 1927) 1:772–779. A. DE SAINT PAUL, *Dictionnaire de théologie catholique,* 15 v. (Paris 1903–50) 9.1:502–503. G. MESTERS, *Lexikon für Theologie und Kirche,* 10 v., ed. J. HOFER and K. RAHNER, (Freiburg 1957–65) 6:1002–1003. B. ZIMMERMAN, *The Catholic Encyclopedia,* 16 v. (New York 1907–14) 9:209.

[K. J. EGAN]

L'HÔPITAL (L'HOSPITAL), MICHEL DE

French statesman and advocate of religious toleration; b. Auvergne, near Aigueperse, 1507; d. Vignay, March 13, 1573. His father was a physician and served also as comptroller of accounts for Charles of Bourbon. His early education was at Toulouse until he was forced to flee France in 1523. For six years he studied law at Padua and then he joined his father in Rome, where he served as auditor of the rota. Upon his return to France in 1534, he practiced law, and he married in 1537. L'Hôpital was appointed counselor to the Parlement of Paris from 1537 to 1547. In 1547 HENRY II sent him to Bologna as his representative to the first session of the Council of Trent. L'Hôpital returned to France in 1548 and became chancellor to Princess Margaret, the king's sister. In 1553 he was appointed master of requests and in 1554 president of the *Chambre des Comptes*. In 1557 he became a member of the privy council. He reached the pinnacle of his career when, through the influence of CATHERINE DE MÉDICIS, he was appointed chancellor of France (1560). He served in this position during a period of religious strife in France over the rise of the HUGUENOTS.

Wars of Religion. In 1561 he appeared before a meeting of the States-General to appeal for greater toleration. The result was the enactment of the Edict of Orléans (1561) and the Edict of January of 1562, which granted improved conditions for the Huguenots. A massacre of Huguenots by soldiers of Francis, the Duke of Guise, took place in March of 1562. In protest, L'Hôpital withdrew to his estates at Vignay until the civil strife was ended through the Edict of Amboise (March 1563), which provided protection for the rights of the Huguenots. Upon his return to court L'Hôpital undertook to strengthen the government of Catherine de Médicis. At his bidding the royal council refused to publish the acts of the Council of Trent because of their conflict with the Gallican liberties of the French Church. He supported the position of the moderate Catholic party in opposition to the rightist Guise position. In 1566 he obtained the enactment of the Ordinance of Moulin, which provided for judiciary reform. No further reforms were possible since religious hostilities broke out again in 1567, and L'Hôpital's influence began to decline. Catherine de Médicis blamed him for policies of moderation that she had supported but that his critics believed responsible for increasing religious strife. As the second phase of the religious wars began, the criticism of his policies increased. The cardinal of Lorraine, the duke of Alva, and others accused him of supporting the Huguenots. In 1568 he was forced to resign his position as keeper of the seals as a result of papal pressure. In return, the papal Curia transferred control of certain Church property to the French government. Shortly thereafter L'Hôpital withdrew from public life, believing that his vacating of his position was essential for the peace of France, although technically he did not resign the chancellorship until forced to do so in February of 1573.

Late Life. L'Hôpital spent the last years of his life in seclusion at Vignay. Here he wrote poems and other short commentaries on his era. In 1570 he addressed to Charles IX a short memoir entitled *Le But de la guerre et de la paix, ou discours du chancelier l'Hospital pour exhorter Charles IX à donner la paix à ses sujets.* In 1585 a grandson published another of his works, entitled *Epistolarum seu sermonum libri sex.*

Although Michel de L'Hôpital was accused of heresy in his own time, he remained a practicing Catholic to the end of his life. His enemies criticized him for the policy of placing the welfare of France above the welfare of a single group. Catherine continued her support of this policy for many years after his death, despite the fact that it was responsible for his fall from power. He deplored the excesses of the Massacre of ST. BARTHOLOMEW'S DAY, which occurred less than a year before his death, and he so indicated in a letter to Charles IX.

Bibliography: *Oeuvres inédites de Michel l'Hospital,* ed. P. J. S. DUFÉY, 2 v. (Paris 1825). A. E. SHAW, *Michel de l'Hospital and his Policy* (London 1905). C. T. ATKINSON, *Michel de l'Hospital* (New York 1900). A. F. VILLEMAIN, *Vie du chancelier de l'Hôpital* (Paris 1874). J. HÉRITIER, *Michel de l'Hospital* (Paris 1943). A. C. KELLER, ''Michel de l'Hospital and the Edict of Toleration of 1562,'' *Bibliothèque d'humanisme et renaissance* 14 (1952): 301–310. A. BUISSON, *Michel de l'Hospital, 1507–1573* (Paris 1950), bibliog. J. LECLER, *Toleration and the Reformation,* tr. T. L. WESTOW, 2 v. (New York 1960). R. NÜRNBERGER, *Die Religion in Geschichte und Gegenwart,* 7 v. (3d ed. Tübingen 1957–) 4:341. S. SKALWEIT, *Lexikon für Theologie und Kirche,* ed. J. HOFER and K. RAHNER, 10 v. (Freiburg 1957–65) 6:1003.

[W. J. STEINER]

LIBELLATICI

Christians in possession of *libelli* or certificates stating that, particularly during the Decian persecution (251–253), they had offered or were willing to offer sacrifice in the prescribed fashion. Copies of the official certificates signed by an imperial commissioner have been discovered in Egypt, though they may have belonged to pagans for whom they posed no moral problem. The term was also applied earlier to requests for pardon (*libelli pacis*) given to the *lapsi* or fallen Christians by incarcerated confessors of the faith demanding that the bishop admit them to reconciliation. Tertullian mentions the practice of the martyrs' granting *libelli pacis* asking pardon for sinners (*Ad mart.* 1.6); but he later condemned their misuse (*De pud.* 22.1–2). The request was based on the notion that the martyrs' sufferings in themselves gave him power to forgive sins, and that the bishop had merely to take note of this fact (CYPRIAN, *Epist.* 21.3). Cyprian of Carthage strongly opposed this movement (*Epist.* 27.1–2) while admitting the value of the martyrs' intercessory prayers and sufferings to abbreviate the time of penance for the *lapsi,* particularly for those seeking reconciliation before death. The practice seems to have been known but early repudiated in Rome; it apparently spread from the Church in North Africa to Egypt and Asia Minor.

Bibliography: H. LECLERCQ, *Dictionnaire d'archéologie chrétienne et de liturgie* (Paris 1907–53) 9.1:78–79. A. D'ALÈS, *l'Édit de Calliste* (Paris 1914). B. POSCHMANN, *Paenitentia secunda* (Bonn 1940). L. FAULHABER, *Zeitschrift für katholische Theologie* 43 (Vienna 1919) 439–466, 617–657. E. BOURQUE, *Histoire de la pénitence-sacrament* (Quebec 1947) 88–92, 98–104. J. R. KNIPFING, ''Libelli of the Decian Persecution,'' *Harvard Theological Review* 16 (1923) 345–390.

[F. HAUSER]

LIBELLI MISSARUM

Leaflets or small booklets containing the prayer formularies (e.g., the collect and other presidential prayers, the preface to the Roman Canon, the introductory formula for the *Hanc igitur*, etc.) that were composed for specific Sundays or feast days. They are significant as the bridge marking the transition from the period of extemporized praying, and the collection and arrangement of presidential prayers into a SACRAMENTARY proper.

It appeared that North African synodal legislation encouraged the individual bishop to write down his formularies of liturgical prayer. During the course of the fifth and sixth centuries individual bishops began to gather together such collections, to which the name *Libelli Missarum* has been given. Some bishops had recourse to the Lateran Archives, which contained the *Libelli Missarum* of many of the popes. Now, from the time of Pope Damasus (366–384), Rome had enhanced the cult of the martyrs. However, such a cult was a strictly local one, the Mass of the martyr being said only in the place of his burial or his church. In the *tituli*, or parish churches, the Mass formularies used were exclusively of the type now in the Roman Missal for use on Sundays. During the pontificate of Leo the Great, the *tituli* began, for some reason unknown to us, to celebrate the feasts of the martyrs—and in the churches of the martyrs they began to make use of the Masses of the Temporal. It was at this time that the first Roman *Libelli Missarum* began to appear. It must be stressed that at this period (mid-fifth century) Rome possessed no Sacramentary for general use—neither during the pontificate of Leo I nor during that of Gelasius. There would have been no call for such a book, since each church had its own small collection of Mass formularies. H. Schmidt has suggested [''De Sacramentariis Romanis,'' *Gregorianum* 34 (1953) 729], and the idea is not without some probability, that Gelasius I gathered together a number of these *Libelli Missarum* and that this collection later formed the nucleus of the official Roman Sacramentary. A study of these prayer formularies is indispensable to an understanding of liturgical development in the Latin rite.

While individual examples of *libelli missarum* are no longer extant in most cases, a single-volume compilation of these *libelli* have survived, and is popularly, though incorrectly known as the LEONINE SACRAMENTARY.

Bibliography: C. VOGEL, *Medieval Liturgy: An Introduction to Sources* (Washington, D.C. 1986). E. PALAZZO, *A History of Liturgical Books: From the Beginning to the Thirteenth Century* (Collegeville, Minn. 1998).

[H. ASHWORTH/EDS.]

listed the various taxes, rates, and dues then owed to the Holy See throughout the Western world. It gave the dues owed by individual churches, monasteries, and others, diocese by diocese and province by province. Such lists were not new, but the *Liber censuum* by its thoroughness, well–ordered arrangement, and subsequent use is one of the outstanding documents of the financial history of the medieval papacy. It remained in use down to Eugene IV (1431–47).

A text of the original survives (MS Vat. lat. 8486), with some additions in the 13th century. Together with the list of dues, the manuscript contains five further pieces: (1) a list of exempt, i.e., papal, bishoprics and abbeys; (2) the *Liber de mirabilibus urbis Romae;* (3) an *Ordo Romanus;* (4) two lists of popes, one to Celestine III and the other to Eugene III; and (5) a cartulary of privileges and donations.

Various sources were used by Censius. There is some doubt as to the exact amount of direct or indirect use he made of the work of Cardinal BOSO, chamberlain to Adrian IV and Alexander III. One of his major sources was the *Gesta pauperis scholaris Albini* (Albinus, Cardinal Bishop of Albano, d. *c.* 1198). But there is no doubt that through these sources Censius took documents from the *Collectio canonum* of DEUSDEDIT (1083–86), the *Liber politicus* of Benedict Presbyter (1140–43), and the tax books of EUGENE III (1145–53) and ADRIAN IV (1154–59).

Certainly the *Liber censuum* was an achievement. But it is a misinterpretation of the facts to regard it as a record of financial success. Censius compiled it at a difficult time in papal financial history. It thus represents the determination of the Curia to keep alive its claims and to provide a basis for future action, especially toward overlordship in central Italy.

Bibliography: Text in P. FABRE and L. D. DUCHESNE, *Le Liber censuum de l'Église romaine,* 3 v. (Paris 1889–1910; v.3 ed. G. MOLLAT, 1952). W. E. LUNT, ed. and tr., *Papal Revenues in the Middle Ages,* 2 v. (New York 1934). H. LECLERCQ, *Dictionnaire d'archéologie chrétienne et de liturgie,* ed. F. CABROL, H. LECLERCQ, and H. I. MARROU, 15 v. (Paris 1907–53) 9: 180–220. M. MICHAUD, *Dictionnaire de droit canonique,* ed. R. NAZ, 7 v. (Paris 1935–65) 3:233–253. A. P. FRUTAZ, *Lexikon für Theologie und Kirche,* ed. J. HOFER and K. RAHNER, 10 v. (Freiburg 1957–65) 6:1012–13. V. PFAFF,''Der Liber censuum von 1192,'' *Vierteljahrschrift für Sozial–und Wirtschaftsgeschichte* 44 (1957) 78–96, 105–120, 220–242, 325–351.

[J. GILCHRIST]

LIBER CENSUUM

Liber censuum is a tax book compiled in 1192 by the papal chamberlain Censius, later Pope HONORIUS III. It

LIBER DE CAUSIS

The *Liber de causis,* ''a book concerning causes,'' is a comparatively short, anonymous, and basically Neoplatonic treatise that most likely was composed in Arabic, and greatly influenced all Western medieval Christian authors once GERARD OF CREMONA (d. 1187) had translated it into Latin at the end of the 12th century. ALAN OF LILLE (d. 1203) was the first Westerner to quote it, and his example was followed by WILLIAM OF AUXERRE, PHILIP THE CHANCELLOR, WILLIAM OF AUVERGNE, ALEXANDER OF HALES, ROLAND OF CREMONA, ALEXANDER NECKHAM, THOMAS OF YORK, BONAVENTURE, ROGER BACON, THOMAS AQUINAS, and ALBERT THE GREAT. Each of the last three wrote a commentary on it. The extent of its popularity is attested by the fact that approximately 150 manuscripts of the Latin text are still extant. The book consists of 32 general propositions, each of which is briefly explained. Modern editions of its Latin version run to little more than 25 pages.

Content. With one exception, to be noted later, the doctrine set down in it is typically Neoplatonic. For the author of the *Liber* as for PLOTINUS and other early Neoplatonists, the universe consists of four strata of reality, hierarchically arranged, within which all existents are located. At the top is God, the First Cause and the Primal One and True; at the bottom is the sensible universe; on the two intervening levels are souls and intelligences. Each stratum below God is subdivided hierarchically. The lowest is headed by heavenly bodies and Time, with material things filling in the lower ranks. On the next stratum the higher division is made up of intellectual souls, with the First Intellectual Soul occupying the lead position and the lower division being constituted by mere souls. On the third stratum divine intelligences make up the more perfect rank, which is headed by the First Divine Intelligence, and mere intelligences form the less perfect.

The relationships within hierarchies are always described by comparing what is higher to what is lower. The higher is joined to what is lower through a middle item, which is similar to each extreme. The higher knows the lower as its effect, while the lower knows the higher as its cause. The higher is in the lower, and the lower in the higher, each in its own way. In the case of an effect produced by both a higher and a lower cause, the higher has more influence than the lower because the higher causes the very causality of the lower, with the result that the efficacy of the Supreme Cause is prior to, present within, and remains after, the efficacy of all other causes. No matter what the basis of comparison may be, the higher is always better than the lower, with the highest completely transcending the order in question.

Such is the hierarchical and Neoplatonic universe described within the pages of the *Liber*—a complex structure whose four tiers are tightly fitted one upon another through mutual resemblance, knowledge, inexistence, and causal influence. The fact that the author espouses a doctrine of creation indicates that, apart from Neoplatonism, he was guided also by divine revelation (through either the Qur'ān or the Hebrew Scriptures). In some form or other the expression, ''to create,'' occurs approximately 45 times in the *Liber*. The common theme of those occurrences is that the First Principle of the universe is a creator, and that his creative casuality extends to absolutely everything—immediately to the First Intelligence and through this latter to all else: to the Soul, to all other eternal and self-subsistent entities, to all heavenly bodies and material things, and even to Time itself. For the author, creation is the bestowal of being upon all (*dare rebus omnibus ens*) as this paraphrase makes clear: ''Every cause makes a unique and characteristic contribution to its effects. Hence, First Being gives being to every being, First Life gives life to self-movers, First Intelligence gives knowledge to knowers. Let us say, then, that the First Being is the cause of causes and, if it confers being on absolutely everything, it does so by creation. On the other hand, First Life confers life on its subsequents not through creation but only after the manner of a form'' [Prop. 18 (ed. Steele) 175].

To create, then, means to bestow being, to cause something to be that before was not. If this interpretation is correct, the author has an accurate notion of creation, and this accuracy indicates that the impact of divine revelation upon him has been strong enough to break through an otherwise rigid Neoplatonism.

Authorship. Although scholars commonly agree that Gerard of Cremona is its Latin translator, the authorship of the *Liber* is still open to question. Until at least the middle of the 13th century the treatise was attributed to Aristotle; in fact, it was at times titled *Liber Aristotelis de expositione bonitatis purae,* and was included among Aristotle's works in the official syllabus of the University of Paris as late as 1255. St. Thomas Aquinas first challenged this attribution shortly after 1268, when he read William of Moerbeke's Latin translation of Proclus's *Elements of Theology* and realized that the ultimate source of the *Liber* was PROCLUS. Aquinas concluded that its author was some Arabian philosopher who was acquainted with Proclus's treatise.

Most modern exegetes attributed it either to ALFARABI (d. *c.* 950), or to David the Jew (ibn Daoud), who worked with DOMINIC GUNDISALVI in Toledo, Spain, translating Arabic and Greek treatises into Latin during the second half of the 12th century. From extrinsic evidence and from the nature and content of the *Liber* itself; this much seems clear: (1) its author was a Semite; (2) he certainly lived before the 13th century and probably as early as the 9th century; (3) he derived his knowledge of creation from divine revelation; and (4) the rest of his theory is Neoplatonic, derived from Arabic versions, certainly of Proclus's *Elements of Theology* and probably of parts of Plotinus's *Enneads.*

See Also: NEOPLATONISM; ARABIAN PHILOSOPHY; SCHOLASTICISM.

Bibliography: O. BARDENHEWER, *Die pseudo-aristotelische Schrift über das reine Gute, bekannt unter dem Namen ''Liber de Causis''* (Freiburg 1882), Arabic text, together with a German translation, plus an edition of Gerard of Cremona's Latin translation. ''Liber de Causis,'' an edition of Gerard of Cremona's Latin tr. in R. BACON, *Opera hactenus inedita,* ed. R. STEELE, fac. 12 (Oxford 1935) 161–87. L. SWEENEY, ''Research Difficulties in the *Liber de Causis,''* *The Modern Schoolman* 36 (1959) 108–15; ''Doctrine of Creation in *Liber de Causis,''* *An Etienne Gilson Tribute,* ed. C. J. O'NEIL (Milwaukee 1959) 274–89. G. C. ANAWATI, ''Prolégomènes à une nouvelle édition du *De Causis* arabe,'' *Mélanges Louis Massignon,* 3 v. (Damascus 1956–57) 1:73–110. H. D. SAFFREY, *Sancti Thomae de Aquino super librum de causis expositio* (Fribourg 1954). M. ALONSO, *Temas filosoficos medievales* (Comillas 1959).

[L. SWEENEY]

LIBER DIURNUS ROMANORUM PONTIFICUM

A book of formulas of the Roman Curia, among the most controversial of medieval sources. The time and place of origin of its three authentic manuscript copies, as well as their subsequent whereabouts throughout the centuries, are as uncertain as are the order and development of its texts. Both the name of the book and its official status have been disputed. However, the latter is now clear. Exact dates and statements concerning places and persons establish beyond doubt the fact that the manuscripts could never have gone back to a private collector remote from Rome. Those objections to the official character of the book that arise from the inclusion of apparently spurious sections ''pertaining to bishops or cloisters'' are not strong in their proof. For with regard to the difficult misinterpreted formulas, the point in question is always what place to assign them with assurance in a papal chancery. That Rome has no further trace of the original official book is understandable, because of the use of papyrus which is subject to deterioration; and considering other losses from archives, it is not surprising.

Manuscripts. The only three copies of this unique source under consideration today are the Roman Vatican Codex V, the Ambrosius A of Milan, and the Cleromontanus C. The last mentioned, formerly preserved at the Jesuit Collège de Clermont in Paris, is now in the care of

the Benedictine Abbey Egmond-Binnen in Holland. V and C belong to the 9th century, whereas A probably first appeared at the beginning of the 10th century. All three copies provide series of different discontinuous sections independent of one another. The numerous former links with an original in the papal chancery office are no longer established.

The writers of these three manuscripts could not possibly have been officials in the papal chancery office. Numerous primitive misspellings, some of them awkward corrections of misinterpreted letter formations or anxious copyings of them, prove that the script of the three manuscripts was not wholly familiar to the copyists. Besides, there is uncertain handling of the word ''ill,'' which is usually employed in a language in many different ways. In addition, there is a lack of familiarity with the commonly occurring abbreviations used in chanceries, and some of the misinterpretations of these are even grotesque. Misunderstood elements of dates, inaccurate forms of Greek tags, mistaken titles of spiritual and worldly hierarchies, and various things prove emphatically that the scribes of the three manuscripts were not officials in the papal chancery. None of the three manuscripts is an example of usage customary in the papal chancery, whereas all three go back to such a manuscript.

In addition to the three fragmentary codices there, are 11 fragments in the canonical Collection of DEUSDEDIT: 2:109–112; 3:145–150; 4:427. Their originals are close to the handwritings of C and A, the stronger similarity being with that of C. The residence of the exarch at Ravenna, the archbishop of that city, papal officials and apocrisiary no longer play a role in these fragments. The German emperor is the addressee; the *dilectissimi fratres domini episcopi* could only have been German bishops. Further changes in materials and in form likewise show that it could have been only the papal chancery that had so lively an interest in the reorganization of the formulas in contrast to the versions of V, A, and C. This new version goes back to the new ordering of political circumstances through the *renovatio imperii* of Otto I.

The real *Liber diurnus* was considered a flexible, changeable work capable of being amended and expanded, a document which, through continual adaptation, would apply to changing conditions and thus remain practicable.

Editions. The widely traveled Lucas Holstenius (1596–1661), a convert from Hamburg, gave to Rome a first edition of the *Liber diurnus* in handwriting V. As a result of the work of opposing forces, it did not have any significant effect. A second one, brought to Paris in 1680 by John Garnier, SJ, based on Codex C, was consigned to a hardly better fate. Even the edition of Rozière (Paris

1869), also based on V, was affected by the delayed aftermath of the great ecclesiastical political disputes that had been so disadvantageous to the earlier ones. Sickel's edition likewise depends on Codex V, which he thought was the only one available; but in addition it depends on the earlier editions of Codex C, which had been lost in the meantime. The existence of A was completely unknown to Sickel at the time of the appearance of his edition.

The many differences of opinion that sentiment and emotion have stirred up in regard to the *Liber diurnus* are not yet entirely settled, not even by the combined edition of H. Foerster containing all three handwritings and the fragments of Deusdedit's collection. This edition has separate printings of the four components of textual transmission and deliberately abandons the constructing of a text that would be valid once and for all, because there has never been only one of the *Liber diurnus*.

Bibliography: *Liber Diurnus,* ed. H. FOERSTER (Bern 1958). A. M. STICKLER, *Historia iuris canonici latini* (Turin 1950) 1:66. A. VAN HOVE, *Commentarium Lovaniense in Codicem iuris canonici I* (2d ed. Mechlin 1945) 1:190–192.

[H. FOERSTER]

Folio of a 12th-century Liber pontificalis with the biography of Leo IV. In the lower margin is a note relative to the fictional Popess Joan.

LIBER PONTIFICALIS

Liber pontificalis (LP) is the name used since the eighteenth century for a work that was titled in the Middle Ages *Gesta Pontificum Romanorum.* The work is a series of career sketches of varying length of the popes. The accounts are not strictly biographical because they rarely contain any information about their subject's prepontifical careers. There is a certain regularity in the information provided for each pope: paternal ancestry, electoral details, major ecclesiastical initiatives, liturgical innovations or reforms, diplomatic engagements, (sometimes) construction and donation records, length of pontificate, and number of ordinations performed. The lives were almost certainly written in the papal administration; some scholars arguing for the *scrinium* and some for the vestiary. Many manuscripts of the LP are preceded by an apocryphal exchange of correspondence between St. Jerome and Pope Damasus. Thus the earliest portion of the work was erroneously attributed to Damasus in the Middle Ages. In the sixteenth century, the LP was attributed to Anastasius Bibliothecarius who may have written some of the mid-ninth century lives. The early papal lives were recorded in several different sources such as the *Catalogus Liberianus* and the *Chronographer of 354.* The LP was prepared in stages beginning under Boniface II (530–532) when the whole series down to Felix IV (526–530) was complied. In the time of Pope Conon (686–687) a second redaction was prepared. From the early eighth century until the death of Leo III (816), the lives were written shortly after each pontificate, but they were usually begun during the pope's reign. Across the ninth century the lives were compiled sporadically. The series then broke off until it was resumed in the time of Gregory VII and carried on in several stages until the end of the twelfth century. Thereafter there were sometimes multiple lives of particular popes and occasional compilations of such lives down to 1479 when Platina prepared the last medieval version of the whole text. Useful and interesting for all periods, the LP is, alongside the papal correspondence, the critical source for papal history between 500 and 900.

Bibliography: L. DUCHESNE, *Le Liber Pontificalis,* 2 v. (Paris 1886-92), v. 3 ed. C. VOGEL (Paris 1957). U. PŘEROVSKÝ, "Liber pontificalis nella recensione di Pietro Guglielmo OSB, e del card. Pandolfo," *Studia Gratiana,* 21-23 (Rome 1978). O. BERTOLINI, "Il 'Liber Pontificalis,'" in *La storiografia altomedievale, Settimane di studio del centro italiano di studi sull'alto medioevo* 17 (1970) 387–455. H. GEERTMAN, *More Veterum* (Groningen 1975). T. F. X. NOBLE, "A New Look at the Liber Pontificalis," *Archivum Historiae Pontificiae* 23 (1985) 347–58.

[T. F. X. NOBLE]

LIBER SEXTUS

The first authentic collection of Church legislation after that of Gregory IX (1234). It was commissioned by Pope Boniface VIII in 1296 and promulgated on March 3, 1298, embracing some 64 years of papal and conciliar legislation. Although the constitutions of the Councils of Lyons (1245, 1274) were in circulation, and some popes had made collections of their own constitutions (e.g., Innocent IV in 1246, 1251, and 1253, and Gregory X when promulgating the 1274 Council of Lyons), there was some uncertainty about the force of much of the papal legislation after 1234. Upon Boniface's election in 1294, the University of Bologna, among others, petitioned its former alumnus (1260–64) to look into the question.

Selecting three seasoned canonists (William Mandagout, Archbishop of Embrun; Bérenger FRÉDOL, Bishop of Béziers; and Richard Petronio, vice-chancellor of the papacy), Boniface gave them a free hand. The new collection, completed within two years, was named *Liber Sextus* (Sext) and, like the decretals of Gregory IX, was divided into five books, with titles and chapters. Of the 15 popes between 1234 and 1294, however, only six were represented (Gregory IX, Innocent IV, Alexander IV, Urban IV, Clement IV, and Nicholas III), being allowed some 108 chapters, while Boniface's own legislation occupied 251 chapters; to a total of 359 chapters some 88 *regulae iuris,* or rules of interpretation of law, were added, mainly from Roman law. The many papal constitutions denied a place were thereby declared null and void for the future; others of a transitory nature were not given in full but noted simply as *reservatae.* Although Boniface accepted all but one of 41 chapters of the third collection of Innocent IV (1253), he recast other decretals, at times retaining only the central idea; on occasion he also modified conciliar decrees, composing, for example, the constitution *Cum ex eo* (Sext 1.6.34) in mitigation of *Licet canon* of Lyons (Sext 1.6.14). It is, indeed, significant that the constitutions of Boniface included in the Sext were written in great part for that compilation. What he intended was, in effect, a codification rather than a collection; in fact any papal decree admitted to the Sext was now universally binding, irrespective of its original scope. Boniface was not simply adding to the decretals but rather, as he put it when explaining his choice of title, advancing Gregory's five books to the state of perfection proper to the number six. Many glosses on the Sext were written, notably by Joannes Monachus (1301) and JOANNES ANDREAE (*c.* 1301), that of the latter becoming *ordinaria.* The Sext was printed many times and is part of the official *CORPUS IURIS CANONICI* of 1582.

Bibliography: L. E. BOYLE, "The Constitution *Cum ex eo* of Pope Boniface VIII," *Medieval Studies* 24 (1962) 263–302. G. LE BRAS, "Boniface VIII: Symphoniste et modérateur," in *Mélanges d'histoire du Moyen Age, dédiés à la memoire de Louis Halphen* (Paris 1951) 383–394. E. GÖLLER, "Zur Geschichte des zweiten Lyoner Konzils und das Liber Sextus," *Römische Quartalschrift für christliche Altertumskunde und für Kirchengeschichte* 10.2 (1906) 81–87.

[L. E. BOYLE]

LIBERAL ARTS

A name given in late Roman times to disciplines that were considered preparatory studies for PHILOSOPHY; they were usually counted seven in number and were grouped as the trivium (grammar, rhetoric, and logic) and the quadrivium (arithmetic, geometry, music, and astronomy). In 20th-century usage, the term has become more general and less precise.

The historical development of the liberal arts tradition, and of its underlying philosophy, is best sketched in terms of its origins in Greek thought, its passage to the West its medieval conception as analyzed by St. Thomas Aquinas, and, finally, its decline in the modern period.

Origins in Greek Thought. From the 8th century B.C., Greek education was based on gymnastics and "music." This latter, eventually called "grammar," included the study of literature and music. These literary studies were expanded during the 5th century by the study of RHETORIC, introduced by the SOPHISTS as they sought to prepare free citizens who could speak in the public assemblies. The Sophist Protagoras about 400 B.C. introduced as a companion to rhetoric the art of debating called eristics, or DIALECTICS, said to have originated with the philosopher ZENO OF ELEA (*c.* 450).

About the same time another Sophist, Hippias of Elis (*see* Plato, *Protagoras* 315C), insisted on the value for public speakers of a broad education in all the arts, including the four mathematical disciplines of arithmetic, geometry, music, and astronomy developed by the Pythagorean philosophers of the previous century.

These seven arts, along with others mentioned from time to time, were called the ἐγκύκλιος παιδεία (general education). This educational practice was explained theoretically in various ways by different schools of philosophy. Thus Isocrates, a leading rhetorician of the 4th century, defends them in his *Antidosis* and *Panathenaicus* as the best preparation of a citizen, since a citizen must lead others by the art of persuasion (rhetoric) and this art requires a broad education.

This sophistic position was vigorously opposed by SOCRATES and PLATO. The latter (especially in *Republic* bk. 7 and *Laws* bk. 7) minimizes the value of both poetry and rhetoric, which lead only to opinion, and emphasizes the importance of mathematics as the first step into the realm of science. Such arts are only a preparation for true wisdom, or philosophy, which Plato believed was to be pursued by dialectics, but which was grasped by intuitive wisdom beyond any method.

Aristotle also opposed the Sophists but did not assign to mathematics the same educational significance as Plato. Instead, he gave the fundamental role to LOGIC, a discipline that he himself developed and distinguished from grammar, rhetoric, and dialectics; the latter are methods of probable reasoning, whereas logic is a method of analysis whereby strictly scientific knowledge can be certified.

Other Greek philosophers tended to minimize the value of the liberal arts. This was true of the skeptics, as seen in the attack on these arts by Sextus Empiricus in his *Adversus Mathematicos* of the 2d century A.D. (*see* SKEPTICISM). It was true The Epicureans reduced logic to their *Canonic*, which was more an epistemological defense of sense knowledge than a true logic. The Stoics, on the other hand, did make important contributions both to grammar and to logic, and it is in the writings of Martianus Capella, a Latin of Stoic tendencies (5th century A.D.), that the traditional list of the seven arts and the term *artes liberales* first appear. Martianus apparently derived his list from that of the Roman encyclopedist Varro (1st century B.C.), which, however, also included architecture and medicine. Yet the Stoics generally took the view expressed by SENECA: "You see why liberal studies are so called: it is because they are worthy of freeborn men. But there is only one really liberal study—that which gives man his liberty. It is the study of wisdom; and that is lofty, brave and great souled. All other studies are puny and puerile" (*Epist.* 88).

Passage to the West. Such studies continued as a matter of course in Byzantine Christianity and were passed on eventually to Islamic education; here there was no marked development except for some advances in mathematics by Arabian writers. In Western Christianity their good repute was established by St. AUGUSTINE, himself a former teacher of rhetoric, who insisted on the importance of these studies as a preparation for the Christian study of the Sacred Scriptures. He began but did not finish an encyclopedia of the arts. From the works *De ordine* and *De musica* it is clear that his conception of these disciplines was essentially Platonic: the order that is found in language, music, and mathematics is a reflection of the perfect order that exists in God. The beginner is led by this sensible reflection of God toward a true vision of Him. For St. Augustine, as a Christian, in this life the vision is possessed only by faith in God's Word.

The detailed transmission of the Greek achievement in these arts came to the West not through Augustine but through BOETHIUS, who attempted, and in part succeeded, in translating into Latin the fundamental Greek works of Aristotle and Euclid. During the Dark Ages these translations, along with various much-abbreviated manuals of the arts, formed the preparation for the study of the Scriptures in the monastic schools (see the *Institutiones* of CASSIODORUS and the *Etymologiae* of St. ISIDORE OF SEVILLE). With ALCUIN and the Carolingian renaissance some real development of these arts began to take place, but it was only in the 12th-century renaissance, with ABELARD and the writers of the School of Chartres, that notable progress was made. The most important works of this period are the *Didascalion* of HUGH OF SAINT-VICTOR and the *Metalogicon* of JOHN OF SALISBURY, both of which, however, still remained within the Augustinian framework.

In the new universities of the 13th century the study of the arts leading to the master of arts degree was the basic faculty that prepared students to go on to law, medicine, or theology or constituted a terminal education. The Augustinian and Platonic view was long dominant and found its finest expression in the *De reductione artium ad theologiam* of St. BONAVENTURE. The introduction of the full Aristotelian corpus, however, gave to the Middle Ages a new conception of philosophy as something distinct from the liberal arts and intermediate between them and the study of theology. It is this view that is found in St. ALBERT THE GREAT, St. Thomas Aquinas, and the later Aristotelian scholastics.

Thomistic Analysis. In his commentary on the *De Trinitate* of Boethius, St. THOMAS AQUINAS attempted to harmonize the complex tradition outlined above and to explain it along Aristotelian lines. Occasional remarks in other works and especially in his commentary on Aristotle's *Posterior Analytics* fill out this theory.

Status as Arts. According to Aquinas the liberal arts are arts only in an analogical sense. [*See* ART (PHILOSOPHY).] An art in the strict sense is *recta ratio factibilium*, i.e., good judgment about making something, where "making" means the production of a physical work. Such a definition applies only to the servile arts; it does not apply to the liberal arts, since these make nothing physical but only a certain "work in the mind," an arrangement of ideas—although, of course, these ideas may be externally expressed by physical symbols. They are called "liberal" precisely because they pertain to the contemplative (speculative) rather than to the active or productive life of man. Many of them, if not all, are true sciences as well as arts because they not only produce a mental work but demonstrate the truth value of this work.

As liberal arts, however, they are not studied for their own truth content but as instruments of other sciences.

Conception of Logic. The clearest example of such a speculative art is logic, which does not deal with any real object but purely with the mental order the mind produces within itself by forming mental relations between one object of thought and another. As Aristotle had seen, however, logic is not a single discipline but a group of related disciplines: (1) demonstrative logic, which analyzes scientific arguments of the strictest type (DEMONSTRATION), wherein the factual evidence is sufficent to yield CERTITUDE; (2) dialectical logic, which analyzes less rigorous types of reasoning such as those involved in discussion, debate, and scientific research, and where only PROBABILITY and OPINION can be obtained; (3) rhetoric, which is similar to dialectics but which also takes into consideration the interests and motives of a particular audience, and which aims at persuasion to action rather than at scientific conviction; and (4) POETICS, which also deals only with probabilities conveyed through stories imitative of human life, whose purpose is the quieting of human passions through the delight felt in contemplating the beautiful. The first two of these logics are instruments for the sciences; the last two, since they deal more with the passions and imagination, are valuable for expressing the truths attained by science or by experience in a way that is ethically effective or pleasing. Although in some respects a very difficult study, logic in its entirety should be taught before the other sciences as the instrument necessary to their perfect functioning.

Grammar, according to Aquinas, is only an auxiliary to these arts and deals with the external expression of thought by verbal symbols. What were later called the fine arts are for him similar to the liberal arts in that they resemble poetics, although they use nonverbal symbols. Those that are purely compositive (the composing of literature or of music) he classified as liberal arts in the strict sense. Those that involve the external execution of a work (such as acting, playing a musical instrument, and the plastic arts) he considered servile disciplines, although the works they produce are liberal in function.

Mathematics. Mathematics, in Aquinas's view, is a science of reality, not merely of mental being. Hence it is markedly distinct from logic; it is deserving of the name of philosophy since it gives insight into the nature of being. Nevertheless, the object with which it deals is abstract QUANTITY; quantity in itself has little dignity because it is a mere accident of things and because it is understood in abstraction rather than in its existence. For this reason mathematics is least among the purely scientific studies. As an instrument, however, it is of great importance for two reasons: (1) since its factual content is slight and its logical rigor great, it is the ideal exemplification of demonstrative logic for the young student whose factual knowledge is limited but who must master the difficult art of demonstrative logic; (2) because it deals with quantities abstracted from their concrete conditions, it is very useful in the natural sciences, which require a study of the quantitative properties of things. Can mathematics then be called a liberal art? Yes, for although it does not make its object (which is real quantity), it does know this object by mental construction, since it studies ideal quantities constructed in the imagination by processes of measurement or counting.

Instruments of Higher Sciences. All these arts are instruments for the higher sciences, which differ from logic in that they deal with real objects, and from mathematics in that they deal with realities considered in their existent condition and not ideally. These real sciences are enumerated by Aquinas as natural science, the moral sciences, and theology, the last of which is divided into natural theology, or metaphysics, and sacred theology. [*See* SCIENCE (SCIENTIA); SCIENCES, CLASSIFICATION OF.]

Decline in the Modern Period. This ideal of a liberal arts education was never actually realized in the medieval universities, where logic and dialectics tended to dominate to the neglect of the other arts. In the 14th century, NOMINALISM brought this logicism to its ultimate extreme. In strong reaction to this, the Renaissance humanists under the influence of Quintilian and Cicero returned to the emphasis on grammar and rhetoric; they thus developed the so-called "traditional classic education," which dominated lower education but did not succeed in destroying Aristotle in the universities. This movement culminated in the work of Rudolphus Agricola and Peter RAMUS, who attempted to replace Aristotelian logic by a new dialectic, which was actually a pedagogical rhetoric, a tool by which received knowledge could be organized simply for memorization.

The really major change began with advances in mathematics in the 16th and 17th centuries, culminating with the proposal of René DESCARTES to adopt the mathematical deductive method as the universal method of all knowledge. This approach, because of its Platonic tendency, came into sharp conflict with the remains of the Aristotelian inductive tradition as proposed by thinkers such as Francis BACON. A kind of reconciliation was effected by Isaac Newton in the form of what has come to be called the "scientific method," wherein a deductive mathematical theory is grounded in observation and experiment.

Such a method, however, proved not very suitable in the "humanities"—the fine arts, philosophy, theology, history, morals, and politics. As a result, as Jacob Klein has pointed out, a second method, the "historical method," was evolved. Having its roots in the development of critical historiography during the religious controversies of the post-Reformation period, this method was developed by philosophers in the romantic and idealistic traditions such as G. VICO, G. W. F. HEGEL, W. DILTHEY, and R. G. Collingwood (1889–1943). Vico emphasized the logic of historical evidence, but added to this the interpretation of the data by a dialectic based on the power of human sympathy; through this dialectic, man is able to see the events of history as an evolution and expression of his own inner tendencies as a man, in contrast to the impersonal and objective approach of the "scientific method." Later this opposition of method was to be reflected in Western culture as a deep division between those trained in science and those trained in the humanities, between an objective and a subjective point of view, and between the two dominant philosophical tendencies, POSITIVISM and EXISTENTIALISM.

Bibliography: P. H. CONWAY and B. M. ASHLEY, *The Liberal Arts in St. Thomas Aquinas* (Washington 1959). P. ABELSON, *The Seven Liberal Arts* (New York 1906). H. I. MARROU, *Saint Augustin et la fin de la culture antique* (Paris 1958); *A History of Education in Antiquity*, tr. G. LAMB (New York 1956). R. P. MCKEON, "Rhetoric in the Middle Ages," *Speculum* 17 (1942) 1–32. W. J. ONG, *Ramus: Method and the Decay of Dialogue* (Cambridge, MA 1958). R. M. MARTIN, *Dictionnaire d'histoire et de géographie ecclésiastiques*, ed. A. BAUDRILLART et al. (Paris 1912—) 4: 827–843. J. KOCH, ed., *Artes liberales: Von der antiken Bildung zur Wissenschaft des Mittelalters* (Leiden 1959).

[B. M. ASHLEY]

LIBERAL CATHOLIC CHURCH

A group or groups within a movement known as "Independent Catholicism." It has roots in the Dutch Old Catholicism and has some theological affinities with Roman Catholicism, such as the meaning of sacraments, but with serious departures both in its theology, ecclesiology, and pastoral practice. In the U.S., there is a Liberal Catholic Church (LCC) that is a regional body within the larger international communion and claims legal title to the name in the United States. There is also a group that splintered from this body in 1947, yet is resident in only America. The latter is called the Liberal Catholic Church International, yet its members simply refer to their church as the LCC. Both entities describe themselves as the Liberal Catholic Church or the Liberal Catholic Church in the Province of the United States and both claim "official" status as the true church. Both the LCC (the international body) and the LCCI (the American body) have similarities and differences, but the critical distinction lies in the succession of bishops. In 2001, Dean Bekken was the presiding bishop of the LCCI with a headquarters

in San Diego, California; James P. Roberts, Jr., was the LCCI regionary bishop in the Province of the United States (New York). In that same year, Ian Richard Hooker was the presiding bishop of the LCC with a headquarters in London, England; Bishop William Downey was the regionary bishop of the LCC in the Province of the United States (Ojai, California).

Both members of the Liberal Catholic movement use the same basic liturgy and both have an open communion table. Both churches acknowledge the laity's freedom of belief. Both churches accept married and celibate clergy. Both churches will remarry the divorced. Neither church ordains women. However, the LCC requires its clergy to accept the basic tenets of theosophy (reincarnation, karma, ascended masters, etc.) as well as Catholic Christianity; the LCCI requires only that its clergy accept the basic tenets of Catholic Christianity (the Holy Trinity, a real Eucharistic presence, etc.). The LCC does not permit its clergy to receive a salary for their religious work. The LCCI permits a salary if a parish is financially able.

History. On April 28, 1908, Arnold Harris Mathew (1852–1919), a former Roman Catholic priest, was consecrated as the Old Catholic Bishop for Great Britain and Ireland (*see* OLD CATHOLICS). By 1915, the movement to convert the English to the Old Catholics of Utrecht was failing. On Dec. 31, 1915, Bishop Mathew left to rejoin the Roman Catholic Church and Bishop Frederick Samuel Willoughby soon followed, but not before consecrating James Ingall Wedgwood a bishop. Theosophists of the Old Catholic Mission in Great Britain rallied behind Wedgwood of the famous tableware china family. In 1916, Wedgwood consecrated a kindred spirit in the noted theosophist Charles Webster Leadbeater regionary bishop of Australasia. Within a year's time, Wedgwood and Leadbeater had compiled the liturgy for the church, which on Sept. 6, 1918, was renamed Liberal Catholic.

In 1917 Wedgwood established the church in the United States. Its growth led him to create (1919) the American province under Bishop I. S. Cooper, who by 1924 had built a procathedral in Los Angeles, California. Cooper was consecrated in July 1919 by Wedgwood and Leadbetter. The St. Alban Theological Seminary was established in America in 1923. It is the LCCI's official seminary, and instructs its seminarians worldwide through distance learning from its base in San Diego, California. It is not an accredited institution, nor does it claim to grant educational degrees. There is also a St. Alban's Press that publishes tracts by its theologian-bishops. Adherents of the LCC are estimated to be around 8,000 worldwide; for the LCCI adherents number approximately 5,000.

In 1947 a controversy arose over what appeared to be a jurisdictional dispute between the American clergy and the then presiding bishop, F. W. Pigott of London, England. As part of the dispute, Bishop Pigott "suspended" the regionary bishop, Charles Hampton, and all the clergy supporting him. A cleft between the U.S. regionary and the presiding bishop resulted in litigation over the control of the church. The result was that Bishop Edward M. Matthews was awarded control of church property as well as the name, though the LCC's international governing body, the General Episcopal Synod, did not acknowledge his authority. While he later reconciled with the LCC, control of the American body fell into the hands of Dean Bekken, whom Matthews ordained a priest, and under whose direction the group came to be known as the LCCI. The schism continues to the present day. The effects of this fracturing have been to surface many scores of claimants to the title of "bishop" for an equal number of "churches."

Belief System. Holding that there are diverse paths to truth, the LCCI does not proselytize. The LCC on the other hand is expansionist and has established itself on every continent. Both groups affirm an apostolic succession through Old Catholicism. Both churches permit laity absolute interpretive license, seeking its members' fellowship in their willingness to worship corporately through a common ritual. While no creedal adherence is demanded from its members, some core teachings resonate with other Christian communities. Among these teachings are a doctrine of the Trinity, creation, Christology (including incarnation, death, resurrection, and ascension), the seven sacraments, and that the church is the mystical Body of Christ. The LCCI also teaches that human beings are all immortal, both before and after physical death, and bodies are vehicles or expressions of human consciousness wherein the Spirit dwells. It does not teach reincarnation.

In the ministry for both groups, minor orders (cleric, doorkeeper, reader, exorcist, and acolyte) are intended primarily to assist the candidate in his own spiritual growth and life. Major orders (deacon, priest, and bishop) are intended primarily to assist the Christian community. Subdeacon is an intermediate stage. The hierarchy comprises regionary bishops over provinces; suffragans over dioceses; and auxiliaries, with various duties; they are all chosen by the general episcopal synod that also selects the presiding bishop. Presiding bishops for the LCC have been J. I. Wedgwood (1916–23), C. W. Leadbeater (1923–34), F. W. Pigott (1934–56), A. G. Vreede (1956–64), Sir H. Sykes (1964–1973), S. H. P. von Krusenstierna (1973–84), E. S. Taylor (1984–93), and J. C. van Alphen (1993–2000). The LCCI claims apostolic succession up through the presidency of Bishop Pigott and then Bishops R. M. Wardell, E. M. Matthews, F. Erwin, W. H. Daw, J. Neth, and since September, 1979,

D. Bekken. The LCCI publishes *Community*, a thrice-yearly journal of news, articles, book reviews and poetry relating to spirituality and religion. The LCC publishes *The Liberal Catholic.*

[E. E. BEAUREGARD/P. J. HAYES]

LIBERALISM, RELIGIOUS

Religious liberalism is a naturalist manifestation, an effort at emancipation from supernatural demands, especially those of a dogmatic kind. It found followers in all positive religions (including Christianity, Judaism, Buddhism, and Islam), but it became widespread only in the 19th and 20th centuries. The phenomenon consists of an opposition between the NATURAL and the SUPERNATURAL; it stems from a desire to establish new relations between the two. In some cases, it endeavors to redefine the supernatural. When this rational ideal reaches its logical consequences, after being generated and developed in a subjective and individualistic manner, its manifestations are very diverse and seemingly contradictory. These include emancipation of the laity in the fervor of their rational adherence to the Church and their apostolic action (Catholic Liberalism); ecclesiastical liberalism; indifferentism; the rationalism of positivism; the subjectivism of fideism; the social engagement of the disciples of traditionalism; the sentimentality of the supporters of modernism.

Origins. Antiquity knew a degree of skepticism concerning Greek and Roman religions. In the early Christian Era, some individuals displayed a parallel tendency. During the medieval period, some laymen, such as the Ghibellines, on the borders of theocracy, affirmed a desire to emancipate themselves in political matters. Ecclesiastical liberalism appeared in the thought of MARSILIUS OF PADUA and others.

Contemporary religious liberalism, especially in western Europe, traces its origins more markedly to the RENAISSANCE. If the Renaissance did not reject the supernatural, it nevertheless produced, in men like MACHIAVELLI, a naturalistic mode of thought and action. Although focused especially on secular areas, it did not neglect religious phenomena, as the lives of ERASMUS and St. Thomas MORE demonstrate.

The Reformation, at the convergence of the preceding currents, developed religious liberalism and strengthened its fabric. By proclaiming the primacy of individual conscience and promoting adherence to an invisible church, LUTHER clearly opened the way to free examination, even in religious matters. This remains true even though Luther's ardent faith seemed to correct what was overnaturalistic in his rationality and overinstinctive in his sentimentality. The individual conscience, which Luther extolled and believed to be moved by the Holy Spirit, did away with the guarantees that dogma, ecclesiastical discipline, and rites might otherwise supply.

Precise delineation of religious liberalism had to await the 18th-century ENLIGHTENMENT, with its strivings for liberty. The philosophy of the Enlightenment, which considered reason the noblest manifestation of human dignity, culminated in the Declaration of the Rights of Man (*See* ENLIGHTENMENT, PHILOSOPHY OF). Its champions had already expressed a desire for liberty. Political circumstances would lead to an even clearer emphasis that human dignity is found in liberty above all. Subjectivist German philosophies, such as that of Immanuel Kant, served to solidify this conviction.

All these currents merged in Hugues Félicité de LAMENNAIS. This publicist sought to establish harmony between God and liberty and thereby to adapt the Church to the contemporary world. His latent rationalism and subjectivism, however, favored the development of all types of religious liberalism. Although he engaged directly in Liberal Catholicism, he did not fail to influence the rationalistic tendencies of 19th-century liberalism. Liberal Catholicism, considered as a new humanism in thought and action, had very close affiliations with Modernism.

POSITIVISM led equally in the same direction. By endeavoring to impose knowledge at the behest of the external object, it approached Kantian subjectivism, which appeared to make knowledge something internal, something which emerged from itself.

Types. These diverse origins resulted in a great variety of forms of religious liberalism, some orthodox, some heterodox.

Liberal Catholicism can be classed among the former. Despite the encyclical *Mirari vos* (1832) of Gregory XVI, and other Roman decisions, some of its adepts consciously or unconsciously accepted modern liberties for themselves, so much so that their adversaries regarded them as heretics. The great majority, however, simply wished to help modernize the Church by this approach. They strongly favored emancipation of the laity in political affairs. This was generally true in France and Belgium; also in Italy, at least during certain periods of the Risorgimento. Some, like DÖLLINGER in Germany and Lord John ACTON in England, advocated autonomy for the laity in doctrinal matters.

Ecclesiastical liberalism, which was displayed especially in Belgium (1840) and Switzerland (1846), reproduced a tendency manifest at the Synod of Pistoia (1786), and partially realized in the CIVIL CONSTITUTION OF THE CLERGY (1792). It sought to introduce democracy into the ecclesiastical hierarchy by having candidates for the episcopacy elected, thereby compromising the rights of the Holy See in the nomination of bishops.

TRADITIONALISM, as advocated by Lamennais was an expression of religious liberalism in the doctrinal domain. It ended by regarding the Church and its teachings not as divine in origin but as one stage in historical evolution.

In its attempt to resolve more precisely the problem of faith, religious liberalism found expression in the theories of HERMES, who considered the act of faith a naturalistic expression of reason and the heart.

Religious liberalism appeared elsewhere in the tendencies of FIDEISM, which, in the manner of ROSMINI-SERBATI, GIOBERTI, and other disciples of ONTOLOGISM, sought to follow the ideas of PLATONISM and discover in faith an intuition, a purely supernatural manifestation inspired by a subjectivism disengaged from rational imperatives.

The subjectivism latent in fideism, and the relativism expressed in traditionalism led to INDIFFERENTISM, which equated, more or less precisely, doctrines of the most diverse, even contradictory, kind, provided they were based on sincerity, the source of certitude and merit.

Enamored with modernity, some tried with more or less good will to impart to dogmas a "historical dimension" and a progressive development. In this class were MÖHLER and others of the Tübingen school.

Others, such as Anton GÜNTHER, turned for inspiration to metaphysics, and derived an explanation of the Trinity and the Incarnation based on reason alone. STRAUSS, RENAN, and others who were devoted to scriptural studies, applied to them positivistic and rationalistic methods and interpreted the sacred books of the Bible as the expression of myths or as merely human language.

Marc SANGNIER and others in France and Italy bore the banner of liberalism into the social domain, where they fought in the name of liberty for the political emancipation and predominance of the working class.

Certain Catholics in the U.S. advanced simultaneously into the terrain of doctrine and of action under the standard of liberty, and engaged in what they termed AMERICANISM. They admitted the activity of the Holy Spirit in souls, but in an individualistic, Lutheran manner. Seeking a new formula of Christian HUMANISM, they attributed to the natural virtues an apostolic efficacy and fecundity superior to that of the supernatural virtues. Active virtues seemed to them better suited to modern times than the passive virtues they conceived to be generally taught in the Gospels.

These types of religious liberalism merged in Modernism, a more precise expression of RATIONALISM. Over and above the reasoning intelligence, it admitted a sort of intuitive and sentimental knowledge which provoked the act of faith. This act, produced more or less by divine grace, was not understood as adherence to a dogma imposed from without, but as the acceptance of a religious truth due to immanent, rational, sentimental, or pragmatic factors. Dogma would, therefore, be described as the effusion of a thinking and emotive soul, and subject, even in its content, to evolution and variation. Modernism penetrated the moral and Biblical sciences, and spread to several countries, notably France, Italy, England, and Germany.

Rationalist tendencies in religious liberalism were equally evident in the thought of Louis SABATIER, Paul SABATIER, and other representatives of Protestant liberalism (*see* LIBERALISM, THEOLOGICAL). They were at work also in liberal Judaism and ZIONISM. After abandoning faith in the divinity of Christ or the Mosaic Law, these intellectual directions moved into AGNOSTICISM.

Papal Condemnations. The Holy See condemned some types of religious liberalism. Its political tendencies were reprobated by Pius IX (*QUANTA CURA*, SYLLABUS OF ERRORS, 1864), and GREGORY XVI (*Mirari vos*, 1832). The latter Pope likewise attacked its rationalistic and fideistic inclinations (*Dum acerbissimas*, 1835), and its ecclesiastical ones (*Quo graviora*, 1833). Leo XIII opposed its activism (*TESTEM BENEVOLENTIAE*, 1899). Its Modernist trends merited from Pius X the severest condemnations of all (*LAMENTABILI* and *PASCENDI*, 1907). Although the protagonists of these movements often protested that Rome did not enunciate their teachings exactly in its condemnations, the Holy See had discovered in all of them an essentially naturalist and rationalist tendency.

Bibliography: C. CONSTANTIN, *Dictionnaire de théologie catholique*, ed. A. VACANT et al., (Paris 1903–50; Tables générales 1951–) 9.1:506–629. R. AUBERT, "L'Enseignement du magistère ecclésiastique au XIXᵉ siècle sur le liberalisme," *Tolérance et communauté humaine* (Tournai 1952) 75–105; *Le Problème de l'acte de foi* (3d ed. Louvain 1958); *Le Pontificat de Pie IX* (Fliche-Martin 21; 2d ed. 1964). J. LEFLON, *La Crise révolutionnaire, 1789–1846* (*ibid.* 20; 1949). W. NIGG, *Geschichte des religiösen liberalismus* (Zurich 1937). H. HAAG, *Les Origines du catholicisme libéral en Belgique, 1789–1839* (Louvain 1950). G. MARTINA, *Il liberalismo cattolico ed il Sillabo* (Rome 1959). A. SIMON, *Rencontres mennaisiennes en Belgique* (Brussels 1963); *L'Hypothèse libérale en Belgique* (Wetteren 1956). É. POULAT, *Histoire, dogme, et critique dans la crise moderniste* (Tournai 1962). P. POUPARD, *Un Essai de philosophie chrétienne au XIXᵉ siècle: L'Abbé Louis Bautain* (Paris 1962). P. SCOPPOLA, *Crisi modernista e rinnovamento cattolico in Italia* (Bologna 1961). J. RIVIÈRE, *Le Modernisme dans l'Église* (Paris 1929); *Dictionnaire de théologie catholique*, ed. A. VACANT et al., (Paris 1903–50; Tables générales 1951–) 10.2:2010–47. H.

J. SCHOEPS, *Israel und Christenheit* (Munich 1961). C. BAUER, *Staatslexikon*, ed. Görres-Gesellschaft (Freiburg 1957–63) 5:370–380. E. DEUERLEIN, *Lexikon für Theologie und Kirche*, ed. J. HOFER and K. RAHNER (Freiburg 1957–65); suppl., *Das Zweite Vatikanishe Konsil: Dokumente und Kommentare*, ed. H. S. BRECHTER et al. (1966) 6:1007–10.

[A. SIMON]

LIBERALISM, THEOLOGICAL

Protestant Christianity was dominated in the 19th and early 20th centuries by liberal theology. This article describes briefly the setting into which it was born, the factors of its coming to be, and its species, insofar as they can be distinguished. In conclusion, it distills out of this description the elements common to the movement.

Setting. In the early 19th century Protestant scholasticism, for a long time on the wane, was in utter disrepute. This was due in great measure to the ascendancy of DEISM and RATIONALISM, but also to the appearance of REVIVALISM, a movement that rejected the dry speculation of the scholastics, but that by the same token did not really meet the problems raised by the champions of the ENLIGHTENMENT. Also on the scene, of course, was the Kantian synthesis, wherein God and immortality were viewed as postulates of moral experience.

Factors. If theological liberalism be viewed, in the first place, as an attempt to conciliate these conflicting forces, it is just to accord F. SCHLEIERMACHER the title Father of Liberal Theology. In fact, his first published work was a sort of apologia for religion, addressed to the adherents of the rationalist school. Schleiermacher's idea about religion, moreover, became the leitmotiv for the entire liberal movement. In *Der christliche Glaube* he articulated these ideas with more precision, indicating that the essence of religion (common to all religions) is the feeling or immediate consciousness of being absolutely dependent upon God, and that the various religions (including Christianity) are peculiar modifications of this feeling. For Christians the attitude of Jesus in this regard is exemplary; and religious beliefs, doctrines, or dogmas are born from reflection on this affective sensibility.

Higher criticism of the Bible was another important factor in the formation of the liberal movement. The so-called *Leben-Jesu-Forschung* was carried on throughout the 19th century (*see* JESUS CHRIST, BIOGRAPHICAL STUDIES OF); and it is present too in contemporary Protestant exegesis. In general the critics of the earlier period abandoned the notion that the Bible is an infallible record of divine revelation; but their outlook concerning the meaning of the Gospel accounts of the life of Jesus varied with the numerous philosophical standpoints open to the liberal school. From a purely rationalist starting point, H. E. G. Paulus did away with everything supernatural in the Bible. D. F. STRAUSS was more under the influence of HEGEL'S IDEALISM; and to him is owed the introduction of the category of "myth" into the Biblical question. [*See* MYTH AND MYTHOLOGY (IN THE BIBLE).] Strauss's French counterpart, E. RENAN, reduced everything supernatural in the Gospels to legend. Another group of German liberal critics attempted, on similar bases, a psychologically oriented description of the historical "personality" of Jesus; and for them He was simply the herald of MESSIANISM, a profound thinker, and the founder, here and now, of the KINGDOM OF GOD (*see* ESCHATOLOGISM).

The contribution of A. RITSCHL to the genesis of the liberal movement is not to be discounted. The main thesis of his theology of moral values is that the gospel is suspended on an ellipse between two foci: JUSTIFICATION and Redemption [*see* REDEMPTION (IN THE BIBLE)], on the one hand (the redemptive work of Christ), and on the other the kingdom of God (the fellowship of redeemed persons). Ritschl also insisted that a genuine understanding of the love of God demands a reevaluation of the doctrine of ORIGINAL SIN—meaning of course an affirmation of the integrity of human nature. These views are characteristically assimilated into liberalism in all its forms.

The dialectic between religion and science is a final factor in the birth of theological liberalism. Among Protestants the notions of DARWIN were applied widely in fields other than that of biology, with the effect of reinforcing the following notions: (1) that God is immanent in the world (*see* IMMANENCE); (2) that Redemption consists in a gradual transformation of man from the state of the brute to a condition of obedient sonship to God; (3) that the relation of the Christian religion to other religions is to be understood in evolutionary terms.

The substance of these tendencies was epitomized in the thought of A. von HARNACK, in whom theological liberalism found its strongest protagonist. In his *Das Wesen des Christentums* Von Harnack made the core of Christianity to consist in the personality and teaching of Jesus. This teaching, moreover, he conceived as susceptible of being summarized in three simple statements: (1) The kingdom of God is coming. (2) God is our Father and thus the value of the human soul is infinite. (3) Christian life consists in perfect righteousness and the fulfillment of the commandment of love. Von Harnack saw that even in primitive Christianity this pure gospel tended to be cast into the alloy of Hellenistic Christianity—the Pauline synthesis. His program, of course, was a return to primitive simplicity, wherein ecclesiastical structures would give way to the real gospel. The contact of Von Harnack with certain figures in the Modernist crisis is well known.

Species. Though it is difficult to categorize so many different currents of thought, theological liberalism seems to be specified by two main emphases. The first of these consists in an assimilation of the theological view of the Enlightenment, which reduced the doctrines of faith to religious and moral principles capable of being discovered and understood by unaided human reason. In this category one may locate the greater number of liberal theologians whose main endeavor was the *Leben-Jesu-Forschung*. Such a view is implicit even in the thought of Schleiermacher, who, however, introduced a notion that became very dear to the liberals: feeling or sentiment as the starting point of religion, from which doctrines might be derived.

The other species of theological liberalism harks back to the Hegelian-inspired theory of the Christian religion's being the fulfillment and crown of the progress of the human spirit. Those who followed this bent make up the so-called *Religionsgeschichtliche Schule*, e.g., D. F. Strauss, A. E. Biedermann, F. C. BAUR (the last named was distinguished also by his debates with the Catholic theologian of Tübingen, J. A. Möhler). They set forth the doctrine of immanence in terms that constitute a denial of the distinction between the natural and the supernatural. In the same vein knowledge of God communicated through Jesus Christ is considered to be quite excellent, but no different in kind from any other knowledge of divine reality.

Common Elements. Throughout the gamut of theological liberalism the same themes occur: a certain confusion of revelation and human reason; the reduction of DOGMA to the philosophy of religion (*see* RELIGION, PHILOSOPHY OF); and the identification of the development of the DEPOSIT OF FAITH with the speculative unfolding of man's self-consciousness. Certain corollaries of these basic principles also appear frequently: a radical distinction between the "Jesus of history" and the "Christ of the creeds"; maximum optimism concerning the status of man in relation to God, with an attenuated doctrine of sin and its effects. And throughout the entire system the constantly recurring note is the exaltation of the faith experience as the ultimate authority in matters of religion.

Bibliography: J. DILLENBERGER and C. WELCH, *Protestant Christianity Interpreted Through Its Development* (New York 1958). A. VON HARNACK, *What Is Christianity*, tr. T. B. SAUNDERS (2d ed. New York 1903). W. LOHFF, *Lexikon für Theologie und Kirche*, ed. J. HOFER and K. RAHNER (Freiburg 1957–65) 6:1005–07. F. MUSSNER, *ibid.* 6:859–864. J. H. NEWMAN, *An Essay in Aid of a Grammar of Assent*, ed. C. F. HARROLD (New York 1947; Image Bk. 1955). F. SCHLEIERMACHER, *The Christian Faith*, ed. H. R. MACKINTOSH and J. S. STEWART (Edinburgh 1928; 2 v. 1963). D. E. ROBERTS and H. P. VAN DUSEN, eds., *Liberal Theology* (New York 1942).

[M. B. SCHEPERS]

LIBERALITY, VIRTUE OF

Liberality is the virtue disposing a person to the observance of a reasonable mean between the opposite extremes of prodigality and stinginess in making expenditures intended for the benefit of others. Although liberality is the virtue that regulates and controls the appetite for external goods, the desire and use of these goods to the benefit of others enters prominently into its concept, and indeed constitutes its principal concern. Generally speaking, men are sufficiently disposed by nature to seek and use such goods to their own pleasure and advantage, and so need no virtue to equip them for this. Moreover, what they spend upon themselves is often spent in the exchange of one kind of possession for another and thus involves no real outlay. What a man needs to be strengthened to is a readiness to use these goods to the benefit of others besides himself. Liberality differs from justice because what is given is not strictly owed; from mercy, because it is not evoked by the need of the beneficiary; from gratitude, because its gifts are not viewed as a return for favors received. Although it differs from charity in that its proximate motive is the inherent fitness of a spirit of generosity in human relationships, it may well be activated at the command of charity, and it is a disposition that lends itself readily to the service of that virtue.

It is characteristic of the liberal man to be generous in giving to others, but his generosity should not be out of proportion to his means, nor should a man let it render him incapable of satisfying the demands of justice, piety, or charity, nor should it entail the sacrifice of other virtuous good. Excess in liberality is the sin of prodigality, but generosity, prudently moderated, becomes the socially developed man and the Christian, and therefore St. Paul urged the Ephesians to labor, working with their hands, that they might have something to share with their neighbors (Eph 4.28). The virtue of liberality in a man is not necessarily measured by the actual quantity of his benefactions, but often depends more upon the disposition with which he gives (Mk 12.41–44).

Bibliography: THOMAS AQUINAS, *Summa theologiae,* 2a2ae, 117–119. B. H. MERKELBACH, *Summa theologiae moralis,* 3 v. (Paris 1949) 2:840–842.

[P. K. MEAGHER]

LIBERATION THEOLOGY

The term ''liberation theology'' covers a diversity of theological movements. Historically and specifically, it refers to a recent theological line of thought within Latin America that focuses on the political, economic, and ideological causes of social inequality and makes liberation rather than development its central theological, economic, and political category. It not only analyzes the concrete Latin-American situation, but it argues that all theology should begin by analyzing its concrete social situation and by returning to its religious sources for means to rectify it. Some of the ideas liberation theology were taken up by the Second General Conference of the Latin American Episcopate (CELAM) that met in Medellín, Colombia in 1968. The Medellín documents describe the institutional violence and the exploitive relations of dependency in the social situation and they point to the need for cultural and economic liberation.

In a more extended sense, liberation theology refers to any theological movement making the criticism of oppression and the support of liberation integral to the theological task itself. Black theology and feminist theology are therefore seen as major types of liberation theology. The term has also been appropriated by other minority groups. Because of its relationship with specific groups, some view liberation theology negatively as simply a specific cultural movement in which specific groups appeal to religious beliefs in order to legitimate their particular agenda and goals.

Common Methodology of Liberation Theologies. In its more fundamental and extended meaning, liberation theology refers to a theological method. Notwithstanding the diversity of liberation theologies they share a common theological methodology. This methodology brings to the fore within theology an awareness of the sociology of knowledge, since it underscores the interrelation between theory and praxis. It outlines the social and cultural conditions of theological concepts and institutional patterns. Therefore, it encourages theology to become more self-reflective about the socio-political basis of its religious symbols and their consequential praxis. It advocates a practical as well as theoretical role for theology as a discipline. Several basic traits constitute the common methodology of liberation theology.

Starting Point. The starting-point of liberation theology is an analysis of the concrete socio-political situation and the uncovering of the discrimination, alienation, and oppression within it. The discrepancy between the rich and poor within individual countries and between the advanced and developing nations leads Latin-American liberation theology to single out the relations of dependency between nations as the cause of this inequality. It therefore censures theories of development reinforcing rather than correcting the exploitation. It therefore demands liberation and not development. Feminist theology argues that the discrimination against women in society and Church is not only factual, but has been given cultural and religious legitimation. Black theology not only points to socio-economic discrimination, but also underscores its cultural causes. All liberation theologies therefore undertake to demonstrate by their analysis of the concrete situation not only the existence of discrimination or oppression, but also its economic and cultural causes.

Reflection on the Religious Tradition. Secondly, liberation theology studies the religious tradition in relation to this contemporary analysis and experience which provides a new perspective for reading and interpreting the tradition. Does the tradition support or allow the unjust situation? Or does it work against it? Much of Latin-American liberation theology examines how the Church's mission has been understood. Has the distinction between priests and laity led to a dichotomy in which the priest has a spiritual mission and the laity a worldly one without much interrelation? Has the Church's mission been bifurcated by separating its salvific function from its concern for the world? Feminist theology describes how masculine language and patriarchal images have specified the religious understanding of God and how anthropological misconceptions have become institutionalized as religious taboos. Black theology not only uncovers how the oppression of blacks has been legitimated in church history, but also shows how fundamental images of blackness and whiteness have led to this oppression. In each liberation theology, therefore, the present experience and analysis of injustices has led to a critique not only of the present but also the past with its cultural and religious traditions.

The Reconstructive Task. Thirdly, liberation theology proposes that theology has the twofold constructive task of retrieval and reinterpretation. Theology should retrieve those forgotten religious symbols or neglected ecclesial practices that could serve to overcome the oppression. It equally proposes a fundamental reinterpretation of traditional religious symbols and beliefs that legitimate oppression or discrimination. Latin-American liberation theology seeks not only to retrieve the public dimension of faith and the political mission of the Church, but also to reinterpret traditional conceptions of sin, grace, salvation history, and eschatology. Sin is reinterpreted as social sin in reference to social structures. Development—political, cultural, and economic—is related to God's Kingdom not merely as sign, image, or anticipation, but as a causal relation that underscores continuity and fulfillment. Black theology discovers in black experience, history, and culture the resources to overcome alienations. It reinterprets traditional conceptions of divine providence, suffering, and salvation. Feminist theology retrieves images of the femininity of God and views of the equality of the sexes within the history of religions and Christianity. It also reinterprets traditional religious symbols and beliefs. It does not simply urge that sexist language be excluded from biblical, liturgical, and theological texts, but seeks to revise dominant images of God. Likewise it suggests that the traditional conceptions of original sin as pride or the desire for power often expresses masculine rather than feminine experience.

Praxis as Criterion. Fourthly, liberation theologies make concrete praxis not only a goal but also a criterion of theological method. Present experience and praxis provide not only a source from which tradition is questioned, but also a criterion by which the truth of theological affirmations can be judged. Much diversity exists among liberation theologians in regard to the norm of theological affirmations. Within Black theology James Cone takes a Barthian position, where J. Deotis Roberts is more Tillichean. Often Latin-American liberation theologies so underscore the primacy of praxis that their positions could be described as a sort of theological consequentialism. Feminist theology along with the others places a premium on personal experience and partisan commitment as a source and criterion of theological affirmations. Since all liberation theologies focus on the relation between theory and praxis, they emphasize the significance of praxis as a source and goal. They demand that theology concern itself with concrete social and political goals. Moreover, these goals should be more than those established by the present structures of society. Instead they should involve a restructuring of society itself. Only if society is restructured and its culture revised, they believe, can their visions of emancipation and liberation be achieved.

Criticisms. Both the individual liberation theologies and the common methodological basis have been criticized, the criticisms centering on the question of criteria and goals. Firstly, since liberation theologies strive to eliminate social discrimination and political oppression, they are criticized for identifying the Church's mission as an immanent socio-political goal rather than as a transcendent, eschatological end. Secondly, since liberation theology appeals to personal experience as a source and norm of theological reflection, it is criticized for replacing objectivity with partisanship. Thirdly, since the goal of liberation is a standard by which the religious tradition is evaluated, it is objected that such a standard is unspecified unless one already has a vision of what constitutes genuine liberation. In response liberation theologians strive to show how precisely the transcendence of the Christian vision contributes to political reform and how this vision provides the ultimate norm of theological reflection and praxis. Its aim is not to eliminate transcendence, but to link this transcedence with social, political, and cultural reform.

Bibliography: General surveys of Latin-American theology and liberation theology: H. ASSMANN, *Theology for a Nomad Church* (New York 1976). J. MIGUEL BONINO, *Doing Theology in a Revolutionary Situation* (Philadelphia 1975). F. FLORENZA, "Latin-American Liberation The-Theology," *Interpretation* 28 n. 4 (1974) 441–457. G. GUTIERREZ, *A Theology of Liberation*, tr. C. INDA and J. EAGLESON (New York 1973). J. SEGUNDO, *A Theology for Artisans of a New Humanity*, tr. J. DRURY (5 v., New York 1973); *The Liberation of Theology*, tr. J. DRURY (New York 1976). History of the movement: E. DUSSEL, *History and Theology of Liberation* (New York 1976). Documents of a conference bringing all liberation theologies of North America together: S. TORRES and J. EAGLESON, *Theology in the Americas* (New York 1976). A. T. HENNELLY, ed., *Liberation Theology: A Documentary History* (Maryknoll, N.Y. 1990). H. MCKENNIE GOODPASTURE, ed., *Cross and Sword: An Eyewitness History of Christianity in Latin America* (Maryknoll, N.Y. 1989). P. C. PHAN, "Method in Liberation Theology," *Theological Studies* 61 (2000) 40–63. L. and C. BOFF, *Introducing Liberation Theology*, tr. P. BURNS (Maryknoll, N.Y. 1986). C. CADORETTE, et al., eds., *Liberation Theology: An Introductory Reader* (Maryknoll, N.Y. 1992). F. E. CROWE, "Bernard Lonergan and Liberation Theology," in W. L. YSAAC, ed., *The Third World and Bernard Lonergan: A Tribute to a Concerned Thinker* (Manila 1986).

[F. SCHÜSSLER FIORENZA]

LIBERATION THEOLOGY, LATIN AMERICA

In Latin America liberation theology is an interpretation of Christian faith out of the experience of the poor (their suffering, struggles, and hope); a theological critique of the injustice in existing society and its legitimizing ideologies; and reflection on criteria for the activity of the Church and of Christians. These aspects are obviously interconnected: e.g., involvement in the struggle for justice sharpens the reading of Scripture, and it is the Biblical vision that makes the critique of existing society theological.

The primary audience addressed by this theology is neither an academic theological community nor the poor themselves, but pastoral agents (priests, sisters, lay) working with the poor. Although the questions arise out of pastoral work, liberation theologians are not concerned with an immediate "how-to" but rather with the theological sense of the experience of poor and struggling Christians. The overall enterprise is aimed at providing a theologically grounded rationale for pastoral work with a liberating orientation. To a degree this involves defending its legitimacy within the Church.

Since its inception in the 1960s this theology has understood "liberation" to mean a process of basic change toward a more just and participatory society, one in which people will be able to live more as brothers and sisters. Liberation theology does not describe in any detail what such a society would be like nor how it would be reached. A frequent theme is that of "integral" liberation: ending the oppression of the poor is a dimension of the total liberation (from sin and death) effected by Christ.

Liberation theology pays particular attention to its context, both sociopolitical and eccesial. Thus far, three such contexts may be more or less clearly discerned. 1) Liberation theology emerged in the late 1960s and early 1970s as Latin Americans concluded that current models of development would not bring most people out of poverty. What was needed was a new model of development—a revolution (not necessarily violent). The 1968 CELAM (Latin American Bishops Conference) meeting at MEDELLÍN, Colombia, was a major catalyst (*see* LATIN AMERICA, CHURCH IN). 2) A wave of military coups led to repressive military dictatorships in most of Latin America during the 1970s. As repression affected pastoral work, church people often found themselves working to defend elemental human rights. Moreover, Archbishop Lopez Trujillo, elected secretary-general of CELAM in 1972, set out to counter liberation theology. 3) Developments beginning in 1978 to 1979 (election of Pope John Paul II; CELAM meeting in Puebla, Mexico; revolution in Central America; gradual return to civilian rule in most of Latin America) signalled a third kind of social and ecclesial context.

Local conditions often varied from these general situations. For example, during the late 1960s and early 1970s, when repression was worst in Brazil, the Peruvian military government was attempting to implement populist programs. The Brazilian church, representing 40 percent of Latin-American Catholics, relied on its own internal structures and paid little attention to CELAM. Finally; at the village or barrio level, conditions often showed little variation, despite larger political shifts. With these qualifications, the sociopolitical and ecclesial context remains important for liberation theology.

Themes. Liberation theologians reflect on the perennial themes: God, creation, Israel, Jesus Christ, the Church, etc. Their concern, however, is not to justify belief in the face of unbelief, but to serve evangelization in a context of oppression. With regard to the "God-question," for example, theologians have retrieved the Biblical category of IDOLATRY. Certain realities, such as wealth, political power, or national security, have taken on an absolute importance, above the welfare and even the life of many human beings, becoming "divinities of death." The Biblical God, however, is a living God who desires that human beings have life—and not only "spiritual" life. Whereas North Atlantic theology seeks to respond to the doubts of its interlocutors, Latin American theology points to a "battle of the gods"—between the divinities of death and the God of life.

While sharing in the larger christological enterprise of biblicists and theologians elsewhere, Latin-American theologians have their own particular emphases. Leonardo Boff, Jon Sobrino, and Juan Luis Segundo, among others, have devoted major attention to Christology. Their central concern however, is not so much to verify with utmost precision what can be known of the "historical" Jesus, as to reflect on the significance of Jesus as a historical actor: his message, his action, the enmity and conflict he aroused, leading eventually to his death; in the Resurrection they see God's vindication of his message and work. The experience of the poor and of persecution of those who struggle for justice has sensitized them to the conflictive aspects of the GOSPEL accounts. They are interested not only in the history lived by Jesus, but in the history-making potential of that history for later generations and especially today. They do not anachronistically seek to make Jesus a first-century revolutionary, but they are convinced that Jesus has revolutionary implications. One central theme is that of the kingdom, the most all-embracing symbol of what Jesus proclaimed. Advances in justice and love are partial realizations of the kingdom, steps toward its definitive consummation. The Church must be ever aware that it is not the kingdom, but is to serve the kingdom.

Latin-American theology is very ecclesial—it grows out of pastoral work and much of the theological writing itself addresses the (specifically Roman Catholic) Church. The notion of the "popular church" is a focus of controversy. Starting in the 1960s, the base-community became a common, though far from universal, model of pastoral work. In Brazil, a nationwide meeting on base-communities coined the expression "church born of the people through the Spirit of God" (1975), usually shortened to "popular church." The intent of the term was not anti-institutional but simply referred to the church "happening," as it were, among the poor masses of the people, when they are evangelized and begin to live their faith at the local level with their own expressions of worship and mutual concern. This is also understood as an ecclesial expression of a process taking place in society as a whole, as poor people become active agents in society, especially in movements to defend their rights. In the period leading up to the CELAM meeting at Puebla (1979) the term became polemical. There the bishops, following Pope JOHN PAUL II, warned against the notion of a "popular church," which they assumed to be in opposition to an "institutional church."

Similarly, the bishops, while supporting base-communities, warned that they were incomplete and stressed that the Church is more fully present in the parish, and even more fully present in the diocese. From this perspective, the base-community is regarded as the lowest subdivision of the world-church. Yet, it is also argued that if the "fullness" of the Church exists where people live the gospel injunction, then it exists fully in the base-community, and in fact, the "higher" levels of the church (parish or diocese) exist to serve the "front lines" where people seek to put the gospel into practice. If the fullness of the Church is there, should it not be expressed eucharistically? If present ministerial structures make that impossible, might they not be changed? It is within this kind of argument that Leonardo Boff raised the question of ordination for married people, including women, at the base-community level.

Most Latin-American liberation theologians operate consciously within the Roman Catholic horizon. They have generally not raised certain questions (papal ofrice and infallibility, sexual morality) commonly discussed in post-Vatican II North Atlantic theology, and they go out of their way to avoid taking on a rebel role, e.g., Boff accepted his silencing (1985). They do not want the central issue of the liberation of the poor to be obscured by ecclesiastical controversies. Their position also reflects a basic acceptance of Roman Catholic eccesiology. For example, in critiquing the "Ratzinger document" [*Libertatis Nuntius* (Aug. 6, 1985)], Juan Luis Segundo explicitly accepted the magisterium, and expressly argued that the authority of Vatican II was higher than that of a Roman congregation (see below).

Although relatively few in number, Protestants have played an important role in the development of liberation theology. Nevertheless, ecumenism is more a matter of practical collaboration than of expressly thematized theological reflection.

Critique of Society—Marxism. There is a consensus that existing development models do not serve the poor majority. PUEBLA spoke of a "grave structural conflict" (i.e., conflict is inherent in existing socioeconomic and political structures) and quoted Pope John Paul II: "The growing affluence of a few people parallels the growing poverty of the masses." Puebla also critiqued ideologies (capitalist liberalism, Marxist collectivism, national security), but as if the Church and its social teaching were above ideology. Liberation theologians question this stance and tend to see ideology as embedded in language and part of the human condition. Moreover, they distinguish between ideologies as all-embracing philosophical systems, such as dialectical materialism, and as limited analytical instruments, means toward an end, specifically for understanding how society functions with a view toward changing it. In this limited understanding they make use of Marxism as do virtually all Latin-American intellectuals who are serious about structural change. Militant grassroots organizations also usually make some use of Marxist categories of analysis.

Nevertheless, Marxism appears rather less frequently in liberation theology than one might expect. Some theologians scarcely mention it, and only a few deal with it head on. Segundo in *Faith and Ideologies* (Maryknoll, New York 1984) has an extended critique. In *The Ideological Weapons of Death* (Maryknoll 1986), Franz Hinkelammert utilizes Marx's concept of fetishism as a major category for uncovering the idolatry present in major Western thinkers and even, he believes, in representatives of Catholic social teaching.

Issues Relating to Practice. Although their questions arise from pastoral work, liberation theologians are not interested in resolving immediate issues, but in elaborating criteria for what the Church and Christians should do. In raising the question of the unity of the Church, for example, John Sobrino was no doubt stimulated by particular conflicts within EL SALVADOR, particularly divisions within the Church over how to respond to the increasing repression and growing popular militancy during the late 1970s. In response, he sought to discern ecclesiological criteria (e.g., that the Church is to serve not itself but the kingdom, and that tension between prophetism and institution is to be expected). He observed that "authority is not the final or sole criterion of discernment," which is rather to be sought in the "communal doing of truth." Unity within the Church will always be "relative, partial, and provisional" and is achieved "through the dialectic of union and conflict." Such a position cautions against an easy reliance on unity with the bishops as a single criterion for Church unity, and suggests a theological basis for living with some tension within the Church, when that tension arises out of the struggle for justice.

The establishment of a revolutionary government in NICARAGUA (1979) raised many questions—practical, but ultimately theological—for Christians, although not a great deal of formal theological writing. People's responses were largely based on a prior political judgement. If one assumed that the Sandinista government was Marxist and that Marxism is ultimately incompatible with Christianity, the Christian response should logically be one of opposition. Numerous Christians, including priests, sisters and theologians, had a different perspective. They argued that discernment should be based not on how the Church would fare institutionally but on the revolution's capability of bringing about a more human

life for the majority of the people. On that criterion, they judged that it was the best feasible alternative, and that Christians should support the revolutionary process. Such support should be critical, but criticism should be made within an overall position of support and participation, not from outside or in a manner that would undermine the revolution itself.

For its part the Sandinista front departed from the precedent of all previous Marxist parties in power when it officially declared that the (Marxist) view of religion as a "machine of alienation" was a product of a particular period in history, and was not true of Nicaragua. This was in effect a rejection of Marx's "opium of the people" dictum as a timeless principle. The Sandinistas furthermore declared that religious belief would not bar anyone form being a Sandinista—a clear break with the practice of Marxist governments in power. As relations between the hierarchy and the Sandinista government worsened, Christians supportive of the revolution maintained that the problem was essentially one of division within the Church over how to respond to the revolution and not a fundamental clash between the Church itself and the revolution.

Liberation Theology and Magisterium. Liberation theology's relationship to official Catholic teaching is complex, and in fact, official Church teaching is close to liberation theology on significant points. The 1971 synod of bishops declared that "action on behalf of justice and participation in the transformation of the world fully appear to us as a constitutive dimension of the preaching of the gospel, or . . . of the Church's mission for the redemption of the human race and its liberation from every oppressive situation," a position echoed at the 1974 synod. Similarly, the Puebla document (1979) shows the effects of liberation theology, especially in its "preferential option for the poor." Latin American theologians welcomed and wrote commentaries on Pope John Paul II's encyclical LABOREM EXERCENS (1981).

Nevertheless, there are numerous disputed points, most of which were expressed in the 1984 Instruction of the Sacred Congregation for the Doctrine of the Faith, headed by Cardinal Joseph Ratzinger. While acknowledging the sincerity of many pastoral workers, and the legitimacy of the theme of liberation, the Instruction points to "deviations and risks" present in some "liberation theologies." (This use of the plural implies that there exist legitimate and illegitimate forms. When leading exponents such as Boff and Gutierrez were summoned to Rome, however, it was unclear who the proponents of a legitimate liberation theology might be.)

Objections can be divided into those against the use of Marxist analysis, and those against what is regarded as liberation theology's hermeneutics. Arguments against Marxism are made on several grounds: that it claims to be "scientific" but in fact overlooks essential aspects, that it promotes "class struggle" and violence, and is committed to atheism. Moreover, existing Marxist regimes, a "shame of our times," are totalitarian and hold millions of people in servitude. As for hermeneutics, liberation theology is said to propose "a novel interpretation of both the content of faith and of Christian existence which seriously departs from the faith of the Church, and in fact actually constitutes a practical negation." Its reading of the Bible is reductionist and it twists the notion of the truth through praxis, making it the criterion for truth. Similarly, it is argued that the Church is "emptied of its specific reality, and its sacramental and hierarchical structure . . . which was willed by the Lord himself." The Instruction is a compendium of charges raised against liberation theology since the early 1970s.

Initially most liberation theologians, such as Gutierrez and Boff, took a benign view of the Instruction, stating that what it presented was a caricature of liberation theology, and that any theologian who held such views would merit censure. They also stated that it reflected a European view, remote from the Latin American experience. Juan Luis Segundo, however, directly confronted the Instruction. In a close reading of the text, and especially the first half, which deals with general principles, he extracted the Instruction's implicit underlying theology, particularly a dualistic pattern of thought that he held was overcome at Vatican II. He noted that PAUL VI, anticipating that some might wonder whether the Church had "deviated toward the *anthropocentric* positions of modern culture," had responded, "Deviated, no; *turned, yes*." In Segundo's assessment, the Instruction is at odds with the theology developed at Vatican II, whose authority is higher than that of a Roman Congregation.

The April 1986 "Instruction on Christian Freedom and Liberation" issued by the same congregation, avoided condemnations, although its tone and style were alien to Latin American thinking. The lifting of Boff's silencing and a cordial meeting between the Brazilian bishops and Pope John Paul II during the same month also signalled a lessening of tension.

Contraction and Expansion. In the 1990s, Liberation Theology experienced both contraction and expansion. The contraction, mainly experienced at home in Latin America, was the result of pressure from both the Vatican and some bishops in CELAM. Nonetheless theologians struggled to prove themselves faithful carriers of Catholic theology and continued to flourish under ecclesiastical activism. Creative expansion of the movement fostered a quieter but even greater impact in a number of

areas and on a global scale. By adhering to their methodological starting point of a careful reading of the "signs of the times" as *Gaudium et spes* recommended, liberation theology expanded its horizons well beyond a Marxist critique and dependency theory to a broader theological critique of culture, a more discerning examination of neo-Liberal economies, and the quest for authentic, integral development in the Third World. The fall of the Berlin wall provided the opening for movement from an ideological posture of confrontation to a more theologically and educationally focused engagement with local, national and global structures. The focus on the suffering poor continued but with a clearer understanding of the impact of globalization, urbanization and technology on that suffering. Following the lead of the founding fathers of liberation thought, Gustavo Gutiérrez and Juan Lois Segundo, José Comblin emphasized the "changing context" but still highlighted the freedom of Christ as "calling and risk." He continued, "It is God's gift, and the Pauline name for the reign of God." It is a gift that never reaches completion on earth but is the fundamental drive that guides the human adventure with its joys and tragedies. That freedom in Jesus Christ constitutes the human calling and vocation. It is that profound sense of freedom which allows for a deeper grasp of poverty. Jon Sobrino's treatment of Jesus Christ as liberator advances this line of thought.

Liberation theology's impact at the beginning of the 21st century had expanded to the whole globe and touched the thorny issues of gender and indigenous cultures. African, Asian, Black, Feminist and Indigenous Theologians were influenced by the methods of liberation theology. A candid and honest cross-fertilization enriched these efforts in contextual theology in a rapidly globalizing world. Likewise, the liberation motif had a positive reaction in other world religions. Liberation theology movements emerged in BUDDHISM, JUDAISM and ISLAM. The imprint of liberation thinking also registered in Catholic social teaching, most notably perhaps, in *Sollicitudo Rei Socialis* (1988) and *Ecclesia in America* (1998) of Pope John Paul II. That same imprint could be deciphered in the important worldwide pastoral efforts surrounding debt relief for underdeveloped countries and faith-based community organizing in the poor inner cities of the United States. Finally, it should be noted that liberation theology, and particularly the "conscientization" approach of Paulo Freire, were singled out as a unique Catholic-Christian contribution to sustainable and integral social-economic development worldwide.

In both its contraction and expansion liberation theology continued, in a modest way, to give a Christian direction for the global pursuit of justice for all peoples.

Bibliography: P. BERRYMAN, *Liberation Theology* (New York 1987); *The Religious Roots of Rebellion* (Maryknoll 1984). L. BOFF, *Ecclesiogenesis* (Maryknoll 1986). J. EAGLESON and P. SCHARPER, eds., *Puebla and Beyond* (Maryknoll 1980). G. GUTIERREZ, *The Power of the Poor in History* (Maryknoll 1983). J. L. SEGUNDO, *Theology and the Church: A Response to Cardinal Ratzinger and a Warning to the Whole Church* (Minneapolis, Minnesota 1985). J. SOBRINO, *The True Church and the Poor* (Maryknoll 1984). J. COMBLIN, *Called for Freedom: The Changing Context of Liberation Theology* (Maryknoll 1998). G. GUTIERREZ, *The Density of the Present: Selected Writings* (Maryknoll 1999). A. T. HENNELLY, *Liberation Theologies: The Global Pursuit of Justice* (Mystic, Connecticut 1995). R. J. SCHREITER, *The New Catholicity: Theology between the Global and the Local* (Maryknoll 1997). I. ELLACURIA and J. SOBRINO, eds., *Mysterium liberationis: Fundamental Concepts of Liberation Theology* (Maryknoll 1993). P. C. PHAN, ''The Future of Liberation Theology,'' *The Living Light* 28/3 (1992) 259–71. M. P. AQUINO, *Our Cry for Life: Feminist Theology from Latin America* (Maryknoll 1993). B. L. SHERWIN and H. KASIMOW, eds., *John Paul II and Interreligious Dialogue* (Maryknoll 1999). G. DE SCHRIJVER, ed., *Liberation Theologies on Shifting Grounds: A Clash of Socio-Economic and Cultural Paradigms* (Leuven 1998). D. BATSTONE, et al., eds., *Liberation Theologies, Postmodernity, and the Americas* (London 1997). J. SOBRINO, *Jesus the Liberator* (Maryknoll 1994); *Christ the Liberator* (Maryknoll 2001). M. ENGELBERT, ''African Liberation Theology,'' L. BOFF and V. ELIZONDO, eds., *Concilium* 199 (Edinburgh 1988). A. PIERIS, *An Asian Theology of Liberation* (Maryknoll 1988). E. MARTEY, *African Theology: Inculturation and Liberation* (Maryknoll 1993). C. S. QUEEN and S. B. KING, *Engaged Buddhism: Buddhist Liberation Movements in Asia* (Albany 1996). A. ENGINEER, *Islam and Liberation Theology: Essays on Liberative Elements in Islam* (New Delhi 1990). O. MADURO, ed., *Judaism, Christianity, and Liberation: An Agenda for Dialogue* (Maryknoll 1991).

[P. BERRYMAN/J. P. HOGAN]

LIBERATORE, MATTEO

Jesuit philosopher and theologian; b. Salerno, Aug. 14, 1810; d. Rome, Oct. 18, 1892. After his studies and ordination in Naples, he was assigned to teach philosophy and later theology at the Jesuit college there (1837–48). He collaborated with C. M. Curci and L. TAPARELLI in founding *Civiltà cattolica* (1850–), which he helped to edit until his death. Having passed from eclecticism to THOMISM about 1850, he used the epistemology of St. Thomas to refute the theories of J. LOCKE, I. KANT, and especially A. ROSMINI-SERBATI. He made a genuine contribution to the traditional understanding of the natural law, and figured significantly in the restoration of Thomism in Italy, defending it against the errors of modern philosophers, with whom he was quite conversant. Among his major works are *Institutiones philosophicae*, 2 v. (Naples 1840–42), published in 11 eds.; *Della conoscenza intellettuale*, 2 v. (Rome 1857–58); *Istituzioni di etica e di diritto naturale* (Rome 1863); *La Chiesa e lo Stato* (Naples 1871); *Dell'uomo*, 2 v. (Rome 1874–75); *Degli universali* (Rome 1883); *Del diritto pubblico ecclesiastico* (Prato 1887); and *Principi di economia politica* (Rome 1889).

See Also: SCHOLASTICISM.

Bibliography: ''Necrologio . . . ,'' *La civiltà cattolica* (ser. 15) 4 (1892): 352–360. A. MASNOVO, ''Le P. Liberatore fut-il thomiste de 1840 à 1850?'' *Revue néo-scolastique de philosophie* 15 (1908): 518–526; *Il neo-tomismo in Italia* (Milan 1923). T. MIRABELLA, *Il pensiero politico del P. Matteo Liberatore . . .* (Milan 1956). P. DEZZA, *Alle origini del neotomismo* (Milan 1940).

[R. M. PIZZORNI]

LIBERATUS OF CARTHAGE

Sixth-century African cleric and theologian; d. after 556. An archdeacon in the Church of Carthage, Liberatus accompanied Bishops Caius and Peter to Rome in 535, carrying a synodal letter from the council held at Carthage after the Byzantine conquest of North Africa (J. D. MANSI, *Sacororum Conciliorum nova et amplissima collectio*, 31 v. [Florence-Venice 1757–98] 8:849). Pope AGAPETUS I mentions him in his response to Bishop Reparatus of Carthage (*Patrologia Latina* 66:45). Liberatus supported his bishop in his strong stand in favor of the Council of CHALCEDON at the beginning of the controversy over the THREE CHAPTERS (544) and followed him to Constantinople (551) when Reparatus was summoned to the capital by JUSTINIAN I. Reparatus was deposed for his intransigence and exiled to the monastery of the Euchaites in Pontus (552). At the close of the Council of CONSTANTINOPLE II (July 553), Liberatus was forced to join him there (Victor of Tunnuna, *Chron.*, an. 552–563). Apparently on the death of Reparatus on Jan. 7, 563, Liberatus returned to Africa. Nothing further is known of his career.

He wrote the *Breviarium causae Nestorianorum et Eutychianorum*, which describes the Christological controversies from the accession of NESTORIUS as patriarch of Constantinople (428) to the condemnation of the Three Chapters (553). Basing his doctrine on the orthodoxy of the Chalcedonian decrees, Liberatus described the intrigues that accompanied the theological disputes regarding the two natures in Christ and the efforts made by the Monophysites to discredit Chalcedon by attacking THEODORE OF MOPSUESTIA, THEODORET OF CYR, and Ibas of Edessa. He said explicitly that it was the partisans of Nestorius who misinterpreted the teaching of Diodore of Tarsus and Theodore in their zeal to combat the teaching of Eunomius and Apollinaris. While he defended the true Antiochene theology and was severe on CYRIL OF ALEXANDRIA because of his methods in dealing with opponents, he proved that the MONOPHYSITES were wrong in the way they interpreted Cyril. His animosity was concentrated on Pope VIGILIUS I, concerning whose career and death he furnished valuable information (c. 22).

Liberatus used excellent sources; for the course of events, he relied on the Tripartite History, which, as he remarked, had recently been translated from the Greek under the care of CASSIODORUS. For Chalcedon (c. 13) he employed the *Gesta synodalia,* the *Epistolae sanctorum patrum,* including the *Gesta Acacii* or *Breviculus historiae Eutychianistarum* (Schwartz, *Acta conciliorum oecumenicorum,* [Berlin 1914–] 2.1–5), as well as a history "that he found written in Greek at Alexandria." This may be the *Ecclesiastical History* of ZACHARY THE RHETOR. For the age of Justinian he used his own and the witness of contemporaries.

Well abreast of the doctrinal issues involved, the *Breviarium* is a valuable witness to the complexity and extent of sixth-century theological development. Its date of composition is difficult to determine. It records the death of Vigilius (June 7, 555) but speaks of Theodore of Alexandria as still living (d. 566 or 567).

Bibliography: *Patrologia Latina,* 217 v. (Paris 1878–90) 68:963–1052. *Acta conciliorum oecumenicorum,* (Berlin 1914–) 2.5:98–144. É. AMANN, *Dictionnarie de théologie catholique,* 15 v. (Paris 1903–50) 9.1:630–631. P. H. HEBRAND, *Historisches Jahrbuch der Görres-Gesellschaft* (1922) 223–232. A. GRILLMEIER and H. BACHT, *Das Konzil von Chalkedon: Geschichte und Gegenwart,* 3 v. (Würzburg 1951–54) 2:159–167. B. ALTANER, *Patrology* (New York 1960) 590. H. RAHNER, *Lexikon für Theologie und Kirche,* 10 v., ed. J. HOFER and K. RAHNER, (Freiburg 1957–65) 6:1012. O. BARDENHEWER, *Geschichte der altkirchlichen Literatur,* 5 v. (Freiburg 1913–32) 5:328–329.

[F. X. MURPHY]

LIBERIA, THE CATHOLIC CHURCH IN

The Republic of Liberia, largely agricultural, is located on the coast of West Africa, bordering the North Atlantic Ocean on the southwest, SIERRA LEONE on the northwest, GUINEA on the north, and CÔTE D'IVOIRE on the east. A tropical region, Liberia has a long coastal plain rising to plateau, with low mountains in the northeast. Dry winters from December to March are punctuated by dusty harmattan winds blowing from the Sahara desert, while summers are rainy. Natural resources include iron ore, diamonds, gold and timber from the region's rain forests; agricultural crops include rubber, coffee, cocoa, cassava, palm oil, sugar cane, rice, bananas and livestock.

Africa's oldest independent republic, Liberia was created out of settlements of liberated American slaves organized by the American Colonization Society. The re-

---

Capital: Monrovia.
Size: 43,000 sq. miles.
Population: 3,164,160 in 2000.
Languages: English; 20 ethnic languages are spoken in various regions.
Religions: 300,790 Catholics (10%), 760,400 Muslims (24%), 759,340 Protestants (24%), 1,343,630 follow indigenous beliefs.
Archdiocese: Monrovia, with suffragans Cape Palmas and Gbarnga.

---

gion, settled after 1822, proclaimed its independence in 1847 and patterned its government on that of the United States. Political and economic power remained largely in the hands of a very small American-Liberian minority, despite the fact that 95 percent of the inhabitants are members of indigenous African tribes such as Kpelle, Bassa, Gio, Kru, Grebo, Mano and Gbandi. An additional 75,000, the Congo people, are descendants of Caribbean slaves who immigrated to the region. A military government during the 1980s was followed by a decade of civil war ending in 1996 when free elections were held in the country. The region's economy and social structure remained unsettled through 2000. Most of the population are agricultural workers; only 39 percent of Liberians can read and write.

Early History. Portuguese missionaries visited the coastal region from the 15th century, and the Jesuits and the Capuchins from Sierra Leone exercised an intermittent apostolate beginning 200 years later. Settlements of blacks, liberated from slavery in the United States, began forming in 1822, and from its founding, Liberia was a stronghold of Protestant missionary activity. The American Catholic bishops and the Congregation for the Propagation of the Faith expressed keen concern for the expatriate Catholic settlers. In 1833, Bishop John England of Charleston, South Carolina, requested of Rome that missionaries be sent to care for black Catholic settlers. Pope Gregory XVI then asked the bishops of Philadelphia and New York each to send a priest. They arrived in 1842: Edward BARRON, an Irish-born priest of Philadelphia, and John Kelly (1802–66), an Irish-born priest of Albany, with Denis Pindar (1823–44), an Irish lay catechist. Barron became the first bishop of the Vicariate Apostolic of the Two Guineas (created 1842), an immense territory comprising all of West Africa from Senegal to the Orange River in Southern Africa. He returned to Liberia in 1844 after recruiting seven priests and three laymen in Europe, but the mission was abandoned before the year's end because the missionaries had either died or were broken in health due to the region's damp climate. Barron resigned his post and returned to the United States.

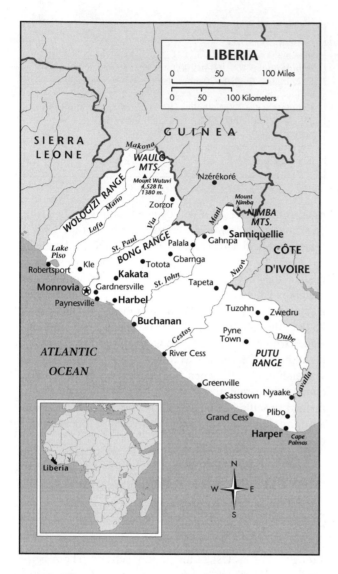

The Holy Ghost Fathers from Sierra Leone established a mission at Monrovia that lasted from 1884 to 1886. When the Prefecture Apostolic of Liberia was created in 1903 (Vicariate in 1934), it was confided to the Montfort Fathers, who remained for a year in the unhealthful climate. The Society of the AFRICAN MISSIONS arrived in 1906, and took charge of the mission. By 1928 there were 3,350 Catholics, mostly among the coastal tribes.

Liberia remained a prefecture apostolic until 1934 when John Collins, SMA, was ordained bishop and appointed vicar apostolic. In 1950 the vicariate was divided when the prefecture apostolic of Cape Palmas was established; this latter jurisdiction was raised to the status of a vicariate in 1962. The first Liberian priest, Patrick Kla Juwle, was ordained in 1946. In 1972 he was ordained as the first Liberian Catholic bishop and was named the Vicar Apostolic of Cape Palmas. The Liberian hierarchy

was formally established in 1981 when Monrovia became an archdiocese and had the diocese of Cape Palmas as a suffragan see. The Metropolitan See of Monrovia was further divided in 1986 when the diocese of Gbarnga was created as a second suffragan. The bishops, all native, belong to the Inter-Territorial Catholic Bishops' Conference of Liberia, Gambia and Sierra Leone.

Fatima College, a Catholic teacher training institution, opened at Cape Palmas in 1952. The Barclay Training Center, a third-level vocational and technical school staffed by the Salesians and indigenous teachers, was established in Monrovia in 1978. Also that year the National Pastoral Center was founded in Gbarnga, its emphasis on the training of lay leaders for parishes and the formation of catechists to assist in the work of evangelization. In 1979 an Inter-diocesan Matrimonial Tribunal was created in Monrovia and an indigenous religious community, the Sisters of the Holy Family, was founded in Cape Palmas. 1982 saw the founding of a Catholic Agricultural Training Center at Sanniquellie in northeast Liberia and in 1992 a nursing school was established in Monrovia. A regional major seminary for the seven dioceses was established in 1972 at Gbarnga; in 1990 it was temporarily relocated to Sierra Leone because of military hostilities.

Civil Unrest. Liberia prospered from the 1920s through the 1970s due to the lucrative market provided for its rubber harvest by the Firestone Rubber Company. The Americo-Liberian elite, which had settled the coastal areas from 1822, ruled the republic after 1947 under the leadership of president W. V. S. Tubman. Tubman's death in 1971 and a shrinking rubber market set the economy into a decline and on April 12, 1980 a violent military coup led by Master Sergeant Samuel Doe gained control of Liberia. The decade that followed was characterized by a great deal of social and political instability, the result of a corrupt and repressive regime. The flagrant disregard for civil liberties sparked confrontation between Church leaders and the military-civilian authorities. The Monrovia-based National Catholic Secretariat defended human rights and civil liberties through a newspaper and radio station; since the Church's position was strong among the indigenous peoples whom the government purported to represent, its voice could not be silenced. The region's growing unrest eventually culminated in civil war. An armed incursion led by Charles Taylor in December of 1989 to unseat the government escalated into a brutal ethnic conflict that had devastating effects in all areas of public life. Over 200,000 people were killed; another 800,000 became refugees or were exiled. As Taylor attempted to build his rebel army, children as young as eight years old were forced to carry arms.

The turmoil seriously hurt Catholic life, particularly since the Church depended heavily on its schools, health-care and social service institutions. Church installations suffered much physical damage; some, including those in the capital city of Monrovia, were totally destroyed. Many religious congregations were dispersed, many missionaries forced to leave. Although not a stated target of either of the military factions, the Church lost one Ghanian missionary priest (1991) and five American missionary sisters (1992) in execution-style killings. In October of 1994, two of the country's bishops were forced to flee, although Archbishop Michael Francis remained, thanks to the protection offered him by a West African peacekeeping force. Lay Catholics kept Catholicism alive among the people during the civil war, especially in those areas where schools had ceased to function. Catholics, working with the ecumenical Liberian Council of Churches, sponsored vigorous programs of humanitarian assistance and social welfare; its work among the refugees, displaced persons and exiles proved consistent and effective. The defense of human rights and the active support of peace and democratic evolution continued to be a focus of the pastoral letters and speeches of Liberia's bishops throughout the civil war, which finally ended in 1997 when free elections brought rebel-turned-President Taylor to power.

Into the 21st Century. By 2000 there were 51 parishes left in Liberia, tended by 52 priests, 26 of whom were religious. Fewer than 100 other religious remained in the country, most of whom tended Liberia's 34 primary and 26 secondary Catholic private schools. Orders active in the region included the Hospitalers of St. John of God, Missionaries of the Immaculate Conception, Salesians and Hospital Sisters of the Sacred Heart of Jesus. The government continued to respect freedom of religion, which was guaranteed under the constitution promulgated in 1986, although tensions were sometimes apparent in its treatment of Liberia's growing Muslim population, which had opposed Taylor during the civil war. Of special concern to many Catholics was the damage wrought on the young, forced to fight in the war, and special schools were planned as a way to help deal with the psychological trauma associated with these disrupted childhoods. In March of 2000 the Church ran afoul of government censors, its Monrovia-based radio station closed down until it agreed to restrict broadcasts to "purely religious matters." However, this action was viewed as politically motivated; Taylor remained a proponent of Christianity, in 1999 firing most of his cabinet after they failed to attend a prayer meeting.

By late 2000 armed conflict in the northern region had resumed amid charges of corruption against Taylor and his administration. Control of the region's diamond deposits was held to be a motivation for control of the government.

Bibliography: *Africa Watch*, v. 5, no. 6, *Liberia: Waging War to Keep the Peace* (New York 1993). M. J. BANE, *The Catholic Story of Liberia* (New York 1950). J. BAUR, *Two Thousand Years of Christianity in Liberia* (Nairobi 1994). BISHOPS OF LIBERIA, *Pastoral Letters* (Monrovia 1980–94). P. CLIFFORD, *Christianity and Politics in Doe's Liberia* (London 1993). P. GANTLY, *African Mission*, 2 vols. (Rome 1991–92). J. C. HICKEY, *A Land Both Old and Young* (Newark 1987). E. M. HOGAN, *Catholic Missionaries and Liberia* (Cork 1981). J. G. LIEBENOW, *Liberia: The Evolution of Privilege* (London 1969); *Liberia: The Quest for Democracy* (Bloomington 1987). SOCIETY OF AFRICAN MISSIONS, *A Missionary Policy for Liberia* (Rome 1992). U.S. COMMITTEE FOR REFUGEES, *Uprooted Liberians: Casualties of a Brutal War* (New York 1992). *Bilan du Monde*, 2:562–565. *Annuario Pontificio* has information on all diocese. For additional bibliography *see* AFRICA.

[R. M. WILTGEN/EDS.]

LIBERIAN CATALOGUE

A list of popes with dates from St. Peter to LIBERIUS (352–366), which forms a part of the compilation of chronological and liturgical data contained in the CHRONOGRAPHER OF 354. It is evidently the earliest version of the *LIBER PONTIFICALIS* and consists of two sections: one dating the pontificates from Peter to 231 (Pontianus 230–235), which was apparently constructed from authentic but faulty traditions; and one from 231–352, which seems to reflect official documentation. This list was probably prepared in 336 under Pope Mark and then revised and published under Pope Liberius as a section of the Chronographer of 354. The catalogue gives 25 years for the reign of St. Peter, and this is repeated by Eusebius-Jerome (*Chronicon* 2, ed. R. Helm, *Die griechischen christlichen Schriftsteller der ersten drei Jahrhunderte* 7:179). But all the dates down to Eleutherius (175–189) are conjectural at best.

Bibliography: *Liber pontificalis*, ed. L. DUCHESNE (Paris 1886–92) 1:vi–x. T. MOMMSEN, ed., *Chronica minora*, 3 v. (*Monumenta Germaniae Historica Auctores antiquissimi* 9, 11, 13; Berlin 1892–98) 1:73–76. H. LECLERCQ, *Dictionnaire d'archéologie chrétienne et de liturgie*, ed. F. CARROLL, H. LECLERQ, and H. I. MARROU, 15 v. (Paris 1907–53) 9.1:527–530. G. BARDY, *Catholicisme* 2:645. O. SEECK, *Paulys Realenzyklopädie der klassischen Altertumswissenschaft*, ed. G. WISSOWA et al. 3.2 (1899) 2477–81. *Epigrammata Damasiana*, ed. A. FERRUA (Rome 1942) 21–45. H. STERN, *Le Calendrier de 354 . . .* (Paris 1952).

[F. X. MURPHY]

LIBERIUS, POPE

Pontificate: May 17, 352 to September 24, 366. Liberius, a native Roman, was elected bishop of Rome May 17 to succeed Pope Julius who had died April 12, 352. He came to the papacy under trying conditions.

Pope Liberius. (Archive Photos)

Arian Controversy. CONSTANTIUS II, sole emperor since the death of his brother Constans (350), was under the influence of the Eastern bishops hostile to the Creed of Nicaea. At the insistence of the Arians, the Emperor wanted the Western episcopate to reject the Nicaean doctrine of the HOMOOUSIOS or consubstantiality of the Father and the Son, and to abandon ATHANASIUS, the most stout defender of the Nicene Creed. Liberius had scarcely been elected pope when he became involved in the controversy and his attitude, which always seemed somewhat contradictory, still poses problems for the historian.

Athanasius. The Eastern bishops hostile to the Nicaean doctrine requested Liberius at the outset of his papacy to revise the decision in favor of Athanasius made by Pope St. JULIUS I (340) and by the Council of Sardica (343). Apparently Liberius summoned Athanasius to Rome to exonerate him before a synod; but instead of appearing in Rome Athanasius sent a memorandum signed by 80 Egyptian bishops. After inspecting this document the Roman synod refused to support the enemies of Athanasius.

As Constantius was then located in Arles, Liberius sent Vincent of Capua and Marcellus, Bishop of Campania, to request the convocation of a council at Aquileia. But Ursacius of Singidunum and Valens of Mursa, the two Illyrian bishops who controlled the ecclesiastical politics of Constantius, induced the Emperor to convene a synod at Arles instead; that assembly confirmed the condemnation of Athanasius. The papal legates gave way under pressure and concurred in this condemnation. The only bishop present who refused to sign was Paulinus of Treves, who was immediately exiled.

Liberius reacted strongly against his representatives and in a letter to EUSEBIUS OF VERCELLI expressed his determination to demand of Constantius the convocation of a council between the Western and Eastern bishops to establish the union that had not been achieved at Sardica (P., *Regesta pontificum romanorum ab condita ecclesia ad annum post Christum natum 1198* 211). This letter contains the first known use of the term ''Apostolic See.'' Liberius then sent a letter to the Emperor through LUCIFER OF CAGLIARI, in which he defended himself energetically against the calumnies brought against him by the Emperor:

> God is my witness that it is in spite of myself that I have accepted this office; but I want to live in it as long as I am in this world without offending God. It is not my own decisions [*statuta*] but those of the Apostle [Peter] that I am to conserve and guard. Following the tradition of my predecessors I have added nothing to the episcopal power of the bishop of Rome; but neither have I allowed it to be diminished in any way. In preserving the faith handed down by the succession of bishops, many of them martyrs, I hope that it will always remain intact [*Ad Constant.*, Jaffé 212].

Council of Milan. The council requested by the Pope was held at Milan in October 355; under the pressure of the Emperor and his court, all the bishops but three (Denis of Milan, Eusebius of Vercelli, and Lucifer of Cagliari) approved the condemnation of Athanasius (Jaffé 216; Athanasius, *History of the Arians* 31–35). A short while later, the imperial eunuch Eusebius arrived in Rome with a threatening letter demanding that the Pope accede to the condemnation of Athanasius. Liberius rejected Eusebius's credentials and when Eusebius attempted to deposit them before the Confession of St. Peter, Liberius had them thrown out. Constantius then had the Pope arrested at night in the papal palace at the Lateran and brought to Milan. Theodoret of Cyrus has preserved the record of the meeting between the Pope and the Emperor. Liberius's stand was noble and spirited (Theodoret, *Historia Ecclesiastica* 2.16; Athanasius, *History of the Arians* 39). Two days later the Pope was exiled to Beroea in Thrace (355).

The Capitulation of Liberius. Toward the end of 357, the Pope left Beroea for Sirmium where the court was in residence, and in 358 he returned to Rome. But what price did Liberius pay for his liberation? There is question of the ''fall'' or the ''capitulation'' of Liberius. Reliable and unanimous contemporary evidence supplied by Athanasius (*History of the Arians* 41; *Apology against the Arians* 89), Jerome (*Chronicon Eusebii Caesariensis* 2365; *De Viris illustribus* 3.37), Hilary of Poitiers (*Contra Constantinus* 11) and the *Collectio Avellana* (1), as well as by ancient historians, such as Sozomen (*Historia Ecclesiastica* 4.11) relate that Liberius was guilty of a culpable failure.

Probably weakened by infirmity and age the Pope could not withstand the rigors of exile nor resist the violent threats of Constantius. He abandoned the cause of Athanasius and subscribed to a document hostile to the Nicene cause. The *Collectio Avellana* speaks of ''perfidy,'' and Jerome charges Liberius with *haeretica pravitas,* while Hilary of Poitiers cites the testimony of four letters, preserved in his *Fragmenta historica,* which he attributed to Liberius.

These letters, written in 357, are addressed to the Eastern bishops, to Ursacius, Valens, Germinius of Sirmium, and Vincent of Capua, whom the Pope had already blamed for the betrayal at the Council of Arles. They explain in an embarrassed fashion the manner in which Liberius had been induced to abandon the cause of Athanasius. They contain the pathetic request that his correspondents intercede with the Emperor so that the exile might return to Rome.

The Formula of Sirmium. Besides the abandonment of Athanasius, what are the nature and character of the concessions Liberius was forced to make? Everything points to the fact that he accepted the doctrine of ''the first formula of Sirmium'' of 351. This symbol is capable of an orthodox explanation, but it avoided the use of the most characteristic expressions of the Nicene faith, particularly the homoousios. Thus while apologists could maintain that Liberius did not teach false doctrine, one must concede that he did not do justice to the full truth. Liberius refused to sign the second formula of Sirmium (357), which is particularly subordinationist in tendency; and in his dealings with Basil of Ancyra, the leader of the Homoiousian party, he occasioned the composition of a formula of Sirmium that contradicted the doctrine of the Anomoeans or radical Arians. Liberius condemned the bishops who denied that the Son was similar to the Father ''in essence and in all things'' (Sozomen, *Historia Ecclesiastica* 4.15). Unsatisfactory though this expression might be, it was a considerable improvement over earlier formulas and checked for a time the triumph of the Arians.

When Constantius returned Liberius to Rome, the bishops gathered in Sirmium wrote to Felix, Liberius'

Pope Liberius traces the plan of the Basilica of Santa Maria Maggiore in the snow, mosaic by F. Rusati, 1308, located in the loggia of the Basilica, Rome.

archdeacon, who had taken the place of the exiled Pope, and to the clergy of the capital that ''the two bishops together should occupy the Apostolic See and assist each other in discharging their episcopal functions'' (Sozomen, *Historia Ecclesiastica* 4.15). Actually Liberius was received with enthusiasm by the Roman populace who greeted him with the acclamation: ''One God, one Christ, one Bishop.'' To avoid a riot, the usurper Felix had to flee the city, and after an attempt to occupy the Julian Basilica in Trastevere, he remained in hiding until his death (November 22, 365).

Last Years of Liberius. Little is known concerning the last years of Liberius. He was not invited personally nor did he send representatives to the Council of Rimini in 359, which approved the Homoiousian doctrine and the displacement of orthodoxy. In 385 Pope Siricius alluded to an ''act'' of Liberius, which set aside the synod of Rimini, and cited a decree forbidding the rebaptism of Arians addressed ''to the provinces'' (Jaffé 220, 255). There is also a letter of Liberius addressed in 362 to the bishops of Italy who had yielded at Rimini, in which the Pope acknowledges his agreement with the orthodox measures taken by a Synod of Alexandria in 362, and grants peace to those who rejected the error of Arius and sustained the faith of Nicaea (Jaffé 223; St. Hilary, *Frag. hist.,* ed. Feder, 156).

Finally in 366, Liberius received a delegation of Eastern bishops including Eustathius of Sebaste, Sylvanus of Tarsus, and Theophilus of Castabala, sent by the Homoiousians who sought the support of the West. He asked them to accept the Creed of Nicaea and to discard the decisions of Rimini before he received them into communion with the Roman church. In a letter written some while later to their leaders, Liberius asserted that the Creed of Nicaea contained the complete truth and contradicted all heresies, and that the homoousios was a bulwark against Arianism. He condemned everyone who adhered to that error. (Jaffé 228; Socrates, *Ekklesiastike historia* 4.12.)

On the Esquiline hill in Rome near the Market of Livia, Liberius had constructed a basilica, which was renovated in the 5th century by Pope SIXTUS III and known as Santa Maria Maggiore. It is probable that the Liberian basilica had been dedicated to the Virgin Mary. On Christmas, probably of 353, in the Vatican basilica, Liberius bestowed the veil of a virgin on Marcellina, the sister of St. AMBROSE. The address that the Pope delivered on this occasion is cited by Ambrose in his *De Virginitate* (3.1–3) but was doubtless revised by the bishop of Milan.

Liberius's character has been sharply discussed; as early as the 6th century legend made him out to be a heretic and a traitor in order to justify his rival Felix (*Gesta Liberii*). Liberius did not have the strength of character of his predecessor JULIUS I, or of his successor DAMASUS I but he was a genuine if weak supporter of the Nicene cause. The troubles that erupted upon the latter's election indicate that the Roman Church had been weakened from within as well as without during the pontificate of Liberius. His name was not inscribed in the Roman MARTYROLOGY.

Bibliography: *Clavis Patrum latinorum,* ed. E. DEKKERS (2d ed. Streenbrugge 1961). B. ALTANER, *Patrology,* tr. H. GRAEF from 5th German ed. (New York 1960) 413–414. É. AMANN, *Dictionnaire de théologie catholique,* ed. A. VACANT et al., 15 v. (Paris 1903–50; Tables générales 1951–) 9.1:631–659. A. L. FEDER, "Die Liberiusbriefe," *Sitzungsberichte der Akademie der Wissenschaften in Wien* 162: 153–183. P. LORIEUX, *Mélanges de science religieuse* 1: 7–34. T.D. BARNES, "The Capitulation of Liberius and Hilary of Arles", *Phoenix* 46: 256–265. E. FERGUSON, ed., *Encyclopedia of Early Christianity* (New York 1997) 2:680. H. JEDIN, ed., *History of the Church* (New York 1980) 2:41–63. J. N. D. KELLY, *Oxford Dictionary of Popes* (New York 1986) 30–31. C. PIETRI, *Roma Christiana* (Rome 1976) 237–268. C. PIETRI, "La question d'Athanase vue de Rome (338–360)," in *Christiana Respublica. Élements d'une enquête sur le christianisme antique* (Rome 1997) 631–664.

[P. T. CAMELOT]

LIBERMANN, FRANÇOIS MARIE PAUL, VEN.

Religious founder; b. Saverne, (Bas-Rhin), France, April 12, 1802; d. Paris, Feb. 2, 1852. He was destined to become a Jewish rabbi like his father Lazarus Libermann, but his reading of the New Testament and the influence of his oldest brother, a convert, led to his own conversion to Catholicism. At his baptism in Paris on Dec. 24, 1826, he changed his name from Jacob to François Marie Paul. In 1827 he entered the Sulpician seminary at Issy, but an attack of epilepsy (1829) shortly before the subdiaconate impeded his reception of Holy Orders. Because of his wholesome influence on the seminarians, he was permitted to remain as part of the staff. While still in minor orders he acted as novice master (1837–39) to the EUDISTS, who were reorganizing after their suppression during the French Revolution. Acquaintance with Creole seminarians inspired Libermann to found the Society of the Immaculate Heart of Mary to evangelize former slaves (1839). In 1840 he went to Rome to win approval for the new society and was ordained there (1841). In 1841 he also opened the society's first novitiate at Neuville, near Amiens. Seven of his missionaries accompanied the Irish-American bishop Edward BARRON to Africa (1843) and were among the first to penetrate the interior. Later the congregation was entrusted with missions in Mauritius, Réunion, and Haiti. At the Holy See's request, Libermann's society merged in 1848 with the HOLY GHOST FATHERS, founded in 1703 but in decline since the French Revolution. Libermann became their eleventh superior general. He continued the educational traditions of the older congregation but infused it with the missionary spirit and apostolic methods of the newer institute. Libermann's spirituality was characterized by concreteness; its essential features were later popularized by St. THÉRÈSE DE LISIEUX as the way of spiritual childhood. The decree approving the heroicity of Libermann's virtues was issued in 1910.

Bibliography: G. LEE, *The Life of the Venerable Francis Libermann* (St. Louis 1911; repr. London 1937). E. LEEN, *The Voice of a Priest* (New York 1946). H. W. HOMAN, *Star of Jacob* (New York 1953). A. L. VAN KAAM, *A Light to the Gentiles* (Milwaukee 1962).

[A. L. VAN KAAM]

LIBERTAS

Encyclical letter of Pope LEO XIII on human liberty, issued June 20, 1888. In what is in effect a miniature philosophical treatise on the nature of human liberty, Leo examined the so-called "modern liberties" and issued certain practical directives to European, especially French, Catholics.

The 19th century had seen the rise of the political and ethical philosophy that came to be called liberalism. Often referred to as continental or European liberalism (to distinguish it from more recent American usage), this philosophy embodied the denial of any divine authority and the refusal to accept it as a law or norm of the human will. Thus, in Leo's words, "What naturalists or rationalists aim at in philosophy, that the supporters of liberalism . . . are attempting in the domain of morality and politics. The fundamental doctrine of rationalism is the supremacy of the human reason, which . . . proclaims its own independence and constitutes itself the supreme principle and source and judge of truth. Hence, these followers of liberalism deny the existence of any divine authority to which obedience is due, and proclaim that every man is the law to himself; from which arises that ethical system which they style independent morality, and which under the guise of liberty, exonerates man from any obedience to the law of God and substitutes a boundless license" (par. 15).

Opposing this doctrine, Leo explains human liberty as it has ever been "cherished by the Catholic Church." He distinguishes between natural liberty, which belongs to man as endowed with intelligence, and moral liberty, which consists in choosing that good only which is in conformity with the judgment of reason. He is primarily concerned with moral liberty. Because the intellect and will of man are defective, law is morally necessary as a guide to knowledge of what is objectively reasonable and unreasonable. But law must be understood adequately. Hence, natural law and human (civil) law are analyzed. Their source is in divine law, which is ultimately "the sole standard and rule of human liberty" (par. 10). True moral liberty, therefore, requires submission to the authority of God commanding good and forbidding evil.

As he had already done on other occasions, Leo discusses the four major "modern liberties": liberty of worship, of speech and press, of teaching error, and of conscience. His purpose is to distinguish between the good and evil elements in these liberties. The Church approves the good, and condemns the evil.

The last part of the encyclical comments indirectly on the situation in France, where a dispute existed between conservative and progressive Catholics. The dispute was as political as it was doctrinal, and the pope encouraged men on both sides of it to strike a balance, pointing out that the Church accepts any form of government that truly promotes the common good, and that Catholics should take part in public affairs.

Bibliography: *Acta Sanctae Sedis* 20:593–613, has the official Latin text.

[D. L. LOWERY]

LIBRI CAROLINI

A Carolingian work in four volumes stating, in CHARLEMAGNE's name, the objections of his circle of theologians to the restoration of images in the Byzantine Church by the Second Council of NICAEA (787). A copy of the council's proceedings was brought by two papal legates to Rome, where an anonymous cleric prepared an imperfect translation that was sent by ADRIAN I to Charlemagne. This garbled version gave rise to the impression at the Frankish court that the Empress IRENE and her bishops had enjoined on all Christians, under pain of anathema, what was taken to be the worship of images. An official protest was planned.

The Nicene acts were read in Charlemagne's presence, and a list of objections drawn up. These became the *capitula* of the projected work and were sent to Adrian; his reply survives. A delegation of bishops took a fair copy of the work, once completed, to Rome. The original, working copy was kept in the imperial archives, where HINCMAR later saw and studied it; he had a copy made at Reims *c.* 850 (now MS Paris Arsenal 663).

This copy was discovered and its contents published (1549) pseudonymously by Jean du Tillet, afterward bishop of Meaux. New controversy now surrounded the work, whose arguments were enthusiastically adopted by Protestant apologists. Catholics rejected it as a forgery, and it was placed on the Index, where it remained until 1900. In 1865 the original copy was found in the Vatican Library (from which, several centuries earlier, the presentation copy made for Adrian I had disappeared); this at last established the work's authenticity.

Debate has continued, however, on the question of its authorship. The traditional attribution to ALCUIN is questionable, since Alcuin was in England from 790 to 793, the period during which the work was composed. New evidence has recently been discovered in its scriptural citations, which contain reminiscences of the Visigothic liturgy. These formulas, unique in Spanish sources, indicate authorship by THEODULF OF ORLÉANS, the only Spaniard at the Carolingian court, who had a natural tendency to quote Scripture in the familiar phrases of his native liturgy. In addition, the orthography—in its original version—displayed many Spanish peculiarities; these were carefully corrected in the SCRIPTORIUM.

Other corrections reflect the roundtable discussions that accompanied final preparation of the work. Official comments by the critics were noted in the margins, at first in minuscule; later these comments were transcribed into Tironian notes and the minuscule notations erased. The Vatican MS (Vat. lat. 7207) now contains 192 folia (it lacks the preface and bk. 4, which may be supplied from Arsenal 663), in a carefully executed early Caroline minuscule. The script is that of the Palace school.

The Carolingian stand on the veneration of IMAGES is conventional; images are "ornaments" in churches and reminders to the faithful of the heroism of the saints. The *Libri Carolini* show that Charlemagne's theologians did not understand the real issues of the controversy over ICONOCLASM in the East. The work has cardinal importance, however, for the history of CHURCH AND STATE in the West. It anticipates Charlemagne's imperial role as protector of the faith and illustrates all the characteristic principles and predilections of his scholars; it is a *summa* of Carolingian thought.

Bibliography: *Libri Carolini,* ed. H. BASTGEN, *Monumenta Germanica Historica* (Berlin 1826–) *Concilia* v. 2 suppl. G. MERCATI, "Per la storia del codice Vaticano dei *Libri Carolini,*" *Bessarione* 37 (1921) 112–119. W. VON DEN STEINEN, "Entstehungsgeschichte der *Libri Carolini,*" *Quellen und Forschungen aus italienische Archiven und Bibliothekan* 21 (1929–30) 1–93; "Karl der Grosse und die *Libri Carolini,*" *Neues Archiv der Gesellschaft für ältere deutsche Geschichtskunde* 49 (1930–32) 207–280. D. DE BRUYNE, "La Composition des *Libri Carolini,*" *Revue Bénédictine* 44 (1932) 227–234. A. FREEMAN, "Theodulf of Orléans and the *Libri Carolini,*" *Speculum* 32 (1957) 663–705. L. WALLACH, "The Unknown author of the *Libri Carolini,*" *Didascaliae: Studies in Honor of Anselm M. Albareda,* ed. S. PRETE (New York 1961) 469–515. *Codices latini antiquiores,* ed. E. A. LOWE (Oxford 1934–) v.1, on Vat. lat. 7207 (and Paris Arsenal 663). A. FREEMAN, "Further Studies in the *Libri Carolini,*" *Speculum* 40 (1965) 203–289.

[A. FREEMAN]

LIBYA, THE CATHOLIC CHURCH IN

The Socialist People's Libyan Arab Jamahiriay, commonly known as Libya, is located in North Africa, south of the Mediterranean Sea. Bordered by the Gulf of Sidra to the north, Libya is bordered on the east by EGYPT, on the southeast by SUDAN, on the south by CHAD and NIGER, and on the west by ALGERIA and TUNISIA. Containing the northeast section of the Sahara, Libya is a desert region, its agricultural areas restricted to its northern coastline. The central region contains highland areas, with oases marking the Hammada al-Hamra, Fezzan, and Murzuch regions to the south. Farm crops include wheat, barley, dates, citrus fruits, and peanuts, while the region's large oil deposits have made crude oil and refined petroleum products Libya's main exports.

Although Libya became independent in 1951, after a coup by the military in 1969 it was transformed into a military dictatorship. Despite the wealth generated by its

---

Capital: Tripoli.
Size: 678,400 sq. miles.
Population: 5,115,450 in 2000.
Languages: Arabic; Italian and English are spoken in urban areas.
Religions: 51,000 Catholics (.9%), 4,961,986 Sunni Muslims (97%), 102,464 (2.1%) other faiths.

---

oil exports, Libyan society was hampered by an undeveloped infrastructure, and mismanagement of its socialist economy led to frequent food shortages and other economic hardships. Most Libyans are of Berber or Arab descent; ethnic minorities include Greeks, Maltese, Egyptians, Pakistanis, Indians, and Italians.

Libya is the name by which the ancient Greeks referred to all of northern Africa except Egypt. The following essay presents the history of Libya from the seventh century to the present.

After the Muslims conquered Egypt in the seventh century, they drove west and occupied Libya in 641. Although Christians there were at first tolerated as DHIMMI, Christianity languished as the older population gradually embraced both the religion and the language of their Arab conquerors. The Islamization of the country was completed in 1067, when the new tribes from Arabia settled in the land. A prefecture was established at Tripoli in 1643, under the care of Italian Franciscans, who in the early days exercised works of charity in the ports, principally among Christians, merchants, and captives, but did little among the nomadic Sanussi tribes of Libya's desert regions.

Libya remained under Turkish rule for the next several centuries, during which time few inroads were made by the Church. In 1912 the Turks were defeated and an Italian administration took over. Soon settlers arrived in the country, attended by priests, and in 1913 Tripoli was raised to the rank of a vicariate, whose territory covered the whole of Libya. As Italian immigration increased, this vast territory became too great for a single ecclesiastical administration, and in 1927 it was divided into the Vicariate of Tripoli, in the west, and that of Cyrenaica, or Benghazi, in the east. In 1939 two more territories were detached from Cyrenaica: the Prefecture of Misurata and the Vicariate Apostolic of Derna. Derna was entrusted to the Salesians, the other territories remaining in the hands of the Franciscans.

Libya was the scene of heavy fighting between German-Italian and British forces during World War II. When war broke out in 1939, the region's European population was significant, but after occupation by the British

in 1943, the Italian administration was expelled, and many settlers left the country. On Dec. 24, 1951, the region achieved independence as the Kingdom of Libya, and within ten years its economy had strengthened due to the exportation of oil. However, the monarchy was short-lived; on Sept. 1, 1969, a military junta under the leadership of Col. Mu'ammar Abu Minyar al-Quadhafi took control and began a reign of terror. Active in efforts to destabilize both capitalism and communism, Quadhafi

at first attempted militancy by invading Chad in the 1980s, but his failure there led him to support the terrorist efforts of others. While Libyan-sponsored terrorism decreased following a U.N.-imposed trade embargo from 1992–99, they remained a source of conflict within the Middle East. However, by 2000 the Libyan government surprised the world when it took an active role in ending a hostage crisis caused by Philippine rebels, even going so far as to pay the ransom money.

Even before Quadhafi's rise to power, changes had taken place in the number and composition of Libya's Catholic clergy; the number of Franciscans gradually diminished, and the Salesians handed over to Benghazi the administration of the Vicariate of Derna. During the late 20th century, Quadhafi established the Islamic Call Society (ICS), a moderate Islamic group that promoted the Libyan government's political and social agenda while also undermining Islamic fundamentalism and establishing relations with Libya's other faiths.

In 2000 the Church maintained apostolic vicariates in Benghazi and Tripoli, as well as an apostolic prefecture in Misurata. In Tripoli the bishop served the Italian community, while Benghazi's bishop administered to the city's predominately Maltese Catholic population. Coptic and Greek Orthodox clergy also worked in the cities of Tripoli and Benghazi. Libya established diplomatic relations with the Holy See in 1997, and as the region' first apostolic nuncio, Bishop Jose Sebastian Laboa defended the courage of the Libyan people during a politically difficult period.

Despite its status as a minority religion in a predominately Muslim nation, the Church took responsibility for a number of charitable and cultural activities, among them hospitals, schools, and homes for the handicapped. Catholic schools, open also to Muslim children, provided education for thousands of Libyan young people. While members of religious orders had been restricted from entering the country during the 1970s and 1980s, this situation was reversed and religious were actively encouraged to enter Libya after U.N.-imposed trade sanctions caused shortages of medical aid and other necessary supplies. While opposing Libya's role in terrorist activities, Pope John Paul II's activism was instrumental in finally lifting the U.N. trade sanctions, thus aiding the region's economy in recovery as Libya moved into the new millennium.

Bibliography: C. BERGNA, *La missione franciscana in Libya* (Tripoli 1924); *La missione franciscana in Tripoli dal 1510 al 1850* (Tripoli 1925). *Conspectus missionum O. F. M.* (Rome 1957) 37–47. *Bilan du Monde* 2:566–569.

[J. CUOQ/EDS.]

LICCIO, JOHN, BL.

Italian Dominican preacher and reformer; b. Càccamo (Palermo), *c.* 1426; d. there, 1511. He received the religious habit at about 15 years of age in the Monastery of Santa Zita in Palermo, where he learned the spirit of religious reform from his superior (Bl.) Pietro Geremia. He preached with success in Sicily, Vicenza, and Naples. In 1469 he established the Monastery of the Holy Spirit

in Polizzi, and in 1487 that of Càccamo, where he was the first vicar until 1494, and then first prior until his death. He was elected vicar-general of the reformed congregation of Sicily in 1488 and ten years later became vicar-general of the entire Sicilian Province and also canonical visitor for the reform of the monasteries of Augusta, Taormina, and Trapani. Miracles occurring during his life and during the transfer of his relics led to his beatification by BENEDICT XIV on April 25, 1753.

Feast: Nov. 14.

Bibliography: *Monumenta Ordinis Fratrum Praedicatorum historica* 14 (1904): 229–230. G. BARRECA, *Vita del beato Giovanni Liccio da Càccamo* (3d ed. Palermo 1953). I. TAURISANO, *Catalogus hagiographicus ordinis praedicatorum* (Rome 1918). M. S. CONIGLIONE, *La Provincia domenicana di Sicilia* (Catania 1937); *Pietro Geremia* (Catania 1952); *Il beato Giovanni Liccio da Càccamo* (Palermo 1955).

[A. L. REDIGONDA]

LICHTENBERG, BERNHARD, BL.

Priest, martyr, provost of Berlin; b. Dec. 3, 1875, Ohlau, Silesia, Poland (then Germany); d. Nov. 5, 1943, Hof, Upper Franconia, Germany.

One of five children of the devout Catholic grocer August Lichtenberg and his wife, Emilie, Bernhard was raised in the predominantly Protestant town of Ohlau. After studying in Prague, Munich, and Innsbruck, he completed his theological studies in Breslau (now Wrocław, Poland), where he was ordained in 1899. He held various parish assignments in Berlin, then in 1914 served as military chaplain. In 1931 he joined St. Hedwig's cathedral chapter in Berlin, where he was appointed to the parish the following year and named provost in January 1938. He was a tireless promoter of the apostolate for priestly vocations.

As early as 1935, Lichtenberg protested from St. Hedwig's pulpit and to the government leaders against the atrocities in the concentration camps. Lichtenberg condemned the elimination of religious instruction in the schools, the secularization of marriage, and the euthanasia practiced against the innocent. Beginning in November 1938, he prayed publicly every day "for the oppressed non-Aryan Christians, for the persecuted Jews, and for prisoners in the concentration camps." Arrested in October 1941 but released shortly thereafter, he continued his prayers and protests. On May 22, 1942, he was sentenced to two years' imprisonment for treason and "misuse of his official position." While in prison Lichtenberg, who was 68 years old, suffered a heart attack. The Gestapo, fearing he would die in Berlin in their custody, put him in a cattle car en route to Dachau concentration camp. At Hof he was so sick that he was unloaded and taken to the city hospital, where he died.

John Paul II declared Lichtenberg a martyr July 2, 1994. Following the beatification rite in Berlin's Olympic Stadium June 23, 1996, during John Paul II's third pastoral visit to Germany, the pope prayed at the martyr's tomb in the crypt of St. Hedwig's Cathedral.

Feast: Nov. 5 (Archdiocese of Berlin).

Bibliography: W. ADOLPH, *Im Schatten des Galgens* (Berlin 1953). A. ERB, *Bernhard Lichtenberg: Dompropst von St. Hedwig zu Berlin,* 5th ed. (Berlin 1968). C. FELDMANN, *Wer glaubt, muss widerstehen: Bernhard Lichtenberg-Karl Leisner,* 3d. ed. (Freiburg 1996). D. HANKY, *Bernhard Lichtenberg. Priester. Bekenner. Martyrer* (Berlin 1994). B. M. KEMPER, *Priester vor Hitlers Tribunalen* (Munich 1996). E. KOCK, *Er widerstand* (Berlin 1996). H. KÜHN, *Blutzeugen des Bistums Berlin* (Berlin 1952). K. MAGIERA, *Bernhard Lichtenberg* (Berlin 1963). O. OGIERMANN, *Bis zum letzten Atemzug* (Leipzig 1983).

[K. I. RABENSTEIN]

LICINIUS OF ANGERS, ST.

Bishop; b. *c.* 540; d. *c.* 610. According to his biographies, one written by an anonymous author of Angers, the other by MARBOD OF RENNES, archdeacon at Angers, Licinius (Lésin) was born of a wealthy, noble family and was educated at the royal court. He was made count of Anjou by Clotaire II (d. 628) and at the urging of the court and his family was about to marry the daughter of a prominent nobleman. By divine intervention, as his biographers insist, the young lady was stricken by leprosy, whereupon Licinius left the court and became a cleric. When the See of ANGERS became vacant, Licinius was chosen bishop, possibly in 592, and fulfilled the duties of this office with great zeal and effectiveness. In 601 Pope GREGORY I THE GREAT wrote a letter to seven Frankish bishops, one of them Licinius, recommending to their charity the monks who were on their way to help AUGUSTINE OF CANTERBURY in England (P. Jaffé, ed. P. Ewald, *Regesta pontificum romanorum ab condita ecclesia ad annun post Christum natum 1198,* 205). The monastery of St. John the Baptist, to which Charles II the Bald later granted some property, was founded by this saintly bishop of Angers. In his last will and testament BERTRAM, bishop of Le Mans, makes mention of the close friendship that existed between him and Licinius (*Dictionnaire d'archéologie chrétienne et de liturgie,* 15 v. [Paris 1907–53] 10:1506, 1519).

Feast: Feb. 13 (Angers); Nov. 1 (Roman MARTYROLOGY).

Bibliography: *Acta Sanctorum* Feb. 2:675–686. *Gallia Christiana,* v. 14–16 (Paris 1856–65) 14:549, 599, app. 146. J. L.

BAUDOT and L. CHAUSSIN, *Vies des saints et des bienheureux selon l'ordre du calendrier ave l'historique des fêtes,* 12 v. (Paris 1935–56) 11:56–58. J. CAMBELL, *Lexikon für Theologie und Kirche,* ed. J. HOFER and K. RAHNER, 10 v. (Freiburg 1957–65) 6:1029. L. RÉAU, *Iconographie de l'art chrétien,* 6 v. (Paris 1955–59) 3.2:805. *Bibliotheca hagiographica latina antiquae et mediae aetatis,* 2 v. (Brussels 1898–1901) 2:4917–4918. J. LEVRON, *Les Saints du pays angevin* (Grenoble 1943) 73–84.

[H. DRESSLER]

LIDANUS, ST.

Benedictine abbot and monastic founder; b. Antina, Italy, *c.* 1026; d. Sezze, Italy, 1118. He is believed to have entered the monastery of MONTE CASSINO at an early age. He was the founder and first abbot of the monastery of St. Cecilia at Sezze. He is especially noted for the part he played in the work of draining the Pontine marshes, where his monastery was located. He is the patron of Sezze, where his relics are venerated.

Feast: July 2 (Sezze); April 27 and July 18.

Bibliography: *Acta Sanctorum* Jul. 1:302–309. *Bibliotheca hagiographica latina antiquae et mediae aetatis,* 2 v. (Brussels 1898–1901) 2:4919–4921. A. M. ZIMMERMANN, *Kalendarium Benedictinum: Die Heiligen und Seligen des Benediktinerorderns und seiner Zweige,* 4 v. (Metten 1933–38) 2:390, 393. V. VENDITTI, *La leggenda medioevale di Lidano d'Antena* (Turin 1959).

[K. NOLAN]

LIDGETT, JOHN SCOTT

English Methodist divine; b. Lewisham, Aug. 10, 1854; d. Epsom, June 16, 1953. After studying at the University of London, he was ordained to the Methodist ministry (1876). He became a noted preacher with a passion for social justice. Lidgett is remembered best for his foundation in 1891 of the Bermondsey Settlement, in which he held the position of warden. He was active in London municipal politics and served as alderman on the London County Council (1905–10) and as leader of the Progressive party (1919–28). He was editor of the *Methodist Times* (1907–18) and president of the Methodist Conference (1908). In 1932 he was instrumental in uniting the Wesleyan Methodist Church with the Primitive Methodist Church and the United Methodist Church, and then he became the first president of the United Methodist Church of Great Britain. At the University of London he sat on the senate (1926–46) and became vice chancellor (1930). His publications include *The Spiritual Principle of the Atonement* (1897), *The Christian Religion: Its Meaning and Proof* (1907), *The Idea of God and Social Ideals* (1938), *God and the World* (1943), and *Salvation* (1952).

LIECHTENSTEIN

0   2   4 Miles

0   2   4 Kilometers

Bibliography: E. W. BAKER et al., *John Scott Lidgett: A Symposium,* ed. R. E. DAVIES (London 1957).

[W. HANNAH]

LIECHTENSTEIN, THE CATHOLIC CHURCH IN

A sovereign principality located on the right bank of the Rhine, the Principality of Liechtenstein is bordered on the west and south by the Swiss cantons of Saint Gallen and Graubünden and the east by the Austrian province of Vorarlberg. A lowland region bordering the Rhine characterizes its west, while the landscape of the princi-

pality rises to mountainous terrain and a portion of the Rhaetian Alps to the south. Liechtenstein's economy depends largely on light industry; agricultural crops include corn, wine and fruit. Farming and stock raising have diminished in importance as the population has become increasingly urbanized. Small machinery, dental products, hardware and pottery now account for much of its exports. One of the smallest nations in the world, Liechtenstein derives 30 percent of its state revenues from the nominal incorporation of foreign companies, which establish "letter box" offices in the principality to benefit from Liechtenstein's low business tax rate. Almost half of the principality's labor force are residents of Austria and Switzerland.

The principality was formed in 1719 from the union of the Barony of Schellenberg with the County of Vaduz; it continued to be part of the Holy Roman Empire until July 12, 1806, when it gained its independence as part of the Rhine Federation. It became wholly independent in 1866, and to preserve its neutrality into the future had abolished its army within two years. The 1921 constitution established a constitutional, hereditary monarchy based on democratic and parliamentary principles. Although once linked to Austria, Liechtenstein has retained close ties with Switzerland since World War I; it uses the Swiss franc as its currency, and is in a customs union with Switzerland, which administers its telegraph and postal systems. Women were given the right to vote in national (but not local) elections in 1984.

History. Christianity entered Liechtenstein in the 4th century. Ecclesiastical jurisdiction over the region was exercised by the Diocese of Chur in SWITZERLAND probably by the 4th century, certainly by the 5th. Chur also covered Zurich and eastern Switzerland. The highland region belonged from the beginning to the deanery of Unter der Landquart (*Capitulum sub Langaro*); the lowland, not until 1370. Previously Liechtenstein was part of the deanery of Walgau (*Capitulum vallis Trusianae*). Beginning in 1717 Liechtenstein pertained to the chapter of Walgau; after its independence in 1816 it gained its own chapter under a local vicar (*Landesvikar*). During the Protestant Reformation Liechtensteiners remained loyal to the Catholic Church, thanks in good part to the attitude of their civil rulers. Historians have argued that, in 1943, German Chancellor Adolph Hitler considered a plan to take control of the Vatican by deporting Pope Pius XII to Liechtenstein, although this scheme was never realized.

The constitution of Oct. 5, 1921 guaranteed freedom of conscience and of religion to all residents. As the national church (*Landeskirche*), the Catholic Church enjoyed the full protection of the government, and was funded in full by the government until the late 1990s, when the relationship between the State and the Church came under renewed scrutiny. While these financial arrangements remained pending through 2002, the government continued to allocate church funds into an escrow account. Other beliefs were granted freedom of worship within the limits of morality and public order, and also received state funding in proportion to their membership. Civil legislation permitted separation from bed and board but not divorce. Pastors were also civil officials. An Evangelical Church was organized in 1881, and in 1961 was formally established in the Principality of Liechtenstein under the patronage of the Reformed Church (*Landeskirche*) of Saint Gallen.

In 1997 the Vatican established a new diocese in Vaduz, to be headed by Bishop Wulfgang Haas, a liberal and somewhat controversial former bishop of Chur. Vaduz, like Chur, was immediately subject to the Holy See. Liechtenstein had ten parishes, administered by 16 secular and ten religious priests (*see* LA SALETTE, MISSIONARIES OF OUR LADY OF). Several MARIST BROTHERS engaged in secondary school teaching, while additional care was offered by the 62 PRECIOUS BLOOD SISTERS, members of both Sisters Adorers of the Most Precious Blood and Sisters of the Precious Blood of Schellenberg, Liechtenstein. Religious training remained compulsory in all public schools, unless a parental exemption was requested. The government supported ecumenical dialogues and funded adult education in religion.

Bibliography: A. FROMMELT, ''Fürstentum Liechtenstein,'' *Helvetia Christiana: Bistum Chur,* v.1 (Zurich 1942) 209–234; ''Das Fürstentum Liechtenstein im Bistumsverband,'' in *1500 Jahre Bistum Chur* (Zurich 1950) 211–221. E. POESCHEL, *Die Kunstdenkmäler des Fürstentums Liechtenstein* (Basel 1950). *Jahrbuch des Historischen Vereins ür das Fürstentum Liechtenstein* (Vaduz 1901–). I. MÜLLER, ''Die Patrozinien des F.L.,'' *ibid.* 59 (1959) 303–327. M. H. VICAIRE and N. BACKMUND, *Dictionnaire d'histoire et de géographie ecclésiastiques,* ed. A. BAUDRILLART et al. (Paris 1912–) 13:213–221, s.v. ''Chur.''

[R. ALLGÄUER/EDS.]

LIÈGE

City on both banks of the Meuse River in east Belgium; capital of Liège Province; and a diocese (*Leodiensis*) comprising Liège and Limburg Provinces, 2,426 square miles in area.

Liège owes its origin to the fact that LAMBERT, Bishop of Maastricht, built near a Merovingian *portus* an oratory where he was murdered. His successor, Hubert, impressed by the miracles that took place, established his see there (717–718), suffragan to COLOGNE. Liège became an ecclesiastical principality under the German Holy Roman Empire *c.* 980 and remained so until the French Revolution. Under the first PRINCE-BISHOP, Notker (972–1008), and his successor, WAZO, the cathedral school flourished, ''the Athens of the North,'' until it gave way to the University of Paris. RATHERIUS OF VERONA (d. 974) and HERIGER OF LOBBES were literary figures associated with Liège. The Peace of God was introduced into the Empire form Liège (1082). JULIANA OF LIÈGE in 1246 had Bishop Robert establish a special feast in honor of the Blessed Sacrament, which Urban IV prescribed for the whole Church. Bishops of the 16th century successfully opposed various Protestant movements.

When new dioceses were created in the Low Countries (1559), the bishop of Liège lost half his see but nonetheless promulgated the reforms of the Council of Trent and founded a seminary. In the 18th century the ENLIGHTENMENT made progress; Bp. François-Charles de Velbruck (1772–84) belonged to the Masons. In 1795 France annexed the town and principality. The CONCORDAT OF 1801 gave Liège its present territory with the collegiate church of St-Paul as cathedral; St-Lambert having been demolished by French Revolutionaries. In 1815 Liège went to the United Kingdom of the Netherlands, and in 1830 became part of Belgium. The city, which in the 16th century had a school of humanities, obtained a university in 1816. The fact that Liège was for many centuries the seat of a diocese and of an ecclesiastical principality explains its riches in churches, abbeys, and convents, as well as the anticlerical feeling of the population.

St-Paul, founded in 969, built in the 13th and restored in the 16th century, the cathedral since 1802, contains the shrine of St. Lambert in gilded silver. The collegiate St-Barthélémy, in part 11th and 12th century, has famous baptismal fonts by Renier de Huy (1111–18). St-Croix, founded by Notker, has a west apse in 13th-century Rhenish Romanesque. St-Denis, with the oldest Romanesque tower in Belgium, has a 14th-century Gothic choir. St-Jacques, rebuilt in 16th-century flamboyant Gothic; has a rich decor and a Renaissance side portal. The palace of the prince-bishops (1526–38), now the Palais de Justice, has an inside court with original composite columns. The church of the Benedictine Abbey of St-Jacques (1015), which was suppressed in the French Revolution, became a parish church.

Bibliography: J. DARIS, *Notices historiques sur les églises du diocèse de Liège,* 17 v. (Liège 1867–99). T. GOBERT, *Liège à travers les âges,* 6 v. (2d ed. Liège 1924–29). J. PAQUAY, ed., *La Collégiale de Saint-Barthélémy à Liège* (Liège 1935). G. DE FROIDCOURT, *François-Charles, comte de Velbruck, prince-évêque de Liège, franc-maçon* (Liège 1936). É. DE MOREAU, *Histoire de l'Église en Belgique,* 5 v. (Brussels 1945–52), 2 suppl. J. LEJEUNE, *La Princip-*

auté de Liège (Liège 1948). J. PHILIPPE, *L'Ancien palais des princes de Liège* (Liège 1949). J. STIENNON, *Étude sur le chartrier et le domaine de l'Abbaye de Saint Jacques de Liège,* 1015–1029 (Liège 1956). L. DEWEZ, *La Cathédrale Saint-Paul à Liège* (Liège 1956). P. HARSIN, *Études critiques sur l'histoire de la principauté de Liège, 1477–1795,* 3 v. (Liège 1956–59).

[M. DIERICKX]

LIÉNART, ACHILLE

Cardinal, bishop of Lille, France; b. Lille (Nord), France, Feb. 7, 1884; d. Lille, Feb. 15, 1973. He studied at the College of St. Joseph in Lille and the Seminary of St. Sulpice in Paris, where he was ordained to the priesthood on June 29, 1907. Remaining in Paris for further studies, he received licentiates in theology from the Institut Catholique and in letters from the Sorbonne. He completed his studies in Rome, receiving a doctorate in theology and a licentiate in Sacred Scripture from the Pontifical Biblical Institute. Upon his return to France, he taught Sacred Scripture at the grand seminary in Cambrai (1910–14) and at the grand seminary of the new diocese of Lille (1919–26). During World War I he served as a volunteer chaplain and received the *Croix de guerre* with six citations. From 1926 to 1928, he was pastor of St. Christopher's parish in the industrial city of Tourcoing. On Dec. 8, 1928, he was consecrated bishop of Lille, where he served until his resignation due to age on March 14, 1968.

As bishop, his two deepest concerns were the care of souls and social justice. He built a new diocesan seminary, completed the Cathedral of Notre Dame de Treille, and called a diocesan synod to draw up the first statutes of the diocese. During a bitter strike in 1929 he sided with the workers and won Vatican support for the right and duty of Catholic workers to form labor unions. The following year, Pope Pius XI appointed him cardinal. A vigorous advocate of Catholic Action as the remedy for social ills, he condemned both atheistic materialism and economic liberalism. He served as president of the Assembly of French Cardinals and Archbishops from 1940 to 1966 and, concurrently from 1954, as director of the Mission of France. During the Nazi occupation, he publicly opposed forced labor and rendered notable assistance to the victims of the war. In 1947 he journeyed to Cameroon, where the first sections of the association *Ad Lucem,* which he established to send lay Catholics to help in mission lands, were located. He took a pivotal role in the Second Vatican Council, where he insisted at the opening session that the council must be master of its own house and not merely the rubber stamp for the work of the preparatory commissions. He was mainly responsible for the revision of the "Schema on the Sources of Di-

vine Revelation" and was a staunch advocate of a strong statement on behalf of the Jews. His many pastoral letters and statements constitute a corpus of contemporary Catholic theology on the whole range of problems facing modern man.

Bibliography: *L'Ame du régiment, l'abbé Thibaut* (Cambrai 1922). *Dans les pas de Jésus* (Paris 1953). *La Semaine Religieuse de Lille* (1928–68). W. ABBOTT, SJ, *Twelve Council Fathers* (New York 1963). P. LESOURD and J. M. RAMIZ, *Achille Cardinal Liénart* (Notre Dame, Ind. 1965).

[F. MURPHY]

LIESBORN, ABBEY OF

Benedictine monastery in the Diocese of Münster, Westphalia, founded in 1131 by monks from Werden. They were invited by Bishop Egbert to replace a community of nuns that, having been founded there *c.* 815, was suppressed by the bishop because of relaxed discipline. By the 13th century the abbey was rich and powerful, but religious life declined and it became a kind of rest home for the nobility. Discipline was restored when it joined the Bursfeld Union in 1465 under Abbot Heinrich of Cleves (1464–90). Under Abbot Johann Smalebecker (1490–1522) it became famous as a center of art and learning, and because of its influence in the reform of other communities it was known as the Bursfeld of the West. The Gothic abbatial church was completed in 1506. In the 16th century decline set in under several unworthy abbots, and the wars of the 17th century caused more disorder. There was a period of improvement after the Peace of Westphalia in 1648, but 18th-century wars caused a new decline. It was deeply in debt when it was suppressed in 1803.

Bibliography: L. SCHMITZ-KALLENBERG, *Monasticon Westfaliae* (Münster 1909). J. LINNEBORN, "Das Kloster Liesborn zur Zeit seiner Aufhebung," *Studien und Mitteilungen* 23 (1902) 309–339. B. SENGER, *Lexikon für Theologie und Kirche,* ed. J. HOFER and K. RAHNER, 10 v. (2d, new ed. Freiburg 1957–65) 6:1048.

[C. FALK]

LIESSIES, ABBEY OF

Former Benedictine monastery near Avesnes (Nord), France, Diocese of Cambrai (patron, St. Lambert). Very little is known of its origin: according to the 11th-century *Vita* of St. Hiltrude, it was founded in the 8th century, *c.* 764, by Count Wibert whose son Guntrade was first superior, and whose daughter Hiltrude lived a holy life nearby. It is quite possible that originally it was a double MONASTERY. The great riches given by its founder disappeared during the following centuries as a result of SECU-LARIZATIONS (of church property) and Norman invasions. When in 1095, Thierry, lord of Avesnes, decided to restore the monastery, it was occupied by only four canons. Its restoration was in fact a refoundation: BENEDICTINES were introduced and the monastery was once again richly endowed. But prosperity was short-lived and Liessies remained in the following centuries a small abbey often experiencing financial difficulties that, in turn, made difficult the practice of regular observance. The great abbot of Liessies was Bl. F. Louis BLOSIUS (1530–66), whose many ascetical treatises record the Benedictine program of asceticism he worked out for his monks; at the same time he reorganized the temporal administration of the abbey with such success that through him material well-being returned to the abbey temporarily and spiritual fervor, permanently. During the French Revolution, the religious were driven away, the goods of the monastery were sold, and the buildings gradually destroyed.

Bibliography: J. PETER, *L'Abbaye de Liessies* (Lille 1912). F. BAIX, *Dictionnaire d'histoire et de géographie ecclésiastiques,* ed. A. BAUDRILLART et al. (Paris 1912–) 9:228–242.

[H. PLATELLE]

LIETBERT OF CAMBRAI-ARRAS, ST.

Bishop of Cambrai; b. Brabant, Belgium; d. June 23, 1076. Lietbert (Liébert, Libert) became bishop of CAMBRAI in 1051, succeeding his uncle Gerard. He labored zealously for the peace and well-being of his people, protecting them from the extortions of Hugo, his bailiff, and those of Jean, castellan of Cambrai, who exiled him. After returning in triumph to his see, Lietbert led a PILGRIMAGE to the Holy Land (1054). He was forced to turn back when he heard that the Saracens had closed the Holy Sepulcher. Upon his return Lietbert gained a reputation as a builder for his establishment of the monastery and basilica of the Holy Sepulcher and for his construction of the churches of St. Croix and Saint-Vaast in Cambrai.

Feast: June 23.

Bibliography: *Acta Sanctorum* June 5 (1867): 498–516. *Bibliotheca hagiographica latina antiquae et mediae aetatis,* 2 v. (Brussels 1898–1901) 1:4928–4929. É. DE MOREAU, *Histoire de l'Église en Belgique* (2d ed. Brussels 1945–) 2:21–25. H. LANCELIN, *Histoire du diocèse de Cambrai* (Valenciennes 1946) 95–98.

[D. S. BUCZEK]

LIETZMANN, HANS

Protestant church historian; b. Düsseldorf, March 2, 1875; d. Berlin, June 25, 1942. Lietzmann spent his youth in Wittenberg, studied in Jena, and studied classical philology and theology at Bonn, coming under the influence of the New Testament scholar Eduard Graf and of Herman Usener for his formation in philology and religious science. Upon earning his licentiate in theology with a dissertation on *Der Menschensohn* in 1896, he taught for a few years. He returned to Bonn in 1900 for specialization in Church history, was called to Jena in 1905, and replaced HARNACK in Berlin in 1924, taking over the chairmanship of the Church Fathers' Commission in 1930. In 1920 he assumed editorship of the *Zeitschrift f. Neutestamentliches Wissenschaft.* He described his life's work as the attempt to "combine classical philology and theology in a unity" (*Autobiographie* 8), which he did by demonstrating an expert competence in Church history, archeology, liturgy, Canon Law, credal study, and papyrology. All these disciplines were employed in his highly influential *Petrus und Paulus in Rom* (1915; 2d ed. 1927). His ability in dealing with New Testament studies extended to both textual and exegetical fields, and his stylistic excellence was extraordinary as were the courage and depth of his judgments. Frequently in small brochures he opened up new approaches to knowledge, as in his *Schallanalyse und Textkritik* (1922) and his *Study of the Mandaeans* (*Beitrag zur Mandäerfrage* 1930). His four-volume *Geschichte der alten Kirche* is likewise a monument to his all-embracing competence (*see* MANDAEAN RELIGION).

Bibliography: H. LIETZMANN, "Autobiographie," *Religionwissenschaft der Gegenwart in Selbstdarstellungen* 2 (1926): 77–117; *Mass and Lord's Supper,* tr. D. H. G. REEVE (Leiden 1953–); *Kleine Schriften,* in *Texte und Untersuchungen zur Geschichte der altchristlichen Literatur* 3 (1958–62) 67,68,74, esp. in late antiquity, New Testament, liturgy, and symbol. H. LIETZMANN et al., eds., *Handbuch zum Neuen Testament,* 22 v. (Tübingen 1917–31). H. LIETZMANN and H. W. BEYER, *Die jüdische Katakombe der Villa Torlonia in Rom* (Berlin 1930). H. BORNKAMM, *Zeitschrift für die neutestamentliche Wissenschaft und die Kunde der älteren Kirche* 41 (1942): 1–12. K. ALAND, "Die Schriften H. Lietzmanns," *ibid.* 12–33. W. ELTESTER, *Die Religion in Geschichte und Gegenwart* 7 v. (3d ed. Tübingen 1957–65) 4:375–376.

[K. ALAND]

LIFE, CONCEPT OF (IN THE BIBLE)

Life, as understood in the Bible, is God's action within a plan of goodness and for a purpose, fully known only to Himself. God lives of Himself. Human life is God's manifest action in man and man's obedient response to God reverently rendered by his action toward his fellow men and, together with them, toward the good of all creation. Man possesses life as a gift, so free that he may choose to act outside God's plan of good and so lose the gift. Action apart from God's purpose is not life but death (Gn 2:17). In the first pages of the Bible one finds man and woman making the choice of death and God mercifully promising to continue His action as a redemptive force that they must use to struggle against death and the instigator of death, whom they have preferred. Addressing the woman, God lets them know that victory, and therefore fullness of life, will not come until one of her seed shall crush the enemy's head (Gn 3:15). The Bible is a record of God's life-giving action from the beginning, as it gradually became known to a people, Israel, the seed of Abraham (Gn 17:4–8). As a record, the Bible gives a full report of life in conflict with death.

In The Old Testament

Walter Eichrodt closes his revised edition of *The Theology of the Old Testament* (Philadelphia 1961) with an affirmation of unity and continuity in the Biblical concept of life and a critique (512–520) of E. von Rad's 1960 edition of *Old Testament Theology* (New York). Von Rad is more impressed by the complications in Biblical thought and does not find a unified theology in the Scriptures. Obviously, one cannot attempt extended observations here. Every tradition of thought that enters into the record takes the Torah, or PENTATEUCH, the divine instruction given to Moses and by him to the people, as its central position. Here one must be content to cite the Biblical texts to show that all traditions agree on the concept of life they find in the Torah. After considering the terminology connected with the OT idea of life, this section treats of Israel's concepts of the living God and man's corporate life and concludes with some remarks on the tensions in the life of the Israelite and his view of a future life.

Terminology. The Hebrew never speaks of life in the abstract. Life is always observable, something possessed. Basically, life is motion. To have life is to possess the power to act, to accomplish a task begun in man by God's *rûah*, His breath, His dynamic spirit (Gn 2:7). The primary meaning of *rûah* is wind; it is mobile and mobilizing. God's breath is the vital, always effective source of energy in men and animals, in all living things [Ps 103 (104):10–30]. Blood coursing through the flesh is the bearer of life in men and animals (Gn 9:4–5). Bubbling water is living water, the symbol of God and of His spirit (Ez 36:25–26; Jer 2:13). Fire is living fire, often a manifestation of God Himself [Ex 3:1–6; 19:16; Ps 17(18):13; 35(36):10]. Israel's conviction that man has breath from God in common with other earthly creatures (Gn 6:17) is never pantheistic monism, which would make all life one physical reality. Animals are different from men [Gn 2:20; Ps 48(49):13; 72(73):22; Jer 50:3]. God's life is ineffable (Ex 15:11; Is 40:25).

The terms translated into English as flesh, spirit, and soul may be used interchangeably to denominate the life of the whole man; yet, each may be used to express some individual manifestation of life that is its primary meaning. The most common names for life are *hayyîm* (life, lifetime, a period of existence), *rûah* (breath), *bāśār* (flesh), *nepeš* (soul), and *'ôr* (light, used metaphorically). "To see the light" is to remain alive, to find life or to return to life, freed from the power of death (Is 2:5; 53:11). Light is life [Mi 7:8; Is 60:1; Ps 12(13):4] and life-giving (Is 60:3). Darkness is evil, confusion, and death (Is 5:20; Lam 3:2). Man's *rûah,* his breath, his spirit, his soul is the principle of life within him, but not in the Greek dualistic sense. *See* SPIRIT (IN THE BIBLE). To the Hebrew, man is one, undivided being.

Flesh (*bāśār*) denotes man's whole being with an accent on his mortality and weakness [Ps 64(65):3]; less often it indicates the outer man only (Nm 19:8; Jgs 8:7). So also *nepeš* (soul, literally "breath": Jb 41:13) may signify life itself (Gn 35:18; Ex 21:23; 2 Kgs 17:21; etc.). The final result of God's act in creating mankind is a *nepeš hayyâ,* a "living soul," i.e., a living being (Gn 2:7). The *nepeš* is thus the being, the person, self [1 Sm 18:1; Ps 102(103):1; etc.]. *See* SOUL (IN THE BIBLE).

After his sin and God's merciful promise (Gn 3:15) man exists as living, but he is always in decline. Death can and does always intrude [Ps 17(18):5–6; 77(78):50; 89(90):10; Prv 13:14; Is 28:15]. The Hebrew speaks of grief, sickness, the calumny of enemies, and other dire afflictions as forms of death. *See* DEATH (IN THE BIBLE). When man overcomes these, he lives again [Ps 70(71): 20; Is 38:15–17].

In Biblical anthropology the heart (Heb. *lēb, lēbāb*) is the seat of man's inner life (Prv 4:20–23), thinking [Ps 13(14):1; 14(15):2; Prv 24:2], remembering (Dt 4:39), and freely moving toward whatever it determines (1 Sm 14:7; Is 10:7), but subject to God's word in the way of salvation (1 Sm 12:20; Prv 3:5). *See* HEART (IN THE BIBLE).

An Israelite "hears" the word of God in inanimate creation [Ps 18(19):2–5; 28(29):3–9] and in the events of history [Ex 19:4–6; Ps 80(81):11–12; Is 9:7–8]. He "sees" what God says to him (Hb 2:1). Vision born of fidelity enables him to assent to God's word [Ps 105(106):12; Ex 4:31] with joyful, confident certainty and self-abandonment [Ps 32(33):4, 20–22; 55(56):5; 72(73):23–28; Jb 42:1–6].

As knowledge and understanding grow in Israel, its record declares with ever greater force that the SPIRIT of God will bring life to fruition (Is 11:2; 42:1; 44:3; Jl 3:1–2). The spirit of the Lord continues to sustain the spirit He gives to men [Ps 138(139):7; Neh 9:20]. Yet in the OT God's spirit is never said to dwell in men. It is poured out upon them to enable them to respond to God's word and carry out His purpose (Is 42:5; 44:3), which they make their own (Is 61:1; 63:11–19).

The Living God. Taking the Bible on its own terms, there is nothing more obvious than that Israel's view of human life issues not from a mystic, other-worldly philosophy or a mystery cult, but from everyday, interpersonal experience within which God acts as Creator, Savior, and Lord (Dt 30:11–14). In the events of the Exodus, in which God led them out of the bondage of Egypt (Ex 13:21), a mixed multitude of people (Nm 11:4), partly Hebrew and partly other, saw God (Ex 4:30; 5:22–6:1; 19:4) in the signs He gave of Himself there. They learned to perceive, know, and acknowledge Him, day by day, as the living God, present in their midst (Ex 33:15), acting to save them (Ex 13:21; 14:30; 15:13; 16:15), merciful (Ex 16:11; Dt 6:20–23), and beneficent (Ex 33:12–17). They saw Him doing what was always good for them (Dt 4:32–40; 8:16), giving them what was fitting to their most urgent needs [Dt 1:25; 8:1–5; Ez 17:8; Ps 85(86):5], and moving them in the depths of their being (Ex 19:5; Dt 6:4–9) to imitate Him in their personal activity toward one another (Lv 19:18; Dt 24:10–22; Mi 6:8) and toward all creation (Gn 1:28–30; Dt 8:6–20; Wis 9:2–3). Guided by their leader Moses, they heard Him in the total outcome of their deliverance, calling, enlightening, and creating in them a life of corporate unity, a will to live in His presence [Ex 19:4–8; 33:16; Dt 4:9–14; 6:1–3; Ps 23(24):6; Lam 3:40] according to the pattern, purpose, and goal that His action had begun in them (Gn 12:3; Ex 3:6–10; 19:4–8; 20:1–17).

It is not in the scope here to show how or when the people reached into the primal fibers of their ancestral tradition to find that the activity of Yahweh was the true object of its myth-making attempts to explain cosmic beginnings. [*See* MYTH AND MYTHOLOGY (IN THE BIBLE)]. The OT authors are content to record, by allusion, that they did so [Gn 1:1–3:24; Is 51:9–10; Jb 3:8; 9:13; 26:12; 38:8–11; 40:25; Ps 32(33):7; 73(74). 12–17; 88(89): 10–11; etc.]. For them Moses was the embodiment of God's word (Sir 45:1–5) brought forward to his time (Sir 44:16–23) and carried forward to their own.

Israel did not know Yahweh's fullness, but they saw that He was not like the gods of other nations (Ex 8:6; 15:11; Is 44:6–8; Wis 15:1–17). He showed Himself as the living cause of all things that had already happened and all things yet to be (Dt 7:7–9; Is 40:26–31; Ez 39:21–29), in full control of all the elements of the earth (Exodus ch. 7–15; Psalm 8), unchanging King, enthroned forever [Ex 15:18; Dt 32:40; Is 40:28; Ps 91 (92); 92(93); 95(96)–98(99)]. He came to them as a person, one who plans and communicates toward a purpose (Dt 4:36–38; Is 45:1–13), and who sends men to communicate His purpose to others (Ex 3:16; Dt 5:5; Is 6:8; Zec 1:6).

The OT does not speak of God as spirit. It has been remarked often that, perhaps, the idea of God as spirit did not seem personal enough. Anthropomorphism, i.e., speaking of God as if He had human characteristics (Gn 2:3; 6:5–6; Ps 2:4; Is 62:5; etc.), is the Bible's way of describing God as living person. In no sense is God identified with men (Nm 23:19; Os 11:9; Is 40:25). Rather, if man lives as a free, knowing, loving, and choosing agent (Dt 11:26–28; Jos 24:14–15; Sir 15:11–20), it is because God is a person (Ex 33:14; Sir 17:1–18). Personal relationship between God, the sovereign Lord, and His people structures all Biblical life and thought (Dt 5:2–4; 6:4–9; Hos 2:9, 16; Am 3:2; Is 38:15–19; 40:1–2; etc.).

Corporate Life. Basic in the OT is the truth that human life is an ordered existence of corporate living, which moves in the direction and in the channels given it by God's command.

Founded on Divine Law. The Pentateuchal PRIESTLY WRITERS place God's word in the form of law. It describes the economy of corporate life in the apodictic commands of the Decalogue, a charter of interpersonal life based on God's absolute dominion over all things (Ex 20:1–17; 24.3; Lv 19:2–18). The DEUTERONOMISTS are more persuasive but nonetheless firm. The Book of Deuteronomy presents Moses as inculcating the observance of God's laws (Dt 4:1–2, 13; 5:1–21), which come from the Lord's personal love for the Israelites (4:37), as shown by the miracles He worked for them (4:9, 32–39). The people are to fix these laws in their heart (4:9) and teach them to their children (4:9–14), in order that they, individually and collectively (4:25–31), may live (4:1, 40). This is not to say that justice founded on law is the cause of life [Dt 7:8; Neh 9:6; Ps 118(119):17; Dn 9:18]. Man does not merit life; it is always God's free gift (Dt 32:6, 18, 39; Is 51:1–6). He acts for the glory of His Name (Is 42:8; 43:7; 62:2). It is to say that man does not truly live except in the way recognized in signs of God's activity and revealed to man's heart as the only way in which human life can operate toward its perfection [Gn 1:27–31; Dt 6:10–19; 7:12–15; 8:1–5; Ps 102(103):5]. This point is very important in view of later developments. Law and order are necessary to life by God's command (Dt 8:20) and by its very constitution, but life itself is the breath of the Lord. God placed life within an order of relation to Himself, which the Torah describes and commands. Man can choose to disobey and to die (Gn 3:6; Dt 32:15–18; Is 5:24; Jer 18:12; Prv 1:24, 33), but God alone has the power to save him [Ps 48(49):8–13; 68(69):14–19; etc.].

Social Life under God. The priestly and Deutero-nomic strains in the Torah are introduced and illustrated in the teaching of Genesis ch. 1 3. It is the evident conviction of the Biblical record that man, created in God's image (Gn 1:27), became aware of his place in life within the orderly manifestation of God's goodness when, upon recognizing the inner reality of living things and giving them names, he found no helper like himself (Gn 2:20) until God gave him woman. Man and woman recognized in things as they found them an order of created good (Gn 1:27–31; see also Jer 5:24; Ps 148:6), in which they had a dominant role (Gn 1:28; see also Ps 8:6–9; Wis 9:2–3) but which they themselves did not set up (Gn 2:8; see also Sir 42:15–43:35; Wis ch. 9). All things were made ready to serve them (Gn 1:28–31). In their interpersonal lives, they found equality of being (Gn 2:23), a common need for one another (Gn 2:18; 3:16b), the common blessing of marriage and children (Gn 1:28; 2:28; see also Gn 9:7), and the land that each must till and keep as his spirit directs (Gn 2:15), while respecting the land of others (Ex 20:15, 17). There is no suggestion here of merely human evolution of thought. Understanding of life is never complete apart from communion with God (Gn 3:8; Jer 12:1, 14–17; Hos 2:10, 16; Wis 1:7; 2:21–23). Communion with God is the living thing that protects the law of human life, while adapting it to changing circumstances (Ex 4:11+17; 19:4–8; 33:7–11; Nm 11:17; 2 Kgs 22:13; Jer 16:19).

In the light of this communion, Moses' people know that life can proceed to fullness only by corporate action. Men and women are to live by manifesting God's love in each generation by their own free giving of themselves in signs of love for one another (Gn 2:24; Ex 23:4; Lv 19:18) and by perfecting all things according to His manifest will as a sign of love for Him (Dt 6:4–9). They are to use all earth's energies as they know them concretely, to bring them to fruition.

In union with Him they are to develop all earth's possibilities, which are also their own (Gn 1:28–30; 2:15–16; Dt 1:8; 11:10–12; Jer 29:5–7; Is 35:1–10). The fact that the Israelites' view of life was totally earthbound is not surprising. Their experience in God's word and, therefore, their knowledge of life was incomplete. They recognized that man lives as viceregent in the KINGDOM OF GOD, but that in every generation, much of life eludes their grasp and understanding (Job ch. 28). When all their work is done, God's faithful must wait hopefully for the full life in the promised land (Lv 26:3–13; Is 30:15, 18; Jer 29:10–14).

Israel in the Family of the Nations. In this view there is no room for dominating nationalism, exaggerated collectivism, or excessive individualism. All men belong to one human family (Gn ch. 10; Lv 19:33–34; Is 2:2–4; Ez 47:22; Zep 3:9–10). The OT as well as the NT extol the faithful of all times and nations (Gn 5:24; 6:9; 14:18; 2 Kgs ch. 5; Is 44:28; Rom 2:12–16) who, though perhaps confusedly, knew God speaking to them through signs in the cosmic order and through the events of history (Acts 17:26–28). The recorded word credits their faith as justice. They live according to God's regal will in spite of sin all around them (Gn 6:9–13; Rom 2:27–29), purified by their submission to God's word as they understand it (Wis 14:6; Mal 1:11). Men of all nations, wicked as well as just, carry forward God's action in Israel's regard (Hb 1:2–11; Is 45:14–15; 2 Chr 36:22). Israel is the servant of the Lord (Is 41:8–10; 49:3) through whom and in final union with whom the nations are to live in the light [Gn 12:2–3; Dt 9:4; Mi 4:1–5; 42:6–7; 66:18–19; Ps 95(96):3–8; 97(98):2].

Israel is God's son, His heir by adoption (Ex 4:22; 19:5–6; Hos 11:1; Bar 3:37), within whose corporate life individual Israelites, also sons and servants (Lv 25:55; Dt 3:24; Is 1:2; 2 Sm 7:5), share all life's gifts and responsibilities (Ex ch. 20–23; Jer 3:19–4:2; Is 27:12). Israelites are brothers in a spirit that transcends the flesh (Lv 19:17–18; Dt 15:7–11). The law of life inevitably binds each to all others and all others to each in good (Nm 14:19–20; Dt 9:5; Sir 17:1–18) and evil [Jdt 8:18–23; Ps 50(51):7]. One who knows what is at stake (Is 49:5) and who is without sin (53:9), if he will spend his life in suffering (Is 53:2–10) rather than give in to evil by doing wrong (Is 49:4; 53:8–10), will therefore die condemned by his fellows (Is 53:8). But if he gives his life and death as an offering for sin, bearing the guilt of many (Is 53:11), he will accomplish the will of the Lord (Is 53:10) and will justify the many (53:11), to rectify the life of the world (53:12).

Those who live justly do so by God's spirit and power projected through their action into every avenue of social existence (Ex 3:13; Nm 11:16–30; Dt 34:9; 2 Sm 23:2; Is 42:1–7; Jer 22:1–5; Ez 34:1–6). Those who respond carry forward the word of life taught by the priests during the corporate remembrance (*zikkārôn*) of cultic prayer (Dt 31:10–13; Jos 22:21–29; Ezr 9:5–38). Here they recognize and accept the gifts and demands of daily living as things of the spirit no less than of the flesh (Dt 26:1–15; Jos 22:2–6; 24:1–28). They offer them together in sign of their corporate fidelity, mutual labor, and self-giving (Ex 24:3–11; Lv ch. 3; Dt 12:4–28), only to receive of them again, replete with the sustaining action of God, who had given them in the first place for the happiness of their life (Ex 24:8; Lv ch. 1–7; 22; Dt 7:13). Whenever the spirit of law and cult remained pure, the worshipers' view of life remained unclouded (Jos 22:24–31; 1 Sm ch. 1; 2 Sm ch. 7; 2 Kgs ch. 23; Ezr

9:5–15) and full of joy (Dt 16:9–15; 1 Chr 15:25; 2 Chr 20:27–28; Ezr 6:22; etc.).

Tensions. God did not make death, and He takes "no pleasure in the death of a wicked man" (Ez 3:11). When through the temptation of the envious devil (Wis 2:24) mankind turned from God and death entered the world (Gn 2:17; 3:1–19), God offered hope of renewed life (Gn 3:15). But following the blind perversity that sin (*hēt'*, erroneous choice) maintains, mankind chose to continue in its own way (Gn 6:11–13; Is 43:27). God continued to speak to man (Gn 4:6–15; 6:13–21; etc.), but the vision of life was hopelessly clouded.

In Israel the forces of sin and death struggled to dominate at its very heart. The nation as a whole, led by faithless priests (Jer 2:8; 7:1–8:3; Hos 4:4–10; 5:1–7; Mal 2:1–9), false prophets (1 Kgs 22:6–25; Mi 3:5–8; Jer 14:13–16; 23:16–40; Ez 13:1–23), and ambitious kings (2 Kgs 16:2–18; 21:1–16; Jeremiah ch. 21–22), gradually fell to mere lip service of God (Is 29:13), when they did not fall into idolatry. Many expected their elect position in God's plan to save them (Jer 14:13; Am 5:18). There was a persistent tendency to legalism, as if life were a thing of *quid pro quo* with God (Prv 10:16, 27; 11:6, 19; 13:6). However, this tendency never reached the proportions found in later Judaism; for faithful priests, prophets, kings, and people combated it consistently. Legalism is not part of the Biblical tradition (Dt 8:3; 9:4–6; Jer 3:19; Hos 11:1–4).

When social injustices of all kinds fell heaviest on the Remnant of Israel that continued to live in obedient love (1 Kgs 21:1–14; Am 5:11–12; 8:4–6; Mi 2:1–10; 3:1–3, 9–11; Is 3:14–15), the anguish of their trial caused them to question God concerning His justice [Ps 72(73):1–22; Jer 15:10–21; 20:7–9]. They received no immediate answer other than a further strengthening of their faith [Ps 16(17):6–9; 20(21):17–22; etc.]. Ecclesiastes, writing late into the record, shows the futility of seeking an answer to the mystery of life by reason alone (Eccl 3:17–22; 8:5–13; 12:13–14).

View of Future Life. During many years God supported the people by His promise of a kingly mediator whom He would anoint with His spirit to a wonderful degree (Is 9:1–6; 11:1–5) and through whose regency He would finally establish a living community of His kingdom in paradisaical peace (Is 11:6–9). Now in the people's darkest hour, Jeremiah, while living still in the messianic tradition (Jer 23:5–8), knows from the Lord that in the Israelites' present state their sin is incurable (Jer 2:25–26). Although bound by the law of life, they do not have the power to keep it. They have forgotten and do not know the Living God (Jer 24:7). But "the days are coming, says the Lord, when I will make a new covenant

with the house of Israel and the house of Judah. . . . I will place my law within them and write it upon their hearts. . . . All, from least to greatest, shall know me" (Jer 31:31–34). They will come to life again (Ez 37:6) when the Lord will sprinkle clean water upon them, to cleanse them of their impurities and place a new spirit within them (Ez 36:25–26).

Deutero-Isaiah (Isaiah ch. 40–55) sees God's plan for man's rebirth that will include man's cooperation. The glory of God and the unfolded manifestation of His power will appear in a new Exodus (40:3–4; 45:1–6; 49:8–12) when He will support the chosen servant, who, although He will be without sin, will willingly identify Himself with His fellows (49:5–7; 53:6) and will accept the death (50:4–6; 52:13–53:9) that sinful men will impose upon Him, in order to give perfect response to God from among them. The will of the Lord will be accomplished through Him; He will justify many and will see the light in fullness of days (53:11).

A number of interpreters see statements of belief in a life of conscious relationship with God after the death of the body and even of resurrected life in Is 26:19; 53:10–12; Ps 72(73):23–27; Wis 3:1–4; 6:18–19. All scholars agree that the doctrine of the RESURRECTION OF THE DEAD is clearly stated in Dn 12:2–3 (from the middle of the 2d century B.C.) and 2 Mc 7:9, 14, 23; 14:46 (from about the same period). In Dn 7:13–27 God's holy ones are symbolized by "one like a son of man coming in clouds of heaven," who, at the throne of God, the "Ancient One," receives everlasting dominion.

The OT concept of life remains consistent. Life is God's action known through signs in His terrestrial domain (Is 41:17–20; 42:10–12). In Is 65:17–20; 66:22–23 the seer beholds, far ahead in the future, a suprahistorical world, where there is life in "the new heavens and the new earth" (66.22).

In The New Testament

Although the NT writers use a Greek terminology concerning life that is essentially the same as the Hebrew terminology of the OT writers, an immeasurably new content is given to these terms in the NT because of the new revelation of the triune life of God and the divine life as possessed by Jesus Christ and consequently of the new concept of the corporate life that Christians have as members of the mystical body of Christ.

Terminology. The NT writers follow Hebrew thought patterns, but with important qualifications in the Greek terms for life (ζωή), body (σῶμα), soul (ψυχή), and spirit (πνεῦμα). The momentum in man that needs nourishment from the TREE OF LIFE (Gn 3:9, 24; Rv 2:7) is the ψυχή, the soul as the seat of natural life, received from Adam (1 Cor 15:45, 49), which became the seat of death when he accepted the reign of death by sin (Rom 5:14). The life made possible to all men by God in Christ (Rom 5:15, 17) is the life of the πνεῦμα, the spirit, spiritual life. The continuity of God's life-giving action, proceeding through Christ and received in man (1 Pt 3:18, 21–22; Acts 2:14–39) is uppermost in all NT thought (Mt 19:29; Jn 3:16; 5:21; etc.).

In the beginning life was given in the WORD, the LOGOS, the Son of God (Jn 1:1–4). It was given also in promise (Gn 15:4–5); the "children of the promise" retained it in all generations (Lk 1:46–55; Rom 9:6–13), but still in promise (Gal 3:14; Heb 11:39–40), until He who was promised had come, the offspring of Abraham, who is Christ (Gal 3:16).

Spirit (πνεῦμα) in man may be the breath of life (2 Thes 2:8.), the soul as the principle of life (27:50), or the seat of man's feelings and thoughts (Mk 2:8; Rom 8:16). But it may also be the state of being produced in man by the divine sanctifying power (2 Cor 4:13; Phil 1:27). In reference to God πνεῦμα may be the third divine person, best recognized by acts proper only to Him (Jn 14:16–17, 26; 16:7, 13–14), or when He is set off from the Father and the Son in Trinitarian formulas (Mt 28:19; 1 Cor 12:4–6; 2 Cor 13:13). Most often, however, πνεῦμα is the Spirit of God (Rom 8:9) or the spirit of Jesus Christ (Phil 1:19) designating God's life-giving power received in man (Lk 11:13; Jn 3:5; Acts 8:19, 29; 16:6; Eph 5:18).

Triune Life of God. In the one God there are three persons who live and act: God, eternal Father, principle of eternal life (1 Jn 1:2; 5:11); who gives all He is to the Son, begotten coequal with Himself (Jn 1:18; 14:10; Col 1:19; 2:9); God, eternal Son, the Father's Word (Jn 1:1–2) and His image (Col 1:15); and God the Holy Spirit, mysterious bond between Father and Son (Jn 14:16–17, 26), who pours forth Their life and love in men through Christ Jesus (Rom 5:5).

Life as Possessed by Christ. The life that Jesus Christ possesses is eternal life, the outward expression of the eternal community of life (1 Jn 1:2; Jn 5:26; Col 1:15–17; Heb 1:2–3), on which all human life is patterned (Eph 1:3–6; 3:14–15; Rom 8:29; 2 Cor 4:4–6; Jn 1:12). He whom the Father sent to identify Himself with men in the conflict between life and death (Gal 4:4–5; 1 Tm 2:5–6; Phil 2:6–8; Rom 5:17; 8:3; etc.) is His Son (Gal 4:4; Rom 1:1–4), His Word (Jn 1:14; 1 Jn 1:1–3), the supreme revelation of the Godhead in human flesh (Jn 1:18; Rom 1:3–4; Col 1:19). Although He was without sin (1 Pt 2:22; 2 Cor 5:21; Jn 8:46), He who is life itself made incarnate (Jn 1:4, 14; 14:6) accepted all the sufferings of death in the flesh (Heb 5:7–9; Rom 5:9) rather than yield to the demands of Satan or the ψυχή (natural life) in Himself or others, in order to redeem all who unite with Him (Mk 3:35) to carry forward God's creative purpose (Col 1:25–27; Eph 1:3–5; Jn 14:2; 16:7).

In Him, the spirit of life prevailed. He laid down His ψυχή only to take it up again (Jn 10:17), filled with power to resist the temptations of Satan (Lk 4:1–13; Heb 2:18; 4:15) and overcome him (Mt 12:29). He gave others power over him (Mk 3:15). As instrument of the Word in the power of the Spirit, the soul of Jesus spent itself in doing good (Acts 10:38; Jn 10:11; Mt 11:3–5) out of compassion for the poor and afflicted (Mk 1:41; Lk 7:13; Mt 9:36; 14:14; 20:34), even to the forgiveness of sin in those who wounded Him and offended His heavenly Father (Lk 23:34; Mk 2:5, 10; Lk 7:36–50; 1 Pt 2:24–25). Death had no power over Him (Jn 10:18); His spirit was free at all times to surrender itself to the will of His Father (Jn 4:34; Lk 23:46). His final surrender was victory (1 Cor 15:54).

Christ now lives, the triumphant Servant of God (Phil 2:7–9), whose life, death, and Resurrection remain the cause of life to many (Jn 10:10b; Rom 4:25; 5:10; 14:9; 2 Cor 5:15). His glorified life is the first fruits of God's eternal plan (1 Cor 15:20, 25; Col 1:15, 18), the life of the new Adam (1 Cor 15:45). When He entered into His glory (Lk 24:26), Christ became a life-giving spirit (1 Cor 15:22, 45); His risen body and soul, impregnated with the Holy Spirit, became the principle of life (2 Cor 3:17–18) in the disciples He had left on earth and those who, through them, would believe in His name (Jn 17:20).

From heaven, Christ, living as Lord of all in the kingdom of God (Acts 2:36; Phil 2:9–11; Eph 1:22; Rv 1:6; 17:14), mediator between God and men (1 Tm 2:5; Heb 8:6), sends the Holy Spirit as a pledge of eternal life in those who believe in Him (Eph 1:12–13, 19), to dwell in the very center of their being (Jn 14:16; 1 Cor 3:16), helping them to assimilate spiritually all that Christ came to teach (Jn 14:25–26; 15:26; 1 Cor 2:10–12), and enabling them to take on Christ's mind (1 Cor 2:16; Eph 4.20–24; Rom 15:6; Phil 2:9) and will (Jn 14:23; 15:12; 17:6), which are the mind and will of the Father (Rom 12:2; Jn 7:17; 14:10; 15:10, 15; 17:7–8), and so by a common bond of likeness, which is eternal life (Jn 17:3), to participate in the divine nature (2 Pt 1:4) as adopted sons of God (Jn 1:12–13; Rom 8:14–23; Gal 4:5–7; 1 Jn 3:1–2). They become the MYSTICAL BODY OF CHRIST (Eph 1:22–23), through whose Spirit (Eph 1:13; 2 Cor 3:17–18) His fullness (Eph 1:23), the fullness of God, is penetrating the earth (Eph 3:19), to reestablish the harmony in which all things were set up in Christ (Eph 1:10) and toward Him (Eph 1:3–10). He lives as head of His body, which is the

CHURCH (Eph 1:22–23). His kingdom is wherever the power of God works in men to bring about in the here and now what He has already accomplished in Christ's life, death, and Resurrection (Col 1:13–14, 22; 2:9–15).

Life of the Redeemed in Christ. Christian life is eternal life in the kingdom of God (Col 1:13), hidden in the hearts of men who bear about in their bodies the dying of Christ (Phil 3:8–11; 2 Cor 4:10; Gal 5:24) for the same reason that He bore His sufferings and death (l Pt 2:21–25; Phil 3:10; Rom 6:8–11) and who abide in the power of His victory (Phil 4:13; 1 Jn 5:4–5). Christian life is a pearl of great price (Mt 13:46), bought by entering into the life of the kingdom through the way of the commandments of God (Mk 10:17–19), and living them (Rom 7:25) in the perfection that Christ gave them (Mt 5:17–48) in the "law of the Spirit of the life in Christ Jesus" (Rom 8:2). The rule of the Spirit is not experienced as command (Gal 5:18), for it frees men from what is purely natural (ψυχικός) in the body of death (Rom 7:23–24; 2 Cor 3:17; Gal 5:16–21) and lifts them into a life of unbounded faith, hope, charity, joy, peace, patience, continency, goodness, and fidelity (Gal 5:22–23).

Corporate life in Christ's body, which is being brought to its fullness (Eph 4:13–16), expresses itself in every avenue of temporal and spiritual responsibility (1 Cor 12:27–31; 2 Cor 8:1–9; Eph 5:21–33; 1 Pt 1:22–25; 2:3–4). In this way the Church gives evidence to all on earth that where the Spirit reigns mankind becomes a new creature (2 Cor 5:17; Eph 2:15). This life of service is echoed and prolonged even now in heaven (Rv 4:4–11; 5:9–14; 7:9–12).

Whereas Paul uses the term body of Christ (Rom 12:5; 1 Cor 12:12–27; Eph 1:23; 2:14–16; 4:4, 12, 16; 5:23, 30; Col 1:18, 24; 2:19; 3:15) to express man's new life relationship to God, John uses the concept of the vine and its branches (Jn 15:1–8) to denote this. Both comparisons serve to express oneness of spiritual being in Christ. The fact that the Spirit is the bond of union between Christ and men, the source of personal intercommunication between Father, Son, Spirit, and men united in Christ, is uppermost in both (Jn 14:16–17, 26; 15:26; 1 Cor 12:12–13; Eph 4:4).

But the rule of the Spirit is not complete even in those who, by Baptism into Christ's death and life (Rom 6:4–11; Col 2:12–13), have accepted it (Phil 3:12) and have nourished it by partaking of the bread of life in His word (Jn 6:28–29, 35–40; Phil 2:16; 1 Pt 1:23–25) and in the Sacrament of His body and blood (Jn 6:55; Lk 22:19–2:0; 1 Cor 10:16–17). Therefore, life in Christ's body is also redemptive. Redemptive help within their own community living is assured to those who believe and who use the effective signs of life and redemption that Christ has left in His Sacraments. Sacramental life is both a pledge of glory (1 Pt 3:21; Jn 6:55) and a sign to the world that the members of Christ's body are still on trial (2 Cor 6:1–2; 13:5), carrying life about in vessels of clay, so that all may see that it is from God and not of themselves (2 Cor 4:7). The total life of the Church is a sign that Christ is dwelling within it, to call sinners to reconcile themselves to the Father (2 Cor 5:20; 6:1–2), to fight the good fight of faith and lay hold of life in heaven (1 Tm 6:11–14; Lk 6:22–23).

The work of perfecting the material creation according to time and circumstance belongs to the Creator (Rom 8:19–22; 2 Pt 3:13). From the beginning God continues to give men ability, desire, time, circumstances, and command to develop earth's possibilities, each in his own personal field of endeavor (Mt 25:14; 1 Cor 7:17). Living in the Spirit, members of Christ's body must accept the challenge of their times (Rom 6:4; 13:13; Eph 5:8–15; Jn 12:35), imaging Christ's principles, thoughts, habits, desires, and loves (Col 3:9–10; Rom 8:29; 2 Cor 3:18), stripped of jealousy (1 Pt 2:1–10), stewards of God's manifold favor (1 Pt 4:10), sowing the seed of God's word (Mk 4:4–20), which, when fallen on good ground, unites men of every status (Col 3:11) in the knowledge of incorruptible existence (1 Pt 2:1–3, 13–17; 5:1), making them recognize that judgment begins here on earth (1 Pt 4:17), and orienting them to Jesus' glorious PAROUSIA (1 Cor 4:1–5; Ti 2:11–14; Mt 25:31–46).

By a mysterious condescension of His mercy, God awaits upon men to "wash their robes in the blood of the Lamb" (Rv 7:14; 22:14) and to assume their life of spiritual responsibility (2 Pt 3:8–10): but in His own time (1 Thes 5:1–3; 1 Tm 6:15; Lk 12:39–40) Christ will come again to bring about the final regeneration (Mt 19:28.). [See REBIRTH (IN THE BIBLE)]. The water of life and the power of the Spirit will flow from the throne of God and of the Lamb (Rv 22:1). The life of heaven will come to earth (Rv 21:22–22:5), to free, renew, and perfect the quality of all creation (Rom 8:19). In it, the children of God, His servants, will reflect Christ's image perfectly, because they will see Him in God as He is (1 Jn 3:2; 1 Cor 13:12), and God will be all in all (1 Cor 15:28).

Bibliography: W. EICHRODT, *Theology of the Old Testament,* tr. J. A. BAKER (Philadelphia 1961–); *Man in the Old Testament,* tr. K. and R. GREGOR SMITH (Chicago 1951). G. VON RAD, *Old Testament Theology,* tr. D. M. G. STALKER (New York 1962–). E. JACOB, *Theology of the Old Testament,* tr. A. W. HEATHCOTE and P. J. ALLCOCK (New York 1958). A. GELIN, *The Religion of Israel,* tr. J. R. FOSTER (New York 1959) ch. 5–8. Y. M. J. CONGAR, *The Mystery of the Church,* tr. A. V. LITTLEDALE (Baltimore 1960). D. MOLLAT, *De notione vitae apud sanctum Joannem* (Rome 1960). M. L. LAMB, "Christian Humanism and St. John's Theology of Life," *Review for Religious* 23 (1964) 149–159. J. J. NAVONE, "In Our Image and Likeness," *Bible Today* 1 (1963) 492–499. F. MUSSNER, ΖΩΗ: *Die*

Anschauung vom "Leben" im 4. Evangelium. . .(Munich 1952); J. HÖFER and K. RAHNER *Lexikon für Theologie und Kirche,* 6:853–856. *Encyclopedic Dictionary of the Bible,* tr. and adap. by L. IIARTMAN (New York 1963), from A. VAN DEN BORN, *Bijbels Woordenboek* 1336–44.

[P. M. COYLE]

LIFE, CONCEPT OF (IN THEOLOGY)

The concept of life plays a central part in theology both in describing the living God and in explaining the created participation in the divine life that man enjoys by GRACE in this world and that constitutes his glory in the next. Hence this article speaks (1) of life in general, (2) of the living God, (3) of Christ our life, (4) of the supernatural life of creatures, and (5) of life in heaven.

Life in General. As such, life in general is not the object of theology; still less is the theologian obliged to tie himself to any particular philosophical or scientific explanation of the nature and origin of life. Where human life is concerned, the theologian must insist on the immediate creation of the individual human SOUL (H. Denzinger, *Enchiridion symbolorum* 3896), but this does not bar him from speculation on the manner in which the soul informs the body or on the place to be ascribed to the evolutionary process in the explanation of the genesis of life. All that immediately concerns the theologian is that life ultimately stems from the divine act of creation and that the rational life of this individual human soul comes into existence through a direct creative act of God.

But if he is to speak of the living God and of man's supernatural organism, the theologian must speak analogically, in terms borrowed from the natural and created life that he sees around him. Indeed, the need for this is clear both from what God reveals of Himself and from the very terms used by Christ in making known to man his supernatural vocation and DESTINY. He, the Way, the Truth, and the Life, came that men might have life and have it more abundantly (Jn 14.6; 10.10). To speak of all SUPERNATURAL life in this analogical way, the theologian must start from created life as he observes it. A living substance he knows as one that is able to move itself, to operate immanently; its life is not so much a quality as the existence proper to such a nature.

The Living God. Hence the question at once arises: Can one speak of life in God? The difficulty, at the level of natural reason, is, as St. Thomas Aquinas points out (*Summa theologiae* 1a, 18.3 ad 1–3), that in God there is no motion and that, in view of God's simplicity, one can in no way speak of any principle of life such as one recognizes among creatures in the intellectual or sensible soul. One must, however, reflect that the fundamental concept of life, purified of its creaturely imperfections, consists not in self-movement considered as a transition from potency to act, nor in an essential composition of body and soul, but in a self-determination in act, an independence of operation that, although found in a limited way in living creatures, is found supereminently and perfectly in PURE ACT alone, the unmoved Mover. One cannot say that God has life; one must simply state that He is Life (just as He is Intellect, Will, Omnipotence, etc.) and that He is the source of all life.

In the Old Testament, God is proclaimed as the living God [*see* LIFE, CONCEPT OF (IN THE BIBLE)]: He is truly living, unlike the inanimate idols worshiped by the pagans; He is the living source of all the life one knows; there is in Him an inexhaustible vitality to save and to deliver, to love and to punish; His life is at the root of His eternal fidelity, whereas idols, lifeless themselves, can do nothing for those who have recourse to them [cf. Psalm 113B(115)]. The wisdom books especially, with their insistence on the power of God's knowledge and will, lead one further into the mystery of the divine life; but only in the New Testament is one presented with the fullness of this mystery in the revelation of the Holy TRINITY, through which one can begin to glimpse the fullness of the interpersonal knowing and loving that *is* the Divine Life.

Christ Our Life. Because He comes to men from the living Father to win them back from the death of sin, to take men up into the sharing of the Trinitarian life of knowing and loving to which God has gratuitously called them, Christ is "our life" (Col 3.4). This sharing in the divine life is to attain its fullness in the BEATIFIC VISION (through the communication of the LIGHT OF GLORY, *lumen gloriae*), but it has its start in this world. By faith and baptism a man is linked to the risen Lord Jesus, now "a life-giving spirit" (1 Cor 15.45), and so shares even now in that "eternal life" of which St. John speaks so frequently. It is through the Holy Spirit, the life-giver, that this union of man with Christ is forged and sustained, and it is to the action of the Spirit that one appropriates both the life of the Church and the supernatural life of the individual Christian.

Supernatural Life of Creatures. Because Scripture (above all St. Paul and St. John) speaks so consistently in terms of new life, REBIRTH, regeneration, when describing the state of the justified Christian, these terms have entered into the common vocabulary of the Church, and theologians have sought to elaborate and synthesize the data of revelation by the analogical application of the fundamental concepts proper to natural, created life. Men are "partakers of the divine nature" and adoptive sons of God because, by their INCORPORATION into the MYSTI-

CAL BODY OF CHRIST and through the divine INDWELL-ING, uncreated GRACE, they receive habitual, or sanctifying, created grace, the vital principle that fits men to know and love God as He is in Himself in a way that is proper to no creature but only to God. Given this fundamental analogy (and its correlative, the death of the soul through mortal sin), it is natural to pursue it through every aspect of the Christian's supernatural life. The VIRTUES (especially the three theological virtues) are seen as the faculties corresponding to the life of grace, immediate principles of supernatural operation by which men are directly conjoined to God's proper knowability and lovability. The Sacraments are the exterior means of the life of grace, either engendering it (Sacraments of the dead) or nourishing it in its various stages (Sacraments of the living). The whole progress of a man toward perfection is, quite simply, his spiritual life.

Life in Heaven. But, as has already been noted, whatever the perfection of supernatural life that may be attained in this world, it is inchoate, imperfect, wholly ordered to the achievement of its consummation in heaven. Only there, in the facial vision of God (strictly supernatural, due to no creature, not even to the angels, though their purely spiritual natural life far exceeds all the created life that man knows), will the supernatural life, the participation in the inner life of the Trinity, which is men's by virtue of their adopted sonship in Christ, reach its fullness. Our life now is hidden with Christ in God (Col 3.3.); "it has not yet appeared what we shall be. We know that, when He appears, we shall be like to him, for we shall see him as he is" (1 Jn 3.2).

Thus life is at the very center and core of the Christian mystery, or rather, a passover from death to life. God reveals to men His innermost Trinitarian life and sends men His Son, the life of the world, that they may receive a gratuitous share in that same life that is proper to Him alone. "God has given us eternal life; and this life is in his Son. He who has the Son has the life. He who has not the Son has not the life" (1 Jn 5.11–12).

See Also: ELEVATION OF MAN; INTELLECTUAL LIFE; MAN, 3; GRACE, ARTICLES ON.

Bibliography: F. MUSSNER, *Lexikon für Theologie und Kirche*, ed. J. HOFER and K. RAHNER (Freiburg 1957–65) 6:853–856. H. FRIES, *Handbuch theologischer Grundbegriffe* (Munich 1962–63) 2:25–30.

[R. L. STEWART]

LIFE, ORIGIN OF

Theories of how life originated on Earth are of two sorts. Biogenetic theories hold that living things always arise through the agency of preexisting organisms. Abiogenetic theories hold that living things arise from inanimate sources. Spontaneous generation, an abiogenetic theory, postulates the origin of lower plants and animals from the slime of Earth and microorganisms from nutrient broth. Biopoesis holds that only the first living form or forms arose in the remote past from inorganic matter by spontaneous generation.

This article will review some of the theories of how life may have arisen on Earth and consider the philosophical problems associated with them. These theories can be categorized under the headings of spontaneous generation, cosmozoic processes, creation, and biopoesis.

Spontaneous Generation. Until the mid-17th century it was generally held that living things could arise spontaneously, as well as by sexual or nonsexual reproduction. In 1668 Francesco Redi provided experimental evidence that maggots thought to be spontaneously generated had actually been produced from the eggs of adult flies. Redi put a snake, eels, a slice of veal, and some fish into two sets of four large, wide-mouthed flasks, covered one set of jars with fine gauze, and left the other set open. Flies entered and left the open jars, and maggots soon appeared in them. No maggots were discovered in the covered jars, although a few fly deposits and maggots appeared on the gauze cover. Redi noticed that the adult flies that finally emerged were like those crawling on the meat before the appearance of the maggots. Redi's experiments discouraged belief in the spontaneous generation not only of maggots, but of macroscopic animals and plants in general.

In the 18th century the controversy over spontaneous generation was reopened when Anton van Leeuwenhoek made a number of important discoveries about microorganisms using a microscope. An Italian abbot, L. Spallanzani, performed hundreds of experiments to show that no animalcules appeared when nutrient broth was heated in phials and sealed off from the air. The English Jesuit John Turberville countered that Spallanzani had heated his liquids too vigorously and had in this way destroyed the "vital force" of the infusions and of the air in the sealed container.

In the 1860s Louis Pasteur ended the debate over whether or not microorganisms developed *de novo* without parents in nutrient solutions. After heating flasks of nutrient materials to the boiling point, he sealed off the necks of some and drew the necks of others out into an S-shaped curve and left them open to the air. In the cases where he sealed the portals of entry no microorganisms appeared, whereas in the open flasks the microorganisms were trapped in the moisture in the S-shaped necks. As a result of Pasteur's experiments many biologists ruled out spontaneous generation as a theory of the origin of life. *Omne vivum e vivo* became the accepted dictum: yet this did not preclude the possibility of life's having arisen spontaneously in the remote past.

Cosmozoic Processes. H. von Helmholtz and Lord Kelvin were among the scientists who speculated that viable spores floating through interstellar space may have accidentally seeded life on Earth when conditions were favorable. Adherents of this theory held that life, like matter, is eternal. Therefore, it was not the origin of life that needed explanation, but the passage of the seeds of life from one planet to another. Helmholtz postulated that live germs were brought to Earth in meteorites. In 1908 S. A. Arrhenius published a similar theory, known as panspermia, which included careful calculations of the pressure of the Sun's rays acting on live germs to bring them to Earth.

At the beginning of the 21st century, the cosmozoic theory draws mixed reactions from scientists. Those in favor of it, such as Francis Crick, point to the rapidity with which life arose on Earth. Earth is approximately 4.6 billion years old. The earliest fossils currently known are 3.5 billion years old, and life is thought to have originated around 3.8 billion years ago. Until about 3.9 billion years ago Earth was bombarded by meteorites, which in some cases may have been large enough to sterilize Earth's surface to the depth of several kilometers. The numerous chemical reactions needed for the first living thing to form on Earth seem incompatible with so short a period. Other scientists, however, think that there may have be more time available than is generally assumed. Their claim is that life may not have had to wait until Earth ceased to be bombarbed, but may have have arisen deep in the subsurface of Earth. Also, it is far from certain that life could not have arisen more quickly than is generally supposed. Thus panspermia does not seem to be the only option. Another objection to panspermia is that the extreme cold, the absence of moisture and oxygen, the intense ultraviolet radiation, and the vast interstellar and interplanetary distances to be traveled make the passage of highly organized living things through space virtually impossible. On the other hand, it must be noted that life forms such as bacteria are amazingly resistant to extreme conditions. For example, *Deinococcus radiodurans* is able to resist 3,000 times the dose of radiation lethal to humans. Bacteria inside a camara left on the Moon were found to still be alive two-and-a-half years later despite the absence of atmosphere on the Moon. Still, proponents of panspermia fail to explain what it is about sites in the universe other than Earth such that one would have reason to believe that life began elsewhere. Panspermia does not solve the problem of the origin of life; it merely locates the origin on another planet or in space, and leaves the question unsolved. At present it is debated whether definite traces of living things have been found in meteorites. Some of the apparent trace fossils in the meteorites examined were ultimately determined to be earthly contaminants (e.g., in the 1969 Murchison meteorite). Examination of meteorite ALH84001 and other Martian meteorites, however, has led some researchers to conclude that the features observed are best explained as biogenic in origin.

Creation. The author of the book of Genesis states that God created the heavens and the earth and that God then said, "Let the earth bring forth vegetation: seed-bearing plants and all kinds of fruit trees that bear fruit containing their seed" (Gn 1.11–12). St. AUGUSTINE (*De Genesi ad litteram* 5.4–5, *Patrologia Latina,* ed. J. P. Migne, 271 v., indexes 4 v. [Paris 1878–90] 34:323–372) interprets Genesis to mean that God created animals and plants only virtually, in the sense that the earth was given the power to bring forth living things in time. Although this idea concurs with modern evolutionary theories, Scripture's purpose is not to pass judgment on scientific theories of the universe. The sacred writer teaches only that a transcendent God called the cosmos into being and set man, made in His own image and likeness, over visible creation. (*See* CREATION.)

Biopoesis. Theories of biopoesis attempt to explain how the first living things evolved naturally from inorganic matter. There is perhaps no other area of investigation in biology in which the words "conjectural," "speculative," and "as yet lacking experimental support" come up so frequently. Despite great advances in biology we remain ignorant of many aspects of the processes carried on by extant living things, and thus it is not surprising that we experience difficulties in explaining the origin of life processes in organisms that may be different from those we can observe. Compounding this difficulty is our lack of certitude regarding the conditions of early Earth at the time that life originated.

One of the earliest theories of the origin of life was that of A. I. Oparin. In 1924 Oparin theorized that the complex properties of living things arose in the natural process of the evolution of matter. In his view, large amounts of complex organic compounds in the oceans of primitive Earth reacted to form yet more complex molecules until one or more evolved that could be designated as alive. Oparin later showed that by mixing solutions of different proteins and other substances of high molecular weight he could produce coacervate droplets that readily adsorb organic substances from the surrounding medium. He proposed that the first primitive cells may have been much like these coacervate droplets. J. B. S. Haldane speculated (1926) that ultraviolet light acting on a mixture of water, carbon dioxide, and ammonia could produce a wide variety of organic compounds in the primitive oceans. If the first living things were formed in such a medium, the nutrient material there would sustain them.

In the 1950s, experimental work to establish the possibility of a prebiological formation of "building blocks" for living things originated in the laboratories of Melvin Calvin of the University of California and of Harold Urey at the University of Chicago. Calvin and his associates treated carbon dioxide and water in a cyclotron and produced formaldehyde and formic acid. S. L. Miller, a student of Urey, then exposed a mixture of water vapor, methane, ammonia, and hydrogen—gases believed to have been present on primitive Earth—to a silent electric discharge for a few days. Analysis of the results by the method of paper chromatography revealed a mixture of amino acids, several of which are essential components of proteins.

By heating concentrated solutions of hydrogen cyanide in aqueous ammonia for several days, J. Oró was able to produce adenine, an essential building block of nucleic acids. C. Ponnamperuma exposed to ultraviolet light a dilute solution of hydrogen cyanide and produced guanine as well as adenine, the only purines found in RNA (ribonucleic acid) and DNA (deoxyribonucleic acid).

One problem with these experiments that produce amino acids abiotically is that they require reducing conditions in order to work. Many scientists no longer think that the atmosphere of early Earth at the time that life is thought to have appeared was a reducing atmosphere. Banded iron formations have been found as far back as the Archean, and it is thought that they could not have formed under reducing conditions. There are other lines of evidence as well pointing to a neutral rather than a reducing atmosphere. Some scientists remain unconvinced by this evidence and hold to a Miller-type scenario. Others turn to outer space as a source of life's building blocks. Ninety different amino acids have been discovered in meteorites, eight of which belong to the set of 20 that are found in organisms on Earth. Meteorites including microscopic ones called micrometeorites may have deposited a substantial amount of organic material on early Earth's surface. Comets and cosmic dust clouds that early Earth passed through may also have been other significant sources of organic materials.

Among those who think that the building blocks of life had a terrestrial source, some suggest that they were formed at other sites on Earth other than its surface, namely, in thermal vents in the ocean floor that provide a reducing environment. Yet other scientists suggest a hot environment even deeper in Earth's crust. Still others propose a cold environment, because high temperature tends to break down protein, nucleic acids, and many of their building blocks. In short, theories abound and there is no consensus.

Even if there were a plausible explanation for how the building blocks of life were generated, there still would remain the question of how they became assembled into the more complex units, the proteins and nucleic acids that are found in even the simplest life forms. A "chicken and egg problem" arises here: in cells amino acids are assembled into proteins on ribosomes following instructions on mRNA that was copied from DNA. Thus to get proteins it seems that there has to be DNA. Nevertheless, in order for the DNA to be transcribed into RNA one needs proteins (proteins are also need for DNA replication). A number of approaches have been taken to get around this problem.

One is to say that originally proteins were assembled by some other means. Sidney Fox had some success in forming proteinlike polypeptides under anhydrous conditions in vitro. With carefully controlled conditions of temperature and hydration he produced proteinlike polymers. The majority of origin of life scientists, however, remain unimpressed, and some find Fox's proteinoids to be more like gunk than proteins. Freeman Dyson is also of the view that proteins arose first, followed by cells that carried on metabolism and reproduced without any genetic material, but simply by breaking in two. Nucleic acids arose independently, and eventually came together with these cells, eventually directing their replication. This gets around the chicken and egg problem, but the questions remain as to how proteins and nucleic acids arose without each other, and then how the two got working together in so highly an orchestrated manner. There are other current theories of abiotic protein formation, such as the thioester hypothesis advanced by Christian De Duve, but even their own authors regards them as speculative.

Another group of scientists holds that proteins did not come first, but rather RNA did. This theory gained popularity when it was discovered that certain forms of RNA can self-replicate as well as catalyze other reactions. This seemed to offer a way out of the protein-nucleic acid dilemma. Recently, however, much of the initial enthusiasm for this theory has been lost, largely because of the failure to discover a way that RNA could be synthesized under plausible abiotic conditions, and because of RNA's instability.

A further question remains as to how these larger units (proteins, nucleic acids) are assembled into cells. Oparin formed coacervate droplets by shaking a mixture of large protein and a polysaccharide. These droplets divide into an interior and exterior phase, and the conditions of interior phase were unlike those in the surrounding medium. Although some scientists find this an attractive model of a precursor of the cell, it is far from being a consensus view. Fox proposed as a better alternative "microspheres" that spontaneously form upon adding water to abiotically formed protenoids. Acccording to Fox microspheres manifested lifelike characteristics. Many scientists, however, remained unconvinced that there are sufficient likenesses between microspheres and cells such that microspheres could have been the precursor of cells.

There are many other theories of how life got started that have not been mentioned, e.g., theories such as those of J. D. Bernal and A.G. Cairns-Smith suggesting that clay initially catalysed the formation of complex biological molecules. This brief review should make it clear that scientists are nowhere close to an abiotic explanation of life's origin. This is only to be expected, however, given the relative newness and the special difficulties of this area of investigation.

Philosophical Problems

Philosophical problems associated with the origin of life are closely related to the definition one adopts for life itself. The lower forms of life have manifest affinities with the nonliving as well as with the higher forms of the living, and depending on which affinities one emphasizes, less or greater difficulty is encountered in explaining the production of life from inorganic matter. What follows is a discussion of the possibility of biopoesis in the context of Thomistic teaching on life and its need for an adequate cause, and the possible role of chance in the biopoesic process.

Possibility. St. THOMAS AQUINAS admitted the possibility of biopoesis. He did not reject St. Augustine's teaching that in the six days of creation Earth received from God the power to produce plants and trees (*Summa theologiae* 1a, 69.2). Thomas Aquinas acknowledged that the potentiality for such living forms could be present in primary matter; what is problematic is identifying an efficient cause of sufficient power to educe such from matter (*see* MATTER AND FORM). Earth does not seem to be an adequate efficient cause of plants, since plants, like all living things, are superior to the nonliving elements in that they are able to move themselves.

Thomas Aquinas appears to offer two different solutions to this problem. One answer is given when he addresses the question of whether the heavenly bodies are animate. In an objection it is argued that since a cause must be superior to its effect, the generation of animals

from decaying materials cannot be adequately accounted for by inanimate causes, but requires an animate cause. Given that decay is caused by the motions of the celestial bodies, especially the Sun, it follows that the celestial bodies must be animate. Thomas Aquinas responds in part by proposing an alternate explanation, namely, that spontaneous generation is caused by spiritual beings who use the celestial bodies as their instruments (*De spiritualibus creaturis* 6 ad 12; *Contra gentiles* 3.23).

Other passages of Thomas Aquinas indicate that he does not categorically reject the notion that natural material agents alone may be sufficient causes of the generation of plants and lower animals. (Following Aristotle, he did not believe that higher organisms could be generated without semen.) He did see living things as differing from nonliving things in performing activities that go beyond those of the nonliving, either simply as to the manner in which they act, or as to what they accomplish as well (*De Anima* 13). Plants stay in existence through their own activities, whereas inanimate things do not. Animals are not only able to do things to maintain their existence, they are also capable of knowing things through their senses. In these ways plants and animals exceed nonliving natural things in perfection. On the other hand, the souls of plants and animals (*see* SOUL) are not forms separable from matter; the activities that plants and animals perform all involve physical interaction. E.g., a life activity proper to higher organisms such as hearing requires both having organs (ears, brain), and the presence of physical entities (sound waves) that interact with the organ. And so Thomas Aquinas in commenting on the verse from Genesis which speak of Earth producing reptiles says that "it seems that the sensitive souls of reptiles and other animals are from the action of the corporeal elements. . . . Souls of this sort do not exceed the principles of natural things. And this is manifest from considering the operation of them." (*De potentia* 3.11, s.c. and corp.) This latter line of thought coincides with some versions of contemporary anthropic reasoning that hold that active principles sufficient for the development of life were built into the universe by an intelligent agent from its very inception.

On either view, it is reasonable to think that Thomas Aquinas would maintain that human intelligence accompanied by our ability to manipulate natural forces may allow us someday to produce life from chemicals by artificial means.

Role of Chance. Can CHANCE account for the origin of life? Charles Darwin wrote in a letter to Asa Gray that the problem of the origin of living things is too profound for the human intellect. Nevertheless he concluded: "I am inclined to look at everything as resulting from designed laws, with the details, whether good or bad, left to the working out of what we may call chance.''

There is much debate about whether the origin of life is fortuitous or necessary, and several confusions. A position at one extreme, emphasizing the contingency of natural things, regards life as a cosmic accident. At the other extreme are those who regard the finality of living things as sufficient evidence that they are the product of design, and who go on from there to deny that there is any element of chance in life's origin. Both extremes regard chance and design as mutually exclusive. This is not, however, always the case. Thomas Aquinas gives the example of a head of the household who wants the maid to meet the butler, and with this in mind sends them to the same place, each with a different task. Since the two intend something other than meeting each other, from their point of view they meet by chance. But from the householder's point of view, the meeting was not chance, but prearranged.

Another common confusion lies in opposing fortuitous occurrences with lawlike occurrences, as Oparin does when he says that ''The origin of life is not a 'fortunate,' extremely improbable event, but quite a regular phenomenon subject to a deep scientific analysis.'' Those who favor this view of the workings of nature hold that, where conditions were favorable, life had to originate. Now chance occurrences are not mere coincidences, such as the Moon undergoing eclipse as one steps into the shower. Chance involves causality in keeping with the laws of nature. When a person fails to notice a small step, and moves his foot upwards, of necessity he stubs his toe. We call that bad luck not because it is not in keeping with the laws of nature, but because it was not his intention to stub his toe. Thus that something be fortuitous does not mean that it is not due to causes knowable through scientific analysis. Moreover, whether life has originated once or a few times or frequently in the universe, adequate efficient causality is in all cases necessary.

Another common misconception is the notion that if a thing arises but once, it must be an unintended fluke. From this some of those who think that life on Earth was intended go on to conclude that life must be abundant throughout the universe. If the first premise was correct, however, then many of the world's great art masterpieces would be accidents, since they are unique.

Thomas Aquinas held that spontaneously produced plants and animals, unlike those that were produced from seeds or semen, were produced by chance (*In Metaphys.* no. 1403). Their production required the causality of the Sun, and the fortuitous coming together of matter not determinately ordered to the production of that life form, in the way that the material in the gametes is. That the Sun gives rise to different spontaneously generated species is due to differences in the matter the Sun shines on (*Summa theologiae* 1a2ae, 60.1). Thus that the Sun any given day causes the production of an individual of this particular species is by chance. In the greater scheme of things, however, the Sun is a universal cause meant to bring into act all the forms that are in the potency of the matter, and from this point of view that it produces individual of various species is not chance, but intended (*In Metaphys.* no. 1403). Thus in a similar way Thomas Aquinas might have held that the exact time life originated in the universe was a matter of chance as to its immediate causes, but that it arise at some given time was not.

Chance is not seen by Thomas Aquinas as opposed to Divine Providence, but indeed as intended by the Creator in order to have a richer universe than one in which all things were necessary. Chance events, however, are, from God's point of view, part of the order of divine providence; in this sense ''nothing in the world happens by chance,'' as Augustine declares (*Summa theologiae* 1a, 103.7 ad 2). Thus Thomas Aquinas would also assert a divine determinism overarching the very real contingencies of nature according to which chance events occur in the production of life and, especially, of human life.

Bibliography: C. DE DUVE, *Vital Dust* (New York 1995). F. DYSON, *Origins of Life* (Cambridge 1999). J. HEIDMANN, *Extraterrestrial Intelligence* (Cambridge 1997). P. D. WARD and D. BROWNLEE, *Rare Earth: Why Complex Life Is Uncommon in the Universe* (New York 2000).

[A. M. HOFSTETTER/M. I. GEORGE]

LIFE AND WORK

Like the Roman Catholic social movement of the late 19th century, the ECUMENICAL MOVEMENT for ''life and work,'' involving a united Christian witness on social issues among Protestants and Orthodox, had its antecedents in the increasing concern for the economic and social problems of an expanding industrial age. After World War I, these hitherto scattered Christian social movements were gathered into an international Christian effort for human welfare and world peace. This movement developed into the Universal Christian Council on Life and Work, largely through the work of Nathan SÖDERBLOM.

The Universal Christian Council on Life and Work was active from 1920 to 1938, when the provisional committee of the World Council of Churches in process of formation came into being. This period of social history included the difficult and fruitless effort of interwar reconstruction, the encounter with revolutionary social movements and ideologies accompanying the economic depression and mass industrial unemployment of the '20s and '30s, the German church struggle, and the deepening international crisis prior to World War II. The ideas that were developed in ecumenical study and discussion provided insight and vitality for a new type of Christian witness and concern that continues to influence Christian thought and action.

The development of Life and Work is best seen through its two great conferences, at Stockholm (1925), and at Oxford (1937). The former was the first contemporary ecumenical conference on social questions. This meeting clarified the need, the possibilities, and the difficulties of an international ecumenical attitude on social issues. It revealed also a lack of theological understanding and agreement on the Christian view of man and society. The Oxford Conference of 1937 went far beyond the 1925 meeting in theological acumen and depth of social analysis. This is reflected in its pronouncements, especially in its *Report on Church, Community, and State in Relation to the Economic Order.* This statement emphasized that the church must exercise its transcendence of all social systems in order to guard its moral and spiritual integrity, and to render a true critique, especially of those Western social systems that it may be inclined to accept or defend uncritically.

This viewpoint became later the basis for a WORLD COUNCIL OF CHURCHES (WCC) definition of the responsible society as a guide for Christian thinking in relation to all social systems. The more subtle statement of Christian social thinking could come about only through an adroit use of the best theological and lay minds in the churches. The preparatory studies directed by J. H. Oldham are classics of ecumenical social thinking.

Life and Work was almost exclusively Western in outlook, a weakness that characterized ecumenical social thinking until 1955, when the WCC, using the Life and Work method, launched a new study program to draw the churches and the social problems of the new nations of Africa, Asia, and Latin America into the ecumenical debate. In WCC these concerns continued to be addressed by the Department on Church and Society and the Commission of the Churches on International Affairs.

Bibliography: Universal Christian Conference of Life and Work, *The Stockholm Conference, 1925,* ed. G. K. A. BELL (London 1926). World Conference on Church, Community and State, *The Churches Survey Their Task: The Report of the Conference at Oxford, July 1937,* ed. J. H. OLDHAM (London 1937). R. ROUSE and S. C. NEILL, eds., *A History of the Ecumenical Movement, 1517–1948* (London 1954). E. DUFF, *The Social Thought of the World Council of Churches* (New York 1956). World Council of Churches, *Statements on Social Questions* (Geneva 1955).

[P. ABRECHT]

LIFE PHILOSOPHIES

Historians of contemporary philosophy (I. M. Bocheński, J. Hirschberger) use the term "life philosophies" to designate the teaching of a group of German and French philosophers and historians including: W. Dilthey, G. Simmel, R. Eucken, E. Troeltsch, K. Klages, H. Bergson, and E. Le Roy. The German writers do not constitute a school. Most of them were NEO-KANTIANS at the start, but they were trained in a wide variety of disciplines: history, sociology, mathematics, psychology, and, in the case of Oswald Spengler, in journalism.

The common bond among these thinkers is the notion that the abstract use of the intellect gives rise to technical and formal conceptual structures that are artificial, and that these structures are, too often, assigned greater importance than the deeper source of life in man that generates them. If we are to understand man, they say, we must turn away from conceptualization and seek to coincide with the fresh, unspoiled upsurge of life before it becomes atrophied in a rigid network of scientific formulas, eternal truths, or metaphysical absolutes. Life is infinitely richer than the conceptual instruments that we invent to interpret it.

Dilthey. Wilhelm DILTHEY (1833–1911) held that the study of the history of culture (morality, art, science, poetry, religion) provides the best approach to the life principle. A reflective study of the past reveals life on the move in its concrete manifestations. Through history man becomes conscious of himself, for he is both subject and object of the study. Such study reveals that there are no absolute scientific laws governing man's progress through time. Each event or decision is unique; each epoch has its own character. The role of the historian or the philosopher of history is to examine the momentary structure of life as it is manifested at a given point of time. This moment can never be repeated, because every event or world view emerges out of a particular context with indefinite ramifications in time and space. Postivists and metaphysicians alike want to "explain" history in terms of scientific or eternalistic ideologies. But this is to interpret life by an offprint of life, by something that is derivative. Life is self-justifying; it does not need "explanation" but "understanding," that is, an immediate insight into what is happening. To acquire an understanding of this kind we must grasp the total situation, using all our human power of sympathy, not just the abstractive faculty that always tries to reduce the particular situation to a universal law or category.

Dilthey's sense of the uniqueness of events did not prevent him from recognizing that life, as manifested in history, is expressed in various moods: the rationalistic, which gives rise to positivist naturalism; the emotional, which tends towards objective idealism; the voluntaristic, which finds expression in idealistic freedom. But these attitudes with their structures well up from below, from life itself; they are not constructs to be imposed from above upon the ongoing flux of history.

Dilthey's insistence on context was one of his great contributions to the study of HISTORY; but his historicism, which includes a rejection of rational explanations, led him into a relativistic position, making any account of the past a maze of particular events with little connection between them.

Spengler, Toynbee, and Simmel. Oswald Spengler (1880–1936) shared Dilthey's skepticism regarding the permanence of values and human institutions. In his pessimistic but brilliantly written *The Decline of the West* (Monaco 1918–22, 2 v.), he distinguishes eight different types of civilization produced by the life principle. Each culture cycle flourishes and then loses its vitality. The technological civilization of the West, and with its democracy and Christian humanism, is already on the way to destruction. The tide of life that lifted it to preeminence has begun to ebb, leaving only a tragic sense of helplessness. History is governed, not by institutions and concepts, but by deeper organic energies that have little regard for the niceties of justice.

Spengler's morose biologism was, no doubt, colored by the disillusionment of an author who wrote after the German defeat in World War I and by a cynical attitude towards conventional morality. But the English historian Arnold Toynbee (b. 1889) in his *A Study of History* (London 1934–54, 10 v.), while covering some of the same ground as Spengler, worked in a far more scholarly manner. In his analysis of the dynamics of history, while dealing with culture cycles, he is less deterministic and leaves ample room for man's voluntary control over his own future.

Georg Simmel (1858–1918), like Dilthey, was impressed by the uniqueness of each historical situation. Every past event is compounded by an unlimited number of infinitesimal forces that we can never know or catalogue in their entirety. The Battle of Marathon, for example, is at best only a tag used to designate a certain unity of vital forces. All such events are fictions, wrenched out of the complex flux of life. If we cannot hope to recover the total situation, even by the most exhaustive analysis of the contributing factors, we can at least resolve events into a set of relations between individuals and societies and in this way discover the "form" of the situation. History, then, is not merely a headlong torrent of evanescent influences; it can be grasped partially in terms of these dynamic structures that express the deeper life principle. In spite of his willingness to con-

cede that there is some immanent logic in history, Simmel's view remains a kind of nominalistic RELATIVISM.

Troeltsch, Eucken, and Driesch. Ernst TROELTSCH (1865–1923), on the other hand, found in his sociological study of history that the life-force receives its highest expression in religion and in the values that it releases. This objective world of religious values corresponds to a deep a priori within us that finds its fulfillment in the divine.

Rudolf Eucken (1846–1926) also recognized an intelligible world of religious values. These values, implicit in the life principle, we project before us as teleological ends for action; and they constitute the one world view that can offer some hope of unifying human striving.

Hans Driesch (1867–1941) was a noted psychologist whose vitalism was influential in turning many German philosophers away from POSITIVISM and physical determinism. He attacked SCIENTISM and its attempt to explain life in terms of chemical and mechanical complexity. There is in every living organism an ENTELECHY, or vital principle, that controls its growth and accounts for its unity. If it is not yet spiritual, it cannot be reduced to the sum of the material parts that it rules.

Klages' Philosophy. Many regard Ludwig KLAGES (1872–1956) as a new NIETZSCHE. His principal work, *Spirit, the Adversary of the Soul* (Leipzig 1929–32, 3 v.), suggests by its very title his cult of the irrational. But he passes over Nietzsche's value theory and stresses the orgiastic, Dionysian outlook of *The Birth of Tragedy* (Leipzig 1872). For Klages, soul is opposed to mind or spirit (*Geist*). The latter is an invention of the Greeks, canonized by Christianity with its postulate of a higher world of spirit. Life is a purely biological force that surges up in the organism. Man must remain passive to its promptings, obedient to its rhythms. Spiritual values curb the innocence and purity of this naked life principle; they are like barbed wire fences that hold vital energies in prison. Man is most true to life when carried along by blood, instinct, sensibility, feeling, and the surge of life. He becomes weak and pale, self-conscious and duty-bound when he lets the conventions of society curtail the unconscious drives of the biological instinct.

Therefore, it is not logic, reason, or calculation that will rule the world, but passion. The constructions of reason are alien to life; technology, economics, and speculation divorce man from his biological roots. We must live by the compulsive image, which engenders a sense of power. The "moral" man is a city divided; he is constantly trying to subject his vital and instinctive self to a world of spiritual values that he represents as an absolute order. But children and savages have no such inhibitions because they do not reason but feel. Theirs is the authentic life because it is experienced passively as something that ''happens'' to them, not as something they try to control or subdue.

There are similarities between Klages' views and the Nazi glorification of blood and power: the conquering barbarian lives according to nature, emancipated from artificial moral conventions. He is the avant-garde of an expansive life-force that must overthrow the superstructure of Christianity and democracy in order to release man from the spiritual framework that crushes joy and the zest for life.

French Thinkers. In France the life philosophies assumed an entirely different character (*see* BERGSON, HENRI; LE ROY, ÉDOUARD; BLONDEL, MAURICE). Far from being a political danger or hostile to religion, they were almost uniformly rooted in a profound sense of the mystery of life, which never excluded but was completed by transcendence. It is true that they too made a sharp distinction between life and the abstract use of the intellect in its discursive operation. But this distinction has behind it a long tradition, beginning with Plato and Aristotle, up through St. AUGUSTINE with his *ratio superior* and *ratio inferior*, and on to the *intellectus* and *ratio* of St. THOMAS AQUINAS. The French remained more solidly in the intellectual current of the past, recognizing the value of conceptualization with its constructions, but warning against the kind of dogmatic scientism that tended to overlook connatural knowledge, or lived rationality, in order to substitute for it notional symbols that owed their validity and usefulness to a more direct and immediate insight into life.

The French life philosophies have nothing of the Faustian demonism in their make-up. They did not constitute an attack on rationality, but on RATIONALISM. During the modernist crisis, some Catholics feared that the French philosophers were moving in the direction of the German twilight of intellect with a corresponding emphasis on emotion and feeling (*see* MODERNISM). But anti-intellectualism and IRRATIONALISM are not congenial to the Gallic temperament. It was EXISTENTIALISM that made its appearance at the very end of the revolt against systematic philosophy, and it bears but slight resemblance to the earlier life philosophies. On the contrary, while existentialism rejects ready-made conceptual systems and all forms of essentialism, it calls on man to structure his own experience and to develop a system of values, whether Christian or agnostic, that engages the will in an almost heroic effort of creativity. Such activism is a far cry from the German emphasis on passivity to impulse such as we find in Klages.

See Also: HISTORY, PHILOSOPHY OF.

Bibliography: For brief summaries of life philosophies, see I. M. BOCHEŃSKI, *Contemporary European Philosophy* tr. D. NICHOLL and K. ASCHENBRENNER (2d ed. rev. Berkeley 1956) 121–128. J. HIRSCHBERGER, *The History of Philosophy,* tr. A. N. FUERST, 2 v. (Milwaukee 1958–59) 2:565–575. Among the English translations of the works of the Germans, one may consult: W. DILTHEY, *Meaning in History,* ed. H. P. RICKMAN (London 1961); *Philosophy of Existence,* tr. W. KLUBACK and M. WEINBAUM (New York 1957). H. A. HODGES, *The Philosophy of Wilhelm Dilthey* (London 1952). R. C. EUCKEN, *Life's Basis and Life's Ideal,* tr. A. G. WIDGERY (2d ed. London 1912); *Main Currents of Modern Thought,* tr. M. BOOTH (London 1912). E. TROELTSCH, *The Social Teaching of the Christian Churches,* tr. O. WYON, 2 v. (New York 1931).

[J. M. SOMERVILLE]

LIGHT, LITURGICAL USE OF

The use of light in the liturgy is derived from four main sources: Jewish custom, pagan and civil ceremonial, practical necessity or convenience, and symbolism, both natural and Christian. This article treats biblical usage, pagan and civil ceremonial, Christian significance, and liturgical use.

Biblical Usage. The Mosaic Law prescribed that a seven-branched lampstand, made of the finest gold, be erected in the temple (Ex 25.31–40). It was also customary for Jews to keep a light burning perpetually in the sanctuary (Ex 27.20–21; Lv 24.2–4). The significance originally attached to this perpetual light is obscure, but the later Talmudists interpreted its burning as an act of reverence for the Torah kept in the Ark of the Covenant.

The custom of burning lights before the tombs of the Prophets was not unknown in Judaism; it was a practice common to all Mediterranean religions to light torches at funerals. A great many lights were used in some of the Jewish festivals as well, notably the Feast of Tabernacles and the Feast of the DEDICATION OF THE TEMPLE, called by Hanukkah or Feast of Lights by modern Jews. The *chaburah* usually called for a ceremony in which a lamp was brought in and blessed with a formula such as: ''Blessed art Thou, O Lord our God, eternal King who createst the lamps of fire.'' This ceremony marked the beginning and the end of the Sabbath and was connected with several Jewish feasts.

Pagan and Civil Ceremonial. It was a popular pagan custom to light lamps and candles both in the sanctuaries and about the doorways of homes on religious festivals. Lights were burned before idols and statues of emperors. Although torches were used to kindle the funeral pyre, they had additional significance. Offering lights to the dead was regarded as a religious act; it was a means of honoring the dead who were thought to be living in the tomb. State functionaries were also honored with lights; for example, Roman consuls had the privilege of being preceded by torches or a thick candle. This was especially the right of the Roman emperors, particularly in the court ceremonial, and the custom was continued into the Middle Ages, both in the imperial court at Byzantium and in the palaces of Western kings.

Christian Significance of Light. Apart from any religious association, light conveys to the human mind a sense of joy, optimism, goodness, purity, beauty, festiveness, dignity, and life, while darkness signifies ignorance, error, sadness, gloom, desolation, death, and evil in general. This is why lights are used so profusely by all peoples in their celebrations, whether civil or religious. Moreover, all religions, using natural symbolism, associate light with goodness and the divinity, darkness with wickedness and the evil spirits. Christianity has special reason to associate light with God, for it would be difficult to find a theme more strongly emphasized by Scripture than God as light.

In the Old Testament, light has already become part of the figurative language used to describe God. His interventions in human history are surrounded by light, fire, and lightning (Ex 3.2; 19.16; Dt 33.2; Is 30.27; 66.15; Hb 3.11; Za 14.7). Yahweh's glory shines with a brilliant light (Bar 5.9; Ez 10.4); He is robed in light (Ps 104.1–2). Thus, light is a symbol of His presence (Ex 13.21; 2 Chr 4.7; 13.11). Indeed His nature is compared to light: "Thou shalt no more have the sun for thy light by day, neither shall the brightness of the moon enlighten thee; but the Lord shall be unto thee for an everlasting light" (Is 60.19). When Yahweh shows His favor to the Israelites, He is said to let His countenance shine upon them (Nm 6.25; Ps 4.7; 89.16). As light is the symbol of devine protection (Jb 22.28; Ps 27.1; Mi 7.8), it is one of the blessings of Messianic salvation (Is 9.1; 58.8). The Servant of Yahweh himself is called a light (Is 42.6; 49.6; cf. Dn 12.3).

It is only natural for this symbolic language to be continued in the New Testament. God is called "the Father of lights (Jas 1.17); He "dwells in light inaccessible" (1 Tm 6.16). In fact, St. John says: "God is light and in Him there is no darkness" (1 Jn 1.5). Thus the Word, who before His Incarnation had engaged in a victorious struggle with darkness (Jn 1.5), is presented as the light-bringer (Lk 1.79; 2.32; Acts 26.23; 2 Cor 4.6), "the light of the world" (Jn 8.12; 9.5; 12.46), "the true light that enlightens every man who comes into the world" (Jn 1.9); His life is the light of men (Jn 1.4). This divine prerogative finally shines through the glorified humanity of Christ (Mt 17.2–5; 28.3; Acts 9.3; 22.6–11; 26.13). Those who believe in Him become the children of light opposed to the children of darkness (Mt 5.14–16; Lk 16.8; Jn 3.19; 5.35; 12.36; Acts 13.47; 2 Cor 3.18; Eph 5.8; 1 Thes 5.5; 1 Jn 1.6–7). Indeed Christ is the light of the heavenly Jerusalem (Rev 21.23–24).

While in theology the LOGOS as light of the Father is explained by way of intellectual generation or procession (*see* PROCESSIONS, TRINITARIAN), the Nicene Creed professes faith in Christ as "light from light."

Liturgical Use. The importance of this light theme in the Christian life is shown in the numerous references to light in the Divine Office, particularly in the hymns of the various hours, which compares the permanence of the Christ-light to the rise and decline of the natural light of day. Vespers, named after the evening star, Vesper, developed out of a combination of the prayer service at the twelveth hour and the Lucernarium, the blessing of the evening lamp.

Christmas. The whole of the Christmas liturgy is centered upon the coming of the divine light into the world, of the light shining in the darkness. The Word, born in light from the womb of the Father, is born again in the obscurity of this world, in the darkness of the fleshly womb of Mary; His human birth is accompanied by the splendor of the heavenly bodies manifested to the sheperds (Lk 2.9) and the Magi (Mt 2.2, 9). There are deeper theological implications than usual behind the profuse display of lights commonly seen in Christmas decorations.

Candlemas. The Feast of Candlemas (Feb. 2) brings a fitting climax to the light theme of the Christmas cycle with the blessing and procession of lighted candles. The original reason behind this feast appears to be the meeting in the temple between the Holy Family and Simeon, who proclaimed the Infant to be "a light of revelation to the gentiles and a glory to the people of Israel" (Lk 2.32). Although a procession at Jerusalem is already mentioned in the fourth–century diary of EGERIA [26; H. Pétré, *Journal de voyage* 21 (Paris 1948) 208], there is no indication that lights were used in it. A procession with lighted candles is certainly attested to in Palestine by Cyril of Scythopolis (d. 565) in his life of St. Theodosius [E. Schwartz, *Kyrillos von Skytopolis* (Leipzig 1939) 236, 24].

Easter. The Easter season, on the other hand, portrays the slow conquest of the darkness of sin by "the light of the world." During Lent He is seen to struggle with the powers of darkness that seem to triumph on Good Friday, but Christ rises from the darkness of the tomb with greater radiance and splendor than ever: "His countenance was like lightning and His raiment like snow" (Mt 28.3). This glorious victory of light over darkness is brought out dramatically in the ceremonies of the Easter Vigil: the striking of the new fire in utter darkness; the lighting of the paschal candle and its gradual dispelling of the darkness of the church building as its flame is extended to the smaller candles of the participants, accompanied by shouts of "Lumen Christi"; the magnificent strains of the Exsultet in praise of the paschal candle, symbol of Christ, the new "pillar of fire" (Ex 13.21–22) who leads redeemed Israel out of the shadow of death.

The fact that the life of the Christian is a life in the Christ-light is brought out most pointedly by the celebration within the Easter Vigil of Baptism, the paschal sacrament par excellence. In Patristic times, catechumens were called *illuminandi* (those to be enlightened) and the newly baptized *illuminati* (the enlightened). It is in this context that we must place the use of light in every baptismal ceremony. The newly baptized is given a candle with the exhortation: "Receive this burning light." After the initiation of the neophyte, the faithful participating in the Easter Vigil renew their baptismal vows, holding their candles, which have been lighted from the flame of the paschal candle. Because the religious life has traditionally been considered a king of second Baptism, it has become common in ceremonies of reception of the habit and profession for the candidate to receive a lighted candle.

Symbols of Honor and Solemnity. The ancient civil custom of honoring state officials with torches and candles was taken over by the Church [T. Klauser, *Der Ursprung der bischöflichen Insignien und Ehrenrechte* (Krefeld 1953) 18]. Candles and torches were carried before popes, and later bishops; by the seventh century, seven candles were carried before such dignitaries and then placed on the pavement about the altar (*Ordo Rom.* 1.46, 52; 2.7; 4.7–8; M. Andrieu, *Les 'Ordines Romani' du haut moyen-âge* [Louvain 1931–61] 2:82, 84, 158). Much later candles were placed on the altar; Innocent III (d. 1216) states that two candles were used for papal Masses (*De sacro altaris mysterio* 2.21; *Patrologia Latina*, ed. J. P. Migne [Paris 1878–90] 217:811). This number mounted to seven by 1254 [E. Bishop, *Liturgica Historica* (Oxford 1918) 310–311]. In the High Middle Ages, the quantity of candles on the altar emphasizes the solemnity of the occasion: seven for solemn pontifical Mass, six for high Mass, and two for low Mass.

It is in this context that we must place the carrying of lighted candles for the proclamation of the Gospel at solemn Mass. The Gospel Book, containing the Word of God, came to be considered as a symbol of Christ Himself and hence was honored with lights of joy (Jerome, *Contra Vigilantium* 7; *Patrologia Latina* 23:345).

Ceremonies Connected with the Dead. At first the Church inveighed against burning lights before the tombs of the dead (Council of Elvira from 301–303, c.34; J. D. Mansi, *Sacrorum Conciliorum nova et amplissima collectio* [Florence-Venice 1757–98] 2:11); in fact Lactanti-

us spoke out against any use of lights in worship because of their pagan implications (*Divinae institutiones* 6.2; *Patrologia Latina* 6:637–639). However, when the pagan and superstitious connotations were no longer a danger, the Church adopted lamps and torches as a popular means of showing respect for martyrs (Jerome, *Contra Vigilantium* 7; *Patrologia Latina* 23:345) and other deceased Christians [see inscriptions in T. Klauser, *Die Cathedra im Totenkult der heidnischen und christlichen Antike* (Münster 1927) 127]. Lights were also carried in the funeral cortege [A. Rush, *Death and Burial in Christian Antiquity* (Washington 1941) 226–227]. It is from this early Christian custom that we derive the practice of burning candles around the coffin during the burial rites in church.

It is obvious that this Christian use of light for the dead has a much deeper significance than in pagan practice. The body of the deceased Christian has been a temple of the Holy Trinity, a tabernacle of the Light that is God; it awaits the day of the resurrection when in its glorified state it will share in "the splendor of the saints." The use of lights recalls the sacredness of the body, the immortality of the soul, and the Beatific Vision to which both are destined and for which the Church prays: "Let perpetual light shine upon him." In this same spirit of respect are lights burned before images of the Blessed Virgin Mary and the saints.

Other Uses. Not every use of lights in worship bears a special significance. Without doubt torches, lamps, and candles were often used to provide the light necessary for functions celebrated at night or in dark churches. Apart from certain solemnizing extras, the ordinary lights in a church serve a purely utilitarian purpose. Nonetheless in some circumstances lights, once needed for functional reasons, have in time taken on symbolic meanings. A typical example of this sort of development is the bishop's bugia, a candle held or placed near the book the bishop reads from in pontifical services. The lack of adequate lighting, together with the difficulty of reading the contracted spelling of ancient manuscripts, once made this candle a practical necessity. When the original utilitarian reason no longer existed, the bugia evolved into a mark of honor for the bishop.

Bibliography: G. DIX, *The Shape of the Liturgy* (2d ed. London 1945). F. J. DÖLGER, *Sol Salutis: Gebet und Gesang im christlichen Altertum* (2d ed. Münster 1925); "Lumen Christi," *Antike und Christentum* 5 (1936) 1–43; *Die Sonne der Gerechtigkeit und der Schwarze* (Münster 1918). A. G. MARTIMORT, *L'Église en prière* (Tournai 1961).

[B. I. MULLAHY/EDS.]

LIGHT, METAPHYSICS OF

The notion of light has greatly influenced centuries of philosophical speculation and led to metaphysical, cosmological, and noetic theories. In the mythologies of early cultures and religions, light was conceived as an important condition not only of life but also of sight and knowledge. Although usually connected with the divine, in many religions light was not so much a constituent as an attribute of the deity—a life-giving factor, a cause of happiness, wealth, health, knowledge, and beauty. Dualistic religions held that light (in man the pneuma or spirit or soul), after separation from the deity, was chained to matter; through purification, however, it could return to its origin.

Greek Thought. Philosophers rationalized the notion of light. In Greek thought, Heraclitus's theory of fire as the first principle of the world initiated an ontology of light that was further developed by the Stoics and the Pythagoreans into a dualism of light and darkness. PARMENIDES assigned this theory to the realm of opinion. Light, he held, is as little related to darkness as being is related to nonbeing.

The nucleus of Plato's teaching is the GOOD; this enlightens the intelligible world just as the sun illumines the sensible world. Thus, for him, the perfect Idea of the Good becomes at once the principle of being and knowing.

ARISTOTLE held that the cosmos consists of five elements: earth, water, air, fire, and ether. He considered ether the finest of all elements, filling the highest spheres of the cosmos and constituting the celestial bodies. Ether, in his view, is not mixed with heterogeneous particles; its purity accounts for the circular (that is, perfect) movement of the heavens in contrast with the less perfect up and down motion of the other elements. During the Middle Ages it was called the *quinta essentia,* light, the clarity of the heavenly regions.

Neoplatonism. Neoplatonic systems are rich in speculations concerning light (*see* NEOPLATONISM). In Philo's teaching, Plato's Idea of the Good is not spoken of figuratively; it is the spiritual light. However, it was PLOTINUS who first developed a metaphysics of light, considering light no longer as a physical substance. From the One emanates immaterial light, radiating outward, growing dimmer and dimmer until it shades off into darkness (a PRIVATION of light), which is matter. From the One also proceeds Nous (thought, mind), which knows all things simultaneously in an eternal now. From Nous emanates the WORLD SOUL; from the latter emanate human souls and finally material beings. They do not lack light completely, for they are illumined by form, which

is considered the exteriorization of the intelligible. Here light starts its ecstatic return to its origin and proves that the sensible and the intelligible are bound together. Such unity allows for mystical and prophetical experience and knowledge.

Medieval Development. Augustine combined the teaching of Neoplatonism and Plato's Idea of the Good with revealed truths. For instance, he applied Genesis 1.3 ("Let light be made") to the creation of the *mundus intelligibilis,* the world of the angels. He accepted the Platonic distinction between sensible and spiritual light. Like Plato, Augustine cautioned men not to trust the sensible realm. Christ is called "Light" in the sense that He enlightens every man, although man is free to turn toward or away from the Light. On such ontological premises Augustine built his theory of ILLUMINATION, which had considerable impact on medieval thought.

Pseudo-Dionysius. The *Hierarchia caelestia* of PSEUDO-DIONYSIUS became the handbook of Christian symbolism. From God, the Father of Lights, comes all radiation. The physical light that attracts bodily beings symbolizes the divine IMMANENCE and TRANSCENDENCE, for it penetrates all things while remaining pure itself. Light is also the forming power within man, leading him upward and uniting him to the Father of Lights.

Arabs and Jews. In later centuries an amalgamation of Christian, Jewish, and Arabian thought led to a fuller development of the metaphysics of light. Some Arabian and Jewish philosophers saw light as a substance or a power. The literature of the Talmud and Midrash speaks of light as the garment of God: God took His garment and spread it like a mantle, thus creating the celestial world. ISAAC ISRAELI taught that in the hierarchy of being, the lower beings proceed from the shadow of the higher, for example, from the shadow of Intelligence originates the *anima rationalis,* from its shadow, the *anima bestialis,* and so on. Through a good moral life, man participates in the light of the Intelligence. Similar doctrines were held by the Arabs, mainly by ALFARABI, AVICENNA, and ALGAZEL, who combined Aristotelian, Neoplatonic, and Oriental thought.

Grosseteste. Influenced by thinkers of his era, ROBERT GROSSETESTE formed an elaborate metaphysics of light. God is the Eternal Light and Exemplary Form of all things. He first created *forma prima* and *materia prima. Forma prima* is a point of light that by its very nature diffuses itself and becomes the corporeal form of matter. In this process *materia prima* is expanded into the three spatial dimensions of the finite universe. As corporeal form, light functions as a principle of distinction and multiplicity and continuity in nature. "All things are one by the perfection of one light." The rarefaction of matter through light is considered the highest actualization of matter; it is exemplified by the firmament, "the first body," which has nothing "in its composition but first matter and first form." Through this expansion of matter by light, nine celestial immutable spheres are built. The innermost of these concentric spheres is the sphere of the moon, which produces through its own light the four infralunar spheres consisting of fire, air, water, and earth. The infralunar regions are subject to change and corruption. Their beings are determined, specified, and perfected by light; and here light becomes also the principle of motion and color. Light gives these bodies form, actuality, movement, and color.

As a consequence of this speculation, optics came to be greatly developed. In its service stood geometry, the study of light diffused from a central point into straight lines, reflected and refracted by angles, and providing a mathematical structure for the universe. Grosseteste's theory had a decisive influence upon the natural philosophers at Oxford (ADAM MARSH and ROGER BACON) and at Paris (ALEXANDER OF HALES, BONAVENTURE, and others). Grosseteste's clear distinction between corporeal and noncorporeal light no longer prevailed in the *De Intelligentiis* of ADAM PULCHRAE MULIERIS, who returned to a light-monism: "*Unumquodque quantum habet de luce, tantum retinet esse divini.*" Unlike these thinkers, St. THOMAS AQUINAS did not accept light as substantial form but understood it as a quality and applied it by analogy to the intelligible realm.

Renaissance and Modern Thought. During the Renaissance a revival of the metaphysics of light occurred in the theories of such philosophers as M. FICINO, G. BRUNO, and J. Böhme. G. PICO DELLA MIRANDOLA, who combined Neoplatonism, medieval Christian theology, and CABALA, spoke of the supernatural light (faith), the natural light, and the light of glory. Man, a microcosm, contains in himself the cosmic sources of light and possesses also the light of the agent INTELLECT.

Francesco Patrici da Cherzo (1529–97) returned to a Neoplatonic doctrine of light in which God is the original, uncreated Light. From Him light emanates as a metaphysical principle of being, causing multiplicity and life as well as the unity of beings. Light is a kind of an intermediary between the purely spiritual and the purely material. Besides light, there are other factors in nature, namely, warmth, space, and fluidity.

Little philosophical work has been done on later theories of light. The scientific current leads to physicomathematical theories, as in Newton's *Opticks* (1704), rather than to metaphysical analysis. Newton postulated an ethereal medium mainly to account for the propagation of light, which he could not explain in purely me-

chanical terms. Light was conceived and spoken of merely in the sensible realm by G. BERKELEY and the British empiricists, whereas F. H. JACOBI applied the term to a supersensible reality open only to intuition. However, contemporary work in the philosophy of science, particularly that associated with interpretations of quantum theory, is more and more directed to investigating the reality that lies behind the physicist's equations.

See Also: ILLUMINISM; PHILOSOPHY AND SCIENCE.

Bibliography: F. C. COPLESTON, *History of Philosophy,* 7 v. (Westminster, Md. 1946–63). J. HIRSCHBERGER, *The History of Philosophy,* tr. A. N. FUERST, 2 v. (Milwaukee, Wis. 1958–59). A. A. MAURER, *Medieval Philosophy* (New York 1962). A. C. CROMBIE, *Robert Grosseteste and the Origins of Experimental Science* (Oxford 1953). R. GROSSETESTE, *On Light,* tr. C. C. RIEDL (Milwaukee 1942). C. BAEUMKER, *Witelo, ein Philosoph und Naturforscher des XIII. Jahrhunderts* (*Beiträge zur Geschichte der Philosophie und Theologie des Mittelalters* 3.2; 1908). J. RATZINGER, "Licht und Erleuchtung: Erwägungen zur Stellung und Entwicklung des Themas in der abendländischen Geistesgeschichte," *Studium generale* 13 (1960) 368–378.

[C. E. SCHÜTZINGER]

LIGHT OF GLORY

The term used in theology to describe the help given the intellect whereby it is enabled to see God face to face. The necessity of this help is a dogma of the Catholic faith, defined in the Council of Vienne against the BEGUINES and Beghards, who held that "the soul does not need the light of glory to elevate it to see God and to enjoy God in blessedness" (*Enchiridion symbolorum*, 895). This definition is based on Scripture passages such as Rv 21.23, which depicts God as a light illuminating the blessed in the heavenly Jerusalem, which has the glory of God (v. 11) "and has no need of the sun or the moon to shine upon it, for the glory of God lights it up" (v. 23).

Fathers. The teaching of tradition on the light of glory is found principally in the commentaries of the Fathers on Ps 35(36).10: "and in your light we see light." Although there is no clear-cut and definite teaching that can be said to be the mind of the Fathers, two affirmations recur in their writings. On the one hand, God Himself is represented as the light that illumines the elect. In addition, the Greek Fathers frequently add that the Holy Spirit will make us capable of seeing God in the Word. Even though this points in the direction of the light of glory being identified with God, a tendency that some scholastics espoused, it is not difficult to find indications in the Fathers, even in texts describing this uncreated light, that this illumination produces a true elevation of the intellectual powers of the elect. It would be pointless, however, to seek passages in the Fathers where they speak of this elevation as due to a principle intrinsically perfecting the intellect; they were content to enunciate the dogma that the blessed must be elevated to see God, without theologizing upon the means whereby this is accomplished.

Theological Speculation. Elaborating on the nature of the light of glory, theological speculation has specified it as a SUPERNATURAL habit permanently perfecting the intellect of the blessed and elevating it to enable them to see God. It is considered a HABIT because it must be permanently possessed by the elect, and a dynamic habit because it enables intellectual creatures to exercise their highest faculty perfectly with respect to its most perfect object.

The necessity of the light of glory is proved from two sources. First, the natural faculty must be elevated to the supernatural operation of the BEATIFIC vision, which totally surpasses the ability of the unaided intellect. Second, the beatific vision presumes an immediate union between the created intellect and the uncreated light, the principle and term of this vision. This union, far from rendering the light of glory superfluous, cannot be explained without it, for two things that are not one cannot be associated with one another unless at least one of them undergoes a change. Since the object seen cannot change, the created intellect must be strengthened for the vision, which strengthening is the light of glory.

Thus the light of glory has a threefold function. It elevates the created intellect to the order of the beatific vision and makes it physically capable of attaining the divine essence; it disposes the intellect to the immediate union with the divine essence necessary for the vision; it concurs actively with the intellect in producing the act of vision itself.

In the Orthodox Churches there is a difference in teaching on the light of glory that goes back to the time of the Palamites (*see* HESYCHASM), who distinguished between the divine essence and an uncreated light, proceeding from it and distinct from it, although not inseparable from it. God is absolutely unknowable and incommunicable in the divine essence, but is knowable and communicable in His operations or energies, chief of which is this uncreated light. Vladimir Lossky says: "This uncreated, eternal, divine, and deifying light is grace, for the word grace belongs to the divine energies in as far as they are given to us and operate the work of our deification. . . . This illumination or divine and deifying grace is not the essence but the energy of God" (95). Thus the light of glory for them, far from being a created habit infused into the intellect, is something in God that is seen in the beatific vision, a concept that seems to contradict the divine simplicity and the dogma that the divine essence itself is

the object of the vision.

See Also: HEAVEN (THEOLOGY OF); PALAMAS, GREGORY.

Bibliography: A. MICHEL, *Dictionnaire de théologie catholique,* ed. A. VACANT et al., 15 v. (Paris 1903–50; Tables générales 1951) 7.2:2370–77. R. SCHNACKENBURG and K. FORSTER, *Lexikon für Theologie und Kirche,* ed. J. HOFER and K. RAHNER, 10 v. (2d new ed. Freiburg 1957–65) 1:583–591. R. GARRIGOU-LAGRANGE, *The One God,* tr. B. ROSE (St. Louis 1943) 364–372. V. LOSSKY, "La Théologie de la lumière chez st. Grégoire de Thessalonique," *Dieu vivant* 1 (1945).

[R. J. BASTIAN]

LIGHTFOOT, JOSEPH BARBER

Anglican scripturist, patrologist, and bishop, known especially for his commentaries on the Pauline Epistles; b. Liverpool, England, April 13, 1828; d. Bournemouth, Hampshire, England, Dec. 21, 1889. After his studies at King Edward's School, Birmingham, he entered Trinity College, Cambridge (1847), where he was a private pupil of B. F. WESTCOTT and worked as editor with F. J. A. Hort on the *Journal of Classical and Sacred Philology* (1854–59). He was appointed tutor of Trinity College in 1857 and was ordained the next year. He then became in turn Hulsean professor (1861), chaplain to the prince consort and honorary chaplain to the queen, Whitehall preacher (1866), canon of St. Paul's (1871), and Lady Margaret professor of divinity (1875). Consecrated bishop of Durham in 1879, he administered this office until his death a decade later. His commentaries on the Epistles to the Galatians (1865), Philippians (1868), and Colossians (1875), by reason of their historical insight, mark a new era in New Testament exegesis in England. His works on the Apostolic Fathers are thorough, painstaking studies much esteemed by patristic scholars. For a bibliography of Lightfoot's principal works, see the *Quarterly Review* 176 (1893): 73.

Bibliography: F. J. A. HORT, *The Dictionary of National Biography from the Earliest Times to 1900,* 63 v. (London 1885–1900) 11:1111–19. *Quarterly Review* 176 (1893): 73–105. A. C. BENSON, *The Leaves of the Tree* (London 1911) 187–211. G. R. EDEN and F. C. MACDONALD, eds., *Lightfoot of Durham* (Cambridge 1932).

[B. VEROSTKO]

LIGUGÉ, ABBEY OF

In the commune of Ligugé (Vienne), France, three miles south of Poitiers. The present Abbaye Saint-Martin de Ligugé was founded in 360 by St. Martin of Tours, who became bishop of Tours in 370. Archeological excavations since 1953 have unearthed the Gallo-Roman villa, dating from the second or third century, that was the saint's first dwelling; a fourth-century exedra and chapel that testify to his coming to Ligugé; the sixth-century church visited by St. Gregory of Tours; and the structures built by Ursinus, abbot at the end of the seventh century. After being ruined during the Arab invasion (732), the monastery revived at the beginning of the eleventh century with the aid of Aumode, countess of Poitou, as a priory of the Abbey of Maillezais (Vendée). The monks ceded the place to chaplains long before it became the property of the Jesuits from Poitiers. Four monks from SOLESMES restored Benedictine life to Ligugé (1853). Under Dom Bourigaud, the second abbot (1876–1906), Ligugé revived the monasteries of Sainte-Marie of Paris, FONTENELLE (Saint-Wandrille) in Normandy, and SILOS in Spain. Expelled by the law of associations (1901), the community settled at Chevetogne, Belgium, until 1923, when it returned. Since then it has prospered under its abbots, Dom Gaugain, Dom Basset, and Dom Le Maître, and has cooperated with the ecumenical movement. The productions of its workshop in enamels are highly esteemed.

Bibliography: P. MONSABERT, *Le Monastère de Ligugé* (Ligugé 1929). J. COQUET, *L'Abbaye de St. Martin de Ligugé* (Ligugé 1948); *Revue Mabillon* 44 (1954) 45–94; 45 (1955) 75–147; 48 (1958) 245–248. H. ROCHAIS, *ibid.* 43 (1953) 138–146, bibliog. L. H. COTTINEAU, *Répertoire topo-bibliographique des abbayes et prieurés* (Mâcon 1935–39) 1:1613. O. L. KAPSNER, *A Benedictine Bibliography: An Author-Subject Union List* (Collegeville, Minn.) 2:224–225.

[H. ROCHAIS]

LIGUTTI, LUIGI G.

Pastor of rural ministry and ecumenist; b. near Udine, Italy, March 21, 1895; d. Rome, Italy, Dec. 28, 1984. He attended primary schools in his native village of Romans and Udine before emigrating to the United States in 1912 and enrolling in St. Ambrose College in Davenport, IA. He completed theological studies at St. Mary's Seminary, Baltimore, and was ordained a priest of the Diocese of Des Moines Sept. 22, 1917. He pursued graduate studies at The Catholic University of America, Columbia University, and the University of Chicago.

After eight years of pastoral ministry he was named pastor of Assumption parish, Granger, IA, where he refined his philosophy of Catholic rural sociology, expressed in the classic work co-authored with John Rawe, SJ, *I Rural Roads to Security*. He gained national prominence by founding the Granger Homesteads, the first national program of housing for lower income families.

In 1937 Ligutti became executive secretary of the National Catholic Rural Life Conference (NCRLC).

Three years later he resigned his parish, moved the headquarters of the Conference to Des Moines and became its first full-time executive secretary. Over the next 20 years he wrote and traveled extensively throughout the United States, speaking before innumerable audiences on the Church and rural life. In his apostolate he joined forces with leaders in the liturgical movement, the National Conference of Catholic Charities, and Catholic Relief Services, making American Catholics more aware of the importance of rural life and its problems. He associated with his counterparts in other Christian churches in promoting these same goals, and thus became one of the earliest ecumenists in the United States. He remained executive director of the NCRLC until 1958 when he subsequently became its director of international affairs.

On July 26, 1948, Ligutti was appointed Vatican Observer to the Food and Agriculture Organization of the United Nations, the first Vatican appointment to any office of the United Nations. What he did for the cause of rural life in the United States he now undertook for the entire globe. In time he became the best known American priest throughout the world. In this office he helped draft the section on agriculture in Pope John XXIII's encyclical *I Pacem in terris*.

Ligutti served as a consultant to the prepatory commission and subsequently to the conciliar commission on the laity of Vatican Council II. The council's statements on rural life, tithing, and migration are chiefly the results of his efforts.

Following the Council he established *I Agrimissio*, an organization to assist missionaries in fostering rural values among underprivileged people throughout the world. The closing years of his life were spent in retirement at his home, Villa Stillman, in Rome. Following his death his body was returned to the United States and buried in Assumption parish cemetery in Granger.

Bibliography: V. A. YZERMANS, *The People I Love: A Biography of Luigi G. Ligutti* (Collegeville, MN 1976).

[V. A. YZERMANS]

LILIENFELD, ABBEY OF

Cistercian abbey in the Diocese of St. Pölten, Lower Austria; founded (1202) by Duke Leopold VI, who is buried there, and settled (1206) from HEILIGENKREUZ. It flourished in the 14th century, declined during the Reformation, and was revived by German-born abbots and monks educated at the Germanicum in Rome (Ignaz Kraft 1622–38 and Cornelius Strauch 1638–50); but there were tensions between German and Austrian monks. Abbot Matthäus Kolweiss (1650–95), an Austrian,

Exterior of the church of the Abbey of Lilienfeld, Austria.

founded St. Joseph Archconfraternity (1653) and regained ZIRC for the Cistercians. Lilienfeld, which successfully resisted the Turks (1683), was suppressed briefly (1789–90) and badly damaged by fire (1810) and war (1945). The large early Gothic church (1230), with baroque furnishings (1730–45), and the 13th-century cloister are of interest. The library, whose main hall was built *c.* 1700, has 34,000 volumes, 119 incunabula, and 226 MSS. The monk Christianus (d. before 1332) was a liturgical poet; Abbot Ulrich (1345–51) compiled the *Concordantia caritatis;* Chrysostomus HANTHALER (1717–54) compiled the *Fasti Campililienses;* Abbot Ladislaus Pyrker (1812–18), later patriarch of Venice, was a poet. The 100 monks of 1330 declined to 43 in 1964. The abbey serves 19 parishes.

Bibliography: N. MUSSBACHER, "Das Stift Lilienfeld," *Heimatkunde Lilienfeld,* v. 1, 2 (Vienna-Lilienfeld 1960–63). L. H. COTTINEAU, *Répertoire topobibliographique des abbayes et prieurés,* 2 v. (Mâcon 1935–39) 1:1614. F. LOIDL, *Lexikon für Theologie und Kirche,* ed. J. HOFER and K. RAHNER, 10 v. (2d, new ed. Freiburg 1957–65) 6:1054.

[N. MUSSBACHER]

LIMA, MANUEL DE OLIVEIRA

Brazilian diplomat and historian; b. Recife, Dec. 25, 1867; d. Washington, D.C., March 24, 1928. Oliveira Lima came from a rich family and received all his education in Lisbon, where he graduated in 1888 in diplomacy, law, and philosophy. In 1890 he was named second secretary to the Brazilian legation in Lisbon and in 1892 was transferred to Berlin. Back in Brazil in 1896, he worked as a journalist for a short time. From 1896 to 1900 he was first secretary of the Brazilian Embassy in the United States; in 1900 he was in London and was then named minister to Japan. In 1903 he was appointed minister to Peru, but did not serve in that office, being almost immediately appointed chief of the Brazilian commission to carry on boundary negotiations with Venezuela. Later he served as minister to Sweden and Belgium. Oliveira Lima became, in fact, the intellectual ambassador of Brazil, in Europe, Japan, the United States, and Spanish America. He became famous as a public speaker and a conversationalist, giving conferences and courses in every country he visited. He was the first Brazilian to be professor at the Sorbonne in Paris. A dozen of the most important universities of the United States invited him to lecture or teach. A lover of books and a serious historian, he searched for rare and precious volumes everywhere and built up one of the most valuable collections of books and documents on Brazilian and Portuguese history. He did much to make his country known in foreign lands. He tried to strengthen cultural links between the Americas and Europe and Japan. He was an admirer of German culture and of monarchy and a pacifist who received a great shock with the outbreak of World War I. Professor at The Catholic University of America in his last years, he donated his library to that university and endowed a chair for Portuguese and Brazilian language and culture. He was an advocate of Pan Americanism and hoped that this would help to unite the Americas and to make The Catholic University in Washington, D.C., an international center of learning.

Among his best scholarly historical works are *D. João VI no Brasil* (Rio de Janeiro 1919), *O Imperio Brasileiro* (São Paulo 1928), and *Historia da Civilização* (São Paulo 1921).

Bibliography: M. DE OLIVEIRA LIMA, *Memórias* (Rio de Janeiro 1937).

[T. BEAL]

LIMA TEXT

A statement of the Faith and Order Commission of the World Council of Churches (WCC) on "Baptism, Eucharist, and Ministry" (BEM) unanimously approved at the Commission plenary meeting at Lima, Peru, on Jan. 12, 1982. It purports to be a statement of convergence rather than full consensus, and is submitted to the churches for their reception and response.

The roots of the Lima Text go back to discussions in the Faith and Order Movement since the First World Conference at Lausanne in 1927, when efforts were made to find common ground on questions concerning sacraments and ministry. The Faith and Order Commission meeting in Louvain in 1971 reviewed earlier consensus statements on the Eucharist and on Baptism dating from 1967 and 1968 and a new draft report on the Ordained Ministry. At the Accra meeting of the Faith and Order Commission (1974) the reports on Baptism, Eucharist, and Ministry were revised and combined in a single brochure. The Nairobi Assembly of the WCC (1975) asked the member churches to submit their reactions to the three reports. Taking account of these reactions, a small committee of experts headed by Max Thurian composed the draft for Lima, which considered and voted on many amendments to produce the final text.

The very dense text cannot be adequately summarized. The language adheres closely to that of previous Faith and Order documents and, in general, that of the Bible. Where there are clear disagreements among the churches, an effort is made to give a fair statement of each position. The disagreements are explained in a running commentary which is part of the official text.

The chapter on Baptism has 23 paragraphs, with commentary. Baptism is described as a participation in Christ's death and Resurrection, as an event of conversion and cleansing, as a bestowal of the Holy Spirit, as incorporation into the Body of Christ, and as a sign of the Kingdom. Infant and adult ("believers") baptism are presented as "equivalent alternatives." The unusual practice of baptizing without water is noted as requiring further study.

The chapter on Eucharist contains 33 paragraphs, with commentary. The Eucharist (or Lord's Supper) is depicted as thanksgiving to the Father, as a memorial of Christ, as invocation of the Holy Spirit, as communion of the faithful, as an anticipation of the eschatological meal. It is described as "the sacrament of the unique sacrifice of Christ," a memorial wherein the Church intercedes in union with the great High Priest. Transubstantiation is mentioned in the commentary, with the remark that many churches do not link Christ's presence so definitely to the consecrated elements. Intercommunion is encouraged as a manifestation of "the catholicity of the Eucharist" (Comm. 19).

The chapter on Ministry (55 paragraphs with commentary) begins with a treatment of the ministry of the whole people of God and states that a special or ordained ministry is constitutive of the life and witness of the Church. The ordained are described as heralds and ambassadors, as leaders and teachers, and as pastors who direct the community. Disagreements about the ordination of women are noted in the commentary.

The threefold pattern of bishop, presbyter, and deacon is recognized as ancient and as holding promise for Church unity. Bishops are portrayed as charged with preserving continuity and unity in the Church and with pastoral oversight of a given area. The apostolicity of the whole Church is held to be served and symbolized by the continuous succession of bishops. Churches that have maintained this succession are, however, urged to recognize the "apostolic content" of the ordained ministry in other churches.

Responses. The Lima text is preceded by a preface (not technically part of the Text) in which all churches are asked to respond officially to four questions: To what extent can you recognize in this text the faith of the Church throughout the ages? What consequences can you draw for relations with other churches? What guidance can you find in the text for your worship, life, and witness? How should Faith and Order make use of this text for its future research? The Vancouver Assembly of the WCC (1983) reaffirmed the request that the churches respond to these questions.

The official response of the the Catholic Church to BEM issued by SPUC on July 21, 1987, was basically positive, characterizing the Lima texts as "perhaps the most significant result of the [Faith and Order] movement so far." "The study of BEM," it asserted, "has been for many Catholics an enriching experience." Noting that "BEM demonstrates clearly that serious progress is being made in the quest for visible unity," the response encouraged Faith and Order "to continue its valuable work of seeking unity in faith as a basis for visible unity."

While observing that BEM converges with Catholic doctrine and practice on a broad range of issues, the response noted that there are occasional passages which suggest options in theology and practice not consistent with Catholic faith. Some of these may here be indicated under the headings of Baptism, Eucharist, and Ministry.

On Baptism, the SPUC found the Lima text to be "grounded in the apostolic faith received and professed by the Catholic Church." The trinitarian, sacramental, and missionary dimensions of Baptism, according to the response, are well stated. But the text was faulted for its failure to treat a number of points that Catholics consider important; e.g., the necessity of Baptism for salvation, original sin, the Baptismal character, and the completion of initiation through Confirmation (as a distinct sacrament) and the Eucharist. The SPUC response also considered that the value of infant Baptism and the importance of nurture in a Christian community should have been given more emphasis.

On the Eucharist the SPUC response praised, among other things, the strong trinitarian and christological dimensions of the text, its use of patristic and liturgical sources, and its rich ecclesiological and eschatological context. The Secretariat, however, found unfortunate ambiguities in the treatment of the Eucharist as sacrifice and in the handling of Christ's real presence through the conversion of the elements, which Catholics regard as a matter of faith. The report also objected that the problem of eucharistic sharing among churches was discussed without sufficient attention to the ecclesial significance of Holy Communion. Lima's treatment of reservation of the consecrated species was also found deficient.

On the Ministry text, SPUC was likewise positive.

Well aware of the complexity of the ecumenical dialogue on ministry, we are grateful for the work achieved on it by the Commission and we appreciate especially the fact that its presentation goes in the direction of the major lines of what we recognize 'as the faith of the Church throughout the ages'.

On the ordination of women, SPUC took the position that this is excluded by apostolic tradition, which the Church has no authority to change. The response expressed regret that BEM is unclear as to whether the threefold ministry of bishop, presbyter, and deacon is a constitutive feature of the Church or a historically contingent disposition. It would have welcomed more emphasis on the collegiality of the bishops and on the papacy as the "focus of unity." While acknowledging that ordination is in effect treated as a sacrament (without the word being used), SPUC took the position that "ordained ministry requires sacramental ordination by a bishop standing in the apostolic succession"—a point not affirmed by BEM. For this reason SPUC considered the proposals of BEM on the mutual recognition of ministries premature.

In proposing future work for Faith and Order, SPUC called attention to three areas needing further treatment: first, sacrament and sacramentality, including (it would seem) the Church as a real and effective "icon of the presence of God and His Kingdom in the world"; second, apostolic tradition, which should be clearly distinguished from the particular "traditions" that develop in the separate churches; and third, authority in the Church, including the power of definite persons and bodies to discern and make binding decisions.

On Aug. 31, 1987, Günther Gassmann, the director of Faith and Order, welcomed this response by SPUC as the first official response ever given by the Catholic Church to an ecumenical document. He interpreted this response as an unambiguous commitment of the Catholic Church to the one ecumenical movement. He also applauded the support given in the response to multilateral dialogue as complementary to the bilateral dialogues that the Catholic Church has vigorously sponsored since Vatican Council II.

Bibliography: *Baptism, Eucharist, and Ministry,* Faith and Order Paper 111 (Geneva 1982). J. GROS, ed., "Baptism, Eucharist, and Ministry and Its Reception in the U.S. Churches," *Journal Ecumenical Studies* 21, no. 1 (Boston 1984). SECRETARIAT FOR PROMOTING CHRISTIAN UNITY, "Baptism, Eucharist, and Ministry: An Appraisal," *Origins* 17, no. 23 (Nov. 19, 1987) 401–16. M. THURIAN, ed., *Ecumenical Perspectives on Baptism, Eucharist, and Ministry,* Faith and Order Paper 116 (Geneva 1983); *Churches Respond to BEM. Official Responses to the "Baptism, Eucharist and Ministry" Text,* 6 v. (Geneva 1986–88). M. A. FAHEY, ed., *Catholic Perspectives on Baptism, Eucharist, and Ministry. A Study Commissioned by the Catholic Theological Society of America* (Lanham, Md. 1986). G. LIMOURIS and N. VAPORIS, *Orthodox Perspectives on Baptism, Eucharist and Ministry,* Faith and Order

The Descent into Limbo, fresco by Fra Angelico, cell 3 in the convent of San Marco, Florence. (©Massimo Listri/CORBIS)

Paper 128 (Brookline, Mass. 1985); also printed in *The Greek Orthodox Theological Review* 30, no. 2 (1985).

[A. DULLES]

LIMBO

A word derived from the Latin *limbus*, literally meaning the "hem or border" as of a garment. The word is not employed by the Fathers, nor does it appear in Scripture. Since the time of Thomas Aquinas theologians have used the term to designate the state and place either of those souls who did not merit hell and its eternal punishments but could not enter heaven before the Redemption (the limbo of the fathers') or of those souls who are eternally excluded from the beatific vision because of original sin alone (the children's Limbo).

The Limbo of the Fathers. Inhabiting the "limbo of the fathers" (our ancestors in the faith) are those who led a righteous life before Jesus' earthly existence and death. They could not enter heaven even though righteous, however, because of Adam and Eve's sin. This is the limbo (the Hebrew *Sheol*, the Greek *Hades*) referred to in the Apostles' Creed—the "hell" into which Christ descended after his crucifixion. Jesus' experience of a true human death included his entering this realm of the dead, but his descent there redeemed the just and brought them to salvation. The "limbo of the fathers" explained how the righteous who died before Christ's death could attain salvation, while maintaining that their salvation depended upon and was effected by Christ's death. The same difficulty is addressed today more generally in the question of the possibility of salvation for the adult non-Christian.

The Limbo of Children. In the patristic era there was apparently little concern with the problem of infants dying without baptism. St. Augustine thought that unbaptized infants went to hell, although he conceded that, due to their lack of personal responsibility and guilt for original sin, the pains of hell were in some way diminished for them. Subsequent theologians distinguished between a pain affecting one's senses (the pain of sense), and the pain caused by the absence of the perfect joy of the Beatific Vision (the pain of loss). The scholastics of the 12th century departed from Augustine's viewpoint. St. Thomas Aquinas freed the doctrine of the idea that unbaptized infants suffer from any pain of sense; indeed, he held that, though deprived of the Beatific Vision, they enjoy a natural bliss. The problem was not handled in any explicit manner by the Council of Trent, though there was some preliminary discussion about the punishment of original sin in the next life.

From Trent to Pistoia. During this period theologians were absorbed in attempting to determine exactly what punishment is allotted to unbaptized infants in the next life. The vast majority believed them immune from the pain of sense and transferred to a special place, or state, called Limbo. Although this was without doubt the common teaching of the period, the question was considered open to discussion. Others believed these infants were consigned to the fire of hell, obviously denying the existence of Limbo. The defenders of the existence of Limbo found their strongest arguments in the teaching of Aquinas and his concept of original sin as a sin of nature and not of the person. As a result they viewed the punishment of original sin and that of personal sin as entirely different. Only personal sin involves a conversion to some forbidden created good that deserves the pain of sense. Traces of this doctrine are found in the teaching of Innocent III in 1201 (H. Denzinger, *Enchiridion symbolorum*, ed. A. Schönmetzer [Freiburg 1963] 780) as well as in that of the Second Council of Lyons (*ibid.* 858) and the Council of Florence (*ibid* 1306).

Pistoia and the Bull *Auctorem Fidei*. The Jansenists in Italy based their idea on the teaching of St. Augustine. They said that Limbo as taught by the scholastics is a fable invented by Pelagius and that the teaching that infants dying without Baptism are condemned to the fire of hell is revealed doctrine. They boldly proclaimed it at the Synod of PISTOIA in 1786, and implied that the defenders of the existence of Limbo are heretics. The reply of Rome is found in Pius VI's bull *Auctorem Fidei* (1794). This is the last declaration of the Church in regard to this problem and the only official document containing the word Limbo. From the history of this document it is certain that the Church merely wished to defend the common teaching from slander. As such it is not a defense of the existence of Limbo. The question of Limbo's existence—openly disputed by Catholic theologians at the time of the bull—was not touched upon directly in any way by Pius VI. The open denial of Limbo by the Jansenists was tolerated and merely their manner of denial censured. *Auctorem Fidei*, in fact, dealt the deathblow to the teaching of St. Augustine. For all purposes, no one defended any longer the opinion that infants who die without baptism are condemned to the fire of hell.

Recent Church Teaching. While limbo was mentioned in a 1951 address given by Pius XII to Catholic midwives, of far greater significance is its absence in recent Church documents in the very context where mention of it might be expected. Examples include the 1979 "On Certain Questions Concerning Eschatology" and the 1980 "Instruction on Infant Baptism," both published by the Sacred Congregation for the Doctrine of the Faith. The *Catechism of the Catholic Church* (CCC) quotes from and affirms the 1980 "Instruction": "As regards *children who have died without Baptism*, the Church can only entrust them to the mercy of God, as she does in her funeral rites for them. Indeed, the great mercy of God who desires that all men should be saved, and Jesus' tenderness toward children which caused him to say: 'Let the children come to me, do not hinder them' (Mk 10:14), allow us to hope that there is a way of salvation for children who have died without Baptism. All the more urgent is the Church's call not to prevent little children coming to Christ through the gift of holy Baptism'' (1261).

Most theologians today regard the "limbo of children'' as a once-popular, but now inert, theological opinion that attempted to resolve the theological tension between the Church's teaching on the necessity of baptism for salvation and the acknowledgment that infants and young children are innocent of personal sin. While some theologians have devised sophisticated theories attempting to reconcile the two (for example, that an infant would receive supernatural knowledge at the moment of death and thus be able to choose for or against God), today most would support the theological and pastoral approach suggested by the CCC. The possibility of an eternal state of natural bliss, separate from the Beatific Vision, is not treated directly in official Church teaching, while among theologians it is addressed more generally in the discussions of the relationship between nature and grace.

Bibliography: G. J. DYER, *Limbo, Unsettled Question* (New York 1964). P. GUMPEL, "Unbaptized Infants: May They Be Saved?" *Downside Review* 72 (1954) 342–458. P. J. HILL, *The Existence of a Children's Limbo According to Post-Tridentine Theologians* (Shelby, Ohio 1961). V. WILKIN, *From Limbo to Heaven* (New York 1961). L. G. WALSH, *The Sacraments of Initiation* (London 1988), 104–109. K. STASIAK, "Infant Baptism Reclaimed: Forgotten Truths about Infant Baptism," *Living Light* (1995): 36–46. C. BEITING, "The Idea of Limbo in Thomas Aquinas," *The Thomist* 62 (1998): 217–244.

[P. J. HILL/K. STASIAK/EDS.]

LIMITATION

The term limitation is used in philosophy and theology to explain why some being or some property of a being is only limited or finite, as in the case of creatures, and not unlimited or infinite, as in the case of God. A principal problem in scholastic philosophy is to explain, in terms of causes or principles, the limitation of one creature compared to another (e.g., man to angels), and more especially of all creatures compared to God.

Thomists usually assign a twofold reason for the qualitative limitation of a given being. First, every limited being requires some external agent or efficient cause to determine its capacity or limit, and to communicate the corresponding degree of perfection. Second, the result or effect in the being of the determining action of its cause is some internal principle of limitation within the being itself. This inner principle of limitation fixes the being's inner capacity for receiving so much and no more of a given attribute or perfection. To borrow an analogy from the quantitative order, if a person wishes to fill a pitcher with water, he must pour so much water; likewise the pitcher (the recipient) must itself have a certain shape or capacity to be able to receive the water. This inner cause or principle of limitation St. THOMAS AQUINAS called a POTENCY for receiving a perfection or ACT (*see* POTENCY AND ACT). Both of these terms he borrowed from ARISTOTLE, the original proponent of potency and act, though Aristotle himself applied his theory only to the problem of CHANGE and not to that of limitation, St. Thomas argues that no positive qualitative perfection, such as knowledge, goodness, or power, can be identically its own limiting principle, i.e., the reason why it is possessed by a particular being to a limited degree and not in its fullness. Therefore, wherever there is limitation there must be an internal duality or real metaphysical distinction of elements within the limited being: one principle to take care of the positive perfection that is received or participated; the other to limit the capacity of the subject that receives or participates. This philosophical doctrine, referred to as the limitation of act by potency, may be summarized thus: No act (or perfection) can be found in a limited state unless it be received into a really distinct limiting potency.

Other scholastic philosophers, such as John DUNS SCOTUS and F. SUÁREZ, agree with St. Thomas on the need for an external agent to determine the limitation of a being, but deny that any internal principle of potency within the limited being need be really distinct from the perfection it limits.

See Also: FINITE BEING; PARTICIPATION; PERFECTION, ONTOLOGICAL.

Bibliography: W. N. CLARKE, "Limitation of Act by Potency," *The New Scholasticism* 26 (1952) 167–194. G. GIANNINI, *Enciclopedia filosofica,* 4 v. (Venice–Rome 1957) 3:54–58.

[W. N. CLARKE]

LINACRE, THOMAS

English physician and priest, founder of the Royal College of Physicians in London; b. Canterbury, *c.* 1460; d. London, Oct. 20, 1524. He was educated at the Priory School in Canterbury under William of Selling (later prior), through whose influence he enrolled in All Souls College, Oxford. He studied also in Florence, Padua, and Rome. In 1488 Henry VII sent Prior Selling to Rome as ambassador to the pope, and Linacre accompanied him. In Florence he met Lorenzo de'Medici, who invited him to share in the instructions given by Angelo Poliziano and Demetrius Chalcondylos to the two young princes Piero and Giovanni de'Medici. Giovanni later became Pope LEO X. Linacre studied medicine in Padua, where he received his M.D. After years of practice on the Continent, he returned to England, where he became royal physician to HENRY VIII and regular medical attendant to many of the highest nobility of the country. He used most of his fortune to found the Royal College of Physicians. The charter for the college was granted by Henry VIII on Sept. 23, 1518, upon the petition of Linacre, several other physicians, and especially Cardinal Wolsey. This charter gave the college the sole power to give medical licenses. His important contribution to medical science was his translation of GALEN's work from Greek into Latin. Linacre was highly esteemed by his contemporaries. He began to receive ecclesiastical preferments, even before he was ordained in 1520. After this he gave up his medical career in order to devote himself to priestly work. Johnson says that he seems to have had no enemies.

Bibliography: J. F. PAYNE, *The Dictionary of National Biography from the Earliest Times to 1900,* 63 v. (London 1885–1900) 11:1145–1150. J. N. JOHNSON, *The Life of T. Linacre,* ed. R. GRAVES (London 1835).

[M. A. STRATMAN]

LINCOLN, ANCIENT SEE OF

The largest and most populous diocese in medieval England, extending from the Humber to the Thames. An old Roman town, it may well have had a bishop in the 4th century; St. PAULINUS OF YORK built a stone church and consecrated Honorius Archbishop of Canterbury there in 627. It became a see in 1072 when Remigius, Bishop of Dorchester-on- Thames, moved his headquarters to Lincoln in obedience to the policy of WILLIAM I and LANFRANC, of erecting sees in fortified towns. In 1086 Remigius began the cathedral, superbly situated on a steep hill; it was added to by Alexander the Magnificent (1123–48) and rebuilt by St. Hugh and his successors. It is probably the finest example of 13th-century Gothic architecture in England. Lincoln was often fortunate in her bishops. St. Hugh's example inspired a series of reforming bishops such as Hugh of Wells (1209–35), ROBERT GROSSETESTE, the pastoral canonist Oliver Sutton (1280–99), and the saintly John Dalderby (1300–20), while Richard Fleming (1420–31) and William ATWATER were among the most devoted bishops of their time. John LONGLAND was confessor to Henry VIII and advised him to seek a divorce from CATHARINE OF ARAGON. Religious houses in the diocese included Peterborough, Bardney, and Crowland (Benedictine); the exempt abbey of St. Albans; Louth Park and Revesby (Cistercian); and several GILBERTINE nunneries. Besides the cult of St. Hugh, whose shrine was in the "Angel Choir," there were popular cults of Remigius, Grosseteste, Dalderby, and "Little St. Hugh," none of whom were ever officially canonized. At the Reformation, the territory of the old diocese was divided among Lincoln, Oxford, and Peterborough.

Bibliography: Registers of: Hugh of Wells (Eng. Publications of the Lincoln Record Society 3, 6, 9; Lincoln 1912–14); Oliver Sutton (*ibid.* 397; Hereford 1948–); Richard of Gravesend (*ibid.* 20; Horncastle 1920); R. Grosseteste and H. Lexington (*ibid.* 11; Lincoln 1914). C.W. FOSTER and K. MAJOR, *The Registrum Antiquissimum of the Cathedral Church of Lincoln* (*ibid.* 27– ; 1931–). A. H. THOMPSON, ed., *Visitations of Religious Houses in the Diocese of Lincoln, 1420–1449* 3 v. (*ibid.* 7, 14, 21; Horncastle 1914–29). J. H. SRAWLEY, *The Story of Lincoln Minster* (London 1933). R.M. WOOLLEY, comp., *Catalogue of the Manuscripts of Lincoln Cathedral Chapter Library* (London 1927). K. MAJOR, "The Finances of the Dean and Chapter of Lincoln," *Journal of Ecclesiatical History* 5 (1954) 149–167. K. MAJOR, ed., *Lincoln Minster Pamphlets* (Lincoln 1948–). A. SCHMITT, *Lexikon für Theologie und Kirche,* ed. J. HOFER and K. RAHNER (Freiburg 1957–65) 6:1061–62.

[H. FARMER]

LINDAU, CONVENT OF

Founded by Count Adalbert of Raetia (Tirol) *c.* 817 for Benedictine nuns. The convent, also known as St. Marien, was generously endowed with lands, privileges, and immunities. In 948 it was destroyed by fire but was rebuilt. The convent enjoyed a spiritual growth in the 11th century and adopted the rule of St. AUGUSTINE in the 12th. A hospital was founded at Lindau sometime before 1237. Around 1470 the abbess of the convent was granted the title "Princess of the Realm." There were, however, jurisdictional disputes between the convent and the city of Lindau that lasted into the 18th century. Despite considerable pressure from the Lindau governors, who had embraced Protestantism, the convent persevered in the old faith. On Sept. 16, 1728, its buildings were once again leveled by fire. Although the convent was secularized in 1805, the convent church, rebuilt during the years 1748 to 1852, has served Lindau's Catholic parish since 1813.

Bibliography: *Liber anniversariorum monasterii Lindaugiensis, Monumenta Germaniae Historica: Necrologia* (Berlin 1826–) 1:179–197. K. WOLFART, *Kurze Geschichte der Reformation in Lindau, Aeschach, und Reutin* (Lindau 1917); ed., *Geschichte der Stadt Lindau am Bodensee,* 2 v. in 3 (Lindau 1909). A. HORN, *Die Kunstdenkmäler von Schwaben: Stadt und Landkreis Lindau* (Munich 1954).

[D. ANDREINI]

LINDISFARNE, ABBEY OF

Former English abbey on Lindisfarne Island, or Holy Island, off the coast near Berwick-upon-Tweed, England. This early abbey and bishop's seat in northern England was of Celtic origin for, although Christianity had first been brought to the north through King ETHELBERT OF KENT's daughter, ETHELBURGA, who had married EDWIN, the pagan king of Northumbria (627), and through her chaplain, Paulinus, who had become the first bishop of YORK, the Queen and Paulinus had fled south to Canterbury when Edwin was slain by the heathen king of Mercia in 632. Edwin's immediate successors apostatized, and the infant church in Northumbria collapsed. But when the Christian, OSWALD, who had been educated in an Irish school, became king of Northumbria, he asked the community of Celtic monks at IONA to undertake the conversion of his Northumbrian domains. One of the monks, AIDAN, was consecrated a bishop and together with a group of missionaries, went to Northumbria (635), where he chose Lindisfarne for his abbey and episcopal seat. Aidan was succeeded (651) as bishop by another monk of Iona, FÍNÁN. His successor was COLMAN, who withdrew to Iona and then to Ireland after the Synod of WHITBY opted for the Roman rather than the Celtic Easter date. By this time the missionaries from Lindisfarne had penetrated even beyond Northumbria into Mercia. In 685 St. CUTHBERT was consecrated sixth bishop; he was a man of the Iona tradition of spirituality, who retired to the neighboring island of FARNE to live as a hermit. Lindisfarne was the first monastery to suffer from Viking attacks, which began in 793. It continued as a bishopric until 875, when raids forced the monks to flee with Cuthbert's body to Chester le Street (*c.* 883). In 995 the see was finally transferred to DURHAM. In the 11th century Lindisfarne Abbey was granted to the Benedictines of Durham, who supplied the island with monks until the suppression in 1536, when the property passed into the hands of the dean and chapter of Durham. The famous Book of Lindisfarne, or LINDISFARNE GOSPELS, dating from *c.* 700, is now in the British Museum, London.

Bibliography: BEDE, *Histoire ecclesiastique* 3.4, 5, 17, 23, 26; 4.17, 27, 28; 5.1, 12, 23. G. F. BROWNE, *The Venerable Bede* (new ed. New York 1919). W. LEVISON, *England and the Continent in the 8th Century* (Oxford 1946). B. COLGRAVE, ed. and tr. *Two Lives of Saint Cuthbert* (Cambridge, Eng. 1940); *Life of Bishop Witfrid by Eddius Stephanus* (New York 1927). J. EARLE and C. PLUMMER, eds. *Two of the Saxon Chronicles Parallel,* 2 v. (Oxford 1892–99). F. L. CROSS, *The Oxford Dictionary of the Christian Church* 811.

[J. RYAN]

LINDISFARNE GOSPELS

The Lindisfarne Gospels is a vellum codex of the four Gospels (British Museum, Cotton MS Nero D IV), with Canon–tables and prefaces, written in a noble Anglo–Saxon majuscule script and splendidly decorated in Hiberno–Saxon style by Eadfrith (bishop of Lindisfarne, 698–721) on the island of Lindisfarne off the northeast coast of England, probably between 695 and 698. Complete and exceptionally well-preserved, it comprises 259 folios (13.8 inches by 9.8 inches). About 970 a word-by-word interlinear translation of the Latin text into the Anglo-Saxon was added by Aldred, a monk of the Lindisfarne community. This is one of the longest Old English texts and a very important linguistic document. Aldred added also a colophon (on fol. 259r) giving details of the making of the Gospels. The binding, now lost, was by Aethelwald (bishop, 721–740) and was enriched with gold, silver, and gems by Billfrith (Bilfrid), an anchorite of the community. The codex was thus made on Lindisfarne in the monastery founded (635) by the Irishman AIDAN but by Saxon hands. The Gospel text is a pure Vulgate of the Italo–Northumbrian family very close to that of the Codex Amiatinus. Its exemplar appears to have come from Naples. Italian influence appears also in the setting–out of the text, in the Canontable arcades, in the Evangelist portraits, and even in the character of the script. Eadfrith is the first known name in British art history. The text was issued in editions by J. Stevenson and G. Waring (1854–65) and by W. W. Skeat (1871–87).

See Also: MANUSCRIPT ILLUMINATION.

Ruins of Lindisfarne Priory, Holy Island, England. (©Patrick Ward/CORBIS)

Bibliography: *Codex Lindisfarnensis,* ed. T. D. KENDRICK et al., 2 v. (Olten 1956–60), color fac. and commentary. S. F. H. ROBINSON, *Celtic Illuminative Art in the Gospel Books of Durrow, Lindisfarne and Kells* (Dublin 1908). E. G. MILLAR, *The Lindisfarne Gospels* (London 1923). F. HENRY, *Irish Art in the Early Christian Period, to 800 A.D.* (Ithaca, N.Y. 1965). J. BACKHOUSE, *The Lindisfarne Gospels: A Masterpiece of Book Painting* (San Francisco 1995).

[R. L. S. BRUCE–MITFORD]

LINDORES, ABBEY OF

Former Benedictine monastery of the Tironian congregation (*see* TIRON, ABBEY OF) in Fifeshire, Scotland, within the Diocese of St. Andrews. Founded and richly endowed in 1191 by David, earl of Huntingdon and grandson of DAVID I, the abbey was colonized from Kelso and dedicated to St. Mary and St. Andrew. Like DUNFERMLINE and BALMERINO, Lindores was popular with, and frequently visited by, English and Scottish monarchs in the 13th century and emerged almost unscathed from the wars of independence. One of its monks, Laurence of Lindores, was a distinguished teacher at the nearby University of St. Andrews in the early 15th century. In 1543 the abbey was sacked and its monks expelled by an army of reformers; and in June of 1559 under John KNOX's leadership they utterly desecrated it. The last abbot, the historian John Leslie, who was also bishop of Ross, died in exile in 1596; and the abbey was erected into a temporal lordship for Patrick Leslie in 1600. It is now a ruin.

Bibliography: *Chartulary of the Abbey of Lindores, 1195–1479,* ed. J. DOWDEN (Edinburgh 1903). J. WILKIE, *The Benedictine Monasteries of Northern Fife* (Edinburgh 1927). D. E. EASSON, *Medieval Religious Houses: Scotland* (London 1957) 60.

[L. MACFARLANE]

LINE, ANNE, ST.

Martyr; b. Dunmow, Essex, late 1560s; hanged Tyburn, Feb. 27, 1601. Her parents, William and Anne Heigham, were ardent Calvinists, enriched by monastic spoils. When Anne was still in her teens, she and her brother William became Catholics with the result that they were disinherited and driven from home. Soon afterward Anne married Roger Line, also a convert of a good family, and they agreed to observe the virtue of continence. In 1585 Roger, then 19 years old, and William were arrested for assisting at Mass. While Roger was in prison, his father or uncle (he was heir to both) sent him a message that if he refused to attend the Protestant Church, his patrimony would go to his younger brother. Roger refused and, like Anne, was disinherited. He was released and sent into exile in Flanders where he died in 1594. William became a Jesuit brother in Spain.

Anne found herself bereft of both husband and brother, and of her home; although young, she was an invalid. When John Gerard, a Jesuit missionary, decided to establish a house for priests in London, he asked Anne to take charge of it. She gladly accepted, although it was a dangerous work. She managed the finances, did the housekeeping, answered inquiries, taught children, and embroidered vestments. The priests called her Mrs. Martha. She longed for martyrdom, and the martyr (Ven.) William Thompson had once promised her that if he should be martyred, he would "pray for her that she might obtain the like happiness."

After Gerard's escape from the Tower in October 1597, Anne moved to another house, for hers had become too well known to be safe. There, she made vows of poverty, chastity, and obedience. On Candlemas Day, 1601, Anne invited an unusually large number of Catholics for Mass which attracted attention, and constables arrived. The celebrant, Francis Page, SJ, escaped, but Anne and some of the congregation were arrested. She came up for trial on February 26 before Lord Chief Justice Popham and was sentenced to death for harboring a priest; but since the priest had not been found, the charge was unproved. The next day, she was drawn from Newgate to Tyburn. (Bl.) Mark Barkworth, OSB, and (Bl.) Roger Filcock, SJ, who had long been a friend and confessor of Anne, were martyred at the same time. The Countess of Arundel, Bl. Philip Howard's widow, lent her carriage for the rescue of Anne's body from the communal grave. Anne was beatified in 1935 and canonized in 1970.

Feast: Feb. 27.

Bibliography: J. GERARD, *The Autobiography of a Hunted Priest*, tr. P. CARAMAN (New York 1952). M. O'DWYER, *Blessed Anne Line* (Postulation pamphlet; London 1961).

[G. FITZHERBERT]

LINGARD, JOHN

English historian; b. Winchester, Feb. 5, 1771; d. Hornby, Lancashire, July 17, 1851. Lingard received a Catholic education at the English College in DOUAI, France, which he left shortly before the final expulsion of the English community during the French Revolution (1793). In England he rejoined a group of Douai professors and students in Durham County, where they dwelt at Tudhoe and then at Crook Hall (1794). After his ordi-

nation (1795), Lingard became vice-president, professor of moral and natural philosophy, and prefect of studies at Crook Hall and from 1808, at Ushaw College, site of the permanent establishment. From May of 1810 until June of 1811, he was acting president of Ushaw College. For the remainder of his life he was a zealous pastor in charge of the mission in Hornby.

Lingard, who came of old English stock, was very proud of English Catholic traditions and wished to retain them. Forthright and intensely English, he was, in his correspondence, critical, at times very critical, of bishops, of Rome, of Italian missionaries to England, and of the pious practices that they introduced. He was distressed because English Catholics remained subject to the penal laws and lacked a clergy with a tradition of learning and culture. The popular concept of the Catholic Church in England as an Italian mission to Irish immigrants disturbed him. In his many writings, his chief aims were to restore the good name of English Catholics and to effect the conversion of that country.

At Crook Hall, Lingard composed his *History and Antiquities of the Anglo-Saxon Church* (2 v. 1806), a valuable work that is still cited frequently by specialists. At Hornby he engaged in controversy with leading Anglican divines and published a version of the New Testament with a critical introduction (1836) and several devotional books. But his fame rests principally on his eight-volume *History of England, from the First Invasion by the Romans to the Accession of William and Mary in 1688* (1819–30; the 5th ed., enlarged, 1849–51, was the last one revised by the author; the much later edition by Hilaire BELLOC added nothing of value). The work was a general history intended to attract non-Catholic readers by its impartiality and accuracy. His method was, as he described it, "to take nothing on trust; to confine my researches in the first instance to original documents and the more ancient writers; and only to consult the modern historians when I have composed my own narrative." Original documents were, however, difficult of access at that time, when scientific history was in its infancy. To obtain them Lingard went to Italy in 1817 and visited Venice, Milan, Florence, and Parma. In Rome he worked for several weeks in the Barberini and Vatican archives; he found there a useful collaborator in Robert Gradwell, rector of the English College, who supplied him with materials for the next ten years. Publication of the first few volumes of the *History of England* established Lingard's reputation as an original and critical historian. Thereafter materials and offers of help came from all parts of Europe. Alexander Cameron and Thomas Sherburne, rectors at the English College in Valladolid, did research for Lingard in the archives of Simancas. The archbishop of Paris aided him in discovering the important dispatches of Simon Renard, Spanish ambassador during the reign of Mary Tudor.

The extensive use of original sources brought the work a success that was immediate and enduring. Lingard was one of the first to utilize diplomatic materials for sixteenth- and seventeenth-century English history. Thereby he was able to present this controversial period in an entirely new light. The *History* was translated into French, German, and Italian and earned its author a European reputation. It was rumored that LEO XII created Lingard a cardinal *in petto* but died before actually conferring the red hat. Today the work is almost in its entirety out of date, particularly for the pre-Reformation period. The treatment of the sixteenth and seventeenth centuries is the best section; the chapters on Queen MARY TUDOR still constitute one of the better studies of this reign.

Lingard's voluminous correspondence, as yet unedited, constitutes an important source for English Catholic history.

Bibliography: M. HAILE and E. BONNEY, *Life and Letters of John Lingard* (London 1911). E. BONNEY, *The Catholic Encyclopedia,* 16 v. (New York 1907–14) 9:270–272, with photo. J. GILLOW, *A Literary and Biographical History or Bibliographical Dictionary of the English Catholics from 1534 to the Present Time,* 5 v. (London-New York 1885–1902) 4:254–278. T. COOPER, *The Dictionary of National Biography from the Earliest Times to 1900,* 63 v. (London 1885–1900) 33:320–323. G. CULKIN, ''The Making of L.'s History,'' *Month* 192 (1951): 7–18. D. MILBURN, *A History of Ushaw College* (Durham 1964).

[G. CULKIN]

LINUS, ST. POPE

Pontificate: 68 to 79; first successor to Peter (*See* CLEMENT I). All early lists of Roman bishops and the Canon of the Roman Mass agree that Linus was the immediate successor of Peter as head of the Roman Church. Possibly he was Peter's ''coadjutor.'' St. Irenaeus (*Adv. Haer.* 3.3) identifies him with a disciple of St. Paul (2 Tm 4.21), which is likely. The epistle's unknown author tried to give his work a Pauline pedigree by addressing it to a known Pauline disciple, by setting it in Rome (1:16-7), and by mentioning Prisca and Aquila (4:19). He probably mentioned Linus because he was known to be a Roman associate of Paul. The dates of his episcopacy vary according to Eusebius (67–79), Jerome (*Chron. a. Abr.,* an. 70), the Liberian catalogue, and the *Liber pontificalis* (56–67), the only source to call him a martyr. The *Annuario Pontificio* of 2001 gives the date of 68 for the beginning of his pontificate. This late date suggests some disorganization in the Roman community following the Neronian persecution of 64 and the deaths of Peter and

Paul. Linus's feast follows the tradition of the *Liber*, which claims that he was a Tuscan and reports that he decreed, at the direction of Peter, and possibly under the inspiration of 1 Cor. 11.1–16, that women must veil their heads in church. Modern excavations under the Vatican do not bear out the account in the *Liber* of his burial next to Peter.

Feast: Sept. 23.

Bibliography: Eusebius, *Historia Ecclesiastica* 3:2, 4, 13, 21; 5:6. *Liber pontificalis,* ed. L. DUCHESNE (Paris 1886–92, 1958) 1:cii, 2, 52, 121. *Acta Sanctorum* Sept. 6:539–545. H. LECLERCQ, *Dictionnaire d'archéologie chrétienne et de liturgie.* ed. F. CABROL, H. LECLERCQ and H. I. MARROU (Paris 1907–53) 9.1:1195–98. É. AMANN, *Dictionnaire de théologie catholique.* ed. A. VACANT et al., (Paris 1903–50) 9.1:772. A. P. FRUTAZ, *Lexikon für Theologie und Kirche,* ed. J. HOFER and K. RAHNER (Freiberg 1957–65) 6:1068. J. N. D. KELLY, *The Oxford Dictionary of Popes* (New York 1986). E. FERGUSON, ed., *Encyclopedia of Early Christianity,* 2d. ed. (New York 1997) 2:682. J. HOFFMAN, ''Linus: erster Bischof von Rom und Heiliger der orthodoxen Kirche'' *Ostkirchliche Studien* (Würzburg 1997) 105–41.

[E. G. WELTIN]

LIOBA, ST.

Anglo-Saxon abbess, aide to Boniface in Germany; b. Wessex, England; d. Schornsheim, near Mainz, Germany, Sept. 28, 782. The daughter of Dynne and Ebba, West Saxons related to St. BONIFACE, she was placed in Thanet Abbey when young and was professed at WIMBORNE ABBEY when she came of age. Literature was for her a world of delight, and she wrote a letter to Boniface that concluded with a poetic passage and asked him to correct her writing and to pray for her. As a result of ensuing correspondence, some of which survives, 30 nuns including Saints Lioba (or Liobgytha), THECLA, and WALBURGA, were sent to Boniface in Mainz. Lioba was placed in charge of a monastic establishment called Tauberbischofsheim (735), and from that base she set up other convents in Germany. She was highly respected by the early CAROLINGIANS and was often invited to attend at court, especially by Charlemagne's wife, HILDEGARD OF KEMPTEN. Boniface's regard for her carried over to his successors, especially to LULL OF MAINZ, and she alone was allowed to enter Fulda to pray, all other women being excluded. She was buried at Fulda at the specific behest of Boniface.

Feast: Sept. 28.

Bibliography: *Vita* by RUDOLF OF FULDA, *Monumenta Germaniae Historica: Scriptores* (Berlin 1826–) 15.1:118–131, Eng. trans. in *The Anglo-Saxon Missionaries in Germany,* ed. and tr. C. H. TALBOT (New York 1954). *Monumenta Germaniae Historica: Epistolae selectae* (Berlin 1826–) 1:nn. 29, 67, 96, 100, letters. W.

LEVISON, *England and the Continent in the Eighth Century* (Oxford 1946) 70, 76–77, 150. T. SCHIEFFER, *Winfrid-Bonifatius and die christliche Grundlegung Europas* (Freiburg 1954) 162–166.

[J. L. DRUSE]

LIPSIUS, RICHARD ADELBERT

German Protestant theologian; b. Gera (Thuringia), Germany, Feb. 14, 1830; d. Jena, Aug. 19, 1892. Lipsius came from a Saxon family long noted for producing theologians. He studied at the University of Leipzig and there became lecturer (1855) and professor (1859). In 1861 he moved to the University of Vienna and in 1865 to Kiel, where the Lutheran bishop attacked him for alleged theological LIBERALISM. From 1871 until his death Lipsius was professor of systematic theology at Jena. Hegelian influences on his thought gave way to a NEO-KANTIANISM that opened a new understanding of SCHLEIERMACHER. But Lipsius never completely shook off traces of the approaches of HEGEL and F. C. BAUR. He found himself constantly in critical dialogue with the old Protestant scholasticism and with RITSCHL. Because of his biblical and patristic studies, along with his interest in practical Church affairs, Lipsius strove to develop a universal speculative theology that would blend scientific and religious perceptions. In this endeavor he did not succeed; he reduced his efforts to the exposition of his concepts of religious cognition as subjective experience. Despite this allowance for "mysticism," he moved close to Ritschl's theology, which eventually overshadowed his own. His principal work, the *Lehrbuch der evangelisch-protestantischen Dogmatik,* demonstrated in its three editions between 1876 and 1893 the development of his thought. Besides his numerous historical studies, his *Apokryphe Apostelgeschichten und Apostellegenden* (2 v. 1883–90) deserves attention, as well as his text edition of *Acta Apostolorum Apocrypha* (1891; new ed. 1959). Lipsius was also a man of action, being a cofounder of the Evangelical Alliance and the Evangelical Prostestant Missionary Union.

Bibliography: M. SCHEIBE, *Allgemeine deutsche Biographie* 52:7–27. J. J. HERZOG and A. HAUCK, eds. *Realencycklopädie für protestantische Theologie,* 24 v. (3d ed. Leipzig 1896–1913) 11:520–524. S. M. JACKSON, *The New Schaff-Herzog Encyclopedia of Religious Knowledge,* 13 v. (Grand Rapids, Mich. 1951–54) 6:493–494. H. WEINEL, *R. A. Lipsius* (Tübingen 1930). H. HOHLWEIN, *Die Religion in Geschichte und Gegenwart,* 7 v. (3d ed. Tübingen 1957–65) 6:385–386. R. BÄUMER, *Lexikon für Theologie und Kirche,* ed. J. HOFER and K. RAHNER, 10 v. (Frieburg 1957–65) 1072.

[D. RITSCHL]

LISBOA, CRISTÓVÃO DE

Missionary and natural historian of Brazil; b. Lisbon, Portugal, *c.* 1590; d. convent of St. Anthony of Curral, April 19, 1652. He was the son of Gaspar Gil Severim, executor-môr of Portugal, and the brother of the celebrated antiquarian Manoel Severim de Faria, chanter of the Cathedral of Évora. He joined the reformed Franciscan province of Piedade, and after four years transferred to the Province of St. Anthony. After ordination he became a noted literary figure and preacher and, after 1640, a favorite of King John IV. Frei Cristóvão held important positions in the Church and order, including that of first custos or vice provincial of the Franciscan vice province of Maranhão–Pará in northern Brazil (1624–36). When the king divided Portuguese America into two independent states in 1621, he also ordered an ecclesiastical division. In lieu of a new bishop, Frei Cristóvão was sent there with quasi-episcopal authority, arriving with 18 friars, 5 of whom were Brazilians. He became the foremost champion of the rights of the indigenous peoples in the area, traveling extensively in both Maranhão and Pará. The difficulties of enforcing the humane *aldeiamento* laws were enormous: he succeeded partially in Maranhão, but not in Pará. He returned to Portugal in 1636 in broken health. In 1644 he was named Bishop of Angola, but he was never consecrated. Among his works are many printed sermons. While in Brazil he wrote and illustrated in color the "Historia dos animais e arvores do Maranhão," which was never published. The only copy is in the Arquivo Histórico Ultramarino in Lisbon.

Bibliography: L. DA FONSECA, "Frei Cristóvão de Lisboa, O.F.M., Missionary and Natural Historian of Brazil," *Americas* 8 (1951–52): 289–303. M. C. KIEMEN, *The Indian Policy of Portugal in the Amazon Region, 1617–1693* (Washington 1954).

[M. C. KIEMEN]

LISMORE, ABBEY OF

Early Irish abbey, County Waterford, Ireland (Gaelic; *Lis Mór;* Latin, *Lismorensis*). According to the *Annals of Inisfallen,* it was founded the year Mo-Chutu was expelled from Raithen (County Westmeath), in 638. The nature of this entry and the obit of Mo-Chutu in the same annals imply that Mo-Chutu was also its founder. The *Annals of Ulster* place Mo-Chutu's expulsion a year earlier and are silent about the foundation of Lismore. It was the principal religious center of the Déissi clan (County Waterford). Although sacked six times by the Scandinavians, it flourished and continued as a center of learning. Many of its community were venerated as saints. In time it became one of the strongholds of the CULDEES. Its later history is that of the origins of the Diocese of Lismore, which was joined to that of Waterford in 1362.

Franz Liszt. (The Library of Congress)

Bibliography: *Annals of Inisfallen,* ed. and tr. S. MACAIRT (Dublin 1951), *Annals of Ulster,* ed. and tr. W. M. HENNESSY and B. MACCARTHY, 4 v. (Dublin 1887–1901). Kenney, this with the indexes to annals cited gives the most reliable synopsis of its history. E. H. L. SEXTON, *Descriptive and Bibliographical List of Irish Figure Sculptures of the Early Christian Period* (Portland, Maine 1946). F. HENRY, *Irish Art in the Early Christian Period* (2d ed. London 1947).

[C. MCGRATH]

LISZT, FRANZ

Romanticist musician whose artistic achievements substantially influenced music history, b. Raiding (Doborján), Hungary, Oct. 22, 1811; d. Bayreuth, Germany; July 31, 1886. His father, Adam, administrator of an Esterházy estate and a skilled music amateur, was presumably of Hungarian descent; his mother, Anna (Laager) Liszt, was of Austrian-German background. Although physically frail, the boy genius was playing in public at nine. His first and most important teachers were Carl Czerny (piano) and Antonio Salieri (theory) in Vienna; later he studied composition and counterpoint with F. Paër and A. Reicha in Paris. His prodigious talent and winning manners made him society's darling, and his father exploited him, though not excessively, in England and on the Continent. Franz produced an opera, *Don Sanche,* in Paris in 1825; it was not successful and he never wrote another, although he figured factorially in operatic history, particularly vis-à-vis Richard WAGNER, as conductor, producer, and promoter. In 1827, upon the death of his father, he began teaching piano in Paris. In 1830 he met BERLIOZ, whom he championed, and in 1831 he heard the violinist Paganini, whose virtuosity changed his whole concept of pianism. In 1832 he met CHOPIN and was strongly influenced by his musical style. From 1839 to 1847 he toured all Europe in concert, acknowledged the greatest of all pianists (albeit something of a showman).

As a youth Liszt had at times desired to enter the priesthood but had been dissuaded by his father. In the 1830s he fell in love with Countess Marie d'Agoult (the writer "Daniel Stern") and became the father of three children: Blandine; Cosima, later Wagner's wife and widow; and Daniel. In 1848 he settled with the Polish princess Carolyne Von Sayn-Wittgenstein in Weimar, where for 12 years he served the court as *Kapellmeister* and produced his major orchestral works. He had hoped to marry the princess in Rome on his 50th birthday, but the union was forbidden by the Church when her existing marriage could not be dissolved. In 1865 he took minor orders from Cardinal Hohenlohe at the Vatican and was thenceforth known as the "Abbé" Liszt. In 1875 he became president of the New Academy of Music in Budapest and thereafter divided his time among Budapest, Rome, and Weimar, as elder statesman in the world of art.

Liszt was one of the great creators and innovators of 19th-century music. He expanded its expressiveness, organized new forms, justified new sources of inspiration, illumined the value of nationalism, and set the pattern of present-day concert life. He wrote a vast amount of original music, some utilizing Hungarian elements and, in later years, dissonance and atonality pointing to 20th-century idioms. His keyboard pieces are daringly emotional and chromatic, if sometimes overly sentimental. He originated the "symphonic poem" and made opulent transcriptions of songs and opera airs. Less familiar is his sacred music; yet he wrote an impressive amount, nonliturgical but of an uncommonly high quality and consonant with his fundamental piety. Two massive oratorios (*Die Legende von der heiligen Elisabeth* and *Christus*) head the list, which includes several Masses, psalms, part-songs, and other religious settings.

His essay "On the Church Music of the Future" (1834), with its thesis of "humanistic religious music," inspired Wagner's later interest in church music, and its exemplification in Liszt's own music led to Wagner's

Parsifal as well as to a Lisztian type of instrumental church composition. Moreover, he took a lively interest in the reform objectives of the CAECILIAN MOVEMENT and corresponded with its leader, F. X. Witt, over the creation of the Kirchenmusikschule in Regensburg. His many books (some of them probably the work of Marie d'Agoult and Princess Carolyne) reflect his broad interest in literature, philosophy, and social reform. During the early 20th century Liszt's music fell into critical disfavor along with the whole corpus of romanticist expression. The current reappraisal of romanticism has, however, returned his work to the honorable place among the scholars that it had never lost in the popular reckoning.

Bibliography: *Gesammelte Schriften*, ed. L. RAMANN, 6 v. in 7 (Leipzig 1881–99); *Briefe*, ed. LA MARA (I. M. LIPSIUS), 8 v. (Leipzig 1893–1905); "Vierzehn Original Briefe Liszts an Witt," *Musica Sacra* 46 (1913) 289–295. E. NEWMAN, *The Man Liszt* (New York 1935). R. HILL, *Liszt* (New York 1949). H. SEARLE, *The Music of Liszt* (London 1954). W. BECKETT, *Liszt* (New York 1956). S. SITWELL, *Liszt* (rev. ed. New York 1956). H. ENGEL, *Die Musik in Geschichte und Gegenwart*, ed. F. BLUME (Kassel-Basel 1949–) 8:964–988. K. G. FELLERER, *The History of Catholic Church Music*, tr. F. A. BRUNNER (Baltimore 1961). R. WOODWARD, *The Large Sacred Choral Works of Franz Liszt* (Doctoral diss. microfilm; U. of Illinois 1964). W. WIDMANN, "Witt und Liszt-Wagner," *Caecilienvereinsorgan* 65 (1934) 192–195. J. M. BAKER, "The Limits of Tonality in the Late Music of Franz Liszt," *Journal of Music Theory* 34 (1990) 145–173. S. GUT, "Le profane et le religieux dans les différentes versions de l'*Ave Maria* de Franz Liszt," *Revue de Musicologie* 76 (1990) 95–102. J. KANSKI, "Problem formy w sonacie h-moll F. Liszta: Przemiany formy sonatowej w okresie romantyzmu," *Studia Muzykologiczne* (1955) 276–294. G. KENNEL, "*Weinen, Klagen, Sorgen, Zagen:* Franz Liszts Variationen—ein musikalischer Trauerprozeß," *Musik und Kirche* 69 (1999) 316–325. W. KIRSCH, "Franz Liszts *Requiem für Männerstimmen*," *Kirchenmusikalisches Jahrbuch* 71 (1987) 93–108. V. MICZNIK, "The Absolute Limitations of Programme Music: The Case of Liszt's *Die Ideale*," *Music and Letters* 80 (1999) 207–240. R. SATYENDRA, "Conceptualising Expressive Chromaticism in Liszt's Music," *Music Analysis* 16 (1997) 219–252. D. SCHMIDT, "Liszt und die Gegenwart: Versuch einer theoretischen Schlußfolgerung aus der Lektüre dreier Analysen zum Klavierstück *Unstern!*," *Musiktheorie* 11 (1996) 241–252. L. R. TODD, "The 'Unwelcome Guest' Regaled: Franz Liszt and the Augmented Triad," *19th Century Music* 12 (1988) 93–115.

[E. N. WATERS]

LITANY

Definition. A litany is a repetitive prayer form, usually characterized by the announcement of varying invocations (e.g. lists of divine titles, names of saints) or supplications by a leader, each of which is followed by a fixed congregational response. Examples of such responses in the Christian tradition are "Lord have mercy," "Pray for us," or "Amen." The genre of litanies as a form of public worship may be distinguished from other responsorial forms by their relative brevity and somewhat insistent quality. The word "litany" also designates a procession of intercessory prayer, such as those used on rogation days. Examples of liturgical litanies are the Kyrie eleison, Agnus Dei, solemn orations of Good Friday, and litany of the saints. This entry discusses the origin and development of litany as prayer.

Origin. Chants resembling litanies can be traced to both Christian and non-Christian religions and cultures. Litanic patterns are found in the Hebrew Scriptures (e.g., Ps 136: *Praise the Lord, who is so good; God's love endures forever,* and Dn 3:52–90: *Blessed are you, O Lord, the God of our ancestors, praiseworthy and exalted above all forever*). These patterns are also discernible in extra-biblical Jewish litanies, such as the *hashanot* procession for the Feast of Tabernacles and the *selichot*. In the first century B.C. papyrus, Tebtunis Papyri 284.9, the Greek noun *litaneia*—derived from the verb *litaneuo,* meaning to "entreat" or "implore"—was used to refer to a pagan prayer. Early Christian writers often used *litaneia* and the related noun *lite* to signify public and corporate rather than private and individual prayer, especially for forgiveness of sins and the general welfare. These prayers were often invoked on occasions of earthquakes, plagues, and other disasters, and they soon came to be associated with public processions. The diverse forms of the term *litaneia* underwent a shift of meaning. In the fifth- and sixth-century documents, for example, an epistle of the Council of Ephesus (431) and a report on the Council of Tyre (518), these word forms seem to connote the procession itself. In the Greek Orthodox Church, the primary meaning of the word *litaneia* remains "procession."

As early as the year 396, the Latin form of *litania* was in use. In medieval Latin, it was spelled *letania* and connoted some meanings not found in the Greek. Due to the fact that processions came to be commemorated on certain fixed days of the calendar, the Latin word was frequently used to indicate the procession days customary in the West, such as the rogation days celebrated on April 25 and the weekdays before Ascension. In a separate development, the word also designated the *te rogamus, audi nos,* the repetitive *prayers* that were chanted during these processions by a deacon or cantor, to which the people would respond: "Kyrie eleison" or "ora pro nobis." This latter meaning becomes the more prominent one in Latin, and it is from this that the final sense of the Western "litany" derives its meaning.

Eastern liturgies. An early manifestation of the litany in the East is in the diaconal liturgies, in which the deacon expresses an intercession and the people respond *Kyrie eleison.* While it may go back as far as the prayer of the synagogues, it was already in use in Antioch in the time of John Chrysostom. This form of prayer still occupies a large place in Eastern liturgies.

Byzantine liturgical rites contain five main types of texts that, according to Western terminology, may be called *litanies*: (1) the *synapte*, (2) the *aitesis*, (3) the *ektene*, (4) the *dismissal litanies*, and (5) the prayers of the *lite*. Each is led by a deacon. *Synapte* (Greek for "joined together") is a Byzantine term in which the deacon proposes petitions and the assembly responds "Lord have mercy" or "Grant this, O Lord." The "great synapte" begins with the deacon chanting "In peace, let us beseech the Lord." Because the first three petitions commence with an intercession for peace, the great synapte is also called the *eirenika*. The "little synapte" is an abridged version beginning with "Again and again in peace let us beseech the Lord."

The *aitesis* (request) is a litany in the Byzantine divine office consisting of two petitions with the response "Lord have mercy," six petitions with the response "Grant it, O Lord," and an acclamation to the Mother of God and to all the saints. It was also called the "Angel of Peace" litany from its characteristic fourth petition.

The *ektene* (fervent supplication) is a unique litany form in that the deacon prays directly to God rather than proposing petitions to the assembly. The deacon sings this litany after the reading of the gospel in the Divine Liturgy and as the conclusion of the daily *orthos* and *hesperinos*. It is called "intense" because the people respond by singing three times "Lord have mercy." Its use at processions and its persistent repetition of the *Kyrie* cause the *ektene* to be perhaps the most typical genre of litany. In the Slavonic rites all litanies are called *ekteniya*, even the *synapte* and *aitesis*.

Reporting on the fourth-century Jerusalem liturgy, Egeria observed that at the *dismissal litany*, unbaptized catechumens were dismissed before the great entrance to the Mass and at the liturgy of the Presanctified. The deacon begins by instructing those being prayed for to pray silently and then asks the already baptized to respond to the litany. Fully developed dismissal litanies are found in the *Apostolic Constitutions* in which the deacon is instructed to mention the name of each individual. After each petition, the assembly, especially children, shouted: *Kyrie eleison. The Apostolic Constitutions* also assign the use of the dismissal litany at every morning and evening prayer. Two other dismissal litanies were included: for those undergoing canonical penance and for those possessed by demons.

In the Byzantine liturgical rite, *lite* is a procession of clergy and people to an appointed church in celebrating a feast for the purpose of intercession or thanksgiving. It sometimes involved a procession at the end of Vespers in which a litany is chanted when the procession pauses in the vestibule of the church. The deacon begins with "O God, save your people and bless your inheritance" and then continues with a long list of prayers for the welfare of the Christian people, often invoking the names of many saints. Depending on the liturgical source one consults, the assembly responds to each group of petitions by answering *Kyrie eleison* as many as three, eight, twelve, forty, or fifty times. Incessant repetition of the Kyrie has a long history in the liturgy of the Eastern churches.

Various other Eastern rites use or formerly used litanies that may appear to be similar in form to Byzantine litanies, but they may be diverse in content. But for a few exceptions, Eastern rite litanies are practiced as public forms of worship. Private litanic prayers are more characteristic of the Western Church.

Western litanies. Some scholars propose a very early date for the use of the *Kyrie eleison* in the West. The fourth century hymn, *Miserere Domine, miserere Christe* by Gauis Marius Victorinus (d. after 363), bears witness to not only the *Kyrie* but also to the *Christe eleison* that was never used in the East. Judging from an anti-Arian tract of uncertain date, there is indication that Greeks, Latins, and Goths each prayed the Kyrie in their own language. The first dateable evidence of the practice of the Kyrie in the West is canon 3 of the Council of Vaison in Gaul (c. 529). The canon directs that since the custom of saying "Kyrie eleison" has been introduced "in Rome, and in all the provinces of Italy and the Orient," it should be introduced in all the churches for morning and evening Office and the Mass, being sure to say it "repeatedly with great sorrow and remorse." This instruction recalls the fervor of the Greek *ektene* and perhaps the council's desire for Latin litanies to be similar in structure to the Greek. Such Latin litanies are called *preces* or *deprecationes*.

There are three witnesses to these *preces* in the litanies of the West. The first is known as the *Deprecatio Gelasii*, used in Rome and attributed to Pope Gelasius (492–496) after whom it is named. The opening phrase of the *Deprecatio* recalls the Greek *ektene*, "Let us all say: Lord, hear and have mercy." This was followed by an invocation to the Trinity, peculiar to the West. The content differs from the Eastern-type petitions, resembling the intentions of the solemn prayers of the faithful of the early Roman liturgy.

The next most important group of *preces* comprises two that were prayed in Milan during Lent, immediately after the entrance chant of the Ambrosian liturgy. These two litanies were prayed on the first two Sundays of Lent, respectively. They closely resembled the Greek *ektene* with "Let us all say: Kyrie eleison," followed by three Kyrie for the first week and one Kyrie for the second week.

The third Western source, the Mozarabic rite, had the most extensive body of *preces*-type litanies. They were used in the Lenten Masses, within the Office on penitential days, and for burial services. This group was the least dependent on Greek models and evidenced great creativity: many are metrical, some are acrostic, and a few even use rhyme. The Good Friday veneration of the Cross recalls the Eastern rite of the Exaltation of the Cross, with its profuse repetitions of "Kyrie eleison".

The most distinctive *preces* was the Tenebrae Service of Holy Week. It incorporated both the responses "Kyrie eleison" and "Domine miserere" with verses referring to the passion of Christ.

Litany of the saints. The Middle Ages witnessed the development of probably the most well known type of litany in the Western Church—the litany of the saints. This litany is composed of a list of holy men and women, each name intoned by a leader, with the assembly's response "Ora pro nobis (pray for us)." Following the list of saints' names came a second list of calamities from which the petitioner sought deliverance, with the response "Libera nos, domine (deliver us, Lord)." A Greek antecedent to the litany of the saints may be seen at the end of the *aetesis*, in which the names of saints were often multiplied after the commemoration of the Virgin Mary.

Seventh-century testimony indicates that the litany of saints was a processional litany, connected particularly with the rogation days. The Greater Litany was the name of the procession for April 25, and the Lesser Litany for the three days preceeding Ascension Thursday. In addition to rogation days, processional litanies took place on many other occasions: Holy Saturday and the Pentecost vigil, fixed days during Lent and other penitential seasons, before stational liturgies in which the bishop and assembly would gather at one church and process to the next church where the Mass was to be celebrated, and in times of drought, famine, earthquake, and other calamities. The particular litany that accompanied the procession was indicative of the interior attitude and intent of the procession itself.

Until an imposed uniformity in 1570, the text of the litany of saints varied greatly from one locale to another in elements such as the number and selection of saints, and other material at beginning and end. Some forms of the litany of the saints had special functions. The *commendatio animae*, for example, was prayed over a dying person. The *laudes regiae* was usually sung at ceremonies at which the bishop or king took part, and was joined to the Kyrie in the beginning of Mass. This litany often began with "Christus vincit, Christus regnat, Christus imperat" (Christ conquers, Christ reigns, Christ commands), and the response to each saint's name was frequently "Tu illum adiuva (you help him)."

The Protestant Reformers of the sixteenth century, espousing a strong belief in justification by faith, rejected the mediatory and intercessory role of the saints and therefore purged the Reformation liturgies of any invocation of the saints. The Anglican archbishop, Thomas Cranmer, greatly influenced by Luther and Zwingli, retained the invocation of the saints initially, but he followed the example of the continental reformers in his 1549 *Book of Common Prayer* and omitted it.

Devotional litanies. Litanies addressed exclusively to the Virgin Mary began to emerge beginning in the twelfth century. Names of saints were replaced with Marian titles such as "Mater purissima" (Mother purest), "Regina apostolorum" (Queen of the apostles), and "Rosa Mystica" (Mystical Rose). The most well known Marian litany is probably the so-called Litany of Loreto, named for the Italian village where a revered house is reported to have been miraculously transported from Palestine by angels.

By the sixteenth century similar devotional litanies developed, such as one for the Holy Eucharist. Succeeding centuries saw the growth of other approved litanies, namely the Litanies of the Holy Name (1862), Sacred Heart (1899), St. Joseph (1909), and Most Precious Blood (1960).

Current liturgical usages. In the Missal of Paul VI, the Kyrie Eleison, long a litanic and musical element in the Mass, is sung after the penitential rite or takes the form of the penitential rite itself. In this case, a short verse (trope) addressed to Christ is interpolated by the minister to which the assembly alternates, "Lord, have mercy, Christ have mercy, Lord have mercy." When it follows the penitential rite, the acclamation is alternated by the assembly and choir or cantor. While it is customary to repeat each acclamation twice, the number of repetitions may be increased according to circumstance (*The General Instruction of the Roman Missal* 52).

The prayer of the faithful, or "general intercessions" have been restored to their original place at the conclusion of the liturgy of the Word. While there is no prescribed form or response stipulated, supplication is to be made for the needs of the Church, public authorities, the salvation of the world, those in need, and the local community (GIRM 45–47). The General Intercessions for Good Friday follow the general order given for all intercessions but are more expansive in scope to include catechumens, those preparing for baptism, the Jewish people and those who do not believe in Christ or in God. Some liturgists suggest that an effective use of sung response, silence, and postures of kneeling and standing, as allowed for in the sacramentary, could greatly enhance this litanic prayer.

The *Agnus Dei* (Lamb of God) is another example of an ancient litany in the Mass. According to a statement from the *Liber Pontificalis* (ed. Duchesne 1:376), Pope Sergius I (687–701) directed that the Agnus Dei should be sung by the presider and people for as long as the consecrated bread was being divided for distribution in Communion. When the extended fraction rite was abandoned, the Agnus Dei was shortened to a litany of three petitions, and came to be reduced to a pre-Communion song. In the Mass of Paul VI, this litany is returned to its original function of accompanying the breaking of bread and the commingling. It may be repeated as often as needed; the final response being "grant us peace" (GIRM 56e).

Formularies of supplication litanies varying in text and melody according to the situation or circumstances are also included in various *sacraments and sacramentals.* Litanies of the saints are prescribed for the sacramental celebrations of adult and infant baptism and the ordination of a deacon, presbyter, or bishop. An intercessory form of litany is prayed during the anointing of the sick, following the Liturgy of the Word. The sacramentals that include a liturgical litany are as follows: religious professions, consecration of virgins, blessing of an abbot or abbess, dedication of a church or altar, Christian burial, and exorcism. In the Morning and Evening prayer, a litanic prayer form called *preces* follows the Gospel canticle.

Popularity of litanies. Between the years of the Council of Trent and Vatican II, popular devotions including various forms of litanies, often provided religious experience to the faithful in a more affective and intelligible manner than did the official services. Litanies were able to be prayed communally by ordinary people without the aid of liturgical office holders. At certain periods of history as well as today, they appealed to a large proportion of church members whatever their religious status and function, or their ethnic, educational, or socioeconomic background.

Contemporary composers, following the norms of the instruction *Musicam Sacram* (March 5, 1967), have retrieved the traditional form of litany to foster liturgical music that both respects the integrity of the rites and promotes active participation. The community of Taizé has taken the lead in composing litanic forms for such Mass parts as the *gloria* and *credo,* as well as hymns appropri-

ate for other parts of the liturgy. Other composers have begun to utilize litanies as a way for assemblies of diverse languages to sing together with refrains and/or invocations of alternating languages. The short and repetitive nature of litanies is also being recognized by church musicians as useful for processional chants.

Bibliography: E. BISHOP, *Liturgica Historica* (Oxford 1962). P. JOUNEL, "Les oraisons du propre des saints dans le nouveau missel," *La Maison-Dieu* 105 (1972): 181–98. A. MARTIMORT, ed., *The Church at Prayer: An Introduction to the Liturgy,* tr. M. O'CONNELL (Collegeville MN 1987). F. RAINOLDI, *Psallite Sapienter* (Rome 1999) 39–40. D. RIMAUD, "The Litany: Biblical and Liturgical Use," *Pastoral Music* 12:6: 32–35. *The Rites of the Catholic Church,* v. 2 (Pueblo 1980) 292–93. L. WEIL, "The History of Christian Litanies," *Liturgy: With All the Saints* 5:2 (Fall 1985): 33–37. M. WHALEN, "The Litany of the Saints—Its Place in the Grammar of Liturgy," *Worship* 65 (1991): 216–223. J. WILKENSON, *Egeria's Travels* (3d ed. Warminster, England, 1999).

[M. A. CLARAHAN]

LITANY OF LORETO

The litany in honor of the Blessed Virgin Mary in common use in the Western Church. It derives its name from its association with the shrine at Loreto, where it was known and commonly used from the mid-16th century. Earlier litanies or comparable series of *laudes,* eulogies, and invocations honoring the Blessed Virgin Mary are known to have existed, a Gaelic example of which was in use as early as the 8th century. The Litany of Loreto did not originate at the shrine, but is traceable, according to the researches of G. G. Meersseman, to the early Middle Ages, and shows the influence of Marian devotion in the East, where lists of titles of the Blessed Virgin Mary were not uncommon. The earliest known manuscript copy of a litany approximating that of Loreto dates from *c.* 1200 [*Der Hymnos Akathistos im Abendland,* 2 v. (Freiburg 1958–60) 2.220–225]. This form of the Marian litany no doubt found favor and displaced others with longer and more elaborate invocations because of its beauty and because its brevity was better adapted to public devotion. When it came into use at Loreto, thousands of pilgrims became familiar with it, and returning to their homes spread its popularity throughout Europe. Its association with the shrine at Loreto was already well established in 1558, when it was printed and published by St. Peter Canisius at Dilligen, Germany, under the title *Letania Loretana.* This is the oldest known printed copy of the litany, and its text, probably taken from an earlier Italian publication, is identical with that in use down to modern times, except for two minor variations in the titles by which the Blessed Virgin Mary is addressed, and its omission, perhaps by editorial oversight, of two titles.

For a short time in the 16th century it appeared that the Litany of Loreto would have to give way to a new version that was drawn up containing invocations taken more directly from the Scriptures and liturgy and thought to be more in accord with the *motu proprio* of Pius V of March 20, 1571, prohibiting unapproved forms of the Little Office and some litanies of the Blessed Virgin Mary. Sixtus V, however, granted his approval to the old form used at Loreto and recommended preachers to propagate its use. In time there were new titles introduced: Pius VII added that of Queen of All Saints on his return to Rome after his long captivity; Leo XIII, the titles Queen of the Most Holy Rosary, Queen Conceived without Original Sin, and Mother of Good Counsel; Benedict XV, during World War I, Queen of Peace; and Pius XII, on the occasion of the definition of the dogma of the Assumption, that of Queen Assumed into Heaven [*Acta Apostolicae Sedis* 42 (1950) 795].

The titles of the litany fall into four categories. In the first 20, after being saluted as Holy Mary, The Blessed Virgin Mary is addressed first as Mother, then as Virgin, by titles indicative of the dignity of her relationship to God and to man, and of her excellence as prototype, after her divine Son, of Christian perfection. She is mother of God, of our Creator and Savior, and hence mother most pure, most admirable, possessed of perfect integrity of heart and perfect harmony of mind and body, of unalloyed goodness and perfect love, wise, powerful, gentle, and true. Then follow 13 beautiful titles associated with Old Testament prophecy and symbolism, and four whose origins are lost in antiquity tell of her power and office. Finally she is addressed 12 times as queen in terms that declare the broad extent and character of her queenship. The litany ends with the Collect from the common Mass of Blessed Virgin Mary, which prays for health of body and spirit and deliverance from present sorrow to a future joy.

In an attempt to draw continuities between the ordinary life of the Blessed Virgin Mary and the lives of women today, some communities have added contemporary Marian invocations that call on the Blessed Virgin Mary as "Mother of the homeless, widowed mother, mother of a political prisoner, oppressed woman, first disciple . . ." Such images can lend dignity to the lives of those devalued by society as well as call attention to God's liberating activity in the life of the Blessed Virgin Mary.

Bibliography: A. DE SANTI, *Le litanie Lauretane* (Rome 1897); *The Catholic Encyclopedia*, ed. C. G. HERBERMANN et al., 16 v. (New York 1907–14) 9:287–290. G. VANN, "Notes on Our Lady's Litany," *Worship* 30 (1955–56) 437–441. J. F. SULLIVAN, *The Externals of the Catholic Church*, rev. J. C. O'LEARY (2d ed. New York 1959) 362–364.

[C. H. BAGLEY/EDS.]

> **Capital:** Vilnius.
> **Size:** 25,170 sq. miles.
> **Population:** 3,620,755 in 2000.
> **Languages:** Lithuanian, Polish, Russian.
> **Religions:** 3,041,435 Catholics (84%), 144,830 Orthodox (4%), 17,680 Muslims (.5%), 37,460 Protestants (1%), 25,350 Jews (.7%), 354,000 without religious affiliation.
> **Archdioceses:** Kaunas, with suffragans Siauliai, Telšiai and Vilkaviškis; Vilnius, with suffragans Kaišiadorys and Panevėžys. A military ordinariate also exists in the country.

LITHUANIA, THE CATHOLIC CHURCH IN

The Republic of Lithuania is located in northeastern Europe, east of the Baltic Sea. The largest of the Baltic States, it is bordered on the north by Latvia, on the east by the Kalinigrad Oblast of Russia, on the south and southeast by Belarus and on the south by Poland. Benefited by a moderate climate, Lithuania is comprised predominately of lowlands, with numerous lakes. Natural resources include peat, while the nation's fertile soil produces such crops as grain, potatoes, sugar beets, vegetables and flax.

A grand duchy from the 13th century until 1795, Lithuania became subjected to Russia until claiming independence in 1918. Except for the years it was occupied by German troops during World War II, between 1940 and 1990, Lithuania was incorporated as part of the Union of Soviet Socialist Republics (USSR). Ethnic Lithuanians are Baltic Indo-Europeans who entered the region before the Christian era. Lithuania is the most nationally homogenous Baltic state: 80 percent of the population is Lithuanian, while the remaining 20 percent are divided between Russian and Polish.

Early History. The early Lithuanians followed a form of ANIMISM, based on belief in the supranatural character of natural phenomena and a cult of the dead. The region's first encounter with Christianity was likely through Western merchants, Christian Danes or Swedes, who at times entered Lithuania. The missionary journeys of Bishop ADALBERT OF PRAGUE and Bruno of Querfurt at the turn of the 10th century ended with martyrdom for both in Prussia. Missionaries and knights came from North Germany *c.* 1200 and evangelized, partly by preaching the Gospels, partly by force. The land of the Prussians, to the west, was given *c.* 1230 to TEUTONIC KNIGHTS, recently expelled from Palestine, to evangelize and colonize. Meanwhile the Lithuanian tribes united and moved eastward into the former Kiev kingdom. Pressure from the German KNIGHTS OF THE SWORD, founded in Li-

vonia in 1202, and from the Teutonic Knights in Prussia (both merged into one order in 1237), threatened the independence of Lithuania and forced Grand Duke Mindaugas to negotiate with the master of the Christian order of Livonia. In 1251 Mindaugas, his family and many of his retinue were baptized, and a delegation sent from Lithuania to Pope Innocent IV. The pope recognized Mindaugas as king and his coronation in 1253, and also established the Diocese of Lithuania immediately subject to the Holy See. Christian, a Teutonic Knight, became the first bishop of Lithuania. In 1257 Vitus, a Dominican, was consecrated as bishop for southern Lithuania. The populace was instructed in the faith by Franciscans, Dominicans and other priests (*see* DACIA).

The desire for power among the Teutonic Knights, dissension among the princes and the strong adherence

to paganism among the masses prevented an easy transition to the new religion. In 1263 a pagan faction murdered Mindaugas and assumed control of the region for the next century. Attempts to Christianize Lithuania during the 13th and 14th centuries were unsuccessful, in part because of the eagerness of the Teutonic Knights for territorial conquest. Lithuanians realized that to become Christian was to lose their freedom. The region's permanent conversion was effected by grand dukes JAGIEŁŁO and Vytautas. In 1385 Jagiełło united Lithuania and POLAND, through his marriage with Jadwiga, heiress to the Polish throne. Baptized with a number of Lithuanian princes, he was crowned King Władysław II Jagiełło of Poland on March 4. Early in 1387 he and his cousin Vytautas went to Vilnius, where nobles as well as many common people converted to Christianity. Jagiełło and his Catholic retinue translated several holy texts into Lithuanian and explained Catholic doctrine to the populace. Jagiełło founded the diocese of Vilnius in 1387; the diocese of Medininkai (later Samogitia) was erected in 1417, the same year all of Lithuania was converted. Both Vilnius and Medininkai were subjected to the metropolitan of Gniezno. Latin dioceses were erected in the eastern part of the grand duchy, along with a few eparchies under the Orthodox metropolitan of Kiev. In 1320 a Latin diocese was established in Kiev and in 1358 another in Vladimir, which was transferred to Lutsk in 1428.

Growth and Danger: 1387–1569. When Catholicism became the state religion, Catholic nobles became leaders in the senate and in the administration of the state, and as a result mixed marriages were forbidden by law. A long period of peace under Kazimieras IV contributed much to the establishment of religion throughout both Lithuania and Poland. Kazimieras' second son, Kazimieras (CASIMIR, d. 1484), was canonized and is venerated as the principal patron saint of Lithuania. Despite the spread of the faith among the upper classes, the small number of churches and priests, the lack of schools for higher education and the influx of the Polish clergy seeking better Benefices but unable to speak the language, left the common people ignorant of their faith and encouraged their reliance on pagan customs.

By the mid-16th century, most of Lithuania's influential noble families had become followers of CALVINISM or ARIANISM, while several merchants and townsmen adopted LUTHERANISM. While most rural folk remained loyal to the Church, they were pressured by their landowners to accept the new beliefs. Soon a vigorous Catholic counteraction began, led by Cardinal Stanislaus HOSIUS, bishop of Ermland. The conversion of Prince Mikalojus Radvilas in 1567 brought many leading noble families back to the Church. Also effective in turning the tide were the JESUITS, who entered East Prussia in 1564 at the invitation of Hosius and arrived in Vilnius in 1569 at the call of Bishop Valerijonas Protasevičius.

Great Development: 1569–1795. The Jesuits opened their first college in Lithuania at Vilnius in 1570; nine years, as a university, it became the only institution of higher learning in northeastern Europe, a situation lasting until 1755. As an important Catholic center of learning, the influence of the University of Vilnius stretched beyond Lithuania to Sweden, Kiev and Moscow. The Lithuanian Jesuits formed their own province in 1608 and continued establishing colleges in the country, with 21 colleges by 1756. Jesuits were also active as theologians, confessors of bishops and princes, preachers and writers of theological, polemical, ascetical and devotional literature. Due to their efforts, Catholic written works such as

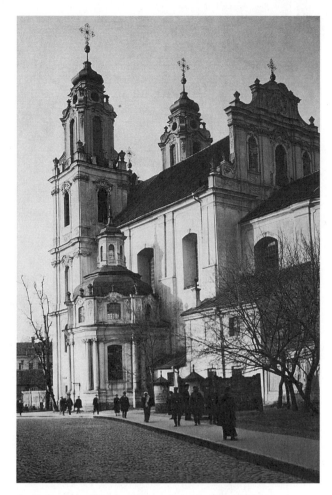

St. Catherine's Church, Vilnius, Poland. (©Hulton-Deutsch Collection/CORBIS)

the catechisms of St. Peter Canisius (1585) and Ledesma (1595) were translated into Lithuanian. The Jesuits also popularized Lithuanian hymns and religious customs, such as the singing of the rosary, the chanting of the Little Office of the Immaculate Conception, solemn processions and pilgrimages. Dramatic productions in Jesuit schools were highly esteemed. Of the other orders engaged in education and in literary work, the PIARISTS, BASILIANS and VINCENTIANS were the most active.

Several bishops played a significant role in the development of the Lithuanian Church. Merkelis Giedraitis, bishop of Samogitia (1576–1609), was responsible for building new churches, teaching the faith to the common people and increasing the number of native clergy. Jurgis Radvilas, bishop of Vilnius (1579–91) and cardinal (1584), founded the first major seminary in Vilnius in I582. In the same year a second seminary, the Seminarium Pontificum, was established there by Gregory XIII to train missionaries for the eastern territories. Seminarians for the Diocese of Samogitia were also trained in Vilnius

Pilgrims from Lithuania pray during a Mass celebrated by Pope John Paul II in Elk, Poland. (Photo by Czarek Sokolowski; AP/ Wide World Photos)

thodox Church through the abolition of Catholic schools, the dissolution of almost all monasteries and religious orders, and continual state interference in religious matters.

In 1798 Czar Paul I created a new church organization with a Catholic Church province of Mogilev containing six Latin-rite and three Eastern-rite Catholic dioceses, among them the existing dioceses of Samogitia and Vilnius. Pope Pius VI could do nothing but give a *post factum* approbation. In those lands incorporated into Prussia, Pius VI created a new diocese with its seat in Vygriai, later moved to Augustavas, and in 1818 to Seinai. At St. Petersburg the Collegium Ecclesiasticum Romano-Catholicum was founded in 1801; a kind of consistory, it was composed of Catholic priests but completely controlled by the government. The Catholic Academia Ecclesiastics, at which many Lithuanian priests studied and taught until 1917, was moved from Vilnius to St. Petersburg in 1842. Although the Holy See tried to help Catholics in Russia by signing a concordat in August of 1847, the agreement went unobserved and Catholics continued to be treated harshly.

The increasingly oppressive czarist regime sparked revolts in Poland and Lithuania in 1831 and 1863, that were brutally suppressed and resulted in even greater restrictions. In 1864 the episcopal seat was moved to Kaunas to allow the czar closer supervision of the bishop. However, these new laws only served to increase Lithuanian nationalism and resistance. Church leaders such as Motiejus Valančius, Bishop of Samogitia (1850–75), stood out as courageous and dauntless champions, promoting the Lithuanian language and culture and helping Lithuanian Catholics survive persecution without suffering great harm.

The Interwar Period: 1918 to 1940. Lithuanian independence was restored by the legislature on Feb. 16, 1918. Poland's seizure of Vilnius two years later caused bitter enmity between the two countries, which had formerly shared a common destiny. Because of the dispute over Vilnius, relations between Lithuania and the Holy See became strained. Normal relations were finally restored in 1925, after Pius XI appointed Archbishop Jurgis Matulaitis (1871–1927) as apostolic visitor to Lithuania, and then established the country as a distinct ecclesiastical province. The Archdiocese of Kaunas became a metropolitan see, with suffragans Telšiai, Panevėzys, Vilkaviškis and Kaišiadorys, and the Prelature *nullius* of Klaipêda (Memel), all created in 1926. (Part of the territory of the Metropolitan See of Vilnius was restored later to Lithuania.) With the signing of a concordat on Dec. 10, 1927, relations with Rome were completely regularized, although tensions remained between the governing party and the Holy See.

until their own seminary was opened, first in the Jesuit college at Kražiai (*c.* 1620), then at Varniai (1740). In 1611, after Smolensk fell to Lithuania, a Latin diocese was established there; in 1636 it received its first bishop. After Smolensk was retaken by Moscow in 1654, there remained only three parishes on the Lithuanian side. Nevertheless, the diocese survived until 1798; the bishops of the diocese resided generally in Vilnius.

For the union with Rome of members of the EASTERN CHURCHES living in Lithuania, *see* BREST, UNION OF; ISIDORE OF KIEV.

Under Czarist Control: 1795–1918. In the partitions of Poland and Lithuania, almost the entire Grand Duchy of Lithuania fell to Russia while lands south of the Nemunas River went to Prussia. The authoritarian attitude of the Russian rulers—even toward the popes—hindered free communication with Rome. To Russianize the Lithuanians, the czars tried to convert them to the Or-

Catholic life now progressed rapidly. Religious education was made compulsory in the country's public schools. There were three seminaries and, from 1922, a Catholic faculty of theology and philosophy at the University of Kaunas. Catholic intellectuals founded the Lithuanian Catholic Academy of Science, while Catholic students and academicians participated from 1910 in public life as members of *Ateitis* (Future). Numerous noteworthy members of the laity also supported the Church.

World War II and Occupation. In 1940 Lithuania became the first Roman Catholic country to come under Soviet rule when it was annexed to the USSR. The new communist government began a policy of secularization that included the abolition of religious instruction in public schools and the end of government support for religious institutions. It also instituted civil marriage, legalized divorce and abolished religious holidays. The Catholic press was closed and Catholic societies outlawed, and priests were recruited to work for the political police. Thousands were arrested or deported, including many active clergy. By 1941 the communist regime had closed virtually all Catholic institutions and confiscated the Theological Seminary in Kaunas.

The Nazi invasion of June 22, 1941 was met by large-scale anti-Soviet uprising in Lithuania. Initially, the Church hierarchy welcomed the departure of the Communists, urging the people to remain calm and carry on under the new occupation. As the Nazis showed relatively little interest in purely religious matters, some seminaries were reopened, and religion was allowed back into the schools. In March of 1942 the Germans deported Archbishop Romuald Jałbrzykowski (1876–1955) of Vilnius, replacing him with Archbishop Mečislovas Reinys (1884–1953) and marking the end of Polish control over this historic diocese.

Nazi genocidal policy posed a moral challenge to the people of the Baltic States. By the end of 1941, the majority of the Jews living in the area, nearly a quarter million from Lithuania's culturally vibrant Jewish community, were dead. Attempts by Church leaders to request German and Lithuanian military commandants to intercede on behalf of the Jews, as well as proposals by the Lithuanian bishops' conference to address the Jewish issue fell on deaf ears. The bishops also protested the forced resettlement policies of the Nazi and in 1943 successfully opposed the planned killing of the disabled and mentally impaired. Hundreds of Lithuanians, many of them Catholic laymen and religious, assisted the persecuted Jews in many ways. However, in the end only several thousand Jews survived the war in Lithuania, and the relative attitude—collaboration, resistance or indifference—of Lithuanian society, as well as that of the Church during the Holocaust, remained a controversial response. The accounts of survivors revealed that many who risked their lives to save Jews were motivated by a desire to do their Christian duty; on the other hand, some clergy did not escape the prevailing anti-Semitic attitudes partly motivated by the widespread belief that Jews had been active supporters of the hated Soviet regime.

The Church under Communism. Following Germany's defeat, Soviet armies returned in 1944 and under Josef Stalin immediately reactivated their atheistic and anticlerical policies. Soviet propaganda portrayed the Church as fascist, and an agent of the West. This spiritual oppression occurred against a backdrop of economic losses and violence within a totalitarian system alien to the religious traditions of Lithuania. The horrors of Stalin's rule represented a nadir in the modern history of the region. Mass deportations between 1945 and 1953 sent hundreds of Catholics, including several bishops, westward, or to Siberia and other remote regions of the USSR. Collectivization and a particularly bitter anti-Soviet guerrilla war raged in Lithuania during the late 1940s and early 1950s. Prohibitive taxes were levied against the Church and religious instruction in churches was banned. Church properties were nationalized and the buildings "leased" to the religious communities. In 1946, after Church leaders spoke out against the government's introduction of a system of government-controlled religious communities designed to subvert the parish system and undermine the clergy, Telšiai Bishop Vincentas Borisevičius was arrested and executed, Archbishop Reinys was exiled and the outspoken Bishop Teofilis Matulionis (1873–1962) of Kaišiadorys was imprisoned. By mid-1947, Kazimieras Paltarokas (1875–1958) was the only active bishop remaining in Lithuania.

Indicative of the greatly altered status of the Church in Lithuania, under Communist rule, was the decline in the number of churches, which dropped from 716 in 1940 to 604 by 1965. In all, about a third of the country's Catholic clergy were imprisoned or deported during the late 1940s. All the 324 chapels open in 1940 and all monastery churches had been closed by 1948. The 1,448 priests that worked in the country in 1940 had dropped to 869 by 1965.

A brief respite from oppression occurred under the government of Nikita Khrushchev (ruled 1953–64). In 1956 two bishops were restored (two others had died in prison); many priests and about 30,000 laymen were allowed to return to Lithuania. In 1955 two new bishops, Petras Maželis (1894–1966) and Julijonas Steponavičius (1911–92) were ordained and assigned to Telšiai and Vilnius respectively. For the first time since the war, limited official contact with the Holy See was permitted, and some Lithuanian clergy—although no bishops—were allowed to attend the Second Vatican Council. Unfortunately, Khrushchev's "thaw," as it was known, was short-lived, and repressive policies were again in place by the late 1950s, albeit without the mass terror of the Stalin years. By 1961 bishops Matulionis, Vincentas Sladkevičius (1920–2000) and Steponavičius were exiled from their dioceses, and a number of priests arrested. Atheist propaganda was reactivated. Even as the Soviet government sought to normalize relations with the Vatican, and the Holy See sought an "opening to the east," the Lithuanian Soviet regime launched an anti-Catholic campaign which reached its height in the 1960s and 1970s.

The Church Resists. In response to Soviet repression, a Catholic dissident movement emerged and gained strength in the 1970s. Its main vehicle was the *Lietuvos Katalikų Bažnyčios Kronika* ("The Chronicle of the Lithuanian Catholic Church"), which was one of the most important samizdat publications in the Soviet Union between 1972 and the late 1980s. Along with the Catholic Committee for the Defense of the Rights of Believers, organized in 1978, it detailed abuses of religious freedom, as well as the violation of human and national rights in Lithuania. Despite arrests, imprisonment and harassment of Catholic activists by the KGB, Soviet authorities were unable to eliminate the dissident movement. Catholic resistance to Soviet religious policy also opened up a split within the Church between elements in the hierarchy and clergy, who favored accommodation with the Soviet regime, and the Catholic dissident movement, which was closely allied to the growing Lithuanian movement to restore national sovereignty.

The upheavals of the Gorbachev era (1985–1991) in the USSR altered the role of the Church in Lithuania. The most egregious restrictions on religion were lifted in the late 1980s and effectively eliminated by 1990. Imprisoned Catholic activists and exiled prelates were released and allowed to resume their work, and Pope John Paul II appointed bishops to the country's diocese. Bishop Sladkevičius, named the country's first modern cardinal in June of 1988, joined other Church leaders in actively advocating for greater religious and national rights as embodied in the Lithuanian reform movement until his death in 2000. The Cathedral of Vilnius, which had been turned into an art gallery by the Soviets, was returned to the Church, and by 1989 virtually all legal restrictions on the Church were removed.

In March of 1990 the Lithuanian government proclaimed independence from the USSR. Under its constitution promulgated on Oct. 25, 1992, freedom of religion was guaranteed and traditional religions were granted government support. Among the new government's tasks, in the wake of decades of communist rule, was the need to restore Church property seized by the Soviet government, although lack of available government funds made this a lengthy process. Meanwhile, Church life began to return to normalcy. The Holy See opened a nunciature in Vilnius in 1992, and in May of 2000 signed accords establishing the juridical status of the Church in Lithuania. In September of 1993, Pope John Paul II visited Lithuania. Catholic instruction was once again permitted in public schools, and a number of private Catholic primary and secondary schools opened during the early 1990s. The Theological Seminary in Kaunas was expanded, and a new seminary opened in Telšiai. A rejuvenated Catholic press issued several popular periodicals, the largest being Katalikų pasaulis (Catholic World). In 1992 the Vatican appointed a career Vatican diplomat, Audrius Bačkis, as archbishop of Vilnius, that archdiocese now recognized as part of the Lithuanian ecclesiastical province.

By 2000 there were 649 parishes tended by 658 diocesan and 951 religious priests, and over 100 brothers and 990 sisters worked actively in the country, although an increase in evangelical Protestant and fundamentalist groups continued to challenge the Church's evangelical efforts. Although their numbers decreased dramatically as a result of the Holocaust, Lithuanian Jews opened a new synagogue in Vilnius in 1990. Reminded by this of their nation's role in the Holocaust, Church leaders publicly apologized in 2000, both for the indifference of some Catholics, as well as for all crimes committed against Jews by the Lithuanian people as a whole. Reemerging into capitalist society provided Church leaders with other causes of concern; during a 1996 statement, the Lithuanian Bishop's conference stated that problems such as organized crime, a declining birth rate, drug use, alcoholism and increased promiscuity would lead to "social depression, distrust of the government, and political indifference." Echoing these words, the pope noted during his 1999 *ad limina* visit with Lithuanian bishops, that after vanquishing communism, their task was now to battle "the seductive power of secularizaed and hedonistic models of life."

Bibliography: General literature. A. ŠAPOKA, *Lietuvos istorija* (Fellbach, Ger. 1950); *Lithuania through the Ages* (2d ed. Los Angeles 1955). C. R. JURGLA, *History of the Lithuanian Nation* (New York 1948). A. VISCONT, *La Lithuanie religieuse* (Geneva 1918). A. ALEKNA, *Kataliku Bažnyčia Lietuvoje* (Kaunas 1936). S. SALKAUSKIS, *Sur les confins de deux mondes* (Geneva 1919). A. M. AMMANN, *Storia della Chiesa russa* (Turin 1948), Ger. tr. (Vienna 1950). J. VAIŠNORA, *Marijos garbinimas Lietuvoje* (Rome 1958). P. RĖKLAITIS, *Einführung in die Kunstgeschichtsforschung des Grossfürstentums Litauen* (Marburg 1962). *Bilan du Monde* 2:890–893. Special topics. W. C. JASKIEWICZ, "A Study in Lithuanian Mythology," *Studi Baltici*, 9 (1952) 65–106. V. GIDŽIŪNAS,

De Fratribus Minoribus in Lituania (Rome 1950). Z. IVINSKIS, "Mindaugas und seine Krone," *Zeitschrift für Ostforschung,* 3 (1954) 360–386. H. JABLONOWSKI, *Westrussland zwischen Wilna und Moskau* (Leiden 1955). O. HALECKI, *From Florence to Brest, 1439–1596* (Rome 1958) 13–444. S. ROSTOWSKI, *Lituanicarum Societatis Iesu historiarum libri decem* (Paris 1877). A. ŠAPOKA, *Lietuva ir Lenkija po 1569 metu Liublino unijos* (Kaunas 1938). S. KOT, "La Réforme dans le Grand-Duché de Lithuanie," in *Pankarpeia: Mélanges Henri Grégoire,* ed. J. MOREAU, 4 v. (Brussels 1949–53) 4:201–261. J. LEBEDYS, *Mikalojus Daukša* (Vilna 1963). L. LESCOEUR, *La Persécution de l' Église en Lithuanie* (Paris 1873). A. BOUDOU, *Le Saint Siège et la Russie, 1814–1883,* 2 v. (Paris 1922–25). M. J. ROUËT DE JOURNEL, *Nonciatures de Russie,* 5 v. (*Studi e Testi,* 166–69, 194; 1922–57). J. PRUNSKIS, *Comparative Law, Ecclesiastical and Civil, in Lithuanian Concordat* (Washington 1945). W. KOLARZ, *Religion in the Soviet Union* (New York 1961); "Catholic Lithuania, Bishoprics and Bishops (1939–1961)," *Expulsus,* 9.2 (Konigstein Taunus, Ger. 1961) 8–19. J. SAVASIS, *The War against God in Lithuania* (New York 1966). A. KUČAS. "JAV lietuviai," in *Lietuviu enciklopedija,* v.10 (Boston 1957) 36–71. *Lithuania under the Soviets,* ed. V. S. VARDYS (New York 1965); "Human Rights Issues in Estonia, Latvia, and Lithuania," *Journal of Baltic Studies,* 12 (fall 1981) 275–98. M. BOURDEAUX, Land of Crosses (Chulmleigh UK 1980). P. DAUKNYS, The Resistance of the Catholic Church in Lithuania against Religious Persecution (Rome 1981). D. KINSELLA and R. TAAGEPERA, "Religious Incident Statistics for Soviet Lithuanian Schools," *Journal of Baltic Studies,* 15 (spring 1984) 27–47. A. LIEVEN, *The Baltic Revolution: Estonia, Latvia, Lithuania, and the Path to Independence* (New Haven, CT 1993). R. J. MISIUNAS and R. TAAGEPERA, *The Baltic States: Years of Dependence 1940–1990* (2d ed. Berkeley 1993). T. REMEIKIS, *Opposition to Soviet Rule in Lithuania* (Chicago 1980). A. E. SENN, *Lithuania Awakening* (Berkeley 1990). S. SUŽIEDĖLIS, *The Sword and the Cross: A History of the Church in Lithuania* (Huntington, IN 1988).

[P. RABIKAUSKAS/EDS.]

LITTA, ALFONSO AND LORENZO

Cardinals from a noble Milanese family; their careers touched the 17th, 18th, and 19th centuries.

Alfonso; b. Milan, 1608; d. Rome, Aug. 28, 1679. He was governor of the Marches under Innocent X; he was created archbishop of Milan in May of 1652, and cardinal on Jan. 14, 1666. An intelligent and energetic prelate, he visited his diocese, held two synods (1659 and 1669), corrected disciplinary abuses of his clergy, and bravely defended ecclesiastical rights against representatives of the king of Spain. During his tenure, the Helvetic College, envisaged by St. Charles BORROMEO, was completed, and its administration reorganized. Alfonso attended the conclave that elected Innocent XI.

Lorenzo, diplomat; b. Milan, Feb. 23, 1756; d. Monteflavio, Sabina, May 1, 1820. After being educated at the Clementine College in Rome, he was ordained in 1789 and made titular archbishop of Thebes on June 23, 1793. When sent to Warsaw in 1794, he persuaded Tadeusz

Kościuszko to respect the rights and liberties of the Church in Poland. In 1796 he attended the coronation of Paul I and was appointed legate to St. Petersburg. Greatly concerned with obtaining guarantees of Church rights, he persuaded Czar Paul to restore the Basilian Order and the Church property confiscated by Catherine II. Six dioceses of the Latin rite and three of the Ruthenian were reorganized, and on Nov. 15, 1798, the metropolitan sees of Mohilev and Polotsk were established. Forced to leave Russia in 1799, Lorenzo returned to Rome, where he held the office of papal treasurer and was made a cardinal by Pius VII on Oct. 23, 1801.

Loyal to the pope and opposed to Napoleon, expelled from Rome by Napoleon, he was exiled to Saint-Quentin on the Seine (1809), following his refusal to attend the second wedding of the emperor. While residing in Saint-Quentin, Fontainebleau, and Nimes, he translated the Bible into Italian and wrote letters refuting the Gallican Articles of 1682, which were published pseudonymously in Lyons (1818) as *Lettres diverses.* In 1814 he returned to Rome, was appointed prefect of Propaganda and suburbicarian bishop of Sabina; later, he became cardinal vicar of Rome (1818).

Bibliography: Alfonso. A. MONTI, *Tre Secoli di Vita Milanese* (Milan 1955). E. CAZZANI, *Vescovi e Arcivescovi di Milano* (Milan 1955) 257–260. A. POSCH, *Lexikon für Theologie und Kirche* ed. J. HOFER and K. RAHNER (Freiburg 1957–65) 6:1083. Lorenzo. M. F. ROUËT DE JOURNEL, *Nonciature de Russie* (*Studi e Testi* 167; 1943). V. MEYSZTOWICS, *De archivio nuntiaturae varsaviensis quod nunc in Archivio Secreto Vaticano servatur* (Vatican City 1944). P. PIERLING, *La Russie et le Saint-Siège,* 5 v. (Paris 1896–1912). A. POSCH, *Lexikon für Theologie und Kirche* ed. J. HOFER and K. RAHNER (Freiburg 1957–65) 6:1083. É. AMANN, *Dictionnaire de théologie catholique* (Paris 1903–50) 9:785–787.

[E. J. THOMSON]

LITTLE, ANDREW GEORGE

British historian; b. Manchester, Oct. 10, 1863; d. Sevenoaks, Oct. 22, 1945. Lecturer and professor of history at Cardiff (1892–1901) and reader in paleography at Manchester (1904–28), he was the founder and general editor of the *British Society of Franciscan Studies.* Between 1907 and its dissolution in 1937 the society published 22 volumes, the last being *Franciscan History and Legend in English Franciscan Art,* which Little edited. His chief works were *The Grey Friars at Oxford* (Oxford 1892); *Initia operum latinorum* (Manchester 1904), a collection of 6,000 *incipit* of medieval manuscripts; *Studies in English Franciscan History* (Manchester 1917); and *Oxford Theology and Theologians 1282–1302* (Oxford 1934, with F. Pelster). He also edited THOMAS OF ECCLESTON's *Tractatus de adventu Fratrum Minorum in*

Angliam (2d ed. Manchester 1951); the *Liber exemplorum,* a medieval Franciscan manual for preachers; part of JOHN PECKHAM's *Tractatus de paupertate;* and some hitherto unknown Leonine material concerning St. FRANCIS that he himself discovered (in *Collectanea Franciscana* 1). Most of the histories of the English friaries in the *Victoria County Histories* were by him, and he contributed to the *Cambridge Medieval History,* v. 6; the *Archivum Franciscanum Historicum;* and *Proceedings of the British Academy;* the *Transactions of the Royal Historical Society;* and the *English Historical Review,* for which, between 1889 and 1945, he wrote 50 articles. His more important essays were republished in his last book, *Franciscan Papers, Lists and Documents* (Manchester 1943). Little was a witty and brilliant teacher and inspired many books besides his own. His kindliness, unselfishness, and generosity won him many friends among his colleagues and pupils and among foreign scholars such as Paul SABATIER and the Franciscans of QUARACCHI.

Bibliography: *Annual Register* n.s. (Toronto 1945) 428–429. F. M. POWICKE, *A. G. Little, 1863–1945* (London 1947).

[D. L. DOUIE]

LITTLE BROTHERS OF JESUS

(LBJ) A religious congregation with simple, perpetual vows, founded in 1933 by Father René Voillaume in South Oran, Algeria. It was made a diocesan congregation in 1936 by Bishop Nouet, Prefect Apostolic of Ghardaïa, Algeria. Its ideals are those of Charles de FOUCAULD. In their apostolate the Little Brothers seek to conform to the economic and social milieu where they live. Their stress is on manual labor among the laboring classes. They dwell in communities of three to five members and work mostly in factories and fisheries, among the poor and marginalized. The Little Brothers had established communities in Europe, Africa, Asia, and South America.

Bibliography: R. VOILLAUME, *Seeds of the Desert,* tr. W. HILL (Chicago 1955); *Lettres aux Fraternités,* 2 v. (Paris 1960). M. CARROUGES, *Le Père de Foucauld et les fraternités d'aujourd'hui* (Paris 1963).

[A. J. WOUTERS/EDS.]

LITTLE COMPANY OF MARY

(LCM, Official Catholic Directory #2270); a papal institute of nursing sisters familiarly known as Blue Nuns, in many parts of the English-speaking world, because of their distinctive blue habit. The sisters have adopted their official title from the small group who stood at the foot of the cross on Calvary in the company of Mary. In union with the maternal heart of Mary, the sisters devote themselves to nurse the sick and the dying with maternal care. The foundress, Mother Mary POTTER, was born in London. In 1877 she and five companions founded the first convent of the Little Company of Mary in an abandoned factory in Hyson-Green, Nottingham, England. From this humble beginning in home nursing, the institute has spread throughout the world and now maintains many modern hospitals in North and South America, Australia, New Zealand, Korea, Scotland, England, Malta, Ireland, South Africa, and Italy, including one at the motherhouse in Rome.

In 1893 the sisters accepted a foundation in Chicago, Ill., where they opened their first U.S. mission. For many years the house in Chicago was the center of busy home nursing activities. In 1930 the sisters transferred to the suburban area of Evergreen Park, where they staffed their first hospital in the U.S., and where the U.S. provincialate is located. The generalate is in London, England.

[M. J. SCHLAX/EDS.]

LITTLE HOURS

Historically, the Divine Office of the Roman Catholic Church comprised the Little Hours of Prime, Terce, Sext, and None. These hours have been so called because they have never had as great an importance in the daily cursus as LAUDS and VESPERS. In fact, for centuries they were commonly not prayed at all outside of monasteries. It was only in the middle of the eighth century that their obligatory recitation by all clerics in the West started.

In the Roman Empire, daytime was divided into twelve hours. These hours varied in length according to the season of the year. The third hour, terce, began at midmorning; the sixth, sext, at midday; and the ninth, none, at midafternoon. Since these were the principal divisions of the day, it was only natural that some effort be made to raise the mind to God at these times.

Terce, Sext, and None are older than Prime. Already at the beginning of the third century Hippolytus (d. *c.* 235) and Tertullian (d. *c.* 220) commended private prayer at these hours. Tertullian cited the example of the Apostles in Acts 2.15, 10.9, and 3.1–7 as justification for consecrating these hours to prayer. Hence, they were frequently called the apostolic prayers. By the fifth century the monks and the *devoti* had turned these prayer times into formal periods of public prayer in many places. The sixth-century Rule of St. Benedict shows that these hours then had practically the same format as they have today. After the usual introductory versicles there is a short hymn, whose content is determined by the time of day for the recitation of that particular hour. The rest of the hour follows the customary pattern: psalmody, a short reading, responsory, and prayer. The three Psalms of each hour are taken in order from the Psalter without reference to the time of day or the festal theme.

Prime was the last hour introduced. John Cassian (d. 435) tells of its introduction in a monastery in Bethlehem. The monks had formed the habit of returning to bed after Lauds until time for Terce. To get them up earlier for the morning work the abbot introduced Prime. Its quasi-private nature was long evident from the fact that it was prayed not in the oratory but in the dormitory. For some time it had the same structure as the other Little Hours. Chrodegang of Metz (d. 766) is the first witness to the addition of the *Officium Capituli*, the appendix that is peculiar to Prime; it was in reality a monastic chapter meeting. The day's martyrology was read, the day's work was distributed, a chapter of the rule was read, and the abbot closed the meeting with his blessing. Thus, as the hymn for Prime indicates, this hour became a consecration of the day's work and activity.

The *Constitution on the Sacred Liturgy* (89) of Vatican Council II decreed a revision of the Office, and ordered the suppression of Prime in the revision. It also said it will be lawful outside choir to select one of the other three Little Hours according to the respective time of day. This change came about because historical studies had pointed up the fact that Prime was an unnecessary duplication of Lauds and, along with the other Little Hours, had not been binding on the secular clergy for a long time.

Bibliography: P. SALMON, *The Breviary through the Centuries*, tr. D. MARY (Collegeville, Minn. 1962). J. A. JUNGMANN, *Pastoral Liturgy* (New York 1962); *Public Worship: A Survey*, tr. C. HOWELL (Collegeville, Minn. 1957). P. PARSCH, *The Breviary Explained*, tr. W. NAYDEN and C. HOEGERL (St. Louis 1952). S. CAMPBELL, *From Breviary to Liturgy of the Hours: The Structural Reform of the Roman Office* 1964–1971 (Collegeville 1995). G. GUIVER, *Company of Voices: Daily Prayer and the People of God* (New York 1988). R. TAFT, *The Liturgy of the Hours in East and West: The Origins of the Divine Office and Its Meaning for Today*, 2d rev. ed. (Collegeville 1993).

[G. SCHIDEL/EDS.]

LITTLE MISSIONARY SISTERS OF CHARITY

(LMSC, Official Catholic Directory #2290); in Italian, *Piccole Suore Missionarie della Carità*, a congregation with papal approval (1957), founded at Tortona, Italy, in 1915 by Don Luigi Orione as a part of his program called the Little work of Divine Providence. The purpose of the congregation was to perform works of charity among the poor, orphaned, aged, and the mentally and physically handicapped. The sisters are engaged in teaching, nursing, and social and catechetical work in Italy, Poland, Spain, England, Argentina, Uruguay, Chile, and Brazil. The sisters first arrived in the U.S. in 1949. The general motherhouse is in Rome. Don Orione founded a cloistered branch within the community when, in 1927, he organized the Perpetual Adorers of the Most Blessed Sacrament. This group is made up of blind persons who live a contemplative life, devoted mainly to prayer before the Blessed Sacrament.

[T. F. CASEY/EDS.]

LITTLE OFFICE OF THE BVM

An abridged version of the Common Office of the Blessed Virgin in the Divine Office that was historically recited on most feasts of Our Lady. It began as a votive office in the early Middle Ages. Alcuin (d. 804) composed and propagated votive Masses for the various days of the week and included a Saturday Mass in honor of Our Lady. A complementary votive office also may have been introduced, for usages adopted during this period of the Carolingian renaissance were longlasting. At any rate, there is 10th-century evidence of the daily recitation of this office by Bernerius, provost of the Cathedral of Verdun, and by Ulric, bishop of Augsburg (d. 973), which would indicate that the devotion was already widespread.

Peter Damian (d. 1072), one of the most influential churchmen of his century, reorganized this office and strongly commended its daily recitation. By the 12th century it was in use throughout Europe and was often made obligatory for both regular and secular clergy except on greater feasts. This office was also the core of the various Books of Hours, the popular prayer books of the laity in the Middle Ages. Pius V (d. 1572) removed all general obligation, limiting it to certain monastic groups. Pius X abolished the obligation. The 1952 revision of this office retained the same psalms, canticles, and hymns, but offered greater variety than the old edition by adding special lessons, responsories, little chapters, antiphons, and collects.

See Also: MARIAN ANTIPHONS

Bibliography: L. EISENHOFER and J. LECHNER, *The Liturgy of the Roman Rite,* tr. A. J. and E. F. PEELER from the 6th Germ. ed., ed. H. E. WINSTONE (New York 1961) 473–474. J. H. MILLER, *Fundamentals of the Liturgy* (Notre Dame, Ind. 1960) 343–344. A. HÄUSSLING, *Lexikon für Theologie und Kirche,* ed. J. HOFER and K. RAHNER, 10 v. (2d, new ed. Freiburg 1957–65) 7:1119.

[G. E. SCHIDEL/EDS.]

LITTLE ROCK, DIOCESE OF

The Diocese of Little Rock (*Dioecesis Petriculana*), upon the recommendation of the Fifth Provincial Council of Baltimore, was erected by Pope Gregory XVI on Nov. 28, 1843. It is coextensive with the boundaries of the state of ARKANSAS, and until 1891 when a vicariate apostolic was established in Oklahoma, it included the Indian Territory. In its early years it was a suffragan see of the Archdiocese of New Orleans, but in 1972 it was transferred to the newly created province of Oklahoma City. In its more than 150 years of existence, Little Rock has only had six bishops, with the sixth assuming his position in 2000.

Bishop Byrne Era, 1844–1866. Arkansas's first bishop, Andrew BYRNE, like his successor, was born in Ireland, but the exact date is unknown. Given that he was baptized Andrew, it is likely that he was born on or near Nov. 30, 1802, the feast day of St. Andrew the Apostle. While still a seminarian, he was brought by Bishop John England to Charleston and the famed South Carolina prelate ordained him to the priesthood on Nov. 11, 1827. Nine years later he left to became a diocesan priest for the New York Diocese, where he founded St. Andrew's Church in Manhattan. Byrne's abilities as a pastor, his connection with Bishop John Hughes of New York, and his previous experience in the South made him the natural choice to be a prelate on the southwestern frontier. Consecrated on March 11, 1844, in old St. Patrick's Cathedral in New York City, Byrne arrived in Arkansas with just two priests. Byrne raised the money necessary to build Arkansas's first Catholic Cathedral at Second and Center Streets in Little Rock and dedicated it on Nov. 1, 1846.

Throughout his 18 years as bishop, Byrne never had more than ten priests to work with him and his diocese, which was sustained basically by the Leopoldine Society in Vienna and the Paris-based Society for the Propagation of the Faith. With funds from these societies, he purchased land near Fort Smith and there placed Arkansas's first Catholic college, St. Andrew's. Byrne judiciously avoided religious disputes with fellow Arkansans, and this was not easy during the Know-Nothing uproar in the 1850s. Byrne owned no slaves and never expressed any views on the peculiar institution, probably accepting it as part of the economic landscape of the American South. Byrne sought to augment his minuscule Catholic flock by attracting immigrants from famine ravaged Ireland. The Religious Sisters of Mercy, a newly formed Irish-based community, answered his call. In February 1851 the first groups of sisters arrived and that fall founded St. Mary's Academy in Little Rock. This Mercy academy became Arkansas's oldest educational institution, celebrating its sesquicentennial in 2001. The Mercy sisters also founded St. Anne's Academy in Fort Smith (1853), and St. Catherine's Academy in Helena (1858).

At first, the Diocese of Little Rock was attached to the archdiocesan province of Baltimore. In 1850 the diocese became part of the newly created province of New Orleans, together with dioceses that then covered the states of Mississippi, Alabama, and Texas, and, after 1853, northern Louisiana. Byrne attended provincial councils in New Orleans early in 1856 and 1860.

The American Civil War brought about the close of Arkansas's first Catholic college in 1861 and Byrne died the next year on June 10, 1862, in Helena. At first buried in the courtyard of St. Catherine's Mercy convent, his remains were removed and placed under a newly constructed St. Andrew's Cathedral in 1881. Due to the exigencies of the Civil War, communications between Rome and the embattled Confederacy were difficult. Arkansas would not see another bishop for almost five years, one of the longest times in American history for a diocese to be without a bishop. Until Rome named a new bishop, it would be the responsibility of New Orleans Archbishop Jean Odin to name an apostolic administrator. Yet Odin was in Europe at that time and was not expected to return until the spring of 1863. It was then up to the senior bishop in the province and that was Bishop Auguste Martin of Natchitoches, Louisiana. Martin appointed Fr. Patrick Reilly, vicar general for the diocese, as the administrator for the Arkansas diocese.

Born on March 10, 1817, in County Meath, Ireland, Reilly was a seminarian in Ireland when he heard Bishop Byrne plead for missionaries for Arkansas. Reilly arrived in 1851 with two other seminarians and the Mercy sisters; the Arkansas bishop ordained him on St. Patrick's Day, 1851. Reilly began serving as vicar general in 1855 and as rector of the Cathedral of St. Andrew in 1858. He tried earnestly to keep the diocese going and its institutions open during the Civil War. All three Mercy academies in Little Rock, Fort Smith, and Helena remained opened throughout the war. Mercy sisters ministered to both Union and Confederate troops in the fall of 1863 when the battle raged around Arkansas's capital. Between 1863 and 1866, there would be only four priests working in the state. News arrived in the summer of 1866 via a Catholic newspaper in Cincinnati that Fr. Edward M. Fitzgerald of St. Patrick's Church in Columbus, Ohio, would become Arkansas's second Catholic prelate. Reilly remained vicar general under the new bishop until poor health moved him to return to Ireland in 1881. He died in his native village on April 29, 1882.

Bishop Fitzgerald Era, 1866–1906. Edward M. FITZGERALD was born in Limerick of an Irish father and a German mother sometime in October 1833. He arrived in America with his family in 1849 and the following year entered St. Mary of the Barrens Seminary in Perryville, Missouri. Two years later he transferred to St. Mary's Seminary in Cincinnati, Ohio, where Archbishop John Purcell of Cincinnati ordained him to the priesthood on Aug. 22, 1857. His only assignment as a priest was at a parish in Columbus, Ohio. On June 22, 1866, he received a letter from the Vatican naming him the second bishop of Little Rock. The 32-year-old priest initially rejected the appointment in a written response two months later. That December he received from Pope Pius IX a mandamus, an order to accept the position under holy obedience. Fitzgerald had by that time already changed his mind after attending the Second Plenary Council of the American Catholic bishops at Baltimore with Archbishop Purcell in October 1866. Consecrated bishop on Feb. 3, 1867, in Columbus, Ohio, Fitzgerald made it to Little Rock by St. Patrick's Day. Barely 33, he was the youngest prelate in the Catholic hierarchy of the United States, if not the world.

In late 1869 Fitzgerald was called to the First Vatican Council and needed financial assistance from Rome to attend. The Little Rock prelate earned a footnote in Catholic history by being one of only two bishops in the whole world—and the only English-speaking bishop—to vote against the declaration of papal infallibility made at this council. He was the first negative vote after 491 affirmations. Immediately after the vote he went to the front and submitted to the council's decision. In a public address a decade later, Fitzgerald explained that while he always believed in the doctrine, he did not think it expedient to declare it as it might hinder Catholic evangelization in the United States. His vote did not damage his career in the church. Pope Leo XIII, successor to Pius IX, offered him the archdioceses of Cincinnati and New Orleans, along with three or four other dioceses. Fitzgerald, however, stubbornly spurned all efforts to promote him or transfer him out of Little Rock.

Fitzgerald's career as bishop was an active one that spanned more than three decades. When he came in 1867 he had only six priests; by 1900 that number was 21 diocesan priests and 22 religious order priests belonging to the Order of St. Benedict or the Congregation of the Holy Ghost. New women's religious orders also arrived; what would become the Fort Smith Benedictines came in 1878, and the women who would become the Olivetan Benedictines arrived late in 1887. By the end of the 19th century, he had four women's religious orders, with 150 religious sisters, serving in the state. He had only two seminarians in 1867; by 1900 he had 25 studying at Subiaco Benedictine Monastery in Logan County, Arkansas. Arkansas's first Catholic hospital, St. Vincent's, opened in Little Rock in 1888, staffed then by the Sisters of Char-

ity from Nazareth, Kentucky; it is still the state's oldest medical facility. The Mercy sisters opened St. Joseph's in Hot Springs in 1888, and the Olivetan Benedictines in Jonesboro opened St. Bernard's in 1900. Five years later, the Mercy sisters would open another hospital, St. Edward's, in Fort Smith. Fitzgerald constructed Arkansas's present St. Andrew's Cathedral at Seventh and Louisiana and dedicated it on Nov. 27, 1881.

Fitzgerald was instrumental in attracting some Catholic migration to the state and attempting to convert African Americans to Catholicism. Fitzgerald opened Arkansas's first black Catholic parish, in Pine Bluff in 1895, and had six black Catholic schools opened by that date, but only two were still operating a decade later. All his efforts yielded few results as the Arkansas Catholic population still stood at just one percent, virtually unchanged since 1860. On Jan. 17, 1900, Fitzgerald's active career came to an end; he suffered a stroke that kept him confined to St. Joseph's Hospital for the rest of his life. He celebrated his fortieth anniversary as bishop from his hospital bed in Hot Springs, just 18 days before he died on Feb. 21, 1907. His remains were placed under the cathedral he had built a quarter century earlier.

During Fitzgerald's confinement, the affairs of the diocese were conducted by Vicar General Fr. Fintan Kraemer, O.S.B. Kraemer was not an apostolic administrator because Fitzgerald was still alive and there was hope that he might recover. When that was no longer deemed likely, bishops of the New Orleans province recommended that the Vatican name his successor. On May 14, 1906, John B. Morris, then the vicar general for the Diocese of Nashville, Tennessee, received word that he was to become coadjutor bishop for Little Rock with right of succession upon Fitzgerald's death.

Bishop Morris Era, 1906–1946. Born near Hendersonville, Tennessee, on June 29, 1866, John Morris's parents were Irish immigrants; his father was a veteran of the Union army. They sent their eldest son to St. Mary College in Lebanon, Kentucky, where he earned a degree in 1887 and a year later entered the seminary to study for the Nashville diocese. Bishop Joseph Rademacher sent him to Rome where he was ordained to the priesthood on June 11, 1892. He returned to Tennessee in 1894. Bishop Thomas S. Byrne named him his personal secretary in 1895 and then rector of the cathedral in Nashville. In 1900 Morris was given the rank of monsignor and made vicar general for the Nashville diocese. Consecrated Arkansas's third bishop in Nashville on June 11, 1906, he was the first native-born Tennessean to be a member of the Catholic hierarchy.

Morris served as coadjutor bishop, running the diocese as soon as he came in the summer of 1906. When

Fitzgerald died the following February, Morris automatically became his successor. Morris inherited a great deal of money from Fitzgerald and he used it to build up many Catholic institutions in the state. He started Little Rock College in 1908 in downtown Little Rock; it moved eight years later to Pulaski Heights, seven miles away. This attempt at Arkansas's second Catholic college would last only 22 years, as the outset of the Great Depression closed it. St. Joseph's Orphanage near North Little Rock opened in the fall of 1909 and it lasted for more than 60 years. Morris launched St. John's Home Mission Seminary in 1911 to train seminarians for both his diocese and others. When Little Rock College closed in 1930, Morris moved the seminary to the campus in Pulaski Heights. During the depression Morris opened St. Raphael's, a black Catholic orphanage near Pine Bluff, in 1932, but the institution was forced to close five years later. Blacks were reluctant to send their children to an organization run by whites and operated by a church to which they did not belong. St. Raphael's operated as a trade school until 1961. One heritage from Morris that has survived is the weekly diocesan newspapers that began publishing in 1911 and continued to operate at the start of the 21st century.

Institutionally, the Diocese of Little Rock grew during the four decades Morris was its bishop. In 1906 there were 60 priests and 200 sisters; four decades later there were 154 priests and 582 sisters. Where in 1906 there 29 schools with 2,702 students, by 1946 there were 80 schools with 7,750 students. And these schools were not only white schools. Morris had found only two black Catholic schools operating in 1906; by 1946 there were nine black Catholic parishes and seven of them had schools. From 1905 to 1945, the number of Catholic hospitals operating in the diocese increased from four to nine, with a bed capacity of a thousand. The number of Catholics in Arkansas did increase somewhat, going from just 1 percent in 1900 to 1.7 percent by 1940.

Known as a gifted orator, Bishop Morris was often asked to make speeches inside and outside of the diocese. In October 1932 he spoke at the dedication of the new building at Xavier University in New Orleans, the only predominately black Catholic college in the United States. In 1937 he gave one of the main addresses on the pope at the 1937 Eucharistic Congress in New Orleans. After an invitation from the American Legion in Arkansas, Morris gave a sharply worded attack on Nazi anti-Semitism after Kristallnacht in November 1938. Although his remarks were hardly noticed outside of Arkansas, no other American Catholic prelate made such a verbal broadside against Nazism at that time.

Morris's declining health forced him to ask for an auxiliary bishop. The Vatican agreed and they named the Little Rock bishop's candidate, Vicar General Albert Lewis Fletcher. Fletcher was born in Little Rock on Oct. 28, 1896. His father was a member of one of Arkansas's most prominent families and his mother was of German background. Both his parents were converts and Albert was their oldest child. His father was a physician who moved his family from Little Rock to Paris (Ark.) in Logan County and Tontitown in Washington County. Albert Fletcher was graduated in 1917 from Little Rock College with a degree in chemistry. He immediately entered St. John's Seminary and was ordained to the priesthood on June 4, 1920. He then attended the University of Chicago, which awarded him a master's degree in chemistry in 1922. He taught chemistry at Little Rock College and eventually served as its president for two years. In 1926 he became chancellor for the diocese and seven years later Morris appointed him vicar general. He was notified of his appointment on Dec. 11, 1939, and, on April 25, 1940, at a ceremony at St. Andrew's Cathedral in Little Rock, he became auxiliary bishop. He was the first native-born Arkansan to be raised to the American Catholic hierarchy.

Morris continued to head the diocese over the next six years, yet day-to-day operations were performed by his auxiliary bishop. The aging prelate lived to witness the centennial of the diocese on Nov. 28, 1943, and he celebrated his fortieth anniversary as bishop in June 1946. He died a few months later on Oct. 22, 1946, and his remains were placed under the cathedral. As auxiliary bishop, Fletcher did not have the right of succession. On Dec. 11, 1946, he was notified by telephone that he was to be the fourth bishop for the Diocese of Little Rock. He was formally consecrated on Feb. 11, 1947, at St. Andrew's Cathedral.

Bishop Fletcher Era, 1947–1972. Both his predecessors, Fitzgerald and Morris, had been builders who had each served as bishop for 40 years. Fletcher, a mild-mannered, soft-spoken gentleman, came to serve as Arkansas's Catholic prelate in a tumultuous quarter century of racial and religious change.

Fletcher's first decade rather quiet, the seminary was expanded, a Catholic bookstore opened, and the number of Catholics in Arkansas topped two percent in 1860 for the first time in history.

A major storm erupted over the integration of Little Rock public schools in the fall of 1957. Though often cautious and slow, Fletcher believed in gradual peaceful integration. He published a catechism deploring racial segregation and discrimination as violations of justice and charity. He oversaw the integration of Catholic schools and hospitals, but one unintended consequence was the closing of several black Catholic parishes and schools between 1962 and 1972.

Fletcher attended all four sessions of the Second Vatican Council, which met during the autumns of 1962–65. While he never addressed the council, he wrote 13 interventions or amendments, and nine were accepted by the council. After the council, Bishop Fletcher and a priest professor at St. John's seminary got into a dispute concerning a series of articles the priest published in the local newspaper. The priest asserted incorrectly in the spring of 1967 that the papacy would change its views of birth control, which would lead to the "demythologizing" of the papal office. Bishop Fletcher suspended him and the priest appealed to Rome, which decided in favor of the bishop the following year. That summer of 1967, Bishop Fletcher closed St. John's because of the difficulty in getting new qualified faculty to teach. The old seminary grounds became home to the chancery, diocesan offices, and the Catholic newspaper.

Like Morris, Bishop Fletcher asked for an auxiliary bishop and the Vatican agreed to name Fletcher's close associate, Lawrence P. Graves to the position. Graves was born in Texarkana, Arkansas, on May 16, 1916. He entered St. John's Seminary in 1936 and was sent to Rome for his theological education in 1938. He returned from Rome in 1940 and was ordained to the priesthood by Bishop Morris in June 1942. Graves eventually went to Catholic University of America to earn a master's degree in 1947 in canon law. He returned to begin teaching in the seminary until 1961 when Bishop Fletcher choose him to travel with him to the Second Vatican Council; Graves was also serving then as chancellor. On April 25, 1969, at St. Andrew's Cathedral, he became the second native Arkansan to become a Catholic bishop. New rules mandated that a bishop retire at the age of 75. Bishop Fletcher submitted his resignation to Rome in January 1972, perhaps hoping that the Vatican would name his auxiliary bishop his successor. History did not repeat itself as Rome named a priest from Savannah, Georgia as Arkansas's fifth bishop. After his retirement, Fletcher lived in his home in Little Rock until declining health forced him to be moved to the rectory next to St. Andrew's Cathedral. He collapsed at a local diner on Dec. 6, 1979, and was rushed to hospital where he was pronounced dead. He was buried with his predecessors under the cathedral. Auxiliary Bishop Graves was later named bishop of Alexandria-Shreveport in 1973, but he had to retire after nine years due to ill health. He died in Alexandria, Louisiana, in January 1994.

Bishop McDonald Era, 1972–2000. Andrew J. McDonald was the 11th of 12 children and was born on Oct. 24, 1923, in Savannah, Georgia; he attended major and minor seminaries in Baltimore. On May 8, 1948, he was ordained a priest for the Diocese of Savannah. He earned a degree in canon law at the Catholic University of America in 1949 and then was sent to Rome for two additional years of theology. Returning to Savannah in 1951, McDonald served as chancellor and pastor at one of the largest parishes in Savannah. Notified of his appointment as bishop of Little Rock on June 11, 1972, he was consecrated bishop at Savannah's St. John the Baptist Cathedral on September 5 of that year.

In time McDonald became noted for his concern for the poor, the unborn, and immigrants, and as one who made a strong effort to better relations with non-Catholic religious groups. In 1982 the Catholic Diocese of Little Rock became a member of the Arkansas Interfaith Conference of Churches and Synagogues. During McDonald's era a lay couple, Fred and Tammy Woell, launched the Little Rock Scripture Study Program in the summer of 1974. Aided by diocesan priests and Benedictine Jerome Kodell, a scripture scholar, they prepared materials for individual and group study. In 1977 Bishop McDonald gave his official approval for the program and it offices moved into the old seminary, the headquarters for the various diocesan agencies. By 1986 the program entered a partnership with the Liturgical Press in Collegeville, Minnesota, which distributes the program across the United States and throughout the English-speaking world. On Nov. 28, 1993, the diocese began a year-long celebration of its sesquicentennial anniversary. Along with the celebration, the diocese published the first history of Catholic Church in Arkansas. On Nov. 1, 1996, Bishop McDonald commemorated the 150th anniversary of the dedication of the first cathedral and the 296th anniversary of the first Mass ever said in the state of Arkansas.

Although Bishop McDonald reached the age of 75 in October 1998, the mandatory retirement age, he continued in office until January 2000, when it was announced that his successor would be the Reverend J(ames) Peter Sartain, a pastor in the Diocese of Memphis. Born June 6, 1952, in Memphis, he began his seminary training in 1971 at St. Meinrad Archabbey in Indiana. He studied theology in Rome and was ordained to the priesthood in October 1978. Up to the time he was named the sixth bishop for the Diocese of Little Rock, Sartain had served in various capacities in Memphis— pastor, chancellor, and vicar general. It would be up to this native of Memphis, Tennessee, to lead the Diocese of Little Rock into the second millennium.

Bibliography: DIOCESAN HISTORICAL COMMISSION, *The History of Catholicity in Arkansas* (Little Rock, Ark. 1925). J. M. WOODS, *Mission and Memory: A History of the Catholic Church in Arkansas* (Little Rock, Ark. 1993).

[J. M. WOODS]

LITTLE SISTERS OF JESUS

An international religious congregation of religious women founded in 1939 in the Sahara at Touggort, Algeria, by Little Sister Magdeleine of Jesus. Characterized as contemplatives living in the world, the sisters pursue a simple life, after the examples of Charles de FOUCAULD. Their spirituality, centered around the adoration of the Blessed Sacrament, is modeled on the hidden life of Jesus at Bethlehem and Nazareth. They do not undertake an organized apostolate, but earn their living by manual labor on farms, in factories, and in hospitals. They live in ordinary dwellings in small communities comprising persons of diverse races and nationalities. Located in many countries throughout the world, the Sisters seek to live especially among the Islamic peoples. The motherhouse is in Rome; in the U.S., the principal house is in Baltmore, Maryland. At the beginning of the 21st century, the Sisters numbered some 1,300 in about 70 countries.

Bibliography: Official Catholic Directory, #2330.

[A.-M. BOUCHER/A.J. WOUTERS]

LITTLE SISTERS OF THE ASSUMPTION

(LSA, Official Catholic Directory #2310); a congregation of nursing sisters who bring relief to the homes of the needy sick, gratuitously, and regardless of race or creed. The congregation was founded in Paris, France, in 1865 and approved by Leo XIII in 1897. The cofounders were Étienne PERNET, an Assumptionist, and Marie Antoinette Fage (1824–83).

Mlle. Fage was a member of the Association of Our Lady of Good Counsel, a charitable society in Paris. When Pernet met her, he put her in charge of the work of nursing the sick poor, which he had inaugurated. Out of this movement the sisterhood grew; Mlle. Fage, as Mother Marie de Jesus, became the first superior. Along with complete nursing care, the Little Sisters also assume the responsibility of the management of the home whenever necessary, and give assistance where family life is threatened with disunity. The community follows the Rule of St. Augustine and is governed by a superior general who resides in the motherhouse in Paris, France. The U.S. provincialate is in Walden, NY.

[J. IONE]

LITTLE SISTERS OF THE HOLY FAMILY

(*Les Petites Soeurs de la Sainte Famille*, PSSF, Official Catholic Directory #2320); a congregation with papal approbation, founded in Canada in 1880 for the purpose of providing domestic help for the clergy. The foundress, Alodie Virginie Paradis (1840–1912), was born in Nova Scotia and joined the Holy Cross Sisters at the age of 13. After 20 years as a teacher, Mother Marie Leonie (her name in religion) was put in charge of the domestic work at St. Joseph's College, Memramcook, New Brunswick. Finding that there were many young women eager to join her in this work, Mother Leonie decided, with the advice and help of Camille Lefebvre, a Holy Cross priest, to form a new community. In 1895 the novitiate was transferred to Sherbrooke, Quebec, where the motherhouse was later established. The sisters devoted themselves exclusively to work in the kitchens, laundries, and sacristies of colleges, seminaries, and episcopal residences. The first foundation in the U.S. was made in 1890. The motherhouse is in Sherbrooke, Quebec. The U.S. headquarters is in Lowell, Mass.

[A. J. ENNIS/EDS.]

LITTLE SISTERS OF THE POOR

The Congregation of the Little Sisters of the Poor (Official Catholic Directory #2340) was founded in 1839 at St. Servan, Brittany, France, by Jeanne JUGAN. The spirit of the Congregation is that of humility, evangelical simplicity, and confidence in Divine Providence. Its apostolate is the care of the elderly poor.

Jeanne Jugan, a 47-year-old Cancalaise woman, founded the Congregation some time during the winter of 1839 when she opened her small St. Servan apartment to an elderly, blind, paralyzed woman who had no one to care for her. Jeanne and Françoise Aubert, a pious woman with whom she shared her apartment, soon welcomed a second woman; by 1843 there were forty old women under their care, and the group had moved to larger accommodations. Three young women came to help with the work, and they were aided materially by sympathetic persons in the community. In 1841 Jeanne herself began the practice of going from town-to-town and door-to-door to beg alms for her poor. In 1842 Jeanne Jugan was elected superior of the young community, which adopted the name ''Servants of the Poor.'' This name changed to ''Sisters of the Poor'' in 1844, and then ''Little Sisters of the Poor'' in 1849.

As the community grew, the work quickly spread to other towns and cities in France and beyond. Formal diocesan approbation was given by the bishop of Rennes in 1852, and papal approbation was accorded by Pope Pius IX on July 9, 1854. At that time the Congregation numbered 500 Little Sisters and 36 houses, including foundations in England and Belgium. The motherhouse was established at La Tour St. Joseph, in the village of St. Pern, in 1856. The Constitutions of the Congregation were approved by Pope Leo XIII on March 1, 1879. Jeanne Jugan died at La Tour St. Joseph on August 29 of the same year. She was beatified by Pope John Paul II in Rome on Oct. 3, 1982.

The first American foundation of the Congregation was made in Brooklyn, New York, in 1868. Within four years, thirteen homes were established in the United States. At the end of the 20th century, there were more than 30 homes in North America. Worldwide, there were about 3,600 Little Sisters caring for the elderly in 30 countries in addition to the United States: Algeria, Argentina, Australia, Belgium, Benin, Canada, Chile, Colombia, Congo, England, France, Hong Kong, India, Ireland, Italy, Kenya, Malaysia, Malta, New Caledonia, New Zealand, Nigeria, Portugal, Scotland, Singapore, South Korea, Spain, Sri Lanka, Taiwan, Turkey, and Western Samoa.

The Little Sisters practice the three traditional vows of chastity, poverty, and obedience, and a special fourth vow of hospitality, by which they devote their lives solely to the care of the aged poor. An association of consecrated lay women, known as the Fraternity Jeanne Jugan, was begun in 1958 for those who wished to collaborate closely with the Little Sisters in their apostolate while retaining their lay status. This collaboration with the laity was expanded in 1998, with the approbation of statutes for a new initiative, the Association Jeanne Jugan, which offers to lay men and women the opportunity of sharing in the spirit and apostolate of the Little Sisters of the Poor and of deepening their Christian faith.

The Congregation is governed by a Superior General and a Council of six Assistants General. Each of the 20 provinces is governed by a Provincial Superior, in close collaboration with the Superior General and her Council. Provincial houses for the United States are located in Queens Village, NY, Baltimore, MD, and Palatine, IL.

[C. CAROLYN]

LITURGICAL ACCLAMATIONS

Origin and history. The word *acclamation* originates from the Latin, *acclamation, adclamation, conclamation, vox,* etc.; and the Greek *euphēmia, euphēmēsis, polychronion, polychronisma.* The term was used to designate a formula pronounced or sung by a group to express a common sentiment or to address a specific person or object. Acclamations, widely used in the ancient world in pagan cults, have also been in evidence in Judaism,

Islam, and Buddhism. In both Western and Eastern Christendom, acclamations developed independently as expressions of homage and recognition of both spiritual and temporal dignitaries. They have been an important element in Christian liturgy throughout its development.

From early usage, acclamations were simple refrains or exclamations which were often sung. Ideally, an acclamation is an expression of the religious unison, or *koinonia,* of the faithful community. Werner identifies three functions of acclamations: (1) demonstrating the active participation of the community; (2) loudly confirming and professing a common faith; and (3) providing outlets for spontaneous expressions of religious emotion.

Several places in the Hebrew Scriptures record the use of ''Amen'' as an expression of affirmation or oath. Examples include Dt 27:15-26 and 1 Chr 16:36 or Ps 72:19 and Ps 106:48. All four Gospels record the public acclamation of ''Hosanna'' with which the crowds greeted Jesus at his triumphal entry into Jerusalem. Early Christians with Jewish roots naturally carried over their use of ''Amen'' in Jewish worship into their celebration of Christian liturgy.

Contemporary Usage. The liturgical renewal begun by Vatican II was instrumental in retrieving the important role of acclamations in Roman Catholic worship. *Music in Catholic Worship* (article 53) describes liturgical acclamations as ''shouts of joy which arise from the whole assembly as forceful and meaningful assents to God's Word and Action.'' Because of their key role in the liturgy and because they enable the assembly's active participation, acclamations are most successful when they are ''rhythmically strong, melodically appealing, and affirmative.'' The primary liturgical acclamations in the Eucharist include the Gospel Acclamation, the Holy or *Sanctus,* the Memorial Acclamation (with its four options), the Great Amen, and the Doxology of the Lord's Prayer. Such responses as ''Thanks be to God'' at the end of the readings and the ''Amens'' at the end of the various prayers are also considered acclamations.

In many ways, liturgical acclamations are an example of liturgical music as truly music *of* the liturgy. That is, acclamations are ritual music in the best sense of the term, providing the assembly with the opportunity to be actively engaged in the liturgical rite and in dialogue with the presider. In this sense, acclamations aptly suit the genius of the Roman Rite in a way that hymnody, for example, does not. This is because acclamations are intimately tied to the liturgical texts and the liturgical action. In fact, all of the important climaxes of the liturgical action are highlighted by the sung acclamations of the people. Through these acclamations, the worshiping assembly actively expresses their faith in the mystery being celebrated.

The General Instruction of the Roman Missal (article 39) and the Introduction to the *Lectionary for Mass* (article 23) also highlight the importance of singing the Gospel Acclamation. Such directives acknowledge the difficulty of uniting a group of people in an enthusiastic and unified expression of faith through mere speech. Indeed, *Liturgical Music Today* (article 17) highlights the musical nature of all of the acclamations when it describes them as "the preeminent sung prayers of the eucharistic liturgy."

Bibliography: G. CHEW, "Acclamation," in *New Grove Dictionary of Music and Musicians* (London 1980) v.1, 35–36. L. DEISS, *Visions of Liturgy and Music for a New Century* (Collegeville 1996). J. GELINEAU, *Voices and Instruments in Christian Worship: Principles, Laws, Applications* (Collegeville 1964). E. WERNER, *The Sacred Bridge: The Interdependence of Liturgy and Music in Synagogue and Church during the First Millennium* (New York 1959).

[J. KUBICKI]

LITURGICAL ART, HISTORY OF

Part 1: Definition of Liturgical Art

The term liturgy is derived from the composite Greek word λειτουργία, meaning a public duty or a work undertaken by a citizen for the state. Today the term liturgy is applied to the public worship of the Church and is generally distinguished from private devotion, which occurs outside of the official community worship. The administration of Sacraments, the Mass, and public ritual are all part of the LITURGY.

The fashioning of objects, such as vessels and vestments for liturgical use, and the programming of worship space, or the planning of the architecture of a church for liturgical worship are commonly designated liturgical art. The use of ritual and devotional objects is common in the rites also of religions other than Christianity and in cult ceremonies that go back to primitive times (*see* ART, 1). This article confines itself to aspects of the use of art in Christian worship.

Terminology. The term liturgical art is often used interchangeably with the term sacred art (*art sacré, ars sacra*). However the term sacred art, in current usage, tends to overflow the boundaries of what is more restrictively called liturgical art. The term liturgical has a precision that is not shared by the obscure term sacred. All liturgical art are sacred, but not all sacred art are liturgical.

The use of the term sacred art is carried over from the Tridentine interest in sacred image when the concern

was more strictly *de sacris imaginibus*. The term was applied to images or representations of sacred subjects that were set aside for devotional purposes; these were distinguished from paintings and images of subjects that were profane (*profanum,* e.g., not devoted to religious ends). The concern of the council was twofold: (1) to uphold the legitimate use of images for devotional purposes and (2) to purge existing abuses (and prevent additional ones) that tended to introduce a questionable iconography into religious art. The council wished to exclude what was profane (*profanum*) and immodest (*inhonestum*) from the churches because pagan iconographic themes became common during the Renaissance and often found their way into churches. It wished, furthermore, to restrict unusual innovations (the *insolitum*) in the representation of dogma (e.g., that of the Trinity) because heretical interpretations easily crept in. The question was not one of style or aesthetics but of subject matter (iconography). It was fidelity to these Tridentine principles that encouraged the extreme caution of the succeeding period regarding innovation in art and architecture. By the end of the 19th century, with fidelity to "historical styles" prevailing, *ars sacra* within the Catholic Church was channeled in a mode of artistic production quite distinct from modern movements of art in general. The separation of general artistic currents from that kind of art used in churches created the understanding that art in the service of religion has a unique character inherent in its style and form that makes it "sacred" as distinct from the "profane."

With the introduction of modern art and architecture into churches, the term sacred came to be applied indiscriminately to elements of art and architecture that serviced the Church. Within the modern liturgical movement both in the U.S. and Europe this usage has been relatively common in descriptive expressions such as "sacred space," "sacred inwardness," and "sacral meaning." Such usage has led some to lodge a sacredness or an undefined sense of the sacred in objects, decoration, and architectural space that has an implied religious value. The term sacred, which was earlier applied to a distinction of subject matter, has come to be applied to the art form itself. The undefined "sense of the sacred" provides a tenuous basis for the scope of usage of the term; as a consequence sacred has been used to include meditative garden sculpture and abstract compositions that, however suitable, may or may not be employed in places of worship (e.g., some works in the *Exposition Internationale d'Art Sacré*, Royan, France, 1964).

More loosely employed are the terms "Christian art" and "religious art," which can be understood only within the context of the intentions and understanding of their users. Generally the term Christian art is applied

Baptismal font carved with Apostles sitting on the shoulders of Prophets, 12th century, in the cathedral at Merseburg, Germany.
(Marburg-Art Reference, Art Resource, NY)

The "Imperial Dalmatic," Byzantine, probably 13th century. (Alinari-Art Reference/Art Resource, NY.)

broadly to artistic production by and for Christians in cultures predominantly Christian; such art might be quite removed from immediate devotional or ritual ends (e.g., a pilgrim's water flask). The term "religious art" is used even more universally and often takes on the sense of *art sacré* in its wider meaning, designating any art that is perceived to have some religious interest. (For consideration of the concept of a Christian art *see* ART, 2.)

The term liturgical art might properly be understood in the same sense as the term sacred art in the constitution issued by Vatican II (chapter 7); it refers to art that is in the service of the official worship of the Church. So understood, the term extends not only to objects and vesture but also to the plastic arts and architecture. Thus a painting by A. Manessier hanging in the Museum of Modern Art in Paris is not a work of liturgical art, but it may be if it is transferred to a sanctuary space as suitable articulation for a sanctuary wall. A medieval water flask may have an ornamental iconographic theme articulated in the same character as that of a chalice; the chalice is proper subject matter to liturgical art whereas the flask is not.

Function. Liturgical art is determined in part by its functions. It serves to create the instruments and places of worship used for the liturgy. The sacred vessels, the altar, and the distribution of elements in the worship space itself are all specified to some extent by their instrumental service. Art may serve also to create the appropriate signs or images related to devotion; these are determined somewhat by their significative functions (cross, icon). Often liturgical items are both instrumental and significative (the baptismal font, the altar). When either the significative or instrumental function of a liturgical object is not realized in the work then it falls short of its characterization as liturgical art. Liturgical art assumes the burden of serving a function that is larger than the specific ends of the art engaged in fashioning it. A fine art engaged for the service of liturgy fills a function proper to worship that is not possible to it, for example, in a gallery. The larger function given to liturgical art is to serve the specific needs of public worship and private devotion. The artist himself may not, by reason of his art, fix the functions of liturgical art, though he might, by the combining of his perception of liturgical needs and his artistic sensibility, create a more complete or useful realization than was earlier employed.

The function of liturgical art may not be known by the disciplines of art and architecture in themselves. Just as the architect expects to be supplied with specific information concerning the needs and purpose of a research laboratory he might build, so also does he rightly expect that the Church will specify the needs and purposes of its liturgy for the church he might build. The architect and artist, understanding these ends, may then create adequate solutions according to their proper creative abilities and skills. It is for this reason that clarifications have been issued concerning the use of image and the functions of elements in the church; these instructions, discussed below have the function of pointing out the needs of the liturgy for the understanding of the pastor, the artist, and the architect.

In recent times such instruction has become necessary since often professional designers and builders are employed from a society that is not oriented to the needs of the Christian community. Furthermore, modern technical abilities along with architectural and artistic theory of the past hundred years have posed problems that have affected religious art considerably.

[R. J. VEROSTKO/EDS.]

Part 2: Legislation before Vatican II

An important piece of legislation published in recent years was the instruction *De arte sacra* issued by the Sacred Congregation of the Holy Office on June 30, 1952. Since this document was meant to be a summary of the legislation on sacred art in force at the time, it may serve as a point of reference for the subject up until its date of issuance.

The opening paragraph of the instruction defined sacred art in terms of its function: "It is the function of sacred art . . . to enhance the beauty of the house of God and to foster the faith and piety of those who gather in the church to assist at the divine service and to implore heavenly favors." The instruction then expressed the same ideas in a negative manner by recalling St. Pius X's remarks in his *motu proprio* on liturgical music, *Tra le sollecitudini* (Nov. 22, 1903): "Nothing should have a place in the church which disturbs or even merely diminishes the piety and devotion of the faithful, nothing which reasonably might be considered in bad taste or be the cause of scandal, nothing which might be unworthy of the house of prayer and the majesty of God."

This pastoral attitude of the Church toward sacred art has been at the core of its instruction throughout the centuries. The instruction *De arte sacra* cited the action of the Council of Nicaea II (787) in condemning the Iconoclasts and confirming the cult of sacred images (*see* ICONOCLASM). It also mentioned session 25 (1563) of the Council of Trent, which issued directives on Christian iconography, as well as the norms of Pope Urban VIII issued on March 15, 1642, providing for the execution of the decrees of the Council of Trent. The council had concluded its exhortation to the bishops with these words: "Let bishops exercise much diligence and care concerning these matters, that nothing disordered may meet the eye, nothing distorted and confused in execution, nothing unfitting and unbecoming, since sanctity belongs to the house of God."

The instruction then listed the canons of the 1917 Code of Canon Law that gathered all the ecclesiastical legislation on sacred art under summary headings: canons 485, 1161, 1162, 1164, 1178, 1261, 1268, 1269.n1, 1279, 1280, 1385, 1399. Special mention was made of the prescriptions of canon 1261, which obliges ordinaries to see that nothing foreign to the faith or not in harmony with ecclesiastical tradition be introduced into divine worship, and canon 1399.n12, which prohibits the production of all images that are foreign to the mind and decrees of the Church. In the event that there be any doubt that contemporary art has a legitimate place in the liturgy, the instruction recalled the words of Pius XI on the occasion of the inauguration of the new Vatican Gallery of Paintings (Oct. 27, 1932): "open wide the portals and tender sincere welcome to every good and progressive development of the approved and venerable traditions, which in so many centuries of Christian life, in such diversity of circumstances and of social and ethnic conditions, have given stupendous proof of their inexhaustible capacity of inspiring new and beautiful forms."

The instruction also adverted to the words of Pius XII in *Mediator Dei* (Nov. 20, 1947) on the place of con-

A wood sculpture of Saint Barbara decorates the altar of the Franciscan mission named for her, Santa Barbara, California. (©Richard Cummins/CORBIS)

temporary art in the liturgy. While confirming the place of modern art in sacred edifices and rites, Pius XII reproved those images and forms that were contrary to Christian piety, but there was no clarification of what forms these might be. After reasserting these points, the instruction proceeded to enumerate a number of nebulous directives of its own, first concerning architecture and then concerning descriptive art.

Besides the instruction issued by the Holy See on sacred art several episcopal directives were formulated after World War II to serve as a guide to church construction. Most important and earliest of these, usually referred to as the directives of the German bishops, was an official document entitled *Richtlinien für die Gestaltung des Gotteshauses aus dem Geiste der römischen Liturgie* (Liturgical Institute, Trier 1947). The document was drawn up by T. Klauser in collaboration with the liturgical commission appointed by the German bishops. This document not only influenced the rebuilding of churches in postwar Germany, but served as a valuable guide to diocesan liturgical commissions elsewhere. The directive clarifies five fundamental purposes of the Christian church and presents 21 concise conclusions based on theological and liturgical principles that bear importantly

Baptismal font in the basilica of S. Maria Maggiore, Rome, designed by L. Valadier in 1825, with figures by Carlo Spagna. (Alinari-Art Reference/Art Resource, NY)

on church architecture. A similar directive based on the German one and resembling it in outline was issued by the diocesan commission at Superior, Wis., in 1957 (*Diocesan Church-Building Directives*). The German document and the Superior document are presented with a brief commentary in the appendix to *Towards a Church Architecture,* ed. P. Hammond (London 1962) 245–262.

In April of 1952 the French hierarchy issued a directive in 11 short articles. This directive, however, was not an instruction on church building like the German one, but concerned itself more with the plastic arts and the role of the artist.

[R. K. SEASOLTZ/R. J. VEROSTKO/EDS.]

Part 3: Twentieth-Century Renewal Efforts

In Western Christian cultures art and architecture in general underwent radical changes following the Counter Reformation. Art was affected not only by the advent of modern technical abilities but also by the shifting of philosophical thought, the growth of the city, mass communications, and modern economic systems. After the mid-19th century the artistic world was in the upheaval of the disagreements between the academies and the in-

dependents, and the force of creative thinking that was to mold 20th-century art and architecture grew independently of institutional patronage, often opposing the Church. The 19th-century revivalisms in church architecture such as that of PUGIN, the attempts to revive the simple purity of Christian fresco painting by the Nazarenes, and the efforts of the later 19th-century BEURONESE school all failed to initiate the regeneration of religious art and architecture.

Separation of Art and the Church. By the turn of the century independent creative thinking had prepared the way for radical innovations in the art and architecture of the 20th century. In architecture F. L. Wright had already built homes on the freely spread ground plan (1890s), and L. H. Sullivan's skeletal structure in the Carson, Pirie, Scott & Company building in Chicago (1899–1904) had already broken with tradition. While skeletal structure and free space were successfully experimented with in America, the early work of T. Garnier (1861–1948) and A. PERRET led to the design of structures of genuine and specific character. Garnier's work in Rome in 1901 was directed toward the new industrial city; it was exhibited in 1904 and published in 1917. Efforts in architecture and industrial design by de Stijl, the Bauhaus, etc. were independent of any ecclesiastical patronage or interest. Similarly the plastic arts had already assimilated the contributions of the Impressionists and the Postimpressionists by the turn of the century; Fauvism, German Expressionism, Cubism, and Futurism all preceded World War I and contributed to a transforming vision that widened the gap between the art world in general and the Church. The failure of the Church to patronize creative art in its places of worship and the seeming indifference of ecclesiastics to the progress being made by modern art and architecture in general shaped a reaction within Christianity early in the century.

Renewal Efforts up to World War II. At the end of the 19th century the Spaniard A. Gaudí undertook at Barcelona the grandiose Sagrada Familia (still under construction), which, beyond its reminders of the past, opened the way to imaginative church construction. At the same time painters, following the insights provided by Gauguin and Cézanne, investigated the possibilities of renewing the treatment of religious themes. This earliest attempt led to the establishment in Paris after World War I of several studios of sacred art; here Maurice Denis and Georges Desvallières attempted to liberate Christian art.

It was not until after World War I that the French architect Auguste Perret built the first decidedly modern church, at Raincy, near Paris. In its construction, reinforced concrete was used on the basis of its functional adaptability and was successfully shaped to fit the needs of a program of worship. Denis and Bourdelle were called on to participate in the realization of the work.

At the same time two German architects contributed their efforts: Dominikus Böhm in the renewal of architectural expressionism and Otto Bartning in that of architectural rationalism.

In Switzerland K. Moser, at Saint-Antoine in Basel, continued the construction principles of A. Perret and trained pupils whose works would contribute to the future of church architecture. The churches that Fritz Metzger and Hermann Baur designed in German-speaking Switzerland from 1930 on, in particular at Zurich and Basel, inspired in other countries a type of rectangular building with plain walls, flanked by a chimney-like bell tower. These churches were characterized by a purity of line, a precision of volume, and a brightness of space, all of which accommodated the liturgical disposition of the interior. They created a style that was often repeated in modern church building.

These churches and certain works of art, such as stained-glass windows, paintings, and statues that were created to be used in them, were the occasion of the first controversies over modern religious art. A quarrelsome climate, with its collision between partisans and adversaries of ''modern sacred art,'' surrounded also the creative work of A. Cingria in French Switzerland; M. Denis, J. Barillet, and Le Chevallier in France; Thorn Pryker in Germany; and Joep Nicolas in Holland. In France and central Europe the movements initiated shortly after the turn of the 20th century (expressionism, Cubism, and even pure abstraction) had made considerable progress by 1914. The artists mentioned above, active after World War I, served only to bridge the gap that separated artistic progress in general from the Church.

Renewal Efforts after 1945. It was not until after World War II that a decisive confrontation took place between modern art and the Church. The periodical *L'Art sacré,* founded in 1935 by Joseph Pichard, which from before the war had been the organ for much activity in modern sacred art, published important postwar studies by the Dominican Fathers P. COUTURIER and P. Régamey. These pointed the way to new possibilities. They encouraged the construction of several chapels, which, while of modest dimensions, quickly acquired worldwide renown because of their bold though sensitive innovations in the retarded area of religious art. At ASSY, in a chapel serving several Alpine sanatoriums, a host of artists was engaged: P. Bonnard, G. Rouault, G. Braque, F. Léger, H. Matisse, Germaine Richier, J. Lipchitz, M. Chagall, and J. Lurçat. At Audincourt, in a working-class neighborhood, Léger and J. Bazaine contributed abstract compositions in stained glass and mosaic to the church

of the Sacred Heart. At the same time Matisse initiated work on the chapel at VENCE that was to contribute to the growing modern sensibility. The architect Le Corbusier began the chapel of RONCHAMP, which provided an unparalleled articulation of sanctuary space and light. Most of these accomplishments were realized (directly or indirectly) through the work of Father Couturier.

It was a time when plans for building or rebuilding churches were being undertaken; many had been seriously damaged or destroyed during the war, especially in France and Germany. Special commissions for historical monuments were able to take charge of the more ancient churches (Romanesque, Gothic) that could be restored. For the others it was necessary to rebuild. At the same time the growth of cities, with the formation on their outskirts of entirely new working-class districts, required the preparation of building programs that included new churches. Especially important as a guide, in regard to contemporary styles and the liturgy, were the directives of the German bishops (1947). Postwar church building was significant in Germany in Cologne, Berlin, and Frankfurt; in France, major churches were rebuilt at Le Havre, Brest, Lorient, Royan, and Baccarat, and many smaller churches were begun; in England, a new COVENTRY CATHEDRAL was constructed.

Two contrasting trends were in evidence in postwar church architecture. On the one hand, the functional rationalism that Perret, Bartning, and the Swiss architects had promoted in the period between the world wars was continued; on the other hand, a search for expressive forms, especially after 1950, developed both in the Americas and in Europe.

Architects who worked in the more functionalist and rationalist style were not only Swiss; there were in France, Le Donné, Pinsard, Pierre Vago, the brothers Arsène and Henry Lods, and Maurice Novarina (who was interested at the same time in regionalism); in the U.S., Eliel and Eero Saarinen, Ciampi, M. Breuer; and in Germany, R. Schwarz and Emil Steffann (who was particularly attached to simple and austere designs).

Among those who introduced the expressive into architecture, Le Corbusier must be given first place as demonstrated in his church of Ronchamp (completed 1955) and later in the monastery of L'Arbresle, near Lyons. These works achieved a new flexibility in concrete disciplined by a mature knowledge of human elements and physical processes (light, structural forces, landscape) and adjusted well to liturgical and monastic needs. Among others who searched for plastic expression were: in France, Guillaume Gillet (Royan), Rouquet (Metz and Nantes), N. Kazis (Baccarat), Bourbonnais, and Perrouin (around Paris); in Germany, Hans Schädel (Berlin), D.

Böhm, and J. Lehmbrock; in Finland, Aalvar Aalto; and in the Americas, Frank Lloyd Wright (U.S.), F. Candela (Mexico), and O. Niemeyer (Brazil).

The plastic arts had preceded architecture in their religious interest, but necessarily followed architecture in actual use within the church. The curiosity and emotion stirred up by the chapels at Assy and Vence provided ground for intelligent inquiry into the appropriate use of modern styles in the Church. At the same time the Church became receptive to modern styles in painting and sculpture (1952 instruction *De arte sacrale*). For more than 50 years artistic movements in general had tended to liberate the plastic arts from any representational function. By the mid-century artists were engaged with pure abstract art that sought expressive value in structure and response to plastic values (color, light, spontaneous calligraphy, etc.). First adaptations of abstraction in churches occurred notably in stained glass, which easily abandoned narration and iconography to concentrate on the creation of a suitable atmosphere through controlled design of light. Abstract reliefs and paintings emerged also in an effort to give plastic articulation to interior and exterior surfaces; J. Bazaine, A. Manessier, Léon Zack, G. Meistermann, P. Szekely, and many others were active in this regard.

The Americas. The efforts to renew liturgical art did not occur in Europe alone. The work of Virgil MICHEL (1890–1938) with the LITURGICAL MOVEMENT led to an awareness of the importance of religious art at ST. JOHN'S ABBEY, Collegeville, Minnesota, which was to make that abbey a center of renewal in the U.S. More important was the work of the LITURGICAL ARTS SOCIETY (founded in 1928). Both before and after the war its publication, *Liturgical Arts,* and the personal efforts of its secretary-editor, Maurice LAVANOUX, served to create a liaison between those interested in renewal in religious art and ecclesiastics. Through the lectures and articles of M. Lavanoux and others a climate had been created for the years following World War II that made significant progress possible. As early as 1946 the renovation of the basilica crypt at ST. VINCENT ARCHABBEY (Latrobe, Pa.) was carried out through the efforts of Father Quentin Schaut, including a remarkable series of 14 stained-glass windows by Emil Frei.

Though the mediocrity of derivative modernism occurred in liturgical ornamentation and church architecture during the 1940s and 1950s, a number of significant projects were undertaken. Most notable of these was the abbey church at St. John's (Collegeville, built in 1960 but planned earlier) by Marcel Breuer. This project included careful planning and articulation of every detail in terms of liturgical need and architectural expression. A number of monastic projects quickly followed the pattern of re-

newal that issued from St. John's: Hellmuth, Obata, and Kassabaum designed the St-Louis Priory of St. Mary Church (1962), and P. Belluschi (b. 1899) designed the Priory of St. Gregory the Great, Portsmouth, R.I. (1961), which includes the sculpture above the altar by R. Lippold. Of note also are the St. Mary Abbey Church and Monastery at Morristown, N.J. (1965), by Victor Christ-Janer, and the new St. Vincent Monastery, Latrobe, Pa., by Tasso Katselis. Contributions in Latin America were made by O. Niemeyer (b. 1907) and L. Costa (b. 1902), F. Candela (b. 1910), and E. de la Mora y Palomar.

Painting and sculpture in the service of church architecture have made less progress in the U.S. than in Europe. In general the postwar tendency has been to employ in churches a kind of pseudomodern articulation of figural work that is partly Cubist or expressionistic and sometimes primitive. With few exceptions the main currents of the artistic world have been either misunderstood or avoided by patrons of liturgical art in the U.S. (e.g., abstract expressionism and recent programmed art). However, the recent consultant work of F. Kacmarcik (St. Paul, Minnesota) has managed to point a direction by engaging J. Albers to design an abstract altar screen (St. Patrick's, Oklahoma City) and stained glass (St. John's, abbot's chapel). Others, not mentioned above, who have contributed promising conceptions are M. Goeritz (Mexico, stained glass), H. Bertoia (Massachusetts Institute of Technology chapel, sculpture), J. Reynal (mosaic), A. Rattner (stained glass), and Sister Mary Corita (illuminated texts).

Bibliography: A. CINGRIA, *La Décadence de l'art sacré* (Paris 1919; new ed. 1930). M. DENIS, *Nouvelles théories sur l'art moderne, sur l'art sacré, 1914–1921* (Paris 1922). J. KREITMAIER, *Beuroner Kunst: Eine Ausdrucksform der christlichen Mystik* (5th ed. Freiburg 1923). M. BRILLANT, *L'Art chrétien en France au XXe siécle* (Paris 1927). E. GILL, *Art-Nonsense and Other Essays* (London 1929). M. A. COUTURIER, *Art et catholicisme* (Paris 1948). R. HESS, *Moderne kirchliche Kunst in der Schweiz* (Zurich 1951). P. R. RÉGAMEY, *La Querelle de l'art sacré: Assy et Vence* (Paris 1951); *Religious Art in the Twentieth Century* (New York 1963). M. OCHSÉ, *La Nouvelle querelle des images* (Paris 1953). J. PICHARD, *L'Art sacré moderne* (Paris 1953). G. J. AUVERT, *Défense et illustration de l'art sacré* (Paris 1956). A. HENZE and T. FILTHAUT, *Contemporary Church Art,* ed. M. LAVANOUX, tr. C. HASTINGS (New York 1956). A. HENZE, *Neue kirchliche Kunst* (Recklinghausen 1958). J. PICHARD, *Images de l'invisible* (Tournai 1958). W. WEYRES and O. BARTNING, eds., *Kirchen: Handbuch für den Kirchenbau* (Munich 1959). M. OCHSÉ, *Un Art sacré pour notre temps* (Paris 1959). W. S. RUBIN, *Modern Sacred Art and the Church of Assy* (New York 1961). A. CHRIST-JANER and M. M. FOLEY, *Modern Church Architecture* (New York 1962), illus., bibliog. with each section. G. MERCIER, *L'Art abstrait dans l'art sacré* (Paris 1964) includes app. of directives, bibliog. 219–228. G. E. KIDDER SMITH, *The New Churches of Europe* (New York 1964). R. SOWERS, *Stained Glass: An Architectural Art* (New York 1965), ch. on content, notes. Periodicals and yearbooks. *Ars sacra* (Basel 1927–). *Jahrbücher der Deutschen Gesellschaft für christliche Kunst* (Munich 1951–). *Kunst und*

Kirche (Berlin 1924–). *L'Art d'église* (Bruges 1932–), Eng. summaries. *L'Art sacré* (Paris 1935–39; 1946–). *Liturgical Arts* (New York 1931–). *Das Münster* (Munich 1947–). *Chiesa e quartiere* (Bologna 1957–). *Arte cristiana* (Milan 1913–). *Art Chrétien* (Paris 1934–). *Catholic Art Quarterly* (Buffalo 1937–59), superseded by *Good Work* (1959–). *Christliche Kunstblatt* (Munich 1904–). *Fede e arte* (Vatican City 1953–). *Módulo* (Rio de Janeiro 1955–). *Formes sacrées* (Lombreuil 1964–), trimestrial.

[J. PICHARD/R. J. VEROSTKO/EDS.]

Part 4: Renewal Societies

The growth of the LITURGICAL MOVEMENT effected the establishment of a number of organizations concerned with the spirit and function of the arts as employed in the service of the Church in the age of 20th-century liturgical renewal. Better known among these renewal societies during this period were: the Central Pontifical Commission for Sacred Art in Italy (founded by Pius XI, 1924; Msgr. Giovanni Fallani, president); the LITURGICAL ARTS SOCIETY, New York (founded 1933, Maurice Lavanoux, secretary); Pro Civitate Christiana (founded 1939, Giovanni Rossi, president); and Istituto internazionale di arte liturgica (International Institute of Liturgical Art), Rome (founded 1954 by Vittorino Veronese). Essentially concerned with the arts (architecture, sculpture, painting, and other liturgical objects, these groups generally attempted to promote a more intelligent church patronage of the arts. Their most common aim was to provide commentary and direction for those engaged in building and decorating places of public worship. Such work has become more meaningful since the publication of the *Constitution on the Sacred Liturgy* (Dec. 4, 1963; ch. 7).

In the U.S. the most important single influence in creating a consciousness of need for renewal in liturgical art until its demise in 1972 was the Liturgical Arts Society (and its active editor-secretary, Maurice Lavanoux); the LITURGICAL CONFERENCE, though not specifically oriented to art, became important for auxiliary conferences and exhibitions at its annual meetings after 1940.

The rise of a more art-conscious public in the U.S. caused groups founded for apostolic purposes at various levels of society to develop, within their structures, committees or sections that concentrated on evangelization through various art media. In the early post-World War II years, the GRAIL (founded in the Netherlands, 1920 and U.S., 1940) encouraged local artists to work in religious themes by providing exhibit space (and consequently forums and markets) in the Grail shops. Associations of professional artists and art educators also attempted to implement the spirit of the Liturgical Movement. Such associations were: the Catholic Art Association (founded 1937), which published the quarterly *Good Work;* the Catholic Fine Arts Society (founded 1955, an association

of college and secondary school educators, and artists); and finally the National Conference of Catholic Art Educators (an offshoot and almost a branch of the National Art Education Association, a secular group of professional art educators).

Bibliography: J. KARLIN, ''Contemporary Art and the Church in Italy,'' *Liturgical Arts* 30.1 (1961) 26–28. See also collective statement of aims issued in the 1960s by the *Istituto internazionale di arte liturgica* (Rome).

[B. T. LUCEY/EDS.]

Part 5: Impact of Vatican II.

As a pastoral guide to the teaching, doctrine, and theory in regard to the promotion and reform of the liturgy the fathers of Vatican Council II issued the *Constitution on the Sacred Liturgy* (Dec. 4, 1963). Chapter 7 of this document concerns itself with the role of liturgical art in the first phase of the Church's reform, the renewal of worship.

There are two other documents that provide a fuller understanding of the meaning of chapter 7 of the constitution. One, usually referred to as the ''appendix,'' contains declarations of the preparatory commission for a clearer explanation of certain constitution articles; the ''appendix'' to article 128 of the *Constitution on the Sacred Liturgy* is of particular importance because it serves as a basis of interpretation for chapter 7 and also as background for other instruction on liturgical art that has been, or will be, issued by the Liturgical Commission. The instruction of Sept. 26, 1964, was issued to implement effectively what was broadly outlined by the council; chapter 5 of this instruction provides the first official implementation of article 128 of the *Constitution*.

Thus three documents are directly relevant to liturgical art and the renewal issuing from Vatican Council II: (1) chapter 7 of the *Constitution on the Sacred Liturgy;* (2) the appendix to article 128 of that *Constitution* (an appended illustration on the meaning of the text); and (3) chapter 5 of the instruction of Sept. 26, 1964, issued by the Liturgical Commission.

In regard to the interpretation and understanding of these documents two factors must be kept in mind: (1) the norms and regulations issued in regard to art in the liturgical renewal attempt to give official expression to the principles and doctrine underlying the structure of the liturgy: (2) meaningful employment of the norms can come only from a study of the reasons for which they were issued in the context of the *aggiornamento*. The practical implications of the ''appendix'' to article 128 and the instruction of Sept. 26, 1964, are discussed under section 5 below.

The *Constitution on the Sacred Liturgy,* (CSL) although chapter 7 on sacred art is brief (articles 122–130), contains a number of valuable clarifications that may be summarized as follows:

1. A strong point concerns style. "The Church has not adopted any particular style of art as her very own"; free scope is to be given to contemporary art of every race and region provided it serves with due reverence the holy rites and the enrichment of sacred buildings (CSL 123).2.

Veneration of images is to be maintained by the faithful but the sacred images placed in the church are to be moderate in number; relative positions of images, when used, are to reflect an order that does not create confusion among Christian people; neither should it foster devotion of doubtful orthodoxy (CSL 125).

3. Noble beauty rather than sumptuous display is to be sought. Works that are mediocre or pretentious and those which offend true religious sense or are repugnant to faith, morals, and Christian piety are to be carefully removed from churches by the bishops (CSL 124).

4. When churches are to be built care is to be taken to implement the celebration of liturgy and the participation of the faithful (CSL 124). Statutes and regulations concerning the building and appointment of furnishings in the church are to be revised for this purpose. "Laws which seem less suited to the reformed liturgy are to be brought into harmony with it, or else abolished; and any which are helpful are to be retained if already in use, or introduced where they are lacking" (CSL 128). The instruction of Sept. 26, 1964, was the first official implementation of this article. Chapter 5 of this instruction concerned itself mainly with the construction of the church and the appointment of its furnishings in order to facilitate the active participation of the faithful. These instructions form a basis for flexibility in building in anticipation of changes yet to come. As a working principle, older legislation and instruction was to be viewed in the light of the reformed liturgy and the instruction issued thus far.

5. Judgments on works of art are not a personal matter. The local ordinary is to give hearing to a diocesan commission on sacred art, which is to include experts on art (CSL 126.44, 45).

6. To facilitate sound judgment and appreciation in matters of sacred art, clerics are to be taught its history and development during their philosophical and theological studies (CSL 129). Bishops are enjoined to have a special concern for artists (CSL 127) and see to it that works of value are preserved (CSL 126).

Summary. In viewing the instruction and legislation of the Church in regard to sacred art it is important to bear in mind the reason for which the instruction was issued. The councils of Nicaea (787), Constantinople (869–870), and the 25th session of Trent (1563) all concerned themselves with problems related to the use of images. Instruction was issued to uphold the legitimate and healthy use of images for devotional purpose against those who would deny their use (*see* IMAGES, VENERATION OF). Where abuses were prevalent, such as iconographic schemes that threatened the understanding of doctrine or excesses of imagery that might introduce superstition and false worship, the Church issued clarifications to protect Christian doctrine and piety. None of this legislation provides judgment of quality or aesthetic and stylistic norms since such judgment is neither the intention nor the province of the fathers. Both older and recent instruction has, at root, a pastoral concern.

More recent instruction has concerned itself with the function of liturgy and the critical role of art in the proper fulfillment of that function. Consequently there is a greater interest in architecture. The concern of the earlier councils over images has been replaced in the 20th century by a concern over the intelligent employment of new artistic abilities in the liturgy. With the advent of abstract art another kind of question has been posed in regard to image. Also new concepts and abilities with regard to architectural space have appeared in church architecture (*see* CHURCH ARCHITECTURE, HISTORY OF, 1). Vatican II clearly did not wish to frustrate healthy progress in the intelligent use of contemporary abilities (LCS 123). Subsequent norms and instructions attempted to maintain a flexibility that embraces the wealth of contemporary creative thought, and in a way that would complement and fulfill the proper function of the liturgy.

Bibliography: K. B. FRANK, *Fundamental Questions on Ecclesiastical Art,* tr. M. NATHE (Collegeville, MN 1962), pt. 2 gives account of instructions up to the 1952 document. "La legislazione ecclesiastica sull'arte," *Fede e Arte* nos. 10–11 (Oct.–Nov. 1957), special issue with pertinent acts of the popes, council decrees, and acts of the Roman Congregation up to 1957. Congregation of the Holy Office, *On Sacred Art* (Instruction, June 30, 1952), *Acta Apostolicae Sedis* 44.10 (1952) 542–546. Vatican Council II, *Constitution on the Sacred Liturgy,* ch. 7, *Acta Apostolicae Sedis* 56.2 (1964) 130–133; Eng. ed. G. SLOYAN (Glen Rock, N.J. 1964). Sacred Congregation of Rites, *Instructio,* ch. 5 (Sept. 26, 1964) *Acta Apostolicae Sedis* 56.14 (Nov. 10, 1964) 897–900. F. R. MCMANUS, "Recent Documents on Church Architecture," in *Church Architecture: The Shape of Reform* (Washington 1965), proceedings of a meeting on church architecture conducted by the Liturgical Conference in Cleveland, Feb. 23–25, 1965, includes app. of the recent documents, 95–104. R. K. SEASOLTZ, *The House of God: Sacred Art and Architecture* (New York 1963).

[R. J. VEROSTKO/EDS.]

Part 6: Church Furnishing

The furnishing of the church is directly related to its architecture since the total ensemble of the edifice and the program of worship elements are necessarily interdependent. Although this mutual reliance of liturgical function and architectural conception has always been important in the appointment of church furniture it has become more relevant since the turn of the century, owing to two almost parallel modern movements: the new phase in the development of architecture and design and renovation within the Church of its liturgy.

Modern Art and Architecture. Modern architecture has an increase of possibilities at its disposal for the articulation of space. The flexibility of reinforced concrete, the visual openness provided by the use of glass, and the strength of steel and new alloys all contributed to a technical facility that enabled designers to add new structural procedures to the old, or in some cases to substitute them. There has been considerable speculation in architectural theory concerning the integrity of form and its relationship to function (L. Sullivan, F. Wright, and Le Corbusier; *see* CHURCH ARCHITECTURE, HISTORY OF, 1). The influence of this thinking on industrial design has been felt especially in the work of the Bauhaus and men such as L. Moholy-Nagy and the Saarinens. Modern theory and technical capacities have contributed to radical changes in the structure and design of architecture, furniture, and mass-produced items. Their effects have been felt also in liturgical art and bear on the design of many elements of the church.

Division of the Arts. Permanent utility elements that were formerly designed by the artists of their separate crafts have become rather the domain of the architect whose architectural forms evolve from the nuances of function and the architect's sensitivity to plastic qualities. Thus the structure, disposition, and design, for example, of altar, confessionals, pews, entry and exit systems, and lighting systems are considered an integral part of the architectural conception. Yet the design of these elements cannot proceed without a clear understanding of their purposes and interrelationship. The role of the liturgist in this regard is discussed below.

Although painting, sculpture, and the minor arts continue to maintain their distinctive abilities and qualities, their interchange on the conceptual level makes the differences between them less discernible. Thus the Rosary Chapel at VENCE by H. Matisse has been referred to as a painter's architecture. The passage from painterly conception to architectural conception is hardly noticeable in the organic totality of the structure. An example of what is referred to at times as architectural sculpture is the shrine chapel at RONCHAMP by Le Corbusier. Light apertures, altar, pew units, and sanctuary cross all participate in the interior sculptural sense; on the outside the water spill, the outdoor altar, and the pulpit are an organic part

of the structure that may be viewed for its sculptural qualities. The metal altarscreen by H. Bertoia in the chapel at the Massachusetts Institute of Technology creates a sanctuary environment from the interaction of architecture and sculpture. The use by A. Manessier of stained glass for a wall in the chapel at Hem is conceived architecturally to create a suitable light environment for the nave.

Because of the interrelationship of artistic conceptualization and liturgical function, the intelligent appointment of furnishings can proceed only on the basis of organic solutions achieved through the cooperation of designer, architect, and liturgist.

Ornamentation and Expression. Modern architects rarely give specific expression to a structure through ornamentation that represents narrative, descriptive, or historical subjects. The artist tends to derive expressive strength from the character of materials and the plastic or spatial articulation of the functions and quality of the structural elements themselves; this is applied to the creation of chalice, tabernacle, church pew, and vestment as well as to architecture.

Function includes the significative and spiritual purposes of specific liturgical elements. Joint efforts of liturgists and architects after World War II (especially in Germany and France) attempted to create a church architecture with all its appointments that would at once serve liturgical needs and be expressive of the purpose of this service. The altar, for example, was given its signification through the architectural disposition and the strength of its form; the main altar in R. Schwarz's church of Maria Königin (Saarbrücken, 1959) receives the focus of light and centrality to the assembly so that its significative presence is seen in the actuality of itself. Without further explication it becomes a fitting symbol of Christ in the strong architectural statement of a table around which the assembly is gathered for the Eucharistic service.

Relevance of the Liturgical Movement. In regard to church furnishing there are two abilities of fundamental importance that must be distinguished. On the one hand, the architect has the special knowledge, sensitivity, and ability necessary to create structures and establish the internal relationship of worship spaces. In doing so he is able to make such relationships meaningful to the degree that he has understood the function of the liturgy he serves. On the other hand the liturgist has the special knowledge of the precise purpose of liturgy, but this knowledge does not give him the ability to perceive how an architectural solution might be best realized. The role of the liturgist in the design and appointment of a specific church building is to relate the total complex of liturgical functions to the particular place where it will be performed; the aim of the architect and designer is to create adequate functional and aesthetic solutions in terms of their special creative abilities.

Just as the arts of architecture, painting, and sculpture are intimately related to the sensibilities of the specific cultural milieu where they are created, so also is the liturgy, which presupposes a dynamic prayer life with a ritual center whose form receives specification from the cultural milieu where it is actualized. The view of the dynamic aspect of the liturgy and thus of its adaptability to modern times grew clearer owing to the LITURGICAL MOVEMENT, which early in the 20th century presented the liturgy as a source for the formation of Christian life. The restoration of this view was initiated by PIUS X (*motu proprio,* Nov. 22, 1903) and received an important impetus through the proposals of Dom Lambert BEAUDUIN at a national Catholic congress at Malines in 1909. In his lecture ("Il faudroit democratiser la liturgie") he explained the importance of taking practical measures to live the liturgy in order to share the life of Christ in His body, the Church. The subsequent work of the Liturgical Movement to create a more effectual liturgy was pioneered in Europe by P. PARSCH, R. GUARDINI, J. JUNGMANN, Odo CASEL, and I. HERWEGEN, and in the U.S. at Collegeville, Minn., by Virgil MICHEL. In his essay *Art Principle of the Liturgy* [tr. W. Busch (Collegeville 1931) 16] Herwegen noted that "the idea of Christian transfiguration is the art-principle of the liturgy." In order to realize the transforming power of the liturgy it was necessary to re-form community worship on livable terms. Work was begun to free the liturgy of irrelevant historicisms, the language barrier (Latin), and burdensome minutiae of rubrics whose functions were no longer meaningful. Concomitant with the advance of the movement was the rediscovery of the Bible and Biblical theology, which complemented the liturgy.

The relevance of the new findings to the programming of the worship elements in the Church was first felt, on a broad scale, in the rebuilding in Europe after World War II, particularly in Germany, where new church construction was greatly affected by the 1947 "Directives for the Building of a Church" approved by the German bishops. Of the 21 succinct articles, the first sums up the several purposes of the building according to their relative importance, noting the Eucharistic celebration as primary. The third article focuses on the problem of crucial importance for liturgist, architect, and designer:

> These various purposes [e.g., Eucharistic celebration] which the church building must serve present a peculiar problem in its construction. The Eucharistic Sacrament requires an arrangement of space different from that required by the administration of the sacraments of baptism and penance; the re-

quirements in the administration of these sacraments differ from those which preaching demands; and differences appear again as between preaching and eucharistic adoration, as between eucharistic adoration and community worship, as between community worship and private devotion. It is the task of the architect to find a solution of the problem which will best satisfy these several purposes of the church edifice.

Before the architect or designer can provide these solutions he must understand the nature of these various functions in the context of the community they serve. The work of the Liturgical Movement provided the groundwork for explicating liturgical functions and making them meaningful. The 1947 directives represented the first joint episcopal recognition of the work of the liturgists on church architecture; their work has been of unquestionable value to patrons and designers.

Vatican Council II. The reform measures taken by VATICAN COUNCIL II in regard to the liturgy were issued in the *Constitution on the Sacred Liturgy* (Jan. 25, 1964). Guidelines for the furnishing of the church were indicated in article 128.

> Along with the revision of the liturgical books, as laid down in Article 25, there is to be an early revision of the canons and ecclesiastical statutes which govern the provision of material things involved in sacred worship. These laws refer especially to the worthy and well planned construction of sacred buildings, the shape and construction of altars, the nobility, placing, and safety of the eucharistic tabernacle, the dignity and suitability of the baptistery, the proper ordering of sacred images, embellishments, and vestments. Laws which seem less suited to the reformed liturgy are to be brought into harmony with it, or else abolished; and any which are helpful are to be retained if already in use, or introduced where they are lacking.

> According to the norm of Article 22 of this constitution, the territorial bodies of bishops are empowered to adapt such things to the needs and customs of their different regions; this applies especially to the materials and form of sacred furnishings and vestments.

In order to implement this article a directive based on the present reformed liturgy and sufficiently flexible to provide for reforms that may come in the future was issued in the form of an instruction on Sept. 26, 1964 [*Acta Apostolicae Sedis* 56 (Nov. 10, 1964) 14]. It is a refinement of the Preparatory Commission's declaration that was added as an appendix to explain certain articles. The "Appendix" relevant to article 128 appeared in *Liturgical Arts* (33.1, February, 1964) and also in *Church Architecture, The Shape of Reform,* (Liturgical Conference, Washington 1965). The fifth chapter of the September 26 instruction, without usurping the domain of architect and designer, provides a clear and flexible directive relevant to the disposition of the major elements in church furnishing; it is the practical explicative in effect at this time (1965) concerning the liturgical intelligence necessary for properly furnishing a church.

This fifth chapter, "The Proper Construction of Churches and Altars in order to Facilitate the Active Participation of the Faithful," taken from the *Instruction for the Proper Implementation of the Constitution on the Sacred Liturgy,* reads as follows:

I. The arrangement of churches

90. In the new construction, repair, or adaptation of churches, great care shall be taken that they are suitable for the celebration of divine services according to the true nature of the services and for the active participation of the faithful (cf. constitution, article 124).

II. The main altar

91. It is proper that the main altar be constructed separately from the wall, so that one may go around it with ease and so that celebration may take place facing the people; it shall occupy a place in the sacred building which is truly central, so that the attention of the whole congregation of the faithful is spontaneously turned to it.

In choosing the material for the construction or ornamentation of the altar, the prescriptions of law shall be observed.

Moreover, the presbyterium or sanctuary area around the altar shall be of sufficient size that the sacred rites may be conveniently celebrated.

III. The seat of the celebrant and ministers

92. The seat for the celebrant and ministers, according to the structure of individual churches, shall be so placed that it may be easily seen by the faithful and that the celebrant may truly appear to preside over the entire community of the faithful.

Nevertheless, if the seat is placed behind the altar, the form of a throne is to be avoided, as this belongs to the bishop alone.

IV. Minor altars

93. The minor altars shall be few in number. In fact, to the extent permitted by the structure of the building, it is highly suitable that they be placed in chapels in some way separated from the principal part of the church.

V. Ornamentation of altars

94. The cross and candlesticks, which are required on the altar for the individual liturgical services, may also, in accordance with the judgment of the local ordinary, be placed next to it.

VI. The reservation of the most holy Eucharist

95. The most holy Eucharist shall be reserved in a solid and inviolable tabernacle placed in the middle of the main altar or of a minor, but truly outstanding, altar, or, according to lawful customs and in particular cases to be approved by the local ordinary, also in some other noble and properly adorned part of the church.

It is lawful to celebrate Mass facing the people even if there is a tabernacle, small but suitable, on the altar.

VII. The ambo

96. It is fitting that there be an ambo for the proclamation of the sacred readings, so arranged that the ministers can be easily seen and heard by the faithful.

VIII. The place of the schola and organ

97. The place for the schola and the organ shall be so arranged that it will be clearly evident that the singers and the organist form a part of the united community of the faithful and so that they may fulfill their liturgical function more suitably.

IX. The places of the faithful

98. The places for the faithful shall be arranged with particular care, so that they may participate in the sacred celebrations visually and with proper spirit. It is desirable that ordinarily benches or seats be provided for their use. Nevertheless, the custom of reserving seats for certain private persons is to be reprobated, in accordance with article 32 of the constitution.

Care shall also be taken that the faithful may not only see the celebrant and the other ministers but may also hear them easily, with the use of present day technical means.

X. Baptistry

99. In the construction and ornamentation of the baptistry, care shall be taken that the dignity of the sacrament of baptism is clearly apparent and that the place is suitable for the community celebration of the sacrament (cf. constitution, article 27).

The first published commentaries on this instruction were those of a meeting on church architecture conducted by the Liturgical Conference in Cleveland, Ohio, Feb. 23–25, 1965 [*Church Architecture, The Shape of Reform* (Washington 1965)].

Although much of the postwar building in Europe revealed a sensitivity to liturgical need, few of the structures are flexible enough in their arrangement to accommodate all the desirable provisions of the 1964 instruction. Churches built before Vatican II (and the 1964 instruction) often present the following difficulties: (1)

The altar in the sanctuary space is usually designed for the celebration of Mass with the celebrant's back toward the people; consequently the space more central to the people and more suited for the altar is occupied by the priest and ministers. (2) The tabernacle is usually placed on the main altar and provision for a repository or a Blessed Sacrament altar is neglected. (3) The place of the ambo for the proclamation of the readings is not clearly articulated architecturally. (4) The seat of the celebrant and ministers in the churches mentioned is not easily adapted to the reformed liturgy.

However problematical the rearrangement of older structures and the development of satisfactory solutions may seem, the 1964 instruction remains a lucid document on questions relevant to the architectural program of the church for the reformed liturgy that were unanswerable at an earlier date.

Bibliography: For specific liturgical objects see bibliog. under subject titles; for legislation on sacred art *see* LITURGICAL ART, 3; for select general bibliography on liturgical and ritual objects see *Encyclopedia of World Art* 9:314–315. General. History and handbooks. R. GARRUCCI, *Storia dell'arte cristiana*, 6 v. (Prato 1872–81), illus. C. ROHAULT DE FLEURY, *La Messe . . .*, 8 v. (Paris 1883–89), illus. F. WIELAND, *Mensa und Confessio*, 2 v. (Munich 1906–12). DACL. V. THALHOFER, *Handbuch der katholischen Liturgik*, 2 v. (2d ed. Freiburg 1912). K. M. KAUFMANN, *Handbuch der christlichen Archäologie* (2d ed. Patterborn 1913). W. F. VOLBACH, *Metallarbeiten des christlichen Kultes* (Mainz 1921). J. BRAUN, *Der christliche Altar in seiner geschichtlichen Entwicklung*, 2 v. (Munich 1924); *Das christliche Altargerät* (Munich 1932). A. MUNIER, *Construction, décoration, ameublement des églises*, 3 v. (Paris 1926) v.2 *L'Église à notre époque, sa décoration son ameublement.* E. TYRRELL-GREEN, *Baptismal Fonts* (London 1928). V. CASA-GRANDE, *L'arte a servizio della Chiesa*, 2 v. (Turin 1932–38). D. DURET, *Mobilier: Vases, objets et vêtements liturgiques* (Paris 1923). L. EISENHOFER, *Handbuch der Katholischen Liturgik* v.1. E. ROULIN, *Nos Églises: Liturgie, architecture moderne et contemporaine, mobilier, peinture et sculpture* (Paris 1938). E. SHORT, *A History of Religious Architecture* (4th ed. London 1955). A. L. DRUMMOND, *The Church Architecture of Protestantism* (Edinburgh 1934). G. W. O. ADDLESHAW and F. ETCHELLS, *The Architectural Setting of Anglican Worship* (London 1948). Contemporary church furnishing. P. R. RÉGAMEY *Religious Art in the Twentieth Century* (New York 1963). A. HENZE and T. FILTHAUT, *Contemporary Church Art,* ed. M. LAVANOUX tr. C. HASTINGS (New York 1956), illus. P. WINNINGER, *Construire des églises* (Paris 1957). R. SCHWARZ, *The Church Incarnate*, tr. C. HARRIS (Chicago 1958), influential theoretical work. W. WEYRES and O. BARTNING, eds., *Kirchen: Handbuch für den Kirchenbau* (Munich 1959), diagrams, illustrations, bibliography. J. CHÉLINI, *La Ville et l'église* (Paris 1958). J. PICHARD, *Modern Church Architecture*, tr. E. CALLMANN (New York 1962), illustrations, commentary and history of modern renewal. P. HAMMOND, *Liturgy and Architecture* (New York 1961), bibliography, illustrations, most useful on relation of liturgy to architecture; ed., *Towards a Church Architecture* (London 1962), illus., app. of useful directives. A. CHRIST-JANER and M. M. FOLEY, *Modern Church Architecture* (New York 1962), includes Protestant and Jewish structures, useful bibliog., illus. for each entry. R. K. SEASOLTZ, *The House of God* (New York 1963), structured after the 1952 instruction but precedes Vatican Council II contributions. G.

MERCIER, *L'Art abstrait dans l'art sacré* (Paris 1964), illustrations, bibliography, appendices with legislation and instruction. G. E. KID-DER SMITH, *The New Churches of Europe* (New York 1964), profusely illustrated, floor plans. R. GIESELMANN and W. AEBLI, *Kirchenbau* (Zurich 1960). R. BIEDRZYNSKI, *Kirchen unserer Zeit* (Munich 1958). E. D. MILLS, *The Modern Church* (New York 1956). F. PFAMMATTER, *Betonkirchen* (Einsiedeln 1948). A. HENZE, *Neue kirchliche Kunst* (Recklinghausen 1958). R. SOWERS, *Stained Glass: An Architectural Art* (New York 1965). A. BIELER, *Liturgie et architecture* (Geneva 1962). *Kirchenbau von heute für morgen*, introd. W. M. Förderer (Sakrale Kunst 7; Zurich 1964).

[R. J. VEROSTKO/EDS.]

Part 7: Liturgical Vessels

This article offers considerations on the artistic structure of the principal vessels used in the liturgy of the Eucharist. For more detailed information on other aspects of liturgical vessels in general, see LITURGICAL VESSELS.

The Chalice. In early Christian times people drank from an ordinary drinking vessel in the celebration of the Eucharist and the Sacrament of the Lord's Supper took place at a citizen's house; the celebrant did not yet wear ritual dress. The architectural structure of the church evolved from existing structures and the priest's vestments from the ordinary garments. In the same way the shape of the chalice developed from the former Roman drinking bowl.

Stylistically the chalice can be traced back by way of the Roman drinking bowl to the Greek two-handled bowl, this in its turn having been derived from the prehistoric cup of Aegean cultural origin. The Greek drinking vessel shows a low base and a broad bowl beneath which a nodelike support is inserted. The most typical features of this bowl were adopted for liturgical use, including the small intermediate section, from which decorative motif the node later developed.

The oldest vessels still extant and which, some assume, served as sacred vessels since early Christian times are Roman quartz bowls set in copper or silver gilt, provided with two handles and set on a small base (St. Mark's, Venice). It would thus appear that the Eucharistic vessel originated in the ordinary drinking bowl without a base.

Old vessels that may have served for the Sacrament were of semitransparent bluish glass; there are still fragments of such vessels showing a picture of Christ melted into the bottom of the bowl (British Museum, London).

From early times up to the late Middle Ages chalices were made of various materials: glass, as mentioned above, metal, horn, and wood. As time went on copper and silver gilt were increasingly employed.

The chalice, just as architecture, painting, and sculpture, underwent the changes of styles and tastes proper to the age of its makers. The handles gradually disappeared, and the node, as we see it on many chalices today, became a functional part of the chalice during the 13th century.

In the Romanesque-Byzantine period the chalice was made low and round in shape; in the Gothic period it was higher with a conical cup and a smaller and narrower base; its stem and node were more frequently ornamented with sexfoils. The node, hitherto mostly spherical, became flatter until the latter part of the 15th century when it was frequently broken up into six projections. The Renaissance altered the composition of the chalice very little, though articulation of detail and ornamental motifs changed. During the 17th and 18th centuries its shape became more fanciful with a clumsy and heavy foot, but a more delicate node, which was most often tripartite. The cup was more cylindrical with a rounded bottom, and the whole chalice was richly ornamented and covered with tracery. In the later baroque era three-quarters of the cup was concealed beneath a filigree basket.

At all times all manual processes related to vessel-making have been employed in the making of chalices—embossing, casting, engraving, enameling, and the application of filigree-work.

The modern chalice is characterized by a large and forceful shape with dignity in its simplicity and lack of ornament. Stress is laid on the most important part, the cup. The size of the foot is limited to that demanded by its function, while the node has tended to disappear in the search for a purer and more harmonious line.

A chalice is typically made of precious metal, usually silver and rarely of gold. The General Instruction to the Roman Missal allows other materials to be used, so long as they are appropriate and tasteful. Since the 1980s, transparent crystal chalices that allowed the faithful to see the wine have been popularized.

The Paten. The paten is the Eucharistic dish; the Latin word is derived from the Greek πατάνε. In early Christian times this vessel was usually of glass (blue molten glass). Copper and silver were used in the pre-Carolingian period. In the early days of the Church a large dish was presumably used to collect the bread brought by the faithful from their homes, but with the introduction of the small hosts in the 11th century the paten became smaller. The oldest extant patens indicate the shape the early patens must have had; they were made large and deep since a big loaf of bread was cut up and placed upon them. Patens from the late Middle Ages until the 16th century were strong and vigorous in line. The hollow in the middle was frequently decorated with sexfoils and richly ornamented. In the late Gothic period patens became flatter and almost dish-shaped.

The modern paten has again become larger, and has a deep hollow; it is free of ornament and has a smooth surface; its shape once more conforms to that of the bread dish. Like the chalice, the paten is mostly in silver gilt. In recent times we often find the surface rhodium-plated or enameled; rhodium does not oxidize and provides a surface that is easily cleaned.

The Ciborium. The name, derived from Latin *cibus* signifying nourishment, refers to the function of the ciborium as a dish for bread.

The ciborium and the paten probably originated in the same vessel, the bread dish. This vessel is assumed to have served in the early days to distribute the consecrated bread among the faithful, and later also for reservation of the Eucharist. Nothing is known of the shape of this vessel in early Christian times. A symbol, fish and bread, found in the Roman catacombs, provides only a vague indication. In very early times it was customary to reserve the Eucharist, and the pyx was made for this purpose.

No vessels from the Middle Ages are extant, or if they still exist we fail to recognize them as such. We know only that containers made of wood, ivory, glass, and parchment served for the reservation of the consecrated bread. The 12th century provides more clarification; extant vessels dating from this period indicate that suspended ciboria were employed. These were flat or spherical in shape, with a very small foot. The 13th century brings further elucidation; in this century were made the enameled copper host containers of Limoges, still to be found in a number of old churches and museums. They are small pyxes, about 2 1/2 to 3 inches in diameter, that seem from their conical lids and the cross top to have evolved from the earlier hanging ciboria. The suspended vessels often in the shape of a dove are also enameled copper work from Limoges. The hanging up of such vessels may well have come from the ancient practice of preserving and protecting foodstuffs in this manner.

Later it would seem that the vessels were kept in the sacristy or in a wall niche that could be closed with an iron or wooden door. In the 15th century the vessels for reservation were of greatly varying types; some resembled a cylinder with a conical lid and were obviously a further development of the Limoges pyx; others were bowl-shaped and had a spherical lid. These vessels, so dissimilar in type, were set upon a stem that became increasingly high in the early Gothic period. The shape of foot, stem, and node varied in detail, but remained parallel with the style of the chalice. The ciborium retained the character of a drinking vessel from the 15th century until the present day, its general structure changing little in the baroque era; only its ornamentation was adapted to the style trend of the time. The small cross already seen on the small medieval pyx has been placed unchanged on almost all ciboria from the 15th century until today.

The fundamental conceptions of modern ciboria differ very considerably. We see ciboria in the usual chalice shape with foot, node, and cup, while at the same time attempts are made to design bowl-shaped vessels of various types. The shape of the modern vessel tends to revert to that of the original bread dish. (*See* CIBORIUM).

The Pyx. The pyx is the name usually given to the vessel used to carry the consecrated host to the sick. The word comes from ancient Greek πυξίς and signifies a container made of boxwood.

The oldest pyxes that would seem to have fulfilled this purpose are the enameled copper vessels from Limoges. Since the 13th century pyxes of the most varying kinds have been made in different countries. They frequently resemble a reliquary or small monstrance. This latter type was customary when the visit to the sick took place in procession and with an escort.

In recent times a small silver-gilt box has become the most generally used, in which the receptacle is enclosed in a small patenlike plate, frequently enameled to facilitate cleaning. (*See* PYX).

The Monstrance. The monstrance or ostensory (ostensorium), is a container used for fixed or processional exposition of the Eucharist. The monstrance was unknown in the early Christian Church; it was introduced in the 14th century with the Feast of Corpus Christi.

The monstrance gradually became more widely used. Its shape developed slowly from that of the pyx, which had hitherto served for liturgical ceremonies and was then partially replaced by the monstrance; as a consequence the latter has taken over part of the function of the pyx. The lid of the pyx vessel is enlarged by decorative elements and raised above the bowl. A receptacle is inserted between vessel and lid.

A similar vessel developed simultaneously from the reliquary, particularly from the type with the vertically inserted glass cylinder. From these forebears came the Gothic monstrance with its typical towerlike superstructure, showing an influence of the architecture of the period. The depository for relics became the sacred vessel, the pyx the ostensory.

There are few monstrances from this early period still extant; however, many 15th-century ones of varied types have survived. Renaissance monstrances have still greater variety. Toward the close of the 16th century the flat disk became increasingly common, and in the baroque period they were more uniform in shape, a richly

ornamented flat surface being usually combined with the ray motif. In the 19th century, when there was a general decline in applied art, all historical forms were reproduced; even monstrances with Romanesque style elements were constructed although this vessel did not exist in the period of Romanesque art.

See Also: MONSTRANCE; CHALICE, PATEN, AND VEIL.

Bibliography: See bibliography under specific vessels. J. BRAUN, *Das christliche Altargerät in seinem Sein und in seiner Entwicklung* (Munich 1932), standard work on vessels and altar furnishings. H. LECLERCQ, *Dictionnaire d'archéologie chrétienne et de liturgie* 2.2:1595–1645; 13.2:2392–2414; 14.2:1983–95. J. BAUDOT, *ibid.* 2.2:1646–51. M. RIGHETTI, *Manuale di storia Liturgica,* 4 v. (Milan 1949–53) 1:461–476. F. N. ARNOLDI, *Encyclopedia of World Art* 9:297–300. W. W. WATTS, *Catalogue of Chalices and Other Communion Vessels: Victoria and Albert Museum* (London 1922). A. HENZE and T. FILTHAUT, *Contemporary Church Art,* ed. M. LAVANOUX, tr. C. HASTINGS (New York 1956). *Sakrale Kunst,* v.1 (Zurich 1957), a yearbook, this issue discusses problems of contemporary sacred vessels. M. BURCH, *Sacred Vessels* (Zurich n.d.), pamphlet, issued as guide to contemporary design problems.

[M. BURCH/EDS.]

Part 8: Liturgical Vestments

The style of liturgical vestments is derived from that of the common secular dress worn in early Christian times. From the fourth to the ninth century, garments became formalized in use, took on symbolic meanings, and, as popular styles changed, became distinct from the dress of the ordinary citizen. Eventually some vestments became insignia of an officiant's rank or function, and prescriptions developed regarding materials, color, use, and design.

The vestments discussed here are the main ones used in Roman rite (chasuble and cope, stole, amice, maniple, dalmatic, tunic, alb, and cincture), but counterparts of these, which had a somewhat different evolution, exist in the Eastern Churches. Contemporary trends represent a return to the original form of vestments, approximating these more closely now than in the past 600 years.

Specific vestments are considered historically and from the aspect of prescribed liturgical use under their specific titles. (*See* LITURGICAL VESTMENTS; ALB; AMICE; CHASUBLE; DALMATIC; MANIPLE; STOLE; SURPLICE; and COPE AND HUMERAL VEIL). For papal vesture (*see* PAPAL CEREMONY AND VESTURE); for episcopal vesture (*see* EPISCOPAL CEREMONY AND VESTURE).

The Principal Vestments. *Alb.* The alb is a straight garment with close-fitting sleeves, hung from the shoulders, and extending to the ankles. Usually it is white linen, although originally it was made of wool, and during the Middle Ages it was any color. The alb was derived from the Roman *tunica alba,* worn during the first and second centuries, and is the most unchanged in form of all the liturgical vestments. Originally a baptismal garment in the early church, it gradually became worn by all grades of clerics and monks. When its use became still more restricted from the 12th century onwards, the rochet and surplice developed to replace it. Ungirt, it was an inconvenient garment to wear and became associated in the ancient world with a life of culture and ease. By the addition of a girdle the folds were more controlled, and it could be shortened by being raised above the girdle.

Cincture. The cincture, *cingulum,* is the girdle that is worn with the alb. It was originally a flat band, secured with a clasp or buckle, and made of leather or cloth. Although included with the linen vestments, it can actually be of wool, linen, or silk, the latter being reserved for prelates. It is usually white but can be the color of the outer vestments.

Amice. The amice is a rectangular piece of white linen, to the two upper corners of which are attached long tapes. It was worn under the alb, around the neck like a muffler and secured by tying the tapes around the body. It serves the functions of protecting the other garments.

Stole. The long narrow scarflike vestment worn around the neck and hanging down the front to the waist or crossed in front, is the stole. Several authorities claim that it evolved from the Greek *homophorion* or *orarium,* a linen drape used as a facecloth and worn around the neck or on the head by people of rank. Stoles gradually became ornamental in insignia, and their practical function was fulfilled by the amice. The stole is conferred on the deacon at his ordination. He wears it on his right shoulder and crosses it under his left arm; the priest and the bishop wears the two sides parallel in front. This is the only vestment indicating rank by the manner in which it is worn. Stoles were enlarged during the Middle Ages, developed wide flanging ends, and were heavily ornamented with embroidery, fringe, gold, and jewels. They seem to have been in general use in Gaul as early as the 6th century and not to have come into wide usage in Rome until the 12th century. Recently there has been a tendency to return to a full length, narrow, less ornate stole. The color of the stole denotes the color of the liturgical season.

Maniple. The Roman *mappula* was a table napkin; the *mappa* was a cloth worn on the arm by women to wipe their faces. Both terms were eventually used to refer to the ceremonial napkin, the prototype of the maniple, which was used by persons of rank in pre-Christian times. This item of personal luxury was employed by officials to signal the beginning of public events. The origins of the maniple were then both practical and ceremonial. It was worn on the left arm and used at the Eucharistic banquet until the 12th century. As it became more ornamental and less useful, its function was assigned to the purificator. Like the stole, it became stiff, ornate, and fringed. Short maniples became inconvenient appendages in danger of dragging on the altar. The liturgical reform of Vatican II rendered the use of the maniple obsolete.

Chasuble. The form of the chasuble, outermost garment of the celebrant, has gone through successive alterations. Liturgical books traditionally referred to it as the *planeta,* the term applied to the earlier *paenula* by the fourth century. By the seventh century it was called the chasuble from a popular nickname associating it with the *casula,* the small tent of shepherds. This term is understandable considering that the early *paenula* and its liturgical derivative was an enveloping cone-shaped garment with an opening at the top, which permitted the head to emerge. Ancient representations of both the secular *paenula* and the early sacerdotal vestment show that it was semicircular in pattern, with the two flat edges sewn together to establish a single front seam and a conical shape. This accounts for the characteristic horizontal drape of the fabric, freeing the arms. It is seen in statues, mosaics, manuscripts, and paintings up to the high Renaissance.

Human clothing has usually consisted of two basic garments, an undergarment draped to the figure in vertical folds, and an overgarment draped horizontally across the body as a cloak for warmth and protection, or as a mark of distinction or pure ornamentation. The ancient mantle, worn over the toga and open in front, was the garment of ordinary citizens. It was both a mark of distinction and a protective garment. This evolved into the cope. The ancient *paenula* was a protective garment also, distinct from the mantle, having a front seam and being made of less refined fabric. It was always colored and was associated with the poor and travelers. Although admitted into Rome by the third century, it never became an imperial garment. Thus the chasuble is derived from the encompassing garment that gave warmth and protection.

As early as the sixth century it began to show changes. They resulted in the loss of its original shape and meaning as a garment, turning it more and more into an elaborate costume. First the sides were shortened, the front was cut to a point, and eventually both front and back were shortened. During the Middle Ages abbreviation of size continued and elaborate embroidery and heavy fabrics began to be used. After changes from the 13th to the 17th century, the chasuble resembled two stiff panels joined at the shoulders. Post-Reformation models evolving into this form exhibited national variations—Italian (Roman), Spanish, French (Gallican), and German. The orphrey, which had originated as a decoration covering the front seam, became enlarged and ornamental, adorning both front and back panels. The so-called "Gothic" chasuble is actually neo-Gothic coming from the period of the Gothic revival. It was an attempt at an ample embracing vestment, made at a time when relationship with the original *paenula* was lost. It was simply a fuller version of the derivative fiddle-back panel form. It has two unadorned shoulder seams allowing for the vertical draping of the fabric, and, compared to the original chasubles, it was considerably abbreviated in length. Often a Y-shaped cross served as the orphrey.

In the wake of the liturgical reforms of Vatican II, the design of the chasuble gradually returned to its traditional origins, a return to the style of the original chasuble developed. Ornamentation, for which there is no regulation, became more simplified and restrained. The enveloping function of the garment and the color of the liturgical season now assumes a primary role in its design.

Dalmatic. The outer garment of the deacon, the dalmatic was derived from a woolen garment originating in the Greek province of Dalmatia; they displaced the awkward Roman toga for general wear during the first half of the 4th century. The early Christians are usually pictured wearing the dalmatic in catacomb paintings. These frequently show two *clavi,* vertical bands of decoration, which, even today, should be the only ornamentation of the dalmatic. The dalmatic was conferred on Roman deacons as early as the 4th century even though it still remained a secular garment for emperors, consuls, and even the French kings through the 7th century. Throughout the 10th century it was usually of white linen or wool; by the 12th century silk prevailed. Today it is prescribed as an outer garment, usually matching the chasuble, and differing from the tunic by being longer and having wider sleeves. In the past the sides were split to facilitate walking, and eventually the split extended to the under seam of the sleeves. Now there is a tendency to restore the normal pattern.

Liturgical Colors. The liturgical colors for vestments are white, red, green, purple, violet, and rose, with gold as a substitute for white and, if necessary, for other festive colors. No shade or tint of these colors is prescribed, and there is no limitation of colors used for ornament or lining. The first color sequence was established by Innocent III in the 13th century, printed in Burckard's *Ordo Missae* in 1502, and made obligatory in the General Rubrics of the Missal of 1570.

Prescriptives and Regulations. As early as the reign of St. Stephen I in the 3d century there were Church regulations regarding the use and appearance of vestments. Today these appear principally in the General Instruction to the Roman Missal, and adaptations by local bishops' conferences.

The Art of Vestments. Throughout history there have been numerous examples of precious vestments. Although some are beautiful in their form as garments, more often it is the ornamentation that distinguishes them, sometimes to the detriment of their symbolism as garments. They combine richness of fabric with refinement of embroidery.

Early Christian. After the Edict of Milan in the early fourth century public services of worship were held more openly, and enriched versions of the dress of the times began to be reserved for the celebration of the Eucharist. There is record of a golden cloth cloak given by Constantine in 330 to a church in Jerusalem for use at Easter. With Constantinople established as the capital of the empire there began a long period of Byzantine influence on the art of the West, extending to the 12th century. An indescribable delicacy and richness of embroidery developed, which harmonized with the glory of the mosaics in church interiors. These, frequently depicting clerics, showed the type, shapes, and decoration of the vestments as well as the woven patterns of the fabrics. Gold and silver threads as well as silk and jewels were used with rich variety. Sometimes the backgrounds were so well filled that the original fabric was almost completely obscured.

Byzantine work at its finest is seen in the Imperial Dalmatic, sometimes known as the dalmatic of Charlemagne or of Pope Leo III. It is probably the most important medieval object in the treasury of St. Peters, and is variously dated from the 9th to the 15th century. It is most likely a work of the 13th-century Byzantine renaissance. The embroidered iconography includes the Transfiguration, Last Supper, and Second Coming of Christ. The design in gold and silver, with some silk, almost obscures the basic steel-blue silk fabric. The cut is that of the Greek *homophorion,* similar to a modern dalmatic.

One of the earliest extant examples of embroidery is a sixth-century roundel, Coptic in origin, in the collection of the Victoria and Albert Museum. It has three figures stitched in silk and is characteristic of the ornamental embroidery and tapestry weavings that were used by the Copts as orphreys, stoles, and ornaments on sacred vesture. Extant fragments indicate a well-developed tradition of the use of figures of Christ, the Virgin, angels, and saints, as well as an interesting variety of symbols.

Romanesque and Gothic. In the West there is sparse evidence of the ornamental development of vestments through the Romanesque period, although manuscripts and sculptures depicting them suggest a vigor comparable to that of the architecture.

But it was during the Gothic age that a flourishing textile production joined with the skill of designers and craftsmen to produce precious and elaborate works of vesture. Large textile centers were frequently attached to monasteries of the Cistercians in England, the Humble Fathers of Saint Michael, who moved from Egypt to Florence, and the great centers at Lyons and Seville. The Benedictines and Humiliates joined forces in Florence making it a powerful textile center. More than 200 communities existed in Florence, where there were 30,000 craftsmen producing 100,000 pieces of cloth per year, exclusive of cotton and linen. In the same period designing skills were applied to objects ranging from the refined manuscript to the sculptures in majestic cathedrals. The embroidered and woven designs of vestments harmonized with the other artistic works of the time. The tradition of the Eastern Churches was well known. Varied fabrics and dyes were available, and embroideries were ingenious. Artists were usually anonymous. Though several persons might be engaged on a piece, apparently individuals often did a single work. Embroidery was undertaken by both men and women, laymen and religious alike. Much time was given to it in certain convents, and gifts were often made by noble ladies.

From 1250 to 1350 the English embroidery that became internationally prized for its perfection was Opus Anglicanum. Successive popes commissioned or were given vestments and copes of Opus Anglicanum, and there are numerous records of such works on inventories in France, Italy, and Spain. Bearing some similarity in design to early manuscripts such as KELLS and LINDISFARNE, the background was originally covered with circles or other geometric figures, which were filled with figures of saints and angels. Later an architectural division of the background into a series of arches radiating from the center of the vestment developed. A characteristic mode of treating figures evolved, which is especially apparent in the manner of embroidering the faces, split stitches being made in spiral patterns on the cheeks and chin, across the forehead and down the nose. The S-curve posture, the folds of drapery, and the gestures are similar to those found in the manuscripts and sculptures of the same period. Although a number of fine examples of Opus Anglicanum vestments, orphreys, and borders exist, the most impressive example is the Butler-Bowden cope, a 14th-century piece in the Victoria and Albert Museum. It is somewhat unusual in that the basic material is not hard surfaced, but is a crimson velvet that has been embroidered with silks, gold, silver gilt, and seed pearls. The whole was covered with a fine material on which the design was first traced. The embroidery was then worked through both layers and the linen backing, the fine material being cut away once the embroidery was completed. Eight figures are embroidered into the orphrey, some of them prelates garbed in full liturgical vesture of the time.

Although the Opus Anglicanum represented advanced development during the medieval period, on the Continent similar work was being done, an especially inventive tradition prevailing in Germany. Many of the continental works lack the gold dominant in the Opus Anglicanum but show greater variety of stitches.

Renaissance to Baroque. From the 13th to the 17th century, vestments changed repeatedly in form and ornamentation. Three major phases of change took place, each a mistake being corrected by an additional error. In the late Middle Ages the magnificent materials used (heavy brocades, elaborate embroideries, gems) were unsuited to the function of the garment and the manner of draping desired. The overweight material was retained in the Renaissance, and the form was sacrificed, being cut away more and more at the shoulders. Finally, in more recent times, the neo-Gothic began to restore the length and shoulder width but neglected the true form and nature of the chasuble.

In the late 14th and in the 15th century embroidery work lost some of its earlier perfection. The figures embroidered into pillar and cross orphreys were less graceful and symbolic emblems were meager. Refinement of design and execution tended to disappear. By the end of the 16th century secular subjects predominated, judging from inventory lists: griffins, columbines, waterlilies, oak leaves, pheasants, and hawks. At the same time new techniques were admitted into textile weaving in the West along with velvets, brocades, and damasks. Embroidered units were worked separately on linen and sewn onto the vestment separately, the edges being broken with rays of gold. Repetitions of design suggests the poverty of inspiration. By the late 15th and the early 16th century, chasubles were generally fiddle-shaped, many of the earlier vestments having been cut down. Sumptuous materials of wearing apparel were often donated for the use of the Church. During the Reformation quantities of vestments were destroyed; some were burned and the gold reclaimed, the jewels removed; others were distributed and cut up for wearing apparel and furnishings.

The amice and alb, when decorated, were adorned by the adding of rich fabrics sewn in strips to the linen. On the amice they formed an outer collar around the neck and outside the chasuble. They served as outer cuffs for the alb and ornamented the center front and back hem. Apparels usually had some embroidery added that harmonized with but did not necessarily duplicate the liturgical color of the outer vestments. Sometimes the stole and maniple matched the apparels. The rise of the lace industry in Europe had its effect on the comparatively untouched alb. Needlepoint lace is first mentioned in an Italian inventory of 1493, and within the next century pattern books for laces appeared. Soon albs were decorated with borders, cuffs, and collars of lace until the border decoration eventually assumed the appearance of an entire skirt of lace. Some of the finest laces adorn such albs: *punto in aria, gros point de Venise,* rose point, and *point de France.* Although these usages constituted a degeneration of the form of the alb, they occasioned exquisite lacemaking. The use of apparels has never been completely lost; they are still found in Milan, Lyons, and Spain.

In the late 16th century, St. Charles BORROMEO tried to prevent the curtailment of the form of vestments, which was already under way. His "Directions" comprise the most copious and detailed prescriptions in the history of liturgical propriety. His prescriptions did not regard shape but were concerned with size, requiring ample, floor-length, simple vestments. Various changes in style that affected the integrity of vestments after his time were optional.

The worldliness of the Renaissance and the elaborate display of the baroque and the rococo caused a fashion of meaningless decor, bountiful flowers, over-high miters, large hoods, over-wide ophreys, stiff and heavy copes, all rendered in gorgeous, brilliant textiles, technically remarkable for raised figures, "needle painting," and shading. The post-Reformation up to 19th-century revivalisms saw the ascendance of a kind of theatrical vestment-making; the flare for display reached its height in the Rococo.

The 20th Century. The Gothic revival was discernible in the neo-Gothic vestment-making of the earlier part of the 20th century. The style did not achieve the goal of restoring the traditional form of vestments, but it did lead to this restoration by replacing the fiddle-back chasuble. The postwar renaissance, especially in continental Europe, had evidenced a return to the classic *paenula* shape; artisans tend to employ modern materials, ample but light, with simple trim and contrasting fabric. These vestments complement the simplicity and clarity of the best of contemporary church architecture. The modern renewal of the liturgy has been supported by the interest of vestment-makers both in Europe and America; however, in general, the vestment has received less attention than architecture. Some European churches, planned with attention to liturgical service, reveal awareness of architectural form that extends to every detail of the church including the appointment of vestments. The harmony is observable in the chapel by H. Matisse at VENCE, St.

Kuris (Bruges), and St. Thérèse (Audincourt). The Abbey of Sainte André in Belgium produced vestments that show awareness of their function, and since 1948 has provided a steady stream of scholarly articles and inspiring illustrations in *L'Ouvroir liturgique,* the regular supplement to *L'Art d'église.* The works of Sister Augustina Flüeler at the Paramentenwerkstätte Sancta Klara in Stans, Switzerland, combine the best elements of both the contemporary and the traditional. Artistic embroidery has been revived at the German Saarbruecker Paramente-Manufaktur of Ella Broesch and encouraged by the works and writings of Beryl Dean in England.

Chapter 7, section 128, of the *Constitution on the Sacred Liturgy* calls for "an early revision of the canons and ecclesiastical statutes which govern the provision of material things involved in liturgical worship," and specifically mentions vestments.

Bibliography: A. W. PUGIN, *Glossary of Ecclesiastical Ornament and Costume* (London 1846). E. E. VIOLLET-LE-DUC, *Dictionnaire raisonné du mobilier français de l'époque carlovingienne à la renaissance,* 6 v. (Paris 1868–75). J. BRAUN, *Die liturgische Gewandung im Occident und Orient* (Freiburg 1907); *Die liturgische Gegenwart und Vergangenheit: Ein Handbuch der Paramentik* (Freiburg 1912). E. A. ROULIN, *Vestments and Vesture,* tr. J. MC-CANN (St. Louis 1931; Westminster, MD, 1950). R. JAMES, *Origin and Development of Roman Liturgical Vestments* (2d ed. Exeter, 1934). P. F. ANSON, *Churches, Their Plan and Furnishing* (Milwaukee, 1948). H. NORRIS, *Church Vestments* (New York, 1950). B. DEAN, *Ecclesiastical Embroidery* (London 1958). R. LESAGE, *Vestments and Church Furniture,* tr. F. MURPHY (New York, 1960). Righetti 1:488–524. *L'Art d'église* (Bruges 1927–), quarterly.

[J. BECKER/EDS.]

Part 9: Episcopal and Abbatial

The origin and development of the use by prelates of the miter, ring, crozier, and coat of arms as marks of dignity and authority, is of interest to the history of forms of art.

Miter. The use of headgear as a symbol of regal, or of priestly status antedates Christianity. The prelatial miter takes its name from the word *mitra,* meaning in Greek a headband, or diadem, also a conical Persian cap, and in Latin, a bonnet secured to the head by a band. From the conical cap of Oriental origin is derived the papal tiara, and, according to Galbreath, the miter shares the same prototype. A distinctive official headdress was not used by bishops before the 11th century. It first appears as a round bonnet secured by a headband, fastened at the sides, the loose ends depending like lappets. Early in the 12th century this bonnet developed lobes, or points to right and left. By the end of the same century the points shifted to back and front, and the lappets fell at the back. In this form the miter appears on the seal of William, Archbishop of Bourges (1201).

Originally of white linen with embroidery (orphrey) the miter was progressively elaborated until three distinct types emerged in the Middle Ages, differentiated by the quality of the materials used in their construction: (1) the *mitra simplex,* of plain white linen or silk damask, with red fillets; (2) the *mitra aurifrigiata,* of silk damask, cloth of silver or gold, embroidered but without jewels, except seed pearls; and (3) the *mitra pretiosa,* adorned with jewels and plates of precious metal. Before the ornamentation of the miter was standardized greater freedom in its adornment was possible. Woodward mentions a Swedish miter of the 14th century from the cathedral of Lenköping bearing plates of silver gilt enameled with figures of saints and with the arms of the bishop and his diocese.

Keeping its essential form the miter has accommodated itself to changing fashions. In early examples the points were comparatively low, but in the later Middle Ages they began to soar until with the advent of the baroque style they reached the exaggerated height that still largely prevails. An example of a modern miter that reflects the taste of an earlier period is the very pleasing abbatial miter used at the Benedictine abbey at Fort Augustus in Scotland, a low miter richly embroidered in designs that recall the intricacies of Celtic illumination. A good example of the late medieval miter of the heightened form appears as part of the reliquary of St. Lambert in the cathedral at Liège.

The abbatial miter was first conceded in 1063 to Engelsinus, abbot of the monastery of St. Augustine at Canterbury. This was no doubt the *mitra simplex.* In 1267 exempt abbots were conceded the use of the *aurifrigiata.* The *pretiosa,* however, was generally reserved to prelates of at least episcopal rank. (*See* MITER.)

Rings. Rings of a distinctly Christian character, bearing symbols of the faith and figures of saints, were in use among the faithful at an early date, but the ring as a mark of episcopal dignity and authority appears to have come into use no earlier than the sixth century. St. Isidore, Bishop of Seville (593–633), mentions the bestowal of a ring as "signum pontificalis honoris," as one feature of the consecration ceremony. The bishop's ring, besides being a mark of honor, stands as a symbol of the espousal by the prelate of the flock over which he presides. Some early prelatial rings appear to have been signet rings. It was only later that the custom of adorning the official ring of bishops and abbots with some semiprecious stone became common. The stone most often used appears to have been the amethyst (*see* RINGS, LITURGICAL USE OF).

Crozier. The crozier as a symbol of spiritual authority antedates both the ring and the miter, its use going back to the 4th century. The nature of this authority is suggested by its form, which is that of the pastoral staff, or shepherd's crook. The earliest examples of the crozier that appear on episcopal and abbatial seals are extremely simple, approximating very nearly the staff actually used by shepherds. With changing fashions in taste, however, the pastoral staff, like the miter, gradually became ornate. Decorative elaboration occurs chiefly on the curved section, or crook. An early example of the tendency to elaborate is the crozier of carved wood used by St. Boniface, the Apostle of Germany (d. 754), which is still preserved at the monastery of Fulda. The curved section of the staff encloses the figure of a lamb surmounted by a cross, presumably a simpler version of the more elaborated Agnus Dei, which in the baroque period is often seen depending from the crook. The crozier, while keeping its essential character of pastoral staff or shepherd's crook, has undergone many accidental changes dictated by the changing taste of successive periods. The transition from late Gothic to baroque produced the type that is in fairly general use today. An example of late medieval taste can be seen in the reliquary of St. Lambert at Liège, mentioned above. An interesting modern crozier designed in the spirit of an earlier period is in use at the Benedictine abbey at Fort Augustus (Scotland). The staff is of a dark wood and the silver crook is elaborated into the form of a dragon, recalling fantasies of medieval illumination.

Episcopal Coat of Arms. Armorial insignia came into fashion in the 12th century. They were adopted at first as a means of identification on the field of battle, where warriors of both sides were encased in nearly identical armor. As a convenient means of identification it began to appear on seals and to serve also as a device for authentication. As such the cognizance of the warrior was adopted by prelates, and in time the custom of displaying a coat of arms as a mark of rank as well as a means of identification became permanently established among churchmen (*see* HERALDRY).

Normally the personal arms only, inherited or assumed, are to appear upon the shield. A deviation from this rule has become customary in the U.S., where the bishop impales his arms with those of his diocese, the abbot his personal coat with that of his monastery. Behind his shield of arms the bishop places the processional cross. This cross in the case of an archbishop has two traverses. Behind an abbot's shield is placed the crozier, with the "sudarium," a sort of protective scarf, attached to the staff. In the U.S. both the bishop and the abbot place a miter on top of the shield to the left; the bishop places a crozier to the right of his cross behind the shield. Above the shield is placed the ecclesiastical hat with its cords and tassels depending to either side. The rank of the prelate is indicated by the color of this hat and the number of tassels depending from it. The hat of the bishop and of the archbishop is green, that of the abbot, black. A bishop's hat has 12 tassels depending, six to either side of the shield, so also that of an abbot. The number of tassels for an archbishop is increased to 20, 10 to either side of the shield. If the bishop, or archbishop, is also a cardinal the hat is red, the number of tassels 30, 15 to either side of the shield.

The prelatial coat of arms, like the miter and crozier, has reflected current trends in taste; fashions in its design range from the vigor and grace of the best heraldic art of the Middle Ages to the overloaded extravagances of the 18th century. In the latter period the shield was often abandoned in favor of the cartouche, usually oval in shape. Prelates of noble birth often placed over the shield, or cartouche, a coronet indicating their secular rank. In recent times this practice has been forbidden by Rome. The prince-bishops and abbots of the *ancien régime,* being temporal as well as spiritual rulers, placed behind their shields of arms a sword crossed in saltire with the crozier. Crests are not normally used by ecclesiastics, but there is a curious exception to this rule to be seen in the arms of a medieval bishop of the Palatine See of Durham, where the crest of the bishop's family appears issuing from the top of the miter.

As an art form the ecclesiastical coat of arms has many decorative uses in the embellishment of vestments, sacred vessels, monuments, churches, and other buildings connected with diocesan activities. It has also a modest place in the liturgy for it is customary to display upon the two small kegs of wine presented by a bishop to his consecrator, the consecrator's arms and his own.

Bibliography: W. SMITH and S. CHEETHAM, *A Dictionary of Christian Antiquities,* 2 v. (Hartford 1880). J. WOODWARD, *Ecclesiastical Heraldry* (London 1894). D. L. GALBREATH, *Papal Heraldry* (A Treatise on Ecclesiastical Heraldry 1; Cambridge, England, 1930). B. B. HEIM, *Coutumes et droit héraldiques de l'église* (Paris 1949). M. RIGHETTI, Manuale di storia liturgica, 4 v. (Milan 1949–55) 1:531–539.

[W. W. BAYNE]

LITURGICAL ARTS SOCIETY

A national organization which existed from 1928 to 1972 for the renewal of liturgical art and aesthetics. The ideals of the society were drawn from the following propositions: (1) the official public worship of the Church has infinite spiritual value and a unique and majestic beauty; (2) this value and beauty demand that the products of artistic endeavor used in the service of the Church embody the highest quality of art and architecture that is free from commercialism and sentimentality. Its principal contribution to the Liturgical Movement among Roman Catholics in the United States was the quarterly journal *Liturgical*

Arts, which served an important role in promoting the renewal of liturgical art and architecture and stimulating conversation among artists, architects, artisans, liturgists and clerics. In its latter years, the society suffered from a chronic lack of funds, leading finally to its demise in 1972.

Bibliography: S. J. WHITE, *Art, Architecture and Liturgical Reform: The Liturgical Arts Society (1928–1972)* (New York 1990).

[M. LAVANOUX/EDS.]

LITURGICAL BOOKS OF THE ROMAN RITE

The term liturgical books means the official books of the ROMAN RITE published by authority of the Holy See. The official text of a liturgical book is contained in what is called a typical edition (*editio typica*), one that is produced by the authority and under the supervision of the Congregation of DIVINE WORSHIP AND THE DISCIPLINE OF SACRAMENTS.

ORIGIN AND HISTORICAL DEVELOPMENTS

It seems clear that in the earliest days the only book used at Christian worship was the Bible from which the lessons were read. The account of Justin Martyr (d. *c.* 165) in his first *Apology* (67; J. Quasten, ed., *Monumenta eucharista et liturgica vetustissima* [Bonn 1935–37] 19–20) speaks of reading the memoirs of the Apostles or the writings of the Prophets before the Eucharist, but for the latter he mentions only that the president offered up "prayers and thanksgivings" to the "best of his power." This means that he improvised in accordance with a central theme, and although such solemn prayers would have been prepared in advance, there does not seem at first to have been any written formula that was used. The first written evidence of a formulary for the Eucharist, or at least for its anaphora (eucharistic prayer), is to be found in the *Apostolic Tradition*, although this, it appears, was not an official book (4; B. Botte, ed., *La Tradition apostolique de saint Hippolyte: Essai de reconstitution* [1963] 10–16). It is possible that certain formulas became more or less stereotyped before they were written down, and after the Edict of Milan and the peace of the Church (313), the development of a systematic liturgy can be discerned. At the end of the fourth century St. Ambrose (*De Sacramentis* 4.5, 6) quotes what is clearly the central part of the Roman Canon.

Early Roman Books. The point had been reached when certain of the formulas were being written down; once this happened formulas naturally tended to become

"The Hours of Jeanne d'Evreux": Folio 154. "St. Louis Receives Breviary in Prison," Folio 155. (©Francis G. Mayer/CORBIS)

fixed. Little books (*libelli*) were provided for some celebrants as a form of *aide-mémoire* and appear to have been used in conjunction with the Roman stational churches and for domestic celebration of the Eucharist. The *libelli* were the immediate forerunners of the Sacramentaries. The most famous collection of Roman libelli is the LEONINE SACRAMENTARY (Veronense), a private compilation of various *libelli missae* collected outside Rome. An interesting feature of this collection is that certain sections of it are made up of *libelli* forming self-contained units that seem to belong to a transitional period, when formulas were gradually becoming fixed. The Old GELASIAN SACRAMENTARY (Vat Reg Lat 316) was an official compilation with both Roman and Gallican elements. In the evolution of the Roman liturgical books, the Sacramentaries are characteristic in that they are books for the use of a person performing a function and contain solely those formulae that were proper to the celebrant. The Sacramentaries contained the rite as used by the bishop in the celebration of the Eucharist, the conferring of Baptism, Orders, etc. The parts read or sung by others—the choir, reader, deacon, etc.— are found in other books and it is these that must now be examined.

Primitively, a Bible was used for the scripture readings. The readings were not yet fixed at this stage; the lec-

tor or reader concluded each reading at a signal from the president. As time went on and the course of Scripture readings tended to become fixed, points of beginning and conclusion were marked so that the PERICOPES could easily be found. This book was called the *Comes* or *Liber comicus;* from this developed the *Evangeliarium* (EVANGELARY or Book of Gospels) and *Lectionarium* (Lectionary) for use by the lector. Similarly there emerged the book containing the parts for the choir (*Antiphonarium Missae, Liber antiphonarius,* or *Gradalis*).

The Biblical lessons for the Office, the sermons of the Fathers, and the acts of the martyrs were gradually collected into separate books. The Lectionary, the Homiliary, the *Legenda,* etc. The last named, distinct from the Martyrology which was primarily a list of anniversaries, contained the account of the sufferings of each martyr; it was read at Rome up to the eighth century at the cemetery basilica of the martyr during the night Office. It was also called the *Passionale.* The Psalter was written out in the order that the Psalms were to be sung, and for the responsories and antiphons there were the *Liber responsorialis* and the *Antiphonarium Officii.* Hymns appeared in the West as part of the Church worship service in the fifth century. They were often included in the Antiphonary, but a separate collection also existed (*Hymnarium*). At a later date when sequences were introduced, they were added to the *Liber antiphonarius* or *Gradualis.* Similarly when parts of the Ordinary of the Mass came to be padded with musical phrases, these pieces were added to the Gradual or Antiphonary, or else contained in a separate book, the Troper, as it was known in medieval England (or *Troparium*); the earliest known example is the tenth-century St. Martial Troper (*Cod. Par.* 1240).

The early liturgical books contained very few ritual or ceremonial directions, although some of the Sacramentaries occasionally add a word or two in this respect. The rubrics were probably the last elements of the liturgy to be written down since tradition governed the ceremonial for some time. With increasing elaboration of the papal ceremonial and the use of the Roman rite all over Europe, particularly in Gaul, it became necessary to provide precise directions. This guidance was provided by the Ordinals (*Ordines Romani*), the first of which was intended as an accompaniment in Gaul of the Gelasian and Gregorian Sacramentaries. There is a series of 15 of these *Ordines,* dating from the seventh to the fourteenth centuries; they were printed first by J. Mabillon in his *Musaeum Italicum* (reprinted in *Patrologia Latina,* ed. J. P. Migne [Paris 1878–90] 88:851–1408; critical edition, M. Andrieu, *Les 'Ordines Romani' du haut moyen-âge* [Louvain 1931–61]) and form the basis for any study of the development of the ceremonial of the Roman rite. The earliest is probably Ordo VII, the greater part of which is to be found in the Gelasian Sacramentary. Ordo I is of great importance and value for its depiction of a papal mass of the Roman Rite circa 700.

Medieval Developments. From around the beginning of the ninth century, the Sacramentary was divided into three books, and thus eventually emerged the Pontifical, Ritual, and Missal, the last named absorbing the parts of all ministers, choir, and people at Mass as well as the celebrant's part. Thus, the whole of the rite was in one book and could be used for low Mass, which was at that time becoming common. The Pontifical contained the complete text of all rites peculiar to a bishop and the Ritual (known also a century or two later as Manuale, *Alphabetum Sacerdotum, Sacerdotale, Pastorale*), those rites ordinarily performed by a priest (*see* PONTIFICAL, ROMAN; RITUAL, ROMAN; AND MISSAL, ROMAN).

On the other hand, the various books required for the Divine Office, by means of an abbreviation of the lessons, were finally contained within the covers of a single volume in the 12th and 13th centuries. Thus emerged the BREVIARY, which, as its name indicates, was an abbreviation (at least of the lessons) of the choir Office, although

it was not long before the shortened lessons were used in the choir also. Side by side with the Missal and Breviary, however, the use of separate books (Psalter, Hymnal, Antiphonary, Gradual) continued in use to provide the musical (plainchant) settings needed for the singing of the Office and Mass.

COUNCIL OF TRENT'S REFORM OF LITURGICAL BOOKS

It would be a mistake to regard the emergence of these various medieval liturgical books as a sign of liturgical uniformity throughout the West. While the general pattern of the Roman rite as it had evolved was followed everywhere, there were great differences in detail: local ''uses'' of the Roman rite in whole provinces, dioceses, or religious orders, proliferated. In addition, the great number of feasts of saints observed in the local calendars, and particularly those of the religious orders, practically obscured the proper celebration of the LITURGICAL YEAR, and the text of the liturgical books in many instances (e.g., lessons at Matins and of the Martyrology) was in a corrupt state. Moreover, there were elements in some of the Breviaries and Missals, hymns and antiphons especially, that were really unworthy of worship in the Church. By the beginning of the sixteenth century the time was ripe for reform.

The Council of Trent decreed the general reform that was needed and appointed a commission to deal with the matter, but when the Council closed (December 1563), the commission had not finished its task; the matter was remitted to the pope, Pius IV. He died (1565) before the work was concluded, and the first of the reformed books of the Roman rite were issued by his successor, Pius V (d. 1572). The Roman Breviary appeared in 1568; the Roman Missal, in 1570. At the same time the pope abolished all rites and uses that could not show a prescription of at least 200 years.

In 1588 Sixtus V established the Congregation of RITES for the purpose of carrying out the decrees of the Council of Trent regarding the public worship of the Church. Since that date this Congregation has been a potent influence for uniformity, particularly in watching over the correction and orthodoxy of text of the liturgical books. The first book to be issued as a result of this Congregation's work was the Roman Pontifical in 1596, which was made obligatory on all bishops of the Roman rite. The Ceremonial of Bishops was published by order of Clement VIII in 1600. The immediate source for this book was the *Ceremoniale Romanae Ecclesiae* of 1516, but as an official liturgical book the Ceremonial of Bishops was an innovation, giving directions for episcopal functions, as well as norms for the daily liturgy in cathedrals and collegiate churches. The reform that Trent initiated was complete with the issuance of the Roman Ritual by Paul V in 1614.

As they were issued in compliance with the instructions of the Council of Trent, the principal books of the Roman Rite remained essentially the same up to the twentieth century. Both Missal and Breviary underwent reform at the hands of Pius X in 1911 and Pius XII in 1955. A further change was the promulgation of Pius XII's Ordinal for Holy Week in 1955 (*Ordo hebdomadae sanctae instauratus*), containing the restored Holy Week services. This necessarily entailed changes in the liturgical books affected. The Code of Rubrics (1960) resulted in the publication of new typical editions of Missal and Breviary in 1962.

VATICAN II'S REFORM OF LITURGICAL BOOKS

The *Constitution on the Sacred Liturgy* of the Vatican Council II, promulgated in 1963, called for revision of the liturgical books of the Roman Rite, with a view to simplifying the rites so that the texts and rites "express more clearly the holy things which they signify" and that "the Christian people, as far as possible, be enabled to understand them [the texts and rites] with ease and to take part in them fully and actively" (21). This reform marked the first revision of the official Roman liturgical books after a lapse of four centuries.

The task of reform through revision of service books was entrusted to the CONSILIUM for the Implementation of the Constitution in 1964, and subsequently in 1969 to the Congregation for Divine Worship. With permission being granted for vernacular translations of Latin *editiones typicae*, bishops' conferences established language groups to facilitate the production and publication of vernacular editions of liturgical books. In the English-speaking world, the INTERNATIONAL COMMISSION ON ENGLISH IN THE LITURGY was established by some dozen English-speaking episcopal conferences. Following the principles set forth in the *Instruction on Translation of Liturgical Texts, (Comme le prévoit)*, ICEL had produced the English version of liturgical texts of the Roman Rite that were adopted by the individual bishops' conferences.

These postconciliar liturgical texts, as all previous official books of the Roman Rite, are published by the authority of the Holy See. However, much distinguishes them from the liturgical books of the past: in variety of options, alternatives, and suggestions; in liturgical theory; in simplicity; and in pastoral concern. Apparent is the conciliar concern for intelligibility and careful restoration, as well as emphasis upon corporate action of the local church.

Bibliography: L. C. SHEPPARD, *The Liturgical Books* (New York 1962). T. KLAUSER, *The Western Liturgy and Its History: Some Reflections on Recent Studies,* tr. F. L. CROSS (New York 1952). C. VOGEL, *Medieval Liturgy: An Introduction to the Sources* (Washington, DC 1986). E. PALAZZO, *A History of Liturgical Books from the Beginning to the Thirteenth Century* (Collegeville, Minn 1998).

[L. C. SHEPPARD/J. A. WYSOCKI/J. M. SCHELLMAN/EDS.]

LITURGICAL CALENDAR, I: CATHOLIC

Although from the beginning of the Christian Era, the Christians followed the Julian solar calendar of 46 B.C. for general purposes, and with it adopted the Roman usage of counting the days of the month in a continuous series in relation to nones, ides, and kalends, they also evolved a specifically Christian calendar, the center of which was the day of the Resurrection.

Easter. Since the majority of the early Christians were Jewish converts, it is understandable that from the outset the Christian calendar was governed by the fact that the death and Resurrection of Christ had taken place at the time of the chief Jewish feast, the Pasch, or Passover, celebrated on the 14th day of the month of Nisan, i.e., at the full moon following the Spring equinox. However, rather than literally follow the Jewish Passover, since this would necessitate the commemoration of the Resurrection on a different day of the week each year, Christian custom (sanctioned at the Council of NICAEA I in 325; *Concilorum occumenicorum decreta* [Bologna-Freiburg 1962] 2–3, n.6) fixed the anniversary of Christ's Resurrection on the actual day of the week (the first day) on which the Resurrection had taken place. As a result, Easter falls on the first day of the week (Sunday) after the first full moon following the spring equinox, and can be as early as March 22 and as late as April 25.

The Christian Week. The Christians also adopted from the Jews the seven-day week, dividing it the Christians much as the Jews did, but with some striking differences. Since Christ had died on the eve of the Passover Sabbath and had risen from the dead on the first day of the week following that Sabbath, the sacred character of the Jewish Sabbath (the last day of their week) was now transferred, in memory of the Resurrection, to "the first day of the week" (Acts 20.7), "the Lord's Day" (Rv 1.10), "the day named after the sun" (St. Justin, *First Apology,* ch. 67; *c.* 150). Likewise the Jewish tradition of a day of rest was transferred from the Sabbath to SUNDAY, becoming law in the fourth century. Again, the traditional Jewish fasts on Tuesday and Thursday were advanced by a day to Wednesday (the day of the betrayal of Christ in Passover week) and Friday (the day of the Crucifixion). Apart from the first day of the week, however, Christian usage retained Jewish designations for all the days of the week, thus the second day (Monday) became *feria secunda* and the Sabbath became *Sabbathum* (Saturday).

Movable Feasts. By the mid–fourth century there was a cycle of commemorations that had evolved around the feast of Easter, again paralleling Jewish usage. Pentecost, the celebration of the descent of the Holy Spirit, was related to Easter much as the Jewish Pentecost (Feast of Tabernacles, or First-Fruits) related to the Passover, and at the same interval of 50 days. Likewise, the penitential period before Easter, said by LEO I (d. 461) to be of apostolic institution, was modeled on that observed by the Jews before the Passover. Ascension Day, however, was determined by the fact that, as the Acts of the Apostles testify (Acts 1.3), the event had taken place 40 days after the Resurrection.

Computation of Easter. In the early centuries the diversity of rules for observing Easter was the cause of much strife among the churches (*see* EASTER CONTROVERSY; COMPUTUS). If various computations of the lunar cycle were current (e.g., those of Alexandria and Rome), the matter was further complicated by the adherence of some Christians (QUARTODECIMANS) to the variable weekday. The Council of Nicaea, however, imposed Sunday as the fixed day of the commemoration of the Resurrection; the universal acceptance of the Alexandrian 19-year cycle or COMPUTUS of Easter is due to the Scythian monk DIONYSIUS EXIGUUS at Rome in 526, although the Celtic Church still clung to the Roman computation until 664 (*see* WHITBY, ABBEY OF). The introduction of a chronological Christian Era is also the work of Dionysius; for, when continuing the Easter tables of CYRIL OF ALEXANDRIA for another 95 years, he counted for the first time the years from the birth of Christ, which, however, he wrongly dated to 754 A.U.C., at least four years too late.

The Dionysian cycle was universally followed until the Gregorian reform, which altered the cycle so as to predict the date of full moons more accurately. Belief in the Nicene origin of the Dionysian cycle was one reason for opposition to the Gregorian reform by the Orthodox Churches which still use the old cycle, making their Easter sometimes differs by as much as five weeks from that of the Latin Church. The full moon computed by the Gregorian cycle may differ from the date of the astronomical full moon, so that occasionally the Gregorian Easter differs from that determined astronomically (e.g., 1962). This was well known to the authors of the reform and is inherent in any form of cyclical computation. It could be avoided by using the astronomical full moon, but this solution was rejected, for it would bring its own difficulties; e.g., full moon may fall on different days on either side of the date line.

The fact that the dates of Easter on the Gregorian and Julian Calendars do not correspond has been perceived as a source of scandal and a sign of disunity among Christians on the holiest of days. In the 1990s, the World Council of Churches made several unsuccessful attempts to come up with a common date for Easter for Orthodox, Catholics, and other Christians.

The Christmas Cycle. A second cycle of feasts, this time a fixed one, was introduced some time after the movable Easter cycle. The earliest mention of an anniversary of the birth of Christ on CHRISTMAS Day (December 25) is in the Philocalian Calendar. The entry, which may be dated to 336, reads: *VIII.kal. Ian. natus Christus in Betleem Iudeae.* Many scholars think that the date was chosen to offset the imperial feast of the *Natalis solis invicti* (the birthday of the unconquered sun). The Christological controversies of the fourth and fifth centuries doubtless contributed to the feast's growth in importance; it also aided in lessening the importance of the feast of the EPIPHANY, originally a more important feast, to the point that it became part of the Christmas cycle, a position that evolved in Africa sometime between 380 and 530, passed from there into Spain, and then to Italy. ADVENT, which now prefaces the cycle, appears to have been introduced at Rome by Pope SIMPLICIUS or Pope GELASIUS I in the second half of the fifth century.

Other Fixed Commemorations. In Asia Minor from the end of the second century and at Rome from at least the third, the anniversary of a martyr's death was kept as a feast, with a liturgical celebration at his tomb. This day was the *dies natalis* of the martyr, possibly meaning his "heavenly birthday." These commemorations, together with a brief indication of the time, place, and circumstances of the martyr's death or burial, were often entered into registers roughly known as MARTYROLOGIES. The oldest extant compilation of this nature occurs in a commonplace book of Furius Dionysius Filocalus. Begun at Rome in 336 and completed in 354, it contains an invaluable list of popes (*Depositio episcoporum*) and martyrs (*Depositio martyrum*), together with indications of other Roman commemorations, e.g., Christmas. From an examination of the three most ancient martyrologies (Philocalian; Syrian, 411; Carthaginian, *c.* 450) and of other martyrologies such as the Hieronymian, the Gallican of Polemius Silvius, the Mozarabic, and the Andalusian, it may be concluded: (1) that although the celebrations of martyrs were occasioned initially by local cultus, the more celebrated of these martyrs soon obtained favor outside their own localities; (2) that from an early date, feasts were granted to the Apostles; (3) that feasts of Our Lady (*see* MARIAN FEASTS) were not general until *c.* 650, although the PURIFICATION OF MARY was kept locally at Jerusalem on Feb. 14 (later Feb. 2) from *c.* 350.

Reforms and Revisions. The multiplication of lists of martyrs (to which non-martyrs were added in time) and the emergence of liturgical books (of the Roman rite) such as sacramentaries, LECTIONARIES, and Gospel books (see: EVANGELARY) contributed greatly to the decline of the ferial day, especially during the Carolingian period, when continuators of the classic martyrology of BEDE (d. 735) rushed to fill in every blank space. The inclusion of new saints and new devotional interests led, well before the end of the Middle Ages, to overcrowded and chaotic calendars. A greater uniformity throughout the Church was ensured by the reformed calendar of PIUS V (1568–70), inasmuch as all churches and religious orders that could not prove a prescription of 200 years were obliged to conform to the new disposition of the calendar. An instruction of the Congregation of Rites of Feb. 14, 1961 [*Acta Apostolicae Sedis* 53 (1961) 168–180], reducing considerably the commemoration of saints, now allows the ferial day much of its original Paschal connotation. However, the most far-reaching reform of the liturgical calendar was effected by the 1969 General Norms of the Roman Calendar, which drastically pruned the number of commemoration of saints from 338 to 191.

Particular Calendars. The General Norms of the 1969 Roman Calendar allow the formation of particular calendars, i.e. the insertion of special celebrations into the general calendar by individual regions, countries, dioceses, and religious families. In June of 1970, the Congregation for Divine Worship issued an instruction giving specific norms for the establishment of such calendars.

Particular calendars may include saints proper to a region or religious community, as well as those saints listed in the universal calendar to whom a higher rank will be given. To insure historical credibility, proper hagiographical studies must, when necessary, be conducted regarding the life and deeds of the saint. Whenever possible, the saint should be commemorated on the day of death; otherwise, on a day of importance in the cult of the saint. If the feast already occurs in the general calendar, it should generally be observed on the same day. Permission is granted for a more solemn celebration of the saint in some parts, rather than in the whole of a diocese or religious family.

In addition to commemorating those saints having a special connection with a particular diocese, the diocesan calendar may include a proper liturgical celebration of the principal and secondary patrons of the diocese, as well as the anniversary of the dedication of the cathedral.

Bibliography: The three earliest martyrologies in H. LIETZMANN, ed., *Die drei ältesten Martyrologien* (Bonn 1903). See additional bibliog. under MARTYROLOGIES, MARTYROLOGY, ROMAN, MARTYROLOGY OF ST. JEROME. L. DUCHESNE, ''La Question de la Pâque au concile de Nicée,'' *Revue des questions historiques* 28 (1880) 5–42. N. NILLES, ed., *Kalendarium manuale utriusque ecclesiae, orientalis et occidentalis,* 2 v. (Innsbruck 1896–97). W. H. FRERE, *Studies in Early Roman Liturgy,* 3 v. (Oxford 1930–35) v.1. B. BOTTE, *Les Origines de la Noël et de l'Épiphanie* (Louvain 1932). H. DELEHAYE, *Les Origines du culte des martyrs* (2d ed. Brussels 1933). P. JOUNEL, ''Le Sanctoral romain du 8ᵉ au 12ᵉ siècles,'' *Maison-Dieu* 52 (1957) 59–88. Sacred Congregation for Divine Worship, ''Normae universales de anno liturgico et de calendario,'' *Notitiae* 46 (Apr.–June 1969) 165–176 (Eng. tr., USCC pub. v-453). ''Instructio de calendariis particularibus atque officiorum et Missarum propriis recognoscendis,'' *Notitiae* 58 (Nov. 1970) 348–370. T. J. TALLEY, *The Origins of the Liturgical Year* (Collegeville, 1991); A. J. MARTIMORT, ed. *The Church at Prayer IV: The Liturgy and Time* (Collegeville 1986); A. ADAM, *The Liturgical Year: Its History & Its Meaning after the Reform of the Liturgy* (New York 1981). J. F. BALDOVIN, ''The Liturgical Year: Calendar for a Just Community,'' in *Liturgy and Spirituality in Context,* ed. E. BERNSTEIN (Collegeville, Minn 1990) 98–114. ''Towards a Common Date for Easter: WCC/MECC Consultation,'' *Saint Vladimir's Theological Quarterly* 41(1997) 235–247. B.L. MARTHALER, ''The Date of Easter, Anno Domini, and Other Calendar Considerations : Chronology or Eschatology?'' *Worship* 73 (1999) 194–211.

[L. E. BOYLE/EDS.]

LITURGICAL CALENDAR, II: ECUMENICAL

The liturgical year is not the result of a direct and conscious arrangement of the annual cycle for pedagogical purposes about some such thematic scheme as the life of Christ or salvation history. Rather, it is the result of a long and complex evolution in which many cultic and cultural forces have shaped times of feast and fast into a pattern that not only celebrates the several dimensions of the Christian kerygma, but constitutes an epitome of the entire Christian tradition. Critically reviewed in the 16th century, with widely divergent results ranging from slight to radical reform, the calendar has received fresh attention since Vatican Council II along lines manifesting more ecumenical convergence. Calendars of Western Christian Churches in the United States today agree in beginning the year with four Sundays of Advent leading to Christmas, and all observe the feast of Epiphany on January 6 or an adjacent Sunday, with the Sunday after Epiphany kept as the Baptism of Christ. Omitting the former three pre-lenten Sundays (Septuagesima, Sexagesima, Quadragesima), all begin Lent on Ash Wednesday and distinguish the days of Holy Week. Easter is celebrated for 50 days, terminated by the one-day celebration of Pentecost, from which the following Sundays are numbered.

Such are the norms for the liturgical year issued with the new Roman Calendar (1969). They were adopted by the Presbyterian *Worshipbook* (1970), the Episcopal *Book of Common Prayer* (1979), and the Lutheran *Book of Worship* (1978). The same norms govern the lectionary prepared for the Consultation on Church Union (1974), now approved for use by the Methodist Church. The Disciples of Christ and the United Church of Christ follow the calendar of the Presbyterian *Worshipbook*. In the United Kingdom, on the other hand, calendar reform began somewhat earlier and along different lines. In 1963 a Joint Liturgical Group composed of representatives of the churches of England, Scotland, Ireland, and Wales (Anglican, Methodist, Presbyterian, Baptist, Congregationalist, and Churches of Christ, with an observer from the Roman Catholic Church) undertook the formulation of a common calendar and lectionary along new lines. The result, published in 1967, arranged the Sundays of the year thematically about three major festivals: Christmas and Easter, each preceded by nine Sundays and followed by six, and Pentecost, followed by 21 Sundays. Although the earlier (1962) calendar of the Church of South India had treated Septuagesima as the Ninth Sunday before Easter, the parallel arrangement before Christmas was an innovation of the Joint Liturgical Group. Traditional themes of Epiphany were set on the first and third Sundays after Christmas, but that feast itself did not appear. Since its publication this radical proposal has undergone further development in a more conservative direction in individual churches. In *The Calendar and Lessons* (1969) the Church of England added feasts of Christ and of the saints, and the *Methodist Service Book* (1975) restored Epiphany and All Saints' Day. Both retain the three pre-lenten Sundays as well as the distinctive nine Sundays before Christmas, although alternative titles show that these are coming to be seen either as Sundays before Advent (Methodist) or as the last five Sundays after Trinity or Pentecost (Church of England). A period preceding Advent has also characterized the Methodist calendar in the United States, the time after Pentecost giving way to a season of Kingdomtide from the last Sunday of August. Roman and Lutheran calendars designate the last Sunday after Pentecost as Feast of Christ the King, and the same lessons are given in other lectionaries.

While the number of observances in the sanctoral cycle has been reduced in the reform of the Roman Calendar, it has been increased in calendars of the Lutheran Church to 127 and of the Episcopal Church to 152; for both the latter these are divided between feasts (Lutheran, 30; Episcopal, 33) and optional commemorations. Like the Roman, the Lutheran Calendar occasionally places more than one optional memorial on the same day. The General Roman Calendar has 33 feasts of fixed date (10 designated Solemnities) with others of moveable date, as well as 64 obligatory memorials. All modern calendars strongly emphasize SUNDAY as a weekly feast of Christ that is accorded precedence over all but the most important feasts of fixed date, an emphasis that casts doubt on the acceptability of any universal calendar reform (such as the World Calendar), which would interrupt the independent cycle of the week.

Bibliography: R. C. D. JASPER, ed., *The Calendar and Lectionary: A Reconsideration by the Joint Liturgical Group* (London 1967). The Standing Liturgical Commission of the Episcopal Church, *The Church Year* (Prayer Book Studies 19; New York 1970). The Inter-Lutheran Commission on Worship, *The Church Year: Calendar and Lectionary* (Contemporary Worship 6; Minneapolis, Minn; Philadelphia, Pa; and St. Louis, Mo. 1973). R. NARDONE, ''The Roman Calendar in Ecumenical Perspective,'' *Worship* 50 (1976) 238–246. H. M. DANIELS, ''Recent Changes in the Presbyterian Celebration of the Liturgical Year,'' *Reformed Liturgy and Music* 16 (Fall 1982) 153–158.

[T. J. TALLEY/EDS.]

LITURGICAL CATECHESIS

Liturgical catechesis seeks to lead communities and individual members of the faithful to maturity of faith through full and active participation in the liturgy, which effects and expresses that faith. As the name itself suggests, liturgical catechesis is only one of several forms of catechesis, although all forms have a liturgical dimension. Liturgical catechesis has certain identifying characteristics. It is trinitarian-paschal, ecclesial, sacramental and transformative. The paschal mystery is the heart of all catechesis, the cornerstone of Christian faith and paradigm of the Christian life, both for individuals and for a community of faith. Liturgical celebration is an ecclesial action. It is not simply a series of actions but the celebration and expression of relationships: relationship to God and to one another in Christ through the Spirit.

Liturgical catechesis takes place in the midst of the community because the Church's faith precedes the faith of those who are invited to believe. Catechesis is the responsibility of the whole church. Liturgical catechesis is sacramental. It aims to initiate people into the mystery of Christ ''by proceeding from the visible to the invisible, from the sign to the signified, from the sacrament to the mysteries'' (CCC, no 1075). The central symbols such as the assembly, the water, wine, oil, imposition of hands, reading and interpretation of scripture and the sign of the cross are constituent of the liturgy and are contextualized within the liturgical year. Liturgical catechesis aims to uncover the meaning of these symbolic actions so that the faithful may gradually realize that by participation in the sacramental action they participate in the saving action of Christ. The liturgy supports conversion, a transformation that takes place throughout the individual's life, that results in a life lived in charity, justice and peace making.

Strictly speaking, liturgical catechesis is MYSTAGO-GY. Mystagogy is a reflection upon the symbols, actions and scriptures of the liturgical rite in terms of one's daily life. It is dependent upon the celebration of the assembly, and the celebration in turn is deepened by a preparation for the liturgy that builds up a lexicon of images, concepts, scriptural stories, ritual action and symbols.

The first dimension, preparation for the liturgy, begins with the human values that are present in the liturgical celebration including ''community activity, exchange of greetings, capacity to listen, to seek and grant pardon, expression of gratitude, experience of symbolic actions, a meal of friendship and festive celebration'' (DMC, 9). Liturgical catechesis fosters reflection on the rites and prayers of the liturgy in the light of these human values. The rites and prayers are seen within the framework of the scriptures, the doctrinal and liturgical tradition, the liturgical year and of necessity include attention to the social and cultural context of the community. The theological principles for catechesis are drawn from the theology in the Introduction to the Rite. Liturgical catechesis takes place within a celebration of the word (RCIA, 85–89). The preparation for the liturgy is essential in building up a storehouse of images, rituals, symbols, gestures, music and sacred space that serve as a source for interpreting the experience of the liturgy and enabling the community to attend to the ways in which the liturgy reveals the presence of God in their lives.

The second phase is catechesis through the liturgy. Liturgy conveys its meaning not through explanation but through participation. Liturgy is experiential and liturgical catechesis opens up and brings to awareness what is known intuitively. The mystagogical reflection, catechesis from the liturgy, occurs after the celebration but the celebration of the rite and mystagogy is all of piece. It takes place in the midst of the community and brings together the human values, the received tradition, and the experience of the individual within the context of the community. Mystagogy is about making meaning. It is a way of interpreting life and responding to the mystery celebrated. The process then, progresses from reflection on the community's experience of the liturgical action in light of human values, to the interpretation of the experience in terms of the Scriptures and the Christian tradition; to an exploration of the meaning in their own lives and its ethical implications for living a life of peace and justice. Celebration followed by reflection, and then action, returns to celebration with new insight and new meaning.

This form of catechesis is not new but rather is a restoration of a relationship between liturgy and catechesis that existed in the early church and is so well illustrated by the mystagogical homilies for example, of St. AM-BROSE, CYRIL of Jerusalem, THEODORE OF Mopsuestia and St. AUGUSTINE. It is again given prominence by the 1963 Constitution on the Sacred Liturgy (48) and other liturgical and catechetical documents such as the 1967 Instruction on the Worship of the Eucharistic Mystery ([*Eucharisticum mysterium*] (14–15), the Apostolic Exhortation of John Paul II, *Catechesis in our Time* (23), The *Rite of Christian Initiation of Adults* (75), the *Catechism of the Catholic Church* (1074–1075) and *The General Directory for Catechesis* (1997).

Bibliography: C. DOOLEY, ''Liturgical Catechesis: Mystagogy, Marriage or Misnomer?'' *Worship* 66 (1992): 386–397. G. OSTDIEK, ''Catechesis, Liturgical'' in *The New Dictionary of Sacramental Worship*, ed. P. FINK (Collegeville: The Liturgical Press, 1990), 163–172. G. OSTDIEK, ''Liturgy as Catechesis For Life,'' *Liturgical Ministry* 7 (1998): 76–82. T. MORRIS, ''Liturgical Catechesis Revisited,'' *Catechumenate* 17 (May 1995): 13–19. G. F. BAUMBACH, *Experiencing Mystagogy: The Sacred Pause of Easter* (New York: Paulist, 1996).

[C. DOOLEY]

LITURGICAL COLORS

All Church vesture achieves its effect by its cut, color, and texture. Color appeals most quickly to the emotions, and the proper use of it can help the priest and people to feel the mood and spirit of a particular feast day. Colors of the spectrum may be associated with two moods: the warm, active, and exciting qualities of red and the cool, passive, and calming qualities of blue, violet and green. Because of these associations, it is not surprising that a color sequence proper to particular feasts of the Church year became the subject of ecclesiastical legislation.

The first such legislation known is that of the 12th-century crusaders written for their Church at Jerusalem. Innocent III (1198–1216) prescribed five colors for liturgical use in the Roman Rite: white, red, green, black, and violet (*De Sacro Altaris Mysterio* 1.65). Although the directive is precise about what colors are to be used, it leaves the choice of shades of these colors to the vestment maker. Innocent III's color scheme forms the basis for contemporary practice. White is worn on Sundays in Eastertide, on solemnities of Our Lord and the Blessed Virgin Mary, and for funeral masses; red is used for Pentecost and the feasts of apostles and martyrs; violet for Advent and Lent; and green for Sundays in ordinary time. From the 13th century onward, the practice of wearing rose-colored vestments on the 3rd Sunday of Advent (*Gaudete* Sunday) and the 4th Sunday of Lent (*Laetare* Sunday) caught on.

Bibliography: W. H. HOPE and E. G. ATCHLEY, *Liturgical Colors* (Society for Promoting Christian Knowledge; London 1918).

[M. MCCANCE/EDS.]

LITURGICAL CONFERENCE

The Liturgical Conference began as the Benedictine Liturgical Conference, under the sponsorship of the Benedictine abbots of the United States in 1940. The first of these meetings, called Liturgical Weeks, was held in Chicago in 1940, and they were held annually in major cities throughout the United States and Canada. In 1943, the leaders of the Benedictine Liturgical Conference decided to dissolve it as a Benedictine enterprise and to reconstitute it on a broader basis. In 1944, the Liturgical Conference was incorporated as a voluntary association of American clergy and laity, formed to promote understanding of the liturgy among Catholics and to assist in leading the people to a full, active participation in the Church's public worship.

The *Instruction on Sacred Music and Liturgy* (Sept. 3, 1958) requiring the active participation of the people in liturgical rites, gave new impetus to the work of the conference. Its activities were expanded to serve the growing needs of parishes and dioceses. Under the presidency of F. R. McManus, a central office was opened in Washington, D.C., in February of 1960. Relations were established with diocesan liturgical commissions, and programs and publications were produced for laity and clergy.

The tremendous impetus given to all movements for ecclesial reform and renewal by the Second Vatican Council led to the expansion of the conference's membership and activities. The Liturgical Weeks drew large crowds of people, peaking at about 15,000. In 1964, the conference launched a major publishing and educational program to promote liturgical renewal and reform. This "Parish Worship Program" (1964) of books, kits, pamphlets was followed by the publication of a popular commentary on the Constitution on the Sacred Liturgy in 1965. Regional groups developed in New England, the Southeast, and the Southwest.

At the same time, ecumenical activity was accelerating. A number of Anglican, Lutheran, and other Christian liturgists became involved in the conference's activities. They participated in the one-day institutes preceding the Liturgical Weeks, and subsequently in the programs of the Liturgical Weeks themselves. Some were nominated and elected to the Board of Directors. Membership became opened to all Christians who share the conference's concerns. The conference's character evolved to one that is consciously and deliberately ecumenical.

The 1970s witnessed a great flourish in the conference's publications and activities. The conference sponsored specialized conferences on church architecture and music, and initiated a number of new periodical services: *Living Worship, Homily Service, Parish Council, Today Songs for Today's People,* and *Major Feasts and Seasons.* Short educational films on liturgical renewal were produced in cooperation with other agencies. Corresponding to the rapid postconciliar development of liturgical renewal and with the evolving ecumenical character of the conference, the range and focus of publications broadened. Problems of adapting reformed liturgical rites were addressed in the *Manual of Celebration* and its supplement; *The Rite of Penance* (a three-volume collection comprising: (1) *Understanding the Document,* (2) *Implementing the Rite,* and (3) *Background and Directions*); *It Is Your Own Mystery: A Guide to Communion Rite; Celebrating Baptism; Children's Liturgies; Signs, Songs and Stories; There's No Place Like People;* and *Parishes and Families.* The conference also produced liturgy resource materials: *Liturgy Committee Handbook* (1971); *The Lector's Guide* (1973); *The Ministry of Music* (1975); *There Are Different Ministries* (1975); *Strong, Loving and Wise: Presiding in Liturgy* (1976); *The Spirit Moves: A Handbook of Dance and Prayer* (1976); and *Touchstones for Liturgical Ministers* (1978). The particular gifts and contribution of the black worship experience in the United States is the subject of *This Far By Faith: American Black Worship and Its African Roots.* Other resource collections included *Simple Gifts* (a two-volume collection of articles from *Liturgy*); *Dry Bones* (a collection of articles from *Living Worship*); *The Rites of People* (a popular study of ritual questions); and the more recent *From Ashes to Easter: Design for Parish Renewal (Years A, N and C)* and *Preaching on Death.*

The Conference continues to publish *Liturgy* and *Homily Service. Liturgy* is now a quarterly resource for parish liturgy planning, with practical aids for clergy, musicians, educators, and planners. *Homily Service* is ecumenical in focus, covering readings from the *Revised Common Lectionary,* the *Book of Common Prayer* and *Lectionary for Mass.*

[J. B. MANNION/R.W. HOVDA/V. SLOYAN]

LITURGICAL GESTURES

Bodily gestures are the principal means by which one expresses the highest forms of one's spiritual, intellectual, and artistic experiences, and the principal ways in which humans communicate with each other. Rite and ceremony have been used by all religions both to intensify and to communicate the interior dispositions of the soul. Gestures, no less than words, are a part of human language, the one appealing to sight, the other to hearing—the two senses closest to the intellect and therefore closest to the spiritual life. Each is a language unto itself, yet normally they depend upon each other for the full expression of one's inner self—words calling upon gestures to give them greater force, intensity, and eloquence, and gestures calling upon words to make their meaning more articulate. Any act or movement of the human body becomes a gesture when it gives expression to meaning within an interpersonal relationship. Liturgical gestures in their turn express specific meanings within the relationship between God and human persons in community celebrations.

Christian Use. Christian prayer demands a profound engagement of the human body because the mystery of the Incarnation—the Word became flesh and gave humanity a share in the social life of the Trinity, expressed in the communal life of the Mystical Body. For Christians, the mystery of the Incarnation is the reason for sacramentalizing the human body. Human gestures play an extensive role throughout the entire liturgy. The use of bodily gesture in the prayer life of the Church is simply an imitation of Christ himself who in prayer lifted his eyes to heaven, prostrated himself, etc.; who used gestures as a means to perform his miracles when a simple word would have sufficed; who taught by means of such gestures as the washing of the feet of his disciples; and who finally offered his entire body in the perfect act of worship on the cross.

In particular, there are three ways in which the human body, through the use of gestures, enters into the liturgical action of the Church: by giving expression to the sentiments and dispositions of the soul, as in extending the hands, bowing, or kneeling; by performing an action upon an external object, as in anointings and blessings; and by being acted upon in such a way that it becomes sanctified, as in baptismal immersion or the laying on of hands.

However, if gestures are to be meaningful and our use of them intelligent, their real significance must be properly understood. For this two extremes must be avoided. One is the excessively allegorical interpretation found in a number of medieval authors, such as AMALARIUS of Metz (d. 850) and Bernold of Constance (d. 1100), which was popular up to the 17th century. Like the allegorical exegesis of the Bible characteristic of some of the early Church Fathers, this method projects into liturgical gesture arbitrary, subjective, mystical, and piously moralistic significance that ignores its actual historical origin or its objective basic symbolism. Thus, to cite only one example, a great variety of meanings were attributed to the gesture of breaking the host into three parts: the Blessed Trinity, the three parts of the Church, the wounds of Christ in the three parts of His body, the three travelers on the road to Emmaus, etc. The other extreme is exemplified by Dom Claude de Vert [*Explication simple, littérale et historique des cérémonies de l'Église,* 4 v. (Paris 1706–13)], who tried to eliminate all symbolism from liturgical ceremonies by explaining their origin in terms of practical necessity or convenience. Later, Pierre Le Brun succeeded in avoiding these two extreme positions by taking into account both symbolic and functional aspects [*Explication littérale, historique et dogmatique des prières et des cérémonies de la Messe,* 4 v. (Paris 1716–25)].

Kinds. In the light of objective and realistic analysis, liturgical actions can be grouped into three main categories. First of all, there are actions that serve functional purposes of utility, convenience, or fittingness, such as the ablutions of the chalice and the fingers of the priest after Communion. Then there are interpretative actions that express the natural human inclination to communicate by combining words and gestures, such as kneeling as a sign of penitence. Third, there are purely symbolic actions, such as the presentation of the white robe and the lighted candle to the newly baptized. It is also possible to divide all liturgical actions into postures and gestures.

Standing. In modern times kneeling has become generally accepted as the most appropriate attitude for prayer. In antiquity, however, and for many centuries in the Church, standing was considered to be the most normal posture, and it is still so considered by the liturgy, except for times and ceremonies that call for a special expression of penance and humble adoration. Even today many of the older basilicas do not have pews or kneelers. Standing was considered by the Jews as the most fitting attitude in praying to the Lord (Ex 33.8, 10; Sir 50.12–13; 1 Sm 1.26; Ps 135.2; Mt 6.5; Mk 11.25; Lk 18.11) and in listening to Him speak (Ex 19.17; Neh 8.5). That the early Christians adopted this custom as the normal attitude for prayer is evident not only from the many images of the ''orante'' in the catacombs and on ancient sarcophagi, but also from the testimony of early ecclesiastical writers: Justin (*Apologia* 1.67; J. Quasten, ed., *Monumenta eucharista et liturgica vetustissima* 19), Tertullian (*De corona militis* 3; *Patrologia Latina*, ed. J. P. Migne, 2:99), and Cyprian (*De dominica oratione* 31; *Corpus scriptorum ecclesiasticorum latinorum* 3.1:289). St. Benedict made standing the official posture for chanting the psalms.

For the early Christians, as for the pagans and the Jews, standing was a natural expression of respect and reverence. But for the Christians, as is evident in the writings of the Fathers, it had the added significance of the new dignity, the liberty of the children of God, the freedom from slavery and sin through Baptism and participation in the Resurrection, which makes it possible to stand confidently before God with eyes and arms uplifted to Him. As the Second Eucharistic Prayer of the Roman Rite puts it: "We thank you for counting us worthy to stand before you and serve you." For Tertullian (*De oratione* 23; *Patrologia Latina* 1:1191) kneeling was a sign of atonement and penance, whereas standing signified joy, and for this reason standing was customary throughout the Easter and Pentecost season; it was contrary to Church discipline to kneel on Sundays (*De corona militis* 3; *Patrologia Latina* 2:99). As a matter of fact, the first Council of NICAEA explicitly made standing obligatory on Sundays and during the Easter season (c.20; J. D. Mansi, *Sacrorum Conciliorum nova et amplissima collectio* 2:719–20). Something of this prescription still exists in the custom of standing for the Angelus on Saturday evening and throughout Sunday, and also for the REGINA CAELI during paschal time. Because the day consecrated to the Resurrection is a kind of image of the future world, the attitude of standing had for the early Christians an eschatological meaning: it was considered the proper attitude for those awaiting with confidence the Parousia. In a very special way, standing was considered proper for the exercise of the priesthood.

Sitting. This is the normal position of an official teacher, of a presiding officer, of a judge, and of a person of special dignity in the presence of others of lower rank. The word "cathedral" comes from the Latin word *cathedra*, a throne or seat, which, as the place where a bishop presides and teaches, symbolizes his jurisdiction and his functions. When the pope teaches infallibility he speaks ex cathedra. And formerly, rubrics provided for the bishop and priests to be seated during certain liturgical functions, but excluded all other ministers, even the deacons, from assuming this position. Sitting is a normal attitude for both speaker and listener. The Child Jesus was found seated in the midst of the doctors of the temple (Lk 2.46). Mary sat at the feet of Jesus listening to His words (Lk 10.39). There are indications in Scripture that, for both the Jews and the early Christians, a sitting position was customary for listening to readings and the sermon, while standing was the usual practice for prayer (Lk 4.16–20; Jn 8.2; Acts 20.9; 1 Cor 14.30). Similar indications are found in Justin (*Apologia* 1.67; *Monumenta eucharista et liturgica vetustissima* 19) and in the *Apostolic Constitutions* (8.6.2; *Monumenta eucharista et liturgica vetustissima* 199). Sitting has become a more common attitude in prayer in modern times, especially since pews were introduced into churches after the 16th century, as a result of the influence of the Reformation, whose services concentrated almost exclusively on the hearing of the Word

of God. More recent rubrics have emphasized the position of sitting as the proper attitude for listening to God's Word, except for the Gospel, when the special dignity of the Word of God calls for the more respectful attitude of standing.

Kneeling. Though it is especially in the last few centuries that kneeling has become the most popular position of the body in prayer, the almost instinctive practice of kneeling at prayer goes back to the Old Testament (1 Kgs 8.54; Dn 6.11) and is found in many pagan religions. This has been especially true in private prayer, and more particularly in times of especially intense prayer. Christ Himself prayed on His knees during the agony in the garden (Lk 22.41); Stephen knelt to pray before his martyrdom (Acts 7.60). The kneeling posture was introduced in the liturgy principally as a sign of humble supplication, sorrow, and a penitential spirit, incompatible with a time of joy, such as Eastertide, but especially suitable for times of fasting (Tertullian, *De oratione* 23; *Patrologia Latina* 1:1191). Reminders of the special connection between kneeling and fasting still exist in the liturgy, as, for example, the *Flectamus genua* of Good Friday. In the course of time, kneeling was reinterpreted more and more a sign of profound adoration, and this is now its most predominant meaning. For this reason the rubrics now prescribe this posture especially for adoration of the Blessed Sacrament. It would seem that the growing practice of adoration of the Blessed Sacrament, resulting from the effort of the Counter Reformation to emphasize the Real Presence, has been one of the main reasons why kneeling, rather than standing, has in modern times become the most characteristic attitude of prayer.

Genuflection. The gesture of bending the knee is of ancient origin dating back to pre-Christian times. Its primary significance among the pagans, especially those of the Roman Empire, was that of adoration and worship, and it was used as a salutation to the gods and to the "divine" rulers, particularly the emperor. Because of this pagan religious significance, it was not used by the early Christians. When, however, it eventually lost this religious significance and began to be used simply as a sign of respect and courtesy for those in high authority, it was first used by Christians as a sign of reverence for popes and bishops [T. Klauser, *The Western Liturgy and Its History* (London 1952) 27], later for the altar, the crucifix, and relics and images of Christ and the saints. During the early centuries the profound bow, rather than genuflection, was prescribed by the Church as the customary act of adoration, and this practice has persisted in the Eastern Churches. In some places in the West, genuflection was explicitly forbidden since it recalled the mockery of Christ in his Passion. In the 11th century, however, it began to be introduced as an act of adoration of the

Blessed Sacrament in reaction to the errors of BERENGARIUS OF TOURS. It was not until the 16th century that it entered the liturgy of the Mass. In 1502 it was introduced into the *Ordo Missae* of John Burchard and 70 years later into the *Missale Romanum* of Pius V.

Bows. Bowing is a gesture that is, in a sense, something between standing erect and genuflecting, and it has, generally speaking, the same significance as the latter: humble supplication and above all adoration when directed toward God, reverence and veneration when directed toward persons of high rank or objects. An instinctive expression of one's inner feelings and a common gesture in ancient pagan rites, it was introduced early into Christian prayer and became one of the most commonly used gestures in the liturgy, often on occasions for which genuflection has now been substituted in the Latin Church. It is used both to express and to intensify a variety of religious sentiments: adoration and reverence in prayer, and respect for sacred objects, particularly the altar and the crucifix.

Prostration. This is a more intense, total, and dramatic way of expressing the same sentiments expressed in genuflection: adoration, penance, and supplication. It was common among ancient peoples and especially the Jews (Gn 17.3; Dt 9.18; Neh 8.6; Tb 12.16; Jdt 9.1; 10.1; 2 Mc 10.4). It is also found in the New Testament (Mt 17.6; 26.29). There are indications that it was a fairly common form of penance during the early centuries of the Church (Tertullian, *De poenitentia* 9.2; *Patrologia Latina* 1:1243–44). For a time and in certain places, it was the customary way of venerating the altar at the beginning of Mass. It is now restricted to only a few ceremonies of special solemnity: the beginning of the Good Friday liturgy (probably a relic of the ancient prostration before Mass), ordination to major orders, the blessing of abbots, and monastic profession.

Facing the East. A special orientation at prayer, particularly in the direction of the rising sun, was extremely common in ancient pagan rites, especially in those which worshiped the sun as a god. The Jews turned toward the Temple in Jerusalem when they prayed (Dn 6.11). In adopting this custom the Christians gave it a number of new meanings: the sun was the symbol of the light that is Christ; He is the *Oriens ex alto* (Lk 1.79), the Sun of Justice; He had ascended into heaven in the east and was expected to return from there (Mt 24.27); the Garden of Paradise was supposed to be located in the east (*Apostolic Constitutions* 2.57.14; *Monumenta eucharista et liturgica vetustissima* 184–85). This practice remained largely Eastern and it gained only a limited and temporary acceptance in the West, through Byzantine and Gallican influences, in the construction of churches oriented toward the east, and in the custom of celebrants facing in that direction while at prayer. It fell gradually into disuse with the lessening of expectancy of the second coming of Christ, though in some places it lingered on in private devotion in the Middle Ages.

The Orans Position. Since it has always been a universal feeling that the dwelling place of God is above the sky, the upward movement of the soul is naturally accompanied by corresponding gesture of standing with outstretched hands, a.k.a. the *orans* position. These gestures were common among the pagans and the Jews (Ex 9.29; Ps 28.2; 63.5; Is 1.15). They were used by early Christians [1 Tm 2.8 Tertullian, *Liber apologeticus* 30 (*Patrologia Latina* 1:422); Clement of Rome, *Epist. 1 ad Cor.* 29 (*Patrologica Graeca*, ed. J. P. Migne, 1:270)].

Among all the organs of the body, the hands, after the tongue, are the most effective instruments for communicating the thoughts and sentiments of the soul. It is not surprising, then, that the liturgy pays a great deal of attention to the movements of the hands and tries to make full use of their capacity to express the relations of the soul with God. Just as the modern practice of kneeling has obscured the fact that standing is the much more traditional attitude, so the modern custom of joining the hands makes us lose sight of the fact that formerly the *orans* position was a much more common gesture. There are evidences that joining the hands was known in private prayer in the 9th century; there are no examples of it in Christian monuments until the 12th century; and it was about this time that it began to be used in the liturgy. It seems to be derived from the Frankish feudal custom for a vassal to present himself to his lord with folded hands, and in that context it signified subjection and submission (M. Righetti, *Manuale di storia liturgica* 1:231). It may also be taken to symbolize recollection and fervor.

Standing erect with arms outstretched was the favorite posture in the early ages of the Church. This gesture was taken to represent the posture of Christ on the cross when He offered the supreme prayer of sacrifice (Tertullian, *De oratione* 14; *Patrologia Latina* 1:1169–70). For this reason, until the end of the 15th century, it was prescribed for the Mass, particularly during the Canon, and more especially during the time immediately following the Consecration. In a somewhat modified form it perdures in the present Mass at the orations, the Canon, and the LORD'S PRAYER. It is also found in the ascetical practices of some religious communities. Thus, through the raising of his hands, one is able to express in an intense manner, one's identification with the sacrifice of Christ, the lifting up of one's whole being to God, one's dependence upon God, and confident waiting for God's answer, and the opening out of one's soul to God.

Imposition of Hands. This gesture is, in a sense, the primary and most important of all the liturgical gestures because of the essential role it plays in the sacramental action of the Church. Though widely used outside its sacramental role, its special importance and dignity is evidenced by the fact that its use has always been restricted to bishops and clerics. The human hands play such an important role in almost all human activities that they have traditionally been considered symbols of strength, power, and dignity, and of the communication of these qualifies. This is why Scripture speaks so frequently of the arm of God and of the right hand of the Lord. The IMPOSITION OF HANDS, not unknown among the ancient pagans, was widely used in the Old and New Testament.

Striking the Breast. Already familiar to the ancient Hebrews and pagans, this gesture is found in the New Testament in the well-known parable of the tax collector (Lk 18.13) and in the reaction of the Jews to the death of Christ on the cross (Lk 23.48). At an early date it became a part of Christian piety as a symbol of sorrow for sin, the root of which was considered to be in the heart (Augustine, *Sermo* 67.1; *Patrologia Latina* 38:433). It is always with this meaning that it is prescribed by the rubrics of the Mass for the Confiteor (I confess).

Vatican II. Vatican Council II in the Constitution on Liturgy gave clear directives that liturgical gestures be expressive of the divine realities that they signify, and at the same time that these gestures be adapted to contemporary needs (*Sacrosanctum Concilium* 21, 62; *Gaudium et spes* 4–10 shows that implementation means more than simply changing a former ritual for a revised one).

It is evident that Baptism by immersion more clearly expresses the inner faith reality of dying and rising with Christ (*Sacrosanctum Concilium* 6) than does Baptism by pouring a trickle of water on the forehead. Christian Initiation admits the non-Christian into the mysteries of Christ and into the faith community as well (ChrInitAd 19, 2). This is expressed very well when celebrant and members of the assembly—at least sponsors and catechists—sign each of the five senses of the candidate when he/she is admitted to the first step of the catechumenate (ibid. 85).

The General Instruction of the Roman Missal also concerns itself with Vatican II's call for more authentic liturgical gestures. The kiss of peace has been reinstated as an expression of the state of full reconciliation and forgiveness (GenInstrRomMissal 56, b). There is mention that "the sign of Communion," as the eschatological banquet, "is more complete when given under both kinds" (ibid. 240). Also "the nature of the sign demands that the material for the Eucharistic celebration appear as actual food" (ibid. 283).

Emphasis on the gesture of laying on of hands in the Sacrament of Reconciliation further carries out the Council's concern for meaningful gestures. The *Praenotanda* of the revised Rite of Penance, give the directive: ". . . the priest extends his hands or at least his right hand, over the penitent and pronounces the formula of absolution" (Rite of Penance Intro 19). This gesture is encouraging as it reassures the penitent in a kindly human way of safety from evil by the power of Jesus' death and resurrection. Such directives on meaningful gestures exemplify the richness of the instructions accompanying the liturgical rites in their revisions since Vatican II.

Bibliography: J. A. JUNGMANN, *The Early Liturgy,* tr. F. A. BRUNNER (Notre Dame, Ind. 1959). C. VAGAGGINI, *Theological Dimensions of the Liturgy,* tr. L. J. DOYLE, 2 v. (Collegeville, Minn. 1959) v.1. B. I. MULLAHY, "The Raising of My Hands," *Orate Fratres* 21 (1946–47) 241–49. L. MITCHELL, *Meaning of Ritual* (New York 1977). H. CAFFAREL, *The Body at Prayer: An Introduction* (London 1978). J. L. LEONARD and N. MITCHELL, *The Postures of the Assembly during the Eucharistic Prayer* (Chicago 1994). E. E. UZUKWU, *Worship as Body Language: Introduction to Christian Worship: An African Orientation* (Collegeville, Minn. 1997).

[B. I. MULLAHY/M. P. ELLENBRACHT/EDS.]

LITURGICAL HISTORY

Early

A survey of the early history of the liturgy reveals great richness in both its plurality and its organic dynamism, defying any neat categorizations of universal linear development. Even the definition of "early" can vary from geographical area to area, ranging from sub-apostolic to anywhere between the 6th and the 10th centuries. For the purposes of this essay, "early" will cover the development of the liturgy from the sub-apostolic period to the 8th century.

LITURGICAL CENTERS AND PRIMARY SOURCES

Modern scholarship on early liturgical history can be described as a movement from the quest for the "original" liturgy to the recognition that the first four centuries represent a movement from tremendous pluriformity to regional uniformity. While the three great branches of Christian liturgy (Greek, Syriac and Latin) are rooted in these early centuries we can also see the regional, cultural and linguistic liturgical rites taking shape by the late third and early fourth centuries.

Jerusalem. From Jerusalem, the birthplace of Christianity, we have evidence of liturgical practices and understandings that reflect the multilingual and multicultural center of Christian pilgrimage, resulting in liturgical practices both influenced by and influential throughout the Christian churches in late antiquity and beyond. The bulk of the written evidence dates from the fourth and fifth century, revealing a marriage of the indigenous Semitic and cosmopolitan Greek influences. The primary texts are those of CYRIL, Bishop of Jerusalem (the *Catecheses* of the mid-4th century and possibly the *Mystagogical Catecheses* of the 380s), and EGERIA, whose travel diary is calculated to date from 381 to 384 and compares in interesting ways to the earlier travel diary of an anonymous pilgrim from Bordeaux (c. 330). In addition, the Armenian and Georgian lectionaries from the first half of the fifth century give evidence of liturgical continuity and change, as does the Georgian chantbook (the *Iadgari*, 7th century). The earliest Eucharistic liturgy (*The Liturgy of Saint James*) with roots in Jerusalem is quite late from a manuscript perspective (9th century) but may reflect late 4th/early 5th century practices of Jerusalem intertwined with those of other Eastern Christian areas. Archaeological work has also contributed to our understanding of the central Christian complex in Jerusalem built around Constantine's *martyrion* (now *Holy Sepulchre*) and how it was used liturgically.

Rome. From Rome, one of the earliest and most prominent centers of Christianity, we have evidence from varied types of sources, but not as comprehensive as those of Jerusalem. First is the valuable description of JUSTIN MARTYR, who defends Baptism and Eucharist to the emperor in his *First Apology*, c. 150. Another voice from a Roman church, although disputed as to authorship and dating, is the church order *Apostolic Tradition*, an edited document probably covering two centuries of information on how to perform different rites, making it one of the earliest *ordines*. In addition, the *Philocalian Calendar*, dating from 354, and the *Liber Pontificalis* of the sixth century both contribute to our understanding of the liturgical calendar. Later resources, such as the sermons of Leo the Great (440–61) and Gregory the Great (590–604) and the earliest collections of liturgical texts (*libelli, lectionaries*, and *sacramentaries*) which emerge in the 6th and 7th centuries, give scholars a clearer sense of the characteristics of liturgy in the city of Rome and its environs. (For further information on the liturgy in the city of Rome, *see* ROMAN RITE.)

Alexandria. Alexandria and Lower Egypt represent another of the great early centers of Christianity and have yielded multifaceted sources for understanding liturgy, but rarely in the form of actual liturgical texts. Two early Christian theologians, CLEMENT OF ALEXANDRIA (c. 150–215) and ORIGEN (c. 185–254), both refer to liturgical practices and reveal a fascination with symbolic meanings, especially in the poetic texts of Clement's hymns. The Trinitarian and Christological controversies that tore the fabric of Coptic Christianity in these early

centuries also contributed to descriptions or clarifications of liturgy, particularly in the writings of ATHANASIUS, sometimes bishop of Alexandria (c. 296–373), whose festal letters help our understanding of the development of Lent and Easter in Egypt and elsewhere. EPIPHANIUS, bishop of Salamis in Cyprus (367–403), contributes to our understanding of the origins of Epiphany and Christmas in 4th century Egypt. From the Egyptian monastic writers, particularly PACHOMIUS (c. 290–346) and CASSIAN (c. 360–435), we have descriptions of monastic daily prayer that contribute to our later understandings of how non-Eucharistic prayer grew. Liturgical texts from Egypt include the *Canons of Hippolytus* (dating disputed, but perhaps as early as mid-4th century), a collection of liturgical directions with clear roots in the *Apostolic Tradition* of Rome. One of the most important documents is the so-called *Sacramentary* (or prayer book) of Sarapion, a 4th-century bishop of Thmuis (lower Egypt). Sarapion's texts include Eucharistic prayers and a number of blessings. The early Egyptian church has also contributed three fragmentary Eucharistic prayers; the first is the prayer included in the *Strasbourg papyrus 254* (late 4th to early 5th century), the related *Anaphora of Saint Mark* (mid-5th century) and finally the *Liturgy of Saint Basil*, possibly 4th century, which could either be indigenous to Egypt and borrowed by Basil of Cappadocia, or brought to Egypt by Basil himself. Egyptian or Coptic liturgical practices are fundamental to the development of the liturgy of Ethiopia, which preserves many similarities in its ancient Ge'ez language rites.

Syria. The liturgies of Syria form a major liturgical family, although differences exist between Western and Eastern Syria. Syria yields some of the earliest liturgical *ordines*, or practical instruction books on how to do liturgy, which parallel the family tree of the Roman document, the *Apostolic Tradition*. The *Didache* (late 1st century), the *Didascalia* (c. 230), the *Apostolic Constitutions* (c. 380), the *Epitome* (5th century) and the *Testamentum Domini* (5th century) are all from the Syrian Christian tradition with links to other Christian centers. Each *ordo* hands down to us valuable information on prayer patterns, initiation, Eucharist, appointment of community leaders and their duties, and eventually the layout of liturgical space and the unfolding of the liturgical year. The related *West Syrian Synodicon* (7th century) contains additional information on the sanctoral cycle. From East Syria, the *Acts of John* (c. 200) and the *Acts of Thomas* (c. early 3d century) offer evidence of different patterns of Baptism and similar patterns of Eucharistic celebration, as does the 5th-century *Armenian Ordo*, which preserves much of the East Syrian liturgical pattern. From the environs of Antioch in West Syria comes a series of episcopal writings which include extensive liturgical descriptions or explanations. JOHN CHRYSOSTOM's (c. 347–407) writings contain information on initiation (including the catechumenate), Eucharist and ordination. THEODORE OF MOPSUESTIA (c. 350–428) also writes extensively of Baptism, Eucharist, and the catechumenate. The letters and sermons of SEVERUS OF ANTIOCH (bishop from 512 to 518) preserve information on the cult of martyrs, the liturgical year and the meaning of Lent. Two Eucharistic liturgies, the *Anaphora of the Twelve Apostles* and the *Liturgy of John Chrysostom*, both have roots in this area, whether or not the two related anaphorae are from the hand of Chrysostom or not. Finally, the *Syrian Martyrology* of 411 provides a parallel liturgical calendar to the *Philocalian* of Rome and helps organize the various sermons preached on the feasts of martyrs. From Eastern Syria, the writings of APHRAATES (early 4th century) and EPHREM (c. 306–73) often reveal in poetic form many of the important images underlying the Syriac Christian understanding of the meaning of initiation and Eucharist (as well as penance, anointing of the sick, and leadership in the churches). The *Anaphora* (Eucharistic prayer) of Addai and Mari, dating perhaps from the 3rd century, reflects some of the key differences in the East Syrian church. Later writings, such as the anonymous *Liber Graduum* (late 4th century) and the *Liturgical Homilies* of Narsai (d. c. 503) deal with the interpretations of meaning for Baptism and Eucharist. The 6th-century *Sogitha on the Temple of Edessa* contains a valuable discussion on the meaning of liturgical space in relation to the liturgical action. Finally, some local Eastern councils contain legislation regarding various aspects of liturgy, especially the *Synod of Laodicea* (c. 370) and the *Canons* ascribed to Maruta of Maipherqat (7th century).

Constantinople. The imperial city of CONSTANTINOPLE was a late but important player in the development of early church liturgy. Beginning in the 4th century with the move of the emperor Constantine to the city, Constantinople became the recipient of a major imperial building project (beginning about 328), which changed the landscape of the city to fit the needs of Christian liturgies and processions. This use of stational liturgy, also seen in Jerusalem and Rome, made the city the church, with processions gathering in public places and moving from dedicated Christian building to building, shifting with the liturgical year. The Great Church, or *Hagia Sophia*, first dedicated in 360, was the heart of the system of stational liturgy and remained so through the rebuilding projects of the emperor Justinian (527–65), who continued developing the ''Christian topography'' of the city. The written sources that tell us how these spaces were used are primarily those of two bishops; GREGORY OF NAZIANZUS (bishop from 379–81), John Chrysostom (bishop from

398–403); two 5th-century church historians, SOCRATES and SOZOMEN; a 6th-century church historian, THEODORE LECTOR; the 7th-century *Chronicon Paschale*, which makes reference to a number of liturgical processions and liturgies from 330 to 533; the Byzantine chronicler THEOPHANES CONFESSOR (752–818); and a number of 10th and 11th-century sources which witness to the continuity of Constantinople's stational liturgy. Within the unique pattern of liturgy in this city, the sources mentioned above yield a rich display of chants, popular religious practices, eucharistic liturgies, the cult of saints, daily office and the unfolding of the year according to the Byzantine liturgy. One notable liturgical text that has its origins in the Constantinopolitan stational liturgy is the *TRISAGION*, a chant originating in the 5th century and spreading from here to many other Christian liturgies.

North Africa. The North African church was crucial to the development of Latin language theology and liturgy because of several extremely influential writers. TERTULLIAN (Christian from c. 195–230) gives us the earliest description of Baptism related to Easter and some of the elements of Baptism (*De Baptismo*), as well as reflecting on Eucharist, agape, evening prayer and other daily prayers. CYPRIAN, bishop of Carthage from 248 to 258, wrote extensively on leadership within the church, particularly the roles of presbyters and bishops, the requirements for an efficacious baptism, the Eucharist as sacrifice and memorial, and what would later be called ''public'' or ''canonical'' penance, the process whereby serious sinners (especially apostates in times of persecution) were to be admitted back into the church. AUGUSTINE, bishop of Hippo from 396 to 430, gives us an extensive collection of sermons from which we know a great deal about the catechumenate, the celebration of the rites of initiation, the seasons of the year, the setting of the Eucharist, the cult of the martyrs, and funerals for Christians, as well as the current theological arguments regarding penance, orders and Baptism. The liturgical information gleaned from these three is corroborated by several local synods; Hippo (393) and Carthage (397, 407 and 419) all of which reflect a growing tendency toward ''official'' prayers and collections of prayers to offset misleading or possibly heretical liturgical texts. Unfortunately, none of these texts in question survives. In addition to these writings, the other important ''voice'' for liturgical information is archeology; there are many remains of churches, baptistries, cemeteries, inscriptions and mosaics. These all contribute to a better understanding of the setting for Baptism and Eucharist, the latter especially as it intersects with funerals and the cult of martyrs.

Northern Italy. A number of bishops from northern Italy provide information on 4th- and 5th-century liturgical practices. The most prominent is AMBROSE, bishop of Milan from 373/374 to 397. Ambrose wrote extensively on Baptism and Eucharist; his *mystagogical catecheses* known as *De Sacramentis* (preached to the newly baptized in Milan c. 391) reveals invaluable information on how he and his community understood the rituals of initiation (anointing, Baptism, chrismation, foot-washing and Eucharist). The practices reveal continuity with some Roman traditions in later centuries and also link to the East. Ambrose was a prolific hymn and antiphon writer also, and his poetic compositions preserve a theology of liturgy with regard to daily prayer, Christmas, Easter and other occasions. The continuation of an extended and elaborate catechumenate and rites of initiation are captured in the writings of other less-known bishops such as CHROMATIUS, bishop of Aquileia (c. 388–407), GAUDENTIUS, bishop of Brescia (c. 397), ZENO, bishop of Verona (362–c. 375), MAXIMUS, bishop of Turin (died c. 423) and PETER CHRYSOLOGUS, bishop of Ravenna (c. 400–50). In addition, several early Western liturgical texts come from the north of Italy, including the *Rotulus* of Ravenna (c. 5th–7th century), and a number of lectionaries, gospel books, or lists of scripture readings for the Eucharist, such as the *Lectionary of Sélestat*, c. 700; *Bobbio Missal*, c. 6th; and the *Gospel Book of Vercelli*, c. 4th–8th centuries.

Spain. The early liturgical evidence from Spain is not as extensive as other geographical centers. Aside from a number of local synods concerned with funerals Eucharists held at the cemetery and the cult of martyrs, it is not until the primary Spanish liturgical books, the *Liber mozarabicus sacramentorum* and the *Liber ordinum*, that we have extensive knowledge of the Mozarabic rite (materials date from the 5th to the 10th centuries). One of the great early poets and hymn writers in the Latin language was a Spaniard, PRUDENTIUS (348–c. 410), whose texts covering the feasts and seasons of the liturgical year are still sung today.

Gaul. The great explosion of liturgical texts from Gaul occurs in the late 7th and 8th centuries, but several different sources inform our knowledge prior to that. The earliest references are from IRENAEUS, Bishop of Lyons (c. 177–200), who, while not a native of Gaul, reflected local practices in his extensive writings on the meaning of Baptism, Eucharist and Christian death. Other early liturgical references come from the canons of local Gallican councils and synods, of which there were many between the 4th and the 7th centuries, and the canonical collection, *Statuta ecclesia antiqua*, of the late 5th century. The writings of various bishops reveal a great deal about liturgical practice, especially those of CAESARIUS OF ARLES (c. 470–542) and GREGORY OF TOURS (bishop from 573–94). A rare source for liturgical detail is the

disputed (as to author and date) *Expositio antiquae liturgiae gallicanae*, perhaps written by Germanus, Bishop of Paris (555–76). The document contains a wealth of information which supports other evidence of the strong Eastern (and particularly Syrian) influences in Gallican liturgy and the cult of the martyrs. There are extensive hagiographical resources from Gaul, including the *Life of Martin of Tours* by Sulpicius Severus (c. 401) and the *History of the Franks, Glory of the Martyrs*, and *Glory of the Confessors* all by Gregory of Tours, which contain information about daily prayer, healing and anointing, Eucharist, Baptism, funerals, the liturgical year and the rise of monastic influence on parish liturgy. Finally, two early lectionaries, the *Wolfenbüttel Palimpsest* (c. 500) and the *Lectionary of Luxeuil* (c. late 7th century) contribute to our understanding of how the developing cycle of the liturgical year was arranged.

Out of this regional variety emerges the great liturgical families of rites in the 5th to 7th centuries: the ROMAN RITE, which in a hybrid form would eventually dominate in Europe; the GALLICAN RITE; the MOZARABIC RITE of Spain; the AMBROSIAN RITE of Milan; the CELTIC RITE; the COPTIC and ETHIOPIAN Rites; the various Syrian Rites (EAST SYRIAN, MARONITE, SYRO-MALABAR); the ARMENIAN RITE; and the BYZANTINE RITE (and later related national rites).

Early Historical Shifts in Initiation and Eucharist. The early history of the church is the setting for some of the most dramatic shifts in the two major liturgical actions of the church, initiating new members and the ongoing center of ecclesial identification, the Eucharist. Without forcing an artificial uniformity in the early rites of initiation, there are still some generalizations which can be made with regard to ritual and interpretation in Christian initiation. The scriptural evidence reveals a simplicity of profession of faith, minimal preparation, water bath and, of course, a changed life. This pattern soon develops from a sequence of more deliberate preparation, water bath and Eucharist (*Didache* and *Justin Martyr*) to the addition of anointings, sometimes multiple (*Tertullian* and the *Apostolic Tradition*) and finally to the large-scale and rigorous catechumenate of the 4th century (see especially the *catecheses* of Cyril of Jerusalem, Ambrose of Milan, John Chrysostom and Theodore of Mopsuestia). As the church moved through the 4th century, the "cost" of baptism began to shift dramatically, from the potential danger of being martyred to the reality that baptism could lead to status and position in worldly affairs. While not outwardly reflected in the rites themselves, certainly this dramatic shift changed the understanding of what was happening in initiation. The elaboration of ritual and ritual process reaches an apex by the 5th centuries, however, at which time the complex rites begin to change, either taking place within a considerably shorted amount of time (Greek and Syrian) or, fractured into distinct actions separated by years (Latin). This shift goes hand in hand with another major change, adults to infants as the subject of the initiation process. This is a shift with wide-ranging ramifications, most notably the reversal of catechesis first-initiation second, to initiation first-weak catechesis second. This shift affects understandings of what initiation does, the role of personal affirmation of faith, the meaning of Lent, and the unity of the rites of initiation, to name just a few. Shifts in Eucharist during the early centuries of the church will also result in dramatic changes in practice and understanding. The textual shift from a preference for blessing in Judaism to a preference for thanksgiving and offering in Christianity will impact the construction of fixed prayers; the shift from domestic settings to public spaces will change the view of who participates and who leads; the move from small groups of people who knew each other to larger and larger gatherings removes Eucharist from the meal setting and changes the fabric of relationships; the legalization of Christianity opens the door to the increasing inculturation of the ritual to the imperial cult, rivaling the glories of the court; the change in design of buildings, removing the action of the Eucharist from access and sight parallels the shift in understanding of Eucharist as meal to Eucharist as awe-filled mystery and sacrifice. In the West, the evolution of language will result in a distancing of comprehension from a liturgical language which did not change, and the stratification of ranks of Christians within the church will affect understandings of access and worthiness. Finally, in spite of great continuity in the shape of the Eucharistic liturgy, reductions in primary rituals and expansions in secondary rituals will result in a liturgy which appears quite different by the late 7th- to early 8th-century description of Roman papal liturgy detailed in the *Ordo romanus primus*. Parallel shifts in the early rites of reconciliation, ordination, anointing of the sick and eventually marriage can be traced through these same pivotal centuries of the church.

Bibliography: J. BALDOVIN, *The Urban Character of Christian Worship* (Rome 1987). P. BRADSHAW, *The Search for the Origins of Christian Worship* (New York 1992). M. JOHNSON, ed., *Living Water, Sealing Spirit* (Collegeville 1995). G. MACY, *The Banquet's Wisdom: A Short History of the Theologies of the Lord's Supper* (New York 1992). E. MAZZA, *The Celebration of the Eucharist: The Origin of the Rite and the Development of Its Interpretation* (Collegeville 1999). F. PAXTON, *Christianizing Death: The Creation of a Ritual Process in Early Medieval Europe* (Ithaca 1990). T. TALLEY, *The Origins of the Liturgical Year* (Collegeville 1986). P. TURNER, *The Hallelujah Highway: A History of the Catechumenate* (Chicago 2000). C. VOGEL, *Medieval Liturgy: An Introduction to the Sources* trans. and rev. by W. STOREY and N. RASMUSSEN (Washington, D.C. 1986). E. YARNOLD, *The Awe-*

Inspiring Rites of Initiation: The Origins of the RCIA (Collegeville 1994).

[L. LARSON-MILLER]

Medieval

For the purposes of this entry, "medieval liturgy" will refer to the development of the liturgy from the mid-8th century to the early 16th century in the Latin West, from the rise of the Carolingian monarchy to the 95 Theses of Martin Luther.

Some trends in the complex history of medieval liturgy may be observed from the outset. The first is that of two broad periods of Romanization: the Carolingian renaissance and the propagation of the liturgy of the Roman curia. The second is a general movement from widely variant customs, through a sense of unity, to the uniformity of a single Roman liturgical practice.

THE PRE-CAROLINGIAN SITUATION

To appreciate the importance of the Carolingian liturgical renaissance, some background is needed. The liturgical centers of the early church developed under the aegis of the Roman Empire. With the fall of Rome in the early 5th century, those provinces whose wellbeing depended on the *pax romana* were thrown into chaos. Moreover, the boundaries of the known world continued to expand North and East into regions lacking historical liturgical centers.

Gaul, nominally Christian since the baptism of Clovis (496), experienced scattered integration of Roman liturgical culture as a result of initiatives of private individuals, primarily monks and pilgrims, bringing back books and mementos from Rome. The Gallican church was organized on a local basis, and with the exception of early conciliar efforts to unify provinces with the same liturgical practice, there was little concern about liturgical unity.

When, with papal approval, the Carolingians usurped the Frankish throne in the mid-8th century, they sought to reorganize church life as an aid to unifying the realm and expanding into pagan territories. They had long sponsored the work of Anglo-Saxon missionaries (e.g., Boniface) who had strong ties to Rome and had restored ecclesiastical discipline via episcopal councils. The organization of a unified liturgical practice in Gaul was more difficult as available liturgical materials were varied and often threadbare. Years of constant warfare had interrupted the output of books by monastic workshops, and the Carolingians turned to Rome for help.

THE FIRST ROMANIZATION OF EUROPE

The Carolingian Synthesis. With the reign of Pippin III (741–768) the church became the focus of the Carolingian renaissance, and the enterprise of Romanization shifted from assimilation to substitution. In attempting a revival of old Roman culture, the Frankish monarchs created something new, a church-state led by an emperor thoroughly reliant upon monks and bishops (e.g., Alcuin, Theodulf). The leadership of the Frankish church took up the task of renewal with great energy and creativity, producing an explosion of liturgical materials. They, like their emperor, set about to restore the Roman liturgy, and ended up producing a hybrid of old and new. With the revival of monasticism, the Carolingians made it possible for Frankish scribes to set about assembling and systematizing liturgical texts. The 9th through 11th centuries were centuries of the book.

Liturgical Books. A significant Carolingian achievement was the development of the *Sacramentaries*, a book containing the words spoken by the liturgy's presider. Sacramentaries evolved from *libelli missarum*, small booklets containing the presider's prayers (excepting the *canon missae*) for one or more masses. Sacramentaries occasionally included ritual comments that became known as rubrics after the custom of writing them in red to distinguish them from the spoken words. By the early 8th century, two principal types of Roman sacramentaries were circulating in Gaul: GELASIAN and GREGORIAN. These types were differentiated both by their origin and organization of material. Gelasians originated in the presbyteral liturgies of the Roman parish churches (*tituli*) and were organized into distinct cycles: Sundays and feasts celebrating events in life of Jesus (*Temporale*), and feasts of the saints (*Sanctorale*). Gregorians were a presbyteral adaptation of the papal liturgy used at St. Peter's, and the materials appeared in a single series according to the movement of the liturgical year. These two types were blended together with older Gallican material to form the so-called Frankish (or, 8th-century) Gelasian Sacramentaries.

To make sense of the confusing proliferation of resources, the Carolingians imported both books and liturgical personnel from Rome. The principal example was Charlemagne's request for "pure" Roman sacramentary from Pope Hadrian (r. 772–795). After considerable delay, the pope sent a book that represented a papal liturgy from the early 8th century. The *Hadrianum*, a type of Gregorian sacramentary, was received with some confusion as it contained no formulae for many Sundays. To provide missing materials and address local circumstances, Frankish liturgists under the guidance of BENEDICT OF ANIANE (d. 821) assembled a supplement of optional texts. Charlemagne issued the *Hadrianum* and its supplement—known by its incipit *Hucusque*—with a decree requiring the use of the former, and recommending the latter. In subsequent copies the division between the sacramentary and the supplement was blurred, and the entire work took on royal authority. The Carolingians had succeeded in cataloging liturgical texts, but not systematizing them. Use of the *Hadrianum* spread sporadically as it was too expensive to replace old manuscripts that were still usable. But the sacramentary was a book for the presider only, and other books, each with its own complex history, were required to conduct the liturgy.

An *ORDO* (pl. *ordines*) contained ceremonial directions for conducting a service (Eucharist, Baptism, Ordination, etc.) and was a necessary accompaniment to a sacramentary. Various *ordines* migrated north of the Alps independently to be gathered into collections by Frankish liturgists. Like the sacramentaries, *ordines* were adapted for local use.

The *lectionary,* a list of readings for specific services, developed in several ways. Readings could simply be noted in the margins of a book of Scripture; a separate list could be made, indicating where readings began and ended (*capitulary*); readings could be written out in full, and assembled in an independent book; or they could be written out in full and assembled with the other texts required for the liturgy. An *EVANGELARY* was a type of lectionary containing only readings from the Gospels.

The *antiphonary* contained all of the things to be sung for either the office or the Eucharistic liturgy. The Roman antiphonary and members of the *schola cantorum* brought from Rome by Pippin were vital to the Frankish liturgical reform as cantors also served as masters of ceremony and liturgical experts. The book of music for the Eucharist was sometimes called the *gradual*.

The *PONTIFICAL* included material needed by a bishop for non-eucharistic services (e.g., Baptism, Ordination). The pontifical—a much later term—was a practical combination of non-eucharistic *ordines* with corresponding prayers from the sacramentary, and took many centuries to evolve into the *Pontificale Romanum* of 1596. An important Carolingian landmark was the *Romano-Germanic Pontifical* (RGP) from about 960. Compiled by Frankish liturgists, it played an important role in the Ottonian reform of Roman liturgical life in the 10th century The development of pontificals illustrates the presumption that the ordinary liturgical presider is no longer the bishop, and we see an analogous development of the *RITUAL*, a resource providing priests with materials needed for the non-eucharistic services for which he was responsible (baptism, penance, marriage, anointing, burial).

The Church's Worship: Calendar. The seasons before and after Easter were the first to develop in most liturgical traditions; Sundays bore a direct connection to the celebration of the Resurrection. By the Carolingian period the unity of the Paschal celebration had begun to break apart, with each of the three days of the ancient *Triduum* developing a distinct character. The ever-present strain of liturgical interest in the course of Jesus' earthly life found great room for growth, and we see the roots of Western drama in the development of liturgical drama (e.g., *Quem quaeritis* and Passion plays). A similar piety will flourish around the Nativity cycle. The Carolingians also introduced the preface *De Trinitate* (Concerning the Trinity) that became the permanent Sunday preface and marked a decisive shift of the Sunday Eucharist from resurrection memorial to doctrinal formulation. The bulk of medieval additions to the calendar were in the Sanctorale, with saints' days providing holidays.

The Church's Worship: Daily Prayer. Two different traditions of daily prayer had developed in the early period, the so-called cathedral and monastic traditions. Meant for different audiences, each was a combination of psalmody, readings, song, and prayer. The *cathedral office* was celebrated morning and evening, ideally in the presence of the bishop, and included large amounts of unchanging material. It was time-related, with the rising sun and the evening lamp becoming images of Christ as the light of the world. Another feature of the cathedral office was a weekly resurrection vigil, held on Saturday evening. By the 12th century, the establishment of parish churches contributed to the demise of the cathedral office as the people were less able to gather at local cathedrals.

The *monastic office* was an eight-fold structure: matins, lauds, prime, terce, sext, none, vespers, compline. The psalter was sung (or recited) weekly, and the office included scripture readings, canticles, hymns, hagiography (histories of saints), patristica (writings by church fathers), prayers, responses, and the Apostles' Creed. Eventually, so-called little offices in honor of Mary and the dead were attached to the daily cycle.

The monastic reforms of Benedict of Aniane were important building blocks of the Carolingian revival. Monasteries served as cultural and educational centers, vital to the production of liturgical books and reflection on liturgical practice. Benedict's reforms were to have an effect on the regular (i.e., non-monastic) clergy as well. At Metz, CHRODEGANG issued a Rule (*c.* 753) requiring priests to live in community and recite the office daily. He even directed them to say the office in private if unable to do so in common. Such a practice, novel for regular priests, set a trend toward a wider privatization of the church's official prayer.

The Church's Worship: Sacraments. *Christian Initiation*. In the Old Gelasian Sacramentary (Frankish redaction *c.*750) we see textual evidence of a central shift in Christian initiation—the presupposition of baptizing children rather than adults. Despite this change, the questions addressed to those being baptized were still aimed at those able to answer for themselves. The ancient multi-year catechumenate had become mostly ceremonial with its various rites all taking place within Lent. To the *traditio* (handing over) of the Gospels, Lord's Prayer and Creed to catechumens, the Carolingians added exorcism and the presentation of the Gospels. Baptism took place at the Easter Vigil or Pentecost, and included the laying on of hands by the bishop and communion. In the *Romano-Germanic Pontifical* (10th century) there was also a new order of Baptism combining many of the pre-baptismal and baptismal rites together for the baptism of children outside of Easter or Pentecost.

Eucharist. The Carolingian reforms had a vast influence on the celebration of the Eucharist in the West. Latin was becoming a specialized religious language, and the liturgical books were in constant flux. In addition to the increasing monasticisation of clerical life, the emperors laid down strict standards of clerical education, including regular examinations. Such particular attention to what the priest said and did at the Eucharist was to have a profound impact. Two immediate results were the rise of Mass commentaries (*expositiones missae*) and Eucharistic controversies.

Expositiones missae, a genre of liturgical exegesis whose origins were found in the mystagogical catecheses, found new life in the Carolingian educational program. The foremost figure was AMALARIUS of Metz (*c.* 775–850), who applied a fully developed vocabulary of symbolic interpretation to such commentaries; his principal work was the *Liber officialis*. Though officially condemned in his own day, Amalarius's work became the cornerstone for most subsequent medieval liturgical expositors, culminating in the *Rationale divinorum officiorum* of William Durandus the Elder (*c.* 1230–1296).

Already in the 9th century questions arose about the Eucharist that would influence the experience and the theology of the sacrament for centuries. Around 825, a Frankish monk at the monastery of Corbie, RATRAMNUS had proposed an understanding of the real presence of Christ in the eucharistic species based on an Augustinian conception of the reality of symbolic presence. His abbot, PASCHASIUS RADBERTUS preferred a more physical conception in the literal sense. BERENGARIUS OF TOURS revived the issue about 150 years later. Prayers by priests to be made worthy to celebrate the Eucharist began to appear at many points in the liturgy. These prayers (*apologiae*) soon formed part of the unchangeable Order of Mass (*ordo missae*) that began to take on the tone of a privatized devotional experience for the priest.

Priests began to fill roles of other liturgical leaders (e.g., deacon, lector, psalmist), often becoming the sole liturgical minister. Increasing attention was paid to the *canon missae* and institution narrative (''words of consecration''), a natural if problematic by-product of the eucharistic controversies. If what happened at the Eucharist was of great concern, when it occurred was equally important. The *canon missae* became inaudible to the people, though most did not understand Latin, and was gradually punctuated with gestures and bells to highlight its solemnity. The increase of such ritual elements throughout the liturgy accompanied the impoverishment of essential elements, e.g., the communion of the faithful.

In this period, we also see the beginnings of the private mass—priests celebrating the Eucharist without a congregation. The exact origins of this practice are unclear but, given the recent proliferation of ordained monks, one possibility is that it might have been monastic in origin. The great Carolingian monastic churches developed around the idea that each church, with its principal altar and many side altars, was a miniature copy of urban Rome with its many churches. While full privatization of the mass would come later, the Carolingian age provided the necessary tools: many priests and many altars. Some scholars have suggested that the side altars grew when pilgrimages to the Holy Land were no longer possible under Muslim rule. The side altars became substitutes, each altar representing a particular pilgrimage shrine. Others have identified the proliferation of side altars with the rise of private solitary masses and the notion of the mass as an *opus bonum* (good work) that each priest was obligated to perform.

Penance. In the pre-Carolingian period, penance was a multi-stage and public experience, including admission to the Order of Penitents, and eventual public reconciliation (cf. Old Gelasian Sacramentary). It was non-repeatable, and was used only for those considered to be in grave sin. Frankish liturgists added elements including vesting in a penitential garment and imposing ashes (cf. *Ordo Romanus* 50). In time, penitents were expelled from the congregation. These developments roughly coincided with the advent of private penance, introduced to the Frankish church by Irish and Anglo-Saxon monks though resisted by the Frankish bishops. In this new system now administered by priests, there was no order of penitents, no communal prayer, no liturgy of penance, and no need for bishops. A tariff system developed along with private penance, wherein certain offences had prescribed penalties, including monetary fines.

Conclusion. The Carolingians imported what they thought was the Roman liturgy into the chaotic liturgical world of 8th century Gaul. Finding it insufficient to their needs they added to it, forming a hybrid European (often known as the Romano-Frankish or Romano-Germanic) liturgy. They also turned their considerable creativity to adapting other remnants of Roman culture: language, music, script, architecture, painting and sculpture. By focusing on educating an increasingly monasticized clergy, they created a highly developed clerical culture that became more insular. This clerical and sacral class became the liturgical representatives of the observing laity. After Charlemagne's death, Carolingian culture declined quickly in the West, but was well preserved in the monasteries of the Eastern (''German'') part of the Empire. It was from here that the Ottonian emperors were able to impose the hybrid European liturgy on Rome in the middle of the 10th century.

THE SECOND ROMANIZATION OF EUROPE: THE LITURGY OF THE PAPAL COURT

The Roman curia. After the Ottonian period, there were great changes in the administration of the church. During the Investiture Controversy, Pope GREGORY VII (pope from 1073 to 1085) vastly increased his authority in relationship to the Emperors. The administrative workings of the church were systematized and, with important developments in canon law, the church became a governmental system with the pope at its head. Rome had long laid claim to the imagination of Western Christians; now it was also the seat of a powerful monarch. In the late 11th century, the papal court (*curia Romanum*) developed to assist in the governmental affairs of the church. Within the Lateran complex, the pope had his own chapel, and the celebration of the liturgy with pope and people of Rome in stational churches gave way to pope and court in the curial chapel. Special books were needed, and it was the European liturgy brought to Rome by the Ottonians that was adapted for this purpose.

Liturgical Books. *Missal.* A number of factors accompanied the growth of the missal, including an increasing number of churches and ordained priests. Additionally, new legislation obliged priests to recite to themselves all the parts of the Mass, even when performed by other ministers (e.g., deacon, psalmist). A practical book, the missal was a combination of sacramentary, lectionary, gradual and ordo. An important exemplar was the missal created for the curial chapel by Honorius III (pope from 1216 to 1227). In the *Missale plenum* (full missal), a later adaptation, texts were combined into mass formularies for each celebration. The *Missale plenum* would evolve into the *Missale Romanum* of 1570. (For a further discussion, *see* MISSAL, ROMAN.)

Pontifical and Ritual. The *pontifical* continued to evolve, heavily reliant on the RGP. The two principal pontificals of the 13th century were that of the Roman curia under the influence of INNOCENT III, and that of William Durandus (*c.* 1230–1296). With additional editing the latter became the *Pontificale Romanum* of 1596. Unlike the pontifical, the *ritual* was more adaptable to local circumstances, and there was considerable cross-pollination with the pontifical for services not reserved to bishops. Sometimes bound with sacramentaries, rituals became discrete books in the 11th century, and were made mandatory for priests from about the 12th century. (For more information, *see* PONTIFICAL and RITUAL, ROMAN).

Breviary. Analogous to the missal, the breviary began to appear in the 11th century, a practical compilation from many sources (*Psalter, Collectar, Lectionary,* and *Antiphonary*). Legislation of the Fourth Lateran Council (1214) bound the entire clergy to recite the Office. Innocent III (pope from 1198 to 1215) compiled the *Ordinale,* a prototype of the breviary, for curial use. Up until this time the Office had been marked by great creativity, and much material was omitted to form the breviary. The mendicant Orders of the 13th century, especially the Franciscans were instrumental in popularizing the breviary.

The Church's Worship: Daily Prayer. *Official Prayer.* From the 8th to the 12th centuries, monastic communities were the principal elaborators and transmitters of the divine office. The new mendicant orders such as those founded by Dominic (1170–1221) and Francis (1181–1226) found the complex monastic liturgical style unsuited to their itinerant lifestyle and pastoral work in urban areas. The liturgical books available at the cathedral of Assisi were those of the papal court and were used as models for a new style of liturgical books carried across Europe by the Franciscans. Still more revisions were made by Favo of Haversham (d. 1244).

In the same era, time demands upon priests attached to the new universities increased the pressure for private recitation. By the 15th century private recitation had become the norm for non-canonical priests. Although no synod before Trent obliged private recitation, the trend toward privatization begun in the Carolingian period had continued to escalate, with the result that the official prayer of the church was seen as an individual obligation of the ordained representative of the faithful.

Popular Prayer and the Saints. In the face of the increasing clericalization of official prayer, popular piety found ever-new modes of expression. Shortened versions of the divine office—especially LITTLE OFFICE OF THE BLESSED VIRGIN MARY and the Office of the Dead—became popular with lay people. Members of the upper classes commissioned sumptuous Books of Hours. New

celebrations of Mary and the saints and their relics continued to be added to the liturgical calendar. The sense of the year's progress and the Mass itself as a dramatic representation of salvation history also contributed to the proliferation of piety that the Council of Trent attempted to address.

The Church's Worship: Sacraments. *Christian Initiation.* Since the Carolingian period, infant baptism had become increasingly normative. The multi-year catechumenal rites, collapsed into Lent by the Carolingian period, had been further folded into one rite. Over the course of the Middle Ages the initiation process was gradually divided into three stages (Baptism, Confirmation, Communion) often separated by numbers of years, and involving different ministers. Several developments contributed to these changes. Eucharistic controversies contributed to misgivings about communing infants, although this varied widely. Additionally, the reigning theology of Baptism had become one of washing away Original Sin, resulting in an urge to baptize children as soon as possible after birth, and a final disconnection from Easter.

From the 14th century on, councils decreed that children be baptized within eight days of birth. Under these circumstances, it was unlikely for a bishop to be present for Confirmation, and later theologians began to assert that Confirmation augmented the grace of Baptism, and determined that it should administered at the age of reason—seven years old. Once Confirmation was an independent rite, more elements were added. Anointing becomes the central act of confirmation.

Eucharist. By the 12th century, the Eucharist had become the domain of the people's ordained representatives, rather than the people themselves. Latin was no longer a vulgar tongue in Europe. The Eucharistic table had become an altar at the east end of the church with only a small space for plate and cup. The faithful had become onlookers and liturgical details with visual interest were introduced. The most important of these was the elevation of the host in the middle of the *canon missae.* Officially prescribed in 1209, the so-called minor elevation spread rapidly. Such a visual focus on the consecrated Host opened the door to a preoccupation with ocular rather than oral communion. The evolution of tabernacles, rites of Exposition and Benediction, stories of miraculous (or bleeding) hosts, and the Feast of Corpus Christi (1264) were extensions of this highly specific and visual eucharistic piety.

Over time, the notion of the Eucharist as *opus bonum* (good work) gave rise to an elaborate stipendiary system, whereby a monetary offering is given to priests to say a mass for a specific intention. An elevated sense of unworthiness on the part of the laity, and the increasing emphasis on the priest celebrating the private mass (*missa privata*) hastened this development. In many places, the stipendiary system evolved into a full-blown system of remuneration for priests. Rich lay persons began to endow chantry chapels, setting up a trust to pay a priest to say a mass a day in perpetuity for the donor's soul.

Penance. By the first half of the 13th century, the tariff system had developed to such an extent that it was possible to exempt oneself from penance (e.g., fasting) with monetary payments (*redemptiones*), often in the form of paying mass stipends. In an attempt to curb such abuses, private confession was introduced into the rite of penance. This new focal point of the rite was soon overshadowed by the priest's absolution. All of this did not do away with the tariff system, and *redemptiones* developed into indulgences.

Conclusion. The liturgy of Rome, imported to Gaul in the 8th century and amended by Frankish liturgists, was re-imported to Rome in the 10th century. This hybrid, European liturgy was simplified for use in the Papal court, and further adapted by the mendicant orders of the 13th century who would popularize it across the face of Europe where it replaced a wide variety of traditions. This loose unity of liturgical practice would become codified at Trent, becoming the obligatory, uniform use of the Roman Catholic Church until the late 20th century.

Bibliography: R. CROCKER, *An Introduction to Gregorian Chant* (New York 2000). G. DIX, *The Shape of the Liturgy*, with notes by P. V. MARSHALL (San Francisco 1982). M. E. FASSLER and R. A. BALTZER, eds. *The Divine Office in the Latin Middle Ages: Methodology and Source Studies, Regional Developments, Hagiography* (New York 2000). J. HARPER, *The Forms and Orders of Western Liturgy from the Tenth to the Eighteenth Century: A Historical Introduction and Guide for Students and Musicians* (New York 1991). J. A. JUNGMANN, *The Mass of the Roman Rite: Its Origins and Development (Missarum sollemnia)*, tr. F. A. BRUENNER (New York 1950). L. LARSON-MILLER, ed., *Medieval Liturgy: A Book of Essays* (New York 1997). R. MCKITTERICK, *The Frankish Church and the Carolingian Reforms 789–895* (London 1977). E. PALAZZO, *A History of Liturgical Books from the Beginning to the Thirteenth Century*, tr. M. BEAUMONT (Collegeville, Minn. 1998). R. W. PFAFF, *Medieval Latin Liturgy: A Select Bibliography* (Toronto 1982). C. VOGEL, *Medieval Liturgy: An Introduction to the Sources*, tr. and rev. W. STOREY and N. RASMUSSEN (Washington, D.C. 1986).

[P. A. JACOBSON]

From Reformation to Vatican II

The period from the Reformation to the beginning of the Second Vatican Council consisted of times of comparative peace and tranquility interspersed with political and religious upheaval, and industrial and economic turmoil. For the Catholic Church, reform took place in the liturgy at the beginning of the period and was followed by several centuries in which little changed. Toward the end of the period it was clear that growing dissatisfaction indicated the need for a rethink and for reforms in the ways that the Church's prayer was celebrated. This entry breaks the period into four reasonably distinct historical sections: the 16th century; the 17th to 19th centuries; and the 19th and 20th centuries, and also considers developments in the Reform Churches.

16TH CENTURY

Liturgical Reforms of Luther and Calvin. It is important to take account of the significance of the Lutheran Reform for the history of liturgy during this time. In his ecclesiology, Martin LUTHER (1483–1546) identified the church as a communion of saints in both spiritual and institutional form. For him, the Spirit was not restricted by the institution but remained free to act. Of particular importance for Luther was his sense of the church as a local community, and so the *assembly* played a much greater role than had been usual before. Naturally, these elements were reflected in their communal prayer and worship, and we find this particularly in the emphasis upon the clarity of the spoken word in the vernacular, the encouragement of the participation of the congregation in all aspects of worship, including the music, and the involvement of the assembly in all other areas of church life. The focus on the word of God in scripture, both proclaimed and preached, is particularly noteworthy. For Luther, good preaching *makes* the church, and the liturgical ministry of greatest merit is that of the preacher, who inspires all Christians to preach the good news through the power of baptism. Turning away from the kind of individual piety that Luther identified as one of the signs of the failure of Christian liturgy up to his time, Luther encouraged fuller participation. His *Formula Missae et Communionis* of 1523 was followed by a much more radical service in the vernacular in 1526, including Communion under both species, hymns, texts and prayers in German, the abandonment of all language referring to sacrifice and the turning of the presiding minister to face the people over the altar table.

Among those who followed Luther in the history of the reform churches, the key figure for liturgical reform was John CALVIN (1509–64) of Geneva, Switzerland. His most influential liturgical work was his *Form of Church Prayers . . . according to the Custom of the Ancient Church*, published in 1542. In this, and in his more formally theological work, the *Institutes* of 1559, Calvin places a great deal of emphasis on the holiness of God and on the primacy of God's will. He emphasizes the importance of discipline, and on the ordered activity of the church community as it moves toward holiness. Calvin's views on liturgy are an important continuation of Luther's ideas, but show the influence of his own theology: baptism is our initiation into saving faith and the Lord's Supper is the symbol of unity of the community; the ministry of the Word of God governs all things; the promotion of good order should govern all liturgical practices, as all other aspects of the life of the faith community: peace and good order are the signs of the presence of a "true" Church; the sacraments and public worship are to be overseen by elected pastors, whose ordination, including the ceremony of the laying on of hands, is given considerable importance; liturgical variation is encouraged, with love as the guide for what is best.

Anglican Liturgical Reforms. Alongside the reform of the liturgy in Lutheran and Reformed Churches, there were important developments in the Anglican liturgy in England, led by the work and inspiration of Thomas CRANMER, Archbishop of Canterbury in 1532. During the short reign of Edward VI, Cranmer saw worship become strongly Protestant, and was responsible for two key texts before his execution in 1556: the BOOK OF COMMON PRAYER of 1549, and its second edition of 1552. Both these texts display important principles of theology for liturgy: the people's offering of themselves is a sacrifice of praise and thanksgiving; the sacrament of the Eucharist is a memorial of the passion and death of Christ; Christ's death on Calvary was to be regarded as unique, perfect, and all-sufficient; we are called to receive the Eucharist in a worthy manner. This second edition suffered under a ban from 1645 and reappeared in revised form in 1662. Another area of influence of Cranmer's liturgical reform was in music. Because of the requirements of the new rite, liturgical music underwent a revolution: paramount in the requirements of the music was to be the transmission of the text, clearly and with no doubt as to its intention; music thus now performed a key role in the proclamation of the word of God. Yes, the music in cathedrals still tended to be sophisticated and more elaborate than that found in most parishes, but the fundamental aim remained in force throughout. From this moment onward, then, we see the clear musical break between the churches of the Reform and Roman Catholicism: the Reform Churches recognized that the primary reason for singing hymns and psalms in the vernacular was as a tool for evangelization and the teaching of theology. This development was to find even greater encouragement through the inspiration of John WESLEY (1703–91) and his Methodist Church.

The Catholic Response: Council of Trent. A careful study of documents of the Council of TRENT reveals some level of pastoral concern on the part of the bishops who participated. Preference was given to "conventual" or communal Masses over private Masses lacking in music and other liturgical ministries; indeed, the solemn sung Mass was to be normative over the ferial "low Mass." Communion received by the lay faithful during the Mass that they had attended was recognized as important, and we even find discussion on the possibility of the assembly's drinking from chalice at Communion.

The seventh session of the council (1547) treated the sacraments, particularly baptism and confirmation, and the canons appear to be primarily directed against Luther and Melanchton. Seven sacraments were affirmed as having been instituted by Christ and containing "the grace which they signify," as opposed to Luther who would eventually affirm only baptism and confirmation as sacraments "instituted by Christ."

The thirteenth session (1551) affirmed the doctrine of transubstantiation, i.e., that at the moment of consecration the bread and wine is converted into the body and blood of Christ, "truly, really, and substantially," and that with the body and blood of Christ are His soul and divinity where the "whole Christ" is contained in its entirety in each species and in every part of each species. The sacrament was also to be reserved in churches for adoration and also for pastoral care of the infirmed.

In 1562 the twenty-first session treated the topic of Communion under both species for the laity, stating that laity and clerics who do not celebrate Mass are not obliged to drink from the chalice. As for the communing of little children, while the ancient practice of small children was not to condemned, it was neither required for salvation "before the age of reason."

The twenty-second session of the council (Sept. 17, 1562) addressed liturgical abuses in its disciplinary decree *De observandis et evitandis in celebratione missae:* the magical treatment of the host was to cease; Mass was to be celebrated only in consecrated oratories or churches; bishops were to better control their clergy regarding the number of Masses celebrated so that they did not profit inappropriately from an excessive number of Mass stipends; superstition around the fixed number of Masses was to stop as was the use of inappropriate liturgical music. Music had been used inappropriately in the liturgy prior to the council (e.g., as background to the priest's silent praying of the canon).

There was, indeed, widespread corruption within the Catholic Church of the 16th century, and much of that corruption centered around the liturgy and sacraments. The priest's Communion had come to be seen as sufficiently symbolic of the whole Church, and Eucharistic adoration became more important than the Eucharistic celebration itself. Some of those abuses might be attributed to ignorance on the part of clergy, since there was a tremendous lack of priestly formation; indeed, it was only at the Council of Trent that each diocese was required to have its own seminary. Whatever the reasons, abuses were rampant. There were problems with the exaggerated cult of the saints, along with an abuse of Mass stipends where some clergy celebrated as many as 30 Masses per day to receive the stipend; in some cases up to 1,000 Masses would be celebrated for a deceased person. Some clergy accepted two or three stipends for the same Mass while repeating the first part of the Mass two or three times up to the preface, but praying the canon only once. The abuse of indulgences and the large numbers of clergy living in concubinage only contributed to a decline in the Church's credibility.

The council's twenty-second session also affirmed the propitiatory nature of sacrifice of the Mass as a response to Protestant reformers who could only affirm that the Mass was a "sacrifice of praise," or a "testament" of God's forgiveness. Rather, Christ offered himself in bread and wine to reveal himself as a priest in the order of Melchizedek. Indeed, the third canon of that session stated that if one holds that the Mass is nothing more than a sacrifice of praise and thanksgiving or a mere commemoration of the sacrifice on the cross and not a proprietary sacrifice, "let him be anathema." Moreover, against the reformers, priests were reminded that water was to be mixed with wine in offering the chalice, as already decreed in the Council of FLORENCE.

The use of the vernacular was another item on the agenda also discussed at length in the twenty-second session. Council records show that some bishops spoke out in favor of the vernacular, at least for some parts of the Mass. They did so out of concern for large numbers of their congregations who were unable to grasp the richness of what was taking place since they were unable to understand Latin. These participants did not deny the centrality of Latin as the official language of the Church, nor did they deny its beauty as a language of mystery, but argued, rather, out of pastoral sensitivity for their constituencies. Thus, in the twenty-second session, it was decided that the liturgical readings and the mystery of the Eucharist should be explained to the people in the local language, at least on Sundays and feast days.

It was in the twenty-fifth session of the council when the reform of the missal and breviary were discussed, but the complexity of such a task and lack of time prompted the council fathers to delegate the task to the reigning pontiff, PIUS IV. He, in turn, delegated the project to a commission whose proceedings are no longer extant. Although the Council of Trent limited its liturgical mandate only to the reform of the missal and breviary, it is appropriate to refer to the subsequent revision of other liturgi-

cal books as part of the Tridentine reform, since those revisions were very much influenced by the council's spirit. In both the breviary and missal reforms, a primary goal was liturgical uniformity. Thus, for the first time, these liturgical books contained carefully prescribed rubrics printed at the beginning of each text, despite requests for regional differences to be respected with variations in the Roman rite to be determined by the local bishops involved. The source for these rubrics was the 1502 *Ritus servandus in celebratione missae* of Johannes Burckard, papal master of ceremonies.

The postconciliar liturgical commission was led by Cardinal Guglielmo Sirleto. In a relatively brief period, revision of the breviary and missal was completed; the breviary the first to be promulgated. Following the publication of a new postconciliar Index (1564) and a new *Roman Catechism* (1566), the Roman Breviary followed two years later in 1568: the *Breviarium romanum ex decreto sacrosancti Concilii Tridentini restitutum Pii V. Pont. Max iussu editum.*

Prior to the council, Pope CLEMENT VII (1523–34) had commissioned the Spanish Cardinal Francisco de QUIÑONES to undertake a revision of the breviary, which he published in 1535. Quiñones intended his edition of the breviary for private use and divided the psalter into weekly segments, eliminating repetitions; saints' legends; votive offices; hymns; and other elements more appropriate to the choral office. Scripture readings were lengthened and read sequentially. The simplicity of the Quiñones text held great appeal and was reprinted 11 times in the first year alone, and more than 100 times in its 30-year history. It was ultimately supressed by the conciliar breviary of 1568. The sanctoral calendar was restructured in the new breviary, bringing about greater balance between ferial days and feasts and a more ordered praying of the psalter. Localized customs that could not demonstrate an ancient tradition of at least two centuries or more were eliminated.

Some of the concerns evidenced in the breviary reform were seen yet again in the reform of the missal. The Roman Missal (*Missale Romanum ex decreto ss. Concilii Tridentini restitutum, Pii V. Pont. Max iussu editum*) was promulgated on July 14, 1570. This was not a new rite of the Mass, but rather a lightly revised edition of the 1474 missal used by the Roman Curia. In the Tridentine revision, the liturgical calendar was restructured. Saints' days were diminished as Sirleto's commission gave priority to the principal liturgical seasons and feasts of the Church year and to those saints' days celebrated in Rome prior to the 11th century; numerous minor (often local) feasts and memorials were excised, resulting in 157 free days on the liturgical calendar with the exception of octaves. Some votive masses and sequences were also removed. Private prayers and gestures of the priest-celebrant that found their way into the Roman Rite through Gallican influence were also reordered.

As the new breviary was to be the primary tool for the centralization of the Divine Office for the Church, so the *Missale Romanum* of 1570 was to be the definitive text for the celebration of the Roman Rite. Like the criteria used for the breviary reform, the new missal was to suppress all other local rites less than 200 years old. Thus, such religious orders as the Dominicans, and certain dioceses (e.g., Milan and Lyon) were given permission to continue using their own missals, each with its own distinctive rites.

Twelve years later, in 1582, the liturgical calendar was revised under Pope Gregory XIII, followed by the revision of the *Roman martyrology* in 1584. Using the 9th-century martyrology of Usuard as the source, hagiographical accretions that were either historically inaccurate or undocumented were removed. The work was completed by a commission of ten, including the noted historian Cardinal Cesare Baronius whose further revisions of the text were published in 1586 and 1589. The martyrology was meant to be read in religious communities during the daily office of Prime. The making of new saints and ongoing research made the martyrology the most revised liturgical book of all, with frequent new editions.

The Congregation of RITES was established by Pope Sixtus V in 1588 along with 14 other congregations. This new congregation was to oversee the celebration of the rites themselves; the restoration and reform of ceremonies; the reform of liturgical books; the canonization of saints and regulation of the office of patron saints; the celebration of feasts; and the reception of dignitaries to Rome. It was also responsible for dealing with liturgical problems raised by local circumstances. While the Congregation of Rites had varied responsibilities, the primary focus of that office was clearly to promote liturgical unification throughout the world and to assure that the newly included liturgical rubrics were carefully followed.

The reform of other liturgical books begun at Trent was continued with the Congregation of Rites. Based on the 13th-century pontifical of French bishop William Durandus, a new *Roman Pontifical* (for the use of bishops) was published in 1956 and made universally mandatory by Pope CLEMENT VIII. The first *Caeremoniale Episcoporum* (a book of rubrics for bishops and Episcopal masters of ceremonies) followed in 1600. The *Roman Ritual* (a pastoral manual for deacons, priests, and bishops) was published in 1614, containing texts for the administration of baptism, penance, marriage, extreme unction, proces-

sions, and for the blessings of persons, places, and things. The source for the 1614 text was largely the 1523 manual for priests by Dominican Alberto Castellani, as well as Cardinal Guilio Antonio Santori's 1601 ritual. The *Roman Ritual* was not obligatory, although its use was encouraged by Pope PAUL V. The fact that the text never received a universal mandate meant that it was hardly known outside of Italy until the middle of the 19th century, and even then, many dioceses had their own appendixes included until Vatican II.

17TH TO 19TH CENTURIES

Revision, Development, and Stagnation. The revision of the Catholic rites after the Council of Trent shows the effects of the theological debates between Catholicism and the Reform Churches. Of particular importance is the emphasis on the nature of Christ's presence in the Eucharist, the significance of the *verba Iesu* during the Eucharistic prayer, and the ecclesial centrality of Rome. Certain texts were removed altogether (for example, all but four sequences were removed) and the list of feast days and saints' days was simplified. Alongside this simplification and regularization came inevitable rubricism, indicating the desire to maintain the rituals and to apply them uniformly across the realm of Catholicism through the use of instructions of great detail. Thus, for the first time, the Missal was printed with an introduction composed by the papal master of ceremonies, providing a detailed list of rules to be followed in the celebration of Mass. There is little doubt that the printing of these texts greatly enhanced the possibility of uniformity in ritual. Only churches with ritual whose provenance could be proved to be more than 200 years old were exempt.

The reforms of the Missal and the Breviary were successful and effective, and these were soon followed by revision of the other books of worship: the Ritual, the Martyrology, the Ceremonial, the Pontifical. This process of reform and development seems to have come to a standstill, and the effectiveness of the reform lasted only about 50 years. As the decades went by, the original aim of simplification of rites and especially of liturgical music, as encountered in the compositions of Palestrina and Victoria for example, was ignored in some places as cathedrals vied with one another for the splendor of their ritual and music. Along with the leap in artistic and musical sophistication, we also see a rise in the number of liturgical feasts. It is during this period (about 1580 to 1903) that we find the introduction of major religious feasts such as Sacred Heart and *Corpus Christi,* the enhancement of the role of Mary with the construction of new rites for the celebration of the Immaculate Heart of Mary and the Immaculate Conception, and the addition of over 100 other feast days. As the rites continued to grow and proliferate, it was clear that further reform was required, but in fact it was only in France that anything significant was achieved. During the 18th century as many as 50 dioceses adopted the reformed Parisian liturgy for Mass and the Divine Office of *c.* 1736. these too, however, came under attack from several influential church figures, including Prosper GUÉRANGER, and the attack was ultimately successful.

Synod of Pistoia (1786). A significant attempt at liturgical reform in the 18th century came with the initiative made by Scipione de' RICCI (d.1810), bishop of PISTOIA. In that Jansenist-influenced synod, the call was made for a return to the pristine liturgy of the early church, encouraging active liturgical participation by the laity and in the vernacular, gathered around only one common altar in every church. There was emphasis on only one principal Sunday Mass where the priest proclaimed the presidential prayers in loud, clear voice. Communion given to the faithful should be consecrated at that Mass and not given from the tabernacle. Baptismal preparation for parents and godparents was insisted upon, and it was preferable that baptisms took place during the Easter Vigil. Marriage preparation was also decreed. The synod was ahead of its time and lacked the movements and years of preparation that preceded Vatican II. De' Ricci was deposed as bishop in 1790 and the synod was condemned four years later by Pope PIUS VI in the bull *AUCTOREM FIDEI.*

19TH AND 20TH CENTURIES

From Solesmes to the Liturgical Movement. More recent centuries saw important development in liturgy throughout Christianity. The reform of the liturgy within the Anglican Church was given much impetus by the Parish and People movement (1949–68) and its most popular cause, the Parish Communion movement. Most prominent among its members was A. G. Hebert, author of *Liturgy and Society* in 1935. The work and inspiration of these groups fostered and ultimately led to the production of the continued adaptations of the *Book of Common Prayer,* the *Alternative Service Book* (1980), and *Common Worship* (2000). (*See* OXFORD MOVEMENT.)

The four key figures during this period in the Catholic Church were Prosper GUÉRANGER (1805–75), founder of the Abbey of SOLESMES, Lambert BEAUDUIN (1873–1960), one of the founding figures of the modern LITURGICAL MOVEMENT, Pope PIUS X (pope 1903–14) and Pope PIUS XII (pope 1939–58). Guéranger's influence on the liturgy in France and across Europe was immense, fostered by the fame of the liturgy at his abbey, continued on through the liturgical prayer in monasteries in Germany (BEURON) and Belgium (MAREDSOUS and Mont César)

and through his publications, principally his *Année Liturgique,* (1841–66). Perhaps Solesmes's greatest influence was its restoration of plainchant to the celebration of the liturgy, mainly thanks to the efforts of André MOCQUEREAU, fostered through the benefits of printing and greatly indebted to the Vatican for its official approval.

PIUS X's motu proprio *Tra le sollecitudini* of 1903 has commonly been credited with starting off the reform of the liturgy toward the possibility of a fuller participation by the assembly, which reached its zenith at the Second Vatican Council. While he limited his aim to the education of the laity in singing Gregorian Chant, it was the statement of the philosophy behind this intention that was so important—they should learn the chants in order to take part in the celebration more fully, and thus to be drawn toward sharing in the Eucharist. Above all, Pius reformed the liturgical laws to enable more frequent Communion (*Sacra Tridentina,* 1905), and recommended the reception of Communion for children. In addition to these important reforms, Pius also regularized the primacy of the celebration of the Lord's Day over other feasts, as well as the order of the recitation of psalms in the Daily Office.

Among those who responded to these reforms by Pius X, the most significant was Dom Lambert Beauduin, of the monastery of Mont César. Beginning with liturgical conferences and courses, Beauduin founded the Centre du Pastoral Liturgique in Paris, published the influential journal *Questions Liturgiques* and founded an ecumenical (Roman Catholic and Orthodox) monastery.

It is important to note the theological atmosphere prevalent at this time. Grave measures were taken to ensure that theological developments were in line with the prevailing notion that theological questions were to be dealt with according to the classic scholastic method. Any theological speculation based on contemporary values or philosophical techniques or discoveries came to be seen as a dangerous threat to the traditional teaching of the Church. The same Pius X who had promoted active participation in the liturgy also issued the decree *LAMENTABILI* and the encyclical *PASCENDI* in 1907, condemning the errors of ''MODERNISM'' and establishing an oath to be taken by all priests and theologians in the Catholic Church, one not rescinded until 1967. Thus speculative or experimental theology became difficult if not impossible, and this may have helped to spur theologians to turn to the tradition and the historical sources. Yet this too was dangerous, if the discoveries made seemed to threaten the status quo: the power of the neo-Thomistic method and the authority of the established tradition. We should therefore admire Beauduin's dogged determination to base his studies of the liturgy on as many historical texts as he could find. Beauduin gradually built up a collection of texts that was to be an important archive of materials concerning the liturgy and many other theological subjects. An important part of Beauduin's approach was that the study of historical texts demanded that one try to understand the intellectual and social milieu of the writer of the original text. Although he did not publish more than a single book, Beauduin's many talks, lectures, and articles in *Questions Liturgiques,* as well as his influence on the many priests he trained about the liturgy, represent an abiding source for the movement toward the reform of the liturgy that came after him. Elements typical to the reforming work and influence of Beauduin were mirrored in Germany through the efforts of Romano GUARDINI (1885–1968), Odo CASEL (1886–1948) and Pius PARSCH (1884–1954), who have left to posterity a much more extensive range and depth of liturgical writing.

For some time during this first half of the 20th century, there was considerable support for the fostering of good liturgy from the Vatican. PIUS XI (pope 1922–39) sought to promote effective liturgy through his Apostolic constitution of 1928, *Divini cults sanctitatem.* PIUS XII was regarded as the primary patron of pastoral liturgy during his pontificate, and paid particular attention to increased participation by the laity in liturgy, the fostering of good liturgical music, congregational singing, and the like. His most important liturgical statement, the encyclical *MEDIATOR DEI* (1947), sought to encourage the fostering of worthy liturgical rites and more frequent Communion. Pius XII's commitment to the process is shown by his creating a special commission to oversee the reform of the liturgy, his acceptance of the need for the use of the vernacular, even if under carefully controlled conditions, and his request for the rubrics to be simplified. Of particular importance was the revision of the rites of Holy Week from 1956 onward. Taking their cue from the Vatican, many dioceses around the world supported the continuing reform, and there was a growing sense that the liturgy would have to be examined in greater detail, fostering another, albeit this time more thorough, "return to the sources." (For a further discussion on the incipient trends in liturgical renewal that formed the basis of Vatican II's Constitution on the Sacred Liturgy, e.g., dialogue masses; *see* LITURGICAL MOVEMENT, I: CATHOLIC.)

The Second Vatican Council and *Sacrosanctum Concilium.* JOHN XXIII's calling of the Second Vatican Council gave the foremost liturgical scholars and historians of the day a powerful forum in which to provide the bishops and other delegates with the fruits of their research and experience, and to ensure that the reforms that were put in place would be far-reaching and effective. The work of the preparatory commission was long and arduous, but resulted in the constitution *Sacrosanctum Concilium,* issued on Dec. 4, 1963.

Bibliography: B. BOTTE, *From Silence to Participation* (Washington, D.C. 1988). A. BUGNINI, *The Reform of the Liturgy: 1948–1975* (Collegeville, Minn. 1990). J. D. CRICHTON, *Lights in the Darkness* (Collegeville, Minn. 1996). H. DAVIES, *Worship and Theology in England,* Combined Edition, Book I, "From Cranmer to Hooker" (Grand Rapids, Mich. 1996). G. DIX, *The Shape of the Liturgy* (London 1945, 1993). E. FOLEY, *From Age to Age: How Christians Celebrated the Eucharist* (Chicago 1992). R. JASPER, *The Development of the Anglican Liturgy, 1662–1980* (London 1989). J. A. JUNGMANN, *The Mass of the Roman Rite: Its Origins and Development,* 2 v. (Blackrock/Dublin 1950). E. KILMARTIN, *The Eucharist in the West: History and Theology,* ed. R. J. DALY (Collegeville, Minn. 1998). D. MACCULLOCH, *Thomas Cranmer* (New Haven, Conn. 1996). A. G. MARTIMORT et al., ed., *The Church at Prayer,* v. 1–2, (Collegeville, Minn. 1986). M. METZGER, *History of the Liturgy: The Major Stages* (Collegeville, Minn. 1997). K. F. PECKLERS, "History of the Roman Liturgy from the Sixteenth to the Twentieth Centuries," *Handbook for Liturgical Studies I,* ed. A. J. CHUPUNGCO (Collegeville, Minn. 1997) 153–178. D. N. POWER, *The Sacrifice We Offer: The Tridentine Dogma and Its Reinterpretation* (Edinburgh 1987). S. A. QUITSLUND, *Beauduin, a Prophet Vindicated* (New York 1973). F. C. SENN, *Christian Liturgy: Catholic and Evangelical* (Minneapolis 1997). G. S WAKEFIELD, *An Outline of Christian Worship* (Edinburgh 1998). J. F. WHITE, *Roman Catholic Worship, Trent to Today* (New York 1995). J. F. WHITE, *Protestant Worship: Traditions in Transition* (Louisville, Ky. 1989). S. J. WHITE, "Christian Worship since the Reformation," *The Making of Jewish and Christian Worship* ed. P. BRADSHAW and L. HOFFMANN (Notre Dame 1991). M. T. WINTER, *Why Sing?: Toward a Theology of Catholic Church Music* (Washington, D.C. 1984).

[A. CAMERON-MOWAT/K. F. PECKLERS]

Vatican II's Program of Liturgical Reform

The program of liturgical reform initiated by the Second Vatican Council was delineated in its *Constitution on the Sacred Liturgy*, promulgated Dec. 4, 1963.

Principles of Liturgical Reform. The paramount purpose of this reform was to restore to the faithful "that full, intelligent, active part in liturgical celebrations which the nature of the liturgy itself requires, and which, in virtue of their Baptism, is their right and duty" (*Sacrosanctum Concilium* 14). This essentially pastoral concern as the supreme norm for liturgical reform is repeated over and over throughout the Constitution, and is given solid doctrinal support in the rich theological introduction on the nature of the liturgy and its importance in the life of the Church (*ibid.* 5–13). This theological and pastoral foundation for reform, likewise prefaced to each of the seven remaining chapters of the Constitution, was to become one of the insistent and increasingly profound characteristics of the major documents of liturgical reform. Posited on the assumption that the liturgy consists of "a part that is unchangeable because it is divinely instituted and of parts that can be changed," the reform clearly involved giving to "texts and rites a form that will express clearly the sacred content they are meant to signify, a form such that the Christian people will be able to grasp this content as easily as possible and share in it in a full, active, congregational celebration" (*ibid.* 21).

Three areas were explicitly singled out for a revision based on an understanding that liturgical services were "not private activities, but celebrations of the Church" (*ibid.* 26): (1) the hierarchical and communal nature of the liturgy, by which the diverse ministerial roles of the entire liturgical assembly were to be fostered (*ibid.* 26–32); (2) the pastoral and didactic nature of the liturgy, by which, through the clear, concise, and simple conjuncture of word and rite, the faith of the participants is nourished (*ibid.* 33–36); (3) the cultural diversity of various groups, regions and peoples, which, while still preserving the "substantial unity of the Roman rite," would profit by "legitimate variations and adaptations" (*ibid.* 37–40). In light of the pastoral and theological objectives of the Constitution, these were the three fundamental directional principles that were to govern the reform of the Eucharistic Liturgy, rites for the other Sacraments and sacramentals, the Liturgy of the Hours, the calendar, church music, and sacred art.

Vehicles of Reform. To carry out this reform, Paul VI established, Jan. 25, 1965, a commission known as the Consilium for the Implementation of the Constitution on the Liturgy, under the direction of Cardinal Giacomo Lercaro. This body of highly-qualified experts retained its quasi-autonomous identity until late in 1969, when it was reconstituted as the Special Commission for the Completion of the Liturgical Reform within the newly created Congregation for Divine Worship, with Cardinal Benno Gut as first prefect. From July 11, 1975, competency for liturgical reform passed to the newly constituted Congregation of Sacraments and Divine Worship, which Pope John Paul II renamed as the Congregation for Divine Worship and the Discipline of the Sacraments in 1982. Whereas the overall revision of the Roman liturgy was centralized under the direction of the Holy See, legitimate adaptation was to be channelled through the competent regional and national episcopal conferences. In the United States the liturgical reform has been under the guidance of the Bishops' Committee on the Liturgy, which, since 1970, has been in consultation with the Federation of Diocesan Liturgical Commissions. The English translations of the Latin *editio typica* of the various reformed liturgies have been provided by a separate entity under the English-speaking episcopate, the International Commission on English in the Liturgy.

Major Achievements of Vatican II's Liturgical Reform. The reform of the liturgical books mandated by

the Constitution (*Sacrosanctum Concilium* 25) is now substantially complete, with the publication of the *editio typica* for the rite of exorcism in 2000. A general assessment of the reform process reveals the following elements.

(1) *The Liturgy, Locus of Encounter.* Fundamental throughout the entire liturgical reform has been the conviction that the Church celebrates in her liturgy, through ritual transposition, the Trinitarian economy of salvation, celebrating, that is, the mysteries "in which are set forth the victory and triumph of Christ's death, and also giving thanks to God for his inexpressible gift in Christ Jesus, in praise of his glory through the power of the Holy Spirit" (*ibid.* 6). The dialogic perception of the liturgy as being the locus par excellence where God speaks to his people through Christ and where they, in return, respond to the Father by actualizing the priestly mission of the same Christ is expressed not only in the Constitution (*ibid.* 7), but also in the theological statements introducing the reformed rites. In this regard, the General Instruction on the Roman Missal, the General Instruction of the Liturgy of the Hours, the General Norms for the Liturgical Year and the Calendar, for example, marked an extraordinary advance over the juridical, rubrical directives of the analogous sections of the unreformed books. This theological understanding of the liturgy as being "the very exercise of the priestly office of Jesus Christ" and therefore "preeminently a sacred action, the efficacy of which no other act of the Church can equal on the same basis and to the same degree" (*ibid.* 7) became the *raison d'être* of the Church's repeated emphasis on liturgical reform.

(2) *Other Theological Aspects.* The *ressourcement* (return to sources) of the reform also brought with it a rediscovery or restoration of certain theological aspects of the Christian tradition which through the centuries had fallen into the background: the totality of the paschal mystery in every liturgical celebration; the multimodal presence of Christ in all of the liturgy and not only in the Eucharistic elements; the Trinitarian economy of prayer to the Father, through the Son, in the power of the Spirit; the role of the Holy Spirit in the formation and sanctification of the Church as People of God set apart to sing praises to God within their liturgical assembly; the eschatological hope of the pilgrim Church awaiting the day of the Lord; liturgical remembrance of the deeds of the Lord of history and their recovery in the Kingdom; the relationship of faith, repentance, conversion, reconciliation and their sacramental realization; the incarnational and worldly dimension of Christian life; and many more areas which have hardly begun to be explored. In no small measure is this theological recovery due to the Constitution's stipulation (*ibid.* 92) that the Scriptures be made

readily accessible in greater fullness, and that patristic and other ecclesiastical writers be represented more authentically.

(3) *The Liturgy, Prayer of the Whole People.* The hierarchical and ecclesial aspect of the liturgy described in the Constitution (*ibid.* 26–32) has restored the precious value that liturgy is not the private province of the clergy, but is indeed the prayer of the whole people who, while under the leadership of the ordained minister, all exercise the shared priesthood of Christ. In this context, the multiple functions of readers, cantors, acolytes, choir and other ministers, as well as the active participation of the congregation are to be regarded as a true liturgical ministry.

(4) *A Pastoral Liturgy.* Regarding the pastoral and didactic nature of the liturgy (*ibid.* 33–36), three reformed areas have produced incalculable benefits: introduction of the vernacular far beyond the expectations of the conciliar Fathers; restoration of the Liturgy of the Word almost to the point of surfeit; and transparency of rite. More than any other change, perhaps, the use of the vernacular has made the liturgy into an active and conscious part of Christian spirituality. In place of the spare rites of the Tridentine liturgy there is now accessible to the people in their own language a copious, amplified liturgy with God's Word poured forth in abundance. The use of the mother tongue consequently makes immediately available the astonishing increase of Scripture reading, not only in the Lectionary at Mass with its three cycles of judiciously selected pericopes and responsorial psalms, but also in the cycle of readings prepared for the Liturgy of the Hours and the sacramental celebrations, so that every liturgy allows God to speak to his people and Christ to proclaim the good news (*ibid.* 33). Drawing upon this source, the HOMILY, regarded as an integral part of the liturgy, becomes "like a proclamation of God's mighty deeds in redemptive history" (*ibid.* 35), with the mystery of Christ always present and at work in the Church. In addition, catechetical insights, brief commentaries, and instructions are encouraged to make of the prescribed liturgy a more cohesive and effective celebration. Finally, the ritual symbolic actions and gestures have been pared down so that the dominant liturgical symbol becomes more immediately understandable, pruned of its former repetitive and allegorical overlayering.

(5) *Adaptation and Inculturation.* The most revolutionary liturgical reform, in comparison with the previous 400-year static uniformity, has been, without doubt, the acceptance of the principle of liturgical adaptation required by the needs and cultural differences of various groups, regions, and peoples (*ibid.* 38), with an even more radical adaptation proposed for mission lands (*ibid.*,

40). Regarding cultural adaptation, the *Praenotanda* of the reformed liturgical books make special provision for regional adjustments to be determined by episcopal conferences working together with the Congregation for Divine Worship and the Discipline of Sacraments. The question of adaptation and inculturation is perhaps the most difficult question to deal with is how to resolve, or keep in creative tension.

Bibliography: D. BONDIOLI et al., "Situazione della liturgia riformata e futuro della pastorale liturgica," *Rivista di Pastorale Liturgica* 13 (1976) 3–36. P. M. GY, "La reforme liturgique de Trente et celle de Vatican II," *Maison-Dieu* 128 (1976) 61–75. H. SCHMIDT, "Liturgy and Modern Society—Analysis of the Current Situation," H. SCHMIDT, ed., *Liturgy in Transition: Concilium 62* (New York 1971) 14–29. H. SCHMIDT and D. POWER, eds., *Politics and Liturgy: Concilium 92* (New York 1974). R. G. WEAKLAND, "The 'Sacred' and Liturgical Renewal," *Worship* 49 (1975) 512–29. P. C. FINN and J. M. SCHELLMAN, eds., *Shaping English Liturgy: Studies in Honor of Archbishop Denis Hurley* (Washington, D.C. 1990). W. J. GRISBROOKE, "Liturgical Reform and Liturgical Renewal," *Studia Liturgica* 21:2 (1991) 136–54. A. A. HÄUSSLING, *The Meaning of the Liturgy* (Collegeville, Minn. 1994). D. N. POWER, "Liturgy and Culture Revisited," *Worship* 69 (1995) 225–43. N. MITCHELL, "The Renewal That Awaits Us," *Worship* 70 (1996) 163–72.

[G. M. COLESS/EDS.]

LITURGICAL LANGUAGES

The Catholic Church uses many languages in its official worship of God, though LATIN is the one most intimately associated with the Roman liturgy. This article will consider primitive practice, the Churches of the East, the Church in the West, and the reforms of Vatican Council II.

Primitive Practice. The earliest liturgical language in the Church was almost certainly ARAMAIC, this being both the native tongue of the Apostles and their first Jewish converts and the one used by the Lord. These first Christians seem never to have adopted a hieratic use of Hebrew, with which they would have been familiar from the reading of the Law and the Prophets in the Temple, nor is there any evidence that the first missionaries attempted to preserve Aramaic as a sacred liturgical language in non-Aramaic–speaking communities. In rural districts people had their own native forms of speech, but in urban areas they used Greek, and this *koine,* the usual cosmopolitan language of everyday affairs, became the foremost language of the liturgy (*see* GREEK LANGUAGE, EARLY CHRISTIAN AND BYZANTINE.).

There is ample evidence that the language of the people to whom Christianity was preached from the beginning was also the language used in their liturgy (cf. O. Korolevsky). Only three languages, however, were of importance in the development of the liturgy: Syro-Aramaic, Greek, and Latin. Syro-Aramaic was used in Jerusalem, in the Judeo-Christian communities of Palestine, and in those territories to the north and east that had not come under Hellenistic influence. Thus EDESSA became the center of a national Aramaic or Syrian Christianity. The Syriac liturgy has survived to the present day, though much of it is a translation from the Greek. Until the 4th century Greek was the lingua franca in the whole of the eastern half of the Roman Empire and was therefore the language of the liturgy in those areas. Even in Rome Greek was the common language. It was not until *c.* 250 A.D. that Latin predominated there and gradually became the official language of the Western Church by the 4th century.

The Churches of the East. In the East the principle of retaining the Byzantine liturgy in Greek as the official liturgical language was not maintained so rigidly as Latin in the West. When the Melkites around Antioch adopted Arabic as their vernacular, their liturgy was accordingly translated into Arabic. The Georgians in the Caucasus used Georgian. The Byzantine liturgy is also celebrated in Hungarian, Finnish, Chinese, and Japanese. Other Oriental liturgies are celebrated in Syriac, Coptic, and Armenian.

"We do not," wrote PIUS XII, "hold the venerable liturgies of the Eastern Church in less esteem; on the contrary these ancient and traditional rites are equally dear to us" (*Mediator Dei* 11). In 1929, when conceding that reconciled Orthodox clergy in Estonia might use their native language in the liturgy, PIUS XI emphasized that as a matter of principle Eastern Catholics must be accorded full liberty to use in the liturgy languages that are suited to the good of souls, once the Holy See approves their use (cf. Korolevsky, 54). On April 1, 1960, JOHN XXIII approved a decision, taken the previous day at a plenary session of the Holy Office, that recognized the right of Byzantine priests to use vernacular, even non-Oriental, languages in celebrating the liturgy anywhere in the world. (For the background to this decision, arising out of an attempt to impose restrictive norms on the use of English in the United States, see Maximos IV Saigh, ed., *Eastern Churches and Catholic Unity* [New York 1963].)

The Church in the West. After the transfer of the imperial capital from Rome to Constantinople, and the political dismemberment of the Western empire, a common understanding of Latin was one of the chief means whereby Christian culture was transmitted to the new barbaric peoples. There is strong evidence that Rome abandoned Greek in favor of Latin some time in the second half of the 4th century, more precisely between 360 and 382. Klauser (469–473) points to DAMASUS I as prob-

ably the most influential person in making the language of Rome the language of the liturgy. Vernacular liturgies were feasible only in the later Middle Ages, as the dialects of the barbaric peoples assimilated the vulgar Latin, admittedly the less thoroughly as they were farther from the Mediterranean, and emerged as modern European languages. For more than 1,000 years Latin remained the language of cultured people and hence was the obvious language for the Church's meetings and quite naturally continued to be the language of the liturgy.

At the Council of TRENT suggestions that Latin should be canonized by name, or that vernacular languages should be indiscriminately approved, were equally rejected, and the Fathers anathematized in a canon those who said "that the Mass must be celebrated only in the vernacular" (H. Denzinger, *Enchiridion symbolorum,* ed. A. Schönmetzer [32d ed. Freiburg 1963] 1759), explaining in the preceding chapter that "although the Mass contains a great deal of instruction for the faithful, it does not seem expedient to the Fathers that it be indiscriminately in the vernacular" (*ibid.* 1749).

The easy identification of the liturgical use of the vernacular with Protestant ideals led to a grave suspicion of heresy, or at least disloyalty, attaching to any tendency among Catholics to champion that use. PIUS VI, in the apostolic constitution *AUCTOREM FIDEI* (1794), spoke of the Synod of PISTOIA's proposal to use the vernacular in the liturgy as "false, temerarious, disruptive of the prescribed manner of celebrating the mysteries, and easily productive of many evils" (H. Denzinger, *Enchiridion symbolorum* 2666). PIUS X, in his motu proprio *Tra le sollecitudini* (1903), reaffirmed that "the language proper to the Roman Church is Latin and hence it is forbidden to sing anything whatsoever in the vernacular in solemn liturgical functions—much more to sing in the vernacular the variable or common parts of the Mass and Office" (7; A. Bugnini, *Documenta pontificia ad instaurationem liturgicam spectantia* [Rome 1953] 18). John XXIII, in the apostolic constitution *Veterum Sapientia* (1962), asked that "no one, moved by an inordinate desire for novelty, should write against the use of Latin either in the teaching of the sacred disciplines or in the sacred rites of the liturgy" (*Acta Apostolicae Sedis* 54 [1962] 133).

In spite of this rigorous official attachment to Latin, the Church occasionally admitted other languages into the Roman liturgy, usually when missionaries from the West had to collaborate with their Eastern counterparts. The best known was the permission given in the 9th century by ADRIAN II (d. 872) and JOHN VIII (d. 882) for the use of Old Slavonic in Moravia. Despite its withdrawal by STEPHEN VI (d. 891), this ancient custom, secured by SS. CYRIL AND METHODIUS, has survived down to our own times in parts of central Europe. Similarly in 1398 BONIFACE IX allowed the Dominican missionaries in Greece to celebrate Mass in the liturgical Greek. The Armenian Catholics of the Order of St. GREGORY THE ILLUMINATOR, an Armenian association (1330–1794) that worked for reunion with the Holy See, celebrated according to the Dominican rite in the classical Armenian tongue, and Carmelite priests also made extensive use of the same language. In the 18th century the Capuchin missionaries in Georgia read the Epistle and Gospel in the vernacular, and the Carmelites in Persia were permitted to celebrate one Mass in Arabic every day. In India councils at Goa (1585) and DIAMPER (1599) authorized private Mass in Syriac.

There is evidence that CLEMENT V, when he established a bishopric at Beijing (1307), gave permission for Chinese in the liturgy. The Jesuit missionaries 300 years later persuaded the Holy Office to support the use of this vernacular, and in 1615 PAUL V granted to Chinese priests a faculty of using their own language for Mass and the Sacraments. Whether the permission had ever been put into effect, it was later withdrawn by the Congregation for the PROPAGATION OF THE FAITH (founded in 1622). In the Caughnawaga and Saint-Regis Indian reservations, not far from Montreal in Canada, a Mohawk Iroquois tongue is still used by the people in their parts of the Mass, thanks to concessions obtained by Jesuit missionaries in the 17th century.

In the West Latin was retained as the liturgical language of the Catholic Church in spite of strong protests at the time of the Reformation. The Council of Trent ruled that "it was not expedient" that Mass should be celebrated in the vernacular language (sess. 22, ch. 8; H. Denzinger, *Enchiridion symbolorum* 1749). The beginnings of a change are discernible in the encyclical *MEDIATOR DEI* (Nov. 20, 1947) which, while reiterating the statement that the use of Latin is a sign of the Church's unity, admitted that the use of the mother tongue was frequently of great advantage to the people. It did not specify what parts of the liturgy could be rendered in the mother tongue, and in fact hardly any permissions were given until after Vatican Council II, with the notable exception of the *Deutches Hochamt* (high Mass) in Germany.

For several centuries German peoples had a custom of singing in their own language at Mass, so that, in Germany and Austria and parts of Switzerland and Luxembourg, the choir and congregation sang many of their parts in German, and the Epistle and Gospel were read in both Latin and German. A similar order using Hindi was approved for the province of Agra in 1958, and in the same year the use of Hebrew was authorized in Israel

for the whole of the Mass before the Offertory. These changes as well as the various approvals given by the Holy See in the first part of the 20th century for the use of bilingual versions of the *Rituale Romanum* are now largely of historical interest only, since they were superseded by the work of liturgical reform accomplished at Vatican Council II.

Vatican Council II. In 1947 PIUS XII had said that "the use of the Latin language prevailing in a great part of the Church affords at once an imposing sign of unity and an effective safeguard against the corruption of true doctrine. Admittedly the adoption of the vernacular in quite a number of functions may prove of great benefit to the faithful. But the Apostolic See alone is empowered to grant this permission" (*Mediator Dei* 60). The conciliar *Constitution on the Sacred Liturgy* goes further. Whereas it insists that "the use of the Latin language is to be preserved in the Latin rites" (36.1), Latin is not called, as some Fathers during the debates in the council had desired, the official language of the Roman rite. And although the principle, familiar in Eastern rites, that the living language can be the normal liturgical language, is not conceded, nevertheless all the practical results of such a concession are made possible. "Since the use of the mother tongue, whether in the Mass, the administration of Sacraments, or other parts of the liturgy, frequently may be of great advantage to the people, the limits of its employment may be extended. . . . It is for the competent territorial ecclesiastical authority . . . to decide whether, and to what extent, the vernacular language is to be used; their decrees are to be approved, that is, confirmed, by the Holy See" (36.2–3). Later it is said that at "Masses celebrated with the people, a suitable place may be allotted to their mother tongue. This is to apply in the first place to the readings and the 'common prayer,' and also, as local conditions may warrant, to those parts which pertain to the people. . . . And wherever a more extended use of the mother tongue within the Mass appears desirable" (54), the competent territorial authority should submit the matter to the Holy See (40). The vernacular language may be used for the entire rites of Sacraments, sacramentals, and for the Divine Office.

The principle behind this reform was well formulated by Vatican II: "In this restoration [of the liturgy], both texts and rites should be drawn up so they express more clearly the holy things they signify; the Christian people, so far as possible, should be able to understand them with ease and to take part in them fully, actively, and as befits a community" (21).

Even the council did not envisage an entire vernacular liturgy. It decreed that though existing special exemptions are to remain in force, the use of the Latin language

LITURGICAL LAWS, AUTHORITY OF

LITURGICAL LAWS, AUTHORITY OF

is to be preserved in the Latin rites. Nevertheless, in view of the advantage accruing to the people through the use of the mother tongue, in the first place the readings and directives and some of the prayers and chants could be translated at the discretion of the competent local authority (*Sacrosanctum Concilium* 36). This decree was later clarified by the Instruction of the Congregation of Rites *Inter oecumenici* (40; *Acta Apostolicae Sedis* 56 [1964] 897–900). It was left to the episcopal conferences to decide which texts were to be translated. Permission was not given for the translation of the Roman Canon until June 29, 1967, with the Instruction *Tres abhinc annos* (*Acta Apostolicae Sedis* 59 [1967] 442–448). Thus gradually in the whole of the liturgy the vernacular became permissible as pastoral needs became evident.

All translations have to be authorized, i.e. confirmed, by the Congregation for Divine Worship before use in the liturgy and on June 25, 1969, the Consilium for the Implementation of the Constitution on the Sacred Liturgy published important guidelines for liturgical translators in an *Instruction on Translation of Liturgical Texts (Comme le prévoit)*. In 2001 the Congregation for Divine Worship issued new guidelines on the translation of liturgical texts, *Liturgicam authenticam*. Among other things, *Liturgicam authenticam* called for a more literal translation of the Latin into vernacular languages.

Bibliography: A classic introductory survey for the general reader is C. KOROLEVSKY, *Living Languages in Catholic Worship*, ed. and tr. D. ATTWATER (Westminster, Md. 1957). C. MOHRMANN, *Liturgical Latin: Its Origins and Character* (Washington 1957). G. T. KLAUSER, "Der Übergang der römischen Kirche von der griechischen zur lateinischen Liturgiesprache," *Miscellanea Giovanni Mercati*, 6 v. (Studi e Testi 121–126; 1946) 1:467–482. S. SMRŽIK, *The Glagolitic or Roman-Slavonic Liturgy* (Cleveland 1959). D. ATTWATER, *Eastern Catholic Worship* (New York 1945). F. E. BRIGHTMAN, *Liturgies Western and Eastern* (Oxford 1896). J. A. JUNGMANN, *The Early Liturgies to the Time of Gregory the Great* (Notre Dame, Ind. 1959). A. A. KING, *Liturgies of the Primatial Sees* (Milwaukee 1957). A. RAES, *Introductio in Liturgiam Orientalem* (Rome 1947). H. SCHMIDT, *Liturgie et langue vulgaire* (Rome 1950). P. D. GARRETT, "Problem of Liturgical Translation: A Preliminary Study," *Saint Vladimir's Theological Quarterly* 22:2–3 (1978) 83–113; "The Problem of Liturgical Translation: An Addendum," *Saint Vladimir's Theological Quarterly* 24:1 (1980) 37–50. N. MITCHELL, "Christine Mohrmann (1903–1988): The Science of Liturgical Language," *Liturgy Digest* 1:2 (1994) 4–43 (with extensive bibliographies). P. F. BRADSHAW, ed., "Liturgical Language" (symposium, 15th Cong of Soc Liturgica, Dublin, Aug. 14–19, 1995), *Studia Liturgica* 26:1 (1996) 119–143. A. A. R. BASTIAENSEN, *The Beginnings of Latin Liturgy* (Louvain 1997). A. CHIROVSKY, ed., "Papers and Discussions of the International Symposium on English Translations of Byzantine Liturgical Texts, Part I," *Logos* 39:2–4 (1998) 155–402.

[C. R. A. CUNLIFFE/H. E. WINSTONE/EDS.]

This article considers the authority of liturgical laws in the Latin church *sui iuris*, since each of the Eastern Catholic churches has its own liturgical patrimony and canonical discipline. Liturgical law may be understood broadly as the law regulating the liturgy. Liturgical laws are mainly ecclesiastical (human) laws, so their promulgation, binding force, interpretation, dispensation, and revocation are subject to the same canonical rules as any other ecclesiastical law. Some liturgical laws are based on divine law, for example, many requirements for the validity of sacraments. No one may dispense a divine law or validly enact a human law contrary to it.

The legislators for the liturgy are the same as those for any other area of ecclesiastical law. The supreme legislator is the pope, acting on his own, or the college of bishops, which exercises its power in an ecumenical council. The Second Vatican Council's Constitution on the Sacred Liturgy established the foundations and directions for the most comprehensive liturgical reform in the history of the Church, which was implemented by the legislation of Popes Paul VI and John Paul II.

Universal and Particular Law. The pope issues universal liturgical laws for the entire Latin church. These are found principally in the introductions and rubrics of the official liturgical books. Universal liturgical laws are also found in the *Code of Canon Law*, in Book IV, "The Sanctifying Office of the Church." Other sources of universal liturgical law are apostolic constitutions and apostolic letters *motu proprio* of the pope, if treating a liturgical matter, and the decrees of the Congregation for DIVINE WORSHIP AND DISCIPLINE OF THE SACRAMENTS (CDWDS) issued by mandate of the pope. Although rare, an administrative document of the Roman Curia may have legislative force by specific papal approval, indicated at the end of a document with the precise words, *in forma specifica approbavit*.

The supreme authority may issue particular law for a part of the Church, but normally particular law is issued by lower legislators. Below the supreme authority is the plenary council and conference of bishops of a nation or other territorial grouping of dioceses. At the next level is the provincial council made up of representatives of the dioceses that comprise an ecclesiastical province. Finally, there is the level of the diocese or equivalent particular church.

Plenary and provincial councils and diocesan bishops are free to enact laws regulating any kind of liturgical matter, provided their laws are not contrary to a higher norm (*ius*), whether this be a higher law, administrative norm, or legal custom (c. 135, §2). There are additional restrictions on the legislative power of conferences of bishops. The conference of bishops may enact laws only for specific matters as permitted in the universal law or by prior authorization of the Holy See. To be binding, the decrees of the conference must be approved by at least two-thirds of the total membership and must obtain the *recognitio* (a kind of approval) of the Holy See (c. 455). The legislative competence of conferences of bishops includes the approval of vernacular translations of the liturgical rites, many liturgical adaptations, and policies on numerous liturgical matters, such as lay preaching, the age for confirmation, holy days of obligation, the catechumenate, etc.

Customs. Unlike laws, which are issued by legislative authorities, customs originate within the community itself (parish, religious community, diocese, etc.). During the first millennium, the liturgy was regulated more by custom than by law, whereas law tended to predominate in the second millennium, especially in the centuries after the Council of TRENT when liturgical development ossified and a mentality of rigid rubricism prevailed. The role of custom is regaining momentum since Vatican II due to the recovered theology of the local church within the communion of churches; the stress on the dignity of all the faithful, their participation in the threefold *munera* of the Church, and their right and duty to participate meaningfully in the liturgy; and the imperative of inculturation. Many aspects of the liturgy are today subject to local customs as well as laws, for example, lay ministers, art and architecture, music and dance, gesture and posture, observances of feasts days and seasons, inclusive language, etc.

The customs of a community obtain the force of law if they are specifically approved by the competent legislator, or if they are observed by the majority of the community for thirty continuous and complete years. This applies both to customs contrary to the law and customs on matters not treated in the law (*praeter legem*). No custom can attain the force of law if it is contrary to divine law or if it is not reasonable (cc. 23–26). A legal custom (one that has the force of law) must be observed in those communities where it is in force, even if it is contrary to the law. Customs with the force of law can be revoked only by the competent legislative authority (c. 28).

Administrative Norms. Executive authorities, especially the congregations of the Roman Curia, may issue general administrative norms within their competence, as does the CDWDS for the liturgy. These norms are contained in non-legislative documents, such as directories, instructions, circular letters, etc. There is no consistent difference between legislative and administrative norms as to their content or style, but laws (*leges*) and legal customs have the greater juridic value. An administrative norm in a document of a Roman dicastery, which is contrary to universal law, is null. A curial document cannot revoke particular laws or legal customs. This can only be done by an act of the competent legislator that expressly revokes the particular law or custom (cc. 20, 28).

Vicars general and episcopal vicars may also issue general administrative norms, including norms for the liturgy, but they would not do this without a mandate from the bishop. The liturgical commissions of dioceses and conferences of bishops have no power to issue binding norms. Their documents are advisory only, except for those provisions within them that are citations of other binding norms.

Bibliography: *A New Commentary on the Code of Canon Law*, ed., J. P. BEAL, J. A. CORIDEN, and T. J. GREEN (New York/Mahwah, NJ 2000). J. M. HUELS, "Assessing the Weight of Documents on the Liturgy," *Worship* 74 (2000) 117–135. J. M. HUELS, "A Theory of Juridical Documents Based on Canons 29–34," *Studia Canonica* 32 (1998) 337–370.

[J. M. HUELS]

LITURGICAL MOVEMENT, I: CATHOLIC

Grounded in the theology of the MYSTICAL BODY OF CHRIST, the Liturgical Movement aimed at recovering full and active liturgical participation for all members of the Church. This part treats the Movement's origin, purpose, and history within the Catholic Church.

Origin. The 19th century was a time of tremendous intellectual activity in Europe. While great thinkers like DARWIN, HEGEL, HUME, MARX, and ENGELS were developing their own theories and philosophies, theological giants like J. M. SAILER, J. HIRSCHER, and especially J. A. MÖHLER and M. SCHEEBEN were calling for a return to the Pauline concept of the Church as the mystical body of Christ. As the biblical movement and biblical theology served to focus the attention of liturgical pioneers on Sacred Scripture and salvation history, the patristic movement recovered a rich understanding of the Church and its communitarian sacramental system. The Liturgical Movement in Europe was born within such a milieu.

The founding of the Liturgical Movement is usually attributed to Dom Prosper GUÉRANGER (1805–75), the restorer of the French Benedictine Congregation at SOLESMES in 1833. It must be stated, however, that even prior to Guéranger, one finds considerable movement toward liturgical reform through efforts at increasing lay participation in the Eucharist and the Liturgy of the Hours. The 17th through 19th centuries in France was a time of great liturgical creativity. Although these innovations began only as minor additions to the Roman liturgy, each diocese in France eventually had its own liturgy. Moreover, proposals for greater participation within the liturgy were voiced by the Fathers present at the Synod of PISTOIA (1786), although without success.

Finally, as we consider the birth of the Liturgical Movement in 19th-century France, similarities with the Anglican Communion's OXFORD MOVEMENT should not be overlooked. Both movements were concerned with a return to the sources; both exerted an influence outside the churches in which they were born; both were influenced to some degree by the Romantic movement; and in the end, both were concerned with a more profound understanding of the mystery of the Church.

The French liturgical movement. It is ironic that Guéranger is usually considered the founder of the Liturgical Movement. His approach was highly subjective, often leading him to inaccurate liturgical conclusions, e.g. calling for a return to the Middle Ages as the period of the highest liturgical development. Moreover, he saw in the French liturgical innovations a lack of fidelity to tradition, attributing the state of the French Church to JANSENISM and GALLICANISM. Thus, rather than continuing the liturgical experimentation found elsewhere in France, the Eucharist and Divine Office at Solesmes were celebrated strictly according to the Roman Rite. Despite Guéranger's fierce critique, however, some of the very innovations he criticized were later incorporated into the liturgical reforms of Pope Pius X at the beginning of the 20th century, and eventually into the Roman liturgy itself. Without denying his limitations, Guéranger's contribution to the liturgical and monastic revival in Europe cannot be underestimated. His goal was to restore the liturgy with the Eucharist as primary focus, making it more central to the cenobitic monastic life. Further, the church year became the paradigm for the daily life and rhythm of the monastery. Accordingly, he developed his famous work *L'Année Liturgique* (begun in Advent of 1841), with the intention of writing a pastoral commentary on the entire liturgical year at the service of parish priests and their parishioners. He completed only nine of the proposed twelve volumes prior to his death. In that same year, he founded *Institutions liturgiques*, a more scholarly journal offering serious articles that would respond to liturgical problems and abuses within France, and offer a solid, proper instruction in the Roman liturgy. Guéranger promoted a return to Gregorian chant as the official liturgical music of the Catholic Church. He encouraged chant in place of popularized liturgical music in vogue at the time. Although the Liturgical Movement in France did not grow until years later, Guéranger's influence held sway throughout the 19th century, not only in France, but also in Germany and Belgium, especially in those monasteries founded by Solesmes.

The German liturgical movement. The German movement began at the Benedictine monastery of BEURON, re-founded in 1863 by the brothers Maurus and Placidus Wolter, who desired to offer the Church in Germany the same spirit of monastic and liturgical reform that Solesmes had offered the Church in France. Maurus Wolter spent several months at Solesmes in 1862, and was impressed both by the monastic observance and the monastic liturgy celebrated there. When he returned to Germany and joined his brother in re-founding the monastery at Beuron the following year, the influence of Guéranger could be seen. A study of the early years at Beuron reveals a great admiration and respect for the classic Roman liturgy, not unlike Solesmes. Both the monastic liturgy and overall governance were strictly controlled by Solesmes in the early years, leaving its distinctive mark on that monastery's life and worship. The nascent Liturgical Movement in Germany soon bore fruit. In 1884 Dom Anselm Schott published the first German-Latin Missal, *Das Messbuch der Hl. Kirche*; the *Vesperbuch* followed in 1893. Each volume contained explanations taken from Guéranger's *L'Année Liturgique*. Beuron was also known for its famous art school founded by Dom Desiderius Lenz, which had tremendous influence on Church art well beyond the shores of Europe. Lenz worked at establishing artistic unity within one liturgical space, thereby fostering a harmonic relationship between liturgy and art.

In 1893, the monks of Beuron re-founded the German monastery of MARIA LAACH (near Cologne) that had been suppressed by Napolean in 1803. Under the leadership of Abbot Ildefons Herwegen and two of his monks, Kunibert MOHLBERG and Odo CASEL, in collaboration with the young diocesan priest, Romano GUARDINI, and with the aid of two professors, Franz J. DÖLGER and Anton BAUMSTARK, the Liturgical Movement in Germany gained momentum. They organized a three-fold series of publications which were begun in 1918: *Ecclesia Orans, Liturgiegeschichtliche Quellen* and *Liturgiegeschichtliche Forschungen*. Moreover, the well-known journal *Jarbuch für Liturgiewissenschaft* was founded at the monastery in 1921. There is no question that Odo Casel (+1948) was the theologian of the German movement and one of its key players. He came under the influence of Herwegen while studying at the University of Bonn, and entered the monastery in 1905, at least in part through Herwegen's mentorship. In the thirty years that followed, he wrote hundreds of articles and a number of books, and not unlike other great minds, his writings were initially considered highly controversial. His classic text, *Das christliche Kultmysterium*, argued that the pagan mystery cults were a preparation for the mysteries of the Christian sacraments. Even though Casel's theory is no longer espoused by sacramental theologians, his work gave way to a rich understanding of the Church as the mystical body of Christ which expresses itself symbolically through sacramental participation. While Maria Laach was known for its cultivation of liturgical science, it did not limit its activities to the academic. With the permission of Abbot Herwegen, the first *Missa recitata* was celebrated in the monastery's crypt chapel on Aug. 6, 1921, under the presidency of Prior Albert Hammenstede. The celebration took place in Latin, but included the praying of the Gloria, Credo, Sanctus, and Agnus Dei in common, as well as responses involving the entire assembly. Those who attended the Mass also participated in the Offertory procession, reviving the ancient practice of bringing their own bread to the altar. Despite episcopal approval for the liturgical experiments, rumors quickly spread in the Rhineland that the monks of Maria Laach were advocating a lay priesthood and attempting to "Protestantize" the Church and its worship.

There was other pastoral involvement registered in those years, thanks to the strength of the German youth movement and related organizations. Johannes Pinsk (+1957), university chaplain in Berlin, and Romano GUARDINI (+1968) at Burg Rothenfels were pastorally involved in promoting participative liturgy, especially for the more significant feasts of the Church years. Leaders like Guardini were also involved in collaborating with leading secular architects of the day in creating liturgical architecture that facilitated participative worship. With the founding of the Liturgical Institute at Trier after World War II, the movement saw other names emerging like Balthasar Fischer and Johannes Wagner. Austrian liturgist Josef Andreas JUNGMANN, S.J. (+1975), did his own part to collaborate with his German colleagues. Liturgical pioneering in Germany was not limited to men, as demonstrated in the recent study by Teresa Berger of Duke University. Aemiliana Löhr (+1972), a Benedictine nun of the Abbey of Holy Cross at Herstelle, was greatly influenced by the monastery's chaplain and her mentor, Odo Casel, and she carried the torch through her own writings—more than three hundred articles, not to mention books. There were other women in that same monastery who, even though trained in philosophy or medicine, soon took up the task of promoting the liturgical renewal upon entrance into the convent. Like their male counterparts, these Benedictine women were encouraged and promoted in their own pioneering and scholarship by monks like Herwegen and Casel.

It must be noted, however, that Germany was not the first country to witness the effect of an organized Liturgical Movement. Prior to the founding of Maria Laach, the monks of Beuron were already planting seeds of liturgical renewal elsewhere in Europe: Maredsous in Belgium, Emmaus-Prague in Czechoslovakia, and Seckau in Austria. Maredsous, and later Mont César (also in Belgium) were the most liturgically significant of these new monastic foundations.

The Belgian liturgical movement. The Benedictine monastery of MAREDSOUS was founded by Maurus Wolter (then Abbot of Beuron) in 1872. It soon became famous for its liturgical publishing and would later inspire the young American Benedictine student Virgil MICHEL to initiate a similar publishing venture in the United States. In 1882 Dom Gérard van Caloen, rector of the Abbey School at Maredsous, published the first French-Latin missal, *Missel des fidéles.* One year later, in a talk at a French Eucharistic congress, he advocated lay participation in the Mass, bringing about his removal as school rector. Two years later, he founded the review *Messager des fidèles* (later *Revue bénédictine*), the first publication intended to be an instrument of promoting the Liturgical Movement. The monastery of Mont César was founded in 1899 by Robert Kerchove (+1942), along with several other monks from Maredsous. The liturgical influence of Solesmes, Beuron, and Maredsous was influential, and liturgical publishing quickly became an apostolate of that new monastic foundation, as well. In 1910 *Les Questions liturgiques* was founded, and in the summer of 1912 the monastery initiated the famous *sémaines liturgiques* held each year—the primary means of communicating the message of the Liturgical Movement.

The Belgian movement is known principally for its pastoral focus, thanks to the leadership of Lambert BEAUDUIN, O.S.B. (+1960). Beauduin had been a labor chaplain with the *Aumôniers du Travail* as a diocesan priest in Liége, and was deeply influenced by the workers whom he served and their social problems. Even prior to his association with the *Aumôniers*, he was known for his strong social consciousness and his compassion for the downtrodden. In 1906 he left his labor chaplaincy and diocese, and entered the monastery of Mont César, where he came into contact with the Irish Benedictine Colomba Marmion (+1923). Like Beauduin, Marmion had also been a diocesan priest prior to entering the monastery. Both monks saw liturgical prayer as foundational to their monastic life and shared a deep love for the liturgy of the hours. Beauduin soon became convinced of liturgy's transformative power within a secularized world and as the necessary grounding for Christian social activism.

The official beginning of the Liturgical Movement in Belgium is usually traced to September of 1909, during the National Congress of Catholic Works at Malines. In fact, many chroniclers of the Liturgical Movement prefer this event to mark the beginning of the European Liturgical Movement, rather than Guéranger and Solesmes. At that conference, Beauduin delivered a talk entitled "*La vraie prière de l'Eglisé*" in which he called for full and active participation of all people in Church life and especially in its worship. He based his remarks on the *Motu Proprio* of Pius X (Nov. 22, 1903) which described the liturgy as the Church's true and indispensable source. During the conference, he met Godefroid Kurth, an historian and prominent Catholic layman at the time, who shared Beauduin's dream of full and active liturgical participation. Together, they devised a practical plan to launch the Liturgical Movement. In 1914 Beauduin published *La piété de l'Eglise* (Louvain, 1914), intended to be a public declaration of the Liturgical Movement with a solid theological and ecclesiological foundation. Beauduin's success as a liturgical pioneer is due in large part to his capacity to integrate his liturgical vision with a healthy pragmatism.

Through Beauduin's efforts and the collaboration of others—among them, his confrére Dom Eugéne Vandeur (+1968), Bernard Botte (+1980), and the Benedictine nuns at the monastery of Ancilla Domini at Wépion (founded in 1917 by Vandeur)—the liturgy in Belgium was restored to the assembly. Complex theological ideas were popularized, providing greater access for ordinary Catholics to the Church's rich theological treasury. Eucharistic adoration during Mass was opposed since it conflicted with the Eucharist being celebrated. Influenced by his experience as a labor chaplain, Beauduin advocated a shorter eucharistic fast allowing for greater participation at the principal sung Eucharist on Sunday mornings. Ahead of his time, he promoted the controversial "dialogue Mass." Beauduin's vision included a great passion for ecumenism, particularly regarding Anglican and Orthodox Christians. He was convinced that the Anglican Church should be invited to return to communion with the bishop of Rome without having to be completely absorbed in the Roman Catholic Church. He suggested that Anglicans might continue to maintain their liturgical and disciplinary autonomy in much the way Eastern Catholics preserved that same autonomy while remaining in communion with Rome. In 1925 he founded a monastery at Amay sur Meuse (later CHEVETOGNE) as a monastic contribution to the unity of the churches, directed to the relationship between eastern and western Christianity.

The Austrian liturgical movement. Under the leadership of Augustinian Canon Pius PARSCH (+1954) the Austrian movement registered similar pastoral concerns as evidenced in Belgium. Greatly influenced by developments at Maria Laach, Parsch gave German liturgical scholarship a pastoral expression, using his own parish church of St. Gertrude (near his monastery of Klosterneu-

burg) as testing ground. Taking the best of the biblical, catechetical, liturgical, and patristic movements, he brought about an integration on the pastoral level that was largely unmatched elsewhere in Europe. In 1923 he initiated *Das Jahr des Heiles*, a pastoral commentary on the Eucharist and Liturgy of the Hours for the entire liturgical year. An even more significant publication was *Bibel und Liturgie*, founded in 1926, as an attempt to encourage wider readership of the Bible among Catholics, and to promote the relationship between liturgy and Scripture. He preached that the Eucharist is a sacrifice offered by the entire parish community and a sacrificial meal eaten in common; he also insisted on a proper and expanded use of Sacred Scripture within the liturgy.

Elsewhere in Europe. In England, significant developments included the founding of the Henry Bradshaw Society (1890), "for the purpose of printing liturgical MSS and rare editions of service books and illustrative documents on an historical and scientific basis"; and the Alcuin Club (1899) with its series of *Tracts* and *Proceedings* that have been an invaluable service to liturgical scholars throughout the entire 20th century. Also in 1899, the classic address of Edmund BISHOP (+1917) at Oxford, "The Genius of the Roman Rite," has had profound impact on liturgical scholarship. Years later, the Society of St. Gregory was founded in 1929 with its periodical *Music and Liturgy* and its summer schools; the English Liturgy Society (1943) founded by Samuel Gosling focused largely on the promotion of vernacular liturgy, and the collaboration of British liturgical pioneers Donald Attwater; Charles Cunliffe; C. C. Martindale, S.J.; and Clifford Howell, S.J..

Italy, Spain, Portugal, and Ireland did not witness the same level of participation as seen in other parts of Europe. There are, however, several key developments worth noting. In 1914, Italian Benedictines at Finalpia, Savona, inaugurated *Rivista Liturgica* as the chief organ of communication for Italian liturgical pioneers. A leading figure in the Italian movement was Abbot Emmanuele Caronti, O.S.B., whose text *La pietà liturgica* (Turin, 1921) promoted an ecclesial piety grounded in a solid liturgical spirituality. An even greater contribution, however, was his *Messale festivo per i fedeli* (Turin, 1921), opening up the riches of the Church's liturgical treasury to large numbers of Italian Catholics. In 1961 Pope John XXIII established the Pontifical Institute of Liturgy at Sant'Anselmo, Rome, for the scientific study of liturgy. Under the leadership of an international faculty, the school continues to grant numerous doctoral and licentiate degrees to students from around the world.

In Spain, the Catalonian Benedictine monastery of MONTSERRAT became a center of liturgical renewal, through the founding of a pastoral liturgical center and publishing, all in the Catalonian language; even there, the influence can be traced back to Maria Laach. During the repressive era of Franco, monks at Montserrat were divided up and sent away to different monasteries for their own safety. Those who were sent to the Rhineland were steeped both in the beauty of the monastic liturgy celebrated at Maria Laach, but also in the rich liturgical theology being done by German monks like Casel and Herwegen. Upon returning to Montserrat, these monks took the best of what they learned and experienced in the Rhineland and applied it to the cultural context of Catalonia. The result was an inculturated form of worship both grounded in the tradition and at the same time, uniquely Catalonian. Even today, visitors to Montserrat are struck by the participative liturgy celebrated daily in Catalan, while in Barcelona, the Center for Pastoral Liturgy continues to blend the best of Catalonian cultural and liturgical traditions in service of the Church.

In Ireland, the Benedictines at Glenstal Abbey (near Limerick) played a leading role in the pastoral liturgical revival after World War II, while at St. Patrick's College, MAYNOOTH, the pastoral journal, *The Furrow*, took up many of the liturgical themes being promoted by Glenstal and did its part in promoting a participative liturgy. Finally, thanks to the leadership of the Rev. Sean Swayne, the founding of the Irish Institute of Pastoral Liturgy at Carlow provided a year-long sabbatical program with diploma for clergy, religious, and laity, interested in a deeper understanding of the liturgy and its pastoral implications.

Switzerland pioneered modern liturgical architecture in the late 1920s by using a one-room type plan in designing liturgical space, creating a living church architecture that rivaled some of the best secular architecture of the day. Early examples include the Church of St. Anthony, Basel (1927) designed by Karl Moser, and Fritz Metzger's St. Charles Church, Luzerne. In the Netherlands, the first Liturgical Congress took place at Breda in 1911. In this century, France, like Switzerland and Germany, led the way in a new type of liturgical architecture. 1923 marks the beginning of the movement in modern liturgical architecture with the church building of Notre-Dame du Raincy, designed by secular architect Auguste Perret; significantly, it was the first church building to use reinforced concrete construction.

For its part, the French Liturgical Movement in this century notes several key events: the founding of the *Centre de Pastorale liturgique* in Paris (1943), and the launching of an important liturgical periodical, *Le Maison-Dieu* (1945). While Dom Gaspar Lefebvre contributed in popularizing the liturgy for French parishes, Bernard Botte, A.G. Martimort, Pierre-Marie Gy, Louis Bouyer, and Joseph Gelineau all made significant contributions to the movement well beyond the confines of that country. France was also a leader in the restoration of the catechumenate and the full implementation of the Rite of Christian Initiation of Adults (RCIA) in places like Paris and Strasbourg, only to be superseded by the Church in the United States and England with active catechumenal programs on the parish level.

The Americas. As German Benedictines initiated the South American Liturgical Movement with their pioneering in Brazil, publishing leaflet missals and pastoral commentaries, it was German Benedictines from ST. JOHN'S ABBEY in Collegeville, Minnesota, who pioneered the renewal in the north. The movement in the United States demonstrates two fundamental elements: 1) a concern for social justice, thus, a strong link with social movements of the day; and 2) the involvement of large numbers of lay people, both women and men.

As a young monk, Virgil MICHEL (+1938) was sent to Rome for studies at the Benedictine university of S. Anselmo. During those several years, he had the opportunity to travel throughout Europe, visiting the great Benedictine monasteries and liturgical centers like Maria Laach and Montserrat, and observing their life and worship. Moreover, during studies at S. Anselmo, he came into contact with Belgian pioneer Lambert Beauduin, who was his professor. Beauduin's passion for justice coupled with his love of the liturgy left a tremendous mark on Michel, and returning to Collegeville in the Autumn of 1925, he founded the Liturgical Movement with the help of William Busch (St. Paul, Minn.), Gerard Ellard, S.J. (St. Louis, Mo.), and German-born Martin Hellriegel (St. Louis, Mo.). Other Germans soon arrived on the scene: Reynold Hillenbrand of German ancestry (Chicago), and Hans Anscar Reinhold, who fled Germany because of the Nazis. The movement was headquartered at St. John's Abbey, Collegeville, with the founding of the liturgical periodical *Orate Fratres* (later *Worship*) and the Liturgical Press (both in 1926). Following Michel's death, the editorship of *Orate Fratres* was taken over by confrere Godfrey Diekmann, O.S.B., later a *peritus* for liturgy at the Second Vatican Council (1962–65).

Unlike its European counterpart, however, the United States' movement soon moved from monasteries into the hands of lay activists who were to play a key role in the movement. Even before Michel arrived on the scene, Justine WARD (+1975) and Georgia Stevens, R.S.C.J., were busy at work at the PIUS X SCHOOL OF LITURGICAL MUSIC, which they founded in 1916 on the grounds of the College of the Sacred Heart in Manhattanville, N.Y. A frequent visitor to Solesmes, Ward was largely responsible for popularizing Solesmes chant in the United States using her "Ward Method." With Ward and Stevens at the helm, the school was a leading force both in the restoration of chant and in liturgical renewal for many years until it closed in 1969. Another example of lay involvement was the founding of the LITURGICAL ARTS SOCIETY in 1928 by Maurice LAVANOUX and several others, drawing the participation of many artists and architects, among them the British artist Eric Gill. Except for their chaplain, Jesuit John La Farge, the group was largely a lay association, attracting women and men dedicated to art and architecture that would assist the participation of the liturgical assembly and give artistic expression to what their participation professed, as seen in their journal, *Liturgical Arts*. The Liturgical Arts Society ended in 1972.

The strong presence of the LITURGICAL CONFERENCE (founded in 1940), famous for its annual liturgical weeks which drew up to 12,000 people each year for the three-day meeting, is another example of lay participation in the movement. Women pioneers like Sara Benedica O'Neill, Elizabeth Johnson, and Mary Perkins Ryan, and artist Adé Bethune were all involved, along with Joseph Morrisey, Gerard Sloyan, William Leonard, S.J., Frederick McManus, Thomas Carroll, Robert Hovda, John Mannion, Virginia Sloyan, Gabe Huck, and Rachel Reeder. The published *Proceedings* of the annual Liturgical Weeks bear testimony to the fundamental role that the Conference played in the American movement. The Conference (now ecumenical) continues today with its journals *Liturgy* and *Homily Service* and is headquartered in Washington, D.C. The St. Jerome Society (later Vernacular Society) was founded in 1946 by H. A. Reinhold during the Liturgical Week in Denver, Colo., to promote vernacular in the liturgy. Reinhold soon persuaded retired Colonel John K. Ross-Duggan, then editor of *Quick Frozen Foods* magazine in Chicago, to assume responsibility for the group. That he did until his death in 1967, leaving his full-time job to devote all his energies to the vernacular cause, launching their periodical *Amen* in 1950; making frequent visits to Rome to meet with Vatican cardinals and bishops, while maintaining a lively correspondence with many others throughout Asia, Africa, and South America. Despite numerous presidents and other officers of the Vernacular Society over the years, Ross-Duggan remained in control. The Vernacular Society merged with the Liturgical Conference in 1965. At its peak, the organization had several thousand members (including 84 bishops); leaders included Dr. Joseph Evans, John Agathen, Irwin St. John Tucker, Dr. Jack Willke, Rev. Joseph Nolan, and Elaine and Reinhold Kissner. Other examples of lay participation included social activists from the CATHOLIC WORKER; CATHOLIC ACTION; FRIENDSHIP HOUSE; the GRAIL; CHRISTIAN FAMILY MOVE-MENT, most notably, Dorothy DAY (co-founder of the Catholic Worker) and the Baroness Catherine De Hueck DOHERTY (founder of Friendship House). Around the country, a number of women opened book stores as a way of promoting the liturgy and educating American Catholics; most famous was the St. Benet's Bookshop in downtown Chicago, under the leadership of Sara Benedicta O'Neill and Nina Polcyn. Places like St. Benet's became centers of activity—either for the praying of compline together on Saturday evenings, or for the occasional lecture when Dorothy Day or Godfrey Diekmann or other well-known figures were passing through. The Vernacular Society held its first organizational meeting in the back of St. Benet's.

The issue of immigration is crucial in evaluating the Movement's growth and success. The Liturgical Movement grew in the German Midwest (St. Louis; Chicago; Collegeville, Minn.) and was less successful on the Irish east and west coasts of the United States. Steeped in congregational participation in Germany, those immigrants often brought with them a rich understanding both of liturgical participation and of social outreach. Not surprisingly, it was Germans who founded the first Church-based social outreach program in 1855, the German Catholic Central Verein. Irish immigrants, on the other hand, were not accustomed to such participation. They had come from an experience of oppression where they were often forced to celebrate the Mass quietly and expeditiously (often behind barns) so as not to be discovered. That tradition was then passed down and gradually found its way into Irish-American parishes in the United States. Thus, when Irish immigrants made their way to these shores, they were quite at home with the "low masses" that had very little congregational singing, if any.

The movement came of age with the founding of academic programs in liturgy. In Indiana, Michael Mathis, C.S.C., founded the Summer School of Liturgy at the University of NOTRE DAME in 1947. In 1965 it was expanded into the graduate program in liturgical studies, an ecumenical program that trained many liturgical scholars from the Catholic Church and other churches. The program continued to thrive, along with a strong graduate program in liturgical studies at the CATHOLIC UNIVERSITY OF AMERICA in Washington, D.C.

Over the years, the Liturgical Movement had its critics. It was not until papal documents like *MYSTICI CORPORIS* or *MEDIATOR DEI* that the movement and its agenda gained respectability. The bilingual *Collectio Rituum* of 1954 was another notable advance, allowing for greater use of the vernacular and containing significant reforms of some of the rites. The 1955 restoration of the Holy Week rites to their proper place pushed liturgical advocates onward toward a participative Conciliar liturgy, which was only several years away. In 1956 liturgical experts gathered at Assisi from all around the world, including Godfrey DIEKMANN, O.S.B., Monsignor Frederick McManus, William Leonard, S.J., and Colonel John K. Ross-Duggan. Expecting a major announcement on the vernacular, delegates were greatly disappointed during their audience in the Vatican with Pope Pius XII, who assured them that Latin would remain the language of the Church's worship. The 1958 "Instruction for American Pastors on Sacred Music and Liturgy" provided renewed hope for a vernacular liturgy with the "dialogue Mass" (*Missa recitata*), but that hope was only to be dashed in 1961 with the Papal document *Veterum Sapientia*, which again upheld Latin as the official language of the Church and cautioned against the vernacular. Indeed, it was following that document that Bishop Mark Carroll of Wichita, Kans., was told by the anti-vernacular apostolic delegate, Archbishop Vagnozzi, that his association with the Vernacular Society was to cease; other members of the clergy also resigned from the group.

The Second Vatican Council. On Dec. 4, 1963, the bishops of the Second Vatican Council, together with Pope Paul VI, solemnly promulgated their first document of Vatican II—the Liturgy Constitution, *Sacrosanctum Concilium*. The formal vote taken that day was 2,147 bishops in favor, four opposed. The Vatican then issued a pastoral instruction on Sept. 26, 1964, to assist with implementing the new document on the local level and gave the first Sunday of Advent 1964 as the effective date for implementation. This was the crowning achievement of the Liturgical Movement and the fulfillment of a dream for liturgical pioneers who were still alive at the time to see the dream come true. While the Constitution endorsed the efforts of the pioneers, it only marked the beginning of work to be undertaken by the whole Church in subsequent years. National liturgical commissions and institutes of pastoral liturgy would be formed; liturgical experts would need to be trained.

The CONSILIUM for the Implementation of the Constitution on the Liturgy—a commission of experts—was established in 1964 to carry out the revisions of the Roman liturgical books. Except for the section of the Roman Ritual on blessings, all of the Church's liturgical books were published before 1978; a number were subsequently revised. Each language group was charged with the task of translating the Latin edition into the vernacular, and the creation of original texts (with the help of linguists, poets, anthropologists, etc.) that reflected the culture and experience of the particular local church. Those liturgical texts had to be approved by each episcopal conference and confirmed by the Congregation for DIVINE WORSHIP AND THE DISCIPLINE OF THE SACRAMENTS.

Actual sacramental formulae were approved by the pope for each language group. In 1963 the English-speaking world formed the INTERNATIONAL COMMISSION ON ENGLISH IN THE LITURGY (ICEL), which was incorporated in Canada (1967) with Washington, D.C., as the site of its secretariat. In the U.S., the Bishops' Commission on the Liturgical Apostolate was formed in 1958 under the leadership of Archbishop Paul Hallinan (Atlanta) and Msgr. Frederick R. McManus (Boston). The Bishops' Committee on the Liturgy (BCL) had a full-time secretariat at the offices of the National Conference of Catholic Bishops in Washington, D.C. As dioceses established liturgical commissions in keeping with the directive of *Sacrosanctum Concilium* (no. 44), the FEDERATION OF DIOCESAN LITURGICAL COMMISSIONS (FDLC) was founded in 1969 to create a network of diocesan liturgy directors, promoting leadership in pastoral liturgy. Two members were elected from each of the twelve regions of the country to serve on its board of directors. Together with the BCL and a local diocese, the FDLC sponsored a national meeting annually. It promoted the appointment of full-time trained liturgical personnel in most large dioceses around the country.

In the area of the arts, a Composers' Forum for Catholic Worship was established in 1970 to promote the composition of new music, but was discontinued in 1977. In 1976, the NATIONAL ASSOCIATION OF PASTORAL MUSICIANS (NPM) was founded by Rev. Virgil Funk to include both pastors and musicians. NPM annual conferences drew thousands of people from around the country and its journal, *Pastoral Music* was widely acclaimed. Another organization on the scene was the Society for Catholic Liturgy, founded in 1995 by Msgr. M. Francis Mannion of Salt Lake City, Utah. This group of 160 Catholic liturgical specialists held annual meetings at the end of September.

Certain places were also designated as centers for liturgical research, among them the Notre Dame Center for Pastoral Liturgy (1970) and the Georgetown Center for Liturgy, Spirituality, and the Arts (Washington, D.C.). The Chicago Office of Divine Worship instituted the widely acclaimed Liturgy Training Publications (now independent) which provided a tremendous service to the Church in publishing excellent liturgical material (both in English and Spanish) that was accessible both to clergy and parishioners alike.

Bibliography: J. ARIOVALDO DA SILVA, *O Movimento Litúrgico No Brasil: Estudo Histórico* (Petrópolis 1983). W. BARUANA, *The Liturgy of Vatican II: A Symposium in Two Volumes* (Chicago 1966). T. BERGER, *Women's Ways of Worship: Gender Analysis and Liturgical History* (Collegeville 1999). B. BOTTE, *Le mouvement liturgique: témoignage et souvenirs* (Paris 1973). English trans. *From Silence to Participation: An Insider's View of Liturgical Re-*

newal (Washington 1988). A. BUGNINI, *The Reform of the Liturgy* (Collegeville 1990). W. R. FRANKLIN, ''The Nineteenth Century Liturgical Movement,'' *Worship* 53 (1979), 12–39. K. HUGHES, *How Firm a Foundation. v. 1: Voices of the Early Liturgical Movement* (Chicago 1990). C. JOHNSON, *Prosper Guéranger, 1805–1875, A Liturgical Theologian: An Introduction to his Liturgical Writings and Work* (Rome 1984). E. B. KOENKER, *The Liturgical Renaissance in the Roman Catholic Church* (Chicago 1954; 2nd ed., St. Louis 1966). L. MADDEN, ed. *The Awakening Church: 25 Years of Liturgical Renewal* (Collegeville 1992). T. F. O'MEARA, ''The Origins of the Liturgical Movement and German Romanticism,'' *Worship* 59 (1985), 326–53. K. F. PECKLERS, *The Unread Vision: The Liturgical Movement in the United States of America: 1926–1955* (Collegeville 1998). R. L. TUZIK, *How Firm a Foundation. v. 2: Leaders of the Liturgical Movement* (Chicago 1990). S. J. WHITE, *Art, Architecture, and Liturgical Reform: The Liturgical Arts Society, 1928–1972* (New York 1990).

[K. F. PECKLERS]

LITURGICAL MOVEMENT, II: ANGLICAN AND PROTESTANT

Since the Reformation, the Anglican and Lutheran traditions have used and cherished liturgies that are essentially revisions of medieval Latin rites. In the Anglican churches these liturgies have always been officially and canonically prescribed; in the Lutheran churches, they have been accepted as models of proper liturgical order, but greater freedom has been allowed to local or regional churches in adapting them to particular times and circumstances. Both the Anglican and the Lutheran liturgies preserve the ancient structures of the sacramental rites—including the traditional propers of collects and readings at the Eucharist, the structure of Morning and Evening Prayer, and the celebration of the principal feasts and seasons of the liturgical year. They have also continued many of the external ceremonies and ornaments and arrangements of liturgical space that existed prior to the Reformation. Thanks to the liturgical renewal shared by all the mainline Protestant churches, and in particular, to a recovery of patristic sources, one finds other churches, e.g. those of the Reformed (Calvinistic) tradition; Methodists etc.; calling for a more frequent celebration of the Eucharist with a ritual structure (use of liturgical vesture etc.) that had largely been unknown in those churches prior to the renewal.

Led by liturgical scholars like John M. Neale, J. Wickham Legg, Walter H. Frere, and F. E. Brightman in Britain and Paul Drews, Julian Smend, and Georg Rietschel in Germany, the Liturgical Movement in Protestantism and Anglicanism focused on the same conditions and concerns that affected the affected the beginnings of liturgical renewal in Catholicism: a desire to recover the ancient liturgical tradition and heritage of the Church.

Anglican Communion. The revival of liturgical interest within Anglicanism must be viewed in light of the growth of the OXFORD MOVEMENT with its own emphasis on the sacraments; an increased frequency in the celebration of the Eucharist; an increase in ceremonial; and a widespread favor for Gothic architecture, Gregorian chant, and popular hymnody that relied heavily on Latin and Eastern sources. The revision of the BOOK OF COMMON PRAYER—the first time since the Reformation—grew within such a milieu, first with the American revision in 1892, then with revisions in Scotland, Canada, England, South Africa, and the United States in the 1920s. Interestingly, one of the leading British Anglican pioneers of the 1930s, A. Gabriel Hebert, attributed his own liturgical influence to the Roman Catholic Benedictine monks at Maria Laach in Germany.

Episcopal Church. The Liturgical Movement in the EPISCOPAL CHURCH in the United States came into its own in 1946 with the Associated Parishes for Liturgy and Mission. Founded by John Patterson (+1988), Rector of Grace Church, Madison, Wisconsin, in collaboration with Massey Shepherd, Samuel E. West, and John H. Keene, Episcopal priests in the movement used their parishes as testing ground for liturgical experimentation and renewal. The fundamental goal of the movement was the restoration of Sunday Eucharist as normative for Episcopal parishes, with congregational participation that included an offertory procession; the gospel proclaimed in the midst of the assembly; liturgical music that invited participation and no choir procession. Public celebrations of Morning and Evening Prayer were restored and baptisms, marriages, and funerals again became public events. Like its Catholic counterpart, Associated Parishes promoted a greater unity between liturgy and social justice. Through the publishing of pamphlets and annual conferences, this organization promoted a renewed liturgy within the Episcopal Church, paving the way for the 1979 revised Book of Common Prayer. It also served as a catalyst for ecumenical efforts by inviting Catholic speakers and others to participate in their liturgical weeks. In recent years, the Associated Parishes Movement expanded its activities to include the restoration of the catechumenate and the diaconate, as well as the defense and promotion of inclusive language within worship. Associated Parishes' quarterly journal ''Open,'' has assisted its efforts.

Lutheran Churches. A similar development can be seen within the Lutheran movement, with its recovery of liturgical orders inspired by the *Kirchenordnungen* of the Reformation era as a reaction against attempts to downplay those orders in the 18th and early 19th centuries, thanks to Pietism and rationalism. Wilhelm Loehe (1808–72) and Theodor Kliefoth (1810–95) led the revival. Loehe's writings influenced those in the United States who produced the 1888 *Common Service* (revised in 1917). By the beginning of the 20th century, Lutherans on both sides of the Atlantic were already forming societies and institutes for the study and reform of liturgy, e.g., the Lutheran Liturgical Association (1907); the Hochkirchliche Vereinigung, founded by Friedrich Heiler (1919); the Berneuchen Circle (1923), from which came the Michaelsbruderschaft (1931) and the Alpirscbacher Circle (1933). Similar societies have emerged in Scandinavia. In the United States, Lutheran liturgical renewal took shape in the 1950s, e.g. with altars being turned toward the people for the Eucharistic celebration. The revised *Lutheran Book of Worship*, (1978) bears testimony to years of fruitful pioneering in Lutheran circles. More recently, the text, *With One Voice: A Lutheran Resource for Worship* (Minneapolis 1995) brings the renewal to full stature.

Reformed Churches. The Reformed (Calvinistic) churches experienced their own liturgical renewal, beginning in the 1840s and 1850s, with the Liturgical Movement of the German Reformed Church in the United States led by Philip Schaaf (+1893) and John Williamson Nevin (+1886) at the seminary in Mercersburg, Pennsylvania. In 1865, the Church Service Society was founded in the Church of Scotland. Its *Euchologion* (many editions since 1867) was quite influential, culminating in the 1928 *Book of Common Order* (revised 1940). Its counterpart among American Presbyterians was the *Book of Common Worship* (1905; revised 1931, 1946). The recently revised edition of 1993 is consistent with the liturgical structure found in the United Church of Christ's 1986 *Book of Common Worship*, the United Methodists' 1992 *Book of Worship*, and the revised service books of the other churches.

Characteristics. The recovery of traditional liturgical structures in the churches separated at the Reformation era was matched during the 20th century by widespread adoption within the "free" Protestant churches of more formal rituals and ceremonials borrowed or adopted from the ancient and classical rites. Most of the major Protestant denominations had official worship commissions responsible for the revision and production of service books and hymnals. As Sunday celebrations of the Eucharist became more frequent, so, too, was the observance of traditional feasts and liturgical seasons (e.g., the celebration of Ash Wednesdays with the imposition of ashes). Standards of liturgical music were greatly improved. The prejudice against formalized worship significantly diminished.

The contribution of biblical scholarship to the Liturgical Movement was significant in the Protestant liturgical renewal as well as regarding ecumenical liturgical collaboration. By 2000 there was much greater agreement among Catholic and Protestant biblical and liturgical scholars on the meaning of worship in the Christian Scriptures and the Patristic period than ever before. Influential Protestant and Anglican leaders included Hans Lietzmann, Joachim Jeremias, Oscar Cullman, Gregory DIX, and Charles H. Dodd. Research produced consensus in two significant areas: 1) the inseparable relationship between word and sacrament as the normative pattern of Christian worship; and 2) the eschatological understanding of sacraments in the context of the Christian scriptures.

Liturgical societies formed in most of the Protestant and Anglican churches in Europe and North America. A long list of Protestant and Anglican liturgical leaders had significant influence on the liturgical reforms of their respective churches, among them Massey Shepherd, Thomas Talley, Geoffrey Wainright, Kenneth Stevenson, Brian Spinks, Paul Bradshaw, James White, Don Saliers, Hoyt Hickman, S. Anita Stauffer, Gordon Lathrop, Frank Senn, and Horace Allen.

Bibliography: R. K. FENWICK and B. D. SPINKS, *Worship in Transition: Highlights of the Liturgical Movement* (Edinburgh 1995). D. GRAY, *Earth and Altar* (Norwich 1986). A. G. HEBERT, *Liturgy and Society* (London 1935). M. H. SHEPHERD, ''The Liturgical Movement in American Protestantism,'' *Yearbook of Liturgical Studies* 3 (1962) 35–61. M. J. TAYLOR, *The Protestant Liturgical Renewal* (Westminster, Maryland 1963). J. F. WHITE, *Protestant Worship: Traditions in Transition* (Louisville 1989).

[M. H. SHEPHERD JR./K. F. PECKLERS]

LITURGICAL MOVEMENT, III: ECUMENICAL CONVERGENCES

Efforts at ecumenical liturgical cooperation began in 1937 when the Edinburgh Conference on Faith and Order established a Commission on Ways of Worship, whose work has continued since the formation of the World Council of Churches at Amsterdam in 1948 through various theological commissions. The reports and papers of these commissions have covered a wide range of topics, including sacramental theology; the relation of word and sacrament in worship; the meaning of priesthood; the significance of Christian Initiation; and the relationship between liturgy and culture. Together, they have squarely faced the often divisive issues of eucharistic presence and sacrifice. Orthodox and Roman Catholic theologians have often made significant contributions to these dialogues.

The Church of South India offers another example. Formed in 1947 from Anglican, Presbyterian, Congregationalist, and Methodist churches, the Church of South India published a first edition of its liturgy in 1950 with the title *An Order for the Lord's Supper or Holy Eucharist*; it has undergone subsequent revisions. It is an interesting rite precisely from an ecumenical perspective.

Following upon the ecumenical initiatives of Vatican Council II, the CONSILIUM for the Implementation of the Constitution on the Sacred Liturgy (*Sacrosanctum Concilium*) invited observers from other traditions to be present in the work of reforming the calendar and lectionary. Moreover, the INTERNATIONAL COMMISSION ON ENGLISH IN THE LITURGY (ICEL), entrusted with the preparation of authorized English translations of the new Latin liturgical documents, was assisted in its work by consultants from other churches to review proposed translations from an ecumenical viewpoint. One of the more important examples of ecumenical liturgical cooperation has been the work of the INTERNATIONAL CONSULTATION ON COMMON TEXTS (ICET), a cooperative drafting of modern English versions of frequently used liturgical texts by representatives of the Anglican, Baptist, Congregational, Lutheran, Methodist, Presbyterian, and Roman Catholic churches in England, Ireland, Scotland, Wales, Canada, Australia, South Africa, and the United States. Begun in 1969, this group of 25 scholars in regular consultation with the bodies represented, both produced and revised texts of the Lord's Prayer, the Creeds, and the ordinary chants of the Eucharist and Liturgy of the Hours, texts which have been widely adopted in recent liturgical reforms. When ICET dissolved in 1975, a new group, the ENGLISH LANGUAGE LITURGICAL COMMISSION (ELLC) was subsequently established to continue ecumenical efforts at common liturgical texts. In addition to these official bodies, the international meeting of SOCIETAS LITURGICA was a forum for Catholic and other Christian liturgical theologians and scholars to meet and collaborate in research and other projects.

Perhaps the greatest ecumenically liturgical document of the century came in 1982 at the historic meeting of the World Council of Churches at Lima, Peru. It was there that the Faith and Order Commission's statement, "Baptism, Eucharist, and Ministry," was agreed upon and accepted by all the member churches represented. Such agreement on issues of baptismal participation; eucharist and sacrifice; and church ministry would have been impossible back in 1937 when the Ways of Worship Commission first met at Edinburgh, but the historical and theological insights of the liturgical movements in all the Christian churches made such doctrinal accord possible. It was precisely the fact that scholars used the same sources for their liturgical revisions that the mainline Christian churches developed a marvelous unity regarding liturgical structure, both in Eucharistic celebrations

and the Liturgy of the Hours, often using the same or very similar texts, thanks to the efforts of ICET and then ELLC.

As ecumenical liturgical cooperation continued to be more the norm than the exception, increasing numbers of Protestant churches are asking for a more frequent (e.g. weekly) celebration of the Eucharist, while Catholics slowly rediscovered non–eucharistic forms of liturgical prayer (e.g. the Liturgy of the Hours) for parochial use. Catholics also recovered the importance of biblically based preaching; congregational singing; and a revival of various liturgical ministries long a mainstay in Protestant churches. The Common Lectionary also held great promise; despite the sad division at the table of the Eucharist, there was no reason why the churches needed to remain divided at the table of God's Word. Indeed, increasing numbers of Christian churches read the same lessons on Sunday morning, and pastoral commentaries that assist preachers in their preparation such as the "Homily Service" published by the ecumenical Liturgical Conference (Silver Spring, Md.) directed their reflections accordingly. On the experiential level, liturgical cooperation was modelled in the prayer rituals organized and hosted by the ecumenical community of Taizé, France. Founded in 1949 and including brothers from a variety of Christian traditions in Europe and North America, Taizé united Christians of many different churches in ecumenical rituals and in the lived experience of Christian community. This was true, not only for the thousands of young people who flocked to Taizé each year for week–long experiences of prayer and meditation, but also for the the many ecumenical experiences of "Taizé Prayer," or "Prayer around the Cross" scheduled in parishes throughout Europe and in North and South America.

The United States had more academically qualified liturgists than any other country representing a wide variety of churches and traditions, and as a result, in 1973, the ecumenical North American Academy of Liturgy (NAAL) was founded by John Gallen, S.J. By 1999 NAAL had grown to over 400 members from Canada and the United States. At the 1999 meeting in Vancouver, B.C., a campaign was launched to seek out qualified candidates from Mexico to better represent its North American identity. The Academy also became interfaith, and enjoyed a growing number of Jewish liturgical scholars, the first of whom was Rabbi Lawrence Hoffman, Professor at Hebrew Union College, New York.

On the international level, *Societas Liturgica* was founded through the initiative of Dutch Reformed pastor Wiebe Vos, when in 1962, he launched *Studia Liturgica* "an international, ecumenical quarterly for liturgical research and renewal." In 1965, Vos called a meeting of

25 liturgists from Europe and North America in Neuchâtel, Switzerland. Chaired by J. J. von Allmen, the group discussed Christian Initiation and agreed to found *Societas*, "an associaton for the promotion of ecumenical dialogue on worship based on solid research, with the perspective of renewal and unity." The first meeting took place in 1967 at Driebergen, Holland, where Vatican II's *Sacrosanctum Concilium* was studied, along with recent liturgical work completed by the Faith and Order Commission of the World Council. Although the over 400 members remained largely from Europe and North America, there was growing interest among the membership to attract new members from Asia, Africa, and South America. *Societas* continued to meet every two years with a particular topic chosen for each congress. The 1999 meeting held in Kottayam, Kerala, India, under the leadership of President Jacob Vellian (Syro–Malabar), addressed the topic of "Liturgical Theology." Proceedings of the biannual meeting were published in *Studia Liturgica*.

Bibliography: T. F. BEST, and D. HELLER, eds. *So We Believe, So We Pray: Koinonia in Worship,* Faith and Order Paper No. 171 (Geneva 1995). T. F. BEST, and D. HELLER, eds. *Eucharistic Worship in Ecumenical Contexts: The Lima Liturgy and Beyond* (Geneva 1998). G. LATHROP, "New Pentecost or Joseph's Britches? Reflections on the History and Meaning of the Worship *ordo* in the Megachurches," *Worship,* 72 (Nov. 1998) 521–538. G. LATHROP, "The Worship Books in Mutual Affirmation and Admonition: Liturgy as a Source for Lutheran–Reformed Unity," *Reformed Liturgy and Worship,* 21(2) (1997) 88–92. F. SENN, *Christian Liturgy* (Minneapolis 1997). WORLD COUNCIL OF CHURCHES, FAITH AND ORDER COMMISSION, *Baptism, Eucharist, and Ministry* (Geneva 1982).

[T. J. TALLEY/K. F. PECKLERS]

LITURGICAL MUSIC, HISTORY OF

PART 1: EARLY CHRISTIAN MUSIC

The historical development of music in Christian worship is intimately connected with the history of liturgy on the one hand and with the general history of music on the other. Until the late Middle Ages there is no history of music except that related to the liturgy. After that time, in addition to liturgical music, religious music that was not intended primarily for public worship can also be found. Such music, then, is a part of the history of church music, although it does not form part of the history of liturgical music.

Music in Apostolic Times. There is no doubt that the early Christian communities simply continued the musical practices of the Jewish synagogues that they had been accustomed to attend. For the Synaxis (Liturgy of the Word) the synagogue practice served as the model. Readings from Scripture were followed by Psalm singing. At least the differentiation between the roles of the

Cantor and congregation was a clear one. The cantor was also permitted a kind of improvised, charismatic song of joy. It is difficult to determine whether in Ephesians 5.19 St. Paul is referring to three different types of musical pieces in the Christian community or using three terms to describe the same phenomenon: ψαλμοῖς καὶ ὕμνοις καὶ ᾠδαῖς πνευματικαῖς. In Colossians 3.16, however, he uses the same division. It must be remembered that the Jewish synagogues in the diaspora had already adopted the Greek language, and Hellenistic musical practices could also have made inroads into the traditional chants.

Theories of Jewish Origins of Gregorian Chant. All critics agree that the descriptions of musical practice in the Jewish temple have nothing in common with the Christian chant. The most difficult problem is to ascertain the degree to which the Gregorian chant as known today has been influenced by Jewish chants, specifically from the synagogue practices of the time of Christ. In answering this question, certain facts must be considered: the first notated sources for the Gregorian chant come from the ninth century (before that time only literary references to music exist); there is no way of finding out the exact nature of Hebrew chants in the early Christian centuries. Even if one assumes that the Gregorian melodies, as written down for the first time in the ninth century, go back in basic form for several centuries as an oral tradition, there is no exact parallel in the Hebrew chant with which to compare it. The assumption that several Jewish groups have retained an oral tradition untampered by Western practice for almost two millennia seems difficult to accept. The Hebrew literary forms, especially the antithetical structure of the Psalms, were carried into early Christian practice. Beyond this, all one can say is that the general musical system common to the Jewish, Syriac and Hellenized communities became the musical system for early Christianity. The fragment of the Oxyrhynchos papyrus (third century), which contains the fragment of a hymn written in classical Greek notation, shows that the musical practice was of the type associated with the Near East basin, i.e., diatonic and based on modal formulas related to the octoechos, and had nothing in common with the descriptions and few musical fragments of classical Greek music that have survived.

Descriptions of Musical Practices in the Early Patristic Period. The improvised, charismatic song—associated especially with the Alleluia—continued in Christian worship, although the dangers of pride and theatricality are often alluded to. A distinction in this regard between the roles of cantor, lector and deacon is often difficult. In the West, it was Gregory who took the melismatic song from the deacon. The general musical practice, however, was of the litany or refrain type (*see* RESPONSORIAL PSALM). After verses of the Psalms sung by a cantor, the congregation sang a simple refrain. In addition to this practice, there is an allusion in St. Basil to the practice of dividing the congregation into two groups for alternating verses of the Psalms; Basil maintains that this practice was not unique to his region. Various sources for the origin of this practice are given, with Ambrose being cited as the originator of the practice in the West (Augustine, *Conf.* 9.7). Although the Eastern Church had developed free hymnody and poetry as a part of the liturgical service (especially St. Ephrem), the West was slower to adopt such a practice. After the time of Ambrose, hymnody became a structural part of the Divine Office in addition to Psalms and Biblical lessons. The first allusion in the West to the manner of Psalm singing, which was to become the standard medieval practice, namely the taking over of the responsorial refrain into the antiphonal or alternating style, is found in Cassian (early fifth century). From the fifth century on, less is known of the manner in which the people participated at services; the reason for this lack of knowledge is that the purpose of the surviving descriptions was to recount monastic and basilical practices.

Attitudes toward Music among the Fathers. The rejection of all musical instruments from Christian worship is consistent among the Fathers. These were associated with pagan, orgiastic rites. For this reason the descriptions in the Old Testament of the temple worship with different kinds of instruments were interpreted allegorically. The heavy influence of Platonic musical aesthetics can be found in the Fathers, especially in Clement of Alexandria and Chrysostom (probably through the writings of Philo). Plato insisted on the need to control the music of the community in order to protect morals. Once the proper number for music was found, it should not be abandoned. The Psalms, thus argued Chrysostom, were divinely given to the Church and were the inspired word. They were the earthly reflection of the divine harmony. In general, the Fathers could be divided into two classes in their attitude toward music: those who accepted it and its beauty, provided the *vox* and *mens* were in agreement (Basil, Cassiodorus and Benedict); and those who feared the pleasures of music as contrary to the ascetical Christian ideal (Jerome is the supreme example).

Families of Chant. Concommitant with the rise of the various families of Western rites there arose families of Western chant: AMBROSIAN, GALLICAN, MOZARABIC and GREGORIAN. They all show musical relationships to the contemporaneous BYZANTINE chant and a certain interdependency among themselves that musicologists have not accurately determined.

Bibliography: H. HUCKE, *Lexikon für Theologie und Kirche,* eds., J. HOFER and K. RAHNER, 10 v. (2d, new ed. Freiburg 1957–65) 4:429–433. T. GEORGIADES, *Die Religion in Geschichte und Gegenwart,* 7 v. (3d ed. Tübingen 1957–65) 4:1207–17. H. LECLERCQ, "Chant romain et grégorien," *Dictionnaire d'archéologie chrétienne et de liturgie,* eds., F. CABROL, H. LECLERCQ and H. I. MARROU, 15 v. (Paris 1907–53) 3.1:256–311. B. STÄBLEIN, "Choral," *Die Musik in Geschichte und Gegenwart,* ed. F. BLUME (Kassel-Basel 1949–) 2:1265–1303; "Frühchristliche Musik," *ibid.* 4:1036–64. E. WERNER, *The Sacred Bridge* (New York 1959). T. GÉROLD, *Les Pères de l'Eacute;glise;et la musique* (Strasbourg 1931). E. WELLESZ, *Eastern Elements in Western Chant* (Oxford 1947). H. ANGLÈS, "Latin Chant before St. Gregory," *New Oxford History of Music,* ed. J. A. WESTRUP, 11 v. (New York 1957–) 2:58–91. J. QUASTEN *Musik und Gesang in den Kulten der heidnischen Antike und christlichen Frühzeit* (Münster 1930).

[R. G. WEAKLAND/EDS.]

Plucked-fiddle players before the Lamb of God, miniature from a manuscript of Beatus' Commentary on the Apocalypse, written for the Abbey of Santo Domingo de Silos, Spain, c. 1091–1109.

PART 2: MONOPHONIC MUSIC TO 1200

The oral traditions of the Christian communities and monasteries (until the invention of musical notation in the ninth century) must have varied greatly one from another. If Pope Gregory the Great at the beginning of the seventh century supposedly attempted to bring some order into the liturgical makeup, it is hardly conceivable, given the lack of means of communication of the times, that any uniformity could have been attained in music. The founding of the Roman SCHOLA CANTORUM and the erecting of monastic chapters at the major basilicas gave life to a Roman chant tradition that became more and more subtle and complex. Darkness still shrouds much of the story, as no musical manuscripts from the period are available. That the reign of the Byzantine popes in the seventh century also had an influence on music can only be surmised.

The Carolingian Period. Before the Carolingian period there was no attempt to keep a musical unity in Christendom, but the concept of Holy Roman Empire included liturgical—and thus musical—imitations of Roman usages. Cantors and liturgical books were brought up to the Carolingian court for diffusion of the Roman practice throughout the empire. The different Gallican usages were to be suppressed in favor of the *cantilena romana,* although Walafrid Strabo (b. 808), a generation later, mentions that those with an ear for music could still recognize the old Gallican tunes in the revised hymnody.

The first Western music that is written down and can be subjected to a critical analysis is GREGORIAN CHANT. Manuscripts containing the chant appear all over the Empire beginning with the late ninth century. Whether it was the original Roman chant brought north, or a hybrid of Roman and local Gallican practices remains a disputed question, although more scholars favor the latter theory. From the theoretical treatises beginning with the mid-ninth century, the actual fragments from the same century, and the full manuscripts of the tenth century, it is clear that the musical repertoire of that time was a vast and highly developed one. The *Ordines romani* show the numerous adaptations of Roman liturgical practice as well as the need for skilled cantors and leaders (called *primicerius* and *secundicerius*). The music recorded is not that sung by the people, but by the trained *scholae* of clerics and monks. The *antiphonale missarum* or Graduale for the Mass chants and the *antiphonale* for the Office chants contained most of the music needed for the complete year. When the teaching of this standard repertoire resulted in considerable inconvenience, *tonaria* were developed. The chants were arranged by modal similarities in them for easier memorization and reading. The special chants reserved to the soloists were written in the *cantatorium.* The survival of many copies of these books from the tenth century onward makes possible an accurate history of liturgical music from that time. However, not only do we know nothing of the music of the people at this point of history, but we are also totally ignorant of nonliturgical or folk music before the 12th century.

Additions to the Standard Repertoire. The chant repertoire was soon augmented by freely composed additions of texts and melodies that gave birth to TROPES and SEQUENCES. The need for new outlets for the creative imaginations of the post-Carolingian cantors must have come as a result of the rigidity of the standard repertoire. The tropes and sequences permitted the introduction on a given feast of more popular elements and more local allusions. Although there is some evidence that a basic repertoire of these new pieces somehow made its way across the Empire, the differences in the extant collections from various abbeys are large. It is clear that the lengthening of the services by long processions and incensations may have contributed to the need for more music not provided by the standard repertoire. St. Martial at Limoges, France, and Sankt Gallen in present Switzerland were renowned sources for this activity.

Liturgical Drama. Out of the dialogue trope, especially that which preceded the Introit, there arose the liturgical drama. Again, it permitted more popular and more didactic elements to enter the liturgy and provided opportunity for freer creativity on the part of the composer. These dramas became larger and larger until they separated entirely from the liturgy.

Other New Compositions. The special talents of the composer from the Carolingian period until the 12th century and beyond also found outlets in the composition of RIMED OFFICES. As new feasts were introduced, experimentation with verse texts and rhythmical patterns found its counterpart in music. The numerous processions connected with monastic services gave birth to a special book called the *processionale.* In it could be found new responsories and antiphons to be sung on special feasts as well as metrical *conductus* or processional hymns. The influence of the growing secular forms that culminated in the troubadours could also be seen in the Latin *planctus* or laments (reaching their peak in those by Abelard) and the new vernacular *laudi, cantigas* and *Geisslerlieder.* These new popular forms became especially prominent after the 13th century. During this entire period new compositions of the Ordinary of the Mass in chant continued, both troped and untroped.

Special Chant Traditions. Within the Gregorian tradition one cannot distinguish families as markedly different as were the Gregorian and Ambrosian, for example, but different religious orders and different localities did develop traits peculiar to themselves. Thus the Beneventan tradition in Italy differed from the German not only in notation but also in many particular usages. In England the early Gregorian practices merged with new elements after the Norman invasion to form a chant dialect called Sarum (*see* SARUM USE). The Cistercian reform also affected music and many of the more elaborate chants were brought into simple patterns. The Dominican chant also has its peculiar flavor.

Gregorian chant continued to be used in services long after the new elements listed above and the use of polyphonic music took over the major interests of composers. As it came down through the centuries, this chant was constantly affected by secular music of the times and by contemporary styles and idioms. Attempts to restore it to its pristine vigor have been constant. It can be said, however, that it reached its apogee in the Carolingian and post-Carolingian period and never regained the subtlety evidenced in the earliest manuscripts of that time. It was only natural that composers, after exhausting the musical means of one style, should have turned so avidly to the possibilities of the new polyphony.

Bibliography: W. APEL, *Gregorian Chant* (Bloomington, Ind. 1958). H. ANGLÈS, "Gregorian Chant," *New Oxford History of Music,* ed. J. A. WESTRUP, 11 v. (New York 1957–) 2:92–127. J. HANDSCHIN, "Trope, Sequence, and Conductus," *ibid.* 128–174. S. CORBIN, *L'Église à la conquête de sa musique* (Paris 1960). A. GASTOUÉ, *Les Origines du chant romain* (Paris 1907). O. URSPRUNG, *Die katholische Kirchenmusik* (Potsdam 1931). P. WAGNER, *Einführung in die gregorianischen Melodien,* 3 v. (Leipzig).

[R. G. WEAKLAND/EDS.]

PART 3: POLYPHONIC MUSIC, ORIGINS TO 1450

The ninth century, the era of the CAROLINGIAN RENAISSANCE, with its palace school and liturgical reforms, had also provided the first example of written counterpoint in the anonymous treatise Musica enchiriadis [M. Gerbert, *Scriptores ecclesiastici de musica sacra potissimum,* 3 v. (Milan 1931) 2:168]. There is no certain evidence as to what extent either written or unwritten part music may have existed before then.

Early Organum. The examples in *Musica enchiriadis* are all syllabic, note against note and very short. They are called organum, the name given until *c.* 1250 to all the various styles of polyphony that involve a liturgical melody and added voice parts. Some, called "strict," proceed in simple parallel motion at the fourth or fifth; others, called "free," have oblique motion as well.

A gap of more than 100 years occurred before the next important treatise, a chapter in GUIDO OF AREZZO'S Micrologus (*c.* 1040), where counterpoint is more firmly established by introducing the concept of planned contrary motion at the cadences (*occursus*): major second or third to unison. Examples reveal also the crossing of parts; and free organum is preferred to strict. Outside the theoretical treatises, the largest number of examples of polyphony—about 164 organa—is found in the 11th-century manuscript Corpus Christi College 473, called the *Winchester Troper.*

The music of *Winchester* confirms the theorists' statements on contrary motion, but the pitches cannot be transcribed accurately since the example are written with staffless (cheironomic) neums. Two other manuscripts, Lucca 603 and Chartres 109, are written with neums on staves; hence their music can be transcribed accurately with regard to pitch but not to rhythm. The striking example from the Chartres manuscript ignores the theorists' rules of perfect consonances in order to build lines with color and strength.

Toward the year 1080, the start of a renaissance that was to last through the 12th century made its appearance with some of the finest Romanesque buildings, the *Chanson de Roland,* the earliest troubadours, and the first substantial growth in polyphony. Four manuscripts from the Limoges district, probably from the monastery of St. Martial [Bibliothèque Nationale lat. 1.1139 (late 11th century), BN 1.3459, 3749 (12th century), and British Museum add. 36881 (early 13th century)] contain polyphonic works. Most are written with neums that are heighted or on a staff (diastematic), so that the pitches are clear. Transcription of rhythm, however, involves so much guesswork that scholars differ widely in their interpretation. The most striking device is the lengthening of the chant, or tenor, notes to sometimes as long as 26 notes of the added voice (as in *Jubilemus exultemus,* BN 1.1139, fol. 41), so that actual perception as melody is excluded. It sounds more like a series of drones at various levels, a method later developed by the Notre Dame school. On fol. 60' of BN 1.1139, the upper voice of the *Benedicamus Domino* is troped, i.e., has its own separate text added to the melody and text of the liturgical tenor (*see* TROPE). This device qualifies it as an example of the early MOTET, a polyphonic form that was to become prominent during the 13th century. In the melismatic passages of many pieces the beginnings of masterful contrapuntal technique appear. These passages alternate sensitively with the note-against-note passages and lose the angularity of more primitive counterpoint. The quality of melody, however, differs from chant, with many melodic sequences and sweeping descents. Extraordinary passages like those below contain some of the earliest examples of exchanged voices, called *Stimmtausch,* as well as imitation.

Another manuscript, copied *c.* 1140, the Codex Calixtinus in the cathedral library in Compostela, Spain, has 20 two-part *organa* and the oldest known three-part piece, *Congaudeant catholici.* The middle voice appears to have been interpolated later; some parts of it function as a filler, being without melodic interest.

The Ars Antiqua (The Old Art). The first contrapuntal school to produce music of international acclaim was that of Notre Dame, which flourished in and near Paris during the late 12th and early 13th centuries. Its music may be found in three 13th-century manuscripts: Florence *Biblioteca Laurenziana* Pl. 29.1 (F), Wolfenbüttel Bibliothek 677 (W¹) and 1206 (W²), each containing over 190 closely written pages of polyphony. As this music was performed in monasteries and cathedrals throughout Europe, large and small collections may be found in 60 or more other manuscripts copied as far away as Spain, England and Bavaria. Although not all the rhythmic problems have been worked out, most of the transcriptions done recently are faithful enough to convey the poetical aspects of the music and warrant performance in church, concert, or recording.

The original Notre Dame collection was called the *Magnus liber organi* (Great Book of Organa), and, according to the English theorist known to musicologists as Anonymous IV [H. Coussemaker, *Scriptorum de musica medii aevi nova series,* 4 v. (Paris 1864–76) 1:342], it included settings for the feast days of the entire ecclesiastical year written by the composer LÉONIN and partly rewritten by his successor, PÉROTIN. Anonymous IV stated that the *Magnus liber* was in use at the cathedral of Paris until his own day (*c.* 1280); this, however, is not proof that it originated there. The Magnus liber has not survived, but the organa common to all three Notre Dame manuscripts, as well as those common to F and W², are considered by Husmann to have belonged to that original collection [*Musical Quarterly* (New York 1915–) 49:311–330]. Léonin and his successors set the Proper rather than the Ordinary of the Mass, together with the solo parts of the Gradual and Alleluia and some responsorial sections of the Office, leaving the choral parts of the service to be sung in unison as on the nonfestive days of the year.

The chief difference between a Saint-Martial and a Notre Dame *organum* was that the latter was organized according to one of six repeated patterns of rhythm called *modi*. These patterns were varied at irregular intervals by omitting a weak beat (*fusio modi*), inserting a rest (*pausatio*), or by breaking a note into several quick ornaments (*fractio modi*); these variations, however, never obscured the patterns. The syllabic sections of the tenor could stretch out beneath the upper melisma in even longer drones than at Saint-Martial, sometimes lasting 40 measures. The added voice or voices crossed and recrossed one another as in the earlier styles of organum, though by Pérotin's time the phrases had become short and clearcut. Phrases usually began and ended on perfect consonances, touching unisons midway. The perfect consonances appeared, too, on most accented beats, the other beats carrying any of the other intervals.

New in Notre Dame was the treatment of the melismatic sections of the chant tenor, reshaped rhythmically into one of the *modi,* often a slower *modus* than that of the added voice. These sections were called discantus or *clausulae.* The measuring of both or all voices, together with the heritage of unifying devices from Saint-Martial and Léonin, made possible the construction of really interesting works in three parts by Pérotin and his contemporaries. Before the turn of the century, Pérotin wrote the first four-part works, *Viderunt* (F, fol. 1) and *Sederunt* (W¹ fol. 1). The *clausulae* form the link with the two later periods of the *Ars antiqua,* as many were transformed into motets by adding texts to the upper voices. Later, original motets were composed. Starting as a sacred form, the motet underwent secular influence, and love songs, often frivolous and imaginative, were added to the liturgical tenors or even combined with sacred verse in another voice. The counterpoint continued to gain its marvelous linear liberty, which combined with increasing vertical subtlety.

The rhythmic changes occurring during the 12th and 13th centuries kept the notational systems in an almost constant state of flux. Among the theorists were John of Garland, Walter Odington, Johannes de Grocheo, as well as the above mentioned Anonymous IV. Two theorists undertook important reforms of notation. In the mid-13th century, FRANCO OF COLOGNE facilitated exactness in reading by assigning definite time values to the conventional note forms then in use (*Ars cantus mensurabilis; Scriptorum de musica medii aevi nova series,* 1:117). At the end of the century, PETRUS DE CRUCE introduced further notational innovations to facilitate distinction among the smaller note values.

The Ars Nova (The New Art). A new musical spirit appeared early in the 14th century. The six rhythmic patterns of the 12th- and 13th-century *modi,* which had long served as means of unification, now became a prison. The musical idea of the 14th century usually found expression in complicated rhythms, often with iambic and trochaic figures in the same phrase. Triple rhythm had been the norm during the time of the *ars antiqua,* with duple as the exception; now both were the norm, with the duple indicated at first by red notation (e.g., manuscript BN 1.146, *Le Roman de Fauvel*), later by time signatures. Sometimes one voice alternated rapidly with rests in the other (the "hocket"). The first musical canon had appeared in France in 1288 and was followed by many others.

The traditional employment of rhythmic figures as unifying devices continued, however, in a new way. The 13th-century patterns (*ostinati*) were replaced by whole complicated phrases, sometimes as long as ten measures, which were repeated several times with fresh pitches (isorhythm). The working out of so much that was new in counterpoint and organization involved a temporary neglect in the setting of words, the latter becoming a mere pretext, sometimes, for the setting of multiple lines.

In a time of profound change it is inevitable that there be modernists and conservatives. Many of the innovations were condemned by the *Docta sanctorum* (1322) of Pope John XXII. Composers were accused of arbitrary interruptions in melody, addition of frivolous vernacular texts to the sacred chants, and, in general, of preferring modern to ancient music. The *Docta sanctorum* went so far as to regulate technical details, permitting only the Pythagorean fourth, fifth and eighth (octave) in counterpoint, over a chant tenor that must be rhythmically unaltered. Although parts of this letter are understandable in view of the bold procedures that were just beginning, it is unfortunate that it was written before the characteristic 14th-century works had appeared. Those who drafted it could not realize how the new style would be made to speak in a work as august as Guillaume de MACHAUT's Mass (transcribed in 1949 by G. Van, in *Corpus mensurabilis musicae,* ed. American Institute of Musicology, 2). This great monument of the 14th century, the first known polyphonic Mass to be written by one person, combines solid tradition, in its isorhythmic foundation, with wild audacity, especially in its astounding rhythms and intervals. The Kyrie, Sanctus, and Agnus Dei have sections with isorhythm in all voices, some contrasting sharply with others in speed. The Gloria and Credo prolong the *conductus* tradition, alternating between marching block chords and held chords. The whole disconcerting and exalting work is united by five or more motifs, some appearing in each movement. Machaut brought high refinement, astonishing melodies, and unexpected chromatics to the other forms that he inherited—the *lai, complainte, virelai, rondeau, and ballade.* His double ballade has two simultaneous texts. His motets, like the Mass, have the traditional base of isorhythm, though in extremely complex phrases, which are sometimes repeated in diminution. His works can be found in over 30 manuscripts, most of them transcribed by Friedrich Ludwig.

Among composer-theorists, two leaders of the new movement were Philippe de VITRY and Johannes de Muris. Vitry introduced the term *Ars nova* (c. 1325) as the title to a treatise that, however, deals mainly with notational rather than musical innovations (see *Scriptorum de musica medii aevi nova series*). In his compositions there are numerous complete chords, some tonal cadences and passages with consecutive thirds. Both composers frequently raised the seventh degree to function as leading tone (*musica falsa*), and sometimes even the fourth degree in the same cadence, as leading tone to the dominant, forming a cadence with a strangely modern

sound (Burgundian cadence). The tracts of Johannes de Muris are available in *Scriptorum de musica medii aevi nova series* by H. Coussemaker, *Scriptores ecclesiastici de musica sacra potissimum* by M. Gerbert and *Source Readings in Music History* edited by O. Strunk.

The period between Machaut and DUFAY, known as that of the mannerists [W. Apel, *The Notation of Polyphonic Music* (4th, rev. ed. Cambridge, Mass. 1949) 403–435], produced much secular and some sacred music with even more complicated rhythms than before, with a tendency for recherché combinations and picturesqueness. Composers in France were Baude Caurdier (fl. *c.* 1400), Jean Tapissier, Cesaris, Grimace and many others.

Some music for religious dance, appearing in a manuscript at Sens, consists of a liturgical Gradual reshaped isorhythmically, with indications for the steps (J. Chailley, 21:18).

In Italy the first part of the 14th century saw French *ars nova* influence, with copies of French works in Italian manuscripts; later there was influence of French on Italian forms. This period is represented by Giovanni da Cascia (1300–50) and Jacopo da Bologna. Little sacred music has survived. Composition in the last part of the century was dominated by the blind organist of Florence, Francesco LANDINI (1325–97), who astonished and moved everyone by the speed and delicacy of his playing on the portative organ and who won the laurel crown reserved for poets and emperors. He introduced some of the complexities of Machaut's style, to which he added an Italian sweetness of melody. His contemporaries were Partolino da Padua, Paolo Tenorista, Ghirardello da Firenze and Johannes CICONIA, among many others. A typical style involved moving two voices together, the upper one with added ornaments, as in Bartolino's setting for the Credo (in G. de Van, *Les Monuments de l'Ars Nova*). The consecutive thirds are noteworthy. For further examples of this music, see N. Pirrotta and L. Ellenwood (in bibliog.). Important manuscripts are manuscript Torino Bibl. Naz. J II 9 (ed. Hopper) and manuscript Firenze Bibl. Laur. Squarcialuppi Pal. 87 (ed. J. Wolf). The chief theorists were Marchettus of Padua, who wrote a comparison of French and Italian notation, *Pomerium musica mensurata* (*Scriptores ecclesiastici de musica sacra potissimum,* 3:121), Prosdocimo de Beidemandis (*Scriptorum de musica medii aevi nova series,* 3:218) and Ugolino of Orvieto (see F. X. Haberl, in bibliog.). Ugolino clarified some of the rules of *musica falsa.*

In 14th-century England, Worcester appears to have been the important center. The chief English contribution was the use of the sixth chord in parallel motion, with the liturgical chant in the lowest voice (discant). There was much reciprocal influence between England and France.

The composer who dominated early 15th-century England was John DUNSTABLE (d.1453), musician and astronomer. His music, although essentially in the style of the French *ars nova,* avoided that school's artificial modernism, having a transparent beauty and naturalness destined later to characterize the works of the early Renaissance. Others of the early 15th-century English school were the insular composers Cooke, Damett and Sturgeon, and the Continental ones, Lionel POWER and Bedingham. A manuscript known as Old Hall, at the Catholic College of St. Edmonds, contains Mass parts and hymns by many of these composers (ed. A. Ramsbotham and H. Collins). Dunstable's complete works were edited by M. Bukofzer for *Musica Britannica.* Also in *Musica Britannica* (v.55) is a collection of 15th-century English carols in two and three parts, which were assembled from a number of manuscripts. Most are in English, the rest in Latin.

Bibliography: F. LUDWIG, *Repertorium organorum . . . et motetorum . . .* (Leipzig 1910), descriptive catalogue of the Notre Dame and allied manuscripts. F. GENNRICH, *Bibliographie der ältesten . . . Motetten* (Darmstadt 1957). *Polyphonia sacra,* ed. C. VAN DEN BORREN (rev. ed. University Park, Pa. 1963). *Music of Fourteenth-Century Italy,* ed. N. PIRROTTA, [*Corpus mensurabilis musicae,* ed. American Institute of Musicology, v.1– (Rome 1947–) 8; 1954]; *Early Fifteenth-Century Music,* ed. G. REANEY, (*ibid.* 11; 1955). *Les Monuments de l'Ars Nova,* ed. G. DE VAN, fasc. 1 (Paris 1938). *The Earliest Motets,* ed. H. TISCHLER, *Corpus mensurabilis musicae,* ed. American Institute of Musicology, v.30 (in press), 12th- and early-13th-century motet collections. F. LANDINO, *Works,* ed. L. ELLINWOOD (Cambridge, Mass. 1939). J. CHAILLEY, *Histoire musicale du moyen âge* (Paris 1950); ''Un Document nouveau sur la danse ecclésiastique,'' *Acta musicological,* 21 (1949) 18–24. W. G. WAITE, *The Rhythm of Twelfth-Century Polyphony* (New Haven 1954), with transcriptions of two-part organa in W¹. H. HUSMANN, *Die Drei- und vierstimmigen Notre-Dame-Organa* (Leipzig 1940), with transcriptions of three- and four-part organa; ''The Origin and Destination of the *Magnus liber organi,*'' tr. G. REANEY, *Musical Quarterly,* 49 (1963) 311–330. E. THURSTON, *The Conductus Compositions in Manuscript Wolfenbuttel 1206* (Doctoral diss. microfilm; N.Y.U. 1954), with transcriptions of *conductus* in W². Y. ROKSETH, *Polyphonies du XIII ᵉ siècle,* 4 v. (Paris 1935–39), with transcriptions of a large 13th-century motet collection. U. KORNMÜLLER, ''Musiklehre des Ugolino von Orvieto,'' *Kirchenmusikalisches Jahrbuch,* 10 (1895) 19–40. F. X. HABERL, ''Biobibliographische Notizen über Ugolino von Orvieto,'' *ibid.* 40–49. J. HANDSCHIN, ''The Two Winchester Tropers,'' *Journal of Theological Studies,* 37 (1936) 34–49, 156–172. L. TREITLER, ''The Polyphony of St. Martial,'' *Journal of the American Musicological Society,* 17 (1964) 29–42. G. REESE, *Music in the Middle Ages* (New York 1940). *New Oxford History of Music,* ed. J. A. WESTRUP, 11 v. (New York 1957–) v.2. W. APEL, *The Notation of Polyphonic Music* (4th, rev. ed. Cambridge, Mass. 1949) 201–202, list of medieval theorists who discussed notation. *Source Readings in Music History,* ed. O. STRUNK (New York 1950). H. COUSSEMAKER, *Scriptorum de musica medii aevi nova series,* 4 v. (Paris 1864–76). M. GERBERT, *Scriptores ecclesiastici de musica sacra potissimum,* 3 v. (Milan 1931). H. HÜSCHEN, *Die Musik in Geschichte und Gegenwart,* ed. F. BLUME (Kassel-Basel 1949–) 1:679–702. H. BESSELER, *ibid.* 702–729.

[E. THURSTON/EDS.]

PART 4: POLYPHONIC MUSIC, 1450–1600

The Middle Ages developed a strong organized and measured rhythm. The 15th and 16th centuries saw this trend enhanced by melodic as well as rhythmic fluidity into a contrapuntal art never surpassed.

Music of Northern France and the Low Countries. With the coming of the Guillaume DUFAY generation, paraphrasing of the chant in Mass compositions became widespread. Often, however, the chant melody was so extensively elaborated as to be hardly recognizable. Composition in the treble-dominated style continued. Complete Mass Ordinaries began to appear in profusion and the cantus-firmus treatment became a chief method of unification. In a *cantus-firmus* Mass of this period, the chosen melody, sacred or secular, was normally presented by the tenor in relatively long time-values, while the other voices wove constantly fresh polyphony about it.

One method of composition much utilized, especially in hymns, was *fauxbourdon,* in which the unwritten middle part moved in parallel fourths with the upper part. The result was largely a series of 6/3 and 8/5 chords, in contrast to later Italian falso bordone, which, commonly applied in 16th-century psalmody, employed mainly chords in root position but was similarly chordal (with florid cadences), recitativelike, and given to repetition. Common cadences in the period were the ''under-third'' (sometimes wrongly called the ''Landini sixth''); the ''octave-leap,'' in which the bass leaps up an octave while the tenor crosses below it, and the so-called ''Burgundian cadence,'' which has two different, simultaneously sounding leading tones. The polyphonic flow might occasionally be interrupted by fermata-marked block-chords to emphasize words of special importance.

Sources. The most extensive sources for sacred polyphony dating from *c.* 1420 to *c.* 1480 are seven codices compiled at Trent, then under Germanic control. They contain over 1,800 compositions, most of them sacred. An example of a more accurate but smaller source (containing 339 works) is the famous manuscript Q15 at Bologna.

Composers. Jean Brassart and Arnold de Lantins joined the papal choir in 1431. Arnold's three-voice Mass is among the early complete settings of the Ordinary after MACHAUT. Guillaume Dufay was one of the greatest exponents of French music, regardless of period. He wrote in all the forms and used all the techniques of his day. His

Mass on *L'Homme armé* may be the first in the long list of *cantus-firmus* Masses based on that celebrated tune. *Cantus-firmus* style gradually replaced the treble-dominated in the Masses of Dufay. His compositions in sequence- and hymn-form illustrate the systematic alternation of plainsong and polyphony, a technique also applied in some of his separate Mass movements.

The tenors of a number of chansons of Gilles Binchois and Antoine Busnois were used as *cantus firmi* in Masses by later composers. Binchois's motets and Magnificats contain much *fauxbourdon*-like writing. Johannes Okeghem, who enjoyed a reputation for excellence among his contemporaries, is the acknowledged master of the latter part of the 15th century, as well as the composer of the earliest surviving polyphonic Requiem setting. Okeghem often conspicuously avoided the clear phrase formation found in compositions by Dufay and Busnois and preferred to keep the flow of polyphony constant. His style is characterized by grand, sweeping melodic lines.

Renaissance Style. The small total range that was typical of medieval polyphony, and abetted the frequent crossing of voices, went hand in hand with a sharp differentiation of the individual parts—whether in rhythm, in melody, or in the timbres of the performing media. As a wider range came into use, crossing became less frequent and differentiation between the voices less sharp. The growing homogeneity of the voices eventually resulted in the establishment of imitation as the standard technique of the late Renaissance. As to form, the larger structures that were widely cultivated included not only the Mass but also the MAGNIFICAT, of which whole cycles were written in all the modes (often two examples of each).

Mass Compositions. During the Renaissance, a tendency developed to write complete Mass Ordinaries. The cyclic Mass, in which the sections are related to each other, resulted from an effort to unify the Mass as a whole. Two main types, the *cantus-firmus* Mass and the ''motto'' Mass (which involves the use of a head motif), were already being used in the early 15th century. The parody Mass, which is based, not on a single melody, but on the several voices of a polyphonic model, came to be favored by 16th-century composers. The 15th and 16th centuries are notable also for the development of the organ Mass. Here, in certain movements, alternate verses were represented by music solely for organ, the other verses being sung in plainsong.

Theorists. The 12 treatises of Johannes Tinctoris (*c.* 1435–1511) form a *summa* that affords insight into the musical theory of the entire Renaissance. Other theorists active *c.* 1480 were Franchino Gaforio, whose important contributions include his eight rules of counterpoint and theory of proportions, the Spanish Bartolomé Ramos de Pareja and the German Adam of Fulda. Pietro Aaron, who wrote in the vernacular, desired consistent indication of accidentals and emphasized practical terminology. The Swiss Henricus Glareanus gave separate identity to the Ionian, the Aeolian and their plagals in the traditional system of ecclesiastical modes. Virtually all these provided equivalents for major and minor. Giuseppe Zarlino recognized the difference in effect of major and minor harmonies. He also gave ten rules for underlying words to polyphonic music. Among other important Renaissance theorists were Francisco de Salinas, Domenico Pietro Cerone and Adrianus Petit Coclico.

Music Printing. The first important printer of music other than plainsong was Ottaviano dei Petrucci of Venice. His sacred publications include some 15 collections of Masses and about 15 of motets and other sacred works, such as lamentations and *laude*.

Franco-Netherlandish Composers (c. 1490–c. 1560). In the period of Josquin DESPREZ practically every basic feature of Renaissance music that did not already exist made its appearance. A fusion of the art impulses of Italian and Franco-Netherlandish music was in process and produced the underlying musical style of the late Renaissance. The characteristic qualities of the new music were molded by a large group of singularly gifted composers, all vigorously active at about the same time. Of these, Jacob Obrecht, Alexander Agricola, Heinrich Isaak, Loyset Compère, Josquin Desprez, Antoine Brumel, Pierre de La Rue, Antoine de Févin, Jean Mouton and Carpentras were outstanding. One of the prominent features of Obrecht's Masses is his breaking of a *cantus firmus* into segments and employing each one repeatedly, reserving a complete consecutive presentation for the tenor or some other voice toward the end. Isaak's monumental *Choralis Constantinus* (*Constantiensis*) is the first comprehensive polyphonic setting of Propers of the Mass spanning the whole Church year. It includes the Propers for all Sundays and for certain feast and saints' days. Of interest among the works of Compère are two ''substitution'' Masses. Such works consist of a series of motets, each intended to replace a liturgical Mass movement. Josquin Desprez was the foremost composer of the early Renaissance, serving also as a transition to the late Renaissance. Although he is at his very best as a motet composer, where he is not restricted to one text, Desprez is still a central figure in the field of the Mass. His works in this form collectively illustrate all the basic Mass techniques of the entire Renaissance. Here, as elsewhere, his technical virtuosity is such that contrapuntal complexity in no way interferes with apparent spontaneity.

Post-Josquin Period. After Josquin's death, his style was further developed and disseminated throughout Europe by Netherlandish composers. The Franco-Netherlandish style took root on foreign soil, producing masters such as Palestrina in Italy, Victoria in Spain, Senfl in Germany and Byrd in England. A general trend toward simplicity in French writing is evident in the post-Josquin period. A distinct tradition that developed in the French Mass showed a tendency toward chordal writing and a resulting clarity of text. "Word painting"—an attempt to depict actual words through musical devices—gained in popularity. All these trends were evident in the works of a group now known as the "Paris school," of which Claude de Sermisy and Pierre Certon, both of the Sainte-Chapelle, and Clément Jannequin were the leading representatives. The three most important composers of sacred polyphony in the period between Josquin and Lasso were Nicolas Gombert, Clemens non Papa and Adrian Willaert. In the sacred music of Gombert, pervading imitation is a pronounced trait. Clemens, a prolific writer of motets, composed three-part settings for the *Souterliedekens,* or "Little Psalter Songs," an extremely popular collection of monophonic settings of the 150 Psalms in Dutch rhymed verse, originally intended for Catholic use outside the church. Willaert spent his last 35 years at St. Mark's in Venice. His main contributions to sacred polyphony in Italy were: (1) the establishment of Franco-Netherlandish technique in church music; (2) the development of choral antiphony; and (3) the cultivation of a "modern" style emphasizing faultless declamation of the text. Other important composers of sacred music in Italy during this period were Costanzo Festa (who spent nearly 30 years in the papal service), Jakob Arcadelt, Nicolò Vicentino, Philippe Verdelot, Jachet Berchem, Jacques Buus and Cipriano de RORE. Claude Goudimel, who remained for the most part in France, composed works for Catholic use prior to his becoming a Huguenot *c.* 1460.

Council of Trent and Church Music. In 1562 a canon was approved at the Council of Trent that banned from church music all seductive or impure melodies, all vain and worldly texts, all outcries and uproars, and decreed that the words be clearly understandable. A minority attempt to restrict the Mass to monophonic setting was rebuffed. Tendencies, already present, toward carefully observing Latin accentuation and curtailing melismas purely on artistic and humanistic grounds, were confirmed by the Commission of Cardinals, which sat following the Council. In response to a need for shorter and simpler polyphonic Masses, the *Missa brevis,* which happened to conform to the requirements of the Commission, became common. The prestige of plainsong temporarily declined, partly owing to a change in musical ideals to which Gregorian chant no longer conformed.

Late Renaissance Music in Italy (c. 1560–c. 1600). Probably one of the influences persuading the Council to retain polyphony in the Church was the frequent performance at its early sessions of the *Preces speciales* of Jacobus de Kerle. Kerle, Palestrina, Animuccia, Lasso and Rosselli contributed to the investigation by composing contrapuntal Masses. Among the works of Giovanni Animuccia are two collections of *laude spirituali. Laude* were canticles of praise to be sung in the evening before the image of the Virgin, a practice dating from the 13th century. The sacred works of Palestrina have long been regarded as embodying the ideal application of polyphony to music for the Catholic Church. They represent the last stage in the development of a style that systematized the handling of dissonance and the use of certain time values in particular rhythmic contexts. Palestrina's predilection for symmetrical structure and quiet harmonies is reminiscent of the Josquin style. Although Palestrina's 105 surviving Masses are, as a group, his greatest contribution, his numerous motets and related works include some of his finest compositions. Among other composers of sacred music active at Rome were the madrigalist Luca Marenzio, Giovanni Maria Nanino, Felice Anerio and Annibale Zoilo.

Other Italian centers made noteworthy contributions. At Modena, Orazio Vecchi wrote sacred works much affected by secular traits. Mantua fostered Giaches de Wert and Giovanni Gastoldi. At Milan, Vincenzo Ruffo, encouraged by Cardinal Borromeo, wrote much in a preponderantly choral style with the specific purpose of meeting the wishes of the Council of Trent, while Orfeo Vecchi, foreshadowing the 17th century, provided his Masses with *basso continuo.* Among other important composers were Marco Antonio Ingegneri at Cremona, Carlo Gesualdo (Prince of Venosa) at Naples and Giovanni Matteo Asola and Costanzo Porta in cities near Venice. The Venetian composers, as a group, dedicated their best efforts to the motet rather than to the Mass. Andrea Gabrieli and his nephew, Giovanni, both organists at St. Mark's, wrote distinguished polychoral motets.

Renaissance in Spain and Portugal. Spanish music in the 15th century was strongly influenced by that of France, and, increasingly, of Italy. The two greatest Spanish composers of sacred music in the late Renaissance were Cristóbal de Morales and Tomás Luis de Victoria. Although Morales based his work on Franco-Netherlandish models, he achieved an individual style marked at the same time by starkness and richness. Victoria belongs stylistically with the Roman school, though his writing tended more toward abrupt and vigorous lines and leaps uncharacteristic of the Palestrina style. Other composers of sacred music in 15th- and 16th-century Spain were Johannes Cornago, Johannes Urredo (actually

Wreede, a Fleming), Juan del Encina, Diego Ortiz, Francisco Querrero and Juan Pablo Pujol.

In Middle Europe. German sacred music with Latin text shows, on the whole, extreme conservatism in the 15th century, while leaning heavily on Franco-Netherlandish precept. Three features characterize the sacred polyphony to about 1500: (1) a tendency to fall into closed, uneven periods, as opposed to the smooth, unceasing flow of Franco-Netherlandish music; (2) continuous activity of all four voices, as opposed to the Western preference for varying the texture by means of passages for two or three voices; and (3) awkwardness in the treatment of rhythm. The most important sacred composer in the early period was Heinrich Finck, who quite transcended the general run. German sacred composition of the 16th century continued to be strongly influenced by Franco-Netherlandish models, and later also by Italian. The leading native Germanic composers of the century were Ludwig Senfl and Hans Leo Hassler. More important and influential, however, was a Walloon at the court of Albert V of Bavaria, Orlando di Lasso. His motets for four or more voices display much chordal writing mingled with the polyphony (the breakdown of pervading imitation being well under way); a feeling for harmonic propriety, made evident by the many chord roots that progress by leaps of fourths and fifths; and the inclusion of the third or fifth of a chord much oftener than in Palestrina. Lasso, unlike Senfl, employed Gregorian chant in very few of his Masses, the great majority of them being parodies of works by himself and other composers. Among the Netherlanders active at the Hapsburg court were Kerle, Jacob Vaet, Philippe de Monte, Jacques Buus, Jacques Regnart and Carl Luython. The Slovene Jacob Händl (Jacobus Gallus), also in Hapsburg employ, was active principally in Bohemia. His *Opus musicum* is a collection of motets for the whole liturgical year. The German Thomas Stoltzer was active mainly in Hungary. By far the most brilliant native musical development in the East was that of the Poles, among whom Waclav of Szamotuł, Nicholas Gomółka and Nicholas Zieleński are outstanding.

Music in England. England was one of the leading musical nations about 1450. After mid-century, however, the English tended increasingly toward an insular conservatism, culminating in the works of William Cornysh, Robert Fayrfax and others. Fayrfax, relying heavily on pure counterpoint, made much less use of imitation than Josquin. The greatest English composer in the early 16th century was John Taverner. The polyphonic lines in his Masses show greater freedom and complexity than those of his contemporaries, yet many of the same technical features are evident—frequent changes in vocal registration, repetition of melodic fragments by varying voice

groups, and instances of *fermata*-marked block chords. Important composers of the period after the formal break between England and the papacy in 1534 were Christopher Tye, Robert White, John Shepard and Thomas Tallis. All wrote works with both Latin as well as English texts, and it is not always possible to tell whether a piece of Tudor church music with Latin text was intended for the Roman Catholic Mass or the Anglican Communion Service, in its earlier stages. The finest Elizabethan composer of Latin Church music was William Byrd. His *Gradualia* is the last of the great Renaissance Proper cycles, the others being those of Isaak and Händl. Among other Elizabethan composers of Latin sacred polyphony were Alfonso Ferrabosco I, Thomas Morley, John Wilbye, Richard Deering and Peter Philips.

Bibliography: G. REESE, *Music in the Renaissance* (rev. ed. New York 1959). *New Oxford History of Music,* ed. J. A. WESTRUP, 11 v. (New York 1957–) v.3. K. G. FELLERER, *The History of Catholic church Music,* tr. F. A. BRUNNER (Baltimore 1961).

[E. THURSTON/G. REESE/EDS.]

PART 5: THE BAROQUE PERIOD

All the music of the baroque period is dominated by opera, which began with the early *favole in musica* of J. Peri (1561–1633), G. Caccini (*c.* 1546–1618) and especially MONTEVERDI (1567–1643) and which, with the opening of the first public opera house in Venice in 1637, became the first music to appeal to large audiences and hence to be influenced by popular taste. Nothing in baroque music, from Monteverdi to J. S. BACH, can be understood without knowing something of the overwhelming popularity of opera and the way in which all other music reflected its influence to a greater or less degree. Baroque style, in the words of W. Apel,

is characterized chiefly by the thorough-bass technique, leading to a texture of two principal contours, melody and bass, with the intervening space filled in by improvised harmony [on a keyboard instrument—organ or harpsichord, the so-called 'continuo']. In Germany, however, the contrasting style of true polyphony not only persisted but reached, in Bach, its very acme of perfection and greatness. A third principle of Baroque [music] style is the *stile concertante,* that is, contrasting effects, a principle which expressed itself in the abrupt changes of the early canzona as well as in the solo-tutti alternation of the concerto grosso and in the echo-effects of vocal and of organ music. Other basic conceptions of Baroque music are improvisation and ornamentation. Lastly, mention must be made of the final establishment of tonic and dominant as the principal chords of harmony . . . . [W. Apel, *Harvard Dictionary of Music,* 1950, 77]

In Italy. Composers of liturgical music in the first decades of the 17th century followed two methods of composition: the *stile antico,* which preserved features of the 16th-century style of choral writing and the *stile moderno.* All the leading composers of the 17th and 18th centuries, from Monteverdi to Antonio Lotti, wrote works in *stile antico.* The *stile moderno* first appeared in G. GABRIELI's polychoral motets for St. Mark's, Venice, which blend and contrast solo, choral and instrumental groups—large-scale motets containing many striking effects of chromatic harmony and instrumental color. A representative collection of liturgical music published by Monteverdi in 1610 includes a Mass in *stile antico* with organ continuo, Vespers of the Blessed Virgin (responsory, five psalms, hymn, and two settings of the Magnificat) and other pieces designed, according to the title page, "for princely halls and chapels." The Vesper items are much influenced by Gabrieli. In the psalms the musical treatment is changed for each verse, the verses being frequently separated by *ritornelli.* Generally the psalm tones are retained as canti firmi, accompanied by vocal and instrumental counterpoints; but they are also set in falso bordone, i.e., reiterated chords under the melody in the rhythm of the words. In the other pieces of the collection the new style of writing for solo voices is evident; virtuoso ornamental passages underlie the meaning and mood of the texts. The *Sonata sopra Sancta Maria* shows the growing importance of instrumental music for church use. Although it is not a liturgical work, the 11-fold repetition of a plainsong by a solo soprano gives it a quasi-liturgical air almost completely belied by the independent music for two violins, viola, cornetti, trombones and organ.

Monteverdi's contemporaries and successors generally abandoned the use of the plainsong *cantus firmus.* They preferred two *concertato* styles: the one using only solo voices with or without instruments, which came to resemble the secular cantata in its forms and its use of instrumental *ritornelli;* and the "grand" *concertato,* employing one or more choirs and groups of instruments, mainly intended for the new baroque churches. André Maugars (*c.* 1600–40), a French viol player visiting Rome in 1624, has left descriptions of performances of such works with as many as eight lofts erected around the nave, each containing its own instrumental or vocal group, and all directed by the composer from the middle of the church. Despite their apparent complexity, these compositions were held together by a very simple, even banal, harmonic structure. The most extravagant work of this sort was the 53-part Mass of Orazio Benevoli (1605–72) for the consecration of Salzburg cathedral, requiring two eight-part choirs, two string ensembles, two of wind instruments, and two of brass.

By the end of the 17th century the operatic styles reigned supreme. The rise of Neopolitan opera saw the introduction of solo arias in the motet, which by this time could mean any piece of music set to a Latin text (other than those of the Mass Ordinary) and often denoted forms that were in fact cantata's of several movements. In the hands of Leo (1694–1744), Durante (1684–1755), Feo (1685–1745) and other 18th-century composers, the Mass was expanded into a huge cantata in which independent choruses and arias were combined with instrumental movements. An overture frequently served as an introduction. The liturgical consequences were disastrous. As J. A. Jungmann describes it:

> The liturgy was not only submerged under this ever-growing art but actually suppressed, so that . . . there were festive occasions which might best be described as 'church concerts with liturgical accompaniment'. . . . Texts which could be chosen at random—as was permitted after the elevation—were transferred to other places in the Mass. On the other side, the celebrant often tried to continue with the offertory even while the choir was still singing the *Credo,* or to restrict the singing of the preface and *Pater noster* to the initial words so as to leave the rest for the music and the organ. [The Mass of the Roman Rite (New York 1951) 1:149]

The church music of the Austrian and south German composers of the baroque was deeply influenced by that of the Italians, many of whom visited or resided for long periods in the chief cities. The works of the Germans, however, and particularly those of J. J. FUX, show a more strongly contrapuntal approach.

In France. The development of church music in France was much influenced by the requirements of the court, the artistic and cultural center of the nation. Louis XIV preferred to attend a low Mass, which did not allow time for elaborate settings of the Ordinary. Yet, since music was considered an essential part of a ritual performed in the King's presense, a compromise was made in the so-called *Messe basse solonnelle:* the performance of motets for voices and instruments during certain parts of the service. The influence of the Italian *concertato* may be seen in the motets of Henri Dumont (1610–84), director of the Chapelle Royale from 1663. From the mid-17th century, Italian styles and forms dominate French music. Marc Antoine CHARPENTIER (1634–1704), a pupil of CARISSIMI and director of the Dauphin's chapel, wrote Masses, motets and *Leçons des Ténèbres* for soloists, chorus and instruments. The Tenebrae settings are a remarkable example of musical interference with the liturgy: texts intended to be chanted by a lector are set as cantatas and drawn out to ten times their length by constant verbal repetition. Jean Baptiste LULLY (1632–87) brought to the motet the pomp and brilliance of the French form of opera, of which he was virtually the sole creator: the *tragédie-lyrique*. His *Miserere* and *Te Deum* are scored for full operatic band including trumpets and drums. Operatic overture, double choirs, solo aria and recitative are blended with instrumental interludes to produce some of the most elaborately brilliant church music ever written. Michel de Lalande (1657–1726) extended the style of Lully's motets to the Mass Ordinary, of which he wrote 12 settings. Despite an almost Handelian grandeur, his music has a seriousness and a perception of the religious meaning of his texts and their relevance to the liturgy that Lully's works lack. François COUPERIN (1668–1733) wrote in the highly ornamental style called rococo (or *stile galante*); his chief works for liturgy are psalms (treated as cantatas, each verse having a separate movement) and *Leçons des Ténèbres*.

Protestant Music. The music for all Protestant churches in this period contrasts sharply with that composed for the Catholic liturgy in that it includes vernacular music for the congregation as an essential part of liturgical worship.

Lutheran Germany. The development of German Lutheran choral music was profoundly influenced by the congregational hymn, or *chorale* (as it came to be called when used in choral compositions). Michael PRAETORIUS (1571–1621) published nine volumes entitled *Musae Sioniae* containing 1,200 of his compositions based on *chorales*, using *concertato* styles, contrapuntal forms and simpler treatments such as duets and solo arias. Johann Schein (1586–1630) and Samuel Scheidt (1587–1654) continued the *concertato* treatment, emphasizing the textual meaning by melodic and harmonic features. The greatest figure before Bach, Heinrich SCHÜTZ (1585–1672), seldom used *chorale* melodies (though he made a book of harmonizations for a metrical PSALTER), preferring, by reason of his Italian training under Gabrieli, a dramatic approach that, while indebted to both Gabrieli and Monteverdi, was profoundly personal and deeply felt. The works in *Sacrae Symphoniae*, published in three volumes (1628, 1647 and 1650), utilize all the techniques of the early Italian baroque, ranging from solo settings of Psalms to mighty polychoral motets.

The Lutheran Church had continued the older method of reciting the Passion narrative to a special chant while punctuating it by polyphonic settings of the "crowd" portions of the text. Later composers developed this into the "oratorio-Passion" by introducing orchestral and organ accompaniments and inserting sections with nonliturgical texts. Stages in this development are represented by the *St. John Passion* (1643) of Thomas Selle (1599–1663); *St. Matthew Passion* (1667)

of Christian Flor (1626–97); and *St. Matthew Passion* (1673) of Johann Theile (1646–1724). Schütz's Passions stand apart: they have no instrumental accompaniment, and, apart from the opening and concluding movements, the chorus sings only "crowd" passages, the rest being sung to a quasi-Gregorian type of recitative.

By the end of the 17th century Italian opera was a strong influence on German church music. The blending of the various choral forms based on *chorale* tunes had produced a large composite type of composition that later came to be called cantata. A Hamburg pastor, Erdmann Neumeister (1671–1756), published texts for what he called "reformed" cantatas. Regarding the cantata as a "fragment of an opera," he discarded all Biblical passages and hymn texts in favor of poetical paraphrases that could be set as recitatives and *da capo* arias. His texts roused much opposition, and many composers mingled them with texts and musical forms from the older style; the cantatas of J. S. BACH are the greatest representatives of this. The Passion story was also given "operatic" treatment and poetical paraphrased texts; such works, however, were no longer liturgical but concert hall music. Bach's Passions represent a compromise between the earlier and the new forms; he retained the complete Biblical text but added *chorales*, choruses, and arias that had non-Biblical texts.

Anglican Music. English composers were slow to incorporate the new vocal styles of the Continent. Up to the civil war, despite some experiments in music for the Chapel Royal by William Child (1606–97) and Monteverdi's pupil Walker Porter (1595–1659), the older polyphonic style continued in the "full" and "verse" forms of the anthem and service. At the Restoration (1660) Charles II imported music "in the French style," with instrumental sections for violins, and had Pelham Humfrey (1647–74), John Blow (1649–1708) and Henry PURCELL (1659–95) trained in up-to-date European techniques. The church music of these men and particularly of Purcell is equal to anything of its period on the Continent in technical expertise, while preserving a peculiarly English type of melody and harmony. After Purcell and with the appearance of Italian opera in London, Anglican church music speedily copied Italian models. HANDEL's Chandos Anthems, while revealing acquaintance with Purcell's work, are wholly Italianate in style and form.

Bibliography: M. F. BUKOFZER, *Music in the Baroque Era* (New York 1947). S. CLERCX, *Le Baroque et la musique* (Brussels 1948). R. HAAS, *Die Musik des Barocks* (*Handbuch der Musikwissenschaft* 3; New York 1928). A. HARMAN et al., *Man and His Music* (New York 1962). P. H. LÁNG, *Music in Western Civilization* (New York 1941). W. APEL, *Harvard Dictionary of Music* (Cambridge, Mass. 1958).

[A. MILNER/EDS.]

PART 6: THE CLASSICAL STYLE

Characteristics peculiar to the classical period emerged around 1750, reached a high point of artistic expression in the works of Haydn and Mozart, and evolved into Romanticism in the works of Beethoven and Schubert.

New Style Sources. Sources of the style were the experiments of the Mannheim composers with new orchestral devices, the interest of the Viennese composers in formal structures, and the melodic and harmonic freedoms of the Italian composers of opera and cantata. The Church composer assimilated all of these styles—often more instrumental and theatrical than religious—and applied them to liturgical texts. The style is basically dramatic, and is founded on a balanced formal structure that permits the tensions inherent in musical contrasts, both tonal and melodic, to evolve in a logical but emotionally moving way. Historically, the style is cast against the intellectual background of the ENLIGHTENMENT: it combines the rational temperament of that movement with its JOSEPHINISM, and reflects both its strained Church-State relationships and its attempts at reform.

The Mannheim School. Musical activity reached tremendous heights throughout Europe. Composition, performance, and circulation of new music in general showed clearly the intense musical life Europe was experiencing at this time. The rise of the Mannheim School in the mid-18th century brought a new orchestral style and performance into music that would be as important as the Viennese interest in sonata form in building the Viennese classical style. Two leading composers of religious music in the Mannheim circle who attempted a combination of formal aspects and high expressiveness were Franz X. RICHTER and George Vogler. The period around 1750 and shortly thereafter provides a transitional stage in Church music from the baroque contrapuntal style with thorough-bass accompaniment to a more expressive vocal and instrumental style that also emerged with national elements. The orchestral concept dominated the Masses, Vespers, litanies, Offertories and psalms written in the new style.

Southern Influences. The influence of Italian opera and cantata conventions moved north during the middle part of the 18th century. The Neapolitan use of simple harmonies with highly ornamented melodic lines rendered the liturgical texts dramatic and full of pathos. Niccolò JOMMELLI, Baldassare GALUPPI, Domenico CIMAROSA and Giovanni PAISIELLO wrote in this style. By building on the foundations of the cantata form and its sectional structure, these Italian composers lost sight of the unity of liturgical texts and imposed on them the concerto principle. Vivid orchestrations, the aria and *bel canto*—all characteristic of the Neapolitan stage—found their way into liturgical music since the same composers who wrote for the theater wrote for the church. It was a simple process to combine this trend with *Empfindsamkeit* (highly expressive technique) of Germany to achieve a new style, neither baroque nor yet fully classical. Typical of the merging of the operatic with the instrumental idioms are the works of Johann Adolph HASSE, a German composer who, like many others, lived and studied in Italy. He wrote his 100 operas in the same style as his many oratorios and Masses. But not all composers favored the new style. Many still wrote in the strict contrapuntal style of "stile antico." For example, Johann ALBRECHTSBERGER and Georg Pasterwitz and others continued to write in the polyphonic idiom of previous generations. Their works show but slightly the influence of the new melodic concept.

The Viennese Classics. A reconciliation of the Italian operatic tendencies with Northern instrumental writing matured in the Viennese composers. Here, the element of balance in a logical form combined with expressionism in melody reached its peak. After 1770 religious music also was affected by these elements. For example, to give balance and unification, parts of the Mass received cyclic treatment, i.e., the music of the first Kyrie would be repeated for the third Kyrie and again for the *Dona nobis pacem* of the Agnus Dei. This created an A-B-A form in the Kyrie and made that Mass a rounded form. The first and final sections of the Gloria and the Credo were treated in similar fashion. Sonata and rondo forms were worked into the larger sections with a fugue acting as a coda. The cantata elements remained, however, and arias were standard fare for the *Et incarnates est,* and the Benedictus; the orchestral accompaniment knits the work into a homogeneous whole. All joined to form in the classical period a definite ecclesiastical style that was both religiously inspired and musically satisfying. These composers were writing church music in their own contemporary style and were using their talent and craft to produce artifacts that were consistent with the philosophy that surrounds the celebration of the liturgy during the Classical period. For this reason they were musically superior to the uninspired, academic compositions of those composers adhering to the old polyphonic style.

Mozart and Haydn. With the emphasis given to symphonic writing, it is not surprising that Classical sacred music found its zenith in Wolfgang Amadeus MOZART and Franz Joseph HAYDN. In early works they were careful to express the general meaning of the text, repeating syllables, words and sections of the text when musical reasons demanded. Haydn experimented with techniques of form and even tapped the store of folk song. In the case of Mozart, one can discern a marked change in his style after he left Salzburg. His first compositions reflected the examples of Johann Eberlin and a stronger influence from chamber music and the Neapolitan style. The Masses he wrote from 1758 to 1782 show a unique ability to blend elements of German classicism and form with Italian lyricism. The unfinished C-Minor Mass (K.427) illustrates the new church style: it is a successful assimilation of the forementioned principles. His great *Requiem* is considered to be the epitome of his church style, if not of all Viennese sacred music. The vocal idiomatic writing that Mozart gave to his religious music can be compared with the symphonic and orchestral principles that Haydn contributed. The vocal solo did not interest Haydn as much as did the vocal quartet. Using remnants of the concerto-grosso form, he contrasted the quartet against the tutti of the full choir. In his earlier works, he had used polyphony infrequently, with the exception of specific choral fugues. After a 14-year lapse, Haydn returned to writing sacred music, using a polyphony integrated into the expanded use of the orchestra. His six monumental Masses written between 1796 and 1802 make extensive use of sonata principles, canon and fugue—all with a full participation of the orchestra. Unlike Mozart, Haydn wrote two oratorios. After his visit in England, he returned to write his *Creation,* a work that reflects the exuberance of Nature, an idea characteristic of the Enlightenment. Although the naïve representation of natural phenomena was criticized, the oratorio was tremendously successful as a combination of symphonic and choral elements. Because of its success, Haydn composed his second, *The Seasons,* that was equally well received. In these last works of Mozart and Haydn the pinnacle of classical sacred music was reached: the emergence of a style that united the polyphonic choir and the symphony orchestra is significant. If operatic traces can be detected, it is only because these elements were necessary parts of the composer's vocabulary.

Beethoven and Schubert. The Viennese classical style was carried on by Ludwig von BEETHOVEN and Franz SCHUBERT. Beethoven's C-Major Mass (1803) is so reminiscent of the Viennese style that it could be called a companion Mass to Haydn's works. It has all the fresh, heroic ideals of Beethoven's early creative period. Even in his *Missa Solemnis* one can see the influence of Haydn's symphonic cohesion. The large individual parts of this Mass are conceived with oratorio principles of grandeur. Schubert, too, participated in this direct stylistic line with the Viennese church style. His early Masses exhibit the sectional treatment of the text, but show the lyrical quality peculiar to all of his works. In his last two Masses (A flat and E flat), the music tends to be Romantic because of the harmonic color and moving lyricism characteristic of Schubert's writing. Classical elements, however, can be seen in the balance and reserve inherent in the structural make-up of the works.

The Influence of Josephinism. The high classical Viennese church style was not without its opponents. The conservatives who favored the "stile antico" have already been mentioned. The restoration of liturgical propriety took place under the decrees of Joseph II of Austria (*see* JOSEPHINISM). As a child of the Enlightenment's philosophy, he wanted to simplify the celebration of the liturgy in Austrian churches. Because of the large number of churches in Vienna, schedules were devised to regulate the hours of worship to avoid duplications. Vespers and Compline were curtailed considerably in diocesan churches together with many popular pious exercises. To establish a vernacular hymnody during the celebration of liturgical functions, a German hymnal was prepared by Johann Kohlbrenner in 1777; it was promulgated in all of Austria by 1783. The German sung mass (*Singmesse*) can trace its origins to this decree. While instrumental church music was not totally restricted, the use of concerted music was regulated. The symphonic Mass was too well rooted to be easily discouraged and dispensations were occasionally granted for its performance. Archbishop Collarcdo (*see* MOZART) suppressed instrumental music in his see, but later (1787) permitted its performance on special feasts. It was under his direction that Michael HAYDN reinstituted the sung Gradual (1782). Haydn composed many Graduals in a simpler chordal style with instrumental accompaniment that replaced the "Epistle sonatas." The whole trend of Josephinism reform of church music was the simplification of the liturgy to encourage better communal worship. It did not deter, however, countless second-rate composers from imitating the Masses of Haydn and Mozart well into the middle of the 19th century.

Bibliography: D. J. GROUT, *A History of Western Music* (New York 1960). K. G. FELLERER, *The History of Catholic church Music,* tr. F. A. BRUNNER (Baltimore 1961). P. H. LÁNG, *Music in Western Civilization* (New York 1941). R. G. PAULY, "The Reforms of Church Music under Joseph II," *Musical Quarterly,* 43 (1957) 372–382; *Music in the Classic Period* (Englewood Cliffs, N.J. 1965). O. URSPRUNG, *Die katholische Kirchenmusik* (Potsdam 1931).

[F. J. MOLECK/EDS.]

PART 7: ROMANTICISM AND ITS AFTERMATH

The revival of religious interest that took place during the opening years of the 19th century is mirrored in the music of the period. The most important romanticist trend was the use of all musical devices to project a subjective attitude toward religion in sacred music. Especially among French and Italian composers opera was the most popular means of musical expression, and the line between what was appropriate for the stage and what for the choir loft was not sharply drawn. The new harmonic resources developed by C. P. E. Bach and Mozart, most clearly evident in Mozart's *Ave Verum Corpus* and *Requiem,* widened the range of emotional expression but also led to secular and sentimental styles. The romanticist interest in exoticism found religion an "effect," as is shown by inclusion of church scenes on the operatic stage or the use of the *Dies Irae* in secular instrumental compositions by Berlioz, Liszt and Rachmaninoff. Although "national styles" in church music were discernible, nationalism as such played a minor role in Catholic church music during this century.

Concerted Mass. The aesthetic of symphonic church music, dominant in the later 18th century, remained in force during most of the 19th. In the typical concerted Mass of these periods, liturgical considerations were subordinated to musical exigencies: the chorus sang to orchestral accompaniment; passages of text were excised, troped, or repeated for subjective emphasis or to round out musical forms; and sections were allocated to soloists whose parts sounded like operatic arias or ensembles. The degree of romanticist content in concerted church music varied from composer to composer. Latent in Mozart's later works, it was developed by Cherubini, Lesueur and Hummel, continued in the music of Schubert and Weber, and reached its peak in the works of Thomas, Gounod and Rossini. Later composers such as Liszt, Franck and especially Bruckner, Dvořák and Fauré, treated the musical devices of the time with more restraint and better taste.

Concerted Masses are objectionable on liturgical grounds because of text repetition, settings of the priest's intonations, virtuoso demands on the musicians, orchestral accompaniment and length—all of which distract the congregation from the action of the Mass; yet the works in this genre by Schubert, Bruckner, Dvořák and Fauré are an integral part of the musical treasure of Catholic-inspired music and are eminently suitable for concert performance. The merits of concerted Masses should be judged by comparison with the Masses of Maillart and Farmer, early editions of *St. Basil Hymnal,* and the *Tantum Ergo* derived from the Sextet in Donizetti's *Lucia di Lammermoor.* The *Missa Solemnis* of BEETHOVEN and the rediscovery of J. S. Bach's *B-minor Mass* inspired the composition of large concerted Masses and similar works for the concert hall rather than for the church. The Requiems of Cherubini, Berlioz, Schumann, Verdi and Dvořák, despite their liturgical texts, should be classed as oratorios.

Oratorio. The rise of choral societies and music festivals during the 19th century provided a steady demand for new oratorios. The founders of the romantic Protestant oratorio were Spohr and Mendelssohn. The sentimental chromaticism of Spohr and the "Victorian" complacency of Mendelssohn's religious music permeates most of these later works. Brahms, with his roots in the older German contrapuntal tradition, created in his *German Requiem* the best Protestant successor to the great works of Schütz, J. S. Bach and Handel. Oratorio was less popular in Catholic countries. Deserving of study are the oratorios of Lesueur, which anticipate those of Dubois, Saint-Saëns, and Massenet. Fauré's *Requiem* is a virtual transfiguration of these intimate oratorios. Gounod's *Rédemption* and *Mors et Vita* (written for England) and Franck's *Les Béatitudes* are the leading large-scale French oratorios. The greatest Catholic oratorios of the period are those by Elgar. Also of interest are "religious" operas such as Saint-Saëns' *Samson et Dalila,* Massenet's *Le Jongleur de Notre Dame,* and d'Indy's monumental *La Légende de Saint Christophe.*

Organ. The rediscovery of J. S. Bach's organ works served to rescue organ music from the virtual desuetude into which it had lapsed during the classical period. Protestant organ music is best represented by the sonatas of Mendelssohn, the late chorale preludes of Brahms and the works of Reger and Karg-Elert. Liszt's organ works are significant among those by Catholic composers. During the latter part of the 19th century, France was the center of organ playing. Though Franck's works stand at the peak, many excellent organ compositions were written by Guilmant, Widor and Vierne. Subsidiary centers of organ composition and performance were in Brussels (Lemmens), Munich (Rheinberger) and Rome (Bossi).

Other Forms. Concerted Masses were generally restricted to court and cathedral churches with professional singers and musicians. In smaller parishes the principal music consisted of the simple *Landmessen* and Masses in the style of Michael Haydn and Hummel of the Viennese classical school. Though Catholic hymns continued to be written during the 19th century, little of enduring value was created. Most of them contain sentimental chromatic harmonies, are operatic in style, or resemble salon romances (e.g., Lambillotte's hymns with piano-style accompaniments); and for these reasons they are proscribed in many U.S. dioceses.

Protestant church music assumed a variety of forms. Spohr and Mendelssohn were the models for the "Victorian" Anglican church music of Goss, Barnby and Stainer. Excellent hymns, especially of the processional type, were written in England. In popular Protestant hymnody the rugged "Sacred Harp" and the sentimental or martial GOSPEL SONGS were peculiarly American contributions (*see* HYMNS AND HYMNALS). A major revival of sacred music occurred in Russia. About 1830 Bortniansky's Italianate anthems began to be supplanted by the Germanic tonal chant harmonizations of Lvov and Bakhmetieff. The influence of Glinka and ''The Five'' (Balakirev, Borodin, Cui, Moussorgsky and Rimsky-Korsakov), especially in their scoring of folk songs, led to modal harmonizations of the traditional chants and of compositions in modal style by Kastalsky, Rachmaninoff, Ippolitov-Ivanov, Grechaninov, and others.

Reform of Catholic Music. Notable attempts were made during the century to reform Catholic church music, chiefly by reintroducing Renaissance sacred polyphony, which had been rediscovered through such sources as Baini's biography of Palestrina; the studies of Renaissance polyphony by Thibaut, Kiesewetter, and Winterfeld; the collections of 16th-century vocal music by Choron, Commer, Proske, Maldeghem and others; and the composition of new music in this restrained contrapuntal style (*see* CAECILIAN MOVEMENT). Munich (Aiblinger, Ett. Rheinberger) and Regensburg (Proske and Haberl) were the focal points of reform, and the Caecilian Society, founded by F. X. Witt in 1868, was the most influential reform group; but parallel movements were found in every land, and the reform ideal was formally approved by Pius IX in 1870. The most enduring monument of 19th-century Catholic musical scholarship was the restoration of Gregorian chant, largely through the labors of the Benedictine monks of SOLESMES under the leadership of Dom Guéranger. The chief legacies of Solesmes are the *Paléographie musicale* (1889–), a collection of facsimiles of early manuscripts; a theory of chant rhythm; and the Vatican edition of the chant (*see* CHANT BOOKS, PRINTED EDITIONS OF).

Musicology. Neither the Caecilian reforms nor the Solesmes studies would have been possible without the emerging discipline of historical musicology. Musicology's task was not to illustrate how music had ''progressed,'' but to investigate the music of the past on its own merits and to publish collections and scholarly studies of early music. Besides the publications cited above in the fields of Renaissance and Gregorian music, other landmarks of 19th-century research and publishing activity were the incomplete general histories by Ambros and Fétis; Fétis's *Biographie universelle* of musicians; Eitner's *Quellen-Lexikon,* a census of music manuscripts; Coussemaker's anthology of medieval treatises on music; and the prolific writings of Riemann. Nationalism stimulated the publication of *Denkmäler* (monuments of music) in the Germanic lands, and in England, France, Italy and Spain.

Although the 19th-century investigations of Renaissance church music were handicapped by an almost total misunderstanding of 16th-century performance practice, this was outweighed by the creation of a climate of opinion in which music of the past was found worthy in its own right and, because of its lack of association with the 19th-century styles of the concert hall, opera house, or salon, was best suited for divine worship. The labors of the musicologists were crowned by Pope St. Pius X when he declared in his motu proprio of 1903 that the most suitable styles of church music were Gregorian chant and Renaissance polyphony—in that order.

The Church Composer. Relations between the Church and the composer, however, had reached a low point by the beginning of the 20th century, and only in organ music was significant creative work produced. On the one hand, the Church was devoting her resources to more urgent educational, missionary and social endeavors; on the other hand, congregational (and too often, clerical) preference was for melodious Masses and sentimental hymns. Then, too, the individualism implicit in romanticism tended to alienate the composer from the emerging emphasis on the doctrine of the Mystical Body, with its corollary in ''collective,'' participated worship. Composers of stature disdained to write for the limited uses of the parish church, and in their sacred compositions they favored Gregorian chant and Renaissance polyphony, thus reflecting both Caecilian ideals and the romanticist penchant for the archaic, but also rejecting the idiom of the day and the role of style-setter of music to come.

Bibliography: K. G. FELLERER, *The History of Catholic Church Music,* tr. F. A. BRUNNER (Baltimore 1961). A. EINSTEIN, *Music in the Romantic Era* (New York 1947). O. URSPRUNG, *Die katholische Kirchenmusik* (Potsdam 1931). A. OREL, ''Die katholische Kirchenmusik seit 1750,'' *Handbuch der Musikgeschichte,* ed. G. ADLER, 2 v. (2d ed. Tutzing 1930; repr. 1961) 2:833–864. A. SCHERING, *Geschichte des Oratoriums* (Leipzig 1911) 382–624.

[R. M. LONGYEAR/EDS.]

PART 8: POST-ROMANTICISM

Post-Romanticism in music signifies, basically, both an idiom (advanced tonal chromaticism) and a historical period of transition. It bridges 19th- and 20th-century styles and ends, approximately, with the death of Gustav MAHLER in 1911. It is therefore introductory to the history of sacred music in the 20th century, which is a period more properly characterized by the development of new technical resources, including atonality and polytonality, and the application to music of such aesthetic concepts as Impressionism and Expressionism. For liturgical music the motu proprio of St. Pius X, *Inter pastoralis officiae* (Nov. 22, 1903), was the key document. Its influence, while profound, was less complete than had been hoped, and attention to its ideal of ''the restoration of all things in Christ" was seriously retarded by World War I. Nevertheless it must ultimately be assessed in terms of its permissive if reserved attitude toward modern music, its effect on later papal pronouncements, and three general developments accelerated by its impetus: (1) the revival of chant as an ideal for choral and congregational singing, (2) the practical study of chant in seminaries, and (3) the establishment of schools for the professional study of chant as well as of church music in other styles.

The "Traditional School." The musical idioms of Romanticism and Post-Romanticism achieved a valid and permanent popularity that impeded any mass espousal of later styles. That a "traditional school" of Catholic church-composers should gain ascendancy was therefore not surprising; but musicians such as Refice, Perosi and Yon, competent and dedicated though they were, remained apart, both from major figures of the era (SCHOENBERG, BARTÓK, STRAVINSKY) and from such minor but still "mainstream" composers as K. Szymanowski (1882–1937), Charles Ives (1874–1954) or VILLA-LOBOS (1887–1959). Contributing further to the Church's loss of vital contact with contemporary trends were: her global concern with problems other than those of an often esoteric new music, the almost total secularization of 20th-century musical art and changing sociological patterns, particularly that of patronage.

In France the transition from a lingering Romanticism to authentically modern liturgical styles was facilitated by continuing interest in the organ as a church instrument. Conservatives such as VIERNE and WIDOR prepared the way for progressive successors as diverse as the gifted but essentially minor Jean Langlais (1907–) and the more controversial but influential Olivier Messiaen (1908–). The latter's organ cycles have attracted particular attention (e.g., *La Nativité du Seigneur,* 1935). He has produced important orchestral, chamber and didactic works and numbered among his composition pupils such members of the later avant-garde as Pierre Boulez (1925–) and Karlheinz Stockhausen (1928–).

After Debussy. Impressionism offered composers of liturgical music a break with Romanticism free from involvement with expressionism and unmitigated dissonance; clear roots in the modality of chant and the structural principles of Gothic polyphony; and seemingly unlimited possibilities of adaptation to a continuing chant revival. Claude DEBUSSY (1862–1918), as the genius of French Impressionism, evolved a highly distinctive, sensuous, musical language, sometimes with neopagan implications (he was once rebuked by the archbishop of Paris for a production of *Le Martyre de Saint-Sêbastien*). "Les Six," following Debussy, Ravel and Satie, developed sophisticated personal styles that were indebted, in part, to the neoclassic elements in the work of Stravinsky. Three of the "Six" took some account of religious values, as can be seen in such works as Darius Milhaud's setting of texts from Pope John XXIII's encyclical *Pacem in terris* (1963); Arthur Honegger's Le Roi David (1921) and POULENC's Mass in G Major (1938), Gloria (1961) and *Sept Répons des Ténèbres* (1963).

Bibliography: P. COLLAER, *A History of Modern Music,* tr. S. ABELES (Cleveland 1961). J. MACHLIS, *Introduction to Contemporary Music* (New York 1961), contains bibliog. of 161 titles and works in Eng. K. G. FELLERER, *Soziologie der Kirchenmusik* (Cologne 1963). J. SCHELL, *Aesthetische Probleme der Kirchenmusik im Lichte der Enzyklika Pius' xii. Musicae sacrae disciplina* (Berlin 1961). *Musical Quarterly,* 51 (Jan. 1965), a special issue: "Contemporary Music in Europe." J. GÉLINEAU, *Voices and Instruments in Christian Worship,* tr. C. HOWELL (Collegeville, Minn. 1964) 199–203. *Liturgy for the People,* ed. W. J. LEONARD, (Milwaukee 1963).

[F. J. BURKLEY/EDS.]

PART 9: UNITED STATES

The history of liturgical music in the U.S., like that of general music, is a study as variegated as the plurality of cultural and religious backgrounds represented in the nation's early settlers and later immigrants. While American music thus was far from being indigenous in its first manifestations, in its development it has exhibited a continuing (if uneven) surge for freedom from its European motherland together with a growing self-awareness and involvement with native sources of inspiration. Colonial America's first music was music related to denominational worship; today, significantly influenced by current liturgical, theological and ecumenical developments, the music of America's churches continues its process of adaptation.

Music in the Missions. The music of 16th- and 17th-century Europe was brought to America by Spanish and French missioners, chiefly Franciscan, Dominican and Jesuit.

In Spanish Domains. Spanish foundations dating from 1598 in New Mexico achieved a high degree of development in the areas of organ music, choir schools and vocal polyphony that involved "note" singing a century before it was practiced on the Eastern seaboard. Fray Cristóbal de Quiñones (d. April 27, 1609) and numerous other friars were responsible for these initial musical endeavors. One of the first collections of authentic Indian melodies was that of Fray Felipe Arroyo de La Cuesta. Again in the California missions the Franciscan padres introduced the music as well as the language and customs of their native Spain. Plainchant predominated, but some figured Masses and motets, also homophonic in structure and with a high incidence of thirds, sixths, dominant sevenths and occasional diminished chords, were in the mission repertory. The absence of ornamental solo sections and of repetitions of text helps to distinguish this mission music from its later liturgical counterpart in Eastern centers. Part-music was written on a single five- or six-line staff, with a system of colored notation to distinguish voice parts: tiple (soprano), white notes outlined in red; contralto, white notes outlined in black; tenor, solid red notes; bass, black notes.

Mission life in the 18th and early 19th centuries dictated the musical usage, since natives were encouraged to live within the mission compound. The daily musical program was scheduled as follows: *Cantico del Alba* (morning prayer), chanted upon rising; the *Alabanza* (the Commandments, Sacraments and other catechetical material recited or sung in Spanish); the Mass in plainsong or figured Latin settings; the *Alabado* (song of divine praise); the *Bendito* (grace before and after meals); and the *Angelus.* At sundown the mission populace gathered for the *Doctrina* and the *Alabado* in the native Indian tongue, and during the day chosen singers chanted the Divine Office. The whole day was thus permeated with sung prayer, and even after sundown an evening of song and dance was common. Instruments used were the violin, viola, cello, bass, flute, trumpet, horns, guitars, drums and triangle. After congregational singing in the form of simple psalm tones and antiphonal chants was established, a formal choir was trained. The repertory consisted of Propers for Sundays and principal feasts (simplified settings by Padre Narciso Durán), Masses in chant or homophonic settings, and Latin hymns for Benediction and special feasts. Padre Durán encouraged instrumental accompaniment to sustain pitch and wrote in simplified scale patterns using the *F* clef with needed accidentals. Although concrete evidence of the music in the Southwest, Texas and Florida is scarce, it may be assumed that the same pattern was followed wherever the Spanish missioners penetrated. With the collapse of the Spanish missions (1833–34) their music fell into obscurity and therefore failed to influence directly the course of church music in America.

In French Domains. The pattern of mission life prevailing on the West Coast was unknown in northeastern U.S. and Canada. The missioner spent his days in the midst of the Native American nations. Tribes remained tribes, not guests of the mission enclosure. As in Spanish territory, however, one of the chief problems was that of communication—especially of religious truths. Often the basic facts were imparted through hymns—either the setting of Christian texts to native melodies or, as later happened, native dialects to European melodies. Various teaching aids were devised, such as the Quipii, a knotted cord signifying certain doctrinal ideas; the Order of

Songs, pictures suggesting the subject of each hymn stanza; the Notched Stick, arbitrary engraved characters used to direct prayers and hymns; and Syllabaries, which were signs used to indicate sounds, thus obviating the task of teaching the natives a foreign tongue. Extant hymnals (1830–70) use the Native American vernacular with the title of the melody indicated in a European language. Contents include Latin hymns, *cantiques* (common tunes), English hymns and some original tunes. In use today is the Huron carol *Jesous Ahatonia,* probably composed by Jean de Brébeuf, one of the NORTH AMERICAN MARTYRS. One Midwestern missioner, the Italian Samuel MAZZUCHELLI, OP, made such headway with his Wisconsin Winnebagos that they learned to chant Sunday Vespers with alternating verses in Latin and their vernacular. Because of the language barrier, however, none of these apostolic-cultural endeavors had any influence on the course of American church music.

Protestant Beginnings (17th Century). The pilgrims of New England relied upon English hymnals for their worship services. The *Ainsworth Psalter* contained unaccompanied unison settings of metrical psalms—one note to each syllable in binary rhythm (*see* PSALTERS, METRICAL; HYMNS AND HYMNALS). When the Salem and Plymouth communities joined the Massachusetts Bay Colony (1691), the BAY PSALM BOOK gained ascendancy and continued to constitute New England's singing staple for the next century. In the Anglican settlements there was a struggle for popularity between the "Old Version" (*Bay Psalm Book*) and the more poetic New Version of the Psalms of David (1696) of Tate and Brady. Both versions were later replaced by the hymnody of English writers, such as Isaac Watts. Two non-English communities, the Ephrata Cloister, near Lancaster, Pennsylvania, and the Moravians (Unity of Brethren) centered in Winston-Salem, North Carolina, maintained a high level of musical activity in the 18th century. Relying heavily on European material, the Ephrata group developed antiphonal singing to an art, whereas the Moravians performed choral, chamber and symphonic works (not necessarily religious) of European masters. Another center of musical activity was the camp meeting. The revival movement among various denominational dissenters generated the folk hymn, a combination of secular folk tune and religious text, as leaders sought to replace the "placid" Puritan psalm with a heartier type of group singing. Folk hymns in turn were succeeded by the popular GOSPEL SONG, a commercial, individually composed hymn.

Catholic Hymnody (18th Century). Formal publication of hymnals for Catholic use was not initiated until 1787. Credit is due to Benjamin Carr (1768–1831), influential musician, teacher, hymn composer and music publisher, for his pioneer publications. Numerous other hymnals, however, came with immigrating Catholics, and with this influx of hymnals came a threefold western European influence: (1) postbaroque concerto style with its specified elements, i.e., melodic and harmonic reiteration, alternation of solo and chorus sections, and ornamentation of melodic lines (in this way a pseudo-Neapolitan *bel canto* style was implanted in the hymnals); (2) Viennese classical form and presentation of thematic material, whose unskilled and inartistic handling resulted in a monotonous tonic-dominant harmony with "Alberti Bass" accompaniment; thus Viennese orchestral idiom was exploited in the form of numerous orchestrated Masses, but, in an attempt to imitate the masters, most composers simply exaggerated the means; and (3) adulation of the self-styled composer who was the enthusiastic and zealous but all too often untrained hymn tune writer and compiler. Catholic hymnody suffered both musically and textually as a result of one or more of these factors. Moreover, the defensive mood of the post-Tridentine period penetrated liturgical music, and at the same time Catholics were deprived of the heritage of the German chorale. Congregational singing was almost entirely replaced by the solo voice, quartet choirs and lengthy organ solos. Degeneration became complete when hymnals proudly displayed "religious" texts set to popular secular compositions.

Nineteenth-Century Trends. The 19th century felt the surge of political and artistic nationalism. Composers, such as GOTTSCHALK, incorporated "American" elements in their works, e.g., Native American melos, spiritual tunes, rag-time rhythms. Arthur Farwell (1872–1952), recognizing the role of imitation in the early stages of creativity, sought freedom from European domination and answered DVOŘÁK's challenge to explore native folk music with the foundation of the Wa-Wan Press for the advancement of American music. Henry Gilbert (1868–1928) shared Farwell's interest, his deep love for all folk music manifesting itself in a heavy reliance on American Indian lore. Gilbert preferred to "seek his own hat" rather than wear "a borrowed crown." An 18th-century predecessor, William Billings (1746–1800), had championed the same cause with an unusual display of musical creativity and his fuguing tunes became basic source material for later composers, such as William Schuman. Charles Ives (1874–1954), successor to Farwell and Gilbert, realized their ideals. Rejecting conventional musical structure, Ives introduced polytonality, polyrhythms, tone clusters, functional intervals and jazz effects, and his use of native folk music as his germinal musical idea initiated a truly creative trend in American music.

Protestant Churches. Protestant church music reflected a twofold trend during the Victorian period: the use of the dignified hymn and the popularity of gospel songs. Three basic elements in the religious milieu are recognizable: (1) the evangelical movement headed by the Wesleys; (2) the OXFORD MOVEMENT, fostering a return to ancient faith and practice; and (3) the Modernist movement, which sought complete involvement of man in liturgical worship. Hymnody drew heavily on the poetry of Cardinal J. H. NEWMAN, E. Caswall, F. W. FABER and John Mason Neale; initially, however, less attention was focused on the music. The Oxford Movement encouraged the revival of the Latin hymns, folk song carols, plainsong hymns and German chorales, which were adopted according to local American needs. A simultaneous concern for performance led to the utilization of secular part-song techniques as evidenced in the works of the English composers J. B. Dykes, J. Barnby and J. Stainer. The Victorian feeling for antiquity led to extreme sentimentalism, musical and religious. Lowell Mason (1792–1872), well known for his hymns "Nearer My God To Thee," "My Faith Looks Up to Thee" and "From Greenland's Icy Mountains," stands in the forefront of American musicians of this period, by reason of his labors for music education in the public schools, with special emphasis on sound choral training. Other major composers included Thomas Hastings (1784–1872) and W. B. Bradbury (1816–68). The oratorios *St. Peter* (John Knowles Paine, 1839–1906) and *Hora novissima* (Horatio Parker, 1863–1919) represent the peak of religious music of the period. The Parker work, for mixed chorus and orchestra, and based on St. Bernard's poem *Contemptor mundi,* was his first internationally recognized success. Critics paid Parker the highest of 19th-century accolades in comparing it with the works of such composers as Palestrina, J. S. Bach and Josquin Despres, while choral societies in England and America performed the work frequently.

Catholic Church. Catholic music of the 19th century seemed as deeply entrenched in European operatic style as ever. The influx of English and Irish Catholics, lacking valid liturgical traditions, continued the deterioration of Church music. Quartet choirs and orchestral ensembles seemed the ideal at this time. Gregorian chant was scarcely known in the U.S. Mass composers of the period assumed the romanticist symphonic style, with no attempt to differentiate between secular and church expression. The CAECILIAN MOVEMENT, initially a reform group in the German-speaking countries, found strong support in German parishes of the Middle West. Restoration of plainsong and classic polyphony was their main concern, and their desire for objectivity of expression challenged the lush romantic composition of the period. While the group fostered revival of the older German hymns, the vernacular hymn was relegated to extraliturgical services.

The movement must be credited with stemming the tide of shallow, operatic church composition; by severing itself from the general musical development of the country, however, it gradually deteriorated to a system of stereotyped reproduction of musical patterns.

Early 20th Century. At the turn of the century, American church musicians resisted the influx of secular tunes as a basis for liturgical music, while leading secular composers have turned to religious themes for their inspiration. Within the churches themselves there has been a multiple development: (1) congregational music using German chorale form and sung in unison; ancient motets adapted to congregational singing; Gregorian chants and hymn settings by contemporary writers; and (2) selections for the trained choir—an artistic repertory capable of expressing meaning congenial to the worship by the larger group. *The Episcopal Hymnal* (1940) contains the old Latin Office hymns in English, hymns by American authors, translations from Orthodox and German Pietist sources and German chorales.

The *motu proprio* of Pope St. Pius X (1903) restated the role of music in Catholic worship, admitting for use "everything good and beautiful . . . in the course of the ages." This decree, on the one hand, gave a final impetus to the revival of Gregorian chant, initiated earlier by the Benedictine monks of Solesmes. On the other hand, it heralded the return of Renaissance polyphony and encouraged modern composition. The LITURGICAL MOVEMENT, through its interest in the congregation's participation, occasioned the reexamination of musical means and materials. The chant has come to be recognized as the highly artistic and difficult work it is, demanding the appropriate assignment to choir or partial use by the congregation. Hymnody received perhaps the closest scrutiny. A purging of 19th-century romanticist endeavors and a reconsideration of the wealth of Reformation and pre-Reformation hymns caused an artistic advance in hymnal publication. Contemporary composers, native and European, began to explore the area of congregational music for Catholic liturgies, a development that hastened after the liturgical reforms of the Second Vatican Council were implemented.

Bibliography: K. G. FELLERER, *The History of Catholic Church Music*, tr. F. A. BRUNNER (Baltimore 1961). W. DOUGLAS, *Church Music in History and Practice* (rev. ed. New York 1962). R. N. SQUIRE, *Church Music* (St. Louis 1962). R. M. STEVENSON, *Patterns of Protestant Church Music* (Durham, N.C. 1953). L. W. ELLINWOOD, *The History of American Church Music* (New York 1953). *Music in America*, eds., W. T. MARROCCO and H. GLEASON, 1620–1865 (New York 1964). H. W. FOOTE, *Three Centuries of American Hymnody* (Cambridge, Mass. 1940, repr. Hamden, Conn. 1961). G. CHASE, *America's Music* (New York 1955). *One Hundred Years of Music in America,* ed. P. H. LÁNG, (New York 1961). *Mission Music of California,* ed. O. DA SILVA, (Los Angeles 1941). J. V. HIGGINSON, "Hymnody in the American Indian Missions," *The Papers of the Hymn Society XVIII,* ed. W. W. REID (New York 1954). *A Short Bibliography for the Study of Hymns,* ed. J. R. SYDNOR, *ibid. XXV* (1964). C. VERRET, *A Preliminary Survey of Roman Catholic Hymnals Published in the U.S. of Amer.* (Washington, D.C. 1964). *Alonso de Benavides' Revised Memorial of 1634,* ed. F. W. HODGE et al., (Albuquerque 1945). L. M. SPELL, "Music Teaching in N. Mex. in the 17th Century," *New Mexico Historical Review,* 2 (1927) 27–36. L. B. SPIESS, "Benavides and Church Music in N. Mex. in the Early 17th Century," *Journal of the American Musicological Society,* 17 (1964) 144–156. L. SAMINSKY, *Living Music of the Americas* (New York 1949).

[C. VERRET/EDS.]

PART 10: PRE-VATICAN II LEGISLATION

Since apostolic times the Church has been careful to regulate the use of music in liturgical worship, encouraging fitting music and prohibiting unbecoming songs and chants.

History of Legislation. The directions of the Church on liturgical music during the early Christian centuries are contained in documents of a liturgical and disciplinary nature, rather than in separate acts of legislation on music. The first successor of St. Peter to write on music was Pope St. Clement (92–101), who regulated the use of chant. Only after Pope Leo IV (847–855) are separate documents on music to be found. In his *Una Res* he commanded Abbot Honoratus of the monastery of Farfa and his monks to sing only Gregorian chants.

In the Fathers. The Fathers of the Church forbade worldly and pagan music but commended worthy Christian songs and chants. They prohibited musical instruments that were associated with pagan music—the harp and lyre—and excluded lascivious and worldly songs as well as chanting by women, since this was a characteristic of pagan worship and was thought to foster sensuality rather than piety. The Fathers sought to encourage spirituality and devotion by the use of psalmody, for this allowed participation of the faithful in the worship of the church.

Conciliar Action before Trent. The Councils and synods of the Church have frequently legislated on liturgical music. Those held before the 14th century concerned themselves with the following questions: the entry of laymen into the office of singing the liturgical chant, the preservation of texts from Sacred Scripture and the exclusion of hymns and songs that contained heretical teachings, the preservation of the traditional chant of the Church, the condemnation of worldly and theatrical songs in church and cemetery (especially on the occasion of vigils and funerals) and the exclusion of worldly dances and themes. Principal among these councils and synods were those at Laodicea (343–381), Braga (561), Tours (567), III Toledo (589), Autun (650), Cloveshoe

(747), Aachen (816), Rome (853), Trier (1227) and Rouen (1235). In 1324–25 Pope John XXII spoke from Avignon in the bull *Docta sanctorum patrum* and warned against the introduction of unbecoming elements in polyphony. Subsequent synods and councils reiterated the need to guard against the introduction of profane songs in the vernacular and unbecoming and worldly texts.

The Council of Trent. The reform of the liturgical books following the Council of TRENT (1545–63) involved the reediting of the missal and breviary. Further, the *Ceremonial of Bishops,* which contains directions for the conducting of pontifical ceremonies, was revised under Clement VIII and published in 1600. It described the rites and ceremonies to be observed at Masses, Vespers and other liturgical functions, as well as the rights of precedence. It contains many references to music.

The legislation of the Council of Trent concerning music was enacted at the 22d, 23d and 24th sessions. The principal points discussed centered upon the nonliturgical character of some church music, the curtailment and unintelligibility of liturgical texts and the insertion of non-churchly vernacular songs, as well as worldly and lengthy organ compositions. These abuses were to be eliminated from the churches and care was to be given to the musical and liturgical education of clerics. Provincial councils were to determine the legislation in these matters, as seemed fitting according to particular circumstances.

After Trent. Legislation following the Council of Trent may be divided into two classes: general laws and particular indults for religious communities or dioceses. Only the laws that had general applicability will be listed here. They are the following: Alexander VII, *Piae Sollicitudinis,* 1657; Congregation of the Apostolic Visitation, 1665; Declaration of Cardinal Carpegna, 1692; Roman Council at the Lateran Basilica, 1725; *Instructio Clementina,* 1731; Clement XII, "Musicians in Pagan Worship," 1733; Benedict XIV, *Annus Qui,* 1749; Pius VI, "Choral Functions," 1791; Declaration of Cardinal Zurla (1824); Cardinal Odescalchi, "Notification," Declaration of Cardinal Patrizi, 1842, and Nov. 18 and 20, 1856; Congregation of Sacred Rites, *Romanorum Pontificum,* 1883; Congregation of Sacred Rites, "Regulations for Sacred Music," 1884; Congregation of Sacred Rites, *Quod Sanctus Augustinus,* 1894; Congregation of Sacred Rites, "Regulations for Sacred Music," 1894; and Congregation of Sacred Rites, encyclical letter to the bishops of Italy, 1894.

It can be said that the sources for the legislation on church music in effect at mid-20th century began with the motu proprio of St. Pius X, Nov. 22, 1903. The important documents between 1903 and the Constitution on the Sacred Liturgy of Vatican Council II are the following:

Canon 1264 of the 1917 Code of Canon Law; *Divini cultus sanctitatem;* Plus XI, Dec. 20, 1928; *Musicae sacrae disciplina,* Pius XII, Dec. 25, 1955; and "Instruction on Sacred Music and Sacred Liturgy," Congregation of Sacred Rites, Sept. 3, 1958.

Spirit of the Legislation. It is the mind of the Church that the faithful take an active part in both sung and recited Masses.

Sung Mass. Specific directions for participation in sung Mass are found in the 1958 "Instruction on Sacred Music and Sacred Liturgy" (par. 24–27), in which these three stages in the progress of the faithful toward active participation are given: (1) chanting of the liturgical responses, (2) singing of the parts of the Ordinary and (3) chanting some of the Proper of the Mass.

Recited Mass. The 1958 instruction (paragraphs 28–34) outlines four stages by which the participation of the faithful in recited Mass may be accomplished: (1) by saying the easier liturgical responses, (2) by answering the parts said by the server, (3) by reciting with the celebrant parts of the Ordinary and (4) by reciting sections of the Proper, i.e., Introit, Gradual, Offertory and Communion. Moreover, participation is to be effected by the singing of "hymns clearly suited to the respective parts of the Mass."

Basic Norms. The pre-Vatican II norms for music used at liturgical services were laid down by Pius X in the *motu proprio* of 1903. They are "holiness, true art, and universality." The specific types recommended are GREGORIAN CHANT, classical polyphony and approved modern compositions. Pope Pius XI repeated these principles in 1928, as did Pius XII in *Musicae sacrae disciplina.* But Pius XII enumerated distinctions between liturgical music and non-liturgical sacred music, and made provision for the performance of sacred music at nonliturgical occasions. The 1958 Instruction clarifies certain points on sacred concerts (par. 55), but in general preserves the norms of Pius X, Pius XI, and Pius XII.

Bells and the Use of Instruments. Pius X opposed the use of instruments in church (*motu proprio,* par.15–21) and Pius XI continued this policy, but Pius XII in *Musicae sacrae disciplina* (par. 58–61) relaxed this prohibition, allowing instrumental music that was executed artistically.

Use of the Organ. The *motu proprio* of Pius X (par. 15–18) encouraged the use of the ORGAN both as an accompaniment for the singing and as a solo instrument. *Divini cultus sanctitatem* (ch. 8) gave specific directions as to the correct manner of playing the organ. *Musicae sacrae disciplina* (par. 58) stated that the organ holds preeminence over all other instruments in church. The 1958 instruction (par. 61–64) distinguishes between the pipe organ, harmonium and electric organ. The electronic organ had previously (July 13, 1949) received a broader sanction from the Congregation of Sacred Rites than was stated in the 1958 "Instruction," according to which "the electronic organ may be tolerated temporarily." The 1958 instruction (par. 80) restricted the playing of the organ during those parts of the Mass when the celebrant prayed in a loud voice, in order that the readings might be heard clearly by the faithful.

Choirs and Women in Choirs. The *motu proprio* of Pius X stated that whatever singing does not pertain to the celebrant and sacred ministers "belongs properly to the choir of clerics, and that if singers are laymen they are substitutes of the ecclesiastical choir." Pius X stated that the singing must be, for the greater part, choral music, and that solos must never absorb the greater part of the liturgical text. In paragraph 13 he stated that "women cannot be admitted to the choir." This law was not well obeyed, especially in the U.S., where, as a result, women sang in choirs with the tacit permission of the bishops. Pius XI refrained from speaking on the subject, but Pius XII in *Musicae sacrae disciplina* (par. 74) modified the legislation of St. Pius X and allowed the use of mixed choirs or choirs of women or girls, so long as they remained outside the sanctuary and behaved in a suitable manner. The 1958 instruction especially mentioned choirs of men and women or of women or girls as being allowed.

Concerning Personnel. The *motu proprio* of Pius X (par. 12–14) described the office of choir members as a liturgical one and mentioned the high moral and spiritual qualities that should be possessed by those who sing in church, since they are substitutes for clerics. Pius X spoke of the proper attire of singers as that of cassock and surplice. He advocated the training of boys for the singing of the soprano and alto parts. Boys were to be trained in choir schools at cathedral and parochial churches, and they were to sing with the men. The 1958 instruction outlined the Christian qualities that should be present in the lives of singers, directors, organists, musicians and composers, as well as the necessary musical and liturgical training required for the proper performance of their duties.

Bibliography: P. M. FERRETTI, *Papal Documents on Sacred Music* (Washington 1928). A. HANIN, *La Législation ecclésiastique en matière de musique religieuse* (Paris 1933). R. F. HAYBURN, *St. Pius X and the Vatican Edition of the Chant Books* (Los Angeles 1964); *Digest of Regulations and Rubrics of Catholic Church Music* (rev. ed. Boston 1966). J. F. MYTYCH, *Digest of Church Law on Sacred Music* (Toledo, Ohio 1959). A. PONS, *Droit ecclésiastique et Musique sacrée,* 4 v. (St. Maurice 1958–61). F. ROMITA, *Jus musicae liturgicae* (Turin 1936). *Les Enseignments pontificaux: La Liturgie,* ed. Moines de Solesmes (Tournai, France 1954). Liturgi-cal Conference, *Manual for Church Musicians,* ed. P. J. HALLINAN (Baltimore, Md. 1964). K. WEINMANN, *Das Konzil von Trient und die Kirchenmusik* (Leipzig 1919). G. REESE, *Music in the Renaissance* (rev. ed. New York 1959). K. G. FELLERER, *The History of Catholic church Music,* tr. F. A. BRUNNER (Baltimore 1961).

[R. F. HAYBURN/EDS.]

PART 11: SECOND VATICAN COUNCIL

Vatican Council II's *Constitution on the Sacred Liturgy* (Dec. 4, 1963) in ch. 4 gives a concise code of sacred music (*musica sacra*), without all the details given in previous Roman documents (notably Pius XII's encyclical *Musicae sacrae disciplina,* Dec. 25, 1955; and the Instruction *Sacred Music and the Sacred Liturgy,* Sept. 3, 1958).

The Role of Music in Liturgy. Chapter 4 begins by reaffirming the role of liturgical music: "The musical tradition of the universal Church is a treasure of inestimable value, greater even than that of any other art. The main reason for this pre-eminence is that, as a sacred song united to the words, it forms a necessary or integral part of the solemn liturgy." Thus any discussion of Catholic Church music must turn in great part on its function. This is described by the *Constitution* as triple: "expressing prayer more delightfully" (*orationem suavius exprimens*), "fostering unity of minds" (*unanimitatem fovens*) and "enriching sacred rites with great solemnity" (*ritus sacros maiore locupletans sollemnitate*). While this division of functions is neither complete nor devoid of overlapping, it does call attention to several values found in music generally, and it relates them to worship: the first suggests the role of music as "true art," insisted on in Pius X's motu proprio of 1903; the second stresses the socializing function of the liturgy; the third is a reminder of the stately and sacral qualities that befit public worship.

The *Constitution* speaks of the "ministerial function of music in the liturgy," rather than of "the handmaid of the liturgy," as Pius X had done earlier. This ancillary role and some of its implications had often been resented by musicians, who were pleased with the more significant term "ministerial." Both words, however, throw light on an obscure area. For while music must not be belittled as something adventitious, neither can its place in liturgy be altogether autonomous. Music for worship must be controlled by the requirements of those who are to use it as a means of prayer. Thus, in the normal heterogeneous parish, if music is to fulfill its ministerial function, it must not be entirely unrelated to the people's preparation of sensitivity. Nor, on the other hand, should the artistic level of liturgical music be low, and this for obvious reasons. It seems evident that this artistic-vs.-popular tension implies a zone of relativity, and can hardly be expected to achieve more than an unstable, shifting resolution.

The Role of the People. At the same time, the *Constitution* insists, more explicitly than its predecessors had done, on the role of "God's people" in the liturgy, recalling also the "hierarchical" (art. 28, 30, 32). Gregorian chant is acknowledged as specially suited to the Roman liturgy (*liturgiae romance proprium*), and "other things being equal" (*ceteris paribus*) should be given "pride of place" (*principem locum*). In this context it is not clear what *ceteris paribus* means; however, in view of the notably smaller stress placed on Gregorian chant in the *Constitution,* as compared with previous documents, it would appear that its place of honor is in great part speculative. At the same time, article 117 expresses the desire for new chant editions and for "an edition containing simpler melodies, for use in small churches."

Article 121 invites composers to "produce compositions which have the qualities proper to the liturgy, not confining themselves to works which can be sung only by large choirs, but providing also for the needs of small choirs and for the active participation of the entire assembly of the faithful." While in previous Roman documents popular hymnody had been allowed and occasionally encouraged, this new statement extends the use of music sung by the people. Following the *Constitution*'s appearance and to fill its demands, a great number of "People's Masses" in the vernacular have appeared.

The Choir. "Other kinds of sacred music, especially polyphony, are by no means excluded from liturgical celebrations" (art. 116). It is evident that such music presupposes choirs, and the *Constitution* insists that "choirs must be diligently promoted" (art. 114). The earlier stress on Palestrina does not appear. To what extent this more elaborate music belongs in the liturgy will depend very much on the choral resources of individual churches; thus, article 114 adds "especially in cathedral churches." The same article insists, too, that "whenever the liturgy is to be celebrated with song, the whole body of the faithful be able to contribute that active participation which is rightly theirs, as laid down in Art. 28 and 30" (these two articles do not specify the parts, though they include at least responses and acclamations).

Instrumental Music. Instrumental music is given a wider range of use, following the severe restrictions set down (but, in subsequent practice, unevenly obeyed) by the motu proprio of Pius X. The special privilege of the pipe organ in the Latin Church is upheld, "for it is the traditional musical instrument which adds a wonderful splendor to the Church's ceremonies and powerfully lifts up man's mind to God and to higher things."

Other instruments require "the knowledge and consent of the competent territorial authority" and may be used "only on condition that the instruments are suitable, or can be made suitable, for sacred use, accord with the dignity of the temple, and truly contribute to the edification of the faithful." This article (120) gives cross references that indicate a deemphasis on uniformity in favor of fostering "the genius and talents of the various races and peoples." This broad missiological principle will need special application when Western countries are had in mind. Accordingly, after the *Constitution* appeared, the use of popular instruments (guitar, percussion and others) arose in several countries.

Bibliography: J. GELINEAU, *Voices and Instruments in Christian Worship,* tr. C. HOWELL (Collegeville, Minn. 1964). J. SAMSON, *Musique et chant sacrés* (Paris 1957). J. QUASTEN, *Musik und Gesang in den Kulten der heidnischen Antike und christlichen Frühzeit* (Münster 1930). C. J. MCNASPY, "The Sacral in Liturgical Music," in *The Renewal of the Liturgy* (New York 1963). J. MCKINNON, *The Church Fathers and Musical Instruments* (Doctoral diss. unpub. Columbia U. 1965). F. ROMITA, *Jus musicae liturgicae* (Rome 1947).

[C. J. MCNASPY/EDS.]

LITURGICAL MUSIC, THEOLOGY AND PRACTICE OF

Introduction. In all official Vatican documents, the term "sacred music" is used to name the music used at, or appropriate for the liturgy. *Musicam sacram* (1967) expanded the current definition of sacred music beyond GREGORIAN CHANT and polyphony to include music indigenous to missionary countries. Like the categories "religious music" and "church music," "sacred music" has a broad and rather nebulous meaning which does not necessarily relate to the liturgy at all. The phrase "liturgical music" was introduced to correct the older understanding. Some liturgists have argued that the term "liturgical music" tends to subordinate liturgy to music, and have suggested an alternative term, "musical liturgy." Another term, "pastoral music," as used by the National Association of Pastoral Musicians, refers to all music used at the parish level (including music used in religious education, evangelization, social ministry, and music education), though the bishops' document *Liturgical Music Today* (1982) restricts the term to a liturgical context (#63–64). In order to clarify music's role in the liturgy, some writers toward the end of the twentieth century settled on the term "Christian ritual music," while others chose "Catholic liturgical music." In this entry, the term "liturgical music" encompasses all types of music used in all Christian liturgies.

This entry covers developments in the theology and practice of liturgical music in the Roman Catholic

Church since the end of the Second Vatican Council. For the history and practice of Roman Catholic church music before Vatican II, *see* LITURGICAL MUSIC, HISTORY OF. The Second Vatican Council had paved the way for an interaction between reflection on liturgical music and the practice of liturgical music which was one of the most creative, challenging, and confusing in the history of church music. The new energy sparked by this interaction was reflected in musical composition and experiments in musical performance as well as in a fundamental shift in understanding both the liturgy itself and, subsequently, the role of liturgical music. That shift was caused not only by the introduction of the vernacular but also by the shift in primary responsibility for music from the choir to the whole assembly, and, more subtly, by the subsequent influence of culture on the music and the rite itself. Finally, this period engaged countless new musicians, trained or simply inspired, in the pastoral practice of church music.

The theoretical reflection on music took place in official documents issued by the Vatican and by the U.S. Conference of Catholic Bishops as well as non-episcopal initiatives, both international and specifically American. The major Vatican documents, reflecting both the theology and practice of liturgical music, include *Sacrosanctum Concilium* (the *Constitution of the Sacred Liturgy*, 1962), the *General Instruction of the Roman Missal* (1969 and revisions), *Musicam sacram* (1967), and *The Roman Liturgy and Inculturation: IVth Instruction for the Right Application of the Conciliar Constitution on the Liturgy* (1994). The U.S. Conference of Catholic Bishops issued, either as a statement by the whole conference or by one of its committees, documents that also reflected both theory and practice. They include: *Music in Catholic Worship* (1972, rev. 1983), *Liturgical Music Today* (1982), and *Plenty Good Room* (1990). Documents issued as non-episcopal initiatives include the *Manifesto of Universa Laus* (1980), the *Milwaukee Symposia for Church Composers: A Ten-Year Report* (1992), and the *Snowbird Statement on Catholic Liturgical Music* (1995).

The theology of liturgical music is embedded in the ecclesiology that is the foundation for Christian liturgy and in liturgical theology built on that foundation. While the development of ecclesiology and liturgical theology, which influenced the theology of liturgical music during this period of renewal, owed a great debt to individual theologians such as Dom Odo CASEL, Edward Schillebeeckx, OP, Karl RAHNER, SJ, and Edward KILMARTIN, SJ, this article examines the theology of liturgical music expressed in the literature described above. The few attempts by individual authors to craft a theology of liturgical music did not significantly influence the practice reviewed in this entry.

As important as the documentary reflection, therefore, was pastoral practice. The opportunities for new compositions, the involvement of new persons in ministry, the shift in a basic understanding of liturgy from the action of the priest, assisted by various ministers, to the action of the gathered assembly were not worked out only on paper; they were shaped and reshaped by pastoral practice. Musical practice significantly influenced both official and non-official documents, and, no doubt, the documents influenced practice. In addition to the major blocks of pastoral practice described here there are less noticed, but equally true, positions articulated in the documentation, including the Vatican documents, that advocate specific pastoral practices.

An Overview of the Theology of Music and Its Practice. Theology is the study of God and, in a Christian context, of God's involvement with humanity, including specific divine interventions on behalf of particular people in certain historical periods. The theological purpose or ultimate end of liturgical music falls within the general purpose of all liturgical action, which is to associate the church with Christ in the "great work wherein God is perfectly glorified and the recipients made holy (*Sacrosanctum Concilium* 7). The end of liturgical music, therefore, is "the glorification of God and the sanctification of the faithful" (SC 112, MS 4). Diverse interpretations of the way music is to accomplish this goal, using diverse approaches to music, have developed within the Catholic Church in the past 100 years. While all of these would agree that the ultimate end (*finem*) of liturgical music is its twofold transcendental and incarnational purpose, the ways in which God becomes personally manifests is widely debated. One approach focuses on an incarnational ecclesiology: By becoming fully human, one achieves the completion of humanity's teleology and reaches, through divine grace, participation in the divinity of God. Another believes that by transcending normal experience through participating, e.g., in an aesthetic experience, one is lifted toward union with the divine.

The function of liturgical music or, to use a scholastic theological term, its proximate end (the way music moves toward achievement of its ultimate end) is also debated among these various approaches. Within the official documents, the function (*munus ministeriale*) has been stated in diverse terms, reflecting the differing approaches to the theology of liturgical music which influenced those developing a particular document. One such approach would maintain that the three elements of holiness, beauty, and universality are key elements of any art used in the liturgy to achieve the transcendent goal of the act, so they are required as well of the musical art form used in liturgical worship. Another would maintain that "sacred music will be the more holy the more closely it is joined to the liturgical rite'' (SC 112), emphasizing an incarnational approach to music. In short, there are disagreements even within the official documents regarding the function or proximate end of liturgical music.

By way of introduction, the theology of liturgical music has been profoundly influenced by ''the doing'' of music. For example, the use from 1907 to 1963 of the *Liber Usualis*, a collection of the official chants for the Eucharist and the daily offices prepared by the Benedictines of Solesmes ''to ensure uniformity in the rendering of the Chant of the Church,'' profoundly determined an understanding by those who used this resource of the purpose (ultimate end) and function (proximate end) of liturgical music—not because of any theoretical statement or a rational reflection on experience, but because of the actual singing of the chants themselves and the experience of God which they created (or failed to create) in the participants. The theology of liturgical music, clearly, is shaped by its pastoral practice.

Second Vatican Council and Its Aftermath (1962–1972). The documentation for this period begins with Chapter VI of *Sacrosanctum Concilium*, the *Constitution on the Sacred Liturgy*, approved by the bishops on Dec. 4, 1962. This chapter reflects two positions on sacred music which existed prior to the Second Vatican Council, drawn from two papal documents—*Tra le sollecitudine* (1903) and *Mediator Dei* (1947)—and especially from pastoral practice influenced by use of the *Liber Usualis*. Chapter VI, as already noted, defines the purpose of sacred music to be ''the glorification of God and the sanctification of the faithful'' (SC 112). The two positions mentioned above dealt with the ritual function (the *munus ministeriale*) of sacred music to achieve that purpose. The first position affirms that the treasury of sacred music is to be preserved and Gregorian chant is be fostered (SC 112, 114); the second states that the people's own songs are to be encouraged and due importance is to be attached to their music (SC 118, 119). So while the basic trust of the Council was to develop full, conscious, and active participation of the whole assembly as ''the aim to be considered before all else'' (SC 14), and despite the encouragement given to new compositions (SC 121), in accord with existing documentation the bishops gave pride of place to music from a treasury containing products of ages that, on comparison with the theology of liturgy articulated in the *Constitution on the Sacred Liturgy*, do not represent an ideal in theological-liturgical thinking. That tension between the liturgical theology articulated at the Council and the recommended musical practices to express that theology did not take long to reveal itself.

In fact, the tension surfaced in 1966, at two important meetings of liturgical musicians in the United States.

The Fifth International Congress on Sacred Music of the Consociatio Internationalis Musicae Sacrae (Milwaukee, Wis., and Chicago, Ill., August 21–28) brought musicians from other nations into contact with liturgists and musicians in the United States for the first time since the Council. Later that year, a joint meeting of The Liturgical Conference and The Church Music Association of the United States (November 29–December 1, Kansas City, Mo.) brought together American liturgists and musicians representing two approaches to liturgical music: a recovery of the treasury of the past and the creation of a new repertoire based on the new theology of liturgy. Both meetings proved to be heated exchanges. The then Abbot Rembert Weakland, OSB, who chaired the U.S. Bishops' Advisory Board on Music, and who was present at both meetings, challenged the participants with an analysis of the Romantic influences underlying the assumptions regarding Gregorian chant and polyphony that existed in past historical documents as well as in Chapter VI of the Constitution on the Sacred Liturgy: ''We cannot preserve the treasures of the past without coming to terms with the false liturgical orientations that give birth to this music, nor can we preserve them according to the false aesthetic judgments of the last century.'' The result of these meetings, particularly of the second, was that church music in the United States was committed to endorsing the innovative aspect of the Second Vatican Council regarding music, namely, the challenge to create a repertoire suitable for assembly participation through music in the vernacular. American musicians took up the challenge, whether they were classically trained composers such as C. Alexander Peloquin, ethnically based musicians such as Rev. Clarence Jos. Rivers, or popularly oriented writers such as Joe Wise and Carey Landry.

The growing struggle over correct application of the Council's principles did not go unnoticed by the Vatican. On March 5, 1967, the Sacred Congregation of Rites issued *Musicam sacram*, whose purpose was to provide clarification regarding ''some problems about music and its ministerial function'' (*munus minsteriale, Musicam Sacram* 2). *Musicam sacram* first reiterated the transcendent and imminent purpose of music, ''for the glory of God and the sanctification of the faithful'' (MS 4), then it expanded the definition of ''sacred music'' by including both Gregorian chant and sacred polyphony as well as the ''sacred, i.e., liturgical or religious, music of the people'' under one heading (MS 4). It thus united paragraphs 114–116 of the Constitution on the Sacred Liturgy with 118–119. Further, it offered a new description of sacred music: ''Music is 'sacred' insofar as it is composed for the celebration of divine worship and possesses integrity of form'' (MS 4). It followed this intentional definition of sacred music with a description of such music functions (or proximate ends) of sacred music (#5). Such music is used: (i) to provide a more graceful expression to prayer; (ii) to bring out more distinctly the hierarchic character of the liturgy and the specific make-up of the community; (iii) To achieve a closer union of hearts through the union of voices; (iv) to raise minds more readily to heavenly realities through the splendor of the rites; (v) to make the whole celebration a more striking symbol of the celebration to come in the heavenly Jerusalem.

Previously, in *Tra le sollecitudine*, Pius X had described the functions of sacred music to be holiness, beauty, and universality which produce an art form. In *MEDIATOR DEI* (1947), Pius XII stated a more emotional and eschatological view:

> A congregation that is devoutly present at the sacrifice, in which our Savior together with His children redeemed with His sacred blood sings the Nuptial Hymn of His immense love, cannot keep silent, for "song befits the lover," and, as the ancient saying has it, "he who sings well prays twice." Thus the Church militant, faithful as well as clergy, joins the Hymns of the Church triumphant and with the choirs of angels, and all together, sing a wondrous and eternal Hymn of praise to the most Holy Trinity (#192).

A close reading of the functions named in *Musicam sacram* in comparison with these earlier statements, especially Pope Pius XII's evocation of the divine nuptial song and the heavenly liturgy, shows how the list of functions reflects an understanding of music that has shifted from Pius X's extra-liturgical measure of liturgical music as an art form to the more intra-liturgical understanding of music as "the more holy the more closely it is joined to the liturgical rite" (SC 112). In addition, *Musicam sacram* added a third element to the discussion, clearly influenced by pastoral practice: "The choice of the style of music for a choir or congregation should be guided by the abilities of those who must do the singing" (MS 9).

The revised *Ordo Missae* of Pope Paul VI and the accompanying *General Instruction of the Roman Missal* were first published in 1969, with a revised edition appearing in 1975. Unhesitatingly, the GIRM affirmed that "great importance should be attached to the use of singing at Mass" (*General Instructions of the Roman Missal* 19). Itself influenced by the experience of the previous five years, the *General Instruction* in turn influenced the developing theology of liturgical music by focusing its directives on a functional approach to music, as to other liturgical elements, providing specific directions regarding practice. This functional approach suggested that the theology and practice of liturgical music was to be determined by the liturgy itself and not by extra-liturgical factors. Therefore, the *Instruction* describes the function or purpose of each section of the liturgy and follows it with a set of practical instructions on how that function is to be expressed. For example, the general aim of the introductory rites is to help the faithful who have come together to "take on the form of a community and prepare themselves to listen to God's word and celebrate the eucharist properly" (GIRM 24). Within that general purpose, the role of the entrance song is "to open the celebration, intensify the unity of the gathered people, lead their thoughts to the mystery of the season or feast, and accompany the procession of priest and ministers" (GIRM 25). Then follows the practical instruction "The entrance song is sung alternately either by the choir and congregation or by the cantor and the congregation, or it is sung entirely by the congregation or by the choir alone . . . etc." (GIRM 26). By establishing a ritual function followed by the celebrative model, the *General Instruction* provides not only specific directives about what should be done but establishes the criteria by which the ritual act may be judged to be accomplished or not. Each element of the liturgy is similarly described in the *General Instruction*, providing criteria based on history and purpose whereby ritual participation can be measured against theological purpose. Slowly, but deliberately, these principles guided the creative development of the rite, freed from a false rubrical rigidity.

Liturgical music practice during this period in the United States was driven by three factors: the official generic encouragement of singing, especially congregational singing, the legal expectation of the *General Instruction* that at least some singing would be normative in the Roman Rite, and the need to discover or create a repertoire with vernacular texts. In the United States at this time, the focus was on English texts, though the need for musical settings of Spanish texts quickly became obvious as well. But there was little or no repertoire with English texts and certainly not settings of official liturgical texts in English. There was a significant effort to adapt Gregorian chant for use with vernacular texts, but it failed, and composers were ill-equipped to launch a massive and coordinated program of creating new music for English liturgical texts. Some settings of biblical texts, such as an English translation that used the psalmody developed by Joseph Gelineau, SJ, were used successfully, but interest soon turned in another direction. Urged on by the social and political climate of change in secular society, the primary influence on composers came from pop-folk music, either as an inspiration for "instant song" that could be readily learned (e.g. Ray Repp's "Here We Are" or "Sons of God") or as a direct borrowing from secular sources for liturgical use (e.g. "Michael, Row the Boat Ashore"). Universal and national legislation in 1969 permitted the use of "another song" for the entrance, presentation, and communion processions in place of assigned liturgical texts and the chant models that existed, e.g., in the *Liber Usualis* (see GIRM 26, 50, 56i; U.S. Appendix 2650, 56i). An available repertoire of such songs, and one that had already been used to a limited extent and masses before Vatican II, was the huge collection of Protestant hymnody, which became the mainstay of worship aids produced to support congregational participation. Once such resources became available, pastoral practice began to reinterpret the Council's call for full participation. While the liturgical documents envisioned participation as an engagement through ritual activity in the divine mysteries, with music as one way to assist such participation, pastoral practice often focused on participation as a call to get the people "more involved" in singing—mistakenly making singing the final end of the liturgy.

The Influence of *Music in Catholic Worship*. In 1972, the U.S. Bishops' Committee on the Liturgy issued the statement *Music in Catholic Worship* (MCW), confirmed by the full Conference of Bishops (and subsequently revised in 1983). This document established a theology of music based on a theology of celebration: "We are Christians because through the Christian community we have met Jesus Christ, heard his word in invitation, and responded to him in faith. We gather at Mass that we may hear and express our faith again in this assembly and, by expressing it, renew and deepen it" (MCW 1). Interior and exterior participation are understood as aspects of one act: "We are celebrating when we involve ourselves meaningfully in the thoughts, words, songs, and gestures of the worshipping community—when everything we do is wholehearted and authentic for us—when we mean the words and want to do what is done" (MCW 2). And, boldly, echoing Pope Pius XII and subsequent documents: "People in love make signs of love, not only to express their love but also to deepen it. Love must be expressed in the signs and symbols of celebration or [it] will die" (MCW 4). Perhaps the most challenging statement for practicing musicians as for other liturgical ministers appeared in MCW 6: "Good celebrations foster and nourish faith. Poor celebrations may weaken or destroy it."

This document had the most significant influence on the American theology of music and its practice in the decades immediately after the Council, because it was profound and practical, and it engaged the American religious imagination. It also offered a threefold practical judgment as a way to "determine the value of a given musical element in a liturgical celebration" (#25): The judgement has three aspects—musical, liturgical, and pastoral: Is it good music? Does it relate to the liturgical function? Does my community sing it? This was, for the Catholic Church in the United States, the first document on inculturation.

As a result of the widespread influence of *Music in Catholic Worship*, pastoral practice began to shift. Whereas some communities had been invited to sing anything at the key processional moments of entrance, preparation, and communion (plus a closing song), now music was more often chosen to accord with the threefold judgment. There was additional attention paid to music with texts rooted in the Bible, especially to new responsorial settings of the psalms. In many parishes, communities began to sing the texts of the liturgy—especially the psalm and gospel acclamation in the liturgy of the word and the acclamations of the eucharistic prayer—and not simply sing at the liturgy.

Compositional practice also changed after 1972. In 1974, for example, the music of the group that came to known as the St. Louis Jesuits—John B. Foley, Dan Schutte, Roc O'Connor, Tim Mannion, and Robert Dufford—began to reshape an understanding of the kind of compositions that used contemporary popular musical idioms. Their texts grew from the Scriptures, poetically adapted but written specifically for use in the liturgy. Their musical craft was used to develop congregational song rather than choral or solo repertoire, and their melodic resonance with many assemblies was often instantaneous.

Through the selection of repertoire they print and distribute it, music publishers contribute significantly to pastoral practice and, therefore, to a developing practical theology of liturgy. In the decades after Vatican II, World Library Publications, later joined to the J. S. Paluch Co.; the Gregorian Institute of America (later GIA Publications); and The Liturgical Press served as the major sources of repertoire for hymnals and for choirs. They were soon joined by North American Liturgy Resources (NALR), the leading publisher of pop-contemporary music, which subsequently merged with Oregon Catholic Press (OCP). The publication of monthly or seasonal worship aids, including the Paluch *Missalette* and similar resources, provided a vehicle for the rapid turnover of repertoire as new approaches developed, but it also firmly established an experience of "disposable" music in many parish communities. Liturgical texts and practices as well as the sacred music repertoire developed a transient character as a result of the multiple ritual changes during these times, which encouraged a kind of congregational approach to the liturgical books: If Rome is changing things so rapidly, then there is little to which we must hold ourselves accountable in ritual practice, and we are free to craft our own approach. This attitude was only reinforced by the changing repertoire which, in turn, reflected a rapidly changing society. The identification of liturgical music with these necessary transitions from Latin and chant to vernacular texts and music, and from a priest-centered to an assembly-centered liturgy, united to the developing performance style of liturgical leadership in which the leaders, aided by sound enhancement technology, sang new materials with which the rest of the assembly was unfamiliar, created an experience of music in the liturgy closely identified with the role of music in secular society.

Eventually, about twenty years after Vatican II, progress toward a more stable repertoire, a better incorporation of the sense of assembly participation, and a focus on singing the liturgy, not just singing at the liturgy, combined with the increasing interest in a more stable parochial liturgical experience, began to shape parish communities in a commitment to ritual unity without uniformity, a stronger and richer understanding of the nature of ritual, and a better appreciation for the unique role that music plays in ritual celebration.

Founded July 1, 1976, in response to the need for training and supporting the growing number of parish musicians needed to serve a liturgy in which "great importance should be attached to the use of singing" (GIRM 19), the NATIONAL ASSOCIATION OF PASTORAL MUSICIANS has emerged as the major U.S. association of liturgical musicians and parish liturgists, providing a national resource for the formation of a wide and diverse range of pastoral musicians at the parish level. Annual meetings provide a forum in which current teaching regarding musical liturgy is presented and new repertoire and resources are reviewed. *Pastoral Music* magazine provides ongoing formation in the development of the theology of liturgical music and the clarification of pastoral practice, as well as providing a venue for identifying and developing leaders in the field of pastoral music.

It cannot be emphasized too strongly that this postconciliar period was faced with several very practical tasks: (1) develop a repertoire in the vernaculars used in the nation; (2) teach the whole assembly—the congregation as well as its ministers—to participate; (3) revise the average parishioners' notion of God, the church, sacraments, and their own baptism. These tasks made use of and reshaped the theology of liturgical music. MCW's musical-liturgical-pastoral judgment provided a guideline for each parish community. Internationally, though it was not expressed by other hierarchies as it had been by the U.S. bishops, this threefold judgment in effect became the standard by which development of liturgical music was measured, though its application was influenced in various nations by tendencies in the national cul-

ture. So, for example, in the German community, with its history of great composers, from Bach through Beethoven and into the modern era, and its familiarity with great musical literature, instinctively approached the task of congregational singing through the use of quality music organically related to its tradition as uppermost in its musical consciousness. The French, on the other hand, with a strong background in contemporary scriptural and liturgical scholarship, enthusiastically took on the task of relating the music to the liturgy and began to emphasize music's ritual function. The Americans, characteristically, took a pragmatic approach, asking: Does the assembly sing it? These different approaches reflect an emphasis on one or another aspect of the threefold judgment as well as an understanding of music for the liturgy as "sacred," "liturgical," or "pastoral."

The International Attempt at a Theology of Liturgical Music (1980 to 1990). In 1980, UNIVERSA LAUS (UL), an international group for the study of singing and instrumental music in the liturgy, published a report of its work since its formal organization in 1966. The first part of the document, "Music in Christian Celebration," contains "points of reference" by which to view the relationships between music and Christian liturgy. The second part of the document—"Beliefs Held in Common"—establishes 45 one-line statements reflecting the international community's view of such music. This document provides a wealth of information regarding the developing theology of Christian ritual music in the 25 years after Vatican II.

First, the document names the "ultimate goal" of this music:

> The demands made by Christian ritual music spring from the ultimate goal of this music, which is to make manifest and make real a new humanity in the risen Jesus Christ. Its truth, worth, and grace are not only measured by its capacity to arouse active participation, nor by its aesthetic cultural value, nor its long history of acceptance in the church, nor by its popular success, but because it allows believers to cry out the Kyrie eleisons of the oppressed, to sing the Alleluias of those restored to life, and to uphold the Maranatha of the faithful in the hope for the coming of the Kingdom" (UL 10.1).

It also draws a conclusion about how one is to judge the appropriateness of music for incorporation into the liturgy. The UL Document and its official commentary explain that "common expressions such as 'sacred music,' 'religious music,' or 'church music' have broad and rather nebulous meanings which do not necessarily relate to liturgy at all." It concludes: "No type of music is itself profane, or sacred, or liturgical, or Christian: but there do exist types of ritual music in Christian worship. Christians do not possess a kind of music separate from other people, but they make use of each type of music in their own particular way.''

The overall theological premise of Universa Laus regarding ritual music is stated in the following terms. (1) Christian worship consists of : (a) the proclamation of salvation in Jesus Christ; (b) the response by the assembly of believers; and (c) the making real, by action, of the Covenant between God and humankind. (2) Music is integrated into these different components of worship: (a) to support and reinforce the proclamation of the Gospel in all its forms; (b) to give fuller expression to professing one's faith, to prayer (intercession) and to the giving of thanks; (c) to enhance the sacramental rite in its dual aspect of action and word (UL, "Points of Reference" 1.2).

Further, the document affirms:

> Music is not indispensable to Christian liturgy, but its contribution is irreplaceable. A celebration is a whole; and all of its elements—musical and non-musical—are interdependent. When music takes place within a rite, it always affects the form and the signifying power of the rite . . . . As a symbolic sign, singing and music play a role above and beyond determined ritual functions (UL, "Beliefs Held in Common," 21–26).

As the new vernacular versions of Roman Catholic worship began to take hold and reshape our understanding and practice of worship, a new era has been opening up in the continuing encounter between worship and culture. This new era has directed the main thrust of UL's work toward the study of "ritual function" within the Roman Rite. But the recognition of the continuing impact of culture has shifted that focus to a deeper study of the effective "functioning" of these same musical moments within particular cultures. Thus, the fields of human behavior, social customs, and cultural differences became a focus for studies of ritual music. This meant that the fields of semiology, cultural anthropology, and sociopsychology had to be incorporated, as well, into a study of music under the sign of faith.

The statement *Liturgical Music Today* (LMT), published by the U.S. Bishops' Committee on the Liturgy in 1982, was an attempt to articulate principles governing the function of music in the liturgy and function and form of various musical elements (LMT 6–11). In fact, *Liturgical Music Today* provided practical directives for new situations which had arisen since the publication of *Music in Catholic Worship*.

This statement appeared at a time when the successes as well as the failures of pastoral practice with the revised rites were causing a re-examination of the experience as well as the theory that was operative before the Council. "On the eve of the Council," LMT summarized the pastoral practice since 1903, "few parishes were performing the authentic repertoire recommended by Saint Pius X in his famous *motu proprio* on music" (LMT 51). Conceding that most parishes used only a limited amount of the chant and polyphony repertoire that had been encouraged by every pope from Pius X to the Second Vatican Council, and many parishes since the Council have failed to embrace this commended repertoire, LMT notes that many parishes are employing diverse styles of liturgical music within the same celebration. Affirming this eclectic approach to repertoire which had grown up in practice, LMT proposed a new understanding of the traditional repertoire and its use. Rather than commending it as high art, and therefore the most appropriate music for Roman Rite liturgy, LMT placed this repertoire in the context of historic faith and worship: "Singing and playing the music of the past is a way for Catholics to stay in touch with and preserve their rich heritage. A place can be found for this music, a place which does not conflict with the assembly's role and the other demands of the rite" (LMT 52). A blend of music from the past and new music composed for congregational participation was proposed as both a pastoral ideal and a practical application of liturgical music's function (*munus ministeriale*).

This was also a time when the Church in the United States and throughout the world was becoming aware of the impact of various cultures on the way liturgy is celebrated. So *Liturgical Music Today* also affirmed the value and significant impact of diverse languages and cultural differences on liturgy in the United States (LMT 54–55).

On the matter of music ministry, LMT begins with a theological statement that would have been highly controverted just twenty years before: "The entire worshiping assembly exercises a ministry of music" (LMT 63). The document then turns its attention to pastoral practice by addressing the musicians in terms of a theology of their ministry:

> Some members of the community, however, are recognized for the special gifts they exhibit in leading the musical praise and thanksgiving of Christian assemblies. These are the pastoral musicians, whose ministry is especially cherished by the Church. What motivates the pastoral musician? Why does he or she give so much time and effort to the service of the church at prayer? The only answer can be that the church musician is first a disciple and then a minister. The musician belongs first of all to the assembly; he or she is a worshiper above all. Like any member of the assembly, the pastoral musician needs to be a believer, needs to experience conversion, needs to hear the Gospel and so proclaim the praise of God.

Thus, the pastoral musician is not merely an employee or volunteer. He or she is a minister, someone who shares faith, serves the community, and expresses the love of God and neighbor through music'' (#63–64).

In these years, pastoral practice in the United States was influenced by more sophisticated composition and by a wide range of styles in musical repertoire. The British St. Thomas More Group, with Christopher Walker and Paul Inwood, brought to the U.S. a new level of craft in popular pastoral music. Together with U.S. composers J. Michael Joncas, Marty Haugen, and David Haas, they introduced into the liturgy music techniques from secular culture, especially from Broadway-style musical forms. More classical forms were also being reshaped based on the renewed liturgical theology and pastoral practice. These included attempts at a new style of chant for use with English texts. Richard Proulx's *Community Mass* and Marty Haugen's *Mass of Creation* began to create an ''American standard'' for common eucharistic acclamations. A wide range of styles setting responsorial psalms was being published, though most compositions followed the pattern of providing an antiphon for the congregation with verses for the cantor or choir. Liturgical music practice was beginning to stabilize in many parishes.

American Attempts at a Theology of Liturgical Music in the 1990s. Following the nation's experience with the civil rights movement, the immigration of Vietnamese and Hmong people following the Vietnam War, Cuban immigration, the arrival of Mexican and other Spanish-speaking immigrants, and a new wave of immigrants from Asian Pacific nations, existing American liturgical practice was severely challenged to develop an appropriate way to deal with multi-lingual and multi-cultural/multi-ethnic expectations for pastoral liturgy. The Vatican Council had directed openness in these matters: ''Even in the liturgy the Church has no wish to impose a rigid uniformity in matters that do not affect the faith or the good of the whole community; rather, the Church respects and fosters the genius and talents of the various races and peoples'' (SC 37).

Though *Music in Catholic Worship* (1972) may be considered the first document to address liturgical inculturation for the Catholic Church in the United States, the first document to address the multi-cultural challenge to worship in U.S. Catholicism appeared in 1990. *Plenty Good Room: The Spirit and Truth of African American Catholic Worship* (PGR, Aug. 28, 1990), produced by the Black Catholic Secretariat of the United States Conference of Bishops, contained reflections on music in the Black Church. It notes, especially, that people of African-American heritage ''do not sing only to make music'' (PGR 3).

Like most of the American Catholic documents, PGR affirms the symbolic nature of liturgy: ''First, one cannot arbitrarily make symbols—they are not merely things. They become symbolic because of their resonating with the members of a given historical, cultural, ethnic, and racial community. They can assume levels of meaning that make sense of birth, life and death—by means of tradition, community and grace'' (PGR 5). The statement applies this symbolic understanding to liturgical music:

> A person may be particularly moved by the singing of a certain hymn . . . Were they asked, ''what do these symbols mean?'' they respond ''I don't know. I didn't even know they were symbols.'' This would not imply that they have not experienced meaning in their symbolic activity. They have, for symbols are truly multi-dimensional phenomena (#9).

In other words, the measure of successful repertoire is not whether a particular piece is a ''hit'' but whether it succeeds in the order of religious symbolism.

As described in PGR, the theology of African American music (PGR #101–104) centers on the active presence of the Spirit and on improvisation. Singing becomes the effective sign of the Spirit's presence and also the ritual act that evokes the Spirit: ''This congregational response becomes a part of the ritualized order of the celebration. The deadly silence of an unresponding assembly gives the impression that the Spirit is absent from the community's act of praise'' (PGR 102).

The function (*munus ministeriale*) of African American sacred song, as Sister Thea Bowman noted, is holistic, participatory, real, spirit-filled, and life giving. She describes those characteristics this way: (i) *Holistic*: Challenging the full engagement of mind, imagination, memory, feeling, emotion, voice and body; (ii) *Participatory*: inviting the worshiping community to join in contemplation, in celebration, and in prayer; (iii) *Real*: celebrating the immediate concrete reality of the worshiping community—grief or separation, struggle or oppression, determination or joy—bringing that reality to prayer within the community of believers; (iv) *Spirit-filled*: energetic, engrossing, intense; and (v) *Life giving*: refreshing, encouraging, consoling invigorating, sustaining.

In part as an attempt to analyze the experience of multi-cultural and multi-repertorial musical liturgy, a group of composers met for ten years in Milwaukee (1982–1992) at the suggestion of Sister Theophane Hytrek, SSSF, and under the sponsorship of Archbishop Rembert Weakland, OSB. On July 9, 1992, they issued *The Milwaukee Symposia for Church Composers: A Ten-Year*

Report (MS). This document brought the elements connected with Christian ritual music contained in the Universa Laus Document to the attention of musicians in the United States and set out to describe a theology of ritual music, since it affirmed that "a theology of Christian ritual music is necessary." While such a theology "may be implicit in some of the official documents," MS states, "there has been little explicit attempt in these documents to fashion such a theology" (MS 10).

MS attempts to establish the major elements of such a theology in articles 11–17. The paschal mystery, of course, is central, though it is to be seen as the climax of the "'liturgy of the world . . . which God celebrates' through the length and breadth of human history" (MS 11). This mystery is expressed and shaped in symbols: "While our words and art forms cannot contain or confine God, they can, like the world itself, be icons, avenues of approach, numinous presences, ways of touching without totally grasping or seizing." Christian liturgy is a symbolic event, and music takes part in that symbolic activity, particularly in four ways: (i) music as sound, the raw material of music, reveals God in a non-localized, symbolic way; (ii) music is rhythmic and, therefore, time-bound; it "underscore[s] the temporality of human existence into which God has intervened." In this temporal aspect, music becomes one with the very nature of the liturgy; (iii) music heightens words. Because word reveals God in the liturgy, music has a heightened role in the liturgy; and (iv) music uniquely unites singer to song, singer to those who listen, and singers with each other: "Christian ritual song joins the assembly with Christ, who is the source and content of the song. The song of the assembly is an event of the presence of Christ. What fuller expression of the sacramental nature of Christian ritual music, especially the song of the assembly?"

In its theology of liturgical music, the Milwaukee Statement abandons the scholastic language of purpose and function. In addressing a wide range of issues connected with pastoral practice, MS reflects the concerns of the composers about liturgical formation, liturgical preparation, liturgical structures and forms, textual considerations, cross-cultural music making, models of music making, and technology. It describes accurately how pastoral practice and the theology of music interacted in the years after the Council:

> First we experienced an effort to translate Latin chants into English. We then moved from vernacular chant to attempts at contemporary composition in popular idioms. Other developments included emphasis on scripturally based texts, the adoption of repertoire from the broader Christian community, and a growing awareness of the need for improved standards in musical and textual

composition. In each of these developments, a primary concern has been music's ministerial role. Increasingly, we are coming to understand how a rite and its sound, its music, are inseparable: serving, enabling and revealing aspects of our belief that would otherwise remain unexpressed" (MS 4).

The statement also offers a way to treat the musical-liturgical-pastoral judgment of MCW as one integrated judgment rather than as three separate judgments (MS 81–86), finally uniting efforts that had previously been divided by a concentration on one aspect of this judgment as primary, leaving the other two as secondary: "An integrated approach to the musical-liturgical-pastoral judgment demonstrates that no single musical element can be evaluated apart from the whole of the liturgical-musical contour" (MS 84).

In 1994, issues raised by inculturation received a formal response from the Congregation for Divine Worship and the Discipline of the Sacraments in the Instruction *The Roman Liturgy and Inculturation* (RLI). This document affirmed the importance of music and singing and reiterated the liturgical importance of music native to "mission lands"(RLI 40). The statement also noted the importance of paying attention to the text that is to be sung: "It is important to note that a text which is sung is more deeply engraved in the memory than when it is read, which means that it is necessary to be demanding about the biblical and liturgical inspiration and the literary quality of texts which are meant to be sung (RLI 40). Recognizing the growth of the church in areas less influenced by European Catholicism and Western music, such as Asia and Africa, RLI commented not only on the use of indigenous "musical forms, melodies, and musical instruments" but also on the incorporation of "gestures and postures" appropriate to the culture, including "hand-clapping, rhythmic swaying, and dance movements on the part of the participants. Such forms of external expression can have a place in the liturgical actions of these peoples on condition that they are always the expression of true communal prayer of adoration, praise, offering and supplication, and not simply a performance" (RLI 42). This document also expressed a growing concern on the part of Vatican officials that an approach to music as "entertainment" was replacing a legitimate respect for religious "delight."

The American dialogue on the purpose and function of music in the liturgy continued with the publication, on Nov. 1, 1995, of a statement by a small group of liturgists and musicians meeting in Utah. Titled *The Snowbird Statement*, this document entered into dialogue with the *Milwaukee Symposia* report and current pastoral practice. *Snowbird* affirmed the category of ritual music as an appropriate way to describe music in the liturgy, but it warned against reducing that category to a kind of practical functionalism.

As a corrective to perceived problems with current practice, the *Snowbird Statement* offers a series of principles that serve to articulate an underlying theology of music in the liturgy. (1) Beauty is essential in the liturgical life and mission of the Church. (2) Standards of excellence in composition and performance must be affirmed. (3) Of the three judgments described in MCW, the musical judgment has not been advanced with sufficient development, indicating a belief by the signatories that an objective judgment may be made about musical quality. (4) While endorsing cultural adaptation, the statement rejects any approach that would inject an entertainment attitude or a therapeutic ethos into the liturgy. The *Snowbird* signatories encourage singing music from the Church's treasury, and they emphasize the need to develop or re-develop choirs for Catholic liturgy.

Many of the points made in *Snowbird* are based on the premise that there is a Catholic liturgical "ethos":

> We believe there exists a characteristic ethos of Catholic liturgical music, although we acknowledge that such is difficult to define. To identify the ethos narrowly with any specific period or genre in liturgical-musical history would be a mistake. The church is not intrinsically limited to any particular "sacred" style of music for the celebration of the liturgy. Still, we believe that a Catholic ethos is discernible, for instance, in music that elaborates the sacramental mysteries in a manner attentive to the public, cosmic and transcendent character of religion, rather than in styles of music that are overly personalized, introverted or privatized. Music employed by countless generations of Catholic Christians is the starting point for discerning the characteristics of a Catholic ethos in liturgical music. In response to the church's developing needs and the many new cultural contexts within which the church worships, the ethos of Catholic liturgical music will continue to find new expressions. This process of development, however, should consult pre-existing forms to a greater extent than has generally been the case in recent decades. We advocate that new forms and styles grow organically from extant forms which display a Catholic ethos (#8).

Conclusion. The theology of church music and its practice have profoundly influenced the period immediately following the Second Vatican Council. More Christian believers have participated in the practice of church music in these years, as ministers and as members of the singing assembly, than in almost any other era of Church life. A perfect solution to linking the treasury of sacred music to the requirement for assembly music has not been found, but there is a great awareness that an organic link to the treasury is beginning to develop. An agreed upon theology of ritual music does not exist, but efforts have been made to begin the process of developing such a theology. A new repertoire for assembly participation is not complete, but it is well on its way. Pastoral practice is by no means stable, but considerable effort has been made toward a workable model, and a large core of competent musicians, skilled at the craft of assembly song, are serving the Church. The theology of liturgical music and the pastoral practice associated with it will continue to develop as we strive to make music for the glory of God and the sanctification of the faithful.

Bibliography: W. M. ABBOTT, SJ, ed. *The Documents of Vatican II* (New York 1966). C. DUCHESNEAU and M. VEUTHEY, *Music and Liturgy: The Universa Laus Document and Commentary*, tr. P. INWOOD (Washington 1992). R. F. HAYBURN, *Papal Legislation on Sacred Music: 95 A.D. to 1977 A.D.* (Collegeville, Minn. 1979). E. HOFFMAN, ed. *The Liturgy Documents: A Parish Resource.* Vol. 1. (Chicago 1991). International Commission on English in the Liturgy. *Documents on the Liturgy, 1963–1979: Conciliar, Papal, and Curial Texts* (Collegeville, Minn. 1982). C. JONES, G. WAINWRIGHT, and E. YARNOLD, SJ, eds. *The Study of Liturgy* (London 1978). The Liturgical Conference and the Church Music Association of America, *Crisis in Church Music?* (Washington 1967). D. A. LYSIK, *The Liturgy Documents: A Parish Resource,* Vol. 2. (Chicago 1999). *The Milwaukee Symposia for Church Composers: A Ten-Year Report* (Washington 1992). "The Snowbird Statement on Catholic Liturgical Music." *Pastoral Music* 20:3 (Feb.–Mar. 1996): 13–19.

[V.C. FUNK]

LITURGICAL RITES

Throughout the ages, the liturgical celebration of the mystery of salvation has received many different ritual expressions, bound historically to various areas of ecclesiastical influence. This article treats the differentiation of rites and the ritual families.

DIFFERENTIATION OF RITES

The starting point in the evolution of Christian liturgical families was necessarily the paschal meal that Christ ate with His Apostles. Despite the simplicity of that scene, the depth and richness of the mystery inaugurated at the Last Supper ultimately accounts for the variety that subsequently adorned its celebration. It is true that up to the fourth century there were no rites in the strict sense of clearly fixed patterns followed by well-defined groups; the extant evidence suggests that extemporization within set patterns was the usual practice (*see* Bouley, *From Freedom to Formula*).

The task of tracing the exact path of evolution in the first three centuries is greatly hampered by incomplete sources, but it is more and more agreed that the fourth century was a time of great importance in the development of the liturgy. The increase of Christians after Constantine's rule necessitated further organization, encouraging a trend toward uniformity. The threat of Arianism and other heresies were further causes for standardizing orthodox forms of worship. These factors were intimately intertwined with another fourth-century phenomenon: the emergence of preponderant centers of authority in matters of Church discipline. These great metropolitan or patriarchal sees became centers of more or less particular liturgical rites, and this in turn intensified the trend toward writing down and gathering together the texts used. Liturgical books were thus created. The saying of improvised prayers gave way to the reading of set formulas, so that the borrowing of texts from one church by another was greatly facilitated; and a mother church could easily impose a fixed order of worship on daughter churches. Liturgical books can thus be seen as instrumental in establishing both uniformity and diversity in the history of the liturgy: uniformity among the churches of a province that came to use the same books, and diversity by that very fact among groups of churches that embraced different collections of texts.

Classification. In this evolution of liturgical families it should be noted that the root principle of diversification was not language or doctrine or nationality, although all of these were influences, but geopolitics. Already at the time of St. Paul, the concentration of Christianity was in the chief cities of the Empire, and these became the great centers already spoken of; in general, rite followed patriarchate.

There are different ways of attempting to classify liturgical families, a fact that can create confusion. It is artificial and misleading to select elements other than their historical origins as the basis, but even when this is agreed upon, the outcome can be different, depending on whether one's chief interest is with the past—what rites have existed—or the present—what rites have survived. In the former approach, for example, the Byzantine liturgical rite appears merely as one of several developments of the Antiochene tradition, while in the latter it is set apart in a class by itself as the greatest, most extensive, and most influential of all the modern Eastern rites.

LITURGICAL FAMILIES

The chief division of liturgical families is the same as the chief geopolitical division of the ancient world: East and West.

Eastern Liturgical Rites. Since Christ lived in the East, the oldest practice of the Christian liturgy is also from the East. With the destruction of Jerusalem in 70 A.D., Christianity in the East centered in Antioch and Alexandria.

Antiochene. The Syrian type of liturgy had two traditions in apostolic times. The more Jewish strain kept the traditional language and, as seems quite likely, ultimately centered in Edessa. This is known as the East Syrian (Mesopotamian, Persian) branch, because its members were outside the Roman and within the Persian Empire. This Edessene liturgy retained many of the Semitic traits and was little influenced by Hellenism. The East Syrian liturgy is used by three churches of the Christian East: the ancient Assyrian Church of the East, the Chaldean Catholic Church, and the Syro-Malabar Church.

The West Syrian branch has been the more influential; it blended a fair amount of Greek influences with other elements borrowed from other liturgical families. The splendor of processions, vigils, and singing that characterizes it gives it a markedly different atmosphere than the more Semitic East Syrian branch.

The fifth century, however, brought a division within the West Syrian branch that had a curious and unfortunate outcome. With the condemnation of Monophysitism at Chalcedon in 451, national instincts and political dislikes for Byzantium contributed to the rejection of the Council by many. These Syrian Monophysites, known as Jacobites, soon adopted Syriac as the liturgical language, and a great period of development followed with the borrowing and creating of numerous compositions. The liturgical rite, called SYRIAN, thus acquired a richness and variety unparalleled elsewhere, boasting more than 70 Anaphoras. However, the group that accepted the orthodoxy of Chalcedon formed themselves into the MELKITE CHURCH. This group retained the Greek language and came more and more under the influence of Constantinople, until in the 12th century it finally lost its particular West Syrian liturgy and adopted the Byzantine as its own liturgical rite.

Another church that uses the West Syrian liturgical rite is the MARONITE CHURCH of Lebanon. Its early history is obscure; never Monophysite, this Church has been in direct contact with Rome since the Crusades, and its liturgy has suffered from heavy latinization, especially since the 18th century, although in the wake of Vatican II, steps have been taken to retrieve its rich ancient liturgical heritage.

Of all the Eastern liturgical families, the Byzantine rite is today the most important by far. This leads many to treat it separately, but historically it belongs to the West Syrian family. Since Constantinople was founded by Constantine in the fourth century, it obviously had no primitive liturgy of its own, but had to borrow or create one. The many ties between Antioch and the imperial city naturally led to the liturgical usages of the former being the principal influence upon the latter, and St. John Chrysostom (native of Antioch, but bishop of Constantinople) had much to do with the process.

The mid–ninth century marked the beginning of a period of unification and regulation of this rite throughout the empire. The two most important developments were (1) its translation into Slavonic by SS. Cyril and Methodius, when it was adopted as the liturgy of the newly converted Slavs, and (2) the Baptism of the prince of Kiev, St. Vladimir, more than a century later, opening to this rite a new province that was to become the huge empire of Russia. Subsequently the Russian missionaries carried it across central Asia as far as Manchuria, China, and Japan. The Byzantine rite thus became the most fully developed liturgy of the East, undergoing an evolution of ten centuries. Drawing into itself elements from many sides in its formation, it subsequently reversed the procedure, pushing out to replace all the rest of the liturgies in the churches within the Empire that remained orthodox after Ephesus and Chalcedon. A further development, one of latinization, took place in those dioceses that recognized papal oversight at the end of the 16th century, resulting in a hybrid liturgy.

Armenian. The distinctive ARMENIAN LITURGICAL RITE has a complex and by no means fully known history. Since the Middle Ages, however, it has been considerably modified, first by the Byzantine influence, and since the Crusades, by the Latin.

Alexandrian. Ever since the days of Alexander the Great (three centuries before Christ), Alexandria, in Egypt, was the rival of Antioch. This was so in the early centuries of the Christian Era too. The development of the Egyptian liturgy, known as the Liturgy of St. Mark, parallels the West Syrian development. The reaction after Chalcedon was much the same: mass desertion to Monophysitism and adoption of the vernacular, in this case Coptic. Yet as in Syria, there may well have been two kinds of liturgies from the start, one in Greek, the other in Coptic. After the Monophysite crisis, monasticism exercised an even greater influence on the evolution of the Coptic liturgy than on the Byzantine.

The liturgy of Ethiopia is derived from the Coptic, but with Syrian elements. Its ancient history has been the subject of much ongoing study. The Ethiopian liturgy is of special interest today, since it reveals some remarkable elements of adaptation to African cultures.

Western. The diversity of liturgical forms thus seen in the East was also found in the West. Rome was the outstanding center, although other cities, such as Milan and Carthage, vied for attention. In the third and fourth centuries there was a change from Greek to Latin, and in contrast to what happened in the East, Latin soon became the sole liturgical language of the West. The evolution of liturgical families in the West, except for Rome, is not so clearly tied to metropolitan sees as in the East. There are two broad families: Gallican and Roman-African.

Gallican. The precise origin of the GALLICAN RITES has long been disputed. Within the heterogeneous group loosely called the Gallican liturgy, the following types are usually enumerated, although they were surely not the only forms of this liturgy that were more or less independent.

The old Spanish, later called (inaccurately) MOZARABIC RITE or sometimes the Visigothic Rite, is exceptional in that it was built according to clearly stated principles. Its sources are obscure, but it was already fully developed by the sixth century. It shows the influence of the battle against the Arian Visigothic invaders of the fifth century. Suppressed by Pope Gregory VII after the Christian reconquest of the Iberian peninsula from the Muslims, the dying liturgical rite was resuscitated by the decision of of Cardinal F. XIMENEZ DE CISNEROS (d. 1517) to preserve this ancient liturgy for use in a chapel of the Toledo.

The CELTIC RITE, the historical liturgical rite used in the British Isles in Ireland and Scotland and propagated by their monks, seems to have had little original about it except its ability to weave together all manner of local and foreign elements. Missionaries and papal legates bearing the Roman Rite dealt a deathblow to this ancient rite, as churches and monasteries were either persuaded or compelled to switch to the Roman Rite.

The GALLICAN RITES, called so because it was used in the Frankish realm, was probably of greater variety than is often supposed. Because of suppression under Charlemagne in favor of the Roman rite, only limited witnesses survive.

Roman-African liturgical rites. The other great Western family is the Romano-African type. Of the liturgy of Africa, however, no complete documents or liturgical books are preserved. Reconstructions from the writings of Tertullian, Cyprian, Augustine, and others show that it was closely allied to the Roman.

Ambrosian. The AMBROSIAN RITE, although permeated with elements of the Roman liturgy, has succeeded in preserving the essentials of its traditional practices and has thus kept alive one of the oldest forms of Western liturgy. Scholars often classify it as a Roman-type Latin liturgical rite, with good reason, since it sometimes preserves elements of older Roman usage abandoned at Rome. Indeed, St. Ambrose of Milan wrote that he followed the Roman usage (rite); however, he insisted that it is reasonable to adopt some practices from other Churches (*De sacramentis*, 3.1.5). Other Italian rites, such as that of AQUILEIA and BENEVENTO, have also flourished.

Roman Rite proper. The earliest liturgical witnesses in Latin of the Roman Rite that are earlier than the seventh century are the LEONINE SACRAMENTARY (Veronense) and Old GELASIAN SACRAMENTARY (Vat. Reg. Lat. 316). Surviving fragments of liturgical texts suggest that the basic text of the Roman Canon was already worked out in the fourth century and the framework of the whole Mass was essentially set by the turn of the fifth. The last major reform, especially of the Mass, was under Gregory the Great. While his name is still connected with the music used in the Roman rite, in reality much of this chant took its origin considerably later in the monasteries of the Rhineland. Whatever the exact nature and scope of his reform, however, this was indeed the golden age of the Roman liturgy, when it was sufficiently evolved to express the manifold aspects of the Christian mystery and was still a rite in which the whole community took conscious active part. It was also the time of its greatest prestige, when it was more and more adopted by other churches. This process of expansion was hastened first by Pepin, then by Charlemagne, who worked energetically to impose it on their whole territory. The pontifical Sacramentary sent by the pope and used as the basis for this unification, the work of supplementing done by Alcuin, the multitude of manuals (*Ordines Romani*) produced in the reorganization, all this is more fully explained in the article ROMAN RITE. The ancient Roman rite was considerably modified. Curiously enough, a few centuries later history reversed itself when the Germanized Roman Pontifical made its way back to Italy, replacing the older usages by the end of the 11th century.

The liturgical reform undertaken by Innocent III marks a turning point in the history of the Roman liturgy. The period was hampered by a preference for allegory and legalism, under which the original meaning of the actions was lost and yet their smallest details prescribed, so that the appreciation of the liturgy as the communal and hierarchical celebration of the whole Church was more and more replaced by juridical preoccupation with the task to be performed. Under the influence of the Mendicants, the sanctoral cycle grew and theological controversy over the Real Presence abetted new currents of Eucharistic piety that brought new rites such as the Elevation of the Host.

Historically, various religious orders had their own liturgical rites that were derivatives of the Roman Rite with some elements borrowed from the Gallican Rites.

(*See* CARMELITE RITE, CARTHUSIAN RITE, DOMINICAN RITE and PREMONSTRATENSIAN RITE.) During the Middle Ages, liturgical usage developed adaptations of the Roman Rite in the British Isles, the most famous of which is the SARUM USE. Other examples include the YORK USE and HEREFORD USE.

The riches of the liturgy remained enshrined in the Roman liturgical sources, awaiting recovery, but the misfortunes of the 16th-century division deterred the Council of Trent's reform from doing much more than solidifying the general *status quo*. Benedict XIV initiated a more critical reform, but it was interrupted, not to be resumed until the 20th century under Pius X, more extensively under Pius XII, and finally on a wholesale basis by Vatican Council II.

Bibliography: A. A. KING, *The Rites of Eastern Christendom,* 2 v. (London 1950); *Liturgies of the Past* (Milwaukee 1959). A. KING, *Liturgies of the Religious Orders* (London 1955). J. A. JUNGMANN, *The Mass of the Roman Rite,* tr. F. A. BRUNNER, 2 v. (New York 1951–55); *The Early Liturgy to the Time of Gregory the Great,* tr. F. A. BRUNNER (Notre Dame, Ind. 1959). D. ATTWATER, *The Christian Churches of the East,* 2 v. (rev. ed. Milwaukee 1961–62). B. BOTTE, ''Rites et familles liturgiques,'' *L'Église en Priere* (Paris 1965). H.A.J. WEGMAN, *Christian Worship in East and West: A Study Guide to Liturgical History* (New York 1985). C. VOGEL, *Medieval Liturgy: An Introduction to the Sources* (Washington, DC 1986).

[J. J. MEGIVERN/T. RICHSTATTER/EDS.]

LITURGICAL THEOLOGY

The theological task arising from Christian worship is multifaceted. Its starting point is neither dogmatic affirmation, nor, strictly speaking, liturgical text, but rather the living Church actively engaged in the worship of God. Likewise, its final goal is not merely to understand the various dimensions of worship, but in addition to return that understanding to the Church's life and prayer.

Place and Character. Liturgical theology must intersect with other branches of theology, e.g., ecclesiology, Christology, and soteriology, particularly insofar as their own theological truth unfolds in the act of worship. It must examine current and past liturgical texts, as expressions of theological understanding and as texts whose meaning and purpose is to be activated as Christian worship. Liturgical theology must engage many disciplines and many methodologies, but its enduring concrete focus on the living worship of the Church is both its unifying principle and its distinguishing characteristic.

As a branch of theology it is both systematic and pastoral. It is systematic in that it explores the doctrines of faith which liturgy articulates in its own way (*lex orandi est lex credendi*) and examines these doctrines in relation to their other formulations. Liturgical theology also explores fundamental theological questions relating faith to prayer and Revelation to proclamation. It is pastoral because liturgical theology always speaks from and to the Church at prayer. It cannot rest content with the inner logic of a reflective methodology. The truth which unfolds in liturgical theology must finally be validated in the experience of worship itself.

Development. Liturgical theology evolves upon several relationships which hold between faith, the liturgical event, and reflective theology. These can be specified as: faith related to liturgy and liturgy related to theology.

Faith and Liturgy. A dialectic relationship exists between faith and liturgy. Vatican Council II in the Constitution on Sacred Liturgy articulated the dual movement of this dialectic when it affirmed that liturgy expresses faith (movement from faith to liturgy) and, at the same time, instructs or informs faith (movement from liturgy to faith) (*Sacrosanctum Concilium* 59). Liturgical theology must engage both movements of this dialectic.

The first movement is addressed in the attempt to understand the inner contours of the faith experience as it comes to expression in symbolic action. This is a complex hermeneutical task, partially fulfilled by phenomenological description, e.g., describing the inner movement of Eucharistic Prayers and the full significance as commitment and surrender of the people's *Amen*. The task is further advanced by anthropological and psychological studies into the nature and behavior of ritual, and by investigations into the power of language to evoke affections, motivation, and commitment. In short, liturgical theology at this point attempts to determine the conditions under which people successfully enter and engage in liturgical prayer, and the dynamics by which faith seeks ever new modes of liturgical expression.

Liturgical theology likewise seeks to understand the effect liturgy has upon faith. Vatican II gives two directions for this investigation: "In the liturgy the sanctification of the People of God is manifested by signs perceptible to the senses, and is effected in a way which is proper to each of these signs. . ." (ibid. 7). *Sanctification* signals all that God in Christ has done and continues to do *for us*. It embraces liberation from sin, growth in holiness, and a promise of final victory over death. Vatican II affirms that this is not a mysterious, behind-the-scenes activity of God. Rather, it is spoken to human awareness and accomplished in human life in recognizable ways.

Liturgical theology seeks therefore to understand the liturgy as accomplishing this twofold function, viz., to *manifest* and *effect* sanctification. For the first, it attempts to understand the nature of proclamation with deep respect for the mystery of God, the evocative thrust of symbolic language, and the cognitive dimension of human awareness. For the second, it investigates the profound truths of the Christian faith, conscious that not only is the liturgy the place where these truths unfold, but that the inner dynamics of the liturgy reveal the process by which they unfold.

Liturgy and Theology. A similar dialectic relationship exists between liturgy and theology, which liturgical theology likewise investigates. The movement toward theology recognizes the liturgy as a privileged source (*locus theologicus*) for understanding the Church, its sacramental actions, and its fundamental creeds. This line of investigation is perhaps the most developed, and represents the original scope of liturgical theology (*see* LITURGICS). The introductions and texts for the revised rites encourage this kind of investigation, since they embody far more of the Church's rich tradition than the liturgical books they replace.

The converse movement toward the liturgy involves the return of theological insight to the Church at prayer. Reflective theology brings forth explanation which, by the very fact that the liturgy continues to be celebrated in the Church, must likewise take on the nature of promise. The truth of theology must be sought in worship, and its function to give faith something to look for in worship needs to be understood well. Theology's return to worship is the final task of liturgical theology.

Bibliography: A. KAVANAGH, *On Liturgical Theology* (Collegeville, Minn. 1992). K. W. IRWIN, *Context and Text: Method in Liturgical Theology* (Collegeville, Minn. 1994). P. F. BRADSHAW, ed., "Liturgical Theology" *Studia liturgica* 30 no. 1 (2000) [entire issue devoted to the papers on "Liturgical Theology" presented at 17th Congress of Societas Liturgica, Kottayam, India, 19–24 August 1999].

[P. E. FINK/EDS.]

LITURGICAL VESSELS

Containers used in liturgical worship. Most of them originated from practical utensils that, because of their use in the liturgy, came to be set apart from non-liturgical use by blessings or consecrations, and were often elaborated artistically. The most important liturgical vessels are the CHALICE AND PATEN, which contain the Eucharistic elements both before and after Consecration at Mass; the CIBORIUM, to contain the consecrated hosts intended for distribution in Communion; the MONSTRANCE, which enables the faithful to venerate Blessed Sacrament at Exposition, Benediction, or during processions; and the PYX, used for taking Communion to the sick. Cruets are vessels used to carry wine and water to the altar. The censer or thurible is used to contain burning incense at high Masses, at Vespers, Benediction, and other services. At first censers were mere pots fitted with perforated lids, but by the 4th century some were made of metal and suspended on chains so that they could be carried in procession and swung.

Bibliography: J. BRAUN, *Das christliche Altargerät* (Munich 1932). R. AIGRAIN, "Les vases sacrés." *Liturgia* (Paris 1930) 261–299, *passim.*

[C. W. HOWELL/A. D. FITZGERALD/EDS.]

LITURGICAL VESTMENTS

In early centuries of Christianity the dress the clergy used for liturgical functions was the same as the ordinary clothes worn by the laity. It was the attire of Greco–Roman civilization: the tunic, an undergarment fastened at the neck and tied with a belt at the waist, and the mantle, an outer garment wrapped around the body. Even in the 4th century, though clerical liturgical vesture was frequently made of better material and in a more refined cut, it actually varied little from ordinary clothing. During the barbarian invasion there came a change in fashion, but the clergy kept to the old style. With the growing difference in costume, liturgical vesture acquired a symbolic value in much the same way that some modern secular modes of dress have become a sign of a particular profession.

In the Middle Ages vestments gradually became more ornate and colorful with the introduction of brocades. These splendid fabrics tended to be so heavy and unyielding that it became necessary to reduce the cut of the outer vestments in order to allow for freedom of movement. This had its disadvantages, however, for abbreviated garments looked less like clothing and deprived the priest of a very important means of setting off his central role in the sacred action. In the 19th century a movement to restore the ample cut was started for purely aesthetic reasons. Whereas at first (1863, 1925) the Congregation of Rites showed little favor to vestments not in current use at Rome, in a decree of 1957 it left the matter to the judgment of ordinaries.

For more information on specific liturgical vestments, *see* AMICE, ALB, STOLE, CHASUBLE, MANIPLE, COPE AND HUMERAL VEIL, DALMATIC, BIRETTA, and SURPLICE.

Bibliography: J. BRAUN, *Die liturgische Gewandung im Occident und Orient* (Freiburg 1907); *Die liturgischen Paramente in Gegenwart und Vergangenheit* (2d ed. Freiburg 1924). E. A. ROULIN, *Vestments and Vesture*, tr. J. MCCANN (Westminster, Md. 1950). R. LESAGE, *Vestments and Church Furniture*, tr. F. MURPHY (New York 1960). E. HAULOTTE, *Symbolique du vêtement selon la Bible* (Paris 1966). C. E. POCKNEE, *Liturgical Vesture: Its Origins and Development* (Westminister, Md. 1961).

[M. MCCANCE/A. D. FITZGERALD/EDS.]

LITURGICAL YEAR IN ROMAN RITE

The liturgical year consists of the series of feasts and seasons celebrated by the Church. It begins at First Vespers of the first Sunday of Advent and ends on the Saturday before the First Vespers of that Sunday. It is inserted into the civil solar year without depending on it, for its principal date, that of Easter, is calculated according to the lunar calendar. Easter is the Sunday after the full moon of the Jewish month (Nisan) after the vernal equinox.

Theology

By means of her liturgical year the Church seeks to redeem time and make it serve humanity's quest for union with God. A feast day, the opposite of an ordinary day, was from the very beginning a holy, sanctified day, a special day intended to focus the attention of the faithful on Christ and the mystery of His salvation so that they can live in accordance with His spirit. The celebration of the liturgical year revolves about the person of Jesus Christ and the paschal mystery of his suffering, death and resurrection. The celebration of Marian feast days and the memorial of the saints and martyrs do not detract from this principal focus of the Church's liturgical year in Christ and the mystery of salvation.

Vatican II's Constitution on the Sacred Liturgy explains the relationship of the liturgical cult of Mary and the Saints to Christ in the liturgical year in the following manner: "In celebrating this annual cycle of Christ's mysteries, holy Church honors with special love the Blessed Mary, Mother of God . . . in whom the Church holds up and admires the most excellent fruit of redemption, and joyfully contemplates, as in a faultless image, what she herself desires and hopes wholly to be. The Church has also included in the annual cycle the memory of the martyrs and other saints. . . . By celebrating the heavenly birthdays of these saints the Church proclaims the paschal mystery achieved in the saints who have suffered and been glorified with Christ. She proposes them to the faithful as examples drawing all to the Father through Christ, and through their merits she pleads for God's favors" (*ibid.* 103, 104).

General Development

In the concrete unfolding of its annual commemorations the liturgical year is identified with the calendar containing the feasts of our Lord (temporal cycle) and of the saints (sanctoral cycle).

Origin of the Calendar. In the beginning the calendar of saints had a strictly local character; it was a catalogue of anniversaries celebrated in a given church or diocese. By means of mutual borrowings of one calendar from another, general calendars arose, thus preparing the way for the 1568 universal calendar of Pius V. Over the centuries saints' feasts were unduly multiplied. Pius V had purged many feasts of saints, retaining only 87 in the Tridentine liturgical calendar, but beginning with Clement VIII (d. 1605) there was an uninterrupted increase of saints' feasts. Despite the recommendations of Vatican Council I, the universal calendar at the beginning of the 20th century listed 266 feasts. In his bull *Divino afflatu* of 1911, Pius X, without touching the content of the calendar, gave precedence to the temporal cycle. Nonetheless, new feasts were added so that in 1955 there were 338. The decree of March 23, 1955, resulted in somewhat of a reduction: 39 semidoubles became simples, while all simples became commemorations, and the number of octaves were cut. The 1969 reform of the Roman Calendar under the mandate of Vatican II pruned the number of feasts from 338 to a more manageable 191.

Classification of Feasts. A whole hierarchy of feasts was gradually elaborated as their number increased. In the first place a distinction is made between feasts of Our Lord and those of the saints (the Blessed Virgin included, *see* MARIAN FEASTS). The dedication of a church is classified as a feast of the Lord; several saints' feasts, however, were introduced on the occasion of the dedication of a church (e.g., St. Michael, Our Lady of the Snows, and SS. John and Paul) and were subsequently regarded as belonging to the category of saints' feasts.

Normally, feasts celebrate the anniversary of an event: an historical mystery of Our Lord or Lady, the dedication of a church, and the earthly birth of only three persons, Christ, Mary, and John the Baptist. For other saints the Church commemorates the anniversary of their death, called ''birthday'' into heaven, sometimes their ''exaltation,'' or the official recognition of their title to veneration, and even occasionally the finding and transfer of their relics.

In the course of centuries idea-feasts have also been introduced. Although once very numerous, only a few remain in the universal calendar: Holy Trinity, Sacred Heart, Corpus et Sanguinis Christi, and Christ the King.

Some feasts are observed on the same day each year; other feasts are movable, as a result of their computation based on the lunar cycle. Among the latter are Easter and feasts that are related to its cycle. Current canonical provisions permit local bishops' conferences, with the approval of the Holy See, to transfer certain solemnities and days of obligations to a Sunday.

Until 1960 feasts were classified as doubles of the first class, doubles of the second class, major and minor doubles, semidoubles, simples, and commemorations. The 1960 reform of liturgical rubrics simplified this system considerably to categories of first, second, third, and fourth class, and commemoration. The 1969 reforms of the Roman Calendar further simplified the system to categories of solemnities, feasts, obligatory memorials and optional memorials.

In a reform promulgated in 1955 the number of octaves—festal celebrations prolonged for eight days—was reduced to three: Easter, Pentecost, and Christmas. Formerly there were 18 in the universal calendar—without counting those in particular calendars—and they were classified in a very complicated fashion. The 1969 reform of the Roman Calendar further reduced the number of octaves to two: Easter and Christmas, the two principal solemnities of our Lord.

Temporal Cycle

The liturgical year actually comprises two principal parts or cycles, the temporal and the sanctoral. Although these two cycles are parallel and intertwined, the temporal, because of its Christological foundations and focus, always takes precedence over the sanctoral.

Over and above the feasts honoring the historical events of redemption and other feasts of Our Lord, this cycle comprises all the Sundays of the year and certain weekday observances.

The Week. Among Christians SUNDAY is nothing else but a weekly celebration of the paschal mystery, that central event of salvation history that marked off for good the first day of the week. Eight days after Christ's Resurrection the apostles assembled to recall the event, and the Jerusalem community remained faithful to this weekly observance. In the beginning Christians participated in the Jewish Sabbath service and had their Eucharistic assembly on Sunday. But toward the end of the 1st century they made the Jewish element a part of the one Sunday observance.

Following the Hebrew idea of sanctifying weeks, the Church designated the days of the week simply by numbers, Sunday being the first day. In reaction to the pagan practice, Christians called them *feriae*. But it is only in the liturgy that this term was preserved; in everyday life names of pagan origin held sway.

Two weekdays stood out in Christian observance, i.e., Wednesday and Friday. At the end of the 1st century the Didache reported them as fast days; in the following century they were also days of prayer. It was thus that Christian antiquity universally observed them. Friday is just as venerable a Christian institution as Sunday; from the very beginning it bore a penitential character recalling the Savior's death. In the West, however, fasting on these two days began to give way between the 6th and 10th centuries. The fasts on Wednesday and Friday of Ember weeks alone remained, but even in this case the fast was mitigated. (*See* EMBER DAYS; FAST AND ABSTINENCE.) They were also days of prayer; at first the prayer was private, but soon it was held in common and enjoyed a variety of forms according to time and place. In most places these liturgical stations (*see* STATIONAL CHURCH) were held without the celebration of Mass; Mass was allowed on these two days in the West beginning only with the 6th century.

The attitudes of the churches toward Saturday were quite divergent. Some areas, out of aversion for Jewish practices, allowed no religious observance at all; others—at least in the West—from the 3d century on made it a fast day in commemoration of the Holy Saturday fast. Beginning with the 10th century there spread in the West the custom of honoring the Mother of God in a special way on Saturday. The votive Mass of the Blessed Virgin for Saturdays was inserted in the Carolingian Sacramentaries. In the 12th century it was to be found in the Missal of the Lateran, and the devotion was definitively approved by Pius V.

Paschal Cycle. The most important celebration of the Liturgical Year is that of Easter. (*See* EASTER AND ITS CYCLE.) In the beginning, Christians commemorated the death and Resurrection of Christ every Sunday, but in the 2d century they began to celebrate this central mystery of redemption on its anniversary. Since the 3d century its celebration has lasted for 50 days, the final day of which, Pentecost, enjoys a solemnity on a par with Easter. Very soon a fast went before and coincided with the observance of Christ's Passion and death. The duration of the fast was lengthened, and thus arose the period of preparation.

Triduum. Originally Thursday of HOLY WEEK was not regarded as part of the Sacred Triduum (three-day observance); only Friday, Saturday, and Sunday were included in this term. The term "Pasch" also has changed meaning; it was not restricted to Easter Sunday. In the first three centuries *Pascha* designated the annual commemoration of the Passion and death of Christ, in the 4th century the EASTER VIGIL too, and in the 5th century, only Easter Sunday. According to A. Baumstark there were

two primitive conceptions of Easter: the Pasch of the cross and the Pasch of the Resurrection (*Comparative Liturgy,* tr. F. L. Cross [London 1958] 168–174; see B. Botte's critique of this in "Pascha," *L'Orient syrien* 8 [1963] 213–226). As O. Casel has shown ("Art und Sinn der ältesten christlichen Osterfeier," *Jahrbuch für Liturgiewissenschaft* 14 [1938] 1–78), Easter was an indivisible feast of the events of salvation; it celebrated the Redemption achieved by both the Passion and the Resurrection. In the course of the centuries the ceremonies of the Easter Vigil were removed from the night of Holy Saturday, and it was then that Thursday came to be regarded as part of the Triduum. This led people to see only the death of Christ in the Triduum and thus to dissociate His death and Resurrection, two aspects of the unique salvific mystery.

Easter Vigil. Until 1951 the rites of the Easter Vigil had been anticipated on Saturday morning. Returned to the night time, they regained their true significance. The two essential parts of the celebration are baptism, by which all peoples are initiated into Christ's Church and the mystery of Christ's dying and rising is realized in them, and the Eucharist, the living memorial of this death and Resurrection. The other ceremonies—the blessing of the new fire, paschal candle and Exsultet, the readings, blessing of baptismal water, the Christian initiation of catechumens and the profession of faith—revolve about these two pivotal points.

Good Friday. The Passion is more specifically stressed in the GOOD FRIDAY celebration. To the elements peculiar to the ancient aliturgical synaxis (the readings and prayer of the faithful) are added the Veneration of the Cross and the Communion service.

Holy Thursday. Holy Thursday was the last day of the 40-day fast, later the first day of the Easter Triduum. The restored rite of 1955, combining elements of both the ancient papal liturgy and the Roman parish liturgy of the 7th-8th centuries, comprises a Mass for the consecration of holy oils and an evening Mass with the *Mandatum,* or washing of feet, and a Eucharistic procession.

Palm Sunday. Eight days before Easter the Church begins Holy Week with a celebration of PALM SUNDAY. In 1955 the special ceremonies of this day too were simplified in order to bring out more pointedly the Messianic theme of Christ bringing victory and life out of defeat and death and to thus set the stage for the dramatic unfolding of the events of Redemption.

Preparation for Easter. In order to take part in the Easter celebration more worthily, the early Christians observed an especially rigorous fast during the Sacred Triduum. Later this fast was gradually extended to three weeks, to the 40 days of LENT (at the end of the 4th century), and to seven weeks beginning with Quinquagesima Sunday (at the start of the 6th century). Toward the end of the 6th century Sexagesima week appeared, and at the beginning of the 7th century Septuagesima week. In addition to the Sundays, the weekdays of Lent were gradually fitted out with liturgical celebrations, first the Wednesdays and Fridays, then (in the 5th century) the Mondays, Tuesdays, and Saturdays. From the 6th century on these synaxes included the Eucharistic celebration, but the Thursdays remained aliturgical until the 8th century. From the very beginning this period had a double aspect: baptismal and penitential. The 1969 reforms removed the Sexagesima and Septuagesima weeks, returning the observance of Lent to its ancient pattern beginning with Ash Wednesday.

Paschal Time. The Easter octave existed already in the 4th century; the formularies of this week center around Christ's Resurrection and the faithful's share in it through baptism. Originally paschaltide was a continuous 50-day celebration of the Resurrection (the word "Pentecost" means 50 days). Formularies of this season pursue the general theme of the divine life coming to the human race through Christ. The jubilation of Easter is manifest in the constantly repeated alleluias, the use of white vestments even on ferias, and—in ancient times—the prohibition against kneeling and fasting. This joyful season is brought to a glorious conclusion in celebrations of Christ's ASCENSION and His sending the Holy Spirit on His Church.

Christmas Cycle. The series of feasts whose object is a special commemoration of Christ's infancy and childhood made its appearance rather late under a variety of influences. (*See* CHRISTMAS AND ITS CYCLE.)

Christmas and Epiphany. These are the two Christian feasts of the winter solstice. The celebration of Christmas is of Roman origin and dates from around 330. It had been customary for Roman pagans to gather at Vatican hill to worship deities of the East; the choice of December 25 (*Natalis Invicti*) and St. Peter's Basilica for the celebration of the feast shows that the Church's aim was to oppose a Christian feast to that of the *Sol invictus* (unconquered sun), the symbol of paganism's resistance. The Feast of EPIPHANY, although arising in similar circumstances, was of Eastern origin. It appeared in the West first in Gaul (*c.* 361), then at Rome. By the middle of the 5th century both feasts had been accepted practically everywhere, for they complemented each other, their themes changing slightly in the process. In both East and West the Christmas season came to a close with the Feast of CANDLEMAS.

Advent. The term was one of profane origin, but for the early Christians (as in the Vulgate) it meant the coming of Christ into the human world: His coming in the flesh to inaugurate the Messianic era and His coming in glory to initiate the eschatological age. Advent designated also the same reality as *natalis* (birthday) and *epiphania* (manifestation). Little by little, however, the term came to be applied to the liturgical period preceding Christmas. During the 5th century there evolved in Spain and Gaul an ascetical preparation for the feast. At Rome Advent made its appearance in the second half of the 6th century as a liturgical institution from the first, and went from six to four weeks. Although it was intended from the start as preparation for Christmas, Advent did not appear as the beginning of the year in liturgical books until the 8th-9th centuries. Today, although it is intended as a joyous preparation for the feast of the Lord's birth, Advent naturally turns the thoughts of Christians toward His glorious return at the end of the world.

Ordinary Time. The term *tempus per annum* (literally, "time through the year," generally translated as "Ordinary Time," or sometimes as "Ordinal Time") is officially used by the Church to designate the days from the day after the Feast of the Baptism of Our Lord (usually January 13) to Ash Wednesday and from Monday after Trinity Sunday to the Saturday before the First Sunday of Advent. Thematically, however, the Sundays after Epiphany really belong to the Christmas cycle. The same cannot be said of the Sundays after Pentecost; the history of the liturgy sufficiently proves that they have no direct link with Pentecost. The system for numbering these Sundays varied from church to church; it was the Carolingian liturgical books of the 9th and 10th centuries that started numbering them as Sundays after Pentecost. Furthermore, the very structure of these Sundays reveals a system of continuous reading of at least the Epistles (*see* PERICOPES). Historically, the ancient processional chants of the Mass are divided into two blocks: those from the 1st to the 17th Sunday are taken from the Psalms according to the order of the Psalter; those from the 18th to the last Sunday are antiphons habitually composed from other books of the Bible. On the other hand, the ancient orations for the 5th to 20th Sundays are borrowings from the older stratum for Sunday Masses in the GELASIAN SACRAMENTARY. Hence one cannot even claim that there is an internal unity that exists the cycle of the post-Pentecost Sundays in Ordinary Time.

Sanctoral Cycle

Alongside the temporal cycle run the feasts of the saints; the series of their anniversaries is called the SANCTORAL CYCLE.

Martyrs. The origin of the cult of martyrs is not to be found in the hero-honor paid heroes and gods in pagan antiquity. Already SS. Jerome (*Contra Vigilantium; Patrologia Latina,* 23:342–343) and Augustine (*Civ.* 22.10; *Corpus Christianorum. Series latina* 48:828) raised their voices against such an interpretation. Early reports show that uppermost in the minds of Christians was the desire to provide a decent burial for the victims of persecution. At least at first the funerals of Christian heroes were not essentially different from those of other deceased Christians; the same is true of the observance of their anniversaries. But after the peace of Constantine, Christian worship underwent a great development, manifested, among other ways, in the celebration of martyrs' feasts. Their names were inscribed on the DIPTYCHS, and the dates of their anniversaries were carefully noted in local calendars.

In the 4th and 5th centuries the veneration of martyrs began to shed its local character as Christian communities began to admire the heroes of other churches. Many factors contributed to this evolution: the diffusion of relics, the panegyrics of great orators of the 4th and 5th centuries, the *Passionaria* of martyrs, the books of their miracles, and pilgrimages. Furthermore, the churches of Gaul, under the influence of Charlemagne, copied the Roman liturgical books and the calendar of saints contained in them.

Confessors and Ascetics. The ancient Church paid a martyr's honors also to those who, even though they had not shed their blood for Christ, had nonetheless suffered torture, imprisonment, or exile for Him; they were called confessors. This broadening of the concept of "martyr" marked the first step in the extension of the cult of saints. From honoring such confessors as martyrs the Church soon went to honoring as confessors first ascetics and then bishops.

When the persecutions were over, generous souls still sought ways and means of attaining to the perfection of charity even though it was no longer possible to shed their blood for the Lord. The Desert Fathers looked upon their isolated and penitential life as a substitute for martyrdom. It is not to be wondered at that upon their death such heroes of asceticism received the same veneration as martyrs.

Virgins and Holy Women. Consecrated virginity is a superior form of asceticism. Hence very early the faithful venerated a number of holy nuns. Widowhood, when spent in the service of the Church, is also a form of asceticism that merits to be honored as martyrdom. For a long time, however, virgins and holy women received the Church's official honors only because they were martyrs, e.g., the two Felicitys, Perpetua, Agnes, Agatha, and Lucy. Others were inserted in the calendar with the title of martyr thanks to legend; still others, as foundresses of

Roman titular churches, came to be thought in time as having suffered martyrdom, e.g., Pudentiana, Praxedes, Sabina, and Cecilia.

Bishops. The great bishops of the first centuries often crowned their episcopal administration by means of martyrdom. Others were ranked among the confessors of the faith because they either suffered torture, undertook their grave responsibilities in time of full persecution, or engaged in heavy, demanding missionary endeavors. St. Gregory the Wonder Worker (d. 270) was the first bishop not a martyr to receive the honors of cult. Other bishops, e.g., SS. Basil, Martin, and Paulinus, attracted the veneration of the crowds mainly because of their monastic activity. Alongside the calendar containing the anniversaries of martyrs, each church kept a distinct list of bishops' anniversaries for celebration. Practically speaking, the difference between these two types of anniversary must have been rather vague, since the title of saint had not yet been clearly determined, and the liturgical formularies were still improvised.

Marian Feasts. Although devotion to Mary began very early, there is no evidence of a feast in her honor until the middle of the 5th century. This is perhaps because liturgical veneration of the saints was always in connection with their tomb; Mary had none.

The octave day of Christmas seems to have been the first feast of Our Lady in the Roman rite, commemorating the Feast of Mary, Mother of God. Although suppressed in the Middle Ages, the feast was restored in the 1969 reform of the Roman Calendar. The emperor Maurice (d. 602) made the Feast of the Assumption obligatory. Pope Sergius I (d. 701) made the Feast of Mary's Nativity one of the four calling for a stational procession.

Marian feasts became increasingly numerous in the course of the centuries. In fact, one even spoke of the "liturgical year of Mary." Idea-feasts became more numerous in honor of Mary than in honor of the Lord, especially in the last few centuries. Many of these feasts were reduced to optional memorials in the 1969 reform of the Roman Calendar.

Vatican II's Reform of the Roman Calendar. *Mysterii paschalis,* the title of the accompanying *motu proprio* of Paul VI, well described the general thrust of the revised Roman Calendar published by decree of the Congregation of Rites on March 21, 1969. In accordance with the terms of reference given in chapter 5 of the *Constitution on the Sacred Liturgy,* the feasts of the Lord that commemorate the mysteries of salvation are given preference over the feasts of the saints. In order that the Proper of the time may truly take precedence, the number of saints' feast days for the universal Church has been sharply reduced. The *Calendarium Romanum* consists of General Norms for the Liturgical Year and the Calendar and the General Roman Calendar, both of which correspond to the revised Roman Missal in which they are reprinted and to the revised Liturgy of the Hours. An unofficial commentary prepared by the Consilium and two simplified forms for the Litany of the Saints are also included in the *editio typica* of the Roman Calendar.

Proper of the Time (Temporal Cycle). The weekly observance of the paschal mystery occurs every Sunday, the first day of the week, the Lord's day, "the original feast day" commemorating Christ's Resurrection. Because of its primordial significance, the celebration of Sunday is replaced only by solemnities and feasts of the Lord, and not even these during the seasons of Advent, Lent, and Easter. Although the liturgical day normally extends from midnight to midnight, the Church following biblical usage observes Sundays and solemnities beginning with the evening of the preceding day: an observance that explains the rationale behind First Vespers and the anticipated Sunday Mass on Saturday evening.

Paschal Cycle. What Sunday is to the week, the solemnity of Easter is to the liturgical year. So that the faithful may properly appreciate the Easter triduum not simply as a preparation for Easter Sunday, but as a unit commemorating in Augustine's words the *sacratissimum triduum crucifixi, sepulti et suscitati*—the total paschal mystery of Christ's Passion and Resurrection, the Easter triduum begins with the evening Mass of the Lord's Supper on Holy Thursday, reaches its high point in the Easter Vigil, and closes with Vespers on Easter Sunday.

The original meaning of the Easter season has been restored: 50 days between Easter Sunday and Pentecost celebrated as one feast day, sometimes called "the great Sunday." The Sundays of this season are reckoned as Sundays of Easter and following the Sunday of the Resurrection are appropriately called the Second, Third, Fourth, etc., Sundays of Easter. In order that Pentecost Sunday might recover its pristine importance as the culmination of the Spirit-filled Easter season, and not specifically the anniversary of the coming of the Holy Spirit upon the apostles, the Octave of Pentecost as well as the celebration of the Vigil of Pentecost on the preceding Saturday morning have been suppressed.

The season of Lent, the 40 days beginning with Ash Wednesday, has been underscored as a time of preparation for Easter with its ancient twin motif of baptismal preparation/recommitment and penitential conversion. To this end the superfluous Septuagesima season and misleading period of Passiontide have been deleted.

Christmas Cycle. Second only to the annual celebration of the Easter mystery is the Christmas season, which celebrates the birth of the Lord and his early manifestations and extends from First Vespers of Christmas until Sunday after the Epiphany or after January 6 inclusive. The Feast of the Holy Family is now celebrated on the Sunday within the Octave of Christmas. The most ancient of Roman Marian feasts, the solemnity of Mary, Mother of God, has been restored as the content of the celebration on January 1, the octave day of Christmas. The Epiphany, January 6, where not a holy day of obligation, is assigned to the Sunday between January 2 and 8. Sunday after January 6 is the Feast of the Baptism of the Lord. The Feast of the Most Holy Name of Jesus, of comparatively recent origin, has been dropped.

The season of Advent is no longer so much a penitential season as one of expectation: a reminder of Christ's second coming at the end of time (from the First Sunday of Advent to December 16) and more immediately a preparation for the memorial of the first coming at Christmas (December 17 to 24).

Season of the Year. In addition to the seasons of Easter, Lent, Christmas, and Advent, the other 33 or 34 weeks of the year celebrate no particular aspect of the mystery of Christ, but rather this mystery in its fullness, especially on Sundays. These Sundays and weeks numbered consecutively constitute the season of the year and thus replace the earlier clumsy arrangement of time after Epiphany and time after Pentecost. The Feast of Christ the King has been assigned to the last Sunday of the Church year. The Rogation and Ember Days have been left to local custom to be determined by the conferences of bishops.

Proper of the Saints (Sanctoral Cycle). Because of the priority given to the temporal cycle and to the feasts of the Lord, there is a considerable reduction in saints' feast days and a simplification of their categories. In addition to the movable solemnities (Trinity Sunday, Corpus Christi, Sacred Heart, Christ the King), there are only 10 "solemnities" corresponding to the earlier feasts of class 1. There are 23 "feasts" corresponding to the earlier feasts of class 2, and 63 "obligatory memorials" or feasts of class 3. The category of "optimal memorials," some 95 in number, round out the reclassification.

Five principles were involved in revising the sanctoral cycle: the curtailment of feasts of devotion or "idea-feasts" that celebrate no particular mystery of salvation; a critical examination of the historicity of the saints; the selection of saints of greater importance; the recognition, wherever possible, of the anniversary day of death or martyrdom; and a more universal or catholic approach to the calendar so as to include saints from all peoples and ages.

National episcopal conferences are to draw up particular calendars that may include local celebrations and "memorials" of local saints, as has been done in this country since 1972 with the inclusion of memorials of Bl. Elizabeth Ann Seton (January 4), Bl. John Neumann (January 5), St. Isidore (May 15), St. Peter Claver (September 9), St. Isaac Jogues and companions (October 19), St. Frances Xavier Cabrini (November 13), and Our Lady of Guadalupe (December 12).

There are also votive masses provided for the civic observances of Independence Day (July 4) and Thanksgiving Day.

Bibliography: *Calendarium Romanum* (Typis Polyglottis Vaticanis 1969). J. DUBOIS, "Les saints du nouveau calendrier: Tradition et critique historique," *Maison-Dieu* 100 (1969) 157–178. P. JOUNEL, "L'organisation de l'année liturgique," *Maison-Dieu* 100 (1969) 139–156. T. J. TALLEY, *The Origins of the Liturgical Year* (Collegeville, Minn. 1991). A. G. MARTIMORT, ed. *The Church at Prayer IV: The Liturgy and Time* (Collegeville, Minn. 1986). A. NOCENT, *The Liturgical Year*, 4 v. (Collegeville, Minn. 1977) J. M. PIERCE, "Holy Week and Easter in the Middle Ages," in *Passover and Easter: Origin and History to Modern Times,* eds. P. F. BRADSHAW and L. A. HOFFMAN (Notre Dame, Ind. 1999) 161–185. A. ADAM, *The Liturgical Year: Its History & Its Meaning after the Reform of the Liturgy* (New York 1981).

[R. VAN DOREN/C. W. GUSMER/EDS.]

LITURGICS

The scientific study of the liturgical rites and ceremonies of Christians and Jews. This field, sometimes called liturgical studies, is comprised of the historical, theological, and pastoral study of public worship activity. Although a great deal of work has been done since the Reformation in the recovery and publication of liturgical sources, liturgics has been a scientific field of research only in the past century or so. The liturgical reform of the Second Vatican Council was itself largely a product of liturgical investigation and in turn spurred further scientific advances both in the Roman Catholic and in other churches. In addition, the Jewish background of Christian worship has been the focus of renewed interest among both Jewish and Christian scholars. Finally, since the council much attention has been paid to the relation between liturgy and theology as well as liturgy and the arts and ritual studies in the social sciences. This last topic as well as the interest in social history has been the most significant advance in liturgics in the past 25 years. Not only the texts but the contexts of worship have been the increasing focus of serious scholars.

Comparative Liturgy. One of the most fruitful paths of liturgics has been the comparative study approach, first inspired by Anton BAUMSTARK (d. 1948).

The study of Catholic worship has been increasingly enriched by scholars plumbing the depths of other liturgical traditions and especially by those who have discerned connections in the historical development of the various liturgical families.

Jewish Liturgy. The Jewish roots of Christian worship have been an important source of liturgical study since the beginning of the 20th century, especially in the contributions of F. Gavin, W. E. Oesterly, G. DIX, C. W. Dugmore, and L. Finkelstein. During the late 20th century Jewish liturgical study was advanced by the ground breaking study of the development of Jewish prayer forms, significant for the development of the eucharistic prayer, by J. Heinemann [*Prayer in the Talmud* (New York 1977)]. Also important for comparative studies is the work of L. A. Hoffman in early and medieval Jewish liturgical worship.

Eastern Liturgy. Baumstark's own comparative work focused on the relations between the Christian liturgical traditions of East and West. His method was advanced in particular by the "school" centering on Juan Mateos of Rome's Pontifical Oriental Institute [M. Arranz, W. Macomber, G. Winkler, and especially R. F. Taft, whose *Beyond East and West: Problems in Liturgical Understanding* (rev. ed. Rome 1997) deals above all with methodology]. The comparative study of eastern and western liturgy was also advanced by I. H. Dalmais, H. J. Schulz [*The Byzantine Liturgy* (2nd ed. New York 1986)] and the publication of the annual conferences of the Saint Sergius Institute in Paris (published as *Ephemerides Liturgicae Subsidia* in Rome). Finally a major aid in the study of the liturgical theology of the Byzantine Church is René Bornert's *Les commentaires byzantins de la divine liturgie* (Paris 1966).

Anglican and Protestant Liturgy. The Second Vatican Council's liturgical reform not only inspired practical liturgical renewal in the Anglican and Protestant churches but also encouraged the further development of liturgics among scholars of those traditions. Names like W. H. Frere, G. Dix, and F. E. Brightman, all early-20th-century scholars, show that this is not a new field for Anglican scholars. Building upon these early scholars were G. J. Cuming, R. C. D. Jasper, and P. Bradshaw in England, and Massey Shepherd, M. Hatchett, L. L. Mitchell, and Louis Weil in the United States who produced important critical studies on Anglican liturgical rites.

On the strictly Protestant side scientific liturgical studies also advanced. Significant here was the publication of the Lutheran *Jahrbuch für Liturgik und Hymnologie* (Kassel, since 1955). In addition a valuable handbook of the liturgy from the point of view of the Lutheran tradition was published as *Leitourgia* in five volumes (Kassel

1954–70). For the English churches an invaluable tool is H. Davies five-volume work, *Worship and Theology in England* (Princeton 1961–75) which treats music, architecture, preaching, worship, and theology in all of the Catholic and Protestant traditions represented there from the Reformation to the mid-20th century. The origins of the Reformed (Calvinist) tradition of worship have long been in need of scientific study. H. O. Old began this task in *The Patristic Roots of Reformed Worship* (Zurich 1975). An important contextual study of Protestant liturgy in one of the Reformation cities was provided by R. Bornert, *La réforme protestante du culte à Strasbourg au xvi siècle (1523–1598)* (Leiden 1981). A little studied field of investigation, the Free Church tradition of worship, was opened up by D. Adams, *From Meeting House to Camp Meeting* (Austin, TX 1979). Increasing ecumenical collaboration between liturgical scholars bore remarkable fruit, with important comparative studies produced by G. Lathrop, F. Senn, S. A. Stauffer, M. Johnson, B. Spinks and J. White.

The Eucharist. Since the beginning of the 20th century, a great deal of attention has been paid to research on the origins and development of the anaphora or eucharistic prayer. The pathbreaking research of J. P. Audet, T. J. Talley, and L. Ligier paved the way for a better understanding of the *berakah* (blessing) form of Jewish prayer, especially the *birkat-ha-mazon* (grace after meals) in relation to the primitive forms of the Eucharistic Prayer. This Jewish form provided the basis for the extended argument of L. Bouyer [*Eucharist* (Notre Dame 1968)] as well as the study of the lexical problems involved in the relation between Hebrew and Greek euchological vocabulary by R. Ledogar [*Acknowledgement: Praise Verbs in the Early Greek Anaphoras* (Rome 1968)]. A significant challenge to understanding the origin of the Eucharistic Prayer solely in terms of the *berakah* was raised by the investigation of an Israelite covenant/thanksgiving formula (*todah*) by C. Giraudo in his *La struttura letteraria della preghiera eucaristica* (Rome 1981). Further studies in the anaphoral developments of the early Church were undertaken by J. Fenwick, A. Tarby, B. Spinks, E. J. Kilmartin, and A. Gerhards [*Die griechische Gregoriosanaphora* (Münster 1984)]. An important study by A. Bouley, *From Freedom to Formula* (Washington, D.C. 1981), deals with the question of the improvisational character of the primitive eucharistic prayers. Other important studies on the eucharistic prayers were carried out by E. Mazza and P. Bradshaw.

The study of the Eucharistic Prayer was also aided significantly by the publication of a number of prayer collections. The most valuable was A. Hänggi and I. Pahl, *Prex Eucharistica* (Fribourg 1968), comprising the classic prayers of the eastern and western traditions. Another

volume, *Coena Domini* (Fribourg 1983), edited by I. Pahl, carried this project through the prayers of the reformation churches. An English translation and introduction to a number of the Eucharistic Prayers appears in R. C. D. Jasper and G. J. Cuming, *Prayers of the Eucharist: Early and Reformed* (3rd ed. New York 1987).

In terms of the liturgical books, the edition of the Roman sacramentaries begun by L. C. Mohlberg was complemented by the magisterial critical edition of the Gregorian sacramentaries by J. Deshusses [*Le sacramentaire grégorien*, 3 v. (Fribourg 1971–82)]. The same scholar together with B. Darragon produced a valuable concordance for the major sacramentaries in six volumes (Fribourg 1982–83). The study of the Milanese or Ambrosian tradition was aided by the edition of a number of its representative sacramentaries, e.g., O. Heiming's *Sacramentarium triplex* (Münster 1964). Work on the Mozarabic rite was furthered by J. Pinell's edition of the *Liber missarum de Toledo* (Toledo 1983). The important 8th century Gelasian sacramentaries were represented by the long-awaited edition of the Gellone Sacramentary by A. Dumas and J. Deshusses [*Liber sacramentarum Gellonesis*, 2 v. (Turnhout 1981)]. The vital Romano-Germanic Pontifical, responsible for the reintroduction of the mixed Roman-Frankish liturgical tradition to Rome in the 10th century, was edited by C. Vogel and R. Elze [*Le Pontifical Romano-Germanique du dixième siècle*, 3 v. (Vatican City 1963–72)]. This represents an important addition to the work of M. ANDRIEU on the medieval pontificals. Another complement to that research was provided by S. J. P. van Dijk and J. H. Walker in *The Ordinal of the Papal Court from Innocent III to Boniface VIII, and Related Documents* (Fribourg 1975) and their *Origins of the Modern Roman Rite* (New York 1960).

Finally, a number of scholars furthered the understanding of the historical development of the eucharistic liturgy. Notable are G. Kretschmar ["Abendmahl" and "Abendmahlsfeier," *Theologische Rëal-Encyclopädie I* (Berlin 1977) 59–89, 229–278)] and E. Cattaneo [*Il culto cristiano in occidente* (Rome 1978)]. Various aspects of the Eucharist were investigated as well, for example by P. DeClerck on the prayers of the faithful [*La prière universelle dans les liturgies des églises latines anciennes* (Münster 1977)], by A. Häussling on the relation between monastery and eucharistic celebration in the early Middle Ages [*Mönchskonvent und Eucharistiefeier* (Münster 1973)], by G. G. Willis on various aspects of the ancient Roman eucharist [*Essays in Early Roman Liturgy* (London 1964) and *Further Essays in Early Roman Liturgy* (London 1968)], by K. Stevenson on the sacrificial aspects of the Eucharistic Prayer [*Eucharist and Offering* (New York 1986)], as well as numerous works by the German scholar K. Gamber. Investigation of the Byzantine tradition of the Eucharist was brought to an extremely sophisticated level by J. Mateos [*La célébration de la parole dans la liturgie byzantine* (Rome 1971)], R. Taft [*The Great Entrance* (Rome 1975)], F. van de Paverd [*Zur Geschichte der Messliturgie in Antiocheia und Konstantinopel gegen Ende des vierten Jahrhunderts* (Rome 1970)], and G. Wagner [*Der Ursprung des Chrystomus liturgie* (Münster 1973)]. The manuscript tradition of the liturgy of St. John Chrysostom has been definitively studied by A. Jacob [*Histoire du formulaire grec de la liturgie de S. Jean Chrysostome* (Louvain 1968)].

Initiation. One of the most effective reforms of the Second Vatican Council was the restoration of the catechumenate and the promotion of the *Rite of Christian Initiation for Adults*. This reform was itself based on the important historical research of the century preceding the council and in turn engendered much further research and theological reflection. The historical texts of Christian initiation were collected and edited by E. C. Whitaker [*Documents of the Baptismal Liturgy* (2nd ed. London 1970)]. The classic mystagogical catecheses of the 4th century were translated by E. Yarnold in *The Awe-Inspiring Rites of Initiation*. In addition, the baptismal homilies of John Chrysostom were made available in P. W. Harkins' *St. John Chrysostom: Baptismal Instructions* (New York 1963). A thorough study of the classic mystagogical homilies can be found in H. Riley's *Christian Initiation* (Washington, DC 1974). Several studies in the Medieval and Reformation texts and practice of Christian initiation were done by J. D. C. Fisher, with an up-date by P. Jagger.

A classic book-length presentation of the various rites of initiation in the early Church were provided by G. Kretschmar in *Leitourgia*, v. 5. One of the more important findings of historical research on initiation in the primitive Church were the discovery of traditions that emphasize the royal anointing and Jordan-event motifs of initiation as opposed to the Pauline and paschal aspects, which so clearly dominate the current western rites. Noteworthy here are the contributions of S. Brock on the Syrian baptismal ordines and especially G. Winkler [*Das armenische Initiationsrituale* (Rome 1982)]. Much of this material was ably summarized by A. Kavanagh and M. Johnson in their studies on the history and practice of the initiation of adults.

Confirmation continued to be the object of both research and perplexity. One of the most important historical studies in this regard was L. A. Van Buchem's *L'Homélie Pseudo-Eusebienne de Pentecôte* (Nijmegen 1967) which deals with the crucial homily of Faustus of Riez and its dissemination in early medieval Gaul. Other important contributions were made by L. L. Mitchell, L. Ligier, J. Ysebaert, P. Turner, and G. Winkler.

Increasing attention was paid after the 1960s to the liturgical development of the various sacraments on the principle that theological development goes hand in hand with ritual history. In the field of research on Penance, a major contribution to historical understanding was made with the publication of C. Vogel's two works of text and commentary *Le pécheur et la pénitence dans l'église ancienne* (Paris 1966) and *Le pécheur et la pénitence au Moyen-Age* (Paris 1969). The Rites of Ordination was the focus of a number of liturgical scholars participating in the 1979 congress of the international Societas Liturgica [W. Vos and G. Wainwright, eds., *Ordination Rites* (Rotterdam 1980)]. A thorough study of the rites of Christian Marriage was undertaken by K. Stevenson [*Nuptial Blessing* (London 1982)]. The rites of anointing, radically transformed by the conciliar reform, was studied by two American scholars, C. Gusmer and J. Empereur. Finally, an extended historical study of the western history of Christian burial rites was published by D. Sicard [*La liturgie de la mort dans l'église latine des origines à la réforme carolingienne* (Münster 1978)].

The Liturgy and Time. Two of the most fruitful areas of scientific liturgical research in the 20th century were the liturgical year and the liturgy of the hours. The question of the origin of the Christian observance of Sunday was hotly debated by W. Rordorf [*Sunday* (Philadelphia 1968)] and C. Mosna [*Storia della domenica dagli origini fino al inizi del quinto secolo* (Rome 1977)]. A radically new theory of the origins of the liturgical year that challenged G. Dix's historicization hypothesis was proposed by T. J. Talley (*The Origins of the Liturgical Year.*) Studies in the sources of the liturgical year have also been aided by the publication of the following: a newly discovered Easter Homily of Origen [P. Nautin, ed., *Origène: Peri Pascha* (Paris 1979)], a new manuscript of the early-5th-century Armenian lectionary, which details the Jerusalem services [A. Renoux, ed. *Patrologia Orientalis*, v. 35–36 (Turnhout 1969–71)], the Easter homilies of the 4th-century Cappadocian Asterios Sophistes [H. J. Auf Der Maur, *Die Osterhomilen des Asterios Sophistes* (Trier 1967)], a new translation and edition of the pilgrimage diary of Egeria by J. Wilkinson in *Egeria's Travels*, and especially helpful for understanding the liturgical year in Constantinople, the *ordo* (*typikon*) of Hagia Sophia in the 10th century [J. Mateos, ed., *Le typicon de la grande église,* 2 v. (Rome 1962–63)]. R. Cantalamessa, W. Rordorf, and A. Strobel provided collections of texts that deal respectively with the early Pascha, Sunday, and the Quartodeciman crisis.

In addition several works on individual aspects of the liturgical year advanced scientific scholarship considerably. Among them: R. Cabié on the great 50 days of Easter [*La Pentecôte* (Paris 1965)], R. Zerfass on the Jerusalem stational services [*Die Schriflesung im Kathedraloffizium Jerusalems* (Münster 1968)], G. Bertonière on the development of the Byzantine paschal vigil [*The Historical Development of the Easter Vigil and Related Services in the Greek Church* (Rome 1972)], and P. Jounel on the sanctoral calendars of the medieval Roman basilicas [*Le culte des saints dans les basiliques du Latran et du Vatican au douzième siècle* (Rome 1977)].

With the renewed interest on the liturgy of the hours as the prayer of the whole Church, a good deal of research went into the historical development of daily prayer. Based on A. Baumstark's distinction between monastic and cathedral (or parochial) office, a number of scholars including M. Arranz, G. Winkler, W. Storey, J. Pinell, and especially J. Mateos investigated the daily office in various traditions. A. Veilleux transformed the understanding of the Egyptian cenobitic liturgy of the hours in his *La liturgie dans le cènobitisme pachomien au quatrième siècle* (Rome 1968). P. F. Bradshaw [*Daily Prayer in the Early Church* (London 1981)] and R. F. Taft [*The Liturgy of the Hours in East and West* (Collegeville, MN 1986)] reflected on contemporary research into the liturgy of the hours in comprehensive studies.

Liturgy and the Arts. Late-20th-century liturgical renewal also spurred interest between worship and other fields of study. While not strictly speaking investigations of the development and nature of liturgy itself, such studies became indispensable for a deeper understanding of the development and meaning of liturgical forms as well as their context. Most prominent among the arts studied in conjunction with liturgy was architecture. The work of R. Krautheimer was most significant for describing and evaluating architectural space on the basis of its liturgical functions, for example, in his *Early Christian and Byzantine Architecture* and the invaluable *Corpus Basilicarum Christianarum Romae,* 5 v. (Vatican City, 1937–77). Krautheimer's student, T. F. Mathews, published an in-depth study of the relation between liturgy and architecture in his *The Early Churches of Constantinople: Architecture and Liturgy* (University Park, PA 1971). J. Baldovin explored the relationship between stational churches and their liturgies in his groundbreaking work, *The Urban Character of Christian Worship in Jerusalem, Rome, and Constantinople from the Fourth to the Tenth Centuries: The Origins, Development, and Meaning of Stational Liturgy* (1982), and a shorter work, *Liturgy in Ancient Jerusalem* (1989). The influence of the architecture and topography of Jerusalem on the medieval Frankish church and its liturgy was investigated by C. Heitz [*Rapports entre architecture et liturgie à l'époque carolingiènne* (Paris 1963)]. J. G. Davies and S.A. Stauffer produced important studies on baptisteries and baptismal fonts.

The relation between liturgy and drama was studied by J. G. Davies and D. Adams; between liturgy and music by R. A. Leaver and E. Routley. In addition, an English translation of J. QUASTEN'S classic, *Music and Worship in Pagan and Christian Antiquity,* appeared (Washington, DC 1983).

Liturgy and Social Science. In terms of new directions for liturgics the most important turn the field took after the Second Vatican Council is undoubtedly an interest in the relation between Christian and Jewish worship and the social sciences. Inspired by sympathetic thinkers like E. Erickson and C. G. JUNG (psychology), V. TURNER and M. Douglas (anthropology), and B. Wicker and D. Martin (sociology), liturgical scholars began to take seriously the date provided by this relatively modern field of research. An early and comprehensive approach to this mode of research was J. Shaughnessy, ed., *The Roots of Ritual* (Grand Rapids 1973), followed by R. Grainger [*The Language of the Rite* (London 1974)], F. Isambert [*Rite et éfficacité symbolique* (Paris 1979)], R. Grimes [*Beginnings in Ritual Studies* (Lanham, MD 1982)], and L. A. Hoffman [*Beyond the Text: A Wholistic Approach to Liturgy* (Bloomington, IN 1987)]. A number of important studies were published by M. Searle, M. Collins, M. M. Kelleher, and N. Mitchell.

In sum, the scientific study of Jewish and Christian worship clearly progressed both in terms of content and methodological turns during the 20th century. Liturgical institutes and programs of study continued to flourish in Rome (San Anselmo and the Pontifical Oriental Institute); Trier, West Germany; Paris (Saint Serge [Orthodox] and the Institut Superieur de Liturgie); Washington, DC; Notre Dame; Collegeville, Minnesota; and Berkeley, California. Updates of ongoing research continued to be published in journals such as the *Archiv für Liturgiewissenschaft* (Regensburg), *Questions Liturgiques* (Mont César, Belgium), and *Studia Liturgica.*

Bibliography: C. JONES, et al., eds., *The Study of Liturgy* (New York 1992). S. MARSILI, ed., *Anamnesis: Introduzione storico-teologico alla liturgia,* 5 v. (Turin 1974–). A. G. MARTIMORT, ed., *The Church at Prayer,* 4 v., tr. M. W. O'CONNEL (rev. ed. Collegeville, MN 1986–87). C. VOGEL, *Medieval Liturgy: An Introduction to the Sources,* tr. and rev. by W. STOREY and N. RASMUSSEN (Washington, DC 1986). H. J. WEGMAN, *Christian Worship in East and West,* tr. G. LATHROP (New York 1985). G. LATHROP, *Holy Things: A Liturgical Theology* (Minneapolis 1993). F.C. SENN, *Christian Liturgy: Catholic and Evangelical* (Minneapolis 1997).

[J. F. BALDOVIN/EDS.]

LITURGY, ARTICLES ON

In this encyclopedia, the two principal articles in this area are LITURGY, which discusses the definition and nature of liturgy, and LITURGICS, which surveys the field of liturgical studies, i.e., the historical, theological and pastoral study of the Church's liturgical rites, ceremonies and other public worship activities. The entry LITURGICAL THEOLOGY treats the systematic and pastoral theologies of liturgical worship. LITURGICAL HISTORY, a comprehensive four-part entry, discusses historical developments in the Church's worship. Other specific issues in liturgical history include EASTER CONTROVERSY. Twentieth-century endeavors to restore the liturgy to its place of primacy in the life of the Church are described in LITURGICAL MOVEMENT; LITURGICAL CONFERENCE; MEDIATOR DEI; and MYSTERY THEOLOGY.

The principal entry on the Mass is EUCHARIST IN CONTEMPORARY CATHOLIC THEOLOGY. Related entries on the various categories of Masses, communion services and eucharistic devotion outside of Mass are: BENEDICTION OF THE BLESSED SACRAMENT; COMMUNION SERVICE; EUCHARIST OUTSIDE MASS, WORSHIP OF THE; EUCHARISTIC DEVOTION; EUCHARISTIC ELEVATION; FORTY HOURS DEVOTION; MASS, DRY; MASSES, VOTIVE; RED MASS; REQUIEM MASS; and TRIDENTINE MASS. The following special treatments of the individual parts of the Mass are provided: AGNUS DEI; ANAMNESIS; ASPERGES; COMMINGLING; CREED IN EUCHARISTIC LITURGY; EMBOLISM; EPICLESIS; EUCHARISTIC ELEVATION; FERMENTUM; GENERAL INTERCESSIONS; HOMILY; INTROIT; KISS OF PEACE; LORD'S PRAYER, THE; ORATIO SUPER POPULUM; PREFACE; SANCTUS; and SEQUENCE.

The use of specific items in the liturgy are covered in the following entries: ASHES, LITURGICAL USE OF; BREAD, LITURGICAL USE OF; DIPTYCHS, LITURGICAL USE OF; INCENSE, LIGHT, LITURGICAL USE OF; PALMS, LITURGICAL USE OF; WATER, LITURGICAL USE OF; and WINE, LITURGICAL USE OF. For general information on various liturgical rituals, ceremonies, actions, formulas, rubrics and laws, see ANTIPHON; APOLOGIES, LITURGICAL; BLESSINGS, LITURGICAL; CONCELEBRATION; DOXOLOGY, LITURGICAL; LITANY; OREMUS; PROCESSIONS, RELIGIOUS; LITURGICAL ACCLAMATIONS; LITURGICAL COLORS; LITURGICAL GESTURES; LITURGICAL LANGUAGES; LITURGICAL LAWS, AUTHORITY OF; ANOINTING OF THE SICK, LITURGY OF; COMMENDATION OF THE DYING; FUNERAL RITES; VIATICUM; and ORDINATIONS IN THE ROMAN RITE.

The liturgical year, calendars and feasts of the Church are covered in LITURGICAL YEAR IN THE ROMAN RITE; LITURGICAL CALENDARS; ALL SAINTS, SOLEMNITY OF; ALL SOULS' DAY; BAPTISM OF THE LORD; CANDLEMAS; CHRIST THE KING, FEAST OF; CHRISTMAS AND ITS CYCLE; CORPUS ET SANGUINIS CHRISTI; EASTER AND ITS CYCLE; EASTER VIGIL; EMBER DAYS; EPIPHANY, SOLEMNITY OF; GOOD FRIDAY; HOLY THURSDAY; HOLY WEEK; LENT; MAR-

IAN FEASTS; MARTYROLOGY, ROMAN; SANCTORAL CYCLE; SUNDAY; TENEBRAE; and TRIDUUM.

The liturgy of the hours is treated in the general articles LITURGY OF THE HOURS; BREVIARY, ROMAN; LITTLE OFFICE OF THE BLESSED VIRGIN MARY; and OFFICE OF THE DEAD. Specific hours are discussed in MATINS; LAUDS; LITTLE HOURS; VESPERS and COMPLINE.

The various roles exercised in the celebration of the liturgy are discussed under ACOLYTE; CANTOR IN CHRISTIAN LITURGY; DEACON; LECTOR; MASTER OF CEREMONIES; PAPAL CEREMONY AND VESTURE; and SACRISTAN. Service books used in the Roman rite receive a general treatment in LITURGICAL BOOKS OF THE ROMAN RITE and specific treatment in CEREMONIAL OF BISHOPS; EVANGELARY (BOOK OF GOSPELS); LECTIONARIES; LECTIONARY FOR MASSES WITH CHILDREN; MISSAL, ROMAN; PONTIFICAL, ROMAN; RITUAL, ROMAN; and SACRAMENTARIES, II: CONTEMPORARY. Historical developments are discussed under their respective titles, e.g., GELASIAN SACRAMENTARY; GREGORIAN SACRAMENTARY; LEONINE SACRAMENTARY; LIBELLI MISSARUM; ORDINALS, ROMAN; PERICOPES; SACRAMENTARIES, I: HISTORICAL; and STOWE MISSAL.

The liturgical families of Christendom are introduced by the overview article LITURGICAL RITES. The liturgical families of the East are treated in ALEXANDRIAN LITURGY; ANTIOCHENE LITURGY; ARMENIAN LITURGY; BYZANTINE LITURGY; COPTIC LITURGY; EAST SYRIAN LITURGY; ETHIOPIAN (GE'EZ) LITURGY; MARONITE LITURGY; RUSSIAN LITURGY; SYRIAN LITURGY; and SYRO-MALABAR LITURGY. The liturgical families of the West are discussed in LATIN RITE; ROMAN RITE; AMBROSIAN RITE; BANGOR USE; CARMELITE RITE, CARTHUSIAN RITE; CELTIC RITE; CISTERCIAN RITE; DOMINICAN RITE; GALLICAN RITE; HEREFORD USE; LYONESE RITE; MOZARABIC RITE; and PREMONSTRATENSIANS (RITE).

The relations between liturgy and culture are treated in the essay INCULTURATION, LITURGICAL. The principal entry on liturgical art is the nine-part essay LITURGICAL ART, while the principal entry on liturgical music is LITURGICAL MUSIC, THEOLOGY AND PRACTICE OF. For a survey of the history of liturgical music, see the 11-part entry, LITURGICAL MUSIC, HISTORY OF. Specific entries on liturgical chant are: AMBROSIAN CHANT; BYZANTINE CHANT; GALLICAN CHANT; GREGORIAN CHANT; MOZARABIC CHANT; and RUSSIAN CHANT.

The church building and all its appurtenances are described in CHURCH ARCHITECTURE, HISTORY OF and related articles such as ALTAR IN CHRISTIAN LITURGY; AMBO; BAPTISTERIES AND BAPTISMAL FONTS; CORNERSTONE, CHURCH; and TABERNACLE. Liturgical vestments are treated in LITURGICAL VESTMENTS; ALB; CHASUBLE; COPE

AND HUMERAL VEIL; DALMATIC; FANON; MANIPLE; MITER; STOLE; and SURPLICE. For information on the liturgical vessels, see the general entry LITURGICAL VESSELS and the specific entries CHALICE, PATEN AND VEIL; CIBORIUM; PYX; and RELIQUARIES.

Biographical information on prominent liturgical scholars and theologians are treated under their respective names. For information on international bodies that have contributed significantly in the production of liturgical texts for the English-speaking world, see: CONSULTATION ON COMMON TEXTS; ENGLISH LANGUAGE LITURGICAL CONSULTATION (ELLC); INTERNATIONAL COMMISSION ON ENGLISH IN THE LITURGY (ICEL); and INTERNATIONAL CONSULTATION ON ENGLISH TEXTS (ICET).

[J.Y. TAN]

LITURGY

Term for the official worship of God by the Church in the West for centuries. In the East, however, the tendency to restrict the word to the Eucharist arose at an early date. This article uses the expression to designate the Church's liturgical worship as distinct from its other devotions, whether practiced by groups or individuals.

Meaning of the Term. Etymologically the word means any service done for the common welfare of the people. It is derived from the Greek λειτουργία, which is a combination of λειτός, an adjective meaning pertaining to the people (λάος), and ἔργον, a noun meaning work.

History of the Word. For the Greeks liturgy designated any public service rendered to the community at personal expense or at least without remuneration: education, entertainment, or defense. The word referred even to forced labor done for the common good and, later, to any action that had repercussions in the social and political sphere.

The term made its way into revealed literature through the Septuagint translation of the Hebrew text of the Old Testament. The translators used it almost exclusively for the chosen people's prime purpose for existence, the worship of Yahweh. The word liturgy was used also, though less frequently, for something done for state (1 Kgs 19.21; 2 Chr 17.19; 22.8).

The same practice was followed by the New Testament writers. Luke, for example, speaks of Zechariah's liturgy in the Temple (1.23). Paul calls himself "the liturgist of Christ Jesus to the Gentiles" (Rom 15.16) and also uses the word liturgy to refer to the collection taken up for the poor in Jerusalem (2 Cor 9.12) and to the services

rendered to his own person (Phil 2.30). The Letter to the Hebrews employs the term for the priestly work of Jesus Christ, liturgy in its specifically Christian sense: "We have such a high priest . . . a minister [λειτουργός, liturgist] of the Holies, and of the true tabernacle which the Lord has erected and not man. . . . But now He has obtained a superior ministry [λειτουργίας, liturgy], in proportion as He is the mediator of a superior covenant, enacted on the basis of superior promises" (8.1–6). This is properly the work of the Christian People of God, for through Christ's liturgy they are able to offer acceptable worship to God and receive from Him the fruits of Christ's redemptive work.

Whereas Christian antiquity applied the term to prayer and sacrifice in general, writers of early centuries made it serve more frequently to denote an official or community service as opposed to devotions of purely private piety [Didache 15.1 (*Enchiridion patristicum*, ed M. J. Rovët de Journel 4); Clement of Rome. *Epist. ad Corinthios*, 40.2–5. 41.1 (*Patrologia Graeca*, ed. J. P. Migne, 1:288–289); Synod of Antioch, chapter 4 (K. Kirch, *Enchiridion fontium historiae ecclesiasticae antiquae*, ed. L. Ueding 490)]. Subsequent development in the East restricted the word to the Eucharist, as in the Liturgy of Saint James or the Liturgy of Saint Basil. During the Middle Ages the West preferred terms such as *ministerium, munus, servitus,* and *officium.* It was left to the Renaissance period to adopt the word liturgy in the titles of collections describing the Church's worship. Since then the term has been thus employed consistently.

Definition. Vatican Council II in The Constitution on the Sacred Liturgy (Dec. 4, 1963) describes liturgy as the carrying out of the work of redemption, especially in the paschal mystery (*Sacrosanctum Concilium* 2, 6); the exercise of the priestly office of Christ (*ibid.* 7); the "presentation of man's sanctification under the guise of signs perceptible by the senses" (*ibid.*); and a sacred action surpassing all others because it is the action of Christ the priest and of his Body the Church (*ibid.*). The liturgy is viewed as a foretaste of the heavenly liturgy (*ibid.* 8), "the summit toward which the activity of the Church is directed"; and the "fount from which all her power flows" (*ibid.* 10). Liturgy is seen as the source of grace and sanctification in Christ as well as the glorification of God (*ibid.*). The Council said also: "Liturgical services are not private functions, but are celebrations of the Church . . . the holy people united and ordered under their bishops. Liturgical services pertain to the whole body of the Church; they manifest it and affect it" (26). Thus the constitution builds upon and goes beyond the classic Thomistic definition of liturgy as "common worship that is offered to God by ministers of the Church in the person of all the faithful" (*Summa theologiae* 2a2ae,

83.12), as well as Pope Pius XII's definition of liturgy as the "public worship of the Mystical Body, Head and members" (*Mediator Dei* 20).

Nature

Sacramental Worship. All liturgical actions are sacramental; that is, they are signs and symbols that give expression to the conferring of divine life by Christ on His Church and the offering to the Father, through Christ, of the homage and worship of His people. The foundational basis of this sacramental quality of liturgical worship is the Incarnation. Christ is the first of all Sacraments. As the Word Incarnate, He clothes in visible, tangible form and shape the unseen and transcendent God; He is the dynamic embodying of the living and life–giving God. The hypostatic union means precisely that the Son of God in person unites to Himself a real human nature, in order, in it and through it, to pervade and transform all human beings with the power and glory of His divinity. Through the Incarnation, Christ's humanity becomes the direct personal instrument of God the Father's eternal plan to redeem the whole human race. Thus Christ is the Sacrament of God in the most perfect sense.

The paschal mystery is the internal content of every liturgical action, for the latter is simply an external sign enabling the worshiper to participate in that supreme act of worship in which God's plan of salvation was brought to fruition by Christ's suffering, death, and resurrection. Without this internal reality of the paschal mystery, liturgical worship would be an empty shell. Although worshippers might be quite sincere in their own interior sentiments, the objective religious action would be incapable of uniting them with God, for saving union with God comes only through Christ's redemptive work. A mere human act of the will does not suffice to make us adopted daughters and sons of God; all must participate in the resurrected body of Christ. It is precisely in the sacramental, liturgical worship of the Church that we are assimilated into Christ's risen body.

This understanding of the liturgy is beautifully expressed by Vatican Council II in its *Constitution on the Sacred Liturgy* (5–7). After speaking of the paschal mystery as the core and kernel of the liturgy, it says that the liturgy is but a complex of "sensible signs through which the sanctification of man is signified and brought about in a way proper to each."

Priestly Worship. The worship of the Church has no meaning except as an action of Christ the Redeemer; from Him it receives its content and efficacy. It is nothing less than Christ's worship of His Father, His worship done through His Mystical Body.

According to the Epistle to the Hebrews, through His transfiguring sacrifice Christ exercised a priesthood, a priesthood that is eternal. "Because He continues forever, He has an everlasting priesthood. Therefore He is able at all times to save those who come to God through Him, since He lives always to make intercession for them" (7.24–25). Through the liturgy Christ's Priesthood becomes a continuous and living reality throughout the ages (*Mediator Dei* 22; *Constitution on the Sacred Liturgy* 7).

This priesthood He chose to share with His followers, so that they would be able to continue Him as the Sacrament of redeeming worship. In his first Epistle Peter urges Christians to draw near to Christ, "a living stone, rejected indeed by men but chosen and honored by God. Be you yourselves as living stones built thereon into a spiritual house, a holy priesthood, to offer spiritual sacrifices acceptable to God through Jesus Christ. . . . You are a chosen race, a royal priesthood, a holy nation, a people purchased by God to proclaim the great deeds of Him who has called you out of darkness to His marvelous light" (2.4, 5, 9). The power of this royal priesthood enables all Christians to associate themselves and their lives with Christ's sacrifice, which alone can make of their act of worship pleasing to God the Father. It is this priesthood of Christ, present and active within the Church, that empowers the Church to be an efficacious sign of the redeeming worship of Christ at the instant of His dying and rising.

In its liturgical worship, then, the Church acts as one, since everything it does is done precisely as the action of the one Body of Christ, with Him as head, as priest. Christ's priesthood, present and active in the members of His body, is so essential that without it there would be no liturgy; in it the members of the Church act as the one people of God in its proper condition of the divinely chosen holy cult community, the single, unified expression of the priestly movement of Jesus Christ back to His Father.

The dignity of the liturgical assembly is no small thing, for it is the concrete realization of the Mystical Body of Jesus Christ, the organ of the Mystical Body, expressing its union with its Head in His most sublime role as mediator between God and humanity. By its very nature, then, the liturgy demands full, conscious, and active participation of all the faithful; and they have a right to participation by reason of their Baptism (*Constitution on the Sacred Liturgy* 14). Since Liturgical functions are not private actions but celebrations that pertain to the whole body of the Church, the Sacrament of unity, the Church officially desires that their communal celebration—with the full active participation of the faithful—be observed as something preferred over what might be called a "private'' use of these functions (*ibid.* 26, 27). In order to bring out externally and more adequately the real and necessary diversity of function in the Church's worship, Vatican Council II insisted that everyone, whether cleric or laity, do all and only those parts that pertain to his or her office by the nature of the rite (*ibid.* 28).

That the liturgy is the source of Christian sanctity follows from its being the divinely intended means for achieving assimilation to Christ and insertion into His redemptive action. Vatican Council II was clear on this. Although the Council admitted that the liturgy does not exhaust all the activity of the Church, ''as the action of Christ the priest and of His body the Church, every liturgical celebration is an action of such excellence that no other action of the Church can equal its efficacy by the same title and to the same degree . . . of piety. . . . The liturgy is the summit toward which the activity of the Church tends, and the fount from which flows all her power'' (*ibid.* 6, 13, 10).

See Also: LITURGICAL BOOKS OF ROMAN RITE; LITURGICAL MOVEMENT; LITURGICAL RITES; LITURGICAL THEOLOGY; LITURGICAL VESTMENTS.

Bibliography: A. G. MARTIMORT, ed. *The Church at Prayer: An Introduction to the Liturgy* (rev. ed. Collegeville, Minn. 1992). A. A. HÄUSSLING, ed., *The Meaning of the Liturgy* (Collegeville, Minn. 1994). A. J. CHUPUNGCO, ed., *Handbook for Liturgical Studies,* 5 v. (Collegeville, Minn. 1997–2000).

[J. H. MILLER/D. W. KROUSE/G. AUSTIN/EDS.]

LITURGY OF THE HOURS

The Liturgy of the Hours (Divine Office), composed of Psalms, hymns, scriptural, patristic, and hagiographical readings, and prayers, is the public liturgical prayer of the Church, destined by her for the sanctification of specific parts of the day. This article treats the meaning, history, and renewal of the Liturgy of the Hours in the Roman rite.

Overview. Without frequent and fervent prayer the life of the Christian soon can easily become directionless and empty. In the absence of *communal* prayer, relying solely on private devotion, Christian witness becomes individualistic and ultimately devoid of any ecclesial sense. The development of the Liturgy of the Hours (or Divine Office) through the ages was predicated on the necessity for Christians to gather as often as possible not only to sanctify the day through the celebration of various hours, but to strengthen the community's capacity and resolve to give witness to Christ as the gathered faithful. So ''like all liturgical celebrations, the Liturgy of the Hours is not a private act. As a public sign of the Church, it belongs

to the whole Church and has impact on all its members'' (*General Instruction of the Liturgy of the Hours* 20). By its very nature the Liturgy of the Hours is a communal action of the Church, since it is the Church's daily round of prayer celebrated in common. Private recitation of any or all of the hours is always exceptional rather than normative. The primary responsibility of ''those in sacred orders or with a special canonical mission'' is to direct and preside over the prayer of the community (*ibid.* 23). As the prayer of the Church, the Liturgy of the Hours is a common prayer that is much more than the sum total of individual prayers of the participants; it is the result of that transcendent reality uniting all the faithful among themselves. During the exercise of this prayer, the *ecclesia* is reunited as such in Christ.

The distribution of the Office throughout the day is the Church's response to the Lord's commandment to pray always (Lk 18.1). The words of the Psalmist, ''Seven times a day I praise you'' (Ps 119.164), inspired development of the hours. The two moments of the rising and setting of the sun were the first chosen for prayers—LAUDS (Morning Prayer) and VESPERS (Evening Prayer). The divisions formerly marking the day served to determine the minor hours of Terce, Sext, and None, at the third, sixth and ninth hour respectively. To imitate Christ's example and to follow His teachings, there was established a night Office (MATINS) divided into several nocturns, a remnant of the ancient divisions of the night. Very early in the Church, the memory of a moment of the Passion was linked with each of these hours; in some countries, the memory of the great stages of salvation history was added to them. Such a prayer retains its full meaning in the traditional organization of the Office when the latter is celebrated at the liturgical hours. However, when it is recited at any time of the day or anticipated before its prescribed time, it loses much of its value and efficacy for those who recite it.

History. The prayer of the first Christians had its roots in Jewish prayer. From the first centuries there were three kinds of prayer: morning and evening prayers, day prayers, and night prayers. Only the first two were practiced regularly by the Christian community; they were liturgical—as the others could have been—when they were celebrated by the local *ecclesia* under the authority of the bishop. These services, inasmuch as they were public, were composed of hymns, prayers, and readings, accompanied by explanations or exhortations. In the 3d century, the Psalms of the Old Testament were permanently adopted and sung in a responsorial manner.

After Constantine recognized the Church's place in society (313), the Church organized her prayer by establishing the times of celebration and determining the formulas to be used. Two tendencies were brought to bear on this. The first came from cathedral or parish communities, the other from monastic communities' and led to two types of cursus for the Office.

The monks who led a cenobitic life were the first to organize a complete Office with determined times for the reunions of the community and with established formulas and the recitation of the whole Psalter. Nocturnal prayer was the most characteristic use of monasticism, whence vigils were introduced in the churches, first in the East and then in the West. The most ancient monastic cursus known to us are those of Jerusalem, Lower Egypt, Palestine, Gaul, St. Basil, St. John Chrysostom, St. Caesarius, St. Columban, the *Regula Magistri,* and St. Benedict. For the last two the Office is complete and daily; the monks are obliged to take part in it, and, if they cannot, they must recite it privately.

In cathedral and parish churches, on the contrary, the community, with the presidency and active collaboration of the different orders of the clergy, celebrated each day a simpler Office (the so-called ''cathedral Office'') that was usually composed of Lauds and Vespers. Between the 5th and 9th centuries, the liturgies received their permanent structure. We know little about the primitive Roman Office, but we must distinguish between that of the *tituli* (the presbyteral churches) and that of the basilicas (cared for by more or less regular communities). The latter Office probably served as model for St. Benedict's Rule. In these basilica communities, the Office was composed of Psalms, antiphons, readings from Scripture and the Fathers, responsories, and, in certain churches as well as in monasteries, of hymns. The anniversaries of martyrs and confessors began to be celebrated at their tombs by means of a votive Office that was without relationship to the Office of the day.

From the end of the 6th century, at the time of St. Gregory the Great, the liturgy of the basilica was spread to the rest of Rome and even further: to Gaul, England, and Germany. The Office of the Roman basilicas thus became that of the clergy of those countries. Then in the middle of the 8th century, the complete cursus of all the hours, including the lengthy Matins, became general practice, and the clerics were obliged to participate in it entirely. The kind of canonical life necessary for this celebration received its organization principally from St. Chrodegang (d. 766) and the Council of Aix-la-Chapelle (816). With Pepin the Short (751 to 768), the Frankish monarchy openly favored, and Charlemagne sought to impose officially, the adoption of the Roman uses in his Empire. Amalarius and the *schola cantorum* of the Church of Metz played an important part in the correction and diffusion of the Antiphonary of the Roman Office.

Taken as a whole, the Office also underwent certain adaptations and additions such as the chapter Office, supplementary psalms after each hour, offices such as those of the dead and the Blessed Virgin, and several commemorations and *preces.* All these additions burdened the Office; decadence was the result. In the 10th century an attempt was made to shorten the old Office, especially by reducing the psalmody and the readings of Matins.

As early as the 11th century there appeared the first signs of a reform that was to be accentuated with the renaissance of the 12th century and the Gregorian reform. On the one hand, the common life of clerics and the solemn choral celebration of the Office were gradually abandoned. On the other hand, the Office of the Papal Curia began to take shape, and all the elements of the Office were gathered in a single book, the BREVIARY. The Office of the Curia was adopted and propagated by the Friars Minor, and private recitation of the Office spread. Little change was made in the old texts, but numerous *ad libitum* sections disappeared. Moreover, trends in spirituality had great repercussions on the evolution of the Office; they were manifest in the multiplying of feasts and historical legends and by the diminishing of the number of readings as well as of certain old elements little in accord with the devotions then characteristic of piety. Finally, in the 13th century, canonists and theologians began to justify the practice of private recitation.

Tridentine Reform. In the 16th century, the necessity for a reform was felt because of all the successive but somewhat confused transformations of the Office. Clement VII gave Cardinal Francisco de QUIÑONES the responsibility of preparing a new breviary with a simpler office that would be more in conformity with tradition and historical truth. His work first appeared in 1535. It contained a completely new organization of the Office, but the old texts were hardly modified, except for the historical readings. However, it was attacked by theologians and suppressed by the Council of Trent. A new edition of the Roman Breviary was prepared by a pontifical commission and was published in 1568 by Pius V who imposed it on all churches that did not possess a liturgy at least 200 years old. The printing press was a powerful instrument for its rapid diffusion. This edition was characterized by a reduction of the calendar, the hour of Prime, the *preces,* and the supplementary offices.

At the end of the 16th century, the Jesuits were the first religious order to abandon the choral celebration of the Office, and their theologian, F. Suárez, taught that the obligation bore directly on private recitation. Thus the latter became the rule for the secular clergy and the modern congregations. In the 17th and 18th centuries, a certain number of churches, especially in France and

Germany, readopted and corrected their old liturgies. Benedict XIV decided to reform the Breviary, but he died before realizing his project.

In 1911 Pius X began a reform of the Office by redistributing the Psalms throughout the week—shortening the lengthy Matins of Sunday, giving Sundays precedence over numerous feasts, and favoring the Office of the feria before that of feasts of inferior rank. The reform was furthered in 1955 and 1960 to favor the "temporal" Office and to obtain greater simplification.

Vatican Council II. In calling for a systematic and comprehensive reform of the liturgy of the Roman rite, Vatican Council II was motivated by deep pastoral concern. The aim of the entire endeavor was to enable Catholics once again to recognize the liturgy of the entire Church as the ritual expression of their union with Christ, and thus be moved to participate in it more actively, intelligently, and fruitfully. The same pastoral solicitude which prompted modification of the Mass, the other Sacraments, and the Calendar, was no less operative in the revision of the Divine Office—now called the Liturgy of the Hours. As plainly stated in the conciliar document *Sacrosanctum Concilium* on the sacred liturgy, the Office was to be reformed in order that it "may be better and more worthily prayed in existing circumstances" (art. 87; Abbott, *Documents,* 164).

In the estimation of the Council fathers, the chief obstacle to prayerful recitation of the Divine Office was the widespread practice of not observing the component Hours at their proper times, thereby frustrating the whole purpose of the Office, which is to sanctify the various moments of the day and night. To some extent this practice was caused by a conflict between the Office as it was then constituted and the demands of active ministry in the modern world. The Hours were simply too numerous to be prayed separately and in order; hence the almost inevitable urge to bundle them together. Furthermore, the length and arrangement of certain Hours militated against their being observed at the appointed times. But an inadequate theology of the Office, coupled with poor understanding of the psalms and other biblical elements, were also responsible for the Breviary being considered merely as an undifferentiated body of official prayers to be read within a 24-hour period by clerics in major orders and solemnly professed religious.

Recognizing this unfortunate state of affairs, the Council stipulated that "the traditional sequence of the Hours is to be restored so that as far as possible they may once again be genuinely related to the time of day at which they are prayed" (*Sacrosanctum Concilium* 88; Abbott, *Documents,* 164). To this end, Lauds and Vespers, consecrating the morning and evening, respectively, were to be celebrated as the two chief Hours around which the rest of the Office turns. Prime, a second morning prayer, was to be suppressed. The minor Hours of Terce, Sext, and None were to be retained only in choir. Outside of choir one of the three was to be selected as a prayer during the work day. It has been termed the Middle Hour. Compline was to be maintained as a prayer before going to bed. Matins, originally a night vigil, and hence the most problematic of all the Hours, was to be transformed into an atemporal Hour, now known as the Office of Readings, suitable for use at any time of day or night. In addition, the Council recommended that the component elements of the various Hours be revised. In particular, psalms were to be distributed over a longer period than I week; readings and hymns were to be more judiciously chosen and arranged.

Responsibility for the actual revision of the Office lay, of course, with the postconciliar liturgical commission and later with the Congregation for Divine Worship. The results of their work were disclosed on Feb. 2, 1971, with the publication of the *General Instruction of the Liturgy of the Hours,* accompanied by the Apostolic Constitution of Pope Paul VI, *Laudis canticum.* The *General Instruction* was placed at the head of the four volumes containing the texts of the new Office. It must not, however, be equated with the General Rubrics which introduced the Breviary of Pius V. Although it describes the external format of the Hours and tells how they should be executed, it also explains their theological significance. By doing so it intends to impart a spirit, to arouse and shape an attitude, to orient an approach to the Office and so facilitate its being prayed more profitably. Fruitful celebration of the Hours was after all the goal toward which the reform was directed. The objective of the *General Instruction on the Liturgy of the Hours,* then, is no different from that of the *General Instruction on the Roman Missal.*

Theology. The renewed appreciation of the Divine Office is unmistakably evident in the new term applied to it by the *General Instruction:* Liturgia Horarum, the Liturgy of the Hours. This designation emphasizes, first, that the Office is a liturgical act in the full sense and, second, that it is intimately bound to periods of time. As liturgy it is by nature a public and communal action of the entire people of God, faithful as well as clergy. Hence private recitation by individual clerics, though praiseworthy, is seen to be far from satisfactory. Besides referring to the action itself, the phrase Liturgy of the Hours also serves as the title of the volumes containing the texts to be employed in the celebration of the Hours. Thus the term Breviary, with all its semantic ambiguity and impropriety, has been resolutely discarded. In the not too distant past praying the Office was habitually spoken of as reading the Breviary. The changed vocabulary of the *General Instruction* clearly implies that the Liturgy of the Hours involves more than dutifully scanning a little book.

Building on the encyclical *MEDIATOR DEI* of Pius XII and the Constitution on the Sacred Liturgy, the *General Instruction on the Liturgy of the Hours* teaches that all Christian prayer is the prolongation of Christ's prayer, the principle characteristics of which are praise and intercession. The Eucharist, the other Sacraments, and the Divine Office are simply various modes whereby the Church, as Spirit-filled body of the risen Lord, is united with its Head in His one great act of glorifying the Father and pleading with Him for the needs of mankind. While the Office is a preparation for the Eucharist as well as an extension of it, it also renders present in its own way the same reality which lies at the heart of the Eucharist: the sacrifice of Christ.

Understood as a continuation of Christ's priestly work in the Church, the celebration of the Hours is no longer considered a form of liturgy belonging primarily to those in Holy Orders or solemn vows. It is recommended to all the faithful on the basis of their baptismal union with Christ. This is a most important development and presumes no slight evolution in ecclesiology. Ecclesial sensitivity is maintained throughout the *General Instruction*. In treating those who celebrate the Liturgy of the Hours, for example, the *Instruction* first discusses communal celebrations involving bishop, priests, and faithful, or various groups within the Church; only then does it take up the subject of private observance by individuals.

The obligation of ordained ministers to pray the Office is likewise presented in an ecclesial perspective:

> The Liturgy of the Hours is entrusted to sacred ministers in a special way so that it is to be recited by each of them—with the necessary adaptations—even when the people are not present. The Church deputes them to say the Liturgy of the Hours in order that at least through them the duty of the whole community may be constantly and continuously fulfilled and the prayer of Christ may persevere unceasingly in the Church [*General Instruction* 28].

This obligation, however, should not be interpreted casuistically. Nor should it engender scruples. In reciting the whole sequence of the Hours each day, ministers should preserve "as far as possible the genuine relationship of the Hours to the time of day" (*General Instruction* 29). Presumably there is no obligation to recite the Hours at inappropriate times. Furthermore, the *Instruction* recognizes that all the Hours are not of equal weight. Lauds and Vespers are more important than the others

and should not be omitted except for serious reason (*General Instruction* 29). The implication is that other Hours may be omitted for less than serious reason.

Structure. With few notable exceptions the general structure of each Hour is the same: opening verse, hymn, psalms, reading, and concluding prayer.

The first office of the day opens with an invitatory consisting of the verse "Lord, open my lips; and my mouth shall proclaim your praise," and Psalm 94. Subsequent Hours begin with the verse "O God come to my aid; Lord, hasten to help me." Instead of being linked to one particular Hour regardless of the time at which it is said, the invitatory now serves as a call to praise at the beginning of the day. This, after all, is its true function.

At every Hour a hymn follows the introductory verse. Besides being particularly well suited to popular participation, the hymn immediately directs attention to the spirit of the Hour or feast. Episcopal conferences are authorized to secure vernacular adaptations of the Latin hymns given in the typical edition of the Liturgy of the Hours and to introduce other appropriate compositions.

Lauds includes a morning psalm, an Old Testament cantitle, and a psalm of praise. At Vespers there are two psalms followed by a canticle from the Epistles or the Book of Revelation. Although Old Testament canticles always found place in the Divine Office, the use of canticles drawn from the Epistles and the Book of Revelation is an innovation. Psalmody at the Middle Hour usually consists of three sections of Psalm 118, or three gradual psalms. The Office of Readings also includes three psalms. One or two psalms expressing trust in God are chosen for Compline each night. Psalms 4, 90, and 133, traditional at this Hour, figure among them.

In keeping with the recommendation of the Council fathers, psalms are now distributed over a period of four weeks rather than one. Compared to the Roman Breviary the number of psalms presently employed at any Hour is reduced. Far from minimizing the importance of the Psalter, the new arrangement is intended to encourage a slower, more prayerful pondering of the sacred texts. The Liturgy of the Hours furnishes three aids for this purpose. First, each psalm bears a title indicating its general theme. A phrase from the New Testament or the Fathers is added to the title in order to evoke a specifically Christian interpretation of the Psalm. Second, a collection of psalm-prayers is provided in a supplementary volume of the Liturgy of the Hours. These prayers enable the content and application of a given psalm to be savored in the form of a short oration. Third, each psalm is prefaced by an antiphon. As explained in the *General Instruction*,

> The antiphons help to illustrate the literary character of the psalm; turn the psalm into personal

prayer; place in better light a phrase worthy of attention which may otherwise be missed; give special colour to a psalm in differing circumstances; while excluding arbitrary accommodations, help considerably in the typological and festive interpreting of the psalm; and can make more attractive and varied the recitation of the psalms [113].

In the past psalmody had been a serious stumbling block on the path of many who took up the Breviary. It would be foolish to think that the aids mentioned above will automatically eliminate the problem. Appreciation of the psalms must be acquired by systematic study, and by surrender to the Spirit who inspired them. This is plainly enunciated in Numbers 100 to 109 of the *General Instruction,* which comment on the role of the psalms and their close relationship with Christian prayer.

Turning to the reading material of the Office, Lauds and Vespers provide a choice between two types of Scripture reading: short and long. The short readings are not mere snippits from the Epistle of the day's Mass as were many *capitula* of the Roman Breviary. They are carefully selected to highlight certain brief but noteworthy sayings which claim less attention when they form part of more ample pericopes. The longer reading is recommended for celebration with the people, in which case, a homily may be added. The Middle Hour and Compline always have short readings. Two long readings are given for the Office of Readings. The first is scriptural; the second is taken from the Fathers, modern authors, or the lives of the saints. At Lauds and Vespers the customary Gospel canticles succeed the readings.

Formerly every Hour of the Office ended in identical fashion: Kyrie, Lord's Prayer, oration of the Mass. The Liturgy of the Hours modifies this pattern. It suppresses the Kyrie, reserves the Lord's Prayer for Lauds and Vespers, and allows considerable diversity in the final oration. The most significant change, however, is the return of intercessions before the Our Father at Lauds and Vespers. Petitions (Latin: preces) on behalf of all were a characteristic feature of morning and evening prayer in ancient times. They took the form of a litany, the response to which was usually *Kyrie eleison.* With the passage of time the intentions disappeared, leaving only a thrice-repeated cry for mercy. Thus the restoration of intercessions is consistent with the suppression of the *Kyrie.*

Parish Catechesis on the Liturgy of the Hours. The obligation of bishops, priests, and deacons to pray the hours is linked to their duty to assure the celebration of this liturgy by local communities, particularly on Sundays and solemnities. Deacons and priests, together with parish liturgy planning teams, were encouraged to devise programs of creative catechesis and implementation of the Liturgy of the Hours, aware of the possibilities and needs of the particular parish. Pastoral adaptation of the hours, as well as parish catechesis on the Office, drew its direction from the General Instruction on the Liturgy of the Hours, a theological and pastoral document.

Parishes learned from experience in the implementation of new liturgical rites that catechesis was not only desirable but necessary before and during that implementation. While the Liturgy of the Hours, particularly Morning and Evening Prayer, did not represent a great innovation, American Catholics did not have much experience with this form of common prayer, especially the common recitation or singing of the Psalms. Experience with the Responsorial Psalm in the Eucharistic Liturgy demonstrated the need for a thorough-going catechesis on the nature of the Psalms, the tradition of their use in the Church's liturgy, and the various forms of singing them. Thus instruction on psalmody benefited the celebration of the Eucharist as well as the Office. The General Instruction of the Liturgy of the Hours provided a sound basis for parish catechesis since it offered a pastoral theology of the praying Church. Central is the relationship between prayer and witness: "When one takes part in the Liturgy of the Hours, he contributes in a hidden way to the growth of God's people, for he makes the apostolate more fruitful" (*ibid.* 18). Frequent communal prayer is therefore intrinsic to parish life, for such prayer strengthens and nourishes the resolve of the Church to persevere in its witness to Christ in the world. "Prayer is of the very essence of the Church. The Church is a community and should express in prayer its communal nature" (*ibid.* 19). Some of the following principles and themes might be included in a parish catechesis:

(1) the relationship of communal prayer and Christian witness (*ibid.* 19);

(2) the consecration of time and the sanctification of the Church (*ibid.* 10–11, 14);

(3) the Liturgy of the Hours as preparation for the Eucharist (*ibid.* 12);

(4) participation in Christ's priestly work of praise (*ibid.* 13, 15–16);

(5) developing the prayer of supplication and intercession (*ibid.* 17);

(6) the Psalms as Christian prayer, and the nature of psalmody (*ibid.* 100–109, 121–139);

(7) the place of God's Word, its reading, and celebration in the life of the Church (*ibid.* 140–158);

(8) the nature of the various hours of prayer, and the intrinsic importance of Morning and Evening Prayer;

(9) the celebration of the liturgical year through the Liturgy of the Hours.

These are only some of the themes with which a pastoral catechesis on the Liturgy of the Hours might deal. The General Instruction is rich in a great variety of subjects that clergy were encouraged to study carefully.

Pastoral Considerations in the Implementation of the Hours. "Perhaps the most difficult and challenging task is to make the liturgy of the hours in fact and practice, as well as in theory and doctrine, the prayer of the entire Church" (United States Bishops' Committee on the Liturty, *A Call to Prayer*). Extraordinary efforts are indeed required to implement the celebration of the communal prayer of the Church. Likewise hard pastoral questions regarding the priority of prayer in individual parishes need to be asked. One such question involves scheduling. Given the pastoral practice of daily Eucharists, for example, when does one schedule and celebrate Morning and Evening Prayer, "the hinges of the Office," in a local parish?

(1) *Scheduling the Hours.* Obviously the most important days for celebrating the hours are Sundays and solemnities; secondarily, feasts and weekdays. The greatest obstacle, oddly enough, is the multiplicity of Masses on those days. Parishes need to reexamine their Mass schedules in order to strike a proper balance between the principles of convenience and the presence of a community at the Eucharist. Too often in large urban or suburban parishes weekday and Sunday Eucharists are multiplied in the name of convenience for the people, when in fact very few people are present at certain celebrations, especially in the early morning hours. The question of stipends and support of the clergy, a legitimate concern, frequently intervenes in the problem of scheduling. The Eucharist needs to be scheduled according to need and the actual presence of an assembly. Once that is accomplished, Morning and Evening Prayer may take their proper places. The liturgical day ought to begin, especially on Sundays, with Morning Prayer and conclude with Evening Prayer. For example, Sundays might begin with Evening Prayer I ("First Vespers") on Saturday before the anticipated Masses and might be celebrated as a vigil to prepare those who are present for the Sunday Eucharist. Late Sunday evening may seem more suitable nowadays for the celebration of Evening Prayer II, rather than late afternoon as in the past. However, this may vary from place to place.

(2) *Which Hours to Celebrate?* As Morning and Evening Prayer are the hinges of the Church's daily round of prayer, they are naturally the most important of all when scheduling the celebration of the hours. However, the other hours of the Office should find some place in a parish's prayer life. Daytime Prayer (mid-morning, midday, or mid-afternoon) and Night Prayer (Compline) are as easily celebrated by small groups as they are by large groups. Rather than beginning a parish meeting "with a prayer," one of the hours might be recited or sung. Thus an evening parents' meeting might end with Night Prayer; a school faculty meeting in the afternoon might end or begin with one of the daytime hours. Even on a diocesan level, those who plan meetings and congresses ought seriously to consider solemn celebration of one of the hours instead of the Eucharist, especially on weekends; in this way people are not taken away from their parish Eucharistic celebration. Even the Office of Readings can be profitably celebrated in a parish on important occasions, since it enables people to delve more deeply into the Scripture and become acquainted with the rich theological tradition which the second reading of that Office represents. Marian, Eucharistic, and other devotions can be carefully joined to the celebration of some of the hours from time to time.

(3) *Who Leads the Celebration of the Hours?* Those who are obliged to the Office also have the responsibility to lead the people in its celebration. Thus priests and deacons, and even the bishop in his cathedral, should lead in the celebration of each of the hours. However, the leadership of prayer in the celebration of the Liturgy of the Hours is not limited to those in Orders. Lay men and women and religious should be trained in the ministry of prayer-leadership to assure the daily celebration of the hours. Families should likewise be encouraged to pray the hours at home, especially Morning, Evening and/or Night Prayer.

(4) *Participation Materials.* The publication of materials suitable for the celebration of the hours is still in process. While the four-volume edition of the Liturgy of the Hours, and its one-volume excerpt, *Christian Prayer,* are available, these are too expensive for most parishes. However, excerpts from the hours are being published (e.g., *Shorter Christian Prayer*) and made available. Parish liturgy committees should investigate what is available.

(5) *Musical Choices.* In celebrating any of the hours, planners ought to keep in mind certain principles with regard to music. Obviously the hymn which begins Morning or Evening Prayer must be sung and must reflect the character of the feast. A choice must be made with regard to PSALMODY, to sing or not to sing the Psalms, to use Psalm tones (e.g. Gregorian, Anglican, Gélineau, etc.), or metric Psalms. If Psalm tones are chosen, then the type of psalmody is important; responsorial, antiphonal, or *in directum.* While the Psalms need not be sung on weekdays, it would seem inappropriate merely to recite them on Sundays and solemnities. In parish celebration consideration ought to be given to the question of using a cons-

tant repertory of Psalms, rather than varying them every day. As with the Eucharist, care, planning and competent musical leadership are required. The simplest of chants are quite accessible to most congregations nowadays and ought not to be rejected out of hand as too difficult or out of date. Music in the Liturgy of the Hours is not ornamental—the Psalms are songs before all else—for the "sung celebration of the Divine Office is the form which best accords with the nature of this prayer" (*General Instruction of the Liturgy of Hours* 268).

(6) *Ritual Elements in the Celebration of the Hours.* The celebration of any of the hours may be as simple or as elaborate as the needs of a particular community or occasion may require. The use of such ritual elements as water, light, incense, flowers, processional banners, vestments, or electronic media (e.g., visuals) ought carefully to be integrated in the celebration of the Office and in the proper places. For example, the use of incense is traditional during the singing of the *Magnificat* or *Benedictus.* At times incense may be used as a penitential act in the celebration of Evening Prayer. A light service or *lucernarium* can sometimes be joined to Evening Prayer as well, just as a rite of sprinkling to recall Baptism might find a occasional place in Morning Prayer.

(7) *Other Occasions in Celebrating the Hours Solemnly.* There are many occasions when the Liturgy of the Hours ought to be celebrated with solemnity, not as an alternative to the Eucharist, but rather as more fitting than the Eucharist. (a) At ecumenical gatherings, such as are held during the Week of Prayer for Christian Unity or on Thanksgiving Day, Christians from many different backgrounds can draw on the common tradition of Morning or Evening Prayer of the various Churches to create a truly ecumenical and unifying service of prayer. Many of the Churches are in the process of revising or already have revised their rites for the Liturgy of the Hours. These revisions, as with the Roman Catholic reform of the Office, are based on the common tradition and demonstrate an already achieved liturgical unity. Thus an ecumenical gathering ought to be celebrated in this Liturgy that all can call their own and in which unity may already be perceived. (b) During the seasons of Advent, Epiphany, Lent, and Easter special celebrations of Morning or Evening Prayer, or even the Office of Readings, might be adapted without prejudice to the normal celebration of the hours or the Eucharist. For example, on the third Sunday of Advent the celebration of Evening Prayer might be lengthened and adapted to resemble a ceremony of lessons and carols. An Evening Prayer in Lent might be joined to a celebration of the Stations of the Cross. Evening Prayer on the feast of the Epiphany might include a dramatic reading or dramatization (through dance, mime, etc.) of the theophany of the Messiah. During Eas-

tertide, a longer Office of Readings might be devised for the neophytes during their *mystagogia,* stressing the communal nature of their newly acquired faith. Such adaptations, of course, ought to be accomplished without doing harm to the course of prayer or the liturgical year as provided in the liturgical books and must be carefully planned.

The Liturgy of the Hours as Family Prayer. The need for families to pray together is important not only that children might grow up in an atmosphere of prayer and devotion, but also because through prayer a family can find nourishment for its faith and strength for its unity. The Liturgy of the Hours does provide, especially in the "little hours" (Daytime Prayer and Night Prayer), a varying form of prayer for parents and children that is adaptable to the needs of each particular family. Members of the family can participate in Night Prayer, for example, in a variety of ways. The Psalm is constant for each day of the week. The *Nunc dimittis* (Canticle of Simeon) is unchanging. After a while these invariables can be learned by heart and become a part of each person's "repertory" of prayer. The Marian antiphons at the end of Night Prayer, like the opening hymn, can be easily sung by a family. Prayerful silence is likewise learned from this prayer, as is a sense of penitence and reflection on the day's activities during the examination of conscience. Instead of a hastily recited formula for grace before meals, Prayer at Midday might be recited in common around the table before the start of Sunday dinner. The celebration of the Liturgy of the Hours by a family has many merits, e.g. familiarity and use of the Psalms as Christian prayer, the singing of simple hymns, but most of all the development of prayer in the life of a child that prepares the child for Sunday worship and eventually for Christian witness.

Communal Prayer and Personal Prayer. The goal of the Liturgy of the Hours is the development and growth of a praying Church, a Church united to the communion of saints who worship in the presence of God. Communal prayer ultimately develops an intense life of personal prayer. The Liturgy of the Hours will always need to be adapted; thus Paul VI noted that the 1971 revision has provided "various forms of celebration that can be accomodated to the various groups, with their differing needs" (Paul VI, *Laudis Canticum* 1). There is no opposition between communal and personal prayer, especially when the latter draws its nourishment from the former. "When the prayer of the the Office becomes real personal prayer, then the bonds that unite Liturgy and the whole of Christian life are manifested more clearly. The whole life of the faithful, during the single hours of the day and the night, constitutes a *leitourgia,* as it were, with which they offer themselves in a service of love to God and to men, adhering to the action of Christ, who, by staying among us and offering himself, sanctified the lives of all men'' (*ibid.* 8).

See Also: COMPLINE; LITTLE OFFICE OF THE BVM; LITTLE HOURS; OFFICE OF THE DEAD; MATINS; LAUDS; VESPERS; BREVIARY, ROMAN.

Bibliography: P. SALMON, *The Breviary through the Centuries,* tr. D. MARY (Collegeville, Minnesota 1962). J. A. JUNGMANN, *Pastoral Liturgy* (New York 1962); *Public Worship: A Survey,* tr. C. HOWELL (Collegeville, Minnesota 1957). P. PARSCH, *The Breviary Explained,* tr. W. NAYDEN and C. HOEGERL (St. Louis 1952). H. ASHWORTH, OSB, ''The New Patristic Lectionary,'' *Ephemerides liturgicae* 85 (1971) 306–22. ''La liturgie des heures: le renouveau de l'office divin,'' *Maison-Dieu* 105 (1971). *Liturgia Horarum,* typical ed., 4 v. (Vatican City 1971). A. G. MARTIMORT, ''L' 'Institutio generalis' et la nouvelle 'Liturgia Horarum,''' *Notitiae* 7 (1971) 218–40. A. ROSE, ''La répartition des lectures bibliques dans le livre de la Liturgie des Heures,'' *Ephemerides liturgicae* 85 (1971) 281–301. W. G. STOREY, ''The Liturgy of the Hours: Principles and Practice,'' *Worship* 46 (1972) 194–203. United States Bishops' Committee on the Liturgy, *A Call to Prayer. The Liturgy of the Hours* (Washington, D.C. 1977). P. BOTZ, ''Praying the Psalms,'' *Worship* 46 (1972) 204–13. Congregation for Divine Worship and the Sacraments, *General Instruction of the Liturgy of the Hours* (Washington, D.C. 1975). J. D. CRICHTON, *Christian Celebration: The Prayer of the Church* (London 1976). PAUL VI, *Laudis Canticum, Acta Apostolicae Sedis* 63 (1971) 527–35; tr. *Laudis Canticum. Apostolic Constitution on the Breviary* (Washington, D.C. 1977). F. C. QUINN, ''Music and the Prayer of Praise,'' *Worship* 46 (1972) 214–19. A. M. ROGUET, *The Liturgy of the Hours: The General Instruction with Commentary,* tr. P. COUGHLAN and P. PURDUE (Collegeville, Minnesota 1974). W. G. STOREY, ''Parish Worship: The Liturgy of the Hours,'' *Worship* 49 (1975) 2–12. W. G. STOREY, et al., eds., *Morning Praise and Evensong. A Liturgy of the Hours in Musical Setting* (Notre Dame, Indiana 1973). P. F. BRADSHAW, *Daily Prayer in the Early Church: A Study of the Origin and Early Development of the Divine Office* (London 1981). G. GUIVER, *Company of Voices: Daily Prayer and the People of God* (New York 1988). R. TAFT, *The Liturgy of the Hours in East and West: The Origins of the Divine Office and Its Meaning for Today* 2nd rev. ed. (Collegeville, Minnesota 1993).

[P. SALMON/P. REGAN/J. A. GURRIERI/EDS.]

LITZ, DAMIAN

Marianist educator and columnist for various Catholic newspapers, whose teaching and writing influenced many German-speaking Catholics in the U.S.; b. Eschenbach, Baden, Germany, Aug. 15, 1822; d. San Antonio, TX., Feb. 24, 1903. He entered the Society of Mary in 1844 in France (*see* MARIANISTS). Five years later he volunteered with three other brothers, Andrew Edel, Maximin Zehler, and John Stintzi, to pioneer the educational work of the Society of Mary in America. For more than half a century he established or consolidated schools conducted by his congregation in ten of the principal cities in the U.S. At St. Michael's in Baltimore, MD, Litz began

a 35-year apostolate of the press, a supplementary work of zeal and instruction. His articles for the German Catholic *Volkszeitung* of Baltimore were so much in demand that Catholic papers in Philadelphia, PA; Cincinnati, Ohio; and later in San Antonio, carried his weekly column. Published under the title *Unter Uns,* they helped spread his literary fame.

Bibliography: J. E. GARVIN, *The Centenary of the Society of Mary* (Dayton 1917). J. W. SCHMITZ, *The Society of Mary in Texas* (San Antonio 1951).

[J. W. SCHMITZ]

LIU ZIYN, PETER, ST.

Lay martyr, potter; b. 1843. Zhujiaxie, Shen County, Hebei (Hopeh) Province, China; d. there, July 17, 1900. At the height of the Boxer persecution, many of the Christians in the predominantly Catholic village of Zhujiaxie sought refuge in Tangqui in Ningcing County. The bachelor Peter Liu Ziyn (also given as Tzu-yü, Tzeu-U, or Zeyu) determined to remain and trust in God. He was captured, ordered to apostatize, and beheaded and disemboweled upon refusal. Because of his courage before his tormentors, he was beatified by Pope Pius XII on April 17, 1955 and canonized on Oct. 1, 2000 by Pope John Paul II with Augustine Zhao Rong and companions.

Bibliography: L. MINER, *China's Book of Martyrs: A Record of Heroic Martyrdoms and Marvelous Deliverances of Chinese Christians during the Summer of 1900* (Ann Arbor 1994). J. SIMON, *Sous le Sabre des Boxers* (Lille 1955). C. TESTORE, *Sangue e Palme Sul Fiume Giallo. I Beati Martiri Cinesi Nella Persecuzione Della Boxe Celi Sud-Est, 1900* (Rome 1955). *L'Osservatore Romano,* Eng. Ed. 40 (2000): 1–2, 10.

[K. I. RABENSTEIN]

LIUTBIRG, ST.

Virgin, anchoress; d. *c.* 876 or 882. Little is known of Liutbirg's origin. Her family appears to have lived in the neighborhood of the Altmühl River (southern Germany). She spent some time in the household of Gisla, daughter of the east Saxon Count Hessi. About 824 she had herself enclosed (*see* ANCHORITES) in a hermitage attached to the cloister at Wendhausen by Bishop Thiatgrim of Halberstadt. She instructed young girls in church music and handiwork. HAYMO OF HALBERSTADT often sought her prayers and counsel. Since the fifteenth century the day of her death has been variously assigned to February 28 and December 22, 30, or 31. She was buried at Wendhausen. In the eleventh century she was venerated in Quedlinberg.

Feast: Feb. 28.

Bibliography: *Acta Sanctorum* Feb. 3:723, 768. O. MENZEL, *Das Leben der Liutbirg* (Leipzig 1937); "Die heilige Liutbirg," *Deutsches Archiv für Geschichte des Mittelalters* 2 (1938): 189–193; "Das Leben der Liutbirg," *Sachsen und Anhalt* 13 (Magdeburg 1937): 78–89. W. GROSSE, "Kloster Wendhausen, sein Stiftergeschlecht und seine Klausnerin," *ibid.* 16 (1940): 45–76.

[M. B. RYAN]

LIUTPRAND OF CREMONA

Bishop of Cremona, historian; b. probably in Pavia, Italy, *c.* 920; d. probably 972. He was a scion of a noble Lombard family, and both his father and stepfather had served as ambassadors from King Hugh of Italy to Constantinople in 927 and 942. Liutprand was admitted to the court school in Pavia and later became a deacon in that city. After the overthrow of King Hugh, the family became partisans of King Berengar II of Italy, who sent Liutprand as an envoy to Constantinople in 949. On his return, Liutprand quarreled with Berengar and fled to the court of the Roman Emperor OTTO I THE GREAT. In Frankfurt am Main (956) Liutprand was encouraged by Bishop Recemundus of Elvira, the ambassador of Caliph Abd ar-Rahman II of Córdoba to Otto the Great, to compose a history of his times, and it was there that he wrote his *Antapodosis* (Retribution). Liutprand took part in Otto's second Italian campaign and was installed as bishop of Cremona by the emperor. He continued in Otto's service and was much in evidence when Otto intervened in affairs of the Holy See in 963 and 965—it was these events he described in his *Historia Ottonis*. In 968 Otto sent Liutprand to Constantinople to obtain a bride for his son and heir, OTTO II; Liutprand's third work, the *Relatio de legatione Constantinopolitana,* describes this unsuccessful mission. There is repeated evidence of Liutprand's presence both at court and in his diocese after he returned home, but the date of his death is not known with certainty. However, the first documented date in the career of his successor is March 5, 973.

Liutprand was no theologian, but his historical works show great rhetorical talent. He mixed verse with his prose in the fashion of the satire of Menippus, probably imitating Boethius's *De consolatione philosophiae* in this matter; he often cited Latin classical writers and delighted in demonstrating his knowledge of Greek, an uncommon achievement in his time. His works reveal a man of turbulent temperament. His pride, his hatred of political opponents, his scorn for clerical and secular Rome as well as for the Byzantine court, led to drastic distortions in his accounts of situations and personalities. Liutprand's political goal was the growth and freedom of the Lombard kingdom. Although he approved of the emperor's intervention in Italy, he was willing to grant the Lombard crown only to the person of Otto, and not to the German king per se. Furthermore, for Liutprand, the office of emperor had only canonical, not civil, function, and its universality derived only from its protection of the Roman church, which was the head of the universal Church.

Liutprand's *Antapodosis* (in six books written between 955 and 962 and left incomplete) claims to portray "the deeds of emperors and kings of all Europe," but in fact it confines itself to events in Germany, Italy, and Byzantium beginning with the year 888. The work lacks chronological detail and is anecdotal in style, but it remains a valuable medieval source. Its initially sober style gives way to violent invective against Berengar II and Queen Willa (hence the title). Beginning in 935, the work is based on personal experience; it breaks off in the midst of the description of the 949 embassy. The *Antapodosis* may well have prompted Adalbert of Magdeburg to write his history of the years from 907 to 967 as a continuation of REGINO OF PRÜM's chronicle. The *Historia Ottonis* (to 964) describes Otto I's clashes with the Roman nobility and with their papal nominees JOHN XII and BENEDICT V. The work is a semiofficial apologia of Ottonian policy for the years from 960 to 964 and is based partly on documents. The *Relatio de legatione Constantinopolitana* is a diatribe against Emperor Nicephorus II Phocas, calculated to incite Otto to a new war against Byzantium in southern Italy. The *Chronicon (Patrologia Latina* 136:967–1134), the *Adversaria (Patrologia Latina* 136:1134–1180), and the *Opusculum de vitis Romanorum pontificum (Patrologia Latina* 129:1149–1256) ascribed to Liutprand are spurious.

Bibliography: Works. *Monumenta Germaniae Historica: Scriptores* (Berlin 1826–) 3:273–363. *Patrologia Latina,* ed. J. P. MIGNE, 217 v. (Paris 1878–90) 136:787–938. *Monumenta Germaniae Historica: Scriptores rerum Germanicarum* (Berlin 1826–) (3d ed. 1915) 41:1–212. L. A. MURATORI, *Rerum italicarum scriptores, 500–1500,* 25 v. in 28 (2d, new ed. Città di Castello 1900–) 2.1:425–489, except for the *Historia Ottonis,* Eng. tr. by F. A. WRIGHT (London 1930). **Literature.** A. POTTHAST, *Bibliotheca historica medii aevi* (2d ed. 1896: repr. Graz 1954) 1:742–744. J. BECKER, ed., *Monumenta Germaniae Historica: Scriptores rerum Germanicarum* (3d ed. Berlin 1915) 41:vii–xl. M. MANITIUS, *Geschichte der lateinischen Literatur des Mittelalters,* 3 v. (Munich 1911–31) 2:166–175. F. C. DAHLMANN and G. WAITZ, *Quellenkunde der deutschen Geschichte* (9th ed. Leipzig 1932) 5946. M. LINTZEL, *Studien über Liutprand von Cremona* (Berlin 1933), reprt. in *Ausgewählte Schriften* 2 (1961): 351–398. S. PIVANO, *Enciclopedia Italiana di scienzi, littere ed arti,* 36 v. (Rome 1929–39, suppl. 1938–) 21:316. A. CUTOLO, ed., *Tutte le opere* (Milan 1945) 1–43. W. WATTENBACH, *Deutschlands Geschichtsquellen im Mittelalter. Deutsche Kaiserzeit* (3d ed. Tübingen 1948) 1.2:318–321. G. E. FONTANA, *Annali di Bibl. govern. e Libreria civica di Cremona* 1 (1948): 75–; 2 (1949): 78–. G. ARNALDI, "Liutprando e l'idea di Roma nell'lato medioevo," *Archivio della Società romana di storia patria* 79 (1956): 23–34. J. E. REXINE, "The Roman Bishop Liutprand and Constantinople,'' *Greek Orthodox Theological Review* 3 (1957): 197–211.

[H. M. KLINKENBERG]

LIUTWIN OF TRIER, ST.

Founder, bishop; d. Reims, Sept. 29, 717–722. Liutwin was descended from Frankish nobility that had considerable prerogatives under the CAROLINGIANS. In 690 Liutwin founded his monastery of Mettlach. Upon the death of his uncle, Basinus, in 705, he succeeded to his See of TRIER. He also became bishop of the dioceses of REIMS and Laon, probably through the grace of CHARLES MARTEL (716–741). Liutwin's son Milo succeeded him as bishop of Trier and of Reims. Liutwin was buried at Mettlach; his remains were translated some time after 1483. His life was written by THIOFRID OF ECHTERNACH (*Monumenta Germaniae Historica: Scriptores* [Berlin 1826–] 15:1261–1268).

Feast: Sept. 29.

Bibliography: L. DUCHESNE, *Fastes épiscopaux de l'ancienne Gaule,* 3 v. (2d ed. Paris 1907–15) v. 3. *Bibliotheca hagiographica latina antiquae et mediae aetatis,* 2 v. (Brussels 1898–1901) 2:4955–4959. A. M. ZIMMERMANN, *Kalendarium Benedictinum: Die Heiligen und Seligen des Benediktinerorderns und seiner Zweige,* 4 v. (Metten 1933–38) 3:115–116. E. EWIG, ''Milo et eiusmodi similes,'' *Sankt Bonifatius: Gedenkgabe zum zwölfhundertsten Todestag* (Fulda 1954) 412–440.

[G. J. DONNELLY]

LIVARIUS OF METZ, ST.

According to a twelfth-century legend, a knight, Livarius (Livier), along with Saints Purgentius and Agentius, was martyred by the Huns at Marsal, south of Metz, in Lorraine, where there is a chapel dedicated to them. Other accounts would place the martyrdom of Livarius at Lyons. If there is any historical basis to the legend, it will most likely be found in the Hungarian incursion of the ninth and tenth centuries. Late in the tenth century the relics of Livarius were removed to the abbey church of Saint-Vincent in Metz by Bishop Theodoric I. In the eleventh century they were translated to the church of Saint-Polyeucte in Metz, which was rededicated to Livarius in the twelfth century.

Feast: July 17.

Bibliography: R. HARMAND, ''Les Miracles de Salival: La Légende de Saint Livier . . . ,'' *Bulletin Mensuel de la Société d'Archéologie Lorraine* 7 (1907): 190–212, notice of this article in *Analecta Bollandiana* 27 (1908): 226–227. H. LECLERCQ, *Dictionnaire d'archéologie chrétienne et de liturgie* 15 v. (Paris 1907–53)

11.1:810–817. J. L. BAUDOT and L. CHAUSSIN, *Vies des saints et des bienheureux selon l'ordre du calendrier avec l'historique des fêtes,* 12 v. (Paris 1935–56) 7:377.

[W. A. JURGENS]

LIZÁRRAGA, REGINALDO DE

Dominican bishop and author; b. Medellín, Extremadura, Spain, 1539; d. Asunción, Paraguay, Nov. 1609. Baltasar de Obando, as he was born, went to America with his parents. In 1560 he became a Dominican in Lima. He went to Chile for the first time as head of the province of St. Lawrence Martyr. His trip from Callao, Peru, to Coquimbo, Chile, was exceptional because it took him only 22 days. His second trip took place in 1587, and he was still in Santiago when Bishop Medellín, a relative of his, died (1593). Later he lived in the Jauja Valley, where he first planned his book. In 1599 he was made bishop of Imperial, Chile, but he remained in Lima until the middle of 1602. His see city had been ravaged by a native uprising begun in 1598, and he had to move to Concepción (1603). He did not stay there long. By the beginning of 1608 he was on his way to the Bishopric in Rio de la Plata, with headquarters in Asunción. Fray Reginaldo was both a man of action and an author. Meléndez, his biographer, mentions six of his works. Only two are extant: one report and the extensive *Descripción breve de toda la tierra del Perú, Tucumán, Rio de la Plata y Chile,* also called *Descripción y población de las Indias* (C. A. Romero, ed., Lima 1908; R. Rojas, ed., Buenos Aires 1916). Caillet-Bois characterizes this work as a ''little encyclopedia of practical knowledge.'' The report entitled ''Una opinión relativa a la guerra contra los indios chilenos,'' written in Lima in 1599, has been published in *Cuerpo de documentos del siglo XVI* (Mexico City 1943).

Bibliography: J. T. MEDINA, *Historia de la literatura colonial de Chile,* 3 v. (Santiago de Chile 1878). R. ROJAS, *Los coloniales,* v. 3, 4 of *Historia la literatura argentina,* 9 v. (4th ed. Buenos Aires 1957). J. CAILLET BOIS, *Historia de la literatura argentina* (Buenos Aires 1958).

[A. M. ESCUDERO]

LLANDAFF, ANCIENT SEE OF

Llandaff, Ancient See of, one of the four ancient Welsh dioceses, near Cardiff, Wales. Like other ancient churches of WALES, Llandaff was founded by the missionary activity of Celtic monks of the 5th and 6th centuries. St. Oudoceus (d. *c.* 590), to whom with SS. Dubricius and Teilo the church was originally dedicated, is believed to have founded Llandaff. Though doubts have been expressed whether it was the seat of the pre-Norman bishops of Morgannwg (modern Glamorgan), there is good reason for thinking it an ancient foundation. But its early history is as much confused as illuminated by *Liber Landavensis*, a 12th-century compilation containing authentic material that purports to tell the history of the diocese but is perhaps chiefly concerned with validating the territorial and other claims of its post-Norman bishops. After the Norman Conquest Llandaff's boundaries were determined, not without bitter controversies, and covered most of the modern counties of Glamorgan and Monmouth. Cathedral dignitaries and capitular organization, archdeaconries, rural deaneries, parish boundaries, and Roman discipline were introduced at the same time. Urban of Llandaff (1107–33), first builder of the cathedral, was the first Welsh bishop to take the oath of canonical obedience to Canterbury. The fortunes of the see were closely controlled by the lords of Glamorgan until 1290, when Edward I asserted royal rights over it. Tension was created in the 14th century by conflict between the claims of the pope, who succeeded in providing many bishops, and those of the king and the almost invariably royal nominees. Much damaged during the Glyn Dwr Rebellion (1400–10), the see remained in poverty-stricken condition during the 15th century. It was valued at £144 in *Valor Ecclesiasticus*, but suffered heavy losses of its possessions under Bp. Anthony Kitchen (1545–63), the only Marian bishop to accept the Elizabethan settlement. Today Llandaff, as well as the Dioceses of Monmouth and Swanseand-Brecon, which were formed from it, is one of the six dioceses of the Church of Wales (*see also* ST. ASAPH; ST. DAVIDS).

Bibliography: *A. Bibliography of the History of Wales* (2d ed. Cardiff 1962). J. C. DAVIES, *Episcopal Acts Relating to Welsh Dioceses, 1066–1272,* 2 v. (Cardiff 1946–48). E. T. DAVIES, ed. *The Story of the Church in Glamorgan, 560–1960* (London 1962). C. BROOKE, ''The Archbishops of St. Davids, Llandaff and Caerleon–on–Isk,'' *Studies in the Early British Church*, ed. N. CHADWICK (Cambridge, England 1958) 201–242. G. WILLIAMS, *The Welsh Church from Conquest to Reformation* (Cardiff 1962).

[G. WILLIAMS]

LLANTHONY, MONASTERY OF

House of CANONS REGULAR OF ST. AUGUSTINE, situated in the remote valley of the Honddu (hence its name Llanhonddu or Church-of-the-Honddu) in the Black Mountains of southeastern Wales. The priory began as the hermitage of William de Lacy, a knight turned hermit in the time of William Rufus (1090–1100). A church was consecrated in 1108 and evolved into an Augustinian priory *c.* 1118. It flourished until the turmoil in WALES following the death of Henry I (1135). A second priory,

The ruins of Llanthony Priory in Gwent, Wales. (©John Heseltine/CORBIS)

Llanthony Secunda, was then founded near Gloucester. At Llanthony Prima new buildings of great beauty were begun *c.* 1175 to 1190 and completed by 1230. The two priories became independent by agreement *c.* 1205. Llanthony Prima, though holding considerable possessions in its own vicinity and in Ireland, suffered a marked decline during the difficult period of the 14th and 15th centuries. In 1481 Henry DEANE, prior of Llanthony Secunda, obtained a royal grant for the merger of Llanthony Prima with his own priory. Abp. William WARHAM visited Llanthony Prima in 1504. It continued to maintain a prior and four canons until the Dissolution, when its income was estimated in *Valor Ecclesiasticus* as £112. On March 10, 1538, the deed of surrender of both priories was signed by Richard, prior of Llanthony Secunda, and David, prior of Llanthony Prima, as well as 23 others.

Bibliography: *A Bibliography of the History of Wales* (2d ed. Cardiff 1962). G. WILLIAMS, *The Welsh Church from Conquest to Reformation* (Cardiff 1962). O. E. CRASTER, *Llanthony Priory* (London 1963).

[G. WILLIAMS]

LLORENTE, JUAN ANTONIO

Spanish historian; b. Rincón del Soto, Aragon, March 30, 1756; d. Madrid, Spain, Feb. 5, 1823. Llorente was educated in Tarragona and continued his studies in Roman law and Canon Law at Zaragoza. He was ordained in 1779, and in 1781 became an advocate at the Council of Castile. The following year the bishop of Calahorra appointed him vicar-general of that diocese. Although in his religious views Llorente was already strongly influenced by JANSENISM and the ideas of the Enlightenment, he was appointed a commissioner of the Inquisition. In 1794 his plan for a reform of the Holy Office was used by the royal minister, Gaspar Jovellanos, and later Manuel de Godoy used it for the initial steps in the establishment of a schismatic church. Llorente's program envisaged the restoration of the Spanish Church to conditions that had prevailed in the sixth and seventh centuries, and this was set forth in his *Collección diplomatica de varios papeles antiguos y modernos sobre dispensas matrimoniales y otros puntos de disciplina ecclesiástica.* During the French occupation of Spain, he gave his allegiance to Joseph Bonaparte and was finally put in charge of the property confiscated from the Church by the French regime. The French defeat in Spain forced Llorente to go to France, and he took with him a good part of the archives of the Aragonese Inquisition. Although he wrote many books, a major part of them polemical in character, his most valuable work is his *Histoire critique de l'Inquisition d'Espagne. . .* (4 v. Paris 1817–18).

[S. J. T. MILLER]

LLOYD, JOHN, ST.

Welsh priest, martyr; b. Brecon, Wales, 1630?; d. Cardiff, July 22, 1679. Nothing is known of his life before he entered the seminary at Valladolid in 1649. He was ordained on June 7, 1653. On April 17, 1654, he left for England, and he worked on the mission in his native Wales. He was marked out as a victim by the Calvinist John Arnold, a justice of the peace, and after the outbreak of the Oates persecution, Lloyd was arrested in Glamorgan, Nov. 20, 1678. It was reported that he used to say Mass at Treivor, Llantilio (where there were many Catholics), and at Penrhos. No other charges were made against him. On his capture he was confined to Cardiff Castle in the same underground dungeon as Philip EVANS, with whom he was later tried and executed. Although many Catholics were brutally treated in an attempt to make them testify that they had witnessed these two priests performing their sacred functions, none did; eventually an old lady and her daughter were bribed into testifying against them. On their false evidence, Lloyd and Evans together were indicted and condemned (May 3, 1679), on the sole ground of their priesthood. They were not executed until July 22. Lloyd had first to witness the barbarous sentence of death carried out on his companion,

Philip Evans. On the scaffold, in Gallows Field, he explained, "I never was a good speaker in my life"; and in a simple manner proclaimed his own faith, asked forgiveness of any persons he may have offended, and urged his fellow Catholics to bear their sufferings with patience. He was beatified by Pius XI on Dec. 15, 1929 and canonized by Paul VI on Oct. 25, 1970.

Feast: July 22; Oct. 25 (Feast of the 40 Martyrs of England and Wales); May 4 (Feast of the English Martyrs in England).

See Also: ENGLAND, SCOTLAND, AND WALES, MARTYRS OF.

Bibliography: T. P. ELLIS, *The Catholic Martyrs of Wales* (London 1933). J. STONOR, *Six Welsh Martyrs* (Postulation Pamphlets; London 1961) 13–14. R. CHALLONER, *Memoirs of Missionary Priests,* ed. J. H. POLLEN (rev. ed. London 1924; repr. Farnborough 1969). A. BUTLER, *The Lives of the Saints,* ed. H. THURSTON and D. ATTWATER, 4 v. (New York 1956) 3:166–167. J. GILLOW, *A Literary and Biographical History or Bibliographical Dictionary of the English Catholics from 1534 to the Present Time* (London and New York 1855–1902) 4:289–290.

[G. FITZHERBERT]

LOAYSA, JERÓNIMO DE

First archbishop of Peru; b. Trujillo or Talavera, Spain, 1498; d. Lima, Oct. 25, 1575. In 1540, eight years after the conquest of Peru, the Spanish found it necessary to enlarge the ecclesiastical organization for the area; the bishopric of Cuzco, the only one created thus far, was not enough. That year the Castillan monarch asked papal approval for the erection of a new diocese in Lima, already the seat of the government and later the capital of the viceroyalty. The pope acted on the request in May of 1541 and appointed as first bishop the Dominican, Jerónimo de Loaysa. Loaysa, born of a noble family, had entered the Dominican convent in Córdoba, probably influenced by family connections with the order: his cousin was Fray García de Loaysa, cardinal primate of Spain, master general of the order, and president of the Council of Indies. After making his profession, he studied humanities in Coria and theology in Seville, completing his theological studies at the Dominican college of San Gregorio in Valladolid under some of the outstanding theologians of the period, who were occupied with the moral problems involved in the conquest of the Indies. This influence, added to his Thomistic background, served him well when he was put in charge of the religious organization of the viceroyalty of Peru. After teaching at Córdoba and Granada and serving as prior in Carboneras, he decided to go to the Indies and devote himself to missionary work. He arrived in the New World late in 1529 or early in 1530, but within the year he was back in Spain as missionary commissary of the order, raising funds for the missions. While there, he was nominated bishop of Cartagena and consecrated in Valladolid in June of 1537. He made his solemn entrance into the diocese at the end of 1538 but was there only a few years until his appointment as bishop of Lima.

Loaysa arrived in Lima on July 25, 1543, in the middle of the civil wars in which the viceroy had just been taken prisoner. The bishop tried in vain to reconcile the quarreling factions. In Panama, he met the new governor, La Gasca, sent by the king to pacify the area, and returned to Lima with him. He then proceeded to the canonical organization of the Church, giving it the same constitutions as those of the Diocese of Seville. The civil wars were hardly over, and he was involved in building the cathedral and laying plans for the conversion of the indigenous peoples, when he received the bulls of Paul II raising Lima to an archbishopric and appointing him first archbishop. In December of 1549 he published a much-needed *Instrucción* in which he set forth in a concrete fashion the means to be followed in missionary work. To further inspire missionary activity and to discuss the problems involved in it, he called the First Provincial Council of Lima in October of 1551. From this council came regulations for systematic evangelization and a code for canonical discipline that remained fundamentally in force until the Third Council of Lima in 1583. With the publication of the Tridentine decrees, Loaysa called the Second Provincial Council in March of 1567 to incorporate them into the ecclesiastical regulations of Peru. This council followed the decrees of Trent very closely, making some attempt to adapt them to the reality of Peru. However, the enforcement of its regulations was negligible.

Bishop Loaysa founded many parishes and furthered the building of many convents. Perhaps his most important work was the founding of the Hospital de Santa Ana, where natives were cared for and given religious instruction. In 1550 he provided for a school there in which the children of caciques were educated. He lived there himself until his death.

Bibliography: M. DE MENDIBURU, *Diccionario histórico-biográfico del Peru*, 11 v. (2d ed. Lima 1931–34) 7:38–66.

[F. DE ARMAS MEDINA]

LOBBES, ABBEY OF

A Benedictine monastery near Thuin in Belgian Flanders, founded between 636 and 654 by St. Landelin in honor of St. Peter. Lobbes (Laubias, Laubacum) en-joyed a period of prosperity until the 9th century, when it fell victim to the custom of appointing laymen as abbots, and its possessions and reputation began to decline. From 885 to 960 the bishops of Liège held the abbatial office, and during this period the abbey's life was disturbed also by invasions of the region by the Normans and Hungarians. In 960 the abbey's independence was restored and it was again allowed to choose its own abbots. Under a succession of great leaders—Folcwin (965–990), Heriger (990–1007), Richard (1020–32), and Hugh (1033–53)—Lobbes again prospered. From its flourishing theological school came future bishops and abbots for other monasteries. Several important historical works were produced during this period: the *Gesta abbatum Lobbiensium*, written by Abbot Folcwin, and the *Annales Laubacenses*, a history of the Carolingian kingdom. The period of prosperity continued until the second half of the 12th century, when a decline set in, accompanied by continual financial difficulties which were not overcome until the accession of William Cordier to the abbacy in 1495. The monastery was almost totally destroyed by fire in 1546, but it was soon rebuilt under the energetic Abbot William Caulier (1520–50). In 1569 Lobbes united with other Benedictine monasteries in the Congregation of Exempt Monasteries of Flanders. When the French revolutionary armies destroyed the monastery and its rich library in 1794, there were still 43 monks in the community.

Bibliography: J. WARICHEZ, *L'Abbaye de Lobbes depuis les origines jusqu'en 1200* (Tournai 1909). J. VOS, *Lobbes, son abbaye et son chapitre*, 2 v. (Louvain 1865). U. BERLIÈRE, *Monasticon belge* (Bruges 1890–) 1:179–228. M. DIERICKX, *Lexikon für Theologie und Kirche*, ed. J. HOFER and K. RAHNER (Freiburg 1957–65) 6:1108–09. L. H. COTTINEAU, *Répertoire topobibliographique des abbayes et prieurés* (Mâcon 1935–39) 1:1632.

[C. FALK]

LOBO, DUARTE

Prominent Portuguese composer; b. Alentejo(?), *c.* 1563; d. Lisbon, Sept. 24, 1646. As a choirboy studying in Évora cathedral with Manuel Mendes, he attracted the attention of Cardinal Henry (archbishop 1574–76), brother of King João III. After serving as chapelmaster for the Hospital Real in Lisbon, he was Lisbon cathedral chapelmaster from *c.* 1594 until his death. During his later years, he was also rector of the Seminário de São Bartolomeu in Lisbon. His numerous pupils included such erudite theorists as António Fernandes (*Arte de Musica*, Lisbon 1626) and João Álvares Frovo; but his own works published at Antwerp—*Natalitiae noctis Responsoria* (1602), *Magnificat* (1605), and books of Masses (1621 and 1639)—indicate less learning than the liturgical collections of Francisco Garro (1609) and Manuel Cardoso (1613, 1621, 1636, 1648). The spread of Lobo's fame is attested by copies, both manuscript and printed, of his works found at Seville and Mexico City cathedrals. Alonso Lobe, sometimes confused with Duarte, was a Spanish contemporary (b. Osuna, *c.* 1555; d. Seville, April 5, 1617) who published *Liber primus missarum* at Madrid (1602) and was chapelmaster at Toledo (1593–1604) and Seville (1604–17).

Bibliography: M. DE SAMPAYO RIBEIRO, *Die Musik in Geschichte und Gegenwart,* ed. F. BLUME (Kassel-Basel 1949–) 8:1073–74. M. JOAQUIM, *Vinte livros de música polifónica* (Lisbon 1953) 57–59. G. BOURLIGUEUX, ''Duarte Lobo'' in *The New Grove Dictionary of Music and Musicians,* vol. 11, ed. S. SADIE (New York 1980) 102–103. D. M. RANDEL, ed., *The Harvard Biographical Dictionary of Music* (Cambridge 1996) 512. N. SLONIMSKY, ed. *Baker's Biographical Dictionary of Musicians,* 8th ed. (New York 1992) 1072.

[R. STEVENSON]

LOBO, JERÓNIMO

Portuguese missionary, travel writer; b. Lisbon, 1595; d. Portugal, 1678. Lobo entered the Society of Jesus in 1609 and was ordained in 1621. He made a dangerous voyage to Goa (1622) and spent the following year completing his theological studies. He began his long missionary work in Ethiopia in 1625; the steps that led to it are necessary as background.

After the Portuguese embassy to Ethiopia, of which Dom Rodrigo de Lima was the head and Francisco Álvares, chaplain, rather close military and ecclesiastical relations between the two Christian nations continued for a century. At first the Portuguese Catholics respected the Ethiopian Eastern rite. Later, however, the Portuguese manifested considerable intolerance, and about 1550, the Jesuits assumed the delicate task of instructing the Ethiopians in ''orthodox'' Christianity. A Portuguese Jesuit, João Nunes Barreto, was consecrated in Lisbon in 1555 as Patriarch of Ethiopia, but, although other Jesuits reached Ethiopia, he never got farther than Goa, where he died in 1562. Growing Turkish pressure in the Red Sea area made access to Ethiopia increasingly difficult for Western missionaries. Finally, in 1603 Father Pero Páez reinforced the earlier Jesuits. Before Páez's death in 1622, the emperor was baptized.

At Páez's suggestion, Father Afonso Mendes became patriarch of Ethiopia on March 4, 1623, the first such prelate since André de Oviedo, Barreto's successor (1562) who died in Ethiopia in 1580. Mendes set out at once for the East, and Lobo joined him in India. They reached Ethiopia in 1625 and began a fruitful apostolate.

The Catholic emperor died in 1632, and the ecclesiastical picture changed at once; in 1634 all the Jesuits were expelled.

Lobo returned to Goa and then went on to report to Madrid and Rome the desperate plight of the Ethiopian mission. He went back to Goa in 1640 and remained there for almost 20 years. He spent the last years of his life in Portugal.

Lobo wrote in Portuguese two unpublished works concerning Ethiopia, one of which, translated into English by Sir Peter Wyche and published in London in 1669, survives in the library of the Royal Society. The other, much more extensive, was lost for many years. A manuscript has recently been discovered, however, and is now being readied for publication. The Abbé Joachim Le Grand translated a different manuscript of this longer work into French (Paris, 1728). Young Samuel Johnson adapted Le Grand's work in his English translation (London, 1735); this early Johnsonian interest in Ethiopia reached full flower in *Rasselas* (London, 1759).

Bibliography: D. M. LOCKHART, *Father Jeronymo Lobo's Writings concerning Ethiopia, Including Hitherto Unpublished Manuscripts in the Palmella Library* (Doctoral diss. unpub. Harvard U. 1958); '''The Fourth Son of the Mighty Emperor': The Ethiopian Background of Johnson's *Rasselas,*'' *Publications of the Modern Language Associations* 78 (1963): 516–528.

[F. M. ROGERS]

LOCATION (UBI)

One of the ten Aristotelian CATEGORIES OF BEING (Gr. ποû, Lat. *ubi*) that answers the question ''where?'' Although ARISTOTLE only gives examples (Cat. 2a 1, 11b 14), St. THOMAS AQUINAS defines location as the state of being in place (*In 11 meta.* 12.2376). By analogy with time (cf. *In 4 phys.* 20.11), this means that location, being in place, is the same as being measured by or commensurate with place (*In 3 phys.* 5.15). The implications of this definition are a subject of controversy among scholastics. There are three fundamental views: that location adds an intrinsic, nonrelative MODE to bodies (F. Suárez); that it adds only a relative mode, based on extrinsic denomination (John of St. Thomas); or that it is a pure extrinsic denomination—considered to be enough to constitute it a true category (modern authors).

See Also: PLACE; SITUATION (SITUS); BILOCATION; IMPENETRABILITY.

Bibliography: R. MASI, *Cosmologia* (Rome 1961). P. H. J. HOENEN, *Cosmologia* (5th ed. Rome 1956).

[P. R. DURBIN]

LOCCUM, ABBEY OF

Cistercian monastery near Nienburg, Lower Saxony, in the former Diocese of Minden; founded by Count Wilbrand of Hallermund and colonized by monks from Volkenrode in 1163. It is the best-preserved monastic structure in northern Germany. The basilica, which has three aisles, was built between 1240 and 1280 (length about 200 feet; height about 60 feet). The east end corresponds to the second church of CLAIRVAUX; its lines are austere and somber. Noteworthy are the gatehouse, with chapel, and the chapter house (both 13th century), the cloister, built *c.* 1300, and the late Gothic refectory. One of its foundations is the monastery at Reinfeld, near Lübeck (1190). Loccum, under the leadership of Abbot (Bl.) Berthold, participated in the evangelization of Livonia, where the abbot died a martyr's death in 1198. The monastery made progress under Abbot John VII about 1593. However, it accepted the Confession of AUGSBURG and became a Lutheran monastery, but in so doing it retained many old monastic traditions, such as the abbot, prior, customs, and the *Opus Dei.* Vespers, now called *Hora,* are still said today in the ancient choir by the community and *hospites* (candidates for the seminary). The abbot of Loccum is the present bishop of Hannover and follows pontifical rubrics at certain solemnities. In the 18th century the learned Abbot Gerhard Molanus (1677–1722) participated in theological discussions with LEIBNIZ, BOSSUET, and SPINOZA in an effort to realize a reunion of the Lutheran and Catholic faiths. The Lutheran Academy, which moved to Loccum in 1952, has won ecumenical acclaim for its annual interconfessional dialogues (*see* ECUMENICAL MOVEMENT).

Bibliography: O. KARPA, *Kloster Loccum 800 Jahre Zisterzienser Abtei* (Hanover 1963).

[A. SCHNEIDER]

LOCI THEOLOGICI

A term made classical by Melchior CANO (d. 1560) in *De locis theologicis,* published 1563. The principles underlying Cano's work were traced by St. Thomas Aquinas (*Summa theologiae* 1a, 1.8 ad 2), but no treatise had ever undertaken such an extensive study of the principles presupposed by the work of THEOLOGY. An argument from authority is essential to theology, since theology is a derivative of supernatural faith. Cano's treatise studies the loci (places) in which this authority may be found. (The term *locus,* reflecting Renaissance interest in classical rhetoric, is commendably flexible as defined by Cano. *See De locis* 1.3: "domicilia omnium argumentorum theologicorum"; Moran, 80). Cano enumerates ten loci. Seven are proper to theology: (1) Sacred Scripture, (2) apostolic traditions, (3) the universal Church, (4) Church councils, (5) the papal magisterium, (6) Church Fathers, and (7) theologians and canonists. Three are borrowed by theology: (8) natural reason, (9) philosophers and jurists, and (10) history and human tradition. Among the proper loci he distinguishes those that are fundamental, containing the deposit of revelation (1, 2), from those that are declarative, articulating the content of the fundamental loci in successive ages. Declarative loci may provide an efficacious argument, since they involve the infallible magisterium (3, 4, 5), or they may provide a probable argument (6, 7). Associated with his loci, Cano developed a code of theological NOTES, employed to categorize the conclusions of theological argumentation (*De locis* 12.6–10).

A notable contributor to theological science, Cano reflects shortcomings of his age (*see* Y. M. J. Congar, *Dictionnaire de théologie catholique,* 15.1:422–423). His distinctions are unquestionably valid, but his neglect of the wisdom character of theology (whereby it preserves its living unity by concerning itself primarily with the mysteries enunciated in its principles and the light they shed one upon the other, rather than with argumentation from the principles) permitted these distinctions to establish a precedent of codification and dissection that has characterized subsequent theology. In particular, Cano and later theologians had a superficial view of the mystery of the Church, a view that has made possible a progressive dissociation of Scripture, tradition, and magisterium. Revived awareness in mid-20th century of the mystery of the Church made possible, in the view of many, a renewal of theology's understanding of the presence in the world of the living Word of God that it must interpret to men (see the debates of Vatican Council II). Moreover, contemporary theology's awareness of historical perspective in revelation and the life of the Church makes it possible to deal with the problem raised by Cano in a more adequate manner.

See Also: DEPOSIT OF FAITH; DOGMATIC THEOLOGY; DOGMATIC THEOLOGY, ARTICLES ON; METHODOLOGY (THEOLOGY); REVELATION, FONTS OF; THEOLOGY, ARTICLES ON; TRADITION (IN THEOLOGY).

Bibliography: A. GARDEIL, *Dictionnaire de théologie catholique,* ed. A. VACANT et al., 15 v. (Paris 1903–50; Tables générales 1951) 9.1:712–747. A. LANG, *Die Loci Theologici des Melchior Cano und die Methode des dogmatischen Beweises* (Munich 1925). G. MORAN, *Scripture and Tradition* (New York 1963), summary of contemporary controversy concerning the two principle loci of Cano, throwing light on the whole question.

[J. THORNHILL]

LOCKE, JOHN

British philosopher, generally regarded as the founder of EMPIRICISM; b. Wrington, near Bristol, Aug. 29, 1632; d. Oates, Essex, Oct. 28, 1704. Locke was educated at home until he attended Westminster school in 1646. He later went to Oxford, where he received the B.A. and M.A. degrees. At Oxford he read philosophy, became interested in physics and chemistry, and took his medical degree (1674); he never practiced medicine, however, turning his attention to public affairs instead. In 1665 he took a position as secretary to Sir Walter Vane and two years later entered the service of Lord Ashley, afterward the first Earl of Shaftesbury. Because of his involvement in political intrigue with Shaftesbury, Locke was forced to flee to Holland. He did not return until 1688, when William of Orange became king of England.

Locke's is a plain historical method by which he hoped to achieve an empirical analysis of knowledge based on EXPERIENCE and devoid of the pretensions of RATIONALISM. He applies this analysis to ethics, politics, and religion.

Theory of Knowledge. As his main work, *The Essay concerning Human Understanding* (1690), indicates, Locke is no radical empiricist. The *Essay* is characterized by a plain, commonsense approach and its rational reflection on ordinary experience. In it, Locke rejects all innate ideas and insists that the sources of knowledge are experiential, viz., sensation and reflection. From sensation the mind derives ideas, while from reflection it becomes aware of such internal operations as thinking, willing, and desiring. Locke divides ideas into two different classes: simple and complex. Simple ideas are produced in the mind in various ways: (1) some are formed by an external object acting on one or more of the external senses, for example, the idea of hardness or sweetness; (2) others are caused by the internal actions of thinking and willing; (3) still others are produced by a combination of internal and external activity, such as the ideas of pain and pleasure. Complex ideas are combinations of simple ideas, and of these Locke lists three different classes: (1) ideas of modes, which are collections of simple ideas conceived of as modifications of substance; (2) ideas of substances; and (3) ideas of relations.

Ideas and Understanding. Whatever the nature of the idea, simple or complex, it is the idea that the mind understands. Man knows ideas, and knowledge is nothing else but an apprehension of the agreement or disagreement of ideas (*Essay*, bk. 4, ch. 1). This conception leads Locke into an almost complete SUBJECTIVISM, against which he struggles in vain throughout the various parts of the *Essay*. The agreement or disagreement of ideas can take various forms: (1) identity and diversity, (2) relation between ideas, (3) coexistence of ideas, and (4) ideas of real existence (*Essay*, bk. 4, ch. 3). It is in examining the different kinds of ideas composing knowledge that Locke discerns the meaning and structure of reality.

Cause of Ideas. Having rejected the doctrine of innate ideas, Locke is forced to posit something as the cause of simple ideas. Hence he argues that things or substances that affect man in certain ways must exist. Since what man knows is the effect on him, substance must remain an unknown that is supposed to exist as a substratum for the various qualities and powers through which the thing is able to act. Here, however, a distinction must be made. Since man experiences certain affections that are consistently the same in relation to all material things, such things must really possess these qualities. All bodies, for example, appear as solid, as having some shape and magnitude, and as being in motion or at rest. These are primary qualities and are real modifications of bodies. There are, however, other affections that differ from individual to individual, such as sweet and bitter, hot and cold. These subjective affections, corresponding to the sensations of the external senses traditionally affirmed—color, taste, odor, touch, and sound—Locke calls secondary qualities. The only objective references such qualities have are the powers bodies have to cause such affections in a sensing subject. From this viewpoint SUBSTANCE is merely a name given to a collection of secondary sense qualities. Gold, for example, means merely a combination of the simple ideas of yellow, hard, shiny, etc. This name is the nominal essence, as distinguished from the real essence, which is supposed to exist beneath the primary qualities and powers, but which can never be known (*Essay*, bk. 2, ch. 23; bk. 3, ch. 6).

Locke, however, always remains a realist—if an inconsistent one—because he never denies the existence of this unknown substratum. He holds, too, the reality of primary qualities and their real power to affect man. He also makes use of several so-called commonsense arguments to establish the reality of a material world distinct from the knowing subject. He refers to the idea of cause as an idea with a foundation in real existence, and he appeals to the real idea of fire as opposed to the imaginary idea of fire. Let one put his hand into a real fire, Locke notes, and he straightway understands the difference (*Essay*, bk. 4, ch. 11).

Divisions of Knowledge. Locke divides the mind's knowledge of ideas on the basis of degrees of intensity. First is intuitive knowledge, which is an immediate apprehension of the agreement or disagreement between ideas; e.g., the idea of bitter is not the same as that of yellow. Then there is knowledge of ideas attained through the mediation of other ideas apprehended intuitively; this is demonstrative knowledge, although Locke is careful to point out that intuition must accompany each step in the demonstrative process. Mathematical knowledge is of this sort. On the level of the natural sciences, however, Locke does not think that necessary connections can be established between ideas. He sees only a *de facto* connection in this area; hence, he does not regard the conclusions of the natural sciences as demonstrable, but only as enjoying high degrees of probability.

Existence of God. Under demonstrative knowledge Locke includes also the knowledge of God's existence. His proof begins with an intuition of one's own existence. Since nothing cannot produce something and since man is aware that he had a beginning, he must have been produced by something else. If there is not some eternal being, the problem simply regresses indefinitely. Therefore, something eternal must exist, and this is God. Furthermore, not only does God produce that which has a beginning, but He also produces it as the kind of being that it is. Again, there are created beings that have intelligence and the capacity to love. Hence, God must also be intelligent and loving and, therefore, a personal being.

Ethical Theory. Locke continues his empiricism in his ethical theory. For Locke, all moral ideas are grounded in experience, but these ideas can be clearly grasped and just as clearly related to one another. They can then serve as norms for judging the morality of activity. Moral good consists in the conformity of voluntary actions to these established norms. From this viewpoint Locke sees no reason why ethics cannot be as clear and certain a science as mathematics.

Norms are of different kinds, and Locke enumerates them as divine law, civil law, and the law of opinion or reputation. In relation to the divine law, actions are judged to be duties or sins. In relation to the civil law, actions are called innocent or criminal. In relation to the law of opinion, actions are judged as praiseworthy or blameful, depending on the manners or customs of the place. Since it is obvious that these laws can and do conflict with each other, Locke holds that the divine law must be the ultimate norm of moral activity. He maintains that this divine law can be known by human reason, and to this extent he seems to hold for the existence of a basic moral absolute, to which man has the obligation to conform.

Political Theory. In his political philosophy Locke attacks both the theory of the divine right of kings and of the nature of the state as understood by T. HOBBES. According to Locke, the original state of nature was not a state of war and license but one of peace, in which natural rights and obligations prevailed. However, because such a situation could not adequately supply man's needs or

protect him from abuses, he entered into a political state, by either explicit or tacit consent; such a state could then make laws for him, as the public good or society required. Hence, sovereignty resides in the people and is delegated by them to their authorities. For him, as for Hobbes, authority in the state is supreme; but, unlike Hobbes, Locke insists that governing authorities are bound by both civil and "natural law." Hence, such authority is validly exercised only as long as it respects the "common good." There is therefore an authority superior to civil authority.

One of the chief goods to be achieved in the state is the right to the acquisition of private property. Locke sees this right as founded in labor. The laborer, in working on the land or on some natural product, contributes something of himself and thus acquires a title to it. Such a right, however, is not unlimited; it is restricted to as much property as a man can reasonably put to use.

Approach to Religion. In his approach to religion Locke gives the impression of being a sincere Christian who sees no discrepancy between reason and Christianity. In bk. 4, ch. 17, of the *Essay,* Locke distinguishes truths according to reason, those above reason, and those contrary to reason. Christianity deals with truths that are above reason, and it is to these that the Christian makes an assent of faith. Such truths must be proposed by God for man's belief, and it is here that Locke encounters difficulty. How is one to know that God is really the author of such truths? Locke's answer refers to the outward signs that accompany them, i.e., miracles. But how is one to know that such signs are really miraculous? It seems that Locke must either settle for some sort of probability here or else have recourse to an intuition of the connection between a given sign and the proposition of faith that it is supposed to justify. In neither case is the solution satisfactory, since it makes faith in the first instance only a probable proposition or, in the second, makes reason itself the criterion of Christian faith. Locke's approach is at best naturalistic and at worst rationalistic, in the sense that it makes reason the ultimate criterion even of truths that are above reason (*Essay,* bk. 4, ch. 19).

Influence. Locke has had a lasting influence on modern philosophy. Berkeley's empirical IDEALISM is a direct outgrowth of Locke's epistemology, as is Hume's later SKEPTICISM. Locke himself attempted to hold a common-sense middle position between these two extremes, but both Berkeley and Hume represent the logical consequences of the position. The systems of D. Hartley and J. S. MILL are clearly indebted to Locke. And through Hume, the Kantian doctrines of the unknown thing-in-itself, the nature of substance, the intellectual categories reveal either Kant's acceptance of Locke or his attempt to overcome what he considered an extreme empiricism.

There is good reason to believe that Locke's theory of government influenced the founders of the American Constitution, and Thomas Jefferson especially. The American people were establishing a government after their successful Revolution, and Locke had sought to justify the Glorious Revolution in England. Some of Locke's ideas—e.g., on natural rights, the rule of the majority, property rights, and the obligation of government to secure and preserve these rights—appear in the Constitution, at times exactly in Locke's phrasing. And 19th-century American laissez-faire individualism was rooted in the Lockean notion of natural rights, indirectly by way of constitutional interpretation.

In contemporary philosophy most systems of naturalism, LOGICAL POSITIVISM, and analytical philosophy are sympathetic to Locke. They generally accept his position on the object of knowledge, the nature of substance, the lack of innate ideas, and the nominalistic interpretation of the function of the idea.

Critique. The basic difficulty with Locke's experiential approach is the assumption from which it begins: what is known is only an affection of the knowing subject. This subjectivism puts Locke into a position where he is forced to prove the reality of an external world and God. He himself recognized the difficulty and strove in vain to overcome it. Berkeley showed him the impossibility of demonstrating the existence of material reality, and Kant made clear the inadequacy of his proof for the existence of God. Such a subjectivism had to end where it began—in the mind. The ease with which such an approach slips into a complete idealism and even into SOLIPSISM is only too apparent in the history of philosophy. Man's basic experience is of things, not of ideas. Any theory of knowledge denying that basic experience is bound to lead to the bankruptcy of all knowledge.

See Also: KNOWLEDGE, THEORIES OF.

Bibliography: *Works,* 10 v. (rev. ed. London 1823); *The Philosophical Works of John Locke,* ed. J. A. ST. JOHN, 2 v. (London 1854); *An Essay concerning Human Understanding,* ed. A. C. FRASER, 2 v. (Oxford 1894); *The Reasonableness of Christianity,* ed. I. J. RAMSEY (Stanford 1958); *Two Treatises of Government,* ed. T. I. COOK (New York 1947); *The Correspondence of John Locke and Edward Clarke,* ed. B. RAND (London 1927); *Selections,* ed. S. P. LAMPRECHT (New York 1928). **Literature.** F. C. COPLESTON, *History of Philosophy* (Westminster, Md. 1959) v.5. A. CARLINI, *Enciclopedia filosofica,* 4 v. (Venice-Rome 1957) 3:96–112. P. K. KING, *The Life of John Locke,* 2 v. (London 1830). R. I. AARON, *John Locke* (2d ed. Oxford 1955). D. J. O'CONNOR, *John Locke* (Baltimore 1952). J. D. COLLINS, *A History of Modern European Philosophy* (Milwaukee 1954).

[H. R. KLOCKER]

LOCKWOOD, JOHN, BL.

Priest, martyr; b. Sowerby, North Riding, Yorkshire, England, *c.* 1555; d. hanged, drawn, and quartered at York, April 13, 1642. John was the eldest son of Christopher Lockwood and Clare Lascelles of Sowerby and Brackenborough Castle, Yorkshire. He and his brother Francis arrived at Rheims on Nov. 4, 1579. John was immediately sent to Douai to study philosophy. While Francis was ordained in 1587, John did not finish his studies at the English College in Rome until Oct. 4, 1595. He was ordained on Jan. 26, 1597, then sent on the English mission, April 20, 1598. He was arrested several times, imprisoned, and even banished (1610), but managed to minister to his flock for 44 years before he was captured at Wood End, Gatenby, the residence of Bridget Gatenby, and executed with Bl. Edmund CATHERICK. He was beatified by Pius XI on Dec. 15, 1929.

Feast of the English Martyrs: May 4 (England).

See Also: ENGLAND, SCOTLAND, AND WALES, MARTYRS OF.

Bibliography: R. CHALLONER, *Memoirs of Missionary Priests,* ed. J. H. POLLEN (rev. ed. London 1924; repr. Farnborough 1969), II, 168. J. FOSTER, *Visitation of Yorkshire* (London 1875) 61, 549. T. F. KNOX, *First and Second Diaries of English College, Douai* (London 1878) 157. J. H. POLLEN, *Acts of English Martyrs* (London 1891).

[K. I. RABENSTEIN]

LOCULUS

Latin diminutive of *locus,* "place"; a small grave or chamber cut out of the rock sides of a gallery, usually in a catacomb. Loculus is the term used to distinguish a small individual grave from the larger and more imposing ones, called *arcosolia,* which were large enough to receive a coffin or sarcophagus. The loculus was a horizontal niche scooped out of the soft rock of the tunnels running through the catacombs. In Roman law, all cemeteries and burial places were certified as *loci religiosi* and, like churches and temples, were inviolable. The term loculus, thus, came to be applied to any small grave sacred to the dead. The term was also applied to the small cavity prepared in an altar stone to receive the relics of martyrs as required for the celebration of Mass. The term sepulcher is also used for loculus in this sense.

Bibliography: H. LECLERCQ, *Dictionnaire d'archéologie chrétienne et de liturgie* (Paris 1934–43) 9.2. E. DIEHL, *Inscriptiones Christianae latinae veteres,* 3 v. (Berlin 1925–31) 222–232.

[E. E. MALONE]

LOCUTIONS

Affirmations or statements supernaturally effected in the external sense, internal senses, or directly in the intellect. They often accompany visions and they are divided in the same manner: corporeal (auricular), imaginative, and intellectual. Auricular locutions are words perceived by the bodily sense of hearing, and are generally caused by supernaturally produced acoustical vibrations. They sometimes seem to emanate from a vision or a religious object such as a statue or crucifix. As extraordinary phenomena they could be caused by God or the devil or proceed from natural causes. Imaginative locutions are words perceived in the imagination during sleep or in waking hours. Since they, too, could be supernatural, diabolical, or natural in origin, the rule for discernment is to study the effects produced in the individual. Locutions of supernatural origin cannot be produced at will; they are distinct, causing fervor, peace, humility, and obedience. Intellectual locutions are words or statements perceived immediately by the intellect without the aid of the external senses or imagination. Sometimes they are directly infused; at other times they are a supernatural coordination of naturally acquired ideas. It is beyond the power of the devil to produce truly intellectual locutions. St. John of the Cross divides intellectual locutions into successive, formal, and substantial.

Successive intellectual locations are a kind of dialogue or conversation between the Holy Spirit and the soul. It is a discursive reasoning rather than an instantaneous intuition, and although it is under the direction of the Holy Spirit, the human intellect plays its part. Therefore the actual functioning of the human intellect in this type of locution requires the operation of the imagination, with the result that error can proceed from the human side of the dialogue. The devil can indirectly affect successive locutions by influencing the imagination. Similar locutions occur in the natural phenomenon of the dual personality, although the effects are noticeably different from the effects of truly supernatural successive locutions.

Formal intellectual locutions are those words or statements which come to the mind from without and do not involve the activity of the intellect itself, except to receive them. Unlike the successive locutions, they may be infused into the mind when it is thinking of something entirely different. When they are truly supernatural, they produce virtuous effects in the soul and impart great illumination and certitude. Although the devil cannot directly influence the intellect, an individual may be deceived by the devil, so that the phenomenon itself cannot easily be distinguished by its effects. St John of the Cross advises that souls should never act according to their own opinions or accept the locutions without much reflection and the counsel of others.

Substantial intellectual locutions are basically the same as formal locutions, but with this difference: what is stated is effected immediately. They are similar to the creative word of God. According to St. John of the Cross, there is no possibility of deception or the influence of the devil in substantial locutions.

Since locutions are often closely associated with visions, the same rules applied to locution (see VISIONS). Locutions are unmerited and freely given graces in the sense that they do not proceed from the normal development of the spiritual life; they differ somewhat from the usual charismatic gifts given for the benefit of others in the sense that they can bring much consolation and many blessings to the soul that receives them. They should not be desired, except for the substantial locutions, of which St. John of the Cross says: ''Blessed is the soul to whom the Lord speaks the substantial locution.''

Bibliography: JOHN OF THE CROSS, *Complete Works*, ed. SILVERIO DE SANTA TERESA and E. A. PEERS, 3 v. (Westminster, MD 1953) v.1 *Ascent of Mount Carmel*, Bk. 2, ch. 28–31. TERESA OF AVILA, *Complete Works,* ed. SILVERIO DE SANTA TERESA and E. A. PEERS, 3 v. (New York 1946) v.1 *Life* ch. 25 R. GARRIGOU–LAGRANGE, *The Three Ages of the Interior Life,* tr. T. DOYLE, 2 v. (St. Louis 1947–48) 2:589–595. J. G. ARINTERO, *The Mystical Evolution in the Development and Vitality of the Church*, tr. J. AUMANN, 2 v. (St. Louis 1949–51) 2:304–333. A. ROYO and J. AUMANN, *The Theology of Christian Perfection* (Dubuque 1962) 658–660. A. F. POULAIN, *The Graces of Interior Prayer,* tr. L. L. SMITH (6th French ed. St. Louis 1950) 266–297. E. UNDERHILL, *Mysticism* (12th rev. ed. New York 1960).

[J. AUMANN]

LOGIC, HISTORY OF

Western formal logic began among the Greeks of the 5th and 4th centuries B.C., who developed syllogistic and prepositional systems. The Greeks of the Hellenistic age and the Romans did nothing to advance these beginnings, but injected a stream of rhetoric that was to plague the subject until quite recent times. It also began a long sequence of sketchy textbooks. After the Dark Ages logic began to revive in the 12th century, and by the middle of the 13th century scholastic logic was well developed. While borrowing much from Aristotle and a little from Roman hints about Stoicism, it developed original methods in propositional and quantificational logic and in regard to logical antinomies. It borrowed rather little from rhetoric but was a good deal influenced by grammar. About mid-15th century the impetus failed and within 100 years had died completely, giving place to a centuries-long crop of incompetent handbooks, often infected with rhetoric, entirely lacking in originality or serious investigation. Only occasionally was the monotonous desert interrupted by something of interest, notably, by the great genius of G. W. LEIBNIZ. In mid-19th century the modern period began with G. Boole and with renewed authority through the immense analytical acumen of G. Frege. Their work brought new understanding of the past and a huge increase in doctrine, presented with an altogether new completeness, strictness, and critical control. One thus has four periods to consider: (1) the Greco-Roman, (2) the medieval, (3) the post-Renaissance, and (4) the modern.

Greco-Roman Period

Aristotle claimed to be the founder of logic, saying that he could find nothing like what he had done among his philosophic predecessors. The claim seems to be justified. One can, of course, find a climate of intense discussion that favored such a development. Both in the school founded by Euclid of Megara, who was a pupil of SOCRATES, and in the Platonic Academy descended from the same source, as also in the tradition of the 5th-century SOPHISTS, discussion was so strongly cultivated that it is not surprising that people should have begun to reflect on the processes of argument, to notice patterns of recurrence, and to generalize in a reflective way about conclusive and inconclusive methods.

Already in PLATO one can see intimations of what would become, in the hands of Aristotle, the syllogism, and, in the hands of the Megarians and Stoics, propositional logic. Roughly speaking, Athens gave birth to the former, Megara to the latter. Plato was surely influential in that he developed the notion of universal law, already in evidence among the pre-Socratics, but it was left for Aristotle to achieve the first conscious, general, explicit system of formal logic, so that Leibniz could say of him that he was the first to write mathematically outside of mathematics.

Aristotelian Logic. The logical works of ARISTOTLE, known as the *Organon,* have been handed down in a systematic order: *Categories,* dealing with the TERM; *On Interpretation,* the PROPOSITION; *Prior Analytics*, the SYLLOGISM in general; *Posterior Analytics, Topics,* and *Sophistical Refutations,* apodictic, dialectical, and sophistical syllogisms, respectively. Surely this list does not represent the order of composition, but attempts to ascertain this through the varying complexity of doctrine are somewhat uncertain, since a thinker's development may not be continuous and homogeneous. Thus the *Topics* and *Sophistical Refutations*, though lacking the doctrine of the syllogism, contain some insights that belong to a more advanced area.

Syllogistic is a theory of whole or partial inclusion between classes, its laws being presented in schematic form, the use of letters instead of words from ordinary language being a brilliant device to secure generality and isolate form. (The device would not be fully exploited until Frege.) Aristotle begins by presenting his syllogisms listwise, classified by patterns called "figures," those that are valid being alternated in each figure with those that are inconclusive, the latter being rejected by counterexample. His incomplete definitions of the figures would give much trouble to later writers, and those who paid more attention to the letter than the spirit would be troubled by the incompleteness of the explicit list. Aristotle reworked his system in several ways, propounding alternative methods of deduction from axioms (thus showing that there is nothing inflexible about a given set of axioms) and making some metalogical statements. The deductions are either direct, by laws of conversion, or indirect, by *reductio ad absurdum.* They are carried out in an intuitive, not in a formalized way, for Aristotle states only two or three laws of propositional inference, though it is noteworthy that he does there consciously use propositional variables.

Especially to be distinguished from the nonsyllogistic laws are some belonging to the logic of relations, e.g., "if knowledge be conceiving, then an object of knowledge is an object of conceiving," a principle that A. De Morgan in the 19th century would adduce against contemporary would-be Aristotelians as unprovable syllogistically. Also from the *Topics* and *Sophistical Refutations* come laws about identity that add up to the "principle of the identity of indiscernibles" commonly ascribed to Leibniz. The presence of such things in Aristotle has been more often ignored than noticed, and they are fragmentary in character. Even the assertoric syllogistic is not treated with the thoroughness and generality currently accorded to the systematic investigation of logical ideas. Aristotle's modal syllogistic is even less fully elaborated and still awaits definitive investigation and assessment. But he got logic off to an astonishingly good start, and in spite of the undoubted merits of some medieval treatises, there is no extant work (in the absence of full Stoic texts) of comparable promise until Leibniz.

Theophrastus. Aristotle was succeeded as head of the Peripatetic school by Theophrastus of Eresos. He is known chiefly for having made explicit the five syllogistic moods later known as *Baralipton, Celantes, Dabitis, Fapesmo,* and *Frisesomorum.* He introduced a non-Aristotelian modal syllogistic in which the assertoric law that the conclusion follows the weakest premise holds; and he offered an extensional proof, perhaps with a spatial model before him, of the convertibility of universal negative propositions. Only fragments of his work remain. They contain references to his work on syllogisms "from hypotheses," i.e., with conditional premises, initiated by his predecessor. It is possible that Theophrastus stimulated the Megarian-Stoic work on propositional logic.

Megarian-Stoic School. Materials exist only in fragmentary and often hostile reports. Among the Megarians, Eubulides of Miletus is credited with the discovery of the PARADOX called "the Liar," or the "Epimenides," noted by Aristotle and much pondered over by Theophrastus and Chrysippus. A new form was claimed as late as 1937, but it has been found to have existed in the Middle Ages. One early version goes: "If you say that you lie, and in this say true, do you lie or speak the truth?" Eubulides is reported to have been hostile to Aristotelian doctrine, thus depriving later Aristotelians of a progressive and complementary influence.

Diodorus Cronus of Iasus (end of 4th century B.C.) held views on modality, the accounts of which have proved difficult for modern interpreters. His definition of the necessary introduced a time variable, "that which neither is nor will be false." Although it is tempting to think that his definition of implication was that at no time ever is its antecedent true and its consequence false, the text does not certainly justify this. He was the author of a "master argument" about the incompatibility of three modal propositions, which it has proved impossible to reconstruct satisfactorily. Stilpo of Megara was influential in drawing new adherents, including Zeno of Citium, who founded the Stoa (*c.* 300 B.C.). Philo of Megara was the first to formulate the truth conditions for the material conditional, true except when its antecedent is true and its consequent false.

The Megaric school seems to have disappeared with the rise of STOICISM, and the logical history of the latter is overshadowed by Chrysippus of Soli, its second founder, who died shortly before 200 B.C. The most important contribution to logic made by the Stoics was a deductive system of propositional logic. It was based on five "indemonstrable moods" (one should not say "axioms," for this word is kept by them for the objective meanings of declarative sentences) and four "themes" or rules, only two of which have been preserved. Instead of letters they used ordinal terms as variables. W. Kneale has suggested a convincing reconstruction of the system, for which the Stoics claimed completeness, but it is not clear what they could have intended by such a claim.

Later Developments. For the remainder of ancient logic, one should mention CICERO—no logician indeed, but his rhetorical syllogism influenced logic in the Renaissance and after; the handbooks of Galen and Apuleius of Madaura (2d century A.D.); the Greek commentators on Aristotle, especially Alexander of Aphrodisias (3d century) and JOHN PHILOPONUS (6th centu-

ry). GALEN was later credited with the invention of a fourth figure of syllogism, but J. Lukasiewicz has shown that this was a mistake. Apuleius gave the square of OPPOSITION, which has become traditional. Alexander showed how to derive a law of conversion from a syllogism and a law of identity by *reductio ad absurdum,* which offered to medievals and to Leibniz new possibilities in syllogistic axiomatics. Philoponus suggested resolving doubts about how to define syllogistic figures by calling the subject (predicate) of the conclusion the minor (major) term and denominating the premises thence. This is the most economical method, but it did not come into general use until the end of the 17th century. Porphyry of Tyre (3d century) contributed his "tree" or scheme of genera and species, of which he took an extensional view, the species being contained in the genus predicated of it (*see* PORPHYRIAN TREE).

Boethius was the great transmitter of ancient logic to the medieval world. He was a peripatetic but preserved some Stoic doctrines, translated most of the *Organon,* and composed works on *Topics* or *Loci,* as had been done in the domain of rhetoric by Cicero and Marius Victorinus (4th century). His translations of the *Categories* and *On Interpretation* constituted the *logica vetus* of the early medievals, the other parts of the *Organon* being the *Logica nova.* The variables in his treatise on hypothetical syllogisms have been taken as propositional, but since the doctrine is basically Theophrastan, and in view of Boethius's Aristotelian convictions, they are probably term variables.

Medieval Period

Study in the field of logic began to revive toward the end of the 11th century, amid a great deal of fruitful activity, of which much remains to be learned through the publication of further texts. The full logic of Aristotle, notably the *Prior Analytics,* became available only in the course of the 12th century. Boethius was influential, as was Cicero, but the grammarians seem to have been more influential than the rhetoricians.

Twelfth Century. ABELARD, remembered by his contemporaries as "the Aristotle of our time, the equal or superior of all logicians there have been," noted that logic is not a science of using arguments but of discerning their validity. In his *Dialectica* he distinguishes "antecedent" and "consequent" as referring both to subject and predicate within simple propositions and to the parts of hypothetical propositions. This and other passages show the emergence of medieval propositional logic in distinction from a logic of terms. Abelard knew that these were different and that there are analogies between them—he reports a view that propositional connectives and their term analogues have the same sense, and he rejects it. The statement that a hypothetical proposition is called both a "consequence" and a "conditional" may raise a doubt whether relations of implication and inference were yet clearly distinguished, and the fact that ALBERT OF SAXONY (14th century) distinguishes *si* and *ergo* only by their positioning should engender caution in viewing the theory of "consequences" in one or the other light. Abelard already has a number of valid consequences, and some are even deduced from others, but the Middle Ages never attained an axiomatized system of propositional logic. One of Abelard's most elaborate consequences is "of whatever hypotheticals the antecedents are concomitant, the consequents are concomitant." This is the theorem that Leibniz would rediscover and call *praeclarum*. One should note the metalogical formulation, a style that would remain standard and that is perhaps derived from the *De differentiis topicis* of Boethius, who distinguished the maxim or metalogical formulation of a class of truths from the instances.

In the 12th century, Adam of Balsham also wrote a highly original work, *Ars disserendi*, in which one sees the rise of a concern with *sophismata* or logical puzzles, which became very characteristic of the period. While, under an inventive hand, *sophismata* could produce a rich body of doctrine, the medium favored the perpetuation of a fragmented treatment rather than a genuinely systematic one. Adam made a rare attempt to begin a logic of questions, in the course of which he reached the conclusion that an infinite set could be equinumerous with a proper part of itself.

Thirteenth Century. The best-known works of the 13th century are the *Introductiones in logicam* of WILLIAM OF SHERWOOD (Shyreswood), the *Summulae logicales* of Peter of Spain (Pope JOHN XXI), and the commentaries on the *Prior Analytics* by St. ALBERT THE GREAT and ROBERT KILWARDBY. This last shows that consequences were already a normal part of logical teaching. Peter of Spain became a standard author throughout the 15th century. Curiously his summary handbook does not have a chapter on consequences, but it does have a well-developed doctrine of *proprietates terminorum*, as does the earlier and similar book of Shyreswood. The origins of this can be faintly detected in the previous century, where more can surely be found. The property that came to be chiefly discussed is SUPPOSITION, the reference that the subject (and later also the predicate) has in a proposition. The *De suppositionibus dialecticis* (1372) of St. VINCENT FERRER shows a wide selection of disparate logical material discussed in this connection, including some points of quantification theory. Once again the necessity of considering numerous examples from ordinary speech favored the fragmented approach.

Later Centuries. WILLIAM OF OCKHAM sparked an intensification of activity, partly because of the very comprehensiveness of his *Summa totius logicae*. His influence can be seen even in those who repudiated his epistemology. WALTER BURLEY, JOHN BURIDAN, Albert of Saxony, MARSILIUS OF INGHEN, the Mertonians, WILLIAM OF HEYTESBURY (HENTISBER) and RALPH STRODE, and Richard Ferabrich were some of the notable writers. Besides the areas already mentioned, they paid much attention to *insolubilia*, or logical paradoxes, developing many versions of the Epimenides, which was already known to Adam of Balsham. Numerous solutions were proposed, including the outlawing of self-referring propositions from meaningful language (*see* ANTIMONY).

The 15th century was unoriginal; toward its end there was the encyclopedic *Logica magna* of Paul of Venice (Paolo VENETO), who with Peter of Mantua and Paul of Pergolae formed a school known to their contemporaries as the *Sorticolae*.

From the 13th century on, syllogistic was considered as a special department and even rather a small one. The supposedly Aristotelian idea that developed in the next period—that valid arguments are always syllogistic—was quite foreign to the medievals. The subject was of course treated at length in the Aristotelian commentaries and required detailed treatment in commentaries on the *Summulae*, but in the more general treatises, syllogisms are just one kind of consequence. The usual method of defining terms was a generalization of that of Boethius, the first premise stated being the major premise by definition, and the extreme term therein the major term. This is quite different from the method of Philoponus, and there are signs that some people could work out its consequences correctly, but again a unified and systematic presentation was lacking. Mnemonics of various kinds were experimented with in the 13th century, and the familiar "*Barbara, Celarent,* etc." occurs in Shyreswood.

Post-Renaissance Period

It was about 1440 that the first recorded voice of the new age, or non-age, in logic made itself heard. L. VALLA, a renowned humanist scholar, then rejected the third figure of the syllogism on the grounds that women, children, and nonlogicians generally, do not argue that way. Perhaps this is the first time that ordinary language was claimed as the standard of logical doctrine. Evidently all sense of syllogistic as a deductive system had been lost; indeed Valla said that conversion, Aristotle's chief means of deduction, is only a "remedy for sick syllogisms." R. Agricola's *De dialectica inventione* swung the ambivalent "topical" tradition firmly into the path of rhetoric, in contrast with Abelard. P. MELANCHTHON, writing in 1521, expounded Cicero's syllogism before Aristotle's. Older doctrines were quickly dropped or ridiculed. G. SAVONAROLA kept telling the 16th century in numerous reeditions that anyone arguing from a conjunction to one of its parts was *dignus explosione.*

Ramist Controversy. In the mid-16th century, vernacular logics began to appear, for example, T. Wilson's *The Rule of Reason* (1551) and the *Dialectique* (1555) of Peter RAMUS. This last writer's views on logical reform provoked widespread and long-lasting controversy. His simplified syllogistic and novel terminology occasioned long commentaries on very little and a new technical scholasticism. Aristotelians found little to discuss besides the iniquities of Ramism and the fourth figure of the syllogism, few recognizing that this was a matter to be settled by definition. Sextus Empiricus appeared in Latin in 1569, but led to no rediscovery of Stoic logic.

There was an occasional break in the clouds. J. Hospinianus (1515–75) thoroughly investigated syllogistic on a combinatory basis, and G. Cardano illustrated his *Dialectica* with geometrical arguments. J. Junge (*Logica Hamburgensis,* 1638) showed a deductive interest in the syllogism and some appreciation of Aristotle's logic of relations. In 1662 A. GEULINCX pleaded for the restoration of medieval doctrines. In that year the "Port Royal Logic" of A. ARNAULD and P. NICOLE was published. Anti-rhetorical and anti-Ramist, the authors idolized geometry and did much to tighten up syllogistic theory. At the same time they opened the way to introducing epistemological and psychological discussions into books of logic. H. Aldrich, in his *Artis logicae compendium* (1691), correctly tabled 24 moods of syllogism in four figures and methodically proved all others invalid.

Leibniz and After. Meanwhile G. W. LEIBNIZ had begun to develop quite new ideas. A polymath famous in philosophy for his *Monadology,* and in mathematics for his invention of the infinitesimal calculus, he was not yet 20 years old when he began to be haunted by the idea that logic might be developed in a mathematical way. Others before him had discerned a kinship (e.g., ROGER BACON), but mathematical notations had not been used. Leibniz experimented with various versions of a logical calculus that he wanted used in association with a rationally constructed universal language. He also envisioned an encyclopedia that would be progressively perfected as the sciences advanced and at any one stage would unify the whole body of achieved human knowledge. In forming these projects Leibniz found his interest caught by J. Wilkins, G. Dalgarno, and other contemporaries for the language, T. Zwinger and J. H. Alsted for the encyclopedia, and Raymond LULL for the calculus. But his own ideals went beyond any of theirs, especially in regard to the analysis of ideas into their simplest parts; this the language would mirror, the encyclopedia present, and the calculus reverse so as to be effective for the discovery of new combinations. Leibniz's efforts with his calculus of logic were frustrated by difficulties with empty terms (which the medievals had also noticed) and by doubts about the relationship between extensions and intensions. He anticipated the circular diagrams of L. EULER and the ruled or dotted lines of J. H. Lambert (1728–77).

After Leibniz a number of attempts were made to construct a satisfactory symbolic calculus, e.g., by Lambert, his contemporary G. J. Holland, and G. F. Castillon. Sir William Hamilton claimed priority in quantifying the predicate, but this had been done by Leibniz and those just mentioned. A real breakthrough was achieved by A. DE MORGAN, whom C. S. Peirce called "unquestionably the father of the logic of relatives."

Modern Period

In the same year (1847) that De Morgan's *Formal Logic* appeared, George Boole published *The Mathematical Analysis of Logic,* which was followed in 1854 by *An Investigation of the Laws of Thought.* From this time on there was a steady clarification of ideas interdependent with the perfecting of a calculus. Thorough systematization and investigation of logical notions became possible as never before.

Boolean Algebra. Boole's algebra, in which $1 - x$ represents the class of objects in the universe of discourse, 1, which are not in the class $x,$ and in which the equation $x (1 - x) = 0$ expresses the principle of noncontradiction, is rich enough for all the traditional modes of class reasoning, though some (e.g., subalternation) require statement that the classes involved are not empty. The system can be interpreted as well in the domain of truth functions or that of probabilities. W. S. Jevons (1835–82) showed that inclusive alternation offered some advantages over the exclusive used by Boole; it gives the law $x + x = x,$ getting rid of coefficients. In 1869 he used the new methods to make a logical machine; the logical diagrams proposed by J. Venn in 1881 also mirror the new methods. C. S. PEIRCE, a very original and inventive thinker, augmented the Boolean algebra with the now customary symbol of inclusion (similar ones had been used by Lambert and J. D. Gergonne), which he also interpreted prepositionally as material implication. In 1885 he devised the truth-table test for the necessary truth of a formula, and by the introduction of essentially new notions, "expanded" the Boolean system into a logic of relations; here he also developed De Morgan's work, with the help of O. H. Mitchell. Peirce also showed how all truth-functional connectives can be defined by joint exclusion (neither . . . nor . . .), which was rediscovered more than 30 years later by H. M. Sheffer. The *Vorlesungen über die Algebra der Logik* of E. Schröder incorporated the various improvements made in Boole's system in the interval and further developed Peirce's ideas about relations. Since this represents the peak of the Boolean line of thought, the resulting system is now known as the Boole-Schröder algebra.

Frege and After. Meanwhile, in 1879 there appeared the *Begriffsschrift* of G. Frege, perhaps the most penetrating and original logical work ever published. Frege was explicitly concerned with banishing all rhetorical and even traditional grammatical influence, on the one hand, and, on the other, providing for an accurate analysis of reasoning in a more thorough way than was possible by means of an equational system such as Boole's. The Boole-Schröder system utilized an unexpressed intuitive logic, as Aristotle's syllogistic had done. This fundamental logic was successfully formalized by Frege, with the use only of the rules of *modus ponens* and substitution for variables to derive valid propositional formulas from axioms (which later were seen to be unduly lavish). Frege's connectives were built out of vertical and horizontal lines; and while his expressions can be read quite mechanically in terms of negation and conjunction, the space they occupy has prohibited their general use. There are more compact notations, for example, the "wheels" of S. Lesniewski, which are diagrammatically closer to the intended meaning and serve calculation more readily. Applying his propositional system to propositional functions, and analyzing such functions, Frege gave rules for the use of quantifiers and discussed the differing nature of variables according to whether they are governed by quantifiers or not. In these systems logic at last reached its maturity.

Frege's aim was to analyze and codify mathematical reasoning in a deductive way. G. Peano actually brought the new methods to bear on mathematics and introduced improvements in symbolism. B. RUSSELL and A. N. WHITEHEAD joined the ideas of Frege and Peano to produce *Principia Mathematica* (1910–13), the most comprehensive exposition of logical and mathematical thought ever effected. In 1917 J. Lukasiewicz announced his first views on many-valued logic (inspired by Aristotle, and published in 1920, when E. Post's independent investigation in the same field also appeared). The natural deduction systems of S. Jaskowski and G. Gentzen, and K. Gödel's proof of the completeness of predicate logic, appeared in 1930. Gödel's epoch-making adaptation of the *Epimenides* in 1931 to show that the system of *Principia Mathematica* is undecidable continues to be adapted to show the same for many other systems, especially

by A. Tarski. In 1936 A. Church showed that the predicate calculus has this property.

See Also: LOGIC, SYMBOLIC; AXIOMATIC SYSTEM.

Bibliography: General. H. SCHOLZ, *Abriss der Geschichte der Logik* (2d ed. Freiburg 1959). I. M. BOCHEŃSKI, *A History of Formal Logic,* tr. and ed. I. THOMAS (Notre Dame, Ind. 1961). W. and M. KNEALE, *The Development of Logic* (Oxford 1962). P. H. NIDDITCH, *The Development of Mathematical Logic* (London 1962). A. N. PRIOR, *Formal Logic* (2d ed. Oxford 1962). J. T. CLARK *Conventional Logic and Modern Logic* (Woodstock, Md. 1952). Ancient Period. J. LUKASIEWICZ, *Aristotle's Syllogistic from the Standpoint of Modern Formal Logic* (2d ed. Oxford 1957). G. PATZIG, *Die aristotelische Syllogistik* (Göttingen 1959). I. M. BOCHEŃSKI, *Ancient Formal Logic* (Amsterdam 1951); *La Logique de Théophraste* (Fribourg 1947). B. MATES, *Stoic Logic* (Berkeley 1953). Medieval Period. P. ABELARD, *Dialectica,* ed. L. M. DE RIJK (Assen 1956). ADAMUS BALSAMENSIS, *Ars disserendi,* ed. L. MINIO-PALUELLO (Rome 1956). P. BÖHNER, *Medieval Logic* (Chicago 1952). E. A. MOODY, *Truth and Consequence in Mediaeval Logic* (Amsterdam 1953). C. VON PRANTL, *Geschichte der Logik im Abendlande,* 4 v. (Leipzig 1855–70; repr. Graz 1955). Post-Renaissance Period. W. RISSE, *Die Logik der Neuzeit* (Stuttgart 1963—) v. 1. W. J. ONG, *Ramus: Method, and the Decay of Dialogue* (Cambridge, Mass. 1958); *Ramus and Talon Inventory* (Cambridge, Mass. 1958). I. THOMAS, "Medieval Aftermath," Oxford Historical Society, *Oxford Studies Presented to Daniel Callus* (Oxford 1964). L. COUTURAT, *La Logique de Leibniz après des documents inédits* (Paris 1901; repr. Hildesheim 1961). J. VENN, *Symbolic Logic* (2d ed. London 1894). C. I. LEWIS, *A Survey of Symbolic Logic* (rev. ed. New York 1960). Modern Period. A. CHURCH, *Introduction to Mathematical Logic* (Princeton 1956—) v. 1; "A Brief Bibliography of Formal Logic," *Proceedings of the American Academy of Arts and Sciences* 80 (1952) 155–172; "A Bibliography of Symbolic Logic," *Journal of Symbolic Logic* 1 (1936) 121–218; 3 (1938) 178–192; additional bibliog. in issues to date. E. W. BETH, *The Foundations of Mathematics* (Amsterdam 1959). H. B. CURRY, *Foundations of Mathematical Logic* (New York 1963).

[I. THOMAS]

LOGIC, SYMBOLIC

A modern version of formal logic, referred to variously as logistic, mathematical logic, and the algebra of logic; it may be described generally as the set of logical theories elaborated since the mid-19th century with the aid of symbolic notation and a rigorous method of DEDUCTION. Symbolic logic differs from traditional logic in its extensive use of symbols similar to those used in mathematics, in its lack of concern with the psychology and epistemology of knowledge, and in its FORMALISM. It is concerned mainly with the analysis of the correctness of logical laws, such as the law of contradiction, that of the hypothetical syllogism, and so on. Symbolic logicians attempt to deduce logical laws from the smallest possible number of principles, i.e., axioms and rules of inference, and to do this with no hidden assumptions or unexpressed steps in the deductive process (*see* AXIOMATIC SYSTEM).

This article provides a brief survey of the history of the discipline and discusses its basic concepts and principal divisions, viz, propositional logic, the logic of predicates and of classes, and the logic of relations.

History. G. W. LEIBNIZ is usually regarded as the forerunner of symbolic logic, largely for his attempt to formulate a *mathesis universalis* and for his discovery of several theorems that later assumed importance. Historians of symbolic logic, mainly of the Polish school (J. Lukasiewicz, J. Salamucha, I. M. Bocheński), have pointed out that the principal concepts utilized in the new logic are to be found in the works of ARISTOTLE, who introduced variables and the idea of the deductive system. Similarly, they have shown that the logic of propositions was extensively treated by the Stoics and by the later scholastics, and that even some aspects of the problem of antinomies had their counterparts in the medieval concern with *insolubilia.* Yet it was not until the mid-19th century, with the work of G. Boole and A. DE MORGAN, that systems of symbolic logic similar to those used in the 20th century were developed. The history of this development may be conveniently divided into three periods, the first (1847–90) dominated by the work of Boole, the second (1890–1930) principally under the influence of G. Frege, and the third (1930–60s) devoted largely to metalogical considerations.

Boolean logic had two characteristics: it was a logic of classes and it was developed using a rigorous mathematical method. It was Boole's intention, in fact, to apply the method of algebra to logic—whence the designation of his system as "the algebra of logic." De Morgan furthered the development, discovering some new laws, doing work on the SYLLOGISM, and making a pioneer study of the logic of relations. C. S. PEIRCE likewise belongs to this period. The most ample development of logic according to Boole's method, however, is to be found in the work of E. Schröder, *Vorlesungen über die Algebra der Logik* (3 v. Leipzig 1890–1905).

The Fregean period was characterized by a more formal development of the new discipline. Frege himself discovered a new logic of propositions and developed the first axiomatic system for such a logic; this has been regarded as a fundamental work on the foundations of mathematics. Improving on Frege's symbolism, G. Peano invented a form of symbolic writing that was later adopted by B. RUSSELL and A. N. WHITEHEAD in their *Principia Mathematica* (3 v. Cambridge, England 1910–13). Another notational advance was made by the Polish logician J. Lukasiewicz, who also invented polyvalent or many-valued logics and did research in the history of formal logic. Also worthy of note, although extending somewhat beyond this period, is the work of the German logicians D. Hilbert and P. Bernays on the foundations of mathematics (*Grundlagen der Mathematik*, 2 v. Berlin 1934–39).

The metalogical period was inaugurated by K. Gödel, who showed that many propositions in the *Principia Mathematica* and in equivalent systems were formally undecidable, i.e., that their truth or falsity could not be proved within the formal structure of the system. Noteworthy in this period is the work of A. Tarski on the semantic definition of truth and that of K. Popper and R. Carnap on the methodology of the exact sciences. Additional applications of the methods of mathematical logic have been made in theology (Bocheński, I. Thomas), in analytical philosophy (A. Church, N. Goodman, W. V. O. Quine, C. G. Hempel), in physics (H. Reichenbach, C. E. Shannon), in biology (J. H. Woodger), and in economics (J. von Neumann, O. Morgenstern). *See* LOGIC, HISTORY OF.

Basic Concepts. A fundamental distinction in symbolic logic is that between constants and variables. Variables are symbols (usually the letters *x, y, z*) that can be replaced by constants (usually the letters *a, b, c*) or by complex formulas. If a constant is replaced by a variable in a sentence, or proposition, the result is a function; this is a schema for a sentence, or proposition, and in itself is neither true nor false. Thus, "*x* is a student" is a function and is neither true nor false, whereas "*a* is a student" and "John is a student" are sentences and may be true or false. Functions may be transformed back into sentences, or propositions, by prefixing a quantifier to them. There are two types of quantifiers: universal quantifiers, of which an example would be "for all *x*,. . ." [written (*x*)]; and existential quantifiers, of which an example would be "there is at least one *x* such that . . ." [written (∃*x*)].

Symbols are generally divided into basic categories and functor, or predicate, categories. The basic categories are either names (substantives) or sentences. Functors, or predicates, are symbols (usually designated by the Greek letters φ, ψ, χ, or by specially invented characters) that determine other symbols, which are referred to as arguments. Thus, "Peter" is the argument of the functor "walks" in the sentence "Peter walks," which may be written "φa," where "*a*" stands for "Peter" and "φ" stands for "walks." Functors are divided in three different ways, each based on a different principle of division. (1) First there is the division into sentence-forming and name-forming functors. Thus, "walks" is sentence forming because "Peter walks" is a sentence, whereas "brilliant" is name forming because "brilliant student" is a name. (2) A second division is that into name-determining and sentence-determining functors. Thus, "walks" is a name-determining functor, as in the example "Peter walks"; on the other hand, "it is not the case that" is a sentence-determining functor, as in the example "It is not the case that Peter walks." (3) Finally, functors are distinguished according to the number of arguments that they determine into one-place, two-place, three-place, or, in general, *n*-place functors. An example of a one-place functor is "walks" in the sentence "Peter walks"—"walks" here determines only one argument, viz, "Peter." An example of a two-place functor is "loves" in the sentence "Paul loves Joan"—here "loves" determines two arguments, viz, "Paul" and "Joan." An example of a three-place functor is "gives" in the sentence "Paul gives Joan a ring"—here "gives" determines three arguments, viz, "Paul," "Joan," and "ring." And so on.

In accordance with these principles of division, symbolic logic may be seen as divided into three main parts: (1) propositional logic, in which all functors are sentence-determining; (2) the logic of predicates and of classes, which treats of name-determining functors; and (3) the logic of relations, which is concerned with special properties of functors that determine two or more arguments.

Propositional Logic. Propositional logic is concerned exclusively with sentences, or propositions, that may be constructed by means of so-called truth functors. Truth functors are sentence-forming, sentence-determining, generally one- and two-place functors that can be used to form sentences whose truth value depends exclusively on the truth value of their arguments and not upon their meanings. Truth value in propositional logic—which is a two-valued logic—is twofold: it may be either the value of truth (usually written *T* or 1) or the value of falsity (usually written *F* or 0). An example of a truth functor is negation, since the value of a negated true sentence is falsity and the value of a negated false sentence is truth, and this independently of the sentences' meanings. The most widely employed truth functors are negation ("it is not the case that . . . ," usually written ~), the logical sum ("either . . . or . . ." in the sense of "either or both"), the logical product (". . . and . . . ," usually symbolized by a period or dot), material implication ("if . . . , then. . . ," usually written ⊃), equivalence ("if and only if . . . , then . . . ," usually written ≡), and disjunction ("either . . . or . . ." in the sense of "not both. . . and . . . ," usually written |).

The truth functor known as material implication is most important for understanding how symbolic logic differs from traditional formal logic. Although material implication is taken to mean "if . . . then . . . ," it has a different significance from the conditional compound of ordinary discourse. Because of its ordination to a truth-value type of VERIFICATION, material implication abstracts from, ignores, or leaves behind some of the ordinary elements of meaning of the conditional compound. Some authors (e.g., H. Veatch) make this abstraction the central point of their evaluation of material implication, arguing that it cannot express the intentional character of the conditional, which must lie in the relation of meaning between the component propositions, viz, the antecedent and the consequent. Other authors, while recognizing differences between the ordinary conditional compound and material implication, attempt to point out an element common to both. Thus I. M. Copi argues that material implication expresses a partial meaning of the conditional. Every conditional whose antecedent is true and whose consequent is false must be considered a false proposition; it is this element of the conditional that is expressed by material implication. Since material implication has a "weaker" meaning than the conditional compound, material implication can always be asserted when a strict conditional obtains, although the converse is not true. The essential value of material implication appears to lie in its permitting one to state that if the antecedent proposition has been assigned the value of truth, the consequent proposition must also be assigned the same value; this makes possible a purely mechanical operation that resembles a deductive process based on the recognition of meanings of what is stated in the antecedent and the consequent.

Using the concept of deduction thus associated with material implication, one may derive all the sentences, or propositions, of propositional logic from very few axioms and rules. Propositional logic is the most completely developed part of symbolic logic; it is regarded by mathematical logicians as the simplest and most basic part of their science, which provides the framework, so to speak, for all other types of logical analysis and deduction.

Logic of Predicates and of Classes. The second branch of symbolic logic falls into two divisions: the logic of predicates, which gives an intensional interpretation of its formulas, and the logic of classes, which gives an extensional interpretation.

In the logic of predicates the sentence is analyzed into a sentence-forming, name-determining functor (usually written φ, ψ, or χ) and a name (usually written as a variable or as a constant). An example of the basic formula would be φx. Formulas of this type are combined by means of sentence-determining functors, i.e., truth functors, and are transformed into sentences by means of quantifiers. Thus the universal proposition "All φ is ψ" may be replaced by the expression "$(x). \varphi x \supset \psi x$," and the particular proposition "Some φ is ψ," or "There is a φ that is ψ," may be replaced by the expression "($\exists$

x). φ*x*. ψ*x*.'' Use of these modes of writing and the deductive methods of the logic of propositions has led to a considerable extension of Aristotelian syllogistics.

The logic of classes is the extensional counterpart of the logic of one-place functors or predicates. A class or set (generally designated by the Greek letters α, β, or γ) is always defined by a predicate; it is the set of all objects that possess a given property. For example, the class of human beings consists of all objects to which the predicate ''is a man'' can be attributed. The most important concept of the logic of classes is that of class membership, ''*x* ε α,'' which is usually read ''*x* is a member of α'' or ''*x* belongs to α.'' Another concept—one that has caused considerable controversy among philosophers—is that of the null class, i.e., the class that contains no elements. On the basis of the definition of class and the theorems of the logic of predicates, as well as those of propositional logic, various combinations of classes can be effected and the relationships between them ascertained.

Logic of Relations. The logic of relations may be described as an extensional counterpart of the logic of predicates (or functors) that determine two or more arguments, just as the logic of classes may be regarded as an extensional counterpart of the logic of predicates that determine one argument. The reason for this is that relations can hold only between two or more arguments. In this branch of symbolic logic, relations are conceived extensionally, i.e., as relating to groups of objects. A relation, in a manner completely analogous to the defining procedure for a class, may be defined by a two-place predicate. Thus one may define the relation ''in love with'' as ''the set of pairs of persons who love each other.'' The symbol usually employed is *R*, which is generally written between the two variables it relates, e.g., *xRy*. Every relation may be conceived as having a converse; thus ''to the right of'' is the converse of ''to the left of,'' and ''the author of'' is the converse of ''the work of.'' It is common also to distinguish various relational descriptions: (1) individual, e.g., the husband of the Queen of England; (2) plural, e.g., the authors of the *New Catholic Encyclopedia*; (3) double plural, e.g., the authors of English poems; and (4) the domain, which is the most general type of relational description, e.g., all authors. Of considerable importance are the concepts used for the purposes of compounding several relations, such as the relative product (e.g., the square of the half, the brother of the mother) and the relative power (e.g., the father of the father, or father ''squared''). Another group of useful concepts is provided by the properties of relations: some are reflexive, i.e., *xRx*; others are symmetrical, i.e., if *xRy* then *yRx*; and still others are transitive, i.e., if *xRy* and *yRz*, then *xRz*. A concept of great use in the investigation of series is that of ancestral relation (R or R^2 or R^3, etc.).

See Also: ANTINOMY; MATHEMATICS, PHILOSOPHY OF; SEMANTICS.

Bibliography: A. CHURCH, ''A Bibliography of Symbolic Logic,'' *Journal of Symbolic Logic* 1 (1936) 121–218; 3 (1938) 178–192, continued in subsequent issues; ''A Brief Bibliography of Formal Logic,'' *Proceedings of the American Academy of Arts and Sciences* 80 (1952) 155–172. History. W. and M. KNEALE, *The Development of Logic* (Oxford 1962). H. SCHOLZ, *Concise History of Logic,* tr. K. F. LEIDECKER (New York 1961). I. M. BOCHEŃSKI, *A Précis of Mathematical Logic,* tr. O. BIRD (Dordrecht, Netherlands 1959), select bibliog.; *A History of Formal Logic,* ed. and tr. I. THOMAS (Notre Dame, IN 1961); *Ancient Formal Logic* (Amsterdam 1951). J. LUKASIEWICZ, *Aristotle's Syllogistic from the Standpoint of Modern Formal Logic* (2d ed. enl. Oxford 1957). P. BOEHNER, *Medieval Logic: An Outline of Its Development from 1250-c. 1400* (Chicago 1952). E. A. MOODY, *Truth and Consequence in Mediaeval Logic* (Amsterdam 1953). Studies. W. V. O. QUINE, *Mathematical Logic* (rev. ed. Cambridge, MA 1958); *From a Logical Point of View* (2d ed. rev. Cambridge, MA 1961). I. M. COPI, *Symbolic Logic* (New York 1958). R. CARNAP, *Introduction to Symbolic Logic and Its Applications* (New York 1958). S. K. LANGER, *An Introduction to Symbolic Logic* (2d ed. New York 1953). I. M. BOCHEŃSKI et al., *The Problem of Universals: A Symposium* (Notre Dame, IN 1956). J. A. LADRIÈRE, *Les Limitations internes des formalismes* (Louvain 1957). H. VEATCH, ''Aristotelian and Mathematical Logic,'' *Thomist* 13 (1950) 50–96; 14 (1951) 238–258; 15 (1952) 624–641.

[W. A. WALLACE]

LOGICAL POSITIVISM

A contemporary philosophical movement that aims to establish an all-embracing, thoroughly consistent empiricism based solely on the logical analysis of language. Because of its anti-metaphysical bias, militantly propagated by its founders and some prominent adherents, the movement constitutes a serious challenge to traditional philosophy and religion. In what follows, consideration is given to its historical development, its principal proponents and some of their antecedents, its philosophical tenets and how these evolved, and a critical evaluation.

Origins with the Vienna Circle. The logical positivist movement began with a small group of philosophers and scientists later known as the Vienna Circle (Wiener Kreis). The group had formed itself around Moritz Schlick, a former physicist who was appointed to the chair of philosophy of the inductive sciences at the University of Vienna in 1922. Meetings to discuss logical and epistemological problems were held regularly. Among those who joined Schlick were Rudolf Carnap, Hans Hahn, Otto Neurath, Herbert Feigl, Philipp Frank, Friedrich Waismann, and Edgar Zilsel. Most of these men had developed an interest in philosophy as an outgrowth of their work in physics, mathematics, or mathematical logic.

In the fall of 1929 the Vienna Circle published a document written by Carnap, Hahn, and Neurath, and dedicated to Moritz Schlick, titled *Wissenschaftliche Weltauffassung: Der Wiener Kreis*. In this statement of "scientific outlook" they set forth the two aims of the group: (1) to establish a firm foundation for the sciences, and (2) to demonstrate the meaninglessness of all metaphysics. The method proposed for accomplishing these aims was the logical analysis of statements.

A decisive influence in the early years of the Vienna Circle was that of Ludwig WITTGENSTEIN, whose *Logisch-Philosophische Abhandlung* had been published in 1921. Although he did not attend the meetings, Wittgenstein was in personal contact with Schlick and Waismann, and his views provided the basis for many discussions.

Convinced that their cooperative efforts were producing results, the members of the Vienna Circle reached out to form alliances with other rising positivist groups in Germany, Scandinavia, Poland, and England. Hans Reichenbach of the Berlin school of scientific philosophy was among those who became closely associated with the growing movement. A series of international congresses was inaugurated in 1929. An existing journal, *Annalen der Philosophie*, was taken over in 1930, renamed *Erkenntnis*, and edited by Carnap and Reichenbach as the organ of the new positivism. Other cooperative publishing ventures were also undertaken.

In the next decade, however, the Vienna Circle disintegrated. Schlick had died in 1936; Hahn, before him. The departure of many original members—among them Carnap, Frank, Waismann, Neurath, and Feigl—for universities in England and the U.S. led to a new development. Its influence all but over in central Europe, logical positivism was to become, along with its variant forms, such as analytical philosophy, the dominant philosophical movement in Scandinavia and the English-speaking world.

Basic Teachings. Logical positivism is not unique in the history of philosophy for its rejection of metaphysics. Early British EMPIRICISM had developed in this direction, culminating in the doctrine of HUME with its decisive influence on KANT. On the European continent, Auguste COMTE had proclaimed the end of the "metaphysical stage" in human intellectual history (*see* POSITIVISM). American pragmatism, in doctrine and spirit, and the whole scientific temper of the 20th century favored a strict empiricism.

What distinctly characterizes the logical positivists is their explicit resolve to eradicate metaphysics and to make empiricism a matter of logical necessity. Not content merely to abandon metaphysics as beyond human grasp, nor to cast it aside as having outlived its usefulness, they set out to show that every attempt to make a metaphysical statement, or even to ask a metaphysical question, results inevitably in nonsense. They questioned not the limits of human knowledge but the limits of meaningful linguistic expression.

Logical Foundations. This approach to philosophy was made possible by the development of modern mathematical logic from Peano and Frege to Bertrand RUSSELL and Ludwig Wittgenstein. Of particular importance to logical positivism is the doctrine of propositions worked out by Russell and Wittgenstein, but based upon earlier suggestions in the writings of LEIBNIZ, Hume, and Kant (*see* LOGIC, SYMBOLIC; LOGIC, HISTORY OF).

Logical positivists, following Wittgenstein, hold that there are two distinct types of propositions: (1) tautologies, which are evidently and necessarily true, but say nothing about the world; and (2) factual propositions, which refer to the world of experience, but are at best probable. These latter are either elementary statements, corresponding to absolutely simple "atomicfacts," or complex statements constructed from, and resolvable into, the first. No logically necessary proposition says anything about reality. The propositions of logic and mathematics, though certain and necessary, arc dcvoid of factual content; they are all tatuologies, that is, so many varied ways of saying *"A is A."*

The function of factual propositions is to enable us to "anticipate the course of our sensations." Unavoidably hypothetical, they must repeatedly be put to the test of experience, and they are verified whenever the observations they lead one to expect are forthcoming. This predictive character is essential to factual propositions.

Verification and Metaphysics. By classifying all genuine propositions into tautologies and those empirically verifiable, logical positivists so define meaningful discourse that metaphysics becomes logically impossible. They proceed, nonetheless, to "demonstrate" the meaninglessness of metaphysical statements by invoking their criterion of meaning, the "verification principle" (*see* VERIFICATION).

The formulation of this key principle has been a continuing point of contention in the logical positivist movement. It was soon recognized that to demand conclusive verifiability for meaningfulness was to exclude empirical hypotheses. So this requirement was quickly abandoned. Another formulation of the principle required that a statement at least be supportable by some elementary statements.

Schlick himself had held that the meaningfulness of a proposition depends upon the "logical possibility" of verification, not upon its actual confirmation. By this he meant that the existence of circumstances in which a statement might be verified must not be contradictory. To state the meaning of a sentence, he held, is to describe the circumstances in which it is to be used, for "the meaning of a proposition is the method of its verification" (*see* SEMANTICS). This assertion is quite fundamental to logical positivism. From it the meaninglessness of any discourse about objects transcending the empirical order follows directly. Thus the term "metaphysical," used by logical positivists to cover all non-empirical attempts to speak about reality, becomes equivalent to "nonsensical." In their understanding, the whole of reality is the exclusive domain of empirical science.

Ethics and Religion. At first logical positivists disagreed on the status of ethics. Schlick held that ethical statements are factual propositions about what people approve or disapprove, their actual standards of behavior, and their actual motives. This would make ethics an empirical science, in no essential way distinct from the physical sciences. Such a position never won general acceptance in the movement.

The view of ethics that gradually prevailed is based upon the notion of "emotive meaning." According to this theory, the normative statements of ethics are cognitively meaningless but have "emotive" significance. This means, in A. J. Ayer's terms, that they are "pure expressions of feeling," "moral sentiments" that "do not say anything." C. L. Stevenson, who later developed the emotive theory at greater length, describes ethical statements as expressions of approval or disapproval that are intended to exert persuasive force upon others.

The majority of logical positivists considered that they had sufficiently disposed of religious and theological questions by their treatment of metaphysics. Ayer, however, applies the positivist criterion of meaning to the question of God's existence in an effort to disassociate the logical positivist position from ATHESIM and AGNOSTICISM. Rather than asserting the nonexistence of God, as does the atheist, or proclaiming himself, like the agnostic, ignorant as to whether or not God exists, the positivist rejects the very question of God's existence as meaningless, and declares the atheist's answer, no less than the theist's, nonsensical. The theist is thus offered the "comfort" of knowing that he can never be accused of saying anything false. Furthermore, there can be no conflict between religion and science, since there are no genuine theological propositions to oppose the propositions of science.

Such complete frankness makes superfluous any further exposition of the incompatibility of logical positivist doctrines with any religious doctrine that is proposed as true.

From the first, logical positivists were aware that their doctrines were being attacked as destructive of religion, morality, and even of philosophy. The charge of opposition to religion they readily admitted, Ayer observing only that this puts them in excellent philosophical company. With morality itself they had no quarrel. Their interest in denying the cognitive significance of ethical propositions concerns simply a point of logic—the distinctness of the emotive from the scientific order.

Role of Philosophy. The question of what function remains for philosophy now that it has lost its former domains never ceased to disturb logical positivists. One answer with support from the start was that philosophy is simply a branch of logic. This was the position of Rudolf Carnap, who declared without hesitation that the only proper task of philosophy is the logical analysis of scientific concepts and propositions.

For Schlick, a "great turning point" came when philosophy ceased to be regarded as a science in its own right with propositions of its own. With nothing to say itself, philosophy becomes the "activity" of making scientific propositions clear, leaving to the sciences the task of stating the truth about things.

This conception of philosophy grew, at least in part, out of Wittgenstein's early teaching that philosophy's total function is negative: it exposes lapses into metaphysical utterance thereby rescuing man's intelligence from its "bewitchment" by language. Philosophical problems are not solved; they just "dissolve." Yet Wittgenstein's final advice to discard even the propositions of his book as nonsense (after having made use of them) disturbed some of his disciples. Carnap charges him with inconsistency, and Ayer suggests that there are philosophical propositions after all, viz, those that constitute books such as Ayer's own. Holding these to be tautologies, Ayer rejoins Carnap in making philosophy a branch of logic.

Critique and Evaluation. This did not end the logical positivists' struggle, in the grip of their own basic principles, to create a role for themselves as philosophers. Friedrich Waismann, prominent in the original discussions of the Vienna Circle, was moved, by 1956, to observe that it is "nonsense" to say that metaphysics is nonsense. Later, considering again the frequently voiced objection that the verification principle is itself unverifiable, Ayer continued to shun the suggestion that it might be nonsense, but could offer little in its defense, He conceded that, if a metaphysical statement is neither a tautology nor a scientific hypothesis, it does not follow that it is meaningless, unless one "makes it follow"—a procedure that, he observes, has proved useful for banishing metaphysicians from the domain of science.

This is a telling observation. It points to the practical concern behind the logical positivist movement and dispels the image of a doctrine growing out of inexorable laws of logic. It calls attention to the circumstance that the early founders of logical positivism were predominantly men of a scientific outlook, chiefly concerned with what they regarded as metaphysical encroachments within science.

Apart from this, however, there are valuable truths to be drawn from the movement. By insisting upon clarity of thought and precision in the use of language, and by calling into question rationalist and idealist modes of philosophizing, logical positivists have served both philosophy and science. Many of them have shown themselves to be exceptionally competent philosophers. Their analyses have, at times, placed them firmly on the side of common sense. But what is more important, by their radical challenge to the survival of traditional philosophy they have compelled those who would resist them to take seriously their obligation to be true philosophers.

None of these factors, however, removes the basic philosophic weaknesses of logical positivism; nor do they mitigate its basic incompatibility with a religion that promises anything to the mind of man.

See Also: METAPHYSICS, VALIDITY OF.

Bibliography: A. J. AYER, *Logical Positivism* (Glencoe, IL 1959); *Language, Truth and Logic* (2d ed. New York 1957). J. R. WEINBERG, *An Examination of Logical Positivism* (New York 1936). C. L. STEVENSON, *Ethics and Language* (New Haven 1944). V. KRAFT, *The Vienna Circle: The Origin of Neo-Positivism,* tr. A. PAP (New York 1953). O. NEURATH et al., *Wissenschaftliche Weltauffassung: Der Wiener Kreis* (Vienna 1929).

[M. F. GRIESBACH]

LOGICISM

The philosophical conviction that logic alone can solve all problems, whether scientific, philosophical, or theological, because these are reducible to logical problem. Although sometimes opposed to PSYCHOLOGISM as a tendency to construct a logic independently of psychology or to reduce psychology to logic, it is more commonly contrasted with mathematicism as an attempt to reduce all of mathematics to logic (*see* MATHEMATICS, PHILOSOPHY OF).

Historically, logicism made its appearance in the 12th century with the efforts of Peter ABELARD to solve

the problem of UNIVERSALS. It later developed into NOMINALISM and SKEPTICISM towards the close of the Middle Ages. In recent times its revival parallels the growth of symbolic or mathematical logic, and the related movements of LOGICAL POSITIVISM and analytical philosophy (*see* LOGIC, SYMBOLIC).

While logic is a universal discipline that has important contributions to make to both science and philosophy, its overemphasis can have harmful effects. One of these is the confusion it generates between method and content. More important is its failure to recognize any distinction between logic and metaphysics. Logic concerns itself with ideas, judgments, laws of reasoning, and their expressions as these exist formally in the mind, whereas metaphysics concerns itself with reality as this exists in itself. Logical beings are actually contents of the mind as universals of second intention that are univocal in meaning; ontological being is transcendental and analogical in meaning. Logic emphasizes the extension of concepts, whereas metaphysics is more concerned with intension and hierarchies of content.

By confusing ontological being with logical being, logicism makes logic overreach itself and thus become indistinguishable from other forms of thought.

See Also: METHODOLOGY (PHILOSOPHY); METAPHYSICS, VALIDITY OF.

Bibliography: E. H. GILSON, *The Unity of Philosophical Experience* (New York 1937). J. MARITAIN, *Distinguish to Unite, or The Degrees of Knowledge,* tr. G. B. PHELAN from 4th French ed. (New York 1959).

[E. Q. FRANZ]

LOGOS

The word Logos (λόγος) has various meanings in Greek: reckoning, account, explanation, reason, narrative, saying, term, word, etc. But it is the use of this word in the expression, λόγος θεοῦ, "Word of God," as employed in the Johannine writings of the New Testament, that makes it a term of prime theological significance.

1. In the Bible

For a better understanding of this term as used by St. John it is necessary to begin with a consideration of its similar usage in the works of PHILO JUDAEUS, who preceded the author of the Fourth Gospel in the employment of this expression.

Logos in Philo. Like most of his thought, Philo's theory of the Logos was a combination of Biblical and Greco-philosophic themes. The developing poetical personification of the WORD OF GOD in the Old Testament [cf. Ps 32(33).4, 6; 106(107).20; 147(147B).15; Wisdom 18.15–16] was the basis for his synthesis. This Biblical personification was augmented in the Targums of the post-Biblical period, works whose contents go back far into the Old Testament oral traditions. In these homiletically expanded translations of the Old Testament the term Memra (Aram. *memrā',* corresponding to Heb. *dābār,* ''word'') was often used as a synonym for the divine name Yahweh. Originally, this was intended to safeguard the transcendence of the divine name, especially when this was used in anthropomorphic contexts. [*See* ANTHROPOMORPHISM (IN THE BIBLE).] Thus the Targum of Genesis 3.8 says that Adam and Eve, ''heard the sound of the Memra walking in the garden.'' From this use of Memra for Yahweh's anthropomorphic seeing, hearing, feeling, becoming angered, etc., the Memra becomes a poetic intermediary between Yahweh and His people. The result is that from its usage as a word created to guard the divine transcendence, it becomes a term that intensifies the divine immanence. The Memra becomes God's instrument in creation and in history, and in the ruling of both. Here the theme of personified Word and personified Memra meet and unite. It is difficult to decide the exact line between poetics and metaphysics in these personifications.

Thus Philo would have found the poetic personification of the word (*dābār*) of Yahweh not only in the Old Testament itself, but united with the rabbinical theories on the Memra in contemporary Judaic tradition. This supplied the Biblical stratum for Philo's theories on the Logos. The Greco-philosophic concept was a combination of the Logos of Heraclitus and the Stoics with the idea world of Plato; it is no wonder that the Logos theory of Philo defies organization into perfectly coherent unity.

Logos as Image of God. The Platonic thesis of the idea world was equated by Philo with the Logos. Plato considered the visible, sensible world an image (εἰκών) of the idea world (*Timaeus* 92); Philo knew from Genesis 1.26 that man was created ''according to the image'' (κατ' εἰκόνα) of God and he took this to mean that man was the image of the Image (εἰκὼν εἰκόνος) of God. The Image, then, must be the Logos (*De opificio mundi* 25). This understanding of the Logos as Image of God seems to be accepted by Philo as a first principle, and this is his ordinary way of describing the relation of the Logos with God: ''the Image of God is the Logos through whom the whole universe was framed'' (*De specialibus legibus* 1.81); ''the divine Logos is Himself the Image of God, chiefest of all beings intellectually perceived, placed nearest, with no intermediary distance, to the truly Existent One'' (*De fuga et inventione* 101); ''it well befits those who have entered into comradeship with knowl-

edge to desire to see the Existent if they may, but, if they cannot, to see at least his Image, the most holy Logos'' (*De confusione linguarum* 97). The Logos, then, is the Image of God; it is the personified divine Reason binding creation to the divine.

Logos Image as Wisdom. At times Wisdom (σοφία) seems greater than Logos (*De fug. et inv.* 109; *legum allegoriae* 1.65; 2.49; *De somniis* 2.242); at other times Logos seems superior to Wisdom (*De fug. et inv.* 97). In reality, however, Logos and Wisdom are but two terms for the same divine Reason as intermediary for creation (*Leg. all.* 2.86; *De fug. et inv.* 51, 101; *De migratione Abrahami* 40 and *De som.* 185; *De fug. et inv.* 109 and *De cherubim* 125–127; *De con. ling.* 146 and *Leg. all.* 1.43). Logos is Wisdom, but this latter term is more ''feminine'' and can be used for divine Reason in a receptive role, e.g., as mother of creation (*De fug. et inv.* 109; *Leg. all.* 2.49).

Logos Image as Divine ''Man.'' In an allegory on Genesis 42.11 Philo explains, ''You have all enrolled yourselves as children of one and the same Father, who is not mortal but immortal—God's man, who being the Logos of the eternal. . .'' (*De con. ling.* 41). In another allegory, on Zechariah 6.12, he identifies the ''man'' with ''the Incorporeal One who differs not a bit from the divine Image'' (*ibid.,* 62). Thus the Logos who is the Image of God, the personified divine Reason (νοῦς), can also be called Wisdom (σοφία) and Man (ἄνθρωπος), divine Man.

Logos Image and the World. The same Logos who is Image (εἰκών) with regard to God is Model (παράδειγμα) in relation to the sensible world (κόσμος). The Platonic theory that the sensible world is the visible image of the idea world (*De con. ling.* 172) is incorporated into Philo's synthesis by the equation of the Logos and the idea world: ''the world discerned only by the intellect is nothing else than the Word of God when He was already engaged in the act of creation'' (*De op. mun.* 15–25). Thus, for Philo, the material universe is the image of the Logos, which is itself the Image of God.

Logos Image and Mankind. Since the world is the image of the Logos, what of man who is himself part of this world? Man has reason (νοῦς), whereby he is a very special part of the universe. This reason of man's, ''which is in the true sense and full sense man, is the image of the Logos, the cast, as it were, of the Image of God'' (*Quis reum divinarum Heres* 230–31; cf., *De fug. et inv.* 68; *De op. mun.* 69). Whatever the term used for man's reason, whether νοῦς, or λόγος, or ψυχή, or some of their derivatives, it is always through this faculty that man is the image of the Logos (*Quod det. pot. insid. sol* 82–84; *De fug. et inv.* 69; *Quis rer. div. Her.* 234; *De mutatione nominis* 223; *De spec. leg.* 1.171; *Leg. all.* 3.95; *De spec. leg.* 1.81; 3.207; *De plantatione* 5). It is here that Philo's Biblical conceptions seem to break through his philosophical framework. At times the Logos intermediary fades from the picture and man becomes directly the Image of God by himself (*De spec. leg.* 3.207; *De somniis* 1.74; *Quod. det. pot. insid. sol* 82–83; *De decalogo* 134). It should be noted that this is never said of the world itself, but only of man.

For Philo, then, the Logos is the poetic personification of divine Reason, the Image of God. Logos is also termed, at times, divine Wisdom and divine Man. The sensible world is the image of the Logos as the creational mind of God, but this point is not too fully developed by Philo; it was possibly too un-Biblical. Finally, man, through his reason, is the image of the Logos, which is divine Reason; it is reason that makes man most perfectly and fully man. Philo's Biblical heritage, however, often makes him ignore the Logos's role in this last point, and he speaks of man as the Image of God Himself.

Logos in St. John. The term Logos appears as a technical term in the Johannine writings. Leaving aside the detailed problems of authorship, it will be here presumed that Revelation, 1 John, and John stem from the same theological mentality and may be studied together.

Logos in Revelation 19.13. The general context of this passage is the eschatological judgment (19.11–21; 20.7–15) and salvation (21.1–22.5) of mankind. The judgment is shown as a battle (19.11–21; 20.7–10), after which sentence of condemnation is passed on the vanquished evildoers (20.11–15). In this battle the forces of the just are led by a Rider on a white horse among whose many names is that of "The Logos of God." This vision is of Christ as the eschatological Victor and Judge. It is obvious that the title Logos in such a context owes nothing to Philo. It is also clear from the description of the Rider in Revelation 19.11–16 that the seer bases his vision on the Old Testament conception of the Logos of Yahweh as an avenging force in history. The destruction of Egypt, whereby Israel was liberated from bondage (Ex 12.23), was later described (Wisdom 18.14–16) as a visitation of the wrathful Logos of God—the Logos as sword of Yahweh (see also Rv 19.15 and 1 Chr 21.16). Thus, the Old Testament theme of God's judgment and God's visitation in wrath (Is 11.4; Ps 2.9) is here given to the Logos as eschatological Victor and Judge. The Logos of God exterminates the unjust.

Logos in 1 John. The problem of chronological sequence of 1 John and John is still disputed; for the present purpose, it is presumed that 1 John preceded John. The prologue of the Epistle describes Christ as the "Logos of life." This sudden and unexplained title probably means

that the first readers of 1 John were already familiar with the oral catechesis that lay behind the later writing of John 1.1–18. In Deuteronomy the Law was preached as a source and way of life, and at times it was simply termed "the word" (*dābār:* 4.1–2; 32.47). The revelation of Yahweh in the Law was the word that gave life to Israel; so 1 John sees the incarnate Christ as the full and perfect revelation and communication of divine life to mankind (1 Jn 1.2; 5.20; Jn 14.6; see also Jn 1.17). The Logos of God vivifies the just.

Logos in John 1.1–18. In his magnificent prologue John mentions the Logos four times under this title; the term is used here without any genitival qualifications. The functions of the Logos as eschatological avenger (Revelation) and as revelatory vivifier (1 John) are here overshadowed as the Logos appears in the fullness of both being and function.

In the Old Testament the hymns to personified Wisdom in the sapiential literature followed a three-point schema: Wisdom was with God from all eternity; Wisdom was with God at creation; Wisdom has come down with gifts to mankind (Prv 8.22–35; Sir 1.1–35; 24.5–31; Wis 9.9–12). In John 1.1–18 the Logos is described in this same pattern except that it is done in inverse parallelism: the Word with God (1–2, 18); the Word at the old and new creation (3, 17); the gifts that the Word brings to men, centered on divine sonship through the Incarnation (4–16). But despite the Wisdom framework, John terms Christ the Logos and not the Wisdom of God. In this, John is reverting to the earlier word-of-Yahweh theology of the Old Testament while including in the term all the activity in creation and history attributed to Wisdom in the sapiential books.

The Logos appears immediately as eternal, already existing when God came to create the world. He was both distinct from the Father ("with God," where the divine name has the definite article, ὁ θεός) and yet one with God ("was God," where God, θεός, lacks the definite article). The Logos's preexistent divine being is at the height of the descent that terminates in the Logos becoming flesh and giving to the people of God a new Tent in which the divine can dwell (1.14).

Logos in Philo and in St. John. One can hardly state that John did not know the thought of Philo on the Logos; yet it is equally difficult to show any real dependence on it or influence from it. The two syntheses described above have their common roots deep in Biblical and rabbinical thinking on the word and the Memra of God, and this is sufficient to explain their similarities. Their differences arise from the fact that Philo depends on Plato to help him develop the theme of the Logos, whereas John develops the theme from what the Spirit reminds him concerning what he had heard, seen, and felt of the Logos become flesh.

Bibliography: PHILO JUDAEUS, *Philo,* tr. F. H. COLSON and G. H. WHITAKER, 10 v. (Loeb Classical Library; London-New York-Cambridge, Mass. 1929–62). É. BRÉHIER, *Les Idées philosophiques et religieuses de Philon d'Alexandrie* (2d ed. Paris 1925). M. E. BOISMARD, *St. John's Prologue,* tr. Carisbrooke Dominicans (Westminster, Maryland 1957). J. STARCKY, *Dictionnaire de la Bible,* suppl. ed. L. PIROT et al. (Paris 1928–) 5:465–75, 479–96. *Encyclopedic Dictionary of the Bible,* tr. and adap. by L. HARTMAN (New York 1963), from A. VAN DEN BORN, *Bijbels Woordenboek* 1364–68.

[D. M. CROSSAN]

2. Theology of

Because it is decidedly Trinitarian in its historical and logical implications, the present question is intimately connected with CHRISTOLOGY as well (*see* GOD [SON]). By way of an introductory definition, the latter may be taken to designate a particular way of understanding and expressing the reality-activity of Jesus of Nazareth—this in terms of a definite function attributed to Him; in the present case, that of Logos, or Word. To view Him in such a perspective is to adopt a frame of reference that was originally Biblical, however much it may have been developed in the course of subsequent Christian thought. Consequently, the proclamation of Jesus as the preexisting, divine, creative Logos on the part of the postapostolic Church had its source not directly and certainly, not exclusively in Hellenistic philosophy but rather in the Jewish-Christian Scriptures. The development of this faith and its understanding in the long ages of meditation on the mystery of God's Word is the subject under consideration here; in other words, the theology of the Logos in the postapostolic Church.

Precondition. The diversity found in the ways Jesus is presented in the New Testament is a fact. One of those Christic theologies—indeed a most important one—is that of the Logos. Preexistent and intimately related to the Father eternally; divine; the Guide or Word of all creation; incarnate among men in time—such is Jesus as Logos according to the Scriptures, especially in the Johannine corpus (Jn ch. 1; 1 Jn ch. 1).

Faith in Jesus—which was also faith concerning Jesus—was formulated in diverse, if mutually compatible, ways within the New Testament, that of the Logos being numbered among them. In view of this, one might consider antecedently probable the occurrence of a similar situation in later times as well. Such was in fact the case.

Of relevance here are such efforts insofar as they terminated in new modes of presenting the Logos doctrine and its implications. These were attempts on the part of individuals or the magisterium to express the same Biblical faith concerning Jesus in terms more immediately familiar to men of post-Biblical times. Implicit in the whole phenomenon were a consciousness and conviction on the part of the Church. It was aware that its mission to preach the one gospel of and concerning Jesus to all men would entail retaining its truth undiluted, though adapted to vastly different mentalities. The Church also came to the conviction that professing the faith in union with all other believers no more involved the necessity of adopting a particular philosophical system than it involved the necessity of conforming one's eating habits to certain dietary prescriptions of the Mosaic Law.

Realization as Continuation. A most noteworthy characteristic found in the early theology of the Logos was that it involved the homogeneous development of a Biblical truth. If in the New Testament Jesus as Logos had truly transcendent qualities, He was nevertheless presented as very much endowed with a cosmic function at once illuminative and productive (*see* WORD, THE). His preexistence with the Father was clearly asserted, but even more in focus were the implications this had regarding the entire universe in its relation of dependence on Him. In this, the scriptural perspective was one of transient or functional interpersonalism. It was this aspect that was elaborated further when Christian apologists came into contact with an intellectual milieu concerned with a logos as the explanation of all order and rationality in the world.

Striking evidence of this is present in the ideological connection they made between the creative word of Elohim in the first chapter of Genesis and Jesus as Logos in the prologue of the Fourth Gospel [Theophilus of Antioch, *Autol.* 2.10, *Patrologia Graeca,* ed. J. P. Migne, 6:1066; Tatian, *Orat.* 5, *Patrologia Graeca* 6:814–818; Justin, *Dial.* 61, *Patrologia Graeca* 6:614–615; Justin, *2 Apol.* 6, *Patrologia Graeca* 6:454; Tertullian, *Adv. Praxean* 5, *Corpus scriptorum ecclesiasticorum latinorum* 47:232–33; Clement of Alexandria, *Str.* 6.7.58.1, *Die griechischen christlichen Schriftsteller der ersten drei Jahrhunderte* (Stählin) 461; Clement of Alexandria, *Str.* 6.5.39.2, *Die griechischen christlichen Schriftsteller der ersten drei Jahrhunderte* 451; Origen, *Hom. 1 in Gen.* 1, *Die griechischen christlichen Schriftsteller der ersten drei Jahrhunderte* (Baehrens) 6.1:1–10]. The grammatical and exegetical presuppositions this involved were commented on by later Fathers too (Hilary, *Tract. in Psalm.* 2, *Corpus scriptorum ecclesiasticorum latinorum* 22.2:39; Jerome, *Liber heb. quaest. in Gen.* 1.1, *Corpus Christianorum. Series latina* 67: 3).

It was a common thing for such writers to distinguish between the eternal reason or mental word of God and its external utterance (Theophilus in the place cited; Justin in the place cited in the *Dial.*; Tertullian in *Adv. Praxean* 6–8, *Corpus scriptorum ecclesiasticorum latinorum* 47:233 and following; Hippolytus, *Noët.* 10, *Patrologia Graeca* 10:818). Here one cannot but note the definite resemblance with the λόγος ἐνδιάθετος-προφορικός of contemporary philosophy, particularly Stoicism. The immanent procession of the Logos in the Godhead and His temporal mission are closely connected; the creative-redemptive οἰκονομία is not divorced from that within the Deity. If the unified picture thus obtained is a decided advantage, there is a difficulty as well. Saving cosmic process threatens to become a necessary element in the divine origin of the Logos. Such theological endeavors were not enthusiastically received by all even at the time (Irenaeus, *Haer.* 2.28.6; Harvey 1:355).

In effect, these efforts to describe the origin of the Logos from the Father were motivated by a desire to win a sympathetic hearing for the faith. Despite its mysterious character, the doctrine of Jesus as Logos was not without any affinity with elements of non-Christian thought prevalent at the time. There was a willingness on the part of the Fathers in question to search out examples or images from daily life to show that the origin of the Logos from God the Father (ὁ θεός) was not *totally* unlike anything man could encounter in the world of his experience. In this way one understands better the intention behind their use of such images as the origin of the external word by which man expresses one already in his mind and also the case of the fire giving rise to another without diminution on its own part.

To put it another way, these Fathers used natural analogues to illustrate one aspect of the Jesus-Logos profession—His distinction from the Father and His creative-illuminative-redemptive relation to the world from the very beginning. Examples from the realm of created being could not but limp when applied to the clarification of a mysterious communication of life from Father to Son-Logos in the Godhead. In this case, the distinction between an eternal word in the mind of God and one uttered in time could be understood to make the Logos temporal in the strict sense and therefore not equal to the Father. Such a procedure errs on two counts.

First, it attributes to the writers in question the intention of doing a great deal more than offering helps to understand the meaning and implications of the faith concerning Jesus-Logos. It assumes they thought they had discovered the real equivalent of this mystery in the everyday life of man. There is not the slightest indication that this was the case; they distinguished between this faith and their attempts to render it more intelligible [Justin, *Dial.* 48, *Patrologia Graeca* 6:579, 582; Tertullian,

De praescr. haer. 7.12–13, *Corpus Christianorum. Series latina* 1:193; Origen, *Princ.*, praef., 2–4, *Die griechischen christlichen Schriftsteller der ersten drei Jahrhunderte* (Koetschau) 5:8–10]. Second, it also takes for granted that these Fathers, besides considering their examples completely adequate, saw as well and immediately the consequences to which the latter would lead. In this case that would amount to the temporal generation of the Son, or utterance of the Word. Such a view is clearly anachronistic.

It also overlooks the fact that these same authors insisted on the Word-Son's equality in dignity with the Father [Justin, 1 *Apol.* 63, *Patrologia Graeca* 6:426; Athenagoras, *Leg.* 10, *Patrologia Graeca* 6:907, 910; Theophilus, *Autol.* 2.22, *Patrologia Graeca* 6:1087; Origen, *Princ.* 5, *Die griechischen christlichen Schriftsteller der ersten drei Jahrhunderte* (Koetschau) 5: 10]. In other words, neither of the two Biblical poles indicating the mystery of Christ as Logos was forgotten. It was very difficult to find the formula to express both simultaneously; emphatic assertion of one seemed to exclude the other. The distinct character of the Logos-Son was presented by use of such examples; His divinity was not for that fact being questioned—at least according to the intent of the authors involved. It may be another question to ask whether there is objective compatibility between the assertion that the Word is not fully generated as Son until time begins and that He is nevertheless always God in the full sense. The way one understands what is meant by God will have much to do with determining the answer. It has been suggested that a philosophical theory of participation (the Logos being God by *sharing in* the Father's substance) and an intellectual attitude at once realist and acritical (permitting *partial appropriation* of the divine reality by the Word-Son) may have influenced men such as Origen and Tertullian respectively in the systematic replies they gave [B. Lonergan, *De Deo Trino 1: Pars dogmatica* (Rome 1964) 45–48, 54–62, 93]. One thing is sure: this era of Christian thought included efforts to achieve a limited understanding of the Biblical doctrine of the Logos as dependent on the Father. Involved was a willingness to use a non-Biblical distinction between immanent word in God's mind and Son or Logos arising fully with reference to creation. Nor is there any doubt that in the minds of those who so reasoned, this was compatible with asserting the transcendence-divinity of the Word.

Realization as Diversity of Perspective. Even in noting the definite continuity the postapostolic theology of the Logos has with the Biblical presentation, one sees that marked differences have appeared as well. The most obvious is this: a growing preoccupation with preexistence. This was definitely among the Biblical data, but there the reason for its introduction was the central, temporal function of the Word. It was almost as if to say that what the Logos incarnate does for man in time is only one part of the truth; that with the Father He has actually been preparing for this from all eternity. That prior state of existence becomes very much the center of attention as Christian reflection on the mystery increases. This was a logical development; it is perfectly understandable that in a culture very much concerned with the supertemporal, the pretemporal aspect of Christ would come sharply into focus.

To put this more concretely, the contrast between the relation of the Logos to the Father and that of other realities (τὰ πάντα) to the same Father became an object of direct concern. That such a contrast exists and is Biblical, there can be no doubt. How it is to be accurately expressed is something else. Sooner or later someone was bound to ask the question whether Jesus in His preexistent state was God or creature in the strict sense. If the first, then the Logos might seem to be no more than another name for the Father (MODALISM), and no real dependence of Jesus on the Father could antedate the Incarnation. Then, too, it would be the Father who suffered (PATRIPASSIANISM), or else merely the man Jesus, no more a son than the rest of His followers (ADOPTIONISM). But if the second, then assertions that before His human birth He was as Logos equal to the Father would appear to be mistaken piety and in reality blasphemous. Such a mode of considering Jesus-Logos was expressed most explicitly and forcibly in the 4th century by ARIUS (*see* ARIANISM). One major difficulty was that he and his followers accepted the entire New Testament. This made it difficult for bishops such as Alexander and later St. ATHANASIUS to show them that asserting the creaturehood of the Logos was at variance with the apostolic faith.

Frustrated and not entirely happy with the alternative such circumstances forced them to accept, the Catholic bishops at the Council of NICAEA I introduced into the structure of a preexisting creed elements asserting the divinity of the Son. He is begotten and *not made* (in counterdistinction to the invisible beings proposed as *made* by the Father), originating from the latter's own being and not from something else or from nothing, consubstantial [H. Denzinger, *Enchiridion symbolorum*, ed. A. Schönmetzer, 125–26; cf. Ortiz de Urbina, *El símbolo niceno* (Madrid 1947) 25–61]. No one can deny that this dogmatic formulation deals with an aspect of the mystery of Jesus as Logos; nor can there be serious question that it views His preexistence in a new frame of reference. The assertions of the Creed of Nicaea I were made contingently in history because of the Arian challenge. They would, however, have been true of the Logos-Son in relation to

the Father whether or not there was ever a world to create, sustain, redeem. This is a definitely new turn in the exposition of the Logos doctrine.

Nature of the Development in Question. The aim of the present study is not to discuss the nature of dogmatic development in general. Still, to ask what precisely took place in this transformation is hardly something indifferent in a consideration of Logos theology.

The first thing is that the progress from the Bible to Nicaea I cannot be reduced to one of deducing a conciliar conclusion from scriptural premises. That is not to say that any laws of deductive reasoning are violated; they are not. But the phenomenon in question was simply not an example of that sort of thought process. This should be clear from the fact that the assertion that would serve as conclusion (conciliar definition of consubstantiality) views Jesus as Son-Logos in a very different frame of reference than is the case with strictly Biblical premises. This would be very much like having four terms in a syllogism. To put it more concretely, the Bible sees Jesus as Logos related to the Father before time—His divinity appears there insofar as He is, in His activity, on the Father's side of the dichotomy between God and τὰ πάντα. In terms of creative function rather than strict metaphysical identity of nature, He is associated with the Father. To speak of a unity of being involving consubstantiality may very well be an equivalent way of stating this doctrine. It is not, however, to remain within the Biblical perspective or frame of reference, nor is it to come to a logical conclusion from two strictly Biblical premises. It is to see the compatibility of what is said about Jesus in relation to the Father in the scriptural exposition with that which the Council of Nicaea I asserts. The former is in terms of *function* regarding men and their salvation; the latter deals rather with *being* in a manner that more closely approximates the systematic and metaphysical.

Clearly a cultural transformation is involved as well. The Semitic becomes Hellenistic. Still the relation of the Logos to the Father was created by neither though variously expressed by each. It was presupposed by both and was there to be formulated in different but non-exclusive ways. The development in question implied more than a change from one culture to another. Consequently, the truth communicated by both will remain when they have left no more than traces of themselves in human history. When man in a religion based on a real divine revelation attempts to theologize, he makes use of the cultural instruments within his reach. What happened in this case was that a Greek culture served to express the answer to a question inspired by a Greek mentality about a revealed relation between Logos and Father. That there are abundant traces of the Hellenistic *Weltanschauung* in the reply should come as no surprise. One has only to recall that recourse to such a mode of thought and expression was had by the Church because a real question about the faith did not seem to be answerable otherwise at the time.

In comparing the doctrine of Jesus as Logos-Son in Bible and conciliar documents of the 4th and 5th centuries, it may serve a useful purpose to say that the same relation is viewed from two different perspectives. In the first the mode of presentation is concrete and historical; the other is systematic, abstracted from and contrasted to cosmic process, and much closer to what could be termed logical-metaphysical. This is by no means to imply that the transit from the first to the second was from the imperfect to the perfect. It is simply asserted that the transit was required at the time to make the Christian message concerning Jesus as Logos relevant, or so at least it seemed to the principals involved. That introduced theological considerations as well as articles of faith.

Nor is it in any way indicated that the prior mode may not in other circumstances be called for in doctrinal pronouncements. If many subsequent examples of the latter imitated the method introduced at Nicaea I (*Enchiridion symbolorum* 150, 250–51, 301–02, 426), no one can deny (prescinding from the question of definitions) that Vatican Council II in the first chapters of its constitutions on the sacred liturgy and Church treated of Christ as Son and Logos in a way far more akin to the Biblical than to that of these earlier Councils [*Constitution on the Sacred Liturgy* 5, *Acta Apostolicae Sedis* 56 (1964) 99; *Dogmatic Constitution on the Church* 2–5, *Acta Apostolicae Sedis* 57 (1965) 5–8].

Strictly Theological Consequences. The previous consideration involved a theology of the Logos that was formulated *pari passu* with a development of faith. There was, however, as well, a development of Logos-theology that did not find for itself a definitive approbation of the Church in a doctrinal pronouncement. It rather dealt with scriptural, patristic, and magisterial expressions of the faith and sought to unify them for the purpose of their assimilative understanding. This attempt characterized the Middle Ages in western Europe. It had its inspiration in Augustine's notion that man is the image of God insofar as he has in his psychological life created representations of the Trinitarian processions of knowledge and love (*Trin.* 12.6.6, 15.11.20; *Patrologia Latina*, ed. J. P. Migne, 42:1001, 1072).

The doctrinal data concerning the Logos—His origin by way of generation; His reality as a relation opposed to paternity and passive SPIRATION; His personal character; His ability to be sent temporally into the world—seem often to be merely juxtaposed in the Scripture and magisterium. Medieval theologians made an effort to see

these aspects of the mystery as one unified whole (cf. Thomas Aquinas, *Summa theologiae* 1a, 27–44). This involved a theologizing that started out with the hypothesis that something not altogether unlike the human process of knowing was found in the Trinity. In the light of it the data in question fell into an intelligible pattern. Thus, reflection on the faith concerning Christ as Logos led to the discovery of something with regard to theological method in general. In confrontation with the certainty of Christian faith, THEOLOGY has the function not merely of repeating old formulas (however true and authentically guaranteed) and of searching for new ones, but also to see the old and new as interrelated and forming one intelligible whole. This shows that theology at least under one of its aspects is a science far more like the natural ones than has often been suspected.

If contemporary theology has turned, like the magisterium itself in Vatican Council II, to a consideration of the Logos in SALVATION HISTORY, modern concerns have made themselves felt in the process. Distinct personal relations to the Logos, Spirit, and Father in the just are one [see P. de Letter, SJ, "The Theology of God's Self-Gift," *Theological Studies* 24 (1963) 402–22]. Another is the question of divine consciousness in the Word [*see* JESUS CHRIST (IN THEOLOGY) (SPECIAL QUESTIONS), 10]; this is closely connected with inquiry concerning the new aspect of perfection that the revelation of the Logos within the Godhead opens to man [B. Lonergan, SJ, *De Deo Trino 2: Pars systematica* (Rome 1964) 186–93, 208–15]. Finally, the question has been raised as to whether assuming that any Divine Person could have become man does full justice to the implications of the fact that only the Son-Logos did [K. Rahner, SJ, "Natur und Gnade," *Fragen der Theologie Heute* (Zurich, Cologne 1958) 218–19].

See Also: CONSUBSTANTIALITY; FILIATION; GENERATION OF THE WORD; JESUS CHRIST IN THEOLOGY; NICENE CREED; PROCESSIONS, TRINITARIAN; SON OF GOD; JESUS CHRIST, ARTICLES ON; TRINITY, HOLY, ARTICLES ON.

Bibliography: C. HUBER, *Lexikon für Theologie und Kirche*, ed. J. HOFER and K. RAHNER, 10 v. (2d, new ed. Freiburg 1957–65) 6:1125–28. J. BARBEL, *Christus Angelus* (Bonn 1941). O. CULLMAN, *Die Christologie des Neuen Testaments* (Tübingen 1957), tr. S. C. GUTHRIE and C. A. M. HALL (rev. ed. Philadelphia 1963). A. GRILLMEIER, *Christ in Christian Tradition,* tr. J. S. BOWDEN (New York 1965). K. RAHNER, "Chalkedon: Ende oder Anfang?," A. GRILLMEIER and H. BACHT, *Das Konzil von Chalkedon: Geschichte und Gegenwart*, 3 v. (Würzburg 1951–54) 3:3–49. P. MCSHANE, "The Hypothesis of Intelligible Emanations in God," *Theological Studies* 23 (1962) 545–68.

[C. J. PETER]

LÖHE, JOHANN KONRAD WILHELM

German Lutheran theologian; b. Fürth, Feb. 21, 1808; d. Neuendettelsau, both near Nuremberg, Bavaria, Jan. 2, 1872. After attending the Melanchthon Gymnasium in Nuremberg, he studied theology at the universities of Erlangen and Berlin. As pastor of several different congregations (1831–37), he became known as a forceful advocate of Lutheran orthodoxy. His ideas on Church government, the efficacy of works, self-denial, and celibacy closely resembled those of Roman Catholicism; so also did his suggestions for liturgical reform, private confession, and frequent communion, which he promoted by scholarly studies and pastoral work. Löhe also labored to provide religious care for German emigrants, particularly those going to the United States, and he was involved in the founding of the Lutheran Missouri Synod. His interest in practical works of charity led him to found a Society for inner mission (1844) and a Society of Deaconesses (1853). In 1854 he established a deaconess motherhouse in Neuendettelsau, where he served as pastor from 1837 until his death.

Bibliography: *Gesammelte Werke,* ed. K. GANZERT, 7 v. (Neuendettelsau 1951–58). S. HEBART, *W. Löhes Lehre von der Kirche, ihrem Amt und Regiment* (Neuendettelsau 1939); H. KRESSEL, *Wilhelm Löhe als Prediger* (Gütersloh 1929); *Wilhelm Löhe als Liturg und Liturgiker* (Neuendettelsau 1952); *Wilhelm Löhe als Katechet und als Seelsorger* (Neuendettelsau 1955). K. GANZERT, *Evangelisches Kirchenlexicon: Kirchlich-theologisches Handwörterbuch,* 4 v. (Göttingen 1956–61) 2:1151–1152.

[L. J. SWIDLER]

LOHELIUS, JOHANN (LOCHEL)

Archbishop of Prague; b. Ohře (Eger), Bohemia, 1549; d. Prague, Nov. 2, 1622. He was educated at the abbey school of Tepl, received the Norbertine habit in 1573, and was ordained in 1576. Much of Lochel's early career was spent restoring the historic Premonstratensian Abbey of Strahov, from 1578 as prior, from 1586 as abbot. He colonized it with monks from other monasteries and rebuilt the church. In 1604 he was appointed auxiliary to Archbishop von Lamberg of Prague, succeeding him in the post in 1612. Lochel showed himself a resolute opponent of Calvinist encroachment, and was driven from his see at the time of the Defenestration (1618). With the imperial victory over the Protestant forces at White Mountain, Lochel was able to return to Prague in 1621. He died the following year.

Bibliography: J. SEIBT, *Lexikon für Theologie und Kirche,* ed. J. HOFER and K. RAHNER, 10 v. (Freiburg 1957–65) 6:1129. K. PICHERT, *Analecta Praemonstratensia* 3 (1927): 125–140, 264–283, 404–22.

[B. L. MARTHALER]

Alfred Loisy. (Corbis/Bettmann)

LOISY, ALFRED

Leading exponent of biblical MODERNISM; b. Ambrières, France, Feb. 28, 1857; d. Paris, June 6, 1940. After theological studies in the seminary at Châlonssur-Marne (1874–79) and ordination (June 29, 1879), he was sent to the Institut Catholique of Paris for higher studies (1881). Abbé L. DUCHESNE became his principal teacher. He remained there as professor of Hebrew and later of exegesis (1884–93) until he was dismissed, somewhat unfairly, because of a controversy over biblical inerrancy. The step seems to have been taken to save his rector embarrassment, and it initiated the bitterness Loisy afterward held toward Church authority. Five of his books were placed on the INDEX OF FORBIDDEN BOOKS (Dec. 19, 1903). With his excommunication as *vitandus* on March 8, 1908, he publicly gave up his Catholic faith and all Christianity, professing a vague ''Religion of Humanity.'' He obtained a professorship of the history of religions in the Collège de France (1909–26) and the École des Hautes Études (1924–27). Active throughout his long life, he kept writing about ''problems of religion'' even after his jubilee (1927) and retirement. The high point of his career (1900–10) was followed by a period of gradual decline into oblivion. He never recanted his positions and died without being reconciled to the Church.

In his *Choses Passées* (1913) and *Mémoires pour servir a l'Histoire religieuse de notre Temps, 1860–1931* (3 v. 1930–31), there is a wealth of information about the history of Modernism and autobiographical details that show the tortured variations of his thought, his difficulties of conscience, and his relationship with scholars and ecclesiastics of his time. He traced everything to a crisis of faith 29 years before his formal excommunication (1886): although practicing his priesthood, he was a complete atheist. He rejected all Christian dogmas in their traditional sense. His concept of God was that of a vague, indefinable Ego furnishing obscure solutions for the mystery of the universe. In these books are seen his independence of mind, his deep-rooted conviction of a lack of intellectual sincerity within the Catholic Church, and a deficiency in solid philosophical formation.

His most characteristic biblical writings concerned the Gospels. *L'Évangile et l'Église* (1902) was his first "little red book." In a critique of A. von HARNACK'S *Essence of Christianity*, he maintained that Christianity underwent a historical evolution that had not been foreseen by its Founder, Jesus Christ. His *Quatrième Évangile* (in which he maintained that the Apostle John is not the author and that everything is purely symbolic) was followed by *Autour d'un petit Livre,* the second "little red book" (both in 1903). The latter is a defense and exposition of the positions taken in the former. His third "little red book," *Simples Reflexions sur le Décret du Saint-Office 'Lamentabili' et sur l'Encyclique 'Pacendi,'* was an expression of insolence and defamation of the authorities in Rome, particularly Cardinal Merry del Val. This was followed by *Les Évangiles Synoptiques* (2 v. 1907–08), which contained some judicious remarks and radical criticism.

Bibliography: J. BONSIRVEN, *Dictionnaire de la Bible,* ed. L. PIROT, et al. (Paris 1935–65) 5:530–544. O. SCHROEDER, *Lexikon für Theologie und Kirche,* 10 v. (Freiburg 1957–65) 6:1134. J. ROTH, *Die Religion in Geschichte und Gegenwart,* 7 v. (3d ed. Tübingen 1857–65) 4:445–446. S. LEBLANC, in *Congrès d'histoire du christianisme: Jubilé de Alfred Loisy,* ed. P. L. CHOUCHOUD, 3 v. (Paris 1928). J. LEVIE, *Sous les yeux de l'incroyant* (Paris 1946) 191–215. F. HEILER, *Der Vater des katholischen Modernismus, Alfred Loisy* (Munich 1947).

[L. A. BUSHINSKI]

LOLLARDS

Lollards is the name given to the English followers of John WYCLIF, the Oxford theologian and heretic who died in 1384. A derogatory term, it was meant to convey the attributes of a *lollaerd* (in Middle Dutch, a mumbler) and a *loller* (in Middle English, an idler). At first the sect was confined to a small group of educated priests, such as Nicholas HEREFORD, Philip REPINGTON, and John Aston, who had known Wyclif at Oxford and had been attracted by his radical views on lordship, grace, the Sacraments, and the temporal power of the papacy. In 1382, however, the Archbishop of Canterbury, William COURTENAY, moved swiftly and firmly to suppress the activities of these Oxford scholars, and in consequence the sect was soon deprived of its vigorous intellectual leaders, and passed into the hands of the more discontented and less literate elements of English society. Such poorly educated, unlicensed preachers as William Swinderby, who for one reason or another had failed to obtain a benefice, then formed the backbone of the movement. Many laymen, including burgesses, small freeholders, artisans, and tradesmen, were attracted by its nonconformist doctrines, and while it would be unrealistic to suppose that these gave much thought to Wyclif's theological ideas, many were seriously perturbed by the practical shortcomings and laxity of church dignitaries, religious corporations, mendicants, and secular clergy in their midst, not to mention the scandal that the contemporary WESTERN SCHISM gave to all the faithful. Thus from the first the movement provided a focal point for the more reactionary antipapal and anticlerical elements within the country, but it also included many sincerely religious people, however illinformed or self-opinionated. On the whole there were few Lollards among the nobility and lesser gentry, for two reasons: first, heresy was by then an offense in English common law, so that if indicted, the higher ranks of society stood to lose more; second, the Lollard belief that dominion or lordship should be exercised only by those in a state of grace appeared to the nobility as a threat to their feudal authority. The one notable exception in this class was the Lollard knight, Sir John Oldcastle, who was finally hanged as a traitor and heretic in 1417. Thus proscribed, discredited, and leaderless, the sect gradually disintegrated and after 1431 ceased to exist effectively. Being popular among semiliterate people, the movement had a literature of its own. Tracts and sermons echoing Wyclif's ideas in simple, forceful English passed rapidly and enthusiastically among Lollards throughout the country, although a more permanent achievement was the English translation of the Bible by Wyclif's followers, which became known as the Lollard Bible.

See Also: HUSSITES.

Bibliography: J. GAIRDNER, *Lollardy and the Reformation in England,* 4 v. (London 1908–13) 1:1–242. J. WYCLIF, *Selected English Writings,* ed. H. E. WINN (London 1929). M. DEANESLY, *The Significance of the Lollard Bible* (London 1951). K. B. MCFARLANE, *John Wycliffe and the Beginnings of English Nonconformity* (New York 1953). V. H. H. GREEN, *The Later Plantagenets* (London 1955) 191–209. M. E. ASTON, "Lollardy and Sedition, 1381–1431," *Past and Present,* 17 (1960) 1–44. J. A. F. THOMSON, *The Later Lollards 1414–1520* (New York 1966). M. ASTON and R. COLIN, eds., *Lol-*

lardy and the Gentry in the Later Middle Ages (Stroud, Eng. 1997). J. I. CATTO, ''Wyclif and Wycliffism at Oxford 1356–1430,'' in *The History of the University of Oxford,* v. 2, ed. B. HARRISON (Oxford 1992) 175–261. M. ASTON, *Lollards and Reformers: Images and Literacy in Late Medieval Religion* (London 1984).

[L. MACFARLANE]

LOMBARD LEAGUE

A federation of north Italian cities formed in 1167 to resist the attempts of the Holy Roman Emperor FREDERICK I BARBAROSSA (1152–90) to organize and consolidate imperial rule in northern and central Italy. It was a defensive alliance of changing membership, and became active during the century and a half following its foundation whenever emperors attempted to enforce imperial rule in Italy. Although the League theoretically never claimed independence of the Empire, its very reason for existence was to defend communal autonomy against the emperor.

At the Diet of Roncaglia (November 1158), Barbarossa made it clear that the reconstruction of imperial administration and rule in Italy constituted a major part of his program for restoring the Empire, shattered by the INVESTITURE STRUGGLE. He undertook military operations against recalcitrant north Italian cities, the foremost among them being Milan. These cities created numerous coalitions to defend their *de facto* autonomy. One of the important confederations, the League of Verona (1164), comprised Verona, Vicenza, Padua, and Venice. Frederick's enemy, Pope ALEXANDER III (1159–81), sided with the allied cities. During the spring and summer of 1167, other alliances which included Cremona, until then a loyal imperial city, were concluded. Earlier historians called the League of Pontida (April 7, 1167) the origin of the Lombard League, but this was only one of many coalitions.

By Dec. 1, 1167, the Lombard League had taken shape. Its 16 members included the adherents of the leagues of Verona and Pontida. The signers protected their individual interests by special provisos, but all were bound to make war, truce, and peace only by unanimous consent. The League arrogated to itself such imperial prerogatives as the right to raise and support an army and to hear judicial cases on appeal. At League meetings each member acted through a rector, ordinarily chosen from among the chief communal magistrates. On Dec. 1, 1168, the League strengthened its organization and established regulations to prevent discord among its members.

In defiance of Frederick, the League founded a new city (1168) named Alessandria in honor of the pope. At Legnano (1176) the League army inflicted a crushing defeat on Frederick. This induced him to negotiate with Al-exander III the Truce of Venice (1177), a six-year truce that included the League members. In 1183 at the ''Peace of Constance'' (technically an imperial privilege, not a ''peace''), although Frederick reasserted some imperial prerogatives, the League and other allied communes won imperial recognition of their autonomy. The regulations of Roncaglia were set aside. The emperor ceded the communes considerable self-government, including authority to exercise regalian rights, raise armies, make alliances, and wall themselves. This concluded the League's greatest era, though it was revived (with fluctuating membership) whenever imperial rule threatened to become a reality in northern Italy. It actively opposed Emperor FREDERICK II (d. 1250) after 1226, and supported his papal opponents GREGORY IX and INNOCENT IV. The military fortunes of the League and its Guelf allies varied. Although defeated at Cortenuova (1237), they received solace from the victory at Vittoria (1248). The League was revived (1310–13) and joined a coalition against the Emperor HENRY VII.

Bibliography: G. VOIGT, *Storia della lega Lombarda . . .* (Milan 1848). C. VIGNATI, *Storia diplomatica della lega Lombarda* (Milan 1867). C. MANARESI, *Atti del comune di Milano fino all'anno 1216* (Milan 1919). E. JORDAN, *L'Allemagne et l'Italie aux XIIᵉ et XIII ᵉ siècles* (Paris 1939). G. TRECCANI DEGLI ALFIERI, ed., *Storia di Milano*, v.4, *Dalle lotte contro il Barbarosa al primo signore* (Milan 1954).

[W. M. BOWSKY]

LOMBARDS

A nation of Germanic barbarians who entered the Italian peninsula in 568. Their kingdom survived until 774, when it fell to Frankish conquest under CHARLEMAGNE. The invading Lombards are thought to have been Arian Christians (although some may still have been heathen), but their settlement among a Catholic population, the influence of a series of Catholic queens (especially the Bavarian Theodolinda), and steady pressure from the papacy produced conversion to the Roman form of Catholicism by the mid-7th century.

Settlement. The Lombards entered the western Roman world at a time when the earlier barbarian invaders of the Empire had been settled on Roman soil for many years and had absorbed a considerable amount of Latin culture. In contrast with these other Germanic peoples, the warlike Lombards were uncouth and barbarous, and they impressed the peoples among whom they settled as well as those with whom they came into less intimate contact as being harsh and cruel—these descriptive terms appear frequently in contemporary records. Such charges, however, were undoubtedly exaggerated, due in

Iron Crown of the Lombards, now in the cathedral at Monza, Italy. (Alinari-Art Reference/Art Resource, NY)

no small part to political opposition from the papacy, fearful of Italian unification under Lombard rule. Most of the northern and central portions of Italy became part of the Lombard kingdom, but the conquest never extended into the extreme southern part of Italy. Even in the northern and central sections the Lombards did not succeed in establishing a consolidated state. It was not until late in the mid-8th century that the Exarchate of RAVENNA fell to Lombard conquest; some of the land in the vicinity of Rome—under the political control of the pope—was never secured by the Lombards, although they did hold the duchies of Spoleto and Benevento immediately to the east and south.

The Lombard kingship was not a powerful institution, and shortly after the death of Alboin, who had led them into the peninsula, the Lombards failed to elect a king for some 12 years. During this interval effective leadership was in the hands of a series of dukes who furthered the conquest by carving out more or less independent duchies for themselves. The weakness of this decentralization soon became apparent, however, and after 584 the Lombards never allowed a regnal vacancy to be prolonged. It should be noted that the Lombard kingship remained elective to the end, although royal heirs were normally preferred.

The Kingdom. The story of the Lombard kingdom is told by the 8th-century Lombard historian, PAUL THE DEACON. Paul's history, together with a series of legal edicts and a number of land charters (dating primarily from the 8th century), provides considerable internal in-

formation about the Lombard kingdom; the *LIBER PONTIFICALIS* and the Frankish chroniclers are the chief external sources. The legal records are especially important: Rothair (636–656) attempted to codify the unwritten customs of the Lombard nation. Liutprand (712–744) issued a long series of supplements that, together with *Rothair's Edict* and a few additional laws issued by Grimwald, Rachis, and Aistulf, make up the body of laws usually known as the *Leges Langobardorum.* These *leges* reveal that the private law of the Lombards was still essentially Germanic, based on wergelds and COMPURGATION, but property law (and to a lesser extent public law) had been considerably influenced by Roman law.

Liutprand was the most important of the Lombard kings. As a Catholic Liutprand favored certain Romanizing influences in the kingdom; as a military leader he reconsolidated the Lombard conquests in Italy and extended them; and as one of the major barbarian rulers of Western Europe he maintained peace and friendship with the Franks and cooperated against the Moors who threatened Provence. During his reign the centralization of the kingdom reached its greatest extent and royal officials successfully counterbalanced the dukes whose interests were primarily local.

When Liutprand died in 744, the Lombard kingdom appeared to have been built into a consolidated whole with a sufficiently centralized administration to ensure its continuing success. Not only had Liutprand subdued the duchies of Spoleto and Benevento, where he installed his own followers, but he had also conquered most of the Exarchate of Ravenna and added its territory to his own. He had expanded the Lombard territory at the expense of the Church lands in the vicinity of the Duchy of Rome and even remained on friendly terms with CHARLES MARTEL and his son PEPIN, the Frankish mayors of the palace, to whom successive popes had appealed in vain for aid against "the most wicked Lombards."

Yet despite the successes of Liutprand and the seeming strength of the kingdom, and despite the fact that his successors Rachis, Aistulf, and DESIDERIUS were fairly able although not very diplomatic rulers, the Lombard kingdom did not long survive. The last Lombard kings proved unable to hold the kingdom together, and upon their final defeat by the Franks in 774, the Frankish ruler, Charlemagne, assumed the Lombard iron crown.

Italy was not incorporated into Francia, however, but remained organized as a separate subkingdom with its own CAROLINGIAN DYNASTY. Thus Lombard influence was preserved (through the continued use of Lombard custom supplemented by Carolingian CAPITULARIES), but the political vitality of the Lombards was gone, and with it any hope of bringing all of Italy under a single unified control.

Lombard King Rachis, depicted in an illumination in the Codex Matrittensis. (©Archivo Iconografico, S.A./CORBIS)

Bibliography: PAULUS DIACONUS, *History of the Lango-bards,* tr. W. D. FOULKE (Philadelphia 1907). *Leges Langobardorum,* ed. F. BLUHME, *Monumenta Germaniae Historica Leges* v.4. *Codice diplomatico Longobardo,* ed. L. SCHIAPARELLI, 2 v. (Rome 1929–33). F. BEYERLE, ed. and tr., *Die Gesetze der Langobarden* (Weimar 1947). T. HODGKIN, *Italy and Her Invaders,* 8 v. in 9 (Oxford 1892–99) v.5–7. L. M. HARTMANN, *Geschichte Italiens im Mittelalter,* 4 v. (2d ed. Stuttgart 1923) v.2. N. F. ÅBERG, *Die Goten und Langobarden in Italien* (Uppsala 1923). G. ROMANO et al., *Le dominazioni barbariche in Italia, 395–888* (3d ed. Milan 1940). G. PEPE, *Il medio evo barbarico d'Italia* (3d ed. Turin 1945). G. P. BOGNETTI, *Santa Maria di Castelseprio* (Milan 1948); G. P. BOGNETTI et al., *Dall'invasione dei barbari al governo vescovile, 493–1002,* v. 2 of *Storia di Milano* (Milan 1953-). E. PONTIERI, *Le invasioni barbariche e l'Italia del V e VI secolo* (Naples 1960).

[K. F. DREW]

LOMBERS, COUNCIL OF

Meeting in May or June 1165, in the French castle of Lombers, about ten miles south of Albi, France. Here, for the first time in Languedoc, the CATHARI, then called *Bonshommes* and later known as ALBIGENSES, were prosecuted for HERESY. Neither a colloquium nor a provincial council, the assembly was a trial conducted by authority of the bishop of ALBI, a suffragan of Bourges, with the bishops and abbots of neighboring Narbonne province, several great nobles, and the local populace in attendance. Assisted by four *assessores,* the bishop of Lodève examined the accused and found them heretical on seven counts. All present approved these findings, although their action did little to check the growth of the movement.

Bibliography: *Sacrosancta Concilia,* ed. P. LABBE and G. COSSART, 17 v. (Paris 1671–73) 10:1470–79, under the year 1176, original ed. of complete *acta; Chronica magistri Rogeri de Houedene,* ed. W. STUBBS, 4 v. (*Rerum Brittanicarum medii aevi scriptores* 51; 1868–71) 2:105–117, xvii–xxii, abr. version under the year 1176. C. DE VIC and J. VAISSETE, *Histoire générale de Languedoc,* ed. E. DULAURIER et al., 16 v. in 17 (new ed. Toulouse 1872–1904) 6:3–5 and esp. 7:1–5, n.1 for place (*not* Lombez) and date. C. J. VON HEFELE, *Histoire des conciles d'après les documents originaux,* tr. and continued by H. LECLERCQ, 10 v. in 19 (Paris 1907–38) 5:1006–10, for bibliog., otherwise unreliable. A. BORST, *Die Katharer* (Schriften der *Monumenta Germaniae Historica* 12; Stuttgart 1953) 95–96, with bibliog.

[R. KAY]

LOMÉNIE DE BRIENNE, ÉTIENNE CHARLES DE

French prelate, minister of Louis XVI; b. Paris, Oct. 9, 1727; d. Sens, Feb. 16, 1794. His family had included ministers of state since the time of Henry III. He studied at the college of Harcourt and at the Sorbonne, which he left in 1751 after sustaining theological theses of doubtful orthodoxy. He was ordained in 1752 and was preferred rapidly, becoming in 1760 bishop of Condom and in 1763 archbishop of Toulouse, where he was an able civil and religious administrator and a philanthropist. Besides the Brienne canal that connects the Garonne with the canal of the Midi, he sponsored other public works, education and libraries, and hygienic reforms. However, his faith came to be suspect at this time. As a friend of the *philosophes* and overly tolerant, he was reputed to be an atheist.

As president of the committee of jurisdiction of general assemblies of the clergy, he worked diligently and exerted a decisive influence, especially beginning in 1766 as part of the committee responsible for the ruinous reform of the religious orders. In 1780 he was replaced by the archbishop of Arles. Joseph II and Marie Antoinette failed to secure his appointment as minister in 1783, but in December of 1787 he replaced Calonne. A few good measures marked a mediocre ministry, and in August of 1788 he was succeeded by J. Necker. He was compensated with the archbishopric of Sens and the rich Abbeys of SAINT-OUEN and CORBIE. He went to Italy, was made cardinal in December of 1788, and returned to France at the end of 1789. He took the oath of loyalty to the Civil Constitution of the Clergy on Jan. 30, 1791, without ceremony, but not without raising a strong reaction. After being reproved by the pope, he resigned his cardinalate and was expelled by the college of cardinals on Sept. 26, 1791. He was then elected bishop of Yonne and passed the last two years of his life at the Abbey of Saint-Pierre-le-Vif. He was twice arrested during the French Revolution, resigned his ecclesiastical income and functions on Nov. 15, 1793, and died, perhaps of apoplexy, while being interrogated. Writers in his own day and since have attacked him with bitterness and contempt, but his clergy at Toulouse and at Sens were fond of him.

Bibliography: J. PERRIN, *Le Cardinal de Loménie de Brienne* (Sens 1896). M. MARION, *Histoire financière de la France depuis 1715,* 3 v. (Paris 1914–21). C. LAPLATTE, *Dictionnaire d'histoire et de géographie ecclésiastiques,* ed. A. BAUDRILLART, et al. (Paris 1912–) 10:693–698, bibliography.

[W. E. LANGLEY]

LONDON, ANCIENT SEE OF

Medieval English diocese with its seat at London; suffragan see of the Archdiocese of CANTERBURY. The earliest unequivocal sign of Christianity in London is the reference to Restitutus, Bishop of London, who attended the Council of ARLES in 314; the lists of his predecessors and successors given by GEOFFREY OF MONMOUTH are worthless. Almost three centuries later, after the Roman withdrawal and the defeat of the Romano-Britons at the hands of the ANGLO-SAXONS, London was designated by Pope GREGORY I THE GREAT as the see from which AUGUSTINE OF CANTERBURY, as archbishop and metropolitan, was to govern the 12 dioceses of southern England just as YORK would govern 12 in the northern province, the primary alternating between York and London. Gregory's scheme, based on memories of Roman Britain, could not be put into effect because London was resolutely pagan in 597 and this Augustine settled on Canterbury as the primatial see. Only in 604 was he able to found the Diocese of London, appointing MELLITUS as its first bishop. Three years later King ETHELBERT of Kent built a cathedral there dedicated to St. PAUL. This see of "London and the East Saxons," however, proved fragile, for with the death of King Ethelbert, Bishop Mellitus and his disciples were driven out by the pagans (617). The see remained vacant until, in 654 (?), it was occupied by the dubious bishop Wini, and it was not until the time of Bishop ERCONWALD (c. 675–c. 693) that the diocese was organized on the dignified lines befitting the city of London. In the preconquest period London's bishops were mainly undistinguishing personages, except possibly for Robert of Jumieges. There has survived from this period a Rule of St. Paul's, which regulated the lives of the canons serving the cathedral and which was probably introduced by Bishop Theodred (926–c. 951). The rule affords a unique insight into the life of an old English cathedral community, disclosing a group of canons living together in chapter and choir, probably sharing a dormitory, yet having jobs to perform outside the cloister, and each enjoying a private stipend. DUNSTAN who was briefly bishop of London (958–960), is supposed to have restored the diocese's WESTMINSTER ABBEY.

In the century after the conquest of 1066, St. Paul's, the heart of the diocese, became very much a center of worldly business, its chapter of 30 prebendaries being regarded as a valuable recruiting ground for royal servants, sheriffs, judges, and curial bishops. Since many of the canons were married, family interests often outweighed pastoral considerations, especially throughout the long dominance by the Belmeis family. Nevertheless, by the middle of the 12th century the diocese was sensibly divided into the four archdeaconries of London, Middlesex, Essex, and Colchester. In many ways in this century the diocese was at the height of its fame, for the burning of the Saxon cathedral (1087) gave Bishop Maurice the opportunity to rebuild his cathedral on a magnificent scale: when completed in 1332 St. Paul's was the largest building in England, its immense spire stretching as loftily as that of Salisbury. It was at this time that the historian of London William FitzStephen (d. c. 1190) wrote: "It was

once a metropolitan see, and will so again . . . if the citizens have their way." In an attempt to have their way the Londoners induced Arcoid, nephew of Bishop Gilbert the Universal (d. 1134), to write a new life of St. Erconwald, whose bones were then translated (1148) to a new and splendid shrine behind the high altar of St. Paul's. This glorification of its history gave some countenance to London's claim to metropolitan status, which was pressed as far as possible by Gilbert FOLIOT (1163–87) in his rivalry with the archbishop of Canterbury, Thomas BECKET. But whatever chance of acceptance this claim might have had was effectively snuffed out by Becket's martyrdom.

For the rest of the medieval period the Diocese of London played a secondary role in the English Church. Its bishops were appointed for their administrative and secular skills rather than for outstanding churchmanship, e.g., RICHARD OF GRAVESEND, SIMON OF SUDBURY, William WARHAM, and Cuthbert TUNSTALL. Nor did it help the diocese that it was comparatively poor, being assessed at £1,000 per annum in the *Taxatio* of NICHOLAS IV (1291). Also, its benefices were particularly easy targets for pluralists and nonresidents, nonresidence being extremely frequent in St. Paul's, from the 12th century in. One exception to the spiritually mediocre bishops of the period was Roger Niger, bishop from 1229 to 1241, who was popularly canonized as "Saint Roger" because of his sanctity and defense of the oppressed. MATTHEW PARIS characterized him as "a man of venerable life and admirable holiness, distinguished for his learning, a brilliant preacher—joyful in speech, urbane in his home, of open and happy countenance." The cathedral later saw great days under the inspiration of its humanist dean John COLET (1466–1519). His efforts to reform the crown of canons, vergers, and chantry priests who had by this time a vested interest in the business conducted in and around St. Paul's were unsuccessful, but he did establish St. Paul's School in the east end of the church, where 153 boys were given free tuition. Up to the early 15th century St. Paul's had its own liturgical rite, the *Usus S. Pauli*, but after 1414 the SARUM rite prevailed.

Edmund BONNER, the last Roman Catholic bishop of London, died in prison in 1569 during the reign of Queen ELIZABETH I. Thereafter Roman Catholics in England relied on priests and sometimes an apostolic vicar appointed by the pope for their guidance. In 1688 Pope INNOCENT XI divided England into four vicariates, including that of London, which eventually acquired jurisdiction over all Catholics in the British possessions of North America and the West Indies. Bishop Richard CHALLONER was one of the memorable apostolic vicars of London, When Pope Pius IX restored the Roman Catholic hierarchy in England in 1850 the London vicariate became the Archdiocese of Westminster and the Diocese of Southwark; some of its area went to the Diocese of Brentwood.

Bibliography: W. S. SIMPSON, *Registrum statutorium et consuetudinum ecclesiae cathedralis sancit Pauli Londinensis* (London 1873). H. WHARTON, *Historia de episcopis et decanis Londiniensibus* (London 1695). E. BESANT, *Medieval London*, 2 v. in 3 (London 1906). W. D. NEWTON, *Catholic London* (London 1950). E. I. WATKIN, *Roman Catholicism in England: From the Reformation to 1950* (New York 1957). W. R. MATTHEWS and W. M. ATKINS, eds., *A History of St. Paul's Cathedral* (London 1957).

[D. NICHOLL]

LONDON CHARTERHOUSE

A former Carthusian foundation formally established by Sir Walter Manny in 1370, the London charterhouse is on land near Smithfield and Aldersgate bought for a chapel and cemetery for victims of the Black Death. It is famous principally for its 18 monks who were martyred in 1535 for refusing to take the oath of supremacy, which recognized HENRY VIII as sole and supreme head of the Church in England. The first prior was John Luscote of Hinton, and the community first numbered ten. Knights and ecclesiastics endowed cells, and by 1532 there were 29 choir monks and 13 lay brothers, 20 of whom were under 38 years of age. They were an unusually distinguished, happy, and fervent community, with a reputation for the especially devout rendering of the Divine Office. They were rich by Carthusian standards, having a fine library and splendid ornaments in the church and an income of £643; notable benefactors were buried in the enclosure. St. Thomas MORE as a young man had lived there for four years as a guest. In 1533 the prior John HOUGHTON accepted the Act of Succession, but soon realized that the subsequent Act of Supremacy involved a denial of the Catholic faith. He prepared his community for the alternative of death or apostasy by a triduum of prayer and penance. The death sentence was passed on him and two other Carthusian priors, April 29, 1535, and in their habits they were dragged on hurdles to the scaffold at Tyburn and hung, drawn, and quartered there on May 4. Before its suppression in 1537, 15 other London Carthusians were martyred; their deaths constitute one of the finest episodes in English monastic history. In the reign of ELIZABETH I, Thomas Sutton refounded the London Charterhouse as an almshouse and school. In spite of extensive war damage during World War II, much still remains of the Tudor buildings, serving as the almshouse. Charterhouse school is now near Godalming in Surrey.

Bibliography: W. H. ST. JOHN HOPE, *History of the London Charterhouse* (New York 1925). E. M. THOMPSON, *The Carthusian Order in England* (New York 1930). M. CHAUNCY, *Passion and Martyrdom of the Holy English Carthusian Fathers,* tr. A. F. RADCLIFFE (New York 1936). D. KNOWLES and W. F. GRIMES, *Charterhouse* (New York 1954). A. QUICK, *Charterhouse: A History of the School* (London 1991).

[H. FARMER/EDS.]

LONERGAN, BERNARD

Theologian, university professor, author, member of the Society of Jesus; b. December 17, 1904, Buckingham, Quebec (Canada); d. Pickering, Ontario, November 26, 1984. The eldest of three sons born to Gerald J., a land surveyor, and Josephine Helen (Wood) Lonergan, Bernard showed himself a precocious youngster. He was educated by the CHRISTIAN BROTHERS at the elementary level in his hometown, and later acquired a solid grounding in classical languages, the humanities, and mathematics at Loyola High and Loyola College in Montreal. He entered the Society of Jesus at age 17 (1922), received his philosophic training at Heythrop College in England (1926–29), and earned an external Bachelor of Arts in classics at London University (1929–30). By his own account, it was the basic honesty and modesty of his Jesuit professors in philosophy that made the greatest impact on him at the time. He was especially influenced by the genial instruction in mathematics he received from his tutor, Charles O'Hara, S.J., and seriousness with which Lewis Watt, S.J. approached questions about economics and morality in the social encyclicals. He confessed that NEWMAN's *An Essay in Aid of a Grammar of Assent,* ''made (him) something of an existentialist'' (*Second Collection,* 271). Letters of the period attest to Lonergan's fascination with methodology; and one can discern his budding interest in cognitional theory from the titles of three of his works from this period: *Blandyke Papers:* ''The Form of Mathematical Inference'' (1928); ''The Syllogism'' (1928); ''True Judgment and Science'' [on Newman's illative sense] (1929).

Early Career and Insight. After a three-year period teaching at Loyola College in Montreal, Lonergan attained a licentiate in theology at the Gregorian University in Rome (1937), where he had been ordained a priest in 1936. There he went on to do doctoral work on THOMAS AQUINAS's theory of grace and human freedom (1938–40), though he was not actually awarded the doctorate until after World War II (1946). The next 13 years were evenly split as professor of theology at Jesuit theologates in Montreal and Toronto. His intensive research on the thought of Aquinas gave rise to an impressive flow of publications in theological journals, principally of his reworked doctoral thesis, ''St. Thomas's Thought on *Gratia Operans,*'' which appeared in installments in *Theological Studies* (1941–1942); and "The Concept of *Verbum* in the Writings of St. Thomas," in five parts in the same journal between 1946 and 1949.

During these years Lonergan labored to find in economics, sociology, and history the theoretic basis that might underpin a concrete realization of the conditions required to achieve the ends envisioned in the great social encyclicals of LEO XIII and PIUS XI. This work is documented in unpublished manuscripts, including the final version of an "Essay on Circulation Analysis" (*c.* 1943–44), a topic to which Lonergan returned in his later works.

In a series of courses taught during the late 1940s at the Thomas More Institute for Adult Education in Montreal (founded by his life-long friend and collaborator, R. Eric O'Connor, S.J.), Lonergan attempted to transpose what he had learned from Aquinas about human understanding and knowledge into the world of the twentieth century, addressing issues in mathematics and sciences undreamt of by St. Thomas. The result was *Insight: A Study of Human Understanding* (1957).

Method in Theology and Post-Method Interests.
In 1953 Lonergan had taken up duties as professor of dogmatic theology at the Gregorian University in Rome during which time he published several works in Latin related to his courses on Christology and the Trinity. He characterized them as products of teaching in a situation that "was hopelessly antiquated" (*Second Collection*, 212). These maps for the 650 students attending his lectures include *De constitutione Christi ontologica et psychologica supplementum* (1956), *Divinarum personarum conceptionem analogicam* (1957), *De Verbo incarnato* (1961, with later revisions), and *De Deo trino* (1964).

The main challenge to which Lonergan responded in his Roman years "came from the *Geisteswissenschaften*, from the problems of hermeneutics and critical history" (*Second Collection*, 277). His concern to take seriously the 19th-century emergence of scholarship and to think out the implications of human being as constituted by meaning in history is most explicitly documented in the notes from his *exercitatio* courses (graduate seminars devoted to specialized topics)—*De intellectu et methodo, De systemate et historia,* and *De methodo theologiae*—as well as in summer courses on topics such as mathematical logic, existentialism, philosophy of education, and method in theology.

After 12 years in Rome, he returned to Toronto to be treated for cancer in 1965. Following his recovery from the surgical removal of one of his lungs, his superiors at Regis College made it possible for him to complete his

Method in Theology. The period after 1964–65 witnessed the reformulation of *Insight*'s preoccupation with experience, direct understanding, and reflective understanding in terms of "intentionality analysis" (*Method,* ch. 1), blossoming into what Lonergon would at last affirm to be the primacy of the practical and existential level of human consciousness on which we evaluate, decide, act and love. This change supplements his sensibility for historical mindedness cultivated in Rome with new developments regarding the role of the dynamic unconscious, feelings, images and symbols, and religious experience.

The sweep of these developments permit Lonergan in *Method* to situate his intentionality analysis of the four-fold cognitional structure of attentiveness, intelligence, reasonableness, and responsibility into ever more concrete and complex contexts. Accordingly, *Insight*'s chapter 18, in which "the good was the intelligent and the reasonable" (*Second Collection*, 277), shifts into the context of "The Human Good" (*Method,* ch. 2) with its elaboration of feelings as intentional responses to vital, social, cultural, religious, and personal values. Again, *Insight*'s idea of meaning as "a relation between sign and signified (x)" gets plunged into "Meaning" (*Method,* ch. 3), with its types, elements, functions, realms, and stages. Similarly, *Insight*'s account of mystery and myth and of God's existence and nature (ch. 19) are shifted into the context of "Religion" (*Method,* ch. 4) where "the question of God is considered more important than the precise manner in which an answer is formulated, and our basic awareness of God comes to us not through our arguments or choices but primarily through God's gift of . . . love" (*Second Collection*, 277).

Both on the way to *Method* and after its publication Lonergan published a series of essays and lectures clarifying, applying, drawing the implications of, and further working out the implications of the 1964–65 shift to the primacy of the practical and existential (*Second Collection* and *Third Collection*). In the academic year of 1971–72 Lonergan was the Stillman Professor at Harvard Divinity School in Cambridge, Mass., where he put the finishing touches on *Method,* which finally came out in 1972. From 1975 until 1983 he taught at Boston College, alternating each year between courses having to do with issues in *Method* and those devoted to the last great preoccupation of his productive years, economics and the dynamics of history.

Of his post-*Method* work most students of Lonergan would probably agree with Frederick E. Crowe, S.J., that the chief fruit is his ever sharper elucidation of the two complementary rhythms of human development with the healing vector moving from above downwards (i.e., of being-in-love with God [with love's eyes of faith], believing, evaluating, judging, understanding, experiencing); and the creative vector moving from below upwards (i.e., experiencing, understanding, reflecting, deliberating, believing, loving). Next in importance would probably be his analysis of the "pure cycle" of the rhythms of money circulation within and between economic factors producing things for producers (surplus circuit of capital formation) and those producing goods and services for consumers (basic circuit). This analysis lays bare the normative intelligibility of exigencies underlying people's free and moral accommodations to the anti-egalitarian and egalitarian flows of money, goods, and services required by industrial exchange economies. Lonergan saw the intelligibility of the economy as dependent upon people's intelligence, reasonableness, responsibility—and so convertedness—in a way unsuspected by and unaccounted for by either Marxist or "supply-side/demand-side" conventions in economic theory.

Achievement. The Christian faith is now undergoing a hermeneutical crisis diagnosed by Lonergan as rooted in Christianity's inability to make the transition to modern society and culture. As a Roman Catholic theologian he was critical of the failure of Catholic philosophy and theology to pass from the fixist norms espoused by a mentality he named "classicist" towards a transcultural normativity compatible with historical consciousness. To be sure, he was no less critical of the historicist or positivist drift towards relativism on the part of those who more or less renounced any kind of normativity along with the heritage of scholasticism. Lonergan's life was dedicated chiefly to helping Christian theology meet this hermeneutical crisis and make the transition to modernity without losing its integrity.

Both Lonergan's execution of this task and the results of his work are profoundly and uniquely hermeneutical, especially in the way his lifework pivots on his nuanced historical relationship to the paradigm-figure of the Middle Ages, Thomas Aquinas. He concluded that "in the practice of Aquinas (theology) was . . . the principle for the molding and the transformation of a culture." The lesson Lonergan learned from St. Thomas' practice was that besides "reflecting on revelation" by "investigating, ordering, expounding, communicating divine revelation," theology "has somehow to mediate God's meaning into the whole of human affairs" (*Second Collection,* 62).

One thing that makes the meaning of "method" for Lonergan so profound and so unprecedented, therefore, is the manner in which his project of method flows out of the way he paid attention to, understood, judged, and appreciated the practice of Aquinas as a theologian. As he insisted in *Method,* such "encounter is the one way

in which self-understanding and horizon can be put to the test" (247). Whereas ordinary ideas about method tend to be technical in the Enlightenment vein of DESCARTES or BACON, and so are focussed on "a set of verbal propositions enunciating rules to be followed in a scientific investigation" (*Second Collection,* 64), Lonergan placed method in the context of Aquinas's dictum that "it is characteristic of the wise person to bring about order in all things." By reconceiving the Thomist viewpoint of highest wisdom in terms of the phenomenological notion of horizon, Lonergan makes method in the most serious sense a matter of at once utmost radicality and complete concreteness. To do method for Lonergan comes down to appropriating and articulating the grounds of theological (and *any*) practice in one's own total and basic horizon.

Hence, on account of his engagement with the thought of Aquinas, method in its plainer but quite important sense of "distinguishing different tasks, and thereby eliminating totalitarian ambitions" (*Second Collection,* 212) was realized by Lonergan to be anchored in the human subject's appropriation of method as 'transcendental'—i.e., the thematization of our own ultimate (and so transcultural) set of operations of experiencing, understanding, reflecting, deliberating, deciding, and loving. Thus, at root, "method" means 1) appropriating the structures of one's own conscious intentionality that specify our horizon as total and basic; and 2) consciously living in accord with one's horizon by following the transcendental precepts: Be attentive. Be intelligent. Be reasonable. Be responsible. Be loving.

The cognitive dimension of consciousness became most clear to Lonergan while writing the *Verbum* articles, especially the implications of the dependency of that dimension of consciousness upon the practical and existential levels. Deliberation, decision, and loving action presuppose and complement knowing, but the way knowing presupposes and complements those operations is even more crucial. Lonergan was increasingly able to express in terms of the notion of intentionality the metaphysical explanation of human freedom and divine grace that he had earlier retrieved in the 1930s and 1940s from St. Thomas.

In *Insight* Lonergan had tended to equate the breakthrough to the total and basic horizon with the appropriation of rational consciousness in one's affirmation of oneself as a knower (ch. 11) (fourth-level rational *self*—consciousness takes center-stage only at ch. 18); with one's clear recognition that knowing is a compound dynamic structure of experiencing, understanding, and judging; and especially with one's ability "to discriminate with ease and from personal conviction between one's purely intellectual activities and the manifold of other 'existential' concerns that invade and mix and blend with the operations of intellect to render it ambivalent and its pronouncements ambiguous'' (intro., xix). Already in his lectures on ''Intelligence and Reality'' (1950–51) he had indicated that the key to *Insight*'s breakthrough was ''radical intellectual CONVERSION'' (27) because it involved a revolution in oneself and a purification of oneself from what he there calls ''inhibiting and reinforcing (i.e., reductively utilitarian) desires'' (19) in order to liberate the pure, disinterested, and unrestricted desire to know being, and to make this desire normative in one's actual living. By the time of writing *Method,* however, what was implicit before was fully explicated: on account of the primacy of the practical and existential levels of conscious intentionality intellectual conversion (as uncovery of one's horizon as total and basic) presupposes both moral conversion (from one's spontaneous likes to the truly good or right) and religious conversion (from stupid self-centeredness to being-in-love with God).

But, as was already altogether clear in *Grace and Freedom,* religious conversion is the result of the gift of God's self-communication, beyond the horizon of finite human knowing and choosing. God's Spirit and Word are sent to make moral and intellectual conversion possible. Those conversions in turn demand the exercise of our liberty by which we reorient ourselves and bring the horizon of our day-to-day living into ever closer attunement with the infinite potentiality of our total and basic horizon. Openness as Gift heals us to transform our sinful closedness and elevates us to the factual, healing and creative openness of divine adoption.

Bibliography: The Lonergan Research Institute, Toronto, has a complete archive of Lonergan's works. The *Collected Works of Bernard Lonergan* is being published by the Lonergan Research Institute and the University of Toronto Press. B. LONERGAN. ''Insight Revisited.'' In *Second Collection* (London 1974). P. BYRNE. ''The Fabric of Lonergan's Thought.'' *Lonergan Workshop* 6 (Atlanta 1986). F. E. CROWE. *Lonergan* (Collegeville, Minn. 1992). J. FLANAGAN. *Quest for Self-Knowledge: An Essay in Lonergan's Philosophy* (Toronto 1997). V. GREGSON. *The Desires of the Human Heart: An Introduction to the Theology of Bernard Lonergan* (New York 1988). R. LIDDY. *Transforming Light: Intellectual Conversion in the Early Lonergan* (Collegeville, Minn. 1993).

[F. G. LAWRENCE]

LONG-SUFFERING

Long-suffering, a moral virtue that perfects the irascible appetite so that one is able to continue in good action over an extended period of time in spite of difficulties arising from external obstacles. It is also called constancy. Long-suffering is very similar to the virtue of PERSEVERANCE; it differs, however, by reason of the difficulties that must be sustained. Perseverance strengthens the appetite against the difficulty that exists simply because a course of action must be continued for a prolonged period; constancy is concerned with withstanding the hardships that may come from external causes when virtuous action is extended over a period of time.

St. Peter attributed long-suffering to God: ''The Lord does not delay in his promises, but for your sake is long-suffering, not wishing that any should perish, but that all should turn to repentance'' (2 Pt 3.9). The human virtue imitates its divine model by a willingness to endure the sufferings imposed from external impediments to the Christian life such as bad example and the onslaught of special temptations from the world. The vices of inconstancy and pertinacity are opposed to the virtue of long-suffering. Inconstancy is the vice of those who are unwilling to endure the tedium of prolonged action in the face of obstacles. They are ''soft'' and easily abandon the pursuit of virtue in the face of exterior difficulties, such as the jibes of others. Pertinacity is the vice of those who refuse to desist from some course of action even after persistence has become unreasonable. Pertinacity is usually found in self-opinionated and stubborn people who, because of vanity, refuse to abandon a position once they have assumed it.

Bibliography: THOMAS AQUINAS, *Summa theologiae* 2a2ae. 137.3. A. ROYO, *The Theology of Christian Perfection*, tr. and ed. J. AUMANN (Dubuque 1962).

[R. DOHERTY]

LONGLAND, JOHN

Bishop of Lincoln; b. Henley-on-Thames, Oxfordshire, 1473; d. Woburn, May 7, 1547. Educated at Magdalen College, Oxford, he was ordained in April of 1500. He became principal of Magdalen Hall (1505), and in 1511 earned the doctorate of divinity. His first major ecclesiastical appointment came in 1514 when he was appointed dean of Salisbury and confessor to HENRY VIII. In 1521 Henry appointed Longland Lord Almoner, and in May of the same year he was elevated to the bishopric of Lincoln. As bishop he continued to exercise severe repressive measures against the LOLLARDS and other heretical groups in his diocese. Cardinal Thomas WOLSEY, however, prevailed upon him to support Henry VIII's divorce proceedings. In 1533 Bishop Longland sat as an assistant judge in the divorce hearings at Dunstable Priory, with Thomas Cranmer, whom less than two months previously he had consecrated archbishop of Canterbury.

Longland's stand on the divorce question and his support of the royal supremacy made him one of the principal targets, after Cranmer himself, of the rebellions that arose shortly, and that had their center in his diocese (*See* ASKE, ROBERT; PILGRIMAGE OF GRACE). Later in life he repented ever having taken part in the king's divorce question.

His sermons, though marked with "rhetorical repetitions" and "prolixity" were powerful and justly famed. ERASMUS dedicated several treatises to Longland; Thomas MORE referred to him as a "second Colet." A *Benedictional* was written for his use and printed in London in 1528 by Richard Pynson; extant copies are at Lambeth and the British Museum. It is edited by R. M. Wooley, *The Benedictional of John Longlande, Bishop of Lincoln* (London 1927). Longland's published works include *Tres conciones; Quinque sermones*; printed by Pynson (London *c.* 1527); *Expositiones concionales*, on the Penitential Psalms; and a *Good Friday Sermon*, spoken before Henry VIII at Greenwich and printed by Thomas Petyt (London *c.* 1536).

Bibliography: A. H. THOMPSON, ed., *Visitations in the Diocese of Lincoln, 1517–1531*, 3 v. (Lincoln Record Society Publications 33, 35, 37; Hereford 1940–47) v. 2–3. P. HUGHES, *The Reformation in England*, 3 v. in 1 (5th rev. ed. New York 1963). J. H. LUPTON, *The Dictionary of National Biography from the Earliest Times to 1900*, 63 v. (London 1885–1900) 12:120–121.

[J. G. DWYER]

LONGO, BARTOLO, BL.

Also known as the "Man of Mary" and "Brother Rosario," Dominican tertiary, founder of the Shrine of Our Lady of Pompeii, and of the Daughters of Saint Rosario of Pompeii; b. Feb. 11, 1841, Latiano, Apulia, southern Italy; d. Oct. 5, 1926, Pompeii, Italy.

Son of a prosperous physician named Bartolomeo Longo and his wife, Antonietta Luparelli, Bartolo Longo received a good education from the Piarists at Francavilla Fontana and Lecce, then studied law at the University of Naples, where he received his degree in 1864. During his university years, Bartolo was influenced by the anticlericalism of the time and involved himself in popular occult spiritism. After a severe depression, Dominican Father Alberto Radente led him to conversion on May 29, 1865. Thereafter he devoted himself to charitable works. Bartolo became a Dominican Tertiary with the name Brother Rosario March 25, 1871.

In 1872, Longo went to Pompeii valley on business for the Countess Marianna Farnararo de Fusco (Feb. 9, 1924), whom he married in 1885. Observing the despair and lack of faith in the region and recalling Father Alber-

to's devotion to the rosary, Bartolo decided to encourage it there, while continuing his works of mercy and teaching the catechism. With much difficulty he established a Confraternity of the Holy Rosary and sought to build a shrine of the Blessed Mother. After several unsuccessful attempts to raise funds, he took up Bishop Formisano of Nola's suggestion to collect a "soldo" (penny) a month from each of 300 donors. The cornerstone was laid in 1876. Fortuna Agrelli provided a major contribution after her miraculous healing in 1884, which led to the consecration of the Shrine of Our Lady of the Rosary May 7, 1891. Pope Pius X raised it to the status of a pontifical basilica in 1894. About 1900, Bartolo was falsely accused of financial mismanagement, but he was later cleared of the charge.

Longo promoted a unique "Rosary of the Fifteen Saturdays" and 54-day Novena Rosary of Our Lady of Pompeii. He also advocated the definition of the Assumption of Mary as dogma and founded the Dominican Daughters of Saint Rosario. He and his wife built an orphanage for girls in 1887, hospices for the children of prisoners in 1892 and 1922, a typesetting workshop and printing press to publish pamphlets, a hospital, music school, and two houses for Dominican tertiaries near the shrine. Other charities have grown up in the "City of Mary" around the shrine where hundreds of miraculous cures are alleged to have occurred. Before his death, Bartolo also wrote *The Fifteen Saturdays*, *Petition* (1883), and began the magazine *The Rosary and the New Pompeii* (founded 1884). His mortal remains now rest in the basilica of Pompeii under the throne of Our Lady's shrine (1983).

He was beatified by Pope John Paul II on Oct. 26, 1980.

Feast: Oct. 6 (Dominicans).

Bibliography: *Bartolo Longo e il suo tempo: atti del convegno storico promosso dalla Delegazione pontificia per il Santuario di Pompei sotto l'alto patronato del Presidente della Repubblica*, ed. F. VOLPE. M. J. DORCY, *Saint Dominic's Family* (Dubuque, Iowa 1964), 580–83. P. M. FRASCONI, *Don Barolo Longo* (Alba 1941). A. ILLIBATO, *L'archivio Bartolo Longo: guida-inventario* (Naples 1986). I. LÜTHOLD-MINDER, *Die Rosenkranzkönigin von Pompei und ihr Advokat Bartolo Longo* (Hauteville, Switz. 1981). N. TAMBURRO, *Bartolo Longo, pioniere di civiltà: nel centenario di Pompei* (2nd ed. Pompei 1975). *Acta Apostolicae Sedis* (1981) 529–32. *L'Osservatore Romano* (English edition) 44 (1980) 10–11.

[K. I. RABENSTEIN]

LOOR, ISIDORE OF SAINT JOSEPH DE, BL.

Passionist priest; b. April 18, 1881, Vrasene, eastern Flanders, the Netherlands; d. Oct. 6, 1916, Kortrijk

(Courtrai) Monastery, Belgium. As the eldest of three children of subsistence farmers, Isidore received six years of elementary education at the local school. At the suggestion of a Passionist missionary, Isidore joined the PASSIONISTS at Ere, Belgium (April 7, 1907) and became brother Isidore of Saint Joseph. After his religious profession in 1908, he served the community as cook, gardener, custodian of the preparatory school, and later (1914) as porter. Intense penitential prayer helped Brother Isidore to cope with several crises: cancer that required the removal of his right eye (1911); the conversion of the monastery into a German military hospital and its abandonment by all but five brothers and three priests during World War I; and the metastasis of cancer to his intestines (1916). This simple, diligent "Brother of the Will of God" suffered his final illness with great fortitude. He was buried next to the Passionist Church, where those remembering him came to pray for his intercession and received his help. The official process for his beatification was opened in 1950, leading to his beatification by Pope John Paul II on Sept. 30, 1984.

Bibliography: *Isidore of St. Joseph* (Kortrijk 1960). M. CLAYES, *The Life of Brother Isidore de Loor* (Chicago 1976). H. GIELEN, *Het diepste lied zingt binnenin: de zalige broeder Isidoor de Loor* (Tielt, Netherlands 1984). C. VAN HEMELEN, *Blessed Isidore de Loor, Passionist* (Dublin 1984). *Acta Apostolicae Sedis* 78 (1986): 965–968. *L'Osservatore Romano*, Eng. ed. 44 (1984): 6–7.

[K. I. RABENSTEIN]

LOOS, CORNELIUS

Theologian; b. Gouda, *c.* 1546; d. Brussels, Feb. 3, 1595. Loos (Callidius) studied at Louvain, received Holy Orders, and became professor of theology at Mainz, where he had an active literary career, upholding the Catholic cause and denouncing the rebellion in the Low Countries. He also wrote *Illustrium Germaniae scriptorum catalogus* (Mainz 1581), a collection of literary biographies. After becoming a professor at Trier, he came under attack for denouncing the burning of witches, and upon the instigation of the nuncio, Ottavio M. Frangipani, he was imprisoned and on March 15, 1592 compelled to recant. He left Trier for Brussels, where he served briefly as a pastor, but again he spoke out against the witchcraft delusion and was twice imprisoned. He died before his third trial. His work on this topic, *De vera et falsa magia*, was printed in Cologne, but the authorities prohibited its publication. His political writings were *De tumultuosa Belgarum rebellione sedanda . . .* (1579) and *Apologia in orationem Philippi de Marnix pro Archiduce Austriae Matthia* (1579).

Bibliography: É. AMANN, *Dictionnaire de théologie catholique*, 15 v. (Paris 1903–50) 9.2:930–933. F. ZOEPFL, *Lexikon für Theologie und Kirche*, ed. J. HOFER and K. RAHNER, 10 v. (Freiburg 1957–65) 6:1139–1140. *Allgemeine deutsche Biographie*, (Leipzig 1875–1910; Berlin 1953–) 19:168–169.

[C. G. NAUERT, JR.]

LÓPEZ, LUDOVICO

Dominican moral and pastoral theologian; place and date of birth unknown; d. Spain, Sept. 27, 1595. He received the Dominican habit and was professed at Atocha, Madrid. Lopez taught theology for many years in Spain and then in the Province of St. Antoninus, Colombia. The encomenderos (plantation owners) persecuted him for championing the rights of the Indians. Apparently he died in Spain while pleading their cause at the court. His principle works are: *Tractatus de contractibus et negotiationibus sive Instructorium negotiantium* (1592) and *Instructorium conscientiae* (1585).

Bibliography: J. QUÉTIF and J. ÉCHARD, *Scriptores Ordinis Praedicatorum* (New York 1959) 2.1:316. M. D. CHENU, *Dictionnaire de théologie catholique*, ed. A. VACANT et al. (Paris 1903–50) 9.1:934.

[R. J. POWERS]

LÓPEZ DE MENDOZA GRAJALES, FRANCISCO

Founder of the first permanent mission in the United States; b. Jerez de la Frontera, Spain, date unknown; d. place and date unknown. He accompanied the expedition of Pedro Menéndez de Avilés, which sailed from Cádiz for Florida on June 29, 1565. On Friday, Aug. 10, 1565, the expedition reached Puerto Rico, where López was offered, but refused, a chaplaincy. Menéndez's fleet reached St. Augustine on the Florida coast on Sept. 8, 1565. After military ceremonies accompanying the landing, solemn Mass was chanted in honor of the Blessed Virgin on the feast of her nativity; the site is marked on the grounds of the Mission of Nombre de Dios, St. Augustine. In 1565 López accompanied a group sent by Menéndez to start a colony at Santa Lucia, on the east coast of Florida. The party was attacked by natives, nearly died of starvation, and was driven back by storms when it attempted to reach Havana, Cuba. Eventually, the expedition was rescued by Menéndez. In 1566 new colonists, including five priests, arrived at St. Augustine. From this date López acted as pastor of the first white settlement in the United States. In a letter to the king of Spain, written on Aug. 6, 1567, López designated himself "vicar of Florida" and "chaplain and vicar." In the same letter he spoke of a slight illness that troubled him. It is not known how long he remained in St. Augustine after this.

Bibliography: F. LÓPEZ DE MENDOZA GRAJALES, "Memoria" in E. RUIDIAZ Y CARAVIA, *La Florida: Su conquista y colonización por Pedro Menéndez de Avilés,* 2 v. (Madrid 1893) 2:431–465.

[J. P. HURLEY]

LÓPEZ Y VICUÑA, VICENTA MARÍA, BL.

Foundress of the Daughters of Mary Immaculate for Domestic Service; b. Cascante (Navarra), Spain, March 22, 1847; d. Madrid, Dec. 26, 1890. Vicenta was reared by her pious, middle-class parents until 1854, when she was sent to Madrid for schooling. She lived there with her aunt, Eulalia de Vicuña, who conducted a hospice for young, unemployed servant girls. This charitable work so attracted Vicenta, that she took a private vow of chastity (1866) and dedicated herself to the welfare of working girls, despite her parents' urging that she marry or join the Visitation Nuns. Together with her aunt and a few others, she lived a communal life (1871–76). Under the guidance of Father Hidalgo y Soba, she drew up a constitution that was approved by the auxiliary bishop of Toledo, Sancha y Hervas (July 1876). With three others, Vicenta pronounced her vows in August of 1878. The work of the congregation was to conduct hospices for working girls and to teach domestic arts. Despite early financial difficulties and the foundress's poor health, the institute flourished in Spain and soon spread to Europe and Latin America. The Holy See gave its approval in 1888. By 1961 the Daughters had more than 2,000 members and 81 houses. Vicenta was beatified on Feb. 19, 1950.

Feast: Dec. 26.

Bibliography: E. FEDERICI, *La Beata Vicenta María Lopez y Vicuña* (Rome 1950). C. TESTORE, *La Beata Vicenta María Lopez y Vicuña* (Isola del Liri 1950). J. L. BAUDOT and L. CHAUSSIN, *Vies des saints et des bienheureux selon l'ordre du calendrier avec l'historique des fêtes,* 12 v. (Paris 1935–56) 12:709–712.

[I. BASTARRIKA]

LORAS, JEAN MATHIAS PIERRE

Missionary and educator, first bishop of DUBUQUE, Iowa; b. Lyons, France, Aug. 30, 1792; d. Dubuque, Feb. 19, 1858. He was the tenth of eleven children of Jean Matthias and Étiennette (Michalet) Loras. His father, one of the councilors of Lyons during the unsuccessful Girondist revolt against Jacobin Paris at the height of the French Revolution, was guillotined on Nov. 3, 1793. Although 16 other relatives also died during the Reign of Terror, the widow Loras continued to shelter fugitive priests and to reject the extremes of the French Revolution.

Early Career. In 1799 Jean Mathias, in the company of his brother-in-law, was received in audience by PIUS VI, in exile in Valence. With his brother Jacques, he enrolled (1803) in the presbytery school of Rev. Charles Balley at Ecully, where he formed a lifelong friendship with his schoolmate (St.) John B. VIANNEY. As a student at St. Irenaeus Seminary, Lyons, he was associated with two future archbishops of Baltimore, Md., Ambrose Maréchal, professor of dogmatic theology, and James Whitfield, an Englishman and fellow student. Although ordained for the Archdiocese of Lyons on Nov. 12, 1815, he continued on at the minor seminary at Meximieux, to which he had been sent as instructor the previous year, and became superior in 1817. In 1824 he was appointed superior of the larger minor seminary at L'Argentière, but he resigned three years later to work as a home missioner in the Lyons archdiocese. When Bishop Michael Portier of Mobile, Ala., returned to his native Lyons in 1828 in search of clergy and funds, Loras decided to volunteer for service in America. He sailed from Le Havre on Nov. 1, 1829, and for seven years worked in Alabama as pastor of the cathedral in Mobile, vicar-general of the diocese, and superior of the newly founded (1830) Spring Hill College.

Bishop of Dubuque. Loras, chosen first bishop of the newly created see at Dubuque, was consecrated on Dec. 10, 1837, by Portier in the cathedral at Mobile. The new bishop did not arrive in Dubuque until April 18, 1839, having spent the intervening months in Europe in search of clergy and funds. Almost immediately he began his long series of missionary voyages among whites and natives living in the isolated outposts of his vast diocese, and in the area east of the Mississippi River provisionally in his charge. During these years, his closest friends were Bishop Joseph ROSATI of St. Louis, Mo.; Joseph CRÉTIN, a former pupil of his at Meximieux, who served as vicar-general of Dubuque and whom Loras nominated as first bishop of St. Paul, Minn.; and the missionary Samuel MAZZUCHELLI, OP, who had come to Dubuque in 1835 and continued to work in the diocese after the arrival of Loras.

When government resettlement of Native Americans outside of Iowa ruined what had at first been a fruitful mission field, particularly among the Winnebagoes at Fort Atkinson, and French Canadian immigration virtually ceased, Loras conceived a plan to people Iowa with Irish and German Catholic settlers. As early as 1841 he sent Judge Charles Corkery and two other Dubuque laymen to establish contacts with Irish immigrants in the East. Although acute tension between the preponderantly French clergy and the Irish laity marked the years from 1843 to 1845, Loras finally succeeded in recruiting Irish missionaries, and the crisis passed. To further assuage the

Irish grievance, Loras in 1853 initiated plans to have Clement Smyth, the prior of the Irish Trappists whom he had induced to settle at New Melleray near Dubuque in 1849, chosen as his successor. Smyth was consecrated coadjutor with right of succession on May 3, 1857.

With generous grants from mission societies in Lyons, Vienna, and Munich, Loras was able to build numerous mission churches and, with unusual foresight, to buy parcels of land for future parishes. As early as 1839, despite a chronic shortage of priests, he had organized a diocesan college with a view to training a native clergy and shortly afterward, a cathedral boys' school, which was matched in 1843 with a cathedral girls' school, staffed by the newly arrived Sisters of Charity of the Blessed Virgin Mary. During 1850 and 1851 he directed the building of Mt. St. Bernard Seminary south of Dubuque.

Although he retained great affection for his native Lyons, to which he paid a final visit during a trip to Europe in 1848 and 1850, Loras nevertheless stoutly rejected the offer of a French bishopric and developed through the years a genuine love and understanding for the United States. His gracious manners and accent were always those of a Frenchman, but his breadth of view and directness reflected the influence of the American frontier. He is buried in the crypt of the cathedral in which he had offered the first Mass on Christmas Day 1857, when his final illness was already upon him.

Bibliography: M. M. HOFFMANN, *Church Founders of the Northwest: Loras and Cretin, and Other Captains of Christ* (Milwaukee 1937); "The Roman Catholic Church in Iowa," *Palimpsest* 34 (Aug. 1953): 337–400.

[W. E. WILKIE]

LORD, DANIEL ALOYSIUS

Teacher, author, editor, composer, playwright, and propagator of the Sodality movement, chiefly among youth; b. Chicago, Ill., April 23, 1888; d. St. Louis, Mo., Jan. 15, 1955. He was one of two sons of George Douglas Lord and Iva Jane (Langdon) Lord. He attended De La Salle parochial school, St. Ignatius High School, and St. Ignatius College, Chicago. In 1909 he entered the Society of Jesus at Florissant, Mo., and he was ordained on June 24, 1923. It is impossible to categorize Lord's talents and work, but certainly it can be said that his superb gift for teaching characterized all his achievements. It is evident in most of his writings: 30 books, almost 300 pamphlets, 66 booklets, 50 plays, 12 musicals, 6 pageants, his syndicated column "Along the Way," and the 900 transcripts he prepared for radio presentation. In his years as editor

of the *Queen's Work* (1925–48), that magazine never failed to face current social issues. He taught at St. Louis University and its corporate high school from 1917 to 1920, working mostly in the English departments; he also co-founded, administered, and taught in the university's department of education.

As time went on, Lord often won praise from experts in the theater and music fields. The *Social Action Follies* (1937) and *Matrimonial Follies* (1939), like his other pageants, employed casts of as many as 1,000 and were viewed by audiences of 17,000 at a time. With his unique combination of talents, it was not surprising that Lord was frequently called on for technical advice by movie producers, among them Cecil B. DeMille. He was coauthor of the original Motion Picture Code, and his ability to get young people to act on their objections to crudity and immorality on the screen had at least an indirect influence on the establishment and success of the National Legion of Decency.

Lord's preeminent accomplishment was the revival of the moribund Sodality movement. He presented the Sodality, not as just another devotional practice, but as a challenge and a way of life wherein one uses every means to bring oneself and one's neighbor to God. He had assisted Edward GARESCHÉ, SJ, in establishing the Sodality magazine, the *Queen's Work,* in 1913. Beginning in 1925, when he himself became editor and national Sodality director, he toured the United States, seeking, as he put it, to make the Sodality the laboratory of the religion class. In the summer of 1928 he organized the first national Leadership School and in 1931, the first Summer School of Catholic Action (SSCA) on a national scale. By the end of 1963, some 190 sessions of the SSCA had been held in all sections of the country, with just under 300,000 participants. In 1948 Lord was cited by PIUS XII for his successful Sodality work. In 1943, still another demand was made on his time and talents, when he was made director of the Institute of Social Order of the Society of Jesus. His article "Cancer Is My Friend" was his characteristic reaction to news of his impending death.

Bibliography: D. A. LORD, *Played by Ear* (Chicago 1956). J. T. MCGLOIN, *Backstage Missionary* (New York 1958). M. FLORENCE, *The Sodality Movement in the United States: 1926–36* (St. Louis 1939). W. B. FAHERTY, "A Half-Century with the *Queen's Work,*" *Woodstock Letters* 92 (1963): 99–114.

[J. T. MCGLOIN]

LORD, THE

There are many important connotations of the name "the Lord" applied to God in both the Old Testament and the New Testament.

In the Old Testament. The term *'ādôn,* a common Hebrew word parallel to *ba'al* (*see* BAAL) and signifying lord or master, is often used of persons having some kind of superiority, e.g., a king (1 Sm 24.11), a husband (Gn 18.12), or a tribal patriarch (Gn 24.10), sometimes as a polite form of address (2 Sm 1.10), but most importantly for this article as a divine epithet. In Israelite tradition there are two distinct usages, namely, as one of God's honorific titles and as a substitute for God's sacred proper name YAHWEH.

As an Honorific Title for God. The word *'ādôn* entered into many theophoric names, e.g., Adonisedec and Adoniram (Jos 10.3; 1 Kgs 4.6), but was not used as a proper name of Israel's God, Yahweh. As a divine epithet it expressed the sovereign power and dominion of God and was often used with the definite article to mean the ultimate Lord [Ex 23.17; 34.23; Is 1.24; Mal 3.1; Ps 113(114).7], Lord of all the earth [Jos 3.11, 13; Mi 4.13], and Lord of lords [Dt 10.17; Ps 135(136).3]; *'ādôn* was preferred to *ba'al* to express God's lordship since the latter was used as the proper name of many Canaanite gods.

In the period of the writing of Prophets, the title was frequently linked to the holy name of Yahweh, e.g., in Amos 19 times and in Ezechiel no less than 122 times. The Prophets thereby emphasized God's supreme authority and the subjection of Israel to God as His servant.

Substitution of the Lord for Yahweh. Because of the destruction of Jerusalem and Solomon's Temple (586 B.C.), the Exile in Babylon, and the continued dispersal of the Jews throughout the Near East, a new place of worship and instruction, the SYNAGOGUE, emerged where Jews faithfully recited their Psalms and had the Scriptures read and explained to them. In this environment the sacred name Yahweh was treated with growing reverence and respect, so that eventually it became too sacred even to be pronounced. When it appeared in the Sacred Text, *'ădōnāy,* the Lord (plural form of *'ādôn* with the first person singular possessive suffix, meaning literally my Lord), was usually substituted. This reverence for the sacred tetragrammaton was so carefully fostered during the postexilic period that Yahweh does not occur at all in Job, Ecclesiastes, Esther, Chronicles, or the second and third collections of the Psalms. The usual substitute, Adonai, itself became so revered that it acquired substitutes of its own, Heaven, Father of Heaven, the name, etc.

Because of this habitual substitution, the pronunciation of Yahweh was gradually lost. In the seventh century A.D. when a complete system of vowel signs was added to the mainly consonantal text of the Hebrew Bible, the vowel signs for the word *'ădōnāy* (a long "ā" to distinguish the sacred word from the profane *'ădōnay,* my lords) were placed under the consonants of Yahweh in ac-

cordance with the Masora and eventually led to the erroneous transcription of Yahweh as JEHOVAH.

A profound theological relationship between the terms Lord and Yahweh was thus established by the reverent usage of the synagogue. The Greek translation of the Hebrew Bible, published during the second century B.C. and known as the Septuagint (LXX), bears witness to this tradition by never transcribing the sacred name but rather writing for it κύριος, the Greek translation of *'ădōnāy.* The usage later led to the frequent *Dominus* for Yahweh in Latin versions and the Lord (usually printed in small capitals) for Yahweh in English Bibles. The substitution's most important result, however, is found in the meaning given to κύριος when it refers to Jesus Christ in the New Testament.

In the New Testament. The authors of the Gospels and Epistles whose Bible was mainly the Greek LXX continued to refer to God as "the Lord" or "Lord" and to substitute κύριος for Yahweh, but they more frequently applied the title in a specific way to Jesus Christ.

Lord Used for God. Jesus Himself and Paul called the Father Creator, "Lord of heaven and earth" (Mt 11.25; Lk 10.21; Acts 17.24), and also "the Lord of lords" (1 Tm 6.15). The title's most frequent usage for God, however, is found in its substitution for Yahweh, either with the definite article, the Lord (Mk 5.19; Lk 1.6; etc.), or without it, as God's name, Lord (Mk 13.20; Lk 1.17, 58; Acts 7.49; etc.). It also substitutes for Yahweh in such expressions as the "ANGEL OF THE LORD" (Mt 1.20; 2.13; 28.2; Lk 1.11; Acts 5.19; etc.), the "glory of Lord" (Lk 2.9), and the "Lord's handmaid" (Lk 1.38). Of course, κύριος appears in place of Yahweh also in citations from the Greek Old Testament (cf. Mt 4.7 with Dt 6.16).

Lord Used for Jesus Christ. In Mark and Matthew Jesus is called "the Lord" only once (Mk 11.3, parallel to Mt 21.3; see Mk 16.19–20, a non-Marcan but inspired appendix). The vocative form κύριε is frequently applied to Him in all four Gospels but may originally have meant only "Sir." Luke refers to Him as "the Lord" (ὁ κύριος) 15 times, but this usage is commonly recognized as coming from a later stage in the Gospel tradition, when Christians began to speak of Jesus while He was on earth with the understanding that they had of Him long after Pentecost. In the fourth Gospel Jesus is called "the Lord" mainly in texts describing post-Resurrection events (Jn 20.2, etc.; "the Lord" of 6.23 and 11.2 appear to follow the Lucan usage mentioned above). Thomas's cry, "My Lord and my God" is intended as a doctrinal climax to John's Gospel, affirming the Lordship of the victorious and glorified Son of Man (Jn 20.28). It is improbable, then, that "the Lord" in its theological connotation was predicated of Jesus before His Resurrection. Until then He was called RABBI, Master, or Sir; "the Lord" was reserved for the risen Jesus.

Jesus is called Lord more than 20 times in the Acts and more than 130 times in the Pauline Epistles. Even in its earliest application there is no hint of any doctrinal innovation in the title. That Jesus is "the Lord" represents the belief of the earliest Christian communities of Jerusalem, Damascus, and Antioch. The Aramaic communities of Palestine used, of course, the title *mārānā'*, Our Lord (1 Cor 16.22; *see* MARANATHA). Jesus received this Lordship, according to St. Paul, because He humbled Himself by becoming obedient even to death on the cross, and therefore God exalted Him and gave Him the name that is above every name, so that every tongue should confess that Jesus Christ is "Lord" for the glory of God the Father (Phil 2.8–11). In this text the name that transcends any other name is not Jesus, which He received at His circumcision, but κύριος, the substitute for the name Yahweh; and thus this ancient hymn affirms Christ's equal rank with the Father.

The Resurrection revealed Jesus to be the victor over death and sin, and to be the Prince of this world (Rom 1.4), and as a result the terms by which He had formerly been designated (SON OF MAN, MESSIAH, Master, Prophet, etc.) were now inadequate to express the new dimension that was manifested by His exaltation. "The Lord," however, was adequate to express Jesus' exaltation to the glory He had with the Father before He became flesh. It recalled Jesus' prediction that He would come with His Father's glory to judge all men (Mt 16.27; 25.31), His conundrum about the Messiah's being David's Lord (Mt 22.41–45), and His confession that He was the mysterious Son of Man who would establish God's final kingdom (Mt 26.64; cf. Dn 7.13). Jesus thus suggested even before His exaltation that His Messiahship was more than that of the awaited Davidic king and that He was Himself the divine judge, the Lord. In the light of the Resurrection His followers understood that He was really the Lord and applied to Him other passages of the Old Testament that they previously referred only to Yahweh [cf. Acts 2.34–36 with Ps 109(110); See Also 1 Cor 10.9, where "Neither tempt the Christ" may well have been the original reading, and cf. Nm 21.5–6; See Also the illation made in Acts 2.14–41, Peter's sermon at Pentecost, between vv. 21 and W. 36–39].

Unlike θεός, κύριος does not express Jesus' divine nature as much as His divine Lordship. A Christian must acknowledge that Jesus is the Lord (1 Cor 12.3) and must recognize that there is only one Lord (1 Cor 8.6). In Paul's doctrine, God the Father and the Lord Jesus are on the same level; both are divine, and the Father acts through the Lord, His Mediator.

The New Testament writers agree on the doctrine of Jesus' Lordship. Unless He was worshiped by them as the divine Lord, at the right hand of the Father, it is impossible to explain how these ardent Israelite monotheists could have attributed to Him the incommunicable name and the functions of the Lord God Yahweh.

Bibliography: P. VAN IMSCHOOT, *Encyclopedic Dictionary of the Bible*, tr. and adap. by L. HARTMAN (New York 1963) 1369–74. L. CERFAUX, *Dictionnaire de la Bible,* suppl. ed. L. PIROT, et al. (Paris 1928–) 5:200–228; *Christ in the Theology of St. Paul,* tr. G. WEBB and A. WALKER (New York 1959). W. EICHRODT, *Theology of the Old Testament,* tr. J. A. BAKER (Philadelphia 1961–). V. TAYLOR, *The Names of Jesus* (New York 1953).

[R. T. A. MURPHY]

LORD'S DAY, THE

The only explicit mention of the Lord's Day in the New Testament occurs in Rv 1.10: "I was in the spirit on the Lord's day ἐν τῇ κυριακῇ ἡμέρᾳ." From this single reference alone, it would be impossible to conclude that the early Christians celebrated the first day of the week, Sunday, as their special day of devotion and rest. However, there are several indications in the New Testament, which, taken in conjunction with other early Christian writings, provide strong cumulative evidence to that effect.

First, there is the clear emphasis in all the Gospels (Mt 28.1; Mk 16.2; Lk 24.1; Jn 20.1, 19) on the fact that the RESURRECTION OF CHRIST took place on the first day of the week. (The quasi-technical expression used by all, μία σαββάτων "number one of the Sabbath," i.e., the week, is explained by most authors as a double Hebraism.) Then, St. Luke in Acts 20.7 connects the first day of the week (μία τῶν σαββάτων) with the "breaking of bread" (κλάσαι ἄρτον), i.e., the celebration of the Eucharist, as appears evident from Acts 2.42, 46; 1 Cor 10.16. Finally, St. Paul indicates the first day of each week (κατὰ μίαν σαββάτον) in his directive for the alms collection in 1 Cor 16.2.

These New Testament allusions, however inconclusive by themselves, find clarification and confirmation from early Christian writings. In the Didache, for example, it is said:

> On the Lord's own day, assemble in common to break bread and offer thanks; but first confess your sins, so that your sacrifice may be pure. However, no one quarrelling with his brother may join your meeting until they are reconciled; your sacrifice must not be defiled. For here we have the saying of the Lord: In every place and time offer me a pure sacrifice; for I am a mighty king, says the Lord; and my name spreads terror among the nations (ch. 14).

See also the references in the Epistle of Barnabas (15.8, 9), St. Ignatius of Antioch (Magn. 9), and St. Justin (1 Apol. 67). These writings provide ample evidence that the Jewish SABBATH was early replaced by the Christian Sunday, the Lord's Day, in honor of the Resurrection of Christ. Exactly how this came about is not clear, but Acts 20.7 indicates that the observance of Sunday may have begun at sundown on Saturday evening as an addition to the Jewish Sabbath, whose observance was eventually discontinued, perhaps upon the destruction of Jerusalem.

For the New Testament Christians, the expression "the Lord's Day" probably suggested a wealth of meanings largely overlooked today: (1) the glorious Resurrection that established Jesus of Nazareth as LORD and Christ (Ps 2.7; Acts 2.36; Phil 2.11); (2) the revelation of Christ as identified with Yahweh, God of Israel and Lord of the earth (Jos 3.11; Rom 1.4); (3) the "DAY OF THE LORD," a day of judgment and salvation, death and resurrection (Jl 3.4–5; Acts 2.20); (4) the unique and universal Lordship of Christ (1 Cor 8.6) as opposed to the "many lords" (1 Cor 8.5) of the pagans; (5) His fullness (πλήρωμα), His headship over His body, the Church, and His lordship over the world to come (Col 1.15–20; Eph 1.20–23). The Lord's Day was, for the early Christian, not simply a day of devotion and rest, but one of renewed commitment and consecration to Christ, Our Lord.

See Also: SUNDAY.

Bibliography: W. FOERSTER, G. KITTEL *Theologisches Wörterbuch zum Neuen Testament* (Stuttgart 1935–) 3:1095–96. *Encyclopedic Dictionary of the Bible*, tr. and adap. by L. HARTMAN (New York 1963) 2362–63. H. RIESENFELD, "Sabbat et Jour du Seigneur," *N.T. Essays: Studies in Memory of T. W. Manson*, ed. A. J. B. HIGGINS (Manchester, Eng. 1959) 210–217. W. RORDORF, *Der Sonntag: Geschichte des Ruhe- und Gottesdiensttages im ältesten Christentum* (*Abhandlungen zur Theologie des Alten und Neuen Testaments* 43; Zurich 1962).

[W. F. DICHARRY]

LORD'S PRAYER, THE

The model prayer, so named because it was taught by Jesus to his disciples. From its first words in Latin it is commonly called the Pater Noster (Our Father). It is treated here according to its form, its contents, and its use in the liturgy.

FORM

The Lord's Prayer is found in the Gospels of Matthew (6.9b–13) and of Luke (11.2b–4), but in different contexts and with considerable variations.

In Matthew. In the first Gospel the Lord's Prayer is part of the Sermon on the Mount, following an instruction on prayer and introduced by the words of Jesus, "In this manner therefore shall you pray" (Mt 6.9a). It is composed of an address and six petitions. The verse numbers are included in parentheses.

> Address: Our Father in heaven (9b), Petitions: 1. hallowed be your name (9c). 2. your kingdom come (10a). 3. your will be done on earth as in heaven (10b). 4. Give us today our daily bread (11). 5. And forgive us our debts, as we also forgive our debtors (12). 6. And do not subject us to the final test, but deliver us from the evil one (13).

Many manuscripts, but not the best nor the oldest, add the words, in variant forms, "For the kingdom, the power and the glory are yours, now and forever, Amen." This doxology was used by the Jews at the time of Christ. In a more elaborate form it already occurs in 1 Chronicles (29.11–13). The Christians in the East added it to the Lord's Prayer when they said this prayer at divine service, as can be seen in the *DIDACHE* (8.2) version of the Lord's Prayer. The Greek scribes, accustomed to this liturgical use of the prayer, gradually introduced it into the text of Matthew's Gospel. It is certain, however, that it is not a part of the Gospel text.

In Luke. In the third Gospel the setting of the Lord's Prayer is the prayer of Jesus Himself (11.1). After seeing Jesus in prayer, the disciples ask Him to teach them also how to pray. The Lukan version has an address and five petitions. The verse numbers are shown in parentheses.

> Address: Father (2b), Petitions: 1. hallowed be your name (2b). 2. Your kingdom come. (2c)[3 not in Lk.] 4. Give us each day our daily bread (3). 5. And forgive us our sins, for we ourselves forgive everyone in debt to us (4a). 6. And do not subject us to the final test (4b).

In his smaller number of phrases Luke may be closer to the original Aramaic than Matthew, who may have added other words of Jesus: for "in heaven" (cf. Mt 6.1; 6.14; etc.), for "your will be done" (cf. Mt 26.42), for "deliver us from the evil one," (cf. Jn 17.15). In some of his wording, however, Luke may be further from the original, for he shows signs of adaptation to a later Gentile audience: in petition (5) he uses "sins" instead of the more Semitic "debts"; in petition (4) he uses the Greek present imperative δίδου, "keep on giving," instead of Matthew's aorist δός, "give (once and for all)." This may show a later emphasis on the present rather than the eschatological needs of the church.

CONTENTS

While the Lord's Prayer contains words used by Jesus himself in prayer, the plural forms indicate that it had already become the liturgical prayer of the Christian community in the first century. Although many of the

Multilingual tablets of prayer on the cloister walls of the Pater Noster Church, Jerusalem, Israel. (©Hanan Isachar/CORBIS)

phrases of the prayer may be found in the Jewish liturgy, there is a new spirit that pervades it. For Christians, Jesus himself was now the way to God. Through the gift of the Holy Spirit, they could now pray to the Father in the same manner he did (Rom 8.15; Gal 4.6). Jesus, however, was not only the way, but the end of the way, the object of hope. So the early Christian community looked forward to his speedy return from heaven. This eschatological atmosphere must be kept in mind for a full understanding of the Lord's Prayer. Lending itself to this interpretation is Matthew's use of the Greek aorist tense with its "once and for all" meaning.

Address. The direct "Father" in Luke translates the original Aramaic *abba* of Jesus. This was his own distinctive and intimate way of speaking with his Father, now shared by Christians (Rom 8.15). The "our" in Matthew shows that the Lord's Prayer has already become a Christian community prayer, since Jesus nowhere addresses God in this manner. "In heaven" (Mt) distinguishes God the Father from any earthly father and may indicate the absence of any localization such as the Temple.

Petitions. *First petition.* The first petition is literally, "may your name be sanctified." However, the passive Greek forms in the first two petitions really represent Se-

mitic reflexives, with the name of God standing for God Himself, so that the sense is: "May God sanctify his Name." The name in Semitic usage indicates the person as he makes himself known to others. The Greek aorist and the eschatological atmosphere of the prayer point to the last times: that God may sanctify all of humanity through the Holy Spirit. The Jewish Kaddish has a similar prayer: "May God's great Name be magnified and sanctified. . . ."

Second petition. Understanding the passive Greek form as above, the sense would be, "May God establish his reign" (*see* KINGDOM OF GOD); Jesus came on earth to establish God's rule (Jn 18.36–37). But the final stage of the kingdom can come only at Jesus' return, when he crushes the power of Satan (2 Thes 2.8). So the early Church prayed for the definitive establishment of God's kingdom at the end of time. The wording resembles the verse of the Jewish Kaddish following the one quoted above: "May God establish his reign during your life. . . ."

Third Petition. Parallel to the second petition, the Church prays that God may accomplish his salvific will, which is to redeem the human race (Eph 1.5–12; Jn 6.39–40). "On earth as in heaven": the Semitic expression, "heaven and earth," means the whole universe. Hence the petition refers to the redemption of the whole cosmos through Christ (Col 1.20).

Fourth Petition. Literally, in Matthew, "Give us today our future (?) bread"; in Luke, "Keep on giving us each day our future (?) bread." The word, ἐπιούσιον (modifier of bread), has no proved parallel in Greek writings. Etymology offers two possibilities: (1) ἐπί (on) plus εἶναι (to be), which could give us "daily" or "for existence," that is, the bread that is needed; (2) ἐπί plus ἰέναι, (to go, come), which could give us "the bread of tomorrow" or "the future bread." The Bohairic and Sahidic versions as well as Marcion have the latter reading, and St. Jerome writes that he saw the reading *māḥār* or "of tomorrow" in the Gospel of the Hebrews. The reading "bread of the future," or "tomorrow," would link with other Gospel references to the coming eschatological banquet (Lk 14.15; Mt 8.11). Words very similar to the petition are found in a Eucharistic context in John 6 (particularly 6.31–35). This would also indicate a Eucharistic interpretation in this petition of the Lord's Prayer. Luke has the present imperative δίδου, "keep on giving," and καθ' ἡμέραν, "each day," in place of Matthew's δός, "give" (once and for all), and σήμερον, "today." He thus draws more attention to that daily nourishment which anticipates the eschatological bread.

Fifth Petition. Literally, in Matthew it is, "and forgive us our debts as we have forgiven our debtors"; in Luke, "and forgive us our sins, for we also forgive our debtors." The perfect tense in Matthew, "as we have forgiven," is the attitude of the Christian awaiting a proximate judgment. All Christians are called upon to beg God's forgiveness while disposing themselves by a generous forgiving of others' debts, knowing that if they do not do so, the words of Matthew 18.35 apply to them: "So will my heavenly Father do to you, unless each of you forgives his brother from his heart." Luke, with his present tense, "as we also forgive," emphasizes forgiveness for the sins of each day as a preparation for the future judgment.

Sixth Petition. Literally, in Matthew and Luke it is, "and lead us not into trial," to which Matthew adds, "but deliver us from the evil one." Before the final judgment, the early Church expected a great time of trial, a final terrible onslaught of the devil (2 Thes 2.1–8). All Christians ask to be delivered from this test, knowing that no human power could withstand such a trial (Mt 24.21–22). Only the power of God can accomplish this (Rv 3.10). This final battle is the same basic struggle that Jesus faced by prayer in Gethsemane, where he asked his disciples to pray they might be spared the same trial (Mt 26.41). "But deliver us from the evil one" (Mt): the

Greek phrase ἀπὸ τοῦ πονηροῦ means either "from evil" or "from the evil one." In John 17.15 Jesus prays, "[I ask] that you keep them from the evil one." Parallels such as this, and the meaning of the first half of the petition, incline us to the second translation, "the evil one." A reference to daily trials and temptations is not eliminated, for these prepare the way for the final test.

USE IN THE LITURGY

The early use of the Lord's Prayer in the baptismal liturgy is witnessed by a variant reading of Luke's second petition as quoted by several Fathers: "May your Holy Spirit come upon us and cleanse us." The *Didache* (8.2–3) has the Matthaean form of the Lord's Prayer where it follows the baptism ceremony and precedes the Eucharist. The Didache instructs Christians to recite it thrice daily (8.3). In the ancient rites of the catechumenate there was a *traditio* of a "handing over" of the Lord's Prayer before baptism. This ancient practice has been revived in the Rite of the Christian Initiation of Adults. The Lord's Prayer is sung or recited at the Liturgy of the Hours, as well as before Communion in the Eucharist.

Bibliography: H. VAN DEN BUSSCHE, *Understanding the Lord's Prayer,* tr. C. SCHALDENBRAND (New York 1963). R. E. BROWN, "The Pater Noster as an Eschatological Prayer," *Theological Studies* 22 (1961) 175–208. M. DROUZEY, "Le 'Pater,' prière du Christ," *La Vie spirituelle* 93 (1955) 115–134. M. E. JACQUEMIN, "La Portée de la troisième demande du 'Pater,'" *Ephemerides theologicae Lovanienses* 25 (1949) 61–76. J. ROCHE, "Que ta volonté soit faite," *La Vie spirituelle* 93 (1955) 249–268. J. B. BAUER, "Libera nos a malo," *Verbum Domini* 34 (1956) 12–15. G. WALTHER, "Untersuchungen zur Geschichte der griechischen Vaterunser-Exegese," *Texte und Untersuchungen zur Geschichte der altchristlichen Literatur* 40.3 (1914). P. J. VAN KASTEREN, *Was Jesus predigte: Eine Erklärung des Vaterunsers,* tr. J. SPENDEL (Freiburg 1920).

[J. A. GRASSI/EDS.]

LORD'S SUPPER, THE

An early name (κυριακὸν δεῖπνον) for the celebration of the Eucharist, found in the New Testament only in 1 Cor 11.20 and perhaps original with St. Paul. The adjective κυριακός (belonging to the Lord, the Lord's) that is employed here in place of the more usual noun in the genitive κυρίου (of the Lord; see also Rv 1.10), is borrowed from Hellenistic governmental and legal language with the meaning "pertaining to the Lord (Emperor); imperial." In Paul's use, the supper "pertains to the Lord" primarily and fundamentally as a liturgical repetition of the LAST SUPPER of the historical Jesus, whom the Christians now recognized as risen Lord ("the Lord Jesus": 1 Cor 11.23). The Jewish PASSOVER meal made ritually

"The Last Supper," c. 1594, painting by Tintoretto in the Church of San Giorgio Maggiore, Venice.

present the past redeeming action of God, and at the same time it was an appeal for the decisive coming of the eschatological kingdom. According to Paul (1 Cor 11.23–26), at the Last Supper Jesus sealed a new covenant in His own sacrificial body and blood; the supper's liturgical reproduction, explained by the "do this in remembrance of me," is a proclamation of the death of the Lord, to be repeated until His final coming.

To exploit the riches of this complex mystery, Paul used Old Testament and even pagan parallels and analogies. In spite of verbal similarities, his pagan converts would not have failed to see the utter opposition between the Christian "table of the Lord," "cup of the Lord" (1 Cor 10.21), and such Hellenistic cult terms as "to sup at the table of the Lord Serapis," "cup of the Good Genius" (see G. A. Deissmann, 299); to partake of the latter was to eat and drink at the "table of demons" (1 Cor 10.20–21; see Dt 32.17). A meal was a favorite Biblical image for eschatological realities; see, e.g., Is 65.13; Mt 8.11–12; 22.1–14; 25.10; Lk 14.15–24; Rv 3.20; 19.9. As the "table of the Lord," the Eucharist is sacrificial food (Mal 1.7, 12; for table, supper in the sense of food, see Dn 1.8, 13, 15). The model for the eschatological "great supper of God" in Rv 19.17 has at the same time a cultic character (cf. Ez 39.17–20, where slaughter has the meaning of sacrificial meal).

Paul underlined the sacrificial nature of the supper; that he was no innovator, however, is shown by the traditional character of the report (1 Cor 11.23), its lapidary liturgical tone, and its conformity with other New Testament accounts where sacrificial and eschatological elements are present also (see, e.g., Mk 14.22–25). That his doctrine was not fundamentally different from that of the primitive Jerusalem community, with its joyous "breaking of bread" (Acts 2.42, 46) is shown by the use of this term in 1 Cor 10.16 and in description of the religious assembly of the Pauline community at Troas (Acts 20.7–11). Thus, at the commemorative and eschatological Lord's Supper, the Eucharistic presence of the Lord who has died and risen is an anticipation of His final presence (PAROUSIA) and already a partial answer to the earnest early Christian prayer "MARANATHA, come Lord!" (1 Cor 16.22; see also Rv 22.20).

See Also: AGAPE.

Bibliography: G. A. DEISSMANN, *Licht vom Osten* (4th ed. Tübingen 1923) 298–99, 304–06. H. SCHÜRMANN, "Herrenmahl," *Lexikon für Theologie und Kirche,* ed. J. HOFER and K. RAHNER, 10 v. (2d, new ed. Freiburg 1957–65) 5:271. P. NEUENZEIT, *Das Her-*

renmahl: Studien zur paulinischen Eucharistieauffassung (Munich 1960).

[C. BERNAS]

LORENZANA, FRANCISCO ANTONIO DE

Archbishop of Mexico City and Toledo, cardinal; b. León, Spain, Sept. 22, 1722; d. Rome, April 17, 1804. After finishing his studies with the Jesuits in León, he became a cleric and at an early age he was given a canonry in Toledo. In 1765 he was named bishop of Plasencia, and in the following year Charles III appointed him archbishop of Mexico. In his New World diocese he displayed great energy in advancing not only the religious but also the scientific and social interests of those under his charge. He is particularly noted for collecting and publishing the acts of the first three provincial councils of Mexico (1555, 1565, 1585), *Concilios provinciales, I, II, III de México* (Mexico 1769–70). In 1771, at royal behest, he held the fourth Mexican provincial council. Although he sent the proceedings of the sessions to Madrid, they were never published; moreover, the acts of this synod have never been approved by the Holy See. Lorenzana brought together valuable historical documents relating to Mexico's history and published them in a richly illustrated work called *Historia de Nueva España escrita por su esclarecido conquistador Hernán Cortés aumentada con otros documentos* (Mexico 1770). In 1772 he was recalled to Spain and made archbishop of Toledo, where he built a fine library for the city and collected and published the works of the principal writers of the Archdiocese of Toledo. These appear in *SS. Patrum Toletanorum opera* (Madrid 1782–83). He also had published, at his own expense, the works of St. Isidore of Seville, and brought out a beautiful edition of the Gothic Breviary and the Gothic Missal. In his diocese he carried on a number of social works and aided the exiled French clergy during the revolutionary period. In 1789 he was created cardinal by Pope PIUS VI, and in 1797 was appointed by Charles IV of Spain as envoy extraordinary from Spain to the Holy See. In this office he supported the pope in the difficult times that followed on the French invasion of Italy by Napoleon Bonaparte. On the death of Pius VI, he made possible the conclave at Venice in December of 1799 by paying the travel expenses of cardinals who were without funds. After the election he accompanied the new pope, Pius VII, back to Rome and in order to assist the pontiff so sorely tried by political conditions, resigned his archiepiscopal See of Toledo in 1800. In Rome he was one of the founders of a new Catholic academy and was considered a great friend of the poor, leaving them 25,000 scudi, a bequest he had received. Lorenzana was a typical regalist Spanish bishop of the eighteenth century.

Bibliography: M. CUEVAS, *Historia de la Iglesia en México,* 5 v. (5th ed. Mexico City 1946–47).

[C. E. RONAN]

LORETTO, SISTERS OF

Officially known as the Sisters of Loretto at the Foot of the Cross (SL, Official Catholic Directory #2360). It was founded in 1812 by Charles Nerinckx, a Belgian priest exiled by the French Revolution. This first native American sisterhood without foreign affiliation had its origin in the educational efforts of Maryland-born Mary Rhodes, who opened a school near St. Charles Church in Hardin's Creek, Ky. With Father Nerinckx's permission, she and Christina Stuart and Anne Havern taught catechism in addition to rudimentary subjects. When the group expressed the desire to live the religious life, Nerinckx received them as novices on April 25, 1812. Two months later, the society was formally organized by the election of a superior according to rule. In the next 12 years the membership increased; six other houses were established in Kentucky, and one in Missouri.

Upon the death of Nerinckx in 1824, Bp. Benedict Flaget of Bardstown, Ky., moved Loretto from its original foundation at Hardin's Creek to St. Stephen's Farm, seven miles distant. The convent and church that the sisters erected there, dedicated in 1826 and totally destroyed by fire in 1858, were replaced by more spacious buildings that included the motherhouse.

Loretto's constitutions were submitted to Pius VII for approval in 1816; in 1851 they were again presented to the Holy See; in 1907 Pius X fully and finally confirmed them. An act of the legislature of Kentucky incorporated the Loretto Sisterhood under the title, Loretto Literary and Benevolent Institution. The Loretto Sisters labored in China from 1923 until their expulsion in 1951. The motherhouse is in Nerinx, KY.

Bibliography: Archives of the Motherhouse of the Sisters of Loretto (Nerinckx, Ky).

[M. BARRETT/EDS.]

LORETTO SISTERS (INSTITUTE OF THE BLESSED VIRGIN MARY)

A community of religious women, without enclosure, founded by Mother Mary WARD for the instruction of youth (IBVM, Official Catholic Directory #2370).

They are popularly known as *Dami Inglesi, Englischen Fräulein,* Loretto sisters, etc., in the countries where they established themselves. In 1609, Mary Ward and seven companions opened a boarding school for English Catholic refugees in St. Omer, Flanders, where they also conducted a free day school. A house was founded in London (1611), and soon the institute spread to Bavaria and Italy. They adopted the rule of the Society of Jesus and received provisional approval from Paul V. Opposition to this novel form of religious life grew and was climaxed by the bull of suppression of Urban VIII in 1631. Soon after, however, Mary Ward was encouraged by Pope Urban himself to open schools in Rome. The foundress then returned to England to encourage her sisters there; she died in York in 1645.

After Mary Ward's death, Mary Poyntz transferred both religious and pupils from York to Paris. Twenty years later Frances BEDINGFELD, a companion of Mother Ward, returned to England and in 1686 opened the Micklegate Bar Convent, York, the first convent founded in England after the Reformation. In 1703 Clement XI granted full approval to the rule. Meanwhile the houses in Germany and Austria had multiplied. The Paradeiser Haus, Munich, having remained open during the suppression by special permission of Urban VIII, was moved to Rome. St. Pölten (1706) became the Austrian generalate, and Mainz, Germany, became an independent motherhouse in 1809. Frances BALL entered the York community in 1814, and in 1821 she became foundress of a house of the same order in Dublin, Ireland. Foundations in Navan and Meath, Ireland (1833), and Australia (1874) were made from Rathfarnham, Dublin. Teresa DEASE established the first North American foundation in Toronto, Canada (1847). In the United States, a convent was opened in Joliet, Ill., in 1880. Pius X in 1909 reinstated Mary Ward to full honor as foundress. Two years later, York and Munich united at Rome, and after World War II they were joined by the St. Pölten and Mainz generalates.

The institute's educational work extends from primary school to university level, in catechetics, adult education, youth ministries, retreats, and pastoral outreach. Despite differences in history and variations in habit and title, there is an essential unity and strength among the many branches of the Institute of the Blessed Virgin Mary stemming from its constitutions and the spirit of its foundress.

The general motherhouse in North America is in Toronto, Canada. The U.S. regional headquarters is in Wheaton, IL.

Bibliography: *Life and Letters of Mother Teresa Dease,* by a member of the community (St. Louis 1916).

[M. F. MADIGAN/EDS.]

LORRAINE, CARDINALS OF

They may be considered according to the two houses to which they belonged.

House of Guise. The first cardinal of this house was John, son of René II of Lorraine, and brother of Antoine, Duke of Lorraine, and Claude, Duke of Guise; b. Bar, April 9, 1498; d. Neuvy-sur-Loire, May 10, 1550. At the age of three he was appointed coadjutor of Metz and at 20 was made a cardinal. Altogether he held 12 bishoprics, including Reims, Lyons, Albi, Narbonne, Toul, and Metz. Having been appointed a member of the royal council in 1530, he presided (1536) over an embassy to Emperor Charles V. Francis I, King of France, used his diplomatic services particularly in dealing with the Holy See.

Charles I, nephew and successor of John, and son of Claude of Guise; b. Joinville, Feb. 17, 1524; d. Avignon, Dec. 26, 1574. He was designated archbishop of Reims in 1538 and consecrated in 1545; he became a cardinal in 1547. In diocesan synods (1548, 1549) he attacked absenteeism and enacted rules for testing candidates for orders; he made a visitation of his diocese and preached frequently, though usually on semipolitical themes. He founded the University of Reims on Jan. 6, 1548. He held several bishoprics and was abbot *in commendam* for 11 abbeys as well as *legatus natus* under Paul IV. He furthered ecclesiastically the cause for the foundation of the Society of Jesus. At the third session of the Council of Trent (1562–63) he promoted Gallican liberties and episcopal residency (*see* GALLICANISM); he led the movement for inviting Protestants, but then he changed this policy because of political circumstances. He was active politically under Henry II and Francis II, who appointed him chancellor. He negotiated the Franco-Papal treaty against Charles V on the Parma question.

Louis I, another son of Claude of Guise was known as the cardinal of Guise; b. Paris, Oct. 21, 1527; d. Paris, May 29?, 1578. He became a cardinal in 1553 and bishop of Metz in 1558. Politically he was less active than his brother Charles, and the estimates of his character vary among contemporary witnesses.

Louis II, son of Francis de Guise and Anne d'Este, nephew of Charles, whom he succeeded as archbishop of Reims in 1574 and as cardinal in 1578; b. Dampierre, June 7, 1555; d. Dec. 24, 1588. He was associated with his brother Henry III, duke of Guise and was involved in the formation of the Holy League, in the Treaty of Joinville, and in the disputes among Henry III of France, Henry of Navarre, and his own brother Henry (*see* WARS OF RELIGION). Henry III of France brought about his death and that of his brother.

Louis III, son of Duke Henry III of Guise, and brother of Charles IV, who succeeded to the dukedom; b. Aug. 11, 1582 (1585?); d. Sainctes, June 21, 1621. Louis was made archbishop of Reims and cardinal in 1615.

House of Lorraine. The earliest cardinal from this house was Frederick, brother of Godfrey I, Duke of Lorraine; b. between 1010 and 1020. Frederick became Pope STEPHEN IX (1057–58).

Charles of Lorraine-Vaudemont, b. No], April 2, 1559; d. Nov. 29, 1587. He became a cardinal in 1578, bishop of Toul in 1580, and also bishop of Verdun in 1585, although he was not ordained and consecrated until 1586. He was noted for piety and ecclesiastical zeal.

Charles II, second son of Duke Charles III of Lorraine; b. Nancy, July 1, 1567; d. Nancy, Dec. 24 (30?), 1607. He was coadjutor to the bishop of Metz, Louis I of Guise, in 1573 and became bishop of Metz in 1578. Ten years later he was made cardinal deacon by Sixtus V; in 1591 he became a cardinal priest and apostolic delegate to the Duchy of Lorraine. He was bishop of Metz, Toul, and Verdun, and abbot of at least four monasteries. His election as bishop of Strasbourg in 1592 in opposition to Johann Georg von Brandenburg, the Protestant candidate, was the cause of sporadic riots. In 1559 a commission awarded the election to Charles and in 1604 the Protestant party relinquished the diocese and the cathedral to the Catholics.

Nicholas Francis; b. Dec. 6, 1609; d. Nancy, Jan. 25, 1670. He became coadjutor to the bishop of Toul in 1620, bishop of Toul in 1625, and a cardinal in 1627. He disagreed with his brother, Duke Charles IV, who was subservient to France and Cardinal Richelieu. In 1634 he renounced all clerical titles, married his cousin Claudia, and proclaimed himself Duke of Lorraine. When expelled from Lorraine by the French, he went into exile in Vienna and Munich. His son, Charles Leopold, succeeded Charles IV as Duke of Lorraine.

Bibliography: H. O. EVENNETT, *The Cardinal of Lorraine and The Council of Trent* (Cambridge, Eng. 1940). H. O. EVENNETT and L. JUST, *Lexikon für Theologie und Kirche*, ed. J. HOFER and K. RAHNER, 10 v. (2d, new ed. Freiburg 1957–65) 6:1146–47.

[J. J. SMITH]

LORSCH, ABBEY OF

More properly called Lorsch on the Bergstrasse, in Hesse, Germany, Diocese of Mainz (Latin, *Laureshamense, Laurissa*), at one time the foremost German BENEDICTINE abbey, later a Premonstratensian monastery. It was founded in 764 by Count Kankor and his mother,

Williswinda, in Altenmünster, and was settled with monks from GORZE. In 772 episcopal EXEMPTION and royal protection were granted by CHARLEMAGNE, and in 774 the cloister was removed to Lorsch. The great numbers who entered, the extraordinarily large grants, the rewards of able administration, the exemplary discipline, and the number of daughter-foundations gave this imperial abbey a vast influence in the 9th century, and for the next 200 years, a period of cultural brilliance. Decline followed in the 12th century, partly because the abbots were so preoccupied with efforts to check episcopal annexation that they were unable to introduce serious reforms within the monastery. Archbishop Siegfried II of Mainz finally secured jurisdiction over Lorsch from Pope Gregory IX in 1229; this was confirmed by Emperor Frederick II in 1232, after which Lorsch became a CISTERCIAN house and sank to the rank of a PRIORY. With the permission of Pope Innocent IV, Abp. Siegfried III in 1244 introduced PREMONSTRATENSIAN canons from Allerheiligen. In 1461 Lorsch was handed over to the Count Palatine. During the Thirty Years' War the monastery was burnt to the ground by Spanish troops (1621). In the 17th century the attempts of the Premonstratensians to return to Lorsch were fruitless, and in 1803 the monastic territory was awarded to the state of Hesse-Darmstadt.

The crypt, which was the burial place of two Carolingian rulers, and which contains two important murals, has been restored since 1927. The catalogue of Lorsch's library testifies to the intellectual greatness of the monastery in the 10th and 11th centuries and clearly suggests that it was the best of the medieval libraries in its time. After 1460 under Palatine control, the still-extensive library was removed to Heidelberg, and in 1632 it was sent to the Vatican; in 1815 part of it was restored to Heidelberg.

Bibliography: *Annales Laureshamenses, Monumenta Germaniae Historica: Scriptores* 1. *Gallia Christiana* 5:695–714. F. KIESER, *Beiträge zur Geschichte des Klosters Lorsch*, 2 v. (Bensheim 1908–09). W. M. LINDSAY, "The (Early) Lorsch Scriptorium," *Palaeographia Latina*, ed. W. M. LINDSAY, 6 pts. in 1 v. (Oxford 1922–29) 3.5–48. L. H. COTTINEAU, *Répertoire topobibliographique des abbayes et prieurés* (Mâcon 1935–39) 1:1656–58. P. SCHMITZ, *Histoire de l'Ordre de Saint-Benoît*, 7 v. (Maredsous, Bl. 1942–56). W. SELZER, *Das Karolingische Reichskloster Lorsch* (Kassel-Basel 1955).

[B. D. HILL]

LOS ANGELES, ARCHDIOCESE OF

Metropolitan see (*Angelorum*) comprising the counties of Los Angeles, Santa Barbara, and Ventura in California, an area of 8,782 square miles. In 2001 there were

4,121,601 Catholics, about 39 percent, in a total population of 10,449,129. When the diocese was erected April 27, 1840, San Diego was constituted the see city; it was moved to Monterey in 1850, and five years later to Santa Barbara. In 1859, after the episcopal residence had been moved to Los Angeles, the title of the diocese was changed to Monterey-Los Angeles. In 1922 it became Los Angeles-San Diego when Monterey-Fresno was constituted a diocese. The Archdiocese of Los Angeles was established July 11, 1936. Its suffragan sees in 2001 were the Dioceses of Monterey, Fresno, Orange, San Bernardino and San Diego.

Early History. Los Angeles is an abbreviated version of the title *El Pueblo de Nuestra Señora de Los Angeles del Rio de Porciuncula,* given to the town founded by Gov. Felipe de Neve on Sept. 7, 1781. The area covered by the archdiocese was originally part of the first Diocese of the Californias, which was created by Gregory XVI in 1840 as a suffragan of the See of Mexico, and comprised the state of California, Lower California, and much of present-day Nevada and Utah. Upper California contained the missions founded by the Franciscan, Junípero SERRA; the missions of Lower California were the work of the Jesuit, Juan Maria SALVATIERRA. The first bishop, Francisco GARCÍA DIEGO Y MORENO, OSF, was consecrated on Oct. 4, 1840, in the Basilica of Our Lady of Guadalupe near Mexico City, and arrived in his episcopal city, San Diego, Dec. 11, 1841. A year later, however, he took up residence at Santa Barbara and administered the diocese from there until his death on April 30, 1846. The first priest ordained in California was Miguel Gomez on June 29, 1842, at Mission Santa Barbara.

Before the California diocese was established, the Mexican government had appropriated the PIOUS FUND, upon which the missions depended for support. Thus, the bishop found 12 of the missions, which had been secularized by 1833, in ruins. These were restored to episcopal control; in 1841 García Diego had 17 Franciscans in Upper California and four Dominicans in Lower California. In 1844, Our Lady of Guadalupe Seminary was opened near Santa Ines (now Santa Barbara County) where it survived for 17 years. Two priests and four students were brought from Mexico.

After the flag of the United States was raised over the custom house in Monterey July 7, 1846, disturbed political conditions between Mexico and the United States and revolts in Italy delayed the appointment of a new bishop. At the time when Father Gonzales Rubio acted as administrator of the diocese (1847–50), the Picpus Fathers, who had been temporarily in the area in the 1830's, returned to California. With the discovery of gold in northern California in January 1848, a new era began,

Serra's statue and church entrance, San Gabriel Mission, Los Angeles. (©Richard Cummins/CORBIS)

trade routes were opened, and California was admitted to the Union as the 31st state Sept. 9, 1850.

1850 to 1896. In 1850, after the Seventh Provincial Council of Baltimore had proposed three names for the vacant California diocese, Joseph Sadoc ALEMANY, OP, was appointed May 31, 1850, and Monterey was designated his official residence.

Alemany. After his consecration in Rome June 30, 1850, and establishment at Monterey early in 1851, Alemany directed his attention principally to the northern part of the diocese. Since his jurisdiction over Lower California was not recognized by the Mexican government, the Holy See removed the Diocese of Monterey from the Province of Mexico in 1851, and a year later Lower California Peninsula was withdrawn from the diocese. On Dec. 18, 1855, a U.S. Land Commission, after a three-year study, decreed the return of the mission properties to the diocese; in the following six years this was gradually accomplished over the signatures of Presidents James Buchanan and Abraham Lincoln.

Replica of "Virgin of Guadalupe," digitally remastered, on tour at Los Angeles Coliseum. (AP/Wide World Photos)

Amat. When, on July 29, 1853, Alemany was transferred to the new metropolitan See of San Francisco, Thaddeus AMAT, CM, was appointed to Monterey and consecrated in Rome March 12, 1854. In November 1855, he took possession of his see, establishing his residence at Our Lady of Sorrows church in Santa Barbara. Besides the Franciscan and Picpus fathers, he had only nine secular priests. Through him the Daughters of Charity of St. Vincent de Paul arrived in Los Angeles Jan. 5, 1856, to establish a school, an orphanage, and the city's first hospital. In 1858, envisioning the growth of Los Angeles, Amat moved his residence there. A year later, during a visit to Rome, the bishop succeeded in having the title of the diocese changed to Monterey-Los Angeles. The old Plaza Church of Our Lady of Angels became the procathedral. When, in May 1862, a diocesan synod was held in Los Angeles, there were 13 parishes with resident pastors.

In 1865 the Vincentian fathers opened a school in Los Angeles; four years later it received its charter as St. Vincent's College. A college for lay students, opened by the Franciscan fathers in 1861, lasted until 1877. In 1869 the Pious Fund was again the object of investigation, and when the members of an American-Mexican commission

failed to agree, an umpire, in the person of the British Ambassador, gave the verdict in favor of the Catholic bishops of California and the vicar apostolic of Colorado and Utah. Amat attended the sessions of Vatican Council I, returning to Los Angeles in December 1870. The following spring, ground was broken for a cathedral, which was consecrated by Archbishop Alemany April 30, 1876, in honor of St. Vibiana, whose relics Amat had obtained from Pius IX on the promise to honor her with a cathedral as the principal patroness of his diocese.

Mora. When Amat died on May 12, 1878, he was immediately succeeded by Francis Mora, his vicar-general and pastor of Our Lady of Angels, who had been consecrated coadjutor on Aug. 3, 1873. Mora, a native of Catalonia, Spain, had come to America as a student with Amat; he was ordained for the diocese March 19, 1856. By the time of his succession the diocese had 31 priests in addition to the Franciscan community at Santa Barbara and the Vincentian community at Los Angeles. The city's population of 10,000 included about 2,300 Catholics, while of the 100,000 throughout the diocese, about one-fourth were Catholics. However, with the inauguration of transcontinental railroads (1885), the discovery of oil (1891), and the development of the citrus industry, the population of city and diocese grew rapidly and the Church's progress was marked.

In 1886 the cathedral school was built and entrusted to the Immaculate Heart Sisters who had come to California and located at Gilroy in 1871. St. Vincent's College moved to a more spacious location in March 1887; St. Vincent's parish, also under the direction of the Vincentian fathers, was erected. Sacred Heart parish and St. Joseph's were established. The Sisters of St. Joseph of Carondelet and the Sisters of the Holy Names joined the diocese and opened academies for girls, and the Sisters of Mercy arrived to found a home for working girls and one for the aged. The Daughters of Charity moved their hospital to a new location in 1884, and in 1890 transferred the orphanage to a site in Boyle Heights. St. Mary's Church was built in 1896.

1896–1936. Failing health led Mora to request a coadjutor, and the chancellor of the Archdiocese of San Francisco, George Montgomery, was consecrated for Monterey-Los Angeles April 8, 1894. Two years later Mora resigned the see, returning to Spain where he died Aug. 3, 1905.

Montgomery. When Montgomery succeeded Mora on May 16, 1896, there were in the diocese 72 parish churches and missions, ten religious communities with 183 sisters, and six orphanages, four hospitals, two colleges, four academies, and 18 parish schools, for a Catholic population estimated at 52,000. During Montgomery's administration, Los Angeles, among other cities, suffered from the anti-Catholic bigotry of the AMERICAN PROTECTIVE ASSOCIATION. Its influence was counteracted to some extent, however, by a series of lectures under the auspices of the Catholic Truth Society. In September 1902 Montgomery was appointed coadjutor to Archbishop Riordan of San Francisco, and left Los Angeles on March 27, 1903.

Conaty. Bp. Thomas J. CONATY, second rector of The Catholic University of America, Washington, D.C., was transferred to Monterey-Los Angeles and took possession of his see June 18, 1903. Two months after his arrival three new parishes were erected in the city. The Claretian fathers took charge of San Gabriel 1908 and the Old Plaza Church in 1910. The St. Vincent de Paul Society was organized. In 1905 the Little Sisters of the Poor arrived in the diocese. By 1911 there were 166 churches and chapels in the diocese, 18 of which were centers of parish life in the city of Los Angeles. Nine new schools had been erected, making a total of 29 parish schools, exclusive of the academies, which still provided elementary school facilities for a number of parishes. The orphanages cared for 1,048 children and the Catholic Indian school at Banning had 118 pupils, while an additional 335 Cath-

olic children attended the two schools for Native Americans in the diocese. Mass was celebrated at least monthly at 43 mission stations. There were five hospitals in the diocese, and three homes for the aged. In 1910 the number of priests had increased to 206, including 73 who were members of the eight religious communities, serving about 100,000 Catholics in the diocese.

Although they retained St. Vincent's parish, the Vincentian fathers gave up their educational work in Los Angeles in June 1911, after 46 years in charge of St. Vincent's College. The Jesuits, who had been in Santa Barbara since 1908, entered the field of education in 1911. Under their direction St. Vincent's College became Loyola University and moved to a new location in 1929. For the benefit of the teaching religious, Conaty inaugurated summer conferences at which educators of national reputation taught the latest methods of administration and instruction. Settlement work in the poorer parts of the city met with immediate success. When religious communities devoted to works of mercy were encouraged, Sisters of the Good Shepherd established a home in Los Angeles. In San Diego and other cities of the diocese new parishes and institutions were founded, and proportionate progress was made. When Conaty died at Coronado, near San Diego, Sept. 18, 1915, the Catholic population of the diocese had grown to 178,000, and the number of priests to 271. The diocese, which remained vacant for two years, was administered by Msgr. Patrick Harnett. Although Bp. Peter J. Muldoon, of Rockford, Ill., was appointed to Monterey-Los Angeles March 22, 1917, he did not take possession of the see, and resigned in June of that year.

Cantwell. On Dec. 12, 1917, John Joseph CANTWELL, vicar-general of the Archdiocese of San Francisco, who had been appointed bishop of Monterey-Los Angeles Sept. 21, 1917, was installed in Los Angeles, after his consecration in San Francisco on December 5. During his 30-year administration, the diocese shed its Mexican-colonial characteristics and took its place as one of the great metropolitan sees of the U.S. The population increase was a prime factor in diocesan development, which included the erection of the Diocese of Monterey-Fresno on Dec. 3, 1922, comprising the 12 northern counties, while the eight remaining counties received the new title of Los Angeles-San Diego. Many Mexicans, fleeing from their native land during the persecution of the Church under President Plutarco Calles, arrived in Los Angeles, where their total grew to more than 300,000, including 129 expelled priests. There, 50 parishes and missions were erected and Spanish-speaking priests were provided.

The growth of the diocese necessitated the better organization of its departments of administration. The

Catholic Welfare Bureau was established in 1919; the Confraternity of Christian Doctrine, in 1922; and the Society for the Propagation of the Faith, in 1924. In November 1920, the Holy Name Union was established, while the Council of Catholic Women had its origin in April 1923. The Catholic Youth Organization, with its club and camp programs, came into being in 1936. To ensure a steady supply of priests, appeals were made to the missionary seminaries of Ireland, and the generous response provided the founders of most of the new parishes for half a century. Religious orders were invited; the Augustinians and Capuchins arrived in 1922, and a year later the Passionists began the lay retreat movement, and the Oblate fathers located in San Fernando. The Dominican fathers were established in Eagle Rock in 1921; the Salesian fathers, in 1919; and the Paulists, in 1925. To provide for native vocations, a junior seminary, under the title of Los Angeles College, was instituted in 1926 as a day school, and a major seminary of St. John's at Camarillo was founded in 1939, both institutions under the direction of the Vincentian fathers.

Archdiocese. When in 1936, four southernmost counties were separated from Los Angeles to form the diocese of San Diego, Los Angeles was elevated to the status of an archdiocese, with Cantwell becoming its first archbishop.

1936 to 1947. Even after the division, the Catholic population in the Archdiocese of Los Angeles was estimated at 650,000. By 1947, the archdiocese had 688 priests, of whom 362 were diocesan. There were 217 parishes with resident pastors, four colleges, 35 high schools, 115 parochial schools with an enrollment of 42,877 pupils, and 36 communities of sisters established in the diocese. Five hundred Confraternity teachers were giving religious instruction to 45,000 pupils.

The Legion of Decency, particularly appropriate in view of the vast motion picture industry in Los Angeles, was established in 1934. Other notable events of Cantwell's episcopate included the convocation in 1929 of the first synod since 1889; the great earthquake of 1933, which did considerable damage to Church properties in the Long Beach area; the consecration of two auxiliary bishops, Joseph T. McGucken on March 19, 1941, and Timothy Manning on Oct. 15, 1946; and the visit of Cardinal Eugenio Pacelli in October 1936. Two historic anniversaries were celebrated, with attendance of over 100,000 in the Los Angeles Memorial Coliseum—on Sept. 6, 1931, the sesquicentennial of the founding of the city of Los Angeles, and Oct. 13, 1940, the centennial of the foundation of the hierarchy. Other developments included the founding of 18 hospitals and health agencies. An unsuccessful statewide effort was made in 1933 to se-

cure tax exemption for private nonprofit schools. A national celebration of Catholic Action was held in Los Angeles in April 1934, the 150th anniversary of the death of Father Junipero Serra.

McIntyre. At Cantwell's death Oct. 30, 1947, McGucken was elected administrator of the diocese until March 19, 1948, when James Francis A. MCINTYRE was installed in St. Vibiana's Cathedral as the second archbishop of Los Angeles. Archbishop McIntyre who since 1946 had been coadjutor archbishop in New York under Cardinal Spellman, brought experience of administering a large archdiocese with him to Los Angeles. Shortly after his installation, he set about reorganizing the archdiocesan curia and administrative structures of the archdiocese. During his episcopacy, a total of 82 new parishes were established. In 1956, McIntyre formally sponsored the establishment of the Lay Mission Helpers Association, the pioneer organization of lay missioners in the nation.

Cardinal McIntyre is credited with using his influence to repeal the burdensome taxation of parochial schools in California, but he was criticized for his silence on interracial issues. In 1964 the bishop of every diocese in California save Los Angeles issued a statement against the repeal of the Rumford Fair Housing Act. The Reverend William DuBay petitioned the pope to remove McIntyre from office because he had forbidden the priests of the archdiocese from addressing the race issue.

In 1960, on the eve of Vatican II, the cardinal convened an archdiocesan synod. He served on the Central Preparatory Commission, attended all the sessions, and took an active role in the deliberations of the Council. And though he spoke in favor of the continued use of Latin, opposed changes in the Mass, and argued against giving juridical status to liturgical conferences, after the Council he moved expeditiously to implementing its recommendations and complying with its spirit. On the other hand, the archdiocese received a national notoriety because of the Cardinal's opposition to renewal measures taken by the Immaculate Heart of Mary Sisters and because of his highly publicized dispute in 1969 with *Catholicos por La Raza*, a radical Mexican rights group. McIntyre resigned the archbishopric in 1970 at the age of 88.

Manning. McIntyre was succeeded by Timothy MANNING, who had been appointed coadjutor to McIntyre in May 19, 1969. Before his installation as Archbishop of Los Angeles on Jan. 21, 1970, Manning had been an auxiliary bishop in Los Angeles (1946–1967) before becoming the first bishop of Fresno (1967–1969). Three years later Manning was named a cardinal. Although his administrative style was less confrontational, Manning pursued the expansionary policies of his predecessor, and energetically supported a host of ecumenical involvements and warmly endorsed the Cursillo movement. He continued to encourage the Lay Mission Helpers that McIntyre had established, visiting missionaries in South Africa, Rhodesia, Ghana, Kenya, Malawi and Uganda. Although a portion of the archdiocese was carved out into a new Diocese of Orange County in 1976, the Catholic population continued to grow rapidly, fueled by massive waves of Mexican and other Latin immigrants. A year later, Manning retired and turned over the reins of leadership over to his successor, Archbishop Roger M. Mahony. Manning remained active in his retirement years. In addition to working a day each in the archdiocesan archives and spending another visiting infirm priests and religious, he traveled widely and gave numerous retreats throughout the west. He passed away on June 23, 1989 in Los Angeles.

Mahony. In 1985, Bishop Roger Mahony of the diocese of Stockton was installed Archbishop of Los Angeles. Pope John Paul II named him a cardinal on June 28, 1991. Mahony's active and highly visible leadership put him at the center of some controversies and at the same time enabled him to reach to the farthest outposts of the most populous diocese in the country. His relationship with Los Angeles's powerful media and film industry, initially testy and filled with mutual suspicion, led him to found Catholics in Media, an organization intended to influence, shape, and reward the entertainment industry. A high priority in Mahony's tenure as archbishop was to erect a new cathedral for Los Angeles. When in 1994 the Northridge earthquake so undermined the Cathedral of Saint Vibiana that repairing it was not an option, Cardinal Mahony obtained a prime location in the Los Angeles Civic Center on which to build the Cathedral Center of Our Lady of the Angels in grand contemporary style.

Mahony's friendship with Cardinal Joseph Bernardin of Chicago and his participation in the latter's Common Ground project expanded his view of the Church's need to interact with contemporary society. His personal friendships with other religious leaders in Los Angeles led to the signing of a covenant among Catholics, Lutherans, and Episcopalians. He worked hard to increase lay involvement in the administration of the archdiocese, expanding the services of the archdiocese while simplifying archdiocesan structures. A pastoral letter on the liturgy, *Gather Faithfully Together,* published on the feast of Our Lady of the Angels, Sept. 4, 1997, served as a call to renewal for the parishes in the archdiocese. The years of Cardinal Mahony's ministry have returned him to his roots in Catholic social activism. He has fostered free and open dialogue in the archdiocese—especially through the expansion of the Los Angeles Religious Education Congress, an annual event that has drawn tens of thousands and became a forum for speakers from all over the Catholic world. Mahony has been a frequent caller on local talk radio, and has used his skill as a ham radio operator to keep in contact with people all around the world. He was quick to grasp the power of the Internet and frequently uses it to hold chat sessions with his people. With funds and friendship he has supported churches in the developing world, especially in Central and South America.

Catholic Higher Education. Los Angeles is home to two Catholic institutions of higher learning, Loyola Marymount University and Mount St. Mary's College. Loyola Marymount University traces its roots to the Jesuit-sponsored Loyola College (established 1911; university status 1930) and Religious of the Sacred Heart of Mary–sponsored Marymount College (established 1933). In 1968, Marymount College moved to the campus of Loyola College as an autonomous institution. At this point, the Sisters of St. Joseph of Orange joined the Religious of the Sacred Heart of Mary as co-sponsors of Marymount College. After five years of sharing faculties and resources, Loyola University and Marymount College merged in 1973 to form Loyola Marymount University, sponsored by the Jesuits, the Religious of the Sacred Heart of Mary, and the Sisters of St. Joseph of Orange. The other major Catholic institution of higher learning in the archdiocese is Mount St. Mary's College, sponsored by the Sisters of St. Joseph of Carondelet.

Bibliography: Archives, Archdiocese of Los Angeles; Archives, Santa Barbara Mission; Archives, University of San Francisco. H. H. BANCROFT, *History of California,* 7 v. (San Francisco 1884–90). R. E. COWAN, *A Bibliography of the History of California and the Pacific West, 1510–1906,* 3 v. (San Francisco 1914; new ed. Columbus, Ohio 1952). Z. ENGELHARDT, *The Missions and Missionaries of California,* 4 v. (San Francisco 1908–15). W. E. NORTH, *Catholic Education in Southern California* (Washington 1936). F. PALOU, *Historical Memoirs of New California* tr. H. E. BOLTON, 2 v. (Berkeley, Calif. 1926). Z. ENGELHARDT, *The Missions and Missionaries of California,* 4 v. (San Francisco 1908–1915). D. WEBER, *The Spanish Frontier in North America* (New Haven and London 1992). L. HAAS, *Conquests and Historical Identities in California* (Berkeley 1995). A. L. HURTADO, *Indian Survival on the California Frontier* (New Haven and London 1988). R. JACKSON and E. CASTILLO, *Indians, Franciscans and Spanish Colonization* (Albuquerque 1995). M. ENGH, *Frontier Faiths: Church, Temple and Synagogue in Los Angeles, 1846–1888* (Albuquerque 1992). F. J. WEBER, *A Biographical Sketch of the Right Reverend Francisco Garcia Diego y Moreno* (Los Angeles 1961). F. J. WEBER, *Thaddeus Amat: California's Reluctant Prelate* (Los Angeles 1964); *Century of Fulfillment: The Roman Catholic Church in Southern California, 1840–1947* (Mission Hills 1990); *His Eminence of Los Angeles: James Francis Cardinal McIntyre,* 2 v. (Mission Hills 1997). J. M. BURNS, ''The Mexican Catholic Community in California,'' *Mexican Americans and the Catholic Church, 1900–1965,* J. DOLAN and G. HINOJOSA, eds. (Notre Dame 1994). F. J. WEBER, comp., *Magnificat: The Life and Times of Timothy Cardinal Manning* (Mission Hills 1999).

[T. MANNING/EDS.]

LOSSKIĬ, NĬKOLAĬ ONUFRIEVICH

Russian philosopher; b. Kreslavka, Province of Vitebsk, Dec. 6, 1879; d. Sainte-Geneviève des Bois, near Paris, Jan. 24, 1965. As a student in the gymnasium he was expelled for spreading atheism and went to Bern to finish his preparatory studies. Returning to Russia, he studied at the University of St. Petersburg, where, later at the age of 29, he was invited to prepare himself for a professorship. Meanwhile, he went abroad again, working under W. Windelband, W. Wundt, and G. E. Müller. In 1903 he received his master's degree for his dissertation on the fundamental doctrines of psychology from the viewpoint of voluntarism and in 1907 his doctorate at the University of Moscow for his dissertation *Obosnovanie intuitivizma* (The Foundation of Intuitivism). Losskiĭ became *docent* and later professor of philosophy at St. Petersburg, a post he held until the fall of 1921. In 1922 he was forced to leave, along with some 125 scholars and writers, including N. A. BERDÎAEV. He settled in Prague until appointed professor at the University of Bratislava (Slovakia). In 1945 he moved to New Haven, Conn., where he commuted to New York in order to teach at St. Vladimir Orthodox Russian Theological Seminary and Academy. In 1951 he moved to Los Angeles, Calif. The last few years of his life he spent in France.

Losskiĭ constructed his own philosophical system, which he referred to as hierarchical personalism. In metaphysics he advocated a concrete ideal realism. His epistemological theory, which differs profoundly from that of H. BERGSON, he named intuitivism. God and the kingdom of God are the starting point for his moral philosophy and aesthetics.

Bibliography: Works. *Die Grundlehren der Psychologie vom Standpunkt des Voluntarismus* (Berlin 1905); *Grundlegung des Intuitivismus* (Halle 1908); *The Intuitive Basis of Knowledge* (London 1919); *Handbuch der Logik* (Leipzig 1927); *The World as an Organic Whole* (New York 1928); N. O. LOSSKIĬ and J. S. MARSHALL, *Value and Existence,* tr. S.S. VINOKOOROFF (London 1935); *Freedom of Will,* tr. N. DUDDINGTON (London 1932); *History of Russian Philosophy* (New York 1951). **Studies.** S. TOMKIEFF, *The Philosophy of N. O. Lossky* (Durham Univ. Philos. Society Proceedings 6; Durham, N.C. 1923). A. S. KOHANSKI, *Lossk'y Theory of Knowledge* (Nashville, Tenn. 1936). *Festschrift, N. O. Lossky zum 60. Geburtstage* (Boon 1932). J. PAPIN, *Doctrina de bono perfecto eiusque in systemate N. O. Losskii personalistico applicatio* (Leiden 1946); "In Memoriam N. O. Lossky" in *Most* 12 (Cleveland 1965), a quarterly for Slovak culture.

[J. PAPIN]

LOS-VON-ROM MOVEMENT

Literally "away from Rome," a term often applied to a number of modern movements whose purpose was to lead Catholics out of the Catholic Church. Its specific reference here is to a movement in the German regions of the Austro-Hungarian monarchy after 1897 that sought to encourage disaffection among Catholics because of the Church's indifference to nationalistic political goals.

As national tensions mounted in Austria and Bohemia, many Germans were fearful that they were threatened by a coalition of the monarchy, the Catholic Church, and the Slavs. A coalition of German clericals and Slavs had been the basis of the Taafe government (1879–93) and was held responsible for the passing of Count Kasimir Badeni's language ordinances in 1897 that required parity between Czechs and Germans in Bohemia. In the face of this blow to German pride and prestige, demonstrations took place, and during one of them in Vienna a medical student, Theodor Rakus, proclaimed the slogan, "Los von Rom."

The Pan-German movement of Georg von Schönerer was quick to adopt it as a part of its program in the hope that a weakening of Catholicism would increase the chances for *Anschluss* with Germany. Protestant missionary organizations in the German empire, especially the Evangelical Union and the Gustavus Adolphus Union, actively encouraged Catholics to become converts to Protestantism. Churches were built in Austria, missionaries were sent from Germany, and a lively propaganda developed, with the newspaper *Die Wartburg* as the movement's chief organ after 1902.

Although the Los-von-Rom movement originated as a political protest, it eventually included a number of people for whom the terms "German" and "Protestant" were identical. An effort to encourage a similar movement among the Czechs by an appeal to their Hussite traditions broke down because of animosity between Czechs and Germans. The movement failed to become widespread; yet 76,000 or more Catholics deserted their Church and joined the Protestants or OLD CATHOLICS between 1897 and 1914. The movement led many others into religious indifference.

During World War I the movement diminished; but it revived under the First Austrian Republic as a form of protest, often without religious overtones, against political Catholicism. German nationalistic feeling was largely responsible for Los-von-Rom, but other factors were involved, such as the huge size of dioceses; the relative scarcity of German priests, which meant that Czech priests often served in German and mixed parishes; and the weakening of adherence to Catholicism among the middle class and the students. Catholic-Protestant relations were strained by this movement. Interaction between churches was not as close to the heart of the movement as was the conflict between one form of European nationalism and a supranational Church.

Bibliography: L. ALBERTIN, *Nationalismus und Protestantismus in der österreichischen Los-von-Rom Bewegung um 1900* (Cologne 1953). F. LAU, *Die Religion in Geschichte und Gegenwart* (Tübingen 1957–65) 4:452–455. K. ALGERMISSEN, *Lexikon für Theologie und Kirche*, ed. J. HOFER and K. RAHNER (Freiberg 1957–65) 6:1153–55.

[W. B. SLOTTMAN]

LOTHAIR I, MEDIEVAL EMPEROR

Reigned: 817–855. b. 795. The oldest son of Emperor Louis the Pious and a key figure, with his brothers, in the civil wars that marked both the later years of his father's reign and the period immediately following his death. In 814, Lothair was appointed king of Bavaria. In 817, his father named him co–emperor and crowned him at Aachen. In conjunction with the coronation, Louis also enacted his *Ordinatio imperrii* by which he designated Lothair as successor and placed the latter's younger brothers, Louis of Bavaria and Pipen of Aquitaine, under his authority. Lothair spent the years 822–825, as regent for Italy, significantly reducing the power and independence of his uncle, King Bernard of Italy (812–817), without actually displacing him. While in Italy, Lothair was also crowned emperor by Pope PASCHAL I at Rome (823).

The *Ordinatio imperii* was apparently intended to preserve the unity of the empire without denying Lothair's siblings their rightful share. In fact, the orderly settlement it envisaged failed to materialize, largely because of the anxiety generated when Emperor Louis remarried and his new wife, Judith, produced yet another son and potential heir. When Judith and her supporters began pressing Louis to allocate a share in the realm to her son, Charles (''the Bald''), the elder siblings rose up in revolt (830). Lothair, whose rights appeared most threatened, took the lead in the rebellion and suffered most heavily when it failed. In the aftermath, his father undertook a new division of the realm that foresaw its division into four roughly equal kingdoms, including one for the young Charles. Lothair was to retain his Italian lands, but lost any authority over his brothers' lands, now understood to be independent realms. This new settlement failed to calm the underlying discontent among the brothers, however, who continued to conspire and vie for greater power and influence. In 833, with Lothair in the lead, the elder siblings rebelled again. This time, they also enjoyed the support of Pope GREGORY IV, but were defeated nonetheless. Lothair continued his resistance, although he was effectively restricted to his Italian lands.

In the civil war that followed the death of Louis the Pious (840), Lothair laid claim to all the rights originally bestowed upon him by the *Ordinatio imperrii* of 817. Any chance of realizing that claim, however, was effectively ended by his crushing defeat at the battle of Fontenoy (July 25, 841). After much negotiation, the brothers concluded the Treaty of Verdun (August 843), a permanent arrangement whereby Lothair retained the title of emperor (though with no authority over his brothers) and rulership over a middle kingdom stretching from Frisia in the north to Sicily in the south. Lothair's territories included the imperial capitals of AACHEN and ROME. In the period following the Treaty of Verdun, fraternal cooperation and the ideal, at least, of unity were maintained through regular meetings between the now more or less equally ranked monarchs. Although there is no reason to think that Lothair's middle kingdom was doomed to failure, it did suffer heavily from external invasions. From 845 on, the northern part of the realm suffered annual attacks by the Vikings, while the Saracens attacked Italy. Lothair delegated the government of Italy to his eldest son, Louis II, whom he also elevated to the rank of co–emperor (850). His younger sons, Charles and Lothair II, received Provence and Lotharingia, respectively. In 855, Lothair I retired to the monastery of Prüm where he died on September 29.

Bibliography: E. HLAWITSCHKA, *Vom Frankenreich zur Formierung der europäischen Staaten—und Völkergemeinschaft, 840–1046* (Darmstadt 1986) 75–80. P. RICHÉ *The Carolingians, A Family Who Forged Europe* (Philadelphia 1983) 141–196. J. NELSON, ''The Frankish Kingdoms, 814–898: The West,'' *New Cambrige Medieval History 2.* ed. R. MCKITTERICK (Cambridge 1995) 110–l41. J. FRIED ''The Frankish Kingdoms, 817–911: The East and Middle Kingdom,'' *ibid* 142–68.

[D. A. WARNER]

LOTHAIR II, FRANKISH KING

Reigned: 855–869; d. Piacenza, Italy; the second oldest son of Emperor LOTHAIR I, and brother of Louis II and Charles of Provence. When his father's kingdom was divided (855), Lothair II received the northern part, between Frisia and the Jura mountains, which included AACHEN. At the death of his brother Charles, Lothair received half of the latter's realm as well. This kingdom of Lothair subsequently came to be known as Lotharingia. Lothair's reign was marked by continual tension with his uncles, Charles the Bald and Louis the German, who sought, among other things, to take advantage of his marital difficulties. Those difficulties arose from the childless state of his marriage to Theutberga, daughter of Hubert, lay-abbot of St Maurice-in-Valais, and more specifically, from the serious question that the absence of a legitimate heir opened with regard to the royal succession. From 857 until the end of his reign, Lothair sought to annul his

Louis the German and Charles the Bald forming alliance against Lothair. (©Bettmann/CORBIS)

marriage to Theutberga in favor of an earlier, less formal arrangement (*Friedelehe*) with a certain Waldrada, by whom he had a son, Hugh (b. 860). A synod held at Aachen annulled his marriage to Theutberga on the basis of incest, thereby permitting Lothair to marry Waldrada in 862. Lothair' plans almost immediately aroused the opposition of Archbishop HINCMAR OF REIMS, who rejected the annulment as fundamentally inconsistent with Christian morality and with the responsibilities of a Christian king. It also violated canon law which had come to strongly favor legitimate marriage (*muntehe*) over any form of combinage. This dispute is particularly noteworthy because of the involvement of the papacy. Pope NICHOLAS I joined with Hincmar in condemning Lothair's illegal divorce. After a synod held at Metz (863) failed to resolve the matter in an acceptable fashion, Nicholas went so far as to suspend from office the archbishops of Cologne and Trier. In 865, Lothair was forced to return to Theutberga, though this in no way hindered his efforts to proceed with his original plan. Under Nicholas's suc-

cessor, Pope HADRIAN II, Lothair was readmitted to communion, a hopeful sign which was voided soon by his own death. In 867, Lothair had traded territory to his uncle, Louis the German, in return for recognition of his plans for the succession. In spite of this agreement, the deceased king's uncles proceeded to divide his realm between them, without regard for the claims of his natural son or his surviving brother (Louis II). As Lothair's brother had also failed to produce an heir, the end of the middle kingdom was a foregone conclusion.

Bibliography: R. KOTTJE, ''Kirchliches Recht und päpstlicher Autoritätsanspruch. Zu den Auseinandersetzungen ueber die Ehe Lothars II.'' *Aus Kirche und Reiche. Studien zu Theologie, Politik und Recht im Mittelalter* ed. H. MORDEK (Sigmaringen 1983) 97–103. E. HLAWITSCHKA, *Vom Frankenreich zur Formierung der europäischen Staaten-und Völkergemeinschaft, 840–1046* (Darmstadt 1986) 80–81. P. RICHÉ, *The Carolingians: A Family who Forged Europe* tr. M. I. ALLEN (Philadelphia 1993) 177–78.

[D. A. WARNER]

LOTHAIR III, ROMAN EMPEROR

Reigned Aug. 30, 1125, to Dec. 4, 1137; Count of Supplinburg; b. 1075; d. Breitenwang, Tirol; buried at Königslutter, Braunschweig, which he founded. He was crowned king in AACHEN on Sept. 13, 1125. Federick, Duke of Swabia, the nephew of the deceased and childless HENRY V, inherited the imperial property and the hereditary claim to the throne, and, as the Hohenstaufen candidate, remained an enemy of Lothair despite his feudal submission. Since the German princes, led by Adalbert I of Mainz, feared the continuation of a Salian ecclesiastical and territorial policy, they decided in favor of a free election.

Lothair seemed to have been the ideal opponent of the Hohenstaufen. His father had fallen in battle against their grandfather, HENRY IV (1075). Appointed Duke of Saxony by Henry V (1106), the once insignificant count diplomatically took advantage of opportunities and increased his power in the duchy and in the border marches through profitable inheritances and successful war against the Slavs east of the Elbe, as well as against the Salians themselves (Welfesholze, 1115). Lothair won over Henry the Black, Duke of Bavaria, by giving his only child, Gertrude, in marriage to the Duke's son, Henry the Proud. As king, he intervened in the Bohemian controversy in 1126 and suffered a military defeat, but by shrewd diplomacy managed nevertheless to attain his goals. Conrad, the younger Hohenstaufen, took advantage of the moment, had himself appointed as rival king, and thus gained a temporary foothold in imperial Italy. The Hohenstaufen, however, had overestimated their strength, although Lothair's wife Richenza and (St.) BERNARD were unable to arrange a settlement before 1135.

Influenced by Bernard during the schism between Anacletus II (*see* PIERLEONI) and INNOCENT II, Lothair decided (1130) in favor of Innocent, from whom he had twice, but in vain, demanded a revision of the Concordat of WORMS. In 1133 Innocent crowned Lothair emperor at the Lateran, since Anacletus had taken possession of St. Peter's. Lothair's recognition of papal dominion over the estates of MATILDA OF TUSCANY occasioned anti-imperial propaganda to construe his action as a recognition of feudal supremacy of the pope over the emperor. In 1136 Lothair campaigned against Anacletus and his Norman vassal ROGER II. He died while returning from Italy. Such historically far-reaching developments as the GUELF AND GHIBELLINE controversy, the revival of German eastern colonization and the missions to the Slavs, the consolidation of the southern Italian Norman state, the surrender of further sacral functions on the part of the Empire, and the decay of the royal duchies (Lower Lorraine) either began or took shape during his reign.

Bibliography: Sources. *Historia Welforum,* ed. E. KÖNIG (Stuttgart 1938). *Annales Patherbrunnenses,* ed. P. SCHEFFER-BOICHORST (Innsbruck 1870). Literature. H. VOGT, *Das Herzogtum Lothars von Süpplingenburg* (Hildesheim 1959). H. WOLTER, *Lexikon für Theologie und Kirche,* ed. J. HOFER and K. RAHNER (Freiburg 1957–65) 6:1156–57, the birthdate is incorrect. E. WADLE, *Reichsgut und Königsherrschaft unter Lothar III. (1125–1137)* (Berlin 1969). K. HAMPE, *Germany under the Salian and Hohenstaufen Emperors* (Oxford 1973). M. L. CRONE, *Untersuchungen zur Reichskirchenpolitik Lothars III. (1125–1137) zwischen reichskirchlicher Tradition und Reformkurie* (Frankfurt am Main 1982). H. FUHRMANN, *Germany in the High Middle Ages, c. 1050–1200,* tr. T. REUTER (Cambridge 1986). T. GROSS, *Lothar III. und die mathildischen Güter* (Frankfurt am Main 1990).

[H. WOLFRAM]

LOTZE, RUDOLF HERMANN

Physician and philosopher; b. Bautzen, Germany, May 21, 1817; d. Berlin, July 1, 1881. The son of a physician, Lotze studied medicine, psychology, and philosophy at Leipzig under E. H. Weber, G. T. Fechner, and C. H. Weisse (1801–66), receiving his M.D. and Ph.D. in 1838. His dissertation in medicine, *De futurae biologiae principiis philosophicis* (Leipzig 1838), gave indication of a special competence in philosophy. In Leipzig Lotze wrote his first *Metaphysik* (1841), became a lecturer in philosophy, and wrote his first *Logik* (1843). In 1844 he was appointed professor at the University of Göttingen, where he composed his *Medizinische Psychologie oder Physiologie der Seele* (Leipzig 1852). His *Mikrokosmus,* 3 v. (Leipzig 1856–58, 5th ed. 1896–1909) is one of the most important documents in modern German philosophy. In 1881 he was called to Berlin and died shortly after his arrival there.

Lotze had an excellent background in the natural sciences and put his knowledge of inductive and experimental methods to use in the modernization of philosophy. At a time when others were hostile to metaphysics, however, he undertook to combine the inductive method of the exact sciences with metaphysical insights, mainly those in the tradition of German IDEALISM. He acknowledged the existence of mechanistic functions in nature, but regarded these as the means by which the Deity actualizes the final good of the entire universe. He also taught the substantiality of the human soul and its freedom of action. The ego, for him, is not merely a logical subject, as it was for I. KANT; rather it is an active principle. Body and soul he conceived to be in constant reciprocal relationship: the body affects the soul (e.g, in perception and feeling), while the soul acts upon the body (e.g., in acts of free will). In this teaching Lotze was opposed to 19th–century determinism. He held that without freedom, morality would have no foundation.

Lotze's impact on contemporary philosophy is perhaps best expressed in his three notions of being, happening, and value. The characteristic of the external world is being (inductive metaphysics); that of man's perception is happening, which is channeled from the without to the within (physiology of the soul); and that of the inner world is thought, truth, and value (axiology). Greatly influenced by Lotze were C. Stumpf, W. Windelband, A. Wenzl, F. BRENTANO, and, through Brentano, E. HUSSERL.

Bibliography: J. HIRSCHBERGER, *The History of Philosophy,* tr. A. N. FUERST, 2 v. (Milwaukee 1958–59) v.2. F. BARONE, *Enciclopedia filosofica* 3:168–170. W. ZIEGENFUSS, ed., *Philosophen–Lexikon,* 2 v. (Berlin 1949–50) 2:80–87. M. WENTSCHER, *Lotzes Leben und Werke* (Heidelberg 1913). S. HALL, *Die Begründer der modernen Psychologie (Lotze . . .)* (Leipzig 1914).

[C. E. SCHÜTZINGER]

LOUGHLIN, JAMES F.

Pastor, educator, author; b. Auburn, N.Y., May 8, 1851; d. Barbados, West Indies, March 17, 1911. He attended the Urban College of the Propaganda, Rome, and was ordained on April 4, 1874, attaining a doctorate in theology. After incardination into the Archdiocese of Philadelphia, Pa., he served a brief curacy and was then appointed to teach moral theology and Canon Law at St. Charles Seminary, Overbrook, Pa. He founded (1886) Our Lady of the Rosary parish in Philadelphia, became chancellor (1892), and was made a domestic prelate (1899). In 1901 he became rector of the important parish, Nativity of the Blessed Virgin, Philadelphia, where he concentrated on raising the intellectual level of his parishioners. He improved parochial and commercial schools and conducted Catholic reading circles, one of which, the Baronius Club, founded in his memory a scholarship at Trinity College, Washington, D.C. Loughlin was one of the founders and a trustee of the Catholic Summer School of America and was its second president; he established the first diocesan cottage at Cliff Haven and frequently lectured on Church history at the school. In the late nineteenth-century school controversy, he opposed Archbishop John Ireland's FARIBAULT PLAN. Loughlin was prominent in the formation of the National Union of Catholic Young Men's Societies, serving as its president as well as being spiritual director of the Archdiocesan Union of Young Men.

He wrote many articles and essays in Church history, of a popular rather than scholarly nature. He was coeditor of the *American Catholic Quarterly Review,* and for several years he contributed sermons to the Saturday edition of a secular newspaper, the *Philadelphia Ledger.* His articles for the old *Catholic Encyclopedia* dealt principally with the lives of medieval popes, local Philadelphia history, and religious sects and included one on the Protestant confessions of faith.

Bibliography: W. LALLOU, "Monsignor James F. Loughlin, D.D.," *Records of the American Catholic Historical Society of Philadelphia* 25 (1914): 277–284.

[H. J. NOLAN]

LOUGHLIN, JOHN

First bishop of Brooklyn, N.Y., diocese; b. County Down, Northern Ireland, Dec. 20, 1817; d. Brooklyn, N.Y., Dec. 29, 1891. His parents, John, a tenant farmer, and Mary (McNulty) Loughlin, immigrated to the United States around 1830 and settled in Albany, N.Y. Loughlin attended Albany Academy, conducted by the classicist Dr. Peter Bullion, and St. Peter's College, Chambly, Montreal, Canada. In February of 1834 he entered the Nyack Seminary, and in October enrolled as a seminarian-tutor at Mt. St. Mary's College, Emmitsburg, Md. After a year at St. Mary's Seminary, Baltimore, he was ordained by Bishop John Hughes in old St. Patrick's Cathedral, New York, on Oct. 18, 1840. He served as curate at St. John's Parish, Utica, until January of 1841, when he was transferred to St. Patrick's Cathedral, where he became rector in 1844 and vicar-general of the diocese in 1849.

On July 29, 1853, Pius IX erected Long Island as the Diocese of Brooklyn and appointed John Loughlin its ordinary. He was consecrated on October 30 in St. Patrick's Cathedral and installed at St. James, Brooklyn, the moth-

er church of the new diocese, on November 9. Loughlin's pioneer work laid a strong foundation for the future importance of his see. He was under constant pressure from immigration, the unceasing demand for churches, schools, and charitable agencies, and a shortage of priests, religious, and financial resources. Although he planned a cathedral with the architect Patrick KEELY, his parishioner, and laid its cornerstone in 1868, the need for orphanages and hospitals prevented its completion.

Loughlin was the second oldest bishop at the Third Plenary Council of Baltimore (1884) and one of very few who had attended the First and Second Councils in 1852 and 1866 respectively. In 1864, 1873, and again in 1880, he was among the candidates proposed by his fellow suffragans for the archiepiscopal See of New York, but each time he declined the honor.

Bibliography: J. K. SHARP, *Priests and Parishes of the Diocese of Brooklyn, 1820–1944* (New York 1944); *History of the Diocese of Brooklyn, 1853–1953,* 2 v. (New York 1954).

[J. K. SHARP]

LOUIS VI, KING OF FRANCE

Reigned from 1108 to 1137; b. 1081. The son of PHILIP I and Bertha of Frisia, Louis studied at the abbey school of SAINT-DENIS, where he became acquainted with SUGER, the future abbot of Saint-Denis, who became Louis's biographer and chief adviser. His marriage to Lucienne de Rochefort ended in annulment in 1107. In 1115 Louis married Adelaide of Maurienne, who bore him several children, including his successor, Louis VII. Although Louis came to the throne at a time when disputes over elections and investitures remained unsettled, overall, he enacted favorable policies toward ecclesiastical institutions. As he extended royal authority beyond the Ile-de-France, he intervened evenhandedly to settle quarrels between ecclesiastics and lay lords. When necessary, he disciplined clerics who had ignored the law, and he punished lay officials who had committed offenses against the church as well. In 1110 Waldric, bishop of Laon, implicated in the murder of Gerard of Quierzy, was tried before the king and exiled. In 1113 Louis forced Arnaud, abbot of Saint-Pierre-le-Vif to return the lands he had unlawfully taken from a royal vassal. In 1122, when William VI, count of Auvergne expelled Amaury, bishop of Clermont, from his bishopric, Louis and his army drove the count from Clermont. Both a benefactor and reformer of monastic houses, Louis favored established Benedictine monasteries such as Saint-Denis and founded the Benedictine convent at Montmartre. He also provided for the establishment of SAINT-VICTOR, which became the center of several Augustinian houses, and gave land to the Premonstratensian abbey at Dilo. Louis's relationship with the papacy remained generally harmonious, especially when the papacy needed an ally against the emperor. Louis allowed Gelasius II to remain in exile at Cluny until the end of his life. In the papal schism of 1130 Louis sided with Innocent II, who had the support of BERNARD OF CLAIRVAUX and the Cistercians. Innocent II crowned the future Louis VII, and with Louis's support returned to the papal see in Rome. Upon his death, Louis's body was interred at St. Denis.

Bibliography: SUGER, *The Deeds of Louis the Fat*, ed. and tr. R. C. CUSIMANO and J. MOORHEAD (Washington, DC 1992). R. FAWTIER, *The Capetian Kings of France*, tr. L. BUTLER and R. J. ADAM (New York 1960). E. HALLAM, *Capetian France* (London 1980).

[P. D. WATKINS]

LOUIS VII, KING OF FRANCE

Reigned from 1137 to 1180; b. 1120. The second son of LOUIS VI and Adelaide of Maurienne, Louis's education at the cathedral school in Paris prepared him for an ecclesiastical career; however, upon the death of his brother, Philip, in 1131, he became heir to the French throne to which he succeeded in 1137. Following their return from the Second Crusade (1147–1149), Louis procured an annulment for his marriage with Eleanor of Aquitaine on the grounds of consanguinity. He then married Constance of Castile and later Adela of Champagne, who produced a long-awaited male heir, PHILIP II AUGUSTUS, in 1165. In May 1152, Eleanor subsequently married the future HENRY II of England (r. 1154–1189), whose possessions in France and powerful ambition became a source of rivalry and conflict for Louis. His contemporaries, including Odo de Deuil, Stephen of Paris, John of Salisbury, and Walter Map praised Louis VII for his piety and his favorable disposition toward the church. He undertook pilgrimages to SANTIAGO DE COMPOSTELA (1154–55), the Grande Chartreuse (1162–63), and to CANTERBURY (1179). Because of a disputed papal election, Alexander III sought refuge in France in 1162, where he received Louis's welcome. Louis's protection of Thomas BECKET, who had fled to France in 1164 to escape the wrath of Henry II, received widespread approval. Louis asserted his rights over the French church, especially regarding episcopal elections in his realm and control over royal churches. To provide continual support for his royal policies, elections to royal bishoprics often went to members of the king's own household or to families loyal to Capetian interests. As a benefactor to the TEMPLARS, Louis gave them the land for their commandery at Savigny, along with sizable rents and privileges. He also made generous grants to smaller monastic houses

Louis VII.

and created several small perpetual chapels. A patron of the CISTERCIAN order, Louis supported CLAIRVAUX through an annual gift, he founded La Bénisson-Dieu in the 1140s, and he established the major Cistercian abbey at Barbeaux, where he was interred in a magnificent tomb.

Bibliography: ODO OF DEUIL, *De prefectione Ludovici VII in Orientem*, ed. and tr. V. R. BERRY (New York 1948). R. FAWTIER, *The Capetian Kings of France*, tr. L. BUTLER and R. J. ADAM (New York 1960). E. HALLAM, *Capetian France* (London 1980).

[P. D. WATKINS]

LOUIS IX, ST. KING OF FRANCE

Reigned Nov. 29, 1226, to Aug. 25, 1270; son of Louis VIII and Blanche of Castile; b. Poissy, April 25, 1214; d. Tunis. He married Marguerite of Provence in May 1234; they had ten children. Until her death in 1252, his mother dominated the King and the government, quickly quelling the baronial opposition during his minority and ruling alone during his absence on his first CRUSADE. Louis's personal government between 1254 and 1270 gave him a deserved reputation for promoting peace and doing right. He became a model to his successors. His sense of duty made him punctilious in the asser-

Frontispiece to a "moralized" Bible, showing Queen Blanche of Castile and King Louis IX enthroned in top quadrants and the "author" (a monk) and scribe of the book in lower quadrants, probably written and illuminated for King Louis in Paris, France, c. 1230.

tion of his rights, and his piety and benevolence were a source of strength and not of weakness to the monarchy.

The Crusades. Louis is best known for his crusades, on the first of which he was accompanied by the Sire de Joinville, who has left a memoir of those years, the earliest intimate picture of a French king. Louis took the cross during an illness in 1244 and carefully prepared his campaign. He tried to reconcile INNOCENT IV and FREDERICK II, excommunicated in 1245, in order to help the crusade, but Innocent refused. Louis left in August 1248. The difficulties of the Hohenstaufen Emperor in Italy had a profound influence on the whole episode. After wintering in Cyprus, the crusaders surprised the city of Damietta in June 1249 and awaited there the arrival of further troops. Louis then advanced on Cairo, but the army, weakened by dysentery, was cut off from Damietta when the Egyptian fleet regained control of the Nile. The crusaders were surrounded and captured at Mansura, April 6, 1250. A palace revolution made Louis's situation very dangerous, but he finally negotiated the release of his whole army in return for the surrender of Damietta and the payment of

a ransom. He went to Acre to await the completion of the treaty and remained in Syria four years. He encouraged the Christians there by building elaborate fortifications, by attempting to exploit the rivalries of Cairo and Damascus, by hoping to convert the Mongols, and by sending for more men and money from the West. His brothers returned to France for this purpose, but they were unable to do much. Finally Louis himself recognized that he, unaided, could achieve nothing more; so he returned to France, arriving in July of 1254.

France had remained relatively tranquil, in spite of the Pastoureaux movement. However, the ambitions of King Henry III to recover his father's lost French possessions; involved Louis in difficult diplomatic negotiations in Spain, Italy, Germany, and Flanders, while his Hohenstaufen alliance was no help to him. He first arbitrated in the Flemish dispute, but Henry III did not agree to terms of peace until his brother Richard became—nominally—king of Germany in 1257. By the treaty of Paris (1259) Henry renounced his claims to the lost provinces, did homage for Gascony, secured the conditional reversion of disputed lands, and obtained a subsidy from Louis. The treaty was unpopular in France and the cause of much later discord. Louis thought that it would promote family concord (the two kings had married sisters); actually it put an end to the immediate danger of English hostility. Louis continued to support Henry III, this time by his arbitration of 1264 against the English barons. He arranged a similar treaty with James I of Aragon at Corbeil (1258), renouncing his claim to the Spanish March in return for James's homage for his French fiefs.

During the 1260s, Louis became increasingly disturbed by Moslem advances in Syria and announced his intention to lead a second crusade in 1267. By the time the crusaders were ready, Louis's brother, Charles of Anjou, had become sole master of Italy, and there was a papal interregnum. Charles is therefore held responsible for the diversion of Louis's crusade to Tunis, to attack Charles' enemy, the emir of Tunis, as a preliminary maneuver. The army was depleted by disease within a month of landing, and Louis himself died. The crusaders promptly returned to France, carrying Louis's bones.

Domestic Policy. Despite the personal example Louis set by his devotion to the crusades, it is arguable that a greater claim to respect was his interpretation of his responsibilities as king, in the light of his faith. After the violence of the two previous reigns, Louis brought peace and promised justice. The greatest troubles were those of the south, where the problem of heresy continued to cause social unrest. Louis's domains in the south were confined to the *senéchausées* of Carcassonne and Beaucaire, but his brother Alphonse became count of Toulouse in 1249, and the two administrations, if not identical, provided similar advantages for each area. Louis had ordered *enquêtes* into abuses in the new provinces in 1247, and on his return from crusade he received numerous petitions for justice. In the light of these, he drew up new regulations for his officials that became the first of a series of reforming *ordonnances,* designed to improve administration, eradicate corruption, and improve the law of his dominions. The latter part of Louis's reign is remarkable for a growing interest in legal affairs. Several attempts were made to write down customary law, and cases coming before the king's court or Parlement were formally recorded after 1254. Louis tried to modify legal procedure by replacing trial by battle with a form of examination of witnesses, a procedure that encouraged the use of written records in the courts. He commissioned several handbooks of political wisdom and composed for his successor his own maxims, the *enseignements.*

His sense of responsibility made him keen to learn from his clergy, but he did not automatically support his bishops, claiming that he had to make his own decisions. Notably, in the important case of Frederick II, Louis refused to recognize Innocent IV's sentence of deposition. Louis was always respectful of the papacy, but he defended royal interests against the popes during episcopal vacancies and protested against papal expectative PROVISIONS. Although his ''PRAGMATIC SANCTION'' is not now considered genuine, Louis did in fact defend what he considered the legitimate interests of the Gallican Church. From his youth he showed a deep and sincere piety. He built the Sainte Chapelle in Paris as a shrine for the crown of thorns; he was a friend and patron of the CISTERCIANS and of the new FRANCISCAN and DOMINICAN orders, from which he selected his confessors; he founded hospitals and patronized learning; he was notable for his humility and his personal examples of Christian service. Many miracles of healing were performed at his tomb at SAINT-DENIS, and after several inquiries, he was canonized in 1297.

Feast: Aug. 25.

Bibliography: J. DE JOINVILLE, *The History of St. Louis,* ed. N. DE WAILLY, tr. J. EVANS (New York 1938). C. PETIT-DUTAILLIS, *The Feudal Monarchy in France and England from the Tenth to the Thirteenth Century,* tr. E. D. HUNT (London 1936). L. BUISSON, *König Ludwig IX, der Heilige, und das Recht* (Freiburg 1954). J. R. STRAYER, ''The Crusades of Louis IX,'' in *A History of the Crusades,* ed. K. M. SETTON (Philadelphia 1955) v. 2. D. O'CONNELL, *The instructions of St Louis: A Critical Text* (Chapel Hill, NC 1979). W.C. JORDAN, *Louis IX and the Challenge of the Crusade: a Study in Rulership* (Princeton, NJ 1979). L. CAROLUS-BARRE, *Le proces de canonisation de Saint Louis (1272-1297): essai de reconstitution* (Rome 1994). J. LE GOFF, *Saint Louis* (Paris 1996). D. H. WEISS *Art and Crusade in the age of St. Louis* (Cambridge and New York 1998).

[D. J. A. MATTHEW]

St. Louis IX.

LOUIS XIV, KING OF FRANCE

Called the Great, or *le Roi Soleil;* b. Saint-Germainen-Laye, Sept. 16, 1638; d. Versailles, Sept. 1, 1715. His reign of 73 years was the longest in European history and marked the political and cultural hegemony of France. As the son of Louis XIII and Anne of Austria, he acceded to the throne at the age of five; he first reigned under the regency of his mother, although real power was exercised by the Italian born protégé of Richelieu, Cardinal Jules MAZARIN. While Louis was still a minor, the civil war known as the Fronde (1648–53) broke out, first manifesting itself as a revolt of the Paris Parlement and subsequently as an uprising of the princes against the Court. This is the last feudal revolt in French history.

Mazarin's Tutelage. At an age when he should have been engaged in formal schooling, Louis was, instead, enmeshed in the tortuous and dangerous maneuvers of Mazarin. A lifelong suspicion and a conviction that all were bent upon lessening his authority are thought to have had their origin in this environment. His education was rudimentary. He became adept at horseback riding, the dance, and the hunt, but measured by even the more modest Renaissance standards he was an ignoramus. He knew no Greek, very little Latin, and history and mathematics were virtually unknown to him. In later life he as-

Louis XIV, King of France.

tounded foreigners with his knowledge of geography, but this he learned from practical experience, not schoolbooks. Louis's religious education was also neglected. The monarch who would be thrust into the midst of the thorniest theological controversies was taught nothing beyond the necessity for pious works and decorous behavior at religious observances. Although his formal, spiritual education was entrusted to Charles Paulin, SJ, more important in Louis's formation was his mother, who frequently attended two Masses a day and spent untold hours at the *prie-dieu*, but disdained formal theology. To her influence are traced the seeming pangs of conscience that followed his youthful amorous adventures. Contemporary witnesses relate his frequent but generally futile efforts to part from his mistresses. Later, FÉNELON characterized Louis's religion as superstitious, devout, and in the Spanish style.

When Mazarin died in 1661, Louis astounded the courtiers by announcing promptly and emphatically that ministerial rule was at an end and that he was taking charge of all affairs of government. His decision was widely acclaimed. For almost four decades, and in violation of the essence of monarchy, France had been ruled by ministers, one of whom had not even been French-born. It was an auspicious moment in the history of France. For the first time in a century and a half, thanks

largely to Richelieu, the monarchy could feel secure against its internal and external foes: the feudal nobility, Huguenots, and Hapsburgs. After imprisoning Nicolas Fouquet, the immensely wealthy superintendent of finances who had been the prime candidate to succeed Mazarin, the 23-year-old Louis turned to the able Jean Baptiste Colbert, to mastermind a program of reform unequaled in the history of the old regime. Both envisaged a France rid of all clumsy feudal survivals, unified and prosperous, united by a fine network of roads and canals, ruled according to the Cartesian ideals of order and method. But the opposition of French society to such a program was too powerful. Louis gradually lost enthusiasm for reform and turned to more bellicose means of ensuring French greatness. Colbert was thrust into the background, as the minister of war; Louvois, emerged as Louis's principal counselor.

Pursuit of Glory. Louis XIV's overriding passion was the pursuit of glory. "The love of glory goes beyond all others in my soul," he once said. He saw himself as Augustus, Constantine, and Justinian, all at the same time. In the internal administration of France, in his patronage of the arts and sciences, and in other ways, this passion had admirable results. In foreign policy, however, it led only to disaster. He fought four wars, all motivated primarily by personal and dynastic considerations. He envisioned himself the acknowledged leader of Christendom, the true successor of Charlemagne. From the start he converted this idea into a principle of international law by inflicting gratuitous humiliations upon the pope, the emperor, and the king of Spain. He also made grandiose plans for a new crusade to destroy the Ottoman power.

Military Ambitions. Louis's principal interest centered in the Spanish Netherlands. Temporarily abandoning his efforts to reestablish his wife's right to the Spanish throne, he fell back on a local right of inheritance, the *droit de dévolution,* which made Maria Theresa the heiress of the Belgian provinces. This provoked the War of Devolution (1667–68) with Spain. Although his armies were successful, Louis was forced to conclude peace and surrender his spoils because of the unexpected anti-French Triple Alliance, formed by Holland, England, and Sweden in 1668. Blaming John de Witt, pensioner of Holland, and further angered by the refuge given in Holland to French political pamphleteers, he declared war on the Dutch in 1672, after extensive military and diplomatic preparations that included the secret Treaty of Dover with England in 1670. After six years of costly war, the Treaties of Nimwegen (1678–79) brought terms of peace in which Spain lost Franche-Comté and lands in the Spanish Netherlands to Louis. At the height of his power, he established the Chambers of Reunion

(1680–83), which exploited the loose terminology of preceding peace treaties so as to acquire additional land along the north and northeast frontiers.

After a short breathing spell, Europe was plunged into the War of the League of Augsburg (1688–97), when Louis laid claim to the Palatinate after the death, without an heir, of the Elector Charles, whose sister was the wife of Louis's brother. Louis committed a major strategic mistake by sending his armies into the Palatinate, thus allowing William of Orange to slip across the channel and receive the English crown, as the exiled James II became the unhappy guest of the French. Years of combat finally ended with the inconclusive Treaty of Ryswick in 1697.

On Nov. 1, 1700, Charles II of Spain died, after making a last-minute will in favor of Louis's grandson, Philip of Anjou, hoping desperately that this move would keep his far-flung empire intact. Instead, the Grand Alliance was renewed and extended, and in the warfare that followed, Louis XIV lost every major battle (Blenheim, 1704; Ramillies, 1706; Malplaquet, 1709). In the Treaty of Utrecht, April 11, 1713, which terminated the war, Louis won recognition for his grandson as King of Spain, but lost Newfoundland, Nova Scotia (Arcadia), and the Hudson Bay territory to England. Louis survived the Treaty of Utrecht by two melancholy years. The old monarch witnessed the death of four members of his family in the direct male line, so that only a frail great-grandson remained as his successor. On his deathbed he admitted to him, "I have loved war too much. Do not imitate me in that nor in the great expenses that I have incurred." His passing caused no great sorrow to an exhausted France.

Gallicanism. Louis's reign is conspicuous for struggles with the papacy over the limitations of ecclesiastical power in France and French power in Rome. Immediately upon his assumption of the government, difficulties arose out of the affair of the Corsican Guard, the Sorbonne thesis defending papal infallibility, and Colbert's efforts to increase the age for final religious vows. But the major quarrel came in the 1670s with the affair of the *régale,* the king's right to dispose of the revenues and benefices of vacant bishoprics. This ancient royal prerogative had never been disputed in the larger part of France. When a few provinces in the south of France claimed exemptions, earlier kings at least tacitly recognized them. Louis, however, intent on uniformity, extended these regalian rights in 1673 to the hitherto exempted provinces. Only two bishops opposed the move, François Étienne CAULET of Pamiers and Nicolas Pavillon of Alet, men of high moral integrity. The latter soon died, leaving the elderly Caulet to face the King's ire. Caulet obtained support in 1678 from Innocent XI, newly elevated to the papal

throne and conscious of the dignity of Rome and past humiliations from Louis XIV. The Pope dispatched a succession of protests to the French monarch, culminating in 1679 with a clear threat of excommunication. This was countered by a declaration of the Assembly of the Clergy in 1680 that they were "bound to His Majesty by ties that nothing can break." Caulet's diocese remained in a virtual state of siege. When Louis convoked the clergy in 1682, there was promulgated the famous DECLARATION OF THE FRENCH CLERGY that, for the rest of the decade, strained relations between Versailles and the Vatican. Only with the death of Innocent XI in 1689 did a compromise become possible. Innocent XII in 1692 received a message from Louis that the "things ordained by my edict of 1682 . . . should not be observed." These Gallican Articles remained legally in force until the end of the old regime, but were a dead letter until revived by Napoleon.

The Huguenots. Louis XIV's relations with the Huguenots center upon his revocation of the Edict of Nantes, by which his grandfather, Henry IV, had granted them religious toleration on April 15, 1598. What motivated Louis's action? The Huguenots were suffering a steady attrition at the start of his reign so that, politically, they were no longer a menace. This had been proved during the Fronde, when the French Protestants remained entirely loyal to the crown. Certainly, the revocation was not the result of any deep religious feeling on the part of the King. The answer probably lies in Louis's conviction that France had to be consolidated. In the same manner that he strove to unify his state politically, economically, and culturally, he had to unify it religiously. The implied challenge of a dissident minority sect could not be tolerated. In justice to Louis XIV it should be acknowledged that the idea of tolerating a religious minority was a strange and unwelcome one in all Europe, and France was no exception. From the start of his reign, Louis was subjected to heavy pressures to solve the Protestant question. As early as 1655, the Assembly of the Clergy demanded a strict interpretation of the Edict of NANTES, meaning that Protestants should be allowed no right not specifically guaranteed. As long as Colbert remained in the ascendency, no great hardships were imposed on the Huguenots. Once he was replaced by Louvois, who was not concerned about the economic impact of the persecution, Louis came under the influence of the zealous Madame de Maintenon, although historical research has absolved her of responsibility for the revocation as it was finally effected. More important were Louis's troubles with Innocent XI. He came perilously close in 1682 to going the way of Henry VIII of England, and it is contended that this anti-Huguenot move was motivated by a desire to prove his orthodoxy to the Catholic world.

In 1682, 68 French prelates issued the *Avertissement Pastoral,* which was, in effect, a last warning, given with Louis's approval, to abandon Calvinism. Immediately, a large number of Protestant churches were destroyed on one pretext or another, but always under the orders of the courts of law. The following year brought a short respite because of the undeclared war that Louis fought with Spain and the Emperor. By the summer of 1684, Madame de Maintenon was writing that "the King has determined to work for the complete conversion of the heretics." Officially, Louis to the end remained a staunch opponent of the use of force. It was Foucault, the obscure intendant of Béarn, who first, and without permission from Versailles, made extensive use of the *dragonnades* to achieve mass conversions, at least on paper. Neighboring intendants took up his example, and by the end of the summer Chancellor Le Tellier could show the King that by simple arithmetic no significant number of Huguenots was left in France. On this basis the King signed the revocation on Oct. 18, 1685, forbidding the exercise of the reformed religion in France. Despite the prohibition of emigration, about 250,000 Huguenots left France, causing serious economic repercussions. One significant consequence of the emigration was the growth of anti-French feeling in many countries of Europe, notably England, Holland, and certain German states, with the daily arrival of Huguenot refugees.

Jansenist Question. The problem of Jansenism during the reign of Louis XIV was no older than the monarch himself. Cornelius Jansen died the year Louis was born, and some of the principal elements of the controversy unfolded while the prince was still a child. The AUGUSTINUS appeared in Paris in 1641 and was condemned by Urban VIII in the bull *In eminenti* in 1642, the same year in which Antoine ARNAULD's *De la Fréquente Communion* attacked what was universally recognized as Jesuit teaching. For the next two decades, Louis was exposed to the confusing and at times meaningless disputes made more tragic by the great goodwill and virtue of the protagonists of both sides. Louis's attitude at this time reflected the view of Cardinal Mazarin, who saw in the Jansenist movement the same elements that opposed him in the Fronde. When Louis assumed personal rule in 1661, he simply intensified Mazarin's policy. As in the case of the *régale,* the furor which the opposition aroused seemed disproportionate to the numbers involved. By the mid-1660s only four bishops, including Caulet of Pamiers and Pavillon of Alet, and a handful of nuns and theologians at PORT-ROYAL refused to sign the formulary against Jansenist tenets. To conciliate both sides, Clement IX, weary from the conflict, drew up a compromise statement that even the four bishops and Antoine Arnauld himself could in conscience sign, thus initiating the Clementine Peace of 1669.

The peace of 30 years terminated with the emergence of the rash and intemperate Pasquier QUESNEL. His widely read *Réflexions morales sur le Nouveau Testament,* restating virtually the whole of Jansenist theology, occasioned an intense battle of pamphlets. Louis XIV saw in revived Jansenism a challenge to his own political authority, since it merged with a movement of growing general criticism aimed at the King. Clement XI was asked by Louis XIV to pronounce formal condemnations, which appeared in the dogmatic constitutions *Vineam Domini Sabaoth* of July 16, 1705, and most notably in the fateful *Unigenitus* of Sept. 8, 1713, which censured 101 verbatim propositions of Quesnel. When the nuns of Port-Royal repeated their earlier intransigence, Louis in 1710 ordered the demolition of their ancient buildings and their dispersion. At Louis XIV's death, 2,000 people were held in jail on charges of Jansenism.

See Also: GALLICANISM; JANSENISM.

Bibliography: P. R. DOOLIN, *The Fronde* (Cambridge, Mass. 1935). D. OGG, *Louis XIV* (London 1933). J. ORCIBAL, *Louis XIV contre Innocent XI* (Paris 1949); *Louis XIV et les Protestants* (Paris 1951). C. GÉRIN, *Louis XIV et le Saint-Siège,* 2 v. (Paris 1894). L. O'BRIEN, *Innocent XI and the Revocation of The Edict of Nantes* (Berkeley 1930). P. GAXOTTE, *La France de Louis XIV* (Paris 1946). W. C. SCOVILLE, *The Persecution of the Huguenots and French Economic Development, 1680–1720* (Berkeley 1960).

[L. L. BERNARD]

LOUIS XV, KING OF FRANCE

Reigned 1715 to 1774; b. Versailles, Feb. 15, 1710; d. Versailles, May 10, 1774. Louis XIV's will left him under the care of Marshall Villeroi and Bishop André FLEURY, but the Duke of Orleans assumed the regency. In 1721 Louis fell seriously ill amid rumors that the regent, and heir-apparent, had poisoned him. He recovered and was crowned in 1722 and declared of age in 1723. In 1722 the four-year-old Spanish infanta came to Versailles as the betrothed of the king, but after the death of the Duke of Orleans in 1723, the new regent, the Duke of Bourbon, sent her back to Spain, needlessly angering Philip V and his queen, Elizabeth Farnese. Louis then married Maria Leszczynska, daughter of the deposed king of Poland. France enjoyed peace and prosperity during the administration of Cardinal Fleury (1726–43), thanks to whom Jansenist opposition to the papal bull UNIGENITUS was silenced in 1730. During the War of the Austrian Succession (1740–48) Louis went to the front but fell ill in Metz. On his recovery he was called *le bien-aimé,* but his decline in popularity dates from the Treaty of Aix-la-Chapelle in 1748.

Mistresses had a fair influence in his reign after 1745. The Marquise de Pompadour favored the alliance with Austria before the Seven Years War. Difficulties between the king and Parlement and between Parlement and the Church were not resolved, nor did Louis take any action against the criticism of the *philosophes*. Du-Barry succeeded Pompadour in 1764 and intrigued against the prime minister, E. F. de Choiseul. The Jesuits were expelled in 1764 and suppressed in 1773. Finances were not repaired, and France lost prestige abroad. Louis died with the Sacraments, repentant of his faults, as his daughter, LOUISE OF FRANCE, had prayed.

Bibliography: P. GAXOTTE, *Louis the Fifteenth and His Times* (Philadelphia 1934). P. MURET, *La Prépondérance anglaise, 1715–1763* (3d ed. Paris 1949). G. P. GOOCH, *Louis XV: The Monarchy in Decline* (New York 1956).

[W. E. LANGLEY]

LOUIS D' ALEMAN, BL.

Cardinal archbishop; b. Arbent-en-Bugey, *c.* 1390; d. Salonne, near Arles, France, Sept. 17, 1450. Educated in theology and Canon Law, he rose rapidly in the Church. Pope MARTIN V attached him to his person and entrusted him with difficult assignments at the Council of Siena. Louis later took a leading role at the Council of Basel, nominating Amadeus VIII of Savoy as antipope Felix V (1439). For this he was excommunicated by EUGENE IV. After the death of the pope, Felix resigned in favor of the newly elected NICHOLAS V, who forgave all connected with the schism. Louis recanted and was restored to his dignities. He died the following year with a reputation for sanctity. He was proclaimed blessed by Pope CLEMENT VII in 1527.

Feast: Sept. 16 (formerly 17).

Bibliography: *Acta Sanctorum* Sept. 5:436–462. *Gallia Christiana* (Paris 1715–85) 3:787–830, 1312–79. G. PÉROUSE, *Le Cardinal Louis Aleman, président du concile de Bâle et la fin du grand schisme* (Paris 1904). A. BUTLER, *The Lives of the Saints,* ed. H. THURSTON and D. ATTWATER, 4 v. (New York 1956) 3:573–575. J. GILL, *The Council of Florence* (Cambridge, England 1959) 67–71, 310–317. J. WODKA, *Lexikon für Theologie und Kirche,* ed. J. HOFER and K. RAHNER, 10 v. (2d, new ed. Freiburg 1957–65) 1:302–303.

[D. S. BUCZEK]

LOUIS OF BESSE

Capuchin pioneer of the social apostolate; b. Besse-sur-Issole, France, Oct. 17, 1831; d. San Remo, Italy, Oct. 8, 1910. Before entering the Capuchins (1851) as alumnus of the Paris province, he was called Alphons Eliseus Chaix. After his ordination (1858) he dedicated himself

Louis XV, King of France. (Archive Photos)

to the service of the working people. In order to foster their cause and protect their interest he instituted societies and popular banks and founded also the periodical *Union économique.* He followed as an ideal the Bl. BERNARDINO OF FELTRE, concerning whose life and social activities he wrote two volumes: *Le B. Bernardin de Feltre* (Tours 1902). At the same time he was interested also in spirituality. In this field he wrote, among other works: *Éclaircissement sur les oeuvres mystiques de S. Jean de la Croix* (Paris 1893), which was translated into English under the title *Light on Mount Carmel* (London 1926); *La Science de la prière* (Paris 1903). The persecution of the religious orders (1903) forced him into exile.

Bibliography: HILAIRE DE BARENTON, *Le P. Ludovic de Besse,* 2 v. (v.1, Paris 1913; v.2, Arras 1935). *Lexicon Capuccinum* (Rome 1951) 994.

[G. GÁL]

LOUIS OF CASORIA, VEN.

Religious founder; b. Casoria (Napoli), Italy, March 11, 1814; d. Posillipo, near Naples, March 30, 1885. After joining the Franciscans (Alcantarines) in 1832, Arcangelo Palmentieri took the name Louis. As a priest he taught physics, mathematics, and philosophy until 1837 when the scope of his apostolic labors broadened. In the following years he established an association for clerical and lay intellectuals to promote a Catholic cultural revival and started the periodical *Carità*. He also opened a hospital for priests, an institute to house street urchins and another in Assisi for blind, deaf, and mute children, a home for elderly fishermen in Posillipo, and many other centers for charitable assistance and Catholic activities throughout the peninsula.

In Florence, he fostered the building of the first church in Italy dedicated to the Sacred Heart. From 1858 he became much interested in missions and went to Egypt for a time. Pius IX and Leo XIII, who both esteemed him highly, entrusted him with diplomatic tasks. To carry on his apostolate, he founded the Brothers of Charity at Naples in 1859; they were called *Frati Bigi* because of their gray attire. Originally the members were laymen without vows, but later the founder admitted priests as well as laymen to help educate poor children. The congregation, approved in 1896 by the Holy See, had 63 members in 1963. Louis of Casoria also founded the Gray Sisters of St. Elizabeth (1862). The decree introducing his beatification cause was issued in 1907.

Bibliography: A. CAPECELATRO, *Vita del ven. p. L. da Casoria* (Naples 1887). L. LE MONNIER, *Vie du père L. de Casoria* (Paris 1892). L. FABIANI, *Vita del ven. p. L. da Casoria* (Naples 1931).

[F. G. SOTTOCORNOLA]

LOUIS OF GRANADA

Dominican spiritual writer; b. Louis de Sarriá, Granada, Spain, 1504; d. Lisbon, Dec. 31, 1588. The death of his father in 1509 left Louis and his mother in such poverty that they had to beg food at the Dominican priory of the Holy Cross. On June 15, 1524, Louis received the Dominican habit at the priory of the Holy Cross and after his year of novitiate he spent the next four years at the same priory, studying philosophy and theology. In 1529 he was sent for advanced study to the college of St. Gregory at Valladolid. Here he changed his name to Louis of Granada. During his stay at Valladolid he was exposed to three influences: Thomistic SCHOLASTICISM, Christian HUMANISM as expounded by Francisco de VITORIA, and zeal for the apostolate of preaching as exemplified by SAVONAROLA. Louis preferred to be a preacher rather than a professor. When he was on the point of being sent to the Americas as a missionary, there was a change of plan, and his provincial assigned him to restore the abandoned Dominican priory at Escalaceli, near Córdoba.

Louis soon became renowned as a preacher in the area of Córdoba and in 1538 he was selected as the Lenten preacher at the cathedral. In 1539 the general chapter of the Dominican Order invited him to a professorship at Valladolid, but Louis declined. Gradually he lost interest in academic life and speculative theology and was drawn more to preaching and writing.

Some time after 1547 Louis became prior at Badajoz and began to preach in neighboring Portugal. The prince cardinal, son of Don Manuel I of Portugal, obtained him as confessor and chaplain in 1551 and Louis soon became confessor to Queen Catherine of Portugal, sister of Charles V. During this period he began to write in earnest, and between 1554 and 1559 he published 12 books. In April of 1556 he was elected provincial of Portugal. Later he was offered the archbishopric of Braga, which carried with it the title of primate of Portugal, but he refused the honor and arranged that it be given to Bartholomew de los Mártires. In 1559, through the efforts of Melchior CANO, books by Louis and his former professor, Carranza, later archbishop of Toledo, were placed on the Index. The books were subsequently approved by Pius IV and in 1562 the chapter of the Dominican Order conferred on Louis the title of master of sacred theology. In his later years, afflicted with failing health and partial blindness, Louis was unwillingly involved in court intrigues in Lisbon. He settled the dispute between Don Sebastian and Queen Catherine in 1568. Shortly thereafter, his book on prayer was again brought before the Spanish Inquisition, but for a second time Louis was exonerated. Queen Catherine died in 1568, and Don Sebastian was killed in battle that same year.

Although the aged cardinal, who had been Louis' penitent, was the successor to the Portuguese throne, the nobility demanded that he abdicate or obtain permission to marry and thus provide a successor. Three pretenders claimed the throne: Catherine of Braganza; Anthony, the natural son of the Infante Louis; and Philip II of Spain. As soon as the cardinal died, Anthony claimed the throne and Philip II sent the duke of Alba to conquer Portugal. A false papal brief was sent to Louis, appointing him vicar provincial, and this action resulted in placing him in disfavor with Philip II. The king pardoned him, however, when he learned of the fraudulence of the document. Another source of distress for Louis was a Dominican nun of Lisbon, Sor Maria de la Visitación, who claimed to have received the stigmata on March 7, 1584. Her statement was accepted by the Inquisition, the master general of the Dominican Order, and even by Gregory XIII. Louis was told to write her biography, which he compiled from documents provided him by the nun and her confessor. But when in 1588 it was discovered that the case involved fraud or delusion, the scandal was the occasion of Louis's last sermon, in which he spoke upon the theme of sinners in public life.

Louis has enjoyed fame as a spiritual writer and especially for his doctrine on the practice of prayer. He was one of the first ascetical writers to formulate a method of prayer for the laity. He used as his sources Sacred Scripture, the Fathers of the Church, Thomistic theology, St. Catherine of Siena, Savonarola, Bautista de Crema, and the spiritual writers of the Rhineland, especially Tauler. Granada's doctrine was primarily Christocentric, and his spiritual methods were seven: the practice of prayer, cultivation of virtue, contempt for the world, contemplation of God in nature, the practice of mortification, obedience to the Commandments and use of the Sacraments, and imitation of the saints. Granada emphasized throughout his writings that all Christians are called to become Christlike and to strive for perfection, and on this point he was condemned by Melchior Cano and the Inquisition. His works are noted for their literary quality. They have been translated into many languages and can be found in every land. The saints who were influenced by his teaching include Charles Borromeo, Francis de Sales, Alphonsus Liguori, Rose of Lima, Teresa of Avila, Louise de Marillac, and Vincent de Paul.

The most important and most widely diffused works of Louis of Granada are *Libro de la oración y meditación* (1544; definitive text, 1566); *Guía de pecadores* (1567); *Memorial de la vida cristiana* (1565); *Adiciones al memorial* (1574); *Introducción del símbolo de la fe* (1583).

Bibliography: E. A. PEERS, *Studies of the Spanish Mystics,* 2 v. (New York 1927–30) 1:31–76. L. DE GRANADA, *Summa of the Christian Life,* tr. J. AUMANN, 3 v. (St. Louis 1954–58) 1:xvii–xxxvii. R. L. OECHSLIN, *Louis of Granada* (St. Louis 1962). A. HUERGA, ''Ascetical Methods of Louis of Granada,'' *Cross and Crown* 3 (1951): 72–91.

[J. AUMANN]

LOUISE DE MARILLAC, ST.

Cofounder of the Daughters of Charity; b. probably at Ferrières-en-Brie, near Meaux, France, Aug. 12, 1591; d. Paris, March 15, 1660. Although she was a member of the powerful de Marillac family and well educated, she led an unhappy childhood as an introspective, melancholy girl of poor health. She was married to Antoine Le Gras on Feb. 5, 1613; in October of the same year, she gave birth to her only child, Michel, who was to cause her much heartache. She was widowed on Dec. 21, 1625. At some earlier time she had come under the influence of St. VINCENT DE PAUL, who was her spiritual director. By 1629 her interior life was firmly established, and Vincent started her in exterior work by sending her to make an inspection tour of the Confraternities of Charity that he had established in the provinces. To better care for the poor, Louise assembled a few country girls in her own home in Paris in 1633, where she trained them in piety and in the service of the poor. Thus began the Daughters of Charity. Louise devoted the rest of her life to the formation of the Daughters of Charity and to the supervision of the works entrusted to her by Vincent: the care of foundlings, galley slaves, aged persons, poor children, and the insane, as well as other charitable activities. Her body now rests under an altar in the motherhouse of the Daughters of Charity, Paris. Having been beatified on May 9, 1920, she was canonized on March 11, 1934, and on Feb. 10, 1960, was named patron of all those who devote themselves to Christian social work.

Feast: March 15.

Bibliography: *Letters of St. Louise de Marillac,* tr. H. M. LAW (Emmitsburg, Md. 1972). *Vincent de Paul and Louise de Marillac: Rules, Conferences, and Writings,* ed. F. RYAN and J. E. RYBOLT (New York 1995). A. RICHOMME, *Sainte Louise de Marillac* (Paris 1961). J. CALVET, *Louise de Marillac: A Portrait,* tr. G. F. PULLEN (New York 1959). M. D. POINSENET, *De l'anxiété à la sainteté: Louise de Marillac* (Paris 1958). M. FLINTON, *Sainte Louise de Marillac: L'Aspect social de son oeuvre,* (Tournai 1957) tr. by Flinton as *Louise de Marillac: Social Aspects of Her Work* (New Rochelle, N.Y. 1992), bibliography. P. COSTE, *Life and Works of St. Vincent de Paul,* tr. J. LEONARD, 3 v. (Westminster, Md. 1952). E. CHARPY, *Petite vie de Louise de Marillac* (Paris 1991); *Spiritualité de Louise de Marillac* (Paris 1995). L. SULLIVAN, *The Core Values of Vincentian education* (Niagara University, N.Y. 1994). K. B. LAFLEUR, *Louise de Marillac* (Hyde Park, NY 1996).

[M. A. ROCHE]

LOUISE OF FRANCE (THÉRÈSE DE ST. AUGUSTIN), VEN.

Daughter of Louis XV of France and Maria Leszczynska; b. Versailles, July 15, 1737; d. St. Denis, Dec. 23, 1787. She was educated at the Convent of FONTEVRAULT as a child, and at 14 came to court where she led a pious life. In 1770, after the death of her mother, she entered the Carmelite Convent of Saint-Denis. As novice mistress and prioress, she devoted herself to penances to bring about the conversion of her father; she was noted for her devotion to the observance of the rule and to the Church. The cause of her beatification was introduced in 1873. Her Eucharistic Meditations and her spiritual testaments for her Carmelite daughters were published after her death, and her letters were published by M. Faucon in 1878.

Bibliography: C. A. GEOFFROY DE GRANDMAISON, *Madame Louise de France* (2d ed. Paris 1925). J. LENFANT, *Chez Madame Louise de France* (Paris 1936). A. HOFMEISTER, *Lexikon für Theologie und Kirche* (Freiburg 1930–38) 6:707. G. MESTERS, *Lexikon für Theologie und Kirche* (Freiburg 1957–65) 6:1202.

[W. E. LANGLEY]

LOUISE OF SAVOY, BL.

Widow, Poor Clare; b. Dec. 28, 1462; d. Orbe, Switzerland, July 24, 1503 (feast, July 24). She was the daughter of Bl. Amadeus of Savoy and Yolanda of France, and thus the granddaughter of King Charles VII and the niece of Louis XI. Louise wished to become a religious but, obedient to her parents' will, married Hugh of Orléans in 1479. They lived an exemplary Christian life together at the Château de Nozeray until Hugh died, July 3, 1490. During the next two years, Louise prepared to retire from the world. After distributing her fortune, she, together with her maids of honor, Catherine de Saulx and Charlotte de Saint–Maurice, entered (June 1492) the monastery of Poor Clares at Orbe, Switzerland, a convent founded by Hugh's mother, and rendered illustrious by the reform of St. COLETTE in 1427. Professed in 1493, she became an exemplary religious and as abbess was noted for her hospitality to the Franciscan friars. Her remains were transferred to Nozeray in 1531 and to the chapel of the royal palace, Turin, in 1842. Gregory XVI confirmed her cult, Aug. 12, 1839.

Feast: July 24.

Bibliography: A.M. JEANNERET, ed., *Vie de très haulte. . . Madame Loyse de Savoye . . . escripte en 1507 par une religieuse* (Geneva 1860). J. L. BAUDOT and L. CHAUSSIN, *Vies des saints et des bienheureux selon l'ordre du calendrier avec l'historique des fêtes*, ed. by the Benedictines of Paris, 12 v. (Paris 1935–56) 7:601–606. A. BUTLER, *The Lives of the Saints* rev. ed. H. THURSTON and D. ATTWATER. 4 v. (New York 1956) 3:518–519. D. STÖCKERL, *Lexikon für Theologie und Kirche*, ed. J. HOFER and K. RAHNER, 10 v. (2d, new ed. Freiburg 1957–65) 6:1202.

[M.G. MCNEIL]

LOUISIANA, CATHOLIC CHURCH IN

Located in the south central United States, Louisiana was admitted to the Union as the 18th state on April 30, 1812. The area now comprising the state was once part of the immense Louisiana Territory claimed in 1682 by Robert Cavelier, Sieur de La Salle, for France and was under the successive control of Antoine Crozat (1712–17), John Law's Company of the West (1717–31), and the French Crown (1731–62); it then became a Spanish possession (1762–1801), was returned to France (1800–03), and was sold to the United States and governed as a territory (1804–12). Baton Rouge is the capital and New Orleans is the largest city.

In 2001 Catholics numbered about 1.3 million, slightly more than 31 percent of the total state population of 4,321,980. The ecclesiastical province of New Orleans coincides with the state boundaries. New Orleans is the metropolitan see and the other six Louisiana dioceses— ALEXANDRIA, BATON ROUGE, Houma-Thibodaux, LAFAYETTE, Lake Charles, and Shreveport—are its suffragans. Catholics are concentrated mainly in the southern part of the state. Lafayette has a higher proportion of Catholics (65 percent) than any other diocese in the United States, and with New Orleans has one of the highest populations of African American Catholics in the nation.

Colonization and Missionary History. The discovery, colonization, settlement, history, and economic growth of the state are associated with its waterways, principally the Mississippi River. Hernando De Soto discovered it in 1541; La Salle went down the Mississippi from the Illinois in 1682; Pierre Lemoyne, Sieur de Iberville, sailed up the river from the Gulf of Mexico in 1699; and his brother, Jean Baptiste Lemoyne, Sieur de Bienville, in 1722 transferred the capital of French Louisiana from New Biloxi on the Gulf Coast to a bend of the river that gives to New Orleans its sobriquet of "Crescent City." The 1718 plans of the city, laid by Adrien de Pauger, provided for a church and presbytery, but divine services were held only in improvised and inadequate quarters until April 1727, when the first substantial St. Louis parish church was finally completed. Franciscan recollects, Zénobe Membré and Anastase Douay, were with La Salle when he reached the mouth of the Mississippi and the territory was placed under the ecclesiastical jurisdiction of the bishop of Quebec. Priests of the Quebec Seminary, connected with the Seminary of Foreign Missions in Paris, worked among the Native Americans of lower Louisiana in the late 1600s and early 1700s. François de Montigny, Antoine Davion, and Jean François Buisson de St. Cosmé were outstanding pioneer missionaries. Buisson, regarded as the first American-born missionary martyr, was killed in 1706 by a party of Chitimacha tribe members a few miles below Donaldsonville on the Mississippi River. In 1717 the Franciscan Antonio MARGIL offered the first Mass in Natchitoches, Louisiana's oldest town (1715), and ministered to its French settlers and Native American inhabitants. In 1724, three years before New Orleans had its own substantial church building, a chapel was erected about 35 miles upstream at present-day Killona on the German Coast (Les Allemands). The first chapel of the state was built in 1700 by the Bayagoula tribe under the supervision of Fr. Paul du Ru at the site of present-day Bayou Goula in Iberville Parish (county), which the Jesuit missionary had reached by way of the Mississippi.

Catholicism made little progress during the five years when Antione Crozat, a French financier, attempted to exploit the region. In 1717 the Council of the Marine recommended turning the colony over to John Law's Company of the West and its successor, the Company of the Indies (or Mississippi Company). In accordance with the charter issued by the regent, Philip II, duke of Orleans, religious affairs were included in the activities of the Company of the West from 1717 to 1731. Occasionally, concession chaplains, Jesuits, Capuchins, Carmelites, and other missionaries traveled up and down the river during the early years of colonization. The first Capuchins were Bruno de Langres, who arrived in New Orleans toward the end of 1722, and Plilibert de Vianden, who took charge of the district from the Chapitoulas. The district extended a few miles above the original boundaries of the city, to Pointe Coupée. It included Les Allemands, the German Coast, and the intervening concessions. Les Allemands had a chapel, dedicated to St. John, on the west bank of the Mississippi as early as 1724. Most land grants were along the Mississippi River and other bodies of water, such as Bayou St. John and Lake Pontchartrain. On the Mississippi, itself, the land grants stretched from Chapitoulas to Point Coupee about 140 miles upstream. From the parochial centers established along the river, priests plied the Mississippi and other streams or pushed into the interior to build chapels and start missions from which emerged the later parishes. At the confluence of the Mississippi River and Bayou Lafourche, Capuchins and, later, Vincentians, descended in pirogues from the Plattenville Assumption Church (1793) and Seminary (1838) to lay the foundation of bayou parishes. In 1722 the Jesuits, who contributed notably to the spiritual and economic well-being of the area, undertook the spiritual jurisdiction of the natives in the colony, a responsibility entrusted to them by Bishop Louis DUPLESSIS-MORNAY of Quebec. Their endeavors were supported in large measure by an extensive indigo and sugar plantation adjacent to New Orleans. In July 1763, while Michel Baudouin was superior, the Jesuits were dispossessed of their property and banished from Louisiana. Their departure, some ten years before the society was suppressed, seriously hampered and retarded the growth of the Church in colonial Louisiana.

The arrival of the French-speaking Acadians, expelled from Nova Scotia in the mid-1750s, was a boon to the state and a blessing to the Church in Louisiana. As early as 1758, Acadians reached Louisiana by way of Georgia, the Carolinas, and Maryland. During the following years several hundred—including groups from New England, the Antilles, and French ports—migrated to the state. They settled in St. Martinville (Les Attakapas) on Bayou Têche, in the Poste des Opelousas, a few miles from the Têche, and along the Mississippi below Baton Rouge. At St. Gabriel, Iberville Parish, they deposited the precious parish registers of St. Charles Church, Grand Pré (1688–1755). Those who settled along Les Allemands soon intermarried with the descendants of the original settlers—almost all Catholics—from the Low

Archdiocese/Diocese	Year Created
Archdiocese of New Orleans	1850
Diocese of Alexandria	1986
Diocese of Baton Rouge	1961
Diocese of Houma-Thibodaux	1977
Diocese of Lafayette	1918
Diocese of Lake Charles	1980
Diocese of Shreveport	1986

Countries, Switzerland, Alsace Lorraine, and the Rhineland. The Acadians and other French-speaking Louisianians generally retained their Catholic faith, despite a dire shortage of priests and churches. With other settlers, who followed them to Les Attakapas and the Opelousas District, they formed a cluster of parishes in St. Martinville (1765); Opelousas (1777); Grand Coteau (1819); Lafayette, formerly Vermilionville (1821); and New Iberia (1838). In the central and northern areas of the state, the Church made smaller gains than elsewhere. Except in the civil parishes of Natchitoches, Avoyelles, and Rapides, the inhabitants were and still are mostly Protestants of Anglo-Saxon descent.

In 1769, Spanish troops took control of New Orleans and the Louisiana Territory which was ceded to Spain by the Treaty of Fontainbleau. After 1776, Church affairs in New Orleans were greatly influenced by the Spanish. Cirillo de Barcelona, chaplain of the Spanish expedition against the British in West Florida, was consecrated auxiliary bishop for the Louisiana colony on March 6, 1785. Shortly before leaving for his consecration in Cuba, he appointed his assistant, Antonio de SEDELLA, temporary pastor of St. Louis. For decades thereafter, Sedella, known as Père Antoine, was the center of controversy in the area.

Church Expansion. When the Diocese of Louisiana and the Floridas was created in 1793, Luis Ignacio de PEÑALVER Y CÀRDENAS was consecrated as first ordinary. He arrived in New Orleans on July 17, 1795, marking the beginning of home government in Church affairs. Peñalver noted in a report to the Spanish government, that of the 11,000 Catholics in New Orleans, only about 400 had performed their Easter Duty. He instituted a number of necessary reforms, combated religious indifference, and Voltaireanism, and established parishes in such places as the Poste des Avoyelles, Many (Nuestra Señora de Guadalupe at Bayou Scie), and Monroe. Meanwhile, the parish church in use since 1727 had been destroyed in the great fire of 1788 and a new structure, the future Cathedral of St. Louis, was completed in 1794. Although renovated several times, it remains substantially the same building, still in use as the cathedral. In December 1964 it became a Minor Basilica.

Cemetery candles on All Saints' Day, Lacombe, Louisiana. (©Philip Gould/CORBIS)

In 1801 Peñalver was transferred to the Archdiocese of Guatemala and jurisdictional quarrels, interdiction, and threats of schism marked the next 15 years in New Orleans. Père Antoine was at odds with Fr. Patrick Walsh and Canon Thomas Hasset, who attempted to administer the diocese during the episcopal vacancy. When Hasset died on April 24, 1804, the last canonical link of the Louisiana Church with Spain was extinguished. Walsh claimed to be vicar-general of Louisiana which precipitated a two-year schism between his followers and those of Père Antoine, who was "elected" pastor of St. Louis Cathedral the following year by the majority of New Orleans's citizens under the direction of the church wardens (marguilliers). To complicate matters further, Spain ceded Louisiana back to France, which in turn, sold it to the United States in 1803. Aware of the territorial transfer, the Holy See decided not to send Bishop-elect Francisco Porro y Peinado to Louisiana, and on Sept. 1, 1805, placed it temporarily under the spiritual supervision of Bishop John CARROLL of Baltimore. Carroll, in time, named the chaplain of the Ursulines, Jean Olivier, his vicar-general, but the latter's authority was openly challenged by Père Antione and the cathedral wardens. Finally, on Aug. 18, 1812, Fr. Louis William DUBOURG was named administrator apostolic by Archbishop Carroll. It

was DuBourg, complying with Andrew Jackson's request, who officiated at a *Te Deum* in St. Louis Cathedral following the U.S. victory over the British at the Battle of New Orleans on Jan. 8, 1815. An all-night vigil before Our Lady of Prompt Succor was held at the Ursuline convent chapel before the battle; Jackson personally thanked the nuns for their prayers at the thanksgiving service presided over by DuBourg.

On Sept. 24, 1815, DuBourg was consecrated in Rome and Louisiana finally had a bishop after an interregnum of nearly 15 years. DuBourg, however, remained in Europe for the next two years enlisting the help of priests and seminarians. He successfully acquired the services of St. Rose Philippine DUCHESNE, who visited New Orleans and the Religious of the Sacred Heart, and helped form the organization that eventually became the Pontifical Society for the Propagation of the Faith. Upon arriving in the United States, DuBourg went to St. Louis, MO, and didn't return to New Orleans until late 1820. The next year he called a synod, which was attended by 20 priests. On March 25, 1824, Joseph ROSATI, C.M. was consecrated as DuBourg's coadjutor, but his administration of the Church in New Orleans amounted to supervision at a distance, since he resided in St. Louis. A significant event of the period was the arrival of the Sisters of Charity from Emmitsburg, MD, to staff the Poydras Asylum in New Orleans. It was the first of numerous educational, social, and health care facilities in Louisiana, including Hôtel Dieu. DuBourg resigned in mid-1826 and returned to France, where he died in 1833 as archbishop of Besançon. A further division of the old diocese took place with St. Louis, MO becoming the see of the northern area, while the Diocese of New Orleans became co-extensive with the state boundaries of Louisiana. DuBourg's resignation left the lower end of the Mississippi Valley without a resident bishop which caused further disorder. Although Rosati visited the area he could not completely control the see. Rosati, appointed bishop of St. Louis in 1827, in time recommended a fellow Vincentian for the See of New Orleans, and Leo de Neckere was consecrated in St. Louis Cathedral on June 24, 1830 at the age of 29. His episcopate was brief, for he was stricken with yellow fever and died on Sept. 5, 1833. A few months before, he had established New Orleans's second parish, St. Patrick's, to accommodate the Irish immigrants and other English-speaking people of the city.

A remarkable period of church expansion coincided with the growing importance of New Orleans as a center of commerce and expanding population. The city, emerging as the fourth largest in the nation, increased in population from 29,737 in 1830 to 102,193 in 1840. The diocese covered the entire state, and had a total population approaching 300,000, served by 26 churches and 27 priests when Antoine BLANC became fourth bishop on Nov. 22, 1835. During the 25 years Blanc administered the see, the number of churches increased to 73 and the number of priests to 92. He established Assumption Seminary on Bayou Lafourche, two colleges, nine academies and schools, four orphanages, a hospital, and a home for girls. Under the guidance of Etienne Rousselon, vicar-general, the Sisters of the Holy Family was founded by a free African–American woman, Henriette Delille, in 1842. It was a community commited to teaching, caring for orphans, and tending to elderly African Americans. The Redemptorist Fathers established themselves (1843) in Lafayette and New Orleans where German, Irish, and French immigrants had settled. Of the Redemptorists, Blessed Francis Xavier SEELOS died and was buried in New Orleans in 1865. In 1836, while abroad recruiting priests and religious for his diocese, Blanc persuaded the Father General of the Jesuits in Rome to release eight members of the society for service in Louisiana, guaranteeing the return of a Jesuit presence to the area after nearly three-quarters of a century. In 1837 they established themselves in Grand Coteau, building St. Charles College for their novitiate. They also took charge of Sa-

cred Heart Church and parish, which embraced a wide territory in the west. The Jesuit Fathers opened the College of the Immaculate Conception in 1849 on a plot of ground that had once formed part of the plantation of which they had been defrauded in 1763. The Congregation of the Holy Cross came in 1849 to stabilize St. Mary Orphan Boys Home, which had been opened by Fr. Adam Kindelon, first pastor of St. Patrick's. Fr. Cyril de la Croix organized the first conference of the Society of St. Vincent de Paul after a layman, William Blair Lancaster, brought a manual of the society to New Orleans (1852).

Blanc called two diocesan synods and two provincial councils. The death of Abbé Louis Moni, pastor of St. Louis Cathedral in 1842, precipitated a three-year struggle between Blanc and the wardens of the cathedral over the right to appoint clergy; the controversy, which caused the withdrawal of the clergy from the cathedral, eventually was settled in the Louisiana supreme court in favor of the bishop, and shaped the pattern of parish establishment for several decades, abolishing the trustee system.

Diocesan Developments. In 1850, Pope Pius IX raised New Orleans to the rank of an archdiocese and created the Province of New Orleans which included all of Louisiana, Mississippi, Arkansas, Alabama, Texas, and part of Indian Territory (Oklahoma). Three years later, the upper part of Louisiana state was erected into the Diocese of Natchitoches with Auguste M. Martin as its first bishop. The new diocese had but five priests and five churches to serve the Catholic population of about 25,000, spread throughout the entire northern half of Louisiana. After Blanc's death on June 20, 1860, the archdiocese was administered by Rouselon until the arrival of Archbishop-elect Jean Marie ODIN from Galveston, TX.

Archbishop Odin took possession of his see only a few days after the bombardment of Ft. Sumter on April 12, 1861. Louisiana had already seceded from the Union and joined the Confederacy. During the Civil War, the archbishop's position was an extremely delicate one, calling for infinite tact and diplomacy; Pope Pius IX appointed Odin and Archbishop Hughes of New York his personal intermediaries for trying to effect a reconciliation between the North and South. The times grew more trying after the city was occupied by Federal troops on May 1, 1862. Union forces wrought considerable damage on Church properties in such places as Vermilionville (Lafayette), Pointe Coupée and Donaldsonville. In addition, the war years witnessed a disruption of religious and educational work in Thibodaux, Convent, Plaquemine, Grand Coteau, and elsewhere. Reconstruction was no less trying, but Odin continued the expansion program of his predecessor. In 1863, Odin went to Europe in search of men and money for his diocese. He convinced the Marist Fathers to come to the U.S. and work in Louisiana. In 1867 the Oblate Sisters of Providence, a Baltimore community of African-American nuns, began staffing a home for dependent children of the newly freed slaves. The Little Sisters of the Poor opened their home for the aged poor after a committee of pious women, called Les Dames de la Providence, asked for their help in maintaining another home for the aged founded in 1840. The Brothers of the Sacred Heart came to New Orleans from Mobile, AL in 1869. The first Benedictine convent in the archdiocese was opened (1870) in the German national parish of Holy Trinity, New Orleans (1847). The nuns arrived from Covington, KY, and later established a motherhouse in Covington, LA. After numerous requests for assistance, Odin finally obtained a coadjutor with right of succession, Napoleon Joseph Perché, who had been chaplain of the Ursulines for many years, founder of the first Catholic newspaper in Louisiana, *Le Propagateur Catholique* (1842), and vicar-general of the archdiocese. He was consecrated in St. Louis Cathedral on May 1, 1870, and succeeded to the see when Odin died in France on May 25, 1870, after attending the First Vatican Council with Bishop Martin of Natchitoches.

Like his predecessors, Perché invited several communities to the archdiocese: the Sisters of the Most Holy Sacrament (formerly Perpetual Adoration), who arrived at Waggaman in 1872; the Sisters of Christian Charity, who established themselves at St. Henry's Convent, New Orleans in 1873; and the Discalced Carmelite Nuns, who arrived in 1877. In addition, Archbishop Perché approved the founding of a diocesan community, the Sisters of the Immaculate Conception, organized on July 11, 1874 in Labadieville with Elvina Vienne as first superior. Soon after his installation as head of the see, Perché also inaugurated a costly program of church building, school construction, and parish foundations that contrasted sharply with the record of his predecessor. These expenses, plus financial aid to families impoverished by the Civil War, caused the archdiocese's debt to soar. Weakened by age and infirmities, and overwhelmed by the tremendous debt, the archbishop asked for a coadjutor. The Holy See appointed François Xavier Leray of Natchitoches, who became archbishop upon Perché's death on Dec. 27, 1883. Bishop Leray was succeeded in Natchitoches by Bishop Antoine Durier, who was instrumental in establishing a Catholic School Board and Catholic schools near every church in his diocese. Leray's chief concern as coadjutor and as ordinary was the reduction of the archdiocese's debt, so his administration was practically without building or expansion programs. The only new community established in the archdiocese was that of the Poor Clare Nuns (1885). Upon his death on Sept. 23,

1887, Leray was succeeded by Francis Janssens, the Dutch-born bishop of Natchez.

The new archbishop received the pallium from Cardinal James Gibbons on May 8, 1889, although he had actually taken possession of the archdiocese on Sept. 16, 1888. He invited the Benedictines of St. Meinrad's Abbey in Indiana to open a seminary for the training of native priests. Fr. Luke Grüwe, O.S.B. established in 1890, what later became St. Joseph Abbey and Seminary at St. Benedict, LA. Janssens dedicated the seminary on Sept. 3, 1891. The archbishop welcomed St. Frances Xavier Cabrini to New Orleans, and encouraged her in 1892 to establish a school and orphanage to assist the children of Italian immigrants; thousands were entering the city. In 1893, he asked the Sisters of the Holy Family to care for dependent or neglected African-American boys, and thus started the present Lafon Home for Boys, one of several institutions named for the local African-American philanthropist, Thomy Lafon.

Janssens was greatly esteemed throughout the archdiocese, which numbered 341,613 in the centennial year of 1893. The celebration that year attracted many dignitaries to Louisiana, including Cardinal Gibbons of Baltimore. He encouraged spiritual ministrations to patients at the leprosarium at Carville, LA. When the hurricane of 1893 swept the Louisiana Gulf Coast, Janssens went among the Italian, Spanish, and Malay fishermen in the island settlements in a small boat to comfort them; he later helped to rebuild their homes. He promoted devotion to Our Lady under the title of Prompt Succor. The structure of the parishes was determined in 1894 when each was legally incorporated with the archbishop, the vicar-general, the pastor, and two lay directors as board members. Janssens was the first ordinary to promote native vocations on a large scale; his predecessors generally had depended on priests and seminarians from Europe, and had leaned heavily on religious to staff new parishes. He sponsored the Catholic Winter School, opened parochial schools, and launched a dozen new parishes. Alarmed at the defections from the faith among African Americans, he established St. Katherine's as an African-American parish, but on a temporary basis, since he did not want to promote racial segregation. He died on June 9, 1897, while traveling to Europe on behalf of the archdiocese.

Placide Louis CHAPELLE, sixth archbishop of New Orleans, was transferred from Santa Fe, NM in February 1898. Concerned about the archdiocese's debt, he ordered the annual contribution of 12 percent of the revenues of each parish for five years. This measure eventually liquidated the longstanding debt, although it aroused the displeasure of some pastors. Chapelle's relationship with the priests in the diocese was strained. Many of them born and educated in France, were upset by his extended, though necessary, absences as Apostolic Delegate to Cuba and Puerto Rico, and later as Apostolic Delegate Extraordinary to the Philippines, where Chappelle was needed to negotiate ecclesiastical problems arising from the Spanish-American War. It was evident that he needed an auxiliary and one was provided when the pastor of Annunciation Church in New Orleans, Gustave Rouxel, was consecrated on April 9, 1899. Archbishop Chapelle opened a theological seminary (1900) with the Vincentian Fathers as professors. Some 12 parishes and missions were established during Chapelle's episcopate and the Dominicans began their ministry in the archdiocese (1903). Chapelle died a victim of yellow fever on Aug. 9, 1905.

The next ordinary, James Hubert Blenk, S.M. was well known to the archdiocese long before his appointment on April 20, 1906. He had served as bishop of Puerto Rico, former auditor and secretary to the apostolic delegation to the West Indies, rector of Holy Name of Mary Church, and president of Jefferson College, Convent, LA. Blenk, an ardent promoter of Catholic education, set up in 1908 the first archdiocesan school board and appointed the first superintendent of schools. In 1914, he hosted the National Catholic Education Association convention in New Orleans, the first major convention of its kind to be held in Louisiana. The preparatory seminary was placed again under the care of the Benedictine Fathers of St. Joseph Abbey, but the theological courses were discontinued in 1907. Most major seminarians of the archdiocese matriculated at Kenrick Seminary in St. Louis and St. Mary Seminary in Baltimore, or studied abroad. In September 1904, the Jesuits started a small college in New Orleans, which in 1911 was amalgamated with the College of the Immaculate Conception and became Loyola University, receiving state charter as a university in 1912. Blenk designated St. Mary's the normal school for women religious engaged in teaching in the archdiocese. In time, St. Mary's Dominican College became an accredited Catholic women's college.

French Benedictine nuns, forced to leave France in 1906, settled in Ramsay under the guidance of Paul Schaeuble, O.S.B., who had become first abbot of St. Joseph Abbey in 1903. The Sisters Servants of Mary, having left Mexico during the Carranza revolution, found refuge also in the archdiocese and in 1914 began their ministrations among the sick and the bedridden in the city. The sisters of the Society of St. Teresa of Jesus, likewise refugees from Mexico, began teaching at St. Louis Cathedral School in 1915. That same year, the archbishop urgently requested St. Katharine DREXEL, foundress of the Sisters of the BLESSED SACRAMENT, to undertake the

education of African-American youth in the city and throughout the archdiocese. Accordingly, in 1915 the sisters opened Xavier High School and ten years later opened Xavier College, the oldest continuing African-American Catholic university in the United States. In 1911, the Brothers of Christian Schools purchased St. Paul's College, Covington from the Benedictine Fathers. In 1912 the Ursulines, under the supervision of their chaplain, François Racine, moved from their third convent building to a new site on State Street, where ten years later, the national shrine of Our Lady of Prompt Succor was erected.

Early in his administration, Blenk strengthened lay groups. He organized the state board of Holy Name Societies in 1906, the Louisiana State Federation of Catholic Societies in 1909, and the Federation of Catholic Societies of Women of Louisiana. He promoted the Catholic Order of Foresters, the Knights of Columbus, and the Knights of Peter Claver.

The growth of the population in the archdiocese, especially in Acadian (Cajun) southwest Louisiana, made a division expedient. Shortly before Archbishop John William Shaw was promoted to the New Orleans See on Jan. 11, 1918, Pope Benedict XV established the Diocese of Lafayette, comprising western Louisiana. He also appointed Jules Benjamin Jeanmard administrator of the archdiocese following the death of Blenk on April 15, 1917. Jeanmard became the first native Louisianian to be raised to the episcopate, its founding bishop.

Meanwhile, in New Orleans, one of Archbishop Shaw's first actions was to invite the Oblates of Mary Immaculate, with whom he had worked closely as bishop of San Antonio, TX to administer St. Louis Cathedral and to take charge of the churches and missions in Livingston parish. In 1919 the Sisters of Charity of the Incarnate Word, from San Antonio, came to teach at St. Francis de Sales parochial school. In 1920 Archbishop Shaw, with his chancellor, August J. Bruening, began to lay plans for a financial campaign for the erection of a major seminary. In September 1923 the Notre Dame Seminary opened and was staffed by the Marist Fathers. That same year, the Sisters of St. Francis of Calais opened Our Lady of the Lake Hospital in Baton Rouge. Franciscan Fathers returned to the archdiocese on July 21, 1925, when they took charge of the newly established parish of St. Mary of the Angels in the city, and the missions of the Lower Coast. The Sisters of the Holy Ghost and Mary Immaculate arrived from San Antonio in September 1926 to teach the African-American children of St. Luke School, Thibodaux. Shaw encouraged the endeavors of Catherine Bostick and Zoé Grouchy to establish the Eucharistic Missionaries of St. Dominic, an organization which would provide religious instruction to children in public schools and offer social relief work. In 1928 the Society of the Divine Word took over the mission stations on both the east and west bank of the lower Mississippi River. In 1931 the Jesuits purchased the old Jefferson College in Convent and converted it into Manresa House, a place for laymen's retreats.

Father (later Bishop) Maurice Shexnayder began Newman club work in 1929 at Louisiana State University, one-third of whose student body was Catholic. Monsignor Peter M. H. Wynhoven established (1925) Hope Haven for orphaned and abandoned boys, later placed under the direction of the Salesian Fathers of St. John Bosco. Opposite Hope Haven, Madonna Manor for small boys replaced St. Mary and St. Joseph Orphanages. Wynhoven, in addition to many other assignments, reorganized the social services and charities of the archdiocese by setting up Associated Catholic Charities in 1924. In 1922 Shaw convoked the sixth synod, the first in 33 years. In 1932 he launched the official diocesan paper, the *Catholic Action of the South*, with Wynhoven acting as first editor in chief. It replaced the *Morning Star*, which had been published between 1878 and 1930. Shaw's last years were burdened by problems brought about by the Depression of the 1930s. Some of the archdiocese's funds were frozen in local banks and several parishes found it difficult to meet the high interest due on monies borrowed during the 1920s. Nevertheless, 33 new parishes were opened between 1919 and 1934. After a brief illness, Shaw died on Nov. 2, 1934, and Jean Marius Laval, who had been consecrated auxiliary to Blenk, became administrator.

In 1935, Joseph Francis RUMMEL of Omaha, NB was transferred to the Archdiocese of New Orleans to become its 13th ordinary and 9th archbishop. Rummel intensified and accelerated existing movements; proposed and promoted new projects; sponsored the eighth National Eucharistic Congress in 1938, the largest public demonstration of Catholic faith ever seen in the city to that time; and endorsed numerous regional and national conventions. He also issued authoritative statements on social problems, such as the 1953 letter, ''Blessed are the Peacemakers,'' which deplored racism. Two years later he ordered the planned desegregation of Catholic schools in the archdiocese. Rummel also launched a series of successful financial campaigns, insisted on a sound fiscal policy for each parish and institution, reorganized and expanded the archdiocesan administration, and promptly implemented decrees of the Holy See.

When Rummel was appointed to New Orleans the Catholic population was estimated at 361,882, out of a total population of nearly one million. At that time, there were 132 resident parishes, 97 missions, and 451 secular and religious priests. By 1960, the entire population (Catholic and non-Catholic) had increased by about 66 percent. The number of parishes had grown by 40 percent, and the number of priests had increased by 25 percent. Insufficient vocations to the priesthood prevented the archbishop from establishing more parishes, even though a growing population brought an increased demand for churches, schools, and other institutions, especially in suburban areas. Nevertheless, well over $100 million worth of building contracts were signed, the majority after World War II, and at least half were for schools, convents, and school-allied buildings. The Youth Progress Program was launched on Jan. 21, 1945 for the expansion of high schools for boys, recreational facilities, and a boy's protectory. Twelve years later, the oversubscribed Diocesan Campaign of Progress made possible the construction of a $2 million seminary at St. Benedict to accommodate 400 students, a new central administration (chancery) building, four centers for Newman Clubs at state and private colleges and universities, and a projected home for the aged. Between these two campaigns, which were carried out by volunteer laymen under the guidance of their pastors, parishes of the archdiocese memorialized Rummel's golden jubilee as a priest in 1952 by contributing $1 million for the erection of St. Joseph Hall of Philosophy, which raised the capacity of Notre Dame Seminary to 150.

In 25 years, the Catholic school population more than doubled, reaching 90,546 in 1961. Contributions to the missions totaled $3.6 million from 1935 to 1960. Under the leadership of Msgr. Edward C. J. Prendergast, Fr. (later Bishop) Robert E. Tracy, and (after 1945) Msgr. (later Bishop) Gerard L. Frey, the Confraternity of Christian Doctrine (CCD) became one of the most dynamic forces in the archdiocese, as did the Cana and pre-Cana conferences to which Rummel gave impetus in 1957.

New communities of men entering the archdiocese were Missionaries of Our Lady of La Salette (1938), the Maryknoll Fathers (1944), and the Brothers of the Good Shepherd (1955). Communities of women returning to the archdiocese, or settling in it for the first time, included the Religious of the Presentation of the Blessed Virgin Mary (1949); the Poor Sisters of St. Francis Seraph of the Perpetual Adoration (1951); the Daughters of Jesus (1952); the Religious of Our Lady of the Retreat in the Cenacle, who opened (1958) Maria Immaculata Retreat House; and the Oblate Sisters of Providence (1958). Rummel organized the Archdiocesan Council of Catholic Men, although in time, its program was more or less assumed by the Archdiocesan Union of Holy Name Societies. The Archdiocesan Council of Catholic Women was even more successful as the Catholic Daughters of America and the St. Margaret's Daughters augmented their courts and circles. New organizations, groups, and agencies established since 1935 have been numerous including Serra Clubs, the Catholic Committees for Boy and Girl Scouts, Catholic Youth Organizations, Catholic Physicians and Nurses Guilds, Ozanam Inn, and the St. Vincent de Paul Store.

In addition to the curial posts, the diocesean administration includes an appreciably expanded ecclesiastical tribunal; commissions for sacred music, ecclesiastical art, and the liturgy; a diocesan building commission, appointed at the time of the seventh diocesan synod in 1949; a Catholic Bureau of Information; directors for the Legion of Decency; the deaf apostolate, and hospitals; and a Catholic Council on Human Relations, an organization of Catholic laymen designed to promote justice and charity, which held its first meeting in March, 1961.

Through the years, Rummel was a staunch champion of the underprivileged and a promoter of social justice. He opposed right-to-work bills introduced in the state legislature during the sessions of 1948 and 1954; led a movement to maintain reasonable rent controls after World War II; accepted African-American applicants at both minor and major seminaries; racially integrated the Archdiocesan School Board, the Councils of Catholic Men and Women, the Sodalities, and the Holy Name Societies; recommended African-American laypersons for Papal honors, and spoke out vehemently against segregation, upholding the Supreme Court decision of May 17, 1954, which ruled segregation in public schools unconstitutional. Regrettably, his stand on these socio–moral issues proved unpopular among many, otherwise, representative Catholic laymen.

On Aug. 14, 1961 Pope John XXIII named Bishop John P. CODY of Kansas City-St. Joseph MO, coadjutor archbishop with right of succession and erected the Diocese of Baton Rouge. He also appointed Robert E. Tracey, formerly auxiliary of Lafayette, its first bishop. The Louisiana bishops departed for Rome in 1962 to attend the Second Vatican Council. Tracey, who later published his well-received council diary, formed his diocese according to the norms of the Council, thereby, making Baton Rouge a model for other dioceses in establishing post-Conciliar administrative structure and consultative process. He placed particular emphasis on liturgical renewal and modern catechetical efforts.

On the 60th anniversary of his ordination to the priesthood, May 24, 1962, Archbishop Rummel announced that Archbishop Cody had been appointed apostolic administrator of New Orleans. Cody succeeded to the see at Rummel's death on Nov. 8, 1964. Archbishop Cody was transferred to Chicago, IL on June 16, 1965

and his successor, Philip M. Hannan, auxiliary bishop of Washington, DC was installed in New Orleans on October 13. Prior to this time, Hannan had been helping the victims of the devastating Hurricane Betsy. The following year, Harold R. Perry, the first African-American bishop since 1875, was consecrated as New Orleans's auxiliary on January 6.

During Hannan's administration the Vatican Pavilion at the New Orleans World Exposition was erected in 1984. The treasures of Catholic art assembled in the pavilion drew hundreds of thousands of visitors to the site. Three years later, New Orleans received its first visit by a reigning pontiff. From Sept. 11 to Sept. 13, 1987 Pope John Paul II made a pastoral visit to New Orleans, highlighted by a prayer service in the cathedral, a visit with the young people of the area at the Superdome, a Mass on the grounds of the University of New Orleans, and an address on education at Xavier University. On Dec. 13, 1988, Archbishop Hannan announced that his resignation as archbishop of New Orleans had been accepted by the Holy See. His 24 years as ordinary was marked by an impressive increase in the number and kinds of social services rendered by the archdiocese. During his tenure, three new diocese were created: Houma-Thibodaux (1977) was carved out of the Archdiocese of New Orleans with Bishop Warren Boudreaux as its founding ordinary. The Diocese of Lake Charles was created from the Diocese of Lafayette (1980) with Bishop Jude Speyer as ordinary. In 1986, the Diocese of Alexandria-Shreveport was divided. Bishop William B. Friend became the first bishop of the new Diocese of Shreveport.

On Feb. 14, 1989 Philadelphia native, Francis Bible Schulte, was installed as twelfth archbishop of New Orleans after serving as bishop of Wheeling-Charleston, WV. Alfred C. Hughes, appointed fourth bishop of Baton Rouge in 1993, was named coadjutor with right of succession to Archbishop Schulte on Feb. 16, 2001.

Catholic Population. The history of slavery accounts for the large number of African-American Catholics in South Louisiana, with New Orleans having the highest number of African-American Catholics in the U.S. The slave trade remained brisk in New Orleans from the time the city was founded up to the Civil War. Most slave owners in Louisiana were Catholic and were bound by the prescriptions of the Code Noir, which demanded that slaves be baptized and instructed in the Catholic religion. The economy of the sugar plantations in South Louisiana depended on slave labor up to the time of the Emancipation Proclamation. There were no separate churches for African Americans until the late 19th century. The first one, St. Katherine's, was established in New Orleans in 1895. In 1897, Fr. Pierre LeBeau began the

Josephite apostolate in Louisiana, and since then, well over 100 separate African-American churches and chapels have been established in the state, most of which are administered by religious communities, most notably the Society of the Divine Word and the Josephites.

National parishes were established in New Orleans shortly after immigrants from France and Germany arrived in the city in the early 1800s, from Ireland in the mid-1800s, from Italy toward the close of the century, and from Lebanon at the beginning of the 20th. The fall of Saigon in 1975 resulted in the emigration of many Catholic Vietnamese refugees to Louisiana, where they found a hospitable climate and the opportunity to continue working in the fishing industry. Louisiana has the third largest concentration of Vietnamese Catholics, after California and Texas. Since the late 1960s, Hispanic Catholics from Mexico, Central and South America, and the Caribbean have reintroduced Spanish settlement to the state, but in much smaller numbers than in neighboring states. The majority of the diocesan clergy in Louisiana are native born and locally educated, in contrast with the situation a few generations earlier, when bishops continued to depend on European and Canadian priests to staff parishes. Just under half of the clergy in the state belong to religious communities, many of these priests are foreign born, coming from India, Africa, and parts of Asia.

Educational Institutions. The Church in Louisiana has had a stake in education since the 1700s. Presently, there are two Catholic universities and one college in New Orleans-Loyola New Orleans. There is also XAVIER UNIVERSITY OF LOUISIANA, Holy Cross College, and Our Lady of the Lake College in Baton Rouge.

Catholic secondary and elementary schools enroll about 22 percent of all children in the state from prekindergarten to 12th grade. Slightly less than half of school-age children, who are Catholic, are in Catholic institutions. The number of students enrolled at Catholic schools remains constant. The Confraternity of Christian Doctrine (CCD) is responsible for the religious instruction of Catholic children in public and nonsectarian private schools. Each diocese has its own superintendent of schools and its own CCD director.

Bibliography: Archives, Archdiocese of New Orleans. Archives, Diocese of Alexandria. Archives, Diocese of Baton Rouge. Archives, Diocese of Lafayette. Archives, Diocese of Shreveport. Archives, St. Louis Cathedral, New Orleans. R. BAUDIER, *The Catholic Church in Louisiana*, (New Orleans 1939). H. E. CHAMBERS, *A History of Louisiana*, (New York 1925) v.1. C. M. CHAMBON, *In and Around the Old St. Louis Cathedral of New Orleans* (New Orleans 1908). G. CONRAD, ed., *Cross, Crozier, and Crucible* (New Orleans 1993). E. A. DAVIS, *Louisiana, the Pelican State* (Baton Rouge 1959). C. L DUFOUR, ed., *St. Patrick's of New Orleans, 1883–1958* (New Orleans 1958) commemorative essays for the 125th anniversary. A. E. FOSSIER, *New Orleans: The Glamour Period, 1800–1840* (New Orleans 1957). M. GIRAUD, *Histoire de la Louisiane francaise* (Paris 1953–58) v.1, "Le Regne de Louis XIV, 1698–1715;" v.2 "Annes de transition, 1715–1717," P. J. KENNEDY AND SONS, *The Official Catholic Directory* (Providence, NJ 2001). E. LAUVRIERE, *Histoire de la Louisiane francaise, 1673–1939* (Paris 1940). T. L. SMITH and H. L. HITT, *People of Louisiana* (Baton Rouge 1952). *Louisiana Digest, 1809 to Date* (St. Paul, MN 1936–).

[H. C. BEZOU/M. G. GUIDRY]

LOUISMET, SAVINIEN

Missionary, mystical writer; b. Sens, France, April 4, 1858; d. BUCKFAST ABBEY, Jan. 19, 1926. Louismet came from a devout Catholic family and attended choir school at Sens and the Petit Séminaire at Auxerre. He was professed as Dom Savinien at the Benedictine Abbey of La Pierrequi-Vire, Yonne, on Nov. 13, 1877, and ordained at Quimper, Brittany, in 1882. As a young priest he was sent to the Benedictine mission in Indian Territory (now Oklahoma) where he labored for 13 years. Ill health brought him back to Europe, and in 1902 he was temporary superior at Buckfast Abbey. There he spent the rest of his life as a simple monk, engaged in preaching missions and retreats, and writing articles for various periodicals. Six or seven short treatises on the mystical life followed each other at short intervals, the most popular of which were: *The Mystical Knowledge of God* (1917); *Mystical Initiation* (1924); *Divine Contemplation for All* (1922); and *The Mystery of Jesus* (1922). Dom Louismet was well read in his special subject, but his judgment was not always well-balanced and lent itself to justifiable criticism.

[J. STÉPHAN]

LOUISVILLE, ARCHDIOCESE OF

The Archdiocese of Louisville (*Ludovicopolitana*), comprising 24 counties in central Kentucky, is the metropolitan see of the states of Kentucky and Tennessee. The Province of Louisville includes the suffragan sees of Covington, Owensboro, and Lexington in Kentucky, and the sees of Nashville, Memphis and Knoxville in Tennessee. Originally created as the Diocese of Bardstown by Pius VII on April 8, 1808, the see was transferred to Louisville on Feb. 13, 1841, and created an archdiocese on Dec. 10, 1937.

When the diocese of Bardstown transferred its see city to the growing municipality of Louisville in 1841, Benedict Joseph FLAGET (1763–1850), the first Bishop of the West, found three churches in his new hometown: one for English speaking, one for Germans and one for French. As Germans and Irish increased rapidly in numbers in the area, anti-immigrant and anti-Catholic feelings exploded in the Bloody Monday Riots of Aug. 6, 1855, when over 20 were killed in mob action.

The earlier history of the city had been (and its subsequent history would be) decidedly more ecumenical. When Louisville's first congregation, Saint Louis, (forerunner to today's cathedral parish) built its primal church in 1811, Protestants made up over half of the contributors. The cornerstone ceremony for the second church building in 1830 was hosted by a Presbyterian congregation. The first resident priest of the parish was Philip Hosten, a Flemish native who died quite young in 1821 as "a victim of his zeal" as his Louisville tombstone reports. He had been nursing his people through the cholera epidemic and succumbed to the disease.

In the years before the Civil War, several traditional aspects of Catholic culture came to the city: a newspaper, *The Catholic Advocate*; the Jesuit Fathers to found a short-lived school; the Xaverian Brothers to make their first American foundation; a large congregation of teaching Ursuline Sisters from Germany, and the Sisters of the Good Shepherd from France to begin their social works ministry.

Spalding. Flaget was succeeded by his coadjutor, Martin J. SPALDING. Three years after Spalding became the second bishop of Louisville in 1850, the Diocese of Covington was erected by separating the eastern part of Kentucky from Louisville. While in Europe that year, Spalding secured from Belgium several priests and a community of Xaverian Brothers, who in 1854 opened a school in Louisville. That year the Saint Vincent DePaul Society was established in Louisville. Spalding introduced the Ursuline nuns in 1858 and the Christian Brothers in 1860; the Franciscans and the School Sisters of Notre Dame also joined the diocese at his invitation. In his 16 years as bishop, eight new churches were built in Louisville and 22 new parishes erected elsewhere, making a total of 85 parishes in the diocese. On May 1, 1858, the *Catholic Guardian* began publication; it suspended publication in July 1862 because of the Civil War. The war years were characterized by a weakening of Know-Nothing and other anti-Catholic movements, especially after the sisters of the diocese became active in nursing the soldiers. In 1862 the army closed Saint Joseph College in order to use the building; Saint Thomas Seminary barely managed to remain open. The war caused an interruption of all progress.

Lavialle. On June 9, 1864, Spalding was transferred to the See of Baltimore; his brother and vicar-general, Benedict J. Spalding, was made administrator until the third bishop, French-born Peter Joseph Lavialle, was consecrated Sept. 24, 1868. The new bishop had been or-

Thomas Merton at the library of the Abbey of Gethsemani.
(©Horace Bristol/CORBIS)

dained to the priesthood in 1844, and then served successively as secretary to Flaget, superior of the diocesan seminary (1849–56), and president of Saint Mary's College (1856–65). During his brief episcopacy, six new churches were started in the diocese; ground for Louis Cemetery was purchased; and a group of Franciscan sisters, formed under the direction of the Trappists, opened a school at Mount Olivet near Gethsemani. Failing health caused Lavialle's retirement to Nazareth where he died, May 11, 1867; he was buried beside Flaget in the crypt of the cathedral.

McCloskey. On March 3, 1868, William George MCCLOSKEY, rector of the American College in Rome, was appointed to the vacancy in Louisville and consecrated in Rome May 24, 1868. Four months later, he arrived in his see city for a turbulent episcopate of 41 years. His first major dispute was with Spalding over the terms of the will of Spalding's brother. Shortly thereafter, some of the older priests had some difficulty with their bishop and turned to Spalding for aid. During these years, many priests left the diocese, led by the bishop's secretary and the chancellor, John Lancaster SPALDING (1840–1916), nephew of bishop Martin John Spalding and later first bishop of Peoria. Moreover, many religious establishments were the objects of episcopal disfavor. McCloskey first suppressed Saint Mary's College; as early as 1869 the abbot of Gethsemani complained that the bishop was hostile to the Trappists; in 1898 the SCHOOL SISTERS OF NOTRE DAME withdrew from the diocese and the Sisters of Saint Francis from Mount Olivet left for Clinton, Iowa, because of trouble with the bishop. Nor were the DOMINICAN SISTERS, the SISTERS OF MERCY, the URSULINE nuns, SISTERS OF LORETTO, and the mens' orders left unvexed.

Despite these difficulties, religious advancement marked the four decades of McCloskey's administration. Six new religious orders came into the diocese: Carmelite Fathers, RESURRECTIONISTS, the Society of Saint Joseph for Foreign Missions, the PASSIONISTS, the Sisters of Mercy, and the LITTLE SISTERS OF THE POOR. In 1870 the seminary was moved from Saint Thomas to a location known as Preston Park, in Louisville. It was closed in 1888, reopened in 1902, and closed again at McCloskey's death. An official diocesan organ, the *Record* was established in February 1879. In the next decade, about 50 priests and 25 churches were added to the diocese and similar progress marked the next ten years. Between 1900 and 1909, the year of McCloskey's death, 14 churches were established or dedicated in Louisville alone, and a like number elsewhere. By 1909 the Catholics of the diocese had increased to 155,000, the number of priests to 201, and there were almost 100 new churches.

O'Donaghue. Denis O'Donaghue, auxiliary bishop of Indianapolis, Indiana, was transferred to Louisville Feb. 7, 1910, and a month later was enthroned. A year later, the Clerical Aid Society was organized, the orphan boys home was moved from Saint Thomas to Louisville, and the Catholic Orphans Society was organized. Saint Joseph's College was reopened under the Xaverian Brothers. Four new parishes were organized; 21 churches built to replace older or smaller ones; nine new schools were established in the city; and 18 schools were built in country parishes. O'Donaghue's failing health caused the Holy See to appoint an apostolic administrator (1921) and a coadjutor (1923). The next year O'Donoghue resigned and was given the titular See of Lebedus. He died Nov. 7, 1925 and was buried in Saint Louis Cemetery.

The Louisville see was elevated to the status of an archdiocese by the action of Pope Pius XI on Dec. 10, 1937. The first archbishop was John A. Floersh (1886–1969), noted both for his piety and business acumen. In his administration, the amazing post-World War II building boom occurred and new institutions and parishes grew rapidly throughout the archdiocese.

Floersh. John A. Floersh, born Oct. 5, 1886, in Nashville, Tenn., was ordained June 10, 1911, in Saint John Lateran, Rome. After a year in Nashville parishes he was called to Washington, D.C., to act as secretary at the apostolic delegation. On Feb. 6, 1923, he was named coadjutor of Louisville and was consecrated in Rome on April 8, 1923, succeeding to the see on July 26, 1924. In December 1937, Louisville was made a metropolitan see with Floersh as its first archbishop. He consecrated his chancellor, Francis R. Cotton, on Feb. 23, 1938 as first bishop of Owensboro. Floersh instituted the Catholic School Board and the Office of Catholic Charities. He brought the Carmelite nuns to Louisville and founded several new high schools as well as Bellarmine College, with Monsignor Alfred Horrigan as first president.

Archbishop Floersh, for reasons of health attended only the first session of the Second Vatican Council in 1962, while his Auxiliary Bishop, Charles Garrett Maloney (consecrated on Feb. 2, 1955) was in attendance at all four. Mary Luke Tobin, at the time President of the Sisters of Loretto was the only American woman to have official status (auditor) at the conciliar sessions. She would remain a major voice in American Catholicism even into the next century. Another figure from the archdiocese, Passionist Father Carroll STUHLMUELLER, was a *peritus* in the years of the Council. Of all the residents of the archdiocese in those years, the most internationally known was Father Louis (Thomas MERTON), monk of the Abbey of Gethsemani. Less than two years after the Council's close, on March 1, 1967, Archbishop Floersh resigned his see. He died June 11, 1968.

McDonough. Thomas Joseph McDonough (born in Philadelphia in 1911) was installed as Louisville's second archbishop on May 2, 1967. His early pastoral letters signaled his encouragement of those engaged in addressing racism, poverty and other social evils. He noted in 1967 (echoing a Merton title) that the church and the world could not be "disinterested bystanders" amid social brokenness.

McDonough's tenure helped to initiate not only social, but also ecclesiastical and liturgical change in the light of the Second Vatican Council. He initiated the restored office of permanent deacon in the archdiocese, beginning in 1976. Sometimes the changes of the era were painful—such as the decision to close down the long tradition of the annual Corpus Christi procession involving in some years over 50,000 people at Louisville's famed Churchill Downs. Dwindling attendance caused its suspension after the 1976 event. McDonough announced his resignation in the autumn of 1981, exiting office with the words: "A good bishop today needs big ears and a small mouth" (*Courier-Journal*, Feb. 4, 1982). He died on Aug. 4, 1998.

Kelly. Dominican Thomas Cajetan Kelly (born July 14, 1931) had seen long service with the National Conference of Catholic Bishops in Washington before he was installed as Louisville's third archbishop on Feb. 18, 1982. Among his first tasks was leading diocesan leaders in the articulation of a mission statement. He also oversaw the restoration of the historic downtown Cathedral of the Assumption through the activity of an innovative, inter-faith Cathedral Heritage Foundation (begun in 1985). The Cathedral was renewed not only architecturally but as a lively inner-city parish where liturgy, the arts, ecumenical understanding and social service—especially to the urban poor—flourish. Visitors to the venerable church have included Dorothy Day, Thomas Merton, Joseph Cardinal Bernardin, Jesuit Karl Rahner, historian Martin Marty, Muhammad Ali, the Dalai Lama and Nobel Laureate Jewish scholar Elie Wiesel.

Kelly encouraged and supported individuals with special leadership skills. In the last third of the 20th century, no fewer than nine clerics, laity and religious of the archdiocese held national presidencies in professional Catholic groups. One, Father Nick Rice, was elected to three separate leadership roles at the national level. At home Renew and other programs enhanced parochial and personal spiritual life.

In 1988, the creation of the new Diocese of LEXINGTON reduced the geographical area of the Louisville archdiocese to 24 counties in central Kentucky. In addition to metropolitan Louisville and the Holy Land counties, this included creative mission programs in southern portions of the diocese where Catholics are few in number. In 2000 the archdiocese had a Catholic population of some 197,000 (about 16% of the total population), served by 112 parishes and 12 missions.

Bibliography: C. F. CREWS, *An American Holy Land* (Wilmington 1987). M. C. FOX, *The Life of the Right Reverend John Baptist Mary David, 1761–1841* (U.S. Catholic Historical Society 9; New York 1925). M. R. MATTINGLY, *The Catholic Church on the Kentucky Frontier, 1785–1812* (Washington 1936). V. F. O'DANIEL, *A Light of the Church in Kentucky . . . Samuel Thomas Wilson, O.P.* (Washington 1932). J. H. SCHAUINGER, *Cathedrals in the Wilderness* (Milwaukee 1952). M. J. SPALDING, *Sketches of the Early Catholic Missions of Kentucky, 1787–1827* (Louisville 1844). B. WEBB, *The Centenary of Catholicity in Kentucky* (Louisville 1884).

[J. H. SCHAUINGER/C.F. CREWS]

LOURDES

Town on the Gave de Pau River, at the foot of the Pyrenees, southwest France. Since 1912 the See of Tarbes (founded *c.* 500, perhaps in the 4th century) has been known as the Diocese of Tarbes and Lourdes.

Lourdes was an obscure village until the Blessed Virgin appeared there to the 14-year-old St. Bernadette SOUBIROUS 18 times between February 11 and July 16, 1858. It has since become the location of one of the most popular Marian SHRINES in the world. Bernadette's visits to the grotto of Massabielle on the riverside were accompanied by crowds that reached 20,000 on March 4; only Bernadette, however, saw the visions. After calling for penance on the 24th, the Lady directed Bernadette to drink and wash at a spring which came forth as soon as Bernadette dug (February 25). The water, which now flows at the rate of 32,000 gallons a day, is used for the bath at Lourdes (which is changed twice daily) and is prized as a sacramental by pilgrims. On February 27 and March 2 Bernadette was instructed to have a chapel built and to have people come there in processions. On March 25 the Lady told Bernadette, in the dialect of Lourdes, "I am the Immaculate Conception." The dogma of the IMMACULATE CONCEPTION had been defined by Pope Pius IX, December 8, 1854. The final apparition occurred on the feast of Our Lady of Mount Carmel. Bernadette, who entered the Sisters of Charity and Christian Instruction at Nevers (1865), died in 1879; she was beatified in 1925 and canonized in 1933.

There was a period of opposition; the grotto and spring were barricaded by the mayor from June to October 1858 "for hygienic reasons." In 1861 the shrine became the property of the See of Tarbes, and in 1862 Bishop Laurence confirmed the apparitions and approved the public cult of Our Lady of Lourdes. Apart from the cures associated with the spring (whose water is chemically the same as Lourdes drinking water), reasons for the approval were the good spiritual effects resulting from the devotion, the evident ecstasy of Bernadette, and the accuracy and veracity of her testimony. In 1862 a marble statue was carved and a Gothic church (in place of a chapel) was begun. In 1871 the first Mass was celebrated in the church, and in 1872 (after the Franco-Prussian War) pilgrims flocked to Lourdes from all parts of France. The church was made a minor basilica and was consecrated by Abp. Guibert of Paris in 1876 in the presence of 100,000 pilgrims, while the statue was crowned by the papal nuncio to France. The increase in the number of pilgrims necessitated another church, the Rosary Basilica with 15 chapels (1883–1901), which became a minor basilica in 1926. Leo XIII, who built a Lourdes grotto in the Vatican gardens, approved an Office and a Mass of Lourdes for the province of Auch (1891), and Pius X extended the feast (February 11) for the whole church (1907). The crypt below the Basilica of the Immaculate Conception and the underground Church of Pope St. Pius X were consecrated by Cardinal Roncalli (later Pope John XXIII) in 1958, a centenary year which attracted six million pilgrims. Two annual PILGRIMAGES, the French national pilgrimage led by the Assumptionists and the Rosary pilgrimage under the Dominicans, date from the 1870s.

The Basilica at Lourdes, France. (©Chris Bland; Eye Ubiquitous/CORBIS)

Development of the Sanctuary. Each year millions of pilgrims visit Lourdes. They come from every continent, every social background and age-group. The sick are particularly prominent. The first cure at Lourdes was reported in 1858, and in 1861 the first commission pronounced 15 of 100 cures miraculous. Of 5,000 reported cures by the end of 1959, 58 were declared miraculous by the Church, but a number of cures are believed not to have been reported. The cures of organic illnesses include the healing of cancers, tuberculosis, and blindness; cases of neurasthemia or nervous disorders are not considered significant. As many cures derive from the processions and the individual blessings of the sick as from the baths and from private prayers at the grotto. Reported cures are first examined at Lourdes by a medical bureau of physicians (since 1882), and valid cases are asked to return a year later. The medical bureau then forwards its conclusions to the International Medical Commission of Lourdes (in Paris) for confirmation. Approved cases then go to a canonical commission in the diocese of the person cured. The bishop of this see pronounces on the miraculous nature of the cure. The sanctuary publishes a monthly magazine translated from the French into four languages that reports news and current events in Lourdes.

Bibliography: R. P. CROS, *Histoire de Notre Dame de Lourdes d'après les documents et les témoins,* 3 v. (Paris 1925–27). D. C. SHARKEY, *After Bernadette* (Milwaukee 1945). B. LEBBE, *The Soul of Bernadette* (Tralee 1946). P. MIEST, *Les 54 miracles de Lourdes au jugement du droit canon, 1858–1958* (Paris 1958). G. SIEGMUND, *De miraculis atque sanationibus Lourdensibus* (Rome 1960). R. LAURENTIN, Lourdes: *Histoire authentique des apparitions de Lourdes,* 6 v. (Paris 1961–66).R. HARRIS, *Lourdes: Body and Spirit in the Secular Age* (New York 1999). R. LAURENTIN, V. MESSORI, and M. J. FURIÓ, *Lourdes: crónica de un misterio* (Barcelona 1997).

[T. F. CASEY/EDS.]

LOUVAIN, AMERICAN COLLEGE AT

The official title is: The American College of the Immaculate Conception of the Blessed Virgin Mary. It was originally founded in 1857 to train European priests for work in the U.S. The project originated with Martin J. Spalding, Bishop of Louisville, Ky., who was in Belgium in 1852 to recruit priests for the U.S. The idea was warmly received by the Belgian hierarchy but opposed by Francis P. Kenrick, Archbishop of Baltimore, who at that time was more interested in establishing an American College in Rome. Political disturbances, however, made the Roman project impossible. The Rev. Peter

KINDEKENS, Vicar-general of Detroit, Mich., who was sent to Rome for that purpose, returned to his native Belgium where he found the Belgian hierarchy still interested in the American College. On his return to the U.S., Kindekens wrote to the American hierarchy pointing out the feasibility of a foundation in Louvain (1) to serve as a seminary for the training of European clergy for mission work in the U.S., and (2) to provide the American bishops with a college to which at least some of their students might be sent to acquire a well-rounded clerical training.

The bishops approved the project but could not offer any financial aid with the exception of Spalding and Peter Paul LEFEVERE of Detroit, who made the project their own and promoted monetary support. In February 1857 Kindekens returned to Belgium as rector, and the college was opened on March 19 in an old Benedictine college that had been founded in 1629. In April 1858 the American College sent its first missionaries to the U.S., two to Detroit and two to Louisville, in gratitude to the two bishops, Spalding and Lefevere, who were regarded as founders.

The students followed the theology courses partly at the College and partly at the University until 1877, when the University course was discontinued and the students attended the lectures in moral theology and Scripture given by the Jesuits. In 1898 the Jesuit courses were discontinued and the Belgian hierarchy established a full course in elementary theology at the University. In 1894 the rules and constitution of the American College were approved; and in 1899 the college was officially affiliated with the University of Louvain.

In 1906 two major events marked the progress of the College: the definitive approval of the rules by Pope PIUS X and the establishment of a department of philosophy. By 1907, the 50th anniversary of its founding, the American College had sent more than 700 priests to the U.S., and counted among its alumni 15 archbishops and bishops. In 1914, under the direction of the rector, Rev. Jules DeBecker, extensive improvements were undertaken—the property was enlarged, and a new building was added. August of 1914 brought the outbreak of World War I, the invasion of Belgium, and a long period of hardship and destruction.

After World War I, DeBecker, with the approval of the American hierarchy, began the reconstruction of the College and classes were resumed in 1919. The first America vice-rector, Rev. Charles Curran of Rhode Island, was named to assist DeBecker, and the first American students arrived—18 in number—in November. From this period onward, the American College passed from a training center for European priests destined for

the American missions to a European center of training primarily for American priests.

During the German occupation of Belgium in World War II, the college building was used as a garrison by the occupying forces, and for a time after the war, the university used the American College as a residence for students. At the time a debate was taking place in the United States as to whether or not the American College had outlived its usefulness. The college had prepared over 1,000 priests for the apostolate and gave five bishops to the Church between 1931 and 1939. In 1949 its rector, DeStrycker, died and the college was closed. In the same year the issue of maintaining the college was presented to the American hierarchy. After much deliberation, the college was reopened and the Rev. Thomas F. Maloney of the Providence diocese was appointed as the first American Rector of the college. Maloney's first task was to regain the use of the college buildings.

Maloney worked closely with Msgr. Honoré van Waeyenbergh, rector magnificus of the university, to negotiate the return of the American College to the American hierarchy. The college officially reopened on Sept. 30, 1952 with seminarians from 20 U.S. dioceses. Classes, open to other seminarians, were conducted in the college by the professors of the University's schola minor of theology, including Joseph Coppens. Philosophy students attended courses at the Higher Institute of Philosophy. Under Maloney's leadership and with the continued support of alumni bishops, the college enrollment continued to grow. With the opening of the 1955–56 academic year, the seminary population had reached 114 students sponsored by 26 dioceses. The number was the largest in the history of the college which now had a full complement of two years of philosophy and four years of theology.

Maloney's rectorship was marked by his friendship with the guardian of the Irish (Franciscan) College and the cooperation of van Waeyenbergh, now a bishop and an influential figure in the International Federation of Catholic Universities. Maloney, named an extraordinary professor of the university, lectured in pastoral theology at the university. In May 1960 Maloney was appointed auxiliary bishop of Providence, where he died on Sept. 10, 1962.

Rev. Paul D. Riedl, a 1935 alumnus of the college and priest of the Springfield, Mass., diocese, succeeded Maloney as rector. The early years of his rectorship (1960–1971) were an exciting period in the history of the college. Several of its university professors served as *periti* during Vatican Council II and many of the American Council Fathers visited the college on their way to or from sessions of the Council. Responsibility for the college was formally entrusted to a committee of the National Conference of Catholic Bishops (NCCB) whose membership consisted of one bishop from each of the 12 episcopal regions in the United States.

The latter years of Riedl's rectorship were a critical period for the college. The rapid decline in the number of American seminarians brought with it a rapid decrease in the number of American seminarians studying in Louvain. The postwar growth of the university and tensions between Belgium's Flemish and Walloon populations threatened and eventually brought about a splitting of the university. Walloon professors hoped that college students would attend classes on the planned campus at Louvain-la-Neuve. Flemish professors of theology, on the other hand, decided to inaugurate a program of theology with courses in English. They would include a number of professors from religious congregations, hitherto barred from university appointment except as "extraordinary professors." The American College remained in Louvain, now commonly called Leuven. Its enrollment of less than 50 seminarians were complimented by a number of priests in graduate studies.

Riedl and the Rev. Clement Pribil, vice- rector of the college, worked closely with university professors in the development of the new English-language theology program. Two alumni of the college, Raymond F. Collins (Providence, '59) and Francis J. Manning (Oklahoma City, '60), were among the four visiting professors appointed in the new program that opened in October of 1969. In 1970, Pribil took over the mantle of leadership from Riedl (d. 1997) who then returned to his Springfield diocese. By that time, Collins had been appointed to succeed Pribil. Pribil's rectorship was marked by efforts to increase the enrollment of the college. In this task he was assisted by his successor, with whom he served as co-rector during the fall semester of 1971.

Collins' appointment resulted from the shared vision of the college's leadership, its NCCB committee, and the university faculty. Ties with the "English faculty" were the hallmark of Collins' tenure as rector. Collins was appointed a university docent in 1972 and was promoted to ordinary professor in 1977. He would remain in that capacity until he assumed the deanship of the School of Religious Studies at the CATHOLIC UNIVERSITY OF AMERICA in 1993. At one point college enrollment passed the century mark, with more than 80 seminarians and a score of priests in graduate studies. Almost 100 men were ordained to the priesthood during the Collins years.

When Collins resigned from the rectorship in 1978, he was succeeded by Rev. William Greytak, a priest of the Helena diocese and professor of history at Carroll College. Greytak brought with him the spirit of the West

with the result that the college was no longer as oriented towards the U.S. northeast as it had been. He sold the villa property outside the city that had belonged to the college and negotiated with university officials for full title to the college's properties. Greytak returned to his post at Carroll College in 1983, entrusting the college rectorship to Rev. John J. Costanzo, a priest of the Pueblo, Co., diocese. Costanzo's rectorship (1983–88) was marked by stability in enrollment and emphasis on a development program, with the assistance of the Rev. Frank E. Lioi, formerly rector of the Rochester, N.Y., seminary.

In 1988, Monsignor Ivory of the Newark archdiocese became the seventh American rector of the American College. Ivory was an alumnus of the college and served as its spiritual director for a five-year period during Riedl's rectorship. Ivory's rectorship was marked by internal strife, resulting in the appointment of Rev. Melvin T. Long, of Salina, Kan., as interim rector in the spring of 1992. Ivory was the last of four successive American rectors of the college to possess an earned doctorate. Long had served as the college's first full-time director of pastoral formation during Collins' rectorship. At the time of his appointment as interim rector, Long was in charge of the Office of the American College located in the recently built NCCB-USCC building in Washington. He returned to the nation's capital in 1993 when Rev. David Windsor, CM, was appointed as rector.

Windsor was the first American rector of the college who had not been an alumnus. His tenure as rector was marked by the increased organization of the college staff, the use of modern technology, and attention to an American advisory board. His concern for the development of the college prompted Windsor to make repeated trips to the United States. Despite his efforts, enrollment continued to decline. When Windsor relinquished the rectorship to his vice-rector, Rev. Kevin A. Codd, an alumnus of the College and a priest of the Spokane, Wash., diocese in 2001, the college had reached its lowest ebb in enrollment.

Bibliography: V. BRANTŜ, *La Faculté de droit de l'Université de Louvain à travers cinq siècles* (Brussels 1917). A. BRUYLANTS, "Louvaina y su Faculdad di Ciencias en el transcuro de los siglos," *Afinidad,* v.22 (Barcelona 1955–56). F. CLAEYS, BOÚÚAERT, *L'Ancienne Université de Louvain: Études et documents* (Louvain 1956). J. COPPENS, ed., *Le Cinquième centenaire de la Faculté de Théologie de l'Université de Louvain, 1432–1932* (Bruges 1932). V. DENIS, *Catholic University of Louvain, 1425–1958* (Louvain 1958); *Supplement* (Louvain 1965). J. VAN DER HEYDEN, *The Louvain American College, 1857–1907* (Louvain 1909). L. VAN DER ESSEN, *L'Université de Louvain, 1425–1940* (Brussels 1945). E. LOUSSE, *L'Université de Louvain pendant la seconde Guerre mondiale, 1939–1945* (Bruges 1945). G. MALENGREAU, "Lovanium, première expérience universitaire au Congo," *Bulletin du Cercle Congo—U.L.B.* (1955–1956). R. PIRET, *La Faculté de Droit de 1922 à 1952* (n.p. 1952). L. DE RAEYMAEKER, "Les Origines de l'Institut supérieur de Philosophie de Louvain," *Revue philosophique de Louvain* 49 (1951) 505–633. E. H. S. REUSENS, *Documents relatifs à l'Histoire de l'Université de Louvain, 1425–1797,* 5 v. (Louvain 1881–1903). J. D. SAUTER, *The American College of Louvain, 1897–1898* (Louvain 1959). R. E. CROSS and E. L. ZOELLER, *The Story of the American College,* extract from *The American College Bulletin* (Louvain 1957). *The American College Bulletin,* v.44 (Louvain 1965).

[V. DENIS/R. F. COLLINS]

LOUVAIN, CATHOLIC UNIVERSITY OF

The Catholic University of Louvain is the popular name in the English- speaking world for the historic Universitas Catholica Lovaniensis, founded in 1425 in the Flemish city of Leuven. It is the oldest university in the Low Countries with six centuries of distinguished contributions in European intellectual tradition. This entry covers its history in four separate phases: (1) the historic "old university" from 1425 to 1797; (2) the state university founded by the Dutch King, William I from 1817 to 1835; (3) the re-established Catholic university from 1834 to 1968; and (4) the division of Leuven into two independent universities in 1968—the Flemish-language Katholieke Unversiteit te Leuven, located in the old university city of Leuven and commonly abbreviated as K.U. Leuven, and the French-language Université Catholique de Louvain, located in the newly established town of Louvain-la-Neuve, commonly abbreviated as UCL. For the American College affiliated with Louvain, *see* LOUVAIN, AMERICAN COLLEGE AT.

First Foundation. Through the personal efforts of John IV, Duke of Brabant, Pope Martin V issued a bull on Dec. 9, 1425, establishing a university in Leuven, the capital of Brabant. The papal bull called for the creation of four faculties: arts, canon law, civil law, and medicine. The first home for the university was on Hogeschoolplein, "High School Square." The first 12 professors came from the universities of Paris and Cologne. In 1432, Pope Eugene IV granted permission for the establishment of a faculty of theology at Leuven. The city of Leuven donated the 14th-century cloth weavers' hall to this faculty of the university. Since its inception, the student population has been diverse and international; by 1450 most European nations were represented.

In the 16th century, a number of outstanding names dominated Leuven scholarship. Adriaan Floriszoon Boeyens (1459–1523), elected as Pope Adrian VI in 1522, had been a student, professor, rector of Leuven, and tutor to Erasmus and to the future Emperor Charles V. In his will, Adrian VI instructed that his house in Leuven

be turned into a college. After it collapsed in 1775, an impressive *Pauscollege* or the "Pope's College" was built on the same site. Theologians of Leuven defended papal precedence over councils at the Council of Basel (1431–1439). Leuven's faculty of theology was the first to condemn Martin Luther openly (Nov. 7, 1519). Several Leuven professors later took active and even directive roles in the work of the Council of Trent (1545–1563), including Michael Baius (1513–1589) and Cornelius Jansenius (1510–1576), not to be confused with his namesake, Cornelius Jansenius (1585–1638) also a Leuven professor, the so-called "founder" of Jansenism.

Suppression and Second Foundation: The State University of King William I. Like its counterparts elsewhere, Leuven fell victim to the frequent economic and social unrest, religious strife, and political and military exigencies that enveloped Europe from the 16th to the 18th centuries. Matters hit a low point with the French conquest of Belgium in 1794. On October 24 of that year, the Revolutionary French Republic suppressed the university, seized its properties, and appropriated some 5,000 volumes from the library, or about one-tenth of the total holdings. In 1797 the university was officially closed. After the successful Dutch revolt against the French in 1813, King William (1772–1843), son of William V the Prince of Orange, became King William I of the United Netherlands, encompassing modern-day Belgium. One of William's actions, a major irritation to Belgians, was the re-opening the university at Leuven as a secular state university in 1817.

Third Foundation: The 19th-Century Revival of the Catholic University. As soon as Belgium obtained its independence from the Netherlands in 1830, the movement to establish a Catholic university gathered momentum. Pope Gregory XVI approved the project in a papal brief on Dec. 13, 1833. In 1834 the Belgian bishops established a Catholic university in Mechlin. The university was transferred to Leuven in 1835. The 19th century was an especially favorable period for the development of the theology and philosophy at Leuven. In 1898, a *Schola Minor* was created to provide preliminary theological training. In the general atmosphere of renewal, characteristic of the pontificate of Pope Leo XIII, theologians from Leuven strove for greater scholastic achievement. The historical-critical methodology that would become the faculty's hallmark, i.e., the close association of positive research and speculative theology, was further developed in each of the disciplines of theological research. A first step was taken in 1889 with the creation of a course entitled "Critical History of the Old Testament" by Albin Van Hoonacker. This course was an early attempt to apply the historical critical method to biblical texts. The appointment of Albert Cauchie as professor of Church History six years later had an even more decisive influence on the renewal of methodology and spirit among Leuven theologians. Cauchie, who founded the *Revue d'histoire ecclésiastique* in 1900, was the inspiration for a scientific approach in the fields of exegesis (as illustrated by the later publications of Lucien CERFAUX and Joseph Coppens), patristics (with the work of Joseph Lebon, the founder of *Spicilegium Sacrum Lovaniense*, and of René Draguet, the dynamic director of the *Corpus Scriptorum Christianorum Orientalium*) and Church history (as seen in the efforts of Albert De Meyer who, in 1928, took over the direction of the *Dictionnaire d'histoire et de géographie ecclésiastiques*). The launching of a new theological journal, the *Ephemerides Theologicae Lovanienses* in 1923 and the inauguration of the *Colloquium Biblicum Lovaniense* after the Second World War, increased the reputation of Leuven theology and bore witness to the continuation of its exegetical tradition. The *Bibliotheca Ephemeridum Theologicarum Lovaniensium* continues to publish, among many other items, the proceedings of the biblical colloquia.

The linking of tradition and contemporary life refection, so important to the Leuven theological tradition, has been equally important for the Leuven philosophical tradition. Founded in 1889, the Institute of Philosophy at Leuven has undergone a steady process of growth and development. During its first decades, the Institute focused on medieval philosophy, especially the thought of Thomas Aquinas. At the same time an ongoing dialogue with the new sciences and their offshoots, positivism and scientism, complemented the study of Thomism.

In his encyclical *Aeterni Patris* (1879), Pope Leo XIII (1810–1903) had recommended the study of Thomas Aquinas as an impetus for the renovation of Christian intellectual life in modern society. Psychology, anthropology, sociology and other new sciences presented themselves as a challenge to Church doctrine. Leo XIII believed that a revised Thomism would provide a framework within which the Church could address the new sciences and integrate them within traditional Christian belief. Before becoming pope, Leo had been papal nuncio in Brussels and had first-hand knowledge of Leuven. In October 1882, under continued pressure from Pope Leo XIII, the reluctant Belgian bishops agreed to establish a chair of Thomistic Philosophy at Leuven. A young professor from the diocesan seminary in Mechlin, Désiré Joseph MERCIER (1851–1926), later to become the archbishop of Mechelen, was the first to be named to the new chair. Mercier combined a profound sense of Thomas with a lively interest in contemporary issues.

In 1887 Mercier proposed that a specialized institute should be established as a center for instruction as well as research. In 1889 Pope Leo approved Mercier's plan and the Leuven "Higher Institute of Philosophy" was established. The foundation of the *Revue Néo-Scolastique* in 1894 gave the Leuven school an international forum for its conception of an "open" Thomism. In order to achieve his project of revitalizing Thomism, Mercier recruited a core of specialists from diverse fields. In 1893 he brought in four young professors to assist him: Désiré Nys (1859–1927) who devoted himself to the natural sciences and worked out an open Thomistic cosmology; Armand Thiéry (1868–1955) who had studied experimental psychology with Wundt in Leipzig; and Simon Deploige (1868–1927) and Maurice DE WULF (1867–1947). Deploige, who succeeded Mercier as president of the Institute (1906 to 1927), was primarily interested in social and political philosophy. De Wulf devoted himself to the study of the history of philosophy. His *History of Medieval Philosohy* was a pioneering investigation into medieval thought.

Leuven in Two World Wars. The city of Leuven and its university suffered greatly in both world wars. The university's greatest physical loss was the August 1914 burning of the university library with its 300,000 volumes, 1,000 or more ancient manuscripts and all its archives. *"Ici finit la culture Allemande"* was the sign the Belgians attached to the walls of the burned-out library, after German troops left town. As a result of the heroic efforts of Paulin Ladeuze (1870–1940), then rector of Leuven, and of the indefatigable Cardinal Mercier, a new library was established with donations from alumni, individuals, other educational institutions, and the government of the United States of America.

World War II brought new destruction to Leuven and to its university. Not only was there a second burning of the university library in 1940, but also its rector, Honoré van Waeyenbergh, was imprisoned in Brussels by German authorities for refusing to turn over lists of student names as well as refusing to accept German professors at Leuven. The key figure who managed the university's affairs during the war, enforcing the policies of Van Waeyenbergh, was the vice-rector Léon Joseph SUENENS, later cardinal archbishop of Mechlin-Brussels. Following World War II, the rector Van Waeyenbergh effectively carried out a major expansion of programs and facilities at the university and established a Catholic University of Lovanium in the Belgian Congo.

Vatican II. Leuven theologians, under the leadership and inspiration of Cardinal Suenens, played a significant role in the deliberations at Vatican II. These periti worked with the Belgian bishops and with their former students, many of whom were present as Council fathers. A Leuven theologian, Msgr. Gerard Philips, was prominent in the deliberations that led to the formulation of the dogmatic constitution *Lumen Gentium*. The years following Vatican II witnessed an attempt by Leuven's theologians to enter into dialogue with scientists and others who engage in the study of the human condition, seeking to develop a theological language faithful to tradition and in touch with the mentality and situation of modern times.

Division into Two Universities. In the 1960s, Leuven was caught up in the crossfire between the French- and Flemish-speaking communities. In the wake of student riots, ethnic unrest, and government upheavals, Leuven was reorganized into separate Flemish-language and French-language universities in 1968—the Flemish Katholieke Universiteit Leuven in the old university city of Leuven and the French Université Catholique de Louvain on an entirely new campus, Louvain-la-Neuve, about 20 miles away from the historic city of Leuven. On May 28, 1970 the Belgian parliament gave separate legal status to each of these two divisions. In 1972 the first faculties were installed in the new university at Louvain-la-Neuve.

Another result of this linguistic separation was the offering of classes, especially in theology and philosophy, in the English language on the old campus in the university city of Leuven. In later years, the French-language university too began to offer some programs in English. Each university, in its own way and to varying degrees, has remained faithful to the original vision and tradition, with a strong international faculty and student presence. Despite the cleave, there came a tremendous growth in student enrollment. By 2000, the student population at Leuven was approaching 26,000, while the student population at Louvain-la-Neuve had reached 21,000.

The tense relations between both universities during the 1970s later gave way to a more congenial and collaborative atmosphere, especially with the joint celebration in 2000 of the 575th anniversary of the first foundation at Leuven. Both universities are united in the common academic tradition of the historic Universitas Catholica Lovaniensis. Although each university has its own rector and academic council, they are united under the archbishop of Mechlin-Brussels, the grand chancellor of each of the universities.

Bibliography: E. LOUSSE, *The University of Louvain during the Second World War* (Bruges 1946). V. DENIS, *Catholic University of Louvain, 1425–1958* (Louvain 1958). *L'opinion publique belge et l'université de Louvain. Enquête sociologique sur les problèmes de l'université et divers* (Louvain 1967). L. DE RAEYMAEKER, *Le Cardinal Mercier et l'Institut supérieur de philosophie de Louvain* (Louvain 1952). J. T. ELLIS, *The Influence of the Catholic University of Louvain on the Church in the United States* (Louvain 1982). U. DHONDT and F. J. BOCK, *Leuven, the Institute of Philosophy (1889–1989)* (Leuven 1989). E. LAMBERTS and J. ROEGIERS, eds., *De Universiteit te Leuven* (Leuven 1986). *Leuven University, 1425–1985* (Leuven 1990). L. KENIS, *The Louvain Faculty of Theology in the Nineteenth Century: A Bibliography of the Professors in Theology and Canon Law: With Biographical Notes* (Leuven 1994). D. AERTS and C. COPPENS, *Leuven in Books, Books in Leuven: The Oldest University of the Low Countries and Its Library* (Leuven 1999).

[J. A. DICK]

LOVE

An affective accord or union with what is in some way grasped as congenial. While almost hopelessly general, this definition has the merit of indicating the dynamic and relational character of all love and of suggesting that its function is to promote wholeness. An effort to specify the levels of wholeness toward which various loves are directed cannot fail to throw light on the ultimate meaning and destiny of human existence. This article considers the various kinds of love, the historical development of theories of love, love at the level of sense, and love at the level of reason.

Kinds of Love

Human beings experience many different kinds of love, corresponding to different levels of existence. The most important distinction is that between sensible and rational love; other types are concupiscent and benevolent love, eros and agape, and appreciative love.

Sensible and Rational. Sensible love, which humanity shares with the animals, is geared to satisfying the needs of biological life. It looks to what is presented by the senses as requisite and congenial to the individual here and now. Since it is intrinsically dependent on matter and consists in the dynamic accord of sensitized potency with what can fulfill it, it is radically subjective.

Rational love, on the other hand, is rooted in human spirituality and openness to BEING. Because he is spiritual, man can grasp the real (both sensible and suprasensible) as independent of the present condition of his organism and affectively relate himself to it on the basis of its own merits. Such love is fundamentally objective. Whereas sensible love is a psychic reaction to stimulus, rational love is a personal response to worth. The first looks to the conservation and promotion of the individual organism or the species. The second looks beyond these to the absolute value of being, which it seeks to promote in all its finite embodiments.

Concupiscent and Benevolent. The fact that rational love is ordered to the continual enhancement of the finite in the light of the infinite leads to a further distinction. For one cannot enhance something without desiring for it whatever is conducive to its growth and development. This facet of love, which is rooted in the limited and potential character of the beloved and seeks goods that will perfect him, is called concupiscent love (*amor concupiscentiae*). On the other hand, the beloved for whom such goods are desired and whose full growth in being is sought is loved with benevolent love (*amor benevolentiae*). Concupiscent love and benevolent love are thus two dimensions or aspects of rational love; although not identical with one another, they are nonetheless inseparable.

Eros and Agape. Another important distinction in the language of love is that between eros and agape. Although sometimes confused with the distinction between concupiscent and benevolent love, this is really quite different. It does not arise from the essential polarity within all human love, but regards instead the different orientations such love may assume. For since man is open to Being as absolute, he can serve such Being anywhere. He is not limited to promoting being in himself only, but can do so in others. When, therefore, he focuses on himself and seeks his own full expansion in being, his love is called eros. When, however, it looks to others and devotes itself to their fulfillment, it is called agape. In either case, both the concupiscent and benevolent aspects of all human love are involved. On the other hand, neither eros nor agape taken separately would seem to be equal to love's total drive, for the distinction between self and other is a distinction within being. A love, therefore, looking to Being Itself could not exclude either without falling short. But more about this later.

Appreciative. Mention should also be made of what is sometimes called appreciative love (C. S. Lewis). For in the presence of what is congenial, it sometimes happens that a person's stance is neither one of desire nor one of benevolence but is more akin to sheer gratitude. From the depths of his soul he appreciates simply the excellence of what he encounters. However, although this may appear to be a distinct mode of love, it seems better to identify it with the openness to being that is the root of all rational love. It is precisely because man can appreciate the consummate excellence of being wherever he finds it that he seeks to promote it in himself and others and desires what furthers this work. And he is able to appreciate it because of that basic affinity to being that is the root of his spirituality.

Historical Development

Theories of love have gone through so long a process of evolution that it is impossible to detail their history in brief compass. [M.J. Adler, ed., *The Great Ideas: A Synopticon of Great Books of the Western World* (Chicago 1952) 1:105–82; R. Eisler, *Wörterbuch der philosophischen Begriffe* (Berlin 1927–30) 2:29–38; *Enciclopedia filosofica* (Venice Rome 1957) 1:173–180.]. Here only the main stages are mentioned, with emphasis focused on the origin of such theories among the Greeks and on their development within Christianity.

Greek Theories. Among the facets of love outlined above, the first to take systematic shape in a full-blown philosophy was that of ἔρος—not eros as contrasted with agape and as one of the two orientations of rational love, but as the overriding dynamism of the soul. Thus PLATO (*Symp.* 210A–E) conceives the soul as ordered from the outset to a wholly satisfying contemplation of the GOOD, which it can reach, however, only gradually and by means of a laborious ascent. Stirred by the ideal reality that makes its presence felt in and through the sensible, the soul is moved with longing for the eternal. Beyond the fleeting forms of beauty and goodness in the world around it, it looks for that which does not fade and whose immutable possession can alone quench its thirst. The Good, therefore, for Plato, however nobly and spiritually conceived, remains a term of desire (concupiscent love). It is not loved for its own sake but for its capacity to satisfy the soul's hunger. Love, on the other hand, is basically a matter of longing. It is not benevolence, a generous impulse to enhance the world; it is flight from the world to a changeless noetic heaven that is seen as the soul's salvation.

ARISTOTLE is more down to earth. His analysis of love is directed largely to the question of FRIENDSHIP and is situated in the context of natural finality (*Eth. Nic.* 1155a–1172a). Like all natural entities, man too has an innate drive toward what will perfect him. This relationship to himself is seen as a kind of friendship, a benevolent attitude aiming at his own promotion in goodness. More importantly, because of man's intellectual nature, he is able to recognize another man as in some sense one with him by likeness and, on the basis of this similarity, to extend the benevolence he has for himself to this other. Friendship is thus a prolongation of self-love and the friend a kind of second self (*Eth. Nic.* 1166a 1–2).

The importance of Aristotle's theory is that it makes room for a love that is more than mere desire. Because of his likeness to the self, the friend is loved for his own sake. Love becomes generous, a matter of giving as well as of getting. This is what will permit a Christian theologian such as St. THOMAS AQUINAS to make considerable use of Aristotle's ideas in the elaboration of a theory of charity. However, it must be pointed out that because of Aristotle's fundamental naturalism and his lack of a doctrine on creation, the individual substance remains ontologically primary and all its activities, including friendship in the case of man, are necessarily subordinate to its own drive for perfection. Benevolence is therefore rooted in a more radical concupiscence; although one's friend is loved for his own sake, the reason that one enters such a relationship is to satisfy a natural need. Friendship is but a good required for human happiness.

Christian Thought. Christianity brought about a basic shift in man's thinking about love. The abundant generosity of love comes to the fore. Instead of rooting love, as Plato did, in man's spiritual poverty or deriving it, with Aristotle, from the needs of nature, Christian thought sees love's source in the infinite perfection and creativity of Divine Being. God Himself is love (1 Jn 4.8). His very substance is a loving community of three divine Persons. He creates the world out of love. And out of love He sends his Son to redeem man. The Word made flesh is Love incarnate who calls man, made in His image, to a share in His life. Man's basic vocation is now one of generous love, agape. His consuming task is to promote God's kingdom on earth, to spend himself in behalf of the Lord who seeks an ever fuller presence in the world He made. In this perspective, even the search for personal happiness is subordinated to pure devotion to God and His glory (cf. Thomas Aquinas, *In 4 sent.* 49.1.2.1 ad 3).

This Christian insight, founded on God's revelation of Himself, represents the high-water mark in man's comprehension of love's scope. Subsequent thinkers, working under its influence, have only partially succeeded in elaborating comprehensive systems consistent with it. Too often, when they have not ignored it and reverted to something inferior, their efforts have resulted only in distorting the sublime vision that Christ's revelation affords.

It is perhaps not too much to say that in the writings of Aquinas, the Middle Ages produced its least unsatisfactory synthesis. Even there, however, some thinkers feel that Aquinas's reliance on Aristotle produced a tension in his thinking on love that he never fully overcame. The other great medieval tradition, represented by RICHARD OF SAINT-VICTOR, though more in tune with contemporary PERSONALISM, is, like the latter, too lacking in comprehensive categories to provide an adequate metaphysics. Both, however, are truer to the Christian concept of love than anything found in modern thought until quite recently. Thus, for example, the Italian Renaissance combined the impersonalism of Platonic eros with the creativity of Christian agape to conceive love as an immanent, all-pervasive cosmic force. The rise of EMPIRICISM, on the other hand, stripped away love's transcendental im-

plications and reduced it to the status of a particular, purely natural instinct. While the romantics absolutized the sexual side of love, the objective idealists, once more recognizing its suprasensible orientation, nevertheless saw it as part of a universal, impersonal dialectic. In reaction to all this, recent years have seen the rise of a new personalism, much enriched by the techniques of PHENOMENOLOGY, but still, it must be said, in search of a metaphysics. If ever there is to be a philosophy adequate to the Christian message, its best hope seems to lie in the restructuring of Aquinas's metaphysics of being along lines that take more explicit account of the central and comprehensive mystery of the personal.

Love at the Level of Sense

The distinction between sensible love and rational love is rooted in the different types of awareness that give rise to them. Sensible love is aroused by the presence to the animal's senses of something congenial to his nature. Its goal is pleasure, a strictly subjective state that is related to the animal's objective good only as a natural sign. For sensible consciousness is not objective. The animal is wholly guided in its actions by feelings of attraction and repulsion that it is unable to distinguish from the realities stimulating them. Hence those other traits of sensible love: the narrowness of its horizon and its lack of freedom, but also, on the brute level, its sureness and apparent innocence.

Role in Man. With man, the picture becomes more complicated. The sensible level of his nature is radically transformed by the spiritual component it embodies. As SPIRIT, man is at once interior to himself and present to the other as other. He enjoys OBJECTIVITY. Unlike the brute, he is not imprisoned within his own psycho-organic nature but can refer his sensations and feelings explicitly to the objects arousing them. They become revelations of the nature of the situation in which he finds himself and of its harmony or discord with his own concrete being. Thus, even though his sensible love has pleasure for its aim, it is pleasure known as such and as distinct from the things that provide it. This is what J. Guitton means when he remarks that in man's "most fundamental states, even the most bestial, there is always a hormone of spirit sufficient to differentiate these states from their animal counterparts" (113).

Granting, however, this transformation of sense life by its integration in man with objective awareness, its role nonetheless remains basically the same. In both man and beast, the attractions things exert are in the service of biological life—the life of the individual and that, too, of the species. Experiencing his own affective accord with certain objects in his environment, of his desires in their absence and of his pleasure in their presence, man, no less than the beast, is induced to satisfy the objective requirements of his psyche-organic nature that the former reactions signify. But whereas for the beast the inducement is compelling, it is not so for man. His self-possession and openness to more comprehensive values leave him free to follow the lead of sense or not to follow it. He cannot suppress the feelings that things arouse in him; but he can, when to yield would conflict with pursuit of a higher good, resist their promptings. Moreover, such regulation by reason is necessary if this vital realm of feelings and emotions, which is meant to sustain and promote human life, is not to disrupt it instead. For since nature has relaxed its grip on man to allow for the emergence of personal freedom, man's fund of emotional energy will dissipate itself in chaotic eruptions unless he personally intervenes to restrain and order it.

Need for Passions. But if man's passionate life apart from spirit's control will lack humanity, his spiritual life will be limp and languid unless fired from below by his passions. This is the truth Aquinas saw when he rejected the Stoic view of the passions as enemies of reason and morality (*Summa Theologiae* la2ae, 24.2). On the contrary, not only does the rational application of passionate energy not diminish spiritual activity; it enhances and presses it onward (*Summa Theologiae* la2ae, 24.3). For just as in man the presence of spirit transforms all the levels below it, so also it needs the support and cooperation of all these lower levels to carry out its own work. Here, perhaps, is the germ of truth in views that reduce all love to the level of sense and even to the sexual instinct (H. Spencer, S. Freud). Because spirit can insert itself effectively in the world only through the mediation of psycho-organic energy and because among all his drives the sexual one in man is the most clamorously insistent, the temptation is strong to simplify matters by collapsing all distinctions. One refutation of these views is simply that, in suppressing manifest distinctions, they impoverish experience instead of explaining it. That there is a difference between sensible love whose goal is pleasure and rational love whose term is being itself should become clear in the following section, which is devoted to the latter. Suffice it to say here that when man makes pleasure his overriding concern, not only does he blind himself to all that is valuable in itself, but by that very fact he makes sadness his constant companion. For he condemns himself to the permanent absence of the only good commensurate with the human heart.

Love on the Level of Reason

The root of rational love is the openness and affinity to Being Itself that defines the realm of spirit. To be spirit is to have access to being-as-absolute, i.e., to a value that

encompasses both oneself and the other and, while grounding each person in his originality, still transcends him on every side. To be spirit is to be-for-being, to exist, even prior to choice, as sharing in that pure devotion-to-being that is being. Whereas the dynamism of sensible nature is the dynamism of POTENCY seeking its own fulfillment, the radical dynamism of spirit is one of ACT, of abundance—it is a pure love of excellence, a pure complacency with perfection, rejoicing in its presence and bent on promoting its reign.

Characteristics. On this basis, the characteristics of rational love, as distinct from sensible love, are clearly discernible. For rational love is the individual's free ratification of this fundamental dynamism of spirit. It is a matter of freely orienting one's life in the direction of service. The element of FREEDOM here is important. The individual, to be sure, is not free on the pre-reflective level to determine what will present itself as good to his intellect. Just as the dynamism of the organism assures that whatever is sensibly present and in harmony with that dynamism will be *felt* as attractive, so also, when what is intellectually perceived presents itself as harmonizing with the spirit's essential drive, it is *known* as a rational good (cf. J. de Finance). But whereas, on the sensible level, the reactions are automatic, the response of spirit is not. For the absolute value of Being is present to spirit only through the mediation of particular forms, and the ways it may be served are seen as limited and often conflicting. Moreover, given the distinction in man between his psycho-organic drives, which look to his fulfillment as a separate individual, and the spirit's thrust toward a generous service that subordinates separate fulfillment to a more comprehensive good, the need for man to assume the direction of his life becomes manifest. What will he do? Will he pursue his own satisfaction on the organic level even if it means sacrificing his spiritual fulfillment, or will he let spirit be his guide even when to do so entails the curtailment of sensible appetites? This is the choice he must make. To decide for the former is to reject spirit's call and to settle for a life that he knows falls short. To opt for the latter is to undertake a life of discipline and hardship, but one in which even frustration serves a purpose and is redeemed by what it promotes. Reason and spirit, to be sure, are involved in either case since, on this level, even failure is a matter of free decision. But only when reason directs its course is a person's love truly rational.

Disinterested Love. What has been said about love in the preceding paragraphs raises an important question about love's disinterestedness. For if it is its harmony with the spirit's drive that recommends a particular course of action as good—much as sensible attractiveness is grounded in the conformity of an object with the psycho-physical dynamism of the organism—then it seems that love of the good on the level of spirit, no less than on the level of sense, is actually and inevitably simply a form of self-seeking. The reason a person dedicates himself to the service of Being is to achieve himself as spirit, just as the pursuit of pleasure looks to his fulfillment as organism. The one may be a higher and more comprehensive goal than the other, but in both cases the good remains subordinate to self-realization. The question then arises: Is a pure and disinterested love of anything, even God, within the bounds of human possibility? If it is not, then the selfishness of man becomes limitless and incurable, since he cannot help making God Himself a mere means to his own happiness. If, however, such love is possible, how can one even begin to understand it—for it seems to imply that a being can tend to something in no way connected with itself (cf. *Summa Theologiae* 2a2ae, 26.3 ad 2).

In their efforts to resolve this dilemma, philosophers have usually succeeded in holding on to only one of its horns. Thus, for example, there developed among some of the mystics of the 12th century an ecstatic conception of love (see Rousselot). From their point of view, love is not love at all unless it is completely pure and disinterested, unless the subject goes completely outside himself and loses himself in the beloved. An echo of this passion for complete disinterestedness comes up later in the writings of I. KANT (e.g., *Critique of Practical Reason*), for whom morality is not genuine if the maxims it proposes are in any way connected with the subject's likes or dislikes or with his drive for fulfillment, even spiritual. ''Duty and obligation are the only names that we must give to our relation to the moral law.'' In both of these views something human is lost. The ecstatic conception maintains a disinterested love at the price of foregoing any attempt to understand it. Kant's doctrine sacrifices love itself to preserve the subject from any touch of EGO-ISM.

On the other hand, there are thinkers who are less interested in idealizing selflessness than in giving a rational account of it. Thus P. ROUSSELOT defends as the doctrine of Aquinas a thinly disguised monism wherein God and creature are interpreted as whole and part and the distinction between them is all but collapsed. In this light, self-love is identically a pure and greater love of God, since to love oneself is at the same time and more profoundly to promote the whole in which the self has its being. Such a position is not much different from that of philosophers who are openly pantheistic. B. SPINOZA, for example, likewise collapses the distinction between creature and God. But instead of identifying self-love with a greater love for God, Spinoza ultimately identifies it with God's own love for Himself.

If moves such as these, which account for selfless love by doing away with the self, are philosophically inadequate, they are less so than the ones that either ignore or deny God in their efforts to explain love. For if the individual self is primary and has no ground beyond itself, then in all its relations with others it must ultimately seek itself. Thus, as has been seen, Aristotle was forced to derive an individual's love for another from his natural love for himself. And centuries later, J. S. MILL preached service to others as a source of deepest satisfaction to oneself. There is, no doubt, truth in both positions. But neither is successful in explaining disinterested love. For all they actually do is to make selfless love reasonable by showing that it is really not selfless.

Love of Self and Others. If a rational account of truly generous love can be given, it will have to proceed along lines similar to the ones indicated in L. B. Geiger's brilliant exposition of the Thomist solution. The foundation of Geiger's position is the analogy of appetite consequent upon the different ways in which the good is present to it. The WILL, or intellectual appetite, seeks the good as presented by intellect. But the INTELLECT is man's faculty for objective knowledge. It knows the real not merely in terms of the person's immediate dealings with it but as it is in itself. It presents to the will, therefore, not merely what is good for the individual but what is good in itself. The will thus is seen as naturally ordered to the real on its own merits. It is true to itself only when it loves what is good in itself for its own sake.

To rephrase this in the language used above, one can say that the spirit in man is dynamically ordered to being as an absolute value. In its very roots it is a love of being for its own sake. The perfection of spirit, therefore, is not a matter of acquisition but of orientation. Its fulfillment is to love generously. It is most itself when it is most *for* the other.

Since, in this light, there is no distinction between self-realization and genuine devotion to being for its own sake, the problem of disinterested love disappears. For now there can be no question of subordinating love for the other to one's own fulfillment (egoism) or of sacrificing that fulfillment to one's love for the other (ecstaticism). Personal fulfillment is identically a matter of generous service. When one loves generously, one is by that very fact fulfilled; one is caught up in Being's embrace. On the other hand, any idea of self-realization as a separate goal to which love is only a means is a misconception. It is to think of the self as something apart from its loving relation to Being and, therefore, able to use this relation for its own advantage. The truth is that the SELF exists only in this relationship and apart from it is nothing at all.

From what has been said, it is clear that no opposition can exist between genuine love of self and genuine love for others. Hence it is misleading to speak of a person's loving God more than himself, as if one could really sacrifice himself for the love of God and not instead be completed by it. What such a phrase means is that, since the root relation of spirit is one of responsiveness to the consummate excellence of Being Itself (God), the created spirit can be concerned for itself only as derivatively sharing in that excellence, not as rivaling, or, much less, surpassing it. So also with the idea that man naturally loves himself more than his neighbor. One can no more subordinate others to oneself than one can sacrifice self to God. On the contrary, one loves himself truly only in willing and spending himself for others.

What lies behind these other views is Aristotle's idea that self-love is the origin of man's love for others—an idea that, in turn, is founded on the Stagirite's conception of the ontological primacy of the individual SUBSTANCE. With one's own substantial reality functioning as the ultimate reason for all one does, it is manifest that one's relation to others must be secondary to the pursuit of one's own perfection. For Aristotle, this is true without qualification. It is only partly so, however, when viewed from the perspective of a metaphysics that takes account of the fact of CREATION. Thus St. Thomas, adopting Aristotle's position regarding man's relations with others who are finite like himself, is nevertheless forced to reverse it when it comes to man's love for God. For God is the ontological ground of man's individual reality and hence is the ultimate reason why man himself is lovable. Hence St. Thomas concludes that naturally man loves God more than himself and himself more than his neighbor. This view is tenable, and indeed irrefutable, so long as finite reality is seen as a collection of individual substances that are only accidentally related to one another. It would not hold, however, if the self is essentially constituted by its relationship to the other. Moreover, this latter position seems to some to be more in line with the Christian contention that love is the root of reality, its first beginning and its last end.

Man's Vocation. Thus, even apart from grace, man's vocation as a person is one of generous love. He completes himself through wholehearted commitment to a work of "reasonable service." The dominant motif of this work is the promotion of being in the beings around him, their continual enhancement in the light of possibilities that the enveloping presence of Being opens up. To this overriding motif, all man's passionate energies must be subordinated. The passions supply the raw material with which spirit works, the vitality it requires for any effective accomplishment. But they must be checked, disciplined, and integrated into the coherent work of love.

Unless spirit truly and vigorously assumes the ascendency, man's lower drives run riot in their strident search for satisfaction. But as part of the larger work of love, even their curtailment and frustration in particular instances can contribute to overall growth. This natural capacity of the person to grow in love and achieve a work of genuine service is what GRACE presupposes and transforms. For the manner and scope of this transformation, which enriches without suppressing what has here been described rather briefly, *see* CHARITY.

See Also: APPETITE; EMOTION; PASSION; PERSON; SEX.

Bibliography: L. B. GEIGER, *Le Problèe de l'amour chez saint Thomas d'Aquin* (Montreal 1952). P. ROUSSELOT, "Pour l'histoire du problème de l'amour au moyen âge," *Beiträge zur Geschichte der Philosophie und Theologie des Mittelatlters* 6.6 (Münster 1908) 1–102. H. D. SIMONIN, "Autour de la solution thomiste du probléme de l'amour," *Archives d'histoire doctinale et littéraire du moyen-âge* 6 (Paris 1931) 174–276. R. O. JOHANN, *The Meaning of Love* (Westminster, Md. 1955). J. DE FINANCE, "La Motion du bien," *Gregorianum* 39 (Rome 1958) 5–42. F. E. CROWE, "Complacency and Concern in the Thought of St. Thomas," *Theological Studies* 20 (Woodstock, Md. 1959) 1–39, 198–230, 343–395. J. GUITTON, *Essay on Human Love,* tr. M. CHANNING-PEARCE (New York 1951). C. S. LEWIS, *The Four Loves* (London 1960). M. C. D'ARCY, *The Mind and Heart of Love* (New York 1947). F. D. WILHELMSEN, *The Metaphysics of Love* (New York 1962).

[R. O. JOHANN]

LOVE (IN THE BIBLE)

To understand the place of love in the Bible, one must begin by examining the Biblical usage of the pertinent Hebrew root and of the Greek stem that corresponds to it in the Septuagint (LXX) and in the NT. Love, then, will be treated under three main headings: vocabulary, in the OT, and in the NT.

Vocabulary. Biblical Hebrew has a root (*'āhab* or *'āhēb*) that corresponds rather closely to the English term love. Like love, it can signify passion, desire, satisfaction, contentment, friendliness, intimacy, attachment, esteem. It regularly implies preference and often vehemence.

Greek has four stems for love: στέργω (affection founded on a natural bond such as family relationship), ἐράω (passionate, possessive love), φιλέω (friendship; intimate, respectful, often tender love), and ἀγαπάω (preference, esteem). The pagan poets and philosophers treat most often of the second (ἔρως) and third (φιλία) the translators and writers of the LXX show marked preference for the fourth (ἀγάπησις or ἀγάπη). Perhaps because ἀγαπάω sounds somewhat like *'āhab* or because, like the Hebrew root, it implies preference, the translators regularly use it, employing φιλέω much less frequently, ἐράω rarely, and στέργω hardly at all.

The NT follows LXX usage: ἀγαπάω is the usual term for love while ἐράω is absent, στέργω almost so, and φιλέω (except in compound words) relatively rare (usually expressive of friendship, but in John of a particularly warm love).

Old Testament. The Hebrew Bible prefers other terms to describe the relationship between God and man. As partner to a covenant with His people, Yahweh shows them loyal attachment (*ḥsd*), fidelity (*'mn*), tenderness (*rḥm*), and active favor (*ḥnn*). But to nuance the notion of covenant, Deuteronomy and Hosea point (ten times) to the gratuitous divine elective love that inspired it and to the enduring character of the divine love that will outlast the repudiation of the covenant at the time of the Exile. Later writers occasionally refer to this strong, gratuitous, preferential, and privilege-conferring divine love for Israel or for certain chosen individuals (e.g., David) or places (e.g., Zion).

The Israelites' relation to Yahweh is one of fear, service, and loyal attachment (the second and third of these terms referring to the COVENANT relationship), but also occasionally of love—most often in the stereotyped formula that usually appears in translation as "those who love Yahweh" but probably means simply "Yahweh's friends." Deuteronomy, however, uses love several times to present the really religious man—the convinced Yahwist—as a man wholeheartedly devoted to the God of the covenant and showing his devotion in obedience to all Yahweh's commands: obedient love is the equivalent of authentic religion.

Love for fellow man appears as a religious duty only three times in the entire Hebrew Bible. In texts that are neither characteristic nor central, it is commanded as the proper attitude toward fellow Israelites and aliens resident within the Israelite community (Lv 19.18, 34; Dt 10.19). The usual terms to designate this proper relation are righteousness (*ṣᵉdāqâ*) and justice (*mišpāṭ*), the former implying active beneficence and coming gradually to signify almsgiving.

The Septuagint contains nothing more than the Hebrew Bible on love for neighbor. It contains several additional references to love for God in the deuterocanonical books, but these are almost always instances of the stereotyped formula referred to above (God's friends). It also contains about twice as many references to divine love because of deuterocanonical usage or the translators' occasional rendering of other terms than *'āhab* by ἀγαπάω. But the idea of divine love in these additional texts is that of the Hebrew books. Most often the participle ἠγαπημένος or the adjective ἀγαπητός occurs, and Israel (or some favored individual) is the object of the Lord's elective love.

New Testament. The stem ἀγαπάω occurs well over 300 times in the NT. It rarely designates reprehensible love. It represents a central notion in the NT conception of divine-human relations. The reason lies in the fact that in the NT the notion of covenant gives place to that of divine paternity. Father is the proper name of the God of Jesus. He is Father of Jesus and of all those who become one with Jesus.

Synoptic Gospels. Crucial texts in Matthew, Mark, and Luke (baptismal THEOPHANY, TRANSFIGURATION, parable of the wicked vinedressers) present Jesus as God's "beloved Son," i.e., His Son in a unique sense ("only" Son—Hebrew *yāḥîd*, Septuagint ἀγαπητός) and the object of His paternal predilection. At the same time Jesus occasionally uses the term love to designate the total devotion to the Father and to Himself that He demands, and He declares Deuteronomy's command to love God (Dt 6.5) the greatest commandment of the Old Law. But above all, with startling originality, He proclaims love of neighbor the second greatest commandment of the Law and like the first; He reinterprets it to extend to all men including religious persecutors; He declares it an imitation of the Father and the behavior that proves a man son of God, and He identifies it as the criterion by which men will be judged.

Pauline Epistles. St. Paul presents the divine beneficence to man as mercy, to emphasize the misery or undeserving nature of its objects; as grace, to underscore its gratuitous character; and otherwise as love (usually thereby implying its magnitude). Christ's Passion-Resurrection is the great manifestation of His own and the Father's love. In imitation of Christ (and God) the Christian, the man who is "in Christ," must love especially fellow Christians but also all men, with a sincere, active, self-sacrificing love. Such love for neighbor is ultimately love for Christ (and God) because of the relation in which the neighbor stands to Christ. Other references to love for God occur rarely, as e.g., the OT cliché, "those who love God" (or "the Lord"). Paul's usual term for man's proper relationship of total surrender to God in Christ is faith. Those who make this surrender then reflect the divine love in their lives by their love for neighbor.

Johannine Writings. St. John almost never uses any term but love for God's beneficence toward men. In His Passion-Resurrection Christ reveals that God is love. The Father shows unique love for the Son, passing on to Him His own glory. The Son shows love for the Father and maintains Himself in the Father's love by obeying His command to show supreme love for the disciples by His Passion-Resurrection. The disciples show love for the Son and maintain themselves in the Son's love by obeying His command to love one another with a self-sacrificing love like His own. Love is a divine reality coming to believers from the Father through the Son, returning from them through Christ to the Father, vivifying them, marking them as Jesus' disciples, and proving the divine origin of His mission.

See Also: FAITH, 1; GRACE (IN THE BIBLE).

Bibliography: *Encyclopedic Dictionary of the Bible*, tr. and adap. by L. HARTMAN (New York 1963), from A. VAN DEN BORN, *Bijbels Woordenboek* 1377–85. C. SPICQ, *Agape in the New Testament*, tr. M. A. MCNAMARA and M. H. RICHTER (St. Louis 1963).

[T. BARROSSE]

LOVE, VIRTUE OF

In classical Catholic theology love was understood as the supernatural or theological virtue of CHARITY and its acts. Through divinely infused charity a person is oriented directly to the goodness of God as he is in himself, and God is loved for his own sake; the self and others are loved inasmuch as they potentially or actually participate in the divine goodness.

Since charity intends God as he is in himself rather than as only Creator of the universe, it was understood to be distinct from natural love of God, based on natural knowledge of him as source of the universe. Accordingly, charity presupposes the supernatural knowledge of God that is faith, which in turn exists only as a response to a free, supernatural, divine revelation.

Even this most rudimentary statement of the meaning of charity in classical theology discloses that the concept, ''charity,'' is inseparably bound to the meanings of such other concepts as natural love, natural knowledge, faith, revelation, the natural and the supernatural. Charity is analyzed and its meaning employed as a part of a theological conceptual system; its meaning is assigned in conjunction with the assignments of other meanings within the system.

The direction of contemporary theology that was established by Vatican Council II has passed from a classical world view and into historical consciousness. That has brought about theological developments of the concepts inseparably bound to the notion of charity in classical theology. The meaning of charity itself, it is therefore clear, must evolve similarly.

In the textbook way of pursuing theology, the principal treatise on charity has traditionally been part of MORAL THEOLOGY, a discipline oriented in the past to the preparation of confessors. The orientation towards *PRAXIS,* it is now generally recognized, was conducive to understanding the Christian life in a minimalistic way. The Christian life as presented in the textbook setting is the life of the precepts or commandments. It is distinct from the life of the COUNSELS, which was classified also as the life of striving for perfection and was studied in another discipline, ascetical theology.

As an element of Christian life, charity did not escape the minimalizing tendency in the science of the life of the precepts. Moral theologians generally maintained that Christ's new law of charity added no moral precepts in a material sense to those already contained in the Decalogue; charity, rather, brought a new ''form'' to acts in accord with those precepts. Thus moral theology tailored charity to fit the life of the precepts. While the face of charity in ascetical theology was generous and self-sacrificing, mirroring the countenance of its crucified Lord, the face of charity in moral theology was often egocentric and self-serving. Moralists saw charity as love, first, for God; secondly, for self; and only thirdly, for neighbor. Since the Christian life studied by ascetical theology was considered to be extraordinary, and since biblical research had not yet come into existence, the moralists' understanding of charity prevailed in classical Catholic theology.

Models for Understanding Charity. Three models or ways of understanding charity are now discernible in theology. They can be called potency-act, I-Thou, and self-transcendence respectively.

Potency-Act Model. The potency-act model of charity prevailed in moral theology from its beginnings as an independent discipline until the period of Vatican Council II. Basic to this model is the notion that love is an act of the intellectual appetite, the WILL. Man desires happiness, and his beatitude in the order of salvation is the beatific vision of the divine essence, in which man's supernaturally elevated intellectual appetite for the perfect good is completely fulfilled. Love for God is radically love for the perfect good, which God in himself is and to which the human intellectual appetite is ordered, at least when supernaturally elevated by charity. The neighbor is loved inasmuch as she or he is related to the divine goodness.

The strength of the potency-act model is its insistence on God's transcendence. If God is understood as the perfect, universal GOOD, which totally satisfies the human appetite and in which alone the beatitude of man consists (*Summa theologiae* 1a2ae, 2.8), there can be no tendency toward the false immanentism inclined to seek God only as present in the neighbor and not also as the transcendent Mystery and to reduce religion to social service in the secular city.

Nevertheless, this model has several limitations. The uniqueness of the person of the neighbor seems to be undervalued and ultimately superfluous. If the neighbor is loved only inasmuch as he or she participates in the divine goodness, it is difficult to explain how the neighbor is loved precisely inasmuch as he or she is not God but a unique person in his or her "otherness" in relation to God. How or why the neighbor can be loved for his or her own sake is not readily explicable, and there is a tendency to regard the neighbor as a means to one's own final end. St. Thomas himself concluded that the perfection of charity essential to beatitude does not necessarily include a perfection of charity for the neighbor: even if there were only one soul enjoying God, it would be perfectly happy (*beata*) without a neighbor to love (ibid. 4.8 ad 3).

Another disadvantage of this model is its anthropocentrism. Man is (OBEDIENTIAL) POTENCY for the BEATIFIC VISION, in which God is apprehended directly. God as the perfect good is seen as man's fulfillment, the fulfillment of the human appetite. The charge of regarding God here as a function of man cannot be completely escaped. A theocentric view of reality, it seems, would see man at the ultimate goal of love as a "function" of God.

A third disadvantage is demonstrated by the history of the use of this model. The model is individualistic and hardly conducive to the development of a social consciousness that strives toward the reign of God in working to ameliorate the social order on earth.

I-Thou Model. The second model of charity, the I-Thou, differs from the first in that it sees the love for "a concrete Thou" (Rahner) rather than an explicit love for God as the primary, fundamental act of charity. The love for a human Thou, according to this model, is the human and moral act par excellence. In it a person comes to himself or herself, fulfills his or her personal nature and freedom, and actuates himself or herself totally as a person in relation to all reality. The genuine love for a human Thou, moreover, is a supernatural act of charity and intends, implicitly and unthematically, God as he is in himself; and this implicit intending of God is the basic act of love for God.

Unlike the potency-act model, the I-Thou model emphasizes that love is an interpersonal relation and that, rather than rationally objectifiable goods, persons themselves in their ultimately mysterious depths are intended by love. This model makes clear also that a person is loved for his or her own sake as the unique individual that he or she is. Hence there is little tendency to regard the neighbor as a means to one's own beatitude. Love is seen here also as issuing from the mysterious core of the human spirit, touched by the Spirit of God, where a person freely disposes of herself or himself. As the notion that love is an act of the intellectual appetite is basic to

the first model, basic to the second is the idea that love is the personal act par excellence of freely disposing of oneself.

A limitation of the I-Thou model, shared in its own way by the first model, is that it seems to portray a "cheap grace" of personal fulfillment. Fulfillment appears to be located prematurely in the I-Thou relation. To be sure, the love for a human Thou is seen as placing the one who loves in an authentic relation to all reality. What is not indicated, however, is that one who stands in authentic relation to all reality must experience an exigency to work toward the transformation of the social order of the world. Precisely because the person loving a human Thou is seen as actuating herself or himself in the totality of her or his person, it is unclear that authentic universal, social community could add anything essential to the personal fulfillment already realized in the I-Thou communion.

Self-Transcendence Model. A third model sees charity as self-transcendence. Whereas the second model emerged in the decade before Vatican Council II, the third began to appear, chiefly in LIBERATION THEOLOGY, only in the decade following the Council. Still undeveloped, the self-transcendence model sees man, somewhat in the manner of Eastern mysticism, as oriented to transcend himself. Its view differs from Eastern mysticism, however, in that personal individuality is won, not lost, in self-transcendence.

While the potency-act model sees man as an active potency for the good, which, when attained, actuates and fulfills him, the self-transcendence model sees him more as a passive potency, capable of being annexed, indeed through his own cooperation, to the reality greater than himself that envelops him. Man needs to be "converted" (Lonergan) to reality; he must allow himself to be annexed to reality through authentic relations to it. Knowledge, according to this model, is less a drawing of reality into the mind and an actuation of the self (*intellectus quodammodo omnia*) and more a process of allowing the self to be annexed or joined, in an authentic (cognitive) relation, to the totality of what is. Similarly, love is seen as a state of CONVERSION to reality, in which a person allows herself or himself to be united, in an authentic personal (affective and effective) relation, to the whole of reality.

Defense of the Self-Transcendence Model. The third model seems to possess the strengths but none of the weaknesses of the other two models. The idea of love as the self transcending itself through authentic personal union with the totality of reality, like the first model, certainly safeguards the transcendence of God. Indeed the third model reverses the ANTHROPOCENTRISM of the first and locates the individual properly within the totality of reality, seeing him or her as ultimately annexed to God himself.

Like the I-Thou model, the self-transcendence model sees love as issuing from the depths of a person, from the core of personal freedom; moreover, it recognizes that the basic act of love is the I-Thou relation and that love is directed to the Thou in the mysterious, nonobjectifiable depths of his or her person. However, the third model also makes it clear that the fulfillment experienced in the love for a human Thou is merely relative and that personal fulfillment is ultimately to be found only in the fulfillment of the totality of reality. Only the self-transcendence model, seeing the individual as called to be annexed authentically to the whole of reality, makes clear that the individual's fulfillment is ultimately inseparable from the beatitude of all mankind. Love according to this model becomes, in a word, the seeking of the KINGDOM OF GOD. It becomes an active concern to transform the world by working to transform society into authentic community. When charity is understood as personal commitment to the reign of God, the unity of love for God and love for neighbor is seen in a new, more intimate and universal dimension, concealed from the eyes of the first and second models.

Bibliography: G. GILLEMAN, *The Primacy of Charity in Moral Theology*, tr. W. RYAN and A. VACHON (Westminister, Md. 1959). B. HÄRING, *The Law of Christ* (Westminster 1964) 2:83–107, 351–469. R. JOHANN, *The Meaning of Love* (Westminster 1959). B. LONERGAN, *Method in Theology* (New York 1972) 101–124, 237–244. K. RAHNER, *Theological Investigations* 5 (Baltimore and London 1966) 439–459; 6 (London and New York 1974) 231–249. N. RIGALI, ''Toward a Moral Theology of Social Consciousness,'' *Horizons: Journal of the College Theology Society* 4 (1977) 169–181. P. TEILHARD DE CHARDIN, *The Phenomenon of Man*, tr. B. WALL (New York 1959) 237–290.

[N. RIGALI]

LOVERS OF THE HOLY CROSS (LHC)

(*Amantes de la Croix, Dòng Mến Thánh Gia*, abbreviated ''L.H.C.,'' Official Catholic Directory, #2390) the first Vietnamese indigenous religious congregation, founded 1670 by Bishop Pierre LAMBERT DE LA MOTTE. This congregation is significant in the history of the Catholic Church in Vietnam for being the mother congregation that gave birth to, or inspired the formation of, all subsequent Vietnamese indigenous women religious congregations, including DOMINICAN SISTERS, Vietnamese Dominican Sisters, and the CONGREGATION OF MARY, QUEEN. The accompanying table lists all the L.H.C. congregations in existence at the beginning of the 21st century.

L.H.C. communities are found in Vietnam, Thailand, Laos, Cambodia, Taiwan, Japan, France, Germany, Norway, Italy, and the United States of America.

THE LOVERS OF THE HOLY CROSS IN VIETNAM

Early History. In his travels in northern Vietnam, Bishop Lambert had come across a group of celibate Vietnamese Catholic women who, on their own initiative, organized themselves into a community and practiced virtuous deeds. Impressed by their faith and perseverence, he decided to reorganize them into a religious congregation. Lambert drafted the original Rule for the fledging congregation, and witnessed the vows of the first two sisters on Feb. 2, 1670. The first community was officially formed at Kiên Lao (Nam Định, Bùi Chu Diocese in northern Vietnam), followed by Bái Vàng (Hà Nam, Hà Nội Diocese) and An Chỉ, Quảng Ngãi. On Aug. 28, 1678, the congregation received the official *recognitio* from the Congregation for the PROPAGATION OF THE FAITH.

Persecutions. The early decades of the young congregation were unsettling times, marked by the Vietnamese rulers' persecutions of Christians (*see* VIETNAM, THE CATHOLIC CHURCH IN). Despite these persecutions, the congregation attracted many new members and convents were established in all dioceses in Vietnam. From its inception, the sisters were engaged in a diverse range of ministries: praying for the success of the missionary enterprise in Vietnam and China in the midst of persecution; teaching catechism; educating Christian and non-Christian girls; caring for widows, the sick, homeless, refugees and the destitute; and baptizing infants and children in danger of death. Often, the sisters were the only Catholic presence in the area, working as catechists and ministering to the religious needs of the local Catholic community when foreign missionaries were either expelled or executed on orders of the Vietnamese emperor. At the height of the persecutions during the mid-19th century, over 30 convents were destroyed, about 2,000 sisters were dispersed and some 200 were martyred. In Huế alone, 56 sisters were burnt alive in the local parish church and two other sisters were buried alive.

Revival, Growth and Reorganization. When persecutions ended, the congregation experienced a renaissance, with many new vocations coming in and new convents established. In the early years of the period of reconstruction, the sisters wore lay clothes and worked in the rice-fields. In 1867, the sisters returned to their apostolic ministries, and began wearing religious habits and working as village catechists. With the promulgation of the 1917 Code of Canon Law, steps were taken to regularize the congregation's various diocesan foundations.

In 1925, the Congregation of Phát Diệm became the first to validate its Rule and regularize its vows according to the 1917 Code. Since then, other congregations sought to regularize their status.

First Great Exodus of 1954. The partition of Vietnam into the communist North and the non-communist South pursuant to the 1954 Geneva Agreement resulted in a massive displacement of the various congregations in the North. Many of these congregations were decimated when most of the sisters joined the exodus of Catholics fleeing the incoming communist government. These sisters were welcomed and helped by the congregations in the South to re-establish themselves, often from scratch. In the South, many congregations collaborated closely with the Catholic Relief Services and Caritas International.

The Fall of Saigon and the Second Great Exodus. The wave of religious persecution that followed in the wake of the fall of Saigon on April 30, 1975 also engulfed the L.H.C. Practically all the properties belonging to the various congregations, especially the schools and centers for social outreach were consfiscated by the communist authorities. Many sisters fled Vietnam, joining the second exodus of refugees fleeing on rickety fishing boats. Those who remained behind faced great hardships. Deprived of all means of support, the sisters returned to the land, working in rice-fields and raising cattle, as was the case in the 1860s. Under such tumultuous conditions, many sisters died from hunger, malnutrition and sicknesses. Those who had survived struggled to minister to the needs of the faithful. The sisters' solidarity with the common folk earned them much admiration, inspiring many Catholics to hold onto their faith despite the intense persecution.

When persecutions eased in the mid-1980s, many congregations were able to regroup and reorganize themselves with financial assistance from the Vietnamese diaspora. Despite continuing restrictive practices such as registration and reporting requirements, the Sisters were able to re-establish their social outreach ministries gradually, setting up childcare centers, kindergartens and orphanages as a result of new vocations and growth.

Reorganization and New Directions. Under the sponsorship of the late Archbishop Paul Nguyễn Văn Bình of Hồ Chí Minh City (Saigon) and under the guidance of Fr. Phi Khanh Vương Đình Khởi, a Franciscan priest, a Studies Committee on Lambertian Spirituality was formed in 1985 from the seven L.H.C. congregations in the Archdiocese of Hồ Chí Minh city. The principal objective of this committee was the carrying out of research and studies for the purposes of facilitating a return to the roots and a better understanding of the Lambertian

Name of Congregations	Diocese	Date of Foundation
Northern Vietnam		
L.H.C. Kiên Lao	Bui Chù	1670
L.H.C. Hưng Hóa	Hưng Hóa	1786
L.H.C. Vinh (Xã Đoài)	Vinh	1844
L.H.C. Phát Diệm	Phát Diệm	1902
L.H.C. Hà Nội	Hà Nội	1928
L.H.C. Thanh Hóa	Thanh Hóa	1932
Central Vietnam		
L.H.C. Huế (Thủ Đô)	Huế	1719
L.H.C. Nha Trang	Nha Trang	1955
L.H.C. Qui Nhơn	Qui Nhơn	1958
Southern Vietnam		
L.H.C. Cái Nhum	Vĩnh Long	1800
L.H.C. Thủ Thiêm	HCM City	1840
L.H.C. Cái Mơn	Vĩnh Long	1844
L.H.C. Chợ Quán	HCM City	1852
L.H.C. Gò Vấp	HCM City	1902
L.H.C. Đà Lạt	Đà Lạt	1932
L.H.C. Khiết Tâm	HCM City	1938
L.H.C. Cần Thơ	Cần Thơ	1958
L.H.C. Tân Lập	HCM City	1960
L.H.C. Tân Việt	HCM City	1963
L.H.C. Tân An	Mỹ Tho	1963
L.H.C. Bắc Hải	Xuân Lộc	1963
L.H.C. Thủ Đức	HCM City	1965
L.H.C. Phan Thiết	Phan Thiết	1983
U.S.A.		
L.H.C. Los Angeles	Los Angeles	1992

charism of the Cross. At the beginning of the 21st century, three important documents were published: The *Biography of Pierre Lambert de la Motte*, the *Manual on Lambertian Spirituality* and the *Constitution of the Lovers of the Holy Cross*. The Constitution was approved by the Vietnamese Bishops and was accepted by most L.H.C. congregations in Vietnam and the United States. At the end of the year 2000, in Vietnam there were about 2,940 perpetual professed, 1,074 temporary professed, 474 novices, and 447 pre-novices. Future plans in Vietnam include the formation of a federation of all diocesan L.H.C. congregations and the pooling of resources for collaborative programs for the training and formation of pre-novices and novices.

THE LOVERS OF THE HOLY CROSS IN THE UNITED STATES

Sisters of the L.H.C. arrived in the United States under terrible, chaotic conditions, their journeys by fishing boats totally unplanned and uncoordinated. The sisters were divided and split into different refugee camps, and were resettled in the United States under the sponsorship of various religious orders. Eventually, the sisters were able to regroup and establish new communities. In compliance with canonical provisions, each community was attached to a Vietnamese L.H.C. congregation.

Despite much hardship coping in a strange land and mastering an unfamiliar language, the sisters were able to settle down and establish new social ministries, healthcare and outreach programs for Vietnamese refugees, as well as religious education programs for Vietnamese children and youth.

The L.H.C. in the United States came of age in 1992, when the motherhouse of the L.H.C. Phát Diệm Congregation in Northern Vietnam, with the approval of the Holy See, granted administrative autonomy to the Los Angeles community, the largest community of L.H.C. in the United States. A new congregation, the L.H.C. Los Angeles Congregation came into existence as an autonomous Institute of Consecrated Life of Diocesan Right under the 1983 Code of Canon Law, with the motherhouse in Gardena, California. The L.H.C. Los Angeles Congregation has continued to maintain close ties with the other Vietnamese congregations, holding steadfastly to the Lambertian charism and spirituality, as well as assisting the Vietnamese congregations by rallying support and raising funds among the faithful in the Vietnamese diaspora for various relief projects.

Bibliography: Published sources on the L.H.C. include the three major works in the Vietnamese language produced by the Studies Committee on Lambertian Spirituality — the *Biography of Pierre Lambert de la Motte*, the *Manual on Lambertian Spirituality*, and the *Constitution of the Lovers of the Holy Cross*. These works were published for the first time in the United States in Thời Điểm Công Giáo, since 1995.

[T. T. PHAN]

LÖW, JOSEPH

Liturgical scholar; b. Vienna, July 23, 1893; d. Rome, Sept. 22, 1962. After having studied at Vienna and Katzelsdorf, Austria, he entered the REDEMPTORIST novitiate at Eggenburg in 1911, took philosophy and theology in the Redemptorist seminary at Mautern, and was ordained July 31, 1919. From 1920 to 1935 he taught liturgy, homiletics, archeology, and history of sacred art at Mautern and Gurk, making three long stays in Rome, where he worked under Johann Peter KIRSCH on the disciplines of Christian antiquity. He contributed valuable assistance in the restoration of the cathedral of Gurk, Carinthia. When called to Rome in 1935, he was named vice relator in the historical section of the Congregation of Rites and worked on hagiographical material, particularly in the preparation of the historical positions for the

confirmation of cult and beatification of Hemma of Gurk, Kateri Tekakwitha, Rose Verini, and Herman Joseph. From 1948 he was employed in the preparation of liturgical reform that eventuated in the restored Easter Vigil (1951) and the new Code of Rubrics (1960). His interest in liturgical reform stemmed from a sane pastoral appreciation, which was for him a most important aspect of liturgical cult. He was named *relatore aggiunto* for the historical section of the Congregation of Rites (Nov. 21, 1959). Meanwhile, he published studies on liturgy, archeology, and the history of the Redemptorists. He was a founder and editor of the *Spicilegium historicum CSSR*.

Bibliography: F. ANTONELLI and A. SAMPERS, *Spicilegium historicum Congregationis Sanctissimi Redemptoris* 10 (1962) 305–322, with complete bibliog. A. SAMPERS, *Ephemerides liturgicae* 77 (1963) 39–45.

[A. SAMPERS]

LOW CHURCH

Low Church is the name applied to the party within the ANGLICAN COMMUNION in general, and the Church of England in particular, that interprets the BOOK OF COMMON PRAYER in a wholly Protestant sense. This large body in the Church of England took its rise with the evangelicals of the 18th century. The Tractarians, with their lofty views on Catholic doctrine and sacerdotal nature of the priesthood, contrasted with the lower views of the evangelical tradition, and the two groups gradually became distinguished as High Church and Low Church. Both designations, however, had been used in the early 18th century. At that time the term Low Church was used as an alternative name for LATITUDINARIANISM. A small group of evangelical divines contemporary with the Tractarian Movement formed the Broad Church. Today the Low Church party within the Anglican Communion represents the Protestant party, in contrast to the Catholic tendencies of the High Church party.

Bibliography: G. R. BALLEINE, *A History of the Evangelical Party in the Church of England,* (London 1933). K. HYLSON-SMITH, *Evangelicals in the Church of England, 1734–1984* (Edinburgh 1988). C. J. COCKSWORTH, *Evangelical Eucharistic Thought in the Church of England* (Cambridge, Eng. 1993). R. T. FRANCE and A. E. MCGRATH, *Evangelical Anglicans: Their Role and Influence in the world today* (London 1993). R. STEER, *Church on Fire: The Story of Anglican Evangelicals* (London 1998). G. CARTER, *Anglican Evangelicals: Protestant Secessions from the Via Media, c. 1800–1850* (Oxford 2001).

[E. MCDERMOTT/EDS.]

LOWE, JOHN

Friar, anti-Lollard bishop; b. *c.* 1382; d. Rochester, Sept. 3, 1467. He entered the AUGUSTINIANS at Droitwich, Worcester, and studied at Lincoln where he was ordained deacon on Dec. 20, 1403. After ordination and the earning of his doctorate at OXFORD, he was affiliated with the great house of his order in London (1420). He was the Augustinian provincial in England (1427–33); was appointed confessor of King Henry VI in 1432; became bishop of SAINT ASAPH in 1433, and of ROCHESTER in 1444. A bitter foe of the LOLLARDS, he contributed to the downfall of Bp. Reginald PECOCK both as a judge, and as adviser to John Bury in the writing of the *Gladius Salomonis.* As a humanist Lowe assisted in the foundation of Eton College (1442) and King's College, CAMBRIDGE UNIVERSITY (1444) and built the library of the Austin Friars in London (*c.* 1456). While bishop of Rochester, he rebuilt the episcopal palace. He was involved in politics as a Member of Parliament. Although he had been the confessor of Henry VI, he joined the opposing Yorkist cause in 1460 and served as an emissary to Henry in Northampton without result. After the second battle of St. Alban's (1461) he was a delegate of the city of London to Edward IV.

Bibliography: A. I. PEARMAN, *Rochester* (Diocesan Histories; London 1897). A. B. EMDEN, *A Biographical Register of the University of Oxford to A.D. 1500,* 3 v. (Oxford 1957–59) 2:1168–69, 3:xxxiii. F. ROTH, *English Austin Friars,* 2 v. (New York 1961) 1:104–108.

[F. ROTH]

LOWE, JOHN, BL.

Priest, martyr; b. ca. 1553 at London, England; d. Oct. 8, 1586, hanged, drawn, and quartered at Tyburn. He was a Protestant minister who was converted to Catholicism and then studied for the priesthood at Douai and Rome, where he was ordained in 1582. He ministered in the London area, where he was a well-known exorcist. He was condemned for his priesthood and executed with BB. Robert BICKERDIKE, John ADAMS, and Robert DIBDALE, who were all beatified by Pope John Paul II on Nov. 22, 1987 with George Haydock and companions.

Feast of the English Martyrs: May 4 (England).

See Also: ENGLAND, SCOTLAND, AND WALES, MARTYRS OF.

Bibliography: R. CHALLONER, *Memoirs of Missionary Priests,* ed. J. H. POLLEN (rev. ed. London 1924). J. H. POLLEN, *Acts of English Martyrs* (London 1891).

[K. I. RABENSTEIN]

LOWELL PLAN

An experiment involving an educational compromise between secular authority and Catholic schools from 1831 to 1852 in Lowell, Mass. The first Catholic school in Lowell, which had been opened between 1823 and 1824, for lack of facilities was run haphazardly. At the annual town meeting of May 3, 1830, the citizens voted to expend "for this year only" $50 "for the instruction of the children of the Irish families in this town." The town meeting of April 4, 1831, voted to establish a public school for the purpose and to make a school district of the "acre" on which the Irish Catholics had become accustomed to living. By 1835 the first school, in the basement of St. Patrick's Church, and another, which had been built at Chapel Hill, were adopted into the public school system. The terms set by the public officials were that a town committee approve teacher qualifications, appoint teachers, and pass on curriculum and texts and that these schools be on the same footing as the other schools of the town concerning examinations, inspection, and general supervision. The Catholic terms, presented by Rev. Peter Conelly, were that the teachers must be Catholic and that the textbooks should contain no statements unacceptable to Catholics (Catholics later approving the books that were already in use).

Though town regulations then required Bible reading and prayer in the schools, this arrangement said nothing about religious instruction. Because Bp. Benedict Fenwick of Boston, under whose jurisdiction the plan was devised, wrote in a letter on this matter (March 26, 1831) that he "would not give a straw for that species of education, which is not accompanied with and based upon religion," it is assumed that the Catholic schools gave religious instruction, presumably after school hours, however, since both state and municipal regulations forbade otherwise.

In 1837 the school committee reported that the plan was "eminently successful," and the mayor lauded "these public nurseries of intelligence, freedom, good order, and religion." By 1839 the plan comprised three grammar and two primary schools with a total enrollment of 752 pupils; and in 1840, because of amalgamation and rearrangement, one grammar school and five primaries. The plan brought more Irish children into school than before, lessened the crime rate, avoided prejudice and exclusiveness, and helped alleviate financial burdens of Catholics.

The picture was not completely bright, however, for by degrees Catholic schools lost their distinctive character, becoming "separate but equal" schools for Irish Catholics. The town, moreover, violated its agreement by employing some non-Catholic teachers. In 1844 dissatisfaction with some teachers caused Catholic parents to petition their removal, and brought about a drop in attendance. In 1849 public authorities named the grammar school after Horace Mann—an insult to the Irish—and at the same time the chairman of the school committee lauded the plan that had been used to bring the Irish under public school instruction. By 1851 there were almost as many Irish in public as in the special schools. The passions of the Know-Nothing movement further complicated matters (*see* KNOW-NOTHINGISM). In 1852 the Catholics under Rev. John O'Brien established St. Patrick's school for girls, staffed by the Sisters of Notre Dame de Namur, and applied for an extension of the town's plan to provide for it. The civic authorities could not legally employ Catholic religious, with the result that the arrangement was abrogated by the town, the Catholics established private schools, and totally nonsectarian public education received another impetus. Had the experiment remained successful, it might have spread and thus might have helped solve the church-public school problem.

Bibliography: S. M. SMITH, *The Relation of the State to Religious Education in Massachusetts* (Syracuse, N.Y. 1926) 191–199. L. S. WALSH, *The Early Irish Catholic Schools of Lowell Massachusetts, 1835–1852* (Boston 1901).

[H. A. BUETOW]

LOYSON, CHARLES

Apostate French priest, sectarian leader; b. Orléans, March 10, 1827; d. Paris, Feb. 9, 1912. He entered the seminary of Saint-Sulpice in Issy (1845) and joined the SULPICIANS (1850). After ordination (1851) he taught philosophy in Avignon and theology in Nantes until he became a curate in the church of Saint-Sulpice, Paris (1856). In 1859 he entered the Dominicans and took the name Hyacinthe. Five months later he transferred to the Discalced CARMELITES. Père Hyacinthe was a dynamic pulpit orator who won wide acclaim for his sermons in the cathedral of Notre Dame, Paris (1864), and also in Rome. His Advent sermons of 1868 and some exaggerated remarks concerning marriage and non-Catholic groups brought him into conflict with his religious superiors. His connection with a religiously pathological woman from the U.S., Emily (Butterfield) Meriman, whom he converted in 1868, contributed to his difficulties. He seized upon the agitation concerning papal infallibility previous to VATICAN COUNCIL I as an occasion to leave the Church. After he was excommunicated (1869), he entered into a civil marriage with Emily in London (1872). He joined the OLD CATHOLICS and became their pastor in Geneva (1873–1874), but his restless and eccentric nature soon alienated him from them. In 1879 he founded in Paris his own church, the Église catholique gallicane, after fruitless attempts to do so since 1872. Despite his great oratorical gifts, he was unable to give life to the movement,

Charles Loyson. (Archive Photos)

which survived precariously until 1893. Periodic efforts thereafter to revive it failed. After journeys in America and in Palestine, Loyson settled in Paris. MODERNISM did not interest him. More and more he tended toward an undogmatic type of mysticism and rationalism that degenerated into a cult of his wife. His principal writings are listed below.

Bibliography: Works. *De la Réforme Catholique*, 2 v. (Paris 1872–73); *Ni cléricaux ni athées* (Paris 1890); *Mon testament . . .* (Paris 1893), Eng. tr. F. WARE, *My Last Will and Testament* (London 1895). *Du sacerdoce au mariage* (letters and diaries), ed. A. HOUTIN and P. L. COUCHOUD, 2 v. (Paris 1927); synopsis by O. KNAPP, *Hochland* 24.2 (1927) 520–531. Literature. G. RIOU, *Le Père Hyacinthe et le libéralisme d'avant le Concile* (Paris 1910). A. HOUTIN, *Le Père Hyacinthe,* 3 v. (Paris 1920–24). M. DE LANZAC DE LABORIE, *Le Correspondant* 25 (April 1925) 240–265.

[V. CONZEMIUS]

LOZANO, PEDRO

Jesuit historian; b. Madrid, Spain, June 16, 1697; d. Humahuaca, Argentina, Feb. 8, 1752. He entered the Society of Jesus on Dec. 7, 1711, and 20 days later left from Cádiz as a member of the expedition of Burges en route to Buenos Aires, where he arrived on April 8, 1712. He was ordained in 1721. After spending nine years assisting the sick and dying in Santa Fe, he was appointed in 1730 historiographer of the province. Lozano gives the impression that he remained in Santa Fe or Córdoba; actually he traveled widely through the La Plata area—in what is now Argentina, Paraguay, and Uruguay. In 1751 his fellow Jesuits appointed him their representative to prepare a reply to the Treaty of Limits, which transferred some of the Jesuit Reductions to Portugal.

Numerous books and other writings by Lozano are known. No matter what judgment may be made of his work, he made good use of the 20 years as provincial historiographer. His chief works are: *Descripción del Gran Chaco Gualamba* (Córdoba, Spain 1733; repr. Tucumán 1941); *Historia de la Compañía de Jesús de la Provincia del Paraguay* (2 v. Madrid 1754–55); *Historia de la conquista del Paraguay, Río de la Plata y Tucumán* (5 v. Buenos Aires 1873–75); *Historia de las revoluciones de la provincia de la Paraguay* (2 v. Buenos Aires 1905).

Bibliography: G. FURLONG, *Pedro Lozano, S. J., y sus "Observaciones a Vargas" (1750)* (Buenos Aires 1959). E. CARDOZO, *Historiografía paraguaya* (Mexico City 1959) 1:285–306.

[H. STORNI]

LUBAC, HENRI DE

Theologian, cardinal; b. Cambrai, Feb. 20, 1896. After the study of law, Henri Marie-Joseph Sonier de Lubac entered the Society of Jesus in 1913 at the novitiate of Saint Leonard (Great Britain). During his study of letters (Canterbury 1919–20), philosophy (Jersey 1920–23), and theology (Ore Place, Hastings 1924–26; Lyon-Fourviere 1926–28) he had as fellow students Yves de MONTCHEUIL (1899–1944) and Gaston Fessard (1897–1978). De Lubac published many of their works after their deaths. Stimulated by their friendship, his thought developed through contact with such great masters as the philosopher Maurice BLONDEL (1861–1949), whose more important correspondence he would later publish, and Léonce de GRANDMAISON (1868–1927), Pierre ROUSSELOT (1878–1915), Joseph MARÉCHAL (1878–1944), and Joseph Huby (1878–1949).

After ordination to the priesthood (1927), and following his tertianship (Paray-le-Monial, 1928–29), de Lubac taught fundamental theology at the Catholic Faculty of Lyon (not at Fourvière, as legend has it), where he succeeded Albert Valensin, brother of Auguste, many of whose works de Lubac also published posthumously [notably *Auguste Valensin: Textes et documents inédits* (Paris 1961)].

Henri de Lubac, Rome, 1969. (AP/Wide World)

The following year, de Lubac founded the chair of the history of religion at Lyon and became acquainted with Jules Monchanin (1895–1957) who initiated him to "Mahayanasutralamkara" and who had a decisive influence over his thought [cf. *Images de l'abbé Monchanin* (Paris 1967)]. While in residence at the Jesuit theologate at Fourvière (Lyons), he founded in 1940, with J. DANIÉLOU the collection *Sources chrétiennes*, which would become famous. Having fought during World War I and been seriously wounded in 1917, he nurtured and enlivened a spiritual resistance movement against Nazism during World War II with his confreres Pierre Chaillet and Gaston Fessard, publishing the journal *Témiognage chrétien* [cf. R. Bedarida, *Les armes de l'espirit: Témiognage chrétien, 1941–1944* (Paris 1977)]. From its inception he collaborated as advisor and author on the collection of monographs *Théologie* published at Fourvière. From 1947 to 1950, he was director of *Recherches de Science religieuse,* a review founded by P. L. de Grandmaison. In 1950, the authorities of his order barred him from teaching (until 1959) and theological research (a measure that would be progressively relaxed). They were not, however, implementing the directive of the encyclical HUMANI GENERIS (1950), but the "mots d'ordre" of a small group of theologians who prosecuted the so-called *Ecole de Fourvière* and *Nouvelle Théologie.* Later this same group attempted to have his theology condemned by the Council. Pope PIUS XII, who did not condemn de Lubac or his ideas, sent him words of encouragement through a letter dictated to his confessor, P. A. Bea, S.J.

In August 1960, Pope JOHN XXIII, who knew of the affair as nuncio at Paris, named him consultor of the preparatory commission to the Ecumenical Council of Vatican II. As a *peritus* on the theological commission, de Lubac participated thereafter in all the work of the council (1962–65). And the same superior general who had prohibited de Lubac from teaching asked him to defend the thought of his friend and confrere, Pierre TEILHARD DE CHARDIN (1881–1955), fearing that it might be condemned by the council. Lubac defense of Teilhard, which demonstrated an exact understanding of his thought, was decisive to his exoneration.

Named as a member of the International Theological Commission (1969–74), de Lubac became a consultor to the Pontifical Secretariats for Non-Christians and for Non-Believers. He sought to understand the true sense of the conciliar teachings, and to guard against a "para-council" which would make Vatican II an absolute point of departure for drawing the Church in an unjustified direction. During this period he traveled through North and South America and received numerous doctorates *honoris causa*. A founding member of the review *Concilium*, from which he retired in November 1965, he also contributed to the foundation of the international Catholic review *COMMUNIO*, with the later Cardinal J. Ratzinger, and Louis Bouyer, M. J. Le Guillou, and H. U. von BALTHASAR and served as a member of the French editorial committee until May 1977. JOHN PAUL II, who developed ties of friendship with de Lubac during the Council, created him cardinal in 1983.

Works. Like the opening of an opera, de Lubac's *Catholicisme* (1938; Eng. 1950) brings to our understanding nearly every theme of his truly "organic" theology. He considers in this book how the Spirit of God works through society and history in order to make humanity the Body of Christ according to the design of the Father, Who has created humanity in His image as persons and who has loved them, from that time on, as they are in themselves. The created and incarnated spirit which is man is henceforward an impulse toward God, who is his origin and calls him to Himself, while the Church, as the Body of Christ, is missionary. Moved by "the natural desire for God," the primordial act of the human spirit is the fundamental "certitude" of the original "faith," which in other words is "the knowledge of God" which envelops and critiques (*via negativa*) affirmations of God.

Correlatively, ATHEISM merits theological reflection. De Lubac treats of oriental and occidental atheism, as well as both the atheism that is anterior to Christ, that of Buddhism, and that which is posterior to Christ and specifically anti-Christian, that of Feuerbach, Nietzsche, and Comte, which he distinguishes from that of Proudhon: this latter is formed through a reaction against a Church dominated by an "unsupportable reactionary narrowness of a certain kind of Catholicism found during the Restoration" (H. U. von Balthasar, *Henri de Lubac,* 65). Concerning anti-Christian atheism, de Lubac discerns the shadow of Joachim of Flora of the twelfth century. The theory of Abbot Joachim, according to which the spirit realizes the design of God apart from the incarnated Word, in effect inspired Lessing and the Enlightenment which would secularize it, as well the progressive movements up to our day. It risks contaminating the Church when it admits an "atheistic hermeneutic of Christianity" (*Athéism et sens de l'homme,* 23 ff.).

With a capacity for both affirming and denying God, the human spirit has a history-determining destiny that he beyond at the same time that it belongs to him. According, in effect, as the human spirit considers itself called to filial adoption by God, as rising to the center of the cosmic becoming, or as receiving the revelation of God through Jesus Christ, the created spirit of man is moved by an identical movement in its own depths: it directs itself and is guided toward an end which is gratuitous. This is respectively, elevation to the SUPERNATURAL life; the Spirit; and Jesus, the Son of God. This end is prepared: with regard to supernatural elevation, it is the natural desire of God; with regard to the spirit, the world; and with regard to Jesus Christ, it is Israel and the chosen people. But because it is gratuitous, this end goes beyond all that has been prepared: the desire for God, the world, Israel, and all that transforms within.

It is well suited to de Lubac's purpose to consider separately the problematic of the spiritual, treated in *Surnaturel* (1946) and *Mystére du surnaturel* (1956), that of anthropogenesis, undertaken during his studies of Teilhard de Chardin, and that of the connection between the old and the new covenant, developed in *Histoire et Espirit* (1950) and in *Exégèse Médiéval* (1959–65). These three problematics clarify one another without ever recurring, though de Lubac treated all three together in his *Pic de la Mirandole* (1974).

This kind of analogy between movement and structure finds its principle and its end in the Lord Jesus. The universe is Christ-like by its constitution and destination, for man finds his final reality in Christ and knows of no movement of the Spirit that could go beyond Christ (*contra* Joachim of Flora). Furthermore, as in clear in *Corpus Mysticum* (1944, 1968), one part of de Lubac's Christology is implicitly eucharistic: in His singular Body through which He places Himself into human history and becomes cosmic, Jesus fulfills the destiny of humanity thanks to the eucharistic offering of Himself through which he is united to the Church, His spouse and body. Consequently, the ecclesiology of de Lubac is also eucharistic. Thence its Marian dimension, the reciprocal interiority of the particular churches within the universal Church is also the human subject who believes in the God of the Trinity, bringing to completion the primordial consciousness of God and the movement of the human spirit toward God; it is in this sense that all believe and become persons [cf. *La Foi chrétienne* (1969, 1970)].

Influence. Henri de Lubac never defended his work as an original theological contribution. He only gave, he said, his voice to the tradition. As a matter of fact, he showed it to be living. The originality of his work is that of the tradition itself. His influence is both discrete and diffuse—not that of a school, but more that of a master. One can see it in the ecclesiology of Vatican II which is eucharistic (J. Ratzinger), and in the dogmatic perspective—not rationalistic—of *Dei verbum*. Instead of imposing from outside the ideas of theological reflection, the apologetic of de Lubac is dogmatic, inviting the scientific study of religion to leave its methodological neutrality, which is fallacious, to abandon the idea of a "transcendent unity of religions," as well as that of a diffraction of the religious into the cultural, and to raise in their proper relief and contrast the great spiritual options, which lead the Christian to better perceive the absolute novelty of Christ. In brief, de Lubac's apologetic is dogmatic in being historic [cf. M. Sales in his admirable *Der Gott Jesu Christi* (Mainz 1982)]. Just as he has overcome the opposition, born in the sixteenth century, between the natural and supernatural ends of the human spirit, de Lubac has also overcome the division between positive and speculative theology, which had appeared in the same century.

Correlatively, all historical questions have been renewed. In effect, de Lubac observes a unity between history and the Spirit everywhere. Exegesis should also become a renewed being [cf. M. van Esbroeck, *Herméneutique, structuralisme et exégèse. Essai de logique kérygmatique* (Paris 1978); P. Piret, *Exégèse et Philosophie* (Brussels 1987)], as should moral theology, which can depart from its positivism and its Kantian transcendentalism thanks to his doctrine of the supernatural. For all of these reasons and in diverse manners it is clear that the Modernist crisis is overcome from within and in principle: history and Spirit are reconciled. If one agrees that this crisis recovered vigor after Vatican II and has not since ceased to rage (cf. G. Chantraine, *Vraie et fausse liberté du théologien* 1969), one will know that de Lubac's work has not ceased to be fertile.

Bibliography: K. N. NEUFELD and M. SALES, *Bibliographie Henri de Lubac, S. J. 1925–1974* (Einsiedeln 1974); "Bibliographie de Henri de Lubac (corrections et compléments) 1942–1989," *Théologie dans l'histoire*, 2:408–416. J. P. WAGNER, *La théologie fondamentale selon Henri de Lubac* (Paris 1997). H. DE LUBAC, *At the Service of the Church: Henri de Lubac Reflects on the Circumstances That Occasioned His Writings* (San Francisco 1993); *Théologie dans l'histoire* (Paris 1990). H. U. VON BALTHASAR, *The Theology of Henri de Lubac: An Overview* (San Francisco 1991). J. A. KOMONCHAK, "Theology and Culture at Mid-Century: The Example of Henri de Lubac," *Theological Studies* 51 (1990): 579–602. S. WOOD, *Spiritual Exegesis and the Church in the Theology of Henri de Lubac* (Grand Rapids, Mich. 1998). *L'homme devant Dieu: Mélanges offerts au père Henri de Lubac*, 3 (Paris 1963–64). D. L. SCHINDLER, ed., "The Theology of Henri de Lubac: Communio at Twenty Years," *Communio* 19 (1992): 332–509.

[G. CHANTRAINE]

LUBIENIECKI, STANISŁAW

Socinian knight, pastor, and historian; b. Raków, Poland, Aug. 23, 1623; d. Hamburg, Germany, May 18, 1675. The son of the pastor in Raków and educated in the academy there, Lubieniecki was appointed traveling tutor to a young count and with him visited Holland and France (1646–48). In 1652 he was ordained in the Minor Church, serving first in Czarków. In 1655 he besought Charles X Gustav of Sweden, whose troops occupied Cracow, for protection of the Minor Church. By 1660 all remaining Socinians were obliged to flee Poland or suffer death (*see* SOCINIANISM). After brief stays in Fredericksburg, Copenhagen, Stralsund, and Stettin, he settled in Hamburg, where he was opposed by the Lutheran clergy. Of his 32 works, two were published posthumously: *Historia reformationis Polonicae* (Amsterdam 1685), a major source of Polish religious history from the point of view of an exiled antitrinitarian leader, and *Theatrum cometicum* (Amsterdam 1688), a history of comets and a demonstration that they had no significance in presaging human affairs.

Bibliography: B. STASIEWSKI, *Lexikon für Theologie und Kirche,* ed. J. HOFER and K. RAHNER, 10 v. (2d, new ed. Freiburg 1957–65) 6:1167. R. WALLACE, *Antitrinitarian Biography,* 3 v. (London 1850) 3:294–306. J. TAZBIR, *Stanisław Lubieniecki: Przywódca ariańskiej emigracji* (Warsaw 1961), with genealogical tables.

[G. H. WILLIAMS]

LUCARIS, CYRIL

Patriarch of Constantinople, theologian; b. Candia, Crete, Nov. 13, 1572; d. Constantinople, June 1638. He studied in Venice, in Padua, and in Geneva, where he absorbed the Calvinist teachings that are reflected in his theological writings. As rector of the Vilna Academy in the 1590s, he strongly opposed the Union of BREST in 1596. Appointed patriarch of Alexandria in 1602, he became patriarch of Constantinople in 1612. He was several times deposed and then reappointed by his Muslim masters, holding office from 1620 to 1623, 1623 to 1630, 1630 to 1633, 1633 to 1634, 1634 to 1635, and 1637 to 1638. The brief intervals in his tenure mark periods of political and religious unrest within the empire. He was often attacked and criticized by his coreligionists because of his Calvinist leanings. Throughout his life he opposed any efforts at reunion with Rome. It was he who gave the *Codex Alexandrinus* to Sir Thomas Roe, the English Ambassador at Constantinople, who presented it to Charles I; it now lies in the British Museum. In 1638 the troops of the Sultan Murad seized and strangled Lucaris, and cast his body into the sea. His theological writings were numerous and important for their Calvinist influence on Orthodox doctrine.

Bibliography: C. EMEREAU, *Dictionnaire de théologie catholique,* ed. A. VACANT et al., 15 v. (Paris 1903–50; Tables générales 1951–) 9.1:1003–19. R. SCHLIER, *Der Patriarch Kyrill Lukaris von Konstantinopel* (Marburg 1927). G. HOFMANN, *Griechische Patriarchen und römische Päpste, Patriarch Kyrillos Lukaris und die römische Kirche* (Rome 1928–).

[F. J. LADOWICZ]

LUCAS, FIELDING, JR.

U.S. publisher and bookseller; b. Fredericksburg, Virginia, Sept. 3, 1781; d. Baltimore, Maryland, March 12, 1854. For almost 40 years Lucas was Baltimore's leading publisher and, after Mathew CAREY's death in Philadelphia (1839), the major U.S. Catholic book publisher. He regularly did business with Carey, with whom he exchanged stereotype plates; historically, Lucas is noted for printing atlases and maps. He began Catholic publications with textbooks written by members of the faculty of Mt. St. Mary's College in Emmitsburg, Maryland. Between 1838 and 1841, the active Lucas catalogue included 154 Catholic titles on popular dogmatic, apologetic, and devotional subjects. Widely circulated in annual editions of 3,000 or more was the *Metropolitan Catholic Almanac and Laity's Directory* (1833–57), a continuation of the *U.S. Catholic Almanac, or Laity's Directory,* acquired (1833) from James Myres, also of Baltimore. Although Lucas attended church services regularly, he became a Catholic only during his last illness.

Bibliography: J. W. FOSTER, "Fielding Lucas, Jr., Early 19th Century Publisher of Fine Books and Maps," *American Antiquarian Society Proceedings* 65 (1955) 161–212.

[E. P. WILLGING]

LUCAS, FREDERICK

Journalist; b. Westminster, March 30, 1812; d. Staines, Middlesex, Oct. 22, 1855. He belonged to a well-known Quaker family, attended London University, and read for the bar, to which he was admitted in 1835. He was received into the Church in 1839, but should not be reckoned among the OXFORD MOVEMENT converts. His great contribution to the revival of Catholic life in England was the foundation of the *TABLET* (1840) as a weekly journal for the educated laity. He did not limit the journal's content to ecclesiastical or religious subjects; the first issue, for example, reported a current murder trial at some length. Lucas's political sympathies were with the Whigs, the party of reform and liberalization, and he was deeply disappointed when Pius IX, after his first liberal phase, became more and more preoccupied with the defense of the temporal power of the Holy See against the rising tide of anticlerical Italian nationalism. The pope became increasingly anxious to keep the friendship of the British government, and the situation in Ireland offered a good bargaining point. Lucas was not an Irishman, but he warmly espoused their cause and was returned to the House of Commons for an Irish seat. He moved the *Tablet* to Dublin (1849) and edited it from there for about three years. The paper's chronic financial difficulties worsened as Lucas could win little English Catholic support for the Irish cause. He was dismayed to discover that the Irish bishops, acting in obedience to Rome, discouraged the clergy from supporting the movement for the repeal of the Union. Lucas went to Rome (1854) to try to get the policy modified, with no success. He returned to England and died in the following year; the *Tablet* was acquired by another convert, John Wallis, who sold it (1868) to the future Cardinal Herbert VAUGHAN.

Bibliography: J. GILLOW, *A Literary and Biographical History or Bibliographical Dictionary of the English Catholics from 1534 to the Present Time,* 5 v. (London-New York 1885–1902; repr. New York 1961) 4:336–343. E. LUCAS, *The Life of Frederick Lucas, M.P.,* 2 v. (London 1886).

[D. WOODRUFF]

LUCCI, ANTONIO NICOLA, BL.

Baptized Angelo Nicola; Conventual Franciscan, bishop; b. Aug. 2, 1682, Agnone, Isernia (near Naples), Italy; d. July 25, 1752, Bovino, Italy.

Angelo was the fifth of the seven children of Francesco Lucci and Angela Paolantonio. The family owned two vineyards and a copper firm, but Francesco worked as a cobbler. Francesco's unexpected death in 1604 led to some financial difficulties, but he had provided for Angelo's education under the Conventual Friars Minor at Agnone until the age of 15. Despite his mother's objections, Angelo entered the order at Isernia in 1697, professed his vows in 1698, and took the name Antonio. He continued his studies at Venafro, Alvito, Aversa, Agnone, and Assisi, and was ordained a priest in 1705.

After receiving his doctorate in theology in 1709, he was assigned to San Lorenzo (Naples), where he taught and ministered. The profundity of his theological insight gained him several positions, including provincial superior of Sant'Angelo (1718), rector of San Bonaventura, Rome (1719–29), theological advisor for two Roman synods, consultor to the Holy See (1725), and spiritual director to Princess Maria Clementina Sobieski. He was consecrated bishop of Bovino Feb. 7, 1729, by Pope Benedict XIII.

Even after his episcopal consecration, Lucci continued to conduct his life according to the Franciscan Rule in poverty, humility, and charity. He emptied his treasury to provide for the poor and was known to give away the clothes off his back. As bishop, he was known for his pastoral zeal, even to teaching children's catechism classes to prepare them for the sacraments. In addition to reforming the clergy and religious and building schools, Bishop Lucci defended the rights of the poor and the vulnerable in response to the problems of the era. He died in the odor of sanctity after 23 years as bishop and was buried in his cathedral at Bovino.

Lucci's cause was initiated shortly after his death: informative process (1758–60), official introduction (1764), apostolic process (1769–70), and publication of the *positios* (1793 and 1835). Pope Pius IX declared Lucci venerable in 1847. His cause was reopened recently when a number of miracles were attributed to his intercession. After one was approved June 18, 1989, Lucci was beatified by Pope John Paul II June 18, 1989.

Bibliography: *Acta Apostolicae Sedis* (1989): 764.

[K. I. RABENSTEIN]

LUCEY, ROBERT EMMET

Second archbishop of San Antonio, TX, founder of the Bishop's Committee for the Spanish Speaking; b. Los Angeles, CA, March 16, 1891; d. San Antonio, TX, Aug. 1, 1977. He was the fifth of John Lucey and Mary Nettle's eight children. Lucey's lifelong and outspoken advocacy of labor causes may be traced to an early childhood experience. When Robert was nine years old, his father, an employee of the Southern Pacific railroad, was killed in a work-related accident for which the family

received only a small compensation from the company. Lucey pursued his theological studies in Rome, where he was ordained on May 14, 1916, and awarded a doctorate in theology.

Lucey returned to Los Angeles and took up the routine of a parish priest until his appointment as diocesan Director of Catholic Charities in 1920. He subsequently acknowledged that this assignment completely changed the direction of his life by giving him direct contact with the poor, an experience that evoked a firm commitment to Catholic social teachings. In 1934, he was ordained bishop of Amarillo, TX, where he remained until his 1941 installation as the sixth ordinary and second archbishop of San Antonio. Lucey remained archbishop until advanced age and conflicts with his priests over his autocratic exercise of episcopal authority forced his retirement in 1969.

Career. During a career that spanned more than four decades in the hierarchy, Lucey earned a solid reputation as a liberal on social issues. In 1941 *Time* magazine hailed him as the "most socially conscious New Dealer in the Roman Catholic hierarchy." In addition to his outspoken advocacy of unpopular social causes, Lucey was one of the hierarchy's staunchest supporters of the Confraternity of Christian Doctrine (CCD), an organization that he regarded as the apostolate of the laity *par excellence* because of its potential to educate informed and socially committed adult Catholics. He served on the Bishop's Committee for the CCD from 1946 to 1969.

The archbishop is further remembered for establishing and directing the Bishops' Committee for the Spanish Speaking from 1945 until 1969. Lucey used his position as chair of this committee to champion the rights of migrant farm workers. His widely publicized efforts in this area won him a 1950 appointment by President Harry Truman to a blue ribbon committee on migrant worker issues. Archbishop Lucey delivered the invocation at the presidential inauguration of Lyndon B. Johnson in 1964. He subsequently served as a member of President Johnson's Advisory Council for the War on Poverty and, more controversially, as a member of the observation team for the 1967 presidential elections in South Viet Nam. The later appointment came in recognition of his strong support for the Johnson administration's unpopular prosecution of the Viet Nam War.

Lucey spent his retirement years promoting the use of telecommunications and space satellites for evangelization and catechesis. In 1969 he hosted an international study week on telecommunications and catechetics that brought recognized experts from all over the world to San Antonio. The last five years of his life were marked by increasingly serious health problems that precluded the retired archbishop's active participation in public life.

Bibliography: S. E. BRONDER, *Social Justice and Church Authority. The Public Life of Archbishop Robert E. Lucey* (Philadelphia 1982). S. A. PRIVETT, *Robert E. Lucey: Evangelization and Catechesis Among Hispanic Catholics* (Arbor, MI 1985). V. A. YZERMANS, *American Participation in the Second Vatican Council* (New York 1967).

[S. A. PRIVETT]

LUCHESIUS OF POGGIBONSI, BL.

First Franciscan tertiary; b. Gaggiano, Tuscany, Italy, *c.* 1181; d. Poggibonsi, between Florence and Siena, April 28, 1260. A tall Guelf soldier turned greedy merchant and grain speculator, Luchesius underwent a change of heart, probably before meeting St. FRANCIS OF ASSISI *c.* 1213. With his wife, Buona dei Segni, he distributed his wealth to the poor, retaining only a field that he farmed himself. He then undertook an apostolate of charity, seeking out and nursing sick paupers and begging food for the hungry. Luchesius and Buona were among the first to whom St. Francis, in 1221, gave the long grey habit and strict rule of his Third Order. Luchesius and Buona died the same day. Luchesius had received the graces of ecstatic prayer and levitation, and after his death acquired fame for miracles. Pope Bl. GREGORY X first approved his cult in 1273 at Poggibonsi, and a basilica was built over his tomb *c.* 1300. The cult was confirmed in 1694. Basilica and town, almost completely destroyed by Allied bombing in 1944, have been rebuilt.

Feast: April 28.

Bibliography: *Acta Sanctorum* Apr. 3:600–616. C. R. HALLACK and P. F. ANSON, *These Made Peace*, rev. and ed. M. A. HABIG (Paterson, N.J. 1957) 2–9, 243. G. DUHAMELET, *Lucchese, Premier tertiaire franciscain, 1180–1260* (Paris 1960). *Quaderni Poggibonsesi* (Poggibonsi 1960). O. ENGLEBERT, *St. Francis of Assisi: A Biography,* tr. E. M. COOPER, 2d augm. ed. by I. BRADY and R. BROWN (Chicago 1966). M. MINGHI, *Poggibonsi: repertorio bibliografico delle località e delle persone* (Poggibonsi 1986).

[R. BROWN]

LUCIAN OF ANTIOCH, ST.

Martyr, theologian, founder of the school of Antioch; b. probably in Antioch, *c.* 240; d. Nicomedia, Jan. 7, 312. Suidas said Lucian was born at Samosata of devout parents and studied under Macarius at nearby Edessa. At Antioch Lucian became involved with the Patriarch PAUL OF SAMOSATA and shared his condemnation (269) for holding that Christ was a mere man. As head of a schismatic group, Lucian remained excommunicated during the episcopates of Paul's three successors at Antioch. He made his submission *c.* 285, was received back into communion, and remained orthodox until his martyrdom.

Few men have had so strong an influence on the history of Christianity. Lucian used his linguistic skill to correct the Septuagint and Gospel texts; and his recension became the common one. He also developed a literal–historical method of exegesis characteristic of the School of Antioch, which he founded (*c.* 260). He held that each passage of Scripture has a literal sense, either proper or metaphorical, and he found the true sense of scriptural metaphor and parables by considering the special features of Hebrew and Greek literature, by comparing similar Biblical passages, and by grammatical and historical examination. He also allowed a typical meaning based on the literal sense and expressing the relationships between OT and NT. His method opposed the allegorizing practice of the Alexandrian School; but in stressing the importance of the letter, his school sometimes neglected the spirit, that is, the divine element in Scripture. Nonetheless, it later produced such exegetes as DIODORE OF TARSUS and JOHN CHRYSOSTOM.

Lucian's influence in theology was less fortunate. He is called Father of Arianism because ARIUS and almost all the fourth-century Arian theologians were his students. Calling themselves Lucianists and Collucianists, they developed his adoptionist and subordinationist tendencies into a full heresy. Lucian's moral life was blameless, however, and he was revered as saint and martyr by Arian and orthodox alike. Both John Chrysostom and EUSEBIUS provide firm evidence of his cult, confirmed by numerous church dedications.

Feast: Jan. 7 (West); Oct. 15 (East).

Bibliography: J. QUASTEN, *Patrology* (Westminster, Maryland 1950) 2:142–144. *Acta Sanctorum* Jan. 1:357–64. G. BARDY, *Dictionnaire de théologie catholique.* ed. A. VACANT et al., (Paris 1903-50) 9.1:1024–31; *Recherches sur s. Lucien d'Antioche et son école* (Paris 1936); ''Le Discours Apologétique de s. Lucien d'Antioche (Rufinus Hist. eccl., IX.6),'' *Revue d'histoire ecclésiastique* 22 (1926) 487–512. C. LATTEY, ''The Antiochene Text,'' *Scripture* 4 (1951) 273–277. PHILOSTORGIUS, *Kirchengeschichte: Mit dem Leben des Lucian von Antiochien und den Fragmenten eines arianischen Historiographen,* ed. J. BIDEZ (Berlin 1981). G. ZUNTZ, *Lukian von Antiochien und der Text der Evangelien,* ed. B. ALAND and K. WACHTEL (Heidelberg 1995).

[P. W. HARKINS]

LUCIE-CHRISTINE

French mystic whose identity is almost completely submerged in her pseudonym; b. France, Feb. 12, 1844; d. France, April 17, 1908. Lucie-Christine married at age 21, had five children, and became a widow after 22 years of married life. During the last 38 years of her life she completed 16 notebooks detailing her spiritual life for her director, the parish priest of the place where she lived. Although he had never known or met Lucie-Christine, Auguste Poulain, SJ, was given the task of editing and condensing these notes because of the prominence of his own book, *The Graces of Interior Prayer.*

Lucie-Christine began to receive extraordinary graces on April 25, 1873, while she sat alone at her needlework. From that day on she became increasingly adept at dovetailing the demands of her duties as wife and mother with the demands of the mystical life. She prayed in the streets of Paris, on trains, at the theater, and while entertaining her children. She contracted conjunctivitis which eventually resulted in total blindness.

Bibliography: A. POULAIN, ed. and tr., *Spiritual Journal of Lucie-Christine* (St. Louis 1915). J. VERBILLION, ''Married Mystic: Lucie-Christine,'' *Cross and Crown* 9 (1957) 148–161.

[J. VERBILLION]

LUCIFER OF CAGLIARI

Bishop of that see (ancient Calaris) in Sardinia; d. *c.* 370. Along with EUSEBIUS, Bishop of Vercelli, Lucifer represented Pope LIBERIUS at the Synod of Milan (355), at which the Emperor CONSTANTIUS exerted strong pressure on the bishops to condemn St. ATHANASIUS. Lucifer opposed the emperor in such vehement terms that both he and Eusebius were sent into exile. Lucifer was banished to Commagene, and subsequently to Palestine and the Egyptian Thebais. Throughout his career he was an uncompromising defender of the letter, rather than the spirit, of the Trinitarian teachings of the Council of NICAEA, and he attacked all opponents—even those who merely questioned these teachings—with a fierceness bordering on fanaticism. While in exile, he wrote five exceedingly bitter polemics: *De non conveniendo cum haereticis, De regibus apostaticis, De S. Athanasio, De non parcendo in Deum delinquentibus,* and *Moriendum esse pro Dei filio.*

Although expecting and hoping to be martyred, he was freed from exile by the Emperor Julian's edict of 362 and was soon embroiled in the religious controversies between the followers of Meletius and Eustathius at Antioch. He was invited by St. Athanasius to attend the Synod of Alexandria, which had been called to reconcile, as far as was possible, the differences between the Catholics and Arians of various understandings. He refused the invitation, but sent two deacons to represent him. Ignoring the conciliatory recommendations of the synod, he proceeded to consecrate Paulinus, a priest of Antioch and an adherent of Eustathius, as bishop, thereby founding the Meletian schism. On his return to Sardinia, he continued to attack all who disagreed with or questioned his uncom-

promising views and ended his career in isolation. That he died in schism is supported by the testimony of St. AMBROSE (*De excessu Satyri* 47) and St. AUGUSTINE (*Epist.* 185.47).

Lucifer was a mediocre theologian and exegete. However, his copious citations from the Old Latin versions of Scripture are an invaluable source of Old Latin readings. His deliberately careless literary style reflects many usages of the spoken Latin of his age. His close adherents, the Luciferians, as a more or less schismatic group, continued his rigoristic views, but disappeared in the early 5th century. They are attacked by St. JEROME in his *Dialogus contra Luciferianos* (*c.* 379).

Bibliography: *Corpus scriptorum ecclesiasticorum latinorum* 14 (1886). G. CERETTI, *Moriendum esse pro Dei filio* (Risa 1940), with comment. J. L. DAVIES, *A Dictionary of Christian Biography,* ed. W. SMITH and H. WACE (London 1877–87) 3:749–751. É. AMANN, *Dictionnaire de théologie catholique.* ed. A. VACANT et al., (Paris 1903–50). 9.1:1032–44, including Luciferians. O. BARDENHEWER, *Geschichte der altkirchlichen Literatur* (Freiburg 1913–32) 3:469–477. U. MORRICA, *Storia della letteratura latina cristiana,* 3 v. in 5 (Turin 1923–35) 2.1:165–181. C. ZEDDA, ''La teologia trinitaria di Lucifero di Cagliari,'' *Divus Thomas* 52 (1949) 276–329. G. THÖRNELL, *Studia Luciferiana* (Uppsala 1934), on L.'s language.

[M. R. P. MCGUIRE]

LUCIUS, ST.

Legendary Christian king in England; fl. second century. The *LIBER PONTIFICALIS* mentions a letter supposedly written to Pope ELEUTHERIUS *c.* 187 by a British king asking the Holy See to send missionaries to convert his people. The monarch's name is given in a passage reporting a letter from *Lucio Britannio rege,* and this is the only extant evidence of his existence. Later, unsubstantiated traditions relate that the king was baptized by St. TIMOTHY, who reportedly was working as a missionary in Gaul at the time, and that he then undertook a missionary journey himself to the area around the Swiss canton of Graubünden. His relics are reputed to have been brought to Chur, and a completely unhistorical life of the saint was written by the end of the 13th century. He has been honored since the Middle Ages as the patron of the Diocese of Chur. The story was taken up by BEDE (*Hist. Eccl.* 1.4; 5.24) and later chroniclers, but it is well to remember that the section of the *Liber pontificalis* in which he appears was not compiled until *c.* mid-sixth century, when he was already popular in Switzerland. It is the opinion of present-day scholars that the word *Britannio* in the text may have been confused by some medieval scribe for *Britio,* which was the location of one of the strongholds of Lucius Aelius Septimius Megas Abgar IX (*see* ABGAR,

LEGENDS OF), an early Christian king of Edessa in Asia Minor who concerned himself with the conversion of his people in mid-second century.

Feast: Dec. 3.

Bibliography: L. P. DUCHESNE, *Liber pontificalis* 1:136. The 13th-century life, ed. B. KRUSCH, *Monumenta Germaniae Historica: Scriptores rerum Merovingicarum* 3:1–7. *Bibliotheca hagiographica latina antiquae et mediae aetatis* 2:5024. A. HARNACK, ''Der Brief des britischen Königs Lucius an den Papst Eleutherius,'' *Sitzungsberichte der Deutschen (Preussischen to 1946)* (1904) 909–916, reviewed by A. H. MATHEW, *English Historical Review* 22 (1907) 767–770; ''Saint Lucien,'' *The Irish Ecclesiastical Record* 4th ser., 22 (1907) 457–474. J. G. MAYER, *Geschichte der Bistums Chur* (Stans 1907) 11–29. H. LECLERCQ, *Dictionnaire d'archéologie chrétienne et de liturgie* 9.2:2661–63. C. J. GODFREY, *The Church in Anglo-Saxon England* (New York 1962) 10.

[B. J. COMASKEY]

LUCIUS I, POPE, ST.

Pontificate: June or July 253 to March 5, 254. With his predecessor Pope CORNELIUS, Lucius was banished from Rome to Civitavecchia by the Emperor Gallus. Valerian (253–260) soon succeeded Gallus, however, and allowed Lucius to return to Rome. Cyprian of Carthage (*Epistolae* 61) salutes him as ''dearest brother'' and praises him as an honored confessor. Cyprian expressed his regret that the pope had not died a martyr and his hope that this might yet happen, but Lucius apparently died a natural death.

Nothing is known of his pontificate. The *LIBER PONTIFICALIS* ascribes to him an order that two priests and three deacons should abide with the bishop as constant witnesses of his conduct, but this source also contains an apocryphal account of his martyrdom. Cyprian (*Epistolae* 6.88) states that Lucius maintained the liberal policy of his predecessor with regard to the *LAPSI* of the Decian persecution, despite the continued opposition of the Novatianists (*see* NOVATIAN AND NOVATIANISM), a schismatic group, to the policy by which *lapsi* were to be readmitted into the church after a suitable penance.

Lucius was buried in the cemetery of Callistus where a portion of his epitaph has been recovered. He is the first bishop whose death is recorded in the *Depositio episcoporum* (on March 5), thus attesting to the commemoration of Roman bishops that was then being celebrated along with that of other heroic Christians, such as the martyrs.

Feast: March 4.

Bibliography: EUSEBIUS, *Ecclesiastical History,* 7:2. DUCHESNE, *Liber pontificalis*, 1:xcvi-xcviii, ccxlviii, 66–69, 153. É. AMANN, *Dictionnaire de théologie catholique*, ed. A. VACANT et al.,

(Paris 1903—50) 9.1:1056–57. G. SCHWAIGER, *Lexikon für Theologie und Kirche*, ed. J. HOFER and K. RAHNER (Freiberg 1957–65) 6:1176. E. FERGUSON, ed., *Encyclopedia of Early Christianity* (New York 1997) 2:698. J. N. D. KELLY, *Oxford Dictionary of Popes* (New York 1986) 19–20.

[E. G. WELTIN]

LUCIUS II, POPE

Pontifcate: March 12, 1144 to Feb. 15, 1145; b. Gerard Caccianemici, Bologna, date unknown. Having been a canon of St. John Lateran, he was named cardinal priest by Honorius II in 1124. As legate to Germany (1125–26) he was present at LOTHAIR III's election and suggested the nomination of (St.) NORBERT as bishop of Magdeburg. INNOCENT II, whom he vigorously supported and whom he also served as legate to Germany, appointed him chancellor. No details of his election are known. Lucius acknowledged the homage, but not the royal title, of Alfonso Henriquez of Portugal. An armistice of seven years temporarily stabilized papal relations with Roger II of Sicily; Roger retained Capua, but promised to refrain from attacking Benevento or other papal lands. Meanwhile, in Rome the senate reconstituted itself under the leadership of Jordan PIERLEONI, brother of the former antipope, Anacletus. Since the new Emperor, CONRAD III, was unable to respond to his pleas for assistance, Lucius personally took charge of an assault on the capital. The pope died during this operation, presumably as a consequence of a wound from a stone. Lucius founded monasteries in Germany and Italy and was especially favorable to the PREMONSTRATENSIANS. He held a synod in Rome in May 1144.

Bibliography: *Patrologia Latina*, ed. J. P. MIGNE (Paris 1978–90) 179:819–938. *Pontificum romanorum . . . vitae*, ed. J. M. WATTERICH, 2 v. (Leipzig 1862) 2:278–281. *Liber pontificalis*, ed. L. DUCHESNE (Paris 1958) 2:385–386. P. JAFFÉ, *Regesta pontificum romanorum ab condita ecclesia ad annum post Christum natum 1198*, ed. S. LÖWENFELD (2d ed. Leipzig 1881–88; repr. Graz 1956) 2:7–19. H. K. MANN, *The Lives of the Popes in the Early Middle Ages from 590 to 1304* (London 1902–32) 9:113–126. P. BREZZI, *Roma e l'Impero medioevale 774–1252* (Bologna 1947). F. X. SEPPELT, *Geschichte der Päpste von den Anfängen bis zur Mitte des 20. Jh.* (Munich 1956) 3:187, 604–607. G. DESPY, ''Les cathares dans le diocèse de Liège au XIIe siècle. À propos de l' 'Epistola Leodiensis' au pap L(?),'' *Christianisme d'hier et d'aujourd'hui. Hommage à Jean Préaux* (1979) 65–75. G. M. FACHETTI, *Ripalta Sicca. Rivolta d'Adda dall'origine all'anno 1300 alla luce delle nuove importanti scoperte* (Rivolta d'Adda 1996). E. SAUSER, *Biograhisch-Bibliographisches Kirchenlexikon* 5 (Herzberg 1993). G. SCHWAIGER, *Lexikon für Theologie und Kirche* (3d ed. Freiburg 1997). F. R. SWIETEK, ''A Savigniac Forgery Recovered: Lucius II's Bull 'Habitantes in domo' of Dec. 5, 1144,'' *Studisorum speculum: Studies in Honor of Louis J. Lekai, Ocist* (Kalamazoo, MI 1993). F. R. SWIETEK and T. M. DENEEN, ''Pope Lucius II and Savigny,''

Analecta Cisterciensia 39 (Rome 1983) 3–25. J. N. D. KELLY, *Oxford Dictionary of Popes* (New York 1986) 171–172.

[M. W. BALDWIN]

LUCIUS III, POPE

Pontificate: Sept. 1, 1181 (consecrated, Velletri Sept. 6, 1181) to Nov. 25, 1185; b. Hu[m]baldus Allucingoli (?), Lucca; d. Verona; cardinal deacon of Sant'Adriano (1138), promoted cardinal-priest of Sta Prassede (1141) by Innocent II, and cardinal bishop of Ostia and Velletri by Hadrian IV (1158); long thought to have been a Cistercian, but seems never to have become a monk.

Lucius participated in drawing up the Treaty of Constance with Emperor Frederick I Barbarossa (March 1153), but was an important member of the "Sicilian party" of cardinals who favored an alliance with the king of Sicily and the Lombard cities rather than with the emperor. He took part in negotiating the Treaty of Benevento with William I of Sicily (June 1156) and was prominent in the curia of Pope Alexander III, undertaking legations to the Sicilian kingdom (1166–7) and Constantinople (1167, 1168–9). He participated in failed negotiations with Frederick in Pavia in 1175 and, after Frederick's defeat at Legnano (1176), was a leading negotiator of the Treaty of Venice (1177) that ended the papal schism of 1160–77.

On accession, he was the only pope of this period who is known to have refused to bestow *beneficia* or gifts on the Romans, a failure to respect custom which contemporaries regarded as contributing to the conflict which led to his exile from the city after only five months. He spent the remainder of his pontificate travelling between towns near Rome and moved north to Verona in the summer of 1184. At first he was aided in fighting the Romans by the imperial chancellor, Christian, archbishop of Mainz, but after Christian's death, sought aid elsewhere.

The most pressing issues of his pontificate were undoubtedly reform after the crisis of the schism and disputes left unresolved by the Treaty of Venice. A controversy over the legacy of Matilda of Tuscany, who had left both allodial and imperial fiefs to the papacy, was not resolved, although an imperial letter records that Frederick offered to hand over a tenth of present and future imperial revenues in Italy to the pope and a ninth to the cardinals, to submit contentious possessions to mutually agreed arbitration, and to meet the pope. Frederick was keen to ensure the Hohenstaufen succession and to have his son crowned during his own lifetime. Lucius may initially have planned to accede to this request, but if so, he later changed his mind. The pope was in Verona

from July 22, 1184 and met in council with Frederick there from mid-October to early November and again in mid-December.

On Oct. 29, 1184 the betrothal took place in Augsburg of the emperor's son Henry to Constance, posthumous daughter of King Roger II and aunt of King William II of Sicily. The pope's attitude to this match is not known. He certainly favored the Sicilian kings, raising the royal Benedictine foundation of Monreale to an archbishopric (1183), and he could not have known that King William II of Sicily would die childless. He may also have hoped for imperial support against the city of Rome, as suggested by the chronicler Robert of Auxerre.

Frederick was prepared to make concessions to the pope, as demonstrated by his acceptance (November 1184) of the pope's request that Henry the Lion, Duke of Saxony, be allowed to return from exile in England. The emperor and pope agreed on support for a crusade to the Holy Land, urgently sought by ambassadors to Verona from Jerusalem.

Frederick also supported the papal bull *Ad abolendam* (Nov. 4, 1184), designed to "eradicate the depravity of heresy," by condemning named heretical groups (Cathars, Patarines, Humiliati, Poor of Lyons, Passagines, Josephines, and Arnaldists) and identifying preaching without authority, or any teaching which differed from that of the Roman church on the sacraments, baptism, forgiveness of sins, and marriage as indicators of heresy. A first attempt at a comprehensive papal policy, the decree charged bishops with seeking out heresy and required temporal rulers to take oaths to aid the church against heretics. Sympathizers with heresy were to be penalized and heretics themselves handed over to secular authority for punishment.

Other issues discussed in Verona were more contentious: Frederick sought the recognition of ordinations bestowed by Alexander's schismatic opponents, but this was referred by the papal side to a later council that never took place. Negotiations broke down over the disputed double election to the archbishopric of Trier. Frederick had called the two candidates to his court in Konstanz, had ordered a second election, and had invested the provost Rudolf. The original victor, archdeacon Folmar, appealed to the pope. Lucius supported Folmar, but no definitive settlement was reached during his pontificate.

This sequence of events may have influenced the pope's attitude toward Henry's coronation: whether at Verona or during 1185, Lucius refused to crown Henry, arguing, according to contemporary chroniclers, that it was not appropriate to have two emperors.

Other acts show Lucius's concern for reform. His bull *Vestra* (X.3.2.7) commended the holy zeal of laypersons who boycotted masses celebrated by notoriously concubinous priests. He remained well-disposed towards the Cistercians: a privilege of November 1184 prohibited bishops from exercising their power of correction over Cistercian houses and forbade the passing of sentences of excommunication, suspension, or interdict against the order. He settled the disputed status of the diocese of Tripoli, allowing that while part of the province of Tyre, it belonged to the jurisdiction of the patriarch of Antioch. On May 17, 1182 he absolved William the Lion, king of Scotland, lifted the interdict on his kingdom which had been imposed because of royal interference in the election of the bishop of St. Andrews, and sent him a golden rose, a mark of papal favor.

His additions to the college of cardinals included four canons and one monk, but he also continued the tradition of his predecessors in appointing *magistri,* and the majority were from the communal milieu of north Italy whence he himself came. He encountered Joachim of Fiore, who interpreted a prophecy in Veroli. His Registers do not survive (but certainly existed), and during his pontificate the *Liber Censuum* was begun. In 1183 he canonized Bruno bishop of Segni (d. 1123), whilst the earliest extant canonization process is that carried out at Lucius's request in 1185 for the lay hermit Galganus (d. 1181). He declined to canonize Anno, archbishop of Cologne, founder of the monastery of Siegburg (d. 1175) but sought further information and recommended that details of the life of the Cistercian Peter, archbishop of Tarentaise (d. 1174) be written down. Both were later canonized. Lucius was buried in the Cathedral of Verona.

Bibliography: J. P. MIGNE, *Patrologia Latina* (Paris 1878–90) 201:1067–1380; IP 7, 247 nr. 8. *Initienverzeichnis und chronologisches Verzeichnis zu den Archivberichten und Vorarbeiten der Regesta pontificum Romanorum,* ed. R. HIESTAND, *Monumenta Germaniae Historica Hilfsmittel,* 7 (Munich 1983) 342–82. P. JAFFÉ, *Regesta Pontificum Romanorum,* ed. S. LOEWENFELD, 2 (Graz 1956) 431–92. J. D. MANSI, *Sacrorum conciliorum nova et amplissima collectio,* 22 (repr. Graz 1961), cc. 173–8, 185, 188, 474–94. *Monumenta Germaniae Historica, Legum Sectio IV, Constitutiones et acta publica imperatorum et regum,* tome I (Hannover 1893; repr 1963) nr. 296. G. BAAKEN, "*Unio regni ad imperium. Die Verhandlungen von Verona 1184 und die Eheabredung zwischen König Heinrich VI. und Konstanze von Sizilien,*" *QFIAB,* 52 (1972), 219–97 (repr. in G. BAAKEN, *Imperium und Papsttum* [Cologne 1997] 81–142). W. MALECZEK, *Papst und Kardinalskolleg von 1191 bis 1216,* Publikationen des Historischen Instituts beim Österreichischen Kulturinstitut im Rom, Abt. 1 Abhandlungen 6 (1984). I. S. ROBINSON, *The Papacy 1073–1198. Continuity and Innovation* (Cambridge 1990). V. PFAFF, "Sieben Jahre päpstlicher Politik: die Wirksamkeit der Päpste Lucius III, Urban III, Gregor VIII," *ZRGKA,* 67 (1981) 148–212. J. PETERSOHN, "Kaiser, Papst und *praefectus Urbis,* zwischen Alexander III. und Innocenz III.," *QFIAB,* 60 (1980) 157–88. S. WEISS, *Die Urkunden der päpstlichen Legaten von Leo IX. bis Coelestin III. (1049–1198)* (Cologne 1995) 145–147, 149, 273–4, 282–86, 389; W. OHNSORGE, *Die Legaten Alexanders III. im ersten Jahrzehnt seines Pontifikats (1159–1169),*

Historische Studien, 175 (Berlin 1928). B. ZENKER, *Die Mitglieder des Kardinalskollegiums von 1130 bis 1159* (1964) 22–25.

[F. ANDREWS]

LUCK

Luck, according to Aristotle, who made the first satisfactory analysis of it, is an accidental cause intervening in things that happen for the sake of an end and according to purpose (see *Phys.* 195b 31–198a 13). It is a species of CHANCE, differing from other fortuitous causes in that it happens only to created agents having the use of intelligence. Luck may be good or bad. Many things commonly attributed to it, such as winning at so-called games of chance, are not, since they are intended, due to luck in Aristotle's sense, for in his view lucky events are neither intended nor foreseen: they happen to agents seeking other ends. Whatever their immediate accidental causes may be, lucky and unlucky events ultimately result from the indetermination and limitation of natural causes, and from the incompleteness of human knowledge. St. Thomas Aquinas adopted and developed Aristotle's teaching on luck, showing its compatibility with Catholic doctrine concerning PROVIDENCE by explaining God's foreknowledge and control of fortuitous events (see esp. *In two phys.* 7–10; *Summa theologiae* 1a, 115.6; 116.1).

Bibliography: C. DE KONINCK, "Chance and Fortune," *Laval theologique et philosophique* 1.1 (1945) 186–191). M. J. JUNKERSFELD, *The Aristotelian-Thomistic Concept of Chance* (Notre Dame, Ind. 1945).

[H. J. FREEMAN]

LUCRETIUS

Roman poet and philosopher; b. *c.* 98 B.C.; d. 55 B.C. Lucretius was probably an aristocrat and a friend of Gaius Memmius, the patron of Catullus and Cinna. According to St. Jerome, he composed his only poem, *De rerum natura* (On the Nature of the Universe), in the lucid intervals between bouts of insanity, and he died by his own hand, the unfinished poem being entrusted to Cicero for publication. Yet Lucretius was a poet of great ability and forged a strong link in the chain of Latin hexameter verse between Ennius and Vergil. His poem had earlier models in the works of Xenophanes, PARMENIDES, and especially EMPEDOCLES ("On Nature"). Indeed, the opening invocation to "kindly Venus" who alone has power to subdue Mars, the god of war, may refer to a wish not only for the end of civil strife in Rome, but also for the reconciliation of the cosmic forces of love and strife found in Empedocles.

The general aim of the poem is the elimination of superstitious fear—whether of the gods, unusual happenings, or death—by an account of nature that will be rational and will exclude any divine interference. Thus the poet's main purpose coincides with that of the EPICUREANISM he professed. In a word it is ethical: it aims at tranquillity and peace of mind. However Lucretius does concentrate upon that division of Epicureanism called physics or philosophy of nature. No capricious agency, but the movement of atoms, eternally falling through the void, accounts for everything. The introduction of an arbitrary swerve (the ultimate source of man's free will) enables them to unite by collision, rebound, and interlinkage. Considerable ingenuity is shown in the naturalistic accounts of the origin of the world, heavenly bodies, man, and speech. Further it is argued that the mind or soul is also corporeal, being composed merely of finer atoms than body, and therefore, equally liable to dissolution. Knowledge comes about through material contact with the effluences or images that are constantly being given off by all things. Explanations of portents and extraordinary phenomena are provided in order to rid the mind of vain fears.

Perhaps, in his lengthy treatment of the emotion of love, Lucretius is speaking from personal experience. He is well aware that it is a pleasure not unmixed with pain and a desire that is sharpened rather than allayed by the attempt to satisfy it. Here he shows evidence of Epicurus's refined critique of pleasure. Man needs to live a life of peace with his soul purged alike from fear and vice, thus imitating the eternal peace and freedom from emotion of the gods, from whom come emanations that announce divine tranquillity.

The attitude of Christians toward Lucretius has been somewhat ambivalent. Early Christian writers, such as ARNOBIUS and LACTANTIUS, although opposed to Epicureanism, borrowed much from Lucretius and even made use of his attacks against the pagan gods. But medieval manuscripts of his work are rare, and the few copies made from one fourth- or fifth-century original seem to owe their existence to the Carolingian literary revival. From the Renaissance onward greater interest was shown, and several printed editions appeared. Although valued as a poet, Lucretius was still opposed on doctrinal grounds; witness the *Anti-Lucretius* of Cardinal Melchior de POLIGNAC—nine books of hexameter verse *De Deo et Natura* (On God and Nature), published in Paris in 1747. Since the nineteenth century, however, Lucretius has been studied sympathetically by many Christians.

Lucretius appears as a sensitive man of genius whose aim was to banish from human life the craven fear of deities, unreasoning terror at so-called supernatural phenomena, and anxiety over death. It is incorrect to call him either an atheist or a hedonist in the normal sense of these terms. His end was tranquillity of soul, a tranquillity that he himself perhaps never achieved. It is the Epicurean doctrine of the noninvolvement of deity within man's world that leads to the mechanistic materialism that he so skillfully describes in hexameter verses of great power and even beauty. Such a viewpoint seemed to him vastly superior to the rank superstition that characterized much so-called religion in the first century B.C. Lucretius excites sympathy as a noble character in an evil world; he never lived to see the advent of a religion characterized by a relationship of love and trust between God and man.

See Also: ATOMISM; MATERIALISM.

Bibliography: Works. *De rerum natura,* ed. and tr. C. BAILEY (Oxford 1947); *ibid.,* tr. W. H. D. ROUSE (*Loeb Classical Library* London-New York-Cambridge 1912); *Titus Lucretius Carus on the Nature of Things,* tr. T. JACKSON (Oxford 1929); *Lucretius on the Nature of Things,* tr. R. LATHAM (Baltimore, Md. 1957). Literature. C. A. GORDON, *A Bibliography of Lucretius* (London 1962). A. D. WINSPEAR, *Lucretius and Scientific Thought* (Montreal 1963). H. HAGENDAHL, ''The Apologists and Lucretius,'' pt.1 of *Latin Fathers and the Classics* (Göteborg 1958). L. ALFONSI, *Enciclopedia filosofica,* 4 v. (Venice-Rome 1957) 3:187–190.

[W. H. O'NEILL]

LUCY, ST.

Martyr in Syracuse, Sicily, 304. A fifth-century Greek inscription attests to her cult in Syracuse; she was later introduced into the Gelasian and Gregorian sacramentaries and in the MARTYROLOGY OF ST. JEROME. Her cult spread to Rome, Milan, and Ravenna in the sixth and seventh centuries; GREGORY I (THE GREAT) probably introduced her name and Agatha's, into the Canon of the Mass. A legendary fifth- or sixth-century *PASSIO* in Greek and Latin tells how in a vision St. AGATHA encouraged her to remain constant to her death in her virginity. Her relics, according to one account, were taken from Syracuse to Abruzzo in the eighth century and from there to Metz in 969, an arm given to Henry III in 1042 going to the monastery of Luitburg. According to the other version, the relics went to Constantinople in 1038 and were brought to Venice in 1204. Lucy, patroness of the eyes, is frequently portrayed with two eyes in a dish. She appears also with a palm of martyrdom, a lamp (or a book), and a sword (or a knife) in her neck. She has frequently been a subject for art. Before the Gregorian calendar reform her feast was the shortest day of the year, and predictions were made for the coming 12 months on the basis of events of the 12 days between her feast and Christmas.

Feast: Dec. 13.

Scene from the Life of Saint Lucy, painting by Jacobello del Fiore, 15th century. (©Archivo Iconografico, S.A./CORBIS)

Bibliography: GUERDAL, *Santa Lucia, attualità di un messaggio: storia, culto, leggenda* (Milan 1976).

[E. G. RYAN]

LUDANUS, ST.

Pilgrim; d. Feb. 12, 1202. Ludanus (Lotten, Luden), who is venerated in the Diocese of Strasbourg, is known only through a 14th-century vita that claims that he was born in Scotland, son of a certain Duke Hiltibold, and that he made a pilgrimage to Rome after the death of his father. He died in Alsace on his return. His tomb in the church of Hipsheim is a fine example of 15th-century Alsatian sculpture, and a popular pilgrimage center of that region.

Feast: Feb. 12 or 16.

Bibliography: *Bibliotheca hagiographica latina antiquae et mediae aetatis* 2:5025. *Acta Sanctorum* Feb. 2:638–639. J. M. B. CLAUSS, *Die Heiligen des Elsass* (Düsseldorf 1935). J. BRAUNER and K. OHRESSER, ''Der Kult des heiligen Ludanus im Elsass,'' *Archives de l'Église d'Alsace* 2 (1947–48) 13–61. M. L. HAUCK, ''Der Bildhauer Conrad Sifer von Sinsheim . . . ,'' *Annales Universitatis Saraviensis. Philosophie-Lettres* 9 (1960) 173–179, the tomb of Ludanus.

[J. CHOUX]

LUDGER OF MÜNSTER, ST.

Bishop, missionary to Frisia and Westphalia; b. Frisia, *c.* 742; d. Billerbeck, Westphalia, Germany, March 26, 809. Ludger became a student of Bp. GREGORY OF UTRECHT and, in 767, of ALCUIN in York, England. The date of a second stay in England is uncertain. In 776 he was made deacon and missionary in Deventer (Netherlands).

After his ordination (777), he spent seven years in Dokkum, West Frisia, which had been Christianized by English missionaries. Bishop Gregory's successor, Alberic of Utrecht, directed Ludger to rebuild the church in Deventer that had been destroyed during a Frisian uprising, and to found a seminary there. However, in 784 the SAXONS under WIDUKIND rebelled against the FRANKS, and Frisia was lost to the Christian faith when the area between the rivers Lauwers and Fli reverted to pagan practices. Ludger was forced to flee and spent more than two years in Rome and Monte Cassino. In 786 CHARLEMAGNE recalled Ludger and sent him to the defeated Frisians. He rebuilt the churches there and, with the emperor's consent, destroyed the pagan places of worship in Helgoland. These drastic measures incited the Frisians on the Continent, and they ravaged the missions, driving out Ludger.

In 792 Charlemagne sent him to Münster (formerly Mimigardeford), Westphalia, where he organized 40 parishes that he visited yearly. In 804 Ludger was consecrated first bishop of Münster. He founded a convent for women at Nottuln and the abbeys of Helmstedt and WERDEN. Ludger was buried in Werden. Pilgrimages are held in his honor at Billerbeck and Werden. He is depicted as a bishop with either a church or two geese.

Feast: March 26.

Bibliography: *Acta Sanctorum*. March 3:626–65. W. WATTENBACH, *Deutschlands Geschichtsquellen im Mittelalter bis zur Mitte des 13. Jh.* (Stuttgart-Berlin 1904) 1:243–245. A. HAUCK, *Kirchengeschichte Deutschlands* (Berlin–Leipzig 1958) 2:361–368, 416–419. H. SCHRADE, *Die Vita des heiligen Liudger und ihre Bilder* (Münster 1960). B. KLÖSSEL, *Vollständige Faksimile-Ausgabe im Original-Format der Vita Sancti Liudgeri* (Graz 1993). R. R. POST, *Kerkgeschiedenis van Nederland in de Middeleeuwen*, 2 v. (Utrecht 1957). *Liudger, 742–809: de confrontatie tussen heidendom en christendom in de Lage Landen*, ed. A. VAN BERKUM et al. (Dieren 1984). W. FREITAG, *Heiliger Bischof und moderne Zeiten: die Verehrung des heiligen Ludger im Bistum Münster* (Münster 1995). K. SIERKSMA, *Liudger Thiadgrimszoon: leven en voortleven van een Christus–prediker* (Franeker 1995). L. VON PADBERG, *Heilige und Familie: Studien zur Bedeutung familiengebundener Aspekte in den Viten des Verwandten—und Schülerkreises um Willibrord, Bonifatius, und Liudger* (2d ed. Mainz 1997). J. L. BAUDOT and L. CHAUSSIN, *Vies des saints et des bienheureux selon l'ordre de calendrier avec l'historique des fêtes* (Paris 1935–56) 3:562–566. A. BUTLER, *The Lives of the Saints*. rev. ed. H. THURSTON and D. ATTWATER (New York 1956) 1:686–688.

[S. A. SCHULZ]

LUDLAM, ROBERT, BL.

Priest, martyr; b. ca. 1551 at Radbourne (near Sheffield), Derbyshire, England; d. July 24, 1588, hanged, drawn, and quartered on St. Mary's Bridge at Derby. Like Bl. Nicholas GARLICK with whom he died, Ludlam (also given as Ludham, Ludleham) studied at Oxford, taught for a time, then engaged in seminary studies at Rheims, where he was ordained (May 1581). After a six-year apostolate in his homeland, he was arrested with Garlick in the home of an ancient Catholic family through the treachery of one of the sons. He and Garlick fortified the flagging faith of their fellow-prisoner, Bl. Richard Simpson. All three were tried, condemned for their priesthood, and executed together. Together they were beatified by Pope John Paul II on Nov. 22, 1987 with George Haydock and Companions.

Feast of the English Martyrs: May 4 (England).

See Also: ENGLAND, SCOTLAND, AND WALES, MARTYRS OF.

Bibliography: R. CHALLONER, *Memoirs of Missionary Priests*, ed. J. H. POLLEN (rev. ed. London 1924). J. H. POLLEN, *Acts* *of English Martyrs* (London 1891). D. DE YEPES, *Historia Particular de la persecución de Inglaterra* (Madrid 1599).

[K. I. RABENSTEIN]

LUDMILLA, ST.

Martyr, patroness of Bohemia; b. *c.* 860; d. Tetin, West Bohemia, Sept. 15, 921. She was a Bohemian princess, and the wife of Bořiwoj (d. *c.* 894), first Christian duke of Bohemia. She and her husband were baptized at Velehrad by St. Methodius (*see* CYRIL AND METHODIUS) in 871. A Christian of great piety and zeal, she became one of the chief promoters of Christianity in Bohemia and was violently opposed by the adherents of national paganism. When her grandson, St. WENCESLAUS, ascended the throne (920) the struggle became particularly acute. He had been raised a Christian by Ludmilla, but since he was still a minor in 920, the regency was exercised by his mother Drahomira, a forceful and ambitious woman in sympathy with the pagan reaction. In her anxiety to eliminate the influence of Ludmilla on the young Wenceslaus, Drahomira instigated Ludmilla's murder at Tetin, where she was living in retirement. Ludmilla was buried at Tetin and later translated to St. George's Church in Prague.

Feast: Sept. 16.

Bibliography: *Passio s. Ludmillae,* ed. O. HOLDER EGGER, *Monumenta Germaniae Historica: Scriptores* 15.1:572–574. *Bibliotheca hagiographica latina antiquae et mediae aetatis* 2:5026–31. J. PEKAR, *Die Wenzels– und Ludmilla–Legenden und die Echtheit Christians* (Prague 1906). A. BUTLER, *The Lives of the Saints* 3:570.

[O. P. SHERBOWITZ–WETZOR]

LUDOLF OF CORVEY, ST.

Abbot of CORVEY; d. Aug. 13, 983. The son of Corvey's bailiff Hoger, Ludolf entered the monastery of Corvey; in 965 he was elected abbot. Under his direction the monastic school flourished, teachers were excellent, and the pupils good. Ludolf was energetic and deeply spiritual. He was devoted to the poor souls and was reputedly endowed with EXTRASENSORY perception. He saw, for example, the bloody head of Margrave Gero lying before him on the altar during Mass at the very moment it was severed by the executioner in Magdeburg. Ludolf made a pilgrimage to Rome by way of Cologne and earned for his church the reputation of being a true and dutiful daughter of the apostolic see. In 973 OTTO II confirmed the prerogatives of the abbey and agreed also to its engaging in profitable trade. Ludolf was active in building, surrounding the monastery by a high, strong wall. In 1100

his remains, together with those of Abbot DRUTHMAR, were solemnly elevated. Later (1662) they were placed in a gilt shrine and transferred to the mausoleum chapel in Corvey. There is a baroque statue of Ludolf in the choir of the monastery church.

Feast: Aug. 13, Feb. 21, June 5.

Bibliography: *Acta Sanctorum* Aug. 3:139–142. *Die Chronik des Bischofs Thietmar von Merseburg,* ed. R. HOLTZMANN (*Monumenta Germaniae Historica: Scriptores rerum Merovingicarum, Scriptores rerum Germanicarum* [new series] 9; 1935). J. L. BAUDOT and L. CHAUSSIN, *Vies des saints et des bienheureux selon l'ordre du calendrier avec l'historique des fêtes* 8:217–218. A. M. ZIMMERMANN, *Kalendarium Benedictinum: Die Heiligen und Seligen des Benediktinerordens und seiner Zweige* 2:567, 570. J. E. STADLER and F. J. HEIM, *Vollständiges Heiligenlexikon,* 5 v. (Augsburg 1858–82) 3:916.

[G. SPAHR]

LUDOLF OF RATZEBURG, ST.

Bishop of Ratzeburg 1236–50; d. Wismar, Mar. 29, 1250. As bishop he continued to observe the PREMONSTRATENSIAN rule and imposed it upon his cathedral chapter. With Prince John of Mecklenburg he established a convent of Benedictine nuns, which in 1319 became a Premonstratensian convent. He is sometimes honored as a martyr because of his conflict with Duke Albert of Sachsen–Lauenburg. During his long struggle the bishop suffered imprisonment, maltreatment, and banishment. His death is attributed to the tortures endured while in prison. His unflinching courage and severe discipline were outstanding. He was canonized in the 14th century, and is venerated at Wismar in Mecklenburg.

Feast: Mar. 30 (formerly 29).

Bibliography: *Acta Sanctorum* March 3:789–791. C. L. HUGO, *S. Ordinis Praemonstratensis annales* (Nancy 1734–36) 2:599–612. A. BUTLER, *The Lives of the Saints* (New York 1956) 1:702.

[M. J. MADAJ]

LUDOLPH OF SAXONY

Carthusian spiritual writer; b. *c.* 1295; d. Strassburg, April 10, 1377. Ludolph began his religious life as a Dominican, but entered the CARTHUSIANS in 1340 at Strassburg. He was prior at Coblenz from 1343 to 1348, then retired to the charterhouse at Mainz, and finally to that of Strassburg.

Ludolph was the author of one of the most widely read books of the later Middle Ages: *Vita Domini nostri Jesu Christi ex quatuor Evangeliis.* In this life of Christ,

Ludolph dwelt at length upon the events and teachings recorded in the Gospels and commented upon them abundantly from the Fathers of the Church and later spiritual authors, such as St. Bernard, Pseudo-Bonaventure, and James of Voragine. St. Ignatius Loyola was influenced in his conversion by reading the *Vita Christi,* and Ludolph's method of meditation left its mark on the one adopted in the *Spiritual Exercises.*

The *Vita* was first printed in 1474 by the Carthusians of Strassburg, and French translations were circulating in manuscript before 1485. During the 16th century there were innumerable editions in several languages. St. TERESA OF AVILA prescribed that a copy of the book should be in every Carmelite house. Ludolph also wrote *Expositio in Psalterium Davidis,* in which he drew most of his material from the commentaries of St. JEROME, St. AUGUSTINE, CASSIODORUS, and PETER LOMBARD. It was first printed at Paris in 1491 and has since been reprinted frequently. In both the *Vita* and the *Expositio* Ludolph's interpretations of Scripture are allegorical and moralizing.

Bibliography: S. AUTORE, *Dictionnaire de théologie catholique,* ed. A. VACANT et al., (Paris 1903–50). 9.1:1067–70. A. PASSMANN, ''Probleme um Ludolph von Sachsen,'' *Archiv für elsässische Kirchengeschichte,* 3 v. (1949–50) 13–34. M. I. BODENSTEDT, *The Vita Christi of Ludolphus the Carthusian* (Washington 1944). E. R. VON FRENTZ, ''Ludolphe le chartreux et les Exercices de Saint Ignace de Loyola,'' *Revue d'ascétique et de mystique* (1949) 375–388.

[B. DU MOUSTIER]

LUDWIG MISSIONSVEREIN (LUDWIG MISSION SOCIETY)

Also known as ''Missio Internationales Katholisches Missionswerk Ludwig Missionsverein,'' or more commonly as ''MISSIO München (Munich),'' with its head office in Munich. The society is one of the two German branches of the pontifical mission society MISSIO that was created by the German Catholic Bishops' Conference in 1972 with the merger of Ludwig Missionsverein (which became MISSIO München) and the St. Francis Xavier Mission Society of Aachen (which became MISSIO Aachen). MISSIO München encompasses the Bavarian region of Germany (covering the sees of Augsburg, Bamberg, Eichstätt, München and Freising, Passau, Regensburg, and Würzburg) and the diocese of Speyer. Together with its sister agency, it promotes and sponsors mission and human development projects in partnership with local churches in the Third World, especially in Africa, Asia, and the Pacific.

History. The society was founded through the efforts of Frederick Résé, a German missionary priest origi-

nally attached to the Cincinnati diocese, at Munich, Bavaria, on Dec. 12, 1838, for the express purpose of giving financial assistance to the Catholic missions of Asia and America. When Résé, encouraged by his recent success in Austria in founding the LEOPOLDINEN STIFTUNG, first approached King Ludwig of Bavaria in 1828, the king thought the time inopportune. Ten years later Résé, now Bishop of Detroit, obtained Ludwig's consent; and the society, which bore the king's name, was established with headquarters in Munich and St. Francis Xavier as patron.

Initially the Ludwig Mission Society collaborated with the Society for the PROPAGATION OF THE FAITH, which had been founded in France in 1822 for the distribution of funds and as a means of obtaining authoritative information about the missions. Mutual dissatisfaction over the allocation of funds led to a complete separation of the two societies in 1844, after which its efforts were directed especially to the needs of German Catholics in the United States. Valuable aid was also rendered to religious orders in the United States, particularly the Redemptorists and Benedictines, and to a lesser degree the Franciscans, Capuchins, and Premonstratensians. The Austrian Jesuit missionary F. X. Weninger, who worked principally with the Germans in the United States, was the recipient of annual allotments from Munich until his death in 1888 at the age of 83. The society contributed annually from 1862 to World War I to the American College at Louvain and helped to develop a corps of German American priests by promoting St. Francis Seminary in Milwaukee. It helped teaching communities such as the School Sisters of Notre Dame, founded in Bavaria in 1833, and in the United States in 1847. Native American missions also benefited and, through Weninger, some pioneer work among African Americans was undertaken.

The society's magazine, *Annalen der Glaubensverbreitung,* published about 300 letters pertaining to the United States before it was supplanted in 1918 by a periodical of the Francis Xavier Mission Society of Aachen. More than 2,000 additional letters are still extant in the society's archives in Munich. In 1922, Pope Pius XI elevated the Ludwig Mission Society to a pontifical mission society.

Bibliography: T. ROEMER, *The Ludwig-Missionsverein and the Church in the United States (1838–1918)* (Catholic University of America, *Studies in American Church History* 16; 1933); *Ten Decades of Alms* (St. Louis 1942).

[B. J. BLIED/EDS.]

LÜFTHILDIS, ST.

Virgin known also as Leuchteldis, Liuthild, Lufthold, or Luchtel; fl. ninth century. Place names, inscriptions, and local devotion testify to the influence exerted by Lüfthildis, of whose life there is no other tangible trace. Tradition has it that she was persecuted by her stepmother because of her generosity to the poor, and eventually retired to a hermitage. Lüftelberg, in the Archdiocese of Cologne, is named for her. As a result of the miracles that occurred after her death, her grave in the parish church there became the center of a cult of which the first evidence is in the work of CAESARIUS OF HEISTERBACH in 1222. Her relics were exhumed in 1623 and enclosed in a marble sarcophagus in 1902. Her aid is invoked by sufferers of head and ear maladies.

Feast: Jan. 23.

Bibliography: *Acta Sanctorum* Jan. 3:750–753. A. STEFFENS, *Die hl. Lüfthildis v. Lüftelberg* (Cologne 1903). A. BUTLER, *The Lives of the Saints*, rev. ed. H. THURSTON and D. ATTWATER (New York 1956) 1:157. J. TORSY, ed., *Lexikon der deutschen Heiligen, Seligen, Ehrwürdigen und Gottseligen* (Cologne 1959) 358. M. FRANK, *Die Volksheilige L. von L. und ihre Attribute in Legende, Kult und Brauch* (Düsseldorf 1959).

[M. B. RYAN]

LUGO, FRANCISCO DE

Jesuit theologian and elder brother of Juan de Lugo; b. Madrid, 1580; d. Valladolid, Dec. 17, 1652. His father sent him to Salamanca to study law, but Francisco entered the novitiate of the Society of Jesus there in 1600. Though he soon made a reputation as a competent theologian, he requested assignment to the foreign missions and was sent to Mexico. Mission work was never to be his task, however, for his superiors, on learning of his academic achievements, appointed him to teach theology. While teaching he managed to write a commentary on the entire *Summa* of St. Thomas. He was then recalled to Spain, but the fleet in which he sailed was attacked by the Dutch and in the battle most of his commentary on the *Summa* was lost. After arriving in Spain he taught both philosophy and theology. His reputation as a theologian grew, and the Jesuit general summoned De Lugo to Rome to be his theologian and censor of books. He was twice rector of the college of Valladolid, where he died well known and respected by the theologians of his time. The confusion of his writings with those of his older brother has led to a certain amount of inaccuracy in theological scholarship. His published works are: the *De Principiis moralibus actuum humanorum* (Elvire 1642), *Theologia scholastica* (Lyons 1647), and *De septem ecclesiae sacramentis* (Venice 1652).

Bibliography: C. SOMMERVOGEL, et al., *Bibliothèque de la Compagnie de Jésus* (Brussels-Paris 1890–1932) 5:175. H. HURTER, *Nomenclator literarius theologiae catholicae* (3d ed., Innsbruck 1903–13) 3:911.

[G. V. KOHLS]

LUGO, JUAN DE

Jesuit theologian and cardinal of the seventeenth century, especially esteemed as a moralist; b. Madrid, Nov. 25, 1583; d. Rome, Aug. 20, 1660. Juan de Lugo, born of noble parents, seems to have been destined for an ecclesiastical career from his earliest years. Before he was ten years old, he had received the tonsure and he had obtained a benefice from PHILIP II of Spain by the time he was 14. Juan received his early education in Seville, where he obtained a bachelor of arts degree in 1598. Then his parents sent him with his older brother Francisco to Salamanca to study civil and canon law. While in Salamanca, Francisco entered the Society of Jesus. In 1603, Juan also became a JESUIT, against the wishes of his father. After his ordination, he taught philosophy and theology in various Jesuit houses of study.

In 1616 De Lugo received his master's degree and was assigned to teach theology at Valladolid. His fame as a theologian spread quickly within the society, and in 1621 or 1622 the general summoned him to Rome. There he taught theology for the next 20 years.

Although urged by his friends to publish his theological treatises, De Lugo refused until 1631, when he was commanded by his superiors to do so. Within 15 years he prepared five major works for publication: *De incarnatione Domini* (Lyons 1633); *De sacramentis in genere, de venerabili eucharistiae sacramento, et de sacrasancto Missae sacrificio* (Lyons 1636); *De virtute et sacramento poenitentiae, de suffragiis et indulgentiis* (Lyons 1638), *De iustitia et iure* (Lyons 1642); *De virtute fidei divinae* (Lyons 1646). Later his *Responsorum moralium libri sex* (Lyons 1651) was published by his former pupil and friend, Cardinal Sforza PALLAVICINO. In addition to these works, De Lugo wrote a number of other philosophical and theological treatises during his long teaching career. A group of these was published in Cologne in 1716 under the title *De Deo, de angelis, de actibus humanis et de gratia*. Other compositions are cited in his published works, such as, *De anima, Philosophia, Logica, De Trinitate, De visione Dei, De scientia Dei, De praedestinatione, De bonitate et malitia humanorum actuum;* the manuscripts of some of these works are still extant in the libraries of Madrid, Salamanca, Karlsruhe, and Mechlin.

The basis of De Lugo's fame as a theologian and of his influence on the development of theology is to be found in his published works, which show him to have been a theologian of considerable stature and an independent thinker. His approach was nonpolemic. It was not his custom to present an exhaustive review of opinion on a topic, nor did he quote many authorities in support of his own position. In direct fashion he stated the question, discussed the problem, and reasoned his way to a solution. In the process he demonstrated his thorough grounding in scholastic philosophy, dogmatic and moral theology, and civil and canon law.

In his discussions the supernatural is seen as built upon the natural order, and moral obligations as flowing from doctrinal truths. He drew the principles of the political order from the nature of man as a social being, but at the same time he pointed out that social life is a most necessary means for the profession of the Christian faith (*De iustitia,* 10). The supreme jurisdiction of the pope in the Church and his infallibility in regard to faith and morals were deduced from the nature of the Church as the agency of salvation founded by Christ (*De virtute fidei divinae,* 1).

A comparison of De Lugo's teaching with the social doctrine of the popes from LEO XIII to PIUS XII shows that there are few points on which the seventeenth-century theologian would have to be corrected because of the subsequent development of Catholic social doctrine. His discussion of the rights of slaves could be used as an exposition of the inalienable rights of man (*De iustitia,* 3). Again, his consideration of the use of torture in judicial processes makes it evident that theologians at the time of the Inquisition were well aware of the moral problems connected with its use.

De Lugo dedicated his fourth work, the monumental *De iustitia et iure,* to Urban VIII. The pope was so impressed with the work and its author that he determined to make the theologian a cardinal. Although the Jesuit tried to decline, the pope commanded him to accept the cardinalate in 1643. Thereafter, De Lugo became active in the work of the Holy Office and the Congregation of the Council.

When the Jansenist Antoine Arnauld published his book, *De la fréquente communion,* a violent theological controversy broke out and there developed a strong trend to condemn the entire Jansenistic movement. In a memorial counseling moderation, De Lugo pointed out that the Jansenists still professed to be Catholics and urged that they be treated with as much kindness as the defense of Catholic principles would allow. In spite of his moderate stand, De Lugo was left out of the committee of cardinals commissioned to evaluate the orthodoxy of Jansenism. Since the Jesuits had been active in opposing the Jansenists, it was felt that he would not be impartial in his judgment.

In the conclave of 1655, King Philip IV of Spain declared Cardinal Sacchetti *persona non grata* and tried to have him excluded as a papal candidate. In the debate that arose among the cardinals of the conclave, it was proba-

bly De Lugo who defended the Spanish king's claim to the right of exclusion.

Bibliography: J. DE LUGO, *Disputationes scholasticae et morales,* ed. J. B. FOURNALS, 8 v. (new ed. Paris 1891–94). J. E. NIEREMBERG, *Varones ilustres de la compañia de Jesús,* cont'd A. DE ANDRADE and J. CASSINI, 9 v. (2d ed. Bilbao 1887–92) v. 5. Pastor. G. BRINKMAN, *The Social Thought of John de Lugo* (Washington 1957).

[G. BRINKMAN]

LUKÁŠ OF PRAGUE

Czech theologian, leader of BOHEMIAN BRETHREN; b. Prague, *c.* 1460; d. Mladá Boleslav, Dec. 11, 1528. He was reared as an Utraquist; he graduated from Prague University in 1481 and soon afterward joined the Unity of Brethren. In the 1490s Lukáš was instrumental in persuading the Unity to abandon its antistate position. In 1494 he was elected to the Narrow Council; in 1500 he was chosen a bishop of the Unity, which he reorganized. He was a prolific writer of theological and liturgical works, hymns, and catechisms. Although he had contacts with Luther in the early 1520s, the two never reached any agreement.

Bibliography: P. BROCK, *The Political and Social Doctrines of the Unity of Czech Brethren* (The Hague 1957). J. WEISSKOPF, *Lexikon für Theologie und Kirche,* ed. J. HOFER and K. RAHNER (Freiburg 1957–65) 6:1207. E. PESCHKE, *Die Religion in Geschichte und Gegenwart* (Tübingen 1957–65) 4:473.

[P. BROCK]

LUKE, EVANGELIST, ST.

St. Luke is called by St. Paul, ''our most dear physician'' (Col 4.14), a description that the vocabulary of the third Gospel and of Acts seems to justify. Luke's medical terms, however, may have been those familiar to any educated man of the period. Paul also calls Luke a fellow worker in Philemon 24. In 2 Tm 4.11 Luke is Paul's only companion shortly before the Apostle's death. These are the only times Luke is mentioned in the NT.

Early Christian tradition identifies him as the author of the third Gospel and the Acts. Luke was a Greek-speaking convert of pagan origin (cf. Col 4.11b with Col 4.14). He was not himself an eyewitness of what he writes (Lk 1.2) and, therefore, not one of the 72 Disciples (Lk 10.1), nor Cleophas's unnamed companion on the road to EMMAUS (Lk 24.8). From the ''we sections'' of the ACTS OF THE APOSTLES, we may conclude that he first met St. Paul at Troas (16.10), rejoined him at PHILIPPI some years later (20.5), accompanied him to Jerusalem

Saint Luke the Evangelist. (Archive Photos)

(21.1–18), and remained with the Apostle during his imprisonment in CAESAREA IN PALESTINE, and Rome (Acts 27.1–28.16).

According to the anti-Marcionite prologue (A.D. 160–180), Luke never married, and lived to the age of 84. After his death in Achaia (or Bithynia or Egypt), his bones were transferred to Constantinople.

In Christian iconography, St. Luke, portrayed either as a man, or a writer, or an ox, appears frequently on various sacred artifacts. The symbol of an ox (Ez 10.14; Ap 4.7), most frequently used for Luke, may have been applied to him because of his calm and strength, or because his Gospel begins and ends in the Temple.

Feast: Oct. 18.

[R. T. A. MURPHY]

LUKE, GOSPEL ACCORDING TO

The third Gospel with the Acts of the Apostles forms a two-volume work about the origins of Christianity. Like the other Gospels that preceded Luke's work, this Gospel follows the outline of the proclamation of the good news (*see* GOSPEL) of salvation that originated with the preaching of the Apostles in Jerusalem. This treatment will be a consideration of three aspects: contents and division; origin; and literary and theological characteristics.

Contents and Division

Luke has added an account of the birth and infancy of Jesus and resurrection appearances to his edition of Mark's Gospel. In addition to the prologue (1.1-4) the Third Gospel contains seven major sections: the Infancy Gospel, the preparation for the public ministry, the ministry in Galilee, the journey to Jerusalem, the ministry in Jerusalem, the Passion, the Resurrection.

The Infancy Gospel (1.5–2.52). The first two chapters recount in parallel order an angelic announcement of the birth of John the Baptist; an announcement by the same Archangel Gabriel of the conception and birth of Jesus; the birth of John and its circumstances; the birth of Jesus (*see* NATIVITY OF CHRIST), the joyful prophecies and revelations surrounding it; and one incident of His hidden life. These two double panels are skillfully woven together by the account of the visit of Jesus' mother to John's mother (*see* VISITATION OF MARY).

In this well-ordered narrative the important places are named: the Temple in Jerusalem (Jerusalem and the Temple will remain central focuses of attention for Luke), Nazareth, the Judean hill-country, David's city of Bethlehem, and again Jerusalem and its Temple. Well-known Jewish customs and rites play important roles in the story: a priest chosen by lot and according to his class to offer incense, the gathering of the people for prayer at the hour of the incense offering, the practice of circumcision on the 8th day, the purification of mothers (*see* PURIFICATION OF MARY), the offering to God in order to redeem a first-born son, and the pilgrim feast of the Passover. Chronological references are given: "In the days of King Herod of Judea. . ." (1.5); "Now in the sixth month. . ." (1.26); Mary's three-month visit with Elizabeth (1.56); the birth of Jesus in the time of Caesar Augustus and during the census under the governor of Syria, Quirinius (2.1–2). [*See* CENSUS (IN THE BIBLE).] The key figures appear in due order: Zachary; Elizabeth, too old to have children; Gabriel; Mary, a virgin engaged to Joseph, a descendant of David; the shepherds; Simeon and Anna; and the Jewish teachers in the Temple. Mary is described as one who "treasured all these words and pondered them in her heart" (2.19, 51).

Preparation for Public Ministry (3.1–4.13). Luke begins the story of salvation against a background of profane history. Seven rulers who then held office, from the

Emperor Tiberius to Caiaphas, are named (3.1–2). The preaching of John the Baptist sets the scene for the appearance of Jesus as God's beloved Son in whom He is well pleased (3.3–22). The GENEALOGY OF JESUS follows. Jesus is the 77th descendant, i.e., the most perfect offspring, from God through the line of Adam (3.23–38). In contrast to Matthew, who traces Jesus from Abraham through David's son, Solomon, and Joseph as Jacob's son, Luke begins his list with Jesus and ascends from Joseph as Heli's son, through David's son, Nathan, to God Himself, the Father of Adam.

Thus, Jesus is represented as the Son of God (*see* BAPTISM OF CHRIST). Under the guidance of the Holy Spirit who descended upon Him at His baptism, Jesus is tested in the desert and proves Himself, in this first passage at arms with the devil, to be the humble, obedient, and completely confident adorer of the Father (4.1–13; *see* TEMPTATIONS OF JESUS). With this victory won, Jesus "returned in the power of the Spirit into Galilee" (4.14) to begin His work (3.23).

Ministry in Galilee (4.14–9.50). Luke's record of the Galilean ministry is marked by a topographical vagueness. The trend of events, however, is clearly indicated. Summarily telescoping what were different and later visits, Luke shows (4.16–30) how the Savior's mission of grace met with rejection at Nazareth; Jesus' reception at Capernaum, where the crowds were enthralled at His teaching and miracles, was more encouraging (4.31–44). With the call of the first DISCIPLES (5.1–11) and the cure of the leper (5.12–16), however, Jesus aroused the attention of the Pharisees and Scribes (5.17) with whom he was soon involved in controversy because of his association with publicans and sinners (5.27–32) and over fasting and the Sabbath (6.1–11). After a night of prayer, Jesus named 12 chosen disciples apostles (6.12–16). Luke follows this with an inaugural sermon, the Sermon on the Plain (6.17–49). It contains much of the same material as is found in Matthew's SERMON ON THE MOUNT (Mt 5–7).

At Capernaum a centurion shows a greater willingness than the Jews to believe in Jesus (7.1–10). Luke depicts Jesus as the Lord with power over death (7.11–17). The doubts of the Baptist and his disciples are dispelled by an appeal to Jesus' miracles and His preaching of the good news to the poor. John is praised as the greatest prophet, but of less worth than the least in the kingdom of God (7.18–30). In contrast to a wicked generation that closes its ears to His message (7.31–35), Luke relates the touching incident of the penitent woman (7.36–50) and mentions the generosity of other women (8.1–3).

Jesus begins to teach in parables (*see* PARABLES OF JESUS). The reason for this new method is given; the para-

St. Luke.

ble of the Sower is explained; and the parable of the Lamp is recounted. We have reached a crisis in faith (8.4–18). Jesus' true relatives are those who hear and keep His word (8.19–21). After demonstrating His power over nature (8.22–25), demons (8.26–39), death and sickness (8.40–56), Jesus sends the Twelve on their first mission (9.1–10). When they return, he feeds 5,000 men (9.11–17). Then Peter, in answer to Jesus' question, proclaims Him to be "the Messiah of God" (9.18–21). The first prediction of the Passion follows immediately, juxtaposed to the conditions for following Jesus and the coming glory of His kingdom (9.22–27). The Transfiguration is recounted with details proper to Luke, a possessed boy is delivered from his affliction, and a second prediction of the Passion is given (9.28–45). A dispute among the disciples about their relative greatness and about an exorcism performed by someone who had not been with them leads to Jesus teaching about humility and a rejoinder that puts them in their place (9.46–50).

The Travel Account, Jesus' Journey to Jerusalem (9.51–19.27). Luke's "great interpolation" or "travel document," as the section from 9.51 to 18.14 is called, fills out a vague reference in Mark 10.1 to a ministry outside of Galilee. In it Luke uses traditional materials not found in Mark but found in Matthew in a different version. The exact sequence of events and their location are

pax hominibuf·bonç uolun
tatis·

"The Nativity," from an 11th-century Lectionary from the Abbey of St. Peter, Salzburg, Austria.

Ministry in Jerusalem (19.28–21.38). On His arrival in Jerusalem, Jesus is accorded a triumphal reception (19.28–40); He predicts the destruction of the Holy City (19.41–44), cleanses the Temple, and continues to preach in the face of mounting opposition (19.45–48). The questioning of his authority, the parable of the vineyard, the trap about tribute to Caesar, a controversy with the Sadducees on the Resurrection and another with the Scribes on the nature of the Messiah, and finally, Jesus' warning against the hypocrisy of the Scribes, lead artfully to the discourse on the destruction of Jerusalem (20.1–21.38).

The Passion Narrative (22.1–23.56). Throughout this section Luke manifests a much greater independence from Mark and manifests many similarities with the Fourth Gospel. Plotting precedes the betrayal of Christ (22.1–6). The Eucharist is instituted in the context of the Jewish Passover meal and the eating of the Passover lamb (22.7–20). Judas's betrayal and Peter's denials are announced (22.21–38). The agony in the garden is narrated with an admirable terseness (22.39–46). Peter's denials occur after the arrest (22.47–62). Sparing in his treatment of violence, Luke gives the impression that Jesus was manhandled only once (22.63–65); the Evangelist dislikes repetition of what has been said already. Christ appears before the Sanhedrin (22.65–23.1) and then before Pilate (23.2–7). He has skillfully prepared for Jesus' appearance before Herod (Antipas) (23.8–12) long before (9.7–9); in similar fashion, the two thieves are introduced before they speak (23.32, 39–42); one of them is promised Paradise (23.43). Jesus' death and burial are succinctly told (23.44–56). [*See* PASSION OF CHRIST, I (IN THE BIBLE); TRIAL OF JESUS.]

The Resurrection Narrative. Luke recounts the empty tomb and the "two men . . . in dazzling raiment" who proclaim the Resurrection to the women; the apostles remain unbelieving (24.1–12). Then, Jesus appears to two disciples going to Emmaus (24.3–35), and to the Eleven gathered in Jerusalem (24.36–43). Next follow Jesus' last instructions to His Disciples (24.44–49) and, very abruptly, the ascension into heaven (28.50–52). *See* ASCENSION OF JESUS CHRIST. The Gospel that struck a note of joy in the first two chapters closes on the same note of great joy: the Disciples are continually in the Temple praising God (24.53). Luke has no mention of a Galilean appearance of Jesus in Galilee.

vague, but there are frequent reminders that Jerusalem is the destination of the journey (9.51, 53; 13.22, 33; 17.11; 18.31). Luke is otherwise content to link things together by "after this," or "in a town," or "in another village," etc.

This section contains Luke's finest contributions: 18 parables of great beauty and six miracles found only in Luke. Whatever order is followed is logical rather than chronological or topographical: artificially grouped polemical discourses (11.14–14.24); vocation sayings (9.57–62); privileges granted disciples (10.17–24); instructions on prayer (11.1–13);a trilogy of parables on divine mercy (15.1–32); good and bad use of wealth (16.1–15, 16–31); social virtues (17.1–19); sayings about the Law taken out of their original context (16.16–18); sayings about the end-time and the "Day" of the Son of Man (17.20–18.8); sayings about humility and detachment, linked to a third prediction of the Passion (18.9–34). It is in this latter section at 18.15 that Luke rejoins Mark, following him until the Passion story, but with some notable additions, e.g., the Zacchaeus story and the parable of the pounds (19.1–28).

Origin

Luke and Acts are two parts of one work that treats of Christian origins. The close relationship of the two parts, so much alike in style, vocabulary, and grammar, points to a single author. Both works open with prologues addressed to Theophilus, the second referring to a "first book,'' which it proposes to continue. Luke concluded his Gospel with an account of the Resurrection and ascension; Acts opens with a brief account of the ascension and continues with a description of the coming of the Holy Spirit and the extension of the gospel to the end of the earth (Acts 1.8). The Gospel sequence from Galilee to Jerusalem is balanced by that of Acts, which describes the spread of the gospel from Jerusalem to Rome. The two works may originally have been a single book separated at a very early date so that the faithful might have the four Gospels in a single convenient codex.

Early Tradition about Authorship. The early tradition that holds Luke to be the author of both the third Gospel and Acts is firm and unswerving. His name (*see* LUKE, EVANGELIST, ST.) appears in neither the two works attributed to him nor in the extant fragments of Papias (*Ecclesiastical History* 3.39.16). The works of Justin Martyr (100–164) which speak (*c.* 155) of the ''Gospels'' read in the liturgical assemblies of the faithful (*Apol.* 1.66.3), works abound with details that presuppose a knowledge of the third Gospel. Marcion's bid (*c.* 145) to establish an authoritative collection of genuine Christian writings included one unnamed Gospel that is clearly Luke's. Irenaeus (135–202) is the earliest Christian writer to mention Luke by name as author of the third Gospel. In his *Adv. Haer.* 3.1.1 (Eusebius, *Ecclesiastical History* 5.8.2), he writes: ''Luke, the companion of Paul, put down in a book the gospel preached by him.'' Irenaeus was obviously stressing the point that even the Gospels written by disciples of the Apostles had apostolic authority behind them. Tertullian (160–250) insists on the apostolic authority of the third Gospel (*Adv. Marc.* 4.2.5). The Muratorian Canon attributes the third Gospel to Luke, the physician who accompanied Paul as a *juris studiosus* (legal consultor?). This fragmentary text states that Luke had never seen Christ in the flesh, nor had he been one of Jesus' disciples. It gives this as the reason why Luke began his Gospel with the announcement of the Baptist's birth. Clement of Alexandria (150–218) frequently quotes the third Gospel and unhesitatingly names Luke as its author (*Strom.* 1.21.145). Later tradition adds nothing more to our knowledge beyond the doubtful detail that Luke was of Antiochean origin (Eusebius, *Ecclesiastical History* 3.4.7).

Place and Time of Composition. The oldest attestation pertinent to the geographical origin of the Third Gospel is an ancient Greek Prologue that states that ''this Luke is an Antiochene, a Syrian.'' Eusebius knows the same tradition, affirming that ''by descent Luke was of those from Antioch'' (*Ecclesiastical History* 3.4, 6). Jerome affirms that Luke was an ''Antiochene doctor'' (*De vir. ill.* 7). This ancient tradition is consistent with what can be gleaned about the provenance of the Gospel from

its contents, namely, that the Gospel shows evidence of a concern for Hellenistic Christians and that was directed to Gentiles (1.3) or to a community in which Gentiles were the majority. No convincing arguments have thus far been advanced as to identify the place of its composition. Sites as diverse as Achaia, Boetia, and Rome have been suggested at various times.

Ancient tradition says that Luke's Gospel was composed after the deaths of Peter and Paul (Irenaeus, *Adversus haereses* 3.1.1). Modern scholarship, which generally acknowledges the dependence of Luke on Mark, holds that the Gospel was written some time after 70 A.D. It was certainly written before Acts (Acts 1.1) but the exact date of composition cannot be determined with any degree of certainty. Most scholars opt for an approximate date in the eighties but some would place the time of its composition in the early nineties.

Sources. Since much of the material contained in the Fourth Gospel is the same as that found in Mark and since Matthew and Luke follow the same sequence of presentation of material only when they share that sequence with Mark, the consensus of contemporary scholarship is that Mark is one of the primary sources of the Third Gospel and furnishes Luke with a narrative framework. Markan material is especially found in five large segments of the Fourth Gospel, 3.1–4.15; 4.31–6.19; 8.4–9.50; 18.15–21.33; and 22.1–24.12. Much of Luke's non-Markan material is found in the Infancy Narratives, the Resurrection stories, and the two interpolations that interrupt Luke's following of the Markan narrative plot, the little interpolation of 6.20–8.3 and the great interpolation of 9.51–18.14.

Scholars generally agree that Luke made use of another source, a Greek-language collection of Jesus' sayings (Q, from the German *Quelle* meaning ''source''). This hypothetical source—for which there is no ancient textual witness—was shared by Luke and Matthew, contributed about 230 verses of discourse material to each of these Gospels, the Sermon on the Plain (6.20–49), among them. In many instances, but not in all, Luke's version of the Q material appears to be closer to the source than Matthew's version.

In addition Luke had his own sources. These special sources are collectively identified as ''L'' but ''L'' is not a single source. It may include some written material as well as oral traditions known to and used by Luke (1.1–4). The stories of the raising of the son of the widow of Nain (7.12–17) and of the visit with Martha and Mary (10.38–42) are examples of material that comes from Luke's special sources. ''L'' is, however, not a source of the Third Gospel in the way that Mark and Q are. Mark and Q are documentary sources; ''L'' is neither a single source nor is it entirely documentary.

In the history of the interpretation of the Gospel mention is frequently made of Mary, the mother of Jesus, as the primary source for the Infancy Narratives (1.4–2.80). Modern scholarship has generally abandoned this suggestion. It attributes little of this material to any of Luke's special sources, preferring to see the Infancy Narratives as the product of Luke's own composition.

Literary and Theological Characteristics. Luke is a fine Hellenistic writer. His work is generally acknowledged to be the best Greek composition in the New Testament. He follows the style of the Hellenistic prologue in 1.1–4, is familiar with the symposium genre (7.36–50; 11.37–54; 14.1–24), and knows how to write a farewell discourse (22.14–38). The Greek of his Infancy Narratives follows the style of the Septuagint, the common version of the Greek Bible. Luke is creative in his use of his sources, skillfully using material from different sources to weave an artful account of a single narrative. He uses parallelism to good advantage, particularly in the juxtaposition of stories about John the Baptist and Jesus (1.5–2.8) and his side-by-side stories about men and women (1.25–38; 15.3–10). Luke provides unity for his narrative with the use of ring construction (literary inclusion), most notably beginning and closing his account with a Jerusalem narrative (1.8–23; 24.13–53).

His narrative uses time and space effectively, as often as not with manifest theological intention. His time is historical time (3.1–2) to the degree that Conzelmann could sum up Luke's theology as "the center of time," biblical history its prelude, the time of the church its sequel. Luke's "today" is the today of salvation (19.9; 23.43). His space draws attention to Jerusalem (9.51) and the temple (18.9–14) in a way that is found in neither Matthew nor Mark. For theological reasons Luke has creatively exploited Mark's geographic scheme, the ministry in Galilee, the Passion and Resurrection in Jerusalem. The story of Jesus ends in Jerusalem; it is retold to the nations (Acts 1.8).

The Infancy Narratives presents Jesus as a Jew who was properly reared in a pious family. Lk 4.16 provides a further indication of the success of his rearing as a devout Jew, but in the ministry itself Jesus appears as a "cultured Hellenistic gentleman" (J. O'Grady's phrase). Luke's christology highlights Jesus as son of God and filled with the Holy Spirit (1.26–38; 3.21–4.13; see 4.14, 18, etc.). The Gospel shows an interest in prophecy (6.23, 26; 11.47–51; etc.) and creatively portrays Jesus as prophet (4.24–27; 7.11–17). Jesus is also the one who explains the scriptures (4.16–21; 24.27, 32).

Luke often portrays Jesus at prayer, particularly at the most significant moments in his ministry (3.21; 6.12; 9.18; etc.) His prayer was so impressive that the disciples

asked him to teach them how to pray. Jesus's response was to teach his disciples the Lord's prayer (11.1–5; see Mt 6.9–13). Luke's emphasis on prayer is without parallel in the other Synoptic Gospels (11.5–13; etc.), giving examples of prayer formularies that continue to be used in the church, the *Magnificat* (1.46–55), the *Benedictus* (2.68–79), the *Nunc Dimittis* (2.29–32), and some words of the "Hail Mary" (1.28, 42).

Jesus' outreach to outcasts and the marginalized appears in the Third Gospel as it does in no other text. The beatitudes proclaim the blessedness of the poor and constitute a prophetic challenge to the rich (6.20–25). Jesus' feeling for the poor and widows (2.37; 4.25–26; 7.12) is expressed in the story of the poor widow with two small copper coins (21.1–4). The poor, the crippled, the blind, and the lame are invited to the Messianic banquet; for Jesus' disciples, they are to be the focus of concern (14.12–24). Jesus tells the story of the good Samaritan (10.29–37); Luke draws attention to the grateful Samaritan (17.16). Jesus' sympathy for the marginalized is particularly evident in the many stories that Luke tells about women, beginning with the story of Elizabeth (1.24–25) and ending with the women's discovery of the empty tomb (24.22–24, see 24.11). Interspersed throughout the Gospel are narratives about Mary (1.26–56), the widow of Nain (7.11–17), Martha and Mary (10.38–42), the woman in the crowd (11.27–28), the women from Galilee who came to Jerusalem with Jesus (8.1–2; 23.55), and so forth.

These themes are skillfully woven together as the expression of God's eternal and mysterious plan of universal salvation through the Savior who was "taken up" from this world by His Passion and Resurrection in Jerusalem (9.51; 24.25–26; 24.50–53). This salvation, once for all times achieved, is proclaimed through the Holy Spirit, the power from heaven (Acts 1.7–8), the gift to His children from God the Father through the intercession of the only Son of God (Lk 11.13). It is this Spirit who guided Luke to the completion of his masterpiece.

Bibliography: R. LAURENTIN, *Structure et théologie de Luc I–II* (*Études bibliques*; Paris 1957). D. L. BOCK, *Luke*, 2 v. *Baker's Exegetical Commentary on the New Testament* (Grand Rapids, Mich. 1994, 1996). R. E. BROWN, *The Birth of the Messiah* (New York, N.Y. 1993). H. CONZELMANN, *The Theology of St. Luke* (New York, N.Y. 1990). C. A. EVANS and J. A. SANDERS, *Luke and Scripture: The Function of Sacred Scripture in Luke-Acts* (Minneapolis, Minn. 1993). J. A. FITZMYER, *The Gospel According to Luke*, Anchor Bible 28, 28A, 2 v. (Garden City, N.J. 1981, 1985). H. FLENDER, *St. Luke: Theologian of Redemptive History* (Philadelphia, Penn. 1967). L. T. JOHNSON, *The Gospel of Luke* (*Sacra Pagina 3* Collegeville 1991). R. J. KARRIS, *Luke: Artist and Theologian* (New York, N.Y. 1985). L. E. KECK and J. L. MARTYN, *Studies in Luke-Acts* (Nashville, Tenn. 1966). J. D. KINGSBURY, *Conflict in Luke: Jesus, Authorities, Disciples*, (Minneapolis, Minn. 1991). M.

A. POWELL, *What Are They Saying about Luke?* (New York, N.Y. 1989).

[R. T. A. MURPHY/R. F. COLLINS]

LUKE-ACTS

One of the overarching issues in modern New Testament criticism is the relationship of the Gospel according to Luke and the Acts of the Apostles. As Biblical studies moves beyond historical criticism, scholars began to treat Luke and Acts as a single, two-volume whole. The Third Gospel is interpreted in light of its sequel Acts, not through its differences from Mark and Matthew, though these remain important clues to Lukan intentions.

In last decades of the 20th century, redaction criticism and stylistic criticism dominated approaches to Luke and to Acts respectively. Stress on Lukan theology theology replaced concern for the historicity of Luke and Acts, often bringing with it negative judgments about the latter. For example, few scholars held any longer that Luke and Acts were written before the destruction of Jerusalem; nor did many think the author was Paul's companion Luke. Not being an eyewitness and writing some 20 years after Paul's death, the author's picture of Christian beginnings seemed idealized and the Paul of Acts scarcely reconcilable with the historical Paul and his theology found in his letters. Acts was more and more ignored in theories of the origins of Christianity or as an interpretive guide to Paul's letters. These negative attitudes especially towards Acts filtered down into religious education on all levels.

Then in the 1980s scholarly unrest with this negative picture grew. In his Anchor Bible commentary, Joseph Fitzmyer dated Luke-Acts in A.D. 80–85. Still, he argued that its author was a companion of Paul, though only on the two later journeys where he signals his presence by using "we" in Acts 16:10 and later passages. The differences between Lukan and Pauline theology do not necessarily mean that Luke never knew Paul. They rather suggest that Luke did not use Paul's letters when he wrote 20 to 30 years later. They imply that Luke had less accurate information about Paul's early career before Luke came to know him than Paul's letters had, that he wrote in a later period when Pauline controversies about justification by faith were no longer burning questions, and that he had his own theological concerns that account for many of his differences from Paul (cf. *The Anchor Bible*, v. 28, 35–57).

Fitzmyer voiced the objection of many to unfair comparisons between Luke and Paul, especially regarding Luke's failure to emphasize Jesus' death as saving,

and his substituting a "theology of glory" for Paul's "theology of the cross" and a bland salvation history for his eschatological urgency. As the reaction against these previous negative comparisons spread, first Lukan theology, then his narrative techniques, were studied in their own right. No longer do many scholars label Luke-Acts by the pejorative term "early Catholic," implying a decline from the Pauline-Johannine gospel of salvation by faith into an institutionalization, legalization, and sacramentalization of Church order and discipleship, as well as "bourgeois ethics."

New Approaches. Within historical criticism, sociological and anthropological approaches tried to fill in more first century cultural background and thus remedy some of the historical deficiencies inherent in mere extrapolations from Lukan changes in presumed Markan and Q sources used to reconstruct the situation of the author and his community or communities. Meanwhile, skepticism toward the historical value of Acts increased, bringing on counter-reactions led by Martin Hengel in Germany and English-speaking Evangelicals who defended the basic historicity of Acts according to the standards of its day and in conjunction with its theological concerns.

Historiography. Study of the rhetoric and historiography of the Hellenistic age was an important factor in moderating some of the extremes in debates about the genre, purposes, and historicity of Luke-Acts. By ancient standards, Luke-Acts is reputable and serious history comparable with contemporary works by historians as diverse as Josephus, Polybius, and Dionysius of Halicarnasus, and with the Biblical books of Sm-Kgs and 1–2 Mc. Luke exhibits terms and methods common in the rhetorical training for writers of that age. His preface uses technical rhetorical terms to indicate his goal to convince his addressee Theophilus of the reliability of what Theophilus had been told about Christian beginnings by structuring an appropriate narrative. This is not a mere chronicle of unrelated facts but an embellishment of these facts in a narrative complete with rhetorical devices like speeches, vivid episodes, prophesies, fulfillments and proofs from prophecy. All ancient historiography had to appeal to general readers, for there was no purely academic history to be read only by historians. Therefore, history had to be interesting and persuasive, not just a factual account. This accounts for the novelistic elements scholars have found in Acts: ancient history did incorporate some such elements.

Comparison of Luke-Acts with both Biblical and Hellenistic forms of history shows its considerable use of elements of both types. Luke was a minor Hellenistic historian who imitated Biblical rather than Attic style because of his special subject matter. The overall structure of Luke-Acts is therefore a "continuation of the Biblical history" to Paul's ministry in Rome, using many Hellenistic motifs and methods familiar to its readers, as 1 and 2 Mc had done. Its universe is the Biblical universe, not that of secular Hellenistic writing. That is, it is dominated by a creator God and his plan of salvation for his people, not by Fate or Chance or a punishing Justice (to which Luke alludes as the thought of pagans on Malta when Paul survived shipwreck and was bitten by a snake; Acts 28:3–4). The events of Luke-Acts fulfill God's promises and prophecies, both from Luke's Greek Bible (OT) and from prophetic figures in the narrative, like John the Baptist, Jesus, Paul, and Agabus.

God as Main Agent. Thus the main driving force in Luke-Acts, as in Gn or 1 Sm, is not Jesus or Peter or Paul but God. God begins the action in the Gospel with his messages to Zachary and Mary, his causing the virgin Mary to conceive Jesus miraculously, his anointing of Jesus with his Spirit and call of him as Son at the Jordan, his raising Jesus from the dead, and the Pentecostal outpouring of his Spirit through the risen Jesus on the community of disciples in Acts. God directs the action by means of his Spirit and prophecies and angels' messages throughout both Luke and Acts, as when he leads Jesus into the desert to be tempted, fills Peter and Stephen with his Spirit to proclaim his word, and forbids Paul to go further into Asia and calls him instead to Macedonia. God continues to work in Luke-Acts the kinds of signs and wonders He had worked through Moses, Elijah, and Elisha. These signs indicate the presence of God's salvation to those healed and raised from the dead especially by Jesus, Peter, and Paul.

Acts traces the spread of God's word from Jerusalem to Judea, Samaria, Asia, Europe, and Rome where it is poised for launching to the end of the earth. The obvious biographical interest and focus on individuals is subordinated to a narrative showing the roots of the contemporary Gentile church in the first community of Jerusalem, and demonstrating God's will in the turn to the Gentiles without requiring the circumcision that would make them first Jews. The narrative demonstrates that after God's people Israel had rejected its prophetic Messiah like Moses, it was restored when thousands of Jewish pilgrims and Jerusalem dwellers accepted the Pentecost preaching (Acts 2:41) and the Jerusalem church grew to "tens of thousands" (Acts 21:20). The narrative also shows that those Jews who rejected the resurrected prophet like Moses preached by the Apostles and Paul were cut off from people and promises (Acts 3:23), thus creating a division among the people and the prophesied "fall and rise of many in Israel" (Lk 2:34). Acts ends with Paul declaring for the third and climactic time, that

as Is 6:9–10 had prophesied to "your fathers," this people's heart has grown dull, but the salvation of God has been sent to the Gentiles. "They will listen" (28:28).

Shifts in Scholarship. Unrest among Biblical scholars over the limitations of historical criticism in general has grown dramatically in the 1980s, leading to the paradigm shift beyond mere historical criticism to more holistic and multi-disciplinary approaches. Thus, canon criticism counteracts the atomizing of the Bible by treating all Scriptures in the context of the OT-NT Christian canon. Against the relating of the Bible primarily to ancient cultures it treats it as appropriated by the Church. For Luke-Acts, this means not emphasizing isolated pre-Lukan stages like the "historical Jesus" or Markan and Q communities, or admitting absolute dichotomies between Luke and Paul, but recovering some of the lost patristic emphasis of the unity amidst the plurality of the Bible.

Another source of dissatisfaction with historical criticism is its failure to relate to contemporary religious and social experience. Critiques come from such vastly different sources as liberationist and feminist theologians and from charismatics of all denominations. Historical critics often resist liberationist analyses and applications as anachronistic. And they tend to dismiss as implausible many Lukan descriptions of phenomena like religious healing, community, deliverance from evil spirits, prophecy, and tongues, which look very similar to contemporary charismatic experience.

But not all of the new approaches shed real insight on Luke-Acts. Structuralism seems to most exegetes to be needlessly arcane. Liberationist and feminist uses of Luke-Acts tend to be more marginal to the main concerns of the text, as when applying Lukan concern for the poor to Marxist readings of Scripture or when focusing exclusively on Luke's treatment of women. And insofar as liberationist exegesis uses a "hermeneutics of suspicion" (e.g., in seeing bias toward the economic or patriarchal *status quo*), it critiques the Lukan Scriptures from nonbiblical standards of authority which are themselves not subjected to criticism, more than it explains their intrinsic meaning.

Narrative Criticism. Literary and narrative criticism of Luke-Acts seems more promising for explaining the aims, limits, and dynamics of the Lukan narratives. First applied to OT narratives, narrative approaches began only in the mid-1980s to be applied to Luke-Acts. These analyze such narrative elements in Luke-Acts as deliberate plot gaps, use of irony, the author and readers implied by the narrative, and different narrators (the usual Biblical "omniscient" third-person narrator in most of Luke-Acts; the historian "I" sifting strands of evidence in Lk 1:1–4; and the ''we'' participating marginally in some passages after Acts 16:10).

These literary and narrative studies have relativized the dogmatism of some historical critics and exposed the lack of evidence and foundation for many popular historical conjectures. Where historical critics have found dichotomies and ''seams'' between not fully compatible sources, literary critics often see the ''gaps'' that are needed for any sophisticated narrative to maintain interest by engaging the reader's imagination. Thus the gaps at the end of both Mark and Acts prod the readers to fill in the gaps with information they had. For deliberate ending before foreshadowed outcomes was a common Greco-Roman narrative practice, as St. John Chrysostom noted in his *Homilies on Acts* 55: ''At this point the historian stops his account and leaves the reader thirsting so that thereafter he guesses for himself. This also non-Christian writers . . . do. For to know everything makes one sluggish and dull'' (Cadbury 322).

Where historical critics conjecture about who wrote Luke-Acts and whether he could possibly have known Paul, literary critics speak more appropriately of the implied author—those aspects of the real author that have been revealed and included in the text. The abrupt switch in style after the prologue, for example, makes a deliberate claim about the implied author. He reveals himself as someone able to write both in cultivated Greek periodic sentences (the prologue) and in the Biblical paratactic style using ''and . . . and . . . and,'' as in Mark's Gospel. Because of the prologue, his imitation of the cruder Septuagint style does not label his work barbarian, as Mark's Gospel was.

While historical critics hypothesize where and to what communities Luke-Acts was written, literary critics content themselves with the implied reader—those aspects of the real readers imagined and addressed by the real author and discoverable from the emphases in the text. Literary criticism has shown that the real author and readers are outside the text (e.g., anyone in any place and time who can read the text's language could be the real reader, such as we are today). The act of writing creates distance from the original author, setting, and auditors, and requires the writer to *imagine* his absent audience (Ong). Historical reasoning beyond the authors and readers *implied* by the text to *real* authors and readers is necessarily conjectural and at best probable.

Narrative critics have also exposed the dogmatism of some historical judgments that the author of Luke-Acts could not have known Paul. They show that the narrative claim made by using a first person narrator in the Lukan prologue (''events among us . . . to me also,'' Lk 1:1–4) and the ''we'' passages of Acts (16:10 and later) is that the real author is analyzing experiences of the community and was present at events narrated with ''we.'' Not all such claims are true (e.g., in Lucian of Samasota's fantastic ''True History''), but they are intrinsic to understanding the narrative as it stands and are not fully explained by source theories like use of an itinerary, or claims that the genre of sea voyages has a conventional use of ''we.'' The switch in narrator is always meaningful in literary criticism and not merely a matter of sources or convention. Regardless of how it originated, the effect of switching from third person omniscient narrator to ''we'' in parts of Acts has been observed from ancient to contemporary times—it claims participation in those events narrated by ''we.''

Infancy Debate. In the context of dissatisfaction with historical criticism can be mentioned the acrimonious debate about the historicity or midrashic (and fictional) character of the infancy narratives between R. E. Brown and R. Laurentin. Both have written major books with suggestions that tend to balance one another, and both seem to have hypothesized beyond the limited evidence. Studies of narrative do undercut the certitude of some of Brown's historical negativity based on style, differences between Matthew and Luke, silence about some facts in other NT authors, or use of OT in describing an event. Beyond their debate, Luke-Acts makes the narrative claim that Lk 1–2 has some basis in fact and Mary's memory preserved in the early Church: ''His mother meanwhile kept all these things in memory,'' Lk 2:51 (NAB), and her presence in the Acts 1 assembly. This claim seems more plausible than to dismiss all historicity of Lk 1–2 as purely Lukan theology in narrative form, as some do who go beyond Brown.

Text Criticism. Narrative and other holistic approaches to Luke-Acts have contributed to text-critical debates about the authenticity of some key Lukan verses. Fitzmyer, e.g., argues on textual grounds for the authenticity of Lk 22:19b–20 (*Luke X–XXIV* 1387–88), which to ''This is my body'' adds ''to be given for you. Do this in remembrance of me'' (NAB), and the covenant in his blood shed for them. The command to do this in Jesus' memory fits the farewell genre perfectly, and reference to his body and blood given ''for you'' provide an apologetic for Jesus' Crucifixion appropriate to that genre. On textual grounds, Fitzmyer rejects Lk 23:34a, ''Jesus said, 'Father, forgive them; they do not know what they are doing''' (NAB). But despite weak manuscript support, most narrative critics consider it more likely to be from Luke than a copyist because of its strongly Lukan language and narrative links with Stephen's dying forgiveness in Acts 7:60b and the ignorance motif in Acts 3:17, 13:27, and 17:30. Fitzmyer also rejects the angel strengthening Jesus and his sweat like blood in Lk

22:43–44 because of its mixed textual evidence (though it is canonical). Besides Duplacy's persuasive textual arguments that these verses are more likely to have been dropped than added because of heresies, Neyrey (pp. 55–65) adds cogent arguments for the narrative appropriateness of their Lukan style, vocabulary and themes, and as the needed follow-up to Lk 4:13 about Satan's return against Jesus.

Lukan Theology. One aspect of the "certainty" about the catechesis of Theophilus that Luke promises to him (Lk 1:4) is the reliability of God's promises and prophecies. Luke-Acts answers a problem of theodicy, defending God's activity in history, by showing that his promises to Israel have not come to naught but have been fulfilled in the events "among us." As in all of Israel's history, some have responded to God's offer of salvation through Jesus, the resurrected prophet like Moses, and many others have rejected and thus excluded themselves from that salvation (Acts 3:23; 7:51–53). Thus Christians like Theophilus can understand how salvation could seem to have passed from God's original people Israel to their Church consisting mostly of Gentiles.

To demonstrate this, Luke-Acts shows that the Biblical history of God's people continues in how Jesus and the community of his followers in Acts fulfill the prophecies. Jerusalem is therefore treated more theologically and literarily than geographically: it is the center, the middle 12 chapters, of the two-volume narrative. The gospel climaxes in Jesus' death and Resurrection appearances in Jerusalem, from where Acts begins and moves out toward Rome and "the end of the earth" (Acts 1:8). Jerusalem provides the paradigmatic expression of the Jewish people's acceptance or rejection of God's prophet (Johnson).

Lukan Christology is subordinated to his demonstration of continuity with Israel through the image of the rejected prophet like Moses. This required stress on Jesus' humanity and prophetic roles of Jesus, rather than on his divinity as in the fourth Gospel's claims against the synagogue.

The image of the Moses-like prophet provides a fundamental structure for Luke-Acts, as suggested by the close parallelism between the story of Moses in Stephen's Acts 7 speech and that of Jesus in Luke-Acts. First God visits his people through this prophet Jesus (e.g., in Lk 7:16 at Naim, "A great prophet has risen among us" and "God has visited his people," RSV). After they reject him, God recalls this prophet to his people a second time (Moses after his exile, Jesus through Resurrection after His Crucifixion). Only those who reject this risen prophet like Moses a second time are cut off from the people's salvation (Acts 3:23), as the generation who rejected Moses a second time by idolatry in the desert (Acts 7:39–43). Thus Paul three times warns Jews who reject his message about Jesus that he will take it to the more receptive Gentiles (Acts 13:46, 18:6, 28:28).

A closely related christological issue is that in God's plan the Christ must (*dei*) suffer and rise from the dead. The OT prophesied a crucified Messiah. In the NT, only Luke has an explicit rhetorical two-part christological proof from prophecy: the Christ must suffer, and therefore Jesus is the Christ (cf. Lk 24:26–27).

The debate over Lukan eschatology continues to rage, but the programmatic Joel quotation in Acts 2:17–21 seems the key. According to the Joel citation with its Lukan modifications, the outpouring of the Holy Spirit is the inauguration of the eschatological "final days" (2:17) leading up to the manifest day of the returning Lord (2:20). These final days are subdivided into periods including persecution, the destruction of Jerusalem, "times of the Gentiles" (Lk 21:12–24), and false teachers in the community (Acts 20:29–30). This periodization of history is more rooted in the text of Luke-Acts than Conzelmann's three epochs of the time of Israel, the time of Jesus, and the time of the Church. Most scholars have also rejected the notion of a Lukan delay of the parousia prolonged into the indefinite future, so that the Church must "settle down" with "bourgeois ethics" for the long haul. Rather, by the end of Acts all the predictions mentioned in Luke-Acts have come true except for the cosmic signs and return of the Son of Man in judgment (Lk 21:25–28; Acts 1:11). Luke has explained a delay of the parousia by separating it from the fall of Jerusalem, but he continues to expect it soon.

Bibliography: Commentaries. Luke. J. FITZMYER, *The Gospel according to Luke I–IX, X–XXIV, The Anchor Bible*, v. 28, 28A (Garden City, N.Y. 1981, 1985). J. ERNST, *Das Evangelium nach Lukas, Regensburger Neues Testament* (Regensburg 1977). C. H. TALBERT, *Reading Luke* (New York 1982). J. KODELL, *The Gospel according to Luke, Collegeville Bible Commentary*, v. 3 (Collegeville, Minn. 1983). Acts. G. SCHNEIDER, *Die Apostelgeschichte, I. Teil, II. Teil. Herders Theologischer Kommentar zum Neuen Testament*, v. 5.1, 5.2 (Freiburg 1980, 1982). E. HAENCHEN, *The Acts of the Apostles* (Philadelphia 1971). W. KURZ, *The Acts of the Apostles, Collegeville Bible Commentary*, v. 5 (Collegeville, Minn. 1983). Studies. E. GÜTTGEMANNS, "In welchem Sinne ist Lukas 'Historiker'? Die Beziehungen von Luk 1, 1–4 und Papias zur antiken Rhetorik," *Linguistica Biblica* 54 (1983) 9–26. E. PLÜMACHER, "Acta-Forschung 1974–1982," *Theologische Rundschau* 48 (1983) 1–56; 49 (1984) 105–169. E. RICHARD, "Luke—Writer, Theologian, Historian: Research and Orientation of the 1970s," *Biblical Theology Bulletin* 13 (1983) 3–15. F. BOVON, *Luc le théologien. Vingtcinq ans de recherches (1950–1975)* (Neuchâtel 1978); "Chroniques du côté de chez Luc," *Revue de théologie et de philosophie* 115 (1983) 175–189. C. H. TALBERT, "Shifting Sands: The Recent Study of the Gospel of Luke," *Interpretation* 30 (1976) 381–395. W. GASQUE, *A History of the Criticism of the Acts of the Apostles* (Tübingen 1975). M. HENGEL, *Acts and the History of Ear-*

liest Christianity (Philadelphia 1979). J. JERVELL, *Luke and the People of God* (Minneapolis 1972). W. KURZ, ''Narrative Approaches to Luke-Acts,'' *Biblica* 68/2 (1987) 195–220. W. ONG, ''The Writer's Audience Is Always a Fiction,'' *Interfaces of the Word* (Ithaca 1977) 53–81. R. DILLON, ''Previewing Luke's Project from His Prologue (Luke 1:1–4),'' *The Catholic Biblical Quarterly* 43 (1981) 205–227. R. F. O'TOOLE, ''Why Did Luke Write Acts (Lk-Acts)?'' *Biblical Theology Bulletin* 7 (1977) 66–76. R. MADDOX, *The Purpose of Luke-Acts* (Edinburgh 1982). J. DUPLACY, ''La préhistoire du texte en Luc 22:43–44,'' *New Testament Textual Criticism* [Festschrift B. M. Metzger], E. J. EPP and G. D. FEE, eds. (Oxford 1981) 77–86. J. NEYREY, *The Passion according to Luke* (New York 1985) R. E. BROWN, *The Birth of a Messiah* (Garden City, N.Y. 1977) 25–41, 235–499. R. LAURENTIN, *The Truth of Christmas beyond the Myths* (Petersham, Mass. 1986) 1–246, 302–562. C. H. TALBERT, ed., *Perspectives on Luke-Acts* (Danville, Va. 1978). C. H. TALBERT, ed., *Luke-Acts: New Perspectives from the Society of Biblical Literature Seminar* (New York 1984). L. KECK and J. L. MARTYN, *Studies in Luke-Acts* (Philadelphia 1980). F. NEIRNYNCK, ed., *L'Evangile de Luc* (Gembloux 1973). J. KREMER, ed., *Les Actes des Apôtres* (Leuven 1979). J. DUPONT, *Nouvelles études sur les Actes des Apôtres, Lectio Divina,* v. 118 (Paris 1984). L. T. JOHNSON, *The Writings of the NT* (Philadelphia 1986) 197–240. D. AUNE, *The New Testament in Its Literary Environment* (Philadelphia 1987) 77–157. H. J. CADBURY, *The Making of Luke-Acts* (London 1968 [1927]). N. A. DAHL, *Jesus in the Memory of the Early Church* (Minneapolis 1976) 66–98.

[W. KURZ/EDS.]

LUKE BELLUDI, BL.

Franciscan; b. probably in or near Padua, *c.* 1200; d. there, after June 9, 1285. A member of the affluent Belludi family, he is thought to have studied at the University of Padua and to have joined the FRANCISCANS at the age of 20, receiving the habit from FRANCIS OF ASSISI himself. He became the admiring disciple and close companion of ANTHONY OF PADUA, accompanied him on his preaching missions, and attended him on his deathbed at Aracoeli (Rome), 1231. Luke's denunciation of the excesses of Ezzelino (1194–1259) brought heavy reprisals that ended only with the tyrant's death. As provincial superior, Luke continued building the great basilica of St. Anthony where his body now rests in the chapel named for him. PIUS XI confirmed his cult in 1927.

Feast: Feb. 17.

Bibliography: *Acta Apostolicae Sedis* 19 (1927) 213–216. B. MARINANGELI, *Cenni sulla vita del b. L. Belludi* (Padua 1929). L. GUIDALDI, *Il Santo* 3 (1930) 59–69. *La cappella del beato Luca e Giusto de' Menabuoi nella basilica di Sant'Antonio,* photos M. TOSELLO, text G. BRESCIANI ALVAREZ (Padua 1988). A. BUTLER, *The Lives of the Saints,* ed. H. THURSTON and D. ATTWATER, 4 v. (New York 1956) 1:359–360. G. FUSSENEGGER, *Lexikon für Theologie und Kirche,* ed. J. HOFER and K. RAHNER, 10 v. (2d, new ed. Freiburg 1957–65) 6:1206.

[M. F. LAUGHLIN]

LUKE OF ARMENTO, ST.

Monastic founder; b. Sicily, early 10th century; d. Armento, Italy, Oct. 19, 993. He entered the Greek monastery of St. Philip of Agira and then retired to a hermitage near Reggio, Calabria, under the spiritual guidance of St. ELIAS OF REGGIO. To escape the Saracen raids, he left Elias about 959 and moved farther north, stopping at Noa in Lucania. There he restored a small church dedicated to St. Peter and organized a monastic community. After seven years full of many charitable activities, he settled near the Agri River at the monastery of San Giuliano, which he restored and enlarged. Not feeling safe even there from the Saracen incursions and the raids of the troops of Otto I, he withdrew to Armento *c.* 969 and remained there till his death. In the course of his travels Luke built and restored many churches and monasteries. He is also credited with having founded the famous monastery of SS. Elias and Anastasius of Carbone.

Feast: Oct. 13.

Bibliography: *Acta Sanctorum* Oct. 6:337–342. G. DA COSTA-LOUILLET, ''Saints de Sicile et d'Italie méridionale aux VIIIᵉ, IXᵉ et Xᵉ siècles,'' *Byzantion* 29–30 (1959–60) 89–173, esp. 142–146. P. E. SANTORO, *Historia monasterii Carbonensis* (Rome 1601). G. ROBINSON, *History and Cartulary of the Greek Monastery of St. Elias and St. Anastasius of Carbone,* 2 v. in 3 (Rome 1928–30).

[M. PETTA]

LUKEWARMNESS

Lukewarmness or tepidity, in spiritual theology, signifies the state of soul to which the warmth and fervor of charity is wanting, but has not yet completely deteriorated into the coldness of indifference and hatred. The classical origin of the word is the warning addressed to the Church of Laodicea (Rv 3.16) that has been so frequently quoted by preachers that it is probably the best-known text of Revelation. The preceding verse—''I know thy works; thou art neither cold nor hot. I would that thou wert cold or hot''—brings out the meaning of lukewarmness in unmistaken fashion. The word χλιαρός, which the Vulgate renders *tepidus*, is natural enough in the language of love; the metaphor is continued in the threat, ''I am about to vomit thee out of my mouth.'' The following verse apparently indicates that the lukewarmness of the Laodiceans was connected with self-complacency: ''because thou sayest, 'I am rich and have grown wealthy and have need of nothing' and dost not know that thou art the wretched and miserable and poor and blind and naked one.''

Whatever the local conditions, physical or moral, that occasioned this stern rebuke, Christian theology has adapted the description to those who, while still living the life of grace, are not advancing in the fervor of charity. Such people have been called "retarded" souls by analogy with physical and mental failure to grow. St. John of the Cross gives a brilliant psychological description of the return of the capital vices in a more subtle, spiritual form in those he calls "beginners," and thus argues for a second conversion in the "night of the senses" at the threshold of contemplation (*Dark Night*, 1.2–6). Nevertheless, tepidity should not be confused with aridity or dryness in prayer, since the Christian experience of grace and charity, although significant, need not correspond completely or perfectly to the reality of their presence and activity. Lukewarmness is apparently caused by venial sins, especially the deliberate variety (*acedia* is frequently mentioned), and "imperfections" that are unheeded. Although charity cannot be directly diminished, the refusal of further sacrifice and, even more so, acts outside charity not only dispose the will to an act against it, but interrupt the dialogue with God (THOMAS AQUINAS, *Summa theologiae* 2a2ae, 24.10).

Bibliography: R. GARRIGOU-LAGRANGE, *The Three Ages of the Interior Life*, tr. M. T. DOYLE (St. Louis 1947–48) 1:461–470. A. TANQUEREY, *The Spiritual Life*, tr. H. BRANDERIS (Westminster, Md. 1945) 592–596. F. W. FABER, *Growth in Holiness* (Westminster, Md. 1960) ch. 25.

[U. VOLL]

LULL, RAYMOND, BL.

Mystic, missionary, Catalan poet and prose writer; b. Majorca, *c.* 1235; d. probably Tunis, 1316. He is revered by the Franciscans as Doctor Illuminatus. Though he has never been canonized, his cultus was confirmed by Pius IX in 1858. He was strongly attracted to both the Dominicans and the Franciscans, but he never took Holy Orders; there is a tradition that he joined the Third Order of St. Francis.

Work. Brought up in the southern court of Majorca, Lull had about him something of the troubadour, and he always retained traces of a courtly and chivalrous formation. An English version of his manual of chivalry was printed by William Caxton. From the large Moorish population in Majorca he acquired a knowledge of Arabic, in which he wrote some of his works (though no Arabic texts by him have survived), and an interest in Oriental mysticism. About 1263 he had five visions of Christ on the cross after which he entered on a religious way of life and formed missionary resolutions for which he prepared himself by study. Fruits of these years were the *Llibre de contemplació* and the *Llibre del gentil e los tres savis;* the first of these is a mystical and encyclopedic work; the second is in the form of a conversation between a Christian, a Muslim, and a Jew, and shows Lull already investigating common ground between the three religions that could be used as a basis from which to persuade unbelievers of the truth of the Trinity and the Incarnation. This was to be the grand aim of the Art. Lull was a pioneer in using a romance language (Catalan) for theological and apologetic works.

About 1272 Lull had an illuminative experience on Mount Randa in which he saw the whole universe in its relation to the divine attributes, and the principles of his Art were revealed to him. Soon after, he produced the first version of the Art, his system for the discovery of first principles of knowledge and the reduction of all knowledge to unity. The rest of his life was spent in tireless propagation of the Art and in attempting to interest rulers and popes in his projects. One of these was the founding of schools of Oriental languages in order to assist missionary work. King James II of Majorca was persuaded to establish such a school and although it lasted only a few years, the idea of such colleges took root. Lull's missionary journeys included several visits to Tunis; he had always desired a martyr's death, and according to pious legend he suffered martyrdom by stoning on the last of these journeys.

As a mystic, Lull was in the Franciscan tradition, and he was also influenced by Sufi mysticism. His most remarkable mystical work, *Llibre d'amic e amat,* has great religious and poetic power, and is well known in English translation as *The Book of the Lover and the Beloved.* As a philosopher, he belongs in the Augustinian tradition, particularly as developed in the twelfth century. Lull is best understood when it is realized that, although his life was passed in the great age of scholasticism, he was in spirit a man of the twelfth century rather than of the thirteenth, a reactionary toward the Augustinian Platonism of St. ANSELM OF CANTERBURY and the Victorines (*see* SAINT-VICTOR, MONASTERY OF; VICTORINE SPIRITUAITY). He was also somewhat tinged with Neoplatonic influences from JOHN SCOTUS ERIGENA. The actual channels through which some knowledge of the Scotist divine names as primordial causes reached Lull have not yet been identified, though HONORIUS OF AUTUN may have been one of the intermediaries.

The Art. Lull evolved many versions of his Art, but its principles remained the same. The Arts were always based on divine attributes or names (*Bonitas, Magnitudo,* etc.), called by Lull the *Dignitates Dei.* These were designated by letters of the alphabet that were placed on revolving concentric wheels: through the revolutions of the wheels, combinations of the letters were obtained. The Art could work on all the levels of creation, the angelic world, the world of the stars, of man and his activities, of the animal and vegetable worlds, by abstracting the essential *bonitas, magnitudo,* etc., on each level. There is a kind of geometrical logic of relation in the Art that uses as its basic figures the triangle, the circle, and the square. The purpose of the Art was always, for Lull, a missionary purpose. By basing the Art on religious conceptions common to Christians, Jews, and Muslims—the divine names or attributes—and on the elemental structure of nature universally accepted in the science of the time, Lull believed that he had an instrument for bringing unbelievers to Christianity. The Trinitarian structure of the Art was its basic characteristic; it was to reflect the Trinity and to be used by all three powers of the soul defined by St. Augustine as the image of the Trinity in man. As *intellectus* it was an art of knowing; as *voluntas* an art of loving; as *memoria* an art of memory.

A large proportion of Lull's extremely numerous works are either expositions of the various forms of the Art or else are related in some noticeable way to it. Even the attractive romances or allegorical novels, *Blanquerna* (*c.* 1284) and *Felix* (*c.* 1288), are, at bottom, popularizations of it. The *Arbre de sciencia* (1295), which was very widely known in its Latin version, presents the whole encyclopedia of knowledge schematized as a forest of trees whose roots are the principles of the Art, which could be done on all subjects. The *Liber de ascensu et descensu intellectus* (*c.* 1305) describes the ascent and descent of the intellect on the ladder of being through the use of the Art.

The vast diffusion of Lullism is only now beginning to be studied in a systematic way. In the Renaissance it took on a new and intense phase of activity, though with a different emphasis, and in the sixteenth century a chair of Lullism was established at the Sorbonne. Lull's use of letter notations for concepts and his attempt to represent movement through his revolving figures are significant features of the Art, the importance of which in the history of method is becoming increasingly realized. Leibniz's schemes for a universal calculus were influenced by the *combinatoria.*

Feast: July 3 (Franciscans).

Bibliography: M. JOHNSON, *The Evangelical Rhetoric of Raymon Lull: Lay Learning and Piety in the Christian West* (New York 1996), bibliography. R. LULL, *Opera Latina, 19,* tr. A. LINARES (Belgium 1993); *Raymond Lull's New Rhetoric: Text and Translation of Lull's "Rethorica Nova,"* tr. M. JOHNSON (Davis, Calif. 1994). L. SALA-MOULINS, *La Philosophie de l'Amour de Raymonde Lulle* (Paris 1974), bibliography. M. PEREIRA, *The Alchemical Corpus Attributed to Raymond Lull* (London 1989). R. HERRERA, "Ramon Lull: Mystic Polymath," in *Mystics of the Book* (New York 1993). E. A. PEERS, *Raymond Lull: A Biography* (New York 1969), bibliography. F. YATES, *Lull and Bruno* (London and Boston 1982).

[F. A. YATES]

LULL OF MAINZ, ST.

Missionary, archbishop; b. Wessex, England, *c.* 710; d. Hersfeld?, Germany, Oct. 16, 786. An Anglo-Saxon like St. BONIFACE, he became a BENEDICTINE at MALMESBURY ABBEY. He made a pilgrimage to Rome, whence Boniface in 738 took him to Germany. There he became associated in Boniface's missionary efforts. In 751 Lull was sent to Rome, where, having been promised succession to Boniface in the See of Mainz by PEPIN III, he was consecrated a CHORBISHOP in 752. When Lull succeeded Boniface as bishop of Mainz in 754, there developed a long dispute between Lull and Abbot St. Sturmi of Fulda. Lull sought—unsuccessfully—to end Fulda's exemption and direct dependence on Rome and to bring it under the jurisdiction of Mainz. He founded the Benedictine monasteries of HERSFELD and Bleidenstadt and enlarged the Diocese of Mainz by absorbing the Sees of Erfurt and Buraburg. Lull received the PALLIUM from ADRIAN I *c.* 781 and was thus the first regular METROPOLITAN of Mainz. He was buried at Hersfeld Abbey.

Feast: Oct. 16.

Bibliography: LAMBERT OF HERSFELD "Life," *Acta Sanctorum,* Oct. 7 (1845) 1050–91. Boniface-Lull letters, *Monumenta Germaniae Historica: Epistolae* (Berlin 1826–) 3:215–433. W. LEVISON, *England and the Continent in the Eighth Century* (Oxford 1946) 223–240. T. SCHIEFFER, *Angelsachsen und Franken* (Abhandlungen der Akademie der Wissenschaften und der Literatur. Geistes- und sozialwissenschaftliche Klasse 20.2; Mainz 1950).

[B. D. HILL]

LULLY, JEAN BAPTISTE

Baroque musician, virtual founder of French opera; b. Florence, Italy, Nov. 28, 1632; d. Paris, March 22, 1687. Brought to Paris in 1644, Lully was chamber boy and musical page to Mlle. de Montpensier. The gifted and energetic youth devoted himself to the tastes of his Monarch, Louis XIV, and achieved a position of power in the cultural life of France through a monopoly on musical theater. His early productions were ballets in which the king danced; collaborations with Molière followed. His career culminated in his operas, of which *Thesée, Atys, Psyché,* and *Armide* were perhaps best known. His great contribution was the handling of the French language, particularly in recitative, and in instrumental writing—specifically the overture, still associated with his name. His church compositions were conservative, following the massive forms of Henri Dumont rather than presaging the newer style. He set for state occasions most of the standard texts, producing a *Miserere,* a *De profundis,* a *Dies Irae,* and a *Te Deum.*

Bibliography: *Oeuvres complètes,* ed. H. PRUNIÈRES, 10 v. (Paris 1930–39), L. DE LA LAURENCIE, *Lully* (Paris 1911). E. BOR-

Engraving of Jean Baptiste Lully.

REL, *Jean-Baptiste Lully* (Paris 1949). W. MELLERS, *The Heritage of Music,* ed. H. J. FOSS, 3 v. (New York 1927–51) 3:32–52. *Histoire de la musique,* ed. ROLAND-MANUEL, 2 v. (Paris 1960–63); v. 9, 16 of *Encyclopédie de la Pléiade* v. 1. D. J. GROUT, *A Short History of Opera,* 2 v. (2d, rev. and enl. ed. New York 1965). N. SLONIMSKY, ed., *Baker's Biographical Dictionary of Musicians* (5th ed. New York 1958) 991–992. G. CHOUQUET, *Grove's Dictionary of Music and Musicians,* ed. E. BLOM, 9 v. (5th ed. London 1954) 5:422–427. J. R. ANTHONY, ''Towards a Principal Source for Lully's Court Ballets: Foucault vs Philador,'' *Recherches sur la Musique française classique,* 25 (1987) 77–104. L. E. BROWN, ''Departures from Lullian Convention in the *tragédie lyrique* of the *préramiste* Era,'' *Recherches sur la Musique française classique,* 22 (1984) 59–78. M. COUVREUR, ''La Collaboration de Quinault et Lully avant la *Psyché* de 1671,'' *Recherches sur la Musique française classique,* 27 (1991/92) 9–34. J. NEWMAN, *Jean-Baptiste de Lully and His Tragédie Lyrique* (Ann Arbor 1979). J. S. POWELL, ''Appropriation, Parody, and the Birth of French Opera: Lully's *Les Festes de L'Amour et de Bacchus* and Molière's *La Malade Imaginaire,*'' *Recherches sur la Musique française classique,* 29 (1998) 3–26. L. ROSOW, ''*Alceste, ou Le triomphe d'Alcide* [*Alcestis, or the Triumph of Alcides,*]'' in *International Dictionary of Opera,* ed. C. S. LARUE, 2 v. (Detroit 1993) 21–22. J. L. SCHWARTZ, ''The *passacaille* in Lully's *Armide:* Phrase Structure in the Choreography and the Music,'' *Early Music,* 26 (1998) 301–320.

[E. BORROFF]

LUNN, ARNOLD

Catholic convert and apologist, England's leading authority on skiing, b. Madras, India, April 18, 1888; d. London, June 3, 1974. His father was Sir Harry Lunn, who was a Methodist missionary in India, later worked for the Thomas Cook travel agency, and in 1906 formed a successful tour business of his own. His mother was an Irish Protestant devoted to Sinn Fein and Irish independence. In 1908 Lunn founded the Alpine Ski Club and from 1919 was editor of the *British Ski Year Book.* He introduced the modern slalom course in Muerren, Switzerland, in 1922, thus creating the modern Alpine slalom race. For 15 years (1924–39) he was a member of the executive committee of the Féderation Internationale de Ski (FIS) and later (1946–49) was chairman of the International Downhill Ski Racing Committee.

In *The Swiss and Their Mountains,* (1963) Lunn credited a particular experience of an Alpine sunset with awakening in him a sense of the spiritual and the supernatural. Lunn's formal education took place at Harrow and at Balliol College, Oxford. He wrote of his conversion in *Now I See* (London 1934). His defense of Catholicism usually involved collaboration with a friend, such as Ronald KNOX, or with friendly foes, such as the Anglican Garith Lean, or the philosopher C. E. M. Joad, or the scientist J. B. S. Haldane. Lunn's books often took the form of debates. In addition to *Difficulties* (1932, with Ronald Knox), there should be mentioned his *Science and the Supernatural* (1935, with J. B. S. Haldane), and *Christian Counterattack* (1969, with Garith Lean). His reputation as a conservative made him especially useful in World War II, when he traveled extensively in Spain, Portugal, Latin America, and the United States as a spokesman for Britain and the defense of Christian civilization against Nazism.

While refusing to become an alarmist after VATICAN COUNCIL II, he was annoyed by some secularist trends, and especially was saddened by events in the United States. He spoke and continued writing against the new morality, e.g., in *The New Morality,* with G. Lean (rev. ed., London 1967), which he viewed as an accommodation of the Christian code to secularist sensibilities, a preoccupation with social problems, and a general revolt against authority. The real division, as he saw it, was not between liberals and conservatives, but between those who are and those who are not intimidated by dominant fashions of secularism. He refused to tone down differences between various Christian communions but was in favor of a militant ecumenism, in which all would band together to reverse the triumphant advance of secularism. He summed up his approach in an article in the *Tablet* dated the day before his death by citing Augustine: ''Love men, slay errors.''

Bibliography: A. LUNN, *Come What May* (Boston 1941). *Tablet* 221 (1967) 90–91, 132–133; 224 (1970) 544; 227 (1973) 654; 228 (1974) 527.

[E. J. DILLON]

LUPOLD OF BEBENBURG

Canon lawyer and political theorist, bishop of Bamberg (1353–63); b. of a Swabian-Franconian ministerial family, c. 1297; d. Bamberg, Oct. 28, 1363. Lupold matriculated in Canon Law at Bologna in 1316, earning the degree of *doctor decretorum* and returning to Germany c. 1324. After holding several canonries he was elected bishop of Bamberg in 1353.

Although an imperial protagonist in the struggle between the AVIGNON papacy and Emperor LOUIS IV (1314–47), Lupold never assumed an extreme antipapal position. His most important work, *Tractatus de iuribus regni et imperii* (1340), dealt with the relationship between German kingship and imperial dignity, and attempted to define the roles of spiritual and secular powers in Christian society. During the following year, he expressed the same ideas in verse form in his *Ritmaticum querulosum et lamentosum dictamen de modernis cursibus et defectibus regni ac imperil Romanorum.* Lupold's third work, *Libellus de zelo christianae religionis veterum principum Germanorum* (1342), emphasizing the prominence of Germany and the Empire in Christendom, and their ancient and close connection with the faith, is a plea for a *modus vivendi* between papacy and Empire.

Lupold served Emperor Charles IV (1347–78) in an advisory capacity. The ideas and some of the phraseology of Lupold's *Tractatus* appear in the GOLDEN BULL of 1356, the constitutional law that, in its broad outlines, regulated the relations between the emperor and the German princes until 1806.

Bibliography: A. SENGER, *Lupold von Bebenburg* (Bamberg 1905). H. MEYER, *Lupold von Bebenburg: Studien zu seinen Schriften* (Freiburg 1909). R. MOST, ''Der Reichsgedanke des Lupold von Bebenburg,'' *Deutsches Archiv für Erforschung des Mittelalters* 4 (1941) 444–485. J. KIST, *Lexikon für Theologie und Kirche*, ed. J. HOFER and K. RAHNER (Freiburg 1957–65) 6:1218.

[W. A. ERNEST]

LUPUS OF SENS, ST.

Bishop; b. Orléanais, France, c. 573; d. Brienon (11½ miles southeast of Sens), Sept. 1, c. 623. Lupus (or Leu or Loup) was educated and ordained by his maternal uncles, the bishops of Orléans and Auxerre. In 609, when the bishop of Sens died, the king, at the request of the people, appointed the saintly Lupus to replace him. As an adherent of Sigebert of Austrasia, Lupus was exiled by Chlotar II (613) to Vimeu in the canton of Picardy, where he converted many pagans. Pardoned by Chlotar the following year, he returned triumphantly to Sens, stopping in Paris for the council of 614. He was buried in the monastery of Sainte-Colombe-lès-Sens, which he had founded in Sens. In 853 his relics were transferred to the new church. His cult was of special renown during the Middle Ages. Among the many churches and monasteries dedicated to him in France are Saint-Leu-Saint-Gilles in Paris (1235), Saint-Loup of Naud (Provins), and Saint-Loup of Esserent, near Senlis. He is invoked by epileptics.

Feast: Sept. 1.

Bibliography: *Vita Lupi, Monumenta Germaniae Historica: Scriptores rerum Merovingicarum* (Berlin 1826–) 4:176–187, late (790) but of value. *Acta Sanctorum* Sept. 1:248–265. G. VIELHABER in *Analecta Bollandiana* 26 (1907) 43–44. H. BOUVIER, *Histoire de l'église et de l'ancien archdiocèse de Sens,* 3 v. (Paris 1906–11) v. 1. J. L. BAUDOT and L. CHAUSSIN, *Vies des saints et des bienheureux selon l'ordre du calendrier avec l'historique des fêtes,* ed. by the Benedictines of Paris, 12 v. (Paris 1935–56) 9:22–24. *Martyrologium Romanum,* ed. H. DELEHAYE (Brussels 1940); v. 68 of *Acta Sanctorum* 374–375.

[P. COUSIN]

LUQUE, CRISANTO

Archbishop of Bogotá and first Colombian cardinal; b. Tenjo, Feb. 1, 1889; d. Bogotá, May 7, 1959. Luque was ordained in 1916, appointed auxiliary bishop of Tunja in 1931, and bishop in 1932. He visited the various parts of his large diocese, built the episcopal mansion, took an interest in the improvement of the seminary and the religious life of the clergy, and undertook important work on behalf of the poor. In 1950 he was named archbishop of Bogotá, primate of Colombia, to succeed Ismael Perdomo. He was made a cardinal in 1953. He was chief chaplain of the Armed Forces and pontifical legate to the Third National Marian Congress, and he took part in the conclave that elected John XXIII. The governments of Colombia, Venezuela, Spain, Ecuador, and Brazil conferred high decorations on him.

While bishop of Tunja, Luque founded, and later protected, the radio schools of Sutatenza that provided the farm workers with lessons in reading and writing and religious and civic training. The radio schools were later extended to other countries and recommended by UNESCO. He founded, in Bogotá, the Parochial Union of the South that brought together parishes of the working-class districts, with their population of half a million faithful, to solve religious and social problems in common. It was an experiment in priestly teamwork that was effective in combatting communism. He convoked and presided over the First National Assembly of Catholic Workers and the First National Pastoral Congress, and encouraged Social Weeks and Congresses of Social Action. He established the Center of Social Research for the guidance of the pastorate. The opening of the new archiepiscopal palace, the creation of numerous parishes, and the intensification of catechistic campaigns were additional achievements of his regime. He was one of the most effective promoters of the CONSEJO EPISCOPAL LATINOAMERICANO (CELAM), and presided over various episcopal conferences with great success, winning united support for his undertakings.

Luque collaborated actively with the various civil government administrations to combat the violence that plagued Colombia. In religion and in politics, his actions were prudent and benefited the public generally. In 1953 General Gustavo Rojas Pinilla led a *coup d'état* that overthrew the conservative Laureano Gómez. The Rojas movement was legalized by the National Constitutent Assembly, and the cardinal, after consulting with the historically important parties, recognized the new government. However, when it took the path of dictatorship, he energetically defended democratic principles and acted on the side of the people and the students, who overthrew the dictator. Luque maintained excellent relations with the new National Front government, headed by Alberto Lleras, and was able through constitutional reform, voted by plebiscite, to secure political recognition of Catholicism as an essential element of the social order.

During his reign, the religious struggle of the parties largely ceased, and the Colombians reconciled themselves somewhat on Catholic principles. Thanks to his work, backed by the bishops, the Church gained prestige, respect, and acceptance. He had a gift for governing and deserved to be called the archbishop of the peasants and the workers.

[R. GÓMEZ HOYOS]

LURIA, ISAAC

Palestinian Hebrew mystic generally acclaimed to be the founder of the school of practical and applied Kabalism and whose doctrines became the *theologia mystica* of Judaism; b. Jerusalem, 1534; d. Safed, Palestine, Aug. 5, 1572. Because the forebears of Isaac ben Solomon Luria had emigrated from Germany, he was surnamed Ashkenazi (German), and to subsequent generations he

was best known by the metonym Ari (Heb. *'arî,* lion), which probably was derived from the first letters of his name in the form of Ashkenazi Rabbi Isaac. When Luria was young, his father died, and he was taken to Cairo to live with a wealthy maternal uncle, the tax farmer Mordecai Francis. He studied assiduously under such men as Bezalel Ashkenazi and David ibn Abi Zimra and, while still in his teens, became extremely proficient in Talmudic and rabbinical literature. At age 15 he married his cousin, but not being required to support either himself or his bride, he continued his studies without interruption.

However, he apparently preferred the world of the mystic and the ascetic to that of the Talmud or married life, for at the age of 22 he became a hermit and lived in solitude along the banks of the Nile. He had become absorbed in the ZOHAR, the Cabalist classic that first appeared in print in 1557. The more he delved into its hidden mysteries, the more he craved seclusion and the less desire he had for contact with men. Only on the Sabbath would he return to his young wife. He conversed very little with people; and when he did, his conversations were always entirely in Hebrew. Soon the labyrinth of Cabalistic thought became as familiar to Luria as his daily devotions. His mode of living, which was nurtured by an active, imaginative mind, led to the inevitable result—Luria became a visionary. He intimated that he was the Messiah ben Joseph, who, according to Jewish legend, would be one of the forerunners of the Messiah ben David; that Elijah the Prophet, who would be the immediate precursor of the Messiah, resolved for him many difficult passages of the Zohar; that by night his soul ascended to heaven and there conversed with the ancient Talmudic sages. His adherents attributed to him supernatural powers, the ability to exorcize demons, perform miracles, and communicate with trees, angels, and birds.

In 1569 Luria settled in Safed, Palestine, where he soon began to propagate his mystical doctrines to a group of devoted disciples, among whom were such men of renown as Moses Cordovero, Hayyim Vital, Solomon Alkabetz, and Joseph CARO. Although he left no written legacy, a great deal of his life and thought is known through the writings of Vital, his biographer. From copious lecture notes that Luria's followers had made, Vital produced numerous posthumous works of Luria that present the Lurianic concepts; the most important of these works is his six-volume magnum opus entitled *'Es Ḥayyim* (Tree of Life).

Luria's system is based primarily on the threefold doctrine of *ṣimṣûm* (originally "concentration," "contraction," better translated in Cabalistic parlance as "withdrawal" or "retreat"), *ševîrat hakk ᵉlîm* (breaking of the vessels), and *'ôlām hattiqqûn* (the "repaired world,'' i.e., the ideal state of the world). Before creation, the *'ên sôph* (the Endless; the Infinite One) was omnipresent and occupied the entire world. Therefore, in order to make creation possible, God had to contract and withdraw into Himself. In the space created by this withdrawal (*ṣimṣûm*) Luria believed a residue (*rešîmô*) or beam of divine light remained, like the residue of oil left in a bottle after most of its contents have been poured out. Creation takes place by the emanation of this light flowing from God. When in its turn the *rešîmô* retreated, a void appeared in the center encircled by ten spheres (*sephîrôt*) or vessels (*kelîm*) that represented the infinite manifestations and radiations of the *'ên sôph.* The return of some divine light to the center caused the breaking of the innermost six vessels and to a lesser degree the seventh. Since the outer three were closer to the *'ên sôph,* they were of purer substance and were able to withstand the light. With the fracturing of the *kelîm,* confusion, evil, and darkness entered the cosmos; and everything, the good and the bad, intermingled.

Primordial man (*'ādām qadmôn*) emanated from the essence of the *'ên sôph* as a consequence of *ṣimṣûm.* Man's soul unites the infinite with the finite. When Adam was created, the soul for each human being was simultaneously created with the organs of Adam's body. Each human being, therefore, is a spark (*nîṣôṣ*) of Adam, and just as there are inferior and superior organs, so there are inferior and superior souls in keeping with the organs with which they are coupled. Because of Adam's sin, men's souls, in their various gradations, were cast into turmoil and could not be distinguished from each other. The purest soul, therefore, has become intermingled with the impure or, as Luria calls it, with the element of *qelippôt* (shells, i.e., forces of evil). No person is any longer entirely good or wholly bad. Man's soul, therefore, cannot find peace by returning to its source until it expiates its imperfections and seeks purification through the process of METEMPSYCHOSIS, that is, by passing through animate and inanimate bodies: humans, animals, wood, and stone. Luria and his followers (known as ''the lion's whelps'') would refrain from killing even worms for fear these carried human souls.

With the separation of the holy from the profane, the *'ôlām hattiqqûn* will be reestablished and the advent of the Messiah will be at hand. This can be accomplished only through the observance of God's Commandments and the study of the Torah.

Bibliography: G. G. SCHOLEM, *Major Trends in Jewish Mysticism* (3d ed. New York 1954). *The Jewish Encyclopedia,* ed. J. SINGER, 13 v. (New York 1901–06) 8:210–212: W. DUCAT, *Universal Jewish Encyclopedia,* 10 v. (New York 1939–44) 7:237–239. M. MARGOLIS and A. MARX, *A History of the Jewish People* (New York 1927; repr. pa. 1958). H. H. GRAETZ, *History of the Jews,* ed. and tr. B. LÖWY, 6 v. (Philadelphia 1945) 4:618–627. E. L. RAPP, *Die Religion in Geschichte und Gegenwart,* 7 v. (3d ed. Tübingen 1957–65) 4:479. K. SCHUBERT, *Lexikon für Theologie und Kirche,* 10 v. (Freiburg 1957–65) 6:1220–1221.

[N. J. COHEN]

LUST

The vice opposed to the virtue of chastity. Called *luxuria* in Latin and commonly referred to as impurity in English, lust always indicates an excessive, that is, irrational, attachment to venereal pleasure. Because of the wide variety of vicious acts and habits it causes, Christian tradition classifies it as one of the seven capital SINS. The malice of lust is shown in the vices to which it leads: blindness of mind, rashness, thoughtlessness, inconstancy, self-love, and excessive attachment to the material world. It destroys man's humanity by subjecting sexual activity not to its proper ends recognized by reason, that is, the procreation of children and the promotion of the mutual love of spouses in marriage, but instead to mere bodily pleasure. This article considers lust (1) as spoken of in Sacred Scripture, (2) in its relation to the natural law, (3) in its opposition to chastity, (4) as a violation of the sexual order, (5) according to its gravity as a sin, (6) in the moral imputability of its acts, and (7) in relation to natural and supernatural remedies.

Scripture. Although Scripture does not provide an exhaustive list of the types of lust and describe the malice of each, both the OT and NT condemn sexual misbehavior in a number of its forms. The OT, for example, condemns ADULTERY, incest, the seduction or rape of a virgin, bestiality, and prostitution, especially the cultic prostitution practiced in the Canaanite sanctuaries. Further, in the Sixth and Ninth Commandments it forbids improper sexual acts and desires. In the NT, the OT teaching is elevated and refined by the delineation of lust as a profanation of a mutual love that can be humanly expressed only in the sanctity of marriage. The profanation is the greater for the dignity of the married union, which is so sacred as to be a symbol of Christ's union with the Church (Mt 19.3–9; Eph 5.25–33). Christ Himself, declaring and reinforcing the primitive inviolable sanctity of the marital bond, brands as adulterous any quasi-marital association of a married person with another man or woman. Paul denounces the ''uncleanness'' of the pagans, declaring that God has abandoned them to ''shameful lusts'' or unnatural vices because of their idolatry (Rom 1.24–28). Among the ''works of the flesh'' that exclude from the kingdom of God are sexual immorality, uncleanness, and licentiousness (Gal 5.19–20); nor shall the kingdom be possessed by adulterers, the effeminate, or sodomites (1 Cor 6.9–10).

"The Fall of Man," oil painting by Hendrick Goltzius, 1616. (© Christie's Images/CORBIS)

In a noteworthy passage (1 Cor 6.12–20) the Apostle points out the immorality of promiscuity, arguing from the dignity conferred on a Christian by his vocation as one destined to rise with Christ, whose members are the members of Christ and the temple of the Holy Spirit, bought at a great price so that he should glorify and bear God in his body.

Natural Law. Paul's strong condemnation of the pagans for their unnatural vices indicates that the natural law itself, written in the heart of man (Rom 2.14), imposes certain essential restraints on the pursuit of pleasures of the flesh. The sex appetite is one of the most powerful of human urges, needing rational control lest the indulgence of it destroy the basis of society. The possibility of such destruction has been shown by the rationalist scholar J. D. Unwin in his statistical survey of more than 80 civilized and uncivilized communities (*Sex and Culture,* Oxford 1934).

Customs concerned with sex and marriage differ widely with various peoples, but their universal existence is irrefutable testimony to the common conviction of mankind that the sex instinct must be controlled and that, therefore, prohibitions of sins of lust are part of the natural law.

Lust as Opposed to Chastity. Integrating into his Christian moral synthesis the Aristotelian concept and catalog of moral virtues, St. Thomas Aquinas designates lust as the vice opposed by excess to chastity (*Summa Theologiae* 2a2ae, 153.3 ad 3), chastity being that part of temperance which moderates the concupiscible appetite in its inclination for the pleasures that go with the use of the generative faculty (*ibid.* 2a2ae, 151.3). In contemporary language, chastity governs the use and the pursuit of the pleasures of sex. Hence lust refers to the unbridled enjoyment of them. In the terminology of Aristotle and St. Thomas, one commits a sin of lust by seeking or enjoying these pleasures in a way that exceeds the measure of right reason; in a Christian context one can add in a way that contravenes the sacred significance of sex and marriage in the order of Redemption.

Thus, on the one hand, chastity controls the enjoyment of sex pleasure according to the dictates of right reason and the Christian moral law, forbidding, permitting, or approving according to circumstances and especially according to the objective and subjective purpose of such pleasure. Lust, on the other hand, indulges in sex pleasure without regard to these necessary controlling factors.

Although this narrows the concept of chastity, and hence of lust, to the use and abuse of sex and of sexual pleasure, the pleasure itself must be considered in a very wide context of human sensations, emotions, and reactions. A lustful action is a disordered use or pursuit of sex pleasure not only because it defeats the biological, social, or moral purpose of sex activity, but also because in doing this it subjects the spiritual in man to values of the grossly material order, acting as a disintegrating force in the human personality.

Against this background one can consider the careful distinctions traditionally made by theologians between pleasure that is merely sensible, pleasure that is sensual, and pleasure that is venereal, only the last being immediately attached to the exercise of sex in its narrow physical sense. Merely sensible pleasure, such as delight in the touch of a soft object, is relevant only insofar as such pleasure can become venereal, as when there is pleasure in physical contact between adult persons of opposite sexes, especially in kisses and embraces, because the deliberate and prolonged seeking of such pleasure is apt to arouse venereal pleasure, even when there is no intention that it should, and cause a danger of consenting to it (cf. Alphonsus Liguori, 1.3 n.416).

Love, especially between members of opposite sexes, can express itself on the three levels of sensible, sensual, and venereal, and lapses into lust only when it expresses itself inordinately on the last of them. The difference is enormous between venereally pleasurable activity when absorbed into the full meaning of sex, and when it escapes from the control of reason and spirit. This difference is due to the nature of the sex drive considered as a creative force. Of itself it reaches out to another person as, under God, a coprinciple of new life. Thus it comes from and tends to the core of man's fruitful nature, understanding the term not only of man's physical power to procreate his kind, but also of his responsibility for the moral and spiritual formation of offspring.

These responsibilities belong to man as a person, one who is made to God's image and recognizes the divinely imprinted pattern of human sexual activity, and the obligation to accept with his reason and execute with his will and its attendant emotions what this pattern requires. Thus sex activity outside the framework that alone provides for the loving and responsible care of children converts the force of sexual activity into one that tends to personal disintegration. In marriage itself, sexual actions must conform to the divine pattern; they have a disintegrating effect when they are performed irresponsibly, most conspicuously when the creative nature of sex is positively defeated by acts that are unnatural or when in varying degrees according to circumstances cogent reasons for avoiding pregnancy are carelessly neglected or when sheer pleasure seeking upsets the balance of intimate friendship. There are no hard and fast rules, but human lovers will know for themselves whether what they do is a descent to a merely animal condition or an ascent to a graciously human dignity and delight.

Distinctions must be made between sex, eros, and agape, indicating respectively the appetite or instinct for sexual pleasure in the narrow sense common to animals and human beings; an affective sympathy toward another human being based on qualities that are psychical and spiritual as well as physical; and a love that is a self-giving and committal to the other. Thus lust, the violation of chastity in the high Christian context emphasized by St. Paul, violates charity, the soul of the Christian order (cf. J. Fuchs, *De Castitate,* 21–22).

Violation of the Sexual Order. Lust as a disordered enjoyment of sexual pleasure generally involves a violation of the sexual order. That it necessarily does so seems the fairly general assumption of moralists. They assume also that chastity is a virtue whose essential function is the protection of the sexual order, i.e., the direction of sex activity to its specific purpose.

Both assumptions have been questioned by J. Fuchs, who introduces alongside chastity another virtue whose scope is the preservation of the right order of sex, whereas chastity is concerned with controlling the appetite for the pleasures of sex. Sex activity is possible without the pleasurable experience normally accompanying it, and the right order of this activity can be preserved even when one enjoys or seeks its characteristic pleasure in a disordered way. He instances the case of a prostitute who plies her trade for monetary gain without any physical enjoyment, and that of a married man enjoying normal conjugal intimacy but with no motive except that of physical pleasure. Thus in one case there is a sin against the sex order without a sin of lust, and in the other a sin of lust without a sin against the sexual order (*loc. cit.* 17–18).

This view can claim a shadow of support in St. Thomas, especially in his *Quaestiones disputatae de malo,* where he distinguishes between inordinate concupiscence in the normal use of marriage and a disorder in the external act, as when there are sex relations outside marriage (*De malo* 15.1). However, in each case he speaks explicitly of a sin of lust. The disorder proper to such a sin is to be found primarily in the failure of the natural appetite for sex pleasure to be guided by man's reason. Reason is the norm truly constitutive of morality, not indeed the highest and transcendent one, which is the eternal law in the mind of God, but a true and proximate norm sharing as man does by his practical reason the directive power of God's mind and will, directing all created activity to its end (cf. *Summa Theologiae* 1a2ae, 19.3). By accepting the objective order of finality whereby sex pleasure is integrated into sexual activity for the sake of this activity, reason as a norm of right action actively ordains both the pleasure and the activity to the purposes for which the latter exists. Thus the moral rightness that gives chastity its specific motive as a controlling and restraining influence on the appetite for sex pleasure is founded immediately on the exigencies of the human sexual order. The fundamental disorder the virtue holds at bay is that of separating sex pleasure from the order to which it belongs by right. This one does essentially as often as he seeks or accepts such pleasure in this disordered way, whether his concupiscence contains itself within the external framework imposed by the objective ordering of sex activity, as when a man performs the normal conjugal act exclusively for pleasure, or whether this disordered concupiscence motivates a disorder in the external act as such which, because performed outside marriage or in a solitary or some other unnatural way, is found deprived of its divine ordination to the generation and education of children (cf. *De malo* 15.1).

At first sight it may be difficult to see how the prostitute plying her trade without seeking or enjoying sex pleasure, which is entirely absent, commits a sin of lust in an isolated and technical sense. There is, however, the consideration that she formally cooperates in the lustful action of her partner; but more fundamentally there seems to be a sin of lust because an action and its proper pleasure are identically related to the moral order, seeing that such pleasure exists for the sake of the action and is included in its total concept (*Summa Theologiae* 1a2ae, 2.6 ad 1). What regulates the pursuit of pleasure is the finality of the action. If, therefore, in a particular and exceptional case the pleasure is lacking, it does not follow that the same virtue does not come into play when the act is performed with a conscious submission to the right order inscribed in its very nature, or that this virtue is not positively violated when this right order is voluntarily disregarded. A woman who is unresponsive to sex stimuli can still have chaste motives for abstaining from sinful sexual actions, as the prostitute can act lustfully by admit-

ting them. A further problem, i.e., the concrete virtue or vice acquired and developed by such actions in accord with or contrary to the norms of chastity, is here irrelevant.

On the other hand, it docs not seem necessary or desirable to discard the ordinary definitions of chastity and lust and to place their essence primarily in a disposition to perform sexual acts only according to their purpose or to abuse them in contravention of that purpose, as do certain modern theologians (cf. Vangheluwe, "De temperantia stricte dicta eiusque partibus subiectivis," *Coll. brug.* 47 [1951] 38–48; Zalba, 1.1372). It is true, indeed, that the nature of the act regulates the morality of the pleasure, but the difficulty to be overcome in the use of sex activity comes precisely from the attractiveness of the pleasure that goes with it. Hence chastity facilitates the practice of a rightly ordered sex life and controls the appetite for sex pleasure. Lust primarily inclines this appetite to rebel against the order imposed by reason. Thus St. Thomas, and with him most moral theologians, teaches that lust consists primarily in the use of venereal pleasure other than according to right reason: "in hoc quod aliquis non secundum rectam rationem delectatione venerea utitur" (*Summa theologiae*, 2a2ae, 153.1, 154).

Gravity of Sins of Lust. It is clear that all deliberately sought sex activity must be properly oriented, and that if it is not, the pursuit or acceptance of its pleasure is sinful.

For centuries theologians have emphasized the essential ordination of sex and its use to the generation and education of children, and from this they deduce the unlawfulness of all deliberate sex activity outside marriage (ST 2a2ae, 154.2). This is confirmed by the magisterium of Pius XI (in the encyclical *Casti connubii,* Dec. 31, 1930; H. Denzinger, *Enchiridion symbolorum* [Freiburg 1963] 3705) and that of Pius XII [cf. *Acta Apostolicae Sedis* 43 (1951) 852].

Recently there has been much emphasis on the personal values of sex, and hence on sexual intercourse as expressing a mutual personal giving. From this some deduce the exclusive right of married partners to exercise it, since without an indissoluble bond between them, this mutual giving cannot be verified. Hence follows the unlawfulness of fornication, adultery, and all sex activity outside marriage as well as anything in marriage that contradicts or sets aside this mutual, complete giving (cf. Hildebrand, 35–42; Häring, 3:296–303). The magisterium of Pius XII recognized this personal aspect of the conjugal act according to the scriptural phrase that man and wife become "two in one flesh" [*Acta Apostolicae Sedis* 43 (1951) 850].

These considerations as well as the strong condemnations of various sins of impurity in the NT make it clear that, in general, acts of lust are gravely sinful.

The common teaching of theologians can be summed up thus: outside marriage, every movement of lust as here defined or pleasure directly provoked or consented to is objectively a mortal sin; but venereal movements foreseen but not intended can be without sin, venially sinful, or mortally so, according to principles governing the permission of an evil effect.

Lustful Movements Directly Provoked or Consented To. Parvity of matter is not possible in the deliberate indulgence of sexual acts that defeat the generative purpose of the sex faculty, as in contraceptive or other unnatural practices; however, there may be slightness of matter when the acts indulged in retain their due ordination to this purpose, even though they might be, as we have seen from St. Thomas, acts of disordered concupiscence because they are sought only for pleasure. The necessary subordination of this pleasure to higher values is present at least implicitly in the ordinary moderate exercise of conjugal rights. On the other hand, a selfish desire for venereal pleasure can be the occasion of serious sins against justice or charity, as when conjugal relations are sought that are gravely injurious or strain the companionship of marriage.

Outside marriage the distinction between complete and incomplete acts is relevant, the former indicating a venereal movement brought to its term usually accompanied by pleasure amounting to a climax, the latter indicating movements or pleasure short of this completion.

The possibility that complete acts might be venially sinful is excluded because there is the full exercise of sex activity or the full enjoyment of its pleasure in a way that contradicts its specific, lifegiving purpose, intended by God Himself, the sole Author of human life. Solitary or other unnatural acts exclude the physical result of conception; moreover, so-called natural sins, such as fornication or adultery, contradict the purpose of sex in human beings, for those who exercise the full normal sex act are responsible for the proper care of any resulting offspring that is effectively guaranteed only by the marital bond (ST 2a2ae, 154.2.11). In both cases, there is introduced into the exercise of a faculty that is for the good of the whole human race a perversion by which it serves the pleasure or interest of an individual only. This subordination of the race to the individual is not a light matter.

In an incomplete act the perversion is still grave, and the best reason for this seems to be the one implied by St. Alphonsus and other classical moralists when they speak of it as the beginning of a complete act—

"quaedam inchoata pollutio, seu motus ad pollutionem" (1.3.416).

This is to be understood in the sense that an incomplete venereal act is of its nature the beginning of a complete act insofar as the actuation of the generative or sexual faculty is one complete, indivisible process. There can be light matter in other sins, such as theft, because a man who steals $1 does not by that fact commence a process whereby he steals $1,000. In sex activity one who performs an incomplete act necessarily begins the process of total actuation, even though he stops before it is complete. Consequently, the complete act is virtually present so that its grave malice is shared by the incomplete act (see authors such as Fuchs and Vangheluwe).

It is to be noted that the Church has condemned a proposition that states that a kiss indulged for the sake of carnal pleasure and that does not involve danger of further consent is only venially sinful (H. Denzinger, *Enchiridion symbolorum* [Freiburg 1963] 2060); recent attempts to defend similar views have been officially censured by the Holy See.

Finally, the gravity of both complete and incomplete venereal acts outside marriage arises from the nature of the normal sex act as a personal intercommunion. But this argument may be inconclusive if it is proposed separately from the argument given above (cf. Fuchs, *De castitate* 38–44).

Lustful Movements Provoked or Willed Indirectly. In speaking of the absence of sin or the presence of light sin only in certain actions (or omissions) whose foreseen but unintended result are venereal movements, it is understood there is no consent or proximate danger of consent by the will to these pleasurable movements themselves. If there is a sufficient reason for performing such an act, the resultant movement is lawfully permitted, a sufficient reason being a motive whose reasonable necessity is such as to counterbalance the evil of a movement that can never be desired in itself. Thus a moderate cause is sufficient to justify the permission of an incomplete movement, for its incompleteness indicates that this cause is not apt to disturb one profoundly; but a grave cause is required if the movement is foreseen as most likely to be complete: thus necessary study for a medical student, the fulfillment of one's duty in looking after the sick. However, as a general rule, attention to the interest of the study itself or the conscientious fulfillment of one's duty tends to diminish the likelihood of gravely disturbing venereal movements.

Actions apt of their nature to arouse only incomplete movements and performed without reason are venially sinful. In individual cases this aptitude, combined with other factors, can form a total cause of complete movements, but in general one can regard things such as reading from mere curiosity matter that is not notably suggestive, or passing embraces that, although sensual, are not venereal in character, as venially sinful only.

Actions apt to arouse full movements, if performed without reason, are serious sins. Usually the mere absence of any sufficient reason tends to make certain acts provocative of full venereal movements. Thus what could be read without any sin by reason of necessary study could be seriously provocative if read from mere curiosity. Similarly, close and prolonged embraces between adult persons for sensual pleasure are apt to cause grave disturbances, which, if the parties are not husband and wife, are not truly expressive of lawful love. Thus they must be regarded as seriously sinful.

Imputability. It is a commonplace in moral theology that strong passion that a person has not himself deliberately aroused tends to diminish or even destroy freedom, and hence the moral imputability for actions in themselves seriously sinful.

This has an obvious application in the matter of lust because of the strong character of the sex urge together with temperamental, psychological, and even psychiatric factors that weaken the resistive power of individuals to unlawful sexual inclinations. It is especially relevant when, as so frequently happens, they are exposed to innumerable external influences concentrating attention on sexual enjoyment.

Modern theologians are inclined to take seriously the claims of contemporary depth psychology that in sexual aberrations one must extend, perhaps considerably, the boundaries of diminished responsibility and admit the possibility of even total lack of imputability. Thus to the extent that actions in themselves seriously sinful are performed not from full deliberation, or to the degree that a man is the victim of uncontrollable forces that impel him so that he is passive rather than active, these are not human actions but actions of a man—*actiones hominis* (cf. *Summa Theologiae* 1a2ae, 1.1). While warning strongly against the tendency to generalize as if it were a universal assumption that sexual sins are never fully imputable, Pius XII accepted in several of his allocutions the practical possibility of diminished or totally absent imputability [radio talk, March 23, 1952, *Acta Apostolicae Sedis* 44 (1952) 275; allocution, April 9, 1953, *Acta Apostolicae Sedis* 45 (1953) 279]. Hence a confessor should not be hesitant to judge as free from mortal sin a penitent who falls into sin by solitary impure actions only after a struggle and because, as he asserts, he felt physically incapable of further resistance, when he is otherwise of good moral dispositions. Such a judgment can be made

even when a penitent of prayerful habits protests that he knew at the time he was committing sin and felt he was sinning freely. However, each case must be taken on its merits.

Remedies. It is usual to list various remedies, natural and supernatural. To the first belong such things as bodily cleanliness, the taking of suitable exercise, cultivating interest in hobbies or study, as well as the avoiding of stimulants and of erotic reading and erotic experiences in general, and self-discipline in food and in the hours of sleep. To the natural order belongs also an intelligent understanding of the significance of sex, and hence of the natural virtue of chastity. It is not necessary to stress the need, imperative in many cases, of medical and psychiatric assistance for one who has difficulty controlling his sexual inclinations.

These means cannot ordinarily be fully effective unless they are supernaturalized; complete chastity is, in the state of fallen nature, practically impossible for the average person without the help of grace. Therefore, the means of grace must be stressed, that a life of prayer and frequentation of the Sacraments. Another remedy is the appreciation of the sublime significance of sex and marriage in the supernatural, Christian order, and hence the need for cultivation of the Christian virtue of chastity.

Because grace truly builds on nature and is not merely superimposed upon it, it is important that natural and supernatural remedies work together as one whole. For want of this integration, supernatural means are sometimes insufficiently effective. When prayer and the Sacraments are used as though they were automatic preservatives, these means of grace flow over the soul, so to speak, without the grace itself finding a point of entry ample enough to take possession of a man's life.

Chastity must be seen and accepted in its natural personal values, but in such a way that these values form at the same time a basis for the supernatural. In this way both the natural and supernatural virtues become integrating parts of one harmonious principle of human action, whereby sex and its pleasures are sought and accepted or generously renounced in accordance with one's vocation in the Mystical Body of Christ.

Bibliography: General treatises. J. ADLOFF, *Dictionnaire de théologie catholique* (Paris 1903–50) 9.1:1339–56. ALPHONSUS LIGUORI, *Theologia moralis,* ed. L. GAUDÉ, 4 v. (new ed. Rome 1905–12) 1:655–707, clearly summarizes and applies to particular cases the classical teaching *de sexto praecepto et nono.* A. VERMEERSCH, *De castitate et de vitiis contrariis: Tractatus doctrinalis et moralis* (2d ed. Rome 1921) 300–413. B. MERKELBACH, *De castitate et luxuria,* rev. G. DANTINNE (8th ed. Brussels 1956). L. WOUTERS, *Tractatus dogmatico-moralis de virtute castitatis et de vitiis oppositis* (rev. ed. Bruges 1932) 23–75. J. FUCHS, *De castitate et ordine sexuali* (Rome 1963) 99–108, with strong emphasis on the antipersonal and the antigenerative aspects of lust. Useful seminary manuals. M. ZALBA, *Theologiae moralis compendium,* 2 v. (Madrid 1958) 1:1372–1509. H. DAVIS, *Moral and Pastoral Theology* (New York 1958) 2:204–221. Scriptural references. H. LESÊTRE, *Dictionnaire de la Bible,* (Paris 1895–1912) 4:436–437. A. VAN DEN BORN, *Encyclopedic Dictionary of the Bible,* (New York 1963) 1056. B. ORCHARD et al., eds., *Catholic Commentary on Holy Scripture* (London 1953), index. Personal aspects. D. VON HILDEBRAND, *In Defense of Purity* (New York 1931; repr. Baltimore, Md. 1962). B. HÄRING, *Das Gesetz Christi,* 3 v. (6th ed. Freiburg 1961). Notion of the sexual order. J. FUCHS, *Die Sexualethik des heiligen Thomas von Aquin* (Cologne 1949). Gravity of matter. J. FUCHS, *De castitate, op. cit.* 138–142. M. ZALBA, *op. cit.* 1382–83. V. VANGHELUWE, "De intrinseca et gravi malitia luxuriae imperfectae," *Collationes brugenses* 48 (1952) 36–44. J. J. LYNCH, "Notes on Moral, Theology," *Theological Studies* 21 (1960) 225–227. G. A. KELLY, "A Fundamental Notion in the Problem of Sex Morality," *ibid.* 1 (1940) 117–129. Imputability. J. C. FORD and G. A. KELLY, *Contemporary Moral Theology* (Westminster, Md. 1958–) 1:174–276. J. S. DUHAMEL, "Moral and Psychological Aspects of Freedom," *Thought* 35 (1960) 179–203.

[A. REGAN]

LUTGARDIS, ST.

Cistercian mystic and stigmatic; b. Tongres, Belgium, 1182; d. Aywières (near Brussels), June 16, 1246. Lutgardis was born of bourgeois parents. She received the habit at the Benedictine convent of Saint-Trond in 1194, was professed about 1200, and was elected prioress there in 1205. Because of the relaxed observance of this community, she transferred to the Cistercian convent at Aywières in 1208. There, sustained only by bread and weak beer, she engaged in three seven-year fasts in reparation for the Albigensian heresy then at its height. In apparitions, Christ usually was represented as showing her his heart, and she was perhaps the first saint in whom the mystical "exchange of hearts" was effected. Her frequent communions antagonized the community. The Passion was the center of her religious life, and in her 29th year she received the spear wound; she carried the scar to her death. She often experienced the sweat of blood. From 1235 she was totally blind, and the ideal of vicarious suffering in reparation for sin was highly developed in her spirituality. She predicted the day of her death.

Feast: June 16.

Bibliography: T. MERTON, *What Are These Wounds?* (Milwaukee 1950). G. HENDRIX, *Ontmoetingen met Lutgart van Tongeren: Benedictines en Cisterciënzerin* 5 v. (Leuven 1996–98). A. BUTLER, *The Lives of the Saints,* rev. ed. H. THURSTON and D. ATTWATER, 4 v. (New York 1956) 2:557–558.

[J. VERBILLION]

Martin Luther. (New York Public Library Picture Collection)

LUTHER, MARTIN

German Reformer; b. Eisleben, village in Thuringia, Nov. 10, 1483; d. there, Feb. 18, 1546. His parents, Hans Luder and Margaret Ziegler, had recently emigrated from the farming community of Möhra, where the Luder family had lived for many generations. As was the practice of the time, the child was baptized the following day by the pastor, Bartholomew Rennebecher; and since it was the feast of St. Martin of Tours, he was named after the sainted Roman soldier.

Early Years. Within a year after his birth the family moved to Mansfield, where the father was employed as a laborer in the copper mines. Luther's father was a strict disciplinarian and in his early childhood the family was beset by poverty. There is little evidence to argue, as Erik Erikson once did, that the atmosphere of the household was abnormal. By the turn of the 16th century his father's financial situation had improved, and in 1511 he became owner in a number of mines and foundries in the area. He had been elected to the city council in 1491. Young Martin was enrolled in the local Latin day school in 1488 and there began the traditional study of Latin grammar. In 1496 he was sent to Magdeburg, where he remained until Easter of the following year at a school conducted by the BRETHREN OF THE COMMON LIFE. The next semester he transferred to Eisenach because he had relatives there.

Student at Erfurt. In April 1501 Luther matriculated at the University of Erfurt and enrolled in the bursa of St. George. Two of his professors, Jodocus Trutvetter and Bartholomew Arnold von Usingen, were followers of the *via moderna*. Whether Luther was deeply influenced by NOMINALISM is still disputed. The picture drawn by Heinrich DENIFLE, OP, that portrays Luther as an ossified Ockhamite is no longer tenable. Although Luther, in his later life, remarked that he belonged to the school of William of Ockham, he did not, on other occasions, hesitate to refer to the nominalists as "hoggish theologians." Nor was Luther, as his Dominican biographer contends, a "crass ignoramus." He received his baccalaureate in 1502 and immediately began the required studies for a master's degree. In January 1505 he passed the examinations after the shortest period of study possible, standing second in his class. Although the young Luther had but a slight knowledge of Greek, he was well acquainted with the classical Latin authors. Ovid, Vergil, Plautus, and Horace were well known to him. He was also fairly well acquainted with humanism. The humanist Hieronymus EMSER had lectured at Erfurt during the summer of 1504; and Luther was familiar with the Eclogues of the Latin humanist Baptista Mantuanus. Grotius Rubeanus, a close friend of young Luther, was painfully shocked at his decision to enter the monastery.

The Call to Religion. In the summer of 1505 Luther, influenced no doubt by his father, began the study of law. Sometime in July of the same year, while returning to Erfurt from a visit to Mansfield, he encountered a severe thunderstorm near the village of Stotternheim; as a lightning bolt threw him to the ground, he vowed to St. Anne in a sudden panic that he would become a monk. To assume that the decision to enter the monastery was as impromptu as it is often depicted does Luther an injustice. His strict religious upbringing, his natural bent toward piety, and above all the experiences of the last few years at the university were unquestionably factors of his move. In 1503 he had severely wounded himself by accidentally cutting the artery in his thigh and had spent many weeks in meditative recuperation. In the same year one of his closest friends, a fellow student, had died suddenly. The plague that struck the city of Erfurt in 1505 made him keenly aware of the preeminence of death. All of this indicates that a call to religion was something that had been in his thoughts for a long period.

Nor is it without significance that he chose to enter the monastery of the Hermits of St. Augustine. The city of Erfurt boasted a Dominican, a Franciscan, and a Servite monastery in addition to the Black Cloister, a member of the Observant, or stricter Augustinian, congregation of Saxony, which was by far the most severe religious house in the city. On July 16, 1505, much

to the chagrin of his parents, who were already selecting a bride for the student of law, Luther entered the novitiate. Soon after his profession, the exact date of which is not known, he was told to prepare himself for the reception of Holy Orders. He was ordained a deacon by the suffragan bishop, Johann von Laasphe of Erfurt, on Feb. 27, 1507; he received the priesthood in the Erfurt cathedral on the following April 4th.

Professor at Wittenberg. Soon after ordination, Luther was sent to WITTENBERG, where the order held two professorships at the Elector Frederick's newly founded university. Johann von STAUPITZ, vicar-general of the Saxon congregation of the Augustinians, held the chair of scriptural theology; Luther was given the chair of moral philosophy in the arts faculty. In addition to lecturing on the *Nicomachean Ethics*, Luther was also obliged to continue his theological studies. He received his baccalaureate in theology in the spring of 1509. The following autumn he returned again to Erfurt, where he continued with his study of the *Sentences* of Peter of Lombard and lectured on philosophy to the Augustinian students there. Luther's studies were interrupted in 1510, when he was chosen to accompany Staupitz to Rome. The vicar-general had for years been identified with the reform group in the order who sought to unite both the observant, or stricter, group in the order with the more numerous conventuals. Luther probably spent a month in Rome, visiting its shrines and churches. He was not edified with the horde of unlettered clergy whom he encountered there, many of whom were unable to hear confessions. He later observed that the priests said Mass in such an irreverent fashion that it reminded him of a juggling act. Yet there is little evidence that the scandals of Rome had any bearing on the gradual religious transformation that was taking place in his mind.

After his return to Erfurt he was again sent to Wittenberg in the late summer of 1511. In October of 1512 he received the doctorate in theology and was assigned to the theological faculty succeeding Staupitz as professor of Scripture. The next five years were of vital importance in the development of Luther's theological ideas. During this period he lectured on the Psalms (1513–15), on the Epistle to the Romans (1515–16), the Epistle to the Galatians, and the Epistle to the Hebrews (1517–18). One gains some idea of the competence of the man in considering that in addition to following a monastic and academic schedule, he also preached at the castle church and held the office of Augustinian vicar of the district of Meissen and Thuringia.

Inner Conflict. If Luther had sought peace of mind in entering religion, he found it illusory. He gradually grew aware of the vast abyss between what he felt himself to be in his innermost self and the demands of God. He was increasingly conscious of the power of sin, and repeated confession brought him no peace. Further, the complacency that he felt at doing good seemed, as he said, ''to poison his soul as the frost nips flowers in the bud.'' There were times when he felt on the brink of hell and the verge of despair. He tells us that while contemplating the righteousness of God in the monastery tower, probably in 1512, a new concept, a new illumination came to him, and ''the gates of paradise were opened.''

The study of the Epistle of Paul to the Romans had convinced him that the justice of God before which he trembled is not exacting, does not condemn, but is wholly beneficent. It is a justice that reinstates the sinner qua sinner in the eyes of God, in virtue of Christ's redemption. In explaining how this phenomenon is produced, Luther logically rejected the traditional teaching of the Church. For justification, no longer an objective transformation, is produced by the word of God, the Gospel. It is in, with, and through the Gospel that God works upon the soul through His Spirit. The soul remains passive and receptive. Thus Luther made an extremely personal experience the center of a new theory of salvation that was no longer in harmony with the one traditionally taught by the Church. These ideas were only gradually formed, but a study of the glosses and the notes kept by Luther's students during the years 1513 to 1518 leaves no doubt that they had formed the basis of his religious thought. They would probably have remained within the depths of his own inner spiritual struggle and never spread beyond the confines of the classroom where he lectured were it not for a series of events that brought the focus of all Christendom on the Wittenberg monk and changed the course of history.

The St. Peter's Indulgence. ALBRECHT OF BRANDENBURG, brother of the elector Joachim, at the age of 23 was elected archbishop of Magdeburg and was, at the same time, given the administration of the diocese of Halberstadt. Both his age and the accumulation of two bishoprics were in direct violation of Canon Law; nor was his personal life beyond reproach. The Holy See condoned the appointment and a year later the same pluralist was elected archbishop of Mainz, a position that automatically made him prince elector, Reich-chancellor, and primate of all Germany. The move was undeniably inspired by political aspirations since it gave the Hohenzollerns two votes in the electoral college. Yet the price was incredibly high. For the dispensation to hold benefices in three dioceses Albrecht had to pay the Curia a sum of 10,000 golden ducats. Another 14,000 was demanded to pay up the arrears in pallium taxes for the See of Mainz. An agreement was made with the Curia whereby, for allowing the Peter's Indulgence to be preached in his epis-

copal territories, the bishop would receive one half of the income and the other half would go toward the construction of St. Peter's.

As principal agent for this sordid simoniacal act, the Fuggers chose the well-known indulgence preacher Dominican Johann TETZEL. Of the indulgence agreement between the House of FUGGER, the Curia, and the archbishop of Mainz, Luther knew nothing. It was only when Tetzel began to preach the indulgence in the towns of Jüterbog and Zerbst on the northern boundary of Saxon territory that Luther felt it his duty to admonish his electoral highness, the archbishop of Mainz and Magdeburg, regarding the difficulties Tetzel was causing. He wrote him on October 31, 1517: ''Papal indulgences for the building of St. Peter's are hawked about under your illustrious sanction. I am not denouncing the sermons of the preachers who advertise them, for I have not seen them, but I regret that the faithful have conceived some erroneous notions about them. These unhappy souls believe that if they buy a letter of pardon they are sure of their salvation; also that souls fly out of purgatory as soon as money is cast into the chest, in short, that the grace conferred is so great that there is no sin whatever which cannot be absolved thereby, even if, as they say, taking an impossible example, a man should violate the mother of God. They also believe that indulgences free them from all guilt of sin.''

The Ninety-five Theses. At the same time as Luther approached Tetzel with his criticisms he also wrote and circulated his attack upon indulgences, the so-called 95 theses, and announced his intention to hold a debate on their value. What had been for years a question in the mind of Luther, a matter of theology, now became a matter of reform. Most of the theses were not opposed to traditional Catholic doctrine.

Tetzel, who was in Berlin at the time the theses were published, was supported by the members of his order, and to confirm their confidence in his theological competence they later gave him an honorary degree in theology from their Roman college. Luther's own attitude toward his antagonist was anything but hostile. Later, when he heard that Tetzel was stricken with a fatal illness, he wrote him a consoling letter stating that the unfortunate affair was in no way the Dominican's responsibility. The roots of the controversy lay much deeper.

In early February 1518, Luther presented the bishop of Brandenburg with a series of *Resolutiones* on the theses, requesting that the bishop strike out whatever he found displeasing. He wrote, ''I know that Christ does not need me. He will show His Church what is good for her without me. Nothing is so difficult to state as the true teaching of the Church, especially when one is a serious sinner as I am.'' He ended his letter of explanation by urging reform of the Church and pointing out that, as recent events proved, namely, the Lateran Council, the reform is the concern not of the pope alone or of the Cardinals but of the entire Christian world. The bishop answered Luther, informing him that he found no error in the *Resolutiones* and that in fact he thoroughly objected to the manner in which indulgences were being sold.

Denunciation from Rome. Rome had already been alerted to the dangers contained in Luther's novel doctrine by the archbishop of Mainz. In view of the recent negotiations between Albrecht and the Curia, it is understandable that his protest was interpreted in terms of declining revenues rather than threatened dogma. However, with the powerful Dominican Order now denouncing the Wittenberg professor, Rome had no alternative but to act. Following an established pattern, the Roman authorities, having failed to silence Luther through his own order, instigated a formal canonical process against him. The provincial of the Saxon province of the Dominicans, Herman Rab, induced the fiscal procurator, Marius de Perusco, to have the pope instigate charges against Luther. At the procurator's request, an auditor of the Curia, Girolamo Ghinucci, was entrusted with the preliminary investigation, and a Dominican, Sylvestro Prierias, Master of the Sacred Palace and *censor librorum* of Rome, was commissioned to draw up a theological opinion on Luther's doctrinal writings.

A thorough Thomist, Prierias handled Luther's writings as if he were conducting a scholastic disputation. His *Dialogus* was nothing more than a polemic tagging the various theses as erroneous, false, presumptuous, or heretical. A citation, which reached Luther on August 7, 1518, was drawn up demanding that he appear personally in Rome within 60 days to defend himself. The citation and the dialogue were dispatched to the general of the Dominican Order, Tommaso de Vio, commonly known as CAJETAN, probably the outstanding theologian of the century.

The Meeting with Cajetan. During the same month, the pope, now informed of Emperor Maximilian's willingness to prosecute Luther, instructed Cajetan, whom he had appointed as his legate to the Diet of Augsburg, to cite the accused to appear before him. An order of extradition was also sent to Frederick the Wise, Luther's territorial sovereign, and also to his provincial, Gerhard Hecker, who was commanded to arrest him. Upon receipt of the citation, Luther immediately moved to forestall his appearance before what he considered anything but an impartial tribunal. Supported by Frederick the Wise, he demanded that his case be tried in Germany and by a group of competent scholars. Frederick

managed to obtain a promise from Cajetan of a fair hearing and pledged safe-conduct to the young monk. On October 12, Luther appeared before the Dominican cardinal and his entourage of Italian jurists. It was Cajetan's hope to obtain recantation by paternal exhortations, but Luther obstinately refused to make an act of revocation, maintaining that he would not do so as long as he was not convinced of his errors on a basis of scriptural proof. He flatly denied the validity of Pope Clement VI's decretal on indulgences, *Unigenitus*. When Luther suggested that the decretal be submitted to the opinion of a Council, Catejan accused him of being a Gersonist. (*See* GERSON, JEAN; CONCILIARISM, HISTORY OF.)

On October 16, Luther informed the cardinal of his willingness to stop commenting on indulgences and his readiness to listen to the Church. He apologized for his violent outbursts against the pope. Yet there was not a word of recantation. To his brethren at Wittenberg he wrote: ''The Cardinal may be an able Thomist, but he is not a clear Christian thinker, and so he is about as fit to deal with this matter as an ass is to play the harp.'' Cajetan, thwarted in his attempt to reconcile Luther, demanded that the Elector Frederick extradite Luther and send him to Rome for trial. On November 28, Luther appealed to a general council. The appeal was actually a legal device intended to stay the civil effects of the excommunication that was now imminent.

Rome and the Impending Imperial Election. The delay of the excommunication of Luther was not a result so much of this legal maneuver as it was of a developing political situation that involved the papacy once again in the affairs of Germany. The Emperor Maximilian had since 1513 been planning the election of his grandson, Charles, Duke of Burgundy and King of Castile and Aragon, as Holy roman emperor. The election of Charles would have constituted a threat to the territorial independence of the pope because of the latter's sovereignty over Naples. Hence the Curia, favoring an election of either Francis I of France or, preferably, Frederick, Luther's sovereign, made efforts to delay any move that would antagonize the elector. To win the support of Frederick, Karl von MILTITZ, a swaggering, alcoholic Saxon, holding the office of papal notary in the Rome court, was sent to the elector with a plan to have Luther tried in a German ecclesiastical court, preferably in Trier. In addition he was to present the elector with the Golden Rose, as well as a letter of legitimization for Frederick's two children. None of the supporters of Luther were, however, deceived by the boastful Saxon. In fact, his presence in Germany supported their conviction that politics, not theology, was behind Rome's denunciation of Luther.

Leo X's Bull of Excommunication. A bull of excommunication, *Exsurge Domine*, was issued in Rome on

June 15, 1520, and Johann ECK, Luther's opponent in his debates with KARLSTADT at Leipzig in July 1519, was commissioned to promulgate it throughout the empire. In September he published the bull in the diocese of Brandenburg and in the diocese of Saxony. Before the 60-day time limit, within which he had to submit, Luther again appealed to a general council. The appeal did not delay, however, the final bull of excommunication, *Decet Romanum Pontificem*, which pronounced sentence on Luther on January 3, 1521. In April of that year he appeared before the Diet in Worms; and although protected by a writ of safe-conduct, he was declared henceforth a criminal in the Empire.

It is one of the strange turns of history that Luther was never officially prosecuted in his own country, although excommunication, by labeling him a heretic, made him liable to the death penalty in the Empire. A number of circumstances combined to render the ecclesiastical and civil penalties ineffective. In the first place there was strong public reaction that rebelled at the prospect of condemning a man who had become the outright spokesman for their own grievances against corruption in the Church. The conviction that until a council had actually pronounced against him, he and his followers were not definitely cut off from the Catholic Church was widespread. Finally, the majority of the German bishops, still influenced by conciliarism, were hardly inclined to stand in the way of a man whose attacks on papal claims to ecclesiastical supremacy expressed their own opposition to Romanism.

Almost everywhere the publication of the bull met with strong opposition. In Luther's home diocese of Brandenburg, the local ordinary, Hieronymus Schulz, did not dare to publish it. The University of Wittenberg brushed it aside as a further example of Eck's skullduggery. There, on Dec. 10, 1520, before an assembly of students, Luther had consigned the bull to the flames together with a copy of Canon Law. In Erfurt the document was cast into the river, and in Leipzig a riot of the students at the University forced the executor to flee the city.

Writings of 1520. During the summer and fall of 1520, Luther wrote what many consider, after the translation of the Bible, to be the most important of his works. In a series of pamphlets, *An Appeal to the Nobility of the German Nation, On the Babylonian Captivity of the Church*, and the *Liberty of a Christian Man*, he outlined what he felt would be a program for reforming and revitalizing the Church. The first edition (some 4,000 copies) of the *Appeal to the Nobility* was sold out between August 18 and 23. In this work he pointed out the three walls the Romanists have built about themselves that constitute

the main obstacles to true reform and are responsible for the decline of Christianity: the claim that civil government has no rights over them, the superiority of papal decrees over Scripture, and, finally, the superiority of the pope over a council.

In early October Luther penned his second famous work, *On the Babylonian Captivity of the Church*. While the first had been an attack on the century-old abuses of the Church and contained little that was novel, this next work openly struck a blow at the sacramental system and the Sacrifice of the Mass. Written in Latin, it was intended for theologians and scholars and opened the eyes of many, for the first time, to the radical elements in his new doctrines. Erasmus declared that it precluded all possibility of peace with the papacy. The third great work of this period, *On Christian Liberty*, continued to strike out at the roots of papal Christianity by emphasizing the primacy of Scripture, the priesthood of the laity, and the doctrine of justification by faith alone. In emphasizing Christian liberty, Luther stresses the freedom expressed in obedience to God and service to one's neighbor. He traces the religious implications of justification by faith and impugns the idea that good works are the mechanical performance of ecclesiastical laws. Rather, they are the fruit of faith from which they flow. Although these three writings in a certain sense epitomize the salient features of the early Lutheran movement, it would be unjust to say that they are the very heart and soul of Luther's doctrine. Neither would it be correct to assert that Luther or his followers felt that they had in any way separated themselves from the Catholic Church by condemning the abuses within it. But the three treatises of 1520, widely circulated in the next decade, did win large numbers of converts for the evangelical movement.

Progress of the Lutheran Reform. While returning from Worms Luther was kidnapped by the agents of Frederick the Wise and placed in hiding at Wartburg, where he continued to pour forth his scriptural and reformatory writings. The years between 1521 and 1525 were the most decisive period in the growth of Lutheranism. Since neither the bull of excommunication nor the Edict of Worms were actually put into effect in the empire, the reform movement continued to flourish. A number of events, however, caused a loss in its original momentum. As a popular uprising it was thwarted by the very forces that Luther had originally hoped to liberate. For several generations the peasants in the south and west of Germany had threatened local governments with grievances arising out of the economic and sociological changes of this transitional period. The doctrines of Luther, particularly his teaching on Christian liberty, were quickly transformed into demands for social reform. Eventually, peasant uprisings broke out in the Black Forest region in

June 1524 and spread throughout Swabia, Franconia, Thuringia, and parts of the Rhineland. Luther firmly opposed the revolt, asserting that rebellion would stir up more ills than it would cure. The subsequent failure of the revolt and the urging of Luther that the civil authorities step in to stop the political anarchy that was threatening large areas of the Empire gave a definite impetus to the formation of territorial or state churches. *See* PEASANTS' WAR (1524–25).

In the fall of 1526 PHILIP OF HESSE summoned a synod in Homberg. There, under the direction of former Franciscan Franz Lambert of Avignon, a new church ordinance was imposed on the territory of Hesse. Monasteries and other ecclesiastical properties were confiscated, Catholic pastors were removed, and the Lutheran adaptation of the Mass was introduced. The following year in Saxony a commission of lawyers and theologians, after a series of visitations to the parishes in the area, published regulations governing divine service and the establishment of schools to instruct the faithful in the new gospel teaching.

To implement the new state church regulations Luther wrote his Large Catechism—a manual of instruction for pastors—and his Small Catechism—both a devotional work and an instruction for the faithful in the fundamentals of the Christian religion.

A loss of humanist support inflicted on the cause of Lutheranism a blow even more severe than that incurred with the disaffection of the peasants. Luther's *De Servo Arbitrio*, an attack upon free will, heightened the difference between his own position and that of his earlier humanist sympathizers. In denying freedom of the will it must not be assumed that Luther intended to deny individual responsibility. Throughout his life, beginning with the theses, his appeal to the Church had been one of repentance. A denial of responsibility would have completely nullified this call.

The Confessio Augustana. The break with humanism and the growing interference of German political leaders turned the attention of the reformer to the more practical implementations of his design. The controversy on the Eucharist that arose at the same time that Luther wrote his *De Servo Arbitrio* made it obvious that some strong clarification of doctrinal position was necessary if the movement was not to dissolve into warring parties. Doctrinal divisions within the reform movement accentuated by the Eucharistic controversy at Marburg in 1529 had their counterpart in the political sphere. Between 1524 and 1529 the political leadership of the Lutheran movement gradually passed from the Saxon electors to the Landgrave Philip of Hesse. At the Diet of Speyer (1526) it was already apparent that a division between the

Catholic and the Lutheran princes within the empire was taking shape. In 1530 at Augsburg, Luther's closest associate at Wittenberg, Melanchthon, who had already attempted to systematize Luther's teachings in his *Loci communes* in 1521, drew up the *Confessio Augustana*, the final embodiment of the basic Lutheran, or reformed, doctrine. An examination of the document gives some insight into the perplexities of the religious situation as it stood after almost 12 years of religious controversy. It also demonstrated the ambivalence that invested the expression "reform" long after the Edict of Worms. Melanchthon maintained the conviction that he had not departed from the teaching of the Catholic Church in a single dogma, and Elector John of Saxony strongly rejected the accusation that the signers of the Confession had separated themselves from the Church. The Confession addressed to the emperor laid down the fundamental points of the new doctrine and repudiated all rival doctrines.

After the Diet of Augsburg in 1530, which Luther was not permitted to attend (being refused safe-conduct by the emperor), he tended to remain more and more aloof from the political developments that continued to detract from the religious aspect of the reform movement. The Augustinian monastery in Wittenberg had become secularized and was finally deeded to Luther in 1532. With few interruptions Luther continued to teach at the university until his death.

Luther's Marriage and Later Years. In 1525 Luther married Katherina von Bora, some 16 years his junior. She came from the town of Lippendorf, near Leipzig, and at the age of five she had been sent to the Benedictine nuns near Brehana. Four years later she transferred to a Cistercian cloister near Grimma, where her aunt was abbess and an older sister, a nun. She took her vows here in 1515 but during the generally troubled times in 1523 joined in the exodus from her convent. Wittenberg had become a refuge for hundreds of monks and nuns who left their monasteries during these years, and it was there that she met Luther. Their marriage caused a great stir in Europe. ERASMUS, in correspondence with Luther at that time on the *Diatribe*, attributed the failure of Luther to answer his letters to his marriage, He wittily remarked that in comedies troubles are wont to end in marriage with peace to all. He added that he felt the marriage was timely as he heard that a child was born ten days afterward. It was his hope that Luther would be milder in his attacks on the Church since even the fiercest beasts can be tamed by their female mates. Later on he apologized for his inference about the child, remarking that he had always been skeptical about the old legend that the antichrist would be born of a monk and a nun. Were this true, there would have been too many antichrists in the world already. The Luther household became a gathering place for needy priests, poor relatives, and indigent students. In addition to his own six children, four of whom survived their parents, Luther brought up eleven orphaned children. Luther's almost reckless hospitality and generosity to friends necessitated income greater than his professor's salary provided. He constantly refused the honorarium demanded of students in the German universities and turned down frequent offers for the sale of his manuscripts.

During these years Luther continued his commentaries on the New Testament and revised many of his earlier writings. During his lifetime he published more than 400 works, which fill more than 100 volumes. With the possible exception of Goethe, no single writer influenced the development of German literature as did Luther.

Luther's support of Philip of Hesse in the celebrated case of bigamy did little to enhance the reformer's cause. He had approved the marriage on March 4, 1540, of the duke to Margaret von der Saal, even though Philip was married to Christina, daughter of Duke George of Saxony. Luther's recommendations to Philip of Hesse were virtually the same as those he had made to Henry VIII of England: he should take a mistress rather than divorce. They were also consonant with the arguments he had made about marriage as early as *The Babylonian Captivity of the Church* in 1520. There he had argued that divorce and annulment were contrary to divine law, but that the problems of a barren marriage might be resolved in the manner of the Old Testament Patriarchs, that is, through the employment of a concubine. In so arguing he was not entirely at variance with many contemporary Catholic theologians, including Cajetan. The convocation of the Council of Trent gave him little hope that any reconciliation between Protestants and Catholics would result. In one of his final works against the papacy he refers to the Council as a juggling contest. Luther died of a stroke on the morning of Feb. 16, 1546, at Eisleben, where he had been attempting to arbitrate a disagreement between the courts of Mansfield.

Evaluation. It is an exaggeration to identify the Reformation solely with the person of Luther and to equate all of Protestantism with his doctrines. Nevertheless, one must admit the enormous influence that he exercised upon the movement. The survival of Luther's own brand of evangelicalism was greatly aided by the rise of numerous reformers elsewhere in Northern Europe, that is, by the rise of figures like Zwingli, Bucer, Calvin, and a host of others. Lutheranism's success as a protest against the Church's dominant teachings concerning salvation, and its later growth as a church independent of Rome, is also in part attributable to Luther's long and productive life.

He continued to exert his stamp upon the evangelical cause for a quarter century after the movements birth. And upon his death in 1546, he had trained large numbers of pastors and theologian who were prepared to carry on his legacy.

Bibliography: His writings are found in several large collections. Wittenberg ed., 19 v. (12 v. in German, 7 v. in Latin; 1539–59); J. G. WALCH ed., 24 v. (Halle 1740–53); Erlangen ed., 105 v. (67 v. in German, 38 v. in Latin; 1826–86); Weimar ed. by J. K. F. KNAAKE et al. (1883–); *Luthers Werke in Auswahl*, ed. O. CLEMEN et al. (5th ed. Berlin 1959–); an Engish ed. by J. PELIKAN and H. P. LEHMANN (St. Louis-Philadelphia 1955–). *Career of the Reformer*, v.31, ed. H. J. GRIMM, v.32, ed. G. FORELL, arranges his writings about his life in chronological order. K. ALAND et al., *Hilfsbuch zum Lutherstudium* (Gütersloh 1957), an analytical listing of all Luther's writings. Literature. K. SCOTTENLOHER, *Bibliographie zur deutschen Geschichte im Zeitalter der Glaubensspaltung, 1517–85*, 6 v. (Leipzig 1933–40) 1:458–629. H. JEDIN, *Lexikon für Theologie und Kirche*, ed. J. HOFER and K. RAHNER, 10 v. (2d, new ed. Freiburg 1957–65); suppl., *Das ZweiteVatikanische Konzil: Dokumente und kommentare*, ed. H. S. BRECHTER et al., pt. 1 (1966) 6:1223–30, bibliog. H. BORNKAMM and H. VOLZ, *Die Religion in Geschichte und Gegenwart*, 7 v. (3d ed. Tübingen 1957–65) 480–495, 520–523, bibliog. J. PACQUIER, *Dictionnaire de théologie catholique*, ed. A. VACANT, 15 v. (Paris 1903–50; Tables générales 1951–) 9.1:1146–1335, bibliog. G. RITTER, *Luther, Gestalt und Tat* (Munich 1959). K. A. MEISSINGER, *Der katholische Luther* (Munich 1952). E.G. RUPP, *The Righteousness of God: Luther Studies* (New York 1954). H. BÖHMER, *Road to Reformation*, tr. J. W. DOBERSTEIN and T. G. TAPPERT (Philadelphia 1946). H. S. DENIFLE, *Luther und Luthertum*, 2 v. (Mainz 1904–09), Eng. *Luther and Lutherdom*, tr. R. VOLZ (Somerset, Ohio 1917–), a polemical, unsympathetic view. H. GRISAR, *Martin Luther: His Life and Work*, ed. F. J. EBLE and A. PREUSS (2d ed. St. Louis 1935; repr. Westminster, MD 1950), a psychological study. P. J. REITER, *Martin Luthers Umwelt, Charakter und Psychose*, 2 v. (Copenhagen 1937–41). R. H. FIFE, *The Revolt of Martin Luther* (New York 1957). E. H. ERIKSON, *Young Man Luther: A Study in Psychoanalysis and History* (New York 1959). E. W. ZEEDEN, *Martin Luther und die Reformation im Urteil des deutschen Luthertums*, 2 v. (Freiburg 1950–52) v.1 tr. R. M. BETHELL, *The Legacy of Luther* (Westminster, Md. 1954). A. HERTE, *Das katholische Lutherbild im Bann der Lutherkommentare des Cochläus*, 3 v. (Münster 1943). J. LORTZ, *Die Reformation in Deutschland*, 2 v. (Freiburg 1949). R. BAINTON, *Here I Stand: A Life of Martin Luther* (New York 1950). J. M. TODD, *Martin Luther* (London 1964). J. P. DOLAN, *History of the Reformation* (New York 1965). M. BRECHT, *Martin Luther*, J. L. SCHAAF, trans. (Philadelphia 1985). G. EBELING, *Luther*, R. A. WILSON, trans. (London 1970). H. A. OBERMAN, *Luther*, E. WALLISER-SCHWARZBART, Trans. (New Haven 1989). D. STEINMETZ, *Luther and Staupitz* (Durham, NC 1980). D. STEINMETZ, *Luther in Context* (Bloomington, IN 1986).

[J. P. DOLAN/EDS.]

LUTHERAN CHURCHES IN NORTH AMERICA

A century after the beginning of the Protestant REFORMATION the first Lutherans migrated from Europe to North America. During the 17th century there were rela-

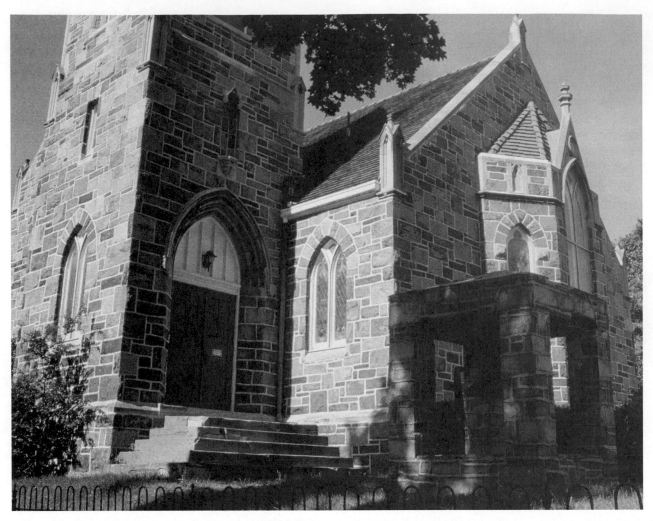

Georgetown Lutheran Church, Georgetown district, Washington D.C. (©Lee Snider/CORBIS)

tively few of them in the New World, but in the next century their numbers increased and they came to be scattered along the entire Atlantic seaboard. In the course of the 19th century and down to the beginning of World War I, large waves of immigration carried even more Lutherans to North America, and many of them settled in the Middle West and then the Far West. As a consequence, Lutheran churches were in time established in all states of the United States and most provinces of Canada.

Just as the appearance and the numerical strength of Lutherans in North America can be accounted for largely by colonization and immigration, so the structures of church life that developed can be understood only against the background of the successive waves of immigration from a variety of European countries. More than any other Protestant family of churches, Lutherans in North America were distinguished by great diversity of national origins. The language and culture of each national group were perpetuated for several generations, and not until

the process of acculturation enabled all to adopt the same tongue and similar patterns of life was it possible to express in unity of ecclesiastical organization the remarkable unanimity that had all along existed in faith and doctrine.

Colonial Beginnings, 1619–1775. Apart from a short-lived settlement of Danes on Hudson Bay (1619), the earliest Lutheran colonists were in New Netherland, on the Hudson River (1623), and in New Sweden, on the Delaware River (1638). In the former there were Norwegian and German as well as Dutch Lutherans, but all accommodated themselves to the Dutch language and Dutch models of congregational organization and worship, although ministers were sent to them from Hamburg as well as Amsterdam. In New Sweden, on the other hand, the colonists were Swedish and Finnish, their ministers were sent to them from Sweden, and the whole complexion of church life was colored by the traditions of the Church of Sweden. After both colonies had been lost to England (1664) and in time became predominantly English in character, the descendants of the early colonists gradually became Anglicized and demanded church services in their adopted tongue. This in miniature is what happened again and again among Lutherans in North America.

More Lutherans made their way to America in the 18th century, and the vast majority were German speaking. Entering the New World through the ports of Halifax, New York, Philadelphia, Baltimore, Charleston, and Savannah, they soon moved inland along water courses and in time established settlements as far west as the Appalachian mountain range. Some colonists, such as the Palatines in New York and the Salzburgers in Georgia, were accompanied by clergymen; but for the most part laymen conducted public worship until clergymen were sent to them. Most ministers came from Halle, in Saxony, the center of German PIETISM, and helped give colonial Lutheranism a pietistic stamp. The recognized leader was Henry Melchior MUHLENBERG, who journeyed often from his home in southeastern Pennsylvania to instill hope and introduce order among his scattered fellow Lutherans. He was a personal link between the descendants of the older Dutch- and Swedish-speaking Lutherans and the newer German-speaking colonists. He made provision for a better supply of ministers and for a form of congregational organization adapted to American conditions. He also helped create the Lutheran Ministerium of North America (1748), intended to unite all the ministers, and through them the congregations, in fellowship and common action. Between 1700 and 1775 the enrolled membership of Lutheran churches increased from an estimated 3,000 to about 40,000, although there were many more nominal Lutherans.

Uncertainty and Compromise, 1775–1855. From the beginning of the American Revolution to about 1830 Lutheran immigration was at a virtual standstill. Contacts with the Old World and its Lutherans became more and more attenuated. Descendants of the German colonists, especially in the larger towns and wherever they were in a minority, adopted English speech by the third generation. As a consequence German services began to be replaced by English services in many churches. The adoption of English often was accompanied by an imitation of practices current in other Protestant churches—a change that was in a measure prepared for by the earlier pietism.

Although there was little new immigration, there was migration westward and northward to new frontiers. Such geographical expansion was accompanied by the reduction of the original ministerium to eastern Pennsylvania and the organization of additional district synods: New

William H. Cardinal Keeler nailing "Joint Declaration on the Doctrine of Justification" on the doors of Christ Lutheran Church in Baltimore. (AP/Wide World Photos)

York (1786), North Carolina (1803), Ohio (1818), Maryland-Virginia (1820), Tennessee (1820), South Carolina (1824), West Pennsylvania (1825), Pittsburgh (1845), Illinois (1851), and Iowa (1855). In order to prevent such a proliferation of synods from destroying Lutheran unity, the General Synod was formed in 1821 as a union of synods. For the training of ministers it established a theological seminary (1826) in Pennsylvania and sent missionaries to fields at home and abroad. Samuel Simon SCHMUCKER was the outstanding leader of this period in educational and missionary projects. Other theological seminaries were founded in New York (1815), Ohio (1830 and 1845), and South Carolina (1830), in addition to a half-dozen colleges. Among other less enduring periodicals a weekly church paper, the *Lutheran Observer,* was launched in 1831, and another, the *Lutheran Standard,* in 1843. Enrolled Lutheran membership rose from about 40,000 in 1775 to approximately 225,000 in 1855.

Confessional Revival, 1855–1914. With the resumption of immigration about 1830, the way was prepared for a new epoch. The tide of immigrants crossing the Atlantic between 1830 and 1914 changed the social and religious complexion of North America in many ways. In addition to the unprecedented influx of Roman

Catholics, probably four million people of at least nominal Lutheran background made their way to the New World from Germany, Norway, Sweden, and Denmark. Toward the end of the period smaller numbers of Icelandic, Finnish, Slovak, and Hungarian Lutherans joined the movement. Although the descendants of Lutherans who had come to America before the Revolution had been developing more effective ecclesiastical organizations and had been erecting educational and other institutions, they were ill prepared for the avalanche of new immigrants. The Americanization in doctrine and practice as well as in language had progressed so far that the newcomers appeared to be not only cultural foreigners but also ecclesiastical strangers.

The consequence was that (apart from the many who were not reached by the church at all) the new immigrants usually established church organizations of their own, especially in the Middle West, where they settled in largest concentrations. The Missouri Synod was formed in 1847 by Lutherans from Germany, under the leadership of Carl Ferdinand William WALTHER. Some withdrew from this synod and founded the German Iowa Synod in 1854, when Walther was charged with undue rigidity in questions of ecclesiastical polity. The Joint Synod of Ohio, which had before been associated with Missouri, also broke away in 1881 after disagreement about the doctrine of predestination, and before this, in 1850, the Wisconsin Synod came into being. Although these four German synods carried state names in their titles, they quickly expanded far beyond the frontiers of the states in which they were organized. Meanwhile several synods were formed by immigrants from Norway; one reflected the opposition of its leader to anything that suggested the state church in his homeland, and another represented greater sympathy with the traditions of the Church of Norway. In 1860 the Augustana Synod was organized by Swedish immigrants under the guidance of Lars P. ESBJÖRN; this body at first included some Norwegians, but it soon became exclusively Swedish. Danish immigrants inherited two divergent tendencies from their homeland and formed separate bodies in America in 1872 and 1896. In 1890 the Suomi Synod was organized among Finnish immigrants, but in this case, too, there were dissidents who established independent bodies. In addition, two Slovak synods and an Icelandic synod were formed.

Two things characterized this proliferation of independent synods. One was the establishment of congregations and then of synods along national lines. This was almost inevitable if the immigrants were to be ministered to in their own languages and in accordance with the practices to which they had been accustomed. A second was a tendency toward separation even within national groups. The absence of ecclesiastical supervision from

Europe and the spirit of free enterprise in America contributed to such division. The fact of the matter is that more of the immigrants would have been lost to the church than was the case if laymen and ministers had not taken initiative and assumed authority to act.

Further division occurred during the Civil War, when Lutheran synods in the South withdrew from the predominantly northern General Synod and in 1863 formed what later came to be called the United Synod in the South. After the Civil War, in 1867, some other synods withdrew from the General Synod and united with several independent synods (notably the Swedish Augustana Synod) to form the General Council in protest against what was regarded as an extreme accommodation in the former general body to American REVIVALISM and puritanism. Another, and looser, federation of synods came into being in 1872, when the Missouri Synod joined with what was to be called the Joint Synod of Wisconsin, a small Norwegian group, and for a time the Joint Synod of Ohio to form the Synodical Conference. These four general bodies of Lutherans—General Synod, United Synod in the South, General Council, and Synodical Conference—continued to exist to the time of World War I. Although many large synods remained outside and independent of them, these general bodies were testimonies, however muted, to a longing for Lutheran unity.

In spite of organizational fragmentation, such unity was actually in the making, although it usually remained concealed under linguistic and other differences that occasionally exploded in controversy. The second half of the 19th century was marked by a recovery, on the part of virtually all Lutherans, of the theology of 17th century orthodoxy and by a reintroduction of the forms of worship of that and the preceding century. The CONFESSIONS OF FAITH included in the Book of CONCORD (1580), especially the AUGSBURG CONFESSION and Luther's Small Catechism, were not only appealed to but diligently studied, and this strengthened the inner bonds of unity. Such confessionalism was combined with pietism, which marked most of the Lutheran immigrants of the 19th century as well as those of the 18th. This combination produced zealous activity in domestic missions, which reached to the Pacific coast, and in foreign missions. In these same years baptized membership increased from about 225,000 to about three million.

Growing Unity and Enterprise in the 20th Century. The unity that was a hope before World War I became more and more of a reality after 1914. By this time the second and third generations of 19th-century immigrants were adopting the English tongue, and the war itself gave a tremendous impetus to the abandonment of languages other than English. The linguistic barriers that had separated English-speaking from German-speaking Lutherans, Norwegian-speaking from Finnish-speaking Lutherans, etc., now broke down. In 1917 all Lutherans were able to join hands in preparation for and the celebration of the 400th anniversary of the Reformation. This commemoration of Martin Luther's posting of the 95 Theses made Lutherans more aware of their common heritage. When the United States became a participant in World War I, most Lutheran bodies joined in the creation of the National Lutheran Commission for Soldiers' and Sailors' Welfare, and in 1918 this agency was enlarged in its scope and transformed into the National Lutheran Council. The Missouri Synod and a smaller synod that were not originally associated in the National Lutheran Council joined their fellow Lutherans in 1967 in a reorganization of the agency, named the Lutheran Council in the U.S.A. This unity, however, lasted for only two years, when in 1969 the Missouri Synod broke away to go on its own.

While these things were happening, a series of mergers reduced the number of Lutheran church bodies from 25 to 3. In 1917 three bodies of Norwegian provenance united to form the Norwegian Lutheran Church, soon called the Evangelical Lutheran Church. The following year the General Synod, General Council, and United Synod in the South merged to establish the United Lutheran Church and were shortly joined by small Icelandic and Slovak synods. In 1930 the Joint Synod of Ohio, the Iowa Synod, and the Buffalo Synod—all of German extraction and predominantly Middle Western—united to form the American Lutheran Church. In 1960 the two bodies that had just come into being through mergers in 1917 and 1930 entered a new union together with smaller synods of Norwegian and Danish origin to comprise the American Lutheran Church. In 1962 the United Lutheran Church merged with the Augustana (of Swedish origin), the Suomi (of Finnish), and the American Evangelical Lutheran (Danish) Churches to form the Lutheran Church in America. In this way, more than 90 percent of the Lutherans in North America in the 1960s and 1970s came to be organized in three churches: the Lutheran Church in America (LCA), the American Lutheran Church (ALC), and the Lutheran Church—Missouri Synod. What was especially significant is that these mergers brought together Lutherans of diverse national origins and ended the previous tendency toward isolation of different language groups.

Hopes for Lutheran unity, however, received a setback when at the 1969 convention of the Missouri Synod the newly organized conservative wing succeeded in electing J. A. O. Preus to the presidency. His election meant an opposition to ecumenism except through confessional agreement. In spite of Preus's opposition the agreement on pulpit and altar fellowship with the ALC was passed. Nevertheless, Preus took his election as a mandate for restructuring the Missouri Synod along conservative lines. This attempt led to a major floor fight at the 1971 convention over how strictly binding were synod doctrinal statements. Preus also saw the agreement of both ALC and LCA on the ordination of women as reopening the whole fellowship question. While the Missouri Synod did not rescind its agreement of fellowship with the ALC, the resulting turmoil pushed the ALC closer to the LCA position on Lutheran unity, i.e., the Lutheran confessions are sufficient basis for unity and extra-confessional agreements are not necessary. As the Missouri Synod's doctrinal position hardened, several churches broke away from the Missouri Synod in 1976 to form the Association of Evangelical Lutheran Churches (AELC).

The gradual rapprochement between the LCA and the ALC sowed the seeds for further developments in Lutheran unity in the early 1980s. On January 1, 1988, three Lutheran churches—the LCA, the ALC, and the AELC—merged to form the EVANGELICAL LUTHERAN CHURCH IN AMERICA (ELCA). The ELCA plays an active role in the Lutheran World Federation, the NATIONAL COUNCIL OF CHURCHES OF CHRIST IN THE U.S.A., and the WORLD COUNCIL OF CHURCHES. In 1997 the ELCA entered into full communion with the Presbyterian Church (U.S.A.), the United Church of Christ, and the Reformed Church in America. This was followed in 1999 by full communion relations with the Moravian Church in America and the Episcopal Church, U.S.A.

Bibliography: A. R. WENTZ, *A Basic History of Lutheranism in America* (Philadelphia 1955). F. W. MEUSER, *The Formation of the American Lutheran Church* (Columbus, Ohio 1958). E. C. NELSON and E. L. FEVOLD *The Lutheran Church among Norwegian-Americans,* 2 v. (Minneapolis 1960). W. O. FORSTER, *Zion on the Mississippi* (St. Louis 1953). G. E. ARDEN, *Augustana Heritage* (Rock Island, Ill. 1963). P. C. NYHOLM, *The Americanization of the Danish Lutheran Churches in America* (Minneapolis 1963). E. SCHLINK, *The Theology of the Lutheran Confessions,* tr. P. F. KOEHNEKE and H. J. A. BOUMAN (Philadelphia 1961). L. D. REED, *The Lutheran Liturgy* (Philadelphia 1960). C. J. I. BERGENDOFF, *The Doctrine of the Church in American Lutheranism* (Philadelphia 1956). F. S. MEAD, S. S. HILL, and C. D. ATWOOD, eds., *Handbook of Denominations in the United States* (Nashville 2001).

[T. G. TAPPERT/J. K. LUOMA/EDS.]

LUTHERANISM

The term, Lutheranism, can mean either the churches that emerge from the reform movement that Martin Luther founded, or the theological doctrines that these churches profess and from which their life and particular forms of piety take their origin. This article will (1)

Luther's grave inside Schlosskirche, the Castle Church, where he posted his 95 Theses. Wittenberg, Germany. (©Dave Bartruff/ CORBIS)

sketch historically the profile of Lutheran church life, including theological development, to the present time; and (2) summarize the fundamental doctrines of Lutheranism as derived from documents recognized as normative by the Lutheran churches themselves.

For information on Lutheran churches in North America, *see* LUTHERAN CHURCHES IN NORTH AMERICA; EVANGELICAL LUTHERAN CHURCH IN AMERICA.

History of Lutheran Institutions and Church Life

Lutheranism came into being in Europe between 1520 and 1570. At the end of this period two-thirds of the people living in what today is modern Germany called themselves Lutherans, and the movement had taken root in several other countries on the Continent.

Germany. The conquest of Germany for Lutheranism was guaranteed by the Peace of AUGSBURG (1555) after much political and religious strife. The various princes were empowered to establish either the Catholic or Lutheran religion within their respective realms. Under the stress of rapid change, Martin Luther and his supporters formed a church polity that made it easy for Lutheran princes to set up state churches where Lutheranism was preached and they themselves remained in control of affairs.

Scandinavia. Outside Germany the most radical and successful dominion of Lutheranism came about in Scandinavia. In Denmark the movement was first supported by Frederick of Holstein (1523–33), who allowed the preaching of Lutheranism in 1527. Two years later it became by royal decree the sole religion of the land; Catholic doctrine and worship were banned. Christian III (1533–59), his successor, seized Church properties and replaced the seven bishops of his state with "superintendents," becoming himself the *summus episcopus*. A church disciplinary code was constructed by Johann BUGENHAGEN in 1537 and promulgated by force throughout the state, which included Norway and Iceland. In Sweden the transformation of the state into a Lutheran religious body was accomplished through the cooperation of a preacher, Olaus PETRI, who had studied in Wittenberg (1516–18), and a politician, Gustavus Eriksson Vasa, who obtained Sweden's political independence from Denmark in 1523 and founded a dynasty, ruling as king from 1523 to 1560. He used Petri, then preaching in

Stockholm, to effect the gradual transformation of the religious life of the people, with the intention of making his own power absolute. In 1527 the Diet of Väterås voted to break with Rome. In the new independent church the title of bishop and the apostolic succession were retained, but the king became its head, with the Lutheran archbishop of Uppsala his first lieutenant. Olaus published the first Swedish service book, *Een Handbock pää Swensko*, in 1529; the Catholic religion was banned from Sweden in 1544. Vasa was able to accomplish a similar change in Finland with the help of Michael Agricola and Peter Särkilathi.

Other Countries. The support of Polish nobles, whose sons had studied in Wittenberg, helped Lutheranism make inroads there. The reform of the Teutonic Knights according to a Lutheran pattern in 1525, under the aegis of its grand master, ALBRECHT OF BRANDEN-BURG-ANSBACH, opened the way to the imposition of Lutheran doctrine and practice along the Baltic. In Bohemia, students who had imbibed the spirit of the Lutheran Reformation, were welcomed by the calixtin descendants of John Hus and Bohemian Brethren. In Hungary, Matthew D. Biro, friend of Philipp MELANCHTHON, promoted Lutheranism among the Magyars until a visit to Switzerland in 1543 inclined him to Calvinism. Italy and the Iberian Peninsula were practically untouched by any form of the Reformation, while the rest of the Continent, especially Switzerland, parts of France, and the Low Countries, came under the almost exclusive sway of Calvinism (*see* REFORMED CHURCHES).

Doctrinal Controversy. During this period of expansion, the doctrinal basis of Lutheran life and belief was being melted down in the crucible of controversy. Its crystallization in the Formula of CONCORD (1577) was achieved after a series of adjustments and disputes that had lasted for almost a half-century from the date of Luther's break with Rome. The antitheses were several, for it was not merely a question of opposing Catholicism, but of finding agreement with non-Lutheran movements of reform, as well as doctrinal unanimity among Lutherans themselves.

As regards the ANABAPTISTS, who were the radicals or enthusiasts among the Reformers, no real controversy arose, for it was clear to those in the mainstream of the Lutheran movement that these were extremist groups. With the Calvinists it was otherwise. Though their orientation was basically the same as that of the Lutherans, disagreement arose particularly over the presence of Christ in the Eucharist. Martin BUCER, the leader of the Reformation at Strasbourg, who was subject to both Lutheran and Calvinist currents, acted as mediator in effecting the Wittenberg Concord (1536). Stauncher Lutherans

A plaque dedicated to Martin Luther in the Schlosskirche, the Castle Church, where Luther posted his 95 Theses and where he is buried. Wittenberg, Germany. (©Dave Bartruff/CORBIS)

opposed the agreement, and their suspicions were voiced in accusations leveled against such advocates of conciliation as Melanchthon. These they branded as Crypto-Calvinists.

Before the death of Luther, controversy had divided his disciples. Most notable of the debates was concerned with the relationship between the law and the gospel. Johann Agricola (J. Schnitter), the first champion of Antinomianism, rejected the Decalogue as unworthy of Christians and stated that faith sets the Christian free of law. Luther, himself, responded that the Commandments are altogether necessary, since the Church includes some not yet reborn, and since those who have experienced rebirth are still sinners. In *Der Grosse Catechismus* (1529) he included a long commentary on the Decalogue.

Resistance to Compromise. The most serious and bitter disputes arose after the death of Luther (1546). They involved two parties: the rigid conservatives led by Nikolaus von AMSDORF and Matthias FLACIUS ILLYRICUS; and the Philippists, who, as disciples of Melanchthon, urged doctrinal compromise and adaptation. The extent, though not the depth, of the disagreements appears in the Formula of Concord, where they were ostensibly resolved. Its structure shows that the contentions concerned mostly soteriological problems, which were the main concern of the Reformers. The articles of the epitome of the Formula treat of original sin, free will, righteousness before God through faith, good works, the law, and the gospel, as well as the Eucharist and questions concerning the Person and the work of Christ.

According to a temporal sequence, the first of the important differences involved the adiaphora. In the two Interims of the year 1548, the Lutherans were called upon to make certain doctrinal and ceremonial compromises in lieu of a final resolution of the problems by an ecumenical council. Melanchthon supported these proposals with the notion that there are certain factors in the Catholic religion that are, at very least, innocuous. As regards the Sacraments, he and other conciliatory theologians held that the rites of confirmation and the anointing of the sick are permissible. They showed similar tolerance for the veneration of the saints and other liturgical ceremonies and customs. The conservatives, proclaiming themselves Gnesio-Lutherans (of a pure and genuine strain), GNESIOLUTHERANISM, rejected Melanchthon's adiaphorism as well as his doctrine of synergism, which stated that man could exercise his innate power to accept or reject the prevenient grace of God. This position was attacked by members of the rigid party, who, appealing vigorously to the authority of the young Luther, stressed the radical corruption of man's nature, which made it necessary for him to receive a new will before he is even capable of accepting grace.

Connected with this basic disagreement in Lutheran doctrine of subjective redemption was the Osiandric controversy. Named after Andreas OSIANDER, it touched the notion of justification itself; is it merely forensic acquittal of man, the sinner; or is it an actual infusion of righteousness? Osiander taught that the sinner is made just by an infusion of the divine nature of Christ. The place of good works in the process of justification brought on the ''Majoristic'' controversy. Georg MAJOR, a disciple of Melanchthon and professor at Wittenberg, taught that good works following justification are necessary for salvation. Amsdorf countered that good works are, on the contrary, dangerous to salvation. Even Melanchthon considered Major's position extreme and preferred to state simply that good works are necessary.

Search for Orthodoxy. In the meantime, the confessional literature of the Lutherans had grown extensively. To the Confession of AUGSBURG and the Apology thereof (written by Melanchthon, with the approval of Luther) were added the Articles of Schmalkald, Melanchthon's treatise on the power of the papacy, and the two catechisms of Luther. None of these documents had been canonically approved, however; and little by little the

leaders of the Lutheran Reformation felt the need for a document, especially since the Lutheran theologians were divided into two camps, those of the University of Jena (the self-styled Gnesio-Lutherans) and those of the University of Wittenberg. The Formula of Concord is, then, the result of the attempt to mediate and unite Lutherans. Its redaction was due in great part to theologians of the Gnesio-Lutheran type, although not of the extreme right: Jakob Andreä (1520–90), Martin CHEMNITZ, Nikolaus Selnecker (1530–92), and David CHYTRAEUS. Paradoxically, although Lutheran orthodoxy had been present in embryo during this formative period, the Formula made it possible for it to develop systematically.

The orthodox theologians aimed at systematizing the established teaching of the confessional writings. The existence of a certain canonized consensus was a prerequisite to such an endeavor. Lutheran orthodoxy, therefore, was born from the apparent resolution of the controversies that took place in the second generation of Lutheranism. Agreement on the Formula of Concord in 1580 effected both a cohesion of the parties previously at odds with each other and a concern for accurate expression of doctrine. The vehicles of this accuracy were biblical proofs and an elaboration of their meaning according to Aristotelian categories. Another factor in the emergence of orthodoxy was the continuing and ever sharper polemic against the Church of Rome and various Protestant groups. The authority of Luther was at high tide; and the paradox of orthodoxy itself consists in its virtual equation of his dicta with those of the Bible. The representatives of this school were not so much interested in him as a person, as in a witness of true doctrine.

The orthodoxy in embryo that was represented by Flacius Illyricus found its full emergence in the works of Johann GERHARD. His *Loci theologici* (9 v. compl. in 1622) is the best specimen of what Lutheran orthodoxy says. It is more than a body of doctrinal writings, and must be understood from its motives. The orthodox theologians were certainly intent on defending the honor of Luther and the truth of his teaching. The rigidity of this defense, however, can only be explained by the fact that the system gradually began to be considered as inviolable. This development eventually jeopardized both the apology for the validity of Luther's vocation to reform the Church and the claims for absolute parity of doctrine. The rigidity soon produced a protest in the form of Lutheran Pietism.

Even during the age of the orthodox ascendancy, the humanist tradition was present in the bosom of Lutheranism, for example, in the person of Georg CALIXTUS, who insisted on the *consensus quinquesaecularis*, the agreement of the Church during the first five centuries on certain fundamental articles of faith. Thus, he evoked the notion of tradition and brought down upon himself from orthodox quarters the accusation of syncretism. The ecumenical labor of Calixtus was stillborn, but it helped maintain a certain awareness within the Lutheran community that the Reformation and its continuation was for the sake of the Church.

Pietism. PIETISM was in great measure a reaction against what seemed to be the unrealistic speculation of orthodox theology, and also against the formalistic church life that followed from it. The need for more vitality was felt, especially at the end of the devastating Thirty Years' War (1618–48). On the other hand, Pietism was also a continuing expression of the humanist strain in German Lutheranism. Veit von Seckendorf (1626–92) and Gottfried W. LEIBNIZ did not belong to any Pietist school, but their lives exhibit an openness that does not accord with the spirit of orthodoxy.

Most representative of the Pietists is Philipp Jakob SPENER. For 20 years (1666–86), he served as pastor for a congregation in Frankfurt am Main; and it was there that the movement came alive. Spener organized small Bible study-circles (*ecclesiolae*), the work of which was almost exclusively ethically oriented. The Scriptures were treated not as the sources of proof-texts for speculative theological conclusions, but as the immediate font of spiritual enlightenment and strength—experience. The name, Pietist, was first given to these groups in derision. Spener later went to Berlin and spent the last ten years of his life at the recently founded University of Halle (1694), which thus became the center of Pietism. To Halle also came August H. FRANCKE, who at Leipzig had organized groups similar to the ones Spener had founded in Frankfurt. The separatism his disciples manifested toward other Lutherans at Leipzig brought friction and eventually caused him to leave. Halle, thus, became to Pietism what Wittenberg had been to the early Reformation.

Lutheran Pietism was never a tightly organized movement; therefore, it took various forms according to the milieu in which it developed. For example, whereas in Halle the Pietists tended to be rigoristic and ecclesiologically separatist, in Würtemberg they were more attached to the Lutheran Church and to deeper theological reflection. Elsewhere, eccentric groups such as the Herrnhuter of Nikolaus L. ZINZENDORF (*see* MORAVIAN CHURCH) emerged from the movement, as did also sectarian assemblies such as the Engelbrüder.

Personal Experiences of Salvation. Pietism was more than a reaction against orthodox rigidity. As with the other manifestations of Lutheranism it accented one of the other principles emphasized by the Reformers. In this case, stress was on the personal experience of salvation. The pessimism concerning human nature that characterized earlier Lutheran thought was softened, and the priority of experience over speculation of any kind was affirmed. At the same time the Pietists departed slightly from a tightly formulated scriptural principle in the direction of the independence of the individual in making his religious judgments and decisions. By this avenue a species of pure subjectivism made its appearance, and, even though the Pietists did give the Bible to the people, by their disregard for dogma they smoothed the way for the *Aufklärung*.

The Enlightenment. What Pietism conceived, the *Aufklärung* brought forth. During this 18th-century period, Lutheranism was besieged by rationalism and was thereby transformed. The object of belief became of less and less moment, for the criterion of religiosity according to the rationalists was conscientiousness. The Lutherans of the *Aufklärung* still revered Martin Luther as their patriarch; not as the expounder of the biblical doctrine of justification by faith, however, but as the patron saint of the principle of the absolute independence of the individual in religious matters. Thus appeared the cleavage within Lutheranism itself, that is implicit in the simultaneous proclamation of biblical doctrine and affirmation of the principle of undetermined independence in its interpretation.

The leaders of the *Aufklärung* did not abandon the Bible; they put it to the test of the kind of criticism that dominated the next century. Johann S. Semler laid the foundation for this new approach to the Scriptures. At the same time Gotthold E. LESSING led the attack against orthodoxy with his notion of a formal Lutheranism, which consisted in the exercise of the right of every man to absolute religious freedom, after the example of Luther. These orientations met the whole-hearted approval of political leaders, including Frederick the Great.

Neo-Lutheranism. The first reaction to rationalism was heralded at the very apex of the *Aufklärung* in the life and work of Johann G. HERDER and Johann G. HAMANN. The "back to Luther" movement that they represented was a revival of the doctrine of justification by faith. These neo-Lutherans, who appeared when the spirit of romanticism was flourishing, appealed to the fundamental beliefs of the Reformation and made them meaningful by providing access to the Bible, as the source of preaching and teaching, without unwarranted concessions to the rationalism of that era.

Liberalism. As a result of the rationalist revolution, however, the spirit of the *Aufklärung* was translated into the liberal theology of the 19th century, represented by Ernst TROELTSCH and Adolf von HARNACK, and thence into the 20th under the leadership of such theologians as Rudolf BULTMANN. At the same time a more conservative line was held by other churchmen and deepened theologically by a more critical view of Reformation sources, e.g., the work of Edmund Schlink.

Thus, the general pattern of the history of Lutheranism has been affected radically by the interaction of two opposing forces that were present from the beginning: Martin Luther's emphasis on religious experience and Flacius Illyricus's penchant for rational systematization of doctrine. Subsequently the former emphasis, always as a reaction against overrationalization, has appeared in Pietism, romanticism, and the more contemporary forms of Lutheran existentialism. The rationalizing tendency has been mostly a reaction against excessive confidence in experience. The Pietists, for example, unwittingly and certainly unintentionally permitted rationalism itself to play a role in the history of Lutheranism; just as romanticism ceded to the more modern attempts to control religion rationally.

Ecumenism. The political upheaval, especially in Europe, after 1850, plus a half-century of ecumenism have continued to modify the status of Lutheranism as an institution. Politics has had its greatest effect in Germany, where the Lutheran churches are no longer state churches. In other countries too, there is evidence of a reconsideration of the relevance of establishment.

The drama of the rise and fall of the Third Reich is a conspicuous factor in the growth of the ecumenical trend among Lutherans. The first effect was the split of German Lutherans into several groups, on the basis of their varied view of the political regime. Common persecution, however, produced a unifying force, especially in the *Una Sancta* movement, which in postwar years has made Germany a lively center of ecumenical activity. Lutherans of such various tendencies as Otto Dibelius, Martin Niemöller, Hanns Lilje, and Franklin C. Fry played important roles in the formation of the WORLD COUNCIL OF CHURCHES. In the dialogue with the Roman Catholic Church, of special significance is a postwar group of Lutheran theologians who have advocated corporate reunion with the Church of Rome. This "League for Evangelical-Catholic Reunion" has no official status within Lutheranism. Its principles have been stated and are currently being developed in the writings of Max Lackmann, Hans Asmussen, and Richard Baumann.

Another effect of ecumenism within Lutheranism was the formation of the Lutheran World Federation (Der Lutherische Weltbund) in 1947. A free association of Lutheran churches, it is bound together by the traditional Lutheran confessional writings. Under its auspices a center of interconfessional research is maintained in Strasbourg.

Fundamental Doctrine of Lutheranism

Historians and theologians alike are accustomed to presenting the Reformation as grounded in a material and a formal principle. The former is the doctrine of justification by faith (*sola fide*); the latter is Scripture, which certifies this doctrine (*sola Scriptura*). They further assign one of the principles to each of the two leaders of the Reformation: Martin Luther as the champion of the *sola fide*, while John Calvin is responsible for the strong scriptural emphasis.

If this simple presupposition were adequate, then a sufficient knowledge of Lutheranism could be found in an analysis of what Luther and his immediate disciples understood by "justifying faith," together with an account of subsequent variations in its understanding. The reality is otherwise, however; for, despite the obvious differences in the orientation of Luther and Calvin, the Reformation represents a certain unity in which several confessions have become interpenetrated. Hence Lutheran doctrine—as the articulation of the particular Lutheran experience—takes in much more than a statement of Martin Luther's insight concerning justification. Nor can it be sealed off from the so-called Calvinist scriptural principle, even though, admittedly, the Lutheran interpretation of this principle appears to be (at least implicitly) more radical than that of either Calvin himself or the majority of his adherents.

On the condition that these cautions are observed, however, it is not impossible to apply the twofold principle to Lutheran doctrine itself. Comprising the material element are such things as justification by faith and the church as the "assembly of believers." Each of these factors is complex. The Lutheran concept of justification presupposes a particular understanding of the condition of the human will (*servum arbitrium*) before the advent of justifying faith. It also includes a comprehension of the relationship between law and gospel as well as the distinctive grasp of the meaning of faith. Likewise, Lutheran doctrine on the church is a complexus of convictions having to do both with factors constitutive of the church and with mutual relationships of the church with other societies. On the one hand, the formal element is the insistence on the primacy of the canonical Scriptures in matters of doctrine, and on the other, it is the right of the individual conscience to determine freely its adhesion to or separation from a given doctrine.

Despite the tensions, if not contradictions, that have occurred in the development of this Lutheran body of doctrine, and have prevented it from achieving a cohesive and changeless form, the main doctrinal points can be described.

Sinful Man before God. The principal concern of all Lutheran theology—and this in accord with the concern of Luther himself—is the relationship of God and man. As a son of Adam, man is under the power of Satan. What is his status before God? The language Lutherans use in answer to this question is very strong. The Formula of Concord approvingly attributes the following statement to Luther himself: "Our free will has no power whatsoever in virtue of which man could prepare himself for justice or even seek it out. On the contrary, blind and captive man gives exclusive obedience to Satan's will and perpetrates thereby things offensive to God" (*Solids declaratio* 2; *Die Bekenntnisschriften der evangelisch-lutherischen Kirche* [BSLK] 889). On this basis alone one might be inclined to use the term "totally depraved" in reference to the Lutheran concept of human nature. That, however, would not be just in light of this further statement: "Fallen man does not cease to be a rational creature . . .; furthermore, in civil and external matters he is able somewhat to discern the good from the bad and even freely to do some things and desist from others" (*ibid.* 879). The entire matter is viewed in a religious context; fallen man, on his own, is absolutely helpless, as far as the God-relationship is concerned. "Before conversion man is, indeed, a rational creature, having intellect and will (though no understanding of divine realities nor will to do what is good and salvific). He is, nonetheless, able to contribute nothing to his own conversion" (*ibid.* 895–896).

A difficulty that pervades the Lutheran synthesis of the God-man relationship appears here. If man is unable to contribute anything to his own conversion, is he really able to be converted? This Lutheran doctrine, as proposed in the confessional writings and traditionally explained by theologians, is susceptible to being understood in a sense consonant with the teaching of the Council of Trent (H. Denzinger, *Enchiridion symbolorum* 1551–53; cf. 1554–55, 1557, 1559), although the accent is indeed heavy upon the notion of human impotence and depravity.

Law and Gospel. The omnipotent Word of God breaks through the impotency of fallen man in two distinct forms: (1) in the preaching of the law, which makes man aware of his sins and the wrath of God, for "the Law, properly so-called, is any divine doctrine wherein is set forth the most just and changeless will of God, concerning the obligations incumbent on man as regards his being, and his thoughts, words, and deeds, with a view towards his attaining God's approval and acceptance" (Formula of Concord, *Solida declaratio* 5; BSLK 957); and (2) in the heralding of the Gospel, which consists exclusively in the proclamation of God's graciousness and clemency, made visible in the forgiveness of sins; this leads to faith, because the Gospel consists in the "doc-

trine which states what a miserable sinner must believe in order to be forgiven his sins by God" (*ibid.* 958).

This is the familiar Lutheran distinction between law and Gospel. Both deserved to be proclaimed, the former as subordinate and directed to the latter. And the force of the Lutheran witness is accented by the observation that to confuse law and Gospel with each other leads to an obscuring of the merit and good works of Christ, and a transformation of Gospel into law, "such as we see has happened under the Papacy" (*ibid.* 961).

The Lutherans protested that in the Church of the late Middle Ages the Gospel was presented as a set of obligations, which, when fulfilled, ensure God's approval and acceptance of man. This charge has been transmitted in the confessional writings, as well as in the thought of contemporary Lutheran theologians. For them, universally, the word productive of faith is the proclamation that "the son of God, our Lord Jesus Christ, took upon himself the burden of the Law's curse; that he offered altogether adequate satisfaction for our sins, in such wise that through Him alone are we reconciled with God, receiving forgiveness of sins through faith, freedom from death and the other punishments of sin and eternal salvation" (*ibid.* 958).

Fiducial Faith. In the process of justification, man's response to God is shown in his firm confidence in the merits of Christ. "Justification calls for three things, and three things only: God's grace, Christ's merit, and faith. Faith, moreover, takes hold of the very gifts which God promises in the Gospel; and on its account the righteousness of Christ is deemed ours. Through it also we have our sins forgiven; we are reconciled with God; and we become his adopted children and heirs of eternal life" (Formula of Concord, *Solida declaratio* 3; BSLK 922). When the Gospel is proclaimed, both the grace of God and the merit of Christ are set forth openly, and this in the form of a promise: the graciousness of God the Father belongs to the man who trusts solely in the merit of Christ. Fiducial faith, then, according to the Lutheran position, is an attitude of total confidence in the merit of Christ; and its correlative is justification or righteousness.

Although this position does not accord altogether with the description of faith as furnished, for example, by Vatican Council I (H. Denzinger, *Enchiridion symbolorum* 3008), in which both the gratuity of this divine gift and the revealed truth to which faith clings are emphasized, still the Lutheran concept of faith is not devoid of reference to the content of the Gospel. "Faith is a gift of God whereby through the word of the Gospel we rightly acknowledge [*agnoscimus*] Christ as our Redeemer and put our trust [*confidimus*] in him . . ." (BSLK 917–918). Thus two elements are necessary, but any mere knowledge (Melanchthon called it *otiosa notitia*) of revealed dogmas is not worthy of the name faith. "Faith is not mere knowledge, but much more the will to receive or take to oneself whatever is offered in the promise concerning Christ" (*Apology for the Confession of Augsburg* 4; BSLK 203). Lutherans, furthermore, distinguish between conversion and justification. The latter involves solely and exclusively the faith described above. Conversion, on the other hand, includes such realities as sanctification and the renewal of one's life—good works. These latter are never thought of as meritorious, but rather, as the natural fruit and sign of true righteousness.

All of the factors of the Christian life set forth by St. Paul and synthesized in the tradition of the Church are present also in the Lutheran doctrine of justification and conversion, but with the additional element that produces the radically different order given to the doctrine, namely, the Lutheran preoccupation with the personal certitude of justification. This accounts for the emphasis upon confidence or trust as an element of faith and the insistence that good works are not properly a part of justification. It also illumines the meaning of the Lutheran slogan, *simul justus et peccator*. In the Lutheran conception, *justus* refers properly to the man of faith who has trust in the promises made in Christ, and not to the man of faith inasmuch as he is "converted," i.e., interiorly, though imperfectly, renewed.

Ecclesiology. Lutheran ecclesiology takes its origin from Martin Luther's interpretation of the common priesthood of the faithful. From it stems the description of the church provided by the Confession of Augsburg, "The assembly of believers where the Gospel is preached in its purity and the sacraments are rightly administered." To be a believer is to be a constitutive member of the holy people of God, whom St. Peter calls "a chosen race [and] a royal priesthood" (1 Pt 2.9). The sense attached to these propositions was affected by the situation in the early years of the Reformation. As it appeared to Luther and his disciples, the crucial hindrance to reform in the Church was the attitude of the bishops, including the Roman Curia. This view took the form of a dilemma; either cede to the bishops and abandon the movement for a reform or proceed without them. By choosing the latter course, Lutherans radically affected their ecclesiology. However, because the Gospel must be preached and the Sacraments administered, the assembly of believers requires "ministering men." These are provided for by choice and ordination in such ways that they are considered representatives of the congregation. There is an ambiguity in such an arrangement, but Lutheran theologians have, for the most part, been satisfied to continue the emphasis upon the common priesthood of the faithful, leaving the doctrinal basis for a ministry uncertain.

Church and State. In 16th-century Germany the bishops of the Church as temporal lords were key figures in determining the balance of political power. Lutheran denouncement of episcopal hegemony in the Church, therefore, constrained them to depend on princes and nobles for the support of their religious views. This led eventually to the *cujus regio ejus religio* settlement of the Peace of Augsburg. More significant was the tendency to put the choice of the ministers of their church into the hands of Lutheran princes and thus to make way for the state church. The Augsburg Confession teaches that "ecclesiastical power and the power of the sword are different one from the other. Furthermore, both of them, according to God's command, are to be revered religiously and treated with honor as the highest gifts of God on earth" (art. 28). In Lutheranism, therefore, political society and the assembly of believers differ, one from the other, but the differences are not explicitly enunciated. As a result of this lack of clarity in doctrine, Lutheran churches became subjected to the control of the "venerable" political authority as state churches, with the restrictions this implies. The condition of Lutheranism in North America and in Germany in the 20th century indicates that it is viable in a more pluralistic society. There is a tendency today to question the relevance of the state church in Europe, which might lead to a reassessment of the notion of the "two powers."

From the Lutheran idea that faith creates the church, it might be concluded that the church is an invisible reality. However, the audible word of the gospel and the visible sign of the Sacraments are to be witnesses to the divine promise—remission of sins through the merits of Christ, whose sacrifice the Father accepts on our behalf. "Just as the word [of the Gospel] falls upon the ear and thus strikes the heart, so the [sacramental] rites are set forth before our eyes also to move the heart . . . . The eyes take in the rite which is a picture of the Word, as it were, signifying the same thing as the Word. So they have exactly the same effect" (*Apology for the Confession of Augsburg* 13; BSLK 292–293).

Therefore the church is visible, but only to those who have this faith in the promises of God. And the real church has as members those who hear the Gospel and see the Sacraments fruitfully. Wherever the Gospel is heard and the Sacraments are seen, faith is conceived in some: this is the church.

Sacramental System. The term sacrament refers to three rites, all of which, according to the Lutheran view, have their divine origin guaranteed in the Scriptures: baptism, penance, and the Eucharist (*Apology for the Confession of Augsburg, loc. cit.*). Notwithstanding the conviction that faith is a requisite factor for the fruitfulness of the Sacraments (*ibid.*), the practice of infant baptism is retained on the grounds that the church owes them the proclamation of the promises on which the church's life is based.

Lutheran doctrine concerning the Eucharist was formulated first in opposition to certain dogmatic positions of the Roman Catholic Church and became more defined in debates with Calvinistic and Zwinglian divines. Thus the following two composite theses are paramount: (1) in the Eucharist the Body and Blood of Christ are present in, with, and beneath [the forms] of bread and wine; and thus they are our souls' real meat and drink; (2) only those who believe actually profit from reception of the Eucharist; and faith is at the same time awakened and bolstered in them. Nonbelievers, moreover, receive the Body and Blood of Christ to their condemnation.

In the 16th century, Lutherans inveighed strongly against the Mass as a sacrifice; their objection was in keeping with the first principle of their ecclesiology, the common priesthood. The debate suffered from misunderstanding concerning the teaching of the Catholic Church on the sacrificial character of eucharistic worship. Hence this has become a lively topic in 20th-century ecumenical dialogue.

Present-day Lutheran theologians are mostly silent about the sacrament of penance; and, although the dicta of the *Apology* stand as such, the practice of confession is rare in the Lutheran churches.

Scripture and Tradition. The "formal" part of Lutheranism is a complex of convictions about the way the doctrinal content of its confession of faith is received, preserved, and developed. The first element of this complex consists in authoritative documents, especially the Old and New Testaments. According to the Formula of Concord, the Scriptures are the one and only rule and norm (*norma normans*), according to which all dogmas and all teachers, living or dead, are to be judged. Other documents are enumerated, but with careful emphasis on their circumstantial and, therefore, temporary character in relation to the Scriptures. Just as the ancient creeds were formulated to combat primitive heresies, so too the Lutheran confessional writings (a list is given in which the Confession of Augsburg and its companion Apology rank first in authority) were necessarily constructed to clarify the religious questions of the 16th century. These latter documents are designated as *normae normatae*. They stand as authoritative but in subjection to the judgment of the Scriptures.

Besides the Scriptures, however, Lutheranism admits a notion of tradition, composed of two factors: (1) the authority of the university professors, who *de facto*

have served as quasi-official interpreters of Lutheran doctrine, and (2) the observation of what has occurred in the Lutheran churches through the centuries, as various influences and currents of thought affected them.

Perhaps this can be understood initially through reflection on Martin Luther's own protest before the Diet of Worms: "Unless I am convicted by Scripture and plain reason—I do not accept the authority of popes and councils, for they have contradicted each other—my conscience is captive to the word of God. I cannot and I will not recant anything, for to go against conscience is neither right nor safe. God help me. Amen." [R. H. Bainton, *Here I Stand* (New York 1950) 195].

The formal element in Lutheranism, therefore, is Holy Scripture as authoritatively interpreted through the Lutheran confessional writings and as understood through the "Lutheran conscience"—however that may be formed in a given epoch, and to the exclusion of any exterior constraining norm. Note that any explicit reference to the "interior testimony of the Holy Spirit" as a normative factor is practically absent from the Lutheran tradition.

Bibliography: K. ALGERMISSEN, *Konfessionskunde* (Celle 1957), extensive bibliog. and full treatment; Eng. tr. J. W. GRUNDNER, of an earlier edition, *Christian Denominations* (St. Louis 1945). *Die Bekenntnisschriften der evangelisch-lutherischen Kirche.* S. GRUNDMANN, *Der lutherische Weltbund: Grundlagen, Herkunft, Aufbau* (Cologne 1957), with bibliog. E. SCHLINK, *Theologie der lutherischen Bekenntnisschriften* (Munich 1946). H. H. W. KRAMM, *The Theology of Martin Luther* (London 1949). J. PELIKAN, *From Luther to Kirkegaard* (St. Louis 1950). W. ELERT, *The Structure of Lutheranism*, tr. W. A. HANSEN (St. Louis 1962—). A. K. SWIHART, *Luther and the Lutheran Church* (New York 1960). L. FUERBRINGER et al., *Concordia Cyclopedia* (St. Louis 1927). G. W. FORELL, *Faith Active in Love: An Investigation of Principles underlying Luther's Social Ethics* (New York 1954). H. WEINEL, *Die Deutsche evangelische Kirche* (Gotha 1933). H. SASSE, *Was heisst lutherisch?* (Munich 1934); *Here We Stand: Nature and Character of the Lutheran Faith*, tr. T. G. TAPPERT (New York 1938); *This Is My Body* (Minneapolis 1959). H. W. GENSICHEN, *Damnamus. Die Verwerfung von Irrlehre bei Luther und im Luthertum des 16. Jahrhunderts* (Berlin 1955). F. UHLHORN, *Geschichte der deutschen—lutheranischen Kirche*, 2 v. (Leipzig 1911). E. G. RUPP, *The Righteousness of God: Luther Studies* (New York 1954). E. M. CARLSON, *The Reinterpretation of Luther* (Philadelphia 1948). *The Book of Concord*, tr. H. T. DAU and F. BENTE (St. Louis 1921). *The Lutheran Churches of the World*, ed. A. R. WENTZ (Geneva 1952). H. E. JACOBS and J. A. W. HAAS, eds., *Lutheran Encyclopedia* (New York 1899). E. ROTH, *Sakrament nach Luther* (Berlin 1952). H. GRASS, *Die Abendmahlslehre bei Luther and Calvin* Gütersloh 1954). H. BORNKAMM, *Luther im Spiegel der Deutschen Geistgeschichte* (Heidelberg 1955). E. W. ZEEDEN, *Martin Luther und die Reformation im Urteil des deutschen Luthertums*, 2 v. (Freiburg 1950–52), v.1 tr. R. M. BETHELL, *The Legacy of Luther* (Westminster, MD 1954). H. ASMUSSEN et al., *The Unfinished Reformation*, tr. R. J. OLSEN (Notre Dame, IN 1961). H. E. JACOBS, *Encyclopedia of Religion and Ethics*, ed. J. HASTINGS (Edinburgh 1908–27) 8:202–204. J. PACQUIER, *Dictionnaire de théologie catholique*, ed.

A. VACANT et al., (Paris 1903–50) 91:1183–1335, with bibliog. F. L. CROSS, *The Oxford Dictionary of the Christian Church* (London 1957) 833–835. K. ALGERMISSEN, *Lexikon für Theologie und Kirche*, ed. M. BUCHBERGER (Freiburg 1930–38) 6:732–739. E. W. ZEEDEN and E. KINDER, *Lexikon für Theologie und Kirche*, ed. J. HOFER and K. RAHNER (Freiburg 1957–65) 6:1231–40. E. W. ZEEDEN and J. P. MICHAEL, *Staatslexikon*, ed. GÖRRES-GESELLSCHAFT (Freiburg 1957–63) 5:475–482. G. EBELING, *Die Religion in Geschichte und Gegenwart* (Tübingen 1957–65) 4:495–520, with bibliog.

[M. B. SCHEPERS/EDS.]

LUX MUNDI

Lux Mundi is the title of a book of theological essays published in 1889 (4th ed. 1890), subtitled *A Series of Studies in the Religion of the Incarnation*. It was edited by Charles GORE, Anglican Bishop of Oxford, and did much to transform the Anglo–Catholic movement in the Church of England (*see* ANGLO–CATHOLICS). The book was written after a group of young Oxford men had become impatient with the superficial "Romanizing" tendencies of the ritualists and the obscurantist fundamentalism in which Edward PUSEY and others would have imprisoned the OXFORD MOVEMENT. This group was also deeply concerned with the social question and with the sense of responsibility for the well–being of all men, including the poor and underprivileged, that Gore had learned from B. F. WESTCOTT, and Westcott from the Christian socialism of F. D. MAURICE. The most memorable pages in *Lux Mundi* occur in the essay "The Holy Spirit and Inspiration," written by Gore himself. This essay marked the beginning of Liberal Catholicism in the Church of England, because its author affirmed that it is not inconsistent with the Catholic faith to accept the reasonable results of higher criticism of the Scriptures and the well–founded discoveries of science. The brief preface to the book, also written by Gore, explained the purpose of this "new look" in Anglo–Catholicism: "We have written in this volume not as 'guessers of truth,' but as servants of the Catholic creed and Church, aiming only at interpreting the faith we have received." All the authors of *Lux Mundi* were extremely conscious of continuity with the Catholic past and also of the need for "great changes in the outlying departments of theology" to meet the "new needs, new points of view, new questions" of the times. Other contributors to *Lux Mundi* were canons H. Scott Holland and Aubrey Moore, J. R. Illingworth, E. S. Talbot, R. C. Mobberly, Arthur Lyttelton, W. Lock, F. Paget, W. J. H. Campion, and R. L. Ottley. *Lux Mundi* was severely attacked by such prominent High Church leaders as Henry Parry Liddon and was publicly assailed in Convocation.

Bibliography: J. K. MOZLEY, *Some Tendencies in British Theology from the Publication of Lux Mundi to the Present Day* (Society for Promoting Christian Knowledge 1951). A. M. RAMSEY, *From Gore to Temple* (London 1960). J. CARPENTER, *Gore: A Study in Liberal Catholic Thought* (London 1960).

[W. HANNAH]

LUXEMBOURG, THE CATHOLIC CHURCH IN

The Grand Duchy of Luxembourg is bordered on the east by Germany, on the south by France and on the west by Belgium. Located in the plateau region of the Ardennes, the region's terrain consists of rolling hills rising to low mountains in the east, and falling to the Moselle river valley in the southeast. Wooded areas abound and natural resources include iron ore, which is no longer mined; agricultural crops, nourished by the region's mild climate and grown on small, family-run farms, include barley, oats, wheat, grapes, fruits and potatoes. Luxembourg exports steel, rubber and chemical products throughout Europe, the United Kingdom and the United States, and was one of the original founders of the European Economic Community (now the European Union). In the late 20th century banking grew into a major component of its economy. In 1999 it entered the agreement to utilize the Euro currency.

Founded in 963 and with its roots in the Holy Roman Empire, the grand duchy passed through German, Spanish and Habsburg control before coming into formal existence in 1815 at the Congress of Vienna. It remained part of the kingdom of the Netherlands until 1839, when a revolt by neighboring Belgium resulted in the loss of half its area to that country. Political control was retained by the Netherlands, and then Germany until World War I. The region—neutral through both world wars— was occupied by German forces from 1940 to 1944, and joined NATO following World War II. Luxembourg is a constitutional monarchy in which legislative power resides in a chamber of deputies composed of one representative for every 5,500 inhabitants. There is an executive council with seven ministers. The Nassau-Weilbourg family, Catholics, have ruled since 1912. Ecclesiastically, Luxembourg has an archdiocese located in the city of Luxembourg that is immediately subject to the Holy See. Our Lady, Comfort of the Afflicted, whose miraculous image has been venerated since 1624, is the patroness of the city and Duchy of Luxembourg. The image continues to attract many pilgrims, especially during the octave of her feast on the 3d to 5th Sundays after Easter.

Catholic Church to 1500. Christian communities established themselves in the region during the 5th and

6th centuries under the influence of the important Christian centers in TRIER and LIÈGE. The consolidation of Christianity continued until the end of the 8th century; it owed much to the activities of St. WILLIBRORD, the English Benedictine missionary. The parish system developed in the 9th century. Most of Luxembourg pertained to the See of Liège and, still more, to the See of Trier; smaller sections belonged to the dioceses of Metz, Verdun, REIMS and COLOGNE.

Monasteries were established early and exercised political and cultural as well as religious influence. Saint Hubert was founded in 687 (occupied by Benedictines in 817), Saint Maximin in Trier in the 7th or 8th century, Prüm in 721 and Münster in the town of Luxembourg in 1083. Orval, founded in 1071 by the Benedictines, passed to the Canons Regular of St. Augustine in 1110 and to the Cistercians in 1132.

The Abbey of ECHTERNACH, founded in 698, gained wide renown for its school of copyists, which flourished in the 11th century, when it produced such masterpieces as the Golden Gospel Books, now in Nuremberg, Uppsala and the Escorial. The church and monastery built (1016–31) over the grave of St. Willibrord in Echternach remained a notable example of early Romanesque architecture. A dancing religious procession continued to take place annually on that site since the 14th century on Whit-Tuesday still attracted thousands of pilgrims into the 21st century.

Soon after their foundation Teutonic Knights and Knights Hospitallers established houses in Luxembourg, as did Dominicans, Franciscans and their respective orders of nuns. The best-remembered medieval religious women are St. KUNIGUNDE (d. 1033), daughter of Duke Siegfried II of Luxembourg and wife of Emperor Henry II, and Blessed Yolanda of Vianden (d. 1283).

Since 1500. In 1354 the Duchy of Luxembourg was created; during the Middle Ages its rulers sometimes attained European significance as heads of the Holy Roman Empire while losing contact with Luxembourg itself. This phenomenon left its mark on the historical development of the Church, as political alliances were arranged with Burgundy (1441–43), the Spanish Hapsburgs (1506) and then Austria (1714). During the FRENCH REVOLUTION the duchy was incorporated into the French Republic as a department. Not until the 19th century would the region's political autonomy prompt the development of a unified diocesan ecclesiastical structure.

During the 15th and 16th centuries abuses invaded many monasteries and lowered the religious and moral life of the clergy. Since Luxembourg was part of the southern province of the Spanish Netherlands and had the

Archdiocese of Trier to the east acting as a spiritual bulwark, it was protected from the influence of the Protestant Reformation. The establishment of Luxembourg as a separate diocese was urged from the time of King Philip II, but the request was not granted partly because of the opposition of the bishops of Liège and Trier, both eager to preserve their feudal rights. The Jesuit College in the town of Luxembourg benefited the entire duchy (1602–1773). The Jesuits had a special devotion to the Blessed Virgin, which they spread by their teaching, preaching and missionary labors.

The 17th-century Gothic Cathedral of Notre Dame in Luxembourg city. (©Carmen Redondo/CORBIS)

In the 17th and 18th centuries priestly vocations, especially to the Jesuits, were numerous. Some of these Jesuits became influential advisers at European courts, notably Karl von Mansfeld and Wilhelm LAMORMAINI. The brothers W. and A. Wiltheim, J. Reuter, C. Lacroix, F. X. de Feller and others gained fame as writers.

Neither JOSEPHINISM nor the ENLIGHTENMENT made much impact on the loyal Catholic Luxembourgers. The French Revolution, however, resulted in the confiscation of almost all the goods of nobles and monasteries. This great political and social upheaval also created a new class, composed often of foreigners with newly acquired wealth, that conducted, mildly at first and then ever more aggressively, a campaign of ANTICLERICALISM, using political means to create a new ideological climate. In the transitional period the intellectual quality of clerical education deteriorated.

Luxembourg fell under first the dioceses of Metz (1801–23) and then Namur (1823–40). Its ecclesiastical status was finally stabilized in 1840 with the creation of the Vicariate Apostolic of Luxembourg. J. T. Laurent, the first vicar apostolic, was a distinguished prelate, firm on matters of principle, who had been exiled from the country (1842–48). The vicariate became a diocese in 1870. Until 1908 it was subject to the Congregation for the Propagation of the Faith, and was recognized by the state in 1873. A state-funded seminary was opened in 1845.

Beginning in the late 19th century, numerous vocations to the priesthood and to missionary religious orders developed in the diocese. From 1880 until World War II diocesan priests traveled to German and French dioceses, to Norway and to the United States. However, vocations dropped sharply after the mid-1900s. By 2000 there were 215 diocesan and 80 religious priests administering to the duchy's 275 parishes, while 17 brothers and 734 sisters performed educational and other social ministrations. Because of the shortage of clergy, the Church began to increase the level of participation among lay Catholics.

In addition to funding private religious schools, the state mandated religious instruction in public primary and secondary schools. A convention signed in 1997 provided local autonomy in such religious education, and allowed parents to choose between Roman Catholicism or ethics. In accordance with the Napoleonic French CONCORDAT OF 1801 and the Luxembourg constitution of Oct. 17, 1868, Catholic churches, as well as churches of other denominations, were funded by the state. Despite its majority status, Catholicism was not a state religion. Protestants in Luxembourg were predominately of Lutheran and Calvinist denominations; minority faiths included Jews, Greek and Russian Orthodox, Muslim and Anglican.

Luxembourg's influential role within the European community was stressed by Pope John Paul II during an ad limina visit by Luxembourg Archbishop Fernand Franck in December of 1997. The pope had special praise for Luxembourg's support of Catholic social doctrines amid a materialist society. Archbishop Franck continued to remain an active voice in Europe's Catholic community, noting at the 1999 European Synod that the focus of the Church in the 21st century should be to assist in the creation of stable "multicultural and multi-religious societies" that would benefit people of all faiths.

Bibliography: C. WAMPACH, *Urkunden- und Quellenbuch zur Geschichte der altluxemburgischen Territorien bis zur burgundischen Zeit,* 10 v. (Luxembourg 1935–55). R. M. STAUD and J. REUTER, *Die kirchlichen Kunstdenkmäler der Diözese Luxemburg* (Luxembourg 1935–). C. J. HERSCHEN, *Manuel d'histoire nationale,* rev. N. MARGUE and J. MEYERS (5th ed. Luxembourg 1947), Eng. tr. A. H. COOPER-PRICHARD (Luxembourg 1950). E. DONCKEL, *Die Kirche in Luxemburg von den Anfängen bis zur Gegenwart* (Luxembourg 1950). A. HEIDERSCHEID, *Aspects de sociologie religieuse du dio-*

cèse de Luxembourg, 2 v. (Luxembourg 1961–62). *Bilan du Monde,* 2:570–572.

[V. CONZEMIUS/EDS.]

LUXEUIL, ABBEY OF

One of the most illustrious Irish foundations of the medieval period in east central France, Archdiocese of Besançon. In *c.* 590 the Irish missionary St. COLUMBAN established a monastic foundation on the site of the old Roman fort of *Luxovium* and dedicated it to St. Peter. He was succeeded as abbot by EUSTACE OF LUXEUIL and then by Waldebert, who introduced the BENEDICTINE RULE at Luxeuil. The abbey became an influential religious and cultural center of eastern France. During the Arabic invasion (732), however, the monastery suffered a lapse and dispersal of its members. This epoch of destruction appears to have been the occasion also of a loss of a number of valuable MSS from the abbey's library. Fortunately, several of them have been recovered and are presently preserved in various libraries. Among these works is the *Lectionary of Luxeuil,* dating from the 7th century and first recognized by the Benedictine scholar Mabillon in 1685. The *Lectionary* (Paris, Bibliothèque Nationale lat. 9427) is important for its evidence of Mozarabic and Bobbian liturgical influences and practices of the time. (*See* P. Salmon's critical edition, *Le Lectionnaire de Luxeuil,* 2 v. Rome 1944–53.) Luxeuil's SCRIPTORIUM seems to have been an important paleographic center, originating a distinctive book known as the ''Script of Luxeuil'' (E. A. Lowe, *Revue Bénédictine* 63:132–142).

The abbey was restored under CHARLEMAGNE but was again subject to incursion, this time from the NORMANS, who sacked it in 888. From the 10th century, the abbots were princes of the empire. The abbey's discipline and economic status declined toward the end of the 15th century as a result of COMMENDATION. This condition of affairs continued until a reformation was instigated in 1631 by Abbot Philip of Baume and the abbey incorporated into the BENEDICTINE congregation of Saint-Vanne. With the coming of the French Revolution, Luxeuil, like most of the religious houses of France, was suppressed (1790). Today, Luxeuil's main buildings still stand and house a diocesan minor seminary. The abbey church, which dates from the 14th century, dominates the scene and has, since 1926, been designated a minor basilica.

Bibliography: *Gallia Christiana* 15:144–162. E. DE BEAUSÉJOUR, *Le Monastère de Luxeuil, l'église abbatiale* (Besançon 1891). H. BEAUMONT, *Étude historique sur l'abbaye de Luxeuil, (590–1790)* (Luxeuil 1895). H. LECLERCQ, *Dictionnaire d'archéologie chrétienne et de liturgie* (Paris 1907–53) 9.2:2722–87. A. BOSSUAT, ''Philippe le Bon et l'abbaye de Luxeuil,'' *Annales de Bourgogne* 9 (1937) 7–23. L. H. COTTINEAU,

Répertoire topobibliographique des abbayes et prieurés (Mâcon 1935–39) 1:1684–85. B. DELLA CHIESA, A. MERCATI and A. PELZER, *Dizionario ecclesiastico* (Turin 1954–58) 2:756. D. MISONNE, *Lexikon für Theologie und Kirche,* ed. J. HOFER and K. RAHNER (Freiburg 1957–65) 6:1246–47.

[B. F. SCHERER]

LWANGA, CHARLES, ST.

One of the 22 UGANDA MARTYRS; b. Buddu County, Uganda, *c.* 1860; d. Namugongo, Uganda, June 3, 1886. Lwanga first learned of the Catholic faith from two retainers in the court of chief Mawulugungu. While a catechumen he entered the royal household of the Kabaka of Buganda in 1884 as the assistant to Joseph Mukasa, the majordomo in charge of the young court pages. On the night of Mukasa's martyrdom by order of the new Kabaka, Mwanga, Lwanga requested and received baptism (Nov. 15, 1885). During the succeeding months, when it was most difficult to communicate with priests, he protected the pages from Mwanga's perverted demands. He instructed and encouraged the youths and, at the moment of crisis, baptized the catechumens. When persecution started anew (May 1886), Lwanga was arrested with the Christian pages, after making with them a public profession of faith. During the march to Namugongo he was roughly treated. He was singled out for a particularly cruel death by slow fire. With 21 others he was beatified (June 6, 1920) and canonized (Oct. 18, 1964). Pius XI declared him patron of youth and Catholic Action for most of tropical Africa (June 22, 1934).

Feast: June 3.

Bibliography: J. P. THOONEN, *Black Martyrs* (London 1941). J. F. FAUPEL, *African Holocaust* (New York 1962). *Acta Apostolicae Sedis* 56 (Rome 1964) 901–912.

[J. F. FAUPEL]

LYING

An act contrary to TRUTHFULNESS, or the virtue of veracity, consisting in the communication to another of a judgment that is not in accord with what the one who communicates thinks to be true.

Nature. In its most common and explicit form, lying involves either spoken or written words; but it is possible to lie in using other forms of communication, for example, in gestures or in actions that involve a pretension to distinguished qualities which a person does not possess. The communication of something other than what one holds to be true is essential to lying, although what is said need not be contrary to objective truth. A lie differs from an erroneous statement. It can exist even though what is said happens to be in accord with fact; on the other hand, despite objective error, a communication is not a lie unless the speaker is aware that what he says is false.

It has been disputed whether the intention to deceive is essential to a lie. Actual deception, of course, is not, since this is the effect of lying rather than the act itself. But as to the intention, some Scotists have taken St. Augustine's words (*De mend.* 4) "with a will to deceive" as equally essential to lying as the other part of his statement, "the enunciation of something false." Judged in its immediate context, as well as in that of his other writings, St. Augustine's statement is a restricted affirmation about harmful lying rather than a definition of lying in general. St. Thomas clearly taught that the will to deceive was not essential to lying (*Summa theologiae* 2a2ae, 110.1), and Scotus appears to have been in accord with this view. Some Scotists, however, claiming the authority of St. Augustine, taught that the intent to deceive is of the essence of lying rather than a property of it. Almost all theologians, nevertheless, follow St. Thomas in his interpertation of St. Augustine upon this point, and affirm that a deliberately false utterance is the essence of a lie, but that the intention to deceive belongs to the perfection of lying, not to its essence.

If deception or the intent to deceive is not essential to lying, there can be a lie that deceives no one, and that is told without an intention to deceive. On the other hand, deception can occur where no lie is actually told. For example, a person could tell a truth with sufficient clarity to avoid making a false statement and sufficient ambiguity and evasiveness to avoid revealing a truth which he wants to keep hidden. The hearer might misinterpret what is said and so be deceived, yet the speaker has not lied (*see* MENTAL RESERVATION).

Kinds of Lying. From the point of view of the virtuous "mean," formally constitutive of truthfulness, lying is opposed to truthfulness by excess or defect. Excess consists in boasting, or in the willful exaggeration of a truth. Defect occurs in disparagement or "irony."

The more important division of the lie is based upon its effect, or the motive of the one who lies. Least among lies is that which is told in jest or for the purpose of amusement (*mendacium iocosum*). If a story is obviously fiction, then there is no lie, since the literary genre of a story requires only internal consistency, not conformity to reality. But if illusion is allowed to substitute for reality, or if a story leaves a reader confusing fact with fiction, there has been a violation of truthfulness.

A more serious offense against truthfulness is the lie whose author intends some useful good, and to achieve

it is willing to speak falsely. Useful and harmless according to strict justice, the so-called "officious" lie (*mendacium officiosum*) is intended to gain some good or to protect oneself or others from harm. The motive in this case could be commendable from a moral point of view. This would mitigate the malice of the act, but if a lie is intrinsically evil, it cannot become a good act, however virtuous its motive, for the end cannot justify the means. The most malicious kind of lie is that which is directly and explicitly intended to do harm to another. This is the "pernicious" lie (*mendacium perniciosum*).

Moral Evaluation

The morality of lying can be considered either from the point of view of authority, or from that of rational argument. In surveying the opinion of moral authorities, profane and sacred, account must be taken of the fact that different authorities, in condemning the lie, may have had in mind some specific form of lying, and not the lie in general.

Plato and Aristotle. Plato, in the *Republic,* appears to have regarded lying as a socially subversive practice when indulged in by private citizens, but that the privilege of lying for the public good should be accorded to rulers (*Republic,* 388). Aristotle, on the other hand, declared that falsehood was of its own nature (intrinsically?) bad and reprehensible (*Eth. Nic.* 4.7).

The Scriptures. The sinfulness of lying is attested to in a number of passages in Sacred Scripture: in the OT, Prv 6.12, 17; Ps 5.7; Sir 7.13; Wis 1.11; in the NT, Eph 4.25; Col 3.9. The scriptural evidence, however, is not satisfactory, because it is not clear that what is condemned is the lie as such, i.e., as unqualified by the malice of injustice. In some cases, at least, the sacred writer must have had in mind only the pernicious lie, since the degree of malice he attributes to it is far greater than traditional doctrine and common sense would allow for a lie that intends or causes no harm. For example: "You destroy all who speak falsehood; the bloodthirsty and the deceitful the Lord abhors" (Ps 5.7). And: "A lying mouth destroys the soul" (Wis 1.11). Thus the ambiguity of the Scriptures upon this matter has left room for debate both in patristic and in modern times.

In Patristic and Scholastic Times. In the patristic age, Clement of Alexandria, Origen, and St. John Chrysostom in the East, and St. Hilary and Cassian in the West seem to have held (but not without some ambiguity) that in certain exceptional cases a lie was justifiable. St. Augustine held to the stricter view that a lie is intrinsically evil. In this he was followed by SS. Thomas Aquinas, Raymond of Peñafort, and Antoninus, as well as by Scotus, Cajetan, Suárez, John of St. Thomas, and by all but a few modern Catholic theologians.

Moral Gravity. Although Christian tradition has, in the main, held firmly to the conviction that a lie is intrinsically evil, the judgment of moralists is relatively lenient with regard to the degree of malice inherent in the lie. The common teaching is that a lie, deliberately told, is per se no more than venially sinful. It is damaging in some degree to man's social good, but it does not strike at the very existence of that good, as do theft, adultery, and murder. However, circumstances might involve the violation of virtues other than truthfulness in a particular lie. For example, the pernicious lie violates justice and charity as well as truthfulness, and for that reason is a grave sin when the damage done or attempted is notable. Similarly, a lie could be a mortal sin because it causes serious SCANDAL, or because it is contrary to faith or to the virtue of religion (see PERJURY), or because, in serious matter, it violates another's strict right to be informed of the truth.

Modern Controversy. Dissatisfied with the theory and the use of mental reservations in order to conceal the truth in difficult cases, some authors have accepted the admissibility of an intentionally false statement whenever the hearer has not a strict right in justice to know the truth. For them the malice of lying is not the violation of a personal obligation to veracity, but a violation of a strict right on the part of another to be informed of a particular truth. H. Grotius and S. Pufendorf, among Protestant thinkers, as well as some Catholics have maintained that in a case of necessity a false statement, *falsiloquium,* may be without moral fault. The *falsiloquium* is for them a "psychological" rather than a "moral" lie, and the latter they continue to reprobate along with all other Christian thinkers. Since the strict obligation not to lie does not depend upon the strict right of another to know a truth but upon one's nature as a rational social being, theologians generally have rejected the distinction between psychological and moral lies as unfounded in sound moral theory, at least if it is made to rest upon the hearer's right to be accurately informed.

Others, acknowledging the obligation to speak the truth, if one speaks at all—and this independently of any right on the part of the one to whom a statement is made—nevertheless point out that a person obliged to speak only the truth may also be under an obligation to conceal a truth, and this latter obligation may in some cases be more urgent and more sacred than the former. If we suppose a case in which the truth, or evasion, or silence, would bring harm upon a neighbor, the obligation in charity to prevent this, they say, would take precedence over the obligation in veracity, and the latter would be suspended and cease for the time being to bind.

However, this theory provides escape from moral perplexity only when a strict obligation exists to conceal

the truth; it does nothing to enable an individual to protect his privacy against prying or intrusive people, a thing that most of those who defend lying in certain circumstances would like to do. But the more important objection to it is that it cannot be adopted without abandoning the traditional doctrine that a lie is intrinsically evil, so that the reaction of the Christian conscience to it is likely to be that of St. Augustine: "He who says that there are some just lies must be regarded as saying that there are some just sins, and, consequently, that some things which are unjust are just. What could be more absurd?" (*C. mend.* 15.31.)

Argument from Reason. The most fundamental argument is that drawn from man's social nature. The social order that human nature requires for its proper development and fulfillment demands that mutual trust and confidence and a general friendly good will should prevail between men. This, however, is undermined not only by the pernicious lie that damages the rights and reputations of others, but also by officious and jocose lies, because if one were under no obligation to refrain from such lies, an individual's confidence in the communications made to him would be considerably lowered. Every statement would have to be weighed with suspicion, and this would, in effect, debase the currency of communication. Man's faculty of speech or communication would be perverted in the sense that the prevalent mendacity would make it impossible or difficult to communicate with others. This is a situation that has in fact come to pass in matters with regard to which "white" or "social" lies are in common use. Words lose their meaning and their capacity to convey thought. Richard Cabot has pointed out the dilemma that physicians create for themselves when, for humane reasons, they lie to patients suffering from incurable disease (see bibliography). When this practice comes to be generally known, the physician has no effective way of reassuring a patient who suspects that he has contracted such a disease and that his physician is concealing this fact.

Difficult Cases

It cannot be denied that the doctrine of the intrinsic malice of the lie can involve a conscientious person in moral dilemmas. However, the frequency and seriousness of these troublesome situations should not be exaggerated, and from most of them escape of one kind or another is available without lying.

The "Social" Lie. In many cases a statement, whose literal sense is not in accord with facts as the speaker knows them, is nevertheless not a lie because social convention permits certain kinds of expressions to be used, and requires people of good sense to understand them, in other than a literal sense. This conventional meaning is not false; ultimately all meaning that attaches to words is determined by convention. No prudent person would take in their strict and literal sense complimentary forms of address such as ''your devoted servant'' or even ''yours.'' Nor would a serious person take seriously many of the amenities common in social intercourse: compliments about dress or appearance, or the remarks about the pleasantness of an evening made by a departing guest.

Similarly the statement made by one answering the door or the telephone that a member of the family is not at home has acquired by general use (or misuse) a certain objective ambiguity. It may either mean that the person is literally not at home, or that, though at home, he does not want to see or talk with the caller, but wishes to signify his refusal in the polite manner sanctioned by social custom. In this situation, however, the status of the person calling could affect the objective sense of the statement. If he is a person who should not be refused, he will be entitled to understand the statement in its literal sense, and if the speaker knows it to be untrue, it will be a lie.

Professional Secrecy. Mental reservation, or the restriction of one's understanding of the meaning of a question put to him, and the sense of his reply, will enable a person to avoid other difficulties. Clergymen, lawyers, physicians, nurses, pharmacists, secretaries, and others are obliged to professional secrecy with regard to certain information that they may possess. This is understood by all reasonably well-informed people. When such a person is questioned about matter he knows only under professional secrecy, he can legitimately (and charitably) interpret the inquiry to mean: Have you any communicable knowledge about this subject? He may, consequently, frame his answer accordingly, and deny that he has knowledge of it. Because of the objective nature of the situation, the hearer ought to understand the statement to be ambiguous. It may be an absolute denial of knowledge, or it may only be a denial of communicable knowledge.

Non-Professional Secrets. It seems unreasonable to restrict the use of this kind of evasion to the protection of professional secrets. Others besides professional people have in their keeping secrets it would be sinful, even gravely so, to reveal. For example, revelation of the hidden sin of another could amount to a mortal sin of DE-TRACTION. Everyone should be aware of the obligation to secrecy that exists in certain cases, and should be sensitive to the possibility that questions he asks might put another in a moral quandary. A well-intentioned and reasonable man can therefore be understood, when he puts a question, to be asking for information that his hearer is

morally free to divulge. Hence a denial of knowledge could reasonably be understood as objectively ambiguous, just as in the case of the professional secret.

Other Dilemmas. There is another type of difficulty in which ambiguity provides no refuge. For example, let us suppose that a man is hidden from a gang of murderers intent upon killing him, and his friend is questioned concerning his whereabouts, or that a person working with the underground in an area occupied by the enemy is interrogated by enemy officials about the resistance movement. No doubt the type of evasion discussed above could legitimately be used in these cases also, but their particular difficulty consists in this that no simple denial of knowledge would be likely to suffice to put the miscreants off the scent. Denials would need to be backed by strong, circumstantial affirmations that no stretch of ingenuity could classify as ambiguous, and perhaps positive misinformation would have to be invented and palmed off for true. If one holds to the doctrine of the intrinsic malice of the lie, there would seem to be no escape possible in these cases, unless it lies in questioning whether, in such circumstances, the idea of true human speech or communication is verified.

A lie is essentially a false communication. A man, speaking falsely to himself, does not lie. Similarly, it could be argued, it is no lie to speak falsely to another when some circumstance prevents one's speech from being, in a true sense of the word, a communication. As has been shown, false communication is immoral because it subverts the mutual trust and confidence that should exist between men, and tends to make communication impossible. Now in the extremely difficult situations being considered, there is no mutual trust or confidence to destroy. In fact, a maximum of distrust prevails between the parties, and no man in such a position could prudently take the words of the other at their face value. In such a case, words would cease, to a degree, to be a medium for the exchange of thought. Communication would be broken down, and to the extent in which the communication of mind with mind has become impossible, it would be equally impossible to realize the idea of a lie. In particular cases the breakdown of communication or its degree might be difficult to determine, but it seems incontestable that if no communication in the ordinary sense of the word is possible, there can be no lie.

However, these cases are altogether exceptional, and if special norms are found to apply to them, these must not be extended to include situations in which one cannot refrain from lying without involving himself (or even others) in trouble and difficulty. The practice of virtue of any kind is likely to require a measure of heroism in some circumstances. At times the obligation to truthfulness may impose some hardship, but the endurance of this is a small price to pay for the blessings which society and individuals enjoy when its members "speak the truth each one with his neighbor" (Eph 5.25).

Bibliography: AUGUSTINE, "Lying" (*De mend.*), tr. M. S. MULDOWNEY, *Treatises on Various Subjects,* ed. R. J. DEFERRARI (Fathers of the Church, 16; New York 1952); "Against Lying" (*C. mend.*), tr. H. B. JAFFEE, *ibid.* THOMAS AQUINAS, *Summa theologiae* 2a2ae, 110; *Quodl.* 8.6.4; *In 5 eth.* 4.15. J. A. DORSZYNSKI, *Catholic Teaching about the Morality of Falsehood* (CUA Stud. Sac. Theol. 2d ser. 16; Washington 1948). J. H. NEWMAN, *Apologia pro vita sua* (Garden City, NY 1956). J. BROSNAN, "The Malice of Lying," *The Irish Ecclesiastical Record* 4 (1914) 377–392. L. GODEFROY, *Dictionnaire de théologie catholique,* ed. A. VACANT, 15 v. (Paris 1903–50; Tables générales 1951–) 10.1:555–569. R. CABOT, *Honesty* (New York 1938).

[D. HUGHES]

LYKE, JAMES PATTERSON

Fourth archbishop of Atlanta, GA; b. Chicago, Illinois, Feb. 18, 1939; d. Atlanta, Dec. 27, 1992; educ. Quincy College, Quincy, Illinois, and Antonianum, Rome. James Patterson Lyke professed in the Order of Friars Minor on June 21, 1963 and was ordained a priest on June 24, 1966. In 1967, St. Joseph's Theological Seminary granted him the Master of Divinity degree. Lyke served from 1972 to 1977 as a member of the committee that drafted the National Catechetical Directory, Sharing the Light of Faith [1979]. He was also president of the National Black Catholic Clergy Caucus. On Aug. 1, 1979, Lyke was ordained bishop to minister as auxiliary in the Diocese of Cleveland, Ohio, and episcopal vicar of its Urban Region. In 1990 the Holy See named Lyke apostolic administrator, sede vacante, for the Archdiocese of Atlanta, and he was installed as archbishop of Atlanta on June 24, 1991.

Lyke's interest in liturgical life spurred him, in 1987, to coordinate the development of a new hymnal, *Lead Me, Guide Me,* which unites Roman Catholic hymnody and the rich tradition of African-American music. He took note of the values that had originated among and been handed down by the Swahili-speaking tribes of Africa, developing them in a pastoral reflection, *Say not, "I am too young!,"* addressed to African-American Catholic Youth. In addition to pastoral letters on the sanctity of the family, "So Stood Those Who Have Gone Down through the Ages," and on the sanctity of the unborn, "Precious Lord, Precious Life," he cooperated with other African-American bishops in a joint pastoral letter, published in 1984, on evangelization in the black community, *What We Have Seen and Heard.*

The strong thread connecting the pastoral efforts of James Patterson Lyke, the pastor and bishop, was his vi-

sion of uniting African-American culture and the Catholic Church. While Lyke's service to the People of God was cut short by cancer, he is remembered as an outstanding leader whose sagacity continues to inspire African American Catholics.

Bibliography: Lyke's writings include: "When the Poor Evangelize the Church," *Origins* 11:3 (June 5, 1980) 33-38; *Say Not "I Am Too Young!,"* (Cleveland 1990); "The Family in the Black Community," *Origins* 16:28 (Dec. 25, 1986) 511-516; "So Stood Those Who Have Gone Down Through the Ages," Pastoral Reflection on the Black Family (Cleveland 1986); "A Black Perspective on the National Catechetical Directory" (Ph.D. diss., Union Graduate School, 1981); in collaboration with others: *What We Have Seen and Heard* (Cincinnati 1984) and *Lead Me, Guide Me: The African American Catholic Hymnal* (Chicago 1987).

[G. DOLAN]

LYNCH, BAPTISTA, MOTHER

Ursuline foundress; b. Cheraw, S.C., Nov. 2, 1823; d. Columbia, S.C., July 28, 1887. Ellen was the daughter of Conlaw and Eleanor (Neison) Lynch, and the sister of Patrick N. Lynch, Bishop (1858–82) of Charleston, S.C. She attended the Ursuline Academy in Charleston. When the community transferred to Ohio, she entered the novitiate in the Ursuline Convent of the Assumption, Banks Street, Cincinnati, in 1848. As Baptista Aloysius, she made her profession on Nov. 15, 1850. This community disbanded and she was transferred to St. Martin's Convent, Fayetteville, Ohio. When Bishop Lynch invited the Ursulines to South Carolina in 1858, she led a group of sisters to Columbia to take over the Immaculate Conception Academy and Convent. The daughters of important Catholic families in the South attended the academy during the Civil War, but it was destroyed when Columbia was burned by Gen. William T. Sherman's army. As refugees, the nuns and their pupils moved to a farm, called Valle Crucis, outside the city of Columbia. Subsistence was difficult, and in an effort to lessen the burden, Mother Baptista sent some of her nuns to open a school in Tuscaloosa, Ala., in 1866. This venture failed and in 1872 a parochial school was begun in Columbia. In 1887 a convent sufficient for the whole community was obtained in the city, and the Valle Crucis Convent was closed. Mother Baptista died ten days after bringing the nuns back to the city.

Bibliography: Archives, Diocese of Charleston.

[R. C. MADDEN]

LYNCH, JOHN JOSEPH

Missionary, archbishop; b. near Clones, County Monaghan, Ireland, Feb. 6, 1816; d. Toronto, Canada,

May 12, 1888. He was educated at the Academy of St. Joseph, Clondalkin, entered the College of the Lazarists at Castleknock (1835), and was sent to France to the Seminary of Saint-Lazare, Paris (1837). After ordination at Maynooth, Ireland, June 9, 1843, he worked as a home missionary until 1847, when he was sent to the U.S. He served as president of St. Mary's of the Barrens (1847–54), a Lazarist college in Missouri, and founded the Seminary of Our Lady of the Angels at Niagara Falls, N.Y. (1856). Lynch was named coadjutor to Bp. Armand F. M. de Charbonnel of Toronto, and consecrated titular bishop of Echynos (Nov. 20, 1859). After succeeding to the See of Toronto in April 1860, he concerned himself with developing education within the diocese. At Vatican Council I (1869–70) he supported immediate definition of papal infallibility. He became the first archbishop of Toronto on March 25, 1870, receiving the pallium at Rome. Under his direction the First Provincial Council (1873) adopted the decrees of the Council of Quebec. He promoted charitable institutions and was active in securing the passage of the Separate School Bill (1863).

Bibliography: *Jubilee Volume: The Archdiocese of Toronto* (Toronto 1892). H. C. MACKEOWN, *The Life and Labours of Most Rev. John Joseph Lynch, D.D. Cong. Miss., First Archbishop of Toronto* (Toronto 1886).

[J. T. FLYNN]

LYNCH, PATRICK NELSON

Third bishop of Charleston, South Carolina; b. County Monaghan, Ireland, March 10, 1817; d. Charleston, Feb. 26, 1882. Lynch was the son of Conlaw Peter and Eleanor (Neison) Lynch, who emigrated to the United States in 1819, settling in Cheraw, South Carolina. He attended the local primary school and then Cheraw Academy until 1829, when he entered the Seminary of St. John the Baptist in Charleston. In 1833, Bp. John ENGLAND sent him to the College of the Propaganda in Rome, where he distinguished himself in languages, on one occasion giving the annual address in Hebrew before the Holy Father. He was ordained in Rome on April 4, 1840, by Cardinal Jacob Fransoni, prefect of the Congregation of the Propaganda.

Lynch was became assistant at the Charleston cathedral, editor of the diocesan paper, the *United States Catholic Miscellany,* and professor at the Seminary of St. John the Baptist. Upon England's death in 1842, Abp. Francis P. KENRICK of Baltimore considered Lynch as a possible successor to England, but he judged his ill health and youth as obstacles. From 1845 to 1847 Lynch was pastor of St. Mary's Church; he then became rector of the cathedral and of the Seminary of St. John the Baptist, a posi-

tion he held until the seminary closed in 1851. In December of 1845 he was appointed, with James CORCORAN and Augustine HEWITT, to collect the writings of John England for publication. He supervised the erection of the Cathedral of St. John and St. Finbar (1850) and was treasurer and chaplain of St. Mary's Relief Hospital, a special project for the aid of fever victims (1852–53). In November of 1854, Bp. Ignatius Reynolds, who was failing in health, appointed him administrator of the diocese, an office he held until he was appointed to the see on Dec. 17, 1857.

Lynch was consecrated in the Cathedral of St. John and St. Finbar, March 14, 1858, by Archbishop Kenrick. During the Civil War, a fire in Charleston on Dec. 11, 1861, destroyed church property, notably the cathedral; the later siege of Charleston and the march of Sherman's army across the state added to the losses. The war brought new duties, no small part of which was attending prisoners of war. In 1864 the Confederate Government prevailed upon Lynch, as special commissioner of the Confederate States, to put its cause before Pius IX. Lynch accepted the commission, hoping his efforts might be conducive to peace. By the time he reached Rome, however, the Confederacy was failing, and he deemed it inadvisable to present his credentials, so he was received by the Holy Father simply as the bishop of Charleston. He was pardoned for his complicity by Pres. Andrew Johnson on Aug. 4, 1865, but he was not able to get back to his diocese until late November.

To repair the losses in his diocese, Lynch proposed to raise the necessary funds by begging in the metropolitan areas of the country, a program that occupied him the rest of his life. The establishment in 1868 of the vicariate of North Carolina relieved him of some of his responsibility. He attended VATICAN COUNCIL I (1869–70) and prepared a series of articles that were published in *Catholic World.* His published work also included many articles in *American Catholic Quarterly Review.*

Bibliography: Lynch Papers, Archives of the Diocese of Charleston.

[R. C. MADDEN]

LYNDWOOD, WILLIAM

Bishop and canonist; b. Linwood, Leicestershire, England, 1375; d. Oct. 21, 1446. Lyndwood was educated at Gonville Hall, Cambridge, where he obtained a doctor's degree in both civil and Canon Law. After ordination in 1407 he held benefices, some concurrently, in various dioceses. On occasions between 1417 and 1441 he was king's envoy to Castile, Burgundy, etc.; in 1432 he became keeper of the privy seal; and in 1442, bishop of St. David's until his death.

Lyndwood's only extant work is his great *Provinciale*, begun in 1422 and completed in 1430; it is a digest with commentary of the synodal constitutions of 14 archbishops of Canterbury, from Langton in 1222 to Chichele (to whom the work is dedicated). As chancellor of the archbishop of Canterbury and an auditor of causes (1414–17), as a prolocutor of the clergy in convocation (1419–21, 1424–26), and as an official of the Court of Canterbury (1417–31), Lyndwood had a wide experience of the workings of the Canon Law in England. His *Provinciale*, therefore, has the practical object of helping lawyers to understand the most frequently quoted texts of provincial legislation, and, in general, of seeing whether and how the edicts of a non-sovereign legislator, such as an archbishop, could be harmonized with a large body of law that the legislator has no power to repeal or to override.

The *Provinciale (seu Constitutiones Angliae)* was printed at Oxford about 1485 to 1490; at Westminster, by Wynkyn de Worde in 1496 and 1499; and then eight times between 1501 and 1534 at Paris, Antwerp, and London. The last and best-known edition is that of Oxford, 1679, to which there was attached JOHN OF ACTON'S gloss on the Legatine Constitutions.

Bibliography: F. W. MAITLAND, *Roman Canon Law in the Church of England* (London 1898) 1–50. A. OGLE, *The Canon Law in Medieval England: An Examination of William Lyndwood's Provinciale in Reply to the Late Prof. F. W. Maitland* (London 1912). C. R. CHENEY, "William Lyndwood's Provinciale," *The Jurist* 21 (1961) 405–434. A. B. EMDEN, *A Biographical Register of the Scholars of the University of Cambridge before 1500* (Cambridge 1963) 379–381, 679. A. B. EMDEN, *A Biographical Register of the University of Oxford to A.D. 1500* (Oxford 1957–59) 2:1191–93.

[L. E. BOYLE]

LYONESE RITE

The historical pre-Vatican II liturgical rite of the Archdiocese of Lyons. This article treats the rite's history and liturgical specialties.

History. Before the 4th century there is no evidence of a stereotyped liturgy in Lyons; the early Christian immigrants from EPHESUS did not initiate the Lyonese rite. Except for some few details, the rite owes nothing to the Gallican rite, even though the latter prevailed in Lyons from the 5th to the 7th century. The Church at Lyons suffered much from the Saracen invasion (725) and the levies of CHARLES MARTEL. For a number of years Lyons did not even have a bishop. While Bishop Ado (*c.* 767–*c.* 797) possibly attempted to introduce the Roman rite, the recognized father of the Lyonese rite was LEIDRADUS

(798–814). Charlemagne directed this monk from his school at Aachen to introduce liturgical worship at Lyons according to the usage of Aachen's chapel. Aachen followed the rite of the Church at Metz, a Roman liturgical center after the return of St. CHRODEGANG OF METZ from Rome in 751. A cleric from Metz assisted Leidradus in his liturgical reforms at Lyons. Hence the Lyonese rite is not Ephesine or Gallican, but Roman in origin.

Leidradus's successor, Bishop Agobard (814–840), maintained local customs and introduced corrections that made the rite a Carolingian variant of the Roman rite. In the 11th century the Romano-German pontifical exerted the last significant influence on the formation of the rite of Lyons. The prototype of the Lyonese liturgical books is the 10th-century Alcuin edition of the Gregorian Sacramentary, which continued to be reproduced with minor variations down to the Missal of Bishop De Marquemont (1620).

The neo-Gallican period for the Lyonese liturgy began with Archbishop C. de Neuville's Breviary (1695). A pandering to neo-Gallican tastes also appeared in Archbishop C. de Rochebonne's Missal (1737). Archbishop A. de Montazet further destroyed Lyons's traditional rite by introducing the liturgical books of Paris (Missal, 1768; Breviary, 1772) while retaining the Lyonese rubrics and sanctoral. In 1776 Parliament's enforcement of these books brought about their general use in Lyons.

The Lyonese liturgy reached its nadir during the FRENCH REVOLUTION. Bishop A. Lamourette established constitutional worship in 1791. His destruction of the cathedral's apse altar and erection of a new altar at the transept confused rubrics in the cathedral ceremonial books until 1936, when the altar was restored to its original position. Pagan worship of the goddess of reason, begun in 1793, was followed by a restoration of the Catholic religion and Montazet's neo-Gallican books in 1799.

Pius IX resolved a three-way controversy regarding the future of the Lyonese liturgy (return to the traditional, Gallican, or Roman liturgy) in favor of Cardinal M. de Bonald's traditional position (1863). Although the 1866 *Missale Romano-Lugdunense* retained many of Montazet's Prefaces, Proses, and Propers, it used Marquemont's Missal (1620) as its model. A revised edition approved by the Congregation of Rites appeared in 1904 as the *Missale Romanum in quo antiqui ritus Lugdunensis servantur*.

In 1864 the Roman Breviary of Pius V, with a diocesan Proper, replaced Montazet's Breviary; the ancient ceremonial for the Office, however, was kept. The Ritual had nothing distinctive about it except for an unusually prolix rite for the Sacrament of the Sick (12 anointings).

Liturgical Specialties. Although basically the same as that of the classical Roman rite, the Lyonese Mass had enough variants to make it distinctive. Such variations could be seen in the shorter prayers at the foot of the altar, in more frequent proses (20), in the slightly varied Offertory prayers with an Epiclesis-like prayer before the *Suscipe, sancta Trinitas.* The 1904 Missal contained, besides the Roman Prefaces, seven others. From the *Unde et memores* to the Canon's doxology, the celebrant assumed a cruciform position. He held the Host over the chalice from the doxology to *sicut in caelo* of the Pater, at which point the little elevation occurred. The Pater's embolism was said or sung aloud. The Agnus Dei preceded the Commingling and was said with the Host particle held above the chalice. Lyons reversed the order of Rome's ablution prayers.

At solemn Mass the three official ministers were assisted by extra priests, deacons, and subdeacons, each properly vested. Each official minister had from two to six co-ministers, depending upon the solemnity of the feast. This ceremonial CONCELEBRATION occurred on important feast days. Between the Epistle and Gospel there was a rite for testing the wine at a pontifical Mass. After the Gospel all the clergy in choir kissed the Gospel book. The subdeacon held the paten as usual but with his maniple. At the beginning of the Offertory the priests offered the celebrant a host; after the incensing of the oblation, chapter members offered a coin. The celebrant incensed above the altar; the deacon incensed below. A solemn blessing followed the Pater's Embolism at a pontifical Mass. After reception of Communion at solemn Mass, the sacristan administered wine as a mouth ablution. The Blessed Sacrament after Communion was carried in procession to a repository altar.

Bibliography: D. BUENNER, *L'Ancienne liturgie romaine: Le Rite lyonnais* (Lyons 1934), the basic work. A. A. KING, *Liturgies of the Primatial Sees* (Milwaukee 1957). L. MOILLE, ''The Liturgy of Lyons,'' *The Month* 151 (1928) 402–408.

[R. X. REDMOND/EDS.]

LYONNET, STANISLAUS

Biblical scholar; b. 1902; d. 1986. He entered the Society of Jesus in 1919, and was ordained a priest in 1934. After taking a licentiate in classics, Lyonnet taught Greek for three years at the Haute-Études (Paris) where he afterwards took up the study of ancient languages under the guidance of two famous linguists, A. Meillet and E. Benveniste. He graduated in 1933 with a doctoral dissertation on ''Le parfait en arménien classique.'' After theological studies at the Jesuit theologate in Lyon-Fourvière, he went to the Pontifical Biblical Institute in Rome. In 1943

he defended his thesis on ''Les origines de la version arménienne de la Bible et le Diatessaron'' (published in 1950). He remained at the Institute, where he was appointed a professor, and taught until 1980.

During his very long and prolific career he wrote several books and many articles. Among his works are *La vie selon l'Esprit, condition du chrétien* (Paris 1965) with I. de la Potterie; *Les étapes du salut selon l'épître aux Romains* (Paris 1969); *Sin, Redemption and Sacrifice: A Biblical and Patristic Study, Analecta biblica* 48 (Rome 1970), with L. Sabourin; *Le message de l'épître aux Romains* (Paris 1971); ''Péché—dans le judaïsme, le Nouveau Testament; péché originel'' *Dictionnaire de la Bible, Supplément,* v. VII (1966) 480–567. He is best known, however, for his translation of the Epistles to the Romans and to the Galatians in the *Bible de Jérusalem* (1953). At a time when most scholars saw the key to the interpretation of the New Testament in the Mysteries and Gnosis, Lyonnet was one of the first to recognize the importance of the Jewish background. Although he did not himself study the Jewish translations (Targumim) and commentaries (Midrashim) of the Old Testament, nevertheless, he introduced some of the famous experts (M. McNamara, J. A. Fitzmyer, R. Le Déaut) to the study of Intertestamental Judaism.

Lyonnet's openness to the views of others was well known but was unacceptable to some of his Roman colleagues who had rejected literary criticism. His articles ''Le sense de *eph'hō* en Rm 5,12 et l'exégèse des Pères grecs,'' *Biblica* 36 (1955) 436–456, and ''Le péché originel et l'exégèse de Rm 5,12–14,'' *Recherches de Science Religieuse* 44 (1956) 63–84, both gave rise to criticisms from conservative scholars. He was at one time suspended from teaching for two years (1962–64), but endured that trial with a sincere obedience and a real spiritual freedom. He took advantage of that period to give many talks to the French-speaking bishops who participated in Vatican Council II, and to assist them in many ways. A few years later, Pope Paul VI appointed him consultor to the Congregation for the Doctrine of the Faith. At the request of Pope John Paul II he gave the annual retreat at the Vatican during Lent, 1982.

[J.-N. ALETTI]

LYONS, COUNCILS OF

Two ecumenical councils held in Lyons, France. The first was concerned chiefly with Frederick II's struggle with the papacy, and the second, 29 years later, with the reunion of the Eastern and Western Churches.

The First Council. Pope INNOCENT IV summoned a General Council to meet at Lyons in June 1245. Innocent had fled from Emperor FREDERICK II, who like Barbarossa was bent on asserting imperial supremacy and had seized much papal territory, not to mention 100 prelates who were captured on their way to a Roman council in 1241. The emperor was ordered to appear at Lyons in order to defend himself from the charge of heresy.

The council opened June 26 and had three sessions: June 28, July 5, and July 17, 1245. In the first public session Innocent addressed an assembly of three patriarchs, 140 bishops, and a number of religious and seculars, including Baldwin II, the Latin emperor of Constantinople. The pope spoke on the "five wounds" of the Church: the sins of the clergy, the loss of Jerusalem, the Greek threat to the LATIN EMPIRE OF CONSTANTINOPLE, the Mongol (Tatar) invasion of Hungary, and especially Frederick's persecution (evident from the fact that few German or Sicilian bishops dared to attend). On July 5, Frederick's ambassador, Thaddeus of Suëssa, ably defended his lord, urging that no one should be condemned for heresy without being heard. Thaddeus could scarcely refute, however, the charge of Frederick's violence toward the bishops. A delay of 12 days (to July 17) was allowed for Thaddeus to consult with the emperor. Innocent spent the interval interviewing the bishops, allowing further time for the emperor's defense. When Frederick did not appear on July 17, the pope reviewed the case, and pronounced sentence of excommunication and deposition; most of the prelates signed the document. MATTHEW OF PARIS states that the electors were left free to choose a successor to Frederick but that the pope would arrange for Sicily (of which he was suzerain).

Plans were made to be ready for the Tatars; taxes were voted to aid the Holy Land as well as the Latin Empire. Some of the 22 constitutions dealt with judicial reform (those against usury and too frequent use of excommunication). The appeal of Thaddeus to a future *general* council met with a rebuke from Pope Innocent. Indeed the First Council of Lyons has been accepted as general only since the time of BELLARMINE (1542–1621).

The Second Council. Pope GREGORY X called the Second Council of Lyons in 1274. Considerable strife accompanied the extinction of the Hohenstaufen line, when Charles of ANJOU became king of Sicily. When Pope CLEMENT IV died in 1268, the cardinals allowed almost three years to pass before they could agree on the election of Teobaldo Visconti, who was away on a crusade in Acre. He returned to Rome to be ordained and crowned, and manifested great zeal for a crusade, reunion, and reform. Emperor MICHAEL VIII PALAEOLOGUS, who had retaken Constantinople in 1261, warmly welcomed legates from Gregory X. Charles of Anjou, however, was bent on a restoration of the Latin Empire in the East. It seemed to Michael that only the pope could control Charles, and that union of the Greeks with Rome was therefore vital to the safety of the Greek Empire. He wrote submissively to Gregory, but at the same time minimized the matter of reunion in dealing with his own churchmen.

On May 7, 1274, Gregory addressed some 200 prelates about the problems of the Holy Land, of union with the Greeks, and of reform, but the Greeks did not arrive until June 24 because of a shipwreck. GERMANUS II, the former patriarch of Constantinople, the archbishop of Nicaea, the chancellor, and others came in the emperor's name. They brought a letter from him giving his views and purporting to represent those of 50 archbishops and hundreds of bishops. At the fourth session (July 6) reunion was formally effected, the Greek representatives raising no objection to the FILIOQUE (defined in the last session), papal PRIMACY, PURGATORY, and the seven Sacraments (cf. H. Denzinger, *Enchiridion symbolorum*, ed. A. Schönmetzer [32d ed. Freiburg 1963] 850–61). Michael's letter read publicly at this session declared his full acceptance of Roman faith, primacy, and the rest, but urged that "the Greek church be permitted to retain its symbol (creed) and its own rites." Gregory's tolerant attitude was appreciated by the emperor, who was convinced that he could gradually overcome the aversion of his clergy and people for Rome. The Franciscan cardinal St. BONAVENTURE, a leader in dealing with the Greeks, died July 15. Some four months earlier THOMAS AQUINAS had died en route to the council.

Gregory strove mightily to finance the crusade by a ten percent tax on clerical incomes. Dealing individually with the bishops he avoided a concerted outcry. The problem of clerical reform involved disputes and bickering between the friars and the bishops, and required judicious handling. The prohibition of 1215 against new religious foundations had been neglected, and restrictions were placed on certain orders, with an exception made for the FRANCISCANS and DOMINICANS, "known for their great service to the church." Another phase of reform emanating from the council was the famous rule of the conclave, meant to obviate delay of election after the death of the pope. It was decided that ten days after the pope dies, the cardinals must assemble to choose a successor. If after three days they have not reached a decision, their diet was to be curtailed. With some modification, the basic regulations of Gregory X are still followed.

The great khan of the Mongols sent legates to ask for help against Egypt. Efforts were made for the spread of the faith into the Far East through missionaries such as JOHN OF MONTE CORVINO. Three bishops were deposed for unworthiness. The union of Greeks and Latins proved unpopular in the East, and lasted until the death of Emperor Michael in 1282 (*see* EASTERN SCHISM). A change of personnel at Rome and Constantinople effected a change of heart; and crusading efforts proved ineffectual.

The 31 decrees usually attributed to Lyons II were actually published several months later (Nov. 1, 1274). H. Finke discovered (1891) that three decrees (13, 14, and 18) were added by Gregory X after the council had ended. He also found and edited the long-lost constitution, *Zelus fidei,* a series of decrees relating to Gregory's proposed crusade. The text of the constitution was further emended by the discoveries of S. Kuttner.

Bibliography: C. J. VON HEFELE, *Histoire des conciles d'après les documents originaux,* tr. and continued by H. LECLERCQ, 10 v. in 19 (Paris 1907–38) 5.2:1633–79; 6.1:153–209. F. VERNET, *Dictionnaire de théologie catholique,* ed. A. VACANT et al., 15 v. (Paris 1903–50) 9.1:1361–91. V. GRUMEL, *ibid.* 1391–1410. R. BÄUMER, *Lexikon für Theologie und Kirche,* ed. J. HOFER and K. RAHNER, 10 v. (2d, new ed. Freiburg 1957–65) 6:1251–52. H. K. MANN, *The Lives of the Popes in the Early Middle Ages from 590 to 1304,* 18 v. (London 1902–32) 14:60–80; 15:361–454. D. J. GEANAKOPLOS, *Emperor Michael Palaeologus and the West, 1258–1282* (Cambridge, Mass. 1959) 258–304. H. JEDIN, *Ecumenical Councils of the Catholic Church,* tr. E. GRAF (New York 1960). F. DVORNIK, *The Ecumenical Councils* (New York 1961). H. J. SCHROEDER, *Disciplinary Decrees of the General Councils* (St. Louis 1937) 297–364, 585–606. H. DENZINGER, *Enchiridion symbolorum,* ed. A. SCHÖNMETZER (32d ed. Freiburg 1963) 830–39, 850–61. *Conciliorum oecumenicorum decreta* (Bologna-Freiburg 1962) 249–307. R. W. EMERY, "The Second Council of Lyons and the Mendicant Orders," *American Catholic Historical Review* 39 (1953–54) 257–71. J. M. POWELL, "Frederick II and the Church: A Revisionist View," *ibid.* 48 (1962–63) 487–97. S. KUTTNER, "Conciliar Law in the Making," *Miscellanea Pio Paschini,* 2 v. (Rome 1948–49) 2:39–81. D. M. NICOL, "The Byzantine Reaction to the Second Council of Lyons, 1274," *Councils and Assemblies,* ed. G. J. CUMING and D. BAKER (Cambridge 1971) 113–46.

[O. MCKENNA]

ISBN 0-7876-4012-3

90000

9 780787 640125

ISBN 0-7876-4012-3

90000

9 780787 640125